THE CAMBRIDGE DICTIONARY OF AMERICAN BIOGRAPHY

THE CAMBRIDGE DICTIONARY OF AMERICAN BIOGRAPHY

Edited by
JOHN S. BOWMAN

CAMBRIDGE
UNIVERSITY PRESS

Published by the Press Syndicate of the University of Cambridge
The Pitt Building, Trumpington Street, Cambridge CB2 1RP
40 West 20th Street, New York, NY 10011-4211, USA
10 Stamford Road, Oakleigh, Melbourne 3166, Australia

© Cambridge University Press 1995

First Published 1995

Printed in the United States of America

Library of Congress Cataloging-in-Publication Data

The Cambridge dictionary of American biography / edited by John S. Bowman.
p.   cm.
Includes index.
ISBN 0-521-40258-1
1. United States – Biography – Dictionaries.   I. Bowman, John
Stewart, 1931–   .
CT213.C36   1995
920.073 – dc20   94-5057
                                                                            CIP

A catalog record for this book is available from the British Library

ISBN   0-521-40258-1 Hardback

CONTENTS

PUBLISHER'S PREFACE

The Cambridge Dictionary of American Biography has been in preparation since 1989. We felt there was a need for an up-to-date volume that covered all the major occupations, professions, and activities of Americans past and present, and that tried to redress the bias that had often operated in the past to exclude women and members of minority groups from such books. Our book had to be large enough to include all the chief figures traditionally covered but had to be comprehensive enough to include also a good many others who are minor only in the sense that they have been traditionally excluded. To fit all this into one volume, we had to keep the entries short but nevertheless hoped to make them readable as prose. We would use few abbreviations and no codes or other shorthand devices in the text. It was a big job, we knew, but in fact it was even bigger and more challenging than we knew at the time. In his Introduction, John Bowman describes some of the main difficulties that had to be overcome.

One of the first things we did after signing up the editor was to invite several distinguished American historians to serve on an editorial board to advise us on policy issues. With the help of the editorial board's advice we decided from the start that although our book was to be essentially a work of American history, it should not be addressed solely to the people of the United States but to a much wider audience. We are innocent or arrogant enough to believe that many people throughout the world have an interest in American history, and accordingly agreed with the editor that the articles should not be written in an insular or parochial way, with allusions to a peculiarly American popular culture that might confound readers from other parts of the world. Indeed, some American readers may wonder why the editor found it necessary to spell out so many things that, to many Americans, need not have been spelled out. That is the reason. While we have assumed that every well-informed person is familiar with the main events of American history, lesser events are identified and briefly described, and all but the most universally understood abbreviations are written out. Though the subject is national, the readership, we hope, will be international.

The editorial board was invaluable in proposing particular people for our team of consultants, the experts in each of the 90-odd fields who recommended the names of the people to be included in the volume. All such consultants are listed in the front matter of this volume, and the publisher deeply appreciates the assiduity and thoughtfulness with which they fulfilled this very difficult task. As the editor describes, it is an assignment that by its nature cannot be done perfectly. The publisher wishes to say quite clearly, however, that we alone are responsible for the final selection, and that no consultant should be held responsible for the omission of any name. For reasons of space, some names recommended by consultants have been dropped. Likewise, some names may have been added. Although our selection has been compiled based on lists provided by our consultants, and although we tried to follow their recommendations as closely as possible, the final selection is ours. The reader should keep in mind, too, that the disciplines covered overlap one another, that many biographees were entered in two or more lists, and that therefore it is often impossible to ascertain which consultant recommended a particular individual.

While we know *The Cambridge Dictionary of American Biography* will not satisfy every authority in every field, we offer it for publication with a sense of satisfaction that it is an original, careful, and honest effort to marshal the best advice available from the community of American scholars, scientists, historians, professionals, and students of the various arts, crafts, trades, sports, and fields of entertainment toward this compilation. The plan was to give brief accounts of the thousands of Americans from all walks of life who have contributed in the past and who contribute now to all the disciplines covered. It is hoped that such profiles, about 9000 in all, will in the aggregate succeed in providing a picture of the entire history of the United States, from the American colonies and the period of early nationhood through the nineteenth and twentieth centuries, up to the very present. About 11 percent of the entries represent people who were born before 1800. At the other end, about 27 percent of the entries represent people who are still living.

We cherish the hope that this first edition will be revised frequently in the years ahead and become a permanent and important resource for readers everywhere who are interested in the history and culture and, most of all, the people of the United States.

The publisher wishes to acknowledge with gratitude the unflagging dedication the editor has demonstrated over a period of more than five years. In spite of it, as the editor would be the first to say, we realize there will be errors and omissions. The publisher, who must take full responsibility for such errors and omissions, welcomes comments and suggestions from readers so that we may consider them for subsequent editions of the book.

There are two indexes at the back of the book. The first, the Occupational Index, lists all the entries in the dictionary according to the occupational field or fields to which they belong. Since an individual may be prominent in several different fields, many entries appear under more than one field.

The second index, the Index of Names, lists the names of all individuals mentioned within any article anywhere in the dictionary. This index takes the place of thousands of cross-references that would otherwise clutter the text; since it includes many names that are not entries, it effectively enlarges the scope of the dictionary by a considerable margin. An explanation of how to use each index will be found at its beginning.

ACKNOWLEDGMENTS

A work of this size and complexity can only be compiled if a great many people talented in various ways contribute to its preparation. The publisher and editor thank all of them for their dedicated effort. We wish to acknowledge in particular the major contributing writers, each of whom wrote at least 350 entries. They are: Barbara Basbinah, Samuel W. Crompton, Rosamond Dauer, Michael Golay, Sydney Johnson, William McGeveran, Marietta Pritchard, Jan Swafford, Pamela White, Janet Bond Wood, and Amy Zuckerman.

Other contributors are: Thomas Aylesworth, John Bollard, Bob Carroll, Lisa Clyde, Sophy Craze, C. Roger Davis, Marilea Polk Fried, Marcia Isserman, Maurice Isserman, Jim Kaplan, Kenneth Kronenberg, Margaret A. Lowe, Sherry Marker, Geoffrey Martin, Amy Mittelman, James Mote, Barry Pritzker, Thomas F. Reney III, Brooks Robards, Robin L. Sommer, Eva Weber, Peter Woodsum, and Joel Zoss.

The following people helped us obtain consultants or assisted the project in various other important ways: Barbara Bannerman of the American Advertising Federation; Gloria Conwell of Springfield, Massachusetts; Professor John Heritage of the University of California, Los Angeles; Professor John H. Lienhard of the University of Houston, Texas; G. Brian McDonald of Springfield, Massachusetts; and Susan Penny of Harcourt Brace Jovanovich.

Our thanks also to Michael E. Agnes and Kenneth R. Greenhall, who assisted the editor during the early and intermediate stages of this project, and to Nancy Feldman. We would also like to thank the staff of Huron Valley Graphics, of Ann Arbor, Michigan, particularly Karen Faletti, Kevin Rennells, Janice Brill, and H.P. Patterson for their careful work in copy editing, proofreading, and marking the copy for the Index of Names, and to Dana Harrison. Finally, and though last not least, we want to thank the staffs of countless libraries who helped our writers in so many ways as they undertook the research for their contributions.

CONSULTANTS, BY SUBJECT

ADVERTISING AND PUBLIC RELATIONS

American Advertising Federation
Washington, D.C.

AERONAUTICS AND SPACE

Dominick Pisano, *Curator*
Department of Aeronautics
National Air and Space Museum
Washington, D.C.

AFRICAN AREA STUDIES

Philip Curtin, *Professor of History*
Johns Hopkins University
Baltimore, Maryland

AGRICULTURE *See* **FOOD SCIENCE.**

AIR FORCE AND AVIATION

William R. Stewart, Jr., *Colonel USAF (Ret.)*
San Antonio, Texas

ANIMAL SCIENCE

Joseph Tritschler, *Professor of Animal Science*
University of Massachusetts at Amherst
Amherst, Massachusetts

ANTHROPOLOGY *See* **PHYSICAL ANTHROPOLOGY;
SOCIAL AND CULTURAL ANTHROPOLOGY.**

ARCHITECTURE

Sarah Bradford Landau, *Associate Professor of
Art History*
Department of Fine Arts
New York University

ARCHITECTURE *See also* **LANDSCAPE ARCHITECTURE.**

ARMY

James M. Morris, *Professor of History*
Christopher Newport College
Newport News, Virginia

ART *See* **ARCHITECTURE; ART HISTORY; COMIC ART
AND CARTOONS; CRAFTS; LANDSCAPE ARCHITECTURE;
PAINTING AND THE ART WORLD; SCULPTURE.**

ART HISTORY

Lee R. Sorensen, *Art Bibliographer*
Lilly Art Library
Duke University
Durham, North Carolina

ASIAN AREA STUDIES

Parks M. Coble, *Professor of History*
University of Nebraska
Lincoln, Nebraska

ASTRONOMY

Steven J. Dick, *Historian*
U.S. Naval Observatory
Washington, D.C.

ATMOSPHERIC STUDIES

Charles L. Hosler, *Senior Vice President for Research*
Dean of the Graduate School
Pennsylvania State University
University Park, Pennsylvania

AVIATION *See* **AIR FORCE.**

BANKING *See* **FINANCE.**

BIBLIOGRAPHY *See* **LIBRARIANSHIP.**

BIOCHEMISTRY AND MOLECULAR BIOLOGY

John T. Edsall, *Professor of Biochemistry and Molecular Biology, Emeritus*
Harvard University
Cambridge, Massachusetts

BIOLOGY *See* **ANIMAL SCIENCE; BIOCHEMISTRY; DEVELOPMENTAL AND CELL BIOLOGY; ZOOLOGY.**

BOOK COLLECTING AND BOOKSELLING

John Tebbel, *Professor of Journalism, Emeritus*
New York University
New York, New York

BOTANY

John Burk, *Professor of Botany*
Smith College
Northampton, Massachusetts

BUSINESS AND INDUSTRY AFTER 1945

Marshall Loeb, *(Former) Managing Editor*
Fortune
New York, New York

Allan T. Demaree, *Executive Editor*
Fortune
New York, New York

Thomas A. Stewart, *Associate Editor*
Fortune
New York, New York

BUSINESS, INDUSTRY, AND FINANCE BEFORE 1945

William J. Hausman, *Professor of Economics*
The College of William and Mary
Williamsburg, Virginia

BUSINESS *See also* **MANAGEMENT.**

CELL BIOLOGY *See* **DEVELOPMENTAL BIOLOGY.**

CHEMISTRY

Wyndham D. Miles
Gaithersburg, Maryland

CHILDREN'S LITERATURE

Rosamond Dauer, *Writer*
Northampton, Massachusetts

CLASSICAL MUSIC

Jan Swafford, *Composer*
Cambridge, Massachusetts

CLASSICAL STUDIES

Sherry Marker
Northampton, Massachusetts

COMIC ART AND CARTOONS

M. Thomas Inge, *Blackwell Professor of the Humanities*
Randolph-Macon College
Ashland, Virginia

COMPUTERS

Paul Ceruzzi, *Curator*
National Air and Space Museum
Washington, D.C.

CONGRESS: SENATORS AND REPRESENTATIVES

Leroy N. Rieselbach, *Professor of Political Science*
Indiana University
Bloomington, Indiana

CONSERVATION AND ECOLOGY

Donald Worster, *Hall Distinguished Professor of American History*
University of Kansas
Lawrence, Kansas

CRAFTS

Linda Seckelson, *Director of Library and Information Services*
Bard Graduate Center for Studies in the Decorative Arts
New York, New York

CRIME *See* **LAW ENFORCEMENT.**

CULTURAL ANTHROPOLOGY *See* **SOCIAL ANTHROPOLOGY.**

DANCE

Claudia Roth Pierpont, *Writer*
The New Yorker
New York, New York

DEVELOPMENTAL AND CELL BIOLOGY

J. T. Bonner, *Professor of Biology*
Princeton University
Princeton, New Jersey

DIPLOMACY

Charles E. Neu, *Professor of History*
Brown University
Providence, Rhode Island

ECOLOGY *See* **CONSERVATION.**

ECONOMICS

Michael Szenberg, *Professor of Economics*
Director of the Center for Applied Research
Lubin Graduate School of Business
Pace University
New York, New York

EDITING AND PUBLISHING

Ezra Greenspan, *Professor of English*
University of South Carolina
Columbia, South Carolina

EDUCATION

John R. Thelin, *Chancellor Professor*
School of Education
The College of William and Mary
Williamsburg, Virginia

ENGINEERING

David F. Channell, *Professor of Historical Studies*
University of Texas at Dallas
Dallas, Texas

ENTERTAINMENT AND SHOW BUSINESS

Don B. Wilmeth, *Professor of Theatre and English*
Brown University
Providence, Rhode Island

ENVIRONMENTAL STUDIES *See* **CONSERVATION.**

EXPLORATION, COLONIAL AND NINETEENTH-CENTURY FRONTIER AMERICA

Samuel W. Crompton, *Instructor in American History*
Holyoke Community College
Holyoke, Massachusetts

FILM

Ray Carney, *Professor of Film*
Boston University
Boston, Massachusetts

FINANCE AND BANKING AFTER 1945

Morris Mendelson, *Professor of Finance, Emeritus*
University of Pennsylvania
Philadelphia, Pennsylvania

FINANCE *See also* BUSINESS.

FOLKLORE AND FOLK CULTURE

Bess Lomax Hawes
Arlington, Virginia

FOOD SCIENCE

Frederick John Francis, *Professor of Food Science*
University of Massachusetts at Amherst
Amherst, Massachusetts

GAMES

Jim Kaplan, *Bridge Columnist*
Northampton, Massachusetts

GENETICS

Richard C. Lewontin, *Alexander Agassiz Professor of Zoology and Professor of Biology*
Harvard University
Cambridge, Massachusetts

GEOGRAPHY

Geoffrey J. Martin, *Professor of Geography*
Southern Connecticut State University
New Haven, Connecticut

GEOLOGY AND GEOPHYSICS

B. F. Howell, Jr., *Professor of Geophysics, Emeritus*
Pennsylvania State University
University Park, Pennsylvania

Eldridge Moores, *Professor of Geology*
University of California, Davis
Davis, California

GEOPHYSICS *See* **GEOLOGY.**

GOVERNMENT *See* **CONGRESS: SENATORS AND REPRESENTATIVES; GOVERNMENT SERVICE; MUNICIPAL GOVERNMENT; STATE GOVERNMENT.**

GOVERNMENT SERVICE

Robert H. Salisbury, *Souers Professor of American Government*
Washington University
St. Louis, Missouri

GRAPHIC ARTS *See* **ILLUSTRATION.**

HISTORY

Frederick J. McGinness, *Lecturer in History*
Mt. Holyoke College
South Hadley, Massachusetts

ILLUSTRATION AND THE GRAPHIC ARTS

Rosamond Dauer
Northampton, Massachusetts

ILLUSTRATION *See also* **CARTOON ILLUSTRATION.**

INDUSTRIAL AND INTERIOR DESIGN

David Revere McFadden, *Curator of Decorative Arts*
Cooper-Hewitt National Museum of Design
New York, New York

INDUSTRY *See* **BUSINESS.**

INTERIOR DESIGN *See* **INDUSTRIAL DESIGN.**

INVENTION AND TECHNOLOGY

Robert C. Post, *Editor*
Technology and Culture
National Museum of American History
Washington, D.C.

ISLAM *See* **MIDDLE EASTERN STUDIES.**

JAZZ *See* **POPULAR MUSIC.**

JOURNALISM, PUBLISHING, AND PRINTING

John Tebbel, *Professor of Journalism, Emeritus*
New York University
New York, New York

JUDAISM

Shuly Rubin Schwartz, *Assistant Dean*
The Albert A. List College of Jewish Studies
Jewish Theological Seminary of America
New York, New York

JUDICIARY

Hiller Zobel, *Associate Justice*
Superior Court of Massachusetts
Boston, Massachusetts

LABOR

Melvyn Dubofsky, *Distinguished Professor of*
History and Sociology
State University of New York at Binghamton
Binghamton, New York

LANDSCAPE ARCHITECTURE

Mary Parker, *Landscape Architect*
Northampton, Massachusetts

LATIN AMERICAN STUDIES

Kempton E. Webb, *Professor of Geography, Emeritus*
Columbia University
New York, New York

LAW

Morris Cohen, *Professor of Law, Emeritus*
Yale University Law School
New Haven, Connecticut

LAW *See also* **JUDICIARY; LAW ENFORCEMENT;**
LEGAL SCHOLARSHIP.

LAW ENFORCEMENT, CRIMINOLOGY, AND PENOLOGY

Franklin Zimring, *Professor of Law*
Director, Earl Warren Legal Institute
University of California, Berkeley
Berkeley, California

LEGAL SCHOLARSHIP

Theodore Steinberg, *Assistant Professor of History*
New Jersey Institute of Technology
Newark, New Jersey

LEXICOGRAPHY

Sidney I. Landau, *Editorial Director*
North American Branch
Cambridge University Press
New York, New York

LIBRARIANSHIP AND BIBLIOGRAPHY

Elizabeth Futas, *Director*
Graduate School of Library and Information Studies
University of Rhode Island
Kingston, Rhode Island

LINGUISTICS

John Algeo, *Professor of English, Emeritus*
University of Georgia
Athens, Georgia

LITERARY HISTORY, CRITICISM, AND THEORY

William H. Pritchard, *Professor of English*
Amherst College
Amherst, Massachusetts

LITERATURE

Albert Gelpi, *Coe Professor of American Literature*
Stanford University
Stanford, California

LITERATURE *See also* **CHILDREN'S LITERATURE; LITERARY HISTORY, CRITICISM, AND THEORY.**

MANAGEMENT

Myron E. Weiner, *Professor of Management, Emeritus*
University of Connecticut
Storrs, Connecticut

MATHEMATICS

Harold M. Edwards, *Professor of Mathematics*
Courant Institute of Mathematical Sciences
New York University
New York, New York

MEDICINE

Martin Kaufman, *Professor of History*
Westfield State College
Westfield, Massachusetts

MEDICINE *See also* **NURSING AND WOMEN IN MEDICINE.**

MIDDLE EASTERN STUDIES AND THE ISLAMIC WORLD

Robert M. Haddad, *President*
American University of Beirut
Beirut, Lebanon

MILITARY *See* **AIR FORCE; ARMY; NAVY.**

MOLECULAR BIOLOGY *See* **BIOCHEMISTRY.**

MUNICIPAL GOVERNMENT

David M. Katzman, *Professor of History*
The University of Kansas
Lawrence, Kansas

MUSIC *See* **CLASSICAL MUSIC; POPULAR MUSIC AND JAZZ.**

NATIVE AMERICAN HISTORY

Peter Iverson, *Professor of History*
Arizona State University
Tempe, Arizona

NAVY

James M. Morris, *Professor of History*
Christopher Newport College
Newport News, Virginia

NEUROBIOLOGY *See* **PSYCHIATRY.**

NURSING AND WOMEN IN MEDICINE

Bar Dee Bond
Marietta, Ohio

OCEANOGRAPHY

James R. Luyten, *Chairman*
Department of Physical Oceanography
Woods Hole Oceanographic Institution
Woods Hole, Massachusetts

Walter H. Munk, *Professor of Oceanography, Emeritus*
Scripps Institution of Oceanography
University of California, San Diego
San Diego, California

PAINTING AND THE ART WORLD

Irma B. Jaffee, *Professor of Art History, Emerita*
Fordham University
New York, New York

PALEONTOLOGY

Leonard Krishtalka, *Curator of Paleontology*
The Carnegie Museum of Natural History
Pittsburgh, Pennsylvania

PENOLOGY *See* **LAW ENFORCEMENT.**

PERFORMING ARTS *See* **DANCE; ENTERTAINMENT; THEATER.**

PHILANTHROPY

Vernon F. Snow, *Professor of History*
Syracuse University
Syracuse, New York

PHILOSOPHY

Terence Moore, *Executive Editor, Humanities*
North American Branch
Cambridge University Press
New York, New York

PHOTOGRAPHY

Glenn Willumson, *Curator of Photography*
J. Paul Getty Center
Santa Monica, California

PHYSICAL ANTHROPOLOGY

F. Clark Howell, *Professor of Anthropology*
Laboratory for Human Evolutionary Studies
University of California, Berkeley
Berkeley, California

PHYSICS

George L. Trigg, *(Former) Editor*
Physical Review Letters
Brookhaven, New York

PIONEERING SETTLEMENTS *See* **EXPLORATION.**

POLITICAL ACTIVISM *See* **SOCIAL REFORM.**

POLITICAL SCIENCE

Nelson W. Polsby, *Director*
Institute of Governmental Studies
University of California, Berkeley
Berkeley, California

POPULAR MUSIC AND JAZZ

Thomas F. Reney III, *"Jazz á la Mode" Host*
Public Radio
Amherst, Massachusetts

PRINTING *See* **JOURNALISM.**

PROTESTANTISM

John F. Wilson, *Professor of Religion*
Princeton University
Princeton, New Jersey

PSYCHIATRY AND NEUROBIOLOGY

Samuel B. Guze, *Spencer T. Olin Professor of Psychiatry*
Washington University School of Medicine
St. Louis, Missouri

PSYCHOLOGY AND PSYCHOTHERAPY

Neil Weinberg, *Instructor in Psychology*
Holyoke Community College
Holyoke, Massachusetts

PUBLIC RELATIONS *See* **ADVERTISING.**

PUBLISHING *See* **EDITING; JOURNALISM.**

PUERTO RICAN CULTURE

Gonzalo Córdova, *Professor of History*
University of Puerto Rico
San Juan, Puerto Rico

Sherry Marker, *Lecturer, American Studies*
Smith College
Northampton, Massachusetts

RADIO *See* **TELEVISION.**

REGIONAL PLANNING *See* **URBAN PLANNING.**

RELIGION *See* **JUDAISM; MIDDLE EASTERN STUDIES
AND THE ISLAMIC WORLD; PROTESTANTISM;
ROMAN CATHOLICISM.**

ROMAN CATHOLICISM

Christopher J. Kauffman, *Catholic Daughters of the Americas*
Professor of American Church History
The Catholic University of America
Washington, D.C.

SCULPTURE

George Gurney, *Associate Curator of American Sculpture*
National Museum of American Art
Washington, D.C.

SENATORS AND REPRESENTATIVES *See* **CONGRESS.**

SHOW BUSINESS *See* **ENTERTAINMENT.**

SLAVIC STUDIES

William Gleason, *Kenneth R. Rossman Professor of History*
Doane College
Crete, Nebraska

SOCIAL AND CULTURAL ANTHROPOLOGY

George W. Stocking, Jr., *Professor of Anthropology*
University of Chicago
Chicago, Illinois

SOCIAL REFORM AND POLITICAL ACTIVISM

Christopher Kimball, *Professor of History*
Augsburg College
Minneapolis, Minnesota

SOCIOLOGY

Gerald Platt, *Professor of Sociology*
University of Massachusetts at Amherst
Amherst, Massachusetts

SPACE *See* **AERONAUTICS.**

SPORTS

Peter Bjarkman, *Writer*
West Lafayette, Indiana

STATE GOVERNMENT

Thad L. Beyle, *Professor of Political Science*
University of North Carolina
Chapel Hill, North Carolina

TECHNOLOGY *See* **INVENTION.**

TELEVISION AND RADIO

Brooks Robards, *Professor of Mass Communication*
Westfield State College
Westfield, Massachusetts

THEATER

Don B. Wilmeth, *Professor of Theatre and English*
Brown University
Providence, Rhode Island

URBAN AND REGIONAL PLANNING

Andrew J. W. Scheffey, *Professor of Landscape Architecture
and Regional Planning, Emeritus*
University of Massachusetts at Amherst
Amherst, Massachusetts

ZOOLOGY

C. Leon Harris, *Professor of Zoology*
State University of New York at Plattsburgh
Plattsburgh, New York

ALPHABETICAL LIST OF CONSULTANTS

John Algeo / Linguistics
Thad L. Beyle / State Government
Peter Bjarkman / Sports
Bar Dee Bond / Nursing and Women in Medicine
J. T. Bonner / Developmental and Cell Biology
John Burk / Botany
Ray Carney / Film
Paul Ceruzzi / Computers
David F. Channell / Engineering
Parks M. Coble / Asian Area Studies
Morris Cohen / Law
Gonzalo Córdova / Puerto Rican Culture
Samuel W. Crompton / Exploration, Colonial, and Nineteenth-Century Frontier America
Philip Curtin / African Area Studies
Rosamond Dauer / Children's Literature; Illustration and the Graphic Arts
Allan T. Demaree / Business and Industry After 1945
Steven J. Dick / Astronomy
Melvyn Dubofsky / Labor
John T. Edsall / Biochemistry and Molecular Biology
Harold M. Edwards / Mathematics
Frederick John Francis / Food Science
Elizabeth Futas / Librarianship and Bibliography
Albert Gelpi / Literature
William Gleason / Slavic Studies
Ezra Greenspan / Editing and Publishing
George Gurney / Sculpture
Samuel B. Guze / Psychiatry and Neurobiology
Robert M. Haddad / Middle Eastern Studies and the Islamic World

C. Leon Harris / Zoology
William J. Hausman / Business, Industry, and Finance Before 1945
Bess Lomax Hawes / Folklore and Folk Culture
Charles L. Hosler / Atmospheric Studies
B. F. Howell, Jr. / Geology and Geophysics
F. Clark Howell / Physical Anthropology
M. Thomas Inge / Cartoon Illustration
Peter Iverson / Native American History
Irma B. Jaffee / Painting and the Art World
Jim Kaplan / Games
David M. Katzman / Municipal Government
Christopher J. Kauffman / Roman Catholicism
Martin Kaufman / Medicine
Christopher Kimball / Social Reform and Political Activism
Leonard Krishtalka / Paleontology
Sarah Bradford Landau / Architecture
Sidney I. Landau / Lexicography
Richard C. Lewontin / Genetics
Marshall Loeb / Business and Industry After 1945
James R. Luyten / Oceanography
Sherry Marker / Classical Studies; Puerto Rican Culture
Geoffrey J. Martin / Geography
David Revere McFadden / Industrial and Interior Design
Frederick J. McGinness / History
Morris Mendelson / Finance and Banking After 1945
Wyndham D. Miles / Chemistry
Terence Moore / Philosophy
Eldridge Moores / Geology and Geophysics

ALPHABETICAL LIST OF CONSULTANTS

James M. Morris / *Army; Navy*
Walter H. Munk / *Oceanography*
Charles E. Neu / *Diplomacy*
Mary Parker / *Landscape Architecture*
Claudia Roth Pierpont / *Dance*
Dominick Pisano / *Aeronautics and Space*
Gerald Platt / *Sociology*
Nelson W. Polsby / *Political Science*
Robert C. Post / *Invention and Technology*
William H. Pritchard / *Literary History, Criticism, and Theory*
Thomas F. Reney III / *Popular Music and Jazz*
Leroy N. Rieselbach / *Congress: Senators and Representatives*
Brooks Robards / *Television and Radio*
Robert H. Salisbury / *Government Service*
Andrew J. W. Scheffey / *Urban and Regional Planning*
Shuly Rubin Schwartz / *Judaism*
Linda Seckelson / *Crafts*
Vernon F. Snow / *Philanthropy*
Lee R. Sorensen / *Art History*
Theodore Steinberg / *Legal Scholarship*

William R. Stewart, Jr. / *Air Force and Aviation*
Thomas A. Stewart / *Business and Industry After 1945*
George W. Stocking, Jr. / *Social and Cultural Anthropology*
Jan Swafford / *Classical Music*
Michael Szenberg / *Economics*
John Tebbel / *Book Collecting and Bookselling; Journalism, Publishing, and Printing*
John R. Thelin / *Education*
George L. Trigg / *Physics*
Joseph Tritschler / *Animal Science*
Kempton E. Webb / *Latin American Studies*
Neil Weinberg / *Psychology and Psychotherapy*
Myron E. Weiner / *Management*
Glenn Willumson / *Photography*
Don B. Wilmeth / *Entertainment and Show Business; Theater*
John F. Wilson / *Protestantism*
Donald Worster / *Conservation and Ecology*
Franklin Zimring / *Law Enforcement, Criminology, and Penology*
Hiller Zobel / *Judiciary*

INTRODUCTION

To offer a collection of biographies these days, with bookstores and libraries heavily stocked with reference books, may seem presumptuous. Yet despite all such books and computer services, it is still difficult for the nonexpert to find essential data about many prominent Americans, past and present. We resolved to try to fill that gap with a book that was broadly conceived to provide extensive coverage, with attention to all periods of American history and in all fields of endeavor. To place it within the means of most people, the work would have to be in one volume. Therefore, given the scope we had in mind, most entries would have to be short. But we wanted our book to be readable, not a dry statistical summary with abbreviations and shorthand codes, but a shaped profile beginning with the basic facts (date and place of birth, and so on) and including also a selection of key activities that made the individual significant.

SCOPE AND CHARACTER OF COVERAGE

Although the difficulties of including entries for the living were formidable, both in selection and obtaining information about them, we felt, and our editorial board concurred, that no book without such entries could purport to present a balanced and comprehensive source of information for those interested in recent American history as well as in the past. After all, many living Americans are notable for accomplishments twenty, thirty, or more years ago. The chess grandmaster Bobby Fischer became world champion in 1972. The best-selling novel by J. D. Salinger, *The Catcher in the Rye,* was published in 1951. To omit any record of such memorable events in the recent history of the United States would hardly do justice to the purpose we had set for ourselves.

The decision to include entries for the living as well as for the deceased presented many challenges. In seeking to be up-to-date, we ran the risk of becoming out-of-date very rapidly. There is no denying that many of the entries on living people may quickly become dated. But we felt that this was outweighed by the value of including hard-to-find information about people in the news now, such as current Nobel prize winners, dramatic artists, and business leaders.

Many of the standard biographical works give thorough coverage to certain areas, such as government and the military, the traditional arts, the academic world, certain sciences, and sports, while neglecting other areas. CDAB includes individuals in all such areas but its range is broader, covering not just the main branches of science, for example, but more specialized areas as well: not just botanists but food scientists, horticulturists, and experts on forests; not just biologists but ecologists and conservationists. This holds true in every field. In the humanities, we include not just the traditional canon of writers but a generous selection of children's book writers as well as some of the better-known popular writers of westerns and detective fiction. In the popular arts and entertainment, we include not just major movie stars and musicians but also a selection of the newer performance artists.

We have sought to go beyond coverage of conventional occupations to profile many people whom it is impossible to categorize, people who in the past for this reason often fell between the cracks. I refer to people like Bill W, founder of Alcoholics Anonymous, or Hannah Dustin, the colonial woman who is said to have scalped ten Indians; or "Get Rich Quick" Ponzi, the Boston financial wizard; or Onesimus, the obscure African-American who may have played a role in developing the smallpox inoculation. We have also included many legendary Americans based on actual persons, such as Molly Pitcher (about whom there is disagreement and either of two people may be the model), Johnny Appleseed, Uncle Sam, Casey Jones, or that archetypal American over-reacher, Sam Patch.

We sought to impart a contemporary outlook to our coverage and treatment. Many of our entries incorporate recent scholarship, new findings, and reappraisals. In some cases this meant rescuing individuals from the obscurity of neglect or ignorance. In other cases it meant using scholarly opinion to cast famous Americans – for example, Thomas Jefferson, Woodrow Wilson, and Thomas Eakins – in a slightly different light from the way they have traditionally been treated, with new shadows and highlights. We have also not scrupled to include people infamous rather than famous if their exploits were widely recognized or written about. We exercised no censorship in our selection, which includes assassins, traitors, thieves, embezzlers, and rascals of every sort. Moreover, we do not seek to conceal the flaws and fumbles of otherwise admirable men and women if these are part of the public record.

We make no claim to be exhaustive in listing awards, honors, degrees, in recording every stage and appointment or all the offices held in a person's life, let alone all the works accomplished or published. We see this dictionary as fulfilling a different role: providing a shaped profile of each individual, one that selects from both personal and professional data, from the private as well as the public life. Nonetheless, our entries do include mention of notable honors and awards. Although we could not begin to include all winners of all Pulitzer prizes, when our subjects did win one, the fact is noted, as it is for winners of an Oscar, an Emmy, a Spingarn (for race relations), a Pritzker (in architecture), a Templeton (in religion), or a MacArthur Foundation award.

There are a few groups who gained automatic inclusion: American winners of a Nobel prize; U.S. presidents, vice presidents, and first ladies; justices of the U.S. Supreme Court. We also chose to include all those represented in the National Statuary Hall Collection on view in the Capitol of the United States. The statuary collection was begun in 1864 when Congress authorized the President to invite each state to send statues of marble or bronze of two individuals most worthy of representing their state. (They did not have to be natives of the state; indeed, several were not even citizens of the United States.) Originally, the statues were set up in the old chamber of the House of Representatives, but by 1933 the collection had outgrown that space and it is now spread throughout the Capitol. All fifty states have at least one statue; all but eight have sent their quota of two. Presumably millions of visitors to Washington, D.C., gaze upon these statues every year. Here they can learn something about the people they honor.

CONSULTANTS AND CRITERIA FOR INCLUSION

As noted in the Publisher's Preface, we started by turning to consultants, initially recommended by our editorial board and by editors of Cambridge University Press, and later by colleagues and associates of consultants already engaged. In many instances, our consultants are prominent figures in their fields. This raises the delicate issue of whether consultants could include their own names. The answer is yes, but in fact very few did (and are included); several others were nominated by consultants in related fields. Being oneself a potential entry was never a prerequisite for being a consultant, and most are not entered. The chief requirement was not fame or accomplishment but knowledge of the field and good judgment. The remuneration for this work, often involving research and always demanding hard decisions, was modest, and I am very grateful to the many busy people who took precious time to compile their lists of recommended names. That a number of quite prominent people in many fields volunteered to help us speaks well for their commitment to their disciplines.

The major criterion for inclusion, as described to our consultants, might be stated thus: We want those individuals whose names would be most likely to show up in a variety of contexts where nonspecialists would encounter them and want to learn more about said individuals. In effect, we tried to establish something like a citation index, an attempt to quantify the importance of a person's work, as though by tracking the number of times it had been cited by others. But whereas citation indexes tend to be linked to uses by specialists in the same field, our hypothetical citations were in contexts where the nonspecialist would come across them.

Another criterion that had to be established was exactly who was and who wasn't an American, and what exactly "American" means. Since the people of the United States of America are traditionally known as "American," we use "American" in this sense in our title. Throughout the text, *U.S.* is used as an adjective except in established names. We chose to adopt broad and flexible criteria of "American" in setting the standards for inclusion for our consultants.

We had to admit people who were not American citizens but who had lived here for many years and who were well known because of their accomplishments in this country. (Incidentally, and unusually in biographical references, we identify when a foreign-born individual came to the U.S.) We rejected any rigid test either requiring citizenship or so many years of residence. Instead, we tried to apply what came to be known as the Baryshnikov vs. Nureyev Rule, after the two Russian expatriate ballet dancers. That is, if the individual really made the United States a home and participated in American life (as Baryshnikov has), then he is included. But if it turned out that the U.S. was merely a way station in the course of a life and career, even if the individual is famous in American history, he is not included. In many cases, the issue was far from clear-cut, but these were our guiding principles.

In general, we did not include the early explorers of this continent if all they did was come ashore, look around, and leave. We required them to settle here. This means that Columbus, Henry Hudson, and Coronado are not here (nor is Amerigo Vespucci), while Father Marquette and Eusebio Kino and Junipero Serra are here. A more difficult problem occurred in the colonial period. We tried to sort out those who settled into American society and became part of American life from those who functioned simply as colonial officials. We did not impose any rigid requirement regarding the number of years a person lived here or whether or not the person died here. Instead we made a judgment based on the entire record. Thus William Bradford and John Winthrop are here, as are Peter Minuit and William Penn, whereas Jeffrey Amherst and "Gentleman Johnny" Burgoyne are not.

In later times, when the issue of becoming an American citizen comes into play, we decided once more against adopting a rigid requirement of citizenship, and we undoubtedly include many who never became U.S. citizens. Some may even have gone back to their native lands in later years. Our criterion was that the individuals became part of American society for a substantial and usually productive period of their lives. Thus we include Einstein (who, as it happens, did become a U.S. citizen) but not only because he spent one third of his life here; he is included because he truly became part of American society while here. So, too, in his own way did a great scientist of another era, Joseph Priestley.

The advice of our consultants often determined our decision in such matters. If a consultant said an individual was regarded as an American by members of his or her profession, we took that as definitive. On the other hand, some consultants nominated individuals who turned out to be regarded by all other sources as Canadian or British; these individuals had to be dropped.

We include a number of expatriates. So long as individuals were born in the U.S. or born to American parents, and are generally identified as Americans, we included them, whether they lived in the United States or not. Thus we have both Lady Astor and the Duchess of Windsor, along with many missionaries and educators. We also have Count Rumford and Whistler, George Hatem and Eddie Constantine, and – even though born abroad – John Singer Sargent.

We made a special effort, as noted in the Publisher's Preface, to include more women and members of minorities, particularly African-Americans, than have heretofore been included in general biographical dictionaries. We asked consultants to "stretch their nets" of recognition so as to capture individuals often overlooked in general compilations. We encouraged consultants to seek out people who deserved to be rescued from the shadows, both men and women, of all ethnic and racial origins. A word about nomenclature may be in order. In general we use *African-American,* as this is the current preferred usage, but when the context would make that awkward, we use the older but still current designation *black,* and in some historical contexts when *black* would be anachronistic, *Negro* is used. We do not identify the race of an individual unless that is relevant to the importance or achievements of the person.

FORM OF THE ENTRIES

Names   We have tried to track down the names given at birth, including middle names and, in the case of females, maiden names. We have also indicated women's married names as well as all assumed names – pen names, stage names, etc. In general, the names listed outside parentheses are the ones that the individual generally used and was known by. In many instances where we had no way of knowing whether an individual generally used a middle name or names, we have left them outside parentheses. When initials only are given, our research was unable to find any source providing full names. Nicknames have been left outside parentheses if that is how the individual was widely known; nicknames that are more like sobriquets ("The Yankee Clipper") are placed within parentheses.

Dates of birth and death   We have tried in every case to establish the exact years of birth and death. When no reliable source could be found, the year is preceded by a question mark. Rarely, when an individual surfaces only for a period and then vanishes into obscurity, especially in the early years of colonial settlement, *fl.* (for *flourished*) may precede a span of years. When there is no death date, the individual was alive, to the best of our knowledge, when this book went to press.

Birthplace   We have in every case tried to establish the exact city and state of birth; in many instances during earlier times, however, no precise information is available. In all cases where an individual was born abroad, we provide the city and country of birth. If the parents were in fact Americans abroad at the time of the birth, this is usually indicated in the entry. As mentioned above, we indicate when the individual came to the U.S.

Relations   If the individual is closely related to another fairly well-known person – usually someone who is also represented by an entry in this dictionary – we have indicated this relationship in parentheses.

FACTUAL CONTENT

Tracking down information about living contemporaries was the most challenging assignment of our writers. In countless instances writers had to track down obscure facts or resolve contradictions by searching out local public records or local newspapers. Facts about academics were often sought from their department offices and in several instances, unexpectedly, from the subjects themselves. In no case did the subject write or approve the entry, however. All that said, we are forced to admit that we are undoubtedly perpetuating some errors and have probably introduced a few of our own. But in general, we feel we have been able to clear up many errors that lurk in biographical sources. We have gone to considerable lengths, for example, to pin down the exact dates of discoveries and inventions, and we hope to have cleared up many matters involving priority claims for inventions and other "firsts."

Years in government service, particularly state and federal elective offices, posed a question that is often dealt with inconsistently in other sources. We tried to deal with it systematically. The confusion results over the difference between the year an individual was elected to public office and the year that the person actually took office. Unfortunately, there is no single or simple rule applied to all levels of government: elections may be held in virtually any year in any state, and the person elected may assume office in that year or in the next year. It is frequently hard to settle such questions, especially since many municipalities and states have changed their terms of office over the years. We have sought to clear up these matters and be precise in our phrasing. In most instances, we provide the actual years the individual served in office, although there are instances where in the course of a narrative it is relevant to state the year of election.

RELATIVE WEIGHT OF ENTRIES

At the beginning of this project, it was assumed that there would be a direct and uniform relationship between an individual's importance and the length of that individual's entry: the more important the person, the longer the entry. In the obvious cases, the principle held up. George Washington and Abraham Lincoln are accorded fuller treatment than Millard Fillmore, or even than John Adams. But apart from the difficulty of determining relative importance, it soon became apparent that it was often easier to sum up the life and accomplishments of many of the more important personages than the lives and careers of others who might be regarded as of lesser importance. Many an individual has led a fascinating and diverse life without it all adding up to a major historical career. Meanwhile, many important statesmen, academics, and scientists may have stuck to the straight and narrow. In the course of writing many entries, we modified the rule that worthiness necessarily bears a direct relationship to number of words. Put another way, the relative importance of two individuals in the same field of endeavor cannot be securely gauged by comparing the lengths of their entries.

CONCLUSION

I hope that the audience for this dictionary will feel that we have accomplished what we set out to do, as expressed in the opening paragraph of this Introduction. In a real sense, this is a work of history. Many aspects of American life can be tracked with the help of the indexes: the history of retailing and department stores, for example, or of most major industrial and manufacturing processes, of inventions and technologies, of agriculture and food processing. The history of many professions and disciplines, from architecture to zoology, can be tracked down, as can broad fields such as aviation or publishing. On a still broader scale, the colonial period is well described, as is the opening of the Western frontier. For the latter, for instance, the reader could start with the appropriate occupational groups in the Occupational Index to find the explorers and trailblazers, the trappers and miners, Native Americans and soldiers, cowboys and lawmen, mountainmen and pioneer settlers, local heroes and national legends.

It is in this spirit that we turn this work over to its users. We hope that it is more than the sum of its parts, that it is a collection of biographies of individual Americans that adds up to a portrait of America.

John S. Bowman

ABBREVIATIONS

DESIGNATIONS FOR STATES AND TERRITORIES

Ala.	Alabama	**Mich.**	Michigan	**Utah**	Utah
Alaska	Alaska	**Minn.**	Minnesota	**Vt.**	Vermont
Ariz.	Arizona	**Miss.**	Mississippi	**Va.**	Virginia
Ark.	Arkansas	**Mo.**	Missouri	**Wash.**	Washington
Calif.	California	**Mont.**	Montana	**W. Va.**	West Virginia
Colo.	Colorado	**N.C.**	North Carolina	**Wis.**	Wisconsin
Conn.	Connecticut	**N.D.**	North Dakota	**Wyo.**	Wyoming
D.C.	District of Columbia	**Nebr.**	Nebraska		
		Nev.	Nevada		

OTHER ABBREVIATIONS

Del.	Delaware	**N.H.**	New Hampshire		
Fla.	Florida	**N.J.**	New Jersey		
Ga.	Georgia	**N.M.**	New Mexico	**b.**	born
Hawaii	Hawaii	**N.Y.**	New York	**CEO**	chief executive officer
Ida.	Idaho	**Ohio**	Ohio		
Ill.	Illinois	**Okla.**	Oklahoma	**Dem.**	Democrat
Ind.	Indiana	**Ore.**	Oregon	**fl.**	flourished
Iowa	Iowa	**Pa.**	Pennsylvania	**Ind.**	Independent
Kans.	Kansas	**Puerto Rico**	Puerto Rico	**m.**	married
Ky.	Kentucky	**R.I.**	Rhode Island	**N.Y.C.**	New York City
La.	Louisiana	**S.C.**	South Carolina	**Rep.**	Republican
Maine	Maine	**S.D.**	South Dakota		
Md.	Maryland	**Tenn.**	Tennessee		
Mass.	Massachusetts	**Texas**	Texas		

A

Aaron, (Henry Louis) Hank (1934–) baseball player/executive; born in Mobile, Ala. Baseball's all-time homerun king, he played 23 years as an outfielder for the Milwaukee (later Atlanta) Braves and Milwaukee Brewers (1954–76). He holds many of baseball's most distinguished records, including most lifetime runs batted in (2,297), most years with 30 or more homeruns (15), and most career homeruns (755). Breaking the latter record, baseball's most venerable since Babe Ruth retired with 714 homeruns in 1935, was both a triumph and a trial for Aaron. He was beseiged by the media and badgered by racist letter-writers who resented Aaron breaking Ruth's record. A complete player whose skills were never fully appreciated until he broke the record in 1974, Aaron was voted the National League Most Valuable Player only once (1957). After retiring as a player, he moved into the Atlanta Braves front office as executive vice-president, where he has been a leading spokesperson for minority hiring in baseball. Nicknamed, "Hammerin' Henry," he was elected to baseball's Hall of Fame in 1982. His autobiography, *I Had a Hammer,* was published in 1990.

Abbe, Cleveland (1838–1916) meteorologist; born in New York City. He worked on the U.S. Coast and Geodetic Survey before apprenticing himself in 1864 at the Russian Pulkovo Observatory, home of the then largest refracting telescope in the world. On his return in 1866 he tried but failed to establish an observatory in New York City. In 1868 he became the director of the Cincinnati Observatory. While there, he implemented a daily weather bulletin for the Chamber of Commerce using telegraphed reports of storms. In 1871 he became scientific assistant to the Weather Bureau of the Signal Corps and continued forecasting until his death. In 1879 Abbe proposed establishing time zones based on the system used by the railroads; this was adopted in 1883 when the U.S.A. was divided into four zones. An author and editor of many publications on the weather, he is credited with setting high standards for the new science of meteorology.

Abbey, Edward (1927–89) author, conservationist; born in Home, Pa. Raised on a Pennsylvania farm, he moved permanently to the Southwest in 1947. He published his first book, the novel *Jonathan Troy,* in 1954. In *Desert Solitaire* (1968), an account of his years as a part-time ranger in the Arches National Monument, Utah, he called for, among other things, a ban on motor vehicles in wilderness preserves. *The Monkey Wrench Gang* (1976), a novel about a gang of ecological saboteurs, was a bestseller and made him a cult hero; although he disavowed such extremists who actually engaged in sabotage on behalf of ecological goals, he became increasingly quirky in his writings and public statements.

Abbey, Edwin Austin (1852–1911) painter, illustrator; born in Philadelphia. In 1872 he worked as an illustrator for *Harper's Magazine,* New York. He later painted murals in Boston (1895–1901) and at the Pennsylvania capitol (1908). Much of his life was spent in England, painting historical subjects.

Abbot, Francis (Ellingwood) (1836–1903) philosopher; born in Boston, Mass. Forced to resign as a Unitarian pastor because of his free-thinking views (1868), he devoted himself to aggressively promoting them: he was president of the National Liberal League (1876–78), editor of *The Index: A Journal of Free Religion* (1870–80), and author of such works as *Scientific Theism* (1885).

Abbott, Berenice (1898–1991) photographer; born in Springfield, Ohio. After a short time at Ohio State University (1917–18) and a few weeks at Columbia University in New York City (1918), she took up the study of drawing and sculpture in New York City (1918–21), Paris (1921–23 – partially under Antoine Bourdelle), and Berlin (1923). Back in Paris she became an assistant to the photographer, Man Ray (1923–25), and then opened her own portrait studio (1926–29); one of her best-known portraits was of James Joyce. Meanwhile, she had discovered the work of Eugene Atget (1857–1927), the French photographer known for his semidocumentary studies of cityscapes and activities in Paris and its suburbs; on his death she acquired his archives and thereafter promoted his work. She went back to New York City and worked as an independent documentary and portrait photographer (1929–68); she occasionally did commissions for *Fortune* and other magazines, but became best known for the series she did for the Federal Art Project (under the Works Progress Administration), a thorough and sensitive documentation of Manhattan during the 1930s, published as *Changing New York* (1939). In 1940 she turned to a new subject, capturing in photographs such scientific phenomena as magnetism, gravity, and motion; some of her work was used to illustrate high school physics texts. She also taught photography at the New School for Social Research (1935–68). Her final major projects included photographing a series on rural California and U.S. Route 1 from Maine to Florida. In 1968 she moved up to Maine where she worked until near her death.

Abbott, George (Francis) (1887–) playwright, director;

born in Forestville, N.Y. During his long and successful career, he often collaborated with other writers, beginning in 1925, with James Gleason on *The Fall Guy,* and later with Richard Rogers and Lorenz Hart. Among his successes were *Three Men on a Horse* (1935), *Where's Charley?* (1948), *Pajama Game* (1954), and *A Funny Thing Happened on the Way to the Forum* (1962). He worked into his 90s.

Abbott, Grace (1878–1939) social worker, activist; born on Grand Island, Nebr. She studied at the Universities of Nebraska and Chicago and in 1908 went to live at Chicago's Hull House to head the Immigrants' Protective League. Author of forceful articles exposing the exploitation of immigrants, she also campaigned for child labor laws, and as director of the federal Children's Bureau (from 1919), she administered grants to provide health care for mothers and children. She was president of the National Conference of Social Workers (1923–24), an adviser to the League of Nations (1922–34), and professor of public welfare at the University of Chicago (1934–39).

Abbott, Lyman (1835–1922) Congregational clergyman, editor; born in Roxbury, Mass. He graduated from New York University (1853) and joined a law firm before turning to the ministry and becoming ordained in 1860. Between 1860–65, he had a parish in Terre Haute, Ind. At the end of the Civil War, he went to New York City, where, in addition to serving a parish, he worked with the American Union Commission for more sympathetic reconstruction policies in the South. He became editor of a new periodical, *The Illustrated Christian Weekly* (1870–76), then joined Henry Ward Beecher at the *Christian Union;* Abbott replaced Beecher as editor in 1881 and the magazine's name was changed to *Outlook* in 1893. When Beecher died in 1890, Abbott took over his Brooklyn parish; he retired in 1899 to devote his final years to editing, writing, and guest preaching and speaking. He was noted for the intelligence, balance, and tolerance that he combined with traditional Christian teachings.

Abdul-Jabbar, Kareem (b. Ferdinand Lewis Alcindor) (1947–) basketball player; born in New York City. After leading the University of California: Los Angeles (UCLA) to three National Collegiate Athletic Association championships (1967–69), the 7'2" center played for the Milwaukee Bucks (1969–75) and Los Angeles Lakers (1975–89), where he was named the Most Valuable Player six times (1971–72, 1974, 1976–77, 1980) and established over 20 all-time records during his 20-year career. He scored the most career points of any player in history (38,387), scored the most playoff points (5,762), played the most games (1,560), and played the most years (20). He led the Bucks to one National Basketball Association title (1971) and the Lakers to five championships (1980, 1982, 1985, 1987–88).

Abel, John J. (Jacob) (1857–1938) biochemist, physiologist; born near Cleveland, Ohio. He studied at Johns Hopkins (1883–84) and in Europe (1884–91), taught at the University of Michigan (1891–93), then returned to Johns Hopkins as a professor of pharmacology (1893–1932), remaining active until his death. He founded several professional journals and made major advances in the fields of endocrinology, toxicology, and tetanus research. His experiments on dialysis of amino acids in blood through cellophane (1914) led to his proposal for construction of an artificial kidney. He is best known for first isolating and naming the adrenal hormone epinephrine (1897), and for his crystallization and analysis of insulin (1927).

Abernathy, Ralph D. (1926–90) Baptist clergyman, civil rights activist; born in Linden, Ala. An early civil rights organizer and leading confidante of Martin Luther King Jr., he was pastor of the West Hunter Street Baptist Church in Atlanta, Ga. throughout his civil rights career (1961–90). He was King's chosen successor as head of the Southern Christian Leadership Conference (SCLC) (1968–77). Although he was a competent leader, the SCLC never regained the influence it had under King. He resigned the SCLC leadership to run unsuccessfully for Andrew Young's congressional seat (1977). Turning away from the civil rights movement, he devoted his attention to the West Hunter Street Baptist Church and the issues of worldwide peace.

Abler, Ronald (Francis) (1939–) geographer; born in Milwaukee, Wis. He was a co-author of a major text on the spatial organization tradition in geography (1971) and editor of a comparative atlas of U.S. metropolitan regions (1976). He was director of the Geography and Regional Science Program at the National Science Foundation (1984–88) and in 1990 became executive director of the Association of American Geographers.

Abourezk, James (George) (1931–) U.S. representative/ senator; born in Wood, S.D. Lebanese-American, he grew up on an Indian reservation. He served in the U.S. Navy (1948–52) and was an engineer before becoming a lawyer in 1966. He was a member of the House of Representatives (Dem., S.D.; 1971–73) and the Senate (Dem., S.D.; 1973–79). He was a spokesman for the Arab cause and the chairman of the Senate's Select Committee on Indian Affairs. He founded the American-Arab Anti-Discrimination Committee in 1980 and worked to ensure fairer treatment of Arabs, particularly as they are portrayed in the media.

Abrams, Creighton W. (Williams), Jr. (1914–74) soldier; born in Springfield, Mass. The son of a railroad repairman, he graduated (1936) in the bottom third of his West Point class but became one of the boldest junior armored commanders of World War II. His tank unit played an important role in the relief of Bastogne, Belgium, during the Battle of the Bulge. In 1962, during racial unrest when James Meredith became the first black to enter the University of Mississippi, Abrams served as chief of staff of federal troops posted in Memphis, Tenn. Appointed to succeed William Westmoreland as U.S. commander in Vietnam in June 1968, he was effectively assigned to do little more than preside over the policy of "Vietnamization" that led to the gradual disengagement and eventual withdrawal of U.S. forces there.

Abrams, Floyd (1936–) lawyer; born in New York City. A graduate of Yale Law School, he was visiting lecturer there (1974–80) and at Columbia Law School (1981–86). At New York's Cahill Gordon & Reindel, he argued more First Amendment and media cases before the U.S. Supreme Court than any other lawyer in history.

Abrams, Meyer (Howard) (1912–) literary critic, educator; born in Long Branch, N.J. A major historical and humanistic critic, his work on the English Romantic poets include *The Mirror and the Lamp* (1953). He taught English literature at Cornell University (1945–83).

Abravanel, Maurice (1903–93) conductor; born in Saloniki, Greece. After conducting in Europe and at the Metropolitan Opera (1936–38), he began a brilliant tenure with the Utah

Symphony (1947–79), where he became known for performing works of American and other contemporary composers.

Abû Mâdî, Ilyâ (?1890–1957) poet; born in Lebanon. He moved to Egypt where he worked as a tobacconist, then emigrated to the U.S.A. (1911). He published several books, notably *Al-Jadawil,* ("*The Brooks*"), (1925). Largely self-taught, he set up a biweekly literary review, *al-Samir,* in New York City (1929). It became a daily in 1936 and he edited it until his death. He was known as a romantic poet, a poet of moods.

Abzug, Bella (b. Savitsky) (1920–) U.S. representative; born in New York City. She was a civil rights lawyer (1944–70) and director of Women Strike for Peace (1961–70) before going to Congress (1971–77). Well known for both her outspoken views and outsize hats, she was an unsuccessful senatorial and mayoral candidate.

Acheson, Dean (Gooderham) (1893–1971) diplomat, lawyer; born in Middletown, Conn. He was educated at Groton School and Yale, and received his law degree from Harvard in 1918. He served in the navy during World War I, then as private secretary to Supreme Court Justice Louis Brandeis (1919–21). After serving briefly as undersecretary of the treasury under Franklin D. Roosevelt (1933), he returned to private practice before becoming assistant secretary of state (1941–43) and a council member of the United Nations Relief and Rehabilitation Administration (UNRRA) (1943). As undersecretary of state (1945–47), he helped formulate America's Cold War "containment" policy vis-a-vis the Soviet Union and was closely involved in the creation of the Marshall Plan and the Truman Doctrine. As secretary of state (1947–53) he was instrumental in the creation of NATO, the rebuilding and rearming of Germany, formulation of atomic policy, and the non-recognition of Communist China. He advised Presidents Kennedy and Johnson and recommended withdrawal from Vietnam. His memoirs, *Present at the Creation* (1969), received a Pulitzer Prize (1970).

Acheson, Edward (Goodrich) (1856–1931) inventor, metallurgist, electrical engineer; born in Washington, Pa. With little formal schooling, he invented a rock-boring machine for coal mines and by 1880 was working in Thomas Edison's lab. In the late 1880s he helped install electrical plants in Europe. Back in America, he made several inventions (including electrical wire insulation), discovered Carborundum, and founded several companies that produced products he pioneered in developing for the electrothermal process – an electric furnace, artificial graphite, lubricants.

Ackerman, Bruce A. (Arnold) (1943–) legal scholar; born in New York City. He taught at the University of Pennsylvania (1969–74), Yale Law School (1974–82), and Columbia University (1982). Known for his liberal views, his work concentrated on social and legal philosophy, as well as constitutional and environmental law.

Ackerman, James S. (Sloss) (1919–) architectural historian; born in San Francisco. A Harvard professor (1960–90), he studied the intellectual and cultural context of Renaissance and Gothic architecture. He published *The Cortile del Belvedere* (1954) and books on Michelangelo (1961) and Palladio (1966, 1967).

Ackerman, Nathan W. (Ward) (1909–71) psychiatrist, family therapist, educator; born in Russia. Brought as a four-year-old to the U.S.A. (he became a citizen in 1920), he took his B.A. (1929) and M.D. (1933) at Columbia University. After serving a residency and on the staff of the Menninger Clinic in Topeka, Kans. (1935–37), he returned to New York City to become chief psychiatrist of the Jewish Board of Guardians (1937–51). In addition to various other teaching and staff posts in the field of psychiatry, he was a professor of psychiatry at Columbia's medical school (1957–71). He was the recipient of many honors and authored numerous articles and books, but he was most widely known and honored for pioneering "family therapy" – namely, the approach that treated individuals with mental illness in the context of their families. To this end he founded the Family Institute in 1960, now known as the Ackerman Family Therapy Institute, in New York City, a major clinical center as well as training ground for therapy that focuses on the psychodynamics of troubled families.

Ackoff, Russell L. (Lincoln) (1919–) systems theorist; born in Philadelphia. He taught at the University of Pennsylvania's Wharton School (1964–86), consulted to major corporations, and founded the Institute for Interactive Management (1986). His many publications on operations research and corporate and economic planning include *The Management of Change* (1970).

Acosta, (Bertram Blanchard) Bert (1895–1954) aviator, aeronautical engineer; born in San Diego, Calif. One of the best-known civil aviators in the 1920s, he helped establish the first transcontinental (North America) mail service (1920) and set a number of early speed and endurance records. He was a member of the crew of the *America* that made the sixth nonstop transatlantic flight (June 1927). Although he made one more brief bid for glory by flying for the Loyalists in the Spanish Civil War in 1936, he was frequently in trouble with the law and his own alcoholism, and he died penniless.

Acuff, (Claxton) Roy (1903–92) country music singer, fiddler, songwriter; born in Maynardville, Tenn. Forced by poor health to abandon a promising baseball career, he polished his skills as a singer and fiddler and began to play publicly in 1932. He performed on radio in the 1930s with the Tennessee Cracklers, then joined the "Grand Ole Opry" in 1938 with the Smoky Mountain Boys, becoming that radio program's first network broadcasting host. During World War II he was immensely popular and became known as "the King of Country Music." In the 1940s he appeared in several films and toured the United States. His unique moaning singing style influenced such musicians as Hank Williams. Among his most famous songs are "The Great Speckled Bird" and "Wabash Cannon Ball." Although his style of country music was somewhat pushed aside by the late 1950s, he continued to appear on "Grand Ole Opry"; he was a co-owner of Acuff-Rose, a music publishing company, and he remained active in Tennessee Republican politics.

Adair, James (c. 1709–c. 1783) pioneer, trader; born in County Antrim, Ireland. He came to South Carolina by 1735 and traded with the Catawba, Cherokee, and Choctaw Indians. In *In The History of the American Indians* (1775) he argued that the Indians were descended from the ancient Hebrew tribes.

Adair, (Paul Neal) "Red" (1915–) oil well problem specialist; born in Houston, Texas. He grew up in poverty, working in a drugstore and for the railroad. He worked for Myron Kinley (1939–59), putting out and capping oil well fires. In 1945, he dug up and disarmed unexploded shells in Japan. He established his worldwide reputation by extinguishing the Devil's Cigarette Lighter, a pillar of flame, fueled by 550 million cubic feet of gas a day, that had burned for six months in Algeria (1962). Fearless, he handled the Occidental Petroleum Company's platform disaster in the North Sea (1988) and extinguished oil well fires in Kuwait (1991).

Adamic, (Alojzij) Louis (?1899–1951) writer; born in Blato, Slovenia, Yugoslavia. He emigrated to America (1913), became a citizen (1918), and served in the United States Army in World War I. He lived in Milford, N.J., and wrote many articles, stories, and books based on his experiences in America and his former life in Yugoslavia, the best known being *The Native's Return: An American Immigrant Visits Yugoslavia and Discovers His Old Country* (1934). Although he supported Tito, he was opposed to Soviet Communism, and when he was found dead of a gunshot wound, there was inconclusive speculation as to whether he had committed suicide or been murdered by Soviet agents.

Adams, Abigail (b. Smith) (1744–1818) First Lady; born in Weymouth, Mass. A minister's daughter, she married John Adams in 1764, beginning a classic partnership that lasted for 54 years. She had no formal schooling but taught herself Latin and then educated her five children, one of whom, John Quincy Adams, became the sixth president. Adams was often away on government business and she ran the family farm in Quincy. She and Adams maintained a long correspondence during those years of separation; her letters displayed a political bent which exceeded that of most Revolutionary period women. She was not overly happy as first lady; she resented both the expense of entertaining and the lack of privacy. She and Adams resided in Philadelphia until 1800, when she supervised the move to Washington, D.C. Following the presidency, she continued her letter writing (Thomas Jefferson was one of her correspondents). She is the only woman to have been both the wife and the mother of U.S. presidents.

Adams, Alvin (1804–87) businessman; born in Andover, Vt. Orphaned as a child, he began working odd jobs at age 16. In 1840 in New York City he formed Adams & Company, an express package business between Boston and New York City. The company prospered, buying routes in New England (1841) and in the west and south as far as St. Louis (1842), eventually opening 35 offices in California (1849). In 1854 the Adams Express Company incorporated and expanded to Europe.

Adams, Ansel (Easton) (1902–84) photographer, conservationist; born in San Francisco. A commercial photographer for 30 years, he made visionary photos of western landscapes that were inspired by a boyhood trip to Yosemite. He won three Guggenheim grants to photograph the national parks (1944–58). Founding the f/64 group with Edward Weston in 1932, he developed zone exposure to get maximum tonal range from black-and-white film. He served on the Sierra Club Board (1934–71).

Adams, Brooks (1848–1927) historian, lawyer; born in Quincy, Mass. (grandson of President John Quincy Adams, son of Charles Francis Adams, brother of Henry Adams). After graduating from Harvard (1870), he served his father as secretary in Geneva and practiced law in Boston. His major historical work, *The Law of Civilization and Decay*

(1895), a cyclical view of history, influenced his brother Henry. He lectured on law at Boston University (1904–11).

Adams, Charles Francis (1807–86) diplomat; born in Boston, Mass. (son of John Quincy Adams, grandson of John Adams). He practiced law in Boston, wrote and edited family histories, and served in the Massachusetts legislature as a Whig. He was a member of the House of Representatives (Rep., Mass.; 1859–61). As ambassador to Great Britain (1861–68), he skillfully lobbied to keep Britain neutral during the Civil War. He declined the presidency of Harvard University, but served as one of the University's overseers.

Adams, Charles Kendall (1835–1902) university president, historian; born in Derby, Vt. As president of Cornell University (1885–92), he established new schools of law and history and political science and recruited a scholarly faculty. Known as a "building president," he greatly expanded enrollments and the campus of the University of Wisconsin as president there (1892–1901).

Adams, Diana (1926–93) ballet dancer; born in Stanton, Va. She studied with Edward Canton and Anthony Tudor and appeared in two Broadway musicals before she joined the Ballet Theatre in 1943. There she performed featured roles in several ballets. She joined the New York City Ballet in 1950 where she created numerous roles until her retirement in the mid-1960s.

Adams, Franklin P. (Pierce) (1881–1960) journalist; born in Chicago. A New York based columnist for four decades through 1941, Adams was better known under the byline "F.P.A." He had top writers vying to contribute to his "Conning Tower" where he also supplied his own crisp, humorous verse and wide-ranging commentary; on a regular basis he substituted a diary of his doings on the New York literary scene, in a style parodying 18th-century English diarist Samuel Pepys. He was a panelist on the popular radio show *Information Please* (1938–48) and he is also remembered for his 1910 verse, "Tinker to Evers to Chance."

Adams, Hannah (1755–1831) compiler of historical data; born in Medford, Mass. Privately educated and in frail health from childhood, she was encouraged by a boarder in her family home to research comparative religions. Her *Alphabetical Compendium of the Various Sects* (1784) was well received and went into several editions in the United States and England. Her other compilations include *A Summary History of New England* (1799), *History of the Jews* (1812), and *Letters of the Gospels* (1824). She is remembered as the first American woman to support herself by writing.

Adams, Henry (Brooks) (1838–1918) historian; born in Boston, Mass. (grandson of President John Quincy Adams, son of Charles Francis Adams, brother of Brooks Adams). After graduating from Harvard and studying law in Germany, he served as secretary to his father during the latter's term as ambassador to England (1861–68). On returning to the U.S.A. he went to Washington, D.C., but, disillusioned by the new government, he turned to teaching both medieval and American history at Harvard (1870–77) (where he is credited with introducing the seminar system into U.S. education). He left teaching and returned to Washington, D.C., where although he had a small circle of elite friends, he remained out of step with the new nation; he expressed this in his novel *Democracy* (1880). He continued to publish biographies and a nine-volume *History of the United States of*

America from 1801 to 1817 (1889–91). After the death of his wife, Marian Hooper (1885), he traveled to many parts of the world but he always returned to Washington. He privately published *Mont-Saint-Michel and Chartres* (1904) and *The Education of Henry Adams* (1907), but their success led to trade editions (1913 and 1918, respectively); the latter, now regarded as an idiosyncratic American classic, was his detached view of his problematic relationship with his times, and he did not have to deal with the irony of its receiving a posthumous Pulitzer Prize (1919).

Adams, Henry Cullen (1850–1906) U.S. representative; born in Oneida County, N.Y. A dairy farmer in Wisconsin, he was Dairy and Food Commissioner of Wisconsin (1895–1902) and a Democratic congressman (1903–06). He championed the National Food and Drugs Act and Meat Inspection Laws.

Adams, Herbert Baxter (1850–1901) historian, educator; born in Shutesbury, Mass. Educated at Amherst College and Heidelberg, Germany, he joined the faculty of Johns Hopkins University at its inception (1876) and played a major role in the professionalization of American history. His *Johns Hopkins Studies in Historical and Political Science* series (1877) set standards throughout the country. He was one of the founders of the American Historial Society (1884) and was its secretary until 1900.

Adams, Herbert Samuel (1858–1945) sculptor; born in West Concord, Vt. He studied in Paris (1885–90), taught at the Pratt Institute, Brooklyn, (1890–98), and settled in New York City and Plainfield, N.H. He is noted for his marble and polychrome sculptures and for the bronze doors of St. Bartholomew's Church, New York City (1902).

Adams, John (1735–1826) second U.S. president; born in Braintree (now Quincy), Mass. He studied at Harvard and settled into law practice in Boston. Although he defended British soldiers after the Boston Massacre (1770), he had also shown "patriot" sympathies by pamphleteering against the Stamp Act in 1765. Having gained prominence as a political thinker and writer, he was sent as a Massachusetts delegate to the First (1774) and Second (1775–77) Continental Congresses; he helped edit Jefferson's Declaration of Independence and led the debate that ratified it (1776). During the American Revolution he chaired several committees and served on many more, was commissioner to France and Holland, and in 1779 drafted the influential Massachusetts constitution. After the war he was ambassador to England (1785–88), where he wrote the *Defense of the Constitution of the United States*. After eight frustrating years as vice-president under Washington (1789–97), he assumed the presidency (1797–1801). The prickly Adams proved less able as a practical politician than as a theorist; his regime was torn by partisan wrangles between Hamiltonian Federalists and Jeffersonian Democrat-Republicans, all of whom he antagonized; his persistence in negotiating peace with France when his fellow Federalists were urging war cost him their support. Meanwhile his Alien and Sedition Acts (1798), which virtually forbade criticism of the government, outraged many citizens. Defeated for reelection by Jefferson in 1800, Adams retired from public life. In later years he pursued an extensive correspondence with many men, including his one-time opponent Thomas Jefferson, and both men died on July 4, 1826, the 50th anniversary of the signing of the Declaration of Independence.

Adams, John (Coolidge) (1947–) composer; born in Worcester, Mass. Harvard-trained, he taught at San Francisco Conservatory during the 1970s. His music, notably the opera *Nixon in China* (1987), is of the "minimalist" school, stressing relentless repetition.

Adams, John Quincy (1767–1848) sixth U.S. president; born in Braintree (later Quincy), Mass. (son of John Adams). Reared for public service, he traveled in childhood on his father's diplomatic missions and at age 14 was private secretary to the American envoy at St. Petersburg. In 1787 he graduated from Harvard and was admitted to the bar in 1790. Successively ambassador to the Netherlands, Great Britain, Portugal, and Berlin, he was elected as a Massachusetts Federalist to the U.S. Senate (1803); in 1806, however, his support of Jefferson outraged New England Federalists and he lost his seat in 1808. In 1809 he was ambassador to Russia; in 1814, a member of the commission to negotiate peace with Great Britain; and from 1815 to 1817, ambassador to Great Britain. As a brilliant secretary of state under President Monroe (1817–25), Adams negotiated with Spain the treaty for the acquisition of Florida and wrote a good deal of the "Monroe Doctrine" (1823). In 1824 he won the presidential election over Andrew Jackson, but only after a close vote in the House of Representatives. Cold in manner and too independent to command a following, he was an ineffective president and lost to Jackson in 1828. In 1831 he entered the U.S. House of Representatives where for the rest of his life he was a champion of the antislavery faction. In 1841 he successfully defended the African mutineers of the slave ship *Amistad*. He suffered a stroke while sitting in the House and died two days later.

Adams, Leason Heberling (1887–1969) geophysicist; born in Cherryvale, Kans. In 1920, he and E. D. Williamson published their invention of a new method of annealing optical glass; Adams gained further reknown for his research in the elastic properties of minerals and rocks at high pressure, especially as related to the composition of the earth. He served as professor of geophysics at the University of California: Los Angeles from 1958 until his retirement in 1965.

Adams, Louisa (Catherine b. Johnson) (1775–1852) First Lady; born in London, England (mother of Charles Francis Adams, grandmother of Henry Adams). Daughter of a Maryland merchant and English mother, she met the young John Quincy Adams in London in 1795 when her father was the first U.S. consul; they were married in 1797. Renowned for her beauty, and accustomed to a more elegant life than were the Adams clan, she stayed by her husband as he pursued his career of public service in Europe and Washington but she often suffered from both physical illness and mental depression. In 1840 she began a memoir, *The Adventures of a Nobody,* but her many letters provide the most revealing glimpse of her world.

Adams, Marian Hooper ("Clover") (1843–85) hostess, photographer; born in Boston, Mass. Her mother died when she was five and she would remain extremely close to her wealthy physician father. Privately educated in Cambridge, Mass., she volunteered for the Sanitary Commission during the Civil War, then traveled abroad (1866), where she met young Henry Adams in London. Back in Cambridge, she and Henry married in 1872, and their home in Boston soon became an intellectuals salon. In 1877 she and Henry moved to Washington, D.C., and now their home on Lafayette Square, across from the White House, again became the gathering place for a lively circle of intellectuals, politicians, and all who aspired to be among the elite. (Her gossipy letters to her father provide a superb view of the Washington of the day.) She had by this time taken up photography and did her own developing. She and Henry were planning a new home on Lafayette Square when her father died in 1885; profoundly depressed, she took her own life with a developing chemical. Henry Adams commissioned Augustus Saint-Gaudens to sculpt the brooding figure that marks her (and his) burial place in Rock Creek Cemetery in Washington.

Adams, Maude (b. Maude Kiskadden) (1872–1953) stage actress; born in Salt Lake City, Utah. She was the daughter of the leading lady of Salt Lake City's stock company. One of the most popular actresses of her day, Adams was best known for her 1905 role as Peter Pan in the J. M. Barrie play. Barrie then cast her in several more of his plays. Graceful and elfin on stage, she was also known among her colleagues as a generous and principled professional.

Adams, Robert McC. (McCormick) (1926–) anthropologist; born in Chicago. He taught at the University of Chicago's Oriental Institute (1955–84) before becoming secretary of the Smithsonian Institution (1984). He studied the history of land use and urban settlement in ancient Babylonia, Iraq, and Mexico; his books include *The Evolution of Urban Society* (1966) and *Heartland of Cities* (1981).

Adams, Roger (1889–1971) chemist; born in Boston, Mass. After completing his graduate studies in Germany, he joined the faculty of the University of Illinois (1916–50s). He was influential in changing the emphasis of chemistry education in the U.S.A. from pure research toward a meshing of academic and industrial needs; the University of Illinois became particularly noted for providing chemists for industry. He is also regarded as one of the founders of the modern field of organic chemistry.

Adams, Samuel (1722–1803), politician, Revolutionary leader; born in Boston, Mass. (second cousin of John Adams). After studying law, he failed at several business enterprises, then devoted himself to politics. One of the first and most outspoken colonists to oppose British laws and policies, in the Massachusetts legislature (1765–74) he promoted corresponding with other colonies' leaders, wrote newspaper articles criticizing British rule, and composed and circulated a declaration of colonists' rights. He helped organize the Boston Tea Party (1773) and by 1774 was advocating open resistance to Britain. He served in the First and Second Continental Congress and signed the Declaration of Independence. At first he backed George Washington as commander-in-chief, but he criticized what he thought was an overly cautious pursuit of the war. Regarded as too radical by many, he resigned from Congress in 1781 but supported the Federal Constitution of 1787. He was governor of Massachusetts (1794–97).

Adams, Sherman (1899–1986) governor, government official; born in East Dover, Vt. A lumber company executive and New Hampshire Republican legislator (1941–44), he served New Hampshire in the U.S. House of Representatives (1945–47). As governor (1949–53), he streamlined government and encouraged business development. As President Eisenhower's domineering chief of staff (1953–58), he resigned under pressure after accepting expensive gifts from businessmen. He later developed a ski resort.

Adams, Walter (Sydney) (1876–1956) astronomer; born in Antioch, Syria. Born to American missionary parents, he studied at Dartmouth College and then worked under George Hale at Yerkes Observatory at the University of Chicago (1900–04). He accompanied Hale to California and helped set up the Mt. Wilson Observatory, becoming its director on Hale's retirement (1923–46); after that he helped design the 200-inch telescope for Mt. Palomar Observatory in California. His own contributions came about from his mastery of mathematics and spectroscopy; his method of spectroscopic parallaxes allowed the determination of stellar luminosities and the distance between stars.

Addams, Jane (1860–1935) social reformer, pacifist; born in Cedarville, Ill. Raised in comfort by her widowed father, a state senator and abolitionist (he was a friend of Abraham Lincoln), she studied at the Women's Medical College of Pennsylvania for a few months before spinal illness and a realization that she was not cut out to be a doctor led her to withdraw (1882). Disturbed by urban poverty and searching for meaningful work, she visited Toynbee Hall, a pioneering settlement house in London, which inspired her, with Ellen Starr, to found Hull House, a settlement house in Chicago (1889). She lived and worked out of Hull House for the rest of her life, developing educational, cultural, and medical programs for the community, while lobbying for improved housing, fair labor practices, and just treatment for immigrants and the poor. Hull House also had great influence beyond Chicago by both inspiring similar institutions in American cities and by training many individuals who became notable reformers. Addams herself was so far in advance of many Americans on social issues in her day that she was attacked by some as a subversive. A staunch supporter of women's suffrage, she served as vice-president of the National American Suffrage Alliance (1911–14). An unwavering pacifist, she was president of the Women's International League for Peace and Freedom (1919–35) and shared the Nobel Prize for Peace (1931). She lectured and published widely; her many books include *Twenty Years at Hull-House* (1910) and *Peace and Bread in Time of War* (1922).

Adderley, (Julian) "Cannonball" (1928–75) jazz musician; born in Fort Lauderdale, Fla. He was an alto saxophonist, a sideman with Miles Davis in 1958–59, and the leader of his own soulful, hard-bop bands thereafter.

Addington, Maybelle See under CARTER FAMILY.

Ade, George (1866–1944) journalist, writer, playwright; born in Kentland, Ind. He was a Chicago newspaperman (1890–1900) whose collected columns, *Fables in Slang* (1899), became a classic of midwestern vernacular satire. He continued to publish more collections of his "fables," and between 1900–10 he wrote a dozen popular Broadway plays and musicals. Collections of his trademark fables, such as *People You Know* (1903) and *Hand-Made Fables* (1920), are the most durable of his voluminous writings. He lived in Indiana after 1904 but traveled widely.

Adelman, Irma (b. Glicman) (1930–) economist; born in Rumania. All her degrees (B.S., M.A., Ph.D.) were from the University of California where she also accepted a professorship (1979). She is best known for developing a system of "factor analysis," integrating social, political, and economic factors to explain economic growth in developing countries.

Adler, Cyrus (1863–1940) educator; born in Van Buren, Ark. A graduate of the University of Pennsylvania, he was named librarian of the Smithsonian Institution in 1892. In 1908 he became president of the new Dropsie College for Hebrew and Cognate Learning, Philadelphia, and in 1924 president of the Jewish Theological Seminary, New York. He edited the *Jewish Quarterly Review* (1910–40). He was a founder (1929) and later president of the American Jewish Committee.

Adler, Dankmar (1844–1900) architect; born in Langsfeld, Germany. A childhood immigrant to America, he trained in Chicago and Detroit, Mich. Adler was the engineering and structural expert in his partnership with Louis Sullivan (1882–95); famous for their midwestern skyscrapers, the pair completed 120 buildings, including the Guaranty Building, Buffalo, N.Y. (1894–95). Adler was largely responsible for the nation's first registration act for architects being passed in Illinois in 1897.

Adler, Elmer (1884–1962) printer; born in Rochester, N.Y. A collector of books and fine prints, he founded Pynson Printers in 1922 to produce works of high graphic quality, and in 1930 founded *Colophon: A Book Collector's Quarterly.* After closing Pynson in 1940, he moved his collection to Princeton University, where he established a department of graphic arts and was a professor and curator.

Adler, (Lawrence) Larry (1914–) harmonica player; born in Baltimore, Md. The world's leading classical harmonica virtuoso, he began concertizing in his teens and commissioned many works for the instrument. He emigrated to Britain after being blacklisted during the 1950s Red Scare and continued his career there as a respected musician.

Adler, Mortimer J. (Jerome) (1902–) philosopher, writer; born in New York City. He taught at the University of Chicago (1930–52), where he helped design the Great Books program (1946), and directed the Institute for Philosophical Research (1952). Adler popularized the great ideas of Western civilization in such works as *Great Books of the Western World,* 54 vols. (1954, revised 1990), *How to Read a Book* (1940, revised 1972) and *Six Great Ideas* (1981).

Adler, (Pearl) Polly (1900–62) madam; born in Avanovo, Russia. Emigrating at age 12, she worked in factories, and in 1920 opened a house of prostitution in New York City. Her clients included politicians, gangsters, and vice squad police, and this was said to be the reason she survived so long. Subpoenaed by the Seabury Commission in 1930, she refused to testify. She closed down in 1943 and moved to Los Angeles. She later graduated from college and wrote *A House is Not a Home* (1953).

Adler, Richard (1921–) composer, lyricist; born in New York City. The son of teacher-pianist Clarence Adler, he attended the University of North Carolina and served in the U.S. Navy before concentrating on composing. He collaborated with lyricist Jerry Ross on the award-winning musicals *The Pajama Game* (1954) and *Damn Yankees* (1955). After Ross's death in 1955, Adler's stage works of the 1960s and 1970s never caught on but he began to write concert music. His symphonic suite *The Lady Remembers* was performed in 1985 in Washington, D.C., honoring the centenary of the Statue of Liberty. Throughout his career he was also successful at composing musical commercials.

Adler, Samuel (1809–91) rabbi; born in Worms, Germany.

He was educated, ordained, and served as a rabbi in Germany (1842–57). In 1857 he came to New York to become rabbi of Temple Emanu-El. He wrote numerous monographs and played a leading role in Reform Judaism; his revision of the prayer book became a model for later Reform prayer books.

Adler, Stephen L. (Louis) (1939–) physicist; born in New York City. He was a fellow at Harvard (1964–66), taught theoretical physics at Princeton (1966–79), then became Albert Einstein Professor at the Institute for Advanced Study in Princeton, N.J., (1979). He has made major contributions to quantum field theory and effective action models for quark confinement.

Adrian (Gilbert) (b. Adrian Adolph Greenburg) (1903–59) fashion designer; born in Naugatuck, Conn. Discovered as a student in Paris by Irving Berlin, he designed costumes for countless Broadway shows and Hollywood films (1920s–1930s). Under his own Beverly Hills label (1941–53), he designed women's couture and quality ready-to-wear; his trademarks included padded shoulders and dolman sleeves.

Agassiz, Alexander (Emmanuel Rodolphe) (1835–1910) oceanographer; born in Neuchâtel, Switzerland. He came to the U.S.A. (1849) to join his father, the naturalist Jean Louis Agassiz. He graduated from Harvard with degrees in engineering (1857) and zoology (1862), then amassed a fortune in the copper mines of Lake Superior (1866–69). He was curator of Harvard's Museum of Comparative Zoology (1873–85), founded by his father. He made numerous oceanographic zoological expeditions, wrote many books, and examined thousands of coral reefs to refute Darwin's ideas on atoll formation.

Agassiz, (Jean) Louis (Rodolphe) (1807–73) geologist; born in Motier-en-Vuly, Switzerland. He received an M.D. in Erlangen, Germany (1830), but preferred his early interest in natural science. He became professor of natural history at Neuchâtel, Switzerland (1832), and combined ichthyology, geology, and paleontology in his five-volume classic, *Récherches sur les Poissons Fossiles* (1833–44). His studies of Alpine glaciers and glacial boulders led to his monumental works, *Études sur les Glaciers* (1840) and *Système Glaciaire* (1847), which demonstrated the existence of a geologically recent ice age. In 1846 Agassiz came to the U.S.A. on a lecture tour, and was appointed professor of natural history at Harvard (1847–73). He founded Harvard's Museum of Comparative Zoology in 1859. With his second wife, Elizabeth Cabot Cary (1822–1907), he conducted a young ladies school in Cambridge; a naturalist and educator herself, she later became president of the Society for Collegiate Instruction of Women and its successor, Radcliffe College (1894). A popular lecturer who opposed Darwin's theories on religious grounds, Agassiz continued to teach, publish, and make zoological expeditions until his death.

Agee, James (Rufus) (1909–55) writer, poet; born in Knoxville, Tenn. He attended St. Andrews School, Tenn., (1914–24), Phillips Exeter (1925–28), and Harvard (1928–32). Based in New York City, he worked for several periodicals, and is known for his study of tenant farmers in Alabama, *Let Us Now Praise Famous Men* (1941), co-authored with the photographer Walker Evans. He is also known for poetry, film scripts, such as *The African Queen* (1952), and his novels, notably *A Death in the Family* (1957).

Agnew, Spiro T. (Theodore) (1918–) vice-president, governor. In his one year as governor of Maryland (1967–68) he enacted liberal policies, but after he assumed the vice-presidency in 1969 he became the Nixon administration's "hard-line" spokesman. In 1973, charged with accepting secret payments while governor of Maryland, he was allowed to plead "no contest" to tax evasion and resigned the vice-presidency.

Aguinaldo, Emilio (1870–1964) Filipino revolutionary. He led the uprising against Spain (1896–98) and later the U.S.A. (1899–1901); captured in 1901, he took an oath of allegiance to the U.S.A. and retired from politics.

Aiken, Conrad (Potter) (Samuel Jeake, Jr., pen name) (1889–1973) poet, writer; born in Savannah, Ga. He was raised in Cambridge, Mass., attended Harvard (B.A. 1907–12), lived in England for various periods, and settled in Brewster, Mass. (1940). He wrote for leading periodicals, and was noted for his rather difficult poetry, such as *The Preludes for Memmon* (1931), and for his demanding novels and short stories.

Aiken, Howard (Hathaway) (1900–73) computer engineer, mathematician; born in Hoboken, N.J. He was educated at the Universities of Wisconsin and Chicago before joining the faculty of Harvard, where he spent most of his professional career (1939–61). With his colleagues at Harvard – and with some assistance from International Business Machines – by 1944 he had built the Mark I, the world's first program-controlled calculator; an early form of a digital computer, it was controlled by both mechanical and electrical devices. Although he went on to build the Mark II (1947) and other computers, they would soon be made obsolete by more advanced electronics. On retiring from Harvard he taught at the University of Miami (1961–73).

Ailey, Alvin (1931–90) choreographer, modern dancer, director; born in Rogers, Texas. He studied with Lester Horton, made his debut with the company in 1950, and became director in 1953. A noted Broadway dancer and choreographer, he formed the Alvin Ailey American Dance Theatre in 1958 and founded a school (1971) and junior troupe (1972). His works, influenced by classical ballet, jazz, Afro-Caribbean, and modern dance, explore a wide range of black experience, from gospel music to social inequality.

Akeley, Carl (Ethan) (1864–1926) **and Mary Lee (b. Jobe)** (1878–1966) naturalists, explorers; Carl born in Clarendon, N.Y.; Mary Lee born in Tappan, Ohio. He worked as a taxidermist in Rochester, N.Y., and then at the Milwaukee Museum. By the time he joined the staff at the Field Museum of Natural History in Chicago (1895), he was perfecting new techniques for making large habitat groups of wild animals – sculpting realistic forms on which real skins, horns, and other bodily parts were placed. He made five trips to Africa (1896, 1905, 1909, 1926) and invented a special motion-picture camera for naturalists to study wildlife (1916). He died in Africa, two years after he married Mary Lee Jobe, his second wife. She had explored in the Canadian Rockies (1913–18) and she continued his African expedition (1926–27). She returned to Africa in 1935 and 1946 and collected further materials for the American Museum of Natural History, New York City. She won international recognition for her work in informing the world of the importance of maintaining primitive and natural life in Africa.

Akeley, Mary Lee See under AKELEY, CARL (ETHAN).

al-Amin, Jamil Abdullah (originally H. Rap Brown) (1943–   ) political activist, author; born in Baton Rouge, La. As chairman of the Student Nonviolent Coordinating Committee (SNCC), he emerged with Stokely Carmichael (1966) as an advocate of black power. He was charged with inciting a riot in Cambridge, Md. (1968), and was convicted in New Orleans on a federal charge of carrying a gun between states. During this period he wrote *Die Nigger Die* (1969). He disappeared (1970) before going to trial in Maryland and was shot (1972) while holding up a saloon in New York City. He was arrested, convicted for the incident, and imprisoned (1974). During his sentence he converted to the Islamic faith and took the name Jamil Abdullah al-Amin. On his release he opened a grocery store in Atlanta. He was a writer/lecturer for *Dial Press* and leader of the Community Mosque, Atlanta.

Albee, Edward (Franklin III) (1928–   ) playwright; born in Washington, D.C. Adopted as an infant by the son of the founder of the Keith-Albee vaudeville circuit, Albee spent two years at college before quitting to work at odd jobs while he wrote plays. *Zoo Story* (1958) and *The Death of Bessie Smith* (1959) gained him considerable reputation. Albee's unhappy families and vision of tangled sexuality are best known to theater and movie audiences through his *Who's Afraid of Virginia Woolf?*, which opened in New York in 1962 and later became a film. Although he won Pulitzer Prizes for *A Delicate Balance* in 1966 and for *Seascape* in 1975, his critical and popular reputation never rose to fulfill its early promise.

Albee, Fred (Houdlette) (1876–1945) orthopedic surgeon; born in Alna, Maine. Starting in 1906 in New York, he pioneered the techniques of bone grafting. By 1911, he had perfected techniques for fusing tubercular vertebrae without using metal. He invented machine tools for his operations (1912). His techniques found widespread use during World War I. After the war, he turned his attention to victims of industrial accidents in New York and New Jersey.

Albers, Anni (1899–   ) weaver; born in Berlin, Germany. She studied her craft at the Bauhaus (1922–29), where she married painter Josef Albers, and where she later taught (1930–33). Their 1933 move to the U.S.A. brought her as a professor to Black Mountain College (1933–49) and later to a career as independent artisan in New Haven, Conn. One of the most influential weavers of her time, she advanced a theoretical approach to textile design through her teachings and writings.

Albers, Josef (1888–1976) painter; born in Bottrop, Germany. In 1933, fleeing from Nazism, he emigrated to America to continue his teaching career at Black Mountain College, North Carolina (1933–49), and at Yale University (1950–60). A series of paintings, *Homage to the Square,* reveals his fascination with color relationships. He was influential in introducing the Bauhaus art school concepts from Germany, which stressed craftsmanship and a functional approach to design.

Albert, Abraham Adrian (1905–72) mathematician; born in Chicago. Known primarily for his work with associative and nonassociative algebras and Riemann matrices, this National Academy of Science member chaired the University of Chicago Mathematics Department (1958–62), fought for government funding of math (1950s–60s), and was vice-president of the International Mathematical Union (1971).

Albert, Carl (Bert) (1908–   ) U.S. representative; born in

North McAlester, Okla. Born in a miner's shack, he picked cotton before going to the University of Oklahoma, where he became a champion debater and wrestler who won a Rhodes scholarship to study law at Oxford University. A lawyer in Oklahoma, he worked for the Federal Housing Authority and the Ohio Oil Company before joining the army in 1941. Returning from the Pacific with a Bronze star, he went to the U.S. House of Representatives (Dem., Okla.; 1947–77) where he became majority whip in 1955 and majority leader in 1962. He created an alliance between northern liberals and southern "boll weevils" to insure passage of President Johnson's Great Society legislation. In 1968, he presided over the disastrous Democratic convention, ruling against the delegates opposed to the war in Vietnam. Succeeding John McCormack as Speaker in 1971, he finally voted against the war in 1973. Faced with Democratic opposition and widespread rumors about his drinking, he retired to McAlester in 1977.

Albizu Campos, Pedro (1891–1964) revolutionary; born in Ponce, Puerto Rico. Educated at Harvard (B.S. 1916, LL.B. 1923), he joined the Nationalist Party in 1924 and was the most prominent *independentista* of his time. He was jailed from 1936–47 for advocating the violent overthrow of the U.S. administration of Puerto Rico. He masterminded a 1950 nationalist uprising in Puerto Rico and was accused of being behind the October 31, 1950, assassination attempt on President Truman at Blair House. After he was sentenced to prison for 53 years, Governor Luis Muñoz Marín offered him a conditional pardon in 1953, but withdrew it after the nationalist attack on the U.S. House of Representatives the next year. Campos spent his final years in prison.

Albright, Horace Marden (1890–1987) conservationist, business executive; born in Bishop, Calif. The son of a millwright, he obtained a law degree from the University of California and was admitted to the bar in 1914. In 1916, as an official of the U.S. Department of the Interior, he helped found the National Park Service. He served as superintendent of Yellowstone National Park from 1919–29 and in 1929 became the second director of the park service. He resigned in 1933 to start a second career in business, as vice-president and general manager of the United States Potash Co. He rose to president of the company in 1946.

Albright, Ivan (Le Lorraine) (1897–1983) painter; born in North Harvey, Ill. He studied at the Art Institute of Chicago (1920–23) and lived in various places until settling in Woodstock, Vt. A former medical draftsman, he drew on this background, both in his preoccupation with decay and in his paintings' macabre surrealistic details – as in *That Which I Should Have Done I Did Not Do* (1931–32). He gained his widest exposure from the painting that was the centerpiece of the movie, *The Picture of Dorian Gray* (1945).

Albright, William Foxwell (1891–1971) archaeologist, biblical scholar; born in Coquimbo, Chile. Son of missionaries, he came to the U.S.A. at age 12. He directed the American School of Oriental Research, Jerusalem (1920–29, 1933–36), and taught at Johns Hopkins (1929–58). An authority on biblical languages and commentator on the Dead Sea scrolls, he brought archaeology and linguistics to bear on biblical studies, identified numerous biblical villages during many Middle Eastern expeditions, and authored 800 publications.

Alcott, (Amos) Bronson (1799–1888) educator, mystic, author; born near Wolcott, Conn. (father of Louisa May Alcott). Largely self-educated, he became an itinerant teacher (1823–33) before settling in Boston to found his own school (1834). By this time he was a mystic and transcendentalist and his radical ideas of educating children – plus his acceptance of a black girl as a pupil – led to the failure of his school (1839). He settled in Concord, Mass., but after an 1842 trip to England, where a school (Alcott House) based on his theories had been set up, he returned to establish a utopian community, Fruitlands, outside Boston (1844). Devoted to vegetarianism as well as to high thinking, the community failed within 8 months. He took his family back to Concord, and although he had to move about to teach and lecture, he spent most of the rest of his life there, the center of the transcendentalists. He was appointed superintendent of schools in Concord (1857) and he is credited with several innovations including the first parent-teacher association. The success of Louisa May Alcott's *Little Women* (1868) gave the family financial security and allowed him to set up his Concord Summer School of Philosophy and Literature (1879). He wrote poetry, several books on his theories of education, a biography of Ralph Waldo Emerson, and an autobiography, but his greatest impact seems to have come through his personal presence and conversation.

Alcott, Louisa May (1832–88) writer; born in Germantown, Pa. She was tutored by her father, Amos Bronson Alcott, until 1848, and studied informally with family friends such as Henry David Thoreau, Ralph Waldo Emerson, and Theodore Parker. Residing in Boston and Concord, Mass., she worked as a domestic servant, a teacher, and at other jobs to help support her family (1850–62); during the Civil War she went to Washington, D.C., to serve as a nurse. Unbeknown to most people, she had been publishing poems, short stories, thrillers, and juvenile tales since 1851, under the pen name of "Flora Fairfield"; in 1862 she also adopted the pen name "A. M. Barnard"; some of her melodramas were actually produced in Boston stages. But it was her account of her Civil War experiences, *Hospital Sketches* (1863), that confirmed her desire to be a serious writer. She began to publish stories under her real name in *Atlantic Monthly* and *Lady's Companion* and took a brief trip to Europe in 1865 before becoming editor of a girls' magazine, *Merry's Museum*, in 1868. The great success of *Little Women* (1869–70) gave her financial independence and also created a demand for more writings. For the rest of her life she turned out a steady stream of novels and short stories, most for young people, and, like *Little Women,* drawing fairly directly on her family life: *Little Men* (1871), *Eight Cousins* (1875), *Jo's Boys* (1886). She also tried her hand at adult novels – *Work* (1873), *A Modern Mephistopheles* (1877) – but did not have the literary talent to attract serious readers. Like so many women of her day and class, she supported women's suffrage and temperance; but she never found much happiness in her personal life. She grew impatient with the demands made on her as a successful writer, she became the caretaker of her always impractical father, and she became increasingly beset by physical ailments that led to a succession of remedies and healers. Sickly and lonely, she died at age 55 on the day of her father's funeral.

Alda, Alan (1936–) television/movie actor; born in New York City. Developing his satirical style with Second City in New York City, he starred as Hawkeye Pierce in the comedy series M*A*S*H (1972–83), winning four Emmies. He has acted occasionally in films, including *Crimes and Misdemean-*

ors (1989), and in 1992 he appeared on Broadway in *Jake's Women*. He has been an outspoken liberal on many social issues, serving, for example, as the cochair of the campaign to pass the Equal Rights Amendment (1982).

Alden, John (c. 1599–1687) Pilgrim; born in England. He was a cooper aboard the *Mayflower* and signed the Mayflower Compact. Although he did marry Priscilla Mullens, there is no basis for the story told in Henry Wadsworth Longfellow's *The Courtship of Miles Standish*. He held several important posts within the Duxbury colony, where he had moved to from nearby Plymouth c. 1627.

Aldredge, Theoni V. (b. Theoni Athanasiou Vachlioti) (1932–) costume designer; born in Salonika, Greece. After attending the American School in Athens, she came to work at the Goodman Memorial Theatre in Chicago in 1949 (where she met her husband, the actor Tom Aldredge) and since her first costume designs there in 1950 she has done the costumes for countless productions, mostly for the New York and London stage but also for some movies and operas.

Aldrich, Larry (b. Orlevitch) (1905–) businessman, art collector; born in New York City. After graduation from high school he made a fortune in the garment industry in New York City. Encouraged by Alfred Barr, director of the Museum of Modern Art, he donated funds to several museums for the work of artists who were then unknown. He acquired and then bestowed his collection of contemporary art in order to fund a series of exhibitions in the museum he founded (1964), the Larry Aldrich Museum of Contemporary Art, Ridgefield, Conn.

Aldrich, Nelson (Wilmarth) (1841–1915) U.S. representative/senator; born in Foster, R.I. After prospering in the wholesale grocery business, he was elected from Rhode Island as a Republican to the U.S. House of Representatives (1879–81) and to the U.S. Senate (1881–1911). A friend of business interests and the high protective tariff, he became a major power in the Republican controlled Senate after 1897; he was known for the Aldrich-Vreeland Act for monetary reform (1908), the Payne-Aldrich Tariff (1909), and the Aldrich Plan for reforming the American banking system. His own investments allowed him to leave a large fortune to his heirs and favored philanthropies.

Aldrich, Thomas Bailey (1836–1907) writer, poet; born in Portsmouth, N.H. He worked in New York City mainly in publishing (1852–65), published poetry, settled in Boston (1865), and was editor of the *Atlantic Monthly* (1881–90). He remains best known for his novel, *The Story of a Bad Boy* (1870).

Aldridge, Ira (Frederick) (1807–67) stage actor; probably born in New York City. He got his start in his teens with the African Theatre, established by William Henry Brown in New York City in 1821 to present all-black casts in a variety of plays. In 1824 Aldridge went to England, where for the next 25 years he became widely known throughout Britain and Ireland. In 1833 he replaced the mortally ill Edmund Kean as Othello at London's Covent Garden Theatre (to mixed reviews). He played both comedy and tragedy and is credited with introducing psychological realism in acting in the 1850s, before his European counterparts. In 1852 he began a series of highly successful appearances in Europe and Russia, receiving several decorations from heads of state. His return to the London stage in 1865 was well received. He died in Poland while on an engagement there.

Aldrin, (Edwin Eugene, Jr.) "Buzz" (1930–) astronaut, science consultant; born in Montclair, N.J. A Korean War fighter pilot (1953), he set a world space-walking record during the Gemini 12 space mission (1966). He was lunar module pilot on Apollo 11 – the first manned lunar landing (1969) – and was the second man to walk on the moon. He became a consultant to the aerospace industry.

Alegría, Ricardo E. (1921–) scholar; born in San Juan, Puerto Rico. He was the driving force behind the creation of the influential Institute of Puerto Rican Culture, which he headed from its foundation in 1955 to 1972. He was director of the governor's Office of Cultural Affairs from 1973 to 1976. In 1976 he launched the Graduate Center for Advanced Studies on Puerto Rico and the Caribbean. In 1993 he was the first Latin-American to win the United Nations Educational, Scientific, and Cultural Organization's Picasso Medal, the same year that President Clinton awarded him the Charles Frankel Award of the Humanities.

Alexander, (Andrew) Lamar (1940–) governor; born in Blount Co., Tenn. A Tennessee lawyer, he served as Howard Baker's legislative assistant (1967–68) and worked for Nixon's congressional relations office in 1969. As a Republican governor (1979–87), he spent his first term dealing with scandals left by outgoing governor Ray Blanton, recovering some prestige with the Knoxville World's Fair in 1982. He became University of Tennessee president in 1988 and served as secretary of education (1991–93) under President Bush.

Alexander, Archibald (1772–1851) Protestant clergyman, educator; born near Lexington, Va. The son of a merchant/farmer, he underwent a religious conversion in 1789, began to evangelize, and proved to be a fluent and persuasive preacher. Ordained in the Presbyterian ministry in 1794, he served two terms as president of Hampden-Sidney College (1796–1801, 1802–07). He became a professor at the newly established Princeton Theological Seminary in 1812 and remained there for the rest of his life. His teaching, along with a series of published essays, reviews, tracts, and sermons, gave him wide influence among the Presbyterians of his time.

Alexander, Clifford (1933–) cabinet member, lawyer; born in New York City. A lawyer, he was executive director of Harlem Youth Opportunities (1962–63), later serving on the National Security Council (1963–64). He served as special counsel to President Johnson (1965–67), chaired the Equal Opportunities Commission (1967–69), then practiced law in Washington (1969–76). As President Carter's secretary of the army (1977–81), he encouraged African-Americans to enlist. He formed Alexander Associates in Washington afterward.

Alexander, De Alva Standwood (1845–1925) U.S. representative, historian; born in Richmond, Maine. A member of the Ohio Volunteer Infantry during the Civil War, he was a teacher and newspaperman in Indiana before becoming a lawyer in 1877. In 1885 he moved his practice to Buffalo, N.Y.; he served this district as a Republican congressman (1897–1911). He wrote a three-volume *Political History of the State of New York* (1906–09) and *The History and Procedure of the House of Representatives* (1916).

Alexander, Grover (Cleveland) (1887–1950) baseball player; born in Elba, Neb. One of baseball's great (righthanded) pitchers, he won 373 games and pitched 90 shutouts during his Hall of Fame career, mostly with the Philadelphia Phillies and Chicago Cubs (1911–30). An epileptic and admitted alcoholic, his life was portrayed in the 1952 film, *The Winning Team,* starring Ronald Reagan.

Alexander, Hattie Elizabeth (1901–68) pediatrician, microbiologist; born in Baltimore, Md. Educated at Baltimore's Goucher College (B.A. 1923), she worked as a bacteriologist for state and federal Public Health Services for three years to save money for medical school. She received the M.D. from Johns Hopkins University in 1930 and specialized in pediatrics at the Harriet Lane Home in Baltimore. She was a research and teaching staff member of New York's Columbia-Presbyterian Medical Center for 37 years. Her studies on influenzal meningitis resulted in a successful treatment for this previously fatal disease (1939). Her 1940s research into DNA made her one of the first geneticists.

Alexander, John (White) (1856–1915) painter; born in Allegheny, Pa. He began as an illustrator for *Harper's Weekly* in New York (c. 1874), studied in Germany and Venice (1877), returned to New York (1879), and moved to Paris (1890–1901). He settled in New York (1901), and was a successful portrait painter using an art nouveau style, as seen in *Isabella; or the Pot of Basil* (1897).

Alexander, Robert J. (Jackson) (1918–) political scientist; born in Canton, Ohio. With a Columbia University Ph.D., he taught at Rutgers University (1947). His works on economic development and the history of labor and radical movements in Latin America include *The Venezuelan Democratic Revolution* (1964) and *Bolivia* (1982). The Bolivian government awarded him the Order of the Condor of the Andes (1962).

Alexanderson, Ernest (Frederick Werner) (1878–1975) electrical engineer, inventor; born in Uppsala, Sweden. He came to the United States in 1901 and went to work for the General Electric Co. the following year. He invented radio receiving and transmitting systems, and by 1930, had perfected a complete television system. He produced a successful color television receiver in 1955.

Alford, Andrew (1904–) electrical engineer, inventor; born in Samara, Russia. He graduated from the University of California in 1924 and held engineering posts at Harvard and in private industry. His main work involved the development of antennas for radio navigation and instrument landing systems. His best-known invention is the "Alford Loop" antenna.

Alger, Horatio (1834–99) author; born in Revere, Mass. He graduated from Harvard Divinity School (1860), and became a Unitarian minister (1864), but resigned and settled in New York City (1866). His inspirational novels such as *Ragged Dick* (1867) made his name synonymous with the American ideal of young men gaining success through hard work. He died impoverished after giving his wealth to the poor.

Alger, Russell Alexander (1836–1907) soldier, politician; born in Lafayette Township, Ohio. A lawyer and lumberman, he was an officer with the Michigan cavalry and fought for the Union in various battles including Gettysburg. He was a Republican governor of Michigan (1885–86) and was head of the Grand Army of the Republic (1889). As secretary of war (1897–99) he was blamed for the U.S. unpreparedness during the opening months of the Spanish-American War and was forced to resign.

Algren, Nelson (b. Nelson Ahlgren Abraham) (1909–81) writer; born in Detroit, Mich. He trained as a journalist after a childhood in the Chicago slums. After working at a variety of jobs during the Depression, he settled in Chicago and became a leading exponent of the Chicago school of realism; his five streetwise novels include *The Man With the Golden Arm* (1949, National Book Award) and *A Walk on the Wild Side* (1956). After 1956 he wrote mostly stories and essays, producing only one novel (1981). In later years he became known for having had an affair with the French intellectual/writer, Simone de Beauvoir.

Ali, Muhammad (b. Cassius Marcellus Clay, Jr.) (1942–) boxer; born in Louisville, Ky. From 1956–60, as Cassius Clay, he fought as an amateur (winning 100 of 108 matches) before becoming the light-heavyweight gold medalist in the 1960 Olympics. Financed by a group of Louisville businessmen, he turned professional and by 1963 had won his first 19 fights. In 1964 he won the world heavyweight championship with a stunning defeat of Sonny Liston. Immediately after that, Clay announced that he was a Black Muslim and had changed his name to Muhammad Ali. After defending the championship nine times within two years, he was stripped of his title in 1967 when he refused induction into the U.S. Army on religious grounds. His action earned him both respect and anger from different quarters, but he did not box for three and one-half years when in 1971 he lost to Joe Frazier. A few months later the U.S. Supreme Court affirmed his right to object to military service on religious grounds and he regained the title in 1974 by knocking out George Foreman in Zaire, Africa. Ali defended his title ten times before losing to Leon Spinks in 1978. When he defeated Spinks later that same year, he became the first boxer ever to regain the championship twice. Famous for his flamboyant manner, his boasting predictions of which round he'd defeat his opponent, and his doggerel verse ("float like a butterfly, sting like a bee"), he was also recognized as one of the all-time great boxers with his quick jab and footwork. He compiled a career record of 56 wins, five losses, with 37 knockouts, before retiring in 1981. During the 1960s and 1970s he was arguably the best-known individual in the entire world due not only to his controversial career but also to his travels and deliberate reaching out to the Third World. In the 1980s it was revealed that he was suffering from a form of Parkinson's disease, but he made occasional appearances to the acclaim of an admiring public.

Alinsky, Saul (David) (1909–72) social activist; born in Chicago. Director of the Industrial Areas Foundation (1939–72), he organized Chicago slum dwellers to demand better housing and education, then trained others to be community organizers. After the 1964 race riots, he brought his organizing skills to urban ghettos. In *Rules for Radicals* (1971), he articulated his principles of social activism.

Allard, Harry A. (Ardell) (1880–1963) botanist; born in Oxford, Mass. He worked for the U.S. Department of Agriculture (1906–46), concentrating his research on the physiology and pathology of tobacco and cotton. In 1920, with Wightman Garner, he discovered photoperiodism, a fundamental botanical law stating that the blossoming and fruiting of plants depends on the amount of exposure to light. Allard was a consummate naturalist whose field explorations to study the plants of Virginia and West Virginia resulted in a variety of publications dealing with the songbirds, amphibians, and the "musical" insects of the region, such as crickets and grasshoppers.

Allen, Clarence Roderic (1925–) seismologist; born in Palo Alto, Calif. A professor of geology and geophysics at the California Institute of Technology (1964), his major research was to evaluate hazards inherent in the fault systems of Southern California and Baja California.

Allen, Ethan (1738–1789) soldier, Vermonter; born in Litchfield, Conn. He and his brothers acquired large landholdings in the "New Hampshire Grants" as Vermont was then known. He formed the Green Mountain Boys, and resisted all efforts by New York and New Hampshire to control the Vermont area. He and Benedict Arnold jointly captured Fort Ticonderoga (1775) but he was then captured by the British during an attack on Montreal. After his imprisonment (1775–78), he returned to the new Republic of Vermont. He sought to represent Vermont as an independent political entity – he even negotiated with the British in pursuit of this goal. He died two years before Vermont achieved statehood.

Allen, Florence Ellinwood (1884–1966) jurist, women's suffrage activist; born in Salt Lake City, Utah. The daughter of the first woman admitted to Smith College, she studied music but decided she lacked the talent to become a concert pianist and took up law instead. Admitted to the Ohio bar in 1914, she served as legal counsel for the suffragist movement, became assistant prosecutor for Cuyahoga County (1919) and was elected a common pleas court judge (1920). In 1922 she won election to the Ohio Supreme Court. Appointed to the U.S. Sixth Circuit Court of Appeals in 1934, she served for 25 years and in 1958 became the first woman named to a federal appellate chief judgeship. She retired from the bench the following year. Despite strong support from women's groups, she never received the U.S. Supreme Court nomination she sought.

Allen, Francis A. (1919–) legal educator, criminal justice consultant; born in Kansas City, Kans. A leading authority on criminal law and juvenile delinquency, he drafted the modern Illinois Criminal Code (1961). He chaired the Committee on Poverty and the Administration of Federal Criminal Justice during the Kennedy Administration and was a member of the National Institute of Law Enforcement and Criminal Justice (1974–78). He was Dean of the University of Michigan Law School (1966–71), named professor emeritus (1986), then joined the faculty of the University of Florida in 1986. He was the author of the *Decline of the Rehabilitative Ideal* (1981) and other books.

Allen, Fred (b. John F. Sullivan) (1894–1956) comedian; born in Cambridge, Mass. Starting as a juggler as a youth, he switched to comedy when he found he was getting more laughs for his quips than applause for his skill. He appeared in vaudeville and Broadway shows in the 1920s and moved into radio in the 1930s. As host of *Town Hall Tonight* (1934–40) and then CBS's *Texaco Star Theatre* (1940–49), he wrote much of his material and was one of the first American comedians to employ situations and a cast of characters that satirized topical events. He converted somewhat reluctantly to television, starring in *The Colgate Comedy Hour* (1953–54) and *Fred Allen's Sketchbook* (1954). The nature of his characteristically wry, ironic, even occasionally mordant humor was expressed in the title of his autobiography, *Treadmill to Oblivion* (1954).

Allen, Frederick Lewis (1890–1954) author, editor; born in Boston. He became editor of *Harper's Magazine* in 1941 and was widely known for his colorful works of social history, including *Only Yesterday* (1931).

Allen, Henry Justin (1868–1950) publisher, governor; born in Pittsfield, Pa. Starting as a reporter in Kansas, he bought his first newspaper in 1895, later publishing the *Wichita Beacon* (1907–28), exposing local corruption. He worked for the American Red Cross in France in 1917–18, returning to be Republican governor of Kansas (1919–23); although he generally supported fairly liberal and reform legislation, he became best known for passing the Kansas Industrial Act to curb striking unions (1920). Briefly a U.S. senator (1929–31), he returned to journalism.

Allen, Mel (b. Melvin Allen Israel) (1913–) sports broadcaster; born in Birmingham, Ala. He was the broadcaster of New York Yankees games from 1939 to 1964, during which time his mellow drawl gained him the nickname "Voice of New York." He was elected to baseball's Hall of Fame in 1978.

Allen, Paula Gunn (1939–) Laguna/Sioux scholar, writer; born in Cubero, N.M. Of mixed Laguna Pueblo, Sioux, and Chicano heritage, she is a poet and novelist who incorporated feminist issues in writing of Indian culture and personal experiences. She was primarily associated with the Native American Studies program at the University of California: Berkeley. Her books include *The Woman Who Owned the Shadows* (1983), *The Sacred Hoop* (1986), and *Spider Woman's Granddaughters* (1989).

Allen, Richard (1760–1831) Methodist minister, church founder; born in Philadelphia. Born a slave, he was sold as a child to a farmer in Delaware. He converted to Methodism as a young man and then converted his owner, who allowed Allen to obtain his freedom. While working at odd jobs, he educated himself and traveled throughout the mid-Atlantic state preaching. By 1874 he was accepted as a Methodist preacher and he returned to Philadelphia to preach (1786–87). After an incident in which white parishioners forced the African-Americans present to segregate themselves, Allen led his black parishioners to form a Free African Society (1787). In 1794 he established a separate Methodist church for African-Americans. In 1816 a number of independent black Methodist churches around the Northeast came together to form the African Methodist Episcopal Church; Allen was ordained its first bishop (April 11, 1816) and led it until his death as it expanded not only as a religious force but also in civil and social activism. This has often been called one of the most enduring institutions ever organized by African-Americans. Allen himself was a strong patriot, even supporting the War of 1812, and he denounced the notion of sending African-Americans to colonize in Africa.

Allen, Terry (de la Mesa) (1888–1969) soldier; born in Fort Douglas, Utah. The famously profane son of a professional soldier, "Terrible Terry" Allen failed to graduate from West Point, and fought as a professional boxer for a time. During World War II, he became the only officer to lead two infantry divisions in battle – the 1st, composed largely of regulars, in Sicily in 1943, and the conscript 104th, which he trained in Oregon and led in France and Germany in 1944–45.

Allen, William (1803–79) U.S. representative, governor; born in Edenton, N.C. He moved to Ohio (1819) and was admitted to the bar in 1827. He served in the U.S. House of Representatives (Dem., Ohio; 1833–35) and in the U.S. Senate (Dem., Ohio; 1837–49). An ardent expansionist, he was chairman of the committee on foreign relations. He acted as a spokesperson for President James Polk during the deliberations on the start of the Mexican War. An antiwar Democrat during the Civil War, he later served as governor of Ohio (1874–76). Ohio placed his statue in the U.S. Capitol.

Allen, (William) Hervey (Jr.) (1889–1949) writer, poet; born in Pittsburgh, Pa. He attended the U.S. Naval Academy but took his B.S. from the University of Pittsburgh (1915). He served briefly on the Mexican border with the National Guard and then with the U.S. Army in France during World War I; his war diary, *Toward the Flame* (1926), was highly regarded in its day. After some graduate study at Harvard, he taught English at a high school in Charleston, S.C. (1919–25) and then at several colleges. During the 1920s he published many volumes of his poetry and lectured on poetry at the Bread Loaf Writers' Conference (Vt.), but his reputation as a poet soon faded. Instead, he is best known for his still-relevant biography of Edgar Allan Poe, *Israfel* (1926), and for a swashbuckling historical novel, *Anthony Adverse* (1933). The popularity of the latter freed him to go on writing historical novels set in the Civil War and the Pennsylvania frontier, but nothing ever repeated the success he enjoyed with *Anthony Adverse*.

Allen, William (McPherson) (1900–85), aircraft manufacturer; born in Lolo, Montana. A Harvard educated lawyer, he worked for the legal counsel of Boeing Aircraft, joining the company's board of directors in 1931. First as president and then chairman and chief executive officer, from 1945 to 1972 he guided Boeing as it became the world's largest commercial jet transport producer.

Allen, Woody (b. Allen Stewart Konigsberg) (1935–) film actor, director, scriptwriter, playwright; born in New York City. He began his career writing jokes for columnists and comedians, then appeared in nightclubs with his own material, establishing the persona that would persist through most of his ensuing works: the flustered neurotic, obsessed with sex and death. His first film, as scriptwriter and actor, was *What's New, Pussycat?* (1965), and he went on to write, direct, and star in a series of films, some lightweight, some heavy, but the best of which – such as *Annie Hall* (1977), for which he won three Oscars – drew on his inimitable brand of verbal-situational absurdism. He is the author of two Broadway hits and collections of humorous essays, many of which first appeared in the *New Yorker,* and is a talented clarinetist who plays regularly in a New York jazz club. Said to be as neurotic in real life as in his scripted roles, he had a long-term relationship with one of his leading actresses, Mia Farrow, with whom he had a daughter. In 1992, their relationship dissolved in recriminations when he acknowledged an attachment with one of her young adopted daughters.

Allibone, Samuel Austin (1816–89) bibliographer; born in Philadelphia. He started out in business, working for an insurance company in Philadelphia. Between 1867 and 1879, as editor of the American Sunday School Union, he published many indices and anthologies, including *An Alphabetical Index to the New Testament* (1868) and *Prose Quotations from Socrates to Macaulay* (1876). His invaluable three-volume *Critical Dictionary of English Literature and British and American Authors* was published in 1858 and 1871.

Allison, William B. (Boyd) (1829–1908) U.S. senator; born in Perry, Ohio. A lawyer by profession, he entered Ohio politics and joined the new Republican Party. In 1857 he moved to Iowa and practiced law before going to the U.S. House of Representatives (Rep., Iowa; 1963–72). Although implicated in the Credit Mobilier railroad scandal of 1870, he went on to serve in the U.S. Senate (1873–1908) where he became one of the leaders of the Republican delegation, renowned for his ability to unite opposing groups. A fiscal conservative, he took moderate stands on currency issues such as the Bland-Allison Silver Act (1878).

Allport, Gordon (Willard) (1897–1967) psychologist; born in Montezuma, Ind. He received his Ph.D. from Harvard in 1922, then spent 1922–24 in Europe on a fellowship. He was instructor of social ethics at Harvard (1924–26) and assistant professor of psychology at Dartmouth (1926–30); he returned to Harvard's psychology faculty in 1930, where he became Cabot Professor of Social Ethics in 1966. His most influential work was *Personality: A Psychological Interpretation* (1937), revised as *Patterns and Growth in Personality* (1961). Among his several innovative approaches to the study of human psychology was his use of individuals' personal writings and artistic creations. He was a guest professor at various institutions, served as president of the American Psychological Association from 1939–40, and was awarded the American Psychological Foundation's gold medal in 1963.

Allston, Robert (Francis Withers) (1801–64) farmer, governor; born in Waccamaw, S.C. A West Point graduate (1821), he spent a year on the Geodetic Coastal Survey when family matters called him home to oversee the rice plantation. An innovative farmer, he improved cultivation methods and developed better varieties of seed, samples of which won medals at the 1855 Paris Exposition. In 1843 he published *Memoir on Rice*. In addition to farming, he was South Carolina's surveyor general (1823–27), a state representative (1828–30) and a state senator (1832–56) until he was elected governor (1856–58). As governor, he emphasized the importance of local taxation to supplement the support of schools.

Allston, Washington (1779–1843) painter; born in Georgetown County, N.C. He spent many years in England (1801–18), studied with Benjamin West (1801–03), became friends with Samuel Taylor Coleridge and Washington Irving, and produced romantic paintings, such as *The Rising of a Thunderstorm at Sea* (1804). He returned to Boston (1818), settled in Cambridgeport, Mass., and continued to paint poetic and narrative subjects, as in *The Flight of Florimell* (1819) and *The Moonlit Landscape* (1819). His most famous pupil was Samuel F. B. Morse.

Almond, Edward Mallory (1892–1979) soldier; born in Luray, Va. A veteran of World War I and World War II, he commanded the amphibious invasion of Inchon, Korea, and captured the South Korean capital, Seoul (1950). When a massive Chinese counteroffensive threw the United Nations' drive into reverse, he led the X Corps in a fighting withdrawal southward from Choisin Reservoir.

Almond, Gabriel (Abraham) (1911–) political scientist; born in Rock Island, Ill. He taught at several universities before joining the faculty at Stanford in 1963, and served as a consultant to the State Department and the U.S. Air Force. He is best known for his work in comparative political studies, international politics, contemporary political systems, and what he called "the civic culture."

Alpers, Svetlana (b. Leontief) (1936–) art historian; born in Cambridge, Mass. She studied at Radcliffe (B.A. 1957), and Harvard (Ph.D. 1965). She taught at several institutions, notably the University of California: Berkeley (1962), and was a consultant to National Public Radio and the National Endowment for the Humanities. She was a specialist in Dutch art of the 17th century.

Alpert, Herb (1935–) musician; born in Los Angeles. A trumpeter, and record and movie soundtrack producer, he began as a songwriter for Sam Cooke in 1958, then established and led the pop instrumental group, Tijuana Brass, from 1963–69. Thereafter he concentrated on executive duties at A&M Records, which he cofounded in 1962.

al-Rayhânî, Amîn (1876–1940) poet; born in Lebanon. He went with his family to New York City (1888) and worked for a time with them as a peddler. He toured with a theater company and turned to poetry. He wrote *Myrtle and Myrrh* (1905) and *The Book of Khalid* (1911), and was often referred to as the "father of prose poetry in Arabic." Always conscious of his position as an ambassador between East and West, he wrote, "Neither Crescent nor Cross we adore/Nor Buddha nor Christ we implore/Nor Muslim nor Jew we abhor/We are free."

Alsop, Joseph (Wright), Jr. (1910–89) journalist; born in Avon, Conn. He wrote a syndicated political column, "Capital Parade" (1937–40) with Robert Kinter. He interrupted his career for wartime service with the U.S. Navy. In 1946 he started a new column, "Matter of Fact," which he wrote with his brother, Stewart Alsop, until 1958, then by himself until 1974. His interest in archaeology led him to write *From the Silent Earth* (1964).

Alsop, Stewart (1914–74) journalist; born in Avon, Conn. A self-described New Deal liberal, he wrote a widely syndicated political column with his brother, Joseph Alsop, from 1946 to 1958. Later a *Newsweek* columnist, he wrote *Stay of Execution* (1973) about his final battle with leukemia.

Altgeld, John Peter (1847–1902) governor; born in Nieder Selters, Germany. Brought to Ohio as a baby, he received little schooling while working on his father's farm. A Union private in the Civil War (1864–65), he then taught school in Ohio, moving to Missouri where he became a lawyer in 1871 and a county attorney (1874–75). Moving to Chicago, he opened his own law practice, making a fortune in real estate. He wrote *Our Penal Machinery and Its Victims* (1884), becoming Superior Court judge (1886–90), then chief justice (1890–91). As the Democratic governor of Illinois (1893–97), he gained sudden fame – and offended the conservative establishment – when he pardoned the remaining Haymarket Riot anarchists, claiming they had not been given a fair trial. He improved prison conditions and reformed trial and parole procedures. He advocated child labor laws and opposed the use of federal troops to end the Pullman Strike in 1894. After campaigning for William Jennings Bryan in 1896, he lost his own re-election campaign, returning to his law practice with his partner, Clarence Darrow. He was penniless when he died but his reputation as a progressive reformer increased over the years.

Altman, Benjamin (1840–1913) businessman, art collector; born in New York City. Much of his early life is obscure and he had little formal education. By 1865 he owned a dry goods store in New York City, and later founded B. Altman & Company (1906), which became one of the country's most stylish department stores. He collected paintings and sculptures among other art works during his many visits to Europe. He bequeathed his collection to the Metropolitan Museum and a legacy to the National Academy of Design.

Altman, Robert (1925–) movie director; born in Kansas City, Mo. After serving in World War II as a pilot, he took up writing for radio and magazines and then produced industrial films. His first feature movie was *The Delinquents* (1957) and he went on to direct plays and series episodes for television. After two forgettable feature films, he gained instant recognition for *M*A*S*H* (1970) and went on to direct and/or produce a series of highly individualistic movies, noted especially for their simultaneous layers of dialogue. Impatient with Hollywood's conservative and commercial approach to moviemaking, he effectively moved to Europe, although he would return to America to make such movies as *Nashville* (1975) and *The Player* (1991).

Altman, Sidney (1939–) biochemist; born in Montreal, Canada. He became affiliated with Yale in 1971 and holds dual citizenship. He showed that the RNA molecule could rearrange itself, thereby altering the material it produces without requiring an enzyme. This was a major breakthrough in our understanding of genetic processes. He and Thomas Cech shared the Nobel Prize for chemistry (1989).

Alvarez, Luis W. (Walter) (1911–88) physicist; born in San Francisco. He spent his career at the University of California: Berkeley (1936–78). He discovered radioactive decay by orbital-electron capture (1938), and described the magnetic properties of the neutron (1939). During World War II he designed aircraft navigational systems and worked on the Manhattan Project. In 1947 he built the first proton linear accelerator. His modification of the bubble chamber to discover new subatomic particles won him the 1968 Nobel Prize for physics. With his geologist son, Walter Alvarez, he proposed the still-controversial theory that the mass extinction of dinosaurs was due to an asteroid or comet striking the earth (1979). Luis Alvarez's many inventions demonstrate ingenious applications of physics to other scientific areas.

Amdahl, Gene (1922–) computer engineer; born in Flandreau, S.D. Working for International Business Machines (IBM) at Poughkeepsie, N.Y., he helped design the IBM 704 in the 1950s and the S/360 series of computers in the early 1960s. In the 1970s, he ran Amdahl Corporation, then the largest manufacturer of IBM-compatible computers. In 1980, he formed Trilogy to build large computers.

Ames, Adelbert (1835–1933) governor; born in Rockland, Maine. A West Point graduate (1861), he saw continuous action, distinguishing himself at 1st Bull Run, Gettysburg, and Petersburg. Governor of the Mississippi military district (1868–70), he served in the U.S. Senate (Rep., Miss.; 1870–74). Returning as governor of Mississippi (1874–76), he was unable to quell widespread disorder, including the Vicksburg riots, and resigned when threatened with impeachment. He moved to New York City, investing in Minnesota flour mills and manufacturing in Lowell, Mass. As a volunteer brigadier general, he saw service in Cuba during the Spanish-American War in 1898, retiring to Lowell afterward.

Ames, Ezra (1768–1836) painter; born in Framingham, Mass. He worked in Worcester, Mass. (1790–93), settled in Albany, N.Y., (1793), and started as a carriage painter and miniaturist. Later he painted portraits, including that of Vice-President George Clinton (1812).

Ames, James Barr (1846–1910) legal scholar; born in Boston, Mass. He was educated at Harvard and taught at Harvard Law School from 1872 until his death. He advanced the case method of instruction by compiling and publishing cases on torts, partnerships, trusts, and equity jurisdiction. He took part in founding the *Harvard Law Review* in 1887 and published *Lectures on Legal History* (1913).

Ames, Jessie Daniel (1883–1972) suffragist, civil rights activist; born in Palestine, Texas. Educated at Southwestern College (1902), she made lynching a southern white women's issue by linking feminism to racial justice. She became director of the Commission on Interracial Cooperation Women's Committee (1929) and founded the Association of Southern Women for the Prevention of Lynching (1930–42). She remained politically active until 1968.

Ames, Oakes (1874–1950) botanist; born in North Easton, Mass. He taught and performed research at Harvard (1898–1941). In 1900 he was instrumental in founding Harvard's Atkins Garden in Cuba. His skilled administration (1937–45) brought Harvard's Botanical Museum to prominence. He amassed a large collection of orchid specimens, his specialty, and made major contributions to studies of their taxonomy and evolution. A pioneer in economic botany, he devised the Ames charts in which plant families were pictured and identified by their economic products. His theory (1930s) that civilization was directly dependent on agriculture – eventually supported by archaeological findings – was summed up in his masterwork, *Economic Annuals and Human Culture* (1939).

Ames, Oakes (1804–73) capitalist, U.S. representative; born in Easton, Mass. At age 16 he began working at Oliver Ames & Co., his father's shovel factory, and when his father retired in 1844, he took over the company with his brother, Oliver Jr. Their business flourished, riding the waves of the California Gold Rush of 1848, the Australian gold rush, the westward exodus, and the Civil War. Active in politics, Oakes served in the U.S. House of Representatives (Rep., Mass.; 1863–73). In 1865 he joined Crédit Mobilier, financiers of the Union Pacific Railroad. In 1872 he was investigated for selling Crédit Mobilier railroad stock to Congressmen below par value in order to influence their votes on behalf of the financial scheme. His actions were condemned by a House resolution in 1873 and he died soon thereafter.

Ammons, A. R. (Archie Randolph) (1926–) poet, teacher; born in Whitehall, N.C. He studied at Wake Forest College, N.C. (B.S. 1949), the University of California: Berkeley (1951–52), worked in New Jersey (1952–61), and began teaching at Cornell University in 1964. He is noted as a poet in the transcendental tradition.

Ammons, Elias Milton (1860–1925) rancher, public official; born in Macon County, Ga. He went to Colorado and entered the cattle business in 1886. A "Silver Republican" after 1896, he was governor of Colorado (1913–15). He was accused of favoring the mine owners during a coalfield strike in 1913–14. He returned to business enterprises.

Amram, David (1930–) composer; born in Philadelphia. His career has involved extensive playing (mostly on French horn) and composing in both classical and jazz styles. His music is eclectic and relatively conservative, with elements of jazz and various ethnic musics.

Amsterdam, Anthony G. (Guy) (1935–) legal scholar; born in Philadelphia. He is known for his expertise in criminal law, especially in its use of psychiatry. He taught at the University of Pennsylvania (1962–69), Stanford (1969–81), and New York University (1981).

Anastasi, Anne (1908–) psychologist; born in New York City. She taught at Barnard College (1930–39), Queens College (1939–46), and Fordham University (1946–79). In 1933 she married psychologist John Porter Foley Jr., a fellow graduate of Columbia University. They were frequent collaborators in research, where she specialized in differential psychology, test construction, and statistics. Her important textbooks include *Differential Psychology* (1937), *Psychological Testing* (1954), and *Applied Psychology* (1964).

Andersen, Dorothy H. (Hansine) (1901–1963) pathologist, pediatrician; born in Asheville, N.C. Discoverer of cystic fibrosis (1938) and related diagnostic tests, she did work on congenital heart defects leading to breakthroughs in open-heart surgery. Working at Babies Hospital at the Columbia-Presbyterian Medical Center (1935–63), she became chief pathologist (1952). Independent and free-thinking, she loved the outdoors and carpentry.

Anderson, Carl D. (David) (1905–91) physicist; born in New York City. He taught and performed research at the California Institute of Technology (1930–77). In 1932 he discovered the positron, for which he received the 1936 Nobel Prize (jointly with Victor Hess). In 1937, he and S. H. Neddermeyer announced their discovery of intermediate-mass subatomic particles called mesons (now muons).

Anderson, Don Lynn (1933–) geophysicist, seismologist; born in Frederick, Md. He received his Ph.D. in geophysics and mathematics from the California Institute of Technology in 1962, and was named director of its Seismology Laboratory in 1967. He was the editor of the periodical *Physics of the Earth and Planetary Interiors;* his research focused on both theoretical seismology and the structure and composition of the earth and planets.

Anderson, Edgar S. (Shannon) (1897–1969) botanist, geneticist; born in Forestville, N.Y. He was a research assistant at Harvard (1920–22), then became a geneticist at the Missouri Botanical Garden (MBG) (1922–30) and a professor at Washington University, St. Louis (1922–31). He then joined Harvard's Arnold Arboretum and lectured at Harvard (1931–35) before returning to Washington University (1935–69) and the MBG (1952–69). He made major contributions to studies of the cytology, crossbreeding, evolution, and classification of flowering plants, especially maize, American irises, and tobacco. He coined the term "introgressive hybridization" (1938) to describe the gradual introduction of genetic material of one species into another due to repeated backcrossing.

Anderson, George W. (Whelan) (1906–) naval officer, diplomat; born in New York City. He was the assistant to the deputy commander of the Pacific Fleet and Pacific Ocean Areas (1944–45). Later he served as chief of naval operations (1961–63) and ambassador to Portugal (1963–66).

Anderson, (James) Maxwell (1888–1959) playwright; born in Atlantic, Pa. After taking an M.A. at Stanford, he served as an editor with the *New Republic* (1918–24) before achieving his first success, collaborating with Lawrence

Stallings on a realistic war drama, *What Price Glory?* (1924). Thereafter he alternated between romantic blank-verse such as *Elizabeth the Queen* (1930) and *Winterset* (1935) and more realistic dramas such as *Key Largo* (1939) and *The Bad Seed* (1954).

Anderson, Joseph R. (Reid) (1813–92) industrialist; born in Botetourt County, Va. An 1836 West Point graduate, he spent five years as an army engineer before joining the Tredegar Iron Company in Richmond, Va. In 1848 he bought the company and turned it into one of the best iron works in the country. As a supporter of the Confederacy, he supplied Southern forces with ordnance and he himself fought in the Civil War until wounded (1861–63). He returned to Tredegar where his expert management kept the works running throughout the war, as both the Confederacy's sole supplier of heavy ordnance and the prime supplier of everything from plates for iron-clad ships to railroad trains. Confiscated by the Union in 1865, the company was returned to him in 1867.

Anderson, Judith (b. Frances Margaret Anderson) (1898–1992) actress; born in Adelaide, Australia. She made her stage debut in Sydney, Australia, in 1915 and launched her American career three years later. Her long association with Broadway began in 1922. Notable for her portrayals of powerful women, her interpretations of Lady Macbeth and of Robinson Jeffers's Medea helped her earn the sobriquet of "First Lady of the American theater." Her credits include 29 motion pictures and many television series, among them *Santa Barbara* (1984–87).

Anderson, Marian (1902–93) contralto; born in Philadelphia. Anderson grew up singing in a church choir, and at age 19 she began formal study. In 1925 she won a major vocal competition in New York City that gained her a career as a recitalist, but was always constricted by the limitations placed on African-American artists. In the 1930s she traveled across Europe and America, finding acclaim as perhaps the greatest living contralto. Her most electrifying moment came in 1939, when she was refused permission to sing in Washington's Constitution Hall because of her race; instead, she sang at the Lincoln Memorial on Easter Sunday, for an audience of 75,000. In 1955 she became the first African-American singer to appear at the Metropolitan Opera. Awarded the Presidential Medal of Freedom in 1963, Anderson spent the next two years in a worldwide farewell tour.

Anderson, Mary (1872–1964) labor leader; born in Lidkoping, Sweden. Emigrating to the U.S.A. at age 16, she became active in union work, becoming an officer of the International Boot and Shoe Workers' Union in Chicago. She was also active in the Women's Trade Union League and worked to obtain equal pay to women for equal work. She was the first director of the Women's Bureau of the U.S. Department of Labor (1920–44).

Anderson, Philip W. (Warren) (1923–) physicist; born in Indianapolis, Ind. He was a member of the technical staff at Bell Telephone Laboratories (1949–84), and concurrently a physics professor at Cambridge University (1967–75) and Princeton (1975). He shared the 1977 Nobel Prize for physics (with J. H. Van Vleck and English physicist Nevill Mott) for his work on the electronic structure of magnetic and disordered systems. In 1987 he published a theory of how some metals become superconductive at higher relative temperatures.

Anderson, Robert (1805–71) soldier; born near Louisville, Ky. A West Point graduate (1825) he served in the Mexican War. As an artillery officer, he commanded the Federal garrison at Fort Sumter, S.C., surrendering there on April 13, 1861, after a 34-hour bombardment that signaled the opening of the Civil War. He spent most of the rest of the war keeping Kentucky in the Union until disabilities forced his retirement in 1863. In April 1865 he returned to Fort Sumter for the raising of the original flag.

Anderson, Robert O. (Orville) (1917–) oil executive; born in Chicago. After taking a B.A. from the University of Chicago, he bought Malco Refineries, Inc., Roswell, N.M., in 1941. As president (1941–62), he added wells and pipelines, creating a large production company that he sold to Atlantic Refining Co., Philadelphia (1962). As Atlantic's largest stockholder he became chairman and CEO (1965–86). With its president, Thornton Bradshaw, he initiated the program of modernization, restructuring, and acquisitions (notably Richfield Oil Corporation, 1966) that made Atlantic Richfield the 12th largest U.S. corporation. He resigned to form Hondo Oil & Gas Co. (1986), which through a merger with Pauley Petroleum, Inc. (1987) became one of the country's largest private oil companies. He became the largest individual landholder in the U.S.A., with ranches totaling one million acres. He was noted for his humanistic interests and long affiliation with the Aspen Institute for Humanistic Studies.

Anderson, Robert (Woodruff) (1917–) playwright; born in New York City. Best known for *Tea and Sympathy* (1953), the story of a schoolboy accused of homosexuality, his later plays include *You Know I Can't Hear You When the Water's Running* (1967).

Anderson, Sherwood (Berton) (1876–1941) writer; born in Camden, Ohio. He was raised in the small town of Clyde, Ohio. After age 14 his schooling was erratic; after a succession of jobs he moved to Chicago. He served in the Spanish-American War (1898–99), then attended an academy in Springfield, Ohio. In 1900 he began working as a copywriter and he established his own mail-order company in Cleveland (1906). From his early years he despised business ethics and resented his dependence on business earnings, and in 1912, suffering from an amnesic nervous breakdown, he walked out on his family and his job managing a paint factory. After his recovery he resumed his Chicago advertising work (1913–22). After publishing two novels (1916, 1917) with the help of Theodore Dreiser and Carl Sandburg, he wrote *Winesburg, Ohio* (1919), the collection of stories that is considered his masterpiece. Subsequent works included his finest novel, *Poor White* (1920); another collection of stories, *The Triumph of the Egg* (1921); and the novels *Many Marriages* (1923) and *Dark Laughter* (1925). He won the first *Dial* literary award (1921). Private patronage after 1922 enabled him to move to a farm in Marion, Va., where he bought and edited two local newspapers (1927–29). Although his standing among his fellow writers remained high, the literary quality of his work declined greatly. Much of his late work, both journalistic and fictional, concerned Southern industrial conditions; roving reportage on the Depression was collected in *Puzzled America* (1935).

Anderson (Terence) Terry (1947–) journalist, hostage; born in Lorain, Ohio. After college he enlisted in the U.S.

Marine Corps and served in Vietnam as a combat journalist. Joining the Associated Press in 1974, he went to cover events in Beirut (1982), where he was kidnapped by Islamic extremists in 1985. He became the longest held American hostage and the last released (December 1991), and was paid tribute by many of his fellow hostages for the strength, humor, and ingenuity he demonstrated in keeping their morale alive.

André, Carl (1935–) sculptor; born in Quincy, Mass. He attended Phillips Academy, Andover, Mass. (1951–53), moved to New York City (1957), and worked as a brakeman and conductor for the Pennsylvania Railroad (1960–64). He became known for his modular sculptures, such as *Pyramids* series (mid-1960s), and his scattered plastic works such as *Spill* (1968).

Andreas, Dwayne (Orville) (1918–) corporate executive; born in Worthington, Minn. He spent 36 years, 20 as chairman and chief executive officer, with Honeymead Products, Cedar Rapids, Iowa (later National City Bancorp). He was later chairman and chief executive officer of the commodities company, Archer Daniels Midland, Decatur, Ill., (1970), which he expanded into international markets. As a government advisor on international trade, he was particularly successful in promoting U.S.-Soviet trade.

Andretti, Mario (1940–) auto racer; born in Trieste, Italy. After spending over three years in a displaced persons camp after World War II, he came to the U.S.A. with his family at age 15. From the time he won the United States Auto Club national driving championship in 1965 and 1966, he emerged as one of auto racing's most versatile drivers. He was the only person to have won the Daytona 500 (1967), the Indianapolis 500 (1969), and the Grand Prix world driving championship (1978). His son, Michael Andretti, also became a championship auto racer.

Andrew, John Albion (1818–67) governor; born in Windham, Maine. He attended Bowdoin College where he was known for his strong antislavery views. A Boston lawyer, he helped to organize the Free Soil Party (1848), became a leader of the new Republican Party, and raised money for John Brown's defense (1859). As governor of Massachusetts (1860–66), he worked indefatigably to raise and equip regiments for the Union cause. Most notably, he successfully worked for the creation of the first regiment (the 54th) of African-Americans in the Union army.

Andrews, Bert (1901–53) journalist; born in Colorado Springs, Colo. As Washington reporter and bureau chief for the *New York Herald Tribune* in the 1940s and early 1950s, he scored many scoops and won a 1947 Pulitzer Prize for articles on government loyalty investigations; he also helped uncover evidence that led to the perjury conviction of Alger Hiss.

Andrews, (Elisha) Benjamin (1844–1917) college president; born in Hinsdale, N.H. A popular teacher of history and political economy, he became president of Brown University (1889–98), where he expanded enrollments and established a new Women's College. As chancellor of the University of Nebraska (1900–08) he added new departments and schools.

Andrews, Frank (Maxwell) (1884–1943) soldier, aviator; born in Nashville, Tenn. The son of a newspaperman, he graduated from West Point in 1906 and served in the aviation section of the Signal Corps during World War I. As the first commander of the army's General Headquarters Air Force (1935–39), Andrews helped develop the B-17 bomber (which would be a key weapon of World War II), and became a prominent advocate of air power as an offensive weapon. Rugged in looks, and firm but softspoken, he campaigned to establish the Air Corps as an independent service. Andrews held senior commands in the Caribbean and the Middle East (1941–43) before succeeding Eisenhower (who had become supreme Allied commander in North Africa) as the head of U.S. forces in Europe (1943). He was killed in an air crash in Iceland on May 3, 1943. Andrews Air Force Base near Washington, D.C., is named after him.

Andrews, John Bertram (1880–1943) labor expert, social reformer, economist; born in South Wayne, Wis. After earning a Ph.D. in history and economics at the University of Wisconsin under labor historian John R. Commons (1908), he became the executive secretary of a new organization he had helped to found, the American Association for Labor Legislation – a promoter of progressive labor legislation. To support its work he would also found and edit the *American Labor Legislation Review* (1911–43). A pioneer in the industrial-hygiene and safety movement in the U.S.A., he wrote a report (1908) that led to federal legislation prohibiting the use of poisonous white phosphorous in matches (1912). His most significant work was on behalf of health and unemployment insurance for working people; he appointed a commission to investigate the feasibility of such insurance (1912); the commission recommended (1915) a compulsory mutual insurance plan modeled on programs operating in Britain and Germany, but this was attacked from all sides – unions as well as insurance companies. He continued to speak out for progressive approaches to issues of employment in the U.S.A., but, accepting that Americans were not willing to go along with this kind of compulsory insurance, he helped develop voluntaristic models; elements of his plan for unemployment insurance were incorporated into the Social Security Act of 1935. In addition to his overt advocacy of his ideas on social reform, he collaborated with his old professor John Commons on several academic texts such as *Principles of Labor Legislation* (1916), and he taught labor law and other social issue courses at Columbia University.

Andrews, LaVerne See under ANDREWS SISTERS, THE.

Andrews, Maxine See under ANDREWS SISTERS, THE.

Andrews, Patti See under ANDREWS SISTERS, THE.

Andrews, Roy Chapman (1884–1960) naturalist, explorer, author; born in Beloit, Wis. Andrews spent his career on the staff of the American Museum of Natural History (1906–42, director 1935–42). He led numerous expeditions, most notably five to central Asia (1922–30), and became famous for his team's discovery in 1928 of 100-million-year-old dinosaur eggs in the Gobi desert (the first ever found). Andrews published many popular accounts of his travels, including *Across Mongolian Plains* (1921) and *Ends of the Earth* (1929), and he was held up to a whole generation of young Americans as a role model for the scientist as adventurer.

Andrews, Stephen (Pearl) (1812–1886) abolitionist, linguist, social thinker; born in Templeton, Mass. A Baptist minister's son, he went to Louisiana at age 18 and studied and practiced law there; appalled by slavery, he became an abolitionist. Having moved to Texas in 1839, he and his family were almost killed because of his abolitionist lectures and had to flee (1843). He went off to England where he failed at his scheme to raise funds to free slaves in America. But he became interested in Pitman's new shorthand writing system and on his return to the U.S.A. he taught and wrote about this new passion while continuing his abolitionist lectures. He also became interested in phonetics and the study of foreign languages, eventually learning 30 including Chinese. By the end of the 1840s he began to focus his energies on utopian communities, establishing Modern Times in Islip, N.Y., (1851), and then Unity Home in New York City (1857). By the 1860s he was propounding an ideal society called Pantarchy, and from this he moved on to a philosophy he called "universology," which stressed the unity of all knowledge and activities. The last two decades of his life saw him at the center of many of the progressive social reform circles in New York City.

Andrews, William Loring (1837–1920) bibliophile; born in New York City. A wealthy businessman, he collected rare books, and from 1865, commissioned limited editions distinguished for their typography, illustrations, and bindings. He was founder of the Grolier Club in New York City.

Andrews Sisters, The popular musical group consisting of **LaVerne** (1915–67); **Maxine (or Maxene)** (1918–); **and (Patricia) Patti** (1920–) all born in Minneapolis, Minn. Of Norwegian-Greek parentage, they formed a harmony trio in 1932, won some local amateur contests, and gained national attention with their recording of "Bei Mir Bist Du Schoen" (1937). They performed on radio with the Glenn Miller Orchestra in the 1930s and 1940s and had another big hit with "Boogie Woogie Bugle Boy" (1940). They appeared as themselves in numerous movies including *Buck Privates* (1941), *Swingtime Johnny* (1943), and *Hollywood Canteen* (1944). After a brief retirement in the mid-1950s, they performed in nightclubs until Laverne's death (1967). Maxine and Patti returned in the early 1970s (with a stand-in for their sister) in a musical, *Over Here,* designed to evoke their earlier appeal.

Andros, Sir Edmund (1637–1714) colonial governor; born in London, England. He became governor of the newly created Dominion of New England (including Massachusetts, Plymouth, Maine, Connecticut, Rhode Island, New Hampshire) in 1686. His aristocratic manner and Anglican sympathies alienated the Bostonians and he was overthrown in a citizens' revolt in 1689.

Anfinsen, Christian (Boehmer) (1916–) biochemist; born in Monessen, Pa. He was affiliated with the National Institutes of Health (1949–62, 1963–82). In 1962, he showed that the structure of active ribonuclease is physiologically the most stable arrangement of amino acids and that the sequence of amino acids determines its function. For this work, begun in the mid-1940s, he shared the Nobel Prize in chemistry (1972). In 1972 he began working on interferon, eventually isolating the substance. He was appointed professor of biology at Johns Hopkins (1982).

Angel, (James Crawford) Jimmy (?1899–1956) adventurer, pilot; birthplace unknown. He joined the Canadian Air Corps at age 16 and during World War I was shot down over France. He became a soldier of fortune and served in China and South America as well as doing stunts in Hollywood. In 1935, seeking a gold mine on Mount Auyantepui, a plateau in southeastern Venezuela, he flew over the highest waterfall

in the world (3,212 feet); as he was the first white person to discover it, the Western world named it Angel Falls. He died in Balboa, Panama Canal Zone, after a stroke suffered during a minor plane accident.

Angel, James (Roger Prior) (1941–) astronomer; born in St. Helens, England. He came to America to teach at Columbia (1967–74), moved to the University of Arizona (1974) and is noted for research on white dwarf stars and quasars. Director of the University of Arizona's Steward Observatory Mirror Laboratory, he assisted construction of the largest American telescope mirror since the 1930s.

Angell, James (Rowland) (1869–1949) educator, psychologist; born in Burlington, Vt. (son of James Burrill Angell). Influenced by such teachers as John Dewey and William James, he completed his graduate studies in Europe and spent a year (1893) as instructor in psychology at the University of Minnesota before going to the University of Chicago where he was a faculty member and an administrator (1894–1919, serving as acting president in 1919). While there he began the new psychology department (1905) that became internationally renowned. A proponent of the "Chicago school" of psychology, known as "functionalism," he espoused a rationalism that was influenced by John Dewey. He wrote *Psychology* (1904), a widely used textbook. He went to New York City to head the Carnegie Corporation (1920–21), then became president of Yale (1921–37); at Yale he established residential colleges, strengthened professional schools and the graduate school of arts and sciences, and greatly increased the endowment. Upon retiring he served as an educational consultant to the National Broadcasting Corporation.

Angell, Joseph K. (Kinnicutt) (1794–1857) legal scholar; born in Providence, R.I. He devoted his life to writing on legal subjects in such classics as *The Law of Private Corporation Aggregate* (1832) and *The Common Law in Relation to Watercourses* (1824).

Angell, Roger (1920–) writer, editor; born in New York City. He graduated from Harvard (1942) and served in the U.S. Air Force (1942–46). He was a senior editor at *Holiday Magazine* (1947–56) and a fiction editor and general contributor to the *New Yorker* (1956). Considered the dean of baseball writers, his books include *The Summer Game* (1972), *Season Ticket* (1988), and *Once More Around the Park* (1991). He received the George Polk Award for commentary (1981).

Angelou, Maya (b. Marguerite Angelou Johnson) (1928–) writer, poet, performer; born in St. Louis, Mo. An activist on behalf of African-American concerns, she settled in California after extensive travel. She had worked as a performer, actress, and teacher. She is known for her poetry and her autobiographical novel, *I Know Why the Caged Bird Sings* (1970).

Anger, Kenneth (1932–) filmmaker, author; born in Santa Monica, Calif. Raised in the Hollywood scene as a child actor, he early rejected conventional movies and by age 15 was making provocative short experimental films. He worked for some years in Europe making outrageous and often inscrutable films, and although he gained a reputation among avant garde filmmakers and buffs, he did not come to wider attention until *Scorpio Rising* (1964). While his films, with their often explicit sexual imagery, were not designed to attract most viewers, he reached a wider public with the publication of *Hollywood Babylon* (1975), his exposé of some of the more shocking aspects of the film world.

Angermueller, Hans (1924–) lawyer, banker; born in Germany. His parents brought him to the U.S.A. at age five. A Harvard graduate (1946), he joined the law firm of Shearman & Sterling in 1950 and was a partner when he left in 1972 to take charge of the lobbying and legal efforts of financial giant, Citicorp. He became vice-chairman of Citicorp's board of directors in 1982.

Angleton, James (Jesus) (1917–87) public official; born in Boise, Idaho. He graduated from Yale and in World War II became a member of the Office of Strategic Services. He was director of counterintelligence at the Central Intelligence Agency (CIA) (1954–74). He came to distrust everyone and pursued Soviet agents within the CIA itself as well as throughout the world. His resignation was demanded (1974) following news that he had conducted clandestine mail-opening and surveillance searches within the agency in pursuit of a Soviet "mole." The quintessential parody of a suspicious intelligence officer, he was said to relax by reading poetry and cultivating orchids.

Annenberg, Walter (Hubert) (1908–) publisher, philanthropist; born in Milwaukee, Wis. Inheriting a communications empire that included the *Philadelphia Inquirer*, the *Racing Forum*, and broadcast stations, he founded *Seventeen* Magazine (1944) and the immensely successful *TV Guide* (1953), and purchased the *Philadelphia Daily News* (1957). A prominent Republican, he served as U.S. ambassador to Britain (1969–74). He assembled a large art collection that he donated to the Metropolitan Museum of Art, and he amassed a huge fortune, some of which he used to endow a graduate school of communications at the University of Pennsylvania.

Anshutz, Thomas (Pollock) (1851–1912) painter; born in Newport, Ky. After studying at the National Academy of Design in New York (1871), he worked with Thomas Eakins at the Pennsylvania Academy of Design (1876), and later became a member of the faculty. His paintings, such as *Steelworkers Noontime* (c. 1884), reveal his study of anatomy and geometric design, and his populist subject matter. He influenced many pupils, including Robert Henri, Charles Demuth and John Sloan.

Anson, (Adrian Constantine) "Cap" (1852–1922) baseball player/manager; born in Marshalltown, Iowa. During his 22-year career as a first baseman for the Chicago White Stockings (1876–97), he compiled a lifetime batting average of .334 and amassed 3,041 total hits. He served as player-manager for Chicago for 19 years (1879–97) and managed the New York Giants in 1898. As prestigious and popular as any player until Babe Ruth, he is generally recognized as having used his influence to bar African-Americans from playing major league baseball from the 1880s. He was elected to baseball's Hall of Fame in 1939.

Antheil, George (1900–59) composer; born in Trenton, N.J. After childhood studies in piano and composition (with Ernest Bloch), he made a sensation on a 1922 European tour with his "ultra-modern" compositions such as *Sonate sauvage*. Becoming a favorite of the influential Parisian avant-garde, Antheil in 1926 premiered his most famous/infamous work, the *Ballet mécanique,* a percussive score including an airplane engine and other noisemakers. Returning to the U.S.A. in 1927, he settled into a long career of

relatively conservative composing, including a number of film scores. His autobiography, *Bad Boy of Music,* appeared in 1945.

Anthes, Richard (Allen) (1944–) meteorologist; born in St. Louis, Mo. Resident meteorologist at the National Hurricane Research Laboratory (1968–71), he taught at Pennsylvania State University (1971–81) before going to the National Center for Atmospheric Research (NCAR). In 1988, he became president of the University Corporation for Atmospheric Research, umbrella organization of NCAR. His work on computer modeling of the atmosphere improved meteorologists' ability to understand climate and predict weather events.

Anthon, Charles (1797–1867) classicist; born in New York City. He was admitted to the bar in 1819 and was made professor of Greek and Latin at Columbia University the next year. He was the first American to prepare critical editions of classical authors (*Horatii Poemata,* 1830). He did the first American edition of *Lempriere's Classical Dictionary,* which he virtually rewrote; his contribution was recognized when the third edition (1833) was called *Anthon's Classical Dictionary.* His nephew Charles Edward Anthon (1823–83) was the numismatist and president of the American Numismatic and Archaeological Society of New York (1869–83).

Anthony, Robert N. (Newton) (1916–) management educator; born in Orange, Mass. He taught at Harvard Business School (1940–42, 1946–83) and was U.S. assistant secretary of defense (1965–68). A specialist in management control of nonprofit organizations, he wrote dozens of books on management control and accounting, including several long-lived accounting texts.

Anthony, Susan B. (Brownell) (1820–1906) women's rights leader; born in Adams, Mass. Raised as a Quaker and observant of the working conditions of the women in her father's cotton mill, she briefly attended Deborah Moulson's Seminary for Females in Philadelphia (1837) and then took up teaching, becoming headmistress at the Canajoharie (N.Y.) Academy (1845–48). Returning to her family – her parents knew the prominent abolitionists and had attended the first women's rights convention in Seneca Falls, N.Y., in 1848 – she met Elizabeth Cady Stanton in 1850. After she was denied a chance to speak at meetings of temperance advocates, she dedicated herself to winning full rights for women. Teamed with Stanton, she gained her first success with the passage of New York State's Married Women's Property Act (1860). An ardent abolitionist, she nevertheless opposed the male-only Fourteenth and Fifteenth Amendments. Between 1868–70 she was publisher of the *Revolution,* a woman suffrage paper. With Stanton, she founded the National Woman Suffrage Association (1869); dissatisfaction with Stanton and Anthony's methods and goals led to a schism within the movement, but in 1890 the two main groups were united as the National American Woman Suffrage Association, of which Anthony served as president (1892–1900). She constantly spoke out against injustices of all kinds but concentrated most of the energies of her final decades in seeking a constitutional amendment to allow women to vote. Although stronger in organizational skills than as a public speaker, she seemed indefatigable in traveling throughout the country to promote her cause. In 1872 she cast a ballot in the 1872 election and was arrested and fined; in 1905 she personally visited President Theodore Roosevelt to urge his support for women's suffrage. She initiated the *History of Woman Suffrage*, seeing the first four volumes into print (1881–1902). As late as 1904 she was in Berlin, Germany, helping to found the International Woman Suffrage Alliance. The ridicule that had greeted her in her first decades was replaced by respect, and she became internationally known as the symbol of the women's rights movement.

Antin, Mary (1881–1949) author, social reformer; born in Polotsk, Russia. She emigrated to the United States in 1894 and was educated at Barnard College. Her books, such as *From Polotzk to Boston* (1899) and *The Promised Land* (1912), detailed immigrant life in America. A lecturer and activist, she campaigned against restrictive immigration legislation.

Antonius, Brother See EVERSON, WILLIAM.

Apgar, Virginia (1909–1974) physician, anesthesiologist; born in Westfield, N.J. Best known for pioneering work in anesthesia relating to childbirth, she developed the Apgar Score to evaluate newborns (1952). She also created the first department of anesthesiology at Columbia-Presbyterian Medical Center (1938–49) where she was the first woman to head a department and to hold a full professorship in anesthesiology (1949). Her deepening interest in maternal and child health eventually led to an executive position with the National Foundation-March of Dimes (1959) where she spent the rest of her life fostering public support for birth defect research. With her fundraising ability, the annual income of the National Foundation increased from $19 million to $46 million by the time of her death. She also made birth defects an academic subspecialty at Cornell University Medical College where she taught (1965–73). Author of scores of papers, she was a much admired teacher most appreciated for her humanitarian qualities.

Applegate, Jesse (1811–88) colonist, cattleman; born in Kentucky. He went to Oregon in 1843 and opened the southern road to that area in 1845. He raised beef cattle in the Umpqua valley and wrote the Western classic *A Day with the Cow Column in 1843* (1876). He was an influential supporter of President Abraham Lincoln and the Union.

Appleton, Daniel (1785–1849) publisher; born in Haverhill, Mass. Starting as a dry goods merchant, he became increasingly involved in bookselling and in 1831 began publishing books, eventually under the imprint D. Appleton & Company, which he passed on to his sons.

Appleton, Nathan (1779–1861) manufacturer, banker; born in New Ipswich, N.H. One of the founders of the cotton-mill industry in Massachusetts, he pursued both profits and attractive working conditions for his employees. As a U.S. representative (Whig, Mass.; 1831–33) he argued for a protective tariff and for the Bank of the United States. He wrote *Currency and Banking* (1841) and was active in Boston's cultural life.

Appleton, William W. (Worthen) (1915–) literary historian, educator; born in New York City. He earned a Ph.D. at Columbia University and spent his academic career teaching there (1945–75). His scholarly works focused on seventeenth- and eighteenth-century English literature and theater and included *A Cycle of Cathay* (1951), *Beaumont and Fletcher* (1956), and books on Charles Macklin and Madame Vestris (1960, 1974).

Arbez, Edward (Philip), S. S. (1881–1967) Catholic theologian; born in Paris, France. Emigrating to the U.S.A. as a seminarian, he studied Near Eastern languages before being ordained a Sulpician priest. While teaching at Catholic University (1928–43) and elsewhere, Arbez earned renown as a biblical scholar; he cofounded the Catholic Biblical Society of America (1936) and chaired the editorial board of the New American Bible.

Arbus, Diane (b. Nemerov) (1923–71) photographer; born in New York City (sister of Howard Nemerov). Daughter of a wealthy department store merchant, she began as a fashion photographer, but from about 1954 on she concentrated on such subjects as deviants, nudists, dwarfs, drug-addicts, and ugly or poor people she might meet on the street.

Arbuthnot, May Hill (1884–1969) educator; born in Mason City, Iowa. While she was principal of the Cleveland (Ohio) Kindergarten-Primary Training School (1922–27), the school was made a department of elementary education at Western Reserve University and she became associate professor. She established the first nursery schools in Ohio, and the Western Reserve Nursery School that she founded became a nationally known center for the study of early education. In 1939 she and William Gray of the University of Chicago produced the *Basic Readers: Curriculum Foundation Series* (1940, 1946), the "Dick and Jane" books used by more than half the children in the U.S.A. Her college textbook, *Children and Books* (1947), became the most widely used textbook on children's literature, largely because of her insistence on high standards of evaluation and the importance of literary quality. Her *Arbuthnot Anthology of Children's Literature* (1953) went into several later editions.

Arcaro, (George Edward) Eddie (1916–) jockey; born in Cincinnati, Ohio. He was a two-time Triple Crown winner with Whirlaway (1941) and Citation (1948), and five-time winner of the Kentucky Derby. During his 31-year career ending in 1962, he rode 4,779 winners.

Archipenko, Alexander (1887–1964) sculptor; born in Kiev, Russia. He studied at the Kiev School of Art (1902–05), in Paris (1908–21), and settled in New York City (1923). He taught at many institutions, including Moholy-Nagy's New Bauhaus School, Chicago (1937–39), and became famous for his combinations of sculpture and painting, as in *Medrano II* (1914).

Arden, Elizabeth (b. Florence Nightingale Graham) (1878–1966) beautician, business executive; born in Woodbridge, Ontario, Canada. She moved to New York City in 1907 and under the name Elizabeth Arden opened a beauty salon that launched an international business empire based on salons, hundreds of "scientifically formulated" beauty products, and an exclusive image – all packaged in her trademark pink. With her rival Helena Rubinstein she made makeup acceptable to "respectable" American women, to whom Arden introduced eyeshadow, mascara, and lipstick tinted to match their outfits. As Elizabeth N. Graham she operated Maine Chance Stables in Kentucky (1930s–early 1960s) where the 1947 Kentucky Derby winner was bred.

Arends, Leslie (Cornelius) (1895–1985) U.S. representative; born in Melvin, Ill. A graduate of Oberlin, and a World War I navy veteran, he worked for the county farm bureau before going to the U.S. House of Representatives (Rep., Ill.; 1935–74). He was minority whip (1939–53) and majority leader (1957–63).

Arendt, Hannah (1906–75) historian, political philosopher; born in Hanover, Germany. Of Jewish ancestry, she received her doctorate in philosophy at Heidelberg (1929) and fled Hitler's Germany for France (1933) and the United States (1940), where she was naturalized in 1951. Her reputation as a scholar and writer was firmly established with the publication of *The Origins of Totalitarianism* (1951), which linked Nazism and Communism to 19th-century imperialism and anti-Semitism. Internationally recognized as the best-known American political theorist of her generation, she was both a prominent member of America's literary and academic elite and a revered mentor. Her teaching career included stints at Princeton (1953, 1959), Berkeley, the University of Chicago (1963–67), Columbia, Northwestern, and Cornell Universities, and the New School for Social Research (1967–75). Her most controversial major work, *Eichmann in Jerusalem, a Report on the Banality of Evil* (1963), suggested that it was simplistic to pin all the guilt for Nazi genocide on functionaries such as Adolf Eichmann; she maintained that other Germans, Western countries, and even the Jews had consented actively or passively to evil as well.

Arensberg, Walter (Conrad) (1878–1954) art collector; born in Pittsburgh, Pa. He studied at Harvard (B.A. 1900; 1903–04), lived in New York City and worked as a newspaper reporter, then married and settled in Boston (1907). He collected works by cubist artists, was a founder of the literary magazine, *Others* (1917), and attempted to prove through the use of cryptology that Francis Bacon wrote the works of Shakespeare. He moved to California (1922), purchased pre-Columbian artworks, and donated his collection to the Philadelphia Museum of Art (1950).

Argall, Sir Samuel (in America 1609–1624) sea-captain, adventurer; born in England. He pioneered a northerly route for sailing from England to Virginia (1609–10). In 1612, he abducted and detained Pocahontas (who later married John Rolfe) to insure safety from Indians raids. In 1613, he eradicated a French Jesuit colony on Mount Desert Island in Maine. He also served what was considered an unsatisfactory term as deputy-governor of Virginia (1617–19).

Argento, Dominick (1927–) composer; born in York, Pa. After studies in the U.S.A. and in Italy, he taught at the University of Minnesota from 1958. He is best known for his operas in a melodious, conservative style, among them *The Aspern Papers* (1988).

Argyris, (Christopher) Chris (1923–) psychologist, sociologist; born in Newark, N.J. He taught at Yale (1951–71) and the Harvard graduate schools of education and business administration (1971). He conducted private consultancies with government organizations. Bringing social science techniques to organizational theory, he specialized in human relations, executive development, and organizational behavior and development. One of his prominent books was *Overcoming Organizational Defenses* (1990).

Àrîda, Nasîb (1887–1946) poet; born in Hims, Syria. He studied at a Russian school before he emigrated to the U.S.A. (1905). Settling in New York City, he worked as a journalist and was a member of the Pen Bond, a group of noted Arab emigré writers. Offended by American materialism, he longed for his homeland. His poems were collected and published as *Al-Arwah, al-Ha'ira*, ("*Troubled Spirits*"), (1946).

Arledge, Roone (Pinckney, Jr.) (1931–) television producer, executive; born in Forest Hills, N.Y. After working for National Broadcasting Company (NBC), he joined ABC in 1960, creating *Wide World of Sports* (1961); he went on to revolutionize sports coverage as president of ABC Sports (1968–86), outbidding the other networks to present Monday night football and the Olympics in 1968, 1972, and 1976. Becoming ABC News president as well (1977), he raided NBC for David Brinkley and CBS for Diane Sawyer. He insured ABC's dominance in news reporting on television by making Ted Koppel *Nightline* host (1979) and Peter Jennings *World News Tonight* anchor (1983). Although he turned over the presidency of ABC Sports in 1986, he was producer for the 1988 Olympics.

Armelagos, George J. (John) (1936–) physical anthropologist; born in Lincoln Park, Mich. He performed field research in the Sudan (1963), then taught at the Universities of Utah (1965–69) and Massachusetts (1969–90) before joining the University of Florida in 1990. He made major contributions to paleopathology in human evolution, especially regarding effects of nutritional stress and infectious disease on bone development.

Armour, (Thomas Dickson) Tommy (1895–1968) golfer; born in Edinburgh, Scotland. After immigrating to the U.S.A. in 1925, he won the U.S. Open (1927), and the British Open (1931). He became a successful teaching pro after retiring from competition.

Armstrong, Edwin (Howard) (1890–1954) electrical engineer, inventor; born in New York City. A 1913 graduate of Columbia University, he studied aircraft detection methods during World War I. His work in the frequency-modulation system of radio transmission, which he pursued while a professor at Columbia (1935–54), virtually eliminated the problem of static interference. Contentious, and much addicted to lawsuits, he took his own life in a fit of depression.

Armstrong, Hamilton Fish (1893–1973) editor, author; born in New York City. He served in the U.S. Army in World War I and became first the managing editor (1922–28) and then the editor (1928–72) of *Foreign Affairs*. He wrote *Europe Between Two Wars* (1934) and *The Calculated Risk* (1947). He often served as a foreign policy advisor to the federal government.

Armstrong, Harry George (1899–1983) physician, airman; born in DeSmet, S.D. After serving a U.S. Marine Corps enlistment, he attended college and medical school, obtained a medical degree, and practiced industrial medicine in Minneapolis, Minn., for several years. Commissioned in the Medical Reserve Corps in 1929, he opted to specialize in the new field of aviation medicine. He was air surgeon, U.S. 8th Air Force, in England during World War II and became surgeon general of the U.S. Air Force in 1949.

Armstrong, Henry (b. Henry Jackson) (1912–88) boxer, minister; born in Columbus, Miss. He is the only professional boxer ever to hold three world titles simultaneously in three different weight classifications: He won the featherweight crown in 1937, and in 1938 he added both the welterweight and lightweight championships. After retiring in 1945, he became a minister and devoted himself to helping underprivileged young people through such organizations as Youthtown in Desert Wells, Ariz.

Armstrong, John (1755–1816) soldier, explorer; born in New

Jersey. He was a militia officer in the American Revolution and then served in the regular army (1784–93). He commanded Fort Pitt (1785–86) and was sent on a secret government exploration mission into Spanish territory and up the Missouri River (1790). He fought heroically in General Harmar's Indian campaign (1790) and later served as treasurer of the Northwest Territory.

Armstrong, Louis (Daniel) "Satchmo" ("Pops") (1901–71) jazz musician; born in New Orleans. He was an innovative trumpeter and singer who was the leading star of jazz throughout his career. Raised by his mother in extreme poverty, at age 12 he served a term for delinquency at the Colored Waifs Home, where he learned to play the cornet. By 1919 he was playing with Kid Ory's band in New Orleans, and also with Fate Marable on Mississippi riverboats. In 1922, he joined his mentor, King Oliver's trailblazing Creole Jazz Band, in Chicago, and in 1924 he spent a year with Fletcher Henderson's pioneering big band in New York, where he also recorded with Bessie Smith and other leading blues singers. Between 1925 and 1929, he made his classic Hot Five and Hot Seven recordings, which shaped the course of jazz for the next two decades. In 1930, his recording of the pop song "Ain't Misbehavin'" became his first show business hit, and for the next 17 years he appeared as a star soloist with various big bands in an increasingly commercial context. In 1947, he formed his All Stars, a Dixieland-style sextet with which he maintained a constant international touring schedule until his death. He appeared in over 50 films as a musician and entertainer, including *New Orleans* (1947), *Paris Blues* (1961), and *Hello, Dolly!* (1969). His autobiography, *Satchmo: My Life in New Orleans,* was published in 1954.

Armstrong, Neil (Alden) (1930–) astronaut, educator, business executive; born in Wapakoneta, Ohio. A U.S. Navy pilot during the Korean War (1949–52), he was a civilian test pilot before joining the astronaut program in 1962. He was the command pilot of the Gemini 8 flight that effected the first successful docking of two vehicles in space. As commander of the Apollo 11 lunar mission, he entered history as the first human being to walk on the moon (July 20, 1969), but afterwards he avoided most public appearances and all attempts to treat him as a hero. He worked for the National Aeronautics and Space Administration (NASA) until 1971, then became a professor of engineering at the University of Cincinnati (1971–79); he went on to become chairman of CTA Inc. (1982), a computer systems company, and continued to avoid the limelight.

Arnall, Ellis (Gibbs) (1907–92) governor; born in Newnan, Ga. A lawyer and Democratic Georgia assemblyman, elected Speaker (1933–37), he became Georgia's attorney general (1939–43). A progressive governor (Dem., 1943–47), he ended prison chain gangs, abolished the poll tax, and restored accreditation of the state university. Founding an Atlanta law firm afterward, he served as President Truman's director of the Office of Price Stabilization in 1952.

Arneson, Robert (1930–) ceramist; born in Benicia, Calif. With a Mills College M.F.A. (1958), he joined the ceramics faculty of the University of California: Davis (1962). A controversial innovator whose intentionally crude sculptural works reflected such modern trends as abstract expressionism, surrealism, pop art, and the funk movement, he helped raise ceramics to an art form through his satirical exploration of themes of sexuality and politics.

Arness, James (b. James Aurness) (1923–) television actor; born in Minneapolis, Minn. He was wounded in the Anzio, Italy, invasion in 1944. After working as a screen actor in the 1940s and 1950s, he took on the role of Marshall Matt Dillon (after John Wayne turned it down), the no-nonsense, good-hearted hero of CBS's *Gunsmoke,* television's first and longest running Western series (1955–75). His brother was the television actor Peter Graves.

Arnheim, Rudolf (1904–) art theorist, psychologist; born in Berlin, Germany. He studied at the University of Berlin, worked in Rome with the International Institute of Educational Films (1933–38), then taught at both the New School for Social Research and Sarah Lawrence College (1943–68), Harvard (1968–74), and the University of Michigan (1974). He taught film history but is most noted as a pioneering theorist of the psychology of the arts; among his influential books are *Art as Visual Perception* (1954, 1974); *Toward a Psychology of Art* (1966) and *Entropy and Art* (1971).

Arnold, Benedict (1741–1801) soldier, patriot, traitor; born in Norwich, Conn. Prior to the American Revolution he was a prosperous trader. He was an outstanding leader in military situations. He captured Fort Ticonderoga (1775) – in conjunction with Ethan Allen – and nearly captured Quebec City, where he was wounded in his leg. In 1776, he delayed a possible British invasion of New York by means of a makeshift fleet on Lake Champlain. In 1777, he inspired American troops and led them to the victory that brought about Burgoyne's surrender at Saratoga (he was again wounded in his leg). He became bitter due to Congressional slights, and he moved into traitorous correspondence with British leaders. In 1780, he attempted to betray vital West Point to the British. Failing in this, he remained in the British camp, conducted raids against both Virginia, and his native Connecticut, and then retired to England where he received some money but no honor for having changed sides. He spent his last years as a not very successful trader in Canada and the West Indies.

Arnold, (Henry Harley) "Hap" (1886–1950) soldier, aviator; born in Gladwyne, Pa. A physician's son, he graduated from West Point in 1907 and served in the infantry before transferring to the Signal Corps. Bored with garrison routine, Arnold volunteered for flight training, receiving instruction from no less an authority than Orville Wright, and obtained a pilot's license in 1911. An ally of air visionary William Mitchell, Arnold became a leading advocate of air power during the 1920s and 1930s. As commander of the Army Air Corps (1938) and, from 1941 onward, as chief of the Army Air Forces, he built a mighty air fleet – 64,000 aircraft and 2.4 million men – and developed strategic and tactical air doctrine, including the massive long-range bombing of Germany and Japan. Arnold retired in 1946, a year before the air force became an independent service. Given a fifth star as a general of the army in 1944, his commission was changed to general of the air force in 1949. Arnold wrote several books, including *This Flying Game* (1936) and *Global Mission* (1949).

Arnold, Thurman (Wesley) (1891–1969) lawyer, government official; born in Laramie, Wyo. Dean of the University of Virginia Law School (1927–30) and iconoclastic law professor at Yale (1930–37), he wrote *The Folklore of Capitalism*

(1937). An assistant attorney general in Washington (1938–43), he spearheaded anti-trust indictments. He served as an appellate judge (1943–45) before returning to private practice.

Arnon, Daniel I. (Israel) (1910–) plant physiologist; born in Warsaw, Poland. Raised in the U.S.A., he spent his career at the University of California: Berkeley (1936–78). His early research (1930s) concerned the role of trace elements in the growth of algae and higher plants. He demonstrated that water (hydroponic) culture of tomatoes, using mineral supplements, produces yields similar to soil crops, but is economically feasible only if the available soil is incapable of supporting growth (1939). His pioneering investigations of photosynthesis began in the late 1940s, when he and colleagues isolated chloroplasts (chlorophyll-containing cell organelles) from spinach cells, and published results of the first photosynthetic process outside the living cell (1954). He also discovered "photosynthetic phosphorylation," which occurs in the absence of carbon dioxide.

Aronson, Boris (1900–1980) set designer; born in Kiev, Russia. Winner of the New York Drama Critics Award in 1964 for *Fiddler on the Roof,* he began his New York career in 1924 working for the Unser Theatre and for the Yiddish Art Theatre. His sets included those for *Three Men on a Horse* (1935), *Detective Story* (1949), and *J.B.* (1958). An admirer of Marc Chagall, he excelled in stylized settings, but he was also capable of straightforward realism.

Arpino, Gerald (1928–) ballet dancer, choreographer; born on Staten Island, N.Y. Trained early in classical and modern dance, he was a leading dancer and resident choreographer with Robert Joffrey's companies from 1956–64. He became assistant director of the Joffrey Ballet in 1965 and artistic director in 1988.

Arrow, Kenneth (Joseph) (1921–) economist; born in New York City. He was recognized early in his career for his "impossibility theorem," a study of collective choice that employs the notational system of logic to illustrate that more than two options in a democratic majority rule leads to a stalemate. He worked to establish the properties of general equilibrium including its existence, significance, and relevance. After a brief period at the Cowles Commission at the University of Chicago, he taught at Stanford University (1949–68 and 1979) and at Harvard University (1968–79). He shared the Nobel Prize in economics (1972) with Sir John Hicks.

Arthur, Chester A. (Alan) (1830–86) twenty-first U.S. president; born in Fairfield, Vt. A lawyer, he joined New York's Republican political machine, which led to a patronage appointment as New York customs collector and an uproar when antipatronage President Hayes removed Arthur. Nominated as vice-president to Garfield in 1880 to pacify party regulars, Arthur became president on Garfield's assassination in July 1881. He surprised all by making solid appointments and signing the Pendleton Civil Service Reform Act of 1883. He lost the 1884 nomination due to his declining health as well as to his having antagonized many Republican politicians.

Arthur, Jean (b. Gladys Georgianna Greene) (1905–91) movie actress; born in New York City. As a teenager she modeled for popular artist Howard Chandler Christy and this led to some small roles in the New York theater. She made her movie debut in *Cameo Kirby* (1923) and continued to appear in unsatisfying roles until 1932 when she went back to act on the New York stage. She returned to films in 1934 but didn't find her true screen persona until 1935 in *The Whole Town's Talking.* From then on, as a husky-voiced, no-nonsense, independent woman, her presence in a series of movies such as *Mr. Deeds Goes to Town* (1936) guaranteed both critical and popular acceptance. Her last major role was in *Shane* (1953) but she appeared in occasional television and theater productions and in 1956 she had her own television comedy series. She taught drama at Vassar and other colleges for several years.

Artin, Emil (1898–1962) mathematician; born in Hamburg, Germany. After emigrating (1937), he taught at the University of Indiana (1938–1946) and Princeton (1946–58), returning to the University of Hamburg (1958). He is best known for work in higher algebra, including the L-series functions, class field theory and hypercomplex numbers. In his spare time he enjoyed astronomy, biology, and old music.

Artzybasheff, Boris (1899–1965) illustrator; born in Kharkov, Russia. He studied in St. Petersburg, Russia (1907–18), emigrated to New York City (1919), and worked as an engraver, illustrator, and set designer. Known for his illustrations of books for adults and children, such as his *Seven Simeons* (1937), he also created surrealistic covers for *Time, Life,* and *Fortune* magazines.

Arzner, Dorothy (1900–79) director, scriptwriter; born in San Francisco. After working on a newspaper, she was hired as a stenographer at Famous Players, rising to the positions of film editor and scriptwriter. Her work was so good that she was promoted to director, making her debut with *Fashions for Women* (1927). She became Hollywood's only female director of the 1930s, directing 15 more movies until 1943; during World War II she made training films for the Women's Army Corps. She was never allowed to direct again and it was not until the 1980s that her pioneering role was recognized.

Asbury, Francis (1745–1816) Protestant religious leader; born in Handsworth, Staffordshire, England. He came to America in 1771 as a missionary. A powerful preacher, he toured the colonies and the Mississippi territory and developed the system of circuit-riding for the frontier ministry. Appointed superintendent of American Methodists in 1772, he fought for many years against British efforts to retain control of the American organization. He appointed himself bishop in 1785 and over the next 30 years established Methodism as one of the leading U.S. denominations.

Asch, Moses ("Moe") (1905–86) record producer; born in Warsaw, Poland. The son of novelist Sholem Asch, he came with his family to the U.S.A. (1909) and grew up in Brooklyn, New York. He studied engineering in Koblenz, Germany. One of his first jobs was installing sound equipment in Yiddish theaters. In 1939 he founded Asch Records to record his father's stories but he soon turned to recording folk singers such as Josh White, Burl Ives, and Pete Seeger, and jazz musicians such as Coleman Hawkins and Mary Lou Williams. In 1948 he founded (with Marion Distler) Folkways Records and in addition to recording songs by Woody Guthrie, Leadbelly, and a large catalogue of folk, jazz, gospel, children's, and other traditional American music, he enlarged the Folkways catalogue to include folk and traditional music from literally every corner of the world. Folkways Records not only provided a service to those specializing in obscure ethnographic music but introduced blues and folk music that influenced several generations of young Americans. Always open to new proposals, Asch also issued unusual novelty recordings, from the sounds of frogs to electronic music; he also cofounded Oak Publications, a music publisher.

Asch, Sholem (or Shalom) (1880–1957) writer, playwright; born in Kutno, Poland. He studied at the Hebrew school in his village, then moved to Warsaw, Poland (1899), where he wrote stories, plays, poems, and novels in Hebrew and Yiddish. He emigrated to New York City (1909), and began as a writer for Yiddish newspapers there. His play, *The God of Vengeance,* enjoyed considerable success in a production in Berlin, Germany (1910) and several other of his plays would be produced in the Yiddish theater in New York. He continued his prolific career as a writer, occasionally in English, but mostly in Yiddish, and although he became a U.S. citizen in 1920 and long maintained a home in Florida, he often lived abroad. Most of his works dealt with Jewish subjects, as in *Mottke the Thief* (1917) and *Three Cities* (1933). His most famous books (to English readers) formed a trilogy – *The Nazarene* (1939), *The Apostle* (1943), and *Mary* (1949) – in which he attempted to portray Jesus, Paul, and Mary in a way that bridged Christianity and Judaism, but he so antagonized some American Jews that he moved to Israel in 1956.

Ash, Roy L. (Lawrence) (1918–) corporate executive; born in Los Angeles. He co-founded Electro-Dynamics Corporation with Charles B. Thornton (1953) and soon bought Litton Industries (president 1961–72). His financial acumen in acquiring high-technology companies turned Litton into one of the first modern international conglomerates. He was director of the Office of Management and Budget (1972–75) and after 1975 headed Addressograph-Multigraph Corporation.

Ashbery, John (Lawrence) (1927–) poet, writer; born in Rochester, N.Y. He attended Harvard (B.A. 1949), Columbia University (M.A. 1951), lived in Paris (1955–65), and settled in New York City. He taught at Brooklyn College beginning in 1974, was a playwright and a literary and art critic, and was known for his visionary poetry, as in *Self-Portrait in a Convex Mirror* (1975).

Ashe, Arthur (Robert) (1943–93) tennis player, author; born in Richmond, Va. He was the first black player ever to win the U.S. championship (1968), the Davis Cup (1968–70), the Australian Open (1970), and Wimbledon (1975). While actively protesting apartheid in South Africa, he was granted a visa in 1973 to become the first black professional to play in that country. He retired from competition after suffering a heart attack in 1979. He wrote a three-volume history of African-American athletes in the U.S.A., *A Hard Road to Glory* (1988). He became a spokesperson for AIDS education after it was revealed in 1992 that he had contracted the AIDS virus from a blood transfusion.

Asheim, Lester Eugene (1914–) library educator; born in Spokane, Wash. A graduate of the University of Chicago, he became a recognized leader in library education and academic and intellectual freedom. He served as dean of the Graduate Library School at the University of Chicago before becoming director of the American Library Association's Office for Library Education, where he was known for his expertise in personnel development. He later joined the faculty of the University of North Carolina where he made significant curriculum changes and inaugurated a doctoral program in library science.

Ashford, Bailey Kelly (1873–1934) physician; born in Washington, D.C. An authority on tropical diseases, he discovered the parasitic hookworm that caused the anemia endemic to agricultural workers in Puerto Rico. He helped wipe out the disease there, thus launching a campaign to wipe it out throughout the world. He organized the Institute of Tropical Medicine and Hygiene, which was administered by Columbia University after 1926. He did research on the American hookworm.

Ashford, Emmett (Littleton) (1914–80) baseball umpire; born in Los Angeles. He became professional baseball's first black umpire in 1951 and major league's first black umpire in 1966. Known for his flamboyant calling of balls and strikes, he umpired American League games from 1966 to 1970.

Ashley, Merrill (b. Linda Merrill) (1950–) ballet dancer; born in St. Paul, Minn. After graduating from the School of American Ballet in 1966, she became one of the New York City Ballet's most acclaimed "Balanchine ballerinas."

Ashmun, Jehuda (1794–1828) colonial agent, author; born in Champlain, N.Y. A graduate of the University of Vermont (1816), he entered the Congregational ministry, then became involved in various educational and journalistic enterprises. In 1822, he shipped from Baltimore to Liberia with a boatload of returning African-American slaves. There he held off an attack by native chiefs and survived the fever that killed his wife. He stayed on and was appointed the American Colonization Society's agent (1824–28). He wrote *The History of the American Colony in Liberia from December 1821 to 1823.*

Asimov, Isaac (1920–92) writer, scientist; born in Petrovichi, Russia. He came to New York City at age three. A Columbia Ph.D., he taught biochemistry at Boston University School of Medicine after 1949. He was an author, lecturer, and broadcaster of legendary prolificacy and astonishing range, but is most admired as a popularizer of science (*The Collapsing Universe* (1977)) and a science fiction writer (*I, Robot* (1950)), *The Foundation Trilogy* (1951–53)). He coined the term "robotics."

Askew, Reubin (O'Donovan) (1928–) governor; born in Muskogee, Okla. After putting himself through college and law school on the G.I. Bill, he served in Florida legislature (Dem., 1959–71), opposing school segregation. As Florida's governor (1971–79) he initiated tax reform, improved the penal system, and established an environmental protection agency. A U.S. representative for international trade negotiations (1979–81), he returned to his law practice afterward.

Astaire, Fred (b. Frederick Austerlitz) (1899–1987) actor, dancer, choreographer, singer; born in Omaha, Nebr. He began dance lessons at the age of five, and by the time he was seven he was touring the vaudeville circuit with his sister Adele as his dance partner. In 1917 they made their Broadway debut in the musical *Over the Top.* When Adele married, Fred was on his own, and made his first film appearance with Joan Crawford in *Dancing Lady* (1933). Then he was paired with Ginger Rogers in *Flying Down to Rio* (1933), and they went on to make 9 more musical films, revolutionizing the film musical with an assortment of original and innovative routines. After Rogers turned to dramatic roles, Astaire made more dance films with several partners. Although not so widely appreciated as a singer, his breezy renditions of certain period pieces are classics of their kind. The urbane, exuberant, sophisticated dancer turned to drama in 1959, in *On the Beach,* and continued in serious roles, winning an Emmy for *A Family Upside Down* (1978). He was the winner of a special Oscar (1949).

Astin, Alexander W. (William) (1932–) higher education researcher; born in Washington, D.C. Professor of higher education (1973) at the University of California: Los Angeles, his many books on assessment and evaluation in higher education include *The College Environment* (1968) and *Assessment for Excellence* (1991).

Astor, Brooke (b. Roberta Brooke Russell) (?1902–) socialite, philanthropist, author; born in Portsmouth, N.H. Largely self-educated, she was a magazine journalist and the author of four books. She married three times (once divorced, twice widowed). Her third husband, Vincent Astor, left her with a fortune that allowed her to become a philanthropist of major proportions. She awarded an average of 100 grants a year ($9 million a year) to civic projects, social projects, and cultural institutions in New York City. She also served on numerous boards, including as trustee of the New York Public Library, one of her major beneficiaries. In her later years, she became the most sought-after guest at New York's charitable and stylish occasions.

Astor, John Jacob (1763–1848) fur trader, real estate investor, millionaire; born in Waldorf, near Heidelberg, Germany. He moved to England at age 16 and then to New York City (1784). He worked at various jobs but soon entered the fur trade and had his own business by 1786. The leading merchant in the North American fur trade by 1800, he gained access to the China trade and invested heavily in New York City real estate. He combined all his fur holdings into the American Fur Company (1808). He planned the Astoria colony in Oregon (1811) but sold the property when it was threatened by the War of 1812. His Manhattan real estate continued to prosper and he sold his fur interests in 1834. He administered his estate wisely and at his death, his worth was at least $20 million, making him the wealthiest man in America. Among his most far-reaching bequests was $350,000 to found a public library in New York City. (The famous New York City hotel named after him, the Waldorf-Astoria, carries on the names of two hotels originally built by his grandsons.)

Astor, John Jacob (1864–1912) financier, inventor; born in Rhinebeck, N.Y. (great-grandson of John Jacob Astor, 1763–1848). He built the Astoria section of the Waldorf-Astoria Hotel in 1897. He served in the Spanish-American War. He invented a bicycle brake and an improved turbine engine. He went down with the *Titanic* after a notable display of courage and gallantry.

Astor, Nancy (b. Nancy Witcher Langhorne) (1879–1964) Viscountess, politician; born in Danville, Va. In 1906 she married the 2nd Viscount Astor, to whose seat in Britain's Parliament she succeeded (Conservative, 1919–45). The first woman to sit in the House of Commons, she promoted temperance and women's rights and wrote an early autobiography, *My Two Countries* (1923).

Astor, William Backhouse (1792–1875) financier; born in New York City (son of John Jacob Astor, 1763–1848). He worked as a clerk for his father, and upon the latter's death, he became the richest man in the U.S.A. He continued the family practice of dealing in New York City real estate and was known as the "landlord of New York." He added to his father's bequest to the Astor Library, which was later absorbed into the main branch of the New York Public Library.

Atanasoff, John V. (Vincent) (1903–) physicist, computer engineer; born in Hamilton, N.Y. He took his Ph.D. in physics at the University of Wisconsin (1930). By 1938, he had developed several concepts that would underlie early computers – that they should be electronic, binary based, and use condensers for memory. Working with Clifford Berry at Iowa State University (1939–42), he built what is regarded as the first electronic digital calculating machine; known as the ABC (Atanasoff-Berry-Computer), it would influence the design of subsequent computers. He built computers for the navy and army (1942–52) and then went into private business.

Atchison, David Rice (1807–86) U.S. senator; born in Frogtown, Ky. Moving to Missouri to practice law, he served briefly as a federal judge (1841–43). He was appointed and then elected to the U.S. Senate (Dem., Mo.; 1843–55). A supporter of slavery, he helped frame the Kansas-Nebraska Act (1854). After losing his seat in the Senate, he went back to Missouri and supported those who attacked the anti-slavery settlers in Kansas. He moved to Texas during the Civil War but returned to Missouri to spend his final years as a farmer.

Atherton, George Washington (1837–1906) land grant lobbyist, college president; born in Boxford, Mass. As president of Pennsylvania State College (later University) (1882–1906) he regenerated a virtually moribund institution. A champion of land-grant colleges, Atherton was instrumental in drafting the Hatch (1887) and Second Morrill (1890) Acts, which established their funding and agricultural research base.

Atherton, Gertrude (Franklin Horn) (1857–1948) writer; born in San Francisco. She began writing during an unhappy marriage, and after being widowed in 1887, continued professionally. She maintained her ties to San Francisco but traveled widely and lived in Europe for many years. Her 56 books include melodramatic historical and society novels, works set in old California (*The Splendid Idle Forties,* 1902), and innovative fictionalized biographies of Alexander Hamilton and others. Many of her novels depict strong-willed women, and her *Black Oxen* (1923) promoted the possibility of rejuvenation through a medical operation.

Atkins, (Chester Burton) Chet (1924–) guitarist, record producer; born near Luttrell, Tenn. In the 1940s he performed with the Carter Family and Red Foley and first appeared in the "Grand Ole Opry." In Nashville in the 1950s he made the electric guitar popular as a solo instrument for country music. As a producer for RCA he promoted such singers as Hank Snow and Waylon Jennings, reviving country music in the 1960s and 1970s. In 1982 he began recording for CBS records.

Atkinson, Brooks (1894–1984) journalist, drama critic; born in Melrose, Mass. He was the erudite, highly influential theater critic for the *New York Times* for over 30 years (1925–42, 1946–60). After a wartime assignment as *Times* correspondent in China and the Soviet Union, he won a 1947 Pulitzer Prize for reporting.

Atkinson, Henry (1782–1842) soldier; born in North Carolina. He entered the army in 1808 and became a colonel after the War of 1812. He led the Yellowstone expedition (1819) and an expedition to the upper Missouri River (1825). He was in general command during the Black Hawk War (1832).

Atlas, Charles (b. Angelo Siciliano) (1894–1972) body-builder, trainer; born in Acri, Italy. Coming to the U.S.A. in 1904, he was anemic and weak as a youth and began to work out at a Brooklyn Young Men's Christian Association gym; there he developed his own system of pitting muscle against muscle – what he later (1921) called "dynamic tension" – and built up his body so that he soon was attracting attention as a strong man at Coney Island; he had meanwhile adopted the name of a statue of the ancient Atlas. Invited to model by sculptors, he posed for several public sculptures (including, it is alleged, George Washington in Washington Square, New York City). In 1922 he won a contest for "the World's Most Perfectly Developed Man," and to capitalize on his reputation, he opened a gymnasium to teach his system. He also launched a mail-order course in body-building, advertising it with his eventually legendary image of the "97-pound weakling" who loses his girl to a bully at the beach. (It is probably apocryphal that Atlas himself experienced this exact event.) This mail-order course became so popular, even throughout the world – it was translated into at least seven languages – that he soon gave up his gymnasium to concentrate on it. A precursor of the modern body-building movement, he maintained his own body so well that in 1938, weighing only 178 pounds, he pulled a 145,000-pound train 122 feet.

Attucks, Crispus (?1723–70) Revolutionary figure; birth-place unknown. Little or nothing is known for sure of his exact origins, but it is generally believed that he was a mulatto and that he was either an escaped or freed slave. (In 1750 a notice for a runaway slave named "Crispus" appeared in a Boston newspaper.) He may well have been a sailor on a whaling ship or at least he worked around the Boston wharves. He was later described as a large man "whose looks was enough to terrify any person," but that may have been the perception of someone uncomfortable with African-Americans. In any case, on March 5, 1770, he evidently joined a group of Boston men and youths who – annoyed at the British authorities trying to enforce new tax laws – had begun to throw snowballs at a lone British soldier guarding the State House. Fearing that the situation was getting out of control, a captain called out a small unit of the guard. As the crowd began to throw stones along with their taunts and push came to shove, the threatened soldiers fired, hitting 11 colonists; five died on the spot or later, and among them was Attucks. Exactly what his role had been is not known but he was quickly made into a hero; he is the only participant in the so-called Boston Massacre whose name has passed into popular legend. In 1888 a statue of Attucks, by the famed Augustus Saint-Gaudens, was dedicated on Boston Common.

Atwater, Caleb (1778–1867) educator, archaeologist; born in North Adams, Mass. An Ohio lawyer and legislator, he founded the Ohio state school system and wrote the important *Essay on Education* (1841). As Ohio's state archaeologist he made the earliest North American archaeological survey (published 1820).

Atwater, Helen Woodard (1876–1947) home economist; born in Somerville, Mass. (daughter of Wilbur Olin Atwater). After graduating from Smith College she assisted her father in his seminal calometric research. She joined the U.S. Department of Agriculture's Office of Home Economics to publicize new findings on nutrition and food preparation to rural women (1909–23), and edited the *Journal of Home Economics* (1923–41).

Atwater, Wilbur Olin (1844–1907) agricultural chemist, educator; born in Johnsburg, N.Y. He was professor of chemistry at Wesleyan University (1873–1907) and directed the first agricultural experiment station in Middletown, Conn., (1875–77). He was involved in fertilizer testing as well as the investigation of nutritional and calorimetric standards.

Atwood, Wallace (Walter) (1872–1949) geographer; born in Chicago. He graduated from the University of Chicago in 1897, thoroughly inspired by Rollin D. Salisbury. He taught at Chicago and Harvard, then assumed the presidency of Clark University (1920–46). He traveled on every continent and wrote much, especially in the area of physical geography.

Auchincloss, Louis (Stanton) (1917–) lawyer, writer; born in Lawrence, N.Y. From New York's upper class, he moved easily through Groton, Yale, and law school. After World War II service with the U.S. Navy, he took up a career as a Wall Street lawyer, a profession he continued to pursue while also gaining a reputation as a writer in the tradition of Henry James. His many civilized and well-crafted novels and short stories are psychological and moral dramas played out among New York's old-money elite.

Auden, W. H. (Wystan Hugh) (1907–73) poet, writer; born in York, England. He studied at Oxford (1925–28), taught, traveled extensively, wrote several plays, and emigrated to New York City (1939), becoming a U.S. citizen in 1946. He taught at many institutions, was an editor for literary periodicals, and is known as a humanist poet, as in *Homage to Clio* (1960). In the 1930s he collaborated with Christopher Isherwood on verse plays, and he later wrote the libretto for Stravinsky's *The Rake's Progress* (1951). One of the most respected men of letters of his time, he returned to England in 1972.

Audubon, John James (b. Jean Jacques ?Fougere) (1785–1851) painter, naturalist; born in Les Cayes, Haiti. The illegitimate son of a French sea captain and merchant, Jean Audubon, and a Creole woman, he was taken to France and legally adopted by Audubon and his wife (1794). He began drawing birds as a teenager (but few now accept his claim that he studied under the great David in Paris). In 1803 he moved to his father's estate near Philadelphia, where he spent his time hunting, experimenting with birds (he is credited with the first banding of wild birds in America), and also drawing the birds he hunted. After convincing her father that he could support her, in 1808 he married Lucy Bakewell; but soon he was going bankrupt operating stores and other business enterprises in Kentucky while he pursued his two real passions: observing and drawing wildlife. To make his finished paintings – for which he used a mix of pastel, watercolor, tempera and, later, oils – he would shoot or trap birds and other wildlife (or sometimes buy dead specimens in the market); at home he set them in lifelike poses by passing wires through the animals. Audubon moved to New Orleans in 1821, and Lucy soon was providing much of their income by tutoring, while Audubon contributed some by doing portraits and teaching art. Determined to publish his bird paintings in a large format, he was advised to go to Europe to find skilled engravers; he went to Great Britain (1826) where, in addition to lining up subscribers, he eventually obtained the help of master engraver Robert Havell, Jr. The great "double elephant" folio edition of *The Birds of America* (4 vols., 1827–38), with hand-colored engravings, enjoyed immediate success; the text was published separately (5 vols., 1831–39) as *Ornithological Biography*. He returned to America (1829–30 and 1831–34) to continue his search for as many species of birds as he could find. He went back to Europe (1834–39), and then settled permanently in the U.S.A. He issued a smaller edition of *The Birds of America* (1840–44), and with the naturalist John Bachman, worked almost until his death on *The Viviparous Quadrupeds of North America* (3 vols., 1845–54). Although criticized for certain scientific and artistic failings, Audubon's work still engages people with its dramatic and detailed images of wildlife.

Auerbach, (Arnold Jacob) "Red" (1917–) basketball coach; born in New York City. During his career as coach of the Boston Celtics (1950–66), his teams won nine National Basketball Association championships, eight of them consecutively (1959–66). Famous for lighting a cigar after each victory, he retired from coaching in 1966 to become the team's general manager.

Augustus, John (1785–1859) pioneer probation officer, philanthropist; born in Boston, Mass. Little is known of his background or early years but by 1841 he was a shoemaker, albeit one who employed several assistants. Attending the Boston Police Court that year, he witnessed a case involving a common drunkard; at Augustus's request, the man's sentence was deferred for three weeks and he was released to Augustus's supervision; at the end of the probationary period the man was able to convince the judge of his reformation and received a nominal fine. After this incident Augustus appeared almost daily in various Boston courts, acting as counsel for prisoners, furnishing bail, and sometimes finding homes for juvenile defenders; his unorthodox approach often brought him into conflict with court officials. He continued to work at his shoemaking business until 1846 when he seems to have acquired enough money to support himself. Between 1842–58, using his own money and some modest contributions from others, he posted bail for 1,946 people. He is regarded as "the father of probation" in the U.S.A.

Austin, Mary (b. Hunter) (1868–1934) writer, naturalist; born in Carlinville, Ill. After graduating from Blackburn College (1888), she moved to California, married, and settled in the Owens Valley; her close observations of desert and Indian life there informed her first book, *The Land of Little Rain* (1903). After separating from her husband (1905), she lived in Carmel, Calif., and New York City; in the latter she became associated with the circle of Mabel Dodge and she was influenced by Dodge to settle permanently in Santa Fe, N.M., from 1924 on. Her move to New Mexico rekindled her interest in the natural world of the desert and Indian culture. Her 32 books and more than 200 articles include poetry, realistic fiction (*A Woman of Genius*, 1912), and pioneering studies of Native American life (*The American Rhythm*, 1923). Her autobiography, *Earth Horizon* (1932), conveys the mystical, feminist, and socialist philosophy that she developed.

Austin, Moses (1761–1821) merchant, colonist; born in Durham, Conn. He managed lead mines in Virginia and Missouri. Following the depression of 1819, he applied for and received a permit from Spanish authorities to settle 300 American families in Texas (1821). He died before going to Texas.

Austin, Stephen (Fuller) (1793–1836) Texas colonist; born in Wythe County, Va. (son of Moses Austin). After varied work experiences in Missouri, Arkansas, and Louisiana, where he also studied law, he founded the first legal settlement of Anglo-Americans in Texas (1822). He went to Mexico City to reconfirm his father's land grant and returned with almost dictatorial powers. He fixed the land system, mapped and charted the province, and encouraged a steady flow of immigrants from the U.S.A. He originally opposed separation from Mexico, but he was imprisoned by Mexican authorities (1834–35) after he attempted to change Texas' status within the Mexican confederation. Freed without a trial, he participated in the Texas Revolution and sought support from the U.S.A. He lost the election for president of the Texas Republic to Sam Houston but served briefly as its secretary of state.

Autio, Rudy (1926–) ceramist; born in Butte, Mont. With an M.F.A. from Washington State University, he became professor of ceramics and sculpture in 1957 at the University of Montana in Missoula. While his early pots reflected abstract expressionism, he is best known for his later figurative work. On anthropomorphic clay forms he superimposed improvisational drawings of women, landscapes, and animals to pictorialize the vessels.

Avedon, Richard (1923–) photographer; born in New York City. A product of the public schools, he was a fashion photographer for *Harper's* (1945–65) and a student of Alexey Brodovitch. Known for his stark portraits of people in unusual poses, he published his first book of celebrity portraits, *Observations,* in 1959. In 1963 he left his studio to photograph the Civil Rights movement and the Anti-War movement, winning a national magazine award for visual excellence in 1976.

Avery, (Frederick Bean) Tex (1907–80) animator; born in Dallas, Texas. One of the creators of Bugs Bunny, he developed the Warner Bros. style of surrealistic fantasy.

Avery, Milton (Clark) (1885–1965) painter; born in Altmar, N.Y. He recorded little information about himself, but it is known that he arrived in New York City in 1925 and devoted himself to painting. His approach, called modernism, linked realism with abstract art. His use of color in paintings such as *Autumn* (1944), *Sailfish in Fog* (1959), and *Dark Inlet* (1963), is inventive and poetic.

Avery, Oswald T. (Theodore) (1877–1955) bacteriologist; born in Halifax, Nova Scotia, Canada. He came to New York City (NYC) in 1887 when his clergyman father began missionary work in the Bowery. He practiced medicine in NYC (1904–07), became a bacteriologist at Hoagland Laboratory, Brooklyn (1907–13), then joined the Rockefeller Institute (1913–48). His career-long studies of the pneumococcus bacterium included the immunological classification of this organism (1917). His discovery that this bacterium's immunospecific substances were polysaccharide capsular type-specific antigens was a breakthrough in the developing science of immunochemistry. His subsequent pneumococcal research, summarized in 1944, indicated that the agent that transforms nonvirulent strains to virulent was DNA, thus demonstrating that DNA is the chemical basis of heredity.

Avery, Samuel Putnam (1822–1904) art connoisseur, philanthropist; born in New York City. He had little formal schooling, worked as an engraver of bank notes, became a wood engraver, and illustrated books. He established an art book publishing company (1865–88), collected engravings and etchings, and was one of the founders of the Metropolitan Museum. He also endowed and built the Avery Architectural Library at Columbia College (1891).

Avery, Sewell (Lee) (1874–1960) corporate executive; born in Saginaw, Mich. He joined the United States Gypsum Co. (1901), which as president (1905–37) and chairman (until 1951) he developed into a major international building materials manufacturer despite the Depression of the 1930s. His effective but autocratic tenure as chief executive officer and chairman of Montgomery Ward and Co. (1931–55) was marked by fights with executives, stockholders and directors. In a highly publicized 1944 episode, federal soldiers literally carried him from his office for noncompliance with a War Labor Board order.

Avram, Henriett D. (Davidson) (1919–) librarian; born in New York City. After studying at Hunter College, she worked in private industry and in government; she held several important positions at the Library of Congress. An information systems specialist, she brought expertise to cataloging and library automation.

Ax, Emanuel (1949–) pianist; born in Lwow, Poland. After studies at Juilliard he made his New York debut in 1973. He went on to become one of the most popular soloists and recitalists of his generation, his repertoire encompassing classics to moderns.

Axelrod, Julius (1912–) pharmacologist; born in New York City. He was a chemist at the Laboratory of Industrial Hygiene (New York City) (1935–45), and a research associate at Goldwater Memorial Hospital (New York City) (1946–49). He became a biochemist for the National Heart Institute (1949–55), then joined the National Institute for Mental Health (1955–84), remaining as a guest worker (1984). His studies of neurotransmission of adrenalin and amphetamines led to his investigations into psychoactive drugs for treatment of mental illness, including schizophrenia. He shared the 1970 Nobel Prize for physiology for his work on chemical neurotransmission and pharmacological interactions.

Ayala, Francisco J. (José) (1934–) zoologist, geneticist; born in Madrid. He came to the U.S.A. in 1961. He performed genetic research at Rockefeller University (1964–65), taught at Providence College (1965–67), then returned to Rockefeller University (1967–71). He moved to the University of California: Davis (1971–87) before joining the University of California: Irvine in 1987. He made major contributions to the studies of evolution and population genetics, including biochemical and molecular evolution. He also published philosophical explorations of the ethical and humanistic issues related to evolutionary biology.

Aycock, Charles Brantley (1859–1912) governor; born in Wayne County, N.C. A Goldsboro lawyer, he was a United States attorney general in North Carolina (1893–97). As Democratic governor (1901–05), he established a literacy test to remove black voters from the rolls, while funding new school construction and teacher training for whites. He returned to his law practice afterward.

Aydelotte, Frank (1880–1956) college president, foundation officer; born in Sullivan, Ind. As president (1921–40) he developed Swarthmore (Pa.) College into an academically outstanding institution with innovations like an honors program. He was director of the Institute for Advanced Study, Princeton (1940–47). Long associated with the Rhodes Trust, he planned the Guggenheim Awards and Commonwealth Fellowships.

Ayer, Edward Everett (1841–1927) book collector; born in Kenosha, Wis. A prosperous railway lumberman, he amassed a book collection rich in materials on American Indians, which he donated in 1911 to Chicago's Newberry Library. He helped found the Field Museum of Natural History and was its first president (1893–98).

Ayer, Francis Wayland (1848–1923) advertising agent; born in Lee, Mass. He founded the Philadelphia advertising firm N. W. Ayer & Son (1869) and transformed the previously unsavory occupation of advertising into a respected profession. His pioneering advocacy of advertisers' interests, use of market research, and development of slogans and trademarks became industry practice; his *American Newspaper Annual and Directory* became a standard reference work. He was also an internationally known dairy stock breeder.

B

Baade, Wilhelm Heinrich (Walter) (1893–1960) astronomer; born in Westphalia, Germany. From overcast Hamburg and its observatory (1919–31) he leapt at the opportunity to join the Mt. Wilson Observatory (1913–58) and Palomar (1948–58) in the clearer skies of California. His classifications of galaxies and stars doubled estimates of the size and age of the universe.

Babbitt, Bruce (Edward) (1938–) lawyer, governor, cabinet officer, environmentalist; born in Flagstaff, Ariz. As a Marshall Scholar he attended the University of Newcastle in England (1962) and studied geophysics. After a brief stint with Gulf Oil, he left petroleum geology to earn a degree from Harvard Law School (1965). He worked for Volunteers in Service to America, marched for civil rights in the South, and then went back to Arizona to practice law. A Democrat, he served as Arizona's attorney general (1975–78) and gained a reputation for fighting organized crime in the state. As Arizona's governor (1978–87), he began to gain a national reputation for his role in Democratic Party and governors' affairs. In 1988 he was an unsuccessful candidate for the Democratic Party's presidential nomination. An ardent outdoorsman, he had been active in many ecological organizations such as the League of Conservation Voters and had received several awards from national environmental groups, so he was well received in many quarters when President Clinton appointed him secretary of the interior (1993).

Babbitt, Irving (1865–1933) scholar, humanist; born in Dayton, Ohio. This Harvard professor (1894–1933) and scholar of French literature espoused the New Humanism, a conservative creed that called politically for self-discipline and restraint, and literarily for a traditional canon of classic authors; it provoked sharp liberal opposition.

Babbitt, Isaac (1799–1862) goldsmith, inventor; born in Taunton, Mass. He became a goldsmith by age 24 and he manufactured the first tableware made of an alloy known as Brittania metal (1824). While superintendent of the South Boston Iron Works, he made the first brass cannon cast in the U.S.A. (1834). He patented (1839) an important part for machinery lined with a soft, silver-white alloy, soon called Babbitt metal. Suffering from overwork and strain, he was committed to an asylum in Somerville, Mass., where he died.

Babbitt, Milton (Byron) (1916–) composer; born in Philadelphia. After studies in both music and mathematics, he joined the Princeton faculty in 1938 and remained there, teaching music and occasionally mathematics. He was among the leading proponents and theorists of serialism, a system of composition that uses mathematical techniques. His works, which often involved the use of electronic media, include *Philomel* for voice and tape (1964) and *Sextets* for violin and piano (1966).

Babcock, George (Herman) (1832–93) engineer, inventor; born near Otsego, N.Y. At age 12 he moved to Westerly, R.I., where he became friends with his future partner, Stephen Wilcox. With his father, Babcock invented the first polychromatic printing press. He and Wilcox later produced an improved type of steam engine. At the same time, the partners designed and produced a water tube boiler that could withstand far greater pressures than earlier types, making possible the development of more powerful steam engines.

Babcock, Orville E. (1835–84) Union soldier; born in Franklin, Vt. An 1861 West Point graduate, he became an aide-de-camp to General Grant in 1864 and soon became a confidant of the commander-in-chief. He was acquitted of fraud charges in the "Whiskey Ring" scandal of the 1870s, largely as a result of Grant's intercession.

Babcock, Stephen Moulton (1843–1931) agricultural chemist; born in Bridgewater, N.Y. He did most of his important work at the Wisconsin Agricultural Station (1888–1913). He is best known for his test for butterfat in milk (1890). In addition, he helped develop the process of cold curing of cheese (1900) and his experiments led to studies that developed the vitamin concept. He is known as "the father of scientific dairying."

Babson, Roger (Ward) (1875–1967) statistician, business forecaster, author; born in Gloucester, Mass. An indifferent student, he was pushed by his father to study bookkeeping and engineering. He set up the Business Statistical Organization, Inc. (1904) and published the *Composite Circular* and the *Babsonchart*, which advised his clients on when to buy and sell their stocks, bonds, and commodities. He established the Babson Institute (later Babson College) in 1919; in 1927 he established Webber College (Florida) to train women for business. His statistical compilations were of great importance to a generation of businessmen during the pre-computer era. He published some 40 books, most of them on statistical and financial matters.

Baca, Elfego (1865–1945) Mexican-American hero; born in Socorro, N.M. A fearless lawman, he protected Mexican-Americans from Texans in New Mexico Territory. In 1884, he arrested a drunken Texas cowboy and killed another Texan who tried to free him; besieged and shot at by a mob of Texans, Baca surrendered, was tried, and was found innocent. He was sheriff of Socorro County and then turned to practicing law (1894–1945).

Bacall, Lauren (b. Betty Joan Perske) (1924–   ) movie actress; born in New York City. Although she had attended the American Academy of Dramatic Arts and appeared in a few Broadway plays, she was called to the attention of movie director Howard Hawks while working as a model. She made her screen debut in *To Have and Have Not* (1944), and nicknamed "the Look," she immediately caught the public's fancy with her feline grace and husky voice. She married her costar, Humphrey Bogart, in 1945 and made three more movies with him. After his death she was married for some years to Jason Robards Jr. (1961–69). Her screen career tended to decline after *Harper* (1966) but she enjoyed a new popularity in musicals on Broadway, particularly *Applause* (1970).

Bacharach, Burt (1929–   ) composer; born in Kansas City, Mo. He played piano in a high school dance band (in Queens, New York City) and studied piano and composition at Mannes School of Music, Berkshire Music Center, and McGill University (Montreal). Drawn to popular music, he played the piano during his army service (1950–52) and then worked as accompanist for Vic Damone and other singers. In 1957 he met Hal David, already a fairly successful lyricist, and they teamed up to write such hits as "Magic Moments" (1957) and "The Story of My Life" (1957). Between 1958–61, Bacharach was musical director for Marlene Dietrich's shows, but he returned to collaborate with Hal David and during the 1960s and early 1970s their music earned singer Dionne Warwick several Grammy Awards and gold records. "Raindrops Keep Fallin' on My Head" (1969) was another of their superhits, while *Promises, Promises* (1968) was their most successful musical. In 1975, Bacharach broke with Dionne Warwick (they were reunited in 1984), Hal David, and his then wife, Angie Dickinson, but he found a new career as performer of his music on tour and television. Starting in the late 1970s he revived his career as a composer with lyricist and wife (from 1982) Carol Bayer Sager.

Bache, Benjamin Franklin (1769–98) journalist; born in Philadelphia (a grandson of Benjamin Franklin). From the age of seven to 16 he lived in France under his grandfather's supervision and learned the printing trade there. On Franklin's death in 1790, Bache inherited a printing house in Philadelphia, where, at the age of 21, he established a newspaper called the *General Advertiser* (later the *Aurora General Advertiser*). He came to be nicknamed "Lightning Rod Junior." Although his paper, unlike others, covered congressional proceedings at length, it was mainly devoted, in the tradition of the time, to virulent and reckless attacks on political opponents – in Bache's case, George Washington (who was accused of having "debauched" the nation as president), John Adams, and the Federalist Party. During the Adams presidency, Federalist sympathizers wrecked Bache's shop on one occasion; on another, he was severely beaten by a Federalist he had slandered. He was also arrested and held briefly on charges of libeling the president. Not long afterward, he fell victim to a yellow fever epidemic.

Bache, Jules S. (Semon) (1861–1944) financier, art collector; born in New York City. He was educated at Charlier Institute, New York City, and in Frankfurt, Germany. He

began his financial career as a clerk for Leopold Cahn & Co. (1880), and by 1892 was head of the banking firm under the new name of J. S. Bache & Co. He made a fortune as a broker, served on many boards, and, assisted by the art dealer, Joseph Duveen, amassed an impressive collection of Old Master paintings. The collection, including works by Titian, Rembrandt, and Velazquez, was given to the Metropolitan Museum in 1944.

Bache, Richard (1737–1811) merchant; born in Settle, Yorkshire, England (son-in-law of Benjamin Franklin). Emigrating to New York City in 1765, he settled in Philadelphia and married Sarah Franklin in 1767. During the Revolution he was on the Board of War and succeeded his father-in-law as postmaster general (1776–82). His family firm issued private insurance policies and engaged in business with the West Indies and Newfoundland.

Bache, Theophylact (1734–1807) merchant; born in Settle, Yorkshire, England (brother of Richard Bache). He came to New York City in 1751 and ran a mercantile firm (in conjunction with his brother Richard after 1765). He was a Loyalist during the American Revolution. His business suffered after 1789. He was governor of New York Hospital.

Bachman, John (1790–1874) clergyman, naturalist; born in Rhinebeck, N.Y. A naturalist and a spiritual thinker from his youth, he was ordained as a Lutheran minister (1814) and led a congregation in Charleston, S.C. (1815–65). He met John James Audubon in 1831; they coauthored *The Viviparous Quadrupeds of North America* (1845–49) and two of Bachman's daughters married Audubon's sons. Unfortunately connected with the movement toward secession (1861), Bachman was forced to leave Charleston at the end of the Civil War, but he was known for his personal kindnesses to African-Americans.

Backus, Isaac (1724–1806) Protestant religious leader; born in Norwich, Conn. He underwent religious conversion during the Great Awakening in 1741 and a few years later founded the conservative New Light Church in Norwich, Conn. He convinced himself that the Scriptures required adult baptism by immersion and joined the Baptist sect in 1751. From 1756 until his death he was pastor of a Baptist church in Middleborough, Mass., where he became a noteworthy defender of religious freedom and the separation of church and state.

Backus, John (1924–   ) mathematician, computer specialist; born in Philadelphia. He was the project leader of the group at International Business Machines (IBM) that developed FORTRAN (1953–57), the first high-level language in data processing. He also worked on the IBM 704 computer with Gene Amdahl during the 1950s and worked on ALGOL 58 and 60.

Bacon, Delia Salter (1811–59) author, lecturer; born in Tallmadge, Ohio. A schoolteacher, she turned her lectures and dramatic readings into public performances in New York and other cities. She devoted her last years to marshaling the case for Francis Bacon's authorship of Shakespeare's plays, a theory that Nathaniel Hawthorne helped her publish in 1857.

Bacon, Leonard (1802–91) Protestant clergyman; born in Detroit, Mich. The son of a missionary, he graduated from Yale in 1820 and, after three years at Andover Theological Seminary, was ordained in 1824. He had planned to return to the western frontier as a missionary, but the First Church of New Haven offered him a pulpit. He accepted and remained there 41 years. An opponent of slavery, in 1848 he helped launch the free soil journal, *The Independent*. He was professor of theology at Yale from 1866–71.

Bacon, Nathaniel (1647–76) colonial leader; born in Suffolk, England. He emigrated to Virginia c. 1674. A landowner and planter, he opposed Governor Sir William Berkeley's Indian policies. In 1676, Bacon attacked the Pamunkey, Susquehanna, and Occaneechi tribes without a commission from Berkeley. After Berkeley denounced him as a traitor, Bacon marched on Jamestown. When a compromise settlement failed, Bacon captured and burned Jamestown. At one point he controlled nearly all of Virginia, but troops were on their way from England to support Berkeley. Bacon died of influenza in October 1676 and the rebellion soon collapsed.

Bacon, Peggy (Margaret Francis) (1895–1987) printmaker, painter, author; born in Ridgefield, Conn. Based in New York City, she studied with John Sloan at the Art Students League, New York (1915–20), and began her work in painting, drypoint etching, and lithography. She illustrated many books for children and adults, and published her witty caricatures of famous literary and artistic personalities, such as *Off With Their Heads* (1934). She participated in the art colony at Woodstock, N.Y., (1920), returned to New York City (1923), then settled in Maine, where she continued her work for periodicals and resumed a painting career (1950s) she had abandoned in 1920.

Badeau, John S. (Stothoff) (1903–) educator, diplomat; born in Pittsburgh, Pa. He became a minister of the Reformed Church of America in 1928 and did civil and sanitary engineering missionary work in Iraq (1928–35). He was a professor of religion (1936–38), dean of the faculty (1938–44) and president (1945–53) of the American University of Cairo. He was ambassador to Egypt (1961–64) and director of the Middle East Institute at Columbia (1964–71). He wrote *The American Approach to the Arab World* (1968).

Badger, Daniel D. (1806–84) iron fabricator; born in Portsmouth, N.H. He pioneered the use of cast-iron building fronts; his New York foundry (established 1846) produced architectural ironwork for New York and Chicago buildings.

Badger, Joseph (1708–65) painter; born in Charlestown, Mass. Beginning work as a glazier and a house and sign painter, he began painting portraits in Boston some time after 1740. Because his portraits were often unsigned, many were previously attributed to John Singleton Copley and Joseph Blackburn. His paintings, characterized by unsophisticated color and naive technique, include *Mrs. Cornelius Waldo* (1750), *Thomas Cushing* (c. 1745), and *James Bowdoin* (c. 1746–47).

Badger, Walter Lucius (1886–1958) chemical engineer; born in Minneapolis, Minn. He was noted for his work on the desalinization of sea water at Detroit Edison (1917–37). He was affiliated with the University of Minnesota (1912–37) and was subsequently an engineering consultant to Dow Chemical Company (1937–44) and numerous other companies.

Badian, Ernst (1925–) ancient historian; born in Vienna, Austria. Educated in New Zealand and England, he came to the United States in 1968 where he taught first at Buffalo State University (1969–71), then at Harvard (1971). Founder of the *American Journal of Ancient History* (1976), he gave the University of California Sather lectures in 1976. His many publications and professional activities made him an important force in his discipline.

Badin, Stephen T. (Theodore) (1768–1853) Catholic missionary; born in Orléans, France. Emigrating after the French Revolution, he studied at St. Mary's Seminary in Baltimore, Md., and became the first priest ordained in America (1793). The hardy, morally rigorous "apostle of Kentucky" labored for over two decades in the frontier region of the Middle West – almost singlehandedly in the early years. He bought land where Notre Dame University now stands and was buried there.

Baekeland, Leo (Hendrik) (1863–1944) chemist, inventor; born near Ghent, Belgium. Apprenticed to a shoemaker at age 13, he disliked the trade, escaped it, and managed to obtain a scientific education at the University of Ghent. He taught chemistry at Ghent and Bruges before emigrating to the U.S.A. in 1890, where he pursued research in synthetic resins and plastics. He invented Velox paper for photographic prints and founded a firm that manufactured it; he sold the company to George Eastman in 1899. In 1909 he discovered the first synthetic resin – named bakelite for him – and established the Bakelite Corp. to produce it in 1910; the versatility of the product's applications opened up the modern age of plastics. In 1939 Union Carbide bought Bakelite Corp.; its founder retired to Florida, where he lived out his last years as a recluse.

Baer, (Arthur) "Bugs" (1886–1969) journalist; born in Philadelphia. His syndicated column of breezy commentary, begun in 1919 for William Randolph Hearst's *New York American,* reached up to 15 million readers and lasted nearly 50 years.

Baer, George Frederick (1842–1914) lawyer, railroad executive; born near Lavansville, Pa. He worked as a printer's devil for, then later owned, a Somerset County, Pa., newspaper. He interrupted law studies to serve in the Civil War (1862–64). He served as legal counsel for the Philadelphia & Reading Railroad, and later was president of the organization that managed all the Reading holdings. An associate of the financier J. P. Morgan, he gained notoriety in 1902 when, taking a hard line on a United Mine Workers strike, he argued that propertied classes rather than labor unions were best fitted to look after workers' interests. He left a fortune of $15 million when he died.

Baer, (Maxmillion) Max (1909–59) boxer; born in Omaha, Neb. He held the heavyweight championship from 1934 to 1935, posting a career record of 65 wins, 13 losses, one no-decision, with 50 knockouts.

Baer, Werner (1931–) economist; born in Offenbach, Germany. He emigrated to the U.S.A. in 1945. A Harvard Ph.D., he taught at Vanderbilt University (1965–74) and the University of Illinois: Urbana (1974). A specialist in Latin American industrialization and economic growth, he wrote such works as *Industrialization and Economic Development in Brazil* (1965) and *The Brazilian Economy* (1979, later revised).

Baez, Joan (Chandos) (1941–) folk singer, songwriter; born in Staten Island, N.Y. She quit Boston University to sing in local coffee houses and gave highly successful performances at the Newport Folk Festival in 1959 and 1960. She added protest songs to her repertory of traditional ballads and became a leading voice of the 1960s with songwriter and associate Bob Dylan. She performed at many benefit concerts for world peace.

Bagley, Sarah G. (George) (1806–?48) labor leader; born in

Candia, N.H. Daughter of a cotton mill operator, she herself went to work in the mills as a young woman. By 1837 she was employed as a weaver in one of the early mills in Lowell, Mass., where she also contributed to *The Lowell Offering,* a literary magazine published by the mill women. In 1844, however, increasingly unhappy with the severe conditions under which the women were working, she helped found the Lowell Female Reform Association. In 1845 she took on the editorship of the *Voice of Industry,* the weekly newspaper of the New England Workingmen's Association. Her major crusade, however, was the so-called Ten Hours Movement – dedicated to limiting the work day to ten hours – and she was regarded as one of the most forceful speakers and writers on behalf of this cause. She also spoke out on the need for reform in other areas of society. But somewhere during 1847, it seems she dropped her crusading activities (perhaps due to illness) and by 1848 she was back working in the mills; when she returned to New Hampshire on her father's death, she vanishes from recorded history.

Bailey, Anna (b. Warner) "Mother Bailey" (1758–1851) heroine; born in Groton, Conn. She figured prominently in heroic situations during the American Revolution and the War of 1812. In 1781, she brought her aunt and cousins to where her uncle lay dying during the battle of Groton Heights (an incident that became a well-known story). She married the local postmaster, Elijah Bailey. In 1813 she gave her flannel petticoat to be used as cartridge wadding, as the town of Groton defended itself against British cannon fire. This episode was celebrated in story and song.

Bailey, Charles P. (Philamore) (1911–93) surgeon; born in Wanamassa, N.J. He took his B.A. at Rutgers, his M.D. from Hahnemann Medical College (Philadelphia) (1932) and went on to earn M.S. and D.Sc. degrees at the University of Pennsylvania. He was chief of thoracic surgery at Hahnemann University Hospital during the 1940s and 1950s; director of cardiovascular surgery at the Deborah Heart and Lung Center in Browns Mills, N.J. (1956–61); professor and director of general surgery at the New York Medical College and Flower-Fifth Avenue Hospitals (1959–62); and held numerous other administrative, surgical, and teaching posts. During the 1940s he pioneered in surgical procedures, techniques, and instruments that made possible direct surgery on the human heart. Admired as an innovative and intrepid surgeon, he was also known for his often volatile temperament and uncompromising ways. In the late 1960s he began studying law in the evenings at Fordham Law School (New York City); after he took his law degree he stopped doing surgery in the mid-1970s and became a consultant to law firms and insurance.

Bailey, F. (Francis) Lee (1933–   ) lawyer; born in Waltham, Mass. Following service as a marine pilot, he was admitted to the bar in 1960. A controversial figure, he gained spectacular success as a defense attorney in the Torso Murder case (1960), the re-trial of Dr. Sam Sheppard (1966), the Boston Strangler case (1966), and many others. His forte was meticulous investigation before a trial and methodical presentation in the courtroom.

Bailey, Frederick See Douglass, Frederick.

Bailey, Gamaliel (1807–59) physician, journalist, abolitionist; born in Mount Holly, N.J. In his early years he worked as a physician, but his true calling was abolitionism. He and James G. Birney edited the *Cincinnati Philanthropist* (1836) – the first anti-slavery organ in the West. He later founded a daily, the *Herald* (1843). He moved to Washington, D.C., to serve as editor-in-chief of the *National Era* (1847–59), the periodical of the American and Foreign Anti-Slavery Society. Tolerant and cool-headed, he stood up to mobs to defend his abolitionist publications, exerting a wide moral and political influence for the anti-slavery movement.

Bailey, Irving W. (Widmer) (1884–1967) botanist; born in Tilton, N.H. (son of astronomer and archaeologist Solon Bailey). He taught and performed research at Harvard (1903–55), beginning his career in forestry in 1909. In 1920 he traveled to British Guiana to study "ant plants," tropical trees whose cavities are home to certain species of ants. This experience in the rain forest engendered his research on tree anatomy and physiology relative to training forest managers in understanding and conserving their resources. During his most productive years (1920s–1930s), he traveled throughout the U.S., Canada, and Europe to become a recognized authority on forest climatology and ecology; his laboratory research at the Carnegie Laboratory at Stanford University (summers, 1930–40) produced major contributions to studies of the microscopy of the cambium, the layer of cells responsible for the secondary growth in woody plants. His suggestions in the "Bailey Report" (1945) for the reorganization of Harvard's botanical museum were instituted in 1935–54 and established his reputation in administration as well as research. After retirement in 1955, he investigated the evolution of flowering plants, especially the cacti and the buttercup/magnolia family.

Bailey, James (Anthony) (1847–1906) showman; born in Detroit, Mich. Proprietor of Cooper & Bailey (1872–81), he took that circus on a world tour, then combined forces with chief rival P. T. Barnum to form Barnum and Bailey's circus (1881–1906).

Bailey, Joseph Weldon (1863–1929). U.S. representative/senator; born near Crystal Springs, Miss. Elected to the U.S. House of Representatives (Dem., Tex.; 1891–1901) and to the U.S. Senate (1901–13), he successfully weathered accusations of wrongdoing in an oil company scandal that arose from his work on behalf of the Hepburn Rate Bill of 1906.

Bailey, Liberty Hyde (Jr.) (1858–1954) botanist, horticulturist; born in South Haven, Mich. He assisted Asa Gray at Harvard (1882–83), became an authority on the hybridization of apples, squashes, and grasses at Michigan Agricultural College (1885–88), then taught at Cornell (1888–1913), where he developed horticulture into a science, and published the four-volume *Cyclopedia of American Agriculture* (1907–09), and the six-volume *Cyclopedia of Horticulture* (1917). He continued research on hybridization, and performed the first experiments in growing plants under continuous electric illumination. He was a dedicated teacher of both college students and New York farmers, and was considered both a naturalist and a rural sociologist. After his retirement from teaching (1913), he devoted his life to world travel, studying and collecting new plant species, and making major contributions to taxonomic research. He coined the term "cultivar" during the 1920s for a plant variant that originates under cultivation. He donated his specimen collection to the Liberty Hyde Bailey Hortorium at Cornell, which he founded in 1935 and directed until 1952. A social philosopher who felt that knowledge of plants was one of the greatest hopes for humanity, Bailey wrote over 65 books and published hundreds of scientific papers.

Bailey, Mildred (b. Rinker) (1907–51) jazz musician; born in Tekoa, Wash. A prototypical jazz singer, she was featured with Paul Whiteman, Benny Goodman, and Red Norvo, and recorded with numerous all-star groups between 1929–48.

Bailey, Pearl (1918–88) vocalist, movie/stage actress; born in Newport News, Va. An irrepressible show business personality, she began as a dancer and won an amateur contest in Philadelphia in 1933, which led to work in touring shows. In 1938 she won a singing contest at Harlem's Apollo Theatre and was subsequently featured with big bands led by Noble Nissle, Edgar Hayes, Cab Calloway, and Cootie Williams, with whom she recorded in 1945. In 1946, she starred in the Broadway musical *St. Louis Woman*. In 1952, she married the drummer-bandleader Louis Bellson, whom she performed with thereafter. Beginning with *Carmen Jones* in 1954, she appeared in numerous films, television, and stage shows, including *Hello, Dolly!* in 1967–69. She hosted her own television variety show in 1970–71. Her autobiography, *The Raw Pearl,* was published in 1968.

Bailey, Stephen (Kemp) (1916–82) educator, foundation official; born in Newton, Mass. A Harvard Ph.D., professor, and academic administrator, he specialized in public administration and frequently advised the government on public policy. His many published works on government and administration include *Congress Makes a Law* (1950) and *The Purposes of Education* (1976).

Bailyn, Bernard (1922–) historian; born in Hartford, Conn. He received his Ph.D. from Harvard University and began teaching there in 1953. His *Ideological Origins of the American Revolution* received Pulitzer and Bancroft Prizes (1968); *Voyagers to the West* received the Pulitzer Prize in 1986. An authority on the American Revolutionary period, he was president of the American Historical Association in 1981 and became director of the Charles Warren Center for Studies in American History in 1983.

Bain, Joe S. (1912–) economist; born in Spokane, Wash. He identified and quantified "barriers to entry" into non-competitive industries by measuring factors such as initial capital requirements, threat of price cutting by established firms, and product differentiation. Except for one year at Harvard University (1951–52), his entire career was spent teaching at the University of California: Berkeley (1939–75).

Bainbridge, William (1774–1833) naval officer; born in Princeton, N.J. He became a captain (1800) after serving in the undeclared naval war with France (1798–1800). In 1803 his ship, the USS *Philadelphia* ran aground and was captured by the Tripolitans; he suggested the raid that later burned the ship. Following his release in 1805 he became the commandant of the Charlestown, Mass., navy yard, and as captain of the USS *Constitution* he won a notable victory over the British *Java* (1812). He organized the first school for U.S. naval officers in 1817.

Baird, Spencer Fullerton (1823–87) zoologist, naturalist; born in Reading, Pa. A protégé of John J. Audubon while a student at Dickinson College in Pennsylvania, he attended medical school before turning to natural history. In 1850 he became assistant secretary (later secretary, 1878–87) of the Smithsonian Institution, where he directed the research and collections program while concurrently publishing a series of monographs, including *Mammals of North America* (1859)

and, with two collaborators, *History of North American Birds* (1875–84). The first U.S. commissioner of fish and fisheries, he founded the marine biological laboratory at Woods Hole, Mass.

Baker, Augusta (Alexander) (1911–) librarian, storyteller; born in Baltimore, Md. After studying at Hunter College, she served as children's librarian and storytelling specialist for the New York Public Library and the public library of Trinidad, British West Indies. Her numerous anthologies for children include several about African-American life.

Baker, (Chesley) Chet (1929–87) jazz musician; born in Yale, Okla. He was a popular trumpeter who emerged with the Gerry Mulligan Quartet in 1952–53. He freelanced thereafter, but his career was hampered by drug addiction and prison sentences in the U.S.A. and Europe.

Baker, Edward Dickinson (1811–61) U.S. representative/senator, soldier; born in London, England. Brought to the U.S.A. as a child, he became a lawyer and practiced in Springfield, Ill., where he became a friend of Abraham Lincoln. After defeating Lincoln in a Whig party primary for the U.S. House of Representatives, he took the seat in 1845 but resigned in 1846 to volunteer for service in the Mexican War. Lincoln (who would name his second son after Baker) took the seat (1847–49) but Dickinson regained it (1849–51) – in part because of Lincoln's opposition to the war. Baker moved out to the West Coast where he practiced law in San Francisco and represented Oregon as a Republican in the U.S. Senate (1860–61), resigning to serve as a colonel with a California volunteer unit. He was killed on October 21 at Ball's Bluff, Va.

Baker, Ella Josephine (1903–86) civil rights activist; born in Norfolk, Va. After graduating from Shaw University in Raleigh, Va. (1927), Baker moved to New York City where she immediately became involved in work to better the conditions in Harlem, joining the Young Negroes Cooperative League and becoming its national director in 1931. In the 1930s she worked for the Workers Education Project of the Works Progress Administration and added a concern with women's rights to her commitment to equal rights for African-Americans. She worked for the National Association for the Advancement of Colored People (1940–46) but was disillusioned by its slow pace. She took an active role in the formative stage of such groups as the Southern Christian Leadership Congress (1948) and the Student Non-Violent Coordinating Committee (1960). She was also active in founding the Mississippi Freedom Democratic Party (1964) and was widely credited with inspiring many of the founders of the Students for a Democratic Society and the Black Panther Party. Although not as well known as some of the other leaders of the civil rights movement, she was highly respected by those inside the movement.

Baker, George F. (Fisher) (1840–1931) banker, philanthropist; born in Dorchester, Mass. He began as a clerk in the state banking department in Albany, N.Y. (1856) and in 1863 he helped found the First National Bank of New York, rising to second president by 1877. In 1908 he established First Security Corporation to buy and sell stocks, bonds, and notes. From 1909–31 he chaired the bank's board and was on the board of directors of 87 corporations. He gave away over $19 million of his personal fortune, including $6 million to the Harvard Graduate School of Business Administration.

Baker, George (known as Father Divine) (?1877–1965) evangelist; born near Savannah, Ga. He began preaching to poor blacks in the rural South, migrated northward, and eventually established himself in New York City, where he launched the Peace Mission movement in 1919. Calling himself Father Divine, he established a large following among African-Americans in New York and Philadelphia. He preached communal living and racial equality, and prohibited tobacco, liquor, and cosmetics. Although more than 170 Peace Mission settlements were established, the movement did not long survive the death of its founder.

Baker, George Pierce (1866–1935) teacher, director; born in Providence, R.I. A professor of drama at Harvard, his course in playwriting led to the formation of the influential 47 Workshop. Eugene O'Neill was among his students.

Baker, (Hobart A. H.) Hobey (1892–1918) hockey/football player; born in Bala-Cynwyd, Pa. He was a football and hockey legend at Princeton University (1911–14). A hockey pioneer in the United States, the college hockey Player of the Year award is named in his honor. He was killed in an airplane crash in World War I.

Baker, Howard H. (Henry), Jr. (1925–) U.S. senator; born in Huntsville, Tenn. From a prominent political family, he served in the U.S. Senate (Rep., Tenn.; 1967–87). He won fame in 1973 as the ranking Republican on the Senate committee investigating the Watergate scandal. Senate minority leader (1977–81) and majority leader (1981–85), he served as President Reagan's chief of staff (1987–88), but never realized his own presidential ambitions. He left public office to practice law.

Baker, James A. (Addison), III (1930–) lawyer, cabinet member; born in Houston, Tex. A shrewd lawyer and personal friend of George Bush, he was undersecretary of commerce (1975–76) and managed George Bush's 1980 campaign for the Republican presidential nomination. He was President Reagan's chief of staff (1981–85), then became treasury secretary (1985–88), stabilizing the dollar overseas. Bush's campaign manager (1988) and secretary of state (1989–92), he achieved his greatest success in advancing Middle Eastern peace negotiations. He resigned in 1992 to take over Bush's flagging presidential campaign and then returned to practicing law.

Baker, Josephine (b. Freda Josephine McDonald) (1906–75) dancer, entertainer; born in St. Louis, Mo. An amateur singer and dancer by age eight, she ran off at age 13 to tour with a vaudeville show. In 1921 she made her Broadway debut in *Shuffle Along* and also began to sing in Harlem's Plantation Club. In 1925 she went to Paris with a show called *La Revue Nègre,* but the show failed and she and many cast members were stranded there. She was hired to appear in an all-black act at the Folies Bergère and became an instant success with her scanty costume, lively dancing, scat singing, and uninhibited cavorting. As the epitome of *"le jazz hot,"* "Josephine" would remain the toast of France for five decades and also gain an international status that reached her homeland largely as a reputation; she would never accept the second-class status assigned to most blacks in America, so she long boycotted the U.S.A., becoming a French citizen in 1937. Her appearances on stage and in public were distinguished by her exotic costumes and outrageous behavior. During World War II she cooperated with the French Resistance movement by providing intelligence she was able to pick up through her privileged travels abroad. After the war she took up the cause of world brotherhood, adopting 12 children of various races and religions and raising them at her estate in France. In 1951, while touring in the States, she was refused service in the Stork Club and this led to false charges by columnist Walter Winchell that she was a communist and had consorted with Nazis during World War II. In the 1950s she took up the cause of racial equality in America, forcing the integration of several theaters and night clubs, and she was among those who addressed the crowds before the Lincoln Memorial at the 1963 March on Washington. Her plans for a "world village" at her estate, meanwhile, collapsed under financial debt and in order to raise money she made a comeback in 1973–75.

Baker, Newton (Diehl) (1871–1937) public official, lawyer; born in Martinsburg, W.Va. Educated at Washington and Lee Law School, he served as city solicitor and progressive mayor (1912–15) of Cleveland, Ohio, and was later appointed secretary of war under President Wilson (1916–21). Accused of pacifism, he nevertheless prosecuted America's war effort with vigor and expertise. He supported the League of Nations and was appointed to the Permanent Court of International Justice (1928).

Baker, Norma Jean See Monroe, Marilyn.

Baker, Oliver (Edwin) (1883–1949) geographer; born in Tiffin, Ohio. Much of his career was spent with the U.S. Department of Agriculture (1912–42). In 1942 he began the department of geography at the University of Maryland. He was the authority on agricultural land utilization in North America; he also had a keen interest in China. He is especially noted for the *Atlas of World Agriculture* (1917), which he coauthored with V. C. Finch.

Baker, Paul T. (Thornell) (1927–) physical anthropologist; born in Burlington, Iowa. He was an internationally-known professor at the Pennsylvania State University (1957–88), and a former UN and U.S. government advisor. He wrote extensively on demographic variables, especially high altitude, as related to human adaptation.

Baker, Ray Stannard (1870–1946) journalist, writer; born in Lansing, Mich. A Chicago journalist, he became a leading muckraking crusader for *McClure's Magazine* (1898–1906) and *American Magazine* (1906–15). He made his home in Amherst, Mass., after 1910. While with the *American Magazine* he began a series of essays under the pen name, "David Grayson"; the first collection, *Adventures in Contentment* (1907), was so popular that he continued publishing eight more volumes. His *Following the Color Line* (1908) collected his pioneering articles on race relations. He became a supporter of Woodrow Wilson and accompanied him to the Versailles peace conference after World War I. His later work included an edition of Wilson's papers (16 vols. 1925–27) and a Pulitzer Prize-winning biography (8 vols. 1927–39).

Baker, Russell (Wayne) (1925–) journalist; born in Loudoun County, Va. Starting as a reporter for the *Baltimore Sun,* he joined the *New York Times* in 1954. In 1962, based in Washington, D.C., he launched his "Observer" column, with its wide-ranging, generally humorous observations on politics and life. He won a 1979 Pulitzer Prize for commentary and a 1983 Pulitzer Prize for his best-selling first volume of reminiscences, *Growing Up.*

Baker, Sara Josephine (1873–1945) physician, public health administrator; born in Poughkeepsie, N.Y. Her efforts led to greatly reduced levels of infant mortality in New York City before World War II and the creation of agencies to foster child health care. A suffragette, she lectured widely on public health (1916–31) and was the author of numerous books and articles.

Balanchine, George (b. Georgi Melitonovich Balanchivadze) (1903–83) ballet dancer, choreographer; born in St. Petersburg, Russia. Trained at the School of Imperial Ballet/State Academy of Dance, he choreographed his first piece in 1922. From 1923–24 he was balletmaster at Petrograd's experimental Maly Theatre. While on a European tour with the Soviet State Dancers in 1924, he defected to the West. His choreography for Diaghilev's Ballet Russe, created between 1925–29, included the masterworks, *Apollo* and *Prodigal Son*. Before immigrating to America in 1933, Balanchine created several ballets for European companies and for his own company, Les Ballets. In 1934, with Lincoln Kirstein, he formed the School of American Ballet, and in 1935, the American Ballet Company, which staged his first American work, *Serenade,* the same year. After the company's financial failure in 1938, Balanchine did the choreography for a number of films and Broadway shows, including *Cabin in the Sky* (1940) and *Song of Norway* (1944), until Kirstein established the Ballet Society in 1946. Soon after the 1948 premiere of *Orpheus,* one of Balanchine's finest works, the company was renamed the New York City Ballet and given a permanent home at New York's City Center. Balanchine, often working with limited funding, revolutionized classical ballet by creating stark, abstract, usually plotless ballets; drawing on serious music, often Stravinsky's, his ballets emphasized "pure" dance and ensemble work. By 1964, when the company moved to Lincoln Center, his reputation was at its peak. In later years he created elaborate "story" ballets such as *Don Quixote, Coppelia,* and the perennial favorite, *The Nutcracker,* demonstrating the remarkable range of his talents. Known for his incredible series of "Balanchine ballerinas," he also created some of his most memorable roles for men. Long before he died, his over 200 works had gained him the reputation as the premier choreographer of the 20th century.

Balch, Emily Green (1867–1961) pacifist, social reformer, economist; born in Jamaica Plain (now in Boston), Mass. Educated at Bryn Mawr College, she taught sociology and economics at Wellesley College (1896–1918). Never one to remain in an ivory tower, she took an active role in labor disputes and other social issues. In 1910 she published *Our Slavic Fellow Citizens,* a pioneering work in its sympathetic view of immigrants. As the impact of World War I spread, she joined others in trying to mediate an end, and she was fired from Wellesley because of her support for dissidents. She turned, somewhat, from advocating economic and socialist solutions, to embracing Quakerism. A founder of the Women's International League for Peace and Freedom (1919), she devoted the remainder of her life to its cause. She shared the Nobel Peace Prize in 1946.

Balchen, Bernt (1899–1973) air force officer, aviator; born in Tveit, Norway. He came to the United States in 1926, becoming a citizen in 1931. He piloted Admiral Byrd's first flight over the South Pole in 1929. During World War II, flying from Sweden, he evacuated several thousand Norwe-gians and 1,000 American airmen. In 1944 he commanded a supply operation for the Norwegian underground.

Baldwin, Billy (1903–84) interior decorator; born in Roland Park, Maryland. In 1935 he joined the New York firm of Ruby Ross Wood, assuming control in 1952. Glossy dark walls and mixed patterns were among his hallmarks.

Baldwin, Evelyn Briggs (1862–1933) Arctic explorer; born in Springfield, Mo. He was the superintendent of city schools in Kansas (1887–91) and an observer for the U.S. Weather Bureau (1892–1900). He made a daring but unsuccessful attempt to reach the North Pole (1901–02). He served in minor government posts (1918–33). He was nearly destitute at the time of his death in an auto accident in Washington, D.C.

Baldwin, Henry (1780–1844) Supreme Court justice; born in New Haven, Conn. He served in the U.S. House of Representatives (Fed., Penn.; 1817–22) and was appointed to the U.S. Supreme Court by President Jackson (1830–44).

Baldwin, James (Arthur) (1924–87) writer; born in Harlem, N.Y. Son of a preacher, as a teenager he himself was a preacher in a Harlem pentecostal church. After high school he began publishing polemical essays on the black experience in journals including *The Nation* and *Commentary*. Supported largely by fellowships, he began writing fiction in Paris (1948–56). His first novels, the autobiographical *Go Tell It on the Mountain* (1953) and *Giovanni's Room* (1956) established him as a promising novelist and anticipated some of the themes dealt with in later works, such as racism and homosexuality. In the U.S.A. (1957–1970s) he became a civil rights activist, and, through his essays, plays, and lectures, something of a celebrity as a spokesman for angry African-Americans. His novels include *Another Country* (1962), *Tell Me How Long the Train's Been Gone* (1968), and *Just Above My Head* (1979). His essays were collected in several volumes including *Notes of a Native Son* (1955), *Nobody Knows My Name* (1961), *The Fire Next Time* (1963), and *The Price of a Ticket* (1985). His plays include *The Amen Corner* (produced 1955), *Blues for Mister Charlie* (1964). He lived in France during his last years, although he returned to the U.S.A. to hold special academic appointments.

Baldwin, Loammi (1745–1807) engineer, soldier, judge; born in Woburn, Mass. A self-educated cabinetmaker, land surveyor, and civil engineer, he used to walk from Woburn to Cambridge to hear lectures on mathematics at Harvard. An opponent of British rule, he fought briefly in the American Revolution, achieving the rank of colonel. He represented Woburn in the Massachusetts legislature (1778–79, 1800–04) and was high sheriff of Middlesex County. He was the chief engineer of the Middlesex Canal that joined Massachusetts' Merrimack and Charles Rivers (1794–1804). He also developed from grafts a hardy variety of apple that is named for him.

Baldwin, Matthias (William) (1795–1866) locomotive engineer; born in Elizabethtown, N.J. A toolmaker and jeweler, he began manufacturing hydraulic and bookbinding machinery about 1825. In 1832 he built the locomotive *Old Ironsides*. He developed tight-fitting steam joints, which allowed high pressures. Baldwin's locomotive works eventually produced over 1,000 locomotives.

Baldwin, Roger (Nash) (1884–1981) social activist; born in Wellesley, Mass. He taught sociology and was chief probation officer in St. Louis, Mo., before serving prison time as a conscientious objector during World War I. He was the director (1920–50) and national chairman (1950–55) of the American Civil Liberties Union (ACLU) that he had helped to found. During this time, the ACLU defended many controversial clients. On retiring, he taught for some years at the University of Puerto Rico.

Baldwin, Roger Sherman (1793–1863) governor, U.S. senator, abolitionist; born in New Haven, Conn. (grandson of Roger Sherman). He served as the Whig governor of Connecticut (1844–46) and as a U.S. senator (Whig, Conn.; 1847–50). Known for his abolitionist sympathies, he was the defense counsel for the African slaves arrested in the *Amistad* case (1841).

Ball, C. (Charles) Olin (1893–1970) food technologist; born in Abilene, Kans. While in graduate school at George Washington University (1919–22) he researched sterilization of canned foods for the National Canners Association. From 1922–41 he worked for the American Can Co. in Illinois and New York where he generated some of his 29 patents, including the basic heat-cool-fill canning method (1936), the method and apparatus for open can sterilization (1937), and processes for canning milk (1938–39). He worked for the Owens-Illinois Glass Co. (1944–46) and taught food science at Rutgers University (1949–63). He was a founding member of the Institute of Food Technology (1939).

Ball, Frank Clayton (1857–1943) industrialist, philanthropist; born in Greensburg, Ohio. Following their father's death, he and his four brothers (Lucius, William, George, and Edmund Ball) entered the business of making tin cans and glass jars to ship oils and varnishes. Moving their firm to Muncie, Ind., the Ball Brothers (incorporated in 1887) expanded into making glass fruit jars and caps that were based on the "Mason jar" (whose patent had expired). They continued to improve their product by their own inventions and by buying exclusive rights to others'. By allowing millions of people to "put up" their own foods in jars, the firm prospered even during the Great Depression. Frank was president of the company (1880–1943). Turning to philanthropy, he and his brothers gave over $7 million to institutions, mostly in Indiana.

Ball, Lucille (Désirée) (1910–89) television comedian, movie actress; born in Celaron, N.Y. Leaving school at age 15 to become a stage actress, her early efforts were unsuccessful; she turned to modeling (as Diane Belmont) which led to her first movie role, in *Roman Scandals* (1934). She appeared in numerous movies and radio shows afterward but didn't become truly successful until 1951, when she teamed up with her Cuban-born, bandleader husband, Desi Arnaz, to play the zany middle-class couple, Lucy and Ricky Ricardo in television's prototypical situation comedy *I Love Lucy*. With near perfect timing and a genius for sightgags, redhaired Ball careened through 179 episodes of the original sitcom as a ditzy housewife; the 1953 episode on which she gave birth to "Little Ricky," filmed to coincide with delivery of her real-life son, was said to attract more viewers than the concurrent inauguration of President Dwight D. Eisenhower. Desilu Productions, which she and Arnaz founded in 1950, was a successful independent producer of television shows before Gulf-Western acquired it. After divorcing Arnaz in 1960, she appeared on Broadway in *Wildcat* (1961) and then soloed in two other successful sitcoms, *The Lucy Show* (1962–1968)

and *Here's Lucy* (1968–73). She continued to appear on television specials almost to her death.

Ball, Thomas (1819–1911) sculptor; born in Charlestown, Mass. He moved to Boston (1837–53), traveled to Italy (1854–57), returned to Boston (1857–64), traveled, then settled in New Jersey (1897). He became known for his naturalistic bronze sculptures, notably the equestrian statue of George Washington in Boston's Public Garden (1864).

Balliett, Whitney (1926–) jazz critic; born in New York City. Upon graduation from Cornell University in 1951, he joined the staff of the *New Yorker* and became its jazz critic in 1957. His writings have been widely anthologized.

Ballou, Adin (1803–90) Universalist clergyman, reformer; born in Cumberland, R.I. A Universalist minister who preached throughout Massachusetts (1823–41), he was founder of the Hopedale Community – one of the first of such American Utopian enterprises – in Milford, Mass., (1841–68). He preached non-resistance throughout the Civil War, then saw his community turned into an industrial center; still he remained pastor of Hopedale Parish (through 1880). Although his efforts at establishing a utopian community failed, he exerted considerable influence on Unitarian and Universalist thought during his almost 60 years as a clergyman.

Ballou, Hosea (1771–1853) Universalist clergyman, theologian; born in Richmond, N.H. Raised in poverty, brought up a Baptist, and self-educated, he was for many years a circuit-riding preacher in Rhode Island and Massachusetts. He settled in Boston, Mass., in 1817 where he helped found the Universalist Church, edited Universalist publications, and developed a liberal theology that denied original sin and the full deity of Christ. From 1827 until his death he was pastor of the Second Universalist Society of Boston.

Baltes, Paul B. (1939–) psychologist; born in Saarlouis, Germany. Educated in Germany, he came to the United States in 1968 and taught at West Virginia University, then at Pennsylvania State University (1974). His research in life-span developmental psychology and gerontology produced important books and papers, including the three-volume *Life-Span Development and Behavior: Advances in Research and Theory,* edited with O. G. Brim (1978–80).

Baltimore, David (1938–) virologist, geneticist; born in New York City. He was a research fellow at the Massachusetts Institute of Technology (MIT) (1963–64) and Albert Einstein College of Medicine (1964–65), then moved to the Salk Institute of Biological Studies (1965–68), where he began investigations of RNA viruses. He returned to MIT (1968–90), where he discovered a tumor virus enzyme he termed "reverse transcriptase" which can transform the host cell's DNA into cancer-causing viral RNA (1970); for this he shared the 1975 Nobel Prize in physiology. In 1972 he synthesized part of the gene for hemoglobin; he then worked on developing synthetic vaccines. An outspoken advocate of self-policing of genetic engineering by scientists, he became president of Rockefeller University in 1990, but resigned in 1991 after an extensive controversy resulted from his attempt to impede an investigation of a paper he had sponsored (1986) by a former MIT postdoctoral researcher who had falsified her data.

Bampton, Rose (1908–) soprano; born in Cleveland, Ohio. American-trained, she sang internationally and appeared at the Metropolitan Opera (1932–43).

Bancroft, Edward (1744–1821) secret agent, inventor; born in Westfield, Mass. He moved to England and was a double agent – working simultaneously for both Benjamin Franklin and the British government – during the American Revolution. He remained in England and made discoveries in textile dyes manufacturing.

Bancroft, George (1800–91) historian, diplomat; born in Worcester, Mass. He tried unsuccessfully to establish a preparatory school for boys before he began writing his 10-volume *History of the United States* (1834–74). His writing showed a marked bias in favor of democracy; he viewed the American political experiment as the highest form of civilization. He supported James K. Polk's "dark horse" candidacy for the Democratic nomination in 1844 and was rewarded with the post of secretary of the navy (1845–46). He established the Naval Academy at Annapolis (1845) and aided the work of the Naval Observatory. He served as ambassador to Great Britain (1846–49) and later to Prussia and Germany (1867–74). After returning to the U.S.A. he spent his final years writing various historical books and articles.

Bancroft, Hubert Howe (1832–1918) historian, publisher; born in Granville, Ohio. Beginning as a bookseller in Buffalo, he founded his own lucrative publishing and mercantile house in San Francisco (1858). After collecting 60,000 source volumes, "The Macaulay of the West," as he has been known, edited and published *The Native Races of the Pacific States* (1875), the first of his landmark 39-volume *History of the Pacific States of America* (1875–1900). He continued publishing until 1916.

Bancroft, Wilder Dwight (1867–1953) physical chemist; born in Middletown, R.I. A professor at Cornell University (1895–1937), he founded and edited the *Journal of Physical Chemistry* (1896–1932). He did research in electrochemistry, colloid chemistry, and contact catalysis. His career was cut short by an accident in 1937.

Bandelier, Adolph (Francis Alphonse) (1840–1914) explorer, archaeologist, author; born in Bern, Switzerland. Brought by his family to Illinois in 1848, he went back to Switzerland to study geology at the University of Bern, then returned to Illinois and worked in a bank. After studying on his own (and a visit to Mexico in 1877), he published several works on the Aztecs (late 1870s). These gained him the sponsorship of the Archaeological Institute of America and he went off to the Southwest in 1880; for the next decade he lived with the Pueblo Indians, studying their ways and history and engaging in some excavations; this work resulted in further publications. In 1892 he went to Peru and Bolivia to continue his researches. In 1903 he came back to the U.S.A. and joined the staff of the American Museum of Natural History in New York and taught at Columbia University. In 1911, having joined the staff of the Carnegie Institution of Washington, he went to continue his researches in Spain and died in Seville. As a scholar he worked to dispose of such legends as Quivira and the Seven Cities of Cibola, but he himself wrote two novels, *The Delight Makers* (1890) and *The Gilded Man* (1893). His early work in the Southwest gained him the distinction of being called the first American archaeologist.

Bandura, Albert (1925–) psychologist; born in Mundare, Alberta, Canada. He studied at the Universities of British Columbia and Iowa and began his long career at Stanford University in 1953. He is best known as a social learning theorist whose research established the concept of imitation, or modeling, on a firm empirical base. His major works include (with R. H. Walters) *Social Learning and Personality Development* (1963), and *Aggression: A Social Learning Analysis* (1973).

Bankhead, John Hollis (1872–1946) lawyer, politician; born in Moscow, Ala. (uncle of Tallulah Bankhead). He graduated Georgetown Law School (1893) and returned to Alabama and the law office of his father's business friend. As a state representative (1903–05), he once wrote a law to disenfranchise African-Americans. In 1930 he ran successfully for the U.S. Senate as a "Jeffersonian Democrat" and embraced New Deal farm programs (Dem., 1931–46). The Bankhead-Jones Farm Tenant Act (1937) established the Farm Security Administration which, among other things, assisted migrant workers. During the war he fought unsuccessfully the president's policy of keeping food prices low. He collapsed during a political battle to prevent the continuation of price controls and died a month later.

Bankhead, Tallulah (Brockman) (1903–68) stage and film actress; born in Huntsville, Ala. Known for her husky, drawling voice and her sultry man-eating roles, she was first noticed in *The Little Foxes* in 1939.

Banks, Dennis (1932–) Ojibwa activist; born in Leech Lake, Minn. Educated in Bureau of Indian Affairs boarding schools, he cofounded, with George Mitchell, the American Indian Movement (1968). He was a leader in such protest actions as the Trail of Broken Treaties (1972) and the occupation of Wounded Knee (1973). Convicted in 1975 on charges stemming from a South Dakota demonstration, he was granted asylum by California governor Jerry Brown the following year, but he returned to South Dakota in 1984 to serve time in prison. In 1992 he appeared in the movie *The Last of the Mohicans*.

Banks, Nathaniel Prentiss (1816–1894) U.S. representative, soldier; born in Waltham, Mass. Largely self-educated, he became a lawyer (1839) but turned to publishing. He then served in the Massachusetts legislature (1849–53) before going to the House of Representatives (Dem., 1853–55; Know-Nothing, 1855–57; he was Speaker of the House (1856–57). Turning Republican, he became governor of Massachusetts (1858–60). Shortly after succeeding George McClellan as head of the Illinois Central Railroad (1860–61), he was commissioned a major general with the Union army. He led Federal forces in several unsuccessful actions against Stonewall Jackson, but succeeded in capturing Port Hudson, La., (1863); however, after the disastrous Red River Campaign of 1864, he resigned from the army. He returned to the U.S. House of Representatives (Rep., 1865–73; Dem., 1875–77; Rep., 1877–79; Rep., 1889–91).

Banneker, Benjamin (1731–1806) astronomer, mathematician; born near Baltimore, Md. Grandson of an Englishwoman and a freed black slave, but son of a slave father and freed black mother, he was allowed to attend a local elementary school where he showed a talent for math and science. As a youth, he made a clock entirely out of wood that kept time for some 50 years. Although his main occupation was farming, he devoted his spare time to applied sciences. Between 1792–1802, he published an almanac that used his astronomical and tide calculations and his weather predictions along with proverbs, poems, and essays contributed by himself and others; this almanac was often cited by opponents of slavery as evidence of African-Americans' abilities. Thomas Jefferson, who knew of Banneker's work, had him hired in 1791 to assist the surveyors laying out the new capital and the District of Columbia. He in turn did not shrink from urging Jefferson to abolish slavery and to adopt more progressive policies for black Americans, of whom he was probably the best known in his day and for some decades.

Bannister, Edward (Mitchell) (1828–1901) painter; born in St. Andrews, New Brunswick, Canada. A prominent Negro painter in his day, he moved to Boston (c. 1848), studied at the Lowell Institute under William Rimmer (1855), and settled in Providence, R.I. (c. 1870). His recently rediscovered landscapes, such as *Fishing* (1881), were painted in the naturalistic Barbizon style, a French approach popular in America (c. 1830–70).

Bara, Theda (b. Theodosia Goodman) (1890–1955) movie actress; born in Cincinnati, Ohio. The daughter of a tailor, she acted briefly in stock companies and then showed up in Hollywood as an extra. The creation of the Hollywood studio machine, she was assigned her new name, billed as the daughter of an Eastern potentate, and turned into an overnight star in *A Fool There Was* (1915). Known as "the Vamp" becamse of her screen portrayals of exotic "man-hungry" women, her famous line, "Kiss me, my fool!" and the offscreen image she cultivated (such as giving interviews while stroking a snake), she made some 40 movies, most by 1919. That year she went to New York to become a Broadway actress, but her reputation did her no good so she returned to Hollywood. By this time, though, changing tastes made her seem absurd, and after a few more unsuccessful movies, she retired in 1926 and effectively vanished.

Baraga, (Irenaeus) Frederic (1797–1868) Catholic missionary; born in Austria. A parish priest, he emigrated to the U.S.A. in 1830 and worked among Chippewa and Ottawa Indians in upper Michigan, where he became vicar apostolic (1853) and ultimately bishop (1865). He published devotional works and a grammar and dictionary of Indian languages.

Baraka, Imamu Amiri (b. LeRoi Jones) (1934–) poet, writer; born in Newark, N.J. He studied at Howard University (B.A. 1953), traveled widely, and taught at many institutions, notably the State University of New York: Long Island (1980). He published a number of works as LeRoi Jones. A revolutionary African-American activist, he became a Muslim and changed his name in 1967. Based in Newark, N.J., he has been a publisher (1958), and founder of a repertory theater (1965), and a community center (1966). In addition to his poetry, such as *Reggae or Not!* (1982), he has written plays, short stories, essays, and nonfiction.

Barber, Edwin Atlee (1851–1916) archaeologist; born in Baltimore, Md. While a West Philadelphia postmaster and Ph.D. student, he became the country's leading authority on ceramics. He was ceramics curator (1901–07) and director (1907–16) of the Pennsylvania Museum and School of Industrial Arts, Philadelphia. He published numerous standard works on ancient and modern ceramics.

Barber, Samuel (1910–81) composer; born in West Chester, Pa. From a musical family, Barber decided on his career in childhood and attended the Curtis Institute of Music from

1924–34. There he wrote the orchestral works *The School for Scandal* and *Music for a Scene from Shelly,* which gained him attention in America and Europe. His *Adagio for Strings,* premiered by Toscanini in 1938, was an immediate hit and remains his best-known score. In the late 1930s Barber joined the Curtis faculty; he left teaching and served in the military from 1942. After the war he settled into a house in Mt. Kisco, N.Y., with composer Gian-Carlo Menotti, who wrote the libretto to Barber's opera *Vanessa* (1958). His music, long popular with listeners, is marked by a classical clarity often joined to a late-Romantic wistfulness; later work, such as the Piano Concerto (a Pulitzer Prize winner in 1963) uses more modernistic techniques without giving up Barber's basic expressiveness. *Antony and Cleopatra,* written for the opening of the new Metropolitan Opera in 1966, was a celebrated failure, although later productions of a revised version fared better.

Barber, (Walter Lanier) "Red" (1908–92) baseball broadcaster; born in Columbus, Miss. He was the broadcaster for the Brooklyn Dodgers and the New York Yankees from 1939 to 1966. Known for his colorful phrases, such as "sitting in the catbird seat," he was elected to baseball's Hall of Fame in 1978. He enjoyed a "revival" in the final decade of his life as a weekly sports commentator on the National Public Broadcasting System.

Barbosa, José Celso (1857–1921) physician, public official, activist; born in Bayamón, Puerto Rico. He was the first black to attend Puerto Rico's prestigious Jesuit Seminary, then the island's only secondary institution. After graduating (1875), he attended the University of Michigan, graduating first in his medical school class (1880). A life-long political activist and Puerto Rico's first prominent black politician, he formed the Republican Party (July 4, 1899) and was the father of the statehood ideology. He established the newspaper *El Tiempo* (1907) and was a member of the Puerto Rican Senate (1917–21).

Barbour, Philip Pendleton (1783–1841); Supreme Court justice; born in Barboursville, Va. He was a member of the Virginia legislature (1812–14) and the U.S. House of Representatives (Dem., Va.; 1814–25, 1827–30). President Jackson named him to a federal district court in Virginia (1830) and to the U.S. Supreme Court (1836–41).

Barchas, Jack D. (1935–) neurologist, psychiatrist; born in Los Angeles. He was professor of psychiatry at Stanford (1967–89) and dean for research development and for neuroscience at the University of California: Los Angeles School of Medicine (1990). His major research dealt with the relationship between behavior and neuroregulators, chemicals that transmit information between nerve cells.

Bard, John (1716–99) physician; born in Burlington, N.J. After practicing medicine in Philadelphia, he moved to New York City (1746). He performed the first recorded dissection of a cadaver in the United States for the purpose of instruction (1750) and the first surgical delivery of a live fetus (1759). He was a precursor of the public sanitation movement in New York City, advocating measures to prevent the spread of yellow fever.

Bard, Samuel (1742–1821) physician; born in Philadelphia (son of John Bard). He studied medicine in London and Edinburgh and remained in New York City as a Loyalist during the American Revolution. He helped found the first medical college in New York State (1765), with which he was affiliated until about 1795. The college was united with Columbia University (1792) and Bard became its dean. He also helped found New York Hospital (1791), the public library, and the New York Dispensary. He was primarily interested in obstetrics and midwifery.

Bardeen, John (1908–91) physicist; born in Madison, Wis. He worked as a geophysicist at Gulf Research and Development Corporation (1930–33) before obtaining a Ph.D. from Harvard (1936). He taught at the University of Minnesota (1938–41), served as a civilian physicist for the Naval Ordnance Laboratory (1941–45), then joined Bell Telephone Laboratories (1945–51). Together with Walter Brattain and William Shockley, he developed the point-contact transistor (1947), for which they shared the 1956 Nobel Prize in physics. Bardeen became a professor at the University of Illinois (1951–75); he shared a second Nobel Prize (1972) with his students Leon Cooper and J. Robert Schrieffer for the Bardeen-Cooper-Schrieffer (BCS) theory of superconductivity. Their research was a breakthrough in electromagnet design, and made Bardeen the first person to win the Nobel Prize for physics twice.

Barker, Jacob (1779–1871) merchant, financier; born on Swan Island, Maine. He followed his brother to New York City at age 16 to become a seaman, but was persuaded to work for a company that sold goods on commission. He acquired part ownership in a fleet of merchant vessels. His first independent business venture (1801) ended in bankruptcy, but he started again as a ship merchant and became wealthy. Although he lost all his ships to the British in the War of 1812, during the war he helped raise money for the American government. In 1815 he founded the Exchange Bank on Wall Street, which failed in 1819. During the depression of 1823, the Life & Fire Insurance Company, of which he was a director, failed; he and six others were indicted for fraud, a charge that he fought in letters and published articles. He moved to Louisiana, became a lawyer, and during the Civil War, even though he had anti-secessionist feelings, he presided over the Bank of Commerce. In 1869, sick and once again poor, he went to live at his son's home in Philadelphia.

Barkley, Alben W. (William) (1877–1956) vice-president, U.S. representative/senator; born in Lowes, Ky. As a U.S. representative and senator, he backed the wartime administrations of Woodrow Wilson and Franklin Roosevelt. In 1949, under Harry Truman, he became the oldest vice-president to take office, and as "the Veep," became something of a humorous figure.

Barlow, Joel (1754–1812) poet, diplomat, writer; born in Reading, Conn. He graduated from Yale (1778), and engaged in various activities before becoming a lawyer (1786); his early writings, including his poem, *The Vision of Columbus* (1787; revised as *The Columbiad*, 1807), made him known as one of the "Hartford [or Connecticut] Wits." Going off to France in 1788 as an agent for a land speculation scheme, he spent the next 17 years there or in London – with time out to serve as U.S. consul in Algiers. He supported himself by writing, and although he had become more sympathetic to radical thinkers, by 1794 he had become rich through his investments. On returning to the U.S.A. in 1805, he settled near Washington, D.C. He was appointed ambassador to France in 1811 and he died in Poland where he had gone in hopes of negotiating a treaty with Napoleon I.

Barlow is probably best known today for his mock epic poem, "Hasty Pudding" (1796).

Barnard, Chester (Irving) (1886–1961) businessman, public official, foundation executive; born in Malden, Mass. After working as an engineer with the American Telephone and Telegraph Company in Boston (1909–22), he moved on to head the Pennsylvania and then New Jersey Bell companies (1922–48). He served on various civic boards and during World War II was president of the United Service Organizations for National Defense (1942–45) and director of the National War Fund (1943–46). After the war he was a U.S. representative on the Atomic Energy Committee and he chaired various science foundations. His later reputation derives from his books, *The Functions of the Executive* (1938) and *Organization and Management* (1948).

Barnard, Edward Emerson (1857–1923) astronomer; born in Nashville, Tenn. Brilliant, but unschooled, he worked for his fatherless family in a photography studio from the age of nine. He later applied his photographic and observational skills to photographing the Milky Way while at the Lick Observatory (1888–95), where he also discovered the 5th moon of Jupiter. At the University of Chicago (1895–1923), he devoted himself to astronomy.

Barnard, Frederick A. P. (Augustus Porter) (1809–89) college president; born in Sheffield, Mass. This mathematician and scientist was president of Columbia College (later University) (1864–89), which he developed into a major university, admitting women (1883; Barnard College is named for him), establishing the Teachers College and the School of Mines, and pioneering the elective system.

Barnard, George Grey (1863–1938) sculptor, collector; born in Bellefonte, Pa. He studied at the Art Institute of Chicago (1880–83), in Paris (1883–87), traveled, and collected medieval antiquities that became part of the Cloisters Museum, New York. Based in New York City from 1896, he was known for his idealized marble sculptures.

Barnard, Henry (1811–1900) educator; born in Hartford, Conn. Raised by his prosperous farmer-father, he went to Yale (B.A. 1830) where he came to feel strongly about the need for education of all classes of Americans. He taught at an academy for a year after graduation, then read law and was admitted to the bar (1835); from 1835–36 he traveled in Europe where he met many prominent individuals. Serving in the Connecticut legislature (1837–39), he set up a board to supervise the common schools of the state and then ended up heading the board; during four years he greatly upgraded the public schools attended by the state's poor. Between 1843–49 he was hired by Rhode Island and effected much the same kind of reforms. By now he was known throughout most of the United States for his advanced views on public education and was much in demand as a speaker. In 1849 he returned to Connecticut to head a new teachers training school and serve as superintendent of the state's public schools. His writings were spreading his views and in 1855 he founded the *American Journal of Education;* as publisher and editor until 1882, he greatly helped to improve public education throughout the United States. Chancellor of the University of Wisconsin (1858–60) and president of St. John's College (Annapolis, Md.) (1866–67), he went on to be the first United States commissioner of education (1867–70). Along with Horace Mann, he earned his status as the foundation-layer of modern public education in America.

Barnes, Albert Coombs (1872–1951) pharmacologist, art collector; born in Philadelphia. He studied at Philadelphia Medical School (M.D. 1892), and interned at the State Hospital of the Insane, Warren, Pa. After study and travel in Europe, he devoted himself to chemical research, developing a new antiseptic, Argyrol (1902), that made him a fortune. By 1905 he began collecting late-19th- and early-20th-century French art, wrote several books on art, and in 1922 established the Barnes Foundation in Merion, Pa., where he housed his collection. Dogmatic in his ideas about art, and ornery in his dealings with art professionals, he allowed only a select few individuals to view his collection during his lifetime.

Barnes, Djuna (Linda Steptoe, pen name) (1892–1982) writer, poet; born in Cornwall-on-Hudson, N.Y. She studied at Pratt Institute and the Art Students League, N.Y., illustrated, and wrote short stories, poetry, and plays. She became an expatriate in Paris (1920–40), then returned to New York City where she lived as a virtual recluse (1940–82). Her best known work is *Nightwood* (1936), a modernist novel praised by T. S. Eliot.

Barnet, (Charles Daly) Charlie (1913–91) bandleader; born in New York City. He was a saxophonist from a New York socialite family who led his first band on the *S.S. Republic* in 1929 and subsequently played on many Atlantic crossings for the Cunard and Red Star lines. In 1933 he formed a big band in New York, and in the following year it became the first white orchestra to appear at the Apollo Theatre in Harlem. His personal wealth enabled him to resist racial and musical barriers, and he became one of the first bandleaders to routinely employ African-American musicians and to perform compositions by Duke Ellington. In 1939 he recorded his hit theme song "Cherokee," and he continued to lead an orchestra until 1949, when he disbanded. He occasionally formed bands for specific engagements in the 1950s and 1960s. His autobiography, *Those Swinging Years,* was published in 1984.

Barney, Joshua (1759–1818) naval officer; born in Baltimore, Md. He served with distinction in the American Revolution (he was three times captured and imprisoned). His management of the flotilla in the Chesapeake Bay and his conduct at the battle of Bladensburg (1814) were outstanding events during the War of 1812.

Barney, Natalie Clifford (1876–1972) hostess, writer; born in Dayton, Ohio. Born into a wealthy family (her grandfather made railroad cars), she was educated at a French boarding school, becoming completely bilingual. She finished her schooling at a private school for girls in New York City (1894), then was introduced into society in Washington, D.C.; her beauty, wealth, artistic talents, and personal charm led to several engagements, but, finding herself attracted to her own sex, she went to Paris in 1898. She soon became one of the most notable lesbians of her time, and while she wrote poetry, plays, fiction, and epigrams, she was mostly admired for the support she gave to other women writers and for her various love affairs with women. Her international salon at her home on rue Jacob attracted the cultivated and artistic from several lands for some 60 years and inspired much of her own writing. Remy de Goncourt addressed his *Lettres à l'Amazone* (1912–13) to her, and one of her volumes of epigrams was called *Pensées d'une Amazone.* (She did most of her writing in French.) Her most enduring relationship (1915–70) was with the American painter, Romaine Brooks. Her memoirs such as *Souvenirs indiscrets* (1960) and *Traits et portraits* (1963) provide an invaluable testimony to the world she inhabited.

Barney, Nora Stanton (b. Blatch) (1883–1971) civil engineer, architect, suffragist; born in Basingstoke, Hampshire, England (daughter of Harriet Stanton Blatch, granddaughter of Elizabeth Cady Stanton). She moved to New York City as a girl. The first female civil engineering graduate from Cornell University, she began in 1914 to design and build houses, and after 1923 became a prominent developer of exclusive houses in suburban Connecticut. She led the fight in New York State for women's suffrage and was a lifelong activist on behalf of feminism and peace.

Barnhart, Clarence L. (Lewis) (1900–93) lexicographer; born near Plattsburg, Mo. Beginning his career at the publishing firm of Scott, Foresman, he joined forces with the educator and psychologist Edward L. Thorndike to edit the Thorndike-Barnhart school dictionaries, for many years the most widely used school dictionaries in the U.S.A. But perhaps his most lasting contribution to lexicography was his editing of the *American College Dictionary* (1947), which introduced the participation of leading linguists and psychologists and was the forerunner of the entire line of Random House dictionaries. With his son Robert he also edited the two-volume *World Book Dictionary* (first published 1963), which is sold as part of the *World Book Encyclopedia.* He was also active in promoting a more linguistically informed approach to reading in association with the linguist Leonard Bloomfield and edited *Let's Read: A Linguistic Approach* (1961). He founded his own publishing company, Barnhart Books, which with his son David published periodic compilations of new words (neologisms), subsequently collected in book form. He is widely regarded as the doyen of American lexicographers of the twentieth century.

Barnum, P. T. (Phineas Taylor) (1810–91) showman; born in Bethel, Conn. The self-proclaimed prince of humbug, he was a publisher when he became intrigued by Joice Heth, a black woman claiming to be George Washington's nurse; he successfully promoted her in the late 1830s. In 1842 he opened his New York museum of natural history and "curiosities," including "the Egress" and the midget, Tom Stratton ("General Tom Thumb"), whom he took to meet Queen Victoria. In 1850 he brought Jenny Lind, the Swedish singer, to America. In 1855 he published the first edition of his autobiography, *The Life of P. T. Barnum.* He knew what the public wanted and how to promote his unique attractions. In 1871 he introduced "The Greatest Show on Earth," a three ring circus which he transported by rail. Joining with rival James Bailey in 1881, he featured exotic animals, including one he advertised as "the last mastodon on earth" (actually, Jumbo the elephant). A liberal Republican, he served in the Connecticut legislature (1865–69) and as mayor of Bridgeport (1875–76).

Baron, Salo (Wittmayer) (1895–1989) educator, author; born in Tarnow, Galicia (now Austria). Educated in Austria, he came to the U.S.A. in 1927. He held the first Miller Chair of Jewish History, Literature and Institutions at Columbia University (1930–63). He edited the *Jewish Social Studies* quarterly, and wrote the 18-volume *Social and Religious History of the Jews* (1937–52). A member of many educational and government organizations, he testified about the history of European anti-Semitism at the 1961 trial of *Adolf Eichmann.*

Barr, Alfred (Hamilton), Jr. (1902–81) art historian, museum administrator; born in Detroit, Mich. He studied at Princeton, Harvard, and in Europe. He taught the first American college course in modern art at Wellesley College (1926). He became the founding director of the Museum of Modern Art in New York City (1929–43) and continued to be affiliated with the museum for the rest of his life. He wrote a number of influential books about modern art and artists, including *What is Modern Painting?* (1943) and *Picasso, 50 Years of His Art* (1946).

Barrett, William (1913–92) philosopher, critic; born in New York City. Educated at the City College of New York and Columbia University, he was associated with the *Partisan Review* group of intellectuals in the 1930s but moved gradually to the right in his political thought. He taught philosophy at New York University from 1950–79. His widely praised *Irrational Man* (1958) explained European existentialism to the general reader. His memoir, *The Truants: Adventures among the Intellectuals,* appeared in 1982.

Barro, Robert (Joseph) (1944–) economist; born in New York City. His principal contributions include promotion of the "new classical macroeconomics," including business cycles and monetary policy. He joined the faculty of the University of Rochester in 1975.

Barron, James (1768–1851) naval officer; born probably in Norfolk, Va. After youthful service in the American Revolution, he became a lieutenant in the U.S. Navy (1798). Commanding the USS *Chesapeake* in its disastrous fight with the British *Leopold* (1807), he was courtmartialed and found guilty of negligence. After five years with the French navy, he returned to the U.S. Navy; convinced that Stephen Decatur was leading an effort to block his career, he challenged and killed Decatur in a duel (1820). Despised by most in the navy, he remained on inactive status until his death.

Barron, William Wallace (1911–) governor; born in Elkins, W.Va. A lawyer and army veteran of World War II, he served in the West Virginia house of delegates, becoming attorney general (1957–61). As Democratic governor of West Virginia (1961–65), he became known for tightening controls over strip mining. He later opened a Charleston, W.Va., law firm, Barron and Davis.

Barrow, Clyde (1909–34) **and Parker, Bonnie** (1911–34) robbers, murderers; Barrow born in ?Houston, Texas; Parker born in Rowena, Texas. They met in 1930 and soon became America's most famous and romanticized outlaws. They killed at least 13 persons and escaped from several police ambushes before they were killed at a roadblock in Louisiana.

Barrow, (Edward Grant) Ed (1868–1953) baseball manager/executive; born in Springfield, Ill. After managing the Detroit Tigers in 1903–1904, he led the Boston Red Sox to a World Series championship as their manager in 1918. He became general manager of the New York Yankees (1921–45), where he shaped the famous pennant-winning teams of Babe Ruth, Lou Gehrig, and Joe DiMaggio. He was elected to the Hall of Fame in 1953.

Barrows, Harlan (Hiram) (1877–1960) geographer; born in Armada, Mich. He was chairman of the department of geography at the University of Chicago (1919–42). His work in historical geography and the conservation of natural resources was widely respected. His presidential address delivered before the Association of American Geographers (1922), "Geography as Human Ecology," remains one of those most quoted.

Barry, John (1745–1803) naval officer; born in County Wexford, Ireland. He went to sea early and settled in Philadelphia by 1760. An ardent patriot, he became a Continental Navy captain (1776) and commanded the USS *Lexington* and *Effingham* (1776–78). He conveyed John Laurens to France aboard the USS *Alliance* and fought a grueling battle on his return voyage. He brought the Marquis de Lafayette back to France after the victory at Yorktown (1781), and captured numerous British vessels in 1782. After the American Revolution, he worked in the merchant trade and retired before being recalled to the naval service in 1794. He became the senior captain in the navy and commanded all U.S. ships in the West Indies (1798–99). He returned to Philadelphia (1801) and remained the senior naval officer until his death.

Barry, Leonora (Marie Kearney) (1849–1923) labor leader; born in County Cork, Ireland. Emigrating to the United States in 1852, she worked in a clothing factory. In 1884 she organized a local assembly of the Knights of Labor. She served as general investigator for the Knights' women's department (1886–90).

Barry, Marion S. (Shepilov) Jr. (1936–) mayor, public official; born in Itta Bena, Miss. He earned a B.A. from LeMoyne College and an M.A. from Fiske University. In 1968 he was co-founder and director of Pride Economic Enterprises. A member of the Washington, D.C., school board (1971–74) and city councillor (1974–78), he was a delegate to the Democratic National Convention in 1980. He was mayor of Washington, D.C., from 1980 to 1991, when he was convicted of cocaine use. In September 1992, upon his release from prison, he won a seat on the Washington City Council and was later re-elected mayor (1995).

Barry, Philip (Jerome Quinn) (1896–1949) playwright; born in Rochester, N.Y. After serving with the U.S. State Department in World War I, he attended George Pierce Baker's "47 Workshop" at Harvard. He spent the rest of his life as a playwright. His greatest success was with light social comedies, including *Holiday* (1928) and *The Philadelphia Story* (1939). But his ambitions toward serious psychological and philosophical theater could be seen in his plays *Hotel Universe* (1930), *Bright Star* (1935), and *Here Come the Clowns* (1938). These more somber pieces, however, did not appeal to his public and he returned to comedy.

Barry, (Richard Francis Dennis III) Rick (1944–) basketball player; born in Elizabeth, N.J. After playing for the University of Miami (Fla.) (1962–65), he played forward for the San Francisco (later Golden State) Warriors, the Houston Rockets, and the American Basketball Association (ABA) New York Nets (1966–80). He is the only player ever to lead both the National Basketball Association and ABA in scoring. He was elected to basketball's Hall of Fame in 1986.

Barrymore, Ethel (1879–1959) stage and film actress; born in Philadelphia. Daughter of Maurice Barrymore and a member of the famous family of actors, she had her first success in *Captain Jinks of the Horse Marines* (1901), and made some early silent films. In 1944 she won an Academy Award for best supporting actress in *None But the Lonely Heart*. She was admired for her portrayal of lovable eccentrics.

Barrymore, John (1882–1942) stage and film actor; born in Philadelphia. Brother of Ethel Barrymore and Lionel Barrymore of the great acting family, he made his debut in 1903 and became a matinee idol. He triumphed as a stage Hamlet in 1922, then turned to films and radio. Married four times, he caricatured his own decadent, alcohol-ridden life in a series of minor comedies, including *The Great Profile* (1940).

Barrymore, Lionel (1878–1954) stage, film, and radio actor; born in Philadelphia. Brother of Ethel Barrymore and John Barrymore of the great acting family, he was known as a fine character actor. His film career included 15 Dr. Kildare movies, as well as *You Can't Take It with You* (1938). He is well remembered for his depiction of Scrooge in the 1936 radio presentation of Dickens' *A Christmas Carol*. Radio became his primary career after he was confined to a wheelchair. Listeners in the 1940s knew him as *The Mayor of the Town*.

Barrymore, Maurice (b. Herbert Blythe) (1849–1905) stage actor; born in Fort Agra, India (father of Ethel, John, and Lionel Barrymore). Giving up a possible law career, he began acting in London in 1872; he became an instant success in New York in 1875 and went on to star in a variety of roles over the next 25 years. In 1876 he married Georgiana Drew, actress-daughter of the famous British-American actors, John and Louisa Lane Drew, thus founding what would become known as "The Royal Family of Broadway."

Barth, John (Simmons) (1930–   ) writer, educator; born in Cambridge, Md. He graduated from Johns Hopkins, where, during a long academic career, he joined the English faculty (1973). His novels, some set on Maryland's Eastern Shore, were distinctive for their formal ingenuity and an existential questioning bordering on nihilism. They include *The End of the Road* (1958), *Chimera* (1972, National Book Award), and *Tidewater Tales* (1988). A major exception was his second novel, *The Sot-Weed Factor* (1960), a long, playful parody written in the style of an 18th century novel.

Barthé, Richmond (1901–89) sculptor; born in Bay St. Louis, Miss. An early African-American artist, he studied at the Art Institute of Chicago (c. 1920–24), and at the Art Students League, New York (1931). Based in St. Anne, Jamaica, he was a painter who became a sculptor of expressive bronze works, such as *Boxer* (1942).

Barthelme, Donald (1931–89) writer; born in Philadelphia. He left Houston, Texas, journalism in the early 1960s to live in New York City as a professional fiction writer. A regular *New Yorker* contributor, he was an influential postmodernist whose deadpan tone, fragmented narrative structure, and linguistic playfulness were widely imitated. His eight volumes of collected stories and four novels include *Come Back, Dr. Caligari* (1964), *Snow White* (1967), *The Dead Father* (1975), and *Paradise* (1986).

Bartlett, (Edward Lewis) "Bob" (1904–68) public official; born in Seattle, Wash. His family moved to Fairbanks, Alaska, soon after his birth. He was a newspaper reporter (1925–33) and a gold miner (1936–39). He was the secretary of Alaska (1939–44) and Alaska's territorial delegate to Congress (1945–59) before becoming one of the new state's

first two U.S. Senators (Dem., Alaska; 1959–68). Alaska placed his statue in the U.S. Capitol.

Bartlett, John (1820–1905) lexicographer; born in Plymouth, Mass. The self-educated Bartlett began his publishing career as a bookseller in Cambridge, Mass. His *Familiar Quotations*, which included American, along with the more traditional British and Biblical selections, was first published in 1855; it continues to this day in revised editions, and "Look it up in *Bartlett!*" is now as famous as many of its contents. He joined Little, Brown and Co. publishers in 1863. He prepared the second American edition of Izaak Walton's *The Compleat Angler* and, in 1894, he and his wife compiled *Phrases and Passages in the Dramatic Works of Shakespeare*.

Bartlett, Josiah (1729–95) physician, governor; born in Amesbury, Mass. A self-taught physician in Kingston, N.H. (1750–79), he reformed medical diagnosis and treatment. A member of the Continental Congress (1775–76, 1778–79), he signed the Declaration of Independence, afterwards serving as common pleas judge. He was chief of justice of the state superior court (1788–90), and New Hampshire's first governor (1790–94).

Bartlett, Paul (Wayland) (1865–1925) sculptor; born in New Haven, Conn. In Paris (1874) he attended the École des Beaux-Arts (1879), worked with Emmanuel Fremiet, and made Paris his home. Specializing in the sculpting of animal figures, he is known for the patina on his bronze sculptures, as in *The Bear Tamer* (1887), and for the equestrian statue of Lafayette (1899–1908).

Bartlett, Robert (Abram) (1875–1946) explorer; born in Brigus, Newfoundland, Canada. He began his Arctic explorations in 1897 and captained Robert E. Peary's ship *Roosevelt* twice (1905–06, 1908–09). He became a U.S. citizen in 1911 and a lieutenant commander in the U.S. naval reserves (1920). He commanded the *Karluk* on Stefansson's expedition (1913–14) and when it was frozen and crushed in the Arctic ice, he walked across the ice to Siberia and returned with rescuers for 13 other members of the expedition. He headed expeditions to various Arctic locations (1925–41), and was especially noted for his scientific work on Greenland. During World War II, he searched for sites for Allied naval bases in the Arctic.

Barton, Bruce (Fairchild) (1886–1967) advertising executive, author, U.S. representative; born in Robbins, Tenn. He was a magazine editor and publicist before founding a New York advertising agency with George Batten, Roy Durstine and Alex Osborn (1919); for more than 40 years he headed what became BBDO, one of the country's largest advertising agencies. He created the character Betty Crocker. The author of numerous inspirational essays, he was best known for his best-selling book, *The Man Nobody Knows* (1925), which presented Jesus Christ as a successful salesman. A conservative and an opponent of the New Deal, he served two terms in the House of Representatives (Rep., N.Y.; 1937–41).

Barton, (Clarissa Harlowe) Clara (1821–1912) nurse, organizer; born in Oxford, Mass. An adventurous and strong-willed farmer's daughter, she nursed an invalid brother as a child, became a teacher at age 15, and worked in the U.S. Patent Office in Washington, D.C., during the 1850s. After the Union defeat at the 1st Battle of Bull Run (July 1861) she advertised for provisions for the wounded and received such a large contribution that she set herself up as a distributing agency. From mid-July 1862 Barton operated as a freelance front-line nurse, distributing comforts and tending the sick and wounded of the Army of the Potomac. In 1864 she served as superintendent of nurses for the Army of the James, her only official connection – she had difficulty taking orders, and preferred to work on her own. After the war Barton worked under the auspices of the International Red Cross in Europe to distribute relief to the French in the Franco-Prussian War. When she returned to the U.S.A. she campaigned for the establishment of an American Red Cross. She headed the agency for 23 years after its incorporation in 1881. Small, slightly built but physically hardy, she expended a large portion of her substantial energies in the field; at age 79 she spent six weeks tending the ill and homeless in Galveston, Texas, after the disastrous flood there. A poor manager, unwilling to delegate, and more unwilling to share authority, Barton resigned under pressure as head of the Red Cross in June 1904, after which the agency experienced a thoroughgoing reorganization.

Barton, Donald C. (Clinton) (1889–1939) geologist; born in Stow, Mass. He taught at Washington University (1914–16), then served as a research geologist in several U.S. oil companies (1916–39). His innovative use of the torsion balance to discover the salt domes that overlie oil deposits, revolutionized the field of petrogeology.

Barton, Ralph (1891–1931) illustrator, caricaturist; born in Kansas City, Mo. At the height of his career during the 1920s, when he was based in New York City but often traveled to Paris, his work was in demand by every magazine and book publisher and he came to epitomize the era he so cleverly caricatured. Often depressed, an insomniac, and a workaholic, he was constantly on the move, and married four times. He was a dandy who knew all the smart people, and could afford all the expensive toys, but ended up committing suicide.

Bartram, John (1699–1777) botanist; born near Darby, Pa. He developed an early interest in botany while growing up on his father's farm. After completing country school at age 12, he taught himself classical languages, medicine, and surgery from books. In 1728 he purchased land at King-sessing, near Philadelphia, which he developed into the first botanical garden in the American colonies and where he conducted the first hybridization experiments in America. Around 1733 he began corresponding with English naturalist Peter Collinson, with whom he exchanged seeds and plant specimens. This relationship led to his correspondence with Swedish biologist and taxonomist Carl Linnaeus, who called Bartram "the greatest natural botanist in the world." By 1750, Bartram was acclaimed throughout Europe. He made frequent collecting expeditions from Canada to Florida, some with his botanist son William Bartram until the early 1770s. In 1743, he became a member of Benjamin Franklin's American Philosophical Society, and in 1765 was appointed botanist to King George III. A naturalist as well as a botanist, Bartram described and collected zoological specimens, proposed geological surveys of North American mineral sites, and argued that fossils be investigated scientifically, rather than exploited as curiosities. A Quaker, he demonstrated his opposition to slavery by freeing his slaves; his outspoken religious opinions caused him to be disowned

by his coreligionists in the Society of Friends. *Bartramia,* a genus of mosses, was named in his honor.

Bartram, William (1739–1823) botanist; born in Kingsessing (Philadelphia), Pa. As a youth he showed a talent for drawing specimens collected by his father, John Bartram, America's first botanist, but he first worked as a merchant and trader (1757–61). In 1765 he accompanied his father on an expedition to Florida, and remained in the American south, drawing natural flora, gathering botanical specimens, becoming an accomplished ornithologist, and befriending both colonial planters and members of indigenous tribes. After his father's death (1777), he returned to Pennsylvania to become a partner with his brother John Bartram to care for his father's botanical garden (1777–1812). He declined a professorship of botany at the University of Pennsylvania (1782), preferring to write on natural history and his observations on Indians; his literary accounts of his travels greatly influenced the 19th-century romantic movement; *Travels through North and South Carolina, Georgia etc.* (1791) is regarded as his masterpiece. In 1786, William Bartram was elected to the American Philosophical Society. He remained active as a botanist, dying suddenly after writing a description of a plant.

Baruch, Bernard (Mannes) (1870–1965) financier, public official, philanthropist; born in Camden, N.C. Starting on Wall Street at $3 a week, he became a multimillionaire by his mid-thirties through his stock investments. He chose to devote himself to public affairs and became a friend of Woodrow Wilson, who appointed him chairman of the War Industries Board (1917) and a member of the president's war council. He participated in the postwar peace conference, and with John Foster Dulles he coauthored *The Making of the Reparation and Economic Sections of the Treaty* (1920). Preferring to act as a personal consultant instead of holding official appointments, he continued to advise every president – and their top appointments – from Wilson through John F. Kennedy. Occasionally he did accept an appointment. During the 1930s, for instance, he advocated that the U.S. prepare and organize itself for the war he saw coming and in 1934 he accepted an appointment by President Franklin Roosevelt to chair a committee on mobilization legislation. After World War II he also accepted an appointment from President Harry Truman – as ambassador to the United Nations Atomic Energy Commission (1946). But for the most part he preferred his near-legendary role as "Mr. Baruch," offering advice from a park bench. He made many gifts to educational institutions, notably his *alma mater,* City College of New York.

Baryshnikov, Mikhail (1948–) ballet dancer; born in Riga, Latvia. After training at the Riga Choreographic School, he performed with the Kirov Ballet from 1966–74. He defected to Canada in 1974 and joined the American Ballet Theater, where his flamboyant style, as well as roles in such movies as *The Turning Point* (1977), propelled him to international stardom. During his tenure as the American Ballet Theater's artistic director (1980–89), he made guest appearances with different companies. In 1990 he began to collaborate with Mark Morris in the White Oak Dance Project.

Barzun, Jacques (1907–) educator, cultural critic, writer; born in Créteil, France. Arriving in the U.S.A. in 1920, he did his undergraduate and graduate work at Columbia University (Ph.D. 1932). He joined the faculty of Columbia in 1927 and remained there as a professor of history and dean, taking emeritus status in 1967. A man of wide-ranging interests, his major professional areas were 19th-century European cultural history, music, and the history of ideas. His many published works, most aimed at a broader public than his professional colleagues, include *Teacher in America* (1945), *Berlioz and the Romantic Century* (1950), *Music in American Life* (1956), *A Catalogue of Crime* (1971), and *Clio and the Doctors* (1974). He served as a consultant or adviser on various publishing projects and was a firm, if sometimes cantankerous, upholder of traditional standards of language usage and educational approaches; he never hesitated to write a letter to the editor, an article, or a book attacking what he regarded as deplorable intellectual trends – not only within his own discipline of history but also in science, the arts, and the publishing world.

Bascove (Anne) (1946–) graphic artist, painter; born in Philadelphia. She studied at the Philadelphia Museum College of Art (1964–68), and was based in New York City. She was a staff artist for the Peabody Museum at Yale University (1970–72), and was known for her illustrations and wood and linoleum block bookcovers for such authors as Dostoyevsky, Virginia Woolf, Thomas Mann, Robertson Davies, and Alice Walker. Her fine art, as in *Summer Fruit* (1990), has also gained recognition.

Basie, (William) Count (1904–84) jazz musician; born in Red Bank, N.J. He received his first piano lessons at age six from his mother and worked as an accompanist to silent films while still in high school. He studied organ informally with Fats Waller, whom he replaced in a New York vaudeville act called *Katie Crippin and Her Kids*. Between 1924–27, he toured on the Keith Circuit with the Gonzelle White vaudeville show until it got stranded in Kansas City, then a bustling center of jazz and blues activity. He played piano at a silent movie theater there, then spent a year with Walter Page's Blue Devils in 1928–29. When this band broke up, he began a five-year association with Benny Moten's orchestra, whose sidemen included blues singer Jimmy Rushing, trumpeter Hot Lips Page, and Lester Young, the highly innovative tenor saxophonist. Upon Moten's death in 1935, these musicians formed the nucleus of Basie's first band. Under his leadership they broadcast from the Reno Club in Kansas City, where a radio announcer dubbed him "Count"; through these broadcasts, he attracted the attention of the well-connected talent scout John Hammond, who set up his first tour. The band played a residency at the Grand Terrace in Chicago, then opened at the Roseland in New York in December 1936. Basie began a prolific series of recordings the following year, and in 1938 he played a long residency at the Savoy Ballroom in Harlem, where his reputation as leader of one of the premier swing bands was firmly established. He led his band on a continual series of U.S. tours throughout the 1940s, but in 1950 economic conditions compelled him to disband and front a sextet for two years. He formed a new 16-piece band in 1952 and began a long association with producer Norman Granz of Verve Records; this outfit established a new and enduring prototype for big bands and radio and television studio orchestras. In 1954, the band undertook the first of its many European tours. During the 1960s, the Basie orchestra accompanied various singers, including Frank Sinatra, Sarah Vaughan, Tony Bennett, and Sammy Davis Jr., on recordings and concert tours. He made numerous appearances with all-star groups in the 1970s, but maintained a regular touring schedule with his band until his death. His autobiography, *Good Morning Blues,* written with Albert Murray, was published posthumously in 1985.

Baskin, Leonard (1922–) graphic artist, sculptor; born in New Brunswick, N.J. He studied at New York University School of Architecture and Allied Arts (1939–41), Yale School of Art, New Haven (1941–43), and in France (1950) and Italy (1951). His sculptures, begun in the 1950s, show his dedication to social humanism, as seen in the wood, bronze, and stone series *Dead Men, Birdmen,* and *Oppressed Men.* His etchings, woodblocks, and graphics exhibit his elegiac and technically sophisticated approach, as seen in *Man of Peace* (1952) and *Angel of Death* (1959). He taught at Smith College, Northampton, Mass. (1953–74). Based in Leeds, Mass., in 1990 he undertook his major work, the long-delayed Franklin Delano Roosevelt Memorial for Washington, D.C.

Bass, George (Fletcher) (1932–) nautical archaeologist; born in Columbia, S.C. He was a pioneer in the field of underwater archaeology, especially known for his work on ancient shipwrecks off the Turkish coast (1960–87). He won the Gold Medal of the Archaeological Institute of America in 1986; his publications include *Archaeology Beneath the Sea* (1976) and *Ships and Shipwrecks of the Americas* (1988). He taught at Texas A&M University (1976) and after founding the Institute of Nautical Archaeology (1972) served as its president (1973–82).

Bass, (Mary) Elizabeth (1876–1956) physician; born in Carley, Miss. She attended local schools and became a teacher (1892–99). As women were then excluded from southern medical schools, in 1900 she enrolled in the Woman's Medical College of Pennsylvania, graduating in 1904. With five female colleagues, she established a free dispensary for the indigent women and children of New Orleans in 1905. In 1911 she and Edith Ballard became the first female faculty members at Tulane University school of medicine, where she taught for 30 years. Her work on behalf of women in medicine opened the doors for many who came after her, internationally as well as locally. She also amassed a major collection of printed materials by and about women in medicine (now part of Tulane's medical library) and she wrote numerous articles and essays on this subject.

Bate, Walter Jackson (1918–) literary critic, educator; born in Mankato, Minn. On the Harvard faculty (1946), he became a prominent spokesman for the humanistic literary tradition, resurrected the study of 18th-century English literature, and wrote Pulitzer Prize-winning literary biographies of John Keats (1963) and Samuel Johnson (1977).

Bates, Edward (1793–1869) public official, cabinet member; born in Belmont, Va. A Missouri state legislator, U.S. congressman (Whig, Mo.; 1827–29) and moderate voice in antebellum politics, he attracted national notice with an 1847 speech. In 1860 he unsuccessfully sought the Republican presidential nomination. He was Lincoln's attorney general (1861–64) – the first cabinet officer from west of the Mississippi – but resigned after his influence eroded because of his opposition to government wartime practices. Back in Missouri he opposed the post-war policies of the Radical Republicans.

Bates, Katherine Lee (1859–1929) poet, writer; born in Falmouth, Mass. Her father died soon after her birth, and her family moved to Wellesley (then Grantville), Mass., where she was schooled locally and graduated from Wellesley (B.A. 1880; M.A. 1891). She taught on the high school level for five years before teaching English at Wellesley (1885–1925). She wrote travel books, children's stories, textbooks, and poetry, as in *America the Dream* (1930). She is best known for her poem, "America the Beautiful" (1895), written after a visit to Pikes Peak and the World's Columbian Exposition in Chicago (1893). Set to the music of Samuel Ward, the poem continues to rival the national anthem in popularity.

Bates, (Theodore Lewis) Ted (1901–72) advertising executive; born in New Haven, Conn. He worked in advertising agencies after graduating from Yale, then founded his own New York advertising agency (1940). The agency grew into the fifth largest in the world through pioneering television advertising in the 1950s and by creating aggressive campaigns for major consumer product manufacturers like Colgate-Palmolive. He created Anacin's headache hammers and the Wonder Bread slogan, "Builds Strong Bodies 12 Ways."

Bateson, Gregory (1904–80) cultural anthropologist; born in Grantchester, England. A scientist's son, he studied biology and psychology before turning to anthropology at Cambridge University in England. He emigrated to the United States and made his career there. His first major work, *Naven,* a study of ritual and symbolism based on fieldwork in New Guinea, appeared in 1936. With Margaret Mead, to whom he was married (1936–50), he was involved in the culture and personality movement. He later studied problems of communication and learning among aquatic mammals and human schizophrenics and published his final work, *Mind and Nature,* in 1978.

Batten, William (Milfred) (1909–) businessman, stock market executive; born in Reedy, W.Va. After graduating from Ohio State (1932), he worked for the Kellogg Company before joining the J. C. Penney Co., where he worked his way up from an assistant store manager to become president, chief executive officer, and chairman (1958–74). He gained credit for a major growth phase of this large retailer. He then became president of the New York Stock Exchange (1976–84), where he tightened and streamlined operations as the Exchange adjusted to changing government regulations and increased competition.

Battle, Kathleen (1948–) soprano; born in Portsmouth, Ohio. American trained, she sang with major orchestras before making her Metropolitan Opera debut in 1978. Her rich, seemingly effortless voice and vivacious interpretations on stage and in concert, made her one of the most popular singers with both critics and the public.

Bauer, Catherine (Krouse) (1905–64) urban planner, housing expert; born in Elizabeth, N.J. After graduating from Vassar and spending a year in Paris, she wrote articles on architecture and worked in publishing in New York where she met Lewis Mumford, who was to become her mentor and lifelong friend. In the 1930s she alternated between Europe and New York, writing influential articles on the progressive social as well as architectural ideas behind European housing communities. Her book *Modern Housing* (1934) called for quality low-cost housing and led to her appointment as executive secretary of the American Federation of Labor Housing Conference, which in turn brought about the first public housing legislation in the U.S.A. She served in the U.S. Housing Authority (1937–40), then went to teach at the University of California: Berkeley. There she met and married the architect William Wurster, and from 1930–50, they lived in Cambridge, Mass., where she continued to teach and work for better housing; they returned to Berkeley in 1950 where she taught until her death. In her teaching, speeches, consultancies, writings, and travels, she moved beyond the simple issues of public housing to become a respected voice on urban planning in the broadest sense. *Shaping an Urban Future* (1969) is a collection of her essays.

Bauer, Harold (1873–1951) pianist; born near London. A student of Paderewski, he pursued an international career, living mainly in the U.S.A. after his 1900 debut there. In 1918 he founded the Beethoven Association in New York.

Baugh, (Samuel Adrian) Sammy (1914–) football player; born in Temple, Texas. After earning All-America honors as a triple-threat tailback at Texas Christian University in 1936, he led the Washington Redskins to National Football League (NFL) championships in 1937 and 1942. The success of his unprecedented pinpoint passing was influential in turning professional football toward a modern aerial style of attack. In his 15-season career, "Slingin' Sammy" led the NFL in passing six times.

Baum, (Lyman) Frank (1856–1919) writer; born in Chittenango, N.Y. A sickly child, he studied at home, became an actor (1870s), worked in the family oil business, then moved to South Dakota. While working as a journalist there, he wrote his first book, *Father Goose: His Book,* published in 1899 after he had moved to Chicago to work on a trade magazine for window decorators (1897–1902). It was successful, but his next book, *The Wonderful Wizard of Oz* (1900), was even more successful; he himself adapted it for the musical stage in 1901. After traveling to Europe, he settled in Pasadena, Calif. (1902), where he turned out 13 more books in the Oz series and many other children's stories – mostly in the fantasy genre – using pen names such as Schuyler Staunton, Laura Bancroft, Captain Hugh Fitzgerald, Suzanne Metcalfe, Floyd Akens, and Edith Van Dyne. Although appreciated primarily as children's tales, the Oz books have also been read as incorporating Baum's views on American society.

Baumol, William (Jack) (1922–) economist; born in New York City. Best known for his work distinguishing sales maximization from profit maximization in industry, he was also known for his clear transcription of business management and operations language into economic terms. He taught briefly at the London School of Economics (1947–49) before joining the faculty at Princeton University. Beginning in 1971 he held a joint appointment with New York University.

Baxter, George Owen See FAUST, FREDERICK SCHILLER.

Bay, Howard (1912–86) set designer; born in Centralia, Wash. Winner of many awards for his sets, he was the designer for *The Little Foxes* (1939), *One Touch of Venus* (1943), *The Music Man* (1957), and *Man of La Mancha* (1965).

Bayard, James Asheton, Jr. (1799–1880) U.S. senator; born in Wilmington, Del. Son of a prominent U.S. senator, Bayard continued the family dynasty with his election to the Senate from Delaware (1851–64). He began as a conservative Democrat but after 1857 became a Republican, although he continued to oppose anti-slavery legislation and resigned in 1864 to protest the test (for anti-slavery) for officeholders. He returned to the Democrats after Lincoln's assassination and was chosen to fill out another term in the Senate (1867–69).

Bayard, James Asheton, Sr. (1767–1815) U.S. representative/senator; born in Philadelphia. Elected to the House of Representatives (Fed., Del.; 1797–1803) and to the U.S. Senate (1804–13), he was a signatory of the Treaty of Ghent, ending the War of 1812.

Bayley, Nancy (1899–) psychologist; born in The Dalles, Ore. She studied at the University of Iowa, then joined the University of California: Berkeley, where she directed the Berkeley Growth Study. This 40-year longitudinal study measured mental and motor development in 74 subjects from infancy into adulthood. She published four books and research aids, including the *Bayley Scales of Infant Development* (1969).

Baylor, Elgin (Gay) (1934–) basketball player; born in Washington, D.C. An All-American from Seattle University, he played for the Minneapolis and Los Angeles Lakers (1958–72) and was a ten-time All-NBA (National Basketball Association) first team forward (1959–65, 1967–69). In 1960 he scored 71 points in a game, and his lifetime scoring average of 27.4 points per game is third best in NBA history. He was elected to basketball's Hall of Fame in 1976.

Bayne-Jones, Stanhope (1888–1970) bacteriologist, medical administrator; born in New Orleans. Known primarily for his work as a medical administrator, he held a series of posts at the University of Rochester (1924–32), was dean of the Yale School of Medicine (1935–40), and was president of the Joint Administrative Board of New York Hospital-Cornell Medical Center (1947–53).

Bazelon, David (Lionel) (1909–93) judge; born in Superior, Wis. His father, a storekeeper, died when he was two and left the family in poverty. Bazelon worked his way through the University of Illinois and Northwestern University and began practicing law in 1932. Confirmed to the bench of the U.S. Court of Appeals, District of Columbia, in 1950, he became chief judge in 1962. He earned a reputation as a strong civil rights advocate, and issued landmark rulings that expanded the scope of the insanity defense in criminal cases. He also issued important rulings that protected the employment rights of homosexuals and that led to a government ban on the pesticide DDT.

Baziotes, William (1912–63) painter; born in Pittsburgh, Pa. Based in New York, he was one of the founders of the Federation of Modern Painters and Sculptors (1940). His calligraphic approach to painting can be seen in such works as *Moon Forms* (1947), and *Pompeii* (1955).

Beach, Amy (Marcy b. Cheney) (1867–1944) composer, pianist; born in Henniker, N.H. After serious piano studies, she made her professional debut in Boston, Mass., in 1884, and appeared the next year with the Boston Symphony. That same year she married Dr. H. H. A. Beach, who encouraged her shift to composing, even though she had little formal instruction in it. Her *Gaelic Symphony,* premiered by the Boston Symphony in 1896, was the first such work by an American woman, as was the Piano Concerto the orchestra premiered four years later (with the composer as soloist). Between 1910–14 she lived in Europe where she again gave piano concerts, usually of her own work. Employing a conservative, Romantic style, she composed over 150 works – many settings of well-known poets' works – and gained some prominence in Europe as well as in America;

but she was continually hampered by the era's resistance to woman composers, expressed perhaps by the fact that she went through most of her public career known as "Mrs. H. H. A. Beach."

Beach, Moses Yale (1800–68) publisher, inventor; born in Wallingford, Conn. Apprenticed to a cabinetmaker at an early age, he later worked on his own and developed several inventions, including rag-cutting machinery that eased the making of paper. In 1838 he bought the *New York Sun* from Benjamin H. Day, his brother-in-law; as its editor until 1848 he organized a news syndicate and, in a competition with James Gordon Bennett's aggressive *New York Herald,* stressed efforts to gather news rapidly. As circulation declined, Beach sold the paper in 1860 to a Christian revivalist, who gave it back after a year; in 1868 he sold it again to Charles Anderson Dana.

Beach, Sylvia Woodbridge (1887–1962) bookseller, publisher; born in Baltimore, Md. In 1919 she established the Shakespeare and Company bookstore in Paris, which became an avant-garde publishing house and mecca for American expatriates. In 1922 she published the first edition of James Joyce's *Ulysses,* which had been rejected by other publishers as pornographic. In 1941 she closed her bookstore in defiance of the German occupation and later she was interned for seven months. She never reopened the store but she was widely honored for her support of Joyce and other authors.

Beadle, Erastus (Flavel) (1821–94) publisher; born in Pierstown, N.Y. Establishing a printing business in 1852, he published popular songbooks and the first "dime novels," inexpensive, paper-bound, fast-paced adventure novels with heroes like Nick Carter and Deadwood Dick.

Beadle, George W. (Wells) (1903–89); geneticist; born in Wahoo, Nebr. As a graduate student at Cornell (1927–31), he revealed that genetic defects relate to abnormal chromosomal behavior during meiosis. He served the California Institute of Technology (Caltech) (1931–36), then moved to Harvard (1936–37), where he induced X-ray mutagenesis in the fruit fly *Drosophilia.* He joined Stanford (1937–46), where, with collaborator Edward Tatum, he began research on the bread mold *Neurospora* to determine that specific genes control the synthesis of specific cellular substances. For this breakthrough, Beadle and Tatum shared half the 1958 Nobel Prize for physiology. Beadle returned to Caltech (1946–61), then joined the University of Chicago (1961–78), where he remained an active educator after his retirement.

Beadle, Wiliam Henry Harrison (1838–1915) educator; born in Parke County, Ind. He studied civil engineering at the University of Michigan and rose to the rank of brevet brigadier general during the Civil War. He went to the Dakota Territory in 1869. As surveyor general for that area, he put all his efforts toward the judicious and cautious use of the public school lands. He wrote the education article in the South Dakota state constitution and was president of the Madison State Normal School (1889–1906). South Dakota placed his statue in the U.S. Capitol.

Beal, Gifford (Reynolds) (1879–1956) painter; born in New York City. A pupil of William Merritt Chase, he lived in New York, summered on the shores of Massachusetts, and painted city and marine scenes, as in *The Albany Boat* (1915), and *Freight Yards* (1920).

Beale, Edward Fitzgerald (1822–93) explorer, naval officer;

born in Washington, D.C. Although a naval officer (1842–51), he made six transcontinental journeys carrying important dispatches (including the first authentic report of gold in California in 1848). He was an Indian agent and the surveyor general for California and Nevada (1851–65). Later, he served briefly as U.S. ambassador to Austria-Hungary.

Beamon, (Robert) Bob (1946–) track and field athlete; born in New York City. In the 1968 Olympics at Mexico City, he set a world long jump record (29 ft. 2½ in./8.90m) that exceeded the previous record by nearly 22 in./0.55m. The mark lasted 23 years, longer than any track and field record in history.

Bean, "Judge" Roy (?1825–1903) frontier figure; born in Mason County, Ky. He left Kentucky for California in 1847, and seems to have spent the next 15 years in such enterprises as goldseeking and cattlerustling. He joined a band of Confederate irregulars during the Civil War and then followed the railroad construction crews as a saloonkeeper and gambler. In 1882 he settled in the Texas camp of Vinegaroon; he had it renamed Langtry after his idol, the English actress Lillie Langtry, then set himself up as justice of the peace, "the law west of the Pecos." Holding court in his saloon, "The Jersey Lily," he threatened to use his six-shooter to enforce his notion of justice. In 1898 he gained national attention for staging a boxing match on a sandbar in the middle of the Rio Grande (to avoid the ban on boxing in Texas), featuring the heavyweight champion, Bob Fitzsimmons.

Bean, L. L. (Leon Lenwood) (1872–1967) outdoor clothing and equipment retailer; born in Greenwood, Maine. A Maine trapper in his youth, he launched a thriving mail-order and retail business in Freeport, Maine, after inventing his rubber-soled Maine Hunting Shoe (1912). Incorporated as L. L. Bean (1934), the company became known for the quality and practicality of its outdoor products, which attracted an international clientele.

Beard, Charles (Austin) (1874–1948) historian; born in Knightstown, Ind. Coming from an independent Quaker background, he edited a local newspaper before going on to DePauw University and becoming exposed to progressive thinkers and social reformers of his time. After graduating (1898) he went on to Oxford University, England, where – with money supplied by a Kansas socialist, Mrs. Walter Vrooman – he helped found Ruskin Hall, a college for workers. After marrying Mary Ritter in 1900, he brought her back to Ruskin Hall and continued developing his ideas on improving society, as expressed in his first book, *The Industrial Revolution* (1901). In 1902 he went to Columbia University to study; he joined the faculty (1904–17) and became one of the leaders in adopting the "new history," a progressive approach to using the past to advance the present. In 1913 he published his seminal work, *An Economic Interpretation of the Constitution of the United States;* highly controversial in its day, it argued that America's "founding fathers" had acted more on economic motives than for abstract ideals. In 1917 he resigned from Columbia to protest the treatment of those opposed to America's involvement in World War I. From then on he never held a regular academic appointment – he lived on his writings, investments, and on the income from a dairy farm in Connecticut – but he remained a prominent public figure as a writer and activist, working for reforms in public administration, speaking out on current affairs, and constantly refining his views about the

past. He collaborated with his wife, Mary Ritter Beard, on several major books, starting with *The Rise of American Civilization* (1927), which emphasized economic forces on American history. In the 1930s he somewhat conditionally endorsed Franklin Roosevelt's New Deal domestic policies, but he definitely rejected Roosevelt's foreign policies and ended up with the isolationists, even charging Roosevelt with having maneuvered Japan into attacking the U.S.A. In his final years he modified his earlier views on the influence of economics on history, and lost some of his standing, but he remains one of the American historians to be reckoned with.

Beard, (Daniel Carter) "Uncle Dan" (1850–1941) illustrator, youth leader; born in Cincinnati, Ohio. He was a surveyor (1874–78) before he became an illustrator. He wrote *What to Do and How to Do It: The American Boy's Handy Book* (1882), the first of his 16 books on handicrafts. He was praised by Mark Twain for his illustrations in *A Connecticut Yankee in King Arthur's Court* (1889). To promote magazines that he edited, he organized the Sons of Daniel Boone (1905) and the Boy Pioneers of America (1909), precursors of the Boy Scouts. When the Boy Scouts of America was formed (1910), he designed the Scout hat, neckerchief and shirt. He wrote and illustrated many articles for the Scout's magazine, *Boys' Life*. As National Scout Commissioner (1910–41), he argued for voluntary leadership within the Scouts and became known as "Uncle Dan" to a generation of American boys.

Beard, James (1903–85) cooking expert, author; born in Portland, Ore. He published his first cookbook in 1940, hosted the first televised food show (1946–47), and founded his own New York cooking school (1955). He championed American cuisine in numerous articles and more than two dozen cookbooks, including *James Beard's American Cookery* (1972) and *The New James Beard* (1981).

Beard, Mary Ritter (1876–1958) historian, social reformer; born in Indianapolis, Ind. (wife of Charles Beard). She met Charles Beard while both were students at DePauw University (Asbury, Ind.) and they married in 1900. She followed him to Oxford University, England, where she became involved in both women's suffrage and working-class education activities; on their return to the U.S.A. (1902), she began graduate school at Columbia University but dropped out in 1904 and thereafter became a self-directed scholar. (She also raised two children.) She continued to work for women's suffrage, labor reforms, and other progressive causes, but by about 1915 she began to concentrate on her writing and lecturing, specifically to bring to light women's contributions to society across the centuries. From her early work, *Women's Work in Municipalities* (1915), to her classic summation, *Women as a Force in History* (1946), she prefigured many of the themes that would be taken up by women's historians and feminists of later generations. She also collaborated with her husband on several influential volumes such as *The Rise of American Civilization* (1927) and *The Basic History of the United States* (1944). Although she managed to inject some of her own findings about women's roles into these collaborations, both this element and her own contribution tended to be overshadowed by her husband's towering reputation, and only in later decades would her own work be truly recognized.

Beardon, Romare (Howard) (?1912–88) painter, collagist; born in Charlotte, N.C. Now regarded as a major American artist, he studied with George Grosz at the Art Students League, New York (1936–37), and at Columbia University (1943). He also studied philosophy and art at the Sorbonne, Paris (1951). He worked in such mediums as collage, oil, graphics, tapestry, and as set and costume designer for the Alvin Ailey Ballet Company, New York (1971). Based in New York City, he founded the Spiral Group (1963), an organization promoting his fellow African-American artists. His collage work, such as *Saturday Morning* (1969) and *Patchwork Quilt* (1970), is influenced by cubism and African symbolism.

Beau, Louis Victor (1895–1986) aviator; born in New York City. An air service veteran of the Western Front in World War I, he commanded the Mediterranean Air Transport Service during World War II. After the war, he became national commander of the Civil Air Patrol, the civilian auxiliary of the air force.

Beaumont, William (1785–1853) physician; born in Lebanon, Conn. He learned medicine as an apprentice to a doctor in Vermont, then became an army surgeon (1812–15, 1820–40). In 1822 he treated Alexis St. Martin, a Canadian victim of a gunshot wound to the stomach; because the wound never completely closed up, he was able to remove and observe gastric juices and the action of the digestive system over a period of years. He published his classic *Experiments and Observations on the Gastric Juices and the Biology of Digestion* in 1833, detailing 238 experiments indicating the presence of what are now known to be enzymes, such as pepsin and hydrochloric acid. His book, which showed for the first time that the stomach is a digestive organ and not a reservoir or grinding organ, marks the start of modern study of the digestive system. After leaving the military, he settled into private practice in St. Louis.

Beauregard, Pierre G. T. (Gustave Toutant) (1818–93) Confederate soldier; born in St. Bernard Parish, La. An 1838 West Point graduate, he was twice wounded in the Mexican War. He resigned from the U.S. service during the secession crisis. He opened the Civil War with the bombardment of Fort Sumter, S.C., commanded the Confederate left wing at the First Battle of Bull Run in 1861, succeeded the mortally wounded A. S. Johnston in command of the Army of Tennessee at Shiloh in 1862, and commanded the Charleston defenses during Union siege operations of 1862–64. Small and animated, Beauregard graded high in defense of static positions but performed less ably on a fluid battlefield. After the war he held several public offices in Louisiana.

Beaux, Cecilia (1855–1942) painter; born in Philadelphia. She was influenced by the work of Thomas Eakins and became a portrait painter. After studying in Paris at the Académie Julien (1887), she set up a studio in New York City (1890). Her sensitive academic work, as in *Dorothea and Francesca* (1898), and *Mother and Daughter* (1898), remains popular.

Bechet, Sidney (1897–1959) jazz musician; born in New Orleans. As a clarinetist and saxophonist, he was a pioneer in establishing jazz as a solo idiom. In 1919, he became the first jazz musician to receive critical attention; in 1926, as a sideman, he made a strong impression on Duke Ellington's emerging style. After spearheading a traditional jazz revival in the 1940s, he settled in France where he was widely honored.

Bechtel, Stephen Davison (1900–89) engineering/construction executive; born in Aurora, Ind. He joined his father's western construction company, W. A. Bechtel Corporation, in 1919, eventually becoming president (1936–60). He built Hoover Dam (1931). His other engineering design and construction companies, consolidated as Bechtel Corporation (1946), became the largest such corporation in the world, building numerous power plants, pipelines, oil refineries, and factories worldwide. His son, Stephen Davison Bechtel, Jr. (born in 1925) spent his career at Bechtel Corporation, overseeing projects including the trans-Alaska pipeline and the Washington, D.C., subway system.

Beck, Aaron T. (Temkin) (1921–) psychiatrist; born in Providence, R.I. Educated at Brown and Yale Universities, he became a fellow of the Austen Riggs Center in Stockbridge, Mass., in 1950, the same year that he joined the faculty of the University of Pennsylvania. He specialized in research on the affective disorders, publishing more than 80 articles and 7 books, including *Diagnosis and Management of Depression* (1978) and *Predictions of Suicide* (1974).

Beck, Lewis Caleb (1798–1853) physician, scientist; born in Schenectady, N.Y. Licensed as a physician in 1818, he used his rural travels to collect natural observations. He taught scientific subjects at Rutgers (1830–31, 1838–53) and elsewhere, and wrote various works, including a *Gazetteer of Illinois and Missouri* (1823).

Becker, Carl (Lotus) (1873–1945) historian; born in Lincoln Township, Iowa. A graduate of the University of Wisconsin, he taught at several colleges before becoming professor of history at Cornell (1917–41). He was a master of both elite and popular thought in 18th-century America and Europe, and his historical writing combined scholarly learning with an accessible style. He was equally honored as a teacher. His best known work was *The Heavenly City of the Eighteenth Century Philosophers* (1932), which reflected his characteristically conservative-skeptical view of modern history. Other works include *The Eve of Revolution* (1918), *Progress and Power* (1936), and *How New Will the Better World Be* (1943), which expressed his views of international relations in the world after World War II.

Becker, Gary (Stanley) (1930–) economist; born in Pottsville, Pa. One of the sharpest economic minds, he often challenged long-established theories and introduced many original ideas into the economic community with his uncanny ability to apply a single, general economic principle to apparently unconnected factors. Except for twelve years at Columbia University (1957–69), he spent his career at the University of Chicago as an active part of the "Chicago School" of economics. His 1957 doctoral dissertation presented model evidence of labor discrimination; it also examined wage differentials between black and white workers by squaring it with the competitive model of labor markets. A later analysis examined crime as an occupation chosen for rational reasons with full consideration of the risks and benefits. In the mid-1960s, he began to concentrate on his "new economics of the family," and in 1965 he explored the division of family labor. His controversial ideas have challenged the singular consumptive nature of the family and instead view the family as a multi-person production unit, producing "joint utility" from the skills and knowledge of different family members.

Becker, Howard (Saul) (1928–) sociologist; born in Chicago. He studied at the University of Chicago (B.A. 1946; M.A. 1949; Ph.D.1951), and photography at the San Francisco Art Institute. He taught at Stanford (1962–65), Northwestern University, Ill. (1965–91), and the University of Washington: Seattle (1991). He is known for his group studies, such as *Boys in White: Student Culture in Medical School* (1961), *Outsiders: Studies in the Sociology of Deviance* (1963), and *Art Worlds* (1986).

Becker, John J. (1886–1961) composer; born in Henderson, Ky. He taught in colleges and administrated for the Works Progress Administration in the Midwest, meanwhile composing, conducting, and promoting modernist music with only occasional success. His pieces include pioneering multimedia works.

Beckman, Arnold (Orville) (1900–) electrical engineer, inventor; born in Cullom, Ill. He worked as a Bell Telephone research engineer and taught at the California Institute of Technology before establishing his own firm, Beckman Instruments, to produce scientific instruments of his own invention. His quartz spectrophotometer made automatic chemical analysis possible. His company developed a long line of products used in medicine, space exploration, and other fields. The Arnold and Mabel Beckman Foundation contributes to the advancement of scientific research.

Becknell, William (?1796–1865) fur trader, explorer; born in Amherst County, Va. He moved to Missouri and became the first American trader to do business in Santa Fe, N.M. (1821). He pioneered the Cimarron cut-off and the Santa Fe Trail (1822). He moved to Texas, fought in the Texas Revolution (1836) and later joined the Texas Rangers.

Beckwourth, (James Pierson) Jim (1798–1867) pioneer, mountain man; born in Fredericksburg, Va. Born a slave but raised free in St. Louis, Mo., by his mulatto mother and white father, Beckwourth participated in the Ashley–Henry fur-trading expeditions into the Rocky Mountains (1823–26) and lived with the Crow Indians (1826–37). Serving as guide, trapper, trader, army scout, and hunter (1837–50), he discovered the pass – later named after him – in the Sierra Nevada Mountains that opened a route to California's Sacramento Valley (1850) and started a ranch nearby. His *Life and Adventures of James P. Beckwourth* (1856) describes the life of the frontiersmen known as mountain men.

Bee, Barnard (Elliott) (1824–61) Confederate soldier; born in Charleston, S.C. A West Point graduate (1845) and Mexican War hero, Bee left his frontier post in 1861 to fight for the Confederacy. At the first battle of Bull Run he inadvertently originated the nickname "Stonewall" for General T. J. Jackson and his brigade when he exhorted his inexperienced troops to rally by crying, "Look at Jackson's brigade – it stands like a stone wall! Rally behind the Virginians." Mortally wounded, Bee survived the battle by one day.

Beebe, (Charles) William (1877–1962) oceanographer, ornithologist; born in Brooklyn, N.Y. He was curator of ornithology for the New York Zoological Park (Bronx Zoo) (1899) and director of the N.Y. Zoological Society's Department of Tropical Research (1899–1962). Of his many books on tropical birds, he is renowned for his monographs on pheasants in Borneo. He made his record-breaking 3,028-foot descent off Bermuda with bathysphere designer Otis Barton (1934). He later abandoned deep dives as having "little scientific value," and concentrated on studying marine wildlife in shallow waters.

Beebe, Lucius (Morris) (1902–66) journalist, author; born in Wakefield, Mass. After graduating from Harvard University (1927) Beebe worked as a journalist, notably for the *New York Herald Tribune* (1929–50), chronicling Manhattan's high society in rococo prose in the syndicated column "This New York." Also an authority on railroads and the West, his books include *High Iron* (1938); *The Overland Limited* (1963); *Legends of the Comstock Lode* (1950); and *San Francisco's Golden Era* (1960). He moved to San Francisco and began the column "This Wild West" for the *Chronicle* in 1960.

Beech, Walter (Herschel) (1891–1950) aviation manufacturer; born in Pulaski, Tenn. In 1932, after serving as a pilot in the U.S. Army, working as a test pilot, and organizing his first company, Travel Air, he founded the Beech Aircraft Company, which incorporated in 1936. During World War II the company produced over 7,000 planes, including Model 18 twin engines.

Beecher, Catherine (Esther) (1800–78) educator, author; born in East Hampton, N.Y. (daughter of Lyman Beecher, sister of Harriet Beecher Stowe). The eldest of eight surviving children, she was educated at home and in private school. In 1821 she began teaching and went through a religious crisis brought on by her father's attempt to force his Calvinist views on her. After her fiance's death in 1823, she founded the Hartford Female Seminary, launching a lifelong campaign as lecturer, author, and advocate for women's education. She left her Hartford school in 1831 and later founded similar schools for young women in Cincinnati, Ohio, and Milwaukee, Wis.; to promote female education in the West she founded the American Women's Education Association in 1852. Her goal was to rescue women who wasted their lives in frivolous "feminine" pursuits as well as those exploited as factory hands, but her ideal woman was one who presided over an intelligent, cultured, well-managed household. Among her many published works was *Treatise of Domestic Economy* (1841), and in 1869 she and her sister Harriet Beecher Stowe collaborated on a new edition, retitled *The American Woman's Home*, which became an immensely influential guide for generations of American housewives. Although she was in the forefront on many social issues of her day, she did not believe that women should be involved in political affairs and she opposed woman suffrage.

Beecher, Henry Ward (1813–87) Protestant clergyman, reformer; born in Litchfield, Conn. One of 13 children of clergyman Lyman Beecher (one of his sisters was author Harriet Beecher Stowe), he graduated from Amherst in 1834 and studied under his father at Lane Theological Seminary in Cincinnati, Ohio. In 1839 he became pastor of the Second Presbyterian Church in Indianapolis, Ind., where he developed a forceful, emotional preaching style. Named the first pastor of Plymouth Congregational Church in Brooklyn, N.Y., in 1847, he crusaded from the pulpit for temperance and against slavery and became one of the most influential public figures of his time. He supported Free Soil political candidates and, later, Republicans; on the outbreak of the

Civil War his church raised and equipped a volunteer regiment. He edited the religious publications *The Independent* and *The Christian Union* (later *Outlook*) during the 1860s and 1870s. He was acquitted on an adultery charge after a sensational trial in 1874. His many books include *Evolution and Religion* (1885).

Beecher, Lyman (1775–1863) Presbyterian minister, revivalist; born in New Haven, Conn. (father of Henry Ward Beecher and Harriet Beecher Stowe). Son of a blacksmith, he attended Yale and its Divinity School, becoming ordained in 1799. Between 1799–1810, he preached at East Hampton, Long Island, N.Y., and then at Litchfield, Conn. (1810–26); his brand of Calvinism called for constant church services and strong opposition to drinking. Invited to Boston in 1826, for six years he preached a fiery evangelicism that at one point inspired a mob to attack a Catholic convent. In 1832 he went to Cincinnati, Ohio, to head the newly founded Lane Theological Seminary and to serve as pastor of the Second Presbyterian Church there. His evangelical zeal and arrogance led to years of strife with more conservative Presbyterians, but he stayed until 1850, when he retired to the Brooklyn home of his son Henry Beecher.

Beene, Geoffrey (1927–) fashion designer; born in Haynesville, La. He studied fashion in New York City and Paris, and in 1949 began a design career noteworthy for unconventional designs even before he started his own New York company (1962). His high-quality ready-to-wear clothing for women and men, subtly colored and distinctively simple, garnered eight Coty Awards.

Beer, George Louis (1872–1920) historian, colonial specialist; born on Staten Island, N.Y. After achieving success in the tobacco business (1893–1903), he retired and wrote three important books on the British colonial system in relation to the American colonies (1907, 1908, 1912). He wrote *The English Speaking Peoples* (1917), and was chief of the colonial division of the American delegation at the Paris Peace Conference.

Beers, Clifford (Whittingham) (1876–1943) founder of mental hygiene movement; born in New Haven, Conn. Trained as a scientist at Yale, he was hospitalized after a mental breakdown (1900–03). As a result of indignities and violence he experienced, he was determined to reform the mental health system. His book, *The Mind That Found Itself* (1908), created a sensation, calling for a true therapeutic approach to mental illness instead of just custodial care. That year he also founded the Connecticut Society for Mental Hygiene; in 1909 he founded the National Commission for Mental Hygiene, which under his lifelong leadership became an international movement that would have a major impact on every aspect of mental health care. Although much of what he advocated would come to be accepted practice, he was greatly honored in his lifetime for his pioneering work.

Beery, Wallace (1889–1949) movie actor; born in Kansas City, Mo. (half-brother of Noah Beery.) After working in the circus and in Broadway musicals, he went to Hollywood and began his long movie career in 1913. At first he played tough villains but with sound movies he assumed a new persona as a rough-edged but lovable character. He won an Oscar for best actor in *The Champ* (1931) and although he did not retain the popularity he enjoyed during the 1930s, he continued in movies until his death.

Beeson, Charles Henry (1870–1949) scholar, medievalist; born in Columbia City, Ind. He took a B.A. (1893) and an M.A. (1895) in classics at Indiana University and taught there as instructor in Latin (1895–96) before going to the graduate school of the University of Chicago to study under William Gardner Hale. He collaborated with Hale and others to produce various Latin readers. He was awarded a Ph.D. by the University of Munich in 1907, where he began to explore the influence of classical Latin language upon medieval writers. He returned to the University of Chicago in 1909 and became professor of Latin. His skill in detecting textual errors led to his work in codes and ciphers for the military intelligence division of the U.S. General Staff during World War I. His standard *Primer of Medieval Latin Grammar* appeared in 1925 and his other scholarly work on medieval Latin texts was wide-ranging.

Behn, Sosthenes (1882–1957) businessman; born on Saint Thomas, Virgin Islands. After being educated in Paris, he immigrated to the U.S.A. in 1898, but immediately left to join his brother Hernand Behn in opening a brokerage house in Puerto Rico. In 1914 the sugar crop failed and Behn Brothers, Inc. acquired the local telephone system as security against a crop loan. The brothers expanded, adding the Cuban telephone system (1916), and in 1919 linked the Cuban system to Florida. In 1920 they incorporated the International Telephone and Telegraph Corporation (IT&T) in Maryland; Sosthenes served as president until 1948, then became chairman of the board (1948–56). There followed a period of rapid growth as IT&T built a network of international cable and local systems in countries throughout the world. As world conditions deteriorated in the 1930s and 1940s, Sosthenes sold local telephone companies to governments and consolidated operations in Great Britain and the United States. He was awarded the Distinguished Service Medal and the French Legion of Honor for service in the U.S. Army Signal Corps during World War I.

Behrman, S. N. (Samuel Nathaniel) (1893–1973) playwright, screenwriter, journalist; born in Worcester, Mass. He studied at Clark University before enrolling at Harvard (B.A. 1916) where he studied in George Pierce Baker's playwriting course. His first sophisticated comedy, *The Second Man* (1927), was a hit. Working with the Theater Guild, he wrote several adaptations for the Lunts, *Amphitryon 38* (1937) and *I Know My Love* (1949). He cofounded the Playwrights' Company in 1938 and wrote the autobiographical drama, *No Time for Comedy* (1939). A writer of screenplays for Hollywood, he was also author of *Duveen* (1952), a profile of the art collector, and *Portrait of Max* (1960), a biography of Max Beerbohm.

Beiderbecke, (Leon) Bix (1903–31) jazz musician; born in Davenport, Iowa. He was a cornetist, pianist, and composer whose meteoric career began in 1923 with the Wolverines and continued with Jean Goldkette, Frankie Trumbauer, Paul Whiteman, and Glen Gray. He was the first important white jazz artist. His early death from pneumonia, complicated by alcoholism, fueled his legend as the romanticized figure depicted in the novel *Young Man With a Horn* (1938).

Beidler, John Xavier (1831–90) vigilante; born in Mountjoy, Pa. A "jack of all trades," he was a saloon owner, a ruthless vigilante, and the collector of customs for Montana and Idaho (1886–90). He was present at the apprehension and the hanging of dozens of outlaws in Montana (1863–65), including the notorious bandit Henry Plummer.

Beissel, Johann Conrad (1690–1768) religious leader, composer; born in Eberbach-am-Neckar, Germany. Fleeing persecution, he came to America in 1720; in 1732 at Ephrata, Pa., he found the Solitary Brethren of the Community of Seventh Day Baptists. Self-trained in music, he wrote many robust, homespun hymns for his community.

Békésy, Georg von (1899–1972) physiologist, physicist; born in Budapest, Hungary. He was concurrently a physicist at the University of Budapest and the Hungarian Post Office, which had charge of Hungary's newly installed telephone system (1923–46). There his work on improving telephone communication led to his later investigations of the mechanisms of human hearing. After the Russian takeover of Budapest, he went to the Karolinska Institute, Stockholm (1946–47), then emigrated to the U.S.A. to join Harvard (1947–66), where he continued his studies of the human ear and how it transmits sounds to the brain. At the University of Hawaii (1966–72), he expanded his research to include other senses. In addition to receiving many awards for his pioneering investigations of aural physiology, he became the first physicist to win a Nobel Prize in physiology or medicine (1961). He left his extensive art collection to the Nobel Foundation.

Belasco, David (b. Valasco or Velasco) (1859–1931) actor, manager, playwright; born in San Francisco. Offspring of a Portuguese-Jewish family, he appeared on stage as a child. His earliest successes as a stage manager in the 1880s were with melodramas in both New York and California. He built a reputation for total theatricality, including highly flamboyant performances in his private life. One of his great interests was in extreme realism on stage, and he used the newest technology to this end. Among his successes were *The Heart of Maryland* (1895), in which Maurice Barrymore performed, *The Music Master* (1904), starring David Warfield, and *The Governor's Lady* (1912), which included a careful onstage representation of Child's restaurant. In 1906 he built a new theater in New York, first called the Stuyvesant, then renamed the Belasco in 1910. The New York Public Library at Lincoln Center houses his extensive theater collection.

Belding, Don (1898–1969) advertising executive; born in Grants Pass, Ore. He worked in the Los Angeles branch of the advertising agency Lord and Thomas (1923–42), which, with Emerson Foote and Fax Cone, he took over and renamed Foote, Cone and Belding (1942). He retired as chairman of this major international advertising agency in 1957.

Bel Geddes, Norman (1893–1958) industrial and theatrical designer; born in Adrian, Mich. After study at the Art Institute of Chicago he became stage designer at New York's Metropolitan Opera in 1918. From 1920 to 1937 his designs for Broadway plays, notably *The Miracle* (1923), and his film sets marked him as an innovator in modern stage lighting. A vigorous self-promoter and visionary, he pioneered industrial design with the 1927 establishment of a firm to create streamlined versions of household appliances, cars, ships, and airplanes.

Belin, David (William) (1928–) lawyer; born in Washington, D.C. Partner in Iowa law firms since 1955, he was counsel to the Warren Commission (on the assassination of President Kennedy) (1964) and led the Rockefeller Commis-

sion (on CIA activities) (1975). His books include *November 22, 1963: You Are the Jury* (1973) and *Creative Estate Planning* (1990), but he was best known for his defense of the Warren Commission's finding that Lee Harvey Oswald was the lone assassin of Kennedy, a view Belin reiterated in *Final Disclosure* (1988).

Belkin, Samuel (1911–76) rabbi, educator; born in Swislicz, Poland. He came to the U.S.A. in 1929. Named a professor at Yeshiva University (New York City) in 1940, he became its president in 1940 and chancellor in 1975. He became dean of Rabbi Isaac Elchanan Theological Seminary in 1941. He was a member of a number of academic and Jewish organizations including the American Academy of Political and Social Science and the Union of Orthodox Rabbis of the U.S.A. and Canada.

Bell, Alexander Graham (1847–1922) inventor, educator; born in Edinburgh, Scotland. The son of an elocution teacher and authority on vocal physiology, he worked as his father's assistant at University College, London, where he pursued research in the techniques of teaching speech to the deaf. His family emigrated to Canada in 1870 and he went to Boston, Mass., in 1871; he obtained a professorship at Boston University two years later. Meanwhile, his interest in the applications of electricity to sound led him to invent a new telegraph system, patented in 1875, and to experiment with methods of transmitting voice sounds. On March 10, 1876, he sent his famous telephone message, the world's first, to his assistant, Thomas A. Watson: "Mr. Watson, come here; I want you." He established the Bell Telephone Company the following year. The telephone assured his fortune; the U.S. Supreme Court upheld his patent rights against various claimants. He pursued other interests after 1880, including research into methods of teaching the deaf to speak. He also made improvements to Thomas A. Edison's phonograph. With Gardiner C. Hubbard, his father-in-law and business associate, Bell founded the journal *Science,* and he was president of the National Geographic Society from 1897–1904. Toward the end of his long life he became interested in aviation; he invented the tetrahedral kite and helped support some of the aircraft development schemes of Samuel P. Langley and Glenn A. Curtiss.

Bell, Chester (Gordon) (1934–) computer engineer; born in Kirksville, Mo. He began at Digital Equipment Corporation in Maynard, Mass., in 1960, where he worked on the PDP series of computers and became a leading expert in minicomputers. He was professor of computer science at Carnegie-Mellon (1966–72), returning to Digital (1972–83) to oversee the production of VAX.

Bell, Daniel (1919–) sociologist; born in New York City. A radical journalist in the late 1930s, he became a moderate liberal spokesman of distinctive intellectual power and breadth. He was labor editor of *Fortune* (1948–58), and spent most of his academic career at Columbia University (1952–69) and Harvard (1969–90). Of his many books, *The End of Ideology* (1960) and *Cultural Contradictions of Capitalism* (1976) attracted the widest attention; he cofounded and edited *The Public Interest* (1965–73).

Bell, Derrick (Albert) Jr. (1930–) legal scholar; born in Pittsburgh, Pa. He is best known for his work combating racism, discrimination, and poverty, as an attorney for the National Association for the Advancement of Colored People (1960–66) and as a deputy director of the National

Office of Civil Rights (1966–68). He taught at Harvard Law School (1969–80), served as dean of the University of Oregon Law School (1981–86), and then returned to Harvard in 1986. In 1990 he took a leave of absence to protest the lack of any African-American women on the Harvard Law School faculty; he was formally fired when he refused to return two years later. He continued with his writing, lecturing, and teaching.

Bell, Eric Temple (1883–1960) mathematician; born in Aberdeen, Scotland. Emigrating to America in 1902, he taught longest at the California Institute of Technology (1926–53). He contributed significantly to numerical functions, analytic number theory, multiple periodic functions, and Diophantine analysis. He published *Men of Mathematics* (1937), 17 science fiction books, short stories, and poetry.

Bell, Griffin B. (Boyette) (1918–) lawyer, judge, U.S. attorney general; born in Americus, Ga. Partner in the Atlanta law firm King & Spalding (1953–61), he appeared to hold the views of conservative white Southerners on racial issues. Appointed to the U.S. Court of Appeals (1961–76), he ruled on many school desegregation cases and was generally regarded as a moderate. A controversial appointee as President Carter's attorney general (1977–81), he again proved to be a moderate. He resumed corporation law in Atlanta.

Bell, (James Thomas) "Cool Papa" (1903–91) baseball player; born in Starkville, Miss. An outfielder for the St. Louis Stars, Pittsburgh Crawfords, and Homestead Grays (black baseball teams of the 1920s and 1930s), he was universally regarded as the fastest player, white or black, ever to play the game. A solid .350 hitter and prolific base stealer, he was elected to baseball's Hall of Fame in 1974.

Bell, John (1797–1869) U.S. senator, cabinet officer; born in Nashville, Tenn. A prominent Tennessee lawyer, he served in the U.S. House of Representatives (1827–41), first as a Democrat, then as a Whig; as the latter, he served less than a year as secretary of war (1841) and then as a moderate U.S. senator from Tennessee (1847–59). Although he owned slaves, he was opposed to the spread of slavery in the new territories and states, and he spent fruitless years trying to fend off the oncoming confrontation over slavery. In 1860 he was presidential candidate for the Constitutional Union Party, in an effort to present a plea against secession that would appeal to those who saw the Republicans as extremists. (He won three states.) But when the Civil War broke out, his last public act was to advise Tennessee to join the Confederacy.

Bell, Lawrence (Dale) (1894–1956) aircraft designer; born in Mentone, Ind. He began as an airplane mechanic, then worked in management for several companies including Glenn Martin. In 1935 he organized the Bell Aircraft Corporation which produced helicopters, guided missiles, and other aircraft. In 1947 he designed the X-1, the first rocket-propelled airplane, in which Chuck Yeager broke the sound barrier.

Bell, Terrel (Howard) (1921–) educator; born in Lava Hot Springs, Ida. After a career in public school administration he was U.S. Commissioner of Education (1974–76); as U.S. secretary of education (1981–84) he consolidated government programs, established the National Commission on Excellence, and sponsored its study, *A Nation at Risk* (1983).

Bell, Thomas Montgomery (1861–1941) U.S. representa-tive; born in Nacoochee Valley, Ga. He was a teacher, a salesman, and a superior court clerk (1898–1904) before going to the U.S. House of Representatives (Dem., Ga.; 1905–31). He became majority whip, returning to Gainsville, Ga., afterward.

Bellah, Robert N. (Neelly) (1927–) sociologist; born in Altus, Okla. He earned a Harvard Ph.D. and taught there (1957–67) before moving to the University of California: Berkeley (1967). A comparative and historical sociologist, he published studies of Asian cultures and explored the relationships between religion and belief, politics, and contemporary culture. His books include *Beyond Belief* (1970), *The Broken Covenant* (1975), and *The Good Society* (coauthored, 1991).

Bellamy, Edward (1850–98) writer; born in Chicopee Falls, Mass. He studied law, then turned to journalism, founding the Springfield (Mass.) *Daily News* in 1880. He also tried his hand at fiction, but he had become increasingly absorbed in contemporary social issues. In 1888 he published a utopian romance, *Looking Backward: 2000–1887,* and its million-copy sales enabled him to devote the ensuing years to refining his notions of state capitalism. The Nationalist Party was established to promote his ideas; he founded *The New Nation* (1891), a journal; and he further expounded his ideas in *Equality* (1897). He died prematurely of tuberculosis.

Bellamy, Joseph (1719–90) Protestant theologian; born in Cheshire, Conn. A farmer's son, he graduated from Yale in 1735, studied theology with Jonathan Edwards, and preached in several churches before becoming pastor in Bethlehem, Conn., in 1738, where he remained for the rest of his life. His influential *True Religion Delineated* (1750) was both a defense of Edwardian theology and a softening of it – he made the possibility of atonement universal rather than limited to the elect.

Bellanca, Dorothy (b. Jacobs) (1894–1946) labor leader, social reformer; born in Zemel, Lativia. Emigrating in 1900, she went to work in a factory at age 13 and became an organizer for the United Garment Workers of America, leading a strike of fellow buttonhole makers in 1912. A founder of the Amalgamated Clothing Workers of America (1914) and member of its executive board (1916–18, 1934–46), she devoted 30 years to organizing campaigns and several major strikes. She also served on committees involved with labor issues and was an active American Labor Party member and supporter of Franklin D. Roosevelt.

Bellanca, Giuseppe Mario (1886–1960) aeronautical designer/manufacturer; born in Sciacca, Sicily. Emigrating to America to join relatives (1912), he became a noted airplane designer when his plane, *Columbia,* set an endurance record (1927) and made a successful transatlantic crossing two weeks after Charles Lindbergh's (June 4–6, 1927). Developer of the single-engine Cruisair passenger series (1930–50), he was viewed as a better designer than a businessman.

Belli, Melvin M. (Mouron) (1907–) lawyer; born in Sonora, Calif. An indifferent student, he went to sea briefly after graduating from college and before entering law school. On graduating (1933) he became an undercover investigator for the National Recovery Administration, posing as a hobo to report on the plight of migrant workers. Setting himself up in private practice, he soon became the flamboyant master of "demonstrative" evidence – dramatic gestures and graphic exhibits designed to sway juries – and over the ensuing decades he won record damages and set legal precedents in numerous cases; such conduct led to his being dubbed "King of Torts." Although his specialty became malpractice and negligence litigation, he was best known to the public for colorful and bizarre cases such as the defense of topless waitresses and of Jack Ruby, the killer of Lee Harvey Oswald. A prolific writer of books for both the legal profession and the public, he appeared in several movies and television shows.

Bellow, Saul (1915–) writer; born in Lachine, Quebec, Canada. Son of immigrant Russian Jews, in 1924 he moved with his family to Chicago, the city with which he was to become most closely identified. He earned a degree in anthropology and sociology from Northwestern University and for most of his life taught intellectual history in universities, including Minnesota (1946–49) and Chicago (1963). During World War II he served in the merchant marine. His first novel, *Dangling Man* (1944), was followed by a steady output of major fiction including the novels *The Adventures of Augie March* (1953, National Book Award), *Henderson the Rain King* (1959), *Herzog* (1963, National Book Award), *Mr. Sammler's Planet* (1969, National Book Award), and *Humboldt's Gift* (1975, Pulitzer Prize). This work, much of which treated with compassion and wit the spiritual crisis of modernism while drawing on his own feelings of alienation from contemporary society, established him as America's most distinguished postwar writer of fiction. He won the Nobel Prize for literature in 1976. His subsequent books included the novels *The Dean's December* (1982) and *More Die of Heartbreak* (1987), and collected stories, *Him With His Foot in His Mouth* (1984) and *The Bellarosa Connection* (1989). He also wrote several plays including *The Last Analysis* (1965).

Bellows, George (Wesley) (1882–1925) painter, lithographer; born in Columbus, Ohio. After studying at the University of Ohio and rejecting the possibility of a career in baseball, he came to New York to study painting with Robert Henri (1904). His life-long interest in athletics was reflected in many of his strongest paintings, such as *Stag at Sharkey's* (1907). He helped to organize the famous Armory Show in 1913 but he continued to work within the more conservative traditions of social realism and family portraiture. Moved by the horrors of World War I, he did a powerful series of anti-war paintings. In 1916 he took up lithography and book illustrations and is credited with reviving these as serious mediums for American artists.

Belluschi, Pietro (1899–) architect; born in Ancona, Italy. He studied at the University of Rome and Cornell University. In his Portland, Oregon, practice and in collaboration (particularly in his later work), he designed more than 1,000 buildings, mostly churches, educational and commercial buildings, in the late International style. Belluschi early mastered the sheer "curtain wall" (Equitable Savings Building (1945–48), Portland, Ore.). He was dean of the architecture school at the Massachusetts Institute of Technology (1951–65).

Belmont, Alva (Erskine Smith Vanderbilt) (1853–1933) socialite, suffragist, reformer; born in Mobile, Ala. Born into a moderately wealthy Southern family, she was educated in France where her family moved after the Civil War. Returning to the U.S.A. with her mother and sisters in the early 1870s, they settled in New York City and by 1875 Alva

was marrying William K. Vanderbilt, grandson of Cornelius Vanderbilt. She immediately set about to advance the Vanderbilts' status by commissioning Richard Morris Hunt to design their mansion on Fifth Avenue – the setting in 1883 of a legendary costume ball. Divorced from Vanderbilt in 1895 on grounds of his adultery, she was awarded a generous annual income as well as their Newport "cottage," Marble House. Having arranged the marriage of her daughter, Consuelo, to the Duke of Manchester (1895), in 1896 she married Oliver Hazard Perry Belmont (the son of August Belmont and Perry's daughter). After her husband's death in 1908, she suddenly put herself and fortune at the service of the struggle for women's suffrage and rights. She opened her Newport mansion to feminist groups, published articles, founded a new suffrage organization, contributed to various feminist groups, and sponsored the 1914 tour of the English suffragist Christabel Pankhurst. She also supported such causes as the Women's Trade Union League and even contributed to keeping the *Masses,* the socialist magazine, from going bankrupt. From 1921–33 she served as president of the National Woman's Party, during which time she actually lived mainly in France where she maintained three elaborate residences. Although her intrusive and aristocratic manner antagonized some of the women's rights leaders of the time, she was sincere in her own way about gaining equality for women.

Belmont, August (1816–90) banker, art collector; born in Alzei, Germany. He began his career sweeping the Rothschild's offices in Frankfurt when he was 14. Showing a talent for finance, he was transferred to Naples and then to Havana to manage the Rothschild branches, but he saw better opportunities in America and in 1837 he established what soon became the highly successful August Belmont & Company on Wall Street, with his first client the Rothschilds. He became a U.S. citizen, married the daughter of Matthew Perry, and became active in the Democratic Party. Although of Jewish descent, he was accepted into New York society due to his charm and wealth. Between 1844–50 he served as consul general for Austria in the United States. President Franklin Pierce appointed him ambassador to the Netherlands (1853–57). Although a Democrat, he opposed slavery and during the Civil War used his influence to obtain support for the Union. He had been a knowledgeable admirer of art since his youth and he acquired a large collection (auctioned off after his death). He also liked horses and racing; New York's Belmont Park was named to honor his years as president of the American Jockey Club.

Belter, (Johann Heinrich) John Henry (1804–63) furniture maker; born in Germany. He was apprenticed to a cabinetmaker in Württemberg, and was trained to be a carver of rich ornamentation. He emigrated to New York City (1844), married, and opened a furniture shop. He designed highly popular Victorian rococo furniture, and patented his invention (1856) for laminating rosewood in thin panels, steaming the pieces in molds, and carving them with fruit and floral motifs. By 1858 he had opened a large factory in New York City. Several years after his death, when there was less demand for his elaborate designs, the factory closed (1867).

Belushi, John (1949–82) comedian; born in Chicago. After appearing with the Second City comedy troop in the 1970s, he achieved national recognition in *National Lampoon's Lemmings* (1973). On the National Broadcasting Company's

Saturday Night Live (1974–79), he portrayed uniquely manic characters. He left to star in films, including *The Blues Brothers* (1980), then died of a drug overdose in California.

Bemelmans, Ludwig (1898–1962) writer, illustrator; born in Meran, Austria (now Merano, Italy). Educated in Bavaria, he emigrated to New York City (1914), worked at various occupations, wrote for periodicals, and became famous for children's books, such as *Madeline* (1939), which he illustrated as well as wrote.

Benacerraf, Baruj (1920–) immunologist; born in Caracas, Venezuela. He moved to Paris with his family (1925) and emigrated to the U.S.A. (1940). After his medical internship and U.S. Army service (1945–48), he joined Columbia University (1948–50). He performed research in Paris (1950–56), relocated to New York University (1956–68), moved to the National Institutes of Health (1968–70), then joined Harvard (1970–91), concurrently serving the Dana-Farber Cancer Institute, Boston (1980). He began studies of allergy in 1948, and discovered the Ir (immune response) genes that govern transplant rejection (1960s). In 1972 he demonstrated the existence of T and B lymphocytes. He shared the 1980 Nobel Prize for his contributions to cellular immunology. He continued his T-cell research and remained active in many professional societies.

Benbridge, Henry (?1743–1812) painter; born in Philadelphia. He worked in Italy and exhibited his *Portrait of Pascal Paoli* (1769) in London before returning to Philadelphia (1770). Settling in Norfolk, Virginia (c. 1800), he was the first teacher of Thomas Sully (c. 1801) and worked as a portrait painter.

Bench, Johnny (Lee) (1947–) baseball player; born in Oklahoma City, Okla. Part Cherokee, often injured, he is regarded as one of the game's greatest catchers. He pioneered the technique of one-handed catching and used a hinged catcher's mitt. He hit 389 career home runs for the Cincinnati Reds (1967–83) and won the Most Valuable Player Award in 1970 and 1972. He was elected to the Hall of Fame in 1989.

Benchley, Robert (Charles) (1889–1945) writer, humorist, actor; born in Worcester, Mass. Onetime editor of the *Harvard Lampoon,* he worked as a journalist and magazine editor. He became the leading humorist of his day as the *New Yorker*'s columnist, "Guy Fawkes," and drama critic (1927–40). A member of the Algonquin Round Table, he became a popular radio personality, film actor, and screenwriter; he performed several of his humorous monologues in short films, including the first such made in the U.S.A., *The Treasurer's Report* (1928). His benign comic sketches were collected in 15 volumes, including *Benchley Beside Himself* (1943).

Bender, (Charles Albert) "Chief" (1884–1954) baseball player; born in Crow Wing County, Minn. A Chippewa Indian, he won 210 games during his 16-year career as a right-handed pitcher (1903–25), mostly with the Philadelphia Athletics. He pitched two no-hitters. He was elected to the Hall of Fame in 1953.

Bender, George Harrison (1896–1961) U.S. representative/senator; born in Cleveland, Ohio. Elected to the U.S. House of Representatives (Rep., Ohio; 1939–49), he was an outspoken critic of the liberal policies of presidents Franklin D. Roosevelt and Harry S. Truman. However, during his brief term in the U.S. Senate (1954–57), he supported President Eisenhower's internationalist policies. He spent a year as a special assistant to the secretary of the interior (1957–58).

Bender, Lauretta (1897–1987) psychiatrist; born in Butte, Mont. She received her M.D. from the State University of Iowa in 1926. She was a senior psychiatrist at New York City's Bellevue Hospital (1930–56) and did important research in childhood schizophrenia and brain injury and devised the Bender Visual Motor Gestalt Test. In 1936 she married her colleague Paul F. Schilder, a highly regarded psychoanalyst who had practiced in Vienna. From 1956 she was principal research scientist at three major New York State mental health facilities. Her four-volume *Bellevue Studies* series (1952–55) was a major contribution to the literature on child psychology.

Bendix, Reinhard (1916–91) sociologist; born in Berlin, Germany. A 1938 emigrant to the U.S.A., he was educated at the University of Chicago and spent most of his academic career at the University of California: Berkeley; from 1947–61, he was with the sociology department, from 1962–91, with the political science department. He wrote many books on the sociology of industrial society, political sociology, and the German sociologist Max Weber, who was an important influence on his own work.

Benedek, Therese (b. Friedmann) (1892–1977) psychoanalyst, author; born in Eger, Hungary. She studied at the University of Budapest (M.D. 1916) and taught pediatrics in Poszony. Her marriage to Tibor Benedek in 1919 took her to Leipzig, Germany, where she became a psychoanalyst and developed a lifelong interest in the psychology of women. She came to the United States in 1936 and joined the Chicago Institute of Psychoanalysis (to 1970). She published five important books, including *Psychosexual Functions in Women* (1952).

Benedict, Kirby (1810–74) judge; born in Connecticut. He read law in Connecticut and was admitted to the bar before 1834. Migrating westward, he established a private practice in Illinois, and later worked as a government attorney there. President Pierce named him a federal judge for the New Mexico Territory in 1853, and he dispensed frontier justice from Taos and Santa Fe until 1866, when he left the bench to return to private practice.

Benedict, Ruth (b. Fulton) (1887–1948) anthropologist; born in New York City. A Vassar College graduate, she earned a Ph.D. in anthropology under Franz Boas at Columbia University, where she joined the faculty and assisted Boas (1923–48). Although deafness limited her fieldwork, she was recognized as America's leading anthropologist after Boas' retirement. Her *Patterns of Culture* (1934) was a classic statement of cultural relativity and one of the most influential modern works of anthropology. In it she argued for cultural determinism; analyzing three Indian tribes in archetypal terms, she concluded that cultures are "personalities writ large," and that psychological normality is culturally defined. Her *Zuñi Mythology* (1935) and *Race* (1940), an anthropologically based denunciation of racism, developed these themes. In her wartime work for the Bureau of Overseas Intelligence (1943–46), she initiated an innovative method of applying anthropological techniques to the study of foreign cultures, developing a series of "national character" studies that bore fruit in *The Chrysanthemum and the Sword* (1946), an analysis of Japanese culture. In this effort, she worked closely with Margaret Mead, who wrote an important study of her friend, *An Anthropologist at Work* (1959).

Benét, Stephen Vincent (1898–1943) poet, writer; born in Bethlehem, Pa. He graduated from Yale (B.A. 1919; M.A. 1920), traveled to France (1926), wrote screen plays in Hollywood, Calif., (1929), and settled in New York City, where he tried to balance his serious writing with necessary hackwork. During World War II he wrote for the Office of War Information. He is known for his poetry, such as the long narrative, *John Brown's Body* (1938), and a short story, "The Devil and Daniel Webster" (1937).

Benglis, Lynda (1941–) sculptor, painter, video artist; born in Lake Charles, La. She studied at Sophie Newcomb College, New Orleans (1960–64), the Brooklyn Museum Art School (1964–65), and is based in California. A feminist artist and educator, she is known for her sculptural pourings, such as *Bounce* (1969), and twisted metallic knot forms, as in *Elnath* (1984).

Benioff, (Victor) Hugo (1899–1968) seismologist, inventor; born in Los Angeles, Calif. He was a physicist at the Carnegie Institution (1924–37) before joining the California Institute of Technology (1937–64). He devised and developed many seismic detection instruments, including a seismograph for measuring travel-time curves of earthquake waves that became the basis for the Geneva Conference nuclear detection system. He was the first to describe the plane of earthquake foci extending from Pacific Ocean trenches to the earth's shallower mantle, now known as the Benioff Zone.

Benítez, Jaime (1908–) educator; born in Vieques, Puerto Rico. He served as chancellor (1941–56) and president (1966–72) of the University of Puerto Rico and as the island's resident commissioner in Washington (1972–76). He was widely credited with finding university positions for scholars who were refugees first from Franco and later from Hitler and other dictators. Thereafter, he brought such distinguished guests as Nobel laureates Juan Ramón Jiménez and Saul Bellow to the university, where he was a strong voice for academic excellence.

Benjamin, Asher (1773–1845) author and architect; born in Hartland, Conn. A Boston businessman and architect, his seven pattern books (1797–1843) spread Georgian, Federal, and Greek Revival styles throughout America. He designed the Charles Street Meetinghouse, Boston, Mass. (1807).

Benjamin, Judah (Philip) (1811–84) lawyer, Confederate cabinet member; born in St. Croix, Danish West Indies. Son of European Jews, he was brought to South Carolina as a child. After attending Yale (1825–27) he settled in New Orleans; he became a widely respected lawyer and served Louisiana in the U.S. Senate (Whig, 1853–59; Dem., 1859–61). Favoring secession, he served the Confederacy as attorney general (1861) and then as secretary of war (1861–62); he was blamed for the Confederate army's lack of equipment, but Jefferson Davis promoted him to secretary of state (1862–65). He favored using slaves as soldiers. With the collapse of the Confederacy he fled to the West Indies and then to England (1866), where he made a brilliant new career as a British barrister, especially in appeal cases. He wrote the *Treatise on the Law of Sale of Personal Property* (1868), which at once became the standard in the field.

Bennett, Floyd (1890–1928) aviator; born near Warrensburg,

N.Y. He quit school at age 17 and ran an automobile garage before enlisting in the U.S. Navy (1917), where he learned to fly. In 1925 he flew with Richard Byrd on an expedition to Greenland, and on May 9, 1926, he was at the controls as the two men made the first flight to the North Pole. He received the Congressional Medal of Honor for this feat and became a national hero, but on the early stage of a long-distance flight he died prematurely of pneumonia.

Bennett, Hugh Hammond (1881–1960) soil conservationist; born in Wadesboro, N.C. Raised on a 1,200 acre farm whose depleted soil made farming difficult, in 1903 he joined the Bureau of Soils at the U.S. Department of Agriculture (USDA) and was soon working on problems of soil erosion. As supervisor of soil surveys (1909–28), he assessed agricultural possibilities in the Panama Canal Zone, inspected the land proposed for a territorial railroad in Alaska, and conducted soil surveys in Cuba. In 1928 he coauthored the USDA report "Soil Erosion, a National Menace," and persuaded Congress to fund an erosion control program (1933). He directed the Soil Erosion Service in the Department of the Interior, and, while a dust storm swept over the capital, he appealed to Congress for more action on soil conservation (1935). Congress enacted the Soil Conservation Act and Bennett became the first chief of the Soil Conservation Service.

Bennett, James Gordon (1795–1872) journalist, newspaper publisher; born in Banffshire, Scotland. Emigrating to Nova Scotia in 1819, he taught school there and in Boston, Mass., before taking up newspaper work in South Carolina, on the *Charleston Courier.* He later became Washington correspondent for the *New York Enquirer,* a party paper, and then associate editor of a paper created by its merger with the *Morning Courier;* but in 1832 he was fired for his views. In 1835, with $500 in capital, Bennett launched the *New York Herald,* a one-penny daily paper aimed at a mass audience, and embarked on the course that made him famous. Its editorials, unlike those of other papers, were not tied to the views of a particular party, and its coverage extended to sports and fashion, as well as to business and finance. Bennett also featured sensational stories focused on sex and crime, made heavy use of illustrations, dispatched correspondents to far-flung regions, and stressed getting the news fast. By the 1860s the *Herald* was the city's most popular paper, though it did not win great prestige. He retired in 1867, to be succeeded by his son.

Bennett, James Gordon, Jr. (1841–1918) newspaper editor; born in New York City. Taking over the *New York Herald* from his father in 1867, he continued a tradition of aggressive news gathering and financed several famous international expeditions, including Henry Morton Stanley's successful search in central Africa for David Livingstone (1869–71). He moved to Paris in 1877, conducting his business from there via cables, correspondence, and the summoning of editors. In 1883, with John Mackay, he founded a company to lay transatlantic cables, breaking Jay Gould's monopoly. Four years later he established the renowned Paris edition of the *Herald.* An avid sportsman, he established international trophies in yachting, automobile, and aeronautical racing.

Bennett, John W. (William) (1915–) anthropologist; born in Milwaukee, Wis. He taught at Washington University, St. Louis, Mo., (1959). His interdisciplinary studies covered a broad range of subjects including human ecology, social and cultural theory, Asian and North American society, and economic development; his books include *Paternalism in the Japanese Economy* (1963), *Northern Plainsmen* (1969, revised 1976) and *Of Time and the Enterprise* (1982).

Bennett, Michael (b. Michael Bennett Di Figlia) (1943–87) dancer, choreographer, stage director/producer; born in Buffalo, N.Y. By age three he was dancing at a dance school in Buffalo; by age 12 he had mastered all forms of dance; at 16 he dropped out of school to join the chorus of a touring company of *West Side Story* and toured Europe for a year. Back in New York City, he danced in choruses until emerging as a choreographer, his first show being *A Joyful Noise* (1966); his first real hit (with eight Tony Awards) was *Promises, Promises* (1968), and he went on to choreograph *Company* (1970) and *Follies* (1971). By this time his reputation was such that he was often called in as a "show doctor" to save struggling productions. Working with a group of so-called "gypsies," chorus dancers, he conceived of a show that would be based on their lives and careers; this became *Chorus Line,* which opened in 1975 and went on to become Broadway's longest running musical. He was hailed as having "reinvented" the American musical, and although some would claim he had tendency to take credit as well as control, he was undeniably an influential choreographer. With some of his profits from the many productions of *Chorus Line* around the world, he bought (1977) an 8-story building on lower Broadway where he established offices and rehearsal spaces that he rented to other dance companies. (He sold the building in 1986.) He had another hit with *Dreamgirls* (1981) but in 1985 he suddenly abandoned a new musical, *Scandal,* and two years later he died of AIDS.

Bennett, Wendell C. (Clark) (1905–53) anthropologist; born in Marion, Ind. He was educated at the University of Chicago. As a staff specialist in Andean archaeology at the American Museum of Natural History in the 1930s, Bennett led many expeditions, publishing, among other important reports of his excavations, *The Tarahumara* (1935). After 1940 he taught at Yale.

Bennett, Willard Harrison (1903–87) physicist, inventor; born in Findlay, Ohio. He received a Ph.D. in physics from the University of Michigan in 1928 and joined the Ohio State University faculty two years later. In the 1950s, he invented a device that produced a model of the Van Allen radiation belt. His radio frequency mass spectrometer, a device that measured the mass of atoms, first went into space in 1957 aboard the Russian satellite Sputnik.

Bennett, William J. (John) (1943–) federal official; born in New York City. Outspoken and controversial, as chairman of the National Endowment for the Humanities (1981–85) he reversed liberal policies; as (1985–88) U.S. secretary of education Bennett promoted a conservative agenda, cutting federal student aid and urging schools to become a force for moral education. As President Bush's "drug czar" (1989–91), he coordinated the "war" against drugs, but resigned in frustration.

Bennis, Warren (Gamaliel) (1925–) psychologist, management educator, consultant; born in New York City. Trained as an economist, he had a varied academic career (including the presidency of the University of Cincinnati (1971–77) before joining the University of Southern California's management faculty (1980). He became well known as a consultant to major corporations. He developed behaviorist-based management theories in his numerous books on leadership and organizational development and change.

Benny, Jack (b. Benjamin Kubelsky) (1894–1974) comedian; born in Chicago, Ill. He dropped out of high school to play violin for vaudeville companies, and discovered his own talent for comedy while appearing in U.S. Navy shows in 1918. Combining his violin with his comic routines, in the 1920s he toured in vaudeville and made a few movies. In 1927 he married Sadye Marks, a clerk in a retail store; she adopted the name Mary Livingstone and became a foil for his comic routines. He went on to become an American institution on radio, first with the National Broadcasting Company (NBC) (1932–48), then with CBS (1948–55), where his own character – a mildly neurotic, self-important tightwad – and a regular supporting cast managed to milk laughs from endless variations on a few themes. He made occasional appearances on television in the early 1950s before settling into the *Jack Benny Show* (1955–65), where to his famous radio shticks – the pregnant pause and the perfectly timed, "Well!" – he added the slow take and the piqued stare. Over his career he had made a score of movies, the most notable being *To Be or Not to Be* (1942). After giving up his regular television show, he continued to appear on television specials, and he made a new career playing his violin in benefit concerts with the nation's symphony orchestras. In real life he was said to have the very opposite of his comic persona – generous, modest, and considerate.

Benson, Ezra Taft (1899–94) government official, religious leader; born in Whitney, Ida. He was President Eisenhower's secretary of agriculture (1953–1961). He became president of the Church of Jesus Christ of Latter-Day Saints (Mormons) in 1985.

Benson, Frank (Weston) (1862–1951) painter, etcher; born in Salem, Mass. He studied at the Boston Museum of Fine Arts (1877–80), and in Paris (1883), settled in Boston to teach at the Museum of Fine Arts (1889–1912), and summered in North Haven Island, Maine. A member of The Ten (1898), he was an impressionist, as in *Summer* (1890), and produced popular wildlife etchings.

Benson, George (1943–) musician; born in Pittsburgh, Pa. A respected jazz guitarist who gained unprecedented success in popular music, he worked as a sideman with Brother Jack McDuff in 1963–65, made his first solo records in 1966, and was a staff musician for CTI Records between 1970–75. In 1976, his recording "Breezin' " became the first of several Top Ten records that he released.

Benson, William Shepherd (1855–1932) naval officer; born in Bibb County, Ga. During a long naval career (1877–1929) he served as chief of staff of the Pacific Fleet (1909–10), and as the first chief of naval operations (1915–19). He published *The Merchant Marine* (1923) and was the first president of the National Council of Catholic Men.

Bent, Charles (1799–1847) trader; born in Charleston, Va. (now W.Va.). He entered the fur trade early, and with his brother, William Bent, and Ceran St. Vrain, built Bent's Fort (1828–32) in present-day La Junta, Colo. He became the civil governor of New Mexico in 1846 but was killed in an uprising of Mexicans and Pueblo Indians.

Bentley, Arthur Fisher (1870–1957) political scientist; born in Freeport, Ill. While employed as a journalist in Chicago, he wrote *The Process of Government* (1908), describing how "pressure groups" influence all governments. Although he wrote several important books including, *Relativity in Man and Society* (1926), *Knowing and the Known* (with John Dewey) (1949), and *Makers, Users, and Masters* (posthumously, 1969), his controversial, often critical views of American government prevented his acceptance by mainstream academia.

Bentley, William (1759–1819) Protestant clergyman, author; born in Boston, Mass. He graduated from Harvard in 1777 and taught school for three years before returning to Harvard as a Latin and Greek tutor. Ordained pastor of East Church, Salem, Mass., in 1783 (where he remained for the rest of his life), he developed an appealing theological and political liberalism and is considered a pioneer of the Unitarian movement. He was a regular contributor to the Salem *Register,* a Freemason, and a correspondent with Thomas Jefferson. His four-volume diary (published 1905–14) provides an illuminating picture of his times.

Bentley, Wilson (Alwyn) (1865–1931) meteorologist; born in Jericho, Vt. He spent his life on a farm in Vermont, collecting data from storms and photographing samples of precipitation. His exhaustive studies show that no two snowflakes are alike because the variables surrounding their formation are infinite. Some 2,000 of his 5,000 snowflake photographs, taken using a microscope and camera, were published by the American Meteorological Society as *Snow Crystals* (1931), with William J. Humphreys as coauthor.

Benton, Thomas Hart (1782–1858) U.S. senator; born in Hillsboro, N.C. A true son of the frontier, he grew up in Tennessee, where after becoming a lawyer, he served a term in the state senate (1809–11). After serving in the War of 1812 – during which he got involved in a brawl with his commander Andrew Jackson – he moved to St. Louis, Mo., where he practiced law and edited the *Missouri Enquirer* (1818–20). His editorials got him elected to the U.S. Senate where he served 30 years (Dem., Mo.; 1821–51). He opposed the national bank and championed "hard money" – for which he earned the nickname "Old Bullion" – and was a supporter of expansion and the small farmer. A moderate on the slavery issue, he lost popularity with his constituents; denied re-election in 1850, he served in the U.S. House of Representatives (1853–55), but lost again because of his opposition to slavery. He was such a loyal Democrat that he opposed his own son-in-law, John C. Frémont, when he ran as a Republican for the presidency in 1886.

Benton, Thomas Hart (1889–1975) painter; born in Neosho, Mo. (grand-nephew of Senator Thomas Hart Benton). Between 1906–12 he studied at the Art Institute of Chicago and in Paris, but he rejected the European approach to art. Drawing on his extensive travels through much of the midwestern, southern, and western U.S.A., he tried to capture his vision of dynamic democracy with an idiom that was dramatic, rhythmic, and populist, often using bright colors and cartoon-like figures. Other hallmarks include his evocation of American legends and his several murals in public buildings. His work is regarded as creating what was known as the Regionalist style or school, seen in such paintings as *Cotton Loading* (1928) and *Country Dance* (1928).

Bentsen, Lloyd Millard Jr. (1921–) U.S. senator, cabinet officer; born in Mission, Texas. He studied law at the University of Texas: Austin and served as a combat pilot in the U.S. Air Force during World War II. He was a member of the U.S. House of Representatives (Dem., Texas; 1948–55) and then built a substantial fortune as president of Lincoln Consolidated Insurance Company. He served in the U.S. Senate (Dem., Texas; 1971–93) and was the Democratic vice-presidential candidate in 1988. Regarded as an influential elder statesman, he served as secretary of the treasury (1993–94) under President Bill Clinton.

Ben-Veniste, Richard (1943–) lawyer; born in New York City. Assistant U.S. attorney in New York (1968–73), he headed the special Watergate task force that analyzed President Nixon's "White House tapes" (1973–75); he wrote about it in *Stonewall* (1977). Partner in a Washington firm (1975–82), he then opened an individual practice.

Berenson, Bernard (b. Valvrojenski) (1865–1959) art historian, connoisseur, collector; born in Biturmansk, Lithuania. He studied at the local synagogue before his family emigrated to Boston (1875), where he studied at Boston University (1883) and Harvard (B.A. 1887). Subsidized by Isabella Stewart Gardner, he studied in Paris, London, Oxford, Berlin, and Italy (1887–88). He settled in an 18th-century Villa I Tatti near Florence and devoted himself to the study and identification of medieval and Renaissance works, specializing in Italian art. An honored scholar and authenticator, he acquired prints and paintings for museums and private collectors, such as Isabella Gardner, and for international dealers, thereby making himself wealthy, and attracting criticism from some quarters for placing his connoisseurship at the service of profit-makers. In addition to the many distinguished critical essays and scholarly works, notably *The Study and Criticism of Italian Art* (1902) and *Drawings of the Florentine Painters* (1903), he published a three-volume autobiography (1949–52). He became famous for his ability to attribute paintings to artists based on specific characteristics of style and technique – even to the point of identifying hitherto unknown painters. At his death, the Villa I Tatti was left to Harvard University as a center for Italian Renaissance studies.

Berg, (Patricia Jane) Patty (1918–) golfer; born in Minneapolis, Minn. She won 57 tournaments during her career, including 15 majors. She was a three-time winner of two majors in a single year (1948, 1955, 1957).

Berg, Paul (1926–) biochemist; born in New York City. After research on the role of tRNA in protein synthesis (1960s), he joined the faculty of Stanford University (1968) and began research on recombinant DNA (c. 1970). Although it occurs naturally, he believed that such DNA could be produced and controlled in a laboratory, and he pioneered techniques for manipulating genes. He shared the Nobel Prize in chemistry (1980).

Berger, Arthur (1912–) composer; born in New York City. After studies at Harvard and with Nadia Boulanger in Paris, he began an active career of composing and criticism. His works show influences ranging from neoclassicism to the atonal tradition.

Berger, Meyer (1898–1959) journalist; born in New York City. As a *New York Times* reporter for over 30 years from 1928, he probed into varied aspects of city life with indefatigable curiosity, winning a 1950 Pulitzer Prize.

Berger, Peter L. (Ludwig) (1929–) sociologist; born in Vienna, Austria. He emigrated to the U.S.A. at age 17 and earned a Ph.D. at the New School for Social Research. He held academic appointments at various institutions including

Boston University (1981). He wrote on modernization, in relation both to Christian beliefs and institutions and to Third World development, in such books as *The Social Construction of Reality* (coauthored, 1966) and *The Capitalist Revolution* (1986).

Berger, Victor Louis (1860–1929) socialist, journalist, U.S. representative; born in Nieder-Rehbach, Austria. After emigrating to America (1878), he settled in Milwaukee, Wis., where he became a public school teacher (1882–92). From 1892 on he dedicated himself to writing about and promoting socialist politics, labor unions, and numerous reform movements. A co-founder of the Social Democrat Party (1898) and executive board member of the new Socialist Party of America (1901), he spread a moderate socialist message through several newspapers he founded. The most important was the *Milwaukee Leader,* which he edited from 1901 (when it was the *Social Democratic Herald*), until his death. From 1911–13, he served in the U.S. House of Representatives, the first Socialist to do so. Harassed for his pacifist views during World War I, he was reelected to the U.S. House of Representatives (1918) but was not allowed to take his seat because he was indicted and found guilty under the Espionage Act. (His conviction was reversed by the Supreme Court in 1921 so he did not go to prison.) Following the war, he served three terms in the House of Representatives as a Socialist (1923–29), and was a highly respected advocate of progressive legislation. He died from injuries when struck by a streetcar in Milwaukee.

Bergh, Henry (1811–88) animal protection pioneer; born in New York City. Manager of his father's shipyard (1837–43), he traveled overseas after his father's death and spent one year in St. Petersburg, Russia (1863–64), as secretary of the United States legation. Resigning because of his wife's ill health, and becoming increasingly concerned with the inhumane treatment of animals, he founded the American Society for the Prevention of Cruelty to Animals (ASPCA) after his return (1866). He later assisted in the formation of the Society for the Prevention of Cruelty to Children (1875). Although he wrote several plays, poetry, and some literary sketches, he is best known for turning the ASPCA into an international movement.

Bergmann, Peter G. (Gabriel) (1915–) physicist; born in Berlin, Germany. He came to the U.S.A. to become Albert Einstein's assistant at the Institute for Advanced Studies, Princeton, N.J. (1936–41). After teaching at several American universities, he became professor of physics at Syracuse University, N.Y. (1946–82). His research in general relativity included studies of wave theory, electron optics, and irreversible processes.

Bergsma, William (1921–) composer; born in Oakland, Calif. After studies at the Eastman School of Music, he composed actively and taught at Juilliard and the University of Washington. His music was neither conservative nor radical, but notable for its lyricism.

Bergson, Abram (1912–) economist; born in Baltimore, Md. At the age of 24, he published a widely recognized article which facilitated a new view of welfare economics. He was one of America's leading experts in Soviet economics, a professor at both Columbia University and Harvard, and a consultant to the Rand Corporation.

Berigan, (Rowland Bernart) "Bunny" (1908–42) jazz musician; born in Calumet, Wis. He was a trumpet soloist in Benny Goodman's 1935 band and the leader of his own orchestra from 1937 until his death from pneumonia.

Berkeley, Busby (b. William Berkeley Enos) (1895–1976) choreographer, film director; born in Los Angeles. He went on the Broadway stage at age five, and by the 1920s was one of the top Broadway choreographers. In 1930 he went to Hollywood to choreograph Eddie Cantor films and Mary Pickford's musical, *Kiki* (1930). A long string of musicals followed that featured his innovative choreography and camera techniques. He later directed complete films, but without much success.

Berkeley, Sir William (1606–77) colonial governor; born in Somerset, England. He became governor of Virginia in 1642, led militia against the colony's remaining Indian tribes, organized a defense that prevented a Dutch landing on the Virginia coast in 1665, and ruthlessly put down a settlers' rebellion in 1676.

Berkman, Alexander (1870–1936) anarchist, author; born in Vilna, Russia. After being influenced by Russian nihilists, he emigrated to America (1887). He became involved with radical Jewish labor groups in New York City and in 1879 began his personal and professional liaison with Emma Goldman that would last to the end of his life. He gained international attention with his attempted assassination of Henry C. Frick (1892); for this he served 14 years in prison (1892–1906). He founded and edited *Mother Earth* with Goldman after his release. The two were arrested and found guilty of opposing conscription during World War I. He went to prison again (1917–19) and then, along with Goldman, was deported to Russia (1919) as a political undesirable. Originally he supported the Communist Revolution in Russia but he changed his views and wrote *The Bolshevik Myth* (1925). He spent his final years in Sweden, Germany, and France before committing suicide in Nice, France.

Berkowitz, Henry (1857–1924) rabbi; born in Pittsburgh, Pa. A graduate of the University of Cincinnati and Hebrew Union College in Cincinnati, he was one of the first four rabbis ordained in the U.S.A. (1883). Rabbi of Rodeph Scholem Synagogue in Philadelphia (1892–1922) and founder of the Jewish Chautauqua Society (1893), he also wrote popular religious literature.

Berle, A. A. (Adolph Augustus) (1895–1971) lawyer, economist, public official; born in Boston, Mass. Educated at Harvard, he practiced law in Boston and New York City before becoming a professor of corporate law at Columbia University in 1927. He joined Franklin D. Roosevelt's "brain trust" for the 1932 presidential campaign and served as an assistant secretary of state (1938–44) and ambassador to Brazil (1945–46). He published several important works on business organization and on Latin America. He retired from Columbia in 1963, but continued teaching as a professor emeritus until his death.

Berle, Milton (b. Milton Berlinger) (1908–) stand-up/television comedian; born in New York City. A child actor in silent films, he appeared in vaudeville and New York musicals like the Ziegfeld Follies, returning to movies in the 1940s. "Uncle Miltie" hosted the television variety show, *Texaco Star Theatre,* from 1948–56; the series' popularity earned him the title "Mr. Television" and helped change the television set from a toy for the wealthy into a family fixture. He continued his career, appearing in occasional movies as well as doing his one-man turns in clubs, but although he retained the admiration of his fans and fellow comedians, he never regained the broad public of his television days.

Berlin, Irving (b. Israel Baline) (1888–1990) composer, lyricist; born in Temun, Siberian Russia. His father was a cantor and the family fled pogroms and emigrated to the United States when he was a child. Living in New York, Irving joined a synagogue choir and at age 14 sang popular songs on street corners and in cafes. A singing waiter in 1906, he taught himself piano and began writing songs; his first song was published mistakenly under "I. Berlin" and from then on he called himself Irving Berlin. He turned out a series of mildly popular songs sung by such fledgling stars as Eddie Cantor and Fanny Brice and wrote his first complete Broadway score in 1914; but it was his song "Alexander's Ragtime Band" (1916) that brought him national popularity. In the army in 1918, he composed a musical performed by army personnel for benefits, *Yip, Yip, Yaphank* (1918), that included "Oh, How I Hate to Get up in the Morning." Throughout the next four decades, he wrote successful stage and film musicals which included many American standards, such as "A Pretty Girl is Like a Melody" (1919), "Blue Skies" (1926), "Puttin' on the Ritz" (1930), and "Easter Parade" (1933). In 1938, on the eve of World War II, he wrote "God Bless America," unofficially adopted as the second national anthem. For the 1942 film *Holiday Inn* he wrote "White Christmas," which became Bing Crosby's signature song. During World War II he wrote another all-soldier musical, *This Is the Army* (1942). His most successful stage musical was *Annie Get Your Gun* (1946) starring Ethel Merman. In 1974 he presented his piano (which he played only by ear and in the key of F-sharp major) to the Smithsonian as a gesture of his retirement. In 1977 he was awarded the Medal of Freedom by President Gerald Ford for his patriotic contributions during the two world wars; but to many people throughout the world he was beloved as the best all-around popular songwriter of the century.

Berliner, Emile (1851–1929) inventor; born in Hanover, Germany. An apprentice printer before he emigrated to the United States in 1870, he became chief inspector of the Bell Telephone Company, and from 1876 on, patented a series of improvements to Alexander Graham Bell's telephone. In 1888 Berliner introduced the first flat disc recording, a marked improvement over Thomas Edison's recording cylinders. He developed the first acoustic tiles in 1915.

Berlitz, Charles (Frambach) (1914–) educator, publisher; born in New York City. A graduate of Yale (1936), he took over the family business of intensive language teaching, founded by his grandfather. During World War II, he restored the fortunes of Berlitz Schools of Languages and Berlitz Publications by getting commissions with the armed services. After the war he offered business courses for overseas employees. Himself a gifted linguist, he was the author and editor of many "Self-Teacher Courses," phrase books, dictionaries, and audio-visual materials.

Berman, Eugene (1899–1972) painter, scenic designer; born in St. Petersburg, Russia. He emigrated to America (1935) and was a scenic designer for ballet and opera. His paintings, such as *Muse of the Western World* (1942), often resemble stage sets.

Bernard, Jessie Shirley (b. Ravitch) (1903–) sociologist; born in Minneapolis, Minn. She collaborated with her husband Luther Lee Bernard (until his death in 1951) on works including *Origins of American Sociology* (1943). Her solo works included *American Family Behavior* (1942) and *American Community Behavior* (1949, revised). After resigning from Pennsylvania State University (1947–64), she was an independent scholar and author of influential feminist analyses such as *Women, Wives, Mothers* (1975) and *The Female World from a Global Perspective* (1987).

Bernardin, Joseph L. (Louis) (1928–) Catholic prelate; born in Columbia, S.C. Ordained in 1952, he did pastoral work and held administrative posts in the Charleston archdiocese before being named auxiliary bishop of New Orleans (1966–68). He later became general secretary of the National Conference of Catholic Bishops (NCCB) (1968–72) and archbishop of Cincinnati, Ohio (1972–82), also serving as NCCB president (1974–77). A progressive, he denounced violence, racism, and poverty, along with abortion, in a "seamless garment" of "pro-life" teaching. He was named archbishop of Chicago in 1982, and became a cardinal the next year.

Bernays, Edward L. (1891–) public relations executive; born in Vienna, Austria (nephew of Sigmund Freud). He was brought to the U.S.A. in 1892. After creating U.S. World War I propaganda, he founded the country's first public relations firm (1919). He and his future wife, Doris E. Fleischman, coined the term "counsel on public relations" for this firm. He was still counseling industrial and government clients after his hundredth birthday. Known as the father of public relations, he pioneered public relations based on social science and market research. He wrote numerous books and articles, including the first book on public relations, *Crystallizing Public Opinion* (1923).

Bernbach, William (1911–82) advertising executive; born in New York City. He was variously president, chairman, and chief executive officer of his own New York advertising agency, Doyle Dane Bernbach (1949–82). A copywriter credited with introducing a low-keyed, often humorous soft sell to advertising (Avis's "We Try Harder"), he heralded the rise of creative New York agencies in the 1960s and 1970s.

Berne, Eric (Lennard) (1910–70) psychiatrist, author; born in Montreal, Quebec, Canada. He studied medicine at McGill University and attended the Yale Psychiatric Clinic (1936–38). He was affiliated with the San Francisco Psychoanalytic Institute (1947–56) and conducted a private practice in psychiatry for more than 30 years. His theory of "transactional analysis" became well known through his book *Games People Play: The Psychology of Human Relationships* (1964).

Bernstein, Aline (b. Frankau) (1881–1955) set and costume designer; born in New York City. After giving up thoughts of being a portraitist, she began her stage career in 1924 with costumes for the Neighborhood Playhouse production of *The Little Clay Cart*. In 1937 she co-founded the Museum of Costume Art. She worked for the Theatre Guild and for the Civic Repertory Theatre in such productions as *The Cherry Orchard* (1928) and *Thunder on the Left* (1933). She is also the "A.B." to whom Thomas Wolfe dedicated *Look Homeward, Angel;* for five years she carried on an extramarital affair with Wolfe.

Bernstein, Carl (1944–) journalist; born in Washington, D.C. With fellow *Washington Post* reporter Bob Woodward, he unmasked the Watergate scandal and cover-up, and coauthored the best-seller *All the President's Men* (1974), about the scandal, as well as *The Final Days* (1976), about the last months of the Nixon presidency.

Bernstein, Elmer (1922–) composer, conductor; born in New York City. After writing music for United Nations radio shows and a brief career as a concert pianist, he began to compose film scores. His music for *The Man With the Golden Arm* (1955) brought widespread acclaim. He wrote over 100 major film scores in a style that drew heavily on jazz; among his scores are those for *To Kill a Mockingbird* (1962), *The Great Escape* (1963), and *My Left Foot* (1989).

Bernstein, Leonard (1918–90) conductor, composer; born in Lawrence, Mass. He played piano from childhood and studied at Harvard and the Curtis Institute of Music, Philadelphia. After becoming a protégé of Koussevitsky as a Tanglewood conducting student in 1940–41, he was named assistant conductor of the New York Philharmonic and in 1943 made a sensation stepping in at the last minute for the indisposed Bruno Walter. There followed an active career as a guest conductor – and occasional pianist – during the 1940s. In that decade he also composed works including the *Jeremiah* and *Age of Anxiety* symphonies and the Broadway musical *Fancy Free*. In 1952 he premiered his one-act opera *Trouble in Tahiti* and 1957 saw the debut of his classical musical *West Side Story*. The next year he began an 11-year tenure as conductor of the New York Philharmonic and a series of televised Young Peoples' Concerts which, combined with his engaging personality and extravagant conducting style, made him the most popular conductor in the country. In later years he guest-conducted worldwide; having spent his early career championing conservative American composers such as Copland, in the 1970s he became the spearhead of the Mahler revival.

Berra, (Lawrence Peter) "Yogi" (1925–) baseball player/manager; born in St. Louis, Mo. During his 19-year career as a catcher with the New York Yankees and Mets (1946–65), he was named Most Valuable Player three times (1951, 1954, 1955). He holds many World Series records, including most series played (14), games played (75), and World Champions titles (10). He managed the Yankees to a league pennant in 1964 and the Mets to a league championship in 1973. Famous for his comical malapropisms, such as, "It ain't over til it's over," he was featured in many commercial endorsements. He was elected to baseball's Hall of Fame in 1972.

Berrigan, Daniel J. (Joseph) (1921–) Catholic priest, social activist, poet; born in Two Harbors, Minn. (brother of Philip Berrigan). He entered the Order of the Society of Jesus (1939), was ordained (1952), and after studying in France (where he was influenced by the worker-priest movement), he taught at Catholic preparatory schools until becoming associate professor of theology at LeMoyne College (Syracuse, N.Y.) (1957–62). His book of poems, *Time Without Number* (1957), won the Lamont Poetry Award. After serving as assistant editor of *Jesuit Missions* in New York City (1963–65), he became associate director of United Religious Work (1966–69). Active in opposing the Vietnam War, he went with professor Howard Zinn of Boston University to Hanoi, North Vietnam, to assist in obtaining the release of three American pilots (1968); the diary he kept during this mission, along with 11 poems, became *Night Flight to Hanoi* (1968). With his brother, Philip Berrigan, he gained national attention for destroying draft registration files in Catonsville, Md. (1968); in 1970 he

was sentenced to three years in prison for this, but he went underground for several months until federal authorities arrested him on Block Island (off Rhode Island). After 18 months in prison, he was paroled in 1972 and participated with his brother in the first Plowshares Action (1980), a protest at the General Electric Plant at King of Prussia, Pa. Living among Jesuits, writing and conducting retreats, he was arrested regularly for his protest actions at weapons manufacturers and other sites (1980–92). He wrote over 50 books, including *The Trial of the Catonsville 9* (1970), an autobiography (1987), and at least four films.

Berrigan, Philip F. (1923–) Catholic priest, activist; born in Two Harbors, Minn. He served in three European campaigns in the U.S. Army (1943–46). He was ordained (1955) and was an assistant pastor in Washington, D.C. (1955–56), a parochial high school counselor in New Orleans, La. (1956–63), director of promotion at St. Joseph's Society of the Sacred Heart in New York (1963–64), and an English instructor at Epiphany College, Newburgh, N.Y. Beginning about 1962, he made the peace movement the focus of his life work, first coming to national attention along with his brother Daniel Berrigan (1968) for destroying Vietnam war draft registration files in Catonsville, Md. He was sentenced to three years in prison, but went underground (1970) and was subsequently captured by federal authorities in a Manhattan church (1970). He married Elizabeth McAlister (1969) but did not formally leave the priesthood. The wedding was publicly announced in 1973, the same year he and his wife founded Jonah House – a community committed to a nonviolent approach to fighting the arms race. Operating a house painting company to survive, he published *Year One*, a newspaper concerned with ongoing resistance to nuclear armament, and conducted the first Plowshare action at the General Electric Plant at King of Prussia, Pa., with his brother Daniel and others (1980). His community staged at least 40 actions at weapons factories and nuclear facilities in the United States, Europe, and Australia and he was indicted over 20 times and served more than six years in prison between 1970–92. He wrote at least five books, including *The Time Discipline: The Beatitudes and Nuclear Resistance* (with McAlister, 1989).

Berrios Martínez, Rubén (1930–93) politician, public official; born in Aibonito, Puerto Rico. He was educated abroad, first in the United States at the University of Georgetown (B.A.) and Harvard (M.A.), and then at Oxford (Ph.D.). An accomplished orator, he was the head of the Puerto Rican Independence Party (1970–93) and a member of the Puerto Rican Senate (1972–73). In 1971 he was jailed for three months for a sit-in on the island of Culebra protesting the U.S. military presence there.

Berry, Brian (Joe Lobley) (1934–) geographer; born in Sedgley, Staffordshire, England. He moved to the United States in 1955 and took professorships at the University of Chicago, Harvard, and Carnegie-Mellon Universities before becoming Founders Professor at the University of Texas: Dallas. He was a prolific authority on urban matters and regional development in advanced and developing countries.

Berry, (Charles Edward Anderson) Chuck (1926–) musician; born in St. Louis, Mo. As a singer-guitarist who drew from blues, rockabilly, and country-and-western styles, and wrote songs about teenage concerns, he was the biggest influence on pre-Beatles rock. He trained as a hairdresser and played with Johnnie Johnson's trio in East St. Louis, Ill., before launching his career with Chess Records in Chicago in 1955. With hit songs such as "School Days," "Rock and Roll Music," and "Johnny B Goode," he appealed to teenagers of all races. In 1962, he began serving a two-year sentence for violating the Mann Act. After his release in 1964, his career never fully recovered, although his 1972 release "My Ding A Ling" was the most successful record of his career. (He served other brief prison terms in 1979 and 1990.) In 1986, he became an inaugural member of the Rock 'n' Roll Hall of Fame. His memoir, *Chuck Berry: The Autobiography,* was published in 1988.

Berry, Edward Wilber (1875–1954) paleobotanist; born in Newark, N.J. When he was fifteen, his formal education ended and he pursued a career as a journalist. He also expanded his childhood interest in botany and geology by reading and making detailed observations. He published scientific articles on the systematic paleobotany of New Jersey fossils, and won a Walker Prize for his book on the diversity and ancestry of the tulip poplar (1901) while working as president, treasurer, and manager of the Passaic, N.J., *Daily News* (1897–1905). He spent the rest of his career at Johns Hopkins (1907–42), serving as dean (1929–42) and provost (1935–42); during most of those years he also worked as a geologist with the U.S. Geological Survey and the state of Maryland. His specialties included taxonomic paleobotany and the paleobotany of South America. His success despite his lack of an advanced education made him antagonistic toward what he perceived as irrelevance in college curricula; he felt that learning should be a lifetime pursuit, and should not end with the obtaining of a degree.

Berry, (Leon) "Chu" (1910–41) jazz musician; born in Wheeling, W.Va. He was an outstanding tenor saxophonist who was featured in the bands of Fletcher Henderson and Cab Calloway until his death in an automobile accident.

Berry, Martha McChesney (1866–1942) educator; born near Rome, Ga. Daughter of a wealthy planter, in the early 1900s she created nondenominational religious schools for Blue Ridge Mountain children with work-study programs that taught students skills useful in their own communities. Supported by benefactors such as Henry Ford, her schools became models for public schools in Georgia and other states. She founded Berry College in 1926.

Berry, Mary Frances (1938–) historian, educator, government official; born in Nashville, Tenn. A graduate of Howard University, she received her Ph.D. from the University of Michigan, taught history at several colleges and was active in the civil rights movement while earning her law degree from the University of Michigan Law School. In 1970 she moved to Maryland as the acting director of Afro-American Studies at the University of Maryland. There she wrote, joined the bar in the District of Columbia, and was promoted to a provost at the College Park campus. In 1976 she became chancellor of the University of Colorado: Boulder; she took a leave of absence to become the assistant secretary for education in the Department of Health, Education, and Welfare at the request of President Jimmy Carter (1977–80). She was the first African-American woman to achieve any one of those positions of leadership. A member of the U.S. Civil Rights Commission (1980), in 1984 she successfully sued President Ronald Reagan, pre-

venting him from firing her from the Commission. Widely honored, she taught at several universities, and published several books including the coauthored *Long Memory* (1982), a history of African-Americans.

Berry, Sara S. (Sweezy) (1940–) economist; born in Washington, D.C. A University of Michigan Ph.D., she taught at Indiana and Boston Universities before joining the Johns Hopkins history faculty (1990). Her works on the economics of development and on property rights and natural resources in western Africa include *Cocoa, Custom and Socioeconomic Change in Rural Western Nigeria* (1975) and *Fathers Work for their Sons* (1985).

Berry, Wendell (Erdman) (1934–) poet, writer; born in Henry County, Ky. He graduated from the University of Kentucky (B.A. 1956; M.A. 1957), taught at various institutions, and at one time was an editor for Rodale Press, Pa. Regarded as a regional writer of novels and essays, he is known for his poetry, as in *The Country of Marriage* (1973), and his deep feeling for rural life and the land.

Berryman, John (McAlpin) (1914–72) poet, writer, teacher; born in McAlester, Okla. He studied at Columbia University (B.A. 1936), at Cambridge, England (B.A. 1938), and taught at various institutions, mainly the University of Minnesota (1954–72). He is known for his almost agonizing self-revealing poetry, as in *Dream Songs* (collected; 1969). He committed suicide in Minneapolis, Minn., and his novel, *Recovery* (1973), appeared posthumously.

Bertoia, Harry (b. Enrico) (1915–78) sculptor, designer; born in San Lorenzo, Italy. He emigrated to the U.S.A. in 1930 and studied (1937–39) and then taught painting and metal crafts at the Cranbrook Academy of Art (in Bloomfield Hills, Mich.) (1939–43). He worked for the Evans Products Company, Venice, Calif., (1943–46), then established his own workshop in Bally, Pa. Although he regarded himself as primarily a sculptor, he was known for his early cubist-influenced silver coffee and tea services, and for his furniture, especially the "Bertoia chair" (1952), with its slender metal legs and frame and mesh-like seat.

Berwanger, (John Jacob) "Jay" (1914–) football player; born in Dubuque, Iowa. A University of Chicago halfback, he won the first Heisman Trophy (1935) and was the first player chosen in the first National Football League player draft (1936).

Bessey, Charles Edwin (1845–1915) botanist; born in Milton Township, Ohio. After growing up on a farm, he founded curricula in botany and horticulture at the Iowa Agricultural College (1870–84), then joined the University of Nebraska (1884–1915), where he became a respected educator and administrator, holding deanships and serving as an officer in many professional botanical and agricultural associations. He was a pioneer in the taxonomy and evolution of angiosperms (flowering plants having enclosed seeds). A dedicated and popular educator, he wrote a series of high school and college textbooks, and introduced the laboratory method (including microscopy) to augment his lectures.

Best, Roy (1900–54) prison warden; birthplace unknown. He was for 20 years the so-called "iron boss" of the Colorado state penitentiary in Canon City (1932–52). There he won a national reputation by instituting an innovative dietary and work regimen that included the liberal use of physical punishment. Acquitted in 1951 and 1952 on charges of embezzlement and flogging prisoners, he died shortly before the end of a 2-year suspension for mismanagement.

Bestor, Arthur Eugene (1879–1944) educator; born in Dixon, Ill. After graduating from the University of Chicago (1901), he taught history and political science at Franklin College (Indiana) and the University of Chicago. Long interested in adult education, from 1905 on he was active in the Chatauqua movement, becoming director of the Chatauqua Institution (1907–15) and then its president (1915–44). He developed its popular home reading courses, gained degree credits for some of its courses, and after World War I he focused on the teacher training programs and cultural events with which Chatauqua would become most closely identified.

Bestor, Arthur (Eugene, Jr.) (1908–   ) educator, historian; born in Chautauqua, N.Y. During a long and varied academic career, he published influential works on American intellectual history (*Backwoods Utopias*, 1950; revised 1970); the "aimlessness" of progressive education in public schools (*Educational Wastelands*, 1953; *The Restoration of Learning*, 1955); and 18th-century American constitutional history.

Bethe, Hans A. (Albrecht) (1906–   ) physicist; born in Strasbourg, Germany (now France). He taught in Germany (1928–33), but since he was half Jewish, he fled Germany's growing Nazi regime and moved to England (1933–34). He came to the U.S.A. to become professor of physics at Cornell University (1935–75), and became director of theoretical physics for the Manhattan Project (1943–46). After World War II, he pursued his earlier research on stellar nuclear energy and the origin of the chemical elements during the generation of the universe. For these pioneering efforts he was awarded the 1967 Nobel Prize in physics.

Bethune, Louise Blanchard (1856–1913) architect; born in Waterloo, N.Y. Showing an early aptitude for designing structures, after graduating high school and two years of teaching, travel, and study, she became an apprentice in a Buffalo, N.Y., architectural firm. There she met a Canadian architect, Robert A. Bethune; they opened their own firm, then were married in the fall of 1881. As the first professional woman architect in America, she designed a variety of buildings – domestic, commercial, and some 18 schools – mostly in the Romanesque Revival style, all in western New York. When a third partner joined the firm in 1890, she went into semi-retirement to have more time for her child and her genealogical research.

Bethune, Mary McLeod (1875–1955) educator, civil/women's rights activist; born in Mayesville, S.C. A child of former slaves, she began her life picking cotton, but a scholarship to Scotia Seminary in North Carolina in 1888 launched her long and distinguished career as educator and activist. Believing that education provided the key to racial advancement, she founded the Daytona Normal and Industrial Institute (Fla.) (1904), which through her persistent direction as president (1904–42) became Bethune-Cookman College in 1929. An activist, she mobilized thousands of black women as leader and founder of the National Association of Colored Women and the National Council of Negro Women. A national figure, she served in the Roosevelt administration as adviser to the president on minority affairs and director of the Division of Negro Affairs within the National Youth Administration (1936–44). Through her efforts to promote full

citizenship rights for all African-Americans and her feminist perspective, she came to symbolize the dual role black women played as activists for the rights of blacks and women.

Bettelheim, Bruno (1903–90) psychotherapist, author; born in Vienna, Austria. He studied with Freud, whom he revered, and graduated from the University of Vienna (1938). During the Nazi regime, he was imprisoned at Dachau and Buchenwald (1938–39); his 1943 article on his experiences and insights would gain him wide recognition. Upon his release, he moved to the United States and worked at the University of Chicago (1939–42, 1944–73). As head of the university's Sonia Shankman Orthogenic School, a treatment center for severely disturbed children (1944–73), he developed a deinstitutionalized environment of total support. He became particularly admired for his work with autistic children – although some of his methods were controversial – and in later years he published advice in the popular media on raising normal children. He published two books on the Nazi death camps, *The Informed Heart: Autonomy in a Mass Age* (1960) and *Surviving and Other Essays* (1979; reprinted in 1986 as *Surviving the Holocaust*). He wrote more than 20 books on psychotherapy, including *Love Is Not Enough: The Treatment of Emotionally Disturbed Children* (1950), *The Children of the Dream* (1969), and *Freud and Man's Soul* (1982).

Bevan, Arthur Dean (1851–1943) surgeon; born in Chicago. Affiliated most of his career with Rush Medical College in Chicago (M.D. 1883; faculty, 1887–1934), he specialized in stomach surgery. As head of the American Medical Association's committees on medical education (1902–16, 1920–28), he made his most important contributions to medical training.

Beveridge, Albert J. (Jeremiah) (1862–1927) U.S. senator, historian; born in Lorain, Ohio. A lawyer by profession, he served in the U.S. Senate (Rep., Ind.; 1899–1911) where he was one of the original "insurgent" Republicans, supporting anti-trust and anti–child-labor legislation as well as naval expansion and imperialist policies. After being defeated for re-election as a Republican, he supported Theodore Roosevelt in the 1912 Progressive Party campaign. He was also known for his historical writings, particularly *The Life of John Marshall* (1916, 1919).

Bevier, Isabel (1860–1942) home economist; born near Plymouth, Ohio. She conducted nutritional research and on the faculty of the University of Illinois (1900–21) helped develop the new field of home economics along scientific rather than utilitarian lines. She became nationally known through such works as *Home Economics in Education* (1924).

Bianco, Margery See WILLIAMS, MARGERY.

Bibb, William (Wyatt) (1781–1820) U.S. representative/senator, governor; born in Amelia County, Ga. Trained at the University of Pennsylvania, he was a doctor in Georgia (1801–13) and a Democratic Party state politician before going to Congress (1805–13). He left to become a senator (1813–16) but resigned because of public opposition to annual salaries for federal representatives. Appointed governor of the Territory of Alabama (1817–20), he helped frame its state constitution before his premature death.

Bickerdyke, (Mary Ann b. Ball) "Mother" (1817–1901) nurse, humanitarian; born in Knox County, Ohio. A farmer's daughter with little formal education, at age 42 she was left a widow with three children. She supported herself by practicing "botanic" medicine, and when the Civil War broke out she volunteered to work in the hospitals at the great Union army base in Cairo, Ill. From then until the surrender at Appomattox, she worked tirelessly as a nurse and caregiver both in battle and behind the lines, taking time out only to give speeches and gain support for the Sanitary Commission. Outspoken in her impatience with military regulations and officials, she became known as "Mother" Bickerdyke and gained the support of men such as Grant and Sherman. After the war, she worked for various social service causes – a Chicago home for indigent women, a project to settle veterans in Kansas, the Salvation Army in San Francisco, and always on behalf of veterans. Receiving a special pension from Congress in 1886, she retired to Kansas in 1887.

Biddle, Francis (Beverley) (1886–1968) lawyer; U.S. attorney general; born in Paris, France. He was secretary to Supreme Court Associate Justice Oliver Wendell Holmes (1911–12), then practiced as a lawyer in Philadelphia. He was first chairman of the National Labor Relations Board (1934) and a strong defender of the Tennessee Valley Authority and other New Deal programs. Solicitor general (1940–41) and attorney general (1941–45) of the U.S.A., he was chief U.S. representative at the Nuremberg war crimes trials. In addition to several books on the law and his autobiography, he wrote one novel, *Llanfear Pattern* (1927).

Biddle, James (1783–1848) naval officer; born in Philadelphia. He joined the navy in 1800 and served in the Tripolitan War and the War of 1812. By leaving a lead plate at the mouth of the Columbia River (1818) he claimed the Oregon Territory for the U.S.A. He helped to negotiate the first treaty between the U.S.A. and China (1846).

Biddle, Nicholas (1786–1844) writer, banker, statesman; born in Philadelphia. A brilliant student and writer, he entered the University of Pennsylvania at age 10; by age 18, he was serving as secretary to the U.S. Minister to France. He returned to the U.S.A. in 1807 and became a lawyer. He wrote part of the *History of the Expedition of Captains Lewis and Clark* (1810–12) but gave the project away when he was elected to the state legislature. Always interested in literature, he became editor of *Port Folio* (1812), the leading literary journal at that time. Drawn to banking by his friend, James Monroe, and to the nation's need during the War of 1812, he eventually became president of the Bank of the United States (1822–36). His attempt to re-charter the Bank failed in the face of vigorous opposition from President Andrew Jackson. In retirement, he made his country home on the Delaware River, "Andalusia," into a center of refined intellectual life.

Biddle, Nicholas (1750–78) naval officer; born in Philadelphia. One of the first five captains commissioned by Congress (1775), he participated in the capture of New Providence Island, Bahamas (1776) and captured several British ships before his death in the explosion of his ship, the USS *Randolph*.

Bidwell, John (1819–1900) pioneer, public official; born in Chatauqua County, N.Y. He moved to Missouri (1839) and then to California (1841). He worked at John Sutter's fort and was active in the short-lived Bear Flag Republic (1846). He found gold on the Feather River and became California's leading rancher. He was in the U.S. House of Representatives (Unionist, Calif.; 1865–67) and was the Prohibition Party candidate for the presidency in 1892.

Bienville, Jean Baptiste le Moyne, Sieur de (1680–1768) explorer, governor; born in Montreal, French Canada. He entered the French navy at age 12 and spent most of his life in the king's service as an explorer and colonial administrator. He founded Mobile, Ala., (1710) and New Orleans (1718) and was the governor of French Louisiana (1701–13, 1717–24, 1733–43). Worn out from Indian wars, he resigned and went to Paris.

Bierce, Ambrose (Gwinett) (1842–?1914) writer, journalist, editor; born in Horse Cave Creek, Ohio. His service in the Civil War provided him with both material for some of his finest stories and the disillusioned attitude that colored much of his writing. After the war he went to San Francisco where he worked as an editor while writing for various magazines (1866–72). He then spent three years in London as an editor (1872–75) and published many stories, old and new. Returning to San Francisco as an editor and newspaper columnist (1887–96), "Bitter Bierce" became the West Coast's leading (and dictatorial) literary arbiter before going to Washington, D.C., as a correspondent for the Hearst newspapers (1897–1909). In 1906 he published the *Cynic's Word Book* (later retitled *The Devil's Dictionary*), a collection of his sardonic-ironic definitions. Never at ease in America, he set off for Mexico in 1913, apparently to find Pancho Villa, the Mexican rebel, and was last seen that December; it is not known exactly when and how Bierce died.

Bierstadt, Albert (1830–1902) painter; born in Solingen, Germany. His parents emigrated to New Bedford, Mass., (1832). After study in Düsseldorf and Rome (1853–57), he returned to America and took part in a survey expedition to the American West; the results were panoramic landscapes such as *The Rocky Mountains* (1863), and *Looking Down Yosemite Valley* (1865). Working mainly in his New York City studio, he was highly regarded in America and Europe until his approach was eclipsed by newer styles. His reputation, however, has recently enjoyed a revival.

Big Foot (b. Si Tanka) (also known as Spotted Elk) (?1825–90) Minneconjou Teton Sioux chief; born in northern Great Plains. One of the first Sioux to raise a corn crop on the Cheyenne River, he traveled to Washington, D.C., as a tribal delegate and worked to establish schools throughout the Sioux territory. He was among those massacred at Wounded Knee in December 1890.

Bigelow, Erastus (Brigham) (1814–79) inventor, engineer; born in West Boylston, Mass. He worked in a cotton mill as a boy and invented a hand loom for weaving webbing. He founded several companies to produce quilts and other items. In the 1840s he developed looms for weaving carpets, the basis for the company long synonymous with American quality carpeting.

Bigelow, Henry B. (Bryant) (1879–1967) oceanographer; born in Boston, Mass. He served Harvard as a professor of zoology and curator of its Museum of Comparative Zoology (1905–50). His committee on the importance of marine research led to the creation of the Woods Hole Oceanographic Institute, Cape Cod (1930). An advocate of keeping oceanography viable by the constant influx of new ideas, Bigelow gained international fame for his research on jellyfish, sharks, and rays.

Bigelow, Jacob (1786–1879) physician, botanist; born in Massachusetts. He took a medical degree at the University of Pennsylvania, then practiced in Boston where he became a professor of *materia medica* at Harvard Medical School (1815–55). Interested in the medical uses of plants, he was the first American botanist to systematize knowledge of New England flora in his *Florula Bostoniensis* (1814). He helped prepare the first *American Pharmacopoeia* (1820) and his *Discourse on Self-Limited Diseases* (1835) was one of the most influential medical books of his era. A progressive influence, he opposed bloodletting and indiscriminate drug dosing. In 1831 he founded Mt. Auburn Cemetery in Cambridge as a public health measure. He was also interested in what he was among the first to popularize as "technology"; he invented a process for reproducing colored plates for his book, *American Medical Botany* (1817–20), and was appointed Rumford Professor of the application of science to useful arts at Harvard College (1816–27).

Biggers, Earl Derr (1884–1933) writer; born in Warren, Ohio. He was a Harvard-educated Boston journalist who achieved widespread popularity with his mystery novel, *Seven Keys to Baldpate* (1913) (adapted for a successful play). His enduring fame, however, rests on his creation of the Hawaiian detective Charlie Chan, the patient, aphoristic hero of six novels beginning with *The House Without a Key* (1925). Chan was popularized through countless comics, radio programs, and films.

Biggs, Hermann M. (1859–1923) physician; born in Trumansburg, N.Y. He was a professor at New York City's Bellevue Medical College and served both city and state as a public health official. He organized the department of pathology and bacteriology at the New York City Health Department (1892) and introduced new bacteriological methods. He introduced diphtheria antitoxin to the United States (1894) and formulated policies aimed at preventing the spread of tuberculosis.

Bikel, Theodore (1924–) actor, singer; born in Vienna, Austria. He emigrated to Palestine in his teens, acted in plays, then went to London where he studied acting and appeared on stage. He came to the U.S.A. in 1954, made his New York stage debut (1955), and a few movies before he was cast as the original Georg von Trapp in Rodgers and Hammerstein's *The Sound of Music* (1959). An American citizen from 1961, he appeared in revivals of such musicals as *Fiddler on the Roof* (1964) and *Zorba* (1968) and played character parts in many movies. He also enjoyed a career as a folksinger-guitarist, noted especially for his renditions of Russian folk and gypsy songs.

Bilbo, Theodore Gilmore (1877–1947) U.S. senator; born in Juniper Grove, Miss. He served as the Democratic governor of Mississippi (1916–20, 1928–32). Popular among the state's poor rural whites, he was a supporter of economic populism and white supremacy. He served in the U.S. Senate (1935–47), where he was a staunch supporter of the New Deal as well as an outspoken racist; he became notorious for his filibustering against legislation aiding African-Americans, instead calling for their deportation to Africa.

Bill W. See WILSON, BILL.

Billings, Frederick (1823–90) lawyer, railroad executive; born in Royalton, Vt. A University of Vermont graduate, he went to California in the gold rush of 1849, and, opening a law office instead of prospecting, became a prominent and powerful San Francisco attorney. An early shareholder in the Northern Pacific Railroad, he raised the capital necessary to complete the road during a term as president (1879–81). He used some of his substantial fortune to build churches in Woodstock, Vt., and the eponymous Billings, Mont.

Billings, John Shaw (1838–1913) surgeon, librarian; born in Switzerland County, Ind. After taking his M.D. from the Medical College of Ohio in 1860, he served as a medical officer with the Union army (1862–64). He then went to the surgeon general's department in Washington, D.C., where he stayed for 30 years (1864–94). While doing research, he was struck by how inadequate the surgeon general's library was; he enlarged it from 600 books in 1865 to more than 50,000 by 1873, and, with Dr. Robert Fletcher, published a 16-volume *Index Catalogue* (1880–95) of the library. In 1873 he was appointed medical adviser for Johns Hopkins Hospital (Baltimore), which he helped found. He was also interested in preventive medicine and was an original member of the American Public Health Association (1872). Because of the work he had done with the surgeon general's library, he was invited to New York City to help consolidate the privately established Astor, Lenox and Tilden Libraries that form the nucleus of the New York Public Library, and he spent his final years at this task (1896–1913).

Billings, Josh See SHAW, HENRY WHEELER.

Billings, William (1746–1800) composer; born in Boston, Mass. Originally a tanner, he studied music on his own and became one of the earliest professional musicians in the Colonies. After publishing his first collection of church music, the *New England Psalm Singer* of 1770 (engraved by Paul Revere), he pursued in Boston a career of composing, reforming church music, and starting musical ensembles, all endeavors that considerably improved New England musical life. His anthems were primitive in technique but vigorous and individual in sound. He founded the continent's first singing class in Stoughton, Mass., (1774) and the first church choir as well. His "Chester," with its text "Let tyrants shake their iron rod . . . New England's God forever reigns," became a favorite of Revolutionary troops and remains his best-known work. Despite his prominence, he was never able to make an adequate living and he died in abject poverty.

Billington, James H. (Hadley) (1929–) historian; born in Bryn Mawr, Pa. Deeply attracted to Russian culture and intellectual life, he earned his Ph.D. on a Rhodes scholarship (1953) and served in the U.S. Army (1953–56) before teaching at Harvard and Princeton. He published three significant books on Russia, including *Icon and Axe: An Interpretive History of Russian Culture* (1966). He was director of the Woodrow Wilson International Center for Scholars (1973–87) and then became the 14th Librarian of Congress in 1987.

Billy the Kid See BONNEY, WILLIAM H.

Binford, Lewis R. (Roberts) (1930–) anthropologist, archaeologist; born in Norfolk, Va. A faculty member of the University of New Mexico (1970), Binford pioneered the anthropologically-oriented "new archaeology," using quantifiable data to study evolutionary processes in Navajo, Eskimo, and Australian aboriginal cultures. His books include *Nunamiut Ethnoarchaeology* (1978), *In Pursuit of the Past* (1983), and *Debating Archaeology* (1989).

Bingham, George Caleb (1811–79) painter; born in Augusta

County, Va. His family moved to Missouri (1819), and he painted scenes from the frontier life surrounding him. Representative examples of his work include *The Fur Traders Descending the Missouri* (1845), and *The Trappers Return* (1851). He was often involved in politics, and his painting, *The County Election* (1851–52) is one of many works reflecting this interest. After studying at Düsseldorf (1856–59), he became an art professor at the University of Missouri (1877). From then on the quality of his work declined.

Bingham, Hiram (1789–1869) missionary; born in Bennington, Vt. He was a missionary to the people of the Sandwich Islands (Hawaii) from 1819–40. He learned the Hawaiian language, devised a 12-letter alphabet and, with others, translated the Bible into Hawaiian.

Bingham, Hiram (1875–1956) explorer, U.S. senator; born in Honolulu, Hawaii (son of an American missionary). Having taken a Ph.D. in South American history, he concentrated on exploring Latin and South America through the early 1920s while teaching at Yale (1907–24). He is noted for discovering the Inca ruins of Machu Picchu (1911) and for writing the first book on Bolivar's march across the northern coast of South America (1909). Earning his pilots wings (1917), he was chief of the Air Personnel Division of the Air Service in Washington during World War I, serving in the same position for the Allied Expeditionary Forces in France. As a senator from Connecticut (Rep., 1924–32) he served on the President's Aircraft Board (1925) and drafted the Air Commerce Act (1926), the first attempt at federal regulation of civil aviation. He later became a director of banks and corporations and president of the National Aeronautic Association (1928–34). Becoming ever more conservative over the years, he headed the Loyalty Review Board of the Civil Service Commission (1951–53) and forced the dismissal of many government employees.

Bingham, Millicent (Todd) (1880–1968) geographer, litterateur; born in Washington, D.C. Even before taking her Ph.D. at Harvard (1923), she had traveled widely (her father, David Peck Todd, was a prominent astronomer whose work took him abroad), published *Peru, Land of Contrasts* (1914), and translated Blanchard's *Geography of France* (1919). Her interest in urban geography later led to her translation of Vidal de la Blanche's *Principles of Human Geography* (1926). After her marriage to the noted psychologist, Walter Van Dyke Bingham (1920), she spent summers on a family-owned island in Maine where, in 1936, they allowed the Audubon Society to establish the first camp for adult conservation leaders. Meanwhile, her mother, Mabel Loomis Todd, had long since taken the lead in publishing the poetry and letters of Emily Dickinson (with whose brother, William Austin, she had carried on a secret affair); in the 1930s, Millicent Bingham shifted her interest to the life and work of Dickinson, and became an authority on her, publishing *Ancestors' Brocades: The Literary Debut of Emily Dickinson* in 1945.

Bingham, William (1752–1804) banker, U.S. senator; born in Philadelphia. He made a fortune in trade and privateering. He founded (1781) and directed the Bank of North America. He founded Binghamton, N.Y., and was president of the Philadelphia and Lancaster Turnpike Corporation. He was a U.S. senator (1795–1801). His wife, Anne Willing Bingham, a leader in Philadelphia society, frequently entertained George Washington.

Binney, Horace (1780–1875) lawyer; born in Philadelphia. For nearly 30 years he was leader of the Pennsylvania bar, and he held several offices, including a term in the U.S. House of Representatives (Whig, Pa.; 1833–35). His two great cases were *Lyle* v. *Richards* (1823) on real property, and *Vidal* v. *Philadelphia* (1844) on the Girard trust, argued against Daniel Webster. He later wrote legal and historical works.

Binns, Charles Fergus (1857–1934) ceramist; born in Worcester, England. After founding a ceramics laboratory at the Royal Worcester porcelain works, he emigrated to Trenton, N.J. (1897), to head a technical school. In 1900 he became first director of what later became the New York State College of Ceramics at Alfred University. Known for his exquisitely glazed stonewares, he was influential as an educator of leading ceramics teachers.

Birch, (Albert) Francis (1903–) geophysicist; born in Washington, D.C. His studies of elasticity of rocks and minerals at high pressures and temperatures contributed extensively to knowledge of the composition of the earth. His proposal (1940) that the earth's innermost core is not liquid, but consists mainly of solid crystalline iron, was confirmed in 1971. Birch became emeritus professor of geology at Harvard University (1974).

Birch, William Russell (1775–1834) engraver; born in Warwickshire, England. He emigrated to Philadelphia (1794), painted miniatures, and became famous for his line engravings as in his series, *Views of Philadelphia* (1798–1800). Later he created etchings of the county seats of the United States (1808).

Birchall, Frederick Thomas (1868–1955) journalist; born in Warrington, England. He rose in the ranks to acting managing editor of the *New York Times* (1926–31); later, as director of the *Times* European news service (1931–41), he perceptively covered Hitler's rise, earning a 1934 Pulitzer Prize.

Bird, Junius (Bouton) (1907–82) archaeologist; born in Rye, N.Y. He rose from field assistant to curator of South American archaeology at the American Museum of Natural History (1931–73), becoming an authority on early cultures of the Western Hemisphere, especially pre-Columbian textiles. His important discoveries include paleo-Indian and mammal remains in southern Chile (1934–37) and textile fragments at Huaca Prieta, Peru (1946–47).

Bird, Larry (Joe) (1956–) basketball player; born in French Lick, Ind. A college player of the year at Indiana State University (1979), he joined the Boston Celtics in 1979 and was a perennial All-NBA (National Basketball Association) first team selection at forward. He led the Celtics to three NBA championships (1981, 1984, 1986), and three times was named the league Most Valuable Player (1984–86). After playing on the 1992 Olympics "dream team," he retired from professional basketball due to recurrent back problems.

Birdsell, J. B. (Joseph Benjamin) (1908–) physical anthropologist born in South Bend, Ind. A professor at the University of California: Los Angeles (1947–75), his long-term research in Australia led to his trihybrid theory (1967) that Australian aborigines derive from three separate circumpacific populations.

Birdseye, Clarence ("Bob") (1886–1956) inventor, food processor; born in Brooklyn, N.Y. He was interested in taxidermy as a child, and he took a cooking course in high school. After briefly attending Amherst College, he worked as a field naturalist for the Biological Service of the U.S. Department of Agriculture (1910–12) before going to Labrador where he engaged in the fur trade (1912–17). Observing how well the natives preserved fish and other foods by freezing them, he experimented with the quick-freezing of foods in the harsh winters there. Back in Gloucester, Mass., he perfected his quick-freezing and packaging process in the 1920s, but it would be the 1940s before the name Birds Eye became a household word through the frozen food firm that he established (in 1927), the General Foods Company.

Birk, Roger Emil (1930–) banker; born in St. Cloud, Minn. He launched a successful career in finance after graduating from St. John's University (New York City) in 1952. President and director of the Federal National Mortgage Association, he became chairman emeritus of the brokerage house Merrill, Lynch & Company and held directorships for a number of major corporations, including Mutual of America.

Birkhoff, Garrett (1911–) mathematician; born in Princeton, N.J. He taught at Harvard (1936–81), and was a National Academy of Sciences member and consultant to General Motors, the Rand Corporation, and Los Alamos Science Lab. His specialties included modern algebra, fluid mechanics, numerical methods, reactor theory, differential equations, and history of mathematics.

Birkhoff, George David (1884–1944) mathematician; born in Oversiel, Mich. A noted Harvard teacher (1912–39) and president of the American Mathematical Society (1925), he focused on differential equations and celestial mechanics, proving Poincaré's "last geometric theorem." He also launched a new era in the theory of dynamical systems, stimulating major advances in topology and global analysis. His geometry work remains standard for today's high school students, and a lifelong interest in music and the arts culminated in his book *Aesthetic Measure* (1933).

Birney, James Gillespie (1792–1857) abolitionist, lawyer, author; born in Danville, Ky. Son of rich slaveholders, he started out as a lawyer and state legislator in Kentucky and then Alabama. Opposition to slavery led him to sell his plantation and most of its slaves; by 1832 he was an agent in the American Colonization Society, but he soon moved from advocating resettlement of slaves to abolitionism. After freeing his last slaves he helped found the Kentucky Anti-Slavery Society (1835) and he attacked slavery as coeditor (with Gamaliel Bailey), of the *Cincinnati Philanthropist* (1836–37). Often harassed for his views, he was indicted for harboring a fugitive slave (1837) but was acquitted. He moved to New York City in 1837 to serve as executive secretary of the Anti-Slavery Society. Birney ran twice for president as a candidate of antislavery parties (1840, 1844). In 1842 he moved to Michigan, attracted by the cheap land; after being severely injured in a riding accident (1845), he settled in an abolitionists' compound in New Jersey.

Bischoff, Elmer (1916–91) painter, teacher; born in Berkeley, Calif. He taught painting at the San Francisco Art Institute (1946–52; 1956–63), and at the University of California: Berkeley (1965–85). A typical example of his work is *Woman With Dark Blue Sky* (1959).

Bishop, Elizabeth (1911–79) poet, writer; born in Worcester, Mass. She graduated from Vassar College (B.A. 1934), traveled widely, was the Consultant in Poetry, Library of Congress (1949–50), spent many years in Brazil (1951–c. 1972), and taught at Harvard (1970–79). She is known for her meditative and personal poetry, as seen in the collection, *North and South – A Cold Spring* (1955).

Bishop, Errett (1928–83) mathematician; born in Newton, Kans. He taught at Berkeley (1954–65) and at the University of California (1965–83). He specialized in the theory of functions of several complex variables, the theory of uniform algebras, and functional analysis.

Bishop, Isabel (m. Wolff) (1902–88) painter; born in Cincinnati, Ohio. She studied at the Arts Students League (1920) with Max Weber. Considered a humanist, she portrayed the people and life of the streets of New York City where she lived. Many of her works have an ethereal, mysterious quality such as, *Men and Girls Walking* (1970), and *Variations on the Theme of Walking* (1979).

Bishop, J. (John) Michael (1936–) virologist; born in York, Pa. After his internship and residency at Massachusetts General Hospital, Boston (1962–64), he performed virology research at the National Institutes of Health (1964–68). He joined the University of California: San Francisco (1968), and became director of the G. W. Hooper Research Foundation (1981). He and colleague Harold E. Varmus received the 1989 Nobel Prize in physiology for their work, begun in the mid-1970s, which demonstrated that external agents, such as viruses or mutagens, may transform a cell's normal genes into cancer-generating oncogenes.

Bishop, John Peale (1892–1944) poet, writer; born in Charles Town, W.Va. He studied at Princeton (1913–17) and published his first book of poetry, *Green Fruit* (1917), before serving in the army (1917–19). After working as managing editor for *Vanity Fair* (1920–22), he traveled in Europe (1922–24), settled in France, and became friends with English and American expatriate writers. He returned to America (1933) and settled in South Chatham, Mass. (1937). He wrote novels, short stories, and literary criticism, but is best known for his lyric poetry as in *The Collected Poems of John Peale Bishop* (1948).

Bishop, William (Howard) (1885–1952) religious leader; born in Washington, D.C. Ordained in the Baltimore archdiocese (1915), he founded the first Catholic diocesan Rural Life Conference (1925), headed the national Rural Life Conference (1928–33), and won approval to found the Glenmary Home Missioners, for pastoral work in sparsely Catholic rural areas (1937).

Bissell, George Henry (1821–84) oilman; born in Hanover, N.H. After graduating from Dartmouth, he settled in New Orleans (1864), working as a journalist and school administrator while studying law at Jefferson College. Ill health forced a return north and he was admitted to the New York bar in 1853. In 1854, after seeing samples of petroleum from Oil Creek, Pa., he and his law partner, J. G. Eveleth, formed the first oil company in the U.S.A., the Pennsylvania Rock Oil Co. A pioneer in boring for oil with the technique used for artesian wells – with "Colonel" Edward Drake supervising the work on site – he became wealthy from his investments in oil-rich lands and spent his later years promoting the use of petroleum.

Bitter, Francis (1902–67) physicist; born in Weehawken, N.J. He taught at the Massachusetts Institute of Technology

(1934–60), and was concurrently a commander in the U.S. Naval Reserves (1943–51). He made significant contributions to the fields of ferromagnetism, nuclear structure, and optics. During the 1930s he invented the Bitter electromagnet, a water-cooled solenoid that produced the first sustained powerful magnetic field.

Bitter, Karl (Theodore Francis) (1867–1915) sculptor; born in Vienna, Austria. He emigrated to New York City (1889), worked with the architect, Richard Morris, and became known for the bronze doors of Trinity Church, New York City (1891–94). He established a studio in Weehawkin, N.J., (1896), and was sculpture director for several American expositions.

Bitzer, (Johann Gottlob Wilhelm) Billy (1872–1944) cinematographer; born in Roxbury, Mass. A former silversmith, he joined and became cameraman of the company that was to become Biograph in 1894. In 1908, he began his association with D. W. Griffith, photographing most of his films until 1920. Some of the best movies photographed by this master innovator were *The New York Hat* (1912), *The Birth of a Nation* (1915), *Intolerance* (1916), and *Broken Blossoms* (1919).

Bjerknes, Jacob (Aall Bonnevie) (1897–1975) meteorologist; born in Stockholm, Sweden. Son of the famous Norwegian meteorologist Vilhelm Bjerknes, Jacob was instrumental in the development of weather prediction in the United States. With his father, he established weather observation stations in Norway during World War I and developed the famous Bergen Institute in Norway. He was visiting the University of California: Los Angeles (UCLA) in 1940 when Hitler invaded Norway, preventing his return home. He joined the faculty of UCLA and became a naturalized citizen in 1946. Bjerknes was instrumental in introducing the concept of weather fronts to United States' forecasters. With phenomenal insight, Bjerknes was able to describe cyclones and the development and dissipation of warm and cold fronts, thus laying the foundation necessary for accurate weather prediction. In the 1950s, his research turned to the ocean. He described the "Niño" effect from the Pacific Ocean and persuaded scientists of the importance of studying the ocean and atmosphere as a single, highly interactive system.

Bjorken, James D. (1934–) physicist; born in Chicago, Ill. He taught and performed research at Stanford (1960–79), moved to the Fermi National Accelerator Laboratory (1979–90), then returned to Stanford (1991). He made major advances in quantum mechanics and studies of quark behavior and was a prolific contributor to professional journals and conferences.

Black Elk (b. Ekhaka Sapa) (1863–1950) Oglala Sioux mystic/medicine man; born near the Little Powder River in present-day Montana or Wyoming. Returning with Sitting Bull from Canadian exile, he traveled with Buffalo Bill's Wild West Show. In 1932 he dictated his autobiography, which provided great insight into Sioux religious beliefs.

Black, Harold Stephen (1898–1983) electrical engineer, inventor; born in Leominster, Mass. After graduating from Worcester Polytechnic Institute in 1921 he went to work for Western Electric, where after six years of persistent research he solved the problem of distortion in telephone communications with the invention of a negative feedback amplifier. His later research centered on developing a negative feedback system for the blind and deaf.

Black Hawk (b. Makataimeshekiakiak) (1767–1838) Sauk and Fox war chief; born in present-day Illinois. A fierce opponent of the spread of white settlers, he attempted to form a pan-Indian alliance to repossess ancestral lands but was defeated in what was called the "Black Hawk War" (1832). Released from prison in 1833, he toured several eastern cities and dictated his autobiography.

Black, Hugo (LaFayette) (1886–1971) Supreme Court justice; born in Harlan, Ala. As a senator from Alabama (Dem.; 1927–37) he supported the policies of President Franklin Roosevelt, who appointed him to the U.S. Supreme Court. Soon after he took his seat, it was revealed that he had once belonged to the Ku Klux Klan; he explained it as a youthful indiscretion and went on to serve one of the longest terms (1937–71). He was noted for holding "absolutely" to the Constitution, especially to the rights set forth in the First Amendment.

Black, Jeremiah (Sullivan) (1810–83) judge, cabinet officer; born in Stony Creek, Pa. Apprenticed to a lawyer in 1827, he was admitted to the Pennsylvania bar in 1830. After 15 years as a judge on the Pennsylvania courts – including the Pennsylvania Supreme Court – he served President James Buchanan as U.S. attorney general (1857–60), defending federal laws and the Democratic Party. In the secession crisis that followed Lincoln's election as president in November 1860, Buchanan appointed Black secretary of state (December 17, 1860–March 4, 1861) and he struggled in vain to maintain the union. He antagonized so many in Congress that the Senate refused to confirm his appointment to the Supreme Court. Always rather temperamental and eccentric, he became despondent as the Civil War spread, but back in Pennsylvania after 1861 he regained fame and fortune in California land cases. Opposed to Lincoln's disregard of civil rights during the war, he was one of President Andrew Johnson's legal advisers during his impeachment. He spent his last years engaging in various public controversies and in trying to regulate the railroads and corporations in his home state of Pennsylvania.

Black Kettle (b. Moketavato) (?1803–68) Southern Cheyenne peace chief; born near the Black Hills in present-day South Dakota. Despite his attempts at accommodation, his band was massacred at Sand Creek, Colo., in 1864. He continued to seek peace but was killed with his tribe in the Washita Valley, Okla., in 1868.

Blackburn, Joseph (?1700–after 1765) painter. It is believed he lived in Boston and Portsmouth, New Hampshire (c. 1750–65). During that time he painted portraits, such as the documented canvas, *Mrs. Nathaniel Barrell* (1762).

Blackburn, Joseph (Clay Styles) (1838–1918) U.S. representative/senator; born in Woodford County, Ky. A Confederate war veteran, he served in the U.S. House of Representatives (Dem., Ky.; 1875–85) and the U.S. Senate (1885–97). He also served as governor of the Panama Canal Zone (1907–09).

Blackmun, Harry A. (Andrew) (1908–) Supreme Court justice; born in Nashville, Ill. He practiced and taught law before President Eisenhower appointed him to the U.S. court of appeals (1959–70); President Nixon appointed him to the U.S. Supreme Court (1970–94), where he became known for his anti-absolutist interpretations, especially of

First Amendment rights. Generally a moderate, his reasoning and writing underlay one of the nation's greatest controversies, the 1973 *Roe v. Wade* decision that guaranteed the right to an abortion.

Blackmur, R. P. (Richard Palmer) (1904–65) literary critic, poet; born in Springfield, Mass. Self-educated, he became a prominent 1920s–1930s New Critic of modern literature, later writing involuted and difficult essays on critical theory. He also published three volumes of poems.

Blackstone, Harry (b. Harry Boughton) (1885–1965) magician; born in Chicago. In a career that began in vaudeville in 1904 and continued on to television in the 1960s, he enjoyed his greatest success touring with a full evening magic show (1920–50). Although he featured elaborate "effects" magic – a floating lightball, a vanishing birdcage – he was also adept at sleight-of-hand and card tricks, all abetted by his distinguished looks and bearing.

Blackwell, Antoinette Louisa Brown (1825–1921) Congregational minister, author, feminist; born in Henrietta, N.Y. Inspired by evangelical revivals, she enrolled at Oberlin College, eventually studying theology, but as a woman was barred from a theology degree. After lecturing on women's rights and occasionally preaching at progressive churches, she was allowed ordination by the First Congregational Church (1853), becoming the first woman minister in an established Protestant denomination, but she soon resigned to become a Unitarian. Married in 1854, she raised a large family but also taught and wrote, especially on behalf of women's rights. From 1908 to 1915 she was pastor of a Unitarian church in New Jersey.

Blackwell, Betty Talbot (?1905–85) editor; born in New York City. As longtime editor-in-chief of *Mademoiselle* magazine (1937–71), she helped bring the world of high fashion to a mass audience.

Blackwell, David H. (Harold) (1919–   ) statistician; born in Centralia, Ill. This noted African-American educator, a National Academy of Sciences member (1965), taught at the Berkeley Department of Statistics (1954) where he chaired the department (1957–61). He was a Rosenwald Fellow at Princeton's Institute for Advanced Study (1941–42), president of the Institute of Mathematical Statistics (1955), and a faculty research lecturer at the University of California (1971), specializing in Markoff chains and sequential analysis.

Blackwell, Elizabeth (1821–1910) physician; born in Counterslip, near Bristol, England. The first woman of modern times to graduate in medicine, she fostered personal hygiene as a means of moral reform and combatting disease. Sister of pioneering physician Emily Blackwell, she emigrated with her family to America at the age of 11 (1832). Educated along with her brothers, introduced to abolitionist and reform activities, she chose to study medicine rather than marry, always maintaining an interest in the arts. She was turned down for entrance by most major medical schools of the time, but was eventually accepted at Geneva College in New York state. Initial student ostracization turned to respect, a pattern repeated throughout her pioneering medical career. After receiving her degree (1849), she was barred from practice in most European and American hospitals (1850–58). Setting up private practice in New York City, she lectured on public hygiene and founded the New York Infirmary for Women and Children (1857). Lecturing in England (1858–59), she became the first female physician

listed in the Medical Register of the United Kingdom. She helped found the U.S. Sanitary Commission (1861) and founded the Women's Medical College of the New York Infirmary (1868–69). Returning to London (1871), she maintained a large practice and was named chair of gynecology at the London School of Medicine for Women (1875).

Blackwell, Emily (1826–1910) physician; born in Bristol, England. Emigrating with her family to America (1832), she was the product of a progressive education for the time and very much influenced by older sister Elizabeth Blackwell, the first woman in modern times to receive a medical degree. Although extremely shy, she followed Elizabeth into medicine. She was turned down by 11 medical schools, including Elizabeth's alma mater in Geneva, N.Y., and was forced to leave Rush Medical College in Chicago (1852) after the state medical society censured the school for admitting a woman. She eventually graduated from Western Reserve University in Cleveland (1854). She is best known for assisting Elizabeth with the development of the New York Infirmary for Women and Children. Noted for her pragmatism and administrative skills, Emily is credited with transforming a clinic into a working hospital. She was left in charge of the institution (1858) when her sister pursued opportunities overseas; later she headed the hospital's medical school (1869), serving as dean and professor of gynecology (1869–99). A believer in coeducation, she disbanded the Women's Medical College when Cornell University Medical College admitted women (1898). Like her sister she was active in the social purity movement and never married.

Blaik, Earl (Henry) "Red" (1897–1989) football coach; born in Detroit, Mich. After coaching seven successful seasons at Dartmouth (1934–40), where he introduced tougher discipline than was customary for Ivy League teams, he went on to West Point. As Army coach (1941–58) he produced two national champions (1944–45) and 13 of his teams were ranked in the top 20 by wire service polls.

Blaikie, William (1843–1904) physical trainer; born in New York City. One of America's pioneer physical educators, he wrote the best-selling *How to Get Strong and How to Stay So* (1879).

Blaine, James Gillespie (1830–93) U.S. representative/senator, secretary of state; born in West Brownsville, Pa. The son of a Scotch-Irish businessman, he taught at the Pennsylvania Institute for the Blind (1852–54), earning his law degree at night. Moving to Maine, where his wife was from, he became an editor of the *Kennebec Journal* and then the *Portland Advertiser*. He championed the new Republican Party in 1854 and became one of its founding members. He served in the state legislature (1858–62), and went to the U.S. House of Representatives (1863–76); he supported black suffrage but opposed the Radical Republicans' harsh reconstruction measures. As Speaker of the House (1869–75) he allied with Western "Half-Breed" Republicans like James Garfield, alienating the powerful New Yorker Roscoe Conkling. Dubbed "The Plumed Knight" because of his image as a crusading liberal, in 1876 he was the leading candidate for the Republican nomination, but he lost out when the Democrats charged him with railroad grafting and Conkling supported Rutherford Hayes. Moving up to the U.S. Senate (1876–81), he lost the 1880 presidential nomination to Garfield, whom he served as secretary of state in

1881. Blaine stayed in Washington to write *Twenty Years of Congress.* The Republican presidential candidate in 1884, he lost to Grover Cleveland. Choosing not to run in 1888, he became President Benjamin Harrison's secretary of state (1889–92) championing Pan Americanism and the annexation of Hawaii.

Blair, Emily Jane Newell (1877–1951) political activist, writer; born in Japon, Mont. She attended college, married, and published fiction before beginning her political career as a suffragist (1914). After rising to national vice-chairman of the Democratic Party (1922–28), she worked to elect women to public office. A prolific writer, she was also appointed to several high-level governmental posts in the 1930s and 1940s.

Blair, Francis Preston (1791–1876) journalist; born in Abingdon, Va. A founding editor of the Washington, D.C. *Globe,* a Democratic party paper, in 1830, he was a member of President Andrew Jackson's "kitchen cabinet" of advisers. For a time he also published the *Congressional Globe,* a predecessor of the *Congressional Record.* Opposed to the extension of slavery, he helped organize the Republican Party and became a close adviser to Abraham Lincoln.

Blair, John (1732–1800) Supreme Court justice; born in Williamsburg, Va. He attended the Constitutional Convention (1787) and signed the U.S. Constitution. Known for his support of a strong national government, President Washington appointed him to the first U.S. Supreme Court (1789–96).

Blake, Eugene Carson (1906–85) Protestant clergyman; born in St. Louis, Mo. Educated at Princeton, he held pastorates in New York and California before becoming a senior administrator of the Presbyterian Church U.S.A. From 1967–72 he was general secretary of the World Council of Churches, in which role he advanced his dream of a "truly reformed, truly catholic, and truly evangelical" church.

Blake, (James Hubert) Eubie (1883–1983) composer, pianist; born in Baltimore, Md. He studied piano as a child and sang outside saloons in a vocal quartet at age 12. While a teenager he began playing piano at bordellos, traveling in minstrel shows, and playing in fine hotels in Baltimore and Atlantic City. He published his first song in 1914; in 1915 he met Noble Sissle, who soon became his lyricist; in 1916 they began their long collaboration, producing many classic ragtime hits and performing as the "The Dixie Duo." They also wrote their first Broadway show, the famous all-black musical, *Shuffle Along* (1921) (including "I'm Just Wild About Harry"). For the next decades, Blake continued his career, writing songs and musicals, sometimes with Sissle, sometimes with other lyricists; Andy Razaf was the lyricist of Blake's signature song "Memories of You" (1930). He led orchestras, toured during World War II, and helped found the Negro Actors Guild; he and Sissle brought an updated *Shuffle Along of 1952* to Broadway, but it flopped. By now Blake had slipped into retirement and was largely forgotten until his music was discovered in the late 1960s and he found himself honored as an American original. The musical *Eubie* (1978) was an anthology of his songs. He performed in public almost until his death.

Blakelock, Ralph (Albert) (1847–1919) painter; born in New York City. He studied medicine but became a landscape painter during the 1860s. He was committed to an insane asylum in 1899. After his release (1916), he never painted again. His moody and evocative pictures, such as *Indian Encampment* (c. 1870), and *Moonlight* (1886) have ensured his reputation.

Blakeslee, Albert Francis (1874–1954) botanist; born in Geneseo, N.Y. After teaching in several American institutions and serving on collecting expeditions in Venezuela (1903) and Europe (1904–06), he became a professor at the Connecticut Agricultural College (1907–15). He then joined the Carnegie Station for Experimental Evolution, Cold Spring Harbor, N.Y. (1912–41, director 1936–41). He moved to Columbia University (1940–52), then Smith College (1942–54). Blakeslee used the chemical colchicine to induce polyploidy (multiplication of the number of chromosomes) to produce extra-large flowers, thus enabling commercial production of seeds for giant blooms. He also investigated sexuality in the common bread mold and mutations in Jimson weed, and he studied the inheritance of taste and smell.

Blakeslee, George H. (Hubbard) (1871–1954) professor, diplomat; born in Geneseo, N.Y. He taught history at Clark University (1903–44). His diplomatic career (1921–46) included participation in the Lytton Commission (1932), which recommended economic sanctions against Japan, and membership in the American delegation to the Far Eastern Advisory Commission (1945–46). He assisted in formulating U.S. policy in Japan after World War II.

Blakeslee, Howard (Walter) (1880–1952) journalist, science writer; born in New Dungeness, Washington Territory. Expelled from the University of Michigan for his student reporting – he later received an honorary degree (1935) – he eventually became a reporter and science writer for the Associated Press (1928–52). He and four colleagues received the 1937 Pulitzer Prize for local reporting. His long career in journalism (1901–52) was highlighted by his pioneering reporting of the growth of science in American life. He reported on the atomic bomb tests at Bikini (1946) and wrote *Atomic Progress, The Hydrogen Race* (1951).

Blakey, (Arthur) Art (1919–90) jazz musician; born in Pittsburgh, Pa. An influential drummer, he performed with Billy Eckstine's big band between 1944–47 and freelanced on numerous recordings. From 1954 until his death, he led the Jazz Messengers, a combo he consistently renewed with outstanding young players. He was a proselytizer for jazz and a leading exponent of "hard bop," an explosive style characterized by a strong backbeat and bluesy lyricism.

Blakey, G. Robert (1936–) lawyer, professor; born in Burlington, N.C. Longtime law professor at Notre Dame (1964–74, 1980), he was chief counsel to the Select House Committee on Assassinations (1977–79). As a member of various commissions charged with reforming federal and state laws, he was the primary architect of wiretap provisions in the Crime Control Act of 1968 and the Racketeer Influenced and Corrupt Organizations (RICO) provision of the Crime Control Act of 1970.

Blalock, Alfred (1899–1964) surgeon, educator; born in Culloden, Ga. From 1925 to 1941 he was head of the surgery department at Vanderbilt University's school of medicine. He conducted experiments to establish that "shock" was the result of drastic loss of blood from the vascular system (1928–30). This led to the practice of treating wounded soldiers with blood substitutes and plasma. He became chairman of the Department of Surgery at Johns Hopkins (1941); there he and his colleagues performed the first total removal of the thymus gland; and in 1944, following through on the idea of Helen Taussig, he performed the first successful heart surgery on a "blue baby."

Blanchard, (Felix Anthony, Jr.) "Doc" (1924–) football player; born in McColl, S.C. A powerful fullback, he paired with halfback Glenn Davis to lead Army to undefeated seasons (1944–46), while earning All-America honors and the 1945 Heisman Trophy.

Blanchard, Kenneth H. (Hartley) (1939–) author, lecturer; born in Orange, N.J. After ten years as a professor of organizational behavior, he founded his own San Diego–based training and development company (1978). His *One-Minute Manager* (with Spencer Johnson, 1982) inaugurated a series of best-selling books and seminars promoting managerial effectiveness through the mastery of a few quickly acquired skills.

Blanchard, Thomas (1788–1864) inventor; born in Sutton, Mass. A clever tinkerer from early age, he devised an automatic tack-making machine and a lathe for turning gun barrels. Working at the U.S. Arsenal in Springfield, Mass., in 1818 he built a lathe that could automatically produce precision interchangeable parts – an essential step in the direction of mass production. He later designed a steam automobile (1825) and several types of steamboats.

Blanda, George (Frederick) (1927–) football player; born in Youngwood, Pa. After an unheralded college career at the University of Kentucky, he became an outstanding professional quarterback and deadly-accurate place-kicker for Chicago, Houston, and Oakland, playing longer than any player had ever before. In a 26-season pro career (1949–58, 1960–75), he passed for 236 touchdowns and scored an all-time league record 2,002 points, all but 54 by kicking.

Blanton, Ray (1930–) governor; born in Hardin County, Tenn. A construction company executive, he served in the U.S. House of Representatives (Dem., Tenn.; 1969–71). As governor of Tennessee (1975–79) he expanded industry and tourism, but left office early after allegedly selling pardons to 52 prisoners. In 1981 he was sentenced to three years in prison for selling liquor licenses while in office.

Blashfield, Edwin (Howland) (1848–1936) painter; born in New York City. He studied in Paris (1867), and returned to America to paint large murals, such as the one commissioned for the Chicago World's Fair of 1893.

Blass, Bill (William Ralph) (1922–) fashion designer; born in Fort Wayne, Ind. He began his New York fashion career in 1946, joining Maurice Rentner Ltd. (1959) (after 1970, Bill Blass Ltd.). Winner of eight Coty Awards, Blass created high-priced, beautifully cut and tailored women's wear, notable for its inventive combinations of patterns and textures.

Blatch, Harriet Eaton (b. Stanton) (1856–1940) women's rights activist; born in Seneca Falls, N.Y. (daughter of Elizabeth Cady Stanton). A graduate of Vassar College (1878), she began to help her mother and Susan B. Anthony compile their *History of Woman Suffrage* (eventually 6 vols. 1881–1922). Upon marrying an Englishman, she lived in England (1882–92) where she became involved in women's suffrage and other progressive causes and came to know many of the leading British socialists. When she and her husband moved to the U.S.A., she launched her own suffrage organization, the Equality League of Self-Supporting Women (1907); in 1908 it was renamed the Women's Political Union in

America and in 1916 it merged with the Congressional Union. During World War I she directed her efforts to organizing women in support of America's role in the war; after the war she wrote *A Woman's Point of View* (1920), in which she called on women to work to prevent any future wars. She continued to support liberal causes including an Equal Rights Amendment for women and the League of Nations, and in the 1920s she ran unsuccessfully as a political candidate for the Socialist Party. Her bluntness, militancy, and insistence on her own goals often left her on the fringe of the mainstream movements.

Blatchford, Samuel (1820–93) Supreme Court justice; born in New York City. Appointed by President Grant to a federal district court (1867), he rose to circuit judge in 1872. President Arthur appointed him to the U.S. Supreme Court (1882–93) where he was known for his expertise in patent law.

Blau, Peter M. (Michael) (1918–) sociologist; born in Vienna, Austria. He emigrated to the U.S.A. in 1939. A Columbia University Ph.D., he taught at the University of Chicago (1953–70), Columbia (1977–88), and the University of North Carolina (1970–77, 1988). A specialist in organizational and social structure, particularly bureaucracy, he wrote among other works *Exchange and Power in Social Life* (1964) and *The American Occupational Structure* (1967).

Blegen, Carl (William) (1887–1971) archaeologist; born in Minneapolis, Minn. He was educated at the University of Minnesota (B.A. 1907) and Yale (Ph.D. 1920). He taught at the University of Cincinnati (1927–57), where he was an emeritus (1957–71). He was director of the American School of Classical Studies during the difficult years of 1948–49. His major excavations included Troy and Acrocorinth, but he is best known for his discovery of the Palace of Nestor at Pylos, with its many Linear B tablets, in the Peloponnese (1939). His *Troy and the Trojans* (1963), although dated, remains a good introduction to the subject. He is buried in Athens.

Blewett, John P. (Paul) (1910–) physicist; born in Toronto, Ontario, Canada. He came to the U.S.A. in 1932, then joined General Electric's research laboratories in Schenectady, N.Y. (1937–46). He was a department head at Brookhaven National Laboratories until his retirement (1947–78). He was an innovative designer of particle accelerators and made major contributions to nuclear fusion.

Bliss, Daniel (1823–1916) Protestant missionary, educator; born in Georgia, Vt. He grew up on farms in Vermont and Ohio, graduated from Amherst in 1852, attended Andover Theological Seminary, and in 1855, went to Syria as a missionary. He founded the Syrian Protestant College (now American University), Beirut, Lebanon, in 1866. President and treasurer of the college until 1902, he continued to teach classes and deliver an occasional sermon after his retirement.

Bliss, Howard Sweetser (1860–1920) missionary, educator; born in Suq al Gharb, Syria. His father, Daniel Bliss (1823–1916) was the founder and the president (1866–1902) of Syrian Protestant College (later renamed the American University of Beirut). Howard Bliss graduated from Union Theological Seminary (1887) and was a Congregational minister in Montclair, N.J. (1894–1902). He succeeded his father as president of Syrian Protestant College (1903–20). During his tenure he increased the size of the non-Christian student body. Through frankness and diplomacy he kept the college intact during World War I. He died in New Hampshire and was buried near Mount Monadnock.

Bliss, Lizzie Plummer (1864–1931) art collector; born in Boston, Mass. Her wealthy family moved to New York City (1866), and she was educated privately. She began her collection of modern American and French art in 1907. A patron of the Armory Show (1913), she was one of the founders of the Museum of Modern Art (1929), and bequeathed much of her collection to that institution.

Bliss, Tasker (Howard) (1853–1930) soldier; born in Lewisburg, Pa. He served as military attaché to Spain, took part in the Puerto Rico campaign (1898), was army chief of staff during the great buildup for World War I (1917–19), and was a delegate to the Versailles Peace Conference (1919).

Blitzstein, Marc (1905–64) composer; born in Philadelphia. A pianist and composer as a youth, in 1924 he enrolled in the newly established Curtis Institute to study composition. He went on to study with Nadia Boulanger in Paris and Schoenberg in Berlin, where he encountered the socially-conscious works of Brecht and Weill. In 1928, he gave his first major performance in New York as composer-pianist (his Sonata for Piano), but in the 1930s he became even more attracted to writing music with explicit social themes and began to focus his efforts on writing for the musical theater. His best known work, *The Cradle Will Rock* (1937), fulfilled this aim and he became a member of the Communist Party (1938–49). After serving in the U.S. Air Force in World War II – which inspired his *Airborne Symphony* (1946) – he returned to writing works for the musical stage; the most ambitious of these was *Regina* (1949), but none of them achieved the success of his adaptation of the Brecht/Weill *Threepenny Opera*. At the time of his death – he was murdered while on holiday in Martinique – he was working on a commission from the Metropolitan Opera, his *Sacco and Vanzetti* (begun in the early 1930s).

Bloch, Ernest (1880–1959) composer; born in Geneva, Switzerland. He studied around Europe before his opera *Macbeth* appeared, to critical grousing over its modernism, in Paris (1910). After teaching in Geneva he emigrated to the U.S.A. in 1917, where he held several teaching posts (his remarkable roster of students included Antheil and Sessions) and gained an international reputation as a composer. He spent most of the 1930s in Switzerland. His works, in a rich late-Romantic vein with touches of modernism and often reflecting his Jewish heritage, include five string quartets and *Schelomo* for cello and orchestra (1915).

Bloch, Felix (1905–83) physicist; born in Zurich, Switzerland. He made pioneering contributions to studies of superconductivity and magnetism while affiliated with several European universities. After Hitler's regime caused his emigration to the U.S.A. (1934), he went to Stanford (1934–41), investigated uranium isotopes for the Manhattan Project (1941–44), performed counter-radar research for Harvard (1944–45), then returned to Stanford (1945–71). He was the first director general of the European Commission for Nuclear Research (CERN) in Geneva (1954–55). He was awarded the 1952 Nobel Prize (with E. M. Purcell) for developing nuclear magnetic resonance, a technique that revolutionized analytical chemistry and medical diagnostics. Several concepts and features dealing with superconductivity have been named after Bloch.

Bloch, Henry Wollman (1922–) **and Richard A.** (1926–) accountants; born in Kansas City, Mo. Sons of a lawyer whose own father came west as a scout for Kit Carson, the brothers founded the tax preparation firm H & R Block in Kansas City in 1955, opening a branch in New York City the following year. By the mid-1980s the firm, with 9,000 offices in North America, prepared 10 percent of all U.S. and Canadian tax returns.

Bloch, Herbert (1911–) classicist; born in Berlin, Germany. He received his D.Lett. in ancient history at the University of Rome (1935) and taught at Harvard (1947–82), where he was Pope Professor of Latin (1973–82). He published widely in epigraphy and ancient and medieval history and historiography and was perhaps best known for his work on Ostia and Monte Cassino.

Bloch, Konrad E. (Emil) (1912–) biochemist; born in Neisse, Germany. When Hitler became chancellor of Germany, Bloch, a Jew, moved to Switzerland and pursued his work with phospholipids in tubercle bacilli. He then came to Columbia University for graduate studies (1936), and joined Columbia's faculty (1938–46). He relocated to the University of Chicago (1946–54), then became Harvard's first professor of biochemistry (1954–82). He shared the 1964 Nobel Prize for physiology for discovering the 36-step biosynthesis of cholesterol and determining both its role in animal cells and its implication in arteriosclerosis. His later research investigated the enzymes involved in fatty acid metabolism.

Block, Herbert (Lawrence) (1909–) editorial cartoonist; born in Chicago. His talent won him a scholarship at the Chicago Art Institute when he was only 12. In 1929 he began his professional life as an editorial cartoonist at the *Chicago Daily News,* signing himself "Herblock." In 1933 he moved to Cleveland to work for the Newspaper Enterprise Association; he won the Pulitzer Prize in 1942. During World War II, he worked in the army's information and education division (1943–46) and his cartoons were famous with soldiers and civilians alike. After the war, he joined the staff of the *Washington Post* (1946), which syndicated his cartoons coast-to-coast, making him the country's best-known editorial cartoonist. He was a strong critic of Senator Joseph McCarthy and won a second Pulitzer in 1954; a third Pulitzer came in 1979. Many collections of his cartoons were published and his works hang in the Corcoran Gallery and the National Gallery of Art in Washington.

Block, Martin (1903–67) radio disk jockey; born in Los Angeles. A traveling salesman while still a teenager, he first worked in radio in Tijuana, Mexico (1931). Hired by WNEW in New York City (1934–54), he was standing by to announce the latest news about the Hauptmann trial, when he played music to divert listeners, explaining it came from "the Make Believe Ballroom." An immediate success, he helped popularize many vocalists including Frank Sinatra and Dinah Shore. With his mellifluous voice, he was a master salesman for sponsors and record companies who vied for him to introduce their products and records. He later broadcast from New York City's WABC (1954–60), leaving for New York City's WOR radio where he produced the *Martin Block Hall of Fame* show.

Bloembergen, Nicolaas (1920–) physicist; born in Dordrecht, Netherlands. After completing his university education at the State University of Leiden in his homeland, he came to the United States in 1946 to take up a post as a research assistant at Harvard. He returned to the State University of Leiden to take his Ph.D. (1947–48) but then came back to Harvard as a junior fellow, joining the faculty in 1951 and becoming the Gordon McKay professor of applied physics in 1951, then the Rumford Professor in 1974, and finally the Gerhard Gade University Professor in 1980. He received numerous honors for his work, including the National Medal of Science (1974). He shared the 1981 Nobel Prize in physics with the American Arthur Schawlow and the Swedish professor Kai Siegbahn. Bloembergen and Schawlow were cited for their contribution to the development of laser spectroscopy; Bloembergen's work in the field of nonlinear optics was especially crucial in explaining and then averting the problems in producing high intensity laser beams.

Bloom, Allan David (1936–92) political scientist, author; born in Indianapolis, Ind. Educated at the University of Chicago, he joined the Chicago liberal arts faculty in 1955, moved on to Cornell and the University of Toronto (1963–79), and returned to Chicago in 1979 to teach political philosophy. He remained an obscure translator of Plato until the publication of his *Closing of the American Mind* (1987), a neoconservative polemic against what he perceived as the politicization of academia and the decline of liberal education in the Western tradition.

Bloom, Harold (1930–) literary critic, educator; born in New York City. He earned a Ph.D. at Yale, where he joined the faculty in 1955. Bloom overturned the humanistic view of literary tradition in *The Anxiety of Influence* (1973). Consistently arguing against deconstruction and most other recent schools of criticism, he developed the theory of "antithetical criticism," which claims that literature itself is an act of criticism. Consistently provocative, his work includes 20 books on the Romantic and modern poets, psychoanalysis, philosophy, and theology.

Bloom, Sol (1870–1949) U.S. representative; born in Pekin, Ill. A self-made man, he learned accounting in a brush factory and supervised construction of the Midway Plaisance at the Chicago World Exposition in 1893. He set up music departments in stores (1849–1910) before going into construction in New York City and becoming a Democratic congressman at age 53 (1923–49). As chairman of the Foreign Affairs Committee (1939–49), he sponsored the Lend Lease Act and the Marshall Plan.

Bloomer, Amelia (b. Jenks) (1818–94) reformer; born in Homer, N.Y. She wrote on current affairs for her husband's newspaper before founding and editing *Lily* (1849–55), a temperance journal that, under the influence of Elizabeth Cady Stanton, also championed women's rights. In *Lily,* her public defense of women's adopting a daring outfit of full trousers under a short skirt became a national cause célèbre, and the costume was nicknamed "bloomers." After she moved to Iowa (1855), her local activism was partly responsible for that state's 1873 equal rights legislation.

Bloomfield, Leonard (1887–1949) linguist; born in Chicago, Ill. After teaching at several universities, he became professor of linguistics at Yale (1940–46), already one of the most influential linguists of the century. He was one of the first to advance linguistics as an empirical discipline, set out first in *An Introduction to the Study of Language* (1914). He developed a method of team-teaching languages and his work on Tagalog and Algonquian languages led to his independent discovery of the phonemic principle that organizes the sound system of a language. He promoted linguistics as a key approach to understanding human behavior and his most important work in this regard, *Language* (1933), is still widely used and studied.

Bloomingdale, Alfred S. (1916–82) corporate executive; born in New York City (grandson of Lyman G. Bloomingdale). He produced plays and movies before founding (1950) a credit card firm which soon merged with Diners' Club. As Diners' Club president (1955–70) and chairman (1964–70), he helped to promote the rapid postwar growth of the credit card industry. He developed Florida and California real estate in his later years.

Bloor, Ella (Reeve) ("Mother Bloor") (1862–1951) radical, labor organizer, feminist; born in Staten Island, N.Y. Married in 1881, she raised a large family while becoming a women's rights activist. After a divorce (1896), she studied at the University of Pennsylvania, remarried, and became increasingly devoted to labor and left-wing causes, joining the Socialist Party in 1902. She adopted the pen name Mrs. Richard Bloor (1906) while doing investigative reporting for Upton Sinclair. After the Russian Revolution she helped found the American Communist Party and later became a longtime member of its Central Committee (1932–48). While electioneering for party candidates in the Dakotas she married her third husband (1932); afterward she traveled in the Midwest organizing farmers and leading farmers' strikes. She lectured widely and wrote several books, including *Women in the Soviet Union* (1938), and a 1940 autobiography, *We Are Many.* In 1938 she ran unsuccessfully for governor of Pennsylvania.

Blough, Roger M. (Miles) (1904–85) lawyer, corporate executive; born in Riverside, Pa. He left a Wall Street law firm to join U.S. Steel (1942–69). As chairman and CEO (1955–69) he directed the world's largest steel manufacturer and the U.S.A.'s third-largest corporation. In 1962 his proposal to increase steel prices after a wage-increase settlement led to a famous confrontation with President John Kennedy. He returned to law practice in later years.

Blount, William (1749–1800) governor, U.S. senator; born in Bertie County, N.C. After fighting in the American Revolution, he served in the North Carolina legislature and then represented North Carolina in the Continental Congress (1782–87). Appointed governor of Tennessee territory in 1790, he became one of the new state of Tennessee's first U.S. senators (1796–97). He was expelled from office when he became implicated in a conspiracy with the British to attack Louisiana and Florida, which then belonged to Spain. After his impeachment was dismissed, he was elected to the Tennessee senate.

Bludhorn, Charles G. (1926–83) corporate executive; born in Vienna, Austria. Educated in England, he emigrated to the U.S.A. in 1942 and started a New York import-export business (1949). In 1957 he bought the first of a number of companies that later merged into Gulf & Western Industries (1958). As chairman of the board and CEO (1960–83) he forged Gulf & Western into a multibillion-dollar conglomerate through diversified acquisitions ranging from New Jersey Zinc to Paramount Pictures.

Bluemner, Oscar (1867–1938) painter, architect; born in Hanover, Germany. He emigrated to America in 1892. A practicing architect (1894–1912), he later devoted his life to painting. His highly individual coloration and his cubist landscapes, using geometric forms, became his trademarks, as may be seen in *Old Canal Port* (1914), and *Composition* (1931).

Blum, Robert (Frederick) (1875–1903) painter; born in Cincinnati, Ohio. He lived in New York City but traveled frequently. He was commissioned to illustrate Sir Edwin Arnold's *Japonica* (1890–91), and the influence of Japan on his work is seen in his major painting, *The Ameya* (1892).

Blumberg, Baruch S. (Samuel) (1925–) epidemiologist; born in New York City. He worked and performed research in New York City hospitals (1951–55), then became a biochemist at Oxford University (1955–57). He moved to the National Institutes of Health (1957–64), where he investigated protein variations in human populations from around the world. In 1963, while studying antibodies in the serum of multitransfused blood recipients, he discovered the "Australian" antigen, which proved to be associated with the hepatitis B virus. This finding led to hepatitis B screening programs by blood banks, and won Blumberg one-half the 1976 Nobel Prize for physiology. At the Fox Chase Cancer Center in Philadelphia (1964) he developed a hepatitis B vaccine (1982) and presented evidence that this disease may lead to liver cancer. While continuing at the Fox Chase Center, he concurrently became a professor at the University of Pennsylvania (1977), clinical professor of epidemiology at the University of Washington: Seattle (1983–89) and Master at Balliol College, Oxford (1989).

Blume, Judy (b. Sussman) (1938–) writer; born in Elizabeth, N.J. She graduated from New York University (1960), married in 1959, and was divorced in 1976. Bored with suburban life, she developed a creative outlet in writing and illustrating children's stories. After many rejection slips, she published *Are You There God? It's Me, Margaret* (1970), *Blubber* (1974), and *Tiger Eyes* (1981) and several other novels for teenagers, that broke new ground in their frank treatment of sensitive issues. She moved into adult fiction with *Wifey* (1978), which graphically described the constraints of sexual roles within a traditional marriage.

Blume, Peter (1906–92) painter; born in Smorgon, Russia. He emigrated in 1911, and after various occupations, became an artist who utilized bizarre imagery in a surrealistic manner. He worked in Italy as an intermittent artist in residence at the American Academy of Rome (1956–73), and thereafter was based in Sherman, Connecticut. His most famous work is *The Eternal City* (1934–37), a denunciation of Fascism in Italy.

Blumenthal, Joseph (1897–1990) printer, book designer, publisher; born in New York City. As head of the Spiral Press, which he founded in 1926, he printed fine editions for the Morgan Library, The Metropolitan Museum of Art, the Grolier Club, and others; he was known especially for his special editions of the poems of Robert Frost. He designed the Spiral typeface, re-named Emerson when it became available commercially. After closing the Spiral Press in 1971, he organized a famous exhibit at the Morgan Library, "The Art of the Printed Book" (1973), and wrote several books on this subject.

Blumer, Herbert (1900–87) sociologist; born in St. Louis, Mo. He earned a Ph.D. at the University of Chicago, where he taught (1925–52) before joining the faculty of the University of California: Berkeley (1952–75). He edited the *American Journal of Sociology* (1940–52). His areas of interest are indicated by his books such as *Movies and Conduct* (1933), *Movies, Delinquency, and Crime* (1933), and *Industrialization as an Agent of Social Change* (1990).

Blunt, Katharine (1876–1954) nutritionist, educator; born in Philadelphia. A University of Chicago Ph.D., she developed a home economics curriculum while on the faculty there (1913–29) and conducted important research on the role of ultraviolet light and vitamin D in nutrition. As president of Connecticut College for Women (1929–43), she strengthened the college academically and extended the curriculum to politics, economics, and business.

Bly, Nellie See SEAMAN, ELIZABETH.

Bly, Robert (Elwood) (1926–) poet, writer; born in Madison, Minn. He studied at St. Olaf College, Minn. (1946–47), Harvard (B.A. 1950), University of Iowa (M.A. 1956), eventually settling in Moose Lake, Minn. He was a magazine founder and editor, and is known for translations as well as for his own poetry. His *Iron John: A Book About Men* (1990), a controversial work propounding his views on the need for modern men to rediscover their essential maleness, unexpectedly if temporarily turned Bly into a cross between a minstrel and a guru as he toured the land strumming his harp and explaining his ideas.

Blythe, David (Gilmour) (1815–65) painter; born in East Liverpool, Ohio. Based in Pittsburgh, Pa., he is known for his genre paintings that satirize everyday life on city streets, as seen in *The Post Office* (c. 1863).

Boas, Franz (1858–1942) cultural anthropologist; born in Minden, Germany. A merchant's son, raised in a liberal environment, he became interested in natural history as a boy and studied geography at the universities of Heidelberg, Bonn, and Kiel. On his first field trip, to the Canadian Arctic (1883–84), he studied Eskimo tribes; from then on his intellectual interests turned to ethnology and anthropology. He emigrated to the United States in 1886, studied the Indian tribes of the Pacific Northwest, and worked in Massachusetts and Illinois before obtaining a post as a lecturer at Columbia University in New York City. Promoted to full professor in 1899, he trained several generations of anthropologists. As a scholar, his emphasis was to draw on ethnology, physical anthropology, archaeology, and linguistics, and to collect data about cultures, especially those passing from the scene. He and his students established new and more complex concepts of culture and race, as outlined in his collection of papers, *Race, Language and Culture* (1940). With the rise of Hitler in Germany he began to speak out against racism and intolerance, and he wrote and lectured widely in opposition to the Nazis. His other works include *The Mind of Primitive Man* (1911) and *Anthropology and Modern Life* (1928).

Bochco, Steven (1943–) television writer, producer; born in New York City. He worked as a screenwriter and story editor for shows like *Colombo* during the 1970s. He created *Hill Street Blues* (1981–87) and *LA Law* (1986) for the National Broadcasting Company, both dramatic series with ensemble acting and overlapping plots. Under contract with ABC, he introduced *Doogie Howser, MD* in 1989 and the controversial *NYPD Blue* in 1993.

Bocher, Maxime (1867–1918) mathematician; born in Boston, Mass. A Harvard University professor (1904–18), this National Academy of Science member concentrated most on differential equations. He served on the editorial staff of

Annals of Mathematics (1896–1900, 1901–07). As president of the American Mathematical Society (1909–10), he also edited the society's *Transactions* (1908–9, 1911–13).

Bochner, Salomon (1899–1982) mathematician; born in Cracow, Austria-Hungary. Fleeing from Nazism, he settled at Princeton University (1933). A pioneer in abstract harmonic analysis, his research preceded the theory of distributions. A noted teacher, he chaired the Rice University Mathematics Department (1969–76) and founded an interdisciplinary institute for the history of ideas.

Bodenheim, Maxwell (b. Bodenheimer) (1893–1954) poet, writer; born in Hermanville, Miss. He lived in Chicago from 1902; after being expelled from high school (1908), he mixed with the literary figures of Chicago before moving to New York City (1915). He published *Minna and Myself* (1918), the first of his 11 volumes of poetry; he also published novels, including *Replenishing Jessica* (1925), which were considered cynical and indecent. As the editor of *Others,* a poetry magazine, he is credited with discovering Hart Crane. Having lived most of his life as a bohemian and alcoholic, he and his third wife were murdered in Greenwich Village.

Boeing, William (Edward) (1881–1956) aircraft manufacturer; born in Detroit, Mich. A lumberman, in 1916 he formed the Pacific Aero Products Company. In 1927 he organized what would become United Aircraft and Transport. In 1934 the federal government divided United Aircraft and Transport into Boeing Aircraft (a major manufacturer of military and civilian aircraft), United Aircraft, and United Airlines, and he retired from business.

Boesky, Ivan (1937–) financier; born in Detroit, Mich. Son of a Russian immigrant milkman who became a restaurateur, he studied law and worked as a tax accountant before moving into securities analysis, forming his own firm in 1975. Credited with (or blamed for) pioneering the junk bond market (later a symbol of the excesses of the 1980s), he had become one of Wall Street's most successful arbitragers when he admitted to insider trading charges in 1986. Fined $100 million, he served time in prison before being given parole for good behavior in 1990, but by 1993 he was claiming to be penniless and was living off alimony from his ex-wife.

Bogan, Louise (1897–1970) poet, writer; born in Livermore Falls, Maine. She studied at Boston University (1915–16), moved to New York City, and served as poetry editor of the *New Yorker* (1931–69). She was an influential critic, as in *Achievement in American Poetry 1900–1950* (1951), and a noted lyrical poet, as in *The Blue Estuaries* (1968).

Bogardus, James (1800–74) inventor; born in Catskill, N.Y. After serving an apprenticeship in watchmaking, he patented the ring-flyer for cotton-spinning machinery (1830), made engraving machines in England (1836–39), and invented the first dry gas meter (patented, 1834). He erected the world's first cast-iron building – a five-story factory at the corner of Center and Duane Streets in New York City (1848) – and later erected many other iron buildings.

Bogart, Humphrey (DeForest) (1899–1957) film actor; born in New York (husband of Lauren Bacall). After serving with the Navy during World War I, he became a stage manager and walk-on actor before making his film debut in 1930. He played the lone wolf – cynical but heroic – for many years, finally winning an Academy Award for *The African Queen*

(1952); but his archetypal role was in *Casablanca* (1942). He died of cancer.

Boggs, Thomas Hale, Sr. (1914–73) U.S. representative; born in Long Beach, Miss. A graduate of Tulane, he practiced law before going to the U.S. House of Representatives (Dem., La.; 1941–43) and served in the Potomac River Naval Command during World War II. He returned to Congress (1947–73) and chaired the Special Committee on Campaign Expenditures in 1951. He became majority whip (1961–71) and was majority leader of the Democrats when his plane disappeared over Alaska.

Bogle, John Clifton (1929–) investment banker; born in Montclair, N.J. He graduated from Princeton in 1951 and attended the Wharton School of Business at the University of Pennsylvania. Joining the Wellington Management Company of Philadelphia in 1951, he rose to become president and chief executive officer from 1967–74. He later founded the Vanguard Group, a marketer of low-cost mutual funds, in Valley Forge, Pa. He served as a director of several investment companies and contributed numerous articles to professional financial journals.

Bogorad, Lawrence (1921–) plant physiologist; born in Tashkent, Uzbekistan. Brought to the U.S.A. in 1923, he taught at the University of Chicago (1948–67), then moved to Harvard (1967). A pioneer in the study of chloroplasts (chlorophyll-containing plant cell organelles), his early studies of chlorophyll synthesis in green algae (1950s) contributed to investigations of the biosynthesis of compounds with similar structure, such as hemoglobin and the cytochromes. He performed major research on accessory plant pigments (1960s) and explored the genetics of chloroplast formation (1960s).

Bohannan, Paul J. (James) (1920–) anthropologist; born in Lincoln, Neb. He taught at Northwestern University (1959–75) and ended his career at the University of Southern California (1982–87). He published studies of African legal and economic anthropology (*Africa and Africans* (with Philip Curtin, 1964, revised 1971), *Tiv Economy* (with L. Bohannan, 1968)) and western middle-class concepts of marriage, family, and divorce (*Divorce and After* (1970)).

Bohlen, Charles E. (Eustis) (1904–74) diplomat; born in Clayton, N.Y. He was the premier Sovietologist in the State Department from 1931. He was liaison officer between the State Department and the White House (1944–46), ambassador to the Soviet Union (1953–57), the Philippines (1957–59), and France (1962–68). He played an important role in several international conferences, including Yalta in 1945.

Bohrod, Aaron (1907–92) painter; born in Chicago. A student of John Sloan in New York, he taught at the University of Wisconsin: Madison (1948–73), where he settled, and was influenced by the 1930s Depression, as in *Landscape Near Chicago* (1934).

Bok, Bart (1906–83) astronomer; born in Hoorn, Holland. He came to Harvard College on a fellowship in 1929 and stayed until he became director of the Mt. Stromio Observatory in Australia (1957–66). At the University of Arizona, he directed the Steward Observatory (1966–70). His classic *The Milky Way* coauthored with his wife, Priscilla Bok, went through many editions.

Bok, Derek (Curtis) (1930–) university president; born in Bryn Mawr, Pa. He taught labor and antitrust law at Harvard Law School, where he was also a reformist dean (1968–71), before becoming president of Harvard University (1971–90). Bok's books include *Beyond the Ivory Tower* (1982), *Higher Learning* (1986) and *Universities and the Future of America* (1990).

Bok, Edward William (1863–1930) editor, author; born in den Helder, the Netherlands. Emigrating to Brooklyn, N.Y., with his struggling family in 1870, he quit school at age 13 to help out, doing office work, writing reviews for the *Brooklyn Eagle,* and eventually editing a church magazine. In 1884, with a partner, he started a syndicate that sold women's features to newspapers; he also wrote and distributed literary pieces of his own. In 1889 he was hired by Cyrus H. K. Curtis (whose daughter he later married) as editor of the *Ladies' Home Journal.* During his 30-year tenure he acquired top authors, from Rudyard Kipling to Theodore Roosevelt, and developed innovative features and services to readers, displaying an intuitive sense for his audience's interests. By 1900 the *Ladies' Home Journal* had the highest circulation of any U.S. magazine. Having accumulated a personal fortune, Bok retired in 1919, devoting himself to writing and philanthropy. His autobiography, *The Americanization of Edward Bok* (1920), was a best-seller and won a Pulitzer Prize.

Boker, George Henry (1823–90) playwright, poet, diplomat; born in Philadelphia. His romantic tragedies were among the few such plays to be successful. Most popular was his *Francesca da Rimini* (1855). He also served as envoy to Turkey and Russia.

Boland, Patrick Joseph (1880–1942) U.S. representative; born in Scranton, Pa. A carpenter and general contractor with Boland Brothers in Scranton, he served in local offices (1905–19) before going to the U.S. House of Representatives (Dem., Pa.; 1931–42), where he became majority whip.

Bolcom, William (Eden) (1938–) composer, pianist; born in Seattle, Wash. After studies in the U.S.A. and Paris, he taught at the University of Michigan from 1973. For many years he also accompanied his wife, the soprano Joan Morris, in performances of American popular songs from all periods. His compositions favored a wildly eclectic style that incorporated popular elements. His 12 New Etudes for Piano won the Pulitzer Prize for music in 1988.

Bolden, (Charles) Buddy (1877–1931) jazz musician; born in New Orleans, La. Subject of myth and fable as the legendary originator of jazz and the "first jazz trumpeter," all that is certain of Bolden's musical career is that he was immensely popular in turn-of-the-20th-century New Orleans, played the cornet, and led bands. He may have contributed toward standardizing the New Orleans jazz ensemble and repertoire; no recordings remain of his work. He was institutionalized in the Jackson Mental Institute from 1907 until the end of his life.

Bolger, (Raymond Wallace) Ray (1904–87) actor, dancer; born in Boston. A rubber-legged dancer who appeared on stage and television, he was the wobbly scarecrow in *The Wizard of Oz* (1939) and received numerous theatre awards including a Tony in 1949.

Bolinger, Dwight (Le Merton) (1907–92) linguist; born in Topeka, Kans. A professor of English and Spanish languages and literature at the Universities of Southern California (1944–60) and Colorado (1960–73) and emeritus professor at Harvard (1973), he advanced numerous linguistic theories, including several on the interconnectedness of intonation and gesture in speech. Among his more popular writings on English is *Language – The Loaded Weapon* (1980).

Bolling, Richard (Walker) (1916–) U.S. representative; born in New York City. A graduate of Vanderbilt University, he worked in educational administration before joining the army (1941–46), fought in the Pacific, and served in Japan under General MacArthur. Awarded a Bronze Star, he was veterans' advisor to the University of Kansas before going to the U.S. House of Representatives (Dem., Mo.; 1949–83). He chaired the Select Committee on Committees and the Committee on Rules, retiring to Crumpton, Md.

Bolt, Bruce A. (Alan) (1930–) seismologist; born in Largs, Australia. Director of the seismographic station of the University of California: Berkeley since his immigration in 1963, he related elastic wave dynamics to earthquakes and nuclear explosions.

Bolton, Henry Carrington (1843–1903) chemist, educator, bibliographer; born in New York City. He taught chemistry at Trinity College (1877–87), then retired to pursue his numerous interests, which included the action of organic acids on minerals. He was a founder of the American Folklore Society and he published papers on that subject as well as on alchemy and the history of chemistry.

Bolton, Herbert (Eugene) (1870–1953) historian; born in Wilton, Wis. This leading historian of Spanish America taught at the University of California: Berkeley (1911–40). A prolific author, he is best known for his explorations in the southwestern U.S.A., his extensive archival research and a massive published guide to Mexican archives (1913), and the "Bolton theory," a controversial hemispheric view of American history.

Bonaparte, Charles Joseph (1851–1921) lawyer, reformer; born in Baltimore, Md. (great-nephew of the Emperor Napoleon I). He was born into wealth but imbued with a sense of high-minded social responsibility by his New England-born mother. He practiced law in Baltimore, where he fought rampant corruption in both the city and state government, and founded the Civil Service Reform Association of Maryland and the National Civil Service Reform League (both in 1881; he served as the latter's chairman, 1901–05). His reform activities led to a friendship with Theodore Roosevelt who, as president, appointed him secretary of the navy (1905) and then attorney general (1906–09). Although he led Roosevelt's anti-trust campaign, he was himself essentially a conservative who had no great faith in the masses. After leaving the Department of Justice, he returned to practice law in Baltimore, and was founder and president of the National Municipal League.

Bond, (Horace) Julian (1940–) civil rights activist, state legislator; born in Nashville, Tenn. His mother was a librarian and his father was a college professor who became president of Lincoln University. Julian led a life relatively sheltered from the worst of discrimination, but in 1960s, while a student at Morehouse College, following the lead of the original sit-in in Greensboro, N.C., he sat in at an Atlanta cafeteria and was arrested. In 1960 he helped to found the Student Nonviolent Coordinating Committee (SNCC) and while working with SNCC as its communications director he took a job with a new African-American owned newspaper, the *Atlantic Inquirer* (1960–61). (He dropped out of college and didn't get his B.A. from Morehouse until 1971.) Elected to the Georgia House of

Representatives in 1965, he was denied his seat because of his objections to the U.S. involvement in the Vietnam War; in 1966 the U.S. Supreme Court ruled that he must be seated; after his years there (1966–75), he served in the Georgia Senate (1975–87). He gave up his seat there to seek the Democratic nomination for the U.S. House of Representatives but lost to John Lewis; shortly thereafter a scandal broke out when his wife charged him with using cocaine and he was named in a paternity suit; he was divorced in 1989. After leaving public office he became a visiting professor at such universities as Drexel (1988–89), Harvard (1989), and American University (1991). Meanwhile he had remained active in various civil rights organizations and events; he helped found the Southern Poverty Law Center (1971); he hosted a television program, *America's Black Forum;* and later narrated the Public Broadcasting System special, *Eyes on the Prize.*

Bond, (J.) Max (Jr.) (1935–   ) architect; born in Louisville, Ky. (son of J. Max Bond). Trained at Harvard, he and Don Ryder co-founded Bond Ryder Associates (1969–90), a Harlem-based firm specializing in urban structures and Bond became a partner in Davis, Brody & Associates (1990). He became dean of the architecture school at the City College of New York (1985).

Bond, William Cranch (1789–1859) instrument-maker, astronomer; born in Portland, Maine. The first director of the Harvard College Observatory (1839–59), he equipped it from his Dorchester-parlor observatory. A donation provided for a 15-inch telescope, for which he designed the dome and chair. A pioneer in celestial photography, he discovered the seventh satellite of Saturn with son George Bond.

Bong, Richard (Ira) (1920–45) aviator; born in Superior, Wis. The greatest American fighter ace of World War II, he shot down 40 Japanese aircraft in three combat tours in the Southwest Pacific (1942–44). He was killed in the crash of an experimental P-80 jet near Los Angeles on August 6, 1945.

Bonior, David (Edward) (1945–   ) U.S. representative; born in Detroit, Mich. A Vietnam veteran and social worker before coming to Congress (Dem., Mich.; 1976), he opposed aid to the Contras in Nicaragua (1983–88); he became majority whip in 1991.

Bonner, J. T. (John Tyler) (1920–   ) developmental biologist; born in New York City. He spent his career at Princeton (1947–90), and remained active there after attaining emeritus status. He published numerous scientific articles on development of the cellular slime molds, served as editor on various scientific journals, and wrote many popular books and articles on morphogenesis and evolution.

Bonner, James (Frederick) (1910–   ) molecular biologist; born in Ansley, Nebr. He was a National Research Council fellow in Switzerland (1934–35), then joined the California Institute of Technology (1936–81). His early research on ribosomes (1950s) led to his major contributions to studies of messenger RNA. Using dormant potato buds, he demonstrated that repressed genes can be "derepressed" by removing their chromosomes' histone protein covering. He was a prolific author of scientific papers, texts on plant physiology and biochemistry, and books on the future of plant physiology and molecular biology.

Bonner, John (1643–1726) mariner, mapmaker; possibly born in London. He came to Boston around 1670. He entered the merchant trade and came to own a number of ships. Three of his vessels were used in the Puritan attack on Quebec (1690) and one was used to carry a flag of truce to Quebec (1706) and then to bring back the "redeemed captive," Reverend John Williams (1707). Bonner was the chief pilot on Admiral Walker's expedition against Canada (1711). Bonner made numerous maps of Boston harbor and the coast of North America. He married four times.

Bonner, Robert (1824–99) newspaper editor; born in Londonderry, Ireland. Emigrating in 1839, he bought the *New York Ledger* in 1851 and made it prosper, attracting articles from literary giants of the day. He was also a well-known race horse owner.

Bonneville, Benjamin Louis Eulalie de (1796–1878) soldier; born in or near Paris, France. He came to the U.S.A. in 1803 and graduated from West Point in 1815. His record of his expedition to the Green River in Wyoming (1832–35) was edited by Washington Irving and published as *The Adventures of Captain Bonneville, U.S.A., in the Rocky Mountains and the Far West.*

Bonney, William H. ("Billy the Kid") (1859–81) outlaw, murderer; born in New York City. Moving with his family to Coffeyville, Kans. (1862), Colorado, and Silver City, N.M. (1868), Bonney allegedly killed his first man at age twelve. After killing three Indians in Arizona (1876) and rampaging throughout the Southwest and Mexico, he led a faction in New Mexico's notorious "Lincoln County [cattle] War" (1878), and killed Sheriff Jim Brady. He continued killing and committing cattle theft with his followers until he was captured and sentenced to hang for Brady's death (1880). He escaped under heavy guard, killing two deputies, and remained at large until fatally shot by Sheriff Pat F. Garrett in Fort Sumner, N.M. (1881).

Bonnie and Clyde See BARROW, CLYDE.

Bonnin, Gertrude Simmons (b. Zitkala-Sa) (1876–1938) Yankton Sioux writer; born at Pine Ridge in present-day South Dakota. She taught with the Indian Service and published her first book, *Old Indian Legends,* in 1901. In 1916, she moved to Washington, D.C., to lobby for her people, and founded the National Council of American Indians in 1926. She was also an accomplished violinist.

Bontemps, Arna (Wendell) (1902–73) writer, anthologist, librarian; born in Alexandria, La. Raised in California, he took his B.A. at Pacific Union College there. He first published his poetry in 1923 in *Crisis,* the magazine of the National Association for the Advancement of Colored People, edited by W. E. B. Du Bois. His *Golgatha Is a Mountain* (1925) won the Alexander Pushkin Award. He spent most of his career as the librarian and public relations director at Fisk University in Nashville, Tenn. He also was a guest lecturer at various universities. He wrote several novels, including *God Sends Sunday* (1931) and *Black Thunder* (1936); the former was dramatized by Countee Cullen as *St. Louis Woman* (1946) and then set to music as *Blues Opera.* He edited *American Negro Poetry* and published several anthologies with Langston Hughes. (Their extensive correspondence was published in 1980.) His *Story of the Negro* (1948) won the Jane Addams Children's Book Award in 1956. He also wrote several children's books with Jack Conroy, including *Sam Patch* (1951).

Bony, Jean (1908–   ) architectural historian; born in Le Mans, France. A scholar of French and English Gothic architecture, his publications include *The English Decorated Style* (1979) and *French Gothic Architecture of the 12th and 13th Centuries* (1983). He joined the faculty of the University of California: Berkeley (1962).

Boone, Daniel (1734–1820) frontiersman; born near Reading, Pa. His parents were Quakers. He learned to hunt and trap by the age of 12. He moved with his family to North Carolina (1750–51) and in 1755 he took part in General Braddock's diasastrous campaign, where he met John Finley, a hunter who told him stories of the Kentucky wilderness. He explored in Kentucky (1767–68, 1769–71) and led the first settlers there in 1775. He founded Boonesborough, a fortified settlement. He was captured by Shawnee Indians (1778) but escaped in time to defend Boonesborough against an Indian attack. Later, his claims to large tracts of Kentucky lands were not validated and he moved to West Virginia (1788), and then to present-day Missouri (1799) where he remained until his death. He has retained his place as the archetypal American frontiersman.

Boorstin, Daniel J. (Joseph) (1914–) historian; born in Atlanta, Ga. Educated at Harvard, Oxford, and Yale (J.S.D. 1940) Universities, he taught at the University of Chicago (1944–69), became director at the National Museum of Natural History (1969–75), and librarian at the Library of Congress (1975–87; librarian emeritus, 1987). Fundamentally conservative, his Pulitzer Prize-winning trilogy *The Americans* (1958–73) reflects his preferences for people, experiences, and inventions over ideology, and his belief in history as enduring literature.

Booth, (Albert James, Jr.) "Albie" (1908–59) football player; born in New Haven, Conn. A tricky runner, adequate passer, and clever punter, "Little Boy Blue" was a legendary, 144-pound tailback for strong Yale teams (1929–31).

Booth, Edwin Thomas (1833–93) actor; born in Belair, Md. He was part of a notable theatrical family: his father, Junius Brutus Booth Sr. and his brothers Junius Brutus Booth Jr. and John Wilkes Booth were all actors, although John Wilkes Booth is best known as the assassin of Abraham Lincoln. Edwin Booth was famous for his classic roles, and became the first American actor to gain an international reputation. In 1864 he played the role of Hamlet in 100 consecutive New York City performances, a record for the time. After New York's Winter Garden was destroyed by fire, he built a new theater, where he opened in 1869 in *Romeo and Juliet* opposite Mary McVicker, who became his second wife. The theater failed and Booth went bankrupt. His own dark temperament was accentuated by family madness and tragedy. In 1918 a statue of him was put up in Gramercy Park, opposite the Players Club, Booth's former house.

Booth, (Evangeline Cory) Eva (1865–1950) Salvation Army general, social worker; born in London, England. She was one of eight children of the founders of the Salvation Army. She became a sergeant at age 15 and field commander of the Army in Canada (1896) where she worked among the Alaskan Indians. She became commander-in-chief of the Salvation Army in the U.S.A. (1904–34) and became a U.S. citizen in 1923. Her social relief efforts captured the public imagination and gained wide support for the Army. After returning to England to serve as general of the entire Salvation Army (1934–39), she retired to Hartsdale, N.Y.

Booth, George G. (1864–1949) newspaperman, philanthro-

pist; born in Toronto, Canada. The wealthy publisher of the *Detroit News,* in the mid-1920s he established the Cranbrook Academy of Art (Bloomfield Hills, Mich.), an experimental art educational community, in collaboration with Eliel Saarinen.

Booth, John Wilkes (1838–65) actor, assassin; born near Bel Air, Md. A member of the well-known Booth family of Shakespearean actors, he was a somewhat erratic, if popular actor. He had come to support slavery and the South, and as a member of a Virginia militia company, had participated in the arrest and execution of John Brown (1859). In the fall of 1864, he hatched a plot to kidnap Lincoln but the scheme failed. He then concocted the plot to assassinate Lincoln, Vice-President Andrew Johnson, and Secretary of State William Seward. Booth's co-conspirators failed with the last two, but he himself shot Lincoln in Ford's Theater (April 14, 1865) before jumping to the stage and evidently crying out, *"Sic semper tyrannis! The South is avenged!"* He was located and killed twelve days later, although it is not certain whether he was killed by his captors or died by his own hand. Rumors inevitably persisted for years that he had escaped.

Booth, Junius Brutus (1796–1852) actor; born in London, England. A success in London, he came to the U.S.A. in 1821. A handsome, eccentric man known for his tragic roles, he fathered three theatrical sons: Junius Brutus Jr., Edwin, and John Wilkes Booth.

Borah, William E. (Edgar) (1865–1940) U.S. senator; born in Fairfield, Ill. Following a celebrated legal career in Boise, Ida., he was elected to the U.S. Senate (Rep., Ida.; 1907–40). Although a supporter of many progressive causes, as chairman of the Senate Foreign Relations Committee (1924–33) he opposed U.S. entry into the League of Nations after World War I. He remained an outspoken isolationist until his death, but he was also a supporter of disarmament, of cooperation with Latin American countries, and of many of President Franklin D. Roosevelt's New Deal measures.

Borchard, Edwin Montefiore (1884–1951) professor of international law; born in New York City. He served as adviser to the U.S. delegation to the international court at the Hague and was law librarian of the U.S. Congress before becoming a professor of international law at Yale University (1917–50). His specialty was the title of his classic text, *Diplomatic Protection of Citizens Abroad* (1915). Between the world wars, he argued for U.S. neutrality on the grounds that international law could settle disputes. He opposed U.S. diplomatic activities in World War II and was suspicious of the Potsdam agreement and the Nuremburg trials. A member of the American Civil Liberties Union, he was a strong advocate for providing restitution to individuals wrongly convicted of crimes.

Borchert, John (Robert) (1918–) geographer; born in Chicago. He taught at the University of Wisconsin (1947–49) and the University of Minnesota (1949–89). His publications include "American Metropolitan Evolution" (1967), "Instability in American Metropolitan Growth" (1983), and *America's Northern Heartland* (1987). He is an authority on U.S. urban and metropolitan growth.

Bordaz, Jacques (1926–) archaeologist; born in France. He earned a Ph.D. at Columbia University and taught at New York University (1964–66) and the University of Montreal before joining the anthropology faculty of the University of Pennsylvania (1972–88). His research focused on the beginnings of village farming, technology, and the crafts of southwest Asia; he is most often associated with his excavation of an early neolithic "hunters' village," Suberde, in southwestern Turkey. Among his publications is *Tools of the Old and New Stone Age* (1970).

Borden, Gail (1801–74) surveyor, inventor; born in Norwich, N.Y. In 1822 he surveyed land in Mississippi, then joined his family at Stephen Austin's colony in Texas where he worked as the official surveyor. During the Texas war for independence from Mexico, he and his brother published the area's only newspaper; he also drew up the first topographical map of the republic and laid out the city of Galveston. Motivated by the problems of obtaining food on the frontier, in 1851 he invented a meat biscuit (pemmican), the first of his food experiments. In 1853 he traveled to New Lebanon, N.Y., to use the Shaker colony laboratory for experiments to condense milk. His patent for "a process of evaporating milk in a vacuum" was granted in 1856. In 1861 a "condensing" factory in Wassaic, N.Y., began production and the milk was used by Union soldiers. He returned to Texas to continue his experiments and was awarded a patent for concentrating juices in 1862.

Borden, Lizzie (Andrew) (1860–1927) alleged murderess; born in Fall River, Mass. She was arrested and tried for the axe-murders of her father and stepmother in 1892. Acquitted in 1893, she was socially ostracized but remained in Fall River until her death.

Borden, (Neil Hopper) Pete (1895–1980) advertising/marketing educator; born in Boulder, Colo. He earned an M.B.A. at Harvard, where he joined the business school faculty and taught advertising and marketing (1922–62). His eight books on advertising, including *The Economic Effects of Advertising* (1942), were influential in developing the fields of marketing and advertising management.

Boreman, Arthur I. (Ingram) (1823–96) governor, U.S. senator; born in Waynesburg, Pa. A Virginia lawyer opposed to secession, he led the Wheeling Convention (1861) to establish a pro-union government in West Virginia, becoming the first governor (Rep., 1863–69) of the new state. In the U.S. Senate (1869–75), he chaired the committee on the territories, returning to the law afterward.

Borge, Victor (1909–) entertainer and pianist; born in Copenhagen, Denmark. A deliciously funny performer who fled the Nazis in 1940, he used his classical training to skew serious music and performers. In 1956 he began to make regular appearances with symphony orchestras.

Borglum, (John) Gutzon (de la Mothe) (1867–1941) sculptor; born near Bear Lake, Idaho Territory. Child of Danish immigrants, he was raised throughout the West; after college he moved to California (1884) where he studied art and took up painting portraits. He met Jesse Benton Fremont, who sponsored his studies in Paris and Spain (1890–92). After working in California and London (England), he settled in New York City (1901). By then he had switched to sculpture; his *Mares of Diomedes* won a gold medal at the St. Louis Exposition in 1904 and was the first American sculpture acquired by the Metropolitan Museum of Art. He was soon winning commissions, including *The Twelve Apostles* for the Cathedral of St. John the Divine in New York City. Asked by the Daughters of the Confederacy to sculpt the head of Robert E. Lee on Stone Mountain, Georgia, he designed an ambitious ensemble portraying Confederate leaders and

hundreds of soldiers; a disagreement led to his quitting in 1924 with only a few figures finished. (The project was revived in 1960.) He had already been asked by South Dakota to carve a "shrine of democracy" there and he chose Mt. Rushmore. He began in 1927 and had finished the 60-foot head of George Washington by 1930, by which time the U.S. Congress had authorized funds. An opinionated man, he feuded with the National Parks Service over money and procedures, but no one questioned his patriotism or energy. He had practically finished the other three heads by his death (and his son, Lincoln Borglum, completed some details shortly thereafter).

Borie, Adolph Edward (1809–80) merchant, financier; born in Philadelphia. His family firm carried on an extensive trade with Mexico, the Caribbean, and the Far East. His friendship with Ulysses Grant led to his brief period as secretary of the navy (1869).

Bork, Robert H. (Heron) (1927–) legal scholar, judge; born in Pittsburgh, Pa. After briefly practicing law (1954–62), he joined the faculty of Yale Law School (1962–81) where he was known for his expertise in constitutional and antitrust law. He was U.S. solicitor general (1971–77) and acting attorney general (1973–74). He was appointed to the federal court of appeals for the District of Columbia (1982–88). President Reagan nominated him to the Supreme Court in 1987, but his conservative views led to his being rejected by a controversial Senate vote. He stepped down from the bench in 1988 to write and lecture on judicial and public policy for the American Enterprise Institute.

Borlaug, Norman (Ernest) (1914–) microbiologist, agronomist; born in Cresco, Iowa. In 1942 he directed pesticide research for E. I. DuPont Nemours and Company in Wilmington, Del. In 1944 he developed a disease-free strain of wheat for the Rockefeller Foundation and the Mexican Agricultural Ministry to remedy the severe Mexican wheat crop failures. In 1954 he crossed a Japanese dwarf wheat strain with the new Mexican strain for a higher-yield strain with a shorter stem; the seeds were distributed to Mexican farmers in 1961. From 1964–79 he directed the International Wheat Research and Production Program at the Centro Internacional de Mejoramiento de Maiz y Trigo (CIMMYT, International Maize and Wheat Improvement Center). During this period, he launched the "green revolution" for which he won the 1970 Nobel Peace Prize for "help(ing) to provide bread for a hungry world." Beginning in 1981 he was a consultant to CIMMYT. In 1984 he became a professor of international agriculture at Texas A & M University and in 1988 he became president of the Sasakawa Africa Association and leader of the Global 2000 Agricultural Programs in Africa. His books include *The Green Revolution, Peace and Humanity* (1971) and *Food Production in a Fertile, Unstable World* (1978).

Boston, Ralph (1939–) track and field athlete; born in Laurel, Miss. He medaled in the long jump in three consecutive Olympics: gold (1960), silver (1964), and bronze (1968).

Botkin, B. A. (Benjamin Albert) (1901–75) folklorist; born in Boston, Mass. He taught at the University of Oklahoma (1921–40), was folklore editor of the Federal Writers' Project (1938–39), and headed the Library of Congress folk song archive (1942–45) before becoming a freelance writer. A collector of folklore, stories, and ballads from throughout the U.S.A., he published many anthologies, including *Treasury of American Folklore* (1944) and *Lay My Burden Down* (1945), a landmark folk history of slavery.

Botta, Anne Charlotte (b. Lynch) (1815–91) writer, salon hostess; born in Bennington, Vt. A writing teacher in the 1840s, she established a New York City salon in her home where writers (including Edgar Allan Poe), editors, actors, politicians, and other prominent people would gather. She continued this salon after her 1855 marriage to the Italian scholar, Vincenzo Botta, and then after his death (when even Andrew Carnegie would show up on an evening). With her own reputation as a minor poet, she wrote *A Handbook of Universal Literature* (1860).

Bottineau, Pierre (c. 1817–95) scout; born in Minnesota. Of part Chippewa descent, he guided many expeditions during 1850–70, including a Pacific Railroad expedition (1853) and a campaign against the Sioux (1863). He was often called the "Kit Carson of the Northwest." He retired to Minnesota in 1870.

Boucicault, Dion (b. Dionysius Lardner Boursiquot) (1820–90) playwright, actor, theater manager; born in Dublin, Ireland. A versatile theatrical personality, he wrote or adapted some 130 plays, including *London Assurance* (1841) and *The Poor of New York* (1857), becoming one of the most popular playwrights of his era. Most of his plays are now forgotten, but *The Octoroon* (1860) is notable for its condemnation of slavery. He came to America in 1853, where, along with George Henry Boker and others, he worked to pass the first American Copyright Law of 1856. He was based in London from 1862–72, then returned to the U.S.A.

Boucot, Arthur James (1924–) paleontologist; born in Philadelphia. Professor of geology (1969) and zoology (1979) at Oregon State University, his research focused on Silurian and Devonian stratigraphy and invertebrate paleontology and rates of animal extinction.

Boudin, Leonard B. (Boudinov) (1912–89) lawyer, civil rights activist; born in New York City (brother-in-law of I. F. Stone). After taking his law degree from St. John's Law School (1936), he joined the law firm of his uncle, Louis (Boudinov) Boudin (1874–1952), a noted Socialist and constitutional lawyer. Specializing at first in labor law, Leonard formed a law firm of his own in the late 1940s, and then became increasingly involved in civil rights cases. He founded (1952) and was general counsel (1952–89) for the National Emergency Civil Liberties Commission. He argued more civil liberties cases before the U.S. Supreme Court than any other constitutional lawyer and won the landmark passport case, *Kent v. Dulles* (1958), establishing the right of all U.S. citizens to have a passport. Among his more celebrated clients were Daniel Ellsberg (the Pentagon Papers case), Julian Bond (denied a seat in the Georgia legislature), Dr. Spock (charged with conspiracy during the Vietnam War), and Jimmy Hoffa (banned from union activities). He also represented Cuba's interest in the U.S.A. during the Castro years, and the Central Bank of Iran during the Iran hostage crisis. He was a visiting lecturer at several major law schools. His son, Michael Boudin, became a U.S. Federal district judge, while his daughter, Kathy (Katherine) Boudin, was a member of the radical Weather Underground and was implicated in the 1970 explosion in a Greenwich Village, New York City, town house that killed three; she

vanished but was captured after participating in a 1981 robbery of an armored car in which two police officers were killed; she pleaded guilty and served almost 20 years in prison.

Boudinot, Elias (b. Galegina) (?1803–39) Cherokee writer, leader; born near Rome, Ga. The first editor of the *Cherokee Phoenix* (1828–34), he was murdered by other Cherokee for his support of Cherokee land cessions. He also wrote a novel and translated part of the Bible into Cherokee.

Boulding, Kenneth (Ewart) (1910–93) economist; born in Liverpool, England. Arriving in the U.S.A. in 1937, he taught at several colleges including the University of Michigan (1949–77) and the University of Colorado (1977). A prolific writer, his major contributions include promoting a social science approach to economics, synthesizing Keynesian and neoclassical economic theory, and work on evolutionary economics and grant economics.

Bourgeois, Louise (b. Goldwater) (1911–) sculptor, painter; born in Paris, France. She studied in Paris (1936–38), and settled in New York City (1938). She became known for her abstract sculptures, such as *The Blind Leading the Blind* (c. 1947–49), and her *Cumul* series, as seen in the marble *Blind Man's Bluff* (1984).

Bourke-White, Margaret (1904–71) photo-journalist; born in New York City. Staff photographer for *Life Magazine* (1936–69), she traveled all over the world to capture people's experiences of historical events, from Nazi camp survivors to world leaders like Gandhi.

Bourne, Randolph (Silliman) (1886–1918) essayist, literary critic; born in Bloomfield, N.J. He was congenitally de-formed (dwarfism) and did not begin college until age 23, but his intellectual range and brilliance were so developed that the same year he graduated from Columbia University (1913), he published his first collection of essays, *Youth and Life*. He traveled in Europe for a year (1913–14) where his optimism was tested by the breakout of World War I; on returning to the U.S.A. he contributed articles about general literacy and cultural issues to the *New Republic*, but his commitment to pacifism led him to publish in the more radical *Masses*. Just as his career as a writer was beginning to expand, he died during the postwar influenza epidemic.

Bouwsma, William J. (James) (1923–) historian; born in Ann Arbor, Mich. He attended Harvard University (Ph.D. 1950) and taught at the University of Illinois (1950–56), the University of California: Berkeley (1956–69), where he was also department chairman and academic vice-chancellor, and at Harvard (1969–71), returning to Berkeley (1971–91) as department chairman and professor emeritus (1991). His influential books on Renaissance history include *Culture of Renaissance Humanism* (1973) and *A Usable Past* (1990).

Bovard, Oliver Kirby (1872–1945) editor; born in or near Jacksonville, Ill. Named managing editor of the *St. Louis Post Dispatch* in 1910, he assembled a top-notch staff and produced outstanding news coverage. He resigned in 1938 after owner Joseph Pulitzer objected to his emerging socialist views.

Bow, Clara (1905–65) movie actress; born in New York City. At age 16 she won a fan magazine beauty contest and by 1922 she was making her first movie. *Mantrap* (1926) was her first major hit and she was suddenly the epitome of the Roaring Twenties, the "It Girl" (referring to her sex appeal), and her kewpie-doll appearance was imitated by thousands of young women; a 1928 poll named her America's most popular female movie star. But by 1930 she was at the center of scandals involving adultery, gambling, drink, and drugs and her career burned out as fast as it began. She married cowboy star Rex Bell in 1931, who later became lieutenant governor of Nevada, but by then she was suffering recurrent breakdowns.

Bowditch, Charles P. (Pickering) (1842–1921) businessman, archaeologist; born in Boston, Mass. A Harvard graduate, he was president of Pepperell Manufacturing Company and Massachusetts Hospital Life Insurance Company while pursuing a career as an amateur archaeologist. After 1891 he planned and financed annual Peabody Museum expeditions to Central America. He wrote a groundbreaking study of Maya hieroglyphics (1910).

Bowditch, Henry Pickering (1840–1911) physiologist; born in Boston, Mass. (grandson of Nathaniel Bowditch). After serving in the Civil War, he studied medicine at Harvard, and in Paris and Leipzig. While studying in Germany in 1871, he discovered the heart's "all or nothing" contractile property and the affect of delphinine on cardiac contractions. He returned to join the faculty of the Harvard Medical School (1871–1906). In 1885, he proved that nerve fiber cannot be tired out and he conducted experiments using curare that led to nerve-blocking during surgery.

Bowditch, Nathaniel (1773–1838) astronomer, mathematician; born in Salem, Mass. Self-taught after age ten, he worked for his father, a barrelmaker, and then in a ship's chandlery, and by age 15 had compiled an astronomical almanac. Between 1795–1803, he went to sea, serving as ship master on his last voyage. He began by correcting errors in the writings of others, especially John Hamilton Moore's *Practical Navigator;* his contributions were so extensive that by 1802 the book became the *New American Practical Navigator* and was credited to him; it has remained to this day the "seaman's bible." Although offered positions in universities, he chose to pursue research on his own and worked all of his adult life as an insurance actuary in Salem or Boston. He published papers on such topics as comets and meteors and translated four volumes of Laplace's *Mécanique céleste,* published (1829–39) with his commentary and updating as *Celestial Mechanics.* He was president of the American Academy of Arts and Sciences (1829–38).

Bowdoin, James (1726–90) Revolutionary statesman, merchant, governor; born in Boston, Mass. A wealthy merchant and property owner, he served in the Massachusetts General Court and Council and although hardly a revolutionary, he did endorse the colonists' economic quarrels with the British. He served as president of the convention that drew up the new constitution for Massachusetts (1779), and then became governor (1785–87). As governor during the period of Shays's Rebellion (1786–87), he responded promptly and vigorously by sending troops to confront and disperse Daniel Shays's followers. He was applauded for this in other states, but his popularity declined in Massachusetts. He was interested in science and literature; Bowdoin College was named for him and was chartered in 1794.

Bowen, Ira Sprague (1898–1973) astronomer; born in Seneca Falls, N.Y. He identified aspects of gaseous nebulae in 1927 while at the California Institute of Technology and continued nebulae research at the Lick Observatory (1938). He directed the Palomar Observatory (1948–64). In retirement,

he made instruments such as the 100-inch DuPont telescope at Las Lampas Observatory in Chile.

Bowen, Louise deKoven (1859–1953) philanthropist, social reformer; born in Chicago. As a youth she enjoyed the privileges of wealth; as an adult she wielded her inheritance to ameliorate social conditions. As Woman's Club director, treasurer, and later president (1893–1944) of Hull House, she created a vital link between Chicago's wealthy and the city's social welfare network.

Bowen, Norman (Levi) (1887–1956) geologist; born in Kingston, Ontario, Canada. He was a petrologist with the Carnegie Institution (1912–18, 1920–37, 1947–52); in the interim years he taught at Queen's University, Ontario (1919–20) and the University of Chicago (1937–47). His pioneer investigations into solid-liquid equilibria of igneous rocks and silicates led to his definitive explanation of the crystallization stages of magma, now known as Bowen's reaction series.

Bower, Marvin (1903–   ) management consultant; born in Cincinnati, Ohio. He earned both law and M.B.A. degrees from Harvard by the age of 27. During a long carreer with McKinsey and Co. (partner 1935–50, managing partner 1950–56, managing director 1956–67), he came to be regarded as the founder of modern management consulting. He made the company international and instituted its trademark entreprenurial culture. He wrote *The Will to Manage* (1966).

Bowersock, Glen (Warren) (1936–   ) classicist, historian; born in Providence, R.I. After graduating *summa cum laude* in classics from Harvard (1957), he went as a Rhodes Scholar (1957–61) to Oxford (D.Phil. ancient history 1962) and then returned to teach at Harvard (1962–80) before becoming professor at the School of Historical Studies, Institute for Advanced Study, Princeton, N.J. (1980). In works like *Greek Sophists in the Roman Empire* (1969) and *Roman Arabia* (1983), he examined areas and epochs previously neglected. His Sather lectures at the University of California (1991–92) were published as *Fiction and History: From Nero to Julian.* His *Hellenism in Late Antiquity* won the James H. Breasted Prize in 1992.

Bowes, Edward (1874–1946) entrepreneur, radio impresario; born in San Francisco. He left school at age 13 and worked as an office boy. He built a flourishing real estate business that was temporarily ruined by the earthquake and fire of 1906. He married Margaret Illington, an actress, and they moved east to run theaters in Boston and New York City. He built the Capitol Theater in New York City, an early movie "palace," and in 1925 became the host of a popular radio program that had originated from there since 1922. In 1934, as manager of New York City's radio station WHN, he began "Major Bowes' Original Amateur Hour," which offered potential stardom and a $10 stipend to contestants during the Great Depression. While he hosted this popular network radio program until 1945, his manner and expressions became known nationwide. He left most of his $4.5 million estate to charity.

Bowie, James (1799–1836) pioneer, soldier; born in Burke County, Ga. A large landholder on the Texas frontier, he was an adventurer whose name was given to a type of knife he allegedly invented. In 1835–36 he led American volunteers against the Mexican Army in Texas and was killed, along with the other 182 defenders, in the siege of the Alamo.

Bowie, William (1872–1940) geodesist; born in Annapolis Junction, Md. As a member of the U.S. Coast and Geodetic Survey (1895–1936), he performed triangulation, leveling, and pendulum measurements in the continental U.S.A., Alaska, the Philippines, and Puerto Rico. His research on the influence of gravity on earth topography led to his seminal book, *Isostasy*, which advanced the concept that the earth's crust is in gravitational balance upon the earth's mantle.

Bowker, Richard Rogers (1848–1933) editor, author; born in Salem, Mass. A founder of the American Library Association and cofounder and editor of *The Library Journal,* he was also publisher and editor of *Publishers' Weekly* and wrote books on public affairs.

Bowles, Jane (b. Jane Sydney Auer) (1917–73) writer; born in New York City. After her marriage to the writer Paul Bowles in 1938, she lived mostly abroad. Her literary reputation rests on a slender output from the 1940s–50s (a novel – *Two Serious Ladies* (1943) – a play, and a volume of stories) notable for its feminism and an oblique experimentalism influenced by Gertrude Stein. A stroke left her unable to read or write for her last 15 years and she died in a hospital in Malaga, Spain, where she spent those years.

Bowles, Paul (Frederick) (1910–) writer, composer; born in New York City. Son of a dentist (whom he never forgave for working so hard on his teeth), he went to Paris in the late 1920s and had his poetry published in *Transition*. After studying with Aaron Copland and Virgil Thomson, he composed theater music, film scores, and opera in the 1930s–1940s. He married the writer Jane Bowles in 1938. His first novel, *The Sheltering Sky* (1949), dealt, like much of his subsequent fiction, with expatriate travelers in non-Western lands. Settling in Tangier, Morroco, in 1952, he collected and translated much Moroccan folklore while becoming something of a cult figure for the international literary set.

Bowles, Samuel (1939–) economist; born in New Haven, Conn. Educated at Yale (1960) and Harvard (Ph.D. 1965), he taught at Harvard before joining the faculty of the University of Massachusetts in Amherst, where he was a professor of economics. He published extensively in the economics of human resources and in Marxist economic theory. His books include *Beyond the Waste Land: A Democratic Alternative to Economic Decline* (1983).

Bowles, Samuel, III (1826–78) editor; born in Springfield, Mass. He was the indefatigable longtime editor of the *Springfield Republican,* which he built into one of the finest papers of the time. His editorials were highly influential; he also published three volumes of correspondence written during travels in the West.

Bowman, Isaiah (1878–1950) geographer; born in Berlin (renamed Kitchener), Ontario, Canada. He studied at Ferris Institute, Big Rapids, Mich., and then at Ypsilanti's Normal College under the tutelage of Mark Jefferson. The latter sent him to Harvard to study for a doctorate with W. M. Davis. Bowman assumed an academic post at Yale University in 1905; in 1915 he accepted the Directorate of the American Geographical Society; and in 1935 he assumed the presidency of Johns Hopkins University. In 1918–19 he had directed the "Inquiry" and then was chief of the American Commission to Negotiate Peace at the Paris Peace Conference; during World War II he was influential with the State Department. His most significant works include *Forest*

Physiography (1911), *The Andes of Southern Peru* (1916), *The New World* (1921), and *Geography in Relation to the Social Sciences* (1934).

Bowne, Borden Parker (1847–1910) philosopher, theologian; born in Leonardsville, N.J. After studying idealist philosophy in Germany, he joined the faculty at Boston University (1876), where he ultimately became head of the philosophy department and dean of graduate studies. He developed a personalistic, religiously oriented idealism through stimulating lectures and in books such as *Personalism* (1908).

Boyd, Belle (1843–1900) Confederate spy; born in Martinsburg, Va. She brought information about Federal troops to Confederate commands, especially to General "Stonewall" Jackson. She was arrested twice (1862, 1863) and was captured on her way to England carrying letters from Jefferson Davis. Capitalizing on her notoriety, she appeared on the London stage (1866) and the New York stage (1868), then took to the lecture circuit after 1886.

Boyd, William (Bill) (1898–1972) movie actor, producer; born in Cambridge, Ohio. He worked at odd jobs until landing his first film role as an extra in *Why Change Your Wife?* (1920). A favorite of Cecil B. DeMille, he revived his faltering career when he played Hopalong Cassidy in a series of popular Westerns. He bought the rights to the character and revived him on television in the 1950s.

Boyden, Uriah (Atherton) (1804–79) engineer, inventor; born in Foxboro, Mass. He helped survey early railroad routes in New England and participated in the construction of several textile mills in Lowell, Mass. In 1844 he designed an improved turbine waterwheel to power industrial machinery. In his late years he occupied himself with problems in pure physics, particularly heat and the velocity of light.

Boyer, Ernest (Leroy) (1928–) foundation executive; born in Dayton, Ohio. He was an innovating chancellor of the State University of New York (1970–76) and U.S. Commissioner of Education (1977–79). As president of the Carnegie Foundation for the Advancement of Teaching (1979) he issued major reports calling for higher teaching and curriculum standards in American high schools (1983) and colleges (1986).

Boyesen, H. H. (Hjalmar Hjorth) (1849–95) writer; born in Frederiksvärn, Norway. He spent much of his childhood with his maternal grandfather in Systrand, Norway, and studied at the University of Leipzig, Germany (Ph.D. 1868). He traveled to America (1869) and worked in Chicago as an editor of the Norwegian weekly, *Fremad,* before becoming a Greek and Latin tutor at Urbana University, Ohio. He wrote *Gunnar* (1874), a popular novel of Norwegian life, that was first serialized in the *Atlantic Monthly*. In 1874 he began teaching in the German department at Cornell, but he moved to New York City where he wrote and taught at Columbia University (1881–95). In his day he was known for such scholarly works as *Goethe and Schiller* (1879) and *Essays on Scandinavian Literature* (1895). In addition to several realistic novels, he wrote children's stories and poetry.

Boyington, (Gregory) "Pappy" (1912–88) marine aviator; born in Coeur d'Alene, Idaho. He led the famous Black Sheep Squadron, which consisted of pilots dismissed from other squadrons for disciplinary and other problems, in the Pacific Theater during World War II.

Boyle, Kay (1903–92) writer; born in St. Paul, Minn. She joined the American expatriate community in Europe (1923–41), returning after the war as the *New Yorker*'s European correspondent (1946–53). A number of her 50 books drew on her European experience. She won two O. Henry Awards for short stories, collections of which include *Thirty Stories* (1946) and *The Smoking Mountain* (1951). A lifelong radical, she taught at San Francisco State University (1963–79) and was outspoken in opposing the Vietnam War.

Boylston, Zabdiel (1679–1766) physician; born in Brookline, Mass. He received medical instruction from his father, but never obtained a medical degree. He was the first colonial doctor to inoculate people against smallpox (1721). He inoculated over 200 people in Boston; only six of those persons died. He and Cotton Mather (who had encouraged the use of inoculation) were both persecuted by angry crowds for their actions. Boylston published his results in London (1726) and then returned to Boston.

Bozeman, John M. (1835–67) explorer; born in Georgia. He pioneered the Bozeman Trail (1863–65), the best route for gold seekers on their way from southeastern Wyoming to Virginia City, Mont. He was killed by Blackfeet Indians at the crossing of the Yellowstone River.

Brace, Charles Loring (1826–90) philanthropist; born in Litchfield, Conn. A relation of the Beechers, he was trained in theology but drawn to assisting the urban poor, particularly children. A pioneer in modern philanthropic methods, he promoted self-help, and during his tenure as founder and secretary of the New York City Children's Aid Society (1853–90), he assisted more than 100,000 immigrant children in finding homes and jobs. Resourceful and tolerant, he gained an international reputation and counted as friends many well-known thinkers and social activists of his time.

Brackenridge, Henry Marie (1786–1871) lawyer, author; born in Pittsburgh, Pa. (son of Hugh Henry Brackenridge). He was raised by his unusual father, who nurtured his frontier roots with his own legal and literary interests; by age seven he had made a voyage down the Ohio River to a village where he learned French, and by age 20 he was admitted to the bar in Pittsburgh. His knowledge of natural history informed the books that were spawned by his travels; his *Views of Louisiana* drew on his years of practicing law there (1810–14); his *Voyage to South America* (1819) grew out of his 1818 trip as a member of a government commission – he had previously urged the policy that became the Monroe Doctrine. He served in the Maryland legislature and held administrative and judicial offices in Florida (1821–32); removed from the bench by President Andrew Jackson, he attacked Jackson in a pamphlet. He served briefly in the U.S. House of Representatives (Dem.-Rep., Pa.; 1840–41) but devoted the final decades of his life to writing memoirs, histories, and political and legal texts.

Brackenridge, Hugh Henry (1748–1816) author, judge; born in Campbeltown, Scotland. He was brought to the U.S.A. at age five. A Princeton-educated chaplain who wrote two patriotic dramas during the American Revolution, he turned to the study and practice of law before settling in Pittsburgh. He later helped establish the first newspaper and bookstore in frontier Pittsburgh. A Pennsylvania assemblyman and Supreme Court justice, he is best known for *Modern Chivalry* (1792–1815), regarded as the first novel based in the American West and still a pertinent satire of the social and political conditions of the era.

Brackett, Charles (1892–1969) movie producer, screenwriter; born in Saratoga Springs, N.Y. He graduated from Williams (1915) and Harvard Law School (1920), his schooling interrupted by his service in World War I. He practiced law and published magazine stories and several novels before becoming drama critic for the *New Yorker* (1925–29). Some of his stories were purchased by Hollywood, which led to his being hired as a writer by Paramount in 1932. In 1938 he began collaborating with Billy Wilder, first as cowriter and then (1943) also as producer, and the two enjoyed a string of popular and critical successes, including *The Lost Weekend* (1945) and *Sunset Boulevard* (1950), winning Oscars for both. They split in 1950, and Brackett continued to produce other movies, winning another Oscar as coauthor of *Titanic* (1953).

Bradbury, (Raymond Douglas) Ray (1920–   ) writer; born in Waukegan, Ill. This Los Angeles-based writer secured a permanent reputation with such works as *The Martian Chronicles* (1950) and *Fahrenheit 451* (1953). Though best known for more than a dozen volumes of science-fiction stories (*The Illustrated Man* (1951), *A Memory of Murder* (1984)), he also wrote novels, drama, essays, and verse. His literary finesse and social criticism did much to make science fiction respectable.

Braddock, James J. (Joseph) (1905–74) boxer; born in New York City. He won one of boxing's greatest upsets when he decisioned world heavyweight champion Max Baer in 1935. In his first defense of the crown, he lost by a knockout to Joe Louis in 1937.

Braden, Spruille (1894–1978) diplomat, consultant; born in Elkhorn, Mont. He studied mining engineering at Yale and directed projects in Latin America. He entered the diplomatic service in 1933 and became known as a crusader for democracy, especially while he was ambassador to Argentina (1945) and assistant secretary of state for Latin American affairs (1946–47). He became a consultant to U.S. companies dealing with Latin American countries.

Bradford, David (fl. 1794) political agitator; birthplace unknown. He was a popular prosecuting attorney in Washington County, Pa. He was the most prominent leader of the movement known as the Whiskey Rebellion (1794). He avoided capture by federal soldiers and fled to present-day Louisiana.

Bradford, William (1590–1657) Pilgrim leader; born in Yorkshire, England. He came from a yeoman family. Although he was not formally educated, he began to read the Bible at age 12, and he joined a separatist congregation (which met at William Brewster's house). He emigrated to Holland (1609–20) before coming to America on the *Mayflower*. He signed the Mayflower Compact, helped to select the location of the Plymouth colony, and was the first elected governor in 1621. He was re-elected thirty times in the next thirty-five years. It was largely because of his honesty, diligence, and administrative ability that the colony survived its difficult early years. He wrote the *History of Plimoth Plantation, 1620–1647,* which gave ample evidence of the moral steadfastness and resolve of the early Pilgrims and ensured their place in American history and folklore.

Bradford, William (1663–1752) printer; born in Leicester, England. Emigrating to Pennsylvania in 1685, he set up the first colonial printing press outside New England and the first colonial paper mill; moving to New York, he founded that colony's first paper, the *New-York Gazette,* in 1725.

Bradley, Joseph P. (1813–92) Supreme Court justice; born in Berne, N.Y. Appointed by President Grant to the U.S. Supreme Court (1870–92), he was active in the legal problems concerning the Reconstruction and cast the deciding electoral vote in the Hayes-Tilden presidential election (1877).

Bradley, Mark E. (1907–) aviator; born in Clemson, S.C. A West Point graduate, he worked on a series of fighter development projects during World War II, including the highly successful P-47 and P-51 programs. After retirement, he became an executive vice-president of Garrett Corp.

Bradley, Milton (1836–1911) manufacturer; born in Vienna, Maine. After various positions as a draftsman, he became interested in lithography and introduced the first lithograph press to Springfield, Mass. (1860). He printed and personally sold a new parlor game, "The Checkered Game of Life," and it was so profitable that he formed Milton Bradley and Company in 1864 to print games and game manuals. In 1869 he published the first book on kindergartens in the United States, *Paradise of Childhood,* by the German kindergarten pioneer, Friedrich Froebel. Bradley followed up with a series of kindergarten materials, newsletters, and children's books. Interested in teaching colors, he wrote and published four books including *Color in the Kindergarten* (1893). In 1893 his company began publishing the *Kindergarten Review,* which became the journal of the International Kindergarten Union. His partners retired in 1878 and he reorganized as Milton Bradley Company, which long retained its position as a leading American manufacturer of games and toys.

Bradley, Omar (Nelson) (1893–1981) soldier; born in Clark, Mo. The son of a schoolteacher, he graduated from West Point in 1915 and rose slowly through the grades in the peacetime army. A protégé of the army chief of staff, George C. Marshall, Bradley succeeded George C. Patton in command of the II Corps in 1943 and led it in the Tunisia and Sicily campaigns. He commanded the U.S. 1st Army in the Normandy landings on June 6, 1944. On August 1 he assumed command of the 12th Army Group in France; with 1.4 million combat troops, it became the largest field command in U.S. history, which he commanded until the surrender of Germany in May 1945. A hard-working, unassuming officer, known as the "GI general" for his concern for the welfare of ordinary soldiers, he earned a high reputation for his handling of large forces in battle. He later served as head of the Veterans Administration (1945–47) and as army chief of staff (1948–49). In 1949 he became the first chairman of the Joint Chiefs of Staff. He retired in 1953, and held a series of public and private posts during his late years.

Bradley, (Thomas J.) Tom (1917–) lawyer, mayor, policeman; born in Calvert, Texas. Educated as a lawyer, he served in the Los Angeles Police Department from 1940–62. He had a private law practice from 1961–63, and served on the city council from 1963–73. He was elected mayor in 1973. He declined to run for a fifth term in 1993, announcing plans to return to the practice of law.

Bradley, Will H. (1868–1962) designer; born in Boston, Mass. He was a special student at Harvard, then worked as a poster and book designer in Chicago (1893–94). He moved to Springfield, Mass. (1895), and later settled in Short Hills,

N.J. He founded the Wayside Press and designed typefaces, furniture, and homes, developing his own style that seemed a cross between the Arts and Craft Movement with Art Nouveau, and bridged the transition from the individual hand craftsman to machine-produced work. Although he did not see many of his designs get built, his illustrations in magazines such as the *Ladies Home Journal* early in the 1900s did influence others. He served as an art director for *Century* magazine and *Collier's* and wrote several children's books.

Bradley, (William Warren) Bill (1943–) basketball player, U.S. senator; born in Crystal City, Mo. A three-time All-American forward at Princeton University (1961–65), he attended Oxford University for two years as a Rhodes Scholar before joining the National Basketball Association New York Knicks (1967–77). Elected to the U.S. Senate (Dem., N.J.; 1979), he gained recognition as an expert in energy conservation and as an advocate for civil rights. Although often mentioned as a potential presidential candidate, he seemed personally reluctant to make the necessary commitment. He was elected to basketball's Hall of Fame in 1983.

Bradshaw, John (1933–) counselor, lecturer, author; born in Houston, Texas. He studied for the Roman Catholic priesthood (1955–63) but left the seminary to become a high school teacher, then a counselor. He became well known in 1986 through the Public Broadcasting System series "Bradshaw On – The Family" and the book of the same title. His concept of reparenting one's "inner child" traumatized by dysfunctional family relationships won him a wide following.

Bradshaw, Thornton F. (Frederick) (1917–88) corporate executive; born in Washington, D.C. He taught at Harvard Business School (1942–52) after earning a Ph.D. there. As an executive and finally president of Atlantic Richfield Co. (ARCO) (1956–81), he developed a national reputation as a long-range strategic corporate planner. He was the last president of RCA (Radio Corporation of America) (1981–85), restoring its profitability before superintending its sale to General Electric.

Bradstreet, Anne (b. Dudley) (c. 1612–72) poet; born in (?)Northampton, England. Educated privately, she married Simon Bradstreet; they were among the first to settle the Massachusetts Bay Colony (1630), of which he would twice serve as governor. She lived in Ipswich (1635–45), then settled in North Andover (1645–72), all the while raising eight children under difficult conditions. She is known as the first English poet in America; her work, *The Tenth Muse Lately Sprung Up in America* (1650), was published in England without her knowledge. Her early poetry was in a derivative literary style but her later poems (published posthumously in 1678) have a more direct, human tone.

Bradwell, Myra (b. Colby) (1831–94) lawyer, editor; born in Manchester, Vt. After marrying a lawyer, James B. Bradwell, she studied the law, originally to help her husband; when she passed the bar exam in 1869, she was denied admission. Meanwhile, in 1868, she established the pioneer weekly *Chicago Legal News.* She got Illinois to grant everyone, irrespective of sex, access to professions (1882) and was finally admitted to the bar (1892). She promoted woman suffrage and women's rights in general and helped secure the World's Fair for Chicago in 1893.

Brady, (James Buchanan) "Diamond Jim" (1856–1917)

financier; born in New York City. He worked for the New York Central Railroad, became a salesman of railroad equipment (1879) and then the only agent in the U.S.A. for the Fox Pressed Steel Car Truck Company of England (1888). Extremely rich and known for living in high style as one of the great Broadway "sports," he wore diamond jewelry estimated at $2 million in value. But he remained a serious businessman, active in several enterprises, and accumulated a large fortune, much of which he gave for urological studies at Johns Hopkins Hospital and New York Hospital. He never married.

Brady, Mathew (B.) (1823–96) photographer; born in Lake George, New York. Studying daguerreotype photography as a teenager, he got an early start, opening his own New York City studio in 1844 where he did portraits of famous Americans. In 1847 he opened a second studio in Washington, D.C.; he published *The Gallery of Illustrious Americans* in 1850. Esteemed by Lincoln, he was the first photographer permitted to film at the Battle of Bull Run in 1861 where he was wounded. Assisted by Alexander Gardner and Tim O'Sullivan, he spent $100,000 to deploy teams of photographers who documented, with bulky silver nitrate plate cameras, the major engagements in the Civil War (1861–65). His images of individuals, groups, and battle scenes were widely reproduced, although Brady did not take many of the pictures attributed to him. Plagued by poor vision, he was forced to sell his war negatives to settle his debts in 1865; he died in poverty.

Brady, William A. (Aloysius) (1863–1950) actor, manager; born in San Francisco. He is best known for the many plays he mounted at various theaters he managed in New York, including the Playhouse, which he built in 1911.

Bragg, Braxton (1817–76) soldier; born in Warrenton, N.C. He graduated from West Point in 1837 and served in the Seminole, Frontier, and Mexican wars. He left the army in 1856 to run a plantation in Louisiana; when war broke out Bragg commanded his state's militia. He led the Army of Tennessee into Kentucky in the summer of 1862 but withdrew after the inconclusive battle of Perryville in October. He won a smashing victory over Union forces at Chickamauga in September 1863; but his defeat at Chattanooga two months later cost him his command. Dour, irritable, and unpopular with his fellow soldiers, he later became a military adviser to President Davis. After the war, he served successively as public works commissioner in Alabama and as chief engineer of the Gulf, Colorado and Santa Fe Railroad.

Bragg, Mabel Caroline (Watty Piper, pen name) (1870–1945) writer, educator; born in Milford, Mass. She taught at the Rhode Island State Normal School (1889–1909), worked in publishing, and embarked on a career in education in Newton, Mass., (1916–30) and Boston University (1930–40). She is also known for her children's books, notably *The Little Engine That Could* (1945).

Braidwood, Robert J. (John) (1907–   ) archaeologist, anthropologist; born in Detroit, Mich. He held appointments at the University of Chicago (1933–76) and directed fieldwork in Iraq, Iran, and Turkey (1947). He pioneered interdisciplinary scientific studies in archaeology; he published widely on the development of agriculture and village society in the Middle and Near East; and he wrote the long-lived textbook *Prehistoric Men* (1951, frequently revised).

Brainard, Daniel (1812–66) surgeon, educator; born in Oneida County, N.Y. He helped found Rush Medical College in Chicago (1843), with which he was affiliated until his death; he taught anatomy and surgery and wrote various medical works including a classic one on fractures (1854). He also helped found the first general hospital in Chicago (1847).

Brainerd, David (1718–47) Protestant missionary; born in Haddam, Conn. An emotional, sickly child, he achieved a religious conversion after much anguish in 1739. He was expelled from Yale in 1742 for making derogatory remarks about a tutor, but he obtained a license to preach and ministered to Indian tribes in Massachusetts, Pennsylvania, and New Jersey. Poor health forced him from the field in early 1747, and he died shortly thereafter. Jonathan Edwards published an account of his life in 1749.

Braithwaite, William Stanley (Beaumont) (1878–1962) writer, editor; born in Boston, Mass. (of West Indian parents). Not formally educated after high school, he helped promote American poetry as literary critic of the *Boston Daily Evening Transcript* (1905–29) and editor of the influential annual *Anthology of Magazine Verse* (1913–29). He encouraged many young African-American writers who would contribute to the Harlem Renaissance, and he himself wrote poetry, criticism, and essays; his *Selected Poems* was published in 1948. He won the National Association for the Advancement of Colored People's prestigious Spingarn Medal (1918). He joined the faculty of the first African-American graduate school at Atlanta University (1935–45).

Brand, Max See FAUST, FREDERICK SCHILLER.

Brand, Stewart (1938–   ) editor, author; born in Rockford, Ill. A graduate of Stanford (1960), he became associated with the Merry Pranksters, a West Coast group of bohemian writers and intellectuals. He then became the founding editor of the counterculture series, *The Whole Earth Catalogue*, from 1968–71; from 1983–85 he was editor-in-chief of *The Whole Earth Software Catalogue*. He became a research scientist at the Media Lab of the Massachusetts Institute of Technology in 1986 and published the account of the lab's work the following year.

Brandeis, Louis D. (Dembitz) (1856–1941) Supreme Court justice; born in Louisville, Ky. During his private practice in St. Louis and Boston (1879–1916), he became known as "the people's attorney" for taking on cases – often for no fee – that fought against the "excesses of capital" in the insurance industry, public utilities, and railroads. His most notable case came in 1908 when he was the first to present to the U.S. Supreme Court what became known as a "Brandeis brief" – an argument (supporting minimum wage legislation) based on sociological, economic, and even physiological data, as opposed to traditional legal arguments. As an outspoken opponent of monopolies and an advocate of reform, he had a direct influence on the economic platform that Woodrow Wilson adopted in his presidential campaign in 1912. In 1914 he published *Other People's Money: and How Bankers Use It,* and when Wilson nominated him to the U.S. Supreme Court in 1916, he was regarded as so radical by many Americans that his nomination was debated for four months by the Senate Judiciary Committee before he was confirmed. He also became the first Jew appointed to the Supreme Court and he would take an active role in the Zionist movement. On the court (1916–39), he criticized the strict, absolutist approach to the Constitution, preferring decisions that took into account social and economic conditions; he even acknowledged that "prevailing public opinion concerning evil and the remedy is among the important facts deserving consideration"; and he was an early proponent of conservation. Such positions often left him with the dissenting minority, especially when President Franklin Roosevelt's New Deal legislation came up for review. Brandeis University (Waltham, Mass.), founded in 1948, was named after him.

Brando, Marlon (Jr.) (1924–) film actor; born in Omaha, Nebr. After being expelled from a Minnesota military academy, he made his Broadway debut as Nels in *I Remember Mama* (1944). The archetypal "method" product of the New York Actors Studio, his naturalistic acting and casual delivery were ideal as the brutish Stanley Kowalski in *A Streetcar Named Desire* (1947), a part he was to reprise in the movie adaptation in 1951. Brando's first film role was as an embittered paraplegic in *The Men* (1950). His first Oscar was earned in *On the Waterfront* (1954). He won the award again in the title role of *The Godfather* (1972), but refused the Oscar in protest of the film industry's treatment of Native Americans. Increasingly quixotic, reclusive, and obese, he ended an eight-year absence from the screen with the anti-apartheid drama *A Dry White Season* (1988).

Brannan, Charles F. (Franklin) (1903–) lawyer, cabinet member; born in Denver, Colo. A Denver lawyer (1929–35) and cattle rancher (1940–48), he was regional director of the Farm Security Administration (1941–44). Assistant secretary of agriculture (1944–48), he became Truman's secretary of agriculture (1948–53), advocating price supports for American farmers and an international wheat agreement. Afterward he practiced law in Denver.

Brannan, Samuel (1819–89) California pioneer; born in Saco, Maine. A journeyman printer, he became a Mormon (1842) and led a Mormon group to California by sea (1846). He published San Francisco's first newspaper, the *California Star,* served on the first city council, and helped to organize the Society of California Pioneers.

Branner, Robert (J.) (1927–73) architectural historian; born in New York City. His many publications on French Gothic architecture include *Burgundian Gothic Architecture* (1960). He taught art history and archaeology at Columbia University (1957–73).

Brant, Gerald Clark (1880–1958) aviator; born in Chariton, Iowa. A 1904 West Point graduate, he served on the Mexican border and in the Philippines before transferring to the air service in 1917. During World War II, he held a senior air force training command in Florida.

Brant, Henry (Dreyfus) (1913–) composer; born in Montreal, Canada. A student of Copland and Antheil, he was a leading avant-gardist of the 1920s and 1930s; he became increasingly interested in music for multiple ensembles separated spatially. He also taught at colleges including Columbia University, Juilliard, and Bennington College.

Brant, Joseph (b. Thayendanegea) (1742–1807) Mohawk chief; born along the Ohio River in present-day Ohio. As a young man, he sided with the British in their war against the French and was befriended by Sir William Johnson, who sent him to a school in Connecticut. Brant converted to Christianity, and returned to his people as a missionary; he translated

the Episcopal Prayer Book and part of the New Testament into Mohawk. During the American Revolution, now fighting with the British against the colonists, he participated in various raids in New York State's Mohawk Valley – including the infamous Cherry Valley Massacre (1778). He ended the war with the British rank of colonel and had to move with his people into Canada. In 1785 he went to England to obtain compensation for the Indians' losses in the war. He built one of the first Episcopalian churches in Canada and although he became an advocate for peace in the 1790s he was not afraid to stand up against those who tried to take away the Mohawks' land.

Brashear, John Alfred (1840–1920) astronomical instrument-maker; born in Brownsville, Pa. A Pittsburgh steel mill mechanic by day, by night he was an amateur telescope maker. Because astronomy was beginning to attract large donations from philanthropists, in 1881 he was able to start the John A. Brashear Company, builders of astrophysical research instruments. He built George Ellery Hale's first spectroheliograph. The company was bought in 1926 by J. W. Fecker of Cleveland.

Brattain, Walter H. (Houser) (1902–87) physicist; born in Amoy, China, to American teachers. He was a researcher at Bell Telephone Laboratories (1929–67), and a visiting professor at Whitman College (1962–72). With J. Bardeen and W. B. Shockley, he developed the point-contact transistor (1947), using a thin germanium crystal. The three men shared the 1956 Nobel Prize in physics for their revolutionary contribution to electronics.

Brauer, Richard D. (Dagobert) (1901–77) mathematician; born in Berlin, Germany. Instrumental in the development of modern algebra, he emigrated to America for professional reasons (1933). A National Academy of Sciences member, he chaired the Harvard Mathematics Department (1959–63), was president of the American Mathematical Society, and was awarded the National Medal of Science (1971).

Braun, E. (Emma) Lucy (1889–1971) botanist; born in Cincinnati, Ohio. She obtained undergraduate and graduate degrees from the University of Cincinnati, and remained there as an educator and researcher (1917–48). With her sister, entomologist Annette Braun, she made extensive field studies of the Ohio area. Emma's knowledge of geology facilitated her analysis of flora of the Appalachians. Her 25 years of exploring the vegetation of Ohio and Kentucky led to her classic ecological study of hardwood forests, *Deciduous Forests of Eastern North America* (1950). She was one of the first American botanists to compare the changes in a particular flora over a historical time period. She fought for saving natural habitats and was elected the first woman president of the Ohio Academy of Science (1933–34) and the Ecological Society of America (1950).

Brautigan, Richard (?1935–84) writer; born in Tacoma, Wash. He became a cult figure in the 1960s as one of the San Francisco poets and embodiment of the 1960s counterculture. He wrote surrealistically random novels and poems about alienation. His books include the novel, *Trout Fishing in America* (1967), and the collection of poems, *The Pill Versus the Springhill Mine Disaster* (1968). Disheartened by public indifference to his later works, he committed suicide in 1984.

Breasted, James Henry (1865–1935) Egyptologist; born in Rockford, Ill. The first teacher of Egyptology in America, he was assistant in Egyptology (1895), assistant director of the Haskell Oriental Museum (1895), instructor in Egyptology (1896), and professor of Egyptology and Oriental history, all at the University of Chicago (1905–35), where he founded the Oriental Institute (1919). He is best known for his monumental *Ancient Records of Egypt* (1906–07), previously unpublished inscriptions with translations, and his translation and editing of the *Edwin Smith Surgical Papyrus* (1930), often referred to as the earliest known scientific document.

Breckinridge, John (Cabell) (1821–75) vice-president, Confederate; born in Lexington, Ky. He served as James Buchanan's vice-president during 1857–61. In 1861, he joined the Confederate cause, and was indicted for treason by the federal government. He became major-general and was Confederate secretary of war in 1865. Following the war, he lived in Europe and Canada until an amnesty was declared in 1868. He returned to Lexington, Ky., and resumed his law practice.

Breckinridge, Mary (1881–1965) nurse/midwife, organization founder; born in Memphis, Tenn. Founder and director of the Frontier Nursing Service in Kentucky and pioneer in American midwifery, she fought successfully to lower infant mortality rates in the South. An effective fundraiser and crusader for women and children, she combined administrative and practical skills with deep spirituality.

Breckinridge, Sophonisba Preston (1866–1948) social worker, educator; born in Lexington, Ky. Reared in a prominent Southern family, she graduated from Wellesley College (Mass.) (1888), became the first woman lawyer in Kentucky (1895), and earned a doctorate from the University of Chicago (1901). In 1907 she went to live at Chicago's Hull House. Soon known for her studies exposing slum conditions, she was also instrumental in professionalizing social work as an administrator and teacher at the University of Chicago (1920–42) and as a founder of the *Social Service Review* (1927), which she edited until her death.

Breen, Patrick (?–1868) pioneer, diarist; born in Ireland. He came to the U.S.A. in 1828. With his wife and seven children, he joined the ill-fated Donner Party. During the winter of 1846–47, he kept a diary of the stark events of deaths, quarrels, and eventual rescue of the surviving members. All members of the Breen family survived the winter and they settled in San Benito County, Calif.

Breit, Gregory (1899–1981) physicist; born in Nikolaev, the Ukraine. He came to the U.S.A. in 1915, and joined the Carnegie Institution (1924–29), then taught at several American universities before moving to the State University of New York: Buffalo (1968–76). A major contributor to the fields of nuclear physics and quantum electrodynamics, he theorized that the hydrogen bomb would not engender an uncontrolled chain reaction resulting in global destruction.

Breitmann, Hans See LELAND, CHARLES GODFREY.

Bremer, Edith Terry (1885–1964) social reformer; born in Hamilton, N.Y. Educated at the University of Chicago (1907), she pioneered immigrant social service work. She gained prominence as founder (1910) and leader of the International Institute movement, which worked to improve the lives of female immigrants. She directed the YWCA Department of Immigration and Foreign Communities (c. 1920–32) and founded the National Institute of Immigrant Welfare (1933–54).

Bren, Donald L. (Leroy) (1932–) real estate developer, art collector, philanthropist; born in Los Angeles. Son of movie producer Milton Bren (and stepson of actress Claire Trevor), he attended the University of Washington and served in the U.S. Marine Corps. His father had already made a small fortune with his real estate investments, and after leaving the service Donald founded the Donald Bren Co., and became a billionaire from his real estate empire, most of it located in Orange County, Calif. His first major project was the Mission Viejo Co., a planned community. In 1977 he took over the Irvine Co., with other investors, to operate the great Irvine property on which they built essentially a new, privately owned city, Irvine, Calif. In 1983 Bren bought out the other investors and then found himself involved for many years in a costly legal dispute with Joan Irvine Smith, the heiress of this property. Although active in supporting the Republican Party, he was generally a private person and lived relatively modestly at Newport Beach, Calif.; twice divorced, he was known to have a major modern art collection, and to be a generous philanthropist.

Brennan, Walter (1894–1974) movie actor; born in Swampscott, Mass. He worked at various jobs while appearing in vaudeville and stock theater, and after serving in World War I, entered Hollywood films as an extra and stuntman in 1923. Over the next 50 years, he appeared in over 100 films as an outstanding character actor, becoming the first actor to win three Oscars – for best supporting actor in *Come and Get It* (1936), *Kentucky* (1938), and *The Westerner* (1940).

Brennan, William J. (Joseph), Jr. (1906–) Supreme Court justice; born in Newark, N.J. He practiced labor law (1932–49) and rose through New Jersey's judicial ranks (1949–56). President Eisenhower named him to the U.S. Supreme Court (1956–90) where he was known for his support of civil and individual rights, particularly for freedom of speech.

Brent, Margaret (1600–71) colonial landowner; born in Gloucester, England. Daughter of an aristocrat, she came to Maryland in 1638 and through connections and business acumen enlarged her original land grant as Maryland's first female landowner. She actively supported military defense of the colony. Upon the death of her brother-in-law, Leonard Calvert, she became executor of his estate; after the Maryland assembly denied her appeal for two votes in the proceedings, one as landowner and one as attorney to the Baltimore family, she moved to Virginia (c. 1651), where she developed another large property. Sometimes cited today as a pioneering protofeminist lawyer, she seems to have acted basically as a strong-willed property owner, making no claims as a woman, nor in any way practicing law.

Brereton, Lewis (Hyde) (1890–1967) aviator; born in Pittsburgh, Pa. A 1911 Naval Academy graduate, he transferred to the army, learned to fly, and saw extensive aerial combat in France during World War I. Japanese bombers virtually destroyed his Far East Air Force on the ground in the opening days of World War II. He commanded the 1st Allied Airborne Army in the unsuccessful Netherlands operation in September 1944.

Breslin, (James) Jimmy (1930–) journalist; born in the New York City borough of Queens. Starting as a sportswriter for the *New York Herald Tribune*, he evolved into a self-described "street reporter"; his columns, for a sequence of New York papers, offered vignettes, character sketches, and commentary, in a scrappy, colloquial style. Also a novelist, he won a 1986 Pulitzer Prize for commentary.

Breuer, Lee (1937–) director, producer, playwright; born in Philadelphia. He was connected with avant-garde theater as cofounder of the Mabou Mines Theatre Group and as director of the LaMama Experimental Theatre Club.

Breuer, Marcel (Lajos) (1902–81) architect and designer; born in Pécs, Hungary. He directed the furniture workshop at the Bauhaus (1924–28); his early furniture designs, such as the Wassily (1925) and Cesca chairs (1928), became modern classics. He joined Walter Gropius at Harvard and in partnership in 1937. His architectural designs, mostly for houses and public buildings, date mainly from his independent practice (established 1947) and include the Whitney Museum of American Art, New York (1963–66).

Brewer, David J. (Josiah) (1837–1910) Supreme Court justice; born in Smyrna (now Izmir), Turkey. His American missionary parents brought him to the U.S.A. at age one. President Benjamin Harrison named him to the U.S. Supreme Court (1890–1910) where he strictly adhered to the limits of federal power as outlined in the U.S. Constitution.

Brewster, William (1567–1644) Pilgrim leader; born in Nottinghamshire, England. Exposed to separatist religious ideas at Cambridge University, he became the leader of the Pilgrims and directed their escape to Holland in 1608. He sailed on the *Mayflower* and then served as a church elder and as adviser to Governor William Bradford.

Breyer, Stephen G. (Gerald) (1938–) Supreme Court justice; born in San Francisco. After graduating from Stanford, he was a Marshall Scholar at Oxford University before taking a degree from Harvard Law School. He served as a law clerk to Justice Arthur Goldberg of the U.S. Supreme Court (1964–65) and spent much of the next 15 years as a lawyer in various federal positions, including the Watergate Special Prosecution Force (1973) and as chief counsel of the Senate Judiciary Committee (1979–80). He also held various teaching posts at Harvard Law School and the Kennedy School of Government at Harvard University (1970–94). From 1980 to 1994 he served as a judge on the First Circuit Court of Appeals, becoming that court's chief judge in 1990. As an authority on government regulation and antitrust legislation, he contributed the legal framework to the deregulation of the airlines in the 1970s. In addition to his numerous articles, he wrote several books including *Regulation and Its Reform* (1982) and *Breaking the Vicious Circle: Toward Effective Risk Regulation* (1993). Widely known both for his grasp of the complexities of the law and for his ability to explain them in clear language, he was appointed to the U.S. Supreme Court by President Clinton in 1994.

Brice, Fanny (b. Fannie Borach) (1891–1951) comedienne; born in New York City. Born on Manhattan's Lower East Side to successful immigrant saloon-keepers, at age fourteen she assumed the name Brice and built a comedic act based on parody, dialect, and physical humor. A perennial *Ziegfeld Follies* attraction after 1910, she attained international stardom in the 1921 *Follies* with her signature torch-song parody, "My Man." Appearing in vaudeville, musicals, drama, movies, and radio throughout her career with such luminaries as W. C. Fields, Eddie Cantor, and Will Rogers, she excelled at lampooning the fake and preposterous. Eschewing jokes about home life, Brice demonstrated that women could succeed in entertainment without exploiting their sexuality or making buffoons of themselves or other women.

Bricker, John W. (1893–1986) U.S. senator; born near Mount Sterling, Ohio. Governor of Ohio (Rep., 1939–45) and U.S. Senator (Rep., Ohio; 1947–49), he was also Republican vice-presidential candidate in 1944.

Brickhouse, (John B.) Jack (1916–) baseball broadcaster; born in Peoria, Ill. He announced Chicago Cubs games on television and radio starting in 1948. In 1983 he was elected to baseball's Hall of Fame.

Bridgeman, Frederick (Arthur) (1847–1927) painter; born in Tuskegee, Ala. He studied with Gérôme in Paris (1866–71), where he lived and produced most of his work. He specialized in archaeological subjects, as in *Funeral of a Mummy* (c. 1877).

Bridger, James (1804–81) fur trader, scout, "mountain man"; born in Richmond, Va. Working with fur companies in the northeast (1822–42), he was the first white man to see the Great Salt Lake (1824). He established Fort Bridger in Wyoming (1843) and discovered Bridger's Pass (1849). After being driven out by Mormons (1853) he guided a federal force in its campaign against the Mormons (1857–58). After serving as a guide to several major expeditions in the West (1859–66), he retired to his farm near Kansas City, Mo.

Bridges, Calvin B. (Blackman) (1889–1938) geneticist; born in Schuyler Falls, N.Y. He did postgraduate research at the Carnegie Institution (1915–19), became a faculty member there (1919–28), then moved to the California Institute of Technology with a group of Carnegie geneticists (1928–38). With mentor and colleague Thomas H. Morgan, he proved the chromosomal theory of heredity and determined the mechanism of sex-linkage in the fruit fly *Drosophila*.

Bridges, Harry (Alfred Renton) (1901–90) labor leader; born in Kensington, Australia. He went to sea at age 16 and entered the U.S.A. after jumping ship in 1920. He knocked about the Mexican oil fields, returned to the sea, then settled down as a longshoreman and waterfront labor organizer in San Francisco. He founded the International Longshoremen's and Warehousemen's Union in 1933 and led a major dock strike the following year. During the 1940s the federal government repeatedly and unsuccessfully tried to deport him as a Communist sympathizer. Although expelled from the Congress of Industrial Organizations in 1950, his union remained a powerful force on the West Coast docks through the 1950s.

Bridges, (Henry) Styles (1898–1961) governor, U.S. senator; born in West Pembroke, Maine. A magazine editor and investment broker, he served on the New Hampshire Public Service Commission (1930–34). As the conservative Republican governor of New Hampshire (1935–37) he spent state money carefully, but he funded relief aid for mothers and dependent children and he appointed the first woman state judge. In the U.S. Senate (1937–61), he opposed the New Deal. After World War II, as chair of the Appropriations Committee (1947, 1953) and Senate minority leader (1952–53), he promoted his ultra-conservative views, supporting the anticommunist campaign of his fellow Republican senator, Joseph McCarthy.

Bridges, Robert (died 1656) iron manufacturer, magistrate; born in England. He came to Massachusetts in 1641 and was the only magistrate in Lynn for many years. He took specimens of bog ore from the Saugus River to London

(1642) and in 1643 formed "The Company of Undertakers for the Iron Works," the first iron works established in America.

Bridgman, Laura Dewey (1829–89) first blind deaf-mute to be successfully educated; born in Hanover, N.H. Scarlet fever left her blind and deaf at age two. She was rescued from total isolation by a dimwitted but gentle handyman, Asa Tenney, who communicated with her by his own system of touch signs. Starting in 1837, Samuel Gridley Howe taught her to read and write at the Perkins Institution (where she remained until her death) using an alphabetic method that prefigured Anne Sullivan's work with Helen Keller, and she became world famous as an object of public interest and scientific and pedagogical study. Unlike Helen Keller, however, she never learned how to talk, she did not develop her intellectual abilities beyond basic literacy, and she could not function in the world outside the institution.

Bridgman, Percy W. (Williams) (1882–1961) physicist; born in Cambridge, Mass. After earning his Ph.D. in physics at Harvard, he stayed on to teach there (1908–54), although he much preferred laboratory research to the classroom. He invented an apparatus to create extremely high pressures, proving experimentally that viscosity increases with pressure; he used this apparatus for such discoveries as a new form of phosphorous and dry ice; his work also made possible the synthesis of diamonds, quartz, and other crystals. For this work he won the 1946 Nobel Prize in physics. In works such as *The Nature of Physical Theory* (1936) he argued that concepts in physics had to be interpreted through experimental operations.

Briggs, Charles Augustus (1841–1913) Protestant clergyman, educator; born in New York City. The son of a prosperous businessman, he served briefly with a New York infantry regiment on the outbreak of the Civil War, then entered Union Theological Seminary. In 1874 he became professor of Hebrew there. Conservative Presbyterians objected to his scholarly work in Old Testament criticism; found guilty in a heresy trial in 1890, he was suspended from the ministry. He later took orders in the Episcopal Church and was restored to his professorship at Union.

Briggs, Lyman (James) (1874–1963) physicist; born in Assyria, Mich. He worked for the U.S. Department of Agriculture (1896–1920), became chief of the Mechanics and Sound Division of the Bureau of Standards, then served as director of the Bureau (1932–45). Effectively the founder of soil physics, in 1939 he headed the committee that investigated the military potential of atomic energy.

Briggs, Robert William (1911–83) developmental biologist; born in Watertown, Mass. He taught at McGill University, Montreal (1938–42), moved to the Institute for Cancer Research, Philadelphia (1942–56), then joined the University of Indiana (1956–74), continuing his scientific writing after his retirement. He made major contributions to studies of nuclear transplantation and nucleocytoplasmic interaction in amphibian eggs and embryos.

Briggs, Winslow R. (Russell) (1928–   ) plant physiologist; born in St. Paul, Minn. He taught and performed research at Stanford (1955–67), moved to Harvard (1967–73), then joined the Carnegie Laboratory at Stanford (1973). He made major contributions to studies of plant growth and the biochemistry and molecular biology of phytomorphogenesis (plant development) and photosynthesis. A dedicated educa-

tor, he was quoted as saying, "With gifted students, remarkable things are possible."

Brigham, Albert (Perry) (1855–1932) geographer; born in Perry, N.Y. He spent a decade in the ministry and some 40 years associated with Colgate University. He was well versed in all branches of the field and published extensively. His role as secretary of the Association of American Geographers in the formative years of that institution is regarded as essential to its success.

Brightman, Edgar Sheffield (1884–1953) philosopher; born in Holbrook, Mass. After studying at Boston University, where he was influenced by Borden Parker Bowne, and in Germany, he returned to teach at Boston University from 1919. His philosophy, systematically presented in the posthumous *Person and Reality* (1958), was an empirically oriented development of Bowne's personalistic theism. He is credited with having inspired many students, including Martin Luther King Jr.

Brill, Abraham A. (Arden) (1874–1948) psychoanalyst, translator; born in Kanezuga, Galicia. He emigrated to the United States at age 15 and took his medical degree at Columbia University in 1903. In 1908 he became the first Freudian psychoanalyst in the United States. He is best known as the translator of Sigmund Freud's works into English, including the compendium *The Basic Writings of Sigmund Freud* (1938).

Brillouin, Leon N. (Nicholas) (1889–1969) physicist; born in Sevres, France. He taught in France before coming to the U.S.A. in 1941. After doing defense research at Columbia University (1943–45), he moved to Harvard (1946–49). A solid-state physicist who specialized in wave theory, he determined that at high frequencies, sound waves approximate thermal waves. He became director of electronics education at International Business Machines in 1949.

Brimmer, Andrew Felton (1926–   ) economist, educator; born in Newellton, La. A sharecropper's son, he served two years in the army before earning a bachelor's degree in economics from the University of Washington, and in 1957, a Ph.D. from Harvard. He worked as an economist for the Federal Reserve Board and taught economics at Michigan State University. In 1966 he became a member of the Federal Reserve Board, where he followed a moderate course on monetary policy, especially on issues involving taxation, government spending, and inflation. He left the board in 1976 to establish his own investment/consultant firm, Brimmer & Co.

Brinton, (Clarence) Crane (1898–1968) historian, teacher; born in Winsted, Conn. Educated at Harvard and Oxford Universities, he became known as a brilliant, cosmopolitan scholar and author as well as a popular teacher at Harvard (1923–68). He worked for the OSS (Office of Strategic Services) in London (1942–45) during World War II. An authority on revolutions and a proponent of "intellectual history," his 15 books include *The Anatomy of Revolution* (1938), *A History of Western Morals* (1959), and *The Americans and the French* (1968).

Brinton, Daniel Garrison (1837–99) physician, cultural anthropologist; born in Thornbury, Pa. He graduated from Yale in 1858, took a medical degree in 1861, and studied abroad for a year before returning to serve as a Union army surgeon (1862–65). He retired from medical practice in 1887 to pursue anthropological research full time. His *American*

Race (1891) was the first systematic classification of the aboriginal languages of the Americas and his studies of the Mayans were landmarks in American archaeology.

Brisbane, Albert (1809–90) social reformer; born in Batavia, N.Y. Son of a wealthy landowner, he had little formal schooling but in 1828 went off to Europe "to solve the mystery of man's destiny." For six years he studied at various universities and met or studied with several great thinkers – Goethe, Hegel, Jules Michelet, and Charles Fourier. It was Fourier's social philosophy, essentially a socialism that called for establishing small cooperative communities, that Brisbane adopted, and after his return to the U.S.A. (1834) he embarked on a phase of writing about and promoting "Fourierism" (which he tended to rename "associationism") through books, articles, and journals that he edited (such as *The Phalanx*, 1843–45). When it came to operating actual utopian communities based on Fourierism, however, Brisbane took little action, and by 1851 – after two other trips to Europe – he had effectively withdrawn from social activism. He concentrated on managing his family's business and on publishing his various ideas on everything from psychology to Fourier's theories (including his major work, the *General Introduction to Social Theory,* 1876); he even suggested new systems for transportation and burials and became an advocate of drinking wine. Although admired in his day, he was generally described as a propagandist, not as an effective leader.

Bristow, Benjamin Helm (1832–96) lawyer, public official; born in Elkton, Ky. A lawyer's son, he worked for a time for his father, then commanded Kentucky Union troops during the Civil War. As a postwar U.S. attorney for Kentucky, he helped suppress moonshiners and Ku Klux Klan activity. As President Ulysses S. Grant's treasury secretary in 1874, he smashed the notorious Whiskey Ring; but some of the distillers were Grant cronies, and they turned the president against Bristow. Forced from office in 1876, he returned to private practice and became president of the American Bar Association in 1879.

Bristow, Joseph (Little) (1861–1944) U.S. senator; born near Hazel Green, Ky. Settling in Kansas (1879), he acquired several newspapers there and rose in the Republican Party, becoming assistant postmaster general (1897–1905); his investigation of corruption in the postal system exposed several Republican legislators and forced their resignation. Aligning himself increasingly with the more progressive wing of the Republicans, he served a term in the U.S. Senate (Rep., Kans.; 1909–15) where his most notable achievement was to help write what became the 17th Amendment, providing for the direct election of senators.

Britton, Nathaniel L. (Lord) (1859–1934) botanist; born in New Dorp, Staten Island, N.Y. Originally a geologist, he was an assistant in geology at Columbia University (1879–86), then taught geology, botany, and ecology there (1886–90). He became a professor of botany at Columbia (1891–96), then resigned to found and direct the New York Botanical Garden (1896–1929), with his wife Elizabeth Gertrude Knight Britton, as its curator of mosses. A rigid taxonomist, he collected and classified plants of the U.S.A. and the West Indies, and wrote and illustrated volumes on flowers, trees, and cacti. He is honored in the names of many plant genera and species; Mount Britton in Luquillo National Park, Puerto Rico, was also named for him.

Brock, (Louis Clark) Lou (1939–) baseball player; born in Hamilton, Ill. During his Hall of Fame career as an outfielder (1961–79), mostly for the St. Louis Cardinals, he stole a total of 938 bases, a record that stood until Rickey Henderson surpassed the mark in 1991. He had 3,023 hits.

Brockway, Zebulon Reed (1827–1920) penologist; born in Lyme, Conn. An acclaimed prison reformer, he introduced courses and manual training at many of the institutions he served. As superintendent at the reformatory at Elmira, N.Y. (1876–1890), he turned the institution into a mecca for criminologists and reformers; he worked for passage of legislation that lightened prison sentences. He wrote *Fifty Years of Prison Service* (1912).

Broder, David S. (Salzer) (1929–) journalist; born in Chicago Heights, Ill. A highly respected Washington political reporter and syndicated columnist, he became an associate editor of the *Washington Post* in 1975 and won, among many awards, a 1973 Pulitzer Prize.

Brodie, Fawn M. (McKay) (1915–81) historian, biographer; born in Ogden, Utah. Raised in one of the preeminent families of the Mormon Church, her first subject following graduation from the University of Chicago (M.A. 1936) was a biography of Joseph Smith, the founder and first prophet of the Church of Jesus Christ of Latter-Day Saints. After the otherwise well-received *No Man Knows My History: the Life of Joseph Smith* was published (1945), she was excommunicated from the Church on charges of heresy. She joined the faculty at the University of California: Los Angeles (1968–77) following biographies of Thaddeus Stevens (1959) and Sir Richard Burton (1967). Her famous biography of Thomas Jefferson (1974) was a featured selection of the Book of the Month Club. In 1967 she was named Fellow of the Year by the Utah Historical Society and in 1975 Woman of the Year by the *Los Angeles Times*. Her biography of Richard Nixon was published posthumously in 1981.

Brodkey, Harold (b. Aaron Roy Weintraub) (1930–) writer, poet; born in Alton, Ill. His mother died when he was very young and he was adopted. He studied at Harvard, but little is known about this reclusive writer except information gleaned from his writings. He is known for his essays, poetry, and short stories, such as *First Love and Other Sorrows* (1957), and *Stories in an Almost Classical Mode* (1988). Noted as a detailed stylist, with, some critics say, an obsessive attachment to his own biography, he spent many years working on a long autobiographical novel, *A Party of Animals*. Excerpts of this novel were published as *Women and Angels* (1985), with additional portions included in *Stories in an Almost Classical Mode.*

Brodovitch, Alexey (1898–1971) art director, teacher; born in Ogolitchi, Russia. After emigrating from Paris in 1930, he became art director of *Harper's Bazaar* (1934–58) and ran design labs (1934–58), training fashion photographers like Avedon to produce striking pictures.

Brodsky, (Iosif Alexandrovich) Joseph (1940–) poet, writer; born in St. Petersburg (then Leningrad), Russia. He studied in Russian secondary schools until 1956, wrote poetry, and was sentenced to a Soviet labor camp for his general refusal to conform. He was expelled from Russia (1972), and emigrated to America. He taught at many institutions, notably as poet-in-residence at the University of Michigan (1972). He was named Poet Laureate by the Library of Congress (1991), and is known for his translations, critical works, and his realistic and lyrical poetry, as in *To Urania* (1988).

Broecker, Wallace S. (Smith) (1931–) oceanographer; born in Chicago, Ill. He began teaching at Columbia University in 1956, and was appointed Newberry Professor of Geology (1977). He made major contributions to chemical oceanography, especially oceanic mixing based on radioisotopic distribution.

Brokaw, (Thomas John) Tom (1940–) TV anchorman; born in Webster, S.D. Starting as a radio reporter in college, he worked in television in Omaha and in Atlanta, before becoming KNBC late-night anchor in Los Angeles (1965–73). As the National Broadcasting Company (NBC) Washington correspondent (1973–76), he covered the Watergate scandal. In 1976 he became *Today* show host, leaving in 1982 to become anchor of the NBC nightly news.

Bromfield, Louis (1896–1956) writer; born in Mansfield, Ohio. The son of a farmer, Bromfield left the family farm in 1914 when he entered Cornell University to study agriculture. His interest in writing led him to transfer to Columbia University's school of journalism (1915). In 1916 he went to France where he served with distinction with the American Ambulance Corps. After the war, he was awarded an honorary B.A. by Columbia and had a series of jobs in journalism before publishing his first novel, *The Green Bay Tree* (1924). The rest of the tetralogy followed swiftly: *Possession* (1925), *Early Autumn* (Pulitzer Prize, 1926), *A Good Woman* (1927). Success allowed Bromfield to return to Ohio, where his farm, Malabar, was a showcase of modern, scientific agricultural methods. He published short stories and novels throughout the 1930s and 1940s, but none received the acclaim of his early works.

Broneer, Oscar (Theodore) (1894–1992) archaeologist; born in Backebo, Sweden. In 1913, he emigrated to the United States where he earned his Ph.D. in 1931. Fittingly, his dissertation was a study of the Roman Odeum at Corinth. A professor of archaeology at the American School of Classical Studies in Athens (1940–52), and at the University of Chicago (1949–60), he spent much of his career at Corinth and his study of Corinthian terracotta lamps produced the first systematic typology of ancient terracotta lamps. He is best known for his work at the important Panhellenic Sanctuary of Isthmia, where he found the temple of Poseidon on the first day of excavation (1952), and was field director (1952–67); he remained closely connected with the site and its museum until his death in his 98th year.

Brooke, Edward W. (William) (1919–) U.S. senator; born in Washington, D.C. A graduate of Howard University and Boston University law school, he served as attorney general of Massachusetts from 1962–66. A Republican, he was elected to the U.S. Senate (1967–79), the first African-American senator elected in the 20th century.

Brooke, John Mercer (1826–1906) naval officer, inventor; born in Tampa Bay, Fla. He served in the U.S. Navy (1841–61) and invented the deep-sea sounding apparatus (1851–53). He joined the Confederate States Navy in 1861 and was largely responsible for the fitting-out of the CSS ironclad *Virginia*. He was chief of the Bureau of Ordnance and Hydrography (1863–65) where he invented the "Brooke" cast-iron rifle.

Brookings, Robert Somers (1850–1932) business executive, philanthropist; born in Cecil County, Md. He had little formal education, but became a successful businessman in St. Louis, first in manufacturing, then real estate, lumber, and transportation. A patron of the arts in St. Louis, he retired from business in 1896 to help found and raise funds for Washington University (St. Louis). He helped found the Brookings Institution in Washington D.C., for the study of public affairs, becoming its first chairman in 1916. He wrote *Industrial Ownership* (1924) and *Economic Democracy* (1929).

Brooks, Alfred (Hulse) (1871–1924) geographer; born in Ann Arbor, Mich. In 1903 he was made chief of the Alaska section of the Geological Survey; he became the authority of this land and published widely on it. *The Geography and Geology of Alaska* (1906) was a comprehensive treatment of the subject. A mountain range in Alaska bears his name.

Brooks, Cleanth (1906–) literary critic; born in Murray, Ky. A long-time Yale professor (1946–75), he was the leading New Critic of the 1940s–1950s, recognized for his critical acuity in close readings of modern literature in *The Well Wrought Urn* (1947) and other essays. He published important works on Milton, Thomas Percy and William Faulkner.

Brooks, Gwendolyn (Elizabeth) (1917–) poet, writer; born in Topeka, Kans. Based in Chicago, she graduated from Wilson Junior College there (1936) and was publicity director for the National Association for the Advancement of Colored People in Chicago (1930s). She taught at many institutions and succeeded Carl Sandburg as poet laureate of Illinois (1968). Her verse narrative *Annie Allen* (1949) won the first Pulitzer Prize awarded to an African-American woman (1950).

Brooks, Louise (1906–85) movie actress; born in Cherryvale, Kans. She began as a professional dancer with the Ruth St. Denis company in 1921. After working on Broadway, she went to Hollywood; her striking good looks created her image as a lightweight but she emerged as a talented actress in such films as *A Girl in Every Port* (1928). Still dissatisfied with the roles she was offered, she went to Germany where she made her finest films, such as *Pandora's Box* (1929), under the direction of G. W. Pabst. Returning to Hollywood in the mid-1930s, she again became disillusioned with the movie world and by the 1940s she had vanished into total obscurity. She was rediscovered living in Rochester, N.Y., by movie buffs in the 1950s and began to write about motion pictures.

Brooks, Noah (1830–1903) journalist; born in Castine, Maine. Journeying west as a young man, he cofounded a California paper, *The Daily Appeal* (1860); later, as Washington correspondent of the *Sacramento Union*, he was a close adviser to President Abraham Lincoln. Subsequently he was editor of the *New York Tribune* and *New York Times* (1871–84). Brooks is also known as the author of two of the earliest boys' novels about baseball, *The Fairport Nine* (1880), and *Our Base Ball Club* (1884).

Brooks, Phillips (1835–93) Protestant religious leader; born in Boston, Mass. He graduated from Harvard in 1855, taught briefly, and was ordained an Episcopal minister in 1859. His famous hymn "O Little Town of Bethlehem" was first sung in 1868. From 1869–91 he served as pastor of Trinity Church and he was university preacher at Harvard. His *Lectures on Preaching* were published in 1877. He died not long after he was consecrated Episcopal bishop of Massachusetts in 1893.

Brooks, Preston (Smith) (1819–1857) U.S. representative; born in Edgefield, S.C. A gentleman farmer, lawyer, and veteran of the Mexican War (1846–48), he served in Congress (Dem., S.C.; 1853–57). When Senator Charles Sumner (Mass.) vilified his uncle, A. P. Butler, in heated debate over the Kansas-Nebraska Bill, Brooks retaliated by smashing Sumner's head with his cane. The 1856 incident became the focus of partisan antagonism between the North and South, and although Congress failed to expel Brooks, he died a year later.

Brooks, Romaine (b. Beatrice Romaine Goddard) (1874–1970) painter; born in Rome, Italy. Child of wealthy and erratic Americans, her mother was in Rome because her husband had deserted her and she was seeking medical help for a mentally disturbed son. Brought to New York City, Romaine was virtually abandoned by her mother at age seven and only rejoined her in London after attending a school in New Jersey (1882–86). After being placed in different European boarding schools, at age 21 she was able to go off to Rome to study painting (with a small allowance forced from her mother). After settling on the island of Capri, she returned to France at her brother's death (1901); with her mother's death in 1902, Romaine became independently wealthy. She then went to England where she was influenced by the work and palette of James McNeill Whistler (and had a brief marriage with an Englishman, John Ellingham Brooks). In 1908 she settled in Paris where (ca. 1915) she met the American expatriate Natalie Clifford Barney; they formed a passionate relationship that lasted over 50 years. She achieved some success with her paintings, particularly her portraits, and came to know many of the artists and writers who came to Paris – she was particularly close to Gabriele D'Annunzio. Her drawings to illustrate her memoirs of her nightmare youth with her mother and brother are considered her strongest work. In 1969 she broke with Barney, who wanted to live with another woman, and although a recluse, she painted almost until her death.

Brooks, Van Wyck (1886–1963) literary critic, biographer; born in Plainfield, N.J. Harvard educated, he emerged as America's most influential cultural and literary critic of the 1930s and 1940s after establishing his reputation with *America's Coming of Age* (1915) and biographies of Mark Twain, Henry James and Emerson. Brooks interpreted the American literary tradition for a wide audience in his prizewinning and influential 5-volume *Makers and Finders: A History of the Writer in America* (1936–52).

Broonzy, (William Lee Conley) "Big Bill" (1893–1958) musician; born in Scott, Miss. He was a versatile guitarist who began his prolific recording career in 1926, was the top-selling male blues singer of the 1930s, and performed at "Spirituals to Swing" at Carnegie Hall in 1938. He conducted several European tours in the 1950s. His autobiography, *Big Bill Blues*, was published in 1957.

Brophy, Thomas D'Arcy (1893–1967) advertising executive; born in Butte, Mont. After a youthful career in marketing he joined the New York advertising agency, Kenyon and Eckhardt (1931), where he was president (1937–49) and chairman (1949–57). In the late 1930s he pioneered professionally written radio advertising and celebrity ad announcers. He founded the American Heritage Foundation (1947), a conservative "think-tank," and was president and chairman until his death.

Brother Antonius See EVERSON, WILLIAM.

Brothers, Joyce (b. Joyce Diane Bauer) (1927–) psychologist, television radio personality; born in New York City. She earned her Ph.D. in psychology from Columbia University (1953). She memorized volumes of information on boxing and then appeared on the *$64,000 Question* (1955) and the *$64,000 Challenge* (1956), which gained her considerable publicity – a female intellectual who knew all about boxing! She soon had her own *Dr. Joyce Brothers* radio program (1958–63) on which she dispensed instant counsel, and over the years she managed to maintain her reputation as a knowledgeable but no-nonsense counselor through years of appearances on radio and television and in a syndicated newspaper column. Her books on popular psychology include *How to Get Whatever You Want Out of Life* (1979) and *What Every Woman Should Know About Men* (1982). Although traditional psychologists were sometimes skeptical, she seemed to satisfy her public audience.

Brougham, John (1810–80) actor, playwright, manager; born in Dublin, Ireland. He began his acting career in London and came to the U.S.A. in 1842. A popular comedian, specializing in stage Irishmen, he wrote over 100 plays, including spoofs such as *Much Ado about the Merchant of Venice* (1869). His adaptation of *Dombey and Son* in 1848 was a considerable success, but his efforts to manage theaters, among them Brougham's Broadway Lyceum, were failures.

Broughton, T. (Thomas) Robert S. (Shannon) (1900–) Roman historian; born in Corbetton, Ontario, Canada. After earning a B.A. (1921) and M.A. (1922) at the University of Toronto, Canada, he acquired his Ph.D. at Johns Hopkins (1928). He spent most of his teaching career in the United States, notably at Bryn Mawr (1928–65) and the University of North Carolina: Chapel Hill (1965–70; emeritus 1970). His *Magistrates of the Roman Republic* (1951–52) and the *Addenda and Corrigenda* (1986) records every known Roman magistrate from 509 B.C. to 31 B.C. This monumental work, largely done by one man working without the help of computer technology, made it possible for historians to apply accurately the techniques of prosopography, the study of relationships between individuals, to the Roman Republic.

Broun, Heywood (Campbell) (1888–1939) journalist; born in Brooklyn, N.Y. Amiable in person and beset with phobias, he was fiery and fearless in print; ousted as a *New York World* columnist in a storm over his criticism of the Sacco-Vanzetti verdict (1928), he showed his concern for social issues as a columnist for the *Telegram* (1928–39). Broun was a cofounder and first president of the American Newspaper Guild.

Brower, David (Ross) (1912–) conservationist; born in Berkeley, Calif. He quit the University of California during his sophomore year, clerked in a candy factory and worked for the National Park Service in Yosemite National Park before joining the University of California Press as an editor in 1941. In 1952 he became executive director of the Sierra Club and soon developed a reputation as a militant environmentalist. Under his leadership, the Sierra Club blocked billions of dollars worth of construction projects in wilderness areas. Sierra Club conservatives forced him from the post in 1969. He then formed the John Muir Institute and Friends of the Earth; the latter group initiated the first Earth Day, April 22, 1969.

Brower, Lincoln P. (Pierson) (1931–) entomologist; born in Summit, N.J. He was a Fulbright scholar at Oxford University (1957–58), then taught at Amherst College (1958–80) before becoming distinguished professor of zoology at the University of Florida (1980). A specialist in studies of migration and protective coloration of monarch butterflies and a producer of ecological films, he made major contributions to research on ecology, evolution, animal behavior, and ecological chemistry.

Brown, Alexander (1764–1834) merchant, banker, early American millionaire; born in County Antrim, Ireland. He came to Baltimore in 1800 and was followed in 1802 by his sons, George, James, and John A. Brown. He began as an importer of Irish linen, then expanded into tobacco, cotton, and other commodities; eventually his international shipping and trading activities turned his firm into a merchant banking house. A model of business acumen, he helped found the Baltimore & Ohio Railroad and he supported Baltimore's civic development.

Brown, Charles Brockden (1771–1810) writer; born in Philadelphia. A Quaker and Philadelphia lawyer who moved to New York City to write (1796), he is regarded as the country's first professional author. His first publication, *Alcuin: A Dialogue* (1798), was on the rights of women. He wrote four groundbreaking American Gothic romances, including *Wieland* (1798) and *Arthur Mervyn* (2 vols. 1799–1800). As these did not earn him much money, he returned to Philadelphia (1801) and worked as a merchant, editor, and translator. He died of tuberculosis.

Brown, Charles L. (Lee, Jr.) (1921–) corporate executive; born in Richmond, Va. Trained as an electrical engineer, he joined American Telephone and Telegraph (AT&T) in 1946. As president (1977–79) and chairman (1979–86), he presided over two sweeping reorganizations, the second after a 1982 antitrust lawsuit forced the breakup of AT&T and the creation of the "Baby Bells."

Brown, Clifford (1930–56) jazz musician; born in Wilmington, Del. He was rapidly establishing himself as one of the greatest trumpeters in jazz history when he was killed in an automobile accident. He played with Lionel Hampton, Tadd Dameron, and Art Blakey in 1953–54. He then co-led a quintet with Max Roach that gained immediate recognition as one of the leading groups in modern jazz.

Brown, Donald D. (David) (1931–) developmental biologist; born in Cincinnati, Ohio. After receiving several research fellowships, he joined the Carnegie Institution (1961), and later served concurrently as a professor at Johns Hopkins (1969). He made major contributions to studies of RNA synthesis as a direct indicator of gene activity, the control of genes during development, and the isolation of genes.

Brown, Earle (1926–) composer; born in Lunenburg, Mass. In the 1950s he began to write highly influential avant-garde works in "open form," giving performers wide choices, the scores sometimes being noteless diagrams. He was also an active teacher.

Brown, Edmund G. (Gerald) "Pat" (1905–) governor; born in San Francisco (father of Jerry Brown). After working his way through law school, he opened practice in San Francisco (1927–43), serving as district attorney there (1943–50) and as California's Democratic attorney general (1950–58). Becoming governor (1959–67), he expanded the state university system and initiated a statewide water project. His most public moment came in 1960 when he decided that California law did not allow him to commute the execution of Caryl Chessman. He retired to his law practice in San Francisco.

Brown, (Edmund Gerald, Jr.) Jerry (1938–) governor, political maverick; born in San Francisco. The son of California governor "Pat" Brown, he studied at a Jesuit novitiate (1956–60). Torn between contemplation and action, he became a lawyer (1964), then served as secretary of state (1970–74) and governor (Dem., 1975–83) of California. As governor, he was known for turning down many perks of office; he would later spend some time in Japan studying Zen Buddhism. During his runs in the 1976 and 1992 Democratic presidential primaries, he campaigned as an "outsider" in politics, stressing the need to eliminate "big money" influence in government, but his populist message was canceled out by what was perceived as his "spacey" manner.

Brown, Eleanor McMillen (1890–) interior decorator; born in St. Louis, Mo. After design study in New York and Paris, in 1924 she opened the first U.S. full-service interior decoration firm, McMillen, Inc. The timeless quality of her designs came from a canny mixing of classical revival styles, attention to architectural detail, and good scale. A 1952 Légion d'Honneur for promoting modern French furniture highlighted a successful career of some 60 years.

Brown, George (1787–1859) railroad promoter; born in County Antrim, Ireland (son of Alexander Brown). He joined his father in Baltimore, Md. (1802). He was influential in the construction of the Baltimore & Ohio Railroad, and was the company's treasurer (1827–34). He was a cautious director of the family firm, Alexander Brown & Sons (1834–59). He gave generously to the House of Refuge and the Peabody Institute of Baltimore.

Brown, George (Scratchley) (1918–78) aviator; born in Montclair, N.J. A 1941 West Point graduate, he flew heavy bombers during World War II, most notably on the raids against the Ploesti oilfields in August 1943. Brown held a series of staff and line appointments during the 1950s and 1960s. As commander of the 7th Air Force in Saigon (1968–70), he was accused of falsifying reports about air strikes in Cambodia in 1969–70. President Richard Nixon appointed him chairman of the Joint Chiefs of Staff in 1974, a tenure punctuated by impolitic comments about Jewish influence in business, journalism, and the Congress.

Brown, H. Rap See AL-AMIN, JAMIL ABDULLAH.

Brown, Hallie Quinn (c. 1845–1949) educator, social reformer; born in Pittsburgh, Pa. Born to former slaves, she graduated from Wilberforce University in 1873 and began a teaching career which ranged from plantation schoolhouses to her alma mater. She was also a public speaker on behalf of African-American culture and a campaigner for temperance. A founder of the National Association of Colored Women, she became its president (1920–24) and remained honorary president until her death.

Brown, Helen Gurley (1922–) editor, writer; born in Green Forest, Ark. Propelled to fame by her best-seller *Sex and the Single Girl* (1962), she became editor of the floundering *Cosmopolitan* magazine in 1965 and gave it a new lease on life, as what some called the woman's counterpart to *Playboy* magazine.

Brown, Henry Billings (1836–1913) Supreme Court justice; born in South Lee, Mass. He practiced law privately and served as a federal judge in Michigan (1875–90) before President Benjamin Harrison named him to the U.S. Supreme Court (1890–1906). He was known for his knowledge of maritime law.

Brown, Henry Kirke (1814–86) sculptor; born in Leyden, Mass. He worked in Boston (1832–36), moved to Cincinnati, Ohio (1836), studied in Italy (1842–46), lived in New York City (1846), then settled in Newburgh, N.Y. (1861). He is known for his bronze works, such as *Aboriginal Hunter* (1846).

Brown, Herbert (Charles) (1912–) organic chemist; born in London, England. He came to the United States in the 1920s and was affiliated with Purdue University (1947–78). He made contributions in the chemistry and synthetic uses of boron derivatives, which led to a wide range of new scientifically and technologically important compounds. He shared the Nobel Prize in chemistry (1979).

Brown, J. G. (John George) (1831–1931) painter; born in Durham, England. He began work in a glassworks, moved to London, emigrated to Brooklyn, New York (1853), and opened a studio in New York City (1860). His genre paintings of street urchins, as in *The Card Trick* (c. 1880), made him a wealthy and popular artist.

Brown, Jacob (Jennings) (1775–1828) soldier; born in Bucks County, Pa. Schoolteacher, surveyor, lawyer, and militia general, he commanded U.S. forces on the New York frontier in the War of 1812, defeating the British at Ogdensburg, Sackett's Harbor, Fort Erie, Chippewa, and Lundy's Lane. From 1821–28 he served as commander of the U.S. Army.

Brown, James (1791–1877) banker; born in Ireland (son of Alexander Brown). He arrived in Baltimore, Md. in 1802 and in 1825 established the New York City branch of his father's firm, Brown Brothers & Company. He guided the banking house through financial crises (1837, 1857) and the Civil War. He gave generously to local institutions and was one of the founders of Presbyterian Hospital. The mayor of New York City ordered all flags on public buildings to fly at half-mast at his death.

Brown, James (1928–) musician; born in Barnwell, S.C. One of the most significant figures in black pop music, he began his singing career in Macon, Ga., with the Gospel Starlighters. In 1954, he formed a vocal group, the Famous Flames, with whom he recorded his first "cry" ballads, "Please, Please, Please" (1956) and "Try Me" (1958). Combining gospel and blues roots with a stage presentation that mixed calculated hysteria and absolute musical precision, he emerged by 1962 as the leading star in rhythm and blues and one of its key innovators. His nicknames included "the Hardest Working Man in Show Business" and "Soul Brother Number One." During the late 1960s, his ambiguous racial politics made him an emblematic figure for both moderate and radical movements. His 1968 recording, "Say It Loud, I'm Black and I'm Proud," became an anthem of the Black Power movement. By the early 1970s, he had become one of the first black entertainers to assume complete control of his own career, and this remains an enduring aspect of his legacy. In 1986, he was an inaugural member of the Rock 'n' Roll Hall of Fame. The following year, his recording "Living in America" won a Grammy for best rhythm & blues performance. In 1988 he was jailed for three years on charges that included aggravated assault. Upon his release in 1991, he resumed his career as a leading concert and recording artist.

Brown, (James Nathaniel) Jim (1936–) football player, movie actor; born in St. Simons, Ga. An All-American at Syracuse University in 1956, his combination of speed and power made him the National Football League's premier running back. He led the league in rushing in eight of his nine seasons, while setting records (since broken) for yards gained in a game, season, and career. In 1966, he retired to pursue a career in action-adventure films.

Brown, John (1800–59) abolitionist; born in Torrington, Conn. Son of an itinerant tradesman, he grew up in Hudson, Ohio, and received little formal schooling. His mother died insane when he was eight years old; several of her nearest relations were also seriously disturbed. He became a tanner, one of his father's trades, then successively a land surveyor, shepherd, and farmer. He married in 1820 and again in 1831 after the death of his first wife, fathering 20 children altogether. He migrated from place to place in the 1830s and 1840s, failing in several businesses and engaging in unprofitable land speculations. He had been an abolitionist from his youth, but he was in his fifties before he began to plot emancipation by main force. By 1855 he and six of his sons and a son-in-law had moved to Osawatomie, Kansas, to participate in the struggle to keep it a non-slave state. After proslavery forces attacked and burned the town of Lawrence, Kansas, Brown led a small force, including four of his sons, to nearby Pottawatomie Creek where on the night of May 24, 1856, they killed five proslavery men; he took full responsibility for the killings. Returning to the East, now dangerously obsessed with abolition through violence, he gained the patronage of northern activists such as Gerrit Smith, who supplied him with money, arms, and moral support. Dreaming of setting up a free state for liberated slaves in the Virginia mountains, he planned a raid on the Harpers Ferry, Va., armory. He and his men seized the armory on October 16, 1859, but were captured when a detachment of U.S. Marines under Col. Robert E. Lee stormed the building. Tried for treason and hanged on December 2, he became the stuff of legend, a martyr to Northern supporters such as Ralph Waldo Emerson, and a dangerous fanatic to most Southerners.

Brown, John A. (1788–1872) banker; born in Ireland (son of Alexander Brown). He came to Baltimore in 1802 and ran the Philadelphia branch of his father's firm (1818–37). He gave generously to Presbyterian churches in Philadelphia.

Brown, John Carter (1797–1874) book collector; born in Providence, R.I. Son of philanthropist-industrialist Nicholas Brown, he assembled a unique library of pre-1800 Americana, eventually housed at Brown University.

Brown, John Carter (1934–) museum director; born in Providence, R.I. He studied at Harvard (B.A. 1956; M.B.A. 1958), at Munich University (with Bernard Berenson) (1958), at the Netherlands Institute of Art History (1960), and at New York University (M.A. 1962). His specialty was 17th-century Dutch art. As the director of the National Gallery of Art, Washington, D.C. (1969–92), he presided over a period of great expansion in the museum's exhibitions and public presence.

Brown, Joseph (Rogers) (1810–76) inventor, engineer,

manufacturer; born in Warren, R.I. He became a machinist in 1827 and set up a shop in 1831 to manufacture tools. In 1858 he began manufacture of sewing machines, forming a company in 1866. Brown invented milling and grinding machines, cutters, and he simplified the Vernier caliper (1852).

Brown, Lee P. (Patrick) (1937–) law enforcement, government official; born in Wewoka, Kans. He became a patrolman in San Jose, Calif. (1960) while still an undergraduate at Fresno State University (B.S. 1961). He earned a masters degree in sociology (San Jose University, 1964) and a doctorate in criminology (University of California: Berkeley, 1970). In 1968, he established the Department of Administration of Justice at Portland State University, and in 1972 he joined the faculty of Howard University. By 1975 he was back in Portland as sheriff of Multnomah County. A proponent of foot patrols and community policing, he was Atlanta's public safety commissioner from 1978–82, the police chief of Houston (1982–90), and from 1990–92 the New York City police commissioner. Author of numerous articles, he coauthored *Police and Society: An Environment for Collaboration and Confrontation*. In 1993, President Clinton made him Director of the Office of Drug Control Policy, a cabinet-level position.

Brown, Lester (1934–) environmentalist, author; born in Bridgeton, N.J. Educated at Rutgers and Harvard (M.A. 1962), he joined the U.S. Department of Agriculture in 1959 as a specialist in food, population, and the environment. He became director of the newly established Worldwatch Institute in Washington, D.C., in 1974. Under the auspices of Worldwatch he lectured and wrote widely on environmental concerns, and the reports issued by the institute have become among the most highly regarded and cited in the field of threats to the environment. His publications include *Building a Sustainable Society* (1981) and *Saving the Planet* (1991).

Brown, Margaret Wise (1910–52) author; born in New York City. She studied in Switzerland (1923–25) and Hollins College, Virginia (1928–32), worked for the Bureau of Educational Experiments (later Bank Street School) as a publisher, edited children's books for William R. Scott (1938–41), and divided her time between New York City and Vinal Haven, Maine. A gifted writer of many innovative books of verse and stories for children, notably *Goodnight Moon* (1947), she died suddenly in France after an operation for appendicitis.

Brown, Mather (1761–1832) painter; born in Boston, Mass. An itinerant portrait painter and miniaturist, he studied with Gilbert Stuart (1773), then left for England and studied under Benjamin West (1781). He stayed in England, painting austere portraits, including those of King George III, the Duke of York, and Charles Bulfinch (1786).

Brown, Michael S. (Stuart) (1941–) biochemical geneticist; born in New York City. He began his close personal and professional relationship with Joseph Goldstein when the two men studied at the Massachusetts General Hospital, Boston (1966–68). Brown investigated digestive system biochemistry at the National Institutes of Health (1968–71), then joined Goldstein at the University of Texas (1971). Together they found that patients with familial hypercholesterolemia have deficient cellular binding sites for low-density lipoproteins (LDLs), and they determined the nucleotide sequence of LDL-receptor genes. For these revolutionary studies in cholesterol metabolism, Brown and Goldstein shared the 1985 Nobel Prize in physiology.

Brown, Moses (1738–1836) manufacturer, philanthropist; born in Providence, R.I. He was a member of one of colonial America's most successful merchant families. In 1774 he became a Quaker, freed his slaves, and helped to start the Rhode Island Abolition Society. He was among the first cotton manufacturers in America and he induced Samuel Slater to set up Arkwright spinning machines in Rhode Island.

Brown, Olympia (1835–1926) suffragist, Universalist minister; born in Prairie Ronde, Mich. Encouraged by her feminist mother, she was educated at Antioch College and the Universalist divinity school at St. Lawrence University. After ordination (1863), she served for 24 years in churches in Massachusetts, Connecticut, and Wisconsin, combining pastoral duties with a militant suffrage activism, and was president of the Wisconsin Woman Suffrage Association (1884–1912) and the Federal Suffrage Association (1903–20). She was publisher of the *Racine Times* (1893–1900), following the death of her husband.

Brown, Paul (E.) (1908–91) football coach; born in Norwalk, Ohio. He achieved success at all coaching levels. His Massillon High School teams (1932–40) won state championships, his 1942 Ohio State University team was voted the national crown, and his professional Cleveland Browns (1946–62) won seven league titles. In 1968, he founded the Cincinnati Bengals. Extremely innovative, he brought classroom techniques to coaching, including detailed playbooks, film study, and intelligence tests.

Brown, Ralph (Hall) (1898–1948) geographer; born in Ayer, Mass. He became a specialist in historical geography; his best known works include *Mirror for Americans* (1943) and *Historical Geography of the United States* (1948). He is regarded as one of the founders of historical geography in North America.

Brown, Raymond (Edward) (1928–) Catholic theologian; born in New York City. A Sulpician priest with doctorates from St. Mary's Seminary (Baltimore, Md.) and Johns Hopkins University, he taught at St. Mary's (through 1971) and then at Union Theological Seminary (New York City), becoming an outstanding biblical scholar. He was president of the Catholic Biblical Association (1971–72) and served on the Vatican Secretariat for Christian Unity (1968–73).

Brown, Rita Mae (1944–) writer; born in Hanover, Pa. She continued her feminist and radical lesbian activism, begun as a student at New York University, into the 1970s, working for national political organizations, then pretty much withdrew to concentrate on her writing. Her zesty, best-selling first novel, *Rubyfruit Jungle* (1973), was followed by other fiction, poems, essays, and screenplays. Later books include *Bingo* (1988).

Brown, (Ronald Harmon) Ron (1941–) cabinet officer, lawyer; born in Washington, D.C. Son of Howard University graduates, he grew up in Harlem. After graduating from Middlebury College (1962) and service with the U.S. Army (1962–66), he earned his law degree at St. John's University School of Law (1970). While working for the National Urban League (NUL) in New York, he was elected district leader of the Democratic Party in Mount Vernon, N.Y. (1971). He was with the Washington, D.C., office of the NUL (1973–79), and he then held a series of positions under Senator Edward Kennedy; he worked for the Democratic National Committee (1981–85). In 1981 he had joined the Washington, D.C., law firm of Patton, Boggs & Blow, thereby becoming its first African-American partner, and for several years he made his name as a corporate lobbyist. By 1988 he was serving as a strategist to Jesse Jackson's presidential campaign, and his role as a unifier at the Democratic Convention led to his being chosen in 1989 to head the Democratic National Committee. Successful handling of the Democratic Party's own factions and of Bill Clinton's campaign in 1992 led to Brown's being appointed secretary of commerce in 1993.

Brown, Sterling (Allen) (1901–89) poet, teacher, writer; born in Washington, D.C. He graduated from Williams College (B.A. 1925), then Harvard (M.A. 1930), and was based in Washington, D.C. He taught primarily at Howard University (1929–69), and is known as a poet and a founder of black literary criticism, as in *Negro Poetry and Drama* (1937); but above all he was an influential teacher and encourager of African-American writers in the decades before they were being widely recognized.

Brown, Tony (1933–   ) television host, producer; born in Charleston, W.Va. A journalist in Detroit, he joined National Educational Television's newsmagazine, *Black Journal,* in 1970, later becoming dean of Howard University's School of Communications (1971–72). He lobbied to keep the show on the air, and as host and executive producer of *Tony Brown's Journal* (1978), he continued to look critically at issues facing African-Americans.

Brown, Trisha (1936–   ) choreographer, modern dancer; born in Aberdeen, Wash. After training in experimental dance, Brown became one of the founders of the Judson Dance Company in 1962. Recognized for her "equipment pieces," she formed her own company in the early 1970s and in 1990 became the first woman choreographer to receive a MacArthur Fellowship.

Brown, Walter Folger (1869–1961) lawyer, politician, postmaster general; born in Massillon, Ohio. Active in Republican politics, he campaigned for Theodore Roosevelt and William Howard Taft, served the administration of Warren G. Harding as chairman of the Joint Congressional Reorganization Committee (1921–24), and was postmaster general under Herbert Hoover (1929–33). He expanded airmail service and tried unsuccessfully to expand passenger air service using airmail contracts as bait.

Brown, William Adams (1865–1943) Protestant clergyman, theologian; born in New York City. The son of a Wall Street banker, he grew up in easy circumstances, graduated from Yale (1886) and Union Theological Seminary (1890) and studied in Germany. Ordained a Presbyterian minister in 1893, he taught at Union from 1898–1936, where he became involved in social causes and the ecumenical movement. He helped found the American Theological Society. He published 15 books, including *Beliefs That Matter* (1928).

Brown, William Henry (fl. 1820s) theater producer, playwright; born in the West Indies. Little is known of his origins except that he arrived in the United States as a seaman and by 1821 was establishing the African Theatre to allow all-black casts to perform mainly plays from the white repertoire, including condensed versions of Shakespeare. But he also staged a sketch that dealt with slavery and in 1823 he produced his own play, *The Drama of King Shotaway* (1823),

evidently drawing on his own personal experience of the 1795 black Caribs' insurrection on the island of St. Vincent. His theater produced the first two notable African-American actors, James Hewlett and Ira Aldridge. Brown may also have founded a theater in Albany, N.Y., but otherwise he passed into oblivion.

Brown, William Wells (b. "William") (c. 1816–84) reformer, writer; born in Lexington, Ky. After adopting the name of the Wells Brown who assisted his escape from slavery (1834), he became a leading abolitionist, lecturing and writing widely on that and other reform causes. His pioneering works of black fiction and history include his autobiography *Narrative of William W. Brown, A Fugitive Slave* (1847) and *The Negro in the American Rebellion* (1867). In 1853 he published in London what was long thought to be the first novel by an African-American, *Clotel, or The President's Daughter;* it was based on the rumor that Thomas Jefferson had fathered a child with a slave woman; when published in the U.S.A. in 1864 it was delicately retitled, *Clotelle: A Tale of the Southern States.*

Browne, Charles Farrar (b. Brown) (Artemus Ward, pen name) (1834–67) writer, humorist; born in Waterford, Maine. In a series of *Cleveland Plain Dealer* letters (1857–59) purportedly written by Artemus Ward, this newspaperman created the blustery character through whom he satirized contemporary society. These letters, followed by an endless series he concocted to describe everything he saw or thought, were part of the ongoing American tradition of "unlettered" colloquial writing that culminated in Mark Twain's work. Browne joined *Vanity Fair's* staff (1859) and after 1861 toured the U.S.A. and England impersonating Ward (and incidentally inventing the comic lecture). He died of tuberculosis while on a lecture tour in England.

Browning, John (1933–   ) pianist; born in Denver, Colo. From a musical family, he studied at Juilliard and won the Leventritt Award in 1955. He became an international soloist, his concerto repertoire stretching from Mozart to Barber.

Browning, John Moses (1855–1926) gunsmith, inventor; born in Ogden, Utah. The son of Mormon parents, he produced his first gun from scrap iron at age 13. He formed Browning Brothers Company and marketed his products through the Colt Company. He patented a breech-loading single-shot rifle (1879) and the Browning automatic pistol (1911). He produced the Browning machine gun (1917) and the Browning automatic rifle (1918) for use in World War I. (It was a Browning pistol that was used to assassinate Archduke Ferdinand in 1914 and so begin World War I.) He expanded his business overseas and died in Belgium.

Brownson, Orestes (Augustus) (1803–76) writer, religious thinker; born in Stockbridge, Vt. Largely self-educated and zealously devoted to social and religious reform, he was, successively, a Presbyterian, a Universalist minister, and a Unitarian pastor, before founding his own sect (1836); he was also associated with the transcendentalist movement. In 1838 he founded and became editor of the *Boston* (later *Brownson's*) *Quarterly Review.* In 1844, with his wife and seven children, he became a Catholic; as an apologist for Catholicism (and for American democracy) thereafter, he was, as always, militant and uncompromising; his works, which attracted controversy from both inside and outside Catholicism, were widely read in his day.

Brubeck, (David Warren) Dave (1920–) jazz musician; born in Concord, Calif. He is one of the handful of modern jazz artists to have achieved mainstream popularity, largely through his recording of "Take Five" in 1962, and his attractive use of unconventional time signatures. A classically-trained pianist who studied with Darius Milhaud, he composed works for ballet, symphony orchestra, and the musical theatre and he toured regularly with his Quartet, which he formed in 1949.

Bruce, David K. (Kirkpatrick) E. (Este) (1898–1977) statesman, diplomat; born in Baltimore, Md. He served in the field artillery in World War I and was admitted to the Maryland bar in 1921. He was with the Foreign Service (1925–27) and then turned his attention to business and farming (1928–40). He helped to organize the Office of Strategic Services (1941). As director of the Economic Cooperation mission (1948–49) he administered the Marshall Plan in France. He was ambassador to France (1949–52), to West Germany (1957–59), and to Great Britain (1961–69). He was a representative to the Vietnam Peace Talks in Paris (1970–71) and liaison officer to Communist China (1973–74). His career culminated with the post of ambassador to NATO (1974–76).

Bruce, Lenny (b. Leonard Alfred Schneider) (1925–66) comedian; born in Mineola, N.Y. He joined the navy at age 16 and served during World War II until 1946. He held various jobs while studying acting in New York. An appearance on the Arthur Godfrey television show brought him national attention. A stand-up nightclub entertainer, his scatalogical language and outrageous, sardonic humor was alternatively called obscene and "radically relevant." Denounced for blasphemy in Australia and banned from performing in England, he was arrested for obscenity after a Greenwich Village show in 1964. Increasingly paranoid, he died of a drug overdose. His autobiography, *How to Talk Dirty and Influence People,* was published in 1965; the play *Lenny* was devoted to him; and he is regarded as having "liberated" a whole new generation of comedians.

Bruch, Hilde (1904–) psychiatrist, author; born in Duelken, Germany. She studied medicine at the University of Freiburg and was active in psychology research and pediatrics until the Nazi occupation of 1933. She emigrated to New York City and taught at Columbia University from 1934 to 1964 while practicing psychoanalysis. In 1965 she joined the Baylor College of Medicine in Houston, Texas. She is best known for her work on eating disorders, including *The Golden Cage: The Enigma of Anorexia Nervosa* (1978).

Brumidi, Constantino (1805–80) painter; born in Rome, Italy. He emigrated to New York City in 1852, escaping from political troubles in Rome. Said to be the first painter of frescoes in America, he decorated many government buildings in Washington, D.C., including *Cincinnatus at the Plow* (1855) in the Agricultural Committee room, and the frieze in the Rotunda of the Capitol (?1875–80).

Brundage, Avery (1887–1975) businessman, athletic administrator, art collector; born in Detroit, Mich. He competed in the 1912 Olympics, and after making a fortune as a building contractor, he gained the presidency of the U.S. Olympic Committee (1929–53) and then the presidency of the International Olympic Committee (1952–72). His tenure was often marked by controversy over his strong opposition to commercialism in amateur athletics and also over his autocratic behavior. His private passion was collecting Asian art, on which he became a respected authority; he left his superb collection to San Francisco's museums.

Bruner, Jerome S. (Seymour) (1915–) psychologist, author; born in New York City. Educated at Duke University and Harvard, he taught psychology at Harvard (1952–72), Oxford (1972–80), and the New School for Social Research in New York City. His book *The Process of Education* (1960) established him as a curriculum innovator whose ideas were grounded in cognitive development. Other influential works included the humanities program, "Man: A Course of Study," in *Toward a Theory of Instruction* (1966). He pioneered techniques for investigating infant perception. Advocating the value of cognitive psychology, he criticized the radical behaviorism of B. F. Skinner as deficient in a proper regard for humanity's primary motivations and problems.

Brunvand, Jan Harold (1933–) folklorist; born in Cadillac, Mich. An Indiana University Ph.D., he taught English and folklore at the University of Utah (1966). His early publications included work on Indiana, Utah, and Alberta folklore; in the 1980s he published several collections of American urban legends, including *The Mexican Pet* (1986).

Brush, Charles (Francis) (1849–1929) engineer, inventor; born in Euclid Township, Ohio. A farmer's son, he took a mining engineering degree from the University of Michigan (1869) and worked as a chemist and an iron merchant before leaving business to devote full time to his electrical inventions. In 1879 the city of Cleveland adopted his Brush arc light. It soon went into use worldwide. The arc light made his fortune, and he devoted his late years to theoretical research and philanthropy.

Brush, George (de Forest) (1855–1941) painter; born in Shelbyville, Tenn. He studied with Gérôme in Paris until 1880, then settled in Dublin, N.H. He is remembered for his American Indian works and tender family paintings, such as *In the Garden* (1906), and *A Family Group* (1907).

Brustein, Robert (Sanford) (1927–) critic, theater director; born in New York City. A wool merchant's son, educated at Amherst College and Columbia University, he gained his first reputation as a drama critic, primarily for *The New Republic* (1959–68). Appointed dean of the Yale Drama School in 1965, he founded the Yale Repertory Theatre in 1966 and helped it gain a national reputation as a semiprofessional company. In 1979 he was released by Yale but he was immediately hired by Harvard as a professor of English and was asked to found a resident professional training company, known as the American Repertory Theatre; he supervised some 200 productions. In addition to his edition of the works of August Strindberg, he published several books on theater and society, including *Who Needs Theatre* (1968) and *Reimagining American Theatre* (1991).

Bryan, John Henry, Jr. (1936–) business executive; born in West Point, Miss. He began his career with his family's business, Bryan Foods, in 1960. He built up the company, then sold it to Consolidated Foods Corporation (later known as Sara Lee Corporation). He joined Sara Lee Corporation and rose to be president, CEO, and in 1976, chairman of the board.

Bryan, William Jennings (1860–1925) political leader, orator; born in Salem, Ill. After practicing law, he was elected to the U.S. House of Representatives (Dem., 1891–95) and began to develop his reputation as "the Great Commoner," using his oratorical skills on behalf of the causes of the common folk. He opposed high tariffs and he called for an income tax, direct popular election of senators, a Department of Labor, prohibition, and women's suffrage. Out of office, he turned to journalism and lecturing and when he showed up at the Democratic national convention of 1896 and delivered his famous "Cross of Gold" speech on behalf of free silver, the agrarian West prevailed over the urban East and he ended up with the presidential nomination. He lost, as he would when he ran again in 1900 and 1908. After helping Woodrow Wilson gain the Democratic nomination in 1912, he became Wilson's secretary of state (1913); devoted to establishing arbitration as the solution to international disputes, he resigned in 1915 rather than go along with Wilson's belligerent warnings to Germany; when America entered World War I, however, he supported Wilson. In 1920 he moved to Florida where, participating in the real-estate boom, he made a fortune; he continued his career as a lecturer, known especially for his support of prohibition and of a literal interpretation of the Bible. It was in this last capacity that he made his final public appearance, speaking for the prosecution at the Scopes anti-evolution "monkey trial" in 1925.

Bryant, Gridley J. F. (James Fox) (1816–99) architect; born in Boston, Mass. (son of railroad pioneer Gridley Bryant). His Boston practice prefigured the large architectural firm and designed primarily commercial and public buildings; he rebuilt 110 of his 152 buildings destroyed in the 1872 Boston fire.

Bryant, Paul (William) "Bear" (1913–83) football coach; born in Moro Bottoms, Ark. At his retirement after the 1982 season, he was college football's winningest coach, with a 323-85-17 record for 38 years. He produced highly ranked teams at Maryland, Kentucky and Texas A&M before returning to his alma mater, the University of Alabama, in 1958. His Alabama teams won six national championships and won or shared Southeastern Conference titles thirteen times.

Bryant, William Cullen (1794–1878) poet, editor; born in Cummington, Mass. He attended Williams College (1810–11), studied law (1811–15), and practiced in Great Barrington, Mass., (1816–25), before settling in New York City and Long Island (1843). An editor of the *Evening Post* (1829–78), he was an opponent of slavery and helped to establish the new Republican Party. During his long years as both a lawyer and editor he continued to write poetry such as "Thanatopsis" (written in 1811, revised in 1821) and "To a Waterfowl" (1821) that gained him the reputation as America's first major poet. He also translated new editions of the *Illiad* (1870) and the *Odyssey* (1871–72).

Bryson, Reid A. (Allen) (1920–) climatologist; born in Detroit, Mich. A major in the Air Weather Service (1942–46), he then joined the University of Wisconsin where he started the meteorology department in 1948. In 1963 he founded the university's Center for Climate Research at which he became the senior scientist. He helped found and chaired the university's Interdisciplinary Committee on the Future of Man. He wrote more than 200 papers, some of which combine original poetry with scientific data, and five books, including *Climates of Hunger* (1977, with J. E. Ross).

Brzezinski, Zbigniew (Kasimierz) (1928–) political scien-

tist, government official; born in Warsaw, Poland. He moved to Canada (1938), studied at McGill University and Harvard, and became a naturalized U.S. citizen in 1958. He taught at Harvard (1953–60) and Columbia University (1969–77). He was director of the Trilateral Commission (1973–76) and national security adviser to President Jimmy Carter (1977–81). He wrote *Political Power: USA/USSR* (1964).

Buatta, Mario (1935–) interior decorator; born in Staten Island, N.Y. Following design study at Parsons, he established Mario Buatta, Inc. (1963). As the inimitable "Prince of Chintz," he was sought after for his interpretation of the English country house style. In the 1980s he began to design textiles and furniture. Together with Mark Hampton he redecorated the Blair House (1985) in Washington, D.C.

Buchanan, Franklin (1800–74) naval officer; born in Baltimore, Md. He became the first superintendent of the Naval School at Annapolis (1845–47). He was captain of Commodore Matthew Perry's flagship during Perry's mission to Japan (1852–53). He joined the Confederate States Navy (1861) and commanded the Chesapeake Bay squadron, became a Confederate admiral (1862), was wounded and captured at Mobile Bay (1864), and was released in a prisoner exchange (1865).

Buchanan, James (1791–1868) fifteenth U.S. president; born near Mercersburg, Pa. Building on a successful law career, he entered politics and served as a Federalist in the Pennsylvania legislature (1815–17) and the U.S. House of Representatives (1821–31), where he went over to the Democratic Party. In 1832–33 he served as ambassador to Russia and returned to serve Pennsylvania in the U.S. Senate (1834–45) until becoming a most effective secretary of state under President Polk (1845–49). After a period of retirement and as ambassador to Great Britain (1854–56), he showed a willingness to accommodate slavery that gained him the presidency in 1856 with the solid backing of the South. During his term (1857–61) he supported laws protecting slavery in the attempt to establish Kansas as a slave state; when pressed by antislavery Americans, he fell back on narrow legal defenses such as the Compromise of 1850 and the Dred Scott decision (1857). All this split the Democratic Party, allowing Lincoln to win the election of 1860. As a "lame duck" president, Buchanan professed the government's helplessness to prevent secession and turned the problem over to his successor. He returned to his Pennsylvania estate but he did support Lincoln throughout the war.

Buchanan, James M. (McGill) (1919–) economist; born in Murfreesboro, Tenn. With his "public choice" theory, an integration of political decision making and economic theory, he attacked the established approach to public sector economics. His interest and analysis of collective choice was strongly influenced by 19th-century European writers on public finance. He taught at several colleges before accepting a professorship at George Mason University (1983). He was awarded the Nobel Prize (1986).

Bucher, Lloyd (Mark) ("Pete") (1929–) naval officer; born in Pocatello, Ida. Orphaned as a child, he spent his early boyhood being shuffled between adoptive parents in Idaho and relatives in California until 1938 when he went to St. Joseph's Children's Home in Culdesac, Ida. From 1941 to 1945 he attended the famous Boys Town (near Omaha, Nebr.); after leaving to spend two years in the navy, he returned to graduate with his class in 1948, then went on to the University of Nebraska, where he majored in geology. In June 1953 he was commissioned in the U.S. Navy Reserve and spent most of his career as a submarine officer. His first command of a surface ship came in May 1967, the *Pueblo,* a small intelligence-gathering ship, and it was on its first tour of duty, off the coast of North Korea, that on January 23, 1968, he surrendered the ship when it came under fire from the North Korean navy (four Americans were wounded, and one later died). He and his crew were imprisoned until December 22, 1968, during which time Bucher and many of his men were forced to sign a letter asking the U.S.A. to admit the ship had been inside North Korea's waters, with the clear implication that they had been spying. In 1969 a naval court of inquiry recommended that Bucher and one other officer be court-martialed, but this was canceled by the secretary of the navy. Bucher never was given a major command and he retired from the navy in 1973; it was 1990 before he and all others on the *Pueblo* were awarded the medals given to other POWs. In his retirement Bucher enjoyed a new career as a painter.

Bucher, Walter H. (Herman) (1888–1965) geologist; born in Akron, Ohio. He taught at the University of Cincinnati (1913–40), joined Columbia University (1940–65), then became a consultant for Humble Oil (1956–65). His theory that mountains are built from contractions of the earth due to cooling and the earth's gravitational field was first proposed in his most famous book, *The Deformation of the Earth's Crust* (1933, revised 1964).

Buchman, Frank (Nathan Daniel) (1878–1961) Protestant evangelist; born in Pennsburg, Pa. The son of devout Lutherans, he graduated from Muhlenberg College in 1899, went on to Lutheran seminary and was ordained in 1902. He was for several years a pastor and social worker in Philadelphia. In the 1920s, in Oxford, England, he founded what would become Moral Rearmament, an ecumenical, conservative, and ultimately anticommunist movement that for a while had a wide international following. An account of his mature views, *America Needs an Ideology,* appeared in 1957.

Buchwald, (Arthur) Art (1925–) journalist; born in Mount Vernon, N.Y. Starting as a columnist for the European edition of the *Herald Tribune,* covering the lighter side of Paris life, he later moved to Washington, D.C., with his syndicated column of wry humor eventually appearing in some 550 papers worldwide.

Buck, Beryl (Elizabeth) H. (Hamilton) (1896–1975) philanthropist; born in Minnesota; **and Leonard W.** (1891–1953) pathologist; born in Vacaville, Calif. Beryl met Leonard at Roosevelt Hospital in Oakland where she was training to be a nurse and he a doctor. They married a year later (1914). Leonard's father died in 1916, and his mother in 1920, leaving the Buck's millionaires with a fortune from oil. They built an estate in Ross (Marin County) (1931), and Leonard, a pathologist, taught at the University of California: San Francisco (1928–51). Leonard died suddenly, leaving all his estate to Beryl. She, in turn, formed the Leonard and Beryl Buck Foundation Trust which, after she died, became part of the San Francisco Foundation, with the stipulation that the money be reserved for Marin County's needy and various nonprofit, educational, religious, and charitable organizations. What was a $15 million bequest became a $253-million trust when the Buck's Beldridge Oil stock was bought by

Shell Oil. Attempts by the San Francisco Foundation to spend money outside the already prosperous Marin County resulted in litigation and a court settlement (1986) establishing the Marin Community Foundation (1987), which administers the trust now valued at more than $500 million for Marin County residents.

Buck, Dudley (1839–1909) organist, composer; born in Hartford, Conn. After studies in the U.S.A. and Europe he held a series of distinguished church-organist positions, meanwhile teaching and composing with equal success.

Buck, (Franklyn Howard) Frank (1884–1950) animal collector, showman; born in Gainesville, Texas. Interested in collecting animals as a boy, he knocked about in his youth and married light-opera star Lillie West (known as Amy Leslie) in 1901; they divorced in 1916. Starting in 1911, he traveled extensively to South America and Asia to buy animals, which he then sold to zoos and circuses in the U.S.A. He soon extended his operations to all continents, began to lead his own expeditions to capture exotic animals, and through his exhibits and lectures became both rich and famous. During the Great Depression he turned to writing adventure books, including *Bring 'Em Back Alive* (1930), which became a movie, starring Buck himself. He published several more books and appeared in several more movies. Popular with adults as well as children, he reportedly received thousands of fan letters.

Buck, Leonard W. See under BUCK, BERYL.

Buck, Pearl (Comfort b. Sydenstricker) (1892–1973) author; born in Hillsboro, W.Va. She was raised among Chinese children by American missionary parents in Chinkiang, China, and apart from attending Randolph-Macon Woman's College in Virginia, lived in China until she was 40. In 1922 she began writing on Chinese life for American magazines. Her second novel, *The Good Earth* (1931), won the Pulitzer Prize; still her best known book, it sold two million copies, established Buck as the foremost Western interpreter of China, and gained her the Nobel literature prize (1938). The literary establishment disdained Buck's prolificacy, sentimentality, and didacticism, and many of Buck's 80 volumes of novels, translations, and memoirs quickly faded; her Chinese fiction in particular lost its immediacy after her move to the U.S.A. (1935); nevertheless, she engendered widespread sympathetic public awareness of China. She established the Pearl S. Buck Foundation (1964) and sponsored humanitarian work on behalf of Asian-American and retarded children.

Buckley, William F. (Frank), Jr. (1925–) journalist, author; born in New York City. Son of a wealthy oilman, he castigated the values of his alma mater in *God and Man at Yale* (1951) and became a leading light of political conservatism as founder (in 1955) and longtime editor of *National Review* magazine, and as a syndicated columnist. Known for his patrician manner and sesquipedalian vocabulary, he hosted a TV discussion program, *Firing Line,* from 1966. His books include a series of popular spy thrillers.

Buckner, Emory (Roy) (1877–1941) lawyer; born in Pottawattamie County, Iowa. After Harvard Law School, he helped reform the New York U.S. attorney's office (1904–10) and New York City's Police Department (1910–13). He then joined with Silas Howland, Elihu Root Jr., and Grenville Clark to establish what became the model for a large New York law firm. In 1925–27, answering the call for a totally independent law officer in New York City, he served as U.S. attorney and prosecuted a series of cases involving prohibition violations and corruption in the government. Zestful and kind, he was an extraordinary mentor to young lawyers who went on to successful careers.

Buckner, Simon Bolivar (1823–1914) Confederate soldier; born near Munfordville, Ky. He graduated from West Point in 1844 and saw extensive action during the Mexican War. Buckner entered Confederate service as a brigadier general in September 1861. In February 1862, after his two senior officers escaped to safety, he surrendered Fort Donelson, Ky., to General Grant after receiving Grant's famous "unconditional surrender" message; exchanged later in 1862, Buckner commanded a wing of Bragg's army at Chickamauga. After the war, he edited a Louisville newspaper and served as Democratic governor of Kentucky from 1887 to 1892.

Buckner, Simon Bolivar, Jr. (1886–1945) soldier; born in Munfordville, Ky. Son of the Civil War general, he commanded the U.S. 10th Army in the invasion of Okinawa in April 1945, and was killed in action on June 18 while inspecting frontline positions there.

Budd, Edward G. (Gowen) (1870–1946) industrialist; born in Smyrna, Del. He apprenticed as a machinist and by 1902 he was general manager at the Hale and Killern Company (Philadelphia), a manufacturer of car seats and other parts for railroads; he introduced pressed steel with oxyacetylene-welded joints. In 1912 he formed the Edward G. Budd Manufacturing Company to put into production his idea for all-steel auto bodies as opposed to some sections of wood used then; his all-steel bodies soon became the standard. In World War I his factory produced military equipment. In 1925 he opened the Budd Wheel Company in Detroit to make steel disk wheels for autos. He continued to experiment with stainless steel, building the first stainless steel airplane in 1931. He also built stainless steel railroad cars called "Buddliners," selling 500 by 1941. During World War II he again retooled for military equipment and in 1946 consolidated his companies into the Budd Company. In 1944 he won the medal of the American Society of Mechanical Engineers.

Budge, (John Donald) Don (1915–   ) tennis player; born in Oakland, Calif. From the time he won his first California junior title (1930) until he turned professional (1939), he proved to be almost unbeatable, taking various national titles and helping to secure several Davis Cups. In 1938 he became the first player ever to win in the same year the four major championships that comprise the Grand Slam of tennis: the U.S., Australian, Wimbledon, and French titles. He won the U.S. professional title in 1940 and 1942, then served in the U.S. Army in World War II, after which he played exhibition matches around the world.

Buell, Don Carlos (1818–98) soldier; born near Marietta, Ohio. An 1841 West Point graduate, he saw combat in the Mexican War, in which he was severely wounded. In mid-1861 he helped organize the Army of the Potomac; he took command of the newly formed Department of the Ohio later in the year. His unopposed entry into Nashville in 1862 followed in the wake of Grant's victories at Forts Henry and Donelson. Buell's forces arrived at Shiloh in April, barely in time to reinforce Grant and assure his victory. After fighting Bragg's Confederate army to a draw at Perryville, Ky., on

October 8, 1862, Buell was relieved of command for failing to pursue the retreating enemy. Regarded as overly cautious, he was never again assigned a field command, so he resigned from the army in 1864. He settled in Kentucky after the war, where he worked with an iron company and as a pension agent.

Buell, Raymond Leslie (1896–1946) editor, writer; born in Chicago. He taught history and government at several colleges during the 1920s. He was the research director (1927–33) and then president (1933–39) of the Foreign Policy Association. An early anti-isolationist, he championed a global policy for the U.S.A.

Buffalo Bill See CODY, WILLIAM FREDERICK.

Buffett, Warren (1930–   ) investment entrepreneur/executive; born in Omaha, Nebr. A stockbroker's son, educated at the University of Nebraska and Columbia University, he formed his own firm, Buffett Partnership, Ltd., in his hometown in 1956. His investment successes, particularly in buying undervalued companies whose stocks shortly began to rise, made him extremely rich and gained him the sobriquet, "oracle of Omaha." He helped rescue Salomon Brothers from corporate raiders in 1987, and took charge of the New York City house in 1992 in the wake of an insider trading scandal.

Buford, John (1826–63) Union soldier; born in Woodford County, Ky. An 1848 West Point graduate, he commanded a cavalry division during the Gettysburg campaign. On July 1, 1863, with a single brigade of dismounted troopers, Buford parried a heavy Confederate attack long enough to allow Union infantry to reach the battlefield. He died of illness later in the year.

Bühler, Charlotte (Bertha) (b. Malachowski) (1893–1974) psychologist; born in Berlin, Germany. She studied at Munich under Karl Bühler, whom she married in 1916. In 1922 they established the Vienna Institute of Psychology, a child study center; her research there resulted in the innovative World Test and major books including *From Birth to Maturity* (1935) and *From Childhood to Old Age* (1938). The Bühlers emigrated to the United States in 1940 because of the Nazi threat, and she worked in the Midwest before settling in Los Angeles in 1945. During the 1960s, her positive view of the course of human development was embodied in humanistic psychology, which emphasized self-determination over biological or environmental determinism.

Buick, David Dunbar (1854–1929) inventor, manufacturer; born in Arbroth, Scotland. His family arrived in Detroit in 1856. He formed Buick and Sherwood (1884), manufacturers of plumbing equipment. He began making gasoline engines and formed the Buick Manufacturing Company (1902); its automobiles were the first to have windshields and a valve-in-head engine. The company failed and in 1903 merged with another to form the Buick Motor Car Company, which built only 53 cars in two years at no profit. Buick left in 1906, pursued oil and gold mining interests, and died an impoverished clerk at a Detroit trade school. The Buick Motor Car Company became part of the General Motors Company that William Durant organized in 1908.

Bukowski, Charles (1920–   ) poet, writer; born in Andernach, Germany. His family emigrated to America (1922), and he grew up in California, attended Los Angeles City College (1939–41), and settled in Santa Barbara. Considered an underground writer, he has produced witty and sardonic poetry, short stories, and novels.

Bulfinch, Charles (1763–1844) architect; born in Boston, Mass. America's first native-born architect, he graduated from Harvard and was inspired by new neoclassical buildings while on a European tour (1785–87). As a member of the board of selectmen (1791–1817) and superintendent of police, he sought to make Boston an American model of classical elegance through town planning and the development of the Federal style, designing numerous row houses, mansions, and commercial and public buildings, including the Massachusetts State House (1795–97), India Wharf (1803–07) and Massachusetts General Hospital (1818–23). Bulfinch became the leading New England architect, his Federal-style public buildings and Adam-like domestic interiors the standard for early republic architecture. Succeeding Latrobe as architect of the U.S. Capitol (1817–30), he completed the western portico, original dome, and landscaping before retiring to Boston. His domed capitol buildings influenced the design of state capitols across the country throughout the 19th century.

Bulfinch, Thomas (1796–1867) banker, author; born in Newton, Mass. Son of the influential architect Charles Bulfinch, he tried his hand at various businesses, then ended up working in a bank (1837–67). This job left him a lot of spare time, which he spent studying natural history and literature. Eventually he began to write books drawing on his extensive reading – *Hebrew Lyrical History* (1853), *The Age of Chivalry* (1858), *Shakespeare Adapted for Reading Classes* (1865). One title in particular, *The Age of Fable* (1855), gained wide fame; known as "Bulfinch's Mythology," it introduced Greek and Roman mythology to generations of Americans who did not read Greek or Latin.

Bullard, Robert Lee (b. William) (1861–1947) soldier; born in Lee County, Ala. The shy, sickly son of a planter, he changed his first name to honor the Confederate commander. An 1885 West Point graduate, he saw combat on the western frontier and in the Philippines (1900–01). In 1918, his 1st Division became the first U.S. division to occupy a section of the front line in France. He retired in 1925 and devoted his remaining years to writing and speech-making, often for conservative and isolationist causes. The last of his three books, *Fighting Generals,* appeared in 1944.

Bullins, Ed (1935–) writer, playwright; born in Philadelphia. He began writing fiction but turned to the theater to reach a wider public. A leader of the 1960s "black arts" movement, he cofounded Black Arts West in San Francisco. He wrote his first play, *Clara's Ole Man,* in 1965, and won three Obie Awards in the 1970s. Although not publishing much after the 1980s, he worked on a 20-play historical cycle about African-Americans. He was associated with several theaters in New York City, including the New Lafayette Theater (1968–73), American Place Theater (1973), and the Surviving Theater (1974) and he taught at, among other institutions, City College of San Francisco (1984).

Bullitt, William C. (Christian) (1891–1967) diplomat; born in Philadelphia. From an affluent family, he worked in Europe as a newspaper correspondent, then joined the State Department (1917). A member of the American delegation to the Paris Peace Conference (1919), he was sent on a secret mission to Russia and returned to advocate recognition of the new Communist government; when this was rejected, he resigned from the State Department and gave testimony before the Senate committee (1919) that influenced the rejection of the Versailles treaty. He left the State Department and lived mainly in Europe; he turned to Freud for therapy and ended up collaborating with him on a highly negative psychological biography of Woodrow Wilson (not published until 1967). In 1932 President Franklin Roosevelt appointed him as a special assistant to the secretary of state and then as the first ambassador to the U.S.S.R. (1933–36); he soon turned against Communism, a position he increasingly promoted in the years ahead. As ambassador to France (1936–40) and a series of other special diplomatic assignments, he was one of President Roosevelt's most trusted advisors; but after the two had a falling out in 1943, Bullitt joined the Free French army (1944–45). Although regarded as a nonconformist, he spent his last years dabbling in international affairs as a respected elder statesman.

Bumbry, (Melzia Ann) Grace (1937–) mezzo-soprano; born in St. Louis, Mo. She made an acclaimed debut at the Paris Opera in 1960 and the next year sang Venus at Bayreuth; her Metropolitan Opera debut came in 1965. She went on to a distinguished international career singing both mezzo and soprano roles.

Bunche, Ralph J. (Johnson) (1904–71) diplomat, statesman; born in Detroit, Mich. He worked his way through college and traveled, wrote (*A World View of Race,* 1937), and taught at Howard University (1928–41). He served in the Office of Strategic Services (1941–44) and then the State Department (1944–47). At the start of his long career with the United Nations (1947–71), he was the acting mediator for the U.N. Palestine Commission (1948, 1949), and won the Nobel Peace prize for this work (1950). He subsequently became under secretary (1955–67) and under secretary general (1967–71) for the United Nations. Most noted for his expertise on colonial affairs and race relations, he directed UN peacekeeping efforts in the Suez (1956), the Congo (1964), and Cyprus (1964). Although he was not an overt activist or spokesman during his public career he was arguably the most prominent role model for his fellow African-Americans until the emergence of Martin Luther King Jr.

Bundy, McGeorge (1919–) educator, public official; born in Boston, Mass. After teaching and serving as a dean at Harvard University, he was special national security adviser to Presidents Kennedy and Johnson (1961–66) and played a prominent role in pursuing the Vietnam War. He went on to become Ford Foundation president (1966–79) and history professor at New York University.

Bunker, Ellsworth (1894–1984) diplomat, executive; born in Yonkers, N.Y. He was an executive in the sugar industry (1927–66) and became a diplomat in 1951. He was ambassador to Argentina, Italy, India, and Nepal (1951–61). He was ambassador to South Vietnam during the crucial stages of the Vietnam War (1967–73) and the chief negotiator of the Panama Canal treaties (1973–78), which became controversial during the 1976 presidential campaign.

Bunshaft, Gordon (1909–90) architect; born in Buffalo, N.Y. He studied architecture at the Massachusetts Institute of Technology and joined Skidmore and Owings in 1937. His public and corporate buildings are characterized by inventive design; especially influential were his skyscraper towers set back in plazas (Lever House (1952), New York City); suburban offices in landscaped parks (Connecticut General Life Insurance Building (1957), Bloomfield, Conn.); and sloping facades (9 West 57th Street Building (1974), New York).

Buntline, Ned See JUDSON, EDWARD ZANE CARROLL.

Bunzel, Ruth Leah (1898–   ) cultural anthropologist; born in New York City. She graduated from Barnard College in 1918 and worked as Franz Boas' secretary before undertaking a study of Zuñi Indian pottery with the encouragement of Boas and Ruth Benedict in 1924. She received a Ph.D. from Columbia University in 1929, the year she published *The Pueblo Potter*. She also contributed important studies of Zuñi ceremonialism. Field trips to Guatemala in the 1930s yielded *Chichicastenango, A Guatemalan Village* (1952). She later taught anthropology at Columbia.

Burbank, Luther (1849–1926) plant breeder, horticulturist; born in Lancaster, Mass. The 13th child of a farmer, he grew up interested in nature, and although he had little formal science education, he was influenced by the ideas of Charles Darwin. Turning to farming to support his widowed mother, by 1870 he was experimenting with improving the varieties of vegetables; his first success was a potato that grew in the stony Massachusetts soil; he sold the rights to it for $150 (to a seed dealer who named it the Burbank). In 1875 he went off to Santa Rosa, Calif., where he began what proved to be a prosperous nursery business; he sold it in 1893 to concentrate on his own experimental farm at nearby Sebastopol. Over the years – by selecting the most desirable specimens or by hybridizing and grafting two or more plants – he developed hundreds of new varieties of vegetables, fruit, and ornamental plants, including the Shasta daisy. He published many catalogues of his plants as well as the multivolume *Luther Burbank, His Methods and Discoveries* (1914–15) and *How Plants Are Trained to Work for Man* (1921). Although he was not truly a scientist and most of his new varieties no longer have commercial value, he remains something of an American legend as a self-taught "tinkerer with nature."

Burchfield, Charles (Ephraim) (1893–1967) painter; born in Ashtabula Harbor, Ohio. Although he attended Cleveland School of Art and briefly lived in New York City (1916), he spent most of his life in small towns in Ohio and upstate New York, and it was not until about 1929 that he could escape the factory jobs to devote himself to art. Known primarily for his watercolors, his works drawn from nature, such as *February Thaw* (1920), often conveyed an almost sinister mood, while his vision of urban America, as in *Black Iron* (1935), seem imbued with a sense of melancholy. His paintings of railroads and mines, commissioned by *Fortune* magazine in the late 1930s, brought his work to a wider public.

Burdett, Allen Mitchell, Jr. (1921–80) aviator; born in Washington, D.C. A 1943 West Point graduate, he helped test newly developed air mobility tactics as commander of the aviation group of the 1st Cavalry Division in Vietnam (1965–66). He subsequently directed the Army Aviation School and commanded the 5th Army before retiring in 1978.

Burger, Warren (Earl) (1907–   ) Supreme Court justice; born in St. Paul, Minn. He had been in private practice since 1931 when President Dwight D. Eisenhower named him assistant attorney general (1953–55) and then to the U.S. Court of Appeals (1956–69). His conservative approach, especially in regard to criminal justice, led President Richard Nixon to name him chief justice of the U.S. Supreme Court (1969–

86). Although generally conservative, he sometimes sided with the liberals on issues of civil rights, and he broke new ground with his outspoken views on the need for administrative reforms of the federal court system. He resigned to devote himself to the bicentennial observation of the adoption of the U.S. Constitution.

Burgess, (Frank) Gelett (1866–1951) writer, humorist; born in Boston, Mass. He attended Massachusetts Institute of Technology (B.S. 1887), and moved to San Francisco (1888), where he worked as a draftsman for the Southern Pacific Railroad (1888–91). He moved to New York City (1897), where he worked as an editor, and, after his marriage to an actress, lived in France to sample bohemian life (1914–18). He is known for publishing *The Lark* (1895–97), a humorous magazine, which carried his famous quatrain, "The Purple Cow." He continued to write, but with little success, and retired to California (1949).

Burgess, John William (1844–1931) political scientist, educator; born in Giles County, Tenn. He almost singlehandedly advanced the field of political science to the academic arena. He chaired the first department of history and political science at Amherst College (1873–76) before moving to Columbia University in 1876. He helped establish Columbia's university status and served as dean (1909–12). A prolific writer and esteemed teacher, he wrote several works that focused on 19th- and early 20th-century U.S. history. He warned against centralized power and stressed the obligation of states to protect individual rights. His lectures are compiled in *Political Science and Comparative Constitutional Law* (1890).

Burgess, Thornton W. (Waldo) (1874–1965) writer; born in Sandwich, Mass. He was a magazine writer and editor (1895–1911) and a syndicated newspaper columnist (1912–60). Drawing on the bedtime stories he told to his son, he published *Old Mother West Wind* (1910) and *Mother West Wind's Children* (1911), the first of his 54 books of stories for children, many featuring a cast of animals that have human names and talk and act like people. (He borrowed the name "Peter Rabbit" from the British author, Beatrix Potter.) He promoted conservationist ideas through his books and his Radio Nature League (founded 1925).

Burk, Martha Jane (Canary) (Calamity Jane) (?1852–1903) legendary frontier figure; born in Princeton, Mo. Raised in Virginia City, Mont. (1864), she became an expert markswoman and rider – dressed as a man – and held her own in rough, mining-town society. Allegedly a pony-express rider and then a scout for Gen. George Custer in Wyoming (1870s), she was companion to "Wild Bill" Hickok and heroine during the smallpox epidemic (1878) in the gold rush town of Deadwood, S.D. In 1891 she wed Clinton Burk(e) in El Paso, Texas, but he soon left her and she died in poverty. She is the heroine of *Deadwood Dick on Deck, or Calamity Jane the Heroine of Whoop Up*, an Edward L. Wheeler dime novel (1884), and is buried beside Hickok in Deadwood.

Burke, Arleigh A. (Albert) (1901–   ) naval officer; born in Boulder, Colo. He entered the navy in 1923 and performed with distinction in World War II. He was a strategic plans director (1952–54) and the chief of naval operations (1955–61). He pursued business interests after his retirement.

Burke, Charles Henry (1861–1944) U.S. representative; born in Batavia, N.Y. A homesteader, lawyer, and realtor, he served in the U.S. House of Representatives (Rep., S.D.;

1899–1907, 1909–15). He became Commissioner of Indian Affairs (1921–29), and returned to dealing in real estate afterward.

Burke, James Edward (1925–) manufacturing executive; born in Rutland, Vt. At Johnson & Johnson (1953–89), the major manufacturer of health care products, he headed the new product division before becoming variously president, CEO, and chairman (1966–89). He introduced important new products like disposable contact lenses and was widely praised for leading the company through two Tylenol-poisoning episodes (1982, 1986) with a sensitivity that increased the company's already high reputation for corporate responsibility.

Burke, James Lee (1936–) writer; born in Houston, Texas. He studied at the University of Southwest Louisiana (1955–57), and the University of Missouri (B.A. 1959; M.A. 1960). He worked as a surveyor, reporter, social worker, teacher, and for the U.S. Forest Service and the Job Corps Conservation Center in Kentucky. A writer of short stories and novels, he is best known for his series of mystery novels featuring his Cajun police detective, Dave Robicheaux, as in *A Stained White Radiance* (1992).

Burke, John (1859–1937) governor, federal official, judge; born in Keokuk County, Iowa. He moved to the Dakota Territory (1888) and served in the North Dakota state senate (1893–95). He was the Democratic governor of North Dakota (1907–12) and treasurer of the United States (1913–21). He served on the North Dakota Supreme Court (1925–37). North Dakota placed his statue in the U.S. Capitol.

Burke, John J. (Joseph) (1875–1936) religious leader; born in New York City. A Paulist priest who was editor of the *Catholic World* (1904–22), he helped during World War I to organize the bishops' group known as the National Catholic War Council. As general secretary (from 1919) of its successor, the National Catholic Welfare Council (later, Conference), he was a respected voice for Catholic interests and social reform. In 1936 he became a monsignor.

Burke, Kenneth (1897–1993) literary critic, poet; born in Pittsburgh, Pa. After dropping out of Columbia University, he began his writing career in New York City, serving as music critic at *Dial* magazine (1927–29). He wrote fiction, poetry, and literary criticism and theory, winning a Guggenheim Fellowship (1935). He taught at various colleges, mainly Bennington (Vt.) (1943–61). A complex writer, he is best known for his philosophy of language articulated in *The Grammar of Motive* (1945) and *Language as Symbolic Action* (1966).

Burleigh, Henry Thacker (1866–1949) baritone, composer, arranger; born in Erie, Pa. He learned African-American songs from his maternal grandfather, born a slave, and his voice gained him entry to the National Conservatory of Music in New York (1892–96). Its director was then Anton Dvořák, who both encouraged Burleigh and learned about the folk music he would use in his own works. He was soloist at St. George's Church in New York City (1894–1946) and sang occasionally at the city's Temple Emanu-El; he also concertized in America and Europe. From 1911 to 1949, he was a music editor at G. Ricordi & Company. He composed many songs and ballads but made his greatest mark through his arrangements of black spirituals such as "Deep River" (1916).

Burlingame, Anson (1820–70) U.S. representative, diplomat; born in New Berlin, N.Y. He was a member of the U.S. House of Representatives (Free-Soil, Mass.; 1855–59, Repub., Mass.; 1859–61). He was ambassador to China (1861–67) where he deeply impressed the Chinese with his integrity and helpfulness. In 1867, China appointed him the head of their first diplomatic mission to Europe. He died in St. Petersburg, Russia.

Burnett, Carol (1936–) television comedian/actress; born in San Antonio, Texas. After studying at the University of California: Los Angeles, she made her Broadway debut in a musical, *Once Upon a Mattress* (1959); she went on to appear in a few other Broadway shows but moved quickly into television, appearing as a regular on the Garry Moore show (1959–62) and on occasional CBS-TV specials. This led to her own comedy-variety show, *The Carol Burnett Show*, which ran from 1967–79. She appeared in several Hollywood movies (such as *Pete 'n' Tillie*, 1972) and television movies (such as *Friendly Fire*, 1979). In 1991 she revived her television comedy series with *Carol and Company*. An accomplished singer and dancer, she is known for her ability to use her expressive face and full-throated voice in playing a variety of broad comic roles.

Burnett, Charles (1944–) film scriptwriter/director; born in Mississippi. Raised in Los Angeles, he attended the film school at the University of California: Los Angeles, where his thesis project, *Killer of Sheep* (1977), received acclaim within the film community and launched his career as a leading African-American independent filmmaker. Often working at odd jobs to support his family, he continued to make critically acclaimed films and he received numerous grants, including a MacArthur Foundation "genius" fellowship; but *To Sleep With Anger* (1990) was his first film to get wider circulation.

Burnett, Francis (Eliza b. Hodgson) (1849–1924) author; born in Manchester, England. Brought up in Manchester, she and her parents emigrated to Knoxville, Tenn. (1865). She wrote for periodicals, traveled to Europe (1875–77), married, and moved to Washington, D.C. After the failure of her marriage, she divided her time between Long Island and England, and wrote her enduring classics for young readers, *Little Ford Fauntleroy* (1886), and *The Secret Garden* (1911). She continued to publish many other books, but her nostalgic approach became unpopular and it is her earlier work that is remembered.

Burnett, Leo (1891–1971) advertising executive; born in St. Johns, Mich. After working on the creative side of midwestern advertising agencies, he founded and chaired his own Chicago agency, Leo Burnett Company, Inc. (1935–67), which became the fifth largest in the world. His books include *Communications of an Advertising Man* (1961).

Burnett, Peter (Hardeman) (1807–95) public official; born in Nashville, Tenn. He went to Oregon in 1843 and led a group of goldseekers to California in 1848 where he briefly served as John A. Sutter's attorney. He was the first governor of California (1849–51) and president of the Pacific Bank in San Francisco.

Burnham, Daniel H. (Hudson) (1846–1912) architect and city planner; born in Henderson, N.Y. He trained with William Le Baron Jenney and later independently, Burnham helped establish the Chicago School with his seminal skyscraper designs beginning with the Montauk Block, Chicago (1881–82). His pioneering city planning (as in Washington, D.C. (1901–2) and Chicago (1909)) launched the "City Beautiful" movement. He was first chairman of the National Commission of Fine Arts (1910–12); he helped found the American Academy in Rome.

Burnham, Frederick Russell (1861–1947) explorer, scout; born in Tivoli, Minn. He moved west with his family and became a horseback messenger with Western Union Telegraph Company at age 13. After two decades of ranging in the Southwest and Mexico, he went to Africa (with his wife and three children); he worked closely with British imperialist Cecil Rhodes who granted him 100 square miles of land in present-day Zimbabwe. He was chief of scouts in the field for the British army during the Boer War and won the admiration of Sir Robert Baden Powell (founder of the Boy Scouts). In 1904 he returned to the U.S.A. and led archaeological and mineral-prospecting expeditions in Mexico before he retired to a cattle ranch near Sequoia National Park (Calif.).

Burnham, Sherburne Wesley (1838–1921) astronomer; born in Thetford, Vt. Trained to be a shorthand reporter, he was an amateur astronomer until he joined the staff of Yerkes Observatory (1897–1914). He reopened the subject of double stars when he counted an additional 1,290 double stars in the northern hemisphere and published his findings in 1900. *His General Catalogue of Double Stars* (1906) listed all 13,665 double stars in the northern hemisphere.

Burns, Anthony (1834–62) fugitive slave; born in Stafford County, Va. He converted to the Baptist faith and became a "slave preacher." He escaped from Richmond on a ship and reached Boston (1854). He was soon arrested and identified, under the provisions of the Fugitive Slave Law (1850). Bostonians fought to keep him free; it took $100,000 and hundreds of soldiers to put down the demonstrations before he was returned to his master in Virginia. Northerners raised $1,200 to purchase his freedom and he studied at Oberlin College (1857–62) and became a Baptist preacher.

Burns, Arthur F. (1904–87) economist; born in Stanislau, Austria. He came to the U.S.A. at the age of ten and went on to receive his university degrees from Columbia University, later teaching there (1933–62). He was a leading expert on business cycles and coauthored *Measuring Business Cycles* (1946) with W. C. Mitchell. He served as an economic adviser to Presidents Eisenhower and Nixon before holding the influential position of chairman of the Federal Reserve (1970–78). He also served as the U.S. ambassador to the Federal Republic of Germany (1981–85).

Burns, John Anthony (1909–75) governor; born in Fort Assineboine, Mont. Having moved to Hawaii, he became a Honolulu policeman (1934–45) and served as vice squad captain and espionage bureau chief during World War II. He was Hawaii's last non-voting delegate to the U.S. House of Representatives, lobbying for statehood in 1956. As Democratic governor of Hawaii (1963–75), he improved services for ordinary citizens and approved a progressive abortion bill.

Burns, Ralph (1922–) musician; born in Newton, Mass. An innovative modern jazz arranger, he attended the New England Conservatory of Music in 1938–39. He began with Charlie Barnet in New York as a pianist-arranger from 1940–43, then played with Red Norvo for a year. He joined Woody Herman in 1944 and served as his staff arranger until 1954, helping to establish the distinctive style of Herman's First, Second, and Third Herds. In the late 1940s, Herman recorded Burns's highly-acclaimed compositions, "Summer Sequence" and "Early Autumn," the latter introducing Stan Getz. In 1955, Burns began working exclusively on commercial recording sessions with singers and for television and film soundtracks.

Burns, William J. (John) (1861–1932) detective; born in Baltimore, Md. As affable as he was determined, he joined the Secret Service (1889–1903) where he gained national attention handling investigations like the Monroehead silver $100 certificate case, which became part of American lore. Working for the Interior Department, he uncovered the Oregon, Washington, and California land fraud cases (1903). After establishing the William J. Burns Detective Agency in New York City (1909), he secured world-wide recognition with the apprehension of the labor union dynamiters (1911).

Burnside, Ambrose (Everett) (1824–81) soldier; born in Liberty, Ind. Recognized more for his famous sidewhiskers than his generalship, he graduated from West Point (1847), served on the frontier, then resigned from the army to manufacture a breechloading rifle of his own design. He returned to service in 1861, became the second commander of the Army of the Potomac (November 1862), and precipitated the Union disaster at Fredericksburg (December 1862), the most one-sided of the major battles of the Civil War. Relieved in January 1863, Burnside led the small army that took Knoxville, Tenn. (1863), before returning east to command a corps in Meade's army. He left on leave after the failure of his assault in the Battle of the Crater (1864) and was not recalled. Burnside was a postwar governor of Rhode Island and a U.S. senator from that state (1875–81).

Burr, Aaron (1756–1836) vice-president, politician, adventurer; born in Newark, N.J. After serving with distinction in the American Revolution, he became a lawyer, engaged himself in some dubious land speculation, and was chosen a U.S. senator (Dem.-Rep., N.Y.; 1791–97). He was nominated in 1800 by the Democratic-Republican Party for vice-president, but because of the process then dictated by the Constitution, he ended up tied with Thomas Jefferson for the presidency. Refusing to concede the election, he forced the House of Representatives to 36 ballots before Jefferson won; Burr received little attention from Jefferson during his vice-presidency (1801–05). Climaxing a 15-year public and private feud with Alexander Hamilton, Burr challenged, dueled with, and killed Hamilton in 1804; after first fleeing south to avoid indictments, he returned to Washington to finish his term as vice-president. He then became involved with James Wilkinson in a still little-understood conspiracy, the goal of which seemed to be to create a new country in the southwest, with New Orleans as its capital. After escaping indictments three times in Kentucky and Mississippi Territory, he was arrested and tried in Virginia for treason, Chief Justice John Marshall presiding. He was acquitted of treason and all other charges. Setting off for Europe in 1808, he continued to try to engage first Britain and then France in his schemes for "liberating" the Spanish colonies in Mexico and America; when this failed, he returned to New York in 1812 and took up the practice of law. Always needing more money, at age 77 he married a wealthy widow, but she divorced him a year later. The last years of this problematic man were spent in relative obscurity.

Burr, Raymond (1917–93) TV actor; born in Westminster, Canada. Coming from Canada to study at Stanford University, he began as a stage actor, appearing in regional theater; he then moved into television dramas and movies. He starred as the burly detective in *Perry Mason* (1957–66) and *Ironside* (1967–75), winning two Emmies. He went on to appear in several TV miniseries and in two-hour versions of *Perry Mason.*

Burritt, Elihu (1810–79) blacksmith, reformer; born in New Britain, Conn. After working as a blacksmith in New Britain, Conn., and Worcester, Mass. (1827–37), and mastering several languages in his spare time, he toured as a lyceum lecturer, becoming known as the "learned blacksmith." In 1844 he founded a newspaper in Worcester, the *Christian Citizen,* especially to propagate his views on Christian pacifism, and he traveled to England (1846) as an "apostle of peace." In 1858 he founded a journal devoted to the cause of buying and emancipating slaves. Despite Burritt's opposition to the Civil War, President Lincoln appointed him consular agent at Birmingham, England, in 1863; he served until 1870.

Burroughs, Bryson (1869–1934) painter, curator; born in Hyde Park, Mass. He is remembered as a curator of painting at the Metropolitan Museum of Art (1909–34), where he discovered and acquired important works, such as *Harvesters* (1565) by Pieter Brueghel.

Burroughs, Edgar Rice (1875–1950) writer; born in Chicago, Ill. Son of a wealthy businessman, he attended the Michigan Military Academy, then served briefly in the U.S. cavalry until he was dropped for being underage. For the next 15 years (1896–1911) he worked at a variety of jobs including as a cowboy and miner, finally deciding to try his hand at writing. He published his first story, "Under the Moons of Mars" (using the pen name "Normal Bean") in the pulp magazine *All-Story* in 1912; it would become the beginning of a serialized novel (published in 1914 as *Princess of Mars*). In the years that followed he wrote several more science-fiction series but he would remain best known for a series of novels he began in 1914 with *Tarzan of the Apes,* a story about an English boy raised by apes in Africa; it was so successful that he went on to write another 27 titles in the Tarzan series. He moved to Hollywood in 1919 to supervise the filming of the first of what would eventually become an extremely popular series of Tarzan movies. The Tarzan story also inspired a comic strip, radio and television programs, and countless other spinoffs, all of which made Burroughs very rich. Although he lost money in early investments, he eventually made enough to buy a large ranch near Tarzana, a suburb of Los Angeles named after his creation. During World War II he served as a war correspondent. Churning out two or three novels a year, he wrote in a rather crude style, but the sheer narrative thrust of the Tarzan story engaged millions throughout the world.

Burroughs, John (1837–1921) naturalist, author; born near Roxbury, N.Y. Raised on a farm in the lower Catskills, intermittently educated, he taught school in Illinois and New Jersey and published his first nature essay in 1860. He took a job as a treasury department clerk in Washington in 1863 and met Walt Whitman there; Whitman provided the title for his first book, *Wake-Robin* (1871). On assignment in England

for the Treasury Department in 1871, he gathered material later used in essays published as *Winter Sunshine* (1875); reviewing the book, Henry James called him "a sort of reduced . . . Thoreau." He returned to the Catskills in 1873, built a house on the west bank of the Hudson near Esopus, N.Y., and turned out a book on the average of one every two years for the rest of his life. Long-bearded and rustic, he became something of a sage, his woodland cabin "Slabsides" the goal of naturalist pilgrims. He traveled widely in later years and formed friendships with Theodore Roosevelt, Thomas A. Edison and Henry Ford. He is credited, more than any other American writer, with establishing the nature essay as an important literary form.

Burroughs, William S. (Seward) (1914–) writer; born in St. Louis, Mo. Heir to the Burroughs business machine fortune, he was a Harvard-educated sometime medical student, private detective, and exterminator. In the late 1950s he became associated with the Beat writers in New York City. He later lived mostly in Paris and Tangier, Morocco, and admitted to being addicted to heroin. His two dozen books controversially blended homosexuality, science fiction, and underworld seaminess; later works experimented radically with language. *Naked Lunch* (Paris, 1959; New York, 1962) remains his best known work.

Burroughs, William (Seward) (1857–98) inventor; born in Rochester, N.Y. His work as a bank clerk led him to develop the first practical adding and listing machine. Exhausting his small capital of $300, he perfected such a machine and received a patent for it in 1888. He developed improved calculators during the 1890s. His Burroughs Adding Machine Company was the forerunner of the Burroughs Corporation, a computer manufacturer.

Burrows, Julius Caesar (1837–1915) U.S. representative/senator; born in Erie County, Pa. A Union war veteran, he served in the U.S. House of Representatives (Rep., Mich.; 1873–75, 1879–83, 1885–94) and in the U.S. Senate (1894–1911).

Burrows, William (Ward) (1758–1805) marine officer; born in Charleston, S.C. A Revolutionary War veteran, he practiced law in Philadelphia during the 1790s and returned to service in July 1798 when President Adams named him first commandant of the newly formed Marine Corps. After overseeing the early development of the service, Burrows retired in 1804.

Burton, Harold (Hitz) (1888–1964) mayor, U.S. senator, Supreme Court justice; born in Jamaica Plain, Mass. Active in Republican politics, he served three terms as mayor of Cleveland, Ohio (1935–40) before he was elected to the U.S. Senate (Rep., Ohio; 1940) and then named by President Truman to the U.S. Supreme Court (1945–58).

Burton, Phillip (1926–83) U.S. representative; born in Cincinnati, Ohio. An air force veteran, he was a lawyer in San Francisco (1956–64) before going to Congress (1965–83) where he led the Democratic reform group to remove old-time committee chairmen.

Burton, Scott (1939–90) sculptor, furniture designer; born in Greensboro, Ala. He and his mother moved to Washington, D.C., where he attended high school and studied with Leon Berkowitz. He studied painting at Hans Hofmann's school in Provincetown, Mass., and attended Columbia University (B.A. 1962) and New York University (M.A. 1963). He was a free-lance art critic for *Art News* and participated in performance art during the 1970s. He is best known for his sculptural furniture constructions.

Burton, Theodore (Elijah) (1851–1929) U.S. representative/senator; born in Jefferson, Ohio. A lawyer, he served in the U.S. House of Representatives (Rep., Ohio; 1889–91, 1895–1909), and the Senate (1909–15). He returned to the House (1921–28), then left to fill a Senate vacancy (1928–29). He also served on waterways and armament commissions.

Burton, William Merriam (1865–1954) inventor; born in Cleveland, Ohio. Trained as a chemist, he went to work for Standard Oil and eventually became a refinery superintendent. He devised the first successful "cracking" process for yielding gasoline from crude oil, an essential step in the development of the automobile industry.

Busch, Adolphus (1839–1913) brewer; born in Mainz, Germany. In 1857 he moved to St. Louis, Mo., and opened a brewing supply store with his brother. In 1861, the brothers married the daughters of customer Eberhard Anheuser; soon thereafter Adolphus became a partner in his father-in-law's brewery (and in 1867 a naturalized citizen). When Anheuser died (1879) Busch renamed the brewery the Anheuser-Busch Brewing Association. He is credited with having developed a new lighter and drier beer that he named "Budweiser." He pasteurized his beer and helped develop mechanical refrigeration so he could ship farther; he built a glass factory to make his bottles; and he founded the St. Louis Manufacturers' Railway to transport coal from his Illinois mines. In 1898 he brought the Diesel engine to the United States from Switzerland. He was a generous donor to a variety of institutions and causes.

Busch, August A. (Anheuser), Jr. ("Gussie") (1899–1989) brewer; born in St. Louis, Mo. He joined the family business, Anheuser-Busch, as a young man; as president (1946–75) he built this small company into the world's largest brewer through massive national advertising. Among his showiest promotional ploys were his introduction of the Budweiser Clydesdale horse team and his acquisition of the St. Louis Cardinals baseball team (1953).

Busch, August Anheuser, III (1937–) brewer; born in St. Louis, Mo. He joined the family firm, Anheuser-Busch, in 1957 and rose through management, becoming vice-president and general manager (1965–74), president (1975–79), CEO (1975) and chairman (1977). He was also chairman and president of Anheuser Busch Companies, Inc. (1979). During his tenure, the firm greatly increased its marketing budget and promotional tactics, became a major advertiser on television and made its Budweiser brand consistently one of the best-selling beers in America.

Bush, Barbara (b. Pierce) (1925–) First Lady; born in Rye, N.Y. She left Smith College to marry George Bush in 1945. She was actively involved in programs to increase literacy and was also honorary chairman of the Leukemia Society.

Bush, Douglas (John Nash) (1896–1983) scholar, literary historian, educator; born in Morrisburg, Ontario, Canada. As an English professor at Harvard (1936–66), he trained generations of literary scholars and published widely on the classical tradition in Renaissance and Romantic literature.

Bush, George (Herbert Walker) (1925–) forty-first U.S. president; born in Milton, Mass. He enlisted as a Navy combat pilot in World War II and was rescued by a submarine when his plane was shot down in the Pacific. He returned to graduate from Yale and then went to Texas in 1948 where he made a fortune in the petroleum industry. He entered politics as a Republican and served two terms in the U.S. House of Representatives (1967–71). After his second failure to gain election to the U.S. Senate, he was appointed U.S. permanent representative to the United Nations (1971–73) and then chairman of the Republican National Committee (1973–74). He became the first chief of the U.S. Liaison Office in China (1974–75) and then director of the Central Intelligence Agency (1975–76). He failed in his run for the Republican nomination for the presidency in 1980 but was picked to be Ronald Reagan's vice-president (1981–89). He won the presidency on his own (1989–93) and proved to be adept at conducting foreign affairs, whether showing restraint as the Communist governments of the Soviet Union and Eastern Europe collapsed or exercising initiative in organizing an international response to Saddam Hussein's invasion of Kuwait. But as the nation slid into a major recession, he failed to take action, and, with the economy in the doldrums, he lost his reelection bid in 1992 and retired to pursue his personal interests in Texas and Maine.

Bush, Vannevar (1890–1974) engineer, government official; born in Everett, Mass. With a varied background in academic studies, private industry (General Electric), and government research (including antisubmarine work for the U.S. Navy in World War I), he became an engineering professor, later dean, at the Massachusetts Institute of Technology (1919–38). During these years he also kept his hand in the private sector as a consulting engineer, among other things founding the company that became the Raytheon Corporation. He also conducted research that led to several inventions including a differential analyzer (1928), a direct ancestor of the modern computer. As early as 1940 he was becoming active in organizing the U.S. scientists and engineers for the imminent war; this was formalized when he was appointed director of the Office of Scientific Research and Development. After the war, he continued to serve as an adviser to various governmental boards and agencies on scientific policies. Through many years (1938–55) he also served as president of the Carnegie Institution. In his later years he published numerous articles and books for a broader public, including *Modern Arms and Free Men* (1949), which called for closer ties between responsible science and public policies.

Bushnell, David (?1742–1824) inventor, physician; born in Saybrook, Conn. After graduating from Yale (1775) he built the first American submarine, *Bushnell's Turtle*, which was tried unsuccessfully against British ships. He was a Continental army engineer (1779–83), spent several years in France, and returned to the U.S.A. (1795) to teach and practice medicine in Georgia.

Bushnell, Horace (1802–76) Congregational minister, theologian; born in Bantam, Conn. After graduating from Yale (1827), he was teaching and reading for the bar when in 1831 he felt called to the ministry. He entered Yale's Divinity School; the rationalistic "new divinity" of Calvinism then in vogue offended his more intuitive spirit but he accepted ordination in 1833, and although not truly a popular preacher, gained a reputation for his fine sermons. Owing to poor health, he went off to Europe in 1845–46 and returned to publish one of his most influential works, *Christian Nurture* (1847). In 1849 he experienced a mystical vision of God and the Gospel; when he revealed this, he was attacked by the more traditional Congregationalists but he continued to preach and write. His weak lungs led him to move to California in 1856; he helped to establish the first University of California at Berkeley, but declining the presidency he returned to Connecticut in 1858. His poor health forced him to resign from a pastorate in 1861, but he continued to publish his sermons and religious speculations. By the time of his death he had carved out a place as one of the most influential of American Protestant theologians with his emphasis on bringing religion into harmony with human experience and nature.

Butkus, (Richard Marvin) Dick (1942–) football player; born in Chicago. An aggressive, 245-pound linebacker, he was chosen All-America at the University of Illinois (1963–64) and All-NFL (National Football League) seven times in nine years with the Chicago Bears (1965–73).

Butler, Benjamin (Franklin) (1818–93) soldier, politician; born in Deerfield, N.H. He supported Jefferson Davis for the Democratic presidential nomination in 1860, but still managed to obtain a senior command in the Union army. Butler led federal land forces against New Orleans in 1862 and became the draconian and allegedly corrupt governor of the occupied city. A postwar member of Congress (Rep., 1866–75; Ind., 1878–82), he was elected governor of Massachusetts in 1882.

Butler, David C. (1829–91) governor; born near Blooming-ton, Ind. A Nebraska cattle trader, he served in the territorial legislature in the 1860's. As Nebraska's first governor (Rep., 1867–71), he developed the railroads and built state office buildings in Lincoln, the new capital. Impeached for appropriating state money for his own use, he returned to stock raising in Pawnee City.

Butler, Howard Crosby (1872–1922) archaeologist; born in Croton Falls, N.Y. He taught art and architectural history at Princeton (1901–22) and led three expeditions to Syria from 1899 to 1909. His supervision of the excavations at Sardis, Turkey, (1910–22), generated his most important published work, including *Sardis* (1922).

Butler, Nicholas Murray (1862–1947) educator; born in Elizabeth, N.J. He graduated from Columbia University and then returned to teach there in 1885. He became a professor of philosophy and education (1895) and then president of the university (1902–45). During his long tenure, he abolished intercollegiate football at Columbia, was active in Republican politics (he advised both Theodore Roosevelt and Howard Taft and sought the 1920 presidential nomination), and made Columbia preeminent in graduate education. He was presi-dent of the Carnegie Endowment for International Peace (1925–45). He was influential in the creation of the Kellogg-Briand Pact for which he shared the 1931 Nobel Peace Prize (with Jane Addams). Because of his many accomplishments he came to be known as "Nicholas Miraculous."

Butler, Pierce (1866–1939) Supreme Court justice; born near Northfield, Minn. In his private law practice (1897–1922), he gained prominence as an expert in railroad law. He was appointed by President Harding to the U.S. Supreme Court (1923–39) and often voted against government interference in business.

Butler, Smedley D. (Darlington) (1881–1940) marine officer; born in West Chester, Pa. A member of a distinguished Quaker family, he fought insurrectionaries in the Far East, Central America, and the Caribbean for more than 20 years, but missed combat in World War I. He caused a diplomatic incident in 1931 when he claimed the Italian dictator Mussolini had killed a child in a hit-and-run automobile accident. Passed over for commandant, he retired in October 1931 and became a prominent isolationist spokesman later in the decade. He was known in the Corps as "Old Gimlet Eye."

Butterfield, Paul (1942–87) musician; born in Chicago. A white singer-harmonica player, he began as a teenager to master the blues style of his hometown through perfor-mances with Muddy Waters and Little Walter. He attended the Universeity of Chicago in 1959–61, then formed the racially integrated Butterfield Blues Band, which pioneered blues-rock, introduced the electric guitarists Mike Bloom-field and Elvin Bishop, and backed Bob Dylan's controver-sial non-acoustic appearance at the Newport Folk Festival in 1965. Butterfield recorded and toured extensively as a bandleader between 1965–75, appearing at the Monterey Pop (1967) and Woodstock (1969) Festivals. He was featured with Muddy Waters at The Band's farewell concert in 1976, which was filmed as "The Last Waltz," and performed sporadically thereafter until his death at age 44.

Butterick, Ebenezer (1826–1903) inventor, fashion business executive; born in Sterling, Mass. With his wife, Ellen Augusta Pollard Butterick (d. 1871), this tailor invented paper clothing patterns for home sewers; they began selling patterns in 1863. He formed E. Butterick & Company, New York (1867–81), established European branches, and founded fashion magazines. He was later secretary of the reorganized Butterick Publishing Company (1881–94).

Button, (Richard) Dick (1929–) ice skater; born in Engle-wood, N.J. He was five-time world champion (1948–52) and gold medal winner in the 1948 and 1952 Olympics. As an innovative competitor and as a commentator for ABC television, he was instrumental in popularizing the sport in the U.S.A.

Bye, A. E. (Arthur Edwin) (1919–) landscape architect; born in Arnhem, Holland. Son of an American art curator and a mother with Dutch family ties, he was brought to America in 1920 and raised in Bucks County, Pa. He attended Pennsylvania State College (now University) and worked for the U.S. Forest Service and National Park Service (1942–45). He taught at various institutions, includ-ing Columbia University (1952–74) and was a visiting professor at Pennsylvania State University (1981). Drawing on the English Landscape tradition, he designed in a style that is distinctly modern in its composition by means of abstraction, and in its relationships between structures and sites; he is particularly known for his use of native flora and his respect for elements in the local natural landscape. Much of his early work was for universities, corporations, and institutions; in later years he did more private estate work, including several projects along the Atlantic coast; his single most notable work is Gainesway Farm, Lexington, Ky. (1974–86).

Byerly, Perry (Edward) (1897–1978) seismologist; born in Clarinda, Iowa. His career at the University of California: Berkeley (1925–64) included the directorship of its seismo-graphic station (1950–62). From examining travel-time curves of western North American earthquake waves, he postulated that the earth's mantle is discretely layered and penetrated by the base structures of mountains.

Byoir, Carl (Robert) (1888–1957) public relations executive; born in Des Moines, Iowa. Among diverse business ventures, including the introduction of Montessori teaching to the U.S.A., he was best known as a public relations specialist. He founded his own public relations agency (1930) that occasionally achieved notoriety: he was charged with Nazi collusion for representing the German Tourist Information Office in the 1930s, and in 1946 he was convicted of violating antitrust laws with another client, A&P.

Byrd, Harry F. (Flood) (1887–1966) U.S. senator; born at Martinsburg, W.Va. As governor of Virginia (1926–30), he established a relatively progressive record, passing the first antilynching law in the South in 1928. He promoted rural electrification while eliminating Virginia's budget deficit. He went on to serve in the U.S. Senate (Dem., Va.; 1933–65). Although initially a Roosevelt supporter, he opposed many New Deal measures in the name of reduced government spending and emerged as a leading southern conservative, often siding with Republicans. After World War II he opposed foreign aid measures abroad and civil rights at home.

Byrd, Henry Roeland See PROFESSOR LONGHAIR.

Byrd, Richard (Evelyn) (1888–1957) aviator, explorer; born in Winchester, Va. (brother of Harry Flood Byrd). Son of the lawyer who founded the Byrd political dynasty in Virginia, he joined the navy's aviation service in 1917, five years after graduating from Annapolis. On May 9, 1926, he and his co-pilot Floyd Bennett made the first flight over the North Pole, flying round trip from Spitsbergen Island. Both men received the Congressional Medal of Honor for the feat. As part of his Antarctic expedition of 1928–30, during which he established the Little America base, Byrd (with Bernt Balchen) made the first flight over the South Pole (November 28–29, 1929). He made four more expeditions to Antarctica for exploration and mapping (1933–35, 1939–41, 1946–47, 1955–56); he directed the U.S. Antarctic program for the International Geophysical Year (1957–58) and was planning future explorations of Antarctica at his death. He published several accounts of his experiences, including *Little America* (1930) and *Alone* (1938).

Byrd, Robert C. (Carlyle) (1917–) U.S. senator; born in North Wilkesboro, N.C. From humble beginnings as a meatcutter and welder, he rose rapidly in politics. Elected to the West Virginia state legislature (1947–52), he moved on to the U.S. House of Representatives (Dem., W. Va., 1953–58) and to the U.S. Senate (1958). Briefly a member of the Ku Klux Klan in his younger days, and a conservative opponent of civil rights and welfare spending in his early career in Washington, he grew more liberal by the 1970s, when he played a role in the Watergate investigation and criticized the continuing war in Vietnam. A master of Senate procedures, he served as majority whip (1971–76), majority leader (1976–80), minority leader (1981–84), a second term as majority leader (1987–88), and then voluntarily went back to being just a senator.

Byrd, William (1674–1744) statesman, author; born in Westover, Va. After being educated in England (1684–92), he became a member of the House of Burgesses and then the Council of State in 1709. He resisted Governor Alexander Spotswood's effort to take away the Council's position as the supreme court in Virginia. From 1704 on, he managed the vast properties and immense fortune inherited from his father. His manuscripts, letters, and diaries provide an intimate look at the life of the gentry in 18th-century Virginia.

Byrne, David (1952–) musician; born in Dunbarton, Scotland. Moving to Landsdowne, Md., at age six, he became a guitarist and songwriter as a teenager. He attended the Rhode Island School of Design, where in 1975 he founded the so-called postmodern rock group, Talking Heads, with three classmates. Beginning in 1983, he became involved in a variety of film and music projects as an actor, director, producer, and ethnomusicologist.

Byrne, Jane (b. Burke) (1934–) mayor; born in Chicago. She worked in Chicago's antipoverty program (1963–68) and then as city consumer sales commissioner under Mayor Richard Daley (1968–77). She defeated the Democratic machine's candidate in the primary and as mayor of Chicago (1980–84) became the first woman to head a major American city. The city experienced serious financial problems during her tenure and she lost in the 1983 Democratic primary to Representative Harold Washington, who became the first African-American mayor of Chicago; he defeated her again in 1987. In the 1991 election, she unsuccessfully challenged Mayor Richard M. Daley Jr.

Byrnes, James F. (Francis) (1879–1972) secretary of state, public official, Supreme Court justice; born in Charleston, S.C. He served the U.S. House of Representatives (Dem., S.C.; 1910–25) and the Senate (Dem., S.C.; 1930–41) where he promoted the passage of landmark legislation such as the Neutrality Act (1935) and the Lend-Lease Act (1941). Appointed by President Franklin D. Roosevelt to the U.S. Supreme Court in 1941, he stepped down after one year to head up the Office of Economic Stabilization (1942) and then the Office of War Mobilization (1943). The title of "assistant president" was bestowed on him by President Roosevelt and he was considered as a running mate both in 1940 and 1944. He accompanied Roosevelt to Yalta (1945) and served as secretary of state under President Truman (1945–47). As governor of South Carolina (1950–55), despite his belief in segregation, he worked to suppress Ku Klux Klan activities and to improve the education of African-Americans.

Byrnes, Robert Francis (1917–) Slavic studies specialist, educator; born in Waterville, N.Y. Known for his work on conservatism in modern Europe and anti-Semitism in modern France, he taught longest at Rutgers (1954) where he was director of the Russian and East European Institute (1971–76). He served concurrently as a distinguished professor of history at the University of Indiana: Bloomington (1967). A consultant for the U.S. Department of Health, Education, and Welfare (1964), he was president of the American Association of Advanced Slavic Studies (1978–79) and author of numerous books and articles.

Byrns, Joseph (Wellington) (1869–1936) U.S. representative; born in Cedar Hill, Tenn. His family moved to Nashville from their farm to provide him, the eldest of six children, with an education. A lawyer in Nashville in 1891, he served in the Tennessee house and senate before going to the U.S. House of Representatives (Dem., 1909–36). As a member of the Committee on Appropriations he championed governmental economy and tariff reductions, although he secured the massive wartime appropriations requested by President Wilson. Faced with a Republican majority in the House, he attacked their economic policies, claiming that their high tariffs had contributed to a world-wide depression. In 1933 he became majority leader, successfully shepherding New Deal legislation through the House, setting aside his fiscal conservatism to support his party. Elected Speaker of the House (1935–36), he managed the Democratic majority through persuasion, using a team of deputy whips to poll congressmen before critical votes.

C

Cabell, James Branch (1879–1958) writer; born in Richmond, Va. After graduating from the College of William and Mary, he worked as a journalist and as a coal miner. With his first novel, *The Eagle's Shadow* (1904), this Virginia-based author launched a prolific literary career producing works ranging from historical short stories to Virginia genealogy. He was known chiefly for his polished romances set in a mythical French province, Poictesme (18 vols. 1913–29), intended as allegories of the modern world. The best known of the series, *Jurgen* (1919), was originally suppressed as being immoral. Highly admired by literary types in his day, Cabell's work failed to speak to later generations.

Cabet, Étienne (1788–1856) Utopian, social reformer, author; born in Dijon, France. Trained as a lawyer, he was a radical member of the French Chamber of Deputies (1831) and founded *Le Populaire* (1833), a publication that promoted the workingmen's cause. In 1834 the government prosecuted him for certain articles and he went into exile in England. Back in France he published a Utopian romance, *Voyage en Icarie* (1839), which outlined what he called the Icarian doctrine, a detailed blueprint for a new society. This and his other writings attracted a large audience and followers for establishing a Utopian community in America; Cabet joined them in 1849 and they established at the abandoned Mormon town of Nauvoo, Ill. But his autocratic rule turned many in the community against him and in 1856 he left for St. Louis, Mo., where he soon died. His death did not stop the creation of Icarian colonies in: Cheltenham, Mo.; Corning, Iowa; and Cloverdale, Calif.; but all were dissolved by 1895.

Cable, George Washington (1844–1925) writer; born in New Orleans. When the Union forces occupied New Orleans in the Civil War, he joined a Mississippi cavalry regiment and fought in a number of engagements. After the war he held several jobs, contributed to a New Orleans newspaper, and in 1873, began to publish stories in *Scribner's Monthly.* The publication in 1879 of *Old Creole Days,* a collection of his stories drawing on the lore of old New Orleans, gained him quick national success and helped to popularize the "local color" movement then emerging in American fiction. Subsequent fictional works with New Orleans settings advanced his standing, but he had in the meantime become interested in the problems of former slaves. The reaction among some Southerners to his *Silent South* (1885), a collection of his essays and lectures calling for reform, led him to move to Northampton, Mass. He continued to publish novels, several

dealing with the contrast between Northern and Southern manners and morals, and on reading tours with Mark Twain, who had expressed admiration for his work, he continued to agitate for equal rights for African-Americans, for prison improvements, and for other reforms.

Cable, Ransom R. (1834–1909) railroad developer; born in Athens County, Ohio. A coal miner for many years in Rock Island, Ill., he became interested in railroads and by 1870 had become president of the Rockford, Rock Island & St. Louis railroad. In 1877 he was elected director of the Chicago, Rock Island & Pacific Railway Company, with which he stayed, rising through the presidency (1883) to become chairman of the board (1898–1902).

Cabot, George (1752–1823) merchant, U.S. senator; born in Salem, Mass. After youthful years at sea (1768–77), he made a substantial fortune as a shipper and merchant; he also worked with his family's cotton mills. As a staunch Federalist, he became a close associate of George Washington and Alexander Hamilton, championing ratification of the Constitution in 1788. He was one of the most prominent members of the Essex Junto, wealthy Federalists from Essex County, Mass. Representing Massachusetts in the U.S. Senate (1791–96), he favored cooperation with Great Britain; he returned to his business afterward. During the War of 1812, he presided over the Hartford Convention (1814), convened to rally Federalist opposition to the war, but he served only as a moderating influence.

Cabot, Godfrey Lowell (1861–1962) industrialist, philanthropist; born in Boston, Mass. He studied chemistry and experimented with carbon black; starting with his first carbon works in West Virginia in 1899, he built up the Cabot Corporation to become the leading producer of that product within the U.S.A., and he prospered through its interests in minerals, energy sources, and industrial research. He traveled widely and was himself a pilot. He directed Boston's puritanical Watch and Ward Society (1920s and 1930s), which blocked certain books, plays, and motion pictures from the public. Among his many philanthropies were large gifts to Harvard and to the Massachusetts Institute of Technology.

Cabot, Hugh (1872–1945) surgeon, educator; born at Beverly Farms, Mass. (brother of Richard C. Cabot). Having taken his medical degree at Harvard, he taught there (1910–19), with some time out to serve as a surgeon with the U.S. forces in France. He introduced innovations in medical education, first at the University of Michigan Medical School (1920–30) and then at the Mayo Clinic and University of Minnesota Graduate School of Medicine (1930–39). He then returned to Boston and private practice. He was an advocate of prepaid group practice and government underwriting of medical care to ensure equitable distribution.

Cabot, John M. (Moors) (1901–81) diplomat; born in Cambridge, Mass. He studied at Oxford and entered the diplomatic service in 1927. He specialized in Eastern Europe and Latin America and was assistant secretary of state for Inter-American Affairs (1953–54). He wrote *The Racial Conflict in Transylvania* (1926) and *Towards Our Common American Destiny* (1955).

Cabot, Richard Clarke (1868–1939) physician, medical reformer; born in Brookline, Mass. (brother of Hugh Cabot). He was affiliated with Harvard Medical School (1899–1932) and Massachusetts General Hospital (1898–1921). He introduced the practice of medical social service so that a physician could treat the whole person. As early as 1913, he advocated prepaid medical group practice. From 1920–34, he taught social ethics at Harvard and he published on a variety of social issues as well as on medical topics.

Cabrini, Frances Xavier (b. Francesca Lodi-Cabrini) (1850–1917) Catholic missionary nun, saint; born in Lombardy, Italy. A devout child who took a vow of chastity at the age of 12, she was trained as a teacher and became director of an orphanage. In 1880 she founded the Missionary Sisters of the Sacred Heart, hoping to spread the faith in China; instead, she was sent by the pope to America (1889); there, battling money problems, she founded schools and charitable institutions to serve poor immigrants in New York and other cities. She also dispatched missionaries to other countries. Naturalized in 1909, she became the first American citizen to be canonized (1946).

Cade, Thomas J. (Joseph) (1928–   ) ornithologist; born in San Angelo, Texas. He was an associate in zoology at the University of California: Los Angeles (1955–58), then took a National Science Foundation fellowship at the University of California: Berkeley (1958–59). He became a professor of zoology at Syracuse University (1959–67), then moved to Cornell (1967–88), where, in the early 1970s, he collected and bred wild peregrine falcons from Canada and the western U.S.A. for release and reestablishment in the eastern U.S.A. He became a professor of biology at Boise State University (Idaho) (1988), where he continued his research on the population biology and behavior of peregrine falcons at the Peregrine Fund in Boise.

Cadman, Charles Wakefield (1881–1946) composer, organist; born in Johnston, Pa. Beginning as a church organist, he became interested in Native American music after reading such ethnologists as Alice Fletcher and Francis La Flesche. He proceeded to incorporate Indian themes in many of his own compositions, such as his opera *Shanewis,* staged at the Metropolitan in 1918. He is best known for such songs as "Land of the Sky-blue Water" (1908).

Cadmus, Paul (1904–   ) painter; born in New York City. Based in Weston, Conn., he was a provocative artist who combined wit and social protest. His most famous (and notorious) paintings are *The Fleet's In* (1934), and *Fantasia on a Theme by Dr. S.* (1946).

Caesar, (Sidney) Sid (1922–   ) television comedian; born in Yonkers, N.Y. He began his career in show business while a teenager, playing saxophone and clarinet for the Shep Fields band. In the Coast Guard during World War II, he made his stage debut in a service show, *Tars and Spars* (1945), appearing in the 1946 film version. Master of pantomine, dialect, and doubletalk, he went on to star on National Broadcasting Company's *Your Show of Shows* (1950–54), a comedy variety series that is regarded as a high point of early television. For some years thereafter his career went into decline and he himself became an alcoholic. He starred in the Broadway musical, *Little Me* (1962–63), and appeared in occasional Hollywood films and television movies in the 1970s and the 1980s. He wrote his autobiography, *Where Have I Been* (1982).

Cage, John (Milton) (1912–92) composer; born in Los Angeles. Cage studied with a number of teachers including Henry Cowell and Arnold Schoenberg, who helped provoke his avant-garde proclivities. He began writing all-percussion pieces in the 1930s and proclaimed the use of noise as the next musical horizon; in 1938 he introduced the "prepared piano," an instrument whose sound is radically modified by various objects placed on the strings. While writing much for prepared piano in the 1940s, notably the Sonatas and Interludes, he also produced some pioneering electronic music. Among the most widely influential elements of his thought was the idea of *indeterminacy,* music that is not strictly controlled, as seen in his 1951 *Landscape No. 4* for twelve radios – the sound of which depends on what happens to be on the air. Later works, especially the notorious *4'33"* (1954), involve complete silence. He continued to develop such concepts and he also produced several quirky, engaging books beginning with the 1961 *Silence*. In his later years he was widely acclaimed as one of the more original of American artists.

Cagney, James (1899–1986) film actor; born in New York City. Graduating from vaudeville to the Broadway stage, he made his film debut in *Sinner's Holiday* (1930). A leading role in *The Public Enemy* (1931) established him as the quintessential screen gangster, and he played thugs through most of the 1930s. His performance in *Yankee Doodle Dandy* (1942), as George M. Cohan, earned him an Oscar. After that movie, he appeared in a variety of roles.

Cahan, Abraham (1860–1951) editor, writer; born in Podberezya, Russia. He continued his youthful revolutionary political activism after emigrating to the U.S.A. (1882), where he taught English to immigrants. He founded (1897) and for 50 years edited the influential Yiddish-language *Jewish Daily Forward*. He also wrote realistic novels of Jewish immigrant life, written variously in English and Yiddish; the best known of his works in English are *Yekl: A Tale of the New York Ghetto* (1896) and *The Rise of David Levinsky* (1917).

Cahill, Holger (b. Sveinn Kristján Bjarnarson) (1887–1960) art authority, author; born in Snaefellsnessysla, Iceland. A childhood emigrant to Canada, he moved to New York City in his teens, determined to become a writer. He studied at New York University, Columbia University, and the New School for Social Research. At the Newark Art Museum (1922–31) he became an authority on American art and wrote the seminal *American Folk Art* (1932). His outstanding leadership of the Federal Art Project (1935–43) – including compiling the Index of American Design – helped nurture a generation of American artists. He wrote fiction in his later years.

Cahn, Sammy (b. Samuel Cohen) (1913–93) lyricist; born in New York City. While a boy he played violin in a Dixieland band and decided to write songs. With pianist Saul Chaplin he wrote many hits of the 1930s. Throughout the 1940s, 1950s, and 1960s he wrote many popular songs for Hollywood, Broadway, and television with composers Jule Styne and James Van Heusen. A prolific lyricist and writer, he published *The Songwriter's Rhyming Dictionary* in 1984.

Cain, James M. (Mallahan) (1892–1977) writer, screenwriter; born in Annapolis, Md. He trained as a singer and worked as a teacher and journalist before achieving fame in the 1930s and 1940s as a Hollywood screenwriter and novelist. His novels, many adapted into popular films, treated criminals, sex, and money with a lean, tough realism; they included *The Postman Always Rings Twice* (1934), *Double Indemnity* (1936), *Mildred Pierce* (1941), and *The Institute* (1976).

Cajori, Florian (1859–1930) mathematical historian; born in St. Aignan, Switzerland. Emigrating to America as a student (1875), he is known best as a mathematical historian. A history of mathematics professor at the University of California (1918–30), this American Academy of Arts and Sciences member wrote a number of texts on the history of math and physics.

Calabresi, Guido (1932–) legal scholar; born in Milan, Italy. Educated in the U.S.A. and England, he joined the faculty of Yale University Law School (1959), serving as dean since 1985. He was an expert in liability law, including medical malpractice and property. He is the author of *The Costs of Accidents* (1970), *Tragic Choices* (1978), and *Ideals, Beliefs, Attitudes and the Law* (1985).

Calamity Jane See BURK, MARTHA JANE (CANARY).

Calder, A. (Alexander) Stirling (1870–1945) sculptor; born in Philadelphia (father of Alexander "Sandy" Calder). He studied at the Pennsylvania Academy of the Fine Arts (1886–90), in Paris (1890), and was based in Pittsfield, Mass., and New York City. He is known for public works, such as the *Swann Memorial,* Philadelphia (1924), and for sculptural portraits.

Calder, Alexander ("Sandy") (1898–1976) sculptor, painter; born in Lawnton, Pa. (son of Alexander Stirling Calder). He studied at Stevens Institute of Technology (1915–19), the Art Students League, New York City (1923–26), and in Paris where he began his famous circus menagerie, *Le Cirque Calder* (1926–61), and the first of his wire sculptures, *Josephine Baker* (1926). By 1927 he was based in New York City, and Roxbury, Conn. (1933), and from 1953 he maintained a home in France. He was an abstract painter, but became most famous for his moving sculptures, named "mobiles" by Marcel Duchamp, as seen in *Big Red* (1959). His stationary sculptures, named "stabiles" by Jean Arp, are often large public works, as in *El Sol Rojo* (1968).

Caldwell, (Charles William, Jr.) Charlie (1901–57) football coach; born in Bristol, Va. One of the last successful single-wing coaches, his undefeated 1950–51 Princeton teams, featuring tailback Dick Kazmaier, were ranked sixth in the Associated Press polls.

Caldwell, Erskine (Preston) (1903–87) writer; born in Moreland, Ga. In his early years he was a Hollywood screenwriter and foreign correspondent. His first novels, *Tobacco Road* (1932) and *God's Little Acre* (1933), were widely banned for obscenity, but they created an enduring portrait of "white trash" and stimulated others to write frankly about the South they knew. He produced 50 volumes of fiction, travel writing, and memoirs, but his literary reputation declined with later works. He collaborated on several books with his wife, photographer Margaret Bourke-White.

Caldwell, Philip (1920–) automobile executive; born in Bourneville, Ohio. He had a long career at Ford Motor Company (1953–85), where he headed truck operations, the Philco division, and international operations (he introduced the Ford Fiesta to Europe) before becoming president (1978–80); he retired as CEO and chairman. He was later senior managing director at Shearson Lehman Brothers, New York (1985).

Caldwell, Sarah (1924–) opera director, conductor; born in Maryville, Mo. After violin studies, she became an assistant to Boris Goldovsky and then, while affiliated with Boston University, formed her own opera company in Boston in 1958. Overseeing every detail of the productions, staging, and music, she was notorious for averting last-minute deadlines and financial crises, but she made her opera company one of the most distinguished and innovative in the U.S.A., especially noted for its productions of modern works such as Schoenberg's *Moses and Aaron.* In the 1970s she began to appear as guest conductor of major orchestras.

Calhoun, John C. (Caldwell) (1782–1850) vice-president, orator; born in Abbeville District, S.C. During a long political career, he was the secretary of war (1817–25) and the secretary of state (1844) and he served as vice-president under two presidents. During the War of 1812, he was a "War Hawk" in Congress. He sought the presidency in 1824, but received the office of vice-president under John Quincy Adams (1825–29). He feuded with Adams and then supported Andrew Jackson in the 1828 elections. He became Jackson's vice-president in 1829–32. He had originally been a nationalist, but by the late 1820s he had become a firm advocate of states' rights – particularly the right of the state to nullify the effects of a federal law within that state's borders. In 1832, the Nullification Crisis in South Carolina led Calhoun to resign the vice-presidency and to accept a vacant Senate seat from South Carolina; he had been frustrated by the rules that prevented a vice-president from speaking out on the issue of nullification. He remained in the Senate until his death, with the exception of a brief period as President Tyler's secretary of state (1844). Although his views on states' rights and slavery have long since been repudiated, no one has ever doubted his sincerity and eloquence.

Califano, Joseph A. (Anthony), Jr. (1931–) lawyer, cabinet member; born in New York City. A Wall Street lawyer, he rose rapidly in the Defense Department (1961–65), becoming Secretary McNamara's assistant. As President Lyndon Johnson's special assistant (1965–69), Califano designed his anti-poverty programs. As Secretary of Health, Education, and Welfare (1977–79), he tried unsuccessfully to reorganize that agency, resuming his legal practice afterward.

California Joe See MILNER, MOSES EMBREE.

Calisher, Hortense (1911–) writer; born in New York City. A Barnard graduate (married to Curtis Harnack), she wrote short stories and novels, typically set among New York's upper middle class but also dealing with a range of subjects including racial conflict. She was best known for her short stories, published in a collected edition in 1975. She held visiting lectureships at many universities.

Calkins, (Earnest) Elmo (1868–1964) advertising executive, author; born in Geneseo, Ill. A talented copywriter, first in Illinois and then in New York City, he was founding president of Calkins and Holden, New York City (1902–31), regarded as the prototypal modern agency for producing integrated advertising campaigns incorporating high-quality copy and art. He coauthored (with Ralph Holden) the first advertising textbook, *Modern Advertising* (1905). In his later years he was an essayist and author; severely hearing-impaired since his youth, he often wrote on the problems of the deaf.

Calkins, Mary Whiton (1863–1930) psychologist; born in Hartford, Conn. She studied at Harvard and taught at Wellesley College (1887–1929). During the 1890s, she conducted research on memorization-by-association at Harvard and was influenced by William James. Often called "the first lady of psychology," she was a personality theorist who described the self as an integral unit that could be studied in its many variables.

Callaghan, Daniel (Judson) (1890–1942) naval officer; born in San Francisco. He was the naval aide to President Franklin D. Roosevelt (1938–41). As rear admiral, he led a brilliant naval battle against Japanese forces off Guadalcanal. He was killed in the action. He was posthumously awarded the Medal of Honor.

Callahan, Daniel (1930–) philosopher, medical ethicist; born in Washington, D.C. After graduating from Yale (1952), he went on to take an M.A. from Georgetown and a Ph.D. in philosophy from Harvard (1965). He served as executive editor of *Commonweal* (1961–68) and then was an associate at the Population Council in New York City (1969–70). Drawing on his experiences there and his formal training in philosophy, in 1969 he cofounded and directed the Institute for Social Ethics and the Life Sciences at the Hastings Center (Briarcliff Manor, N.Y.), a research and educational organization dedicated to examining ethical issues of medicine, biology, and the professions. His particular concerns are reflected in the title of the over 30 books he has written or edited, including *Ethics in Hard Times* (1982), *Setting Limits: Medical Goals in an Aging Society* (1987), and *Abortion: Understanding Differences* (with his wife, Sidney Callahan, 1984). His prominence and authority made him one of the most interviewed and quoted individuals on such controversial topics and have gained him membership in the Institute of Medicine of the National Academy of Sciences, as well as membership on the Task Force on Life and Law of New York State and the Advisory Council of the Office of Scientific Integrity, U.S. Department of Health and Human Services. He was a guest professor at numerous universities and a consultant to various governmental and private committees dealing with his areas of expertise.

Callahan, Harry (1912–) photographer, teacher; born in Detroit, Mich. A pioneer in color photography (1944–64), he shot 8 × 10 pictures, supporting himself with grants until he went to teach at the Rhode Island School of Design (1961–77).

Callas, Maria (b. Maria Anna Sofia Cecilia Kalogeropoulos) (1923–77) soprano; born in New York City. Callas studied voice in Athens and made her operatic debut there in 1938. Her European career blossomed in the late 1940s; from then until her retirement from the stage in 1965, she was celebrated less for a glorious voice than for her electrifying dramatic gifts – as seen in roles such as Medea and Norma – and her equally dramatic temperament and romantic life, including a long liaison with Greek shipping magnate Aristotle Onassis.

Calley, William L. (Laws), Jr. (1943–) soldier; born in Miami, Fla. A college dropout, he worked as a dishwasher and railroad switchman before enlisting in 1966. Commissioned a lieutenant through Officers Training School, he was posted to South Vietnam. On March 16, 1968, he led a platoon into the hamlet of My Lai and supervised his men as they massacred some 500 elderly men, women, and children. In 1971 he was convicted of the murder of 22 Vietnamese and was sentenced to life imprisonment; President Richard Nixon commuted the sentence, first to 20 years and, in 1974, to time served. Calley slipped back into civilian life as an insurance agent, and many came to feel he had been made a scapegoat for all the atrocities of the Vietnam War. General Westmoreland probably summed it up best when he said, "Had it not been for educational deferments . . . Calley probably would never have been an officer. The Army had to lower its standards."

Callimachos, Panos Demetrios (b. Demetrios Paximadas) (1879–1963) priest, author; born in Madytos, Dardanelles, Turkey. A Greek Orthodox priest, he was a voluntary chaplain during the Balkan War (1912–13). He came to the U.S.A. (1914) and while serving as a priest in a Greek Orthodox church in Brooklyn, he also edited the Greek *National Herald* (1915–18, 1922–44). He encouraged Greek-Americans to maintain their Greek heritage in the United States. He opposed the restoration of the Greek monarchy (1935) and denounced the Greek Left at the end of World War II.

Calloway, (Cabell) Cab (1907–94) jazz musician; born in Rochester, N.Y. A versatile song and dance man, he led a succession of outstanding big bands between 1928–53. He was featured in the 1979 movie *The Blues Brothers*.

Calvert, Leonard (1606–47) colonial governor; born in England. The son of George Calvert, the first Lord Baltimore, he arrived in Maryland with the first colonists in 1634 and served as the first governor of Maryland during 1637–47.

Calvin, Melvin (1911–) organic chemist; born in St. Paul, Minn. He became a professor of chemistry at the University of California (1947–71) and head of its Lawrence Radiation Laboratory (1963–80). By combining the techniques of carbon-14 testing and paper chromatography, he traced the intermediate reactions in carbon dioxide assimilation and oxygen release in plants during photosynthesis. He was awarded the Nobel Prize in chemistry (1961) for this work.

Cameron, Simon (1799–1889) businessman, politician; born in Lancaster County, Pa. Orphaned at age nine and largely self-educated, he began as a manager of newspapers, then bought the Harrisburg, Pa., *Republican* (1824); this gained him influence in politics, which in turn gained him lucrative contracts as the state printer; he then branched out into other businesses including railroads and banking. He served Pennsylvania in the U.S. Senate, first as a coalition Democrat (1845–49), then as a Republican (1857–61). He threw his support to Lincoln at the Republican convention in 1860 and was rewarded with the post of secretary of war, but he proved to be so corrupt and inefficient that in January 1862 Lincoln appointed him ambassador to Russia. He returned to run for the Senate in 1863 and lost, but, regaining control of the Republican party, he held the seat for 10 years (1867–77), resigning to let his son, James Donald Cameron, succeed him.

Camp, Walter (Chauncey) (1859–1925) football pioneer and coach; born in New Britain, Conn. He was called "The Father of American Football" because, more than any other person, he was responsible for transforming the U.S. game into a unique contest, different from its soccer and rugby roots. He starred as a rugby runner and kicker at Yale (1876–81) and represented Yale at the intercollegiate football conventions (1877–1925). The following are among the rule changes he championed: reduction of players per side from 15 to 11 (1879); creation of the scrimmage in which one team holds undisputed possession of the ball (1880); the system in which a team must gain a specified number of yards within a specified number of downs to retain possession (1882); and the point system of scoring (1883). Through his writings, his position as Yale's advisory coach, and his annual All-America selections, he remained American football's premier authority until his death.

Campbell, Alexander (1788–1866) Protestant religious leader; born near Ballymena, Northern Ireland. He emigrated to the U.S.A. in 1809 to join his father, succeeding the elder Campbell as pastor of an independent Protestant church at Brush Run, Pa., in 1813. An exponent of a primitive Christianity based wholly on the Scriptures, he allied his church in 1832 with other disaffected sects to form the Disciples of Christ. He published a translation of the New Testament in 1826 and in 1840 founded Bethany College in West Virginia, serving as its president until his death.

Campbell, Earl (Christian) (1955–) football player; born in Tyler, Tex. At the University of Texas, he was the 1977 Heisman Trophy winner after leading the nation in rushing and scoring. He was then the National Football League's leading rusher for three straight years (1978–80).

Campbell, George (Washington) (1817–98) horticulturalist, inventor; born in Cherry Valley, N.Y. He moved to Ohio as a child and trained for newspaper work, but from the mid-1850s he turned his full energies to fruit-growing. His wide-ranging experiments with seedlings and crosses fostered the development of American grape-culture. He considered his Campbell Early, which bore its first fruit in 1892, to come the closest to his professed ambition to create the perfect grape.

Campbell, Helen Stuart (b. Helen Campbell Stuart) (1839–1918) author, reformer; born in Lockport, N.Y. In the 1860s she published fiction, some under the name of Helen Stuart Campbell, which she eventually adopted. She later created widespread public awareness of poverty with *The Problem of the Poor* (1882), *Prisoners of Poverty* (1887), and *Women Wage-Earners* (1893).

Campbell, John Archibald (1811–89) Supreme Court justice; born near Washington, Ga. An experienced lawyer, he was appointed by President Millard Fillmore to the U.S. Supreme Court in 1853. Known for his independence and strict interpretation of the Constitution, he was attacked by abolitionists for supporting the Dred Scott decision. He opposed secession but when Georgia seceded he resigned from the court (1861) and served as assistant secretary of war for the Confederacy (1862–65). After the war he took up private practice in New Orleans.

Campbell, Joseph (1904–87) mythologist, educator; born in New York City. A professor of literature at Sarah Lawrence College (1934–72), he entranced students with his analysis of comparative mythology, writing *The Hero with a Thousand Faces* (1949) and the four-volume *Masks of God* (1959–68). Although his scholarship has been criticized, he attained the status of a virtual guru through a series of television interviews by Bill Moyers in 1985–86.

Campbell, Robert (1804–79) trapper, capitalist, born in Aughlane, Ireland. He arrived in St. Louis, Mo. by 1825 and, with William Sublette, formed the company Sublette and Campbell. He became a hotel owner and bank president and served as an Indian commissioner in 1851 and 1869.

Campbell, William Wallace (1862–1938) astronomer; born in Hancock County, Ohio. Author of *The Elements of Practical Astronomy* (1899), he deduced that the Martian atmosphere could not support life (1894). He worked at California's Lick Observatory (1890–1923), becoming its director in 1901. Working with the Mills spectrograph he measured stellar radial velocities and published them (with Joseph Moore) in a catalogue (1928). He presided over the University of California: Mt. Hamilton (1923–30) and the National Academy of Sciences (1931–35).

Camras, Marvin (1916–) electrical engineer, inventor; born in Chicago. He developed a successful wire recorder in the 1930s and in a long career at the ITT Research Institute received some 500 patents in the field of electronic communications. His inventions are used in magnetic tape recorders, motion picture sound equipment, and videotape recording.

Canby, Edward Richard Sprigg (1817–73) soldier; born in Kentucky. A West Point graduate (1839), he fought in the Seminole War and the Mexican War. He commanded the Union's Department of New Mexico and defeated a Confederate attempt to take California. He went to Washington, D.C., as the Assistant Adjutant General, and then commanded troops in New York City. As commander of the Military Division of Western Mississippi, he captured Mobile, Ala.; as commander of the Department of the Gulf, he accepted the surrender of the last two Confederate field armies in May 1865. Modoc Indians murdered Canby, who had been sent to negotiate peace with the tribe, in northern California.

Canby, Henry Seidel (1878–1961) editor, author; born in Wilmington, Del. A teacher of English at Yale University for over 20 years, he helped found the *Saturday Review of Literature* and as its first editor (1924–36) made it into a top literary magazine; he also wrote literary biographies and criticism, and a three-volume autobiography.

Candler, Asa (Griggs) (1851–1929) manufacturer; born in Carroll County, Ga. He left the family farm to become a doctor in Atlanta, but switched to pharmacy in 1873. In 1887 he bought sole rights to John S. Pemberton's original formula for Coca-Cola and formed the Coca-Cola Company (1890). Marketing and manufacturing the soft drink until 1919, he sold the company after a long federal suit over Coca-Cola's healthfulness. He had meanwhile invested heavily in real estate, and as a public-spirited citizen he now served as Mayor of Atlanta. He also became a major donor to many causes and institutions; his gifts to Atlanta's Emory University included funding of a teaching hospital for its medical school.

Canfield, Cass (1897–1986) editor, publisher; born in New York City. Associated with Harper & Brothers from 1924 until his death, he was an active editor who attracted such notable authors as John Gunther, Thornton Wilder, and John F. Kennedy; he became the company's president in 1931 and was chairman of the board from 1945 to 1955.

Caniff, (Milton) Milt (1907–88) cartoonist; born in Hillsboro, Ohio. He was the creator of the action-adventure newspaper comic strips *Dickie Dare* (1933–34) and *Terry and the Pirates* (1934–46), and his *Steve Canyon,* featuring the adventures of an ex-pilot, made its first appearance in 1947. His work was greatly admired for its realistic detail in the drawings and storyline.

Cannon, Annie Jump (1863–1941) astronomer; born in Dover, Del. Although deaf, she was a gifted pianist and amateur photographer, and after graduating from Wellesley she studied astronomy at Radcliffe College. In 1896 she was hired at the Harvard College Observatory, remaining there for her entire career. Devising a system for classifying stellar spectra, she reorganized the classification of stars in terms of surface temperature and catalogued over 225,000 stars. She was the first woman honored with a doctorate at Oxford and the only woman member of the Royal Astronomical Society.

Cannon, Clarence Andrew (1879–1964) U.S. representative, historian; born in Elsberry, Mo. A professor of history and a lawyer, he clerked for the U.S. Speaker of the House (1915–20). He served in the U.S. House of Representatives (Dem., Mo.; 1923–64) and wrote *Cannon's Procedure* (1928).

Cannon, Joseph G. (Gurney) (1836–1926) U.S. representative; born in New Garden, N.C. A country lawyer with only six months of law school, as state's attorney in Danville, Ill. (1861–68) he dismissed a charge of theft against Lincoln's stepmother. A conservative Republican congressman (Ill., 1873–91), his racy language and uncouth manners earned him the nickname "Uncle Joe." He voted against appropriations for the Civil Service Act in 1882 and was a minority member of the Committee on Rules. Defeated in 1890, he returned to the House (1893–1913) and chaired the Committee on Appropriations; he offended fellow committee members by putting through a $50,000 national defense bill in 1898 for President McKinley without consulting them. Elected Speaker of the House (1903–11), he began "cannonising" procedures to benefit Republicans. When congressmen protested, he kept them off desirable committees. In 1910, Democrats and Republicans led by Champ Clark were finally able to break his arbitrary control of the Rules Committee, but he remained in the House until 1913, then returned in his eighties (1917–23).

Cannon, Walter B. (Bradford) (1871–1945) physiologist; born in Prairie du Chien, Wis. As a medical student at Harvard (1896–1900), he devised the use of radiopaque chemicals for X-ray diagnosis of the gastrointestinal system (1897). He joined Harvard's faculty (1900–42), and investigated the physiology of digestion until 1911. Inquiries into the physiological effect of emotions (1911–17), including studies of surgical trauma during World War I, led him to postulate that the adrenals' action on the sympathetic nervous system is responsible for an animal's "fight or flight" response. He coined the term "homeostasis" (1926) to describe an organism's tendency to maintain physiological stability; he expounded this concept in his book, *The Wisdom of the Body* (1932). In the 1930s, he began his pioneering work on chemical neurotransmission; his "sympathins 1 and 2" are now known as epinephrine and norepinephrine. A visiting professor at numerous institutions and a member of many international societies, he was an antitotalitarian activist who believed that a scientist should also be a world citizen.

Cantor, Eddie (b. Isidore Itzkowitz) (1892–1964) singer; born in New York City. A rolling-eyed actor with a high-pitched singing voice, who often performed in black-face, Cantor appeared in *Kid Cabaret* (1912) with George Jessel. He worked for Florenz Ziegfeld (1916–28) where he sang his best known songs, including "Making Whoopee." A radio host and movie actor in the 1930s, he helped to found actors' unions and to promote the March of Dimes.

Cantwell, Dennis Patrick (1939–) child psychiatrist, educator; born in East St. Louis, Mo. He became professor of child psychology at the University of California: Los Angeles School of Medicine (1980). His area of expertise included communication and learning disorders, disruptive behavior and mood disorders, eating disorders, suicide, and pervasive developmental disorders.

Cantwell, Robert (Emmett) (1908–78) editor, writer; born in Little Falls (now Vader), Wash. His long career in magazine publishing included editorships at *New Outlook, Newsweek,* and *Sports Illustrated* (1956–73). Best known for such proletarian novels of the 1930s as *The Land of Plenty* (1934), he also wrote biographies, (including lives of Nathaniel Hawthorne (1934) and the ornithologist Alexander Wilson (1961), and the historical study, *The Hidden Northwest* (1972).

Capen, Samuel (Paul) (1878–1956) educator; born in Somerville, Mass. He was the first director of the American Council on Education (1919–22) before becoming president of the University of Buffalo (1922–50), where he introduced undergraduate tutorials and further strengthened professional programs. He championed high academic standards and was an authority on university planning and administration.

Caplan, Arthur L. (1950–) philosopher, biomedical ethicist; born in Boston, Mass. After taking his B.A. at Brandeis (1971), he took an M.A., M.Phil., and Ph.D. (1979) at Columbia University. While at Columbia he served on the faculty of the university's medical school, school of public health, and journalism school. He also taught at the University of Pittsburgh (1986). He then joined the Hastings Center (Briarcliff Manor, N.Y.) as associate for humanities (1977–84), becoming associate director (1985–87). He became director of the Center for Biomedical Ethics at the University of Minnesota, where he was also a professor of philosophy (1987–94). He went on to become director of the Center for Bioethics at the University of Pennsylvania (1994). He has edited or written some 18 books and more than 300 articles on topics in biomedical ethics, health policy, and the history and philosophy of health care; among his best known titles are *When Medicine Went Mad: Bioethics and the Holocaust* (1992) and *If I Were a Rich Man Could I Buy a Pancreas* (1992). He served as a consultant to many organizations, including the National Institutes of Health, the Office of Technology Assessment, and the Clinton Health Policy Task Force Ethics Working Group (1993). His primary areas of research interest were in the use of new technologies in health care, transplantation, resource allocation, the termination of treatment, genetics, human experimentation, and long-term care. He wrote a syndicated column on bioethics, carried in some 40 newspapers in the U.S.A. and abroad, and was a frequent guest and much-quoted spokesperson in the national media whenever issues of bioethics came to the fore.

Capone, (Alphonse) Al (1899–1947) gangster; born in Brooklyn, N.Y. He became the leader in Chicago bootlegging, gambling, and prostitution during the Prohibition Era. His involvement in gang and liquor wars left hundreds of people dead in Chicago and its suburbs. Increasingly implicated in the corruption of political, law enforcement, and labor officials, he was convicted of income-tax evasion (1931) and sentenced to 11 years. He was released in 1939 because, infected with syphilis, his mental condition was deteriorating.

Capote, Truman (b. Truman Persons) (1924–84) writer; born in New Orleans. He took his stepfather's surname in childhood. A high school dropout, he came to New York City in 1942 and worked for awhile as an office boy at *The New Yorker*. His first novel, *Other Voices, Other Rooms* (1948), launched a literary career that peaked with his innovative "nonfiction novel" *In Cold Blood* (1966). Resident in New York and Switzerland, he cultivated celebrity and was famous in later years for his jetsetting lifestyle as well as his writing.

Capper, Arthur (1865–1951) publisher, U.S. senator; born in Garnett, Kans. A newspaper and magazine publisher, he was elected governor of Kansas (Rep., 1915–19) and U.S. senator (1919–49). A New Deal supporter in domestic politics and an isolationist in foreign policy, he was not an especially outspoken leader in the Senate.

Capra, Frank (1897–1991) film director; born in Palermo, Sicily. His family moved to California when he was six, and he began to earn money by selling newspapers, playing the banjo, and working other odd jobs. After receiving a degree in chemical engineering at the California Institute of Technology in 1918, he joined the army as a private. Discharged as a lieutenant, he had other odd jobs until he talked his way into directing a one-reeler, *Fultah Fisher's Boarding House* (1922), in San Francisco. He spent time learning the film business, and then became a gag writer for *Our Gang* comedies and for the comedian Harry Langdon. He directed some Langdon films and some two-reel comedies. His most renowned work as a director celebrated the decency and integrity of the common man as he combats corruption in high places, and he earned Oscars for *It Happened One Night* (1934), *Mr. Deeds Goes to Town* (1936), and *You Can't Take It With You* (1938). The film that would eventually become his most popular, *It's A Wonderful Life* (1947), did not receive any special attention at its initial release.

Carder, Frederick (1863–1963) glassmaker; born in Staffordshire, England. In 1903 he came to the U.S.A. to manage Steuben Glass Works. With a grounding in chemistry and metallurgy, he perfected numerous glassmaking techniques including enameling, etching, intarsia and *cire perdue* ("lost wax"). He created over 8,000 designs, many of them in art nouveau style comparable in quality to Tiffany's works. He is considered a founder of the modern glass movement.

Cardin, Shoshana (1926–) volunteer, philanthropist; born in Tel Aviv, Palestine (now Israel). She came to this country in 1927. A 1946 graduate of the University of California: Los Angeles, she received her M.A. from Antioch University in 1979. She was named Woman of the Year by B'nai B'rith Women of Maryland and the outstanding citizen by the city of Baltimore in 1969. President of the Council of Jewish Federations of New York (1984–87), she was active in a number of other philanthropic, civic, and religious organizations.

Cardozo, Benjamin (Nathan) (1870–1938) Supreme Court justice; born in New York City. After attending Columbia Law School (although he never bothered taking a law degree), he began to practice in 1891 and was highly regarded among the legal community when he was elected to the New York Supreme Court (1913). Only six weeks later he was named to the New York Court of Appeals, becoming its chief judge in 1926. His genius at combining a mastery of the law with a philosophic bent was apparent not only in his legal opinions but also in a series of books such as *The Nature of the Judicial Process* (1921) and *Law and Literature* (1931). By the time President Hoover appointed him to the U.S. Supreme Court (1932–38) he was one of the most admired legal minds in the nation. Broad in his approach to the law, generous in his interpretation of the Constitution, and sensitive to social contexts, he was often in dissent as the Court resisted the sweeping agenda of President Franklin Roosevelt's administration. Seemingly shy, even humble in his manner, he would go down in history as one of the truly great individuals to have served on the Supreme Court.

Carey, Henry (Charles) (1793–1879) economist, publisher; born in Philadelphia. Skipping college, he began working in business and by age 24 was a partner in his father's Baltimore publishing business, learning by reading manuscripts submitted for publication. At age 42, he sold the company to write about economics, publishing his *Essay on the Rate of Wages* (1935). He espoused laissez-faire economics in the 3-volume *Principles of Political Economy* (1837, 1838, 1840) and protectionism in *Harmony of Interests: Manufacturing and Commercial* (1851). He continued to write and publish regularly into the 1870s.

Carey, James (Barron) (1911–73) labor leader; born in Philadelphia. He helped organize and was first president of the United Electrical, Radio and Machine Workers of America (UE) (1935–41). At odds with the UE's Communist leaders, he was elected president of the rival International Union of Electrical, Radio and Machine Workers (IUE) (1949–65).

Carey, Joseph Maull (1845–1924) U.S. senator; born in Milton, Del. A prosperous rancher and a judge on the Supreme Court of Wyoming (1872–76), he was elected territorial representative to Congress (Rep., Wyo.; 1885–90). Having introduced the bill for admitting Wyoming as a state, he then became its first U.S. senator (1890–95) and finally its governor (Dem., 1911–15).

Carey, Mathew (1760–1839) publisher, bookseller; born in Dublin, Ireland. Fleeing to the U.S.A. in 1784 to escape prosecution for anti-British publications, he settled in Philadelphia, where he became an important publisher and wrote widely on economics and other subjects. In 1785 he founded the *Pennsylvania Herald*, noted for its detailed coverage of the legislature. He also founded the Hibernian Society and the nation's first Sunday school.

Carey, Ronald (1936–) labor leader; born in New York City. A United Parcel Service driver, he was elected president of a local chapter of the International Brotherhood of Teamsters in 1968. A longtime dissident within a union beset by charges of corruption, he was elected Teamsters president in 1991.

Carlisle, John Griffin (1835–1910) U.S. representative/senator, cabinet officer; born in Kenton County, Ky. A self-educated lawyer, he was elected to the U.S. House of Representatives (Dem., Ky.; 1877–90). He served as Speaker of the House (1883–90) before being appointed to the U.S. Senate (1890–93). He served as secretary of the treasury (1893–97) under President Grover Cleveland. A renowned orator, he was so outspoken in support for free trade and "sound money" that he antagonized his fellow Kentuckians, so he spent his last years practicing law in New York City.

Carlson, Chester (Floyd) (1906–68) inventor; born in Seattle, Wash. A physics graduate of the California Institute of Technology (1930), he took a law degree and worked as a patent lawyer in an electronics firm. He experimented on his own time with photocopying processes and by 1938 had discovered the electrostatic "xerography" process, which he patented two years later. Xerox Corporation's development and marketing of Carlson's invention made him a multi-millionaire.

Carlson, Curtis LeRoy (1914–) corporate executive; born in Minneapolis, Minn. He was founding president of the Gold Bond Stamp Company, Minneapolis (1938–84), and chairman of other construction, real estate, and hospitality companies including the Radisson Hotel Corporation and TGI Friday's. Carlson Companies was one of the largest privately owned companies in the U.S.A.

Carlson, Evans F. (Fordyce) (1896–1947) marine officer; born in Sidney, N.Y. Service in China in the 1930s left him with a great admiration for the Communists there; he patterned his Carlson's Raiders, a famous World War II marines unit, after the Red Chinese Army. After the war, he argued forcefully for peaceful coexistence with the Soviet Union, and after his death was attacked by red-baiting Senator Joseph R. McCarthy.

Carlton, (Stephen Norman) Steve (1944–) baseball player; born in Miami, Fla. During his 23-year career as a (left-handed) pitcher (1965–87), mostly with the Philadelphia Phillies, he won 329 games and won the Cy Young Award four times. He was inducted into the Hall of Fame in 1994.

Carlucci, Frank Charles (1930–) diplomat, government official; born in Scranton, Pa. He studied at Harvard and Princeton and then fought in the Korean War. He was a foreign service officer (1956–69), ambassador to Portugal (1975–78), and deputy director of the Central Intelligence Agency (1978–81). He worked at Sears World Trade and then was national security adviser (1986–87) and secretary of defense (1987–89).

Carmack, George Washington (1860–1922) prospector; born near San Francisco. He went to Alaska in 1884 and married a Tagish Indian woman. He is credited with being the first to discover Alaska's gold in 1896. He returned to California and invested his money in mines and real estate. He abandoned his Indian wife and married a white woman around 1900.

Carmichael, (Hoagland Howard) Hoagy (1899–1981) composer, performer; born in Bloomington, Ind. Tutored in ragtime piano, he played in small bands while in college, where he studied law. After briefly practicing law, he quit to work as a bandleader and arranger. In 1927 he composed the melody that became "Star Dust" when lyrics were later added; it became one of the most widely performed and recorded popular songs of all time. In 1930 he made a series of recordings for RCA Victor with the Dorsey brothers, Jack Teagarden, Gene Krupa, Benny Goodman, Joe Venuti and Bix Beiderbecke. During the 1930s, 1940s, and 1950s he wrote songs and composed film scores; he also occasionally acted in movies, appearing either as himself or a character like himself, playing the piano with a cigarette dangling from his mouth. During the 1940s and 1950s he briefly hosted two radio shows and a television variety show, *Saturday Night Revue*. In the early 1960s he acted in a weekly television western and was a frequent guest on other television shows. He was elected to the Songwriter's Hall of Fame in 1971.

Carmichael, Stokely (1941–) radical activist; born in Trinidad. A carpenter's son, he emigrated to America (1952) and was shocked by the racism he encountered. Involved in civil rights while attending Howard University (1960–64), he was elected leader of the Student Nonviolent Coordinating Committee (SNCC) and changed the group's focus from integration to "black liberation." Gifted, handsome, and articulate, he popularized the phrase "black power" and as a Black Panther came to symbolize black violence to many whites. He came to favor forging alliances with radical whites and resigned from the Panthers over this approach (1968). He and his wife, South African singer Miriam Makeba, moved to Guinea (1969), where he supported Pan-Africanism. He eventually returned to the U.S.A., but he dropped out of all civil rights activities.

Carnap, Rudolf (1891–1970) philosopher; born in Rondsdorf, Germany. After earning a doctorate from the University of Jena, he taught at the University of Vienna (1926–31) and became a leader of the Vienna Circle of logical positivists. Emigrating to the U.S.A. in 1935 to escape Nazism, he held posts at the University of Chicago (1936–52), the Institute for Advanced Studies at Princeton (1952–54), and the University of California (from 1955). A pioneer in the rigorous analytic tradition, he wrote such works as *The Logical Syntax of Language* (translated 1937), *Meaning and Necessity* (1947), and *Logical Foundations of Probability* (1950).

Carnegie, Andrew (1835–1919) iron/steel manufacturer, philanthropist; born in Dunfermline, Scotland. Although he had only a primary-school education, he grew up in a family that valued ideas and books as well as progressive social and economic reforms. His father was a handloom weaver and he brought his family to the U.S.A. in 1848 where they joined relatives in Allegheny (now Pittsburgh), Pa. Young Andrew quickly moved from bobbin boy in a factory to a telegraph operator (and was one of the first to learn to read messages "by ear"); he then became an assistant to Thomas Scott of the Pennsylvania Railroad (1853–65); during the Civil War he was not in military service but he helped improve the Federal army's telegraph communications. He left the Pennsylvania Railroad in 1865 to concentrate on his own businesses, first the Keystone Bridge Company, then making iron and steel. Everything he took up made him wealthier, and the secrets of his success seemed to be that he surrounded himself with intelligent men, invested heavily in new equipment, and managed to keep majority ownership in his companies so that he did not have to answer to stockholders. As he prospered, he broadened his interests, traveling abroad and deliberately seeking to exchange views with leading individuals in Great Britain as well as America; he would count Matthew Arnold and Mark Twain, William Gladstone and Theodore Roosevelt among his friends; he wrote several books, including *Triumphant Democracy* (1886), setting forth his optimistic views about the role of capitalism and democracy; he built a great estate in Scotland where he often entertained prominent people. Although progressive in some respects, he was essentially a benevolent dictator; he had little patience with the burgeoning labor movement, and the blackest mark on his career was the Homestead strike of 1892, when he allowed his assistant, Henry Clay Frick, to take steps that led to violence. (Carnegie himself was in Scotland during the strike.) By 1889 his Carnegie Steel Company had become one of the world's largest; when he sold his business to J. P. Morgan in 1901 for some $260 million profit for himself, he was one of the richest men in the world and could devote himself to his philanthropies. He had started donating money as a young entrepreneur; in 1889 he published an article, "Wealth," in which he argued that the wealthy were obligated to distribute their fortunes to improve the world. He had begun by helping communities build libraries and helping churches buy organs; he established pension funds for teachers, eventually setting up the Carnegie Foundation for the Advancement of Teaching (1905) to support this as well as other programs; he helped support various scientific undertakings, eventually establishing the Carnegie Institution of Washington (1902) to support such; he set up the Carnegie Hero Funds (1904) to recognize individuals who had performed heroic acts; he donated to many institutions of higher learning in Scotland as well as in America and set up the Carnegie Institute of Technology in Pittsburgh (and its sister school, Margaret Morrison); he set up the Carnegie Endowment for International Peace in 1910 and helped build the international court of justice at the Hague. It is estimated that he eventually gave away $350 million, but his money failed to buy what he most wanted, world peace, and he died before the U.S.A. rejected the League of Nations he had long dreamed of establishing.

Carnegie, Dale (b. Carnagey) (1888–1955) author, public speaker; born in Maryville, Mo. Devoted to public speaking from his teen years, he was unsuccessful as a salesman. Moving to New York City, he gave classes in public speaking at the Young Men's Christian Association (1912). Soon he was developing courses on his own, and writing pamphlets he would eventually publish as books. After serving in the army in World War I he managed Lowell Thomas's lecture tour, then turned to his own tour to promote his ideas about success through public speaking. In the early 1930s he was known for his books and a radio program, when he published *How to Win Friends and Influence People* (1930), which enjoyed immediate success and would remain one of the best-sellers of all time. This led to demand for him as a lecturer and writer: he began a syndicated newspaper column and he organized the Dale Carnegie Institute for Effective Speaking and Human Relations, with branches all over the world; he lived to see the day when his name became virtually synonymous with the very kind of self-help-to-success that he promoted.

Carnegie, Hattie (b. Henrietta Kanengeiser) (1886–1956) fashion designer; born in Vienna, Austria. A childhood immigrant to New York City, she appropriated Andrew Carnegie's surname for her first hat shop (1909). Creating a major fashion house, Carnegie reinterpreted French *haute couture* for Americans; she popularized the "little Carnegie suit" and the simple black cocktail dress. She married John Zanft in 1927 but did not use his name in her public or professional life.

Carney, (Arthur William Matthew) Art (1918–) television comedian, stage/movie actor; born in Mount Vernon, N.Y. After working as "second banana" for Fred Allen, Edgar Bergen, and Bert Lahr, he served in the U.S. Army and was wounded during the Normandy landing in June 1944. He returned to act on Broadway and television, gaining his greatest success as Jackie Gleason's sewer-cleaner sidekick, Ed Norton, in *The Honeymooners* (1955–56). He created the role of slovenly Oscar in Broadway's *The Odd Couple* (1960) and after recovering from a mental breakdown, he returned to work on stage and in television and screen films, winning the best actor Academy Award for *Harry and Tonto* (1974).

Carnovsky, Leon (1903–75) librarian, educator; born in St. Louis, Mo. He received an A.B. from the University of Missouri (1927) and a Ph.D. from the Graduate Library School of the University of Chicago (1932), where he remained as a professor until his retirement in 1971. From 1941 to 1963 he was managing editor of the *Library Quarterly*. He became known as a surveyor of libraries and library problems and he conducted surveys of libraries throughout the U.S.A. For the United Nations Educational, Scientific, and Cultural Organization he produced reports of library education in Israel (1957) and Greece (1962). Particularly important among his many journal articles is "The Obligations and Responsibilities of the Librarian Concerning Censorship" (1950), which has been frequently reprinted and which arose from his position as chairman of the American Library Association Intellectual Freedom Committee.

Carnovsky, Morris (1897–1992) stage and film actor; born in St. Louis, Mo. Primarily a stage performer, he was a founding member of The Group Theater. After 1956 he was mainly seen in Shakespearean roles.

Carothers, Wallace (Hume) (1896–1937) chemist, inventor; born in Burlington, Iowa. A teacher's son, he taught chemistry at several universities before concentrating on industrial research. Working for the Du Pont Company, he produced neoprene, the first synthetic rubber, and followed that success with the discovery of nylon. He committed suicide, and the patent for nylon went posthumously to Du Pont.

Carpenter, John Alden (1876–1951) composer; born in Park Ridge, Ill. A student of John Knowles Paine at Harvard and Edward Elgar in England, he pursued a business career while composing actively. He was noted for basing his music on urban subjects, with reference to jazz and popular culture, as in his ballets *Krazy Kat* (1922) and *Skyscraper* (1926).

Carpenter, Matthew Hale (b. Decatur Merritt Hammond Carpenter) (1824–81) lawyer, U.S. senator; born in Moretown, Vt. Having moved to Wisconsin where he practiced law, he was elected to the U.S. Senate (Rep., Wis.; 1869–75, 1879–81). An abolitionist sympathizer, he supported the Union and emancipation for the slaves during the

Civil War. He was so highly regarded as a lawyer that he was employed by William Belknap (1876) after he was charged with corruption as secretary of the treasury and by Samuel Tilden in his unsuccessful appeal before the Electoral Commission (1876).

Carpenter, William T. (1936–) psychiatrist; born in Jacksonville, Fla. His major professional interest since about 1966 was schizophrenia, which he approached within the context of a broad medical model, integrating biological, psychological, and social data. He provided expert testimony in the *U.S. Government* v. *John Hinckley* case, and studied the political use of psychiatry in the Soviet Union (1989).

Carr, (Archibald Fairly, Jr.) Archie (1909–87) herpetologist; born in Mobile, Ala. He spent his career at the University of Florida: Gainsville (1933–87), with concurrent affiliations at the Escuela Panamericana Honduras (1945–49) and the American Museum of Natural History (1951–87). He made major contributions to the ecology of fishes, amphibians, and reptiles of Florida. His classic conservationist book, *The Windward Road* (1956), which won the O. Henry Award for best nonfiction short story that year, became the beginning of his worldwide campaign to protect sea turtles from human predators, ocean pollution, and extinction. This book inspired the creation of the Caribbean Conservation Corporation (1959), where he served from 1961 to 1987.

Carr, Benjamin (1768–1831) organist, singer, composer, publisher; born in London, England. He came to Philadelphia in 1793 and established important early American music stores and publishing houses there and in New York and Baltimore.

Carr, Emma Perry (1880–1972) chemist, educator; born in Holmesville, Ohio. She was assistant professor and then professor of chemistry at Mount Holyoke College (1913–46), where she was not only an inspiring teacher but also an innovator in research programs. Over several decades she herself made significant contributions to both empirical and theoretical problems of analyzing organic molecules with ultraviolet absorption spectroscopy. Her research laboratory produced not only many theses and scientific papers but also inspired numerous young women to take up careers in science.

Carrier, Willis (Haviland) (1876–1950) engineer, inventor; born near Angola, N.Y. Raised on a farm, he attended local schools, won a scholarship to Cornell University, and graduated from there with an engineering degree in 1901. The following year, working for the Buffalo Forge Company, he designed a humidity-control machine for a New York printing plant. He went on to become the pioneer of modern air-conditioning systems, with over 80 patents; he also long dominated the manufacturing of air conditioners with the company he headed, Carrier Corporation (1915–48). By 1930 Carrier air conditioners were cooling more than 300 theaters, and in 1939 he invented a practical air-conditioning system for skyscrapers.

Carroll, Anna Ella (1815–93) political writer; born near Pocomoke County, Md. Descended from old Maryland families, she seems to have been taught primarily by her father, Thomas Carroll, who served as governor (1830–31); the family fell on hard times by 1837 and for some 15 years her activities are vague. But in 1854 she emerged as a supporter of the Know-Nothing Party, publishing books and articles attacking the Catholics. During the Civil War, she

enlisted her pen in the Union cause with such pamphlets as *War Powers of the Central Government* (1861), but her claims for large payments were denied. After the war she claimed she had suggested Grant's successful Tennessee River strategy of 1862, and she spent her remaining years and energy trying to get compensation from the government. Her cause was taken up by some but most students have decided that the "Carroll Plan" did not influence Grant.

Carroll, Charles ("of Carrollton") (1737–1832) Revolutionary leader, U.S. senator; born in Annapolis, Md. (cousin of John Cardinal Carroll). Son of a wealthy, land-owning Catholic family, he was educated at Jesuit schools in France and read law in London, then returned to Maryland in 1765 and took over the family estate, Carrollton. He devoted himself to developing the property until he got drawn into politics in 1773 and ended up as spokesman for the patriot cause. In 1776 he accompanied Benjamin Franklin, Samuel Chase, and his cousin, John, on a failed mission to persuade Canada to join the revolting colonies. As a member of the Continental Congress (1776–78) he signed the Declaration of Independence; later he was a member of the U.S. Senate (Fed., Md.; 1789–92). Active in trade, land development, and with the Baltimore & Ohio Railroad, at his death he was said to be the wealthiest man in America as well as the last surviving signer of the Declaration of Independence.

Carroll, Diahann (1935–) actress, singer; born in New York City. A nightclub singer and model, once married to Vic Damone, she first appeared on Broadway in *The House of Flowers* (1954), working in films during the 1950s as well. Star of *No Strings* (1962), she appeared in the movie *I Know Why the Caged Bird Sings* (1979). When she appeared in *Julia* (1968–71) and *Dynasty* (1984–87) she was the first African-American woman to star in her own television series.

Carroll, James (1854–1907) bacteriologist; born in Woolwich, England. Having first emigrated to Canada, he enlisted in the U.S. Army in 1874. After nine years in the infantry and 15 years as a hospital steward (1883–98), he studied medicine and bacteriology; in 1895 he became an assistant to Walter Reed at the Army Medical School. In 1900, he was appointed to the Yellow Fever Commission to study the disease in Cuba. To test the theory of mosquito transmission, he let himself be bitten and contracted the disease; although he recovered, complications of yellow fever would cause his early death. He succeeded Walter Reed as a professor at the Army Medical School and at Columbian University (Washington, D.C.).

Carroll, John (1735–1815) bishop; born in Upper Marlboro, Md. Born to a family of prosperous Catholic Maryland planters, he studied in Europe, where he entered the Jesuit order (1753) and was ordained. In 1774, a year after the Jesuits' suppression, he returned to Maryland to do pastoral work as a secular priest. A supporter of the patriot cause, he joined in an unsuccessful mission to obtain a promise of Canadian neutrality in the American Revolution (1776). Named head of the U.S. Catholic clergy (1784), Carroll was consecrated as the first American Catholic bishop (of Baltimore) in 1790; he was named an archbishop in 1808. As the church's leader during a crucial early period, he brought in European missionaries, cofounded a college that became Georgetown University (1789), started three seminaries, and labored to establish internal order and counter anti-Catholic discrimination, in part by stressing Catholic commitment to democratic ideals.

Carroll, Vinnette (1922–) stage actress, director; born in New York City. She made her professional debut in *The Little Foxes* in 1948. Artistic director of the Urban Arts Corps, she had a long career as a director and teacher.

Carson, (Christopher) Kit (1809–68) guide, trapper, soldier, Indian agent; born in Madison County, Ky. His father died when he was nine and he received no schooling. He was apprenticed to a saddlemaker (1825) but ran away to join an expedition to Sante Fe, N.M. He became an experienced trapper and Indian fighter and around 1836 married an Arapaho woman he called Alice. After her death, he met John C. Frémont and served as the guide for Frémont's first expedition (1842). He married again (1843) and served as a guide on Frémont's second expedition (1843–44). After Frémont's third expedition and the conquest of California (1846–47), he was selected to carry the reports back to Washington. When the Senate refused to confirm a commission in the regular army, he served as an agent for the Ute Indians (1853–61) and dictated the narrative of his life and adventures. During the Civil War he led the 1st New Mexican Volunteer Infantry, mostly in battles against Native American peoples; his most famous episode involved leading captured Navahos on a 300-mile "long walk." Breveted to rank of brigadier general, he remained in the army and was assigned to command Ft. Garland in Colorado (1866–67) but his health soon failed.

Carson, (John William) Johnny (1925–) television talk show host; born in Corning, Iowa. Raised in Nebraska, he sent away for a magic kit at age 12, and "The Great Carsoni" gave his first performance two years later. After serving in the U.S. Navy (1943–46), he graduated from the University of Nebraska (1949) and went to work in radio in California (1950), where he worked for various radio and television shows. Moving to New York City in 1956, he hosted the television quiz show *Who Do You Trust?* (1958–63), making it ABC's top daytime program. He first appeared on the *Tonight Show* in 1958, and as permanent host from 1962 to 1992, he turned it into one of National Broadcasting Company's biggest moneymakers. His talk show personality combined midwestern innocence with cosmopolitan wit. He portrayed a series of outrageous American types in occasional skits but the program's appeal was its familiar formula: sidekick Ed McMahon introduced him by announcing, "Heeeere's Johnny!"; then Carson did a monologue followed by guest interviews – usually showbiz celebrities – punctuated by Doc Severinsen's music. In private life, Carson was almost the opposite of his spontaneous, charming onstage personality; he was married four times and was reputed to be rather distant, even cool in his dealings with most people. He formed his own production group in 1980 and became immensely wealthy from his own and other shows, and by the time he retired in 1992, he was almost regarded as a national institution.

Carson, Rachel (Louise) (1907–64) marine biologist, environmentalist, writer; born in Springdale, Pa. She grew up close to nature on a Pennsylvania farm, graduated from the Pennsylvania College for Women (now Chatham College) in 1929, and went on to do advanced study at Johns Hopkins University. She taught at the University of Maryland for five years before joining the U.S. Fish and Wildlife Service in 1936. Her first book, *Under the Sea-Wind* (1941) described marine life in clear, elegant, and non-technical prose. She retained her government job through the 1940s, in part because she had taken on the responsibility of supporting her mother and her sister's two orphaned daughters. In 1951 she published *The Sea Around Us;* it became an immediate bestseller and freed her from financial worry. During the 1950s she conducted research into the effects of pesticides on the food chain. It led to the publication of her most influential work, *Silent Spring* (1962), which condemned the indiscriminate use of pesticides, especially DDT (later banned). The book led to a presidential commission that largely endorsed her findings, and helped shape a growing environmental consciousness.

Carter, A.P. (Alvin Pleasant) See under CARTER FAMILY.

Carter, (Bennett Lester) Benny (1907–) jazz musician; born in New York City. His career spanned eight decades as an outstanding alto saxophonist and freelance arranger. He led his own bands in the U.S.A. and Europe during the 1930s, and settled in Hollywood, Calif., in 1943 where he spent the next 40 years as a composer for movies and television. He remained active in jazz on a periodic basis, appeared as an artist-in-residence at Princeton, Cornell, and other universities in the mid-1970s, and resumed a regular concert and recording schedule as a soloist in the 1980s.

Carter, Elliott (Cook, Jr.) (1908–) composer; born in New York City. Encouraged by Charles Ives to pursue composition, he graduated from Harvard and for three years studied with famed pedagogue Nadia Boulanger in Paris. He spent the 1940s teaching, writing on music, and composing relatively conservative music with modest success. Then his 1951 First String Quartet, a bold departure, brought him into the international avant-garde. He explored increasingly complex rhythmic ideas with a series of works including three more string quartets and the 1961 Double Concerto.

Carter, Gwendolyn Margaret (1906–91) political scientist; born in Hamilton, Ontario, Canada. A Harvard Ph.D., she was naturalized in the early 1940s and taught at Smith College (1943–64), Northwestern University (1964–74), and Indiana University (1974–84). After 1948 she focused on Africa, particularly on apartheid; her books include *The Politics of Inequality* (1958, later revised) and *Which Way is South Africa Going?* (1980).

Carter, James Coolidge (1827–1905) lawyer; born in Lancaster, Mass. Throughout 52 years with Davies & Scudder in New York, he defended the evolution of common law, and in 1871, helped prosecute "Boss" Tweed. A founder – and for nine years president – of the National Municipal League and a president of the American Bar Association, he was U.S. chief counsel in the Bering Sea controversy (1893).

Carter, (James Earl) Jimmy (1924–) thirty-ninth U.S. president; born in Plains, Ga. He graduated from the U.S. Naval Academy (1946) and served in the navy until 1953; part of that time he worked under Admiral Hyman Rickover on the naval nuclear reactor project. Carter left the navy to take over the family's peanut business, which he built up. He served two terms as a Democrat in the Georgia legislature (1963–67). After serving as a liberal governor of Georgia (1970–74), he began campaigning for the presidency and won the Democratic nomination of 1976, narrowly beating Gerald Ford in the election. In contrast to recent administrations, he had promised an open and progressive government responsive to the public; despite a Democratic Congress, however, his presidency was notable more for good intentions than achievements. He did effect the Panama Treaty and the historic Camp David agreements between Israel and Egypt (1979), but his initial popularity waned during 1979–80 as a result of mounting economic difficulties and the seizure of U.S. hostages in Iran. He lost the 1980 election to Ronald Reagan. Back in private life he was active in national and international social concerns, taking a hands-on approach to everything from building homes for poor Americans to mediating between hostile parties (as in Haiti).

Carter, John Mack (1928–) editor, publisher; born in Murray, Kans. As editor of the *Ladies' Home Journal* (1965–74) and *Good Housekeeping* (from 1974), he played a major role in shaping women's magazines.

Carter, Nick See STRATEMEYER, EDWARD L.

Carter, Robert "King" (1663–1732) colonial official, landowner; born in Lancaster County, Va. He served in the Virginia Assembly (1691–92, 1695–99) and the Council (1699–1732). A large landowner himself, he became the agent for the wealthy Fairfax family in 1702 and used his position to become one of the wealthiest men in the colonies. His political and economic position earned him the title of "King Carter" or "King Robin."

Carter, Rosalynn (b. Smith) (1927–) First Lady; born in Plains, Ga. She married Jimmy Carter in 1946. After helping him run his family peanut farm, she campaigned actively for him in 1976. An active First Lady, she spoke out on human rights, traveled abroad, and sat in on many cabinet meetings. Deeply hurt by Carter's failure to be reelected, she recovered to join him in his post-presidential activities.

Carteret, Philip (1639–82) first governor of New Jersey; born in Isle of Jersey, England. After arriving at Elizabethport (1665) he instituted a government and summoned the first New Jersey legislature (1668). Following a challenge to his government by Sir Edmund Andros (1680) he was reinstated as governor, but he relinquished his office and died soon afterward.

Carter Family, The, consisting of **Carter, A. P. (Alvin Pleasant)** (1891–1960), born in Scott County, Va.; **Sara Dougherty** (1898–1979), born in Wise County, Va.; **Maybelle Addington** (1909–79), born in Nicklesville, Va.; country music singers, songwriters. After A. P. Carter married Sara Dougherty in 1915, they often sang for friends and relatives; when Maybelle Addington married A. P.'s brother Ezra in 1926, she joined in and proved to be especially good on the guitar, banjo, and autoharp. They made their first records for Victor Company in 1927 (at the same session where Jimmie Rodgers debuted) and soon they were becoming known to a broader audience with their recordings, live radio broadcasts, and personal appearances. With a repertoire of both traditional folksongs, gospel music, and their own compositions ("Wildwood Flowers," "Will the Circle Be Unbroken"), they embodied the authentic mood and style of southern folk music. The original trio broke up in 1943 (A. P. and Sara had separated in 1933) and Maybelle began to perform with her daughters Helen, June, and Anita as Mother Maybelle and the Carter Sisters; they were a popular fixture on Grand Ole Opry (1950–67). When June married Johnny Cash in 1968, the group toured with his show until 1973. A. P. and Sara had pretty much retired in 1943 but they joined their children, Joe and Janette, to make recordings in 1952 and 1956. Maybelle and Sara made an album, *An Historic Reunion,* in 1967. The abiding influence of the original Carter Family trio on several generations is now recognized by all who perform and enjoy American country and folk music.

Cartwright, Alexander (Joy), Jr. (1820–92) baseball pioneer; born in New York City. A bank teller, onetime bookstore-stationery owner, and volunteer fireman, in the early 1840s he joined other young men in New York City in playing an early form of baseball. In the 20th century, he would be credited with "inventing" baseball, including such regulations as 9 players to a team and bases 90 feet apart; what is certain is that in September 1845 his Knickerbocker Base Ball Club drew up the first rules for what would eventually evolve into the modern game of baseball. In 1849, at the news of the gold finds in California, he traveled overland to San Francisco, but almost immediately sailed to Hawaii, where he spent the rest of his life, prospering as a businessman and introducing baseball to the inhabitants. He was elected to the Baseball Hall of Fame in 1938.

Cartwright, Peter (1785–1872) Protestant religious leader; born in Amherst County, Va. He moved with his family to frontier Logan County, Ky., in 1790 and converted to Methodism at age 16. As a traveling preacher from 1803–24, he denounced drinking, gambling, and rival sects on the circuit in Kentucky, Tennessee, Ohio, and Indiana. A committed opponent of slavery, he was twice elected to the Illinois legislature; in 1846 he lost the election to the U.S. House of Representatives to Abraham Lincoln. *The Backwoods Preacher,* his account of frontier religious life, appeared in 1869.

Carty, John (Joseph) (1861–1932) electrical engineer; born in Cambridge, Mass. He worked for Bell Telephone in Boston in 1879 and was in charge of the cable and switchboard departments at Western Electric from 1887–89. He joined American Telephone and Telegraph Co. in 1907, becoming vice-president in 1919, and retiring in 1930. He contributed to the development of telephone wires and technology.

Carus, Paul (1852–1919) philosopher; born in Ilsenburg, Germany. Emigrating to the U.S.A. in the early 1880s because of his liberal views, he preached reverence for science and espoused a monistic philosophy with pantheistic overtones in such works as *Philosophy as a Science* (1909). A prolific writer, he also helped found two important journals, *The Open Court* (1887) and the *Monist* (1890), and was director of the Open Court publishing company in Chicago.

Carver, George Washington (c. 1861–1943) agricultural chemist, educator, botanist; born near Diamond Grove, Mo. Born to slave parents, he began his education at age 14 and earned a B.S. and M.S. in agriculture (1894, 1896) from Iowa State College. He directed the agricultural research department at Tuskegee Institute, Alabama (1896–1943), teaching and pioneering an extension program of "movable schools" to train black farmers in agriculture and home economics. Aiming to revitalize and conserve depleted soil, Carver influenced the southern shift from single-crop to diversified agriculture by developing hundreds of products made from peanuts, sweet potatoes, and other crops, many of them commercially viable. He developed a hybrid cotton and was a noted collector of fungi. Working with severely limited resources outside the white scientific establishment,

Carver published little more than his 44 Tuskegee Experiment Station bulletins (1898–1942) and, wishing his work to be widely available, obtained only three patents; nevertheless he became a researcher of international stature. He chose not to challenge the system of segregation that existed during his lifetime, but he became one of the chief models of what African-Americans could accomplish.

Carver, Raymond (Clevie), Jr. (1938–88) writer, poet; born in Clatskanie, Ore. He studied at Humboldt State University (now California State University: Humboldt) (B.A. 1963), University of Iowa (1963–64), and worked at various low-paying jobs. Later he taught at many institutions and was based in Port Angeles, Wash. He is known as a writer of spare and realistic poetry and short fiction, as in *Will You Please Be Quiet, Please?* (1976).

Cary, Elisabeth Luther (1867–1936) writer; born in Brooklyn, N.Y. She was educated privately, studied art for many years, and was the owner and editor of *The Script,* an art magazine (1905–08). She then became the first full-time art critic for the *New York Times* (1908–27). She also wrote many translations from the French, and critical studies of such writers as Emerson and Rossetti.

Case, Francis Higbee (1896–1962) U.S. representative/senator; born in Everly, Iowa. He settled in South Dakota in 1922 to work as a newspaper editor and then owner. He was elected to the U.S. House of Representatives (Rep., S.D.; 1937–51) and to the U.S. Senate (1951–62). Primarily interested in domestic issues, such as water conservation and farm surplus programs, he initiated the Renegotiation Act of 1942 which was intended to recover excessive defense contract profits.

Case, Jerome (Increase) (1818–91) manufacturer; born in Williamstown, N.Y. He got his start in the threshing business, running his father's horse-drawn machine. In 1842 he bought six threshers and moved to Racine, Wis., where he sold five and operated the sixth. In 1844 he combined a thresher and a chaff separator and by 1880 had incorporated as the J. I. Case Threshing Machine Company. A founder of two banks, he also served as mayor of Racine and helped found the Wisconsin Academy of Science, Art, and Letters.

Casey, James E. (1888–1983) corporate executive; born in Candelaria, Nev. At age 19 he cofounded a Seattle messenger service; renamed United Parcel Service (1919), it grew into an international industry leader known for innovations in operations and corporate practices such as profit sharing. He was variously president, CEO, and chairman.

Casey, William J. (Joseph) (1913–87) lawyer, government official; born in Elmhurst, Queens, N.Y. A lawyer, he supervised spy missions for the Office of Strategic Services in Europe (1941–46). Returning to corporate law, he focused on his stock investments, then served as a tough chairman of the Securities and Exchange Commission (1971–73). As President Reagan's director of the Central Intelligence Agency (1981–87), he was known for extremely aggressive and sometimes questionable policies when it came to pursuing communists; he allegedly supported illegal aid to the Nicaraguan Contras, but died before giving formal testimony.

Cash, Johnny (1932–) musician; born in Kingsland, Ark. A singer, guitarist, and songwriter, he was born into a poor cotton farming family and became one of the greatest stars of country music. He began writing songs while serving in the

air force between 1950–54, and worked as a door-to-door salesman before recording his first Sun Records hits, "I Walk the Line" and "Folsom Prison Blues," in 1956. He appeared regularly on the "Louisiana Hayride" and "Grand Ole Opry" radio broadcasts through the early 1960s. In 1960 he performed the first of many free jailhouse shows in San Quentin Prison. His collaborations with Bob Dylan in the late 1960s underscored his interest in the counter-culture's music. In 1968 he married June Carter, a member of the famous "first family" of country/folk music. In 1969, he began hosting his own television program, "The Johnny Cash Show." Cash also appeared in numerous dramatic roles in movies and television. In 1980, he was inducted into the Country Music Association Hall of Fame.

Casilear, John William (1811–93) painter; born in New York City. He studied with Asher B. Durand (1831), became a banknote engraver, traveled in Europe (1840–43 and 1857–58), and worked in New York (1854). He specialized in Hudson River School scenes, as in *Lake George* (1857).

Cass, Lewis (1782–1866) soldier, U.S. senator, public official; born in Exeter, N.H. He practiced law in Ohio and served with distinction in the War of 1812, rising to brigadier general. He was the military and civil governor of the Michigan Territory (1813–31) and President Andrew Jackson's secretary of war (1831–36); in both offices he spent much of his time dealing with Native Americans. He was ambassador to France (1836–42) and a U.S. Senator (Dem., Mich.; 1845–48, 1849–57). A strong nationalist, he favored the Mexican War and was the unsuccessful Democratic nominee for U.S. president in 1848. As secretary of state (1857–60) he secured from Great Britain an end to all search and seizure rights at sea. He resigned when President James Buchanan refused to respond decisively to South Carolina's secession and, having earlier supported compromise over slavery, called for support of the Union. His last years were spent writing accounts of his experiences.

Cassatt, Mary (Stevenson) (1845–1926) painter; born in Allegheny City, Pa. Born into a well-to-do family, she studied at the Pennsylvania Academy of Fine Arts (1861–65) but found it old fashioned; between 1866–74 she studied and painted in Paris, Italy, Spain, and Holland, finally settling in Paris, her home for the rest of her life. Befriended by Degas, she was soon characterized an impressionist painter in both style and subject matter; in fact by 1883 she was emphasizing more the linear aspect. Another influence on her style was an 1890 exhibition of Japanese prints in Paris. She never married, but her own family gravitated to her in Paris; from 1910 on, her increasingly poor eyesight virtually put an end to her serious painting. She is best known for her luminous portraits of women and children such as *The Morning Toilet* (1886) and *Mother Feeding a Child* (1898). A less recognized legacy was her influence in getting many Americans to acquire Impressionist and other contemporary French paintings now in U.S. museums.

Cassavetes, John (1929–89) actor, director, screenwriter; born in New York (husband of Gena Rowlands). After graduating from Colgate University, he studied acting and then went into stock. He made his film debut in *Taxi* (1953) and became a fine, intense actor in movies and on TV. He used his earnings from a television detective series to finance his first directorial effort, *Shadows* (1961), which broke new ground with its improvised scenes and free-moving cinematography. He continued to make semi-improvised movies until he wrote and directed *A Woman Under the Influence* (1974).

Cassidy, Frederic G. (Gomes) (1907–) linguist, lexicographer; born in Kingston, Jamaica. After immigrating to the U.S.A. with his family in 1919, he attended Oberlin College and the University of Michigan (Ph.D. 1938) and began a long teaching career at the University of Wisconsin (1939). An authority on Jamaican English and pidgin and creole languages, he also served as a fieldworker for the Linguistic Atlas of the U.S. survey. In 1962 he was appointed editor of the American Dialect Society's dictionary project, which has resulted in the monumental and ongoing *Dictionary of American Regional English* (Vol. 1, A–C, 1985; Vol. 2, D–H, 1991). He is also the editor (with R. B. LePage) of *Dictionary of Jamaican English* (revised 1980).

Cassini, Oleg (Loiewski-Cassini) (1913–) fashion designer; born in Paris, France. The son of an emigré Russian countess, he came to the U.S.A. in 1936. He began by designing costumes for Hollywood movies before establishing his own New York firm (1950). His trademarks included provocative sheaths, cocktail dresses, and, in the early 1960s, his widely copied "Jackie Kennedy" look. His dashing good looks, urbane manner, and associations with various glamorous women made him as much a fixture in society and gossip columns as in the fashion section of the media.

Casson, Lionel (1914–) classicist; born in New York City. He graduated from New York University (NYU) (1934), earned his Ph.D. there (1939), and, beginning as an assistant professor in 1936, spent the rest of his professional career at NYU. A specialist in nautical matters in the ancient world, he wrote *Excavations at Nessana* (1950) and *The Ancient Mariners* (1959), as well as *Daily Life in Ancient Rome* (1975) and *Daily Life in Ancient Egypt* (1975). He was a member of the advisory boards of *American Neptune* and *Archaeology.*

Castaneda, Carlos (1931–) cultural anthropologist, author; born in Sao Paulo, Brazil. Educated at the University of California: Los Angeles (B.A. 1962; Ph.D. 1970), he published *The Teachings of Don Juan: A Yaqui Way of Knowledge* (1968), which he claimed was based on his five-year apprenticeship with a Yaqui Indian sorcerer. (The Yaqui live in northwestern Mexico and bordering U.S. states.) Because Castaneda was so elusive, and because the book was taken up by young people at a time when numerous such mystical traditions were in fashion, many professionals cast doubt on the authenticity of the book's contents. When he followed it with a series of equally popular books, including *A Separate Reality* (1971) and *Tales of Power* (1975), even more questions were raised as to how much of his work was true anthropology and how much was his own creation.

Castaneda, Carlos E. (Eduardo) (1896–1958) historian; born in Camarga, Mexico. Emigrating to the U.S.A. at age ten, he studied at the University of Texas, where (from 1927) he was Latin American librarian, then history professor. He wrote widely on Latin American history and translated the first known play written in the Americas (1935), by a Spanish priest and friend of the explorer Hernando Cortez.

Castelli, Leo (b. Krauss) (1907–) art dealer; born in Trieste, Italy. He adopted his mother's maiden name (Castelli) in 1919, graduated from the University of Milan, emigrated to New York City, and studied at Columbia University (1941–43). From 1957 he was the director and owner of the Leo Castelli Gallery and Castelli Graphics. He specialized in avant-garde American paintings, sculptures, and graphics, and was an important force in modern American art.

Castle, Wendell (1932–) furniture maker; born in Emporia, Kans. With a 1961 M.F.A. in sculpture from the University of Kansas, he developed a method of laminating wood to make organic-shaped furniture. In 1970 he started a production line to make limited editions of his designs, and went on to explore more traditional styles using exotic woods and pieces with illusionistic carvings. He established the Wendell Castle Workshop in 1980.

Castner, Hamilton (Young) (1859–99) chemical engineer; born in Brooklyn, N.Y. In 1890, he developed a method for producing sodium by electrolysis of molten caustic soda, which was used in making aluminum, a method rendered obsolete by another's invention. Later he developed a cell for making high-purity caustic soda, which proved important in aluminum production.

Catesby, Mark (c. 1679–1749) naturalist; born in Sudbury, Suffolk, England. He studied natural history in London and first came to America in 1712. He lived in Virginia for seven years and diligently sent collections of plants and seeds to England, whence he returned in 1719. In 1722 he returned to America, traveling in the Carolinas, Georgia, and Florida to observe the region's natural life. Returning to England in 1726, he wrote and illustrated *The Natural History of Carolina, Florida and the Bahama Islands,* published at intervals from 1731–48.

Cather, Willa (Sibert) (b. Wilella Cather) (1875–1947) writer; born in Back Creek Valley (later Gore), Va. Raised on the Nebraska prairie and educated at the University of Nebraska, she went to Pittsburgh, Pa., where she worked as a journalist and teacher while beginning her writing career. In 1906 she moved to New York City to work on *McClure's* magazine (1906–12) before turning to full-time writing. (She published her early works as "Willa Sibert Cather.") Her spare, imagistic novels of pioneer life, several involving independent heroines in Nebraska or in Southwestern settings, include *O Pioneers!* (1913), *My Antonia* (1918), and *Death Comes for the Archbishop* (1927). She won a Pulitzer Prize for *One of Ours* (1922). She continued to produce a respected body of work, including such novels as *The Professor's House* (1925), *Shadows on the Rock* (1931), and *Sapphira and the Slave* (1940), and several decades after her death she would be revived by feminists who saw anticipatory themes in both her life and work.

Catlett, Elizabeth (1919–) sculptor; born in Washington, D.C. She graduated from Howard University (1936) and the State University, Iowa (M.F.A. 1940). As an African-American she was a social activist as well as an artist. Based in Morelos, Mexico, she has taught at the School of Fine Arts, National University of Mexico (1958–76), and is known for her wood sculptures such as *Black Unity* (1968).

Catlin, George (1796–1872) painter; born in Wilkes-Barre, Pa. Beginning as a portrait miniaturist in Philadelphia (1820–25), he lived with American Indians (1832–39), and became a visual historian, as in *Old Bear* (1832), and *Bull Dance* (c. 1832–36). He traveled in Europe and South America (1839–70) with his paintings and a group of Indians, and returned to Jersey City, N.J., when his funds ran out.

Catron, John (c. 1786–1865) Supreme Court justice; probably born in Wythe County, Va. Elected to an early Tennessee court (1824–34), he was named to the U.S. Supreme Court (1837–65) by President Jackson when the Court was enlarged from seven judges to nine. Known as a "Jacksonian jurist," he argued vehemently for states rights.

Catt, Carrie Clinton (b. Lane) Chapman (1859–1947) woman suffrage leader; born near Ripon, Wis. Raised on a farm in the frontier tradition of independence, she taught school for a year before attending Iowa State College (B.A. 1880). She became a principal of an Iowa high school in 1881 and by 1883 was superintendent of schools in Mason City, Iowa. She married a newspaper editor, Les Chapman, and after he died (1886), she worked for a year on a San Francisco newspaper, then returned to Iowa and became involved in the Woman Suffrage Association. By 1890 she was a delegate to the National American Woman Suffrage Association (NAWSA) convention. That same year she married George Catt, a civil engineer and constructor; they lived in Seattle until 1892, then moved to New York City. He supported her goals and activities, and when he died in 1905, the money he left her allowed her to devote herself to promoting women's right to vote. She had emerged in the 1890s as one of the most capable and convincing of the woman suffragists, and with the retirement of Susan B. Anthony, Carrie Catt became president of NAWSA (1900–04); she returned to the presidency (1915–47) and by promoting the so-called "Mrs. Catt's Winning Plan " – which combined efforts at both the state level and the federal amendment – she is credited with a major role in getting the 19th Amendment adopted in 1920. She was also active in promoting woman suffrage on the international level, serving as president of the International Woman Suffrage Alliance (1902–23). She was one of the founders of the League of Women Voters (1919) and she campaigned to promote peace and disarmament.

Catton, Bruce (1899–1978) historian; born in Petoskey, Mich. Before becoming America's most popular historian of the Civil War, he worked as a newspaperman in Boston, Cleveland, and Washington, and held posts with the U.S. Department of Commerce (1945–46; 1948). His best-selling *A Stillness at Appomattox* (1953) earned him a Pulitzer Prize and National Book Award in 1954. Editor and senior editor of *American Heritage Magazine* from 1954 until his death, he produced ten more books on the Civil War, ending with *Grant Takes Command* (1968).

Cauthen, Steve ("the Kid") (1960–) jockey; born in Covington, Ky. Born into a farming and horse-raising family, he was riding ponies at age two and began to race professionally at age 16. In 1977 he set a new American record by riding 487 winners and earning $6 million in purses. In 1978 he won the Triple Crown – the Kentucky Derby, the Preakness, and the Belmont Stakes – on Affirmed; within a few months he hit a slump and went 110 races without a winner. Somewhat disillusioned with the publicity and pressures that attended him, in 1979 he accepted the invitation of a wealthy British horseowner and went to Britain where he spent the rest of his racing career; he settled in Berkshire County – although he returned to Kentucky each winter – and became highly popular with the British. He won the Epsom Derby (1985, 1987), the Irish Derby (1989), and the French Derby (1989), thereby becoming the only jockey ever to win both the Kentucky Derby and the Epsom Derby. Three times champion jockey of Britain (1984, 1985, 1987), he rode a total of 1,704 winners there. In 1992 he retired as a contract jockey with the stable of Sheik Mohammed of Dubai and moved back to Kentucky with his wife (since 1991).

Cavell, Stanley (Louis) (1926–) philosopher; born in Atlanta, Ga. After studying music at the University of California he earned a doctorate in philosophy from Harvard (1961). He taught at the University of California (1956–62) and then at Harvard, winning prominence for his wide-ranging writings in value theory, aesthetics, and other areas.

Cavett, (Richard) Dick (1936–) television host; born in Gibbon, Nebr. Originally a television comedy writer, he hosted ABC's *This Morning* in 1968, taking over ABC television's late night show (1969–74). Despite critical acclaim, he ran third in the ratings behind Johnny Carson and Merv Griffin, which resulted in less and less frequent airings of the show. Subsequently he attracted a loyal following with *The Dick Cavett Show* on WNET, New York City's Public television station (1977–82). While making commercials and occasional theater appearances, he joined the roster of evening talkshow hosts on General Electric's cable channel, CNBC (1989).

Cayce, Edgar (1877–1945) psychic medium; born near Hopkinsville, Ky. He had little education and went into photography. He had a nervous collapse at age 19 and began to experience visions and "receive" messages prescribing ways to heal other people. Over a period of 40 years, he performed "life readings" for and diagnosed over 30,000 people; essential to his therapy was his belief that everyone has had previous existences, some going back thousands of years to Atlantis. Many of his reports were transcribed and preserved by the Association for Research and Enlightenment in Virginia Beach, Va.; these and Cayce were largely forgotten until publicized by best-selling books in the 1960s.

Cayton, Horace Roscoe (1903–70) sociologist, cultural anthropologist; born in Seattle, Wash. The son of a newspaper editor, he was a sailor for four years before entering the University of Washington (B.A. 1932). He taught at Fisk University and later headed a Works Progress Administration research project in Chicago that formed the basis of the landmark study *Black Metropolis* (1946), which he coauthored with St. Clair Drake. He became a professor at the University of California: Berkeley in 1959.

Cazneau, Jane Maria Eliza (b. McManus) Storms (1807–78) adventurer, journalist, publicist; born near Troy, N.Y. The daughter of a lawyer (and U.S. representative, 1825–27), she assisted her father in a failed scheme to establish a colony of German settlers in Texas (1833–35). (Afterward, Aaron Burr's second wife accused him of committing adultery with her. Jane had meanwhile ended her brief marriage (1825–31) to Allen B. (or William F.) Storms.) Settling in New York City, she became a journalist, writing mainly for the New York *Sun;* in 1846 (because she spoke Spanish) she accompanied its editor, Moses Beach, on a secret peace mission to Mexico during the war and is said to have provided crucial information to Gen. Winfield Scott. She went on to Washington, D.C., and New York City where she lobbied for annexing all of Mexico, advocated the expansionist views summed up by "manifest destiny," and promoted the liberation of Cuba from Spain. By 1850 she was married to William L. Cazneau, a Texas politician and fellow adventurer, and they would devote much of the next 20 years trying to get the U.S.A. to annex the Caribbean island of Santo Domingo; they also encouraged William Walker's filibustering in Nicaragua. Apparently as indefatigable as she was irrepressible, she wrote several books (all using the pen name Cora Montgomery) promoting her views about U.S. expansion in the Caribbean, including *The Queen of Islands and the King of Rivers* (1870) and *Our Winter Eden; Pen Pictures of the Tropics* (1878). When their plan to annex Santo Domingo was finally rejected by the U.S. Senate (1870), she and her husband retired to Jamaica. She was lost at sea off Cape Hatteras on a return trip to Jamaica.

Cech, Thomas R. (1947–) biochemist; born in Chicago. At the University of Colorado (1977) he showed that RNA could have an independent catalytic function, aiding a chemical reaction without being consumed or changed. This discovery had major implications for genetic engineering as well as for understanding how life arose. He and Sidney Altman shared the Nobel Prize in chemistry (1989).

Celler, Emanuel (1888–1981) U.S. representative; born in Brooklyn, N.Y. After graduating from Columbia University Law School in 1912, he practiced law in New York City, serving as an appeal agent on the draft board during World War I. A Democrat in the U.S. House of Representatives (1923–73), he was chairman of the Committee on the Judiciary. After his defeat by reform Democrats, he joined a commission to revise the federal appellate courts (1973–75) and resumed his law practice.

Cerf, Bennett (Alfred) (1898–1971) publisher, editor, writer; born in New York City. After successfully marketing reprint classics under the Modern Library imprint, he cofounded Random House in 1927, serving as its president for nearly 40 years. An editor of humor and other anthologies, he also wrote a syndicated newspaper column and appeared regularly on television.

Cermak, Anton (Joseph) (1873–1933) mayor; born in Kladno, Bohemia. He came to the U.S.A. as an infant. He started his working life as a coal miner, and eventually became a prosperous businessman. A power in Chicago Democratic politics, he served four terms as a state legislator, beginning in 1903, as well as other state and city offices. Elected mayor of Chicago in 1931, he was killed in 1933 by a gunman aiming at President-elect Franklin Roosevelt as they were riding in a car in Miami, Fla.

Cesnola, Luigi Palma di (Count) (1832–1904) archaeologist; born in Rivarolo, Italy. He was educated at the Royal Military Academy in Turin (1843–48) and fought in the Austrian, Crimean, and – immigrating to the U.S.A. in 1860 – American Civil Wars. After he took American citizenship (1865), he became U.S. consul in Cyprus. There he conducted many archaeological excavations. His outstanding collection of antiquities, the fruits of these excavations, were given to the Metropolitan Museum in New York, where he was director from 1879 to his death.

Cessna, Clyde (Vernon) (1879–1954) airplane manufacturer; born in Hawthorne, Iowa. He built and flew his first plane in 1911. In 1925 he and others organized the Travel Air Company. In 1928, having built the first cantilever plane in the country, he created Cessna Aircraft to produce them. Affected by the Depression, plant operations were sus-

pended in 1931. Although business resumed in 1934, he retired.

Chadwick, George Whitefield (1854–1931) composer; born in Lowell, Mass. After studies in the U.S. and Germany he settled in Boston, Mass., teaching privately and at the New England Conservatory. His music, in a late-Romantic idiom, was part of the era's "Boston classic" school.

Chadwick, Henry (1824–1908) sportswriter, baseball executive; born in Exeter, England. After immigrating to the U.S.A. at an early age, he became a sportswriter for the *New York Times* in 1856 and wrote some of the earliest articles about baseball, which included his modern version of a baseball box score. For the next fifty years, he wrote prolifically about the game, served on rules committees, compiled official statistics, and published books on baseball. Known as "The Father of Baseball," he was elected to baseball's Hall of Fame in 1938.

Chafee, Adna (Romanza) (1842–1914) soldier; born in Orwell, Ohio. Determined and able, he served for more than a quarter-century on the southwest frontier, led a brigade in Cuba during the war with Spain, and commanded the U.S. contingent in the advance on Peking during the Boxer Rebellion of 1899–1900.

Chaffee, John H. (Hubbard) (1922–) governor, U.S. senator, secretary of the navy; born in Providence, R.I. He was a liberal Republican governor of Rhode Island (1963–69) and the secretary of the navy in the first Nixon administration (1969–72). He was a Senator from Rhode Island (1977).

Chaffee, Roger B. (1935–67) naval officer, astronaut; born in Grand Rapids, Mich. He joined the navy in 1957, was promoted to lieutenant commander, then became an astronaut. He died in a fire aboard Apollo I in 1967.

Chaffee, Zechariah (1885–1957) lawyer, educator; born in Providence, R.I. He graduated from Brown in 1907 and later from Harvard Law School, and joined the law faculty at Harvard in 1916. His book *Freedom of Speech* (1920) established him as a leading legal thinker on civil liberties issues. He later served on national and international commissions on freedom of the press.

Chamberlain, Henry Richardson (1859–1911) journalist; born in Peoria, Ill. Regarded as an expert on the European scene, he achieved distinction as London correspondent for the *New York Sun* from 1892 until his death.

Chamberlain, Joshua (Lawrence) (1828–1914) soldier, educator; born in Brewer, Maine. The defender of Little Round Top at Gettysburg (July 2, 1863), he commanded the force that accepted the formal surrender of the Army of Northern Virginia (April 1865). He served as governor of Maine (1866–71) and was president of Bowdoin College (1871–83).

Chamberlain, Owen (1920–) physicist; born in San Francisco. He worked on the Manhattan Project (1942–46) and at the Argonne National Laboratory (1946–48) before joining the faculty of the University of California: Berkeley (1948). He was awarded the 1959 Nobel Prize in physics, jointly with his colleague Emilio Segrè, for research on the antiproton.

Chamberlain, Richard (1935–) television actor; born in Los Angeles, Calif. Trained as a dramatic actor, he appeared in television series like *Gunsmoke* in the 1950s, then gained great popularity as the lead in *Dr. Kildare* (1961–66). Desiring to change his image as a lightweight television actor, he moved to England where he played serious roles, including Hamlet, in various British stage productions. He then returned to the U.S. to assume the role as a romantic leading man in television films and mini-series including *Shogun* (1980), *The Thorn Birds* (1983), and *The Bourne Identity* (1988).

Chamberlain, (Wilton Norman) Wilt "The Stilt" (1936–) basketball player; born in Philadelphia. An All-American at Kansas University, he played for the Harlem Globetrotters for a year (1958) before joining the National Basketball Association (NBA) Philadelphia Warriors (1959–65), Philadelphia 76ers (1965–68), and Los Angeles Lakers (1968–73). A seven-foot center, he led the NBA in scoring seven times and rebounding eleven times, and he was named the NBA's Most Valuable Player four times (1960, 1966–68). He scored a record 100 points in a game against the New York Knicks in 1962 at Hershey, Pa., and in 1960 he pulled a record 55 rebounds in a game against his chief rival, Bill Russell, of the Boston Celtics. In 1978, Chamberlain was elected to basketball's Hall of Fame and he is generally conceded to be one of the greatest basketball players of all time. In later years he devoted himself to promoting volleyball, in which he also excelled.

Chamberlin, Edward Hastings (1899–1967) economist; born in La Couner, Wash. His book, *Theory of Monopolistic Competition* (1933, eighth and final edition 1962) is regarded as one of the most influential economic books of the 20th century. He spent many years at Harvard University, first as a doctoral student and then in a teaching capacity until his death in 1967. He served as chair of the department of economics during its "Golden Age" (1939–43) when it included several renowned economists. *Theory of Monopolistic Competition* is a market analysis that incorporates such factors as advertising, product differentiation, style and brand preference, and locational advantages. His interpretation concluded that monopolistic ventures lack long-term advantages to the sellers in the industry and that only normal profits will be realized. His so-called "tangency solution" was the major empirical implication of monopolistic competition theory. A collection of his other papers, *Towards a More General Theory of Value,* was published in 1957.

Chamberlin, T. C. (Thomas Chrowder) (1843–1928) geologist; born in Mattoon, Ill. He taught at Beloit College (1873–82), then served the Wisconsin (1876–82) and U.S. (1882–1904) Geological Surveys. He was president of the University of Wisconsin (1887–91), then became head of the geology department at the University of Chicago (1892–1919). His Alpine and North American glaciological and climatological studies were basic to his later research on the origin of the earth and the solar system.

Chambers, Julius L. (Levonne) (1936–), lawyer; born in Montgomery County, N.C. Partner in a Charlotte, N.C. law firm (1964–84), and a civil-rights advocate, he was named director-counsel of the National Association for the Advancement of Colored People (NAACP) Legal Defense and Education Fund in 1984 and was a trustee of several national institutions. Both with his private firm and as head of the NAACP's Fund, he won numerous landmark cases involving the education, employment, and civil rights of African-Americans.

Chambers, Whittaker (b. Jay Vivian Chambers) (1910–61) journalist, writer, Soviet agent; born in Philadelphia. He studied at Columbia University, gained a modest reputation as a writer, and later translated several works, notably *Bambi,* into English. He was an active American Communist (1925–29, 1931–38), writing for the *Daily Worker* and editing the *New Masses.* Along the way he became an actual agent of Soviet intelligence and passed classified government information to Moscow. Disillusioned by Stalin's purges, he became a virulent anticommunist and edited *Time* Magazine's foreign affairs section. In 1948, he testified that many executive branch officials were Communist sympathizers and said that Alger Hiss had given him classified materials; this brought about a libel suit by Hiss, who was found guilty; the Hiss-Chambers trial remains a symbol of the whole era that extended from the idealism of Communism in the 1930s to the disillusionment of the late 1940s. Chambers was also an editor of the *National Review* (1957–60).

Champney, Benjamin (1817–1907) painter; born in New Ipswich, N.H. He worked as a lithographer in Boston, Mass., became a portraitist (1841), traveled to Europe (1841 and 1846–48), and exhibited panoramas in Boston and New York (1848–50). He wintered in Massachusetts, spent summers in North Conway, N.H., and painted landscapes, such as *Picnic on Artist's Ledge Overlooking Conway Meadows, N.H.* (1874).

Chance, Britton (1913–) biophysicist, biochemist; born in Wilkes-Barre, Pa. He spent his professional career at the University of Pennsylvania, while concurrently serving as an adviser to many committees and institutions. From 1936–46 he invented many automatic control systems, precision-timing circuits, and optical instruments used for radar and ship-steering in World War II. His best-known work is his demonstration of the existence of the complex formed between an enzyme and its substrate (1943). He described the mechanism of action of the enzyme peroxidase, and made major contributions to studies of enzyme kinetics, spectroscopy, and mitochondrial function.

Chancellor, John (1927–) television correspondent/anchorman; born in Chicago, Ill. Originally a Chicago *Sun Times* copy boy, he became a television reporter for National Broadcasting Company (NBC) local WMAQ in the 1950s. By 1958, he was NBC Vienna bureau chief, covering Soviet-American relations. Briefly *Today* show host (1961–62), he was the first working journalist to serve as Voice of America director (1965–67). He became NBC nightly news anchor (1970–82), appearing subsequently as a commentator.

Chandler, (Albert Benjamin) "Happy" (1898–1991) public official, baseball commissioner; born in Corydon, Ky. He served as governor of Kentucky (1935–39) and U.S. Senator (Dem., 1939–45) before being named as baseball's second commissioner (1945–51). He presided over the game during the breaking of baseball's color line by Jackie Robinson in 1947. He was known as a "players" commissioner because he took an interest in all aspects of the game. He served a second term as governor of Kentucky (1955–59). In 1982 he was elected to baseball's Hall of Fame.

Chandler, Charles Frederick (1836–1925) industrial chemist; born in Lancaster, Mass. Affiliated with Columbia University for most of his career (1864–1910), he was cofounder and dean of its School of Mines and later head of the chemistry department. Known as an inspiring teacher, he was unusually broad even for his time in encompassing chemistry, geology, and minerology as well as sanitation, oil refining, and social causes. In 1877, he began addressing the issues of food and water supplies for New York City and he became a pioneer in municipal milk control. He also fought abuses by slaughterhouses and gas companies and established a program of compulsory vaccination.

Chandler, Raymond (Thornton) (1888–1959) writer; born in Chicago. Taken to England by his mother at age nine, he was educated there and on the Continent. He worked as a journalist for English magazines and served in the Canadian army in World War I. Settling in the U.S.A. in 1919, he worked as a businessman, including ten years with the oil industry (1922–32), but with the publication of his first crime story in *Black Mask* magazine in 1933, he concentrated on writing. He created his hard-boiled sleuth, Phillip Marlowe, and tawdry underworld settings for his first novel, *The Big Sleep* (1939); Marlowe reappeared in subsequent works, including *Farewell, My Lovely* (1940) and *The Long Goodbye* (1954), which helped establish the American conventions of the genre. He moved between California and London in his later years.

Chandler, Robert F. (1907–) agronomist; born in Columbus, Ohio. He was state horticulturalist to the Maine Department of Agriculture (1929–31) until returning to his alma mater, the University of Maine, for his doctorate (1934). He taught at Cornell University (1935–47) and then the University of New Hampshire (1947–54) where he also directed the Agricultural Experiment Station and headed the College of Agriculture. He was appointed president of the University of New Hampshire in 1950. At the Rockefeller Foundation (1954–75) he established the International Rice Research Institute in the Philippines; there (1959–72) he developed varieties of tropical rice that more than doubled traditional yields and averted a famine predicted for Asia in the 1970s. In Taiwan (1972–75) he was the Foundation's first director of the Asian Vegetable Research and Development Center. Back in the United States, he wrote a history of the Rice Institute, and served as an international consultant on rural agricultural development.

Chandler, William Eaton (1835–1917) lawyer, U.S. senator; born in Concord, N.H. As secretary of the navy (1882–85) he began a program of building steel warships. He served as a senator from New Hampshire (1887–1901).

Chandler, Zachariah (1813–79) U.S. senator; born in Bedford, N.H. He moved to Michigan in 1833 where he prospered in business. A Whig and prominent abolitionist, his home in Detroit became a stop on the underground railroad and he was a founder of the Republican Party. Elected to the U.S. Senate (Rep., Mich.; 1857–75, 1879) he supported Radical Republican positions during the Civil War and Reconstruction. He also used his influence in the Senate to exert control over affairs in Michigan. President Grant appointed him secretary of the interior (1875–77).

Chandrasekhar, Subrahmanyan (1910–) astrophysicist; born in Lahore, India (now Pakistan). As a fellow at Trinity, Cambridge University (1933–37), he developed his theory of white dwarfs, "collapsed" stars of enormous density, such that their mass does not exceed 1.4 times the mass of the sun (the Chandrasekhar limit). Since such a small, dense body allows no radiation to escape, Chandrasekhar's theory predicted the existence of what are now known as "black holes." When his ideas were publicly derided by the respected English physicist Arthur Eddington, the distraught Chandrasekhar emigrated to the University of Chicago (1937), and remained there until his retirement (1980). His theory was vindicated, and he continued his research on relativistic astrophysics, winning the 1983 Nobel Prize for his contribution to knowledge of evolution of the stars.

Chaney, (Alonso) Lon (1883–1930) movie actor; born in Colorado Springs, Colo. Child of deaf-mute parents, he honed his skills as a silent-film actor by having to communicate with them. He toured as a song-and-dance man before making his first movie (1914). After the success of *The Miracle Man* (1919), he went on to play a series of spine-chilling grotesques such as *The Hunchback of Notre Dame* (1924) and *The Phantom of the Opera* (1925). His skill at makeup and miming gained him the name, "the Man of a Thousand Faces." He died of throat cancer right after completing his first talkie, *The Unholy Three* (1930).

Chang, Kwang-Chih (1931–) anthropologist, archaeologist; born in Beijing, China. He came to the U.S.A. in 1955, earned a Ph.D. at Harvard, and taught at Yale (1961–77) and Harvard (1977). A specialist in Far East Asian prehistory, he wrote important works including *The Archaeology of Ancient China* (1963, frequently revised), *The Chinese Bronze Age* (2 vols. 1983–90), and *Shang Civilization* (1980).

Chang, M.-C. (Min-Chueh) (1909–91) reproductive biologist; born in Taiyuan, China. Emigrating to England to study animal husbandry at Cambridge University, he received a degree in animal husbandry from the University of Edinburgh (1939) with a concentration on artificial insemination. After earning a doctorate at Cambridge (1945), he joined the staff of the fledgling Worcester Foundation for Experimental Biology in Worcester, Mass., where he began work with Dr. Gregory Pincus and Dr. John Rock on creation of an oral contraceptive for women. The birth control pill was ready for human testing (1956) and was marketed as Enovid (1960). Chang is also credited for the discovery of *in vitro* fertilization through work he conducted in the 1950s, as well as a process known as the capacitation of sperm. He was named to the National Academy of Sciences (1990).

Channing, William Ellery (1780–1842) Unitarian theologian; born in Newport, R.I. He graduated from Harvard in 1798 and was tutor for 18 months to a Richmond, Va., family, where he became an opponent of slavery. Ordained in 1803, he accepted the pulpit of the Congregational Federal Street Church in Boston; he retained this pastorate until his death. Broadly liberal, he took part from 1815 on in the controversy over Calvinist doctrine and became a leader of the newly emerging Unitarians, calling their doctrine "a rational and amiable system"; he, as much as any single man, brought about the founding of the American Unitarian Association in 1825. Channing Unitarianism, as his beliefs came to be called, influenced the intellectual development of Emerson and many others in the English-speaking world. A pacifist and proponent of public education and labor reforms, he threw his considerable prestige behind the temperance and antislavery causes. Among his published works were an *Essay on National Literature* and *Negro Slavery*.

Chanute, Octave (1832–1910) aerial navigator; born in Paris, France. Brought to America when his family emigrated in 1838, he went on to a successful career as a civil engineer, building iron railroad bridges. His favorite pastime, however, was the study of aerial navigation; he conducted the first scientific experiments in America on gliding (1896–97) and then built a biplane glider that the Wright Brothers used as a model for their first glider. In addition to actually flying gliders, he wrote pioneering works about the engineering and navigational problems of flight.

Chapelle, Dickey (b. Georgette Louis Meyer) (1918–65) pioneer pilot, adventuress, journalist; born in Shorewood, Wis. After attending Massachusetts Institute of Technology for a year, she acquired expertise as a barnstorming pilot and photojournalist and worked as a war correspondent in World War II. After a year as an editor of *Seventeen* (1946–47), she and her husband, photographer Tony Chapelle, spent six years documenting damage from World War II. In 1956–57, while photographing Hungarian refugees, she was imprisoned for seven weeks in Hungary, but she continued to visit any ongoing war zones – in Algeria, Lebanon, Korea – and photographed Fidel Castro's revolution in Cuba. She won a George Polk Award (1962) for her war reporting and was killed by a mine explosion while covering the war in Vietnam.

Chapin, Charles Value (1856–1941) epidemiologist, public health official; born in Providence, R.I. Not caring for the private practice of medicine, he served as superintendent of health of Providence (1884–1932) and became a pioneer in public health. He started the first municipal bacteriological lab (1888), tested water filters and disinfectants, and conducted field studies to show the correlation between unsanitary conditions and disease. His field studies, hospital work, ideas and publications – including *The Sources and Modes of Infection* (1910) and *Report on State Public Health Work* (1916) – provided the foundations of the public health movement in the 20th century.

Chapin, Henry Dwight (1857–1942) pediatrician, social reformer; born in Steubenville, Ohio. He entered medical practice in 1884 in New York City and began to teach on children's diseases at the New York Post-Graduate School (1885–1920) and at the Women's Medical College of the New York Infirmary for Women and Children (1885–90). His particular work was in the area of proper nutrition for infants. Pioneering home care through trained social workers, he founded the Speedwell Society to encourage foster care (1902) and was a charter member and president of the American Pediatric Society (1910–11). With his wife, Alice Delafield, he actively secured adoptions for 1,700 children over the course of their mutual careers; their work led to what is today known as the Spence-Chapin Adoption Service in New York City. A reader of philosophy, he played the violin, loved travel, and enjoyed vintage wines.

Chapin, Roy Dikeman (1880–1936) automobile executive, cabinet officer; born in Lansing, Mich. He left the University of Michigan in 1901 to join Olds Motor Works and later that year attracted wide publicity by making the first automobile trip from Detroit to New York. In 1906, in partnership with designer Howard Coffin, he became general manager of E. R. Thomas Detroit Company, later Chalmers-Detroit Motor Company. He soon sold the firm and organized Hudson Motor Car Company. As president (1910–23, 1933–36) and chairman (1923–33), he introduced the successful popular-priced "Essex" (1919) and his new, cheaper closed cars (introduced 1922) hastened the demise of the open touring car. In his second term as president he restored the ailing company's financial fortunes. As chairman of the highway transport committee of the Council of National Defense during World War I, he promoted the use of cars to ease railroad congestion. Briefly U.S. secretary of commerce (1932–33), he spearheaded Herbert Hoover's reemployment strategy for stimulating recovery from the depression.

Chaplin, (Charles Spencer) Charlie (1889–1977) movie actor, producer, screenwriter, director, composer; born in London, England. The son of music hall entertainers, his mother had a nervous breakdown and his father died when Charlie was five; he became a street urchin, along with his half-brother, Sydney, dancing for pennies in the street. After a time in an orphanage, he joined a troupe of child dancers and later had small roles on the London stage. At age 17 he joined a troupe of players that toured the United States, where in 1912 he joined the Keystone company to appear in his first movie, *Making a Living* (1914). Chaplin made 35 films in one year at Keystone, many of which he also wrote and directed, meanwhile honing his character of "The Little Tramp"; despite the appearance of spontaneity and improvisation, he worked out every last detail of his films. He joined Essanay in 1915, making his first masterpiece, *The Tramp*, that year. He became one of the founders of United Artists in 1919. At First National, he made *The Kid* in 1921, which made him an international star. He went on to make his major works – *City Lights* (1928), *Modern Times* (1936), *The Great Dictator* (1940), *Limelight* (1952) – after which there was a distinct falling off. Over the years he had been criticized for his many romantic affairs, often with younger women; he also had never applied for U.S. citizenship. In 1952, on a ship to England, he was informed that he might not be permitted back into the States because of his alleged leftist views, so he settled in Switzerland with his wife Oona, daughter of Eugene O'Neill, with whom he had eight children. He did not return to the U.S.A. until 1972 when he accepted a Special Academy Award. In 1975, by then regarded as one of the few individuals to be a true genius of motion pictures, he was knighted by Queen Elizabeth II.

Chaplin, Ralph Hosea (1887–1961) editor, poet, commercial artist; born in Ames, Kans. Of New England colonial stock, he studied art while working as a commercial artist in Chicago. He illustrated Jack London's *The Dream of the Debs* (1912), and wrote a number of poetry volumes. A socialist since his teens, he joined the International Workers of the World (IWW) in 1913, wrote the words to "Solidarity Forever" (1915), and edited the IWW newspaper, *Solidarity*. He was jailed (1921–23) for conspiracy to violate the wartime espionage and sedition acts. He joined the Communist Party in 1919, but broke with his Communist friends in 1928 and from then on worked to combat Communism in organized labor. His autobiography, *Wobbly: The Rough and Tumble Story of an American Radical* (1948), vividly describes his political and social beliefs.

Chapman, Frank (Michler) (1864–1945) ornithologist; born in Englewood, N.J. He completed his formal education in 1880, chose not to go to college, and began working in a New York City bank (1880–86). In his spare time, he continued his childhood interest in birds by doing ornithological field studies and surveys. His specimens and notes dealing with birds of Florida so impressed the American Museum of Natural History that he began an assistantship there in 1888, became curator in 1908, and remained at the museum until his retirement (1942). He was the first museum official to build exhibits of bird species in their natural habitats; he was also an accomplished nature photographer who enjoyed educating the public in avian behavior and conservation. Under his leadership, the museum's ornithology department became the finest in the world. He wrote numerous scientific papers and popular books, discovered many new species, and was a pioneer in researching the geography and climatology of different bird groups.

Chapman, John (Gadsby) (1808–89) painter; born in Alexandria, Va. A portrait and historical painter who divided his time between New York and Washington, D.C., he painted the famous mural, *Baptism of Pocahontas* (1837–42), in the Rotunda of the Capitol Building in Washington, D.C.

Chapman, John Jay (1862–1933) man of letters; born in New York City. Independently wealthy, he published poems, plays, translations, and essays renowned for critical power and stylistic grace. Edmund Wilson called him "the best writer on literature of his generation."

Chapman, John, (real name of "Johnny Appleseed") (1774–1847) horticulturalist, missionary; born in Leominster, Mass. Little is known of his youth. He appeared in Ohio in 1800 and began to plant nurseries with apples he brought from western Pennsylvania. He traveled throughout Ohio (1800–12) planting and then pruning his orchards. A mystic, he read aloud from the Bible and the works of Emmanuel Swedenborg, and was credited with many extraordinary acts of kindness to both men and animals. During the War of 1812 he warned isolated farmers of the danger of Indian raids. He carried his planting and missionary work into Indiana in 1838 and died of pneumonia near Fort Wayne, Ind.

Chappell, Warren (1904–1991) typographer, book illustrator, graphic artist; born in Richmond, Va. After studying at the Art Students League in New York, he set up a studio there in 1932 and pursued a joint career as graphic artist/book illustrator and typographer/book designer. As the former, he illustrated many classic texts; as the latter, he designed two admired typefaces, Lydian and Trajanus. He wrote several books on typography and ended his career as artist in residence at the University of Richmond, his alma mater.

Charles, Ray (b. Ray Charles Robinson) (1930–) singer, pianist, composer; born in Albany, Ga. He lost his sight (from glaucoma) when he was six and attended a school for the blind where he learned to read and write music in braille and play piano and organ. Orphaned at age 15, he left school and began playing music to earn a living, moving to Seattle, Wash., in 1947. Dropping his last name, he performed at clubs in the smooth lounge-swing style of Nat "King" Cole. After some hits on Swing Time Records, he switched to Atlantic Records in 1952 and began to develop a rougher blues and gospel style. For New Orleans bluesman, Guitar Slim, he arranged and played piano on "The Things I Used To Do" (1953); the record sold a million copies. He went on to record his own "I've Got a Woman" in 1955 with an arrangement of horns, gospel-style piano, and impassioned vocals that led to the gospel-pop and soul music of the 1960s and to his hit "What'd I Say" (1959). Possessing a multifaceted talent, he recorded with jazz vibist Milt Jackson, made a country and western album that sold 3 million copies (1962), and continued to release a variety of pop hits, Broadway standards, and blues, gospel, and jazz albums. A major influence on popular black music during his early years, he gradually reached out to influence both white musicians and audiences. And although he had been convicted of using drugs in the 1950s, he lived to see the day when he was so acceptable to mainstream Americans that he became virtually the chief image for promoting Pepsi-Cola and he was asked to perform at many national patriotic and political events.

Charney, Jule Gregory (1917–81) meteorologist; born in San Francisco. The son of Russian immigrants, he is remembered as the "father of modern meteorology" for his use of computers to generate forecasts (numerical weather), his mathematical models to describe weather and climate, and his theories of baroclinic instability. Following his doctorate, he studied with the famous Carl-Gustaf Rossby before traveling to the University of Oslo in Norway as a National Research Fellow. At the Institute for Advanced Study in Princeton, New Jersey (1948–56), he and others pioneered the first computer-generated weather forecast using the ENIAC (Electronic Numerical Integrator and Calculator). This success prompted his establishing a Joint Numerical Weather Prediction Unit in Maryland, which generated daily predictions of gross climate and weather patterns. At the Massachusetts Institute of Technology (1956–81) he chaired the Committee on International Meteorological Cooperation and helped organize the Global Atmospheric Research Program; their findings are expected to significantly advance understanding of the atmosphere.

Charren, Peggy (b. Walzer) (1928–) consumer activist; born in New York City. The mother of two children, she founded an art prints store (1951) and ran Quality Book Fairs (1960–65) in Newton, Mass. In 1968, upset at the violence and other defects she saw on children's television programs, she founded Action for Children's Television in her suburban home. Her watchdog group became a national organization that worked strenuously to improve the quality of children's television. She disbanded the organization (1992) because the passage of the Children's Television Act (1990) incorporated the results of many of her goals. She wrote *Changing Channels: Living Sensibly with Television* (1983) and was a visiting scholar at the Harvard Graduate School of Education (1987).

Chase, Agnes (b. Mary Agnes Meara) (1869–1963) botanist, agrostologist; born in Iroquois County, Ill. Her early formal education was limited. After her one-year marriage ended with her husband's untimely death (1889), she worked at various jobs to pay his debts. She began cataloging her own collection of wildflowers in 1897; she worked at the Field Museum of Natural History (1901–03), the U.S. Department of Agriculture (1903–39), and the Smithsonian Institution (1939–49). An ardent suffragette, she was twice jailed for her protests (1915, 1918) and forcibly fed. Her long association (1905–36) with Albert S. Hitchcock resulted in their collaborating on several books and eventually led to her updating his work, *Manual of the Grasses of the United States* (1951). She collected over 12,000 sets of plants, most of them grasses, and published a revised index of grass species (3 vols. 1962).

Chase, Edna Woolman (1877–1957) editor; born in Asbury Park, N.J. Hired by *Vogue* in 1895, she was its editor from 1914 to 1956 and helped build it into an elegant top-fashion magazine.

Chase, Gilbert (1906–92) musicologist; born in Havana, Cuba. Chase wrote music criticism in the 1930s and in the next decade worked for the Library of Congress and for

National Broadcasting Company radio; thereafter he taught and administrated at various schools including the University of Oklahoma, Tulane, and the University of Texas. He was a noted specialist in the music of the Americas, and his books include the classic history *America's Music* (3rd ed. 1987).

Chase, Lucia (1907–86) ballet dancer, ballet company administrator; born in Waterbury, Conn. After pursuing a career in theater and music, she took ballet lessons with Mikhail Mordkin and performed in his company from 1937–40. A charter member and dancer with the American Ballet Theatre, she became codirector in 1944. Totally involved in the company, especially fundraising, until her retirement in 1980, she helped it become one of the world's greatest dance troupes.

Chase, Salmon P. (Portland) (1808–73) cabinet member, Supreme Court chief justice; born in Cornish, N.H. A lawyer in Cincinnati, Ohio, he was an active abolitionist, known as "the attorney general for runaway Negroes." He served as governor of Ohio (1855–60) and was twice elected to the U.S. Senate (Dem./Free-Soil, 1849–53; Rep., 1860–61). He resigned to serve as Lincoln's secretary of the treasury during the Civil War (1861–64). A vocal cabinet member who often disagreed with Lincoln over slavery issues and military matters, he attempted to resign three times before Lincoln accepted his fourth offer (1864) after a radical faction called for Chase to replace Lincoln as the Republican candidate. Upon his re-election and despite their differences, Lincoln appointed him chief justice of the Supreme Court (1864–73). Despite his strong personal antipathy to slavery and secession, he made a number of impartial decisions during the Reconstruction and reluctantly but scrupulously presided over the impeachment trial of President Andrew Johnson.

Chase, Samuel (1741–1811) Supreme Court justice; born in Somerset County, Md. A member of the Continental Congress and a signer of the Declaration of Independence, President Washington named him to the U.S. Supreme Court in 1796. President Jefferson attempted to impeach Chase because of his independent stance (1804), but Congress rejected the proposition in a move that secured the strength of the judiciary.

Chase, William Merritt (1849–1916) painter; born in Williamsburg, Ind. Showing a natural talent for painting, he was sent abroad in 1872 to study, funded by a group of St. Louis businessmen. Although he studied at the Munich Royal Academy, when he returned to America he had converted to the French Impressionist style and in 1878 he began teaching at the Art Students League in New York City. Both there and at his own summer school at Shinnecock, Long Island, he produced a large body of sensuously colored, detailed work, such as *Lady with the White Shawl* (1893), and taught a whole generation of American painters.

Chauncey, Isaac (1772–1840) naval officer; born in Black Rock, Conn. He commanded the naval forces on Lakes Ontario and Erie during the War of 1812. He commanded the Mediterranean squadron (1816–18) and later held important administrative posts within the navy.

Chauncy, Charles (1705–87) Protestant religious leader; born in Boston, Mass. A 1721 Harvard graduate, he became pastor of the First (Congregational) Church of Boston in 1727 and remained for 60 years. A leader of theological liberalism in New England, he was in constant conflict with his Calvinist contemporary, Jonathan Edwards. A political liberal, too, he was an ardent patriot during the Revolution.

Chavez, Cesar (Estrada) (1927–93) labor leader; born in Yuma, Ariz. A migrant farmworker in his youth – he attended 65 elementary schools and never graduated from high school – he became a community and labor organizer of agricultural workers in the 1950s. In 1962 he started the National Farm Workers Association, based in California and the Southwest among the mainly Chicano (Mexican-Americans) and Filipino farmworkers; in 1966 this union would be chartered by the American Federation of Labor and Congress of Industrial Organizations as the United Farm Workers of America; he remained its president until his death. He first attracted national attention when in 1965 he struck the table grape growers in California by calling for a national boycott; this first such strike and boycott lasted five years and ended with the first major victory for migrant workers in the U.S.A. He continued his struggles, both with the Teamsters Union that tried to take over his workers and with the large growers that refused to improve their wages and working conditions; at the time of his death he was leading yet another national boycott of grapes to protest the use of pesticides harmful to workers. He went on three hunger strikes – 25 days in 1968, 24 days in 1972, and 36 days in 1988 – and it was believed that these produced physical damage that hastened his death.

Chavez, Dennis (1888–1962) U.S. representative/senator; born in Los Chavez, N.M. Although he never finished high school, he worked as a clerk in the U.S. Senate and graduated from Georgetown University Law School (1920). He served in the U.S. House of Representatives (Dem., N.M.; 1931–35) and in the U.S. Senate (1935–62). An advocate of integrating minorities, he opposed Navajo Indian autonomy and proposed making English the language of Puerto Rico. He worked tirelessly to create the Fair Employment Practices Commission. New Mexico placed his statue in the U.S. Capitol.

Chávez, Edward (Arcenio) (1917–) painter, sculptor; born in Wagonmound, N.M. A Mexican American, he studied at the Colorado Springs Fine Arts Center with Boardman Robinson (1930s), traveled in Europe, and was based in New York City and Woodstock, N.Y. He has worked in graphics, painting and sculpture, and his abstract paintings, such as *Mirage* (1961), have secured his reputation.

Chavis, Benjamin (Franklin), Jr. (1948–) Protestant minister, civil rights activist; born in Oxford, N.C. From a long line of preachers, he took a degree in chemistry at the University of North Carolina. In 1971, participating in a protest against school segregation in Wilmington, N.C., he was arrested; he eventually spent four years in jail and by the time his conviction was overturned by a Federal court in 1980, he had earned a degree in divinity from Duke University. He went on to become not only a minister for the United Church of Christ but an activist for its Commission for Racial Justice, fighting for civil rights in a variety of arenas. In 1993, after a highly publicized search, he was selected as the executive director of the National Association for the Advancement of Colored People (NAACP); he was charged with reviving that organization's flagging image, specifically with making it more appealing and relevant to the concerns of young African-Americans. In 1994 he was dismissed following allegations of unauthorized use of NAACP funds.

Chayefsky, (Sidney) Paddy (1923–81) screenwriter, television dramatist; born in the Bronx, New York City. As a youth, he was a stand-up comic, then wrote his first play while recovering from injuries received in World War II. After the war, he began writing radio and television dramas, usually realistic depictions of the lives of ordinary people. In Hollywood, he won Oscars for his screenplays for *Marty* (1955), *The Hospital* (1971), and *Network* (1976). He also wrote several Broadway plays.

Chayes, Abram (Joseph) (1922–) legal scholar; born in Chicago. He taught at Harvard Law School (1955–61, 1965) and served as a State Department advisor (1961–64). He is considered an authority on international law and served as chairman of the International Nuclear Fuel Cycle Evaluation Committee (1977–80).

Cheever, John (1912–82) writer; born in Quincy, Mass. He published his first short story at age 17 and never graduated from college. Resident in New York and its suburbs, he wrote Chekhovian satires of upper middle-class suburban life that appeared regularly in the *New Yorker* after the 1930s. He became a recognized master of the genre; a final collected edition of his short stories (1978) won the Pulitzer Prize. He also wrote screenplays and five novels, including *The Wapshot Chronicle* (1957, National Book Award).

Chenery, Hollis (Burley) (1918–) economist; born in Richmond, Va. A key figure in development economics, he demonstrated that self-sustaining economic growth depends on industrialization and declining agricultural export. After teaching at Harvard (1965–70), he moved to the World Bank where he served as vice-president in charge of development policies since 1972.

Cheney, Frances Neel (1906–) reference librarian; born in Washington, D.C. A professor and administrator in the library division of the George Peabody College for Teachers in Nashville, Tenn., she compiled annotated bibliographies of American poetry and Japanese reference materials.

Chenier, Clifton (1925–85) musician; born in Opelousas, La. The "King of Zydeco," he was an accordianist and singer who pioneered zydeco, a fusion of blues and the French Cajun music of Louisiana. He led his own band from the 1950s, playing locally until he gained wide recognition through a series of European tours beginning in the early 1970s.

Chennault, Claire (Lee) (1890–1958) aviator; born in Commerce, Texas. A schoolteacher, he obtained an infantry commission in 1917, transferred to the Signal Corps and became a pilot. Forced out of the service in 1937 because of deafness, Chennault went to work for the Chinese Nationalists, recruiting some 50 U.S. pilots and equipping them with P-40 aircraft for operations against the Japanese. In a brief career of seven months in 1941–42, Chennault's "Flying Tigers" became the most publicized flying unit of World War II. Chennault went on to hold senior U.S. commands in China, retiring in 1945. He continued to serve the Nationalists as an air consultant until the year of his death.

Chesnut, Mary (Boykin Miller) (1823–86) diarist; born near Camden, S.C. Daughter of a former South Carolina governor, she married James Chesnut, a wealthy planter, defender of slavery, and staunch secessionist; joining the U.S. Senate (Dem., S.C.) in 1859, he resigned in 1860 to lead in forming the Confederacy. He then served with the Confederate army, leaving his wife to write her journal of life on the southern homefront (especially in Richmond, Va., and South Carolina) from 1861–65. First published in 1905 as *A Diary from Dixie,* it is recognized as a lively and compelling contribution to the literature of the Civil War.

Chesnutt, Charles W. (Waddell) (1858–1932) lawyer, writer; born in Cleveland, Ohio. Son of North Carolina-born free blacks, he returned to his parents' native state after the Civil War to attend a teacher's training college in Fayetteville; he stayed on to teach there and become its principal (1872–83). Lack of opportunity to advance led him to go to New York City where he worked as a journalist while studying law. He moved back to Cleveland in 1887 and eventually established a successful law practice. He began writing fiction about 1887; in 1889 he published his first collection of short stories, *The Conjure Woman,* and in 1890 his first novel, *Behind the Cedars.* Along with his critical essays on other African-American writers, his works of fiction – some of which dealt realistically with the effects of racial discrimination on American society – gained him the reputation of being the first serious African-American writer. His later years were marked by ill health.

Chess, Leonard (1917–69) recording executive; born in Poland. The founder of Chess Records, he was raised in Chicago, where his immigrant family settled in 1928. In 1939 he and his brother Phil Chess opened the Macombo Lounge, a nightclub catering to African-American patrons on Chicago's South Side. In 1946, the brothers formed Aristocrat Records and recorded several local blues artists, notably Muddy Waters. In 1950, Aristocrat was succeeded by Chess Records, which they operated until its sale in 1968. Throughout its operation, Chess featured the major figures of Chicago blues, including Waters, Little Walter, Howlin' Wolf, Sonny Boy Williamson, and Willie Dixon, and this is its chief legacy. But by 1955, it had diversified to include rock 'n' roll pioneers Chuck Berry and Bo Diddley, and in the 1960s its most popular artist was the soul singer Etta James. In 1963 he purchased radio station WVON ("Voice of the Negro") in Chicago, and by the time of his death from a heart attack, his firm, L & P Broadcasting, owned additional stations in Chicago and Milwaukee.

Chessman, Caryl (Whittier) (1922–60) convict, author; born in St. Joseph, Mich. Convicted on 17 counts of kidnapping, robbery, and rape, he was sentenced to death in 1948. He managed to delay his execution for 12 years and wrote books against capital punishment, including *Trial by Ordeal* (1956). His articulate manner and the fact that he had never actually killed anyone led to an international protest against his execution.

Cheves, Langdon (1776–1857) U.S. representative; born in Rocky River, S.C. Home-schooled, he became a lawyer in Charleston, S.C., in 1797. He was the South Carolina attorney general (1808–10) before being appointed to the U.S. House of Representatives (1810–15); he succeeded Henry Clay as Republican Speaker of the House (1812–15). He declined cabinet and supreme court appointments to become president of the Bank of the United States (1819–22), returning to South Carolina to cultivate rice in 1829.

Chevrolet, Louis (1878–1941) race car driver, automobile designer; born in La Chaux de Fonds, Switzerland. He emigrated to the U.S.A. in 1900 to race cars, and in his first race defeated Barney Oldfield. In 1905 he drove a record mile in 52.8 seconds. In 1911, with the backing of William Crapo Durant, he founded the Chevrolet Motor Company and designed its first car. He sold out his interest in 1915 and concentrated on making racing cars; his cars won the Indianapolis 500 in 1920 (with brother Gaston Chevrolet driving) and 1921. In 1929 he formed (with another brother, Arthur Chevrolet), the Chevrolet Brothers Aircraft Company, but this venture failed and he went back to building racing cars.

Chicago, Judy (b. Judith Cohen Gerowitz) (1939–) painter; born in Chicago. A feminist painter, she is most famous for her room-sized installation of *Dinner Party Project* (1979), a vision of a female Last Supper, which used several mediums including ceramics and woven materials. This well-attended traveling exhibit created controversy, but was acclaimed by many critics.

Chidlaw, Benjamin Wiley (1900–77) aviator; born in Cleves, Ohio. A West Point graduate with training in aeronautical engineering, he helped develop engine modifications for high altitude flight and, during World War II, he supervised the design and construction of the first U.S. jet aircraft. In 1954, he became the first commander of the Continental Air Defense Command.

Chihuly, Dale (1941–) glass maker; born in Tacoma, Wash. He took his M.F.A. at the Rhode Island School of Design and, as his own work began to receive recognition, founded the Pilchuck Glass School near Seattle, Wash. (1971) to stimulate others to take up the craft of blowing glass. He has become internationally recognized as an innovative creator of colorful blown-glass abstract sculptures and architectural installations.

Child, C. D. (Clement Dexter) (1868–1933) physicist; born in Madison, Ohio. He taught at Cornell (1893–97) and Colgate (1898–1933) Universities. He determined that the electric current between ions is proportional to voltage, and published his findings in his book *Electric Arcs* (1913).

Child, Charles M. (Manning) (1869–1954) developmental biologist; born in Ypsilanti, Mich. He taught and performed research at the University of Chicago (1895–1934), spending summers at various institutions for marine biology. After his retirement, he moved to Stanford University (1939–54), where he remained active in both education and scientific publishing. He made major contributions to studies of the origin and development of the invertebrate nervous system. He is best known for his "gradient theory" of regeneration (1911), which states that the dominant section of the regenerating part is developed first. He founded the journal *Physiological Zoology* in 1928.

Child, Francis James (1825–96) philologist; born in Boston, Mass. He graduated first in his class at Harvard (1846), where with the exception of two years' study in Germany he remained on the faculty until his death, teaching rhetoric, oratory, and English literature. Child's most important scholarly contributions include his 5-volume edition of Spenser's *Poetical Works* (1855), for many years the authoritative text, and seminal papers on the language and versification of Chaucer (1863) and Gower (1873). Working from variant manuscript sources, he pioneered a comparative approach to folklore in his *magnum opus, English and Scottish Popular Ballads* (10 vols. 1883–98); known as the "Child ballads," this comprehensive collection provided the basis for ballad studies and remains the most complete work of its kind.

Child, Julia (b. McWilliams) (1912–) chef, author; born in Pasadena, Calif. She trained in Cordon Bleu cooking schools in Paris. Her 2-volume *Mastering the Art of French Cooking* (coauthored, 1961–70) became a classic, and several popular television series demystified French cooking for Americans and established Child as a celebrity treasured – and often parodied – for her forthright manner and hearty humor. Her other cookbooks include *The Way to Cook* (1989).

Child, Lydia Maria (b. Francis) (1802–80) abolitionist, writer; born in Medford, Mass. After teaching for a time she began writing fiction (1824) and started a children's educational periodical, the *Juvenile Miscellany;* then came her popular domestic advice books, notably *The Frugal Housewife* (1829), and biographical essays about women. Following her marriage to attorney David Lee Child (1828), she wrote a classic antislavery tract (1833) that offended many and depressed sales of her other books; she also joined in abolitionist activities and was editor of the *National Anti-Slavery Standard* (1840–44). After a hiatus devoted to other writing, including widely read newspaper columns on arts and society, she returned to her antislavery polemics shortly before the Civil War; she also turned to such causes as women's rights and civil service reform.

Childs, George William (1829–94) publisher, philanthropist; born in Baltimore, Md. He opened a bookstore in Philadelphia in 1847, started a publishing business, and built the Philadelphia *Public Ledger* into a popular newspaper.

Chin, Robert (1918–) psychologist; born in New York City. This social psychologist taught at Boston University (1947–88). His research focused on group conflict, attitudes, and political behavior, public opinion in China, and organizational development, and yielded such works as *Psychological Research in Communist China* (coauthored, 1969) and *The Planning of Change* (coedited, 1969).

Chipman, Nathaniel (1752–1843) jurist; born in Salisbury, Conn. He negotiated the admittance of Vermont to the Union and sat on Vermont's Supreme Court intermittently (1787–1816). During those years he also served in Vermont's legislature, as well as a term as a federal judge (1791–93), and a term in the U.S. Senate (Fed., Vt.; 1799–1805). He lectured at Middlebury College (1816–17), but deafness limited him thereafter.

Chisholm, Roderick (Milton) (1916–) philosopher; born in North Attleboro, Mass. After earning a Harvard doctorate (1942), he taught philosophy at Brown University (from 1946), specializing in theory of knowledge and philosophy of science; his works include *Perceiving: A Philosophical Study* (1957).

Chisholm, Shirley (b. Anita St. Hill) (1924–) U.S. representative, social activist; born in New York City. A teacher and then an educational consultant to New York City's Bureau of Child Welfare (1959–64), she became the first black congresswoman (Dem., N.Y.; 1969–83). She ran for the Democratic nomination for president in 1972. A champion of minority education and employment opportunities, she taught at Mount Holyoke College (1983–87).

Chisolm, Jesse (?1806–?1868) trader; birthplace unknown. Of part Cherokee descent, he blazed a trail between Texas and Kansas (1864–66) which became the main cattle trail between those states.

Chisum, John Simpson (1824–84) cattleman; born in Hardeman County, Tenn. He moved to Texas in 1837 and entered the cattle business in 1854. By 1866 he had begun to remove his ranching operations to New Mexico where he settled (1873) and took the lead in imposing law and order. At his peak, the "cattle king of America" owned 60,000–90,000 head of cattle. His role in the Lincoln County War (1878–79) is a subject of dispute.

Chittenden, Russell H. (Henry) (1856–1943) biochemist, educator; born in New Haven, Conn. As a senior at Yale (1874), he created the first American course in physiological chemistry (later known as biochemistry). He remained at Yale until 1922, bringing Yale's Sheffield Scientific School into prominence as its director (1898–1922), while concurrently lecturing at Columbia University (1898–1903). He made pioneering studies in the enzymatic digestion of proteins and starch, and isolated glycogen ("animal starch") in 1875. He began his advocacy of a low-protein diet for humans in 1907 and investigated the toxicology of human alcohol and chemical addiction (1903–15). After his retirement, he concentrated on writing histories of both biochemistry and the Sheffield School.

Chittenden, Thomas (1730–97) governor; born in East Guilford, Conn. A Vermont farmer, he was a member of the council of state that drew up Vermont's first request for statehood (1777) after it had declared itself an independent republic that year. When the Continental Congress rejected the request, he became governor of the republic (1778–89, 1790–91). After Vermont began negotiating with the British commander in Canada, the adjacent states of New York and New Hampshire settled their territorial disputes with Vermont and it was accepted as the 14th state (March 4, 1791). Chittenden served as its first governor (1791–97).

Choate, Joseph H. (Hodges) (1832–1917) lawyer, diplomat; born in Salem, Mass. President of many clubs and cultural organizations in New York, he argued landmark antitrust, libel, admiralty, and income tax cases over a 55-year legal career. He achieved major success as ambassador to Great Britain (1899–1905) and as a leader at the Second Hague Conference (1907).

Chomsky, (Avril) Noam (1928–) linguist, social/political theorist; born in Philadelphia. Son of a distinguished Hebrew scholar, he was educated at the University of Pennsylvania, where he was especially influenced by Zellig Harris; after taking his M.A. there in 1951, he spent four years as a junior fellow at Harvard (1951–55), then was awarded a Ph.D. from the University of Pennsylvania (1955). In 1955 he began what would be his long teaching career at the Massachusetts Institute of Technology. He became known as one of the principal founders of transformational-generative grammar, a system of linguistic analysis that challenges much traditional linguistics and has much to do with philosophy, logic, and psycholinguistics; his book *Syntactic Structures* (1957) was credited with revolutionizing the discipline of linguistics. Chomsky's theory suggests that every human utterance has two structures: surface structure, the superficial combining of words, and "deep structure," which are universal rules and mechanisms. In more practical terms, the theory argues that the means for acquiring a language is innate in all humans and is triggered as soon as an infant begins to learn the basics of a language. Outside this highly rarefied sphere, Chomsky early on began to promote his radical critique of American political, social, and economic policies, particularly of American foreign policy as effected by the Establishment and presented by the media; he was outspoken in his opposition to the Vietnam War and later to the Persian Gulf War. His extensive writings in this area include *American Power and the New Mandarins* (1969) and *Human Rights and American Foreign Policy* (1978).

Chopin, Kate (b. Katherine O'Flaherty) (1851–1904) writer; born in St. Louis, Mo. She returned to St. Louis to write professionally after the death of her husband, a Louisiana planter (1882). Her Creole tales (*Bayou Folk* (1894), *A Night in Acadie* (1897)) established her as a leading "local color" author. But after her novel *The Awakening* (1899) was attacked for its honest portrayal of a woman's unrepentant sexual passion, she virtually stopped publishing and was not rediscovered until the 1960s.

Chouteau, René Auguste (1749–1829) trader; born in New Orleans. He assisted in the founding of St. Louis, Mo., (1764) and enjoyed a monopoly of trade with the Osage Indians (1794–1802). He became a colonel of the St. Louis militia (1808) and negotiated treaties with the Sioux, Iowa, Sauk, and Fox (1815). He was a financial backer of much of the business and trade of St. Louis.

Christensen, Lew (1909–84) ballet dancer, choreographer; born in Brigham City, Utah. The first of George Balanchine's leading American male dancers in the 1930s, he became chief choreographer and, in 1952, director of the San Francisco Ballet.

Christian, Charlie (Charles) (1919–42) jazz musician; born in Dallas, Texas. He was a pioneering and influential electric guitarist and modern jazz innovator who played with Benny Goodman from 1938 until his death from tuberculosis.

Christie, William (1944–) harpsichordist, conductor; born in Buffalo, N.Y. A 1966 Harvard graduate, he studied music at Yale and taught at Dartmouth for a year before moving to France, where in the 1970s and 1980s he established himself as the leader in the field of French Baroque music. He established the ensemble *Les Arts Florissants* in 1978 to revive 17th- and 18th-century French music, including opera and ballet. He also taught early music at the Paris Conservatory.

Christopher, Warren M. (Minor) (1925–) lawyer, government official; born in Scranton, N.D. In 1950, he joined the Los Angeles law firm O'Melveny & Myers. In the 1960s, he analyzed race riots and aided international textile negotiations. Deputy attorney general (1967–69) and deputy secretary of state (1977–81), in 1980–81 he led successful U.S. negotiations for release of 52 hostages held in Iran. He remained a respected voice in the Democratic Party in the following years and President Bill Clinton appointed him secretary of state (1993).

Christy, Edwin Pearce (1815–1862) singer; born in Philadelphia. Founder of the Christy Minstrels show, he started singing with two assistants in public houses in Buffalo, N.Y. in 1842. He enlarged his troop of black-faced minstrels, performing in New York and London. He is credited with creating many of the features of the classic minstrel show – the white-faced Mr. Interlocutor, the end men, Tambo and Bones, and the semi-circle of blackface musicians. He commissioned Stephen Foster to compose songs for the group, which was still popular when he retired in 1855. Subject to depression, he committed suicide during the Civil War.

Christy, Howard Chandler (1873–1952) painter, illustrator; born in Morgan County, Ohio. He was an illustrator, and his patriotic poster, *Fight or Buy Bonds* (1917), was distributed throughout America during World War I.

Christy, June (b. Shirley Luster) (1925–90) vocalist; born in Springfield, Ill. A singer associated with West Coast jazz, she began with prominent Chicago society bands before joining Stan Kenton's orchestra in 1945. After Kenton disbanded in 1949, she worked as a single and recorded her classic album *Something Cool* in 1953. She toured occasionally in the U.S.A. and abroad until her retirement in the late 1960s.

Chrysler, Walter P. (Percy) (1875–1940) manufacturer; born in Wamego, Kans. He left the American Locomotive Company in 1912 to become works manager of the Buick Motor Company; he was Buick's president from 1916 to 1921, when he became president of the Willys-Overland and Maxwell Motor Company; this became the Chrysler Corporation in 1925. In 1928 he bought Dodge Brothers, Inc., and introduced the Plymouth car which had the industry's first high compression engine. When he retired in 1935, Chrysler Corporation was the second largest auto manufacturer in the world. His autobiography, *The Life of an American Workingman,* was published in 1937.

Chryssa (b. Varda Chryssa) (1933–) sculptor; born in Athens, Greece. She studied in Paris (1953–54), attended the California School of the Arts (1954–55), and settled in New York City (1955). She is known for her abstract letter form sculptures, such as *Cycladic Books* (1955), her neon-light tubing, as in *Five Variations on the Ampersand* (1966), and her mixed media work, *Gates of Times Square* (1964–66).

Chu, Steven (1948–) physicist; born in St. Louis, Mo. He was a member of the technical staff of Bell Telephone Laboratories (1976–78) and head of the quantum electronics and research department of American Telephone and Telegraph Co. Bell Laboratories (1983–87) before becoming a physics professor at Stanford (1987). He made major contributions to laser spectroscopy, analysis of positronium atoms, and studies of gaseous sodium at temperatures approaching absolute zero.

Chung, (Constance Yu-hwa) Connie (1946–) television journalist; born in Washington, D.C. She began her career as a newswriter in 1969, becoming the highest paid local anchor in the nation at CBS's KNXT-TV in Los Angeles (1976–83). She then joined National Broadcasting Company News (1983–89) as a correspondent and anchor for various shows, including *News at Sunrise.* Returning to CBS in 1989, she anchored *Face to Face with Connie Chung,* an investigative news magazine (1990) and in 1993 became coanchor of the *Evening News* with Dan Rather.

Church, Alonzo (1903–) mathematician/philosopher; born in Washington, D.C. A professor of philosophy and mathematics at the University of California: Los Angeles (1967), he was author of *Introduction of Mathematical Logic.* He was editor of the *Journal of Symbolic Logic* (1936–79) and a member of the National Academy of Sciences.

Church, Benjamin (1639–1718) soldier, Indian fighter; born in Plymouth, Mass. In 1676 he led the fight at Mount Hope, R.I., that resulted in the death of King Philip. Later he led five different raids against the French and Indians in the areas of Maine and Nova Scotia.

Church, Frederick (Edwin) (1826–1900) painter; born in Hartford, Conn. Considered a member of the Hudson River School, he studied with Thomas Cole (1844–46) and traveled in Europe and South America. By 1870 he began construction of his exotic mansion, Olana, on the Hudson River. His panoramic scenes reveal his dramatic use of lighting and naturalistic details, as seen in his famous paintings *Niagara* (1857), and *The Heart of the Andes* (1859).

Church, Thomas (1902–78) landscape architect; born in Boston, Mass. Influencing a generation of architects, he combined modern designs with traditional craftsmanship in his California firm (1920–76) to create gardens which were like an outdoor living room.

Churchman, C. (Charles) West (1913–) systems theorist; born in Philadelphia. He earned undergraduate and graduate degrees at the University of Pennsylvania and joined the business school faculty at the University of California: Berkeley (1958). He specialized in systems, operations, and decision-making. His books include *The Systems Approach* (coedited, 1968, later revised).

Chwast, Seymour (1931–) graphic designer; born in New York City. Based in New York, he studied with Will Barnett at Cooper Union, New York (1948–51), was a cofounder (with Milton Glaser) of Push Pin Studios, New York (1954), and was publisher and editor of *Push Pin Graphic* magazine (1974–81) and Push Pin Press (1976–81). His eclectic approach to design is also exemplified in the television series *I, Claudius* (1977).

Ciardi, John (Anthony) (1916–86) poet, writer, teacher; born in Boston, Mass. He attended Bates College (1934–36), Tufts (B.A. 1938), and the University of Michigan (M.A. 1939). He taught at many institutions, was director of the Bread Loaf Writers Conference, Vt. (1956–72), and was poetry editor of the *Saturday Review* (1956–72). Based in Metuchen, N.J., in his later years, he was known as a lecturer and etymologist as well as for his poetry and translations.

Ciccone, Madonna Louise See MADONNA.

Cicotte, (Edward Victor) Eddie (1884–1969) baseball player; born in Detroit, Mich. He was one of eight Chicago White Sox players who allegedly conspired to "fix" the 1919 World Series; an outstanding (right-handed) pitcher, he lost two games in that Series. In 1921 he was barred from baseball for life for his part in the "Black Sox" scandal.

Cisneros, Henry (Gabriel) (1947–) mayor, cabinet official; born in San Antonio, Texas. As mayor of his native city (1982–90) he gained a national reputation for being both a Latino and a progressive in charge of a good-sized American city. He wrote several books, including *Target '90: Goals & Decisions for San Antonio's Future.* In 1993, President Bill Clinton named him secretary of Housing and Urban Affairs.

Civiletti, Benjamin R. (Richard) (1935–) lawyer, U.S. attorney general; born in Peekskill, N.Y. After two years as a U.S. attorney in Maryland (1962–64), he joined one of Baltimore's most prestigious law firms, Venable, Baetjer & Howard (1964–77). Brought in as an assistant attorney general in the new Carter administration in 1977, he was promoted to deputy attorney general (1978) and then to attorney general (1979–81). He pursued white-collar crime, sought release of American hostages in Iran, and handled a number of politically sensitive issues. On leaving the government he returned to his Baltimore law firm, and in 1987 he became managing partner.

Claflin, Tennessee Celeste See under WOODHULL, VICTORIA CLAFLIN.

Claiborne, Craig (1920–) chef, author; born in Sunflower, Miss. A lover of food, an accomplished cook, and trained journalist, he was food editor of the *New York Times* (1957–88); his stylish but impartial restaurant reviews set a new standard for food reporting. His cookbooks include the best-selling *New York Times Cook Book* (1961) and *Craig Claiborne's Southern Cooking* (1987).

Claiborne, Liz (Elisabeth Claiborne Ortenberg) (1929–) fashion designer, business executive; born in Brussels, Belgium. She was raised in New Orleans, returning to Europe to study art instead of finishing high school. After 25 years as a New York designer she founded her own firm (1976), which she built into a billion-dollar-a-year business, first designing stylish, moderately priced sportswear that freed working women from plain, dark suits, then expanding into menswear, accessories, and perfume. She retired from active management in 1989.

Claiborne, William (c. 1587–c. 1677) colonist, agitator; born in Westmoreland County, England. A Virginia colonist, he feuded with the Lords of Baltimore over the right to a settlement on Kent Island in the Chesapeake Bay. He incited an insurrection and held control of Maryland during 1644–46.

Clark, Alvan (1804–87) astronomer; born in Ashfield, Mass. A moderately successful portrait painter and engraver, he developed an interest in optics at age 40 when his son George was studying engineering. This led to the founding, with his sons George Bassett Clark (1827–91; b. Lowell, Mass.), and Alvan Graham Clark (1832–97; b. Fall River, Mass), of Alvan Clark & Sons, makers of optical lenses for telescopes, some of unsurpassed quality. His company represented the first significant American contribution to astronomical instrument making. They tested the lenses themselves, seeking difficult-to-find double stars. In 1862, Alvan Graham won the Lalande Prize for discovering the companion of Sirius.

Clark, Bobby (1888–1960) actor; born in Springfield, Ohio. An intelligent comic, whose unique walk and leer predated Groucho Marx, he teamed up with straightman Paul McCullough in vaudeville, burlesque, and films (1900–36).

Clark, Edna McConnell (1886–1982) philanthropist; born in Atlanta, Ga. She was born the very year her father, David Hall McConnell, founded a perfume company in California that, changing its name to Avon in 1950, would grow into the Avon Products empire, the largest cosmetics company in the world. She graduated from Smith College and married W. Van Alan Clark, who would be associated with the company for 55 years, until his death in 1976. As heir to her father's fortune and share in the company, she established the Edna McConnell Clark Foundation (1950); eventually it had an endowment of $200 million, and she took an active role in administering its generous grants to a variety of institutions and causes throughout her life.

Clark, Edward (1811–82) lawyer, entrepreneur; born in Athens, N.Y. He began practicing law in Poughkeepsie (1833), and moved his practice to New York City in 1836 to form Jordan and Clark with his father-in-law, the state's attorney general. It was to this firm that sewing machine inventor Isaac Merritt Singer turned for help in his defense against a patent infringement suit brought by Elias Howe (1854). Clark became a partner in the I. M. Singer Company and organized the first American patent pool, the Singer Machine Combination, which licensed 24 companies before expiring in 1877. Clark also established the principle of installment buying which the Singer Company pioneered, thus making it possible for modest homemakers to purchase the expensive sewing machines. Clark took over as president of the company in 1875 when Singer died. By 1882, the company had manufacturing plants in Glasgow (Scotland), Montreal (Canada), and Elisabethtown, N.J.

Clark, Eugenie (1922–) ichthyologist; born in New York City. She was an assistant ichthyologist at the Scripps Institute of Oceanography (1946–47) and the New York Zoological Society (1947–48), then relocated to the American Museum of Natural History (1948–66) while concurrently serving as executive director of marine biology at the Cape Haze Marine Laboratory, Sarasota, Fla. (1955–66). Her popular autobiography, *Lady With a Spear* (1953), conveyed her spirited and independent nature as well as her enthusiasm for marine organisms in their own environment. She became an associate professor of biology at City University of New York (1966–67), then moved to the University of Maryland (1969). She made many trips to the Red Sea for field study, performed extensive investigations on the behavior of sharks, and made major contributions to studies of the reproductive behavior, morphology and taxonomy, and isolation mechanisms of fishes.

Clark, Francine Clary See under CLARK, ROBERT STERLING.

Clark, George Rogers (1752–1818) surveyor, soldier; born near Charlottesville, Va. A surveyor by profession, he had explored the Ohio River region. At the outset of the American Revolution, he was commander of the Kentucky militia; taking the offensive with a small force, he conducted an epic campaign, which involved incredible overland marches and the capture of several British outposts, climaxing in the "Night of the Long Knives" at Fort Sackville, Vincennes, Ind. (1779). He continued to fight the British and their Indian allies, and by the end of the Revolution he had secured the old Northwest (Michigan, Indiana, Illinois) for the new United States – a military reality the politicians recognized in the Treaty of Paris (1783). After the war he participated in a military expedition against the Wabash Indians, and because he took some goods, he lost favor with the government in Virginia and with George Washington. After two failures with French military expeditions, from 1803 he was engaged mainly in supervising land allotments in the new territory he had secured.

Clark, Grenville (1882–1967) lawyer, peace advocate; born in New York City. He practiced law in New York and was a founder of the Military Training Camps Association during World War I. In 1940 he helped to draw up the Selective Service Act in anticipation of America's involvement in World War II. He believed in limitations on national sovereignty and he wrote *A Federation of Free Peoples* (1939). With Louis B. Sohn, he coauthored *World Peace Through World Law: Two Alternative Plans* (1958). He continued to work to advance civil rights.

Clark, (James Beauchamp) Champ (1850–1921) U.S. representative; born in Lawrenceburg, Ky. A graduate of Bethany College in West Virginia and of Cincinnati Law School, he moved to Missouri in 1876 where he was a newspaper editor and city attorney in Louisiana and Bowling Green, Ohio, before serving as prosecutor for Pike County (1885–89) and member of the Missouri legislature (1889–91). Elected to Congress (Dem., Mo.; 1893–1921) he served on the powerful Foreign Affairs and Ways and Means Committees, supporting the Spanish-American War, yet opposing annexation of Hawaii. A forcible orator and minority leader, he led the fight to wrest arbitrary control of legislative procedures from the Republican Speaker, Joseph Cannon. Elected Speaker of the House in 1911, he was an enormously popular candidate for president in 1912 who led Woodrow Wilson through 14 ballots at the Democratic Convention.

Clark, John Bates (1847–1938) economist; born in Providence, R.I. He pioneered the marginal productivity theory and engaged in a lifelong debate with the Austrian economist Bohm-Bawerk regarding the fixed status of capital funds. He taught at Smith College (1881–93) and Johns Hopkins (1893–95) before moving to Columbia University, where he remained until his retirement in 1923.

Clark, Joseph S. (Sill) (1901–90) U.S. senator; born in Philadelphia. A crusading mayor of Philadelphia (1951–56), he was elected to the U.S. Senate (Dem., Penn.; 1957–69), where he sponsored antipoverty legislation.

Clark, Kenneth (Bancroft) (1914–) psychologist; born in the Panama Canal Zone. Emigrating to New York City with his mother (1919), he was educated at Howard University (1935) and Columbia University where he earned a Ph.D. in psychology (1940). Teaching at City College of New York (1942), he aided Gunnar Myrdal with his monumental study of America's racial problems. Clark later founded the Northside Center for Child Development to work with ghetto children and he published a report (1950) that unmasked the psychological effects of racial segregation in schools. The report was prominently cited in the 1954 Supreme Court ruling, *Brown* vs. *Board of Education,* that outlawed segregation nationwide. He helped found Harlem Youth Opportunities Unlimited, served as a consultant to private and government bodies, was named the first black member of the New York State Board of Regents (1966), and founded Kenneth B. Clark & Associates (1986), a consulting firm for racially related issues. Besides *Dark Ghetto* (1965), he published numerous books and articles on the condition of African-Americans.

Clark, Mamie Phipps (1917–83) psychologist; born in Hot Springs, Ark. While attending Howard University she married psychologist Kenneth B. Clark (1938) and in 1946 they founded the Northside Center for Child Development in New York City. They made the first, now classic, studies of personality development in black children (1939–50) (the studies cited by the U.S. Supreme Court in the landmark desegregation decision, *Brown* v. *Board of Education*). She served as associate director of the center for 33 years (to 1979).

Clark, Mark (Wayne) (1896–1984) soldier; born in Madison Barracks, N.Y. The son of a career army officer, Clark graduated from West Point in 1917 and fought in France the following year. He served in a succession of staff and operational posts through the 1930s. On November 8, 1942, he convinced Vichy Admiral Darlan to order French forces in North Africa to cease resistance to the Allied landings in Morocco and Algeria. Clark commanded the 5th Army in the Salerno landings in September 1943; after a winter of hard fighting, his troops entered Rome on June 4, 1944. As commander of the 15th Army Group, he received the surrender of 230,000 Axis troops in the Alps in April 1945. Clark commanded United Nations forces in Korea (1952–53) and signed the armistice that ended the fighting there.

Retiring from the army in 1953, he was president of The Citadel, the military college in South Carolina, from 1954–65.

Clark, Ramsey (William) (1927–) attorney general, political activist; born in Dallas, Texas. Son of former Supreme Court justice Tom C. Clark, he was named attorney general (1967–69) during the raucous anti-Vietnam War years. Although he prosecuted activists such as the Berrigan brothers, Clark was known to be a liberal who moved further to the left in his beliefs and causes after returning to private practice. Twice an unsuccessful candidate for U.S. Senate from New York (1970s), he returned to public prominence (1980–90s) as an outspoken critic of two Republican administrations. He himself was roundly criticized for support of extremist politicians like Lyndon LaRouche – regarded by most as an ultra-right extremist – and Iraqi dictator Saddam Hussein, and he became a mystery to former backers.

Clark, (Richard Wagstaff) Dick (1929–) television host, producer; born in Mt. Vernon, N.Y. Originally a radio disc jockey in the 1950s, he was the host of a "record hop," *American Bandstand,* on Philadelphia local WFIL-TV, which moved to ABC (1957–89). He also hosted daytime game shows like *$10,000 Pyramid* (1973), which over the years (and in a new network) grew to the *$100,000 Pyramid.* He formed Dick Clark Productions to produce television movies, variety shows, and special programs on which he often appeared as host.

Clark, Robert Sterling (1877–1956) born in New York City, **and Francine Clary Clark** (1876–1960) born in France; art collectors. An heir of the Singer sewing machine fortune, he was the grandson of Edward Clark, the business partner of Isaac Singer. Robert graduated from Yale (1899), served in the army until 1905, and led a scientific expedition to China (1908–09). He settled in Paris as an art collector (1911), and married Francine (1919). Little is known of Francine's early life. The Clarks moved to New York City (1920s), then settled in Williamstown, Mass. (1949), where they continued to own racehorses and add to their collection of Old Master and 19th-century American paintings, and more especially works by Degas and Renoir, among other French Impressionists. In 1955 the Clarks established the Sterling and Francine Clark Art Institute in Williamstown and both are buried beneath the front steps of the original marble building.

Clark, Tom C. (Thomas Campbell) (1899–1977) Supreme Court justice; born in Dallas, Texas. He joined the Department of Justice and rose to assistant attorney general (1943). As attorney general under President Truman (1945–49), he supported the anticommunist movement. Truman named him to the U.S. Supreme Court (1949–67) where he supported a strong federal government, especially in matters of national security.

Clark, William (1770–1838) soldier, explorer; born in Caroline County, Va. (brother of George Rogers Clark). He entered the U.S. Army (1789) and fought under General Anthony Wayne. He resigned from the army (1796) and tended to his family's estate. He shared command of the famous Lewis and Clark expedition (1804–06) with Meriwether Lewis; among his various contributions to its success were his fine maps and his illustrations of the animals of the territory. He was brigadier general of militia and superintendent of Indian affairs for the Louisiana Territory (1807–13) and governor of the Missouri Territory (1813–20). He established Fort Shelby, the first U.S. post in Wisconsin (1814), and negotiated treaties with various Indian tribes. He was surveyor general for Illinois, Missouri, and Arkansas (1824–25).

Clark, William Andrews (1839–1925) mining operator, U.S. senator; born in Fayette County, Pa. The family moved to Iowa in the 1850s and he began to teach school in Missouri until the Civil War drove him to Colorado to mine gold quartz. By 1863 he was in Montana panning for gold, which he used as capital to start a store in Virginia City. In 1867 he got the mail concession between Missoula, Mont., and Walla Walla, Wash., through which he became wealthy. In 1872 he bought three mining claims in Butte, Mont., studied mining at Columbia University for one year, and returned to form the Colorado and Montana Smelting Company and the Butte Reduction Works. In addition to buying more mines around Butte, he bought the United Verde Mine and its smelter in Arizona. His business interests were vast and included railroads, newspapers, timber, and a sugar refinery in Los Angeles. He established the first water and electrical systems in Missoula and Butte. After much political drama around the forming of the state constitution and selection of its capital, he was elected to the U.S. Senate (Dem., Mont.; 1901–07), where he opposed President Theodore Roosevelt's conservation policies.

Clark, William Smith (1826–86) agriculturist, educator; born in Ashfield, Mass. He graduated from Amherst College (1848) and after taking his Ph.D. from Göttingen, Germany (1852), he returned to teach chemistry, zoology, and botany at Amherst College (1852–61). After serving with the Union army during the Civil War, he became a moving force behind establishing and the first president of the Massachusetts Agricultural College (1867–79), where he also taught botany and history. (It would become the University of Massachusetts in 1947.) When the governor of Hokkaido, the northernmost island of Japan, visited the college, he was so impressed with Smith's work that he invited him to help start what became the Imperial College of Agriculture at Sapparo on Hokkaido. Clark spent a year there (1876–77) to get it started (and also held Bible study classes in his spare time). He has been revered ever since by the Japanese (who in particular repeat his parting advice, "Boys, be ambitious"); Massachusetts and Hokkaido now enjoy a "sister-state" relationship that attracts many Japanese to study at the state's university.

Clarke, Edith (1883–1959) electrical engineer; born in Howard County, Md. Using her inheritance to attend Vassar, she went on to study engineering at the University of Wisconsin and then worked for American Telephone and Telegraph Co. (1912–18) before becoming the first woman to receive an M.S. in electrical engineering from the Massachusetts Institute of Technology (1919). She worked at General Electric from 1922–45, focusing on large electrical power systems, and she developed a calculating device that predicted the electrical behavior of these systems. She postponed her retirement on a farm in Maryland by teaching at the University of Texas: Austin (1947–56).

Clarke, Francis Devereux (1849–1913) educator of the deaf; born in Raleigh, N.C. He served in the Confederate navy as a teenager and trained as an engineer while teaching at New York Institution for the Deaf. As superintendent of Arkansas Institute for the Deaf (1885–92) and Michigan State

School for the Deaf (1892–1913) he expanded both institutions and revised their curricula.

Clarke, James Freeman (1810–88) Protestant religious leader; born in Hanover, N.H. He graduated from Harvard in 1829, was pastor of the Unitarian Church in Louisville, Ky., and edited the *Western Messenger* from Louisville (1836–39), in which he published articles by, among others, Emerson and Hawthorne. He returned to Boston and founded the Unitarian Church of the Disciples in 1841. He taught at Harvard Divinity School from 1867–71. A supporter of temperance, the abolition of slavery, and women's suffrage, he was the author of many books, including *Ten Great Religions* (1871).

Clarke, James Paul (1854–1916) governor, U.S. senator; born in Yazoo City, Miss. A lawyer in Helena, Ark., he was active in state politics, serving as Democratic governor (1895–97). Going to the U.S. Senate midterm (1904–16), he supported Philippine independence, regulation of the railroads, and workmen's compensation insurance; he served as temporary president of the Senate (1913–16).

Clarke, John H. (Hessin) (1857–1945) Supreme Court justice; born in New Lisbon, Ohio. He was appointed to the federal district court (1914–16) and to the U.S. Supreme Court (1916–22) by President Wilson. A renowned peacemaker, he stepped down from the bench in 1922 to campaign, albeit unsuccessfully, for the League of Nations.

Clarke, Mary Francis (1803–87) religious foundress; born in Dublin, Ireland. Emigrating to the U.S.A. in 1833, she overcame financial woes to found a school in Philadelphia. She also formed a teaching community, the Sisters of Charity of the Blessed Virgin Mary, which she relocated to a frontier region in Iowa (1843).

Clarke, Shirley (1925–) director; born in New York City. A former dancer, she began making films in the 1950s. Often using the *cinéma vérité* technique, she made movies such as *The Connection* (1962) and *Portrait of Jason* (1967), notable for their gritty realism.

Clarke, Thomas Benedict (1848–1931) art collector; born in New York City. He studied at Washington Collegiate Institute, New York City, and by 1869 he began buying and selling paintings and Chinese porcelains. He is noted for his collection of Hudson River paintings and early American portraits, which were purchased by the A. W. Mellon Educational and Charitable Trust after his death. He also endowed the Clarke prize, given annually by the National Academy of Design.

Clarkson, John (Gibson) (1861–1909) baseball player; born in Cambridge, Mass. During his Hall of Fame career as a (right-handed) pitcher (1882–94), mostly for the Chicago White Stockings and Boston Red Stockings, he led the league in games won three times, winning as many as 53 games in 1885.

Claude, Albert (1898–1983) cell biologist; born in Longlier, Belgium (to American citizens). He performed cellular research in Europe (1928–29), then joined the Rockefeller Institute (now Rockefeller University) (1929–72). A citizen of both Belgium and the U.S.A., he concurrently directed the Jules Bordet Institute, Brussels (1948–72), and was a professor at the Université Libre, Brussels (1948–69). Claude is considered the founder of modern cell biology, and shared the 1974 Nobel Prize in physiology for his many pioneering contributions. He devised the differential centrifugation technique to separate cell components, identified the Rous sarcoma virus from chicken tumors as an RNA virus, discovered the cell organelles known as mitochondria and also the endoplasmic recticulum, and was the first to use electron microscopy in cellular research.

Clausen, Alden Winship (1923–) banker; born in Hamilton, Ill. Son of a weekly newspaper publisher, he graduated from Carthage College (Ill.) (1944) and served two years as an air force meteorological officer before obtaining a law degree from the University of Minnesota: Duluth (1949). He went to work for the Bank of America (BofA) the following year and rose through the corporate ranks to become president in 1970. Under his leadership, BofA became the most profitable commercial bank in the world. He left BofA in 1981 to become president of the World Bank, then returned as chief executive officer from 1986–90, by which time the bank's fortunes had begun to ebb.

Clausen, Jens (Christian) (1891–1969) botanist; born in North Eskilstrup, Denmark. He performed genetic research in Copenhagen (1921–31), where his work in violets led to his recruitment by taxonomist Harvey Monroe Hall to join the Carnegie Institution's laboratory at Stanford University (1931–69). There Clausen became the cytologist, geneticist, and unofficial leader of climatological transplant studies over two decades. With colleagues David Keck and William Hiesey, he demonstrated that new species can result from rapid experimental environmental changes. He made major contributions to studies of hybridization, race ecology, plant evolution, and studies of world forest compositions.

Clausen, Wendell (Vernon) (1923–) classicist; born in Coquille, Ore. He was educated at the University of Washington (B.A. 1945) and the University of Chicago (1948) and taught at Harvard (1959). He was perhaps the most respected American textual critic of his generation of classicists, known for his *Appendix Vergiliana* (1966) and *Persi et Iuvenalis Saturae* (1959).

Clay, Cassius See ALI, MUHAMMAD.

Clay, Cassius Marcellus (1810–1903) abolitionist; born in Madison County, Ky. (cousin of Henry Clay). He was the son of a wealthy slaveholding planter, but while at Yale, he heard abolitionist William Lloyd Garrison speak and was converted to abolitionism. Returning to Kentucky, he studied law, then served in the state legislature. Clay freed his own slaves in 1844, and the next year founded a newspaper, *The True American* (later the *Examiner*), to combat slavery. Honored for valor in the Mexican American War, he was appointed ambassador to Russia in 1861 but delayed his departure to help strengthen the defenses of Washington, D.C.; he went to Russia, returned to the U.S.A. in 1862 when named a major general in the Union army, then went back to take up his diplomatic post in Russia (1863–69) and participated in the purchase of Alaska. On his return he was active in Republican politics but he became increasingly erratic and reclusive; he was judged insane in his final months.

Clay, Henry (1771–1852) U.S. representative/senator; born in Hanover County, Va. With little formal education, he studied law, and, after being admitted to the bar in 1797, moved to Kentucky to practice law. Elected to the state legislature (1803–06), he was then chosen to fill unexpired terms in the U.S. Senate (1806–07; 1810–11). In 1810 he was elected as a Democratic-Republican to the U.S. House of Representatives, where he served with brief interruptions (1811–14, 1815–21, 1823–25); such was his reputation that he was Speaker of the House for all except a few months of his years there. He became known in Congress as a nationalist and defender of western regional interests. He was a "war hawk" in the period leading into the War of 1812 and served as a member of the delegation that negotiated the Treaty of Ghent in 1814 that ended that war with Britain. After the war he argued for the "American System," which sought to ensure American self-sufficiency through economic development; he favored a protective tariff, the establishment of a national bank, and internal improvements such as roads and canals. More as a firm supporter of the preservation of the Union than as an opponent of slavery, in 1820 he sponsored the Missouri Compromise, which admitted Missouri as a slave state and Maine as a free state. In 1824 he was one of four who ran for the U.S. presidency; when no candidate received a majority of the electoral votes, the election was sent to the House of Representatives; he threw his support to John Quincy Adams, securing his election over Andrew Jackson. When Adams appointed Clay as secretary of state, the two were accused of having made a "corrupt bargain." When Adams was defeated by Jackson in 1828, Clay returned to Kentucky, where his prosperous law practice allowed him to make his estate, Ashland, near Lexington, Ky., into a showplace, with its fine sheep and cattle and prize-winning race horses. He was back in Washington as a U.S. senator (1831–42). By then he was a leading figure in the newly organized Whig Party and became its presidential candidate in 1832 and 1844; he lost the former because of his support of high tariffs, and the latter because of his refusal to take a stand on the annexation of Texas. In the Senate he authored a compromise tariff (1833) that helped resolve the nullification crisis that had again raised the specter of disunion and war. Out of office in the mid-1840s, he returned for a final U.S. Senate term (1849–52). His last major legislative achievement again involved the issue of slavery. He submitted the Compromise Act of 1850 that, although appeasing both pro- and antislavery sides, only postponed the Civil War. He died in office, well before that event, and although his eloquent defense of the Union earned him his nickname "The Great Compromiser," that has remained the extent of his reputation.

Clay, Lucius (DuBignon) (1897–1978) soldier; born in Marietta, Ga. A 1918 West Point engineering graduate, he served in a succession of engineering posts in the 1920s and 1930s, many involving water and hydroelectric projects. As a deputy chief of staff from 1942 to 1944, Clay oversaw the army's vast production and procurement programs. In November 1944 he went overseas to command the Normandy base and the port of Cherbourg, which supplied the Allied forces in their drive through France and Germany. After Germany's surrender, Clay helped establish a military government in the U.S. zone of occupation, and served as military governor from 1947 to 1949. As commander of U.S. forces in Europe, he organized the Berlin airlift of 1948, a massive supply effort that ultimately broke the Soviet blockade of the German capital. He retired in 1949 and began a second career as a business executive and Republican Party activist. President Kennedy chose him to be his personal representative in Berlin during the 1961 Berlin

Crisis. From 1968–74, he was chairman of Radio Free Europe.

Clayton, John Middleton (1796–1856) U.S. senator, cabinet officer; born in Dagsboro, Del. He graduated from Yale (1815) and was admitted to the bar (1819). He served in the U.S. Senate (National Rep., Del.; 1829–36), then resigned to become chief justice of Delaware. He returned to the U.S. Senate (Whig, Del.; 1845–49), resigning again to serve as secretary of state under President Zachary Taylor (1849–50). His major achievement was to negotiate the so-called Clayton-Bulwer Treaty with Great Britain; it dispelled the increasing rivalry between the two nations in Central America by agreeing to a neutralized international canal in that region. Clayton resigned as secretary of state when Taylor died and returned to the U.S. Senate (1852–56).

Clayton, Paula Jean (1934–) psychiatrist; born in St. Louis, Mo. She became professor and head of the department of psychiatry at the University of Minnesota Medical School (1980). Her main areas of research were psychiatric diagnosis and the symptomatology and course of normal bereavement.

Clayton, Powell (1833–1914) governor, U.S. senator; born in Bethel County, Pa. A civil engineer, he fought with Kansas regiments during the Civil War (1861–65), buying a plantation in Arkansas afterward. As Arkansas governor (Rep., 1868–71), he attacked the Ku Klux Klan and issued $6,900,000 in bonds for railroad construction. Indicted for corruption, but never convicted, he served in the U.S. Senate (Rep., Ark.; 1871–77), later becoming U.S. ambassador to Mexico (1897–1905).

Cleary, Beverly (b. Bunn) (1916–) writer; born in McMinnville, Ore. She graduated from the University of California: Berkeley (1938), worked as a librarian (1939–45), and settled in Carmel, Calif. She is known for her popular children's books, such as *Henry Huggins* (1950) and *Ramona the Pest* (1968).

Cleaver, Eldridge (1935–) social activist, author; born in Wabbeseka, Ark. Convicted on a marijuana charge (1954), he began a 12-year cycle of prison terms. During this time he obtained a high school diploma, converted to the Black Muslim faith, and began to write. He was a staff writer for *Ramparts* magazine (1966) and became a much-publicized college lecturer after the release of *Soul on Ice* (1968), a seminal work on the black experience. He fled the United States (1969) to escape a prison sentence resulting from an alleged shoot-out with the Oakland police. Living in several third-world countries, including Algeria, he returned to the U.S.A. (1979) after battling the Algerian authorities over his connection with an alleged skyjacking incident. Pleading guilty to assaulting an Oakland police officer, he was placed on probation and ordered to do 2,000 hours of community service. He became a "born-again" Christian and by 1982 had become an ardent supporter of the U.S.A.

Cleburne, Patrick (Ronayne) (1828–64) Confederate soldier; born in the County of Cork, Ireland. A one-time ranker in the British army, he immigrated to America and prospered as a druggist, and later as a lawyer, in Helena, Ark. One of the hardest-hitting division commanders in Confederate service, Cleburne fought at Shiloh, Perryville, Chickamauga, and Chattanooga; he was killed in battle at Franklin, Tenn., on Nov. 30, 1864.

Cleckley, Hervey Milton (1903–84) psychiatrist; born in Augusta, Ga. For most of his professional career he was associated with the Medical College of Georgia (1937–84). He wrote *The Mask of Sanity* (1946), a highly influential work on the psychopathic personality. With colleague Corbett Thigpen, he wrote *Three Faces of Eve* (1957), the first exhaustive description of a multiple personality, which was made into a movie. He also wrote the less well-known, but equally important book, *The Caricature of Love* (1957).

Cleland, Thomas Maitland (1880–1964) book designer; born in Brooklyn, N.Y. One of the best craftsmen of his day, he illustrated works from textbooks to a deluxe edition of *Tom Jones* and was art director of *McClure's* magazine.

Clemens, Samuel Langhorne (Mark Twain, pen name) (1835–1910) writer, journalist, lecturer; born in Florida, Mo. Growing up along the Mississippi River, he left school at age 12 and worked as a printer (1847–57), then as a Mississippi riverboat pilot (1857–61). In 1863 he took as his pen name the call used when sounding the river shallows, "Mark twain!" referring to two fathoms. In 1861, after a few unhappy weeks as a Confederate volunteer, he went to Nevada where he tried gold mining and then edited a newspaper. In 1864 he went to San Francisco as a reporter and achieved his first success with "The Celebrated Jumping Frog of Calaveras County" (1865). In 1866 he visited the Sandwich Islands (Hawaii) on a newspaper assignment and his articles gained him some reputation, which in turn launched his career as a lecturer. In 1867 he took a trip to Europe and the Holy Land, and his humorous description of his experiences in *The Innocents Abroad* (1869) broadened his reputation; he would repeat its success with later travel books: *Roughing It* (1872); *A Tramp Abroad* (1880); and *Life on the Mississippi* (1883). On his return to America in 1867, he settled in the East, marrying Olivia Langdon, daughter of a wealthy New York coal merchant (1870); they had four children. In 1871 he moved to Hartford, Conn., and built a distinctive house (now open to the public) at the center of a community of artists known as Nook Farm. He collaborated with one of them, Charles Dudley Warner, on a novel satirizing post-Civil War America, *The Gilded Age* (1873). He won wide popularity with *The Adventures of Tom Sawyer* (1876), *The Prince and the Pauper* (1882), and *A Connecticut Yankee in King Arthur's Court* (1889), but it was *The Adventures of Huckleberry Finn* (1884, England; 1885, U.S.A.) that eventually became regarded as a seminal work of American literature. Poor investments wiped out most of his earnings by 1894, but a world lecture tour and sales of his books restored some of his wealth. Beneath his humor there had always been a layer of disillusion and pessimism; the loss of two daughters (1896, 1909) and his wife (1904) hardened this attitude, expressed in such works as *What is Man?* (1906) and *The Mysterious Stranger* (1916). In his final years he was greatly honored (especially in England) and his opinions on everything were sought out by the public, but the posthumous publication of his autobiography (1924) revealed the dim, indeed dark view he held of his fellow humans.

Clement, Frank (Goad) (1920–69) governor; born in Dickson, Tenn. A lawyer, FBI agent, and army veteran, he fought for reduced rates as Tennessee Public Utilities Commission counsel (1946–50). As Democratic governor of Tennessee (1953–59, 1963–67), he supported funding for education and public health and proclaimed his opposition to segregation, but in 1964 he refused to sign a fair practices code.

Clemente, Roberto (Walker) (1934–72) baseball player; born in Carolina, Puerto Rico. During his 18-year career with the Pittsburgh Pirates (1955–72), he compiled a lifetime batting average of .317 and was considered baseball's premier defensive outfielder. After he obtained his 3,000th hit in the last game of the 1972 season, his life was tragically cut short when an airplane loaded with supplies for earthquake victims in Managua, Nicaragua, crashed off the Puerto Rican coast. He was elected to the Hall of Fame in 1973.

Clements, Earle C. (1896–1985) U.S. representative/senator; born in Morganfield, Ky. A Democrat, he served Kentucky as a U.S. representative (1944–47), governor (1947–50), and U.S. senator (1950–56). In the Senate he served as party whip.

Clements, Frederick Edward (1874–1945) botanist, ecologist; born in Lincoln, Nebr. He graduated from the University of Nebraska in 1894, took a Ph.D. there in 1898, and stayed on to teach botany until 1907, when he left for the University of Minnesota. He gave up teaching in 1917 to concentrate on research, working at Carnegie Institution laboratories in Arizona, California, and Colorado. He was one of the first to emphasize the scientific importance of the study of life and the environment – ecology. His best-known work, *Plant Succession: An Analysis of the Development of Vegetation,* appeared in 1916. During the 1930s he worked as a consultant on projects to restore the U.S. western grasslands damaged by prolonged drought.

Clements, William Lawrence (1861–1934) book collector; born in Ann Arbor, Mich. Longtime president of a railway equipment manufacturing firm, he assembled an impressive collection of colonial and Revolutionary Americana, which he donated to the University of Michigan.

Cleveland, Frances (b. Folsom) (1864–1947) First Lady; born in Buffalo, N.Y. One of the youngest and most admired of all first ladies, she married Grover Cleveland in the White House in 1886; she was 21 and he was 49. She held numerous public receptions and her hairstyle and clothing were widely imitated. She married again after Cleveland's death and was active in poor relief during the 1930s Depression.

Cleveland, Horace, W. S. (1814–1900) landscape architect; born in Lancaster, Mass. Trained in agriculture, civil engineering, and horticulture, he was an established architect who bid against Frederick Olmsted to design Central Park in 1856. An advocate of open space design to reduce the problems of urbanism, he moved to Chicago in the 1860s, designing parks for newly developing cities and suburbs from Providence, R.I. to Omaha, Nebr. until the late 1890s.

Cleveland, James L. (1932–) gospel singer, composer; born in Chicago, Ill. He sang in choirs as a boy and began writing songs while a teenager. In the 1950s he sang with several gospel groups and composed many songs including "He's Using Me" (1955). He released over 50 albums and won two Grammy awards. In 1968 he formed the Gospel Music Workshop of America, which had 500,000 members by the mid-1980s.

Cleveland, (Stephen) Grover (1837–1908) twenty-second/twenty-fourth U.S. president; born in Caldwell, N.J. Basically self-educated, he was admitted to the bar in Buffalo, N.Y., in 1859 and began to work his way up the political ladder as a Democrat, becoming a reformist mayor in 1881 and New York governor the next year. His efficiency, honesty, and independence from the state political machine

took him to the presidency in 1884. During his first term he pursued civil service reform and lowered a protective tariff that was hurting labor. The latter, however, gained him the enmity of big-business interests; their man, Benjamin Harrison, won the close election of 1888. Cleveland came back to beat the ineffectual Harrison in 1892, but his second term was troubled by economic problems and ensuing unrest, during which Cleveland alienated workers and most Democrats. Losing the nomination in 1896, he retired to pursue business interests but he maintained his status as a respected statesman.

Cliburn, (Harvey Lavan, Jr.) Van (1934–) pianist; born in Shreveport, La. He soloed with orchestras as a teenager before being catapulted to fame as the first American to win Moscow's Tchaikovsky Prize (1958). He embarked on an international solo career, specializing in the 19th-century standard repertoire, but in 1978 largely ceased performing for personal reasons. The piano competition he began in Fort Worth, Texas, in 1962 became an important international event.

Clifford, Nathan (1803–81) Supreme Court justice; born in Rumney, N.H. He served the U.S. House of Representatives (Dem., Maine; 1839–43). President James Polk named him attorney general (1846) and sent him to negotiate an end to the Mexican War (1848). President James Buchanan named him to the U.S. Supreme Court (1858–81).

Clift, (Edward) Montgomery (1920–66) film actor; born in Omaha, Nebr. After ten years as a stage performer, he went to Hollywood for his role in *The Search* (1948). Four times nominated for an Academy Award, this brooding, intense actor usually played an outsider. Rumors of heavy drinking, drug use, and homosexuality surrounded him, and a car accident left him scarred, but the disfigurements seemed to give him added strength and pathos.

Clifton, James (1927–) anthropologist; born in St. Louis. He received a Ph.D. from San Francisco State in 1960 and taught at Colorado and Kansas before becoming codirector of the Developmental Change Program at the University of Wisconsin: Green Bay. The author of *Cultural Anthropology* (1967), his research fields were cultural change, urbanization, and culture and personality.

Cline, Howard Francis (1915–71) historian; born in Detroit, Mich. Harvard-trained, he directed the Hispanic Foundation at the Library of Congress (1952–71). A pioneer ethnohistorian, he studied social and ethnic history, particularly of Mexico, the subject of two of his major works: *The United States and Mexico* (1953, later revised), a standard history, and *Mexico: Evolution to Revolution* (1962).

Cline, Patsy (b. Virginia Patterson Hensley) (1932–63) country music singer; born in Winchester, Va. She played the piano and began singing country music while a teenager; she adopted the last name of her first husband and retained it after divorcing him. In 1957 she won the *Arthur Godfrey Talent Scouts* contest and went on to record such hits as "I Fall to Pieces" (1960) and "Crazy" (1961). One of the first country performers to achieve success on both the popular and country music charts, her music used innovative vocals and arrangements. She died in a plane crash.

Clinton, Bill (b. William Jefferson Blythe) (1946–) forty-second president of the United States; born in Hope, Ark. His father, William Blythe, died in an auto accident three months before he was born. He was adopted by his stepfather, Roger Clinton. As a youth, he thrilled to John F. Kennedy's promise, especially when he shook Kennedy's hand in the Rose Garden in 1963. He went to Georgetown University and then to Oxford as a Rhodes Scholar and received what would become a controversial draft deferment during the Vietnam War. He graduated from Yale Law School (1973) and married Hillary Rodham, a fellow Yale law student (1975). A committed Democrat, he was attorney general of Arkansas (1977–79) and then won the governor's seat in 1978. Defeated for reelection in 1980, he went through a period of soul-searching and made a comeback in 1982, becoming governor again; he went on to reelection in 1984, 1986, and 1990 and was named "the most effective" by his fellow governors. Overcoming serious charges involving alleged extramarital affairs and questions about his avoiding the draft, he won the Democratic presidential nomination in 1992. He was accused of "waffling" in his campaign speeches, but he kept the pressure on incumbent George Bush by focusing on the economic plight of many Americans. He won the three-way presidential race with 43% of the popular vote and 370 out of 525 electoral votes. His inauguration was notable for the participation of rock stars, poets, and the public at large, all of which led many to see his administration as the passing of the torch to a new generation, but he faced an enormous national debt and a country fragmented by social strife.

Clinton, De Witt (1769–1828) governor, public official; born in Little Britain, N.Y. A Columbia University graduate, in 1787 he published a series of letters – signed "A Countryman" – protesting the federal government's power under the proposed constitution. A lawyer, he learned about politics as private secretary to his uncle, Governor George Clinton (1790–95). He then served in the New York assembly (Dem.-Rep., 1797–98) and senate (1798–1802) where he blatantly dispensed political patronage from the governor's Council of Appointment. Briefly in the U.S. Senate (1802–03), he became mayor of New York (1803–07, 1808–09, 1811–15), organizing the city's first public school, helping found the New York City Hospital, and removing political restrictions on Roman Catholics. As New York's canal commissioner (1810–24), he took the lead in promoting construction of the Erie Canal. In 1812 he ran for president on a coalition ticket of anti-war Democratic-Republicans and Federalists, narrowly losing to James Madison. As governor (1817–23, 1825–28) his terms were marred by intra-party feuding, but completion of the Erie Canal in 1825 assured New York's economic dominance. Although he expended much of his talents and energies on partisan politics, he had also made significant contributions to the natural sciences and above all to the advancement of public education.

Clinton, George (1739–1812) vice-president, governor; born in Little Britain, N.Y. He was a brigadier general during the American Revolution and governor of New York seven times. He opposed the new Constitution in 1787. He was generally considered to be a poor vice-president during his tenure, first under Thomas Jefferson (1805–09), then under James Madison (1809–12).

Clinton, Hillary Rodham (1947–) lawyer, First Lady; born in Park Ridge, Ill. The daughter of a prosperous fabric store owner, she graduated from Wellesley College (1969) and Yale University Law School (1973). In 1975 she married Bill Clinton, a fellow Yale Law School graduate. She practiced law while he became attorney general and then governor of Arkansas, and during this time gained a national reputation for her contributions to issues of women's and children's rights and public education, through her publications, public advocacies, and court cases. (In 1991, before most Americans had heard of her, *The National Law Journal* named her one of the 100 most powerful lawyers in America.) During the 1992 presidential campaign, she emerged as a dynamic and valued partner of her husband, and as president he named her to head the Task Force on National Health Reform (1993). Inevitably there were charges of everything from old-fashioned nepotism to new-fashioned feminism, and she became the butt of both good-natured humor and vicious accusations, but less partisan observers recognized her as simply an example of the new American woman.

Cloninger, Claude Robert (1944–) psychiatric researcher, educator; born in Beaumont, Texas. He became affiliated with the Washington University School of Medicine in St. Louis, Mo., in 1973, becoming head of the department of psychiatry in 1989. A specialist in the genetic epidemiology of psychiatric disorders, his areas of interest included personality disorders, schizophrenia, and alcoholism. In the 1990s, he undertook molecular genetic linkage studies of the inheritance of alcoholism.

Close, (Charles Thomas) Chuck (1940–) painter; born in Monroe, Wash. He studied at the University of Washington School of Art, Seattle (1960–62), Yale University (1962–64), and in Vienna, Austria (1964–65). A photo-realist painter of large portraits, as in *Phil* (1969), he was based in New York City beginning in 1967, and taught at several universities. Paralyzed from the neck down since 1988, he taught himself how to paint using mechanical and electronic aids.

Clurman, Harold (Edgar) (1901–1980) director, theater critic; born in New York City. One of the founders of the Group Theatre in 1931, he directed his first play, Clifford Odet's *Awake and Sing,* for the Group in 1935, and became its manager in 1936. He directed many important Broadway productions including *Member of the Wedding* (1950), *Bus Stop* (1955), and *A Touch of the Poet* (1958). From 1949 on, he was a theater critic and author of books.

Coase, Ronald (Harry) (1910–) economist; born in London, England. Educated in England, he worked as a statistician in the British War Cabinet before emigrating to the U.S.A. in 1951. After teaching at the University of Virginia (1958–64), he taught at the University of Chicago Law School from 1964 until his retirement in 1979. He is known for arriving at his theories by visiting work sites and for advancing his views in straightforward English as opposed to abstruse mathematics. Two journal articles in particular are the basis of his widespread influence: "The Nature of the Firm" (*Economics,* November 1937) analyzed the economics of "transaction costs," secondary expenses such as those involved in negotiating contracts and in other activities that affect business operations and decisions; and "The Problem of Social Cost" (*Journal of Law and Economics,* October 1960) spawned two subdisciplines: the economics of property rights and the economics of law. He was awarded the Nobel Prize in economics (1991).

Coatsworth, Elizabeth (Jane) (1893–1986) writer, poet; born in Buffalo, N.Y. She graduated from Vassar College, (1915) and Columbia University (M.A. 1916). She wrote popular books for young readers, including *The Cat Who Went to*

Heaven (1930) and *The Sod House* (1954), a story of immigrants who move to Kansas. She married Henry Beston, the naturalist, and settled in Nobleboro, Maine (1932).

Cobb, Frank Irving (1869–1923) editor; born in Shawnee County, Ky. Joining Joseph Pulitzer's *New York World* as editorial page editor and heir apparent in 1904, he was editor in chief from 1911 until his death; he spoke forcefully for liberal causes and became a close adviser to President Woodrow Wilson.

Cobb, (Tyrus Raymond) Ty (1886–1961) baseball player; born in Narrows, Ga. During his 24-year career as an outfielder for the Detroit Tigers and Philadelphia Athletics (1905–28), he compiled a lifetime batting average of .367, the highest in major league history. He batted .400 or higher in a season three times, and 12 times he led the American League in batting average, a major league record. He possessed exceptional speed and stole 892 bases in his career, the major league record until Lou Brock surpassed it in 1977. His 4,191 lifetime hits was the major league record until Pete Rose surpassed it in 1985. A ferocious competitor, Cobb's intense manner provoked controversy on and off the field. He managed the Tigers for six years (1921–26), but never finished higher than second place. Having made shrewd investments while a player, including the purchase of Coca-Cola stock, he lived comfortably throughout his retirement. Nicknamed "The Georgia Peach," he was the first player elected to baseball's Hall of Fame in 1936.

Cobbett, William (1763–1835) journalist, publicist; born in Surrey, England. After exposing corruption in the British Army, he fled in 1793 to the U.S.A. to avoid a court-martial. There he opened a bookshop, displayed royalist and Federalist sympathies, and under the pen name Peter Porcupine sharply attacked opposing politicians and journalists in a publication called *Porcupine's Gazette*. Often assailed by libel actions and threats of deportation, he overreached himself in attacking the influential Dr. Benjamin Rush for treating yellow fever through bleedings and purges; he lost a libel suit brought by Rush and was assessed $5,000, but fled before the verdict had been delivered. Back in England in 1800, he published a reform-minded newspaper, the *Register*. Returning to America in 1817, he farmed on Long Island and avoided political journalism; in 1819, after his house burned down, he again sailed to England, where he became an extremely influential voice for reforms to help the working class.

Coblentz, W. W. (William Weber) (1873–1962) physicist; born in North Lima, Ohio. He was a research associate at the Carnegie Institution (1903–05), then became chief of radiometry for the National Bureau of Standards (1905–45). He applied radiometry to astrophysics, infrared spectroscopy, and the standardization of ultraviolet light for medical purposes.

Coca, Imogene (1908–) television comedian; born in Philadelphia. Doe-eyed and pixieish, she enjoyed an extensive career in vaudeville and on Broadway before teaming up with Sid Caesar for *Your Show of Shows,* the acclaimed National Broadcasting Company comedy-variety series that ran from 1950 to 1954. She did not sustain her popularity after the Caesar-Coca partnership dissolved; in 1958 they reunited for a series that failed, as did her situation comedy *Grindle* (1963). She made rare appearances in later years.

Cochise (?1812–74) Chiricahua Apache chief; born in present-day Arizona or New Mexico. Initially friendly toward whites, he embarked on a campaign against them in 1861 after he had been imprisoned on the false charge of having kidnapped a white child. With the murder of his father-in-law, Mangas Coloradas, in 1863, he became the main war chief of the Apaches. For many years he engaged in a series of violent actions against white settlers and the U.S. Army, but he was gradually isolated in a smaller and smaller mountainous region. After winning assurances from the U.S. government that he and his band could remain in the Chiricahua Mountains, he surrendered in 1872.

Cochran, Jacqueline (1910–80) aviator; born in Pensacola, Fla. An orphan, her first career was as an owner of a profitable cosmetics company. Receiving her pilot's license in 1932, she was the first woman to fly in the Bendix transcontinental race three years later. She won the Bendix Trophy in 1938. The first woman to pilot a bomber across the Atlantic in World War II, she directed the Women's Air Force Service Pilots. In 1953 she became the first woman to fly faster than sound; in 1964 she flew faster than twice the speed of sound. At her death she held more flight records than any other pilot.

Cochrane, (Gordon Stanley) "Mickey" (1903–62) baseball player; born in Bridgewater, Mass. As a high-spirited catcher for the Philadelphia Athletics (1925–33) he helped them to three pennants and two world championships in 1929–31. With the Detroit Tigers as the manager/catcher (1934–37), "Black Mike" helped them to two pennants and one world championship. Early in the 1937 season, he was beaned at the plate; his skull fractured in three places, he remained unconscious and close to death for 10 days, but he gradually recovered; he never played again, but he remained as manager into August 1938.

Cocke, John (1925–) electrical engineer; born in Charlotte, N.C. Working at International Business Machines' Thomas J. Watson Research Center (1956), he invented RISC, the Reduced Instruction-Set Computer (1974–75). RISC technology enabled telephone-switching networks to handle 12 million instructions per second. His major research contributions were in systems architecture, hardware design, and program optimization.

Coddington, William (1601–1678) colonist; born in Boston, England. He came to Massachusetts in 1630. He protested against the trial of Anne Hutchinson (1637) and moved to Aquidneck (in Rhode Island) where he later became the governor. He also founded Newport, R.I., in 1639.

Codman, Ogden (1863–1951) interior designer; born in Boston, Mass. Following a youth in France and architecture studies, he opened an office in Boston (1891) and one in Newport (1893), where Edith Wharton hired him to decorate her house. Together they wrote the influential *Decoration of Houses* (1897), which promoted simplicity and suitability. His work on other Newport mansions was characterized by 18th-century French good taste.

Codrescu, Andrei (Betty Laredo, Maria Parfeni, Urmuz, pen names) (1946–) poet, writer; born in Sibiu, Romania. He studied at the University of Bucharest (B.A. 1965) and emigrated to America in 1966. He taught at numerous institutions, such as Johns Hopkins (1979–80), the University of Baltimore (1982–84), and Louisiana State University (1984). His first poetry collection, *License to Carry a Gun*

(1970), brought him critical acclaim, and his subsequent works of poetry and prose reveal a provocative, humorous, and surrealistic stylist. He produced several series for National Public Radio (NPR), and has been a commentator for NPR's "All Things Considered," and for Radio Free Europe. Among other editorial and journalistic positions, he was the editor of *Exquisite Corpse: A Monthly Review of Books and Ideas* (1983). A cross-country trip he took in his 1986 Cadillac convertible resulted in a movie, *Road Scholar* (1993).

Cody, John (Patrick) (1920–82) Catholic prelate; born in St. Louis, Mo. After ordination (1931) and service in the Vatican Secretariat of State, he held administrative posts in the U.S.A. Appointed coadjutor bishop of New Orleans (1961), he implemented the school integration plan of ailing Archbishop Joseph Rummel, succeeding to the see (1964) after Rummel's death. Named archbishop of Chicago (1965) and a cardinal (1967), he alienated clergy by his allegedly authoritarian policies. An investigation into charges that he had diverted church funds to benefit a female friend was suspended after his death.

Cody, (William Frederick) "Buffalo Bill" (1845–1917) frontiersman, showman; born in Scott County, Iowa. After his father died when he was 12, and with little formal education, he worked as a wagoner, trapper, and prospector before joining the Pony Express at age 14. During the Civil War, he served as a scout for the Union army's Ninth Kansas Cavalry (1863) and then with the Union forces in Tennessee and Missouri (1864–65). After the war he tried various ventures – running a hotel and freighting business, working on railroad construction – until in 1867–68 he became a buffalo hunter, supplying meat to the Kansas Pacific Railroad and gaining the nickname "Buffalo Bill." (He killed 4,280 buffalo by his own count.) He then became a civilian scout for the Fifth Cavalry (1868–72), fighting the Sioux and Cheyenne. (He was even awarded the Congressional Medal of Honor but it was revoked in 1917 because he had not been in the military.) In 1872 he appeared in a stageplay by E. Z. C. Judson, who under the pen name "Ned Buntline," also began to feature Buffalo Bill in a series of dime novels. Cody went back to the plains to raise cattle and scout again for the military (he was said to have killed and scalped the Cheyenne chief, Yellow Hand), but in 1883 he decided to capitalize on his fame by organizing "Buffalo Bill's Wild West Show." With himself as the star and with other talented marksmen and riders – including Annie Oakley – and featuring a mock battle with Indians, the show toured before appreciative audiences throughout America and Europe for 30 years. Financial troubles then closed his own show in 1913 but he went on performing for others almost to his death. Meanwhile, in the 1890s he had settled on a large tract given him by the state of Wyoming in the Bighorn Basin (later the site of Cody). He died unexpectedly in Denver and is buried on nearby Lookout Mountain, one of the archetypal American legends.

Coe, Michael D. (Douglas) (1929–) anthropologist, educator; born in New York City. He earned a Harvard Ph.D. and joined the faculty at Yale (1960). Author of numerous studies on pre-Columbian Mexico and Central America, including the *Atlas of Ancient America* (1986), he was advisor to the Robert Woods Bliss Collection of Pre-Columbian Art at Dumbarton Oaks (1963–80).

Coffin, Charles A. (Albert) (1844–1926) manufacturer; born in Somerset County, Maine. A shoe manufacturer in Lynn, Mass. he helped form the Lynn Syndicate (1883) to purchase the American Electric Company in Connecticut; the company was moved to Lynn as the Thomas-Houston Company. In 1892 it merged with the Edison Electric Company (N.Y.) and Coffin was elected president of the new firm, called General Electric Company (1892–1913). From 1913 to 1922 he chaired the board. Under his leadership the company grew to a million-dollar-a-day business. During World War I he created the War Relief Clearing House, later consolidated with the Red Cross. The Charles A. Coffin Foundation awards research fellowships to college students.

Coffin, Henry Sloane (1877–1954) Protestant clergyman, educator; born in New York City. He graduated from Yale in 1897 and studied abroad for two years before taking a divinity degree at Union Theological Seminary in 1900. An evangelical liberal, he held Presbyterian pastorates from 1904–26. As president of Union Seminary from 1926–45 he promoted open inquiry into theological issues. He retired in 1945 but remained active as a lecturer and preacher. His *Religion Yesterday and Today* appeared in 1940.

Coffin, William Sloane, Jr. (1924–) Protestant clergyman, social activist; born in New York City. He interrupted his studies at Yale to serve the U.S. Army as a liaison officer with the French and Russians (1943–47), then took his B.A. from Yale in 1949. He attended the Union Theological Seminary (New York City) (1949–50), then served abroad with the Central Intelligence Agency as a specialist on Russian affairs (1950–53). Ordained as a Presbyterian minister in 1956, he served as a chaplain at Phillips Andover Academy and Williams College before becoming the youngest chaplain in the history of Yale (1958–75). During his tenure there, he was one of 11 Freedom Riders to Montgomery, Ala. (1961), and was arrested on several occasions during the civil rights struggles of the 1960s. He was one of five individuals (Dr. Benjamin Spock was another) who were sued by the U.S. Department of Justice for conspiring to counsel draft resistance during the war in Vietnam (1968); the charges were dropped in 1970. (Yale graduate Garry Trudeau would lightly satirize him in his "Doonesbury" comic strip as the hip minister, "Rev. Scot Sloan.") He left Yale and became the senior minister at the Riverside Church in New York City (1977–87), where his social activism – offering sanctuary to Central American refugees and providing shelter to homeless people – again made him controversial. He resigned from the Riverside pastorate to become director of the SANE/FREEZE Campaign for Global Security (1988). The author of such works as *Civil Disobedience: Aid or Hindrance to Justice?* (with Morris L. Leibman, 1972), he described himself as a man having "a lover's quarrel with the United States."

Cogswell, Joseph Green (1786–1871) librarian; born in Ipswich, Mass. A graduate of Harvard (1806), he traveled for various merchant ventures, studying for a time at Göttingen, Germany. In 1820 he was named librarian of Harvard Library and professor of geology there; he reclassified the library on the Göttingen model. He helped establish the Round Hill School in Northampton, Mass. (1823), edited the *New York Review,* and was superintendent of the Astor Library in New York (1848–61).

Cohan, George M. (Michael) (1878–1942) actor, playwright, director; born in Providence, R.I. Author, composer, director, and often the high-spirited star of 20 musicals, he wrote many patriotic songs, including "You're a Grand Old Flag," "Give My Regards to Broadway," and "Over There." He began his career in vaudeville as a child with his family, one of The Four Cohans. His first Broadway production was *The Governor's Son* (1901); his first successful show was *Little Johnny Jones* (1904). Other shows include *Forty-five Minutes from Broadway* (1906), *Broadway Jones* (1912), *Hello, Broadway* (1914), and *The Song and Dance Man* (1923). He also adapted other people's works for the stage, including the mystery novel *Seven Keys to Baldpate.* He made successful appearances as an actor in Eugene O'Neill's *Ah, Wilderness!* (1934) and as the president in *I'd Rather Be Right* (1937). He wrote an autobiography, *Twenty Years on Broadway* (1925). His career inspired the movie *Yankee Doodle Dandy* (1942), starring James Cagney.

Cohen, Benjamin V. (Victor) (1894–1983) lawyer, government official; born in Muncie, Ind. A brilliant New York corporate lawyer (1922–33) he joined Roosevelt's "brain trust," co-drafting New Deal legislation including the Securities Act of 1933 and plans for the Tennessee Valley Authority. He helped to write the Lend-Lease plan (1941) and served in the United Nations (1948–52) before returning to private practice.

Cohen, Carolyn (1929–) biophysicist; born in Long Island City, N.Y. She was a Fulbright scholar in London (1954–55) and a researcher at the Children's Cancer Research Foundation (CCRF), Boston, Mass. (1955–56). After teaching at the Massachusetts Institute of Technology (1957–58), she returned to CCRF (1958–74) while concurrently performing research at various Boston area institutions and becoming a professor at Brandeis University (1972). She used electron microscopy and X-ray diffraction to elucidate sites of cell protein synthesis and to demonstrate both contractile proteins in muscle and fibrous protein development during blood coagulation.

Cohen, Gerson D. (1924–91) rabbi, historian; born in New York City. A graduate of City College of New York, he became librarian of the Jewish Theological Seminary of America (1950–57), then professor of history. He was also professor of Semitic languages at Columbia University. While he was chancellor of the seminary (1972–86), the first women were admitted to its Conservative rabbinical program.

Cohen, Joel (Israel) (1922–) lutenist, conductor; born in Providence, R.I. After studies at Brown and Harvard, and with Nadia Boulanger in Paris, in 1968 he became leader of the Boston Camerata, a leading early-music ensemble.

Cohen, Morris R. (Raphael) (1880–1947) philosopher; born in Minsk, Russia. Emigrating to the U.S.A. in 1892, he graduated from City College of New York (1900), earned a Harvard doctorate (1906), and taught at City College (1912–38) and the University of Chicago (1938–41). A magnetic teacher, he exhibited his naturalism and pragmatism in such works as *Reason and Nature* (1931) and made contributions to legal, political, and social philosophy. He often wrote for a general audience.

Cohen, Paul J. (Joseph) (1934–) mathematical logician; born in Long Branch, N.J. A National Academy of Sciences member, he taught longest at Stanford University (1964). Recipient of the Bocher Prize (1964) and National Medal of Science (1967), he included among his specialities axiomatic set theory, harmonic analysis, and partial differential equations.

Cohen, Stanley (1922–) cell biologist; born in New York City. He taught at the Universities of Michigan (1946–48) and Colorado (1948–52) before joining Rita Levi-Montalcini's laboratory at Washington University (St. Louis, Mo.) (1953–59). He discovered the epidermal growth factor from mouse tissue extract, which accelerated the maturation of newborn mice. He continued his studies of this substance at Vanderbilt University (1959–86), determining its amino acid sequence and action on cells and wound healing. In 1986, he and Levi-Montalcini received the Nobel Prize in physiology for their fundamental contributions to cell and organ development.

Cohen, Stephen F. (1938–) educator, Russia expert; born in Indianapolis, Ind. Known as a consultant and commentator on the former Soviet Union for National Broadcasting Company TV News, he served on the editorial board of *Slavic Review* and as associate editor of *World Politics.* He was also a member of the advisory council on the Soviet Union and Eastern Europe for the National Academy of Sciences, and of the board of directors of the American Committee on U.S.-Soviet Relations, among others. Teaching longest at Princeton in the Center for International Studies (1969), he directed the Russian Studies Program (1973–80) and was the author of many books and articles on Eastern Europe.

Cohn, Edwin J. (Joseph) (1892–1953) biochemist; born in New York City. A pioneer in protein chemistry, he spent his career at Harvard Medical School (1920–53). He performed research on pernicious anemia (1926–32), which led to the eventual isolation of vitamin B12 by other scientists. During World War II, he planned and directed blood fractionation programs for the armed forces; after the war he continued his research on medical uses of such blood components as plasma, gamma globulin, and albumin.

Cohn, Harry (1891–1958) movie executive; born in New York City. After a youth filled with odd jobs, including a short-lived vaudeville act with composer Harry Ruby, he became the personal secretary to Carl Laemmle, founder of Universal Pictures. In 1920, Cohn and his brother Jack Cohn (1889–1956) and Joseph Brandt started their own company, which in 1924 became Columbia Pictures. Regarded as ruthless and vulgar, Harry Cohn ruled the studio in a way that inspired fear and hatred, while personally developing stars like Rita Hayworth. Although he came to be known as "White Fang," he made Columbia Pictures one of the most successful studios.

Cohn, Mildred (1913–) biochemist, biophysicist; born in New York City. She performed research at Cornell (1938–46), then moved to Washington University (St. Louis, Mo.) (1946–60). She joined the University of Pennsylvania (1960–82), and remained active after retirement, serving the Institute for Cancer Research (Philadelphia) (1982–85) and lecturing as a visiting professor at various institutions. She made major advances in enzymology, the use of stable isotopes in metabolic studies, and in biophysical investigations of electron spin and nuclear magnetic resonance.

Cohn, Roy M. (Marcus) (1927–86) lawyer; born in New York City. Admitted to the N.Y. bar at the age of 21, he became assistant U.S. attorney for subversive activities and soon special assistant to the U.S. attorney general. Brilliant and arrogant, the "boy wonder" performed energetically at the Julius and Ethel Rosenberg spy trial. As chief counsel to Sen. Joseph McCarthy's Communist-hunting U.S. Senate permanent investigations subcommittee (1953–54), he was an often celebrated, often denigrated national figure. From 1954 to 1986, he became a political power broker and much-sought legal talent with Saxe, Bacon & Bolan (and predecessor firms) in New York City. Known as a loyal advocate, he gave lavish annual parties for his famous, fashionable clients and friends at his Greenwich, Conn., estate. Thrice tried and acquitted on federal charges of conspiracy, bribery, and fraud, he was disbarred two months before his death. He admired dogs and had an extensive collection of stuffed animals.

Colbert, Claudette (b. Claudette Lily Chauchoin) (1905–) movie/stage actress; born in Paris, France. Immigrating to New York City at age six, she studied to become a fashion designer but ended up acting on Broadway in 1923. Her screen debut came in *For the Love of Mike* (1927) and she went on to star in movies in many genres, reaching her peak in the sophisticated comedy, *It Happened One Night* (1934), for which she won the Academy Award for best actress. When she was no longer offered film roles to her taste, she returned to Broadway and starred in several popular plays.

Colbert, Lester (Lum) (1905–) automobile executive; born in Oakwood, Texas. A Harvard-trained lawyer, he practiced briefly in New York before joining Chrysler Corporation as an attorney; in his 30 years there (1933–65), he was president of the Dodge division (1946–51), president and chairman of Chrysler (1950–61), and chairman of Chrysler Corporation of Canada (1961–65).

Colburn, Zerah (1832–70) mechanical engineer, author; born in Saratoga Springs, N.Y. He worked on several railroads in the 1840s and 1850s. In 1850 he published *The Locomotive Engine* and later contributed numerous articles to journals. He was sent to research European railways, and the information he garnered led to significant improvements in U.S. railroad technology.

Colby, Charles (Carlyle) (1884–1965) geographer; born in Romeo, Mich. At the University of Chicago (1916–49), he became an authority on the economic geography of North America; three editions of his *Source Book for the Economic Geography of North America* were published (1921, 1922, 1926). His "Centrifugal and Centripetal Forces in Urban Geography" was published in 1933.

Colby, William Edward (1875–1964) lawyer, conservationist; born in Benicia, Calif. Trained as a lawyer, he specialized in forest and mining law. In his first important conservation battle, he joined John Muir in a failed effort to block the Hetch Hetchy Reservoir in Yosemite National Park. He campaigned for the expansion of Sequoia National Park and the creation of King's Canyon and Olympic National Parks and headed the California State Park Commission from 1927–37. He was a director of the Sierra Club for 49 years.

Colden, Cadwallader (1688–1776) physician, scientist, public official; born in Ireland. Of Scotch parentage, he studied at the University of Edinburgh and then studied medicine in London. He came to Philadelphia in 1710 and engaged in business while practicing medicine, then in 1718 moved to New York City where he took on several posts with the British colonial government. He continued to pursue his varied interests and wrote pioneering works about the Native

Americans, botany, physics, medical subjects such as cancer and yellow fever, psychology, and mathematics. As New York's lieutenant-governor (1761–75) he was a loyalist; upon refusing to sign a request from certain colonists to repeal the Stamp Act (1765), he was burned in effigy. He did his best to conduct government evenhandedly until the battle of Lexington signaled that history was taking a different course, so he effectively retired to his estate on Long Island.

Cole, Johnnetta Betsch (1936–) cultural anthropologist, academic administrator; born in Jacksonville, Fla. A graduate of Oberlin College, she received a Ph.D. from Northwestern in 1967 and taught at the University of California: Los Angeles, Washington State (where she headed the black studies program), the University of Massachusetts, and Hunter College (New York City). She became president of Spelman College, Atlanta, in 1987. She was author/editor of *All American Women* (1986) and *Anthropology for the Nineties* (1988).

Cole, Nat "King" (b. Nathaniel Adams Coles) (1917–65) musician; born in Birmingham, Ala. He was raised in Chicago, where he made his recording debut in 1936 with Eddie Cole's Solid Swingers, a sextet led by his brother. He toured with a *Shuffle Along* revue in 1937, then settled in Los Angeles where he played solo piano for a year. In 1939, he began recording for Decca with his original King Cole Trio, whose piano-bass-guitar instrumentation was widely copied by combos in the 1940s and 1950s. The group played in Hollywood and New York nightclubs until 1943, when it had its first national hit, "Straighten Up and Fly Right," featuring solo singing by Cole. Starting with "The Christmas Song" in 1946, he augmented his trio with a studio orchestra and gradually reduced the prominence of his piano playing, which had been highly influential among jazz musicians. By 1950, he had become the first black male to attain mainstream acceptance as a popular singer, and he released a continual series of hit records over the remainder of his career. In 1956–57, he was the first African-American to host his own network television show, but it failed to attract a national sponsor and was not renewed. In 1958 he portrayed W. C. Handy in the film biography *St. Louis Blues,* one of several motion pictures in which he appeared. A biography, *Unforgettable,* by Leslie Course, was published in 1991.

Cole, Thomas (1801–48) painter, poet; born in Lancashire, England. He and his family emigrated to Philadelphia (1819) to escape the industrial revolution. A founder of the Hudson River School, he influenced many artists, especially his pupil, Frederick E. Church. With his mastery of precise detail, his landscapes quickly brought him fame and comparison with his predecessor, Washington Allston. Notable paintings from this period include *The Oxbow* (1836), a view of the Connecticut River near Northampton, Mass., and *View on the Catskill, Early Autumn* (1837). After two trips to Europe (1829 and 1841), he moved between New York City and his home in Catskill, N.Y. His paintings became increasingly allegorical in nature, as in the series called *The Voyage of Life,* which includes *Childhood* (1839), *Youth* (1840), *Manhood* (1840), and *Old Age* (1840), and the five-painting series *The Course of Empire* (1836). His poems, now forgotten except for "The Lament of the Forest," appeared in periodicals of his day.

Coleman, Charles (Caryl) (1840–1928) painter; born in

Buffalo, N.Y. He studied in Europe (1866), and later lived on the Island of Capri, where he painted volcanic scenes.

Coleman, Cy (b. Seymour Kaufman) (1929–   ) composer; born in New York City. In the 1950s, with such collaborators as Carolyn Leigh, Betty Comden, Bob Fosse and Neil Simon, he began to write hit songs and scores for several landmark Broadway musicals including *Wildcat* (1960), *Sweet Charity* (1966), *On the Twentieth Century* (1978, Tony Award) and *Barnum* (1980). In the 1980s he wrote film scores and composed the music and lyrics for the Broadway musical *Welcome to the Club* (1989).

Coleman, James S. (Smoot) (1919–85) political scientist; born in Provo, Utah. He taught after 1953 at the University of California: Los Angeles, there founding the African Studies Center (1960). He is known for his studies of 20th-century Nigerian political history and middle African political elites, including the classic "Nationalism in Tropical Africa" (1954), *Nigeria* (1958), and the pioneering *Politics of the Developing Areas* (1960).

Coleman, James (Samuel) (1926–   ) sociologist, educator; born in Bedford, Ind. A Columbia University Ph.D., he taught at Johns Hopkins and the University of Chicago (1973). His landmark "Coleman Report," *Equality of Educational Opportunity* (1966), spurred school desegregation and higher federal funding. His many works on adolescence and youth include *High School Achievement* (1982).

Coleman, Ornette (1930–   ) jazz musician; born in Fort Worth, Texas. An iconoclastic saxophonist and composer, his experiments in free-form improvisation sharply divided the jazz establishment upon his emergence in 1959. Largely self-taught, he played in rhythm-and-blues bands before settling in Los Angeles in 1951, where he gradually formed a quartet of musicians who were receptive to his unorthodox ideas. He first recorded in 1958 and made his New York debut the following year. He made a series of important recordings in 1959–61 that shaped the direction of jazz for the next twenty years. A sporadic performing artist after the early 1960s, he occasionally led both a conventional jazz quartet and the rock band Prime Time, but turned increasingly to composition, producing several works for symphony orchestra in accordance with his "harmolodic theory."

Coleman, William (1766–1829) journalist; born in Boston, Mass. In 1801 he cofounded the *New York Evening Post*, which he edited under the supervision of Alexander Hamilton; its vituperative pro-Federalist editorials attracted many lawsuits, none of them successful.

Coleman, William T. (Thaddeus), Jr. (1920–   ) lawyer, cabinet officer; born in Philadelphia. Although his family was solidly middle class, he experienced his share of racial bigotry in his youth. His Harvard Law School education was interrupted by World War II service in the Army Air Corps (1943–45), but he returned to graduate first in his class. He joined one of Philadelphia's most prestigious law firms in 1952, becoming a full partner in 1956. He specialized in corporate, transportation, and civil rights law; in the latter, his chief contributions were in *Brown* v. *Board of Education* (banning school segregation) and *McLaughlin* v. *Florida* (allowing interracial marriage). He took on many part-time assignments for the federal government but turned down several offers of full-time appointments until he accepted President Gerald Ford's request to serve as secretary of transportation (1975–

77) – only the second African-American to hold a cabinet post. He then practiced corporate law in Washington.

Coles, Robert Martin (1929–   ) psychiatrist, author; born in Boston, Mass. Beginning in 1960 he was affiliated with the Harvard University Medical School, becoming professor of psychiatry and medical humanities in 1978. He devoted his professional life to the psychology of children and wrote the Pulitzer Prize-winning series *Children of Crisis* (1967–1978), which details the resilience and courage of young children in various "crisis" situations throughout the world.

Colfax, Schuyler (1823–85) vice-president, U.S. representative; born in New York City. He was a newspaperman and U.S. representative (Rep., Ind.; 1855–69). He and Ulysses Grant easily won the 1868 election. He was implicated in the Credit Mobilier scandal in 1872. He defended his receipt of 20 shares of the Credit Mobilier stock, but his reputation was ruined – only the near end of his term prevented a possible impeachment.

Colgrass, Michael (Charles) (1932–   ) composer; born in Chicago. American-trained as a composer and percussionist, he was already known internationally when he won the Pulitzer Prize in 1978 for his orchestral work *Déjà Vu*.

Collamer, Jacob (1792–1865) judge, U.S. representative/senator; born in Troy, N.Y. He served in the War of 1812 and then practiced law in Vermont (1813–33). He was judge of the Vermont Superior Court (1833–42, 1850–54). He served in the U.S. House of Representatives (Whig, Vt.; 1843–49) and was U.S. postmaster general (1849–50). As a U.S. senator from Vermont (Rep., 1855–65) he played an important role in granting broad powers to the federal government in fighting the Civil War. Vermont placed his statue in the U.S. Capitol.

Collier, John (1884–1968) social reformer, government official; born in Atlanta, Ga. He worked primarily as a social worker with immigrants in New York City (1908–19) before moving to California and focusing his interests on Native Americans. As founder and head of the American Indian Defense Association (1923–33), he gained a reputation as an outspoken proponent of Indians' rights. This led President Franklin Roosevelt to appoint him commissioner of Indian Affairs (1933–45); he obtained passage of the Indian Reorganization Act of 1934, which ended the hated land-allotments policy, and generally promoted more progressive policies for Native Americans. He was president of the National Indian Institute (1945–50), one of the founders of the Inter-American Institute of the Indian in Mexico City (1940), and organizer and president of the Institute of Ethnic Affairs in Washington, D.C., (1947–68). He taught at City College of New York (1947–54) and Knox College in Illinois (1955–56). He wrote several books, including *Indians of the Americas* (1947) and *From Every Zenith* (1963).

Collins, Edward Knight (1802–78) shipowner; born in Truro, Mass. He moved to New York City and worked in the shipping business from the age of 15. In 1831 he took over and improved lines that shipped to Vera Cruz and New Orleans. In 1836 he launched his transatlantic Dramatic Line, naming the sailing ships after actors. In 1847, with a Congressional subsidy and supervision by the U.S. Navy, he began building five steamships to compete with the British Cunard steamships and formed the United States Mail Steamship Company. The first ship was launched in 1850 and proved faster than Cunard's ships. In 1854 all passengers – including Collins' wife, son, and daughter – drowned when his *Artic* collided in fog with a small French steamer off Cape Race and sank. After the *Pacific* was lost at sea in 1856, Congress gave six months notice that it was canceling its subsidy. He sold his remaining three ships (1858) and turned to coal and iron interests in Ohio.

Collins, (Edward Trowbridge) Eddie, Sr. (1887–1951) baseball player; born in Millerton, N.Y. As a second baseman for the Philadelphia Athletics and Chicago White Sox (1906–30), he compiled a lifetime batting average of .333. An honest member of the 1919 "Black Sox" team that deliberately lost the World Series, he was elected to the Hall of Fame in 1939.

Collins, J. (Joseph) Lawton (1896–1987) soldier; born in New Orleans. Commanding the 25th Infantry Division, he cleared Japanese forces from Guadalcanal in January 1943. Transferred to the European Theater, he took the VII Corps ashore at Utah Beach, Normandy, on June 6, 1944, and led the Corps, often in the vanguard of the American troops, to a junction with the Russians on the Elbe in the spring of 1945. He served as Army chief of staff from 1949–53.

Collins, Michael (1930–) astronaut, museum director; born in Rome, Italy. As an astronaut he performed two space walks on the Gemini 10 mission (1966) and piloted the Apollo 11 command module, which circled the moon as the first manned vehicle landed there. Director of the Smithsonian Institution's National Air and Space Museum (1971–78), and vice-president of LTV Aerospace and Defense Co. (1980–85), he founded his own firm (1985). He authored *Carrying the Fire* (1974), an account of his experiences in the space program.

Colman, Benjamin (1673–1747) Protestant clergyman; born in Boston, Mass. He graduated from Harvard in 1692 and later studied theology there. After a period in England, he returned to Boston to become pastor of the Brattle Street Church, which had been organized on more liberal principles than those of the city's three established churches. He was an enthusiastic supporter of the Great Awakening revival movement and wrote prolifically on religious subjects.

Colman, Samuel, Jr. (1832–1920) painter; born in Portland, Maine. He studied with Asher B. Durand in New York, and then abroad (1860–62 and 1871–75). Based in Newport, R.I., he painted Hudson River views as well as western landscapes, such as *Ships of the Plains* (1872).

Colt, Samuel (1814–62) inventor, manufacturer; born in Hartford, Conn. An indifferent student, he worked in his father's dye and bleaching establishment (1824–27, 1831–32) and was sent away to sea (1830–31). While at sea, he made a wooden model of an automatically revolving breech pistol and on returning to the U.S.A. he made metal models. To support his work he went on a tour as "Dr. Coult," lecturing on the marvels of chemistry. By 1836 he had patents on his pistol in England, France, and the U.S.A. and began to manufacture them in Paterson, N.J. His factory was one of the most innovative in its use of mass-production technique, and the Colt "six shooter" caught on with individuals – especially in the American West – but not with the U.S. Army. The company failed in 1842. Colt turned his attention to developing underwater mines and telegraph cable. When the Mexican War began (1846), the army placed an order for 1,000 revolvers; he had to subcontract the work to Eli Whitney's factory (in Whitneyville, Conn.) but by 1848 he was making the revolver in his own grand factory in Hartford, Conn. He directed Colt's Patent Fire Arms Manufacturing Company until his death.

Colter, John (?1775–1813) trapper, explorer; born in or near Staunton, Va. He served on the Lewis and Clark expedition (1804–06) and then explored the Yellowstone area alone. He was wounded in an Indian fight (1808) and returned to St. Louis, Mo.

Colton, Frank Benjamin (1923–) chemist, inventor; born in Bialystok, Poland. He emigrated to the U.S.A. in 1934, was educated at Northwestern University (Ill.) and the University of Chicago and, as a researcher at the Mayo Foundation, helped develop an improved synthesis of cortisone. His pioneering work in steroid chemistry led in 1960 to the development of Enovid, the first oral contraceptive, for which he was patentee. He worked for G. D. Searle and Company from 1951 until his retirement in 1986.

Coltrane, John (William) (1926–67) jazz musician; born in Hamlet, N.C. Originally an alto saxophonist, he moved to Philadelphia after graduating from high school, where he had received his first formal training. He played with a local group in 1945, then spent part of his military service from 1945 to 1946 in a U.S. Navy band stationed in Hawaii. He studied woodwinds at the Granoff Studios and the Ornstein School of Music in Philadelphia during the late 1940s. Initially a disciple of Charlie Parker, he played alto and tenor saxophones in a succession of bands led by King Kolax, Eddie "Cleanhead" Vinson, Dizzy Gillespie, Earl Bostic, and Johnny Hodges between 1947 and 1954. By 1955, when he joined Miles Davis's celebrated quintet, he was playing tenor saxophone exclusively and gaining recognition for his distinctive "sheets of sound" style. He left Davis in 1957, began a series of free-lance recordings under his own leadership, and played a formative engagement with Thelonious Monk at the Five Spot in New York for six months. After a period of permanent rehabilitation from drug and alcohol addiction, he rejoined Davis from 1958 to 1960 and was profoundly influenced by the trumpeter's experiments in modal improvisation. In May 1960, following the critical acclaim of his recording *Giant Steps,* he began leading his own quartet. Later that year, his recording *My Favorite Things,* featuring his first use of the soprano saxophone, was a major jazz hit. For the next five years, while his quartet maintained a continual touring schedule in the U.S.A. and Europe, his quest for musical self-renewal made him one of the most revered and controversial figures in jazz. He embraced the new generation of free jazz exponents, and his music gradually reflected his interest in Eastern music and philosophy on such recordings as *Om, Ascension,* and *A Love Supreme.* He also emerged as the most influential and widely imitated saxophonist in jazz, his intensely emotional attack and dense flow of notes becoming hallmarks of the next generation of saxophone players. He led a variety of ensembles during the last two years of his life, working only sporadically while suffering from the liver cancer that claimed him at age 41.

Combs, (Bertram Thomas) Bert (1911–) governor; born in Manchester, Ky. A lawyer, he served on General MacArthur's staff (1942–46), prosecuting Japanese war criminals. Returning to his law practice in Prestonburg, Ky., he became Court of Appeals judge (1951–55). As Democratic governor (1959–63), he instituted a merit system for state employees and reformed election procedures. Returning to his law practice afterward, he also served as U.S. Court of Appeals judge (1967–70).

Combs, Moses (Newell) (1753–1834) manufacturer, philanthropist; born in Morris County, N.J. A Revolutionary War veteran and tanner and shoemaker, he became known as the "Father of Newark industries." He opened an evening school that was probably the first in the U.S.A. and which later became tuition-free. He was also a religious leader in the Newark community.

Comden, Betty (1915–) librettist, lyricist; born in New York City. With lyricist Adolph Green and the Revuers, she performed original songs and sketches at New York clubs in the 1930s and 1940s. She and Green established a reputation as librettists and lyricists of the musical *On the Town* (1944), in which they also appeared. For over four decades they collaborated on librettos and/or lyrics for a string of other Broadway hits or Hollywood musicals such as *Wonderful Town* (1953) and *The Bells are Ringing* (1956). They enjoyed their last hit with the lyrics for *The Will Rogers Follies* (1991).

Comiskey, (Charles Albert) Charlie (1859–1931) baseball player/executive; born in Chicago. After his 13-year career as one of baseball's great pioneer players (1882–94), he became owner of the Chicago White Sox from its inception in 1901 until his death in 1931. Although "The Old Roman," as he was known, financed the building of a palatial stadium, Comiskey Park, in 1910, it was his penuriousness with salaries that provoked eight of his players to "fix" the 1919 "Black Sox" World Series, the only blemish on his Hall of Fame career (elected 1939).

Commager, Henry Steele (1902–) historian; born in Pittsburgh, Pa. He was educated at the University of Chicago (Ph.D. 1928) and the Universities of Copenhagen, Cambridge, and Oxford. He taught at New York University (1926–38), Columbia University (1939–56), and Amherst College (1956). His best-known book, *The Growth of the American Republic* (1931), coauthored with Samuel Eliot Morison, remains a standard undergraduate text. *Documents of American History* (1934) marked the beginning of the editing and publishing of anthologies of source materials of the American historical record, for which Commager was a pioneer. He became a strong critic of 1950s anticommunist conformity, writing in *Civil Liberties under Attack* (1951), "The great danger that threatens us is neither heterodox nor orthodox thought, but the absence of thought." He continued to argue for free speech and enquiry during the Vietnam era, asserting that the idealism of the 1960s was a renaissance, not a repudiation, of American Revolutionary ideals. Unlike many of his professional colleagues, he also wrote for more popular media and often spoke out on contemporary issues. He was also noted for a lucid style that combined a keen critical viewpoint with an absence of cant and jargon.

Commoner, Barry (1917–) biologist, educator, environmental activist; born in New York City. A graduate of Columbia University, with a Ph.D. from Harvard (1941), he taught at Washington University (St. Louis) (1947–76) before becoming head of the Center for the Biology of Natural Systems, a New York City energy and environmental research center. Through lecturing and writing he had a wide influence as an environmentalist; *Time* magazine called him "a professor with a class of millions." He became increasingly more outspoken on behalf of environmental causes and ran for president of the U.S.A. in 1980 on the Citizen's Party ticket. His book *Making Peace with the Planet* appeared in 1990.

Commons, John Rogers (1882–1945) economist; born in Hollandsburg, Ohio. He was both an economic theorist and a renowned labor historian. Without ever completing his graduate studies, he was able to secure teaching positions including a professorship at the University of Wisconsin in 1904. An active policymaker, he drafted early employment and union legislation in Wisconsin and then at the federal level.

Como, Perry (1912–) popular singer; born in Canonsburg, Pa. As a young man he worked as a barber. He sang with the Ted Weems band for six years and recorded many hit records in the 1940s and 1950s, including "Temptation" (1945). His popularity on radio and on his television show, *The Kraft Music Hall*, earned him the nickname "Mr. C." Known for his smooth baritone crooning, he released the hit song "It's Impossible" in 1970 and was one of the most commercially successful popular singers.

Compton, Arthur H. (Holly) (1892–1962) physicist; born in Wooster, Ohio. He studied and taught at Cambridge and several American universities before joining the University of Chicago (1923–45). He shared the 1927 Nobel Prize in physics for his determination of the increased wavelength of X-rays and gamma rays due to photon and electron scattering, now known as the Compton effect. In spite of his religious doubts, he played a major part in developing the atomic bomb. Compton became chancellor of Washington University, St. Louis, Mo. (1945–54), and remained there until 1961.

Comstock, Anthony (1844–1915) reformer; born in New Canaan, Conn. A Civil War veteran, he worked as a shipping clerk and retail salesman (1865–73), eventually in New York City, and pursued legal actions against book dealers selling allegedly obscene material. In 1873 he won passage of federal legislation prohibiting the mailing of obscene material. From 1875 on, as secretary to the New York Society for the Suppression of Vice, he zealously opposed activities he considered immoral, often conducting sensational raids. His targets included writers and publishers, abortionists, dispensers of contraceptives, and art galleries with "indecent" pictures; although not as well known for this in later years, it is also true that he fought quacks and purveyors of patent medicines and as such was a precursor of the consumer protection movement. He lost a legal battle to ban a production of George Bernard Shaw's play *Mrs. Warren's Profession* in New York (1905); it was Shaw who coined the word "comstockery" from Comstock's name. Comstock boasted of having destroyed "160 tons of obscene literature" in his lifetime and driven 15 people to suicide.

Comstock, Henry (Tompkins Paige) (1820–70) prospector; born in Trent, Ontario, Canada. He went to Nevada in 1856 and claimed the ground where (1859) was found the silver lode that was given his name. He sold his right for a small sum and turned to prospecting and road-building elsewhere.

Conant, James Bryant (1893–1978) chemist, diplomat, educator; born in Dorchester, Mass. A Harvard-educated organic chemist noted for his work on chlorophyll and hemoglobin, he taught at Harvard (1916–33) and was president there (1933–53), where he strengthened the professional schools, increased the geographic and social diversity of students, opened the university to women, and introduced curricular reforms. Conant chaired the National Defense Research Committee (1941–46), which developed the atomic bomb, and was instrumental in the targeting of Hiroshima, Japan. He helped found the National Science Foundation (1950). His diplomatic career in the 1950s included four years as high commissioner and ambassador to West Germany. Finally turning toward the reform of public education, Conant conducted an extensive Carnegie Corporation study of American high schools which resulted in *The American High School Today* (1959). His many other educational contributions include *Slums and Suburbs* (1961), *The Education of American Teachers* (1963), and *The Comprehensive High School* (1967).

Conant, Kenneth (John) (1894–1984) architectural historian; born in Neenah, Wis. Himself Harvard trained, he taught generations of architectural historians at Harvard (1920–55) and wrote *Carolingian and Romanesque Architecture 800–1200* (1959); he devoted decades to research on the monastic church at Cluny, France. His object-oriented, technical historiography fell out of fashion after the 1940s.

Conboy, Sara (Agnes McLaughlin) (1870–1928) labor leader; born in Boston, Mass. She started factory work at age 11 and became a skilled weaver. She led a carpet factory strike (1909–10) and became an organizer, and later the secretary-treasurer of the United Textile Workers. She was one of five women who were appointed to the Council of National Defense in World War I. She was the first woman to be an American delegate to the British Trades Union Congress (1920) and the first woman bank director in New York State (1923).

Condit, Carl W. (Wilbur) (1914–   ) architectural historian; born in Cincinnati, Ohio. A professor at Northwestern University (1945–82), this historian of building technology published important studies of 19th- and 20th-century American buildings and the Chicago School (1964), and technological histories of Chicago, Cincinnati, and the Port of New York.

Condon, (Albert Edwin) Eddie (1905–73) jazz musician; born in Goodland, Ind. He was a wit and a raconteur, a nightclub proprietor, a guitarist, and a member of Chicago's fabled "Austin High Gang" of the 1920s.

Condon, E. U. (Edward Uhler) (1902–74) physicist; born in Alamogordo, N.M. He taught at Princeton (1928–37), then worked at Westinghouse Laboratories (1937–45), where he took leave to be assistant director of the Manhattan Project. While at the National Bureau of Standards (1945–51), he was attacked by Congress for being a "weak link" in atomic security (1948), but was later vindicated by President Truman. He worked at Corning Glass (1951–54), was a professor at Washington University, St. Louis, Mo. (1956–63), then became an astrophysicist at the University of Colorado (1963–70). He made major contributions to nuclear and solid state physics, and Air Force-sponsored UFO research.

Cone, Claribel (1864–1929) **and Etta** (1870–1949) art collectors; both born in Jonesboro, Tenn. Their family moved to Baltimore (c. 1870), and their brothers founded the Cone Mills, a textile business. The sisters studied locally, and Claribel attended the Woman's Medical College of Baltimore, Md., then worked in the pathology laboratory of the newly founded Johns Hopkins Medical School (1894–1903). Together the sisters established an artistic salon and began collecting antiques, textiles, and modern paintings. They were friends of Gertrude and Leo Stein, who briefly lived in Baltimore (1891), and the sisters became frequent guests of the Steins in France. The sisters amassed an impressive collection of modern and contemporary French art during their trips abroad. After both sisters died, funds and their collection were bequeathed to the Baltimore Museum of Art.

Cone, (Fairfax Mastick) Fax (1903–77) advertising executive; born in San Francisco. He worked at the advertising agency Lord and Thomas (1929–42), which he took over with Don Belding and Emerson Foote (1942). As chairman and president he helped to build Foote, Cone and Belding into a major international agency. A copywriter known for directness, he created among other campaigns the long-running Clairol "Does she . . . or doesn't she?" slogan.

Cone, James Hal (1938–   ) Protestant theologian; born in Fordyce, Ark. He graduated from Philander Smith College (1958), received a Ph.D. from Northwestern, and taught at two small colleges before becoming a professor of theology at Union Theological Seminary in New York City in 1976. His *A Black Theology of Liberation* (1970) contained an angry critique of the presuppositions of white theologians. A more measured statement of his views, *God of the Oppressed*, followed in 1975; his autobiographical *My Soul Looks Back* appeared in 1987.

Cone, Moses H. (Herman) (1857–1908) merchant, manufacturer; born in Jonesboro, Tenn. He left his father Herman Cone's wholesale grocery in Baltimore in 1891 to form the Cone Export & Commission Company in New York City, a marketer of Southern cloth mill-goods. When the company grew to 40 clients, Herman dissolved his grocery and joined Moses. In 1893 they moved to Greensboro, N.C., where Moses built a denim mill (1895). In 1901 he bought a 3,750-acre estate at Blowing Rock, N.C., and began raising apple trees.

Conklin, Edwin G. (Grant) (1863–1952) developmental biologist; born in Waldo, Ohio. He was a professor at Ohio Wesleyan (1891–94), then moved to Northwestern (1894–96) and the University of Pennsylvania (1896–1908). He joined Princeton (1908–33), remaining active in national and international academic affairs after retirement. A specialist in the embryology of marine organisms, he stressed the importance of the cytoplasm during the development of the fertilized egg. He was both a religious person and an avid evolutionist who interpreted Darwin's theories to lay and scientific audiences.

Conklin, George T., Jr. (1914–   ) financial executive; born in Merrick, N.Y. He graduated from Dartmouth in 1937 and took an advanced degree from New York University in 1943. Director of the Guardian Life Insurance Company (New York City), he served as chairman of the National Bureau of Economic Research.

Conkling, Roscoe (1829–1888) U.S. representative/senator; born in Albany, N.Y. Son of a prominent judge and himself a lawyer, he served in the U.S. House of Representatives (Rep., N.Y.; 1859–63, 1865–67) and the U.S. Senate (1867–81). Famed for his florid oratory, he was one of the most influential politicians of his day, leader of the powerful New York Republican machine and an open foe of civil service reform. Nominated and confirmed for a Supreme Court seat after his resignation from the Senate in 1881, he declined and instead became a corporate lawyer.

Connally, (Thomas Terry) Tom (1877–1963) U.S. representative/senator; born near Waco, Texas. A lawyer, he served in the U.S. House of Representatives (Dem., Tex.; 1917–29) and the U.S. Senate (1929–53). He was a conservative on domestic policy, supporting Southern business interests and opposing anti-lynching legislation; but he was an influential internationalist on foreign policy issues, supporting U.S. participation in the United Nations and the North Atlantic Treaty Organization.

Connell, Evan S. (Shelby), Jr. (1924–) writer; born in Kansas City, Mo. After graduate study at Columbia, Stanford, and San Francisco State Universities, he lived in California, edited *Contact* magazine (1959–65), and wrote a wide range of verse, realistic fiction, and nonfiction. His many books include the novels *Mrs. Bridge* (1959) and *Mr. Bridge* (1969), and the best-selling historical work *Son of the Morning Star* (1984).

Connelly, (Marcus Cook) Marc (1890–1980) writer; born in McKeesport, Pa. A transplanted Pittsburgh drama critic, he was prominent in New York's literary and theatrical world in the 1920s as a founder of the *New Yorker* (1925) and member of the Algonquin Round Table. He collaborated with George S. Kaufman on half a dozen hit plays and musicals (1921–24) and wrote radio scripts, screenplays, and drama (including *Green Pastures* (1930, Pulitzer Prize)). He wrote his last play for Helen Hayes in 1977.

Connelly, Mother Cornelia (b. Cornelia Augusta Peacock) (1809–79) Catholic religious foundress; born in Philadelphia. She converted to Catholicism (1835), as did her husband, an Episcopalian priest. They separated, he became a Catholic priest (1845), and she founded the Society of the Holy Child Jesus, moving to England to begin its work (1846). The order also started schools in the U.S.A., which she visited. Her husband later renounced his conversion and sought unsuccessfully to regain marital rights.

Conner, Bruce (1933–) independent filmmaker; born in McPherson, Kans. Also an artist and art teacher, he specialized in 16mm films, such as *Cosmic Ray* (1962) and *America Is Waiting* (1981).

Conner, David (1792–1856) naval officer; born in Harrisburg, Pa. He served with distinction in the War of 1812. As commander of the Home Squadron (1843–47) he meticulously planned the amphibious landing of General Winfield Scott's troops at Veracruz. His plans were later studied as a precedent for World War II amphibious landings.

Conner, Fox (1874–1951) soldier; born in Slate Springs, Miss. An 1898 West Point graduate, he served in a series of staff positions in a long career, including assistant chief of staff for operations, American Expeditionary Force, in France (1917). As a writer on military subjects, he achieved a reputation as a thoughtful student of the military problems of his time.

Connolly, Maureen (Catherine) (1934–69) tennis player; born in San Diego, Calif. In 1953 she became the first woman to win in the same year the four major championships that comprise the Grand Slam of tennis: the U.S., Australian, British, and French titles. Nicknamed "Little Mo," a horse riding accident in 1954 ended her career in active competition.

Connolly, (Thomas Henry) Tom (1870–1961) baseball umpire; born in Manchester, England. His family moved to Natick, Mass., when he was 13. As an American League umpire (1901–31), he umpired the first ever American League game in 1901 and the first ever World Series game in 1903. He was elected to baseball's Hall of Fame in 1953.

Connors, (James Scott) Jimmy (1952–) tennis player; born in Belleville, Ill. A left-hander who specialized in the two-handed backhand, he won Wimbledon twice (1974, 1982), the Australian Open (1974), and the U.S. Open five times (1974, 1976, 1978, 1982–83). In 1984 he became the first player ever to win 100 singles titles. Noted in his early years for his boisterous behavior that defied the traditionally decorous manners of tennis, he played on for so many years that he came to seem almost mellow.

Conolly, Richard L. (1892–1962) naval officer; born in Waukegan, Ill. Following destroyer service in World War I, he commanded the task force which recaptured Guam in 1944. He was president of the Naval War College (1950–53) and of Long Island University (1953–62).

Conover, Harry (Sayles) (1911–65) modeling agency founder; born in Chicago. A radio performer and model throughout the 1930s, he founded a New York modeling agency (1939). The fresh-faced beauty of "Conover Cover Girls" (a term he invented) graced leading magazines until a financial scandal closed his business (1959).

Conover, Willis (Clark, Jr.) (1920–) broadcaster; born in Buffalo, N.Y. Beginning in 1939, he promoted concerts and hosted jazz and classical programs at radio stations in Washington, D.C. In 1955, his jazz program, *Music USA*, began daily broadcast on the Voice of America. Although unheard and little-known in the U.S.A., he eventually attracted the largest audience of any continuing international broadcast in history, and served as the primary source of jazz for listeners in the Soviet Union, Eastern Europe, and Cuba throughout the cold war. He emceed the Newport Jazz Festivals between 1954–63, and in 1969 he produced and narrated the White House concert celebrating Duke Ellington's 70th birthday. He was instrumental in the establishment of a jazz panel on the National Endowment for the Arts in 1975.

Conroy, Jack (Jack Wesley) (1899–1990) editor, writer; born near Moberly, Mo. After working as a migrant laborer in the 1920s, he began writing for magazines about Depression-era unemployment. In 1933 he published the semi-autobiographical book, *The Disinherited* (1933), which remains a classic proletarian novel. He was founding editor of the leftist journals, *The Anvil* (1933–37) and *The New Anvil* (1939–41). He was senior associate editor of *New Standard Encyclopedia,* Chicago (1947–66).

Constantine, Eddie (1917–93) movie actor, singer; born in Los Angeles. The son of a Russian immigrant opera baritone, he studied voice in Vienna and sang in the chorus at Radio City Music Hall before following his wife, dancer Helene Mussel, to Paris where he established himself as a nightclub singer, and later, as an actor. He became widely known as protégé and friend of Edith Piaf. His film credits include a series of French action thrillers in which he played a tough, hard-drinking American private eye, Lemmy Caution. He also wrote a novel, *La Proprietaire,* published in English in 1976 as *The Godplayer.*

Converse, Edmund Cogswell (1849–1921) inventor, philanthropist; born in Boston, Mass. He invented a lock-joint for tubing and brought millions of dollars in business to his father's National Tube Works in Pennsylvania. He was active in the 1899 merger into the National Tube Company. He was president and director of many corporations (1903–14). He gave generously of his $30 million estate to both institutions and individuals.

Converse, Harriet (Arnot) Maxwell (1836–1903) author, defender of Indian rights; born in Elmira, N.Y. She lived in New York City after 1866, writing essays and romantic verse. Devoting herself after 1881 to studying and preserving Iroquois culture, she published works no longer highly regarded, but, more lastingly, she collected Indian artifacts for major museums and successfully defended Native Americans' property rights in several lawsuits.

Converse, Philip E. (Ernest) (1928–) political scientist; born in Concord, N.H. Beginning in 1960 he taught at the University of Michigan, becoming the Angell Distinguished Professor of Political Science and Sociology in 1975. He endorsed a behavioral approach to political science and had a special interest in political elections.

Conway, Jill Ker (1934–) historian, educator; born in Hillston, Australia. Raised on a sheep ranch, she became a historian at the University of Sydney, Australia, leaving in 1960 for Harvard. She taught women's history at the University of Toronto (1964–75), becoming Smith College's first woman president (1975–85). A visiting professor at Massachusetts Institute of Technology, she wrote a best-selling memoir, *The Road from Coorain* (1989) and continued her academic contributions to women's history.

Conwell, Russell (Herman) (1843–1925) lawyer, Baptist minister, lecturer; born in South Worthington, Mass. Raised on his family farm, which was a station on the Underground Railroad, even as a youth he was an impassioned orator on the rights of all men and women. He volunteered for the Union army and was commissioned as "the boy Captain" at age 19. Severely wounded at the battle of Kenesaw Mountain in June 1864, he was left for dead and later credited the experience with converting him to Christianity. He was admitted to the bar in 1865 and moved to Minneapolis, Minn., where he established a law practice and founded a daily newspaper. Returning to Massachusetts, he became pastor of a moribund Baptist church in Lexington. In 1882 he took charge of the Grace Baptist Church in Philadelphia; his enormous Baptist Temple opened there in 1891. In 1888 the night school he founded under the church auspices became Temple College. A well-known lecturer on the Chautauqua circuit, his most famous lecture was his optimistic, platitudinous "Acres of Diamonds," which he delivered some 6,000 times, thereby earning millions of dollars that he left to endow Temple College.

Cooder, (Ryland Peter) Ry (1947–) musician; born in Los Angeles. A versatile studio session guitarist, beginning in 1965 he recorded with many leading rock bands, including the Rolling Stones. In 1978 he began a second career as a motion picture soundtrack composer and producer for such movies as *Crossroads, The Long Riders,* and *Paris, Texas.*

Cook, Frederick Albert (1865–1940) explorer, physician; born in Calicoon Depot, N.Y. He was the surgeon and ethnologist on Robert E. Peary's Greenland expedition (1891–92) and he returned to Greenland in 1893, 1894, 1897, and 1901–02. He claimed to have made the first ascent of Mount McKinley (1906) and to have reached the North Pole on April 21, 1908 (one year before Robert E. Peary). An investigative committee discredited both of these claims. He

led an expedition around the world (1915–16), founded a Texas oil company, and was imprisoned (1925–29) for mail fraud. He received an unconditional pardon from President Franklin D. Roosevelt just before his death.

Cook, Joe (1890–1959) comedian; born in Evansville, Ind. A vaudeville star, he was a whirlwind of activity on stage, playing instruments, juggling, and doing sight gags on Broadway in the 1920s and 1930s.

Cook, Will Marion (1869–1944) composer, conductor; born in Washington, D.C. Son of the first African-American lawyer in Washington, D.C., he studied composition and the violin in the classical tradition at Oberlin Conservatory of Music (Ohio) and under Josef Joachim and Anton Dvorak in Europe. Convinced that he would not be taken serious as a classical musician because of his race, he turned to composing works that drew on the idioms and themes of African-American folklore and music. Throughout the 1890s and 1900s, he composed for the stage shows of Bert Williams, the leading black comic and vaudevillian. In 1889 Cook produced and wrote the music for *Clorindy, the Origin of the Cakewalk,* the first musical comedy written, directed, and performed entirely by African-American artists; it enjoyed success on Broadway and in London. He went on to compose the music for a number of popular black musicals, including *In Dahomey* (1903) and *Abyssinia* (1906), but his reliance on ragtime left him behind the changing tastes. He led his Southern Syncopated Orchestra, a huge ragtime and concert ensemble, and composed "I'm Coming, Virginia" and "Mammy" in the 1910s. In 1919, on its last tour of Europe before disbanding, the orchestra and its saxophonist Sidney Bechet received enthusiastic reviews from Ernst Ansermet for an emerging jazz style. Cook free-lanced thereafter with New York music publishers and was an influence on Duke Ellington's early work as a composer. His wife, Abbie Mitchell Cook (1884–1960), was a soprano who had a career first in his shows and then in other productions. Their son, Mercer Cook (1903), was a noted scholar at Howard University and served as U.S. ambassador to Nigeria and Senegal.

Cooke, (Alfred) Alistair (1906–) journalist, television host; born in Manchester, England. After studying at Yale, he was naturalized in 1941, broadcasting *Letter from America* for British Broadcasting Corporation Radio, also writing for *The Guardian* (1948–72). Urbane host of the cultural television magazine *Omnibus* (1952–60), he created the National Broadcasting Company series *America: A Personal History of the United States* in the 1970s. He hosted Public Broadcasting System's *Masterpiece Theatre* (1971–92) and became such a fixture on television that he was often the subject of genial parodies.

Cooke, Jay (1821–1905) financier; born in Sandusky, Ohio. In 1839 he went to work for the Philadelphia banking house of E. W. Clark and Co., becoming a partner at age 21. As head of Jay Cooke & Co. (1861–73), he gained acclaim for selling $500 million worth of Civil War bonds for the U.S. Treasury Department in 1862, then repeating this in 1865. His attempts to finance the Northern Pacific Railway failed, triggering the panic of 1873. By 1880 he had recovered his wealth by investing in Utah mining interests.

Cooke, John (Esten) (1830–86) writer; born in Winchester, Va. He earned a national reputation with historical romances set in old Virginia, such as *The Virginia Comedians* (1854).

His Civil War service with the Confederate army inspired him to write war novels and biographies of "Stonewall" Jackson (1863) and R. E. Lee (1871). Returning to Virginia after the war, he wrote idealized novels of the antebellum South and a distinguished colonial state history (1883).

Cooke, Josiah Parsons, Jr. (1827–94) chemist, educator; born in Boston, Mass. As a professor at Harvard (1849–94), he legitimized the practice of lab instruction in chemistry combined with demonstration experiments and is considered the founder of Harvard's department of chemistry. His own specialty was the classification of elements by atomic weights.

Cooke, Morris (Llewellyn) (1872–1960) mechanical engineer; born in Carlisle, Pa. After graduating from Lehigh University (1895) he worked as a machinist in a shipyard and foundry in Philadelphia. There he became interested in scientific management and, with reservations, accepted Frederick Taylor's theories. From 1911–16 he was director of the Department of Public Works of Philadelphia. His pamphlet, "Snapping Cords," helped force a reduction in electricity rates charged by Philadelphia Electric to rural users, a landmark in the movement for cheap power. In 1923 he became head of the Giant Power Survey to study ways to get cheap electricity in Pennsylvania. In 1932, President Roosevelt appointed him chairman of the Mississippi Valley Committee and from 1935–37 he administered the Rural Electrification Administration. During 1940–41, he was technical consultant to the government, and he initiated a program to subcontract military orders to small companies, which helped revive local economies. In 1950, Truman appointed him chairman of the Water Resources Policy Commission.

Coolbrith, Ina (Donna) (1842–1928) writer; born near Springfield, Ill. A Californian from childhood until her death, she lived after 1865 in San Francisco, where she was Bret Harte's coeditor on *Overland Monthly*. Thirty years a librarian, she published three volumes of distinctively simple lyrical verse between 1881 and 1895 that were to earn her selection as the state's first poet laureate (1915).

Cooley, Charles Horton (1864–1929) sociologist; born in Ann Arbor, Mich. He joined the University of Michigan faculty after earning a Ph.D. in political economy, and in a 35-year career there, he pioneered the teaching of the new discipline of sociology and the practice of social psychology. Like other early sociologists he took a philosophical approach to his subject; although the discipline later became empirically based, he made lasting theoretical contributions that laid the foundation for later work. In *Human Nature and the Social Order* (1902), he introduced the concept of "the looking-glass self," the self as defined by social interaction. He developed this view further in *Social Organization* (1909) and *Social Process* (1918), a Darwinian social analysis.

Cooley, Denton Arthur (1920–) surgeon; born in Houston, Texas. He studied medicine at Johns Hopkins University, where he also did his surgical internship and residency (1944–50). He spent the next year in England at the Brompton Hospital for Chest Diseases. In 1951 he joined the Baylor University medical faculty and began performing heart surgery at Texas Children's and St. Luke's Episcopal Hospitals. A pioneer in open-heart and heart-transplantation surgery, he left Baylor University (1954–62) to found the world-renowned Texas Heart Institute in Houston (1962) where he became surgeon-in-chief.

Cooley, Thomas (McIntyre) (1824–98) jurist, scholar; born near Attica, N.Y. Michigan Supreme Court justice (1864–85) and first chairman of the U.S. Interstate Commerce Commission in 1887, he authored several definitive law works.

Coolidge, Archibald Cary (1866–1928) historian; born in Boston, Mass. He taught history at Harvard from 1893. As director of the Harvard Library (1910–22), he oversaw the establishment of the Widener Library (1913–15). He wrote *The United States as a World Power* (1908) and was editor-in-chief of *Foreign Affairs* (1922–27). He was the chief of mission in Paris and Vienna (1919) and the Red Cross negotiator with the Soviet Union in 1921.

Coolidge, Elizabeth (Penn) Sprague (1864–1953) music patron; born in Chicago. Daughter of a wealthy wholesale grocer, she began studying piano at age 11, and started composing music in the 1890s. Following the deaths of her husband, father, and mother in 1915, she used her inheritance to sponsor the South Mountain (later Berkshire) Chamber Music Festival (1918–24), then established the Elizabeth Sprague Coolidge Foundation at the Library of Congress (1925) to fund festivals, composers, and musicians. In the 1940s her foundation commissioned works by modern composers, including Aaron Copland, Sergei Prokofiev, and Igor Stravinsky, introducing them to Americans through radio broadcasts and concerts.

Coolidge, Grace (Anna b. Goodhue) (1879–1957) First Lady; born in Burlington, Vt. She taught at a school for deaf children before she married Calvin Coolidge in 1903. Socially active and personally lively, she was a great asset to the taciturn Coolidge. She was popular as first lady but she suffered from the tragedy of the death of her younger son from blood poisoning.

Coolidge, (John) Calvin (1872–1933) thirtieth U.S. president; born in Plymouth, Vt. After graduating from Amherst College (1895), he became a lawyer in Northampton, Mass. As a Republican, he held a series of local and state offices until becoming governor of Massachusetts (1919–20); he gained national attention for using the state militia to suppress a police strike. Elected vice-president in 1920, he succeeded to the presidency on Warren Harding's death in 1923. He was reelected the next year. A popular and deliberately hands-off president in prosperous times, he was noted more for what he did not do and say than for what he did (although among his oft-quoted phrases is his 1925 remark, "the business of America is business."). In his private life he was equally noted for his taciturn, thrifty ways. After leaving the White House, he retired to Northampton and wrote various articles promoting his conservative views as well as his autobiography (1929).

Coolidge, William David (1873–1975) physical chemist; born in Hudson, Mass. He graduated from Massachusetts Institute of Technology (1896) and received his Ph.D at Leipzig (1899). He worked at General Electric, beginning in 1905 as a research physical chemist, then succeeding Willis Whitney as director of research in 1932; he became a vice-president in 1940. In 1910, he invented a process for the production of carbon-free tungsten filament, which revolutionized the production of light bulbs. His experiments with tungsten led to his most significant invention, the X-ray tube (which became known as the Coolidge tube), as well as to the tungsten target in X-ray machines. During World War I, he assisted in the production of X-ray equipment for the army and later in the development of submarine detectors. During World War II, he advised the government on the feasibility of building an atomic bomb. He retired after the war, but continued consulting for General Electric until about 1965.

Coon, Carleton (Stevens) (1904–81) anthropologist; born in Wakefield, Mass. Educated at Harvard, he taught there (1934–48) and at the University of Pennsylvania (1948–63). His many expeditions led him to discover the remains of Aterian fossil man (in North Africa in 1939) and the second Jebel Ighoud man (Sierra Leone in 1965). His books include *The Seven Caves* (1957) and *Origin of Races* (1962). In his later years his ideas were regarded by many as racialist and were discredited because he contended that the Negroid race had not evolved as far as other races.

Cooney, Joan Ganz (1929–   ) television executive; born in Phoenix, Ariz. After working as a teacher, she became a newspaper reporter in Arizona, then a National Broadcasting Company publicist (1954–62) before producing documentaries for public television (1962–67). She created Public Broadcasting System's *Seasame Street* (1968) for preschoolers. As president of the Children's Television Workshop (1970–88), then chairperson, she produced other children's educational programs including *The Electric Company, 3,2,1 Contact* and *Square One TV*.

Cooper, Gary (b. Frank James Cooper) (1901–61) actor; born in Helena, Mont. Son of English parents who had settled in Montana, after graduating from Grinnell College, Iowa, he worked as cartoonist and at various other jobs before getting into movies in 1925 as an extra in a Western. His role as the laconic cowboy in *The Virginian* (1929) launched him as a star. Initially better known for his offscreen romantic escapades than his acting, he settled down after his marriage to socialite Veronica Balfe (1933). Whether as a cowboy or a peace-loving, but determined character, he came to personify the archetypal American for many around the world, winning Academy Awards for his work in *Sergeant York* (1941) and *High Noon* (1952), as well as an honorary Oscar in 1960.

Cooper, James Fenimore (1789–1851), writer; born in Burlington, N.J. Raised in prosperous circumstances in his father's frontier settlement at Cooperstown, N.Y., he attended Yale University (but was expelled for a prank) and spent several years in the navy (1806–11). Living as a country gentleman, he wrote his first novel, *Precaution* (1820), allegedly after his wife challenged his claim that he could write a better one than what she was then reading. His second, *The Spy* (1821), is regarded as the first major American novel. He moved to New York City and achieved great popular success with *The Pilot* (1823) and his first three Leatherstocking tales, *The Pioneers* (1823), followed by *The Last of the Mohicans* (1826) and *The Prairie* (1827), a series that offered for the first time a heroic vision of the American frontier. From 1826 to 1833 he lived in Europe, where he wrote several American and European romances and other works revealing his deep homesickness for an unspoiled American wilderness. But his return to Cooperstown in 1834 was followed by years of bitter disillusionment with the U.S.A. He wrote many satires and virulent criticism that were largely ignored by readers; he also engaged in libel suits against some of his critics and this only further alienated the

American public. The prolific output of his last years included a scholarly history of the U.S. Navy (1839), and, among other novels, two final Leatherstocking tales, *The Pathfinder* (1840) and *The Deerslayer* (1841).

Cooper, Kenneth H. (Hardy) (1931–   ) physician, author; born in Oklahoma City, Okla. He designed pioneering aerobics programs for astronauts and pilots as a U.S. Air Force doctor (1960–70); his *Aerobics* (1968) helped launch the 1970s fitness craze. (In some countries outside the U.S.A. the term "to cooper" actually came to refer to aerobics.) Founder of the Aerobics Center, Dallas, Texas (1970), in later years he turned to promoting preventive medicine.

Cooper, Leon N. (Neil) (1930–   ) physicist; born in New York City. At the University of Illinois (1955–57), he collaborated with Bardeen and Schrieffer to develop the BCS theory of superconductivity, which won the three scientists the 1972 Nobel Prize in physics. He moved to Brown University (1958), where he predicted the low-temperature pairing of electrons now known as Cooper pairs. His later investigations include research on memory organization in the brain.

Cooper, Peter (1791–1883) engineer, manufacturer, philanthropist; born in New York City. With little formal education, he worked in various trades, laying the basis for his fortune by making glue and isinglass. In 1828 he started an iron works in Baltimore, Md., where he built the first steam locomotive in the U.S.A., *Tom Thumb;* although it lost a famous race with a horse-drawn train in 1830, Cooper helped advance the spread of railroads. His many business interests – mostly involving iron mining and manufacturing – included the telegraph company that laid the first transatlantic cable. Quick to adopt the latest technology such as the Bessemer process, he himself invented several labor-saving devices including a washing machine. Having greatly prospered, in 1859 he founded Cooper Union in New York City to provide free education to adults in art and technical-scientific subjects; it still functions as the Cooper Institute. He was active in civic affairs and in 1876 was the Greenback Party's candidate for president.

Cooper, Thomas (1759–1839) social agitator, scientist, educator; born in Westminster, England. Trained as a lawyer and doctor, with a smattering of chemistry and philosophy, he espoused radical ideas that closed off advancement in England; so in 1794 he emigrated to the U.S.A. with Joseph Priestley. He practiced both law and medicine in Pennsylvania but also became a pamphleteer in support of Thomas Jefferson; attacking the Sedition Law, he was briefly imprisoned and fined $400 (1800). Between 1801–04 he served as a Luzerne County (Pa.) commissioner and then as a Pennsylvania state judge (1804–11); by then he was becoming more conservative and, disgusted with politics, he turned to teaching chemistry, first at Carlisle (now Dickinson) College (1811–15), then at the University of Pennsylvania (1815–19). Moving on to South Carolina College (now the University of South Carolina), he soon became its president (1820–34) while teaching the sciences and political economy; he helped open the first medical school and insane asylum in the state. His strong individualism and libertarianism led him to become a defender of states' rights and he promoted the southern view on the tariff, nullification, and even slavery; following his own logic, he was one of the first to argue for secession.

Coors, Adolph (1847–1929) brewer; born in Barmen, Prussia, Germany. He came to the U.S.A. in 1868. After working in a Denver brewery, he founded Adolph Coors Brewing Company in Golden, Colo. (1873). He was president of the company after its incorporation in 1914. He steered the company successfully through most of the Prohibition period. He left the firm to his sons to develop from a regional brand into one of the most successful American breweries.

Coover, Robert (Lowell) (1932–) writer; born in Charles City, Iowa. After studying at several universities he served in the U.S. Navy (1953–57) and then taught philosophy at several colleges. His first novel, *The Origin of the Brunists* (1966, Faulkner Award), established him as a postmodernist who recombined elements of mythology, Bible stories, and popular culture. His fiction, which often explored dogmatic extremism, included *The Public Burning* (1977) and *A Political Fable* (1980). He lived mostly in England and Spain from the 1960s, returning frequently to the U.S.A. to teach.

Cope, Edward Drinker (1840–97) zoologist, paleontologist; born in Philadelphia. Although his postsecondary education was limited to one year's study with Joseph Leidy at the University of Pennsylvania, Cope went on to found (along with Leidy and O.C. Marsh) the science of American vertebrate paleontology. On numerous western American expeditions he discovered more than 600 fossil species, mostly of cold-blooded vertebrates and extinct mammals, whose discovery significantly pushed back the age of mammals. His published descriptions laid the groundwork for the classification of North American fishes, amphibians, and reptiles. A believer in the inheritability of acquired characteristics, he became America's foremost neo-Lamarckian evolutionary theorist. The ambitious Cope struggled for primacy in his new and fertile field in a famous 25-year feud with his archrival O.C. Marsh, with whom he publicly traded vitriolic accusations of inaccuracy and unethical conduct. Cope's massive published output included more than 1,500 titles. He owned and edited *American Naturalist* (1878–97) and was professor at the University of Pennsylvania (1889–97).

Cope, Thomas Pym (1768–1854) merchant, philanthropist; born in Lancaster, Pa. A Quaker merchant, he established the first regular line of packet ships between Philadelphia and Liverpool (1821). He was also active in constructing canals and railroads. He was president of Philadelphia's Board of Trade (1852–54) and gave generously to the Zoological Society and the Institute for Colored Youth. He was a close friend of Stephen Girard.

Copeland, Charles W. (1815–95) naval engineer; born in Coventry, Conn. He designed the machinery of the USS *Fulton,* the first steam war-vessel constructed under naval supervision (1836). He also designed transatlantic merchant steamers.

Copland, Aaron (1900–90) composer; born in New York City. In his teens he studied in New York with Rubin Goldmark; in France during 1921–24, he worked with the later-famous pedagogue Nadia Boulanger. Returning to New York, he began the wide-ranging activities that would characterize his career: composing painstakingly, performing as a pianist, promoting new music, and teaching. His first successes came from the performances of such important conductors as Walter Damrosch, who premiered the Symphony for Organ and Orchestra in 1925, and Serge Koussevitsky, who became a leading champion of the composer. Meanwhile, he helped create and performed in forums for new works including the Yaddo Festival (which began in 1932). He also helped found organizations including the American Composers Alliance and Cos Cob Press, taught at schools including Tanglewood (1940–65), and wrote a series of books beginning with the 1939 *What to Listen for in Music.* After his early jazz-inspired works such as *Music for the Theater* (1925), and a few severe, avant-garde pieces such as the Piano Variations (1930), his most famous works began with the *El Salón México* of 1936; this and later pieces, among them the much-loved *Appalachian Spring* of 1944, are marked by a warm and rhythmically lively style based on a sophisticated adaptation of American folk material. He largely retired from composing in the 1970s.

Copley, John Singleton (1738–1815) painter; born in Boston, Mass. (stepson of Peter Pelham). Considered the foremost portrait painter in colonial America, he settled in England (1775) at the urging of Sir Joshua Reynolds and Benjamin West. Although his family was Loyalist, he himself remained neutral during the American Revolution. He was successful in England, as seen in his historical subjects, such as *Death of Major Peirson* (1782–84). His reputation is based on his early American work, as in *Boy with Squirrel* (1765), a portrait of his half brother, Henry Pelham. *Watson and the Shark* (1778) is his most famous narrative painting.

Copley, Lionel (?–1693) colonial governor; born in England. He was the governor of Maryland (1691–93). He concluded three different Indian peace treaties. He discovered that it was impossible to serve the king without infringing upon the territorial rights of the Lord of Baltimore.

Coppin, Fanny Marion Jackson (1837–1913) educator, missionary; born in Washington, D.C. Purchased out of slavery as a girl, she went on to graduate from college and as head principal of the Institute for Colored Youth, Philadelphia (1869–1902), she pioneered training for urban blacks. Active in the missionary movement, she spent nearly ten years after 1902 in South Africa.

Coppola, Francis Ford (1939–) movie director; born in Detroit, Mich. A disciple of Roger Corman, he began directing in 1961. The phenomenal success of *The Godfather* (1972) led him to set up his own production company and studios, but most of his subsequent movies fared poorly with either the critics or the public, and the colossal expense of his Vietnam War film, *Apocalypse Now* (1979), all but drove him into bankruptcy. He would recover to continue directing his own movies and supporting those by other young filmmakers but the baroque extravagance of movies such as *Bram Stoker's Dracula* (1992) did little to advance his reputation. His Oscars include awards for *Patton* (1970, for screenwriting) and three for *The Godfather Part II* (1974, for direction, screenwriting, and best picture).

Corbett, (James John) "Gentleman Jim" (1866–1933) boxer; born in San Francisco. A bank teller, he became a professional boxer in 1884. He became the first heavyweight champion under the modern padded gloves rules when he knocked out John L. Sullivan in 1892. After losing his crown in 1897 to Bob Fitzsimmons, he failed twice to regain the championship against James J. Jefferies in 1900 and 1903. His career record was 20 victories, five losses, six draws, with two no decisions. Between 1895–97, he also played baseball with minor league teams. On retiring from boxing he went on to appear on the stage and in movies. He wrote his autobiography, *The Roar of the Crowd* (1925).

Corbin, Arthur Linton (1874–1967) lawyer; born in Linn County, Kans. Educated at the Universities of Kansas and Yale, he spent most of his career at Yale where he transformed the law school's educational system. His major interest was contract law, a field in which he was the national leader, and his major work was the 12-volume, *A Comprehensive Treatise on the Working Rules of Contract Law* (1950). He also wrote on cases as well as scholarly articles, and was an adviser for the American Law Institute on revision of the Uniform Sales Act (1942–45).

Corbin, Margaret (b. Cochran) (1751–c. 1800) American Revolution heroine; born in Franklin County, Pa. When she was five, her father was killed in an Indian raid in which her mother was taken captive, and she was raised by an uncle. Her husband, John Corbin, enlisted in the American Revolution, and she accompanied him as cook, laundress, and nurse for the troops. During the battle of Harlem Heights in September 1776, John Corbin was mortally wounded; she took over his battle station and was wounded, suffering permanent loss of use of one arm. After the battle, she was accorded some of the benefits accorded to veterans (money, clothing, food, and alcohol rations), thereby becoming the first woman pensioner of the United States. She apparently remarried, but vanished from view about 1783. Years later she was mistakenly identified as the "Captain Molly Pitcher" who had fought at Monmouth (Mary Ludwig Hays McCauley).

Corbitt, Ted (1920–   ) long-distance runner; born in Dunbarton, S.C. Called "the father of American distance running," Corbitt's exploits in marathon running and ultramarathons (distances longer than 26 miles, 385 yards) contributed substantially to the popularity of long-distance running in the United States. When few dreamed of running distances longer than the marathon, Corbitt trained for and ran in international races of 40 to 100 miles, often against much younger men, and almost always finished among the top five, often setting American records in the process. By profession a physical therapist, he maintained his fitness long after most have given up competitive efforts. His stamina and longevity are legendary and are not likely to be equaled. At age 54, he ran his 175th marathon in Boston in the time of 2:49.16, less than a minute slower than his first marathon 23 years earlier. (His fastest marathon time was 2:26.44, in 1958.) He held the American record at 25 miles, at the marathon distance, and at 40 and 50 miles.

Corboy, Philip H. (Harnett) (1924–   ) lawyer; born in Chicago. After serving as assistant corporate counsel of Chicago (1949–50), he was in private practice 32 years (1950–82) before founding Corboy & Demetrio. He was recognized as one of America's leading personal injury attorneys and his firm became a training ground for many successful trial lawyers, winning over 100 personal injury suits worth over $1 million each. In 1990, he was named general counsel of the Illinois Democratic Party.

Corcoran, James (Andrew) (1820–89) Catholic theologian, editor; born in Charleston, S.C. A prominent theologian at church councils, he coedited (1846–61) the *United States Catholic Miscellany* and (from 1876) edited the *American Catholic Quarterly Review*. He was also a pastor in the 1860s in Wilmington, N.C., where he went to assist during a yellow fever epidemic. He was named a monsignor in 1883.

Corcoran, Thomas (Gardiner) (1900–81) lawyer, government official; born in Pawtucket, R.I. A protégé of Felix Frankfurter, he was a New York corporate lawyer (1927–32) before joining the Reconstruction Finance Committee in 1932. As President Roosevelt's legislative aide (1933–41), he codrafted New Deal legislation including the Securities Act (1933) and the Fair Labor Standards Act (1938). He returned to private practice afterward.

Corcoran, William Wilson (1798–1888) banker, art collector, philanthropist; born in Georgetown, Wash., D.C. He studied at Georgetown College (now Georgetown University) (c. 1814), joined his brothers in a dry goods business (1815), and later established a banking firm, Corcoran & Riggs (1840). He retired from banking in 1854, and devoted himself to collecting 19th-century American works of art. A supporter of the South during the Civil War, he lived abroad during that time. As a philanthropist he donated substantial sums to many educational, religious, and charitable institutions in America. He founded the Corcoran Gallery of Art in 1859 and it was moved to its present location in 1897; his collection still forms the nucleus of the museum.

Cord, Errett Lobban (1894–1974) manufacturer; born in Warrensburg, Mo. A racing car mechanic and driver, he became president of Auburn Automobile Company in Auburn, Ind., which in 1926 acquired the Duesenberg Motor Company in Indianapolis. In 1929 the Auburn plant introduced the Cord L-29, the first successful front-wheel drive car; it remained in production until 1932. Manufacture of all Cords and Duesenbergs ceased in 1937 because of the Depression.

Cordero, Angel, Jr. ("Junior") (1942–   ) jockey; born in San Juan, Puerto Rico. He began his career as a groom at El Commondante racetrack, to which he returned as a trainer after retiring as a jockey in the early 1990s. He broke many records and was the only jockey to win more than $5 million per season six times. In 1982 he won four stakes in three days at three tracks separated by 3,000 miles, and also won the Eclipse Award. In 1983 he was the fourth jockey to have more than 5,000 career victories (including the Kentucky Derby in 1974, 1976, and 1985) and the third to have won more than $72 million.

Cordier, Andrew W. (Wellington) (1901–75) United Nations official, educator; born in Canton, Ohio. He taught history and political science at Manchester College (1923–44) and was executive assistant to the United Nations secretary general (1946–62). As acting president (1968–69) and president (1969–70) of Columbia University, he helped to restore order to the campus.

Cordiner, Ralph Jarron (1900–73) corporate executive; born near Walla Walla, Wash. He spent virtually his entire career at General Electric, where variously president, chairman of the board, and CEO (1950–63), he implemented an innovative and widely copied decentralized management structure. He explicated his management philosophy in *New Frontiers for Professional Managers* (1956).

Corey, Elias J. (1928–   ) molecular chemist; born in Methuen, Mass. He was affiliated with the University of Illinois (1951–59) and Harvard (1959). He was known for the technique called retrosynthetic analysis, whereby a chemist plans the molecule to be synthesized and studies its theoretical structure. The technique is used in synthesizing complex pharmaceuticals. He was awarded the Nobel Prize in chemistry (1990).

Corey, Lewis (b. Luigi Carlo Fraina) (1892–1953) Marxist theorist, economist; born in Galdo, Italy. He emigrated to New York City with his family (1894). Largely self-educated, he was a reporter for the *New York Journal* and the socialist *Daily People*. He founded and led the Bolshevik Bureau of Information (1917) and was international secretary for the Communist Party of America (1919). In Russia (1920–22), he became disillusioned with Communist politics and turned to economics. He wrote *The Decline of American Capitalism* (1934) and helped to found the Union of Democratic Action (1940), which later became Americans for Democratic Action. Without a high school education, he became professor of economics at Antioch College (1942–51). He wrote *Meat and Man* (1950) and was about to be deported as a Communist by the FBI at the time of his death.

Corey, Martha (died 1692) victim of witchcraft hysteria; date and place of birth unknown. The wife of Giles Corey of Salem Village (now Danvers) in colonial Massachusetts, she was accused by two emotionally aroused young girls of witchcraft. Refusing to confess, she was hanged (and her husband was crushed to death under a rock); her chief accuser and the trial judge later publicly admitted their error.

Cori, Carl F. (Ferdinand) (1896–1984) biochemist; born in Prague, Czechoslovakia. He was a pharmacology assistant in Vienna (1920–22), then emigrated with his wife Gerty to work at the State Institute for the Study of Malignant Disease (Buffalo, N.Y.) (1922–31). He moved to Washington University (St. Louis, Mo.) (1931–66), where he and his wife collaborated on investigating the biochemistry of the glucose-glycogen cycle and determining the mechanism of action of insulin. They became the third husband-and-wife team to receive the Nobel Prize when they won half the 1947 award in physiology for their research on glucose metabolism and its requisite enzymes. After Gerty Cori's death in 1957, Carl Cori remarried and continued an active teaching and research career at both Washington University and Harvard Medical School (1966–84).

Cori, Gerty T. (Theresa) (b. Radnitz) (1896–1957) biochemist; born in Prague, Czechoslovakia. She received her M.D. in 1920, and married her classmate Carl Cori that same year. The couple moved to Vienna, where Gerty Cori investigated thyroid deficiency in children. Both Coris came to the U.S.A. to work at the State Institute for the Study of Malignant Disease (Buffalo, N.Y.) (1922–31). They moved to Washington University (St. Louis, Mo.) (1957), where they shared the 1947 Nobel Prize in physiology for their collaborations on glucose-glycogen metabolism. Gerty Cori went on to make major contributions to studies of inherited glycogen-storage diseases. She died in 1957 from myelosclerosis.

Corigliano, John (Paul) (1938–) composer; born in New York City. After some years working in television and radio, he taught in New York and from 1987–90 was composer-in-residence of the Chicago Symphony. His music has been described as polished, popularistic avant-gardism; his Symphony No. 1 won a 1992 Grammy.

Corliss, George Henry (1817–88) inventor, manufacturer; born in Easton, N.Y. Educated in local schools and at Castleton Academy, Vt., he opened a boot store in Greenwich, N.Y., in 1842. Two years later he went to work for a steam engine manufacturer in Providence, R.I. He designed many improvements – in particular, a governor to control valves – that led to greater efficiency and economy of operation in steam engines. In 1848 he established his own company to make the products of his inventiveness; the Corliss Steam Engine Co. built many of the country's largest engines. His 1,400-horsepower Corliss Engine powered the Philadelphia Centennial Exposition of 1876, driving all the exhibit machinery during six months of continuous operation.

Cormack, Allan MacLeod (1924–) biophysicist, nuclear physicist; born in Johannesburg, South Africa (to Scottish immigrants). At the University of Cape Town (1946–57), he began research in radiology. He emigrated to Harvard (1956–57), then joined Tufts University (1957), where he tested mathematical models fundamental to the development of computerized axial tomography (CAT, or CT scanning), then pursued research in particle physics. For his contributions to CAT scanning as a diagnostic tool for tumor diagnosis, Cormack shared one-half the 1979 Nobel Prize in physiology or medicine.

Corman, Roger (1926–) movie director, producer; born in Los Angeles. He made his film debut as a director in 1955 and went on to specialize in cheapie horror movies, graduating to more expensive films such as *The Masque of the Red Death* (1964). Although long ignored by serious students of the movies, he gained almost cult status with the recognition that his movies had anticipated various themes of "pop culture" and had served as both a training ground and/or inspiration for a whole generation of Hollywood moviemakers.

Cornell, C. (Carl) Allin (1938–) civil engineer, seismologist; born in Mobridge, S.D. A research professor at Stanford University beginning in 1982, he specialized in applying probability theory to structural (especially earthquake) engineering.

Cornell, Ezra (1807–74) capitalist, philanthropist; born at Westchester Landing, N.Y. Originally a carpenter and millwright, he developed a way to insulate telegraph wires attached to wooden poles, then directed the installation of the first telegraph line, from Washington to Baltimore (1844). He joined with other businessmen to form the Western Union Telegraph Company (1855). He built the public library in Ithaca, N.Y., established a model farm, and gave $500,000 for the creation of Cornell University (opened in 1868).

Cornell, Joseph (1903–72) assemblage/collage artist; born in Nyack, N.Y. He attended Phillips Academy, Andover, Mass. (1917–21), worked for his father's textile company, and after his father's death, moved to Utopia Parkway, Flushing, New York City, where he spent the rest of his life. Something of a recluse, he collected ephemera, books, and objects. Often regarded as a Surrealist, he was influenced by Max Ernst's *La Femme 100 Tetes*, a collage-novel (1929). His work consisted of small boxes for walls or tables, as in *Homage to the Romantic Ballet* (1942). His compartmentalized boxes, such as *Multiple Cubes* (1946–48), led to other works, as seen in the *Eclipse* (c. 1960–62) and the *Clay Pipe* (c. 1962) series. He is considered the master of miniature worlds that become magic reincarnations of the past.

Cornell, Katharine (1898–1974) stage actress; born in Berlin, Germany. Her first appearance in this country was with the Washington Square Players in 1916; her first New York hit was *A Bill of Divorcement* (1921). She married, then formed a successful team with her producer-director husband, Guthrie McClintic. She was known for her performances in many theater classics including the role for which she was best known, Elizabeth Moulton-Barrett in *The Barretts of Wimpole Street* (1931). *The Barretts* was produced on television in 1956. She also played in *Saint Joan* (1936) and *The Three Sisters* (1942). One of the first American performers to form her own repertory company, she took several entire New York productions on the road. In 1959 she played Mrs. Patrick Campbell in Jerome Kilty's *Dear Liar*. In 1961, after her husband's death, she retired from the theater.

Corning, Erastus (1794–1872) businessman, U.S. representative; born in Norwich, Conn. He moved to Albany, N.Y. (1814), where he began to manufacture iron. He bought a foundry and eventually founded a partnership with metallurgy genius John F. Winslow; their product became renowned throughout the U.S.A. He promoted an extension of the Mohawk & Hudson Railroad and was the president of the Utica and Schenectady Railroad (1833–53); he took the lead in consolidating the various New York railroad lines into the New York Central and served as its first president (1853–64). He founded the Corning Land Company (1853) and served four terms as the mayor of Albany (1834–37). He served in the New York state senate (1842–45) and in the U.S. House of Representatives (Dem., N.Y.; 1857–59, 1861–63).

Cornplanter, (b. Gaiant-wa'ka), also known as John O'Bail (?1735–1836) Seneca chief; born along the Genessee River in present-day New York. He fought with distinction for the British during the American Revolution and for the U.S.A. during the War of 1812. An accommodationist, in his old age he renounced cooperation with whites.

Corrigan, Michael (Augustine) (1839–1902) Catholic prelate; born in Newark, N.J. Ordained in 1863, he taught theology at Seton Hall University (1864–68) where he was president (1868–76) before being named coadjutor bishop (1880) and later archbishop (1885) of New York. Considered a conservative, he opposed the Knights of Labor and suspended the liberal priest, Edward McGlynn, for political activities.

Corso, Gregory (Nunzio) (1930–) poet; born in New York City. He spent three years in prison as a juvenile, then worked as a manual laborer, reporter, and merchant seaman (1950–53). Based in New York City, he was a central member of the Beat poetry movement (1960s), as seen in *The Happy Birthday of Death* (1960). He taught at the State University, Buffalo, N.Y.

Corson, Juliet (1841–97) cookery educator; born in Roxbury (now Boston), Mass. Daughter of a prosperous wholesale produce merchant, she largely educated herself by reading at home until, at age 16, she took a job in a library in New York City. She soon began to contribute articles and poems to newspapers; by 1873 she was a secretary for the Women's Educational and Industrial Society of New York. In 1874–75 she lectured during cooking classes by chefs and then in 1876 opened her own New York Cooking School in her home. Within a few years she was enjoying wide success as a pioneer advocate of better foods and cooking for poor families, writing pamphlets (such as *Fifteen Cent Dinners for Families of Six*, 1877), and lecturing throughout the Northeast; within the next decade she was internationally recognized as an expert on such innovations as teaching dietetics and educating groups such as nurses on the need to know about cooking. Her numerous publications include *Family Living on $500 a Year* (1887) and several cookbooks such as *Juliet Corson's New Family Cookbook* (1885). After achieving recognition at the World's Columbian Exposition (1892), she was forced by her poor health to restrict her activities to writing.

Cortissoz, Royal (1869–1948) art critic; born in Brooklyn, N.Y. He was educated locally, and worked for the architectural firm of McKim, Mead, and White. He then became the art critic for the *New York Tribune* (1891–1944). A classicist by training and nature, he was opposed to modernism, as seen in such publications as *Art and Common Sense* (1913) and *American Artists* (1923).

Corwin, Edward Samuel (1878–1963) political scientist; born near Plymouth, Mich. A longtime professor at Princeton (1905–46) and a government adviser, he is best known for his expertise in constitutional law. He served as an adviser to the Public Works Administration (1935) and as an assistant to the attorney general (1936–37).

Corwin, Thomas (1794–1865) governor, U.S. representative/senator; born in Bourbon County, Ky. A lawyer, he served in the U.S. House of Representatives (Whig, Ohio; 1831–40), then became Ohio's governor (1841–43). In the U.S. Senate (1845–50), he denounced the Mexican War, predicting that acquisition of more territory would fan regional conflict. President Millard Fillmore's treasury secretary (1851–53), he joined the Republican Party, becoming Lincoln's ambassador to Mexico (1861–64).

Cosby, (William Henry, Jr.) Bill (1937–) comedian, author, television producer; born in Germantown, Pa. Rather than repeat the tenth grade, he left school and joined the navy. While attending Temple University on an athletic scholarship, he appeared at New York's Gaslight Cafe (1962) where his comic narratives were so successful that he left college to pursue his career. In 1965 he became the first African-American actor to star in a weekly television dramatic series, *I Spy* (1965–68), winning two Emmys as an undercover Central Intelligence Agency agent. Subsequent series were *The Bill Cosby Show* (1969–71), *The New Bill Cosby Show* (1972–73), and *Fat Albert and the Cosby Kids* (1972–84). His interest in children and education led him to earn M.A. and Ed.D degrees at the University of Massachusetts and to incorporate many of his ideas and ideals in his work. As obstetrician Cliff Huxtable in *The Cosby Show* (1984–1992), he projected a new image of middle-class African-American families and the program was one of the most popular and lucrative in television history. His gentle, wry clowning appealed to both children and adults, leading to a series of successful television commercials, comedy records, and books, and making him one of the wealthiest individuals in the history of the American entertainment industry. Only his movies failed to be money-machines. In later years he became a generous contributor to various causes and institutions, particularly Atlanta's Spelman College, and was often seen at track-and-field meets for amateur athletes, to which he also contributed.

Cosell, Howard (b. Howard William Cohen) (1918–) sports broadcaster; born in Winston-Salem, N.C. After a brief career as a lawyer, he became a sportscaster for ABC in 1956 and was the boxing announcer throughout Muhammad Ali's career. Famous for his signature remark, "Telling it like it is," his opinionated broadcasts for *Monday Night Football* won him fans and detractors alike.

Coser, Lewis A. (Alfred) (1913–) sociologist; born in Berlin, Germany. A 1941 immigrant to the U.S.A. and a Columbia University Ph.D., he taught at Brandeis University (1951–68) and State University of New York: Stony Brook (1969–87). His books in the areas of social conflict, the sociology of politics, and history include *Sociological Theory* (coauthored, 1957, several times revised), *The American Communist Party* (with Irving Howe, 1957, later revised), and *Refugee Scholars in America* (1984).

Cotton, John (1584–1652) Puritan clergyman, author; born in Derby, England. He arrived in Boston, Mass. (1633), and soon became the teacher of the Boston Church. He originally supported Anne Hutchinson, but he joined her persecutors when he discovered that he was alone in support of her. A tireless worker, he wrote *Spiritual Milk for Babes* (1646), a standard textbook for New England children, and numerous books and pamphlets including *The Way of the Congregational Churches Cleared* (1648). In later years he became hostile toward religious dissenters and favored the power of civil authorities over the individual.

Cottrell, Frederick Gardner (1877–1948) chemist; born in Oakland, Calif. He was affiliated with the University of California (1902–11) and held a number of government posts until 1930. He invented electrostatic precipitators for the removal of suspended particles from gases (c. 1911). He founded the Research Corporation (1912), which eventually held over 750 patents. He helped develop a process for separation of helium from natural gas and helped establish the U.S. synthetic ammonia industry.

Coues, Elliott (1842–99) ornithologist; born in Portsmouth, N.Y. He moved to Washington, D.C., with his family at age 11 and became interested in birds after making the acquaintance of Smithsonian Institution naturalists. He enlisted in the Union Army as a medical cadet in 1862 and was appointed an assistant surgeon in 1864. He served in various western posts until 1881, and during those years made collections and compiled information about local bird life. His *Birds of the Colorado Valley* (1878) is considered a classic. An ardent theosophist, he helped found the American Society for Psychical Research. He also edited several volumes of early travel in the American West.

Coughlin, Charles E. (Edward) "Father Coughlin" (1891–1979) activist, Catholic priest; born in Ontario, Canada. Longtime pastor of the Shrine of the Little Flower in Michigan (1926–66), he won a huge audience in the 1930s for his radio broadcasts. At first a supporter of Franklin D. Roosevelt, he later adopted ultraconservative views and anti-Semitic rhetoric and opposed U.S. entrance into World War II. In 1942 the Catholic hierarchy ordered him to stop broadcasting, and his inflammatory magazine, *Social Justice*, was barred from the mails as violating the Federal Espionage Act.

Coulter, John Merle (1851–1928) botanist; born in Ningpo, China. A child of missionary parents, he was taken to Indiana by his mother in 1853 after his father's death. Originally a geologist, he brought back plant specimens after serving with the U.S. Geological Survey in the Rocky Mountains (1872–73). He became a professor of botany at Hanover College (1874–79), and founded the *Botanical Gazette* (1875), which became a leading American journal.

He joined Wabash College (1879–91), then moved to Indiana University (1891–93), but resigned after differing with the politics of fundraising. He became president of Lake Forest University (1893–96), but he felt that administrative duties interfered with his botanical studies, so he moved to the University of Chicago (1896–1935), where he concentrated on plant physiology, morphology, and ecology. Called the "dean of American botanists," he wrote many books and monographs on North American flowering plants, although his greatest influence was as an educator. He became adviser to the Boyce Thompson Institute for Plant Research, Yonkers, N.Y. (1925–28).

Councilman, William T. (Thomas) (1854–1933) pathologist; born in Pikesville, Md. He was affiliated with Johns Hopkins (1885–92), becoming resident pathologist, and he then became a professor of pathology at Harvard Medical School (1892–1921). He confirmed the discovery of and described *Plasmodium malariae* (1893–94), the sporozoan parasite that causes malaria, and investigated amoebic dysentery.

Counts, George S. (Sylvester) (1889–1974) educator; born in Baldwin City, Kans. A professor at Teachers College, Columbia University (1927–56), Counts was also a government advisor and an impassioned critic of American schools, whose primary function, he argued, should be to promote democratic values. His books include *The American Road to Culture* (1930) and *Education and American Civilization* (1952).

Courant, Ernest D. (David) (1920–) physicist; born in Goettingen, Germany. He came to the U.S.A. in 1934. He taught and performed research in theoretical and atomic physics in several U.S. universities and in Canada before joining the Brookhaven National Laboratories (1948). He made major contributions to the "strong-focusing" of magnetic fields used in particle accelerators.

Courant, Richard (1888–1972) mathematician; born in Lublintz, Poland. A highly decorated officer in the German Army (1914–19) and recipient of the Order of Merit, he came to America (1933) to head the mathematics department at New York University (NYU) (1934–58); he founded an advanced mathematical department, later named the Courant Institute. A prominent educator and National Academy of Sciences member, he was professor emeritus and science advisor at NYU (1958). With H. Robbins he wrote *What is Mathematics?* and several other texts.

Cournand, André F. (Frederic) (1895–1988) physician; born in Paris, France. He served in the French army (1915–19), received his M.D. degree, then emigrated to the U.S.A. (1930) and joined the staff of Columbia University/Bellevue Hospital (1930–64). A specialist in cardiac surgery, he shared the 1965 Nobel Prize in physiology or medicine with his collaborator Dickinson Richards and German physician Werner Forssmann for developing the technique of cardiac catheterization. Cournand later expanded his work to include research on the lungs. After 1964, he trained physicians for research in his field and developed educational programs on the history and social responsibility of science.

Courtney, Charles (Edward) (1849–1920) rower; born in Union Springs, N.Y. He won the Association single sculls in 1875 and the doubles in 1875–76. He was the Cornell University crew coach (1885–1920).

Cousins, Norman (?1915–90) editor, humanitarian, author; born in Union Hill, N.J. As editor of the *Saturday Review of*

Literature (later simply *Saturday Review*) (1942–71, 1973–77), he broadened its scope to include all the arts and many social concerns, thus expanding its audience. He himself was active in promoting various educational, humanitarian, and world-peace initiatives. His popular book, *Anatomy of an Illness* (1979), described his experience in drawing on his emotions – specifically laughter – to overcome illness; he took up the cause of holistic health, even teaching at the medical school of the University of California.

Cousy, (Robert Joseph) Bob (1928–   ) basketball player; born in New York City. One of basketball's greatest playmakers and passers, he was an All-American at Holy Cross. He played guard for the Boston Celtics (1950–63), where he was a ten-time All-NBA (National Basketball Association) first team selection. Between 1957 and 1963, he led the Celtics to six NBA titles in seven years. An author of basketball instructionals and a broadcaster after retiring from the game, he was elected to basketball's Hall of Fame in 1970.

Couzens, James (1872–1936) industrialist, U.S. senator, philanthropist; born in Chatham, Ontario, Canada. Moving to Detroit in 1890, he became one of the original investors in Ford's motor company. As general manager of the Ford Motor Company, he was a major factor in the company's early success and he retired a wealthy man in 1915. He was Detroit's mayor from 1918 to 1922. As a Progressive Republican in the U.S. Senate (1922–36), he advocated graduated income taxes and public ownership of utilities. The Republicans denied him renomination in 1936. His philanthropies included hospitals and other medical organizations.

Cowell, Henry (Dixon) (1897–1965) composer; born in Menlo Park, Calif. Largely self-taught as pianist and composer, in his teens he gravitated to radical musical experiments including his trademark use of tone-cluster harmony. From the 1920s he pursued an international career as composer, concert promoter, and pianist, specializing in his own and others' "ultra-modern" music; he also taught and wrote books including the 1919 *New Musical Resources*, and in 1927 founded the historic *New Music Quarterly*. In his own music, progressive ideas appear alongside traditional material; his works include 20 symphonies.

Cowles, Henry Chandler (1869–1939) botanist, ecologist; born in Kensington, Conn. An Oberlin College graduate (1893), he took his Ph.D. at the University of Chicago (1894). He taught at Gates College (Nebraska) (1894–95), spent the summer of 1895 as a field assistant to the U.S. Geological Survey, then joined the faculty of the University of Chicago (1898–1934). His work emphasized the relations between vegetation and geology, and his scholarly studies – including *The Plant Societies of Chicago and Vicinity* (1901) – helped establish the new scientific discipline of ecology. He made major contributions to studies of the vegetation in the forests, dunes, and prairies of the region around Lake Michigan and northern Illinois; he was instrumental in establishing forest reserves in Illinois; he co-founded the Ecological Society of America in 1915, serving as its president in 1918; he was coauthor of the once standard *Textbook of Botany for Colleges and Universities* (2 vols. 1910–11); and he edited the *Botanical Gazette* from 1925 until his retirement from the Chicago faculty.

Cowley, Malcolm (1898–1989) literary critic, editor; born in Belasco, Pa. He interrupted his studies at Harvard to serve with the American Ambulance Corps in World War I. Returning to France for graduate studies (1921–23), he got to know some of the American writers he would write of in his first widely recognized book, *Exile's Return* (1934). Meanwhile, he worked as a free-lance writer, contributing book reviews and critical essays, translating French works, and composing his own poetry. As associate editor of the *New Republic* (1929–44) he promoted contemporary American writers. As literary advisor to Viking Press (1948–85) he edited popularly available editions of selected works of writers from Hawthorne and Whitman to F. Scott Fitzgerald and Hemingway; it is generally recognized that his *Viking Portable* edition of William Faulkner (1946) was responsible for launching Faulkner's serious reputation. Cowley encouraged later generations of writers such as John Cheever, Jack Kerouac, and Ken Kesey and continued writing and lecturing to promote American literature until his final years.

Cox, Allan V. (Verne) (1926–87) geophysicist; born in Santa Ana, Calif. He was a professor of geophysics at Stanford University (1967), then dean of their School of Earth Sciences (1979). His paleomagnetic research substantiated evidence of periodic reversals in the earth's magnetic field, confirmed plate tectonic theories of continental drift and sea floor spreading, and led to publication of a new geologic time scale (1982).

Cox, Archibald (1912–   ) professor of law, solicitor general; born in Plainfield, N.J. A widely published expert on labor law and long time professor at Harvard (1946–61, 1965–84), he served as solicitor general of the United States under Presidents John F. Kennedy and Lyndon B. Johnson (1961–65). He became widely known as director of the office of the Watergate special prosecution force (1973); he was fired when he demanded that President Richard Nixon turn over possibly incriminating tapes. In 1980 he became chairman of Common Cause.

Cox, Edward Eugene (1880–1952) U.S. representative; born in Mitchell County, Ga. A circuit court judge and lawyer in southwest Georgia, he went to congress (1925–52), becoming a member of the powerful Rules Committee and leading the Southern Democrats opposed to the New Deal. When the Federal Communications Commission charged him with violating federal law in 1943, he demanded their links to Communism be investigated. Despite public outrage, he remained in Congress, successfully blocking progressive legislation.

Cox, George Barnsdale (1853–1916) political boss; born in Cincinnati, Ohio. A Cincinnati saloon keeper, active in Republican politics, he consolidated his power on the Board of Public Affairs, doling out state jobs. His political machine controlled the Republican Party in Ohio (1888–1910). Indicted for missing bank payments, he was cleared, but he retired from politics in 1911, investing in theater afterward.

Cox, James Middleton (1870–1957) editor, publisher, U.S. representative, governor; born in Jacksonburg, Ohio. A successful reporter, he bought the struggling *Dayton Evening News* in 1898 – first building block in the eventual Cox Enterprises newspaper conglomerate. A liberal Democratic congressman (1909–12), then three-term governor of Ohio, he was a friend of labor and foe of Prohibition. Nominated for president in 1920, he lost the election to Warren Harding.

Cox, Kenyon (1856–1919) painter, art critic; born in Warren, Ohio. An academic painter, he studied at the Pennsylvania

Academy of the Fine Arts (1876), and with Gérôme in Paris (1878–82), before returning to New York City. He painted Augustus St. Gaudens, the famous sculptor, in 1908. His art criticism, such as *Painters and Sculptors* (1907), was widely read.

Coxey, Jacob (Sechler) (1854–1951) businessman, monetary reformer; born in Selinsgrove, Pa. Owner of a silica sand company in Massillon, Ohio (1878–1951), he sought to promote non-metal-based legal-tender currency. In the 1890s he championed make-work projects for the unemployed, to be financed by "greenbacks." Inspired by Carl Browne, a sideshow medicine man who injected the theme of reincarnation of souls into the crusade, Coxey marshaled a group of 100 unemployed to march on Washington to raise awareness of the greenback issue (1894). Numbering 500 by the time it reached Washington, "Coxey's army" was allowed to march down Pennsylvania Avenue, but not to the Capitol itself. Coxey made a dash for the Capitol steps and was seized; he was sentenced to 20 days in jail. Between 1894 and 1943 he constantly ran for major offices, from the Ohio governorship to president of the U.S.A.; the only office he held was mayor of Massillon, Ohio (1932–34).

Coyle, Joseph T. (1943–) psychiatrist; born in Chicago. He became chairman of the department of psychiatry at the Harvard Medical School in 1991. His research was focused on the basic neurological mechanisms responsible for Alzheimer's disease and Huntington's disease. He pioneered studies on the development of brain neurotransmitter systems and showed their relevance to psychiatric disorders.

Cozzens, James Gould (1903–78) writer; born in Chicago. He was first published in *Atlantic Monthly* at age 16; his first novel appeared in 1924. Often promoting socially conservative views, his novels focused on the world of male professionals; his best-known works are carefully crafted character studies such as *Guard of Honor* (1948, Pulitzer Prize) and *By Love Possessed* (1957). Although his popularity peaked in the 1950s, he continued to publish into the late 1960s.

Craig, Harmon (1926–) oceanographer; born in New York City. He served the University of Chicago (1951–55), then joined the University of California: San Diego (1955–65) and its Scripps Institute of Oceanography (1965). He made major contributions to the chemical relationships of lakes and oceans, the atmosphere, and land formations.

Craig, Malin (1875–1945) soldier; born in St. Joseph, Mo. Son of a career cavalry officer and a 1898 West Point graduate, this hardworking, colorless officer carried out an extensive modernization as army chief of staff in the late 1930s. At his direction, the army upgraded mobilization plans, updated armored equipment and doctrine, and improved communications.

Cram, Donald (James) (1919–) chemist; born in Chester, Vt. He became affiliated with the University of California: Los Angeles in 1947. He elucidated mechanisms of molecular recognition, working most notably on the properties of crown ether molecules. He shared the Nobel Prize in chemistry (1987) for this work.

Cram, Ralph Adams (1863–1942) architect and author; born in Hampton Falls, N.H. In partnership in Boston with Bertram Goodhue and then with Frank William Ferguson (1892–1913) he became identified with the Gothic Revival style, particularly in church (the Cathedral of St. John the

Divine (1915–41), New York) and collegiate architecture (West Point (1903–10), Princeton University (1907–29)). Cram directed architecture studies at the Massachusetts Institute of Technology (1914–19) and published several books on Gothic architecture and medieval-based social systems.

Cranch, William (1769–1855) jurist; born in Weymouth, Mass. Nephew of John Adams, classmate of John Quincy Adams, he served 54 years on the U.S. Circuit Court of the District of Columbia, the last 50 (1805–55) as its chief justice. He was also reporter of the U.S. Supreme Court (1802–17), and his clear and accurate reports remain important for understanding many of Chief Justice John Marshall's important decisions. He published decisions of his own court (1801–41) in six volumes (1852–53).

Crandall, Prudence (later Philleo) (1803–90) educator, abolitionist; born in Hopkinton, R.I. Her short-lived attempt to train young black women as teachers in her Canterbury, Conn., boarding school (1833–34), provoked passage of a local "black law" and harassment ranging from arrest to violent attacks. Crandall worked for women's rights and temperance throughout her life.

Crane, Carl J. (1900–82) aviator; born in San Antonio, Texas. He was commissioned in the Air Corps in 1924 and, over a long career, proved himself to be an engineering innovator, particularly the development of blind flight and automatic flight and landing instruments. He was coauthor of *Blind Flight in Theory and Practice* (1932).

Crane, Charles Richard (1858–1939) internationalist, philanthropist; born in Chicago. He was the heir to the Crane Company plumbing supplies fortune. He traveled at an early age and met the British adventurer, Richard Burton, in Damascus. He sold his interest in the family company to a brother (1912) and was the largest single contributor to Woodrow Wilson's campaign in 1912. At the end of World War I, he coauthored (with Henry Churchill King) the Crane-King report on what to do with the various lands belonging to the defeated Turkish Ottoman Empire; although ignored at the time, their warning that Palestine was largely an Arab land would in later years be drawn into the controversy over the establishment of Israel on this territory. He was ambassador to China (1920–21). He gave generously to the Marine Biological Laboratory at Woods Hole, Mass., and to the American Colleges in Istanbul. He created the Institute of Current World Affairs (1925). He had an extremely large number of international friends and connections.

Crane, (Harold) Hart (1899–1932) poet; born in Garrettsville, Ohio. Educated in Cleveland, Ohio, he worked in a shipyard, at his father's drug store, and in advertising before moving to New York City (1923) where he worked briefly for a publishing firm. He is known for his visionary and symbolic poetry, as in *The Bridge* (1930). He led a dissolute life and traveled widely; returning from a trip to Mexico (1931–32), he apparently jumped off the ship and drowned.

Crane, (Robert) Bruce (1857–1937) painter; born in New York City. He studied with A. H. Wyant (c. 1877) in New York, and in France (1882). A respected color tonalist and impressionist, as in *December Uplands* (1919), he maintained a studio in Summit, N.J., and lived in Bronxville, N.Y.

Crane, R. S. (Ronald Salmon) (1886–1967) literary critic, educator; born in Tecumseh, Mich. A professor at the

University of Chicago (1935–52) and founder of the Chicago School of literary criticism, he energetically upheld humanistic values in literature against the New Critics.

Crane, Stephen (Townley) (1871–1900) writer, poet; born in Newark, N.J. He studied at Claverack College and Hudson River Institute, near Hudson, N.Y. (1888–90), and briefly at Lafayette College, Pa., and Syracuse College, N.Y. (1891). He moved to New York City (1892), worked as a journalist, published his first novel, *Maggie: A Girl of the Streets* (1893), and wrote poetry. In 1895 he published his most famous work, *The Red Badge of Courage,* a novel concentrating on a young Civil War soldier. He traveled widely as a journalist and war correspondent but in 1898 settled in England where he became friends with several important writers including Joseph Conrad. Crane died prematurely of tuberculosis, but he left a body of work that has secured him a place as an American master.

Cranston, Alan (MacGregor) (1914–   ) U.S. senator; born in Palo Alto, Calif. Elected to the U.S. Senate (Dem., Cal.; 1968–92), he ran unsuccessfully for the presidential nomination in 1984. He supported disarmament and liberal domestic policies.

Crapsey, Adelaide (1878–1914) poet; born in Brooklyn Heights, N.Y. She attended Vassar (1897–1901), studied archaeology in Rome (1904–05), taught school in America (1902–04; 1908), and lived in Rome (1908–13). Using an innovative verse form called cinquains, she anticipated the Imagist poets, as seen in her *Verses* (1915). She died of tuberculosis at a sanatorium in Saranac Lake, N.Y.

Crater, Joseph Force (1889–?1930) lawyer, judge; born in Easton, Pa. He graduated from Lafayette College (1910) and Columbia Law School (1913), practiced law in New York City, and became active in Tammany Hall Democratic politics. Chosen to fill an unexpired term on the New York Supreme Court in 1930, he disappeared after dinner at a restaurant on August 6 of that year. Despite an extensive investigation, no trace of him was ever found; he was declared dead in July 1937. Some speculated that his disappearance was connected with Tammany corruption, but no such link could be established.

Craven, Wayne (1930–   ) art historian, writer; born in Pontiac, Ill. He graduated from Indiana University (B.A. 1955; M.A. 1957), and Columbia University (Ph.D. 1958–60). Regarded as a leading historian of American sculpture, he taught at the University of Delaware (1960) and published numerous works, including *Sculpture in America: The Colonial Period to the Present* (1984).

Crawford, Cheryl (1902–86) actress, director, producer; born in Akron, Ohio. One of the founders of the Group Theatre in 1931, she began her career acting with the Theatre Guild. She also helped found the American Repertory Theatre in 1946, the Actors Studio in 1947, and became a director of the American National Theatre and Academy (ANTA) series. She produced *One Touch of Venus* (1943), *Brigadoon* (1947), and *Sweet Bird of Youth* (1959).

Crawford, Francis Marion (1854–1909) writer; born in Bagni di Lucca, Italy (son of Thomas Crawford). He was educated in the U.S.A. and at European universities. Soon after the immediate success of his first novel, *Mr. Isaacs* (1882), he moved to Italy. An inveterate traveler, he used foreign settings in dozens of popular historical romances and adventure novels, many of which he adapted for the stage.

He wrote the drama *Francesca da Rimini* (1902) especially for Sarah Bernhardt.

Crawford, Frederick C. (Coolidge) (1891–   ) corporate executive; born in Watertown, Mass. A Harvard-trained civil engineer, he worked for Thompson Products, Inc., Cleveland, Ohio (1916–59, president after 1933). A leader of the U.S. industrial war effort, he converted production to aircraft during World War II; he formed the conglomerate TRW (1958). He was an outspoken opponent of organized labor.

Crawford, Joan (b. Lucille Fay Le Sueur) (1906–77) film actress; born in San Antonio, Texas. A chorus girl, she came to Hollywood in 1924, worked as an extra, and then was featured in *Pretty Ladies* (1925). She was usually cast as a working-class girl with her eyes set on wealth, later becoming the other woman. She won an Oscar for *Mildred Pierce* (1945). Her daughter, Christina Crawford, wrote a scathing attack on her domestic tyranny in *Mommie Dearest* (1978).

Crawford, (John Wallace) "Captain Jack" (1847–1917) scout, author; born in County Donegal, Ireland. He came to the U.S.A. in 1854 and worked as a coal miner. He served with the Union forces in the Civil War and as a scout in campaigns against the Sioux and Apache Indians. He established a ranch in New Mexico and wrote books and plays, including *The Poet Scout* (1879).

Crawford, (Samuel Earl) Sam (1880–1968) baseball player; born in Wahoo, Nebr. As an outfielder for the Cincinnati Reds and Detroit Tigers (1899–1917), he hit more triples (312) than any player in history. Nicknamed "Wahoo Sam," he was elected to the Hall of Fame in 1957.

Crawford, Thomas (1813/14–57) sculptor; born in New York City (or Ireland). He was a woodcarver (c. 1827) and a stone cutter (c. 1832), attended the National Academy of Design (c. 1832), and settled permanently in Rome (1835). Essentially an imitator of classical sculpture, he created several marble and bronze sculptures in Washington, D.C., including *Progress of Civilization* (1853) for the U.S. Senate.

Crawford-Seeger, Ruth (1901–53) composer; born in East Liverpool, Ohio. Among her teachers was Charles Seeger, whom she later married. Her first works, such as the 1931 String Quartet, show great innovative imagination and have been successfully revived. She gave up composing for nearly ten years to raise her family and contribute to her husband's work in folksong.

Cray, Seymour R. (1925–   ) computer designer; born in Chippewa Falls, Wis. Educated at the University of Wisconsin, he established himself at the forefront of large-scale computer design through his work at Engineering Associates, Remington Rand, UNIVAC, and Control Data Corporation. In 1972 he founded Cray Research in Colorado Springs and established the standard for supercomputers with the introduction of the CRAY-1 (1976) and CRAY-2 (1985). He resigned as chief executive in 1981 (but remained as consultant director) to devote himself to computer design. He made significant contributions in vector register technology and cooling systems.

Crazy Horse (b. Tashunka Witco) (?1842–77) Oglala Sioux chief; born near the Black Hills near present-day South Dakota. His mother was a sister of Brulé Chief Spotted Tail and his father was an Oglala medicine man who often spoke of the need for a leader to unite the Sioux and drive out the whites. As a youth, Crazy Horse was solitary and meditative – the Sioux called him "Strange One" – but also an accomplished hunter and fighter. He participated in all of the major Sioux actions to protect the Black Hills against white intrusion, believing himself immune from battle injury. In 1865 he was selected as a "shirt wearer," or protector of the people, in recognition of his valor and achievement and he took part in the main battles of Red Cloud's war (1865–68). In 1876 he was named supreme war and peace chief of the Oglalas, uniting in struggle most of the Sioux still free. In January 1876 he led the Sioux and Cheyenne to victory at the battle of Rosebud; that July he led these same tribes' warriors in defeating Custer's forces at Little Bighorn. Pursued by U.S. forces, with his band of some 1,000 facing starvation, he surrendered in May 1877. White fear and Indian jealousy led to intrigue against him and finally to his death at the hands of a U.S. soldier – allegedly while resisting being forced into a jail cell. He is regarded as a symbol of the heroic resistance of the Sioux and as their greatest leader, and a gigantic figure of Crazy Horse has been sculptured (by Korczak Ziolkowski) out of mountain in the Black Hills of South Dakota.

Crazy Snake (b. Chitto Harjo) (1846–1912) Creek chief; born in the Indian Territory (present-day Oklahoma). In 1897, he set up the "Snake Government," a traditional body designed to counter the legal dissolution of tribal governments. A Snake-led uprising (1901) proved unsuccessful. He was a great orator and advocate for the traditional ways of his people.

Creel, George (1876–1953) journalist, government official; born in Lafayette County, Mo. A self-educated muckraking journalist who founded the Kansas City *Independent* (1898–1909), he wrote exposés for *Cosmopolitan* and attacked child labor in *The Children of Bondage* (1914). During World War I, President Wilson named him head of the Committee on Public Information (1917–20), responsible for both propaganda at home in support of the war, and information abroad about America. In later years he turned to writing popular history and columns for *Collier's*.

Creeley, Robert (White) (1926–) poet, writer; born in Arlington, Mass. He studied at Harvard (1943–46), Black Mountain College (B.A. 1955), and the University of New Mexico (M.A. 1960). After extensive travel, he taught at New York State University: Buffalo (1966). Known for his poetry, as in *Mirrors* (1983), he also wrote criticism and fiction.

Creelman, James (1859–1915) journalist; born in Montreal, Canada. A leading reporter for the *New York World, New York Journal,* and other publications, he was known for his intrepid coverage of wars and insurrections around the globe.

Creighton, James Edwin (1861–1924) philosopher; born in Pictou, Nova Scotia. In 1892, after study in Germany, he earned a doctorate from Cornell University and joined the faculty of Cornell's new Sage School of Philosophy (1889–1924). He also became coeditor and (from 1902) editor of the new *Philosophical Review,* American editor of *Kant-Studien* (from 1896), and a cofounder and first president (1902–03) of the American Philosophical Association. His own philosophy was idealistic; a volume of his essays appeared posthumously (1925).

Cremin, Lawrence (Arthur) (1925–90) historian, educator; born in New York City. A professor at Teachers College,

Columbia University (1948–90), Cremin was president of Teachers College (1974–84) and the Spencer Foundation (1985–90). His major published works include a Pulitzer Prize-winning 3-volume history of American education (1970–80) and *Popular Education and its Discontents* (1990).

Cressey, Donald R. (1919–87) sociologist of crime; born in Fergus Falls, Minn. An authority on juvenile delinquency, organized crime, embezzlement, and other white-collar crimes, he was one of the foremost practicing sociologists of crime. After teaching at the University of California: Santa Barbara (1962–86), he assumed the presidency of the Institute for Financial Crime Prevention after retirement. He served as an adviser to national and state agencies concerned with formulating law and policy and was the author of numerous books and texts.

Cressey, George (Babcock) (1896–1963) geographer; born in Tiffin, Ohio. He spent a total of ten years in Asia (much of it in China) from which came *China's Geographic Foundations* (1934), *Asia's Lands and Peoples* (1944), *Land of the 500 Million: A Geography of China* (1955), and many other books and articles.

Cressman, George (Palmer) (1919–) meteorologist; born in West Chester, Pa. He founded the joint numerical weather prediction unit at the U.S. Weather Bureau in 1954 and was instrumental in developing worldwide weather prediction capabilities. Director of the U.S. Weather Bureau from 1965–79, he won many awards including the Robert M. Losey award in 1965.

Cret, Paul Philippe (1876–1945) architect and educator; born in Lyons, France. He studied at the École des Beaux-Arts, Paris and emigrated to Philadelphia in 1903. Particularly prolific during the 1920s, he designed civic and memorial buildings in a modern classical style adapted to steel-frame construction; his work includes the Folger Shakespeare Library, Washington, D.C. (1928–32). Cret was professor of design at the University of Pennsylvania (1903–37). He received the American Institute of Architects' Gold Medal (1938).

Crèvecoeur, (Michel-Guillaume) Jean de (1735–1813) essayist, farmer; born near Caen, France. He fought on the French side in the French and Indian War and then moved to New York State (1759); after travels through various colonies, he settled to farm in Orange County, N.Y. (1769–80). Drawing on his experiences of and insights into frontier life, he wrote one of the classic accounts of life in colonial America, *Letter from an American Farmer* (1782), as well as what would in 1925 be published as *Sketches*. He introduced alfalfa to American soil and became a naturalized citizen (1765). Between 1783–90, he was the French consul in New York City and then returned permanently to France.

Crile, George Washington (1864–1943) surgeon; born near Chili, Ohio. After taking his medical degree at the University of Wooster (Ohio) and studying in Europe, he taught at Wooster (1889–1900) and then was affiliated with the Western Reserve School of Medicine (Cleveland) (1900–24). He founded the Cleveland Clinic (1921). Interested in the phenomenon of "shock" subsequent to blood loss, he popularized the use of the blood pressure cuff. He demonstrated the importance of measuring peripheral and venous pressures during surgery and developed safer surgical techniques.

Crippen, Hawley Harvey (1862–1910) physician, murderer;

born in Michigan. In 1896 he settled in London with his second wife, whom he poisoned and buried in his cellar in 1909. With his secretary-lover, he fled on an Atlantic liner, but was arrested on board, becoming the first person ever to be apprehended with the help of radio. Tried and found guilty, he was executed in November 1910.

Crisp, Charles (Frederick) (1845–96) U.S. representative; born in Sheffield, England. Although his actor parents were visiting England at his birth, they raised their son in Georgia which he left at age 16 to join the 10th Virginia Infantry. After three years of service and one year in Morris Island prison, he returned to Georgia in 1865 to study law. Appointed solicitor general of the southwestern superior court region from Americus, Ga., in 1872, he also served as judge there for five years. Elected to Congress (Dem., Ga.; 1883–96), he mastered parliamentary procedure and became Democratic leader and Speaker of the House (1891–95). He championed the Interstate Commerce Act (1887) and supported the introduction of silver currency, running for the Senate against Hoke Smith, President Cleveland's secretary of the interior, who advocated maintaining the gold standard. Although Georgia voters supported Crisp, he died before the election.

Crittenden, John J. (Jordan) (1787–1863) lawyer, U.S. senator, cabinet officer; born in Versailles, Ky. After graduating from William and Mary (1807), he returned to Kentucky to practice law. He became a prominent defense attorney before serving several terms in the U.S. Senate (Whig, Ky.; 1817–19, 1835–41, 1842–48, 1854–61). In between his time in the Senate, he served as governor of Kentucky (1849), and U.S. attorney general (1841, 1850–53). After his proposed Crittenden Compromise (1860) – extending the Missouri Compromise line to the Pacific, thus allowing but restricting the spread of slavery – failed to avert the Civil War, he moved over to the U.S. House of Representatives (1861–63), where he continued to press for Kentucky's neutrality, the containment of the Union's expanding war aims, and for restraining radicals on both sides.

Crocker, Charles (1822–88) merchant, railroad builder, capitalist; born in Troy, N.Y. His family moved to Indiana (1836) where he established an iron forge (1845); he sold this when he went to California where he took up gold mining. He soon realized that the real money lay in selling goods, and the store he opened in Sacramento in 1852 made him rich within a few years; by 1860 he was elected to the state legislature. Joining forces with Mark Hopkins, Leland Stanford, and C. P. Huntington, he formed the Central Pacific Railroad and personally supervised its construction from California across the Sierra Nevada to its junction with the Union Pacific in Utah (1863–69). In 1871 he assumed the presidency of the Southern Pacific Railroad and he merged it with the Central Pacific in 1884. He was also active in banking, real estate, irrigation, and other projects.

Crocker, Chester (Arthur) (1941–   ) diplomat; born in New York City. He studied at Johns Hopkins University and worked as a journalist on the *Africa Report* (1965–66, 1968–69). He served on the National Security Council (1970–72) and then returned to academic life at Georgetown University. As assistant secretary of state for African affairs (1981–89) he pushed for a policy of "constructive engagement" with South Africa. He was on the board of directors of the U.S. Institute of Peace (1991).

Crockett, (David) "Davy" (1786–1836) frontier figure, U.S. representative; born near present-day Rogersville, Tenn. He was a poor farmer but an excellent hunter and scout. He served under General Andrew Jackson in the Creek War (1813–14). He was a justice of the peace and a Tennessee legislator, and served in the U.S. House of Representatives (Dem., Tenn.; 1827–31, Whig, Tenn.; 1833–35). With little formal education, he was not especially well informed on public issues and he was always ready to take a break from public service to go bear hunting. He made a celebrated tour of the major northern cities (1834). Failing in his re-election effort in 1834, he went to Texas to aid the Anglo-Americans in their struggle for independence. He was killed in the defense of the Alamo.

Croghan, George (?1720–82) Indian agent; born near Dublin, Ireland. He came to Philadelphia in 1741, learned Indian languages and soon built a trade empire on the Pennsylvania frontier. When the start of the French and Indian War (1754) ruined his trade, he became the deputy superintendent of northern Indian affairs (1756–72). He brought about the treaty which ended Pontiac's revolt (1766). During the American Revolution he was unjustly suspected of Loyalist sympathies; he also lost the fortune he had accumulated through trading and land speculation.

Croker, Richard (1841–1922) political boss; born in County Cork, Ireland. His family came to New York City when he was three years old. He worked as a machinist and led a street gang (and was a prize fighter) and became involved in Democratic Party politics by serving as an aide to John Kelly of Tammany Hall. Croker was elected alderman in 1868, and when Kelly replaced the ousted (1871) "Boss" Tweed as the boss of New York City by 1874, Croker also gained influence. When Kelly retired in 1884, he left control of Tammany Hall to Croker. Although Croker held only one formal office during this period – city chamberlain (1889–90) – for the next 17 years, he had a large say in who was elected mayor of New York and controlled patronage. With the election of the reform candidate Seth Low in 1901, Croker lost influence and in 1903 he returned to Ireland, where he purchased a large estate and bred race horses, one of which won the coveted English Derby. He married twice, the second time to a Cherokee Indian.

Croly, Herbert David (1869–1930) editor, author; born in New York City. He was the son of David Goodman Croly, a prominent Irish-born journalist, and Jane Cunningham Croly, also a journalist and an activist for equal rights for women. He interrupted his studies at Harvard between 1886 and 1899 to work as an editor in New York City and to study abroad. From 1900 to 1906 he was editor of the *Architectural Record,* but he left to write *The Promise of American Life* (1909); this and its sequel, *Progressive Democracy* (1914), were extremely influential in their day by calling upon thoughtful Americans to reexamine the true nature and goals of their society. His reputation led Willard Straight, a wealthy diplomat and financier, to found the *New Republic* in 1914, expressly so Croly could edit it to further his ideas. Although aligned with Progressives, it endorsed President Woodrow Wilson's position on entering World War I, then opposed Wilson's acceptance of the Treaty of Versailles. This cost the *New Republic* many readers and in his final decade, having lost his influence in political circles, he took up religious and philosophical questions.

Cromwell, Dean (Bartlett) (1879–1962) track and field coach; born in Turner, Ore. As a track and field coach for the University of Southern California (1909–48), he trained athletes who won gold medals in every Olympiad between 1912 and 1948.

Cromwell, William N. (Nelson) (1854–1948) lawyer; born in Brooklyn, N.Y. Beginning as an accountant in the New York law firm of Algernon S. Sullivan, he joined it after completing law school, becoming a partner in 1879. As Sullivan and Cromwell, it soon became one of New York's most successful firms, specializing in business law. He consolidated 16 concerns into the National Tube Company, concluded the battle over the Illinois Central Railroad, promoted the Panama Canal, and established the "Cromwell plan" – forerunner of "Chapter 11" bankruptcies – allowing insolvent firms to continue operations. After World War I, he devoted himself to charitable causes and he left his large estate to legal and other philanthropies.

Cronin, James W. (Watson) (1931–) physicist; born in Chicago, Ill. He worked at Brookhaven National Laboratories (1955–58), then moved to Princeton (1958–71). In 1963 he and Val Fitch collaborated to discover violations of the symmetry principle in the decay of the kaon, a subatomic particle; for this work the two scientists received the 1980 Nobel Prize in physics. He joined the University of Chicago (1971), where he continued his research in elementary particles.

Cronkite, Walter (Leland, Jr.) (1916–) television journalist; born in St. Joseph, Mo. Raised in Houston, Texas, he decided to become a journalist after reading a magazine article about a foreign correspondent. He left the University of Texas to work for the *Houston Post* in 1935, later working for Midwestern radio stations. During World War II, he covered the European front for United Press and served as chief United Press correspondent at the Nuremberg trials. Joining Columbia Broadcasting System (CBS) News in 1950, he worked on a variety of programs, and covered national political conventions and elections from 1952 to 1981. He helped inaugurate the *CBS Evening News* in 1962, and anchored it until his 1981 retirement; "And that's the way it is" was his nightly closing epithet. The hallmarks of his style were honesty, objectivity and level-headedness; identified in public opinion polls as the man Americans most trusted, he provided a voice of reason during the Vietnam and Watergate eras. After retiring, he hosted CBS's *Universe* (1982), coproduced *Why in the World* (1981) for Public Broadcasting System, and hosted *Dinosaur!* (1991) for Arts and Entertainment Cable television.

Cronquist, Arthur (John) (b. Franklin Arthur Beers) (1919–92) botanist; born in San Jose, Calif. He was a staff member at the New York Botanical Garden (1943–46), taught at the University of Georgia (1946–48), moved to the State College of Washington (1948–52), then returned to the New York Botanical Garden (1952–92). He made major contributions to the taxonomy of American species of composite flowers, the systematics of flowering plants, and studies of the flora of the U.S.A. and southern Canada. His system of classifying plants by their evolutionary relationships (1968), known as the Cronquist system, has become the definitive taxonomic reference for botanists.

Cronyn, Hume (1911–) stage and film actor; born in London, Ontario. While studying law at McGill University, he enjoyed success as an actor in Montreal, so he came on to New York (1934) and soon gained a reputation as a character actor, first on the stage and, starting in 1943, in many movies. Over the years he often teamed with his wife (since 1942), Jessica Tandy. He wrote film and stage adaptations and directed for the theater.

Crook, George (1829–90) soldier; born near Dayton, Ohio. A tough, fearless soldier and an efficient commander, he graduated from West Point in 1852 and survived the uninspiring routines of 1850s garrison life to obtain several important commands during the Civil War. He led a Union brigade at Antietam, Md., in 1862 and a corps under Sheridan in the Shenandoah Valley in 1864, where he fought at Winchester, Fisher's Hill, and Cedar Creek. It is as an Indian fighter, however, that Crook is remembered. He pacified Apaches under Cochise from 1871 to 1873 and, during the Sioux War of 1876, was defeated by Crazy Horse at Rosebud Creek. Crook's forces remained in the field for nearly a year during the Sioux campaign, an epic of hardship and endurance. In 1882 and 1883 he fought Geronimo's Apaches in Arizona. For all his fierceness in battle, Crook was "more prone to pardon than to punish," according to one authority; unlike many fellow officers, he respected his Indian adversaries and believed they should be granted the full privileges of citizenship.

Cropsey, Jasper (Francis) (1823–1900) painter; born in Staten Island, N.Y. He studied architecture, but after traveling in Europe (1847 and 1856), he settled in Hastings-on-Hudson, N.Y. (1864), and concentrated on landscape painting. Considered a member of the Hudson River School of painting, his theatrical and naturalistic canvases, such as *View of the Kaaterskill House* (1855), and *Autumn on the Hudson River* (1860), reveal his romantic approach to nature.

Crosby, Caresse (b. Polly Jacob) (1892–1970) publisher, poet; born in New York City. Married to Harry Crosby in 1922, she shared with him the life of an American literary expatriate in Paris. She wrote poetry and collaborated in establishing the publishing imprint of Editions Narcisse and then Black Sun Press, which she continued after his death in 1929.

Crosby, (George Robert) Bob (1913–93) band leader; born in Spokane, Wash. (brother of Bing Crosby). He became leader of a big-band that was internationally popular in the late-1930s, and members such as Matty Matlock, Nappy Lamare, and Bob Haggart also played in the Bob Cats, a famous small band. Crosby served in World War II and later performed on radio and television and formed reunion bands for special performances.

Crosby, (Harry Lillis) Bing (1904–77) popular singer, movie actor; born in Tacoma, Wash. Beginning as a vocalist-drummer with a combo while in college, he went on to sing with the Rhythm Boys for the Paul Whiteman Orchestra (1926–30). In 1931 he went solo and after appearing in nightclubs he signed a recording contract and appeared in eight Mack Sennett movie shorts. (By this time he had adopted the name "Bing," reportedly from a comic strip character.) This led to his fabulously successful career, with his own radio program (his theme song was "Where the Blue of the Night"), recordings, movies, and television appearances. As a singer, he borrowed from diverse styles including jazz and became one of the earliest crooners who established a clear split between classical and popular singing. His smooth, casual, almost "talking" approach to a melody and subtle use of embellishments highlighted the text of a song and inspired many singers who followed. He sang his signature song, "White Christmas," in the film *Holiday Inn* (1942). Before this he had appeared during the 1930s in several light musicals; in the 1940s he carved out a new career as the wisecracking companion of Bob Hope in the seven "Road" pictures; he also made several serious movies and won the Academy Award for his role in *Going My Way* (1944). He joined Louis Armstrong in the film *High Society* (1956) and on the album *Bing Crosby-Louis Armstrong* (1960). Returning to his roots in jazz, he was accompanied on later world tours by a quartet that included jazz players Joe Bushkin and Milt Hinton. He had become extremely wealthy from his career and investments but later revelations showed that he had been less successful as a father.

Crosby, (Henry Sturgis) Harry (1898–1929) publisher, poet; born in Boston, Mass. An eccentric, flamboyant figure, he was prominent, along with his wife, Caresse Crosby, in Parisian literary and artistic circles during the 1920s until his suicide. He published works of distinguished contemporaries, as well as his own verse and that of his wife; his diaries were published posthumously.

Cross, Amanda See HEILBRUN, CAROLYN.

Cross, Samuel Hazzard (1891–1946) Slavic language specialist, diplomat; born in Westerly, R.I. Known for greatly expanding the Slavic studies curriculum, he served from the end of World War I through 1926 in a variety of diplomatic posts. These included commercial attaché to the American embassy in Belgium (1921–25) and then chief of the European Division of the Bureau of Foreign and Domestic Trade. He resigned in 1926 and after a time in the securities business, he began in 1928 to lecture in history and German language at Harvard and Tufts. In 1930 he became professor of Slavic languages at Harvard, a post he held until his death. Irascible and energetic, he was known for his brilliant linguistic skills. He was an avid fan of Russian architecture and ballet.

Cross, Wilbur (Lucius) (1862–1948) academic, governor; born in Gurleyville, Conn. Educated in a one-room schoolhouse, he studied English literature at Yale, receiving his Ph.D. in 1889. He taught English at a private school in Pittsburgh, Pa., returning to teach at Yale (1894–1930). Becoming editor of the *Yale Review* in 1911, he transformed it into a national quarterly of literature and public affairs. As dean of the Yale Graduate School (1916–30), he attracted scholars and built a graduate school quadrangle. He published several important works including *The Development of the English Novel* (1889), *The Life and Times of Laurence Sterne* (1909), and *The History of Henry Fielding* (1918). After retiring, he was elected Democratic governor of Connecticut (1931–39), much to the amazement of professional politicians. He sponsored public works and relief programs, reduced utility rates, reorganized state government, and established a highway system. Scandals connected with construction of the Merritt Parkway led to his defeat, although he was not the person charged with wrongdoing. While governor, he also headed the American Academy of Arts and Letters (1931–41).

Crosser, Robert (1874–1957) U.S. representative; born in Holytown, Scotland. Emigrating as a boy, he became a lawyer and Ohio state representative before going to the U.S. House of Representatives (Dem., 1913–19, 1923–55). He chaired the Committee on Interstate and Foreign Commerce.

Crossfield, (Albert) Scott (1921–) aeronautical engineer; born in Berkeley, Calif. He served in the United States Navy as a pilot during World War II. While working at North American Aviation as a test pilot and engineer (1955–67), he flew the X-15 rocket airplane and directed the Apollo, Saturn S-II, Hound Dog, and Paraglider projects.

Crossley, Archibald M. (Maddock) (1896–1985) public opinion analyst; born in Fieldsboro, N.J. With Elmo Roper and George Gallup, in the 1920s he pioneered scientific polling techniques using statistically representative population samples. He founded the New York market research firm Crossley, Inc. (later Crossley Surveys) in 1926, retiring in 1962. He was the first to measure radio audiences (1929) and was until 1952 a prominent presidential election pollster.

Crothers, Rachel (1878–1958) playwright; born in Bloomington, Ill. She began as an actress but gave that up to teach, writing her first play in 1904. Her first success on Broadway was *The Three of Us* (1906) and for the next 30 years she wrote a Broadway hit virtually every season, usually producing and directing as well. Her last success was *Susan and God* (1936). Her witty plays were often concerned with the relations between the sexes and with the consequences of inequality and the struggle for women's rights. She founded the Stage Women's Relief during World War I. In 1940 she took the lead in organizing the American Theatre Wing that ran the Stage Door Canteen for service people during World War II.

Crow, (Fred) Trammel (1914–) real estate developer; born in Dallas, Texas. Starting with Dallas warehouses in the late 1940s, he became the nation's largest private developer and landlord, eventually managing 650 corporations and property in nearly every major U.S. city. He developed such high-profile urban shopping precincts as Peachtree Center, Atlanta, Ga. (early 1960s), and Embarcadero Center, San Francisco (early 1970s).

Crow, (Herbert) Carl (1883–1945) author; born in Highland, Mo. A journalist who founded a newspaper at age 19, he worked after 1911 for newspapers in Shanghai and Tokyo and owned a Shanghai advertising agency (1919–37). His popular books about Far Eastern travel, customs, and markets include an early guidebook to China (1912).

Crow, Jim See RICE, THOMAS DARTMOUTH.

Crow Dog (b. Kargi Sunka) (?1835–?1910) Brûle Sioux chief; born in the northern Great Plains. His conviction for the murder of Chief Spotted Tail was set aside by a landmark U.S. Supreme Court ruling, which stated that the U.S. government had no jurisdiction over crimes committed on Indian lands. In the 1880s he joined the Ghost Dance movement.

Crowell, Henry P. (Parsons) (1855–1944) grain merchant; born in Cleveland, Ohio. In 1881 he bought the Quaker Mill in Ravenna, Ohio, and in 1888 he formed the Buckeye Foundry Company (forerunner of Perfection Stove Company of Cleveland) to make oil stoves. He moved to Chicago where he became the senior executive of the American Cereal Company, forerunner of the Quaker Oats Company

(1901), whose board he chaired from 1922–44. A devout man, he presided over the Moody Bible Institute board of trustees (1904–44).

Crowninshield, (Francis Welsh) Frank (Arthur Loring Bruce, pen name) (1872–1947) editor; born in Paris, France. After various editorial posts, including editorship of *The Bookman* (1895–1900), he edited *Vanity Fair* magazine (1914–35), molding it into a slick, sophisticated journal of society and the arts.

Crowninshield, George (1766–1817) yachtsman; born in Salem, Mass. Member of a prominent Salem family that prospered as sea captains and merchants, he went to sea as a ship's clerk and then worked in his family's countinghouse. When the family firm dissolved (1815), he retired and pursued an interest in yachting. He built the first American yacht, the *Jefferson*. He built the more elaborate *Cleopatra's Barge* and took her on a trip to the Mediterranean, where it gained much attention in foreign ports. He died suddenly after his return from the voyage.

Cruess, William (Vere) (1886–1968) food scientist; born near San Miguel, Calif. Born to an impoverished farm family, he worked his way through the University of California: Berkeley where he also taught from 1911 to 1954. From 1938–48 he chaired the Division of Fruit Products. He developed the technology for processing fruit culls, formerly considered waste, and is credited with inventing the canned fruit cocktail.

Crumb, George (Henry, Jr.) (1929–) composer; born in Charleston, W.Va. After studies in the U.S.A. and Germany he taught at the University of Pennsylvania from 1965. His work is noted for its expressive use of novel playing and singing techniques.

Crumb, R. (Robert) (1943–) cartoonist; born in Philadelphia. While living in the Haight-Ashbury district in San Francisco during the hippie movement of the 1960s, he created the classic underground "comix" series, *Zap* (1967), and *Snatch* (1968), featuring the overtly sexual escapades of Mr. Natural, the grotesquely voluptuous Angelfood McSpade, the sexually repressed suburbanite Whiteman, and many others. He was the creator of the cartoon symbol of an era, the strutting hippie over the slogan, "Keep On Truckin'," which he failed to copyright. His comic series, *Fritz the Cat*, was adapted to an X-rated animated feature in 1972.

Crump, (Edward Hull) "Boss" (1874–1954) mayor, U.S. representative, political boss; born in Holly Springs, Miss. A self-made man, he began his political machine as Memphis, Tenn., councilman in 1905. As Democratic mayor of Memphis (1911–17), he took over public utilities and opposed the Ku Klux Klan, but resigned after failing to enforce prohibition. Establishing E. H. Crump Insurance in 1920, he served in the U.S. House of Representatives (1931–35) and controlled state Democrats until 1948.

Cubberley, Ellwood Patterson (1868–1941) educator; born in Antioch, Ind. He was professor (1898–1933) and dean (1917–33) of the new school of education at Stanford. Cubberley's view of public schools as instruments of social engineering was controversial; but in more than 30 books he helped to make education an academic discipline and to professionalize public school teaching and administration.

Cudahy, Edward A. See under CUDAHY, MICHAEL.

Cudahy, Michael (1841–1910) meatpacker; born in Callan, County Kilkenny, Ireland; **and Edward A. (Aloysius)**

(1859–1941) meatpacker; born in Milwaukee, Wis. The brothers' family came to Milwaukee in 1849 and at age 14 Michael began working for meatpackers. By 1869 he was supervising the Plankinton & Armour Packing House and by 1875 was a partner of Armour & Company in Chicago. During the 1870s, Michael brought refrigeration into warehouse packing plants. In 1887 the brothers – Edward had started working as a meatpacker at age 12 – bought a packing plant near Omaha, Nebr. with Philip D. Armour. The Armour-Cudahy partnership broke up and the plant became the Cudahy Packing Company (1890). Under Edward's supervision the company expanded significantly; his son, Edward A. Jr., was kidnapped in 1900 and held in chains for $25,000 ransom. Subsequently the son entered the family's business in 1905, and became president in 1926.

Cuffe, Paul (1759–1817) seaman, reformer; born in Cuttyhunk, Mass. His father was of African descent, and his mother was a Native American. While a seaman, he and his brother John appealed to the courts of Massachusetts to consider why those denied suffrage had to pay taxes (1780). Although unsuccessful at the time, their concerns were reflected in the act of 1783 by which African-Americans acquired legal rights and privileges in Massachusetts. Through a series of successful voyages, he became ship and property owner (1806), settling on the Westport River where he built a public schoolhouse and served as a minister among the Quakers. He founded the Friendly Society and led a voyage to help 38 African-Americans emigrate to Sierra Leone (1815), but died before he could make a second trip.

Cugat, Xavier (1900–90) violinist, bandleader; born in Barcelona, Spain. Raised in Cuba, he first became popular in the United States in the 1920s with his tango orchestra; in the 1930s he introduced other Latin dance rhythms including the Cuban rumba. In the 1940s he appeared in many musical films, such as *You Were Never Lovelier* (1942). He promoted the popularity of Latin music in the United States.

Cukor, George (1899–1983) movie director; born in New York City. Originally a stage director, he made his screen debut with *Grumpy* (1930). Specializing in sophisticated comedy, he often worked with Katharine Hepburn, and won an Academy Award for directing *My Fair Lady* (1964).

Culbertson, Ely (1891–1955) bridge authority; born in Romania. The son of an American mining engineer and a Russian woman, he developed contract bridge's first successful bidding system and established himself as the world's best player in a 1931–32 win. A revolutionary as a youth, he devised a 1940 peace plan including ideas later adopted by the United Nations.

Culbertson, Josephine (b. Murphy) (1899–1956) bridge authority; born in New York City. The first woman to play on a Vanderbilt Cup-winning team (1931), she convinced her then-husband and partner Ely Culbertson to concentrate on bridge and helped him devise the dominant Culbertson bidding system. In 1922–30 she was reputedly the world's highest-paid bridge teacher.

Cullen, Countée (b. Countée L. Porter) (1903–46) poet; born in New York City. Raised by foster parents, he studied at New York University (B.A. 1925) and Harvard (M.A. 1926). Having achieved some recognition for his poetry while still a student, as an African-American he was regarded as contributing to the so-called Harlem Renaissance of the 1920s, but his particular style – as seen in such works as *Color* (1925) and *Copper Sun* (1927) – was more derived from European traditions than from African-American idioms and has not survived his era. Awarded a Guggenheim fellowship in 1928, he spent most of the next six years in Paris. On returning to New York City he taught at a junior high school (1934–46); he also edited a magazine, *Opportunity.* In addition to his poetry, he wrote a novel (*One Way to Heaven,* 1932) and stories for children.

Cullom, Shelby M. (Moore) (1829–1914) U.S. representative/ senator; born in Kentucky. A lawyer in Springfield, Ill., he became a Republican in 1858. He served Illinois in the U.S. House of Representatives (1865–67), as governor (1877–83), and as U.S. senator (1883–1913). He helped establish the Interstate Commerce Commission in 1887.

Cumming, Rose Stuart (1887–1968) interior decorator; born near Sydney, Australia. Caught by World War I in New York, she opened an antiques and decorating shop in 1921. During a 45-year career, her eclectic, exotically colorful and theatrical designs attracted clients such as Mary Pickford and Marlene Dietrich.

cummings, e. e. (Edward Estlin) (1894–1962) poet, writer, painter; born in Cambridge, Mass. He studied at Harvard (B.A. 1915; M.A. 1916). As a volunteer ambulance driver in World War I, he got in trouble with the French who kept him in a detention camp for six months; he described the experience in *The Enormous Room* (1922). He traveled widely but was based in New York City. He is known for his idiosyncratic and typographically inventive poetry, such as *Tulips and Chimneys* (1937, complete edition). He wrote various works for the stage and was an accomplished painter.

Cummings, Homer (Stillé) (1870–1956) U.S. attorney general, author; born in Chicago, Ill. Known as an incisive, dramatic trial lawyer, as well as an astute and loyal supporter of Democratic candidates, he was named attorney general by President Franklin Roosevelt (1933–39). During his tenure, one of the longest in that office, he established uniform rules of practice and procedure in federal courts. He and Roosevelt backed the failed "court-packing plan" to increase Supreme Court justices. He was the author of several books and a golf enthusiast.

Cunningham, Glenn (1909–88) track athlete; born in Elkhart, Kans. After overcoming severe leg burns suffered in a childhood accident, he established a world record for the mile in 1934 and won the silver medal in the 1500 meter race in the 1936 Olympics.

Cunningham, Harry (Blair) (1907–92) retail executive; born in Home Camp, Pa. After 30 years with S. S. Kresge he became president and CEO (1959–72). In 1962 he opened the first Kmart discount store; by 1990 the corporation, renamed Kmart Corporation (1977), was the country's second largest retailer. He is credited with early recognizing and developing the potential of discount retailing.

Cunningham, Imogen (1883–1976) photographer; born in Portland, Ore. She took a degree in chemistry from the University of Washington: Seattle and then went to work in the Seattle studio of Edward Curtis. After eight years assisting Curtis, she went to Dresden, Germany, to study photographic chemistry (1909–10), then returned to Seattle to set up her own commercial portraiture studio. She and her husband moved to San Francisco in 1917 (they had three children and were divorced in the 1930s) and there she spent most of the rest of her life; she continued working until only

a week before her death. She was a founding member of Group f/64, which had its first exhibit at the M. H. de Young Memorial Museum (San Francisco) in 1932, and her work was often shown in galleries and museums throughout the U.S.A. Working in the realistic or "straight" school of Ansel Adams and Edward Weston, she was not especially a technical innovator but she is admired for her sharply focused black-and-white images, particularly her portraits and her nature studies.

Cunningham, J. V. (James Vincent) (1911–85) poet; born in Cumberland, Md. He studied at Stanford (B.A. 1934; Ph.D. 1945), and taught at many institutions, primarily at Brandeis University (1953–85). He was a Renaissance scholar, an essayist, and an epigrammatic poet, as in *The Helmsman* (1942).

Cunningham, Kate Richards O' Hare (b. Kathleen Richards) (1876–1948) social activist; born near Ada, Kans. Drought drove her family to Kansas City where her father became part owner of a machine shop. Kate trained as a teacher in Nebraska and taught one winter, but in 1894 she went to work as a machinist's apprentice in her father's shop. She joined the union, was active as a temperance worker, and soon exchanged her Christian faith for the ideals of socialism as preached by such as "Mother" Jones. She joined the Socialist Party (1899), married a fellow socialist, Francis O'Hare, and spent the next 15 years as a socialist lecturer and organizer in the Midwest. She published articles and wrote a novel, ran unsuccessfully for Congress (1910), was a delegate to the Second International in London (1913), and generally gained a reputation for linking socialist goals with concerns of average Western Americans. Speaking out publicly in opposition to U.S. participation in World War I, she was sentenced to five years in jail but served only one (1919–20). On her release she led the campaign for release from prison of others held for their views, and, somewhat discouraged by Socialism and vehemently opposed to Communism, dedicated herself to prison reform. In 1922 she joined a cooperative colony in Louisiana where she published a socialist paper and tried to start a college for workers' education; by 1924 this all failed and she and her husband went to Arkansas. Divorced from O'Hare in 1928, she married Charles Cunningham, a San Francisco lawyer, and went to live in California. She remained active in progressive politics and as assistant director of the California Department of Penology (1939–40) she reformed the state's prison system.

Cuomo, Mario (Matthew) (1932–) governor; born in Queens County, N.Y. His parents were Italian immigrants. An excellent athlete and student, he played minor-league baseball before going to law school and receiving his degree (1956). He first gained public recognition when he represented community groups in New York City during the 1960s. Entering politics, he became the secretary of state (1975–79), lieutenant governor (1979–83), and finally governor (1983–94) of New York after losing a New York City mayoral race to Ed Koch (1977). As governor, he emerged as the spokesman for the traditional Democratic Party and its supporters. An eloquent speaker, he gave the nominating speech at the 1984 Democratic National Convention and the keynote speech in 1992. He debated running for the presidency himself, but declined both in 1988 and 1992.

Curley, James Michael (1874–1958) mayor, U.S. representative; born in Boston, Mass. Selling newspapers to survive as a poor Irish-Catholic in Boston, he left high school, continuing his education in the public library. A powerful and colorful orator, he campaigned against Democratic political bosses, serving in the Boston common council (1900–01), then becoming an alderman (1904–09). Serving in the U.S. House of Representatives (Dem., Mass.; 1911–14), he left to run for mayor of Boston, defeating Rose Kennedy's father, "Honey Fitz" Fitzgerald. As mayor (1914–18, 1922–26, 1930–34), he funded massive public works projects, draining the city's treasury to employ the poor. As governor of Massachusetts (1935–39) he championed social welfare legislation while bribery charges against him were investigated. Convicted in 1937, he received contributions from Bostonians to pay his fine. Indicted for influence peddling while back in the U.S. House of Representatives (1943–45), he left to become mayor of Boston again (1945–49), serving five months in jail midterm, until pardoned by President Truman. His political career finished, he wrote *I'd Do It Again* (1957), defending himself, and he inspired Edwin O'Connor's novel, *The Last Hurrah* (1956).

Curran, Charles E. (Edward) (1934–) Catholic theologian; born in Rochester, N.Y. After being ordained and earning advanced degrees in Rome, he taught at a diocesan seminary (1962–65), counseling couples on the side. He then taught at Catholic University (Washington, D.C.), also writing on moral theology. His increasingly liberal views on sexual morality caused controversy, especially after a 1968 encyclical condemning birth control. In 1979 the Vatican began investigating him; in 1986 he was barred from teaching at Catholic University.

Curran, Joseph (Edwin) (1906–81) labor leader; born in New York City. A seaman since 1922, he joined the International Seaman's Union (ISU) in 1935. He led a strike in defiance of the ISU (1936) and led 35,000 members of the ISU into his new National Maritime Union (NMU), which he served as president (1937–73). The NMU's membership grew to 100,000 during World War II. He was also vice-president of the Congress of Industrial Organizations (1940–73).

Currier, Nathaniel (1813–88) lithographer; born in Roxbury, Mass. After apprentice years under William S. and John Pendleton in Boston, Philadelphia, and New York City, he established his own firm, issuing his first print in 1835. He made James Ives his partner in 1857 and the firm Currier & Ives became a household name, their hand-colored prints portraying a wide spectrum of 19th-century American life. Although relatively cheap in their day, they sold in quantities that made Currier and Ives quite prosperous. Currier retired in 1880, his son William carrying on the business with Ives.

Curry, Jabez (Lamar Monroe) (1825–1903) U.S. representative, educator; born in Lincoln County, Ga. He studied law at Harvard and was deeply inspired by two men: John C. Calhoun and Horace Mann. He served in the U.S. House of Representatives (States Rights Democrat, Ala.; 1857–61) and then in the Confederate Congress (1861–63). As president of Howard College (1865–68), agent of the Peabody Fund (1881–1903), and director of the Southern Education Board (1901–03), he pursued his life goal of assuring universal education in the South, for blacks and whites. He was ambassador to Spain (1885–88). Alabama placed his statue in the U.S. Capitol.

Curry, John (Steuart) (1897–1946) painter; born in Jefferson County, Kans. He studied at the Art Institute of Chicago (1916–18), made drawings for the Ringling Brothers Circus in 1932, and later became artist in residence at the University of Wisconsin (1936–46). *Tornado Over Kansas* (1933) is a fine example of his populist subject matter, and *The Mississippi* (1935), demonstrates his sensitivity to social issues.

Curtice, Harlowe H. (Herbert) (1893–1962) automobile executive; born in Petrieville, Mich. In a 44-year career at General Motors he began as a bookkeeper, headed the AC Spark Plug and Buick divisions, and became president of the company, the largest U.S. corporation, during the post-World War II boom years (1953–58). He was known for his single-minded focus on sales and national advocacy of corporate issues.

Curtin, Philip (De Armond) (1922–) historian; born in Philadelphia. He pioneered the study of African economic history and helped mainstream African history in American curricula. He founded the African studies program (1961) while at the University of Wisconsin (1956–75) before joining the Johns Hopkins University faculty (1975). He wrote prolifically on the African colonial period, the slave trade, and, in his later work, black demographic and medical history.

Curtis, Benjamin R. (Robbins) (1809–74) lawyer, U.S. Supreme Court justice; born in Watertown, Mass. From an old Massachusetts family, he was left fatherless as a youth and his mother had to help put him through Harvard College and Law School by running a students' boarding house. He entered a Boston relative's law firm and specialized in commercial law (1834–51). He was appointed to the U.S. Supreme Court in 1851 and although he opposed the Free Soil Party and had once argued that a slave-owner should be able to restrain his slave when temporarily in a free state, he gained his place in American legal history by being one of the two justices who dissented in *Scott v. Sandford* (1857). Opposing Chief Justice Taney, Curtis argued that Dred Scott had acquired freedom by residing in free territory. When Curtis published his opinion prematurely, Taney revised his own to counter its arguments; the ensuing correspondence led Curtis to resign from the Supreme Court (1857). (What is usually overlooked in this, however, is that Curtis's brother, George Curtis, had defended Dred Scott.) He took up his lucrative private practice and continued to argue many cases before the Supreme Court. On the approach of the Civil War he reversed himself again, asking Massachusetts to repeal its law against the return of fugitive slaves, evidently in order to placate Southern states. During the war he attacked President Lincoln for suspending the writ of habeas corpus and for issuing the Emancipation Proclamation. His last moment on the public stage was as chief counsel of President Andrew Johnson in his impeachment trial.

Curtis, Charles (1860–1936) vice-president, U.S. representative; born in North Topeka, Kans. He claimed to be one-eighth American Indian and made much of this in his political career. He became Herbert Hoover's vice-president after 34 years in Congress. He supported the Republican policies even as the impact of the Great Depression became more evident.

Curtis, Cyrus Herman K. (Kotzschmar) (1850–1933) publisher; born in Portland, Maine. He founded *The Ladies' Home Journal* in 1883 and in 1897 bought *The Saturday*

Evening Post, which he developed into another highly successful magazine. His newspaper holdings included the *New York Evening Post* and the *Philadelphia Inquirer.*

Curtis, Edward (Sheriff) (1868–1954) photographer; born in White Water, Wis. From 1896 to 1930 he traveled across North America to take stylized portraits of Native Americans from 80 different tribes in traditional dress, publishing 20 volumes and portfolios of photos (1930–54).

Curtis, George Ticknor (1812–94) lawyer, historian; born in Watertown, Mass. Harvard educated, he practiced law in Worcester and Boston and was patent attorney for, among others, Samuel F. B. Morse. He opposed slavery and served as defense attorney in the Dred Scott case (1857), in which the U.S. Supreme Court held slaves were not citizens and thus had no constitutional protection. He wrote two studies vindicating failed Union General George B. McClellan (1886, 1887) and later produced important works on constitutional history.

Curtis, George William (1824–92) social reformer, author, editor; born in Providence, R.I. Influenced by Ralph Waldo Emerson at Brook Farm (early 1840s), he traveled in Europe and the Middle East (1846–50) and published two travel books (1851, 1852) and several popular novels. Back in New York City, he wrote literary essays for several magazines and became known for his "Easy Chair" pieces in *Harper's Weekly.* He spoke out increasingly on public affairs, both as a lecturer and (from 1863) as an editor for *Harper's,* advocating abolitionism (and later, black equality), women's rights, civil service reform, and restraint of corporate power. He turned down an ambassadorship to England (1877) to continue at *Harper's* where he remained influential as an editor and independent voice in national affairs.

Curtis, Natalie (1875–1921) ethnomusicologist; born in New York City. Intending a career as a concert pianist, she went to Europe to study with Busoni and others, but on return (about 1900) she visited Arizona and became so entranced by Native Americans' culture that she decided to record their music. With the support of President Theodore Roosevelt, she gained access to Indian reservations from Maine to the Southwest – although most of her work would be with the Plains and Pueblo tribes – and won the cooperation of individual Indians. At first she recorded with a phonograph but she turned to transcribing the songs with pencil on paper; she also photographed many subjects. Her first book, *The Indians' Book* (1907), included folklore, poetry, and religious texts as well as songs, and her work contributed to gaining a new respect for Native American culture. Meanwhile she had also become interested in preserving African-Americans' music; she helped found the Music School Settlement for Colored People in Harlem (1911), arranged a Carnegie Hall concert by African-American musicians (1914), and set about transcribing African-American songs; she published *Hampton Series Negro Folk-Songs* (4 vols. 1918–19). She was killed by a taxicab in Paris where she had gone to address an international congress on art history. For all its limitations, her record of both Native American and African-American music remains a basic historical source.

Curtiss, Glenn (Hammond) (1878–1930) aviator, inventor; born in Hammondsport, N.Y. Starting with a youthful interest in racing and improving bicycles, he moved on to motorcycles; he had his own motorcycle factory by 1902 and in 1905 he set a world speed record of 137 mph on a self-

designed motorcycle; that same year he helped to build the first dirigible for the U.S. Army. In 1908, in his *June Bug,* he was the first American to make a public airplane flight over one linear kilometer; a competitor of the Wright Brothers, he continued to set many new records for flight. In addition to gaining the patent in 1911 for the aileron, he effectively invented the hydroplane and flying boat; in 1919 the NC-4 he built for the U.S. Navy made the first transatlantic flight. During World War I his Curtiss Aeroplane and Motor Company produced over 5,000 "Jennies" (JN-4's). Recognized as one of aviation's major pioneers, in his later years he moved on to working with automobiles, designing a streamlined trailer, and developing real estate in Florida.

Curtiz, Michael (b. Mihaly Kertész) (1888–1962) film director; born in Budapest. He was a stage actor from 1906, then became a film actor and director in 1912. By the time he came to Hollywood in 1926, he had directed some 60 films in Europe. Working in every film genre, he made some 125 Hollywood films, winning an Academy Award for *Casablanca* (1943). Known for his fractured English and regarded as a production-line director, he would later gain from reappraisals of his best work.

Cushing, Caleb (1800–79) lawyer, public official; born in Salisbury, Mass. After serving in the Massachusetts legislature and the U.S. House of Representatives (Whig, 1835–41; Dem., 1841–43), he was appointed commissioner to China, where he negotiated the commercial treaty of Wang Hia (1844). An advocate of "manifest destiny," he volunteered and served in the Mexican War. President Franklin Pierce appointed him attorney general (1853–57) and he spoke out on many issues beyond the law. He had long been a Democrat and was opposed to the abolitionists, but he was also opposed to slavery itself and to secession, and when Lincoln won the election of 1860 he became a Republican and served as a legal consultant to Lincoln and his cabinet. Under President Grant, he carried through several notable diplomatic-legal negotiations; in 1873 Grant nominated him to be chief justice of the U.S. Supreme Court, but partisan attacks led Cushing to withdraw his name. Instead, he wound up his long and varied career of public services as the popular U.S. ambassador to Spain (1873–77). An accomplished orator and linguist, as a lawyer he was most admired for his expertise at summarizing evidence. He was also extremely well read – Emerson called him the most eminent scholar of his day – and he wrote many articles as well as several books.

Cushing, Frank Hamilton (1857–1900) ethnologist; born in North East, Pa. A boyhood fascination with Indian artifacts was fulfilled with his appointment at the Bureau of American Ethnology (1879–1900). Regarded as a genius of interpretation, he made major contributions to the young field by living among the Zuni for five years (he was initiated into the tribe as Ténatsali) and excavating Hohokam and Seminole sites.

Cushing, Harvey (Williams) (1869–1939) neurosurgeon; born in Cleveland, Ohio. The fourth generation in his family to become a physician, he showed great promise at Harvard Medical School and in his residency at Johns Hopkins Hospital (1896–1900), where he learned cerebral surgery under William S. Halsted. After studying a year in Europe – on his return, he introduced the blood pressure sphygmomanometer to the U.S.A. – he began a surgical practice in Baltimore while teaching at Johns Hopkins Hospital (1901–11), and gained a national reputation for operations such as the removal of brain tumors. From 1912–32 he was a professor of surgery at Harvard Medical School and surgeon in chief at Peter Bent Brigham Hospital in Boston, with time off during World War I to perform surgery for the U.S. forces in France; out of this experience came his major paper on wartime brain injuries (1918). In addition to his pioneering work in performing and teaching brain surgery, he was the reigning expert on the pituitary gland since his 1912 publication on the subject; later he discovered the condition of the pituitary now known as "Cushing's disease." On retiring from Harvard he spent his final years at Yale as professor of neurology and director of studies in the history of medicine; his bequest of his books on this latter field form the basis of Yale's medical history library. America's most admired surgeon in his day, he was a man of many talents, even winning the Pulitzer Prize (1926) for his biography of the man who had greatly influenced his career, *The Life of Sir William Osler.*

Cushing, John Perkins (1787–1862) merchant, philanthropist; born in Boston, Mass. (nephew of Thomas H. Perkins). Circumstances made him at age 16 head of Perkins & Company, his uncle's trading company in China. He conducted business affairs admirably (1803–30) and returned to Boston with a Chinese manner as well as Chinese servants. He built a conservatory, and his yacht, *The Sylph,* won the earliest recorded American yacht race (1832). He left an estate of $2 million.

Cushing, Richard J. (James) (1895–1970) Catholic prelate; born in Boston, Mass. Ordained in 1921, he worked for the Society for the Propagation of the Faith and was Boston's auxiliary bishop (from 1939) then archbishop (1944). He established numerous schools and charitable institutions; he also founded the Missionary Society of St. James the Apostle, which sends priests as missionaries to South America. Cushing was made a cardinal in 1958. Blunt-spoken, making no claim to be a conventional scholar-priest, he was also known for his close ties to the Kennedy family.

Cushing, William (1732–1810) Supreme Court justice; born in Scituate, Mass. Originally a judge for the English crown, he supported the American Revolution and became a prominent judge in Massachusetts (1777–89). He was the first associate justice appointed by President Washington to the U.S. Supreme Court (1790–1810).

Cushman, Charlotte (Saunders) (1816–76) stage actress; born in Boston, Mass. One of the first major native-born American actresses, she began as an opera singer but turned to acting after she overstrained her voice; the vocal damage left her with a husky, veiled quality that she used to great advantage, often playing male roles. Her earliest triumph was as Lady Macbeth in 1836. By 1842 she was managing as well as starring at the Walnut Street Theater in Philadelphia. Earnest and ambitious, she went off to England on her own and in 1845 instantly became the toast of the London stage, although some found her style exaggerated. She acquired a large range of classic roles – including Romeo and Hamlet – but her most popular role was as Meg Merrilies in an adaptation of Scott's *Guy Mannering.* Until 1870, she lived in England or Rome, only appearing in America on tour; returning to the U.S.A., she performed occasionally, climaxing with a triumphal farewell tour in 1874–75.

Cushman, Pauline (1833–93) actress, Union spy; born in New Orleans. Of Spanish and French descent, she was raised in a frontier settlement with Indian children. She joined the New Orleans "Varieties" (1851); by 1852, she had come to New York City where she gained some reputation as an actress. She was in Kentucky with a traveling show in 1863 and, although secretly working for the Federal espionage branch, she pretended to be sympathetic to the South. This allowed her to move about and observe Confederate troop movements; during the Tullahoma, Tenn., campaign of June 1863, she was caught with compromising papers on her; court-martialed and sentenced to be hanged, she was saved by the arrival of Union troops. To capitalize on her notoriety, she began to lecture, wearing a Federal uniform. She eventually went back to acting, but her life was not happy; she had been married three times and she killed herself by taking an overdose of morphine.

Custer, George Armstrong (1839–76) soldier; born in New Rumley, Ohio. The son of a blacksmith, he graduated last in his West Point class of 1861 but went on to become a Civil War cavalry commander of deadly and aggressive efficiency; often flamboyant in appearance and behavior ("like a circus rider gone mad!" said a fellow officer), he participated in virtually every battle in northern Virginia from First Bull Run to Lee's surrender; at the head of Sheridan's cavalry, he led the pursuit to Appomattox in April 1865, and the Confederate flag of truce, passing through the Union lines, came first to him. Although wounded only once, he had 11 horses killed under him and his brigade sustained the highest casualties of any cavalry unit of the Federal army; he was made a brigadier general by age 23. Returned to his rank of captain, and later promoted to lieutenant colonel, he served on the frontier with the Seventh Cavalry Regiment; in 1867 he was court-martialed for leaving his post but he was restored to duty in 1868 and gained even more fame fighting the Plains Indians. A more thoughtful side of Custer emerged in his memoirs of war service and life on the plains (1874) and in his efforts to combat corruption in the Bureau of Indian Affairs. Participating in the government's campaign to force the Cheyenne and Sioux onto reservations, he came across a large encampment of Indians along the Little Bighorn River in Montana territory; dividing his forces, on June 25, 1876, he ordered an attack; Custer and the over 200 men in his command were annihilated by the vastly larger force. The controversy that shadowed his military career has never truly subsided, as people debate the proportions of bravery, egotism, and folly to assign him.

Cutler, Lloyd N. (Norton) (1917–) lawyer; born in New York City. A partner in Washington, D.C., law firms from 1946, during the ensuing decades he served on numerous national commissions dealing with everything from North African land-lease, Latin American liquidation, and civil rights to ethics, violence, Canada, and strategic forces. His most prominent post was as the chief counsel to President Jimmy Carter (1979–81), which solidified his reputation as the consummate Washington "insider."

Cutler, Timothy (1684–1765) Protestant clergyman; born in Charlestown, Mass. He graduated from Harvard at age 17 and was ordained a pastor in the Congregational Church of Stratford, Conn., in 1710. Appointed rector of Yale in 1719, he was forced to resign three years later when he converted to the Church of England. In 1723 he became rector of Christ Church, Boston, where he remained to the end of his life.

Cutter, Charles (Ammi) (1837–1903) librarian; born in Boston, Mass. After graduating from Harvard Divinity School, he became librarian of the Boston Athenaeum (1869–93) where he compiled that library's influential *Catalogue*. His multipart Expansive Classification system, which was designed to help growing libraries expand without completely reclassifying, influenced the Library of Congress system. With his life-long rival, Melvil Dewey, and others, he founded the American Library Association (1876).

Cutting, Bronson M. (Murray) (1888–1935) journalist, U.S. senator; born in Oakdale, N.Y. A journalist, he used his Santa Fe, N.M., newspaper to crusade for progressive causes. Appointed to the U.S. Senate in 1927 (Rep., N.M.), he served until his untimely death in 1935, and won a reputation as a supporter of the New Deal and independence for the Philippines.

Czolgosz, Leon (1873–1901) assassin; born in Detroit, Mich. The fourth child of Polish immigrants, he worked in a wire mill and attended socialist meetings. Following a mental breakdown in 1898, he shot President William McKinley in Buffalo, N.Y. (1901) and was electrocuted that same year.

D

Dabrowski, Joseph (1842–1903) Catholic priest; born in Poland. Fleeing because of his anti-Russian political activities, he was ordained in Rome (1869) and went to Wisconsin to do pastoral work among Polish Americans. He founded the Seminary of Saints Cyril and Methodius in Detroit (1887), becoming its first rector.

Daché, Lilly (1892–1989) fashion designer; born in Bèigles, France. Apprenticed to her milliner aunt at age 12, she emigrated to the U.S.A. as a teenager. She owned the House of Daché in New York (1920s–1968), where her thousands of hat designs came to identify her indelibly with hats, particularly her signature turbans, half-hats, and snoods.

Dade, Francis Langhorne (?1793–1835) soldier; born in King George County, Va. A career officer, he received an infantry commission in 1813. A force of Seminoles and blacks surprised and nearly annihilated his 115-man force in Florida on December 28, 1835. Dade fell dead in the first volley, and only three of his soldiers survived to tell the story of the "Dade Massacre." Florida would later name a county after him.

Dahl, Ingolf (1912–70) composer, teacher, pianist; born in Hamburg, Germany. He came to the U.S.A. in 1935 and had a distinguished teaching career at the University of Southern California. His works, in a modernist idiom, include a saxophone concerto.

Dahl, Robert A. (Alan) (1915–) political scientist; born in Inwood, Iowa. After government service during World War II, he joined the faculty at Yale (1946). He authored many articles and books that examine democratic systems of government, including *A Preface to Democratic Theory* (1956) and *Democracy and Its Critics* (1989).

Dahlberg, Edward (1900–77) writer; born in Boston, Mass. Illegitimate son of a woman barber, he was sent to an orphanage in Cleveland, Ohio, as a boy, but he ran away. After studying at the University of California and Columbia University, he joined the expatriate community in Paris in the 1920s. He wrote pioneering proletarian novels in the 1930s (*Bottom Dogs,* 1929; *From Flushing to Calvary,* 1932), then faded from notice, reemerging in the 1960s as a prolific writer of bitter social and literary criticism, verse, and a highly regarded autobiography, *Because I Was Flesh* (1964). He taught at the University of Missouri: Kansas City (1964–77).

Dahlgren, John (Adolphus Bernard) (1809–70) naval officer, inventor; born in Philadelphia. Classically educated, he joined the navy as a midshipman in 1826 and served in the Mediterranean; he served later as an assistant in the U.S. Coast Survey. From 1847 on, as ordnance officer at the Washington Navy Yard, Dahlgren experimented with naval weaponry; by 1851 the yard had begun to produce a cannon of his own design. His 11-inch Dahlgren smoothbore guns were carried aboard many U.S. warships, including the famous ironclad *Monitor.* As a rear admiral, he commanded the Union's South Atlantic Blockadina Squadron (1863–65) and was commandant of the Washington Navy Yard at his death.

Dale, Chester (1883–1962) banker, art collector; born in New York City. He was educated locally, worked as an office boy on Wall Street, and studied until he became a member of the New York Stock Exchange (1918). He became a wealthy man, specializing in utility bonds. With his first wife, Maud Murray Thompson Dale (1875–1953), he collected American and French art. He was a trustee of many museums and donated the bulk of their collection to the National Gallery.

Dale, Richard (1756–1826) naval officer; born in Norfolk County, Va. After an adventurous career at sea, including two imprisonments by the British, he served as first lieutenant under John Paul Jones on the *Bonhomme Richard* in the battle with the *Serapis* (1779). After 1783 he alternated between merchant ships and the U.S. Navy, commanding the squadron that blockaded Tripoli (1801–02), then retired to a quiet life in Philadelphia.

Daley, Arthur (John) (1904–74) sportswriter; born in New York City. He was a sportswriter for the *New York Times* from 1926 until his death in 1974. He wrote over 10,000 "Sports of the Times" columns from 1942 to 1974.

Daley, Richard (Joseph) (1902–76) mayor; born in Chicago. He served in the Illinois House of Representatives (1936–38) and the state senate (1939–46). As mayor of Chicago (1956–76) and chairman of the Cook County Democratic Party, he headed a powerful political machine that effectively dominated much of Chicago. Though efficient, he was often accused of unscrupulous practices, including "throwing" the Illinois vote to John Kennedy in 1960; more visibly, his police brutally subdued demonstrators at the 1968 Democratic National Convention.

Dalgarno, Alexander (1928–) physicist; born in London, England. He taught at Queens University, Belfast (1951–66), then came to the U.S.A. to teach astronomy and astrophysics at Harvard (1967). He made major contributions to studies of atomic and molecular physics, the interstellar medium, and gaseous nebulae.

Dall, William Healey (1845–1927) naturalist; born in Boston, Mass. He studied natural sciences with Louis Agassiz. Dall led the Western Union Telegraph Expedition to Alaska (1865–68) and joined the U.S. Coast Survey of Alaska (1871–84) and the U.S. Geological Survey (1884–1923). He wrote *Alaska and its Resources* (1870) and the *Pacific Coast Pilot* (2 vols. 1879–83) and he published extensively on mollusks. Dall's sheep, a bighorn sheep found in northwestern North America, is named after him.

Dallas, Alexander James (1759–1817) lawyer, public official; born on the island of Jamaica. The son of a physician, he attended Edinburgh University, worked as a merchant clerk, returned to the West Indies, and began practicing law there. In 1783 he emigrated to the United States, settling in Philadelphia. A journalist as well as a lawyer of repute, he became U.S. attorney for the eastern district of Pennsylvania in 1801, serving 13 years. From 1814–16 he was secretary of the treasury in the Madison administration.

Dallas, George (Mifflin) (1792–1864) vice-president, U.S. senator; born in Philadelphia. He came from a wealthy Philadelphia family. A Jacksonian Democrat, he was mayor of Philadelphia and a senator before winning the vice-presidency in 1844 under James Polk. He promoted the view that a vice-president should always support his administration's policies, regardless of his own political beliefs.

Dallin, Cyrus (Edwin) (1861–1944) sculptor; born in Springville, Utah. He grew up in the West, studied in Boston, Mass. (c. 1880–82), in Paris (1888), and settled in Arlington Heights to teach at the Massachusetts State Art School (1900–40). He is known for his American Indian subjects, such as *The Appeal to the Great Spirit* (1908), which stands in front of Boston's Museum of Fine Arts.

Dalrymple, Jean (1910–) theater producer, publicist; born in Morristown, N.J. She is best known for her association with the New York City Center, where she was producer and publicist starting in 1953. From 1957 to 1968, she was director of the City Center Light Opera Company.

Daly, (John) Augustin (1838–99) theatrical manager and playwright; born in Plymouth, N.C. Although purists criticized him for rewriting standard works, including Shakespeare, he became one of the most admired theatrical personages of his day, with approximately 100 plays to his credit. He founded and managed theaters named for him in both New York and London. His greatest hits were plays he adapted from foreign sources, but he was disappointed when audiences turned away from new American plays. In the 1880s he built an excellent company, including Ada Rehan and John Drew, insisting that his players demonstrate considerable versatility, rather than being type-cast. His first New York success in 1863 was S.H. von Mosenthal's *Deborah as Leah, The Forsaken*. Later productions included *Twelfth Night, Frou-Frou, The School for Scandal,* and *The Big Bonanza, The Railroad of Love,* and Tennyson's *The Foresters*.

Daly, Marcus (1841–1900) miner, businessman; born in Ireland. He came to the U.S.A. in 1856 and worked as a mining prospector. He worked the Anaconda, Mont., silver and copper mines and became a millionaire several times over. He was active in Montana Democratic politics.

Daly, Mary (1928–) theologian, feminist writer; born in Schenectady, N.Y. She studied at the College of St. Rose (Albany, N.Y.) (B.A. 1950), Catholic University of America (M.A. 1952), St. Mary's College (Notre Dame, Ind.) (Ph.D. 1954), and the University of Fribourg (Switzerland) (Ph.D. 1965). She taught at Cardinal Cushing College (1954–59), the University of Fribourg (1959–66), and Boston College (1966). A social critic of the antifeminist position of the Catholic Church and of society in general, she is known for such works as *Gyn/Ecology: The Metaethics of Radical Feminism* (1978), and *Pure Lust: Elemental Feminist Philosophy* (1984).

Daly, Reginald Aldworth (1871–1957) geologist; born in Napanee, Ontario, Canada. He came to the U.S.A. to study at Harvard (1892), then returned to Canada to serve the Canadian International Boundary Commission (1901–07). He taught at the Massachusetts Institute of Technology (1907–12) before joining Harvard (1912–42). He was an authority on igneous rocks and the geological structures of the earth's crust.

Damadian, Raymond (Vahan) (1936–) biophysicist, inventor; born in Forest Hills, N.Y. He studied violin and mathematics before taking a medical degree and doing postgraduate work in biophysics at Harvard. He also served in the U.S. Air Force. His invention of the magnetic resonance imaging (MRI) scanner revolutionized the field of diagnostic medicine. His Fonar Corporation manufactures the device for distribution worldwide.

D'Amboise, Jacques (1934–) ballet dancer, choreographer; born in Dedham, Mass. After training with the School of American Ballet, he joined the New York City Ballet in 1949. For more than 30 years he performed leading roles in such Balanchine classics as *Apollo*. He began choreographing works in 1963. In 1977 he formed the National Dance Institute to teach dance to children in inner-city schools. The winner of a MacArthur Foundation award, he trained and staged performances involving over 100,000 children nationwide.

Dameron, (Tadley Ewing) Tadd (1917–65) musician; born in Cleveland, Ohio. Mainly active in the 1940s, he was a pianist and bandleader, an arranger for Count Basie and Dizzy Gillespie, and the composer of several modern jazz standards.

Damien, Father (b. Joseph Damien de Veuster) (1840–89) Catholic priest, missionary; born in Belgium. A member of the Fathers of the Sacred Heart of Jesus and Mary, he went to Hawaii as a missionary (1864). In 1873 he asked his order to send him to the island of Molokai, Hawaii, where there was a leper colony. He served as both priest and doctor to the lepers there. In 1884 he discovered that he himself had leprosy but he stayed on and died there. Hawaii placed his statue in the U.S. Capitol.

Damrosch, Leopold (1832–85) conductor, violinist, composer; born in Posen, Prussia. A friend of Liszt and Wagner, he played and conducted widely in Germany before coming to the U.S.A. in 1871. He founded several ensembles including the New York Symphony, conducted pioneering Wagner performances at the Metropolitan Opera, and introduced much music by Brahms and others.

Damrosch, Walter (Johannes) (1862–1950) conductor, composer, educator; born in Breslau, Prussia (son of Leopold Damrosch). He came to the U.S.A. with his family in 1871 and was largely trained in music by his father. When his father died, he took over his post as conductor of the New York Symphony Society (1885–1903). He also began an assistantship at the Metropolitan Opera (1885–91), during which time he helped to promote German opera. When he left he began his own company, the Damrosch Opera Company (1895–99), mainly to do Wagner's operas. He also produced his own opera, *The Scarlet Letter* (1896); his second, *Cyrano de Bergerac,* was done by the Metropolitan Opera in 1913. Meanwhile, he took over as director of a reorganized New York Symphony Society (1903–27), turning away from opera to orchestral works. During World War I he conducted for the troops in France and his contacts led to the establishment of a summer music school at Fontainebleau that would train many American musicians over the ensuing decades. He also took his New York Symphony to Europe in 1920, the first American orchestra to be heard there. When his orchestra merged with the Philharmonic, he retired but from 1927 to 1947 he was the music adviser to National Broadcasting Company radio; among his achievements was the Music Appreciation Hour for young people, which he narrated and conducted after opening each session with, "Good morning, my dear children." Although forgettable as a composer, he retains a special place in America's musical life for introducing generations to the music of Wagner in particular and serious music in general.

Dana, Charles Anderson (1819–97) newspaper editor; born in Hinsdale, N.H. After serving as managing editor of Horace Greeley's *New York Tribune* (1849–62) and assistant U.S. secretary of war (1863–64), he purchased the then floundering *New York Sun* in 1868 and revived it financially and editorially. Under his guidance for three decades, the paper stressed human interest and crime stories and became known for its brisk, often cynical editorials and its lively style and wit.

Dana, James D. (Dwight) (1813–95) geologist; born in Utica, N.Y. His observations as scientist on the U.S. expedition to the Pacific and Antarctic (1838–42) under Charles Wilkes formed the basis for much of his later writing on zoology and mineralogy. With his father-in-law, Benjamin Silliman, he edited the *American Journal of Science* (1846–95). His writings include manuals of geology and mineralogy, two treatises on corals, and a text on Hawaiian volcanoes.

Dana, John Cotton (1856–1929) librarian, author; born in Woodstock, Vt. He graduated from Dartmouth College and held a series of positions before becoming head of the Denver (Colo.) Public Library (1889) where he established the nation's first children's reading room. While working in the Newark, N.J., library system (1902–29) he established the "Newark charging system," a simplified lending process, and cofounded the business library. He also helped found the Newark Museum Association and the Port of New York Authority. He wrote over 500 books and articles on librarianship and museum operations.

Dana, Richard Henry (1815–82) author, lawyer; born in Cambridge Mass. The son of poet and essayist Richard Henry Dana (1787–1879), he took time off from Harvard College to work as a seaman on a merchant ship (1834–36); his account of his adventures, *Two Years Before the Mast* (1840) is regarded as a minor classic of its genre. His *The Seaman's Friend* (1841), was long the standard manual on maritime law. He practiced law and in 1867–68 served as a U.S. counsel in the trial of Jefferson Davis. He never completed his own planned study of international law but he edited Henry Wheaton's *Elements of International Law.* Although not an avid abolitionist, he helped found the Free-

Soil Party. He died while in Rome where he is buried in the Protestant Cemetery with Keats and Shelley.

Dandy, Walter Edward (1886–1946) neurosurgeon; born in Sedalia, Mo. On the staff of Johns Hopkins Medical School and its hospital from his internship (1910) until his death, he started as an assistant to the great Harvey Cushing but the two had a falling out; although Cushing would go on to Boston and Harvard in 1912, the two great neurosurgeons of their day never resolved their quarrel. Dandy developed a number of important diagnostic and neurosurgical techniques, including the use of ventriculography and the treatment of hydrocephaly; he pioneered in the surgical treatment of tic douloureux and Ménière's disease; he demonstrated the significance of ruptured vertebra disks to low back pain and pioneered in spinal surgery. Through all this he found time to enjoy a weekly game of golf.

Dane, Nathan (1752–1835) legal scholar; born in Ipswich, Mass. His long career of public service includes being a delegate to the Continental Congress (1785–87) and election to the Massachusetts state senate (1790–98). He revised many Massachusetts laws and wrote *General Abridgment and Digest of American Law* (8 vols. 1823).

Daniel, Peter V. (Vivian) (1784–1860) Supreme Court justice; born in Stafford County, Va. He served the Virginia legislature (1812–35) and as a U.S. district judge (1836–41). President Van Buren named him to the U.S. Supreme Court (1842–60), where he supported Jeffersonian principles.

Daniels, Josephus (1862–1948) newspaperman, politician, public official; born in Washington, N.C. Prominent progressive Democratic editor of the Raleigh *News and Observer,* he instituted reforms as secretary of the navy (1913–21) and was ambassador to Mexico (1933–41).

Daniels, Robert (Vincent) (1926–   ) Slavic specialist, politician, author; born in Boston, Mass. Teaching longest at the University of Vermont (1964), he directed the Center for Area Studies (1962–65), chaired the history department (1964–69), and was director of an experimental program of the College of Arts and Sciences (1969–71). A Vermont state senator (1973–82), he focused his concerns on health care and served on the Democratic National Platform Committee (1980). He was the author of numerous books and articles on Eastern Europe.

Dannay, Frederic (b. Daniel Nathan) (1905–82) **and Lee, Manfred B. (Manford Lepofsky)** (1905–71) (Ellery Queen and Barnaby Ross, joint pen names) writers; both born in New York City. First cousins, they grew up only five blocks from each other. After collaborating to win a detective short story contest in the 1920s, they decided to become full-time writers and in 1929 they published their first "Ellery Queen" novel, *The Roman Hat Mystery.* Eventually they would publish 33 Ellery Queen detective novels, and four others under the name of "Barnaby Ross." Their works sold over 100 million copies and were made into several movie series, a long-running radio program, and occasional television movies. In 1941 they founded *Ellery Queen's Mystery Magazine,* to publish both current mystery stories and reprint classics. They also edited numerous anthologies. They always refused to disclose their exact writing methods, but evidently they took turns in developing the plots and writing the stories.

Dantzig, George B. (Bernard) (1914–   ) operations researcher; born in Portland, Ore. A chief combat analyst during World War II, and father of linear programming, he taught longest at Stanford University (1966). A National Academy of Sciences member (1977), he is the author of *Linear Programming and Extensions* (1963) and *Compact City* (1973).

D'Aquino, Iva Ikuko Toguri (1916–) traitoress; born in California. Of Japanese descent, she went to Japan in 1941 to visit her sick aunt. Caught there by the outbreak of World War II, she became one of the voices on Tokyo Radio known to American soldiers as "Tokyo Rose." She was convicted of treason (1949) and spent six years in prison. She was pardoned in 1977 and worked in a Chicago gift shop.

Dare, Virginia (1587–?88) born in Roanoke, Va. She was the first English child born in North America. Her parents were Ananias Dare and Elinor White. She disappeared along with the 117 Roanoke colonists in 1588.

Dargue, Herbert (Arthur) (1886–1942) aviator; born in Brooklyn, N.Y. A 1911 West Point graduate, he developed a broad vision of the uses and importance of air power in the 1920s and 1930s. Dargue commanded the 1st Air Force at Mitchell Field, N.Y., at the time of his death.

Darin, Bobby (b. Walden Robert Cassato) (1936–73) popular singer, songwriter; born in New York City. His first hit song, "Splish Splash" (1958), was followed by the 1959 hits "Dream Lover" and "Queen of the Hop." In the 1960s he was a popular nightclub performer who was able to skillfully sing in such diverse styles as rhythm-and-blues, country-pop, and folk-rock.

Darley, Felix (Octavius Carr) (1822–88) illustrator; born in Philadelphia. He worked in a mercantile house (1836), became an illustrator (1842), moved to New York City (1848), and settled in Claymont, Del. (1859). He is known for illustrating books by Washington Irving and James Fenimore Cooper.

Darnton, Robert (Choate) (1939–) historian; born in New York City. Educated at Harvard and Oxford (D.Phil. 1964), he began as a reporter for the *New York Times* in New York and England before commencing a teaching career at Harvard (1965–68) and Princeton (1968). His interest in the social history of ideas resulted in a series of studies of books, authors, and public opinion in pre-Revolutionary France, including *The Great Cat Massacre and Other Episodes in French Cultural History* (1984).

Darragh, Lydia (b. Barrington) (1729–89) nurse, midwife; born in Ireland. She married William Darragh (1753) and they emigrated to Philadelphia where she became known as a skillful nurse and midwife. During the American Revolution, she became a "Fighting Quaker," who rejected her sect's extreme pacifism. In 1777, she left Philadelphia and warned the American army leaders of a coming surprise attack by the British. She was suspended from the Quakers' Meeting in Philadelphia in 1783 but was reconciled to them by the time of her death.

Darrow, Charles B. (Brace) (1889–1967) game designer; born in Cumberland, Md. A heating engineer reduced to selling stoves in 1930, he is generally credited with devising "Monopoly," the board game in which players compete to purchase real estate and wipe out their opponents. (Some claim that he only adapted a similar game, based on "The Landlord's Game," devised about 1900 by Elizabeth Magee of Virginia.) At first rejected by Parker Brothers, the toy firm bought it in 1935 after he enjoyed great success in selling it himself. He made over $1 million from it but his subsequent invention, "Bulls and Bears," was a failure.

Darrow, Clarence (Seward) (1857–1938) lawyer, social reformer, author; born in Kinsman, Ohio. Admitted to the bar in 1878, he began as a small-town Ohio lawyer, but moved to Chicago in 1887. Political involvement with reform-minded Democrats led to a successful civil practice, then to two decades of labor law, ending in 1913. He gained a national reputation defending Eugene V. Debs and other railway union leaders in connection with the 1894 Pullman strike. Later came sensational criminal cases that displayed his eminence as a defense lawyer, especially the Loeb-Leopold kidnap, murder, and ransom case (1924) and the Scopes anti-evolution "monkey trial" (1925) in which he argued against William Jennings Bryan. (This is the case celebrated in Jerome Lawrence's play, *Inherit the Wind*.) He opposed capital punishment and was a popular public speaker on religious, social, political, scientific, and literary issues. One of his law partners (1903–11) was the poet Edgar Lee Masters. His many books include *Crime: Its Cause and Treatment* (1922).

Dassin, (Julius) Jules (1911–) movie director; born in Middletown, Conn. (husband of Melina Mercouri). Beginning as a short subject director, he then made slice-of-life features such as *The Naked City* (1948). Forced into exile by the McCarthy witch hunt of the early 1950s, he directed such films as *Rififi* (1955) and *Never on Sunday* (1960).

Daugherty, Harry (Micajah) (1860–1941) lawyer, politician; born in Washington Court House, Ohio. As campaign manager whose prediction originated the term "smoke-filled-room," and as attorney general (1921–24) for President Harding, he figured in several scandals including the Teapot Dome but managed to avoid criminal indictment.

Davenport, Guy (Mattison, Jr.) (1927–) writer, translator, educator; born in Anderson, S.C. A Harvard Ph.D., he joined the University of Kentucky English faculty (1963). His writing, distinctive in its erudition and allusiveness, encompassed essays, poetry, and experimental fiction. He is also known for his translations from Heraclitus, Menander, Sappho, and other ancient Greek authors.

Davenport, John (1597–1670) clergyman, author, colonist; born in Coventry, England. He became an Anglican minister in 1625 but was attracted to the Puritan faith and became a full dissenter by 1632. He resigned his post and preached briefly in Holland before emigrating to Boston (1637). With his boyhood friend, Theophilus Eaton, he founded the New Haven Colony in 1638. He was the pastor of the church there (1638–67). He sheltered the English regicides, Edward Whalley and William Goffe, in 1661. He opposed the Half-Way Covenant and the merging of New Haven into the Connecticut colony. He left for Boston in 1667 and was briefly the pastor of the First Church there.

David, John Baptist (Mary) (1761–1841) Catholic bishop; born in France. A Sulpician priest, he emigrated to the U.S.A. in 1792 and, after pastoral work and teaching, became bishop coadjutor of Bardstown, Ky. (1819). Known for his austere piety in the continental tradition, he served briefly as bishop of the diocese (1832–33), then resigned to teach and write.

Davidson, Donald (1917–) philosopher; born in Springfield, Mass. After earning a doctorate from Harvard (1949), he taught at Queens College (1947–50), Stanford (1950–67),

Princeton (1967–69), Rockefeller University (1970–76), and the University of Chicago (from 1976), before joining the University of California: Berkeley in 1981. In *Inquiries Into Truth and Interpretation* (1983) and other influential works, he analyzed the semantic structures of ordinary languages and made contributions to philosophy of mind.

Davidson, George (1825–1911) geodesist, geographer, astronomer; born in Nottingham, England. Coming to America as a child, he worked for 50 years with the U.S. Coast Survey, mapping the Pacific coast for marine navigation. An avid astronomer, he published catalogues of star positions and began the first observatory in California (1897). In 1898 he was appointed honorary professor of geography and astronomy at the University of California.

Davidson, Gordon (1933–) theater director and producer; born in New York City. Beginning in 1965 he directed the Mark Taper Forum in Los Angeles, where he has done world premieres of important plays including *The Trial of the Catonsville Nine* in 1970.

Davidson, Jo (1883–1952) sculptor; born in New York City. He studied at the Art Students League (c. 1899), Yale Art School (c. 1890), worked in New York, lived primarily in Paris (1907–c. 1940), and settled in Lahaska, Pa. (1940). He is known for his sculptured portraits of Woodrow Wilson (1916), Gertrude Stein (1920), and those of Allied war leaders (1918–19).

Davies, Arthur (Bowen) (1862–1928) painter; born in Utica, N.Y. Although he was a decorative painter, he is remembered as the president of the Association of American Painters and Sculptors, an organization that produced the influential Armory Show in New York (1913). This exhibition presented the current work of American and European artists and created significant interest in contemporary art.

Davies, Samuel (1723–61) Protestant clergyman, educator; born in New Castle County, Del. Ordained in 1747, he led the Great Awakening revival in Virginia, where he became a stout defender of the freedom of religious sects from the authority of the colony's established church. He attracted a large following as a preacher, and his sermons were widely published. In 1759 he succeeded Jonathan Edwards as president of the College of New Jersey (later Princeton) and served there until his death.

Davis, Alexander J. (Jackson) (1803–92) architect; born in New York City. Trained as an architectural illustrator, he collaborated with Ithiel Town (1829–43) and then worked independently in New York. Davis promoted a picturesque romanticism in a wide range of buildings and styles, but favored neoclassical styles with his signature multistory windows for public buildings; in the 1830s he designed a number of state capitols. His *Rural Residences* (1837), country villa designs, and contributions to Andrew Jackson Downing's books (1839–50) greatly influenced American house design.

Davis, Alice Brown (1852–1935) Seminole leader; born near Park Hill in present-day Oklahoma. The co-owner of a trading post, she journeyed to Mexico (1890s) as an interpreter for Seminoles seeking a new home. In 1906 she became superintendent of the Seminole girls' school. After the loss of official tribal identity (1907), she often represented her people in court and served in many ways as a chief.

Davis, Allison (1902–83) cultural anthropologist; born in Washington, D.C. A graduate of Williams College, he studied at Harvard and the London School of Economics before taking a Ph.D. at the University of Chicago in 1942. He taught and was a research associate at Harvard, Dillard, and Chicago, and became an assistant professor of education at Chicago in 1942, where he spent the rest of his academic career. He authored or coauthored eight scholarly works, including *Children of Bondage* (1940) and *Cultural Deprivation* (1964).

Davis, Angela (1944–) author, activist; born in Birmingham, Ala. Influenced by the civil rights movement and her graduate training with Herbert Marcuse, she became a controversial activist and Communist Party member. In a trial that received worldwide attention, she was acquitted of all charges in connection with the Soledad Brothers murders (1971–72). A prominent lecturer and teacher, she wrote *Women, Race and Class* (1980).

Davis, Anthony (1951–) composer, jazz pianist; born in Paterson, N.J. A leader of avant-garde musicians at Yale, in 1973, with trombonist George Lewis, he formed Advent, a free-jazz group. He played in several ensembles that bridged jazz and classical forms. His compositions are structured around complex, atonal lines, though meditative simplicity is also achieved through repetition. His opera, *X,* based on the life of Malcolm X, was premiered in Philadelphia in 1985.

Davis, Arthur Vining (1867–1962) industrialist, philanthropist; born in Sharon, Mass. Working with Charles Martin Hall at the Pittsburgh Reduction Company, he poured the first commercial aluminum in 1888. By 1907, as director of the company, he converted it into the Aluminum Company of America (Alcoa), which he served as general manager, president, and chairman of the board until retiring in 1958. As the nation's premier manufacturer of aluminum, he often had to fend off antitrust suits from the government. He gave most of his $400 million estate to the Davis Foundation, which supports educational, scientific, and cultural institutions.

Davis, Benjamin (Oliver), Jr. (1912–) aviator; born in Washington, D.C. Son of a career soldier who became the first black general in the U.S. military, he organized the all-black 99th Fighter Squadron and served with distinction in North Africa, Sicily, and Italy. Davis held a series of staff and line posts during the 1950s and 1960s; he had finished a tour as deputy commander, U.S. Strike Command, when he retired in 1970. In 1971 Davis became director of public safety for the city of Cleveland, Ohio.

Davis, Benjamin Oliver, Sr. (1887–1970) soldier; born in Washington, D.C. Commissioned in 1901, a long-serving soldier during a difficult era for African-Americans, Davis helped prepare the way for the desegregation of the U.S. services in 1947. Promoted brigadier general in 1940, he was the first African-American to reach general's rank.

Davis, Bette See Davis, (Ruth Elizabeth) Bette.

Davis, Charles Henry (1807–77) naval officer, scientist; born in Boston, Mass. He surveyed the waters around Nantucket and contributed to the establishment of the *American Ephemeris and Nautical Almanac* (1849). He commanded the Upper Mississippi Flotilla and captured Memphis (1862).

Davis, (Daisie) Adelle (1904–74) nutritionist, author; born in Lizton, Ind. After taking a graduate degree in biochemistry from the University of California Medical School, she continued her training in dietetics at hospitals in New York

City, then settled in California to work as a consulting nutritionist, planning diets for thousands of individuals suffering from various diseases and ailments. In 1954 she published *Let's Eat Right to Keep Fit,* which quickly gained a devoted following for her emphasis on a proper diet as the crux of both emotional and physical well-being. What particularly distinguished this and her subsequent books from most popular books on food – in addition to her footnotes and citations of scientific studies – was her claim that one's diet, especially one rich in vitamins and minerals, could actually prevent or cure diseases. For this she was often criticized and even derided by the medical establishment and she died not long before her broad views, if not all her details, began to be accepted by many in the fields of medicine and health.

Davis, David (1815–86) Supreme Court justice; born in Cecil County, Md. A close friend to Abraham Lincoln, he served as a circuit court judge in Illinois (1848–62) until President Lincoln named him to the U.S. Supreme Court (1862–77). A presidential hopeful in 1872, he stepped down from the court to serve the U.S. Senate (Dem., Ill.; 1876–83).

Davis, Dwight (Filley) (1879–1945) public official, sportsman; born in St. Louis, Mo. While still a student at Harvard, he was the U.S. national doubles champion (1899–1901). Independently wealthy, in 1900 he donated the Davis Cup, a silver bowl awarded each year to the national team that wins the world's men's tennis championship. He was active in St. Louis affairs until World War I when he volunteered for military service. He was assistant secretary of war (1923–25) and the secretary of war (1925–29). As governor general of the Philippines (1929–32), he introduced various educational and economic reforms. A trustee of the Brookings Institution from its founding in 1927, he served as its chairman (1937–45).

Davis, Elmer (Holmes) (1890–1956) journalist, broadcaster, author; born in Aurora, Ind. A prominent radio news commentator (1939–42, 1945–53), he was noted for his straightforward style and dry humor. He headed the War Information Office during World War II (1942–45); his books include *Not to Mention the War* (1945) and two short story collections.

Davis, (Ernest) Ernie (1939–63) football player; born in New Salem, Pa. A three-time All-America halfback and 1961 Heisman Trophy winner, he set yardage and scoring records at Syracuse University. His pro career was curtailed by leukemia.

Davis, Frances (b. Elliot) (?1882–1965) nurse, community leader; born in Shelby, N.C. Through quiet persistence she became the first African-American nurse to be enrolled officially by the American National Red Cross. As a nursing supervisor, administrator, and visiting nurse in Detroit, Mich., she encouraged African-American education and promoted nursing efforts there and nationally.

Davis, Garrett (1801–72) U.S. representative/senator; born in Mount Sterling, Ky. He served Kentucky in its legislature and at its constitutional convention. He was elected to the U.S. House of Representatives by a Whig majority he served from 1839–47. A renowned orator, he was sent to the U.S. Senate in 1861, where he served until his death. Although a supporter of the Union, he grew critical of Lincoln's policies and was elected to his second term as a Democrat.

Davis, Glenn (Woodward) "Junior" (1924–) football player; born in Burbank, Calif. An exceptionally fast halfback, he and fullback "Doc" Blanchard led Army to undefeated seasons (1944–45). He won the 1946 Heisman Trophy.

Davis, Hallie Flanagan See FLANAGAN, HALLIE.

Davis, Jefferson Columbus (1828–79) Union soldier; born in Clark County, Ind. He shot and killed his commanding officer after an argument in a Louisville hotel in September 1862, but through political influence went unpunished. He returned to duty and led a corps in Sherman's march to the sea.

Davis, Jefferson (Finis) (1808–89) president of the Confederate States of America, U.S. senator, cabinet member, soldier; born in Fairview, Ky. After graduating from West Point (1828) he served on the frontier for seven years. Then, shattered by the death of his wife of three months (she was the daughter of Zachary Taylor), he secluded himself on his Mississippi plantation. He married Varina Howell in 1845. He served in the U.S. House of Representatives (Miss., Dem.; 1845–46), but resigned to volunteer for service in the Mexican War and was credited with securing the victory at Buena Vista. He returned to serve in the U.S. Senate (1847–51) and then as U.S. secretary of war (1853–57). He returned to the U.S. Senate in 1857 but resigned in 1861 when Mississippi seceded from the Union. Expecting to be given command of the Confederate armies, he was instead chosen president of the Confederate government (provisional, 1861–62; elected, 1862–65). He drew much criticism for intervening in the military's policies and for assuming near-dictatorial executive powers. His intolerance of disagreement, inability to build a national consensus, and failure to select quality subordinates further handicapped his effectiveness as a war president. Nevertheless, historians have judged him the best candidate for a difficult if not impossible job, for he constantly found himself opposed by Southerners who embraced extreme states' rights positions. He fled the capital, Richmond, rather than surrendering, but was captured in Georgia on May 10, 1865; after two years' imprisonment (the first months in shackles), he was released without trial. He retired to his Mississippi plantation, traveled some in Europe, and failed at various business ventures. Refusing to request amnesty, he resolutely defended the Southern cause in speeches and books including *The Rise and Fall of the Confederate Government* (2 vols. 1878–81).

Davis, John William (1873–1955) lawyer, public official; born in Clarksburg, W.Va. He practiced law with his father before winning election to the U.S. House of Representatives (Dem., W.Va.; 1911–13). In 1913 he joined the Wilson administration as solicitor general and became ambassador to Great Britain in 1918. Davis returned to private practice, served as president of the American Bar Association (1922–24), and in 1924 was the surprise Democratic presidential nominee, winning on the record 103rd ballot of a deadlocked convention. Coolidge beat him by a landslide in the general election. Davis later became a strong supporter of the United Nations. In his last major case, he defended atomic scientist J. Robert Oppenheimer, who was accused of being a security risk.

Davis, Katherine Bement (1860–1935) social worker, penologist; born in Buffalo, N.Y. Forced by her family's financial situation to teach during her twenties, it was 1892 before she took her degree from Vassar. She took graduate courses in food chemistry and nutrition at Columbia University, and after teaching and demonstrating domestic economy in 1893, she turned to social work, running a settlement house in Philadelphia (1894–97). She then attended the University of Chicago, taking a Ph.D. in political economy in 1900. She became the superintendent of the Reformatory for Women at Bedford Hills, N.Y. (1901–14) and pioneered in various progressive ways of treating prisoners. On a trip to Europe in 1909, she gained international recognition for her efforts to help the Sicilians recover from the great Messina earthquake of that year. Appointed New York City's first female commissioner of corrections, she introduced several reforms during her brief tenure (1914–15), then became chairperson of the city's parole board (1915–17). She moved on to become general secretary of the Bureau of Social Hygiene, a branch of the Rockefeller Foundation (1917–28), and extended her interests to such matters as prostitution and public health. She worked both during and after World War I to relieve suffering of women and children. She published many articles in professional journals and found time to work for various other social causes before retiring to California in 1928.

Davis, Miles Dewey (1926–91) jazz trumpeter; born in Alton, Ill. He was raised near St. Louis, Mo., in a prosperous African-American family and played with local bands. After brief classical studies at the Juilliard School in 1944, he played in Charlie Parker's trailblazing bebop quintet until 1948. Between 1949–69, he was at the forefront of jazz, developing or advancing several significant and contrasting styles and trends, all of which highlighted his intensely personal sensibilities. These included cool jazz, hard bop, modal jazz, fusion, and several innovative orchestral collaborations with Gil Evans. As a bandleader, he was a discerning recruiter of new talent, including John Coltrane, Bill Evans, and Herbie Hancock. He was widely admired for his cool demeanor and sartorial elegance, but his embrace of an electrified commercial approach during the last 20 years of his career, a period in which he performed irregularly, found little favor with his original audience.

Davis, Natalie (Ann) Zemon (1928–) historian; born in Detroit, Mich. Educated at Smith and Radcliffe Colleges and the University of Michigan (Ph.D. 1959), she taught at Brown University (1959–63), the University of Toronto (1963–71), the University of California: Berkeley (1971–78), and Princeton (1978). A foremost practitioner of the "new social history," she engaged in almost anthropological research into the lives of the artisans, laborers, and peasants of 16th-century France, resulting in such works as *The Return of Martin Guerre* (1983) (which was used as the basis for French and American movies).

Davis, Nathan Smith (1817–1904) physician; born in Greene, N.Y. He settled in Chicago in 1849 where he practiced medicine and taught at Rush Medical College until his death. An early advocate of higher standards of medical education, he had put forward proposals in 1843 at a session of the Medical Society of the State of New York that led to the founding of the American Medical Association (1847), and for this reason he is sometimes known as its "father."

Davis, Ossie (1917–) stage/film/television actor, playwright, director; born in Cogdell, Ga. Some of his best-

known roles were in *The Joe Louis Story* (1953) and *Purlie Victorious* (1963). He was married to Ruby Dee.

Davis, Owen (1874–1956) playwright; born in Portland, Maine. He achieved critical acclaim with *The Detour* in 1921 and a Pulitzer Prize for *Icebound* in 1923, but most of his career was devoted to writing financially rewarding melodramas.

Davis, Rebecca Harding (b. Rebecca Blaine Harding) (1831–1910) writer; born in Washington, Pa. (mother of Richard Harding Davis). Largely self-educated, she first attracted attention with "Life in the Iron-Mills" (*Atlantic Monthly,* 1861) and her realistic Civil War stories. Her novels portraying the bleak lives of factory workers (*Margaret Howth,* 1862) and African-Americans (*Waiting for the Verdict,* 1868) have gained her the reputation as a pioneer of American naturalism. After 1863 she lived in Philadelphia, the setting of much of her later work.

Davis, Richard Harding (1864–1916) journalist, writer; born in Philadelphia. Starting as a newspaper reporter in Philadelphia and then New York (1886–91), Harding was managing editor of *Harper's Weekly* from 1891 to 1893 but spent most of his later career as a freelance, traveling and writing articles, as well as fiction and drama. One of the most popular reporters of his day, he covered half a dozen conflicts, including the Spanish-American War, the Boer War, and World War I, and reported on such events as the 1889 Johnstown (Pa.) flood and Queen Victoria's diamond jubilee (1897), in a colorful style bordering on the sensational. His short story "Gallegher" (1890) brought him instant renown as a fiction writer, and he wrote many more, often focusing on a gentleman-adventurer as hero. Also popular were his novels, including *Soldiers of Fortune* (1897), and several plays. His work was considered somewhat superficial and is not well-known today.

Davis, Russ E. (Erik) (1941–) oceanographer; born in San Francisco. A faculty member of the University of California: San Diego since 1967, he became professor of oceanography at its Scripps Institute in 1977. He made major contributions to studies of fluid dynamics.

Davis, (Ruth Elizabeth) Bette (1908–89) film actress; born in Lowell, Mass. After studying drama she was fired from a stock company in Rochester, N.Y., and then appeared with the Provincetown Players off-Broadway in 1928. She made her Broadway debut in *Broken Dishes* (1929), and her Hollywood debut in *Bad Sister* (1931). By 1932 she was becoming known as a dedicated actress with an electrifying style. Able to bring an emotional honesty to the screen, she became a prime box-office attraction between 1935 and 1946 and was nominated for an Oscar ten times, winning it twice in *Dangerous* (1935) and in *Jezebel* (1938). An independent woman, she fought her studio for better parts, and got them. Married and divorced four times, she was still active until 1978.

Davis, Sammy, Jr. (1925–90) singer, dancer; born in New York City. A short, multi-talented entertainer, he began his career tapping and singing at the age of four with his family. He was working in night clubs in 1954, when a near fatal car crash changed his life. He converted to Judaism and made his Broadway debut in *Mr. Wonderful,* which led to a film career (1956–89). He recorded 40 albums but in later years was best known for his appearances at Las Vegas and on television.

Davis, Stuart (1893–1964) painter; born in Philadelphia. Son of artists, he grew up knowing some original members of the Ashcan School; when his father, an art editor, moved to New Jersey, he left school at age 16 to study painting with Robert Henri in New York. He first painted everyday life under the influence of the Ashcan School but the Armory Show of 1913 (in which he had 5 watercolors) turned him to more modern styles, first like the French Fauvists, then more Cubist. Eventually he developed his own distinctive style based on his theory of "color-space logic," using bold colors and flat, often geometric forms – as in *Lucky Strike* (1921) – to capture every possible aspect of the American scene. He loved the early styles of jazz and remained influenced by African-American music. Although he spent two years in Paris (1928–30) and often visited the Massachusetts coast, he spent most of his career in New York. During the late 1930s he did a remarkable series of mural paintings, such as *Swing Landscape* (1938). Eventually recognized as having anticipated certain elements of Pop Art, his work continued to increase its reputation after his death.

Davis, William (Morris) (1850–1934) geologist, geographer; born in Philadelphia. He studied at Harvard College, then spent three years (1870–73) as assistant at the National Observatory, Cordoba, Argentina. After working for his father, assisting Harvard's Nathaniel Shaler, and touring the world, he accepted an appointment in 1878 as Harvard instructor in physical geography and meteorology. He was extremely prolific throughout his lifetime, and bequeathed a still-relevant literature to his field, including *Elementary Physical Geography* (1902), *Geographical Essays* (1909), *The Lesser Antilles* (1926), and *The Coral Reef Problem* (1928). Creating a disciplined framework for a mass of data is regarded as his most enduring contribution.

Davisson, Clinton J. (Joseph) (1881–1958) physicist; born in Bloomington, Ill. He taught at the Carnegie Institution (1911–17), then joined Bell Telephone Laboratories (1917–46). In 1927 he demonstrated that electrons could behave as waves as well as particles; for this breakthrough, he shared the 1937 Nobel Prize in physics with G. P. Thomson. After leaving Bell, Davisson became a visiting professor at the University of Virginia until 1954. He continued research in electron optics and contributed to the development of the electron microscope.

Dawes, Charles G. (Gates) (1865–1951) vice-president, financier, Nobel Prize winner; born in Marietta, Ohio. During World War I, he was the chief purchasing agent for the American Army. In 1923, he became chairman of the Allied Reparations Committee, which reduced German reparations payments and restructured the German economy; for this "Dawes Plan" he shared the Nobel Peace Prize in 1925. He served as Calvin Coolidge's vice-president (1925–29) and then as ambassador to Great Britain (1929–32).

Dawes, Henry Laurens (1816–1903) U.S. representative/senator; born in Cummington, Mass. A lawyer, he was elected to the U.S. House of Representatives (Rep., Mass.; 1857–75) and to the U.S. Senate (1875–93); in the latter he served as chairman of the senate committee on Indian affairs. He wrote the Dawes Severalty Act of 1887 which granted homesteads and citizenship, after 25 years, to those Native Americans who renounced their tribal holdings. He then served as chairman of the Dawes Commission (1893), which was set up to resolve problems with the Five Civilized Tribes who lived in the Indian Territory.

Dawkins, Henry (active 1753–86) engraver; born in England. He emigrated to New York City (c. 1753), worked as an engraver, moved to Philadelphia (c. 1757), and returned to New York (1774). He is known for his early engravings, such as *Pennsylvania Hospital* (1761), and *The Paxton Expedition* (1764).

Dawson, John M. (Myrick) (1930–) physicist; born in Champaign, Ill. He was a researcher at Princeton (1956–73), then moved to the University of California: Los Angeles (1973), while concurrently serving as consultant to several major research institutions. He made significant advances in studies of plasma, atomic, and molecular physics.

Dawson, William Levi (1886–1970) U.S. representative; born in Albany, Ga. The grandson of slaves, he worked as a bellhop while earning his law degree in Chicago in 1920. A Chicago alderman (1933–39), who became a Democrat, he served in Congress (1943–70). Although he opposed the poll tax and worked for fair employment practices, he was more of a party loyalist than civil rights activist, supporting Richard Daley over a reform mayor in 1955, and delivering Chicago's black vote to President Kennedy in 1960.

Day, Arthur L. (Louis) (1869–1960) geophysicist; born in Brookfield, Mass. While serving on the U.S. Geological Survey (1900–07), he investigated melting temperatures of igneous rocks, and developed the measurement of temperatures above 1150° Celsius. He directed the Carnegie Institution's Geophysical Laboratory (1906–36), where his research included temperature and gas measurements of volcanoes and hot springs, seismological studies, and radioactivity disintegration determinations of the age of ocean core samples. He contributed to the Corning Glass Works' large-scale manufacturing techniques for producing optical glass.

Day, Clarence (Shepard, Jr.) (1874–1935) writer; born in New York City. He studied at Yale (B.A. 1896) before becoming a stockbroker and partner in his father's firm (1898). Soon after his service in the Spanish-American War (1898), he became progressively crippled by a form of arthritis. Forced to withdraw from the stockbrokerage business, he devoted himself to writing and illustrating. He wrote book reviews, stories, and verse, and was cofounder of the Yale Press, but is most famous for his humorous books based on his childhood memories, notably *Life With Father* (1935).

Day, Doris (b. Kapplehoff) (1924–) singer, actress; born in Cincinnati, Ohio. Borrowing her stage name from a song ("Day by Day"), she sang with the Bob Crosby band and with Fred Waring but it wasn't until her recording of "Sentimental Journey" with Les Brown's band (1944) that she gained national popularity. Her singing was sweet, smooth, and intimate, and because she looked like everyone's ideal "girl next door," she was soon making light romantic comedies, 39 movies altogether. In 1968, on the death of her third husband and manager, Marty Melcher, she discovered he had either mismanaged or embezzled her life's earnings, so she went back to work on television with the "Doris Day Show." In 1974 she was also awarded some $22 million in damages from the lawyer who had helped her husband-manager.

Day, Dorothy (1897–1980) social activist; born in New York City. A radical activist and writer, initially Marxist, she became a Catholic in 1927. In 1933, with Peter Maurin, she founded the Catholic Worker movement, devoted to aiding the poor through "hospitality houses" and other facilities and promoting a philosophy of personal Christian social activism, as represented in the *Catholic Worker* newspaper. Deeply spiritual, she was widely regarded as a modern-day saint. Her writings include a 1952 autobiography, *The Long Loneliness*.

Day, Fred Holland (1864–1933) photographer; born in Norwood, Mass. A wealthy eccentric, he did photographic re-creations of mythological and biblical scenes in the 1890s and sponsored the first exhibit of American photographers in Europe.

Day, William Rufus (1849–1923) diplomat, Supreme Court justice; born in Ravenna, Ohio. As secretary of state under McKinley, he helped to negotiate peace in the Spanish-American War (1898). President Theodore Roosevelt named him to the U.S. Supreme Court (1903–22).

Day(e), Stephen (c. 1594–1688) printer; born in London, England. He emigrated to New England in 1638, under contract to work for the Reverend Jesse Glover, who, however, died en route. A press was set up in Cambridge, Mass., where Glover's widow settled. Day is believed to have managed it until 1649, when Samuel Green took over.

Dayton, Jonathan (1760–1824) U.S. representative/senator; born in Elizabeth-Town, N.J. A captain at Yorktown, he served in the New Jersey assembly (1786–87), leaving to attend the Federal Convention. He served in four congresses (Fed., N.J.; 1791–99), supporting Alexander Hamilton's banking policies. A one-term senator (1799–1805), his federal career ended abruptly when he was indicted for treason in 1807 with his friend Aaron Burr. Never prosecuted, he subsequently held local and state offices in New Jersey.

Dean, Arthur H. (Hobson) (1898–1987) lawyer, government official; born in Ithaca, N.Y. He interrupted his undergraduate studies at Cornell to serve with the U.S. Navy in World War I, and then went on to take a law degree from Cornell Law School (1923). He joined the New York City law firm of Sullivan & Cromwell in 1923 and would remain with them – with many years off for government service – until 1976. From the beginning he was involved in international law, particularly financial transactions, but he was also directly involved in drafting federal legislation involving the securities and financial markets. During World War II he served with the Coast Guard Reserve, and in 1953, as special deputy secretary of state, he was the chief U.S. negotiator to end the Korean War. He served on other U.S. delegations to conferences on international sea law, a nuclear test ban, and disarmament. He is credited with helping persuade President Lyndon Johnson to stop the bombing of North Vietnam in 1968.

Dean, James (Byron) (1931–55) film actor; born in Marion, Ind. Raised on an Iowa farm, after high school he attended college in California, where he joined a little theater group and did occasional television commercials and bit part film appearances. Arriving in New York in 1952, he got a part in *See the Jaguar* on Broadway. He had bit parts on television and acted on Broadway in *The Immoralist* (1954), which got him a Hollywood screen test. He starred in only three movies – *East of Eden* (1955), *Rebel Without a Cause* (1955), and *Giant* (1956) – but this moody actor was instantly acclaimed as the epitome of the mid-fifties, representing the alienated American youth of the time, the true rebel without a cause. On September 30, 1955 he was killed in a highway crash while driving his Porsche to compete in a racing event. He became a cult figure, and for many years after his death remained a symbol of youthful alienation and rebellion.

Dean, (Jay Hanna) "Dizzy" (1911–74) baseball player, broadcaster; born in Lucas, Ark. One of baseball's most memorable personalities, he won 30 games and the Most Valuable Player award in 1934 as a (right-handed) pitcher for the world champion St. Louis Cardinals. When his career ended in 1947, he became a baseball broadcaster and was known for his colorful, if ungrammatical use of the English language. He was elected to the Hall of Fame in 1953.

Dean, William (Frishe) (1899–1981) soldier; born in Carlyle, Ill. He became one of the first heroes of the Korean War when he was captured commanding the 24th Infantry Division in action against a heavy North Korean assault at Teajon (1950). He described his three-year ordeal in a Communist prisoner of war camp in the best-seller, *General Dean's Story* (1954).

Deane, Silas (1737–89) diplomat, legislator; born in Groton, Conn. He was the first diplomat sent abroad by the united colonies. He went to France in 1776 and managed to persuade the French government to send cargoes of military supplies to the colonies under the guise of a holding company. He also obtained the services of Europeans such as Lafayette, Johann Kalb, Casimir Pulaski, and Baron von Steuben. In concert with Arthur Lee and Benjamin Franklin, he negotiated and signed two treaties with France (1778). Following this triumph, he was recalled to America after insinuations of disloyalty and embezzlement were made against him. Lacking documentary proof of his transactions, he went back to Europe. He became embittered and advocated reconciliation with the British. After the American Revolution he lived as an impoverished exile in Belgium and then London. In 1842, Congress reexamined the evidence in his case and made restitution of $37,000 to his heirs.

Dearborn, Henry (1751–1829) soldier; born in Hampton, N.H. A Revolutionary War veteran, he served as secretary of war during Jefferson's two terms (1801–09). Assigned command of the critical northeast theater at the outbreak of the War of 1812, he managed affairs so incompetently that he was removed in July 1813.

DeBakey, Michael (Ellis) (1908–) cardiologist, surgeon; born in Lake Charles, La. While he was still a medical student, he invented a major component of the heart-lung machines (1932) that made open heart surgery possible. He joined the faculty at Tulane University in 1937. During World War II he helped the Surgeon General develop mobile army surgical hospitals (MASH units). He returned to Tulane for two years and then joined Baylor University's medical school (1948). In the early 1950s, he became proficient in treating aortic aneurysms by replacing the section with a graft of blood vessels. He performed the first of 12 heart transplants (1968); the procedure was stopped until 1984 when controls on organ rejection were improved. He became president (1969) and then chancellor (1978) of the Baylor College of Medicine (Waco, Texas). A prolific writer, he published *The Living Heart* (1977) and *The Living Heart Diet* (1984).

De Bary, William Theodore (1919–) historian, educator; born in New York City. He took undergraduate and graduate degrees at Columbia University, where he taught Chinese and Japanese history (1949) and directed the Heyman Center for the Humanities (1990). A prolific author, he wrote among other works *Sources of Japanese Tradition* (1958) and *The Liberal Tradition in China* (1983).

de Blois, Natalie (1921–) architect; birthplace unknown. She joined Skidmore, Owings, & Merrill soon after graduating from Columbia University in 1944, and in her 30-year career there she worked closely with Gordon Bunshaft. As a senior designer she exerted a major but anonymous influence on many of the firm's most famous office developments, including the Connecticut General Life Insurance Building in Bloomfield, Conn. (1957), and the Pepsi-Cola (now Olivetti) (1959) and Union Carbide (1960) buildings, both in New York City. She joined Neuhaus & Taylor, Houston (1975).

Debreu, Gerard (1921–) economist; born in Calais, France. Educated in France, he immigrated to the U.S.A. in 1950. He moved from the Cowles Commission from the University of Chicago to Yale in 1955 but left to take a professorship at the University of California: Berkeley (1960). He collaborated with Kenneth Arrow to produce a definitive mathematical method to prove the existence of equilibrium among prices, production, and consumer demand. In 1959, he published *Theory of Value,* restating traditional economic price theory using set theory and topology. He received the Chevalier of the French Legion of Honor (1976) and the Nobel Prize in economics (1983).

Debs, Eugene V. (Victor) (1855–1926) labor leader, political activist; born in Terre Haute, Ind. At age 15 he went to work on the railroads. After serving as secretary of his local of the Brotherhood of Locomotive Firemen (1875–80), he became the union's national secretary and editor of its magazine (1880–92). He served in the Indiana legislature (1886–88). Championing the cause of industrial unionism, he organized the American Railway Union in 1892, and led the boycott of all Pullman cars during the great strike of 1894; for defying the government's injunction he was jailed for six months. Converting to socialism while in jail, he helped found the Social Democratic Party in 1897, which merged in 1901 with another group to form the Socialist Party (SP). In 1905 he helped found the Industrial Workers of the World, which he eventually disavowed because of its use of violence. He ran for the U.S. presidency in 1900, 1904, 1908, and 1912 as the SP's candidate, winning over 900,000 votes, 6% of the total cast, in the 1912 election. During these years he supported himself by lecturing and writing. In 1918 he spoke out against the trials being conducted under the 1917 Espionage Act, under which individuals opposed to America participating in the world war were being charged with sedition; he himself was then tried for sedition and sentenced to ten years in jail. While there in 1920, he again ran for president on the Socialist ticket; he received his largest vote ever. Public protest persuaded President Harding to release him in 1921, but Debs never ceased working for the cause of Socialism.

de Burgos, Julia (1914–53) poet, teacher; born in Carolina, Puerto Rico. One of Puerto Rico's leading 20th-century poets, influenced by Pablo Neruda, she was a prominent member of the literary Vanguard movement in San Juan in the late 1930s. Her best-known poem, "Río Grande de Loíza," was written before she moved to New York City, where she spent her last years. Over the years, she supported herself with a variety of jobs, including teaching. In addition, she was often supported by the wealthy men in her life.

Debye, Peter (Joseph William) (b. Petrus Josephus Wilhelmus Debje) (1884–1966) physicist, chemist; born in Maastricht, Holland. He held a series of teaching posts at Swiss, Dutch, and German universities while he pursued his research in physical chemistry. In 1912–13 he introduced the concept of the molecular electric dipole moment, which led to new understandings of ionization and molecular structure. He was awarded the Nobel Prize in chemistry (1936). He emigrated to the U.S.A. in 1940 and headed the chemistry department at Cornell University (1940–50), where he concentrated on research in the light-scattering process.

De Carava, Roy (1919–) artist, photographer; born in New York City. While working as a commercial artist (1944–56), he switched over to photography and was the first African-American awarded a Guggenheim in 1952. In 1955, he published *The Sweet Flypaper of Life* with pictures of blacks in Harlem. A successful freelance photographer working for advertising agencies and magazines (1959–75), he organized workshops for African-American photographers and was a professor at Hunter College (1979).

Decatur, Stephen (1779–1820) naval officer; born in Sinepuxent, Md. He became a midshipman (1798) and joined the Tripoli Squadron as a first lieutenant in 1801. He led a daring raid into the harbor of Tripoli and burned the captured USS *Philadelphia* (1804). He held various commands in home waters (1805–12) and served on the court-martial that suspended Captain James Barron (1808). He led the USS *United States* to a thrilling victory over the British *Macedonian* (1812). In 1815 he surrendered the *President* after fighting against a much larger British naval force. He commanded the squadron that ended corsair raids from Algiers, Tunis, and Tripoli (1815) and returned home to give a famous toast, "Our country! In her intercourse with foreign nations may she always be in the right; but our country, right or wrong." He was a member of the newly created Board of Naval Commissioners (1815–20) until his death in a duel with Captain James Barron.

Decatur, Stephen (1752–1808) naval officer; born in Newport, R.I. (father of Stephen Decatur, 1779–1820). He commanded five different privateer vessels during the American Revolution and became a captain in the U.S. Navy in 1798. In command of the USS *Delaware,* he captured the first prize in the undeclared war with France.

Decker, Mary See SLANEY, MARY.

de Creeft, José (1884–1982) sculptor; born in Guadalajara, Spain. He worked in Barcelona (1898), studied in Madrid (1900) and Paris (1906–07 and 1911–14), then emigrated to New York City (1929). He is known for carving directly into stone and for sculptures, as *Alice in Wonderland* (1960).

Dee, Ruby (b. Ruby Ann Wallace) (1923–) stage/film/television actress; born in Cleveland, Ohio. She played a wide range of roles, from Shakespeare's Cleopatra to Lutiebelle in *Purlie Victorious.* She was married to Ossie Davis.

Deere, John (1804–86) inventor, manufacturer; born in Rutland, Vt. He worked as a blacksmith until 1837, when he moved to Illinois. With a partner he designed a series of new plows; these sold modestly during the 1840s. On his own, he designed the first cast steel plow, a major advance that made it substantially easier for farmers to break and turn the heavy soil of the Great Plains. By 1855 his factory was selling more than 10,000 steel plows a year. He continued to manage Deere and Company, manufacturers of plows and other agricultural implements, until his last illness.

Dees, Morris (Seligman), Jr. (1936–   ) lawyer, activist; born in Shorter, Ala. While at the University of Alabama he founded Fuller & Dees Marketing Group, a nationwide specialty direct-market-sales publishing house (1960). One of the largest publishing houses in the South, and a pioneer in sex education books for children, it was sold to the Times Mirror Corporation (1969). Partner in the firm of Levin & Dees (1969–71), he became chief trial counsel of the Southern Poverty Law Center, Montgomery, Ala., which he founded (1971) with Joseph J. Levin Jr., and Julian Bond. The center would become involved in wide-ranging lawsuits from the defense of Joan Little in North Carolina to the battle to integrate the Alabama State Troopers. Active as a fund raiser for the Democratic Party, he was national fund raising director for the "McGovern for President" campaign (1972), national finance chairman for the "Carter for President" campaign (1976), and national finance chairman for the "Kennedy for President" campaign (1980). He originated the idea of a Civil Rights Memorial that was dedicated in Montgomery, Ala. (1989) and concentrated on suing white supremacist groups (1990s). His autobiography, *A Season for Justice* (1991), was made into a television special (1992).

Deetz, James (John Fanto) (1930–   ) anthropologist, archaeologist, museum administrator; born in Cumberland, Md. He was educated at Harvard through the Ph.D. His early work focused on North American Indians, and in his studies of residence patterns and ceramic decoration as a reflection of social organization, he was one of the first American contributors to the scientific methodology that created the so-called "new archaeology"; his most notable publication in this area was *The Dynamics of Stylistic Change in Arikara Ceramics* (1965). While teaching at Brown University (1967–78), he served as the assistant director of Plimouth Plantation in Massachusetts (1967–78) and participated in the excavations and historical research that led to the restored site's becoming a major tourist attraction. By this time he had become one of the American leaders of historical archaeology and he went on to teach at the University of California: Berkeley (1978–93) before moving to the University of Virginia (1993). He became an authority on the colonial American gravestones as well as on the artifacts and customs of colonial Americans and he wrote widely on early colonial life in such works as *In Small Things Forgotten* (1977) and *Flowerdew Hundred: The Archaeology of a Virginia Plantation, 1619–1864* (1993).

De Forest, John William (1826–1906) writer; born in Seymour, Conn. After several years abroad, he wrote *Oriental Acquaintance* (1856) and *European Acquaintance* (1858). After serving in the Civil War and staying on in the army until 1868, he settled in New Haven, Conn., and became a prolific writer of short stories and novels, many of which drew on his military experiences. He pioneered realistic fiction with such works as *Miss Ravenel's Conversion from Secession to Loyalty* (1867) and *Kate Beaumont* (1872).

De Forest, Lee (1873–1961) electrical engineer, inventor; born in Council Bluffs, Iowa. He earned his Ph.D. from Yale in theoretical mathematical physics and electricity (1899). While working for Western Electric Company, he made the first of his inventions. He started a radio broadcasting company (1902) and made the first broadcast of live opera, Enrico Caruso singing at the Metropolitan Opera (1910). Although he invented a number of things crucial to radio, including a microphone and a three-element vacuum tube, or triode, his corporate enterprises failed and he worked briefly with the Federal Telegraph Company (1912). In 1913 he sold his triode invention to the American Telephone and Telegraph Company; the triode made transcontinental telegraphy possible and revolutionized military communications during World War I and would eventually become the basis of modern electronics. He used his profits from the triode to establish a firm in New York City, which he then sold in 1923. He went on to work in telephony and sound motion pictures, but, due partly to his prickly personality, he continued to experience financial and legal complications in each field. Although he eventually held more than 300 patents and was called the "Father of Radio," he died with an estate of only $1,200.

DeGaetani, Jan (b. Janice Reutz) (1933–89) soprano; born in Massillon, Ohio. After studies at Juilliard in New York City, she gravitated to modern music and found fame performing challenging works such as Crumb's *Ancient Voices of Children*, one of many works written expressly for her by major composers. Sometimes called "Queen of the Avant-Garde," she actually had a vast repertoire and was an outstanding interpreter of many types of music from the Renaissance on. Known for the intelligence she brought to music as well as for her rich voice, she also taught at the Eastman School of Music and at the Aspen (Colo.) summer festivals.

Degler, Carl N. (Neumann) (1921–   ) historian; born in Orange, N.J. He received his Ph.D. from Columbia University (1952) and taught at Stanford University (1968). Combining sociological, economic, and cultural analysis with historiography, he received the 1972 Pulitzer Prize for *Neither Black nor White: Slavery and Race Relations in Brazil and the United States* (1971). His works on women include *Women and Economics* (1966) and *Women and the Family in America from the Revolution to the Present* (1980).

DeGolyer, Everette Lee (1886–1965) petroleum geophysicist, oil company executive; born in Greensburg, Kans. His use of the reflection seismograph in petroleum field explorations and his investigations into the relationship of salt dome formations to oil deposits revolutionized the burgeoning science of applied geophysical petroleum engineering. He served in field and executive capacities for oil companies in Mexico and the U.S.A. before founding his own consulting practice in Dallas, Texas (1936). He was chief technical adviser to President Franklin D. Roosevelt at the Teheran Conference (1943).

DeGraff, Robert Fair (1895–1981) publisher; born in Plainfield, N.J. In 1939, with backing from Simon & Schuster, he issued the first Pocket Books, cheap paperback reprints of popular works, revolutionizing the book publishing industry.

Dehmelt, Hans G. (Georg) (1922–   ) physicist; born in Goerlitz, Germany. He came to the U.S.A. to perform research at Duke University (1952–55), then moved to the University of Washington (1955). A pioneer in the field of particle physics, he shared the 1989 Nobel Prize (with Wolfgang Pauli) for his work on trapping and separating ions and subatomic particles.

Dekanawida (?1550–?1600) Huron prophet; born near present-day Kingston, Ontario, Canada. With Hiawatha, he is credited with founding the Great League of the Iroquois, joining in a confederacy the Mohawks, Oneidas, Cayugas, Onondagas, and Senecas. Considered the theoretician of the two leaders, he was also one of the first of the Pine Tree Chiefs, chosen by merit rather than by heredity.

de Kooning, Willem (1904–) painter; born in Rotterdam, Holland. He came to America in 1926, and is considered, along with Jackson Pollock, a leader in abstract expressionism, the New York-based school of painting that rejected naturalistic content. Examples of this period include his dramatic *Black Paintings* (1946–48), which were limited to black-and-white colors using enamel and oil paints. His later work became increasingly figurative, and *The Woman* series, beginning in 1950, brought him notoriety due to his brutal and often erotic treatment of his subject matter.

Delahanty, (Edward James) Ed (1867–1903) baseball player; born in Cleveland, Ohio. One of five brothers who played major league baseball, he was one of baseball's first genuine sluggers during its dead ball era. He was an outfielder for 16 years (1888–1903), mostly with Philadelphia. He died when, possibly drunk, he fell off a bridge and was swept over Niagara Falls. He was elected to the Hall of Fame in 1945.

DeLancey, James (1703–60) Colonial official, judge; born in New York City. He was the chief justice of the New York Supreme Court (1733–60) and the lieutenant-governor of New York (1753–60). He became unpopular when he tried to influence the outcome of the trial of John Peter Zenger (1735). His political followers – who were identified as aristocratic and Episcopalian – became known as members of the "DeLancey party."

Delano, William Adams (1874–1960) architect; born in New York City. His New York partnership with Chester Holmes Aldrich (1903–41) was noted for designing private estates for wealthy clients. Delano received the American Institute of Architects Gold Medal (1953).

Delany, Martin Robison (1812–85) journalist, African-American activist; born in Charles Town, Va. (now W.Va.) Born of a freed black woman and a slave father, he apprenticed himself to a doctor in Pittsburgh (1831); years later (1850) he was admitted to Harvard Medical School but had to leave because of classmates' protests. He founded a black weekly magazine, *Mystery* (1843–47), and helped Frederick Douglass publish his abolitionist organ, the *North Star* (1847–49). In an 1852 tract, Delany advocated emigration of blacks, and he traveled to Africa (1859) seeking lands for resettlement. During the Civil War, after recruiting African-Americans to serve in Union regiments, he was commissioned as a major to carry out a scheme for recruiting a black guerrilla army to arm slaves, but the war ended before he could do anything. He criticized the Reconstruction while working as a customs house inspector in Charleston, S.C.; he was nominated for lieutenant governor of South Carolina on the Independent Republican ticket (1874) but lost. He moved to Xenia, Ohio, when the Reconstruction ended. Although never as well known as certain African-American leaders, he has been recognized as a precursor of more militant Black Nationalist movements.

de la Renta, Oscar (1932–) fashion designer; born in Santo Domingo, Dominican Republic. Trained by European couturiers, he settled in New York City where by 1965 he became a partner in Jane Derby, Inc. (later, Oscar de la Renta Couture). He designed luxury women's ready-to-wear, most notably sophisticated, European-styled daywear and lavish, romantic evening gowns. Like several other modern fashion designers, he came to move in the fashionable circles of the very people he clothed.

Delbrück, Max (1906–81) geneticist, virologist; born in Berlin, Germany. Trained as a physicist, he performed research in Europe, where he devised mathematical proofs for the chemical bonding of lithium and published two scientific papers on quantum mechanics. He began his fundamental investigations on bacteria and their viruses (bacteriophages) after coming to the U.S.A. to join the California Institute of Technology (Caltech) (1937–39). He continued his bacteriophage research through his years at Vanderbilt University (1940–47), where he showed that viruses can recombine genetic material (1946). Delbrück returned to Caltech (1947–76), where he later turned his interest to sensory physiology. With fellow bacteriophage researchers Salvador Luria and Alfred Hershey, he won the 1969 Nobel Prize in physiology for his contributions to viral genetics.

DeLee, Joseph (Bolivar) (1869–1942) obstetrician, gynecologist; born in Cold Spring, N.Y. After taking his medical degree from the Chicago Medical College, he went to Europe to advance his knowledge of obstetrical practices. He opened the Chicago Lying-in Dispensary in 1895 to offer the latest in maternity care. He taught at Northwestern University Medical School (1896–1929); when his maternity clinic became affiliated with the University of Chicago Medical School, he joined the latter's faculty (1929–34). A pioneer in modern obstetrical methods and deviser of many new obstetrical instruments, he devoted all his talents to preventing death in childbirth.

De Leon, Daniel (1852–1914) socialist advocate; born on the island of Curaçao. He studied in Europe before he emigrated to New York City (1874), becoming a lawyer (1878) and lecturer on Latin-American diplomacy at Columbia University (1883–86). Joining the Socialist Labor Party (1890), he was named its national lecturer (1891) and editor of its organ, *The People* (1892), and was an unsuccessful candidate for governor and Congress. A lifelong leader of the party, antagonistic to existing trade unions, his intransigency eventually led to formation of a splinter group, the Socialist Party of America. In 1905 he also assisted in the formation of the Industrial Workers of the World (IWW), which soon splintered; he was ousted from the IWW and formed his own Workers' International Industrial Union. To opponents he was a disruptive fanatic; to supporters a man of incorruptible integrity. Lenin praised his writings as incorporating the germ of the Soviet system.

Delille, Henriette (1813–62) Catholic religious foundress; born in New Orleans. She cofounded (1842) and directed the Sisters of the Holy Family, African-American Catholic nuns devoted to charitable work among the poor.

DeLillo, Don (1936– ;) writer; born in New York City. He was briefly a New York advertising copywriter before becoming a professional fiction writer. Starting with his first novel, *Americana* (1971), his social satires are known for their precise language and pervasive sense of anomie and have earned him a reputation as a writer's writer. His books included *Ratner's Star* (1976), *White Noise* (1985, American Book Award), and *Libra* (1988).

Dell, Floyd (James) (1887–1969) author, editor, social critic; born in Barry, Ill. Growing up in poverty, he joined the Socialist Party at age 16, and worked as a reporter and editor at several publications in Iowa and Chicago (1905–13). His Chicago studio was a gathering place for many of the literary figures who contributed to the "Chicago Renaissance." Moving in 1913 to New York City's Greenwich Village, he edited *Masses* (1914–17), wrote plays for various left-wing clubs and earned a reputation as a bohemian after an affair with Edna St. Vincent Millay. When the government suspended *Masses* because of its opposition to America's role in World War I, he was indicted under the Espionage Act (1918) but never convicted. He became an editor of the *Liberator* (1918–24) and then *New Masses* (1924–29). He also wrote a succession of novels about those who sacrifice idealistic dreams for conventional realities. From 1935 to 1947 he worked in Washington, D.C., for various government agencies, and then vanished from public view.

Dellinger, David (1915–) pacifist, peace activist, editor, author; born in Wakefield, Mass. A descendant of old New England families, he graduated from Yale University (1936) and studied at Oxford University, Yale Divinity School, and Union Theological Seminary (1939–40). His passionate pacifism would lead him to the forefront of militant, nonviolent activism. Jailed in 1940 and again in 1943 for draft resistance, upon his release in 1945 he formed the Libertarian Press printing cooperative. In 1956 he became editor and publisher of *Liberation*, a major voice of radical pacifism. As an opponent to American involvement in Vietnam, he was a major link to the North Vietnamese government and facilitated the release of American prisoners of war. He was arrested as a leader of the antiwar demonstration that erupted in riot at the Democratic National Convention in Chicago (1968) and was sentenced to seven years (conviction overturned). Emphasizing the need for radical change as well as nonviolence, he became editor of *Seven Days* magazine (1975–80). In the 1980s he moved to Vermont to teach and write. His books include *Revolutionary Nonviolence* (1970), *More Power Than We Know* (1975), and *From Yale to Jail* (1993).

Dello Joio, Norman (1913–) composer; born in New York City. A prolific composer in a lyrical and mildly modernist idiom, he had his major successes in the 1940s and 1950s.

Dellums, Ronald (Vernie) (1935–) U.S. representative; born in Oakland, Calif. An ex-marine and social worker, in Congress (Dem., Cal.; 1972) he championed civil liberties and opposed military aggression while serving on the Armed Services and Intelligence Committees. As an African-American, he was often a harsh critic of the white power establishment.

Delmonico, Lorenzo (1813–81) restaurateur; born in Marengo, Switzerland. He came to New York in 1832, opening the first of a number of successful restaurants that introduced European standards to New Yorkers. Delmonico's offered fresh foods, a large menu, and long hours, widely copied innovations that promoted a restaurant culture in American cities.

De Long, George Washington (1844–81) naval officer, explorer; born in New York City. He entered the navy in 1865 and became interested in Arctic exploration. He commanded the *Jeanette* in an attempt to reach the North Pole via the Bering Strait (1879–81). He died on the Siberian coast after his ship was crushed and sank.

De Lorean, John (Zachary) (1925–) automobile executive; born in Detroit, Mich. He was an engineer who in a meteoric career in the Pontiac and Chevrolet divisions of General Motors (1956–73) introduced the Tempest, Firebird, and Vega, obtained many patents for innovative engineering, and was influential in shifting U.S. manufacturers to smaller cars in the 1960s. A number of later ventures, including his De Lorean Motor Co. (founded 1974), failed. In 1982 he was arrested and subsequently convicted on drug trafficking charges, but he maintained he had been entrapped.

Deloria, Ella Cara (b. Anpetu Wastewin) (1889–1971) Yankton Sioux scholar, writer; born in Wakpala, S.D. She worked with Franz Boas (1929) at her alma mater, Columbia University, on a study of Siouan language. Her most important books are *Dakota Texts* (1932), *Speaking of Indians* (1944), and the novel *Waterlily* (1988).

Deloria, Vine, Jr. (1933–) Standing Rock Sioux educator, writer, lawyer, activist; born at Pine Ridge, S.D. Born into a prominent family descended from a Yankton chief and a French fur trader, he graduated from Iowa State – after two years in the U.S. Marine Corps – and took a master's degree in theology with the intention of becoming a Lutheran minister. He went on instead to become executive director of the National Congress of American Indians (1964–67), a position that greatly affected his views on the situation of his fellow Native Americans. Deciding to take a more activist role, he took a law degree (1970) and meanwhile gained national recognition with his book, *Custer Died for Your Sins* (1969), which was sharply critical of white Americans' traditional treatment of Native Americans. From then on – through his subsequent books and in his teaching at the University of Arizona – he remained in the forefront of those demanding that U.S. governments live up to treaty responsibilities while Native Americans be allowed to develop along their own lines.

del Rey, (Ramon Felipe San Juan Mario Silvio Enrico) Lester (1915–93) writer, editor; born in Clydesdale, Minn. He studied at George Washington University (1931–33) and during World War II was a sheet-metal worker for McDonnell Aircraft Corp. (1942–44). He moved to New York City and became a well-known fantasy and science fiction writer; he was so prolific that he used many pen names – among others, John Alvarez, Cameron Hall, Marion Henry, Philip James – and sometimes collaborated with other writers under such names as Edson McCann and Charles Satterfield. He taught fantasy fiction at New York University (1972–73) and as editor of the del Rey imprint at Ballantine Books he was credited with promoting a revival of serious fantasy and science fiction. A sampling of his own work is in *The Best of Lester del Rey* (1978).

Delson, Eric (1945–) physical anthropologist; born in New York City. A professor at Lehman College (1973), he made major contributions to the comparative evolution of fossil African, Asian, and European monkeys. He is a specialist in primate classification and systematics.

Del Tredici, David (Walter) (1937–) composer; born in Cloverdale, Calif. After studies at Princeton he taught at

Harvard and Boston University. He is best known for his series of neo-Romantic orchestral works based on *Alice in Wonderland*.

De Lue, Donald (Harcourt) (1897–1988) sculptor; born in Boston, Mass. He studied in Boston and Paris, established a studio in New York City (1938), and lived in Leonardo, N.J. He is known for his heroic and large sculptures, as in his bronze, *The Rocket Thrower* (1964–65).

DeMar, Clarence (Harrison) (1888–1958) marathon runner; born in Madeira, Ohio. Nicknamed, "Mr. Marathon," he won the Boston marathon seven times (1921–24, 1927–28, 1930), placed second three times, and third twice. He won the bronze medal in the 1924 Olympic marathon. He continued to run the Boston marathon until the end of his life and since this was still a time when the race was regarded as fit for only a relatively small elite group of men, he was regarded as a physical phenomenon.

De Menil, Dominique (b. Schlumberger) (1908–) art collector, philanthropist; born in Paris, France. She studied at the University of Paris (B.A. 1927), then studied mathematics and physics. An heir to the Schlumberger fortune, she emigrated to America (1941) and began collecting art (1945), particularly contemporary African art, surrealist work, and antiquities. She and her husband, a wealthy Frenchman, established the De Menil Foundation in Houston (1954), and beginning in 1968, she served as director of the Institute of Arts, Rice University, Houston.

de Mille, Agnes (George) (1905–93) choreographer; born in New York City. The daughter of the playwright William C. de Mille and niece of movie producer Cecil B. De Mille, she made her dancing debut in 1928. During the 1930s she worked in America and Europe as a dancer and actress. In 1936 she had her first commission as a choreographer, creating the dance sequences for an English film version of *Romeo and Juliet*. This led to her joining the New York Ballet Theater, for which she choreographed *Rodeo* (1942). In the 1940s she choreographed a series of hits both on Broadway and in the subsequent films, including *Oklahoma!* (1943), *Carousel* (1945), *Brigadoon* (1947), and *Gentlemen Prefer Blondes* (1949). She founded her own ballet company, toured widely, and was regarded as one of the preeminent 20th-century American choreographers. Her books include *Dance to the Piper* (1952) and *The Book of the Dance* (1963).

De Mille, Cecil B. (Blount) (1881–1959) film director; born in Ashfield, Mass. He made his Broadway acting debut in 1900. As a director, he made the first Hollywood picture, *The Squaw Man* (1914) becoming the creative force behind Paramount and a major contributor to Hollywood's rise to eminence. He became the master of the film spectacle, with moral themes enlivened by violence and sex. Two of his greatest triumphs were *The Ten Commandments* (1923 and remade in 1956) and *The Greatest Show on Earth* (1952). In addition to producing and directing at least 70 films (and being involved in many others), he directed and hosted "Lux Radio Theatre" (1936–45), which featured adaptations of movies and plays.

Deming, W. (William) Edwards (1900–93) statistician, management consultant; born in Sioux City, Iowa. He studied electrical engineering at the University of Wyoming, worked briefly at Western Electric's Hawthorn plant (outside Chicago), took a Ph.D. at Yale in mathematical physics (1927), and then went to work for the U.S. Department of

Agriculture. Over the ensuing years he developed statistical sampling techniques that were first used in the 1940 U.S. census. He served as a consultant to the U.S. War department during World War II and at the end of World War II, he had begun to develop broader concepts of efficient management; in 1947 the American occupation authorities brought him to Japan to lecture the Japanese on this subject. He made such an impression that in 1950 the Japanese business community invited him back and from then on he became a constant visitor to Japan, preaching the gospel of quality control through the statistical control of manufacturing processes. He is considered to have contributed significantly to that country's industrial resurgence since World War II; since 1951 the Deming Award has been Japan's highest honor for the business community, and in 1960 he was awarded Japan's Second Order Medal of the Sacred Treasure. Although he taught occasionally at New York University and Columbia business schools, major American companies were slow to recognize the value of his techniques, but starting in the 1980s he found himself giving countless seminars to many American businesses. Although he has been called the "messiah of management" and "curmudgeon of quality," his business card read simply, "Consultant in Statistical Studies." His several books include *Quality, Productivity and Competitive Position* (1982).

de Montebello, Philippe Lannes (1936–) museum director; born in Paris, France. Descendent of a distinguished French family, he was brought to New York City by his parents in 1950. He studied at Harvard (B.A. 1958) and at New York University (B.A. 1963; M.A. 1976). He worked as assistant curator of the Metropolitan Museum of Art (1963–69); from 1969 to 1974 he was director of the Museum of Fine Arts, Houston; he returned to the Metropolitan as its vice-director of curatorial and educational affairs (1974–78). He became acting director of the museum (1977–78), and then its director (1978).

Demorest, Ellen Louise Curtis (1824–98) fashion arbiter; born in Schuylerville, N.Y. A successful milliner, she invented mass-produced tissue-paper dressmaking patterns and with her husband, publisher and reformer William Jennings Demorest, established a company to sell and a magazine to promote them (1860). The Demorests adapted the latest French fashions for ordinary women, greatly influencing American fashion.

Dempsey, (William Harrison) Jack (1895–1983) boxer; born in Manassa, Colo. He worked in the copper mines and boxed in the mining camps of Colorado before becoming a professional boxer in 1912. He fought in more than 100 semi-pro and professional bouts before winning the heavyweight championship in 1919 by knocking out Jess Willard. He successfully defended his title five times before losing to Gene Tunney in an upset in 1926. In the rematch in 1927, Dempsey knocked Tunney down in the seventh round but delayed going to a neutral corner, so the referee gave the controversial "long count" (estimated from 14 to 21 seconds) and Tunney went on to win on points. Although one of the most popular and well-paid boxers ever, Dempsey effectively retired from professional boxing and moved on to devote himself to sports promotion and various businesses, the best known of which was the restaurant he opened on Broadway, New York City. Nicknamed "The Manassa Mauler," he retired with a professional record of 62 wins (49 knockouts), six losses, ten draws.

Dempster, A. J. (Arthur Jeffrey) (1886–1950) physicist; born in Toronto, Ontario, Canada. He came to the U.S.A. to study at the University of Chicago (1914). He spent his teaching and research career there (1917–50), except for the years that he worked on the Manhattan Project (1941–45). He made major contributions to the field of mass spectroscopy and was the discoverer of uranium-235 (1935).

Demuth, Charles (1883–1935) painter; born in Lancaster, Pa. He worked in water colors and studied at the Pennsylvania Academy of the Fine Arts under Thomas Anshutz (1905–08), at the Académie Julian, Paris (1912–14), and lived in New York City. From 1910–14 he painted illustrations for several writers, including Emile Zola and Henry James. Lame and diabetic, he illustrated the joys of physical life, as in *Circus Riders* (1916), and *Acrobats* (1919). His later work was a combination of cubism and realism, as in the grain elevators of *My Egypt* (1927).

Denby, Edwin (1870–1929) lawyer; born in Evansville, Ind. His tenure as secretary of the navy (1921–24) was tainted by his alleged involvement in the Teapot Dome scandal. Although not impeached, he resigned his office after encountering widespread criticism.

Denby, Edwin (1903–83) dance critic, poet; born in China. Son of the American consul in Shanghai, he was educated at Harvard and the University of Vienna where he studied dance. Although he regarded himself as a poet, he earned his living as a dance critic, writing for *Modern Music* (1936–42) and the *New York Herald Tribune* (1942–45). Thereafter he was a freelance writer for such magazines as *Dance Magazine* and *Nation,* and was known for his striking metaphors and exacting reviews. An early supporter of Balanchine's choreography, he wrote *Looking at the Dance* (1949) and *Dancers, Buildings and People in the Street* (1965). He also published four volumes of poetry including *Collected Poems* (1975). In failing health, he committed suicide when he was 80.

Denfeld, Louis (1891–1972) naval officer; born in Westboro, Mass. He served as a lieutenant in World War I. During World War II he was the assistant chief of the Bureau of Navigation, was promoted to rear admiral, and commanded Battleship Division 9 in the Pacific. Chief of naval operations (1947–49), he was removed because of his vigorous defense of naval independence during the process of unifying the armed forces.

De Niro, Robert (1943–) film actor; born in New York. After studying acting with Stella Adler and Lee Strasberg, he worked off-Broadway before entering films and gaining acclaim in *Bang the Drum Slowly* (1973). A versatile actor who strived for intense authenticity, he won an Academy Award for *The Godfather Part II* (1974). Graduating to leading man status, he received another Oscar for *Raging Bull* (1980).

Dennett, Daniel (Clement) (1942–) philosopher; born in Boston, Mass. After earning an Oxford degree (1965) and teaching at the University of California (1965–71), he became a professor at Tufts, specializing in philosophy of mind and of the social sciences. He won prominence for such studies as *Consciousness Explained* (1991).

Dennie, Joseph (1768–1812) journalist; born in Boston, Mass. Known initially for his "Lay Preacher" essays on manners and morals, he edited the *Farmer's Weekly Museum*

(1796–99) and, under the traditionalist name Oliver Oldschool, *The Port Folio* (1801–12), a successful pro-Federalist literary and political journal. In 1805 he was acquitted on sedition charges for allegedly anti-democratic writings.

Dennis, Eugene (b. Francis X. Waldron) (1905–61) Communist Party leader; born in Seattle, Wash. Joining the Communist Party in 1926, he was arrested for organizing lettuce workers in California's Imperial Valley in 1927–28. He attended a Communist Party school while in Moscow (1931–35) and on return to the U.S.A. he held a series of posts in the Communist Party, becoming its general secretary (1945–51, 1955–59). He was imprisoned (1951–55) for violation of the Smith Act. He was chairmam of the Communist Party of America when he died.

Dennis Wolf Bushyhead (b. Unaduti) (1826–98) Cherokee chief; born near Cleveland, Tenn. He headed the Cherokee National Commission in 1848, was elected tribal treasurer in 1871 and principal chief from 1879–1887. An advocate of accommodation, he defended the Dawes Act (1887), which called for the elimination of Indian tribal land holdings.

Densmore, Frances (Theresa) (1867–1957) ethnomusicologist; born in Red Wing, Minn. Trained as a pianist, after 1893 she pioneered ethnomusicology by recording, transcribing, and analyzing American Indian music. In 40 years of fieldwork for the Bureau of American Ethnology, she recorded the music of more than 30 tribes. Her important published studies include *Teton Sioux Music* (1918).

Denton, Jeremiah A. (Andrew), Jr. (1924–) navy pilot, prisoner of war, U.S. senator; born in Mobile, Ala. After moving frequently during his first 14 years, he settled into a normal high school life, then went to Annapolis. He became a highly skilled navy pilot but as a commander flying off the aircraft carrier USS *Independence* was shot down on a mission over North Vietnam in July 1965. During almost 8 years of captivity – including four in solitary confinement – he demonstrated incredible bravery in the face of torture; he gained fame when he blinked that very word in Morse code when his captors forced him to appear in a public interview. After his release in 1973 and his return to active duty, he became concerned about what he regarded as mounting immorality and disunity in the U.S.A. and in 1977 he founded the Coalition for Decency to promote traditional values of the family and citizenship. Running as a Republican in 1980, he won one of Alabama's seats in the Senate (1981) where he continued to work for a conservative agenda.

DeNunzio, Ralph Dwight (1931–) investment banker; born in White Plains, N.Y. A 1953 Princeton graduate, he joined the investment house, Kidder, Peabody & Co., after college, rising to chief executive officer (1980–87). He chaired the board of governors of the New York Stock Exchange in 1971–72 and served as a Princeton trustee and as a director of several major firms, including the Federal Express Corp. and Nike Inc.

de Paola, (Thomas Anthony) Tomi (1934–) writer, illustrator; born in Meriden, Conn. He graduated from Pratt Institute, New York (1956), the California College of Arts and Crafts (M.A., 1969), and settled in New London, N.H. He started as a freelance designer, illustrator, and writer in 1956, and is known for his books for young readers, such as

Helga's Dowry (1977) and *Pancakes for Breakfast* (1978), which he illustrated as well as wrote.

Depew, Chauncey Mitchell (1834–1928) lawyer, businessman, public official; born in Peekskill, N.Y. He worked as a lawyer after graduating from Yale (1856) and participated in Republican Party affairs. He was the first American ambassador to Japan (1866). Rising through the Vanderbilt industrial-financial empire, he became president of the New York Central Railroad in 1885. Depew served in the U.S. Senate from 1899–1911 (Rep., N.Y.). He was a famous orator and after-dinner wit. "I get my exercise acting as pallbearer to my friends who exercise," he once quipped, explaining his good health and long life.

DePree, Max O. (Owen) (1924–   ) furniture manufacturing company executive; born in Zeeland, Mich. Dropping out of college to join the Army Medical Corps in 1943, he went to work afterward (1947) at his father's Michigan company, Herman Miller (named after his mother's father), which produced furniture by renowned designers like Charles Eames. Taking over as chief executive officer (1980–87), then chairman, he increased sales dramatically through his distinctively worker-friendly management style. His book, *Leadership is An Art* (1989), has been reprinted in ten languages.

DePreist, James (Anderson) (1936–   ) symphony conductor; born in Philadelphia (nephew of Marian Anderson). After taking a degree at the University of Pennsylvania (1958) and completing his musical studies at the Philadelphia Conservatory of Music (1961), he served with the U.S. State Department as a specialist in American music and as a conductor in Bangkok, Thailand (1963–64). He won first prize in the Mitropoulos competition in 1964 and that year made his American debut as a conductor with the New York Philharmonic. He went on to conduct many major symphony orchestras, making his European debut with the Rotterdam Philharmonic in 1969, and enjoying special associations with the National Symphony in Washington, D.C., and L'Orchestre Symphonique de Québec. His latest position was with the Oregon Symphony (1980).

De Priest, Oscar Stanton (1871–1951) U.S. representative; born in Florence, Ala. Son of freed slaves, he moved north as a boy after a neighbor was lynched. Working as a painter in Chicago at age 17, he had his own decorating firm by 1905. A Republican realtor, he became the first African-American member of the city council (1915–17), resigning because of alleged mob connections. A shrewd politician, he fought against Jim Crow laws in the U.S. House of Representatives (1929–35), returning to Chicago politics and real estate afterward.

Derby, Elias Hasket (1739–99) merchant, shipowner; born in Salem, Mass. He inherited his father's merchant business and used his vessels as privateers during the American Revolution. He became very wealthy and expanded his business to the farthest ends of the globe after the Revolution; his skippers were among the first Americans to reach the Baltic, India, the East Indies, and China. Although he never went to sea himself, he chose his captains wisely and he only lost one vessel during his career. He remains known to this day for the fine homes and furniture he and his family commissioned from the leading architects and cabinetmakers of their day.

Deringer, Henry, Jr. (1786–1868) gunsmith; born in Easton, Pa. The son of a German gunmaker, he served as apprenticeship in Richmond, Va., and then opened his own shop in Philadelphia (1806). He made rifles for the U.S. Office of Indian Trade (1830s). He turned to making pistols, and his pocket pistol, the "Deringer Phila," found a ready market during the 1850s and 1860s, especially on the frontier. He died a wealthy man, with real estate and coal land holdings. The "Derringer" (the extra "r" was inserted by mistake) became infamous for its use by John Wilkes Booth in the assassination of President Lincoln.

de Rivera, José (b. José A. Ruiz) (1904–85) sculptor; born in West Baton Rouge, La. His family moved to New Orleans (1910). He adopted his maternal grandmother's name and worked in foundries. He moved to Chicago (1924), where he attended The Studio School (1928–31), and settled in New York City (1930). He is known for his lyrical abstract metal sculptures, as in *Construction #190* (1980).

Dershowitz, Alan M. (Morton) (1938–   ) lawyer, professor, author; born in New York City. Admitted to the bar in 1963 after a brilliant career at Yale Law School, he served as a clerk to U.S. Supreme Court justice Arthur Goldberg and is credited with composing the legal memo that underlay the court's opinion that the death penalty, as then applied, constituted "cruel and unusual punishment." Becoming Harvard Law School's youngest ever tenured law professor at age 28, he would remain there throughout his career, often spicing up his standard curriculum with courses on legal issues of the Vietnam War or psychiatry and the law. Meanwhile, he soon began to take on cases having to do primarily with First Amendment, or free speech issues, defending those such as Dr. Benjamin Spock in his antiwar actions, the radical lawyer William Kunstler, the porno star Harry Reems of *Deep Throat*, and the racist genetic theorist William Schockley. As these cases inevitably brought considerable publicity, he became known as one of the nation's leading defense and appeal lawyers, but he always insisted that he accepted cases primarily because they involved issues of civil liberties or constitutional rights; he also replied to charges that he sought out high profile cases by pointing out his donation of time and talents to many unreported cases, including those involving prisoners on death row. His most celebrated case was the successful appeal and subsequent acquittal of Claus von Bulow; Dershowitz told the story of this case in his *Reversal of Fortune* (1986), which was subsequently made into a movie (in which he played a bit part). An outspoken critic of what he saw as flaws in the legal system, and nearly an absolutist on behalf of every imaginable form of free speech, he wrote in defense of his aggressive tactics in *The Best Defense* (1982). In addition to various professional texts and other books, he wrote a widely syndicated newspaper column on the law and he has been a frequent guest on television programs involving legal matters.

De Seversky, Alexander (Prokofieff) (1894–1974) airplane manufacturer; born in Tiflis, Russia A Russian war hero in World War I, he flew more than 50 combat missions after he had lost a leg. An assistant naval attaché at the Russian embassy in Washington, he decided to stay in the U.S.A. following the Russian Revolution. He founded Seversky Aero Corporation (1922), which became Republic Aviation (1939), and designed bombsights and landing gear for seaplanes and flying boats. He became a naturalized U.S. citizen (1927) and wrote *Victory Through Air Power* (1942), controversial at the time for arguing that the Allies could win World War II primarily through air superiority.

Deskey, Donald (1894–1989) industrial designer; born in Blue Earth, Minn. After study at the Art Institute of Chicago, California School of Arts, and in Paris, he founded the design firm of Donald Deskey Associates, New York (1926–75). His work encompassed almost all areas, including advertising, exhibits, graphics, furniture, interiors, appliances, and new products. His most famous commission was the interior of Radio City Music Hall (1931). He also founded and taught at New York University's School of Industrial Design.

De Smet, Pierre Jean (1801–70) Jesuit missionary; born in Termonde, Belgium. He came to the U.S.A. in 1821 and in 1838 began his career as a missionary to the Indians of the Plains and the Northwest. He founded mission stations, helped to negotiate peace after the Mormon War (1857–58) and effected a truce with Sitting Bull (1868). The Indians trusted him and called him "Blackrobe."

Dethier, Vincent G. (Gaston) (1915–93) entomologist; born in Boston, Mass. He was an entomologist at the G. W. Pierce Laboratory in Franklin, N.H. (1937–38), then an assistant at the Cruft Physics Laboratory, Harvard University (1939). While researching the plant-feeding choices of swallowtail butterfly caterpillars (1930s), he became the first to prove that caterpillars select their food by the plant's taste and smell, not its nutritional value. He taught biology at John Carroll University (Cleveland, Ohio) (1939–41), served the Army Chemical Corps as a research physiologist (1946), then became a professor at Ohio State University (1946–47) before moving to Johns Hopkins (1947–58), where he investigated chemoreception in black blowflies. He became a professor of zoology and psychology at the University of Pennsylvania (1958–67) and concurrently was an associate at the Institute of Neural Science School of Medicine (1958–67). After serving as a professor at Princeton (1967–75), he joined the faculty of the University of Massachusetts (1975). In addition to his major contributions to insect physiology and the life history of *Lepidoptera,* he published (and occasionally illustrated) popular books and short stories for adult and juvenile readers.

de Tolnay, Charles Erich (b. [Vagujhelyi] Karoly Tolnai) (1899–) art historian, painter; born in Budapest, Hungary. He studied at the Universities of Berlin (1920–21), Frankfurt (1922), and Vienna (Ph.D. 1925), and continued postdoctoral studies at the University of Rome. He emigrated to America (1939), and became a citizen (1945). He worked as a lecturer in art and archaeology for many institutions in Europe and America, such as the Sorbonne, (1934–39), the Institute for Advanced Study, Princeton (1939–48), in Germany, and in Italy, where he eventually settled. As a scholar he is most noted for his *History and Technique of Old Master Drawings* (1943) and for his six-volume study of Michelangelo (1943–67).

Dett, R. (Robert) Nathaniel (1882–1943) composer, pianist, conductor; born in Niagara Falls, Ontario, Canada. He was the first African-American student to graduate from Oberlin Conservatory (1908); later he would study music at Columbia University, Harvard, Eastman School of Music, and with Nadia Boulanger in France. He was director of music at Hampton Institute from 1913 to 1931 where he conducted a nationally acclaimed choir, and was an active composer, a

concert pianist, and an editor of collections of spirituals. As a composer, his piano works were in the 19th-century romantic style, but in his choral works, such as "Listen to the Lamb" (1914) and *The Ordering of Moses* (1937), he drew on black spirituals.

Deutsch, Babette (1895–1982) poet, writer; born in New York City. She studied at Barnard College (B.A. 1917), and lived in New York City. She lectured at the New School for Social Research (1933–35), Columbia University (1944–71), and at many other institutions. She is known as a translator of Russian poetry, often in collaboration with her husband, Avrahm Yarmolinsky, as an editor and critic, and as a writer of adult and juvenile fiction. Most importantly, however, she is praised as an intelligent and perceptive poet, as in *The Collected Poems of Babette Deutsch* (1969).

Devens, Charles, Jr. (1820–91) soldier, jurist; born in Charlestown, Mass. An 1838 Harvard graduate, he practiced law and took a keen interest in the militia. Commanding Union volunteers, he fought on the Peninsula and at Fredericksburg and Chancellorsville and led the advance on Richmond in April 1865. After the war, he served on the Massachusetts Superior Court (1867–73) and Supreme Court (1873–77; 1881–91) with time out to serve as Rutherford B. Hayes's attorney general (1877–81).

Devers, Jacob (Loucks) (1887–1979) soldier; born in York, Pa. In charge of U.S. armored forces during a developmental period from 1941–43, he led combat troops in North Africa (1944) and served as commander of the 6th Army Group in southern France (1944–45).

Devine, Edward Thomas (1867–1948) social worker, editor; born near Union, Hardin County, Iowa. After earning a doctorate in economics (1893), he was secretary of the American Society for Extension of University Teaching (1894–96). Named general secretary of the New York Charity Organization Society (1896–1917), he played a major role in the development of social work as a profession. Pragmatic, temperate and experimental in attitude, he helped establish the precursor to the Columbia University School of Social Work (1898) and was a force in improving the conditions in urban slums. On a national level, he assisted in disaster relief, served on the United States Coal Commission (1922–23), and was director of the New York Housing Association (1930) along with emergency relief agencies.

De Vinne, Theodore Low (1828–1914) painter; born in Stamford, Conn. In 1877 he became full owner of a print shop that produced high-quality materials, reproducing illustrations with particular success, and made important innovations in typography. He wrote the influential four-volume *Practice of Typography* (1900–04).

DeVos, Richard (Marvin) (1926–) marketing executive; born in Grand Rapids, Mich. As a 10-year veteran of direct selling, he cofounded with Jay Van Andel the Michigan-based Amway Corporation (1959). A manufacturer and direct sales distributor of household products, Amway became a billion-dollar international corporation while attracting controversy for its pyramid sales structure and cultist motivational techniques.

DeVoto, Bernard (Augustine) (1897–1955) author, critic, historian; born in Ogden, Utah. He taught marksmanship in the army during World War I, then graduated from Harvard in 1920. He taught school in Utah, held an instructorship at

Northwestern University, and published three novels before joining the Harvard faculty in 1929. His critical study, *Mark Twain's America,* appeared in 1932. In 1936 he left Harvard to become editor of *The Saturday Review of Literature* (until 1938). From 1943–52 he published three surveys of the exploration and settlement of the American West, and produced an edition of the journals of Lewis and Clark (1953).

DeVries, Peter (1910–93) editor, writer; born in Chicago. After an extremely varied early career he became editor of *Poetry* (1938–44), then joined the *New Yorker* editorial board (1944–87) as a protégé of James Thurber. He wrote some two dozen witty novels known for their relentless puns and sophisticated satire of suburban life. His best-known works include *Tunnel of Love* (1954), *Reuben, Reuben* (1964), and *Consenting Adults* (1980).

de Weldon, Felix (1907–) sculptor, painter; born in Austria. Son of a wealthy textile manufacturer, he studied sculpture and by age 17 was getting commissions; he went on to study in Paris, Rome, and Madrid, and in the 1930s settled in England, where he became known for his many portrait busts. By the early 1940s he had moved to Canada, and in World War II he enlisted in the U.S. Navy and was assigned as a combat artist. While stationed at Patuxent Naval Air Station (Md.), he saw the photograph (by Joe Rosenthal of the Associated Press) of the U.S. Marines raising the flag at Iwo Jima on February 23, 1945; he set to work at once to make a 3-foot-high model; his commanding officer recognized its impact and asked him to make a 9-foot model (of plaster and stone) for a war bond drive; this then led to a commission to make (during six years) the 78-foot-high, 100-ton statue, cast in bronze in Brooklyn and dedicated in 1954 as the Marine Corps War Memorial in Alexandria, Va. He served on the U.S. Fine Arts Commission under presidents Truman, Eisenhower, and Kennedy. Known for his many portrait busts of presidents, kings, and other notables, he also did some 2,000 public sculptures – 30 works are on view in and around Washington, D.C. – and reproductions of his works sell well; among his most popular is *Humanity* – a concave head of Christ with eyes that seem to follow you wherever you move.

Dewey, Bradley (1887–1974) chemical engineer; born in Burlington, Vt. He designed and produced gas masks during World War I. In 1919 he formed Dewey & Almy Chemical Company to manufacture sealing compounds, wraps, bags, soldering fluxes, and the like. Following World War II, he became involved in the U.S. guided missile program and atomic bomb test evaluation.

Dewey, George (1837–1917) naval officer; born in Montpelier, Vt. He served under David Farragut during the Civil War, then followed the standard career of a peacetime naval officer. In 1897 he was assigned command of the Asiatic Squadron, and in May 1898 he directed the action in Manila Bay that totally defeated the Spanish fleet (during which he is said to have commanded his flagship's captain, "You may fire when you are ready, Gridley.") Dewey stayed on for over a year to oversee the American takeover of the Philippines, then returned to a tremendous hero's welcome. He was honored with a special rank, admiral of the navy, and urged to run for U.S. president; but he settled for presidency of the General Board of the Navy Department, serving as an adviser on naval affairs to his death.

Dewey, John (1859–1952) philosopher, psychologist, educator; born in Burlington, Vt. After graduating from the University of Vermont, he taught high school before taking his Ph.D. at Johns Hopkins. He taught philosophy at the Universities of Minnesota and Michigan and gained some reputation for his book *Psychology* (1887) before going to the University of Chicago (1894–1904) where in 1896 he established a Laboratory School to put his educational theories into practice. His best known innovation was what he called learning by "directed living," with an emphasis on workshop-type projects so that learning was combined with concrete activity and practical relevance. Although not really the first to promote this kind of schooling, he would long be regarded by Americans as the father of progressive education. After a falling-out with the Chicago administration, he went to Columbia University as professor of philosophy (1904–30). He was by this time gaining a reputation as one of the leading exponents of pragmatism, the school of philosophy that stresses the practical application of ideas. At Columbia, he helped move its Teachers College into the forefront of American education by imbuing several generations of educators with his theories of progressive education and pragmatism. When it came to staking out positions on political and international affairs, he did not always make predictable choices, supporting progressive and socialist candidates, then opposing President Franklin Roosevelt's New Deal; he was always opposed to Marxism and communism, however, and he never abandoned his faith in the individual and democracy. As an author of numerous books (*The School and Society* (1899), *Experience and Nature* (1925), *Experience and Education* (1938), *Freedom and Culture* (1939)), as an advisor to various countries' educational systems, as an officer of various professional societies, and as an intellectual consulted and quoted on a wide range of issues, he played a role in public life that few philosophers in American history have known.

Dewey, Melvil (orig. Melville) (Louis Kossuth) (1851–1931) librarian, cataloguer; born in Adams Center, N.Y. He studied at Amherst College (A.B. 1874) and his experience as a student working in the college library led him to propose his decimal-based system of classifying books; he published this as *A Classification and Subject Index for Cataloguing and Arranging . . . a Library* (1876). He was a founding member of the American Library Association (1876), founding editor of the *Library Journal* (1876–80), and an activist in the spelling reform and metric system movements. He was appointed librarian of Columbia College (now Columbia University) (1885–88) in New York, where he founded the first professional school of library services (1887). When he moved to Albany, N.Y., to become director of the New York State Library (1888–1905), he took the library school there. In 1893 he and his second wife, Emily Beal, created the Lake Placid (N.Y.) Club, which pioneered recreational winter sports.

Dewey, Thomas E. (Edmund) (1902–71) governor, presidential candidate, lawyer; born in Owosso, Mich. His record of investigating and prosecuting vice and racketeering led to his election as district attorney in New York City (1937–41) and wide support as a possible Republican nominee for president in 1940. He served as governor of New York (1943–55) and was the unsuccessful Republican candidate for president in 1944 and 1948; in the latter contest he seemed like such a sure winner that the *Chicago Daily Tribune* went to press too early with the headline "DEWEY DEFEATS TRUMAN." He also earned another place in American legend when, because of his bland demeanor, Dorothy Parker said that he looked "like the man on the wedding cake." After leaving the governor's office, he returned to private law practice.

Dewhurst, Colleen (1926–91) stage/television actress; born in Montreal, Quebec, Canada. A powerful character actress, she made her Broadway debut in 1952 in *Desire Under the Elms*. She was the winner of two Tony and two Obie awards.

Dewing, Thomas (Wilmer) (1851–1938) painter; born in Boston, Mass. He studied in Paris (1879), settled in New York City, and painted ethereal scenes of isolated women, as in *The Recitation* (1891).

de Wolfe, Elsie (Lady Mendl) (1865–1950) interior decorator; born in New York City. She adapted the fashion sense of her acting years (1890–1904) to a career as America's first professional woman decorator. The 1898 transformation of her own house from gloomy, cluttered Victorianism to light, airy neoclassicism led to freelance work on New York's Colony Club, the Frick mansion, and houses of the wealthy. The restoration of her own Villa Trianon in France and her marriage to a British diplomat marked her 1920s and 1930s. World War II brought the Mendls to Los Angeles. A self-promoting eccentric, she claimed the introduction of blue-tinted hair, white upholstery, and leopard chintzes.

D'Harnoncourt, René (Count) (1901–68) museum director; born in Vienna, Austria. He studied chemistry at the University of Graz (Austria) (1918–20), and attended the Technische Hochschule, Vienna. During economic troubles in Austria, he emigrated to Mexico, became interested in Mexican folk art, and illustrated children's books. He organized major traveling exhibitions of Mexican art to America. He settled in New York City (1932), dropped the use of his title (1939), and became known as an authority on primitive art. He became director and manager of the Indian Arts and Crafts Board, U.S. Department of Interior, Washington, D.C. (1937–66), and was the art director of the Museum of Modern Art (1949–68).

Diamond, David (1915–) composer; born in Rochester, N.Y. After studies in America and with Nadia Boulanger in Paris, he became a prolific composer of large and small works in a genteel modernist idiom; his music seemed to go cyclically in and out of fashion.

Diat, Louis Felix (1885–1957) chef, author; born in Montmarault, France. He trained at the Paris and London Ritz Hotels before emigrating to the U.S.A. to become chef at the Ritz-Carlton Hotel (1910). Throughout its years of operation (1910–51) "Monsieur Louis" oversaw the superb French cuisine that emerged from New York's most ambitious restaurant kitchen (where he created vichyssoise). He popularized French cooking in his cookbooks (*Cooking à la Ritz*, 1941) and *Gourmet* magazine columns.

Diaz, Justino (1940–) bass; born in San Juan, Puerto Rico. He made his operatic debut in Puerto Rico in 1957 and his Metropolitan Opera debut in 1963. He became a leading bass at the Met and sang internationally.

Dick, A. B. (Albert Blake) (1856–1934) inventor, businessman; born in Bureau County, Ill. An agricultural implements salesman, in 1884 he opened a lumber company in Chicago. To ease the paperwork involved with inventorying stock, he invented a method for duplicating originals called the "autographic stencil." He sold the lumber yard in 1887 to collaborate with Thomas Edison in the invention of the Edison-Dick mimeograph. The A. B. Dick Company devoted all its resources to improving the machine; by the time of his death the mimeograph machine was almost entirely automatic and it dominated the field of office copying until the introduction of the xerographic process.

Dick, Gladys (Rowena b. Henry) (1881–1963) microbiologist, physician; born in Pawnee City, Nebr. After taking her B.S. from the University of Nebraska (1900), she overcame her mother's objections and attended Johns Hopkins Medical School. Turning to biomedical research, specifically into blood chemistry, she went to the University of Chicago (1911) where she met her future husband, George Frederick Dick, who was working on the etiology of scarlet fever. In 1914 the newly married Dicks joined Chicago's John R. McCormick Memorial Institute for Infectious Diseases where she remained until her retirement in 1953. Working together, the Dicks made major contributions to the prevention and treatment of scarlet fever – in 1923 identifying the streptococcus bacterium as the cause and developing the "Dick test" for susceptibility. This led to a long series of lawsuits over their attempts to secure patents for their methods of producing toxins and antitoxins (which some believe cost them a Nobel Prize). In addition to her medical research, she was active in child welfare and founded the Cradle Society in Evanston, Ill., one of the first American professional organizations to supervise adoptions of children.

Dick, Philip K. (Kindred) (1928–1982) writer; born in Chicago. His career as a science fiction writer comprised an early burst of short stories (1952–55) followed by a stream of novels, typically character studies incorporating androids, drugs, and hallucinations. His dozens of books include *The Man in the High Castle* (1962, Hugo Award) and *The Transmigration of Timothy Archer* (1982). He lived in San Francisco.

Dicke, Robert H. (Henry) (1916–) physicist; born in St. Louis, Mo. He taught at the Massachusetts Institute of Technology (1941–46) before becoming a professor at Princeton (1946–84). He made major contributions to the relativistic theory of gravity, the "big bang" theory of the universe, and quantum-mechanical radiation.

Dickenson, Mother Clare Joseph (1755–1830) Catholic religious foundress; born in England. Emigrating to the U.S.A. with other Carmelite nuns in 1890, she helped found the first Carmelite convent in the U.S.A., near Port Tobacco, Md.

Dickey, James (Lafayette) (1923–) poet, writer; born in Atlanta, Ga. He studied at Vanderbilt (B.A. 1949; M.A. 1950), worked in advertising, was consultant to the Library of Congress (1966–68), and taught at many institutions, including the University of South Carolina (1969). He is known for his metaphysical poetry, as in *Buckdancer's Choice* (1965), and his award-winning novel, *Deliverance* (1970).

Dickey, (William Malcomb) Bill (1907–93) baseball player; born in Bastrop, La. One of baseball's greatest catchers, he posted a lifetime batting average of .313 in his 17-year career with the New York Yankees (1928–46). He also managed the Yankees during most of the 1946 season. An eleven-time All-Star, he was elected to the Hall of Fame in 1954.

Dickinson, Anna Elizabeth (1842–1932) orator, lecturer;

born in Philadelphia. Her youthful impassioned speeches on abolition and women's rights launched her on a public career that encompassed Republican political speeches during the Civil War and progressive lyceum lectures afterwards. After unsuccessful attempts at playwriting and acting, she spent her last 40 years in obscurity in New York.

Dickinson, Emily (Elizabeth) (1830–86) poet; born in Amherst, Mass. She attended Amherst Academy (1840–47), Mount Holyoke Female Seminary (1847–48), and lived in Amherst all her life. She met the Reverend Charles Wadsworth in Philadelphia (1854), and he may have been the inspiration for some of her love poems. Thomas Wentworth Higginson, a former minister and author, seems to have been her literary mentor, as indicated in an extended correspondence beginning in 1862. Speculation continues regarding her personal life, but it is noted that she became a recluse c. 1862, and apparently died from the complications of uremia. Only two of her poems were published in her lifetime; her sister, Lavinia Dickinson, discovered hundreds of her poems after her death and they were published in selections from 1890 on. The first authoritative edition, *The Poems of Emily Dickinson* (3 vols.), edited by Thomas H. Johnson, did not appear until 1955. She is known for her poignant, compressed, and deeply charged poems, which have profoundly influenced the direction of 20th-century poetry and gained her an almost cultlike following among some.

Dickinson, John (1732–1808) statesman; born in Talbot County, Md. A prominent lawyer, with practices in both London and Philadelphia, he espoused the colonial cause, but worked for reconciliation with England. He was a member of the Stamp Act Congress (1765) and the First and Second Continental Congresses. He voted against and declined to sign the Declaration of Independence, but he then served in the American Revolutionary militia. As a member of the Constitutional Convention (1787) he supported ratification of the Constitution. His numerous political writings earned him the title of "Penman of the Revolution."

Dickinson, Preston (1891–1930) painter; born in New York City. He traveled widely, often visited Quebec, Canada, and died in France. A Precisionist, he focused on fact and rejected emotional responses. His intellectual approach is seen in *The Factory* (1924). His later work became more sensuous, as in *Plums on a Plate* (1926), and *Still Life with Yellow-Green Chair* (1928).

Dickman, Joseph (Theodore) (1857–1927) soldier; born in Dayton, Ohio. An 1881 West Point graduate, he saw action on the western frontier and in Cuba during the Spanish-American War, led a division and later a corps in France in 1918, and commanded the U.S. 3rd Army during the brief post-war occupation of Germany.

Dickson, Leonard Eugene (1874–1954) mathematician; born in Independence, Iowa. A National Academy of Sciences member, he taught longest at the University of Chicago (1901–54). He published 18 books and hundreds of articles on finite linear groups. Focusing largely on number theory, he published a three-volume *History of the Theory of Numbers*. President of the American Mathematical Society (1916–18), he was the recipient of its Cole Prize (1928).

Diddley, Bo (b. Otha Ellas McDaniel) (1928–) musician; born in McComb, Miss. A guitarist, he was a street-corner gospel and blues singer before beginning his recording career

in 1955 for Chess Records. He became one of the earliest black stars of rock 'n' roll, making numerous television appearances and touring widely through the mid-1960s. Although his popularity as a recording artist dipped thereafter, he remained a celebrated rock pioneer and concert artist and was inducted into the Rock 'n' Roll Hall of Fame in 1987.

Didion, Joan (1934–) writer; born in Sacramento, Calif. She was associate feature editor of *Vogue* (1956–63). Returning to California, she began to write the essays and articles that became her special genre: highly personal commentaries on contemporary events that offer a generally apocalyptic view of social disintegration in the U.S.A. Her books of essays, fiction, and reportage included *Slouching Towards Bethlehem* (1968), *A Book of Common Prayer* (1977), and *Salvador* (1983). She collaborated with her husband John Gregory Dunne (married 1964) on screenplays.

di Donato, Pietro (1911–92) writer; born in West Hoboken, N.J. His father was killed on a construction site when he was 11, but he became a bricklayer. By 1937 he was concentrating on writing and his semiautobiographical novel, *Christ in Concrete* (1939), brought him instant fame. He continued to write fiction, mostly naturalistic portrayals of the hard lives of Italian working-class immigrants in the U.S.A. such as *Three Circles of Light* (1960) or *The Penitent* (1962), but none of his subsequent work ever gained near the attention of *Christ in Concrete*.

Didrikson, Babe See ZAHARIAS, MILDRED ELLA.

Diebenkorn, Richard (Clifford, Jr.) (1922–93) painter; born in Portland, Ore. He studied at the University of California (1940–43), taught at the California School of Fine Arts, San Francisco (1947–50), and lived in California from 1952. Influenced by Willem de Kooning, he began as an abstract painter and, later, became more representational, as in *Man and Woman in Large Room* (1957).

Diego, José de (1866–1918) poet, public official; born in Aguadilla, Puerto Rico. He early showed signs of his two great passions, poetry and politics, and was imprisoned at age 17 for political verses he wrote while studying in Spain. Returning to Puerto Rico, he was a founder of the Autonomist Party (1887) and cofounder (with Luis Muñoz Rivera) of the Unionist Party (1904). From 1907–18 he was president of the House of Delegates, Puerto Rico's first legislative body under American rule. In his later years, he became an advocate of independence. Works such as "A Laura" and "Postuma" won him a lasting reputation as Puerto Rico's finest love poet. He died reciting his own poetry.

Dies, Martin, Jr. (1900–72) U.S. representative; born in Colorado, Texas. A lawyer and rancher in Jasper, Texas (1920–31) before going to the U.S. House of Representatives (Dem., 1931–45), he chaired the notorious Special Committee to Investigate Un-American Activities. He returned to the House (1953–59), then retired to Jasper.

Dietrich, (Maria Magdalene) Marlene (1901–92) film actress, singer; born in Berlin, Germany. Abandoning an early ambition to be a violinist, she became a chorus girl, then studied acting; by 1923 she had launched her career in German films. She gained international attention in *The Blue Angel* (1930) and moved to Hollywood with its director, Josef von Sternberg, who starred her in six films that enforced her persona of enigmatic sexuality. Eventually she moved on to a variety of admired roles in dramas and comedies. Resisting requests by the Nazis to return to Germany, she became a U.S. citizen in 1939 and during World War II made extensive tours, often into combat zones, to entertain Allied troops. After the war, she began a new career as a singer, gaining a new following with her husky, sophisticated renditions. Linked romantically with many men, but married only once (in 1924, to Rudolf Sieber), she spent her last years in Paris.

Dietz, Howard (1896–1983) librettist, lyricist; born in New York City. He served in the U.S. Navy during World War I, then went to work in public relations for Metro-Goldwyn-Mayer. At the same time, he began to write lyrics for Jerome Kern and other composers before beginning a long collaboration in 1929 with composer Arthur Schwartz. He wrote lyrics for their successful revue *The Little Show* (1929) and the musical *The Band Wagon* (1931), which included "Dancing in the Dark," their most famous song. His work was curtailed after he developed Parkinson's disease in 1954 but he collaborated with Schwartz on *Jennie* (1963).

Dietz, Robert Sinclair (1914–) geophysicist; born in Westfield, N.J. He served as oceanographer for various institutions (1937–77) before becoming a geology professor at Arizona State University (1977). A pioneer in the field of plate tectonics, he also contributed to studies of the mineralogy of meteorite craters and the ocean floor.

Diggs, Charles Coles, Jr. (1922–) U.S. representative; born in Detroit, Mich. Interrupting his studies to enlist in the army in 1942, he attended Wayne College of Mortuary Science afterwards, working in the House of Diggs, Inc. A Democratic member of the Michigan senate (1951–54), he served in the U.S. House of Representatives from 1955 until resigning in 1980. He founded and chaired the Congressional Black Caucus (1969–71) and chaired the Committee on the District of Columbia.

Dilg, Will (1867–1927) conservationist; born in Milwaukee, Wis. A well-known writer for outdoor magazines, he established the Izaak Walton League in 1922 to lobby for environmental protection and wilderness preservation. As president of the league (1922–26), he fought to save Superior National Forest in Minnesota from commercial exploitation and set up a fund to save starving elk in Jackson Hole, Wyo.

Dille, John Flint (1884–1957) newspaper syndicate executive; born in Dixon, Ill. The son of an educator, he attended the University of Chicago before founding the National Newspaper Syndicate (1917), which distributed the work of prominent journalists at low cost to newspapers. Credited with originating the "Buck Rogers" comic strip – he saw the possibilities in a novel, *Armageddon 2419 A.D.,* by Philip Nowlan and commissioned Richard Calkins to draw the strip – he introduced the long-running science fiction adventure in 1929. At its peak of popularity, 287 newspapers in 40 countries carried the feature.

Diller, Burgoyne (1906–65) painter, sculptor; born in New York City. He lived in New York, studied with Hans Hofmann, and was influenced by Piet Mondrian. A member of the American Abstract Artists, a group that emphasized nonrepresentational work, he created spare, flat-surfaced work, as in *First Theme* (1933–34). His sculptures are an extension of his painting style.

Dillinger, John (1902–34) robber; born in Indianapolis, Ind. He terrorized Indiana, Illinois, and Ohio with bank robberies (1933–34) and became the FBI's "public enemy number one." Betrayed by a woman friend, he was killed by FBI agents in Chicago.

Dillon, Sidney (1812–92) railroad builder; born in Northampton, N.Y. He left his impoverished family farm at age seven to work as a water boy on railroad construction sites; he progressed to overseer and foreman. In 1840 his bid was accepted to build a small section of the Boston & Albany Railroad. This job launched his railroad career, which included becoming the major contractor for the Union Pacific Railroad; he served as director of the Union Pacific from 1864–92, and as its president, from 1874–84 and 1890–92. He wrote "Historic Moments: Driving the Last Spike of the Union Pacific" published posthumously in *Scribner's* magazine (August, 1892).

Dillon, (Thomas Church) Tom (1915–86) advertising executive; born in Seattle, Wash. He was a copywriter who, during a 42-year career with the New York advertising agency BBDO, created advertisements for such clients as Cream of Wheat and Northern Pacific Railway. He rose to be the agency's president (1964–75), chief executive officer (1967–77), and chairman (1975–80).

DiMaggio, (Joseph Paul) Joe (1914–) baseball player; born in Martinez, Calif. One of baseball's most graceful players, he spent his entire career as an outfielder for the New York Yankees (1936–51), during which he was named the American League Most Valuable Player three times (1939, 1941, 1947). Although he hit 361 lifetime homeruns and posted a career batting average of .325, he is most remembered for hitting in a record-setting 56 consecutive games in 1941. His brothers, Vince and Dom DiMaggio, also played major league baseball. He was married briefly to actress Marilyn Monroe and appeared in many television commercials after his retirement from baseball. Nicknamed, "Joltin' Joe" and, "The Yankee Clipper," he was elected to baseball's Hall of Fame in 1955.

Dine, (James) Jim (1935–) painter, sculptor; born in Cincinnati, Ohio. He studied at the Boston Museum School (1953–55), moved to New York City (1958), traveled to London (1967), and settled in Putney, Vt. (1970). Known as a new realist, he used many mediums, including "happenings" (a type of spontaneous performance), constructional sculpture, collage, and painting. He is noted for his preoccupation with hearts and bathrobes, as in his paintings, *Untitled (Gloves)* (1970–71), and *So Many Different Colors* (1976).

Dingley, Nelson (1832–99) U.S. representative; born in Durham, Maine. A Dartmouth College graduate, editor of the *Lewiston Evening Journal,* he was a protectionist Republican congressman from Maine (1881–99) who sponsored the Dingley Tariff, imposing heavy import taxes.

Dinkins, David (1927–) mayor; born in Trenton, N.J. Trained as a lawyer, he rose slowly and quietly in New York City's Democratic Party political machine until he was elected mayor of New York City (1990–93). As the city's first African-American mayor, he was particularly stung by charges of insensitivity to the city's racial problems and of inaction on other problems confronting the city's poor, but he persisted on his own slow, quiet course.

Dinsmoor, William Bell (1887–1973) classical archaeologist; born in Windham, N.H. He graduated from Harvard (1906), becoming a student, then excavator and restorer at the

American School of Classical Studies in Athens. He taught at Columbia University (1919–63), first as a professor of architecture, then archaeology. He was chairman of the Committee for the Protection of Cultural Treasures in War Areas during World War II. His book, *Architecture of Greece* (1950), is considered definitive.

Dinwiddie, Robert (1693–1770) colonial administrator; born near Glasgow, Scotland. He served as lieutenant-governor of Virginia (1751–58). He sent George Washington to warn the French to stay out of western Pennsylvania in 1753–54. After the defeat of Braddock's army (1755) he had the almost impossible task of defending the extended frontier from Indians' raids; the danger was finally eliminated by the capture of Fort Duquesne in 1758.

Dirksen, Everett (McKinley) (1896–1969) U.S. representative/senator; born in Pekin, Ill. A twin, he was named after President McKinley, one of his father's Republican heroes, and distinguished himself as an orator even in high school. After serving in the army, he worked in family businesses before entering local politics in 1926. In the U.S. House of Representatives (Rep., Ill.; 1933–51), he satisfied his constituents by supporting the New Deal domestic programs while championing isolationist foreign policy. A political pragmatist, he drafted the Legislative Reorganization Act of 1946, running for the Senate in 1950 with the endorsement of *Chicago Tribune* editor Colonel Robert McCormack. In the Senate (1951–69) he was a conservative McCarthyite until 1956 when he became an Eisenhower loyalist and moderate, chosen as Republican whip in 1957 and Republican leader in 1959. Ironically the high point of his career came during the Kennedy and Johnson presidencies when he delivered key Republican support for the Test Ban Treaty of 1963 and the Civil Rights acts of 1964, 1965, and 1968.

Disney, (Walter Elias) Walt (1901–66) movie animator, producer, showman; born in Chicago. He spent most of his boyhood on a farm in Missouri, and at age 16 went to Chicago to study art. From 1920–22 he was in Kansas City, Mo., where, under the pioneer animator Ub Iwerks, he made simple cartoon advertisements that were shown in movie theaters. He moved to Los Angeles in 1923 to open his own animated cartoon studio; very quickly, too, he found that his great talent lay in conceiving new images and projects and then directing others in bringing them into being – he actually did little of the animation. His first series – *Alice in Cartoonland* (1924–26) and *Oswald the Rabbit* (1926–28) – were not especially successful but in 1928 he introduced Mickey Mouse in the first sound cartoon, *Steamboat Willie.* Always quick to adopt the latest technology, his *Flowers and Trees* (1932) was the first film of any kind made in complete Technicolor. From 1929–39, he produced a series of full-color animated cartoons, *Silly Symphonies,* that featured his soon-to-become famous characters, Donald Duck, Goofy, and Pluto. In 1937 he released the first full-length cartoon feature, *Snow White and the Seven Dwarfs,* to enormous financial and critical success; it would be followed by others such as *Pinocchio* (1940), *Fantasia* (1940), *Dumbo* (1941), and *Bambi* (1942). During World War II his studio made educational films for the U.S. government. After the war, he began to produce *True-Life Adventures,* a series of short films showing hitherto unseen close-ups of animals in natural settings; his first full-length nature film was *The Living Desert* (1953).

He also began to produce movies with live actors; his first was *Treasure Island* (1950), followed by others including *Davy Crockett* (1955) and *Mary Poppins* (1964). In 1954 he also launched a successful television series for children; it featured many of his studio's creations. In 1955 he opened Disneyland, in Anaheim, Calif., an amusement park heavily drawing on his studio's productions; Disney World, in Orlando, Fla., did not open until 1971. Greatly honored in his lifetime, with numerous Oscars – including a special award for Mickey Mouse in 1932 – and an honorary degree from Harvard, he remains acknowledged as a true genius of popular entertainment.

Di Suvero, Mark (1933–) sculptor; born in Shanghai, China. His family moved to California (1941) where he attended the University of California. He settled in New York City (1957), founded the SoHo Cooperative Gallery (1962–67), and began work on large outdoor sculptures, as in *Tower of Peace* (1966). Based in Europe (1971), he also lived in the Netherlands and France.

Ditmars, Raymond (Lee) (1876–1942) herpetologist; born in Newark, N.J. Rather than pursuing his parents' wish that he attend West Point, he became assistant curator of entomology at the American Museum of Natural History (1893–98), where he began his personal collection of snakes from around the world. After serving as a court reporter for the *New York Times* (1898–99), he became curator of reptiles at the New York Zoological Park (Bronx Zoo) (1899–1920), then took charge of the zoo's mammals (1910–42). He began lecturing in New York City schools in 1896; from 1910 on he supplemented his lectures with educational movies on animal behavior made in his own home studio. In later years he became interested in the medical uses of snake venom and the behavior of vampire bats. A general naturalist, field explorer, and popularist for reptiles, he wrote many books on reptiles, zoology, and natural science.

Ditson, Oliver (1811–88) music publisher; born in Boston, Mass. He began in 1835 the business that developed into the Oliver Ditson & Company, music publishers.

Divine, Father See BAKER, GEORGE.

Dix, Dorothea (Lynde) (1802–87) reformer, nurse; born in Hampden, Maine. She left an unhappy home at age ten to live with her grandmother in Boston; by age 14 the resourceful and determined Dix was on her own and teaching school in Worcester, Mass. In 1821 she established her own school in Boston, running it successfully until 1834, when a tubercular illness, a recurring affliction, forced her to give it up. After a period of invalidism, she dedicated herself to the quiet study of conditions of insane asylums, prisons, and alms houses, at first in Massachusetts and eventually in many states, Canada, and Europe. What she found appalled her: men and women chained to the walls of tiny, dark and fetid rooms, ill-clothed and -fed and treated brutally when they were noticed at all. Remaining in the background, Dix used influential political leaders to broadcast her findings. From 1842–45 she traveled more than 10,000 miles on her investigations. The results were a gradual and continuing improvement of conditions. New asylums were built in many states, and others improved; more humane methods of caring for the insane were adopted. In June 1861 Dix became superintendent of women nurses for the federal government, in which role she oversaw the recruitment, training, and placement of some

2,000 women who cared for the Union war-wounded. After the war she resumed her work among the insane, traveling widely in Europe and Japan. Hardworking, dedicated to the humanitarian cause in spite of continuing illness, she could seem cold and even distant; "I have no particular love for my species," she once said, "but own to an exhaustless fund of compassion." She died in a Trenton, N.J., hospital she herself had founded.

Dix, Dorothy See GILMER, ELIZABETH.

Dixon, Dean (1915–76) conductor; born in New York City. As a talented African-American child, he was helped by Eleanor Roosevelt. Although he studied at Juilliard and Columbia University, and founded the American Youth Orchestra in 1944, racial conditions in the U.S.A. led him to concentrate on a career in Europe, where he was widely admired.

Dixon, Franklin W. See STRATEMEYER, EDWARD L.

Dixon, George Washington (1808–61) minstrel performer; birthplace unknown but he died in New Orleans. He was one of the first performers to act out skits and songs in blackface and is credited with creating the first "black play", *Love in a Cloud* (1829). His performances in New York in the early 1830s first raised interest in minstrel shows. In the 1840s his career waned and he became an adventurer in Yucatan and the editor of a New York scandal sheet.

Dixon, (William) "Billy" (1850–1913) frontiersman, scout; born in Ohio County, W.Va. He was a government mule driver (1865–69) and a famous buffalo hunter and Indian fighter. After the desperate battle with Indians at Adobe Walls, Texas (1874), he and his four fellow survivors all received the Congressional Medal of Honor.

Djerassi, Carl (1923–) chemist, inventor; born in Vienna, Austria. A refugee immigrant to the United States in 1939, he became a research chemist, and eventually, professor of chemistry at Stanford. While working for a little-known firm in Mexico City in 1951, he was involved in the testing of the oral contraceptive – "the pill" – that for the first time made birth control a simple matter for millions of women. Although he made claims to being the prime developer of the birth control pill, these claims have been disputed by the scientific community. He did make important contributions to other areas of steroid research, and he was noted for his efforts at promoting international cooperation.

Dobie, J. (James) Frank (1888–1964) author, folklorist; born in Live Oak County, Texas. The most important Texas writer of his generation, he collected and published 30 volumes of southwestern lore and history from *A Vaquero of the Brush Country* (1929) to *Cow People* (1964), often collaborating with his wife, Bertha McKee Dobie. His long tenure as a professor of English at the University of Texas (1922–47) was marked by legendary political battles, frequent leaves, and finally dismissal. He won the presidential Medal of Freedom (1964).

Dobzhansky, Theodosius (Grigorievich) (1900–75) geneticist; born in Nemirov, Ukraine. He taught zoology in Russia, and emigrated to the U.S.A. (1927) because of Stalinist repression of genetic science. He was a professor and researcher at the California Institute of Technology (1928–40), where he published his seminal book, *Genetics and the Origin of Species* (1937). He relocated to Columbia University (1940–62), joined Rockefeller University (1962–71), then moved to the University of California: Davis (1971–75). He demonstrated that the genetic variability in a population is large, including many potentially lethal genes that nevertheless confer versatility when the population is exposed to environmental change. A prolific and internationally acclaimed writer, his work on population evolution in both fruit flies and humans gave the experimental evidence that linked Darwinian theory with Mendel's law of heredity.

Dock, Lavinia Lloyd (1858–1956) nurse, social reformer; born in Harrisburg, Pa. Born into a prosperous family, she chose to train as a nurse at New York City's Bellevue Hospital (1884–86); after serving as a visiting nurse among the poor, she compiled the first, and long most important, manual of drugs for nurses, *Materia Medica for Nurses* (1890). After stints at Johns Hopkins (Baltimore) and Cook County (Chicago) hospitals, she joined the Nurses' Settlement in New York City (1896–1915); working closely with Lillian Wald, she strove not only to improve the health of the poor but also to improve the profession of nursing through her teaching, lecturing, and writing. She played a major role as a contributing editor to the *American Journal of Nursing,* and she linked American nurses' goals to similar efforts in England. She also did most of the work for *A History of Nursing* (2 vols., 1907; 2 more vols., 1912; later revised and abridged). Although she gave up nursing as a practice around the age of 50, she dedicated her energies to outspoken activism on controversial social issues of the day – improved working conditions, the elimination of prostitution and venereal diseases, and women's rights, especially women's right to vote. (She was jailed briefly three times for taking part in militant suffrage demonstrations.) Never one to avoid unpopular positions, she spoke out against World War I and she was an early advocate of birth control. She retired to her home in Pennsylvania about 1922, but in her long remaining years maintained her interest in and ties to the causes she had fought for.

Doctorow, E. L. (Edgar Lawrence) (1931–) writer; born in New York City. He published his first novel in 1960 while working as a literary editor and nine years later began to write professionally. *The Book of Daniel* (1971) established his reputation with its trademark mingling of fictional and historical characters. Later novels include *Ragtime* (1975) and *World's Fair* (1985). He taught at Sarah Lawrence College (1971–78) and New York University (1982).

Dodd, S. C. T. (Samuel Calvin Tate) (1836–1907) lawyer; born in Franklin, Pa. Admitted to the Pennsylvania bar in 1859, the year oil was discovered in the state, he specialized in corporate law. Having become the general solicitor for Standard Oil Company in New York City (1881), he proceeded to write a trust agreement for the nine trustees of the 40-some companies that made up Standard Oil; he then represented the company through two major court battles – the Ohio Supreme Court (1892) and the U.S. Supreme Court (1911) – arguing against the government's antitrust concerns. In both cases the government prevailed. He wrote several books, including *Uses and Abuses of Combinations* (1888) and *History of Standard Oil* (1888).

Dodd, William Edward (1869–1940) historian, diplomat; born near Clayton, N.C. He studied in the U.S.A. and in Germany before teaching history at Randolph-Macon College (1900–08) and the University of Chicago (1908–33). He wrote extensively about the antebellum South, the Civil War, and Woodrow Wilson. He was ambassador to Germany (1933–37).

Dodge, Augustus (Caesar) (1812–83) U.S. representative/senator, diplomat; born at Ste. Genevieve, Mo. Settling in Iowa in 1838, he went to the U.S. House of Representatives as a territorial delegate (Dem., Iowa; 1840–46) and was then one of Iowa's first U.S. senators (1848–55). He then served as ambassador to Spain (1855–59).

Dodge, (Ethel) Geraldine R. (Rockefeller) (1882–1973) philanthropist, dog breeder; born in New York City. The daugher of William and niece of John D. Rockefeller, she loved dogs and became an accomplished horsewoman. In 1907 she married Marcellus Hartley Dodge, an heir to the Remington Arms fortune. Established near Morristown, N.J., at Giralda Farms, she lavished her attention on dogs as a breeder, shower, judge, and author. She founded the largest one-day dog show in the world (Morris & Essex Dog Show, 1927–57) as well as St. Hubert's Giralda, an animal shelter (1937). Her only child, Hartley Dodge, died in an automobile accident in 1930; her husband predeceased her by ten years. Her estate was incorporated into the Geraldine R. Dodge Foundation (1975), devoted especially to preventing cruelty to animals and encouraging art.

Dodge, Grenville (Mellen) (1831–1916) engineer, soldier; born in Danvers, Mass. A railroad surveyor in the West, and a merchant in Iowa (after 1854), he volunteered in the Civil War, rising to command a Union army division. Although he saw considerable action and was wounded twice in battle, his greatest contribution to the Union's victory came from his ability to build or rebuild damaged railroads and bridges. After the war he became chief engineer of the Union Pacific Railroad (1866–70) – he fit in one term in the U.S. House of Representatives (Rep., Iowa; 1867–69) – and he oversaw the construction of the Union Pacific transcontinental rail line, completed in 1869. After 1871 he served as chief engineer with other railroads in the Southwest; after the Spanish-American War he helped build railroads in Cuba. He is credited with having built over 10,000 miles of railroad and surveying many more miles. He headed the so-called Dodge Commission (1898–1900) that investigated the U.S. Army's conduct during the Spanish-American War and led to organizational reforms.

Dodge, Henry (1782–1867) pioneer, soldier, U.S. representative/senator; born at Post Vincennes, Ind. He moved to Spanish Louisiana (1796), to Illinois, and eventually to present-day Wisconsin. He served in the War of 1812 and the Black Hawk War. He was governor of the Territory of Wisconsin (1836–41, 1845–48) and served in the U.S. House of Representatives (Dem., Wis.; 1841–45) and the U.S. Senate (Dem., Wis.; 1848–57) where he voted against the Kansas-Nebraska Act. He was known for his fairness and toughness in his relations with the Native Americans.

Dodge, Henry Chee (?1860–1947) Navajo principal chief; born at Fort Defiance in present-day Arizona. Due in part to his English skills, he became the official Navajo interpreter and was appointed political successor to the great chief Manualito in 1884. A successful trader and rancher, he was elected chair of the new Navajo Tribal Council (1923–28) and reelected in 1942. Much of his life he worked to improve the living conditions of the Navajo, both by holding off the intrusions of private white enterprises and by bringing in U.S. government services.

Dodge, Horace (Elgin) See under DODGE, JOHN.

Dodge, John (Francis) (1864–1920) **and Horace (Elgin)** (1868–1920) automobile manufacturers; born in Niles, Mich. They began as bicycle manufacturers in Ontario, Canada, then moved to Detroit (1901) to open a machine shop for the manufacture of automobile parts. In 1914 they expanded to make their own automobiles. Their innovations included the use of conveyor belts in manufacturing, and the technique for baking enamel on steel bodies. They produced the first car with an all-steel body. During World War I they made their factory available to the war effort and designed the machinery to build the French recoil gun. This technology was later used for making car cylinders. The brothers were very close, and while both contributed to mechanical innovation, John was more the businessman, and Horace more mechanically inclined.

Dodge, Joseph M. (Morrell) (1890–1964) banker, government official; born in Detroit, Mich. He rose from an impoverished childhood to become chairman of the Detroit Bank, later Detroit Bank and Trust (1933–63). He was a U.S. government financial advisor in Germany (1945–46). In Japan under General Douglas MacArthur (1949–50), he designed an economic stability plan that was responsible for Japan's postwar industrial rehabilitation. He was director of the federal budget (1952–54).

Dodge, Mary Elizabeth (b. Mapes) (1831–1905) writer, editor; born in New York City. She was editor of the popular *St. Nicholas Magazine* for children, from its inception in 1873 to 1905, and wrote children's books, including the classic *Hans Brinker, or the Silver Skates* (1865).

Doe, Charles (1830–96) jurist; born in Derry, N.H. The son of a well-to-do landowner, he graduated from Dartmouth College (1849) and was admitted to the New Hampshire bar in 1854. He built a thriving law practice in Dover, N.H., and became active in Democratic politics, but converted to Republicanism as the secession crisis boiled over in the late 1850s. As an efficient, reforming associate justice of the New Hampshire Supreme Court (1859–74), the hardworking Doe – he boasted that he had read but one novel in his life – saw his reputation rest on innovative rulings on judicial procedure rather than on interpretations of law. An insomniac and an eccentric who craved fresh air, he habitually ordered all the windows of his courtroom raised, even on the coldest days. In 1876, after a politically inspired court reorganization, he became the state's chief justice.

Dohan, Edith Hayward Hall (1877–1943) archaeologist; born in New Haven, Conn. She graduated from Smith College (1899), then studied archaeology and Greek at Bryn Mawr College, spending 1903–05 at the American School of Classical Studies in Athens. One of the first American women in the field of archaeology, her doctoral dissertation was titled *Decorative Art of Crete in the Bronze Age* (1907). She taught at Mount Holyoke College (1908–12), then went to the University of Pennsylvania and became assistant curator of the museum there. After an interruption to start a family (1915–20), she returned to the museum, becoming its curator in 1942. From 1932 to her death, she was editor of the *American Journal of Archaeology,* specializing in her later years in Etruscan graves.

Doherty, Henry Latham (1870–1939) utilities executive/engineer; born in Columbus, Ohio. Forced by family circumstances to leave school at age 12, he started working as an office boy for the Columbia Gas Company. By 1896 Emerson McMillin & Company, the New York banking firm that owned several utilities including Columbia Gas, had made him chief engineer and general manager of all the McMillin properties. In 1900 Doherty presented a famous paper on utility rates to the National Electric Association. In 1905 he formed his own company to provide various services to utilities and in 1910 he formed Cities Service, a holding company for his own acquisitions, numbering 53 companies in 1913 alone. He continued his engineering innovations in natural gas development and oil production, earning 140 patents in his lifetime, and he was equally ingenious in his financial transactions.

Doisy, Edward A. (Adelbert) (1893–1986) biochemist; born in Hume, Ill. He was an assistant in biochemistry at Harvard Medical School (1915–17), then moved to the Washington University (St. Louis, Mo.) School of Medicine (1919–23). He joined the St. Louis University School of Medicine (1923–65), while concurrently serving as administrator and director of St. Mary's Hospital, St. Louis (1924–86). In collaboration with American embryologist Edgar Allen, he developed the Allen-Doisy vaginal smear for assaying estrogen potency; the two scientists also purified several female sex hormones (1929–35). In 1939 Doisy isolated two forms of the coagulant vitamin K. For this contribution to the treatment of hemorrhagic disorders, he shared the 1943 Nobel Prize for physiology. He also made major advances in antibiotic research, the biochemistry of bodily buffer systems, and the purification of insulin and the placental hormone chorionic gonadotropin.

Dole, Elizabeth (Hanford) (1936–) lawyer, cabinet member (wife of Robert Dole); born in Salisbury, N.C. Originally a Democrat, she was a Washington consumer protection lawyer in the 1970s. President Reagan's secretary of transportation (1983–87), she promoted auto safety. As President Bush's secretary of labor (1989–90), she ended the Pittsdown Coal Strike. She became American Red Cross president in 1991.

Dole, Robert (1923–) U.S. representative/senator; born in Russell, Kans. After serving in the army during World War II (during which his right arm was permanently crippled in combat), he became a lawyer. He was elected to the U.S. House of Representatives (Rep., Kans.; 1961–69), and to the U.S. Senate (1969). From 1971–73 he served as national chairman of the Republican Party, in which office he defended President Nixon's Vietnam War policies and his role in the Watergate Scandal. Generally conservative, he was Gerald Ford's running mate in 1976, and ran unsuccessfully for his party's presidential nomination in 1988. As Senate majority leader (1985–87), he backed the Reagan administration's foreign and domestic policies. He became minority leader after Republicans lost control of the Senate and majority leader again when they regained it (1995).

Dole, Sanford (Ballard) (1844–1926) judge, public official; born in Honolulu, Hawaii. The son of American missionaries, he studied at Williams College and became a leading lawyer on the Hawaiian islands. Long active in efforts to reform the native Hawaiian government, he became a leader after the revolution had overturned the Hawaiian monarchy (1893) and became president of the Republic of Hawaii (1894–98). He worked vigorously for annexation by the U.S.A. and served as the first territorial governor (1900–03) and as a judge in the U.S. district court (1903–15).

Dolphy, Eric (Allan) (1928–64) jazz musician; born in Los Angeles. He was an influential multi-instrumentalist who played with Chico Hamilton, John Coltrane, and Charles Mingus before his death from a brain tumor.

Domar, Evsey D. (David) (1914–) economist; born in Lodz, Russia (now Poland). Initially educated in China, he completed his education in the U.S.A. He taught at several universities before accepting a professorship at the Massachusetts Institute of Technology (1958). He is the co-inventor of the "Harrod-Domar model" of dynamic equilibrium in economic growth.

Domino, (Antoine) "Fats" (1928–) musician; born in New Orleans. A singer and pianist, he was one of the first black rhythm & blues artists to attract a wide following among white youth. He played in New Orleans honky-tonks from his early teens, and in 1950 he recorded "The Fat Man," which became his first million-seller. Between 1954–68, he headlined many rock 'n' roll package shows on the strength of such hits as "Ain't That a Shame" (1955), "Blueberry Hill" (1956), and "Blue Monday" (1957). He had his last hit record in 1968 and worked sporadically thereafter. In 1987, he was honored with a Grammy Lifetime Achievement Award.

Donaldson, Walter (1893–1947) composer; born in Brooklyn. He composed many hit songs of the 1920s and 1930s that were used in Broadway shows, films, and by big-name bands. He wrote Al Jolson's signature song "My Mammy" (1918) and the score for the musical *Whoopee* (1928), which starred Eddie Cantor and contained the hit "Makin' Whoopee." In the 1930s and 1940s he was a composer-arranger of Hollywood films.

Donaldson, William Henry (1931–) financial executive; born in Buffalo, N.Y. He graduated from Yale in 1953 and served two years in the Marine Corps before launching a career in business, government, and education. He was an undersecretary of state (1973–74), dean of the Yale graduate school of management (1975–80), and a Ford Foundation trustee (1968–80). His firm, Donaldson, Lufkin & Jenrette, Inc., founded in the mid-1950s, became well known for innovative approaches. In 1991, he became chairman and chief executive officer of the New York Stock Exchange.

Doniphan, Alexander William (1808–87) lawyer, soldier; born in Mason County, Ky. A successful lawyer, he served as militia commander and led a Missouri brigade in a skirmish with Mormons, but refused to carry out an order (that was later rescinded) to execute the prophet Joseph Smith and others captured with him. He commanded a Missouri militia regiment in the Mexican War, arriving at Chihuahua after an epic 12-month, 3,000-mile march. He returned after the war to the practice of law, which he continued until his death. He opposed secession in 1861, favored Missouri's neutrality, and took no part in the Civil War.

Donnelly, Ignatius (1831–1901) social reformer, politician, author; born in Philadelphia. A lawyer with utopian aspirations, he moved to Minnesota (1856) to promote a land development scheme known as Nininger City; when that failed, he switched to farming and also to politics. Said to have been a spellbinding speaker, he joined the Republican Party because of its stand against slavery and got himself elected to the U.S. House of Representatives (Minn., 1863–69). He supported the Radical Republicans in their harsh policy to the defeated Confederate states and was instrumental in establishing the National Bureau of Education to help people of all color obtain an education. In the years that followed, he became ever more radical and erratic as he jumped between causes and parties, attacking capitalists for exploiting the masses, joining the Grange, forming the Independent Anti-Monopoly Party (1877), forming the Populist Party (1891), running unsuccessfully for Congress, attacking the South for preserving "the color line," calling for a graduated income tax, denouncing anti-Semitism, and predicting class warfare. He was ahead of the times on many of these issues but he lacked the ability to get things done. Through it all, he published several remarkable books, including a futuristic novel, *Caesar's Column* (1891), predicting a 20th-century U.S.A. dominated by the rich and corrupt. He also wrote the highly popular *Atlantis: the Antediluvian World* (1882), a mishmash of pseudoscholarly "evidence" for the lost Atlantis, and *The Great Cryptogram* (1888), in which he "proved" that Francis Bacon wrote the plays of Shakespeare.

Donnelly, Russell J. (James) (1930–) physicist; born in Hamilton, Ontario, Canada. He came to the U.S.A. to study at Yale (1952), then taught at the University of Chicago (1956–57) before joining the University of Oregon (1957). He made major contributions to studies of low-temperature superfluidity.

Donovan, Hedley (Williams) (1914–90) editor; born in Brainerd, Minn. Starting as a reporter for the *Washington Post* (1937–42), he joined *Fortune* magazine in 1945 and rose to managing editor (1953–59); becoming chief deputy to Henry Luce, he succeeded him as editor in chief of *Time,* Inc. (1964–79), with responsibility for all its publishing ventures. On retiring in 1979, he served as an advisor to President Carter (1979–80), then taught at Harvard and Oxford.

Donovan, William (Joseph) (1883–1959) soldier, public official; born in Buffalo, N.Y. A much-decorated World War I veteran, he was an assistant to the U.S. attorney general (1925–29) and served as an unofficial observer for the government in Italy, Spain, and the Balkans (1935–41). Assigned to head the U.S. Office of Strategic Services (1942–45), "Wild Bill" Donovan had responsibility for espionage, counterespionage, and clandestine military operations during World War II. He was ambassador to Thailand in 1953–54.

Dooley, Thomas (Anthony, III) (1927–61) physician, author; born in St. Louis, Mo. He interrupted his education to serve as a U.S. Navy medical corpsman (1944–46); after taking his medical degree, he served with the U.S. Navy (1953–56). Assigned to a ship helping Vietnamese fleeing north to south, he set up a refugee camp near Haiphong; his account of this work, *Deliver Us from Evil* (1956), gained him national attention. He resigned from the navy and went to Laos where he established two medical clinics; his account of this experience, *The Edge of Tomorrow* (1958), plus his lectures, attracted still more financial support for his efforts. He helped found the Medical International Cooperation Organization (MEDICO) and returned to set up other clinics in Southeast Asia; he wrote about one in Laos in *The Night They Burned the Mountain* (1960). He died prematurely of cancer.

Doolittle, Hilda (H.D.; also John Helforth, pen names) (1886–1961) poet, writer; born in Bethlehem, Pa. She attended Bryn Mawr (?1900–06), moved to Europe and England (1911), and was based in Switzerland (1924). A friend of Ezra Pound, she was a major imagist poet, and also wrote plays, novels, and children's stories.

Doolittle, James (Harold) (1896–1993) aviator; born in Alameda, Calif. Commissioned in the Army Air Corps in 1920, he pioneered instrument landing techniques as a test pilot during the 1920s. Doolittle resigned from the regular service in 1930 to join the Shell Oil Company as an executive. Pursuing his interest in aircraft development, he set a world speed record in 1932. Recalled to active duty in 1940, Doolittle led the famous 1942 attack on Tokyo and other Japanese cities by 16 B-25 bombers flying off the aircraft carrier USS *Hornet,* a daring operation that gave a terrific boost to morale on the home front. He commanded the 12th Air Force during the North Africa campaign (1942–43), the 15th Air Force in Italy (1943), and the 8th Air Force during the intensive bombing offensive against Germany (1944–45). Doolittle returned to Shell after the war and was a vice-president and director of the company until his retirement in 1959.

Dorati, Antal (1906–88) conductor; born in Budapest, Hungary. Making his debut as an opera conductor at 18, he worked at opera houses in Budapest, Dresden, and Münster before emigrating to France in 1933. In 1940 he arrived in the U.S.A., where he conducted the symphonies of Dallas (1945–49) and Minneapolis (1949–60); after work in Europe, he conducted the National Symphony in Washington (1970–77) and the Detroit Symphony (1977–81). He was noted as an efficient and workmanly conductor; by 1980 he had made some 500 recordings.

Doriot, Georges F. (Frederic) (1899–1987) management educator, venture capitalist; born in Paris, France. He came to the U.S.A. (1921) to attend Harvard Business School, where as a professor of industrial management (1926–66) he influenced several generations of top U.S. executives. He was founding president of the American Research & Development Corporation (ARD Investment) (1946–72), the first publicly traded venture capital company. Its loans included start-up funding for Digital Equipment Corporation (1960).

Dornbusch, Rudiger (1942–) economics educator; born in Krefeld, Germany. Educated at the University of Geneva, he came to the U.S.A. in 1967 and earned a Ph.D. at the University of Chicago in 1971. In 1977 he became Ford International Professor of Economics at the Massachusetts Institute of Technology. He wrote several works on economics, including *Dollars, Debts and Deficits* (1987).

Dorr, John Van Nostrand (1872–1962) chemical engineer, metallurgist; born in Newark, N.J. While managing a cyanide mill in South Dakota in the early 1900s, he developed the Dorr classifier for extracting ore, which became a practical method for the separation and chemical treatment of fine solids suspended in liquid. His technology was used in sewage treatment, water purification, desilting projects, and sugar production. He founded the Dorr Company in New York City (1916) and the Dorr Foundation (1950).

Dorr, Thomas (Wilson) (1805–54) lawyer, political reformer; born in Providence, R.I. Admitted to the bar in 1827, he was elected to the Rhode Island assembly in 1834. Taking the lead in efforts to establish a state constitution that would abolish such anti-democratic practices as the requirement that only adult males who owned a fair amount of land could vote, he formed a "People's Party" that adopted a constitution. He then got himself elected governor (1842), and in the ensuing "rebellion" against the established government, a minor civil war broke out in Rhode Island. Arrested and charged with treason, he was sentenced to life imprisonment (1844) but was released in 1845. He retired in poor health but a new constitution at least embodied some of his goals.

Dorrance, John T. (Thompson) (1873–1930) food manufacturer; born in Bristol, Pa. He took his doctorate in organic chemistry from the University of Göttingen in Germany but turned down prestigious academic posts to work in his uncle's canning factory, the Joseph Campbell Preserve Company, in Camden, N.J. In 1897 he outfitted a laboratory on the company premises with the idea of replicating the soups he had enjoyed in Europe, but in condensed form. By 1904 his soups had begun to dominate company sales. By 1910 he was general manager and the company was making only soups and pork and beans. His uncle retired in 1914. Dorrance became president and, by 1915, sole owner of Campbell Soup; he turned the company into a major international producer of canned soups.

Dorsen, Norman (1930–) lawyer, professor; born in New York City. Briefly in private practice (1958–60), he was president of the American Civil Liberties Union (1976–91) and a professor at New York University law school (1961). His many books include *Our Endangered Rights* (1984) and *The Evolving Constitution* (1987).

Dorsett, (Anthony Drew) Tony (1954–) football player; born in Rochester, Pa. The first college player to rush for over 6,000 career yards and the 1976 Heisman Trophy winner at the University of Pittsburgh, he gained 12,739 yards in twelve professional seasons.

Dorsey, (Thomas) Tommy (1905–56) musician; born in Shenandoah, Pa. He was a Swing Era bandleader who began with local dance bands in Scranton, Pa. He moved to New York City in 1925 and engaged in free-lance radio and recording work as a trombonist and trumpeter. In 1927–28, he was a sideman with Paul Whiteman. In the late 1920s and early 1930s, he and his brother Jimmy Dorsey (1904–57), a saxophonist, coled a succession of recording bands. In 1934, they launched a full-time orchestra which played a long residency at the Glen Island Casino (New Rochelle, N.Y.). After a dispute with Jimmy in 1935, Tommy split and took over Joe Haymes' orchestra, building it into one of the most popular and versatile Swing bands. He led this orchestra, which featured Frank Sinatra in 1940–42, until the early 1950s. He appeared with Jimmy in the 1947 Hollywood feature film *The Fabulous Dorseys,* and in 1953 they formed a new band together. In 1955–56, they cohosted their own television program, *Stage Show,* on CBS. His premature death was caused by strangulation on food particles.

Dorson, Richard M. (Mercer) (1916–81) folklorist, historian; born in New York City. A Harvard-educated academic, he taught after 1957 at the University of Indiana, where he founded the Folklore Institute (1963). He was instrumental in establishing folklore as a scholarly discipline by advancing fieldwork techniques, helping to establish academic programs, and developing scholarly approaches to American folklore. His many works include a pioneering textbook, *American Folklore* (1959).

Doubleday, Abner (1819–93) soldier; born in Ballston Spa, N.Y. A West Point graduate (1842), he fought in the Mexican War and against the Seminoles in Florida. He commanded the Federal troops that fired the first shot in defense of Fort Sumter as the Civil War commenced and then distinguished himself at the battle of Gettysburg. He retired from the army in 1873 and wrote many newspaper and magazine articles as well as two accounts of his war experiences, drawing on his 67 volumes of diaries. Although in nothing he wrote does he ever mention baseball, nor does his *New York Times* obituary, in 1908 a commission eager to establish American origins of baseball credited him with being its inventor on the basis of a dubious letter from one Abner Graves, who claimed to have been present in Cooperstown, N.Y., on the day in 1839 that Doubleday laid out the field and rules. Although the claim has long since been recognized as popular folklore – even by the Baseball Hall of Fame in Cooperstown – Doubleday remains synonymous with baseball to most Americans.

Doubleday, Frank Nelson (1862–1934) publisher; born in Brooklyn, N.Y. He rose in the ranks at Charles Scribner's Sons and in 1897, with Samuel S. McClure, founded Doubleday & McClure. An aggressive businessman, he attracted top authors; the firm, which he headed amid various partnership changes and mergers, became a top U.S. publishing company. He also started a chain of bookstores.

Doubleday, Neltje de Graff (1865–1918) naturalist, writer; born in Chicago. She married Frank N. Doubleday, the publisher, saw her first book in print in 1894, and went on to write several volumes of nature studies of flowers and birds, including *The American Flower Garden* (1909). Her work has been described as charming but lacking in scientific significance. Active in charitable work, she died in Canton, China, while on assignment for the American Red Cross.

Dougherty, Sara See under CARTER FAMILY.

Doughty, Thomas (1793–1856) painter; born in Philadelphia. Based in Philadelphia, he was a leather merchant until 1820, painted landscapes, and was associated with the Hudson River School. He is remembered for his treatment of light in paintings such as *In Nature's Wonderland* (1836).

Douglas, Donald (Wills), Sr. (1892–1981) aeronautical engineer/manufacturer; born in Brooklyn, New York. After graduating from the Massachusetts Institute of Technology (1912) and working for Glenn Martin as chief engineer, in 1920 he formed his own company. Building on the success of the twin engine D-3 (1936), Douglas Aircraft dominated domestic commercial air traffic until Boeing introduced the jetliner in 1958.

Douglas, James Henderson, Jr. (1899–1988) government official; born in Cedar Rapids, Iowa. A graduate of Princeton and Harvard Law School, he practiced law and was an investment banker before serving in Army Air Force administrative posts during World War II. As Air Force secretary in the second Eisenhower administration during the late 1950s, he helped establish the U.S. Air Force Academy at Colorado Springs, Colo. He also reaffirmed the guilty verdict in the 1925 court-martial of air power visionary William ("Billy") Mitchell.

Douglas, Jesse (1897–1965) mathematician; born in New York City. He taught at a number of American universities, including Columbia (1920–26), the Massachusetts Institute of Technology (1930–36), and New York City College (1955–65). Concentrating largely on geometry, his specialty was the problem of Plateau. He wrote over 50 papers on geometry and group theory.

Douglas, Lloyd C. (Cassel) (1877–1951) clergyman, writer; born in Columbia City, Ind. He was a Congregational minister and author of religious essays who turned to popular fiction in the 1920s. He wrote full-time after the early 1930s, living first in Los Angeles, then Las Vegas. His three major inspirational novels, *Magnificent Obsession* (1929), *The Robe* (1942), and *The Big Fisherman* (1948), sold millions of copies and were made into successful movies.

Douglas, Marjory Stoneman (1890–) author, conservationist; born in Minneapolis, Minn. She graduated from Wellesley College in 1912 and worked as a journalist and educator in Miami. Her book, *The Everglades: River of Grass* (1947), sounded an early warning of the environmental perils facing the Florida Everglades. She cofounded Friends of the Everglades in 1969 and is widely credited with helping to slow the destruction of the swamp ecosystem. She is also the author of several works of juvenile literature.

Douglas, Paul H. (Howard) (1892–1976) U.S. senator, economist; born in Salem, Mass. An economist, he taught at the University of Chicago, and studied wage theory before his election to the U.S. Senate (Dem., Ill; 1949–67). A liberal, he shaped much of the Civil Rights legislation of the 1960s, and was concerned with urban and housing issues. He returned to an academic career after leaving the Senate.

Douglas, Robert L. (1882–1979) basketball coach, promoter; born in St. Kitts, British West Indies. He was brought to the U.S.A. at age four, and although drawn to athletics as a youth, did not have the advantage of high school or college. In 1922, he organized the Renaissance Five, a basketball team composed entirely of African-Americans. Soon known as "the Rens," the team was based in New York City but spent most of the time on the road where it had to endure racial discrimination and outright antagonism; it inspired the formation of other all-black teams – including the Harlem Globetrotters – and gradually became one of the winningest teams ever, winning 2,318 games in their 22 years and taking the first World Tournament in Chicago in 1939. Douglas was legendary for his integrity and leadership and was elected to the Basketball Hall of Fame in 1971.

Douglas, Stephen A. (Arnold) (1813–61) U.S. representative/senator; born in Brandon, Vt. Admitted to the Illinois bar in 1834, after a distinguished career in state politics Douglas was elected to the U.S. House of Representatives (Dem., Ill.; 1843–47) and to the U.S. Senate (1847–61). Known as the "Little Giant" to his followers (because he was short and dynamic) he supported sectional compromise to avoid the threat of disunion in the 1850s. In the 1858 senatorial campaign, he debated Republican politician Abraham Lincoln seven times in what became known as the "Lincoln-Douglas debates." Although he won reelection to the Senate, his increasingly inconsistent positions on the slavery issue would cost him the support of many Democrats. In 1860, as the Northern Democrats' candidate for president, he was defeated by Lincoln. He at once called for support of Lincoln in his efforts to preserve the union, but, exhausted by his speaking tour, he died of typhoid fever less than two months after the Civil War began.

Douglas, William O. (Orville) (1898–1980) Supreme Court justice, author; born in Maine, Minn. He taught corporate law at Columbia University (1925–28) and Yale (1928–36), and published several business law casebooks before joining the Securities and Exchange Commission (1936–39). When he was appointed to the U.S. Supreme Court by President Franklin D. Roosevelt in 1939, he was considered a young nominee. He served an unprecedented 36½ years on the bench (1939–75) during which time he was considered a liberal justice with controversial opinions. He interpreted the courts' judiciary powers broadly and he vehemently defended civil liberties. He held absolutely to the freedoms espoused in the Bill of Rights, especially that of free speech. Drawing on his many travels, he penned some 30 books on legal matters and on nature and conservation; they include *Of Men and Mountains* (1950), *An Almanac of Liberty* (1954), *Democracy's Manifesto* (1962), and *A Wilderness Bill of Rights* (1965).

Douglass, Andrew Ellicott (1867–1962) astronomer; born in Windsor, Vt. A researcher at the Lowell Observatorry in Flagstaff (1894), he became a physics and astronomy professor at Arizona University (1906) and later directed the Stewart Observatory (1918–38). He investigated the relationship between sunspots and climate by examining the growth rings of ancient Arizona pine and sequoia and established the Laboratory of Tree Ring Research in 1937. He coined the term "dendrochronology" (tree-ring dating) in his *Climatic Cycles and Tree Growth* (3 vols. 1919–36), and it soon became an invaluable means for archaeologists to date prehistoric remains.

Douglass, Frederick (b. Frederick Augustus Washington Baily) (1817–95) abolitionist, author, public official; born near Tuckahoe, Md. Born into slavery (his father was white, his mother was part American Indian), he was taught to read as a household servant but at age 16 was sent out to work as a field hand. In 1836 he was apprenticed to a shipyard in Baltimore, Md., but he escaped in 1838 and settled in New Bedford, Mass., where he assumed the name by which he would thereafter be known. After he made a speech before the Massachusetts Anti-Slavery Society in 1841, he was hired as an agent and he lectured throughout the North; because his intelligence and speaking abilities led some to question whether he had been a slave, he published *Narrative of the Life of Frederick Douglass, an American Slave* in 1845. Then, fearing for his freedom, he fled to England where he lectured with such effect that the British contributed a generous sum of money that, added to money contributed by Americans, helped him buy his freedom when he returned to the U.S.A. in 1847. He went to Rochester, N.Y., where he cofounded (with Martin Delany) the abolitionist periodical *North Star,* which he edited for 16 years (in 1851 changing its name to *Frederick Douglass's Paper*). In 1859 he took refuge in Canada for a short time because he was falsely accused of aiding John Brown. He took a more gradualist approach to ending slavery but never wavered as the leading voice of African-Americans' call for freedom and equality. During the Civil War he urged President Lincoln to emancipate the slaves and he helped recruit African-American troops. After the Civil War, he also spoke out for other social reforms such as woman's suffrage. He also held a series of government posts – assistant secretary to the Santo Domingo Commission, marshal of the District of Columbia (1877–81), district recorder of deeds (1881–86), and ambassador to Haiti (1889–91). He issued a final revision of his autobiography as *Life and Times of Frederick Douglass* (1881).

Dove, Arthur (Garfield) (1880–1946) painter; born in Canandaigua, N.Y. He traveled in Europe (1907–09), and in

1910 had his first exhibit with Alfred Stieglitz. As an abstract painter, he used natural forms, which may be seen in his well-known painting, *Fog Horns* (1929). He also created collage constructions, such as his homage to his friend in *Portrait of Alfred Stieglitz* (1925).

Dove, Rita (1953–) poet; born in Akron, Ohio. She began writing verse as a youngster but only became serious about poetry while attending Miami University, Ohio. She studied a year in Germany (her husband, Fred Viebahn, was a German playwright/novelist), then earned an M.F.A. at the University of Iowa. She joined the English faculty at the University of Virginia (1989). Her poetry – such as the 1987 Pulitzer Prize-winning *Thomas and Beulah* – and her novels – such as *Through the Ivory Gate* (1992) – blend the lyrical and personal with the precise and the contemporary, and although she tended not to write explicitly about her African-Americanness, her work drew on that experience in subtle ways. In 1993 she became the first African-American poet laureate of the Library of Congress.

Dow, Henry (Herbert) (1866–1930) chemist, inventor, industrialist; born in Belleville, Ontario, Canada. He came to the U.S.A. with his family as an infant. He began experimenting with brines while a student at Case School of Applied Science (now part of Case Western Reserve University) in Cleveland, Ohio, and ultimately built a great chemical empire upon them. He invented a simple electrolytic method for extracting bromine from brine, and his use of a direct current generator in the process is regarded as the foundation of the electrochemical industry in the U.S.A. He established the Dow Chemical Company in 1897. The company produced bromine, used in medicines and dyes, and soon added chlorine, bleaching powder, insecticides, and pharmaceuticals to the product list. Dow later introduced the first process for making synthetic indigo and was the first to extract iodine from brine. During World War I, he served as a member of the advisory committee of the Council of National Defense.

Dow, Lorenzo (1777–1834) Protestant evangelist; born in Coventry, Conn. He began preaching in 1794 as an independent and later established a connection with the Methodists, for whom he evangelized in the southern U.S. In company with his wife, he made a notorious round trip from Boston to Natchez on the Mississippi River in 1807. He retired afterward to a farm in Connecticut, where he wrote contentious pamphlets and worked up accounts of his travels.

Dow, Neal (1804–97) temperance reformer; born in Portland, Maine. A businessman devoted to the temperance movement, he helped win passage in Maine of the first state prohibition law (1846), banning sale of alcohol by the drink. After being elected mayor of Portland (1851), he won passage of landmark state laws extending the ban to virtually all alcohol sales and providing imprisonment for offenders. A riot in Portland (1856) led to the repeal of prohibition, although Dow won passage of a milder law after being elected to the state legislature in 1858. In later life he toured the United States and Britain preaching prohibition; he ran for president in 1880 as candidate of the Prohibition Party.

Downes, (Edwin) Olin (1886–1955) music critic; born in Evanston, Ill. Writing for the *Boston Post* (1906–24) and *New York Times* (from 1924), Downes became one of the nation's most prominent critics.

Downey, Sheridan (1884–1961) U.S. senator; born in Laramie, Wyo. A lawyer, he began his political career as a Republican district attorney in Wyoming; then, having moved to California, he emerged as a liberal Democrat. Elected to the U.S. Senate (Dem., Calif.; 1939–50), he supported old age pension plans, restrictions on the military, land reclamation projects, and state control of offshore oil resources.

Downing, Andrew Jackson (1815–52) landscape gardener, horticulturist; born in Newburgh, N.Y. He learned horticulture in his family's nursery and would later write the standard text, *The Fruits and Fruit Trees of America* (1845). Before that, his views on designing both landscape and buildings – conveyed in *A Treatise on the Theory and Practice of Landscape Gardening* (1841) and in *Cottage Residences* (1842) – had become widely influential. He was editor of *The Horticulturist* (1846–52) which further promoted his views of improving properties. He himself was somewhat influenced by then current English ideas and he brought Calvert Vaux from England in 1850; together they designed various projects until Downing's untimely death in a steamboat disaster.

Downing, Major Jack See SMITH, SEBA.

Dows, David (1885–1961) businessman; born in Irvington, N.Y. From a wealthy family, he graduated from Yale (1908) and became a four-goal polo player at the Meadow Brook club. He worked at Naylor & Co., where he perfected two processing techniques for iron ore and supervised building plants in England, Italy, France, and Russia. During World War I he was captain of the 60th Field Artillery in France. For W. R. Grace Co., in 1918, he studied various industries in Paraguay, Chile, and Argentina. In 1931 he left business for politics and horse and cattle raising. He was elected sheriff of Nassau County, Long Island, and was a member of the New York State Racing Commission (1945–49).

Doyle, Sarah Elizabeth (1830–1922) feminist, educator; born in Providence, R.I. A 36-year Rhode Island high school teacher and principal, she helped found the coeducational Rhode Island School of Design (1877) and was instrumental in the mid-1890s in permanently funding Brown University's new Women's College.

Dozier, Edward (1916–71) Santa Clara Pueblo/Tewa anthropologist; born in New Mexico. After receiving a Ph.D. from the University of California: Los Angeles (1952), he specialized in studying Native Americans and the peoples of northern Luzon, Philippines. He wrote several books and articles, including *The Hopi Tewa of Arizona* (1954).

Drake, Charles (Lum) (1924–) geophysicist; born in Ridgewood, N.J. He taught at Columbia University (1955–65) before joining Dartmouth College (1967). He elucidated the impact of geosciences on critical energy resources, and advanced the study of plate tectonics with research on the earth's continental margins, crust, and upper mantle.

Drake, Daniel (1785–1852) physician, author; born near Plainfield, N.J. He studied medicine in Cincinnati, Ohio, and spent most of his life in practice and teaching there. He founded the Ohio Medical College in Cincinnati (1819) and served as its president on occasion. He is chiefly known for his two-volume encyclopedic work *A Systematic Treatise, Historical, Etiological and Practical, on the Principal Diseases of the Interior Valley of North America* (1850, 1854).

Drake, Edwin L. (Laurentine) (1819–80) oilman; born in

Greenville, N.Y. He worked a succession of jobs in the Midwest and East after leaving the family farm at age 19, ending up as a conductor for the New York & New Haven Railroad (1850–57). In the late 1850s he bought some stock in George Bissell's Pennsylvania Rock Oil Company, and in 1857 (taking advantage of his conductor's job to travel free) he traveled to see the land near Oil Creek (Titusville), Pa., where surface oil was being collected. Having observed the drilling of artesian wells in New York and Pennsylvania, he shared Bissell's idea of borrowing from that technology to drill for oil in Titusville. The Seneca Oil Company was formed with now "Colonel" Drake as president. He secured a lease and began experimenting in 1858, striking oil at 69 feet on August 27, 1859 – effectively the first true oil well. He neglected to patent his drilling invention, a pipe liner for the drill hole, and proved to be a poor businessman, losing all his savings to oil speculation in New York City (1863). He drifted for several years, then moved back to Pennsylvania in 1870, ill and impoverished. The citizens of Titusville collected some money for him and he was voted an annuity by the state legislature in 1876.

Drake, Frank (Donald) (1930–) astronomer; born in Chicago. His was the first organized search for extraterrestrial intelligence radio signals at the National Radio Astronomy Observatory in West Virginia (1958–63). While on the Cornell University faculty (1964–84), he also directed the world's largest radio telescope at Arecibo, Puerto Rico. At the University of California: Santa Cruz (1984), he displayed a stained-glass representation of the "Arecibo message" to extraterrestrials sent from Puerto Rico (1974).

Drake, (John Gibbs) St. Clair (1911–90) sociologist, cultural anthropologist; born in Suffolk, Va. Son of a West Indian immigrant who became a Baptist preacher, he graduated from Hampton Institute in 1931 and participated in Quaker peace and racial justice campaigns as a young man. With Horace Cayton, he coauthored *Black Metropolis* (1946), a landmark study of Chicago's south side ghetto. He taught at Dillard, Roosevelt, and Stanford Universities, advised leaders of newly independent African nations, and helped develop training programs for Africa-bound Peace Corps volunteers.

Draper, Charles Stark (1901–87) engineer, inventor; born in Windsor, Mo. A generalist with degrees from Stanford, Harvard, and the Massachusetts Institute of Technology (MIT), he became head of MIT's instrumentation laboratory in 1939. There he developed gyroscopes for weapons systems and, eventually, guidance systems for missiles and spacecraft, including the Apollo moon project.

Draper, Dorothy (1889–1969) interior decorator; born in Tuxedo Park, N.Y. Starting her own company in 1925, she created flamboyant neo-baroque hotel and restaurant interiors, and wrote a syndicated newspaper column.

Draper, John William (1811–82) chemist; born in St. Helens, Lancashire, England. He emigrated to Virginia in 1832. He was a pioneer in photography as early as 1837 and was the second American to make a photographic portrait (1839); that of his sister (1840) may be the oldest extant portrait. In 1850, he took the first microphotographs. He made major contributions to the study of chemical effects of radiant energy. He was affiliated with New York University (1839–82); at its School of Medicine, he granted some of the first Ph.D.s in the U.S.A. (1867–72).

Draper, Lyman Copeland (1815–91) historical scholar, librarian; born in Hamburg, N.Y. He interviewed surviving Western pioneers and collected materials illuminating their history, leaving his voluminous notes and acquisitions to the Wisconsin Historical Society, of which he was the longtime secretary (1854–86). He founded and was first editor of *Wisconsin Historical Collections.*

Dreier, Katherine (Sophie) (1877–1952) painter, patron; born in Milford, Conn. She, Marcel Duchamp, and Man Ray founded the New York City based Société Anonyme (1920), and she became a famous promoter and patron of modern artists. The society was significant in that it had the first public collection of modern art in America, and it became a model for the Museum of Modern Art in 1929. As a painter, Dreier had a dynamic style, as seen in her most important work, *Abstract Portrait of Marcel Duchamp* (1918).

Dreier, Mary Elisabeth (1875–1963) labor reformer, suffragist; born in Brooklyn, N.Y. Privately educated, she devoted her life to improving working conditions for women. President of the New York Women's Trade Union League (WTUL) (1906–14), she worked for National WTUL until its demise (1950). A vigorous political activist, she campaigned for suffrage, the Progressive Party, world peace, and nuclear disarmament.

Dreiser, Theodore (Herman Albert) (1871–1945) writer; born in Terre Haute, Ind. Raised in poverty and in a German-speaking environment, he left home for Chicago at age 16. After a period of odd jobs and a year at the University of Indiana he became a Midwestern newspaper reporter, and, in New York after 1894, a magazine feature writer. *Sister Carrie* (1900), his first and still highly regarded novel, was withheld from general distribution because of its supposed amorality; its commercial failure plunged him into financial distress and mental breakdown (1904). He reestablished himself as a magazine editor, however, and self-published a second, successful edition of *Sister Carrie* (1907). The success of the novel *Jennie Gerhardt* (1911) allowed him to write full time; *The Financier* (1912) and *The Titan* (1914) followed. These novels were ungainly in style but groundbreaking in their naturalism and critique of American capitalist society. The withdrawal from distribution, on moral grounds, of his autobiographical novel, *The Genius* (1915), ignited a national anticensorship campaign supported by most of the leading literary figures of the day. His next decade, marked by an energetic output of plays, stories, memoirs, and travel books, culminated in *An American Tragedy* (1925), a major popular success despite its bleak view of American values. He publicly supported left-wing causes through the 1930s and 1940s and propounded socialist ideas in his late works, joining the Communist Party shortly before his death. He had also returned to writing novels, two of which – *The Bulwark* (1946) and *The Stoic* (1947) – were among his various works published posthumously. As insensitive in his treatment of the English language as he was of many women in his life, he seems destined to survive as a major American writer.

Dressler, Marie (b. Leila Koerber) (1869–1934) stage/film actress; born in Coburg, Canada. This versatile comic actress begin her career at age 14 with a touring theatrical company, and for many years she performed in vaudeville, plays, and musical productions, enjoying her greatest success with the song, "Heaven Will Protect the Working Girl." In 1910, she began a film career that went from Mack

Sennett comedies – including *Tillie's Punctured Romance* (1914) with Chaplin – to *Anna Christie* (1930) and *Min and Bill* (1931), for which she won an Oscar. Never very attractive and always on the plump side, she ended up as one of the most popular film stars of her day.

Drew, Charles (1904–50) medical researcher; born in Washington, D.C. He grew up in modest circumstances in a black ghetto, but his academic and athletic accomplishments gained him a scholarship to Amherst College. After graduation (1926), he taught and coached at Morgan College (now Morgan State) in Baltimore, Md., for two years before attending medical school at McGill University in Montreal. By the time he graduated (1932), he had decided to be a medical researcher, concentrating on the problems of blood transfusion. He had also decided to identify himself as an African-American, even though his light complexion, red hair, and facial features would have allowed him to "pass" as a white. After completing his residency in Montreal General Hospital (1935), he went to Howard University as an instructor, then took a two-year fellowship at Columbia University (1938–40) before returning to Howard as head of the department of surgery. Meanwhile, his research had succeeded, first in finding the best way to "bank" whole blood, and then to store only the plasma. In 1940–41 he went to New York City to head the Plasma for Britain program, so vital with World War II now underway. This led to his being appointed head of the U.S. National Blood Bank program (1941), but when he learned that only Caucasians' blood was wanted – and that any African-Americans' blood collected could be given only to other blacks – he publicly denounced this and quit, returning to Howard University. By 1944 he was appointed chief of staff of the Freedman's Hospital affiliated with Howard; as a result of his years at Howard, African-Americans increasingly came to be accepted in the medical profession. Greatly honored by now, he died prematurely in an automobile accident.

Drew, Daniel (1797–1879) capitalist; born in Carmel, N.Y. He moved rapidly from a successful cattle-driving business (1829) to competing against Cornelius Vanderbilt (1834) in the steamboat business, to opening the brokerage firm of Drew, Robinson & Company on Wall Street (1844). A millionaire, he earned a reputation for being unscrupulous during the "Erie War" with Cornelius Vanderbilt (1866–68) over control of the Erie Railroad and other stock and bank deals which brought ruin to thousands. In 1870 his former associates dealt against him and the panic of 1873 furthered his decline. Bankrupt, he became dependent on his son during his last years.

Drew, John (1827–62) actor, comedian; born in Dublin, Ireland. He debuted in 1846 in New York, but most of his career and that of his wife, Louisa Lane Drew, centered on his repertory company at the Arch Street Theatre in Philadelphia.

Drew, Louisa Lane (1820–97) actress, theater manager; born in London, England. She came to the U.S.A. as a child. Known as a character actress, she managed the Arch Street Theatre in Philadelphia after the death of her husband, John Drew.

Drexel, Anthony Joseph (1826–93) banker; born in Philadelphia. He joined his father's banking house, Drexel & Company, in 1847 and helped the company expand rapidly after the death of his father, Francis Martin Drexel (1792–

1863). When Anthony's brother died in 1885, he took over the firm, which continued to prosper and expand. He dabbled in real estate and publishing. A philanthropist, his largest gift established the Drexel Institute at Philadelphia (1892) to promote industrial education.

Drexel, Mother Katharine Mary (1858–1955) Catholic religious foundress; born in Philadelphia. Inheriting a fortune from her banker father, she used it lavishly to fund mission schools and churches for Indians and African-Americans. Entering a novitiate at the pope's urging, she founded her own order (1891), the Sisters of the Blessed Sacrament for Indians and Colored People, and directed it for over 40 years. She was beatified in 1988.

Dreyfuss, Barney (1865–1932) baseball executive; born in Freiburg, Germany. Son of an American citizen residing in Germany, he came to the U.S.A. in 1881. Working as a bookkeeper in a distillery in Paducah, Ky., he bought an interest in the Louisville baseball team, eventually prospering and moving on to acquire the Pittsburgh Pirates in 1900. He helped to establish the modern World Series by letting his Pirates play the new American League champions, the Boston Red Sox, in 1903. He owned the Pirates until his death.

Dreyfuss, Henry (1903–72) industrial designer, author; born in New York City. After designing for the stage, he opened his own industrial design firm (1929). Pioneering in anthropometrics and ergonomics, he made safety and utility rather than mere style central to his creations such as the model 300 Bell telephone (1930), the Twentieth Century Limited locomotive, Hoover appliances, RCA televisions and air conditioners, and Lockhead aircraft interiors. He wrote *Designing for People* (1955) and *The Measure of Man* (1960).

Driscoll, Alfred (Eastlake) (1902–75) governor; born in Pittsburgh, Pa. A Republican lawyer, he served in the New Jersey senate (1939–41), focusing on social legislation. As governor (1947–54), he instituted constitutional reforms, including a bill of rights, and levied monies to create the New Jersey Turnpike. President of Warner Lambert Pharmaceuticals (1954–67), he later chaired the New Jersey Turnpike Authority (1970–75).

Drucker, Peter (Ferdinand) (1909–) writer, management consultant; born in Vienna, Austria. He emigrated to the U.S.A. in 1937. He had a varied early career as an economist, journalist, and philosophy professor before settling into a career teaching management and social sciences (New York University (1950–71), the Drucker School of Management (Claremont, Calif.) (1971)) and consulting to major corporations. He wrote prolifically on a wide range of topics from social and political issues to business analysis. He is best known, however, for changing the teaching and practice of management and helping establish management as a professional discipline through his numerous books, articles, films, and audiocassettes, including *Practice of Management* (1954) and *Management: Tasks, Responsibilities, Practices* (1974). These reached a wide audience, and many of his ideas – business as the representative institution of industrial society, marketing as central to management's task, management by objectives as superior to management by control – have become commonplaces.

Druckman, Jacob (Raphael) (1928–) composer; born in Philadelphia. After studies at Juilliard and in Paris, he taught at Juilliard and Yale. He is best known for his colorful, rather tumultuous orchestral music in a modernist idiom.

Drum, Hugh (Aloysius) (1879–1951) soldier; born in Fort Brady, Mich. After obtaining a commission in 1898 in memory of his father, one of the few officers killed in action during the Spanish-American War, he fought in the Philippines (1889–1901). In World War I he played an important role as chief of staff of the American First Army. A new style manager/soldier, he excelled in staff and administrative assignments during the ensuing years, but was passed over for army chief of staff in 1939 in favor of George C. Marshall. He commanded home front units until his retirement in 1943, when he became president of the Empire State Corporation.

Dryden, Hugh (Latimer) (1898–1966) physicist, NASA administrator; born in Pocomoke City, Md. Known for his scientific contributions to fluid mechanics and boundary layer phenomena, he became director of research for the National Advisory Committee for Aeronautics (1947–58). He gained wide recognition as the first deputy administrator of the National Aeronautics and Space Administration (NASA) (1958–65). He was consultant to the Science Advisory Committee to President Johnson (1965) and a contributor to many technical journals.

Dryden, John Fairfield (1839–1911) insurance executive, U.S. senator; born near Farmington, Maine. Forced from Yale by ill health, he settled in Newark, N.J., in 1873. In 1875 he wrote the first policy of his new firm, the Prudential Friendly Society (named the Prudential Insurance Company in 1878). He became president of the company in 1881 and pioneered in writing industrial policies. In 1902 he was chosen for the U.S. Senate (Rep., N.J.; 1902–07) but ill health prevented him from pursuing reelection.

Dryer, Charles (Redway) (1850–1927) geographer; born in Victor, N.Y. He practiced medicine and taught biology and physical science before teaching geology and geography at the Indiana State Normal School (Terre Haute) (1893–1913). A charter member of the Association of American Geographers, he urged the humanizing of geography and was a keen exponent of the regional concept.

Drysdale, (Donald Scott) Don (1936–93) baseball pitcher; born in Van Nuys, Calif. A ferocious competitor, the tall right-hander won 209 games in 14 seasons with the Brooklyn and Los Angeles Dodgers (1956–69). Nicknamed, "Big D," he became a television broadcaster after retiring from the game. In 1984 he was elected to baseball's Hall of Fame.

Duane, William (1760–1835) journalist; born near Lake Champlain, N.Y. After living in Ireland, where he learned printing, and in India, where he founded an outspoken paper that led to his being deported, he joined Benjamin Franklin Bache's vituperatively anti-Federalist *Aurora,* which he edited from 1798 to 1822. Tried and acquitted of sedition in 1799, he was charged a second time, but the charges were dropped after Thomas Jefferson's election in 1800.

Duane, William (1872–1935) physicist; born in Philadelphia. He taught at Harvard (1893–97) and the University of Colorado (1898–1907), then became a researcher at the Curie Radium Laboratory, Paris, before returning to Harvard (1913–34). A pioneer in biophysics, he made major contributions to the use of X-rays in treating cancer.

Dubinsky, David (b. Dobnievski) (1892–1982) labor leader; born in Brest Litovsk, Russia. Beginning his labor activism in Russia, for which he was exiled to Siberia, he escaped and emigrated to the United States in 1911. He joined the International Ladies' Garment Workers' Union (ILGWU) in New York as a cloak cutter and was elected its president (1932–66). He served as labor adviser to the National Recovery Administration (1933–35). Under his leadership the ILGWU became one of the most successful unions in America – financially solid yet honest, powerful but personal, progressive yet anti-communist. An early supporter of the Congress of Industrial Organizations (CIO), he led the ILGWU back into the American Federation of Labor (AFL) in 1940. When the AFL and the CIO merged (1955) he became a member of the new executive council and then a vice-president of the AFL-CIO. He was active in the international labor movement, representing the AFL at the International Labor Organization and in the UN Economic and Social Council. He also played an active role in areas outside unions, helping to form the American Labor Party (1936), the Liberal Party (1944), and Americans for Democratic Action (1947).

Dublin, Louis Israel (1882–1969) health statistician; born in Kovno, Lithuania. His family emigrated to New York (1886). He turned a zest for biology and mathematics into a career as an actuary at the Metropolitan Life Insurance Company (1909–51). He influenced the keeping of accurate birth and death statistics across the country and wrote prolifically, including a once-popular book on suicides, *To Be or Not To Be* (1933).

DuBois, Cora (1903–) cultural anthropologist; born in New York City. A Barnard College graduate, she received a Ph.D. from the University of California; Berkeley in 1932 and studied the Indian tribes of northern California and Oregon while teaching at Berkeley. Fieldwork in Indonesia in the late 1930s led to her landmark culture and personality study, *The People of Alor* (1944). She was director of research for the Institute of International Education from 1951–54 and taught at Radcliffe from 1954–69.

du Bois, Guy Pène (1884–1958) painter; born in Brooklyn, N.Y. He studied with William Chase and Robert Henri in New York (1905). Beginning as a member of the Ashcan school of painting, which stressed social realism, he later changed his style. This more elegant and satirical approach may be seen in *The Opera Box* (1926).

Dubois, John (1764–1842) Catholic prelate; born in Paris, France. Ordained in 1787, he emigrated to the U.S.A. during the French Revolution, ministered to widely scattered Catholics in Virginia, and founded Mount St. Mary's Seminary in Emmitsburg, Md. (1809), a training ground for early Catholic church leaders. He also helped establish and guide the Sisters of Charity, founded by Mother Seton. In 1826 he became the third bishop of New York.

Du Bois, W. E. B. (William Edward Burghardt) (1868–1963) editor, historian, sociologist, political activist, author; born in Great Barrington, Mass. Supported by the local school headmaster and the Congregational Church in Great Barrington, he was educated at Fisk University (1885–88), where he was shocked by the racial segregation he experienced in the South. He went on to take a Ph.D. at Harvard (1895), with two years at the University of Berlin (1892–94). Under the auspices of the University of Pennsylvania, he studied black life in the Philadelphia ghetto, writing *The Philadelphia Negro* (1899). A professor of economics, history, and sociology at Atlanta University (1898–1910), he sponsored an annual conference for the Study of the Negro Problem and wrote essays, compiled in *The Soul of Black Folk* (1903), calling for an activist African-American middle class to change racial politics. Founding the Niagara Movement (1905) to fight segregation, he also organized its official magazine, *Horizon: A Journal of the Color Line* (1907–10). He resigned from teaching (1910) to serve as director of publications and research for the National Association for the Advancement of Colored People (NAACP) in New York, editing *Crisis: A Record of the Darker Races* (1910–34), a magazine that was credited with encouraging many early civil rights activists. However, when he argued that African-Americans should voluntarily segregate themselves to organize economically during the Great Depression of the 1930s, he alienated the NAACP leadership, so he resigned in 1934. He returned to Atlanta University to chair the sociology department (1934–44), where he founded a scholarly journal, *Phylon: A Review of Race and Culture* (1940–44), and completed his autobiography, *Dusk of Dawn* (1940). Forced to retire at age 76, he returned to the NAACP, serving as director of special research (1944–48), leaving when his Marxist politics became a liability. Chairman of the Peace Information Center, an antinuclear weapons group, he was indicted as a foreign agent in 1951 and although acquitted, his passport was revoked (1952–58). He later toured Europe, China, and the Soviet Union, where he received the Lenin Peace Prize (1959). After joining the Communist Party (1961), he moved to Accra, Ghana, becoming a naturalized citizen just before he died.

Dubos, René J. (Jules) (1901–82) bacteriologist, author; born in Saint-Brice, France. He came to the U.S.A. in 1924, and spent his career at Rockefeller University (1927–71), except for two years at Harvard (1942–44). He expanded his original studies of soil bacteria to include investigations of bacterial enzymes and toxins, infectious diseases, and the relationship between microbes and other life on earth. In 1939 he isolated tyrothricin, the first commercially-produced antibiotic. A prolific author of both scientific and popular books, his *Bacterial and Mycotic Infections of Man* (1948) became a much-reprinted text. In 1969 Dubos won the Pulitzer Prize for *So Human an Animal* (1968).

Dubourg, Louis William (Valentine) (1766–1833) missionary bishop; born in Santo Domingo. After studying and teaching in France, where he was ordained a Sulpician (1788), he came to America (1794) where he became president of Georgetown College (1796–99) and superior of the Sisters of Charity. As bishop of Louisiana (from 1815) he played a key role in the infancy of American Catholicism. He returned to France in 1826.

Duchamp, Marcel (1887–1968) artist; born in Blainville, France (brother of Raymond Duchamp-Villon and half brother of Jacques Villon). He became famous by exhibiting *Nude Descending a Staircase, No. 2* (1912) at the New York Armory Show (1913), and by being a founder of the Société Anonyme, New York (1920), an organization promoting nonobjective art. An intermittent visitor to New York, he led the American Dada movement that tried to convey the absurdity of life. He was also among the first to use mobile works and found (junk) objects. His glass, wire, and painted foil construction, *The Bride Stripped Bare by Her Bachelors, Even* (1915–23), was one of his last major works; he virtually

abandoned art in his final decades and concentrated on playing chess. One of his most famous pieces was *L.H.O.O.Q,* a reproduction of Leonardo's *Mona Lisa* to which he added a moustache and goatee. He became a U.S. citizen in 1955.

Duchesne, Rose Philippine (1769–1862) Catholic religious foundress and saint; born in Grenoble, France. A member of the Order of the Sacred Heart, she emigrated to the U.S.A. (1818) hoping to work among the Indians. Instead her group was sent to Missouri, where she founded Catholic orphanages and schools. In 1841 she was allowed to spend a year among the Potowatami Indians, who called her "the woman who always prays." Known for her austerity and zeal, she was beatified in 1940 and canonized in 1988.

Duckert, Audrey R. (Rosalind) (1927–) linguist, lexicographer; born in Cottage Grove, Wis. A professor of English at the University of Massachusetts (1959), her fields of concentration include regional English, American dialects, and place names.

Duckworth, Ruth (b. Windmuller) (1919–) ceramist; born in Hamburg, Germany. She came to the University of Chicago in 1964 to teach ceramics. Her work ranged from delicate porcelain forms, to large roughly textured pots, to massive stoneware murals.

Dudley, Joseph (1647–1720) colonial governor; born in Roxbury, Mass. (son of Thomas Dudley). He served as temporary governor of Massachusetts (1686) and became notorious for upholding the policies of King James II. He served as Massachusetts governor (1702–15) and came into severe conflict with the General Court. A true imperial thinker, he sought to serve the British-speaking world, not just his own colony.

Dudley, Thomas (1576–1653) colonial governor; born in Northampton, England. He served as Massachusetts Bay governor for four terms and was deputy-governor thirteen times. He was present and active in nearly all of the important actions undertaken by the colony (including the creation of Harvard College).

Duer, William (1747–99) merchant, financier; born in Devonshire, England. He came to New York City in 1773–74 and quickly became an ardent patriot and prosperous merchant. He was a delegate to the Continental Congress (1777–79) and thwarted the Conway Cabal conspiracy in 1778. He was briefly assistant secretary of the U.S. Treasury (1789–90). Often involved in financial and land speculations, he was imprisoned for debt (1792–99, except for a short period in 1797), an event that brought about the first financial panic in New York's history.

Duerk, Alene (Bertha) (1920–) naval officer; born in Defiance, Ohio. She served as a naval nurse during World War II and the Korean War. She became a captain (1967), director of the Navy Nurse Corps (1970), and the first woman admiral (1972).

Duesenberg, (Frederick Samuel) Fred (1877–1932) car manufacturer; born in Lippe, Germany. He came to Iowa in 1885 and manufactured bicycles during the 1890s; he also raced bicycles and competed on them against horses. He patented an efficient gasoline motor (1899), improved upon it, and patented it again (1913) with his brother, August S. Duesenberg. Fred established the Mason Motor Company (1905). The Duesenberg motor was used in racers, called Duesenbergs. Starting in 1914, his cars won three 500-mile victories in the Indianapolis Speedway. The Duesenberg Motor Corporation was incorporated (1917); Fred was the chief engineer. He died from injuries sustained when his car overturned.

Duffy, (Bernard Cornelius) Ben (1902–72) advertising executive; born in New York City. A media specialist, he spent his 43-year advertising career at BBDO, New York City, the advertising agency that as president (1946–56), he led through a period of major growth. He wrote the long-standard *Advertising Media and Markets* (1939, many times revised) and directed publicity for Eisenhower's presidential campaigns.

Duffy, Clinton T. (1898–1982) penologist; born in San Quentin Prison, San Francisco. Inspiration for the movie *Duffy of San Quentin,* he was the son of a San Quentin guard; born and raised within the prison gates, he became warden (1940–52). Known for his humanitarian reforms, he abolished airless cells and physical punishment, fired guards for cruelty, and introduced a night school, a cafeteria, and a prison newspaper. He campaigned ceaselessly against the death penalty. Author of several books, his work was widely imitated by other penologists.

Duffy, Francis P. (Patrick) (1871–1932) Catholic chaplain; born in Ontario, Canada. A progressive-minded theology professor at St. Joseph's Seminary in Yonkers, N.Y. (1898–1912), and longtime New York City pastor, he earned fame for heroism in World War I as chaplain in France to the 69th Regiment of the New York National Guard. A memorial to him was erected in New York's Times Square.

Duffy, Hugh (1866–1954) baseball player; born in Cranston, R.I. During his 17-year career as an outfielder (1888–1906), mostly with the Boston Nationals, he posted a lifetime batting average of .328. He established the major league record for the highest batting average in a season (.438) in 1894. He was elected to baseball's Hall of Fame in 1945.

Dukakis, Michael (Stanley) (1933–) governor; born in Brookline, Mass. An army veteran (1956–58) and lawyer, he served in the Massachusetts House of Representatives (Dem., 1963–71). As governor (1975–79, 1983–91), he initially reduced the budget deficit and attracted business to Massachusetts, but the recession of the late 1980s left the state in a financial crisis. Resoundingly defeated by George Bush in the 1988 presidential campaign, he retired from politics in 1991 to practice law and lecture on government at various universities.

Duke, James (Buchanan) (1856–1925) businessman, philanthropist; born near Durham, N.C. He grew leaf tobacco on his father's farm and saved his family from post-Civil War poverty. He turned to manufacturing cigarettes in 1881 and opened a branch factory in New York City in 1884. He formed the American Tobacco Company in 1890 and competed with the British Imperial Tobacco Company. He also founded the Southern Power Company (1905) to develop hydroelectric power. In 1924 he put his fortune into a trust to be given to various charitable and educational institutions, in particular to Trinity College (North Carolina), which was re-named Duke University.

Duke, Vernon (b. Vladimir Alexandrovich Dulkelsky) (1903–69) composer; born in Russia. Trained at the Kiev Conservatory, he came to New York City, and, wanting to be a serious composer, wrote a piano concerto for Arthur Rubenstein in 1922. In Paris two years later he wrote a ballet

for Sergei Diaghilev and from 1926 to 1929 he wrote stage music in London. (From this point on he tended to use his original Russian name for his serious music and his adopted name for his more popular works.) Back in New York (he became a U.S. citizen in 1936) he became well-known for his stage and film scores; his best-known song was probably "April in Paris" for the revue *Walk a Little Faster* (1932) while his best-known musical was *Cabin in the Sky* (1940). He continued to write his music in the classical forms and his concert music was promoted by Serge Koussevitzky.

Dukelsky, Vladimir See DUKE, VERNON.

Dulany, Daniel (1722–97) lawyer, public official; born in Annapolis, Md. Educated in England at Eton and Cambridge, he returned to Maryland in 1747 and established a thriving law practice. He served several terms in the Maryland assembly. He published a tract opposing the Stamp Act (1765), but remained loyal to Britain after 1776. U.S. officials confiscated his property in 1781, and he spent the remainder of his life in obscurity.

Dulbecco, Renato (1914–) virologist; born in Catanzaro, Italy. He performed research at Turin (1940–47), then came to the U.S.A. as a bacteriologist at the University of Indiana (1947–49), where he worked with his former Turin colleague Salvador Luria on bacterial viruses. He moved to the California Institute of Technology (1949–63) at the invitation of Max Delbrück, under whose direction Dulbecco conducted research on polioviruses that contributed to the development of a polio vaccine. In the early 1950s he began studies of mammalian tumor viruses. His discoveries of virus-induced cell transformation led to the discovery of the enzyme RNA transcriptase by his students Howard Temin and David Baltimore. Dulbecco shared the 1975 Nobel Prize in physiology with Temin and Baltimore for his contribution to the study of cellular changes due to cancer-inducing viruses. Dulbecco joined the Salk Institute for Biological Studies (1963–72), relocated to London to the Imperial Cancer Research Fund (1972–77), became a professor at the University of California: San Diego (1977–81), then returned to the Salk Institute (1977), of which he became president (1988).

Dulles, Allen (Welsh) (1893–1969) diplomat, public official; born in Watertown, N.Y. (brother of John Foster Dulles). After serving in the U.S. Foreign Service (1916–26), he became a lawyer. In 1947 he assisted drawing up the legislation establishing the Central Intelligence Agency (CIA); he became its first civilian director (1953–61). Responsible for several notorious covert operations, he was forced to resign after the failure at Cuba's Bay of Pigs. He served on the Warren Commission (1963–64) investigating President Kennedy's assassination.

Dulles, John Foster (1888–1959) lawyer, diplomat, public official; born in Washington, D.C. (brother of Allen Dulles). A prominent international lawyer, he became President Eisenhower's secretary of state (1953–59). Advocating "Christian" ideals, he was the principal architect of cold war anti-Soviet/Chinese foreign policy. He strengthened NATO, established the Southeast Asia Treaty Organization (SEATO), and authored the "massive retaliation" nuclear weapons policy and "brink of war" diplomacy strategies to "contain" what he considered the moral evil of communism.

Dull Knife (b. Wahiev, also Tamela Pashme) (?1810–?83)

Northern Cheyenne war chief; born near the Rosebud River in present-day Montana. At first friendly to the whites, he turned to war following the Sand Creek (Colo.) massacre (1864). After his people were forced from their homeland into the Indian Territory (1870s), he led a dwindling group on an epic and ultimately successful journey back to the north country.

Dummer, Jeremiah (1645–1718) silversmith, engraver, painter; born in Newbury, Mass. Known as the first American-born silversmith, he completed a Boston apprenticeship with John Hull and went on to make some of the finest silver pieces of his time. He is said to have introduced the ornamentation known as gadrooning, curved flutings cut on the surface of silver.

DuMont, Allen B. (Balcom) (1901–66) electrical engineer, inventor, manufacturer, broadcaster; born in New York City. After working as an electrical engineer for Westinghouse Lamp Company (1924–28) and the DeForest Radio Company (1928–31), he set up a laboratory in his home and developed a cathode-ray tube that was used to tune radio receivers. He incorporated the DuMont Laboratories in 1934 and made cathode-ray oscilloscopes, and he was involved in early experimental telecasts (1941). After World War II he set up a small television network and fostered much of the industry's early programming and business talent; it was incorporated as the Metropolitan Broadcasting Company in 1959, later known as Metromedia. His television assembly plants were the first to make all-electronic television sets.

Dumont, Margaret (b. Margaret Baker) (1889–1965) movie actress; born in Brooklyn, N.Y. She began her career as a singer and became a regular player with the Marx Brothers in stage comedies of the 1920s. As the classic "straight" foil to their antics, she appeared in seven Marx Brothers movies, including *The Cocoanuts* (1929), *Animal Crackers* (1930), and *Duck Soup* (1933). She also appeared in several film comedies of W. C. Fields, Laurel and Hardy, and Jack Benny. Her last movie was *What a Way to Go!* (1964).

Dun, R. G. (Robert Graham) (1826–1900) businessman; born in Chillicothe, Ohio. In 1850 he joined the office of Tappan & Douglass, the first mercantile agency in New York City, and he became partner in 1854. By 1861 he was sole owner of R. G. Dun & Company, a credit-rating agency that had domestic branches in several cities. After the war his offices were the first to use typewriters and other print information innovations. In 1893 he instituted *Dun's Review,* a weekly overview of international business conditions. Later Dun's firm merged to form Dun & Bradstreet, a major business credit-rating and financial services publishing company.

Dunbar, Helen Flanders (1902–59) psychoanalyst; born in Chicago. She received the M.D. at Yale University in 1930, then taught and conducted research at Columbia University (1931–39). She made major contributions to psychosomatic theory and holistic medicine and was an instructor at the New York Psychoanalytic Institute (1941–49). A practicing clinician, she wrote four books, including *Psychiatry in the Medical Specialties* (1959).

Dunbar, Paul Lawrence (1872–1906) poet, writer; born in Dayton, Ohio. The son of former slaves, he attended public schools, worked as an elevator operator (1891–93), and spent most of his life in Dayton. He paid to publish his first book of poems, *Oak and Ivory* (1893), but his second book, *Majors and Minors* (1895), gained him the enthusiastic support of William Dean Howells, who wrote a preface to his third volume, *Lyrics of Lowly Life* (1896). This led to a public for his readings and lectures, which even took him to England (1897). He continued to publish various collections of poetry, short stories, and novels, and was widely recognized as one of the first African-Americans to convert the experiences of their people into forms appreciated by the white majority.

Dunbar, William (1749–1810) planter, scientist; born near Elgin, Scotland. He came to western Florida (1773) and built a plantation near Natchez, Miss. A correspondent of Thomas Jefferson, and the first surveyor general of his area, he undertook explorations of the Ouachita and Red River areas (1804–05) in present-day Texas, Arkansas, and Louisiana.

Duncan, David Douglas (1916–) photographer, author; born in Kansas City, Mo. After graduating from the University of Miami (Fla.) (1938), he became a photojournalist and then spent some years abroad. During World War II he served with the U.S. Marines as a combat photographer (1943–46), then joined *Life* magazine as a staff photographer (1946–56); he became especially well known for his powerful pictures of soldiers in combat during the Korean War and published in his book, *This is War!* (1951). He also worked on assignments in Israel, Greece, and Indochina. In 1966 he became a free-lance photographer and worked throughout the world; from 1967 to 1968 he was in Vietnam as a photo-correspondent for ABC-TV. A man of broad interests and friendships, he was particularly close to Pablo Picasso, the subject of six of Duncan's books.

Duncan, Isadora (1878–1927) dancer; born in San Francisco. Her parents were divorced shortly after her birth and she was raised by her poor but romantic mother, who filled her children with the sounds of music and notions of unconventionality. Isadora showed an early talent for dance and by age ten left school to teach dancing. She soon began to dance in public and in 1896 she went with her mother to New York City where she joined Augustin Daly's theater company as a dancer and actress. She disliked doing traditional dances, so in 1898 she began to perform her own free-style dances. In 1900 she made her debut in London, where she became interested in recreating what she perceived as the ancient Greek dances. By 1902 she was performing her own dances on the Continent to great acclaim. She also started a dance school in Berlin, tried to start a "Temple to the Dance" in Greece (1903–04), had a child by Gordon Craig, the British stage designer, and performed in Russia (1905, 1907, 1908). Wherever she went she gave lecture-demonstrations of what she called "the dance of the future," based on her improvised movements intended to unite music, poetry, and nature; she usually performed barefoot in revealing Greek tunics and with flowing scarves. Her American tour in 1908 was not successful but she went back to Europe and more acclaim. She also had another child, this one by Paris Singer, heir to the sewing machine fortune; when both her children drowned while in a car that accidentally rolled into the Seine (1913), her life not unnaturally became even more erratic although she showed a new profundity in her dances. In the following years she moved about – to the U.S.A., South America, San Francisco, Athens (Greece) – dancing and teaching with mixed success, and in 1921–22 she tried to start a school in Moscow. She married the much younger Russian poet, Sergei Essenin in 1922; mentally unstable, he drank his way through her money; her U.S. tour in 1923 led to charges of her being a Bolshevik, and they fled back to Russia with no money; Essenin deserted her in 1924 and committed suicide in 1925. Her school for young dancers had been taken over by others and she was penniless, so she went to France, where she gave one legendary final performance in Paris and wrote her autobiography, *My Life* (1927). She died in Nice, France, as dramatically as she had lived, when her long scarf caught in the spokes of a car wheel, breaking her neck. Although her influence on dance and the arts is debated, to some in her day and since she seemed one of the greatest spirits who had ever lived.

Duncan, Otis D. (Dudley) (1921–) sociologist; born in Nocona, Texas. He taught at the Universities of Chicago (1951–62), Michigan (1962–73), Arizona (1973–83), and California: Santa Barbara (1983–87). He collaborated regularly with his wife Beverly Duncan. His many works on population, demographics, and urban sociology include *The American Occupational Structure* (coauthored, 1967) and *Notes on Social Measurement* (1984).

Duncan, Robert (Edward) (b. Edward Howard Duncan) (1919–88) poet, writer; born in Oakland, Calif. Adopted when young, and given the name Robert Edward Symmes, he assumed his new name in 1941. He studied at the University of California: Berkeley (1936–38; 1948–50), taught at Black Mountain College (1956–57), and became associated with the San Francisco Bay area group of poets, as seen in *The Opening of the Field* (1960). He was also an editor, playwright, and artist.

Duncan, Robert Kennedy (1868–1914) chemist, writer; born in Brantford, Ontario, Canada. He came to the United States about 1892. After a period of teaching, he was sent to Paris by a magazine to report on the Curies' work (1901). He became a popular interpreter of science. In 1906, he decided to devote himself to the creation of a system of industrial fellowships at universities (notably at the University of Pittsburgh with help from the Mellon family) to mesh academia with the needs of industry.

Duncanson, Robert (Scott) (?1817/22–72) painter; born in Seneca County, N.Y. He was based in Cincinnati, Ohio, and is considered the first internationally acclaimed African-American artist. His luminous landscape, *Blue Hole, Flood Waters, Little Miami River* (1851), reveals his talent.

Dundes, Alan (1934–) anthropologist, folklorist; born in New York City. An Indiana University Ph.D., he joined the University of California: Berkeley faculty in 1963. His first book, *The Morphology of North American Indian Folktales* (1964) was followed by important work on the history and (mostly psychoanalytic) interpretation of diverse folklore from Cinderella and sick jokes to corporate folklore and the Flood.

Dunglison, Robley (1798–1869) physiologist, medical educator, author; born in Keswick, England. After he had made a reputation in medical circles in Europe, President Thomas Jefferson invited him to teach at the University of Virginia in 1825. In 1833 he went to the University of Maryland and he then joined the faculty of the Jefferson Medical College, Philadelphia (1836–68). His books include *Human Physiology* (1832) and *A New Dictionary of Medical Science and Literature* (1833).

Dunham, Ethel Collins (1882–1969) pediatrician; born in Hartford, Conn. A problem solver, organizer, and effective mediator, her main contribution was the establishment of nationwide standards for the care of newborns and premature infants (1948). Besides teaching at Yale University's Medical School (1924–35), she conducted landmark studies for both the United States Children's Bureau and the American Pediatric Society.

Dunham, Katherine (1912–) modern dancer, choreographer; born in Chicago, Ill. A University of Chicago graduate who went on to earn a doctorate in anthropology, she started her first school in Chicago (1931), later becoming dance director for the Works Progress Administration's Chicago theater project. A flamboyant performer, she is best known for her choreography in musicals like *Cabin in the Sky* (1940) and motion pictures, notably *Stormy Weather* (1943). She studied dance forms in the Caribbean, especially Haiti, where she lived for several years; she toured with her company during the 1940s, 1950s, and into the 1960s. In 1967 she founded a performing arts center for inner-city youths in East St. Louis, Ill. She went on a hunger strike in 1992 to protest the American deportation of Haitian refugees.

Duniway, Abigail Jane (b. Scott) (1834–1915) suffragist; born near Groveland, Ill. She moved with her family to Oregon (1852) and taught school briefly. She married a farmer in 1853 but in 1863 her husband was injured and became an invalid. She supported their six children as a teacher and by running a millinery shop and became keenly aware of inequality between the sexes. She organized the Equal Rights Society in Oregon (1870) and, with the help of her six children, published the weekly newspaper *The New Northwest* (1871–87) and continued to work for women's rights. She drafted the resolution that gave the vote to women in Washington Territory (1883) and was instrumental in winning the suffrage in Idaho (1896), the state of Washington (1910), and Oregon (1912). In her day she was noted for disagreeing with many other national leaders over linking the women's right to vote with other reforms such as the prohibition of alcohol. In addition to her account of the suffrage movement in the Northwest (1914), she published two novels and poetry.

Dunlap, William (1766–1839) painter, playwright, theater manager; born in Perth Amboy, N.J. He began as a painter and went to London (1748) to study with Benjamin West, but on his return (c. 1787) he took up writing gothic romances, such as *The Father* (1789) and *Fountainville Abbey* (1795). He then was attracted to the theater, and in the ensuing decades he wrote or adapted some 56 plays (about half of which were translations or adaptations of Continental writers). From 1796–1805 he also served as proprietor and manager of the John Street and Park Theaters in New York City, where he produced many of his own plays, including *Andre* (1798), based on Major Andre's dealings with Benedict Arnold in the American Revolution. He worked to get the government to support the theater to help lift it from its commercialism and he tried to encourage indigenous American plays and actors over the prevailing Anglophile snobbery. For his many contributions, he would later become known as "the father of American drama," but when his theater work led to bankruptcy, he returned to painting; he gained a reputation with his portraits but he maintained his romantic approach in works such as *Count of Death* (1818). He also wrote several histories and biographies including the *Life of Charles Brockden Brown* (1815) and *History of the American Theatre* (1832). He was one of the founders of the National Academy of Design (1826) and wrote *History of the Arts of Design in the United States* (1834).

Dunlop, John Thomas (1914–) economist, labor arbitrator; born in Placerville, Calif. His primary interests were labor markets, wage systems, and industrial organizations. His teaching career at Harvard University was temporarily interrupted by his service on the National War Labor Board (1943–54) and as U.S. secretary of labor (1975–76).

Dunmore, John Murray, earl of (1732–1809) royal governor; born in Scotland. As Virginia governor (1771–76) he offended patriot sympathies by twice dissolving the House of Burgesses. He led a campaign against the Shawnee Indians (1774) which was called Lord Dunmore's War. In 1775 he tried unsuccessfully to oppose the patriot movement in Virginia.

Dunn, L. C. (Leslie Clarence) (1893–1974) geneticist; born in Buffalo, N.Y. He was a geneticist at the Agricultural Experiment Station, Storrs, Conn. (1920–28), and served there as a consultant (1930–74) after moving to Columbia University (1928–62). His research on chromosomal changes in mouse embryos led to major contributions to studies of the effects of recombination and lethal genes. His books on human population genetics express his belief that race is merely one state in human evolution.

Dunne, Finley Peter (1867–1936) journalist, humorist; born in Chicago. As a Chicago journalist he created the fictional Mr. Dooley (1892), a garrulous Irish barkeeper whose rogue – and brogue – commentaries on current events were nationally syndicated and reprinted in eight volumes (1898–1919). He moved to New York (1900) and was associated with *Collier's, American Magazine* and the socialist *Metropolitan* before retiring in 1927.

Du Ponceau, Peter Stephen (b. Pierre Étienne Du Ponceau) (1760–1844) lawyer, philologist, author; born at Saint Martin, Ile de Ré, France. Educated for the French priesthood, he decided it was not his vocation. His knowledge of English gained him the post of secretary to Baron von Steuben, whom he accompanied to America in 1771; with von Steuben's appointment as major general, Du Ponceau was made a captain and Steuben's aide-de-camp (1778–79). His health forced him to leave the army but he became under secretary of foreign affairs (1781–83). After studying the law for two years (1783–85), he practiced international law in Philadelphia; his command of European languages plus his cosmopolitan background soon made him much in demand in this field. In his later decades, he published works on a variety of legal, historical, and linguistic subjects. He became particularly well known for his studies of the languages of Native Americans.

du Pont, Alfred I. (Irénée) (1864–1935) industrialist; born near Wilmington, Del. (son of Eleuthère Irénée du Pont II). At age 20 he left the Massachusetts Institute of Technology to work at the family explosives firm. After studying a new European gunpowder for the U.S. Ordnance Department (1889), he won the contract for its American manufacture. With cousins Coleman and Pierre du Pont he bought E. I. du Pont de Nemours & Company, the Delaware-based family company, in 1902. As general and operating manager he designed new machinery, and among other advances, developed gunpowder for U.S. large-caliber guns. He was forced

out of the company after a family stock dispute in 1915; the family feud continued in later years as he sought to thwart his relatives' political careers. After World War I he founded Nemours Trading Corporation, an exporter of American goods to Europe that lost millions of dollars during the depression of the 1930s. Later business interests included ownership of the *Wilmington Morning News* (1911–20), Delaware and Florida banks, and real estate. Late in life he was a prominent advocate of social security.

du Pont, E. I. (Eleuthère Irénée) (1771–1834) manufacturer; born in Paris, France. He worked under the great Lavoisier at France's royal gunpowder works, and with his father, the publisher and economist Pierre Samuel du Pont de Nemours. E. I. and several in the family left France in the wake of the Revolution and settled in the U.S.A. in 1799. His father joined them and they had plans to develop land in western Virginia; on the advice of Thomas Jefferson, they instead established a commission house in New York City, but that proved unprofitable. An avid hunter, E. I. had noticed the poor quality and high price of American gunpowder; by 1802 he had established a powder works at a site along Brandywine Creek near Wilmington, Del., and with machinery imported from France the E. I. du Pont de Nemours & Company was selling gunpowder by 1804. The U.S. government was the major client and the War of 1812 firmly established the company. E. I. was a director of the Bank of the United States and was active in the American Colonization Society.

du Pont, Henry Francis (1880–1969) businessman, museum founder; born in Winterthur, Del. (son of Henry Algernon du Pont). He studied at Harvard (B.A. 1903), and became a director of the family chemical business, E. I. du Pont de Nemours & Co., Wilmington, Del. (1915–69). He is most noted for founding the Henry Francis du Pont Winterthur Museum (1951) that features displays of early American decorative arts, furniture, and horticultural gardens.

du Pont, Margaret Osborne (1918–) tennis player; born in Joseph, Ore. She won five French, seven Wimbledon, and an unprecedented 24 U.S. championships, in singles, doubles, and mixed doubles, between 1941 and 1962.

du Pont, Pierre S. (Samuel) (1870–1954) industrialist; born near Wilmington, Del. After graduating from the Massachusetts Institute of Technology, he joined his family's Delaware-based explosives company. Disenchanted with its lack of innovation, he left to join his cousin Coleman du Pont's street railway business (1899). In partnership with another cousin, Alfred du Pont, they purchased the family firm in 1902 to prevent its sale to outsiders. As treasurer he negotiated a series of takeovers and management and production reorganizations that concentrated the American explosives industry under du Pont's control. With his deputy, John Raskob, he developed new accounting practices (including financial forecasting and calculating rates of return on capital investment) that later became standard corporate practice. He led the buyout of Coleman du Pont's share in the firm in 1914 that provoked a generation-long family feud. He was president of the company through World War I (1915–19, chairman 1919–40), when it amassed large profits. He retired in 1919 but soon assumed management of the struggling General Motors (president 1920–23, chairman 1923–29), where he introduced modern management, production, and marketing techniques that saved the corporation. In retirement after 1929 he created the extensive gardens on his Longwood estate and devoted millions of dollars to the improvement of Delaware's public schools.

du Pont, Pierre Samuel, IV (1935–) governor, U.S. representative; born in Wilmington, Del. He served as technical representative for Du Pont Nemours & Company (1963–70), going to the U.S. House of Representatives (Rep., Del.; 1971–77). As governor of Delaware (1977–85), he promoted business development by relaxing banking and credit laws, and opposed capital punishment. He practiced law in Washington afterward.

du Pont, Samuel Francis (1830–65) naval officer; born in Bergen Point, N.J. (grandson of Pierre Samuel du Pont de Nemours). He commanded Commodore Robert Stockton's flagship in California operations during the Mexican War. In 1861 he became the commander or "flag-officer" of the South Atlantic blockading squadron. He led a successful fleet assault that captured Port Royal, South Carolina (1861). After failing to capture Charleston using the same methods, he turned over his command (1863). Du Pont Circle in Washington, D.C., is named for him.

du Pont, (Thomas) Coleman (1863–1930) capitalist, U.S. senator; born in Louisville, Ky. He started work in his father's Kentucky coal mines after graduating from the Massachusetts Institute of Technology and developed Central Coal & Iron Company into a major business. After a brief period managing a steel company, he bought a Pennsylvania street railway company and constructed and managed street railways. With his cousins, Alfred and Pierre du Pont, he purchased the family's Delaware-based explosives company and assumed its presidency (1902–15). He masterminded the takeover of some one hundred competitors and the reorganization of the business into a huge holding company, E. I. du Pont de Nemours Company of New Jersey. The company became the sole U.S. producer of military gunpowder and the country's dominant explosives manufacturer; in 1907 the government successfully sued du Pont for antitrust violations. Having sold his stake in the firm in 1914, he shifted his business interests to real estate, insurance, and hotels; he owned among other hotels, the McAlpin and Waldorf-Astoria in New York City and the Willard in Washington, D.C., and built the Equitable Life Building, New York, then the city's largest office building. He sat in the U.S. Senate (Rep., Del.; 1921–28).

Durand, Asher B. (Brown) (1796–1886) painter, engraver; born in Maplewood (then Jefferson Village), N.J. He was an engraving apprentice (1812), and later a partner (1817) of Peter Maverick, and engraved banknotes and received important commissions, such as the engraving of John Trumbull's painting, *Declaration of Independence* (1820). After 1835 he devoted himself to portraits, figure studies and, after study in Europe (1840–41), to landscapes. He was a founder of the Hudson River School and the National Academy of Design (1826). His most famous work is *Kindred Spirits* (1800), in which his two friends, Thomas Cole and the poet William Cullen Bryant, survey a romantic landscape.

Durand, William (Frederick) (1859–1958) educator, marine/ aeronautic engineer; born in Beacon Falls, Conn. He was an authority on the dynamics of ship and airplane propellers and developed ways of minimizing loss of propulsive efficiency. He taught engineering at Lafayette College, and

Cornell and Stanford Universities, retiring in 1924. He was an advisor on the Boulder and Grand Coulee Dam projects.

Durant, Ariel See under DURANT, (WILLIAM JAMES) WILL.

Durant, Henry (1802–75) college president; born in Acton, Mass. He left his Congregational ministry in Massachusetts for the California gold rush (1853). He prompted the chartering of the College of California (1855) and was one of its first faculty members; on its reorganization as the University of California (1870), he became its first president.

Durant, William C. (Crapo) (1861–1947) manufacturer; born in Boston, Mass. He was raised in Flint, Mich., where he left high school to work in his grandfather's lumberyard and various other jobs. In 1885 he organized the Flint Road Cart Company which became a leading manufacturer of horse-drawn carriages. In 1904 he invested in the failing Buick Motor Car Company, which he expanded to the General Motors Company (GMC) (chartered in New Jersey in 1908) by acquiring several firms such as Buick, Cadillac, and Oldsmobile, as well as parts manufacturers. GMC was taken over by a banking house in 1910 and Durant joined Louis Chevrolet to form the Chevrolet Motor Company (1911); its success enabled him to regain control of GMC as president in 1916. The company again ran into trouble under Durant's insistent involvement in all facets of the organization. In 1920 Pierre du Pont, president of General Motors, paid off Durant's debts in return for his resignation. The next year Durant opened Durant Motors, which built the low-priced "Star," but failed in 1933. Bankrupt by 1935, he listed only his clothes as assets. World War II stymied his last business venture, a chain of bowling alleys in Flint.

Durant, (William James) Will (1885–1981) historian; born in North Adams, Mass.; **and Durant, Ariel (b. Chaya Kaufman)** (1898–1981) historian; born in Proskurov (now Khmelnitski), Ukraine. After working as a reporter, he went to Seton Hall College (now University) in New Jersey to teach and to study for the Catholic priesthood, but he left in 1911 and took up radical politics in New York City. He became director of the Labor Temple School in 1914 while taking a Ph.D. at Columbia University (1917). When his lectures on philosophy at the Labor Temple School were published as *The Story of Philosophy* (1926), it became such a best-seller that he was able to quit and write full time. After publishing various books, in 1935 he came out with *Our Oriental Heritage,* the first of his long-planned multivolume *Story of Civilization.* He moved to Los Angeles and for the next 40 years largely devoted himself to this project; the 11th and final volume appeared in 1975. Chaya (or Ada) Kaufman Durant had been assisting him for some years and she was credited as coauthor of the last five volumes. The 10th volume received the Pulitzer Prize in 1968 and the Durants received the Presidential Medal of Freedom in 1977. Academic historians faulted the books on various grounds but their texture and narrative – a colorful tapestry of history, culture, and biographies – made the series one of the most successful popularizations of all time and introduced millions of readers to intellectual history.

Duranty, Walter (1884–1957) journalist; born in Liverpool, England. Joining the *New York Times* in 1913, he became its Moscow correspondent (1922–41) and won a 1932 Pulitzer Prize for reporting. Regarded by some as an expert, he has been soundly criticized for pro-Stalinist bias.

Durocher, Leo (Ernest) (1905–91) baseball player/manager;

born in West Springfield, Mass. As a major league shortstop for 17 seasons (1925–45), he played in two World Series and was an integral member of the St. Louis Cardinals' "Gas House" teams of the 1930s. During his 24-year career as a manager (1939–73), he managed the Brooklyn Dodgers, New York Giants, Chicago Cubs, and Houston Astros. (He was forced to sit out the 1947 season because of "conduct detrimental to baseball.") His irascible style of managing earned him the nickname, "The Lip," and inspired his teams to three league championships and a World Series victory in 1954. Among his many unprintable words, his most often quoted – "Nice guys finish last!" – were probably never spoken by him, at least in such an aphoristic form. He was inducted into the Baseball Hall of Fame in 1994.

Durstine, Roy (Sarles) (1886–1962) advertising executive; born in Jamestown, N.D. He began his 50-year advertising career as a pioneering political publicist for Theodore Roosevelt's 1912 presidential bid. With Bruce Barton and others he founded what became the major New York agency BBDO (1918), where he pioneered radio and institutional advertising and became a leading industry figure. He resigned to head his own agency (1939–62).

Duryea, Charles E. (Edgar) (1861–1938) manufacturer; born near Canton, Ill. He built bicycles in Peoria until his attention was caught by a gasoline-powered engine at the 1886 Ohio State Fair. By 1891 he had drawn plans for a carriage and engine and moved to Springfield, Mass., where his bicycles were manufactured, and where, with his younger brother J. Frank Duryea, he built a car. Disagreement later arose between the two brothers about who did what, but in 1893 the *Springfield Evening Union* reported the Duryea car had been driven on city streets – the first American gasoline-powered automobile. The brothers successfully raced an improved version against European models and formed the Duryea Motor Wagon Company in Springfield, which in 1896 sold the first American automobiles. The brothers left that company in 1898. Charles organized the Duryea Power Company of Reading, Pa., manufacturing three-cylinder cars until 1914. (J. Frank Duryea made the Stevens-Duryea model, 1903–14.) He was president of the American Motor League and author of *The Handbook of the Automobile,* a 1906 correspondence-school textbook.

Duryea, (James) Frank (1869–1967) inventor; born in Washburn, Ill. He and his brother Charles Duryea grew up with an interest in mechanics, and in 1892 they designed an automobile together. Frank worked over his brother's engine design – the first of many conflicts between them – and is generally credited with producing America's first gas-powered highway automobile, which had its trial run on September 21, 1893. Frank Duryea produced the luxury Stevens-Duryea automobile until 1915, when he sold his interest in the company and began a retirement that lasted 52 years.

du Simitière, Pierre (Eugène) (1736–84) painter; born in Geneva, Switzerland. He came to America (1765) and became the curator of the American Philosophical Society, Philadelphia (1776–81). Remembered as a collector of historical objects, he also painted George Washington (1779).

Dustin, Hannah (1657–?1736) colonial heroine; born in Haverhill, Mass. She married Thomas Dustin, a bricklayer and farmer, and they had 12 children. In 1697, during King

William's War, Indian raiders captured Hannah, her youngest child, and a nurse. Fearing what their fate might be, Hannah and a captive boy killed 10 sleeping Indians with hatchets. She scalped the Indians, and the former captives returned to Haverhill, where they received a bounty for the scalps. She left many descendants through her 9 surviving children and two monuments were later erected in her memory (1874, 1879).

Dutton, Clarence Edward (1841–1912) geologist; born in Wallingford, Conn. He joined the U.S. Army in 1862 and retired as a major in 1901. Assigned to the U.S. Geological Survey (1875–90), he made major contributions to geologic and volcanic studies of the western U.S.A. and Hawaii.

Duvall, Gabriel (1752–1844) Supreme Court justice; born in Prince George's County, Md. He fought in the American Revolution and served the U.S. House of Representatives (Va., 1794–96). He was a judge on the Maryland Supreme Court (1796–1802) and President Jefferson's comptroller of the treasury (1802–11) before President Madison appointed him to the U.S. Supreme Court (1811–35).

Duvall, Robert (1931–) movie actor; born in San Diego, Calif. He began as a stage actor and made his film debut in *To Kill a Mockingbird* (1963). Regarded as one of the finest character actors in movies, he won an Oscar for *Tender Mercies* (1983).

Duveneck, Frank (b. Frank Decker) (1848–1919) painter; born in Covington, Ky. He adopted his stepfather's name and studied at the Royal Academy in Munich, Germany (1870). His style consisted of broad brushstrokes, somber brown backgrounds, and an energetic approach, as seen in *Whistling Boy* (1872). Beginning in 1900, he taught at the Cincinnati Art Academy for many years.

Du Vigneaud, Vincent (1901–78) biochemist; born in Chicago. He was affiliated with Cornell University (1937–75). He synthesized penicillin (1946) and isolated and then synthesized the hormone oxytocin, elucidating its structure. He was awarded the Nobel Prize in chemistry (1955) for his work on biochemically important sulphur compounds.

Dwiggins, William Addison (1880–1956) book designer; born in Martinsville, Ohio. An associate of Frederic Goudy, he bought his own press in 1910 and produced a seriocomic magazine, *The Fabulist* (1915–21). He coauthored an influential pamphlet decrying American books as poorly made; as a designer, especially for Alfred A. Knopf, he produced some of the finest books of his time. His analysis of typefaces in *Layout in Advertising* (1928) was a classic. From 1929 on he designed many distinctive typefaces for the Mergenthaler Linotype Company.

Dwight, John Sullivan (1813–93) music critic; born in Boston, Mass. Harvard-educated, he served as a minister and lived for a while at the socialistic Brook Farm Community before returning to his early love of music. In 1852 he founded *Dwight's Journal of Music,* which over the next three decades was an effective, high-minded, and notably conservative voice in promoting European-oriented classical music in the U.S.A.

Dwight, John Wilbur (1859–1928) U.S. representative; born in Dryden, N.Y. A lumberman and owner of Dwight Farm and Land Company, he served as majority and minority whip in the U.S. House of Representatives (Rep., N.Y.; 1902–13), leaving to head the Virginia Blue Ridge Railway Company (1913–28).

Dwight, Timothy (1752–1817) educator, Congregational minister, poet; born in Northampton, Mass. (grandson of Jonathan Edwards). He studied at Yale (1766–69), was a tutor there (1771–77), and was chaplain for the Connecticut Brigade during the American Revolution (1777–79). A member of the Massachusetts Legislature (1781–82), he served as a Congregational minister (1783–95), then became president of Yale (1795–1817). He was a conservative Federalist and Calvinist, and his verse is noted for its early use of American settings and its scorn of contemporaries' behavior he regarded as indicative of a decline in values.

Dworkin, Ronald (Myles) (1931–) legal scholar; born in Wooster, Mass. He is considered one of the clearest, most brilliant theorists of jurisprudence; his work challenges strict adherence to the letter of the law in favor of individual liberties and moral principles in books as *Taking Rights Seriously* (1977), *A Matter of Principle* (1985), and *Law's Empire* (1986). He taught at Yale (1962–69), then at Oxford University (1969), and concurrently at New York University since 1975.

Dyer, Mary (b. Barrett) (?–1660) Quaker martyr; born in England. She and her husband, William Dyer, emigrated to Massachusetts in 1635. She sympathized with Anne Hutchinson's religious views and moved to Rhode Island in 1638. During a period in England (1650–57) she became a Quaker. Upon her return to the colonies, she was arrested three times by Massachusetts colonists and warned to keep out of that colony because of her faith. She returned a fourth time in 1660 and was hanged. Her death led to the easing of anti-Quaker laws in Massachusetts.

Dyer, Wayne W. (Walter) (1940–) counselor, educator, author; born in Detroit, Mich. He received the Ed.D. from Wayne State University (1966) and worked as a teacher, counselor, and therapist from 1967. In 1973 he published the first of three books on individual and group counseling, followed by the best-selling *Your Erroneous Zones: Bold But Simple Techniques for Eliminating Unhealthy Behavior Patterns* (1976).

Dyer-Bennett, Richard (1913–91) folk musician; born in Leicester, England. He came to the U.S.A. in 1925 and after studying voice and guitar, he made his New York City debut in 1944 as a performer of mainly Anglo-American ballads. Calling himself a "minstrel or troubadour," he performed in many locales and foreshadowed the folk music revival of the 1960s; he eventually had a large repertoire that included everything from African-American spirituals to Schubert's songs. He was the first to admit that he had succeeded in "spite of my voice rather than because of it." He recorded about two dozen albums (many on his own label), composed some 100 songs, and wrote articles and books on music. He joined the faculty of New York State University in 1970, but a severe stroke in 1972 ended his career as a performer.

Dylan, Bob (b. Robert Allen Zimmerman) (1941–) folk/rock songwriter, singer; born in Duluth, Minn. He imitated Little Richard on piano at high school dances, changed his name, and dropped out of college to perform folk and country songs at local coffee houses. (Over the years he gave various explanations of the origin of his last name; one was that originally it was "Dillon" after the popular television western lawman, and only later did its spelling change to reflect his admiration for the Welsh poet, Dylan Thomas.) In 1960 he moved to New York and began visiting legendary folksinger Woody Guthrie in the hospital. He was soon playing his own and Guthrie's songs on guitar in small folk clubs; in the latter he met Joan Baez, who helped advance his career. He achieved a huge following with the albums *Freewheelin' Bob Dylan* (1963), with its hit "Blowin' In The Wind," and *Times They Are A-Changin'* (1964), which established him as the premier folk balladeer of his generation as well as its voice for social protest. Influenced by the Beatles, in 1965 he released *Highway 61 Revisited* backed by a full rock band; the album included the hits "Mr. Tambourine Man" and "Like a Rolling Stone." A prolific songwriter and gifted lyricist, he went on to write many great folk-rock songs of the 1970s and 1980s and to sell many gold albums in rock, country, and even gospel styles. In 1985 he sang at benefit concerts for African famine relief and in 1986 he toured Japan, Australia, and the United States with rock star Tom Petty. He continued to make occasional appearances at benefits and special concerts.

Dziewonski, Adam Marian (1936–) seismologist; born in Lwow, Poland. He performed seismological research in Poland before joining the Southwest Center for Advanced Studies at the University of Texas in 1965. He was a member of the Center for Earth and Planetary Physics at Harvard University, and was chairman of Harvard's Department of Geological Science (1982–86). He utilized seismic wave movement and geomagnetic soundings to determine physical properties of the earth's crust.

E

Eads, James (Buchanan) (1820–87) engineer, inventor; born in Lawrenceburg, Ind. The self-educated son of a nomadic, not very prosperous merchant, he found work as a purser on a Mississippi River steamboat in 1838. In his free hours he invented a diving bell and, in 1842, went into the salvage business, recovering cargo and machinery from sunken river steamboats. This venture brought Eads a fortune. After President Lincoln personally asked for his help, in 1861 he built, in 100 days, eight ironclad gunboats that helped Union forces take control of the Kentucky-Tennessee River systems. His Eads Bridge across the Mississippi River at St. Louis (1867–74) contained a 520-foot-long central span. That bridge, together with his engineering and navigation improvements to the mouth of the Mississippi (1875–79), raised him to the front rank of engineers of his era.

Eagle, Harry (1906–92) medical biologist; born in New York City. After taking his medical degree at Johns Hopkins, he taught and researched there (1927–47), then went to the National Institutes of Health (1947–61) where he headed various sections; he then joined the faculty of the Albert Einstein College of Medicine (1961–88). Perhaps the best known achievement of his productive career was his formulation (in 1959) of the essential compounds needed to sustain the reproduction of human and other mammalian cells in test tubes; known as "Eagle's growth medium," it opened the way for new research on viruses, cancer, and genetic defects. He also made notable discoveries about the process of blood clotting, the treatment of arsenic poisoning, and a cure for African sleeping sickness.

Eaker, Ira (Clarence) (1896–1987) aviator; born in Field Creek, Texas. Commissioned in 1918, he entered the Signal Corps and learned to fly. He was part of a pilots' relay that kept a Fokker monoplane aloft over Los Angeles for a record 150 hours; in 1936 he made the first transcontinental flight using instruments only. On August 17, 1942, Eaker led the first B-17 bombing attack on continental Europe. He went on to command the 8th Air Force in England and, in 1944–45, the Mediterranean Allied Air Forces. He retired in 1947 and worked as an aircraft industry executive during the 1950s.

Eakin, Richard M. (Marshall) (1910–) zoologist; born in Florence, Colo. After doing postgraduate research in Europe (1935–36), he spent his career at the University of California: Berkeley (1936–77). He made major contributions to studies of the electron microscopy of photoreceptors in vertebrates and invertebrates, and was editor of several professional journals. To convey his enthusiasm for science to his students, he would appear in the classroom costumed as famous biologists, and lecture in the appropriate character and manner on relevant topics. These popular impersonations led to producing and starring in his own educational films about the life and work of renowned scientists such as Darwin, Pasteur, and Mendel.

Eakins, Thomas (Cowperthwait) (1844–1916) painter, photographer, sculptor; born in Philadelphia. After studying painting at the Pennsylvania Academy of the Fine Arts (1861–66), he studied in Paris (1866–70) under Jean Léon Gerôme. During his travels in Europe he was profoundly influenced by the Spanish painters, Velázquez and Ribera. He returned to Philadelphia (1870), and studied anatomy and dissections at Jefferson Medical College, a pursuit which strongly affected his work. He began teaching at the Pennsylvania Academy (1876) and created a crisis when he insisted on using nude male models in the art classroom. When asked to use loincloths, he refused and resigned in 1886. He worked as a photographer, continuing his study of anatomy in a series of figure-motion studies, and as a sculptor, but he is remembered for his paintings. His work exhibits his mastery of observation and perspective, as well as his stylized but precise realism. Noted for his portraits, scenes of drama, and outdoor activities, such as *Max Schmitt in a Single Scull* (1871), *The Clinic of Dr. Gross* (1875), *The Writing Master* (1881), a portrait of his father, and *The Swimming Hole* (1884–85), he is honored for his unsentimental approach to humanity and nature. Recent exhibitions and newly discovered information concerning Eakins continue to reveal the life of this enigmatic and important artist.

Eames, Charles (1907–78) architect, designer; born in St. Louis, Mo. After early studies and practice in architecture, he taught at Cranbrook Academy of Art (1937–40). There he collaborated on modern furniture design with the Saarinens and student Ray Kaiser (c. 1916–1988), whom he married in 1941. Initially a painter and sculptor, Ray Kaiser Eames formed an innovative design partnership with her husband (1941–78) that produced molded plywood chairs, modular storage units, knock-down furniture, graphics, interiors, exhibit displays, and experimental films. Their 1941 California move led to a workshop designing military leg splints, Metro-Goldwyn-Mayer, Inc. film sets, and in 1947 their own landmark Santa Monica house of prefabricated parts. The 1956 molded plywood, leather-upholstered, pedestal-mounted Eames Lounge Chair 670 with ottoman was their most enduring creation.

Earhart, Amelia (Mary) (1897–?1937) aviator; born in Atchison, Kans. During World War I, Earhart worked as a nurses' aide in Toronto, Canada. She then attended several schools including two stints at Columbia University, held odd jobs in California, and became a settlement house worker in Boston in 1926. She had first flown in Los Angeles in 1920 and within a year made a solo flight. In 1928 she participated in a transatlantic flight with Wilmer Stultz and Louis Gordon, becoming the first woman to fly the Atlantic. In 1932, flying solo, she set a transatlantic record of 14 hours, 56 minutes. In the following year she flew two more record-setting transatlantic flights. In 1937, by now a public favorite, she embarked on an equatorial world trip. She ceased communications on July 2, shortly after leaving New Guinea with her navigator Frederick Noonan. Several extensive searches revealed nothing. Her husband, George Putnam, posthumously published her autobiography, *Last Flight* (1938).

Earl (or Earle), Ralph (1751–1801) painter; born in Worcester County, Mass. He spent most of his life in Connecticut, except for a stay in England (1778–85), and became a leading portrait painter, rivaled only by John Singleton Copley, who influenced his work. His paintings have a folk quality, as in *Portrait of Elijah Boardman* (1789).

Earle, Pliny (1809–92) physician, psychiatrist; born in Leicester, Mass. He wrote extensively on current practices in mental institutions in Europe and the United States, and headed institutions in Frankford, Pa. (1840) and New York City (1844). He was a cofounder of the American Medical Association (1847).

Earls, Felton James (1942–) psychiatrist; born in New Orleans. He designed and directed studies at the Judge Baker Children's Center in Boston, Mass., to determine how violent behavior is produced. He also investigated various other aspects of behavior in preschool children, mental health in children of alcoholic parents, and risk factors for violence and HIV infection in adolescents.

Early, Jubal (Anderson) (1816–94) soldier, lawyer; born in Franklin County, Va. A year after his graduation from West Point (1837), he resigned his commission to take up the law, although he had fought briefly against the Seminoles and then again in the Mexican War. He opposed secession but accepted the colonelcy of the 24th Virginia at the outset of the war and participated in many of the war's major battles. Early's July 1864 raid on Washington advanced to within three miles of the capital and caused a panic there, but on his retreat through the Shenandoah Valley he was defeated by Sheridan. At the war's end, he fled abroad until 1869, then returned to his law practice and to work with the Louisiana lottery. He served as president of the Southern Historical Society and his *Autobiographical Sketch and Narrative* was published in 1912.

Eastland, James O. (Oliver) (1904–86) U.S. senator; born in Doddsville, Miss. A wealthy cotton planter, he was originally appointed to the U.S. Senate but was thereafter reelected (Dem., Miss.; 1943–78). A fervid anti-communist, he served as chairman of the Internal Security Subcommittee, attacking alleged subversives in the Civil Rights movement, education, and the arts. As chairman of the Judiciary Committee, he opposed Civil Rights legislation.

Eastman, Charles (b. Ohiyesa) (1858–1939) Santee Sioux physician, author; born at Redwood Falls, Minn. He received a B.A. from Dartmouth (1887) and an M.D. from Boston University (1890). He established 32 Indian Young Men's Christian Association groups and helped to found the Boy Scouts and Campfire Girls. An advocate for Indians' rights, he also wrote several books and lectured widely in the U.S.A. and England.

Eastman, George (1854–1932) inventor, manufacturer, philanthropist; born in Waterville, N.Y. Interested in photographic processes from an early age, he abandoned banking for photography and produced a flexible role film (1884) and the "Kodak" box camera (1888). His experiments with Thomas Edison made motion pictures possible. Eastman formed the Eastman Kodak Company in 1892 and introduced the legendary Brownie camera eight years later. Aggressive and hard-driving, he bought out rivals or drove them out of business, and his company soon dominated the industry. One of the nation's leading philanthropists, he founded the Eastman School of Music in Rochester, N.Y., and supported various other educational institutions. His home in Rochester, N.Y., is a major photography museum.

Eastman, Joseph Bartlett (1882–1944) social reformer, public official; born in Katonah, N.Y. The "watchdog" secretary of Boston's Public Franchise League (1905–15), he investigated municipal utilities. An independent member and twice chairman of the U.S. Interstate Commerce Commission (1917–44), he earned respect for his fairmindedness, but often lost his fights to regulate railroad rates. He coordinated rail traffic as director of Defense Transportation (1941–44).

Eastman, Linda Anne (1867–1963) librarian; born in Oberlin, Ohio. For 50 years she worked in the Cleveland Public Library. She edited an important annotated new-book list and was an advocate for handicapped readers.

Eastman, Max (Forrester) (1883–1969) journalist, writer; born in Canandaigua, N.Y. The editor of two prominent left-wing publications, *The Masses* (1913–17) and *The Liberator* (1918–22), he later became a critic of Marxism in his writings, lectures, and broadcasts.

Eastman, P. D. (Philip Dey) (1909–86) author, illustrator, film producer; born in Amherst, Mass. He studied at Amherst College and at the National Academy of Design, New York, worked for Warner Brothers and Disney Studios, Calif., and created the *Gerald McBoing Boing* series for United Productions (UPA). He moved to New York City (1950s), lived in Westport, Conn., wrote children's books, notably *Are You My Mother?* (1960), and collaborated with Theodor Geisel on *The Cat in the Hat Dictionary* (1964).

Eastwood, Clint (1930–) movie actor, director; born in San Francisco. He began as a bit-player in low-budget movies, then gained a minor following for the television Western series, *Rawhide*. Appearing in three Italian-made "spaghetti Westerns" (1964–66), he found himself becoming an international star as a laconic if deadly gunslinger, "the man with no name." Returning to Hollywood, he made his directorial debut with *Play Misty for Me* (1971), but carved out another superstar role for himself in several "Dirty Harry" Callahan movies. Incredibly popular throughout the world and able to command among the highest fees for his appearances, he expanded his range of roles in later years to adventure movies, comedies, and dramas but his greatest came with another Western, *Unforgiven* (1992), for which he won

Academy Awards for best director and best picture. As tightlipped and unorthodox in real life as in his movies, he surprised everyone by becoming mayor of Carmel, Calif. (1987–89).

Eaton, Amos (1776–1842) botanist; born in Chatham, N.Y. He graduated from Williams College (1799) and was admitted to the bar (1802), but gave up law to study botany at Yale. After 1810, he gave public lectures in New England and New York and wrote a botany textbook. Then in 1817 he published his major work, *Manual of Botany for the Northern States,* which had its last edition in 1840. He became professor of natural history at the Medical School in Castleton, Vt., joining the Rensselaer School (now Rensselaer Polytechnic Institute) (1824–42). His voluminous writings were later found to be more enthusiastic than accurate.

Eaton, Charles Aubrey (1868–1953) U.S. representative; born in Nova Scotia, Canada. Coming to America for theological studies, he was a pastor and newspaper editor in both countries. He served on the Foreign Affairs Committee in the U.S. House of Representatives (Rep., N.J.; 1925–53).

Eaton, Daniel Cady (1835–95) botanist; born in Fort Gratiot, Mich. He was influenced by his grandfather, botanist and educator Amos Eaton, and by his father's interest in natural history. He served with the army commissary in New York City during the Civil War (1860–64), then became a professor of botany at Yale (1864–95). A specialist in ferns (and later in mosses), he performed much field work, wrote botanical definitions for *Webster's International Dictionary,* and authored the classic *The Ferns of North America* (1877–80).

Eaton, (Margaret O'Neal or O'Neill) "Peggy" (1779–1879) hostess; born in Washington, D.C. Daughter of a tavern-keeper, she married John Timberlake (1816–28), a sailor; while he was at sea she often worked at her father's tavern where she met John H. Eaton, a Tennessee senator and friend of Andrew Jackson. When her husband died at sea, she married Eaton (1829–56), who soon thereafter was appointed secretary of war by newly elected President Jackson. Her low social origins led to her being snubbed by Vice-President John Calhoun's and other cabinet members' wives; President Jackson sided with the Eatons and this led to a split within his party's leadership. Eaton finally resigned his post (1831) and was sent to govern Florida (1834–36) before being named ambassador to Spain (1836–40), where Peggy Eaton enjoyed great social success. Following Eaton's death (1856) she married Antonio Buchignani, a 19-year-old dance instructor (1859). He defrauded her of her fortune, divorced her in 1866, and eloped with her granddaughter (1868). Peggy died as humbly as she began.

Eberhart, Richard (Ghormley) (1904–   ) poet, teacher; born in Austin, Minn. He studied at the University of Minnesota (1922–23), Dartmouth College (B.A. 1926), Cambridge (England) (B.A. 1929), and Harvard (1932–33). He worked as a floorwalker, deckhand, and tutor (1930–33), then as a teacher (1933–41) and, after service in World War II, for a family business (1946–52). He taught at Dartmouth (1956–70) and was a consultant in poetry, Library of Congress (1959–61). His poems in volumes such as *Undercliff* (1953) and *Shifts of Being* (1968) are distinguished by his direct yet occasionally unexpected responses to the basic experiences of human life. He also published his *Collected Verse Plays* (1962).

Eberle, (Mary) Abastenia St. Leger (1878–1942) sculptor; born in Webster City, Iowa. She was raised in Ohio and Puerto Rico, and went to study at the Art Students League in New York City (1899–1902), where she spent most of the rest of her life (she studied in Naples, Italy from 1907–08). Ahead of many of her generation, she rejected the classical tradition and espoused the view that the artist should portray the realities of contemporary society. She specialized in small bronzes depicting the people of the lower east side, as in *Windy Doorstep* (1910), but her most provocative statue was *The White Slave* (1913), intended as a protest against prostitution.

Eccles, Marriner (Stoddard) (1890–1977) businessman, government official; born in Logan, Utah. A Morman, he parlayed family money into a Rocky Mountain real estate and banking empire, Eccles Investment Company (1916–34). As governor, then chairman, of the Federal Reserve Board (1934–51), he used the Banking Act of 1935 to centralize federal control over banking and currency, returning to business afterward.

Echols, Oliver P. (1892–1954) aviator; born in Charlottesville, Va. Commissioned in the army in 1916, he was chief of aviation for the U.S. 1st Army Corps in France during World War I. As chief of the Army Air Force's matériel division from 1940–45, he helped build the largest and most powerful air force the world had seen. He retired in 1949 to become chairman and chief operating officer at Northrop Aircraft.

Eckbo, Garrett (1910–   ) landscape architect; born in Cooperstown, N.Y. Influenced by Gropius, he specialized in clean, clear spaces for public use, designing university campuses and gardens on the West Coast (1940–65). He began to focus on ecology in 1980.

Eckert, J. (John) Presper (1919–   ) computer engineer, inventor; born in Philadelphia. A University of Pennsylvania graduate in electronic engineering, he and John W. Mauchly developed the first practical electronic digital computer, the Electronic Numerical Integrator and Calculator (ENIAC) (1942–46); it weighed several tons and used thousands of valves and resistors. In 1951 an improved version of their computer, the UNIVAC I, became one of the first commercially sold computers. Eckert had more than 85 patents for his various electronic inventions.

Eckert, Wallace (John) (1902–71) computer engineer; born in Pittsburgh, Pa. An astronomer by training, he was early intrigued by the possible application of computers to astronomical calculations. He established a computation lab at Columbia University and encouraged International Business Machines to support computer research (1933). He developed techniques for linking tabulating and adding equipment and was director of the Watson Laboratory at Columbia (1945–67), where he helped develop the Selective Sequence Electronic Calculator (1948).

Eckhardt, Edris (1907–   ) glass maker; born in Cleveland, Ohio. Originally a ceramist, in 1953 she turned to glass, rediscovering ancient glass processes and experimenting with lamination techniques. Her stained glass work won her a Tiffany fellowship.

Eckstein, Otto (1927–84) economist; born in Ulm, Germany. He fled Nazi Germany with his family in 1938, first to England, then to the U.S.A. Educated at Princeton and Harvard, he joined the Harvard faculty in 1955. A pioneer of econometric models of the U.S. economy, he helped found the economic analysis firm, Data Resources, and in the 1960s served the Johnson Administration on the Council of Economic Advisers (1964–66). He returned to Harvard after his government service to become the Paul M. Warburg Professor of Economics (1966–84).

Eckstine, (William Clarence Eckstein) Billy (1914–93) jazz musician; born in Pittsburgh, Pa. He emerged as a ballad specialist with Earl Hines between 1939–45, led a trail-blazing modern jazz orchestra until 1948, and freelanced as a popular nightclub singer thereafter.

Eddy, Henry (Turner) (1844–1921) educator, engineer; born in Stoughton, Mass. From 1868, Eddy was a professor of mathematics and engineering at several universities. He served as president of Rose Polytechnic Institute in Terre Haute, Ind., (1890–94) then returned to being a professor of engineering. Eddy's main focus was on research in reinforced concrete flat slabs.

Eddy, Mary Baker (1821–1910) founder of the Church of Christ, Scientist; born in Bow, N.H. Rather sickly and emotionally unstable as a child, she showed an early interest in poetry and religion. In 1843 she married George Washington Glover but he died within seven months; the son she bore was raised by foster parents. During the next decade she taught school occasionally but she was mostly preoccupied with the basic concerns of her life: medical problems, her own writings, and spiritual issues. In 1853 she married Dr. Daniel Patterson, a dentist, but her medical and psychological condition left her virtually an invalid. In 1862 she went to Portland, Maine, to seek relief from Phineas Parkhurst Quimby (1802–1866), a self-taught "healer" who had come up with his own "science of health": with its emphasis on the mental approach to curing all ailments, and with its strong Christian element, he effectively anticipated many of her later tenets. After Quimby died in 1866, she gradually took upon herself to advance and adapt his ideas, and for ten years she moved about New England, writing down and promoting her own version of "Christian science." In 1875 she took three crucial steps: she acquired a house in Lynn, Mass., where she began to teach her ideas to a circle of followers; she held her first public service in a local hall; and she published the first edition of her *Science and Health*. She had divorced Patterson in 1873 and in 1877 she married Asa Gilbert Eddy, a sewing-machine salesman who would become a valued assistant as her movement spread. In 1879 the Church of Christ, Scientist was formally chartered in Massachusetts, and from then on her movement and her own role expanded greatly and she became ever more famous and wealthy. She continually revised and republished her *Science and Health,* adding in 1883 the *Key to the Scriptures,* her interpretation of the Bible; in 1889 she set up the "Mother Church" in Boston to control the burgeoning movement; in 1908 she founded a newspaper, the *Christian Science Monitor*. She seldom appeared in Boston or public in the final 19 years of her life but she exercised rigid control over her organization; she was constantly engaged in controversy and legal suits, from fighting off the charge that she had stolen all her ideas from Quimby (she had in fact modified them significantly) to resisting efforts by various others to take over her church. She was probably psychosomatic, certainly charismatic, but the church she founded remains a witness to her central tenet of the power of mind over matter.

Eddy, Nelson (1901–67) baritone; born in Providence, R.I.

After working at various jobs, he won a contest to sing with the Philadelphia Civic Opera. A concert tour and radio appearances in the early 1930s led to a contract with Metro-Goldwyn-Mayer, Inc. and he proceeded to make a series of operetta-like films with Jeanette MacDonald, including *Naughty Marietta* (1935) and *Rose Marie* (1936); extremely popular at the time, the movies gained them the billing, "America's Sweethearts." After their last movie, *I Married an Angel* (1942), his career faltered, although he continued to tour and sing; he died after collapsing while on stage in Australia.

Edel, (Joseph) Leon (1907–) biographer; born in Pittsburgh, Pa. He taught at New York University (1953–73), devoting his scholarly career to Henry James. Edel wrote a magisterial 5-volume biography of James (1953–85) and published numerous editions of his letters and other writings.

Edelman, Gerald M. (Maurice) (1929–) immunologist; born in New York City. He practiced medicine at both Massachusetts General Hospital, and the hospital of Rockefeller University (1957–60). He joined the faculty of Rockefeller (1960–81), and became director of their Neurosciences Institute (1981). He shared the 1972 Nobel Prize in physiology for his investigations of the structure of the primary human antibody, immunoglobulin G. He then focused his research on cellular immune responses and intercellular communication in the immune system and the brain.

Edelman, Marion (b. Wright) (1939–) social activist; born in Bennettsville, S.C. After serving as a legal defense fund attorney for the National Association for the Advancement of Colored People (1963–68), she founded the Washington Public Policy Research Center (1968–73). In 1973 she began the Children's Defense Fund, lobbying for children's rights to decent education and health care. She wrote *The Measure of Our Success: A Letter to My Children and Yours* (1992). As a longtime personal and professional associate of Hillary Clinton, she was assumed to have some influence on the Clinton administration's policies in her areas.

Edelstein, David Norton (1910–) judge; born in New York City. He graduated from Fordham University and Law School, N.Y., and worked as a government attorney before being appointed a U.S. district judge for the Southern District of New York in 1951. He was chief judge from 1971–80. He issued important rulings on antitrust cases. He was active in professional organizations and on judicial blue-ribbon committees, and served on the boards of various social service agencies.

Ederle, Gertrude (Caroline) (1906–) swimmer; born in New York City. After winning three medals in the 1924 Olympics, she became the first woman to swim the English channel (1926); her time of 14 hours, 31 minutes broke the existing men's record by two hours.

Edes, Benjamin (1732–1803) journalist; born in Boston, Mass. A planner of the Boston Tea Party, he cofounded, with John Gill, the pro-Patriot *Boston Gazette and Country Journal* (the third paper so named) in 1775. It declined after the American Revolution and shut down in 1789; Edes spent his last years in poverty.

Edge, (Mabel) Rosalie (1877–1962) reformer, conservationist; born in New York City. A campaigner for women's suffrage, she turned her attention to conservation after women were granted the vote in 1920. From 1929–59 she was the crusading leader of the Emergency Conservation Committee. She lobbied successfully for the creation of King's Canyon and Olympic national parks and for the establishment of the Hawk Mountain Sanctuary for predator birds in Pennsylvania.

Edge, Walter Evans (1873–1956) governor, U.S. senator, ambassador; born in Philadelphia, Pa. A self-made advertising millionaire, he served in the New Jersey senate (Rep., 1911–16); as New Jersey's governor (1917–20), he reformed prison administration. In the U.S. Senate (1920–29), he supported founding the bureau of the budget; he left to become ambassador to France (1929–33). Governor of New Jersey again (1944–47), he fought for state constitutional reforms.

Edgerton, Harold (Eugene) (1904–90) electrical engineer; born in Fremont, Nebr. He became professor of electrical engineering at the Massachusetts Institute of Technology in 1934. A pioneer in stroboscopes and high-speed photography, he developed a krypton-xenon gas arc, used to photograph capillaries in the eye.

Edgerton, Sidney (1818–1900) U.S. representative, governor; born in Cazenovia, N.Y. After much self-education, he went to Ohio (1844) where he taught and also studied law. A firm abolitionist, he was a delegate to the Free-Soil Convention (1848) and the first Republican National Convention (1856). As a member of the U.S. House of Representatives (Rep., Ohio; 1859–63) he advocated abolition of slavery and the establishment of a transcontinental railroad. He was chief justice of the Idaho Territory (1863–64) and first governor of the Montana Territory (1864–65). He then resumed his law practice in Ohio.

Edison, Charles (1890–1969) cabinet member, governor; born in Llewellyn Park, N.J. (son of Thomas Alva Edison). Joining Edison Illuminating Company in 1914, he improved working conditions, becoming president in 1926. A Democrat, he cochaired the New Jersey State Recovery Board (1933–36) and as assistant navy secretary (1936–39), then secretary (1939–40), he reorganized the fleet. New Jersey's governor (1941–44), he challenged boss Frank Hague, returning to the Edison Company afterward.

Edison, Thomas (Alva) (1847–1931) inventor; born in Milan, Ohio. Raised in Ohio and Michigan, he was taken out of school at age seven after only three months in the classroom – his constant questioning led some teachers to consider him retarded – and was educated by his mother. He showed an early curiosity for explanations of how everything worked and was especially interested in chemistry. At age 12 he went to work selling newspapers and snacks on the railroad; he also printed his own little paper on the train and experimented with chemicals in the baggage car until he caused a fire. Limited to selling papers at railroad stations, he learned how to operate a telegraph and during the Civil War worked as a telegraph operator. Working for Western Union in Boston in 1868, he tried to sell his first invention, an electric vote-recording machine, but legislatures did not want it; he is said to have decided at that point to work only on inventing things people would buy. In New York City in 1869, as a supervisor in a stock-ticker firm, he made improvements on the stock-ticker. With the profits from the sale of an electrical-engineering firm that held his patents, he opened his own laboratory in Newark, N.J., where he made important improvements in telegraphy and on the typewriter, and invented the carbon transmitter that made Alexander Graham Bell's telephone practical. In 1876 he moved his laboratory to Menlo Park, N.J., where he invented the first phonograph (1877) and the prototype of the commercially practical incandescent electric light bulb (1879). These and other inventions led to his being internationally known as "the wizard of Menlo Park" – although in 1887 he moved to a larger laboratory in West Orange, N.J. By the late 1880s he was contributing to the development of motion pictures, and by 1912 he was experimenting with talking pictures. His many inventions include a storage battery, a dictaphone, and a mimeograph. Meanwhile, he had become interested in the development of a system for widespread distribution of electric power from central generating stations. In 1892 his Edison General Electric Co. merged with another firm to become General Electric Co., of which he was a major stockholder. During World War I he conducted research for the U.S. military on such devices as submarine periscope and torpedo mechanisms. The holder of over 1,000 patents, he lived out his final years in a round of awards and honors. Henry Ford would move his original Menlo Park laboratory to the Greenfield Village museum in Dearborn, Mich. In 1962 his laboratory and home in West Orange, N.J., would be designated a National Historic Site. Although he was personally acquainted with many important men of his era, he never had much time for family or friends due to his dedication to his work. Only later would some point out that had he known a bit more about scientific theory and mathematics he might not have endorsed the definition of genius attributed to him: "one percent inspiration and 99 percent perspiration." In fact, he made only one true scientific discovery (1883), "the Edison effect," for which he could see no commercial applications but which anticipated the vacuum tube that would become the basis of the radio. But using his own methods, he had spent his life inventing many of the devices that shaped the modern world.

Edman, Irwin (1896–1954) philosopher; born in New York City. He taught at Columbia University from 1920 to 1954 and wrote several books, including *Four Ways to Philosophy* (1937) and *Philosopher's Holiday* (1938), a collection of informal reminiscences. He frequently wrote on issues of the day for a general audience and was often heard on radio.

Edmonds, Francis (William) (E. F. Williams, early pseudonym) (1806–63) painter; born in Hudson, N.Y. Based in New York City, his genre paintings were influenced by William Sidney Mount, as in *All Talk and No Work* (1855–56).

Edmondson, William (?1882–1951) sculptor; born in Nashville, Tenn. Born of former slaves, he picked cotton, worked at railroad shops and as a janitor (1908–31), began sculpting in limestone (c. 1931), and lived in Nashville. Noted for his modern-primitive art, he specialized in worldly and religious works, as in *Mary and Martha* (1938).

Edmunds, George F. (Franklin) (1826–1919) U.S. senator; born near Richmond, Vt. A lawyer, he went to the U.S. Senate (Rep., Vt.; 1866–91) where he was author of the Civil Rights Act of 1875 and coauthor of the Sherman Antitrust Act.

Edsall, David Linn (1869–1945) physician, educator; born in Hamburg, N.J. He took his medical degree at the University of Pennsylvania and stayed on to teach there until 1910. He was ahead of his time in his concentration on causes of disease such as inadequate nutrition, metabolic failures, and occupational conditions. With the release of the Flexner

Report in 1910, he moved into the vanguard of those wanting to reform medical education; after a frustrating year at Washington University School of Medicine (Mo.) (1910–11), he went to Harvard Medical School (1912–35), becoming its dean in 1918. In 1922 he also became dean of the Harvard School of Public Health.

Edsall, John T. (Tileston) (1902–) biochemist; born in Philadelphia. He spent his professional career at Harvard (1928–73), remaining active after achieving emeritus status. From the 1960s he made major contributions to studies of the physical chemistry of proteins, peptides, and amino acids, including red cell enzymes and proteins involved in blood coagulation. After 1970 he devoted his time to writings on the history of biochemistry and molecular biology. He has received international acclaim as an author, editor, and adviser to scientific organizations.

Edson, Merritt A. (1897–1955) marine officer; born in Vermont. An aggressive commander with a deceptively soft voice that rose to a near bark in the stress of combat, he received a marine commission in 1917 and served in France toward the end of World War I. He led the 1st Raider Battalion and, later, the 5th Marines during some of the bloodiest fighting of the Guadalcanal campaign in 1942.

Edwards, Harry (1943–) sociologist, civil rights activist, sports consultant; born in East St. Louis, Ill. He attended San Jose State College (Calif.) where he played basketball and was a discus thrower. As a young African-American graduating into the 1960s and well aware of racial injustice, he chose to combine an academic career with that of an activist. By 1968 he had gained national attention by urging African-American athletes to boycott the summer Olympics; he failed in this goal but was widely credited with influencing two sprinters, Tommy Smith and John Carlos, to give the Black Power salute on the victory stand. By 1970 he had joined the sociology faculty at the University of California: Berkeley, (becoming a tenured professor in 1977) and along with his academic career, which included such books as *The Sociology of Sports* and *The Revolt of the Black Athlete,* he served as a consultant to the San Francisco 49ers football team and the Golden State Warriors basketball team. In 1987, after Al Campanis made his racially insensitive remarks on national television, Edwards was hired by Peter Ueberroth, the commissioner of baseball, as a special assistant to promote the hiring of African-Americans, Latinos, and women in more administrative and managerial jobs in organized baseball. Edwards was in demand on the lecture circuit and on television on all issues relating to minorities in sports, and despite his somewhat intimidating appearance – he was 6 feet 8 inches tall, had a shaved head, and often spoke intensely – he never actually changed his simple and reasonable message: that African-Americans and other minorities get a fair deal in sports and elsewhere in society.

Edwards, Jonathan (1703–58) Protestant clergyman, theologian; born in East Windsor, Conn. He entered Yale at age 13, graduated in 1720, and studied theology there for two years. He was a pastor in New York City briefly before returning to Yale as a tutor. In 1726 he became an assistant to his grandfather Solomon Stoddard as minister of the Northampton, Mass., Congregational Church; he succeeded Stoddard after his death in 1729. Imbued with an almost perversely stern Calvinist doctrine, he was a powerful preacher and is regarded as the greatest theologian of the extreme form of American Puritanism. His best-known sermon, "Sinners in the Hands of an Angry God," declared man's baseness and vividly described the conditions of damnation. In the early 1740s he helped inspire the religious revival ironically known as the Great Awakening. Dismissed from the Northampton pulpit in 1750 for overzealousness, he became a missionary to the Indian tribes around Stockbridge, Mass. In 1757 he was appointed president of the College of New Jersey (later Princeton), but died (from a smallpox inoculation) only a few weeks after taking office.

Edwin, James (1797–1861) explorer, naturalist; born in Addison County, Vt. The botanist, geologist, and surgeon for Major Stephen Long's expedition of exploration (1820) he was one of the first three white men to climb Pike's Peak (1820). He compiled several Amerindian spelling books and translated the New Testament into the Ojibwa language (1833). An ardent abolitionist, he ran a station of the Underground Railroad in Iowa.

Egan, William (Allen) (1914–84) governor; born in Valdez, Alaska. Owner of the Valdez general store, he served in the territorial house of representatives (Dem., 1941–43, 1945–56), sponsoring Alaskan statehood. President of the constitutional convention (1955–56), he drafted the state charter, lobbying for congressional approval afterward. Alaska's first governor (Dem., 1959–67, 1971–75), he worked to harness the state's vast natural resources.

Eggan, Fred (1906–91) anthropologist; born in Seattle, Wash. He took a Ph.D. from the University of Chicago in 1933 and became a specialist in Hopi Indian society. Among his published works is *Social Organization of the Western Pueblos* (1950). A leader of professional anthropology organizations, he was named an emeritus professor in 1974 after a long teaching career at the University of Chicago.

Ehrenreich, Barbara (1941–) sociologist, author; born in Butte, Mont. An independent writer, she became known for her outspoken feminist-socialist analyses of contemporary issues, particularly health and the politics of gender and class. In addition to numerous articles in both popular and professional publications, she wrote books including *For Her Own Good* (coauthored, 1978) and *The Worst Years of Our Lives* (1990). She cochaired the Democratic Socialists of America (1983).

Ehrlich, Paul R. (Ralph) (1932–) entomologist, ecologist; born in Philadelphia. He was an entomologist at the University of Kansas (1953–59) and concurrently a research associate at the Chicago Academy of Science (1957–58). He made major contributions to field research on Arctic insects and parasitic mites (1950s), then performed extensive studies of butterflies after moving to Stanford (1959). He became a crusader for human conservation of natural resources after a 1966 trip to India made him aware of the ecological effects of poverty and overpopulation. His best-selling book, *The Population Bomb* (1968), predicted worldwide famine and advocated the concept of zero population growth. He became Bing Professor of Population Studies at Stanford (1976), and, in 1990, won Sweden's Craafoord Prize and became a MacArthur Fellow for his work in population biology and conservation of biological diversity.

Eichelberger, Clark M. (Mell) (1896–1980) international relations specialist; born in Freeport, Ill. He was a U.S. Army corporal in World War I and a Chautauqua lecturer

(1922–28). He was director of the League of Nations Association (which became the American Association for the United Nations) (1934–64). He wrote several books on international cooperation and world peace.

Eichenberg, Fritz (1901–90) illustrator, printmaker; born in Cologne, Germany. He studied graphics in Leipzig, emigrated to the United States (1933), settled in New York City, taught at the Pratt Graphics Center (1956–63), and retired to Rhode Island. He is known for his scathing socio-political wood engravings and illustrations, such as *Beastiarium Juvenile* (1965).

Eickemeyer, Rudolf (1831–95) inventor; born in Altenbamberg, Bavaria. The son of a forestry official, he fought with German revolutionary forces in 1849 and emigrated to America the following year. In 1854 he founded a machine shop in Yonkers, N.Y., and perfected the first in a series of labor-saving devices, among them a leather hatband folder, that revolutionized the hat-making industry. He later designed an efficient electric motor. Active in civic affairs, he served for many years on various boards in Yonkers.

Eidlitz, Leopold (1823–1908) architect; born in Prague, Bohemia. In New York after 1843, he designed churches, and public and commercial buildings. His functional and organic approach to architecture influenced Frank Furness and Louis Sullivan through his *Nature and Function of Art* (1881).

Eilshemius, Louis (Michel) (1864–1941) painter; born near Newark, N.J. Based in New York City, he traveled widely. His work is surrealistic, haunting, and shows the influence of Albert Pinkham Ryder, as in *New York at Night* (c. 1917).

Einhorn, David (1809–79) rabbi; born in Dispeck, Germany. He came to the U.S.A. in 1855 and was minister to congregations in Baltimore, Philadelphia, and New York City. Active in the antislavery movement, he was the leading theologian of the extreme Reform wing of Judaism of the time; but because he preached in German, his influence in this country was limited.

Einstein, Albert (1879–1955) physicist; born in Ulm, Germany. He was an undistinguished student in Germany, but flourished near Zurich, Switzerland. He requested Swiss citizenship in 1901 and took a post with the Swiss patent office (1902–5). By the time he received his Ph.D. (1905), he had achieved world fame for his publications on Brownian movement of molecules, his photoelectric theory that light and other radiation can behave as both waves and particles, and for his revolutionary special theory of relativity, which related matter and energy in the famous equation, $E = Mc^2$. He developed his general theory of relativity (1915), which displaced Newtonian mechanics as the cornerstone of physics and introduced the concept of space-time. In 1921 he received the Nobel Prize, specifically for his ideas on photons and the photoelectric effect. He taught at several European institutions (1909–33), but after Hitler came to power, Einstein, a Jewish pacifist, emigrated in 1933 to the U.S.A. and accepted a post at the newly created Institute for Advanced Studies at Princeton, N.J. He became a U.S. citizen in 1940, and remained in Princeton after his retirement in 1945. Fear of Nazi expansion caused him to sign a letter to President Franklin Roosevelt in 1939 urging America to develop an atomic bomb. Einstein himself took no part in the bomb's construction and spent the remainder of his life promoting peace and humanitarian

causes. He continued his unfulfilled search for a unified theory to combine quantum mechanics and relativity into one all-encompassing equation. A shy and gentle man, he was an accomplished violinist, and he made the world smirk when he once made an error while helping a young student with math homework.

Einstein, Alfred (1880–1952) musicologist; born in Munich, Germany. He was a newspaper music critic in Munich and Berlin before he left Germany in 1933. Arriving in the U.S.A. in 1938, he taught at Smith College, Columbia University, the University of Michigan, and Hartt College. He was an influential writer on music, his books including *Greatness in Music* (1941), *Music in the Romantic Era* (1947), and *Schubert* (1951).

Eiseley, Loren (Corey) (1907–77) cultural anthropologist, writer; born in Lincoln, Nebr. A hardware salesman's son, he graduated from the University of Nebraska (1933) and took his Ph.D. from the University of Pennsylvania (1937). He taught anthropology at the University of Kansas (1937–44) and Oberlin (1944–47) before returning to the University of Pennsylvania (1947–61); he also became the curator of early man at the university's museum (1948–61) and served as university provost (1959–61). In the 1930s he did field work in the American West to investigate the remains of the earliest humans to inhabit North America, but he would become most noted for his highly polished writing style. (As a student he published poetry and short stories and was an editor of *The Prairie Schooner,* a noted literary magazine.) In books such as *The Immense Journey* (1957), *Darwin's Century* (1958), *The Unexpected Universe* (1969), and *Night Country* (1971), he moved from straightforward explanations of matters such as evolution to increasingly more literary and personal ruminations. His autobiography, *All the Strange Hours,* appeared in 1975.

Eisenhart, Luther Pfahler (1876–1965) mathematician; born in York, Pa. Teaching at Princeton his entire career (1923–45), he focused largely on two aspects of differential geometry – surfaces (deformations, systems), and after 1921 on generalization of Riemannian geometry. A prolific author of textbooks, he also wrote on historical topics.

Eisenhower, Dwight D. (David) (1890–1969) thirty-fourth U.S. president; born in Denison, Texas. After graduating from West Point in 1915, he undertook further military studies and became a fast-rising staff officer in Washington, D.C.; from 1935–39 he was an assistant to Gen. Douglas MacArthur in the Philippines. As World War II progressed, he continued to rise in rank and responsibilities and was assigned to command the allied forces during their invasions of North Africa, Sicily, and Italy (1942–43). His talent for both strategic planning and staff coordination led him (December 1943) to be named supreme commander of the allied invasion of Normandy and he directed the campaign from D-Day (June 6, 1944) to the surrender of Germany (May 1945). After commanding the U.S. occupation forces in Germany, he returned to the U.S.A. to serve as army chief of staff (1946–48) before retiring from active duty. He served as president of Columbia University (1948–50) and head of the North Atlantic Treaty Organization (1951–52) before the Republicans drafted him as their presidential candidate in 1952; under the motto "I like Ike," he won by a landslide over Adlai Stevenson and did the same in 1956. His record as president was mixed, but in the years following, his low-profile approach came to seem more attractive. He established a truce in the floundering Korean War in 1953, but still maintained American presence as the main bar to communist expansionism; with the "Eisenhower doctrine" he promised aid to Middle Eastern nations resisting communism; in 1956 he sent troops to restore order in racially troubled Little Rock, Ark. At the same time, he did little to restrain the Cold War machinations of Secretary of State John Foster Dulles or the red-scare.

Eisenhower, (Marie Geneva b. Doud) Mamie (1896–1979) First Lady; born in Boone, Iowa. Daughter of a wealthy Denver meatpacker, she met Dwight Eisenhower when he was a young officer at Fort Sam Houston; they were married in 1916. Uninterested in politics, she became known as the national model for femininity. She used pink colors in redecorating the White House and sometimes conducted "white-glove" inspections.

Eisenman, Peter D. (David) (1932–) educator, author, architect; born in Newark, N.J. Founder/director of the Institute for Architecture and Urban Studies, New York (1967–82), Eisenman espoused a linguistic theory of architecture, becoming a controversial but internationally influential deconstructivist theoretician. His later work included such large institutional projects as the Wexner Center (1983–89, with Richard Trott), Ohio State University, Columbus, Ohio.

Eisenstaedt, Alfred (1898–) photographer; born in Tczew, Poland. Arriving in America at age 37 with his high-speed Leica camera, he became a pioneer photojournalist at *Life* magazine (1936–62), capturing telling moments in history with a glance or gesture, reproducing them on 90 *Life* covers.

Eisner, Thomas (1929–) entomologist; born in Berlin, Germany. As a child in Germany, he showed an early interest in what he termed "biophilia," the love of living creatures, and was always fascinated by insects and odors. When his Jewish father left Germany in 1933, Eisner emigrated with his family to Barcelona, Spain, then France, then Uruguay. He came to the U.S.A. in 1948, and was a research associate at Harvard (1955–57), where he worked with sociobiologist E. O. Wilson. Eisner joined Cornell (1957) where he made major contributions to studies of insect physiology, adaptation, and behavior, particularly web-making communication in spiders, and the spraying defenses of the bombardier beetle. He referred to insects as "master chemists," and was an authority on their pheromones and chemical ecology. In addition to being an accomplished photographer of insects and the author of five books and over 250 scientific articles, he was an advocate of human rights, an opponent of nuclear war, and an active environmentalist and conservationist.

Eisner, (William Erwin) Will (1917–) cartoonist; born in New York City. After studying at the Arts Students League in New York City, in 1937 he created the action-adventure newspaper comic strips, *The Three Brothers, K-51,* and the successful *Hawk of the Seas,* a swashbuckling tale of buccaneers. In 1940 he created a comic book insert for Sunday newspapers featuring his most popular work, *The Spirit,* which also became a long-running newspaper comic strip.

Eitner, Lorenz (Edwin Alfred) (1919–) art historian; born in Brunn, Czechoslovakia. He became an American citizen and studied at Duke (B.A. 1940), and Princeton (M.F.A. 1948; Ph.D. 1952). He served in the Army with the Office of Strategic Services (1943–46), and in the Office of Chief of Prosecution, Nuremberg War Crimes Trials (1946–47). A specialist in 18th- and 19th-century European paintings, he taught primarily at Stanford (1963), and wrote many scholarly books and articles.

Ekholm, Gordon F. (Frederick) (1909–87) anthropologist, archaeologist; born in St. Paul, Minn. He was curator of anthropology at the American Museum of Natural History (1937–74), where he oversaw the permanent installation of the Hall of Mexico and Central America (1970). He promoted the theory of pre-Columbian Asian migration to North America.

Elders, M. (Minnie) Joycelyn (1933–) pediatric endocrinologist, U.S. Surgeon General; born in Schaal, Ark. Born of an impoverished family, the eldest of eight children, she attended Philander Smith College, joined the army in 1952, and became a certified physical therapist. She attended medical school at the University of Arkansas Medical School (UAMS), Little Rock, (1954–60), and interned and was a resident at the University of Minnesota. Teaching at UAMS in 1964, she became a pediatrics professor by 1976, and a certified pediatric endocrinologist in 1978. In 1987 she became director of the Arkansas Department of Health, a post she held until 1993 when President Clinton appointed her United States Surgeon General, the first African-American in that post. Her confirmation was delayed because many senators objected to her outspoken advocacy on such matters as abortion, AIDS, and sex education, and her tenure proved to be short. After the Republicans gained a majority in Congress in 1994, she resigned under pressure following criticism of her response to a question in a public forum about masturbation.

Eldridge, (David) Roy "Little Jazz" (1911–89) jazz musician; born in Pittsburgh, Pa. He was a passionate and original stylist and a major influence on trumpeters between 1935–45. He emerged in New York after 1930 as a featured soloist with Teddy Hill and Fletcher Henderson. He led his own band in 1939, and rose to national prominence with Gene Krupa and Artie Shaw in the 1940s. From 1950, he toured regularly with Jazz at the Philharmonic.

Eliade, Mircea (1907–86) religious scholar, mythographer; born in Bucharest, Rumania. The son of a Rumanian army officer, educated in Rumania and India, he left his native country in 1940, taught in Western Europe and Scandinavia through the early 1950s, and emigrated to the U.S.A. in 1956, where he became a professor at the University of Chicago. His three-volume *History of Religious Ideas* (1979–85), in which he searched out what he called "the 'secrets' of religious history, and of man's destiny on earth," is considered definitive. He also published novels, novellas, and short fiction.

Elion, Gertrude B. (Belle) (1918–) pharmacologist; born in New York City. She taught in the New York City secondary school system and worked as a research chemist for several New York City companies before joining the Burroughs Wellcome Company (1944–83). There she began a 23-year professional collaboration with pharmacologist George Hitchings. Elion considered that she and the more dominating Hitchings could work as a team to discover drugs for immunosuppression, gout, and bacterial, parasitic, and viral diseases; their anti-herpes treatment, acyclovir, was a breakthrough in antiviral research. Elion and Hitchings won one-half the 1988 Nobel Prize in Physiology for their many contributions to pharmaceutical research.

Eliot, Charles (1859–97) landscape architect; born in Cambridge, Mass. (son of Charles William Eliot). After graduating from Harvard University, he studied horticulture before becoming an apprentice to Frederick Law Olmsted in 1883. Taking a year off to study European landscape design, he came back to open his own Boston firm in 1886, creating parks for small New England and midwestern cities like Youngstown, Ohio. A regular contributor to *Garden and Forest Magazine* in 1890, he wrote *Waverly Oaks,* outlining a strategy for conserving a stand of virgin trees (in Belmont, Mass.) and existing flora elsewhere; this led to formation of the Massachusetts Trustees of Public Reservations in 1891, the first state-funded conservation group. Joining the Olmsted brothers in 1893, he formulated a forestry plan to include existing growth in the firm's design for the Boston Metropolitan Parks Commission, before his untimely death in 1897. In 1900 Harvard University established the first university course in landscape architecture in his memory.

Eliot, Charles William (1834–1926) educator; born in Boston, Mass. Trained as a mathematician and chemist at Harvard and in Europe, he taught at Harvard (1854–63) (where he introduced written examinations) and the Massachusetts Institute of Technology (1865–69) before assuming the presidency of Harvard (1869–1909). Having signaled his progressivism and grasp of educational issues in "The New Education" (1869), he presided over a period of intense growth and reform at Harvard in which he increased the number of faculty tenfold, quadrupled enrollment, began teaching women (1879) and established Radcliffe College (1894), introduced the elective system, and liberalized the curriculum. He raised the standards of graduate and professional schools, most notably reforming the law and medical schools, and added graduate schools of arts and sciences, applied science, and business administration. His landmark report on secondary schools (1892) led to the standardization of public school curricula and the foundation of the Board of College Entrance Examinations (1901). In later years he became widely known as the editor of the Harvard Classics, a set of significant books that were said to provide a complete education in "a five-foot shelf."

Eliot, John (1604–90) missionary; born in Widford, England. He emigrated to Boston in 1631 and settled in Roxbury, Mass. He became deeply interested in the Indians of Massachusetts and learned their language in order to preach to them. He wrote and published numerous books in English and Indian languages. He translated the Bible into the Indian language (1661–63), the first Bible printed in any language in North America. He organized fourteen villages of converted "praying" Indians, but the hatred and fear engendered by King Philip's War (1675–76) reduced the number to four villages, and those eventually dwindled away. He continued his work until his death, in spite of the great setback brought about by the war.

Eliot, T. S. (Thomas Stearns) (1888–1965) poet, critic, playwright, editor; born in St. Louis, Mo. Descended from an old Massachusetts and Unitarian family, he studied philosophy at Harvard (B.A. 1909; M.A. 1910), the Sorbonne (1910–11), and Oxford (1914–15). He remained a permanent resident of England but made occasional visits to the U.S.A. He took British citizenship in 1927, the same year he joined the Church of England and embraced Anglo-Catholicism. While teaching school in England (1915–17) and working as a bank clerk (1919–22), he reviewed books and was an editor of the literary magazine the *Egoist* (1917–19) and a founder-editor of the *Criterion* (1922–39). His main career was as an editor at the English publishing firm, Faber and Faber (1926–65), in which capacity he discovered and supported many modern writers. Although in some respects out of step with his century – being deeply religious and conservative, antisecular and antiromantic – he had an astonishing impact on his times. His literary criticism, in such works as *The Sacred Wood* (1920) and *Homage to John Dryden* (1924), set forth the literary tastes of a whole generation, while his own early poetry, such as *Prufrock and Other Observations* (1917) and "The Wasteland" (1922), virtually defined an era; later poems, such as *Four Quartets* (1935–42), although greatly admired, spoke to a smaller public; although several dealt with esoteric themes, his verse plays, such as *Murder in the Cathedral* (1935) and *The Cocktail Party* (1950), proved to be surprisingly popular. He personally remained aloof from most public events and political developments, but in 1948 he was awarded the Nobel Prize in literature, formal recognition of his widespread influence.

Elkin, Stanley (Lawrence) (1930–) writer, educator; born in New York City. A University of Illinois Ph.D., he served in the U.S. Army (1957–59) and taught at several colleges before joining the English faculty of Washington University (St. Louis) (1968). He published many short stories and over half a dozen novels, skewering contemporary American life with his elusive plots and allusive language, from *Boswell* (1964) to *George Mills* (1982) and *The Magic Kingdom* (1985). *Stanley Elkin's Greatest Hits,* a collection of his shorter works, appeared in 1980. He suffered from multiple sclerosis for much of his adult life.

Elkins, Stanley M. (Maurice) (1925–) historian; born in Cambridge, Mass. Educated at Harvard (A.B. 1949) and Columbia (Ph.D. 1958) Universities, Elkins taught at the University of Chicago (1955–60) and at Smith College (1960–68; Syndenham Clark Parsons Professor of History Emeritus, 1968). Prominent among the students of Columbia's Richard Hofstadter and a leading authority on African-American history, his many publications include *Slavery: A Problem in American Institutional and Intellectual Life* (1959) and *The Age of Federalism* (with Eric McKitrick) (1993).

Ellery, William (1727–1820) Revolutionary statesman; born in Newport, R.I. He was admitted to the bar in 1770. He served Rhode Island as a delegate to the Continental Congress (1776–81, 1783–85). He signed the Declaration of Independence. He was collector of the port of Newport (1790–1820).

Ellet, Charles, Jr. (1810–62) civil engineer; born in Bucks County, Pa. In 1842 he built a wire suspension bridge across the Schuylkill River in Pa., and went on to build numerous bridges, canals, and railroads. In 1853 he advocated using dams and reservoirs to control the flooding of major U.S. rivers. In 1854 he proposed using ships with reinforced prows and iron rams for assaulting coastal forts and harbors in wartime. After the successful debut of the Confederacy's *Merrimack,* the Union commissioned the "Ellet Ram Fleet." In June 1862 it opened the Mississippi River from Memphis to Union ships, but Ellet was killed in the action.

Ellington, (Edward Kennedy) Duke (1899–1974) composer, orchestra conductor, jazz musician; born in Washington, D.C. Raised in a moderately well-to-do family, his father being a White House butler and later a blueprint-maker for the U.S. Navy, he studied piano and painting from age six and acquired his nickname from a boyhood friend. He began subbing for ragtime pianist Lester Dishman at a Washington cafe in 1914, and while there he wrote his first composition, "Soda Fountain Rag." He won a poster design contest sponsored by the National Association for the Advancement of Colored People in 1917; this prompted him to leave high school before graduation to operate his own sign-painting business, but a year later he declined a scholarship from the Pratt Institute (Brooklyn) and devoted himself exclusively to music. He first established his name in Washington by supplying bands for parties and dances and as a sideman in others' bands. In 1923 he and hometown associates Sonny Greer and Otto Hardwick moved to New York City and began working as "the Washingtonians." Ellington assumed leadership of the ensemble, which in 1924 made its first recordings and began a three-year residency at a Broadway speakeasy. In 1925 he wrote the score for the *Chocolate Kiddies,* a revue that ran for two years in Germany. He also began to attract significant sidemen to his band, including such colorful, blues-oriented players as Johnny Hodges and Cootie Williams; they helped form Ellington's signature style and propel his output as a composer. In December 1927 the Duke Ellington Orchestra made its decisive opening at the Cotton Club, the showplace of Harlem speakeasies; his composing flourished there and he remained in residency until 1932. By this time, through radio broadcasts and many recordings for U.S., English, and French labels, he was internationally renowned as the foremost jazz composer and bandleader. In 1930 he performed with his orchestra in the Amos and Andy movie, *Check and Double Check,* the first of many such movie appearances. In 1933 he led his 14-piece band on its first tour of England and Europe, and for the next 40 years he maintained a near-constant touring schedule, broken only by perennial residencies at clubs in New York, Chicago, Los Angeles, London, and Paris. Between 1930 and 1942, Ellington was at his most creative, composing a series of pieces that highlighted the distinct musical personalities of his loyal sidemen. In 1938 he hired composer-arranger Billy Strayhorn, an essential collaborator whose 1941 composition "Take the 'A' Train" served thereafter as the band's theme. During this period Ellington also produced several of his most enduring works, including "Mood Indigo," "Sophisticated Lady," "In a Sentimental Mood," and "Don't Get Around Much Anymore." In 1943 he introduced his celebrated extended work, *Black, Brown, and Beige,* at Carnegie Hall, where he premiered other ambitious works at annual concerts through 1948. During the early 1950s Ellington was virtually alone among jazz orchestra leaders in keeping his band intact, though he suffered several key personnel changes and a reduction in the quality of his bookings. In 1955 Johnny Hodges rejoined the band after a four-year absence and during the next five years Ellington's popularity underwent a dramatic renewal, encouraged by a successful appearance at the Newport Jazz Festival in 1956, the recording of which became his biggest-selling album. In 1959 his soundtrack for *Anatomy of a Murder* was the first commissioned from an African-American composer for a major Hollywood movie. His overseas tours in the 1960s and 1970s inspired several large-scale suites, and in his final decade he also wrote liturgical music for concerts he presented in cathedrals in the U.S.A., England, and Germany. Increasingly recognized as a major American composer, he received numerous honorary degrees and awards after 1963, including the Presidential Medal of Freedom in 1969. In 1971 he became the first jazz musician inducted into the Royal Academy of Music in Stockholm, Sweden. His autobiography, *Music Is My Mistress,* was published in 1973. He led his band until a couple of months before his death from cancer, when it was taken over by his son, Mercer Ellington.

Elliot, Walter (Hackett Robert) (1842–1928) Catholic priest, writer; born in Detroit, Mich. A lawyer and Civil War veteran, he was inspired by a sermon of Father Isaac Hecker to become (1872) a Paulist priest. His books included an 1891 biography of Hecker that in translation caused a furor in France and led to papal condemnation of modernism.

Elliott, Jesse Duncan (1782–1845) naval officer; born in Hagerstown, Md. He commanded the USS *Niagara* during the battle of Lake Erie (1813). He was accused of failing to promptly aid Commodore Oliver Perry's flagship; the ensuing controversy, however, did not prevent him from holding numerous other commands in the navy.

Elliott, Maxine (b. Jessie Dermot) (1868–1940) stage actress; born in Rockland, Maine. Described as beautiful and dignified, she took up acting mainly as a way to earn money, and was popular in romantic roles. She debuted in New York in 1890 in *Middleman,* and later performed with her husband Nat Goodwin. She opened her own theater in New York in 1908, then officially retired in 1911, appearing occasionally thereafter.

Ellis, Albert (1913–) psychologist, author; born in Pittsburgh, Pa. He studied at Columbia University (Ph.D. 1947), taught at Rutgers University (1948–49), and practiced clinical psychology from 1950. He published many books on psychology and sexual behavior, and is best known as the developer of Rational-Emotive Psychotherapy, which rejects Freudian theories to assert that emotions come from conscious as well as unconscious sources. His books include *Sex Without Guilt* (1966).

Ellis, Carleton (1876–1941) chemist, inventor; born in Keene, N.H. He cofounded Ellis-Foster Company (1907) in New Jersey and Florida to carry on petrochemical research and he invented important methods of cracking crude oil (1919–30) as well as methods for synthesizing isopropyl alcohol and acetone. He invented lacquers for automobile paints and developed processes for applying plastics. In all, he was granted 753 U.S. patents. He was also an early proponent of hydroponic plant growth (1938).

Ellis, Earl H. ("Pete") (1880–1923) marine officer; born in Iuka, Kans. The eccentric, hard-drinking son of teetotaling parents, he enlisted in 1900, received a commission the following year, and became a leading proponent of Marine Corps amphibious doctrine. Ellis died in suspicious circumstances on the island of Koror in May 1923 while secretly surveying Japanese fortifications in Micronesia.

Ellis, Edward (Sylvester) (1840–1916) writer; born in Geneva, Ohio. He studied at the State Normal School of New Jersey, and settled in Upper Montclair, N.J. Under multiple pen names, he wrote many popular dime novels about the West, such as the Davy Crockett series.

Ellis, Harvey (1852–1904) furniture designer; born in Rochester, N.Y. Originally an architect, he worked with Henry H. Richardson on the design of the New York State capitol in Albany. In the 1880s Ellis worked in the Midwest, then returned to Rochester. In 1902 he began to design furniture for Gustav Stickley's United Crafts shop in Syracuse, N.Y.; in 1903 he began to publish brilliant designs for textiles and interiors as well as furniture in *The Craftsman*. He seems to have been solely responsible for the Stickley workshop's production of ornamental inlaid furniture.

Ellis, John Tracy (1905–) Catholic church historian; born in Seneca, Ill. A priest with a doctorate in history from Catholic University (Washington, D.C.), he spent most of his career on its faculty. A longtime executive secretary of the American Catholic Historical Association and editor of the Catholic Historical Review (1941–62), he wrote widely on church history and won particular notice for his 1955 essay deploring an anti-intellectual "ghetto mentality" among American Catholics. He was named a monsignor in 1955.

Ellison, Ralph (Waldo) (1914–94) writer; born in Oklahoma City, Okla. He studied music at Tuskegee Institute before moving to New York City to study sculpture. A protégé of Richard Wright, whom he met in 1937, he wrote reviews, essays, and short stories. He spent seven years writing *Invisible Man* (1952, National Book Award), and although it was his only novel it gained him a place as a respected American writer and remains one of the central texts of the African-American experience. His other major work, *Shadow and Act* (1964), is a collection of his essays and interviews. After teaching at various universities, he became the Albert Schweitzer Professor in the Humanities at New York University (1970–79). He was awarded the Presidential Medal of Freedom in 1969.

Ellmann, Richard (1918–87) literary critic, educator; born in Highland Park, Mich. A scholar of 19th- and 20th-century Irish literature who lectured widely and taught at Northwestern (1951–68) and Oxford (1970–84) Universities, he wrote among other works definitive biographies of James Joyce (1959) and Oscar Wilde (1987).

Ellsworth, David (1944–) wood craftsman/artist; born in Iowa City, Iowa. After starting as a folksinger/guitarist, he attended architecture school but took his degrees in fine arts at the University of Colorado. Opening a woodturning studio in Boulder, Colo., in 1975, he soon became bored with making production pieces and began to experiment with making thin-walled wooden vessels, more like those made by potters, basketmakers, or glassblowers than traditional woodturners. These distinctive pieces – made with tools of his own devising and designed to exploit the natural features of wood – gained him a wide public, many exhibits, and numerous awards and honors. In 1991 he moved on to a new phase with his "Solstice Series," in which he applied both fire and paints to the natural surface of wood, further extending his craft into the more creative area of art.

Ellsworth, Lincoln (1880–1951) explorer, engineer; born in Chicago (son of James William Ellsworth). After studying at Yale and Columbia University, he worked in the Canadian and American West as a surveyor, prospector, and mining and railroad engineer. He received army flight training during World War I and was the first person to fly over both the North Pole (1926, in a dirigible) and the South Pole (1935, in an airplane). He claimed some 380,000 square miles of Antarctic territory (Ellsworth Land) for the U.S.A. as a result of his overflights (1935, 1939). In 1941 he led an expedition to Peru.

Ellsworth, Oliver (1745–1807) public official, Supreme Court chief justice; born in Windsor, Conn. A lawyer prominent in Connecticut politics, he served in the Continental Congress (1777–83) and was a major figure at the Constitutional Convention in 1787, contributing to the Connecticut Compromise, under which the Senate represents states and the House represents population. As one of Connecticut's first two senators (1789–96), he played a major role in proposing the Bill of Rights and other fundamentals of the American government, such as the rules by which the Senate operates and the regulations behind the nation's judicial structure. President Washington appointed him chief justice of the U.S. Supreme Court (1796–1800); while serving, he went to Paris to negotiate a treaty that averted a war with France (1799). Poor health forced him to resign in 1800.

Elman, Mischa (1891–1967) violinist; born in Talnoy, Ukraine. He made his public debut at age five, and after studies at the St. Petersburg Conservatory, made his professional debut in Berlin, at age 13. Making his first appearance in the U.S.A. in New York in 1908, he settled there in 1911 to pursue an international career as one of the most beloved violinists of the time, especially admired for his lush treatment of the Romantic repertoire.

Elmslie, George Grant (1871–1952) architect; born near Huntley, Scotland. He emigrated to Chicago in 1884. In a Minneapolis partnership (1909–22) with William Gray Purcell (1880–1965) he designed Prairie School banks and houses, later practicing solo in Chicago.

Eltinge, Julian (1883–1941) actor; born in Newtownville, Mass. A leading female impersonator, he charmed audiences with his elegant appearance and deft wit, touring in vaudeville (1906–32) with brief appearances on stage and screen.

Ely, Eugene (1886–1911) aviator; born in Williamsburg, Iowa. He worked as a chauffeur before learning to fly in California in 1909. The next year, he was the first person to fly to and from a warship. An exhibition pilot, he died while attempting a dip at the state fairgrounds, Macon, Ga.

Emerson, Ralph Waldo (1803–82) essayist, poet, lecturer; born in Boston, Mass. Son of a Unitarian minister, he was eight years old when his father died leaving six young children. At age 14 Ralph entered Harvard where he ran messages for the president and waited tables. He also began the journal that he kept up for 50 years, the source of many of his poems, essays, and lectures. Unhappy teaching (1821–25), he tried the Divinity School in Cambridge, Mass., and in 1826 began to guest preach in Unitarian pulpits, but his liberal ideas led him to break with the Unitarians in 1832. At the end of the year he went to Europe where he sought out many of the major literary-intellectual figures – in particular, Thomas Carlyle, his lifelong correspondent – and began to develop his own philosophy, a compound of German idealism, Neo-Platonism, Asian mysticism, and Swedenborgianism. Back in America in 1833 he took up guest preaching again, but he gradually abandoned that for public lectures. His first wife having died (1831), he remarried

(1835) and settled in Concord, Mass., where he spent mornings writing and afternoons walking in the woods and fields; he enjoyed his four children and among his circle of friends was Henry David Thoreau. His famous Phi Beta Kappa oration at Harvard in 1837, "The American Scholar," was a humanist manifesto, stressing Americans' distinctive traits; and in place of traditional Christianity, he subscribed to a philosophy known as Transcendentalism, stressing the ties of humans to nature. Hardly an activist, he did support the abolitionists and the Civil War. Although he published many volumes of essays and poetry – *Nature* (1836), *Representative Man* (1850), *The Conduct of Life* (1860) – his main source of income as well as of his popular reputation came from the lectures that he gave throughout America and in England. He made a final trip to Europe and Egypt (1872–73) and continued to lecture and publish, but his mind clouded over during his final decade. Never accepted solely as a poet, philosopher, or creative writer, he has survived as one of America's most unique voices and influences.

Emerson, Rollins A. (Adams) (1873–1947) geneticist; born in Pillar Point, N.Y. He served the U.S. Department of Agriculture (1897–98), taught horticulture at the University of Nebraska (1899–1914), then moved to Cornell University (1914–42). He made many rigorously detailed studies of the genetics of maize, and influenced many subsequent maize geneticists, including Nobel Prize winner Barbara McClintock.

Emerson, William Ralph (1833–1918) architect; born in Alton, Ill. An inventor of the Shingle style, this Boston architect became influential through numerous 1870s and 1880s designs for New England houses, incorporating Queen Anne and Colonial Revival details.

Emmerich, André (1924–) art dealer; born in Frankfurt, Germany. He studied in the Netherlands, emigrated to America (1940), and studied at Oberlin (B.A. 1944). He was a writer and editor for *Time-Life International* (in New York City) (1944–53) and *Réalités* (Paris) (1944–53). He founded the André Emmerich Gallery (1954), specializing in contemporary art and classical antiquities.

Emmett, Daniel (Decatur) (1815–1904) composer; born in Mount Vernon, Ohio. A pioneering member of blackface comedy troops (1842–98), he composed songs for minstrel shows, including "Dixie," (1859) which became the Southern anthem.

Emmons, S. F. (Samuel Franklin) (1841–1911) geologist; born in Boston, Mass. He served the U.S. geological exploration of the 40th parallel, then became a geologist for the newly created U.S. Geological Survey (1879–1911). He made major contributions to studies of mining and the origin of ore deposits.

Emory, William H. (Hemsley) (1811–87) army officer, explorer; born in Queen Annes County, Md. He was a West Point graduate in the Topographical Engineers who helped survey the U.S.–Canada (1844–46) and the U.S.–Mexico (1848–57) boundaries. He commanded the Indian Territory (1861), held western commands during the Civil War, and retired as a brigadier general (1876).

Endecott, John (c. 1589–1665) colonial official; born in Chagford, England. He landed at Salem and was in charge of the settlement there (1628–30) until the arrival of John Winthrop. He led a punitive expedition against the Indians (1636) which helped to bring on the Pequot War. As governor (1655–65), his Puritan intolerance and lack of tact

led to a number of persecutions and executions of religious dissenters.

Enders, John F. (Franklin) (1897–1985) virologist; born in West Hartford, Conn. He spent his career at Harvard (1929–67) and the Boston Children's Hospital (now Boston Children's Medical Center) (1947–80). He investigated bacterial infections and immunity (1930–37), then began research on viruses, improving the tissue culture techniques needed for their cultivation. After he founded the Infectious Diseases Research Laboratory at Boston Children's Hospital (1947), he, with students Thomas Weller and Frederick Robbins, grew mumps virus in continuous culture. In 1948, Enders, Weller, and Robbins cultivated poliovirus in human tissue cells; this breakthrough made possible the development of a polio vaccine, and won the three scientists the 1954 Nobel Prize in physiology. In 1962, Enders developed an effective measles vaccine. He remained active at Harvard until age 80, and spent his last four years studying the AIDS virus.

Engelbart, Douglas C. (1925–) computer engineer; born in Portland, Ore. A pioneer in the design of interactive computer environments, he invented the "mouse" (1963). He created the first two-dimensional editing system and was the first to demonstrate the use of mixed text-graphics and shared screen viewing. He was director of the Augmentation Research Center in Palo Alto (1959–77). He founded the Bootstrap Project at Stanford University (1989).

Engelberger, Joseph F. (Frederick) (1925–) roboticist, manufacturer; born in New York City. Considered the father of robotics, he and inventor George Devol founded Unimation, Inc., (1958–83) and produced the first industrial robot for General Motors (1961). He founded Transitions Research Corporation (1984), which, while continuing to develop industrial robots, has also designed and built service robots for hospitals, laboratories, nursing homes, and other applications.

England, John (1786–1842) Catholic prelate; born in Cork, Ireland. He became prominent in Ireland as a pastor, preacher, editor, and defender of Irish rights before being consecrated bishop of the missionary diocese of Charleston, S.C., (1820), embracing the Carolinas and Georgia. A progressive, widely known for his efforts to counter anti-Catholic prejudice and champion the separation of church and state, he founded and became editor (1822) of the nation's first Catholic weekly, the *United States Catholic Miscellany.*

Englebright, Harry (Lane) (1884–1943) U.S. representative; born in Nevada City, Calif. A mining engineer with the California Conservation Commission, he served in the U.S. House of Representatives (Rep., Cal.; 1926–43), and as minority whip (1933–43).

Enthoven, Alain (1930–) economist, systems analyst, health care reformer; born in Seattle, Ore. Son of an English father and French mother, the family settled in Seattle. He majored in economics in Stanford and was a Rhodes Scholar at Oxford, then took a Ph.D. in economics at the Massachusetts Institute of Technology (1956). He worked with the Rand Corporation (1956–61) where he pioneered in the multidisciplinary approach to problems known as "systems analysis." He then joined the Defense Department and began what became the Office of Systems Analysis (1961–69); originally applied to defense problems, systems analysis soon was adopted by many branches of government. While also serving as a director of Georgetown University in the late 1960s, he became involved in creating the university's new health maintenance organization (HMO). Switching his focus from defense to health issues, he joined Litton Industries in California in 1969; by 1971 he was president of Litton Medical Products. In 1973 he joined Stanford's Graduate School of Business (1973); he also took on a consulting position with Kaiser-Permanente, the nation's largest HMO. At this time, too, he had begun to meet regularly with the so-called Jackson Hole Group, started by Dr. Paul Ellwood, a Minneapolis (Minn.) pediatric neurologist, who periodically assembled health care professionals at his condominium in Jackson Hole, Wyo., to discuss reforming America's medical delivery system. In the years that followed, Enthoven became acknowledged as one of the prime analysts of health care reform and in particular became a proponent of the approach known as "managed competition."

Epstein, (Sir) Jacob (1880–1959) sculptor; born in New York City. He studied in New York (1896–1902), in Paris (1902–04), and then moved to London (1905), where he lived for the rest of his life. His early religious subjects, such as *Genesis* (1930), were attacked as both indecent and blasphemous, and his busts of contemporary notables were done in a moderately modernist style. The English generally held him in higher regard than did American critics and he was knighted in 1954.

Erdrich, (Karen) Louise (1954–) Ojibwa writer; born in Little Falls, Mont. A child of the Bureau of Indian Affairs boarding schools, she received her B.A. at Dartmouth (1976) and an M.A. at Johns Hopkins University (1979). Her writing has won many prizes and awards, and her books include *Love Medicine* (1984), *The Beet Queen* (1986), *Tracks* (1988), and *Crown of Columbus* (1991).

Erickson, Milton H. (Hyland) (1901–80) psychiatrist; born in Aurum, Nev. He conducted experiments in hypnosis under psychologist Clark Hull at the University of Wisconsin, where he received the M.D. (1925). He carried on research at the Worcester (Mass.) State Hospital and the Wayne County (Mich.) General Hospital and taught at Wayne State University (1934–48). In 1979 he entered private practice in Phoenix, Ariz. He founded the American Society of Clinical Hypnosis in 1957 and became the nation's best-known practitioner of hypnotherapy.

Ericsson, John (1803–89) engineer, inventor; born in Varmland County, Sweden. He served as a topographer and a captain in the Swedish army. He moved to London and worked as an independent engineer (1826–39), developing the idea of placing a ships' engine below the waterline; his *Novelty* was the world's first propeller-driven commercial ship. He came to New York in 1839 with a commission to build a ship for the U.S. Navy. His propulsion system was used by commercial steamers and by the USS *Princeton* (1844), the world's first screw-propelled war vessel. He became a U.S. citizen in 1848. The advent of the Civil War brought a demand for his talents; he designed and built the USS *Monitor* in a 100-day period (1861–62). Following the battle between the *Monitor* and the CSS *Virginia* (formerly the *Merrimac*) he continued to design and build ironclads. He launched a ship capable of firing underwater torpedoes (1878) and continued his experiments to find better methods

of utilizing heat energy, even looking into solar energy. He died in New York and his remains were returned to Sweden (1890) at the request of the Swedish government.

Erikson, Erik H. (Homburger) (1902–94) psychoanalyst, author; born in Frankfurt, Germany (of Danish parents). He entered analysis with Anna Freud during the 1920s and graduated from the Vienna Psychoanalytic Institute in 1933. After emigrating to the United States (1933), he held positions at Harvard, Yale, the Austen Riggs Center (Stockbridge, Mass.), and the University of California: Berkeley. From 1960–70 he was a professor at Harvard. His major research in developmental psychology led to his theory of eight psychosocial stages in the life cycle, from infancy through adulthood; it was Erikson who introduced the term and concept of "identity crisis." His first major book, *Childhood and Society* (1950; revised edition, 1963), remained among his most widely read and influential works, and unlike some of his colleagues he applied his ideas to subjects of more popular interest, as in his psychohistorical studies, *Young Man Luther* (1958) and *Gandhi's Truth: On the Origin of Militant Nonviolence* (1969).

Erikson, Kai T. (Theodor) (1931–) sociologist; born in Vienna, Austria (son of Erik Erikson). A childhood emigrant to the U.S.A., he earned a Ph.D. at the University of Chicago and joined the faculty at Yale (1966), where he edited the *Yale Review* (1979–89). His books include *Wayward Puritans* (1966) and *Everything in Its Path* (1976).

Erlanger, Joseph (1874–1965) physiologist, administrator; born in San Francisco. He was an instructor at Johns Hopkins (1900–06), then moved to the University of Wisconsin (1906–10) where he performed experiments on intracardiac nerve impulses. He joined Washington University (St. Louis) (1910–46), where he reorganized its medical school and brought the university to scientific prominence. With former student Herbert Gasser, he modified the cathode-ray oscilloscope to facilitate the two scientists' research on electrophysiology of the nervous system. Erlanger and Gasser were joint winners of the 1944 Nobel Prize in physiology for their work on nerve impulse transmission. Erlanger continued to publish research papers and accounts of the history of physiology after his retirement.

Ernst, Max (Maximillian) (1891–1976) painter; born in Brühl, Germany. He studied philosophy at the University of Bonn (1911), traveled widely, lived in the U.S.A. during the 1940s, and settled in France (1953). A surrealist and Dadaist, he used the subconscious as his inspiration, as seen in *Oedipus Rex* (1921) and *Polish Rider* (1954).

Erskine, John (1879–1951) educator, novelist, musician; born in New York City. As a youth he showed serious talent as a pianist (studying under Edward MacDowell) but after taking his Ph.D. from Columbia University (1903), he became a professor of English; most of his academic career was at Columbia (1909–37), where his emphasis on studying the classic texts gave rise to the "great books" programs adopted by many educational institutions. As a literary scholar, his editions (1915–22) introduced Lafcadio Hearn's writings to the West and he coedited the *Cambridge History of American Literature* (1917–21). Another reputation was launched with *The Private Life of Helen of Troy* (1925), the first of his satirical novels treating legendary individuals in modern settings. He had kept up his interest in music, giving occasional public concerts, and he was active in the new

Juilliard School of Music, serving as its president (1928–37). On retiring from Juilliard and Columbia in 1937, he devoted himself to writing critical and historical works and his memoirs.

Ertegun, Ahmet (Munir) (1923–) recording producer, song publisher; born in Istanbul, Turkey. Son of the Turkish ambassador to the U.S.A., he and his brother Nesuhi Ertegun effectively grew up in Washington, D.C., and were greatly attracted to American jazz and popular music. Ahmet attended St. John's College (Md.) and studied for a doctorate at Georgetown University, but he abandoned a conventional career when in 1947 he cofounded Atlantic Records (with Herb Abrahmson). Nesuhi Ertegun concentrated on producing jazz records with the likes of John Coltrane and Ornette Coleman, while Ahmet worked with such musicians as Big Joe Turner, the Drifters, Professor Longhair, and the Rolling Stones; he would also play a role in bringing such Southern musicians as the Allman Brothers into the mainstream of popular rock. The cosmopolitan Ahmet was at home among the jet set but he also had a hands-on role in producing many records, and the Atlantic label became one of the most important in the history of 20th-century music because of the support – technical, financial, and personal – the company gave to several generations of emerging musicians.

Ervin, (Samuel James) Sam, Jr. (1896–1985) U.S. senator; born in Morganton, N.C. An expert on constitutional law, he served in the U.S. House of Representatives (Dem., N.C.; 1946–47) and as a judge before going to the U.S. Senate (1954–74). In the Senate, he opposed civil rights legislation, supported the Vietnam War, and generally favored conservative causes. He won his greatest fame for presiding over the Watergate committee investigation (1973), where his impassioned speeches on the Constitution's restraints on the government raised the hearings and himself above partisan politics and ideology.

Erving, Julius (Winfield) (1950–) basketball player; born in Hempstead, N.Y. One of basketball's greatest and most acrobatic players, he gained national attention while playing for the University of Massachusetts. He played forward for the American Basketball Association (ABA) Virginia Squires and New York Nets (1972–76), and for the National Basketball Association (NBA) Philadelphia 76ers (1977–87). His combined ABA and NBA lifetime points scored (30,026) is third best in history. Nicknamed "Dr. J," he was an All-NBA first team selection six times.

Esau, Katherine (1898–) botanist; born in Ekaterinoslav, Russia. She emigrated with her family to Germany (1919), finished college there (1922), then moved to the U.S.A. in 1922 to further her education. She taught botany at the University of California: Davis (1931–63), then moved to the University of California: Santa Barbara (1963–65). She made major contributions to the light and electron microscopy of virus-infected plants, and determined that certain viruses are transported with the plant's food via the phloem (food-conducting tissue). As a necessary adjunct to her studies of pathological anatomy, she made fundamental studies of vascular plant anatomy, phloem structure, and differentiation. After her retirement, she remained an active lecturer at many American institutions.

Esherick, Wharton (1887–1970) wood worker, artist, sculptor; born in Philadelphia. He studied at the Pennsylvania Academy of Fine Art and in his early work as a painter and sculptor he explored the different styles of the early 20th century. Influenced by the theories of Rudolph Steiner and several European artists/designers, he came to develop a style that emphasized twisted organic forms that seemed to grow naturally, and he turned increasingly to working with wood. In the 1930s he handcrafted his studio and house in Paoli, Pa., that in its individualistic details remains a landmark (and museum), and, as factory-produced furniture was attracting other major designers, he continued to make his one-of-a-kind pieces. Many artist-craftsmen in the late-20th-century woodworking movement would be influenced by his unique free-form, sculptural, often asymmetrical designs.

Espy, James (Pollard) (1785–1860) meteorologist; born in Westmoreland County, Pa. He was the first to correctly describe how clouds form and the first to use the telegraph to send weather reports to the U.S. War and Navy Departments (1843–45). He wrote *Philosophy of Storms* (1841) and was dubbed "the storm king." His storm-making fire experiments produced the requisite "rarefied air," but no storms.

Estes, Richard (1936–) painter; born in Evanston, Ill. He studied at the Art Institute of Chicago (1952–56), and became a member of the super realists, who focused on industrial landscapes and a photographic approach to art. His eerie street scenes, such as *Victory Theatre* (1968) and *Canadian Club* (1974), are typical of his work.

Etheridge, Anna (1844–?) nurse; born in Wisconsin. A visitor in Detroit when the Civil War commenced, she enlisted as an army nurse with a Michigan unit and tended Michigan regiments throughout the entire conflict. She came to be known as "Michigan Annie" and "Gentle Anna," was once wounded, and earned the Kearny Cross for bravery. After the war she worked in a federal government office.

Ettinghausen, Richard (1906–79) art historian, museum curator; born in Frankfurt-on-Main, Germany. He studied at the University of Frankfurt (Ph.D. 1931), the University of Munich, and at Cambridge, England. He emigrated to New York City (1934), worked at the American Institute of Persian Art and Archeology, New York City, (1934–37), and at the Institute for Advanced Study, Princeton (1937–38). He was associated with several prestigious institutions, including the Smithsonian's Freer Gallery, Washington, D.C. (1944–67). A noted scholar of Islamic art, he wrote many books on the subject.

Etzioni, Amitai (Werner) (1929–) sociologist; born in Cologne, Germany. Raised in Palestine, he emigrated to the U.S.A. in 1957. He taught at Columbia University (1958–80; Center for Policy Research director after 1968) and George Washington University (1980). He wrote prolifically for both scholarly and popular audiences, often on organizational analysis; his books include *A Comparative Analysis of Complex Organizations* (1961, later revised) and *The Moral Dimension* (1988).

Evans, Charles (1850–1935) librarian, bibliographer; born in Boston, Mass. He cofounded the American Library Association (1876) and created the 12-volume *American Bibliography,* an index of material printed in America from 1639 to the early 1800s.

Evans, Daniel Jackson (1925–) governor, engineer, educator; born in Seattle, Wash. A naval reservist (1943–46, 1951–53), he served on the Armistice Commission at Panmunjon,

Korea. After serving as a Washington state representative (Dem., 1956–65), he founded an engineering firm in 1959. Washington's only three-term governor (1965–77), he improved the state college system and initiated "Education for All" to serve the disabled. In 1977, he became president of Evergreen State College.

Evans, Frederick William (1808–93) reformer, editor, Shaker elder; born in Leominster, Worcestershire, England. Having been influenced by the Owenites and a group of freethinkers and reformers in England, he sailed to America (1820) with family members. He edited with his brother several publications devoted to radical reform. After visiting a Shaker community in Lebanon, N.Y., he joined it, spending 57 of his last 63 years with the community as elder. A born leader and natural orator, he became one of the nation's most influential Shaker leaders and published much on this topic.

Evans, Gil (b. Ian Green) (1912–87) jazz musician; born in Toronto, Canada. He was a pianist and arranger whose landmark orchestrations for Miles Davis included "The Birth of the Cool," "Porgy and Bess," and "Sketches of Spain."

Evans, Maurice (1901–89) stage/movie/television actor; born in Dorchester, England. After his professional stage debut in London in 1926, he enjoyed his first success with *Journey's End* (1929); he went on to the Old Vic, then made his Broadway debut in *Romeo and Juliet* (1936) with Katharine Cornell. Thereafter he settled in the U.S.A., playing mainly in Shakespeare, Shaw, and such classic plays but also making several movies and appearing on television, most regularly in "Bewitched." During World War II he was in charge of the U.S. Army's Entertainment Section in the Central Pacific and performed a famous modern-dress version of Hamlet for the troops.

Evans, Oliver (1755–1819) inventor, manufacturer; born near Newport, Del. Self-taught, a natural mechanic, he invented a high-speed machine for carding wool in 1777. By 1785, despite a chronic shortage of funds, he had designed and built automatic machinery that made it possible to mill grain in one continuous process. He became America's first steam engine builder, improving on James Watt's invention with several advanced models, including an amphibious steam-powered dredging machine (1804), America's first self-propelled land vehicle. In 1807 he established the Mars Iron Works; at the time of his death, the company had produced some 50 steam engines.

Evans, Robley (Dunglison) (1846–1912) naval officer; born in Floyd Court House, Va. Known as "Fighting Bob," he was commander of the Atlantic Fleet (1905–07). He commanded the first segment of the round-the-world cruise of the American battle fleet (1907–08).

Evans, Walker (1903–75) photographer; born in St. Louis, Mo. Originally an architectural photographer, he took pictures of rural poverty for the Farm Security Administration (1935–40). In 1941, his starkly detailed pictures of Appalachian poor families appeared in *Let Us Now Praise Famous Men*. An editor for *Fortune* magazine (1945–65), he photographed industrial landscapes. He was a professor of graphic arts at Yale University from 1964 to 1974.

Evans, (William John) Bill (1929–80) jazz musician; born in Plainfield, N.J. He was a classically-trained pianist whose delicate, introspective style established him as one of the few major white innovators in jazz history. Beginning in 1955, he played with George Russell, Charles Mingus and Miles

Davis, collaborating on the latter's historic 1959 recording "Kind of Blue." From 1961 until his death, he led a succession of highly interactive trios.

Evarts, William Maxwell (1818–1901) lawyer, cabinet officer, U.S. senator; born in Boston (grandson of Roger Sherman). At Yale he founded the *Yale Literary Magazine* but he took up the law and was admitted to the New York bar in 1841. He soon became one of the most prominent lawyers in the country, and although personally opposed to slavery he would argue the constitutionality of the institution when clients engaged him to return escaped slaves. Originally active in the Whig Party, he joined the new Republican Party in 1854. In 1863–64 he went to England on diplomatic missions to try to stop the British from supplying the Confederate navy. He was the chief counsel for President Andrew Johnson in his impeachment trial, after which Johnson named him the attorney general (1868–69). Returning to New York City, he led the fight against the corrupt Tweed Ring. Among his other celebrated cases, he was counsel for the U.S.A. in the arbitration of the *Alabama* claims (1871–72), defense lawyer for Henry Ward Beecher in the adultery trial (1875), and chief counsel for the Republican Party in the Hayes-Tilden presidential dispute (1877). After the last-named, Hayes appointed him secretary of state (1877–81). He served New York in the U.S. Senate (Rep., 1885–91) and was forced to retire because of poor eyesight. In addition to the high esteem he earned as a lawyer and public servant, he was noted as a public speaker, and on July 4, 1876, he delivered the principal address at the Philadelphia centennial of the Declaration of Independence.

Everett, Edward (1794–1865) U.S. representative/senator, educator, orator; born in Dorchester, Mass. A Harvard valedictorian (1811), he served as pastor of the Brattle Street Church in Boston (1814–15), then, after studying abroad, became a professor of Greek literature at Harvard (1819–25). He was a U.S. representative (Ind., Mass.; 1825–35), governor of Massachusetts (Whig, 1836–39), U.S. ambassador to England (1841–45), president of Harvard (1846–49), secretary of state (1852–53), and U.S. senator (1853–54). He turned to lecturing and, as an advocate of compromise over slavery, he ran as vice-president on the Constitutional Union Ticket in 1860; when the war broke out, however he became an ardent speaker on behalf of the Union and he delivered the two-hour keynote speech at Gettysburg in November 1863, the one that was followed (and his historical reputation unfairly eclipsed) by Lincoln's Gettysburg Address. He continued his public lectures almost to the end of his life.

Evergood, Philip (1901–73) painter; born in New York City. Educated at Cambridge University, England, he came to New York City (1923) to study with George Luks at the Art Students League. Influenced by the Depression of the 1930s, he painted scenes of social protest. He is best remembered for his surrealistic paintings, such as *Lily and the Sparrows* (1939).

Evers, (James) Charles (1922–) civil rights leader, mayor; born in Decatur, Miss. After serving in the U.S. Army during the Korean conflict, he took over his family's considerable business interests in Philadelphia, Miss. (mid-1950s) and then moved to Chicago (1957) where he was a successful nightclub owner, real estate agent, and disc jockey. He returned to Mississippi after the assassination of his brother Medgar Evers (1963) and assumed Medgar's post as field director of the National Association for the Advancement of Colored People (NAACP) in Mississippi. He was elected mayor of the town of Fayette, Miss. (1969) – the first black mayor elected in a racially mixed southern town since the Reconstruction – and published his autobiography (1971). He was reelected mayor (1973) after an unsuccessful attempt for the governorship on an independent ticket (1971). In 1978 he failed in his bid to become a U.S. senator.

Everson, William (Oliver) (Brother Antonius, pen name) (1912–) poet; born in Sacramento, Calif. He studied at Fresno State, Calif. (1931, 1934–35), and was a conscientious objector during World War II. He became a Dominican lay brother (1951–71), left the order, and settled in Davenport, Calif. Associated with the Beat poets, he wrote erotic and mystical poetry.

Evert, (Christine Marie) Chris (1954–) tennis player; born in Ft. Lauderdale, Fla. Between 1974 and 1986, she won at least one Grand Slam singles championship every year, a record. She won the French singles championship seven times, Wimbledon three times, the U.S. Open six times, and the Australian twice. During her career, she won 157 professional singles titles, including many memorable competitions with her chief rival, Martina Navratilova. Her coolness under pressure on the courts earned her the nickname "Ice Maiden."

Ewell, Richard Stoddart (1817–72) soldier; born in Georgetown, Wash., D.C. An 1840 West Point graduate, he saw action in the Mexican War. He resigned his U.S. commission in 1861 to serve the Confederacy. In command of an army corps during the Gettysburg campaign, he defeated Union forces north of the town on July 1, 1863, but failed to press his advantage. Able and aggressive, the bald, high-domed Ewell bore, according to one of his biographers, "a striking resemblance to a woodcock."

Ewing, (William) Maurice (1906–74) oceanographer, seismologist; born in Lockney, Texas. He taught at Lehigh University (1930–43), then at Columbia University (1944–72), where he became founding director of its Lamont (now Lamont-Doherty) Geological Observatory in 1949. He left the observatory to join the Marine Biomedical Institute of the University of Texas (1972–74). A pioneer in oceanography, his gravity and seismographic surveys (1935–39) determined the vast thickness of continental margin sedimentary rocks, while his Atlantic explorations in the 1940s demonstrated the relative thinness of the earth's subocean crust. His later marine seismographic research (1956) indicated that the Mid-Atlantic Ridge is part of a continuous global submarine system, and that geological activity at its deep central rift supported the sea-floor spreading hypothesis of H. H. Hess. Ewing's controversial hypothesis of ice age periodicity, based on freezing and thawing of the Arctic Ocean, remains unproven.

Ewry, (Raymond Clarence) Ray (1873–1937) track and field athlete; born in Lafayette, Ind. Though afflicted with polio as a child, he won more Olympic gold medals (10) than any athlete in history. At the 1900, 1904, 1906, and 1908 Games, he won the standing broad jump and the high jump. He won the standing long jump at the 1900 and 1904 Games.

Exner, John E. (Jr.) (1928–) psychologist; born in Syracuse, N.Y. A Cornell University Ph.D. in clinical psychology, he taught psychology at, among other institutions, Long Island University (1969–84). He directed the Rorschach Workshops, Asheville, N.C. (1969). His *Rorschach* (1978, later revised) established standard postulates for use in interpreting the widely used Rorschach test.

Eyre, Wilson (1858–1944) architect; born in Florence, Italy. He came to America as a student and in Philadelphia, alone and in partnership with John G. McIlvaine (1912–39), designed over 350 houses and other buildings.

F

Fagan, Garth (1941–) choreographer, dance teacher; born in Jamaica. Son of Jamaica's chief education officer, he began dancing with the National Dance Company of Jamaica, went on to the Dance Theater of Detroit, and then began teaching dance at the State University of New York (SUNY): Brockport (near Rochester). Working with mostly disadvantaged African-American students, he formed an amateur ensemble in 1970 that soon became known as the Bucket Dance Theater; in the years following, the troupe gained a widening reputation for its exciting blending of Afro-Caribbean with modern dance styles. He maintained his post at SUNY while giving increasing amounts of time to his now internationally recognized dance company. *Griot,* his 1992 collaboration with composer and trumpeter Wynton Marsalis, gained Fagan a wider national exposure.

Fagan, Mark (Matthew) (1869–1955) mayor; born in Jersey City, N.J. The Republican mayor of Jersey City (1902–08), he ran against the Democratic machine and for progressive reform. Although he was named honorary mayor under the new commission government in 1913, he turned his back on politics and returned to his family's funeral business.

Fainsod, Merle (1907–72) Russia specialist, educator; born in McKees Rocks, Pa. Teaching government at Harvard (1932–72), he was director of the Russian Research Center (1959–64) and directed the university library (1964–72). In addition to his academic work, he held several government posts: staff member of President Franklin Roosevelt's Committee on Administrative Management (1936); price executive for the U.S. Office of Price Administration (1941–42); and director of the department's retail trade and services division (1942–43). His many books and articles focused largely on Russia and the Soviet Bloc.

Fairbank, John K. (King) (1907–91) historian; born in Huron, S.D. After graduating from Harvard he spent six years traveling in China, teaching himself Chinese in order to read the country's 19th-century archives. He taught at Harvard (1936–77), where he developed a pioneering modern East Asian history program with his colleague Edwin O. Reischauer and directed (1955–73) the East Asian Research Center. Fairbank created the field of modern Chinese history and became the dean of American Chinese scholars. A target of Senator Joseph McCarthy's anticommunist hearings in the 1950s, he went on to become a leading advocate of normalizing relations with communist China in the 1960s. His more than two dozen books include *The United States and China* (1948) and *China: A New History* (1992).

Fairbank, William M. (Martin), Sr. (1917–89) physicist; born in Minneapolis, Minn. He taught at Amherst College (1947–52), Duke (1952–59), and Stanford (1959–85). He made major contributions to studies of low-temperature superconductivity, was the first to provide experimental evidence of the existence of quarks (1977), and devised a gyroscopic method of testing Einstein's theory of general relativity during space shuttle missions.

Fairbanks, Charles (Warren) (1852–1918) vice-president, attorney; born near Unionville Center, Ohio. A prominent attorney, specializing in railroad disputes, he became a senator in 1898, and vigorously supported President McKinley. He served as Theodore Roosevelt's vice-president (1905–09) but had little impact upon that administration. He ran unsuccessfully for the vice-presidency in 1916.

Fairbanks, Douglas, Sr. (b. Douglas Elton Ulman) (1883–1939) movie actor; born in Denver, Colo. He made his stage debut at age 12. In 1915 he went into films, and in 1920, after divorcing his first wife, he married the popular movie star, Mary Pickford. Swashbuckling hero parts were his specialty, as in *The Three Musketeers* (1921), *Robin Hood* (1922), and *The Thief of Baghdad* (1924), in which he did all his own stunts. Also a producer and screenwriter, he was a cofounder of United Artists (1919). His career dimmed with the arrival of "talkies" and after he and Mary Pickford were divorced in 1936, he married Lady Sylvia Ashley of England.

Fairchild, David Grandison (1869–1954) botanist, agricultural explorer; born in Lansing, Mich. After studies in Italy and Germany he embarked on travels all over the globe, usually under the sponsorship of the U.S. Department of Agriculture or the Smithsonian Institution. He introduced more than 20,000 species of plants into the U.S.A., including the soybean (1898), the nectarine (1902), and bamboos (1903). He established the Fairchild Tropical Garden near Miami, Fla., and described his gardens in *The World Grows Round My Door* (1947).

Fairchild, Sherman (Mills) (1896–1971) inventor, businessman; born in Oneonta, N.Y. (son of George W. Fairchild). An heir to the IBM fortune, he invented a flash camera (1916) and an aerial camera for the U.S. War Department (1916). He started his own company in 1920 to manufacture the aerial camera; he also founded an aerial survey company and became known as the "father of aerial mapping photography." He also started an airplane factory and developed the first U.S. planes to have enclosed cockpits; he later designed the C-119 transport plane with its rear cargo doors. In 1953 he invented the Fairchild Flight Analyzer Camera, the first to take non-distorted pictures of an object in a continuous sequence of action. He invented a radio compass and introduced such innovations as wing flaps, hydraulic brakes, and retractable landing gear. Eventually his companies were grouped under Fairchild Industries (Farmington, N.Y.) and he remained chairman until his death.

Fairfax, Thomas (1693–1781) British peer, landowner; born in Denton, England. He succeeded to his title (Lord Fairfax of Cameron) in 1709. He came to Virginia (1735) to defend his proprietary rights to the "Northern Neck," the area between the Potomac and Rappahannock Rivers. His claim was upheld (1745) and he immigrated permanently (1747), the only British peer who resided in the New America. He was justice of the peace and a friend of the young George Washington (whose half-brother, Lawrence, was married to a Fairfax). During the American Revolution, he was unmolested and his estate remained intact until his death.

Fairless, Benjamin F. (Franklin) (b. Benjamin Franklin Williams) (1890–1962) industrialist; born in Pigeon Run, Ohio. He changed his name to Fairless when he was adopted as a young boy. Trained as a civil engineer, he rose to be president during 17 years at Central Steel Company before joining U.S. Steel (president, 1938–55; chairman and CEO, 1952–55), which he directed through decades of modernization and expansion and four major strikes. He was a prominent champion of big business.

Falk, Peter (1927–) movie/television actor; born in New York. After serving in the merchant marines, he earned an M.B.A. at Syracuse University and worked for the Connecticut budget bureau. Taking up amateur theater, he made his stage debut off Broadway in 1955. He began in films in 1958 and enjoyed a modest success in such movies as *The In-Laws* (1979) and in various television dramas. Having lost the use of his right eye in an accident at age three, he usually played urban types – gangsters or working-class men – but his most popular role was as the star of the television detective series, *Columbo,* in which he employed his rough-hewn mannerisms to create a beloved character.

Falwell, Jerry (1933–) Protestant evangelist; born in Lynchburg, Va. He studied engineering, then turned to religious studies after a conversion. In 1956 he founded a Baptist church in Lynchburg. He later launched an extremely popular television program, "The Old-Time Gospel Hour," and established Liberty Baptist College. From 1979 onward his Moral Majority became a political force for advancing the social agenda of the religious right, although after 1990 he withdrew from the more public and political sphere to concentrate on his preaching. He wrote *Listen, America!* (1980) and *Wisdom for Living* (1984).

Faneuil, Peter (1700–43) merchant; born in New Rochelle, N.Y. Of Huguenot descent, he went to Boston and became the favorite of his uncle, Andrew, from whom he inherited a large fortune (1738). He offered to donate a public marketplace to Boston. The hesitant townspeople approved the gift by a vote of 367 in favor, 360 opposed (1740). He died as the building was being completed.

Fankhauser, Gerhard (1901–81) embryologist; born in Burgdorf, Switzerland. He taught in Switzerland (1925–29),

then came to the U.S.A. in 1929 for fellowships at the University of Chicago (1929–30) and Yale (1930–31). He spent the remainder of his career at Princeton (1931–69, emeritus 1969–81). He was a popular teacher who made major contributions to research on hormone manipulation and crossbreeding in amphibian embryos. He demonstrated that cell size is directly proportional to the number of chromosomes the cell contains.

Farber, Sidney (1903–73) oncologist; born in Buffalo, N.Y. He began as a pathologist at the Children's Hospital in Boston and taught at Harvard (1929). His life's work revolved around cancer therapy, research, and patient care. In 1947 he founded the Children's Cancer Research Foundation (now, in his honor, the Dana-Farber Cancer Center) and achieved the first remissions in childhood leukemia by using chemotherapy.

Fargo, William George (1818–81) expressman; born in Pompey, N.Y. By 1843 he had become the Buffalo (N.Y.) agent for an express firm, Pomeroy & Company. In 1844 he became part owner of the first express company west of Buffalo, Wells & Company (named after Henry Wells, 1805–78; born in Thetford, Vt.); in 1850 it merged with two other companies to become the American Express Company with Wells and Fargo as officers. The two men then organized Wells, Fargo & Company in 1852 for business in California and elsewhere in the Far West; it gradually consolidated with rival companies and by 1866 it monopolized transportation in the West. Fargo remained based in Buffalo where he served as Democratic mayor (1862–66). He served as president of Wells, Fargo (1870–72) and as president of American Express (1868–81).

Farley, (James Aloysius) Jim (1888–1976) businessman, public official; born in Grassy Point, N.Y. He was a bookkeeper and company correspondent before he formed a building supplies company. His affable nature gave him a boost when in 1912 he began his career as a Democratic Party functionary. As he became increasingly prominent in New York State Democratic politics, he worked for Al Smith and then Franklin D. Roosevelt. He managed Roosevelt's first run for governor of New York and backed him at the 1932 and 1936 Democratic Conventions. He was rewarded with the positions of chairman of the Democratic National Committee (1932–40) and postmaster general (1933–40). He broke with Roosevelt in 1940 over the issue of a third term, and failing to get the Democratic nomination for himself, he went back to business. He was a board chairman of Coca-Cola Export Corporation (1940–73).

Farmer, Fannie (Merritt) (1857–1915) home economist; born in Boston, Mass. She became interested in food preparation while working as "mother's helper," and enrolled (1887) in the Boston Cooking School. She stayed on and became its director in 1894, resigning to open Miss Farmer's School of Cooking (1902) to teach practical food preparation. She turned increasingly to diets for the sick and convalescent, teaching nurses and dieticians. Although well known in Boston, she became nationally famous for her *Boston Cooking School Cook Book,* first published in 1896 (at her expense because the publisher thought it was too risky); now called "Fannie Farmer's" it is still going strong some 12 editions later. She spent her later years lecturing throughout the country and cowriting a monthly column for *Women's Home.*

Farmer, James (Leonard) (1920–   ) civil rights activist; born in Marshall, Texas. A founding member of the Congress of Racial Equality (CORE) in 1942, he led student sit-ins and Freedom Bus rides, becoming CORE national director (1961–66). After serving as the executive director of the Coalition of American Public Employees (1972–82), he published *Lay Bare the Heart: An Autobiography* (1985), and became a professor at Mary Washington College (Fredericksburg, Va.).

Farmer, Moses (Gerrish) (1820–93) inventor; born in Boscawen, N.H. He left Dartmouth College because of poor health and he taught school in Maine and New Hampshire. Curious and clever, a compulsive tinkerer, he built a model electric train, designed a fire alarm system adopted by the city of Boston (1851), and devised a multiplex telegraph system (1855). In 1868, a decade before Edison introduced his electric light bulb, Farmer outfitted a house in Cambridge, Mass., with a dynamo and 40 incandescent lamps of his own invention.

Farnham, Russel (1784–1832) fur trader; born in Massachusetts. A member of the Astoria expedition to Oregon (1810–13) he later traveled across Siberia on foot (1814–16). He managed John Jacob Astor's American Fur Company (1817–19) and then took up farming in Missouri.

Farnham, Thomas Jefferson (c. 1804–48) traveler, writer; born in Vermont. He traveled to Oregon in 1839 and wrote *Travels In the Great Western Prairies* (1841). He moved to San Francisco in 1846 and practiced law.

Farragut, David (b. James) (Glasgow) (1801–70) naval officer; born near Knoxville, Tenn. After being adopted by Commander David Porter, he became a midshipman at the age of nine. His naval career progressed slowly until 1861; he was chosen to command the West Gulf blockading squadron. He ran his ships past Confederate forts and captured New Orleans in 1862; the victory made him the outstanding leader of the Union navy. He blockaded the Gulf coast and contributed to the fall of Vicksburg (1863). In 1864 he led an assault on the Confederate port, Mobile Bay. Disregarding the loss of one ironclad ship to a mine, he is said to have cried out, "Damn the torpedoes – Full speed ahead!" and proceeded into the bay where he captured the Confederate flotilla. This famous victory brought his promotion to vice-admiral in 1864 and to admiral in 1866 (the rank was especially created for him).

Farrakhan, Louis (b. Louis Eugene Walcott) (1933–   ) Black Muslim leader; born in the Bronx, N.Y. He grew up in Roxbury, Mass., and was converted to the Nation of Islam by Malcolm X. Following Malcolm X's defection (1963–64), Farrakhan became the national representative for Elijah Muhammad. When Elijah Muhammad's son allowed whites to join the movement (after 1975), Farrakhan split away and formed a revitalized movement, Final Call to the Nation of Islam. An eloquent and persuasive speaker, he continued to work for black separatism and black economic power. Although he denied being antiwhite or anti-Semitic, he often employed an abrasive rhetoric that alienated such groups, as when he made derogatory statements about Jews during the 1984 presidential primaries on behalf of Reverend Jesse Jackson. In the 1990s, however, Farrakhan began to soften his message and image, and, reviving a talent he had as a young man, even began to play the violin in classical concerts to show that he was not totally opposed to whites and their culture.

Farrand, Beatrix (b. Jones) (1872–1959) landscape architect; born in New York City (niece of Edith Wharton). Tutored at home, she traveled frequently to Europe with her mother, and in 1893 studied horticulture with Charles Sargent at the Arnold Arboretum near Boston. She began her career in her mother's New York home in 1895, winning her first major commission the following year. In 1899, she founded the American Society of Landscape Architects with ten other designers. Unfortunately none of her early gardens have survived, but at Dumbarton Oaks in Washington (1921–47), she transformed the Bliss family farm into a masterpiece of asymmetrical design, with formal walkways leading off into planted areas, and a combination of impressionist use of color with formal garden beds. She designed the Memorial and Silliman College quadrangles and the Marsh Botanical Garden for Yale University (1922–45), part of a series of college commissions. From 1945 she worked on Reef Point Gardens in Bar Harbor, Maine, creating a native flora garden, herbarium, and research library.

Farrar, Geraldine (1882–1967) soprano; born in Ridgefield, Conn. Daughter of a baseball player, she began vocal studies in Boston and went to Europe for further training at age 17. After a successful debut in 1901 at the Berlin Opera, she appeared with Caruso in *La Bohème* at Monte Carlo in 1903. Her American debut came three years later at the Metropolitan in New York; she remained there for 16 seasons, her famous roles including the lead in *Madame Butterfly,* which she sang over 100 times. An erratic singer but a vivacious personality with a cult following among young women, she also appeared in a number of silent films beginning with the *Carmen* of 1915. She retired from opera in 1922 and from recitals in 1931.

Farrell, Eileen (1920–   ) soprano; born in Willimantic, Conn. Her rich, hearty voice made her a popular radio performer in the early 1940s and from there she moved on to serious recitals. From 1958 she sang with the San Francisco Opera, and the Lyric Opera of Chicago, and in the 1960s with the Metropolitan Opera. Later she taught at colleges in Indiana and Maine. She liked her distinction as one of the few serious opera singers who also enjoyed success singing and recording popular and jazz music.

Farrell, James T. (Thomas) (1904–79) writer; born in Chicago. He grew up in the Irish-Catholic milieu of Chicago, attended the University of Chicago, held a variety of jobs, visited Paris, and then settled in New York City (1931) where he became involved with left-wing politics. At the same time, he began writing naturalistic urban fiction, of which the *Studs Lonigan Trilogy* (1932–35) remains his best-known work; for almost two decades, by which time far more explicit works left it looking tame, it was considered almost raunchy. It was also seen as a radical indictment of American society. Farrell continued his critique in a steady stream of fiction – in all, 50 novels and 13 volumes of short stories – but he rejected Marxist communism by the 1950s and his reputation waned.

Farrell, Suzanne (b. Roberta Sue Fricker) (1945–   ) ballet dancer; born in Cincinnati, Ohio. Her mother encouraged ballet lessons as a cure for "tomboyishness." Noticed by a scout for the School of American Ballet, she auditioned for George Balanchine on her 15th birthday and won a scholarship to the school. After only six months in the New

York City Ballet's corps de ballet, she became a featured dancer (1962); by 1965 she was a principal dancer. Called one of Balanchine's muses, he choreographed several dances for her including *Variations* (1966). She taught a masters class at the University of Cincinnati, and on her retirement from the Ballet at age 44, she taught at the School of American Ballet until she was fired in 1993.

Farson, Negley (1890–1960) journalist; born in Plainfield, N.J. An intrepid adventurer, he reported from Western Europe, the Soviet Union, Egypt, and India for the *Chicago Daily News* (1924–35), in a vivid, unanalytical style. His memoirs were a 1936 best-seller. He spent his declining years in England.

Farwell, Arthur (1872–1952) composer; born in St. Paul, Minn. After studies in the U.S.A. and Europe, he taught widely while pursuing studies in American Indian, African-American, and other native music, which contributed to his own highly eclectic style.

Fasanella, Ralph (1914–) painter, laborer; born in New York City. After many years as a union organizer for the United Electrical Workers, he took up painting in 1944; entirely self-taught, he began to gain some recognition for his primitivist/populist scenes of city life; to have more time for himself he switched to running a gas station. In his later work, such as *The Iceman Crucified* (1958), he tried more symbolism; but his simple city scenes were what kept his work and name alive.

Fast, Howard (Melvin) (1914–) writer; born in New York City. As a professional writer after 1932, he became a leading proponent of left-wing views. He was blacklisted for a decade for his Communist Party membership (1944–1956), but in 1957 he declared his disenchantment with the Communism of Stalin in *The Naked God*. Of his dozens of novels, children's books, biographies, and plays he was best known for his historical novels, including *Freedom Road* (1944), *Spartacus* (1952), and *The Immigrants* (1977).

Father Divine See BAKER, GEORGE.

Faulk, John Henry (1913–90) folklorist, radio performer; born in Austin, Texas. He was a folksy southern storyteller whose radio and television career, by then based in New York City, was destroyed by the McCarthyism of the 1950s when he was falsely accused of little more than being opposed to anticommunists. His successful libel suit (1962) effectively ended blacklisting in the entertainment industry. He wrote *Fear on Trial* (1964) about his experiences and in later years lectured on First Amendment issues.

Faulkner, William (Cuthbert) (b. Falkner) (1897–1962) writer; born in New Albany, Miss. He lived in nearby Oxford, Miss., nearly all his life, writing, farming, and hunting. The scanty education he had after the tenth grade included fitful attendance at the University of Mississippi after his World War I service with the Canadian Air Force. (The war ended while he was still in training.) A writer from adolescence, he published his first poems in his early twenties, and during the next few years spent time in New Orleans, where he was encouraged by Sherwood Anderson. When his first book of poems, *The Marble Faun* (1924), was published, he added the "u" to his name. He traveled to Europe later in 1925, before returning to Oxford. His first published novels were *Soldier's Pay* (1926) and *Mosquitoes* (1927). *The Sound and the Fury* (1929) was the first of the complex stream-of-consciousness novels for which he was to become known. In the same year, *Sartoris* was published, the first of a series of novels centered on the Sartoris family in a fictionalized Oxford. He married Estelle Oldham Franklin in 1929. Over the years he created a historical saga centered on five families in his fictional Yoknapatawpha County. His famously complex and difficult prose brought to life characters of the South, by turns degenerate, cruel, and macabre, and a major theme of his work was the toll taken by white Southerners' treatment of African-Americans. Other early fiction included *As I Lay Dying* (1930), *Sanctuary* (1931), *Light in August* (1932), *Absalom, Absalom!* (1936), *The Unvanquished* (1938), *The Hamlet* (1940), and *Go Down Moses* (1942). Never that popular, he had to earn money by writing Hollywood screenplays in the 1930s, and, by that time, was known to drink heavily and habitually. By the middle 1940s his critical reputation was in eclipse; his rediscovery as a major writer began with the publication of *The Portable Faulkner* (1946), edited by Malcolm Cowley. Faulkner won the 1949 Nobel Prize in literature; his *Collected Stories* (1950) won a National Book Award (1951); and *A Fable* (1954) won a National Book Award and a Pulitzer Prize (1955). He was writer in residence at the University of Virginia (1957; 1958). Later works include *The Town* (1957), *The Mansion* (1959), and *The Reivers* (1962). He died of a heart attack in Mississippi.

Fauset, Jessie R. (Redmon) (1882–1961) writer; born in Fredericksville, N.J. She graduated Phi Beta Kappa from Cornell University and studied at the Sorbonne, Paris. She had a long career teaching high school in Washington, D.C., and New York, later joining the faculty of the Hampton Institute (1949). As literary editor of the National Association for the Advancement of Colored People's magazine *Crisis* (1919–26), she was influential in promoting black Francophone and Harlem Renaissance writers. She wrote four novels (1924–34) featuring strong black heroines, and herself was one of the first African-American women to receive recognition as an intellectual.

Faust, Frederick Shiller (Max Brand, pen name) (1892–1944) writer; born in Seattle, Wash. He published the first of his 100 "Max Brand" Westerns in 1917. Using 18 additional pseudonyms for an estimated 30 million words' worth of detective stories, thrillers, and screenplays, he earned the sobriquet "king of the pulp writers." His most famous works were *Destry Rides Again* (1930) and the *Dr. Kildare* film series. He also wrote serious poetry, published in such collections as *Dionysus in Hades* (1931). He lived in Italy (1926–38) and was killed there in action as a war correspondent.

Fearing, Kenneth (Flexner) (1902–61) poet, writer; born in Oak Park, Ill. He studied at the University of Wisconsin (B.A. 1924), and settled in New York City (1924). A freelance writer, he was concerned with themes of social justice, as seen in his poetry, and in the novel *The Big Clock* (1946).

Feenberg, Eugene (1906–77) physicist; born in Fort Smith, Ark. He taught at several American universities, including New York University (1938–46), before coming to Washington University, St. Louis (1946–74). His 1939 publication describing his splitting of the uranium atom made him a pioneer in the development of the theory of atomic energy.

Feiffer, Jules (1929–) cartoonist, playwright; born in New York City. His satirical cartoons first appeared in the *Village*

Voice in 1956 and immediately established themselves as the quintessential images of bohemian/neurotic New Yorkers; the cartoons became nationally syndicated in 1959; and in 1992 he became a regular contributor to *The New Yorker*. He also wrote several plays, including *Little Murders* (1967), and filmscripts, notably *Carnal Knowledge* (1971).

Feinstein, Moshe (1895–1986) rabbi; born in Uzda, Russia. He studied and was ordained in Russia, and came to the U.S.A. in 1937. He was dean of Mesifta Tifereth Jerusalem in New York (1938–86), which became a leading yeshiva under his guidance. He was president of the Union of Orthodox Rabbis of the U.S.A. and Canada from 1968–86. He published many books on Jewish jurisprudence and Talmudic analysis.

Fejos, Paul (1897–1963) movie director, documentary filmmaker, anthropologist; born in Budapest, Hungary. A member of an aristocratic family, he took his M.D. before serving in the Hungarian cavalry and air service in World War I. He made several feature movies in Hungary before moving to New York City (1923), and after working as a researcher with the Rockefeller Institute, he made an experimental movie about suicide, *The Last Moment* (1928). This led to a brief career as a movie director in Hollywood, but in the early 1930s he went back to Europe and directed a number of feature movies. By the late 1930s he began to make ethnographic films in Madagascar, Indonesia, and Thailand and began to develop an interest in anthropology; in the 1940s he headed an expedition to Peru where he applied his knowledge of anthropology to film the documentary, *Yagua* (1941). In 1941 he became director of research for the Viking Fund; later it was renamed, after its principal benefactor, the Wenner-Gren Foundation for Anthropological Research, and Fejos headed it from 1955–63. He became a consulting professor of anthropology at Stanford (1943–63) and taught at such institutions as Yale, Columbia, and Fordham.

Feke, Robert (?1705–?50) painter; born in Oyster Bay, N.Y. He was painting in Boston by 1741, and specialized in portraits. Influenced by John Smibert, he was an acclaimed formula painter, who was noted for his use of color and his depiction of textiles. His painting trademarks include women with similar faces and men who dominate the background, as seen in *Isaac Royall and Family* (1741).

Feld, Elliot (1943–) choreographer, dancer; born in New York City. Trained early at the School of American Ballet, he joined the American Ballet Theatre in 1963. He was a lead soloist and choreographer for the company until he formed his own, the American Ballet Company, in 1969. After that group dissolved, he founded the New York Feld Ballet in 1974, one of the most successful small dance companies.

Feldman, Sandra (1939–) union leader; born in New York City. Growing up poor – she would later credit the public school system for "saving my life" – she graduated from Brooklyn College and took an M.A. in English literature from New York University (1964). As a young woman she joined the Congress of Racial Equality (CORE) and was arrested several times on civil rights marches in the South. She began as a substitute teacher in the New York public schools and in 1963 got a full-time appointment, teaching 4th grade. In 1966 she became a field representative for the United Federation of Teachers; by 1981 she became the union's executive director; by 1983 she was its secretary; and by 1986 she became its president, succeeding Albert Shanker (who had long praised her as the effective administrator). She was the first woman to head this union, the largest local union of any kind in the U.S.A., representing some 85,000 teachers, guidance counselors, and teachers aides, and she became known as a tough and dedicated advocate of the labor union movement and the cause of public education. She was married to Arthur H. Barnes, onetime president of the New York Urban Coalition; they had no children. She collected art and was an avid reader of fiction.

Feldstein, Martin S. (1939–) economist; born in New York City. His contributions range from analysis of health and welfare economics to the economics of taxation. He served on President Reagan's Council of Economic Advisers (1982–84) and was a professor at Harvard beginning in 1967.

Feller, (Robert William Andrew) Bob (1918–) baseball pitcher; born in Van Meter, Iowa. One of the fastest throwing pitchers in baseball history, the right-hander won 266 games and pitched three no-hitters in 18 seasons with the Cleveland Indians (1936–56); during 1942–44, he served in the U.S. Navy. Nicknamed "Rapid Robert," he was elected to baseball's Hall of Fame in 1962.

Feller, William (1906–70) mathematician; born in Zagreb, Yugoslavia. Fleeing Nazism (1939), he settled at Brown University and was the first editor of *Mathematical Reviews*. A specialist in pure mathematics, he also enjoyed statistics and genetics. Best known for *An Introduction to Probability Theory and its Applications* (1950–66), he was also admired as a lecturer.

Fellers, Carl R. (Raymond) (1893–1960) bacteriologist; born in Hastings, N.Y. He worked at several jobs including researching the safety of canned foods for the National Canners Association in Seattle (1921–24) before settling at Massachusetts State College (now the University of Massachusetts) and Agricultural Experiment Station in Amherst in 1926. He helped found the Institute of Food Technology (1939). In 1953 he led efforts to establish a fisheries school and laboratory at the University of Massachusetts. In 1957 he retired to private consulting. He invented methods for pasteurizing dried foods and canning Atlantic crab and he encouraged the cranberry industry to use culls for processed cranberry products.

Felling, (Arthur H.) "Weegee" (1899–1968) photojournalist; born in Zloczew, Poland. He was often first to crime scenes in Manhattan, selling his stark, graphic photos to dailies and the wire services (1936–45). He went to Hollywood in 1947 as a technical adviser for films.

Felsenthal, Bernhard (1822–1908) rabbi; born in Münchweiler, Germany. He came to the U.S.A. in 1854 and served the Sinai and Zion Congregations in Chicago (1861–87). A moderate leader of Reform Judaism in the Midwest, he was an early Zionist. He was a founder of the Jewish Publication Society of America and the American Jewish Historical Society.

Fenneman, Nevin (Melancthon) (1865–1945) geographer; born in Lima, Ohio. Associated with the University of Cincinnati for much of his life, he concentrated on the study of physical geography. He divided the U.S.A. into 25 physiographic provinces (1916), and elaborated upon them in *Physiography of Western United States* (1931) and *Physiography of Eastern United States* (1938).

Fenno, John (1751–98) journalist; born in Boston, Mass. From 1789 he published and edited the pro-Federalist *Gazette of the United States,* backed by Alexander Hamilton; it was a vitriolic partisan paper, though perhaps less cutting, and less expert, than a rival paper edited by Philip Freneau.

Fenno, Richard F. (Francis), Jr. (1926–) political scientist; born in Winchester, Mass. He taught at Wheaton College (Norton, Mass.) (1951–53), Amherst College (1953–57), and the University of Rochester (1957) and is considered an expert in the activities of Congress.

Fenollosa, Ernest Francisco (1853–1908) orientalist, art historian; born in Salem, Mass. He lived for 14 years in Tokyo (1876–90), teaching political economy and philosophy and studying Japanese culture (taking the Buddhist name Tei-Shin and the Japanese name Kano Yeitan Masanobu). On his return he became America's leading orientalist as oriental art curator at the Boston Museum of Fine Arts (1890–97). After another stay in Tokyo as professor of English (1897–1900), he spent his last years writing and lecturing. His major work was *Epochs of Chinese and Japanese Art* (2 vols. 1911). His literary executor, Ezra Pound, edited a number of his works posthumously.

Ferber, Edna (1885–1968) writer; born in Kalamazoo, Mich. A midwestern reporter, she moved to New York City in 1912. She is remembered for her popular fiction featuring strong heroines as in *So Big* (1924, Pulitzer Prize) and *Giant* (1952); *Show Boat* (1926), which was transformed into a classic musical; and several witty stage comedies written in collaboration with George S. Kaufman including *Dinner at Eight* (1932) and *Stage Door* (1936).

Ferber, Herbert (1906–91) sculptor, dentist; born in New York City. He attended Columbia University (B.S. 1927; D.D.S. 1930), and studied at the Beaux-Arts Institute, N.Y. (1927–30). A practicing dentist as well as abstract sculptor, he is noted for his environmental rooms, such as *Sculpture to Create an Environment* (1961).

Ferguson, Homer (1889–1982) judge, U.S. senator; born in Harrison City, Pa. After serving on the Michigan circuit court, he was elected to the U.S. Senate (Rep., Mich.; 1943–55). He was appointed ambassador to the Philippines in 1955.

Ferguson, James Edward (1871–1944) governor; born near Salado, Texas (husband of "Ma" Ferguson). Self-educated, he was a laborer and farmer before becoming a lawyer in Temple, Texas, in 1900. Campaigning as a populist, he won two elections as a Democratic governor (1915–17). He opposed prohibition and women's suffrage but worked to improve rural education. Impeached for misusing state funds and forbidden ever to hold public office, he helped his wife become governor and then governed through her.

Ferguson, "Ma" (b. Miriam Amanda Wallace) (1875–1961) governor; born in Bell County, Texas (wife of James Ferguson). A housewife – although she had attended college – she entered politics to clear her husband's name. After his impeachment in 1917 on charges of mishandling funds and interfering in the university, he was forbidden ever to hold any state office. So in 1924, she ran and was elected, first to serve (1925–27) and then later to a second term (1933–35). In many ways she was merely a "front" for her husband (who had an office beside hers in the state house), promoting

his essentially populist conservative agenda – including pardoning large numbers of prisoners, but opposing the Ku Klux Klan. Her last term was marked by charges of graft in the Highway Commission, and she retired to Austin and remained out of public life.

Ferlinghetti, Lawrence (Monsanto) (b. Lawrence Ferling) (1919–) poet, writer; born in New York City. He attended the University of North Carolina (B.A. 1941), Columbia University (M.A. 1948), and the Sorbonne (1948–51). He settled in San Francisco (1951), taught French (1951–53), and was a founder of City Lights (1952), a bookstore and publishing house. He was regarded as a founder of the Beat poetry movement, as in *A Coney Island of the Mind* (1958), and was also a playwright and novelist.

Fermi, Enrico (1901–54) physicist; born in Rome, Italy. His precocity in physics and mathematics was encouraged by a family friend throughout his education. While a lecturer at the University of Florence (1924–27), he developed a new form of statistical mechanics to explain the theoretical behavior of atomic particles (1926). At the University of Rome, he and his colleagues split the nuclei of uranium atoms by bombarding them with neutrons, thus producing artificial radioactive substances. For this breakthrough, Fermi received the 1938 Nobel Prize in physics. Fearing for his Jewish wife because of Mussolini's anti-Semitic legislation, Fermi went directly from the prize presentation in Stockholm to Columbia University, where he became a professor (1939–42). His suggestion to the U.S. Naval Department to develop weapons utilizing atomic chain reactions led to his move to the University of Chicago (1942–54), where he constructed the first American nuclear reactor. On December 2, 1942, he initiated the atomic age with the first self-sustaining chain reaction, after which he became known as "father of the atomic bomb." The element fermium is named for him.

Fernald, Merritt L. (Lyndon) (1873–1950) botanist; born in Orono, Maine. He spent his career at Harvard (1891–1947), serving as curator and director of their Gray Herbarium (1935–47) and as professor of botany. A major contributor to systematic botany, he wrote over 900 monographs and scientific papers on the geographical relationship of the plants of temperate North America. He proposed the controversial "nunatak theory," which refuted the theory that northern North America was completely covered by a thick ice sheet; his theory argued that certain plants survived Pleistocene glaciation on nunataks (promontories which project above the surface of a glacier). He edited the journal *Rhodora* (1899–1928), and published his greatest achievement, the totally revised eighth edition of *Gray's Manual of Botany,* in 1950.

Fernow, Bernhard Eduard (1851–1923) forester, educator; born in Inowrazlaw, Germany (now Poland). The son of a Prussian government official, he emigrated to the U.S.A. in 1876 and, after publishing a series of articles about forestry, helped found the American Forestry Congress in 1882. Four years later he became chief of the new Division of Forestry in the U.S. Department of Agriculture. In 1898 he resigned to establish the New York State College of Forestry at Cornell University, the first such in the U.S.A.; he later organized forestry schools at Pennsylvania State College and at the University of Toronto, Canada. He founded the journal *Forestry Quarterly* (later, *Journal of Forestry*) and was its editor until 1922.

Ferraro, Geraldine (Anne) (1935–) lawyer, U.S. representative; born in Newburgh, N.Y. The daughter of Italian immigrants, she graduated from New York Law School and established a successful law practice. She was assistant district attorney for Queens, N.Y. (1974–78), and served in the House of Representatives (Dem., N.Y.; 1979–85). In 1984, she was selected by Walter Mondale as his vice-presidential running mate – the first woman to run for this office with a major party. She engaged in a lively debate with her Republican opponent George Bush, but the threat of scandal from her husband's business affairs undermined her value to the Democratic ticket; she and Mondale lost the election overwhelmingly. She made an unsuccessful attempt to win the Democratic nomination for the U.S. Senate in 1992.

Ferré, Luis Antonio (1904–) industrialist, politician, patron of the arts; born in Ponce, Puerto Rico. After making his fortune in the family-owned cement and iron works, he bought the newspaper *El Nuevo Día* (1944) and founded the Ponce Museum of Art (1958). He participated in the constitutional committee that made Puerto Rico a commonwealth in 1952, then served in the U.S. House of Representatives (1953–56). He spearheaded the statehood campaign in the 1967 plebiscite and founded the New Progressive Party in 1967. After several previous unsuccessful attempts, he was elected governor and served from 1968–72. A lifelong worker for statehood and the GOP, he was awarded the Medal of Freedom by President George Bush in 1991. In 1993 the San Juan Center for the Performing Arts was renamed the Ferré Center in his honor.

Ferrel, William (1817–91) meteorologist; born in Fulton County, Pa. Largely self-taught, he is credited with moving meteorology from a descriptive science to a quantitative science. He was the first to describe mathematically the significance of the earth's rotation on its surface bodies. Known as Ferrel's Law, it states, "if a body is moving in any direction, there is a force, arising from the earth's rotation, which always deflects it to the right in the northern hemisphere and to the left in the southern hemisphere." He taught school in the midwest before joining the *American Ephemeris and Nautical Almanac* in Cambridge, Mass., in 1857. From 1867–82 he worked on the U.S. Coast and Geodetic Survey. As a member of the Signal Service (1882–86), he invented a tide machine, the first to predict maximum and minimum tides. His publications include *Popular Essays on Movement of the Atmosphere* (1882).

Ferris, George (Washington Gale) (1859–96) engineer; born in Galesburg, Ill. He was an engineer on a number of bridge projects during the 1880s and 1890s. He created a huge revolving observation wheel for the 1892 World Columbian Exposition in Chicago, the original "Ferris wheel."

Ferry, Elisha Peyre (1825–95) governor; born in Monroe, Mich. A successful lawyer in Waukegan, Mich., he was a member of the Illinois constitutional convention (1862). A colonel in the Civil War, he befriended General Grant who, as President, appointed him governor of the Washington Territory (1872–80). Staying in Seattle, he practiced corporate law and banking. After he helped to establish Washington as a state, he was elected its first governor (1889–93).

Ferry, Orris Sanford (1823–75) U.S. representative/senator; born in Bethel, Conn. A Yale graduate, he served in Congress (Rep., Conn.; 1859–61) and became a brigadier-general in the Union army (1861–65). He was a moderate reconstructionist in the Senate (1867–75).

Feshbach, Herman (1917–) physicist; born in New York City. He spent his career at the Massachusetts Institute of Technology, where he taught and performed research investigating intranuclear forces and statistical theories of nuclear reactions.

Fess, Simeon Davidson (1861–1936) educator, U.S. senator; born near Lima, Ohio. President of Antioch College (1907–17), he was elected to the U.S. House of Representatives (Rep., Ohio; 1913–23), where he championed women's suffrage. In the Senate (1923–35), he proved to be extremely conservative.

Fessenden, Reginald (Aubrey) (1866–1932) engineer, inventor; born in East Bolton, Quebec, Canada. A clergyman's son, educated in Canada, he met Thomas Edison in New York in 1886 and became his chief chemist. As an electrical engineer at the University of Pittsburgh (1893–1900), Fessenden carried out important early research in radio communication. His invention of amplitude modulation enabled him to broadcast what is regarded as the first radio program, speech and music, from a transmitter at Brant Rock, Mass., on Christmas Eve, 1906. Some of his other inventions contributed to telegraphy, the radio, sonic depth finding, and the radio compass. Long interested in the classics, he published a study of the origins of myth, *The Deluged Civilizations of the Caucasus* (1923).

Fessenden, William Pitt (1806–69) lawyer, U.S. representative/senator; born in Boscawen, N.H. He graduated from Bowdoin College (1823) and was admitted to the Maine bar in 1827. He rose in the Whig Party and served Maine in the U.S. House of Representatives (Whig, 1841–43). As a strong opponent of slavery and the Kansas-Nebraska Bill, he became one of the founders of the Republican Party (1854) and then went to the U.S. Senate (Rep., 1854–64). As a member of the Senate Finance Committee (chairman after 1861) he was a staunch proponent of fiscal responsibility, arguing for taxes if necessary to support the Union forces. President Lincoln appointed him secretary of the treasury (1864–65), where he continued his conservative fiscal policies. Returning to the U.S. Senate (Rep., Maine; 1865–69), as chairman of the Joint Committee on Reconstruction he supported severe treatment of the defeated South and opposed President Andrew Johnson and his policies. But as a man of principle and law, Fessenden was convinced that Johnson had been impeached (1868) for political motives and so voted "not guilty" after the trial even though it led to his being attacked by his party and constituents.

Festinger, Leon (1919–89) social psychologist; born in New York City. Educated at the State University of Iowa, he taught at Rochester University, the Massachusetts Institute of Technology, and the Universities of Michigan and Minnesota. At Stanford University (1955–68), and the New School for Social Research (1968) he was increasingly recognized for his theory of cognitive dissonance, whereby people are unable to tolerate conflicting thoughts and beliefs over time and must resolve such conflicts by rejecting or devaluing one or more of the cognitions. His major work was *A Theory of Cognitive Dissonance* (1957).

Fetterman, William Judd (?1833–66) soldier; born in (?)New London, Conn. He survived combat in the Civil War only to be killed, along with his entire 80-man command, in an Indian ambush near Lodge Trail Ridge, Wyo., in 1866.

Fewkes, J. (Jesse) Walter (1850–1930) ethnologist, archaeologist; born in Newton, Mass. Fewkes turned from zoology to ethnology in the 1880s and joined the staff of the Bureau of American Ethnology (1895–1928, chief 1918–28). He founded and edited the *Journal of American Ethnology and Archaeology* (1890–95). An early scholar of the Hopi and Pueblo Indians, he pioneered the integration of current anthropological studies with archaeological evidence and the opening of ancient sites to the public.

Feynman, Richard (1918–88) physicist; born in Far Rockaway, N.Y. He worked on the Manhattan Project at Princeton (1941–42) and Los Alamos (1942–45), while continuing to pursue his interest in quantum electrodynamics. Accepting Bethe's offer to join Cornell University (1945–50), he developed pictorial representations of space-time behavioral probabilities of particle interactions, now known as Feynman diagrams. He moved to the California Institute of Technology (1951–88), where he continued to apply his quantum electrodynamic theories to the "superfluidity" of liquid helium. With colleague Gell-Mann, he developed the Conserved Vector Current hypothesis of weak subatomic particle interactions (1958). Feynman shared the 1965 Nobel Prize with Schwinger and Tomonaga for fundamental developments in quantum electrodynamics. He applied his dynamism, curiosity, and intuition to linguistics, music, art, and teaching, and was an outspoken critic of NASA's laxity in constructing the ill-fated space shuttle *Challenger*. His free-spirited personality engaged a wide public with his memoir, *Surely You're Joking, Mr. Feynman* (1984).

Fichandler, Zelda (b. Zelda Diamond) (1924–) theater producer, director; born in Boston, Mass. A cofounder of the Arena Stage in Washington, D.C., in 1950, she was responsible for presenting a wide array of European and American plays. Premiere performances under her auspices include *The Great White Hope* (1967). She received many awards including a special Tony award in 1967 for theatrical work outside New York City.

Fiedler, Arthur (1894–1979) conductor; born in Boston, Mass. Trained as a violinist in Boston and Berlin, he joined the Boston Symphony (1915–30), first playing violin, then viola. Determined to conduct, he founded his own chamber orchestra, the Boston Sinfonietta, in 1924. In 1929 he launched the Esplanade summer series, free concerts by the Boston Symphony, along the Charles River. In 1930 he took over the Boston Pops Orchestra and for almost a half century he was the most beloved conductor of light-classical music in the U.S.A. Active in promoting music through various mediums, he was also made an honorary fire chief because of his practice of chasing every major fire, day or night, and became a familiar figure to Bostonians at the scene of the fires.

Fiedler, Fred E. (Edward) (1922–) psychologist; born in Vienna, Austria. He emigrated to the U.S.A. in 1938. He taught at the University of Illinois (1951–69) and the University of Washington (1969). Among his works on industrial and organizational psychology and organizational behavior are *A Theory of Leadership Effectiveness* (1967) and *New Approaches to Effective Leadership* (coauthored, 1987).

Fiedler, Leslie (Aaron) (1917–) literary critic, educator; born in Newark, N.J. His trilogy beginning with *Love and Death in the American Novel* (1960) analyzed American fiction in terms of its embodied archetypes and cultural myths; his later work located such myths in popular art. A University of Wisconsin Ph.D., he taught at the University of Montana (1941–64) and in 1964 joined the faculty of the State University of New York at Buffalo.

Field, Cyrus W. (West) (1819–92) businessman, financier; born in Stockbridge, Mass. (brother of David Dudley Field and Stephen Johnson Field). By 1854 he had become wealthy from his paper manufacturing company and he retired to concentrate on promoting the first telegraph cable across the Atlantic. He organized the New York, Newfoundland, and London Telegraph Company in 1854, and the Atlantic Telegraph Company in 1856. After four attempts, success was signaled by Queen Victoria's telegraph to President James Buchanan (1858), but the cable broke within weeks. Criticized by many, and personally in debt, Field raised money for additional attempts that were made after the Civil War and finally resulted in success in 1866. He then spent many years promoting the laying of submarine cables elsewhere in the world. Having bought control of the New York Elevated Railway Company in 1877, he served as its president for three years and helped to bring rapid-transit to New York City. In his later years he suffered severe financial losses and he died practically impoverished.

Field, David Dudley (1805–94) legal scholar; born in Haddam, Conn. (brother of Cyrus West Field and Stephen Johnson Field). He was a leading legal reformer; he chaired a New York State commission that wrote a Code of Civil Procedure (1848) which was adopted by other states and countries. His *Outlines of an International Code* (1872) was translated into several languages.

Field, Erastus (Salisbury) (1805–1900) painter; born in Leverett, Mass. He was a student of Samuel F. B. Morse (1824), and became an itinerant portrait painter. His naive paintings of children, such as *Girl Holding Rattle* (c. 1835), are charming. He is most famous for the mystical architectural towers in his last major work, *Historical Monument of the American Republic* (c. 1876–88).

Field, Eugene (1850–95) writer, poet; born in St. Louis, Mo. He was brought up by a cousin in Amherst, Mass. (1856), attended several colleges, and became a reporter and journalist for newspapers in the Midwest. He wrote the column "Sharps and Flats" for the *Chicago Morning News* (1883–95), and wrote sentimental poems for children, such as "Little Boy Blue" (1888).

Field, Marshall (1835–1906) merchant; born in Conway, Mass. A shop clerk in Pittsfield, Mass., he moved to Chicago (1856) where he continued in retail. By 1867 he headed Field, Leiter & Company which in 1881 became Marshall Field and Company, soon recognized as one of the world's largest, most progressive emporia. As a philanthropist, he gave to many causes, from the land on which to establish the University of Chicago to a library for his hometown. In 1893 he gave a million dollars for the Columbian Museum at the Chicago World's Fair; it is now known as the Field Museum of Natural History.

Field, Marshall, III (1893–1956) newspaper publisher; born in Chicago. The grandson of Marshall Field, he founded the

Chicago Sun in 1941 and bought the *Chicago Daily News* in 1947.

Field, Martha A. (Amanda) (1943–) legal scholar; born in Boston, Mass. She taught at the University of Pennsylvania (1969–72) and at Harvard (1978). She is known for her knowledge of administrative and constitutional law and her writings on women's issues, surrogate motherhood, and civil rights of the mentally retarded.

Field, Sally (1946–) film actress; born in Pasadena, Calif. Pert and diminutive, she began on television sitcoms, then switched to films, winning Academy Awards for *Norma Rae* (1979) and *Places in the Heart* (1984).

Field, Stephen J. (Johnson) (1816–99) Supreme Court justice; born in Haddam, Conn. (brother of David Dudley and Cyrus W. Field). He served on California's state legislature (1850–57) and supreme court (1857–63) before President Lincoln named him to the U.S. Supreme Court (1863–97). A staunch conservative, he frequently dissented from the court's majority opinion.

Fields, Dorothy (1905–74) lyricist; born in Allenhurst, N.J. Daughter of Broadway comedian and producer Lew Fields, she taught dramatic arts and published poetry before working with composer Jimmy McHugh on her first hit, "I Can't Give You Anything But Love, Baby," from the 1928 musical *Blackbirds of 1928*. They also wrote "On the Sunny Side of the Street" (1930). She spent most of the 1930s in Hollywood, then returned to Broadway where she continued to write lyrics (*Sweet Charity,* 1966) and librettos (*Annie Get your Gun,* 1946) for composers such as Cole Porter, Arthur Schwartz, and Cy Coleman until her death.

Fields, James Thomas (1817–81) author, publisher; born in Portsmouth, N.H. Known for both literary and business acumen, he became head of the Ticknor & Fields publishing firm and was editor of *The Atlantic Monthly* from 1861 to 1870. His own literary works include *Poems* (1849) and *Yesterdays With Authors* (1876).

Fields, Lew See WEBER, JOSEPH (MORRIS).

Fields, W. C. (b. William Claude Dukenfield) (1879–1946) movie actor, screenwriter; born in Philadelphia, Pa. Son of a cockney-English immigrant, he had little education but learned of life on the streets and took up juggling. By age 14 he was working professionally and he soon began to appear in vaudeville and in Europe as "The Tramp Juggler." From 1915–21 he was one of the stars in the *Ziegfeld Follies,* but his comic patter was becoming as important as his juggling skills and in 1924 he had his first Broadway role as a comic actor. He began to make silent films, and went on to major stardom in the talking films and radio where his inimitable raspy voice completed his characterization of a bulbous-nosed, child-hating, habitually tipsy misanthrope. In fact, his real-life personality was not unlike the one he cultivated in the movies – he deeply distrusted most established institutions and sentiments, going so far as to keep his money in savings accounts in scores of banks and under fictitious names. Author of the screenplays for many of his movies, his still popular classics include: *You Can't Cheat an Honest Man* (1939), *My Little Chickadee* (1940), *The Bank Dick* (1941), and *Never Give a Sucker an Even Break* (1941). His popularity has survived his demise and he remains one of the archetypal American comedians.

Filene, Edward A. (Albert) (1860–1937) merchant, reformer; born in Salem, Mass. In 1881 he abandoned plans to attend Harvard and joined his ailing father and younger brother, Lincoln Filene, in a new venture, a clothing store in Boston. In 1891, as president, Edward launched a series of successful retail innovations including the "Automatic Bargain Basement," and a charge-plate system with cycle billing. He built William Filene's Sons into a prosperous department store but in 1928 he lost control to partners when he tried to turn over management to an employees' cooperative. For most of his life he believed that America's future lay in what he called "companionate prosperity" – cooperation among all levels and areas of society so that all would prosper. He was an avid supporter of Chambers of Commerce, and a proponent of credit unions. In 1909 he invited Lincoln Steffens to help reform Boston's government and municipal services. In 1919 he formed and endowed the Cooperative League (later the Twentieth Century Fund) to research national economic issues. Interested in cooperatives, he organized the Consumer Distribution Corporation in 1935 and also the Good Will Fund, Inc. (1936) to research public affairs enterprises. He wrote several books including *Next Steps Forward in Retailing* (1937). A bachelor, he left most of his fortune to the Twentieth Century Fund.

Fillmore, Abigail (b. Powers) (1798–1853) First Lady; born in Stillwater, N.Y. She was a schoolteacher and Millard Fillmore was originally one of her students; they married in 1826. She started the first White House library. She died of bronchial pneumonia shortly after the presidency began.

Fillmore, Charles (1854–1948) Protestant religious leader, businessman; born near St. Cloud, Minn. The son of a merchant who traded with Indians, he worked as a clerk and muleteer and speculated in real estate in Oklahoma, Colorado, and Texas before turning to religious matters in the late 1880s. With his wife Myrtle he launched the Unity movement, based on a practical Christian doctrine they claimed could overcome physical, mental and financial problems. He wrote a series of books explaining the beliefs of Unity; one book, *Prosperity,* argued that Christianity fostered business success and that the Great Depression was the consequence of negative thinking.

Fillmore, Millard (1800–74) thirteenth U.S. president; born in Cayuga County, N.Y. Largely self-educated, he read law in an office and was admitted to the bar (1832). He became comptroller of New York State (1847) and served in the U.S. House of Representatives (1833–35, 1837–43) as a Whig. Elected vice-president in 1848, he ascended to the presidency on the death of Zachary Taylor in 1850. As president, he sent Commodore Matthew Perry to Japan and tried with little popular success to steer a moderate course through the threatening slavery issue. His support of the Fugitive Slave Law as part of the Compromise of 1850 cost him the Whig nomination in 1852. He ran for president on the Know-Nothing (American) Party in 1856, then retired to Buffalo, N.Y., where he devoted himself to local affairs.

Filson, John (?1747–88) explorer, author; born in Chester County, Pa. He entered Kentucky in 1783 and wrote *Discovery, Settlement, and Present State of Kentucke* (1784) to attract settlers. (The so-called "autobiography" of Daniel Boone first appeared in this book.) He was killed by an Indian while helping to lay out the settlement of Cincinnati.

Finch, Vernor (Clifford) (1883–1959) geographer; born near Tecumseh, Mich. He was a faculty member at the University of Wisconsin (1911–1951). With O. E. Baker he coauthored the *Atlas of World Agriculture,* used for decades as a text for agricultural geography. He contributed much to the dot-map technique and the "fractional" method of representation of landscapes.

Finck, Henry Theophilus (1854–1926) music critic; born in Bethel, Mo. After studies at Harvard and in Germany, he wrote for papers including the *New York Evening Post* (1881–1924); a notable champion of Wagner and Dvořák, he resisted later innovators.

Fine, Henry Burchard (1858–1928) mathematician; born in Chambersburg, Pa. He was dean of the Princeton science departments until 1928 and during Woodrow Wilson's leave to run for president in 1912 Fine was interim president of Princeton. He was a founding member of the American Mathematical Society (1891), serving as its president in 1911–12.

Fine, Irving (1914–62) composer; born in Boston, Mass. After studies at Harvard and with Nadia Boulanger in France, he taught at Harvard and Brandeis. He was admired for his cosmopolitan style marked by a delicate lyricism.

Fine, Vivian (1913–) composer; born in Chicago. After studies with teachers including Cowell, Sessions, and Szell, she taught at schools including Bennington (1964–87). She was a prolific composer of modernist works with a broad, expressive range.

Fingers, (Roland Glen) Rollie (1946–) baseball pitcher; born in Steubenville, Ohio. Sporting a handlebar mustache, he was baseball's premier relief pitcher during his 17-year career with the Oakland Athletics, San Diego Padres, and Milwaukee Brewers (1968–85). By retirement, the right-hander had saved more games (341) than any pitcher in major league history (a record surpassed in 1992 by Jeff Reardon). He was elected to baseball's Hall of Fame in 1992.

Fink, Albert (1827–97) engineer, statistician/economist; born in Lauterbach, Germany. He emigrated to Baltimore, Md., in 1849. As a structural engineer for the Baltimore & Ohio Railroad, he invented the so-called Fink truss bridge (c. 1852), which soon became widely used on American railways. From 1857–75 he worked for the Louisville & Nashville Railroad, where he rose to become vice-president (1869). His ability with statistics and record-keeping resulted in the important "Fink Report on Cost of Transportation" (1874), which helped stabilize the transportation industry of the day, and inaugurated the application of economics to railroads for the future.

Fink, Max (1923–) psychiatrist, psychiatric educator; born in Vienna, Austria. He came to this country in the late 1930s and would become professor of psychiatry at State University of New York: Stony Brook (1972). In the 1950s and 1960s he and coworkers pioneered the field of pharmaco-electroencephalography, the EEG analysis of the effects of drugs. He also became an authority on electroconvulsive therapy and coauthored the principal texts on the subject.

Fink, Mike (?1770–1823) frontier figure; born at Fort Pitt (now Pittsburgh), Pa. A masterful scout, marksman, and wrestler, he became the "king of the keelboatmen." He died on a trapping expedition to the Rocky Mountains. His popularity as a folk hero endured until the Civil War period.

Finkelstein, Louis (1895–1991) rabbi, educator; born in Cincinnati, Ohio. He graduated from the City College of New York and earned a Ph.D. from Columbia University in 1918. A professor of theology at the Jewish Theological Seminary of America from 1920, he was its chancellor from 1951–72. A member of many Jewish religious and cultural organizations, he is the author of a number of scholarly and popular books, including *Faith for Today* (1941).

Finley, James (1762–1828) civil engineer; born in Pa. He was a judge when he conceived of building a suspension bridge with masonry towers and wrought-iron chains. His first bridge was completed in 1801, and in 1810 he built a 244-foot span across the Merrimack River at Newburyport, Mass. Finley's bridges are known for their solidity.

Finley, John H. (Huston), Jr. (1904–) classicist; born in New York City. He was educated at Harvard (B.A. 1925, Ph.D. 1933), where he taught from 1942–76 and was Eliot Professor from 1942–74. It has been said of Finley that he studied the minds of ancient Greeks and modern undergraduates. As master of Eliot House and an immensely popular teacher whose general lectures in humanities drew standing-room-only crowds, he was an influential mentor and teacher. He was vice-chairman of the faculty committee that wrote the influential Harvard Report, "General Education in a Free Society" in 1946. His *Thucydides* (1963) and *Three Essays in Thucydides* (1967) were highly regarded, as was his skill on both the squash and tennis courts.

Finley, M. I. (b. Moses Finklestein) (1912–86) historian; born in New York City. A victim of the McCarthy era, he was fired by Rutgers in 1952 and emigrated to Cambridge, England, where after changing his name he became lecturer (1955–70), professor (1970–79), and master of Darwin College (1976–82). He became a British subject in 1962 and was knighted in 1979. Trained in history and law, and greatly influenced by Marx and Weber, he wrote pioneering works in social and economic history including *The World of Odysseus* (1954), *Early Greece: The Bronze and Archaic Ages* (1970), *The Ancient Economy* (1973), and *The Use and Abuse of History* (1975).

Finley, Robert (1772–1817) Presbyterian clergyman, educator, organizer; born in Princeton, N.J. Ordained a Presbyterian minister, he served the parish at Basking Ridge, N.J., with great devotion and success (1795–1817). In connection with his pastoral work, he conducted a school for boys that was considered one of the best in the nation. He was also trustee of the College of New Jersey (now Princeton) (1807–17). His concern for the condition of African-Americans caused him to be a prime mover in the American Colonization Society (1816) with the encouragement of Henry Clay and President Madison. He was named president of the University of Georgia (1817).

Finn, Chester Evans, Jr. (1944–) educator; born in Columbus, Ohio. A professor of education at Vanderbilt University (1981), he was a top educational policymaker for Republican administrations and a major contributor to the "America 2000" education plan (1991). An advocate of national testing and federal aid to parochial schools, his books include *We Must Take Charge* (1991).

Finney, Charles Grandison (1792–1875) Protestant religious leader, educator; born in Warren, Conn. Raised on the verge of the frontier in Oneida County, N.Y., he studied for the bar but turned to evangelism after an emotional religious conversion in 1821. He was ordained a Presbyterian minister in 1824 and shortly afterwards launched an eight-year revival campaign that carried him through New York, New England, and the mid-Atlantic states. Named pastor of the Second

Free Presbyterian Church in New York City in 1832, he resigned two years later to become pastor of Broadway Tabernacle, a Congregational church organized especially for him. In 1835 he became professor of theology at Oberlin College in Ohio, beginning an association that would continue for the rest of his life. Two years later he accepted the pastorship of the First Congregational Church in Oberlin. He was president of Oberlin College from 1851–66. His *Memoirs,* about his lifetime of teaching, preaching, and evangelism, appeared the year after his death.

Finney, Ross Lee (1906–) composer; born in Well, Minn. After studies with Nadia Boulanger in Paris and at Harvard he began a teaching career, meanwhile continuing studies with Roger Sessions and with Alban Berg in Europe; he taught at the University of Michigan from 1948. His style showed a wide variety of influences from neoclassicism to 12-tone while remaining individual.

Firestone, Harvey (Samuel) (1868–1938) manufacturer; born in Columbiana, Ohio. In 1896 he left his uncle's Detroit buggy company and moved to Chicago to open his own business selling rubber buggy tires. In 1900 he moved to Akron, Ohio, and founded Firestone Tire and Rubber Company to make rubber tires for all kinds of horse-drawn vehicles, but by 1903 he shifted to making rubber tires for the burgeoning automobile market. Firestone's innovations included the pneumatic automobile tire and the "dismountable rim," which made possible spare tires. By 1918 he had begun promoting the use of trucks to haul freight and he continued to lobby for improved highways. He defeated the British rubber cartel in 1924 by establishing his own rubber plantations in Liberia; his company would eventually be criticized for its poor treatment of workers as well as for meddling in Liberia's economy. In the U.S.A., too, he was notorious for being anti-union and for paying low wages. By the time he died, his company supplied some 25 percent of tires used in the U.S.A.

Fischer, Carl (1849–1923) music publisher; born in Buttstadt, Germany. Trained as a musician, he emigrated to the U.S.A. in 1872 and opened a music store in New York City. He sold instruments and other firms' scores but soon found a market for reproducing music; by 1880 he was moving to larger quarters and the Carl Fischer firm went on to become one of the major American publishers of a wide spectrum of music – band, choral, instructional, as well as the classical and contemporary composers. The firm also published *The Metronome* (1885) for bandleaders and the *Musical Observer* (later *Musical Courier*).

Fischer, Edmond H. (Henri) (1920–) biochemist; born in Shanghai to Swiss parents. He taught at the University of Geneva (1946–48), then became a Swiss Foundation fellow (1948) and privatdocent (1950–53), before coming to the U.S.A. to spend the rest of his career at the University of Washington: Seattle (1953–90). There, working with biochemist Edwin Krebs, he drew on his early experience with plant enzymes to demonstrate that the chemical regulation of all cellular processes, including hormonal mechanisms, growth, and metabolism, is fundamental to all living cells. For this contribution to biology, Fischer and Krebs were awarded the 1992 Nobel Prize in physiology.

Fischer, (Robert James) Bobby (1943–) chess player; born in Chicago. Raised in Brooklyn after his parents divorced in 1945, he learned to play chess when he was six

and won the U.S. junior and senior titles at age 14. In 1972 he captured the world championship from Boris Spassky in Reykjavik, Iceland, while competing for what was then the largest purse ($250,000) offered in any sport outside boxing. Amid praise for his "classicist" style, the win set off a short-lived U.S. chess boom. A longtime nemesis of tournament officials for his tantrums and phobias, he failed in 1975 to agree to terms for a title defense against Anatoly Karpov and was stripped of his crown by FIDE (Fédération Internationale des Echecs). Afterwards he refused to compete in public, lived in virtual seclusion in the Los Angeles area, and was briefly active in the fundamentalist Worldwide Church of God.

Fish, Hamilton (1808–93) lawyer, cabinet member, legislator; born in New York City. He was admitted to the New York bar (1830). He served in the U.S. House of Representatives (Whig, N.Y.; 1843–45), as governor of New York (1849–50), and as U.S. senator (Whig, N.Y.; 1851–57). As secretary of state (1869–77), he signed the Washington Treaty (1871), which provided for arbitration in the *Alabama* case, and negotiated with Spain over problems arising from a rebellion in Cuba.

Fishbein, Morris (1889–1976) physician, journal editor, author; born in St. Louis, Mo. He was a doctor based in Chicago, but had little patient contact after 1913, when he became assistant editor of the *Journal of the American Medical Association* (1913–24) and then editor (1924–49). This forum gave him enormous influence in American medical politics, and he became known as the "voice of the AMA." He was an outspoken critic of medical quackery and unorthodox medical procedures as well as the public's right to basic medical knowledge. To this latter end, he wrote numerous syndicated newspaper columns, the magazine *Hygeia* (1924), and books for the lay public, including *Modern Home Medical Advisor* (1935), long a fixture in many homes. He was a vocal advocate of traditional fee-for-service medicine and an opponent of compulsory national health insurance or any government involvement. In 1949 the journal's trustees stripped him of his editorial forum, limiting his comments to scientific subjects.

Fishburne, Larry (Laurence John, III) (1961–) actor; born in Augusta, Ga. He made his film debut at age 15 in *Apocalypse Now* and won a Tony Award for his performance in the Broadway play *Two Trains Running*. He had starring roles in the movies *School Daze* and *Boyz N the Hood* and has also appeared on television.

Fisher, Clarence Stanley (1876–1941) archaeologist; born in Philadelphia. A trained architect, Fisher turned to archaeology after accompanying expeditions to Nippur (1898–1900) and Samaria (1908–10). He stayed in the Middle East directing digs and teaching at the American School of Oriental Research, Jerusalem (1925–41). Best known for his Palestinian excavations, Fisher published important reports on Nippur (1905–6), Samaria (1924), and Armageddon (1929). He is noted for his pioneering precision in the surveying and mapping of sites, the drafting of plans of all structures, and the recording of locations of all recovered objects.

Fisher, Donald G. (1928–) retail executive; born in San Francisco. He earned a B.S. in business administration from the University of California: Berkeley (1950). With his wife, Doris, he cofounded the Gap Stores, Inc. in California in

1969. As chairman and CEO, he built Gap into a major retail chain famous for its casual clothing, with more than 1,200 outlets worldwide. Fisher served on President Reagan's Advisory Council for Trade Negotiations.

Fisher, Dorothy Canfield (b. Dorothea Frances Canfield) (1879–1958) writer; born in Lawrence, Kans. She became a writer after earning a Columbia University Ph.D. in Romance languages. She published her early fiction and later nonfiction under her maiden and married names respectively. Among other contributions to education she popularized the Montessori teaching method in the U.S.A. in the 1910s. She was a founding member of the Book-of-the-Month editorial board (1926–50).

Fisher, Frederick John (1878–1941) automobile body manufacturer; born in Sandusky, Ohio. He learned carriage making from his father and in 1902 he moved to Detroit to be a draftsman for the C. R. Wilson Carriage Works. Superintendent by 1907, he was joined by his brothers, Charles T. Fisher, Alfred J. Fisher, Lawrence P. Fisher, William A. Fisher, and Edward F. Fisher. In 1908 he and his brother Charles formed the Fisher Body Company in Detroit. They were soon joined by the other brothers in a very successful business that custom built bodies for cars. In 1910 they built 150 closed bodies for Cadillac and formed the Fisher Closed Body Company (1912) as well as a Fisher Body Company in Wilkerville, Ontario, Canada. In 1916, with profits over $1 million, the companies merged into the Fisher Body Corporation with an annual capacity of 370,000 units – the largest company of its kind. In 1919 General Motors (GM) and William C. Durant bought a 60 percent interest and agreed to buy almost all of its auto bodies from Fisher for the next ten years. The Fisher family retained managerial control of the firm and after World War I built the world's largest auto body factory in Cleveland. In 1926 Fisher Body became a division of GM and each of the brothers had a post within the corporation. Frederick Fisher was a director of about 20 corporations and contributed to various educational and cultural institutions. He and his brothers remained one of the most closely bonded families in business history.

Fisher, Irving (1867–1947) economist; born in Saugerties, N.Y. One of the most colorful economists, he is remembered for his brilliant and enduring exposition of economic theory. From 1892 until his retirement in 1935, he taught at Yale University. His contributions include crystallizing the distinctions between stocks and flows, clarifying the science of accounting at the individual level, and for explaining the economy as a whole. His invention of a visible index file system led to considerable financial success but he suffered heavy losses in the stock market crash of 1929. In his later years he also became known for his promotion of nutritional cures for diseases.

Fisher, M. F. K. (Mary Frances Kennedy) (1908–92) food writer; born in Albion, Mich. She grew up in Whittier, Calif., where her father owned the local newspaper. She attended several colleges – Illinois, Whittier, and Occidental Colleges, and the University of California: Los Angeles. She married a graduate student, Alfred Fisher, and moved to Dijon, France. In the course of three marriages, she lived in California, Switzerland, and France. She created a new literary genre with 18 volumes of witty, erudite essays evoking the pleasures of food and places. Her 1949 translation of Brillat-Savarin's *Physiology of Taste* is consid-

ered a classic. She also wrote a novel, a screenplay, and travelogues.

Fisher, Ralph (Talcott), Jr. (1920–) Russian specialist, educator; born in Washington, D.C. Specializing in the history of Russia and Eastern Europe, Soviet education and indoctrination, and Russian social history, he worked as a resident in Soviet culture at the American Museum of Natural History (1949). He was a professor of history and director of the Russian and Eastern European Center at the University of Illinois: Urbana-Champaign (1960). His books include a *Dictionary of Russian Historical Terms* (1970) and a *Source Book for Russian History from Early Times to 1917* (1972).

Fisk, James (1835–72) capitalist; born in Bennington, Vt. A flamboyant peddler and stock dealer, in 1869 he opened Fisk & Belden, a brokerage house, with the financial support of Daniel Drew. In the so-called "Erie War" between Drew and Cornelius Vanderbilt, Fisk stymied Vanderbilt's attempt to purchase Erie Railroad Company stock and with Jay Gould took over and looted the company. Fisk and Gould's attempt to corner the gold market resulted in the Black Friday panic of September 24, 1869. In the Congressional investigation that ensued, Fisk gained minor immortality with two oft-quoted remarks; he said that the money he had made had "gone where the woodbine twineth" (i.e. "up the spout," vanished) and that "nothing is lost except honor." Known as the "Barnum of Wall Street" for his fraudulent business practices and notorious for his sybaritic lifestyle, he died after being shot by Edward Stokes during a dispute over business matters and a mistress.

Fiske, Bradley Allen (1854–1942) naval officer, inventor; born in Lyons, N.Y. As a naval officer (1874–1916) he developed over sixty patents, including those for submarine protection devices, telescopic sights for naval guns, and the mechanism for launching a torpedo from a plane (1912). He resigned from the navy after a series of disagreements with the secretary, Josephus Daniels.

Fiske, Daniel Willard (1831–1904) book collector; born in Ellisburg, N.Y. A librarian and language professor at Cornell University (1868–83), he inherited a fortune on his wife's death; on retiring he moved to Italy and pursued literary interests abroad, collecting books on Dante, Icelandic culture, and the Rhaeto-Romantic languages, which he donated to Cornell along with a fund of over $500,000.

Fiske, Fidelia (1816–64) Protestant missionary; born in Shelburne, Mass. The daughter of a farmer, she developed religious interests as a child and volunteered for mission service after graduating from Mount Holyoke Seminary in 1842. Sent to Persia, she founded a girls school and ministered among women and children. Ill health forced her to return to the U.S.A. in 1858; she did not recover sufficiently to return to the field. Her book about the founder of Mt. Holyoke, *Recollections of Mary Lyon*, was published posthumously in 1866.

Fiske, Haley (1852–1929) lawyer; born in New Brunswick, N.J. In 1873 he began working for a New York City law firm with the Metropolitan Life Insurance Company as his client. He became so knowledgeable about insurance that in 1891 he was made vice-president of the insurance company. There he instituted new programs including a national health campaign for policy holders (1909) and investing the company's capital in housing developments. In 1919 he became president of the company, by that time one of the largest financial institutions in the world.

Fiske, John (b. Edmund Fisk Green) (1842–1901) historian, philosopher; born in Hartford, Conn. A precocious child, he changed his name to John Fisk at age 13, to Fiske at 18. After graduating from Harvard University (1863), he tried his hand at law and became a lecturer (1869–79) and librarian (1872–79) at Harvard. A prolific author, he then embarked on a career as one of America's most celebrated lecturers on history. He popularized and championed contemporary scientific, philosophic, and historical thought, especially the theory of evolution. A synthesizer rather than an originator of ideas, he attracted many distinguished scholars to historical studies. In his later years he turned to writing about American history, and from 1884–1901, he taught American history at Washington University in St. Louis.

Fiske, Minnie Maddern (b. Mary or Marie Augusta Davey) (1865–1932) stage actress; born in New Orleans. The daughter of a theatrical family, she made her stage debut in her mother's arms at age three. In her many child roles, including Little Eva in *Uncle Tom's Cabin,* she was praised as mature beyond her years. She graduated to ingenue parts, then eventually reached stardom as Stella in an 1885 adaptation of Sardou's *In Spite of All.* She was described as a short, magnetic redhead whose acting was full of subtlety and finesse. After her marriage to Harrison Grey Fiske, she briefly retired and wrote plays, but returned to the stage in 1893 to act in serious roles including Nora in *A Doll's House* and Tess in *Tess of the D'Urbervilles.* Partly in response to a conflict with the Theatrical Syndicate, which tried to block their enterprises, she and her husband bought the Manhattan Theatre in 1901 where they produced several big successes.

Fitch, Aubrey (Wray) (1883–1978) naval officer; born in St. Ignace, Mich. He commanded one of the two task forces in the battle of Coral Sea (1942). He was superintendent of the Naval Academy (1945–47) and retired with the rank of admiral in 1947.

Fitch, James Marston (1909–) architectural preservationist, historian; born in Washington, D.C. Trained as an architect at Tulane, he moved to New York City, where, working as an architectural editor (1936–53), he embraced modernism but developed an interest in the social concerns of architecture. His early support of "progressive" urban renewal gave way in the late 1940s to a commitment to historical preservation. He taught at Columbia University (1954–77), where in 1964 he founded the nation's first historic preservation program. At the same time Fitch published widely and influentially on historic preservation and American buildings; his works included *American Building: The Environmental Forces that Shape It* (1947) and *Architecture and the Aesthetics of Plenty* (1961). After his retirement from Columbia he became director of historic preservation at the architectural firm of Beyer Blinder Belle, New York (1979), where recent projects have included the renovation of Ellis Island.

Fitch, John (1743–98) inventor; born in Windsor, Conn. A gunsmith by trade, he supplied American forces during the American Revolution. From 1786–90 he built four steam vessels propelled by paddles, and a few years later he conducted some early experiments in screw propulsion. His projects were commercial failures and, disillusioned, he poisoned himself.

Fitch, Val L. (Logsdon) (1923–) physicist; born in Merriman, Nebr. He first utilized his knowledge of theoretical physics with the Manhattan Project (1943–46), then taught at Columbia University (1953–54) before joining Princeton (1954). For their 1963 studies on the behavior of the kaon, an unstable subatomic particle, Fitch and colleague J. W. Cronin were awarded the 1980 Nobel Prize in physics.

Fitch, (William) Clyde (1865–1909) playwright; born in Elmira, N.Y. He began by writing plays based on historical figures – Beau Brummel (1890), Nathan Hale (1898), and Barbara Freitchie (1899) – but he soon moved toward social comedy, at which he was immensely successful (although modern critics complain about their contrived endings). Among his popular works were *The Moth and the Flame* (1898), *Captain Jinks of the Horse Marines* (1901), and *The City* (1909).

Fitzgerald, Ella (1918–) jazz musician; born in Newport News, Va. She was discovered at an amateur show in 1934 and went on to become one of the most celebrated and influential singers in her field. She began her career with the Chick Webb Orchestra and assumed its leadership in 1939. After 1945, she worked mainly with her own trio on a continual series of concert tours, television appearances, and recordings.

Fitzgerald, F. (Francis) Scott (Key) (1896–1940) writer; born in St. Paul, Minn. He spent four years at Princeton, but left before graduating to join the army during World War I. His first novel, *This Side of Paradise* (1920), was blatantly autobiographical and made him temporarily rich and famous. Later that year he married Zelda Sayre, an aspiring writer he had met while stationed in Alabama. A glamorous and witty couple, they lived a legendarily extravagant life in New York City that he unsuccessfully attempted to support with his writing – stories collected in *Flappers and Philosophers* (1920) and *Tales of the Jazz Age* (1922), a novel, *The Beautiful and the Damned* (1922) and a failed play, *The Vegetable* (1923). Knowing they could live more cheaply in Europe, they moved there in 1924; he became friendly with Ernest Hemingway and other expatriates and wrote *The Great Gatsby* (1925), a critical but not financial success, and a volume of stories, *All the Sad Young Men* (1926). The continuing social round deteriorated into debts, alcoholism, and, in 1930, the first of Zelda Fitzgerald's mental breakdowns. They returned to the U.S.A. that year, and the commercial failure of *Tender is the Night* (1934) led to his own breakdown, described in essays later collected in *The Crack-Up* (1945). He wrote screenplays in Hollywood (1937–40) and with Zelda now confined to a mental hospital in North Carolina, he became involved with the columnist Sheila Graham. He died in her apartment of a heart attack, leaving an unfinished novel, *The Tycoon* (1941).

Fitzgerald, John Francis ("Honey Fitz") (1863–1950) businessman, mayor; born in Boston, Mass. (father of Rose Kennedy). After serving as a state senator and U.S. Representative (Dem., Mass.; 1895–1901) and running a newspaper, he became the colorful, popular mayor of Boston (1906–08, 1910–14). His administrations were plagued by charges of corruption and political patronage; his subsequent attempts to be elected as governor and senator failed. He was the grandfather of John, Robert and Edward Kennedy.

Fitz-Gibbon, Bernice Bowles ("Fitz") (?1895–1982) advertising executive; born in Waunakee, Wis. She developed a specialty in retail advertising at Macy's (1923–35), John Wanamaker (1936–40), and Gimbels, New York (1940–54), where as publicity director she was one of the highest paid women in advertising. She wrote such famous slogans as "Nobody, but nobody, undersells Gimbels." She later headed her own advertising consultancy (1954–76).

Fitzhugh, William (1651–1701) lawyer; planter; born in Bedford, England. He came to Virginia about 1670 and became a very successful planter and exporter. Originally trained as a lawyer, he served in the House of Burgesses and prepared (1692) a digest of Virginia's laws. His surviving letters are known by scholars for revealing the business operations of late-17th-century America.

Fitzpatrick, Thomas (c. 1799–1854) trapper, guide, Indian agent; born in County Cavan, Ireland. He came to America by 1816 and served as a guide to pioneer groups, John C. Frémont's second expedition (1843–44), and to military groups just prior to and during the Mexican War (1845–46). He negotiated peace treaties with the Comanche, Kiowa, and Kiowa Apache (1851–53). The Indians trusted him and called him "Broken Hand."

Fitzsimmons, (James Edward) "Sunny Jim" (1874–1966) horse trainer; born in New York City. He trained horses for the Belair stable (1923–55) and conditioned such champion thoroughbreds as Gallant Fox, Omaha, Granville, and Nashua.

Fitzsimmons, (Robert Prometheus) Bob (1862–1917) boxer; born in Helston, England. He grew up in New Zealand and he began his professional boxing career there and in Australia. After immigrating to the U.S.A. in 1890, he went on to win three world titles: middleweight (1891–97), heavyweight (1897–99), and light heavyweight (1903–05). He continued boxing until the age of 52. His career record was 40 victories (32 knockouts), 11 losses.

Flaget, Benedict (Joseph) (1763–1850) Catholic prelate; born in Contournat, France. A Sulpician priest, he emigrated to the U.S.A. after the French Revolution and, after pastoral work and teaching theology, served (from 1811) as first bishop of Bardstown (later Louisville), Ky. He traveled tirelessly throughout his far-flung territory, which was ultimately carved into 35 dioceses in seven states; he was influential in building up and staffing the early American church.

Flagg, Ernest (1857–1947) architect; born in Brooklyn, N.Y. In his New York practice (established 1891) he promoted American adoption of Beaux-Arts principles, pioneered tenement housing with his influential light-court plan (1894), and developed small-house design and wrote *Small Houses* (1922).

Flagg, James Montgomery (1877–1960) illustrator; born in Pelham Manor, N.Y. Based in New York City, he studied at the Art Students League (1893), and in England and France. Working in pen and ink, watercolor, and oils, he was a prolific illustrator for periodicals including *St. Nicholas, Life,* and *Judge*. He is known for his World War I posters, including the "I Want You" portrait of Uncle Sam, and for his popular images of young women of the time, commonly called "Flagg Girls."

Flagg, Josiah Foster (1788–1853) dentist, anatomical artist; born in Boston, Mass. In Boston, he designed the first variable forceps for tooth extraction (1828) and produced the first "mineral teeth" (1833), artificial teeth made out of porcelain. He was also an anatomical artist of note, contributing illustrations to numerous works.

Flagler, Henry M. (Morrison) (1830–1913) capitalist, philanthropist; born in Hopewell, N.Y. He met John D. Rockefeller in Ohio in 1844 before he made his own modest fortune in the grain business. He then went to Michigan, where he engaged in a failed venture to manufacture salt. Returning to Ohio, he took up the grain business, but when Rockefeller came to him with plans for developing the new oil business, he formed the firm of Rockefeller, Andrews and Flagler (1865), which became Standard Oil in 1870. Flagler stayed with the company until 1911 and made a fortune, but he left the operations to Rockefeller and turned his own attention to Florida. He organized the Florida East Coast Railway (1866), which eventually extended to Key West (1913), built numerous hotels along Florida's coast, and helped establish agriculture and fruit-growing in Florida. In addition to his $40 million in commercial investments in Florida, he donated large sums to build schools, hospitals, and churches.

Flaherty, Robert J. (Joseph) (1884–1951) documentary filmmaker; born in Iron Mountain, Mich. From 1910 to 1916 he made a series of expeditions in northern Canada as an explorer and mining prospector. He returned to Eskimo country in 1920 with his camera and equipment, and the result was *Nanook of the North* (1922). He went on to make *Moana* (1926), a South Seas documentary; *Man of Aran* (1934), in Ireland; *Elephant Boy* (1937), in India; and *Louisiana Story* (1948), shot in the bayous of that state. His wife, Frances Flaherty assisted him on several films, but his attempts at collaborating with other directors on feature films – except with Zoltan Korda on *Elephant Boy* – did not pan out. Recognized as a pioneer in his day – the word "documentary" was first applied to his *Moana* – he came to be regarded more as a romantic interpreter of his subjects than as a "pure" documentarian.

Flanagan, Edward (Joseph) (1886–1948) Catholic priest; born in Roscommon, Ireland. Emigrating to the U.S.A. in 1904, he was ordained after studies in Europe. In 1914 he opened a home for derelicts in Omaha, Nebr.; convinced that rehabilitation can be effective if begun early, he went on to found Boys Town near Omaha, to house and reform troubled boys (1922). World famous for his work, he went by the adage "There is no such thing as a bad boy."

Flanagan, Hallie (Mae Ferguson) (1890–1969) theater organizer, teacher, playwright; born in Redfield, S.D. She took her B.A. from Grinnell College in Iowa (1911) and within about 18 months she was married. Her husband died in 1919, leaving her with two children to support. She had done some teaching and play directing and when a play of hers won a local prize, she was accepted into George Pierce Baker's famous 47 Workshop at Harvard. She decided, however, that she could not afford to pursue a career as a playwright, and with her M.A. from Radcliffe (1924), in 1925 she accepted a position to teach drama at Vassar. In 1926 she had a Guggenheim fellowship to visit the theaters of Europe and on her return she founded the Vassar Experimental Theatre, which soon gained a reputation for restaging classical dramas. Even more noticed was her 1931 production, *Can You Hear Their Voices?,* a play about Arkansas farmers that she coauthored and staged with innovative techniques. In

1934 she married Philip H. Davis, a classics professor at Vassar. In 1935 she was invited to head what became the Federal Theatre Project (FTP) and she soon had thousands of theater professionals producing a variety of works, eventually seen by more than 25 million Americans, many of whom had never seen live theater before. Her most famous contribution was the so-called *Living Newspaper,* documentary dramatizations of pressing social issues of the day. In a legendary hearing before the U.S. House of Representatives Committee on Un-American Activities, however, she was accused of promoting leftist ideas and the FTP was halted in 1939. She returned to Vassar and directed the writing of *Arena* (1940), an account of the FTP. In 1942 she became dean (until 1946) and professor of theater at Smith College (until 1955), continuing her lifelong efforts at relating theater to both educational and social concerns.

Flanagan, Tommy (Lee) (1930–) jazz musician; born in Detroit, Mich. A distinctive modern jazz pianist, he accompanied Ella Fitzgerald and other singers throughout the 1960s and 1970s, and led his own trio after 1980.

Flanders, Ralph (Edward) (1880–1970) mechanical engineer, U.S. senator; born in Barnet, Vt. While working at a machine tool factory, he got himself an education; after contributing articles to machine shop journals, he became an editor of *Machine* in New York City (1905–10). Returning to Vermont, he joined a machine tool company and rose to become its president. During World War II he was on the War Production Board and then became president of the Federal Reserve Bank of Boston (1944–46). Going to the U.S. Senate (Rep., Vt.; 1947–59), he was a moderate and sat on several important committees. He became best known for introducing the resolution that censured Senator Joseph McCarthy (1954).

Flannagan, John Bernard (1895–1942) sculptor; born in Fargo, N.D. He studied at the Minneapolis Institute of Arts (1914–17), traveled to Ireland (1930 and 1932–33), and thereafter was based in New York City. He used birth and death themes, as in *Triumph of the Egg* (1937). He committed suicide after an incapacitating accident in 1939.

Flannery, Kent V. (Vaughn) (1934–) anthropologist, archaeologist; born in Philadelphia. An expert on prehistoric human ecology and cultural evolution, he joined the University of Michigan faculty (1967). Flannery is known for describing what he calls the "broad-spectrum revolution," the shift from hunting and gathering to the exploitation of wild resources. His publications include *The Early Mesoamerican Village* (1976).

Flavin, Dan (1933–) sculptor; born in Jamaica, N.Y. He attended the New School for Social Research, N.Y. (1956), and Columbia University (1957–59). Based in Garrison, N.Y., he became known for his minimalist and architectural installations using electric and fluorescent lights, as in *Pink and Gold* (1968).

Fleagle, John G. (Gwynn) (1948–) physical anthropologist; born in Burlington, N.C. He was a consultant at Harvard (1973–74) before joining the State University of New York at Stony Brook (1975). He wrote extensively on the evolutionary biology and adaptive radiation (a specialized migration pattern) of primates.

Fleischer, Leon (1928–) pianist, conductor, teacher; born in San Francisco. After studies in the U.S.A. and with Schnabel in Europe, Fleischer appeared with the New York Philharmonic at age 16 and began a brilliant solo career. Falling victim to a right-hand ailment in 1964, he thereafter played left-hand piano literature while conducting and teaching at Peabody and the Berkshire Music Center.

Fleming, John A. (Adam) (1877–1956) geophysicist; born in Cincinnati, Ohio. He joined the Department of Terrestrial Magnetism of the Carnegie Institution of Washington, D.C. (1904), became its director (1910–46), and continued to serve as an adviser in international scientific relations after his retirement. During his directorship, he designed geomagnetic observatories in Huancayo, Peru, Watheroo, Australia, and Kensington, Md. He took charge of the Institution's World War II contracts dealing with radio communications, ordnance devices, magnetic instruments, and ionospheric research to advance knowledge of the earth's magnetic field. Fleming was one of the first officers of the American Geophysical Union, serving as general secretary and editor of their periodical (1925–47). He expanded the field of geomagnetism by inventing or modifying both terrestrial and oceanographic geomagnetic instruments, designing innovative isomagnetic world charts, and contributing to research in solar and lunar physics.

Fleming, Peggy (Gale) (1948–) ice skater; born in San Jose, Calif. A skater from age nine, she won the world championship three times (1966–68), and an Olympic gold medal in 1968 in Mexico City, where her elegant style won her worldwide acclaim. After skating in professional revues, she served as a commentator for ABC television.

Fleming, Richard H. (Howell) (1909–89) oceanographer; born in Victoria, Canada. He came to the U.S.A. to teach and perform research at the Scripps Institution of Oceanography (1931–46). He served the Hydrographic Office of the Navy (1946–50), then became a professor at the University of Washington (1950–80). He made major contributions to the physics and chemistry of oceans, and to naval applications of oceanography.

Fleming, Victor (1883–1949) movie director; born in Pasadena, Calif. Beginning in Hollywood in 1910 as an assistant cameraman, he worked at times under D. W. Griffith and filmed several of Douglas Fairbanks' films. He was hired as official cameraman of President Woodrow Wilson's trip to Europe (1918–19) and on his return made his directorial debut, launching a three-decades-long career as one of the more reliable directors, working primarily for Metro-Goldwyn-Mayer. Although many of his movies were fairly routine adventures, several have survived as classics, particularly *The Wizard of Oz* (1939) and *Gone With the Wind* (1939); he received an Oscar for the latter though it has since been revealed that several people had a hand in directing parts of that movie.

Fleming, Williamina Paton Stevens (1857–1911) astronomer; born in Dundee, Scotland. Although her formal schooling ended when she was about 15, she served as a teacher until she married James Fleming in 1877. They immigrated to Boston in 1878 but separated in 1879. Forced to support herself, she worked as a housekeeper for Edward Pickering, director of the Harvard College Observatory. Convinced that women could perform research as well as men, he hired her to do clerical and computing work but soon allowed her to take on more responsibilities around the observatory. Eventually she proved to be a decisive administrator of the large observatory staff and served as editor of publications from the observatory. Her truly epic achievement, however, was the classification of stars based on their photographed spectra – she eventually classified 10,351 stars (published in her *Draper Catalogue of Stellar Spectra,* 1890) – and the discovery of more variable stars and novae than any single astronomer up to then. She was named the official curator of astronomical photographs (1898), the first appointment of any woman by the Harvard Corporation; by 1910 she had catalogued some 200,000 plates. She was honored by astronomical societies internationally as well in America, including being the first American woman elected to England's Royal Astronomical Society.

Fletcher, Alice Cunningham (1838–1923) ethnologist, humanitarian; born in Havana, Cuba. Beginning with an interest in the archaeology of American Indians, from 1876 on she became active in working for better treatment of the living Indians of the West. This led to her becoming the first and best informed student of American Indian music. Her major scholarly work was *The Omaha Tribe* (1911) but her most popular work was *Indian Story and Song from North America* (1900). One of the more remarkable women of her era, she combined energetic activism with scholarly pursuits.

Fletcher, Frank J. (Jack) (1885–1973) naval officer; born in Marshalltown, Iowa. He commanded the combined USS *Yorktown* – USS *Lexington* task forces at the battle of Coral Sea (1942), the first sea battle fought entirely in the air. He was the tactical commander at Midway (1942) and commanded the North Pacific naval forces (1943–45).

Fletcher, Horace (1849–1919) author, lecturer; born in Lawrence, Mass. A San Francisco-based businessmen, he cured himself of overweight and chronic dyspepsia and after 1895 became a proselytizer for his own nutritional system. The most important element of his common-sense regimen prescribed chewing food until it was thoroughly mashed, a process once widely known as "fletcherism."

Fletcher, John Gould (1886–1950) poet, writer; born in Little Rock, Ark. He studied at Harvard (1903–07), lived in England (1908–14; 1916–33), and settled in Arkansas (1933). He was associated with the Imagist poets and Southern Agrarian writers.

Flexner, Abraham (1866–1959) educational reformer; born in Louisville, Ky. After a 19-year career as a secondary school teacher he earned a Harvard A.M. in psychology (1906). His Carnegie Foundation report on medical education in the U.S.A. and Canada (1910) exposed the abuses of a profit-driven system lacking standards for students, curricula, or facilities; the report sparked a revolution in American medical education. While on the staff of the General Education Board of the Rockefeller Foundation (1913–28), Flexner made a further major contribution to medical education reform when he disbursed $50 million in funding for medical education, attracting hundreds of millions of dollars more to establish medical school research faculties. He also campaigned for improvements to secondary education and championed the German university model of intellectualism and research against the American vocationalism. He was the founder and first director of the Institute for Advanced Study, Princeton (1930–39), a pure research institution to which he recruited Albert Einstein among other eminent scholars.

Flexner, Simon (1863–1946) microbiologist, medical administrator; born in Louisville, Ky. (brother of Abraham Flexner). After researching and teaching as a pathologist at Johns Hopkins (1890–99), he went to the University of Pennsylvania (1899–1903); during this period he took time away to isolate a strain of the dysentery bacillus in the Philippines (1899) and to investigate the bubonic plague in San Francisco (1901). He joined the newly created Rockefeller Institute for Medical Research in 1901 to direct the research laboratories but soon became the institute's *de facto* administrator; he served as its official director from 1924–35. He was the editor of the *Journal of Experimental Medicine* (1904–23), and during World War I he was commissioned in the Army Medical Corps and charged with inspecting its medical laboratories in Europe. He made several other important contributions to his field, including developing a serum for cerebrospinal meningitis (1907) and laying the groundwork for the development of polio vaccines. He wrote *The Evolution and Organization of the University Clinic* (1939).

Flexner, Stuart Berg (1928–90) lexicographer; born in Jacksonville, Ill. After studying and teaching briefly at Cornell University, he moved to New York City, where he worked for several publishing firms. He was coauthor, with Harold Wentworth, of the *Dictionary of American Slang* (1960), and at Random House, where he became a vice-president and editor-in-chief of the reference division, he edited *The Random House Dictionary of the English Language,* Second Edition (1987). He also wrote several works on language for popular consumption, including *How to Increase Your Word Power* (1968), *I Hear America Talking* (1976), and *Listening to America* (1982).

Flint, Austin (1812–86) physician; born in Petersham, Mass. After taking his M.D. at Harvard (1833), he practiced and taught in Boston and Buffalo, N.Y., where in 1847 he founded Buffalo Medical College. He thereafter concentrated on hospital medicine and teaching at various medical schools, including the University of Louisville and New Orleans Medical College. In 1861 he helped found Bellevue Medical College in New York City, and taught there and at Long Island College Hospital for many years. An authority on pulmonary and respiratory diseases, he popularized the use of the binaural stethoscope. He wrote numerous textbooks, of which *Treatise on the Principles and Practice of Medicine* (1866; many revised editions) was the best known.

Flipper, Henry Ossian (1856–1940) soldier, engineer; born in Thomasville, Ga. The son of slave parents, he endured four years of harassment to become, in 1877, the first African-American graduate of West Point. Dismissed in 1882 after a court martial on trumped-up charges involving commissariat funds, he campaigned the rest of his life for reinstatement. He pursued a long and successful civilian career as an engineer; 36 years after his death the army granted him an honorable discharge dated June 30, 1882.

Flom, Joseph H. (Harold) (1923–) lawyer; born in Baltimore, Md. Beginning in 1948 as an associate in what would become Skadden, Arps, Slate, Meagher & Flom, he led the firm to become New York's largest, specializing in corporate law. A trustee of Barnard and New York University Medical Center, he is known for his charitable and community works.

Flood, (Curtis Charles) Curt (1938–) baseball player; born in Houston, Texas. An outfielder for 15 years (1956–71), mostly with the St. Louis Cardinals, in 1969 he unsuccessfully brought legal action against baseball's reserve clause, which binds a player to a team through a self-renewing contract. Although the Supreme Court upheld the lower courts' rulings favoring organized baseball, Flood's suit eventually led to the establishment of free agency for all players in 1976. Frustrated by the publicity his suit created, Flood retired from baseball in 1971 and went to Majorca, an island off Spain, and ran a bar. He returned to California in 1976 and worked for several years as a sportscaster but never truly profited or recovered from his revolutionary action.

Flores, Patricio (Fernandez) (1929–) Catholic prelate; born in Ganado, Texas. The first Mexican-American bishop, he was ordained in 1956 and did parish work in the Houston diocese before being appointed auxiliary bishop of San Antonio (1970). In 1977 he became bishop of San Antonio, which in 1979 was made an archdiocese.

Flory, Paul John (1910–85) physical chemist; born in Sterling, Ill. He was a pioneer in polymer chemistry, making major discoveries in the physical chemistry of macromolecules while employed at Goodyear Tire and Rubber Company (1943–48). He was awarded the Nobel Prize in chemistry (1974) for this work. He was affiliated with Cornell (1948–56) and Stanford (1961–75).

Floyd, Carlisle (1926–) opera composer; born in Latta, S.C. Teaching at Florida State from 1947, he had a nationwide success with his third opera, *Susannah* (1955). He continued to compose operas, all marked by directness of style and a strong nationalistic element.

Flynn, Elizabeth Gurley (1890–1964) labor leader, social reformer; born in Concord, N.H. Daughter of Irish nationalists, she showed an early talent for public speaking on social issues; dropping out of school by 1907, she became an organizer for the Industrial Workers of the World. She was involved in many famous strikes including the 1912 Lawrence strike. She also worked for women's suffrage, peace, and other progressive causes, and was one of the founders of the American Civil Liberties Union (ACLU) (1920). (Expelled from the ACLU in 1940 because of her Communist Party activities, the expulsion was rescinded in 1978.) Between 1912–25, she was romantically and professionally involved with Carlo Tresca, the Italian anarchist; she worked for such causes as the release of civilians imprisoned during World War I on war-related charges, and then worked to free Sacco and Vanzetti. A heart ailment kept her out of action for a decade but in 1936 she joined the Communist Party and became one of its most outspoken leaders in the U.S.A.; she served two years in prison (1955–57) under the Smith Act, charged with advocating the overthrow of the U.S. government. From 1961–64 she served as chairperson of the Communist Party of America. She died in Moscow where she had gone to work on her autobiography.

Flynn, Errol (1909–59) actor; born in Hobart, Tasmania. Son of an Australian biologist/zoologist, he was schooled in England and Australia. From 1924–33, he led an adventurous life around the Pacific before showing up in England where he took up acting; this led to his debut in the film *In the Wake of the Bounty* (1933). He arrived in Hollywood in 1935 and with *Captain Blood* (1935) launched his career as a handsome swashbuckling star. His heavy drinking, drug-taking, and womanizing caused his career to falter by the late-1940s, even though he was acquitted of statutory rape charges of two teenage girls on his yacht; his final decade was spent in desperate attempts to revive his career and bank account. At his best he was the epitome of a movie star.

Fodor, Jerry A. (1935–) philosopher; born in New York City. After earning a Princeton doctorate (1960) he taught at the University of Illinois (1962–69), Massachusetts Institute of Technology (from 1969), and Rutgers, specializing in philosophical psychology and psycholinguistics. His works include *Psychological Explanation* (1968).

Fofonoff, Nicholas Paul (1929–) oceanographer; born in Queenstown, Alberta, Canada. He was a scientist at the Pacific Oceanographic Group (Canada) (1954–62) before coming to the U.S.A. to join the Woods Hole Oceanographic Institute (1962). He was concurrently a professor at Harvard (1968–86). He made major contributions to the fluid dynamics of ocean circulation.

Fogel, Robert W. (William) (1926–) economic historian; born in New York City. Son of Russian immigrants, he organized Communist youth in New York before enrolling in Columbia University to study statistics (A.M. 1960). A brilliant maverick, he helped found *cliometrics,* a discipline that applies economic statistics to history. He wrote several books challenging historical assumptions such as the relevance of railroads to the American west's economic development. He also wrote *Time on the Cross* (1974), which raised such a controversy about his views on slavery in America that he wrote a more accommodating second book, *Without Consent or Contract* (1989). He taught at several universities before joining the faculty at the University of Chicago in 1981. In 1993 he and Douglass C. North were awarded the Nobel Prize in economics for their contributions to economic history.

Foley, Thomas (Stephen) (1929–) U.S. representative; born in Spokane, Wash. A lawyer in Spokane, Foley was 35 when he defeated the Republican incumbent and entered congress in 1965. A Democratic reformer, he became chairman of the Agriculture Committee in 1974, party whip in 1980, and majority leader in 1986. Although a skilled party strategist, he did not always vote the Democratic party line and his preference for consensus cost him support on key bills. He served as Speaker of the House (1989–95).

Folger, Emily Clara (b. Jordon) (1858–1936) Shakespeare collector; born in Ironton, Ohio. A Vassar graduate, in 1885 she married Standard Oil executive Henry Clay Folger, who collected Shakespeare folios. Living relatively simply, in 50 years they amassed 100,000 books and manuscripts, primarily on the Elizabethan period. She became a Shakespearean scholar, authenticating and cataloguing their purchases; after her husband's death (1932) she oversaw the building of the Folger Library in Washington, D.C. (1932).

Folger, Henry Clay (1857–1930) book collector, philanthropist; born in New York City. An industrialist who was president and then chairman of the board of Standard Oil (1911–28), he assembled an outstanding Shakespeare collection and, in 1928, established the Folger Shakespeare Library in Washington, D.C., to house it.

Folin, Otto (Knut Olof) (1867–1934) biochemist; born in Asheda, Sweden. He emigrated to the U.S.A. in 1882 to join his brother in Minnesota. He taught chemistry at the University of West Virginia (1899–1900), performed research at McLean Hospital (Waverly, Mass.) (1900–07), then became the first professor of biological chemistry at Harvard Medical School (1907–34). He was a pioneer in practical colorimetry and chemical urinalysis (1900–04), then expanded his work to include analyses of blood and tissues.

With Hsien Wu, he developed the classical Folin-Wu method of assaying glucose in protein-free filtrates of blood (1919). Folin's interest in color reactions formed the basis of quantitative clinical chemistry. He founded the *Journal of Biological Chemistry* (1905).

Follett, Mary Parker (1868–1933) social worker, management theorist; born in Quincy, Mass. She graduated *summa cum laude* from Radcliffe College in 1898. In the next decade she founded several Boston boys' and young men's clubs, including the Roxbury League, which pioneered the use of schools as community centers. A believer in using community organizations to foster understanding among different social and occupational groups, she proposed in *The New State* (1918) that community-based groups rather than political parties underpin democratic political organization. Vocational guidance work with the Boston school board and elsewhere led her to industry. In her later years she wrote and lectured widely on industrial relations and management, propounding an advanced theory of management based on the motivation and coordination of group process and laying the groundwork for modern management practices. She coined the terms "togetherness" and "group thinking." After 1924 she lived and worked in England.

Folsom, James (Elisha) (1908–87) governor; born near Elba, Ala. After serving in the merchant marine, he directed the Alabama Relief Administration (1933–36), then formed the Emergency Aid and Insurance Company (1937–46). As Democratic governor of Alabama (1947–50, 1955–59), "Big Jim" was a racial moderate, who legally removed the Ku Klux Klan's hoods and met secretly with Martin Luther King Jr. to resolve the Montgomery bus boycott. He returned to his insurance business afterward.

Fonda, Henry (1905–1982) movie/stage actor; born in Grand Island, Nebr. (father of Jane and Peter Fonda). His involvement with the Omaha Community Playhouse led to Broadway and a film career in which his self-effacing manner and dry, flat tones projected honesty and decency. His movie debut in *The Farmer Takes a Wife* (1935) led to more than 100 screen appearances, culminating with his Oscar-winning role in *On Golden Pond* (1981). He also appeared occasionally on Broadway, as in *Mister Roberts* (1948). Married five times, he was said to be a moody, remote man and did not always enjoy the best of relationships with his children.

Fonda, Jane (1937–) movie actress; born in New York City. She attended Vassar College, left to study art in Paris, returned to New York to dabble in modeling, and then began a stage career; in 1955 she costarred with her father, Henry Fonda, in an Omaha, Nebr., production of *The Country Girl*. Her screen debut was in *Tall Story* (1960). She had a brief phase as a sexpot under the direction of her French filmmaker husband Roger Vadim, but after divorcing him she commenced an entirely new phase as a serious actress and committed radical. She married the political militant, Tom Hayden, took a lead in opposing the Vietnam War – earning the nickname "Hanoi Jane" because she traveled to the Communist capital and posed for pictures there – and became increasingly identified as a spokesperson on issues of civil rights and women's rights. At the same time she continued her screen career and won Oscars as best actress in *Klute* (1971) and *Coming Home* (1978). One of her finest moments came when she produced and appeared in *On Golden Pond* (1982), which gave her father his Oscar-winning

role. In the 1980s she seemed to take yet another tack with her life, becoming immensely successful with a series of aerobic-exercise videos, divorcing Tom Hayden, and, after marrying media-mogul Ted Turner, turning her attention to environmental issues.

Foner, Eric (1943–) historian; born in New York City. Educated at Oxford, England (B.A. 1965) and Columbia University (Ph.D., 1969), he taught at Columbia (1969–73; 1982) and the City College of New York (1973–82). He soon gained prominence as a proponent of the new sociological approach to history, which he applied in such works as *Politics and Ideology in the Age of the Civil War* (1980), where he looked beneath the traditional explanations to posit control of African-American labor as the basic issue of Reconstruction.

Fontanne, Lynne (b. Lillie Louise) (1887–1983) stage actress; born in Woodford, England. A woman of great glamor and sophistication, she was best known for her many collaborations in modern comedies with her husband Alfred Lunt. After studying in England with Ellen Terry, she settled permanently in the United States in 1916, the same year that she met Lunt when they both performed in *A Young Man's Fancy*. The couple first appeared as husband and wife in 1924 in *The Guardsman*, and thereafter they often performed together in Theatre Guild productions, including *Arms and the Man* (1925), *Pygmalion* (1926), and *The Brothers Karamazov* (1927). In the 1930s, she and Lunt were in several plays with roles written for them, including Elizabeth and Essex in *Elizabeth the Queen*. In 1958 they opened in *The Visit* in New York's former Globe Theatre, newly named the Lunt-Fontanne Theatre. In 1964 the couple received the U.S. Medal of Freedom.

Foote, (Albert) Horton (Jr.) (1916–) screenwriter; born in Wharton, Texas. Originally a television scriptwriter, he later won Academy Awards for the scripts of *To Kill a Mockingbird* (1962) and *Tender Mercies* (1983).

Foote, Andrew Hull (1806–63) naval officer; born in New Haven, Conn. His naval career (1822–62) was highlighted by his antislavery book *Africa and the American Flag* (1854) and the abolition of the naval grog ration in 1862.

Foote, Arthur (William) (1853–1937) composer; born in Salem, Mass. A student of John Knowles Paine at Harvard, he taught and played organ and wrote a good deal of late-Romantic music noted for solid craftsmanship; he was one of the "Boston Classic" school.

Foote, Henry Stuart (1804–80) U.S. senator, governor; born in Farquier County, Va. Elected to the U.S. Senate (Dem., Miss.; 1847–52), he resigned to serve as governor of Mississippi (1852–54). A Union-Democrat, he later represented Tennessee in the Confederate Congress, resigning to protest Jefferson Davis's policies. After the war he was appointed superintendent of the U.S. Mint in New Orleans.

Foote, Shelby (1916–) historian, novelist; born in Greenville, Miss. He attended the University of North Carolina (1935–37) and served in the Army (1940–44) and Marine Corps (1944–45). After establishing himself as a novelist with five well-received books, he spent twenty years crafting his epic, 2,934-page, three-volume *The Civil War: A Narrative* (1958, 1963, 1974). His even-handed but moving military account of the Civil War is generally considered history-as-literature at its best. He became familiar to television viewers as consultant and talking head on the Ken Burns series *The Civil War* (1990).

Foraker, Joseph Benson (1846–1917) U.S. senator, governor; born in Rainsboro, Ohio. A Civil War hero, he was a lawyer and judge in Ohio. A Republican, he was elected governor of Ohio (1886–90) and U.S. Senator (1897–1908). Accused of accepting money from Standard Oil, he was forced to resign.

Forbes, Esther (1891–1967) writer; born in Westborough, Mass. She studied at the University of Wisconsin (1916–18), and worked as an editor for Houghton Mifflin in Boston (1920–26, 1942–46). Although she wrote some straightforward history works for adults, she is best known for her historical novels for young readers, such as *Johnny Tremain* (1943).

Forbes, John Murray (1813–98) capitalist; born in Bordeaux, France. At age 15 he entered his uncles' counting house business, Perkins and Company, and worked in their China office for seven years. A wealthy and accomplished businessman, he returned to the U.S.A. in 1846 and began investing in railroad building in the Midwest. During the Civil War he helped organize African-American regiments in Massachusetts, and, along with his brother Robert Bennet Forbes, assisted the U.S. Navy with his maritime expertise. After the war he continued to apply both financially sound and socially responsible methods to his railroad interests. He was active in the Republican Party.

Forbes, Malcolm (Stevenson) (1919–90) publisher; born in New York City. In 1957 he became editor and publisher of *Forbes*, a then-floundering business magazine founded by his father 40 years before. Circulation and profits soared, making him a multimillionaire; he became known for his extravagant parties and colorful hobbies, from hot-air ballooning to collecting Fabergé eggs.

Forbes, Robert Bennet (1804–89) merchant, author; born in Jamaica Plain, Mass. (brother of John Murray Forbes). He entered the China-trade business of his uncles James and Thomas H. Perkins at age 13 and stayed with the company when it merged to become Russell & Company (1830). In 1839 he became head of the Company and ignored the British boycott of Canton during the Opium Wars. Owner of several ships, he supported innovations in marine safety and ship design that included the first iron-hulled tugboat. During the terrible famine of 1847, he personally commanded a ship that took food from Boston to Ireland. During the Civil War he organized a short-lived "Coast Guard." A prolific pamphleteer, he wrote about the China trade and marine matters. His memoirs are titled *Peronal Reminiscences* (1876; 3rd ed., 1892).

Forbes, Stephen Alfred (1844–1930) naturalist; born in Silver Creek, Ill. A farmer's son, he served in an Illinois cavalry regiment during the Civil War, then attended medical school and had nearly finished when he dropped out to study natural history. His research specialty, the food of birds and fish, gave him a broad perspective on biological interrelationships; he is credited with being one of the founders of the discipline of ecology. He worked for Illinois state institutions for most of his career, and was state entomologist from 1882–1917.

Force, Juliana Rieser (b. Reiser) (1876–1948) museum director, art supporter; born in Doylestown, Pa. Born into a "poor but proud" family, she became a secretary at an early age and then directed a secretarial school. Moving to New York City (early 1900s) she became the private secretary to the wealthy Helen Hay Whitney; in 1912 Rieser married Willard B. Force, a dentist. Mrs. Whitney's sister-in-law was the sculptor and art patron, Gertrude Vanderbilt Whitney, and in 1914 she asked Juliana Force to help run her Whitney Studio, a new art gallery in Greenwich Village that was to promote the more progressive American painters. Although she had no background in art, Force seemed to have an instinctive feel for what Whitney and the best young American artists were seeking to achieve and she would spend the rest of her life advancing their cause. She helped Whitney in founding the Friends of the Young Artists (1915), which evolved into the Whitney Studio Club (1918), both designed to support the new artists with exhibits, purchases, and social contacts. Whitney continued to use her fortune to promote art in various other ways, including subsidizing the influential magazine *Arts,* and Force was the active executor of most of these projects. From 1928–30 Force ran the Whitney Studio Galleries but by then Whitney was convinced that a museum was needed; the foundation of the Whitney Museum of American Art was announced in 1930, and with Force as director it opened (originally in Greenwich Village) in 1931. She continued to expand her support of American artists, helping to organize the federal art program under the Public Works of Art Project (1933–34), heading a 1945 committee that got the New York State legislature to earmark funds to purchase art for public buildings, and becoming one of the first women to participate in museum professionals' organizations.

Ford, Betty (Elizabeth Bloomer b. Warren) (1918–) First Lady; born in Chicago, Ill. Trained as a dancer, she spent a few years in the 1930s with the Martha Graham company. Her first marriage ended in divorce and she married Gerald Ford in 1948. A most outspoken first lady, she endorsed the Equal Rights Amendment and women's right to abortion. Following the presidency and her own problems with alcohol and drugs, she helped establish a highly publicized treatment center in California.

Ford, (Edward Charles) "Whitey" (1926–) baseball pitcher; born in New York City. During his 16-year career with the New York Yankees (1950, 1953–67), the left-hander won 236 games and the Cy Young award in 1961. He had more appearances (22), pitched more innings (146), had more strikeouts (94) and won more games (10) than any pitcher in World Series history. He was elected to baseball's Hall of Fame in 1974.

Ford, Gerald R. (Rudolph, Jr.) (1913–) thirty-eighth U.S. president; born in Omaha, Nebr. He grew up in Grand Rapids, Mich., and graduated from the University of Michigan (1935) and Yale Law School (1941). He began to practice law in Michigan but enlisted in the U.S. Navy during World War II. Elected to the U.S. House of Representatives (Rep., Mich.; 1949–73), he became a minority leader in 1965 and was regarded as a moderate if routine politician. On the resignation of vice-president Spiro Agnew in 1973, he was named Nixon's vice-president. When Nixon resigned in 1974 due to the Watergate scandals, Ford became president. A Democratic Congress resisted Ford's economic initiatives in a time of recession; weakened by that, his pardon of Nixon, and a general desire by Americans to put Watergate behind them, Ford lost the 1976 election to Jimmy Carter and retired from politics.

Ford, Henry (1863–1947) industrialist, innovator; born near Dearborn, Mich. Son of a farmer, he left school at age 15 and worked at a series of jobs where he enlarged his mechanical skills and knowledge of engines. By 1892 he had built his own "gasoline buggy" and by 1896 was driving an improved model in public. In 1899 he left a secure post as engineer of the Edison Illuminating Company in Detroit to start an automobile company. It went out of business in 1900 and he concentrated on making racing cars. In 1903, realizing that the future of automobiles lay in making them faster and cheaper, he established the Ford Motor Company with $100,000 from investors. His firm's early models sold well but his big breakthrough came with the introduction of the Model T in 1908, the first car designed for average people's use. Its low price, in turn, depended on his company's adoption of innovative production methods such as assembly-line operations and standardized parts. A paternalistic employer, he introduced the $5-a-day wage in 1914 and generally paid wages above industry standards, but he fiercely resisted unionization (United Auto Workers did not appear in his plants until 1941). He became so widely admired that the term "Fordismus" was coined to describe his brand of capitalism – efficient production, good pay, and mass distribution. He had also taken to promoting his views in articles and books, including *My Life and Work* (1922) (which, like most of his writing, was the work of a hired hand). Blinded by his early successes, he tended to isolate himself from new advances in technology and design – for years his cars were available only in black, and his Model A, introduced in 1927, lagged years behind in its technology. By the mid-1930s, his company slipped behind other American car manufacturers. By then he himself was fabulously rich and although he continued his autocratic control of the company, he turned over much of the operations to his only son, Edsel. Meanwhile, he had already begun to devote himself to other pursuits. He had strongly opposed World War I, and after he lost a race for the U.S. Senate in 1918, he blamed the war and his defeat on "international bankers" and "the Jews," revealing a side he would never live down, provincial at best, bigoted at worst. At one stage he even expressed admiration of Hitler and he urged Americans not to get involved in World War II. Meanwhile, he devoted considerable time and money to establishing the historical village and museum in Dearborn. (His oft-quoted remark, "History is bunk," was intended to mean that, as conventionally taught in books, history failed to capture the true story of people in the past.) In 1936 he established the Ford Foundation, and with the bequests of his and his family's stock, it became one of the world's largest philanthropic institutions. Although not universally admired by the time of his death (and later biographies would further chip away at his image), he was undeniably one of the most influential men of the century.

Ford, Henry, II (1917–87) automobile maker; born in Detroit, Mich. (grandson of Henry Ford, 1863–1947). Upon the death of his father, Edsel Bryant Ford, he gained control of the Ford Motor Company from his grandfather and his Rasputin-like assistant, Harry Bennett. As president (1945–60) and chairman (1960–80), he reorganized and revitalized the company, making it into the second leading automobile maker in the U.S.A.

Ford, James A. (Alfred) (1911–68) archaeologist; born in Water Valley, Miss. He was curator of North American archaeology at the American Museum of Natural History (1947–63). A specialist in prehistoric culture of the Americas, he did fieldwork in Alaska, the lower Mississippi Valley, and the Andes and he pioneered the seriation method of dating artifacts.

Ford, John (b. Sean Aloysius O'Feeney or O'Fearna) (1895–1973) film director; born in Cape Elizabeth, Maine. He left Maine for Hollywood in 1913 and worked as a set laborer and propman. He began directing in 1917, and was to turn out over 125 features, making his debut with a western, *The Tornado*. Over the years, he developed his own little stock company, which featured John Wayne, Ward Bond, James Stewart, Henry Fonda, and many others. Adept at all genres, he frequently explored his Irish roots, but achieved his greatest renown for poetic visions of the American West – its rugged heroes, pioneering families, and sense of male camaraderie. He won Academy Awards four times for directing features – *The Informer* (1935), *The Grapes of Wrath* (1940), *How Green Was My Valley* (1941), and *The Quiet Man* (1952) – and two others for World War II documentaries. He received the first American Film Institute Life Achievement Award in 1973.

Ford, Wendell H. (1924–) U.S. senator, governor; born in Daviess County, Ky. Kentucky's Democratic governor (1971–74), he was elected to the U.S. Senate in 1974. There he staunchly defended the interests of the tobacco industry. He was elected Democratic whip in 1990.

Fordney, Joseph Warren (1853–1932) U.S. representative; born in Hartford City, Ind. A lumberman and alderman before going to the U.S. House of Representatives (Rep., Mich.; 1899–1923), he chaired the Committee on Ways and Means. He resumed lumbering afterward.

Foreman, George (1949–) boxer; born in Marshall, Texas. Coming from a broken home, he joined the Job Corps (1965–67) while training and boxing as an amateur. He won the gold medal as a heavyweight at the 1968 Olympics, then turned professional in 1969. He held the world heavyweight championship (1973–74) until he was defeated by a resurgent Muhammad Ali in Zaire, Africa. He became an ordained minister in 1977 and devoted his money and energies to community work among poor African-Americans in Texas. Needing more money for his projects, he made a comeback as a heavyweight (1987) that was noted less for his being a serious threat and more for his becoming everyone's favorite boxer. In 1994 he knocked out Michael Moorer in a fight sanctioned by two of the three main boxing organizations to become the oldest heavyweight champion in history.

Foreman, Percy (1902–88) lawyer; born in Cold Springs, Texas. Son of a Texas sheriff, he quit school at age 15, then put himself through the University of Texas Law School and went on to become one of America's best known trial lawyers. Notorious for high fees and courtroom theatrics, he was often ridiculed for his clothing and disorganization, but he was a respected master of tactics. He lost only 53 of 1,500 death-penalty cases. His most famous client was James Earl Ray, killer of Martin Luther King Jr.

Foreman, Richard (1937–) director, producer, playwright; born in New York City. An avant-garde dramatist, he was the founder of the Ontological-Hysteric Theatre in New York in

1968. He designed sets for New York's Public Theatre, among others.

Forepaugh, Adam (1831–90) showman; born in Philadelphia. A horse trader who became circus owner by default in 1862, he thrived in the business until his death, drawing crowds with the great clown Dan Rice, and rivaling P. T. Barnum.

Fornes, Maria Irene (1930–) playwright, director; born in Havana, Cuba. After attending the public schools in Havana, she emigrated to the U.S.A. in 1945. In 1954 she went off to Europe to be a painter, then returned to New York City in 1957 to work as a textile designer. By the early 1960s, she had turned to writing experimental plays and musicals and she began to get them produced off Broadway – often under her own direction. Her first notable success was a musical, *Promenade* (1965), but her major success came with *Fefu and Her Friends* (1977), which brings a feminist perspective to female friendship and women's roles in a patriarchal society. She won an Obie (off Broadway theater) award for both those plays and would win four more, including one for *Eyes on the Harem* (1979); in 1982 she won a special Obie for her "sustained achievement." The quintessential off Broadway playwright – with a combination of zany, whimsical humor; innovative, cinematic stagecraft; and strong ideological themes – in later years took up directing the classic repertoire as well as writing and directing her own avant-garde plays.

Forrest, Edwin (1806–72) actor; born in Philadelphia. He was a strikingly handsome, flamboyant man who excelled in tragic roles. A great favorite among ordinary theater-goers, his acting style was seen as a breath of fresh air in contrast to the more tightly restrained British model. But he was criticized by those who found vulgar his tendency to show off his physique and powerful voice. His first stage role was in 1817 when he stood in for an actress in the small role of a harem girl; his true debut was in 1820 in *Douglas*. After this he toured for a time, then made his extremely successful New York debut as Iago in *Othello* (1826). A pugnacious character who had numerous financial and marital problems, his rivalry with actor William Macready led to the 1849 Astor Place Riots, in New York City, where 30 were killed during a fight between the actors' adherents. Forest fell out of favor as new styles of performance became popular. His last performance was in 1872 at the Globe Theatre in Boston.

Forrest, Nathan Bedford (1821–77) soldier; born in Bedford County, Tenn. With little formal education, he became a wealthy livestock dealer, planter, and slave trader. When the Civil War commenced, he enlisted as a private, but by October 1861 he was a lieutenant colonel in command of his own troop of cavalry. He participated in many of the early battles including Shiloh, but soon began to operate on his own, using his cavalry as a "strike force." His motto was the phrase attributed to him: "Git there fustest with the mostest." Aggressive and daring – he stabbed a would-be assailant to death after taking a near-fatal gunshot wound – he struck hard and often at Union lines in Tennessee and Kentucky from 1862–64; troops under his command carried out an infamous massacre of black Union troops at Fort Pillow, Tenn. After the war, he had to rebuild his fortune through planting and railroading. He served as grand wizard of the newly organized Ku Klux Klan (1867–69) but resigned in protest of some of its tactics.

Forrestal, James (Vincent) (1892–1949) cabinet officer; born in Matteawan (now Beacon), N.Y. After making a fortune as an investment banker, he became the undersecretary (1940) and then the secretary of the navy (1944). Although originally opposed to uniting the armed services into one department, he became the first secretary of defense (1947–49); he advocated hard-line anticommunist policies and strengthened the armed forces. Increasingly beset by interservice rivalries, questions of combat strength, and appropriations, he resigned in 1949; convinced that he had failed to protect his country, he took his life.

Forsythe, William (1949–) choreographer; born in New York City. He trained with the Joffrey Ballet School and performed with the company from 1971–73. In 1973 he went to the Stuttgart Ballet, becoming resident choreographer in 1976. He was appointed artistic director of the Frankfurt Ballet in 1984.

Fortas, Abe (1910–82) Supreme Court justice; born in Memphis, Tenn. After teaching at Yale Law School (1933–37), he served in a series of several government agencies (1937–45) before becoming an adviser to the U.S. delegation to the organizational meeting of the United Nations (1945) and to the first session of the General Assembly (1946). He then began to practice law privately in Washington, D.C., combining a corporate practice with cases in defense of civil liberties. For years he had been an unofficial adviser to Lyndon Johnson, who in 1965 appointed him to the U.S. Supreme Court and then nominated him for chief justice in 1968; conservatives who opposed him during the Senate confirmation proceedings forced him to withdraw. In 1969 it was revealed that he had been accepting money from a foundation set up by a man convicted of stock manipulation, and Fortas became the first man ever forced to resign from the Supreme Court. He returned to private practice.

Forten, James (1766–1842) sailmaker, social activist; born in Philadelphia. A free African-American, he joined the Continental navy at age 15 and was among those taken prisoner when his ship, the *Royal Louis,* was captured by the British. After being released, he returned to Philadelphia and was apprenticed to sailmaker Robert Bridges. By 1786 Forten was a foreman there and in 1798, when Bridges died, he took over control of the sail loft; he became wealthy and was a leader of the black community of Philadelphia. In 1814 he helped enlist 2,500 African-American volunteers to protect Philadelphia during the War of 1812. Active in promoting temperance and peace, he devoted much energy and money to abolishing slavery and gaining the civil rights of African-Americans: he opposed the American Colonization Society and its plans to send blacks out of the U.S.; he provided financial support to William Lloyd Garrison's paper, *The Liberator;* and he refused rigging to slave-trade vessels. Although all but forgotten in ensuing decades, he was arguably the most extraordinary African-American of his era.

Fortune, Timothy Thomas (1856–1928) journalist, editor, civil rights activist; born in Marianna Township, Fla. Freed from slavery in only 1865, he witnessed his father's stormy career as a Reconstructionist politician in Florida. Timothy learned the printer's trade and when he moved to Washington, D.C. (1876), he worked on an African-American newspaper and became friendly with Frederick Douglass. In 1880 he moved to New York City where for the next 34 years he worked on, founded, or edited a succession of newspapers, mostly concerned with protecting and advancing the rights of African-Americans; the most influential of these were *The Globe* (1882–84) and *The New York Freeman* (1884–87), renamed *The New York Age* (1891–1907). Because he at times criticized the Republican Party and argued for self-help among African-Americans, he was regarded by some as too conservative. But he was the first to propose the founding of the Afro-American League and was its first chairman and later president (1890–93); although it did not last long, the League was the forerunner of the National Association for the Advancement of Colored People. He was also active in founding several other African-American professional organizations, and he worked closely with Booker T. Washington. For several years his career was sidetracked by a drinking problem, but by 1910 he was active again as an editor and organizer. From 1923–28 he edited *The Negro World*, the organ of Marcus Garvey's "back to Africa" movement. Although he would never attain the status of a major leader of the African-American community, he was recognized by many contemporaries as an important figure.

Fosbury, (Richard) Dick (1947–   ) track and field athlete; born in Portland, Ore. After revolutionizing the high jump with his back-first "Fosbury Flop," he won a gold medal in the 1968 Olympics.

Fosdick, Henry Emerson (1878–1969) Protestant religious leader; born in Buffalo, N.Y. He graduated from Colgate University (1900) and the Union Theological Seminary and was ordained in 1903. As a professor at Union he opposed credal restrictions; he later helped lead liberal Protestant forces during the conflict with Fundamentalism in the 1920s. As pastor of the interdenominational Riverside Church in New York City from 1925–46 he was the acknowledged spokesman for modern liberal Christianity, and he wrote, lectured, and broadcast widely. He published an autobiography, *The Living of These Days*, in 1956.

Foss, Joseph (Jacob) (1915–   ) marine aviator, governor; born in Sioux Falls, S.D. He led the marine Fighting Squadron 121 – "Joe's Flying Circus" – on Guadalcanal Island during heavy fighting there in 1942, and shot down a total of 26 Japanese aircraft. He served as governor of South Dakota from 1955 to 1959.

Foss, Lucas (b. Fuchs) (1922–   ) composer, conductor, pianist; born in Berlin, Germany. A precocious talent, he studied at the Curtis Institute and with Hindemith at Yale, and was a Koussevitzky protégé at Tanglewood. First gaining fame as a pianist, he established himself as a composer with conservative "Americana" works such as *The Prairie* for orchestra (1943); later he turned to an avant-garde idiom, often with improvisatory elements. He conducted widely, leading the Buffalo Philharmonic (1963–70) and the Brooklyn Philharmonic (1971–90), meanwhile working for shorter terms with orchestras in Jerusalem and Milwaukee, Wis.

Fosse, (Robert Louis) Bob (1927–87) choreographer, dancer, director; born in Chicago. He began his career in vaudeville as a child, performing as one of the "Riff Brothers" at age 13. After dancing in films, such as *Kiss Me Kate* (1953), he won Tony Awards for choreography of *The Pajama Game* (1956) and *Damn Yankees* (1957). He created a new title on Broadway, director/choreographer, winning Tony Awards for *Redhead* (1958) and *Sweet Charity* (1966).

Directing musical films as well, he won an Oscar for *Cabaret* (1972). Subsequent Broadway shows, most notably *Dancin'* (1978), and films such as the semiautobiographical *All That Jazz* (1979), secured his reputation as one of the most innovative and influential director/choreographers in musical theater and film.

Fossey, Dian (1932–85) primatologist; born in San Francisco. She was interested in animals from childhood, but changed college majors from preveterinary studies to occupational therapy. She moved to Louisville, Ky., to be director of the Kosair Crippled Children's Hospital occupational therapy department (1955–56), but felt compelled to satisfy her long-standing desire to visit Africa. On her first trip to Africa (1963), she met paleontologists Mary and Louis S. B. Leakey, who encouraged Fossey's dream to live and work with mountain gorillas. When Louis Leakey somewhat facetiously suggested that Fossey have her appendix prophylactically removed before living in a remote area, her having the operation so convinced Leakey of her determination that he invited her to begin field work in 1966. She lived among the mountain gorillas in the Republic of the Congo (now Zaire) until civil war forced her to escape to Rwanda. She established the Karisoke Research Foundation (1967), alternating her time between her field work there and obtaining a Ph.D. based on her research (Cambridge University, 1976), accepting a visiting associate professorship at Cornell (1980), and writing her best-selling book, *Gorillas in the Mist* (published 1983). She was considered the world's leading authority on the physiology and behavior of mountain gorillas, and portrayed these animals as dignified, highly social, "gentle giants," with individual personalities and strong family relationships. Her active conservationist stand against game wardens, zoo poachers, and government officials who wanted to convert gorilla habitats to farmland caused her to fight for the gorillas not only via the media, but also by destroying poachers' dogs and traps. She was found hacked to death, presumably by poachers, in her Rwandan forest camp in December 1985.

Foster, Abigail Kelley See KELLEY, ABBY.

Foster, (Andrew) Rube (1878–1930) baseball player, manager, executive; born in Calvert, Texas. Nicknamed "Rube" for outpitching Hall of Famer Rube Waddell, Foster rose through the ranks from star player (1902–17) to club owner, emerging as the dominant figure in black baseball after pitching and managing his 1910 Leland Giants, who dominated African-American baseball for the following decade, to a 126–6 record. Friend and confidant of major league managers including John McGraw, as a manager (1910–23) his skills achieved legendary proportions; several of his strategies became standard in major league ball. In 1920 he created the Negro National League, which placed black baseball on a solid footing for the first time and gained him the reputation of being "the Father of Black baseball." As president, his fifteen-hour days contributed to a nervous breakdown (1926) from which he never recovered. He was named to the Baseball Hall of Fame in 1981. His half-brother, "Big Bill" (William Hendrick) Foster (1904–78), also compiled an outstanding pitching record in the black leagues (1923–37).

Foster, John (1648–81) printer; born in Dorchester, Mass. He graduated from Harvard University (1667), established the first printing office in Boston (1675–81), and is known for the earliest woodblock engraving in America, a portrait of Reverend Richard Mather (1670).

Foster, Stephen Collins (1826–64) composer, lyricist; born in Lawrenceville, Pa. (now part of Pittsburgh). By the time he was eight he was teaching himself piano and flute, and he learned African-American spirituals from Olivia Pise, a household slave. At age nine he put on minstrel shows for family and friends. After only a week in college, he quit to devote himself to music, and published his first song in 1844. He wrote some of his first songs for a men's club that met at his home in 1845, including "Oh, Susanna," later popularized by blackface minstrel shows and pioneers heading west during the gold rush of 1849. Back in Pittsburgh in 1848, after having abandoned a bookkeeping job his father wanted him to take, he signed a contract with a prominent New York publishing house and within about a year he began living on royalties (although due to his poor business sense, he would never profit very much). The well-known blackface troupe, the Christy Minstrels, began performing such songs as "Camptown Races" (1850) and "Old Folks at Home" (also called "Swanee River") (1851), one of the most popular songs ever published (although it would be 1879 before he would get his own name on the sheet music). He also wrote such nonminstrel songs as "Jeanie With the Light Brown Hair" (1854), dedicated to his wife even though she had little liking for his heavy drinking and bohemian ways. Songs such as "My Old Kentucky Home" (1853) and "Old Black Joe" (1860) brought him further popularity and some financial reward; but during the Civil War his popularity waned, despite his steady output of sentimental and war songs. In 1860 he moved his family to New York City and he was soon reduced to writing imitative songs. When he began drinking heavily, his wife and daughter returned to Pittsburgh and he died alone and in squalor in 1864.

Foster, William Z. (Zebulon) (1881–1961) Communist leader; born in Taunton, Mass. An itinerant laborer in his youth, he joined the Socialist Party (1901) and worked as a labor organizer for the next two decades; he gained fame by organizing the 1919 steel strike. In 1921 he joined the American Communist Party, serving as secretary general until 1930; he was the party's presidential candidate in 1924, 1928, and 1932. Poor health limited his activities in the 1930s, but he remained an ardent Communist and advocate of total loyalty to the U.S.S.R. In 1945 he regained chairmanship of the party from the less rigid Earl Browder, holding the post until 1956. Indicted with 11 others under the Smith Act (1948), on charges of advocating the overthrow of the U.S. government, he was excused from trial because of ill health. He died in Moscow shortly after going there for medical treatment. Although lacking formal education, he wrote many essays and books.

Foulois, Benjamin D. (Delahauf) (1879–1967) soldier, aviator; born in Washington, Conn. He left his father's plumbing business to enlist to fight the Spanish in 1898, was commissioned in 1901, and transferred to the Signal Corps in 1908. He learned to fly two years later; he was assistant chief of the American Expeditionary Force's air service in France in 1917. As chief of the Army Air Corps from 1931–35, Foulois overcame tight budgets and official indifference to improve training, equipment, and doctrine. He retired in 1935, the year in which the establishment of General Headquarters Air Force gave the flying service a measure of autonomy.

Fowle, Elida Barker (b. Rumsey) (1842–1919) relief and welfare worker; born in New York City. During the Civil War she was a private hospital visitor, fundraiser, and field nurse, nationally celebrated for her youth, energy, and initiative. With her fiancé she founded the Soldier's Free Library, Washington, D.C. (1862). Noted for her beautiful voice, she sang in hospitals and to raise money for the troops; after her marriage in the nation's Capitol – in the presence of members of Congress and hundreds of spectators – she sang "The Star Spangled Banner." Her postwar life was devoted to her family and charitable works in New York and Massachusetts.

Fowler, William Alfred (1911–) astrophysicist; born in Pittsburgh, Pa. As a civilian, he first participated in military ordnance research at the Kellogg Laboratory in Pasadena, Calif., during World War II. He then turned his attention to the energy in stars. An emeritus professor of physics at the California Institute of Technology since 1982, he shared the 1983 Nobel Prize in physics for his studies of how chemical elements are formed in the universe.

Fox, Dixon (Ryan) (1887–1945) college president, historian; born in Potsdam, N.Y. A Ph.D. from Columbia University, he taught American social history there (1913–34) and wrote *The Decline of Aristocracy in the Politics of New York* (1919). He was president of Union College, Schenectady (1934–45). As president of the New York State Historical Society (1929–45), he sponsored important scholarly publications.

Fox, Gustavus Vasa (1821–83) naval officer; born in Saugus, Mass. He served in the navy (1841–56) and later became assistant secretary of the navy (1861–66). He was an early advocate of the USS *Monitor* and gave indispensable assistance to Secretary Gideon Welles during the Civil War.

Fox, Matthew (b. Timothy James) (1940–) priest, theologian; born in Madison, Wis. He nearly lost his legs to polio at age 12; upon his recovery he became devoted to the Catholic Church. He studied in Chicago and Paris, was ordained (1967), and began to follow a path of Christian mysticism in the tradition of Meister Eckhart and Thomas Aquinas. He directed the Institute in Culture and Creation Spirituality in Oakland, California (1983). Convinced that original blessing was greater than original sin, he promoted his vision of a vibrant, sensual faith. He wrote *On Becoming a Musical, Mystical Bear: Spirituality American Style* (1972), *Meditations with Meister Eckhart* (1983), and *The Coming of the Cosmic Christ* (1988).

Foxx, (James Emory) Jimmie (1907–67) baseball player; born in Sudlersville, Md. During his 20-year career (1925–45), mostly with the Philadelphia Athletics and Boston Red Sox, the powerfully built first baseman (he also caught and played other positions) hit 534 homeruns and won the league Most Valuable Player award three times (1932, 1933, 1938). Nicknamed "Double X" and "The Beast," he was elected to baseball's Hall of Fame in 1951.

Foxx, Redd (b. John Elroy Sanford) (1922–91) comedian, television actor; born in St. Louis, Mo. A gravelly voiced and furrow faced comedian, for years he had a near legendary reputation for his scatalogical humor to be heard only in venues frequented by African-Americans. Then the television sitcom "Sanford and Son" (1972–77) catapulted him to fame and fortune. Although he retained his popularity with audiences, no other show ever fared as well; he fell into heavy debt and died while filming another television sitcom, "The Royal Family."

Foy, (Edward Fitzgerald) Eddie (1856–1928) actor, dancer; born in New York City. He started dancing in saloons as a kid to support his family, then added a blackface routine as a teenager for circuses and minstrel shows. On the Western circuit for years, he achieved success in costume fantasies before returning home to Broadway in 1901. In 1903 he was appearing at Chicago's Iroquois Theatre when fire broke out; although he did his best to calm the audience, 602 died in the panic that ensued. Known for his facial expressions and pantomime, he achieved his greatest success with *The Seven Little Foys* (1910–23), a vaudeville act featuring his seven children.

Foyt, A. J. (Anthony Joseph, Jr.) (1935–) auto racer; born in Houston, Texas. He drove a miniature car at age four and midget cars at age 11. He began to race professionally in 1953. He won the Indianapolis 500 (1961, 1964, 1967, 1977) and the U.S. Auto Club Championship (1960, 1961, 1963, 1964, 1967, 1975, 1979). Although he suffered accidents in 1965 and 1966, they did not deter him from his career. He also bred and trained horses.

Francis, James (Bicheno) (1815–92) engineer; born at Southleigh, England. He emigrated to America in 1833. The son of a railroad engineer, he worked on numerous railroad projects in New York and New England. He harnessed the power of the Merrimac River in Lowell, Mass. (1845–50), and contributed to other power projects before retiring in 1885.

Francis, (Samuel Lewis) Sam (1923–) painter; born in San Mateo, Calif. After recovery from tuberculosis (1944–47) and extensive travel, he settled in Los Angeles, Calif. He is noted for his abstract expressionist paintings, as in *White Painting* (1950), where the color is amorphous; later the coloration is brilliant, as in *Polar Red* (1973).

Franey, Pierre (1921–) chef, author; born in Tonnerre, France. French-trained Franey emigrated to the U.S.A. (1939) and worked his way up to chef at New York's Le Pavillon Restaurant. He collaborated with Craig Claiborne on cookbooks and food articles in the 1970s–80s and independently wrote two cookbooks based on his *New York Times* "60-Minute Gourmet" column.

Frank, Jerome (1889–1957) judge, legal philosopher; born in New York City. After graduating from the University of Chicago, and before attending its law school, he served as secretary to his political science professor, Charles E. Merriam. He handled corporate reorganizations in Chicago (1912–29) and New York (1929–33) before serving as counsel to several New Deal agencies. He then joined the Securities and Exchange Commission (1937–41) and went on to serve on a U.S. Circuit Court of Appeals (1941–57). His book *Law and the Modern Mind* (1930) argued for "legal realism," with an emphasis on the psychological forces at work in legal matters, and his *Courts on Trial* (1949) stressed the uncertainties and fallibility of the judicial process.

Frank, Jerome David (1909–) psychiatrist, educator; born in New York City. He was associated with Johns Hopkins University School of Medicine (1942), where he became professor of psychiatry in 1959. His major research interest was the shared healing features of all forms of psychotherapy, especially the psychotherapeutic relationship, the arousal of hope, enhancement of the patient's sense of mastery, and the arousal of the patient's emotions.

Frank, John P. (Paul) (1917–) lawyer, author; born in Appleton, Wis. A legendary appellate lawyer with Lewis & Roca in Phoenix, Ariz., (1954), he taught at several law schools (1946–72) and was the lead winning counsel in *Miranda* v. *Arizona* (1966). In addition to his heavy load of corporate cases, he was active in fighting for what he regarded as the rights of the legal profession. His eleven books include *Lincoln as a Lawyer* (1961).

Frank, Mary (b. Lockspeiser) (1933–) sculptor; born in London, England. She and her American mother settled in New York City (1940), where she studied dance with Martha Graham (1949). She lived with her photographer husband, Robert Frank, in New York and the Catskills, before their divorce. She became known for her clay assemblages, drawing on evolutionary and mythological themes, as seen in *Swimmer* (1978).

Frank, Robert (1924–) photographer, filmmaker; born in Zurich, Switzerland. A free-lance fashion and film photographer in Zurich (1943–47), he emigrated to New York in 1947 where he was befriended by Alexey Brodovitch, Art Director at *Harper's Bazaar*. A successful free-lancer (1947–51), he did fashion and advertising photography for *Harper's* and *The New York Times* among others, traveling on assignment to South America and Europe. In 1953 he collected and selected work for Steichen's exhibition, *Post-War European Photographers*, at the Museum of Modern Art. The first European to receive a Guggenheim in 1955, he spent the next two years traveling across America to capture images of daily life with his 35mm camera, publishing *The Americans* in 1959. In 1958 he collaborated with the painter Alfred Leslie and author Jack Kerouac to film the free-swinging *Pull My Daisy*. One of the founders of the New American Cinema Group, he spent most of his time making films until 1966, when he virtually gave up photography. In 1969 he moved to Cape Breton, Nova Scotia.

Frank, Tenney (1876–1939) classicist, historian; born near Clay Center, Kans. He was educated at the Universities of Kansas (B.A. 1898, M.A. 1899) and Chicago (Ph.D. 1903) and taught at Bryn Mawr (1904–19) and Johns Hopkins (1919–38). Often called the finest American historian of Rome of his time, he was appropriately the first American classicist to hold the Eastman Professorship at Oxford (1938–39). Editor of the *American Journal of Philology* (1936–39), and University of California Sather professor in 1930, he published fifteen books (including *An Economic Survey of Ancient Rome*, 1920 and 1933), more than 150 articles, and many reviews.

Frank, Waldo (David) (1899–1967) writer; born in Long Branch, N.J. A Yale graduate, he was founding editor of the short-lived, pacifist little magazine *Seven Arts* (1916–17). After the 1930s he was a left-wing activist whose large literary output included politically inspired fiction and Marxist social analysis. He wrote and lectured widely on Latin America; his works include *Virgin Spain* (1926, revised 1942) and *America Hispana* (1931). He lived in Truro, Mass. and New York City.

Frankenthaler, Helen (1928–) painter; born in New York City. She studied with many teachers, including Hans Hofmann (1950), and was married to Robert Motherwell (1958–71). Based in New York City, she taught in numerous places and is known for her staining technique using thinned oils and acrylics on unprimed canvases. Her optical effects first gained public acclaim with *Mountains and Sea* (1952).

Frankfurter, Alfred (Moritz) (1906–65) art critic; born in Chicago. He studied at Princeton and with Bernard Berenson in Italy. He returned to New York City (1927) and worked as an editor and a free-lance art critic, then became editor of *Art News* (1936–65). In his capacity as an editor, he became an influential force in the art world of the time.

Frankfurter, Felix (1882–1965) Supreme Court justice, presidential adviser; born in Vienna, Austria. He emigrated to the U.S.A. at age twelve and graduated from Harvard Law School in 1906. He briefly practiced law and served as an assistant district attorney in New York before joining the faculty at Harvard Law School (1914–39). While at Harvard, he served as a legal adviser to President Wilson at the Paris Peace Conference (1919). An early contributor to *The New Republic,* he helped found the American Civil Liberties Union (1920) and argued in favor of Sacco and Vanzetti's right to a new trial. He advised President Franklin D. Roosevelt on many New Deal programs and, in 1939, Roosevelt named him to the U.S. Supreme Court (1939–62). His tenure on the court tamed his liberalism. His opinions reflected his belief in judicial restraint: that the law should emanate from the people and the legislative process rather than the court. In 1963 he was awarded the Presidential Medal of Freedom.

Frankl, Paul T. (1887–1958) furniture designer; born in Vienna, Austria. Already an established designer in his native land when he emigrated to New York City in 1914, he became an important promoter of modern design through writing and lecturing. His book *New Dimensions* (1928) was important for disseminating the art deco style. He also continued to design furniture; memorable among his own work is his 1920s "skyscraper style" furniture – extremely elegant in its use of exotic woods with lacquers or gold and silver leaf.

Frankl, Viktor (Emil) (1905–) psychiatrist, author; born in Vienna, Austria. He studied at the University of Vienna (M.D. 1930) and was imprisoned by the Nazis during World War II. After his release, he taught at Vienna from 1947. He came to the United States during the 1960s, when his concept of logotherapy, an existentialist approach to psychotherapy, became well known. He published several dozen books, including *Man's Search for Meaning: An Introduction to Logotherapy* (1963) and a revised and enlarged translation of *From Death-Camp to Existentialism: A Psychiatrist's Path to a New Therapy,* published in German in 1946.

Franklin, Aretha (1942–) soul singer; born in Memphis, Tenn. Daughter of Detroit clergyman C. L. Franklin, she sang in church choirs as a child and at age 14 joined her father's traveling gospel revue. Although she began recording at age 18, it was at Atlantic Records beginning in 1966 that she worked with experienced rhythm-and-blues musicians and was encouraged to use her gospel roots. In 1967 she gained fame with the release "I Never Loved a Man the Way I Love You." This and four subsequent number one hits ensured a large following. In the 1980s, recording for Arista, she overcame a creative slump and added 3 Grammies and 2 gold records to the many she has earned during her career. Her passionate virtuoso singing and tight arrangements give her music an eloquent intensity. In 1986 she starred in the retrospective television special, *Aretha!* and in 1989 she was the subject of a documentary video, *Aretha Franklin: Queen of Soul.* Her highly flamboyant live performances, such as that in the Radio City Music Hall in 1990, never failed to draw full audiences.

Franklin, Benjamin (1706–90) printer, writer, scientist, statesman; born in Boston, Mass. The 15th child in his family, he went to work at age ten in his father's chandlery, then in a brother's printing house. Ambitious and intent on self-improvement, he became a skilled printer while reading widely and developing a writing style. In 1723, at age 17, he left for Philadelphia; starting with no capital, he advanced rapidly and, after a brief stint as a printer in London, had by 1730 become sole owner of a business that included the *Pennsylvania Gazette.* In 1732 he began compiling and publishing the annual *Poor Richard's Almanac;* with its pithy sayings espousing industry, frugality, and other homely virtues, it attracted a large readership and made Franklin's name a household word. Active in the community, he founded a discussion group called the Junta (1727) that evolved into the American Philosophical Association and helped establish the first U.S. lending library (1731), as well as an academy (1751) that evolved into the University of Pennsylvania. Appointed in 1736 as a clerk in the Pennsylvania Assembly, he held a seat from 1751 to 1764. He served as a city deputy postmaster (1737–53); subsequently, as joint deputy postmaster for the colonies (1753–74), he improved postal efficiency and made the postal service solvent. In 1748, his business having expanded and flourished, Franklin retired, turning it over to his foreman in return for a regular stipend, thus gaining more time for scientific pursuits. In the early 1740s he had developed the fuel-efficient Franklin open stove. Later he conducted a series of experiments, described in his *Experiments and Observations on Electricity* (1751–53), which brought him international recognition as a scientist. In 1752 he conducted his famous kite experiment, demonstrating that lightning is an electrical discharge, and he announced his invention of the lightning rod. A later invention for which Franklin is well-known was the bifocal lens (1760). In 1754, Franklin represented Pennsylvania at the Albany Congress, called in response to the French and Indian Wars. From 1757 to 1762 and from 1764 to 1775, he pursued diplomatic activities in England, obtaining permission for Pennsylvania to tax the estates of its proprietors, securing repeal of the Stamp Act, and representing the interests of several colonies. He associated with eminent Britons and wrote political satires and pamphlets on public affairs. In 1776 he went to France to help negotiate treaties of commerce and alliance, signed in 1778. Lionized there, he remained as plenipotentiary, won financial aid for the American Revolution, and then helped negotiate a peace treaty with Great Britain, signed in Paris in 1783. Returning to the U.S.A. in 1785, he was a conciliating presence at the Constitutional Convention (1787). In his last years he corresponded widely, received many visitors, and invented a device for lifting books from high shelves. His posthumously published *Autobiography,* written for his son William Franklin, became a classic.

Franklin, C. L. (Clarence LeVaughn) (1915–84) clergyman, civil rights activist (father of Aretha Franklin); born near Indianola, Miss. He attended the seminary at Greenville Industrial College. Moving to Detroit in the early 1950s, he founded the New Bethel Baptist Church; there and through 30 years of radio broadcasts his powerful sermons reached a wide audience. In June 1963 he and Martin Luther King, Jr. led a large civil rights march in Detroit that prefigured King's more famous march on Washington, D.C.

Franklin, Edward Curtis (1862–1937) chemist, educator; born in Geary City, Kans. After studying in Germany and teaching at the University of Kansas (1899–1903), he joined the faculty at Stanford University (1903–29). He is known for his work on the ammonia system of acids, bases, and salts, as well as on the structure of nitrogenous compounds.

Franklin, John Hope (1915–) historian; born in Rentiesville, Okla. He took his B.A. from Fisk University and did his graduate work at Harvard, taught at colleges in North Carolina, and then in 1947 – the same year he published his pathbreaking study, *From Slavery to Freedom: A History of American Negroes* – he joined the faculty of Howard University. He then became chairman of the history department of Brooklyn College (1956–64), professor at the University of Chicago (1964–82), and professor at Duke University (1982–85). He was the first African-American to become president of the American Historical Association, and as the history of African-Americans finally gained its place among the serious fields of inquiry, he became recognized both as the nestor of the discipline and as a valued voice in the chorus of all American historians. Among his other publications are *Reconstruction after the Civil War* (1961), *The Emancipation Proclamation* (1963), and *Racial Equality in America* (1976).

Frasch, Herman (1851–1914) chemist, engineer; born in Gaildorf, Germany. Emigrating to America in 1868, he discovered a new way of refining paraffin in 1876. Between 1885–94 he developed a desulfurization process for petroleum. He made other important discoveries, notably a method for mining sulfur directly by injecting superheated water into the mine. His own Union Sulfur Company led the U.S.A. to become a major exporter of sulfur.

Fraser, Douglas (Andrew) (1916–) labor leader; born in Glasgow, Scotland. He came to the U.S.A. in 1922 and became an auto worker. He was elected president of Local 227 of the United Automobile Workers (UAW) in 1943. He co-led the bargaining committee that won the UAW's historic early retirement program (1964). He was vice president (1970–77) and president (1977–83) of the UAW.

Fraser, Gretchen (Claudia Kunigk) (1919–) skier; born in Tacoma, Wash. She won the first ever Alpine skiing gold medal for the United States when she won the giant slalom in the 1948 Olympics. She also won a silver medal in the combined downhill and slalom race in the 1948 Games.

Fraser, James Earle (1876–1953) sculptor; born in Winona, Minn. He lived in the Dakota territory, Minneapolis, and Chicago, where he sculpted *The End of the Trail* (1894), a popular image of the American Indian. He studied at the École des Beaux Arts in Paris (1895–99), was an assistant of Augustus Saint-Gaudens (1898–1902), and settled in New York (1902). He created many public monuments and designed medallions and coins, including the buffalo nickel (1913).

Frazee, John (1790–1852) sculptor; born in Rahway, N.J. Born on a farm, he was apprenticed to a mason, became a stonecutter, moved to New Brunswick, N.J. (1814), and opened a stone carvers shop in New York City (1818). He is

considered the first sculptor of a marble bust in America, that of John Wells (1824), and was a founder of the National Academy of Design (1826). He was also the architect and superintendent of the New York Custom House (1834–41).

Frazier, Lynn Joseph (1874–1947) governor, U.S. senator; born in Steele County, Minn. A successful North Dakota farmer, he was endorsed by the Nonpartisan League and became the Republican governor of North Dakota (1917–21), establishing a state run bank and grain processing system. Recalled in 1921 by opponents of the bank and his increasingly progressive policies, he went to the U.S. Senate (1923–41), where he sponsored the Frazier-Lemke Amendment (1934), which postponed farm mortgage payments for three years. His opposition to U.S. involvement in World War II ended his political career.

Fredendall, Lloyd R. (1883–1963) soldier; born in Cheyenne, Wyo. As a corps commander, he led U.S. troops in the North Africa landings in November 1942; he went on to command the U.S. Second Army.

Frederic, Harold (1856–98) writer; born in Utica, N.Y. He spent most of his journalistic career as the *New York Times* London correspondent (1884–98); his news accounts of Russian Jews and William II were reprinted in book form. His ten novels were early examples of Mohawk Valley "local color" and historical fiction and included *Seth's Brother's Wife* (1887) and *The Damnation of Theron Ware* (1896). He died after a paralytic stroke.

Frederick, Pauline (c. 1906–90) journalist; born in Gallitzin, Pa. An award-winning broadcast news correspondent, notably as United Nations correspondent for the National Broadcasting Company (1953–74), she was noted for her coverage of international affairs.

Fredericks, Marshall (Maynard) (1908–) sculptor; born in Rock Island, Ill. After studying at the Cleveland School of Art and with the Swedish sculptor Carl Milles, he settled in Michigan, teaching at Cranbrook Academy, Bloomfield Hills (1933–42). Working in the symbolic-realistic tradition then current, he is best known for his public commissions such as those for the city of Detroit and for U.S. Post Offices in River Rouge, Mich., and Sandwich, Ill. Other of his works are in museums at Cranbrook Academy and the University of Michigan.

Freed, Alan (1922–65) disk jockey; born in Palm Springs, Calif. In the 1940s and 1950s he worked for radio stations in Ohio, Pennsylvania, and New York where he stirred controversy by playing African-American rhythm-and-blues records for white audiences and by sponsoring integrated concerts. In 1962 he pleaded guilty to commercial bribery during a broadcasting industry scandal; some believe he was scapegoated for sponsoring black performers.

Freed, Arthur (b. Arthur Grossman) (1894–1973) lyricist, movie producer; born in Charleston, S.C. Beginning in vaudeville (he appeared at times with the Marx Brothers), he started to write songs and in 1929 was hired as a lyricist by Metro-Goldwyn-Mayer (MGM). For the next ten years he wrote the lyrics for numerous films. In 1939 he became a producer and for two decades helped to make MGM the leading studio for musicals, surrounding himself with talented directors like Vincente Minnelli, Busby Berkeley, and Stanley Donen, and shaping the careers of many Hollywood legends including Judy Garland and Gene Kelly. He also continued writing songs, such as "Singing in the Rain." Two of his films won best picture Oscars, *An American in Paris* (1951) and *Gigi* (1958).

Freedberg, Sydney Joseph (1914–) art historian; born in Boston, Mass. He studied at Harvard (B.A. 1936; M.A. 1939; Ph.D. 1940), and taught at many institutions, notably at Harvard beginning in 1953. An author of many books on Renaissance art, he was a curator and director of several museums, including the National Gallery of Art, Washington, D.C. (1983).

Freedman, Daniel X. (1921–93) psychiatrist, educator; born in Lafayette, Ind. Pioneering in the study of drugs and behavior, he researched the brain mechanisms in allergy at the University of California: Los Angeles (1983) and discovered the link of hallucinogens to brain transmitters. With colleagues, he found similar effects of environmental stress and identified hyperserotonemia in autism. He also did research on indole metabolism and brain receptors for hallucinogens.

Freeman, Douglas Southall (1886–1953) editor, historian; born in Lynchburg, Va. He was a longtime editor of the *Richmond News Leader* (1915–49) and wrote two Pulitzer Prize-winning works; a four-volume biography of Robert E. Lee (1934–35) and a multi-volume biography of George Washington (1948–58).

Freeman, John Ripley (1855–1932) engineer; born in West Bridgeton, Maine. He worked primarily on water projects, consulting on water power, drainage, and municipal water supply in Boston. In 1903 he was chief engineer on the Charles River Dam in Boston Harbor and was later involved in projects in Los Angeles and other cities.

Freeman, Mary (Eleanor) (b. Wilkins) (1852–1930) writer, poet; born in Randolph, Mass. She lacked formal schooling and moved to Metuchen, N.J., when she married (1902). She drew inspiration from her New England background, and wrote poetry, novels, a play, and stories, as in her collection, *A New England Nun* (1891).

Freeman, Morgan (1937–) actor; born in Memphis, Tenn. The son of a barber and a school teacher, raised in Chicago and Mississippi, he served in the air force and attended Los Angeles City College. He made his Broadway debut in 1967 in an all-black production of *Hello, Dolly.* His movie credits include *Street Smart,* for which he received an Academy Award nomination, and *Glory.* He is perhaps best known for his role as Hoke Colburn, the chauffeur in the movie *Driving Miss Daisy* (1989).

Freeman, Thomas (?–1821) engineer, astronomer; born in Ireland. He came to the U.S.A. in 1784. He was one of the surveyors of Washington, D.C. (1794–95) and explored the Arkansas and Red Rivers (1806). As surveyor of the public lands of the American south (1811–21), he opposed land speculation.

Freeman, Walter Jackson (1895–1972) neurosurgeon; born in Philadelphia. For most of his career he was affiliated with George Washington University, St. Louis (1927–54). He introduced psychosurgery in the United States (1936) and took part in more than 2,800 lobotomies. Performed well into the 1960s, the procedure was largely discredited because of its severe side effects and because it was replaced by drug therapy.

Freer, Charles Lang (1856–1919) art collector, businessman; born in Kingston, N.Y. After graduation from high school he worked as a clerk, paymaster, and accountant for various railroads. In 1879 he moved to Detroit and was a founder of the American Car & Foundry Company (1899). He traveled often to Europe and collected oriental art, ancient glazed pottery, 19th- and early-20th-century paintings, and most notably, the work of James McNeill Whistler. He donated funds and his collection to the Smithsonian Institution for the construction of the Freer Gallery (1906).

Freleng, (Isadore) Friz (1906–) animator; born in Kansas City, Mo. He joined Disney in 1927, moving in 1930 to Warner Bros. to work on Looney Tunes shorts. Such creations as Yosemite Sam, Sylvester, and Speedy Gonzales won him three Oscars.

Frelinghuysen, Theodorus Jacobus (1691–1748) Protestant clergyman; born in Lingen, Germany. He received a classical education and was ordained in the Dutch Reformed Church in 1717. Sent to America in 1719 as a missionary, he established several churches in the Raritan Valley of New Jersey from 1720 on and is considered a leading force in the establishment of the Dutch Reformed faith in the new world. All five of his sons became ministers.

Frémont, John (Charles) (1813–90) soldier, explorer; born in Savannah, Ga. He mapped the route of the Oregon Trail as a young army engineer (1842) and became widely known as "The Pathfinder" when he published an account of his subsequent explorations in the Pacific Northwest, Nevada, and California (1843–44). In California in 1846, he supported Californians in revolting against Mexico; in 1847 he commanded the small U.S. force that captured Los Angeles during the Mexican War. He left the army the following year in a dispute over command in California. The gold strikes of the late 1840s made him rich; he briefly served as a senator (Calif., 1850–51); his fame as an explorer and his antislavery convictions led the newly formed Republican Party to choose him as its first presidential candidate (1856). Re-entering the army on the outbreak of the Civil War, he commanded Union forces in Missouri for a short time but was relieved and ordered east; Jackson outgeneraled him during his brilliant Shenandoah Valley campaign of 1862; Frémont resigned from the army later in the year. He lost most of his fortune in a failed railroad venture (1870), served as territorial governor of Arizona from 1878–83, and published his memoirs in 1887.

French, Daniel Chester (1850–1931) sculptor; born in Exeter, N.H. He grew up in Cambridge and Concord, Mass., and studied anatomy with William Rimmer (in Boston, early 1870s) and drawing with William Morris Hunt. He also studied briefly in New York City with John Quincy Adams Ward and then in Italy (1874). He returned to Washington, D.C. (1876) and became the most popular American sculptor of the period, known for his elegant academic and historical work, as in the *Minute Man* (1873–75), the seated bronze of John Harvard (1882), and Abraham Lincoln (1918–22) in the Lincoln Memorial, Washington, D.C. He was based in New York City after 1888 and at a summer home, Chesterwood, in Stockbridge, Mass., which is now a museum exhibiting much of his work.

Freneau, Philip Morin (1752–1832) poet, journalist; born in New York City. A major early American poet, he won renown as "poet of the American Revolution" for his burning anti-British satires at the Revolution's outbreak. After a hiatus in the West Indies, where he wrote lyric verse with Romantic elements, he was captured by the British at sea and imprisoned under harsh conditions described in *The British Prison-Ship* (1781). He was a sea captain later in the 1780s and wrote some of his best verse, including *The Hurricane* and *The Wild Honey Suckle*. In a new phase of his life, Freneau became editor of the *New York Daily Advertiser* in 1789; then from 1791 to 1793, backed by Thomas Jefferson, he capably edited the fiercely democratic *National Gazette*, in rivalry with John Fenno's Federalist paper. In later years, his reputation besmirched by enemies, he earned a meager living as a sea captain, farmer, and tinker.

Freund, Ernst (1864–1932) legal scholar; born in New York City (during a visit of his German parents). He was educated in Germany and emigrated to the U.S.A. in 1892, teaching first at Columbia University (1892–94) and then at the University of Chicago (1894–1932). He was especially noted for helping legislators write uniform laws.

Freund, Paul (Abraham) (1908–) law educator; born in St. Louis, Mo. After serving as a clerk to Justice Louis Brandeis (1932–33), he held a series of legal positions with the government in Washington, D.C. (1933–39). Longtime member of the Harvard Law School faculty (1939–76), he wrote *On Understanding the Supreme Court* (1949), *The Supreme Court of the United States* (1961), and many articles. An authority on constitutional law, he received over twenty honorary degrees and fellowships in several prestigious societies.

Frey, John (Philip) (1871–1957) labor leader; born in Mankato, Minn. He moved to Massachusetts as a young man and apprenticed as an iron molder. He joined the International Molders and Foundry Workers Union (1893) and went on to serve as its long-time vice-president (1900–1950). He was an aide to Samuel Gompers. A conservative unionist, he defended craft union "purity" and held unskilled workers in disdain. He vigorously opposed any union between the American Federation of Labor and the Congress of Industrial Organization, which did occur after his death.

Frey, Viola (1933–) ceramist; born in Lodi, Calif. With an M.F.A. from Tulane University, she joined the faculty of the California College of Arts and Crafts (1965). Exploring avenues of fantasy, kitsch, and stereotype, her large assemblages of cast ceramic objects and massive figures brought the recognition of a 1984 solo exhibition at the Whitney Museum.

Frick, Ford (Christopher) (1894–1978) baseball executive; born in Wawaka, Ind. A New York *American* sportswriter for many years (1922–34), he also made radio sports broadcasts (1930–34). He served as National League president (1934–51) and commissioner of baseball (1951–65). He was elected to baseball's Hall of Fame in 1969.

Frick, Henry C. (Clay) (1849–1919) industrialist, art collector, philanthropist; born in West Overton, Pa. With slight formal education, he worked at various jobs. He organized Frick and Company in 1871 to build and operate coke ovens near Pittsburgh, Pa.; by 1889 he controlled two-thirds of the capacity in the area. By 1882 Frick was associated with Andrew Carnegie and he became chairman of Carnegie Steel (1889–1900). Frick led the company through the Homestead (Pa.) labor strike of 1892, during which he was shot and stabbed by Alexander Berkman; Frick calmly telegraphed Carnegie (who was in Scotland) before seeking treatment. In 1901 he became director of U.S. Steel Corporation. A serious art collector, he bequeathed his New York City home and his art as a public museum. He also gave large sums of money to various educational and medical institutions and donated a large park to Pittsburgh.

Frid, Tage (1915–) furniture maker; born in Denmark. After studying and working in Copenhagen, in 1948 he came to the U.S.A. where he became a professor at Rhode Island School of Design. He is noted for the precise workmanship and sculptural elegance he brought to his handmade furniture. His fellow Danes have honored him with the title of master craftsman.

Friday, Nancy (1937–) writer, popular psychologist; born in Pittsburgh, Pa. She attended Wellesley College and became a journalist and free-lance writer. She published several books based on her research into selected subjects of popular psychology, including *My Secret Garden: Women's Sexual Fantasies* (1973), *My Mother/My Self: The Daughter's Search for Identity* (1978), and *Jealousy* (1985).

Friedan, Betty (Naomi Goldstein) (1921–) author, feminist leader; born in Peoria, Ill. A *summa cum laude* graduate from Smith (1942), she was awarded fellowships for working toward a doctorate in psychology but abandoned this under the influence of what she would later call "the feminine mystique." She married in 1947 and for almost the next 20 years lived the life of a conventional suburban housewife/mother. (She had three children; she would get divorced in 1969.) As a result of surveys of female college graduates, she came to identify certain problems that women were experiencing in their lives, and after several years of research she published *The Feminine Mystique* (1963), an exposé of the traditional roles assigned to women in modern industrial societies; although not an especially profound critique, it became an international best-seller and is credited with generating the so-called second wave of modern feminism. In 1966 she was one of the founders of the National Organization for Women (NOW) and served as its first president (1966–70), moving on to other activities promoting the advancement of women. Through her writings, lecturing, organizational work, and outspokenness, she became one of the most influential feminist leaders of the late 20th century. In 1982, feeling that some individuals and elements of the feminist movement had gone off into extreme positions, she published *The Second Stage*, calling for a more balanced approach in the women's movement, and in 1993 she published *The Fountain of Age*, about the ways that older people can find satisfaction in their lives.

Friedlaender, Israel (1876–1920) scholar; born in Kovel, Ukraine. He came to New York in 1930 to teach biblical literature and exegesis at the Jewish Theological Seminary of America. A specialist on the relation between Islam and Judaism, he was murdered in the Ukraine while serving as commissioner for the Joint Distribution Commission of America.

Friedlaender, Walter (1873–1966) art historian; born in Berlin, Germany. He studied Sanskrit at the University of Berlin (Ph.D. 1898), then studied art history and lived in Italy for several years. Beginning in 1914 he taught at the University of Freiburg, was dismissed by the Nazis (1933), and emigrated to New York City (1935). He taught at New York University beginning in 1935, and specialized in subjects ranging from the mannerist style of the Renaissance to 19th-century art.

Friedlander, Lee (1934–) photographer; born in Aberdeen,

Wash. An East Coast free-lance commercial photographer and teacher, he used snapshot style photographs to capture surrealistic qualities in everyday life in the 1960s and 1970s.

Friedman, Esther Pauline See LANDERS, ANN.

Friedman, Jerome I. (Isaac) (1930–) physicist; born in Chicago, Ill. He taught at the University of Chicago (1956–57) and Stanford University (1957–60) before joining the Massachusetts Institute of Technology (1960). He was awarded the 1990 Nobel Prize in physics (with R. E. Taylor and H. W. Kendall) for experiments (1967–73) confirming the existence of the quark.

Friedman, Milton (1912–) economist; born in New York City. He is one of the most publicly familiar U.S. economists through his economics column in *Newsweek* and his television series "Free to Choose." His intellectual achievements are highly esteemed, especially his analysis of inflation and the role of monetary policy, his permanent income theory of consumption, and the concept of a "natural rate of unemployment." He helped form "the Chicago School" of economic thought during his years at the University of Chicago (1948–79) and also served as an adviser to presidential candidate Barry Goldwater, President Richard Nixon, and the Reagan administration. He received the Nobel Prize in economics (1976).

Friedman, Pauline Esther See VAN BUREN, ABIGAIL.

Friedman, William Frederick (1891–1969) cryptologist; born in Kishinev, Russia. His family emigrated to the United States in 1893. Originally trained as a geneticist, he headed a genetics lab in Geneva, Ill. (1915–17, 1919–20). He had become interested in cryptology and during World War I he set up a cryptology school with his wife for military personnel. Soon recognized by the U.S. government as being in the forefront of such work, he was made head of the Signal Intelligence Service (1930) and he broke the Japanese "Purple" code (1937–40), thus allowing Americans to read much of Japan's secret messages during World War II. He continued to be involved with American intelligence until 1955, by which time he began to receive wider recognition as one of the world's major cryptologists.

Friedrich, Carl J. (Joachim) (1901–84) political scientist; born in Leipzig, Germany. Educated in Germany, he emigrated to the U.S.A. in 1922 and began his long teaching career at Harvard (1926–71). A prolific writer on comparative political thought, his analyses of totalitarianism and communism were particularly controversial. His book, *An Introduction to Political Theory* (1967), concluded that people favor a minimum rather than a maximum of freedoms. He served as a government adviser to Germany (1946–49), and to Puerto Rico (1950s).

Friedrichs, Kurt O. (1901–82) mathematician; born in Kiel, Germany. Emigrating to America to teach at New York University (NYU) (1937), he later directed NYU's Courant Institute (1966–67). A National Academy of Sciences member, recipient of the National Medal of Science (1977), and author of several books, he conducted groundbreaking work in pure and applied mathematics and mathematical physics.

Friendly, Fred W. (b. Fred Wachenheimer) (1915–) television producer; born in Providence, R.I. A broadcast journalist who helped develop the television documentary format, he worked with Edward R. Murrow on *See It Now* (1951–58) and produced *CBS Reports* (1958–64). He resigned as CBS News president in 1966 when the network refused to air Senate hearings on Vietnam. He thereafter produced various television specials and series on public affairs and became a journalism professor at Columbia University (1981).

Fries, Charles C. (Carpenter) (1887–1967) linguist; born in Reading, Pa. He taught at the University of Michigan where he developed programs in both theoretical and applied linguistics. He and his wife, Agnes Carswell, developed the university's English Language Institute (1941), which pioneered methods and materials for teaching English to foreigners. Among his many books are dictionaries of Early and Middle English.

Fries, John (1750–1818) revolutionary insurgent; born in Montgomery County, Pa. An itinerant auctioneer, he became captain of a revolutionary militia company in Bucks County, Pa., (1775). In 1794 he participated in the so-called Whiskey Rebellion, when Pennsylvania farmers resisted federal efforts to impose a tax on their whiskey production. Then in 1799 he took the lead in resisting a federal property tax of 1798; he signed a petition denouncing the tax and led a band of 50 men to eject persistent collectors and to liberate prisoners in federal custody. Stopped by federal militia, he was twice sentenced to death for treason but was pardoned by President John Adams.

Frieseke, Frederick (Carl) (1874–1939) painter; born in Owosso, Mich. Going to Paris in 1898 to study at the Academie Julien, he became an Impressionist after 1901 and settled at Giverny, although he seems more influenced by Renoir than Monet. He spent the rest of his life in France, often painting female nudes or women outdoors in his garden or indoors in his house.

Frietschie or Fritchie, Barbara (b. Haver) (1766–1862) heroine; born in Lancaster, Pa. Her father was a hatter and she married John Casper Frietschie, a glovemaker, in 1806. According to legend, on September 6, 1862, at the age of 95, she boldly displayed the Union flag as Confederate soldiers passed by her home in Frederick, Maryland. In tribute to her bravery, she was not harmed. When an account of the incident reached John Greenleaf Whittier, he immortalized it in his poem: " 'Shoot, if you must, this old gray head / But spare your country's flag,' she said." A replica of her house was built in 1926.

Friml, (Charles) Rudolf (1879–1972) pianist, composer; born in Prague, Austria-Hungary (now the Czech Republic). He studied under Dvorák at the Prague Conservatory and as a pianist and composer he settled in the U.S.A. in 1906 (becoming a citizen in 1925). His completion of *The Firefly* (1912) for Victor Herbert initiated his long series of highly successful Broadway operettas (1912–34) containing such standards as "Indian Love Song" from *Rose Marie* (1924), "Some Day" from *The Vagabond King* (1925), and "The Donkey Serenade" from the film version of *The Firefly* (1937). He also contributed to the *Ziegfeld Follies* (1921–25). After settling in Hollywood (1934) he scored numerous films, and at age 92 he became an original member of the Songwriter's Hall of Fame.

Frishmuth, Harriet Whitney (1880–1980) sculptor; born in Philadelphia. After study in Paris with Rodin (1900), she worked in Berlin, settled in New York City, and studied with Gutzon Borglum. She moved to Philadelphia, became known for graceful figure studies, as in *The Vine* (1821), and retired to Southbury, Conn.

Fritz, John (1822–1913) mechanical engineer; born in Chester County, Pa. A blacksmith and mechanic, by 1849 he was superintending the building of the Cambria Iron Works (by 1860 the Bethlehem Iron Works) in Johnston, Pa. As an early and innovative "iron master," he designed new machinery and introduced new techniques, such as the Bessemer process, and open-hearth furnaces.

Fritzshe, Hellmut (1927–) physicist; born in Berlin, Germany. He came to the U.S.A. in 1952, and taught at Purdue (1955–57) before joining the University of Chicago (1957). An adviser for the *Encyclopaedia Britannica,* he made major contributions to studies of the electronic and optical properties of amorphous and crystalline semiconductors and metals.

Frohman, Charles (1860–1915) theatrical agent, manager; born in Sandusky, Ohio (brother of Daniel Frohman). Interested in the theater from his youth, he settled in New York and worked at a variety of theaters and agencies, setting out as an independent manager in 1883 and then as a booking agent. He soon built up his Empire Stock Theatre Company, developing such notable actors as John Drew, Maude Adams and Ethel Barrymore, and he produced an endless series of plays in New York and London, encouraging new playwrights such as J. M. Barrie, Clyde Fitch, and Somerset Maugham. Less admirable was his Theatrical Syndicate, which dictated to many theaters throughout the U.S.A. and even in London. Extravagant as a personality and in his productions, he died while still active when he went down with the torpedoed *Lusitania.*

Frohman, Daniel (1851–1940) theater manager; born in Sandusky, Ohio (brother of Charles Frohman). He managed a number of New York theaters, including the Madison Square, the Lyceum, Daly's, and his own 1902 reconstruction of the Lyceum, where he had a stock company. He was also one of the first producers of moving pictures.

Fromm, Erich (1900–80) psychoanalyst, social philosopher; born in Frankfurt, Germany. He studied at the Universities of Frankfurt, Heidelberg, and Munich, and at the Berlin Institute of Psychoanalysis. After emigrating to the United States in 1933, he established a private practice in psychiatry and taught at New York University and the National University of Mexico. His major writings explored those needs that he identified as uniquely human – relatedness, transcendence, rootedness, identity, and a frame of orientation. His works, several of which reached wide audiences, include *Escape from Freedom* (1941), *Man For Himself* (1947), *The Heart of Man* (1964), and *The Anatomy of Human Destructiveness* (1973).

Fromm-Reichmann, Frieda (1889–1957) psychiatrist, psychoanalyst; born in Karlsruhe, Germany. She emigrated to the United States in 1935 and became a disciple of Harry Stack Sullivan. She pioneered psychotherapeutic methods with schizophrenic patients and contributed to the understanding of the psychic assets of the mentally ill. For some years (1926–42) she was married to the philosopher and psychologist Erich Fromm.

Frost, Robert (Lee) (1874–1963) poet, teacher; born in San Francisco. He studied at Dartmouth College (1892) and Harvard (1897–99) but never took a degree. He was a mill worker and teacher (1892–97), a farmer in New Hampshire (1900–12), and lived in England (1912–15); his first volume of poems, *A Boy's Will,* was published there (1913). Upon his return to New Hampshire he settled on a farm but he taught at many universities and colleges in the ensuing years. He was a founder of the Bread Loaf School, Middlebury, Vt., (1920) and was poetry consultant to the Library of Congress (1958). He was often honored for his work, and in later years he cultivated the image of America's poet laureate; this climaxed when he read his poem "A Gift Outright" at the inauguration of President John F. Kennedy (1961). Although those who knew him best admitted that he could be prickly, even nasty, none denied his achievements as a poet. His work is distinguished by its everyday language, New England settings, and the natural world, as in *North of Boston* (1914). Individual poems, such as "Stopping by Woods on a Snowy Evening," "Mending Wall," and "The Death of a Hired Man," have ensured his popularity as well as critical acclaim.

Frothingham, Octavius Brooks (1822–95) religious leader, author; born in Boston, Mass. He graduated from Harvard in 1843, studied divinity there and was pastor of North Church, Salem, Mass., for eight years before leaving in a dispute over his antislavery activities. In 1859 he became pastor of the Third Congregational Unitarian Society in New York City. A theological liberal, he founded the Boston Free Religious Association in 1867 and headed it for 11 years. He published a biography of Theodore Parker, a study of New England transcendentalism, and a summary of his own religious thought, *The Religion of Humanity* (1876). He retired from the ministry in 1879 and was in poor health for the rest of his life.

Fruton, Joseph S. (Stewart) (1912–) biochemist; born in Czestochowa, Poland. He came to the U.S.A. in 1923, and became an assistant in biochemistry at Columbia University (1933–34). He moved to Rockefeller University (1934–45), then joined Yale (1945–82). He made major advances in studies of proteolytic enzymes for over 30 years; in the late 1960s, he devoted his time to writing and lecturing on the history of science.

Frye, (William John) Jack (1904–59) airline executive; born near Sweetwater, Texas. Contributing to the rise of commercial aviation, he encouraged construction of fast, comfortable, modern equipment and devices for safe all-weather flying. As President of Trans World Airlines (1934–47) he fostered international flight. Involved briefly in the film industry, he died in a car crash in Tucson, Ariz.

Frye, William Pierce (1831–1911) U.S. representative/senator; born in Lewiston, Maine. A Republican lawyer from Maine, he helped simplify House rules as a congressman (1871–81), and avidly supported protectionist tariffs and expansionist foreign policy as a senator (1881–1911).

Fuchs, Joseph (1900–) violinist; born in New York City. A Kneisel student, he was concertmaster of the Cleveland Orchestra 1926–40 and thereafter pursued an active solo and teaching career.

Fuertes, Louis Agassiz (1874–1927) artist-naturalist; born in Ithaca, N.Y. He showed an affinity for painting birds in childhood, and after graduating from Cornell University (1897), he studied with the nature painter Abbott H. Thayer. A tireless field worker, he traveled all over the world collecting and sketching birds. His paintings appeared in such field guides as *Coues' Key to North American Birds* (1903) and *Birds of New York* (1910). During the 1920s, he lectured on ornithology at Cornell and designed habitat groups for New York's American Museum of Natural History.

Fuglister, Frederick C. (Charles) (1909–87) oceanographer;

born in New York City. He served the Woods Hole Oceanographic Institution as physical oceanographer (1940–67) and senior scientist (1960–67). He made major contributions to the study of Gulf Stream currents.

Fujita, Tetsuya or Theodore (1920–) meteorologist; born in Kitakyushu City, Japan. He came to the University of Chicago in 1953 to teach and research the prediction of severe local storms using satellites and aerial photography. He described the wind shear phenomenon called the microburst. He became a U.S. citizen in 1968.

Fulbright, (James) J. William (1905–) U.S. representative/ senator; born in Sumner, Mo. A graduate of the University of Arkansas and a Rhodes Scholar at Oxford, he taught law and then became president of the University of Arkansas (1939–42). He served a term in the U.S. House of Representatives (Dem., Ark.; 1943–45). In 1944, he traveled to London as a member of a United Nations delegation to discuss postwar education. He went on to serve Arkansas in the U.S. Senate (1945–74) and immediately sponsored a bill to establish international scholarly exchanges (1945), a program still known by his name. Appointed chair of the Senate Foreign Relations Committee in 1959, he performed a difficult balancing act by having to satisfy his conservative southern constituency and his own more liberal inclinations. He conducted six days of nationally televised hearings before the committee in February 1966 about the rapid escalation of the war in Vietnam; the hearings marked a turning point in public discussion of the war issue, lending legitimacy to the antiwar movement.

Fuller, George (1822–84) painter; born in Deerfield, Mass. He worked in Boston (1842–47) and New York (1847–59) as an itinerant painter, studied at the National Academy, New York (1847), traveled in Europe (1859), and returned to work the family tobacco farm in Deerfield. There he painted visionary landscapes and figure studies, such as *Winifred Dysart* (1881).

Fuller, Henry Blake (Stanton Page, pen name) (1857–1929) writer; born in Chicago. He was educated at local Chicago schools before beginning his travels in Europe. After his father's death (1885), he returned to Chicago. Influenced by the contrast between European and American cultures, he wrote both romantic novels, such as *The Chevalier of Pensieri-Vani* (1890), and realistic works, such as *The Cliff-Dwellers: A Novel* (1893), a scathing commentary on Chicago's apartment-dwelling social climbers. He also wrote satiric verses attacking President McKinley, a travelogue, *Gardens of This World* (1929), and plays.

Fuller, (Marie Louise) Loie (1862–1928) dancer, choreographer, stage lighting innovator; born in Fullersburg, Ill. She began to entertain in public as early as two and a half, and throughout her childhood she acted and toured. By 1883 she was acting on Broadway and by 1888 she was touring with her own company. It was in an 1891 play that she was expected to dance, and, wanting to make herself exotic, she took a skirt of Chinese silk and proceeded to flit about the stage while waving the material under the stage lighting. Seeing its effect on the audience, she worked up a solo routine that relied more on the special lighting and the billowy silk than on any particular dance steps. It made such a sensation in a New York show in 1892 that she took her "serpentine" dance to Europe that year; she would spend the rest of her life there, with only brief visits to the U.S.A. (She

appeared at the Metropolitan Opera House in 1910.) Her main base was Paris, where she had first appeared at the Folies-Bergère in 1892 and where she was celebrated by artists and intellectuals. She toured with her company of young women – Isadora Duncan danced with her in 1902 – and founded a dance school in Paris in 1902. Although essentially an entertainer, she was an innovator in stage lighting effects, being among the first to use luminous phosphorescent materials, to dance on glass lit from below, and to employ silhouette-and-shadow effects.

Fuller, Melville W. (Weston) (1833–1910) Supreme Court chief justice; born in Augusta, Maine. He was active in Illinois politics but unknown nationally when President Cleveland named him chief justice of the U.S. Supreme Court (1888–1910). He was known as an able and moderate jurist.

Fuller, (Richard) Buckminster (1895–1983) inventor, designer, futurist; born in Milton, Mass. (great-nephew of Margaret Fuller). Leaving Harvard early, he largely educated himself while working at industrial jobs and serving in the U.S. Navy during World War I. One of the century's most original minds, he free-lanced his talents, solving problems of human shelter, nutrition, transportation, environmental pollution, and decreasing world resources, developing over 2,000 patents in the process. He wrote some 25 books, notably *Utopia or Oblivion* (1969) and *Operating Manual for Spaceship Earth* (1969). A professor at Southern Illinois University from 1959 on, he became in his later decades a popular public lecturer, promoting a global strategy of seeking to do more with less through technology. His inventions include the 1927 Dymaxion House, the 1933 Dymaxion Car and, foremost, the 1947 geodesic dome. He has the distinction of having both his names used for a scientific entity, the "fullerene" (also known as a "buckyball"), a form of carbon whose molecule resembles his geodesic dome.

Fuller, (Sarah) Margaret (1810–50) feminist, literary critic; born in Cambridgeport, Mass. Her father, Timothy Fuller, was a prominent Massachusetts lawyer-politician who, disappointed that his child was not a boy, educated her rigorously in the classical curriculum of the day. Not until age 14 did she get to attend a school for two years (1824–26) and then she returned to Cambridge and her course of reading. Her intellectual precociousness gained her the acquaintance of various Cambridge intellectuals but her assertive and intense manner put many people off. Her father moved the family to a farm in Groton, Mass. (1833), and she found herself isolated and forced to help educate her siblings and run the household for her ailing mother. From 1836 to 1837, after visiting Ralph Waldo Emerson in Concord, she taught for Bronson Alcott in Boston, and then at a school in Providence, R.I. All the while she continued to enlarge both her intellectual accomplishments and personal acquaintances. Moving to Jamaica Plain, a suburb of Boston, in 1840, she conducted her famous "Conversations" (1840–44), discussion groups that attracted many prominent people from all around Boston. In 1840, she also joined Emerson and others to found the *Dial,* a journal devoted to the transcendentalist views; she became a contributor from the first issue and its editor (1840–42). Her first book, based on a trip through the Midwest (1840–42), was *Summer on the Lakes* (1844) and this led to her being invited by Horace Greeley to be literary critic at the *New York Tribune* in 1844. She published her feminist classic, *Woman in the Nineteenth Century* (1845). In addition to writing a solid body of critical reviews and essays, she became active in various social reform movements. In 1846 she went to Europe as a foreign correspondent for the *Tribune*. In England and France she was treated as a serious intellectual and got to meet many prominent people. She went on to Italy in 1847 where she met Giovanni Angelo, the Marchese d'Ossoli, ten years younger and of liberal principles; they became lovers and married in 1849, but their son was born in 1848. Involved in the Roman revolution of 1848, she and her husband fled to Florence in 1849. They sailed for the U.S.A. in 1850 but the ship ran aground in a storm off Fire Island, N.Y., and Margaret's and her husband's bodies were never found.

Fulper, William H. (1872–1928) potter; born in Flemington, N.J. In 1909 at the family pottery, he introduced Vasekraft, a successful and award-winning line of art ware with exquisite glazes, notably the *famille rose* glaze.

Fulton, Robert (1765–1815) engineer, inventor, artist; born in Lancaster County, Pa. He worked as a jeweler's apprentice, gunsmith, and a painter in Philadelphia before he went to England in 1786 to study under the artist Benjamin West. He remained abroad for the next 20 years, abandoning painting for his interest in mechanical and engineering inventions. Fascinated by water transport systems, he published *A Treatise on the Improvement of Canal Navigation* (1796). During a long stay in France (1797–1806), he got some encouragement from Napoleon and developed the *Nautilus* diving boat (1800). Failing to receive research funds from either the French or British governments, he returned to the United States, and with the support of Robert R. Livingston, completed the steamboat *Clermont*, which made its first trial run on the Hudson River in August 1807; although not really the inventor of the steamboat, his was the first to be commercially successful in America. He later developed the *New Orleans*, the first steamboat on the Mississippi River, and constructed a steam-powered warship to defend New York harbor during the War of 1812.

Funk, Isaac K. (Kauffman) (1839–1912) lexicographer, publisher; born in Clifton, Ohio. Serving as a Lutheran minister from 1861 to 1872, he resigned to travel and returned to editorial work for the *Christian Radical*. In 1876 he started his own business in New York, supplying materials and books to ministers. He was joined in 1877 by A. W. Wagnalls. The company, later renamed the Funk & Wagnalls Company (1891), published the *Homiletic Review* and various religious and secular reference works. In the 1880s Funk published the *Voice*, an influential temperance periodical, and in 1890 he founded the *Literary Digest*. He planned, supervised, and served as editor-in-chief of the noteworthy unabridged dictionary, *Standard Dictionary of the English Language* (1893), and of the *New Standard Dictionary of the English Language* (1913), which he had nearly completed before his death.

Funston, Frederick (1865–1917) soldier; born in New Carlisle, Ohio. Son of a farmer and a five-term congressman known as "Fog Horn" Funston, he was trained as a botanist. In 1896–97, he served as a volunteer with the Cubans revolting against Spain. As a volunteer in the U.S. Army, he fought in the Philippine insurrection that followed the Spanish-American War (1899–1901). Promoted to brigadier general, he led a small unit that captured the Philippine leader Emilio Aguinaldo in his camp in March 1901. He commanded the U.S. Army forces that in 1914 seized Veracruz during the revolutionary unrest in Mexico. He spent the remainder of his career commanding troops on the U.S. border with Mexico.

Funston, (George) Keith (1910–92) business executive, college president; born in Waterloo, Iowa. A banker's son, he worked his way through Trinity College and Harvard Business School before becoming a salesman for American Radiator, and later, Sylvania. From 1945–51 he was president of Trinity College (Hartford, Conn.), where he managed to increase the college endowment by 50 percent. He led the New York Stock Exchange through a period of revival and sustained expansion from 1951–67 before ending a varied career as part-time chairman of the Olin Mathieson Chemical Company (1967–72).

Furman, Bess (1894–1969) journalist; born in Danbury, Nebr. As a Washington correspondent for the Associated Press in the 1930s, she covered Eleanor Roosevelt and became one of the best-known woman journalists of the day. She later reported from Washington for the *New York Times* (1943–61).

Furness, Frank (1839–1912) architect; born in Philadelphia (son of William Henry Furness). He trained with Richard Morris Hunt, then fought in the Union cavalry in the Civil War, winning a Congressional Medal of Honor. Returning to Philadelphia, he practiced first with John Fraser and George W. Hewitt and after 1881 with Allen Evans. He was an outstanding exponent of the picturesque eclectic style, which blended colors, textures, and ornamental details from foreign styles of every period. Among his nearly 400 corporate, public, and institutional buildings, mostly in the Philadelphia area, were the Pennsylvania Academy of the Fine Arts (1871–76), and the building now regarded as his masterpiece, the Library (now the Furness Building) (1888–91) at the University of Pennsylvania. He was reduced to obscurity in his later years, a victim of the new neoclassicism made fashionable by McKim, Mead and White. Furness's reputation revived in the 1960s and 1970s, when postmodernists found inspiration in the decorative richness of his style.

Furth, Harold P. (Paul) (1930–) physicist; born in Vienna, Austria. He came to the U.S.A. in 1941. He performed research in nuclear radiation at the University of California: Berkeley (1955–67) before moving to Princeton (1967). A world leader in the fields of plasma physics and controlled thermonuclear fusion, he became widely known for his refutation of the claim that fusion can be achieved at room temperature in a glass of water.

Furuseth, Andrew (b. Anders Andreassen Nilsen) (1854–1938) labor leader; born in Romedal, Norway. He came to the U.S.A. in 1880, and as a seaman helped to organize the Sailor's Union of the Pacific, becoming its secretary in 1887. From then to the end of his life he was dedicated to improving the working conditions and lives of sailors. He fought for passage of various federal laws culminating in the La Follette Seamen's Act of 1915, and as president of the International Seamen's Union (1908–38) he worked to get other nations to adopt equally progressive laws on behalf of seamen. Austere in his idealism, he never married, took only the wages of a seaman, and lived much of his life in a cheap hotel room. He sailed first class for the first time in his life in 1913, as President Wilson's delegate to the London Conference on Safety at Sea. His ashes were scattered over the Atlantic.

G

Gable, (William) Clark (1901–60) movie actor; born in Cadiz, Ohio. Leaving school at age 14, he worked at various jobs, from oilfield handyman to telephone repairman. In 1918 he was drawn to the stage and for several years he acted in productions from New York City to Oregon. In 1924 he got into Hollywood movies as an extra, then enjoyed a hit on Broadway in *Machinal* (1928); he returned to launch his movie career in 1931 when he became a hit in *The Painted Desert* and made 11 other movies that year. Although his large ears had made some people wonder if he would ever be a romantic lead, he combined his rugged masculinity with a casual charm that allowed him to play both "bad guys" and heroes and after he won an Academy Award for *It Happened One Night* (1934), he became "King of Hollywood" and everybody's choice for Rhett Butler in *Gone with the Wind* (1939). After his third wife, Carole Lombard, died in a plane crash in 1942, he joined the air force and flew bombing missions. On returning to Hollywood, he never quite got his career back on track, although he remained popular with older fans. He died shortly after *The Misfits* (1961) was finished.

Gabo, Naum (b. Neemia Pevsner) (1890–1977) sculptor; born in Bryansk, Russia. He studied medicine, engineering, and art in Munich (1910–14), then changed his name to distinguish himself from his artist brother, Antoine Pevsner. He and his brother created theories of spatial sculpture in Scandinavia during World War I and published the *Realist Manifesto* (1920). Naum lived in Berlin (1922–32), Paris (1932–35), and London (1939–46) before settling in Connecticut (1946). He was noted for his constructed sculptures, such as *Linear Construction* (1943).

Gabrieski, Francis Stanley (1919–) aviator; born in Oil City, Pa. He was a top fighter ace of World War II. After retiring from the air force as a colonel in 1967, he became assistant to the president of Grumman Aerospace Corp.

Gabrilowitsch, Ossip (Solomonovitch) (1878–1936) pianist, conductor; born in St. Petersburg, Russia. After a solo career in Europe and America, he became conductor of the Detroit Symphony in 1918, but is mainly remembered as a matinee-idol pianist.

Gaddis, William (1922–) writer; born in New York City. He attended Harvard and briefly joined the staff of the *New Yorker* (1946–47). He worked as a free-lance corporate writer until the 1970s and details of his personal life remained all but unknown, even in literary circles. His first novel, *The Recognitions* (1955), did not gain much popular or critical attention at first but gradually attained an almost "cult" following as well as critical respect; his second novel, *JR* (1975), won a National Book Award. Both works were encyclopedic "meganovels," but his third, *Carpenter's Gothic* (1985), was more conventional. He continued to shun the spotlight and was only briefly observed when he was awarded a MacArthur fellowship in 1982.

Gadsden, Christopher (1724–1805) Revolutionary leader; born in Charleston, S.C. He called for colonial unity in response to the Stamp Act (1765). He became the leader of the radical faction in South Carolina politics, and served as a delegate to the First and Second Continental Congresses (1774–76).

Gadsden, James (1788–1858) soldier, businessman, diplomat; born in Charleston, S.C. (grandson of Christopher Gadsden). He graduated from Yale (1806) and served in both the War of 1812 and conflicts with the Seminole Indians. He was president of the Louisville, Cincinnati, and Charleston Railroad (1840–50) (renamed the South Carolina Railroad in 1842) and was a major proponent of a southern route from the eastern U.S.A. to the Pacific. While U.S. ambassador to Mexico (1853–56), he was authorized to purchase a huge section of northern Mexico in order to provide for a direct southern route. He succeeded in buying a smaller tract of land for $10 million, known as the Gadsden purchase (1853).

Gaine, Hugh (1726–1807) journalist; born in Belfast, Ireland. Emigrating in 1745, he founded the *New-York Mercury* in 1752 and continued it for some 30 years. The paper wavered in its politics before the American Revolution. When the British occupied New York, Gaine at first removed the paper to Newark, N.J., then returned to New York and adopted a strongly pro-Tory stance. After the Revolution the paper folded.

Gaines, Ernest J. (James) (1933–) writer; born in Oscar, La. The son of a plantation worker, he graduated from San Francisco State College. His simple fictional accounts of the struggles of Southern blacks were influenced by the oral traditions of rural Louisiana, and included *The Autobiography of Miss Jane Pittman* (1971) and *A Gathering of Old Men* (1983). He was writer in residence at the University of Southwestern Louisiana (1983).

Gajdusek, D. (Daniel) Carleton (1923–) virologist; born in Yonkers, N.Y. After serving pediatric residencies and performing research on infectious diseases in the U.S.A. and abroad, he joined the National Institutes of Health (NIH)

(1958). In 1957 he began a series of expeditions to the Fore tribe of eastern New Guinea. While investigating *kuru*, the endemic fatal degeneration of the central nervous system, he found that the disease was due to a slow-acting protein virus transmitted by ritual funeral cannibalism. His work with *kuru* and other slow-acting viral neuropathologies won him one-half the 1976 Nobel Prize in physiology. Gadjusek, who is also a comparative child behaviorist, anthropologist, and collector of primitive art, adopted and facilitated the education of 29 Pacific island children. He alternated NIH work in the U.S.A. with field trips to New Guinea, Micronesia, and Melanesia.

Galanos, (James) "Jimmy" (1924–) fashion designer; born in Philadelphia. He worked for Paris and New York City designers before opening Galanos Originals, Los Angeles (1951). Often named as America's greatest designer, he specialized in cocktail and evening dresses, famous for their exquisite construction and high prices.

Galbraith, John Kenneth (1908–) economist; born in London, Ontario, Canada. Emigrating to the U.S.A. in 1931, he pursued a diverse career that led him through academic and government positions including that of a Harvard professor (1949–75), U.S. ambassador to India (1961–63), personal adviser to President Kennedy, and best-selling author. His serious academic work focused on a critical analysis of interactions between economics and power in U.S. society. His broader reputation derives from his often acerbic and openly partisan critiques of national political as well as economic policies.

Gale, Robert (Peter) (1945–) physician; born in New York City. At the University of California: Los Angeles beginning in 1972, he established a major bone marrow transplant center. In 1986 he attained international renown when he traveled to Chernobyl (Ukraine), then in the Soviet Union, to treat victims of a nuclear power plant accident. A prolific writer, he coauthored *Final Warning: The Legacy of Chernobyl* (1988).

Gale, Zona (1874–1938) writer; born in Portage, Wis. She spent most of her life in Wisconsin. She worked briefly as a journalist, but attracted attention as a writer with her early "local color" stories of village life. The fiction of her middle years was realistic; her best-known work, *Miss Lulu Brett* (1920), was notable for depicting the harshness of Midwestern life. In her later fiction she dealt with more abstract themes and in later years she was a public advocate of pacifism and women's suffrage.

Gall (b. Pizi) (?1840–95) Hunkpapa Sioux war chief; born near the Morrow River in present-day South Dakota. As a young warrior he was adopted by Sitting Bull as a major Sioux war chief. He fought with Red Cloud in the 1860s and was a leader in the Battle of the Little Bighorn (1876). He retreated with Sitting Bull to Canada but returned in 1880 and settled on the Standing Rock reservation. He came to accept white rule, even advocating land cessions, and in 1889 he became a judge on the Court of Indian Offenses. He broke with Sitting Bull and refused to support the Sioux uprising that culminated at Wounded Knee.

Gall, Joseph G. (Grafton) (1928–) cell biologist; born in Washington, D.C. He taught at the University of Minnesota (1952–64), became a professor at Yale (1964–83), then joined the Carnegie Institution (1983), becoming American Cancer Society professor of developmental genetics (1984).

His work included major contributions to studies of chromosome structure and function, nucleic acid metabolism, gene structure, and cellular organelles.

Gallatin, (Abraham Alfonse) Albert (1761–1849) financier, diplomat, political leader, ethnographer; born in Geneva, Switzerland. Of noble birth and inspired by Rousseauian idealism, he arrived in America at the age of 19. After teaching French at Harvard and working as a trader and land speculator, he settled on the Pennsylvania frontier and entered public life. He was elected to the U.S. Senate (1793–94) and served in the House of Representatives (Dem.-Rep., Penn.; 1795–1801). A leader among Jeffersonian Republicans and with rare mastery of public finance, he served Presidents Jefferson and Madison as secretary of the treasury (1801–14) and worked hard to retire the public debt. In 1814 his Treaty of Ghent laid the basis for permanent peace with England. He then served as minister to France (1816–23) and minister to England. He was an expert on American Indian and Indian languages, was author of important ethnographic works, was president of the National Bank of New York, and was a cofounder of New York University.

Gallaudet, Edward Miner (1837–1917) educator; born in Hartford, Conn. (son of Thomas Hopkins Gallaudet). He was a founder and superintendent of Columbia Institute for the Deaf and Dumb, Washington, D.C. (1857–1910) (renamed Gallaudet College for his father in 1894). There he introduced a combined manual and oral method of teaching the deaf and established the first U.S. college program for the deaf.

Gallaudet, Thomas (Hopkins) (1787–1851) educator; born in Philadelphia. He studied European methods of deaf education before becoming the founding president of the first American free school for the deaf in Hartford, Conn. (1817–30). A pioneer in training teachers of the deaf, he also actively promoted the education of African-Americans and women. Gallaudet College, Washington, D.C., is named for him.

Galli-Curci, Amelita (1882–1963) soprano; born in Milan, Italy. Galli-Curci began studying piano in Milan, then taught herself to sing. After her operatic debut in 1909 she toured Europe before making a triumphant American debut in Chicago in 1916. Four years later she began a legendary decade-long career at the Metropolitan Opera in New York. After recital tours she retired in 1936, settling in America (where she had been a citizen since 1921).

Gallier, James, Sr. (1798–1866) builder/architect; born in Ravensdale, County Louth, Ireland. He arrived in New Orleans in 1834 and, collaborating with Charles and James Dakin among others, dominated that city's architecture with his Greek Revival buildings until retiring in 1850.

Gallinger, Jacob H. (Harold) (1837–1918) U.S. representative/senator; born near Cornwall, Ontario, Canada. A printer's apprentice in Canada, he emigrated to study medicine in Ohio in 1855, opening a practice in Keene, N.H. (1860). He served in the U.S. House of Representatives (Rep., N.H.; 1885–89) and in the U.S. Senate (1891–1918), where he supported high tariffs.

Gallo, Ernest (1910–) vintner; born near Modesto, Calif. The son of an immigrant Italian grape grower, he and his brother **Julio Gallo** (1911–93) took over the family's Modesto vineyards (1933) and learned to make wine. With Julio Gallo as president and Ernest Gallo as chairman, E.

and J. Gallo Winery became the world's largest winery through vertical integration and aggressive marketing, gradually upscaling its image, as its Thunderbird fortified wine of the 1950s gave way to Bartles and Jaymes wine coolers in the 1980s, and its "jug wines" were supplemented by vintage varietals. The Gallos are generally credited with improving the quality of American table wine.

Gallo, Julio See under GALLO, ERNEST.

Gallo, Robert C. (Charles) (1937–) medical scientist; born in Waterbury, Conn. Inspired to do medical research after his sister's death from childhood leukemia, he graduated from Providence (R.I.) College (1954) and then from Jefferson Medical College (Philadelphia) (1963). He became an investigator at the National Cancer Institute (Maryland) in 1965 and was named chief of the Laboratory of Tumor Cell Biology in 1972. In 1978 he identified the first retrovirus to be found in humans, the HTLV-1, linked to leukemia, for which he won the Lasker Award. When the Acquired Immune Deficiency Syndrome (AIDS) was first recognized in the early 1980s, he immediately set about to identify its cause. In a 1984 paper, he claimed to have discovered and isolated the HIV retrovirus; for this and for developing a test to detect the AIDS virus in the blood system, he shared another Lasker Award (1986). His co-sharer was Luc Montagnier, a French researcher at the Pasteur Institute in Paris, who claimed that in fact he and his staff had first identified the virus and the test. In 1987 Gallo and Montagnier reached a legal compromise on their claims, but in January 1993 a professional review committee found Gallo guilty of "scientific misconduct" in his 1984 claims of priority. Gallo continued to defend himself from all such charges, but even his supporters agreed that his well-known reputation for asserting and advancing himself was at least part of his image problem.

Galloway, Joseph (c. 1731–1803) colonial statesman, Loyalist; born in West River, Md. He served in the Pennsylvania assembly (1756–64, 1766–76) and was a delegate to the First Continental Congress in 1774. He believed that the creation of a written constitution for the British empire would solve the existing political problems in the colonies. He joined the Loyalist camp and became the civil administrator for Philadelphia during its occupation by British soldiers (1777–78). He spent his last 25 years in England.

Gallup, George (Horace) (1901–84) statistician, public opinion analyst; born in Jefferson, Iowa. While directing research at the New York advertising agency, Young and Rubicam (1932–47), he founded the Princeton, N.J. based Gallup Poll (1935), which became internationally influential for its regular public opinion polls on social and economic issues and current events. He pioneered scientifically based opinion polling supported by representative population samples and he popularized opinion polling worldwide.

Galston, Arthur W. (William) (1920–) botanist; born in New York City. He taught and performed research at the California Institute of Technology (1943–55), then joined Yale (1955–90). An authority on light and hormones as major influences in plant development, he made influential contributions to studies of plant growth hormones, photobiology, circadian rhythms, and the biochemistry of photoperiodism. He was one of the first American scientists to enter the People's Republic of China, from where he explored the ecological effects of herbicides in Indochina, especially Vietnam.

Galvin, (James Francis) "Pud" (1856–1902) baseball pitcher; born in St. Louis, Mo. One of the game's great pioneers, the stocky right-hander won 361 games during his 14-year career (1879–92), mostly with Buffalo and Pittsburgh. He was elected to baseball's Hall of Fame in 1965.

Galvin, Robert W. (William) (1922–) electronics executive; born in Marshfield, Wis. (son of Paul V. Galvin). The son of Motorola's founder, he joined the firm at age 18 as a stockroom apprentice and spent the rest of his career there. Named executive-vice president (1949) and president (1956), CEO (1964–86), and chairman (1964–90), he masterminded Motorola's revival as a company known for innovation and quality products. He adeptly responded to heightened foreign competition after the 1970s by selling aging product lines such as television and car radios to concentrate on new ones like cellular telephones; concentrating on high technology areas such as semiconductors and microprocessors; moving production offshore; and establishing joint ventures with foreign firms. As an executive he was known for his egalitarian style, decentralized management structure, and commitment to profit-sharing. At the same time he was a vociferous proponent of protective tariffs on imported manufactured goods and was a major player in the semiconductor trade agreement (1986) which opened the Japanese market to U.S. manufacturers.

Gamow, George (1904–68) physicist; born in Odessa, Russia. His European research on radioactivity and atomic fission gained him an international reputation that preceded his arrival at George Washington University (1934–56). He and Edward Teller formulated their rule for beta decay in 1936. He postulated that primordial matter existed prior to the origin of the universe (1948), he developed the theory of red giant stars, and he was a major proponent of the "big bang" theory of the origin of the universe. He correctly theorized that DNA structure forms a code that directs protein synthesis. He became a professor at Colorado (1956–68), where he wrote and illustrated most of his many books for nonscientists.

Gannett, Frank Ernest (1876–1957) newspaper publisher; born near Rochester, N.Y. He founded the Gannett Group, which at his death embraced 22 papers and seven broadcasting stations. Gannett bought his first paper, the *Elmira (N.Y.) Gazette,* in 1906; he was known for his skill in acquiring papers, streamlining their operations, and making them successful while editorially autonomous.

Gannett, Henry (1846–1914) geographer; born in Bath, Maine. Sometimes referred to as the father of American mapmaking, he produced *Scribner's Statistical Atlas of the United States* (1885), "A manual of topographic methods" (1893), and *Commercial Geography* (with Carl L. Garrison and Edwin J. Houston) (1905).

Gans, Carl (1923–) zoologist; born in Hamburg, Germany. He came to the U.S.A. in 1939 and worked as an engineer for the Babcock and Wilcox Company, N.Y. (1947–55). He was a fellow in biology at the University of Florida (1957–58), and taught and performed research in biology at the State University of New York: Buffalo (1958–71) before becoming a professor at the University of Michigan (1971). He concurrently served as a researcher and consultant to many zoological museums and universities worldwide. Using a biomechanical approach to vertebrate biology, he made major contributions to the systematics of reptiles and amphibians, vertebrate motor coordination studies, shark anatomy, electromyography, and research on the early evolution of vertebrates.

Gantt, Henry Laurence (1861–1919) industrial engineer; born in Calvert County, Md. From 1887–93, Gantt worked with Frederick W. Taylor in the scientific management of Midvale Steel and Bethlehem Steel. He later originated the "task and bonus" system of wage payment and developed methods of assessing worker efficiency and productivity. He served as a consultant until his death.

Garbo, Greta (b. Greta Louisa Gustafson) (1905–90) film actress; born in Stockholm. A shop-girl who won a bathing beauty contest at age 16, she made some publicity shorts and studied acting before gaining international recognition in Mauritz Stiller's Swedish film, *The Story of Gosta Berling* (1924). She came to Hollywood (1924) with Stiller, her mentor and companion, and they worked together on *The Torrent* (1926) but he soon returned to Sweden while she stayed on to become known as "The Swedish Sphinx," reflecting her aloofness and cool beauty. Promoted by the resources of Metro-Goldwyn-Mayer, she became an international star, especially after her first talkie, *Anna Christie* (1930); although she made only 13 more films and retired abruptly in 1941, she came to personify all that was most alluring yet unattainable about movie stars. She became an American citizen in 1951, and in 1954 was awarded a special Oscar. Although linked with several men, she never married and became almost a recluse in her final decades.

Garcia, (Jerome John) Jerry (1942–) band leader, guitarist, songwriter; born in San Francisco. Son of a Spanish immigrant who became a band leader popular in the San Francisco area, he studied piano as a boy but turned to the guitar in his teens. He dropped out of school at age 17 and served nine months in the U.S. Army before being discharged for poor conduct. He began to play folk and blues guitar, alone or with pickup groups, in clubs in the San Francisco area while working as a salesman and music teacher in a music store (1959–65). In 1965 he formed a band, the Warlocks, but on discovering another group with that name, it was changed to the Grateful Dead in 1966. Closely involved with the San Francisco hippie movement and the use of drugs such as LSD, the band first played "psychedelic" rock but moved on to a more diverse repertory of rock styles in the 1970s. About 1974 the band's members began to go their own ways, and Garcia made solo appearances and albums. In the 1980s he became heavily addicted to drugs and after being arrested in 1985 he was sent to a treatment center; after emerging from a diabetic coma, he decided to turn his life around. He and his band made a comeback in 1987 with a hit single, "Touch of Gray" and an album, *In the Dark.* Although the group made over two dozen albums, they experienced their greatest success in live concerts; their loyal fans, known as "Deadheads" – the aging original ones now joined by a new generation – continued to flock to the band's concerts, gathering like hornets at the performance sites. Garcia himself also enjoyed taking a break from his group's "classic hits" by performing occasionally with bands that played other music.

Garden, Mary (1874–1967) soprano; born in Aberdeen, Scotland. Garden came to the U.S.A. at age six with her family and early studied voice, violin, and piano. After five years of vocal study in Paris she debuted in 1900 at the Opéra-Comique; there her historic creation of the first Mélisande in Debussy's *Pelléas et Mélisande* (1902) made Garden world famous. In 1907 she made her New York debut in *Thaïs,* which would become her most celebrated role, demonstrating her mastery of both singing and acting. In 1910 she began two decades with the Chicago Opera. Retiring from the stage in 1934, she sang in recitals for two decades more. Her memoirs, *Mary Garden's Story,* appeared in 1951.

Gardiner, Lion (1599–1663) military engineer, colonist; born in England. He emigrated to Connecticut in 1636. He ably defended the Saybrook settlement during the Pequot War (1637) and purchased the Isle of Wight (now called Gardiner's Island) in Long Island Bay from the Indians. He received a grant for this land from the Earl of Stirling and in 1686 the island became a manor with full manorial rights. The property has remained in the hands of the Gardiner family.

Gardner, Alexander (1821–82) photographer; born in Paisley, Scotland. Technical innovator and skilled manager of Mathew Brady's Washington studio (1856–63), he left to take documentary photographs and run his own studio (1863–82) when Brady refused to give photo credits to his war photographers.

Gardner, Erle Stanley (1889–1970) writer, lawyer; born in Malden, Mass. He moved to California as a child, obtained a high school education, knocked about as a professional boxer, studied law on his own, was admitted to the bar in 1911, and quickly established a reputation as a fine courtroom lawyer. He then turned to writing, launching the career of the brilliant, unconventional lawyer-detective Perry Mason in *The Case of the Velvet Claws* in 1933. The character inspired several movies and a popular television serial, and the Mason series of books sold tens of millions of copies worldwide. He also wrote a series involving "the D.A.," Doug Selby, and under the pen name A. A. Fair he wrote the Bertha Cool mystery series. In 1947 he established the Court of Last Resort, a panel of experts to help people unjustly accused in the courts.

Gardner, Isabella Stewart (1840–1924) art collector; born in New York City. Daughter of David Stewart, a wealthy New York City importer and mining investor, she was schooled privately, toured Europe (1856–58), and married John Lowell Gardner (1860) with his proper Bostonian pedigree. She settled in Boston but was not accepted by its old society; when the death of her two-year-old son (1865) was followed by a miscarriage, she and her husband went to Europe; after they returned in 1868, "Mrs. Jack" soon established herself as the most flamboyant and sought-after hostess in Boston. At first her energies went into entertaining, interior decoration, gardening, traveling, and collecting friends and odds-and-ends, but by the late 1880s she set out seriously to collect great art. Assisted by – and subsidizing – Bernard Berenson, just out of nearby Harvard College, she began to purchase mainly works of the European Renaissance. (She had inherited a large fortune when her father died in 1891.) To house her growing collection, she built an ambitious Italianate *palazzo,* Fenway Court; incorporated as the semiprivate Isabella Stewart Gardner Museum in 1902, it was opened to the first select guests in 1903. She continued to add objects over the next few years and stipulated that everything must stay exactly where she placed it. Regarded as somewhere between an exotic aesthete and a Jamesian heroine, she defined herself with her oft-quoted motto, "C'est mon plaisir."

Gardner, John (Champlin, Jr.) (1933–82) writer, educator; born in Batavia, N.Y. He earned a Ph.D. at Iowa State University and taught at several institutions, including the State University of New York: Binghamton (1978–82). In addition to scholarly works – chiefly medieval translations and editions – he wrote poetry, criticism, and fiction, including *Grendel* (1971), *October Light* (1976, National Book Critics Circle Award) and *Mickelsson's Ghosts* (1982). He died in a motorcycle accident.

Gardner, John (William) (1912–) educator, social activist; born in Los Angeles. Gardner exerted a powerful innovative influence on math teaching, civil rights, and children's television as president of the Carnegie Corporation and the Carnegie Foundation for the Advancement of Teaching (1955–65) and as Secretary of Health, Education, and Welfare (1965–69). He founded the citizens' lobby Common Cause and the volunteer coalition Independent Sector.

Gardner, Martin (1914–) writer, mathematical games editor; born in Tulsa, Okla. After graduating from the University of Chicago (B.A. 1936), he became a reporter for the *Tulsa Tribune*, then worked in public relations for the University of Chicago. Becoming a contributing editor of *Humpty Dumpty* magazine (1952–62), he took on the work for which he was undoubtedly best known, a regular column with *Scientific American* (1957–81), "Mathematical Games," which for a quarter-century covered a broad range of intellectual diversions. Collecting and adding to these columns, he published a seemingly endless stream of books on mathematical puzzles, logical brainteasers, and philosophical and literary diversions. His first book, *In the Name of Science* (1952), sounded another of his favorite themes – his exposure of cults, fads and fallacies in the sciences over the centuries; a practicing magician (as well as musical saw player), he also attacked those who misused magical tricks to suggest some supernatural powers. Still another interest were editions of well-known texts with his own footnotes explaining esoterica and curiosities: *The Annotated Alice* (1960), by Lewis Carroll; *The Annotated Ancient Mariner* (1965) by Samuel Taylor Coleridge; and *The Annotated Casey at the Bat* (1967), by Ernest L. Thayer. He also wrote serious books on science, including *Philosophical Foundations of Physics* (1966), and a "metaphysical novel," *The Flight of Peter Fromm* (1973).

Gardner, (Oliver Maxwell) O. Max (1882–1947) governor; born in Shelby, N.C. A lawyer and wealthy investor, he served in the state legislature before becoming North Carolina's lieutenant governor (Dem., 1916–21). As governor (1929–33) he re-established state credit, consolidating the highway and university systems. He then began to practice law in Washington, D.C., where he won a reputation as a lobbyist and trusted adviser of President Franklin Roosevelt. He served on various federal boards, then chaired the Office of War Mobilization (1944–46) and was undersecretary of the treasury (1946).

Garfield, James A. (Abram) (1831–81) twentieth U.S. president; born in Orange, Ohio. Born in poverty, he worked his way up to an education at Williams College and careers as a lay preacher and a lawyer, then moved into politics. He served briefly in the Ohio senate (1859–61) before taking a commission in the Civil War, during which he led units with distinction. He left the army to enter the U.S. House of Representatives (1863–80), representing Ohio as a conservative Republican leader. In 1880 he won the presidential nomination as a compromise candidate in a convention torn among several factions; with his running mate, Chester A. Arthur, he won a close election over war hero Winfield Scott Hancock. Garfield then proceeded to outrage many Republicans with his patronage appointments; the immediate result was his being shot by Charles Guiteau, a deranged office-seeker (July 1881); with a bullet in his back, Garfield lingered for 79 days before dying.

Garfield, John (b. Julius Garfinkle) (1913–52) movie/stage actor; born in New York City. A one-time juvenile delinquent, he gained a reputation acting with the leftist Group Theater in New York City, then enjoyed both critical and popular acclaim for his first featured role in the movie *Four Daughters* (1938). He went on to play a series of aggressive or embittered characters in such movies as *The Postman Always Rings Twice* (1946) and *Body and Soul* (1947). He was blacklisted in the 1950s for refusing to give a government committee the names of friends who had been Communists, but he died prematurely of a heart attack before it could have much effect on his career.

Garfield, Lucretia (b. Rudolph) (1832–1918) First Lady; born in Hiram, Ohio. A former student of James Garfield at Hiram College, they were married in 1858. She was a great believer in education and was more interested in the Library of Congress than in Washington society.

Garfinkel, Harold (1917–) sociologist; born in Newark, N.J. He took his B.A. from the University College: Newark (a part of Rutgers) and his M.A. at the University of North Carolina (1942). After serving with the U.S. Army in World War II, he took his Ph.D. from Harvard (1952). He taught at several universities but spent most of his career at the University of California: Los Angeles (1954–87); he was affiliated with the U.S. Public Health Service (1957–66). In works such as *Studies in Ethnomethodology* (1967), he pioneered the now internationally influential field of ethnomethodology, the study of methods used by ordinary people to describe and analyze their own activities.

Garfunkel, Art See under SIMON, PAUL.

Garland, (Hannibal) Hamlin (1860–1940) writer; born in West Salem, Wis. A largely self-educated farm worker, he went to Boston in 1884 and was encouraged in his writing by William Dean Howells. He returned to the Midwest in 1887 determined both to depict and better the life there, and some of his novels were little more than tracts promoting his political and economic views. He first gained attention for his stories and sketches collected in *Main-Travelled Roads* (1891) and became best known for his bleak novels debunking the pastoral image of farm life, including the semiautobiographical *A Son of the Middle Border* (1917) and *A Daughter of the Middle Border* (1921, Pulitzer Prize). Living in New York City after 1916 and in Los Angeles after 1929, he wrote little in his later years.

Garland, Judy (b. Frances Gumm) (1922–69) singer, actress; born in Grand Rapids, Minn. (mother of Liza Minnelli). Her vaudeville act with her sisters led to a film contract. Bright and vivacious, with a vibrant singing voice, she starred in films (1939–54) including *The Wizard of Oz* (1939) and *Meet Me in St. Louis* (1944). The emotional power of her singing on stage won her an ecstatic following, despite her well-documented struggles with alcohol and drugs.

Garn, Stanley M. (Marion) (1922–) physical anthropologist; born in New London, Conn. He was a professor at Antioch College (1952–68) before becoming a professor of nutrition and fellow of the Center for Human Growth and Development at the University of Michigan (1968). An evolutionist and specialist on human races, he has made major contributions to pediatrics and gerontology with research on the interaction of genetics with bone development and aging.

Garner, Errol (Louis) (1923–77) jazz musician; born in Pittsburgh, Pa. He was the composer of "Misty" and an exhilarating pianist who emerged in 1946 and developed an international following as a concert performer.

Garner, John Nance (1868–1967) vice-president, businessman; born near Detroit, Texas. During his two terms as vice-president under Franklin Roosevelt (1933–41), he became alarmed at the increase of the executive powers. He unsuccessfully opposed Roosevelt's renomination in 1940.

Garner, W. W. (Wightman Wells) (1875–1956) botanist; born in Timmonsville, S.C. He was an instructor and research assistant at Tufts (1900–03), then joined the U.S. Department of Agriculture (1904–45), where he performed landmark research on the pathology and mineral nutrition of tobacco. While investigating a strain of Maryland mammoth tobacco, he and codiscoverer Harry Allard observed that the length of day is a major regulator of a plant's growth and flowering (1920); Garner named this fundamental principle of botany "photoperiodism."

Garretson, A. B. (Austin Bruce) (1856–1931) labor leader; born in Winterset, Iowa. He apprenticed as a wheelwright but then became a railroad brakeman and eventually a conductor. He joined the Order of Railway Conductors in 1884 and served as chief conductor (1906) and president (1907–19) of that union. He campaigned successfully for the eight-hour day for railroad workers and served on the Federal Commission on Industrial Relations (1912–15).

Garrett, Finis (James) (1875–1956) U.S. representative; born in Ore Springs, Tenn. A newspaperman and lawyer before going to the U.S. House of Representatives (Dem., Tenn.; 1905–29), he was a fiscal conservative but an internationalist who supported the League of Nations. Deprived of a federal judgeship in 1921 by the Republican majority in Congress, he championed the Democratic party on nationwide speaking tours. He became a judge of the Federal Court of Customs and Patent Appeals (1929–55).

Garrett, Robert (1783–1857) financier; born in Lisburn, Ireland. The family emigrated to a farm in Cumberland County, Pa., in 1790. At age 17 he moved to Baltimore to clerk in a produce and commission house. By 1820 he had founded Robert Garrett & Sons, a wholesale grocery and commission business. Interested in developing trade with the American West, he promoted the Baltimore & Ohio Railroad as well as the city of Baltimore. A director of several utility companies and banks, he developed two hotels. In 1848 he built the steamship *Monumental City* to link Baltimore with San Francisco.

Garrison, William Lloyd (1805–79) journalist, abolitionist, social activist; born in Newburyport, Mass. With little formal education, he was a printer by trade who became editor of several small New England papers (1824–28). Turning his attention away from temperance to slavery, in Boston (1829) he delivered the first of his innumerable and inflammatory public addresses against slavery; later that year he joined Benjamin Lundy in Baltimore to help edit the *Genius of Universal Emancipation*. If not the first abolitionist, Garrison was one of the earliest to demand the "immediate and complete emancipation" of slaves. Founder/editor of *The Liberator* (1831–65), he continued his uncompromising attacks on slavery despite threats and harassment from pro-slavery opponents and often disagreement and dismay from other less absolute abolitionists. Cofounder and agent for the New England Anti-Slavery Society (1831) and its president (1841–63), he favored a peaceful separation of the North and South. To dramatize his contempt for the U.S. Constitution's acceptance of slavery, he publicly burned a copy in Framingham, Mass. (1854), but as a pacifist he opposed the actions of John Brown and others who supported violence. With the end of the Civil War and slavery, he turned his passions and energies to crusading for such reforms as prohibition, the plight of Native Americans, and, above all, women's rights. In 1840, when the world's antislavery convention met in London, he had refused to attend sessions because women were excluded.

Garrity, (Wendell) Arthur, Jr. (1920–) judge; born in Worcester, Mass. The son of a lawyer, he graduated from Holy Cross (1941) and, after serving with the U.S. Army in World War II, from Harvard Law School (1946). He served as a government lawyer (1948–50), and went into private practice in Boston (1950–61); active in Democratic politics, he worked on John F. Kennedy's successful 1958 senate campaign. He became U.S. attorney for Massachusetts (1961–66) and was appointed to the federal bench for Massachusetts in 1966. In 1974 he came to national prominence when he ruled that Boston's school officials had deliberately maintained a segregated school system, and he placed the entire system under federal control. During the next 13 years he handed down some 400 orders that had major impact on the conduct of the schools – particularly in the matter of bussing. In 1987 an Appeal's Court ruled that the Boston system no longer needed to be supervised by a federal judge, but Garrity continued to hand down specific rulings as late as 1990.

Garroway, (David) Dave (1913–82) television host; born in Schenectady, N.Y. Originally a disk jockey on Chicago radio, he appeared in his own variety show, *Garroway-at-Large* (1949–51) on National Broadcasting Company (NBC)-TV. The first *Today* host (1952–61), he later hosted *Wide, Wide World* (1955–58), also on NBC. Retiring after his wife's death, he later worked on National Educational Television's show, *Exploring the Universe* (1961–62).

Garvey, Marcus (Moziah) (1887–1940) social activist; born in St. Ann's Bay, Jamaica. Largely self-educated, he worked as a printer in Jamaica, edited several short-lived papers in Costa Rica and Panama, then founded the Universal Negro Improvement Association (UNIA) in Jamaica (1914). In 1916 he moved to New York City, where he established UNIA headquarters and started up the *Negro World,* a popular weekly newspaper that con- veyed his message of black pride. Launching several other African-American capitalist ventures, he presided over an international convention of black people in New York (1920), where he called for freedom from white domination in Africa. His later life, however, was anticlimatic. In 1923 he was convicted of mail fraud when selling stock in his failed Black Star steamship line, which was launched for maritime trade between black nations; he was sentenced (1923) to a five-year prison term. Other ventures also failed, including an attempt to foster black colonization to Liberia. After his release from prison (1927) he was deported to Jamaica; he moved to London in 1934 and never regained prominence. However, in stirring African-Americans with his message of pride in ancestry and prospects of self-sufficiency, he prefigured a later generation of African-American leaders such as Malcolm X.

Gary, Elbert Henry (1846–1927) lawyer, financier; born near Wheaton, Ill. In 1871 he joined his brother's Chicago law firm, Gary, Cody & Gary, and prospered while specializing in corporate law. He served two terms as county magistrate (1882–90), and was thereafter always known as "Judge" Gary. He was president of the Chicago Bar Association (1893–94). In 1898 he went to New York City to become president of the Federal Steel Company. In 1901, at the request of J. P. Morgan, he helped organize the United States Steel Corporation; he became chairman of its board in 1903 and led the corporation in various capacities until 1927. Although he was generally fair in dealing with his employees, and some of his policies were fairly progressive for the time – he abolished the 12-hour, seven-day work week in U.S. Steel plants – he was adamantly against organized labor unions and his opposition provoked the major steel strike of 1919. The company town U.S. Steel built around its Indiana plant was named after him.

Gass, William (Howard) (1924–) writer, teacher; born in Fargo, N.D. He studied philosophy at Kenyon College (B.A. 1947) and Cornell (Ph.D. 1954). He taught philosophy and English at the College of Wooster, Ohio (1950–54), Purdue (1954–69), and Washington University, St. Louis (1969). He won numerous literary awards and is noted for his aesthetic concern for language and metaphor, both in fiction such as *Willie Masters' Lonesome Wife* (1971) and in his nonfictional work such as *On Being Blue* (1975).

Gasser, Herbert S. (Spencer) (1888–1963) neurologist; born in Platteville, Wis. He taught at the University of Wisconsin (1911–16), then moved to Washington University (St. Louis, Mo.) (1916–31) on the invitation of his former professor, Joseph Erlanger. For their pioneering experiments on electrophysiology of mammalian nerves and their demonstration that nerve impulse velocities depend on the thickness of the nerve fibers through which they pass, Gasser and Erlanger were awarded the 1944 Nobel Prize in physiology. After his retirement, Gasser expanded his research to include electron microscopy of nerve tissue.

Gates, Daryl F. (1926–) police chief; born in Glendale, Calif. He rose through the ranks of the Los Angeles police force to become its chief (1978–92). An adviser on crime to presidents and top government officials, he pioneered both the nation's first SWAT team – now an international model – and the use of helicopters to combat street crime. His reputation was tarnished after the notorious Rodney King beatings by members of the Los Angeles Police Department (1991). He defended his force against charges of racism throughout the trial that followed, but retired (1992) not long after quelling

massive riots in Los Angeles following a jury's acquittal of the officers in question.

Gates, Frederick T. (Taylor) (1853–1929) clergyman, businessman; born in Maine, N.Y. A Baptist minister, his first church was in Minneapolis, Minn. (1881). In 1888 he resigned and became secretary of the American Baptist Education Society, in which position he helped reorganize the University of Chicago. In doing so he earned the respect of John D. Rockefeller, the principal benefactor of the new university, and in 1891 he was engaged by Rockefeller to aid in managing his philanthropic activities. In this capacity Gates set up the General Education Board and the Rockefeller Institute for Medical Research and helped establish the Rockefeller Foundation (1913). Gates also found himself becoming involved in some of Rockefeller's business enterprises. Through his own personal integrity and manner, Gates also helped Rockefeller gain a more favorable public image.

Gates, Henry Louis, Jr. (1950–) educator; born in Keyser, W.Va. He graduated from Yale (1973) and was the first African-American to receive a Ph.D. from Cambridge University, England (1979). Sometimes called a "literary archaeologist," he unearthed, edited, and compiled important African-American texts, especially from the slavery period. In addition to his scholarly work, he increasingly wrote and spoke about broader issues relevant to African-Americans and their relations to society at large. His fame made him the subject of "bidding wars" between major universities; he taught at Yale (1979–85), Cornell (1985–90), Duke (1990–91), and Harvard (1991).

Gates, Horatio (c. 1728–1806) soldier; born in Maldon, England. He entered the British army as a boy and saw action in America during the French and Indian War. After ten years back in England, he settled in western Virginia in 1772. Appointed brigadier general in the Continental Army in June 1775, he proved himself a capable administrator and played a major role in the American victory at Saratoga in 1777. But he had a tendency to quarrel with his fellow officers – General Schuyler at Ticonderoga, Benedict Arnold after Saratoga – and in 1778 he permitted his name to be associated with the "Conway Cabal," a plot to have Gates supplant Washington as commander in chief; although not formally implicated, Gates never truly regained Washington's friendship or trust, and for two years he had little role in the action. Finally restored to command in the South on August 16, 1780, he commanded the militia at Camden, S.C., that was routed by the British; Congress demanded an investigation but no court of inquiry ever convened. He played little role in the final actions of the war and retired to his Virginia plantation in 1783. Ever the outsider, he freed his slaves in 1790 and passed his last years as a gentleman farmer on Manhattan Island, New York City.

Gates, Thomas S. (Sovereign) (1873–1948) banker, university president; born in Germantown, Pa. He was a partner at Drexel and Company (1918–30) and J. P. Morgan and Company (1921–30) before assuming the presidency of the University of Pennsylvania (1930–44). He reorganized the university's finances, brought athletics under administrative control, and raised educational standards.

Gates, (William H.) Bill (1955–) computer engineer, entrepreneur; born in Seattle, Wash. At age 15, he constructed a device to control traffic patterns in Seattle. In 1975, he cowrote a compiler for BASIC and interested the MITS company in it. He dropped out of Harvard in 1975 to spend his time writing programs. In 1977, he cofounded Microsoft to develop and produce DOS, his basic operating system for computers; when in 1981 International Business Machines (IBM) adopted DOS for its line of personal computers, his company took a giant step forward; by 1983 he had licensed DOS to more than 100 vendors, making it the dominant operating system. A brilliant and ruthless entrepreneur, and a benevolent if unorthodox employer, by age 35 he had become one of the wealthiest men in America.

Gatling, Richard Jordan (1818–1903) inventor; born in Money's Neck, N.C. The son of a planter, he taught school and ran a country store, but he was observant of the agricultural practices all around him and spent his time inventing such devices as a rice-sewing machine (patented 1839) and a steam plow (1857). By 1862 he had received a patent for a rapid-fire multibarrel weapon; technically speaking it was not a machine-gun because it had to be powered by a hand crank in the early models (and an electric motor in the improved model). Only a few "Gatling guns" were put into use at the end of the Civil War but it was adopted by the U.S. Army in 1866. It could fire about 600 rounds per minute and was used by the army and navy up through the Spanish-American War. Gatling worked on its improved versions but then went back to working on agricultural machinery, inventing a motor-driven plow in 1900.

Gaudin, Juliet (1808–87) Catholic religious foundress; born in Cuba. Emigrating to New Orleans with her parents, she became a friend of Henriette Delille and with her she cofounded the Sisters of the Holy Family (1842), a community of African-American Catholic nuns.

Gault, Stanley C. (Carleton) (1926–) manufacturing executive; born in Wooster, Ohio. At General Electric (1948–79) he specialized in consumer products and major appliances. He was later chairman of the board and CEO of Rubbermaid (1980–91), where he instituted rigorous management shakeup and quality controls to make the company a market leader. In 1991 he became CEO of Goodyear Tire & Rubber Company.

Gavin, James (Maurice) (1907–90) soldier; born in New York City. An orphan, he grew up in coal mining towns in Pennsylvania, enlisted in the army, and won an appointment to West Point, from which he graduated in 1929. In August 1944 "Jumping Jim" Gavin became commander of the 82nd Airborne Division – the youngest division commander of World War II. During the 1950s he developed a reputation as a strategist of limited war; in 1961 President Kennedy appointed him ambassador to France. His memoir, *On to Berlin,* appeared in 1978.

Gay, Ebenezer (1696–1787) Protestant clergyman; born in Dedham, Mass. He graduated from Harvard at age 18 and taught school while preparing for the ministry. Named pastor of the First Parish Church, Hingham, Mass., in 1718, he remained there for 69 years and became one of the most influential New England clergymen. A liberal in theology, he was a forerunner of the Unitarians. He remained loyal to Britain during the Revolutionary era. He died on a Sunday morning as he made ready to preach.

Gay, Peter (Jack) (b. Peter Froelich) (1923–) historian; born in Berlin, Germany. Emigrating to the U.S.A. as a youth (and changing his name that in German means "joyous," "gay") he took degrees in political science and history (Ph.D. Columbia University, 1951); later he would take a degree in psychoanalysis (1983). He taught at Columbia (1947–69) before becoming Sterling Professor of History at Yale (1969). He is known for his often controversial reassessments of broad topics such as the Enlightenment, 19th-century middle-class culture, and the art and politics of imperial and Weimar Germany. He presents his findings in books that reach out beyond the academic disciplines and community, such as his two-volume history, *The Enlightenment: An Interpretation* (1966, 1969) and his two-volume study, *The Bourgeois Experience* (1984, 1985). He also had a lifelong interest in Sigmund Freud, climaxing in his biography, *Freud: A Life for Our Time* (1988).

Gaye, Marvin (Pentz, Jr.) (1939–84) singer, composer; born in Washington, D.C. Composer of "I Heard It Through the Grapevine" and other soul classics, he sang gospel music in his father's church before joining a doo-wop group, the Rainbows, when he was 15. In 1957, he recorded with the Marquees in Washington, and in 1959 with the Moonglows in Chicago. After moving to Detroit in 1960, he began working as a drummer and back-up vocalist at Motown Records. The following year, he married Motown president Berry Gordy's sister, Anna Gordy, and recorded an album of ballads. In 1962, he scored his first chart success with "Stubborn Kind of Fellow," and for the next seven years he released a continual series of hit records and made regular concert tours in the U.S.A. and abroad. In 1971, the album *What's Going On* marked a breakthrough for Gaye as a socially-conscious songwriter. He found success with this new style for the next ten years, a period in which he was also beset by financial, mental, and drug problems, which culminated in his shooting death by his father.

Gaynor, William (Jay) (1849–1913) mayor, jurist; born near Oriskany, N.Y. In 1909 he retired from the New York Supreme Court to run for mayor of New York City, a post he held until his death in 1913. Backed at first by Tammany Hall, he soon lost their support when he proved to be a strongly reform-minded mayor, working against private gain and public corruption.

Gear, John Henry (1825–1900) governor, U.S. representative/senator; born in Ithaca, N.Y. A home-schooled, self-made groceryman, he became a leading Republican in Iowa, serving as governor (1877–79), congressman (1887–95), and senator (1895–1900). An advocate of fiscal responsibility in government, he supported protective tariffs.

Geary, John White (1819–73) soldier, mayor, governor; born in Westmoreland County, Pa. A Mexican War veteran, he was the first mayor of San Francisco (1850) and he pacified "Bloody Kansas" as territorial governor there in 1856–57. He commanded a Union division at Chancellorsville and Gettysburg (1863), during the Chattanooga campaign (1863), and in Sherman's March to the Sea. He was Republican governor of Pennsylvania from 1867–73.

Geertz, Clifford (James) (1923–) cultural anthropologist; born in San Francisco. He studied at Antioch College and Harvard, taught anthropology at the Universities of California (1958–60) and Chicago (1960–70), and became a professor of social science at the Institute for Advanced Study in Princeton, N.J. (1970). His expeditions to Java (1953–54) and Bali (1957–58) resulted in a series of works on environment and economy, social change, and religion, including *The Religion of Java* (1960), *Agricultural Involution* (1963), *Peddlers and Princes* (1963), and *Person, Time and Conflict in Bali* (1966). In the 1960s and 1970s he made several field trips to Morocco, from which he developed a comparative approach to religion, as outlined in *Islam Observed* (1968), and to processes of social change. His theoretical essays on themes ranging from art and ideology to politics and nationalism were collected in *Interpretation of Cultures* (1973) and *Local Knowledge* (1983). In those works he advocated an interpretive approach, in which cultures could be compared to literary texts.

Gehrig, (Henry Louis) Lou (b. Ludwig Heinrich Gehrig) (1903–41) baseball player; born in New York City. Baseball's "iron horse," the left-handed first baseman played in a major league record 2,130 consecutive games during his 17-year career with the Babe Ruth-led New York Yankees (1923–39). Twice named the American League Most Valuable Player (1927, 1936), he posted a .340 lifetime batting average and slammed 493 career homeruns (including 23 grand slams, a major league record). His career and incredible games-played streak came to an end when he was afflicted with the incurable disease, amyotrophic lateral sclerosis (now also known as "Lou Gehrig's Disease"). His emotional farewell to baseball in 1939, in which he proclaimed himself "the luckiest man on the face of this earth" was powerfully portrayed in the 1942 film, *Pride of the Yankees,* starring Gary Cooper. In 1939, Gehrig was elected to baseball's Hall of Fame.

Gehry, Frank O. (1929–) architect; born in Toronto, Ontario, Canada. Trained at the University of Southern California and Harvard, he opened his own Los Angeles firm (1962), gaining a reputation as the most inventive architect on the West Coast. Sculptural design, "brutalist" combinations of materials like corrugated metal and chain-link fencing in residential applications, and undefined interiors characterize his work.

Geiger, Roy S. (Stanley) (1885–1947) marine officer; born in Middleburg, Fla. The restless son of a school superintendent, he abandoned the law to enlist in 1907, rose through the ranks and trained as an aviator. In 1945, on Okinawa, he commanded the U.S. 10th Army, composed of marine and army units – the first marine to command such a large unit.

Geiringer, Karl (1899–1989) musicologist; born in Vienna, Austria. He served as custodian of Vienna's *Gesellschaft der Musikfreunde* archives before fleeing the Nazis. After lecturing at London's Royal College of Music (1939–40), he came to the U.S.A. and taught at Boston University (1941–62) and the University of California: Santa Barbara (from 1962). He is best known for his biographies of Austro-German composers, including Haydn (1932), Brahms (1934, 3rd ed. 1981), and Bach (1966).

Geisel, Theodor Seuss (Dr. Seuss, Theo. LeSieg, Rosetta Stone, pen names) (1904–91) author, illustrator; born in Springfield, Mass. He graduated from Dartmouth College (1925), attended Lincoln College, Oxford, England (1926), became a cartoonist for American periodicals, was a writer and animator in Hollywood, and settled in La Jolla, Calif. A winner of many awards, he is famous for his zany, inventive books for children, such as the popular *Horton Hatches the Egg* (1940), *The Cat in the Hat* (1957), and other books for adults, such as *You're Only Old Once!* (1986), and *Oh, the Places You'll Go!* (1990).

Geldzahler, Henry (1935–94) museum curator; born in Antwerp, Belgium. He emigrated to America and studied at Yale and Harvard. Beginning in 1960 he was on the staff of New York City's Metropolitan Museum of Art and became somewhat controversial for his acquisitions of contemporary American art. He was commissioner of cultural affairs, N.Y.C. (1978–82), and wrote books on contemporary art.

Gell-Mann, Murray (1929–) physicist; born in New York City. While at the University of Chicago (1952–55), he formulated new physical laws to explain apparently anomalous behavior for newly created subatomic particles. At the California Institute of Technology (1955), he organized these "strange" particles into eight-member "families" consisting of fractionally charged particles, which he named "quarks" (after a word in James Joyce's *Finnegan's Wake*). He received the 1969 Nobel Prize for these revolutionary contributions to particle physics. He continued his studies of quantum mechanics, dispersion theory, and theories of strong and weak particle interactions.

Geneen, Harold (Sydney) (1910–) communications executive; born in Bournemouth, England. He emigrated to the U.S.A. with his parents in infancy. A New York University graduate in accounting, he worked from 1934 to 1956 for various accounting and manufacturing companies. As a Raytheon executive (1956–59) he developed the management structure for which he was later famous, which featured semiautonomous divisions subject to strong central fiscal controls and strict accountability. As president (1959–72) and CEO (1959) of International Telephone and Telegraph (ITT), he introduced the same now-legendary accounting structure while presiding over ITT's transformation into one of the largest conglomerates in the world by means of some 350 mergers and acquisitions in 60 countries. His major acquisition, Hartford Fire Insurance Co. (1970), prompted a Justice Department antitrust suit, and under his watch ITT was also investigated for tax fraud and securities manipulation. He was also linked with the CIA's interference in the reelection of Chilean president Allende.

Genovese, Eugene D. (Dominick) (1930–) historian; born in New York City. Educated at Brooklyn College and Columbia University (Ph.D. 1959), he adopted a Marxist approach to analyzing history. He is best known for his works on American slavery, particularly *Roll Jordan Roll: The World the Slaves Made* (1974), winner of the Bancroft (1975) and other awards, and notable for its account of the slaves' daily life. He taught at Rutgers, Sir George Williams University (Montreal), and the University of Rochester (1969).

George, Harold Huston (1892–1942) aviator; born in Lockport, N.Y. A World War I "ace," he commanded U.S. air mail stations during the 1930s and in 1941 took command of U.S. air forces in the Philippines, where he directed the air defense of Manila, Bataan, and Corregidor. He escaped the islands with MacArthur and was killed in a ground accident shortly after his arrival in Australia.

George, Harold Lee (1893–1986) aviator; born in Somerville, Mass. A test pilot and instructor in the early era of flight, he directed the U.S. Army Air Transport Command during World War II. His responsibilities included delivering troops and matériel to all the world's combat zones and mobilizing U.S. airlines to deliver war passengers and freight.

George, Henry (1839–97) social reformer, economist; born in Philadelphia. Although not a truly original or systematic economist, he was perhaps the most influential 19th-century U.S. social analyst, renowned for his fervent writing and magnetic speaking style. His book, *Progress and Poverty* (1879), was one of the most widely read books of that time; it sparked many heated debates among intellectuals, and was translated into several languages. Primarily self-taught, his formal schooling ended at age 14 and he worked as a sailor, a journalist, and a printer before embarking on *Progress and Poverty,* which he wrote while working as a state gas meter inspector in California. The book was his reaction to the great disparity he saw between the wealthy and the poor. In order to abolish poverty and all economic crises, his theory called for a "single-tax" on land, exclusive of improvements, that would be sufficient to finance all government expenses. His popularity as a lecturer in the U.S.A. and abroad and his association with the single-tax movement led him to run, albeit unsuccessfully, for mayor of New York City in 1886.

George, James Zachariah (1826–97) soldier, jurist, U.S. senator; born in Monroe County, Ga. He moved to Mississippi and passed the bar in 1847. He served in both the Mexican War and in the Confederate army during the Civil War. He was a reporter for the Mississippi Supreme Court and then chief justice for the court (1879–81). He served in the U.S. Senate (Dem., Miss.; 1881–97) where he was the only Democrat to share in the framing of the Sherman Anti-Trust Law (1890). He strove always to protect his state and the South from federal interference. Mississippi placed his statue in the U.S. Capitol.

George, Walter F. (Franklin) (1878–1957) U.S. senator; born in Preston, Ga. A lawyer and judge, he went on to the U.S. Senate (Dem., Ga.; 1922–57). Although opposed to many of President Franklin Roosevelt's domestic policies, he supported U.S. participation in World War II, the United Nations, and NATO. As chairman of the Senate Foreign Relations Committee (1954–57), he maintained his internationalist stance.

Georgescu-Roegen, Nicholas (1906–) economist; born in Constanza, Rumania. After earning a mathematics degree from the University of Bucharest and a doctorate in statistics from the University of Paris, he emigrated to the U.S.A. in 1947. He spent two years teaching at Harvard before accepting a professorship at Vanderbilt University where he remained until his retirement in 1976. His early achievements were based on highly technical mathematical economics, largely in utility theory and input-output analysis. He wrote on a number of other subjects including production theory, the nature of expectations, agrarian economies, and the Marxist prediction of capitalist breakdown. He later explored the area of growth modeling and attempted to formulate the principles of "bioeconomics," a new style of "dialectical" economic thinking to replace the "mechanical" mode. The ideas behind bioeconomics are best explored in his article, "Energy Analysis and Economic Evaluation" (*Southern Economic Journal,* April 1979).

Gephardt, Richard Andrew (1941–) U.S. representative; born in St. Louis, Mo. A lawyer and Democratic alderman in St. Louis, Mo., he went to the U.S. House of Representatives in 1977. He ran for the Democratic nomination as president in 1986, losing to Michael Dukakis, and became house majority leader in 1989.

Gerber, (Daniel) Frank (1873–1952) baby food manufacturer; born in Douglas, Mich. After high school he joined the family tannery at age 16 and rose to partner and manager until the business closed in 1905. In 1901 he helped found the Fremont Canning Company to market local produce; he became president in 1917. The company started manufacturing baby foods at the behest of his son Daniel (Frank) Gerber (1898–1974) who, in 1927, was assistant general manager of the company and himself a new father. The Gerbers tested batches of baby food on Daniel's daughter Sally and other babies. By 1941 the baby food line was outselling adult food products and in 1943 the Gerber Products Company dropped its adult foods. Frank Gerber died in the midst of an expansion that saw the company opening plants in California, New York, and Ontario.

Geronimo (b. Goyathlay) (1829–1909) Chiricahua Apache war chief; born along the Gila River in present-day Arizona. Growing up during a time when his people were actively fighting the European settlers from Mexico and the U.S.A., he became a raider after his own family was killed in 1858. He was eventually confined to various reservations but he periodically escaped and led several raids against white settlers, often operating out of Mexico. When his most violent campaign began in 1885, U.S. Army troops were dispatched, but it took some 5,000 of them 18 months to capture Geronimo and about 35 warriors. He was first confined in Florida but was eventually allowed to settle on the Comanche and Kiowa reservation near Fort Sill, Okla. He became a successful farmer, converted to Christianity, appeared at the Louisiana Purchase Exposition (1904) and rode in President Theodore Roosevelt's inaugural parade (1905). He dictated his autobiography (published in 1906). In a tribute to his reputation as a fearless warrior, American military parachute troops have adopted his name as their "battle cry" as they jump from airplanes.

Gerry, Elbridge (1744–1814) vice-president, politician; born in Marblehead, Mass. He served in the Continental Congress and signed both the Declaration of Independence and the Articles of Confederation. He unsuccessfully ran for governor of Massachusetts four times before being elected in 1810. In 1812, he signed a bill for senatorial redistricting; the term "gerrymander" arose from the salamander-like shape of a district he carved out to favor his Republican Party. He served as James Madison's vice-president in 1813–14 and was an outspoken proponent of the War of 1812.

Gerry, Peter (Goelet) (1879–1947) U.S. representative/ senator; born in New York City. He served in the U.S. House of Representatives (Dem., R.I.; 1913–15) and in the U.S. Senate (1916–29, 1934–47).

Gershwin, George (1898–1937) composer; born in New York City. From a Russian-Jewish immigrant family, he began playing both popular and classical piano in childhood and soon was writing tunes. He left school in 1913 to pursue music, becoming a Tin Pan Alley song plugger and composer. His first hit song, "Swanee," dates from 1919; the same year saw his first Broadway musical, *La, La, Lucille.* During the next 18 years, he produced an astonishing amount of music including – in collaboration with his lyricist brother, Ira Gershwin – a celebrated series of musicals such as *Lady Be Good* (1924), *Funny Face* (1927), *Girl Crazy* (1929), and the Pulitzer Prize-winning *Of Thee I Sing* (1931). For the stage and otherwise, he composed some of the most sophisticated American popular songs, among them "I Got Rhythm," "They Can't Take That Away From Me," and "Someone to Watch Over Me." Beyond his immense achievements in popular music, however, he also pursued an ambitious goal of uniting commercial and classical genres (at one point even seeking to study under Ravel); the result was his historic jazz-oriented concert works such as *Rhapsody in Blue* (1924) and *An American in Paris* (1928), as well as the "folk opera" *Porgy and Bess* (1935). Despite his premature death, he left a body of work whose sheer melody and inventiveness guarantee its appeal to music-lovers of all persuasions.

Gershwin, Ira (b. Israel Gershvin) (1896–1983) lyricist; born in New York City (brother of George Gershwin). Showing a youthful talent for writing and drawing, he wrote humorous columns while in high school. But after two years at the City College of New York, he dropped out to work at odd jobs and to concentrate on his writing. He sold his first magazine piece in 1917 and became a reviewer of vaudeville shows. That same year he began to write song lyrics and in 1918 he began his long collaboration with his brother, George; at first Ira used the name "Arthur Francis," but beginning in 1924 he took on his own name. Ira occasionally collaborated with other composers but primarily with his brother; together they created such classic hits as "The Man I Love" (1924), " 'S Wonderful" (1927), and "Of Thee I Sing" (1931) (all from stage musicals rich in other fine songs); Ira also contributed lyrics to George's *Porgy and Bess* (1935) and they wrote original scores for a number of movie musicals. After George's death (1937), Ira retired from songwriting for four years but returned to collaborate with such composers as Kurt Weill (*Lady in the Dark,* 1941), Jerome Kern, and Harold Arlen ("The Man That Got Away," 1954). He wrote an account of his work, *Lyrics on Several Occasions* (1959), and retired for good in 1960; his health incapacitated him after 1970 but he maintained an active role in the Gershwin properties and even revised his own lyrics. He was shy and introspective and content to let his younger brother take the limelight, but later generations have not failed to realize how much his words contribute to the success of the Gershwin songbook.

Gesell, Arnold (Lucas) (1880–1961) pediatric psychologist; born in Alma, Wis. Coming to Yale first as a psychologist in 1911, when he founded the Yale Clinic for Child Development, he graduated from Yale's medical school (1915) and remained affiliated with it until 1948. He was a pioneer in establishing normal ranges of child development and behavior, and to this end in 1924 he initiated the use of movie cameras in recording children's actions; in 1930 he introduced a one-way observation dome that allowed researchers to observe children's behavior unseen. He trained several generations of students of infant and child development. Among his various publications are *The Mental Growth of the Pre-School Child* (1925) and *Atlas of Infant Behavior* (1934). In 1950 Yale established the Gesell Institute of Child Development to carry on his work.

Gesell, Gerhard (Alden) (1910–93) judge; born in Los Angeles. (brother of Arnold Gesell). A graduate of Yale and Yale Law School (1935), he worked for several years as a government lawyer before joining a private Washington firm. He had been in private practice for 25 years when President Lyndon B. Johnson appointed him a U.S. district judge for Washington, D.C., in 1968. He ruled in 1971 that *The Washington Post* had a First Amendment right to publish the leaked government documents known as the "Pentagon Papers." (In that famous case, first *The New York Times* and later *The Post* published documents that disclosed official misinformation and duplicity regarding U.S. policy in Vietnam.) He was eventually upheld by the Supreme Court.

Getty, J. (Jean) Paul (1892–1976) business executive; born in Minneapolis, Minn. He graduated from Oxford in 1913 and the following year entered into oil production as a wildcatter in Oklahoma with his father, George F. Getty. He made his first million dollars by 1916. His father died in 1930, leaving $15,000,000. During the Depression, he added to the fortune by acquiring other oil companies. He drilled for and discovered enormous quantities of oil in Saudi Arabia in the 1950s. In 1953, to display his collection of art, he founded the J. P. Getty Museum on an estate in Malibu, Calif. He retired to England in 1959. Married and divorced five times, he was known for his increasingly bizarre behavior such as refusing to pay ransom for a grandson even when the kidnappers sent him a piece of the youth's ear, and for installing a pay phone in his mansion for guests to use.

Getz, (Stanley) Stan (1927–91) jazz musician; born in Philadelphia. He was a tenor saxophonist whose cool, lyrical beauty established him as one of the most celebrated stylists in modern jazz. He was a sideman with Jack Teagarden and Benny Goodman before his emergence with the Woody Herman Orchestra in 1947–49. He led his own small groups from 1951 until his death. In the 1960s, he helped to popularize the bossa nova jazz style.

Ghormley, Robert Lee (1883–1958) naval officer; born in Portland, Ore. He was responsible for the planning and execution of the invasion of Guadalcanal and Tulgai (1942). As commander of U.S. naval forces in German waters (1945), he administered the demobilization of the German navy.

Giacconi, Riccardo (1931–) astrophysicist; born in Genoa, Italy. He came to Indiana University as a Fulbright Fellow in 1956 after teaching physics at the University of Milan. He went on to teach at Harvard (1973–82) and Johns Hopkins University (1982). He directed the Space Telescope Science Institute in Baltimore (1981) and specialized in X-ray astronomy.

Giaevar, Ivar (1929–) physicist; born in Bergen, Norway. He came to the U.S.A. to do research for General Electric (1957–88). He and Leo Esaki shared one-half the 1973 Nobel Prize in physics for their work on tunneling in semi- and superconductors. In 1988 he became concurrently a professor at Rensselaer Polytechnic Institute and the University of Oslo.

Giamatti, A. (Angelo) Bartlett (1938–89) educator, baseball executive; born in Boston, Mass. A scholar of Renaissance literature, at age 40 he became the youngest person in 200 years to serve as president of Yale University (1978–86). Long known as a baseball fan, he became president of the National League (1986–89), then took over as commissioner of baseball in April 1989, a position he held for only five months before his untimely death. He presided over Pete Rose's banishment from baseball after an investigation into the player's gambling activities. In addition to his scholarly writings, his *Take Time for Paradise: Americans and Their*

Games (1989) eloquently expressed his appreciation of baseball.

Giannini, Amadeo P. (Peter) (1870–1949) banker; born in San Jose, Calif. Child of Italian immigrants, from 1883 to 1901 he worked in his stepfather's produce business; made a partner by 1889, he retired at age 31. His father-in-law died intestate (1902) and as manager of the estate he started the Bank of Italy (1904), primarily as a lender to small, underserved businesses; throughout his career he would continue to promote liberal loan policies. The bank soon began to expand to other cities in California and by 1918 he had developed the first statewide branch-banking system in the United States. He retired as president of the Bank of Italy in 1924 but remained active in its parent holding company, Transamerica Corporation. In 1930 he combined the Bank of Italy and others to establish the Bank of America National Trust and Savings Association, which survived the Depression to become by 1934 one of the world's largest commercial banks. During the Depression he was sometimes criticized for his bank's excessive holdings of farm mortgages, and was accused of encouraging the exploitation of migrant farm workers. By the time of his death, his Bank of America was the largest bank in the U.S.A. and the largest privately held bank in the world. In 1927 he donated $1.5 million to the University of California to establish the Giannini Foundation of Agricultural Economics; after his death much of his fortune went to a foundation for medical research.

Giauque, William (Francis) (1895–1982) chemist; born in Niagara Falls, Ontario, Canada. Both parents were United States citizens. At the University of California: Berkeley (1920–62), he researched the behavior of substances at extremely low temperatures, approaching 0° Kelvin. He was awarded the Nobel Prize in chemistry (1949) for his contributions in the field of chemical thermodynamics.

Gibbard, Allan (Fletcher) (1942–) philosopher; born in Providence, R.I. After earning a Harvard doctorate (1971), he taught at the University of Chicago (1969–77) and (from 1977) at the University of Michigan: Ann Arbor, specializing in metaphysics, ethics, and social choice theory.

Gibbons, Cedric (1893–1960) movie art director; born in Dublin, Ireland (husband of Dolores Del Rio). The most celebrated and influential art director in the history of Hollywood, he worked for Edison (1915–17), Goldwyn (1918–23), and Metro-Goldwyn-Mayer (from 1924). He designed the Academy Award statuette and won it 11 times, from *The Merry Widow* (1934) to *Somebody Up There Likes Me* (1956).

Gibbons, Floyd (1887–1939) journalist; born in Washington, D.C. A veteran war correspondent, he was known for his colorful style and trademark eye patch, worn because of a World War I wound; in 1929 he became a radio commentator, earning a reputation as the fastest talker on the air.

Gibbons, James (1834–1921) Catholic prelate; born in Baltimore, Md. Gibbons was a pastor and Civil War chaplain before becoming secretary to the archbishop of Baltimore (1865), bishop and apostolic vicar of North Carolina (1868), and bishop of Richmond (1872); in 1877 he was named archbishop of Baltimore, becoming a cardinal in 1886. For several crucial decades he was the preeminent leader of American Catholicism. He presided over a national church council that established Catholic University (1884), and he

became the university's first chancellor. A prudent leader as archbishop, he discouraged ethnically separate parishes, circumvented church condemnation of the Knights of Labor, and acted as an interpreter between the Vatican and American Catholicism. In 1911 two U.S. presidents joined in observing the 50th anniversary of his ordination. His writings included *The Faith of Our Fathers* (1876), a simple exposition of beliefs, which became a Catholic best-seller.

Gibbs, J. (Josiah) Willard (1839–1903) mathematical physicist; born in New Haven, Conn. He was the seventh generation of a family of scholars and educators, and the son of Yale divinity professor Josiah Willard Gibbs. After receiving his Ph.D. from Yale (1863), he taught Latin and natural philosophy there for three years. He then studied mathematics and physics in Paris (1866–67), Berlin (1867–88), and Heidelberg (1868–69). Returning to New Haven, he became a professor at Yale (1871–1903). In the 1870s, Gibbs published influential papers on the geometrical analysis of the thermodynamics of fluids and surfaces, which clarified the concept of entropy. His classic memoir, *On the Equilibrium of Heterogeneous Substances* (1876, 1878), integrated chemical, physical, electrical, and electromagnetic phenomena into a cohesive system, and introduced the "phase rule" that formed the basis for modern physical chemistry. He developed his system of vector algebra (1880–84), which, he felt, superseded the older system of quaternions. From 1882 to 1889 he published numerous articles on the electric properties of light. A quiet, dignified person who wrote predominantly from memory, he was respected by students and colleagues, and was internationally recognized for his elegant contributions to mathematics and physical science.

Gibbs, James Ethan Allen (1829–1902) inventor; born in Rockbridge County, Va. (great-grandnephew of Ethan Allen). He worked in the machine-carding and the wool-carding businesses before he experimented with sewing machines. He patented the chain-stitch single-thread sewing machine (1857). In partnership with James Wilcox (1858–60, 1865–90) he concentrated on improving his device. He made gunpowder for the Confederate army (1861–65) and retired to his farm (1890), which was eventually named "Raphine" ("to sew" in Greek).

Gibran, Khalil (1883–1931) poet, painter, novelist; born in Bechari, Lebanon (now Syria). His mother emigrated to the United States in 1894 and settled in Boston. He traveled to Lebanon to study with the Maronite (Christian) clergy (1897–99), then returned to Boston, where he was befriended by Mary Haskell, a wealthy patroness of the arts. After studying art in Paris, he settled in New York City, where he painted, sculpted, and wrote plays and poetry in Arabic and English. His best-known book, *The Prophet* (1923), attracted only modest attention during his lifetime but later became an inspirational classic. Poetic and mystical, his work conveyed a longing to transcend the human condition.

Gibson, Althea (1927–) tennis player; born in Silver, S.C. The first black player to win a major tennis championship, she won the Italian (1956–57), Wimbledon (1957–58), and the U.S. Open (1957–58). After retiring from tennis, she became a professional golfer on the ladies' tour.

Gibson, Charles (1920–85) historian; born in Buffalo, N.Y. A Yale Ph.D., he ended his teaching career at the University of Michigan (1965–85). His groundbreaking ethnohistorical studies of the colonial period greatly broadened the scope of Latin American historical studies. His books include *The Colonial Period in Latin American History* (1958) and *The Aztecs under Spanish Rule* (1964).

Gibson, Charles Dana (1867–1944) cartoonist, illustrator; born in Roxbury, Mass. After studying at the Arts Students League in New York City, he contributed free-lance pen and ink society cartoons to *Life* and *Puck* magazines. He soon developed a bold photographic style that featured handsome men and the ideal American woman – a delicate, tousled-haired beauty that became universally known as "The Gibson Girl." His cartoons were featured in countless advertisements and inspired the fashions and manners of an entire generation.

Gibson, (Joshua) Josh (1911–47) baseball player; born in Buena Vista, Ga. As a catcher for the Pittsburgh Crawfords and Homestead Grays of the 1930s and 1940s black baseball leagues, he was known as "the black Babe Ruth." One of the most powerful homerun hitters in the game's history (he is unofficially credited with almost 800), he was elected to baseball's Hall of Fame in 1972.

Gibson, Paris (1830–1920) Montana pioneer, U.S. senator; born in Brownfield, Maine. He moved to Montana in 1879 and raised the first large flock of sheep there. He planned the city of Great Falls and was deeply connected with the waterpower, coal mining, and railroad development in that town. He was a U.S. Senator (Dem., Mont.; 1901–05).

Gibson, (Robert) Bob (1935–) baseball pitcher; born in Omaha, Nebr. During his 17-year career with the St. Louis Cardinals (1959–75), the right-hander won 251 games and the league Most Valuable Player award in 1968; in that season, his earned-run average (1.12) was the fourth lowest in major league history. A ferocious competitor, he was elected to baseball's Hall of Fame in 1981.

Giddings, J. (James) Louis, Jr. (1909–64) anthropologist; born in Caldwell, Texas. He earned a Ph.D. at the University of Pennsylvania and taught at Brown University (1956–64), where he was director of the Haffenreffer Museum of the American Indian. He pioneered dendrochronology; his many Alaskan excavations led to such works as *Ancient Men of the Arctic* (1967).

Gifford, (Francis Newton) Frank (1930–) football player, sports broadcaster; born in Santa Monica, Calif. The recipient of a full-tuition scholarship, he graduated from the University of Southern California (1952) and became a star running back and pass receiver for the New York Giants (1952–65). Even while an active player, he would do sports broadcasts on radio and television, first on CBS, then ABC. From 1971 on, he became a regular on ABC-TV, doing *Monday Night Football* and *Wide World of Sports* as well as occasional specials. He wrote or coauthored several books on football. The winner of many awards, he was elected to the National Football Foundation Football Hall of Fame in 1975 and he won an Emmy for outstanding sports personality (1977).

Gifford, Sanford (Robinson) (1823–80) painter; born in Greenfield, N.Y. He studied at the National Academy of Design (c. 1845), and was influenced by the work of Thomas Cole. A founder of the American luminism school of painting, he specialized in the effects of light, as seen in his major work, *Kauterskill Falls* (1862).

Gilbert, Cass (1859–1934) architect; born in Zanesville,

Ohio. Trained in St. Paul, Minn., and at the Massachusetts Institute of Technology, he worked with McKim, Mead and White (1880–82) and James Knox Taylor in St. Paul (1884–92). In New York (1900–30) he became known for Americanized beaux arts designs, including the U.S. Custom House (1899–1907) and the Woolworth Building (1908–13). He was president of the American Institute of Architects (1908–09) and the National Academy of Design (1926–33).

Gilbert, G. K. (Grove Karl) (1843–1918) geologist; born in Rochester, N.Y. He served on geological explorations of Ohio and the western U.S.A., became chief geologist for the U.S. Geological Survey (1889–92), then devoted his time to lectures, research, and writing. He formulated many of the laws of geological processes and introduced technical terms to the literature. His writings include a definitive report on the Henry Mountains, Utah (1877), a history of the Niagara River (1895), and his greatest work, a study on the extinct Lake Bonneville of Nevada and Utah (1890).

Gilbert, Henry F. (Franklin Belknap) (1868–1928) composer; born in Somerville, Mass. A student of MacDowell, he absorbed African-American music and was one of the first to use this and other American material in concert works, opera, and ballet.

Gilbert, Walter (1932–) molecular biologist; born in Boston, Mass. He earned degrees in physics at Harvard and mathematics at Cambridge University, England. In his long career at Harvard (1959), he taught successively physics, biophysics, biochemistry, and molecular biology, and was named Carl M. Loeb university professor (1987). He identified the entire sequence of nucleotides in the DNA of a digestive protein produced by the E. coli bacterium (1977); the technique he developed (with Allan Maxam) for rapidly sequencing genes earned him a share of the Nobel Prize in chemistry (1980) and was critical in launching the new field of genetic engineering. In the 1980s he contributed to efforts to identify the basic components of proteins. He founded Biogen, a genetic engineering firm (1978; CEO 1981–84) and was a major force in launching the Human Genome Project in the late 1980s, designed to map all the genes on human chromosomes.

Gilbreth, Frank (Bunker) (1868–1925) engineer, management consultant; born in Fairfield, Maine. Originally a bricklayer's apprentice, he rose to become a successful general contractor in Boston (1895–1911). In collaboration with his wife, Lillian Evelyn Gilbreth (1878–1972), he devised processes for breaking jobs into discrete segments, thus contributing to the foundation of modern time-and-motion studies. He established Frank B. Gilbreth, Inc., consulting engineers (1911), and conducted a summer school of scientific management in Providence, R.I. With his wife, he wrote *A Primer of Scientific Management* (1911) and *Fatigue Study* (1916).

Gilbreth, Lillian (Evelyn b. Moller) (1878–1972) consulting engineer, household efficiency expert; born in Oakland, Calif. She and her husband, Frank Gilbreth, pioneered the application of motion studies in industry (1910–24); they served as consultants to numerous firms in America and abroad, and collaborated on several books and many articles. She wrote four books on her own; she taught at various colleges including Purdue, Bryn Mawr, Rutgers, and Newark College of Engineering; and she served on various governmental committees. She was a pioneer in making the environment easier for the physically handicapped. She also sought to apply business methods to home economics and the management of the home; this aspect of her and her husband's interest was amusingly captured in a best-seller written by two of her 12 children, *Cheaper by the Dozen* (1949).

Gilder, Richard Watson (1844–1909) editor, writer; born in Bordentown, N.J. As editor of what became the *Century Magazine* (1881–1909) he helped make it one of the most distinguished literary magazines of its time; he also was a prolific poet and wrote several studies of Abraham Lincoln.

Gildersleeve, Basil (Lanneau) (1831–1924) classicist; born in Charleston, S.C. A child prodigy who read widely in Latin by the age of six, he received his B.A. from the College of New Jersey (later Princeton) at age 17 and his Ph.D. from the University of Gottingen at 22. Thought of as the greatest American classicist of his day, his *Latin Grammar* (1867), *Pindar: The Olympian and Pythian Odes* (1885), and *Greek Syntax* (1900) were used by generations of American students. He founded the *American Journal of Philology* (1880), was twice president of the American Philological Association (1878 and 1909), and greatly shaped the Johns Hopkins graduate school, where he taught from 1856–1915.

Gill, Irving (John) (1870–1936) architect; born in Tully, N.Y. After training with architects in Syracuse and Chicago (including Dankmar Adler and Louis Sullivan), he worked in San Diego and Los Angeles designing primarily houses, and educational and institutional buildings. He developed an avant-garde cubist style that introduced and refined concrete tilt-slab construction; his unornamented, abstract designs were based on mission and pueblo traditions and fell out of fashion about 1915, after which his output diminished.

Gillars, Mildred (b. Mildred Elizabeth Sisk) (1901–88) Axis propagandist; born in Portland, Maine. She went to Europe in the 1920s, changed her name, and by 1934 was an English-language radio broadcaster in Berlin. During World War II she broadcast Nazi propaganda aimed to demoralize American troops, who nicknamed her "Axis Sally." Convicted of treason, she spent 12 years in jail. She was a teacher in later years.

Gillespie, (John Birks) "Dizzy" (1917–93) jazz musician; born in Cheraw, S.C. After working in the swing bands of Teddy Hill, Cab Calloway, and Earl Hines between 1937–41, he emerged as a leading exponent of bebop and as the most influential trumpeter in the new idiom. In the late 1940s he helped to introduce "Afro-Cuban" jazz to the U.S. From 1945 he alternated between leading small and big bands. In 1956 he led an orchestra on two international tours as cultural missions for the U.S. State Department. He was featured at the White House jazz party hosted by President Carter in 1979, and he received numerous official honors from the U.S. and European governments. His autobiography, *To Be Or Not To Bop*, was published in 1979.

Gillett, Frederick Hunting (1851–1935) U.S. representative/senator; born in Westfield, Mass. A graduate of Amherst College and Harvard University law school, he began practicing law in Springfield, Mass., in 1877. An assistant state attorney general and state senator, he went to the U.S. House of Representatives (Rep., 1893–1925) where he championed the freedman's civil rights and denounced Tammany Hall's election practices. Chairman of the committee on civil service (1900–11), he initiated merit-based

reforms with Civil Service Commissioner Theodore Roosevelt. Appalled by slipshod economic planning while on the Appropriations Committee (1902–18), he lobbied for an independent bureau of the budget, succeeding with the Budget Act of 1921. Elected Speaker of the House (1919–25), he won praise for his impartiality from both Democrats and Republicans, and he reluctantly gave up the position to run for the Senate (1925–35), where he supported the World Court. In 1934 he published *George Frisbie Hoar,* a biography of that senator, but died before completing his own memoirs.

Gillette, King C. (Camp) (1855–1932) inventor, businessman; born in Fond du Lac, Wis. An inveterate "tinkerer," he worked for hardware concerns in Chicago, New York, and Kansas City, and as a traveling salesman. Advised to invent a product for which there would be a continual demand, by 1895 he had made a crude version of a disposable razor blade; by 1901 he founded the Gillette Safety Razor Company in Boston, Mass., to make his razor and blades. In 1904 he sold 90,000 razors and over 12 million blades. Although he remained president of the company until 1931, he retired to Los Angeles in 1913. A utopian, he wrote four books translating his business experience into social theories, culminating with *The People's Corporation* (1924).

Gillette, William (1855–1937) actor, playwright; born in Hartford, Conn. Best known for his authoritative, striking presence in plays that he had himself adapted from other works, he made an extremely successful Sherlock Holmes in 1899, later performing the role in England and frequently reviving it throughout his career. His original plays include two successful Civil War dramas, *Held by the Enemy* (1886) and *Secret Service* (1896).

Gilligan, Carol (1936–) psychologist; born in New York City. She studied English at Swarthmore (B.A. 1958), psychology at Radcliffe (M.A. 1961), and clinical psychology at Harvard (Ph.D. 1964). After working as a lecturer at the University of Chicago (1965–66), she began teaching at Harvard (1967). She is best known for investigations of how women develop their self-identities and values in a society dominated by patriarchal values, as in her publications, *In a Different Voice: Psychological Theory and Women's Development* (1982), and *Meeting at the Crossroads: Women's Psychology and Girls' Development* (with Lyn Mikel Brown, 1992).

Gillin, John P. (Philip) (1907–73) anthropologist; born in Waterloo, Iowa. He founded the anthropology Ph.D. program at the University of North Carolina (1946–59) and the anthropology department at the University of Pittsburgh (1959–72). He directed a pioneering field study of southern American culture (1946), did extensive fieldwork in Central and South America, and contributed to the U.S. government's Latin America policy.

Gillis, James M. (Martin) (1876–1957) Catholic religious editor, broadcaster; born in Boston, Mass. Ordained a Paulist priest in 1901, he taught theology at a seminary, conducted parish missions, and edited *Catholic World* magazine (1922–48). He was widely known for his syndicated religious column and his radio broadcasts on *The Catholic Hour.*

Gilman, Alfred G. (Goodman) (1941–) pharmacologist, educator; born in New Haven, Conn. His interest in science began at age 10 when his father, Dr. Alfred Gilman, took him to his laboratory at Albert Einstein University in New York. He went on to Yale (B.S., 1962) and then took his Ph.D. at Case Western Reserve University (1969). Pursuing his specialty of pharmacology, he did research at the National Institutes of Health (1969–71) before joining the faculty at the University of Virginia (1971–81). In 1981 he went to the University of Texas Southwestern Medical Center. He is the editor of *The Pharmacological Basis of Therapeutics* (1990, 8th edition), a leading textbook on pharmacology originated by his father. In 1994 Gilman shared the Nobel Prize in medicine or physiology with Martin Rodbell for their discovery of G proteins, substances inside all the body's cells that transmit and modulate signals from both within the body and the outside environment. If the G proteins are not in a proper balance, it can affect vision and smell or cause diseases from cholera to cancer.

Gilman, Arthur D. (Delavan) (1821–82) author, architect, planner; born in Newburyport, Mass. His landmark articles and lectures (1843–44) denouncing classical revival styles launched an architectural career in Boston (1843–66) and New York (1868–82), noted for its embrace of contemporary European influences.

Gilman, Charlotte (b. Perkins) (1860–1935) writer, social reformer; born in Hartford, Conn. Despite her ancestry in the well-known Beecher family, she experienced near-poverty after her mother was abandoned by her father, and she was educated irregularly. During a ten-year marriage to Charles Stetson, which ended in divorce (1894), she suffered a mental breakdown, described in thinly veiled fiction in her now classic story, "The Yellow Wall-Paper" (1892). Between 1885–1900 she lived mostly in California or New York City, supporting herself by writing and editing, and by lecturing on various social issues; she also traveled to England where she came to know the British Fabian socialists. In 1898 she published what was and is regarded as her major work, *Women and Economics* (1898), which focused on the need for women to gain economic independence. In 1900 she married George Gilman of New York, and she continued to write, to edit her own magazine, *Forerunner* (1909–16), and to lecture, usually promoting her own rather advanced feminist views. Afflicted with cancer, she committed suicide in 1935.

Gilman, Daniel Coit (1831–1908) geographer, university administrator; born in Norwich, Conn. A graduate of Yale (1852), he returned to help create Yale's Sheffield Scientific School (1856), later becoming professor of physical and political geography there (1863–72). He then became president of the University of California: Berkeley (1872–75). At the recommendation of the presidents of Harvard, Cornell, and Michigan, he was chosen to be the first president of Johns Hopkins University (Baltimore, Md.) (1875–1902). Stressing the importance of graduate schools, he founded Johns Hopkins Medical School (1893), which immediately attracted leading physicians and top-ranked students. After retiring, he helped found the Carnegie Institute in Washington, D.C. (1902–05).

Gilman, Lawrence (1878–1939) music critic; born in Flushing, N.Y. He studied art but then gravitated to music, teaching himself the fundamentals and taking up criticism. He wrote for a number of periodicals, among them *Harper's Weekly* (1901–13), *North American Review* (1915–23), and the *New York Herald Tribune* (1923–39); from 1923 he also wrote program notes for the New York Philharmonic and the Philadelphia Orchestra.

Gilmer, Elizabeth Meriwether (Dorothy Dix, pen name) (1861–1951) journalist, women's rights pioneer; born in Montgomery County, Tenn. She had a difficult youth due to the illness and early death of her mother and the strains of the Civil War. After a bit of formal schooling, she married George Gilmer (1882); their 47-year marriage was most unhappy; often sick, he became incapacitated and died in a mental hospital. She lived apart from him for many of those years and turned to writing fiction and sketches for newspapers. She joined the staff of the *New Orleans Daily Picayune* (1894–1901), beginning a weekly column under the name "Dorothy Dix" in 1895; among the mixture of topics she wrote about were some on women's situations, and women began writing to her. In 1901 she was hired by William Randolph Hearst to report on Carry Nation and that year she went to New York to work for Hearst's *New York Journal* (1901–17). She became nationally known for her reporting on sensational cases while also continuing her columns that attracted letters that she personally answered. During these years she also came to take an increasingly active part in the women's suffrage cause. In 1917 she joined the Wheeler Newspaper Syndicate, returned to New Orleans, and continued writing her nationally syndicated column based on letters from readers and her responses; with an estimated 60 million readers who wrote her 400–500 letters a day, she continued her column until 1949, personally answering much of her mail and also writing seven books. Dismissed by some as a "sob sister," she has come to be recognized for providing an important outlet for ordinary women to air their concerns.

Gilmer, John Adams (1805–68) U.S. representative; born in Guilford County, N.C. Educated in farm schools, he was a lawyer and Whig Party activist, serving in the North Carolina senate (1846–56) and in the U.S. Congress (1857–63), opposing secession until war was inevitable.

Gilmore, Patrick (Sarsfield) (1829–92) bandmaster; born near Dublin, Ireland. Having been taught music and the cornet by his town's regimental bandmaster, he toured with the band to Canada in 1846. Several years later he came to Massachusetts where he founded Gilmore's Band. During the Civil War he headed all the Union army's bands in the Department of Louisiana and it was in New Orleans in 1864 that he presented the first of his monster concerts. He continued to organize these "jubilees" – with thousands of instrumentalists, singers, various bells, and cannons – while touring the U.S.A., Canada, and Europe with his own band. He also composed many band numbers, dance melodies, and popular songs, including the famous "When Johnny Comes Marching Home Again" (1863). He died while conducting his band at the St. Louis Exposition.

Gilpin, Charles Sidney (1878–1930) stage actor; born in Richmond, Va. Introduced as a boy to amateur theatricals, he left school at age 14 to become a vagabond vaudevillian, although he often had to support himself with odd jobs. In 1907 he joined the all-black Pekin Stock Company of Chicago and later acted at theaters in Harlem; for several years he managed the all-black Lafayette stock company in Harlem. His performance of the slave Custis in the Broadway production of John Drinkwater's *Abraham Lincoln* (1919) led to the title role in the first production of O'Neill's

Emperor Jones (1920) – effectively the first starring role by an African-American in mainstream American theater. Unable to cope with the sudden fame and racial prejudice he then confronted, he began to drink and cut off his career.

Gilpin, William (1813–94) territorial governor; born in Brandywine, Pa. He accompanied John C. Frémont's expedition (1843) and engaged in Indian fighting in the Rocky Mountains (1847–48). He wrote *The Central Gold Region* (1860) and as Colorado's first territorial governor (1861–62) he helped save Colorado for the Union.

Gimbel, Isaac (1856–1931) retailer; born in Vincennes, Ind. (father of Bernard Gimbel). His father, Adam Gimbel, was a German immigrant who opened "The Palace of Trade" in Vincennes, Ind., in 1842 and attracted clientele with the promise of "customer satisfaction." Adam moved to Philadelphia in 1865, leaving the store to his eldest son Jacob; Isaac, the second son, began clerking at age 13. All eight of Adam's sons went into the retail business together, opening successful stores, called Gimbel Brothers, in Milwaukee (1889) and Philadelphia (1894). They expanded to New York City (1910), where Isaac became manager. In 1922, persuaded by Isaac's son Bernard (1885–1966), the brothers incorporated as Gimbel Brothers, Inc., with Isaac as president until succeeded by Bernard in 1927. Bernard persuaded Gimbel Brothers to acquire two Saks & Company stores (1922), which kept their name, and Pittsburgh's Kaufmann & Baer (1925). By Isaac's death, the Gimbels owned seven stores, with $123 million in sales and 20,000 employees.

Gimbel, Peter (Robin) (1928–87) explorer, filmmaker; born in New York City. He served in the U.S. Army of Occupation in Japan (1946–47), and graduated from Yale (1951). After a year at one of the family Gimbel's department stores, he joined his identical twin brother, David Alva Gimbel, in the investment firm White, Well & Co. (1952–60). A deep-sea diver since childhood, Peter became fascinated by the *Andrea Doria* that sank in 1956; the photographs he took during an exploration of the ship the day after it sank were published in *Life* magazine (August 6 and 13, 1956). In 1957 and 1958 he became a trustee of the New York Zoological Society and the American Museum of Natural History. In 1959 he also became executive director of Gimbel Brothers' Inc., the family firm. With the sudden death of his brother at age 29, Peter made significant life changes. He quit Wall Street, enrolled in Columbia University to study sciences (1960–62), and devoted himself to the life of an explorer. In 1963, he led an exploration of the uncharted Vilcabamba Range in the Peruvian Andes. He formed the Blue Meridian Company and made the film *Blue Water, White Death* (1971) about the great white shark. His continued fascination with the allegedly "unsinkable" *Andrea Doria* led to repeated dives and the films, *Mystery of the Andrea Doria* (1976) and *Andrea Doria: The Final Chapter* (1984).

Gingrich, (Newton Leroy) Newt (1943–) U.S. representative, teacher, author; born in Harrisburg, Pa. Raised in a peripatetic military family, he received his Ph. D. from Tulane University (1971) and taught European history at West Georgia College. Elected to the U.S. House of Representatives (Rep., Ga.; 1979), he became Speaker of the House in 1995 with the promise of enacting a new conservative agenda. Characterized as cocky and brusque, but also as intelligent and effective, he described himself as a "conservative futurist." *Window of Opportunity: A Blueprint for the Future* (1984), written with his second wife, Marianne Gingrich, and David Drake, a science fiction writer, elucidated his philosophy.

Ginsberg, Allen (1926–) poet; born in Newark, N.J. After studying at Columbia University (B.A. 1948), he held numerous jobs, traveled widely, lived in the Far East (1962–63), but resided mainly in New York City. He was personally associated with Jack Kerouac, William Burroughs, and others in founding the Beat movement in New York and San Francisco (1950s and 1960s); his best known work was published in *Howl and Other Poems* (1956). In 1971 he became a director of the Committee on Poetry Foundation, N.Y., and the Kerouac School of Poetics, Colo. In later years he assumed the mantle of a gentle guru through his many lectures and as a practitioner of Eastern meditation.

Ginsburg, Charles P. (1920–92) electrical engineer, inventor. He worked for a radio station after graduating from San Jose State University in 1948. In the early 1950s, as a researcher for the Ampex Corporation, he led the team that invented the modern videotape recorder, first used by a television network in 1956. He was vice-president for advance development at Ampex from 1975 until his retirement in 1986.

Ginsburg, Ruth Bader (1933–) Supreme Court justice; born in New York City. She studied law at Harvard and earned her J.D. at Columbia Law School (1959). She taught at Rutgers University Law School (1963–72) and Columbia University Law School (1972–80). She was a circuit judge on the U.S. Court of Appeals for Washington, D.C. (1980–93). She led the Women's Rights Project while at Columbia and she won several important cases before the Supreme Court during the 1970s. Nominated and confirmed as a justice of the Supreme Court (1993), she was the second woman (after Sandra Day O'Connor) to sit on the nation's highest bench.

Ginzberg, Louis (1873–1953) rabbi, scholar; born in Kovno, Lithuania. He studied in Lithuania and Germany. After coming to the U.S.A. in 1899, he was named rabbinical literature editor of the *Jewish Encyclopedia* in 1900. From 1903 until his death he was professor of Talmud at the Jewish Theological Seminary of America. A leader in the Conservative movement, he was a much-published scholar, with special interest in the Palestinian Talmud. He also wrote popular books, including *Legends of the Bible* (1956).

Giovanni, (Yolande Cornelia, Jr.) Nikki (1943–) poet, writer; born in Knoxville, Tenn. She studied at Fisk University, Tenn. (1960–61; B.A. 1964–67), the University of Pennsylvania (1967), and Columbia University (1968). Based in Cincinnati, she taught at many institutions, including Mount St. Joseph on the Ohio (1985). An African-American activist, she spoke out on family issues, as in *The Woman and the Men* (1975).

Gipp, George (1895–1920) football star; born in Laurium, Mich. The son of a Congregational minister, he went to Notre Dame on a baseball scholarship and there discovered his great talents in playing football. He died of pneumonia and is said to have been cited in 1928 by Notre Dame coach Knute Rockne when he exhorted a losing team with "Let's win one for the Gipper!" Ronald Reagan starred as Gipp in the 1940 movie, *Knute Rockne: All American*.

Girard, Stephen (1750–1831) merchant, financier, philanthropist; born in Bordeaux, France. He went to sea at age 14 and settled in Philadelphia in 1776. He ran a successful international shipping business, then moved into banking, insurance, and real estate. During the 1793 yellow fever epidemic in Philadelphia, he managed a fever hospital and personally nursed the ill. He started the "Bank of Stephen Girard," which greatly assisted the federal government during the War of 1812 and afterward with loans and stock purchases. He left nearly $7 million to charities, especially for the education of poor, white male orphans; Girard College was opened for this purpose in 1848 (and began to admit African-American youths in 1968).

Girty, Simon (1741–1818) soldier; born near Harrisburg, Pa. Illiterate and brutal, he deserted the Continental army in 1778 to fight with the British and their Indian allies in the Northwest Territory. Known as "the great renegade," Girty had many atrocities charged to him, including the burning at the stake of a captured American officer. He fled to Canada after the war, from where he continued to foment Indian resistance to European settlement in Ohio and Michigan.

Gish, Lillian (b. Lillian de Guiche) (1896–93) film actress; born in Springfield, Ohio. "The First Lady of the Silent Screen" made her stage debut when she was five, and her screen debut in 1912. A discovery of D. W. Griffith, she starred in *The Birth of a Nation* (1915) and went on to play waif-like heroines with indominable spirits. Intelligent and strong-willed, she exerted considerable control over her films and she directed one, *Remodelling Her Husband* (1920), starring her sister, Dorothy Gish. She returned to the stage in 1930, but continued to make occasional films. She received a special Oscar in 1970. She wrote her autobiography, *The Movies, Mr. Griffith and Me* (1969).

Gist, Christopher (?1706–59) frontier explorer, guide, Indian agent; born in Maryland. Nothing much is known for his first decades but by 1750 he had enough reputation to be hired by the Ohio Company to explore and map the Ohio River valley and northeastern Kentucky – the first Englishman to do so. In 1753 he established a settlement near (present-day) Brownsville, Pa. During the French and Indian War, he became a guide to Major George Washington and twice saved his life on the expedition to Fort LeBoeuf (1753–54); he was also with Washington at the surrender of Fort Necessity (1754) and in the disastrous campaign under Braddock (1755). In 1756 he appeared in Tennessee as an Indian agent, but he died within a few years.

Gist, George See SEQUOYAH.

Giuliani, Rudolph W. (1944–) lawyer; born in New York City. He was with the attorney general's office, U.S. Department of Justice (1975–77, 1981–83), then became the U.S. Attorney for the Southern District of New York (Manhattan) (1983–89). After failing in his first bid as the Republican candidate for mayor of New York (1989), he went into private practice, then was elected mayor in 1993.

Glackens, William (James) (1870–1938) painter; born in Philadelphia. After studying in Philadelphia under Robert Henri, he worked in New York as an illustrator for magazines until about 1905 when he devoted himself to painting. A member of The Eight, who emphasized realism and modernism, his own work – such as *Nude with Apple* (1910) – tended toward impressionism.

Gladden, (Solomon) Washington (1836–1918) Protestant religious leader; born in Pottsgrove, Pa. Raised on an uncle's farm in New York state, he graduated from Williams College (1859), served several New England Congregational churches and was religious editor for *The Independent* (1871–75). In

1882 he accepted the pastorship of the First Congregational Church of Columbus, Ohio, where he remained for the rest of his life. An advocate of the "social gospel," he believed enlightened Christians could ameliorate social and economic ills. He was the author of more than 40 books, including an autobiography, *Recollections* (1909).

Gladwin, Harold S. (Sterling) (1883–1976) stockbroker, archaeologist/anthropologist; born in New York City. After making his fortune as a New York City stockbroker (1908–22), he devoted himself to his enthusiasm, New World archaeology, and anthropology. He participated in the excavation of Casa Grande in Arizona (1927), and he and his wife, Winifred Gladwin, directed the restoration of Gila Pueblo (near Globe, Ariz.) as a research institution and museum (1927–50); his synthesis of his work was published as *A History of the Ancient Southwest* (1957). Although he made some serious contributions to his discipline, he became best known for promoting such questionable theories as that of "multitudinous migrations" into the Americas and the related concept of cultural diffusionism: that is, the New World was inhabited by a succession of peoples, including Pygmies from Africa, Australoids from Australia, and Greeks and Middle Easterners stranded on the Persian Gulf by Alexander the Great, all of whom introduced their cultures into the New World. By promoting such views in articles and books, including *Men Out of Asia* (1947), he lost the respect of many professional Americanists.

Glaser, Donald A. (Arthur) (1926–) physicist; born in Cleveland, Ohio. While at the University of Michigan (1949–60), he developed the "bubble chamber" for observing the paths of atomic particles, for which he won the 1960 Nobel Prize in physics. He became a professor of biology and physics at the University of California: Berkeley (1960), where he diversified into investigations of cell growth and molecular genetics.

Glaser, Milton (1929–) graphic designer, illustrator; born in New York City. He studied at Cooper Union, New York City (1948–51), and at the Academy of Fine Arts, Italy (1952–53). Based in New York, he was a founder, with Seymour Chwast and Edward Sorel, and president of Push Pin Studios (1954–74). He was also a founder of *Push Pin Graphic* magazine (1955–74), and was vice-president and design director of the *Village Voice*, New York City (1975–77). In 1974 he became president of his own graphics/design firm, Milton Glaser, Inc., New York City. The recipient of many awards, he is known for his eclectic experiments with graphics, typefaces, and magazine designs.

Glasgow, Ellen (Anderson Gholson) (1873–1945) writer, poet; born in Richmond, Va. She was schooled privately, traveled periodically to Europe, and became progressively deaf beginning in 1889. Based in Richmond, she wrote poetry, essays, and short stories, but her reputation rests on her novels that deal with the social fabric of the South, as in *Barren Ground* (1925) and *The Sheltered Life* (1932).

Glashow, Sheldon L. (Lee) (1932–) physicist; born in New York City. He worked at Copenhagen (1958–60) and several California institutions before joining Harvard (1967). He won the 1979 Nobel Prize in physics (shared with A. Salam and S. Weinberg) for his contributions to theories of electrodynamic forces and to the quantum chromodynamic theory of quarks. He continued to teach and pursue electrodynamic interactions.

Glaspell, Susan (Keating) (1882–1948) playwright, novelist; born in Davenport, Iowa. Starting as a reporter in Des Moines, Iowa, she became known first as an author of short stories for magazines; her novels were never very successful. One of the founders in 1916 of the Provincetown Players with her husband George Cook Cram, she wrote several one-act plays for the troupe. In 1930 she won a Pulitzer Prize for *Alison's House,* a play about a spinster poet based in part on the life of Emily Dickinson. She wrote *The Comic Artist* with her second husband, Norman Matson; after its New York failure in 1933, she retired from the theater.

Glass, Carter (1858–1946) newspaper publisher, U.S. representative/senator; born in Lynchburg, Va. Starting at age 14 as a printer's assistant on his father's newspaper, he became an editor and by 1895 owned three newspapers. An active Democrat, he served in the Virginia senate and then in the U.S. House of Representatives (1902–18); there he sponsored the act that established the Federal Reserve System (1913). He served as secretary of the treasury (1918–20), leaving to fill a vacancy in the U.S. Senate, where he served until his death (1920–46). A fiscal conservative and a defender of states' rights, he often opposed New Deal legislation, but he supported the League of Nations and the U.S. role in World War II.

Glass, Hugh (fl. 1823–33) trapper, frontier legend; birthplace unknown. He first appeared when he joined William Henry Ashley's second Missouri River expedition (1823). Attacked and wounded by a grizzly bear, he was abandoned by his companions, Jim Bridger and a man named Fitzgerald. He recovered and crawled over 100 miles to Fort Kiowa. He caught up with his former companions and lectured them soundly, but after recovering his rifle from Fitzgerald, he declared the account closed. He continued on trapping expeditions and was renowned for his skills and eccentricities. He was killed by Blackfeet Indians.

Glass, Philip (1937–) composer; born in Baltimore, Md. After composition studies at Juilliard, Glass went to Paris in 1964 to study with Nadia Boulanger and later spent time in India studying that culture's traditions. Back in New York in the late 1960s, he organized a group to play his stripped-down, relentlessly repetitive music that was dubbed (along with that of Steve Reich and others) "minimalist." With works including his opera *Einstein on the Beach* (1976), Glass gained a large following, many from the ranks of rock fans.

Glazer, Nathan (1923–) sociologist; born in New York City. A faculty member at Harvard's Graduate School of Education (1968), he wrote widely on contemporary American society, at first from a Zionist and socialist perspective, and after the 1960s as a neoconservative. His books include the classics *The Lonely Crowd* (with David Riesman, 1950) and *Beyond the Melting Pot* (coauthored, 1963, later revised) and a controversial work opposing affirmative action, *Affirmative Discrimination* (1976, later revised).

Gleason, Andrew M. (Mattei) (1921–) mathematician; born in Fresno, Calif. A specialist in topological groups and Banach algebras, he was a Harvard professor of mathematics and natural philosophy (1969). A National Academy of Sciences member, he was the recipient of the Cleveland Prize (1952) and was president of the American Mathematical Society (1962–63).

Glendon, Mary Ann (1938–) legal scholar; born in Pittsfield, Mass. She taught at Boston College (1968–86) and Harvard (1986). She was an expert in comparative law and served as chief editor of the *International Encyclopedia of Comparative Law* (vol. 4).

Glenn, John (Herschel), Jr. (1921–) astronaut, U.S. senator; born in Cambridge, Ohio. A decorated World War II and Korean War fighter pilot, he piloted the first non-stop supersonic flight from Los Angeles to New York (1957). As one of the first group of the National Aeronautics and Space Administration astronauts (1959), he was the first American to orbit the earth in space; it was a three-orbit flight in the Mercury "Friendship 7" capsule (1962). Vice-president and director of Royal Crown Soda (1962–74), he was elected senator from Ohio (1975); although frequently promoted as a presidential candidate, he was never nominated.

Glick, George Washington (1827–1911) governor; born in Fairfield County, Ohio. He was admitted to the bar in Ohio (1850) and he moved to Kansas in 1859. He served eight terms in the Kansas legislature and became the first Democratic governor of Kansas (1883–85). He later served on the state board of agriculture. Kansas placed his statue in the U.S. Capitol.

Glidden, Joseph (Farwell) (1813–1906) inventor; born in Charlestown, N.H. He worked on the family farm and taught school before moving west in 1844 and gradually acquiring large landholdings in Illinois and Texas. Glidden patented an improved type of barbed wire in 1874. He sold his interest in the Barb Fence Company in 1876. By 1880 the factory was turning out 80 million pounds of wire a year, and his invention ultimately fenced in vast areas of the western range.

Glover, Danny (1947–) movie actor; born in San Francisco. After attending San Francisco State, he appeared on the stage. He made his film debut in *Places in the Heart* (1984) but gained his first major success in *The Color Purple* (1985). A versatile actor, he played villains and heroes in all types of movies.

Gluck, Alma (b. Reba Fiersohn) (1884–1938) soprano; born in Bucharest, Rumania. Brought to America as a child, she received her musical training in America and went on to become a favorite at the Metropolitan Opera (1909–12) before pursuing a successful concert and recording career.

Glueck, Eleanor Touroff (1898–1972) social worker, juvenile delinquency reformer; born in New York City. A champion of youthful offenders, she worked as a research assistant in criminology for Harvard Law School (1953–64). She was co-director of a longterm study on the causes, treatment, and prevention of juvenile delinquency (1929–64), served on the delinquency committee at a White House Conference on Children and Youth (1960), and wrote many articles in conjunction with her husband, Sheldon Glueck.

Glueck, Nelson (1900–71) archaeologist, educator; born in Cincinnati, Ohio. An ordained rabbi, he earned a Ph.D. at the University of Jena, Germany, returning to the U.S.A. in 1928 to teach at Hebrew Union College, of which he was later president (1947–71). He discovered 1,500 biblical sites in four decades of work in Transjordan and the Negev, including King Solomon's mines, Khirbet Nahasr, and the possible site of King Solomon's seaport at Ezion-geber.

Glueck, Sheldon (1897–1980) criminologist; born in Warsaw, Poland. Emigrating to America at the age of six, he served as an ordnance sergeant in the American Expeditionary forces

(World War I) and became the first Roscoe Pound professor of law at Harvard (1950). A pioneer in the study of crime and juvenile delinquency, he and his wife, Eleonor Touroff Glueck, wrote scores of articles and books on criminal law and prison practices. He was named professor emeritus at Harvard (1963).

Goddard, George William (1889–1987) aviator; born in Tunbridge Wells, England. He enlisted as a Signal Corps private in the 1930s and went on, in the 1930s and 1940s, to develop pioneering techniques in night, color, high altitude, and stereoscopic aerial photography. He retired in 1953 and became a senior executive at Itek Corp.

Goddard, Robert (Hutchings) (1882–1945) rocket and space pioneer; born in Worcester, Mass. On March 16, 1926 this maverick physicist, once described as a "Yankee inventor-tinkerer," launched the world's first liquid-fuel rocket in Auburn, Mass., and became the father of modern rocketry. Said to have been inspired by H. G. Wells's *War of the Worlds*, he laid the basis for his lifelong work with studies at Worcester Polytechnic Institute and Clark University, where he taught (1914–27) and headed the physics department (1923). Reticent in public, his warm personal nature won him a number of backers throughout his career: the Smithsonian Institution funded his early work in solid-fuel rocketry; at Charles Lindbergh's urging, philanthropist Daniel Guggenheim funded his testing laboratory in Roswell, N.M. (1927–37); but ahead of his time in his theories and experiments, he never developed an operational rocket. As a lone engineer-experimenter unwilling to collaborate with others, he was eventually surpassed by German rocket engineers and military rocket laboratories, but he produced 214 patents crucial to rocket technology.

Goddard, Sarah (b. Updike) (1700–77) printer; born in Cocumscussuc, R.I. Wellborn and well-educated by the standards of the times, when her doctor husband died, she backed her son William Goddard in starting the first printing firm and newspaper in Providence (*The Gazette*) in 1762. In 1765 she took over the enterprise herself; in 1768 she sold the firm and followed her son to Philadelphia where she provided both financial and administrative support to his printing operations.

Godel, Kurt (Friedrich) (1906–78) mathematician/logician; born in Brunn, Austria-Hungary (now Brno, Czechoslovakia). He studied and taught in Vienna; starting in 1933 he began an association with the Institute for Advanced Study at Princeton but he did not immigrate to the U.S.A. until 1940. He stimulated a great deal of significant work in mathematical logic as well as in set theory and general relativity. In 1931 he propounded one of the most important theorems in modern mathematics, Godel's proof: simply stated, in any formal system of mathematics there must be some formally undecidable, or logically uncertain, elements. Personally idiosyncratic and reclusive, he was the first recipient of the International Congress of Mathematicians' Einstein Award (1951) and was elected to the American Academy of Arts and Sciences.

Godey, Louis Antoine (1804–78) publisher; born in New York City. Educated largely in newspaper editorial offices, he was a middle-class tastemaker in fashion, music, and literature as the publisher of *Godey's Lady's Book* (1830–77), the largest circulation magazine of its time. Its illustrations not only influenced women's fashions of the time but

would become documents for social historians and prized items for collectors. A publisher also of children's and music journals, Godey was among the first to copyright magazine contents.

Godkin, Edwin Lawrence (1831–1902) editor; born in County Wicklow, Ireland. Graduating from Queen's College, Belfast, he became a journalist and worked as a war correspondent in the Crimea for the *London Daily News* (1853–55). He emigrated to New York in 1856 and wrote for the *News* and other publications. In 1865 he became editor of *The Nation*, shaping it into a crusading journal of reformist ideas. He sold this small, ailing, high-quality magazine in 1881 to the *New York Evening Post*, of which it became a weekly supplement. Two years later, he became editor of the *Evening Post*, exercising great influence through his powerful, widely quoted editorials; he retired in 1900. A liberal not allied with any party, Godkin earned respect for his broad knowledge, independent-mindedness, and moral purpose, and for his incisive style.

Godowsky, Leopold (1870–1938) pianist; born near Vilna, Lithuania. After establishing an international reputation he settled in the U.S.A. in 1914; he performed widely, composed for the piano, and taught; his scientific ideas of technique became highly influential.

Goebel, William (1856–1900) governor; born in Carbondale, Pa. A lawyer in Covington, Ky., he served as a Democrat in the Kentucky senate (1888–99), supporting regulation of the railroads and election reform, thereby feuding with members of his own party. In 1900, while contesting results of the governor's election, he was shot but was legally declared governor before his death.

Goeppert-Mayer, Maria (1906–72) physicist; born in Kattowitz, Germany (now Katowice, Poland). She married American chemical physicist Joseph Mayer, and accompanied him to Johns Hopkins (1930–39). The couple moved to Columbia University (1939–45), where Goeppert-Mayer separated uranium isotopes for the Manhattan Project. At the University of Chicago (1946–60), she developed her concentric shell theory of the atomic nucleus, with each completed shell having its own "magic number" of protons and neutrons. For this contribution, Goeppert-Mayer and colleague J. Hans D. Jensen shared one-half the 1963 Nobel Prize in physics. She continued her research at the University of California: San Diego (1960–72), even after being partially incapacitated by a stroke.

Goethals, George Washington (1858–1928) engineer, soldier; born in Brooklyn, N.Y. A West Point graduate (1880), he worked with the Corps of Engineers on various harbor, canal, and river projects. In 1907, President Theodore Roosevelt gave him full responsibility for every aspect of constructing the Panama Canal. Facing immense engineering and personal problems – he supervised some 30,000 workers – he completed the job six months ahead of schedule in 1914. He remained as governor of the Canal Zone until 1916, when he retired from the army. He was recalled in 1917 to serve as quartermaster general of the U.S. Army. Retiring again in 1919, he headed an engineering firm until his death from cancer.

Goetz, Cecelia H. (Helen) (c. 1918–   ) lawyer; born in New York City. She served in the Department of Justice (1943–46, 1952–53) and as counsel with the Office Chief of Counsel for War Crimes, Nuremberg, Germany (1946–48) before practicing with three New York law firms (1953–78). She was named judge of the U.S. Bankruptcy Court, Eastern District, N.Y., in 1978.

Goff, Bruce (Alonzo) (1904–82) architect; born in Alton, Kans. Mentored by Frank Lloyd Wright, he was known primarily for his diverse late Prairie School midwestern houses incorporating unusual materials and inventive use of space.

Goffman, Erving (1922–82) sociologist; born in Manville, Alberta, Canada. Educated at the University of Toronto and Chicago, he taught at the University of California: Berkeley (1958–68) and the University of Pennsylvania (1968–82). He was known for his work on patterns of human communication and language, particularly his analyses of routine social interactions such as the ways people walk past one another in public spaces. His books include *Stigma* (1963), *Relations in Public* (1972), and *Forms of Talk* (1981).

Goizueta, Roberto (Crispulo) (1931–) food and beverage company executive; born in Havana, Cuba. A Yale-educated engineer, he joined Coca-Cola as a quality control and research specialist in 1954. As president, chairman, and CEO (1980), he proved an aggressive and successful marketing and corporate strategist. He stunned the country in 1985 by changing Coke's formula, a decision reversed within weeks after a public outcry.

Gold, Ben (1898–1985) labor leader; born in Bessarabia, Russia. Emigrating to the United States in 1910, he worked in the fur industry and joined the radical movement. A Communist, he led a 1926 strike of New York fur workers. He led the fur workers into the Congress of Industrial Organizations (CIO) and was elected president of the International Fur and Leather Workers in 1939. The union was expelled from the CIO in 1950 because of its pro-Communist stance supported by Gold.

Gold, Michael (b. Itzok Isaac Granich) (?1893–1967) writer, editor, journalist, playwright; born in New York City. The son of Romanian- and Hungarian-Jewish immigrants, he left school at age 12 and worked for the Adams Express Company (1905–12). Drawn to radical-Marxist thought, he published articles and short stories in socialist publications and saw three of his one-act plays produced by the Provincetown Players in New York. He went to Mexico to escape the draft during World War I and returned to New York to work as an editor on the *Liberator* (1920) and then founded and edited the *New Masses* (1926–c. 1935). He also contributed columns to the Communist newspaper, the *Daily Worker* (1933–67), and in defending Stalinism against the Trotskyites, he attacked fellow American leftist-liberal writers he felt had betrayed the cause. His own preference was for "proletarian literature," a term he coined, and his best-known novel, *Jews Without Money* (1930), is in that genre.

Gold, Thomas (1920–) astronomer; born in Vienna, Austria. He served in the British Admiralty (1942–46) and proposed the steady state theory of cosmology (with Bondi and Hoyle) before coming to Harvard College in 1956. At Cornell University (1959–81), he directed the Center for Radio Physics and Space Research, studied pulsars, and named the magnetosphere (1959).

Goldberg, Arthur J. (Joseph) (1908–90) public official, diplomat, Supreme Court justice; born in Chicago. He practiced law privately before serving the Office of Strategic Services during World War II. He often represented the interests of organized labor in strike negotiations and litigation; he served as general counsel to the United Steelworkers of America and helped merge the American Federation of Labor and the Congress of Industrial Organizations (AFL-CIO). After serving as a presidential campaign adviser (1960), he was appointed by President John F. Kennedy to be secretary of labor (1961–62). He was nominated by President Kennedy to the U.S. Supreme Court and served from 1962–65. He resigned from the court at the request of President Lyndon B. Johnson in order to replace Adlai Stevenson as the U.S. delegate to the United Nations (1965–68). He ran unsuccessfully for governor of New York (1970) and left New York to teach and practice law in Washington, D.C.

Goldberg, Leo (1918–87) astronomer; born in New York City. A tragic fire left his Polish immigrant family motherless and impoverished; academic promise resulted in his obtaining a scholarship to Harvard. He taught at the University of Michigan (1938–60), Harvard (1960–71), and directed the Kitt Peak National Observatory in Tucson (1971–77). He taught himself Russian to foster communication between Soviet and Western astronomers during the height of the Cold War.

Goldberg, (Reuben Lucius) Rube (1883–1970) cartoonist; born in San Francisco. Originally an engineer, he began his career as a sports cartoonist in San Francisco in 1905. He created the syndicated newspaper comic strips, *Boob McNutt* (1916–33) and *Lala Palooza* in the 1930s. His most whimsical character was Professor Butts, whose complicated inventions to achieve simple ends – using ropes, pulleys, buckets, and small animals – allowed Goldberg to satirize modern technology; he also gave his own name to the language to describe any complicated device that achieves some simple goal. Hired as a political cartoonist by the *New York Sun* in 1938, he won a Pulitzer Prize in 1948 for his cartoon, "Peace Today."

Goldberg, Whoopi (b. Caryn Johnson) (1955–) movie actress, comedian; born in New York City. Raised in a Manhattan housing project, she dropped out of high school and became active in the civil rights movement. In the mid-1970s, she cofounded the San Diego Repertory Theatre. During that time she changed her name in order to protect her privacy and to promote her comic persona. Her one-woman show, *Whoopi Goldberg*, ran on Broadway (1984–85). Her movie credits include *The Color Purple* (1985) and *Ghost* (1990), for which she won an Academy Award.

Goldberger, Joseph (1874–1929) epidemiologist, medical researcher; born in Giralt, Hungary. He came to the United States as a child. After taking his M.D. at New York City's Bellevue Hospital Medical College (1895), he joined the Public Health Service in 1899. He investigated the mechanisms of spread of measles, typhus, typhoid, yellow fever, and other infectious diseases. Most notably, he demonstrated that pellagra, then common in the South, was caused by a vitamin B deficiency.

Goldenweiser, Alexander Alexandrovich (1880–1940) cultural anthropologist; born in Kiev, Russia. The son of a lawyer who brought his family to America in 1900, he graduated from Columbia University in 1902, studied with Franz Boas, and received a Ph.D. in 1910. He helped launch the multivolume *Encyclopedia of the Social Sciences,* and lectured and wrote on race, sex, cultural diffusion, and psychoanalysis, but he never held a full-time academic post. His principal works were *Early Civilization* (1922) and *History, Psychology and Culture* (1933).

Goldhaber, Maurice (1911–) physicist; born in Lemberg, Austria. As a fellow at Cambridge, he discovered the nuclear photodisintegration effect with collaborator James Chadwick (1934). He came to the U.S.A. to join the University of Illinois (1938–50), where he and his wife, Gertrude Scharff-Goldhaber, demonstrated the identity of beta rays with electrons. At Brookhaven National Laboratory, Goldhaber continued to make major contributions to studies of elementary particles.

Goldin, Horace (b. Hyman Goldstein) (1874–1939) magician; born in Vilna, Russia. Emigrating to the U.S.A. as a teenager, he was an illusionist. One of the first to "saw" a woman in half, he switched to a buzz saw when others copied him.

Goldman, Emma ("Red Emma") (1869–1940) anarchist, propagandist; born in Kovno, Lithuania. She moved with her family to St. Petersburg, Russia (1882), where she worked in a glove factory and absorbed the prevailing radical-revolutionary ideas. She emigrated to America (1885), worked in a Rochester, N.Y., garment factory, and was briefly married to a fellow worker. Angered by the execution of those connected with the Haymarket bombing in Chicago (1886), she began to identify with anarchists; she moved to New York City, became a disciple of Johann Most, and became intimately involved with the anarchist Alexander Berkman, whom she also assisted in planning his failed assassination of Henry Frick (1892). She was jailed in New York City (1893) for allegedly inciting the unemployed "to riot" and "take bread." On her release, she took up nursing – studying briefly in Vienna (where she attended lectures by Freud) – and in 1896 began working as a nurse and midwife in American urban slums; but increasingly she was away on lecture tours during which she gained even her enemies' respect for her sharp intelligence. Still, when President McKinley was assassinated in 1901, she was jailed for two weeks without any evidence linking her to the deed. With Berkman out of prison in 1906, he and Goldman founded and edited the anarchist monthly *Mother Earth* (1906–17). Meanwhile she had a new lover, Ben Reitman, who also became her tour manager; her radical speeches continued to draw crowds – and the law; she spent two weeks in jail in 1916 for disseminating birth control information. Then in 1917 she and Berkman were arrested for aiding draft resisters opposed to the U.S. entering the World War; they were sentenced to two years imprisonment; on their release in 1919, they were deported to the Soviet Union. Soon disillusioned with the Bolshevik government, they left and moved about Europe and Canada, finally settling in France; there she finished her autobiography, *Living My Life* (1931), a powerful testament. She was allowed to return to the U.S.A. in 1934, but only for a three-month lecture tour. With Berkman's death in 1936, she gave the last of her remarkable energies to one more cause – antifascists and the foes of Franco in the Spanish Civil War. She died in exile in Canada.

Goldman, Hetty (1881–1972) archaeologist; born in New York City. She earned an A.B. at Bryn Mawr College and her A.M. and Ph.D. at Radcliffe. She turned to fieldwork while in Athens on a fellowship, specializing in prehistoric archaeology of the Greeks and other eastern Mediterranean peoples. She was one of the first female directors of an archaeological excavation (at Halae, Greece, 1911–14) and went on to direct numerous excavations for the Fogg Museum and Bryn Mawr in Greece, Asia Minor, and Yugoslavia at sites including Eutresis, Greece (1924–27) and Colophon (1922, 1925) and Tarsus (1934–39, 1947, 1948), Turkey. She had a reputation as an unusually systematic and accurate fieldworker; published accounts of her digs such as *Excavations at Eutresis in Boeotia* (1931) and *Excavations at Gozlu Kule Tarsus* (3 vols. 1950–63) became classics. She was the first female professor at the Institute for Advanced Study, Princeton (1936–47).

Goldmark, Peter (Carl) (1906–77) electrical engineer, inventor; born in Budapest, Hungary. After studies at the universities of Vienna and Berlin, he immigrated to the U.S.A. in 1933 and went to work in the laboratories of CBS. By 1940 he had developed the first practical color television transmission system. He later built a camera that, carried aboard a lunar orbiting vehicle, transmitted very high definition pictures of the moon's surface back to earth.

Goldovsky, Boris (1908–) pianist, conductor, opera producer; born in Moscow, Russia. German-trained in music, he soloed on piano with the Berlin Philharmonic at the age of 13. In 1930 he came to the U.S.A. to concertize and teach but by the end of the decade he had diverted his talents and energies to producing operas. He ran the opera program at Tanglewood (1942–62) and founded the New England Opera in 1946 and the Goldovsky Opera Institute in 1963, both Boston-based; in 1977 he became head of the opera department at the Curtis Institute. He was well known to a broad public as a commentator for the Metropolitan Opera broadcasts but to several generations of American opera singers he was known for promoting opera in English and for demanding that singers be truly able to act their roles.

Goldsborough, Louis (Malesherbes) (1805–77) naval officer; born in Washington, D.C. He commanded the Atlantic and North Atlantic blockading squadrons during the Civil War. In conjunction with General Burnside's troops, he captured Roanoke Island (1862).

Goldschmidt, Richard B. (Benedict) (1878–1958) zoologist; born in Frankfurt, Germany. After teaching and performing research on Germany, he left due to Nazi pressure on Jewish scientists and emigrated to the U.S.A. in 1936. He became a professor of zoology at the University of California: Berkeley (1936–48), where he remained until his death; he concurrently served as Silliman Lecturer at Yale (1939–40). An internationally renowned scientist and writer, he belonged to twelve countries' professional societies, and made major contributions to studies on worms and fruit flies. His 25 years of research on moths included investigations of their physiology and genetics, degrees of intersexuality, embryology and evolution, and geographic variations. He was a pioneer in population genetics who wrote popular books on science in addition to many scientific books on evolution and heredity in both German and English.

Goldsmith, Grace Arabell (1904–75) physician; born in St. Paul, Minn. She earned an M.D. at Tulane University, where, on the medical school faculty (1936–75), she pioneered nutritional training for medical students. Her research on nutritional deficiency diseases, B-complex vitamins, and vitamin enrichment of foods were important contributions to public health.

Goldstein, Joseph L. (Leonard) (1940–) biochemical geneticist; born in Sumter, S.C. He was a biochemist for the National Heart Institute (1968–70) and a research fellow at the University of Washington (1970–72), before joining the University of Texas (1972). Clinical observations of patients with high cholesterol levels and circulatory impairment stimulated him to study the genetic relationship of high cholesterol and triglyceride levels to heart disease. He invited his close friend and professional colleague, Michael Brown, to Texas; in 1973, the two scientists discovered the cellular receptor molecules that control the blood level of low-density lipoproteins, the cholesterol-transporting substances which are associated with heart disease. For this work, Goldstein and Brown shared the 1985 Nobel Prize in physiology. Goldstein continued to make major advances in protein and lipid biochemistry.

Goldstein, Max Aaron (1870–1941) physician, educator of deaf; born in St. Louis, Mo. He was a St. Louis general practitioner whose technological advances in deaf education included introducing the Viennese method of amplifying sound and inventing the Simplex tube. He founded the Central Institute for the Deaf, St. Louis, (1914), a leading center for teacher training, clinics, and audiology research.

Goldwater, Barry M. (Morris) (1909–) U.S. senator; born in Phoenix, Ariz. Grandson of an immigrant peddler in the Western mining camps, he inherited a prosperous department store business of which he became president in 1937. An active sportsman, he was one of the first white men to navigate the Colorado River through the Grand Canyon. During World War II, he was a pilot in the U.S. Air Force (1941–45). A conservative Republican, he served in the U.S. Senate (Ariz., 1953–65, 1969–87). He was chairman of the Armed Services Committee. He ran for the presidency (1964) but was defeated in a landslide by Lyndon B. Johnson. Although he espoused traditional, Republican values, he often surprised his ideological opponents by his maverick positions; in 1993, he advocated opening the armed forces to homosexuals.

Goldwater, Robert (1907–73) art historian; born in New York City (husband of Louise Bourgeois). He studied at Columbia University, Harvard (Ph.D. 1937), and New York University. He taught at New York University (1934–39), and at Queens College (1939–56). A noted art historian of primitivism and contemporary art, he was the first director of the Museum of Primitive Art, New York City (1957–73).

Goldwater, Sigismund (Schulz) (1873–1942) hospital/public health administrator; born in New York City. His first studies were in sociology, economics, and political science, but he then earned an M.D. from the Bellevue Hospital Medical College (New York City) (1901). Appointed superintendent of Mt. Sinai Hospital (New York City) in 1903, he was one of the first medically trained hospital administrators in the U.S.A. He established Mt. Sinai's social service department in 1906 and introduced other reforms, and later he served as the director (1917–28). As commissioner of hospitals in New York City (1934–40), he completely reorganized and improved the municipal health system. He went on to direct the city's Blue Cross hospital insurance organization.

Goldwyn, Samuel (b. Samuel Goldfish) (1882–1974) film producer; born in Warsaw, Poland. He ran away to London

at age 11, and at age 13 he came to America. He became a glovemaker and salesman, then in 1913 he went into the film business, producing *The Squaw Man* (1914). The founder of Samuel Goldwyn Productions in 1923, this great showman produced such quality films as *Dead End* (1937), *The Best Years of Our Lives* (1946), and *Guys and Dolls* (1955). Famous for his "Goldwynisms" ("include me out"), he won the Irving G. Thalberg Memorial Award in 1946.

Golub, Leon (Albert) (1922–) painter; born in Chicago. He studied at the Chicago Art Institute (1949–50), and became a painter of mythological subjects who rejected the abstract painting of the era. His major work consists of large sculptural figure paintings of nude men fighting, a series he has called *Gigantomachies*.

Gomberg, Moses (1866–1947) organic chemist; born in Elisavetgrad, Russia. He emigrated to Chicago (1884) and was associated with the chemistry department of the University of Michigan (1893–1936). He created the first stable free radical, triphenylmethyl (1900), and carried on studies of organometallic compounds. During World War I, he worked on gases for chemical warfare and on high explosives and smokeless powder.

Gompers, Samuel (1850–1924) labor leader; born in London, England. Born to Dutch-Jewish immigrant parents in London, Gompers left school at age ten to begin work as a cigar maker. He emigrated to New York in 1863, where he joined Local 15 of the Cigarmakers' International Union (CMIU) in 1864. Elected CMIU vice-president in 1886, he was a founder of the American Federation of Labor (AFL), and served as its president (1886–95, 1896–1924). A Marxist in his early days, he turned against the socialists in the AFL, championing a "pure and simple" trade unionism that was hostile to independent labor political action, industrial unionism, and government intervention in the sphere of labor relations. As unions in general and the AFL in particular gained in power and status, he himself became the major figure in the American labor movement and a highly respected figure in American public life. He served as a member of the Advisory Commission to the Council of National Defense (1917–18), and as a member of the American delegation to the Paris Peace Conference in 1919. His important autobiography, *Seventy Years of Life and Labor,* was published in 1925.

Gonzales, (Richard Alonzo) "Pancho" (1928–) tennis player; born in Los Angeles. He was the dominant professional player during the 1950s, when tennis was still largely an amateur sport. In 1969, at age 40, he played in the longest ever match at Wimbledon, a 112-game, 5-hour and 12-minute marathon victory over Charlie Pasarell.

Goode, John (Paul) (1862–1932) cartographer, geographer; born near Stewartville, Minn. In 1903 he helped found the department of geography at the University of Chicago. His work in cartographic representation and "projections" was a great boost to American geography in the first third of the century. He also displayed great knowledge of economic geography.

Goode, (Willie) Wilson (1938–) mayor; born in Seaboard, N.C. The son of a sharecropper, he earned a B.A. from Morgan State College and an M.P.A. from the Wharton School. He worked as a probation officer, a building supervisor, and an insurance claims adjustor. He became the first African-American mayor of Philadelphia (1985–91). A meticulous, sober man, he was much criticized for allowing police to bomb the headquarters of MOVE, an armed radical group. During the last part of his tenure, the city suffered serious financial troubles.

Goodhue, Benjamin (1748–1814) U.S. representative/senator; born in Salem, Mass. A prosperous merchant, he was chosen to represent Massachusetts in the U.S. House of Representatives (Fed., 1789–96) and the U.S. Senate (1796–1800), where he served as chairman of the Committee on Commerce.

Goodhue, Bertram Grosvenor (1869–1924) architect; born in Pomfret, Conn. An eclectic architectural stylist, he became a leading Gothic church architect in partnership with Ralph Adams Cram (1892–1913) and later embraced modernism. He designed additions to West Point (1903–10) and the Nebraska State Capitol (1920–32).

Goodlad, John (Inkster) (1920–) educator; born in North Vancouver, British Columbia, Canada. Goodlad was professor and director of the University of California: Los Angeles Elementary School (1960–85) and dean of the Graduate School of Education (1967–83). In his major study, *A Place Called School* (1984), he criticized public schools' failure to teach analytical thinking.

Goodman, (Benjamin David) Benny (1909–86) jazz musician; born in Chicago. He was raised in a poor immigrant family, received early clarinet lessons at Hull House, and studied privately with Franz Schoepp. He joined the musicians' union and began playing professionally at age 13, and in 1925 he joined Ben Pollack's orchestra, working with it in California, Chicago, and New York until 1929. He played with Red Nichols from 1929 to 1930, and for the next four years he worked as a Broadway and radio-studio musician, and appeared on numerous free-lance jazz recordings, including several under his own leadership. He formed his first regular orchestra in 1934 for Billy Rose's Music Hall, which broadcast weekly from New York on the *Let's Dance* coast-to-coast radio show. In August 1935, near the end of an otherwise uneventful national tour, the band began a residency at the Palomar Ballroom in Los Angeles; this was to prove the turning point in Goodman's career and a cornerstone of the Swing era. Playing before wildly enthusiastic audiences, he achieved national fame, and through constant media attention, was dubbed the "King of Swing". In 1936 the band made its first film appearance, *The Big Broadcast of 1937,* and during that year Goodman introduced his trailblazing, racially-integrated quartet, featuring Teddy Wilson and Lionel Hampton, as an adjunct to his big band. In 1937, his engagement at the Paramount Theatre in New York was phenomenally successful, and in 1938 he played his celebrated Carnegie Hall Jazz Concert with guest artists from Duke Ellington and Count Basie's bands. His big band and small groups remained peak attractions until 1944, when he disbanded and for several years led a series of combos in a bop-oriented style. During the 1940s, he also moved increasingly into the world of classical music, playing concerts with José Iturbi in 1942 and commissioning Bela Bartok to write "Contrasts for clarinet, violin, and piano" in 1947. Throughout the 1950s, 1960s, and 1970s, he led his own highly successful big bands and small groups on regular national and international tours. In 1955, he recorded the soundtrack for the Hollywood motion picture, *The Benny Goodman Story,* which featured Steve Allen in the title role.

In 1962, under the sponsorship of the U.S. State Department, his orchestra became the first American jazz ensemble to tour the Soviet Union. He reduced his touring schedule by the 1980s, but continued to play brilliantly on all-star concert appearances and with a small group of young musicians up to his death.

Goodman, Morris (1925–) physical anthropologist; born in Milwaukee, Wis. A pioneer in molecular anthropology, he was associated with several midwestern medical institutions before joining Wayne State University (1966). His comparative immunological research on primate proteins demonstrated the close genetic similarity of humans to gorillas and chimpanzees. Goodman's globin, enzyme, and DNA nucleotide sequencing studies have advanced and clarified the evolutionary classification of primates and other animals.

Goodman, Nelson (1906–) philosopher; born in Somerville, Mass. After earning a Harvard Ph.D. (1941), he taught at Tufts University (1945–46), the University of Pennsylvania (1946–64), and Brandeis University (1964–77). In 1977 he became an emeritus professor at Harvard. A leading analytic philosopher, he made key contributions to theory of knowledge, psychology, and aesthetics in works that included *The Structure of Appearance* (1951) and *Languages of Art* (1968).

Goodman, Paul (1911–72) author, lecturer, psychotherapist; born in New York City. His prodigious outpouring of poetry, fiction, city planning, social criticism and gestalt therapy consistently articulated a vision of humanistic anarchism that made him the "father figure of the New Left." His best-selling *Growing Up Absurd* (1960) defended dropping out of school, an institution he found repressive of individuality.

Goodnight, Charles (1836–1929) cattleman; born in Macoupin County, Ill. He was a guide and scout in Texas, where he served with the Texas Rangers during the Civil War. He pioneered the movement of cattle ranching into New Mexico (1866) and established the Goodnight and the New Goodnight trails. With John Adair he developed the JA Ranch in Texas (100,000 head of cattle on one million acres) and crossed Angus cattle with buffalo to produce the cattalo. He remained the dominant figure in western Texas until his death.

Goodnow, Frank Johnson (1859–1939) political scientist, educator; born in Brooklyn, New York. An expert in constitutional and administrative law, he served as an adviser to President William Taft (1911–12) and to the Republic of China (1913–14). He taught at Columbia University (1883–1914) but left to serve as president of Johns Hopkins University (1914–29) where he was instrumental in dramatically increasing the endowment, enrollment, and curriculum. He wrote several important books including *Municipal Problems* (1897), *Politics and Administration* (1900), and *Municipal Government* (1909).

Goodrich, Annie W. (Warburton) (1866–1954) nursing educator; born in New Brunswick, N.J. Institutor of the first bachelor's degree in nursing while dean of the Yale University School of Nursing (1919–34), her drive and convictions led to the professionalization of nursing training in America. Known for her brilliance, wit, and vitality, she was a leader in state and federal nursing organizations.

Goodrich, Benjamin F. (Franklin) (1841–88) physician, industrialist; born in Ripley, N.Y. A surgeon during the Civil War, he opened a private practice in Jamestown, N.Y. (1864), which he quit for the real estate business. With his partners, he controlled the rubber company that manufactured Charles Goodyear's products (1867). This venture failed, leading to a second factory purchase in 1868, which also failed. In 1870 Goodrich settled in Akron, Ohio, as Goodrich, Tew & Company, which was forced to reorganize in 1874 as Goodrich & Company. Success came in 1879 with new money (principally from G. W. Crouse) and reorganization as the B. F. Goodrich Company (1880).

Goodrich, Chauncey Allen (1790–1860) lexicographer, scholar, theologian; born in New Haven, Conn. (son-in-law of Noah Webster). As professor of rhetoric and later of theology at Yale College, he wrote several influential works on Greek and Latin grammar. He also prepared an English-language edition of the Bible. He supervised the abridgment of Noah Webster's *American Dictionary of the English Language,* prepared by Joseph E. Worcester in 1829, and served as the chief editor of the revised and enlarged edition of Webster's dictionary (1847), the first in the continuing series published by G. & C. Merriam.

Goodrich, Lloyd (1897–1987) curator, art critic; born in Nutley, N.J. He studied at the Art Students League and the National Academy of Design, and was an editor in New York City (1923–31). He wrote extensively on such artists as Thomas Eakins and Winslow Homer, and was curator and director of the Whitney Museum of Art (1935–71).

Goodrich, Samuel Griswold (Peter Parley, pen name) (1793–1860) publisher, writer; born in Ridgefield, Conn. Beginning as a bookseller and publisher in Hartford, Conn. (1816), he traveled often before settling in Boston (1826), where he edited and published *The Token* (1828–42), a giftbook annual where many of Nathaniel Hawthorne's tales appeared. Adopting the persona of a kindly old man and the pen name of "Peter Parley," he imparted sugarcoated instruction to children in over 100 books – such as *The Tales of Peter Parley About America* (1827) – many probably written by collaborators. He established *Parley's Magazine* (1833). In both England and America his work was often imitated and pirated.

Goodspeed, Edgar Johnson (1871–1962) biblical scholar and educator; born in Quincy, Ill. A distinguished teacher at the University of Chicago (1902–37), he was renowned for his expertise in biblical exegesis and Greek papyrology. His relatively more vernacular *New Testament: An American Translation* (1923) was a milestone.

Goodwin, William Watson (1831–1921) classicist; born in Concord, Mass. He was educated at Harvard (B.A. 1851) and then took his Ph.D. at the University of Gottingen, Germany (1855). He taught at Harvard (1856–1901) and was the first director of the American School of Classical Studies in Athens (1882–83). His publications include *Syntax of Moods and Tenses of Greek Verb* (1878) and *Greek Grammar* (1892), both frequently reprinted and still used today.

Goodyear, Anson Conger (1877–1964) industrialist, art collector; born in Buffalo, N.Y. He studied at Yale (B.A. 1899), joined the family lumber business in Buffalo, became vice-president (1907), and then president (1911). He was president of the Great Southern Lumber Company, Bogalusa, La. (1920–38); served as vice-president of the Buffalo and Susquehanna Railroad (1907–10); and was president of the New Orleans Great Northern Railroad Company (1920–30). He also became chairman of the board of the Gaylord Container Corporation (1937–52), later to merge with the Crown Zellerbach Corporation. He was an avid collector of late-19th- and early-20th-century American and European art, and, after he moved to New York City, he was president of the Museum of Modern Art (1929–39). After his death, his collection was bequeathed to the Buffalo Museum of Fine Arts.

Goodyear, Charles (1800–60) inventor; born in New Haven, Conn. He followed his father into the hardware business but went bankrupt in 1830 and remained in arrears – he went to prison for debt more than once – for the rest of his life. He began experimenting with rubber in 1834, persevering despite poverty and ridicule. By 1844 he had patented a process (vulcanization) to prevent India rubber from melting in heat; he discovered it by accident (1839) when he dropped a chunk of rubber and sulphur mixture onto a hot stove and, although charred, it did not melt. Goodyear foresaw many applications for vulcanized rubber, although never its use for tires. Although he received patents and honors in Europe, he spent any profits on defending his patent rights, and he left more than $200,000 in debts when he died.

Gordis, Robert (1908–92) rabbi, scholar; born in New York City. He graduated from the City College of New York and earned a Ph.D. from Dropsie College (Philadelphia) in 1929. He was rabbi of Temple Beth-El, Rockaway Park, N.Y. (1931–68) and professor of religion at Temple University, Columbia University, and the Jewish Theological Seminary. His many publications include *Conservative Judaism – An American Philosophy* (1945) and *Judaic Ethics for a Lawless World* (1986).

Gordon, Anna Adams (1853–1931) temperance reformer; born in Boston, Mass. An indefatigable crusader for world prohibition and author of numerous inspirational songs and books, Gordon was the chief aide of Woman's Christian Temperance Union (W.C.T.U.) president Frances E. Willard (1888–98), W.C.T.U. president (1914) and world president (1921–25).

Gordon, Caroline (1895–1981) writer, teacher; born in Trenton, Ky. She graduated from Bethany College, W.Va. (B.A. 1916), and married Allen Tate (1924; divorced 1954). She worked as a reporter in Tennessee (1920–24), taught at several institutions, including the University of North Carolina and Columbia, and long lived in Princeton, N.J. She is known for her novels of the American South, as in *Penhally* (1931).

Gordon, Cyrus H. (Herzl) (1908–) orientalist, educator; born in Philadelphia. His varied academic career ended with a professorship of Near Eastern studies at Brandeis University (1956–73) and the Gottesman professorship of Hebrew studies at New York University (1973–89). His scholarly publications on Near Eastern and Semitic studies included many works on Ugarit, but he was more widely known for his controversial theories about the Semitic sources of early Cretan and pre-Columbian North American inscriptions.

Gordon, Dexter (Keith) (1923–89) jazz musician; born in Los Angeles. He was an influential saxophonist and the leader of his own groups from 1945. He won acclaim for his portrayal of a jazz musician in the 1986 film *Round Midnight*.

Gordon, George Angier (1853–1929) Protestant clergyman, author; born in Aberdeenshire, Scotland. An estate overseer's son, he worked several manual trades before emigrating to America in 1871. He graduated from Bangor Theological Seminary, then from Harvard (1881). From 1884 until his death he was pastor of Old South Church, Boston. His *The Christ of Today* (1895) expressed a liberal theological doctrine, and he became an important champion of religious freedom.

Gordon, Robert W. (1941–) legal scholar; born in Boston, Mass. He taught at the State University of New York: Buffalo (1971–77), the University of Wisconsin: Madison (1977–83), and Stanford University (1982). His contributions include work on the history of legal theory and American private and corporate law.

Gordy, Berry, Jr. (1929–) record producer; born in Detroit, Mich. He began writing songs as a teenager and earned a living as a professional boxer and auto worker. In the 1950s he went to New York and sold some songs that became rhythm-and-blues hits for Jackie Wilson. Forming Motown Records in 1959, he created the "Motown sound" with such artists as Smokey Robinson, Marvin Gaye, Diana Ross, and the Jackson Five; his success helped to make African-American music part of the popular music industry. In 1970 he began producing films such as *Lady Sings the Blues* (1972). He sold Motown Records in 1988.

Gore, (Albert Arnold) Al, Jr. (1948–) vice-president, U.S. senator; born in Washington, D.C. His father, Albert Gore, was a Democratic representative and senator from Tennessee. Albert Jr. graduated from Harvard (1969) and served as an army reporter in Vietnam. He served in the House of Representatives (Dem., Tenn.; 1977–85) and the U.S. Senate (Dem., Tenn.; 1985–93). He made an unsuccessful run for the 1988 Democratic presidential nomination; in 1993 he became vice-president under Bill Clinton. Especially noted for his interest in environmental issues, he wrote *Earth in the Balance: Healing the Global Environment* (1992). He also worked to cut back on government bureaucracy.

Gore, Thomas Pryor (1870–1949) U.S. senator; born in Walthall, Miss. Despite his near blindness (he was known as the "Blind Orator") he practiced law. Settling in Oklahoma Territory (1901), he became the most influential politician there, and after leading the territory to statehood, he became one of its first two U.S. senators (Dem., 1907–21). A populist in domestic matters, he opposed U.S. entry into World War I and the League of Nations. He lost the Democratic primary in 1920, but was reelected in 1930. In his final term (1931–37), he opposed much of the New Deal except for legislation supporting farmers.

Gorelik, Mordecai (1899–1990) set designer, director; born in Shchedrin, Russia. Beginning in 1924 with *King Hunger* he designed more than 40 stage and film productions and taught drama at a number of universities.

Goren, Charles (Henry) (1901–91) bridge player, author; born in Philadelphia. Abandoning his law practice for bridge in 1936, he transformed the game by inventing the point-count valuation and Standard American bidding style. Known as "Mr. Bridge," he led master point winners in 1944–62, authored more than a dozen books, and wrote a widely syndicated daily newspaper column.

Gorey, Edward (St. John) (Eduard Blutig, Mrs. Regera Dowdy, Raddory Gewe, Hyacinthe Phypps, Edward Pig, Ogred Weary, among many pen names) (1925–) illustrator, writer, designer; born in Chicago. He graduated from Harvard (1950) and by 1953 was working in New York City as a magazine staff artist. To publish his own distinctive work with its macabre subjects, gothic illustrations, and

black humor, he established his own Fantod Press (1962). As his books garnered a wider public, he was able to divide his time between New York and Cape Cod, Mass. In later years he became a stage designer – as for the play *Dracula* (1977).

Gorgas, Josiah (1818–83) soldier; born in Dauphin County, Pa. While in command of the U.S. arsenal near Mobile, Ala., he married an Alabama girl; meanwhile, he had come to loathe abolitionists, and with the secession he resigned his commission and joined the Confederate army as chief of ordnance. He set up a series of arsenals and organized the production of arms and ammunition so that Confederate forces were amazingly well supplied to the very end of the war. From 1869–78, he taught engineering at the University of the South (Sewanee, Tenn.); elected president of the University of Alabama in 1878, he never served because of poor health.

Gorgas, William Crawford (1854–1920) soldier, sanitary physician; born near Mobile, Ala. (son of Josiah Gorgas). Trained as a doctor, he joined the Army Medical Corps (1880). Having survived an attack of yellow fever, he was assigned to the yellow fever camp in Cuba during the Spanish-American War (1898); appointed chief sanitary officer of Havana, he rid that city and much of the island of the mosquitoes and fever; he then went on to do the same for the Panama Canal Zone (1904–10), despite opposition from many in authority. He was the army's surgeon general during World War I (1914–18). He died in England while en route to Africa to investigate yellow fever there.

Gorky, Arshile (b. Vosdanig Manoog Adoian) (1904–48) painter; born in Khorkom Vari Haiyotz Dzur, Armenia. He emigrated to Rhode Island (1920), and settled in New York City (1924), then in Sherman, Connecticut (1945). He combined the abstract modernism of Europe and a form of organic surrealism. Influenced by Picasso, his most famous work is *The Liver is the Cock's Comb* (1944).

Gorman, R. C. (Rudolph Carl) (1931–) artist; born in Chinle, Ariz. Descended from generations of Navaho craftsmen, holy men, and tribal leaders, he was encouraged by a teacher at a mission school to develop his talent for art. After several years in the U.S. Navy, he attended Arizona State College (now Northern Arizona University), but it was a visit to Mexico in 1958 and then a year at the Mexico City College (now University of the Americas) that fixed his desire to be an artist. After spending several years in San Francisco developing as a painter, he came to Taos, New Mexico; in 1965 he received a one-man exhibition in the Manchester Gallery there, and by 1968 his work was enjoying enough success that he bought the gallery, changed its name to Navajo Gallery, and began to exhibit and sell his own and other artists' work; it would remain for many years as his residence, studio, and gallery, where he was often present to deal personally with the growing numbers of other artists and the public who came by. From the 1970s on, as his reputation spread throughout the U.S.A. and abroad, he moved on from working with oil, acrylic, and pastel to lithographs, ceramics, and occasional sculptures; although he usually drew on southwest Native American themes, he transformed them by his art into more universally significant – and aesthetic – subjects. Reputed to be a genial, accessible man, known to be interested in food and cooking, and someone at home in the worlds of both his ancestors and international museums and academies, he is arguably the first Native American artist to be internationally recognized as simply a major American artist.

Gorrie, John (1803–55) physician, inventor; born in Charleston, S.C. He graduated from the College of Physicians and Surgeons in New York City (1833) and took up residence in Apalachiola, Fla. Around 1840, he conceived the idea of cooling the air in sick rooms and hospitals; in 1851 he received the first patent for mechanical refrigeration in the U.S.A. Unable to raise money to manufacture his new machinery, he suffered a nervous collapse and was unable to resume his work. Florida placed his statue in the U.S. Capitol.

Gorton, Samuel (c. 1592–1677) colonist; born in Gorton, England. He came to Boston in 1637 and encountered resistance to his heretical ideas about church doctrine. He was imprisoned and banished several times before he sought redress in England. He returned (1648) with a letter from the Earl of Warwick ordering Massachusetts to leave him in peace. He moved to Shawomet, R.I., and renamed it Warwick.

Gosnold, Bartholomew (?1572–1607) navigator, colonizer; born in England. Looking for a western passage to Asia, he led an expedition in the *Concord* which went to Cape Cod, Martha's Vineyard, and Elizabeth's Isle, all of which he named (1602). He was vice-admiral of the original Virginia Company fleet (1606–07) and died of malarial fever in Jamestown.

Gossard, Arthur C. (Charles) (1935–) physicist; born in Ottawa, Ill. He was a member of American Telephone & Telegraph Co. Bell Laboratories (1960–87) before joining the University of California: Santa Barbara (1987). He made major contributions to solid state physics, ferromagnetism, and studies of quantum structures and crystal lattices.

Gotbaum, Victor H. (1921–) labor leader; born in New York City. He became involved in union activities while working as a teenager, and by age 19 was working as a pressman in a printing shop owned by an uncle. He was drafted into the U.S. Army and served in World War II and afterwards attended Brooklyn College (B.A. 1948). He then took his M.A. at the School of International Affairs at Columbia University (1950). He briefly taught government at Brooklyn College, then became a foreign affairs officer with the State Department for a few years before working for the U.S. Department of Agriculture. In 1955 he became assistant education director of the Amalgamated Meat Cutters in Chicago, the first of several union jobs that took him to several cities. He returned to New York City to organize the hospital workers. By 1965 he had become head of District Council 37 of the American Federation of State, County and Municipal Employees, which he built into the largest municipal employees union in the U.S.A. while gaining a reputation as both a forceful yet responsible advocate for his union's members. He retired from that position in 1986 and went on to teach, research, and consult on labor-management policies and related social issues at the City University of New York. In 1993 he was selected by Mayor David Dinkins to serve on New York City's Board of Education. Gotbaum's wife, Betsy Brearley, was commissioner of parks and recreation under Dinkins.

Gottheil, Richard James Horatio (1862–1936) scholar; born in Manchester, England. He came to the U.S.A. in 1873 when his father Gustav Gottheil became rabbi of a New York temple. He was professor of rabbinical literature and Semitic languages at Columbia University from 1892 until his death. In 1896 he became chief of the Oriental Division of the New York Public Library. He was founder of the Federation of American Zionists.

Gottlieb, Adolph (1903–74) painter; born in New York City. He studied at the Art Students League with Robert Henri (1919–21) and John Sloan (1923–24) and was a co-founder of the New York City based avant-garde group, The Ten (1935–40). By 1941 he was painting compartmentalized canvases containing symbolic animal and plant forms, called pictographs, as seen in *Dream* (1948). His later work favored cosmic bursts of color, as in *Chrome* (1965).

Gottschalk, Alfred (1930–) rabbi, educator; born in Oberwesel, Germany. He came to the U.S.A. in 1939 and was ordained at Hebrew Union College in Los Angeles in 1957, where he then was dean (1959–71). In 1971 he became president of the Hebrew Union College-Jewish Institute of Religion. He belonged to a number of Jewish, academic, and civic organizations including the Zionist Organization of America and the American Civil Liberties Union.

Gottschalk, Louis Moreau (1829–69) composer; born in New Orleans, La. A keyboard prodigy, he was sent at age 13 to study in Paris, where his playing and his compositions were admired by Chopin and Berlioz and became the rage of Europe. He was among the first Americans to feature nationalistic elements in his music, such as the piano piece *Bamboula* (1845), based on a New Orleans slave dance. After sensational success in Europe, Gottschalk returned to the U.S.A. in 1853, to be wildly applauded for his playing and his nationalistic pieces such as *Le Banjo* (1855). After tours in the Americas and many hastily-written piano pieces (usually brilliant and facile, often over-sentimental), in 1865 he fled an amatory indiscretion in the U.S.A. and spent the rest of his career in South America. Exhausted by his incessant exertions, he died of yellow fever in Rio de Janeiro.

Goudy, Frederic William (1865–1947) type designer, printer; born in Bloomington, Ill. After learning the printing trade in small shops and working as an accounting clerk in a Chicago bookstore, Goudy devoted himself to typography. His first venture, Camelot Press, soon failed; a second, Village Press, was suspended after a 1908 fire, but revived after World War I and a second fire in 1939. Goudy designed many popular typefaces, including one that bears his name. His books include *A Half Century of Type Design and Typography* (1946).

Gould, Benjamin Apthorp (1824–96) astronomer; born in Boston, Mass. Son of the principal of the Boston Latin School, he graduated from Harvard and studied in Germany. He founded the *Astronomical Journal* (1849) and worked with the U.S. Coast Survey (1852–67). His major interest was in the stars of the southern hemisphere and to this end he helped found the National Observatory in Cordoba, Argentina (1865). Serving as its director (1870–85), he headed a staff that catalogued thousands of stars. On returning to the U.S.A., he spent his final years measuring the star clusters he had photographed there. His *Uranometry of the Southern Heavens* complemented star studies of the northern hemisphere.

Gould, Chester (1900–85) cartoonist; born in Pawnee, Okla. He created the newspaper comic strip, *Fillum Fables,* in 1924 for Hearst's Chicago *American,* and in 1931 he created for syndication a strip featuring a square-jawed police detective named *Dick Tracy.* The strip encouraged citizen involvement in crime prevention and a strong adherence to the law. In 1990 the strip was adapted to a full-length film starring Warren Beatty as Tracy.

Gould, Gordon (1920–) physicist, inventor, manufacturer; born in New York City. After taking his B.S. from Union College (N.Y.) (1941), he did graduate work in physics at Yale, leaving to work on the atomic bomb for the Manhattan Project during World War II (1943–45). In the postwar years he worked for various private engineering firms while teaching at different institutions – City College of New York (1947–54), Columbia University (1954–57), Brooklyn Polytechnic Institute (1967–74). While working at Columbia with Charles Townes and others, he contributed to the development of the laser; Gould would claim greater credit for the laser than others have been willing to grant him, but he was named inventor of the year (1978) by the Patent Office Society for his laser amplifier, and he does hold patents on many of the laser devices used for industrial and medical applications. In 1974 he founded Optelecom Inc., which specializes in optical communications; he retired from that firm in 1985.

Gould, James L. (1945–) animal behaviorist; born in Tulsa, Okla. He joined the Princeton faculty (1975) and became a full professor of biology there (1983). In 1974 he demonstrated that bees use a "waggling dance" to show other bees the location of food. An authority in animal communication, learning, and orientation behavior, he extended his research to include learning behavior in human infants and the development of human language.

Gould, (Jason) Jay (1836–92) financier; born in Roxbury, N.Y. A surveyor by training, he wrote *History of Delaware County, and Border Wars of New York* (1856). He became a tanner and leather dealer in New York (1857–60) and began speculating in small railways on the stock market. He, along with associates James Fisk and Daniel Drew, fought and beat Cornelius Vanderbilt for control of the Erie Railroad (1867–68). Having used bribery to gain control, Gould and his partners did not hesitate to loot the railroad's treasury by stock manipulation. His attempt to corner the gold market caused the Black Friday panic (September 24, 1869). Ejected from his Erie Railroad post in 1872, he gained control of several western railroads and extracted a $10 million profit by threatening the Union Pacific. He also owned the *New York World* (1879–83) and most of New York City's elevated railroads, and controlled Western Union Telegraph Company. The epitome of the "robber baron," he died "unlamented" but worth over $100 million.

Gould, Morton (1913–) composer, pianist, conductor; born in New York City. In the 1930s and 1940s Gould worked as pianist and conductor of popular and light-classical music at Radio City Music Hall and National Broadcasting Company radio, among other jobs, meanwhile writing his nationalistic, often jazz-influenced works, including the *American Symphonette* series and the well-known ballet *Fall River Legend* (1948). He guest-conducted many orchestras, specializing in American music.

Gould, Stephen Jay (1941–) paleontologist, author; born in New York City. Influenced by a visit at age five to the Museum of American History, he became interested in

biology and evolution. He took his B.A. from Antioch College (1963) and his Ph.D. from Columbia University, doing his dissertation on the fossil land snails of Bermuda. He joined the Harvard faculty in 1967 as a professor of geology; he would spend his entire career there, becoming full professor (1973) as well as curator of invertebrate paleontology at Harvard's Museum of Comparative Zoology. The world's leading authority on the land snails of the West Indies, he is also known for espousing a modification of the traditional Darwinian theory of evolution, what he called "punctuated equilibria"; namely, that new species occasionally appear more quickly than the slow, steady, gradual process of Darwinian natural selection accounts for. Although he wrote many articles and a couple of books for his fellow specialists, including *Ontogeny and Phylogeny* (1977), he is best known for his regular column, "This View of Life," (since 1974) in *Natural History* magazine, essays on aspects of biology that are understandable – and pleasurable – to a general public. These are periodically collected in such volumes as *Ever Since Darwin* (1977), *The Panda's Thumb* (1980), and *The Flamingo's Smile* (1985). He also wrote a book, *The Mismeasure of Man* (1981), attacking the kind of biological determinism that uses false science to categorize people by "intelligence" testing. Known for his breadth of interests – from Bach to baseball – he also revealed in the late 1980s that he was suffering from a particularly virulent form of cancer.

Gould, William B. (Benjamin) IV (1939–) legal scholar; born in Boston, Mass. Before his position at Stanford University (1972) he taught at Wayne State University (1968–71) and served as counsel to the United Automobile Workers (1961–62) and the National Labor Relations Board (1963–65). He is best known for his knowledge of labor law and arbitration, comparative labor law, and employment discrimination.

Grabar, Oleg (1929–) art historian; born in Strasbourg, France. He emigrated to America (1948) and studied at Harvard (B.A. 1950), the University of Paris (1950), and Princeton University (Ph.D. 1955). He taught at the University of Michigan (1954–69) and at Harvard (1969), and is known for his critical works on Islamic art and archaeology.

Grace, Virginia (Randolph) (1901–94) archaeologist; born in Plainfield, N.J. Her life work on stamped amphora handles evolved from her Ph.D. thesis (Bryn Mawr, 1934) on the same topic. She catalogued more than 150,000 stamped amphora handles from throughout the Greek world, providing an invaluable chronology that was useful in archaeological dating and tracing ancient trade routes.

Grace, William Russell (1832–1904) international businessman, capitalist; born in Queenstown, Ireland. Prevented by his father from joining the Royal Navy, he ran away to sea and then to Peru where he and his brother, Michael Grace eventually formed Grace Brothers & Company, a trading company. His health forced him to leave Peru in 1860, and after traveling around, he settled in New York City in 1865 and set up W. R. Grace & Company. He conducted a vastly successful trade with Peru and after 1890 he profited from concessions received for funding Peru's national debt. By 1895, the William R. Grace & Company had expanded throughout Latin America and he had moved into mining, mills, international banking, and trading; he also started two steamship companies. Although known as "the pirate of

Peru," he served two terms as mayor of New York City (1880–88).

Grady, Henry Woodfin (1850–89) journalist, orator; born in Athens, Ga. As editor and co-owner of the *Atlanta Constitution* (1880–89), he helped raise morale in the postbellum South through positive proposals for redevelopment; his philosophy was embodied in his classic speech on "The New South" (first given in 1886).

Graffman, Gary (1928–) pianist; born in New York City. He began studying at the Curtis Institute at age eight and two years later made his New York debut. His ensuing international career, mainly playing the Romantics, was cut short by a hand ailment in 1979. He went on to teach at Curtis.

Grafton, Sue (1940–) writer; born in Louisville, Ky. She studied at the University of Louisville (B.A. 1961). Based in Santa Barbara, Calif., she was married three times, and worked as a screenwriter while writing successful detective novels. Her popular work features Kinsey Millhone, a no-nonsense private detective, as seen in her alphabetical series, *"A" Is for Alibi* (1982), and *"B" Is for Burglar* (1985).

Graham, Bill (b. Wolfgang Grajonca) (1931–93) rock music promoter/manager; born in Berlin, Germany. His Russian-Jewish parents fled the Nazis and he arrived in the U.S.A. in 1941, becoming a citizen in 1953. He served with the U.S. Army in Korea, then drove a taxi to pay for his business studies. In 1965 he began as the manager of the San Francisco Mime Troupe and moved on to present rock bands in concerts in his own venues, first a San Francisco club hall renamed the Fillmore, then the Carousel Ballroom in San Francisco renamed (1967) the Fillmore West. A mixture of hard-driving entrepreneur and idealistic counter-culturist, by 1968 he was so successful with his concerts that he opened the Fillmore East in a former movie house in New York City. In 1971 he closed his theaters and shifted to managing various groups and stars and promoting large arena concerts and tours, many of them featuring the biggest names in popular music including the Band and the Rolling Stones. Throughout the 1980s he continued to produce various concerts including a big 4th of July 1987 rock concert in Moscow.

Graham, Evarts Ambrose (1883–1957) surgeon; born in Chicago. After taking his M.D. from Rush Medical College (Chicago) (1907), he spent most of his career as chairman of the department of surgery at Washington University (St. Louis) (1919–51). An expert thoracic surgeon, he was the first to successfully remove a lung in fighting cancer (1933) and he developed the technique of cholecystography. Insisting on high standards in the medical profession and with no tolerance for mediocrity, he took a stand in private practice against unethical medical practices such as fee splitting. He was instrumental in founding the American Board of Surgeons (1937) and he was active as a medical editor and writer.

Graham, Katharine (b. Meyer) (1917–) publisher; born in New York City. After the suicide of her husband, Philip Graham (1963), she became president of a communications empire (formerly owned by her father, Eugene Meyer) that included the *Washington Post* and *Newsweek* magazine, among other interests. As *Post* publisher (1969–79) she helped broaden the paper's circulation and reputation.

Graham, Martha (1894–1991) modern dancer, choreographer; born in Allegheny (now Pittsburgh), Pa. Prevented by her strict father from going to dance school when a girl, after he died she enrolled in the Denishawn School of Dancing in Los Angeles in 1916. She then toured with their company, making her professional debut in 1920. From 1923 to 1925 she appeared with the Greenwich Village Follies, a dance group in New York City, and taught at the Eastman School of the Theatre in Rochester, N.Y. For some years she had been working out her own ideas about choreography and she gave her first solo recital in 1926, in New York City. From then on, working at first with pick-up groups, and by the 1930s with a fairly regular company, she began to develop a radically new approach to dance: spare and angular in certain movements yet using exotic costumes far removed from classical ballet; improvised through tapping inner feelings and psychology, yet controlled down to the last facial expression and finger movement. The music for many of the early pieces was composed by Louis Horst, her longtime collaborator (1926–48); later she would commission new works from major composers such as Aaron Copland and William Schuman, just as she would commission sets from artists such as Isamu Noguchi and Alexander Calder. In the 1930s she choreographed several works drawing on Mexican Indian themes, such as *Primitive Canticles;* she then turned to works inspired by the lives of historical women, such as Joan of Arc (*Seraphic Dialogue*) and Emily Dickinson (*Letter to the World*); from 1946 on she did a number of works derived from Greek mythology – most powerfully, the evening-long *Clytemnestra* (1958). By the 1950s she was internationally recognized as the leading American choreographer of interpretive dancing, yet she always considered herself a dancer first and usually cast herself as the central figure in her works until her final performance in 1969. She continued as a teacher and choreographer almost to her death. Demanding and autocratic, she nevertheless inspired a devoted following, among both her students and public; she was the recipient of continual financial grants and personal honors. Many of the most prominent dancers and choreographers of the 20th century got their start in her company, including her first husband, Erick Hawkins.

Graham, Otto (Everett, Jr.) (1921–) football player; born in Waukegan, Ill. A tailback at Northwestern, he switched to T-quarterback as a professional. In a career that lasted only ten years, he was named all-league nine times. He led the Cleveland Browns to four straight All-America Football Conference championships (1946–49) and three National Football League titles (1950, 1954–55). A smooth ball-handler and determined leader, he was his league's top passer six times.

Graham, Patricia Albjerg (1935–) educator; born in Lafayette, Ind. She directed the National Institute of Education (1977–79) and joined the faculty of Harvard (1979), where she became dean of the Graduate School of Education (1982). An authority on women's education and educational history, she wrote *Community and Class in American Education* (1974).

Graham, Sylvester (1794–1851) author, reformer; born in West Suffield, Conn. He was a temperance lecturer whose programs came to include advocacy of vegetarianism, fresh foods, cold showers, lighter clothing, and exercise; from his recommended coarsely ground whole wheat flour, known as "graham flour," he developed the graham cracker. His popularity in the 1830s attracted faddists whose extreme pronouncements unfairly drew ridicule on Graham's own commonsensical regimen. Much of his agenda for healthier living would be endorsed by the late 20th century.

Graham, (William Franklin, Jr.) Billy (1918–) Protestant evangelist; born near Charlotte, N.C. A farmer's son, he converted to fundamentalism at a revival meeting at age 16. He studied at Bob Jones University and the Florida Bible Institute (now Trinity College) and was ordained a Southern Baptist minister in 1940. He graduated from Wheaton College, Ill., with an anthropology degree in 1943 and was pastor of a Baptist church in Illinois before beginning his career as a traveling evangelist. In his first high-profile crusade, in Los Angeles in 1949, he preached to 350,000 people. A vigorous, magnetic preacher, he toured the world with his crusades; he claimed – through his preaching and subsidiary broadcasting, films, and books – to have converted millions of people to his version of Christianity. His Billy Graham Evangelistic Association raised millions of dollars, and was considered a model of financial accountability. He published several accounts of his religious views, including *Peace with God* (1952) and *World Aflame* (1965). From President Eisenhower on, it became almost obligatory for the U.S. president to be seen at least once in the company of Graham.

Grainger, Percy (Aldridge) (b. George Percy Grainger) (1882–1961) composer, pianist; born in Melbourne, Australia. A child prodigy on piano, he studied in Australia and Germany; after 1900 he was a famed traveling virtuoso based in London. Making a sensational American debut in 1915 with his "signature" work, the piano concerto by his friend Edvard Grieg, he remained in the U.S.A. for most of the rest of his life. Most of his compositions are marked by his interest in traditional folk music, yet he had an experimental streak and was among the first to compose for electronic instruments.

Gramatky, Hardie (1907–79) author, illustrator; born in Dallas, Texas. He worked as a logger, bank teller and deckhand, studied at the Chouinard Art School, Los Angeles (1928–30), and became head animator for Walt Disney productions, Hollywood (1930–36). He moved to New York City, worked for *Fortune* magazine (1937–39), and settled in Westport, Conn. He is remembered for his tugboat series for children, notably *Little Toot* (1939).

Grange, (Harold Edward) "Red" (1903–91) football player; born in Forksville, Pa. His many spectacular runs made him a three-time All-America halfback at the University of Illinois (1923–25) and the most famous football player of his time. Against the University of Michigan in 1924, he scored four touchdowns in the first 12 minutes. He turned professional with the Chicago Bears in 1925 after his last college game and drew record crowds to the National Football League.

Grant, Cary (b. Archibald Alexander Leach) (1904–86) film actor; born in Bristol, England. Running away from home at age 13, he became a song-and-dance man, first arriving in New York in 1920 with an acrobatic troupe. Returning to London in 1923, he began appearing in musical comedies where he was discovered by stage producer Arthur Hammerstein, who brought him back to New York. He made his movie debut in *This Is the Night* (1932) and went on to become one of the most popular actors of his time, a suave, debonair, seemingly ageless performer in comedies, romances, and adventure films. Offscreen he had five wives and one daughter and was alleged at various times to have been everything from a cheapskate to a user of LSD. Retiring in 1966, he received a special Academy Award in 1970.

Grant, (Hiram) Ulysses S. (1822–85) eighteenth U.S. president; born in Point Pleasant, Ohio. The son of a tanner, he gained a place at West Point in 1839, from which he graduated with little distinction, except as a horseman. (It was at West Point that he was accidentally assigned the middle initial "S"; it is assumed it referred to his mother's maiden name, Simpson.) He served with considerable bravery in the Mexican War of 1846–48, but afterward languished in remote posts on the West Coast, taking to drink and finally resigning in 1854. He then spent six frustrating years in Missouri, farming and in other pursuits. When the Civil War began, he found a commission as a colonel and was promoted to general in August 1861. Soon he had proved himself the ablest of Northern leaders, winning a string of brilliant victories from 1862–63 that culminated in the capture of Vicksburg, Miss. After he had broken an apparently hopeless siege of Union forces in Chattanooga in late 1863, he was appointed by Lincoln to overall command of Union armies. In that post he created for the first time a single plan for the Union war effort; the main elements were Sherman's campaigns in Georgia and Grant's offensive against Lee in Virginia. After a year of brutal fighting, Lee surrendered to Grant in April 1865 and the Confederacy collapsed. The Republicans seized this war hero as their presidential candidate in 1868; he won a narrow victory in the popular vote. As president, he was out of his element; a cabinet of cronies and political contributors proved largely incompetent and corrupt, and Grant had no overall vision for the country. He managed to gain reelection in 1872 despite the Credit Mobilier and Whiskey Ring scandals and other sensations that would leave his administration – though not his personal integrity – tarnished. Grant left office to make a triumphant world tour, but did not succeed in his hopes for regaining the presidency. Having been swindled by a friend, he took to writing his memoirs to regain his fortune, finishing them a few days before his death.

Grant, Julia (b. Boggs Dent) (1826–1902) First Lady; born in St. Louis, Mo. Sister of a West Point classmate of Ulysses S. Grant, they were married in 1848. She helped Grant cope with his bouts of depression and hard drinking. The public admired her style in the White House. She later wrote an autobiography, not published until 1975.

Grant, Peter R. (Raymond) (1936–) ornithologist, zoologist; born in London, England. He first came to the U.S.A. to be a zoology fellow at Yale (1964–65), then taught at McGill University in Canada (1965–77), where he began his studies on finches in 1973. He joined the University of Michigan (1977–85) before relocating to Princeton (1985), where he continued his ornithological investigations. He won the 1983 Brewster Award for his research on Darwin's finches of the Galapagos Islands. In addition to writing two books on finches with his wife, Rosemary Grant, he made major contributions to studies of interspecific competition in rodents, and the evolutionary importance of animal interactions relative to ecology, behavior, systematics, and genetics.

Grant, W. T. (William Thomas) (1876–1972) retailer; born in Stevensville, Pa. The family moved to Massachusetts where he worked several jobs including a brief stint as a prize fight promoter. In 1906 while clerking in a store he noticed how quickly the 25-cent items sold. He opened a large store in Lynn, Mass., with 21 departments, all selling items for 25 cents or less. W. T. Grant's, with Grant controlling all the buying, was an immediate success. In 1908 he expanded to Connecticut, and in 1913 to New York City. By 1917 he had 30 stores and topped prices at $1. He went public in 1928. By 1940 he had stores in 44 states and no limit on prices. He resigned as chairman of the board in 1966; three years after his death, his company made retail history by filing for bankruptcy. In 1936 he established the Grant Foundation for children.

Granz, Norman (1918–) jazz producer; born in Los Angeles. Beginning in 1944, he operated the touring concert package "Jazz at the Philharmonic," and such record labels as Clef, Verve, and Pablo.

Grasso, Ella (b. Tambussi) (1919–89) U.S. representative, governor; born in Windsor Locks, Conn. A Mt. Holyoke graduate, she served in the state house of representatives (Dem., 1953–55), becoming Connecticut's secretary of state (1958–70). In the U.S. House of Representatives (1971–75) she sponsored the Emergency Employment Act of 1971. The first woman elected governor of any state in her own right (1975–80) she was fiscally hampered from pursuing progressive legislation.

Gratz, Barnard (1738–1801) merchant; born in Langensdorf, Upper Silesia (now Poland) (brother of Michael Gratz). He came to Philadelphia in 1754. Working with his brother Michael, he helped open the American West to trade and supported the American Revolution. In 1782 he laid the cornerstone of the first synagogue in Philadelphia.

Gratz, Rebecca (1781–1869) philanthropist; born in Philadelphia. The daughter of Michael Gratz, who prospered in trade, she helped found the Philadelphia Orphan Society in 1815. In 1838 she founded the first Hebrew Sunday School Society and was its president until 1864. She is said to have been the inspiration for Rebecca in Sir Walter Scott's *Ivanhoe*.

Graupner, Johann (Christian Gottlieb) (1767–1836) musician, composer; born near Hanover, Germany. An oboist who had played under Haydn, he came to the U.S.A. in 1795. In Boston he opened a music store, published, taught, played, and composed. He founded the pioneering Boston Philharmonic Society in 1810 and, in 1815, the still-extant Handel and Haydn Society. He has been called "the father of American orchestral music."

Graveley, Samuel Lee, Jr. (1922–) navy officer; born in Richmond, Va. He had begun college when he left to enlist in the U.S. Naval Reserve (1942); upon completing midshipman school at Columbia University (1944), he became the first African-American to be commissioned as an ensign in World War II. After service in the war, he was released from active duty and completed college at Virginia Union University (B.A. 1948). He was recalled to active duty in August 1949 and saw sea and shore duty during the Korean War. He transferred to the regular navy in 1955 and in 1961 became the first African-American ever to command a U.S. Navy ship. Various promotions followed and in 1971 he became the first African-American to attain the rank of rear admiral. His specialty was naval communications, and after service as commander of the 3rd Fleet (1976–78), he became director of the Defense Communications Agency (1978–80). When

he retired as a highly decorated vice-admiral in 1980, he was the first African-American to attain three stars in the navy. He became a consultant to defense contractors and served on various corporate boards of directors.

Graves, Michael (1934–) architect; born in Indianapolis, Ind. After training at the University of Cincinnati and at Harvard, he joined the architecture faculty at Princeton (1962) and established an independent practice (1964). His designs for museums, residences, and housing and urban planning projects have put him at the forefront of postmodernist architecture. His work frequently incorporated color as architectural metaphor; his works include the Fargo-Moorehead Cultural Center Bridge (1977), which joins Fargo, N.D. and Moorehead, Minn.

Graves, Morris (Cole) (1910–) painter; born in Fox Valley, Ore. He traveled in Japan and China (1928–30), and was influenced by Eastern philosophy, as seen in his gouache, *Bird in the Spirit* (c. 1941). Long based in California, he evolved an abstract technique using delicate and hypnotic images in his famous work, *Flight of Plover* (1955).

Graves, Nancy (Stevenson) (1940–) sculptor, painter; born in Pittsfield, Mass. She studied at Yale School of Art (B.F.A. 1961; M.F.A. 1964), worked in Paris (1964–65) and Florence (1965–66), then settled in New York City (1966). She is known for her Bactrian camel series of the late 1960s, her biomorphic and moon films (1971–74), camouflage and aerial photo paintings, and also for her fanciful sculptures.

Gray, Alfred M. (1928–) marine officer; born in Point Pleasant Beach, N.J. A combat veteran of Korea and Vietnam and a thoughtful marine who contributed articles on defense issues to professional journals, he enlisted in 1950 and rose through the ranks to a series of senior commands.

Gray, Asa (1810–88) botanist; born in Sauquoit, N.Y. He received his M.D. in 1831, but relinquished medicine after a year's practice to pursue his interest in botany. He taught high school science in Utica, N.Y. (1832–35), making botanical expeditions to southern New York and New Jersey during his summers. He moved to New York City to join his friend and fellow botanist John Torrey (1836), published his first textbook, *Elements of Botany* (1836), and collaborated with Torrey to publish the first two (and only) volumes of their projected multivolume *Flora of North America* (1838, 1843). He accepted a position to be professor of botany at the new University of Michigan; when this did not materialize due to the institution's financial difficulties, he relocated to Harvard (1842–73). There he created Harvard's department of botany and brought it to international prominence, while educating many students who became the next generation's leaders in plant science. And as the author of over 350 books, monographs, and papers, he both popularized and professionalized the study of botany in America. By replacing the classical rigid Linnaean system with a more natural classification of plants by type specimen, Gray became the leading taxonomic botanist in the U.S.A. Charles Darwin so admired Gray's work that he shared his theory of natural selection in a letter to Gray (1857) before the theory was published; while Gray had some reservations about the theory, he became an ardent Darwinist, championing natural selection and refuting ideas that Darwinism could not coexist with Protestant Christianity. After retirement, Gray continued to take charge of his specimen collection in Harvard's Gray Herbarium. Among his many writings is the classical treatise, *Manual of the Botany of the Northern United States* (1848, still known as "Gray's Manual.")

Gray, Bowman (Jr.) (1907–69) cigarette executive; born in Winston-Salem, N.C. In 1930 he joined R. J. Reynolds Tobacco (of which his father was president), and served variously as president, chairman, and CEO (1959–69). A prominent apologist for the tobacco industry, he was responsible for developing the Winston and Salem brands and diversifying the company into the food industry.

Gray, Elisha (1835–1901) inventor, manufacturer; born in Barnesville, Ohio. He worked as a blacksmith, a boat-builder, and a carpenter before starting a small concern to make telegraphic equipment of his own invention. His little business eventually became the Western Electric Co., and Gray's some 70 patents included one for a multiplex telegraph. He claimed to have invented the telephone in the 1870s, but lost the patent rights to Alexander Graham Bell in a case eventually decided in the U.S. Supreme Court.

Gray, Glen (b. Glen Gray Knoblaugh) ("Spike") (1906–63) bandleader; born in Roanoke, Ill. He played saxophone in the Orange Blossom Band in Toronto in 1928. In New York City in 1929 the band became the Casa Loma Orchestra with Gray as leader. The band's singer Kenny Sargent was a top romantic vocalist of the 1930s and 1940s and guitarist-arranger Gene Gifford's arrangements helped usher in the swing era. In 1956 Gray initiated a series of all-star albums, recreating the sounds of big bands.

Gray, Hanna (b. Holborn) (1930–) educator; born in Heidelberg, Germany. Emigrating from Germany in 1934, she received her doctorate in Renaissance history from Harvard (1957). A professor at Northwestern (1960–72), she became dean of arts and sciences there (1972–74). The first woman provost at Yale (1974–77), she became the first woman to head a major research university when she served as president of the University of Chicago (1978–93). During her administration she both cut costs and increased undergraduate and minority enrollments. She returned to teaching at the University of Chicago (1993).

Gray, Harold (Lincoln) (1894–1968) cartoonist; born in Kankakee, Ill. After serving as an assistant on Sidney Smith's newspaper comic strip, *The Gumps,* from 1921 to 1924, he created his own strip in 1924, *Little Orphan Annie.* For the next 45 years, he worked ceaselessly on his widely syndicated strip. *Little Orphan Annie* was adapted to a hit Broadway musical *Annie* (1977), and a film based on the musical was released in 1982.

Gray, Harry (Jack) (1919–) industrialist; born in Milledgeville Crossroads, Ga. After an early career in sales, he worked for Litton Industries (1956–71). As president, CEO, and chairman (1971–86) he transformed United Aircraft into United Technologies, a conglomerate of companies poised to take advantage of massive research and development expenditures, particularly in microelectronics. He was later chairman and CEO of American Medical Holdings, Dallas, Texas.

Gray, Horace (1828–1902) Supreme Court justice; born in Boston, Mass. He was active in Massachusetts politics as an organizer of the Free-Soil and then Republican parties. He served on the Massachusetts Supreme Court (1864–81) and was named by President Chester Arthur to the U.S. Supreme Court (1882–1902).

Gray, John Chipman (1839–1915) lawyer, professor; born in Brighton, Mass. Judge advocate major for the Union army in the Civil War, afterwards he joined John C. Ropes in a successful Boston law practice (still an active law firm, Ropes & Gray) and simultaneously taught at Harvard Law School (1869–1913). He helped found and edit the *American Law Review* (1866–70). His works on real property and legal theory are authoritative.

Gray, Robert (1755–1806) navigator, explorer; born in Tiverton, R.I. A naval veteran of the American Revolution and then a merchant seaman, he became a fur trader in Boston. He commanded the *Columbia* for most of its 42,000-mile voyage (1787–90), the first American ship to circumnavigate the globe. After a refitting in Boston, he took the *Columbia* around to the Northwest coast near Vancouver Island; in the course of his explorations, he discovered a large river (1792) that he named the Columbia (after his ship); later his discoveries in the region became the basis of the U.S. claim to the Oregon territories. He died at sea on a voyage to Charleston, N.C.

Gray, William H. (Herbert), III (1941–) U.S. representative, Baptist minister, organization executive; born in Baton Rouge, La. Son and grandson of clergymen, he took degrees at Drew Seminary (1966) and Princeton Theological Seminary (1970), then did postgraduate work at several universities. Between 1964 and 1972 he also served as pastor of the Union Baptist Church in Montclair, N.J.; in 1972 he became senior minister at Bright Hope Baptist Church in Philadelphia, where his father and grandfather had previously been ministers. Deciding that he could do more good for African-Americans in the political arena, he represented the largely-black second district of Philadelphia in the U.S. House of Representatives (Dem., 1979–91); he chaired the House Budget Committee (1982–88) and became the House majority whip (1989–91). Thought to have prospect of even higher political office, he surprised everyone when in 1991 he left Congress to become president of the United Negro College Fund.

Grayson, David See BAKER, RAY STANNARD.

Greatbatch, Wilson (1919–) electrical engineer, inventor; born in Buffalo, N.Y. A World War II veteran, he earned a degree in electrical engineering from Cornell University in 1950 and went on to invent the first implantable cardiac pacemaker. He subsequently developed advanced pacemakers and pacemaker power sources. His Greatbatch Enterprises manufactures the majority of the world's pacemaker batteries.

Greeley, Andrew M. (Moran) (1928–) Catholic priest, sociologist; born in Oak Park, Ill. Ordained in 1954, he earned a sociology doctorate from the University of Chicago while doing parish work (1962); he then joined the university's National Opinion Research Center. His studies convinced him that the Catholic hierarchy was out of touch with the attitudes and needs of priests and laity. Besides sociological studies and writings on moral and religious topics, he turned out salty popular novels, increasing his reputation as a maverick within the church.

Greeley, Horace (1811–72) journalist, politician; born in Amherst, N.H. After working as a job-printer and typesetter in New York, he started a literary and news journal and then edited two weekly Whig publications. He founded the *New York Tribune* in 1841 and, aided by a fine staff, built it into a highly regarded, prosperous paper, but also a mouthpiece for his broadly liberal views, often expressed in signed editorials. Greeley served briefly in the U.S. House (1848–49), but later repeatedly failed to win election to Congress. An abolitionist and supporter of the Free Soil movement, he became a prominent Republican but failed to support Lincoln for a second term in 1864 and bucked Northern public opinion by signing a bail bond for the imprisoned Jefferson Davis in 1867. The indefatigable Greeley traveled widely and often made speeches at lyceums and local gatherings; he was a familiar figure known for his shambling appearance, absentminded manner, and blend of seeming naivete and homespun wisdom. His words of advice, "Go West, young man," became famous. In 1872 he was nominated for president by Republican liberals and endorsed by the Democratic Party, but in a bitter campaign he was badly defeated by the regular Republican candidate, Ulysses S. Grant. He also lost effective control of the *Tribune*. Devastated as well by his wife's death, he died soon afterward in an unbalanced state of mind.

Greely, Adolphus Washington (1844–1935) soldier, explorer; born in Newburyport, Mass. He served as a volunteer in the Civil War and in the regular army (1865–1908). He led an expedition to Smith Sound in the Arctic (1881–84) to set up a meteorological station; only 6 men out of 25 survived this so-called *Proteus* expedition, and although originally blamed for the disaster, Greely was later recognized as having prevented a worse one. He directed the U.S. Weather Service (1887–91) and was the U.S. Army's chief signal officer (1887–1906).

Green, Al (b. Albert Greene) (1946–) soul singer, songwriter; born in Forrest City, Ark. He sang in a gospel quartet with his brothers when he was nine, and at age 16 he formed the Soul Mates. In 1969 he began writing and recording for Hi Records. His hit "Tired of Being Alone" (1971) made him widely popular and was soon followed by several other hits. Returning to his gospel roots, in the late-1970s he became a church pastor and thereafter recorded and performed only religious music.

Green, Arthur (1941–) rabbi, educator; born in Paterson, N.J. He graduated from Brandeis University and earned a Ph.D. there in 1975. He taught religious studies at the University of Pennsylvania (1973–84) and was named dean of the Reconstructionist Rabbinical College in 1984.

Green, Constance (McLaughlin) (1897–1975) historian; born in Ann Arbor, Mich. Her *Holyoke, Massachusetts: A Case History of the Industrial Revolution in America* (1939), based on her Yale Ph.D. dissertation, established her as a pioneer in urban history. *Washington: Village and Capital, 1800–1878* (1962) received the Pulitzer Prize in history (1963). She served as a military historian in Washington (1948–54) and on several civic and institutional boards.

Green (Henrietta Howland) Hetty (b. Robinson) (1834–1916) financier, eccentric; born in New Bedford, Mass. She attended a Quaker school and inherited approximately $10 million from her father and aunt. She married Edward Green, a silk trader; they had two children but the couple kept their finances entirely separate. Independent of her husband, she became a noted operator on the New York Stock Exchange and invested heavily in real estate. Although the press exaggerated her miserliness – she was dubbed "the witch of Wall Street" – there was no denying her shrewdness and eccentricities: she lived out her later

years in cheap lodgings in Hoboken, N.J., then died, the richest woman in America, leaving an estate valued over $100 million.

Green, James Stephen (1817–70) U.S. representative/senator; born in Rectortown, Va. A lawyer, he served in the U.S. House of Representatives (Dem., Mo.; 1847–51), and was chargé d'affaires for Colombia (1853–54). In the Senate (1857–61), he sponsored the statehood of Kansas.

Green, (John W.) Johnny (1908–89) composer, arranger, bandleader, pianist; born in New York City. "Hooked" on music from the time he saw a band concert at age three, he began studying piano at age five; by 13 he knew the basics of composition and orchestration. He enrolled at Harvard at age 15, and while there, commenced his career as an orchestra leader and composer; his "Coquette" (1927), words by Gus Kahn, was a hit even before he took his B.A. (1928). He quit a job in his uncle's brokerage firm in 1928 and dedicated himself to music. At first he worked as a music arranger for the movies, conducted orchestras, and accompanied singers. From the 1930s on he collaborated with such lyricists as E. Y. Harburg and Edward Heyman on many standards including "Body and Soul" (1930). He continued to conduct orchestras on tours and on radio and he was with Metro-Goldwyn-Mayer (MGM) (1942–58), first as a composer-conductor-arranger, later as music director; he was in charge of several successful MGM film musicals, winning Oscars for *Easter Parade* (1948) and *An American in Paris* (1951). A serious musician, he also composed and conducted orchestral music for the concert stage and films, conducted many symphony orchestras, and was lecturer and artist-in-residence at Harvard in 1979 and 1981.

Green, Julien (Hartridge) (1900–) writer; born in Paris, France. Son of Americans living in France, he spent his entire youth in France except for three years at the University of Virginia (1919–22); later he visited the United States for extended periods. He grew up speaking English at home but French in all other situations; he wrote all but two of his works in French, even those set in America, such as his drama, *South* (1953) and the Civil-War trilogy that began with *The Distant Lands* (1989), as well as his multi-volume diaries. Most of his works – such as *Adrienne Mesurat* (1927) and *Moira* (1950) – are somber psychological studies of individuals set in grim households marked by thwarted passions, madness, and death, and are regarded as covertly expressing the tension caused by his Catholicism and homosexuality. In 1972 he became the first American elected to the Academie Française.

Green, Paul (Eliot) (1894–1981) playwright; born near Lillington, N.C. After interrupting his studies at the University of North Carolina – where he was a student of Frederick Koch – for service in World War I, he began to write plays about Southern rural people, often dealing with the problems of African-American as well as white poor folk. He won a Pulitzer for *In Abraham's Bosom* (1926), which ends in a lynching. His antiwar play, *Johnny Johnson* (1936), had music by Kurt Weill. He made a dramatization of Richard Wright's *Native Son* (1941) in collaboration with the author. Meanwhile, he had effectively invented what he called a "symphonic form of drama," which used music, dance, mime, lighting, costumes, and any other theatrical elements to capture some episode or theme in American history. His first such work, *The Lost Colony* (1937), about the Lost

Colony of Roanoke Island, N.C., would remain his best known; he would write a number of these historical pageants, usually produced outdoors only at the relevant site, but in frequent performances. In addition to his plays, he wrote novels, essays, and film scripts while teaching at the University of North Carolina (1923–44) and serving as president of the American Folk Festival (1934–45).

Green, Samuel (1615–c. 1701) printer; born in England. Emigrating to Massachusetts around 1633, he was a bookseller in Boston and in 1649 became manager of the Cambridge press. The only colonial printer active at the time, Green is known to have been responsible for about 275 imprints, including Indian-language Bibles, several editions of the Bay Psalm Book, and official works printed for the colony.

Green, Theodore (Francis) (1867–1966) U.S. senator, governor; born in Providence, R.I. A lawyer by training, he went on to work in the financial sector (1912–27). His initial bids to become governor and a U.S. representative failed, but he eventually became governor of Rhode Island (Dem., 1933–37). He went on to a long career in the U.S. Senate (1937–61) and made his major mark with the Senate Foreign Relations Committee (1938–59; chairman 1957–59). By the end he was the oldest man ever to serve in the U.S. Senate.

Green, William (1873–1952) labor leader; born in Coshocton, Ohio. A coal miner from age 16, he rose in the union ranks and served in the Ohio senate (1911–15). He was secretary-treasurer of the United Mine Workers of America (1913–24) and then succeeded Samuel Gompers as president of the American Federation of Labor (1924–52). He helped to shape the National Industrial Recovery Act (1933) and the National Labor Relations Act (1935). An opponent of industrial unionism, he forced out the unions that then formed the Congress of Industrial Organization (CIO); he would struggle with the CIO to the end of his life. He was the epitome of the respectable, responsible labor leader who chose to restrain the more radical approach to management and labor relations. He attended a conference in London (1949) that formed the International Confederation of Free Trade Unions to promote non-Communist labor unions in Europe.

Greenaway, Emerson (1906–90) librarian; born in Springfield, Mass. He worked at several libraries before becoming the director of the Philadelphia Free Public Library in 1951.

Greenberg, Blu (1936–) author, volunteer; born in Seattle, Wash. She earned bachelor's degrees from Brooklyn College and Yeshiva University, as well as an M.A. in clinical psychology and an M.S. in Jewish history. Active with a number of Jewish educational and activist groups, her writings include *How to Run a Traditional Jewish Household* (1983). She won the 1981 B'nai B'rith Literary Award.

Greenberg, (Henry Benjamin) Hank (1911–86) baseball player; born in New York City. During his 13-year career as a first baseman for the Detroit Tigers and Pittsburgh Pirates (1930–47), he hit 331 homeruns and twice won the league Most Valuable Player award (1935, 1940). In 1938 his 58 homeruns nearly eclipsed Babe Ruth's single season record of 60. As one of the first major leaguers to enlist in the military during World War II, Greenberg lost almost four full seasons of playing time (1941–45). Upon his retirement, he served as general manager of the Cleveland Indians (1948–

57), and vice-president of the Chicago White Sox (1959–63). He was elected to baseball's Hall of Fame in 1956.

Greenberg, Irving (1933–) rabbi, educator; born in New York City. A Harvard graduate, he earned a Ph.D. there in 1960. He was the rabbi of the Riverdale Jewish Center (New York) (1965–72). He taught history and Jewish studies at Brandeis University, Yeshiva University, and at the City University of New York (1972–79). In 1979 he became president of CLAL (the National Jewish Center for Learning and Leadership) in New York.

Greenberg, Jack (1924–) lawyer, educator; born in New York City. As assistant counsel, then director-counsel of the National Association for the Advancement of Colored People Legal Defense and Education Fund (1949–84), he argued many important civil rights cases before the Supreme Court. He taught at Columbia University's law school (1970–84) and served as vice-dean before becoming dean of Columbia College (1989). His books include *Judicial Process and Social Change* (1976).

Greenberg, Joseph H. (Harold) (1915–) anthropologist, linguist; born in New York City. He directed the West African Languages Survey (1959–66) and taught at Stanford University (1962–85). He used "multilateral comparison" in his groundbreaking and sometimes controversial work on the classification and typology of Amerindian and African languages. His books include the now-standard *Languages of Africa* (1963), *Anthropological Linguistics* (1967), and *Languages in the Americas* (1987).

Greenberg, Noah (1919–66) conductor, musicologist; born in New York City. After private musical studies in the merchant marine (1944–49), he conducted choruses in New York and in 1952 founded the New York Pro Musica Antiqua, one of the pioneering early music ensembles in the U.S.A. Presenting original instrument versions of medieval and Renaissance music to worldwide acclaim, Greenberg was best known for his rediscovery and performance of *The Play of Daniel* (1958).

Greenblatt, Stephen (1943–) literary historian; born in Newton, Mass. After taking both his B.A. and Ph.D. at Yale – with two years on a Fulbright scholarship at Cambridge University, England – he joined the faculty of the University of California: Berkeley (1969). He soon emerged as the most brilliant proponent of a new school of literary historians-critics that uses an interdisciplinary approach to studying texts; this approach came to be known as the "new historicism" because of its emphasis on interpreting literary texts by placing them in often complex historical contexts; he also saw the study of texts as yielding insights into the conflicts that concern current society. Among his most highly regarded works is *Shakespearean Negotiations* (1988). In 1983 he was also one of the founders of *Representations*, a journal that advances the "new historicist" approach to cultural criticism.

Greene, Charles Sumner (1868–1957) **and Henry Mather Greene** (1870–1954) architects; brothers born in Brighton, Ohio. They attended the manual training program at Washington University, St. Louis, and then studied at the Massachusetts Institute of Technology. In partnership in Pasadena and Los Angeles (1893–1922), they drew on influences ranging from Japanese art to mission style and became the foremost American proponents of the Arts and Crafts movement, collaborating with artisans on a series of custom wood-construction California bungalows that integrated architectural, interior, and landscape design and dominated Pasadena architecture in their day.

Greene, Henry Mather See under GREENE, CHARLES SUMNER.

Greene, John Holden (1777–1850) builder-architect; born in Warwick, R.I. He changed the face of Providence, R.I., by designing and building 50 buildings, chiefly residential, in the Federal, Georgian, and Greek Revival styles (1806–30).

Greene, Leonard Michael (1918–) inventor; born in New York City. His airplane stall warning device, developed for the Grumman Aircraft Company during World War II, has been called as important a lifesaving device as the parachute. He invented and manufactured other flight safety instruments. In 1974 he founded the Institute for Socioeconomic Studies in White Plains, N.Y. He published *Free Enterprise without Poverty* in 1981.

Greene, Nathanael (1742–86) soldier; born in Warwick, R.I. Raised a Quaker, he was expelled by the Society of Friends for his preoccupation with military matters. His militia experience, however, served his country well at the outbreak of the American Revolution; as a brigadier general, he fought at Trenton, Brandywine, Germantown, and Monmouth. Assigned to command Continental forces in South Carolina in October 1780, Greene fought a series of battles that forced the depleted British to withdraw into their fortifications at Yorktown, Va. After the war, he retired to an estate near Savannah, Ga.

Greenhow, Rose O'Neal (?–1864) Confederate spy; born in Washington, D.C. The widow of a prominent physician, Robert Greenhow, she passed information on Union battle strategy to Confederate generals. She was tried for treason (1862) and exiled. She went to England and amassed gold for the Confederate cause. She died in a shipwreck off North Carolina.

Greenleaf, Simon (1783–1853) lawyer, professor; born in Newburyport, Mass. He read and practiced law in Maine beginning in 1806. When Maine became a state, he was the reporter to its supreme judicial court (1820–32). He then became a professor of law at Harvard (1833–48). Always deliberate and thorough, as seen in his widely hailed three-volume *Treatise on the Law of Evidence* (1842–53), he is regarded, along with Joseph Story, as one who contributed the most to shaping Harvard Law School.

Greenough, Horatio (805–52) sculptor; born in Boston, Mass. Drawn to painting and sculpture from his boyhood, he was encouraged by the painter, Washington Allston, before graduating from Harvard (1825). He went off to study sculpture in Rome, the first American to do so, but malaria forced him home (1827) where he worked on portrait busts. In 1828 he went to Florence, Italy, where he maintained a studio until 1851 and took on many commissions from prominent Americans. (James Fenimore Cooper was a major patron.) He became known for his heroic and idealized sculptures, culminating in the ancient-Roman style statue of George Washington (1832–40), originally in the Capitol rotunda in Washington, D.C., but now in the Smithsonian Institution. In 1851 he returned to the U.S.A., settling in Newport, R.I., writing *Aesthetics in Washington* (1851) about his artistic principles.

Greenspan, Alan (1926–) economist, government official; born in New York City. His firm, Townsend-Greenspan (1953–87), provided economic forecasts to corporations. He chaired the National Commission on Social Security Reform (1981–83), saving that system from bankruptcy. Chairman of the Federal Reserve Board (1987), he fought inflation with a tight money policy, keeping the federal discount rate high.

Greenstein, Jesse Leonard (1909–) astrophysicist; born in New York City. A research fellow at the University of Chicago's Yerkes Observatory (1937–39), he also taught there and worked at the McDonald Observatory (1939–48). He moved to the California Institute of Technology where he taught while observing at the Hale Observatory from 1948–80. He wrote about the nature of interstellar matter.

Greenway, John Campbell (1872–1926) mining engineer; born in Huntsville, Ala. He graduated from Yale (1895) and served in the Spanish-American War with the Rough Riders (1898) and was a brigadier general during World War I. He was a mining superintendent in Minnesota (1905–10). He moved to Arizona (1910) and managed a mining company, a lead company, and a railroad. Arizona placed his statue in the U.S. Capitol.

Greenwood, Arthur Herbert (1880–1963) U.S. representative; born in Plainville, Ind. A lawyer and prosecuting attorney (1916–18), he served in the U.S. House of Representatives (Dem., Ind.; 1923–39) becoming majority whip in 1937. Rejected by the voters, he went back to work as a lawyer, banker, and farmer.

Gregg, John Robert (1867–1948) educator, publisher; born in County Monaghan, Ireland. Developing a system of shorthand, he taught it widely in England; emigrating to the U.S.A., in 1893, he founded a chain of schools to teach his system and a publishing company to produce manuals for students.

Gregg, Josiah (1806–50) trader, author; born in Overton County, Tenn. He made frequent journeys along the Santa Fe Trail (1831–41) and wrote a frontier classic, *Commerce of the Prairies* (1844). He served in the Mexican War and died of exposure after crossing the Coast Range of California.

Gregory, Cynthia (1946–) ballet dancer; born in Alhambra, Calif. She studied with the San Francisco Ballet and graduated into the company at age 19. In 1965 she joined the American Ballet Theatre, where she performed leading roles until her retirement from the company in 1991. She continued for some years to choreograph and teach ballet.

Gregory, Herbert (Ernest) (1869–1952) geologist, geographer; born in Middleville, Mich. He was responsible for building geography into the Yale University Geology Department (1898–1915). From 1919 until 1936 he was director of the Bishop Museum, Honolulu, Hawaii. He was highly regarded as a hydrologist and for his knowledge of the American West.

Gregory, Horace (Victor) (1898–1982) poet, writer; born in Milwaukee, Wis. (husband of Marya Zaturenska). He studied at the University of Wisconsin (B.A. 1923), became a free-lance writer in London and New York (1923–34), and taught at Sarah Lawrence College (1934–60). In addition to his own elegant poems, he is known for his translations of Catullus and Ovid and his critical studies of poets, writers, and painters.

Gregory, (Richard Claxton) Dick (1932–) comedian, civil rights activist, nutritionist; born in St. Louis, Mo. Known for his ground-breaking use of socially conscious racial humor, Gregory overcame his origins in extreme poverty to become the first African-American comedian to perform for white audiences. After attending Southern Illinois University on an athletic scholarship and serving in the U.S. Army (1953–56), he rose to national prominence at the Chicago Playboy Club (1961). Throughout the 1960s his fame as a civil rights activist and nightclub performer made his name synonymous with progressive social and political causes. He ran in Chicago's mayoral race (1966) and for the U.S. presidency (1968) to publicize human rights issues. Embracing vegetarianism through his commitment to non-violence, he became a radical nutritionist and nutritional proselytizer and founded Dick Gregory Health Enterprises (1984). Famous for using fasts and marathons as activist tools, his many popular records and writings include *Nigger: An Autobiography* (1964, 1970).

Gregory, Samuel (1813–72) medical educator; born in Guilford, Vt. An advocate of medical education for women, he founded the Boston Female Medical School (1848), which merged with Boston University School of Medicine (1874), becoming one of the first coeducational schools in the world. As a doctor, he attacked the use of microscopes, thermometers, and test tubes.

Gregory, W. K. (William King) (1876–1970) paleontologist, ichthyologist; born in New York City. Educated at Columbia University (A.B., A.M., Ph.D.), he assisted Henry Fairfield Osborn (1899–1913) before joining the staff of the American Museum of Natural History (1911–44), where he became curator of ichthyology and comparative anatomy. Gregory specialized in anatomy and the development of teeth in fish and mammals; among his hundreds of publications are *The Orders of Mammals* (1910) and *The Origin and Evolution of Human Dentition* (1920–22).

Gregory, Waylande (Desantis) (1905–71) ceramist; born in Baxter Springs, Kans. He studied with sculptor Lorado Taft and began working in bronze before he went to work at the Cowan Pottery (near Cleveland) and shifted to ceramics. He is known for his art deco figurines and his monumental ceramic figures (1938) for which he developed the technique of inner modeling.

Gresham, Walter Q. (Quintin) (1832–95) jurist, public official; born near Lanesville, Ind. A Civil War veteran and friend of Ulysses S. Grant, he served as federal district judge (1869–83), postmaster general (1883–84), and secretary of the treasury (1893–95). Having fallen out with the Republicans over tariff policy, he threw his support to the Democrats in 1892 and was rewarded by being appointed secretary of state (1893–95).

Grew, Joseph Clark (1880–1965) diplomat; born in Boston, Mass. His career with the foreign service began in 1905 (Theodore Roosevelt sponsored him because he had shot a Chinese tiger). After World War I, he was secretary to the U.S. Commission to the Versailles Peace Conference and helped to negotiate a treaty with Turkey (1922–23). He was ambassador to Denmark (1920), Turkey (1927–32), and Japan (1931–41). While in Japan, he worked artfully to maintain good relations between the two countries; his work was frustrated and he was isolated by the attack on Pearl Harbor. Repatriated in 1942, he was director of the Far Eastern Affairs division of the State Department. He wrote *Sport and Travel in the Far East* (1910) and *Ten Years in Japan* (1944).

Grey, (Pearl) Zane (1872–1939) writer; born in Zanesville, Ohio. A graduate of the University of Pennsylvania, he

practiced dentistry in New York City from 1898 to 1904, when he married and left his practice to concentrate on his writing. In 1907 he made his first trip to the West and this inspired him to start writing the "dime novels" that would make him one of America's all-time most popular authors. His Westerns, such as *Riders of the Purple Sage* (1912), featuring stereotypical characters in adventure-laden plots, helped establish the conventions of the genre; over 100 movies have been based on his writings. He lived in California and was an avid hunter and fisherman; his nearly 80 books included several on fishing.

Gridley, Charles (Vernon) (1844–98) naval officer; born in Logansport, Ind. As a Naval Academy student, he was assigned to active duty in the Civil War; for over 30 years he filled the standard posts of a career officer. Assigned as captain to the *Olympia,* he found himself in Manila Bay on May 1, 1898, when Admiral George Dewey gave the famous command, "You may fire when you are ready, Gridley." Evidently under great strain from the battle, he was invalided home but died en route in Kobe, Japan.

Grier, Robert C. (Cooper) (1794–1870) Supreme Court justice; born in Cumberland County, Pa. He served as president judge of the district court of Allegheny County, Pa. (1833–46) when President James Polk appointed him to the U.S. Supreme Court (1846–70). He concurred with the Court in the Dred Scott decision (1857).

Grierson, Benjamin Henry (1826–1911) soldier; born in Pittsburgh, Pa. The son of Irish immigrants, he taught music before joining an Illinois regiment shortly after the outbreak of the Civil War. Although he claimed to despise horses, he accepted a transfer to the 6th Illinois Cavalry; Grant chose him to lead what became the most famous federal cavalry raid of the war. Leaving LaGrange, Tenn., on April 17, 1863, he took 1,700 troopers on a 600-mile gallop of destruction through Mississippi (arriving in Louisiana on May 2), an effective strategic diversion for Grant's Vicksburg Campaign. He saw long postwar service on the frontier, retiring as a brigadier general in 1890.

Griffes, Charles Tomlinson (1884–1920) composer; born in Elmira, N.Y. After beginning his music studies in the U.S.A., he studied piano and composition in Berlin, returning to the U.S.A. in 1907 to teach in a boys' school in Tarrytown, N.Y., where he remained until his untimely death. Developing slowly and composing painstakingly, he had begun to achieve a highly colorful and personal style in works such as the *Pleasure Dome of Kubla Khan* (1920). He is remembered as the great might-have-been of American music.

Griffin, Archie (Mason) (1954–) football player; born in Columbus, Ohio. The only player to win two Heisman Trophies (1974–75), he gained over 5,000 yards as a four-year starting halfback and three-time All-American at Ohio State.

Griffin, Donald R. (Redfield) (1915–) animal behaviorist; born in Southampton, N.Y. He taught and performed research at Harvard (1938–45), moved to Cornell (1946–53), returned to Harvard (1953–65), then joined Rockefeller University (1965–86). Interested in bird and bat migration since his youth, he made major contributions to studies of echolocation in bats, and communication in animals as a means of ascertaining their cognitive processes. He was a visiting lecturer at Princeton (1987–89) before becoming an associate at Harvard's Museum of Comparative Zoology (1989).

Griffin, Marion (b. Mahony) (1871–1961) architect; born in Chicago. Trained at the Massachusetts Institute of Technology, she was a designer and delineator for Frank Lloyd Wright (1895–1910), becoming known for her renderings and interior designs and for producing the drawings published in Wright's so-called Wasmuth Portfolio (1910). Problems of attribution in her work with Wright continued in her close collaboration with her husband Walter Burley Griffin; in Australia (1914–35), though uncredited, she is known to have contributed decisively to the designs for Canberra (1912), Castlecrag Community (1921–35), Sydney and the Capitol Theatre, Melbourne (1924). After her husband's death she established an independent practice in Chicago (1938).

Griffin, (Mervyn Edward) Merv (1925–) television host, businessman; born in San Mateo, Calif. Originally a singer, he appeared on *The CBS Morning Show* in 1956, then hosted game shows like *Keep Talking* for ABC. He hosted the *Merv Griffin Show* (1965–86), producing *Wheel of Fortune* and *Jeopardy* in the 1980s. He invested in gambling casinos, becoming chairman of Resorts International, then was forced to sell his business to Coca-Cola in 1986 when he experienced financial difficulties.

Griffin, Robert P. (Paul) (1923–) U.S. senator; born in Detroit, Mich. He served in the U.S. House of Representatives (Rep., Mich.; 1957–66) and in the U.S. Senate (1966–79). He was Republican whip from 1969–77.

Griffin, Walter Burley (1876–1937) architect, landscape designer, city planner; born in Maywood, Ill. In his early career he practiced independently and simultaneously worked closely with Frank Lloyd Wright, his work stressing indigenous materials and community planning. Collaborating with his wife Marion Mahony Griffin in Australia after winning the competition to plan Canberra (1914–35), he introduced the ideas of Wright and Louis Sullivan to that country.

Griffith, Clark (Calvin) (1869–1955) baseball player/manager/executive; born in Clear Creek, Mo. During his remarkable baseball career, he was one of the game's great (right-handed) pitchers for 21 years (1891–1914), a manager for 20 years (1901–20), and the president of the Washington Senators American League club for 26 years (1920–55). He was elected to baseball's Hall of Fame in 1946.

Griffith, D. W. (b. David Lewelyn Wark Griffith) (1875–1948) film director; born in La Grange, Ky. The son of a Confederate cavalry hero, he grew up in poverty in Louisville, Ky., and in 1897 began a stage career. He wrote poetry and dramas, then found work with the Edison film company in New York, where he starred in a short film, *Rescued from an Eagle's Nest* (1907). He then became a writer and actor at Biograph; his first directorial effort was *The Adventures of Dollie* (1908). By 1909 he was the general director of Biograph. While there he developed undercutting, crosscutting, parallel action, mobile cameras, close-ups, and other techniques now common in filmmaking. He also assembled a "stock company" that was to include Mary Pickford, the Gish Sisters, and others. Feeling restricted, he left Biograph in 1913 to join Reliance-Majestic, where he began work on *The Birth of a Nation* (1915). Still regarded as one of the most influential movies ever made, it was also

criticized for its bias in favor of the South in the Civil War. Griffith's next work was the epic *Intolerance* (1916), four separate stories about inhumanity throughout history. A founder of United Artists (1919), he continued directing until 1931 but nothing went right after 1924. Although he received a special Academy Award in 1935, he died alone and almost forgotten.

Griggs, David T. (Tressel) (1911–74) geophysicist; born in Columbus, Ohio. He taught at Harvard (1934–41) and was a section chief at Project Rand, Douglas Aircraft Corporation (1946–48), before becoming a professor of geophysics at the University of California: Los Angeles in 1948. He proposed that crushing convection currents in the earth's interior led to mountain (and possibly continent) formation. He is also known as an advocate of peaceful uses of atomic energy.

Griliches, (Hirsh) Zvi (1930–) economist; born in Lithuania. Educated in the U.S.A., his contributions include work in econometric methods, agricultural economics, and the economics of technological change. He taught at the University of Chicago (1956–69) before joining the faculty at Harvard (1969).

Grimké, Angelina Emily (1805–79) abolitionist, women's rights advocate; born in Charleston, S.C. (sister of Sarah Grimké). Daughter of a slave-owning judge and educated by tutors, she came to dislike the institution and practice of slavery and in 1829 she followed her older sister Sarah to Philadelphia. There she adopted the Quaker religion and turned to teaching, but she soon was devoting herself to the abolition of slavery and to promoting the rights of women. In 1836 her *Appeal to the Christian Women of the South,* published by the American Anti-Slavery Society, brought the name Grimké to the fore and she was warned not to return to the South. She and Sarah moved to New York City in 1836. She soon became a noted speaker against slavery, but controversial even in the North for speaking before "mixed" audiences of men and women, and soon she was drawn into the related struggle for women's rights in general. In 1838, she married the abolitionist Theodore Weld and thereafter she concentrated on circulating antislavery petitions and publishing antislavery documents. In 1840 the Welds moved to Belleville, N.J., and from 1848–62 they ran a school there. In 1863 they moved to Massachusetts, where Angelina took up teaching (1864–67). Angelina suffered a stroke after her sister Sarah's death in 1873.

Grimké, Sarah Moore (1792–1873) abolitionist, women's rights activist; born in Charleston, S.C. (sister of Angelina Grimké). Daughter of a slave-owning judge and educated by tutors, she had from an early age become uncomfortable with the practice of slavery. Visiting Philadelphia in 1819, she was moved by the Quakers' rejection of slavery and in 1821 she moved there and joined the Society of Friends. For several years she confined herself to religious and charitable causes, but when her younger sister Angelina joined her in 1829 and went public with her own attacks on slavery (1835), Sarah spoke out against the Philadelphia Quakers' own discrimination against African-Americans and moved to New York City (1836). She then published her first work on slavery, *Epistle to the Clergy of the Southern States* (1836), in which she attacked the argument that slavery was justified because it was recognized in the Bible. The Grimké sisters then themselves became controversial by their insistence on speaking before "mixed" audiences of men and women, and soon Sarah was writing *Letters on the Equality of the Sexes and the Condition of Women* (1838). After Angelina married the abolitionist Theodore Weld in 1838, Sarah lived with them and followed them on their moves first to New Jersey and then to Massachusetts, where she helped raise their three children. She ceased lecturing in public but continued to write and petition against slavery, and for many of the years between 1848 and 1867, she taught to help support their family. The sisters did not publish much against slavery after 1839 but they continued to identify with the women's rights movement.

Grinnell, George Bird (1849–1938) naturalist, author; born in Brooklyn, N.Y. An 1870 Yale graduate, he worked as a banker for four years before joining a Black Hills expedition (led by Lt. Colonel George Armstrong Custer) as a naturalist. In 1876 he became an editor with *Forest and Stream* magazine; as editor-in-chief from 1880–1911, he made it the country's leading natural history journal. A founder of the Audubon Society (1886) and the New York Zoological Society, he tirelessly promoted national parks and wildlife preserves. Glacier National Park (1910) was created owing largely to his efforts. He published several books on Indian lore, hunting, and natural history, as well as a series for boys about the outdoors.

Grinnell, Henry (1799–1874) merchant, philanthropist; born in New Bedford, Mass. He was a clerk in New York City (1818–25) and then joined two of his brothers in founding a shipping company (1825). He retired from business (1850) and pursued his interest in Arctic voyages. He entirely financed two expeditions (1850, 1853–55) which went in search of the lost expedition of Sir John Franklin. He was one of the founders and then president (1862–63) of the American Geographical and Statistical Society. Grinnell Land, or Peninsula, in Canada's Northwest Territories, and a genus of red algae (*Grinnellia*) are named after him.

Grinnell, Josiah (Bushnell) (1821–91) abolitionist, clergyman; born in New Haven, Vt. A self-described pioneer, farmer, and radical, he did much to build Iowa agriculturally and through introduction of the railroads, and was a leading abolitionist. After being forced from his Congregational pulpit in Washington, D.C., for delivering antislavery sermons, he followed the advice of his friend Horace Greeley to "go West." Moving to Iowa, he was cofounder of the town of Grinnell (1854) and planned the future Grinnell College. He fought forcefully for temperance and against slavery. Elected Congressman (Rep., Iowa; 1863–67), he vigorously supported Lincoln and suffrage and lost the Republican nomination for governor (1867).

Griswold, Alfred Whitney (1906–63) university president; born in Morristown, N.J. He was educated at Yale (B.A., Ph.D.), where he joined the history faculty (1933) and served as president (1950–63) in a term that strengthened the university's financial position and concentrated its focus on a liberal arts curriculum.

Griswold, John A. (Augustus) (1818–72) manufacturer, U.S. representative, philanthropist; born in Nassau, N.Y. After several commercial ventures, he became head of the Rensselaer Iron Works, the Bessemer Steel Works, and other blast furnaces in Troy, N.Y. An ardent Unionist and advocate of armored ships, he oversaw the manufacture of the iron plates for the *Monitor* and six more such ships for the Union navy. He was one of a group of Americans who in 1864 acquired the Bessemer patents from England, enabling significant developments in America's iron and steel industry. Elected mayor of Troy in 1855, he served in the U.S. House of Representatives (Dem., N.Y.; 1863–67).

Griswold, Rufus Wilmot (1815–57) anthologist, editor, literary critic; born in Benson, Vt. After an obscure period of journalism and editorial work beginning in 1830, he obtained a license as a Baptist minister, though he seems never to have taken a regular pulpit. He edited various periodicals and campaigned against capital punishment and imprisonment for debt. With William Leggett and others he established a library in the New York City Prison. He was a strong opponent of Americanism in literature and published an anthology of *The Poets and Poetry of America* (1842). He succeeded Edgar Allan Poe as editor of *Graham's Magazine* (1842–43) and edited additional literary collections, including *The Prose Works of John Milton* (1845, 1847), *The Prose Writers of America* (1847), and *The Female Poets of America* (1848). He wrote a rather harsh obituary of Poe (1849), even though Poe had named him as his literary executor. He published a flawed edition of Poe's works (1850–56) and included a rather scandalous memoir. He edited the *International Monthly Magazine* (1850–52) and P. T. Barnum's *Illustrated News* (1852–53). He wrote a lengthy and remarkably destructive review of the Duykinck's *Cyclopedia of American Literature* in the *New York Herald* (Feb. 1856).

Grof, Stanislav (1931–) psychiatrist; born in Prague, Czechoslovakia. Educated at Charles University and the Czechoslovak Academy of Sciences, he practiced in Prague until 1960, when he came to Johns Hopkins University as a research scientist and professor of psychiatry (to 1973). His interest in unusual states of consciousness, and his research at California's Esalen Institute (from 1973), resulted in the book *Realms of the Human Unconscious: Observations from LSD Research* (1975).

Grofé, (Ferdinand Rudolph von) Ferde (1892–1972) composer/arranger; born in New York City. An arranger for Paul Whiteman's "symphonic jazz" orchestra, Grofé orchestrated Gershwin's *Rhapsody in Blue* and composed works expressing American locales, notably the *Grand Canyon Suite* (1931).

Gronlund, Laurence (1846–99) lawyer, author, lecturer; born in Denmark. Emigrating to America (1867), he practiced law for a number of years. Originally influenced by Pascal, he turned Socialist and wrote the widely-read *Cooperative Commonwealth* (1884), a blend of Marxism and Christian idealism that called for the end of capitalism. Lecturing throughout the country on this theme, he edited a socialist paper, briefly held a position with the Labor Department, and then returned to lecturing and publishing. He was elected to the executive committee of the Socialist Labor Party (1888), and in the final year of his life he was on the staff of the *New York Journal*, in charge of labor news.

Grooms, Red (b. Charles Roger Grooms) (1937–) sculptor, painter, performance artist; born in Nashville, Tenn. He studied at the Art Institute of Chicago, the New School for Social Research, N.Y., and the Hans Hofmann School, Mass., then settled in New York City (1957). He founded Ruckus Productions (1963), a multi-media environmental and performance company, and is known for both his lifesize installations and impromptu happenings and other theatrical events.

Gropius, Walter (Adolph) (1883–1969) architect, educator; born in Berlin, Germany. He directed the Bauhaus (1919–28) and practiced in Berlin and London. He came to the U.S.A. in 1937 and headed the architecture school at Harvard (1938–52), where he replaced the beaux arts curriculum with modern training. He founded The Architects Collaborative (1945). An internationally influential functionalist theoretician and practitioner, Gropius was adventurous in his use of concrete, glass, and steel in his houses and corporate and public buildings; he investigated standardized, prefabricated housing. He designed the Pan American Building (with Pietro Belluschi, 1962), New York.

Gropper, William (1897–1977) painter; born in New York City. He studied with Robert Henri and George Bellows (1912–13), and became a cartoonist for various periodicals. He was often compared to Honoré Daumier, for his art is satirical and expressionistic. His famous work, *The Senate* (1935), provides a scathing commentary on his subject.

Grosman, Tatyana (b. Aguschewitsch) (1904–82) printmaker; born in Ekaterinburg, Siberia, Russia. She studied at the Dresden Academy of Arts and Crafts, Germany, and settled in France (1931). She and her husband, Maurice, escaped from the Nazis by walking across the Pyrenees to Italy; from there they emigrated to New York City (1943). She founded the Universal Limited Art Editions (ULAE) workshop in East Islip, Long Island (1957), and encouraged such famous New York school artists as Larry Rivers, Jasper Johns, Grace Hartigan, Helen Frankenthaler, Jim Dine and Robert Motherwell to take up printmaking.

Gross, Chaim (1904–91) sculptor, teacher; born in Wolow, Galicia (now Poland). During World War I he and his family fled to Budapest (c. 1914), and he emigrated to New York City (1921), where he studied at the Educational Alliance Art School (1921) and the Beaux-Arts (1922–26). He taught at many institutions and was known for his wood and stone expressionistic figures, such as *Strong Woman* (1935).

Gross, Harold (Royce) (1899–1987) U.S. representative; born in Arispe, Iowa. Educated in rural schools, he served in the Mexican border campaigns of 1916 and overseas during World War I. After graduating from the Missouri School of Journalism, he worked as a newspaperman (1921–35) and radio news commentator (1935–48). He served in the U.S. House of Representatives (Rep., Iowa; 1949–75).

Gross, Samuel David (1805–84) surgeon, author; born near Easton, Pa. After taking his M.D. from Jefferson Medical College (Philadelphia), he set up practice in Philadelphia; he translated and wrote several important works on anatomy and surgery. He went on to teach at Cincinnati Medical College and the University of Louisville before returning to Jefferson Medical College as professor of surgery (1856–82). He had an international reputation as both a teacher and practitioner of surgery, and he continued to be a prolific author; several of his texts were classics, among them *Elements of Pathological Anatomy* (1839) and *System of Surgery, Pathological, Diagnostic, Therapeutic and Operative* (1859). His specialties included operations for bladder stone and intestinal wounds; he invented new techniques and instruments. He was one of the founders and most influential members of the American Medical Association (1847). Thomas Eakins portrayed him in a famous painting, *The Clinic of Dr. Gross* (1875).

Grossman, Albert B. (1926–86) popular music manager, impresario, recording executive; born in Chicago, Ill. Best known for managing Bob Dylan (1962–69), Grossman graduated in economics from Roosevelt College and worked for the Chicago Housing Authority before opening the seminal Gate of Horn folk music club in Chicago in the mid-1950s. Moving to New York City, he codirected the first Newport Folk Festival (1959) and created the group Peter, Paul and Mary. During the 1960s he revolutionized personal management, winning major increases in artists' royalties and control of publishing rights and elevating folk singers into the pop field. He managed Janis Joplin to stardom (1968) and, after her death (1970), moved to Bearsville, N.Y., where he established Bearsville Studio and Records and opened two restaurants. The most influential and respected manager of his day, his stable included The Band, Paul Butterfield, the Electric Flag, Gordon Lightfoot, and Richie Havens.

Grosvenor, Gilbert (Hovey) (1875–1966) editor, naturalist, geographer; born in Constantinople, Turkey. Son of an American professor of history, he returned to the U.S.A as a teenager. After graduating from Amherst College, he became an editorial assistant in 1899 at the *National Geographic* magazine; in 1903 he became its editor, a position he held until 1954. He married Alexander Graham Bell's daughter in 1900. From 1920–54 he also served as president of the National Geographic Society, parent organization of the magazine. By using more engaging illustrations and approaching geography in the broadest possible manner, he made the magazine more accessible to lay readers than it had originally been. During his tenure, membership in the Society also increased from about 1,000 to over 4 million. The increased revenue was used to sponsor scientific teams and exploration expeditions all across the globe and under the oceans, so that instead of just reporting on the world, he and his magazine were instrumental in opening it up. Grosvenor Lake in Alaska, Gilbert Grosvenor Range in Antarctica, and Grosvenor-filliet, a mountain in the Svalbard islands off Norway, are named after him.

Grosz, George (1893–1959) graphic artist, painter; born in Berlin, Germany. He studied art in Dresden and Berlin and served in the German army in World War I. After years of producing drawings that bitterly satirized middle-class complacency, militarism, and Nazism, he emigrated to New York City in 1932, eventually establishing his studio on Long Island. Early associated with Dadaism, the movement that embraced the absurdity of life, he became known as the printmaker and painter who was a sophisticated realist; his later oils were more symbolic in nature. In 1959 he returned to Berlin where he died.

Grotell, Maija (1899–1973) ceramist; born in Helsinki, Finland. In 1927 she emigrated to New York to teach pottery. In 1938 she began some 30 years as head of the ceramics department at Cranbrook Academy of Art near Detroit, and was regarded as an innovative and gifted teacher, as well as a pioneer in glaze technology. Her own works, ever experimental, ranging from simple vessels with art deco motifs to later ones with craterous glazes, brought her 25 major awards and acclaim as the "mother of American ceramics."

Groves, Leslie (Richard, Jr.) (1896–1970) soldier; born in Albany, N.Y. The son of an army chaplain, he graduated from West Point in 1918, entered the Corps of Engineers and worked on various large construction projects during the 1930s and 1940s. He directed the design and construction of the Pentagon before moving on to more important work. As chief of the deceptively named "Manhattan Engineer District" (1942–47), he oversaw the building of facilities for the development, testing, and production of the first atomic weapons, including the laboratories at Oak Ridge, Tenn., Los Alamos, N.M., and Hanford, Wash. Upon retiring from the army, he became vice-president in charge of research for Sperry Rand's Remington division (1948–61).

Grow, Galusha Aaron (1822–1907) U.S. representative; born in Ashford, Conn. He represented Pennsylvania in the U.S. House of Representatives in two periods (Free-Soil Democrat, 1851–57; Rep., 1857–63; Rep., 1894–1903). He was Speaker of the House (1861–63) and was influential in the passage of the Homestead Act (1862). He engaged in various business interests during his long hiatus from Congress (1863–94).

Grueby, William H. (1867–1925) potter; birthplace unknown. He trained in Chelsea, Mass., under John G. Low, and then set up his Grueby Faience Company in 1894 (incorporated in 1897). His hand-thrown pottery won many awards internationally and the L. C. Tiffany Company bought Grueby bases for its stained glass lampshades. His success did not bring him wealth; numerous competitors flooded the market with imitations. He also founded Grueby Pottery (incorporated, 1907).

Gruelle, (John) Johnny (1880–1938) author, illustrator, cartoonist; born in Arcola, Ill. His family moved to Indianapolis, and he worked as a cartoonist for newspapers in Indianapolis and Cleveland before moving to New York City to work for the *New York Herald* (1913–21). He became famous for the Raggedy Ann and Andy series he began in 1918, and for *Beloved Belindy* (1926), among other books for young readers. In 1931 he settled in Miami Springs, Fla.

Gruen, Erich S. (Stephen) (1935–) historian; born in Vienna, Austria. Educated at Columbia University (B.A. 1957), Oxford (Rhodes Scholar; B.A. 1960) and Harvard (Ph.D. 1964), he taught at Harvard (1962–66) and the University of California: Berkeley (1966). His *Last Generation of the Roman Republic* (1974) was nominated for a National Book Award and his *Hellenistic World and the Coming of Rome* (1988) won that year's James H. Breasted Prize. He was president of the American Philological Association (1992).

Gruening, Ernest (1887–1974) U.S. senator; born in New York City. He graduated from Harvard Medical School but then proceeded to write and edit (1912–34). He edited the *Nation* (1920–23) and was territorial governor of Alaska (1939–53). He worked to get Alaska accepted as a state, writing *The State of Alaska* (1954), and became one of the new state's first two U.S. senators (Dem., Alaska; 1959–69). He cast one of the two votes in opposition to the Gulf of Tonkin resolution (1964) that committed the U.S. to pursuing the war in Vietnam, and he opposed U.S. policies there to the end. Alaska placed his statue in the U.S. Capitol.

Grumman, Leroy (Randle) (1895–1982) aeronautical engineer; born in Huntington, N.Y. As general manager of the Loening Aeronautical Corporation (1921–29) and president of Grumman Aircraft Corporation (1930–46), he developed a series of successful Navy aircraft. These included the "Wildcat," "Bearcat" and "Tiger Cat." He was enshrined in the Aviation Hall of Fame (1972).

Grundy, Felix (1777–1840) U.S. representative/senator; born in Berkley County, Va. Home-schooled, he served in the Kentucky legislature (1801–06) before becoming a successful criminal lawyer in Nashville, Tennessee (1807–40). A Whig representative (1811–15) and senator (1827–38), he resigned to become President Martin Van Buren's attorney general.

Guare, John (1938–) playwright; born in New York City. His first success came with *The House of Blue Leaves* (1970), a sardonic comedy about how the Pope's visit to New York affects a zookeeper's family. He wrote several plays for Joseph Papp's Public Theater and had his second major hit with *Six Degrees of Separation* (1990).

Guermonprez, Trude (1910–76) weaver; born in Danzig, Germany. She came to the U.S.A. in 1939 to teach at Black Mountain College and later in California. Known for experiment with on-loom weaving techniques, she also explored unusual materials.

Guess, George See SEQUOYAH.

Guffey, Joseph F. (Frank) (1870–1959) U.S. senator; born at Guffey's Landing, Pa. Entering the family business, he became president of several oil companies. A strong supporter of Woodrow Wilson, he financed Wilson's 1919 national speaking tour. Elected to the U.S. Senate (Dem., Pa.; 1935–47), he backed New Deal legislation and measures regulating the oil and coal industries, but he practiced machine politics when it came to the Democratic party in his home state.

Guggenheim, Daniel (1856–1930) industrialist, philanthropist; born in Philadelphia (son of Meyer Guggenheim). He studied the making of embroidery and lace in Switzerland (1874–84) and then turned to the new family business of mining and metals processing. As head of the American Smelting and Refining Company (1901–19) he extended its operations into Alaska, Africa, and South America. Among his many philanthropic interests, he subsidized free band concerts in New York City and promoted safe flying through the Daniel Guggenheim Fund for the Promotion of Aeronautics.

Guggenheim, (Marguerite) Peggy (1898–1979) art collector, patron; born in New York City (niece of Solomon R. Guggenheim). She graduated from the Jacobi School, New York City, (1915), became a radical bohemian, and settled in Paris soon after the end of World War I. She married young, was divorced (1930), and then was married to Max Ernst (1941–46). She opened a modern art gallery in England, the Guggenheim Jeune (1938), where she exhibited and collected works by avant-garde artists. In 1939 she was in France buying modern works suggested by the art critic, Herbert Read. She escaped the German invasion of Paris and arrived in New York City with her children and her art collection (1941). She opened a new art gallery, Art of This Century (1942). In 1946 she divorced Ernst, moved to Venice, and established a new gallery in her villa there. Her memoirs, *Out of This Century* (1946) and *Confessions of an Art Addict* (1960), were notorious for the details of her love life. Her collection and the Venice gallery were donated to the Solomon R. Guggenheim Foundation.

Guggenheim, Meyer (1828–1905) financier; born in Langnau, Switzerland (father of Simon and Solomon Guggenheim). He met his wife while emigrating to the U.S.A. in 1848 – they would have seven sons. He began as a manufacturer of stove polish, then turned to importing and selling Swiss needlework with his own firm, M. Guggenheim's Sons (1881). By 1888 he had shifted his interest to the mining and smelting of metals. With the aid of his sons, he captured a large share of the world business. He formed the Philadelphia Smelting and Refining Company and won an economic war against the giant American Smelting & Refining Company; his company merged with that giant trust on his own terms in 1901. His sons carried on his tradition of business success and generous philanthropy.

Guggenheim, Simon (1867–1941) business executive, philanthropist; born in Philadelphia (son of Meyer Guggenheim). He worked for his father's large mining and metal-processing firm, eventually becoming president of the American Smelting and Refining Company (1919–41). Having settled in Denver, he served as a U.S. senator from Colorado (Rep., 1907–13). As one of the heirs of the massive Guggenheim fortune, he donated large sums to various educational and medical institutions. He is best known for setting up the John Simon Guggenheim Foundation, which gives annual grants to scholars and creative individuals.

Guggenheim, Solomon Robert (1861–1949) businessman, art collector; born in Philadelphia (son of Meyer Guggenheim). After study in local schools and in Zurich, he became a partner in his father's Swiss embroidery import business. He returned to America (1889), worked in the family mining industry in Colorado and New Mexico, then returned to the business headquarters in New York City (1895). He was a director of many family companies and a founder of the Yukon Gold Company in Alaska before retiring from business in 1919. With the assistance of Hilla Rebay, he collected important modernist paintings and established the Solomon R. Guggenheim Foundation (1937). This was the source of funds for the temporary Museum of Non-Objective Paintings (1937), and for the permanent Solomon R. Guggenheim Museum (1959) designed by Frank Lloyd Wright.

Guglielmi, Louis (O.) (1906–56) painter; born in Cairo, Egypt. He and his family emigrated to New York City (1914), and he studied at the National Academy of Design (1920–25). His painting of people under a glass bell in the desolate streets of New York, *Terror in Brooklyn* (1941), is typical of his combination of surrealism and social commentary.

Guilday, Peter (Keenan) (1884–1947) Catholic historian; born in Chester, Pa. A priest with a doctorate from Louvain, he taught at Catholic University (from 1914), was principal editor of the *Catholic Historical Review* (from 1915), and cofounded the American Catholic Historical Association (1919). His writings established him as the period's leading scholar in Catholic church history. He became a monsignor in 1935.

Guillemin, Roger (Charles Louis) (1924–) neuroendocrinologist; born in Dijon, France. He was an anti-Nazi resistance fighter in France during World War II, then received his M.D. from Lyons in 1949. He emigrated to the University of Montreal (1951–53), then came to the U.S.A. to join Baylor University (Texas) (1953–70). He collaborated with pioneer endocrinologist Andrew Schally on hypothalamic hormones which regulate the pituitary (1955–62), then continued independently at Baylor and the Salk Institute for Biological Studies (1970–89) where he isolated additional pituitary hormones and investigated the action of endorphins. For his many contributions to neuroendocrinology, Guillemin shared one-half the 1977 Nobel Prize in physiology with his former colleague Schally. He continued his work on brain chemistry and hypothalamic hormones at the Whitter Institute for Diabetes and Endocrinology, La Jolla (1989).

Guinzburg, Alfred (Kleinert) (1899–1961) publisher; born in New York City. He cofounded Viking Press in 1925 and headed it until his death, acquiring such authors as James Joyce, D. H. Lawrence, and August Strindberg. In 1926 he founded the Literary Guild book club.

Guiteau, Charles Julius (1841–82) assassin; born in Freeport, Ill. He dabbled in law, newspaper work, and preaching. He unreasonably expected to be offered a diplomatic post by the administration of President James Garfield. Failing in this, he shot President Garfield (1881) and called out, "I am a Stalwart and Arthur is president now!" Despite behaving like a madman at his trial, he was found guilty and hanged in 1882.

Gulick, Luther (Halsey) (1865–1918) physical education/youth leader; born in Honolulu, Hawaii. A child of Congregational missionaries, he took an M.D. from what is now New York University. While training physical education teachers at the Springfield, Mass., Young Men's Christian Association (YMCA) Training School (1886–1903), he contributed to developing the new game of basketball. He also designed the YMCA's official triangle emblem. Moving to New York City, he became director of physical education for New York City's public schools and organized the Public Schools Athletic League. Head of the Russell Sage Foundation's child hygiene department (1907–13), he promoted physical health through books and speeches. In 1910 he founded the Camp Fire Girls with his wife, Charlotte Vetter Gulick.

Gumbel, Bryant (Charles) (1948–) television sports commentator/anchorman; born in New Orleans, La. Editor of *Black Sports* magazine after college, he worked as sportscaster for KNBC in Los Angeles (1972–80). He also covered professional sports for the National Broadcasting Company, winning an Emmy for his 1976 Olympic coverage. Hired by the *Today* show in 1980 to do sports commentary, he became coanchor in 1981.

Gumperz, John (1922–) linguist; birthplace unknown. He studied at the Universities of Cincinnati and Michigan (Ph.D. 1954). A specialist in linguistic anthropology, his extensive list of publications includes *Language in Social Groups* (1971) and *Discourse Strategies* (1982). He was a professor of anthropology at the University of California: Berkeley.

Gunther, Gerald (1927–) legal scholar; born in Usingen, Germany. He emigrated to the U.S.A. in 1938 where he received his education. He worked briefly as a law clerk before joining the faculty at Columbia University (1956–62) and then Stanford University (1962). An expert in constitutional law, he wrote *Individual Rights in Constitutional Law* (1970).

Gunther, John (1901–70) author, journalist; born in Chicago. A graduate of the University of Chicago (1922), he worked as a correspondent for the *Chicago Daily News* and for the

National Broadcasting Company. His best-selling book, *Inside Europe* (1936), was followed by a series of *Inside . . .* books, including *Inside U.S.A.* (1944), combining personal observation with historic documentation. The books sold well, but were criticized for their superficiality. His other books include *Death Be Not Proud* (1949), a memoir of his young son's death, and *A Fragment of Autobiography* (1962).

Guralnik, David B. (Bernard) (1920–) lexicographer; born in Cleveland, Ohio. With Joseph H. Friend, he edited *Webster's New World Dictionary* (1953) for the World Publishing Company and thereby established a major new line of college dictionaries in the American market. As editor-in-chief of the Webster's New World Dictionaries (subsequently published by Simon & Schuster), he edited the *Second College Edition* (1970) and for nearly forty years was one of the leading lexicographers in the U.S.A. He retired at the end of 1985 but remained active as a consultant.

Gurney, (Daniel Sexton) Dan (1931–) auto racer; born in Port Jefferson, N.Y. One of the first U.S. drivers to use rear-engine race cars, he won the Le Mans race (1967), and finished second in the Indianapolis 500 twice (1968–69).

Guston, Philip (1912–80) painter; born in Montreal, Canada. He came to California with his family (1916), and his early paintings combined realism and surrealism, as seen in *Martial Memory* (1941). Later in his career he lived in Woodstock, Vt., and his work had a cartoon-like quality, as in *The Studio* (1969).

Gutenberg, Beno (1889–1960) seismologist; born in Darmstadt, Germany. During his graduate studies at the University of Goettingen, Germany, he made the first known correct determination of the size and composition of the earth's inner core. He left Germany in 1930 to join the seismology laboratory at the California Institute of Technology, where he collaborated with Charles F. Richter to develop the definitive scale of earthquake magnitude, then continued research on earth structure, seismic waves, and stratospheric temperatures.

Guthrie, Janet (1938–) race car driver, pilot; born in Iowa City, Iowa. The daughter of an airline pilot, she flew her first Piper Cub at age 13; she worked as a commercial pilot and flight instructor while attending the University of Michigan (B.A. 1960), then worked as a research and development engineer for Republic Aviation Corp. (1961–67). In 1961 she bought her first Jaguar XK 120 for racing; in 1964 she placed sixth at the Watkins Glen 500 and won two Sports Car Club of America races. On her way to becoming the premier woman car racer, she took 12th-place finishes at the Daytona 500 and the Richmond 400 (1977) and was named the North American Road Racing champion in 1973. Then in 1977, as the first woman to compete in the Indy 500 – where women had been banned from even the repair and refueling pits as recently as 1971 – she finished 29th; in 1978 she finished 9th. She was named to the Women's Sports Hall of Fame in 1980.

Guthrie, Ramon (1896–1973) poet; born in New York City. He was educated in France (1919–23), and taught French at several institutions, notably at Dartmouth College (1930–

63). He is known for lyrical and humanist poetry, as in *Maximum Security Ward* (1970).

Guthrie, (Woodrow Wilson) "Woody" (1912–67) folk musician; born in Okemah, Okla. (father of Arlo Guthrie). Son of an alcoholic, he was farmed out to relatives and friends while still a teenager after his mother was hospitalized for Huntington's chorea. During the 1930s he lived a hobo's life, traveling with his guitar until 1937, when he became a successful radio personality with *Here Comes Woody and Lefty Lou* on KFVD in Los Angeles. Drawing from his travels, he wrote or adapted more than 1,000 songs, performing at political rallies and on picket lines. Ethnomusicologist Alan Lomax began recording his songs in the 1940s, including his most famous, "This Land is Your Land" (1940), and introduced him to other folksingers in New York, like Pete Seeger, with whom Guthrie performed in the Almanac Singers. Guthrie wrote an autobiography, *Bound for Glory* (1943), and served in the U.S. merchant marine (1943–45). A hero to protest singers like Bob Dylan and Joan Baez in the 1960s, he spent his last 15 years in hospitals, ravaged by Huntington's chorea.

Gutman, Herbert (George) (1928–85) historian; born in New York City. Educated at Queens College, Columbia University, and the University of Wisconsin (Ph.D. 1959), he emerged as a social historian who advocated study of the "faceless masses who worked to make America what it is today" for the goal of empowering social change. At the City University of New York after 1972, his influential books include *The Black Family in Slavery and Freedom, 1750–1925* (1976). He served on the National Historical Publications and Records Commission (1974–78).

Guyot, Arnold (Henry) (1807–84) geographer, natural scientist; born in Boudevilliers, Switzerland. A pioneer in the study of Alpine glaciation, in 1848 he traveled to the U.S.A. to give lectures at the Lowell Institute, published as *The Earth and Man* (1849). In 1854, he joined the faculty of the College of New Jersey (later known as Princeton University). Also knowledgeable in meteorology and topography, he founded the U.S. weather station system and measured the altitudes of the Applachian mountains from Maine to South Carolina.

Guze, Samuel Barry (1923–) psychiatrist, educator; born in New York City. He was affiliated with Washington University in St. Louis, Mo. (1946), becoming president of its Medical Center (1971–89). He was a recognized expert in the fields of alcoholism and substance abuse, the psychology of criminal behavior, and the evaluation and treatment of psychiatric disorders.

Gwathmey, Charles (1938–) architect; born in Charlotte, N.C. He formed a New York partnership with Robert Siegel (1968), designing primarily houses, and corporate and institutional buildings that Americanized the International style.

Gwathmey, Robert (1903–88) painter; born in Richmond, Va. After studying art at the Pennsylvania Academy of Fine Arts (1926–30), he participated in the New York art scene. He is especially noted for his sympathetic paintings of rural African-Americans, as in *Singing and Mending* (1945).

H

Haas, Mary (1910–) linguist; born in Richmond, Ind. She earned a Ph.D. at Yale (1935) and taught for many years at the University of California: Berkeley. She specialized in linguistic prehistory and in Thai and American Indian languages. She is the author of *Spoken Thai* (1946) and *Prehistory of Languages* (1969).

Haas, Walter A., Jr. (1916–) business executive; born in San Francisco. Son of Walter A. Haas, head of Levi Strauss, he was vice-president, president, on the board of directors, and then chairman of the board during his career with the world's leading maker of blue jeans (1946–71). In 1980 he purchased the Oakland Athletics baseball team.

Haberle, John (1853–1933) painter; born in New Haven, Conn. Based in New Haven, he prepared paleontological specimens for Yale University, began painting in 1887, and became known for his mysterious and humorous *trompe l'oeil* compositions such as *A Bachelor's Drawer* (1890s).

Habib, Philip C. (Charles) (1920–92) diplomat; born in New York City. Of Lebanese descent, he served in the U.S. Army (1942–46) and was a foreign service officer (1949–80). He was a U.S. delegate to the Vietnam War negotiations in Paris (1968–71) where he was noted for his skill and flexibility. He was ambassador to the Republic of Korea (1971–74), assistant secretary of state for East Asian and Pacific affairs (1974–76) and under secretary of state for political affairs (1976–78). He left the service due to health reasons, but returned to the diplomatic scene as President Reagan's personal representative to the Middle East (1981–83) where he negotiated for an end to the crisis in Lebanon. He was also a special presidential envoy to the Philippines in 1986.

Hadas, Moses (1900–66) classicist, translator; born in Atlanta, Ga. He was educated at Emory (B.A. 1922) and Columbia (M.A. 1925, Ph.D. 1930) Universities; he taught at Columbia from 1925–28 and 1930–66. His best known publications include *History of Greek Literature* (1950) and *History of Latin Literature* (1952); his translations, such as Jacob Burckhardt's *The Age of Constantine the Great* (1949), and *Three Greek Romances* (1954), introduced works in German and Greek to English readers.

Hadley, Arthur Twining (1856–1930) economist, university president; born in New Haven, Conn. A brilliant teacher of political economy at Yale (1879–99), he became a nationally recognized expert on operating and financing railroads with *Railroad Transportation* (1885). During his presidency (1899–1921) Yale expanded into a great international university.

Hagen, Walter (Charles) (1892–1969) golfer; born in Roches- ter, N.Y. One of golf's great pioneers, he won the U.S. Open twice (1914, 1919), the Professional Golfers' Association (PGA) championship five times (1921, 1924–27), the British Open four times (1922, 1924, 1928, 1929), and many other lesser titles. Nicknamed, "The Haig," he was the U.S. Ryder Cup team captain six times between 1927 and 1939.

Haggin, James Ben Ali (1827–1914) lawyer, businessman; born in Harrodsburg, Ky. He studied law in his father's office and was admitted to the bar in 1845. Emigrating west in 1850, he opened (with Lloyd Tevis) a Sacramento law office that over the following decades became one of the chief financial powers of California. His interests included mining and agricultural development. His Kentucky horse farm produced a series of champion racers in the 1880s.

Hague, Frank (1876–1956) political boss; born in Jersey City, N.J. Initially running as a reformer, he was a Democratic Jersey City commissioner (1913–17) who created a political machine that allowed him to serve as mayor from 1917 to 1947. Despite charges of corruption, he controlled New Jersey Democrats, handpicking governors from 1919 to 1941; he also served as vice-chairman of the National Democratic Party (1924–52). Constitutional reforms ended his control of state elections and dissatisfied voters rejected his mayoral successor in 1947.

Haig, Alexander (Meigs, Jr.) (1925–) soldier, public official; born in Philadelphia. He graduated from West Point (1947), served in Korea and Vietnam, and became military aide to Henry Kissinger (1969). President Nixon appointed him vice-chief of army staff and chief of White House staff (1973). Four-star General Haig was commander of NATO (1974–79); after retiring from the army, he was president of United Technologies (1979–81). President Reagan named him secretary of state (1981), but after feuding with other cabinet members over Middle East policy, he resigned under pressure in 1982.

Haines, Allan See under LOCKHEED, MALCOLM.

Haines, Helen Elizabeth (1872–1961) editor, bibliographer, library educator; born in New York City. Educated entirely by her mother and private tutors, she took a position in 1892 with R. R. Bowker, the bibliographic publishers, where she assisted in the production of the *Library Journal, Publisher's Weekly*, the *American Catalogue, State Publications,* and the *Annual Literary Index*. She was appointed managing editor of the *Literary Journal* in 1896 and she served on the executive board of the American Library Association. Because of ill health she resigned her positions in 1908 and settled in Pasadena, Calif., where she lectured on literature and librarianship at the University of Southern California and the University of California: Los Angeles. The second edition (1950) of her most important work, *Living with Books: the Art of Book Selection* (1935) attracted criticism for her advocacy of the representation of divergent points of view and her opposition to censorship.

Halas, George (Stanley) "Papa Bear" (1895–1983) football player, coach, owner, pioneer; born in Chicago. In 1920 he formed the Decatur (Ill.) Staleys, which was one of the 11 original teams in the newly founded American Professional Football Association. This became the National Football League (NFL) in 1922, the same year Halas moved his team to Chicago and renamed it the Bears. While coaching the team (1920–29) he played end; he returned as coach only for 1933–42, 1946–55 and 1958–68; during all those years the Bears won seven NFL championships and he amassed a league-record 325 coaching wins. He is credited with several innovations that led to modern football and for his sideline histrionics. He was elected to the NFL Hall of Fame in 1963 and he owned the Bears until his death.

Haldeman, H. R. (Harold Robbins) (1926–93) advertising executive, government official; born in Los Angeles. An executive with J. Walter Thompson in Los Angeles (1949–69), he had served on Richard Nixon's campaigns since 1956. Campaign manager in 1968, he became Nixon's chief of staff (1969–73), and was fired by Nixon as a "fall guy" for stonewalling the Watergate investigation. Convicted of perjury in 1975, he served a year in prison, publishing his version of the events in *The Ends of Power* (1978). He began a career in commercial real estate afterward.

Haldeman-Julius, Emanuel (b. Emanuel Julius) (1889–1951) publisher, author; born in Philadelphia. A lifelong freethinker, socialist and iconoclast, after his youthful years as an activist reformer, he started a Socialist newspaper in Girard, Kans., in 1919. That same year he began publishing his "Little Blue Books," a series of cheap, little paperback reprints, sales of which eventually rose to 500,000 each year. In addition to publishing such magazines as *American Freeman* and *Agnostic,* he wrote numerous books of his own, ranging from literary studies to a "How To" series, plus his 2-volume autobiography (1949, 1950).

Hale, Clara (b. McBride) "Mother" (1905–92) childcare activist; born in Philadelphia. Widowed in 1932, she supported her family by offering home child care, becoming a foster mother to some 40 children. In 1968, living in Harlem, New York City, with the encouragement of her daughter Dr. Lorraine Hale, she began to take in babies suffering the effects of birth to drug-addicted mothers. In 1973 she formally founded Hale House to put her program on a sounder financial basis. By the 1980s an increasing number of the babies were afflicted with AIDS. President Reagan awarded her the Medal of Freedom in 1985.

Hale, Edward Everett (1822–1901) author; born in Boston (great-nephew of Nathan Hale, nephew of Edward Everett). He graduated from Harvard (1839), became a Unitarian minister in Boston (1846), and was chaplain of the U.S. Senate (1903–09). A prolific author of historical and biographical works for adults as well as stories for younger readers, he is remembered today almost solely for his story published during the Civil War to encourage patriotism, "The Man Without a Country" (1863).

Hale, Eugene (1836–1918) U.S. representative/senator; born in Turner, Maine. A conservative, he was elected to the U.S. House of Representatives (Rep., Maine; 1869–79) and the U.S. Senate (1881–1911). He was a reliable supporter of business interests and although he helped to modernize the U.S. Navy, he opposed the spirit of imperialism that followed the Spanish-American War.

Hale, George Ellery (1868–1938) astronomer; born in Chicago. Doctors thought him too intense and anxious as a child (and he would suffer three breakdowns in his lifetime). While a student at Massachusetts Institute of Technology, he made astronomical observations at his own "Kenwood Observatory" at his home. In 1889, while on a Chicago trolley, he got the idea for the spectroheliograph, an instrument for measuring solar prominences in the daytime. His main work as an astronomer was in solar research and he wrote some 450 articles and books. Cognizant of the importance of institutions in fostering science, he cofounded the *Astrophysical Journal* (1895), held the organizing meeting of the American Academy of Sciences (1899), and established the National Research Council (1916). His most enduring monuments are the three observatories he established. First he built a 40-inch telescope for the Yerkes Observatory, in Chicago, which he directed (1892–1904). Then he built a 100-inch telescope for Mt. Wilson, near Pasadena, Calif., which he directed (1904–23). His poor physical condition forced him to retire from Mt. Wilson but in 1928 he returned to lead the construction of a new observatory for the California Institute of Technology at Mt. Palomar, near San Diego, Calif., for which he designed a 200-inch telescope; it was not installed until 1948, when it was named the Hale telescope. In 1970 the two California observatories were named The Hale Observatories in his honor.

Hale, Lilian (b. Westcott) (1881–1963) painter; born in Hartford, Conn. She studied with William Merritt Chase and at the Boston Museum of Fine Arts with Edmund Tarbell and Philip L. Hale, whom she married. Based in Dedham, Mass., she worked in charcoal, pastels, and oil, and is known for her impressionistic landscapes and portraits, such as *Zeffy in Bed* (c. 1912).

Hale, Nancy (1908–88) writer; born in Boston, Mass. She studied art at the Boston Museum of Fine Arts (1927, 1928) and with her artist father, Phillip L. Hale. She worked as an editor for *Vogue* (1928–32) and *Vanity Fair* (1932–33), and was the first woman reporter for the *New York Times* (1935). A lecturer at Bread Loaf Writers' Conference, Middlebury, Vt. (1957–65), she was based in Charlottesville, Va. She wrote plays, critical essays, a biography of Mary Cassatt, novels, and memoirs, as in *A New England Childhood* (1958). She is best known for her short stories, as in *The Pattern of Perfection* (1960).

Hale, Nathan (1755–76) soldier, martyr; born in Coventry, Conn. He graduated from Yale (1773) and became a Continental Army captain in 1776. He was captured by British soldiers while disguised as a schoolmaster and hanged. His famous declaration "I only regret that I have but one life to lose for my country" became a symbol of the Revolutionary spirit.

Hale, Philip (1854–1934) music critic; born in Boston, Mass. Writing for the *Boston Herald* (1903–33) and as a Boston Symphony Orchestra program annotator, he was a Boston legend with his conservative tastes in music and the arts.

Hale, Philip Leslie (1865–1931) painter, critic; born in Boston, Mass. Going to Paris in 1887 and joining Monet's Impressionist circle at Giverny, he returned in 1890 as "the boldest of the American Impressionists." Despite his openness to new styles in his painting and writings, he never gained much acclaim and is best known for his critical study, *Jan Vermeer of Delft* (1913).

Hale, Sarah Josepha (b. Buell) (1788–1879) editor, writer; born in Newport, N.H. She was editor of *Ladies' Magazine* (1828–37), the first successful U.S. women's magazine, and *Godey's Lady's Book* (1837–77), with which it merged. She also wrote verse, a popular cookbook, and other material aimed at women. Though largely a traditionalist, she energetically promoted female education.

Hale, William Gardner (1849–1928) classicist; born in Savannah, Ga. He was educated at Harvard (B.A. 1870) and taught at Cornell University (1880–1892) and the University of Chicago (1892–1919). He was influential in founding the American School of Classical Studies at Rome (now the American Academy at Rome) and was its first director (1895). His *Art of Reading Latin* (1887) was enormously influential, but his life's work was the preparation of an edition of the Catullus manuscript (known as "R"), which he found in the Vatican library.

Hale, William Jay (1876–1955) chemical engineer; born in Ada, Ohio. During World War I, Hale conducted research on mustard gas for the U.S. government. In 1919 he became director of organic chemical research at Dow Chemical. He made contributions to the production of phenol, indigo, chloracetic acid, and phenyl alcohol.

Haley, (Alexander Murray Palmer) Alex (1921–92) journalist, writer; born in Ithaca, N.Y. He grew up in Henning, Tenn., studied at Elizabeth City (N.C.) Teachers College (1937–39), and became a journalist while serving in the U.S. Coast Guard (1939–59). Retiring from the service, he established himself in Los Angeles as a free-lance writer, distinguished by his *Playboy* interviews. He first gained some national attention as the collaborator-editor of *The Autobiography of Malcolm X* (1965). His highly acclaimed work, *Roots: The Saga of an American Family* (1976, Pulitzer Prize) turned out to be a mixture of fact and fiction but was definitely based on his African-American roots; he had spent 12 years researching his ancestry and claimed to trace it to a Kunte Kinte, brought as a slave to America from Gambia in 1767. The book was the basis of a phenomenally successful television miniseries (1977), for which he received a special Pulitzer Prize and the Spingarn Medal. A sequel, *Queen* (1993), also appeared as a book and television miniseries.

Haley, Jay (1923–) psychologist, family therapist; born in Midwest, Wyo. He was educated at the University of California: Berkeley and Stanford; at the latter he was a research associate at the Project for Study of Communications. As a director of family experimentation at the Mental Research Institute in Palo Alto, Calif., he did influential work in family therapy and published (with Lynn Hoffman) *Techniques of Family Therapy* (1967). He was the director of family research at the Philadelphia Child Guidance Clinic (1967–74) and in 1974 became the director of the Family Therapy Institute in Chevy Chase, Md.

Haley, (William John) Bill (1925–81) musician; born in Highland Park, Mich. A pioneering rock 'n' roll singer, he led country-and-western bands around Philadelphia between 1942–52, when he formed the rhythm and blues-styled Bill Haley & His Comets. In 1954, his recordings of "Rock Around the Clock" and "Shake, Rattle & Roll" were among the earliest rock 'n' roll hits. He had his last hit record in 1956, but continued to record and tour in rock 'n' roll revival shows until 1980.

Hall, Asaph (1829–1907) astronomer; born in Goshen, Conn. A carpenter at age 16, he went to Harvard College Observatory in 1857 and became an expert computer of orbits. From 1862 until 1891, he worked at the naval observatory in Washington, D.C. In 1877, he discovered and named the two satellites of Mars, Deimos and Phobos.

Hall, Charles Francis (1821–71) Arctic explorer; born in Rochester, N.H. Restless as a blacksmith, stationer, and engraver, he made two notable search expeditions in the Arctic (1860–62, 1864–69) for Sir John Franklin's lost expedition of 1847. Congress authorized his attempt to reach the North Pole in 1871. He died of an apoplectic stroke while on the journey.

Hall, Charles Martin (1863–1914) engineer, manufacturer; born in Thompson, Ohio. In 1886, shortly after graduating from Oberlin College, Hall developed a new means of producing aluminum. In 1888 he organized the Pittsburgh Reduction Company to manufacture aluminum. Because he greatly reduced its cost, Hall is credited with making the metal a staple of the U.S. economy.

Hall, David (1930–) governor; born in Oklahoma City, Okla. An air force veteran and lawyer, he served as Tulsa County attorney (1962–66), becoming a University of Tulsa law professor in 1968. As Democratic governor of Oklahoma (1971–75), he reorganized the grand jury system and built new state agency offices. Convicted in 1975 for extortion and bribery while in office, he served a three-year prison sentence.

Hall, Donald (Andrew, Jr.) (1928–) poet; born in New Haven, Conn. (husband of Jane Kenyon). He studied at Harvard (B.A. 1951), Oxford University (B. Litt. 1953), and Stanford (1953–54). He taught at the University of Michigan (1957–75), became a free-lance writer in 1975, and worked as a television and radio broadcaster. He wrote plays, literary criticism, children's stories, books about baseball, and a memoir, *String Too Short to Be Saved* (1961). An editor of numerous poetry anthologies, he is best known as a tough, witty lyric poet, as seen in *The Museum of Clear Ideas* (1993). He and his wife lived in Wilmot, N.H.

Hall, Edward Twitchell, Jr. (1914–) cultural anthropologist; born in Webster Groves, Mo. Educated at the University of Denver and Columbia University (Ph.D. 1940), he began studying communications among the Hopi and Navajo Indians in the 1930s. After army service during World War II, he taught at Bennington, Illinois Tech, and Northwestern. He developed his theories of nonverbal communication and popularized them in *Silent Language* (1959). Other important works were *Beyond Culture* (1966) and *The Dance of Life* (1983). With his wife, he operated a consultancy that interpreted foreign cultures for business and government officials by drawing on his knowledge of gestures, body movement, and other types of nonverbal "languages."

Hall, Edwin H. (Herbert) (1855–1938) physicist; born in Great Falls (later North Gorham), Maine. He discovered the electromagnetic potential difference of conductors, now known as the "Hall effect," while a graduate student at Johns Hopkins (1879). He continued his thermoelectric research at Harvard (1881–1921), where he also wrote numerous physics textbooks and laboratory manuals.

Hall, (Granville) Stanley (1846–1924) psychologist, philosopher, educator; born in Ashfield, Mass. A Harvard Ph.D. also trained in Germany in physiology and experimental psychology, he established at Johns Hopkins what became the country's leading experimental psychology laboratory (1882). He was the first president of Clark University (1888–1920), originally modeled on German lines as an institution for scientific research. A founder and leader of the child-study movement in such works as *The Contents of Children's Minds* (1883) and *Adolescence* (2 vols. 1904), he was also a prolific and influential writer on secondary and higher education and, particularly after 1911, psychology, and he strongly influenced the development of educational psychology in America. He founded the *American Journal of Psychology* (1887) and the American Psychological Association (1891).

Hall, Gus (b. Arvo Kusta Halberg) (1910–) Communist Party leader; born in Iron, Minn. His parents were Finnish immigrants and charter members of the Communist Party, U.S.A. He worked as a lumberjack and steelworker, then went to Russia and studied at the Lenin Institute (1931–33). He joined the Communist Party, U.S.A. (1934). He served in the U.S. Navy (1942–46). He went to federal prison (1951–57) for conspiring to teach and advocate the violent overthrow of the U.S. government. He was national secretary (1950–59) and general secretary (1959) of the Communist Party, U.S.A. He was the Communist Party candidate for president of the United States (1972, 1976) and wrote numerous pamphlets and books, including *For a Radical Change: The Communist View* (1966) and *Fighting Racism* (1985).

Hall, James (1793–1868) lawyer, author; born in Philadelphia. He saw combat in the War of 1812, then quit the army in 1818 after a dispute with his commanding officer. Settling in Shawneetown, Ill., he practiced law, was elected state treasurer (1828), and edited the *Illinois Monthly Magazine* (1830), an early midwestern literary journal. He moved to Cincinnati in 1832, and, while working as a banker there, he wrote a series of books on the early frontier, including *The Romance of Western History* (1857). He also collaborated with Thomas L. McKenney in writing *History of the Indian Tribes of North America* (1836–44; 1884).

Hall, James, Jr. (1811–98) geologist, paleontologist; born in Hingham, Mass. Educated at Rensselaer Polytechnic Institute, he became both the leading stratigraphic geologist and invertebrate paleontologist of his day and an unparalleled collector of geological specimens. He published *Geology of New York,* Part 4 (1843); as New York state paleontologist (1843–98) and director of the New York State Museum (1871–98) he trained many younger paleontologists (including George B. Simpson and Charles Schuchert) and published the 13-volume *New York State Natural History Survey: Paleontology* (1847–94).

Hall, J. C. (Joyce Clyde) (1891–1982) greeting card manufacturer; born in David City, Nebr. A teenage entrepreneur, he was soon selling his "Hallmark" brand greeting cards nationwide from his Kansas City headquarters. Hallmark pioneered independent display racks, special occasion cards, and decorative gift wrap and by 1953 was the largest greeting card company in the world. With a reputation for running one of the firms in America most favorable to employees, he retired as Hallmark's president and CEO in 1966.

Hall, Richard Leland (1923–) food scientist; born in Roseland, Nebr. In 1950 he joined McCormack & Co., Inc. as director of research, in charge of investigating the flavor and odor constituents of spices. In 1965 he was made vice-president of research and development and in 1975 vice-president of science and technology. In 1988 he retired to become a consultant. He was active in the International Union of Food Science and Technology of which he was president (1983–87).

Hall, Rosetta S. (b. Sherwood) (1865–1951) physician/missionary; born in Liberty, N.Y. Besides conducting groundbreaking medical and educational work in Korea, she also championed the education of sight- and hearing-impaired persons there (1890–1933). She was the founder of both the Baldwin Dispensary, later to become the Lillian Harris Memorial Hospital (1892), and the Women's Medical (Training) Institute in Seoul (1928).

Halleck, Charles (Abraham) (1900–86) U.S. representative; born in Demotte, Ind. An infantryman during World War I and an Indiana University graduate, he became prosecuting attorney in Rensselaer, Ind. (1924–34). A Republican member of the U.S. House of Representatives (1935–69), he served as majority leader for six years and minority leader for four years, appearing in weekly television press conferences with Senator Everett Dirksen in the 1960s. In 1960 he was named permanent chairman of the Republican National Convention.

Halleck, Fitz-Greene (1790–1867) poet; born in Guilford, Conn. He was educated in public schools, was a store clerk (1806–11), bank clerk (1812–30), and personal secretary to John Jacob Astor (1832–49) in New York. He was noted for his satiric verse, such as *Fanny* (1819), but is now best known for his historical poems such as "Marco Bozzaris."

Halleck, Henry (Wager) (1815–72) soldier; born in Westerville, N.Y. An 1839 West Point graduate, he established a reputation as an authority on military defense before serving in California (1847–53). He resigned to study law (1854) and wrote two once-important books on mining law. Highly successful in both law and business, he accepted a commission as a major general when the Civil War broke out (1861). He was named general-in-chief of the Union armies (1862–64); overly devoted to details, and cold in his dealings with others, he proved indecisive and ineffectual in engagements and was effectively demoted when Grant became supreme commander in March 1864. Despite his lack of success in the war, he stayed on in various commands almost to his death.

Hallgren, Richard E. (1932–) meteorologist; born in Kersey, Pa. His award-studded career was dedicated to improving the administration of organizations to enhance the development of meteorology. He directed the National Weather Service (1979–88) and held posts in the National Oceanic and Atmospheric Administration before becoming executive director of the American Meteorological Society (1988).

Hallidie, Andrew (Smith) (1836–1900) engineer, inventor; born in London, England. An inventor's son, he emigrated to California with his father in 1852 and became a mining engineer. He later designed and built many bridges in California. In 1871 he perfected the invention for which he is remembered, the cable railroad. He introduced San Francisco's famous cable cars in 1873.

Hallowell, Alfred Irving (1892–1974) cultural anthropologist; born in Philadelphia. He graduated from Pennsylvania's Wharton School of Finance and was a social worker before turning to the study of anthropology. An authority on the Northern Ojibwa Indians, he published many studies of the tribes and made important contributions to culture-and-personality theory. His *Culture and Experience* appeared in 1955.

Halmos, Paul R. (Richard) (1916–) mathematician; born in Budapest, Hungary. Emigrating to America to study (1934), he specialized in pure mathematics. A noted teacher, his most recent post was Santa Clara University (1984). He was a member of the Hungarian Academy of Sciences and author of an autobiography.

Halpert, Edith Gregor (b. Fivoosiovitch) (1900–70) art dealer, collector; born in Odessa, Russia. She and her mother emigrated to New York City (1906), and she attended the National Academy of Design (1914–15). She worked in banking, and as a reorganizer of department stores before opening the Downtown Gallery of Contemporary Art with her husband, Samuel Halpert (1926); the gallery became one of the earliest supporters of modern American artists. She later expanded her space to include the American Folk Art Gallery (1929). She is known for assembling collections at the Williamsburg (Va.) and Shelburne (Vt.) museums, and for sponsoring exhibitions of unknown as well as well-known artists.

Halprin, Lawrence (1916–) landscape architect, writer; born in New York City. A disciple of Thomas Church, he founded his West coast firm in 1949, focusing on people's "spatial experience" of open areas and redesigning urban spaces like Ghiradelli Square in San Francisco to attract pedestrians, using multiple levels and fountains.

Halsey, William "Bull" (Frederick) (1882–1959) naval officer; born in Elizabeth, N.J. He served on the USS *Kansas* during the world cruise of the battle fleet (1907–09), commanded destroyers in World War I, and was the naval attaché at several European embassies (1922–24). He was promoted to rear admiral (1938) and vice-admiral (1940). In the aftermath of Pearl Harbor, he led the first offensives in the Pacific. He escorted the USS *Hornet* which brought Captain James Doolittle's B-52 squadron to within striking distance of the Japanese mainland (1942). He led the South Pacific force in the crucial naval battle of Guadalcanal (1942) and was promoted to admiral. He worked in tandem with General Douglas MacArthur, following the strategy of "island hopping." He was commander of the Third Fleet (1944–45) and began preparations for an assault on the Japanese mainland (1945). He became a fleet admiral (1945).

Halsted, William Stewart (1852–1922) surgeon; born in New York City. For most of his career he was affiliated with Johns Hopkins Hospital (1889–1922), where he trained many surgeons. In 1881, he administered what is thought to be the first blood transfusion in the United States. He devised successful operative techniques for breast cancer and inguinal hernia and discovered the anesthetic use of cocaine (1884).

Halston (b. Roy Halston Frowick) (1932–90) fashion designer; born in Des Moines, Iowa. He was chief custom milliner for Bergdorf Goodman (1959–68) before heading his own fashion house (1968–84). He dressed many socialites and entertainers in the trademark understated designs that earned him four Coty Awards.

Hamann, Donald R. (Robert) (1939–) physicist; born in Valley Stream, N.Y. He began working at Bell Telephone Laboratories in 1965. His contributions to solid-state physics include studies of the electronic structure of semiconductor surfaces, and investigations of the structure, spectra, and length of chemical bonds.

Hambridge, Jay (Edward John) (1867–1924) painter, theorist; born in Simcoe, Ontario, Canada. He ran away from home (1882), settled in New York City, and became an illustrator. He is known for his artistic theory of dynamic symmetry, which is based on the principle of organic growth.

Hamburg, David Alan (1925–) psychiatrist, educator; born in Evansville, Ind. He was professor and chairman of the department of psychiatry and behavioral sciences at Stanford (1961–72) and a member of many policy advisory boards. He conducted research in the areas of psychological stress and endocrine function; adaptive behavior under stress; psychotherapy in crisis; and the genetic basis of behavior.

Hamburger, Viktor (1900–) embryologist; born in Landshut, Germany. He taught in Germany (1926–32), then received a fellowship to the University of Chicago (1932–35). He moved to Washington University, St. Louis (1935–66), remaining active after achieving emeritus status in 1969. His microneurosurgical transplant experiments on chick embryos demonstrated the intrinsic properties of nerve fibers and their modification by environmental manipulation.

Hamill, Dorothy (Stuart) (1956–) ice skater; born in Riverside, Conn. In 1976 she won the world championship and a gold medal in the Olympics at Montreal, where her beauty and charisma won her worldwide acclaim. After her amateur career, she toured extensively with the Ice Capades.

Hamilton, Alexander (1757–1804) cabinet officer, political thinker; born in Nevis, British West Indies. Son of a Scottish merchant and a French Huguenot mother who died when he was 11, he went to work in a store that same year because his father's business was failing. He showed an early talent for writing and an ambition to gain an education, so aunts sent him to America in 1772; he entered King's College (now Columbia University) in 1773. Although always a moderate in his political views, he soon aligned himself with the anti-British patriots, writing lengthy pamphlets that left many amazed at the knowledge and writing skills of a 17-year-old. With the outbreak of the American Revolution, he joined the army and by early 1776 was fighting under George Washington's command. By March 1777 he was Washington's secretary and aide-de-camp and soon assumed considerable responsibilities that extended well beyond organizing Washington's communications and affairs – setting forth plans to reorganize not only the present army but the government that would follow the fighting. After a minor quarrel with Washington, he got himself reassigned to head an infantry regiment that he led at the siege of Yorktown. After a term in the Continental Congress (1782–83), he went into private law practice in New York City. As one of New York's delegates to the Constitutional Convention in Philadelphia in 1787, he did not exercise much influence as his ideas on the organization of a government were too conservative; but he signed the new constitution and in October he published the first of the so-called "Federalist papers" endorsing the new government. (Of the 85 "papers" – actually open letters, most signed by "Publius" – he wrote 51 and collaborated with James Madison on 3 others; Madison and John Jay wrote the remaining 31.) Hamilton also played a most crucial role in applying the power of his oratory and arguments to persuade New York State to adopt the Constitution. Selected by Washington as the first secretary of the treasury (1789–95), he proceeded boldly to structure the new nation's fiscal system, setting up a national bank and national mint and taking on the national debt. But the very aggressiveness that served to strengthen the new government also contributed to the divisiveness – particularly between Thomas Jefferson and himself – that led to the emergence of two opposing political parties, the Federalists led by Hamilton and the Democratic-Republicans led by Jefferson. Hamilton resigned in 1795 and returned to private law practice in New York City and remained recognized as head of the Federalists, but when Jefferson and Aaron Burr ended up in a tie in the presidential election of 1800, Hamilton used his influence to get the House of Representatives to choose Jefferson because he believed Burr to be a dangerous man. In 1804 Hamilton then used his influence to help defeat Burr's candidacy for the governorship of New York. Burr then challenged Hamilton to a duel and although he was opposed to dueling – his own son having been killed in one in 1801 – he met Burr early in the morning of July 11 at Weehauken, N.J.; Hamilton fired into the air but Burr mortally wounded Hamilton, who died the next day. Widely admired for his intellect, Hamilton was less popular for a certain arrogance in pursuit of his own beliefs. And if some of his ideas now seem less than congenial – especially his outspoken distrust of common people – he was probably the right man in the right place at the right time, giving form to many of the elements that allowed for the endurance of the government of the United States of America.

Hamilton, Alice (1869–1970) physician/social reformer; born in Fort Wayne, Ind. (sister of Edith Hamilton). A pioneer in industrial toxicology and a nonconformist who valued personal liberty above all else, she became a leading American authority on lead poisoning and one of the handful of worldwide specialists on industrial diseases by 1916. Her reports on lead – and later on rubber and munitions – led to improved safety standards nationwide. The product of an intellectually stimulating if socially protected environment, she chose medicine as the only way to be both independent and socially useful. It was during her more than a decade as a resident of Chicago's famous settlement house, Hull House, and her ensuing friendship with reformer Jane Addams that she coupled scientific research with her latent reformist zeal. Focusing on industrial diseases, she became a special investigator for the United States Bureau of Labor (1911), Harvard University's first professor of public health (1925), and she eventually published hundreds of studies on industrial toxicology, several books, and an autobiography.

Hamilton, Andrew (?1676–1741) lawyer, legislator; probably born in Scotland. He immigrated to Virginia about 1700. After serving as the steward of an estate, he married the widow of its owner; she seems to have backed him in buying a large property in Maryland, where he took up the practice of law and served in the assembly. After visiting England (1712–13), he returned to settle in Philadelphia, where he became attorney general, did valuable work for the colony's proprietors, and served in its general assembly (1727–39). A man of many talents, he helped design Province House in Philadelphia (now known as Independence Hall). His greatest moment came when in 1735 he was asked to come to New York City to defend John Peter Zenger against the charge of seditious libel; Hamilton's legal techniques and eloquent speech won this landmark case in the history of the freedom of speech.

Hamilton, Charles (1913–) autograph authority; born in Ludington, Mich. He grew up in Flint, Mich. and made his first acquisition (a Rudyard Kipling autograph) at age 12. He served in the U.S. Army Air Corps (1942–45) and in 1952 began to specialize in identifying handwriting and autographs. He established Charles Hamilton Galleries, Inc., in New York City in 1963, the first American auction gallery devoted exclusively to autographs. He wrote numerous books, including *The Signature of America: A Fresh Look at Famous Handwriting* (1979). An expert at spotting forgeries, he became engaged in several notable controversial cases.

Hamilton, Charles (Memorial) (1840–75) U.S. representative; born in Clinton County, Pa. A lawyer, he enlisted in the Union army in 1861 and went with the military government to Florida in 1865, serving as a Republican representative (1868–71), once Florida was readmitted to Congress.

Hamilton, Edith (1867–1963) classicist, author; born in Dresden, Germany (sister of Alice Hamilton). Born to Americans visiting abroad, she learned Latin and Greek while a child. She was educated at Bryn Mawr (B.A., M.A. 1894) and then served as the headmistress of the Bryn Mawr School (Baltimore, Md.), the first U.S. school designed to prepare young women for college (1896–1922). Under considerable strain, she retired to what would be a life devoted to literature and writing. She began with a series of articles on ancient drama in *Theatre Arts Monthly* (1927–29) and then made a sudden impact with *The Greek Way* (1930). She continued to publish articles and other books such as *Mythology* (1942) that, if not taken that seriously by scholarly specialists, made her one of the 20th century's best-known popularizers of the classical tradition. In her late years she was the recipient of many honors such as honorary citizenship of Athens and an invitation from President Kennedy to his inauguration.

Hamilton, George Heard (1910–) art historian; born in Pittsburgh, Pa. He studied at Yale (B.A. 1932; M.A. 1934; Ph.D. 1942), and Cambridge (M.A. 1971). He taught at Yale (1936–66), Williams College (beginning in 1963), and became the director of the Sterling and Francine Clark Art Institute, Williamstown, Mass. (1966–77). He specialized in the history of 19th- and 20th-century art.

Hamlin, Hannibal (1809–91) vice-president, U.S. senator; born in Paris Hill, Maine. He became Lincoln's vice-president in 1861 but did not play an active role. A vigorous opponent of slavery, he was advocating such harsh views of the South that he was not renominated. He later served in the Senate and was identified with the radical Republicans and with the harsh policies of Reconstruction.

Hamlin, Talbot (Faulkner) (1889–1956) architect, architectural historian; born in New York City. He was a practicing architect (1914–34) and Columbia University professor of architectural theory (1916–54); his writings such as *The*

American Spirit in Architecture (1926) awakened popular interest in American architecture.

Hamlisch, (Frederick) Marvin (1944–) composer; born in New York City. A prodigy, he was admitted to the Juilliard School of Music at age seven. In 1974 he won Oscars for the title song and score from *The Way We Were* (1973) and for his adaptation of Scott Joplin's ragtime music in the *The Sting* (1973). He composed the music for *A Chorus Line* (1975), the longest running musical in Broadway history. He also performed and conducted with major symphony orchestras.

Hammer, Armand (1898–1990) industrialist, art collector, philanthropist; born in New York City. His father, Julius Hammer, was a Russian immigrant who was a doctor, a socialist activist, and a founding member of the American Communist Party. While earning his medical degree at Columbia University, Armand made his first million dollars running his father's pharmaceutical business. In 1921 he went to the new Soviet Union to help combat a typhus epidemic; realizing that starvation was also a problem, he hit upon the idea of trading American grain for Soviet furs and other goods. By this time he had gained the support of Lenin, who gave Hammer certain commercial concessions, and he made even more millions in manufacturing and trade. Back in the U.S.A. by 1930, his many business ventures in the 1930s and 1940s included trading in whiskey, cattle, and priceless art works acquired in Russia. In 1956 he bought the near-bankrupt Occidental Petroleum; in his 33 years as chairman and CEO he turned it into a billion-dollar conglomerate through a series of oil strikes and rights deals and the acquisition of fertilizer, chemical, and coal companies. He championed U.S.-Soviet relations throughout the cold war, promoting cultural and commercial exchanges and representing the U.S.A. in trade talks; as one of the few Americans trusted by the Soviet leaders, he became an unofficial ambassador and liaison during difficult moments. (In 1986 he personally paid for a team of physicians to rush to Russia in the wake of the Chernobyl nuclear disaster.) Immensely rich, he supported many philanthropies through the Armand Hammer Foundation and made major donations to Columbia University, the National Gallery, and the Metropolitan Museum of Art. His own extensive art collection was left to the Armand Hammer Museum that he established in Los Angeles in 1990.

Hammerstein, Oscar (1846–1919) theatrical impresario; born in Stettin, Germany. Grandfather of Oscar Hammerstein II, he built several theaters, including the Manhattan Opera House in 1906, and brought many fine singers to the U.S.A.

Hammerstein, Oscar, II (1895–1960) lyricist; born in New York City (grandson of Oscar Hammerstein). The writer of words for *Show Boat* in 1927 with composer Jerome Kern, he is considered one of America's foremost song writers. His greatest successes were with Richard Rodgers. Together they created *Oklahoma!* (1943), *Carousel* (1945), *South Pacific* (1949), and *The Sound of Music* (1959). His singable lyrics include "Ol' Man River," "Oh, What a Beautiful Morning," and "Climb Every Mountain."

Hammett, (Samuel) Dashiell (1894–1961) writer; born in St. Mary's County, Md. After serving in the army in World War I, he went to San Francisco where he became a Pinkerton detective and advertising copywriter, then, after the success of his first novels, a Hollywood scriptwriter. He published

some short stories in *The Black Mask* but most of his work came out in a five-year period, starting with *Red Dust* (1929) and ending with *The Thin Man* (1934). He effectively invented hard-boiled detective fiction with his lean prose style and cynical detective, Sam Spade, and his work was praised by many serious writers and critics. Long identified with left-wing politics, in 1951 he spent six months in jail for refusing to testify about the Civil Rights Congress, of which he was a trustee. In 1953, after refusing to answer questions from Senator Joseph McCarthy's committee, he was blacklisted by Hollywood. He lived the last 30 years of his life with the writer Lillian Hellman.

Hamming, Richard W. (Wesley) (1915–) computer scientist; born in Chicago, Ill. Head of the Computing Science Research Department, Bell Laboratories (1946), he specialized in problem-solving on large-scale computers and computer design. Editor of several journals, he wrote *Numerical Methods for Scientists and Engineers* (1962) and is founder of the Association for Computing Machinery.

Hammon, Jupiter (1711–c. 1790–1806) writer, poet born in Oyster Bay, Long Island, N.Y. Little is known of his life, but it is known that he was born a slave, worked as a clerk for the Lloyd family, and was reportedly educated by missionaries from England. His first published poem, "An Evening Thought" (1761), preceded the work of Phillis Wheatley by six years, thus earning him the distinction of being the first African-American to be published. He later moved to Hartford, Conn., with Joseph Lloyd when the British invaded Long Island (1776). His work was published by the Quakers and includes religious essays, sermons, and poetry. A collection of his work, *America's First Negro Poet: The Complete Work of Jupiter Hammon of Long Island,* was published in 1970.

Hammond, George H. (Henry) (1838–86) meatpacker; born in Fitchburg, Mass. After working as a butcher and a mattressmaker, he moved to Detroit in 1854. There, fire destroyed his mattress factory so in 1857 he opened a meat market and slaughter house. He was the first to envision refrigeration cars and sent the first load of refrigerated beef to Boston (1868–69). By 1885 he had over 800 refrigeration cars in use. He expanded his operation to Omaha, Neb., and Hammond, Ind. (named after him).

Hammond, John (Henry, Jr.) (1910–87) music producer; born in New York City. A member of a wealthy and socially prominent family, he attended Hotchkiss and left Yale before graduation in 1931 to pursue a multifaceted career in music. In 1931 he acquired ownership of a theater in New York in which he showcased black jazz and theatrical performers. In 1932 he produced a recording by Fletcher Henderson's Orchestra, and for the rest of the decade he was associated with the British and American operations of Columbia Records. As a talent scout and record producer, he helped launch the careers of Benny Goodman, Billie Holiday, Teddy Wilson, Count Basie, and Charlie Christian. An ardent civil libertarian, he covered the Scottsboro Boys trials for the *New Republic* and the *Nation* in 1933 and 1935, promoted Goodman's trailblazing interracial band in 1935, joined the board of the National Association for the Advancement of Colored People in 1937, and produced the *Spirituals to Swing* concerts at Carnegie Hall in 1938–39. He served in the U.S. Army during World War II, and worked as a producer of classical and jazz recordings for Vanguard and

Columbia between 1946–60. In 1962–63 he produced Bob Dylan's first two releases, and for the next 20 years he guided the early careers of a second wave of popular music figures, including Aretha Franklin, George Benson, Bruce Springsteen, and Stevie Ray Vaughan. His autobiography, *John Hammond on Record,* was published in 1977.

Hammond, Norman (1944–) archaeologist, anthropologist; born in England. He was educated through his Ph.D. at Cambridge University, England, where he taught until joining the Rutgers University faculty (1977). A fieldworker of wide range, he became best known for his work on Maya settlements and structures; his books include *Ancient Maya Civilization* (1982) and *Nohmul . . .* (1985).

Hammond, William A. (Alexander) (1828–1900) neurologist, army doctor; born in Annapolis, Md. As army surgeon general from 1862–64, he reformed and reorganized the army medical department to meet the burden of tens of thousands of wounded and sick Union soldiers; he supervised more than 230 army general hospitals. Secretary of War Edwin Stanton dismissed Hammond on trivial charges (1864), but a review board exonerated him in 1879. As a civilian, he taught at medical schools, started medical journals, wrote a great deal – including the pioneer text, *Treatise on Diseases of the Nervous System* (1871) – and generally advanced the treatment of nervous and mental diseases.

Hampden, Walter (b. Dougherty) (1879–1955) stage actor; born in Brooklyn, N.Y. A romantic presence, he performed both classic and commercial theater, appearing several times in the title role of *Cyrano de Bergerac.*

Hampton, Lionel (Leo) (1909–) jazz musician; born in Louisville, Ky. Originally a drummer, he later introduced the vibraphone into jazz on a recording with Louis Armstrong in 1930. He came to prominence as a member of Benny Goodman's small groups in the late 1930s. He formed his first big band in 1942, continuing as a leader until the 1990s, and presenting his entertaining blend of musicianship and showmanship on many tours.

Hampton, Mark (1940–) interior decorator; born in Plainfield, Ind. With an M.F.A. from New York University's Institute of Fine Arts and following employment with Mrs. Henry Parish II and with McMillen, Inc., he established his own New York practice (1976). His historical re-creations brought commissions to restore Gracie Mansion (1984) and to redecorate Blair House (1985).

Hampton, Wade (1751–1835) soldier, politician; born in Halifax County, Va. He fought in the American Revolution and afterwards served two terms in Congress. Reentering the army in 1808, Hampton received a share of blame for the failed U.S. expedition to Montreal (1813) during the War of 1812. At one time he was said to be the wealthiest plantation owner in the U.S.A.

Hampton, Wade (1818–1902) Confederate soldier; born in Charleston, S.C. The son and grandson of wealthy planters, he raised and commanded "Hampton's Legion" and succeeded J. E. B. Stuart as commander of Confederate cavalry in 1864. Hampton was a postwar governor (1876–79) then U.S. senator (1879–91) from South Carolina.

Hancock, (Herbert Jeffrey) Herbie (1940–) jazz musician; born in Chicago. He was a classically-trained pianist who emerged with Miles Davis in 1963 and began leading his own stylistically wide-ranging groups in 1968.

Hancock, John (1737–93) merchant, patriot; born in Braintree, Mass. He inherited his uncle's merchant business in 1764, and entered the patriot ranks in 1765 in opposition to the Stamp Act. He engaged in smuggling and one of his ships was seized in 1769. He served as the president of the Massachusetts Provisional Congress (1774–75) and as president of the First and Second Continental Congresses (1775–77). He was the first member to sign the Declaration of Independence. Following his period in Congress (1775–80), he helped to frame the Massachusetts constitution and was elected as the first governor of that state (1780–85; 1787–93). He presided at the state convention which ratified the Constitution and he died during his ninth term as governor.

Hancock, Thomas (1703–64) merchant; born in present-day Lexington, Mass. He established himself in bookselling and in the merchant trade. He furnished supplies to British forces in Nova Scotia (1746–58) and the ships for the removal of the Acadians (1755). He left his estate to his nephew, John Hancock.

Hancock, Winfield Scott (1824–86) soldier; born in Montgomery Square, Pa. A West Point graduate (1844), he served in the Mexican War, Seminole War, and on the western frontier. Commissioned a brigadier general in 1861, he helped General George McClellan organize the Army of the Potomac, and then fought at Fredericksburg, Chancellorsville, and Gettysburg. It was at this last battle that he achieved his greatest fame for reforming the shattered federal forces and repulsing two crucial Confederate attacks. Tall, handsome, and dignified, he fit the 19th-century image of a soldier nearly to perfection; McClellan called him "Hancock the Superb." After the war he held various army commands and then ran as the Democratic candidate for president in 1880, losing by the narrowest of margins to James A. Garfield.

Hand, Augustus Noble (1869–1954) jurist; born in Elizabethtown, N.Y. The son of a lawyer, he graduated from Harvard in 1890 and from Harvard Law School in 1894 before joining his uncle's law firm. Woodrow Wilson appointed him a U.S. district judge for the Southern District of New York in 1914, where he served with his cousin, the jurist Learned Hand. Named to the U.S. Court of Appeals in 1927, Augustus earned a reputation for open-mindedness. He is remembered for his pungent comment about James Joyce's novel *Ulysses,* calling it "a swill pail tragedy of the human soul at low ebb"; he did, however, join in the majority opinion that ruled the book was not obscene. In a 1943 ruling, he upheld the notion that Congress could limit exemptions from military service to those with strictly religious objections. He remained on the federal bench until the year of his death.

Hand, (Billings) Learned (1872–1961) jurist; born in Albany, N.Y. The son and grandson of judges (and cousin of Augustus Hand), he graduated from Harvard in 1893 and from Harvard Law School three years later. A bookish boy, he grew into a skeptical, open-minded adult. He practiced in Albany and in New York City until 1909, when he received an appointment as U.S. district judge for the Southern District of New York. In a 52-year career as district judge (1909–24), appeals court judge (1924–39), and chief judge (1939–51) of the 2nd U.S. Court of Appeals, he issued some 3,000 opinions touching virtually every area of law. His opinions were so highly regarded that he became known as the 10th judge of the U.S. Supreme Court. In 1944, in a neat summary of his own intellectual approach, he declared: "The spirit of liberty is the spirit which is not too sure that it is right." In a series of lectures at Harvard near the end of his life, he warned the judiciary not to exceed its constitutional authority by attempting to legislate from the bench.

Handlin, Oscar (1915–) historian; born in New York City. He taught at Harvard University (1938). His doctoral thesis, *Boston's Immigrants 1790–1865* (1941), updated as *The Uprooted* (1951), won a Pulitzer Prize and established him as an authority on immigration. With his wife, sociologist Mary Flug Handlin, he wrote *Commonwealth* (1947). Other works include *Race and Nationality in American Life* (1957) and *The Distortion of America* (1981).

Handsome Lake (b. Kaniatario) (?1735–1815) Seneca political/religious leader, half-brother of Cornplanter; born near present-day Avon, N.Y. After experiencing a series of visions (1799), he began preaching the traditional values of sobriety, family, and community. Elected a tribal leader in 1801, he convinced the U.S.A. to guarantee Iroquois land boundaries and to stop liquor sales on the reservation; he also urged his people to take up farming. His principles, subsequently influenced by Quakers, were published in 1850.

Handwerker, Nathan (1891–1974) food merchant; born in Poland. He arrived in New York in 1912 and worked as a roll slicer for Charles Feltman (sometimes credited as the "inventor" of the hot dog in America). Taking advice form Jimmy Durante and Eddie Cantor, and assistance from his fiancée Ida, he opened a sidewalk stand on Coney Island in 1916, selling his hot dogs for a nickel, half of what Feltman charged. His stand grew and in 1925 he incorporated as Nathan's Famous. Further expansion occured in 1957 when son Murray Handwerker (born 1921) persuaded his father to open a second store in Ocean Side, Long Island; soon thereafter they began franchising. Nathan's Famous went public in 1967 and began selling products to supermarkets in the early 1970s.

Handy, (William Christopher) W. C. (1873–1958) composer, born in Florence, Ala. He was one of the first composers to incorporate the blues idiom into song forms and orchestrations. He published his first song in 1912, and subsequently wrote such famous songs as "St. Louis Blues" and "Beale Street Blues." In 1918, he founded an early black-owned music publishing business. His autobiography, *Father of the Blues,* was published in 1941.

Hanfmann, George M. A. (Maxim Anossov) (1911–88) archaeologist; born in St. Petersburg, Russia. After his family fled Russia in 1917, he was educated first in Lithuania and then at the University of Berlin, Germany, where he earned his doctorate in 1934. Fleeing Hitler's Germany for the United States, he taught at Harvard (1935–82), after earning a second doctorate at Johns Hopkins (1935). His monumental work, *The Seasons Sarcophagus at Dumbarton Oaks* (1951), was a seminal work in the iconography of ancient sarcophagi, but he is best remembered as the director of the excavations at Sardis, Turkey (1958–82) and for his restoration of that site's Roman bath-gymnasium-synagogue complex.

Hanford, William Edward (1908–) chemist, inventor; born in Bristol, Pa. He received a Ph.D. from the University of Illinois and joined E. I. du Pont de Nemours & Company as a research chemist. He and Donald F. Holmes, a colleague at du

Pont, developed polyurethane in 1942. Hanford later became director of research for M. W. Kellog and, in 1957, vice-president for research and development at Olin Industries.

Hanke, Lewis (Ulysses) (1905–) historian; born in Oregon City, Ore. Educated at Northwestern (B.S. 1924; M.A. 1925) and Harvard (Ph.D. 1936), he taught at the University of Texas (1951–61), Columbia University (1961–67), the University of California: Irvine (1967–69), and the University of Massachusetts (1969–75; professor emeritus, 1975). He directed the Hispanic Foundation of the Library of Congress (1939–51), was special assistant to the U.S. Secretary of State for Latin American Affairs, and member of the U.S. National Commission for the United Nations Educational, Scientific, and Cultural Organization (UNESCO) (1952–54). Often credited with establishing Latin American history as a viable academic discipline in the U.S., his international reputation is reflected by his numerous international honorary degrees. His personal scholarship focused on the Spanish viceroys and Dominican missionary Bartolome de Las Casas, and he organized massive sources into usable forms. His five volume *Guide to the Study of United States History Outside the U.S., 1945–1980* (1985), reveals how foreigners study the United States. He received the Nebrija Award, one of Spain's highest cultural honors, in 1992.

Hanna, Edward (Joseph) (1860–1944) Catholic prelate; born in Rochester, N.Y. After studies and ordination in Rome and teaching posts in classics and theology, he was named auxiliary bishop (1912) and then bishop (1915) of San Francisco, also serving (from 1917) as a spokesman for the Catholic War Council and (from 1919) as a leader of its successor, the National Catholic Welfare Council (later Conference). A progressive attacked by some Catholics for "Americanism," he stressed interfaith cooperation and helped settle a major longshoreman's strike (1934). In 1935 he retired and moved to Rome.

Hanna, (Marcus Alonzo) Mark (1837–1904) businessman, U.S. senator; born in New Lisbon, Ohio. He prospered in the grocery business, coal mining, the iron industry, and shipping and also acquired the *Cleveland Herald* before embarking on a career in politics. After getting his friend William McKinley elected governor of Ohio (1892–96) he engineered McKinley's nomination as the Republican candidate for president in 1896 and then managed his victory in the most expensive and best organized campaign ever seen until then. As chairman of the Republican National Committee (1897) he got himself appointed to the U.S. Senate (Rep., Ohio; 1897–1904). In his first years he devoted most of his energies to promoting his party's goals, but when Theodore Roosevelt succeeded to the presidency in 1901, Hanna took on a surprisingly more statesmanlike, if still conservative role; he admittedly endorsed "standpattism" but he also supported the right of labor to organize unions.

Hanna, William (Denby) (1910–) film animator/producer; born in Melrose, N.M. and **Barbera, Joseph (Roland)** (1911–) film animator/producer; born in New York City. Hanna had been working in Hollywood as a story editor, lyricist, and composer since 1930 when in 1937 he went over to Metro-Goldwyn-Mayer (MGM). That same year Barbera joined MGM after having worked as an accountant and free-lance magazine cartoonist. Hanna and Barbera, working with producer Fred Quimby, soon created the Tom and Jerry cartoon characters and went on to make some 100 short cartoons featuring the cat and mouse – winning 7 Academy Awards along the way. In 1957 they left MGM and set up their own production company, Hanna-Barbera, concentrating on cartoon series for television, including *The Flintstones, Yogi Bear,* and *Huckleberry Hound.*

Hansberry, Lorraine (1930–65) playwright; born in Chicago. She is best known as the author of *A Raisin in the Sun* (1959). A Broadway success and later a movie, the novel explored the struggles of a black family to escape from the ghetto. Hansberry died prematurely, before she was able to fulfill her promise as an eloquent spokesperson for African-Americans' trials and aspirations.

Hänsch, Theodor W. (Wolfgang) (1941–) physicist; born in Heidelberg, Germany. He came to the U.S.A. to teach and do research at Stanford University (1970). He advanced the field of optics with his studies of lasers and spectroscopy of atoms and molecules.

Hansell, Haywood Shepherd, Jr. (1903–88) aviator; born in Fort Monroe, Va. The son of an army surgeon, he graduated from Georgia Institute of Technology (1924) and worked as a boilermaker before enrolling as a flying cadet in 1928. One of a group of officers that believed air power alone could win a war, he reported on the German Blitz from London and later, commanding B-17s, participated in the bombing campaign against Germany. As chief of staff of the 20th Air Force in 1945, he helped plan the long-range strategic bombing of Japan. He became an executive for the General Electric Company after his retirement from the service in 1955.

Hansen, Alvin Harvey (1887–1975) economist; born in Viborg, S.D. He was instrumental in promoting Keynesian economic theory in the U.S.A. During his years at Harvard (1937–57), he also served as an adviser to the Council on Social Security (1937–38) and the Federal Reserve System (1940–45) and he contributed to the creation of the Full Employment Act of 1946.

Hansen, Marcus Lee (1892–1938) historian; born in Neenah, Wis. He received his Ph.D. from Harvard University (1924) and taught at the University of Illinois (1928–38). His study of cross-Atlantic immigration took him to European archives (1925–27); his data on the ethnic composition of the United States in 1790 was used in formulating immigration quotas. Published posthumously, his *Atlantic Migration 1607–1860* received the 1941 Pulitzer Prize in history.

Hansen, William Peat (1923–) petrochemical engineer; born in Waco, Texas. He directed the building of gas, oil, and petrochemical facilities in Saudi Arabia for Aramco (1974–79), as well as oil refinery projects in Alberta, Canada, for Esso (1979–81). After retiring in 1987, he became a consultant to the petroleum and petrochemical industry.

Hanson, Ann (b. Coffin) (1921–) art historian; born in Kinston, N.C. She studied at the University of Southern California (B.F.A. 1943), the University of North Carolina (M.A. 1951), and Bryn Mawr College (Ph.D. 1962). She was a consultant and director for several museums and taught at various institutions, notably at Yale (1970). She specialized in 19th-century French paintings, and 15th-century Italian sculpture.

Hanson, Howard (1896–1981) composer, conductor, educator; born in Wahoo, Nebr. He studied and taught in the U.S.A. before winning the Rome Prize in 1921. He returned

from Italy in 1924 to become director of the Eastman School of Music in Rochester, N.Y., remaining there until retirement in 1964. His compositions, including seven symphonies and the opera *Merry Mount* (1934), typically reflect both his Swedish family background and a conservative, Romantic spirit. He was also an important conductor and promoter of American composers, both conservative and innovative.

Hanson, John (1715–83) colonial and Revolutionary official; born in Charles County, Md. He served in the Maryland Assembly almost continuously from 1757 to 1779. He signed the Association of the Freemen of Maryland (1775), which approved armed resistance against the British. Elected to the Continental Congress in 1779, he signed the Articles of Confederation (1781) and then served as president of the Congress of the Confederacy – some historians have therefore called him "the first president of the United States." He worked to free the public lands to the west from the control of individual states, especially Virginia.

Hapgood, Isabel Florence (1850–1928) translator; born in Boston, Mass. She spent ten years learning every Germanic and Romance language before starting her career in 1886 as a translator, essayist, and reviewer. From her voluminous output she is best remembered for her many translations of Russian masterpieces, particularly Turgenev's novels and stories (16 vols. 1905).

Hapgood, Norman (1868–1937) editor, author; born in Chicago. Particularly successful as the muckraking editor of *Collier's Weekly* (1903–12), he later edited *Harper's Weekly* (1913–16) and *Hearst's International Magazine* (1923–25); he was also a drama critic and wrote several biographies.

Happer, William, Jr. (1939–) atomic physicist, optical engineer; born in Vellore, India, to an American medical missionary and a Scottish medical military officer. His mother brought him home to North Carolina in 1941. Happer worked in Columbia University (1964–80), where he invented the miniaturized resonance magnetometer (1977). He joined Princeton (1980–91), then moved to the U.S. Department of Energy (1991). He made major contributions to the fields of optics, laser spectroscopy, and spin polarization.

Harbach, Otto (b. Otto Abels Hauerbach) (1873–1963) librettist, lyricist; born in Salt Lake City, Utah. Educated at Knox College, he taught English and worked as a journalist and advertising copywriter. He made his Broadway debut as lyricist for *Three Twins* (1908) and went on to write musicals with composers such as Karl Hoschns and Rudolf Friml in the next decade. After 1920 some of his best work was in collaboration with Oscar Hammerstein II, libretti and lyrics for such shows as *Rose Marie* (1924). He also contributed to *No, No, Nanette* (1925). Among his most popular songs are "Indian Love Call" (1924) and "Smoke Gets in Your Eyes" (1932).

Harbison, John (Harris) (1938–) composer; born in Orange, N.J. After studies at Harvard, Princeton, and in Berlin, he taught at the Massachusetts Institute of Technology from 1969. He is admired for writing communicative music with an eclectic blend of techniques.

Harburg, (Edgar) E. Y. "Yip" (1896–1981) librettist, lyricist; born in New York City. Showing an early talent for acting and writing, he attended a high school for gifted students where he met Ira Gershwin; they both went to the City College of New York where they collaborated on a column for the college newspaper. Harburg contributed light verse to the newspapers, but it was hearing Gilbert and Sullivan's *H.M.S. Pinafore* that made him want to be a lyricist. Needing to support himself, he worked for a business that took him to South America (1918–21). He returned to start an electrical appliance business and had his first lyrics performed on Broadway in 1926. The stock market crash of 1929 forced him to take up writing full time and in the ensuing years he wrote a number of standards, including "Brother, Can You Spare a Dime?" (1932). He collaborated with several composers but enjoyed his greatest success with Harold Arlen; they wrote many standards for film and stage musicals including "Over the Rainbow" (1939). In 1947 he was blacklisted in Hollywood for left-wing sentiments, and he returned to Broadway, collaborating on the book and writing lyrics for several musicals, the most successful being *Finian's Rainbow* (1947). He continued to work in theater until 1977 and was killed in an automobile crash just before he was to be honored with a television tribute and receive an award from the Songwriters Hall of Fame.

Harcourt, Alfred (1881–1954) publisher; born in Ulster County, N.Y. In 1919 he cofounded the firm that eventually became Harcourt Brace Jovanovich. As its president until 1941, he used his acumen and taste to acquire fine authors and make the company prosper.

Hardee, William Joseph (1815–73) soldier; born in Savannah, Ga. An 1838 West Point graduate, he served on the frontier and in the Mexican War and then was commandant of cadets at West Point (1856–61). He also wrote the standard pre-war manual of infantry tactics. Having joined the Confederate army when his native state seceded, he commanded a corps at Perryville, Ky. (1862), Stone's River, Tenn. (1862), and Chattanooga (1863). He ordered the evacuations of Savannah and Charleston, S.C., as Sherman approached, and surrendered to Sherman in April 1865.

Hardin, Garrett (James) (1915–) ecologist, educator; born in Dallas, Texas. Educated at the University of Chicago and Stanford (Ph.D. 1941), he joined the faculty of the University of California: Santa Barbara in 1946 and became an emeritus professor there in 1978. Originally a plant biologist, he became increasingly interested in genetics, evolution, and the problems of pollution and population growth. In such books as *Nature and Man's Fate* (1959) and *Exploring New Ethics for Survival* (1977) he argued that disease, starvation, and social disorder will result unless human population growth is curbed. He campaigned for legalized abortion during the 1960s and was president of the Environmental Fund in 1980–81.

Harding, Florence (b. Kling DeWolfe) (1860–1924) First Lady; born in Marion, Ohio. A divorcee and five years older than Warren Harding, after their marriage (1891) she became a major influence in advancing his career. Following his untimely death, she ignored rumors that she had poisoned him. She later destroyed personal papers that might have told more about the marriage.

Harding, Warren G. (Gamaliel) (1865–1923) twenth-ninth U.S. president; born in Corsica (now Blooming Grove), Ohio. After three years at Ohio Central College, he went to work for a Marion, Ohio, newspaper, then bought the *Marion Star* (1884); as its editor he became prominent in the local Republican party. He served two terms in the state senate (1899–1903) and one term as lieutenant governor (1903–05). Known mainly for his old-fashioned oratory and his genial

compliance with the Republican machine, he was elected to a term in the U.S. Senate (1915–21), where his record was distinguished only by his adherence to conservative Republican policies. Back-room politics – engineered by his longtime Ohio mentor, Harry M. Daughtery – secured him the presidential nomination and a confusing campaign gained him a victory in November 1920. Having promised war-weary Americans a "return to normalcy," he proved as lax and shallow as his previous record indicated. Although not personally corrupt, he allowed corruption to permeate his administration; he left most initiatives to Congress and his cabinet while he played poker with his "Ohio gang" in the White House. As a Senate investigation into what proved to be the Teapot Dome scandal began, he went on a tour to Alaska; there he received a coded message informing him of the corruption about to be exposed; en route home, in San Francisco, he became mysteriously ill, allegedly from food poisoning, and suddenly died. The best that historians have been able to say of Harding as president is that he was a man who was in over his head.

Hardison, O. B. (Osborn B.) (1928–90) historian, professor, librarian; born in San Diego, Calif. After taking a Ph.D. at the University of Wisconsin (1956), he taught for a short while at the University of North Carolina before being appointed director of the Folger Shakespeare Library in Washington, D.C. (1969–83). While there he founded the Folger Theater Group (now the Shakespeare Theater at the Folger), introduced the Folger Consort, specializing in medieval and Renaissance music, improved the facilities for the care of the Folger rare book collection, and made the Folger a center for international scholarship. In 1984 he became professor of English at Georgetown University. His books, on a wide range of topics, include *Christian Rite and Christian Drama in the Middle Ages* (1965), *Prosody and Purpose in the English Renaissance* (1989), *Disappearing through the Skylight: Culture and Technology in the Twentieth Century* (1989), and two volumes of poetry, *Lyrics and Elegies* (1958) and *Pro Musica Antiqua* (1977).

Hardy, Oliver See under LAUREL AND HARDY.

Hare, David (1917–) sculptor; born in New York City. He studied at several schools (1923–39) before becoming a medical photographer. Based in New York City, he came under the influence of European surrealists. The publisher and founder of the surrealist periodical *VVV* (1942–44), he used metal forms in his sculptures, as in *Suicite* (1946). In 1965 he also began to work as a painter.

Hare, (James H.) Jimmy (1856–1946) photojournalist; born in London, England. Shortly after arriving in the United States, he became a news photographer in New York (1890–1931), covering five wars and taking the first aerial photos.

Hare, Raymond A. (Arthur) (1901–) diplomat; born in Martinsburg, W.Va. Following consular appointments in the Middle East, he became ambassador to Saudi Arabia (1950), Lebanon (1953), Egypt (1956–60), and Turkey (1961–65). He was director-general of the Foreign Service (1954–56) and assistant secretary of state (1965–66). He was president of the Middle East Institute in Washington, D.C. (1966–69).

Hare, Robert (1781–1858) chemist, educator; born in Philadelphia. Self-taught, he became professor of chemistry at the University of Pennsylvania (1818–47). In 1801, he found the means of producing high temperatures by burning hydrogen and oxygen and invented the blowtorch.

Harken, Dwight E. (1910–93) surgeon, medical innovator; born in Osceola, Iowa. He took his B.A. and M.D. at Harvard, and won a fellowship to study medicine in London, where he began devising his innovative surgical approaches to treat heart infections. During World War II he served with the U.S. Army Medical Corps in London; in removing bullets and shrapnel from the hearts of some 130 soldiers without a single fatality, he became the world's first surgeon to have such success in operating on hearts. After the war he taught at Tufts Medical School (1946–48), then went to Harvard Medical School (1948–70); during those years he was also chief of thoracic surgery at Peter Bent Brigham Hospital in Boston and Mt. Auburn Hospital in Cambridge, Mass. He continued to pioneer in the technology and procedures of surgery to treat malfunctioning hearts. In the 1960s he developed and implanted the first device to assist the heart's pumping and the first internal pacemaker; he was among the first to implant artificial valves. In 1951 he opened the world's first intensive care unit at Brigham Hospital, an approach that was soon adopted for patients in all kinds of life-threatening conditions. His original support group for cardiac patients evolved into Mended Hearts, now an international organization, and he was a cofounder of Action on Smoking and Health (ASH). He wrote or edited more than 200 articles and several books and was active in various medical organizations.

Harkins, Paul Donal (1904–84) soldier; born in Boston, Mass. A 1929 West Point graduate, he served as a staff officer in Italy and France during World War II. In his last assignment before retirement, he commanded the U.S. Military Assistance Command in South Vietnam during the early years (1962–64) of the American build-up there.

Harkness, Georgia Elma (1891–1974) educator, author; born in Harkness, N.Y. Raised on a farm, she graduated from Cornell University (1912), taught high school for several years and took a Ph.D. from Brown in 1923. She taught philosophy and religion at Elmira College, N.Y., from 1923–37, meanwhile turning out books that developed her evangelical liberal ideas. *Holy Flame,* the first of her several volumes of devotional poetry, appeared in 1935. She later taught at Mount Holyoke and at the Pacific School of Religion in Berkeley, Calif. Retiring to Claremont, Calif., in 1961, she continued to publish a book a year until her death. Among her 38 books was *The Dark Night of The Soul* (1945), in which she wrote about the religious meaning of suffering.

Harkness, Sara (b. Pillsbury) (1914–) architect; born in Swampscott, Mass. After taking her master's degree in architecture from Smith College (1937), she worked for several architectural firms. In 1946, she cofounded the Architects' Collaborative, where she took a principal role designing among other projects the Fox Lane Middle School, Bedford, N.Y. (1966), and Schlecter Auditorium, Dickinson College, Carlisle, Pa. (1971).

Harlan, James (1820–99) U.S. senator, college president, cabinet member; born in Clark County, Ill. He grew up on the frontier and was admitted to the bar in 1850. He was president of Iowa Conference University (now Iowa Wesleyan University) (1853–55, 1869–70). A U.S. senator from Iowa (Free Soil Party, 1855–61; Rep., 1861–65), he supported Lincoln (whose son, Robert Lincoln, later married Harlan's daughter). He was secretary of the interior (1865–66), in which capacity he is most noted for dismissing Walt Whitman from a clerical post. Returning to the U.S. Senate (Rep., Iowa; 1867–73), he voted for the impeachment of President Andrew Johnson. He failed in subsequent runs for senator and governor, but his long and sometimes controversial political career was rewarded when Iowa placed his statue in the U.S. Capitol.

Harlan, John Marshall (1899–1971) Supreme Court justice; born in Chicago (grandson of Supreme Court justice John M. Harlan, 1833–1911). He held a number of public positions before President Eisenhower named him to the U.S. Court of Appeals for the Second Circuit (1954–55) and then to the U.S. Supreme Court (1955–71).

Harlan, John Marshall (1833–1911) Supreme Court justice; born in Boyle County, Ky. Active in Kentucky politics, he served as state attorney general (1863–67) and twice ran unsuccessfully for governor (1871 and 1875). He was instrumental in Rutherford Hayes's presidential campaign (1876) and subsequently President Hayes named him to the U.S. Supreme Court (1877–1911).

Harlan, Josiah (1799–1871) soldier, adventurer; born in Newlin Township, Pa. (brother of Richard Harlan). During 17 years in the Far East (1823–41) he was a Bengal Artillery medical officer, secret agent in Afghanistan, and Punjabi governor; he told his story in *A Memoir of India and Avghanistaun* [sic] (1842). He was a Union cavalry commander during the Civil War and afterwards a San Francisco physician.

Harland, Henry (Sidney Luska, pen name) (1861–1905) writer, editor; born in New York City. He posed as a Russian-Jewish immigrant schooled in Europe and Harvard. The only truth to his story was that he attended the Harvard Divinity School for a brief period (c. 1882). He studied at City College (1877–80), and using his pen name, wrote novels about Jewish immigrants, such as *The Yoke of the Thorah* (1887). He moved to Paris (1889), wrote additional novels under his real name, and settled in London (1890). He was the founder and editor of the literary and artistic journal, *The Yellow Book* (1894–97), and wrote romantic novels such as *The Cardinal's Snuff-Box* (1900).

Harland, Thomas (1735–1807) watchmaker, clockmaker, silversmith; born in England. He came to Norwich, Conn. (1773) and made fine watches and clocks. By 1790, he had apprentices all over the U.S.A. and his shop was producing 240 watches and clocks per year.

Harlow, Bryce N. (Nathaniel) (1916–87) lobbyist, government official; born in Oklahoma City, Okla. An army veteran and House Armed Services Committee chief clerk, he was President Eisenhower's congressional liaison and speech writer (1951–61). Chief lobbyist for Proctor and Gamble, he worked briefly for Richard Nixon in 1968. He received the Presidential Medal of Freedom in 1981.

Harlow, Harry (Frederick) (1905–81) ethologist, primate researcher; born in Fairfield, Iowa. Educated at Stanford University, he taught at Wisconsin University (1930–74) and directed its Regional Primate Center (1961–71). His experiments in animal behavior led to his discovery of the process whereby an animal "learns to learn," which provides a valid index to its intelligence. His work with infant monkeys and their surrogate mothers (terrycloth dummies) demonstrated the crucial importance of bonding between primate mothers and infants for emotional health and growth. Highly acclaimed at the time of his original work (early 1960s), these experiments would later become controversial both for some of their procedures as well as conclusions.

Harlow, Jean (b. Harlean Carpenter) (1911–37) actress; born in Kansas City, Mo. Married at age 16 to a wealthy young businessman, she moved to Beverly Hills with him and began appearing in minor roles in movies in 1928. Millionaire playboy and movie producer Howard Hughes discovered her and propelled her into overnight stardom in *Hell's Angels* (1930). With her platinum-blonde hair, her slim but sexy body, her casual, slightly vulgar manner, she quickly dominated the movies and the headlines. She showed a flair for comedy in such films as *Dinner at Eight* (1934) and was able to spoof her own sex-driven image in *Bombshell* (1933). Her private life, however, was not as lighthearted; she divorced her first husband in 1932, and her second husband committed suicide only months after their marriage; a third marriage was unhappy; and while engaged to William Powell and filming *Saratoga,* she died of a cerebral edema. Her life would provide a number of eerie parallels to Marilyn Monroe's.

Harmar, Josiah (1753–1813) soldier; born in Philadelphia. Quaker-educated, he fought under Washington (1778–80) and on the southern front (1781–83) during the American Revolution. From 1784–91 he headed the new nation's one-regiment military establishment. His 1790 expedition against Indians in Ohio was a notable failure. Harmar resigned in 1792 and served as the Pennsylvania adjutant general from 1793–99.

Harnett, William (Michael) (1848–92) painter; born in Clonakilty, Ireland. He came to America as a child, moved to New York (1871), was an engraver until 1874, and then devoted himself to still life painting. His realistic work, such as his *After the Hunt* (1885), prompted many imitators who worked in the "trompe l'oeil" tradition, a photographic-like depiction of objects.

Harney, (Benjamin Robertson) Ben (1872–1938) ragtime songwriter, performer; born in Louisville, Ky. Trained in classical piano, at age 17 he composed one of the earliest ragtime songs, "You've Been a Good Old Wagon But You've Done Broke Down," which became a big hit. He moved to New York in 1896 and performed the new musical style. Before suffering a heart attack in 1928, he toured the United States, Europe, and the Far East. With the rise of jazz, ragtime declined and he died in poverty.

Harper, Fletcher (1806–77) publisher; born in Newton, N.Y. Youngest of the Harper brothers, he joined the family publishing firm in 1825 and played a key role in its expansion, notably by creating *Harper's Weekly* (1857) and *Harper's Bazaar* (1867).

Harper, Frances Ellen Watkins (1825–1911) social reformer, lecturer, poet; born in Baltimore, Md. Born free in a slave city, she was raised by an abolitionist uncle and was well enough educated that by 1845 she published her first volume of poetry. She took up teaching sewing by 1850, but in 1854 she gave her first antislavery lecture; she would continue to give such lectures throughout the Northeast. She also gave recitations of her poems, and published her second volume, *Poems on Miscellaneous Subjects* (1854), which soon made her the best-known African-American poet of the era. She also published articles against slavery and a short story, "The Two Offers" (1859), probably the first such published work by any African-American. After her husband of four years

(1860–64) died, she returned to lecturing on a variety of social causes, stressing the need for temperance, education, and morality among her fellow African-Americans. She was active in various organizations, including the formation of the National Association for the Advancement of Colored Women (1896), and in her later years, she also took up the cause of women's rights. Her extensive writings – including more volumes of poetry, a travel book, and a novel – no longer have much literary status but they were important in providing a new image of and for African-Americans.

Harper, James (1795–1869) publisher; born in Newton, Long Island, N.Y. In 1817, with his brother John Harper, he established the firm that, with his younger brothers as partners, became Harper & Brothers, one of the world's leading publishing companies. Besides publishing books, the company launched popular magazines, including *Harper's Bazaar* in 1867, and pioneered in printing technology. Harper also served a one-year term as reform mayor of New York City (1844–45).

Harper, Michael (Steven) (1938–) poet, writer; born in New York City. He studied at City College (1954), California State: Los Angeles (B.A. 1961; M.A. 1963), the University of Iowa (M.A. 1963), and the University of Illinois (1970–71). He taught at many institutions, notably at Brown University (1983), and lived in Providence, R.I. He wrote poems linked to the sensibilities of African-Americans, as in *Healing Song for the Inner Ear* (1985).

Harper, Mike (Charles Michael) (1927–) food company executive; born in Lansing, Mich. He spent 20 years at Pillsbury Company before moving to ConAgra, Inc., Omaha (1974). As variously president, CEO, and chairman of the board (1976) he rescued ConAgra from near-bankruptcy; through acquisitions such as Banquet Frozen Foods and Armour Foods, he created one of the largest food companies in the country.

Harper, Robert Goodloe (1765–1825) lawyer, public official; born near Fredericksburg, Va. He served briefly during the American Revolution, graduated from the College of New Jersey (now Princeton) in 1785, and settled in Ninety Six, S.C., where he practiced law, taught school, and entered politics. He became a prominent Federalist leader in the U.S. House of Representatives (S.C., 1795–1801) before leaving public service in 1801 to practice law in Baltimore. A founding member of the American Colonization Society (1817), he suggested the name Liberia for the proposed African colony for freed slaves.

Harper, William (1944–) jeweler, metalworker; born in Bucyrus, Ohio. A professor at Florida State University: Tallahassee (1974), he is known for his innovative jewelry and metal objects using anthropological and religious imagery.

Harper, William Rainey (1856–1906) educator, Hebraist; born in New Concord, Ohio. A Yale Ph.D. at age 18, this widely published and brilliant teacher of Semitic languages and literature planned and served as the first president of the University of Chicago (1891–1906), which he created as a great research university, recruiting a brilliant faculty and establishing its extension system, cooperative programs, graduate schools, and university press.

Harrigan, Edward (1845–1911) actor, playwright, manager; born in New York City. Beginning as a vaudeville performer, he formed a highly popular team with Tony Hart. His songs and short sketches eventually grew to full-length musicals, featuring comic characters broadly drawn from American working-class life, including African-American and European immigrants. His shows include *The Mulligan Guards' Ball* (1879) and *Cordelia's Aspirations* (1883).

Harriman, Edward H. (Henry) (1848–1909) financier, railroad executive; born in Hempstead, N.Y. Starting as an office boy on Wall Street, by 1869 he became a member of the Stock Exchange. His marriage to Mary Averell (1879), daughter of a railroad president, led to his life-long career running railroads. By 1883 he was director of the Illinois Central, becoming vice-president in 1887. In 1895 he took the lead in reorganizing the Union Pacific and by 1903 was its president. He was investigated by the Interstate Commerce Commission (1906–07) for speculating with the resources of the Union Pacific. These charges, along with his ruthless approach to all of his business operations – which included banks, insurance companies, and a steamship line – gained him the reputation of one of the worst of the "robber barons." In 1899 he took 25 prominent scientists to Alaska; the results of that expedition are published in 14 volumes called the *Harriman Alaska Series* (1902–14).

Harriman, (William) Averell (1891–1986) financier, public official, diplomat; born in New York City. Son of railroad tycoon Edward Henry Harriman and chairman of the board of the Union Pacific Railroad (1932–46), he was a close friend of President Franklin D. Roosevelt and prominent in the National Recovery Administration (1934–35). In 1941 he was special war aid representative in England and traveled to Moscow with Lord Beaverbrook and with Prime Minister Winston Churchill (1942). He was ambassador to the U.S.S.R. (1943–46) and to Britain (1946), then secretary of commerce (1946–48). As special assistant to President Truman (1950–51), he helped organize NATO. From 1951–53 he directed foreign aid under the Mutual Security Agency. Twice losing the Democratic presidential nomination, he was elected governor of New York (1955–59). He served as undersecretary of state in the Kennedy and Johnson administrations (1961–65) and as ambassador-at-large for Johnson he headed the American delegation during negotiations with North Vietnam in Paris (1968–69).

Harrington, John Peabody (1884–1961) linguist, anthropologist; born in Waltham, Mass. His interest in the languages of Native Americans began while an undergraduate at Stanford University (B.A. 1905). From 1909–15 he studied Indian languages as an ethnologist at the School of American Archaeology in Santa Fe, N.M., and in 1915 he joined the Smithsonian Institution's Bureau of Ethnology, from which he retired in 1954. His respect for the American Indian's knowledge of their world lent credence and support to the study of that knowledge. He is especially remembered for the accurate, voluminous, and valuable notes he took on more than 90 languages, mostly Native Americans.

Harris, Benjamin (fl. 1673–c. 1720) journalist; born in England. Frequently arrested for his activities as a publisher, he fled to America in 1685 and set up a bookstore in Boston; there he published a popular almanac, the *New England Primer,* and other books, as well as *Publick Occurrences Both Foreign and Domestick* (on September 25, 1690), the first American newspaper (which was, however, suppressed after the first issue). In 1695 he returned to England, where he remained active.

Harris, Chauncy (Dennison) (1914–) geographer; born in

Logan, Utah. He took a doctorate from the University of Chicago in 1940, remaining there to teach; he also served as dean of social sciences (1955–60) and director of the Center for International Studies (1966–84). Appointed Samuel N. Harper Distinguished Service Professor (1973), he became vice-president for academics (1975–78), retiring in 1984. With J. Fellman he compiled the *International List of Geographical Serials* (1960, 1971, 1980), and he wrote *Cities of the Soviet Union* (1970). He was active in national and international geographical organizations, holding several offices with the International Geographic Union.

Harris, George Washington (Sugartail, pen name) (1814–69) journalist, humorist; born in Pittsburgh, Pa. Raised from age four in Tennessee, he had little formal schooling but was apprenticed to a jeweler; showing mechanical ability, he wrote articles for the *Scientific American*. He took up writing political pieces in 1839; starting in 1843, and using the pen name "Sugartail," he began to contribute humorous "sporting" sketches to *Spirit of the Times,* published in New York City. In the years that followed, he held several jobs – running a foundry and glass factory, steamboat captain, railroad engineer – and drawing on his varied experiences, he wrote his one published work, *Sut Lovingood Yarns* (1867), a genially boisterous series of tales about a typical Tennessee countryboy of the time. Although hardly high art, they are regarded as a precursor of the work of Mark Twain and others in the American colloquial vein.

Harris, Joel Chandler (1848–1908) writer; born near Eatonville, Ga. As a boy he worked as a printer's assistant (1860–62) on a newspaper published by Joseph Addison Turner, who also encouraged Harris to read and write; Turner owned a plantation and Harris became acquainted with the African-American slaves and their speech, stories, and customs. He then became a journalist for newspapers in Macon and Savannah, Ga., and in New Orleans before settling in Atlanta to work for the *Atlanta Constitution* (1876–1900), which carried the first of his "Uncle Remus Stories," "The Story of Mr. Rabbit and Mr. Fox" in 1879. Its popularity led to a long series of tales, published over the next quarter century in various collections, starting with *Uncle Remus: His Songs and His Sayings* (1880). The tales feature Uncle Remus, an African-American and former slave who tells the tales to the son of the family he now serves; many of the stories feature animals such as Brer (Brother) Rabbit and Brer Fox, and draw on the folklore of African-Americans as well as reproduce their speech, so that the tales are regarded as providing at least glimpses of authentic folklore. Harris also wrote other stories and novels about life in the South; his *On the Wing of Occasions* (1900) is a collection of stories featuring Billy Sanders, the Sage of Shady Dale, a character who expresses the views of average Georgians of the day.

Harris, Julie (b. Julia Ann Harris) (1925–) stage actress; born in Grosse Pointe, Mich. The tiny, intelligent, husky-voiced actress played a wide range of roles, including Emily Dickinson in *The Belle of Amherst* (1976).

Harris, (Louis) Lou (1921–) public opinion analyst; born in New Haven, Conn. He worked with Elmo Roper as a political pollster for ten years before founding Louis Harris and Associates (1956), a New York City firm that became known for its sophisticated qualitative public opinion polls for industrial and political clients. He was associated as a pollster with President John F. Kennedy's administration and with CBS and ABC News (1962–80); he also wrote a syndicated newspaper column (1963).

Harris, Marvin (1927–) cultural anthropologist, author; born in New York City. He was educated at Columbia University (B.A. 1949; Ph.D. 1953) and joined the faculty there in 1952. He was chairman of the anthropology department at Columbia (1963–66) before becoming professor of anthropology at the University of Florida. Occasionally controversial for his claims, such as that the Aztecs gained much of their necessary protein from eating sacrificial victims, he gained a reputation as a "comparative" anthropologist by studying the findings and issues common to the work of his fellow anthropologists in many areas; he then demonstrated an ability to relate these professional matters to concerns of a broader public in such works as *Cannibals and Kings* (1957) and *Our Kind: Who We Are, Where We Came From, Where Are We Going* (1990).

Harris, Paul Percy (1868–1947) lawyer, founder of Rotary International; born in Racine, Wis. He grew up in Vermont and then went to Iowa where he received his law degree (1891). He moved about for five years and then settled in Chicago and practiced law. As a non-native who felt isolated, he began to bring three Chicago business acquaintances together for informal meetings; in 1905 he called their meetings the "Rotary Club" because they originally met in rotation at their offices. The idea spread to other cities and by 1910 the National Association of Rotary Clubs was founded, with Harris as its president (1910–12; emeritus president to his death). He tirelessly preached a secular gospel of sociability and service and the clubs spread throughout the world until Rotary International was founded in 1922.

Harris, Rollin Arthur (1863–1918) oceanographer; born in Randolph, N.Y. He spent his career (1890–1918) with the U.S. Coast and Geodetic Survey. He wrote extensively on ocean (especially Arctic) tides and hydrodynamics, and invented instruments pertinent to his research.

Harris, Roy (Ellsworth) (1898–1979) composer; born in Lincoln County, Okla. Taking up music in his twenties, he studied with Nadia Boulanger in Paris (1927–28) and returned to quick success in the U.S.A. He taught in a number of colleges while composing steadily. His Symphony No. 3 (1939), permeated by American folk idioms, was a sensational success and popular through the 1950s; his later music, eventually including 15 symphonies, never quite recaptured the inspiration or success of that highly influential work.

Harris, (Stanley Raymond) "Bucky" (1896–1977) baseball player/manager; born in Port Jervis, N.Y. As an outstanding second baseman for the Washington Senators, he was made a player-manager in 1924 at age 27, earning him the title of "boy wonder." During his 29 years as manager (1924–56), mostly with the Senators and Detroit Tigers, he won three league pennants and two world championships. He was elected to baseball's Hall of Fame in 1975.

Harris, T. George (1925–) magazine editor, author; born in Simpson County, Ky. While serving with the army in World War II, he received a battlefield promotion during the Battle of the Bulge. He began at the University of Kentucky but took his B.A. degree in psychology from Yale (1949), with a period at Oxford University, England, in 1948. He worked on the editorial staff of *Time* magazine (1949–62). He went on to start a short-lived magazine, *Careers Today,* with Peter Drucker, the management consultant, and then became the editor of *Psychology Today* (1969–76), which he converted from a publication with fairly "dry" technical articles to one with a more popular approach and eye-catching graphics. Between 1976–81 he served as a consultant and free-lance editor for various publications. In 1981 he founded *American Health,* which he sold to the Reader's Digest Corporation in 1988. After serving as editor of publications on children's health and as a consultant for various magazines, he became editor of the *Harvard Business Review* in August 1992; fired in January 1993 over policy differences, he concentrated on his own writing.

Harris, William Torrey (1835–1909) philosopher, educator; born in North Killingly, Conn. The leading American exponent of German philosophy, he was founding editor of the *Journal of Speculative Philosophy* (1867–93) and author of works on philosophy and education. He pursued educational reform as St. Louis school superintendent (1867–80) and as U.S. Commissioner of Education (1889–1906).

Harrison, Anna (b. Symmes) (1775–1864) First Lady; born in Walpack Township, N.J. She married William Henry Harrison in 1795. She never saw the White House; she was ill in early 1841, and missed Harrison's inauguration and his one month as president.

Harrison, Benjamin (?1726–91) governor; born in Charles City County, Va. (father of William Henry Harrison). He served in the Virginia House of Burgesses (1749–75), later leading resistance to the British. In the Continental Congress (1774–77), he presided over debates which led to the Declaration of Independence, which he signed. A member of Virginia's House of Delegates (1777–81, 1784–91), and Virginia's governor (1781–84), he championed the Union and the Bill of Rights.

Harrison, Benjamin (1833–1901) twenty-third U.S. president; born in North Bend, Ohio. Grandson of a U.S. president and son of a U.S. senator, he took up law practice in Indianapolis in 1854. During the Civil War he raised a regiment and led it with distinction. Active thereafter in Republican politics, he made two unsuccessful bids for the Indiana governorship before gaining a seat in the U.S. Senate (1881–87), where he supported civil service reform and a protective tariff. In 1888 he rode the tariff issue into the presidency with the support of big business. As president he signed the high McKinley Tariff and the Sherman Silver Purchase Act (both highly unpopular) as well as the Sherman Antitrust Act; he also supported several international conferences. His association with high tariffs was the main element in his loss to Grover Cleveland in 1892. He returned to legal practice in Indianapolis, regaining respect for his responsible views on national and international issues.

Harrison, Byron (Patton) (1881–1941) U.S. representative/senator; born in Crystal Springs, Miss. After losing his father at age seven, he hawked newspapers and drove mules, later teaching school while he earned his law degree. In the U.S. House of Representatives (Dem., Miss; 1911–19) and the Senate (1919–41) he supported President Wilson's internationalism. Chairman of the Finance Committee (1932–41), he secured passage of New Deal legislation, although after 1937 he became selectively supportive of Roosevelt.

Harrison, Caroline (Lavinia b. Scott) (1832–92) First Lady; born in Oxford, Ohio. She and Benjamin Harrison were married in 1853. She was well-educated and had artistic and musical talents. She fell ill with tuberculosis during the 1892 election campaign and died two weeks before Harrison lost that election.

Harrison, Carter Henry (1825–93) businessman, mayor; born near Lexington, Ky. Having made a fortune in Chicago real estate, he turned to public service, becoming a U.S. representative (Dem., Ill.; 1875–79). A gifted speaker, the author of several books, a man of personal integrity, and a popular campaigner, he won the support of business people, moderate socialists, and immigrants alike as mayor of Chicago (1880–88, 1893). He was assassinated by a young man whom he had turned down for a job. His son, Carter Henry Harrison Jr., was a five-term mayor of Chicago (1898–1906, 1912–14).

Harrison, John, Jr. See under SURRATT, MARY EUGENIA.

Harrison, Lou (1917–) composer; born in Portland, Ore. A Schoenberg student, he became a prolific composer concerned with new instruments and techniques, later composing Asian-influenced music, often for homemade instruments.

Harrison, Peter (1716–75) architect; born in York, England. Settling in Newport, R.I. (1740), he introduced Palladianism to New England in public buildings designed for Newport, Boston, and Cambridge (1748–61) and assembled the colonies' most important private architectural library.

Harrison, Ross G. (Granville) (1870–1959) developmental biologist; born in Germantown (Philadelphia), Pa. He taught at Bryn Mawr College (1894–95), then joined Johns Hopkins (1886–1907). He moved to Yale (1902–38, emeritus 1938–59), then became chairman of the National Research Council (1938–46). He performed extensive transplantation experiments in frog embryos to investigate nerve fiber development (1897–1910). He devised the hanging drop microscopy technique to observe living cells (1907). In the same year he demonstrated that nerve cells cultured outside the body will undergo normal differentiation, thus proving that the cell is the fundamental developmental unit of the multicellular organism. He designed elegant experiments using salamander larvae to demonstrate interspecific grafting, and also investigated eye development, the embryological implications of the neural crest, and alterations of limb symmetry. He was a calm and judicious person, who, after his retirement, served on many scientific and academic committees, and was acclaimed as a visiting lecturer.

Harrison, William Henry (1773–1841) ninth U.S. president; born in Charles City County, Va. Wellborn and well-educated, Harrison opted for the army and in the 1790s fought Indians in the Northwest Territory under Anthony Wayne. As governor of the new Indian Territory (1800–12), he extracted millions of acres from the Indians and fought Tecumseh's rebels in the battle of Tippecanoe (November 1811); though the battle was inconclusive, it made Harrison a hero. Commanding regular army forces in the Northwest during the War of 1812, he reoccupied Detroit in 1813 and soundly defeated the British and Indians at the Thames River in Ontario, Canada (October 1813). He went on to serve Ohio in the U.S. House of Representatives (1817–19) and in the U.S. Senate (1825–28). After an unsuccessful presidential campaign in 1836, Harrison won (as a Whig) with Tyler as vice-president in 1840, on a campaign of ballyhoo and mudslinging, with its slogan, "Tippecanoe and Tyler too." An exhausted Harrison caught a cold at the inauguration and he died of pneumonia a month later.

Harsanyi, John C. (Charles) (1920–) economist, educator; born in Budapest, Hungary. After completing his studies through the Ph.D. (1947) at the University of Budapest, he immigrated to Australia in 1950. There he took an M.A. at the University of Sydney (1953) and was a lecturer in economics at the University of Queensland (1954–56). In 1956 he came to the United States as a Rockefeller Fellow at Stanford University. He became a research associate with the Cowles Foundation at Yale University (1957) and took a Ph.D. at Stanford (1959). He went back to Australia to become a senior fellow at the Australian National University (1959–61), then returned to the U.S.A. to become a professor of economics at Wayne State University (1961–63). In 1964 was appointed a visiting professor of economics at the Haas School of Business at the University of California: Berkeley; he became a full professor in 1965, later also becoming the Flood Research Professor in Business Administration, positions he held until taking emeritus status in 1990. One of his main areas of work involved the formal study of rationality in human affairs, specifically in taking ethical positions or making moral judgments. His other area was game theory, the application of mathematics to formulating rational behavior in conflicts among rational persons. His various publications include *Rational Behavior and Bargaining Equilibrium* (1977) and (with Reinhard Selten) *A General Theory of Equilibrium Selection in Games* (1988). For his contributions to game theory, Harsanyi shared the 1994 Nobel Prize in economic science with John F. Nash, an American, and Reinhard Selten, a German.

Hart, Charles Henry (1847–1918) lawyer, art expert; born in Philadelphia. Educated privately when young, he graduated from the law school of the University of Pennsylvania (1869), and practiced in Philadelphia (1869–94). After a serious accident (1894), he became an authority on historical portraits – particularly the work of Gilbert Stuart – and was known for exposing fraudulent works of art.

Hart, Doris (1925–) tennis player; born in St. Louis, Mo. She won six Grand Slam tournaments between 1949 and 1955, including the French and U.S. twice, and the Australian and Wimbledon once each.

Hart, Edwin Bret (1874–1953) biochemist; born in Sandusky, Ohio. A University of Michigan graduate, he was professor of agricultural chemistry at the University of Wisconsin (1906–44), where he researched the chemistry of dairy production and animal nutrition and metabolism. He discovered the role of iodine and copper in preventing goiter and anemia, and the importance of vitamins in animal nutrition.

Hart, Frederick E. (1943–) sculptor; born in Atlanta, Ga. Starting out as a painter, he was attracted to sculpture and decided he should learn the craft of stonecutting; in 1967 he got himself a job with the on-going construction of the National Cathedral in Washington, D.C., and within a couple of years was an apprentice stonecutter, rendering ornamental decorations. In 1971, he opened his own studio to work out his ideas for the west facade, and in 1974 his design for the main entrance won an international competition; the finished work, carved from Indiana limestone in a traditional romantic-realist style – most notably the tympanum, *Ex Nihilo* – was dedicated in May 1990. Before this, he had placed third in the competition for the Vietnam War Memorial; in the uproar that followed the choice of My Lin's wall, he was awarded a second commission, and his realistic bronze, known variously as "Three Servicemen" or "Three Fighting Men," was dedicated in 1984. He later served on the board of the President's Commission on Fine Arts and took it upon himself to attack what he regarded as a lack of spiritual values in much modern art, although he himself worked in lucite and other plastics.

Hart, Gary (Warren) (b. Hartpence) (1936–) lawyer, U.S. senator; born in Ottawa, Kans. He studied both law and divinity at Yale and became a lawyer in Colorado. He managed George McGovern's presidential campaign (1972) and served in the U.S. Senate (Dem., Colo.; 1976–84). He made a strong run for the Democratic presidential nomination in 1984 and began in 1988 as the frontrunner. He had to abandon his 1988 campaign amid allegations of infidelity, prompted by his presence aboard the vessel *Monkey Business* in the company of a model, Donna Rice. He returned to Colorado to practice law.

Hart, George (Overbury) "Pop" (1868–1933) painter, etcher; born in Cairo, Ill. Based in New York and New Jersey, he used water colors and was an etcher and lithographer. He recorded genre scenes during his travels throughout the world.

Hart, (Milton) Lorenz (1895–1943) lyricist; born in New York City. He studied journalism and wrote poetry at Columbia University and translated plays for the Shuberts before meeting composer Richard Rodgers in 1918. They collaborated on four songs for *Poor Little Ritz Girl* (1920) and did their first complete score for *The Garrick Gaieties* (1925). During the next 18 years they collaborated on a string of successful Broadway and Hollywood musicals – among them *On Your Toes* (1936), *The Boys from Syracuse* (1938), and *Pal Joey* (1940). Although they created many popular songs, including "With a Song in My Heart" (1929), "Blue Moon" (1934), and "My Funny Valentine" (1937), Hart's show lyrics were distinguished by their clever wordplay, intricate internal rhymes, and often sardonic attitude. Dissatisfied with his life, he went on a drinking binge and died of pneumonia.

Hart, Philip A. (Aloysius) (1912–76) U.S. senator; born in Bryn Mawr, Pa. He was admitted to the Michigan bar in 1938. He served in the U.S. Army and was wounded on D-Day (1944). He was the district attorney for Michigan and then lieutenant governor of that state (1955–59). As a U.S. senator (Dem., Mich.; 1959–76) he was considered by his colleagues the "conscience of the Senate." He advocated civil rights, antipollution, and antitrust legislation. He sponsored the Truth in Packaging Act (1965) and the Truth in Lending Act (1966).

Hart, Thomas (Charles) (1877–1971) naval officer; born in Davison, Mich. He commanded the Asiatic fleet (1939–42) and was supreme commander of the ABDACOM (American-British-Dutch-Australian Command) (1941–42). He served on the General Board (1942–45) and filled an unexpired Senate term (Rep., Conn.; 1945–46).

Hart, William S. (Surrey) (1870–1946) movie actor, director; born in Newburgh, N.Y. Learning about the West through youthful travels with his father, he went on the New York stage at age 19 and achieved considerable fame as a Shakespearean and serious actor. He made his first movie at age 44 and was soon directing (and occasionally writing) his

own films, usually Westerns in which he tried to convey the authentic Old West, with realistic sets and costumes as well as plots and character, but with little action and less romance. Although immensely popular and critically acclaimed for a decade, he sued United Artists after making *Tumbleweeds* (1925) and this put an abrupt end to his film career. He spent his later years writing Western novels and an autobiography.

Hartack, (William John Jr.) Bill (1932–) jockey; born in Ebensburg, Pa. Between 1956 and 1969, he won the Kentucky Derby five times, the Preakness three times, and the Belmont once. He served as an occasional television commentator after 1981.

Harte, Bret (b. Francis Brett Harte) (1836–1902) writer, consular official; born in Albany, N.Y. Moving to California at age 18, he worked at various jobs before becoming a journalist. He became an official of the U.S. Mint in San Francisco (1863–70) but worked at his own writing and coedited the *Overland Monthly* (1868–70), for which he commissioned some articles by Mark Twain. Harte's stories and poems on western themes helped launch the "local color" movement and he achieved a meteoric national celebrity with his collection of stories, *The Luck of Roaring Camp and Other Sketches* (1870). He moved to the East to be part of the literary world, but his reputation soon faded and he became U.S. consul in Germany (1878–80) and at Glasgow (1880–85). Settling in London for the rest of his life, he continued to write short stories and he hobnobbed with the literati, but he never again knew the success of his San Francisco days.

Hartford, George Huntington (1833–1917) grocery store magnate; born in Augusta, Maine. His father was a farmer and merchant. After working as a store clerk in Boston, he went to St. Louis where he worked in a store owned by George F. Gilman (1858). The men went to New York City where they opened the first of their stores known as the Great American Tea Company; Hartford took charge of selling quality teas at below average prices. As the company expanded to other cities, in 1869 it was renamed the Great Atlantic and Pacific Tea Company. Hartford had moved to Orange, N.J., where he served as mayor (1879–91). Gilman retired from the business in 1878 but Hartford's sons – George Ludlum Hartford (1864–1957) and John Augustine Hartford (1872–1951) – joined the firm; at Gilman's death (1901) the Hartfords acquired complete ownership. They began to expand the variety of items sold, added to the chain (4,700 stores by 1951, by then known as the A&P), and even began to process and manufacture food and products for their stores under their own brand name. In 1915 Hartford turned over control of the business to his sons; George concentrated on the company's finances while John managed the business operations.

Hartigan, Grace (1922–) painter; born in Newark, N.J. Based in New York City until 1960, she then settled in Baltimore, Maryland. She was an abstract painter who focused on the human figure, as in *River Bathers* (1953). She also depicted urban landscapes, as seen in *City Life* (1956).

Hartley (Edmund) Marsden (1877–1943) painter; born in Lewiston, Maine. Although he lived in New York City when he was young and studied with William Merritt Chase, he was based in Maine and traveled constantly. He used many styles, admired Albert Pinkham Ryder, and is known for his expressionistic, almost mystical approach, as in *Evening Storm, Schoodic, Maine* (1923).

Hartley, Fred (Allen), Jr. (1903–69) U.S. representative; born in Harrison, N.J. After serving in local offices, he became the youngest member of the U.S. House of Representatives (Rep., N.J.; 1929–49). After the Republican victory in 1946, he became chairman of the Labor Committee, drafting the antilabor Taft-Hartley Act of 1947, which outlawed closed shops and required an anticommunist oath from labor officials. His write-in campaign for the Senate in 1954 failed and he retired to cattle farming.

Hartline, H. (Haldan) Keffer (1903–83) physiologist; born in Bloomsburg, Pa. He was a National Research fellow at Johns Hopkins (1927–29), then became a biophysicist at the University of Pennsylvania (1931–48), taking the year 1940–41 to teach at Cornell. He returned to Johns Hopkins (1949–53), then joined Rockefeller University (1953–74). He won the 1967 Nobel Prize in physiology (shared with colleague Ranger Granit and George Wald) for his 40 years of research on vision, particularly for his investigations of the electrical activity of the optic nerve at the cellular level.

Hartmann, Carl Sadakichi (?1867–1944) writer, art critic; born in Nagasaki, Japan. His Japanese mother died shortly after his birth, and he was brought up by his uncle in Hamburg, Germany. He emigrated to Philadelphia (1882), became Walt Whitman's assistant (1884–85), then returned to Europe, where, among other activities, he was associated with Mallarmé. He became an American citizen in 1894, and settled in California. Known as the "King of Bohemia," he sired many children by various women, and died in poverty. He wrote a number of free-verse plays, poetry, and art criticism.

Hartmann, Heinz (1894–1970) psychoanalyst; born in Vienna, Austria. He studied with Sigmund Freud and expanded upon many of his theories. With Anna Freud and Ernst Kris, he founded the *Psychoanalytic Study of the Child* (annual publication). He served as president of the International Psycho-Analytical Association (1951–57) and was honored by the American Psychoanalytical Association in 1958, when he received its Charles Frederick Menninger Award.

Hartshorne, Richard (1899–) geographer; born in Kittanning, Pa. He completed a doctorate at the University of Chicago in 1924, then taught at the University of Minnesota (1924–40) and the University of Wisconsin (1940–70, with war-time interruption). In the 1930s he published some important articles concerning political geography. In 1939 he wrote *The Nature of Geography,* a monumental work that investigated the literature of several countries to synthesize what had been thought and written concerning the nature of geography. The book became required reading in many U.S. graduate schools. Twenty years later, in 1959, Hartshorne published *Perspective on the Nature of Geography,* which provided the benefit of 20 years' further thought and reflection by the author. In 1989, on its fiftieth anniversary, the Association of American Geographers published *Reflections on Richard Hartshorne's The Nature of Geography.*

Hartt, C. Fred (Charles Frederick) (1840–78) geologist, paleontologist; born in Frederickton, New Brunswick, Canada. He was an early explorer and collector in New Brunswick and Nova Scotia in the early 1860s. The leader of several expeditions to Brazil (1865–66, 1867, 1870), author

of *The Geology of Brazil* (1870), and director of Brazil's Geological Survey (1875–78), he founded geological work in that country, where he died of yellow fever. He taught at Cornell University (1868–78).

Hartt, Frederick (1914–91) art historian; born in Boston, Mass. He studied at Columbia University (B.A. 1935), and New York University (M.A. 1937; Ph.D. 1950). He specialized in Italian Renaissance art, and taught at many institutions, notably at the University of Virginia beginning in 1967.

Harvard, John (1607–38) benefactor; born in London, England. He became a teaching elder in the church at Charlestown, Mass. He left half his estate – including his 400-volume library – to the college which was named after him in 1639.

Harvey, E. (Edmund) Newton (1887–1959) cell biologist; born in Philadelphia. He taught physiology at Princeton (1911–56), while concurrently traveling the world as a visiting lecturer. During World War II, he made important contributions to studies of decompression sickness and wound ballistics. He made major advances in the fields of neurophysiology and cell regeneration but is most noted for his pioneering research on bioluminescence in plant and animal cells.

Harvey, Frederick Henry (1835–1901) restaurateur; born in London, England. He emigrated to the U.S.A. about 1850. He expanded his first railroad depot restaurant in Topeka, Kans., (opened in 1876) into a chain of restaurants, hotels, and dining cars associated with the new Atchison, Topeka, and Santa Fe Railroad. Harvey's restaurants were famous for fresh linens, fine food, and highly trained waitresses known as "Harvey Girls."

Harvey, Paul (b. Paul Harvey Aurandt) (1918–) radio journalist; born in Tulsa, Okla. Hired as a radio announcer while still in high school, he worked in various Midwestern stations until he began his daily newscasts in Chicago in 1944. His syndicated commentaries were aired nationally beginning in 1951. Descended from Baptist preachers, he designed his colorful broadcasts, *Paul Harvey News* and *The Rest of the Story,* to reach into the heartland. His distinctive delivery style consisted of dramatic pauses and inflections; he is also known for his somewhat more dubious practice of making his commercials and endorsements blend with the news.

Harwell, (William Ernest) Ernie (1918–) baseball broadcaster; born in Washington, Ga. He was an announcer for the Brooklyn Dodgers (1948–49), New York Giants (1950–53), Baltimore Orioles (1954–59), and the Detroit Tigers (1960–91).

Haskell, Norman (Abraham) (1905–70) seismologist; born in Alton, Ill. He was a U.S. Air Force research scientist who specialized in underwater ballistics and deformation of granitic rocks. He served as a technical adviser to the U.S. delegation at the Geneva Conference (1968).

Haskins, Charles Homer (1870–1937) medievalist, historian; born in Meadville, Pa. One of the leading medievalists of his generation, he shed light on Norman contributions to medieval English government and on the impact of Greek and Arabic scientific materials on Western Europe. A noted teacher, as well as scholar, he taught longest at Harvard University (1902–28). During World War I he was a member of "the Inquiry," where he provided intelligence on Germany and later participated in the Paris Peace Conference

(1918–19). A progressively severe case of paralysis agitans forced him to retire from teaching (1931).

Hassam, Childe (Frederick) (1859–1935) painter; born in Dorchester, Mass. He began his career as an illustrator for magazines, but after a trip to Paris in 1885 he took up the impressionist style. Returning to America in 1889, he settled in New York City and soon became known for his colorful scenes of city life, figure studies, and natural settings such as *Celia Thaxter in her Garden* (1892). During World War I he painted the "flag series," reflecting current events with the American and other flags on display.

Hastie, William Henry (1904–76) judge, public official; born in Knoxville, Tenn. A 1925 Amherst graduate, he taught for two years before going on to Harvard Law School. He taught briefly at Howard University, worked for a private firm and, from 1933–37, served as a U.S. Interior Department attorney. He returned to Howard as dean of the law school (1939–46). He was a consultant on race relations to the secretary of war but resigned in 1943 to protest continued discrimination against African-American servicemen. In 1949 he became the first Afrrican-American jurist appointed a judge of the U.S. Circuit Court of Appeals. He later became an appellate chief judge for the Philadelphia circuit. He retired from the bench in 1971.

Hastings, Alcee (Lamar) (1936–) lawyer, judge, U.S. representative; born in Altamonte Springs, Fla. After taking his B.A. at Fisk (1958) he earned his law degree in Florida A&M (1963). He had a private law practice in Fort Lauderdale, Fla. (1963–77) before becoming a circuit court judge for Broward County (1977–79). He then became a federal judge for the Southern District of Florida (1979–89) and by this time he was one of the most popular and active African-Americans in his part of Florida, participating in countless community affairs and receiving countless honors. By the early 1980s, charges surfaced that he had accepted bribes to influence sentences; tried in 1983, he was acquitted by a jury. But in October 1989 he was impeached by the U.S. Senate on eight articles and forced off the federal bench – the sixth federal judge so removed. Returning to private practice, he sought popular vindication and in 1992 was elected to the U.S. House of Representatives.

Hastings, Thomas (1860–1929) architect; born in Mineola, N.Y. At the École des Beaux-Arts, Paris, in the early 1880s he met John Merven Carrère (1858–1911, born in Rio de Janeiro, Brazil), with whom he later formed a highly successful New York partnership (1885–1915) that became identified with Beaux-Arts architecture in its public and corporate buildings, houses, and country estates. Their buildings included the Ponce de León Hotel, St. Augustine, Fla. (1888), and the New York Public Library (1902–11), Manhattan Bridge (1904–11), and the Henry Clay Frick House (1913–14), all in New York. Hastings was the chief designer, favoring the French classical style. Among the many large office buildings dating from the end of his career were the Standard Oil Building, New York (1926).

Hatch, Carl A. (1889–1963) U.S. senator; born in Kirwin, Kans. A lawyer in Mexico, he went to the U.S. Senate (Dem., N.M.; 1933–49). He was best known as the author of the Hatch Acts of 1939 and 1940, which curtail the political activities of federal employees in national elections. A supporter of farm and labor legislation and land reclamation projects, he also supported President Truman on such

international policies as the Marshall Plan. On leaving the Senate he served as a federal judge in Mexico (1949–63).

Hatcher, John Bell (1861–1904) paleontologist; born in Cooperstown, Ill. His leadership of numerous expeditions in the U.S.A. and Patagonia (1896–99) established him as a major American collector of fossils. He discovered the first fossil remains of *Triceratops* (1889).

Hatcher, Richard (Gordon) (1933–) lawyer, mayor; born in Michigan City, Ind. Much involved in Gary, Ind., politics as deputy prosecutor and city councilor (1963–66), he became the city's mayor (1968–88), one of the first African-American mayors of a large city. In 1988, he became president of R. Gordon Hatcher & Associates. He failed in a 1991 bid to regain the mayoralty.

Hatem, George (Ma Haide, Chinese name) (1910–88) physician; born in Buffalo, N.Y. After training in Beirut and Geneva he moved to Shanghai and in 1936 became physician to the communist army. After 1949 he headed China's massive public health program; his eradication of venereal disease and leprosy saved millions of lives and rates as one of the greatest ever achievements in public health. He is also one of a relatively few Westerners ever to have been fully integrated into Chinese society.

Haugen, Einar Ingvald (1906–94) linguist; born in Sioux City, Iowa. As professor of Scandinavian languages at the University of Wisconsin (1931–75) and as emeritus professor at Harvard University (1975), he wrote extensively on the teaching of Scandinavian languages, particularly Norwegian, and on bilingualism and language contact. Among his works are a *Norwegian-English Dictionary* (1965), *Language Conflict and Language Planning* (1966), and *The Scandinavian Languages* (1976). He is also known for his scholarship on the plays of Henrik Ibsen.

Haugen, Gilbert (Nelson) (1859–1933) U.S. representative; born in Rock County, Wis. Son of a Norwegian farmer, Haugen bought land at age 18 and later went into banking. Active in Iowa Republican politics, he served in the state senate before going to the U.S. House of Representatives (1899–1923). Chairman of the Agriculture Committee (1919–31), he sponsored farm relief measures, including the McNary-Haugen bill to send agricultural surpluses abroad.

Haughton, Percy (Duncan) (1876–1924) football coach; born in Staten Island, N.Y. A former Harvard tackle, he coached two years at Cornell University (1900–01), then entered business. Lured back to coaching by Harvard alumni, he brought the Crimson to its greatest football heights (1908–16). His teams were noted for their use of tricky, open-style play rather than brute force. After military service in World War I and several years in business, he returned to coaching at Columbia University in 1923.

Haupt, Herman (1817–1905) engineer, soldier, inventor; born in Philadelphia. Chief engineer of the Pennsylvania Railroad from 1853–56, he served as head of the strategically vital U.S. military railroads during the Civil War. Author of *General Theory of Bridge Construction* (1851), and inventor of a pneumatic drill (1858), he worked with railroads and other companies after the Civil War.

Hauptman, Herbert (Aaron) (1917–) biophysicist; born in New York City. At the Naval Research Laboratory (1965–70), he and Jerome Karle developed a mathematical method for determining three-dimensional crystal structures of hormone, vitamin, and antibiotic molecules, using X-ray crystallography. They shared the Nobel Prize in chemistry (1985) for this work. After 1970 he worked at the Medical Foundation of Buffalo, Inc.

Hauser, (Benjamin) Gayelord (b. Helmut Eugene Benjamin Gellert Hauser) (1895–1984) nutritionist; born in Tübingen, Germany. He studied nutrition in Europe and became famous in the 1920s promoting health foods and vegetarianism. Based in California after 1930, Hauser advised celebrity clients and published a series of books, including *Look Younger, Live Longer* (1950), whose popularity defied scientists' skepticism about his program.

Havemeyer, Henry O. (Osborne) (1847–1907) sugar refiner; born in New York City (second cousin of William F. Havemeyer). Born into the family that owned the North River Sugar Refining Company, he began working in the refinery in his adolescence. In 1887, with his brother Theodore Havemeyer, he consolidated 15 other refineries in the area to form the Sugar Refineries Company. After this so-called "sugar trust" lost a N.Y. state antitrust suit (1890), the corporation reorganized in New Jersey as the American Sugar Refining Company, which by 1907 had more than 25 plants. Extremely wealthy, Havemeyer collected European paintings, many of which were bequeathed to New York's Metropolitan Museum of Art.

Havemeyer, Louisine Waldron (b. Elder) (1855–1929) art collector, suffragist; born in New York City. Daughter of a wealthy sugar refiner, she studied in Paris (1873), met Mary Cassatt there, and began to purchase works by the Impressionists. In 1883 she married Henry Havemeyer, who also made a fortune in sugar, and they lived a luxurious life in New York City. She and her husband became discerning collectors of art, traveling through Europe and personally buying what they liked; they especially collected the Impressionists but also such under-appreciated artists as El Greco. After her husband's death, she devoted herself to social causes, and was a founder of the Congressional Union for Woman Suffrage (later the National Woman's party) (1913). She lectured – and once exhibited her painting collection – for the suffrage movement, but her most dramatic moment came in 1919 when she burned an effigy of President Woodrow Wilson on the White House lawn; she was jailed for three days, after which she set off on the "Prison Special," a train that toured the country for a month to promote woman suffrage. Most of her vast art collection went to the Metropolitan Museum of Art after her death.

Havemeyer, William Frederick (1804–74) businessman, mayor; born in New York City. A successful sugar refiner, he retired in 1842 and became the Democratic mayor of New York (1845–46, 1849–50). He then turned to business and banking, becoming president of two important banks. After the Tweed ring's financial scandals, Havemeyer defeated the Tammany candidate for mayor in 1872. But after some scandals of his own, the public turned against him. He died in office.

Haviland, John (1792–1852) architect; born in Gundenham Manor, Somerset, England. He emigrated to Philadelphia (1816) and published *The Builder's Assistant* (1818–21). His innovative radial-plan Eastern State Penitentiary in Philadelphia (1821–37) influenced jail design worldwide.

Havlicek, John (1940–   ) basketball player; born in Martin's Ferry, Ohio. After playing in three National Collegiate Athletic Association basketball finals at Ohio State (1960–62), he was drafted by the Cleveland Browns to play football. He was cut from the team so he went to the Boston Celtics who had also drafted him as their number one pick. He played forward for the Boston Celtics (1962–78), where he led the club to eight National Basketball Association titles. Nicknamed, "Hondo," he was a superb defensive player, and in 1983 he was elected to basketball's Hall of Fame.

Hawes, Harriet (Ann) Boyd (1871–1945) archaeologist, educator, social activist; born in Boston, Mass. After graduating from Smith College (1892), she went off to Greece to continue her studies; in 1897 she worked as a nurse during the Greco-Turkish war. She went to Crete in 1900, and with the encouragement of Arthur Evans, began to excavate a Minoan site at Kavousi; from 1901–05 she led a large team that excavated the Minoan town of Gournia, thereby becoming the first woman to head a major archaeological dig. She also became the first woman to lecture to societies of the Archaeological Institute of America (1902). She married the English anthropologist Charles Henry Hawes in 1906 and in 1908 published her monumental work on Gournia. During World War I she went over to Corfu in 1916 to help nurse the Serbians; in 1917 she organized a unit of Smith College graduates and directed their relief efforts in France, where she stayed until June 1918. From 1920–36 she was on the faculty of Wellesley College. Always involved in one political and social cause or another, she worked for woman suffrage, protested the Sacco-Vanzetti executions, became involved in labor and economic issues during the Depression, personally protested the Germans' annexation of Czechoslovakia, called for the U.S.A. to go to Europe's defense in World War II, and was a strong advocate of an international body to promote unity and peace.

Hawes, Josiah Johnson (1808–1908) photographer, inventor; born in East Dudbury, Mass. A pioneer in daguerreotype photography, he manufactured camera equipment at Southworth and Hawes (1843–60) and invented new products like the Grand Parlor Stereoscope viewer.

Hawkes, John (Clendennin Burne, Jr.) (1925–   ) writer, poet, playwright; born in Stamford, Conn. He studied at Harvard (B.A. 1949), worked for Harvard University Press (1949–55), and taught at Harvard (1956–58). He then went to teach at Brown University (1958) and was a visiting professor at many institutions. He published poetry and plays, but is best known for his avant-garde surrealistic narratives, such as *Second Skin* (1964) and *Virginie* (1982).

Hawkins, Augustus (Freeman) (1907–   ) U.S. representative; born in Shreveport, La. Moving to Los Angeles as a boy, he graduated from the University of California and established a real-estate business. He served as a Democratic member of the California State Assembly (1935–62) before going to the U.S. House of Representatives (1963–89). He chaired the Committee on House Administration and the Committee on Education and Labor during the Reagan Administration.

Hawkins, Benjamin (1754–1816) U.S. senator, Indian agent; born in Bute County, N.C. He served as George Washington's aide and translator (with Indians) during the American Revolution and as a member of the Confederation Congress (1781–84, 1786–87). He also served as one of North Carolina's first two U.S. senators (Fed., 1789–95). His most important work was as a commissioner who negotiated treaties with various Indian tribes, including the treaty of Coleraine with the Creeks in 1796. President Washington then appointed him general superintendent of all Native Americans south of the Ohio River. Known as "Beloved Man of the Four Nations," he worked especially closely with the Creeks.

Hawkins, Coleman (1904–69) jazz musician; born in St. Joseph, Mo. He was a tenor saxophonist who brought his instrument into prominence and was its most influential voice until the 1950s. He played with Fletcher Henderson's orchestra between 1924–34, then spent five years performing in Europe. Upon his return to the U.S.A. in 1939, he recorded his classic version of "Body and Soul." He remained a prolific recording artist and concert performer until the mid-1960s.

Hawkins, Erick (1909–) modern dancer, choreographer; born in Trinidad, Colo. He trained with the School of American Ballet and performed in the company (1935–37). After performing with Ballet Caravan, he joined the Martha Graham Company in 1938 as its first male dancer; he was briefly her husband (1948–50). He formed his own company in the early 1950s, performing abstract compositions with elaborate costuming, often in collaboration with the composer, Laura Dlugoszewski.

Hawks, Howard (1896–1977) film director, screenwriter, producer; born in Goshen, Ind. A plane and car racer in his teens, he worked as a prop boy in Hollywood during college vacations. He served with the Army Air Corps in World War I; returning to California to work in an aircraft factory, he soon decided to try the new film industry where he held a variety of jobs in the production field before moving on to writing and producing movies. His directorial debut was with his own script, *The Road to Glory* (1926), which launched a career that spanned 45 years and a broad spectrum of genres, from gangster films (*Scarface*, 1932) and Westerns (*Red River*, 1948) to screwball comedies (*Bringing Up Baby,* 1938) and musicals (*Gentlemen Prefer Blondes,* 1953). Not much of an innovator but in total control of his movies, he was a no-nonsense teller of strong stories, and he came to be highly regarded by French students of film and was awarded an honorary Oscar (1974).

Hawley, Joseph Roswell (1826–1905) journalist, soldier, U.S. representative/senator; born in Stewartsville, N.C. An abolitionist and founder of the Republican Party in Connecticut, he edited the *Hartford Evening Press* (1857–61). During the Civil War he attained the rank of major general in the Union army. He served as governor of Connecticut (1866–67) and then as editor of the *Hartford Courant* (1867). He went on to serve in the U.S. House of Representatives (Rep.; 1872–75, 1879–81) and then in the U.S. Senate (1881–1905). He also served as president of the Centennial Commission in 1876.

Hawthorne, Charles (Webster) (1872–1930) painter; born in Lodi, Ill. He established the Cape Cod School of Art in Provincetown, Mass. (1899), and painted scenes of the area.

Hawthorne, Nathaniel (b. Hathorne) (1804–64) writer; born in Salem, Mass. A descendant of a judge in the Salem witch trials, he spent a solitary, bookish childhood with his widowed and reclusive mother. After graduating from Bowdoin College, he returned to Salem and prepared for a writing career with 12 years of solitary study and writing interrupted by summer tours through the Northeast. After privately publishing a novel, *Fanshawe* (1828), he began publishing stories in the *Token* and *New England Magazine.* These original allegories of New England Puritanism, including such classic stories as "The Minister's Black Veil," were collected in *Twice-Told Tales* (1837). A brief period of paid employment, including the compilation of popular children's works and a stint at the Boston Custom House (1839–41) – thanks to his friend, Senator Franklin Pierce – was followed by a half-year's residence at the transcendentalist community, Brook Farm. In 1842 he married Sophia Amelia Peabody, also a transcendentalist, and they moved to Concord, Mass., where he began a friendship with Henry David Thoreau. Financial pressures forced his return to Salem (1845–49) where he secured another political appointment, this time as surveyor of the port of Salem (1845–49). During these years he continued to publish Puritan tales ("Young Goodman Brown," "The Birthmark"); collections of his stories included *Mosses from an Old Manse* (1846) and *The Snow Image* (1851). His dismissal from the surveyorship initiated the brief period of his greatest novels: *The Scarlet Letter* (1850), *The House of the Seven Gables* (1851), and *The Blithdale Romance* (1852). He also wrote two children's classics: *A Wonder-Book* (1852) and *Tanglewood Tales* (1853). His campaign biography of Franklin Pierce (1852) was rewarded with the U.S. consulship at Liverpool (1853–58). He then went to live in Italy (1858–59) where he began *The Marble Faun,* which he published after returning to the U.S.A. in 1860. Back in Concord, he published his last major work, *Our Old Home* (1863), which drew on his experiences in England, but by then he was becoming ill and disillusioned.

Hay, John (Milton) (1838–1905) journalist, historian, poet, diplomat; born in Salem, Ind. After working in a law office next to Abraham Lincoln's in Springfield, Ill., he served President Lincoln in the White House as assistant private secretary from 1861–65 in a close relationship that has been described as resembling that of father and son. He then served at diplomatic posts in Paris (1865–76), Vienna (1867–68), and Madrid (1869–70). His widely-known ballads were collected in *Pike County Ballads* (1871), and from 1870–75 he was staff editorial writer at the New York *Tribune.* After serving as assistant secretary of state (1879–81), he completed with George Nicolay his monumental *Abraham Lincoln: A History* (1890), making him a sort of political poet laureate. In 1897 he was successful as ambassador to Britain. As secretary of state (1898–1905), Hay authored the Open Door policy, instituted regular press conferences, and paved the way for the building of the Panama Canal, making his office and American foreign policy of worldwide influence.

Hayden, Charles (1870–1937) financier, philanthropist; born in Boston, Mass. He graduated from Massachusetts Institute of Technology (MIT) (1890) and formed the Hayden, Stone & Company brokerage firm in 1892. Specializing at first in copper stocks, he diversified, especially during World War I, and made a fortune. An exceptional judge of men and finances, he was elected to an extraordinary number of boards of directors (58 at the time of his death). He became interested in boys' work and left about $50 million to establish the Hayden Foundation which assisted boys clubs and the Boy Scouts. He also gave generously to MIT and the Red Cross and he was the principal donor to the American

Museum of Natural History's new planetarium, named after him.

Hayden, Ferdinand V. (Vandiveer) (1829–87) geologist; born in Westfield, Mass. After working on surveys in the northwest U.S.A. (1853–62), he became professor of geology at the University of Pennsylvania (1865–72). He was director (1867–79), then geologist (1879–86), of the U.S. Geological Survey. He was influential in securing the establishment of Yellowstone Park.

Hayden, Melissa (b. Mildred Herman) (1923–) ballet dancer; born in Toronto, Canada. After training in Toronto and New York, she joined Ballet Theatre (1945). She joined the New York City Ballet (1950) and performed leading roles until her retirement (1973).

Hayden, Robert (Earl) (b. Asa Bundy Sheffey) (1913–80) poet; born in Detroit, Mich. He studied at University of Michigan (1938; 1942; M.A. 1944), and taught there beginning in 1969. He wrote powerful poetry, sometimes using African-American themes, as in *The Night-Blooming Cereus* (1972).

Hayden, Sophia (c. 1868–1953) architect; born in Santiago, Chile. Raised in Boston, this first woman graduate (1890) of the Massachusetts Institute of Technology's architecture course designed the Women's Building at the World's Columbian Exposition of 1893, her only completed work in a career cut short by a nervous breakdown.

Hayden, Tom (1939–) radical activist, state legislator, author; born in Royal Oak, Mich. One of the best-known student radical leaders of the 1960s, he was a cofounder of the Students for a Democratic Society (SDS) (1961), president of SDS (1962–63), cofounder of the Economic Research and Action Project (1964), and leader of the Newark Community Union Project (1964–67). Married to actress Jane Fonda, he ran for U.S. Senate in California (1976), was founder of the Indochina Peace Campaign, founder and chairman of the California Campaign for Economic Democracy (1977), and chairman of the California SolarCal Council (1978–82). He was elected to the California State Assembly (1982) and was author of several books, including *The American Future* (1980).

Hayes, Carlton J. H. (Joseph Huntley) (1882–1964) historian, diplomat; born in Afton, N.Y. He took all his degrees at Columbia University (B.A. 1904; M.A. 1905; Ph.D. 1909) and then remained there as a professor (1910–50). He became one of the leading authorities on modern nationalism, writing about it in such works as *Essays on Nationalism* (1926) and *Nationalism: A Religion* (1960); he was also the author of a long-standard college history textbook, *Political and Social History of Modern Europe* (1916, many editions). A convert to Roman Catholicism (1924), he became a cofounder of the National Association of Christians and Jews and was its Catholic cochairman (1928–46). He served as U.S. ambassador to Spain (1942–45), with the express goal of dissuading Spain from assisting the Axis powers; he described this mission in *Wartime Mission in Spain* (1945).

Hayes, Helen (b. Brown) (1900–93) stage/film actress; born in Washington, D.C. Best known in roles that combined apparent pliability with inner steel, she made her debut at the age of five. In the 1920s she seemed to be type-cast as a flapper, but she soon graduated to more substantial roles such as Cleopatra in *Caesar and Cleopatra*. In 1928 she married playwright Charles MacArthur. She won an Acad-

emy Award for the 1932 film, *The Sin of Madelon Claudet,* but her most famous role was in Laurence Housman's *Victoria Regina* (1935), where she played the queen as she aged from a young woman to an elderly widow. Her longest New York run was *Happy Birthday* (1946). After 1958 she performed mainly in revivals in the U.S. and Europe. In 1964 she formed the Helen Hayes Repertory Company to sponsor Shakespeare readings in universities. She officially retired from the stage in 1970 after playing Veta Louise Simmons in *Harvey.*

Hayes, Ira (1932–55) Pima war hero; born in Sacaton, Ariz. He was one of five marines photographed raising the U.S. flag on Mt. Suribachi, Iwo Jima (1945). Unable to deal with the adulation that followed the photograph's wide publication, he returned to the reservation where he died of alcoholism and exposure.

Hayes, Isaac Israel (1832–81) physician, Arctic explorer; born in Chester County, Pa. He was the surgeon for Elisha Kent Kane's second Arctic expedition (1853–54) and wrote *An Arctic Boat Journey* (1860). He led another Arctic expedition (1860–61) and served as an army surgeon in Philadelphia during the Civil War. He made a third Arctic expedition in 1869 and gave an accurate description of Greenland in *The Land of Desolation* (1871).

Hayes, Lucy (Ware b. Webb) (1831–89) First Lady; born in Chillicothe, Ohio. She married Rutherford B. Hayes in 1852. She was well-educated and committed to emancipation for black slaves and to temperance. She sometimes accompanied her husband when he was an officer during the Civil War. As first lady, she was known for her simplicity and frugality. She banned alcohol from the White House. Following the presidency, she worked for charitable activities.

Hayes, Peter Lind (b. Joseph Conrad Lind) (1915–) radio/television comedian, actor; born in San Francisco. Abandoned by his father, he occasionally joined his mother (whose maiden name he adopted) in vaudeville skits at the age of nine and appeared with her at New York's Palace Theater in 1932. From 1932–42 he performed his comedy routines at his mother's nightclub in the San Fernando Valley, Calif., and he made several movies. In the U.S. Army Air Corps in World War II (1942–45), he performed in hundreds of service shows. He made his nightclub debut in New York City in 1946 and was instantly acclaimed for his character impersonations. He then toured with his new wife, actress Mary Healey, in a singing-comedy act. In 1951 he had his own television show, *The Star of the Family,* and he and his wife then became the permanent guest-hosts on the *Arthur Godfrey Show* (1953–58), a contractual arrangement that limited them to doing only radio shows, but where he could at least employ his own brand of wry, satiric humor. He then went on to produce and host the *Peter Lind Hayes Show* for ABC-TV, (1958–66), thereafter making only occasional appearances, as in *When Television Was Live* (1975). He had written songs when he was younger and he published his poetry, *Peter's Poems* and *Hayseed* in 1982.

Hayes, (Robert Lee) Bob (1942–) track and field athlete, football player; born in Jacksonville, Fla. A gold medal winner in the 100 meter and 4 × 100 meter relay in the 1964 Olympics, he starred as a pass receiver and kickoff return specialist for the National Football League Dallas Cowboys (1965–74) and San Francisco 49ers (1975).

Hayes, Roland (1887–1977) tenor; born in Curryville, Ga. A son of former slaves, he studied in the U.S.A. and Europe before his 1917 Boston debut. In the 1920s he concertized across Europe and the U.S.A. and was acclaimed for both his performance of classical lieder and his Negro spirituals; his farewell performance was at Carnegie Hall in 1962.

Hayes, Rutherford B. (Birchard) (1822–93) nineteenth U.S. president; born in Delaware, Ohio. After graduating from Ohio's Kenyon College in 1842 and attending Harvard Law School in 1845, he practiced law in Cincinnati. He took a military commission at the beginning of the Civil War, in which he served with modest distinction. In 1864 he won a seat in the U.S. House of Representatives as a Republican but did not take it until after the end of the Civil War (1865–67). He became governor of Ohio (1868–76) and resigned to run for president against Samuel J. Tilden in 1876. The election was so close that a special commission had to decide the issue; the outcome in favor of Hayes was apparently due to the commission's Republican majority and promises to southern Democrats to restore power to the whites. He proved to be a competent and mildly reformist president, but alienated many supporters by insisting on ending patronage appointments and by pursuing civil service reform. Having pledged not to seek reelection, he left office in 1881; his later years were devoted to humanitarian and reform efforts.

Hayes, (Wayne Woodrow) "Woody" (1913–87) football coach; born in Upper Arlington, Ohio. Known for his conservative, "three yards and a cloud of dust" offense, he won national titles in 1954 and 1968 at Ohio State (1951–78).

Hayes, William Henry ("Bully Hayes") (1829–77) trader, adventurer; possibly born in Cleveland, Ohio. The hazy details of his birth and early life are balanced by many stories about his later career as a slave trader, swindler, raider, and confidence trickster throughout the Pacific. He was famous for his undocumented cargoes, braggadoccio, and ability to escape arrest. He was killed by a mutinous sailor.

Hayford, John F. (Fillmore) (1868–1925) geodesist; born in Rouses Point, N.Y. He clarified the U.S.-Mexican boundary (1892–93); helped define the Alaskan boundary (1894); was appointed by U.S. Supreme Court Chief Justice Edward Douglass White to settle the boundary dispute between Panama and Costa Rica (1913); and served on President Woodrow Wilson's advisory committee on aeronautics. His astronomical and mathematical contributions to the U.S. Geodetic Survey helped bring that organization to international prominence.

Hayne, Robert Young (1791–1839) U.S. senator, governor, railroad promoter; born in Colleton District, S.C. A prosperous lawyer, he held various state offices in South Carolina before going on to serve in the U.S. Senate (Dem.-Rep., 1823–32). A staunch defender of states' rights, he came to national prominence as the chief adversary of Daniel Webster in the Senate's debates (1830–32) over the issue of whether a state could "nullify" Federal legislation it did not approve of. Hayne resigned from the Senate, and as South Carolina's governor (1832–34), he led in the adoption of the nullification ordinance and then called for troops to resist any efforts by President Andrew Jackson to force South Carolina to back down. After Henry Clay managed a compromise, Hayne rescinded the ordinance. Leaving public office, he directed his energies to establishing railroad links between the South and the West; in 1836 he formed the Louisville, Cincinnati & Charleston Railroad Company and

became its president, but the financial panic of 1837 ended his ambitious scheme.

Haynes, Elwood (1857–1925) manufacturer; born in Portland, Ind. He graduated from Worcester Polytechnic Institute (1881). By 1891 – allegedly to make his job as a field supervisor for an Indiana utility company easier – he began to develop a gasoline-powered automobile. With the help of Elmer and Edgar Apperson, he built a one-cylinder car that was first demonstrated in Kokomo, Ind., on July 4, 1894 (it is now on display at the Smithsonian Institution). In 1898 they formed the Haynes-Apperson Automobile Company that produced one of the most successful of the early cars. By 1908 the Appersons left in a dispute over who deserved credit for designing the original car, but Haynes continued to make his cars until the 1920s. Meanwhile he had turned his interest to metal alloys and he developed several including Stellite, a cobalt chromium alloy that would not rust and kept its hardness when heated (1907), and stainless steel (1919). He formed Haynes Stellite Company in 1915, then sold it to Union Carbide and Carbon Corporation in 1920.

Haynes, Marquis (1926–   ) basketball player; born in Sand Springs, Okla. Considered the "world's greatest dribbler," he played for the famous Harlem Globetrotters (1947–53) and later for his own touring club, "The Fabulous Magicians."

Haynes, Richard (1927–   ) lawyer; born in Houston, Texas. Tough if short, shrewd if flamboyant – dubbed "Racehorse" by a coach – he excelled in jury selection and became a legendary criminal defense attorney in Houston. He wrote *Blood and Money* (1970), the true story of a plastic surgeon accused of murdering his wife. His celebrated trials include that of oil tools heir T. Cullen Davis (1979).

Hays, Arthur Garfield (1881–1954) lawyer, author; born in Rochester, N.Y. An often controversial but highly admired lawyer in his day, he was unusual in making several fortunes as a successful corporation lawyer while simultaneously fighting for many unpopular causes. During and after World War I, when anti-German feeling was high, he defended the commercial rights of Germany. Then in 1933 he took on perhaps his most unusual case when he went to Germany and assisted in the defense of the Communist accused of setting fire to the Reichstag. Many of his most notable cases came during his tenure as general counsel for the American Civil Liberties Union (1921–54), when he participated in the Scopes "monkey" trial (1925), the Sacco-Vanzetti defense (1927), and other controversial cases. The underlying motive of all his work was his hatred of suppression and his dedication to the freedom of all. His several books include *Trial by Prejudice* (1933).

Hays, (John Coffee) "Jack" (1817–83) soldier, public official; born in Little Cedar Lick, Tenn. As a captain in the Texas Rangers, he reputedly introduced Samuel Colt's revolving pistol – the six-shooter – to the frontier. He moved to California (1849) and served as the sheriff of San Francisco. He also had large real estate and banking interests in Oakland.

Hays, (William Harrison) Will (1879–1954) movie executive; born in Sullivan, Ind. A lawyer (1922), former chairman of the Republican National Committee, and Postmaster General under President Harding, he was appointed head of the new Motion Picture Producers and Distributors of America, Inc. (MPPDA), created by the movie industry itself to counter increasing public protests against Hollywood scandals and risqué films. In 1930 the MPPDA set forth its Production Code (soon known as the Hays Code) – detailed listing of what was or was not allowed in movies – and in administering the Code (until 1945), Hays exercised great influence over American movies.

Hays, William Shakespeare (1837–1907) song composer; born in Louisville, Ky. He wrote over 300 songs, many quite popular, including *Evangeline* and *My Southern Sunny Home*.

Haywood, William Dudley ("Big Bill") (1869–1928) labor leader; born in Salt Lake City, Utah. A miner at age nine, he worked at other jobs but kept returning to mining. Joining the Western Federation of Miners (WFM) (1896) and elected secretary-treasurer (1900), he led the WFM through several violent years of labor strife. In 1905 he cofounded the Industrial Workers of the World (IWW) with the goal of eventually uniting all unions in "one big union." Later that year he was accused of involvement in the murder of an antilabor former governor of Idaho, Frank Steunenberg; defended by Clarence Darrow, he was acquitted and became a hero to labor. But his continued radicalism, including a call to destroy capitalism, led the WFM to withdraw from the IWW, and, in 1918, to dismiss Haywood. A member of the Socialist Party from 1901, he was also dropped from that party's councils for advocating violence (1912). He gained a new following when he championed the organizing of unskilled workers and led textile strikes in Lawrence, Mass. (1912), and Paterson, N.J. (1913). Convicted of violating wartime alien and sedition acts, he was sentenced to 20 years in jail (1918) but jumped bail and fled to the Soviet Union (1921).

Hayworth, Rita (b. Margarita Carmen Cansino) (1918–87) movie actress; born in New York City. Child of then well-known Latin dancer, Eduardo Cansino, she began dancing in public at age six and began her movie career in her teens, dancing as a sultry señorita. She took some acting lessons, changed her name, and (with her now red hair) started a new career. She proved to be a versatile performer, at home in musicals (although her singing was dubbed), more than able-bodied as a sex goddess (as in *Gilda*, 1946), and maturing into a creditable actress in such movies as *Separate Tables* (1958). Her offscreen life had its own glamour, what with her marriages to Orson Welles and Aly Khan, but two more unhappy marriages and Alzheimer's disease clouded her final years.

Hazard, Geoffrey C., Jr. (1929–) legal scholar; born in Cleveland, Ohio. He taught at the University of California: Berkeley (1958–64), the University of Chicago (1964–71), and Yale (1971). His interest was in civil procedure, legal ethics, and the sociology of law. His major publications are *Ethics in Practice of Law* (1978) and *Law and Ethics of Lawyering* (with S. Koniak) (1990).

H.D. See DOOLITTLE, HILDA.

Head, Edith (1907–81) costume designer; born in Los Angeles, Calif. Educated at the University of California: Los Angeles and Stanford University, she taught languages and art before joining Paramount studios during the 1930s. She was head designer there until 1967, when she moved to Universal. As Hollywood's best-known designer, she worked on dozens of movies, including *She Done Him Wrong* (1933), *All About Eve* (1948), *A Place in the Sun* (1951), *The Ten Commandments* (1956), *The Sting* (1973), and *The Big Fix*

(1978). She received eight Academy Awards for her costumes.

Heade, Martin (Johnson) (1819–1904) painter; born in Lumberville, Pa. The son of wealthy farmers, he studied with Edward Hicks (c. 1838), moved to New York City (1866–81), traveled widely, and finally settled in St. Augustine, Florida (1885–1904). His dramatic seascape, *Approaching Storm: Beach near Newport* (c. 1860) is considered his masterpiece, but his later botanical paintings are also highly acclaimed.

Healy, George (Peter Alexander) (1813–94) painter; born in Boston, Mass. He gained an international reputation as an academic painter of important figures of the time, such as Abraham Lincoln and King Louis-Philippe.

Healy, James Augustine (1830–1900) Catholic prelate; born in Jones County, Ga. The son of a black slave woman and white plantation owner, he graduated from Holy Cross College (1849) and was ordained in Paris (1854). After serving as a pastor and administrator in the Boston archdiocese, he was named bishop of Portland, Maine (1875). The nation's first African-American Catholic bishop, though not widely known as such, he was an effective orator, builder of churches, and benefactor of the needy.

Healy, Patrick F. (Francis) (1834–1910) Catholic priest, educator; born in Jones County, Ga. A onetime slave, he was a brother of Bishop James Healy and, like him, was sent north to be educated in freedom; he was ordained a Jesuit (1864) after studying abroad. Besides teaching philosophy at Georgetown College (1866–69), he served (1873–82) as its president, greatly expanding the college through fund-raising. He largely concealed his background from contemporaries.

Hearn, (Patricio) Lafcadio (Tessima Carlos) (1850–1904) writer, translator; born on the island of Lefkas, Greece. Son of a Greek mother and an Irish doctor with the British army, after age six he was raised in Ireland, England, and France. He came to the U.S.A. in 1869 and, settling in Cincinnati, became a journalist and translator (of French). In 1877 he went to New Orleans and as a journalist and translator, also began to publish his own stories, usually involving the exotic or macabre and drawing on local lore. From 1887–89 he lived on Martinique in the West Indies. In 1890 Harpers' *New Monthly Magazine* sent him to Japan to write a series of articles. He would stay in Japan for the rest of his life – becoming a teacher, marrying a Japanese woman, and taking citizenship there as Koizumi Yakumo. He published a series of books that offered the West its first thoughtful, sympathetic view of Japanese culture, most memorably *Japan: An Attempt at Interpretation* (1904).

Hearst, Patricia (Campbell) (1954–) heiress; born in San Francisco, Calif. The daughter of newspaper tycoon Randolph Hearst, she was kidnapped in 1974 by the radical Symbionese Liberation Army. After brainwashing, she assumed the name "Tania" and joined in their bank robberies. She was captured in 1975, tried, and sentenced to prison in 1976. Paroled in 1979, she married her bodyguard and wrote an autobiography, *Every Secret Thing* (1982).

Hearst, William Randolph (1863–1951) publisher, editor, politician; born in San Francisco. Son of George Hearst, publisher of the *San Francisco Examiner*, he left Harvard without taking a degree and in 1887 took over the ailing paper. Combining sensationalism with a civic reform campaign, he made the paper highly profitable, and in 1895 he bought the

New York Morning Journal and successfully fought a circulation war with Joseph Pulitzer's *New York World;* again, his approach combined the sensational elements (giving rise to the phrase, "yellow journalism") with a populist stance. He is regarded as having aroused the public opinion that called for war with Spain in 1898. Hearst then moved on to start or acquire other newspapers in Chicago (1902), Boston and Los Angeles (1904), and many other cities; he also built such magazines as *Cosmopolitan, Good Housekeeping, Town and Country,* and *Harper's Bazaar* into profitable successes; at its peak, his empire included 20 major newspapers, telegraphic news facilities, radio stations, and news and motion picture syndicates. Meanwhile, he had turned his ambition to a political career, but although he served two terms as U.S. Representative (Dem., N.Y.; 1903–07) he could never attain the other offices he sought, including the presidential nomination in 1904 and the nomination for senator from New York in 1922. Fairly progressive in his early years, he had become increasingly conservative – isolationist, jingoist, and just plain ornery, eventually becoming a staunch anticommunist. In 1927 he gave up on New York and moved to his enormous estate in California, San Simeon, where he built a fabulous castle and assembled art and architecture from all over the world – including whole buildings he had dismantled and sent to him. During the Depression he had to sell some of his art collection and he spent his final years as a recluse. Ironically, he would take on a new life as the man who tried to suppress *Citizen Kane* (1941), in the movie Orson Welles had based on him.

Heaton, Maurice (1900–90) glass designer; born in Neuchâtel, Switzerland. Arriving in New York in 1914, he worked with his father in architectural stained glass and later turned to designing glass tablewares, murals, screens and lighting in the art deco-modernist style.

Hebert, Felix (1874–1969) U.S. senator; born near St. Hyacinthe, Quebec, Canada. He served one term in the U.S. Senate (Rep., R.I.; 1929–35) and was party whip from 1933–35.

Hecht, Anthony (Evan) (1923–) poet; born in New York City. He studied at Bard College, N.Y. (B.A. 1944), Columbia University (M.A. 1950), and has taught at many institutions, notably at Rochester University, N.Y., beginning in 1967. His poetry is distinguished by its classical and mythological images, as in *Millions of Strange Shadows* (1977).

Hecht, Ben (1893–1964) screenwriter, director, playwright; born in New York City. After youthful forays as a concert violinist and circus acrobat, he went to Chicago at age 16 and became a newspaper reporter. He was a foreign correspondent in World War I; back in Chicago he tried his hand at more serious fiction and started the *Chicago Literary Times* (1923–25). During the next 40 years he was one of the most sought after and admired scriptwriters in Hollywood, writing, alone or in collaboration, close to 100 screenplays (many for which he received no credit). He did receive Oscars for *Underworld* (1927) and *The Scoundrel* (1935); the latter he cowrote and codirected with Charles MacArthur, his collaborator on various other films and plays, including *Front Page* (1928) and *Twentieth Century* (1932). Because of his open support of the Jewish struggle against the British in Palestine, his name was removed from all his films shown in Britain during the late 1940s. He wrote his autobiography *A Child of the Century* (1954).

Heck, Nicholas H. (Hunter) (1882–1953) geophysicist; born in Heckton Mills, Pa. He had a lifetime career with the U.S. Coast and Geodetic Survey (1904–44). He located earthquake foci in submarine, coastal, and mountain regions, applied radio acoustics to find undersea objects, and developed wire drag techniques to locate pinnacle rocks.

Hecker, Isaac (Thomas) (1819–88) religious leader; born in New York City. After briefly joining the Brook Farm community, he became a Catholic (1844), studied abroad, and was ordained a Redemptorist priest (1849). He conducted missions and won approval for his own congregation (1858), the Missionary Priests of St. Paul the Apostle – widely known as the Paulists – devoted to communications and evangelizing among non-Catholics. He started a publishing house and founded *Catholic World* magazine (1865), which he then edited. In such works as *The Church and the Age* (1887) he advanced a relatively liberal vision of the church. A biography of him published posthumously in France led to controversy and eventual papal condemnation of "Americanism," though the ideas proscribed were not specifically attributed to Hecker.

Heckscher, August (1848–1941) mining executive, real estate owner, philanthropist; born in Hamburg, Germany. He came to New York City in 1867 and taught himself English. Through diligence and good fortune, and after managing coal mines in Pennsylvania, he acquired New Jersey land that contained the richest zinc deposits in the U.S.A.; he fought a famous legal battle to keep the land (1887–97). He profited greatly in New York real estate (after 1904). He established the Heckscher Foundation for Children (1921) and donated to day nurseries, dental clinics, parks, and playgrounds.

Hedberg, Hollis Dow (1903–88) geologist; born in Falun, Kans. He worked for several U.S. and Venezuelan oil companies (1926–64) while concurrently serving as a geology professor at Princeton (1959–71). He published over 150 papers on petroleum geology, sedimentary rocks, stratigraphy, and the oceans.

Hedge, Frederic Henry (1805–90) Unitarian clergyman, translator; born in Cambridge, Mass. He graduated from Harvard in 1825 and was ordained in 1829. He held Unitarian pastorates in Massachusetts, Maine, and Rhode Island from 1829–72 and was a lifelong leader of the Unitarian movement. He edited the *Christian Examiner* (1857–61) and taught at Harvard Divinity School (1857–76). His translation of Goethe's *Faust* appeared in 1882.

Heffelfinger, (William Walter) "Pudge" (1867–1954) football player; born in Minneapolis, Minn. A four-year starting guard for Yale (1888–91), he was named to the first three All-America teams. He enabled Yale to defeat Princeton's famous "flying wedge" by leaping over the blockers and landing on the runner. In 1892, he accepted $500 from the Allegheny Athletic Association to play a game in Pittsburgh, Pa., and thus became the first professional player.

Heflin, James (Thomas) (1869–1951) U.S. representative/senator; born in Louina, Ala. A lawyer and state representative, he filled vacancies in the U.S. House of Representatives (Dem., Ala.; 1904–20) and the Senate (1920–31), afterward working for the Federal government in Alabama.

Hefner, Hugh (Marston) (1926–) publisher, entrepreneur; born in Chicago. Brought up by straitlaced parents, he did postgraduate work in psychology and, after working at

Esquire magazine, gathered $10,000 capital to found *Playboy* (1953), a sophisticated erotic magazine for men that offered articles of high standards, along with advice on sexual problems, men's talk, and a nude "Playmate of the Month" centerfold. With a boost from the sexual revolution, *Playboy* flourished, enabling Hefner to live a playboy-style life in an opulent Chicago mansion; later he transferred his hedonistic menage to Los Angeles. He also founded a chain of restaurant-nightclubs featuring scantily uniformed Playboy "bunnies" as waitresses. By the mid-1980s his clubs and publishing empire began to decline, and when he finally married a former "playmate" in 1989, it appeared the Hefner revolution had ended.

Heifetz, Jascha (1901–87) violinist; born in Vilna, Lithuania. Son of a violinist, he began playing at age three, entered music school the next year, and made his first public appearance at age five. After completing his studies and establishing his reputation in Europe and Russia, he made a triumphant American debut at Carnegie Hall in 1917. Remaining in the country, he became a U.S. citizen in 1925 and bought houses in Connecticut and California. For the rest of his long career the almost supernatural perfection of his playing made him generally considered the greatest violinist of his time as well as one of the most popular. In the 1950s he gradually reduced his public appearances but continued to play and record into the 1970s, meanwhile teaching at the University of Southern California.

Heiland, C. A. (Carl August) (1899–1956) geophysicist; born in Hamburg, Germany. After his emigration (1925), he prospected for water and metals in the western U.S. He became president of Heiland Research Corporation in 1934.

Heilbrun, Carolyn (b. Gold) (Amanda Cross, pen name) (1926–) writer, teacher; born in East Orange, N.J. She studied at Wellesley (B.A. 1947) and Columbia University (M.A. 1951; Ph.D. 1959). She was a visiting lecturer and professor at many institutions, and taught English at Brooklyn College (1959–60) and Columbia (1960–93). She published scholarly works, but is best known as a writer of popular mystery novels featuring Kate Fansler, also an urban college professor, as seen in *A Trap for Fools* (1989).

Heilmann, Harry (Edwin) (1894–1951) baseball player; born in San Francisco. During his 17-year career as an outfielder for the Detroit Tigers and Cincinnati Reds (1914–32), he posted a lifetime batting average of .342. One of the first players to become a broadcaster after retiring from the game, he was elected to baseball's Hall of Fame in 1952.

Heilprin, Angelo (1853–1907) geologist, paleontologist, traveler; born in Satoralja-Ujhely, Hungary (son of Michael Heilprin). He was brought to the U.S.A. in 1856 but returned to Europe for his college and university education. From 1880–1900 he held a series of professorships, curatorships, and club presidencies in Philadelphia scientific institutions. From 1903–07 he was a professor of geography at Yale. Best known as a traveler and explorer, he went with Robert Peary on his Arctic expedition in 1891. His most spectacular moments came when he photographed the Mont Pelée volcano at close range while it was erupting in 1902. He wrote numerous books, including *Principles of Geology* (1890), *The Earth and Its Story* (1896), and *Mont Pelée and the Tragedy of Martinique* (1903); a talented painter, he illustrated some of his own works. On a 1906 expedition up the Orinoco River in British Guiana, he contracted some tropical disease; but he died of a heart problem the next year.

Heilprin, Michael (1823–88) scholar, encyclopedist; born in Piotrow, Poland. Educated solely by his father, he showed an early propensity for learning. His family removed to Hungary in 1842 to escape Russian oppression and he soon mastered Magyar. His revolutionary poetry was widely popular before the 1848 Hungarian Revolution and after the collapse of the Revolution he fled to avoid imprisonment. He emigrated to the U.S.A. in 1856 and took an interest in politics and the abolition of slavery. He was engaged in 1858 to work on the *New American Cyclopaedia;* the thorough revision of the *American Cyclopaedia* (1872–76) owes much to his scholarship. He wrote regularly for the *Nation* and contributed notably to its reputation for accuracy. Because much of his writing was anonymous, his own reputation, though excellent, was limited in extent. His only published book is a two-volume study of Old Testament poetry, *The Historical Poetry of the Ancient Hebrews* (1879–80).

Heimlich, Henry (Jay) (1920–) physician; born in Wilmington, Del. While a New York City thoracic surgeon (1950–69), he developed a procedure to reconstruct the esophagus, followed by the Heimlich valve to help chest drainage. Moving to Cincinnati, Ohio, he devised the antichoking "Heimlich maneuver" in 1974. He wrote *Dr Heimlich's Home Guide to Emergency Medical Situations* (1981).

Heinecken, Robert (1931–) photographer, teacher; born in Denver, Colo. An instructor at the Univirsity of California: Los Angeles (1960), he taught drawing and printmaking before introducing photography into the curriculum in the mid-1960s. He then began combining photography with 3 dimensional surfaces to create photo-sculptural collages. He has taught advanced workshops at the George Eastman House, the Arts Institute, and Howard University while continuing to experiment with combining photography and other media.

Heineman, Ben (Walter) (1914–) railroad executive, lawyer; born in Wausau, Wis. He had a 20-year law career in private practice and government service in Chicago, Washington, and Algiers before reviving the fortunes of the Chicago & North Western Railway Co. as chairman and CEO (1956–72) by streamlining and modernizing its Chicago commuter lines. He was founder, chairman, and CEO of Northwest Industries (1968–85).

Heinemann, Edward H. (1908–91) aircraft design engineer; born in Saginaw, Mich. He worked as a designer and engineer for Morland Aircraft Corporation and Northrop before going to work for Douglas Aircraft in 1936. He left in 1958, becoming vice-president for engineering at General Dynamics Corporation in 1962. He retired in 1973.

Heinlein, Robert (Anson) (Anson MacDonald, Lyle Monroe, John Riverside, Caleb Saunders, Simon York, pen names) (1907–88) writer; born in Butler, Mo. He studied at the University of Missouri (1925), graduated from Annapolis (1929), and did graduate work in physics at the University of California: Los Angeles (1934). Among other endeavors he worked as an engineer, owned a silver mine, and was the announcer for the Apollo lunar landing (1969). He began writing science fiction in 1947, and is noted for his technical knowledge and detailed settings, as in *Stranger in a Strange Land* (1961).

Heinrich, Anthony Philip (Anton Philipp) (1781–1861) composer; born in Schönbüchel, Bohemia. After a banking career in Germany, he came to the U.S.A. in 1810 and first pursued music as a conductor and teacher. Later he embarked on an ambitious and pioneering series of nationalistic compositions such as the symphony *Manitou Mysteries* (c. 1845). Despite some successes and being hailed as the "Beethoven of America," he died in poverty.

Heinrich, Bernd (1940–) zoologist, ecologist; born in Bad Polzin, Germany. He came to the U.S.A. in 1950 when his parents moved to Maine. After doing research as a zoology fellow at the University of California: Los Angeles (1970–71), he was an entomologist at the University of California: Berkeley (1971–80) before becoming a professor of zoology at the University of Vermont (Burlington) (1980). His early research made major contributions to studies of ravens and owls. In 1970 he began studying temperature regulation and energy economics in bumblebees, and postulated that these bees maintain a body temperature above the ambient environmental temperature; he wrote *Bumblebee Economics* (1979) for both the scientist and lay reader. He was a marathon runner who called the bumblebee a "supreme endurance athlete."

Heinz, Henry John (1844–1916) food manufacturer; born in Pittsburgh, Pa. When he was 8 years old he began peddling surplus home-grown vegetables to neighbors; by 1860 he was making three wagon deliveries of his vegetables a week to Pittsburgh grocers. In 1869 he formed his first partnership selling grated horseradish; by 1875 they were bankrupt. The next year the F. & J. Heinz Company was launched with his brother and cousin as partners (providing the initials in the company's name) and himself as manager, manufacturing pickles and condiments: their tomato ketchup, still a best-seller, was introduced in 1876. In 1888 the company was reorganized as the H. J. Heinz Company and by 1896 Henry had invented the phrase "57 varieties." The company incorporated in 1905 with Henry as president. By his death he was employing thousands of employees at 25 separate factories and processing the harvest from over 100,000 acres.

Heinz, Howard (1877–1941) business executive, philanthropist; born in Pittsburgh, Pa. (son of Henry John Heinz). He entered his father's food company in 1900 and became president in 1919. His leadership of H. J. Heinz Company produced excellent advertising and large numbers of traveling salesmen. He directed food relief in southeastern Europe and Turkey after World War I, and among other philanthropies he endowed the Howard Heinz Students' International Fund at Yale University.

Heiser, Charles B. (Bixler) (1920–) botanist; born in Cynthiana, Ind. He taught at Washington University, St. Louis (1944–45), then joined the herbarium (1945–46) and the botanical experiment station (1946–47) at the University of California: Davis. He moved to Indiana University (1947–86), where he remained as herbarium director (1986). He made major contributions to the systematics and cytogenetics of flowering plants, studies on the evolution of cultivated plants, and investigations on the relationship of food plants to human populations.

Heisman, John (William) (1869–1936) football coach; born in Cleveland, Ohio. He began coaching in 1892 at Oberlin College and was successful at several schools. His longest tenure was at Georgia Tech (1904–19), where he produced undefeated teams from 1915–17. A supreme innovator, he invented numerous plays and championed the legalization of the forward pass. The Heisman Trophy, awarded annually since 1935 to college football's outstanding player, is named after him.

Heizer, Robert F. (Fleming) (1915–79) archaeologist, anthropologist; born in Denver, Colo. A pioneer in ecologically-oriented archaeology, Heizer taught at the University of California: Berkeley (1946–75). He was a leading authority on pre-Columbian Californian archaeology and Mexican and Central American prehistory. He reported (with J.A. Graham, 1976) revolutionary evidence of Maya civilization originating on the Pacific coast of Guatemala.

Held, Al (1928–) painter; born in New York City. He studied at the Art Students League, New York (1948–49), in Paris (1950–52), and was based in New York City. After experimenting with a style similar to that of Jackson Pollock, his approach became increasingly geometric. He is known for his large acrylic alphabet paintings (1963–65), with their bold colors and chunky formations.

Held, John, Jr. (1889–1958) cartoonist, illustrator, sculptor; born in Salt Lake City, Utah. He sold his first cartoon to *Life* magazine while still an adolescent. He worked for the *Salt Lake City Tribune* before moving (1912) to New York City to contribute cartoons to *Vanity Fair*. In 1918 his satirical cartoons depicting vacuous Jazz-age flappers made their first regular appearance in the *New Yorker;* his work came to epitomize the Roaring Twenties. In later life, he turned to sculpting and was an artist-in-residence at Harvard University and the University of Georgia.

Heller, Joseph (1923–) writer; born in New York City. He studied at the University of Southern California, New York University (B.A. 1948), Columbia University (M.A. 1949), and Oxford, England (1949–50). He became an advertising writer and promotion manager in New York City (1952–56), and taught at various universities, notably at City College of New York, until 1975. He wrote for television, movies, and theater, but is best known for several novels, most notably his famous antiwar work, *Catch-22* (1961).

Heller, Maximilian (1860–1929) rabbi; born in Prague, Bohemia (now Czech Republic). He came to the U.S.A. in 1879. He was rabbi of Temple Sinai in New Orleans (1887–1927). A leader in Reform Judaism and an early Zionist, he was professor of Hebrew language and literature at Tulane University (1912–28).

Hellman, Lillian (1905–84) playwright; born in New Orleans. After studying at New York and Columbia Universities, she worked in publishing and as a book reviewer and play-reader before attaining her first success with the play, *The Children's Hour* (1934). Concerned with social, political, and moral issues along with more personal ones, she wrote a number of successful plays including *The Little Foxes* (1939) and *Toys in the Attic* (1960). She also wrote many film scripts and adapted the works of others for film and the stage. She published several memoirs, including *Scoundrel Time* (1976), and she wrote the book for Leonard Bernstein's musical, *Candide* (1956). For some 30 years she lived with Dashiell Hammett and shared his commitment to radical political causes; her appearance before the House Committee on Un-American Activities (1952) resulted in her being blacklisted in Hollywood. Her last years were tainted by a feud with Mary McCarthy and allegations that she had often lied in her memoirs.

Helms, Richard (McGarrah) (1913–) government official; born in St. Davids, Pa. He was a journalist before he joined the U.S. Navy in 1942. He joined the Central Intelligence Agency (CIA) (1947) and served as its director (1965–73). He was convicted of lying before a congressional committee (1977); he countered that his oath as head of the CIA required him to keep certain secrets. He was an international consultant (1977) and president of Safeer Company in Washington, D.C. (1977).

Helmsley, Leona (Mindy) (b. Rosenthal) (1920–) business executive; born in New York City. Herself a real estate executive, she married real estate tycoon Harry Helmsley (1972), who owned hotels, apartment buildings, and commercial properties. She became president of Helmsley Hotels (1980) and appeared as the "Queen" in high-profile, high-ego ad campaigns. She was convicted of tax evasion, received a four-year sentence (1989), and went to jail in 1992; she was released in 1994.

Hemingway, Ernest (Miller) (1899–1961) writer; born in Oak Park, Ill. Son of a doctor (who would commit suicide), he never attended college but became a journalist for the *Kansas City Star* (1917–18). He served with the Red Cross Ambulance Corps in France (1917–18) and was wounded while accompanying the Italian army into battle. He worked as a journalist, covering the Greco-Turkish war for the *Toronto Star* (1920). In Chicago, he married (his first of four wives) and went back to Europe to serve as a foreign correspondent (1921–24). He made frequent trips to Spain and the Austrian Alps but for the most part was based in Paris where he fell in with the expatriate circle centered around Gertrude Stein. His first published work was *Three Stories & Ten Poems* (1923), followed by *In Our Time* (1925), consisting of 15 stories that clearly drew on his own youthful experiences; already his distinctive voice was in evidence – simple sentences, enigmatic dialogue, precise description. His first novel, *Torrents of Spring* (1926), was more a satire of Maxwell Anderson, but *The Sun Also Rises* (1926) gained him instant acclaim and seemed to capture what Stein labeled "the lost generation." *Men Without Women* (1927), another collection of stories, maintained his reputation, while his next novel, *A Farewell to Arms* (1929), advanced him to the front ranks of contemporary writers. He had returned to the U.S.A. in 1927 but would never stay long in one place, seemingly always in need of adventure – deep-sea fishing off Key West, Fla., big-game hunting in Africa. He had long been dedicated to Spanish bullfighting – his nonfictional work, *Death in the Afternoon* (1932), effectively introduced it to the non-Spanish world – and when the Spanish Civil War broke out, he went off to cover it (1936–38); he identified with the anti-Fascists, and his only play, *The Fifth Column* (1938), and one of his better novels, *For Whom the Bell Tolls* (1940), came out of this experience. By now he was more than a well-known writer – he had become one of the great celebrities of the century, his every word, activity, drink, and clothing style reported on in magazines such as *Life*. In 1940 he bought a house in Cuba that was to be a fairly regular stopover (and which Fidel Castro and the Cubans treated as a historical site). In World War II, he is said to have aided in espionage in the Caribbean under cover of deep-sea fishing; he then went to England to report on the

Royal Air Force and he accompanied the Allied forces on their drive to liberate Paris. After the war, his talents as a writer seemed to have dulled, but he recaptured both popular and critical audiences with his short novel, *The Old Man and the Sea* (1952), and ended up with the Nobel Prize in literature in 1954. Restless and unable to complete new writing projects, he became prone to various physical ailments, mental depression, and eventually a form of paranoia; he committed suicide by shooting himself at his home in Ketchum, Idaho. A series of works, including *A Moveable Feast* (1964), appeared posthumously. Hemingway's terse prose style, self-promoted macho image, and stress on the search for physical challenges have all lent themselves to imitation and parody; but at their best his writing, life, and themes ensured him a role as one of the century's major literary figures.

Hempel, Carl (Gustav) (1905–) philosopher; born in Oranienburg, Germany. A prominent logical positivist of the Berlin school, he emigrated to the U.S.A. in 1937 because of Nazism. He was naturalized in 1944. He taught at Queens College (1940–48), Yale (1948–55), and Princeton (1955–73). In 1973 he became emeritus professor at Princeton; from 1977 he was a professor at the University of Pittsburgh. His works include *Concept Formation in Empirical Science* (1952).

Hemsley, Sherman (1938–) television comedian; born in Philadelphia, Pa. Originally a stage actor, he appeared on Broadway in *Purlie* (1970). He was a regular on *All in the Family* (1973–75), then starred in CBS's spin-off show, *The Jeffersons* (1975–85), about a black middle-class family. He played the black deacon in the National Broadcasting Company's comedy, *Amen* (1986–91).

Hench, Philip S. (Showalter) (1896–1965) rheumatologist; born in Pittsburgh, Pa. He worked with the Mayo Clinics at the University of Minnesota (1921–57). He was a pioneer in the pathology and therapy of gout before devoting his career to research on rheumatoid arthritis (RA). He coined the term "cortisone" for biochemist Edward Kendall's "compound E" isolate from the adrenal cortex, and devised treatments using cortisone (1948) and adrenocorticotropic hormone (ACTH) (1949) for patients with RA. Hench and Kendall received one-half the 1950 Nobel Prize in physiology for their work on structure and behavior of adrenocortical hormones. Hench also published articles on the history of medicine and was considered an authority on yellow fever.

Henderson, Archibald (1785–1859) marine officer; born in Virginia. In a long career of mostly peacetime service he was commandant of marines from 1820 until his death, and oversaw important reforms in the corps' organization. Commissioned in 1806, Henderson saw service during the War of 1812. He led marines in combat in the Seminole War in Florida in 1837. Brevetted brigadier general for gallantry in that conflict, he became the first general officer in the corps.

Henderson, David (Bremner) (1840–1906) U.S. representative; born in Old Deer, Scotland. Emigrating to America as a child, he grew up on a farm in Iowa and left college to serve as a private in the Union Army. A leg amputation ended his military career in 1863 and he became a lawyer in Dubuque, Iowa (1866–82). A Republican congressman (1883–1903), he served as Speaker of the House for two terms (1899–

1903); fought for veterans' benefits and supported protective tariffs.

Henderson, (James) Fletcher (1897–1952) jazz musician; born in Cuthbert, Ga. He was a pianist and a pioneer of big band jazz, leading his own orchestra between 1924–37 and intermittently thereafter. His bands featured many of the early stars of jazz, including Louis Armstrong and Coleman Hawkins, and his style served as a prototype for the Swing Era. Between 1937–39, he worked as an important arranger for Benny Goodman.

Henderson, Lawrence J. (Joseph) (1878–1942) biochemist, physiologist; born in Lynn, Mass. He spent his career as a research physician at Harvard (1904–42). His quantitative measurements of bodily buffer systems (1907–10) were expanded logarithmically by Danish biochemist K. A. Hasselbach to produce the Henderson-Hasselbach equation describing acid-base equilibria. He founded the department of physical chemistry at Harvard (1920) and established Harvard's Fatigue Laboratory (1927) to study chemical changes due to environmentally-induced stress. Further investigations of oxygen-carbon dioxide exchanges in blood led to his seminal book, *Blood: A Study in General Physiology* (1928). A philosopher and scholar with varied interests, Henderson related Vilfredo Pareto's classic writings on sociology to his own homeostatic approach to the buffering capability of the blood; his lectures on Pareto influenced numerous young sociologists.

Henderson, Loy W. (Wesley) (1892–1986) diplomat, educator; born near Rogers, Ark. He worked for the Red Cross in Europe (1918–21) and entered the Foreign Service in 1922. He was ambassador to India (1948–50) and Iran (1951–55). He was President Eisenhower's chief advisor on Middle East policy. He taught international relations at American University (1961–68).

Henderson, Richard (1735–85) promoter, colonizer; born in Hanover County, Va. He was a lawyer and an associate justice of the North Carolina Superior Court (1768–73). He retired as a judge to form a land development company, the Richard Henderson & Company, and sent Daniel Boone as his agent to explore Kentucky. He organized the Louisa Company (renamed Translyvania company) in 1774 and tried to set up a proprietary colony on land between the Kentucky and Cumberland Rivers (present day Kentucky) he had bought from the Cherokee Indians. He himself established the settlement of Boonesborough, but the American Revolution cost him the support of England necessary for legalizing his colony. In 1779–80, he established a settlement at French Lick (now Nashville), Tenn.

Henderson, Rickey (Henley) (1957–) baseball player; born in Chicago. An outfielder for the Oakland Athletics and New York Yankees (1979), he was known for his sometimes highstrung temperament and his always prolific base-stealing; his 130 stolen bases in 1982 set a new major league record, and in 1991 he broke Lou Brock's lifetime record (938). A solid .290 hitter with power, he was one of the game's greatest leadoff hitters.

Hendricks, (John Carl) Jon (1921–) jazz musician; born in Newark, Ohio. He was a singer and the principal lyricist with (Dave) Lambert, Hendricks, & (Annie) Ross, the vocal trio that popularized "vocalese" in the late 1950s.

Hendricks, Thomas A. (Andrews) (1819–85) vice-president, senator; born in Zanesville, Ohio. As a senator, he opposed Lincoln's leadership during the Civil War. He was elected Grover Cleveland's vice-president in 1884, but died after serving for only eight months.

Hendrix, (James Marshall) Jimi (1942–70) musician; born in Seattle, Wash. One of the tragic figures of 1960s popular music, he was a highly innovative blues-rock guitarist, and one of the handful of black musicians to gain wide popularity in rock. Upon discharge as an air force paratrooper in 1961, he appeared as a sideman with Little Richard, Ike & Tina Turner, and the Isley Brothers. In 1965 he formed Jimmy James and the Blue Flames in New York. The following year, he moved to London where he formed the Jimi Hendrix Experience and recorded his first hit album, *Are You Experienced?* Between 1967 and his death from an overdose of barbiturates, he was a major recording artist and concert attraction.

Henie, Sonja (1912–69) ice skater, film actress; born in Oslo, Norway. Starting in 1927, she won seven European championships, ten world championships, and gold medals in the 1928, 1932, and 1936 Olympics; she is credited with introducing music and dance-based movements into free-skating and thus greatly broadening the public for what had been a previously technical event. She turned professional in 1936 and made her first Hollywood movie, *One in a Million* (1936). She began touring with her ice show in 1937, and went on to make a series of immensely popular movies such as *Sun Valley Serenade* (1941), light romantic musicals designed to show off her skating artistry. Her film career faded in the late 1940s but she continued with her touring until 1952. She had become an American citizen in 1941 but lived her final years in her native Norway.

Heninger, George Robert (1934–) psychiatrist, neurobiologist; born in Los Angeles. He was affiliated with Yale University from 1966, becoming professor of psychiatry and director of the Ribicoff Research Facilities (1978). An expert in the field of depression, antidepressant therapies, and psychopharmacology, he was a consultant to government and numerous pharmaceutical companies.

Henley, Ernest M. (Mark) (1924–) physicist; born in Frankfurt, Germany. He came to the U.S.A. in 1939 and worked in various engineering laboratories and universities before joining the University of Washington (1954). He made major contributions to theoretical nuclear particle physics and symmetries.

Henne, Frances E. (Elizabeth) (1906–85) library educator; born in Springfield, Ill. A professor of library science at both of her alma maters, the University of Chicago and Columbia University, she wrote extensively on children's literature and libraries. She helped establish national guidelines for libraries and edited the American Library Association's *Standards for School Library Programs* (1960).

Hennock, Frieda B. (Barkin) (1904–60) lawyer, public official; born in Kovel, Poland. Emigrating from Poland at age ten, she became a criminal lawyer at age 21, later joining a New York City corporate law firm. The first female member of the Federal Communications Commission (1948–55), she worked to reserve television channels for educational programming. She practiced law in Washington afterward.

Henri, Robert (1865–1929) painter, teacher; born in Cincinnati, Ohio. He studied at the Pennsylvania Academy of the Fine Arts with Thomas Anshutz, and in Paris (1888). As a painter and a teacher he influenced a whole generation of artists, and became the founder of the so-called Ashcan school of painting, which stressed contemporary urban reality. In opposition to the restrictions of the National Academy, he set up an independent exhibition called "The Eight" (1908), whose members included John Sloan and George Luks. Although an academic painter, his teaching methods were considered radical at the time.

Henry, Andrew (c. 1775–1833) trapper, lead miner; born in York County, Pa. He moved to present-day Missouri (1800) where he engaged in lead mining. He joined the St. Louis Missouri Fur Company (1809) and led the first party of American fur trappers west of the Rocky Mountains (1810–11). He became a hero among trappers for this event and for his exploits with William Ashley's trapping expedition in the west (1822–24).

Henry, Edward (Lamson) (1841–1919) painter; born in Charleston, S.C. He was a popular genre painter and illustrator who specialized in simple scenes, such as *Carriage Ride on a Country Lane* (1906).

Henry, Joseph (1797–1898) physicist; born in Albany, N.Y. He worked as a tutor, then as a surveyor (1825–26) before becoming a professor at his alma mater, Albany Academy (1826–32). He began research on electromagnetism (1827), constructed the first electromagnetic motor (1829), and discovered electrical induction independent of English physicist Michael Faraday. The "henry" unit of inductance is named after him. He continued his research after transferring to Princeton (1832–46), demonstrating the oscillatory nature of electrical discharges (1842), and diversifying into the fields of astronomy, galvanometry, and telegraphy. In 1846 he was named first secretary and director of the Smithsonian Institution; through his leadership (1846–77), the Smithsonian supported internationally cooperative scientific research. While administrative duties left him little time for the "pure" scientific endeavors he favored, Henry introduced a system of weather forecasting, investigated the propagation of light and sound waves by lighthouses, and encouraged the museum's patronage of anthropology and ethnology.

Henry, O. See PORTER, WILLIAM SYDNEY.

Henry, Patrick (1736–99) orator, political leader; born in Hanover County, Va. He took up law in 1760 after failures in business and farming. He vigorously opposed the Stamp Act (1765). He was a delegate to the First and Second Continental Congresses. In 1775, he proposed revolutionary motions to the Virginia assembly, including one for the arming and training of militiamen. He carried the day with a speech that included "I do not know what course others may take, but as for me, give me liberty or give me death." He was governor of Virginia (1776–79, 1784–86) and he opposed the new Constitution (1787) because he felt it endangered individuals' and states' rights. He retired from public life in 1788 and refused several offers of posts in the federal government. He was influential in the creation of the Bill of Rights (1791). Although he became reactionary in his later years, his dramatic presence was considered to be integral to the early patriot cause.

Henry Roe Cloud (b. Wonah'ilayhunka) (1884–1950) Winnebago leader, Presbyterian clergyman; born in Nebr. The first Native American to receive a B.A. from Yale, he eventually earned an M.A. and founded the American Indian Institute (1915). He was appointed U.S. supervisor of Indian education in 1936.

Henson, Josiah (1789–1883) social activist, minister; born in Charles County, Md. He was sold at auction at an early age and endured great hardships in slavery; nonetheless, he became a land superintendent and a Methodist preacher while still in slavery. He and his family escaped north to Canada (1830) and settled in Ontario; there he tried to develop a community for African-American escapees but it failed to attract a significant number. He returned to the south and liberated other slaves. He told his story to Harriet Beecher Stowe and was the reputed original for her novel *Uncle Tom's Cabin* (1852). He published his autobiography in 1849. He made three trips to England and was honored by Queen Victoria (1876).

Henson, Matthew (Alexander) (1866–1955) explorer; born in Charles County, Md. An African-American who went to sea at age 12 or 13, he met Lt. Robert E. Peary in 1887 and became his valet and assistant for 22 years. He, Peary, and four Eskimos reached the North Pole on April 6, 1909. Henson worked in the New York Customhouse (1913–33) and never profited from his achievement. Not until the final years of his life did he receive recognition for his role in Peary's expeditions, for Peary, although friendly enough in private, shunned Henson in public. Only in the 1980s was it revealed that both men had fathered children by Eskimo women while on their Arctic expeditions.

Hepburn, Katharine (Houghton) (1909–) film actress; born in Hartford, Conn. Strong-willed and outspoken, she began her career on Broadway, but came to Hollywood in 1932. She won Academy Awards for *Morning Glory* (1933), *Guess Who's Coming to Dinner* (1967), *The Lion in Winter* (1968), and *On Golden Pond* (1981). Her 27-year off-screen romance with Spencer Tracy lasted until his death.

Hepburn, William (Peters) (1833–1916) U.S. representative; born in Wellsville, Ohio. A lawyer in Marshalltown, Iowa (1855–61) and Republican party activist, he joined the Union Army in 1861, becoming a lieutenant colonel. After the war, he returned to his law practice in Iowa and was elected to Congress (1881–87) where he championed military pensions. Reelected (1893–1909) he set a rate law for the railroads, and cosponsored the Pure Food and Drug Act of 1906.

Herb, Raymond G. (George) (1908–) physicist; born in Navarino, Wis. He designed and developed high-voltage proton accelerators while teaching at the University of Wisconsin: Madison (1935–72). He founded the National Electrostatic Corporation (1965) to manufacture his revolutionary pelletron accelerators, and resigned from academia to devote full-time service to his business (1972).

Herbert, (Donald Jeffry) Don ("Mr. Wizard") (1917–) television science educator, producer; born in Waconia, Minn. He served as a pilot in the U.S. Air Force during World War II. He combined his interests in science and drama when he went into radio work in Chicago. He created and starred in *Watch Mr. Wizard* (1951–65, 1971–72), an informal educational television program that popularized scientific principles by demonstrating simple experiments. He also produced the adult science series *How About* (1979–86).

Herbert, Frank (Patrick) (1920–86) writer; born in Tacoma, Wash. He studied at the University of Washington (1946–47), and worked as a journalist. He became a full-time science fiction writer after the publication of his first novel, *Dune* (1965). He continued to write many other books while living in Townsend, Wash., and is considered a master of the genre.

Herbert, Hilary Abner (1834–1919) secretary of the navy; born in Laurens, S.C. As a confederate officer he fought in numerous Civil War battles (1861–64). He became a congressman (1877–93) and the secretary of the navy (1893–97). He promoted the construction of battleships and torpedo boats.

Herbert, Robert Louis (1929–) art historian; born in Worcester, Mass. He studied at Wesleyan University (B.A. 1952), in Paris (1951–52), Yale (M.A. 1954; Ph.D. 1957), and on fellowships in England, Paris, and New Haven, Conn. He worked in a variety of museums in Europe and America, arranging exhibitions and producing catalogs. He also taught at Yale (1954–68), his specialty being 19th- and 20th-century French art.

Herbert, Victor (1859–1924) operetta composer, conductor; born in Dublin, Ireland. When he first came to the United States in 1886, he had the reputation of a serious cellist who had played under Johannes Brahms and Anton Rubenstein. As conductor of the Pittsburgh Symphony from 1889 to 1904, he premiered several of his own orchestral works (and his cello concerto continues to be played). In 1894 he launched a second career as a composer of light operas; among his approximately 50 popular operettas (with their still beloved melodies) are *Babes in Toyland* ("March of the Toys"), *Mlle. Modiste* ("Kiss Me Again"), *Naughty Marietta* ("Ah, Sweet Mystery of Life") (1910), and *Eileen* ("Thine Alone"). He was so versatile that he could write the music for several Ziegfeld Follies and also write one of the first American operas, *Natoma* (1911). (He had become an American citizen in 1902.) He was also a founder of the American Society of Composers, Authors and Publishers (ASCAP).

Herblock See BLOCK, HERBERT (LAWRENCE).

Herbst, Josephine (Frey) (1892–1969) writer; born in Sioux City, Iowa. From a poor family, she worked at odd jobs as she went from college to college, finally taking her B.A. from the University of California: Berkeley (1918). She moved to New York City and fell in with the literary set, had an affair with Maxwell Anderson, and then went off to Berlin and Paris to write. She returned to the U.S.A. in 1924 with the writer, John Hermann, whom she married and then settled with in a farmhouse in Erwinna, Pa. During the next several years she published a series of novels on which her reputation rests, including *Pity is Not Enough* (1933), the first volume of her trilogy based on her own family's history from the Civil War to the Great Depression. During the 1930s, the world's economic, political, and social problems led her to writing journalism and to identifying with radical views and circles; she went to Spain briefly in 1937 to report on the civil war there and she was on the fringes of the American Communist Party; in 1942 she was fired from a government job because of her leftist associations. In the postwar years, divorced from 1940, she at first became almost a recluse in her Erwinna home, but as she resumed her writing she gained a new circle of admirers.

Hergesheimer, Joseph (1880–1954) writer; born in Philadelphia. He studied at the Pennnsylvania Academy of the Fine Arts. After a trip to Italy, he settled in West Chester, Pa., and wrote a series of novels, notably *Java Head* (1919). He

continued to write, but his mannered prose was not well received.

Hering, Constantine (1800–80) homeopathic physician; born in Oschatz, Saxony, Germany. He studied medicine in Leipzig, Germany, under Dr. Samuel Hahnemann, the founder of homeopathy, namely, the theory that minute doses of a substance that produces disease symptoms in a healthy person will cure a person sick with the same symptoms. Hering came to America in 1831, settled in Philadelphia (1933), and organized the first school of homeopathy in the U.S.A. at Allentown, Pa. (1835). In 1848 he cofounded the Homeopathic Medical College of Pennsylvania, which merged with the Hahnemann Medical College of Philadelphia when he founded the latter in 1867. He set forth the basics of homeopathy in English with his 10-volume work, *Guiding Symptoms* (1878–91).

Herkimer, Nicholas (1728–77) soldier; born near what is now Herkimer, N.Y. A veteran of the French and Indian War, he was made brigadier general of militia when the American Revolution began and was given responsibility for defending the Mohawk Valley of upstate New York against the British troops, the Loyalists, and their Indian allies. Wounded in an ambush near Oneida, N.Y., in August 1777, he rallied sufficiently to cheer his men on during the subsequent battle near Oriskany; but his force had to retreat and he died of his wounds at home on August 16.

Herlihy, David (Joseph) (1930–91) historian; born in San Francisco. After receiving his doctorate from Yale University (1956), he became the first prominent medievalist to write about women's roles in medieval history. He taught at the university level for over 30 years and held professorships at the universities of Wisconsin, Harvard, and Brown. His books include *The Tuscans and Their Families* (1984) and *Women and Work in Medieval Europe* (1989).

Herman, (Gerald) Jerry (1933–) composer, lyricist; born in New York City. Majoring in drama at the University of Miami, he won the Snark's award for playwriting; his college revue, *I Feel Wonderful*, had an off Broadway run. His first successful Broadway musical, *Milk and Honey* (1961), was followed by the Tony Award-winning hits *Hello Dolly* (1964), *Mame* (1966), and *La Cage aux Folles* (1983), the first Broadway musical to portray a homosexual relationship.

Herman, (Woodrow Charles) Woody (1913–1987) jazz musician; born in Milwaukee, Wis. He was a clarinetist and singer who began his career with the Isham Jones Band in 1934 and assumed its leadership two years later. Regrouping in the early 1940s, he led a succession of "Herds," the first of which premiered Stravinsky's "Ebony Concerto" in 1946. The Second Herd, or "Four Brothers" band of 1947–48, included Stan Getz and other promising modernists. He continued to lead ensembles of various sizes until his death.

Hernández, Rafael (1892–1965) composer; born in Aguadilla, Puerto Rico. He was one of the most important figures in 20th-century popular Puerto Rican music, dividing his career between Puerto Rico, the U.S.A. (where he had the first "Latin" band in New York after World War I), Cuba, and Mexico. Works such as the "Lamento borincano," "Capullito de Alelí," and his masterpiece "Preciosa" were thought to express the soul of Puerto Rico.

Herne, James A. (b. Ahearn) (1839–1901) actor, playwright; born in Cohoes, N.Y. He began as an actor, then turned to writing melodrama in collaboration with David Belasco. His later, more serious plays were strongly influenced by Ibsen, and were often better esteemed by literary critics than by audiences. Among his most important failures was *Margaret Fleming* (1891), a play that deals with the consequences of a husband's infidelity.

Herres, Robert Tralles (1932–) aviator; born in Denver, Colo. A 1954 Naval Academy graduate, he transferred to the Air Force and served in Germany, France, and Thailand. In the 1970s he directed the Strategic Air Command's command and control center and the Air Force Communications Command. After three years as head of the Air Force Space Command, he became vice-chairman of the Joint Chiefs of Staff in 1987.

Herriman, George (1880–1944) cartoonist; born in New Orleans. In 1910 he created his first successful newspaper comic strip, *The Dingbat Family,* which included animal characters that eventually evolved into the strip *Krazy Kat* (1913), the first comic strip to achieve acclaim for its oblique intellectual and subtle literary qualities.

Herring, E. (Edward) Pendelton (1903–) political scientist; born in Baltimore, Md. He taught at Harvard (1928–47) before embarking on a second career as president of the Social Science Research Council (SSRC) (1948–68). He solicited leading social scientists to the SSRC's committees, enlarged the operating budget, and made data more accessible to policy makers.

Herring, (William) Conyers (1914–) physicist; born in Scotia, N.Y. He was a research fellow at the Massachusetts Institute of Technology (1937–39), then taught at Princeton (1939–40) and the University of Missouri (1940–41). He performed war research at Columbia University (1941–45) before joining Bell Laboratories (1946–78). His work at Bell on spin wave theory was one of the first studies of collective excitations in metals. His research during the 1940s and 1950s on transform phenomena in semiconductors was basic to present understanding of solid state theory. From 1978 to 1981 he was a professor at Stanford.

Herrmann, Alexander (1843–96) magician; born in Paris, France. A success in Europe and America, where he emigrated as an adult, he created the popular image of a magician, elegantly dressed with dark beard and goatee.

Herrmann, Bernard (1911–75) composer, conductor; born in New York City. After studies at Juilliard he began conducting and composing for Columbia Broadcasting System Radio, where he met Orson Welles. Herrmann's 1940 score for Welles' *Citizen Kane* was the first of his 61 film scores, including several classic ones for Hitchcock. He wrote concert works as well.

Herron, Carrie Rand (1867–1914) socialist; born in Hagerstown, Md. Daughter of philanthropist Caroline (Amanda Sherfey) Rand, she and her mother were long involved in social causes and in the development of Iowa College in Grinnell (later Grinnell College). While her mother helped fund creation of departments at Grinnell, Carrie was a physical education instructor (1893–1909), "principal of women" (1894), and helped fund construction of the E. D. Rand Gymnasium for Women (1897). She turned all her attention to the Socialist Party after marrying longtime associate, the Rev. George Davis Herron (1901). Hounded for their socialist activities and liberal social attitudes, they moved to Florence, Italy (1904), returning briefly to the United States to create the Rand School of Social Science in New York City (1906) at the bequest of the late Mrs. Rand who had died in Florence (1905). The school, which trained people for leadership in socialist and labor causes, went out of existence in 1956. Carrie and her husband returned to their villa in Florence where they entertained international socialists during her remaining years.

Herschbach, Dudley R. (Robert) (1932–) chemist; born in San Jose, Calif. While at the University of California: Berkeley (1959–63) and Harvard (1963), he worked with others to elucidate the mechanisms of chemical reactions, detailing the sequence of events and energy release. He shared the Nobel Prize in chemistry (1986).

Hersey, John (Richard) (1914–93) journalist, writer; born in Tientsin, China. His parents were missionaries and after his early education in China he attended Yale (B.A. 1936) and Clare College, Cambridge, England. He was briefly Sinclair Lewis's personal secretary (1937), then went to work as a journalist and editor for several New York magazines. During World War II he saw considerable action as a correspondent and he drew on his experiences for several of his works, including the novel *A Bell for Adano* (1944) (which also became a play and a movie). His greatest impact came from his documentary-style account, *Hiroshima* (1946), the first work to reveal to the general public the true horrors of a nuclear war. He taught at Yale for many years starting in 1950 and continued to publish his fiction and nonfiction.

Hersh, Seymour (Myron) (1937–) journalist; born in Chicago. An aggressive, highly successful investigative reporter, who worked variously for the Associated Press, the *New York Times,* and the *Atlantic Monthly,* he played key roles in exposing evidence of the My Lai massacre in Vietnam, domestic spying by the Central Intelligence Agency, and other stories, winning a 1970 Pulitzer Prize and many other major awards. His books include *The Price of Power* (1983), a scathing portrait of Henry Kissinger.

Hershey, Alfred D. (Day) (1908–) geneticist; born in Owosso, Mich. He began research on bacteriophages (viruses which infect bacteria) while at Washington University (St. Louis) (1934–50), and in 1943 joined the informal "phage group" forum begun by Max Delbrück and Salvador Luria. Hershey then moved to the Carnegie Institution's laboratory in Cold Spring Harbor, N.Y. (1950–74). He and geneticist Martha Chase discovered (1952) that bacteriophage DNA alters genetic replication of the host bacterium, thus proving that DNA is the genetic material of the virus. For his work on viral structure and genetic replication, Hershey (with Delbrück and Luria) was awarded the 1969 Nobel Prize in physiology. Hershey preferred a quiet life after retirement to allow younger scientists to continue advancements in viral genetics.

Hershey, Lewis (Blaine) (1893–1977) soldier; born near Angola, Ind. A serving officer from 1917–73, he directed the Selective Service System (1941–70), the agency that drafted millions of American young men into military service during the 1940s, 1950s, and 1960s.

Hershey, Milton (Snavely) (1857–1945) candy manufacturer, philanthropist; born in Derry Township, Pa. His father moved so frequently, Milton attended seven schools in eight years, never progressing beyond grade four. He apprenticed to a Lancaster, Pa., confectioner (1872–76) and then opened his own candy store in Philadelphia. By 1886 he was back in

Lancaster where he soon found success making caramels using fresh milk but by 1900 had sold his caramel business to concentrate on chocolate. In 1903 he built a factory near his birthplace to manufacture five-cent chocolate bars; the business so prospered that "Hershey" became virtually synonymous with chocolate in the U.S.A. and he branched out to dominate the cocoa and syrup markets. In order to maintain his constantly expanding need for reliable workers, he began to build a complete town near the factory, including stores, schools, recreational facilities, and a large amusement park. In 1909 he built a trade school for orphan boys. Although often criticized for his paternalism and for running a "company town," he did expand the town's building program during the 1930s depression and he left his vast fortune to various philanthropies including a medical center.

Herskovits, Melville J. (Jean) (1895–1963) anthropologist; born in Bellefontaine, Ohio. He studied with Franz Boas at Columbia University and went on to become a leading cultural relativist and the dean of American Africanists. He spent his academic career at Northwestern University, where he founded the first American university program in African studies (1951). He pioneered the cultural anthropological study of American blacks by identifying them as a distinct cultural group in such early works as *The American Negro* (1928). His fieldwork in the West Indies and Africa contributed to his contention that, despite the American blacks' period of enslavement, their culture remained linked to its African origins; this thesis, propounded in *The Myth of the Negro Past* (1941) and other works, was highly controversial. Other important books include *Man and his Works* (1948) and *The Human Factor in Changing Africa* (1962). He married Frances Shapiro (1924), who frequently collaborated on his fieldwork and publications.

Herter, Christian (1840–83) furniture maker; born in Stuttgart, Germany. Around 1860 he joined half brother Gustav Herter's New York firm, which in 1866 was renamed Herter Brothers. After studying design in Paris, Christian bought out Gustav's share in 1870 and abandoned the firm's historical revival furniture in favor of pieces akin to the English arts-and-crafts style. Clients such as the Vanderbilts and J. P. Morgan commissioned suites and interiors from him.

Herzberg, Fred (Frederick) (1923–) psychologist; born in Lynn, Mass. He taught at Western Reserve University (1957–72) and the University of Utah business school (1972). An authority on motivation and the nature of work, he advocated using job enrichment as a motivator. His books include *The Motivation to Work* (1959) and *Work and the Nature of Man* (1966).

Hesburgh, Theodore (Martin) (1917–) clergyman, university president; born in Syracuse, N.Y. An ordained Roman Catholic priest, Hesburgh became indelibly identified with Notre Dame University, where he was president (1952–87) in a term that secularized and integrated the university and brought the athletic department under administrative control. He was a charter member of the Civil Rights Commission (1957–72).

Heschel, Abraham Joshua (1907–72) educator, author; born in Warsaw, Poland. He studied and taught Jewish theology in Germany until 1938, when he was deported to Warsaw. He came to the U.S.A. in 1941. He became professor of Jewish ethics and mysticism at the Jewish Theological Seminary of America (1946–72). A spokesman on issues of social injustice, he wrote many scholarly and popular books including *Unknown Documents on the History of Hasidism* (1952) and *The Problem of the Individual* (1958).

Hess, H. H. (Harry Hammond) (1906–69) geophysicist; born in New York City. While serving with the U.S. Navy in the Pacific during World War II, Hess not only located submarines with sounding gear, but was the first to report the existence of the truncated seamounts known as guyots. He led Project Mohole, the first expedition to drill through the earth's oceanic crust to the mantle beneath (1961–66). His long-term interest in the igneous rock peridotite led to his proposal that this high-temperature substance was basic to investigations of island arc formation, gravity anomalies, mountain building, and the earth's deeper crustal structure. While Chairman of Princeton's geology department (1950–66), he accurately theorized that spreading of mid-ocean ridges was the source of new mantle-derived continental material. As an adviser to the National Aeronautics and Space Administration (NASA), Hess was one of the first scientists to examine lunar rocks.

Hesse, Eva (1936–70) sculptor; born in Hamburg, Germany. She and her family escaped Nazism and emigrated to New York City (1939), where she attended Pratt Institute (1952) and Cooper Union (1952–55). After a trip to Germany (1964–65) she specialized in organic surrealistic images, as in *Untitled* (known as *Seven Poles*) (1970). Based in New York City, she died of a brain tumor.

Hesselius, Gustavus (1682–1755) painter; born in Falun, Sweden. He emigrated to an American colony on the Delaware River (1711), and was an important religious and secular painter. His sympathetic and dignified portraits of American Indians, such as *Chief Lapowinska* (1735) and *Chief Tishcohan* (1735), have ensured his reputation.

Hesselius, John (1728–78) painter; born in either Philadelphia or Maryland (son of Gustavus Hesselius). Although not as famous as his father, he is remembered for his portraits, notably the charming and straightforward *Charles Calvert and a Colored Slave* (1761).

Heston, Charlton (b. John Charlton Carter) (1923–) film actor; born in Evanston, Ill. He studied at Northwestern University, starring in a student film version of *Peer Gynt* (1941) before entering the Air Force in World War II. After Broadway and television work, this strapping actor, with his aquiline profile and sonorous voice, made his Hollywood debut in *Dark City* (1950). Usually playing larger-than-life heroes, he won the Academy Award in the title role of *Ben Hur* (1959). He served six terms as president of the Screen Actors Guild and in later years became a frequent spokesman for Republican Party positions as well as for public service causes.

Heuser, Herman J. (1852–1933) Catholic priest, editor; born in Potsdam, Germany. Emigrating to the U.S.A. at age 17, he was ordained in the Philadelphia archdiocese (1876) and taught for over 50 years at the archdiocesan seminary. In 1889 he founded the *American Ecclesiastical Review*, a professional journal for priests, which he actively edited until 1914; in 1927 he gave it over to Catholic University in Washington, D.C.

Hewins, Caroline Maria (1846–1926) children's librarian; born in Roxbury, Mass. After graduating from the Normal School of Boston (1866), she worked as a librarian at the

Young Men's Institute in Hartford and established a small branch library at Hartford's North Street Settlement, where she lived among the poor for 12 years. During her 50-year tenure as librarian of the Hartford (Conn.) Public Library she advanced cooperation between the Library and local public schools. She founded the Education Association, a forerunnner of the PTA (Parent-Teacher Association).

Hewitt, (Donald S.) Don (1922–) producer; born in New York City. After writing for *Stars and Stripes* during World War II, he became United Press photo editor in 1947. At CBS, he directed *Douglas Edwards with the News* (1948–62), making the news more visually exciting, then became executive director for the *Evening News with Walter Cronkite* (1963–64). Fired by Fred Friendly, he produced CBS documentaries, then created *60 Minutes* (1968), the first and still most successful television magazine news show.

Hewitt, Henry (Kent) (1887–1972) naval officer; born in Hackensack, N.J. He was responsible for the successful amphibious landings in Morocco (1942), Sicily (1943) and southern France (1944). He was the naval representative on the United Nations military staff committee (1946–49).

Hewlett, James (fl. 1821–31) stage actor; birthplace unknown. A free African-American, he was a tailor by trade who in 1821 became a principal actor in William Henry Brown's newly formed African Theatre in New York City. He starred as Richard III, Othello, and as the Carib chieftain King Shotaway in Brown's own drama on the revolt on St. Vincent. The African Theatre soon folded, and Hewlett began to give one-man performances in which he imitated leading actors of the day in their celebrated roles. He enlivened his recitations by singing songs accompanied by his wife on the piano. He is known to have performed in New York City and Pennsylvania and may have also performed in London, England.

Hewlett, William R. (1913–) electrical engineer; born in Ann Arbor, Mich. He graduated from Massachusetts Institute of Technology (1936). With his friend, David Packard, he formed Hewlett-Packard in 1939 in Palo Alto, Calif., first producing resistance-capacitance audio oscillators in a garage. He was actively involved in the company until 1987.

Heyward, (Edwin) DuBose (1885–1940) writer; born in Charleston, S.C. He was educated and lived in Charleston. He worked in a hardware store and as a checker in a cotton warehouse, a crucial experience. Although not African-American, he drew on the life of South Carolina blacks for much of his writing. He and his wife dramatized his first novel, *Porgy* (1925), and it was the basis for George Gershwin's opera, *Porgy and Bess* (1935). He also wrote poetry and other fictional works.

Heywood, Charles (1839–1915) marine officer; born in Waterville, Maine. Appointed colonel commandant in 1891, he improved Marine Corps administration and oversaw an expansion in which the service quadrupled in size – to 7,800 officers and men.

Hiawatha (b. Heowenta) (?1525–?75) legendary Mohawk leader; born in present-day New York State. Although he is known only through Iroquois mythology and legend, it is now generally accepted that he was a real person who was influential in founding the Five Nations League, or Long House, an alliance of five (later six) Iroquois tribes that ended intertribal feuding from sometime about 1550 (some claim as early as 1400) to 1775. (Although it is claimed that

elements of the confederacy influenced the composition of the U.S. Constitution, scholars believe that any influence was at most indirect.) Longfellow used Hiawatha's name for the hero of his poem (1855) but set the action in Minnesota and used only elements of the legendary Hiawatha and other Indian stories for his essentially romantic tale.

Hibbard, Howard (1928–84) art historian; born in Madison, Wis. He studied at the University of Wisconsin (B.A. 1949; M.A. 1952), and at Harvard (Ph.D. 1958). He taught art history primarily at Columbia University beginning in 1966, and worked as editor-in-chief of *The Art Bulletin* (1961–78). He specialized in Renaissance and Baroque Italian art and architecture.

Hickok, (James Butler) "Wild Bill" (1837–76) frontier figure; born in Troy Grove, Ill. He was a stagecoach driver on both the Santa Fe and Oregon trails. As a spy and scout for the Union Army, he was captured and escaped more than once. He was marshal of Hays City (1869) and of Abilene (1871). He killed a number of men in both towns, always in self-defense or in the line of duty. He toured with Buffalo Bill's Wild West Show (1872–73) and was shot from behind by Jack McCall while holding the "Dead Man's Hand" in poker.

Hickok, Laurens Perseus (1799–1888) clergyman, philosopher; born in Bethel, Conn. Ordained a Presbyterian minister in 1823, he was a pastor in Connecticut for 13 years, taught theology at Western Reserve College (1836–44) and Auburn Theological Seminary (1844–52), and was associated with Union College (Schenectady, N.Y.) as philosophy professor (1836–68) and president (1866–68). His works, including *Rational Psychology* (1849), defended Christian theology through a "constructive realism" influenced by Kant.

Hicks, Edward (1780–1849) painter; born in Attleborough (now Langhorne), Pa. A Quaker minister, he also earned a living by painting signs, carriages, and, most importantly, primitive folk scenes. The series of paintings he called *The Peaceable Kingdom,* based on the eleventh chapter of Isaiah, where the animal kingdom lives in harmony together, occupied him for much of his painting life and has brought him continuing fame.

Hicks, Sheila (1934–) weaver; born in Hastings, Nebr. With an M.F.A. from Yale (1959), she studied the textiles of ancient Andean cultures. A pioneer in non-loom weaving techniques, she established a Paris workshop in 1967.

Hicks, Wilson (1897–1970) photo editor; born in Sedalia, Mo. Picture editor at the *Kansas City Star,* he came to New York in 1928 where he became executive editor of the Associated Press. Photographic editor at *Life Magazine* (1937–1950), he built the staff from 4 to 40 photographers, making assignments and developing the photo essay for which *Life* became famous. He was a professor of photojournalism at the University of Miami from 1955 to 1970.

Hiesey, William M. (McKinley) (1903–) botanist; born in Denver, Colo. He joined the Carnegie Institution's laboratory at Stanford University in 1926, where he worked with Jens Clausen and David Keck on a comprehensive comparative study of California flora from contrasting environments. As the plant physiologist of this group, Hiesey performed extensive research at field stations investigating the ecological differences of various plant races, resulting in the group's classic six-volume work, *Experimental Studies on the Nature* *of Species* (1940–58). He joined the department of plant biology at Stanford University in 1951.

Higgenbotham, A. Leon, Jr. (1928–) judge; born in Trenton, N.J. He graduated from Antioch College (1949) and Yale Law School (1952) and served as assistant district attorney for Philadelphia County. In 1954 he entered private practice. He returned to public service as a member of the Federal Trade Commission (1962–64). From 1964–77 he was a federal judge for the Eastern District of Pennsylvania. He was then promoted to the U.S. Circuit Court of Appeals, Philadelphia (1977). As one of the most prominent African-American jurists, he gained attention when in 1992 he publicly rebuked newly appointed Supreme Court Justice Clarence Thomas for his perceived failure to speak more forcefully for the interests of their fellow African-Americans.

Higgins, Eugene (1874–1958) painter; born in Kansas City, Mo. He studied with Gérôme in Paris (1894–1904), and became a member of the Ashcan school, the New York based group who painted urban scenes in a realistic style.

Higgins, George (Vincent) (1923–) lawyer, writer; born in Brockton, Mass. He studied at Boston College (B.A. 1961; J.D. 1967) and Stanford (M.A. 1965). After working as a journalist (1962–64), he made an impressive career as a criminal trial lawyer in the Boston area, where he lived. He also taught at Boston Law School (1973–74; 1978–79). He wrote many crime novels, and is noted for his extensive use of dialogue, as in *The Friends of Eddie Coyle* (1972).

Higgins, Marguerite (1920–66) journalist; born in Hong Kong, China. An intrepid and resourceful war correspondent, she covered the Seventh Army in Europe during 1944 and won a Pulitzer Prize for her Korean War coverage. Later a correspondent for the *New York Herald Tribune,* she contracted a fatal tropical disease while visiting Southeast Asia in 1965. Her 1965 *Our Vietnam Nightmare* criticized the U.S. role in the fall of the Diem regime.

Higginson, Henry L. (Lee) (1834–1919) banker, philanthropist; born in New York City (cousin of Thomas W. Higginson). In 1837 the family moved to Boston where his father was a commission merchant. On an 1852 tour through Europe, Henry became enthralled by music. He returned to work in a merchant office but an inheritance from his uncle in 1856 allowed him to return to Europe to take up music (piano and composition); an injury combined with a lack of talent impeded his success. Returning to Boston in 1860 he fought with the Union army in the Civil War. After an unsuccessful utopian experiment running a cotton plantation by paying the former slaves (1866–67), he joined his father's Boston banking house (1868) and prospered. In 1881, his love of music unabated, he founded the Boston Symphony Orchestra and remained its sole underwriter until 1918 (paying out an estimated $1 million). He left much of his fortune to Harvard, Radcliffe, and other colleges.

Higginson, Thomas Wentworth (Storrow) (1823–1911) Unitarian minister, soldier, writer; born in Cambridge, Mass. After graduating from Harvard (1841), he taught, then returned to take a degree from Harvard Divinity School (1847). In his first parish in Newburyport, Mass., he was more interested in social issues than in theology, usually preaching for women's suffrage and against slavery, and in 1848 he ran unsuccessfully for Congress as a Free-Soiler. Too radical for even his Unitarian congregation, he moved on to become pastor of the Free Church in Worcester, Mass.

(1852–61), but continued to devote much of his energy to abolitionism; he engaged in the forceful release of slaves, traveled to Kansas to fight slavery, and befriended and supported John Brown. With the outbreak of the Civil War, he left the ministry to captain a company of Massachusetts volunteers, then becoming the commanding colonel of the 1st South Carolina Volunteers, the first African-American regiment of the Union Army (1862–64); he would write of this experience in *Army Life in a Black Regiment* (1870). After the war he settled in Newport, R.I. (1865–78) and wrote for the *Atlantic Monthly* and other leading magazines of the day; he also wrote popular histories of the U.S.A. Moving back to Cambridge in 1878, he served uneventfully in the Massachusetts legislature (1880–81) and then went back to writing magazine articles and biographies. He is now best known for the fact that his magazine articles inspired an unknown young woman in Amherst, Mass., Emily Dickinson, to send him some of her poems in 1862; they maintained a correspondence until her death – they met twice – but although he encouraged her to continue writing, he advised her not to publish; after her death (1886), however, he helped to prepare for publication the first (1890) and second (1891) volumes of her poetry.

Highet, Gilbert (1906–78) classicist; born in Glasgow, Scotland. He taught at Oxford (1932–37), where he took a double first (1932), before going to Columbia University (1937), where he was an exceptionally popular teacher until his retirement (1972). Books such as *The Classical Tradition* (1949) and *The Art of Teaching* (1950), as well as his posts as chief literary critic for *Harper's Magazine* (1952–54), judge of the Book-of-the-Month Club (1954–78), and host of weekly radio talks, *People, Places, and Books* (1952–59), made him the country's most widely known popularizer of classics. His bibliography of 1,000 items includes his translation of Werner Jaeger's *Paideia* from German into English. He was married to the novelist Helen MacInnes.

Highsmith, (Mary) Patricia (b. Plangman) (Claire Morgan, pen name) (1921–) writer; born in Fort Worth, Texas. She was raised by her grandparents until she was six, then lived with her mother and stepfather, Stanley Highsmith. She studied at Barnard (B.A., 1942), and worked as a comic strip artist. Her first novel, *Strangers on a Train* (1950), was made into a film (1951) directed by Alfred Hitchcock with a screenplay by Raymond Chandler. A prolific writer, she is considered a master of the suspense novel and is praised for her psychological insights. She spent much of her adult life in Europe and was based in Switzerland.

Hill, Ambrose (Powell) (1825–65) soldier; born in Culpeper, Va. An 1847 West Point graduate, he served in Mexico, on the frontier, and in Washington, D.C., before resigning in March 1861 to enter Confederate service. His Light Division, so-called for its swiftness on the march, participated in most of the major battles in northern Virginia. He intervened decisively at Antietam (1862) when he rushed it to the battlefield in time to prevent a federal breakthrough. As a corps commander, he initiated the battle at Gettysburg on July 1, 1863. Aggressive and unafraid to take risks, "Little Powell" Hill was killed in battle near Petersburg a few days before Lee's surrender.

Hill, Anita (Faye) (1956–) lawyer, professor; born in Lone Tree, Okla. After Yale Law School, she worked in Washington (1981–83) then taught law at Oral Roberts (1983–88) and the University of Oklahoma (1988). Her testimony at the confirmation of Supreme Court Justice Clarence Thomas (1991) put sexual harassment on the national agenda.

Hill, David Jayne (1850–1932) college administrator, diplomat; born in Plainfield, N.J. As president of Bucknell University (1879–88) and the University of Rochester (1888–95), he increased the endowment of both institutions. He was assistant secretary of state (1898–1902) and ambassador to Switzerland, the Netherlands, and Germany (1903–11). He opposed the League of Nations and the World Court. His best known book was *A History of Diplomacy* (1905, 1914).

Hill, George William (1838–1914) mathematical astronomer; born in West Nyack, N.Y. A recluse, this National Academy of Sciences member was a master of mathematical astronomics and a contributor to advances in dynamic astronomy. He worked on tables of lunar and planetary motion and developed Hill's equation. He lectured on celestial mechanics at Columbia University (1898).

Hill, James J. (Jerome) (1838–1916) railroad executive, financier; born near Rockwood, Ontario, Canada. He moved to St. Paul, Minn., in 1856 where he worked in the offices of a steamboat line and a railroad. In 1872 he formed the Red River Transportation Company with partner Norman Kittson; they prospered in the Manitoba fur trade. In 1875 Hill bought the Northwestern Fuel Company, and in 1878, with three others including Kittson, he bought out the bankrupt St. Paul & Pacific Railroad. This launched what became the Great Northern Railway, which extended west from St. Louis and Chicago to Seattle and north to Winnipeg. Hill led this successful and important railroad in various capacities from 1879 to 1912 and was one of the few railroad entrepreneurs who took a hands-on approach to the details of the operation. He became known as "Hill the empire builder" because of his important contributions to developing the Northwest.

Hill, J. (Joseph) Lister (1894–1984) U.S. representative/ senator; born in Montgomery, Ala. Elected to the U.S. House of Representatives (Dem., Ala.; 1923–38) and to the U.S. Senate (1939–69), he helped shape the Tennessee Valley Authority project, the GI bill, and the Hill-Burton Hospital Act.

Hill, Joe (b. Joel Emmanuel Hägglund) or Joseph Hillstrom (1879–1915) labor leader, songwriter; born in Gäyle, Sweden. Little is known of his early life (even his Swedish name is in dispute), but he apparently worked as a seaman and arrived in the U.S.A. about 1901. Joining the Industrial Workers of the World (IWW) ("Wobblies") in 1910, he participated in organizing and strike actions in California and Mexico. While he seems to have led a hobo-like existence, he contributed letters and essays to the Wobblies' publications. He also became known for his protest songs – especially "The Preacher and the Slave," which introduced the phrase "pie in the sky"; these were collected in *The Little Red Song Book*. Arrested for double murder in Salt Lake City (1914) and convicted on dubious evidence, he was executed by a firing squad despite international protests. The night before his death he told "Big Bill" Haywood, "Don't waste any time in mourning. Organize." His body was cremated and its ashes were distributed to IWW locals all over the world. He was one of the best-known "martyrs" of the radical labor movement, which would adopt as one of its anthems, "I Dreamed I Saw Joe Hill Last Night" (words by Alfred Hayes, music by Earl Robinson).

Hill, Patty Smith (1868–1946) educator, composer; born in Anchorage, Ky. Director of the Louisville Training School for Kindergarten and Primary Teachers (1893–1905), she wrote songs for children, one of which became "Happy Birthday to You." Joining Columbia University's Teachers College faculty (1905–35), she initiated curriculum reform, stressing the value of less structured classroom activities and of children's ability to learn through play.

Hill, William (1741–1816) ironmaster, soldier; born in Ireland. He settled in South Carolina (1762) where he operated iron mines and established ironworks for making farm tools, kitchenware, and cannon. He served in the American Revolution and in the South Carolina legislature.

Hillenbrand, Reynold (Henry) (1904–79) activist Catholic priest; born in Chicago. Ordained in 1929, he studied further in Rome, where he was influenced by papal social teachings. While a seminary teacher and rector (through 1944) and pastor (through 1970) in the Chicago archdiocese, he encouraged lay leadership and liturgical reform and played a key role in forming Catholic Action cells and promoting the Christian Family Movement.

Hillerman, Tony (1925–) writer; born in Sacred Heart, Okla. Although he was raised among the Pottawatomie and Seminole Indians and studied at an Indian boarding school, he was not a Native American. He attended Oklahoma State University (1943), the University of Oklahoma (B.A. 1946), and the University of New Mexico (M.A. 1966). He worked as a journalist in Texas, Oklahoma, and New Mexico (1948–63), lived in Albuquerque, and taught journalism at the University of New Mexico (1976–85). He wrote numerous mystery novels drawing on Native American culture, the most successful featuring Sergeant Jim Chee of the Navajo Tribal Police.

Hillier, James (1915–) physicist, inventor; born in Brantford, Ontario, Canada. Son of a mechanical engineer, he began developing the electron microscope with a graduate student colleague at the University of Toronto in 1937. He emigrated to the U.S.A. in 1940 and shortly thereafter designed the first practical electron microscope. This soon became an essential tool in scientific and medical research. He took U.S. citizenship in 1945. From 1942 on he held senior research posts at RCA and was executive vice-president and senior scientist at RCA Labs when he retired in 1978.

Hillis, Margaret (1921–) choral conductor; born in Kokomo, Ind. A student of Robert Shaw at Juilliard, she is best known for organizing the Chicago Symphony Orchestra Chorus (from 1957) and building it into a major ensemble. She also conducted opera and orchestras.

Hillman, Sidney (1887–1946) labor leader; born in Zagare, Lithuania. A labor activist in Russia, he was imprisoned for participation in the abortive revolution of 1905. Upon his release, he emigrated in 1907 to the United States, settling in Chicago. A garment worker, he emerged in the 1910 Hart, Schaffner and Marx strike in Chicago as one of the leaders of the United Garment Workers (UGW) and negotiated a new contract that was regarded as a model of labor-management relations. In 1914 he went to New York City where he led a split from the UGW that resulted in the formation of the Amalgamated Clothing Workers of America (ACWA); he was elected its first president (1914), an office he held until his death. By 1940 his union dominated the manufacture of men's clothing and had pioneered such reforms as the 40-hour week and industry-wide wage scales. A strong backer of the New Deal, he was appointed as a labor adviser to the National Recovery Administration in 1933, and to several war production boards during World War II. A founder of the Congress of Industrial Organizations (CIO), he was the first chairman of the CIO's Political Action Committee (1943–46), and a vice-chairman of the newly founded World Federation of Trade Unions (1945–46). As an advocate of cooperation instead of confrontation between labor and management, he pioneered in such advances as his union's lending money to companies and providing research to improve efficiency. His premature death left many feeling that American society as well as the labor movement had suffered an irreplaceable loss.

Hillquit, Morris (b. Hillkowitz) (1869–1933) lawyer, author, reformer; born in Riga, Latvia. He emigrated to the U.S.A. in 1886, dropped out of high school to go to work and helped found the United Hebrew Trades (1888). He graduated from New York University Law School in 1891. He helped found the Socialist Party of America (1900) and afterward defended many Socialists, including those prosecuted in 1917–18 for antiwar activities. He failed in several bids for elective office. A moderate who tried to adapt European Socialism to the American situation, he published several works on socialism, including *Socialism in Theory and Practice* (1909).

Hillyer, Robert (Silliman) (1895–1961) poet, teacher; born in East Orange, N.J. He studied at Harvard (B.A. 1917) where he was a publisher of *Eight Harvard Poets* (1917), a volume including the work of Hillyer, e. e. cummings, and John Dos Passos, among others. After graduation, he and Dos Passos served in the ambulance corps in France. Hillyer taught at Harvard (1919–20), wrote essays, novels, and many volumes of reflective poetry, notably *The Seventh Hall* (1928). He taught at Trinity College (1926–28), returned to Harvard (1928–45), became a visiting professor at various institutions, then taught at the University of Delaware (1952–61). Traditional in his own work and conservative in his tastes, he often found himself at odds with the prevailing literary modes and movements.

Hilprecht, H. V. (Herman Volrath) (1859–1925) archaeologist; born in Hohenerxleben, Germany. He came to the U.S.A. as a young Ph.D. versed in theology, philology, and law to join the University of Pennsylvania faculty (1886–1911). An authority on cuneiform and Babylonian antiquities, he was scientific director of four expeditions to Nippur, Iraq, the source of more than a dozen volumes of Babylonian texts. His latter years were clouded by scholarly controversies.

Hilton, Conrad (Nicholson) (1887–1979) hotel executive; born in San Antonio, N.M. After World War I service he began buying Texas hotels, graduating by the 1930s–40s to such grand establishments as Chicago's Palmer House (1945) and the Waldorf-Astoria, New York (1949). He formed Hilton Hotels Corporation (1946) and Hilton International (1948) and by the time of his death he controlled the largest hotel organization in the world.

Himes, Chester (Bomar) (1909–84) writer; born in Jefferson City, Mo. He studied at Ohio State University (1926–28), was convicted of armed robbery (1928), and spent six years in prison. After his release he worked as a journalist in Cleveland, as a writer for the labor movement, and at various other jobs. His early novels, such as *Lonely Crusade* (1947), tended to focus on racial issues in contemporary America. By 1953 he had moved abroad and he lived thereafter in Paris and Spain. Because he was an African-American writer he found both he and his work were more appreciated in Europe than in America. He is best known for his series of crime novels featuring the detective, "Grave Digger" Johnson (1957–80).

Himes, Joshua Vaughan (1805–95) Protestant religious leader; born in North Kingstown, R.I. He worked as a cabinetmaker before joining the ministry of the Christian Church in 1827. In 1839 he fell under the spell of William Miller, who predicted the imminent Second Coming of Christ, and he became chief publicist for the Seventh Day Adventist movement. Disappointed by the failure of Miller's prophecy, Himes migrated westward. In 1876 he returned to the Episcopal Church, the faith of his parents, and took charge of Episcopal missions in South Dakota.

Hinckley, John W. (Warnock), Jr. (1955–   ) criminal; born in Evergreen, Colo. The son of an oil executive, he drifted aimlessly in southern California before focusing on the actress Jodie Foster and President Ronald Reagan. He shot Reagan and three other men in Washington, D.C. (1981). A jury found him not guilty of the attempted assassination by reason of insanity and he was placed in a mental institution.

Hinds, Asher Crosby (1863–1919) U.S. representative; born in Benton, Maine. Orphaned as a boy, he graduated from Colby College in 1883 before joining the *Portland Daily Advertiser* as a printer's apprentice. By 1885 he was a reporter for the *Portland Daily Press,* covering the Maine legislature where he attracted the attention of Republican leader Thomas Reed, who briefly appointed him Speaker's clerk in the U.S. House of Representatives in 1889. Once the Republicans were in control of the House again, he returned as clerk of the Speaker's table (1895–1911), studying parliamentary law and procedure, while serving under Speakers Reed, Cannon, and Clark. During that time he wrote *Hinds' Precedents of the House of Representatives of the United States (1907–08),* which expanded into five volumes and covered the entire history of the House. Elected to the House (Rep., Maine; 1911–17) he was an undistinguished representative, in failing health, and unable to write a projected biography of Speaker Reed.

Hine, Lewis (Wicks) (1874–1940) photographer, social reformer; born in Oshkosh, Wis. Trained as a sociologist, he used photographs to inspire reform. In 1905 he documented immigrants on Ellis Island, publishing his photos with his own text. His work as the official photographer for the National Child Labor Committee (1911–16) influenced passage of the child labor laws. Chief photographer for the Works Progress Administration (1936), he documented the Tennessee Valley Authority project.

Hines, Duncan (1880–1959) publisher, author; born in Bowling Green, Ky. A traveling salesman, he published years' worth of notes in *Adventures in Good Eating* (1936). This pioneering restaurant guide promoted higher standards of food preparation and hygiene in American restaurants and launched Hines as a guide and cookbook publisher and sponsor of the packaged food products by which he is best remembered.

Hines, Earl (Kenneth) "Fatha" (1903–83) jazz musician;

born in Duquesne, Pa. He was the first widely influential jazz pianist, showcasing his "trumpet-style" on solo recordings and with Louis Armstrong and Jimmie Noone in 1927–28. Between 1928–40, he became established as a major Swing era bandleader at the Grand Terrace in Chicago. He continued to lead a big band until 1948, working thereafter in small groups until the 1970s.

Hines, Frank (Thomas) (1879–1960) soldier, administrator; born in Salt Lake City, Utah. As head of the army's embarkation service (1918–19), he sent more than 2 million U.S. soldiers to Europe during World War I. Hines served as long-term head of the Veterans Bureau (1923–30) and its successor, the Veterans Administration (1930–45).

Hines, John Leonard ("Birdie") (1868–1968) soldier; born in White Sulphur Springs, W.Va. The son of Irish immigrants, he graduated from West Point (1891) and served with distinction in the Spanish-American War. Taken by Gen. Pershing to France in 1917, he became the first American soldier since Stonewall Jackson to lead in combat successively a regiment, brigade, division, and corps. Hines later served a term as army chief of staff (1924–26).

Hirsch, Emil Gustav (1851–1923) rabbi; born in Luxembourg. He came to the U.S.A. in 1866. After graduating from the University of Pennsylvania (1872), he studied in Germany, then served as rabbi in several U.S. cities. In 1880 he was named rabbi of the Sinai Congregation in Chicago (1880–1923), and in 1892 he became professor of rabbinic literature and Jewish philosophy at the University of Chicago. Active on behalf of the Reform movement and of social justice, he advocated radical reforms in Jewish practice, including the observance of the Sabbath on Sunday.

Hirsch, Maxmilian (Justice) (1880–1969) horse trainer; born in Fredericksburg, Texas. He trained winners of 1,933 races, including such champion thoroughbreds as Bold Venture, Assault, and Middleground.

Hirschfeld, Al (Albert) (1903–) graphic artist, caricaturist; born in St. Louis, Mo. Based in New York City, he studied at the Art Students League (c. 1918), worked for David Selznick (1921) and Warner Brothers (1921–24), New York, and established a studio in Paris (1924–25). He became the theater correspondent for the New York *Herald Tribune* in Moscow (1927–28), then worked for the *New York Times* from 1929. A consummate traveler, he is famous for his stylized and perceptive caricatures of theater and public personalities. Beginning in 1945 he concealed his daughter's name, Nina, in almost every drawing.

Hirschman, Albert O. (Otto) (1915–) political economist; born in Berlin, Germany. He studied in Paris, London, and Trieste before coming to the University of California: Berkeley in 1941. He served in the U.S. Army (1943–45) and worked as an economist with the Federal Reserve Board (1946–52). He taught at Yale, Harvard, and Columbia Universities before joining the Institute for Advanced Study in Princeton, N.J. (1974–85). He advised the government of Columbia (1952–56). In *The Strategy of Economic Development* (1958, later revised) and other works, he rejected a "balanced growth" strategy for Third World countries, proposing instead a new model of economic planning – illustrated in his various studies of Latin American nations – that became internationally influential.

Hirshhorn, Joseph H. (Herman) (1899–1981) financier, art collector; born in Mitvau, Latvia. His widowed mother emigrated to Brooklyn, N.Y. (1907), worked in a sweatshop, and became ill. He and his brothers and sisters were scattered among neighboring families and he became a newsboy. After studying on his own, he became a stockbroker (1916), amassed a fortune, and liquidated his holdings just prior to the crash of 1929. He made other fortunes in gold and uranium mines in Canada, and invested much of his money in art, especially in sculpture, but ranging from Etruscan art to modern American paintings; by the 1960s he owned some 4,000 works. He donated his entire collection to the United States to be administered by the Smithsonian Institution (1966). Funds were donated by Hirshhorn and appropriated by Congress for building the Joseph H. Hirshhorn Museum and Sculpture Garden, Washington, D.C., which opened in 1974.

Hiss, Alger (1904–) lawyer, government official; born in Baltimore, Md. A lawyer who had clerked with Justice Oliver Wendell Holmes, he went to work for President Roosevelt's New Deal, eventually joining the State Department. He rose rapidly in the State Department (1936–45), going with President Roosevelt to Yalta. He was President of the Carnegie Endowment for Peace (1945–49) when Whittaker Chambers accused him of having been a spy for the Russians. Convicted of perjury in 1950, he went to prison for four years, writing and lecturing in his own defense afterward. In 1992 a Russian with access to Soviet files announced that Hiss had never been a Soviet agent, but this seemed unlikely to put a complete end to the controversy that had surrounded Hiss since 1948.

Hitchcock, Edward (1793–1864) geologist, educator; born in Deerfield, Mass. An ordained Congregational minister (1821–25), he remained a lifelong classicist and theologian after resigning his pulpit to become professor (1825–64) and president (1845–54) of Amherst College. He concurrently served as trustee and lecturer at Mount Holyoke Female Seminary (now College) (1836–64). Hitchcock's research as state geologist of Massachusetts (1830) and Vermont (1857–61) resulted in his major contributions to the geology, glaciology, and paleontology of New England. His pioneer studies of fossil dinosaur footprints founded the science of ichnology.

Hitchcock, Ethan Allen (1798–1870) soldier, author; born at Vergennes, Vt. (grandson of Ethan Allen). He graduated from West Point (1817) and commenced upon a remarkable military career. While commandant of cadets at West Point (1829–33), Robert E. Lee, Jefferson Davis, Edgar Allan Poe and others were among his pupils. He served in Florida and on Indian duty in the Northwest (1837–40). He wrote a scathing report on the frauds against the Cherokee Indians (1841–42) and he served in the Mexican War – although his diary indicated his distaste for that conflict. He retired in 1855, but then returned to duty in the Civil War and served as a Union commissioner for exchange of prisoners and as a major general of volunteers. He wrote numerous books on alchemy, religion, and spirituality, especially on Emanuel Swedenborg. He left an unpublished memoir, *Fifty Years in Camp and Field*, which was published in 1909.

Hitchcock, H. (Hugh) Wiley (1923–) musicologist; born in Detroit, Mich. After studies at Dartmouth College and the University of Michigan, he joined the Brooklyn College faculty in 1971 and became director of the important

Institute for Studies in American Music. He was coeditor of the *New Grove Dictionary of American Music* (1986).

Hitchcock, Henry-Russell (1903–87) architectural historian; born in Boston, Mass. He trained at Harvard. Regarded as the founder of modern architectural historiography, Hitchcock combined rigorous scholarship, an acute critical eye, and a physical love of buildings in a stream of publications on an unparalleled range of art historical subjects. Early in his career he brought European modernism to America; *Modern Architecture* (1929), the first English-language book on the subject, was followed by his seminal International Style (he is credited with coining the term) exhibition at the Museum of Modern Art and his accompanying book (with Philip Johnson, 1932) and monographs on H. H. Richardson and Frank Lloyd Wright. He published volumes on 19th- and 20th-century architecture before turning to Rococo German and Austrian architecture and the German Renaissance late in his career. Hitchcock influenced generations of architects as well as younger scholars through his many years of teaching (among them twenty years (1948–68) at Smith College) and his leading role in the Society of Architectural Historians.

Hitchcock, Lambert H. (1795–1852) furniture maker; born in Cheshire, Conn. Starting out making furniture by hand, in 1818 he set up a factory in Barkhamsted, Conn., that would soon employ some 100 workers, turning out the parts for chairs that furniture makers could assemble. (The village was named Hitchcockville but changed its name to Riverton in 1866.) The basic Hitchcock chair (essentially a simplified version of the Windsor chair) was made of simple turned legs, rungs, and back posts (the legs and back being slightly bent); had a broad back rail; usually a rush seat (sometimes cane or wood); and was painted solid black (over a red base) with designs stenciled in gold or colors. As the chairs became popular, in 1825 he greatly expanded his factory space and began to manufacture the completed chairs (as well as other types of furniture). In its own way this was a pioneer effort in the factory/mass production system, but his output got so far ahead of his shipping and sales capacities and his profit per chair was so low that he went bankrupt in 1829. He was rescued by a man who would then marry Hitchcock's sister, and the factory continued for some years. Hitchcock served in the Connecticut state legislature (1840–41). The factory was revived by John T. Kenney as the Hitchcock Chair Company in 1946 to make the chairs and other traditional American furniture.

Hitchcock, (Thomas, Jr.) Tommy (1900–44) polo player, aviator; born in Aiken, S.C. Son of a 10-goal polo player – the highest ranking – he became an outstanding polo player by age 16. In World War I, he volunteered to fly in the Lafayette Escadrille; shot down behind German lines in March 1918, he escaped and made his way back to his squadron, which finished the war as a unit of the U.S. Air Service. After graduating from Harvard, he entered banking but concentrated his energies on polo. Between 1922 and 1940 he was rated as a 10-goal player 18 times and he secured his reputation as the greatest American polo player, arguably the greatest in the world. In 1942 he was commissioned as lieutenant colonel in the Army Air Corps; assigned command of a fighter group, he died while testing a P-51 in England.

Hitchings, George H. (Herbert) (1905–   ) biochemist, pharmacologist; born in Hoquiam, Wash. He taught at Harvard (1928–39) and Western Reserve (1939–42), then joined the Burroughs Wellcome Company, N.C. (1942–75). In 1945 Hitchings began a professional, and often competitive, relationship with Gertrude Elion; the two scientists formed a team that discovered drugs for treatment of leukemia, gout, infective diseases, autoimmune disorders, and transplant rejection. Although Nobel Prizes are rarely awarded to employees of pharmaceutical companies, Hitchings and Elion were awarded one-half the 1988 Nobel Prize in physiology for their many contributions to drug therapy.

Hitti, Philip K. (Khuri) (1886–1978) educator, historian, author; born in Shimlan, Lebanon (then part of Syria). He graduated from the American University of Beirut (1908) and went to the U.S.A. in 1913. He earned his Ph.D. at Columbia University (1915) and became a naturalized citizen in 1920. He was founder of the Syrian Education Society (1916) and he taught Arabic literature at Princeton (1926–54). He wrote widely acclaimed books, including *History of the Arabs* (1937) and *A Short History of the Near East* (1966).

Hoan, Daniel Webster (1881–1961) mayor; born in Waukesha, Wis. He left school early and worked as a cook before he resumed his education and became a lawyer (1908). A convinced Socialist, he became Milwaukee's city attorney (1911–17) and then mayor (1917–41). In what remains the longest continuous Socialist administration in U.S. history, he enacted progressive changes including the building of low-cost housing units, called Garden Homes. In 1944 he left the Socialist Party, and as a Democrat, he ran unsuccessfully for governor (1944, 1946), mayor (1948), and the U.S. Senate (1952).

Hoar, Ebenezer Rockwood (1816–95) judge, public official; born in Concord, Mass. (Son of Samuel Hoar). He graduated from Harvard in 1835 and studied law with his father, a prominent attorney. Active in the antislavery movement, he coined the term "Conscience Whig" for his wing of the party. He was a justice of the Massachusetts Supreme Court from 1859–69, and served a brief term as Grant's attorney general (1869–70). In 1870 the Senate rejected his nomination for a U.S. Supreme Court seat because his views offended some senators. He left public service after a single term in the U.S. House of Representatives (Rep., Mass.; 1873–75) and devoted his later years to Harvard alumni affairs.

Hoar, George (Frisbie) (1826–1904) U.S. representative/senator; born in Concord, Mass. A lawyer and a founder of the Republican Party in Massachusetts, he served in the U.S. House of Representatives (1869–77) and the U.S. Senate (1877–1904). In the Senate he served on the Judiciary Committee and helped draft the Sherman Antitrust Act. He opposed nativism, sponsored legislation to curb gambling, and was a critic of President McKinley's policies in the Philippines.

Hoar, Samuel (1778–1856) lawyer, U.S. representative, public official; born in Lincoln, Mass. He graduated from Harvard in 1802 and worked for a time as a tutor in Virginia before returning north to practice law. He served eight years in the Massachusetts legislature and a single term in the U.S. House of Representatives (Whig, 1835–37) where he passionately opposed slavery. His appearance in a Charleston, S.C., court to argue on behalf of free blacks in 1844 nearly touched off a riot, and his expulsion from the city provoked outrage in the north. In 1854–55 he helped found the Free Soil Party in Massachusetts.

Hoard, William Dempster (1836–1918) editor, dairyman, governor; Munnsville, N.Y. The son of a Methodist circuit rider, he learned dairying on his grandfather's farm. In 1857 he moved to Wisconsin, left the Methodist Church and turned to woodcutting and teaching singing and violin. In 1861 he joined the Union Army and participated in the capture of New Orleans. Back in Wisconsin he edited the weekly *Jefferson County Union* (1870) where he speculated that dairying might be the answer to Wisconsin farmers with depleted soil. He founded the Jefferson County Dairyman's Association (1871) and the Wisconsin State Dairyman's Association (1872). He also introduced alfalfa and promoted such advances as silos and tuberculin tests for cattle. In 1885 he started *Hoard's Dairyman,* which gained an international circulation. He was elected governor of Wisconsin as the "Jersey Cow candidate" (Rep., 1888–91) and established a state dairy and food commission.

Hoban, James (c. 1762–1831) architect; born in County Kilkenny, Ireland. Immigrating to America (1785), he designed the state capitol in Columbia, S.C. (1790–91). After a competition to design public buildings in Federal City, the new capital of the U.S.A., he designed the White House (1792–1801) and rebuilt it after the destruction in the War of 1812. He served as supervisor of construction of the U.S. Capitol (1793–1803) and designed the State and War Department offices.

Hobart, Garret A. (Augustus) (1844–99) vice-president, businessman; born in Long Branch, N.J. He served in several areas of New Jersey state government before gaining the vice-presidency in 1896 in William McKinley's first term. He was a firm advocate of the gold standard. As vice-president, he presided over the Senate capably and fairly.

Hobbs, Alfred Charles (1812–91) lock expert; born in Boston, Mass. He tried several trades before he turned to manufacturing locks. Famous for picking the locks of other companies to demonstrate their inadequacy, he formed Hobbs, Ashley & Company in London, England, and Hobbs, Hart & Company in the U.S.A.

Hobbs, William (Herbert) (1864–1953) geologist, geographer; born in Worcester, Mass. He was responsible for founding the department of geography at the University of Michigan in 1923. He contributed widely to the disciplines of geology and geography and was a specialist in glaciology and mineralogy. He wrote 15 books and more than 400 articles.

Hobby, Oveta Culp (1905–   ) public official; born in Killeen, Texas. A lawyer and journalist, she took charge of the Women's Auxiliary Army Corps in October 1942. Some 100,000 women served under her leadership as clerks, cooks, and chauffeurs. A postwar publisher of *The Houston Post,* she was active in Texas Republican politics and became the first secretary of the Department of Health, Education, and Welfare (1953–55).

Hobby, William Pettus (1878–1964) publisher, governor; born in Moscow, Texas. Starting as a clerk at the *Houston Post,* he became managing editor by 1905. Democratic lieutenant governor of Texas (1914–17) he became governor mid-term (1917–20). He updated the highways, regulated gas and oil, and supported women's voting rights, but also got 90% of Texas to prohibit alcohol. He returned to

publishing afterward, becoming president (1924) then owner (1939) of the *Houston Post.*

Hobson, Richmond (Pearson) (1870-1937) naval officer; born in Greensboro, Ala. He became a naval hero during the Spanish-American War. He served as a U.S. representative (Dem., Ala.; 1907–15) and wrote several books including *America Must Be Mistress of the Seas* (1902).

Hochschild, Arlie Russell (1940–   ) sociologist; born in Boston, Mass. She earned graduate degrees at the University of California: Berkeley, where she later joined the faculty (1971). Her work on sex roles, retirement, and the psychology of work includes *The Unexpected Community* (1973, later revised), *The Managed Heart* (1983), and *The Second Shift* (coauthored, 1989).

Hock, Dee Ward (1930–   ) business executive; born in Utah. He grew up in North Odgen, Utah, and was largely self-educated. He found his niche in financial services and became the CEO of the newly formed National Bank-Americard Inc. (1970) which he renamed Visa International in 1977. He foresaw a global electronic data network and he led Visa past both Mastercard and American Express in the bank-card industry. He pioneered electronic bank transfers, magnetic strips on cards, and the internationalization of financial services. After having revolutionized his industry, he retired in 1984.

Hocking, William Ernest (1873–1966) philosopher; born in Cleveland, Ohio. Born into a devout family of modest means, he spent a decade working his way through college, then studied philosophy at Harvard under Josiah Royce and others. His 1904 dissertation grew into his major work, *The Meaning of God in Human Experience* (1912), which expounded a religiously oriented idealistic metaphysics opening toward mysticism; he also wrote on political philosophy, notably in *The Spirit of World Politics* (1932). After teaching at Yale (1908–14) and elsewhere, he spent most of his career at Harvard (1914–43); during a long retirement in the New Hampshire countryside he continued to philosophize.

Hodge, Charles (1797–1878) Protestant theologian; born in Philadelphia. The son of a Continental Army surgeon, he graduated from Princeton (1815) and Princeton Theological Seminary (1819) and taught at the Princeton seminary from 1820 on. A powerful advocate for conservative Presbyterian doctrine, he edited the *Princeton Review* for more than 40 years. His influential *Systematic Theology* appeared in 1871–72.

Hodges, Courtney (Hicks) (1887–1966) soldier; born in Perry, Ga. The son of a newspaperman, he enlisted in the U.S. Army in 1906, received a commission three years later, and served with great distinction in World War I. During the next two decades he rose in rank as he moved up through the standard staff and command posts. In World War II he took command of the U.S. First Army from General Omar Bradley and led it across France to the liberation of Paris (August 1944), through the Battle of the Bulge, across the Rhine to encircle the Ruhr, and on to the Elbe River in Germany and victory. Promoted to full general, he commanded the First Army until retiring in 1949.

Hodges, (John Cornelius) Johnny "Rabbit" (1906–70) jazz musician; born in Cambridge, Mass. He was an outstanding and influential alto saxophonist, a prolific freelance recording artist, and a prominent member of Duke Ellington's Orchestra between 1928–70.

Hodur, Francis (1866–1953) religious founder; born in Zarki, Poland. Emigrating to the U.S.A. as a seminarian and ordained in 1893, he became pastor (1897) of a Scranton, Pa., church independently built by Polish Catholics chafing under a largely German and Irish hierarchy; the next year he was excommunicated. Additional groups joined together to form a Polish National Catholic Church (PNCC), which he led, becoming a bishop (1907). The PNCC adopted a Polish vernacular liturgy, among other changes; at Hodur's death there were 270,000 adherents.

Hoe, Richard March (1812–86) inventor, industrialist; born in New York City. Son of a British-born manufacturer of printing presses, he joined his father's company at age 15 and, with a cousin, took over the business three years later. His Hoe rotary press, which printed on a cylinder instead of a flat plate, went into operation at the *Philadelphia Public Ledger* in 1847. By 1865 a competitor had developed a rotary press that printed on a continuous roll of newsprint, but within six years Hoe had produced a new design using all the main features of his rivals.

Hoe, Robert (1839–1909) manufacturer, bibliophile; born in New York City. Succeeding his uncle, Richard Hoe, as head of a firm manufacturing printing equipment, he introduced key innovations in newspaper presses. He assembled an impressive personal library of over 20,000 titles and was a founder and first president of the Grolier Club, formed to foster arts relating to book production.

Hoffa, (James Riddle) Jimmy (1913–?1975) labor leader; born in Brazil, Ind. He became an organizer for the International Brotherhood of Teamsters (IBT) in 1934, rising rapidly through the union's ranks. He was elected IBT president in 1957 and gained notoriety for his aggressive tactics against all who opposed him, both inside and outside the labor movement. Target of a 1957 U.S. Senate investigation into union corruption, he was later convicted of jury tampering, fraud, and conspiracy, and sent to prison in 1967. His sentence was commuted in 1971, and he was rumored to be trying to regain power within the IBT when in 1975 he disappeared. Rumors as to how he died continued to surface but his body was never found.

Hoffer, Eric (1902–83) writer; born in New York City. Unschooled and temporarily blind as a child, he read voraciously after recovering his sight at age 15. At age 18 he went to California and took up work as a migrant farmer writing on the side; from 1943 he was a dockworker. His writings, starting with *The True Believer* (1951), a study of fanaticism and mass movements, won recognition for their pungent, aphoristic style and perceptivity. Hoffer retired from the docks in 1967 but continued to be widely celebrated as "the longshoreman philosopher."

Hoffman, Abbie (1936–89) radical activist, author; born in Worcester, Mass. After graduating from Brandeis University (1959) and earning a masters in psychology from the University of California: Berkeley (1960), he joined civil rights workers in the South before returning to Worcester to work as a salesman for a pharmaceutical company. He cut his teeth as an activist in Worcester (roughly 1960–66) where he especially assisted minority youth. Moving to New York City (1966), he ran a theater and helped organize "hippies" in the East Village. He came to national prominence as a Yippie leader during the violent antiwar demonstrations – "days of rage" – in Chicago (1968) and the much-publicized Chicago

Seven trial (1969). Arrested for possession of cocaine (1973), he went underground (1974) and assumed the name Barry Freed in Fineview, N.Y., where he worked on environmental concerns. Resurfacing on the television show "20/20" (1980), he surrendered to authorities and spent less than a year in prison. He was the author of several books, including *Steal this Book* and *Revolution for the Hell of It*. His last public demonstration (1986) was in support of an anti-Central Intelligence Agency protest at the University of Massachusetts: Amherst, along with President Jimmy Carter's daughter, Amy Carter. Evidently in a bout with depression, he committed suicide (1989).

Hoffman, Charles Fenno (1806–84) writer, editor; born in New York City. He lost his right leg in an accident (c. 1817), studied law at Columbia (1821–24), became an avid sportsman, and made a long journey by horseback in the Northwest Territory (1833). He never seriously practiced law, but turned to editing and journalism, serving as the editor of several prominent magazines of the day. For several years in the 1840s he also held various U.S. government jobs in New York City. He wrote poetry, but is best known for *Greyslaer: A Romance of the Mohawk* (1839), a novel based on a Kentucky murder. It was reported that he became insane after a servant used his most recent manuscript to light the fires in his lodgings in New York City; in any case he was committed to the State Hospital, Harrisburg, Pa. (1850) and spent the rest of his life institutionalized.

Hoffman, Dustin (1937–) movie actor; born in Los Angeles. He dropped out of Santa Monica State College to become an actor and by 1961 was getting small parts in plays and television. By 1965 he seemed stalled off Broadway, but his role in *The Graduate* (1967) catapulted him to stardom. Noted for his versatility, his perfectionism, and his occasionally heavy-handed role in productions, he gained Oscars as best actor in *Kramer v. Kramer* (1979) and *Rainman* (1988). He returned to the theater for a run as Willy Loman in *Death of a Salesman* (1984).

Hoffman, Lynn (1924–) family/marriage therapist; born in Paris, France. Child of American parents – her mother was Ruth Reeves, a noted textile designer – she grew up in a New York artists' colony. She graduated from Radcliffe (1946) and held a series of jobs before she began to concentrate on family therapy (1963) in a program influenced by the ideas of Gregory Bateson. She took a master's degree from the Adelphi School of Social Work (1971) and worked for family therapy organizations in Philadelphia, New York City, Massachusetts, Vermont, and Connecticut. She conducted workshops and addressed many conferences around the world, and taught at the Smith College School of Social Work (1983). Among her publications, *Foundations of Family Therapy* (1981) is recognized internationally as an important textbook.

Hoffman, Malvinia Cornell (b. Grimson) (1885–1966) sculptor; born in New York City. She studied at the Art Students League (c. 1909), traveled to Paris to study with Rodin (1910–14), and returned to New York City. She became known for her sculptures of famous personalities, such as *Mask of Anna Pavlova* (1924), and for 100 figures, *Races of Man* (1929–33), commissioned by the Field Museum, Chicago.

Hoffman, Paul (Gray) (1891–1974) industrialist, government official. Starting as a salesman at Studebaker in 1910, he led that company out of bankruptcy in 1935. An economic adviser to President Roosevelt, he later administered the Marshall Plan (1948–50) to speed economic recovery in Europe after World War II. He also led the Ford Foundation (1951–53) and the United Nations Development program (1966–72).

Hoffmann, Roald (b. Roald Safran) (1937–) chemist; born in Zloczow, Poland (now Zolochëv, Ukraine). He came with his family to the United States in 1949 and joined the faculty of Cornell in 1965. By providing mathematical rules that predict when and where a particular chemical reaction will result in a product of greater bonding and stability than the starting reagents (1970), he changed the way chemical experiments are designed. He shared the Nobel Prize for chemistry (1981).

Hofmann, Hans (1880–1966) painter, teacher; born in Weissenberg, Germany. He settled in America (1932) and in the 1950s became well-known as an abstract expressionist, an approach to painting that stressed nonrepresentational form and color as a means of expressing emotional content. He taught at the University of California: Berkeley in 1930–31 and began his own school in New York (1934), influencing such artists as Burgoyne Diller, Louise Nevelson and Helen Frankenthaler. He used many styles, but remained true to his search for what he called "the inner life of things." His distinctive approach is seen in such notable works as *Effervescence* (1944), and *Fantasia in Blue* (1954).

Hofmann, Josef (1876–1957) pianist; born near Cracow, Poland. A sensational child prodigy, he played Beethoven with the Berlin Philharmonic at age ten and made his American debut the following year. After further study with Anton Rubenstein and others, he resumed in 1894 the career as a virtuoso that he pursued the rest of his life. After 1898 he largely lived in the U.S.A.; from 1926–38 he was director of the Curtis Institute.

Hofstadter, Richard (1916–70) historian; born in Buffalo, N.Y. An interdisciplinary pioneer and major seminal influence in American intellectual and political history, he received his doctorate from Columbia University (1942) and taught at Columbia from 1946 until his early death, training a generation of graduate students. His doctoral thesis, *Social Darwinism in American Thought, 1860–1915* (1944), won the Beveridge Award from the American Historical Society (1942). *The American Political Tradition and the Men Who Made It* (1948) sold over one million paperback copies. Both *The Age of Reform: From Bryan to F.D.R.* (1955) and *Anti-Intellectualism in American Life* (1963) won Pulitzer Prizes. The last of his 13 books, *The Idea of a Party System* (1969), explored the slow acceptance of party politics in America.

Hofstadter, Robert (1915–90) physicist; born in New York City. He performed research at Princeton (1939–40), then taught at the University of Pennsylvania (1940–41) and City College, N.Y. (1941–42). After working for the National Bureau of Standards (1942–43) and Norden Laboratories Corporation (1943–46), he returned to teaching at Princeton (1946–50), then Stanford (1950–80). He shared the 1961 Nobel Prize in physics for his pioneering research on the structure of protons and neutrons.

Hogan, (William Benjamin) Ben (1912–) golfer; born in Stephenville, Texas. One of golf's most dominant players during the late 1940s and early 1950s, he learned the game while working as a caddy at age 11. He turned professional at age 19, and between 1946 and 1953 he won four U.S. Open tournaments, two Masters, two Professional Golfers' Association (PGA) titles, and the British Open. In 1949 he was involved in a near-fatal automobile accident, but he recovered to win the U.S. Open in 1950. A movie based on his courageous recovery, *Follow the Sun,* was released in 1951, starring Glenn Ford.

Hoge, Mrs. A. H. (Abraham Holmes) (b. Jane Currie Blaikie) (1811–90) relief and welfare worker; born in Philadelphia. She was a lifelong charity worker. During the Civil War she and Mary Livermore directed the Chicago branch of the Sanitary Commission, coordinating 1,000 local aid societies, improving field distribution of supplies, and raising funds through extensive lecture tours and the great Chicago Sanitary Fair (1863).

Holborn, Hajo (1902–69) historian; born in Berlin, Germany. He taught in Germany until he emigrated to the United States and joined the Yale University faculty (1934–69). Respected as an authority on the Reformation and the Weimar Republic, he served the Office of Strategic Services (OSS) in Washington (1943–45) and in the State Department (1946–48). His *History of Modern Germany* (3 vols. 1968) covered Germany from the Middle Ages to Hitler's fall.

Holden, Edward Singleton (1846–1914) astronomer; born in St. Louis, Mo. A West Point graduate (1870), he taught mathematics for the United States Navy (1873–81), directed the Washburn Observatory in Wisconsin (1881–85), and designed and directed the Lick Observatory in California (1888–98). In 1901 he became the librarian of the U.S. Military Academy and wrote several books, including three collections of children's stories.

Holden, William Woods (1818–92) journalist, governor; born in Orange County, N.C. A self-educated Whig political writer, he became Democratic editor of the *North Carolina Standard* in 1843, advocating secession from the Union. Switching parties again, as North Carolina's Republican governor (1868–70) he pandered to carpetbaggers, using the militia to suppress his opposition. Impeached for corruption, he returned to journalism.

Holder, Geoffrey (1930–) dancer, choreographer, artist; born in Port-of-Spain, Trinidad. He started dancing at age seven in his brother's dance group, which Geoffrey later brought to Puerto Rico (1952), there attracting the attention of choreographer Agnes de Mille. He made his Broadway debut in *House of Flowers* (1955), and after his marriage to dancer Carmen de Lavallade, he danced with the Metropolitan Opera Ballet (1957). A talented painter, he won a Guggenheim grant (1957) and became an avid collector of folk art. He created costumes and scenery for dance companies such as Alvin Ailey's. He won Tony Awards for costume design and direction of *The Wiz* (1975), he choreographed *Timbuktu* (1978), and later played Punjab in the movie, *Annie* (1981). With his varied talents and standing six feet six inches tall, he often seemed larger than life, while his distinctively resonant voice became familiar to millions through several television commercial series he made.

Holiday, (Eleanora) Billie "Lady Day" (1915–59) jazz musician; born in Baltimore, Md. She is the most widely celebrated and influential singer in jazz history, but also one of its most tragic figures, her career hampered by drug addiction, prison sentences, and racial injustice. Between 1933–42, she made a brilliant series of small group recordings featuring Teddy Wilson and Lester Young and appeared with the big bands of Count Basie and Artie Shaw. Her 1939 recording of "Strange Fruit," which depicted a lynching, was a *cause célèbre*. She appeared in several films, including *New Orleans* (1946), but by the end of the 1940s her voice had begun to deteriorate, taking on a fragile huskiness that initially added to her emotional appeal. She continued to record and appear as a nightclub performer until 1959. Her autobiography, *Lady Sings the Blues,* was published in 1956 and was the basis for a 1973 film biography.

Holladay, Ben (1819–87) stagecoach operator, financier; born in Carlisle County, Ky. He moved to Missouri and operated a store and hotel. He furnished supplies for the U.S. Army during the Mexican War and bought oxen and wagons for bargain prices at the end of that conflict. He entered into trade with Salt Lake City and then with California. He bought the Central Overland California and Pike's Peak Express for $100,000. He reorganized these stagecoach expresses and held the mail contracts. His business suffered from Indian uprisings (1864–65) and he sold it to Wells Fargo and Company (1866). He entered into steamship and railroad companies but he was devastated by the Panic of 1873. He retired in 1876. Two of his daughters married titled Europeans.

Holland, Clifford (1883–1924) civil engineer; born in Somerset, Mass. He graduated from Harvard (B.S. 1906) and became the tunnel engineer (1914–16) and the division engineer (1916–19) for the Public Service Commission. As chief engineer (1919–24) for the New York State and New Jersey Interstate Bridge and Tunnel Commissions, he planned and built the first twin-tube, subaqueous vehicular tunnel, named for him in 1924 and opened in 1927, crossing under the Hudson River between lower Manhattan and New Jersey.

Holland, John Philip (1840–1914) inventor; born in Liscannor, Ireland. With his plan for a submarine, he emigrated to the U.S.A. in 1873. After rejection by the U.S. Navy, his work was sponsored by expatriate Irish nationalists. Not until 1900 did the navy accept his *Holland* as their first submarine. He built submarines for various navies but got into financial trouble and ended up experimenting with airplanes.

Holland, Josiah Gilbert (1819–81) writer, editor; born in Belchertown, Mass. Although he graduated from the Berkshire Medical College in 1844, he left medicine first for teaching and then for publishing. He spent most of his career as an editor at the *Springfield Republican* (Mass.), where he worked under Samuel Bowles, son of the founder-publisher of the same name. Holland worked full-time at the *Republican* from 1849 to 1857, after which he concentrated on his writing. His many books, many collections of *Republican* columns, include *A History of Western Massachusetts* (1885) and *Timothy Titcomb's Letters to Young People* (1858), as well as volumes of poetry and a number of novels. In 1870 he was a founder and the first editor of *Scribner's Monthly* (later the *Century*). Widely read during his lifetime, he has been little read since then.

Hollerith, Herman (1860–1929) engineer, computer inventor; born in Buffalo, N.Y. Working as a statistician for the U.S.

census of 1880, he became aware of the need for automation in the recording and processing of vast amounts of data. Working first at the Massachusetts Institute of Technology and then at the U.S. Patent Office (1884–90), he invented a tabulating machine that was fed data via electrical contacts controlled by the holes in punch cards. His machine won a contest for the best data-processing equipment for the U.S. census of 1890 and he organized the Tabulating Machine Company (1896) to make improved versions that soon were being used by other countries. His company merged with others to become the Computing–Tabulating–Recording Company (1911) which adopted the name of International Business Machines Corporation in 1924. Although he was early praised for revolutionizing statistical processing, it was only decades later that he was recognized as having anticipated the modern computer.

Holley, Alexander Lyman (1832–82) mechanical engineer, metallurgist; born in Lakeville, Conn. While still in college he devised improvements for steam locomotives; after working in locomotive plants, he published (1855–57) *Holley's Railroad Advocate.* He wrote many technical articles (usually under the name "Tubal Cain"). In 1863 he went to England to purchase the American rights to the Bessemer process, and then supervised construction of the first such U.S. plant at Troy, N.Y. For his work in engineering other steel plants, he became known as "the father of modern American steel manufacture" and his statue was placed in New York's Washington Square.

Holley, Robert W. (William) (1922–93) biochemist; born in Urbana, Ill. He was a chemist at Cornell University (1942–44, 1946–47), then spent a year at Washington State College. He returned to Cornell (1948–68), where he taught organic chemistry and investigated the biochemistry of botanical substances. During research from 1956–63, he secured the first pure sample of a transfer RNA and elucidated its complete molecular structure, for which he was awarded one-third of the 1968 Nobel Prize in physiology. He moved to the Salk Institute for Biological Studies (1968), where he explored the growth of malignant and nonmalignant mammalian cells.

Holly, Buddy (nickname of Charles Hardin Holley) (1936–59) musician; born in Lubbock, Texas. An early rock 'n' roll star, he began as a country-and-western singer and gradually added rhythm-and-blues elements to his innovative style. With his band, the Crickets, he established the standard rock instrumentation of two guitars, bass, and drums. He toured the U.S.A. extensively for two years before his death in a plane crash in Iowa. He became one of rock's most enduring cult figures and much of his material was released posthumously.

Holm, Eleanor (1913–) swimmer, entertainer; born in Jamaica, Long Island, N.Y. She began swimming off Long Island, N.Y., at age 13; at 15 she competed in the 1928 Olympics (placing 5th in the 100-meter backstroke); in the 1932 Olympics she won the gold in the 100-meter backstroke. Under contract to Warner Bros., she appeared in a few minor roles but quit when the studio asked her to swim in movies (which would have compromised her amateur status). She married the bandleader-singer Keith Jarrett and toured with him as a singer, all the while training for the 1936 Olympics. On the ship to Europe with the Olympics team, she was already a celebrity and spent much of her time socializing in 1st Class; when she was reported to have been drinking champagne and staying up late, she was dropped from the U.S. team by Avery Brundage, head of the American Olympic Committee. She went on to Berlin and covered the Olympics for Hearst's International News Service (although her articles were largely ghost-written by other reporters); she also met Hitler, who expressed disbelief that she had been banned for such a minor infraction. On returning to the States, she was an even bigger celebrity than before. She turned professional in 1937, appeared in *Tarzan's Revenge* (1938), and swam in Billy Rose's "Aquacade," first at Cleveland's Great Lakes Exposition and then at the New York World's Fair (1939, 1940). Divorcing Jarrett, she married Billy Rose in 1939; they were divorced in 1954 and she took up with Tommy Whalen, a Texas entrepreneur, marrying him in 1974.

Holm, Hanya (b. Johanna Eckert) (1893–1992) modern dancer, choreographer; born in Worms, Germany. After studying with Mary Wigman in Dresden, she came on tour to New York in 1931, where she opened the Wigman studio, renamed the Hanya Holm Studio in 1936. Forming her own company, she performed her most famous work *Trend* (1937), later establishing a dance center in Colorado Springs. In the late 1940s she began choreographing on Broadway, most notably *Kiss Me Kate* (1948), going on to create dances for 13 musicals. She also directed and choreographed operas such as *The Ballad of Baby Doe* (1956). She was still teaching in her nineties.

Holm, Saxe See JACKSON, HELEN HUNT.

Holman, Eugene (1895–1962) oil executive; born in San Angelo, Texas. Trained as a geologist, he spent his career in the oil industry, and after 1919 he rose through the ranks of Standard Oil Company of New Jersey. As president (1944–60) and chairman and CEO (1954–60) he launched Standard Oil (later Exxon) as a major player in the Middle East by buying a share of the Saudi Arabian oil fields.

Holman, (Nathan) Nat (1896–   ) basketball player/coach; born in New York City. One of basketball's pioneers, he helped the Original Celtics win 720 of 795 games between 1921–28. A coach at City College of New York for 37 years (1920–52, 1955–56, 1959–60), he was elected to basketball's Hall of Fame in 1964.

Holmes, Donald Fletcher (1910–80) chemist, inventor; born in Woodbury, N.J. Educated at Amherst College and the University of Illinois, he and William E. Hanford, a colleague at E.I. du Pont de Nemours & Co., developed polyurethane in 1942. He spent his entire career with du Pont, working in the company's textile divisions.

Holmes, John Clellon (1926–88) writer; born in Holyoke, Mass. He studied at Columbia University (1943; 1945–46) and the New School for Social Research (1949–50). He wrote novels and essays describing the Beat Generation, as seen in *Nothing More to Declare* (1967). He also published poetry, was a lecturer at writing workshops, and taught at the University of Arkansas beginning in 1977.

Holmes, John Haynes (1879–1964) Unitarian minister, social reformer; born in Philadelphia. Ordained as a Unitarian minister (1904), he helped found the Unitarian Fellowship for Social Justice (1908) while conducting a radical social ministry at the Church of the Messiah, New York City. He helped found the National Association for the Advancement of Colored People (NAACP) (1909), serving as national vice-president for over 50 years, and he helped organize the American Civil Liberties Union (ACLU) (1918–19). An ardent pacifist, he left the Unitarians to protest their support of America's entry into World War I and founded the Community Church in New York City. As a prohibitionist, a supporter of striking workers, a Zionist, editor of *Unity* magazine (1921–46), and chairman of the New York City Civic Affairs Committee that exposed municipal corruption (1929–38), he made his Community Church in New York City into a model for a pluralistic congregation. A leading U.S. proponent of Gandhi, he led early public protests against Hitler (1933), was named chairman of the ACLU (1939), and later fought McCarthyism. He wrote over 20 books, including his autobiography, *I Speak for Myself* (1959).

Holmes, Oliver Wendell (1809–94) physician, poet, writer; born in Cambridge, Mass. The son of a Congregational minister, he was his class poet at Harvard College; he stayed on to study law but changed to medicine; he spent two years studying medicine in Paris, then returned to take his M.D. from Harvard (1836) and start a private practice; from 1838–40 he taught anatomy at Dartmouth, but then he returned to Boston to practice medicine. He invented an early stethoscope; suggested the term "anestesia" (from the Greek for "no feeling") for the state induced by the new gases; published two influential medical works, *Homeopathy and Kindred Delusions* (1842) and *The Contagiousness of Puerperal Fever* (1843); and became Parkman Professor of Anatomy and Physiology at Harvard (1847–82). But long before this he had been gaining a parallel reputation as a poet and writer. In 1830 his poem "Old Ironsides" galvanized national sentiment to save the USS *Constitution* from destruction. While still a graduate student he published two essays in the *New England Magazine* under the title "The Autocrat at the Breakfast Table" and in the late 1850s, *The Atlantic Monthly*, which he had founded in 1857 with James Russell Lowell, began to publish his essays and poems. The essays were collected in a book, *The Autocrat at the Breakfast Table*, and this led to several other collections of his essays. Two of his poems were household classics in their day – "The Chambered Nautilus" and "The Deacon's Masterpiece." He also wrote three novels about psychologically disturbed characters, of which *Elsie Venner* (1861) was the most successful. He wrote a biography of his friend, Ralph Waldo Emerson (1885).

Holmes, Oliver Wendell, Jr. (1841–1935) Supreme Court justice; born in Boston, Mass. (son of Oliver Wendell Holmes, 1809–94). Raised among Boston's intellectual community, he fought for the Union in the Civil War and was seriously wounded three times. After the war, he entered a private law practice in Boston and edited the *American Law Review* and the twelfth edition of James Kent's legal classic, *Commentaries on American Law* (1873) as well as penning the essays that comprised his seminal work, *The Common Law* (1881). He served the Massachusetts Supreme Court (1882–1902), as chief justice from 1899. President Theodore Roosevelt named him to the U.S. Supreme Court (1902–32), where he was known as "The Great Dissenter" for the clarity and verve with which he wrote his frequent dissenting opinions. Although since revered by liberals for his opinions on such issues as free speech, during his tenure on the Supreme Court he promoted judicial restraint, believing that lawmaking was better left to the constituents and the legislature. He retired from the bench at the age of 91.

Holmes, William Henry (1846–1933) archaeologist, artist; born near Cadiz, Ohio. He was a geologist and outstanding illustrator who turned to archaeology while working for the U.S. Geological Survey (1875) and became an expert on southwestern Indian art and prehistoric ceramics and stone implements. His works include the standard *Handbook of Aboriginal American Antiquities* (1919). He was chief of the Bureau of American Ethnology (1902–09) and director of the National Gallery of Art (1920–32).

Holt, Bertha Marian (1904–) adoption activist; born in Des Moines, Iowa. Along with her husband Harry Holt (d. 1964), who had served in the U.S. Army in Korea, Holt sought special legislation from the U.S. Congress to enable them to add eight G.I.-Korean orphans to their family of six children (1955). Realizing that they could not adopt all the children in need, the Holts founded the Holt International Children's Services, which has placed more than 50,000 orphans from around the world – including Korea, Latin and South America, Russia, and India – in U.S. homes. Known to these children as "Grandma Holt," her many honors include Mother of the Year (1966) and Woman of the Year (1973). She wrote *Seed from the East, Created For God's Glory,* and *Bring My Sons from Afar* about her experiences.

Holt, Edwin Bissell (1873–1946) psychologist; born in Winchester, Mass. He studied at Harvard with William James and taught there until 1919, when he moved to Princeton (to 1936). His research was directed toward giving a completely physiological account of motivation and learning. His best-known work is *Animal Drive and the Learning Process: An Essay Toward Radical Empiricism* (1931).

Holt, Elizabeth Basye (B. Gilmore) (?1906–87) art historian; born in San Francisco. She studied at the University of Wisconsin (B.A. 1928), Radcliffe (M.A. 1930), and the University of Munich (Ph.D. 1934). She taught at several institutions, and specialized in the history of art ranging from the Middle Ages to the 19th century.

Holt, Henry (1840–1926) publisher, author; born in Baltimore, Md. Obtaining a law degree in 1866, he formed a publishing company with Frederick Leypoldt, organized in 1873 as Henry Holt & Company. His writings include the popular novels, *Calmire, Man and Nature* (1892) and *Sturmsee, Man and Man* (1905), and a highly regarded memoir, *Garrulities of an Octogenarian Editor* (1923).

Holt, John (Caldwell) (1923–85) educational reformer; born in New York City. A teacher turned writer and lecturer, his best-selling *How Children Fail* (1964, revised in 1982) and *How Children Learn* (1967, 1983) called for educational reform to nurture children's creativity. In the 1970s Holt became a leader in the home-schooling movement.

Holtfreter, Johannes (Friedrich Karl) (1901–) embryologist; born in Richtenberg, Germany. He taught in Germany (1928–38), emigrated to McGill University, Montreal (1942–46), then came to the U.S.A. to join Rochester University (1946–69). After over 40 years investigating morphogenesis and differentiation in amphibian, avian, and mammalian embryos, he concluded that development of specialized organs from the undifferentiated early embryo is the result of both directed cell movement and separations and reassociations controlled by selective cell adhesion.

Holyoke, Samuel (1762–1820) teacher, composer; born in Boxford, Mass. He graduated from Harvard College in 1789 and that same year contributed songs to the *Massachusetts Magazine.* He first compiled hymns in *Harmonia America* in 1791 and his *Columbian Repository of Sacred Harmony,* copyrighted in 1802, contained over 700 tunes for hymn books, including many of his own such as "Arnheim." Living in Salem in the 1800s, he conducted singing schools and concerts and published several music collections.

Homans, George (Casper) (1910–89) sociologist; born in Boston, Mass. He earned an M.A. at Cambridge University, England, and taught at Harvard (1946–80). An authority on social behavior of small groups, he posited group behavior to be the result of individual behavior and wrote such books as *The Human Group* (1950), *Sentiments and Activities* (1962), and *Certainties and Doubts* (1987).

Homar, Lorenzo (1913–) artist; born in Puerta de Tierra, Puerto Rico. He grew up in New York City, where he attended the Brooklyn Museum Art School and studied metalwork at Cartier's. In 1950 he returned to Puerto Rico where he was active in the graphic arts, was a founder of the Puerto Rican Arts Center, and received a Guggenheim in 1957. His lithographs, posters, and paintings hang in New York's Museum of Modern Art and at the Library of Congress. He was one of the first in Puerto Rico to see the potential for the poster as an affordable art form.

Homer, Louise (b. Beatty) (1871–1947) contralto; born in Pittsburgh, Pa. Trained in America and France, she sang opera at the Metropolitan and internationally to great acclaim, pursuing a concert career after 1927.

Homer, Sidney (1902–83) economist, broker, author; born in West Chester, Pa. The son of musicians, he graduated from Harvard in 1923, and, in the midst of the Great Depression, set up his own bond trading house in 1932. He joined Salomon Brothers in 1961, organized the firm's first bond research department, and retired as a partner and chief economist in 1972. He became known as "the Bard of Wall Street" for his colorful treatment of usually dry economic subjects. His *History of Interest Rates: 2000 B.C. to the Present* appeared in 1963.

Homer, Winslow (1836–1910) painter; born in Boston, Mass. Largely self-taught, he began his career as a lithographer and then became an illustrator for popular magazines. *Harper's Weekly* sent him periodically to cover the Civil War (1861–65), and the resulting drawings and paintings revealed his draftmanship, realism, and unsentimental approach to his subjects, as seen in *Prisoners from the Front* (1866). His early genre work, such as *Snap the Whip* (1872), ensured his popularity, and he spent more time on his own work. By 1875 he was using water color, his primary medium, as a method of quickly capturing a dramatic moment in nature. He traveled often, producing many fine works as a result of his journeys to such places as Bermuda, Florida, and Petersburg, Virginia. His series of paintings of African-Americans, such as the well-known *The Cotton Pickers* (1876), and *The Carnival* (1877), exhibit his superb design capabilities and a striking use of paint. After traveling to England (1881–82), he settled at Prouts Neck, Maine, in 1883 and the sea and the men and women who lived near the shore became the main focus of his art. He began a series of oils and water colors that built his reputation as a major artist. His seascapes, such as *Northeaster* (1895) and *Early Morning after a Storm at Sea* (1902), reveal the vitality and power of his genius.

Hood, John Bell (1831–79) soldier; born in Owingsville, Ky. A doctor's son, he graduated from West Point (1853) near the bottom of his class and served in California and Texas. Resigning to join the Confederate service, he commanded a brigade at 2nd Bull Run and Antietam (both 1862) and a division at Gettysburg, where he was seriously wounded. Wounded again at Chickamauga (1863), he recovered from the amputation of his right leg in time to succeed Joseph E. Johnston in command of the army facing Sherman before Atlanta. Promoted beyond his capabilities he was no match for Sherman. Forced out of Atlanta, he marched north while Sherman moved east to the sea; his ill-advised attacks at Franklin and Nashville, Tenn. (1864), shattered his army. Hood went into business in New Orleans after the war, but his ventures were unsuccessful. He died in poverty, the victim, along with some of his large family, of a yellow fever epidemic.

Hood, Raymond M. (Mathewson) (1881–1934) architect; born in Pawtucket, R.I. He graduated from the Massachusetts Institute of Technology and the École des Beaux-Arts, Paris, before establishing a solo practice in New York (1914). His reputation made by the Chicago Tribune Tower (1923–25, with J. M. Howells), he rapidly produced a series of landmark skyscrapers, including Rockefeller Center (1930–33, with others) and the McGraw-Hill Building (1931, with Godley and Fouilhoux), both in New York City and still regarded as masterworks in the art deco style.

Hook, Sidney (1902–89) philosopher; born in New York City. A 1923 graduate of City College of New York, he earned a 1927 doctorate from Columbia University, where he became a disciple of John Dewey, and taught at Columbia until 1972, chairing the philosophy department from 1932 to 1968. He wrote a seminal study of Dewey (1929). Radical as a student, he also wrote influential expositions of Marx's thought (1933, 1936), but he soon revolted against Marxism and became an early "neoconservative," championing free speech, the cold war against Communism, and liberal social programs. After retiring, he became a senior research fellow of the Hoover Institution at Stanford, Calif.

Hooker, John Lee (1917–) musician; born in Clarksdale, Miss. A blues singer and guitarist, he began his career in Detroit in 1948 with the release of "Boogie Chillun," the biggest of his several hit records and a staple of both the blues and rock repertoires. He toured continually, and among "deep blues" artists, enjoyed an unusually successful career, appearing in concerts and on recordings with many of the leading figures in rock. He was inducted into the Rock 'n' Roll Hall of Fame in 1991.

Hooker, Joseph (1814–79) soldier; born in Hadley, Mass. He graduated from West Point (1837), served with distinction in Mexico (1846–47), and left the army in 1853 to farm in California. Recalled on the outbreak of Civil War, he led a corps at Antietam and Fredericksburg (both 1862) and in January 1863 succeeded Ambrose Burnside as commander of the Army of the Potomac. He had a reputation as an aggressive commander, although his nickname, "Fighting Joe," resulted from a dropped hyphen in a news dispatch (that was supposed to have read, Fighting – Joe Hooker) rather than from action in the field. (The claim that "hooker" as the term for a prostitute is derived from the campfollowers he allegedly tolerated is a completely false attribution.) Confident, efficient, and boastful, Hooker

reorganized the army, improved soldiers' conditions, and promised to defeat Lee. Instead, the Confederate commander overmastered him at Chancellorsville (1863). Lincoln accepted his resignation on the eve of Gettysburg. He later held corps commands in the West under Grant and Sherman, and retired as a regular army major general in 1868.

Hooker, Philip (1766–1836) architect; born in Rutland, Mass. An upstate New York architect, as Albany city surveyor (1819–32) and city superintendent (1821–27) he designed many of the neoclassical public buildings that transformed Albany into an ambitious state capital.

Hooker, Thomas (1586–1647) religious leader; born in Leicestershire, England. He emigrated to Holland (1630) and then to Massachusetts in 1633. After falling out with the leaders of the Massachusetts Bay colony, he led a group of his parishioners to Connecticut and helped to establish Hartford. His political ideas were embodied in the Fundamental Orders (1639), which was Connecticut's first constitution.

Hooks, Benjamin (Lawson) (1925–) judge, public official, civil rights reformer; born in Memphis, Tenn. A lawyer as well as an ordained minister, he was pastor of the Middle Baptist Church of Memphis (1956–72), cofounder and vice-president of the Mutual Federal Savings and Loan Association (1955–69), and the first black judge to serve in the Shelby County Criminal Court (1965–68). He gained national recognition as the first African-American to serve on the Federal Communications Commission (FCC) (1972–77), where he became a driving force to improve both the portrayal of and employment opportunities for African-Americans in the electronic media. He succeeded Roy Wilkins as executive director of the National Association for the Advancement of Colored People (NAACP) (1977–93) and pushed the organization to be more vocal and activist in pro-black concerns. He served as producer and host of a number of television shows airing racial issues.

Hooper, C. E. (Claude Ernest) (1898–1954) broadcast audience analyst; born in Kingsville, Ohio. While working in advertising he developed techniques to research radio audiences and in 1938 he founded his own New York firm. His "Hooperatings," based on telephone pollings of listeners, soon became the industry standard, attracting controversy over their methodology and effect on program quality. He sold his national ratings service to A. C. Nielsen in 1950.

Hooten, Earnest (Albert) (1887–1954) physical anthropologist; born in Clemansville, Wis. He was a professor at Harvard, where his laboratory became a center for training physical anthropology specialists. His many popular books introduced human anatomical evolution to a non-academic readership. His occasionally controversial research concentrated on classifying human races and relating physical characteristics to behavior.

Hoover, Herbert (Clark) (1874–1964) thirty-first U.S. president; born in West Branch, Iowa. A successful mining engineer, he came to fame heading national and international relief efforts during and after World War I and served Republican administrations as secretary of commerce (1921–28). Having demonstrated remarkable organizational skills, he easily defeated Democrat Al Smith for the presidency in 1928. However, when the stock market crashed in October 1929 and the nation slid into depression, his opposition to governmental activism made him ineffective in managing the disaster and he became increasingly unpopular. In the 1932 election Franklin Delano Roosevelt won by a landslide. After retiring to private life, Hoover reappeared in a series of public appointments, notably coordinating European economic relief programs after World War II and chairing the so-called Hoover Commissions that helped streamline the U.S. government.

Hoover, J. (John) Edgar (1895–1972) director of the Federal Bureau of Investigation, lawyer, criminologist; born in Washington, D.C. He attended night classes at George Washington University while working as a clerk at the Library of Congress. After being admitted to the District of Columbia bar (1917) he became special assistant to Attorney General A. Mitchell Palmer and led the controversial "Palmer Raids" against alleged seditionists. Advancing from assistant (1921) to director (1924) of the Bureau of Investigation (which became the FBI in 1935), he remained director under every president from Coolidge to Nixon. Hoover emphasized modern technological investigative techniques, improved training, and obtained increased funding from Congress. During the 1930s, FBI exploits against notorious gangsters made him a national hero. In the 1940s and 1950s he became well-known for his anti-Communist and antisubversive views and activities. In the 1960s he became a problematic political figure due to his lack of sympathy for the civil rights movement and the Kennedy administration. His reputation declined in later years following revelations concerning his vendettas against liberal activists, notably Martin Luther King Jr., and widespread illegal FBI activities.

Hoover, Lou (b. Henry) (1874–1944) First Lady; born in Waterloo, Iowa. She was the first woman to major in geology at Stanford, where she met Herbert Hoover. They were married in 1899. Well-educated, and extremely well-traveled, she was popular in 1929–30, but like her husband, she lost much public favor during the Great Depression.

Hoover, William Henry (1849–1932) industrialist; born near North Canton, Ohio. He ran a tannery business (1870–1907). In 1907 he bought the patent of an electric cleaning machine from James Murray Spangler. He formed the Electric Suction Sweeper Company in 1908 (renamed Hoover in 1910). He manufactured his "vacuum cleaner" and marketed it around the world, making his name virtually synonymous with the device. He was a Sunday school teacher for 50 years.

Hope, (Leslie Townes) Bob (1903–　) comedian; born in London, England. Emigrating to Cleveland at age 4, he joined the Fatty Arbuckle review in his teens, doing songs, patter, and eccentric dancing. Featured on Broadway in *Roberta* (1933), where he met his wife, Dolores Reed, he made his first film the following year. His ski-slope nose, lopsided grin, and impeccable timing endeared him to audiences. He hosted *The Bob Hope Pepsodent Show* on radio (1939–48) while acting the cowardly braggart in a string of films (1940–62) including the classic "Road" films with Bing Crosby and Dorothy Lamour. He put his boundless energy to good use, entertaining the troops overseas in every U.S. war since World War II and golfed for charity, sponsoring the Bob Hope Desert Classic. A star on television, with frequent network specials, he was the jester to presidents and the author of nine humorous books. In

1985 he won the Kennedy Center Honors for Lifetime Achievement in the Arts.

Hopkins, Arthur (Melancthon) (1878–1950) theater producer; born in Cleveland. He began his career as a journalist, but soon moved to the theater. As a Broadway producer, he was most interested in bringing out new talent. He did so with the Barrymores: John in *Richard III* (1920), Ethel in *Romeo and Juliet* (1922), and Lionel in *Macbeth* (1921). His successes ranged from *The Poor Little Rich Girl* (1913) to *The Magnificent Yankee* (1946).

Hopkins, Cyril George (1866–1919) agronomist; born in Chatfield, Minn. After earning his Ph.D. from Cornell (1898) he studied at the University of Göttingen, Germany. In 1900 at the University of Illinois he classified Illinois soils as to their type, their chemical composition, and methods of management. In 1918 he directed the agriculture rehabilitation program in Greece at the request of the Red Cross. Among his books are *The Story of the Soil, From the Basis of Absolute Science and Real Life* (1911) and *The Farm That Won't Wear Out* (1913).

Hopkins, Esek (1718–1802) naval officer; born in Scituate, R.I. He was commander-in-chief of the Continental navy (1775–77). He disregarded congressional orders to attack British ships in the Chesapeake Bay; he instead attacked and captured New Providence, Bahamas (1776). Following a difficult year for the new navy in 1776–77, Congress dismissed him from the naval service.

Hopkins, Harry (Lloyd) (1890–1946) social worker, public official; born in Sioux City, Iowa. He held administrative positions in welfare organizations (1913–32), including the Red Cross and the New York Tuberculosis Association. In 1931 Governor Franklin D. Roosevelt appointed him director of New York's Temporary Emergency Relief Administration. When Roosevelt became president, Hopkins became federal emergency relief administrator (1933), director of the Works Progress Administration (1935), and helped set up various relief and rehabilitation programs, distributing over $8.5 billion in unemployment relief (1933–1938). From 1938–40 he was secretary of commerce. Throughout World War II he was Roosevelt's closest confidante, personal aide, and chief liaison to foreign governments, supervising the Lend-Lease program, chairing the Munitions Assignment Board, and attending conferences from Casablanca to Yalta. Winston Churchill dubbed him "Lord Root of the Matter." In 1945 he successfully represented President Truman as special assistant in Moscow and at the San Francisco United Nations Conference.

Hopkins, Johns (1795–1873) merchant, philanthropist; born in Anne Arundel County, Md. In 1812 he left the family tobacco plantation for his uncle's Baltimore commission house. In the 1820s he formed Hopkins Brothers, a grocery store (which at times accepted whisky in payment and sold it under the name "Hopkins' Best") As he continued to prosper, his interests diversified into banking, insurance companies, steamship lines, and railroads. In his will, he left $7 million to establish in Baltimore the present world-class hospital and university that bear his name.

Hopkins, Mark (1802–87) educator, theologian; born in Stockbridge, Mass. (brother of astronomer Albert Hopkins). At Williams College he was a revered teacher of moral philosophy (1830–87) and president (1836–72). A trained physician and ordained minister, Hopkins published numerous philosophical essays and sermons and was president of the American Board of Commissioners for Foreign Missions (1857–87).

Hopkins, Mark (1813–78) businessman, railroad developer; born in Henderson, N.Y. Son of a merchant, he read law but got involved in business. When he heard of the gold discovery in California in 1848, he moved there intending to run a mining company, but he soon discovered that money was more easily made by supplying the needs of the miners. He expanded his business operations and in 1854 joined with Collis P. Huntington to open an iron and hardware store in Sacramento. The two men participated in an informal group – including Leland Stanford and Charles Crocker – that discussed the political issues of the day, and when Theodore Judah appeared with his plan for a railroad linking the East and West, Hopkins and the other three formed the Central Pacific Railroad (1861). Hopkins served as the line's treasurer throughout the construction phase and until his death, and although not as well known or colorful as his three colleagues, he was highly regarded for providing the necessary legal and business acumen. He left a fortune of $20 million (and his name to a well-known hotel in San Francisco).

Hopkins, Samuel (1721–1803) Protestant clergyman, theologian; born in Waterbury, Conn. He graduated from Yale in 1741 and studied theology privately with Jonathan Edwards before becoming pastor of the Congregational church in Great Barrington, Mass., in 1745. His modifications of Edward's orthodoxy, known as Hopkinsianism, were influential. Parishioners, tiring of his stern sermons, dismissed him in 1769; he accepted a pulpit in Newport, R.I., and remained there for the rest of his life. An early opponent of slavery, he worked to establish religious missions in Africa.

Hopkinson, Francis (1737–91) public official, author, musician, judge; born in Philadelphia. The first graduate of what is now the University of Pennsylvania, he became a lawyer, operated a dry goods store, then moved to New Jersey and returned to practicing law. He represented New Jersey at the First Continental Congress and signed the Declaration of Independence. He helped design the first national flag (1777). He also published many political satires and pamphlets, most aimed against the British. A minor poet, he was an accomplished harpsichordist; he wrote music for this instrument and is arguably the first native-born American composer of classical music. After serving on the Pennsylvania admiralty court (1779–89), he was a U.S. district judge in Pennsylvania from 1789 until his death.

Hoppe, (William Frederick) Willie (1887–1959) billiards player; born in Cornwall-Landing-on-Hudson, N.Y. Suave in manner and cool in competition, he won 51 world titles in pocket and three-cushion billiards between 1906 and 1952. In 1911 he became the first billiards player to give an exhibition at the White House.

Hopper, Edward (1882–1967) painter; born in Nyack, N.Y. He studied under Robert Henri (1900–06) and traveled in Europe (1906–10), but his etchings, watercolors, and oils over the next 50 years would reflect little of the current art trends. He supported himself as a commercial illustrator until recognition in the mid-1920s. His vision of realism, using moody light and buildings, created a world of human isolation, as in such famous paintings as *Early Sunday Morning* (1930) and *Night Hawks* (1942).

Hopper, Grace Murray (1906–92) mathematician, computer programmer, naval officer; born in New York City. She graduated from Vassar College and earned a Ph.D. in mathematics at Yale, then taught math at Vassar. She joined the navy in 1943 and was assigned in 1944 to the Bureau of Ordnance Computation Project at Harvard where she wrote programs for the Mark I computer. In 1949 she joined Eckert-Mauchly Corporation where she helped design UNIVAC I. In the 1950s she developed a high-level language, FLOWMATIC, with which she wrote the first COBOL compiler. She helped standardize COBOL. Known as a combative, unorthodox personality, she retired from the navy reserve in 1966, but returned the following year as a rear admiral to oversee the navy computer programs.

Hopson, Howard C. (Colwell) (1882–1949) financier, utilities executive; born in Fort Atkinson, Wis. A lawyer by training, he began working for the Interstate Commerce Commission in Washington, D.C. By 1915, after seven years with the New York Public Service Commission, he set up H. C. Hopson and Co. to serve as a consultant to public utilities. In 1921, with help from his sisters, he acquired the holding company, Associated Gas and Electric Co. By selling stock in this company, he bought utility companies until by 1925 he had at least 250 companies providing utilities to people from the Philippines to the Canadian Maritime Provinces. His financial wizardry was defeated by the stock market crash of 1929, the Public Utilities Holding Company Act of 1935, and the suit for fraud brought against him by Associated stockholders after the company filed bankruptcy in 1941. Found guilty of defrauding stockholders of $20 million, he was sentenced to prison.

Hormel, George A. (Albert) (1860–1946) meatpacker; born in Buffalo, N.Y. After working in various jobs throughout the midwest, he settled in Austin, Minn., where he opened a butchers and meat packers partnership (1887). That dissolved and in 1891 he opened George A. Hormel and Company. His meat packing business not only flourished but he was among the leaders in the U.S.A. in providing better wages and hours for his workers. In 1927 he retired to Bel Air, Calif., turning the company over to his son Jay Catherwood Hormel (1892–1954), who brought about significant innovations in products, introducing canned ham, beef stew, and in 1937, "Spam."

Hornaday, William Temple (1854–1937) naturalist, conservationist; born near Plainfield, Ind. Raised on farms in Indiana and Iowa, he pursued a childhood interest in wildlife at the Iowa State Agricultural College. A self-taught taxidermist, he built up substantial fauna collections for the National Museum in Washington, D.C. In 1896 he became the first director of the New York Zoological Park – the Bronx Zoo – and was an effective spokesman for wildlife protection to the end of his life.

Hornbeck, Stanley K. (1883–1966) diplomat; born in Franklin, Mass. A Rhodes scholar and the author of eight books, he had a distinguished career in government service. He was chief of the State Department Division of Far Eastern Affairs (1928–37), a special adviser to Secretary of State Cordell Hull (1937–44) and ambassador to the Netherlands (1944–47).

Hornblower, Josiah (1729–1809) inventor, public official; born in Staffordshire, England. Hired by Col. John Schuyler, he emigrated to New Jersey (1753), bringing engine parts that were later assembled into the first steam engine in America (1755); it was used to pump water from a copper mine. He was a member of the New Jersey legislature (1779–81), the Continental Congress (1785–86), and judge of the Essex County Court (1798–1809).

Horne, Lena (Calhoun) (1917–) singer, actress; born in New York City. Raised by her actress mother, by age 16 she was dancing at Harlem's Cotton Club; with her stunning looks and electric voice, she soon became a popular singer with bands such as those of Noble Sissle and Teddy Wilson, and she performed in the musical *Blackbirds of 1939*. By 1938 she was making movies and she became the first African-American to be signed to a long-term contract (although her scenes were sometimes excised for distribution in the South). The title song of the movie *Stormy Weather* (1943) became her signature. She was blacklisted in the early 1950s for little more than her friendship with Paul Robeson and her outspokenness about discrimination, but she performed in the musical *Jamaica* (1957) and later made several movies. She toured Europe and the United States as a nightclub singer, spoke out increasingly against racism, and published her autobiography, *Lena* (1965).

Horne, Marilyn (1934–) mezzo-soprano; born in Bradford, Pa. She studied with Lotte Lehman and others in California, making her operatic debut in Los Angeles in 1954. From 1956 she sang several years in Europe, then appeared in San Francisco in 1960, where her Marie in *Wozzeck* was acclaimed. She settled into an active career on stage and in recitals, making her Metropolitan Opera debut in 1970. Her other well-known roles include Carmen.

Horner, Charles Albert (1936–) aviator; born in Davenport, Iowa. In an Air Force career that began in 1958, he served in various operational and staff posts and became commander of the 9th Air Force in 1987. He directed U.S. air operations in the war against Iraq in 1991.

Horner, Henry (b. Levy) (1878–1940) governor; born in Chicago. A Chicago lawyer, he served as Cook County probate judge (1914–32), demanding fair fees from undertakers and probate lawyers. As Democratic governor of Illinois (1932–40), he rescued the state from bankruptcy and improved schools and roads. He rejected the machine Democrats' bill, which led to bitter primary battles weakening his health.

Horney, Karen (b. Danielsen) (1885–1952) psychiatrist, psychoanalyst; born near Hamburg, Germany. Raised by a strict Norwegian father and a more liberal Dutch mother, she lived out tensions in her youth that would provide many of the themes of her later work. While a medical student in Germany, she married a fellow student (1909) and they had three children. Her personal/emotional life was already under great strain by 1915 and she underwent Freudian analysis with Karl Abraham. She herself began to take on patients for analysis in 1919 and would be affiliated with the Berlin Psychoanalytic Clinic and Institute until 1932, when she was invited to the Chicago Institute for Psychoanalysis; separated from her husband, feeling the Berlin psychoanalytic atmosphere too oppressive, fearing the threat of Nazism, she went to Chicago. Meanwhile, during the 1920s she had already begun to publish a series of papers that would take issue with some of the major tenets of orthodox Freudianism and she would continue her often lonely fight, in particular to have women's distinctive psychosexual issues

considered. During the 1930s she would also develop theories about the importance of sociocultural factors in human development, as opposed to purely intrapsychic ones, theories since incorporated into contemporary psychology but which at the time were considered heretical by many Freudians. After two years in Chicago (1932–34), she moved to New York City, where she built up a private practice while teaching at the New York Psychoanalytic Institute and the New School for Social Research. She soon fell out with the orthodox Freudians there, and with Clara Thompson, Erich Fromm, and other prominent psychoanalysts, she founded the Association for the Advancement of Psychoanalysis (1941), which also established its own training institute and professional journal, the *American Journal of Psychoanalysis,* of which she served as an editor (1941–55). These institutions became the base of her influence, in turn communicated by her magnetic lectures and such books as *Our Inner Conflicts* (1945) and *Neurosis and Human Growth* (1950). A difficult woman to get close to – usually reserved but occasionally insensitive to others – she remained at the center of the storm in New York and international psychoanalytical circles, but in the years following her death she has been recognized as a major figure in the psychoanalytical movement.

Hornsby, Rogers (1896–1963) baseball player; born in Winters, Texas. During his 23-year career as a second baseman, mostly with the St. Louis Cardinals and Chicago Cubs (1915–37), he posted a lifetime batting average of .358, the second highest in major league history. Three times he batted over .400 in a season, his 1924 average of .424 being the highest ever in modern major league baseball. An outspoken and controversial player, he also managed the Cardinals, Cubs, Boston Braves, and St. Louis Browns between 1925 and 1953. Nicknamed, "The Rajah," he was elected to baseball's Hall of Fame in 1942.

Hornung, Paul (Vernon) (1935–) football player; born in Louisville, Ky. A Heisman Trophy-winning quarterback at Notre Dame, he became an All-NFL (National Football League) halfback with the Green Bay Packers, scoring a season-record 176 points in 1960.

Horsford, Eben Norton (1818–93) chemist; born in Moscow (now Livonia), N.Y. He was professor at Harvard (1847–63) and developed one of the first labs in America for analytic chemistry. He invented baking powder and founded Rumford Chemical Company in 1856 to produce it. He also made rations composed of grain and meat for the military during the Civil War.

Horsmanden, Daniel (1694–1778) jurist; born in Purleigh, England. Admitted to the Middle Temple in London in 1724, he had emigrated to New York by 1731. He used contacts from England to obtain a seat on the New York Supreme Court. Known as a "political jurist," he lost all his offices in a shift of political fortune in 1747. He recoverd lost ground, however, and returned to the New York Supreme Court in 1753. He became its chief justice in 1763, though in his later years illness prevented him from carrying out his duties.

Hosack, David (1769–1835) physician; born in New York City. He became professor of materia medica at Columbia University (1797–1811) and taught the theory and practice of medicine at New York's College of Physicians and Surgeons (1811–26). He was one of the first physicians to use the stethoscope and to advocate vaccination; he was the first

American surgeon to ligate the femoral artery (1808). In 1804, he was attending surgeon at the Aaron Burr-Alexander Hamilton duel. He helped found Bellevue Hospital (1820).

Hosler, Charles (Luther, Jr.) (1924–) meteorologist, university administrator; born in Honey Brook, Pa. He spent his entire academic career at Pennsylvania State University, joining the faculty in 1948, becoming a full professor in 1958. In 1985 he became senior vice-president for research and dean of the graduate school, retiring in 1992. His meteorological research focused on cloud physics and dynamics for the purpose of weather modification.

Hosmer, Harriet Goodhue (1830–1908) sculptor; born in Watertown, Mass. Raised as a tomboy by her father, she attended school in Lenox, Mass., where she made lifelong friends who encouraged her to study sculpture and anatomy. She lived and worked in Italy and England (1852–1900), creating sentimental works – such as *Puck* (1856) and *Zenobia* (1862). She kept a large studio of stonecutters busy with commissions from American, English, and European patrons, and was the first and most successful American female sculptor of her era. She returned to Watertown, Mass., in 1900.

Hotchkiss, Benjamin Berkeley (1826–85) inventor; born in Watertown, Conn. He worked with his brother, Andrew Hotchkiss, to develop an improved type of cannon shell. He manufactured the shells in New York City and received more orders from the Union army (1861–65) than all other manufacturers combined. He invented the Hotchkiss revolving-barrel machine gun (1872). He spent the final years of his life in France (1871–85) where he organized Hotchkiss and Company (1882). He was the most expert artillery engineer in the world and his magazine rifle (1875) became the standard in both the British and French armies.

Hotelling, Harold (1895–1973) economist; born in Fulda, Minn. He was a pioneering economic and statistical theorist who taught at Stanford (1924–31) and Columbia University (1931–46) before establishing a department of mathematical statistics at the University of North Carolina in 1946. His reputation was based on relatively few published articles, but they launched many ideas regarding the economics of location and the "new" welfare economics. His paper, "The Economics of Exhaustible Resources," (*Journal of Political Economy*, April 1931) was "rediscovered" after the oil crisis of 1973.

Houdini, Harry (b. Ehrich Weiss) (1874–1926) magician, escapologist; born in Budapest, Hungary. The son of a rabbi, he emigrated to Appleton, Wisconsin, and borrowed the name of a French magician. An established vaudeville star in England and America by 1900, he specialized in escaping from padlocked chains, cells, straitjackets, and underwater boxes. His escapes in public locales were covered in the international press and in 1910 he started a company to film his feats. Founder of the Society of American Magicians, he campaigned against mind readers and mediums who claimed to possess supernatural powers, but he encouraged attempts to contact him through a medium after his death.

Houdry, Eugene Jules (1892–1962) chemical engineer, inventor; born in Domont, France. By 1927 he had developed a method for extracting high-quality gasoline by catalytically "cracking" low-grade crude oil. In 1930 he emigrated to America to advance this "Houdry process," which soon revolutionized the production of gasoline around the world. During World War II he developed a method for producing synthetic rubber. Holder of over 100 patents, he also founded the Oxy-Catalyst company to research cancer.

Hough, Jerry F. (1935–) political scientist; born in Salina, Kans. Teaching at the University of Illinois: Urbana (1961–68), the University of Toronto (1968–73), and Duke University (1973), he was named a staff member of the Brookings Institute (1979) and director of Investment & Communication at Duke's Center on East-West Trade (1987). His research focused mainly on Eastern European governments and their transition in the latter part of the 20th century. His books on this theme include *Soviet Leadership in Transition* (1980) and *The Polish Crisis: American Policy Options* (1982).

Houghton, Henry (Garret) (1905–87) meteorologist; born in New York City. At the Massachusetts Institute of Technology (1928–87) he helped found the National Center for Atmospheric Research in 1960 and was the first chairman of its parent organization, the University Corporation for Atmospheric Research. He trained meteorologists during World War II and researched atmospheric radiation.

Houghton, Henry Oscar (1823–95) publisher; born in Sutton, Vt. In 1848 he launched Riverside Press printers and in 1864 started the distinguished publishing firm that evolved into Houghton, Mifflin; the company, a descendant of Ticknor & Fields, published such authors as Henry Wadsworth Longfellow, Nathaniel Hawthorne, Robert Browning, and Charles Dickens.

House, (Edward Mandell) "Colonel" (1858–1938) diplomat; born in Houston, Texas. Born into wealth and successful in business, he devoted himself to Democratic politics, refusing all public offices. A close adviser to Texas governors (1892–1904), he became President Woodrow Wilson's closest adviser, first attempting mediation during World War I (1914–17), then handling all important dealings with the Allies (1917–18). He helped formulate Wilson's Fourteen Points and assisted Wilson in the postwar peace negotiations, but their relationship was severely strained when Wilson proved far less willing to compromise than was House. After Wilson returned to the U.S.A. (1919) and became ill, he never again met with House. Although House maintained his personal contacts with many prominent people at home and abroad, he never again exercised much influence on public affairs.

House, John Henry (1845–1936) missionary, educator; born in Painesville, Ohio. A Congregational minister, he devoted his life to missionary work. In Bulgaria (1874–91) he directed the American College and Theological Institute; in Salonika, Greece (1894–1931) he was founding director of the American Farm School (1902–27), which is still an important institution for training young Greeks in methods of modern agriculture.

House, Royal (Earl) (1814–95) inventor; born in Rockland, Vt. Raised in Pennsylvania, he had no formal education but showed great mechanical aptitude at an early age. In 1844, after several years of effort, he perfected a telegraph that printed out messages in the alphabet; improved Morse systems gradually superseded his printing telegraphs during the 1850s. He later designed efficient glass insulators.

Houseman, John (b. Jacques Haussman) (1902–88) stage and film director, producer, and actor; born in Bucharest,

Rumania. Educated in England, he arrived in America in 1925 representing his father's grain business. He began to devote himself to writing and translating, then moved over to the theater, coming to notice with his directorial debut, *Four Saints in Three Acts* (1934). He joined the Federal Theater Project, then cofounded with Orson Welles the Mercury Theatre (1937) and was closely associated with several of Welles's early productions, including *Citizen Kane*. After serving during World War II as chief of the overseas radio division of the Office of War Information, he commuted between Hollywood and New York as a producer and director. In the early 1970s he served as director of the new acting school and touring company of the Juilliard Academy and then enjoyed an unexpected new life as an actor after his role as the acerbic law professor in *The Paper Chase* (1973).

Houser, Allen C. (?1915–   ) Chiricahua Apache sculptor; born in Apache, Okla. The great-great-grandson of Geronimo, he garnered numerous honors and awards and exhibited widely around the world. In 1962 he was appointed head of the department of sculpture at Santa Fe's Institute of American Indian Arts.

Houston, Charles H. (Hamilton) (1895–1950) lawyer; born in Washington, D.C. A graduate of Amherst College (1915) and Harvard Law School (1922), he taught and served as vice-dean at Howard University (1915–35) and practiced law in Washington (1924–50). He initiated the strategy for many celebrated civil rights cases brought before the U.S. Supreme Court by the National Association for the Advancement of Colored People, and through his position at Howard, he guided and inspired several generations of African-Americans who would go on to prominent legal careers.

Houston, (Samuel) Sam (1793–1863) Texas leader, public official; born near Lexington, Va. He received little schooling and lived for three years among the Cherokee Indians (1809–12). He served in the War of 1812 (1813–14) and studied law. He served in the House of Representatives (Dem., Tenn.; 1823–27) and was governor of Tennessee (1827–29). He resigned the governorship and again lived among the Cherokee Indians. Attracted to the struggle for Texan independence, he led the Texan army at the battle of San Jacinto (1836) and became the first president of the Republic of Texas (1836–38, second term 1841–44). After the admission of Texas as a state, he became a senator (Dem., Texas; 1846–59). He was the governor of Texas (1859–61) but was deposed (1861) when he refused to swear allegiance to the Confederate States of America.

Hovenden, Thomas (1840–95) painter; born in Dummanway, Ireland. He emigrated to America in 1863 and was based in Philadelphia. A deeply sympathetic man, he is known for his genre studies of black Americans, such as *Breaking Home Ties* (1890). He died trying to save a young girl from an onrushing train.

Hovhaness, Alan (b. Chakmajian) (1911–   ) composer; born in Somerville, Mass. Of Scottish as well as Armenian descent, he showed an early interest in both composing and mysticism. He studied at the New England Conservatory in the 1920s and added an awareness of the music of India to that of his Armenian heritage; later he would spend time in Asia and add yet another strand to his own often exotic compositions. Legendarily prolific, usually working with commissions or grants, he went through several periods or styles but most of his work has a religious element and is mellifluous if distinctive.

Hoving, Thomas (Pearsall Field) (1931–   ) museum director, editor; born in New York City. He studied at Princeton (B.A. 1953; M.F.A. 1958; Ph.D. 1959). He began his career as an assistant curator at the Cloisters (1959–60), then progressed to assistant curator at the Metropolitan Museum (1960–63), associate curator (1963–65), curator (1965–66), and director (1967–77). His one year away from the Metropolitan was to serve as administrator of New York City's department of Recreation and Cultural Affairs (1966–67). He was editor-in-chief of the magazine, *Connoisseur* (1981–92). He is credited by some with revitalizing the acquisition program of the Metropolitan Museum and putting together extravagant and popular exhibitions, but others criticized his approach as having compromised too much the interests of the serious art lover. In addition to his early scholarly articles, he published popular works such as the memoir, *Making the Mummies Dance: Inside the Metropolitan Museum* (1993).

Hoving, Walter (1897–1989) retail executive; born in Stockholm, Sweden. He emigrated to the U.S.A. as a child. During his long career in merchandising he became known for his impeccable taste and high standards. He was president of Lord & Taylor, New York (1936–46), then founded Hoving Corporation (1946), which owned Bonwit Teller and Tiffany and Co. As chairman of Tiffany's (1955–80) he restored the store's faded cachet and profitability.

Howard, Bronson (Crocker) (1842–1908) playwright; born in Detroit, Mich. He was one of the first Americans both to use indigenous subjects and to make a living as a playwright. One of his best-known plays is *The Young Mrs. Winthrop* (1882).

Howard, Charles P. (Perry) (1879–1938) labor leader; born in Harvel, Ill. A printer, he was elected president of the International Typographical Union (1923, 1926–38). A proponent of industrial unionism, he was a founder of the Congress of Industrial Organizations.

Howard, Jacob Merritt (1805–71) U.S. representative/senator; born in Shaftsbury, Vt. A lawyer in Detroit, Mich. (1833–62), he was a Whig congressman (1841–43) who later helped organize the new Republican Party. As a senator (1862–71) he favored harsh reconstruction measures.

Howard, Oliver Otis (1830–1909) soldier; born in Leeds, Maine. He graduated from Bowdoin College and then West Point (1854). Stonewall Jackson's famous flank attack routed Howard's XI Corps at Chancellorsville (May 1863), and his command gave way before Confederate assaults on the first day at Gettysburg two months later. Transferred to the West, he led a wing of Gen. William Sherman's army in the March to the Sea (1864). An officer of strong humanitarian and religious convictions, Howard headed the Freedman's Bureau (1865–72). He helped found Howard University in Washington, D.C., which is named for him, and he served as its first president (1869–74). He took part in the Nez Perce Indian war (1877) and served as superintendent of West Point (1881–82). After retiring from the army (1894), he was involved in various educational and religious projects. He also wrote on historical and military subjects and published a two-volume autobiography.

Howard, Richard (Joseph) (1929–   ) poet, critic, translator; born in Cleveland, Ohio. As a poet he became known for his historical dramatic monologues; *Untitled Subjects* (1969) won a Pulitzer Prize. His many translations introduced modern French fiction to American audiences; his verse translation of Baudelaire's *Les Fleurs du mal* (1983) won an American Book Award.

Howard, Sidney (Coe) (1891–1939) playwright; born in Oakland, Calif. His career had many ups and downs, although his first commercial success, *They Knew What They Wanted* (1924), a comedy about grape growers, won a Pulitzer Prize. He also wrote numerous screenplays, including that for *Gone With The Wind* (1939).

Howe, Elias (1819–67) inventor; born in Spencer, Mass. As a boy, he tinkered with the machinery in his father's sawmill; in 1835 he went to work as an apprentice in a Lowell, Mass., cotton mill. He later built and patented the world's first sewing machine (1846) but no U.S. manufacturer was interested. He attempted with some success to introduce his machine to the English market; returning to the U.S.A. in 1847, he found his patent had been infringed. After a five-year court fight his patent rights were restored (1854), and he earned a fortune – sometimes as much as $4,000 a week – from his invention. During the Civil War he served as a private in a New England regiment he recruited and equipped.

Howe, George (1886–1955) architect; born in Worcester, Mass. He graduated from Harvard and the École des Beaux-Arts, Paris. At first designing fashionable arts and crafts-inspired houses with Mellor and Meigs, Philadelphia, in 1928 he reevaluated his work and in partnership with William Lescaze (1929–34) introduced the International Style to America in such buildings as the Philadelphia Savings Fund Society Building (1929–32), Philadelphia. Howe further promoted modernism by sponsoring the journals *T-Square* and *Shelter*.

Howe, Irving (1920–93) literary critic, biographer; born in New York City. He was educated at City College (where he joined the faculty in 1963) and was associated with the "New York intellectuals" in the 1940s. Howe's career is notable for blending socialist activism and literary and cultural criticism. Founder and editor of *Dissent* (1954), his numerous essays and books concern most notably the American novel, the position of literary intellectuals in modern America, and New York's Jewish immigrants.

Howe, James Wong (b. Wong Tung Jim) (1899–1976) cinematographer; born in Canton, China. In the U.S.A. from the age of five, he entered films in 1917 and became a director of photography in 1922. A meticulous lighting cameraman, he was renowned for his low-key lighting and was a pioneer in hand-held cameras and deep focus. He won Academy Awards for his photography in *The Rose Tattoo* (1955) and *Hud* (1963) before turning to directing.

Howe, Julia Ward (1819–1910) writer, reformer, poet; born in New York City. She was educated privately, married Samuel Gridley Howe (1843), and lived mainly in Boston. A social reformer, she and her husband edited *The Commonwealth,* an antislavery paper in Boston, and she was a tireless worker, writer, and lecturer for social causes, particularly for the woman-suffrage international peace movements. She also wrote poetry, but is known today for only one poem, "The Battle Hymn of the Republic" (1861), which she wrote after visiting Union troops camped outside Washington, D.C.

Howe, Louis M. (McHenry) (1871–1936) presidential adviser; born in Indianapolis, Ind. A brilliant, chronically ill New York journalist, he ran Franklin Delano Roosevelt's state senate campaign in 1912, thereafter serving as his secretary (1913–35). He is credited with convincing Roosevelt to remain in politics after polio crippled him in 1921, training Mrs. Roosevelt to campaign, and devising the strategy for his gubernatorial races. When Roosevelt assumed the presidency, Howe continued to be one of the most intimate advisers with influence exceeding his job title of White House secretary.

Howe, Oscar (1915–83) Yankton Sioux painter; born in Joe Creek, S.D. He served as art director at the Pierre (S.D.) Indian School (1953–57) and as professor and artist-in-residence at the University of South Dakota (1957–81). His many exhibitions and illustrated books won numerous awards. In 1960 he was named South Dakota Artist Laureate.

Howe, Samuel Gridley (1801–76) physician, social reformer; born in Boston, Mass. Immediately after taking his M.D. from Harvard (1824), he sailed for Greece to serve as a surgeon during the Greeks' independence struggle against the Turks; he stayed in Greece until 1830 to help build the new nation. Back in Boston, in 1832 he became the first director of a new school for the blind and remained as its head until his death; it became the Perkins Institute for the Blind and he achieved international acclaim for helping educate the blind deaf-mute Laura Dewey Bridgman. He supported Horace Mann's efforts on behalf of public education, helped Dorothea Dix in her campaign for humane treatment of the mentally ill, and fought for prison reform; in the late 1840s he founded the Massachusetts School for Idiotic and Feeble-Minded Youth (now the Walter E. Fernald State School). An opponent of slavery, he and his wife, Julia Ward Howe, whom he married in 1843, published the *Commonwealth* (1853), an abolitionist newspaper; he actively supported the Underground Railway, vigorously opposed the Kansas-Nebraska Act (1854), and secretly aided John Brown. He also continued to work on behalf of the Greeks, returning to Crete in 1866–67 during an uprising against the Turks. But for all his progressive views, he was a man of his time who opposed his wife's public activities and their marriage was strained during its early decades to the point that divorce was considered.

Howell, Albert Summers (1879–1951) inventor, camera manufacturer; born in West Branch, Mich. He was an apprentice machinist and a tool and die technician in Chicago (1905–07). He joined with Don J. Bell to form the Bell and Howell Company (1907). He designed a 35-millimeter movie projector (patented in 1907) and camera (patented 1909), and a continuous printer to reproduce films that made the mass distribution of movies possible (1911). He created the first inexpensive camera for the amateur photographer (1922) and continued to develop new equipment after his official retirement in 1938. Along with Thomas Edison and George Eastman, he was elected an honorary life member of the American Society of Cinematographers.

Howell, F. (Francis) Clark (1925–) physical anthropologist; born in Kansas City, Mo. A professor at the University of Chicago (1955–70) before becoming a professor at the University of California: Berkeley (1970), he wrote extensively on African ecology and paleoanthropology. His expedition to Ethiopia (1969) revealed teeth and jaw fragments demonstrating that human australopithecoid ancestors existed four million years ago, rather than two million, as previously believed.

Howells, William Dean (1837–1920) writer; born in Martin's Ferry, Ohio. He was self-educated, worked in his father's print shop, and became a journalist and editor for the *Ohio State Journal,* Columbus, Ohio (1856–61). After writing a biography of Abraham Lincoln, he was appointed U.S. consul in Venice, Italy (1861–65), then returned to live near Boston. There he was associated with the *Atlantic Monthly* as assistant editor (1866–71), and as editor in chief (1871–81). He moved to New York City to write columns for *Harper's Monthly* (1886–91; 1900–20), and he wrote novels, poetry, plays, literary criticism, travel books, and short stories. As a literary critic he stressed the need for realism, morality, and edification. His major novels – *The Rise of Silas Lapham* (1885) and *A Hazard of New Fortunes* (1890) – exhibited these qualities and have retained their status as fine examples of their kind.

Howells, William W. (White) (1908–   ) physical anthropologist; born in New York City. He served the American Museum of Natural History (1932–43), and was a professor at the University of Wisconsin (1939–54) before becoming a curator at the Peabody Museum, Harvard (1955–74). He made major contributions to mathematical anatomic analyses of the human head. His craniometric and historical studies in Oceania (1966–72) resulted in his popular book, *The Pacific Islanders* (1973). He opposed Carleton Coon and Franz Weidenreich by claiming that contributions of Neanderthal genes to modern humans are virtually negligible.

Howison, George Holmes (1834–1916) philosopher; born in Montgomery County, Md. After graduating from an Ohio seminary (1855), he became a teacher; while teaching political economy at Washington University in St. Louis (1866–69) he was attracted to idealist philosophy and went to study in Europe (1880–82). From 1884 to 1911 he headed a new philosophy department at the University of California: Berkeley. His books include *Limits of Evolution, and Other Essays Illustrating the Metaphysical Theory of Personal Idealism* (1901).

Howlin' Wolf (nickname of Chester Arthur Burnett) (1910–76) musician; born in West Point, Miss. A blues singer, bandleader, and larger-than-life personality, he was one of the giants of post-World War II electric blues whose songs were a staple of rock's early repertoire. He toured extensively between 1955–75, including concert and television appearances with the Rolling Stones in 1965, the year after the release of his only pop hit, "Smokestack Lightning." He was inducted into the Rock 'n' Roll Hall of Fame in 1991.

Howze, Hamilton Hawkins (1908–   ) aviator; born in West Point, N.Y. A West Point graduate, he directed the Army Tactical Mobility Board (1962) that developed a new doctrine of air mobility that U.S. forces tested in Vietnam during the 1960s. After retiring in 1965 he became an executive and later a consultant for the Bell Helicopter Co.

Hoxie, Vinnie (b. Ream) (1847–1914) sculptor; born in Madison, Wis. She studied at Christian College, Columbia, Mo., lived in Washington, D.C., and, the first woman sculptor to be commissioned by the U.S. government, she created a marble statue of Lincoln for the rotunda in Washington, D.C. (1866–71).

Hoyt, Charles Hale (1860–1900) playwright; born in Concord, N.H. A successful writer of farces, he later moved more toward social satire, lampooning the railroads in *A Hole in the Ground* (1887), and prohibition in *A Temperance Town* (1893).

Hoyt, Jesse (1815–82) businessman; born in New York City. He worked as a grocery clerk until 1838 when he formed, with his father, James M. Hoyt & Son, a flour and grain commission house. At his father's death in 1854, the hugely successful business was renamed Jesse Hoyt & Co. Interested in developing the west, in 1851 he began buying large tracts of timberland in the Saginaw Valley of Michigan where he established a lumber company, a small town, and a ship yard. He discovered and mined the abundant salt deposits and promoted the development of several railroads in the western Great Lakes area.

Hrdlička, Aleš (1869–1943) physical anthropologist; born in Humpolec, Bohemia (now Czechoslovakia). He arrived in the U.S.A. in 1882. After earning two M.D. degrees (1892, 1894) he was on the staff of the American Museum of Natural History (1899–1903) before moving to the National Museum of Natural History (1903–43, curator from 1910). His extensive anatomical research – specifically, comparative studies of bodily and skeletal measurements of living and dead populations – led to his being one of the first to argue that North and South American Indians derived from a racial stock that originated in Asia and migrated to the Americas across the Bering Strait. But for decades he used his authority and reputation to oppose all evidence that the first Americans had come over before about 4,000 years ago.

Hrdy, Sarah (C.) Blaffer (1946–   ) primatologist; born in Dallas, Texas. She was an instructor in anthropology at the University of Massachusetts (1973), then became a lecturer and fellow in biology at Harvard (1975–78). She became an associate at Harvard's Peabody Museum (1979), and concurrently joined the University of California: Davis as a professor (1984). She made major contributions to studies of the evolution of primate social behavior, including feminist interpretations of female primate reproductive strategies in evolution and history.

Hubbard, Bernard Rosecrans (1888–1962) Jesuit priest, explorer, photographer; born in San Francisco. Called the "Glacier Priest," between 1927 and the mid-1950s he made countless expeditions to Alaska. He led the first winter ascent of Mount Karmai (1932) and lived with Eskimos on King Island (1937–38). His lectures, writings, and photography introduced the little-known territory of Alaska to Americans.

Hubbard, Elbert (1856–1915) writer, craft colonist; born in Bloomington, Ill. After years as a successful businessman, he established in 1893 the Roycrofters, a craft community in East Aurora, New York. Following the ideals of William Morris, the artisans produced mission style furniture and art nouveau household accessories in metal and leather. Hubbard edited the Roycrofters monthly, *The Philistine,* in which appeared "A Message to Garcia" (1899), embodying his ideas on a community of workers.

Hubbard, Gardiner Greene (1822–97) lawyer, businessman; born in Boston, Mass. The son of a Massachusetts judge, he was an 1841 Dartmouth graduate and practiced law in Boston and Washington, D.C. A civic leader, he helped introduce gaslight to Cambridge, Mass., took a leading role in building one of the country's first streetcar lines, and helped develop and expand telephone service. His daughter's deafness led to his interest in problems of the deaf and he was president of a school for the deaf in Northampton, Mass. He served 12 years on the Massachusetts Board of Education and, with his son-in-law Alexander Graham Bell, founded the journal *Science.* He was founder and first president (1888–97) of the National Geographic Society.

Hubbard, (Lafayette Ronald) L. Ron (1911–86) science fiction writer, cult leader; born in Tilden, Nebr. He studied at George Washington University (1930–34) and then pursued a variety of activities, including exploring, but he mostly concentrated on his writing, usually science-fiction (often under pen names such as Winchester Remington Colt, Eldron, Frederick Englehardt, Michael Keith, and Tom Esterbrook). He attended Princeton in 1945. In 1950 he published *Dianetics,* a system of attaining mental health he developed. Its success led to his founding of the Church of Scientology in 1954; as this began to attract increasing numbers of believers, he began to receive as much as $100 million a year in sales and donations; by 1966 he had taken refuge on a large yacht and became ever more elusive in his whereabouts and motives. In 1980 the Internal Revenue Service challenged the tax-exempt status of his "church of scientology." Rumors continued to swirl about him in his final years, as his followers regarded him as a brilliant prophet and therapist, and his detractors saw him as a con man and charlatan.

Hubbert, M. (Marion) King (1903–89) geologist; born in San Saba, Texas. He taught geology at Columbia University (1931–41), worked as a researcher and consultant for Shell Oil (1943–63), and became a geophysicist for the U.S. Geological Survey (1964–76) while concurrently serving as a visiting professor at major U.S. universities. His studies on the physics of subterranean fluid movement led to revolutionary changes in oil and gas production technology.

Hubble, Edwin (Powell) (1889–1953) astronomer; born in Marshfield, Mo. A high school athlete in Wheaton, Ill., he lettered in basketball and track at the University of Chicago. A Rhodes scholar at Oxford, he read law and boxed in an exhibition match against the French champion, George Carpentier. After one year of practicing law in Louisville, Ky. (1913), he went back to the University of Chicago and took up astronomy. In 1917 George Ellery Hale, attracted by Hubble's observational skill, offered him a post at the Mt. Wilson Observatory at Pasadena, Calif.; but with the American entry into World War I, Hubble enlisted in the infantry. After serving as a ballistician in France, he joined Hale at Mt. Wilson and began observing with the newly installed 100-inch telescope (1919). By 1924 he had established that there are galaxies other than the Milky Way. In 1929, he was able to demonstrate that the galaxies were receding from ours, thus proving that the universe was still expanding. (The numerical relationship between a galaxy's distance and the speed of recession is known as "Hubble's Constant.") These and other of his findings had major impact on the study of cosmology. By 1948 he shifted to the still larger (200-inch) telescope on Mt. Palomar, where he worked until his death. The Hubble Space Telescope, deployed in space in 1990, was named after him.

Hubel, David H. (Hunter) (1926–) neurophysiologist; born in Windsor, Ontario, Canada. He worked at Montreal Neurological Institute (1952–54), then came to the U.S.A. to join Johns Hopkins (1954–55). He moved to the Walter Reed Army Institute for Research (1955–58), then to the Wilmer Institute of Johns Hopkins (1958–59), where he met vision specialist Torsten Wiesel. Hubel moved to Harvard (1959) to continue collaborating with Wiesel on studies relating retinal function to visual perception as interpreted by the brain. For their discoveries, Hubel and Wiesel received one-half the 1981 Nobel Prize in physiology.

Hudson, Fredric (1819–75) journalist; born in Quincy, Mass. Called the "father of modern journalism," he skillfully supervised coverage of the Civil War by the *New York Herald,* with which he was associated from 1837 to 1866.

Hudson, J. L. (Joseph Lowthian) (1846–1912) merchant; born in Newcastle-on-Tyne, England. His family moved to Grand Rapids, Mich., from Canada in 1860. By 1866 he was managing his father's clothing store. In 1881 he opened J. L. Hudson, an innovative men and boys clothing store in Detroit that offered moderate prices, immediate delivery, and customer returns. He incorporated in 1891 and expanded into other midwestern cities. Active in business and civic affairs, he founded the Detroit Municipal League. By 1912 his was the largest retail store in Michigan, with sales of $3.5 million.

Hudson, Manley Ottmer (1886–1960) lawyer, educator, judge; born in St. Peters, Mo. He graduated from William Jewell College (1906) and Harvard Law School (1910), then taught law at the University of Missouri (1910–19). In 1919 he joined the Harvard Law School faculty and took part in the Versailles Peace Conference as an adviser on international law to the U.S. delegation. Active in League of Nations affairs in the 1920s, he joined the World Court in 1936–46 and, from 1948–53, served as chairman of the United Nations' International Law Commission.

Hufstedtler, Shirley (Ann) (b. Mount) (1925–) lawyer; born in Denver, Colo. A champion of civil liberties as a federal appellate judge in California, she served briefly as the first Cabinet-level U.S. Secretary of Education (1979–81) before returning to private practice in Los Angeles.

Huggins, Charles B. (Brenton) (1901–) oncologist; born in Halifax, Nova Scotia, Canada. He came to the U.S.A. to attend Harvard Medical School (1920), then taught surgery at the University of Michigan (1926–27). At the University of Chicago (1927–62), he specialized in clinical urology, and discovered hormonal therapy for prostate cancer, for which he won one-half the 1966 Nobel Prize in physiology. He became head of Chicago's Ben May Laboratory for Cancer Research (1951–69), and Chancellor of Acadia University, Nova Scotia (1972–79). He also made major contributions to studies of bone formation, serum enzyme biochemistry, breast cancer, and treatment of leukemia.

Huggins, Miller (James) (1879–1929) baseball player/manager; born in Cincinnati, Ohio. As a second baseman, he played with the Cincinnati Reds and St. Louis Cardinals (1904–16). As manager of the New York Yankees from 1918 to 1929, he led Babe Ruth and the famous "murderer's row" clubs to six league pennants and three world championships in 12 years. He was elected to the Hall of Fame in 1964.

Hughes, Charles Evans (1862–1948) Supreme Court justice and chief justice; born in Glens Falls, N.Y. He served as governor of New York (1906–10) and was first nominated to U.S. Supreme Court by President Taft in 1910. He left the court in 1916 to run for president against Woodrow Wilson. He served as secretary of state under President's Harding and Coolidge (1921–25); he excelled in international diplomacy. President Hoover named him chief justice of the U.S. Supreme Court (1930–41), where he gained respect for balancing the conservative forces of legal procedure with the progressive forces unleashed by the Depression.

Hughes, Harold E. (1922–) governor; born in Ida Grove, Iowa. An army veteran of World War II, he served on the Iowa Commission of Commerce (1946–58). As Democratic governor of Iowa (1963–69), he increased school funding, established a Civil Rights Commission, and strengthened consumer protection programs. Resigning to go to the U.S. Senate (1969–75), he dropped out of politics because of his problems with alcohol; he later opened the Hughes Centers for Alcoholism and Drug Treatment.

Hughes, Howard (Robard) (1905–76) industrialist, aviator, movie producer; born in Houston, Texas. In 1924 he inherited the Hughes Tool Company worth $650,000; eventually it became a multimillion dollar corporation, making him fabulously rich. He went to Hollywood and produced movies such as *Hell's Angels* (1930), *Scarface* (1932), and *The Outlaw* (1943); during these years he was involved with a succession of actresses; from 1948–55 he owned RKO, Hollywood's fifth largest studio. He had learned to fly, and from 1935 to 1938 he established three major speed records, receiving a Congressional Medal of Honor in 1941. Over the years, his business dealings led to much litigation and he became increasingly more eccentric and reclusive; from 1966 until his death he lived in "germ-free" hotel suites. In 1971 Clifford Irving claimed to have written an "authorized" biography of Hughes, but it was subsequently acknowledged as a fraud. Hughes's death led to a spate of lawsuits over attempts to establish his true will and heirs.

Hughes, (James Mercer) Langston (1902–67) poet, writer, playwright, librettist; born in Joplin, Mo. After publishing his first poem, "The Negro Speaks of Rivers" (1921), he attended Columbia University for one year (1921), but left, working on a freighter to travel to Africa, living in Paris and Rome, and supporting himself with odd jobs. After his poetry was promoted by Vachel Linday, he attended Lincoln University (1925–29); while there his first book of poems, *The Weary Blues* (1926), launched his career as a writer. As one of the founders of the cultural movement known as the Harlem Renaissance – which he practically defined in his essay, "The Negro Artist and the Radical Mountain" (1926) – he was innovative in his use of jazz rhythms and dialect to depict the life of urban blacks in his poetry, stories, and plays. Having provided the lyrics for the musical *Street Scene* (1947) and the play that inspired the opera *Troubled Island* (1949), in the 1960s he returned to the stage with works that drew on black gospel music, such as *Black Nativity* (1961). A prolific writer for four decades – in his later years he completed a two-volume autobiography and edited anthologies and pictorial volumes – he abandoned the Marxism of his youth but never gave up protesting the injustices committed against his fellow African-Americans. Among his most popular creations was Jesse B. Semple, better known as "Simple," a black Everyman featured in the syndicated column he began in 1942 for the *Chicago Defender*. Because he often employed humor and seldom portrayed or endorsed violent confrontations, he was for some years disregarded as a model by black writers; but by the 1980s he was being reappraised

and was newly appreciated as a significant voice of African-Americans.

Hughes, John (Joseph) (1797–1864) Catholic prelate; born in County Tyrone, Ireland. Emigrating to the U.S.A. in 1817 and ordained in 1826, he did pastoral work in Philadelphia, and after becoming coadjutor bishop of New York (1838), succeeded four years later to the see, which was made an archdiocese in 1850. He founded St. John's (now Fordham) College (1841), set up an ambitious parochial school system, helped found the American College in Rome, and began construction of St. Patrick's Cathedral (1858). In 1861 he went on a mission to France seeking friendship for the North in the Civil War. He is now recognized as having played a crucial role in both securing Catholics' rights in the U.S.A. and in helping Catholics become integrated into American society.

Hughes, Richard (Joseph) (1909–92) governor, judge; born in Florence, N.J. A lawyer, he served as a New Jersey county and superior court judge before opening his own practice in 1957. As Democratic governor (1962–70), he fought unsuccessfully for a state income tax to improve the education system. As New Jersey Supreme Court chief justice (1974–79), he presided over the historic case that allowed Karen Ann Quinlan's parents to terminate her life-support system.

Hughes, Vernon W. (Willard) (1921–) physicist; born in Kankakee, Ill. He taught at Columbia University (1949–52) and the University of Pennsylvania (1952–54) before joining Yale (1954). He made significant contributions to radiofrequency and spectroscopy of atoms and molecules, and to studies of particle physics.

Hulett, Alta M. (1854–77) lawyer; born in Rockford, Ill. As a 17-year-old she studied law in a prominent Illinois lawyer's office and soon passed the required examination, but her application for admission to the bar was simply ignored by the Illinois court. She turned to teaching but drew up a bill rejecting sex-based discrimination in employment (except in the military and on juries); the Illinois legislature passed it in 1872. She moved to Chicago, spent another year studying law, and ended up at the head of her class (all others males). After this, in 1873 she became the first woman admitted to practice law in Illinois and had a successful practice during her last few years.

Hull, Clark L. (Leonard) (1884–1952) psychologist; born in Akron, N.Y. Educated at the Universities of Michigan and Wisconsin, he constructed an influential theory of behavior through research at Yale's Institute of Human Relations (1929–52). His theory identified the variables that intervene between stimulus and response, as outlined in his book, *A Behavior System* (1952).

Hull, Cordell (1871–1955) political leader, statesman; born in Overton County, Tenn. A Tennessee legislator and judge, Democratic national committee chairman, U.S. representative (1907–31) and senator (1931–33), he became the longest-termed secretary of state ever under President Franklin Roosevelt (1933–44). A strong advocate of free trade and of the "Good Neighbor" policy with South America during the 1930s, he early advocated strong support for the Allies, attended most of the great wartime conferences, and promoted international cooperation and the UN, for which he received the Nobel Peace Prize (1944).

Hull, Isaac (1773–1843) naval officer; born in Huntington (now Shelton), Conn. (nephew and adopted son of General

William Hull). He served in the undeclared naval war with France and the Tripolitan War. As commander of the USS *Constitution* (1810–12) he won an outstanding victory over the British *Guerrière* (1812), earning the *Constitution* the nickname of "Old Ironsides." During the next 30 years he alternated between commands of naval yards and overseas squadrons.

Hull, John (1624–83) merchant, goldsmith; born in England. He came to Boston in 1635. He became the mintmaster for Massachusetts (1652), coined the colony's pine tree emblem shillings (1662) and served as the colony's treasurer (1676–80).

Hull, William (1753–1825) soldier; born in Derby, Conn. A Yale graduate, he joined the Revolutionary forces in 1775 and saw action at White Plains, Trenton, Saratoga, and Monmouth. After the war he practiced law in Newton, Mass.; in 1805 he accepted Jefferson's offer of the governorship of the Michigan Territory. In 1812 Hull led a small army into Ontario, but retreated on the appearance of a combined British and Indian force; he withdrew into the fortifications of Detroit, where he surrendered his entire force without a battle on Aug. 16, 1812. Tried for cowardice, found guilty, and sentenced to be shot, he received a presidential reprieve and retired into obscurity.

Hulman, (Anton, Jr.) Tony (1901–77) auto racing executive; born in Terre Haute, Ind. In 1945 he purchased the Indianapolis 500 Speedway, and, after extensive renovations to the facility, he promoted the annual 500-mile race into the largest sporting event in the world.

Hulse, Russell A. (1950–) physicist; born in New York City. His discovery of a binary pulsar while a graduate assistant to Joseph Taylor, astronomy professor at the University of Massachusetts: Amherst, helped to confirm the existence of gravitational waves as predicted by Albert Einstein in his theory of relativity. For this 1974 discovery, he and Taylor were awarded the Nobel Prize in physics in 1993. At the Princeton University Plasma Physics Laboratory from 1977, Hulse studied hydrogen fusion.

Humes, Helen (1913–85) jazz musician; born in Louisville, Ky. She was a vocalist with the Count Basie Orchestra between 1938–41, a rhythm and blues stylist in the late 1940s, and a popular nightclub attraction thereafter.

Humphrey, Doris (1895–1958) modern dancer, choreographer; born in Oak Park, Ill. A student and performer in the Denishaw Company in her early years, she formed a company in New York with Charles Weidman in 1927. She staged 83 works with her company – including *The Pleasures of Counter-point* (1932) – and taught at several performing arts high schools and colleges. After retiring from performance in 1943, she served as artistic director of the José Limon Company (1946–58). An innovative influence on modern dance, she was best known for her "fall and recovery" technique; she set forth her ideas in *The Art of Making Dance* (1959).

Humphrey, George (Magoffin) (1890–1970) industrialist, cabinet member; born in Cheboygan, Mich. A lawyer, he became president of the Hanna iron ore company, and in 1929 he created National Steel which flourished despite the depression. President Eisenhower's surprising choice for secretary of the treasury (1952–56), he checked inflation and balanced the budget before returning to National Steel.

Humphrey, Hubert H. (Horatio) (1911–78) vice-president, U.S. senator; born in Wallace, S.D. He worked as a registered pharmacist before studying political science. He was mayor of Minneapolis (1946–49) and a U.S. senator (1949–64). He worked for civil rights and welfare programs while in the Senate and ran unsuccessfully for the Democratic presidential nomination in 1960. In 1964, he was chosen by Lyndon Johnson as his running mate, but as vice-president, he was handicapped by Johnson's insistence on his loyalty in all policy matters. In 1968, he won the Democratic presidential nomination but was defeated narrowly in the election by Richard Nixon. He returned to the Senate in 1971. He ran again for the Democratic nomination in 1972 but was defeated. He was diagnosed with cancer in 1976, but still returned to the Senate. His optimism won admiration during the period before his death in 1978.

Humphrey, William (1924–) writer; born in Clarksville, Texas. He studied at Southern Methodist University and the University of Texas, and then, feeling the need for literary contacts, moved to New York City in 1953. His first novel, *Home from the Hills* (1958), was well received; it is set in the Red River country of northeast Texas, the locale of most of his fiction thereafter. *The Ordways* (1965) was his second novel; a later one was *Hostages to Fortune* (1984). In addition to short stories, critical articles, and a memoir, he published many articles on his activities as an outdoorsman and two books on fishing. He lived for awhile in Italy, then returned to the U.S.A. and began the serious American writer's usual round of teaching at various colleges and universities; his longest stay was at Bard College (New York) and this led him to settle for many of his later years in Hudson, N.Y.

Humphreys, Joshua (1751–1838) shipbuilder, naval architect; born in Delaware County, Pa. Congress named him to refit eight merchant vessels as the first Continental naval vessels (1775). He was the first naval constructor (1794–1801); he designed five of the first six United States frigates and he personally supervised the building of the USS *United States* (launched in 1797).

Humphries, (George) Rolfe (1894–1969) poet, teacher; born in Philadelphia. He studied at Stanford (1912–13) and Amherst (B.A. 1915), where, after a career of teaching Latin, he returned to teach English (1957–65). He wrote poetry, but is best known for his translations, notably of Virgil, Ovid and Federico García Lorca.

Huneker, James Gibbons (1860–1921) critic, musician; born in Philadelphia. Switching from law to musical studies, he became a teacher at the National Conservatory of Music in New York City (1886–98). Meanwhile, in 1887 he had begun to write for the *Musical Courier* and he would continue to write for a series of newspapers and periodicals until his death, broadening his subjects to include drama, art, literature, and the cultural scene in general. He also published over a dozen books, including some serious studies of musicians such as *Chopin: The Man and His Music* (1900), – but mostly wide-ranging commentaries, such as *Ivory, Apes and Peacocks* (1915). In his day he was greatly admired for his keen wit, erudition, iconoclasm, and brilliant style – an American G. B. Shaw; but his tastes in art remained conservative and later generations found his prose old fashioned.

Hunsaker, Jerome (Clarke) (1886–1984) aeronautical engineer; born in Creston, Iowa. He was designer of the flying boat NC-4 – which made the first transatlantic flight (1919) – and the dirigible *Shenandoah*. He also founded the first college course in aeronautical engineering at the Massachusetts Institute of Technology (1914); while teaching there (1912–52) he developed the first modern wind tunnel in America. In charge of American naval aircraft design during World War I, he served for many years as an industry consultant.

Hunt, George (Wylie Paul) (1859–1934) governor; born in Huntsville, Mo. Settling in the silver mining town of Globe, Ariz., in 1881, he worked for the Old Dominion Commercial Company, becoming its president in 1900. He also acquired a ranch on the nearly Salt River. Supported by the silver miners union, he served on the territorial legislature and presided over the constitutional convention that led to statehood. He then became Arizona's first governor (1912–19) and returned to office twice more (1923–29, 1931–33). Although a prosperous businessman, as governor he was noted for policies that favored labor and prison reforms; alternately popular and hated, he became a nearly legendary figure in Arizona.

Hunt, H. L. (Haroldson Lafayette) (1889–1974) oil executive; born in Ramsey, Ill. He became rich from land speculation, oil lease trading, and drilling in Arkansas, Oklahoma, and Louisiana in the 1920s. After acquiring the first East Texas oil site, he founded the Dallas-based Hunt Oil Company (1936), eventually the country's largest independent oil producer. He founded Facts Forum (1951–56) and Life Line (1958) to promote his ultraconservative political views.

Hunt, Richard (Howard) (1935–   ) sculptor; born in Chicago. Based in Chicago, he studied at the Art Institute there (1953–57) and taught at many institutions. He is known for his lithographs and sculptural constructions using found objects and cast metal forms, as in *Organic Constuction #10* (1961).

Hunt, Richard Morris (1827–95) architect; born in Brattleboro, Vt. The first American admitted to the École des Beaux-Arts, Paris (1846), he worked with Hector Martin Lefuel on the Pavillion de la Bibliothèque of the Louvre (1854–55). He opened a practice (1855) and an atelier in New York, training among others Frank Furness and George B. Post. An eclectic stylist, Hunt designed numerous houses and university and public buildings in New York, including the Presbyterian Hospital (1872), the Tribune Building (1873), and Lenox Library (1877). After the 1880s he designed luxurious mansions by which he is best remembered, among them Marble House (1892) and The Breakers (1895), Newport, R.I., and the 225-room Biltmore House Asheville, N.C. (1895), the last of several Vanderbilt family commissions. A founder and third president of the American Institute of Architects (1888–91), Hunt is called the "dean of American architecture" for advancing the education and professional standards of architects.

Hunt, Ward (1810–86) Supreme Court justice; born in Utica, N.Y. He served on the New York state legislature (1838) and as mayor of Utica (1844). An early Republican Party organizer, he was elected to the U.S. Court of Appeals (1865–72) and was appointed to the U.S. Supreme Court by President Grant (1873–82).

Hunt, William Henry (1823–84) jurist, secretary of the navy; born in Charleston, S.C. He practiced law in New Orleans (1844–78). As secretary of the navy (1881–82) he appointed the first naval advisory board. He was ambassador to Russia (1882–84).

Hunt, William Morris (1824–79) painter; born in Brattleboro, Vt. (brother of Richard Morris Hunt). He studied in Germany (1845–46) and Paris (1846–56) before settling in Boston in 1862. His work was influenced by French artists of the time, and his genre paintings are romantic and somewhat sentimental, as seen in *The Bathers* (1877).

Hunter, Evan (b. Evan Lombino) (Ed McBain, Hunt Collins, Richard Marsten, pen names) (1926–   ) writer; born in New York City. He studied at Hunter (B.A. 1950), taught high school briefly in New York City, and held various other jobs. Extremely prolific, he wrote short stories, plays, and film scripts, but he is best known for his novels dealing with contemporary social issues; *The Blackboard Jungle* (1954), based on his teaching experience, was his greatest success. His 87th Precinct crime novels, written under the name of Ed McBain, have also been popular.

Hunter, (Wiles) Robert (1874–1942) socialist, social worker, writer; born in Terre Haute, Ind. Appalled by the misery of the depression of 1893, he decided to become a social worker. He was organizing secretary of Chicago's Board of Charities (1896–1902) and lived at Hull House (1899–1902). He wrote a survey of working-class housing for the City Homes Association (1901). A man of independent means, he became head worker at the University Settlement on Rivington Street, New York City (1902), directing their successful campaign to enact child labor laws (1903). He published his most important book, *Poverty* (1904), the first general statistical survey of America's poor. Declaring himself a socialist (1905), he was elected to the first executive board of the Intercollegiate Socialist Society. He was Socialist candidate for the New York state assembly (1908), he represented American socialism at the Third International in Stuttgart (1907), and having moved to Noroton, Conn., he ran as Socialist candidate for the governorship of Connecticut (1910). Antipathetic to violence and unrestrained radicalism, he published an indictment of the Industrial Workers of the World, *Violence in the Labor Movement* (1914), then left the party disillusioned because socialism had failed to prevent the outbreak of World War I. He moved to California (1918) where he lectured on economics and English at the University of California: Berkeley (1918–22). Moving to Pebble Beach, he wrote *Links* (1926), a book on golf course design, and he laid out several West Coast courses. By the end of his life, he had turned right-wing, repudiated the New Deal, and wrote *Revolution* (1940), which rejected Marxism and revolutions.

Huntington, Anna Vaughn (b. Hyatt) (1876–1973) sculptor; born in Cambridge, Mass. She studied in Boston (1890s), at the Art Students League, N.Y., with Gutzon Borglum (c. 1903), and collaborated with sculptor Abastenia St. Leger Eberle (1904). After visits to France and Italy, she and her philanthropist husband, Archer M. Huntington, founded Brookgreen Gardens near Charleston, S.C. (1931), a nature retreat and sculpture garden, now a state park. They settled in Redding Ridge, Conn. (1939) and she became famous for animal works, such as *Fighting Stallions* (1950).

Huntington, Collis P. (Potter) (1821–1900) railway builder; born in Harwinton, Conn. Starting as a peddler, he became a store owner in Oneonta, N.Y. (1842–49). With the Gold Rush, he moved to Sacramento, Calif., where he opened a store; taking on Mark Hopkins, it soon prospered as a mercantile business, Huntington & Hopkins. In 1863, he joined Leland Stanford, Charles Crocker and Hopkins to win the rights to build the western section of the transcontinental railroad; Huntington went to Washington, D.C., and New York City to arrange for financing and by 1869 their Central Pacific Railroad was linking with the Union Pacific in Utah. Known as "Huntington's group," the men launched more enterprises including the Southern Pacific Railway (1884), of which Huntington succeeded Stanford as president in 1890. Huntington remained largely in the East where he ruthlessly lobbied for his railroad's interests, with little regard for his competitors, the government, or the public. He extended his own interest to eastern transportation projects including the Chesapeake & Ohio Railway and the steamship business, becoming ever more wealthy if disreputable.

Huntington, Frederic Dan (1819–1904) Protestant clergyman; born in Hadley, Mass. He graduated from Amherst (1839) and attended Harvard Divinity School before accepting the pulpit of the South Congregational Church (Unitarian) in Boston in 1842. He taught at Harvard from 1855–60. In 1859 he joined the Episcopal church and served as rector of Emmanuel Church, Boston. In 1869 he became the first bishop of the newly created Diocese of Central New York. A reformer in politics, he opposed American imperial expansion and supported women's suffrage.

Hurd, Nathaniel (1729/30–77) engraver, silversmith; born in Boston, Mass. He worked in Boston as a silversmith and as a copperplate etcher of armorial bookplates and college seals. An early and skillful engraver, he had his portrait painted by John Singleton Copley (c. 1765).

Hurewicz, Witold (1904–56) topologist; born in Lodz, Russian Poland. Emigrating to America to teach at the University of North Carolina (1937–1945) and the Massachusetts Institute of Technology (1945–1956), he discovered higher homotopy groups and exact sequences and did major work on fiber spaces. Charming and absentminded, he died after falling off a pyramid in Uxmal, Mexico.

Hurley, Patrick J. (Jay) (1883–1963) lawyer, diplomat; born in Choctaw Nation territory (near present-day Lehigh, Okla.). Of Irish descent, he became a millionaire through his law practice and real estate investments. As secretary of war (1929–33) he dealt severely with rioting U.S. war veterans and with the Philippine independence movement. He negotiated a settlement of claims between Sinclair Oil Company and Mexico (1940) and was ambassador to China (1944–45). He became a crusading anticommunist and attacked President Truman's China Policy.

Hurok, Sol (1888–1974) impresario; born in Pogar, Russia. Coming to the U.S.A. in 1905, he began producing concerts; he became famous for managing European artists including Pavlova and Artur Rubenstein, and he helped bring to the U.S.A. Russian ensembles including the Bolshoi Ballet.

Hurst, Fannie (b. Danielson) (1889–1968) writer; born in Hamilton, Ohio. She studied at Washington University, Mo. (B.A. 1909) and Columbia University (1910–12). Settling in New York City, she held a variety of jobs ranging from working in restaurants and factories, to small acting parts in plays. Starting in 1920, she wrote an endless succession of novels, plays, screenplays, short stories, and articles. An immensely popular writer for several decades, she is best known for such novels as *Lummox* (1923), *Back Street*

(1931), and *Imitation of Life* (1933). Serious critics dismissed her work as sentimental and lacking style, but she tried to deal with women's lives and in later years she became quite outspoken in calling for reforms in many areas of contemporary society.

Hurst, James Willard (1910–) legal scholar; born in Rockford, Ill. A teacher at the University of Wisconsin: Madison (1937–80, emeritus 1981), he studied the relationship between law and society, and between the legislative and judicial processes. His books on American legal history include *Law and the Conditions of Freedom in the 19th Century U.S.* (1956) and *Law and Economic Growth* (1964).

Hurston, Zora Neale (1903–60) writer, anthropologist, folklorist; born in Eatonville, Fla. She studied at Howard University (1923–24), Barnard College (B.A. 1928), and did graduate work at Columbia University. She spent much of her life collecting folklore of the South (1927–31; 1938–39) and of other places such as Haiti (1937–38), Bermuda (1937–38), and Honduras (1946–48); she published her findings in such works as *Mules and Men* (1935). She lived in New York City and held a variety of jobs, such as teacher, librarian, and assistant to Fannie Hurst. She was associated with the Harlem Renaissance of the 1920s, and would later influence such writers as Ralph Ellison and Toni Morrison. She is best known for *Their Eyes Were Watching God* (1937), a novel celebrating the lives of African-Americans. In 1950 she moved to Florida and became increasingly conservative and alienated from her fellow African-Americans, taking a stand even against school integration. She died in poverty and was all but forgotten, but by the 1970s her works were being rediscovered and recognized for their insights.

Hussey, Obed (1791–1859) inventor, mechanical engineer; born on Nantucket Island, Mass. He invented a mowing and reaping machine, first used successfully in 1833. Cyrus McCormick sued him for patent infringment, but the patent office ruled in Hussey's favor. Although Hussey made improvements on his reaping machine and won the Great Exhibit of 1851, McCormick eventually became the leading manufacturer of reapers.

Huston, John (1906–87) film director, screenwriter, actor; born in Nevada, Mo. (son of Walter Huston; father of Anjelica Huston). After his acting debut off Broadway in 1925, he held various jobs (including a hitch in the Mexican cavalry) until 1938, when he became a scriptwriter in Hollywood; his hits included *Jezebel* (1938) and *Sergeant York* (1941), plus *The Maltese Falcon* (1941) with which he began his directorial career. After making three documentaries with the Signal Corps in World War II, he made his masterpiece, *The Treasure of the Sierra Madre* (1947), for which he won Academy Awards for best director and best screenplay. Later films he both directed and wrote include *The Asphalt Jungle* (1950), *The Red Badge of Courage* (1951), *The African Queen* (1952), and *Moby Dick* (1956). A noted *bon vivant,* gambler, sportsman, and ladies' man, he made his base in Ireland from 1952. In his later years he returned to acting in films, and he died while directing *The Dead* (1987).

Hutcheson, William (Levi) (1874–1953) labor leader; born in Saginaw County, Mich. A carpenter, he became president of the United Brotherhood of Carpenters and Joiners of America (1915–52). Active within the American Federation of Labor (AFL), he was such a conservative that he opposed

President Roosevelt's New Deal. And as a staunch proponent of craft unions, he fell out with his fellow AFL leaders over attempts to get together with the Congress of Industrial Organizations.

Hutchins, Robert Maynard (1899–1977) university president; born in New York City. He earned a B.A. and LL.B. from Yale. He made a name as one of the country's foremost – and youthful – educational innovators. He rejuvenated Yale Law School as dean (1927–29) and at the University of Chicago (president 1929–45, chancellor 1945–51), he introduced the "Chicago Plan," which included the Great Books program, the admission of high school students, and the abolition of course credits and compulsory attendance. His concentration on bolstering Chicago's undergraduate education was profoundly controversial at the primarily graduate institution. Hutchins was long associated with the Ford Foundation's Fund for the Republic and Center for the Study of Democratic Institutions (1954–74). His many books include *The Higher Learning in America* (1936) and *The University of Utopia* (1953).

Hutchinson, Abby See under HUTCHINSON FAMILY, THE.

Hutchinson, Anne (b. Marbury) (1591–1643) religious liberal; born in Alford, England. After emigrating to Boston in 1634, she began to hold discussions of sermons in her home. Eventually, she preached about a "convenant of grace" rather than the more traditional "covenant of works." She originally received support from Governor Sir Henry Vane, John Cotton, and others, but after John Winthrop became governor (1637) she was banished from Massachusetts and formally excommunicated. She and her family moved to present-day Rhode Island and then to New York, where she and most of her family were killed in an Indian raid.

Hutchinson, Asa See under HUTCHINSON FAMILY, THE.

Hutchinson, Jesse See under HUTCHINSON FAMILY, THE.

Hutchinson, John See under HUTCHINSON FAMILY, THE.

Hutchinson, Judson See under HUTCHINSON FAMILY, THE.

Hutchinson, Thomas (1711–80) colonial governor; born in Boston, Mass. (great-great grandson of Anne Hutchinson). As chief justice of the Massachusetts Superior Court, he upheld the legality of the Stamp Act (1765). He was governor of Massachusetts during the eventful period preceding the American Revolution (1771–74) and then he moved to England where he wrote a valuable history of the Massachusetts Bay colony.

Hutchinson Family, The singers; from Milford, N.H. The parents were Jesse and Mary (Leavitt) Hutchinson who had 11 living sons and two daughters, all of whom at one time sang in the family ensemble. They were originally known as the Hutchinson Family or "Tribe of Jesse" when they performed locally, singing the popular songs of the time. By 1841, however, a son, **Jesse** (1813–53), had settled in Boston, and he became the musical director and manager of a quartet made up of four of his siblings: (**Adoniram**) **Judson** (1817–59), **John** (1821–1908), **Asa** (1823–84) and **Abby** (1829–92). (Another brother, Joshua, occasionally substituted for a missing member.) They began to travel throughout New England and New York State (occasionally using the name "Aeolian Vocalists.") They soon changed their name to the Hutchinson Family and it was by that name that they performed in New York City (1842) and Great Britain (1845–46). Although not limiting their appearances to such groups, they often performed before socially progressive gatherings – temperance, aboli-

tionists, women's rights groups – or in prisons and almshouses. The brothers Judson and Jesse composed most of their songs. Judson moved to Minnesota in 1855 and helped found the town of Hutchinson. With the death of Judson (1859), they split into two ensembles – the "Tribe of John" and the "Tribe of Asa" – but both still billed themselves as the Hutchinson Family. During the Civil War they popularized such tunes as "The Battle Cry of Freedom" and "Tenting Tonight on the Old Camp Ground." In 1861 Gen. George McClellan barred their appearing in the army camps in Virginia because their antislavery songs were said to anger many soldiers; after President Lincoln had the offending verses read to him in a cabinet meeting, he said, "It is just the character of song that I desire the soldiers to hear," and the Hutchinsons were allowed to perform before the servicemen. The two Hutchinson groups – by this time including children and grandchildren of the original members – continued performing into the 1880s.

Hutton, Laurence (1843–1904) bibliophile, editor, writer; born in New York City. Left with a modest legacy, he devoted himself to amassing a fine rare book collection and writing on travel, the theater, and other congenial topics. He was literary editor of *McClure's Magazine* (1886–93) and a lecturer at Princeton University (1901–04).

Huxtable, Ada Louise (b. Landman) (?1921–   ) architectural critic; born in New York City. As architecture critic and columnist of the *New York Times* (1963–82) she denounced the despoliation of American cities by banal new buildings and property speculation; her work helped change zoning laws and promote historic preservation. She won the first Pulitzer Prize for distinguished criticism in 1970. She was named a MacArthur Fellow in 1981.

Hyatt, John (Wesley) (1837–1920) inventor; born in Starkey, N.Y. An energetic apprentice printer, he embarked on a long career as an inventor with a knife sharpener in 1861. He later developed a water filter, a multiple-needle sewing machine, and the Hyatt roller bearing, which he began producing in his own factory in 1892. His best-known discovery, made in the search of a substitute for the ivory used in billiard balls, was the plastic celluloid, which he created in 1869–70 by mixing pyroxylin, camphor, and alcohol.

Hyman, (George) Earle (1926–   ) stage actor; born in Rocky Mount, N.C. He graduated from high school in Brooklyn, N.Y. (1943), and having joined the American Negro Theatre, he appeared in their first hit, *Anna Lucasta* (1944), both on Broadway and in London. He would later study with the Actors Studio in New York, but he was most drawn to classic roles, first playing Hamlet in 1951, eventually playing Othello in productions in several countries, and appearing in ten other roles with the American Shakespeare Theatre at Stratford, Conn. Although he would occasionally find choice parts in the professional New York stage – *Mr. Johnson* (1956), *Driving Miss Daisy* (1989), *Pygmalion* (1991) – and appeared infrequently in American television and movies, he felt that his skin color denied him a full range of roles in the American theater and he spent many years acting in Europe, particularly in Norway, Sweden, and Denmark (in their languages). He won the State Award in Oslo, Norway, for instance, for his portrayal in *Emperor Jones* (1965).

Hyman, Libbie (Henrietta) (1888–1969) zoologist; born in Des Moines, Iowa. She performed research on lower invertebrates such as hydra and planaria, while working for the celebrated biologist Charles Manning Child at the University of Chicago (1916–31), and wrote the widely-used *Laboratory Manual for Elementary Zoology* (1919) and *A Laboratory Manual for Comparative Vertebrate Anatomy* (1922). She preferred working with invertebrates, and became an authority on invertebrate taxonomy. After resigning from Chicago, she spent 15 months traveling to European scientific centers, then relocated to New York City to begin writing the first of her comprehensive 6-volume reference, *The Invertebrates* (1940–68). The American Museum of Natural History offered her a research associateship (1937), which she held until her death, taking time to visit marine laboratories in the U.S.A. and South America. She lived and worked alone, and, while she often intimidated others due to her undiplomatic manner and her forceful but well-founded opinions, she held the respect of fellow scientists for her elegant research and writing. Because of ill health, she was unable to complete *The Invertebrates* to include higher mollusks and arthropods, although the finished volumes are classic examples of unspeculative research in comparative morphology and physiology.

Hymes, Dell (Hathaway) (1927–) sociolinguist; born in Portland, Ore. He graduated from Reed College in 1950, took a Ph.D at Indiana University in 1955, and taught at Harvard and Berkeley before becoming professor of folklore and linguistics at the University of Pennsylvania in 1972. He accepted a professorship of anthropology and English at the University of Virginia in 1987. An authority on the use and functions of language, he is the author of *Language and Culture in Society* (1964) and other scholarly works.

I

Iacocca, (Lido Anthony) Lee (1924–) automobile executive; born in Allentown, Pa. He had a long career at Ford Motor Co. (1946–78), where he introduced the best-selling Mustang. Fired from Ford's presidency (1970–78), he became president, CEO, and chairman of the failing Chrysler Corporation (1978–92), which through layoffs, cutbacks, hard-selling advertising (including his personal "pitches"), and a government loan guarantee he restored to profitability. He became the national model of a "can-do" executive; his autobiography, *Iacocca* (1984), was a best-seller.

Icahn, Carl C. (Celian) (1936–) financier, entrepreneur, airline executive; born in Queens, N.Y. Son of a lawyer who wanted to be an opera singer, he took a philosophy degree from Princeton (1957), dropped out of medical school after three years, and learned the broker's trade on Wall Street before establishing his own brokerage firm, Icahn & Co. (1968). One of the most notorious corporate "raiders" of the 1980s, he enriched himself and his partners by his takeovers, while, so his defenders claimed, making money for ordinary stockholders. He also engaged in what was called "greenmail"; threatening to take over corporations such as Marshall Field and Phillips Petroleum, he would sell his stocks at the end and walk off with a sizeable profit. In 1985 he bought Transworld Airlines (TWA), and as its chief executive officer, brought it back from near bankruptcy; but in 1992, despite sinking $100 million of his own money into it, he was forced to relinquish control of TWA to its employees.

Ickes, Harold L. (LeClaire) (1874–1952) lawyer, public official, journalist, author; born in Frankstown Township, Pa. After graduating from the University of Chicago, he reported for Chicago newspapers (1897–1900) but soon became involved in Republican reform politics and a civic-minded law practice. Prominent in the Progressive Party (1912–16), he changed affiliation, backed Franklin D. Roosevelt in 1932, and was appointed interior secretary (1933–46). As Public Works Administration director (1933–39) he angered private utilities by curbing their power and providing low-cost public utilities and housing. Blunt and outspoken, he often quarreled with journalists and fellow officials. During World War II he was administrator of solid fuels, petroleum, fisheries, and coal mines. In 1946 he resigned in protest of President Truman's appointment of an oilman as navy undersecretary. He supported Truman's reelection, joining the staff of *The New Republic* in 1949. His

books include *Autobiography of a Curmudgeon* (1943) and *Secret Diary of Harold L. Ickes* (1953–54).

Ide, John (Jay) (1892–1962) aeronautical engineer/administrator; born at Narragansett Pier, R.I. Sent to Europe to represent the new National Advisory Committee for Aeronautics (NACA) (1921), he connected American and European aeronautical communities for nearly 20 years. He served on the command staff of the U.S. Naval forces (1943–45) and was vice-president of the International Aeronautic Federation (1948–50).

Ignatow, David (1914–) poet; born in New York City. He graduated from high school and worked in his family's butcher shop before working in a book bindery that he later owned and managed. Beginning in 1932 he was a journalist for the Works Progress Administration (WPA). He began his teaching career at the New School for Social Research (1962–64), and went on to teach at such institutions as Vassar College (1967–68), Columbia University (1968), and City University (1968–84). He is praised as a lyrical autobiographical poet, as seen in *New and Collected Poems (1970–85)*. He lived in East Hampton, N.Y.

Imbau, Fred E. (1909–) criminologist, scholar; born in New Orleans, La. A noted criminal law researcher and trainer of police legal advisers, he taught longest at Northwestern University School of Law (1945–77). Named professor emeritus at Northwestern, he founded Americans for Effective Law Enforcement, a national organization to improve crime-fighting efforts. He coauthored dozens of books, including a widely used casebook on both criminal law and procedure, and books on criminal law and evidence for police and laypeople.

Imbrie, Andrew (Welsh) (1921–) composer; born in New York City. After studies with Nadia Boulanger in France and Roger Sessions in the U.S.A., he taught at the University of California: Berkeley. His music is noted for a firmly controlled use of modernist materials.

Imlay, Gilbert (c. 1754–?1828) adventurer; probably born in Monmouth County, N.J. Significant gaps exist in his historical record. He was a lieutenant in the American Revolution and a deputy surveyor in Kentucky (1783–85), but he fled when his land dealings got him in trouble with the law. He next appeared in Europe, and he approached the leaders of Revolutionary France with plans of how to take Louisiana from Spain. He lived with Mary Wollstonecraft, the English feminist, and they had a daughter, Fanny. He disappeared again in 1798 and only resurfaced at the time of his death on the Island of Jersey. He is also known as the author of *A Topographical Description of the Western Territory of North America* (1792) and a novel, *The Emigrants* (1793).

Ince, Thomas H. (Harper) (1882–1924) film producer, director, screenwriter, actor; born in Newport, R.I. He made his stage debut at age six, and later appeared on Broadway and in films. In 1910 he began directing Mary Pickford movies. He used detailed, tightly structured scripts, which he often wrote himself. By 1916 he devoted himself to producing and writing. He is best remembered for *Custer's Last Fight* (1912), *Civilization* (1916), and *Human Wreckage* (1923).

Indiana, Robert (b. Robert Clark) (1928–) painter; born in New Castle, Ind. Based in New York City from 1954, he was a major force of the pop art movement of the 1960s, an avant-garde approach that used hard-edge abstraction and ordinary objects seen in advertising and other popular mediums. His most famous images, some of which resemble road signs, include his paintings based on the word "LOVE."

Ingalls, John James (1833–1900) U.S. senator; born in Middleton, Mass. Settling in Kansas territory in 1858, he was among the framers of the Kansas state constitution and was elected to the U.S. Senate (Rep., Kans.; 1873–92). Renowned for his oratory, he was president pro tem of the Senate from 1889–91.

Inge, William (Motter) (1913–73) playwright; born in Independence, Kans. He studied at the University of Kansas (B.A. 1935) and the George Peabody College for Teachers (M.A. 1938). He worked as an actor before teaching at the high school level (1937–38) and the college level (1938–46). He became a movie, music, and drama critic in St. Louis, Mo. (1943–46), taught intermittently, and moved to New York City where he became famous as a screenwriter, television playwright, and Broadway dramatist. He is best known for his plays *Come Back, Little Sheba* (1950), *Picnic* (1953), *Bus Stop* (1955), and *The Dark at the Top of the Stairs* (1957). Ill and plagued by alcoholism, he committed suicide.

Ingersoll, Robert (Green) (1833–99) lawyer, orator; born in Dresden, N.Y. This son of a Congregational minister had little formal education; he read law on his own and was admitted to the Illinois bar in 1854. He commanded a volunteer cavalry regiment during the Civil War; from 1867 to 1869 he served as Illinois attorney general. He then took to the lecture circuit to promote a secular religion of scientific rationalism that Thomas H. Huxley called "agnosticism." Many of his lectures such as "Superstition" were widely reprinted. He was also active in the Republican Party and at the 1876 convention he nominated James G. Blaine as "the Plumed Knight." He moved to Washington, D.C., in 1879 and to New York City in 1885, continuing to practice law and propound his social views until his death.

Ingersoll, Royal (Eason) (1883–1976) naval officer; born in Washington, D.C. He was the communications officer for the U.S. delegation to the Versailles Peace Conference (1918–19). He was commander of the Atlantic Fleet (1942–44), and the landings in North Africa (1942) were carried out under his general authority.

Ingraham, Prentiss (1843–1904) writer; born in Adams County, Miss. He studied at Jefferson College (Miss.) and at Mobile Medical College. After service with the Confederate army in the Civil War, he became a soldier of fortune in Mexico, Austria, Crete, Africa, and Cuba. He became a writer of popular historical "dime novels" for the Beadle series; he also wrote plays, short stories, and poetry. He was best known for writing a highly romantic biography of his friend, William Cody, that created his reputation as "Buffalo Bill." At various intervals he lived in London, New York City, and Chicago.

Inkpaduta (?1815–?78) Santee Sioux chief; born at the Watonwan River, present-day South Dakota. As chief of his band (1848), he led them on a massacre of whites near Spirit Lake, Iowa, in March 1856. He was never caught, and his violent ways were instrumental in turning many whites against the Santee Sioux.

Inman, Henry (1801–46) painter; born in Utica, N.Y. A portrait and genre painter, he was one of the founders of the National Academy of Design in New York (1826).

Inman, John Hamilton (1844–96) financier; born in Jefferson County, Tenn., and **Inman, Samuel Martin** (1843–1915) merchant; born in Jefferson County, Tenn. Their father's plantation business was ruined by the Civil War, in which each brother fought with the Confederate army. Samuel opened a cotton commission office with his father in Atlanta, Ga. (1867), which, named S. M. Inman and Company after his father returned to Tennessee in 1870, became one of the largest cotton dealers in the world. His brother John worked in a bank before going to a New York City cotton house at which he became partner. In 1870 he organized Inman, Swann and Company and was one of the organizers of the New York Cotton Exchange, soon so influential he was called the "Cotton King." With his fortune and influence, John began redeveloping the South, discovering mineral deposits and promoting railway building and further industrialization. He was one of the directors and organizer of the Tennessee Coal, Iron and Railroad Company, later absorbed by U.S. Steel. He and his brother Samuel helped organize the Southern Railway System that incorporated many of the interterritorial railways in the south in the 1880s. In 1881 Samuel was treasurer of the International Cotton Exposition in Atlanta; in 1895 he was an organizer of the Cotton States and International Exposition in Atlanta. Samuel was a supporter of the Georgia Institution of Technology and Oglethorpe and Emory Universities. John was a director on several banks and insurance companies.

Inman, Samuel Martin See under INMAN, JOHN HAMILTON.

Inness, George (1825–94) painter; born near Newburgh, N.Y. His family moved to Newark, N.J. (1829), where his schooling was interrupted by epilepsy. He traveled often to Europe (1847–74), and finally settled in Montclair, N.J. (1887). His early work was related to the Hudson River School, as in *Peace and Plenty* (1865), but by the 1890s he had developed an expressive approach similar to impressionism with such paintings as his haunting view of trees and water, *The Home of the Heron* (1893).

Innis, (Emile Alfredo) Roy (1934–) civil rights activist; born in St. Croix, Virgin Islands. Emigrating to Harlem, New York City (1946), he dropped out of high school to join the army, then worked for a New York City research laboratory (1963–67). He joined the Congress of Racial Equality (CORE) in 1963 and advocated black separatism and community school boards; in 1968 he became CORE's national president. Promoting community development corporations, he founded several black business groups and was coeditor of the *Manhattan Tribune*. Never fully accepted by established African-American civil rights leaders because of his unpredictable positions and personality, he was dogged by charges from associates of being too dictatorial; the New York attorney general's office investigated him for alleged misuse of contributions and he was forced to pay back $35,000 to CORE (1981). In the 1980s he twice ran unsuccessfully for the U.S. House of Representatives. In 1988 he made controversial appearances on the Geraldo Rivera and Morton Downey Jr. television shows that led to scuffles on camera.

Inouye, Shinya (1921–) cell biologist; born in London, England. He came to the U.S.A. in 1948 as a graduate student. He taught and performed research at the University of Washington School of Medicine (1951–53), Tokyo Metropolitan University (1953–54), the University of Rochester (1954–59), Dartmouth Medical School (1959–66), and the University of Pennsylvania (1966–89). He was concurrently affiliated with the Woods Hole (Mass.) Marine Biology Laboratory beginning in 1961. He made major contributions to submicroscopic cell morphology and physiology, and held several patents in optical equipment.

Insull, Samuel (1859–1938) public utilities executive; born in London, England. A bookkeeper for one of Thomas Edison's agents in England, he came to America in 1881 to be Edison's personal secretary. By 1889 Insull was vice-president of Edison General Electric Company in Schenectedy, N.Y. In 1892 he became president of Chicago Edison Company, and by 1907 all of Chicago's electricity was being generated by Insull's Commonwealth Edison Company, a tribute to his economic management. He pioneered in unifying rural electrification and also in supplying gas. His vast empire of utility companies had been financed by the sale of stock, and after the stock market collapsed in 1929, his empire also went under. In 1932 he fled to Greece but he was forced to return to Chicago in 1934. He was tried on mail fraud, bankruptcy, and embezzlement charges but was acquitted. Some felt he had been made the scapegoat for the whole stock market debacle. Bankrupt, he was reduced to living off modest pensions during his final years in Europe.

Ipatiev (or Ipatieff), Vladimir (Nikolaevich) (1867–1952) chemist; born in Moscow, Russia. As an officer in the Russian army he taught chemistry in St. Petersburg (1898–1906) and headed Russia's chemical warfare program in World War I. He established new means of synthesizing isoprene, the first synthesis of a basic monomer of rubber (1892–96); he was the first to synthesize methane from carbon and hydrogen; he applied high pressure to organic reactions, developing methods of separating metals from water (1909). He came to the United States in 1930 and as director of Northwestern University's Catalytic High Pressure Laboratory (1931–35) he developed a process for making high-octane gasoline. He held over 200 patents.

Iredell, James (1751–99) Supreme Court justice; born in Lewes, England. He emigrated to North Carolina at age 17 and became active in the revolution against England. He served as a North Carolina judge (1777–78) and as state attorney general (1779–81). At age 38, he was the youngest of the original six U.S. Supreme Court justices when chosen by President Washington, serving from 1790–99.

Ireland, John (1838–1919) Catholic prelate; born in County Kilkenny, Ireland. Emigrating to the U.S.A. with his parents (1849) and settling in St. Paul, Minn., he later studied in France and was ordained a priest (1861). He was a Civil War chaplain and cathedral rector before being named coadjutor bishop of St. Paul (1875). In 1884 Ireland became bishop of St. Paul, which was made an archdiocese four years later. Regarded as a liberal and possible target of an 1899 papal encyclical condemning "Americanism," he took stands on many controversial issues, as in his "Faribault plan" for state support of parochial schools.

Irving, John (Winslow) (1942–) writer; born in Exeter, N.H. He studied at the Universities of New Hampshire (B.A. 1965), Iowa (M.F.A. 1967), Pittsburgh (1961–62), and Vienna (Austria) (1963–64). He taught at Mount Holyoke (1967–72), the University of Iowa (1972–75), and at Bread Loaf Writers Conference, Middlebury, Vt. He is considered an inventive writer who combined elements of tragedy and antic comedy, as seen in his popular novel, *The World According to Garp* (1978). He is also widely praised for several later novels, including *The Hotel New Hampshire* (1981), and *The Cider House Rules* (1985). He lived in Dorset, Vt.

Irving, Washington (1783–1859) writer; born in New York City. He was educated privately, studied law, and began to write essays for periodicals. He traveled in France and Italy (1804–06), wrote whimsical journals and letters, then returned to New York City to practice law in a haphazard way. He and his brother William Irving and James Kirke Paulding wrote the *Salamagundi* papers (1807–08), a collection of humorous essays. He first became more widely known for his comic work, *A History of New York* (1809), written under the name of Diedrich Knickerbocker. In 1815 he went to England to work for his brothers' business; when that failed he composed a collection of stories and essays that became *The Sketch Book,* published under the name "Geoffrey Crayon" (1819–20); they included "Rip Van Winkle" and "The Legend of Sleepy Hollow." In 1822 he went to the Continent, living in Germany and France for several years. In 1826 he went to Spain and became attaché at the U.S. embassy in Madrid; while in Spain he did the research for his biography of Christopher Columbus (1828) and his works on Granada (1829) and the Alhambra (1832). He was secretary of the U.S. legation in London between 1829–32. He would return to Spain as the U.S. ambassador (1842–46) but he spent most of the rest of his life at his estate, "Sunnyside," near Tarrytown, N.Y., turning out a succession of mainly historical and biographical works – including a five-volume life of George Washington. Although he never really developed as a literary talent, he has retained his reputation as the first American man of letters.

Irwin, Will (William Henry) (1873–1948) journalist; born in Oneida, N.Y. An outstanding reporter for the *San Francisco Chronicle,* the *New York Sun,* and *McClure's Magazine* (1901–07), he won renown for his knowledgeable coverage of the San Francisco earthquake (1906). Later a World War I correspondent for the *Saturday Evening Post,* he also wrote fiction, biography, and other works.

Irwin, (William) Bill (1950–) comedian; born in Santa Monica, Calif. Patterning himself after silent film greats, he studied acting and clowning. He brought his gravity defying pantomimes to Broadway in 1981, inspiring a new generation of performance and "new vaudeville" artists.

Isaacs, John D. (Dove) (1913–80) oceanographer; born in Spokane, Wash. He worked as an engineer before joining the Scripps Institute of Oceanography (1948–74). He was named director of the University of California's Institute of Marine Research in 1971. A marine ecologist and U.S. government and military adviser, he developed deep-moored unmanned instrument stations, and devised the dating of prehistoric oceanographic events by investigating marine sediments.

Isard, Walter (1919–) economist; born in Philadelphia. He was the first modern economist to apply the economics of location, also known as "regional science," to industry. He taught at the University of Pennsylvania (1956–71) before moving to Cornell University as professor of Regional Science and Peace Science.

Iselin, Columbus O'Donnell (1904–71) oceanographer; born in New Rochelle, N.Y. He served the Woods Hole Oceanographic Institution (1932–70), while concurrently teaching at the Massachusetts Institute of Technology (1959–70) and Harvard (1960–70). He developed the bathythermograph and other deep-sea instruments responsible for saving ships during World War II. He made major contributions to research on ocean salinity and temperature, acoustics, and the oceanography of the Gulf Stream.

Isham, Ralph Hayward (1890–1955) manuscript collector; born in New York City. A business executive, he devoted his leisure to tracking down and acquiring manuscripts and papers of English author James Boswell. He published an 18-volume edition of his collection (1928–34) and sold the originals to Yale University in 1949.

Isham, Samuel (1855–1914) painter, author; born in New York City. Although a painter, he is best remembered for the publication of his book, *A History of American Painting* (1905).

Isherwood, Benjamin (Franklin) (1822–1915) naval officer, engineer; born in New York City. He entered the naval engineer corps in 1844 and became the chief engineer in 1848. His observations and experiments led to his *Experimental Researches in Steam Engineering* (1863, 1865) which became a standard text. As chief of the Bureau of Steam Engineering (1862–70) he facilitated the growth of the steam navy.

Ishi (?1860–1916) Yahi tribesman; born near Mt. Lassen, Calif. The sole survivor of his tribe, he was found half dead in 1911 and taken to live at the Museum of Anthropology in Berkeley, Calif. He was the subject of a book by Alfred Kroeber and renowned as the "last of the Stone Age people" in North America.

Istomin, Eugene (George) (1925–) pianist; born in New York City. After studies at the Curtis Institute he won the Leventritt Award in 1943 and went on to a distinguished international solo career, meanwhile often appearing with the Istomin-Stern-Rose Trio.

Iverson, Ken (Francis Kenneth) (1925–) industrialist; born in Downers Grove, Ill. He worked in industrial research, technology, and marketing before joining what became Nucor Corporation (1962) (president and CEO 1965–85, chairman and CEO 1985). His introduction of high technology in the first U.S. "mini"steel mill in Darlington, S.C. (1969) and in an innovative flat-rolled steel plant (1989) revitalized the American steel industry.

Ives, Burl (b. Burle Icle Ivanhoe) (1909–) folksinger, songwriter, movie actor; born in Hunt Township, Ill. As a child he sang and played banjo in community shows, and after attending Eastern Illinois State Teacher's College, he briefly played professional football. He set out to travel across the U.S.A., working at odd jobs and singing with his guitar to support himself, adding to his repertoire of traditional American folksongs. In the 1940s he performed in several Broadway shows, including Irving Berlin's *This Is the Army* (1942). In the 1950s he made several best-selling recordings of folksongs; as "The Wayfaring Stranger" he had a popular radio program; he toured around the world and would go on to produce educational films and publish collections of folksongs – all foreshadowing the folksong revival of the 1960s. Meanwhile, he had been appearing in several movies as a singer, but with his role in *East of Eden* (1955), he began to show a talent for dramatic acting that culminated in his role as Big Daddy in *Cat on a Hot Tin Roof* (1958). He would continue to appear in (or provide the voice for) numerous movies.

Ives, Charles (Edward) (1874–1954) composer; born in Danbury, Conn. An organ prodigy, he was first trained by his bandmaster father, who also instilled a penchant for musical experiment. At Yale (1894–98) he learned much from the conservative Horatio Parker, but in view of his advanced musical ideas he decided not to pursue a career in music. After college he entered the insurance business in New York and over the next three decades he would rise nearly to the top of that profession. At the same time, after leaving his last church-organist job in 1902, he began a perhaps unprecedented period of creative isolation for a major composer; for twenty years, in his spare time, he composed prolifically and with growing confidence and maturity, although during those years his music was rarely heard in public. His important works, all marked by a unique blend of prophetic experiment and familiar American material, include the *Concord* Sonata, *Three Places in New England,* the *Holidays* Symphony, and the Fourth Symphony. Following a serious heart attack in 1918, his health and productivity declined; his last new pieces date from the mid-1920s. He lived his last decades as an invalid in New York City and West Redding, Conn., promoting his music as best he could and revising pieces; meanwhile, various enthusiasts gradually spread his music into the world.

Ives, Chauncey Bradley (1810–94) sculptor; born in Hamden, Conn. Beginning as a woodcarver, he worked in Boston (1837–c. 1841) and New York City (c. 1841–44), studied in Florence, Italy (1844–51), then settled in Rome. He is known for his classical marble figures, such as *Egeria* (1876).

Ives, Frederick Eugene (1856–1937) inventor; born in Litchfield, Conn. He served a printing apprenticeship (1870–73) and then headed the photographic laboratory at Cornell University (1875–79). He invented (1878) and improved (1885) the half-tone process in photography. He turned his attention to color photography and printing after 1890 and pioneered natural colors for motion pictures after 1912.

Ives, James (Merritt) (1824–95) publisher; born in New York City. Better educated in literature and the arts than Nathaniel Currier, he was hired as Currier's bookkeeper in 1852. Soon he was not only overseeing the various artists who produced the original drawings but he himself would make some of his own. He was made a partner in 1857 and from then on the name Currier & Ives appeared on hundreds of different prints, posters, and handbills.

Ives, Joseph Christmas (1828–68) explorer, soldier; born in New York City. He commanded an exploration of the

Colorado River (1857–58) and wrote a classic description of that area. He was the engineer and architect of the Washington National Monument (1859–60) and he served as an engineer and aide in the Confederate army (1861–65).

Ivory, James (1928–) film director; born in Berkeley, Calif. As a student at the University of Southern California he directed a short subject, *Four in the Morning* (1953), and was then commissioned by the Asia Society to go to India to make a documentary (1960). There, in partnership with a local producer, Ismail Merchant, he made a series of Indian-based films, climaxing with *Shakespeare Wallah* (1965), which Ivory also coscripted. Basing their company in the U.S.A. from the early 1970s, the Ivory-Merchant team enjoyed its greatest success with relatively pure adaptations of literary works, such as Henry James's *The Europeans* (1979) and E. M. Forster's *A Room With a View* (1987).

Iwerks, (Ubbe) Ub (1901–71) animator; born in Kansas City, Mo. After starting an unsuccessful art studio with Walt Disney, he remained in Kansas City doing film animation until Disney brought him to Hollywood in 1923 to help draw *Alice in Cartoonland* (1923–26). He developed many special effects for animated movies, winning Academy Awards in 1959 and 1965 for his technical contributions to motion pictures.

Izard, Ralph (1742–1804) diplomat, U.S. senator; born in Charlestown, S.C. As a diplomat in Paris, he secured warships for the American revolutionaries. A member of the Continental Congress (1782–83), South Carolina elected him to the first U.S. Senate (1789–95).

J

Jackson, Andrew (1767–1845) seventh U.S. president; born in Waxhaw, S.C. Reared in a frontier settlement and largely self-educated, he was admitted to the bar and in 1788 was named public prosecutor in Nashville, in North Carolina territory. When the territory became the new state of Tennessee, he became its first U.S. representative in the House (1769), its senator (1797–98), and a judge on its supreme court (1798–1804). Meanwhile, he had established his estate, "the Hermitage," near Nashville and married Rachel Robards (twice, for they discovered she had not been formally divorced the first time). Named major-general of Tennessee militia during the War of 1812, in September 1814 he defeated the Creek Indians, who were British allies, at Horseshoe Bend. Commissioned a major-general in the regular army, he stormed Pensacola, Fla., and then routed the British in the Battle of New Orleans (January 1815). Retaining his army commission as commander of the Southern District, he created some controversy when in 1818 he invaded Florida on a campaign against the Seminoles and executed two British subjects for stirring up the Indians. Now the South's hero, known everywhere as "Old Hickory," he was elected to the Senate (Dem.-Rep., Tenn.; 1823–24) and in 1824 narrowly lost the presidency to John Quincy Adams when the election was thrown into the House of Representatives. Winning the election of 1828, he set a precedent for the "spoils system" by filling hundreds of offices with his supporters. As president (1829–37), he walked a tightrope between the issues of slavery, nullification, and states' rights; in the name of the latter he suppressed the Bank of the U.S.A. Among his more problematic achievements was his relentless removal of many Indians to west of the Mississippi. In the long run, Jackson's main legacy was the new strength his personality bequeathed to the office of the presidency for the future; also, the new Democratic Party formed around him and his popular image as champion of the common man, even though he himself had little patience with the wishes of most people. On leaving the presidency, he retired from public life and spent his declining years at "the Hermitage."

Jackson, Charles Thomas (1805–80) chemist; born in Plymouth, Mass. After graduating from Harvard Medical School, he continued his studies in Paris, then returned to Boston and established the first lab in analytical chemistry to accept students (1836). Of wide-ranging interests – he did major geological surveys of New England – he became increasingly paranoid. In 1832 he had suggested to Samuel F. B. Morse the idea of an electric telegraph and in 1844 he had suggested to William Morton the use of ether as an anaesthetic; when both men were hailed as the discoverers of the true functional applications of these concepts, Jackson devoted himself to his claims to priority. By 1873 he had evidently become insane and he spent his final years in a mental institution.

Jackson, Chevalier (1865–1958) physician; born in Pittsburgh, Pa. He studied at Jefferson Medical College (Philadelphia) and became a professor there; by 1930 he also held positions at three other medical schools in Philadelphia – the University of Pennsylvania, Temple, and the Women's College of Pennsylvania; he was president of the latter from 1935–41. A specialist in laryngology, he devised an instrument that could remove lodged articles from the larynx (1890). In 1899 he invented a bronchoscope, and in 1902 he placed a tiny light on the end of it.

Jackson, Dugald (Caleb) (1865–1951) electrical engineer, educator; born in Kennett Square, Pa. In 1887 he began building electrical power plants and street railway systems. As an innovative educator (University of Wisconsin, 1891–1907; Massachusetts Institute of Technology, 1907–35), he introduced problem-solving as preparation for the needs of industry.

Jackson, Helen (Maria) Hunt (b. Fiske) (Saxe Holm; H. H., pen names) (1830–85) writer, poet; born in Amherst, Mass. She was schooled briefly in Massachusetts and New York City, and was a neighbor and good friend of Emily Dickinson. She married Edward Hunt (1852). Following his death (1863), she turned to writing poetry, stories, and essays. She married William Jackson (1875) and they settled in Colorado Springs, Colo. She is best known for her novel *Ramona* (1884), an indictment of the U.S. government's treatment of Native Americans.

Jackson, Henry M. (Martin) (1912–83) U.S. senator; born in Everett, Wash. He served in the U.S. House of Representatives (Dem., Wash.; 1941–53) and in the U.S. Senate (1953–83). Known as the "Senator from Boeing," he was a staunch supporter of the interests of his state's defense industry; he also advocated an anti-Soviet foreign policy. He was an unsuccessful presidential candidate in 1972 and 1976.

Jackson, Howell E. (Edmunds) (1832–95) Supreme Court justice; born in Paris, Tenn. He was elected to the Tennessee state legislature (1880) and to the U.S. Senate (Rep., Tenn.; 1880). He rose through the federal court system before his appointment to the U.S. Supreme Court by President Harrison (1893–95).

Jackson, Jesse (Louis) (1941–) civil rights activist, Baptist minister, presidential candidate; born in Greenville, S.C. Son of an Alabama sharecropper (he adopted his stepfather's last name), he was a good enough athlete in high school to be offered a contract by the Chicago White Sox, but he turned it down because a white player was given so much more money; he also turned down an athletic scholarship at the University of Illinois when he was told that as a black he could not expect to play quarterback. He attended the mostly black Agricultural and Technical College of North Carolina in Greensboro; in addition to being a standout athlete, student, and campus leader, he took a lead in protests that forced Greensboro, N.C., to integrate its restaurants and theaters. He trained for the ministry at Chicago Theological Seminary, and in 1965, having joined the protest movement led by Martin Luther King Jr., and the Southern Christian Leadership Conference (SCLC), he was named head of the Chicago branch of Operation Breadbasket, becoming its national head in 1967; Operation Breadbasket was the SCLC's program to persuade American businesses to hire blacks and to get companies to sell products made by blacks, and Jackson proved highly successful in this for several years. He also helped create the Chicago Freedom Movement (1966) to press for integrated schools and open housing. He was beside King when he was assassinated (1968) and although Jackson was viewed by some as the potential successor to King as the leader in the struggle for rights, he never quite gained the full support of all elements of the black community. Ordained a Baptist minister in 1968, he concentrated his fight for rights in Chicago, and after a falling-out with the SCLC removed him from Operation Breadbasket (1971), he founded his own organization, PUSH (People United to Save Humanity), which would continue to work for improving African-Americans' lives on a variety of fronts. Increasingly more active on the political scene, in 1972 he led a group that successfully challenged Mayor Richard J. Daley's slate of delegates at the Democratic national convention; and in 1984 and 1988, backed by yet another of his organizations, the Rainbow Coalition, he ran in the Democratic presidential primaries, gaining enough votes to make him a presence at the convention. And although his occasionally extreme rhetoric and sometimes angry demeanor seemed to frighten off the broadbased support he sought, he constantly won favor with surprising constituencies as he inserted himself into a variety of events – rushing off to Syria to gain the freedom of an American pilot, joining picket lines at all kinds of labor actions. As controversial as he was charismatic, he continued to be named whenever there was talk of the need for a new African-American leader – whether a mayor of Chicago or the first senator of Washington, D.C., if it became a state – and if this very omnipresence also suggested he might be diluting his energies and abilities, he undoubtedly remained one of the more striking figures in American public life in the late 20th century.

Jackson, John B. (Brinckerhoff) (1909–) landscape historian; born in Dinard, France. Of American parentage, he was educated in New England and Europe. He was in the U.S. Army (1940–46) and during World War II worked with maps for intelligence in Europe. He founded and edited *Landscape*

(1951–68), a magazine published in Sante Fe that promoted his appreciation of the American scene based on the value structures have to those who build and use them, not on a comparison to European developments. This was the basis of his best-known concept, "the vernacular landscape," which he came to appreciate through travels on his motorcycle and which he expressed in essays collected in such books as *The Necessity for Ruins* (1980) and *Discovering the Vernacular Landscape* (1984). Between 1961–77, he taught at Harvard and Berkeley; he also taught at other universities and was resident at the American Academy in Rome (1983). Often opposed by conventional designers as well as conservationists, he was a loner by temperament, eloquent in his writings, and widely regarded as altering the way students of the American landscape perceived the interactions between human beings and natural environments.

Jackson, (Joseph Jefferson) "Shoeless Joe" (1887–1951) baseball player; born in Brandon Mills, S.C. During his 13-year career as an outfielder (1908–20), mostly with the Cleveland Indians and Chicago White Sox, he posted a lifetime batting average of .356, third highest in major league history, before being banned from baseball in 1921 for his involvement in the 1919 "Black Sox" scandal. Along with seven other White Sox players, he was accused of conspiring to lose the 1919 World Series to the Cincinnati Reds (even though he hit .375 in the Series). According to folklore, a youngster pleaded to him, "Say it ain't so, Joe," after his testimony at the "Black Sox" trial. Regarded as baseball's greatest "natural" hitter, he remains ineligible for election to the Hall of Fame due to his permanent banishment from baseball.

Jackson, Laura Riding See RIDING, LAURA.

Jackson, Mahalia (1911–72) gospel singer; born in New Orleans. Raised in the Baptist Church, she secretly listened to the blues recordings of Bessie Smith and Ma Rainey. Moving to Chicago in 1927, she joined a Baptist choir; in 1928 she joined the Johnson Gospel Singers and sang and acted in "religious plays" while touring with the group for some years. By the mid-1930s she had joined Thomas A. Dorsey and would tour with his gospel group until the late-1940s. Although she had recorded four sides for Decca in the late-1930s, none gained any notice; it was her 1947 recording of "Move Up a Little Higher" that sold a million copies and soon gained her the "queen of gospel" crown. She appeared on radio and television and by 1952 commenced touring in Europe. She sang at an inaugural party for President John F. Kennedy, at the 1963 March on Washington, and at the funeral of Martin Luther King Jr. She appeared in several movies but refused to sing in nightclubs or to sing secular songs (although she recorded Duke Ellington's "Come Sunday" in 1958). She is credited with having inspired a whole new generation of gospel singers and making gospel become appreciated throughout the world.

Jackson, Martha (b. Kellogg) (?1907–69) art dealer; born in Buffalo, N.Y. She studied at Smith College (1925–28) and at Moore College of Art, Philadelphia (1969). She married twice and was the owner and director of the Martha Jackson Gallery, New York City (1953–69), and president of Red Parrot Films (c. 1964–69). She was known as an early supporter of the paintings and sculptures of abstract expressionists.

Jackson, Maynard (Holbrook) (1938–) mayor; born in

Dallas, Texas. A 1956 graduate of Morehouse College, he received his J.D. from North Carolina Central State School of Law. He was an attorney and director of community relations for the Emory Neighborhood Law Office in Atlanta (1968–69) and a senior partner at Jackson, Patterson & Parks (1970–73). He served as mayor of Atlanta, Ga., from 1974–82 and again from 1990.

Jackson, Michael (1958–) popular singer, songwriter; born in Gary, Ind. He was a child star with his brothers in a popular Motown soul group, the Jackson Five, and had his first solo hits in the early 1970s. He began producing and songwriting when the group left Motown in 1976, becoming the Jacksons, and he collaborated with Quincy Jones on his first best-selling solo album, *Off The Wall* (1979). His second solo album, *Thriller* (1982), sold over 30 million copies and made him a superstar. As his recordings and videos continued to attract an ever larger public and gain him ever more millions of dollars in sales, commercial endorsements, and contracts, he moved beyond being another popular singer to become more an entertainment phenomenon, known for his unusual choreography (including the "moon walk"), elaborate special effects, mannered performances, and occasional tours before frenzied crowds. Meanwhile, his offstage life also became increasingly bizarre: he transformed his face with plastic surgery, became chummy with celebrities such as Elizabeth Taylor, and lived in a secluded estate rumored to be like an amusement park/zoo. In 1993 his private and public careers collided when he was accused of sexual abuse of minor boys; although he was never legally charged, his somewhat ambiguous sexual persona and relations with young children, on and off stage, lost some of their appeal.

Jackson, Patrick Tracy (1780–1847) cotton manufacturer; born in Newburyport, Mass. Originally a merchant sea captain (1799–1808), he joined Francis Cabot Lowell (his brother-in-law), Nathan Appleton, and others to organize the Boston Manufacturing Company in Waltham, Mass. (1813). He was influential in the founding of Lowell, Mass. (1820) and built the Boston & Lowell Railroad.

Jackson, Rachel Donelson Robards (1767–1828) wife of Andrew Jackson; born in Brunswick (now Halifax) County, Va. She married Jackson in 1791, then remarried him in 1794 to prevent confusion stemming from her previous marriage to Lewis Robards. She died just before Jackson's inauguration; he believed that political slights directed against her and their marriage had caused her death.

Jackson, (Reginald Martinez) Reggie (1946–) baseball player; born in Wyncote, Pa. During his 21-year career as a flamboyant and often controversial outfielder (1967–87), mostly with the Oakland Athletics and New York Yankees, the left-handed slugger hit 563 homeruns and won the league Most Valuable Player award in 1973. He also holds the major league record for the most strikeouts (2,597). Known as "Mr. October," for his post-season heroics, he hit three homeruns in one game in the 1977 World Series. He was elected to the Hall of Fame in 1993.

Jackson, Robert (Houghwout) (1892–1954) Supreme Court justice; born in Spring Creek, Pa. He served as counsel to the Bureau of Internal Revenue (1934–36) and to the Department of Justice (1936–40). He was U.S. attorney general (1940–41) when President Franklin D. Roosevelt appointed him to the U.S. Supreme Court (1941–54). After World War II, he served as chief prosecutor at the Nuremberg war crimes trials (1945–46).

Jackson, Shirley (1919–65) writer; born in San Francisco. She studied at the University of Rochester (1934–36), and Syracuse University (B.A. 1940). Based in North Bennington, Vt., she wrote novels, short stories, and radio and television scripts. She became famous for her haunting fiction after the publication of her disturbing short story, "The Lottery" (1948). She was known for her ability to write humorous domestic works as well as horror novels, such as *The Haunting of Hill House* (1959).

Jackson, (Thomas Jonathan) "Stonewall" (1824–63) soldier; born in Clarksburg, Va. After his parents died in poverty, he was raised by an uncle who helped him obtain an appointment to West Point. Following graduation (1846), he served in the Mexican War, then resigned from the army (1852) to accept a professorship at Virginia Military Institute (VMI); there he became noted for his dedication to his Presbyterian faith. He commanded a detachment of VMI students at the hanging of John Brown (1859). When the Civil War broke out, he did not hesitate to sign on with the Confederates. Appointed a brigadier general, he organized a brigade of Virginians that fought at 1st Bull Run; it was here that the unit was described as standing its ground like a "stone wall," and though the brigade, which fought with him to his end, was officially named this, the name became forever attached to Jackson. His Shenandoah campaign of 1862, a strategic diversion that prevented the federals from reinforcing McClellan on the Virginia Peninsula, is graded a military masterpiece. He mysteriously faltered during the Seven Days' Battles on the Peninsula (June–July 1862), but by 2nd Bull Run (August 1862) he and Lee had perfected their brilliant partnership. They triumphed at Fredericksburg, and Jackson's famous flank march at Chancellorsville (1863) made Lee's victory there possible. But within hours after he had routed the Union right, he was accidentally shot by one of his own men while riding by in the dusk. He died eight days later, and Lee said simply, "I know not how to replace him." Not an easy man to know or warm up to, he fought with an intellignece, ferocity, and singleness of purpose perhaps equaled only by Sherman.

Jackson, William Henry (1843–1942) photographer; born in Keesville, N.Y. Photographer for seven U.S. Geological Surveys of the Territories (1870–78), he traveled by mule to take the first pictures of Pike's Peak, Yellowstone, and Mesa Verde Mountain.

Jacobi, Abraham (1830–1919) pediatrician; born in Westphalia, Germany. After taking his M.D. from the University of Bonn (1851) he was imprisoned for treason in the German Revolution of 1848. He escaped (1853) and eventually made his way to New York City, where he established a famous pediatrics practice. The first professor of diseases of children in America (1860, New York Medical College), he opened the first free clinic for children. From 1870–1902 he was a professor of pediatrics at the College of Physicians and Surgeons, New York. In 1873 he married the equally admired physician, Mary Putnam. He had published many articles and books but a fire at his summer home (1919) destroyed valuable documents and notes and hastened his own death.

Jacobi, Mary Corinna Putnam (1842–1906) physician; born in London, England. Her father was the famous New York book publisher, George Putnam. After serving as a medical aide during the Civil War and graduating from the Female Medical College of Pennsylvania (1864), she became only the second woman to take a degree from the École de Médicine, in Paris, (1867–71); while there she contributed articles to various American magazines and newspapers, including some about the siege of Paris and the Paris Commune. Back in New York City she joined the Women's Medical College of the New York Infirmary for Women (1871–1889) and through her lectures, clinical practice, extensive publications, and varied organizational activities, she soon became recognized as not only the leading female physician in America but also one of New York's most influential. She was elected to most of the professional medical organizations (except the Obstetrical Society), among them the Medical Society of the County of New York, whose president, Dr. Abraham Jacobi, she married in 1873. Among her most consistent campaigns was to get women admitted to the leading medical schools such as at Johns Hopkins. She also was in the forefront of those recognizing the need to change social, working, and environmental conditions if the health of the masses was to be improved. A suffragist, her *"Common Sense" Applied to Women's Suffrage* (1894), was reprinted and used for the battle that eventually gained women the vote.

Jacobs, Harriet Ann (1813–97) escaped slave, author; born in Edenton, N.C. Born in slavery, she was threatened by the sexual advances of her owner, Dr. James Norcom; later she had two children by a white man. She escaped from slavery and hid for seven years in her grandmother's attic. She made her way to New York City and worked there as a domestic servant. Under the pen name Linda Brent, she wrote the story of her experiences in *Incidents in the Life of a Slave Girl, Written by Herself* (1861). She worked as a nurse during the Civil War and then lived in Washington, D.C. Her book was long forgotten until discovered in the 1980s.

Jacobs, Jane (b. Butzner) (1916–) urban theorist, author; born in Scranton, Pa. Associate editor of *Architectural Forum* (1952–68), she gained a reputation for attacking urban planners for destroying diverse older neighborhoods with expressways and housing projects; her most influential work was *The Death and Life of Great American Cities* (1961). She served on the New York Community Planning Board and was active in trying to save communities such as Greenwich Village. In 1968 she moved to Toronto, Canada, where her architect-husband, Robert Hyde Jacobs Jr., had accepted a position. There she was briefly a consultant to the urban-legal program of the University of New York Law School, but she concentrated on her own writings such as *Cities and the Wealth of Nations* (1989) and *Systems of Survival* (1992).

Jacobsen, Alfred (1890–1967) oil executive; born near Copenhagen, Denmark. He spent 20 years gaining oil company experience in Mexico before joining Amerada Petroleum (1926–65). Variously president, CEO, and chairman of the board, he helped to make Amerada one of the leading oil search companies in the country.

Jacquet, (Jean Baptiste) "Illinois" (1922–) jazz musician; born in Broussard, La. An outstanding tenor saxophonist, he emerged with Lionel Hampton in 1942, toured with Jazz at the Philharmonic between 1944–47, and led his own bands thereafter.

Jacuzzi, Candido (1903–86) businessman, inventor; born in Casarza della Delizia, Italy. His family emigrated to Berkeley, Calif., where the Jacuzzi Brothers, Inc., produced an airplane propeller for use during World War I. Candido was the general manager and then the president of Jacuzzi Brothers. In response to his son's rheumatoid arthritis, he designed a pump that produced a whirlpool effect in a bath; the "Jacuzzi" became a status symbol of well-to-do Americans.

Jaeger, Werner (Wilhelm) (1888–1961) classicist; born in Lobberich, Germany. He received his Ph.D. at the University of Berlin, where he studied with Wilamowitz, in 1914. Afterward, when only 26, he assumed the chair at the University of Basel, Switzerland, a position once held by Friedrich Nietzsche. In 1921 he returned to the University of Berlin and took up Wilamowitz's chair. Although his works on Aristotle and the Cappadocian Church Father Gregory of Nyssa are still highly regarded, he is best known for the less scholarly *Paideia* (1933, 1943, 1944), which examines the educational, intellectual, and spiritual development and achievements of the Greeks. He began the *Paideia* in Germany and finished it in the United States, where he taught at the University of Chicago (1936–39) and Harvard (1939–58) and strongly influenced such classicists as John H. Finley and Gilbert Highet.

Jaffe, Lionel F. (Francis) (1927–) cell biologist; born in New York City. After studying marine biology on several fellowships, he became an assistant professor at Brandeis University, Mass. (1956–60). He joined the University of Pennsylvania (1960–67), then Purdue (1967–84). He invented the vibrating probe for measuring natural electric currents through living cells (1974). He became director of the National Vibrating Probe Facility at Woods Hole, Mass. (1982), and adjunct professor of biology at the University of Massachusetts (1990). He made major contributions to studies of bioelectric and ionic aspects of development, cellular tropism, and calcium ion waves and gradients.

Jahn, Helmut (1940–) architect; born in Nuremberg, Germany. He emigrated in 1966 and joined C. F. Murphy Associates, Chicago (1967–81) (which became Murphy/Jahn in 1981), designing primarily midwestern commercial buildings, making extensive use of glass sheathing.

James, Alice (1848–92) writer; born in New York City (sister of Henry and William James). She had little formal schooling, lived in Europe when young, and settled in Cambridge, Mass., with her parents. A neurasthenic, she moved to England (1884) with her friend Katharine Loving after the death of her parents; she lived much of her brief life as an invalid. She is known for her personal reflections in *Journal* (1844; 1934), later published as *The Diary of Alice James* (1964).

James, Charles (1880–1928) chemist; born at Earls Barton, England. He emigrated to the U.S.A. in about 1906 and was associated with New Hampshire College in Durham for 22 years. He did extensive research of rare-earth elements, such as cerium, terbium, and yttrium (1907–26).

James, Daniel, Jr. ("Chappie") (1920–78) aviator; born in Pensacola, Fla. He joined the Army Air Corps in 1943 and served as a fighter pilot and instructor. He saw combat in Korea and Vietnam, headed the North American Air Defense Command (1975–78), and became the first African-American to attain four stars in the U.S. military.

James, Edwin Leland (1890–1951) journalist; born in Irvington, Va. Joining the *New York Times* in 1915, he was a war correspondent and European correspondent. As managing editor from 1932 he stressed objectivity in reporting; he was also an influential columnist.

James, Harry (b. Hagg) (1916–83) jazz trumpeter; born in Albany, Ga. As a boy he worked in a circus act – his father was in the band, his mother was a trapeze artist – and as a teenager he took up the trumpet and led the circus band. He played with Ben Pollack for a year before joining Benny Goodman's band in 1937, where he soon became known for his virtuoso playing; he ranks as one of the first of the great modern trumpeters due to his stamina, range, richness of tone, and boldness. In 1938 he formed his own band, which performed through the 1970s although it could not maintain the success it enjoyed in the "big band era" of the 1940s and 1950s. He made about 16 feature movies, both with and without his orchestra, usually playing himself, and several with his wife, Betty Grable. He supplied the actual trumpet music played by Kirk Douglas in the movie *Young Man With a Horn* (1950).

James, Henry (1843–1916) writer, critic; born in New York City (brother of Alice and William James). Son of the wealthy amateur philosopher, Henry James Sr., he was educated by private tutors until 1855; the family spent most of the years 1855–60 traveling in Europe, where Henry continued his education, then settled in Newport, R.I. (1860–62) where he apparently suffered an unspecified injury in a stable fire. He attended Harvard Law School (1862–63), then withdrew to devote himself to writing. Starting in the mid-1860s his essays and critical reviews began appearing in *The North American Review,* while his first novel, *Watch and Ward,* was published in *Atlantic Monthly* (1871). He divided his time between Cambridge, Mass., and Europe (1869; 1872–74; 1875); in Paris in 1875 he came to know Turgenev and Flaubert among other European writers. In 1876 he settled in England, where he would spend most of the rest of his life, chiefly in London and in Rye, Sussex; he never married but he was a sociable man, often in the company of other writers such as Edith Wharton. He traveled frequently on the Continent, and published several notable travel books between 1875 and 1909. His first novels – of the so-called international period, dealing as they do with interactions between Americans and Europeans – include *The American* (1877), *The Europeans* (1878), *Daisy Miller* (1879), and *The Portrait of a Lady* (1881). The works of his second period stressed psychological and social relationships and include *Washington Square* (1881), *The Bostonians* (1886), *What Maisie Knew* (1897), and *The Sacred Fount* (1901). During the 1890s he also wrote plays but he never found much success in the theater. He continued his examination of intricate psychological realities in works of his final period that include his three masterworks, *The Wings of the Dove* (1902), *The Ambassadors* (1903), and *The Golden Bowl* (1904). In 1904–05 he visited the U.S.A. where he traveled, lectured, and arranged for the New York Edition of his works (1907–09), for which he made numerous revisions. His account of his visit, *The American Scene* (1907), was not always appreciative of his homeland; he returned to the U.S.A. in 1910–11. In 1915 he became an English citizen to show his solidarity with Britain during World War I and he became involved in war relief and the American volunteer ambulance corps. Soon thereafter he suffered several strokes, and he died shortly after receiving Britain's Order of Merit.

He had been writing almost to the end, and in his long career, in addition to his many novels and travel books, he had written many classic short novels ("The Turn of the Screw," 1898), short stories ("The Beast in the Jungle," 1903) and critical essays ("The Art of Fiction," 1885) as well as two memoirs. His intricate and complex sentence structure and delicately nuanced perceptions have never appealed to all readers but ultimately they became the models for one "school" of modern fiction and James has become recognized as one of the supreme writers of all time.

James, Henry, Sr. (1811–82) religious philosopher; born in Albany, N.Y. Heir to a large fortune, he left Princeton Theological Seminary in 1837 and abandoned institutional religion. He was at first attracted to Sandemanism, a pietistic sect encountered on a trip to England, but his writings were more permanently influenced by the teachings of Emanuel Swedenborg, which interpreted human nature as a collective spiritual being identified with God. James became better known as father of William and Henry James, whose European education he supervised in the 1850s; William edited his posthumous *Literary Remains* (1886).

James, Preston (Everett) (1899–1986) geographer; born in Brookline, Mass. A graduate of Harvard (M.A.) and Clark (Ph.D.) Universities, he taught at the University of Michigan (1923–41), leaving to serve with the Office of Special Services in Washington, D.C. (1941–45). Professor of geography at Syracuse University (1945–70), he was a keen advocate and practitioner of fieldwork, concentrating on Latin America. His text, *Latin America* (1942), went through four revisions and dominated the classroom for four decades.

James, William (1842–1910) philosopher, psychologist; born in New York City (brother of Henry James). After a broad education in Europe and a brief try at becoming an artist, he completed Harvard Medical School in 1869. Plagued by ailments and depression, he never practiced but did recover his energies, partly by placing faith in free will. He joined the Harvard faculty in 1872, teaching physiology, then psychology. He established America's first psychology laboratory and took twelve years to complete his massive *Principles of Psychology* (1890), which evocatively described mental and physical processes while summing up the current state of psychology and introducing new theories. As a philosophy professor (from 1880) he sought to reconcile his empiricism with religious faith, largely by a "pragmatic" theory that made the truth of beliefs depend on their consequences. He made a respectful study of psychological aspects of religion in lectures published as *Varieties of Religious Experience* (1902) and developed his theory of reality as "pure experience" in articles (1904–05) published posthumously as *Essays in Radical Empiricism* (1912). His vivid style, broad sympathies, and concern for basic issues have kept him a central figure in American thought.

Jamison, Judith (?1943–) modern dancer, choreographer, artistic director; born in Philadelphia. She trained early in dance and music and at the Philadelphia Dance Academy before performing with American Ballet Theatre in 1964. She joined Alvin Ailey in 1965 and performed leading roles created especially for her, as in *Cry* (1971). In 1980 she left the company to perform in the Broadway musical, *Sophisticated Ladies,* and her first choreography, *Divining,* was staged in 1984. She dissolved her own Jamison Project, formed in 1988, when she became artistic director of the Alvin Ailey Company shortly after Ailey's death in 1989.

Janauschek, (Franczziska Magdalena Romance) Fanny (1830–1904) stage actress; born in Prague, Czechoslovakia. Already a star in Europe, this powerful tragedienne first performed in German in her American debut in 1867; by 1870 she had learned enough English to appear in *Mary Stuart*. Settling in America in 1880, she lost her standing due to her old fashioned style.

Janeway, Edward Gamaliel (1841–1911) physician; born in New Brunswick, N.J. His career revolved around New York City's Bellevue Hospital, first as curator (1866), then as visiting physician (1871), and finally as professor of pathological anatomy and dean of the consolidated New York University and Bellevue Hospital medical colleges (1898–1905). He held publicity-seeking in low regard and made few contributions to medical literature, but he was highly regarded by his peers as a diagnostician.

Janeway, Theodore Caldwell (1872–1917) physician; born in New York City (son of Edward Gamaliel Janeway). He followed his father's footsteps, eschewing study abroad for work in his father's office. He is credited with pioneering the clinical use of a patient's blood pressure in *The Clinical Study of Blood Pressure* (1904), and with introducing sphygmomanometers.

Janis, Byron (b. Yankelevitch) (1928–   ) pianist; born in McKeesport, Pa. After private studies he made a successful debut in 1943 with the National Broadcasting Company Orchestra. He went on to a distinguished international career, later playing despite severe arthritis.

Janis, Elsie (b. Bierbower) (1889–1956) singer; born in Columbus, Ohio. Pushed on stage by her mother at age 8, she delighted audiences in Europe and America with her singing and impersonations of other celebrities like Will Rogers (1900–32). She worked as both writer and production supervisor of movies in the early 1930s.

Janis, Sidney (1896–1989) art dealer, author; born in Buffalo, N.Y. He attended school locally, was a vaudeville dancer, worked in his brother's store, and became a shirt manufacturer in New York City (1925). He retired in 1939 and devoted himself to collecting contemporary and primitive art. Later he specialized in the work of abstract expressionists and established the Sidney Janis Gallery (1948–67). His collection was donated to the Museum of Modern Art (1967). He wrote several books on modern art.

Jansky, Karl Guthe (1905–50) radio astronomer; born in Norman, Okla. He initiated the field of radio astronomy when he detected radio waves coming from various places in the Milky Way while investigating short-wave radio telephone interference for Bell Laboratories (1928–31). His published papers (1933–35) established that this "star-noise" was radiation originated in distant space. This led to investigations that have taken astronomy billions of light years beyond the capability of optical telescopes. The *jansky*, a unit of radio emission strength, honors his work.

Janson, H. W. (Horst Woldemar) ("Peter") (1913–82) art historian; born in St. Petersburg, Russia. He studied at the Universities of Hamburg and Munich before he emigrated to the U.S.A. He earned his Ph.D. at Harvard (1942) and taught at numerous institutions, notably New York University (1949–74), where he chaired the Department of Fine Arts and made it one of the finest in the century. He

published many books on art history, ranging from cave paintings to 19th-century art. His *History of Art* (1969, several revisions) was for many years the standard text for college art history courses.

Janzen, Daniel H. (Hunt) (1939–   ) entomologist, ecologist; born in Milwaukee, Wis. He taught at the University of Kansas (1965–68), moved to the University of Chicago (1968–72) and the University of Michigan (1972–76), then joined the University of Pennsylvania (1976). A dynamic teacher who took selected students on field trips, he spent summers in Costa Rica researching moths and the effects of moth caterpillars on tropical plants. He wrote two books on Costa Rican natural history, and made major contributions to studies of the interaction of plants and animals, particularly in tropical areas. He won Sweden's Crafoord Prize in 1984 for evolutionary ecology.

Jarmusch, Jim (1953–   ) film scriptwriter/director; born in Akron, Ohio. Son of a businessman and journalist, he attended Columbia University in New York City; after discovering European films in France, he became acquainted with Nicholas Ray and then set about making his first film, *Permanent Vacation* (1981); this was never released and it wasn't until *Stranger Than Paradise* (1984) that he gained both critical acclaim and a devoted if small following. *Down by Law* (1986) and *Mystery Train* (1989) increased his reputation as a maker of offbeat films, noted for their "European sensibility" – seemingly improvised, often antic elements, and a personalism that does not so much attack mainstream America as divert it.

Jarrell, Randall (1914–65) poet, literary critic; born in Nashville, Tenn. He was a student of John Crowe Ransom and Robert Penn Warren at Vanderbilt University. His academic career was interrupted by his service with the Army Air Corps in World War II (1942–46). His war poems attracted national attention in the 1940s; *The Woman at the Washington Zoo* (1960) won a National Book Award. *Poetry and the Age* (1953), a reevaluation of modern American poets, established Jarrell as a critic with unfailing judgment and a witty style, while his one novel *Pictures from an Institution* (1954), is regarded as a minor classic of the academic-novel genre. Most of his career he taught at the University of North Carolina (1947–51; 1953–54; 1961–65). He was consultant in poetry to the Library of Congress (1956–58). His premature death resulted from his being hit by a car.

Jarrett, Keith (1945–   ) jazz musician; born in Allentown, Pa. A highly original piano stylist, he played with Art Blakey, Charles Lloyd, and Miles Davis between 1965–70 and was the leader of his own groups thereafter.

Jarves, James Jackson (1818–88) editor, art critic, collector; born in Boston, Mass. Born to wealth, he was educated privately, traveled extensively, and was the editor of the first weekly newspaper in the Hawaiian Islands, *Polynesian* (1840–48). He returned to America (1848), but in the 1850s he settled in Florence, Italy, where he collected and wrote about art. He served as the U.S. vice-consul there (1880–82). In addition to his superb collection of early Italian paintings (which he donated to Yale), he collected Venetian glass and textiles among other artifacts.

Jarvis, Edward (1803–84) physician; born in Concord, Mass. He left private practice in 1843 to open a house for the insane in Dorchester, Mass. An "alienist" – as psychiatrists of the time were called – he wrote a 600-page report on the numbers and conditions of the insane and idiots that resulted in a new state facility. His love for statistics led to collaborations with and reforms by census reporters, and the collection of an international library that was donated to the American Statistical Association.

Jastrow, Marcus (Mordechai) (1829–1903) rabbi, scholar; born in Posen, Poland. Educated in Germany, he was active in the Polish revolutionary cause, for which he was imprisoned and then exiled by the Russians. He came to the U.S.A. in 1866 as rabbi of the Rodeph Shalom congregation in Philadelphia. In support of Conservative Judaism, he helped found (1867) and then taught at Maimonides College. A productive scholar, his greatest accomplishment was his enormous dictionary of Jewish literature (1886–1903).

Jastrow, Robert (1925–   ) physicist, writer; born in New York City. Involved in the theoretical aspects of space exploration and the early development of the National Aeronautics and Space Administration, he was director of the Goddard Institute for Space Studies (1961–81). He joined the faculty of Dartmouth College (1973) and became director of the Mt. Wilson Institute, Calif. (1990). His books include *Red Giants and White Dwarfs* (1963) and *Journey to the Stars* (1989).

Javits, Jacob K. (Koppel) (1904–86) U.S. senator; born in New York City. A liberal Republican, he served a district of New York City in the U.S. House of Representatives (1947–54), as New York state's attorney general (1954–57), and in the U.S. Senate (1957–81). Although initially a supporter of the Vietnam War, he introduced the legislation that became the War Powers Act, restricting the president's power to commit troops abroad.

Jaworski, Leon (1905–82) lawyer; born in Waco, Texas. Child of Polish and Austrian immigrants, he became the youngest person ever admitted to the Texas bar (1925). In 1931 he joined the Houston firm that became Fulbright & Jaworski. During and after World War II, as chief of the war crimes trial section of the Judge Advocate General's Corps, he prosecuted Nazi war criminals. He headed many organizations, including the American Bar Association (1971–72). He directed the Watergate Special Prosecution Force (1973–74) that led to the resignation of President Richard Nixon, then returned to private practice.

Jay, John (1745–1829) diplomat, statesman; born in New York City. He practiced law before entering the First Continental Congress (1774). Originally opposed to outright independence, he changed his view after the Declaration of Independence (1776). He wrote New York's first constitution (1777) and served as president of the Second Continental Congress (1778–79) before becoming ambassador to Spain. He was unsuccessful in his attempt to persuade Spain to recognize American independence. In conjunction with Benjamin Franklin and John Adams, he negotiated and signed the Treaty of Paris (1783) which ended the American Revolution. He then served as secretary of foreign affairs (1783–89) and as the first chief justice of the Supreme Court (1789–95). In 1794, he negotiated and signed "Jay's Treaty" with Great Britain. He also served as governor of New York (1795–1801) before retiring to his farm in Bedford, N.Y.

Jeffers, (John) Robinson (1887–1962) poet, writer; born in Pittsburgh, Pa. He attended six colleges and universities in Europe and America, studying medicine and forestry among other subjects. He began writing in 1912, and, from 192_ lived in seclusion by the ocean near Carmel, Calif., wher_ built his own stone house. He is known for his mythical ly_ and narrative poems, as in *Roan Stallion, Tamar, and Ot_ Poems* (1925), most of which promoted his pessimistic vie_ of humanity in the larger scheme of an impersonal cosmos_

Jeffers, (William Martin) Bill (1876–1953) railroad executive_ born in North Platte, Nebr. He worked for the Union Pacific Railroad for 63 years, starting as a callboy at age 14, eventually becoming president (1937–46) and vice-chairman (1947–53). He introduced low-cost passenger service and made the Union Pacific profitable through his legendary dedication to the railroad and his hands-on management style. During World War II he directed the synthetic rubber industry for the War Production Board (1942–44).

Jefferson, "Blind" Lemon (1897–1929) musician; born near Dallas, Texas. He was born blind into a poor sharecropping family in east Texas, where he eventually won his first following as an itinerant blues singer and guitarist. Throughout the 1920s he performed on the streets and in juke joints in Texas, Oklahoma, and the Deep South. Between 1927–29, he was the most commercially successful country blues artist, making over 90 records for the Paramount label in Chicago, including the widely-imitated classics "Matchbox Blues" and "Black Snake Moan." His recorded legacy represents one of the most comprehensive and influential accounts of African-American life in the South in the early 1900s. He was found frozen to death in a snowdrift after leaving a party following a recording session in Chicago in December 1929.

Jefferson, Joseph (1829–1905) actor; born in Philadelphia. Third in a line of that name, he was part of an old theater family. Following his debut at age four mimicking Thomas D. Rice, singer of "Jim Crow," he had a career that spanned 71 years. He became America's preeminent comedian, describing his own profile as "pure nutcracker type." In 1856 he visited Europe, then returned to join Laura Keene's company where he played Dr. Pangloss in *The Heir-at-Law* and Asa Trenchard in *Our American Cousin*. His greatest success was his own version of *Rip Van Winkle,* a role he played solely between 1865 and 1880. In fact, there were critics who said that all of his characterizations were identical with his Rip Van Winkle. He succeeded Edwin Booth as president of the Players in 1893. His last performance was in 1904 in *Cricket on the Hearth,* after which he lectured widely and published his autobiography. Four of his sons continued the family tradition as actors.

Jefferson, Mark (Sylvester William) (1863–1949) geographer; born in Melrose, Mass. He interrupted his studies at Boston University (B.U.) in 1883 to work at the National Observatory in Cordoba, Argentina, graduating from B.U. in 1889. He then taught in Massachusetts public schools, becoming superintendent of schools in Lexington (1893–96); he earned his Harvard M.A. in 1898. From 1901 to 1939 he was in charge of geography at Ypsilanti's Normal College (now Eastern Michian University). A skilled linguist, enthusiastic fieldworker, and prolific writer, he published numerous articles and books; among his better known books are *Men in Europe* (1924), *Principles of Geography* (1926), and *Man in the United States* (1933).

Jefferson, Martha (b. Wayles Skelton) (1748–82) wife of Thomas Jefferson; born near Richmond, Va. Daughter of a lawyer, she was a young widow when she [...] omas Jefferson in 1772 and settled at Monticello. [...] ture death left Jefferson devastated; it was said he [...] her he would never marry again, and he did not. [...] eir children, Martha and Mary, survived to maturity [...] ted their father as hostesses in the White House.

[...], Thomas (1743–1826) third U.S. president; born in [...] arle County, Va. Son of a surveyor-landowner and a [...] r who was a member of the distinguished Randolph [...] y of Virginia, he graduated from the College of William [...] Mary (1762) and read law under George Wythe. After [...] veral years of law practice, Jefferson was elected to the [...] Virginia House of Burgesses (1769–75) and sided with the revolutionary faction, writing an influential tract, *A Summary View of the Rights of British America* (1774). In 1770 he began designing and building Monticello, which would occupy him on and off for some 35 years. Here in 1772 he brought his new wife, Martha Wyles Skelton; together they had six children, only two of whom survived into maturity; she herself died in 1782. Jefferson was among those who called the First Continental Congress in 1774; as a delegate to the Second Congress (1775–77), he was the principal drafter of the Declaration of Independence, adopted on July 4, 1776, which embodied some of his ideas on the natural rights of certain people. Jefferson then returned to Virginia, where as a member of its legislature (1776–79), he took the lead in creating a state constitution and then served as governor (1779–81); during this time he proposed that Virginia abolish the slave trade and assure religious freedom, but he did not achieve this. He was not very successful in organizing Virginian resistance to the British military operations there and would come under criticism for his lack of leadership. Returning to the Continental Congress in 1783, Jefferson drafted the policy organizing the Northwest Territory and secured the adoption of the decimal system of coinage. He was sent to France in 1784 with Benjamin Franklin and Samuel Adams to negotiate commercial treaties and the next year succeeded Franklin as ambassador there. In 1789 George Washington appointed Jefferson secretary of state. In that position he became head of the liberal Democratic-Republican faction – as it was then called – and worked against the more conservative Federalist policies of Hamilton, Madison, and Washington. Jefferson resigned as secretary of state at the end of 1793 to devote himself to his estate at Monticello. (There is no denying, either, that he retained about 150 slaves there, selling or "giving" them to others, treating them as property; he could accept this along with his high ideals because he regarded Africans as inferior beings.) In 1796 Jefferson was elected vice-president under Federalist John Adams. After four troubled years in that position (1797–1801), he beat Adams and, barely, Aaron Burr for the presidency, thanks in large part to the fact that his arch rival, Hamilton, supported him when the Electoral College vote was tied. Among the events of his triumphant first term (1801–05) were the successful war against Barbary pirates, the Louisiana Purchase (which more than doubled the size of the U.S.A.), and the Lewis and Clark Expedition. His second term (1805–09), however, was marred by vice-president Burr's trial for treason and Jefferson's highly unpopular embargo on trade with England and France. In 1809 he retired to his estate at Monticello, continuing his scholarly and scientific interests and helping to found the University of Virginia (1825). The campus he designed for the latter, the masterpiece of his periodic architectural endeavors, ushered in the Classical Revival in the United States; he also designed the Virginia state capitol and several fine homes. In 1813 he began what became an extended and remarkable exchange of letters with his old political adversary, John Adams; both died on July 4, 1826, the 50th anniversary of the adoption of the Declaration of Independence. A complex man, happier when at intellectual pursuits than as an elected politician (he made no reference to his presidency on his tombstone), Jefferson was more admired abroad in his day than at home, where he was charged by some with everything from godlessness to fathering a child with his black servant girl. (This last charge has never been proved.) In the 20th century he has assumed the status of one of the greatest of all Americans, respected for his many achievements, from pioneering work in several disciplines to prophetic insights into such issues as freedom of the press.

Jeffrey, Richard (Carl) (1926–) philosopher, logician; born in Boston, Mass. After earning a Princeton doctorate in philosophy (1958), he taught engineering at Massachusetts Institute of Technology (1959–60) and philosophy at Stanford (1960–64), City College of New York (1964–67), and the University of Pennsylvania (1967–74), then became a professor at Princeton. His specialties included decision and probability theory.

Jeffries, James J. (Jackson) (1875–1953) boxer; born in Carroll, Ohio. After winning the heavyweight championship in 1899 (in only his 13th professional fight) with a knockout of Bob Fitzsimmons, he defended his title seven times before retiring undefeated in 1905. In 1910 he lost in a comeback bid as the "great white hope" against Jack Johnson, who knocked him out in the fifteenth round. Jeffries's career record was 20 victories, one loss, and two draws. On retiring he promoted amateur boxing.

Jelavich, Charles (1922–) historian, Slavic specialist; born in Mt. View, Calif. Teaching longest at the University of Indiana: Bloomington (1962), he chaired the history department's East European Field Committee (1974–75). Working both nationally and internationally to promote Slavic studies, he served on the U.S. Committee on International Exchange of Persons (1971–74), was on the editorial board of both the American and East European editions of *Slavic Review,* and wrote numerous books and articles on the history of the Balkan states.

Jelliffe, Smith Ely (1866–1945) neurologist, psychoanalyst, editor, author; born in New York City. After starting out as a civil engineer, he switched to medicine, taking his M.D. in 1889; that same year he cofounded the important *Journal of Nervous and Mental Disease,* becoming sole owner and managing editor (1902–45). Meanwhile, he had also shown an interest in pharmacology, teaching it at the New York College of Pharmacy and editing the *Journal of Pharmacology* (1897–1901). In 1907 he became a clinical professor of mental diseases at Fordham University Medical School (1907–13); while there he invited Carl Jung for a famous lecture series in 1912. Jelliffe himself began to practice Freudian psychoanalysis, eventually earning the sobriquet, "father of psychosomatic medicine." His greatest influence, however, probably came from his work as an editor and as coauthor of *Diseases of the Nervous System* (6 editions, 1915–35).

Jennewein, Carl Paul (1890–1980) sculptor; born in Stuttgart, Germany. He emigrated to New York City (1907), studied at the Art Students League, returned to Europe (1913–14), studied in Rome (1916), and returned to New York to specialize in stylized and decorative sculptures, such as *The Greek Dance* (1926). In 1963 he became president of Brookgreen Gardens, S.C., a sculpture garden and nature preserve.

Jenney, William Le Baron (1832–1907) architect and engineer; born in Fairhaven, Mass. He founded the Chicago school of architecture, pioneering the development of steel-frame construction in prototype skyscrapers like the Home Insurance Building (1884–85) and training among others Louis Sullivan and Daniel Burnham.

Jennings, Herbert S. (Spencer) (1868–1947) protozoologist; born in Tonica, Ill. He held several teaching and research positions before completing his higher education, then studied physics and psychology in Germany (1896–97). There he began his controversial studies on stimulus-response behavior of unicellular organisms and lower invertebrates. He taught at Montana State Agricultural and Mechanical College (1897–98), moved to Dartmouth (1898–99), then became a professor at the University of Michigan (1900–03). He joined the University of Pennsylvania (1903–05), then relocated to Johns Hopkins (1906–38), where he made major contributions to studies of the genetics and sexual reproduction of protozoa. After retirement, he lectured and performed additional genetic research on paramecia at the University of California: Los Angeles (1939–46). His speeches and writings on the philosophy of biology were popular with both scientists and nonprofessionals.

Jensen, Arthur R. (Robert) (1923–   ) psychologist; born in San Diego, Calif. An educational psychologist at the University of California: Berkeley (1958), he concluded in an explosive *Harvard Education Review* article (1969) that on average whites are more intelligent than blacks; his subsequent report (1979) that intelligence tests are not race biased further stoked the controversy surrounding his work.

Jensen, Jens (1860–1951) landscape architect; born in Dybbol, Denmark. Coming to America at age 24, he became a gardener in the Chicago West Parks in 1886, and rapidly rose to become superintendent of Humboldt Park, a position he held until 1900 when he was fired because he exposed graft in the Chicago parks system. Creating the "prairie style of landscape design," he distributed local plants along broad lawns for midwestern parks (1900–35), retiring to run Clearing, a rustic school of landscape design in Wisconsin.

Jensen, Peter Laurits (1886–1961) audio engineer; born near Stubbekobing, Denmark. He came to the United States in 1909. With Edwin Pridham, he developed the first dynamic horn loudspeaker, called "Magnavox" (1914–15). He helped found the Magnavox Company in 1917. During World War I, he developed an antinoise microphone that could be heard over engine roar. In the 1920s he worked on improving sound fidelity. In 1943 he founded Jensen Industries.

Jepson, Willis Linn (1867–1946) botanist; born near Vacaville, Calif. He spent his career at the University of California: Berkeley (1899–1937), which now holds his extensive notes, library, and herbarium. Known as the "dean of California botanists," he wrote over 200 scientific papers and eight books, including the classic *A Manual of the Flowering Plants of California* (1925) and the uncompleted *A*

Flora of California (published 1909–43). He was a taxonomic conservative whose writings emphasized using the living plant as a model and making detailed field observations. An outspoken conservationist, he founded the California Botanical Society (1913) and the Save the Redwoods League (1918). His dedication and erratic emotionalism caused him to be either admired or resented by his associates. A genus of flowering herbaceous plants, *Jepsonia,* is named for him.

Jervis, John B. (Bloomfield) (1795–1885) engineer, railroad developer; born in Huntington, N.Y. He helped survey and build the Erie Canal (1819–25). He then joined the Delaware & Hudson Company for which he not only built the first railway in the United States, but also drew up the specifications for the first locomotive to run in the U.S.A., the "Stourbridge Lion" (1829). In 1830 he became chief engineer for the Mohawk & Hudson Railway and continued upgrading railroads and equipment. He designed the locomotive "Experiment," which obtained the fastest speeds in the world at the time. He was chief engineer for the Chenango (N.Y.) Canal (1833) and the Croton Aqueduct; he consulted to Boston, Mass., on a new water supply (1846); and he helped build four other railroads. He wrote several books including *The Question of Labour and Capital* (1877).

Jessup, Philip Caryl (1897–1986) law professor, government official; born in New York City. He taught international law at Columbia University in the 1930s. He helped in planning post-World War II relief, in founding the United Nations and Israel, and in ending the Berlin blockade. He was accused by Senator Joseph McCarthy of being pro-Communist but was completely absolved by a senate committee (1951). He resumed teaching at Columbia (1953) and sat on the International Court of Justice (1961–70).

Jewett, Charles Coffin (1816–68) librarian, bibliographer; born in Lebanon, Maine. He graduated from Brown University in 1835 and became the school's first academic librarian. In 1843 he published a *Catalogue of the Library of Brown University* and this led to his appointment as first librarian of the Smithsonian Institution. At the Smithsonian much of his work was devoted to developing methods of cataloguing the holdings of various libraries, with an ultimate goal (never realized) of producing a national union catalogue of all the libraries in the country. His hopes to make the Smithsonian primarily into a reference library brought him into conflict with the Secretary, Joseph Henry, and Jewett left Washington in 1854 to become librarian and then superintendent of the Boston Public Library (1855–68). Perhaps his most familiar and lasting innovation was the use of separate slips rather than a bound ledger to keep track of individual library loans.

Jewett, Frank Baldwin (1879–1949) electrical engineer; born in Pasadena, Calif. In 1904 he began working for American Telephone & Telegraph Co. as an electrical engineer. He later worked under John J. Carty and played a major role in transcontinental telephone transmission. Jewett founded the Bell Telephone Laboratories (1925), where he was president (1925–40) and chairman of the board (1940–49).

Jewett, (Theodora) Sarah Orne (A. D. Eliot, Alice Eliot, Sarah C. Sweet, pen names) (1849–1909) writer; born in South Berwick, Maine. She graduated from Berwick Academy in 1866. Remaining in her home town, she spent her time writing short stories, poetry, children's books, and novels that drew on her intimate knowledge of provincial life. She is considered a major American writer of regional fiction, and is best known for her novel, *The Country of the Pointed Firs* (1896).

Jewett, William (?1789/92–1874) painter; born in East Haddam, Conn. He moved to New York City (c. 1820), created academic portraits, and was the painting partner of Samuel Waldo.

Jewett, William Cornell (1823–93) publicist, peace advocate; born in New York City. His early history in the West was obscure and there were those who questioned the source of his fortune. But after settling in California and then Colorado he was wealthy enough to dedicate his life to pacifism. His first appearance in this regard was as a delegate from Pike's Peak at a Colorado peace convention (1861). During the Civil War he traveled to Europe to plead for peaceful resolution of the war. Known as "Colorado Jewett," he made forays back and forth across the Atlantic to lobby for his cause, issuing a universal appeal for peace (1864). He attempted to negotiate an end to the war by bringing representatives from the North and South to Niagara Falls (July 1864), but the war proceeded despite his intervention.

Jobs, Steven (Paul) (1955–) computer engineer, entrepreneur; born in Los Altos, Calif. Educated at Reed College (Portland, Ore.) in the early 1970s, he and Stephen Wozniak built their own microcomputers in a garage. By the mid-1970s, they had built the first Apple I. In 1976–77, they formed Apple Computer Company, with Jobs as chairman. The company did phenomenally well, introducing a succession of increasingly more sophisticated McIntosh computers known for their "user-friendliness." In 1985, he resigned from Apple after losing a power struggle with president John Sculley; Jobs later founded NeXT, Inc.

Joffrey, Robert (b. Abdullah Jaffa Anver Bey Kahn) (1930–88) dancer, choreographer, teacher, artistic director; born in Seattle, Wash. Of Afghan descent, he trained at the High School of Performing Arts, New York City, and the School of American Ballet, and made his debut in 1949. He taught dance and choreographed ballets before forming his first company in 1954. The City Center Joffrey Ballet, which he founded in 1965, revitalized ballet with multimedia works such as *Astarte* (1967), and became a major force in the world of dance.

Jogues, Isaac (1607–46) Catholic missionary, saint; born in Orléans, France. A Jesuit priest sent to North America in 1636, he worked among the Huron Indians, journeying as far west as Sault Ste. Marie (now in Michigan). In 1642 he and his companions were captured by Iroquois; he was tortured, enslaved, and held captive at Ossernenon (now Auriesville, N.Y.), where he eventually escaped, reaching New Amsterdam with aid from the Dutch. Following a period in France, he returned to North America (1644); in 1646 he was captured by Mohawks near Ossernenon and murdered soon afterward. A National Shrine to the North American Martyrs was later erected at Auriesville. Jogues and seven other martyred missionaries to the Indians were canonized by the church in 1930.

Johannesen, Grant (1921–) pianist; born in Salt Lake City, Utah. One of the leading American pianists of his time, he made his New York debut in 1944 and thereafter performed internationally, including three successful Russian tours.

Johanson, Donald C. (Carl) (1943–) physical anthropologist; born in Chicago, Ill. He was curator of physical anthropology at the Cleveland Museum of Natural History (1972–81) before becoming founding director of the Institute of Human Origins, Berkeley, Calif. (1981). His explorations of the Afar Triangle, Ethiopia, led to his revolutionary discovery of "Lucy" (1974), the oldest (c. 3.5 million years) and most complete human skeleton fossil known to anthropologists.

Johnny Appleseed See CHAPMAN, JOHN.

Johns, Jasper (1930–) painter; born in Allendale, S.C. After studying at the University of South Carolina, he settled in New York City (1952). By 1955 he had transformed the direction of abstract expressionism by using everyday objects and reinterpreting them. His series of paintings of flags and his mixed media images of targets represented a return to the object as art. He worked in encaustic, a mixture of pigment and beeswax, which, when applied with heat, creates a strong, glossy surface. Known as an intellectual artist and a precursor of pop art, he continued to produce original works and gain in reputation long after the pop art movement faded.

Johnson, Alexander Bryan (1786–1867) philosopher; born in Gosport, England. Emigrating and settling in Utica, N.Y., in 1811, he became an industrialist and banker, while writing philosophic works that anticipated aspects of 20th-century analytic philosophy, as in *The Philosophy of Human Knowledge* (1828). He also wrote on political and economic topics.

Johnson, (Alonzo) Lonnie (1899–1970) jazz musician; born in New Orleans. A versatile blues guitarist, he recorded with Duke Ellington and Louis Armstrong in the 1920s and accompanied dozens of blues singers between 1925–45.

Johnson, Andrew (1808–75) seventeenth U.S. president; born in Raleigh, N.C. Poor, self-educated but ambitious, he moved to Tennessee in 1826 to pursue the tailor's trade. He saved enough money and soon entered politics, becoming an advocate of labor and popular democracy against the claims of birth and wealth. Beginning as an alderman, he worked his way up to represent Tennessee in the U.S. House of Representatives (Dem.; 1843–53), and became governor (1853–57), then U.S. senator (1857–62). Although he had defended slavery, he refused to accept secession; his courageous stand led Lincoln to appoint him military governor of Tennessee and then to select him as vice-president for the 1864 election; his presence on the ticket undoubtedly helped the beleaguered Lincoln get reelected. Becoming president on Lincoln's assassination in 1865, Johnson attempted to pursue the conciliatory reconstruction policies Lincoln had envisioned but Johnson was increasingly thwarted by Radical Republican desires for revenge. The conflict finally led to an 1868 congressional impeachment of Johnson, but he survived by one vote. He left office embittered and in disgrace, but later found a measure of exoneration, and, five months before his death, regained his Senate seat.

Johnson, Clarence L. ("Kelly") (1910–90) aircraft designer; born in Ishpeming, Mich. After receiving a master's degree in aeronautical engineering from the University of Michigan, he went to work for Lockheed Corporation in 1933. Beginning as a tool designer he held positions as flight test engineer and stress analyst before becoming chief research engineer in 1938. He was involved in designing over 40 airplanes, including the U-2 high-altitude reconnaissance plane, the F-104 Starfighter, and the P-38 Lightning plane used during World War II. He also helped develop several high-speed long-distance airplanes. During his years at Lockheed he became best known for his leadership of the "Skunk Works," the company's advanced development unit. In 1943, in only 143 days, the group produced the nation's first operational jet fighter, the P-80 Shooting Star. Awarded the Medal of Freedom in 1964, Johnson retired in 1975 but remained a senior adviser to Lockheed until his death.

Johnson, (Claudia Alta b. Taylor) Lady Bird (1912–) First Lady; born in Karnack, Texas. She studied journalism before she married Lyndon Johnson in 1934. She borrowed from her inheritance to help finance his first election campaign. As first lady, she supported the "war on poverty," the Headstart Program, and worked for the "beautification" of Washington, D.C. Following the presidency, she wrote *White House Diary* and remained active in beautification projects.

Johnson, Douglas (Wilson) (1878–1944) geomorphologist, geographer; born in Parkersburg, W.Va. After earning his Ph.D. from Columbia University, he taught at the Massachusetts Institute of Technology (1903–07) and Harvard University (1907–12) where he met William M. Davis, the leading expert in geomorphology, then returned to teach at Columbia. Intensely patriotic, he was commissioned a major by army intelligence during World War I and studied the effect of land formation on military strategy in Europe. A professor at Columbia (1919–44), he published *The Shore Processes and Shoreline Development* (1919) and *New England-Acadian Shoreline* (1925), later founding the *Journal of Geomorphology* (1938–42).

Johnson, (Earvin, Jr.) "Magic" (1959–) basketball player; born in Lansing, Mich. After leading Michigan State University to a National Collegiate Athletic Association championship in 1979, he played 12 years as a guard for the Los Angeles Lakers (1980–91). He was named to the All-NBA (National Basketball Association) team nine times (1983–91), and was voted the league's Most Valuable Player three times (1987, 1990, 1991). He established records for most career assists and most playoff assists. He retired from the NBA in 1992 because of testing positive for the HIV virus. In the 1992 Olympics, he was a member of the "dream team" that won the basketball gold medal.

Johnson, Eastman (1824–1906) painter; born in Lovell, Maine. He studied in Germany and France (1849–55), and returned to America to continue his career as a genre and portrait painter. His series of canvases focusing on harvesting cranberries, such as *The Cranberry Pickers* (c. 1875), remains his most famous work.

Johnson, Edward (1598–1672) historian; probably born in Canterbury, England. He was trained as a joiner, then emigrated to Boston (1630). He traded with the Indians and settled in Charlestown, Mass. (1636). A founder of Woburn, Mass. (1640), he worked at a variety of civic positions. He is best known for his work extolling the attractions of the colonies in America, *The Wonder-Working Providence of Sion's Savior in New England* (1653), published in England in 1654 as *A History of New England*.

Johnson, Edward Crosley, III (1930–) financial executive; born in Boston, Mass. Born into a prominent Beacon Hill family, he graduated from Harvard in 1954 and joined his father's firm, Fidelity Management & Research Corp., rising to president and chief executive officer from 1972–77. In 1977 he became chairman and CEO of Fidelity's parent,

FMR Corp., which he built into one of the nation's largest money management concerns, particularly by aggressive marketing of mutual funds.

Johnson, Eldridge Reeves (1867–1945) inventor, business executive; born in Wilmington, Del. He was apprenticed to a machinist in Philadelphia. Following a trip out West, he developed a spring-driven motor for the gramophone (1896) and founded the Victor Talking Machine Company (1901). His advertising trademark, "His Master's Voice." became famous worldwide. His company's fortunes declined during the 1920s; in 1927, Victor was merged with the Radio Corporation of America. He gave generously to the University of Pennsylvania.

Johnson, Eliza (b. McCardle) (1810–76) First Lady; born in Leesburg, Tenn. Marrying Andrew Johnson in 1827, she educated her husband at home. Later she suffered from tuberculosis and made only two public appearances while in the White House.

Johnson, Frank (Minis), Jr. (1918–) judge; born in Winston County, Ala. After taking his law degree at the University of Alabama (1943), he served in World War II as an infantry captain (1943–45). He went into private practice (1946–55) before becoming a U.S. district judge in Alabama (1955–79), the youngest sitting federal judge at that point. In his first opinion from that bench (1956), he declared segregation on Alabama city buses unconstitutional, and from then on he found himself at the center of the civil rights storm centered in Alabama. Drawing always on the Constitution and the true spirit of laws, he effectively desegregated Alabama's schools, bus terminals, and public facilities of all kinds; in 1960 he became the first federal judge to draw up a court-ordered legislative reapportionment; in 1962 he put an end to discriminatory voter registration; in 1965 he ordered that Martin Luther King Jr. be allowed to lead the march from Selma to Montgomery. He soon found himself ostracized by many in Alabama; his mother's house was bombed; a cross was burned on his front yard; Governor George Wallace, a law school classmate, called him an "integrating, carpet-bagging, scalawagging bold-faced liar." In 1977, President Carter nominated him to head the FBI, but health problems prevented him from accepting. He did accept appointment to the U.S. Court of Appeals – 5th Circuit (1979–81), then 11th circuit (1981–91) – and he came to be honored, even in the South, as a major force in breaking down the old forms of discrimination and injustice in the U.S.A.

Johnson, Hiram W. (Warren) (1866–1945) reformer, governor, U.S. senator; born in Sacramento, Calif. A leading figure in Progressive reform politics, he was elected governor of California on the Republican ticket (1911–17). As governor he supported women's suffrage, the abolition of child labor, and railroad regulation. In 1912 he ran as vice-presidential candidate on Theodore Roosevelt's "Bull Moose" ticket. Elected to the U.S. Senate as a Republican (1917–45), he was known as a staunch isolationist.

Johnson, Howard (Deering) (1896–1972) business executive; born in Boston, Mass. Uneducated beyond elementary school, he developed 28 flavors of ice cream for his Wollaston, Mass., drugstore soda fountain and by 1929 was franchising his name and products. He won exclusive catering rights on thousands of miles of East Coast highways and built the country's largest private food distribution corporation before retiring in 1959.

Johnson, Hugh (Samuel) (1882–1942) army officer, government official; born in Fort Scott, Kans. He graduated from West Point (1903) and held several posts including superintendent of Sequoia National Park. He earned a law degree (1916) and served with Pershing in Mexico (1916). He helped to draft the Selective Service Act (1917). He became a brigadier general at age 35 (the youngest such since the Civil War), but World War I ended before his division sailed for France. He retired from the army (1919). He worked for Bernard Baruch (1927–33). A member of Franklin Roosevelt's "brain trust," he headed the National Recovery Administration (1933–34) but his autocratic manner offended virtually everyone he dealt with and he had to resign. As a syndicated newspaper columnist and radio commentator, he opposed Roosevelt over the "packing" of the Supreme Court and the issue of a third term.

Johnson, (James Louis) "J. J." (1924–) jazz musician; born in Indianapolis, Ind. He emerged as an influential trombonist in the mid-1940s; in the 1960s, he became one of the first African-Americans to work as a film and television composer.

Johnson, James P. (Price) (1891–1955) jazz musician; born in Brunswick, N.J. An important influence on Duke Ellington, he emerged in New York after 1912 as the leading exponent of the stride piano school. He wrote over 200 songs, including "Charleston," scored several musical revues, including *Runnin' Wild* in 1923, and premiered his extended work "Yamecraw" at Carnegie Hall in 1928. He made numerous piano rolls and small group recordings between 1917–51.

Johnson, James Weldon (1871–1938) lawyer, lyricist, writer, social activist; born in Jacksonville, Fla. After graduating from college, he organized a system of secondary education for African-Americans in Jacksonville. The first African-American to be admitted to the Florida bar through examination in a state court (1897), he moved to New York City (1901) to pursue his love of music and theater. He, his brother J. Rosamond Johnson, and Bob Cole formed a song-and-dance act that was famous in America and Europe for several years. He collaborated with his brother as a lyricist on some 200 songs, including "Under the Bamboo Tree" and "The Congo Love Song"; they also wrote "Lift Every Voice and Sing," long considered the "black national anthem." Black Republicans in New York enlisted his services in Theodore Roosevelt's presidential reelection campaign (1904); in return he was appointed a consul in Venezuela (1906) and Nicaragua (1909), where he helped maintain peace and order during the revolution of 1912. He resigned from the consular service after the Democratic Senate rejected him as consul to the Azores. Turning to writing, he anonymously published a novel, *Autobiography of an Ex-Colored Man* (1912), and a volume of poetry, and he became editor of the *New York Age,* the oldest black newspaper in America. During the 1920s he was one of the leading contributors to and interpreters of the so-called Harlem Renaissance and he published anthologies of African-American poetry and spirituals, critical essays, and his own works such as *God's Trombones* (1927), "Negro folk sermons" in verse. Meanwhile, he had become field secretary for the National Association for the Advancement of Colored People (NAACP) (1916). He greatly expanded NAACP membership, investigated lynchings, and championed black causes nationally. Named NAACP executive (1921), he lobbied for passage of the Dyer Anti-Lynching Bill and helped awaken Americans to the enormity of lynching. He resigned from the NAACP (1930) after seeing the U.S. Supreme Court condemn white primary laws. Returning to his literary career, he wrote and edited poetry, documented black life in America, and wrote his autobiography, *Along This Way* (1933). He also taught at Fisk University and New York University. Although his reputation would be eclipsed by more outspoken African-Americans, he had provided a role model for several generations by the sheer vitality and diversity of his achievements.

Johnson, (John Arthur) Jack (1878–1946) boxer; born in Galveston, Texas. The first black to win the world heavyweight title, he was one of boxing's greatest and most controversial champions. He worked as a janitor, dockhand, and stableboy before becoming a professional boxer in 1899. After winning the title in 1908 with a knockout of Tommy Burns, he defended the championship against a succession of "great white hopes," including former champion James J. Jeffries, who came out of a six-year retirement in 1910 only to be knocked out in the 15th round. Because of his flamboyance and self-confidence – and his marriage to a white woman – Johnson incurred the wrath of racist politicians and religious leaders who successfully secured a Mann Act conviction against him in 1913. He took sanctuary in Europe and lost the championship in 1915 to Jess Willard by a knockout in the 26th round. Johnson later returned to the U.S.A. to serve his sentence and to fight in boxing exhibitions. He spent his final years operating nightclubs and working in carnivals. He posted a career record of 78 wins, eight losses, and 12 no-decisions, with 45 knockouts. A play (1968) and motion picture (1970) based on his life, *The Great White Hope,* starred James Earl Jones.

Johnson, John Graver (1841–1917) lawyer, art collector; born in Philadelphia. He graduated from the University of Pennsylvania Law School (1863) and became a corporation lawyer in Philadelphia. During his career he built an impressive collection of 19th-century English and French paintings, as well as early work by Old Masters. He bequeathed his collection to the city of Philadelphia, where it is housed in the municipal museum in Fairmount Park.

Johnson, John Harold (1918–) publisher, consumer products executive; born in Arkansas City, Ark. He founded Johnson Publishing Co. (1942) and launched the *Negro Digest* (1942), a successful compilation modeled on *Reader's Digest* but aimed at African-Americans. That was followed by *Ebony* (1945), a breakthrough vehicle for national advertisers to target black middle-class markets. His other corporate interests included radio stations, books, and cosmetics, and for many years he was known as the richest African-American.

Johnson, John J. (1912–) political scientist, historian; born in White Swan, Wash. He taught at Stanford University (1946–77) and the University of New Mexico (1980–85). He wrote such influential works as *Political Change in Latin America* (1958), *The Military and Society in Latin America* (1964), and *A Hemisphere Apart* (1990), a study of the Latin American policy of the United States government.

Johnson, Joshua See JOHNSTON, JOSHUA.

Johnson, Louis (Arthur) (1891–1966) administrator; born in

Roanoke, Va. A West Virginia lawyer and army colonel in World War I, he commanded the American Legion (1932–33). As assistant secretary of war (1937–40), he modernized the army. Finance chairman for President Truman's 1948 campaign, he became secretary of defense (1949–50), but his plans for restructuring the military forces angered navy admirals and the administration, forcing his return to law practice.

Johnson, Lyndon Baines (1908–1973) thirty-sixth U.S. president; born near Stonewall, Texas. Son of schoolteachers, he taught school briefly after graduating from Southwest Texas State Teachers College (now Southwest Texas State University) (1930), then gravitated to Democratic politics. After serving as President Franklin D. Roosevelt's administrator of the National Youth Administration in Texas, he went on to the U.S. House of Representatives (1937–49) and was quickly marked by his strong support of New Deal programs. A member of the Naval Reserve, he enlisted for active duty within hours after Pearl Harbor – the first Congressman to do so; he served in the Pacific until President Roosevelt ordered all Congressmen back to their elective office in July 1942. He won a narrow race for the U.S. Senate (1948) and served two terms (1949–61). As Democratic whip and then majority leader (1955–61) – and as the consummate arm-twisting deal-maker – he helped pass some of the most progressive social legislation of the century, including the civil rights acts of 1957 and 1960. Elected John F. Kennedy's vice-president in 1960, he became president on Kennedy's assassination in November 1963; in 1964 he was returned to office by a landslide. He proclaimed a "Great Society" program to fight poverty and racism, achieving passage of the Civil Rights Act (1964) and the Voting Rights Act (1965), plus a slate of social-welfare programs including Medicare. At the same time, he led the U.S.A. into an increasingly bloody and unpopular war in Vietnam. Declining support from his own high-level appointees and increasing divisiveness around the country led to his decision not to run in 1968. He retired to his Texas ranch and to writing his memoirs. Larger than life in his public behavior but more than vulgar in his private speech, sensitive to the plight of many less-fortunate Americans but insecure in his dealings with the Eastern Democratic Establishment, he ended as something of a tragic figure because of his overreaching ways.

Johnson, Magnus (1871–1936) agrarian reformer, U.S. senator/representative; born near Kalstad, Sweden. Immigrating to Wisconsin (1891), he settled in Minnesota (1894) and took up farming. Active in the farmers' cooperative movement, as a Farmer Labor Party candidate he served in the Minnesota legislature, in the U.S. Senate (1923–1925), and in the House of Representatives (1933–35).

Johnson, Martin See under JOHNSON, OSA.

Johnson, Martin W. (Wiggo) (1893–1984) oceanographer; born in Chandler, S.D. He was an associate of the University of Washington (1933–34) before joining the Scripps Institution of Oceanography (1934–61). He made major contributions to biological and military science by investigating invertebrate-produced underwater sounds and acoustic signal reflections.

Johnson, Nelson Trusler (1887–1954) diplomat; born in Washington, D.C. While a student at George Washington University, he took his first position as an interpreter (of Chinese) for the State Department. He was assistant secretary

of state (1927–29), envoy to China (1929–41), and the wartime ambassador to Australia (1941–45). His long career in the State Department (1907–52) culminated with his position as secretary-general of the Far Eastern Commission.

Johnson, (Nicholas) Nick (1934–) government official, broadcast activist; born in Iowa City, Iowa. A University of Texas Law School graduate, he fought for broadcast reform as a Federal Communications Commissioner (FCC) (1966–73). He authored *How to Talk Back To Your TV Set* (1970), a manual for consumer advocates, and headed the National Citizens Communication Lobby in 1975. After leaving the FCC, he taught law at various universities, most notably the University of Iowa (1981).

Johnson, Nunnally (1897–1977) screenwriter, movie producer/director; born in Columbus, Ga. After many years as a newspaper reporter and then short story writer, he went to Hollywood and began writing scripts in 1933. Over the following years he wrote countless scripts, ranging from such distinguished films as *The Grapes of Wrath* (1940) to lighter fluff such as *The Dirty Dozen* (1967). Between 1935 and 1960, he also produced and directed films, but as these never garnered much acclaim, he returned to scriptwriting in his later years.

Johnson, Osa (b. Leighty) (1894–1953) born in Chanute, Kans.; **and Martin (Elmer)** (1884–1937) born in Rockford, Ill.; photographic explorers, lecturers. Martin had been drawn to travel as a youth; he became a decent photographer and got himself engaged by Jack London to sail on the *Snark* cruise that ended abruptly with London's illness (1907–09). On his return to the U.S.A., Martin opened a theater in Independence, Ill., where he showed pictures of his trip as he lectured; it was after attending such a showing that Osa met him. They were married in 1910 and soon began their travels that took them to the South Pacific and Africa, where they photographed the native peoples and wildlife. They took up flying and were the first people to fly over Africa's Mt. Kilimanjaro and Mt. Kenya and to photograph them from the air. The Johnsons produced some 20 motion pictures to accompany the lectures they gave throughout the U.S.A. Although nothing more than travelogues and lacking sophistication in everything from anthropology or zoology, the films did provide many Americans with their first view of these exotic places. Martin died in an airplane crash in Los Angeles. Osa visited Africa (1938) and wrote a best-selling account of their lives, *I Married Adventure* (1940), and many children's books, including *Osa Johnson's Jungle Friends* (1939). She married again (1939) but was divorced, and she retained her fascination with Africa to the end.

Johnson, Philip (Cortelyou) (1906–) architect and author; born in Cleveland, Ohio. His groundbreaking book, *The International Style* (1932, with Henry-Russell Hitchcock), coined the term and promoted the style. After studying with Walter Gropius and Marcel Breuer in the early 1940s, he designed small modernist houses and institutional buildings; in partnerships after the late 1960s, he turned to large, urban buildings that ushered in postmodernist architecture by incorporating historical references. His prescient designs and widely published writings have combined to make him uniquely influential in contemporary architecture.

Johnson, Rafer (Lewis) (1934–) track and field athlete; born in Hillsboro, Texas. After placing second in the decathlon in the 1956 Olympics, he won the gold medal in the 1960 Games. After retiring from competition, he was active in youth and community affairs in Los Angeles.

Johnson, Reverdy (1796–1876) lawyer, public official; born in Annapolis, Md. He graduated from St. John's College (1811), and was admitted to the bar in 1816. He became a nationally prominent authority on constitutional law. He sat in the U.S. Senate (Whig, Md.; 1845–49) and was briefly attorney general. He successfully argued in the Dred Scott case (1857) that as a slave Scott could not be a citizen and therefore had no legal standing. A pro-Union Democrat during the Civil War, he returned to the Senate from 1863–67. He defended Mary Surratt and others against charges of complicity in the assassination of Lincoln and worked to save President Johnson from impeachment. As U.S. ambassador to Great Britain (1868–69), he negotiated several important agreements.

Johnson, Robert (1911–38) musician; born in Hazelhurst, Miss. A singer-guitarist, he was the most celebrated and legendary of the Mississippi Delta bluesmen. An itinerant performer, he played on street corners and in juke joints throughout the Deep South before he was poisoned to death at the age of 27. In 1936–37, he recorded 29 songs in Dallas and San Antonio, most of which are staples of the blues and rock repertoires. Johnson's musical brilliance and tormented sensibility were ascribed to his Faustian bargain with the devil, a myth that remains at the heart of the blues. In 1990, a retrospective collection of Johnson's recordings became a million-selling album. The movie *Crossroads* is one of numerous attempts at elucidating his obscure life.

Johnson, Robert Underwood (1853–1937) editor, poet; born in Washington, D.C. Raised in Centerville, Ind., he graduated from Earlham College and in 1873 joined the staff of *Scribner's Monthly*. Named associate editor of the magazine in 1881, by then called *Century*, he edited the famous *Century* series of Civil War recollections that later became the four-volume *Battles and Leaders of the Civil War* (1887). A leading conservationist, he published John Muir's articles and lobbied for the establishment of Yosemite National Park. *Century* went into decline after 1900 and Johnson resigned the editorship under pressure in 1913. He was ambassador to Italy in 1920–21. A lifelong versifier, he published *Poems of Fifty Years* and two successor volumes in the 1930s.

Johnson, Robert Wood (1845–1910) businessman, philanthropist; born in Carbondale, Pa. He worked as a druggist in New York and organized Seabury and Johnson (1874) and then Johnson and Johnson (with his brother James W. Johnson) in 1886. Inspired by the British surgeon, Joseph Lister, he pioneered advances in surgical dressings, medical supplies, and antiseptic practices. He made bequests to colleges of pharmacy and Episcopal churches, and the foundation established in his name is one of the wealthiest in America, with particular interest in financing medical research.

Johnson, Samuel (1822–82) Protestant religious leader, author; born in Salem, Mass. A physician's son, he graduated from Harvard and Harvard Divinity School, and in collaboration with a friend, he published a hymnal in 1848. Initially a Unitarian, he became minister of the Free Church in Lynn, Mass. He opposed slavery, was a mystic and poet, and in the 1870s he published a series of scholarly studies of Oriental religions.

Johnson, Samuel William (1830–1909) agricultural chemist; born in Kingsboro, N.Y. After studying at Yale and completing his graduate work in Germany, he returned to become a professor at Yale (1856). His own research on soils, crop rotation, soil analysis, plant nutrition, fertilizers, and food adulteration advanced scientific agriculture in the U.S.A. He is also known as a pioneer in agricultural regulation (1850s) and he was one of the first to organize an American agricultural experiment station, establishing Connecticut's in 1875 and serving as its director (1877–99).

Johnson, Sargent (Claude) (1888–1967) sculptor, printmaker; born in Boston, Mass. The son of a Swedish father and a mother of Cherokee and African-American ancestry, he was based in San Francisco, and, beginning in 1915, studied at the California School of Fine Arts. He worked in wood with lacquered and painted layers of gesso and linen, as in *Forever Free* (1933).

Johnson, Sir William (1715–74) colonial baron, Indian agent; born in Smithtown, Ireland. He gained the full confidence of the Iroquois tribes, especially Mohawks. He became their agent in 1754 and led militiamen and Iroquois in a victory over the French at Lake George in 1755 (for which he was knighted). He retained his influence with Indian tribes until his death.

Johnson, Thomas (1732–1819) Supreme Court justice; born in Calvert County, Md. He represented Maryland at the First Continental Congress (1774) and served as Maryland's first governor (1777–79). He was chief judge on Maryland's general court when President Washington named him to the U.S. Supreme Court (1791–93).

Johnson, Tom Loftin (1854–1911) businessman, U.S. representative, mayor; born near Georgetown, Ky. Moving about the South during the Civil War, he had little formal education. Settling in Louisville, Ky., he worked for the street railroad owned by members of the du Pont family and gained their respect when he invented the first farebox for coins. The du Ponts then financed a series of Johnson's business ventures – taking over the street railroad in Indianapolis (1875); building a street railroad in Cleveland (1879); and then branching out into the steel business, where he made a fortune during the 1880s. After the great flood in Johnstown, Pa. (1889), he gained national attention by directing relief efforts. Meanwhile, he had become a supporter of Henry George and his single-tax doctrine, and Johnson was determined to devote himself to reforming the government. He served two terms in the U.S. House of Representatives (Dem., Ohio; 1891–95) where he supported free trade. He then served four terms as mayor of Cleveland (1902–08), where he battled for municipal reform against Mark Hanna and local business interests by combining the "grandstanding" of the populist with the "scientific" methods of the progressive. He improved the services available to the city's poor, started sanitary measures, and encouraged civic spirit. He also fought for home rule and more equitable taxation, for public ownership of utilities, and for public works and social services. Although some regarded his reforms as radical, most Americans respected them as a model of good government for cities, and Johnson's reputation would survive his premature death.

Johnson, U. (Ural) Alexis (1908–) diplomat; born in Falun, Kans. He graduated from Occidental College (1931) and entered the Foreign Service in 1935. He was praised for his role in the Korean truce negotiations. He became ambassador to Czechoslovakia (1953–58), Thailand (1958–61), and Japan (1966–69). An expert on Far Eastern affairs, he was undersecretary of state for political affairs (1969–73) and the chief U.S. delegate at the Strategic Arms Limitation Talks (1973).

Johnson, Virginia (b. Eshelman) (1925–) journalist, researcher, sexologist; born in Springfield, Mo. Educated at Washington University (St. Louis), she was a journalist and market researcher who dabbled in country music. In 1957 she joined Dr. William Masters' research group at Washington University School of Medicine and by 1959 she and Masters were founding the Masters and Johnson Institute to investigate the physiology of sexual intercourse and physiology. Their first popular publication, *Human Sexual Response* (1966), caused a major uproar with its explicit descriptions. She stayed on with Masters, helped operate their sexual therapy service, and married him in 1971. Later she and Masters published *On Sex and Human Loving* (with Robert Kolodny, 1986). Her marriage to Masters ended in 1992.

Johnson, Walter (Perry) (1887–1946) baseball pitcher; born in Humboldt, Kans. During his 21-year career with the Washington Senators (1907–27), he won 416 games, the second highest in major league history, and pitched 110 shutouts, a major league record. One of the fastest throwers in the game's history, the right-hander led the league in strikeouts 12 times. Nicknamed, "The Big Train," he was elected to baseball's Hall of Fame in 1936.

Johnson, William (1771–1834) Supreme Court justice; born in Charleston, S.C. He served in the South Carolina legislature (1794–98) and the state's high court (1798–1804) before President Jefferson named him to the U.S. Supreme Court (1804–34). He often dissented from the opinions of Chief Justice John Marshall, thereby establishing the model for recording dissenting court opinions.

Johnson, William Eugene (1862–1945) social reformer; born in Coventry, N.Y. He was a journalist and then a special officer in the U.S. Indian Service (1908–11). He received his nickname, "Pussyfoot," from his sneaky method of raiding gambling saloons in the Indian territory in Oklahoma. During the prohibition movement, he was a prominent speaker in the U.S.A. and around the world, lecturing in favor of temperance. In 1919, he lost an eye when he was struck and dragged by medical students from a lecture platform in London.

Johnson, William H. (1901–70) painter; born in Florence, S.C. After a childhood of poverty, he went to Harlem at age 17 and for five years studied painting at the National Academy of Design, then went to Europe where he lived mainly in Denmark and Norway, absorbing some European influences and gaining a reputation through exhibitions. He had married a Danish weaver and potter, Holche Krake, in 1930 and in 1938 he and his wife returned to New York where he began to produce perhaps his most important work. In 1943 he lost everything in a fire, then his wife died, and by 1947 he was placed in a mental institution. Virtually all of his surviving output – some 800 paintings and watercolors and 400 drawings and prints – was given to the National Museum of American Art in 1967, limiting its visibility. His work is, however, becoming recognized for its original fusion of such disparate strains as Van Gogh and African sculpture, Constructivism and African textiles, all united to convey a personal vision that is both modern and vernacular.

Johnson, (William Julius) Judy (1899–1989) baseball player; born in Snow Hill, Md. As a third baseman for the Homestead Grays, Pittsburgh Crawfords, and other teams of the 1920s and 1930s black baseball leagues, he was one of the great clutch hitters of the game. He hit over .300 during most seasons. In 1975 he was elected to baseball's Hall of Fame.

Johnston, Albert Sidney (1803–62) soldier; born in Washington, Ky. The son of a doctor, he graduated from West Point (1826) and served in the regular army until 1834. He commanded irregular forces in Texas in 1837–38 and led Texas troops during the Mexican War. He reentered the U.S. Army in 1849 and served until April 1861. Given command of Confederate forces between the Appalachians and the Mississippi river, he surprised Grant's army at Shiloh on April 6, 1862, but was killed in action there, perhaps enhancing his reputation as one of the greatest of all soldiers and the general who might have saved the Confederacy.

Johnston, Henrietta Deering (?1670–?1728/9) painter; born in England. Little is known of her life before she emigrated to Charleston, S.C., in 1705. She is considered one of the first important women painters in America. Her work consisted of pastel portraits, which lacked depth perception but were simple and charming, as seen in *Anne Broughton* (1720).

Johnston, Henry Simpson (1867–1970) governor; born near Evansville, Ind. A lawyer, he served on the Oklahoma Territorial Council (1897–1904), becoming a state senator in 1907. As Democratic governor of Oklahoma (1927–29), he clashed with the legislature over state highway commission appointments, invoking martial law to neutralize his opponents. Impeached in 1929, he served in the Oklahoma senate (1932–36), returning to the law afterward.

Johnston, John Taylor (1820–93) businessman, art collector; born in New York City. He studied in Edinburgh when young, graduated from New York University (1839), and studied law at Yale (1839–41). After travel abroad (c. 1843–45), he became a railroad executive and the founder of what was to become the New Jersey Central Railroad. He collected paintings (many of which were sold during financial reverses in 1876) and became the first president of New York City's Metropolitan Museum of Art (1870). He left some art to the Metropolitan and a considerable sum of money to New York University.

Johnston, Joseph Eggleston (1807–91) soldier; born in Prince Edward County, Va. An 1829 West Pointe graduate, he fought in the Mexican War and was the army's quartermaster general when the Civil War broke out. He resigned when Virginia seceded, and commanded a wing of the Confederate army at 1st Bull Run; but he had feuded with Jefferson Davis and did not obtain the position he felt he deserved. Wounded on the Virginia Peninsula in June 1862, he had the distinction of being succeeded by Robert E. Lee. During the long months that followed, he held a series of senior commands but failed to win a major battle, and during Sherman's Atlanta Campaign, Johnston was effectively in retreat; he surrendered to Sherman in North Carolina on April 26, 1865. After the war, he went into the insurance business and then served in the U.S. House of Representatives (Dem., Va.; 1879–81) and as commissioner of U.S. railroads (1885–91). He died of pneumonia brought on by standing hatless in the rain at the funeral of Gen. Sherman.

Johnston (or Johnson), Joshua (?1765–?1830) painter; birthplace unknown, but often taken to be Baltimore, Md. Virtually no biographical details are known of Johnston, often referred to as the first African-American portrait painter. He has been variously identified as a West Indian immigrant and a former slave. The Baltimore City Directory during the period of his greatest activity (c. 1796–c. 1824) lists his studio at eight different addresses in and around Baltimore. Many critics think he was influenced by, and some suggest he may have studied with, Charles Peale Polk, a relative of Charles Willson Peale, and one of the members of the talented family of painters. Johnston painted the Maryland and Virginia gentry; *Portrait of a Cleric* is his only work thought to depict an African-American. Virtually unrecognized until 1939, he was the subject of a retrospective exhibit at the Peake Museum in Baltimore (1948) and his work hangs in most major American museums.

Johnston, Thomas (c. 1708–67) engraver, born in Boston, Mass. He engraved maps, scenes of battles and cities, bookplates, and was also a japanner and organ builder. He is known for his *Plan of Boston* (c. 1727–29), and the earliest engraving of an American historical event, *The Battle of Lake George* (1755).

Jolson, Al (b. Asa Yoelson) (?1886–1950) popular singer, movie actor; born in Srednice, Lithuania. In 1894 he emigrated to Washington, D.C., with his family to join his father, a rabbi and cantor. He began singing on street corners, then went to New York City and made his debut as an extra in *Children of the Ghetto* (1899). By age 15 he was touring in vaudeville and minstrel shows as a boy soprano and whistler; by 1906 he was in San Francisco performing a solo act. His earliest success came with Lew Dockstader's Minstrels in 1909; he sang "Mammy" in blackface and thus launched his career and the stereotype with which he would forever be associated (and imitated); musically he blended a vaguely African-American style with his own expressive Jewish tradition. He was also known for whistling improvised melodies in the style of jazz musicians. In 1911 he made his first recording and starred in *La Belle Paree* in New York; he went on to star in a series of Broadway musicals, his last being *Hold on to Your Hats* (1940). In 1926 he sang three songs in an experimental sound short, *April Showers,* and then he starred in the first full-length "talkie" film, *The Jazz Singer* (1927). By 1932 he had his own radio program; during the 1930s his records were extremely popular and he appeared in several movies. He entertained troops during World War II, but changing tastes in music effectively ended his career until the release of the biofilm, *The Jolson Story* (1946), for which he dubbed the singing; this led to a brief revival of popularity (and imitations). His signature songs include "Swanee," "Sonny Boy," and "California, Here I Come."

Jones, (Benjamin Allyn) "Plain Ben" (1882–1961) horse trainer; born in Parnell, Mo. He trained for the Calumet Farm (1939–61) and conditioned such Triple Crown-winning thoroughbreds as Whirlaway (1941), and Citation (1948).

Jones, Bill T. (1952–) choreographer, dancer; born in Steuben County, N.Y., or Bunnell, Florida. He is the son of migrant farmers and sources differ on his place of birth. He attended the State University of New York: Binghamton (1970–72), where he studied dance. By 1973 he cofounded, with Arnie Zane, Lois Welk and Jill Becker, the American Dance Asylum. He and his companion and dancing partner,

Arnie Zane, formed the Bill T. Jones/Arnie Zane & Company (1982), and created many coproductions, such as *History of Collage* (1988). After Zane died of AIDS (1988), Jones continued to create controversial and acclaimed dance works, notably *Last Supper at Uncle Tom's Cabin/The Promised Land* (1991). In addition to choreographing and dancing with his permanent company, he did some teaching, writing, and opera-directing as well as fundraising to keep his company alive.

Jones, Casey (legendary name of John Luther) (1863–1900) railroader, folk hero; born in southeastern Missouri. He grew up in Cayce, Ky., and became a railroad engineer. On April 30, 1900, he was driving the *Cannonball Express* southward when he saw a freight train on the track ahead (and there is some question as to whether he was at fault for going so fast at this point). Instead of jumping, he stayed in the cab and tried to brake the train, giving his coworker a chance to jump free and saving others aboard from serious injuries while he himself was killed in the crash. Wallace Saunders, an African-American railroad worker, celebrated Luther's heroism in a ballad that was eventually picked up by the commercial music world and performed in vaudeville. Casey Jones soon become a symbol to railroad men in particular and to the labor people in general.

Jones, Catesby Ap Roger (1821–77) Confederate naval officer; born in Fairfield, Va. (nephew of Thomas Ap Catesby Jones). He served in the United States Navy (1836–61) and the Confederate States navy (1861–65). He commanded the CSS *Virginia* (ex-*Merrimac*) during the three-hour indecisive contest with the USS *Monitor* (1862).

Jones, (Charles) Chuck (1912–) animator; born in Spokane, Wash. At Warner Bros., he helped create such characters as Bugs Bunny and Daffy Duck. His work won eight Academy Awards.

Jones, Clara (1913–) librarian; born in St. Louis, Mo. When named director of the Detroit Public Library (1970–78), she became the first African-American to direct a major public library.

Jones, D. F. (Donald Forsha) (1890–1963) agriculturalist; born in Hutchinson, Kans. He left the Arizona Agricultural Experiment Station (1911–13) for the Connecticut Agriculture Experiment Station (1915–60) where in 1917 he developed a hybrid corn that increased yields and made commercial production more practical. In 1924 he introduced the first hybrid sweet corn. He also developed a genetic method for transmitting pollen, thus eliminating the need to detassel corn in the field. He was also associate editor of *The Rural New Yorker* for many years. At retirement he started Seed Producers Advisory Service in Connecticut.

Jones, E. (Ernest) Lester (1876–1929) geodesist; born in East Orange, N.J. After working in various businesses, he joined the U.S. Coast and Geodetic Survey, where he introduced aerial photography to mapmaking. He served as a lieutenant colonel in World War I (1917–19), and founded the American Legion (1919). He surveyed the Alaska-Canada boundary for the International Boundary Commission (1921).

Jones, E. (Euine) Fay (1921–) architect, educator; born in Pine Bluffs, Ark. He taught at the University of Arkansas (1953) while designing artisan-built houses incorporating organic design and native materials. He designed Thorncrown Chapel, Eureka Springs, Ark. (1981), and won the American Institute of Architects Gold Medal in 1990.

Jones, George (Glenn) (1931–) musician; born in Saratoga, Texas. One of the stars of country music, he was born into a poverty-stricken family and raised in Beaumont, Texas, where he began singing on the streets as a teenager. After serving in the U.S. Marine Corps, he made his first record in 1953, appeared on the Louisiana Hayride in 1955, and scored his first hit, "Why Baby Why," in 1956, the first of over 60 singles that he placed on the Country Top-10 charts over the next four decades. He moved to Nashville in 1957 where he joined the Grand Ole Opry. His songs increasingly reflected the turbulence of his four marriages and his struggles with alcohol and drugs, and his skill at conveying heartbreak and headache established the standard against which modern country music is measured.

Jones, Harry Clary (1865–1916) physical chemist, educator; born in New London, Md. He was connected with Johns Hopkins (1894–1916) and was a pioneer promoter of physical chemistry in the U.S.A. His own work was on solutions and solvents.

Jones, James (1921–77) writer; born in Robinson, Ill. He served as an enlisted man in the U.S. Army (1939–44), at one point attending the University of Hawaii (1942); after the war he attended New York University (1945). His first novel, *From Here to Eternity* (1951), won over both readers and critics by its sheer narrative force – and was also made into a popular movie (1953) – but his subsequent work, with the exception of *The Thin Red Line* (1962), was not that well received in literary circles. He lived his later years in Paris, France, and Sagaponack, N.Y.

Jones, James Earl (1931–) stage/film/television actor; born in Arkabutla, Miss. Son of an ex-prizefighter-actor, he attended the University of Michigan, and after Army service, studied acting in New York, making his Broadway debut in 1957. After his first major role in *The Great White Hope* (1966), he went on to star in a wide variety of classic and contemporary plays. His varied film career included lending his distinctive resonant voice (only) to Darth Vader in *Star Wars* (1977).

Jones, Jesse Holman (1874–1956) businessman, government official; born in Robertson County, Tenn. A lumber and real-estate magnate based in Houston, Texas, he provided financial support for the Democrats. Head of the Reconstruction Finance Committee (1932–40) he set loan terms for banks and corporations, becoming secretary of commerce (1940–45). Afterward he published the *Houston Chronicle*.

Jones, John Paul (b. John Paul) (1747–92) naval officer, Revolutionary hero; born in Kirkcudbrightshire, Scotland. He went to sea at age 12 and commanded merchant ships in the West Indies. No saint, he engaged in the slave trade and added "Jones" to his name to avoid pursuit after the death of two sailors he had flogged. He went to Philadelphia at the start of the American Revolution and became a senior lieutenant in the Continental navy (1775). Successful in capturing ships while in command of the *Providence,* he was given command of the *Ranger.* He sailed to France in 1777 and captured the British *Drake* (1778), the first enemy warship to surrender to an American vessel. Sailing from France in the *Bonhomme Richard* (1779), a refitted merchant ship, he fought the British *Serapis* off Flamborough Head, England, in a legendary battle that included his defiant cry, "I have not yet begun to fight!" Following his victory, he was made a chevalier of France and received the

thanks of Congress (1781). He fought no more battles for America but he did go to France and Denmark to negotiate for the return of U.S. ships. He visited the United States for the last time in 1787 and served as a Russian rear admiral (1788–89) before returning to Paris. His remains were returned to the United States in 1905 and placed in a chapel crypt at the U.S. Naval Academy in Annapolis, Md.

Jones, John P. (Percival) (1830–1912) miner, U.S. senator; born in Hay, Wales. Brought to Cleveland, Ohio, as a child, he went to California in the gold rush of 1849, then moved to Nevada where he made his fortune in silver mining. Elected to the U.S. Senate (Rep., Nev.; 1873–1903), he inevitably supported silver coinage.

Jones, Joseph (1833–96) physician; born in Liberty County, Ga. He enlisted in the Confederate cavalry, but was transferred to the medical corps since he was a doctor. In 1872 he joined the faculty at the University of Louisiana and was elected to the State Board of Health (1880–84) where he worked to improve sanitary conditions in New Orleans. Throughout his life he studied diseases endemic to the American South and he wrote on a wide range of subjects.

Jones, Leonard (Augustus) (1832–1909) legal scholar; born in Templeton, Mass. A prolific writer, his many works remain standard texts of law and are respected for their clarity and continued pertinence. He practiced law privately and served as a judge on the Massachusetts Land Court (1898–1909).

Jones, LeRoi See BARAKA, IMAMU AMIRI.

Jones, (Lindley Armstrong) "Spike" (1911–65) bandleader; born in Long Beach, Calif. His zany band, the City Slickers (1942–61), committed musical mayhem with popular tunes, augmenting normal instruments with assorted noisemakers, including washboards and cowbells. The band toured regularly and appeared in movies and on television, where he often had his own show (1951–61). A serious musician, in his last years he took up Dixieland jazz.

Jones, Louis C. (Clark) (1908–) folklorist; born in Albany, N.Y. He was a literature professor before becoming founding director of the Cooperstown (N.Y.) Farmers' Museum (1946–72), which he developed into a leading museum of rural life. There he originated the Seminars on American Culture (1948). A specialist in New York state folklore, 18th-century social history, and American folk art, he directed the State University of New York's Cooperstown graduate programs (1964–82).

Jones, Mary (b. Harris) ("Mother Jones") (1830–1930) labor leader; born near Cork, Ireland. Emigrating to Canada and then the United States as a child, she was widowed at age 37 when her husband, iron molder George Jones, and four children died of yellow fever (1867); she also lost her home in the Chicago fire (1871). She resumed earlier work as a dressmaker, worked with the Knights of Labor as an organizer, and beginning in the 1890s, after the decline of the Knights, organized coal miners and strikes for the United Mine Workers in Virginia, West Virginia, and Colorado. A legend in her time, known for her bold tactics, she fought on for decades; at age 89 she joined in a major steel walkout, earning a jail term. Her fame revived in the 1960s with the establishment of a socially conscious periodical named after her, *Mother Jones Magazine*.

Jones, Mary Cover (1896–1987) psychologist; born in Johnstown, Pa. She studied at Vassar and Columbia University, where she met fellow psychologist Harold Ellis Jones. They were married in 1920. She did important research in developmental psychology and worked with behaviorist John B. Watson. In 1924 she published a landmark study on deconditioning fear. She and Jones conducted research at the University of California: Berkeley (from 1927) and organized the long-term Oakland Growth Study on adolescents.

Jones, Quincy (Delight, Jr.) (1933–) composer, record producer; born in Chicago. A multifaceted jazz and pop figure, he began with his Seattle teenage friend Ray Charles, who interested him in arranging. He played trumpet and arranged for Lionel Hampton between 1951 – 53, then worked as a free-lance arranger on numerouous jazz sessions. He served as musical director for Dizzy Gillespie's overseas big band tour in 1956, worked for Barclay Records in Paris from 1957–58, and led an all-star big band for the European production of Harold Arlen's blues opera, *Free and Easy* (1959). Returning to New York, he composed and arranged for Count Basie, Dinah Washington, and Sarah Vaughan while holding an executive post at Mercury Records and producing his own increasingly pop-oriented records. In the mid-1960s he began composing for films and television, eventually producing over 50 scores and serving as a trailblazing African-American musician in the Hollywood arena. In 1975 he founded Qwest Productions, for which he arranged and produced hugely successful albums by Frank Sinatra, Michael Jackson, and other pop figures.

Jones, Reginald Harold (1917–) business executive; born in Stoke-on-Trent, Staffordshire, England. He was a childhood immigrant to the U.S.A. He joined General Electric (GE) in 1939, worked in finance and manufacturing divisions, and became president (1972–73) and chairman and CEO (1972–81). He was instrumental after the early 1970s in focusing GE on high-technology markets in the nuclear reactor, jet engine, and consumer products sector; in leading the company's diversification into financial and industrial services through a program of acquisitions; and in expanding overseas operations. Under his leadership GE developed such products as CT scanners and industrial plastics. He developed a reputation as a superior financial planner. His peers voted him the country's most influential executive in 1979. As the head of the world's largest manufacturer of electrical equipment, he was also vocal in the public policy arena.

Jones, Robert Edmond (1887–1954) set designer, producer, director; born in Milton, N.H. Beginning in 1915 with his set design for *The Man Who Married a Dumb Wife*, he was in rebellion against the trend toward realism. Eliminating unnecessary detail, he created symbolic and expresionistic settings that were much admired. Critic John Mason Brown described him as a designer who understood "the poetry of the undecorated." In 1926 he both designed and directed *The Great God Brown* by Eugene O'Neill, whose early plays he worked on with the Provincetown Players and at the Greenwich Village Playhouse. He designed settings for productions of Shakespeare (*Othello*, 1937) as well as many modern plays. He was the coauthor with Kenneth Magowan of *Continental Stagecraft* in 1922.

Jones, Robert Trent, Sr. (1906–) golf course architect; born near Ince, England. He came to the U.S.A. in 1911 and studied at Cornell University (1927–30). He worked in partnership with the Canadian architect, Stanley Thompson, during 1930 to 1940 and then worked on his own (1940). He designed more than 400 of the world's outstanding golf courses. He wrote *Great Golf Stories, Golf's Magnificent Challenge* (1988). His son, Robert Trent Jr., worked in the same field, designing more than 100 golf courses.

Jones, (Robert Tyre, Jr.) Bobby (1902–71) golfer; born in Atlanta, Ga. One of golf's greats during the 1920s "golden age" of sports, he became the only player ever to win a recognized Grand Slam in golf (four major championships in a single year) when he won the U.S. and British Opens, and the U.S. and British Amateurs in 1930. From 1922 to 1930 – while earning his B.A. from Georgia School (now Institute) of Technology, another B.A. from Harvard, and his law degree from Emory – he won the U.S. Open four times, the U.S. Amateurs five times, and the British Open three times. An amateur throughout his career, he retired from golf in 1930 to practice law. He designed the course at the Augusta (Ga.) National Golf Club where he helped found the Masters tournament (1934). After a spinal injury in 1948 he was confined to a wheel chair but he continued with his business interests.

Jones, Rufus (Matthew) (1863–1948) philosopher, historian, social reformer; born in South China, Maine. Child of devout Quaker parents, he attended Haverford College (B.A. 1885; M.A. 1886) and chose to devote himself to understanding and promoting Quakerism. He taught at Quaker preparatory schools before returning to join the faculty of Haverford to teach philosophy (1893–1933). He was a minister of the Society of Friends from 1890 on and was much in demand as a preacher and speaker. Among several Quaker periodicals he edited was one he also founded, the *American Friend* (1893–1912). A prolific author, he was best known for the four volumes he published (between 1905–21) on the history of Quakerism and related religions. A militant pacifist, he became widely admired for his work with the American Friends Service Committee (AFSC), which he helped found in 1917. (He was its first chairperson, 1917–28, then again from 1935–44.) He succeeded in having overseas service with the AFSC count as an alternative to American military service. He directed the AFSC's many projects in the years between World War I and World War II – helping refugees, sufferers from famine, and those caught up in revolutions. The AFSC was one of the few non-Jewish organizations that intervened to help Jewish victims of the Nazis and Jones himself went to Germany in 1938 to obtain some cooperation from the Gestapo. During World War II he directed the AFSC's many activities on behalf of refugees; for this work the AFSC shared (with its British counterpart) the Nobel Peace Prize in 1947. By the end of his career he had effectively reinvigorated the American Quaker community through both his activities and intellectual efforts.

Jones, Sam Houston (1897–1978) governor, lawyer; born near Merryville, La. A World War I veteran, he practiced law in Beauregard Parish, La., serving as district attorney (1925–34). As Louisiana's governor (Dem., 1940–44), he cleaned up Huey Long's excesses, and instituted a civil service system that resulted in a 15 million dollar surplus. He returned to his law practice, serving on Louisiana's first biracial commission in 1965.

Jones, Samuel Milton (1846–1904) inventor, manufacturer, reformer; born in Carnarvonshire, Wales. He was brought to America by his family (1849) and began to work for a living at the age of 10. He went into the oil fields (1865) as a driller, pumper, tool-dresser, and pipe-liner and entered the oil business for himself (1870). He moved to Lima, Ohio (1885), where he pioneered in the development of newly discovered oil fields. In Toledo, Ohio (1892–93), he invented some improvements for oil well appliances and organized the Acme Sucker Rod Company (1894), which earned him a fortune. Concerned about workers' conditions, he established major reforms in his factory including an eight-hour day and vacations with pay. He hung a "Golden Rule" placard in his plant, earning him the nickname "Golden Rule" Jones. He wrote a book proposing a fair social order (1899) and an autobiography, and was elected mayor of Toledo for four successive terms (1897–1904). Business and establishment leaders opposed his reform efforts and the police complained of his lax law enforcement standards, but he made a respectable showing as an independent candidate for governor of Ohio (1899).

Jones, Thomas Ap Catesby (1790–1858) naval officer; born in Westmoreland County, Va. His naval career (1805–50) included service in the War of 1812 and the drawing up of a treaty with King Kamehameha III of the Sandwich (now Hawaiian) islands in 1826. He was temporarily relieved of his command after he seized Monterey, Calif., in 1842 before formal hostilities had begun between the U.S.A. and Mexico. He served in the Mexican War, but was court-martialed in 1850 for the misuse of funds.

Jones, Thomas P. (1774–1848) engineer, publisher; born in Herefordshire, England. Emigrating to America as a youth, he ended up in New York City. There he was cofounder (1825), publisher, and editor of *American Mechanics Magazine*. When he accepted a post teaching at the Franklin Institute in Philadelphia (1826) he merged his magazine with that of the Institute; in 1828 its new title became the *Journal of the Franklin Institute*. He retained his post as editor until his death, even when he moved to Washington, D.C., to serve as superintendent (1828–37) then examiner (1837–38) of the U.S. Patent Office.

Jones, Wesley L. (Livsey) (1863–1932) U.S. senator; born near Bethany, Ill. Elected to the U.S. House of Representatives (Rep., Wash.; 1899–1909) and to the U.S. Senate (1909–32), he supported prohibition, the merchant marine, and law enforcement.

Jones, William Richard (1839–89) engineer; born in Scranton, Pa. As a youth he worked in iron foundaries and other trades, then went off and served with distinction in the Civil War. After the war, he went on to become one of Andrew Carnegie's most expert and trusted steel mill superintendents, both because of his knowledge of steel production and his ability to manage the men. He introduced many innovations to the industry, such as the Jones mixer and armor-plated hoses.

Jong, Erica (b. Mann) (1942–) writer, poet; born in New York City. She studied at Barnard College (B.A. 1963), and Columbia University (M.A. 1965; School of Fine Arts 1969–70). She taught at a variety of institutions in New York City, and in Heidelberg, Germany, as a faculty member of the Overseas Division of the University of Maryland. She wrote volumes of poetry and novels, and achieved some celebrity with *Fear of Flying: A Novel* (1973), a story of sexual fantasies that some read as a liberating text for women.

Joplin, Janis (Lyn) (1943–70) blues rock singer; born in Port Arthur, Texas. When she was 17 she performed with bar bands in Texas and California, then moved to San Francisco in 1966 where she joined Big Brother and the Holding Company. Their best-selling album, *Cheap Thrills* (1968), ensured her reputation as a unique blues and rock stylist. With the Kozmic Blues Band in 1969 and the Full Tilt Boogie Band in 1970 she released best-selling albums before her death by a heroin overdose.

Joplin, Scott (1868–1917) composer, pianist; born in Texarkana, Texas. Originally a self-taught and itinerant musician, he studied at the George R. Smith College in Sedalia, Mo., to advance his musical skills (1896). He played piano in disreputable dives but used his musical knowledge to help other itinerant musicians notate their own compositions, just as he was doing with his. He then joined with a music publisher, John S. Stark of Sedalia, and began to receive both credit and money from his own "rags," especially after the success of his "Maple Leaf Rag" (1899). He toured throughout the Midwest, billed as the "King of Ragtime" as he played dozens of his own original ragtimes on the piano, among them "The Easy Winners" (1901) and "The Entertainers" (1902). By 1905 he had settled into Harlem in New York City and began an attempt to "elevate" ragtime. He had already used the ragtime style with dance beats – a waltz, a habanera – and had evidently tried a ragtime "opera" (*A Guest of Honor*, 1903 – now lost), but in New York he composed an ambitious opera drawing on folk music themes, *Treemonisha* (1915); it was never performed beyond the rehearsal stage. (It was first produced on stage in Atlanta, Ga., in 1972.) It is believed that the collapse of the original production helped to cause his premature death. He and his music were largely forgotten until several of his rags were selected for the soundtrack of the popular movie, *The Sting* (1973), and this in turn led to a revival of interest in more of his music.

Jordan, Barbara (Charline) (1936–) U.S. representative; born in Houston, Texas. A Boston University Law School graduate, she practiced law in Houston (1960–67), entering Democratic politics in the Texas Senate (1967–72), continuing in the U.S. House of Representatives (1973–79). A compelling orator, she electrified the 1976 Democratic convention before illness cut short her political career. She became a professor at the Lyndon B. Johnson School of Public Affairs at the University of Texas in Austin.

Jordan, David Starr (1851–1931) biologist, educator; born near Gainesville, N.Y. He was (1891–1913) the first president of Stanford University, and as a prominent advocate of world federalism and peace, was president of the World Peace Congress (1915). He formulated "Jordan's Law" on the geographical distribution of species and published widely on biology, education, and peace.

Jordan, June (1936–) poet, writer; born in New York City. She studied at Barnard College, N.Y. (1953–55; 1956–57), the University of Chicago (1955–56), and taught at many institutions, notably at State University of New York: Long Island (1981). She was influenced by mainstream poetry as well as by the Black arts movement (1970s), and she also wrote books for children.

Jordan, Louis (1908–75) musician; born in Brinley, Ark. A saxophonist, singer, and show business natural, he was the most popular "race" recording artist throughout the 1940s. He began his career in the mid-1920s with local Arkansas bands and toured with the Rabbit Foot Minstrels before emerging in New York as a sideman with Chick Webb's

Orchestra in 1936–38. He formed his own innovative combo, the Tympany Five, in 1938 and recorded a string of hit records in his irrepressible jump blues style. Other musicians frequently recorded his songs such as "Choo Choo Ch'Boogie," "Caldonia," and "Ain't Nobody Here But Us Chickens," thus earning him the nickname "King of the Jukeboxes." He remained active in the 1960s and 1970s, touring the U.S.A. and Europe, but recording only sporadically. He is widely cited as a seminal influence among blues and rock artists.

Jordan, Michael (Jeffrey) (1963–) basketball player; born in New York City. He played for the University of North Carolina (1982–84) and in 1982 led them to a National Collegiate Athletic Association Division I championship. In a National Basketball Association (NBA) career that began in 1985, he became one of basketball's most exciting players as a guard for the Chicago Bulls. In 1991 he led the Bulls to a NBA championship and was the league Most Valuable Player. He played for the 1984 U.S. Olympic team and for the "dream team" of the 1992 Olympics, taking the gold medal both times. His basketball fame won him numerous commercial endorsements throughout the world. Jordan shocked the basketball world by retiring from the game in 1993, after which he pursued a professional baseball career.

Jordan, Vernon (Eulion), Jr. (1935–) civil rights leader; born in Atlanta, Ga. One of the most visible and influential civil rights activists, he was director of the Voter Education Project of the Southern Regional Council (1964–68) and executive director of the United Negro College Fund (1970). As executive director of the Urban League (1971–81), he forged links between the black community and the Nixon and Carter White Houses, pushed voter registration, a full employment plan, and school desegregration, and strengthened the League's traditional social service role. Although he fully recovered from a sniper attack (1980), he left the League to practice law and served on a number of major corporate boards. He played an important role as a member of President-elect Clinton's transition team (1992).

Jordy, William H. (Henry) (1917–) architectural historian; born in Poughkeepsie, N.Y. A faculty member of Brown University (1955), his contributions to 20th-century architectural history include the comprehensive *American Buildings and their Architects* (with William H. Pierson, 1970–72) and the standard study, *Louis Sullivan* (1986).

Jorgenson, Dale W. (1933–) economist; born in Bozeman, Mont. Originator of a neoclassical theory of investment and the neoclassical theory of development of a dual economy, he taught at the University of California: Berkeley (1959–69) before accepting a professorship at Harvard in 1969.

Joseph, Chief (b. Hinmaton Yalatkit) (?1835–1904) Nez Percé chief; born in the Wallowa Valley of present-day Oregon. A peaceful leader of a peaceful tribe, he was forced into a state of war in 1877 and helped lead 750 of his people on a 1,500-mile flight to Canada. Within 40 miles of the border, his people starving and freezing, he surrendered in October 1877, delivering an oft-quoted speech at the event. After being held in Oklahoma, he returned to the northwest (1885), where he encouraged his people to get an education and to abstain from drinking and gambling.

Joseph, Jacob (?1840–1902) Orthodox rabbi; born in Vilnius, Lithuania. He was brought from Vilna, Russia (now Vilnius, Lithuania) in 1888 by the Association of Orthodox Congregations to become the Chief Rabbi of New York City. His presence was desired by the Orthodox Jews who were trying to resist Americanization by founding a Jewish community that would retain Eastern European Jewish institutions. These efforts were largely successful only with the older generation.

Joseph, Mother (b. Esther Pariseau) (1823–1902) nun, architect, pioneer; born in St. Elzear, Quebec, Canada. She joined the Sisters of Charity of Providence (1843) and was sent to Vancouver, Canada, in 1856. She had learned carpentry from her father, who was a carriage-maker. She became an all-purpose architect in the creation of 11 hospitals, seven academies, five Indian schools, and two orphanages. She traveled throughout the Rocky Mountains into the United States and conducted "begging tours" to raise money from miners. Long after her death, she was called the "first architect of the American Northwest." The state of Washington placed her statue in the U.S. Capitol.

Josey, E. J. (Ellonie Junius) (1924–) librarian; born in Norfolk, Va. He planned teacher-librarian curricula at Savannah State College (Ga.) and became a recognized expert in research library services. He headed the New York State Education Department's Bureau of Academic and Research Libraries (1976–86) before moving to the University of Pittsburgh School of Library and Information Services (1986). A prominent civil rights activist, he founded the American Library Association black caucus.

Joslin, Elliott P. (1869–1962) physician; born in Oxford, Mass. An early interest in diabetes became a passion when his mother became his eighth case (1900). He dedicated his life to all aspects of the disease – research, treatment, and education. Based in Boston, he established a clinic for affordable in-patient care and education (1953) and the Diabetes Foundation for charitable donations (1953); he also helped establish a summer camp for diabetic children at Clara Barton's birthplace in Oxford, Mass.

Jouett, Matthew (Harris) (?1787/88–1827) painter; born in Mercer County, Ky. He studied with Gilbert Stuart in Boston (1816), and became a noted portraitist of the era. He spent most of his life in Lexington, Ky., and his subjects included the Marquis de Lafayette and Henry Clay.

Jovanovich, William (Iliya) (1920–) publisher; born in Louisville, Colo. Starting as a salesman for Harcourt, Brace & Company in 1947, he rose to president by 1955 and firmly guided its transition to the large, publicly held conglomerate, Harcourt Brace Jovanovich.

Joy, James F. (Frederick) (1810–96) railroad builder; born in Durham, N.H. A graduate of Harvard Law School (1836), he moved to Detroit and negotiated with a group of northeast capitalists to purchase the Michigan Central Railroad from the state (1846). Continuing to promote railroads as counsel and president of several companies, he built up the combine of western railroads long known as the "Joy System." He also supported the canal company that built the first ship canal at Sault Ste. Marie (1853–55). He served in the Michigan legislature (1861–62) and was president of the *Detroit Post and Tribune* (1881–84).

Joyner-Kersee, (Jacqueline) Jackie (1962–) track and field athlete; born in East St. Louis, Mo. One of the greatest female athletes in history, she won a silver medal in the heptathlon in the 1984 Olympics and gold medals in the 1988 and 1992 Games. She won a gold medal in the long jump in 1988 and a bronze at the 1992 Olympics.

Judah, Theodore (Dehone) (1826–63) engineer, railroad builder; born in Bridgeport, Conn. He studied engineering and worked for the railroads of the Connecticut Valley area until 1854. He went west and became the chief engineer of the Sacramento Valley Railroad. Traveling in the California mountains, he developed the idea of a transcontinental railroad. He wrote a pamphlet (1857) and persuaded Collis Huntington, Leland Stanford, and others to join him in organizing the Central Pacific Railroad Company (1861). The Huntington group bought him out for $100,000 (1863). He died of typhoid fever before the project was completed.

Judd, Donald (Clarence) (1928–) sculptor; born in Excelsior Springs, Mo. He studied at the Art Students League, N.Y. (1947–53) and Columbia University (B.S. 1953; graduate work, 1958–61). Based in New York City, he began as a painter, then became a sculptor (1961), specializing in abstract and geometric forms in various mediums, as in *Untitled* (1965), one of his stacked rectangular metal works.

Judd, Lewis Lund (1930–) psychiatrist, educator; born in Los Angeles. An authority in the fields of biological psychiatry and clinical psychopharmacology, he was the first active scientist named director of the National Institutes of Mental Health (1988). There he promoted research into schizophrenia, child and adolescent mental disorders, and brain function.

Judson, Adoniram (1788–1850) Protestant missionary; born in Malden, Mass. He graduated from Brown in 1807, taught for a year, studied at Andover Theological Seminary, was ordained in 1812 and went to Burma in that year as a Baptist missionary. He was married three times, in each case to women who were missionaries in their own right. He was imprisoned as a spy during the Anglo-Burmese War (1824–26). He translated the Bible into Burmese and claimed to have converted thousands to Christianity. He died a few days after leaving Burma on a voyage for his health.

Judson, Edward Zane Carroll (Ned Buntline, pen name) (1823–86) adventurer, writer; born in Stamford, N.Y. His adventuresome life was obscured by his own fabrications but he seems to have run away to sea as a youth and after some soldiering and trapping in the American West he tried to launch a career in 1844 as a publisher/editor in New York City. That venture failed and he may have escaped a lynching after being accused of a murder in Nashville, Ky. (1846). Back in New York City, he started up another magazine, *Ned Buntline's Own,* and began publishing the first of some 400 "dime novels," most published under the name "Ned Buntline." He then spent a year in jail for his role in starting the Astor Place riot in May 1849. In the 1850s he was one of the organizers of the American Party, the so-called "Know Nothings," who were opposed to "foreigners" and Catholics. He enlisted in the Union army in 1862 but was apparently dishonorably discharged in 1864. About this time he met William F. Cody, and christening him "Buffalo Bill," began to write books featuring his exploits. Judson also wrote a play, *Scouts of the Plains* (1872) that Cody – and later "Wild Bill" Hickok – starred in. He spent his last years back in Stamford, N.Y. A genuine 19th-century rogue, he preached temperance, wrote hymns, and went through four wives while achieving his dubious feats and writing his crude tales.

Judson, Margaret Atwood (1899–1991) historian, educator; born in Winstead, Conn. Educated at Radcliffe College (Ph.D. 1933), she taught at Rutgers University (1928 – 67; professor emeritus, 1967–91), where she was chairwoman of the history and political science department (1955–63) and acting dean (1966–67). Her *Crisis of the Constitution: An Essay in Constitutional and Political Thought in England, 1603–45* (1949), is widely respected. She published *Breaking the Barrier: A Professional Autobiography by a Woman Educator and Historian before the Women's Movement* in 1984.

Juilliard, Augustus D. (1836–1919) businessman; born at sea to French immigrants. A wealthy New York cotton merchant, he bequeathed twenty million dollars to aid the development of music in the U.S.A. The resulting Juilliard Music Foundation established the Juilliard School of Music in New York (1905).

Julia, Raul (1944–94) actor; born in San Juan, Puerto Rico. After graduating from the University of Puerto Rico (1964), where he majored in drama, he moved to New York City to pursue a stage career. In the 1960s and 1970s he appeared in a number of Broadway productions as well as working steadily for the New York Shakespeare Festival. In the 1970s he began his movie career, which brought him great success in films such as *Kiss of the Spider Woman* (1985), *Tequila Sunrise* (1988), and *The Addams Family I* and *II* (1991, 1993). In addition to his successful stage career, Julia frequently appeared as a spokesperson for Puerto Rican tourism.

Julian, Percy (Lavon) (1899–1975) chemist, inventor; born in Montgomery, Ala. The grandson of a former slave, he graduated from DePauw University in Indiana, pursued graduate studies at Harvard, and taught chemistry at Howard University. Denied a professorship at Harvard because of his race, he returned to DePauw. There, in 1935, he synthesized the drug physostigmine, used to treat glaucoma. In 1936 he became director of research for the soya products division of the Glidden Company in Chicago. He and his associates developed scores of soya derivatives, most notably cortisone, used in the treatment of arthritis and other afflictions. He left Glidden in 1953 to establish Julian Laboratories. From 1964 until his death he headed the Julian Research Institute and served as a consultant to the National Institute of Arthritis and Metabolic Diseases.

Just, Ernest E. (Everett) (1883–1941) cell biologist; born in Charleston, S.C. He taught and performed research at Howard University (1907–41). Concurrently, he began studies at the Woods Hole (Mass.) Marine Biological Laboratory (1909), and returned there nearly every summer for 20 years. He made pioneering contributions to studies of the cytology and embryology of marine organisms. In 1925 he demonstrated the cancer-engendering effects of ultraviolet radiation on cells. By 1929, however, the diminishing number of African-American graduate students, his disenchantment with Howard's attitude toward his need for research facilities, and his feeling that Americans regarded him – an African-American – with more curiosity than respect caused him to take a leave of absence and pursue his studies in Europe. He died of cancer shortly after his return to the U.S.A. His scholarship and dignified bearing earned him the sobriquet "Black Apollo of Science."

K

Kabotie, Fred (b. Nakavoma) (1900–86) Hopi painter, silversmith; born in Shungopavi, Ariz. Internationally recognized as a leading interpreter and creator of Hopi art, he published and illustrated numerous books and received commissions and held exhibitions around the world.

Kadanoff, Leo P. (Philip) (1937–) physicist; born in New York City. He taught at the University of Illinois: Urbana (1962–69) and Brown University (1969–78), before joining the University of Chicago (1978). He made major contributions to solid state physics, quantum statistical mechanics, and pressure- and temperature-induced changes in matter.

Kadish, Sanford (Harold) (1921–) law educator; born in New York City. After briefly practicing law in New York City (1948–51), he turned to teaching and writing on criminal law. He taught longest at the University of California: Berkeley (1961–64) where he was dean of the law school (1975–82). He was author of several books, including *Blame and Punishment – Essays in the Criminal Law* (1987), and of numerous articles.

Kael, Pauline (1919–) film critic, writer; born in Petaluma, Calif. She studied philosophy at the University of California: Berkeley (1936–40) before working at a variety of jobs, including writing movie reviews. She moved to New York City (1965) and worked for *Life* magazine. Beginning in 1968, she reviewed movies for the *New Yorker;* she left briefly to work for Paramount Pictures in California but returned to review for the *New Yorker* until her retirement in 1991. Known as a knowledgeable, intelligent, and enthusiastic reviewer of films, she consistently treated movies as a respected art form even when her idiosyncratic or waspish views aroused controversy. Her reviews were unusual in gaining a second life in a series of collections such as *When the Lights Go Down* (1980).

Kagan, Jerome (1929–) psychologist; born in Newark, N.J. Educated at Rutgers and Yale, he did research in developmental psychology at Ohio's Fels Institute (1957–64) before taking up his teaching career at Yale. He conducted extensive research on child development, documented in such books as *Personal Development* (1971), *Growth of the Child* (1978), and *The Nature of the Chilld* (1982). He suggested that both sides involved in the nature/nuture controversy were too rigid – that the parameters of personality formation were still obscure.

Kahanamoku, Duke (Paoa) (1890–1968) swimmer, surfer; born in Hawaii. He revolutionized sprint swimming by introducing the flutter kick, and for 20 years was an international freestyle champion. A member of Olympic teams from 1912 to 1932, he won gold medals in 1912 and 1920. In addition, he is generally regarded as having introduced surfboarding (practiced for centuries by Pacific islanders) to the West, starting with Australia and California about 1912. After a brief movie career, he was sheriff of Honolulu (1932–61).

Kahane, Meir (b. Martin David Kahane) (1932–90) rabbi, Jewish activist; born in New York City. At age 15, he was arrested in a protest against the British policy on Jewish immigration to Palestine. Ordained as an Orthodox rabbi, he earned a law degree from New York University. He was a synagogue rabbi and editor of the *Jewish Press*. In the 1960s he founded the Jewish Defense League, which advocated the use of violence to defend Jewish rights. After moving to Israel in 1971, he founded Kach, a movement aimed at removing Arabs from Israel. He earned a seat in the Israeli parliament in 1981, but his party was later barred from office. He was assassinated in New York, and his alleged assailant, an Egyptian-born American citizen, was found not guilty. He was the author of *The Jewish Stake in Vietnam* and *Never Again.*

Kahn, (Gustav Gerson) Gus (1886–1941) lyricist; born in Coblenz, Germany. His family settled in Chicago in 1891, where he began to write lyrics. From his first published song in 1906 until his death, he collaborated on many hit songs with such composers as Egbert Van Alstyne, Walter Donaldson and Isham Jones for Broadway, Hollywood, and big-name performers. He and Donaldson wrote the score for the popular Broadway show *Whoopee* (1928), starring Eddie Cantor.

Kahn, Julius (1861–1924) U.S. representative; born in Baden, Germany. Emigrating as a child, he was an actor and lawyer before going to Congress (Rep., Cal.; 1899–1924) where he sponsored the Selective Draft Act of 1917.

Kahn, Louis I. (Isadore) (1901–74) architect; born in Ösel, Estonia. He emigrated to Philadelphia with his family as a boy and graduated from the University of Pennsylvania. An important architectural theorist bridging the international style with postmodernist and rational architecture, he championed functionalism, one of his key ideas being that "servant" (structural) and "served" (activity) spaces should be esthetically integrated even if physically separate. His buildings are characterized by their emphasis on space and volume as ordering elements and on their use of daylight. Among his buildings are the Salk Institute for Biological

Studies, La Jolla, Calif. (1959–65), the Kimbell Art Museum, Fort Worth, Texas (1966–72), and the Yale Center for British Art and Studies, New Haven, Conn. (1969–74). He taught architecture at Yale University (1947–57) and the University of Pennsylvania (1957–74). He was awarded the Gold Medal by the American Institute of Architects (1971).

Kahn, Otto (Herman) (1867–1934) financier, art patron; born in Mannheim, Germany. He trained as a banker and worked in the London branch of the Deutsche Bank before emigrating to New York City (1893); there he formed Kuhn, Loeb & Company in 1897, an investment banking firm. He owed much of his wealth to financing railroads, in particular from helping Edward H. Harriman in his operations. A generous supporter of the arts, Kahn was a major supporter of the Metropolitan Opera Company, serving as its chairman (1911–31) and president (1918–34). He lived luxuriously in New York City and at Cold Springs Harbor, Long Island, and collected valuable works of art, concentrating on Byzantine gold enamels and Italian Renaissance art. He suffered huge financial losses in the depression that began in his final years and his major art works were sold off to private collectors.

Kahn, Robert L. (Louis) (1918–) psychologist, systems theorist; born in Detroit, Mich. He earned a Ph.D. from the University of Michigan, where he taught (1948–76) and directed the Survey Research Center. His research ranged over organizational and social psychology and survey methodology; his varied published works include books on electoral politics, unions, and surveys.

Kaiser, Henry J. (John) (1882–1967) industrialist; born in Canajoharie, N.Y. Leaving school at age 13, he became a photographer's apprentice, then bought the business at age 20. In 1907 he moved west to work for a Spokane, Wash., construction company. In 1914 he started his own construction business in Vancouver, Canada, and began a career building government-funded projects including 300 miles of highway in Cuba. In 1931 he organized the combine that built the Hoover Dam; he built the piers for the Oakland-San Francisco Bay Bridge; he built the Parker, Bonneville, and Grand Coulee Dams; and he produced the cement for the Shasta Dam (1939). In 1939 he began building ships in Seattle and Tacoma. During World Ward II his shipyards built some 1,460 Liberty ships for the U.S. Navy with great technical innovation and speed. He founded his own steel company, an aircraft company with Howard Hughes, Kaiser Aluminum, and Kaiser Community Homes Corp. The automobile company he formed with Joseph W. Frazer in 1945 produced some models but ceased production in the U.S.A. in 1954. He excelled at labor relations, and in 1942 founded what has become the largest American health maintenance organization in the country, now known as Kaiser Permanente.

Kaiser, Robert (G.) (1943–) editor, author; born in Washington, D.C. Joining the *Washington Post* as a summer intern (1963), he worked his way up through the reporting/editorial ranks; over the years he distinguished himself as an overseas correspondent in London (1964–66), Saigon (1969), and Moscow (1971–74), and on the national staff (1975–82). Named assistant managing editor of national news (1985), then deputy managing editor (1990), he was the author of several books on the former Soviet Union including *Russia from the Inside* and *Why Gorbachev Happened.*

Kalb, Johann (Baron de) (1721–80) soldier of fortune; born

in Hüttendorf, Germany. Of peasant ancestry, Kalb became a French infantry lieutenant by age 22. Styling himself "Jean de Kalb" or "Baron de Kalb," after serving with distinction in the Seven Years War his search for glory led him on a secret mission to America for the French government (1768). He returned to America with his friend the Marquis de Lafayette (1777) and served under him before wintering as a revolutionary major general under Gen. George Washington at Valley Forge (1777–78). While serving under Gen. Horatio Gates in South Carolina, he was mortally wounded near Camden in a battle against Cornwallis' troops.

Kalisch, Gilbert (1935–) pianist; born in New York City. In the 1960s he came to prominence as a brilliant performer of contemporary music, later extending his repertoire into the past.

Kallman, Chester (Simon) (1921–75) poet, librettist; born in New York City. He studied at Brooklyn College (B.A.) and at the University of Michigan. He was praised for his volumes of poetry such as *Absent and Present* (1963), but is best known for writing, in collaboration with W. H. Auden, the libretto for Stravinsky's opera *The Rake's Progress* (1951).

Kalmus, Herbert T. (Thomas) (1881–1963) born in Chelsea, Mass., **and Natalie Mabelle (b. Dunfee)** (1883–1965) born in Norfolk, Va. inventors. Married in 1902, she studied art while Herbert earned his B.S. from the Massachusetts Institute of Technology (MIT) (1904). They went to Europe (1905–06) where both continued their studies. He taught at MIT (1907–15) and formed Kalmus, Comstock and Westcorr, Inc., in 1915. The firm developed an early form of Technicolor by 1915 and it was used in the motion picture *The Gulf Between* (1917). The couple secretly divorced in 1921 but continued to work together and Natalie is generally recognized as having played a significant role in developing Technicolor. Herbert moved his operations to Hollywood (1927) and the three-color technology was used in what is regarded as the first full-color movie, *Becky Sharp* (1935). Natalie sued Herbert in the late 1940s, seeking half his assets; the court upheld the 1921 divorce and she received only a pension of $11,000 a year. Herbert was sued by the U.S. Justice Department in an antitrust action (1947), but he retained control of Technicolor until he retired in 1959.

Kalmus, Natalie (Mabelle Dunfee) See under KALMUS, HERBERT T.

Kaltenborn, H. V. (Hans von) (1878–1965) radio commentator; born in Milwaukee, Wis. After working as a journalist, specifically for the *Brooklyn Eagle* (1902–05), he took time off to attend Harvard, then returned to the *Brooklyn Eagle* (1909–30). Known for his analyses of foreign affairs, he was hired by CBS in 1930 and became widely known as the first American radio news analyst. He broadcast from a haystack during the Spanish Civil War. From 1940–55 he broadcast for National Broadcasting Company radio; his clipped Oxford-style diction was a favorite of imitators and parodists.

Kamehameha I ("the one set apart," his adopted name) (b. Paiea) (?1758–1819) Hawaiian unifier and king; born on Kohala, District of Hawaii, then known as the Sandwich Islands. Following the death of the chief of Hawaii, his uncle Kalaniopu'u (1782), Kamehameha conquered the island. After other victories on Maui, Oahu, Kauai, and the other islands, he formed the Kingdom of Hawaii by 1810. He stimulated Hawaiian trade but kept intact the customs and the religion of his people. Hawaii placed his statue in the U.S. Capitol.

Kamisar, Yale (1929–) legal scholar; born in New York City. He taught at the University of Minnesota (1957–65) before joining the University of Michigan: (1965). He is best known for his work on criminal law and procedure; his major publication is *Modern Criminal Procedure* (with LaFave and Israel, 1965).

Kandel, Eric Richard (1929–) neurobiologist, educator; born in Vienna. He emigrated to the United States in 1939. He became a professor at Columbia University in 1983 and senior investigator at Columbia's Howard Hughes Medical Institute in 1984. During the 1970s and 1980s he worked on cellular and molecular mechanisms of three basic forms of learning, habituation, sensitization, and classical conditioning; his findings suggest that learning produces changes in behavior by modulating the strength of neural connections.

Kander, (Harold) John (1927–) composer; born in Kansas City, Mo. After earning a master's degree at Columbia University, he worked in the 1950s as a rehearsal pianist, dance arranger, and conductor for Broadway musicals. His first Broadway score was for *A Family Affair* (1961). With lyricist Fred Ebb he wrote the score for the hit musicals *Cabaret* (1968), *Chicago* (1975), and *Woman of the Year* (1981); they also contributed songs to the musical films *Funny Lady* (1975) and *New York, New York* (1977). In the 1980s he composed music for nonmusical films.

Kander, Lizzie Black (1858–1940) settlement founder, cookbook writer; born in Milwaukee, Wis. She was president of the Milwaukee Jewish Mission and its successor, the Settlement (1896–1918). Her *Settlement Cook Book* (1901), compiled in conjunction with a Settlement cooking class, sold over a million copies and funded the Milwaukee Jewish Center.

Kane, Elisha Kent (1820–57) physician, explorer; born in Philadelphia. As a surgeon with the U.S. Navy, he traveled widely and served with distinction in the Mexican War. He was the surgeon and naturalist for an Arctic expedition (1850–51) and he commanded a second one (1853–55), which discovered Kennedy Channel. His goal was to find a route to the North Pole but he died prematurely in Havana, Cuba.

Kane, John (1860–1934) painter; born in West Calder, Scotland. He emigrated to America in 1879 and became a steelworker. An untrained artist, he began painting freight cars and houses. It was only late in his life (1927) that he started exhibiting his documentary paintings of Pittsburgh. A symmetrically balanced primitive work, his *Self-Portrait* (1929) is considered his most famous painting.

Kanin, Garson (1912–) playwright/screenwriter, stage/movie director, author; born in Rochester, N.Y. He commenced his show business career in the late-1920s as a jazz clarinetist/saxophonist, then became a vaudeville comedian. He studied at New York's American Academy of the Dramatic Arts, made his acting debut in 1933, and, after serving as assistant director under George Abbott, directed his first play, *Hitch Your Wagon* (1937). In Hollywood from 1938 he directed several movies; during World War II he made documentary films for the government, the most ambitious being the award-winning *True Glory* (1945), which he codirected (with Carol Reed). After 1946 he divided his time between Broadway and Hollywood. The

best known of his many original stageplays is *Born Yesterday* (1946); he directed such stage works as *The Diary of Anne Frank* (1955) and *Funny Girl* (1964). Among his many movie credits are those for screenplays (sometimes in collaboration with his wife since 1942, Ruth Gordon), including *Adam's Rib* (1949) and *Pat and Mike* (1952). In 1950 he wrote a new English libretto for and collaborated in the direction of the Metropolitan Opera Company's *Die Fledermaus*. He also published several works of fiction and memoirs, including *Tracy and Hepburn: An Intimate Memoir* (1971) and *Moviola* (1979).

Kaplan, Mordecai (Menahem) (1881–1983) rabbi, educator; born in Swenziany, Lithuania. He came to the U.S.A. in 1889. In 1909 he became dean, and later professor, at the Teacher's Institute of the Jewish Theological Seminary. He founded the Reconstructionist Movement in 1935, which holds that Judaism is an entire civilization, not just a religion. He was chairman of the editorial board of the *Reconstructionist* (1935–59). In 1922 he initiated the Bat Mitzvah ritual for young Jewish girls. A widely published author, he wrote *The Future of the American Jew* (1948) and *Judaism Without Supernaturalism* (1958).

Kapor, Mitchell (David) (1950–) computer software designer; born in New York City. He founded Lotus Development Corporation in Cambridge, Mass. (1982), and designed the spreadsheet Lotus 1-2-3 with Jonathan Sachs. He resigned from Lotus (1986) then founded and directed ON Technology (1987–90). He founded the Electronic Frontier Foundation (1990), a public interest organization dealing with computer issues and civil liberties.

Kappel, Frederick R. (Russell) (1902–) communications executive; born in Albert Lea, Minn. Trained as an engineer, he earned a reputation as an able administrator in the Midwestern Bell telephone system before becoming president of its subsidiary Western Electric (1954–56) and of American Telephone and Telegraph Co. (1956–61, chairman and CEO 1961–67). His innovations include the first transcontinental coaxial cable and the first cross-country microwave transmission facility. He was awarded the Presidential Medal of Freedom (1964).

Kaprow, Allan (1927–) painter, theorist, performance artist; born in Atlantic City, N.J. Based in New York City, he studied at the Hans Hofmann School, N.Y.C. (1947–48), with John Cage (1956–58), and at Columbia University. He is known for his assemblage and collage constructions, but is most famous for inventing "happenings," unconventional theatrical events utilizing audience participation, as in *18 Happenings in 6 Parts* (1959).

Karcher, J. C. (John Clarence) (1894–1978) geophysicist; born in Dale, Ind. He worked in several geophysical research companies before founding the Dallas oil firms, Comanche Corporation (1945–50), and Concho Petroleum Company (1950). He conceived and developed the principle of reflection seismography, a technique of locating structures more than five miles below the earth's surface, using seismic instruments to measure reflection of dynamite-induced shock waves. First used in Oklahoma to reveal oil deposits (1928), Karcher's method revolutionized the natural gas and petroleum industries.

Karfiol, Bernard (1886–1952) painter; born in Budapest, Hungary. Born of American parents, he studied in New York (1900) and Paris (1901–06), and lived in Irvington-on-

Hudson, N.Y. He is known for his modernist studies of the human figure, as in *Seated Nude* (1929).

Karle, Jerome (1917–), chemist; born in New York City. He joined the Naval Research Laboratory in Washington, D.C. (1946), becoming chief scientist of the Laboratory for the Structure of Matter (1968). He and Herbert Hauptman developed a mathematical method for determining three-dimensional crystal structures of hormone, vitamin, and antibiotic molecules. He shared the Nobel Prize in chemistry for this work (1985).

Karloff, Boris (b. William Henry Pratt) (1887–1969) actor; born in Dulwich, England. After years of touring as an actor in Canada (where he adopted his stage name) he settled in Hollywood in 1919 where he acted in silent films. His role as the monster in *Frankenstein* (1931) typecast him as a horror movie villain – in real life he was a gentle, refined person – and when he returned to the stage, as he occasionally did, it was also as some menacing character, such as Captain Hook in *Peter Pan* or the villainous brother in *Arsenic and Old Lace*. He also created the stereotype of the mad scientist in such movies as *Isle of the Dead* (1945).

Kármán, Theodore (Todor) von (1881–1963) physicist, aeronautical engineer; born in Budapest, Hungary. While spending most of his early career at German educational institutions, he advised many governments and firms on issues of aerodynamics and applied mechanics. Having visited the U.S.A. on two occasions, he came again in 1930 to direct the Guggenheim Aeronautical Laboratory at the California Institute of Technology; when the Nazis forced him to resign his post in Germany, he stayed in the U.S.A. and remained as the director until 1949. He was a founder of the Aerojet Engineering Corporation (1942), the RAND Corporation (1948), and the Jet Propulsion Laboratory, and gave direction to the early stages of the American rocket and space programs. He received the first National Medal of Science in 1963.

Karp, Ivan C. (1926–) gallery director, writer; born in New York City. He attended public school, became the director of the Leo Castelli Gallery (1959), and director and president of the O. K. Harris Gallery in 1969. He was called the "father of pop art," and wrote one of the first pop art novels, *Doobie Doo* (1966). He was also involved in saving architectural fragments from restored or demolished buildings.

Karst, Kenneth L. (Leslie) 1929–) legal educator; born in Los Angeles. He earned a Harvard law degree and joined the law faculty at the University of California: Los Angeles (1965). A scholar of constitutional and comparative law, he wrote among other works *Latin American Legal Institutions, Law and Development in Latin America* (co-authored, 1975) and *Belonging to America* (1989).

Kasebier, Gertrude (b. Stanton) (1852–1934) photographer; born in Des Moines, Iowa. A peer of Stieglitz and Clarence White, she had her own portrait studio in New York (1897–1926) and traveled to photograph Buffalo Bill and the sculptor Rodin.

Kates, Robert (William) (1929–) geographer; born in New York City. He taught at the graduate school, Clark University (1962–88). In 1986 he became director of the Brown University World Hunger Program. His particular interests are reflected in the titles of the books that he coauthored: *The Environment as Hazard* (1978), *Climate Impact Assess-*

ment (1985), *Perilous Progress* (1985), and *Hunger in History* (1989).

Katz, Alex (1927–) painter; born in New York City. He studied at Cooper Union, N.Y. (1946–49) and at the Skowhegan School of Painting and Sculpture, Maine (1949–50). Based in New York City, he painted stylized large-scale oil portraits, such as *Ada and Alex* (1980).

Katz, Daniel (1903–) psychologist; born in Trenton, N.J. His academic career culminated at the University of Michigan (1947–74). He produced classic studies of racial stereotyping and prejudice and attitude change; his pursuit of the connections between individual psychology and social systems helped to found the field of organizational psychology. An important methodological contribution was his open system theory, presented in *The Social Psychology of Organizations* (1966, later revised).

Katzenbach, Nicholas (de Belleville) (1922–) attorney general; born in Philadelphia, Pa. A prisoner of war in Germany (1943–45) and a Rhodes Scholar (1947–49), he was admitted to the New Jersey bar (1950), and became a member of the law firm, Katzenbach, Gildea & Rudner, in Trenton, N.J. He was general counsel to the Secretary of the Air Force while serving part-time as associate professor of law at Yale University (1952–56). He then taught at the University of Chicago (1956–60) and went to Switzerland (1960) to pursue an international law project as a Ford Foundation Fellow. He joined the Justice Department in 1961 as assistant attorney general in charge of the office of legal counsel (1961). As deputy attorney (1962–64), he fought to set an active agenda for the Justice Department, focusing on civil rights, antitrust litigation, and the war on crime. He was a major force in the integration of the Universities of Mississippi and Alabama and he helped draft the Civil Rights Act of 1964. He succeeded Robert Kennedy as attorney general (1965–66) and George Ball as undersecretary of state (1966–69). Leaving government service, he became senior vice-president and general counsel to IBM Corp. (1969–79); later he became a member of its board and worked on external relations (1984–86). Returning to private practice (1986), in 1991 he was named chairman of Bank Credit and Commerce International (BCCI) with orders to cut American ties from the tainted international banking system.

Kauffman, Ewing M. (Marion) ("Mr. K.") (1916–93) pharmaceutical executive, philanthropist; born near Garden City, Mo. After graduating junior college, and four years in the navy, he founded Marion Laboratories (1950), a pharmaceutical firm made successful in part by his talented salesmanship. In 1989 it merged with Merrell Dow Pharmaceuticals (a unit of Dow Chemicals Company) to become Marion Merrell Dow, Inc. In 1968 he became the first and sole owner of the Kansas City Royals, the American League baseball team. In 1966 he and his wife founded the Kauffman Foundation, a $1-billion organization with two current foci: youth development programs such as Project Choice (1988), which offers scholarships to vocational or college education for certain graduates of selected schools in Kansas City, Mo. and Kans.; and the Center for Entrepreneurial Leadership (1992). Widely honored, he received the Horatio Alger Award, the Southern Christian Leadership Award for his company's support of civil rights (1986), the Harry S. Truman Good Neighbor Award, and was named one of President Bush's "1000 points of light."

Kaufman, Barry Neil (1942–) psychotherapist; born in New York City. He studied at Ohio State University, Hunter College, and the New School for Social Research. He was president of the Communications Quorum in New York City (1968–74) and founded the Option Institute in Sheffield, Mass., to teach nontraditional methods of self-realization through changed attitudes that fostered trust and healing. His books include *Son-Rise* (1976), *Giant Steps* (1979), and *A Land Beyond Tears* (1981).

Kaufman, George S. (Simon) (1889–1961) playwright, director; born in Pittsburgh, Pa. After brief periods studying law and as a salesman, he began to contribute humorous material to newspapers; by 1915 he was writing for the theater section of the *New York Tribune,* moving to the *New York Times* (1917–30). His first successful play, *Dulcy* (1921), was in collaboration with Marc Connelly, and during the next 35 years he enjoyed almost unparalleled success, writing a string of sophisticated satires of contemporary life for the stage and movies in collaboration with others – Marc Connelly, Edna Ferber, Ring Lardner, Moss Hart, Alexander Woolcott, Robert Sherwood; his only success by himself was *The Butter and Egg Man* (1925). After 1928 he staged most of his own plays, and although Hollywood constantly beckoned, he was never really comfortable there. With Morris Ryskind he wrote one of the most successful Marx Brothers scripts, *A Night at the Opera* (1935). He shared two Pulitzers – with Ryskind, for the book to the musical, *Of Thee I Sing* (1931), and with Moss Hart for the play, *You Can't Take It With You* (1936).

Kaufman, Henry (1927–) investment counselor; born in Wennings, Germany. The son of a Jewish meat merchant who took his family out of Nazi Germany in 1936, he studied economics (Ph.D., New York University) before joining Salomon Brothers investment banking house in 1962. He rose to become a general partner by 1967. As Salomon's chief economist, he became known as "Dr. Gloom" for his bearish, though often accurate, forecasts of trends in the U.S. economy.

Kaufman, Irving (Robert) (1910–92) judge; born in New York City. He graduated from Fordham University and Fordham Law School, worked for a private firm, and, as a government attorney in the mid-1930s, prosecuted several notorious New York City cases and became known as the "boy prosecutor." He was named to the federal bench for the Southern District of New York in 1949. In March 1951 Julius and Ethel Rosenberg were tried in his court and found guilty of passing atomic secrets to the Soviets. He sentenced both to death, the first such peacetime sentences in U.S. history. After a series of appeals, the Rosenbergs were executed. Kaufman was elevated to the U.S. Court of Appeals bench in 1961.

Kay, Herma Hill (1934–) legal scholar; born in Orangeburg, S.C. A professor at the University of California: Berkeley (1960), she is best known for her work in family law and sex discrimination. Her major publications are *Law in Culture and Society* (1969) and *Text, Cases, Comments, Questions* (with Cranston and Currie, 1987).

Kay, Hershy (1919–81) composer/arranger; born in Philadelphia. A Broadway and screen arranger who often worked for Leonard Bernstein, he composed and arranged ballets including Balanchine's *Western Symphony*.

Kay, Ulysses (Simpson) (1917–) composer; born in Tuscon, Ariz. One of the first prominent African-American composers, he studied with Hindemith and Hanson and wrote mildly modernist works that won numerous prizes.

Kaye, Danny (b. David Daniel Kominski) (1913–1987) comic actor; born in New York City. Dropping out of school at age 13, he began as a comic in the "Borscht Circuit" in the Catskills, then worked as a singer and dancer in nightclubs and vaudeville until he made his Broadway debut in 1939. With his genius for mimicry, controlled slapstick, and patter song delivery, he appeared in a series of successful films from *Up in Arms* (1944) through *The Court Jester* (1956), all concocted primarily as vehicles for his versatility. He continued to appear in movies through 1969, and he had a popular variety show on television (1963–67), but increasingly he gave his energies to charitable causes, especially as a fundraiser for UNICEF, and often by appearing as a mock guest conductor of symphony orchestras. He received a special Academy Award in 1954 for "his service . . . to the motion picture industry and the American people."

Kaye, Nora (b. Koreff) (1920–87) ballet dancer; born in New York City. After her youthful training with the Metropolitan Opera Company's dance corps, Kaye performed in musical comedies in the late 1930s and became a founding member of Ballet Theatre in 1939. She was known for her dramatic performances of Anthony Tudor's choreography, especially *Pillar of Fire* (1942), and except for a few years at New York City Ballet (1951–54), she performed with Ballet Theatre until she retired from performance in 1961. She was executive or coproducer of seven films including *The Turning Point* (1977) and she served as associate artistic director of Ballet Theatre (1977–83).

Kazan, Elia (b. Elia Kazanjoglous) (1909–) stage and film director; born in Constantinople (now Istanbul), Turkey. His family emigrated to New York City when he was four. He studied at Williams College and Yale University, and began as an actor on Broadway and in Hollywood. With Lee Strasberg, he founded the Actors Studio in New York in 1947. He directed his first stage play in 1935 and began directing feature films in 1945 with *A Tree Grows in Brooklyn,* and was to divide his time between New York and Hollywood until 1964. Kazan's films often had a social or political theme – anti-Semitism and racism, megalomania, corruption – and he was known for getting actors to perform at levels they could not match before or after. He won two Academy Awards as best director for *Gentleman's Agreement* (1947) and *On the Waterfront* (1954), but his own favorite movie was *Viva Zapata* (1952), which he considered his first true film. In later years he turned to writing fiction.

Kazin, Alfred (1915–) literary critic, autobiographer; born in New York City. He was educated at City College and Columbia University, and with Irving Howe belonged in the 1940s to the "New York Intellectuals." Kazin became famous for *On Native Grounds* (1942), his classic study of modern American prose, a literature he would reinterpret in *An American Procession* (1982). He taught and lectured widely and reached a popular audience with an autobiographical trilogy beginning with *A Walker in the City* (1951).

Kazmaier, (Richard William, Jr.) Dick (1930–) football player; born in Toledo, Ohio. One of the last single-wing tailbacks, "Kaz" starred at Princeton (1949–51), earning unanimous All-America honors and the Heisman Trophy in 1951.

Keane, John (Joseph) (1839–1918) Catholic prelate; born in County Donegal, Ireland. Emigrating with his parents (1846), he settled in Baltimore, studied for the priesthood, and after ordination did parish work. In 1878 he became bishop of Richmond. Regarded as a liberal, he earned a national reputation as a cofounder and first rector (1889–97) of Catholic University in Washington, D.C. He held Vatican posts in Rome (1897–99), and after fund-raising for the University, served as archbishop of Dubuque, Iowa (1900–11).

Kearny, Lawrence (1789–1868) naval officer; born in Perth Amboy, N.J. He joined the navy in 1807 and became a captain in 1832. While commanding the East India Squadron (1840–42) he conducted diplomatic initiatives that led to the Open Door Policy and the first American-Chinese treaty (1844).

Kearny, Philip (1814–62) soldier; born in New York City (nephew of Stephen W. Kearny). The son of wealthy parents, he insisted on a military career against family opposition. He became a cavalry officer and served on the western frontier and then with the French army in Algiers. During the Mexican War he lost his left arm in battle, but this did not stop him from serving with the French Imperial Guard at the battles of Magenta and Solferino (1859). Returning to the U.S.A. at the outbreak of the Civil War, he was commissioned a brigadier general in the Union Army of the Potomac and commanded first a brigade, then a division through some dozen battles before being killed in action at Chantilly.

Kearny, Stephen Watts (1794–1848) soldier; born in Newark, N.J. The youngest of 15 children, he joined the army as the War of 1812 approached. From 1819 on he served on the western frontier, where he achieved a reputation as a tough disciplinarian. He conquered the territory of New Mexico shortly after the outbreak of war with Mexico, and then led a small force westward. After joining in the fighting that led to the taking of Los Angeles in early 1847, he engaged in jurisdictional conflicts with other Americans in California. He later served as military governor of Vera Cruz and Mexico City, and died of a disease he contracted there.

Keaton, (Joseph Francis) Buster (1895–1966) film actor, screenwriter, producer; born in Piqua, Kans. The son of medicine show performers, he joined their acrobatic comedy act at age three; they moved on to vaudeville when he was six and already an accomplished acrobat. He entered films in 1917 with *The Butcher Boy,* and after brief service in World War I, he made a series of short movies, along with his first feature, *The Saphead* (1920). By 1923 he was exercising complete artistic control over his films and he had established his persona as a deadpan and agile Everyman undaunted by the most extreme situations. Some of his productions were almost surreal, such as *Sherlock, Jr.* (1924), in which he played a film projectionist who became involved in the action on the screen; other masterworks include *The Boat* (1921), *The Navigator* (1924), and *The General* (1927). After Keaton signed with Metro-Goldwyn-Mayer, Inc. in 1928 he lost some control over his films, and not only did his marriage to Natalie Talmadge break up, but he was also troubled by alcoholism and mental illness. He

hung on at the margins of the Hollywood film world, but it was his appearances at the circus in Paris in 1947 and then in Chaplin's *Limelight* (1952) that led to the reappreciation of his comic artistry. His last decade saw him all but overwhelmed by the constant demands on his time and tributes to his genius.

Keats, Ezra Jack (1916–83) author, illustrator; born in New York City. He was based in Brooklyn, attended the School of Visual Arts (1947–48), worked as muralist for the Works Progress Administration (WPA) during the Depression of the 1930s, and became an illustrator. He is known for writing and illustrating many books for young readers, notably *The Snowy Day* (1962), in which he used the collage medium to feature a black boy named Peter.

Keck, David D. (Daniels) (1903–) botanist; born in Omaha, Nebr. He was on the staff of the Carnegie Institution of Washington (1926–50) and a member of that institution's division of plant biology at Stanford University (1929–50). There, with colleagues Jens Clausen and William Hiesey, Keck served as the group's taxonomist in a long-term study of the climatology, morphology, physiology, genetics, and hybridization of western U.S. plants of various elevations. He continued his taxonomic studies at the New York Botanical Garden (1951–58), then became program director of systematic biology at the National Science Foundation (NSF), Washington, D.C. (1958–62), and continued at NSF as division director of biological and medical sciences (1962). His methods of experimental botanical systematics revised many genera of western U.S. flowering plants.

Keckley, Elizabeth (Hobbs) (c. 1824–1907) dressmaker; born in Dinwiddie, Va. She purchased her freedom from slavery in 1855. By 1860 she was a Washington, D.C., dressmaker; she attracted the notice of Mary Todd Lincoln, to whom she became a companion and confidante. Keckley lost her clientele after publishing details of the Lincolns' private lives in *Behind the Scenes* (1868) and she spent her last forty years in obscurity.

Keeler, James Edward (1857–1900) astronomer; born in La Salle, Ill. He directed the Allegheny Observatory (1891–98) and the Lick Observatory from 1898. He established that Saturn's rings consist of meteoric particles and he carried out important spectroscopic work on 120,000 nebulae.

Keeler, (William Henry) "Wee Willie" (1872–1923) baseball player; born in Brooklyn, N.Y. During his 19-year career as an outfielder (1892–1910), mostly with the Baltimore Orioles and New York Yankees, he posted a lifetime batting average of .345, fifth highest in major league history. A diminutive player, his batting style was, as he put it, "To hit 'em where they ain't." He was elected to baseball's Hall of Fame in 1939.

Keeley, Edmund (Leroy) (1928–) translator, academic; born in Damascus, Syria. Son of an American career diplomat, he came to the U.S.A. in 1939, earned a D.Phil. at Oxford University, England, and joined the Princeton faculty (1954). When Princeton formed its Hellenic Studies Committee, he became its head. Often in collaboration with Philip Sherrard, he translated numerous modern Greek literary works by such as C. P. Cavafy, Yannis Ritsos, and George Sefaris. His books include *The Salonika Bay Murder* (1989), about the murder of CBS news reporter, George Polk (1948). His brother Robert Keeley served as U.S.

ambassador to Greece (1985–89), where his father had once served as a counselor at the U.S. embassy.

Keeley, James (1867–1934) journalist; born in London, England. Emigrating in 1883, he began as a reporter for the *Kansas City Times;* in his first big story, he tracked down and apprehended a murder suspect in a swamp. As general manager of the *Chicago Tribune* from 1898, he shaped it into an omnibus newspaper with many features, including an innovative "Friend of the People" column for readers with grievances.

Keene, Carolyn See STRATEMEYER, EDWARD L.

Keene, Donald (Lawrence) (1922–) literary, critic, translator, educator; born in New York City. A Columbia University Ph.D., he joined its faculty (1954) and became the leading western expert on Japanese literature. His critical and historical studies and translations introduced westerners to Japanese writing and earned Keene the Japanese Order of the Rising Sun (1976).

Keene, Laura (b. Mary Frances Moss) (?1820–73) actress, theater manager; born in London, England. She came to the U.S.A. in 1852, and after instant success in comedies, became the first woman to manage a theater in the U.S.A. (1855), encouraging American playwrights. She was performing at Ford's Theatre in Washington, D.C., when Lincoln was assassinated.

Keeshan, (Robert James) Bob (1927–) television producer, host; born in Lynnbrook, N.Y. Starting as a National Broadcasting Company page, he later played Clarabell on *Howdy, Doody* (1947–52). After developing ABC's *Time for Fun* (1953–55), he produced *Captain Kangeroo* (1955–85) on CBS, starring as the grandfatherly host who teaches through the humorous antics of animal puppets, aided by Mr. Green Jeans. In 1989 he published *Growing Up Happy.*

Keeton, William T. (Tinsley) (1933–80) animal behaviorist; born in Roanoke, Va. He taught at Virginia Polytechnic Institute (1954–56), was an instructor at Redford (Virginia) College (1965), then moved to Cornell (1958–80). From 1955 to 1965 he performed research on taxonomy, zoogeography, and the development of millipedes. His contributions to ornithology include studies of avian migration as influenced by the moon and by the earth's magnetic field, especially as demonstrated by homing behavior in pigeons. He was a dedicated educator whose *Biological Science* (1967) and *Elements of Biological Science* (1968, 1973, 1980) became popular texts. He also served as a consultant to the New York State Department of Education on proficiency tests for high school and college students.

Kefauver, (Carey) Estes (1903–63) U.S. senator; born in Monroe County, Tenn. Elected to the U.S. House of Representatives (Dem., Tenn.; 1939–49), he sponsored the so-called GI Bill, which gave various benefits to veterans of World War II. Elected to the U.S. Senate (1949–63), he was an internationalist and civil rights advocate. He won national fame as head of the "Kefauver Committee," which investigated organized crime. His presidential ambitions were frustrated in the 1950s.

Kegan, Robert G. (1946–) psychologist; born in St. Paul, Minn. He earned a Ph.D. in developmental psychology at Harvard, where he joined the human development faculty of the Graduate School of Education (1977). He was also on the faculty of the Massachusetts School of Professional Psychology, Dedham (1977). Of the Piagetian bent, his studies of cognitive development have appeared in numerous books and journals; in later years he broadened his concerns to embrace life-span development.

Keillor, (Gary Edward) Garrison (1942–) radio host, writer; born in Anoka, Minn. Raised in a strictly religious home, he began hosting a morning music show for Minnesota Public Radio in 1968 and publishing fiction pieces in the *New Yorker* in 1969. With a voice as folksy and mesmerizing as an old-time preacher, he rode to fame on a public radio variety show, *A Prairie Home Companion* (1974–87), set in the imaginary Minnesota town of Lake Wobegon. After a break to concentrate on writing – he produced many fiction pieces and essays, some for the *New Yorker,* and a novel: *WLT: A Radio Romance* (1991) – he returned to public radio with another variety show, *The American Radio Company* (1989).

Keith, B. F. (Benjamin Franklin) (1846–1914) performer, theater manager; born in Hillsboro, N.J. Part of an effort to make vaudeville more respectable, he developed a chain of theaters and formed the United Booking Office.

Kellar, (Harold) Harry (1849–1922) magician; born in Erie, Pa. A protegé of Houdini, he involved audiences in his sleight-of-hand tricks, slipping out of knots they had tied and handing out roses he "created" on stage.

Keller, Helen (Adams) (1880–1968) author, lecturer; born in Tuscumbia, Ala. She became blind and deaf at 19 months, and in a breakthrough made famous by subsequent popular dramatizations, was taught to speak, read, and write when she was seven years old by Anne Sullivan, known as "Teacher" to Keller and "the Miracle Worker" among the general public; Sullivan remained Keller's interpreter and companion until her death in 1936. Keller received communications by lipreading, braille, and finger-spelling using a manual alphabet; she expressed herself through finger-spelling, typewriting, and speech. She achieved international celebrity as a child, graduated from Radcliffe College (1904), and as an adult lectured and published widely on both her own experiences and political, social, and educational issues; she promoted socialism and women's suffrage and raised funds for the American Foundation for the Blind. She remains a model of achievement among the severely disabled.

Keller, James (Gregory) (1900–77) religious leader; born in Oakland, Calif. A Catholic priest, he was the founder (1945) and director (through 1969) of the Christophers, a nondenominational movement urging individual action to improve the world, under the motto "It is better to light a candle than to curse the darkness."

Kelley, (Abigail) Abby (1810–87) abolitionist; born in Pelham, Mass. Inspired by her Quaker faith, by 1835 she was becoming active in the antislavery movement in Lynn, Mass., where she was a teacher. Her first major public address on the subject, at the second women's antislavery convention in Philadelphia (1838), was so effective that she was persuaded by abolitionist leaders to devote herself to being an antislavery lecturer. She left teaching and proceeded to spend the next 20 years traveling throughout the Northeast, not only promoting the message of the abolitionists, but by her very presence and strength advancing the cause of the equality of women. She aligned herself with the more radical of the abolitionists and in 1845 she married one of these, Stephen Symonds Foster; he would often stay at home with their daughter while she went off lecturing. By 1859 she had broken with William Lloyd Garrison with whom she had been closely associated in both the abolition and nonresistance movements since 1835. After the Civil War she devoted herself to advancing women's rights while also finding time for some of the medical, dietary, and spiritual fads of the era. Although she could be something of a fanatic, she was also extremely courageous and is credited with inspiring a whole generation of women to become abolitionists and feminists.

Kelley, Emmett (1898–1977) clown; born in Sedan, Kans. He was over 40 when his sad-faced hobo in oversized rags, "Weary Willie," found a home under the Ringling Brothers big top (1942–55) and made Kelley the most celebrated American clown of his era.

Kelley, Florence (Molthrop) (1859–1932) social reformer; born in Philadelphia, Pa. Raised in a middle-class family and influenced by the Quakers, she was educated mainly at home before attending Cornell (B.A. 1882). Denied entry to the University of Pennsylvania graduate school because of her sex, she taught for awhile and then studied at the University of Zurich, Switzerland. There she adopted Socialism and translated Friedrich Engel's *Condition of the Working Class in England in 1844*. She also married a Russian medical student, Lazare Wischnewetzky; they came to New York City in 1886 and became involved in the Social Labor Party, but they separated in 1891; she moved to Illinois, got a divorce, adopted her maiden name, and gained custody of their three children. She joined the Hull House (1891–99) and played a major role in calling attention to working conditions of children and women. Impatient with the prosecution of violations of new laws, she got a law degree at Northwestern University (1894) and continued working for improved conditions. In 1899, she became the general secretary of the newly founded National Consumers' League and moved to New York City, and for the rest of her life she dedicated herself to using public pressure to force reform in labor practices. Her best-known book was *Some Ethical Gains Through Legislation* (1905) and she played a prominent role in federal legislation for child labor minimum wages. In 1909 she helped form the National Association for the Advancement of Colored People (NAACP); in 1919 she helped form the Women's International League for Peace and Freedom. After World War I she worked so hard to promote child labor legislation that she was often accused of being a communist.

Kelley, Francis Clement (1870–1948) Catholic prelate; born on Prince Edward Island, Canada. A small-town pastor in Michigan and a chaplain in the Spanish American War, he founded the Catholic Church Extension Society (1905) to introduce and maintain Catholicism in far-flung rural areas of the U.S.A. He led the society until being named bishop of Oklahoma in 1924. He became a monsignor in 1915.

Kelley, Hall J. (Jackson) (1790–1874) teacher, Oregon propagandist; born in Northwood, N.H. A graduate of Middlebury College (1813), he became a Boston public school director (1818–23), turning to engineering in Palmer, Mass., after his dismissal. He organized the American Society for Encouraging the Settlement of the Oregon Territory (1831), abandoning his family in 1832 to make the arduous trek by land and sea alone, and arriving near death in Ft. Vancouver, Oregon, in 1834. Returning by boat in

1836, he spent the rest of his life as a hermit in Three Rivers, Mass., supported mainly by his neighbors. Although he was something of a fanatic, his "Memoir" (1839), printed in a Congressional report, influenced the eventual American occupation of Oregon.

Kelley, Oliver Hudson (1826–1913) farmer, founder of the Grange; born in Boston, Mass. He worked in Illinois and Iowa before moving to Minnesota (1840) where he traded with Dakota Sioux and farmed. In 1864 he became a clerk in the Bureau of Agriculture, wrote articles for the *National Republican* on the greatness of Minnesota and undertook the Bureau's survey of agriculture conditions in Minnesota (1865). In 1867 he and six other men founded the National Grange of the Patrons of Husbandry of which he was secretary; he touted the benefits of the Grange in the agricultural press, and by 1874 there were more than 20,000 granges. (Originally activist/reformist organizations for farmers' rights, they would survive more as social/community clubs.) In 1875 he moved his family to Louisville, Ky., where he established the Grange secretary's office. In 1878 he resigned his office and became a land speculator in northern Florida, founding the town of Carrabelle. He wrote *Origin and Progress of the Order of the Patrons of Husbandry* (1875).

Kelley, William Darrah (1814–90) U.S. representative; born in Philadelphia. Apprenticed to a jeweler at age 13, he became a lawyer in 1841, and helped found the Republican Party in 1854. In Congress (Rep., Pa.; 1861–83) he favored high tariffs.

Kellogg, Frank (Billings) (1856–1937) U.S. senator, cabinet member; born in Potsdam, N.Y. A self-educated Minnesota corporate lawyer, he joined Theodore Roosevelt's administration as a special prosecutor and won several government antitrust cases, notably against Standard Oil (1906–11). A senator (Rep., Minn.; 1917–23) and ambassador to Great Britain (1923–25), he became secretary of state (1925–29), masterminding the multinational Kellogg-Briand pact renouncing war (1928), for which he received the 1929 Nobel Peace Prize. He returned to practicing law, and served on the World Court at the Hague (1930–35).

Kellogg, John Harvey (1852–1943) surgeon, food reformer; born in Tyrone Township, Mich. (brother of Will K. Kellogg). Born into a Seventh Day Adventist family, he took a course in a "hygieotherapeutic" school. He rejected this approach and took regular medical training, finishing at Bellevue Hospital Medical College (New York City) but with a thesis claiming that disease is the body's way of defending itself. He had become editor of the Adventist monthly, *Health Reformer* (which he renamed *Good Health* in 1879), and on returning to Battle Creek, he became superintendent of the Western Health Reform Institute, which Sister Ellen Harmon White had already established to promote ideas about health much like Kellogg's. He renamed it the Battle Creek Sanitarium and began to apply his theories about "biologic living," or "the Battle Creek idea," which stressed the role of "natural medicine" such as a vegetarian diet and a Spartan spa-like regimen. He was also much in demand as an expert surgeon and would donate his fees to the sanitarium for indigent patients. During the 1890s he set up a laboratory to develop more nutritious foods; his brother, Will, had joined him and they developed a dry wheat flake that soon became so popular as a breakfast cereal that they began to sell it through a mail-order business; later they developed a rice flake and a corn flake and set up the Sanitas Food Company to produce and sell these new products. As the food business continued to expand, the brothers became legal adversaries and by 1906 Will gained the exclusive rights to sell the products under the name of W. K. Kellogg; John set up the Battle Creek Food Company and developed other health foods such as coffee substitutes and soybean-derived milk. Meanwhile, John had fallen out with the Adventist leaders who felt he and his Battle Creek enterprise had become too big and had drifted too far from the church; in 1907 the Adventists excommunicated him but he fought to retain control of the sanitarium and his food laboratory. He wrote over 50 books promoting his ideas and also founded the Race Betterment Foundation to pursue his theories about eugenics. Although he would never become as rich or well-known as his brother, Will, John Kellogg had actually instituted a major revolution in the human diet.

Kellogg, Paul Underwood (1879–1958) editor, social reformer; born in Kalamazoo, Mich. After working as a journalist, he went to New York City (1901) to study at Columbia University and then joined the editorial staff of *Charities,* a magazine devoted to philanthropic activities. In 1907 he left the magazine to commence an in-depth study of every aspect of life in Pittsburgh, the first such social survey of an American urban community; it was published as the *Pittsburgh Survey* (1910–14) and became a model for sociological investigation, stimulating national calls for housing, workmen's compensation, and other reforms. In 1909 he returned to his old magazine, now retitled *Survey;* as its editor (1912–52), he forged it into America's leading journal of social work and a major force in social reform, and during the 1930s he saw many of his concerns addressed by President Franklin Roosevelt's New Deal. In 1939 he was president of the National Conference of Social Work. In addition to advocating many social reforms that have since become widely accepted, he was active in a variety of progressive causes: he helped found the American Civil Liberties Union (1917) and the Foreign Policy Association (1918), he participated in the defense of Nicola Sacco and Bartolomeo Vanzetti, and he supported the Spanish republicans agains Franco.

Kellogg, W. K. (Willie Keith) (1860–1951) cereal manufacturer, philanthropist; born in Battle Creek, Mich. After working as a broom salesman, he worked with his brother, Dr. John H. Kellogg, during the 1890s to develop new ways to prepare grain for breakfast cereals. After their first success with a flaked wheat, they developed a corn flake and in 1905 Will went on his own to form the Battle Creek Toasted Corn Flake Company. It was soon renamed the W. K. Kellogg Company, and although he achieved great financial success with his line of breakfast foods and revolutionized the world's breakfast-eating habits, he had to fight a long legal battle with his brother over the right to use the family name on his products. He was a pioneer in large national advertising campaigns to promote a product. He retired as president in 1929 but remained chairman of the board until 1946. In 1930 he established the W. K. Kellogg Foundation, which became one of America's richest philanthropic organizations.

Kellogg, William Pitt (1831–1918) U.S. senator/representative; born in Orwell, Vt. A Union veteran, he was elected to the U.S. Senate (Rep., La.; 1868–72, 1877–83). As one of the so-called carpetbaggers, he won a disputed election to governor of Louisiana (1873–77) that nearly led to civil war in the state. He also served in the U.S. House of Representatives (1883–85).

Kelly, Edward (Joseph) (1876–1950) mayor; born in Chicago. As chief engineer of the city's sanitary district, he was indicted on various corruption charges. A leader of Chicago's corrupt Democratic Party machine, he was appointed to fill Anton Cermak's term and served as Democratic mayor from 1933–48. He oversaw many public improvements, but his office was tainted by scandals.

Kelly, Ellsworth (1923–) painter, sculptor; born in Newburgh, N.Y. He studied at the Boston Museum School under Karl Zerbe (1946–48), in Paris (1948–54), and then returned to New York. Influenced by Jean Arp, he worked in a variety of mediums, and his sculptures are composed of curved metal planes. He was preoccupied with objects as art, color patterns, and random collages, and his shaped canvas, *Two Panels: Blue, Red* (1968), reveals his exploration of color as emotion.

Kelly, (Eugene Curran) Gene (1912–) movie actor, dancer, director, choreographer; born in Pittsburgh, Pa. A dance instructor and manual worker with a degree in economics, he became a Broadway chorus boy before he starred in *Pal Joey* (1939). He made his film debut in *For Me and My Gal* (1942); as an athletic dancer with a breezy disposition, he went on to star in several comedies and dramas, but made his irrepressible mark in musicals such as *Singin' in the Rain* (1952). The director of *Hello Dolly!* (1969), he was given an honorary Oscar (1951).

Kelly, Grace (Patricia) (1928–82) film actress; born in Philadelphia. A coolly elegant beauty, she studied at the American Academy of Dramatic Arts, then appeared on Broadway and television. Her short but highly successful film career began in *Fourteen Hours* (1951). She received an Academy Award for *The Country Girl* (1954). She retired in 1956, when she married Prince Rainier III, becoming Princess Grace of Monaco. She died in an automobile accident.

Kelly, Howard Atwood (1858–1943) gynecologist, surgeon; born in Camden, N.J. After taking his medical degree at the University of Pennsylvania (1882), he made several visits to Europe to learn about the more advanced gynecological methods. He founded the Kensington Hospital for Women in Philadelphia. He went to Baltimore in 1889 to be gynecologist-in-chief at the new Johns Hopkins Hospital, then also became a professor of gynecology at Johns Hopkins Medical School (1893–1919), making Baltimore one of America's premier gynecology centers. He developed several new surgical techniques and diagnostic procedures, was one of the first American doctors to use radium to treat cancer, and wrote or edited several books on medical subjects.

Kelly, (John Brendan) Johnny (1889–1960) rower, building contractor; born in Philadelphia. After being denied the prize at Britain's Henley rowing regatta because he worked for a living (the race was for "gentlemen"), he got his revenge by winning gold medals in Olympic singles and doubles sculls in 1920 and in the doubles in 1924. A self-made man, he became a very wealthy contractor and was active in Democratic party politics. His daughter Grace

Kelly was the actress and then Princess of Monaco. His son John B. Kelly Jr. competed as a rower in four Olympiads.

Kelly, (Michael Joseph) "King" (1857–94) baseball player; born in Troy, N.Y. One of baseball's first superstars, he combined power and speed during his 16-year career as an outfielder/catcher (1878–93), mostly with the Chicago White Stockings and Boston Red Stockings. The once-popular song, "Slide, Kelly, Slide!" (1889) was inspired by the fans' chanting that accompanied his frequent stolen bases. Handsome and flamboyant, he was known as baseball's "king of the diamond." In 1945 he was elected to baseball's Hall of Fame.

Kelly, (Walter Crawford) Walt (1913–73) cartoonist; born in Philadelphia. After working as an animator for Walt Disney Studios from 1935 to 1941, he created in 1943 the newspaper comic strip, *Bumbazine and Albert the Alligator,* which featured characters in Okefenokee swamp and eventually evolved into the classic strip, *Pogo,* in 1948. In this strip, which was noted for its sharp political commentary, Pogo Possum provides the frequently quoted aphorism, "We have met the enemy and he is us."

Kelly, William (1811–88) iron manufacturer, inventor; born in Pittsburgh, Pa. In Kentucky in the 1840s and early 1850s, he built and operated iron furnaces and was making wrought-iron articles. By 1850 he had discovered that a blast of air blown through molten iron removes many of the impurities found in cast iron of the day, leaving a stronger and more ductile metal. Using what he called this "air-boiling" process, he built seven "converters" between 1851–56 and was effectively making steel. But in 1856 the Englishman, Henry Bessemer, who had independently discovered much the same process, was given a U.S. patent, so Kelly was forced to convince the U.S. Patent Office of the priority of his claim; Kelly's claims were recognized in a patent of 1857. Although subsequent refinements of Kelly's process would contribute greatly to the new "age of steel," Kelly himself went bankrupt in the panic of 1857 and it was the Bessemer converter that achieved commercial success.

Kelsen, Hans (1881–1973) legal scholar, philosopher; born in Prague, Czechoslovakia. A distinguished law professor who drafted the 1920 Austrian constitution, he fled Nazism, eventually going to the U.S.A., where he taught at Harvard (1940–42) and the University of California (1942–52). He contributed to legal philosophy in such works as *Principles of International Law* (1952).

Kendall, Amos (1789–1869) journalist, public official; born in Dunstable, Mass. A Dartmouth graduate, he became editor of *The Argus of Western America* (1816–28) in Frankfort, Ky., championing Andrew Jackson, whom he followed to Washington. As treasury auditor (1828–34) and postmaster-general (1834–40), he rooted out corruption, and as an intimate friend/adviser, he wrote many of Jackson's speeches. He returned to journalism and farming and then became rich as inventor Samuel F. B. Morse's business agent (1845–59). He devoted his final decade to church and philanthropic projects including the school for deaf-mutes in Washington, D.C. (now Gallaudet College).

Kendall, Donald M. (McIntosh) (1921–) food products executive; born in Sequim, Wash. He distinguished himself as a bomber pilot in the Pacific in World War II and after the war became a New York City salesman for Pepsi-Cola. He rapidly rose in the corporate sales management hierarchy.

As president of Pepsi-Cola International (1953–63) he tripled overseas sales and caused a sensation by arranging for Soviet premier Nikita Khrushchev to be photographed drinking Pepsi (1959). Under his aggressive and often ruthless leadership as president and CEO of the U.S. parent company (1963), PepsiCo initiated its famous "Pepsi Generation" (1964) and "Pepsi Challenge" (1975) advertising campaigns, both greatly increasing its sales to challenge those of archrival Coca Cola. The firm's acquisitions (Frito-Lay, Pizza Hut, Kentucky Fried Chicken) made it the country's largest snack/fast food company and 29th largest industrial corporation. Pepsi became the first U.S. consumer goods manufacturer to set up Soviet production operations (1974).

Kendall, Edward C. (Calvin) (1886–1972) endocrinologist; born in South Norwalk, Conn. He was a research chemist with the Parke, Davis and Company (Detroit) (1910–11) and a hormone biochemist at St. Luke's Hospital (New York City) (1911–14). After moving to the Mayo Clinic (1914–51), he isolated and named thyroxin, the principal thyroid hormone (1916). Of his six hormonal isolates from the adrenal cortex, one (cortisone) was used by his colleague, Philip Hench, for the successful treatment of rheumatoid arthritis. Kendall (with Hench and Swiss adrenal specialist Tadeus Reichstein) received the 1950 Nobel Prize in physiology for his contributions to endocrinology. From 1951 to 1972 he was a visiting professor and researcher at Princeton (1951–72).

Kendall, Henry W. (Way) (1926–) physicist; born in Boston, Mass. He taught and performed research at Stanford (1956–61) before returning to his alma mater, the Massachusetts Institute of Technology (1961). He and colleague Jerome Friedman shared the 1990 Nobel Prize in physics with Richard Taylor for their experiments confirming the existence of quarks.

Kenedy, P. J. (Patrick John) (1843–1906) bookseller, publisher; born in New York City. On his father's death (1866) he inherited and successfully expanded the venerable Catholic book publishing firm, incorporated in 1904 as P. J. Kenedy & Sons.

Kenkel, Frederick P. (Patrick) (1863–1952) Catholic social reformer; born in Chicago. Turning to religion after the death of his first wife (around 1900), he became influential as managing editor of the German Catholic newspaper *Amerika,* and from 1908 he directed the social reform program of the Central Verein, the largest German-Catholic organization of the time. After World War I, however, the organization and Kenkel's conservative social views waned in influence.

Kenna, John (Edward) (1848–93) U.S. representative senator; born in Kanawha County, Va. A confederate veteran and lawyer before going to the U.S. House of Representatives (Dem., Va.; 1877–83) and the Senate (1883–93), he opened the Kanawha River to commercial shipping.

Kennan, George (1845–1924) explorer, journalist; born in Norwalk, Ohio. Without a college education, he became an expert telegrapher and writer. He traveled extensively in Russia and wrote *Tent Life in Siberia* (1870) and *Siberia and the Exile System* (1891). His reputation for integrity made him the White House telegrapher during President Garfield's final weeks of life after being shot (1881).

Kennan, George F. (Frost) (1904–) diplomat, historian;

born in Milwaukee, Wis. Educated at Princeton (B.A. 1925) and at the Berlin Seminary for Oriental Languages (diploma, 1930), he served as U.S. foreign service officer (1926–53) in Geneva, Hamburg, Berlin, Estonia, Latvia, Moscow, Vienna, Prague, Lisbon, and London; he also served as U.S. ambassador to the U.S.S.R. (1952) and Yugoslavia (1961–63). In 1947, using the pen name "Mr. X" (because he was then with the State Department), he wrote a famous article in *Foreign Policy,* "The Sources of Soviet Conduct," that effectively spelled out what would be the West's policy of "containment" toward Soviet Communism for the next 40 years. His first book, *American Diplomacy, 1900–1950* (1951), was praised on both literary and historiographical grounds and he won Pulitzer Prizes for two later works, *Russia Leaves the War* (1956) and *Memoirs: 1925–1950* (1967). His subsequent publications continued to stir interest because his views, if sometimes out of step with official U.S. policy – including his prediction of the demise of the U.S.S.R. – were often vindicated by history; even when events contradicted his views, he was recognized for having raised the level of public debate. He opposed the division of Germany after World War II, the development of the H-bomb, American participation in the Korean and Vietnam Wars, and reliance on nuclear weapons for national defense. His campaign against instruments of mass destruction made him a hero of the antinuclear movement; his 1980 plea to the great powers to abolish such weapons articulated the fears and frustrations of an era. In 1956 he became a professor at the Institute for Advanced Study in Princeton, N.J.

Kennedy, Adrienne (1931–) playwright; born in Pittsburgh, Pa. Her *Funnyhouse of a Negro,* about the sufferings of a racially mixed woman, won an Obie award in 1964. She also wrote *In His Own Write* (1967), based on John Lennon's writings.

Kennedy, Anthony M. (McLeod) (1935–) Supreme Court justice; born in Sacramento, Calif. He practiced law privately (1961–75) before he was named to the U.S. Court of Appeals, ninth circuit (1975). Known for his conservative views, he was named by President Reagan to the U.S. Supreme Court (1988) after the Senate refused to confirm the more controversial Robert H. Bork.

Kennedy, Edward M. (Moore) ("Ted") (1932–) U.S. senator; born in Boston, Mass. (brother of John F. Kennedy). Raised in a family that placed a high priority on achievement, he had a Harvard classmate take an exam for him and was suspended; after serving in the army, he finished Harvard and went on to graduate from the University of Virginia Law School (1959). Only 30 years old when he ran for the U.S. Senate seat his brother John had vacated, he began his long term (Dem., Mass.; 1963). A staunch liberal, he sponsored bills on immigration reform, criminal code reform, fair housing, public education, health care, AIDS research, and a variety of programs to aid the poor; on the Senate judiciary committee, he upheld liberal positions on abortion, capital punishment, and racial bussing. After the assassinations of his brothers John (1963) and Robert (1968), he was widely regarded as a potential president, but his chances were damaged by his behavior after a car accident in Chappaquiddick, Mass., in which a young woman companion drowned (1969); his hopes were finally dashed when in 1980 he failed to wrest the Democratic nomination away from incumbent President Carter.

He continued to be one of the most outspoken advocates for liberal positions, and by the time of his second marriage in 1992 he seemed to have matured and mellowed in his personal life.

Kennedy, Eugene P. (Patrick) (1919–) biochemist; born in Chicago. He was a chemist at Armour and Company (1941–47), then became a fellow at the University of California: Berkeley (1949–50). He taught and performed research at the University of Chicago (1951–60), before joining Harvard Medical School (1960). He determined the enzymatic pathways for biosynthesis of triglycerides and phospholipids (1950s). His later investigations of membrane function demonstrated the genetically-mediated role of proteins in lactose transport in the colon bacillus.

Kennedy, (Florynce Rae) Flo (1916–) lawyer, activist; born in Kansas City, Mo. After working at various odd jobs, she moved to New York City (1942), earned her B.A. at Columbia University, and then graduated from its law school (1951). Her New York practice included Billie Holiday (and her estate), Charlie Parker's estate, and H. Rap Brown, and she became increasingly disillusioned with the racism she saw in the justice system. Broadening her approach, in the 1960s and 1970s she spoke out forcefully in many forums on behalf of not only African-Americans but women, the poor, homosexuals, prostitutes, and minorities of all kinds. To fight racism in the media she founded the Media Workshop (1966) and she formed the Feminist Party when she grew impatient with the National Organization of Women. In the 1970s she became particularly active in promoting women's right to abortions. Noted for her often outrageous outspokenness, she published her autobiography, *Color Me Flo* (1976).

Kennedy, Jacqueline See Onassis, Jacqueline Kennedy.

Kennedy, John F. (Fitzgerald) (1917–63) thirty-fifth U.S. president; born in Brookline, Mass. Descended from Irish-Americans who had shown a talent for politics, he studied at Harvard; his senior thesis became the best-selling *Why England Slept* (1940). (His 1956 *Profiles in Courage* would win the Pulitzer Prize.) He enlisted as a seaman in the U.S. Navy and after Pearl Harbor was commissioned as an ensign, given command of a PT boat, and assigned to the South Pacific. He was wounded when his boat was cut in two by a Japanese destroyer. (The public would never really be aware of the extent of his various medical problems.) Returning to Massachusetts after the war, he was elected as a Democrat to the U.S. House of Representatives (1947–53) and the U.S. Senate (1953–61). Having failed in his 1956 bid for the Democratic vice-presidential nomination, in 1960 he became the youngest man, and first Catholic, to be elected U.S. president. His short term in office would become one of legendary high hopes that was not always matched by tangible accomplishments. His liberal slate of social programs, called the "New Frontier," largely faltered in Congress, although he gradually did actively support desegregation. In 1962 he went to the brink of nuclear war in the Cuban missile crisis, but in 1963 he secured an important nuclear test ban treaty with the U.S.S.R. He also established the Alliance for Progress and the Peace Corps, and above all he inspired a whole new generation to seek to better their world through government service. Kennedy's maturing command of his powers was cut short by his assassination by Lee Harvey Oswald, as determined by the Warren Commission. Revelations in later years of Kennedy's steady series of sexual liaisons with women tarnished his image in the minds of some Americans, but most people around the world continued to think of him as the fallen prince of Camelot.

Kennedy, John Pendleton (Mark Littleton, Mephistopheles, pen names) (1795–1870) politician, writer; born in Baltimore, Md. He graduated from Baltimore College (1812) and became a lawyer (1816). He devoted himself to both politics and writing; his most highly regarded novels include *Swallow Barn* (1832) and *Rob of the Bowl* (1838). He served in the House of Representatives (Whig, Md.; 1838–39, 1841–45). As secretary of the navy (1852–53), he organized several naval expeditions, notably that of Commodore Matthew Perry to Japan.

Kennedy, Joseph (Patrick) (1888–1969) financier; born in Boston, Mass. (father of John Fitzgerald Kennedy). A Boston banker and movie financier (1926–30), he made millions on insider stock deals, but set tough standards as President Roosevelt's chairman of the Securities and Exchange Commission (1934–35). Recalled in disgrace as a pro-German ambassador to Great Britain (1938–40), he retired from public life but financed the careers of his charismatic sons.

Kennedy, Robert F. (Francis) (1925–68) attorney general, U.S. senator; born in Boston, Mass. (brother of John F. Kennedy and Edward Kennedy). One of the large family of Rose and Joseph Kennedy, he took his law degree at the University of Virginia Law School and was admitted to the Massachusetts State Bar (1951). He became an attorney with the Justice Department's criminal division (1951–52). He managed John F. Kennedy's campaign for election to the United States Senate (1952) and was named assistant counsel to the Hoover Commission, in Washington, D.C. He then became assistant counsel to the Senate Permanent Subcommittee on Investigations (1953), chaired by Senator Joseph R. McCarthy. After several more posts as a legal counsel, he became chief counsel to the Senate Select Committee on Improper Activities in the Labor or Management Field (1957). Although later considered a liberal, through such appointments in the 1950s he was associated with the redbaiting and union-smashing tactics being pursued by the committees he represented. He managed his brother's campaign for the presidency of the U.S. (1959–60), and as attorney general (1961–64) and closest adviser to President John F. Kennedy (1960–63), he exerted considerable influence on the nation's domestic and foreign affairs. To supporters he was charming, brilliant, and sincere in his concern for the downtrodden; to detractors, he was described as calculating, ruthless, overly ambitious, and inconsistent. He was able to use the Kennedy name to win election to the U.S. Senate from New York (Dem., 1965–68) – a state to which he previously had few ties. He jumped into the 1968 presidential election only after Senator Eugene J. McCarthy had proven President Lyndon Johnson's political vulnerability. Even so, to many Americans he appeared the hope for the future, to embody his slain brother's ideals, until he himself was assassinated (June 6, 1968, by Sirhan Sirhan, a Jordanian immigrant) immediately after winning the California Democratic presidential primary.

Kennedy, William (1928–) writer; born in Albany, N.Y. He studied at Siena College (B.A. 1949) and had a long career in journalism in Glen Falls, Albany, San Juan, Miami, and Puerto Rico. Beginning in 1974 he taught at State University of New York: Albany. His early novels, such as *Legs* (1975) and *Billy Phelan's Greatest Game* (1978), part of his Albany series, remained largely unnoticed until the publication of *Ironweed* (1983). In 1984 he was awarded the Pulitzer Prize for fiction and his previous novels were reissued. A projected series based in New York City, *Quinn's Book,* was published in 1988.

Kennelly, Arthur Edwin (1861–1939) electrical engineer; born in Bombay, India. Raised in England, he left school at age 13 and taught himself physics while working as a telegrapher. He emigrated to the U.S.A. in 1887 to become Edison's electrical assistant; he left in 1894 to be a consulting engineer, then taught at Harvard (1902–30) and occasionally at the Massachusetts Institute of Technology. He was a pioneer in the use of mathematical models to explain electrical phenomena. He explained the path of radio waves and deduced the existence of an atmospheric ionized reflecting layer, the Kennelly-Heaviside layer.

Kenney, George (Churchill) (1889–1977) aviator; born in Yarmouth, Nova Scotia. He attended the Massachusetts Institute of Technology and worked as a railroad engineer before enlisting in the U.S. Army in 1918. Trained as a pilot, he shot down two German aircraft on the western front. He served in a succession of staff and line posts before taking command of the 5th Air Force, MacArthur's air arm in the Southwest Pacific, in September 1942. After the war, Kenney commanded the Strategic Air Command (1947) and the Air University at Maxwell Air Force Base, Ala. (1948–51). He retired in 1951.

Kenrick, Francis (Patrick) (1796–1863) Catholic prelate; born in Dublin, Ireland. After studies in Rome he was ordained (1821) and headed a seminary in Bardstown, Ky., becoming a leading Catholic theologian. As coadjutor bishop of Philadelphia (from 1830) he asserted church power over lay trustees, founded a seminary, for which he wrote theology textbooks, and promoted calm during the 1844 anti-Catholic riots. As archbishop of Baltimore (from 1851) he promoted parochial education and introduced the Forty Hours devotion into the U.S.A.

Kensett, John (Frederick) (1816–72) painter; born in Cheshire, Conn. (son of Thomas Kensett). He began his career as an engraver, printing maps and banknotes in New York City. In 1840 he traveled in Europe with Asher B. Durand and Benjamin Champney, among others, and returned to New York in 1847. From then on he painted the detailed and luminous landscapes that made him a leader of the Hudson River school from 1850–70, as seen in *Lake George* (1869).

Kent, Allegra (1938–) ballet dancer; born in Santa Monica, Calif. On her toes at the early age of 11, at age 13 she moved to New York City for scholarship study at the School of American Ballet where she attracted George Balanchine's attention. In 1953 she joined the New York City Ballet and became a principal dancer at age 18. One of six ballerinas known for their "Balanchine style," for the next three decades she was one of the stars of the New York City Ballet. In later years she danced in a number of companies including the Ballet of Los Angeles (1990).

Kent, Jacob (1726–1812) soldier, public official; born in Chebacco (now Essex), Mass. Veteran of the French and Indian War, and a founder of the state of Vermont, he led militia forces during the American Revolution, participating in the series of battles that led to the British surrender at Saratoga in October 1777.

Kent, Jacob Ford (1835–1918) soldier; born in Philadelphia. After graduating from West Point in 1861, he saw combat during the Civil War. He served on the frontier for nearly 30 years, and commanded the 1st Infantry Division in the storming of San Juan Hill outside Santiago, Cuba, in July 1898.

Kent, James (1763–1847) legal scholar; born in Southeast, N.Y. A staunch Federalist, he was chosen by John Jay and Alexander Hamilton to be Columbia College's first professor of law (1793–98). In 1798 he was appointed to the New York State Supreme Court and rose to become its chief justice (1804–14). He became chancellor of the New York State court of chancery (1814–23) where his decisions and written opinions often implemented equity jurisdiction, dubbing him "the American Blackstone." His compulsory retirement from the bench at age 60 led to his return to Columbia. There he wrote America's first legal classic, *Commentaries on American Law* (four vols. 1826–30), which provided the first systematic, clear approach to Anglo-American law.

Kent, Joseph (1779–1837) U.S. representative, governor, senator; born in Calverty County, Md. A congressman (Fed., Md.; 1811–15, 1819–26), then Republican governor (1826–29), and senator (1833–37), he raised money for the Chesapeake and Ohio canal and the Baltimore and Ohio Railroad.

Kent, Rockwell (1882–1971) painter, graphic artist; born in Tarrytown, N.Y. He studied with William Merritt Chase in New York (1897–1900), and worked in many mediums, including oil, water color, pen and ink, wood block, and lithography. He traveled widely and was involved in many progressive social causes. His work was noted for its strong geometric composition and his bold use of light and dark, as in *Toilers of the Sea* (1907). He became most widely known for his book illustrations.

Kenton, (Stanley Newcomb) Stan (1912–79) musician; born in Wichita, Kans. He was raised in Los Angeles, where he played piano in several lesser-known big bands throughout the 1930s and with Vido Musso in 1938–39. In 1940, he formed his own orchestra which won wide acclaim for its unusual theme song, "Artistry in Rhythm," and its mild experimentations in a self-described "progressive jazz" style. He disbanded in 1947 and spent three years in retirement. He attracted notoriety in 1950–52 with a 40-piece orchestra which he billed as "Innovations in Modern Music," playing composed avant-garde works as well as jazz. From 1952 until his death, he led a standard jazz big band, although his 1964 recording, *Kenton Plays Wagner,* and his 1966 Neophonic Orchestra were further experiments in symphonic jazz. He was also a pioneer in jazz education, conducting over 100 clinics annually throughout the 1960s and 1970s.

Kenyon, (Jennifer) Jane (1947–   ) poet; born in Ann Arbor, Mich. (wife of Donald Hall). She studied at the University of Michigan (B.A. 1970; M.A. 1972). As translator of *Twenty Poems of Anna Akhmatova* (1985), she gained critical approval, but she is best known for her own perceptive and finely crafted poetry, as in *Let Evening Come* (1990). She lived in Wilmot, N.H.

Kenyon, Josephine Hemenway (1880–1965) pediatrician, columnist; born in Auburn, N.Y. She graduated from Johns Hopkins University Medical School (1904) in a class of 3

women and 42 men. While maintaining a private practice in New York City (1911–45) she was active in the Young Women's Christian Association during World War I. She wrote a monthly column on child care for *Good Housekeeping* (1924–52) and the book *Healthy Babies Are Happy Babies* (1934). She gave thorough information to her readers, but still urged them to see their own pediatricians regularly.

Kenyon, William Squire (1869–1933) U.S. senator, judge; born in Elyria, Ohio. A lawyer, he served in the U.S. Senate (Rep., Ohio; 1911–22), where as a progressive he supported labor and the "farm bloc." Appointed a U.S. circuit judge (1922–23), he canceled the leases that Secretary of Interior Albert Fall had granted in what was known as the Teapot Dome scandal.

Keppel, (Francis) Frank (1916–90) educator; born in New York City. At Harvard's Graduate School of Education (dean 1948–62), Keppel developed an M.A. program in teaching and fostered classroom innovations like team teaching, programmed learning, and television. As U.S. Commissioner of Education (1962–66) he enforced the Civil Rights Act (1964) and oversaw passage of the Elementary and Secondary Education Act (1965).

Keppler, Joseph (1837–94) caricaturist, publisher; born in Kieligenstadt, Austria. After studying art in Vienna, he joined his father in the U.S.A. in 1867 where he soon founded a German-language journal of humor, *Die Vehme.* In 1870 he founded *Puck,* also printed in German; it was revived in New York in 1877 in an English-language version. His intricate cartoons lampooned Tammany politicians, Prohibition, and other issues of the day. He also created several cartoon icons, notably a bewhiskered Uncle Sam.

Kerby, William (Joseph) (1870–1936) Catholic priest, sociologist; born in Lawler, Iowa. Ordained in 1892, he earned a doctorate from Louvain and taught at Catholic University (1906–17); as an official of the National Catholic Welfare Conference, he promoted "scientific charity," or professionalism in the church's administration of social programs. He became a monsignor in 1934.

Kern, Jerome (1885–1945) composer; born in New York City. After a start in Broadway theaters as a song-plugger and rehearsal pianist, he began contributing songs to musical shows. With librettist Guy Bolton, he wrote his first hit show, *Very Good, Eddie* (1915), which brought a new sophistication to musical theater by connecting songs and story more closely than the popular shows of the time. With lyricist Oscar Hammerstein II, he wrote his most important work, *Show Boat* (1927), in which he further integrated lyrical text with the dramatic demands of plot and character to create the first American musical play. In 1939 he moved to Hollywood and wrote only for films. One of the most influential songwriters in American musical theater, he is credited with over 1,000 songs in 104 stage and film productions, including such standards as "Ol' Man River" (1927), "Smoke Gets in Your Eyes" (1933), and "All the Things You Are" (1939).

Kern, John W. (Worth) (1849–1917) U.S. senator; born in Alto, Ind. Active in state politics, and an unsuccessful Democratic vice-presidential candidate in 1908, he was elected to the U.S. Senate (Dem., Ind.; 1911–17). As Senate majority leader he supported progressive initiatives such as child labor legislation.

Kerner, Otto, Jr. (1908–76) governor; born in Chicago. A Chicago corporate lawyer (1934–47) and distinguished World War II veteran, he was Illinois attorney general (1945–54), becoming Cook County judge in 1954. As governor (Dem., 1961–68), he effected fiscal and administrative reforms, leaving to chair the National Advisory Committee on Civil Disorders; the Committee's report (1968) became known as "the Kerner Report" and played a major role in redirecting Americans' thinking about their society's racial problems. A U.S. Court of Appeals judge (1968–74), he was sentenced to a three-year jail term (1974) for racetrack fraud.

Kernighan, Brian W. (1942–) computer scientist; born in Toronto, Canada. He came to the United States about 1965 and joined Bell Laboratories in Murray Hill, N.J., in 1969. He was instrumental in the development of UNIX in the early 1970s, actually giving the operating system its name. He also worked on document preparation software, programming languages (most notably AWK) and software tools.

Kerouac, Jack (b. Jean Louis Lebris de Kerouac) (Jean-Louis, Jean Louis Incognito, John Kerouac, pen names) (1922–69) writer; born in Lowell, Mass. He studied at Columbia University (1940–42), and served in the merchant marine (1942; 1943) and the navy (1943). Later he studied at the New School for Social Research (1948–49). He lived with his mother in Lowell, held a variety of jobs, and traveled throughout the United States and Mexico. The publication of *On the Road* (1957), a semiautobiographical tale of his wanderings with Neal Cassady, instantly established his reputation as a spokesman for the Beat Generation. His friends, Allen Ginsberg and William Burroughs Jr., were strongly supportive when conservative critics of the day were upset by the subject matter of the book and by what Kerouac called his "spontaneous prose." Although his new-found fame helped to promote his previously unpublished books, he was profoundly disturbed by his loss of privacy. He lost his gift for high-speed writing, drank heavily, and tried to escape his notoriety by living in California. His last major work, *Big Sur* (1962), described the price he paid for success, and he lived out his final years back in Lowell with his mother.

Kerr, Clark (1911–) university president, economist; born in Stony Creek, Pa. A widely published labor economist and labor arbitrator, he presided over rapid growth at the University of California (chancellor 1952–58, president 1958–67), coined the term "multiversity," and wrote the controversial *Uses of the University* (1963). He chaired the Carnegie Commission on Higher Education (1967–73).

Kerr, Robert Samuel (1896–1963) oil producer, governor, U.S. senator; born in Ada, Oklahoma. Owner of the Kerr-McGee Oil Company, he served as governor of Oklahoma from 1943–47 and was elected to the U.S. Senate (Dem., Okla.; 1949–63). Liberal on many issues, he opposed civil rights legislation and regulation of the oil industry.

Kertész, André (1894–1985) photographer; born in Budapest, Hungary. A photographer with the Austro-Hungarian army during the First World War, he came to Paris in 1925 where he inspired French photojournalists like Cartier-Bresson. Brought to New York by Keystone studios in 1936, he became a free-lance fashion and interiors photographer, landing a contract with Condé Nast (1949–62). In 1963, he returned to photojournalism, winning the New York City Mayors' Award in 1977.

Kesey, Ken (Elton) (1935–) writer; born in La Junta, Colo. He attended the University of Oregon (B.A. 1957), and studied writing at Stanford (1958–59). He volunteered for drug experiments and was a psychiatric attendant for the Veterans Administration Hospital, Menlo Park, Calif. (1961). This experience was directly related to his best-known work, *One Flew Over the Cuckoo's Nest* (1962). Living and farming in Pleasant Hill, Ore., he was never able to repeat the success of that work, but he retained his image as an inspiration for many young mavericks.

Ketchall, Ephraim (1788–1877) social scientist, geographer; born in Old Mystic, Conn. He made numerous explorations in the Mississippi Valley and Mexico, where he measured the size of pyramids and buildings. By using his figures as a measure of the advancement of nations, he had anticipated later archaeologists' ideas about the size of cities as a measure of their significance.

Ketchel, Stanley (b. Stanislaus Kiecal) (1886–1910) boxer; born in Grand Rapids, Mich. Ranked the greatest middleweight of all time, he held the title from 1908 until his death in 1910, posting a career record of 49 wins, four losses, with 46 knockouts.

Kettering, Charles (Franklin) (1876–1958) engineer, inventor; born near Loudonville, Ohio. A 1904 graduate of Ohio State University, he worked for the National Cash Register Co. until 1909, when he and a partner, Edward A. Deeds, set up the Dayton Engineering Laboratories Co., later known as Delco. Kettering developed the first electrical ignition system and the first self-starter for automobiles, a device that made him famous as an inventor. He sold Delco to General Motors (GM) in 1916. In 1920 he became president and general manager of the General Motors Research Corp., a GM division, and for the next 30 years he led teams that developed improved motor fuels, shock absorbers, variable speed transmissions, safety glass, and the refrigerant Freon. Kettering retired from GM in 1947. With Alfred Sloan, he endowed the Sloan-Kettering Institute for Cancer Research.

Kety, Seymour Solomon (1915–) neuroscientist; born in Philadelphia. He spent most of his professional career at the National Institutes of Mental Health, where he became a senior scientist in 1983. In the 1940s he developed the methods for measuring cerebral metabolism and blood flow. In 1953, he and coworkers produced the first autoradiographic images of cerebral blood flow. He also made major contributions in the study of biological aspects of schizophrenia.

Kevorkian, Jack (?1928–) medical pathologist; born in Pontiac, Mich. He was serving his residency in medical pathology at the University of Michigan Hospital when in 1953 he was dismissed because of his proposal that death-row inmates simply be rendered unconscious (instead of executed) so that their bodies could be used for certain medical experiments. After completing his internship at Pontiac (Mich.) General Hospital (1955), he joined the pathology department of the Pacific Hospital, Long Beach, Calif. (1955–82). Again he was let go because of his controversial views, and now unable to find a staff job, he moved to a small apartment in Royal Oak, Mich., and began to support himself (he was unmarried) by writing for European medical journals – often on issues regarding euthanasia. By 1989 he had invented his first "suicide machine," but the American medical establishment would not deal with him. He reached out to the public by appearing on such shows as *Phil Donahue* in 1990, but did not attain complete national prominence until June 4, 1990, when he used his apparatus to help a 54-year-old woman commit suicide. Using variations of his original apparatus, he thereafter proceeded to help a series of individuals commit suicide while defying the Michigan law passed specifically to stop him. In so doing he gained the nickname "Dr. Death" along with immense publicity, but whatever his motives, manners, and methods, he was forcing several important issues onto the public stage.

Key, Francis Scott (1779–1843) lawyer, poet; born in Carroll County, Md. He began practicing law in 1801 and soon became a successful attorney in Georgetown, D.C. After witnessing the British attack on Fort Henry, Baltimore, in 1814 – while being held in custody by the British on a boat offshore – he wrote a set of verses describing the event. Wildly popular, his lines were matched to an English tavern tune to create "The Star Spangled Banner," the unofficial national anthem until Congress formally adopted it in 1931. Key, who wrote little other poetry of note, was U.S. attorney for the District of Columbia from 1833–41.

Key, Valdimer Orlando, Jr. (1908–63) political scientist; born in Austin, Texas. His early writing focused on corruption in government and his later work on federal grant aid to states. He taught at several universities before settling at Harvard (1951–63). He served on the National Resources Planning Board (1937–38) and the Bureau of the Budget (1942–45).

Keys, Clement (Melville) (1876–1952) journalist, financier, aviation executive; born in Chatsworth, Ontario, Canada. His financial and organizational skills boosted the development of modern airline corporations like Trans World Airlines. He moved to New York to work for the *Wall Street Journal* (1901–06) and eventually founded North American Aviation (1928), a holding company that assisted in the creation of Curtiss-Wright (1929) out of the two greatest pioneering names in aviation.

Keyserling, Leon H. (1908–87) lawyer, government official; born in Charleston, S.C. Senator Robert Wagner's legislative aide in the 1930s, he drafted the Social Security and Labor Relations Acts. A liberal member of Truman's Council of Economic Advisors (1946–52), he advocated full employment. Afterward he served as legal counsel to public employee unions.

Kharasch, Morris (Selig) (1895–1957) organic chemist; born in Kremenets, Ukraine. He emigrated to the U.S.A. in 1908. He taught at the University of Maryland (1922–27). His own pioneering research in organic chemistry contributed to developing plastics and synthetic rubber. He was a founder of the *Journal of Organic Chemistry.*

Khorana, Har Gobind (1922–) molecular biologist; born in Raipur, India (now Pakistan). He was a research fellow at the Swiss Federal Institute of Technology (1948–49) and Cambridge University (1950–52) before moving to the University of British Columbia (Vancouver) (1952–59). There he received international recognition for improving the method of synthesis of acetyl coenzyme A, necessary for cellular metabolism. At the University of Wisconsin (1960–70), he determined the sequence of DNA nucleotide triplets which code for 20 amino acids. This research won Khorana (with molecular biologists Robert Holley and Marshall

Nirenberg) the 1968 Nobel Prize in physiology. In 1970 he synthesized the first artificial gene; he then relocated to the Massachusetts Institute of Technology (1970), where he continued to make major contributions to molecular biology.

Kicking Bird (b. Tene-angop'te) (?1835–75) Kiowa chief; born on the central Great Plains. Advocating peace with whites as a means of Indian survival, he signed his tribe's first treaty (1865), establishing the Kiowa reservation. He later worked to promote peace and as an advocate for education.

Kidd, Michael (b. Milton Greenwald) (1919–) choreographer, dancer, producer-director; born in New York City. While in high school, he attended a performance by a modern dance group that inspired him to take dance lessons. Although he went on to City College of New York and studied chemical engineering, by the end of his third year he dropped out to dedicate himself entirely to dance. He attended the School of American Ballet and made his stage debut in the chorus of Max Reinhardt's production of *The Eternal Road* (1937). He toured for three years with Ballet Caravan (1937–40) and began to dance leading parts with the Dance Players (1941–42) and the Ballet Theatre (1942–47). His first original ballet, *On Stage!,* premiered in 1945, and this led to his becoming choreographer of the Broadway musical, *Finian's Rainbow* (1947). From then on he enjoyed a series of successes as choreographer for such stage musicals as *Love Life* (1948), *Guys and Dolls* (1950), and *Can-Can* (1953), eventually earning five Tony Awards for his dynamic and inventive dances. He also choreographed such movies as *Seven Brides for Seven Brothers* (1954). He broadened his scope to acting and dancing in the movie *It's Always Fair Weather* (1955), directing the Danny Kaye comedy film, *Merry Andrew* (1958), and producing and staging as well as choreographing the musical *L'il Abner* (1956); in later years he composed the choreography for such movies as *Star* (1968) and *Hello, Dolly!* (1969).

Kidd, (William) Captain (?1645–1701) pirate; born in Greenock, Scotland. He established himself as a sea captain in New York (1690) and was commissioned by the English government to fight pirates off Madagascar (1695). He turned to piracy around 1697 and was taken prisoner while ashore in Boston (1699). He was hanged in London.

Kidder, Alfred (Vincent) (1885–1963) archaeologist; born in Marquette, Mich. He led major advances in American archaeology by developing a typology for southwestern American Indian pottery (1914) and introducing large-scale systematic stratigraphic field techniques, notably in his excavations at Pecos, N.M. (1915–29). At the Carnegie Institution (1927–50) he directed interdisciplinary research on the Maya. His nearly 200 titles include the classic *Introduction to . . . Southwestern Archaeology* (1924). The American Anthropological Association's premier award bears his name.

Kidder, Daniel P. (Parish) (1815–91) clergyman, educator; born in South Pembroke (now Darien), N.Y. In his twenties he spent three years as a missionary in Brazil, an experience which yielded among other books the long-standard *Brazil and the Brazilians* (coauthored, 1857). As secretary of the Sunday School Union (1844–56), he reorganized Methodist Sunday schools, then taught at Garrett (1856–71) and Drew (1871–81) Theological Seminaries.

Kieft, Willem (1597–1647) Dutch governor; born in Amsterdam, Netherlands. He was the fifth governor of New

Netherland (1637–45). He governed in a dictatorial manner and his lack of diplomacy led to constant battles with the Indians. He was replaced by Petrus Stuyvesant (1645) and died in a shipwreck while returning to the Netherlands.

Kienholz, Edward (1927–) sculptor; born in Fairfield, Wash. A self-taught artist, he studied at Whitworth College, Spokane (1945–52), moved to Los Angeles (1953–73), then divided his time between Berlin, Germany, and Hope, Ida. He worked with wooden relief painting (1950s), then created assemblage constructions using found objects, as in the mixed media sculpture, *The State Hospital* (1966).

Kiesler, Frederick John (1896–1965) architect, sculptor; born in Vienna, Austria. He studied architecture in Vienna, emigrated to New York City (1926), and became known for his innovative architectural designs in Europe and America, including the design for the Art of This Century Gallery (1942). He is also known for his environmental and surrealistic sculptures, as in *Galaxy* (1951).

Kilby, Jack S. (1923–) electrical engineer; born in Jefferson City, Mo. He developed thick film hybrid circuits and compatible transistors (1947–58). Working for Texas Instruments (1958–70), he invented the monolithic integrated circuit in 1958 and later the first hand-held calculator. In 1970, he became an independent inventor and consultant.

Kiley, Dan (1912–) urban designer; born in Boston, Mass. An early proponent of "site specific design," he worked with prominent modern architects since the 1940s, designing landscapes suitable for monumental urban buildings like Dulles Airport.

Kilgore, Carrie (b. Caroline Sylvester Burnham) (1838–1909) teacher, lawyer; born in Craftsbury, Vt. She taught school in Vermont and Wisconsin, then studied medicine in New York and Boston (1863–65). In Philadelphia, she introduced gymnastics into the schools and promoted women's rights. She read law under Damon Kilgore – whom she married in 1876 – and began to work for women's suffrage. Initially denied admission to the bar, she finally was admitted to the University of Pennsylvania law school and became its first woman graduate (1883). She carried on a practice for many years and in 1908 rode in the first balloon ascension of the Philadelphia Aeronautical Recreation Society.

Kilgore, Harley M. (Martin) (1893–1956) U.S. senator; born in Brown, W.Va. A liberal West Virginia judge, he went on to serve in the U.S. Senate (Dem., W.Va.; 1941–56). He chaired the so-called "Kilgore committee" that oversaw U.S. mobilization efforts for World War II and helped to set up the War Mobilization Board (1943). On the influential Appropriations Committee, he helped to establish the National Science Foundation (1950).

Kimball, (Sidney) Fiske (1888–1955) architectural historian; born in Newton, Mass. Director of the Philadelphia Museum of Art (1925–55), he brought a historical approach based on the use of primary documents to his published work on colonial American architecture. As a leading restoration architect he was involved with the restorations at Monticello and Colonial Williamsburg.

Kimmel, Husband Edward (1882–1968) naval officer; born in Henderson, Ky. He was the commander in chief, U.S. fleet, during the surprise attack on Pearl Harbor. He was suspended from command and a presidential board of inquiry found him guilty of dereliction of duty (1942), but a naval court found no blame or mistakes in his judgment (1944). He published his side of the controversy in *Admiral Kimmel's Story* (1955).

Kincaid, Jamaica (b. Shawn) (1949–) writer; born in St. John, Antigua, West Indies. She emigrated to New York City and became a staff writer for the *New Yorker* in 1976. She has won recognition for her collections of short stories, such as *At the Bottom of the River* (1983), and *Annie John* (1985), a short story cycle. Her work is noted for its telling detail and poetic diction.

Kincaid, Thomas (Cassin) (1888–1972) naval officer; born in Hanover, N.H. He took command of the USS *Enterprise* after the attack on Pearl Harbor. He took part in the battles of the Coral Sea, Midway, and the eastern Solomons. As Douglas MacArthur's naval commander (1943–45), he participated in the New Guinea and Philippines operations. He fought the battle of Leyte Gulf (1944) and landed American troops in Korea in 1945.

King, Carole (1941–) composer-lyricist; born in New York City. Inspired by 1950s rock, she began writing songs in high school. Working with husband-lyricist Gerry Goffin, she wrote some of the biggest hits of the pre-Beatles era including "Will You Still Love Me Tomorrow?" (1960) and "Up On The Roof" (1962). In 1970 she began performing her own songs and went on to make several gold albums, including *Tapestry* (1971), winner of four Grammy Awards, and *Carole King – Her Greatest Hits* (1978).

King, Charles (Bird) (1785–1862) painter; born in Newport, R.I. He studied with Benjamin West in London (1805–12), and became friends with Washington Allston and Thomas Sully. Upon his return he settled in Washington, D.C., and worked diligently as an artist. His most famous work, a still-life summation of his career, is *The Artist's Dream* (1830).

King, Clarence (1842–1901) geologist; born in Newport, R.I. After graduating from Yale (1862), he crossed the U.S.A. on horseback and joined the California Geological Survey (1863–66). He then took charge of a survey of territory from eastern Colorado to California (1866–67). His observations while directing the U.S. exploration of the 40th parallel (1867–78) resulted in his classic volume, *Systematic Geology* (1878); he is credited with introducing the use of contour lines on maps to indicate topographic features. He was instrumental in forming the U.S. Geological Survey and was then appointed its first head (1879–81). He entered private practice as a mining engineer (1881–93). Even his geological writings displayed his literary talents and he collected a series of *Atlantic Monthly* articles in *Mountaineering in the Sierra Nevada* (1872). While in Washington, D.C., he had become one of the so-called "Five of Hearts," an elite circle including Henry Adams and his wife, Marian Adams, and John Hays and his wife, Clara Hays. Only after his death did it come out that King had completely hidden from even his closest friends that in 1887 he had begun an affair with an African-American woman, Ada Copeland, in Brooklyn; he used the name John Todd with her and explained his frequent absences by claiming he worked as a railroad porter; eventually he married her and had five children with her. His classy friends, once they recovered from the shock of discovery, helped the family after his death.

King, Ernest J. (Joseph) (1878–1956) naval officer; born in Lorain, Ohio. He graduated from the Naval Academy in 1901 and took part in the occupation of Veracruz, Mexico (1914).

He was on the staff of the Atlantic Fleet during World War I and undertook aviation training in 1928. He was chief of the Bureau of Aeronautics (1933–38) and served on the General Board (1939–40). In 1941 he became commander-in-chief of the U.S. Fleet; he also became the chief of naval operations in 1942. He commanded the U.S. Navy throughout World War II and served as President Roosevelt's chief naval adviser. He became a five-star admiral (1944, confirmed in 1946) and went on inactive status in 1945. He returned to limited duty in 1950 as an adviser to the president, the secretary of the navy, and the Department of Defense.

King, Henry Churchill (1858–1934) theologian, educator; born in Hillsdale, Mich. He graduated from Oberlin College (1879) and then Oberlin Theological Seminary (1882). He studied in Berlin (1983–94) and was influenced by German philosophy. He taught theology at Oberlin and was president of the college (1903–27). As president, he worked for the development of the "whole man" and Oberlin came to emphasize music, the fine arts, morals, and religion. At the end of World War I he coauthored (with Charles R. Crane) the Crane-King report on what to do with the various lands belonging to the defeated Turkish Ottoman Empire; although ignored at the time, their warning that Palestine was largely an Arab land would in later years be drawn into the controversy over the establishment of Israel on this territory. His health failed soon after that and he retired in an enfeebled condition.

King, Larry (1933–) radio/television host; born in New York City. A radio broadcaster in Miami at age 25, he wrote entertainment columns for the *Miami Herald* in the 1970s. In 1978 he began a national late-night radio show on the Mutual Network. He was host of CNN TV's *Larry King Live* (1985), an interview/call-in show, most famous for being the occasion where Ross Perot announced his presidential intentions in 1992.

King, Martin Luther, Jr. (b. Michael L. King) (1929–68) Baptist minister, civil rights leader; born in Atlanta, Ga. Grandson and son of Baptist ministers (in 1935 his father changed both their names to Martin to honor the German Protestant), young Martin graduated from Morehouse College (Ga.) (1948) and Crozer Theological Seminary (1951) and then took a Ph.D. from Boston University (1955), where he also met his future (1957) wife, Coretta Scott, with whom he had four children. Ordained a minister in 1947 at his father's Ebenezer Baptist Church in Atlanta, he became pastor of the Dexter Avenue Baptist Church in Montgomery, Ala., in 1953. Relatively untested when Rosa Parks refused to give up her seat in a bus in December 1955, he led the boycott of Montgomery's segregated busses for over a year (eventually resulting in the Supreme Court decision outlawing discrimination in public transportation). In 1957 he was chosen president of the newly formed Southern Christian Leadership Conference (SCLC) and he began to broaden his active role in the civil rights struggle while advocating his nonviolent approach to achieving results; he would base his approach on the ideas of Henry David Thoreau and Mohandas Gandhi as well as on Christian teachings. He moved to Atlanta in 1959 to become copastor of his father's church and in the ensuing years gave much of his energies to organizing protest demonstrations and marches in such cities as Birmingham, Ala. (1963); St. Augustine, Fla. (1964); and Selma, Ala. (1965). During these years he was arrested and

jailed by Southern officials on several occasions, he was stoned and physically attacked, and his house was bombed; he was also placed under secret surveillance by the FBI due to the strong prejudices of its director, J. Edgar Hoover, who wanted to discredit King as both a leftist and a womanizer. King's finest hour came on August 28, 1963, when he led the great march in Washington, D.C., that culminated with his famous "I have a dream" speech at the Lincoln Memorial. At the height of his influence, he was awarded the Nobel Peace Prize in 1964 and he used his new-found powers to attack discrimination in the U.S. North. Meanwhile, as the Vietnam War began to consume the country, he also broadened his criticisms of American society because he saw the impact of the war on the country's resources and energies. In the spring of 1968 he went to Memphis, Tenn., to show support for the striking city workers and he was shot and killed as he stood on the balcony of his motel there. (James Earl Ray would plead guilty to the murder, although he would later insist that he was innocent.) With his oratorical style that drew directly on the force of the Bible, with his serene confidence derived from his non-violent philosophy, he had advocated a program of moderation and inclusion, and although later generations would question some of his message, few could deny that he had been the guiding light for 15 of the most crucial years in America's civil rights struggle.

King, Richard (1825–85) steamboater, rancher; born in Orange County, N.Y. He escaped from a jewelry apprenticeship and worked as a steamboatman for some 20 years. In 1852, he purchased 15,500 acres in southern Texas; by the end of his life, he had expanded the property to include over 600,000 prime acres and 100,000 head of cattle. Although he was said to be ruthless and autocratic in acquiring and running the King Ranch, he was also known for his hospitality. His heirs eventually expanded the King Ranch to some 1,000,000 acres (larger than Rhode Island) but these were divided in 1935.

King, (Riley B.) B. B. (1925–) musician; born in Itta Bena, Miss. A singer and guitarist born into a sharecropping family, he became one of the best-known blues performers, an important consolidator of blues styles, and a primary model for rock guitarists. Following U.S. Army service, he began his career as a disc jockey in Memphis, Tenn., where he was dubbed "The Beale Street Blues Boy," soon shortened to B. B. He made his first recording in 1949. The following year he began a 12-year-long association with Kent/RPM/Modern, for which he recorded a string of rhythm and blues hits. He also toured the nightclub circuit continuously, averaging over 300 shows annually for nearly 30 years. In 1962, he signed with ABC Records, which released *Live at the Regal*, a benchmark blues concert album. In 1969, he released his biggest hit single, "The Thrill is Gone." In 1979, he became the first bluesman to tour the U.S.S.R. By this time he had also become the first bluesman to enter the pop mainstream, making regular appearances in Las Vegas, Nev., and on network television. In 1987, he was inducted into the Rock 'n' Roll Hall of Fame.

King, Rufus (1755–1827) politician, diplomat; born in Scarboro, Maine (then part of Mass.). A lawyer, he represented Massachusetts at the Continental Congress (1784–87) and the Constitutional Convention (1787) where he played an influential role in arguing for a strong central government. Having moved to New York City, he became a U.S. senator (Fed.; 1789–96), continuing his eloquent advocacy of Federalist positions. He resigned to serve as ambassador to Great Britain (1796–1803), then returned to run unsuccessfully for the vice-presidency (1804, 1808). He returned to the Senate (Fed., N.Y.; 1813–25) and was the last Federalist to run for the presidency (1816). In the Senate, he continued his lifelong opposition to the spread of slavery, resisted the Missouri Compromise of 1820, and even supported the emancipation of the slaves. Retiring from the Senate, he went back to Great Britain in 1825 as the U.S. ambassador, but illness forced him to come home (1826) where he soon died.

King, Samuel (Archer) (1828–1914) aeronaut; born in Tinicum, Pa. Credited with encouraging transatlantic flight that led to successful dirigible crossings, he made his first balloon ascent at Philadelphia (1851). He never managed to cross the Atlantic via balloon, but he made hundreds of ascensions and several successful flights to gain wind and temperature data for the Army Signal Service (1885).

King, Stephen (Edwin) (Steve King, Richard Bachman, John Swithen, pen names) (1947–) writer; born in Portland, Maine. He graduated from his state university and continued to live in Maine, at first supporting himself with odd jobs while establishing his writing career. The success of his first horror novel, *Carrie* (1974), enabled him to publish earlier work under the pseudonym Richard Bachman (1977–84), a ploy which disguised the true extent of his prolific output of novels, short stories, and screenplays until the ruse became public knowledge and he abandoned it. His own name became synonymous with best-selling novels blending horror, fantasy, and science fiction into a consistently scary mix. His books sold more than one hundred million copies worldwide and included *Salem's Lot* (1975), *The Shining* (1977), *The Dead Zone* (1979), *Misery* (1987), *Needful Things* (1991), and *Gerald's Game* (1992). Several were made into successful movies and he himself tried his hand at directing movies.

King, Thomas Starr (1824–64) Unitarian minister, lecturer; born in New York City. He worked as a teacher, principal, and bookkeeper to support his mother and siblings. Largely self-taught, he became a Unitarian minister in Boston (1846). He went to San Francisco (1860) where his orations helped to keep California in the Union during the Civil War. He died of diphtheria. California named two mountain peaks for him and his statue was placed in the U.S. Capitol.

King, William (1768–1852) shipowner, governor; born in Scarboro, Maine (then part of Massachusetts). He moved to Bath, Maine (1800), and became an important shipowner and a leading citizen. He was a major-general of militia in the War of 1812. Following Maine's admission to the Union, he became the first governor of Maine (1820–21). He was a commissioner for the Adams-Onis Treaty with Spain (1821–24) and lost a race for the governor's seat in 1835. Maine placed his statue in the U.S. Capitol.

King, William R. D. (Rufus Devane) (1786–1853) vice-president, politician; born in Sampson County, N.C. He was elected vice-president under Franklin Pierce in 1852. Ill with tuberculosis, he traveled to Cuba and took the oath of office there. He returned to his Alabama plantation and died, having served only 25 days as vice-president, none of them in Washington, D.C.

King Philip See PHILIP, KING.

Kingsley, Sidney (b. Kirschner) (1906–) playwright; born in Philadelphia. His first play, *Men in White* (1933), won a Pulitzer Prize. Most of his plays, including *Detective Story* (1949), continued to look at serious contemporary themes.

Kingston, Maxine (Ting Ting) Hong (1940–) writer; born in Stockton, Calif. She studied at the University of California: Berkeley (B.A. 1962; teaching certificate 1965). She married Earll Kingston (1962), taught at a variety of high schools in Hawaii and California (1965–69), and at the college level (1970). She divided her time between Hawaii and Studio City, Calif. She often blended legend and autobiography in her nonfiction books, such as *The Woman Warrior: Memoirs of a Girlhood among Ghosts* (1976) and *China Men* (1980). She also wrote many stories and articles for periodicals.

Kinnell, Galway (1927–) poet, writer; born in Providence, R.I. He studied at Princeton (B.A. 1948), and the University of Rochester (M.A. 1949), traveled widely, and taught at many colleges. Based in Sheffield, Vt., he was a translator and essay writer, but is best known for his direct and precise poetry, as in *Selected Poems* (1982).

Kino, Eusebio Francisco (c. 1645–1711) missionary, explorer; born in Segno, Italy. He entered the Jesuit order in 1665 and arrived in Mexico City in 1681. He founded missions in present-day Sonora, Mexico, and southern Arizona (1687–1711), and established cattle and horse breeding there. His explorations established that Lower California was a peninsula, not an island.

Kinoshita, Toichiro (1925–) physicist; born in Tokyo, Japan. He came to the U.S.A. in 1952 to work at Princeton (1952–54), then became a researcher and teacher at Columbia University (1954–64) before joining Cornell (1964). He made significant contributions to quantum electrodynamics and invariance (symmetry law).

Kinsey, Alfred (Charles) (1894–1956) entomologist, sexuality researcher; born in Hoboken, N.J. He joined the faculty of Indiana University (1920) where he remained throughout his career, making himself a reputation as the world's leading expert on the gall wasp (1919–36). In 1938, students at the university petitioned for a course on marriage, which he volunteered to help organize. Soon realizing that there was little sound biological information on the subject, he began conducting his own study; in 1942 he founded the Institute for Sex Research and with grants he began interviewing thousands of subjects from all over the country about their sexual conduct. Out of this came two best-sellers, *Sexual Behavior in the Human Male* (1948) and *Sexual Behavior in the Human Female* (1953) – books that in their day burst like nuclear devices on the American scene. True to his training in biology and taxonomy, he quantified and classified sexual variation in a nonjudgmental, value-neutral fashion. This approach incensed conservative critics, and they made it difficult for him to obtain grant money; meanwhile, some sociologists questioned his methods. Among the books' controversial findings were that certain so-called perversions were actually practiced quite widely, and that women have a much greater range of sexual response than had previously been accepted. He died prematurely before he was able to witness the "sexual revolution" that, it is generally conceded, he helped to bring about.

Kip, Arthur F. (Frederic) (1910–) physicist; born in Los Angeles, Calif. He taught and performed research at the Massachusetts Institute of Technology (1939–51) and the University of California: Berkeley (1951–76). His achievements in solid state physics include studies of microwave resonance, cyclotron resonance in semiconductors and metals, and designing microwave linear accelerators.

Kiphuth, Robert (John Herman) (1890–1967) physical educator; born in Tonawanda, N.Y. Perhaps the greatest swimming coach in history, Kiphuth retired after 41 years at Yale with a 528–12 dual meet record and 38 eastern intercollegiate and 14 national championships. He also coached American Olympic swimming teams (1928–48). He was awarded the Medal of Freedom (1963).

Kiplinger, Willard Monroe (1891–1967) journalist, publisher; born in Bellefontaine, Ohio. He graduated from Ohio State University's new journalism program (1912) and worked for the Associated Press (1914–20). He started with a one-page weekly, *The Kiplinger Washington Letter* (1923), and added a series of newsletters focusing on economic and business affairs. In 1947 he started the monthly magazine *Changing Times*. He organized the Washington Journalism Center in 1965.

Kirby-Smith, Edmund See SMITH, EDMUND KIRBY.

Kirchner, Leon (1919–) composer; born in New York City. A student of Roger Sessions and Schoenberg among others, he taught at Harvard from 1961. His music is modernist in a German vein but nonetheless personal and intensely expressive.

Kirchwey, George Washington (1855–1942) law educator, criminologist, penologist; born in Detroit, Mich. He taught at Columbia Law School (1891–1916) before heading the New York School of Social Work's criminology department (1918–32). He helped elevate criminology to a scientific discipline while fighting for prisoner rehabilitation through state and national prison reform commissions. One of the first presidents of the American League for the Abolition of Capital Punishment (1927), he was also a pacifist and cinema enthusiast.

Kirk, Rahsaan Roland (1936–77) jazz musician; born in Columbus, Ohio. He was an exhilarating multi-reed player, a sideman with Charles Mingus in 1960, and the leader of his own groups until suffering a stroke in 1976.

Kirkbride, Thomas Story (1809–83) physician; born near Trenton, Pa. Raised in a Quaker farming family, he was physician to the Friends' Asylum for the Insane near Philadelphia (1832), before joining Philadelphia's Pennsylvania Hospital to supervise treatment of the mentally ill (1833). Heading the Pennsylvania Hospital for the Insane from 1840, his care and leadership mounted a "renaissance in psychiatry"; he insisted that insanity was illness and sufferers should be treated with respect and care.

Kirkland, Gelsey (1952–) ballet dancer; born in Bethlehem, Pa. She joined the New York City Ballet at age 15, its youngest member. At age 17 she danced the lead role, specially choreographed for her, in George Balanchine's new production of *Firebird*. Her talent inspired many choreographers. In 1974 she joined the American Ballet Theatre as partner to Mikhail Baryshnikov. An ambitious perfectionist, she proved difficult to dance with and, by 1984, left the ballet with severe physical and emotional problems. These she chronicled, along with scathing criticisms of Balanchine and

the dance world, in the memoirs *Dancing on My Grave* (1986) and *The Shape of Love* (1990). Considered a "pariah" in the New York ballet community, she danced her comeback with London's Royal Ballet, including a command performance before Queen Elizabeth (1986). By 1992 she was back in New York teaching at the American Ballet.

Kirkland, (Joseph) Lane (1922–) labor leader; born in Camden, S.C. A merchant marine pilot during World War II, he joined the staff of the American Federation of Labor in 1948, and worked his way up the staff hierarchy. He was elected secretary-treasurer of the American Federation of Labor and Congress of Industrial Organizations (AFL-CIO) in 1969, and president in 1980. He was regarded as one of the new breed of labor leaders – moderate, articulate, even cerebral, and more at home in the board room than on the shop floor.

Kirkpatrick, Jeanne (b. Jordon) (1926–) political scientist, government official; born in Duncan, Okla. A professor at George Washington University (1967–81), she was a Democratic activist, who wrote *Political Woman* (1974). Opposed to President Carter's foreign policy, she switched parties, becoming America's first woman ambassador to the United Nations (1981–85), often strongly attacking communist governments. She returned to teaching in 1985.

Kirkpatrick, Paul H. (Harmon) (1894–) physicist; born in Wessington, S.D. He taught physics in Hangchow, China (1916–18), served in World War I, then became a professor at the University of Hawaii (1923–31). He joined Stanford (1931–60), where he developed X-ray optical instruments, invented the X-ray microscope, and was a pioneer in holography. A dedicated supporter of students' rights to education, he remained active at Stanford after his retirement.

Kirkwood, John G. (Gamble) (1907–59) physical chemist; born in Gotebo, Okla. He performed research in Europe (1931–32), and at the Massachusetts Institute of Technology (1931–34), then taught chemistry at Cornell (1934–47), and the University of Chicago (1937–38). He moved to the California Institute of Technology (1947–51), then became professor of chemistry at Yale (1951–59). Kirkwood's elegant mathematical approach to research made him a leader in investigations of electrical properties of gases and liquids, and an innovator in the field of protein electrophoresis.

Kirkwood, Samuel Jordon (1813–94) governor, cabinet member; born in Harford County, Md. A lawyer and flour mill owner, he served as Iowa's governor (Rep., 1859–63), using his own money to equip the Iowa Union volunteers, and quashing proslavery "Copperheads" with homeguard troops. A two-time U.S. senator (1866–67, 1877–81), he was briefly governor between terms (1876–77) and Garfield's secretary of the interior afterward (1881–82).

Kirschner, Marc Wallace (1945–) cell biologist; born in Chicago, Ill. He taught biochemistry at Princeton (1972–78), then moved to the University of California: San Francisco (1978). He performed extensive research on cellular microtubule assembly, embryonic induction, and biochemical investigations of nucleic acids and cellular proteins.

Kirstein, Lincoln (Edward) (1907–) writer, impresario; born in Rochester, N.Y. Heir to a Filene (department store) fortune, he fell in love with the theater as a child and was profoundly inspired by Anna Pavlova in 1920. After graduating from Harvard, he reviewed dance and theater for *Horn* *and Hound,* which he cofounded. In 1933 he recognized George Balanchine's talents, sponsored his emigration to the United States, and, to provide vehicles for Balanchine's talents, founded the School of American Ballet in 1934 and the American Ballet Company the following year. The American Ballet became attached to the Metropolitan Opera the following year, when Kirstein also ran Ballet Caravan. In 1946 Kirstein and Balanchine founded the Ballet Society, and in 1948 they moved to New York's new City Center as the directors of what became one of America's top-ranking companies, New York City Ballet. Officially retired in 1989, Kirstein remained a presence in the American dance world and intellectual life. He wrote several books, including *Dance* (1935) and *Movement and Metaphor* (1970), as well as poetry, and was founder-editor of *Dance Index Magazine* (1942–48).

Kirsten, Dorothy (1917–92) soprano; born in Montclair, N.J. After studies at Juilliard and in Rome, she debuted with the Chicago Opera in 1940 and at the Metropolitan in 1945, singing her final performance there (as Tosca) in 1975. Among her noted roles were as Mimi in *La Bohème.*

Kissinger, Henry (Alfred) (1923–) political scientist, public official; born in Fuerth, Germany. He fled the Nazis to New York City with his parents in 1938. Even before he became professor of government at Harvard (1962–71), his book *Nuclear Weapons and Foreign Policy* (1957) had gained him national attention, and he served occasionally as adviser to presidents Eisenhower, Kennedy, and Johnson. As special national security adviser, National Security Council executive secretary (1969–71), and secretary of state (1971–76), he was chief architect of foreign policy in the Nixon and Ford administrations, emphasizing *realpolitik* and détente with China and the USSR, and negotiations between Arabs and Israelis. Although he had been a "hawk" in pursuit of the war in Vietnam, he received a Nobel Peace Prize (1973) for his role in the Vietnam cease-fire. Following revelations of his role in secret bombings in Cambodia, illegal wiretaps, and covert Central Intelligence Agency operations in Chile and elsewhere, his reputation suffered but he retired to a lucrative career as a lecturer and consultant. He headed a bipartisan committee on Central America for President Ronald Reagan in 1983. In later years he appeared occasionally on television as a commentator on world affairs, and he returned to his earlier role as a student of political history with such works as *Diplomacy* (1994).

Kistler, Darci (1964–) ballet dancer; born in Riverside, Calif. Determined to be a dancer from age 5, she studied with Irina Kosnovsha in Los Angeles, then went to New York City Ballet at age 14 to become the last of George Balanchine's great ballerinas, and, at age 17, the youngest principal dancer in that company's history. From 1982–85 she was sidelined due to a fractured ankle, but by 1989 she had fully recovered and returned to dancing with her peculiar mix of physical fearlessness and apparent effortlessness.

Kitaj, R. B. (Ronald Brooks) (1932–) painter; born in Cleveland, Ohio. His family moved to Troy, N.Y. (1943), he studied at Cooper Union, New York (1950–51), and in Germany (1951–53) and England (1957–c. 62), where he settled permanently and gained a major reputation. Using many mediums, he created surrealistic images of tormented people, as in *If Not, Not* (1975–76).

Kitchin, Claude (1869–1923) U.S. representative; born in Scotland, N.C. Son of a representative, he was a lawyer before going to the U.S. House of Representatives (Dem., N.C.; 1901–23). A brilliant debater, his support of the Payne-Aldrich tariff won him appointment to the Ways and Means Committee. Its chairman in 1915, he initially opposed Wilson's declaration of war against Germany, but he secured passage of revenue bills to support the war effort.

Kitt, (Earth Mae) Eartha (?1928–) singer; born in North, S.C. Originally a dancer with the Katherine Dunham troupe, she stayed in Paris after a tour and gained a reputation as a club singer. Returning to Broadway in 1952, she lent her cat-like voice and demeanor to a number of stage and film roles over the next 30 years but her mannered style made her an exotic.

Kittel, Charles (1916–) physicist; born in New York City. He was a physicist with the U.S. Navy (1940–45), then performed research at the Massachusetts Institute of Technology (1945–46) and Bell Telephone Laboratories (1947–50), before becoming a professor at the University of California: Berkeley (1950–79). A leader in the application of microwave resonance methods to investigations of solid state ferromagnetism, Kittel was also honored for his improvements in the college physics curriculum.

Kittredge, George Lyman (1860–1941) philologist, Shakespeare scholar, educator; born in Boston, Mass. Kittredge was inextricably identified with Harvard, where he was educated and later taught (1888–1936). At Harvard "Kitty" inaugurated the study of English romance literature and taught English 2 (1896–1936), his famous course on Shakespeare. He was an international authority on *Beowulf,* Chaucer, and particularly Shakespeare. His seminal *Chaucer and his Poetry* (1915) laid the foundation for American Chaucer studies.

Kitzinger, Ernst (1912–) art historian; born in Munich, Germany. He studied at the University of Rome (1931–32), the University of Munich (Ph.D. 1934), and at Swarthmore, Pa. (D.Litt. 1969). He worked in England at the British Museum (1935–40), emigrated to America (1941), and taught at Harvard beginning in 1979. He also taught at the Institute for Advanced Study, Princeton (1966–67, 1980, 1982). He specialized in early Christian, Byzantine, and early medieval art.

Kizer, Carolyn (Ashley) (1925–) poet; born in Spokane, Wash. She studied at Sarah Lawrence (B.A. 1945), Columbia University (1945–46), and the University of Washington: Seattle (1946–47), and settled in Port Townsend, Wash. A founding editor of *Poetry Northwest* (1959–65), she taught at many institutions. She is known for her feminist poetry, as in *Mermaids in the Basement: Poems for Women* (1984).

Kleberg, Robert J. (Justus), Jr. (1896–1974) rancher; born in Corpus Christi, Texas. In 1916 he joined the King Ranch in Texas, the country's largest producer of beef, then owned by his father, who had married Alice King. He became president and CEO of the giant King Ranch (1924–74). On his more than 12 million acres, "Mr. Bob" bred grasses, quarter horses, and Santa Gertrudis, the country's first breed of cattle (1940). He was the owner of a string of champion racehorses.

Klein, Anne (Hannah) (b. Hannah Golofski) (?1921–74) fashion designer; born in New York City. A student at the Traphagen School of Fashion, she started her career at age 15 as a free-lance sketcher in a wholesale fashion house. In

1948 she launched her Junior Sophisticates and in 1968 opened Anne Klein & Company. Named to the Coty American Fashion Awards Hall of Fame in 1971, she was known for her sophisticated, practical sportswear for young women and for recognizing the need for coordinated separates, matching blazers, skirts, and slacks.

Klein, Calvin (Richard) (1942–) fashion designer; born in New York City. He graduated from New York's Fashion Institute of Technology in 1962. After gaining practical experience in New York, he set up his own firm in 1969, Calvin Klein, Inc., of which he was president and designer. A recipient of the Coty Award for 1973, 1974, and 1975, among other important fashion awards, he was known for his understated lines and the simple but sophisticated style of his clothing, including "designer jeans."

Klein, (Charles Herbert) "Chuck" (1904–58) baseball player; born in Indianapolis, Ind. During his 17-year career as an outfielder, mostly with the Philadelphia Phillies (1928–44), he posted a lifetime batting average of .320 and hit 300 homeruns. He is the only player in the 20th century to collect 200 or more hits in each of his first five major league seasons. He was elected to baseball's Hall of Fame in 1980.

Klein, Donald Franklin (1928–) psychiatrist, educator; born in New York City. A leader in the fields of biopsychiatry and neuropsychopharmacology, he was a consultant to the National Institute of Drug Abuse (1992) and served as an adviser to the Alcohol, Drug Abuse, and Mental Health Administration.

Klein, Lawrence Robert (1920–) economist; born in Omaha, Nebr. After teaching at the Universities of Chicago (1944–47) and Michigan (1949–54), he became a professor at the University of Pennsylvania (1958). He is noted for the development of large multi-equation econometric models used to forecast the performance of an economy. These mathematical models simultaneously estimate hundreds of equations regarding economic activity such as consumer spending, public and private investment, exports, imports, capital flows, and monetary supplies. He was awarded the Nobel Prize in economics (1980).

Klem, (William Joseph) Bill (1874–1951) baseball umpire; born in Rochester, N.Y. He was a National League umpire (1905–41) and chief of the National League umpiring staff (1941–51). Considered by many the greatest umpire in baseball history, he was elected to baseball's Hall of Fame in 1953. Known as "The Old Arbitrator," he has been credited with introducing the arm signals that indicate strikes and fair or foul balls.

Klemin, Alexander (1888–1950) aeronautical engineer; born in London, England. Emigrating to America to study at the Massachusetts Institute of Technology (1915), he designed the first American amphibian landing gear (1921). He headed the Research Department of the Army Air Service, Dayton, Ohio, during World War I and was in charge of the Daniel Guggenheim School of Aeronautics at New York University (1924–41).

Kleppner, Daniel (1932–) physicist; born in New York City. He taught and performed research at Harvard (1959–66) and at the Massachusetts Institute of Technology (1966). In 1960 he helped develop the first hydrogen maser clock, an instrument 100,000 times more accurate than any atomic clock previously constructed. He continued research with atomic hydrogen, utilized lasers to examine dimagnetic spectra or atoms, and made quantum electrodynamic investigations of atomic structures.

Klerman, Gerald Lawrence (1928–92) psychiatrist; born in New York City. Between 1956–85 he held various academic appointments at Harvard, Tufts, and Cornell. An authority on depression and schizophrenia, he did research on the effectiveness of combining drug treatment and psychotherapy (1960s–92) and conducted a study that found depression increasing and occurring earlier among people born since 1935.

Kline, Franz (Josef) (1910–62) painter; born in Wilkes Barre, Pa. After attending Boston University (1931–35), he traveled to London and studied at Heatherly's Art School (1937–38). Upon his return to America he settled in New York City. After progressing through a variety of styles, he became famous by 1950 for his black-and-white paintings. His abstract expressionist approach, utilizing a furiously energetic line, as seen in *Wanamaker Block* (1955), became instantly recognizable throughout the art world.

Kluckhohn, Clyde (Kay Maben) (1905–60) cultural anthropologist; born in LeMars, Iowa. After early training in the classics, he studied at Princeton, Wisconsin, Vienna, and Oxford before joining the Harvard faculty in 1935. His chief research interest was the culture of the Navajo Indians; his classic study, *Navaho Witchcraft*, appeared in 1944. A major contributor to culture theory, he set out his views on culture patterns and value systems in the popular work, *Mirror for Man* (1949).

Kluge, John W. (Werner) (1914–) businessman, philanthropist; born in Chemnitz, Germany. He came to the U.S.A. in 1922 and grew up in Detroit, where his mother remarried. He worked on the Ford Motors assembly line before going to Columbia University in New York City; he earned a B.A. in economics (1937). He went to work for a small paper company and then served with the Army Intelligence in World War II. After the war he worked as an executive with radio broadcasting companies, and as his own investments in various enterprises grew, he acquired and built so many radio and television stations that his Metromedia became the largest independent broadcast network; Metromedia also had an advertising division; in 1963 he acquired the Ice Capades and in 1976 the Harlem Globetrotters. When he sold Metromedia in 1985 it was for $2 billion. By 1989 he was regarded as the richest American, with his personal fortune estimated at some $5.5 billion. He had never been in the public spotlight until in 1981 he married for the third time, a 32-year old who had appeared nude in an English "skin mag"; he divorced her in 1990 but had to pay her $80 million a year in alimony. Although known for his generosity to a variety of causes – in 1960 he gave a rare white tiger to President Eisenhower as a "gift to the children of America," he had supported the United Cerebral Palsy Research and Educational Foundation, and in 1992 he singlehandedly subsidized the exhibit of works from the Vatican Library – his philanthropies had not been greatly publicized until 1993 when he gave $60 million to Columbia to provide scholarships for minority students; added to the $50 million he had previously donated to Columbia, it made Kluge one of the largest single benefactors of any American educational institution.

Kneeland, Abner (1774–1844) Protestant clergyman; born in Gardner, Mass. The son of a Revolutionary War veteran, he preached as a Baptist. Appointed to a Universalist pulpit in Charlestown, Mass., in 1812, he soon grew to doubt the divine origin of the Scriptures. Becoming increasingly radical, he moved to Philadelphia and later New York before breaking with the Universalists in 1829. In 1838, after a series of failed appeals, he was jailed for blasphemy. He migrated westward to Iowa the following year, but his plans to found a free-thinking colony there never materialized.

Kneisel, Franz (1865–1926) violinist, teacher; born in Bucharest, Rumania. He graduated at age 14 from the Bucharest Conservatory and studied and played in Austria and Germany until he emigrated to the U.S.A. in 1885, to become concertmaster of the Boston Symphony. The next year he organized the Kneisel Quartet, which achieved worldwide fame. He left the orchestra in 1903 and dissolved the quartet in 1917; from 1905 he taught at New York's Institute of Musical Art.

Knerr, Hugh Johnston (1887–1971) aviator; born in Fairfield, Iowa. A 1908 Naval Academy graduate, he transferred to the army, and in 1917, joined the air service. An associate of William ("Billy") Mitchell, he argued for air power as the primary U.S. strategic weapon. He held a series of senior administrative posts in the U.S., England, and continental Europe from 1942–45, and was inspector general of the newly independent U.S. Air Force from 1948–49.

Knievel, (Robert Craig) "Evil" (1938–) motorcycle stunt performer; born in Butte, Mont. Raised by his grandparents in Butte, a copper-mining town, he began doing motorcycle stunts as a teenager. He embarked on an incredibly varied career (1956–1965) that included professional hockey, a stint in the U.S. Army, work in the copper mines, and eventually crime – safecracking and holdups. He "went straight" in 1965 and formed Evil Knievel's Motorcycle Devils (1965). He performed numerous dangerous and thrilling stunts and became a hero to schoolchildren of the 1970s. After he retired, he managed the stunt career of his son, Robbie Knievel.

Knight, Frank Hyneman (1885–1972) economist; born in McLean County, Ill. His book, *Risk, Uncertainty, and Profit,* remains a classic that accounts for profits under perfect competition and distinguishes risk from uncertainty. He spent many years on the faculty of the University of Chicago (1927–55).

Knight, Philip H. (Hampson) (1938–) footware entrepreneur; born in Portland, Ore. A former college miler and Stanford M.B.A., he began importing Japanese running shoes in 1967 in partnership with coach Bob Bowerman. Their Nike brand (1972) took off after the introduction of an innovative waffle sole (1975) and became the dominant athletic shoe of the decade through constant technological improvement and heavy advertising by professional athletes.

Knight, (Robert) Bobby (1940–) basketball coach; born in Massillon, Ohio. He played on the Ohio State 1960 National Collegiate Athletic Association (NCAA) champion team, then became assistant coach (1963) and head coach (1965–70) at West Point. He became coach at Indiana University in 1971 and led his team to three NCAA championships (1976, 1981, 1987); his Indiana teams never had a losing season. He coached the American team that won the Olympic gold medal in basketball in 1984 and the U.S. team that won the gold medal in the 1979 Pan American Games. He emphasized discipline and defense on the court, and his passion for

winning occasionally got him into trouble; in 1979, as coach of the U.S. team at the Pan-American Games in San Juan, Puerto Rico, he was charged with aggravated assault against a police officer in the gymnasium; at the 1981 NCAA "final four," he put a bothersome Louisiana State University supporter in a trash can.

Knoll, Florence (Florence Margaret Schust Knoll Bassett) (1917–) designer; born in Saginaw, Mich. After architecture and design study and work with Eliel Saarinen, Walter Gropius, Marcel Breuer and Mies van der Rohe, she joined the Hans G. Knoll furniture company (1943) where she perfected such office features as the executive table desk and the boat-shaped conference table. Fabric walls and natural materials in her institutional and commercial interiors humanized the International style. Marrying Knoll in 1946, she headed the company after his death (1955–59). In 1965 she started a private practice.

Knopf, Adolph (1882–1966) geologist; born in San Francisco. He worked with the U.S. Geological Survey (1906–45) while concurrently teaching at Yale (1920–51). He then became a visiting professor at Stanford (1951–57). He made major contributions to mineralogy and mining, radioisotopic geochronology, and igneous petrology as exemplified by investigations of the Boulder batholith in Montana.

Knopf, Alfred (1892–1984) publisher; born in New York City. He founded his own firm in 1915, and with the aid of his wife, Blanche, made it successful while retaining a commitment to high literary excellence; his authors included 16 Nobel Prize laureates and 26 Pulitizer Prize winners. Although the firm eventually became a division of Random House, he headed it until his death.

Knopoff, Leon (1925–) geophysicist; born in Los Angeles. A professor of physics (1955) and research musicology (1961) at the University of California: Los Angeles, he combined knowledge of wave behavior gained from both fields to make major contributions to studies of wave propagation, the acoustics of solids, seismology, and the physicochemical structure of the earth's interior.

Knott, Sarah Gertrude (1895–1984) folk festival director; born in Kevil, Ky. She attended drama schools in Pittsburgh and Chicago and organized community theater groups in North Carolina (where she had worked under Frederick Koch and Paul Green) and St. Louis. She was the founding director of the National Folk Festival, the first of which was held in St. Louis in 1934; until her retirement in 1970, she was the moving force behind the showcase of American folk culture which she also developed into an international festival. She participated in the creation of many other organizations and events that presented the folk cultures of the U.S.A. and foreign lands.

Knowland, William F. (Fife) (1908–74) publisher, U.S. senator; born in Alameda County, Calif. A conservative newspaper publisher, he was initially appointed and then elected to the U.S. Senate (Rep., Calif.; 1945–59). He served as majority leader from 1953–55, and minority leader from 1955–59. He ran unsuccessfully for governor of California in 1958. He committed suicide.

Knox, Bernard (MacGregor Walker) (1914–) classics scholar, author; born in Bradford, England. After taking his B.A. at St. John's College, Cambridge (England) (1936), he went to Spain and fought (and was wounded) with the International Brigade in the Civil War. He came to the

U.S.A. in 1939. While serving with the U.S. Army in Europe during World War II (1942–45), he became an American citizen (1943), and was awarded two Bronze Stars and the French *croix de guerre*. He earned his Ph.D. at Yale (1948) and taught classics there (1948–61). He then served as director of the Center for Hellenic Studies in Washington, D.C. (1961–85). Among various honors and awards, he was the 1963 Sather lecturer at the University of California: Berkeley and received the 1978 George Jean Nathan Award for drama criticism. In addition to his articles, reviews, and translations, his books include *The Heroic Temper, Studies in Sophoclean Tragedy* (1980), *Word and Action: Essays on the Ancient Theatre* (1980), and *The Oldest Dead White European Males* (1993). He wrote the script for and performed in four films for educational television on Sophocles' *Oedipus the King;* these films are used in classrooms throughout the U.S.A. He was the assistant editor and a contributor to Volume I of the *Cambridge History of Classical Literature* (1985) and he was editor of *The Norton Book of Classical Literature* (1993).

Knox, Henry (1750–1806) soldier, bookseller; born in Boston, Mass. One of ten sons of a shipmaster who died when Henry was 12, he worked as a bookseller. Having joined the Boston Grenadier Corps (1772), he became knowledgeable about military tactics and artillery, and he volunteered for the Revolutionary forces at the outbreak of war with England. He soon became a trusted friend and adviser to George Washington and was appointed to command the Continental army's artillery in November 1775; it was Knox who overcame incredible difficulties in getting the pieces of artillery from Fort Ticonderoga to force the British to evacuate Boston (March 1776). From then on he was with Washington in nearly every major engagement of the war, including the crossing of the Delaware to take Trenton, the winter of 1778–79 at Valley Forge, and the final victory at Yorktown. His suggestion led to the establishment of a military academy at West Point and he was a founder of the Society of the Cincinnati (1783). He served as secretary of war from 1785–94, afterward retiring to an estate in Maine, where he lived in great style. He died of complications after swallowing a chicken bone.

Knox, Philander Chase (1853–1921) lawyer, cabinet member, U.S. senator; born in Brownsville, Pa. He practiced industrial law in Pittsburgh, Pa. (1877–99). As McKinley's attorney general (1901–04), he filed an antitrust suit that prevented J. P. Morgan's western railroad monopoly. A midterm senator (Rep., Pa.; 1904–09), he became secretary of state (1909–13), initiating "dollar diplomacy" to protect American investments overseas. He returned to the Senate (1917–21).

Knox, Rose Markward (1857–1950) food products manufacturer; born in Mansfield, Ohio. In 1883 she married Charles Briggs Knox, a glove salesman, and they started a profitable gelatin business together. Following his death in 1908, she ran the Knox Gelatin Company, based in Jamestown, N.Y., and turned it into a market leader. She sponsored research, directed the advertising toward women, emphasized nutritional values and sanitary production, and created a market for food-quality gelatin by publishing recipe books. She was also a progressive employer, pioneering in the five-day work week and paid sick and vacation leave. She was the first woman on the board of directors of the American Grocery

Manufacturers' Association (1929) and became known as the grand old lady of American business, relinquishing the presidency at age 90, but remaining as chairperson of the company.

Knox, (William Franklin) Frank (1874–1944) journalist, cabinet member; born in Boston, Mass. One of Teddy Roosevelt's Rough Riders in Cuba, he worked as a journalist in Michigan before becoming co-owner of the influential New Hampshire *Manchester Union* (1912–27). A brilliant administrator, he bought and revitalized the *Chicago Daily News* (1931–40). Although a Republican, he was Franklin Roosevelt's secretary of the navy (1940–44).

Knudsen, William S. (b. Signius Wilhelm Paul Knudsen) (1879–1948) industrialist, government official; born in Copenhagen, Denmark. Emigrating to America at age 21, he mastered bicycle and auto parts production, and when Ford purchased his auto-parts firm, he was soon running assembly line production for Ford (1913–20). Hired by Ford's archrival Chevrolet in 1922, he was outselling Ford by 1927 and became president of General Motors in 1937. He resigned from General Motors in 1940 to serve first on the National Defense Advisory Commission and then with the Office of Production Management, expediting war-related production. From 1942–45 he accepted an army commission as lieutenant general to supervise production for the War Department and Army Air Force. After the war he worked with the Hupp Corporation.

Knuth, Donald E. (Ervin) (1938–) computer science professor; born in Milwaukee, Wis. A professor of computer science and electrical engineering at Stanford University (1977), he also served as a consultant to Burroughs Corp. (1968–69). A National Academy of Sciences member, he specialized in algorithms, programming languages, digital typography, and history of computer science.

Knutson, Harold (1880–1953) U.S. representative; born in Skien, Norway. Emigrating at age six, he grew up on a Minnesota dairy farm, which he left to become a newspaper man and publisher of the *Pioneer Journal*. An isolationist congressman (Rep., Minn.; 1917–49), he opposed the New Deal and launched personal attacks on President Franklin Roosevelt. A member of the National Committee to Keep America Out of War in the 1940s, he opposed the war effort and the Marshall Plan.

Koch, Edward I. (Irving) (1924–) mayor; born in New York City. He interrupted college to serve in the U.S. Army from 1943 to 1946, winning two Battle Stars. In practice as a lawyer beginning in 1949, he was a member of the New York City Council (1967–8), then served in the U.S. House of Representatives (1969–74). He served as Democratic mayor of New York from 1978–90; his reelection in 1981 was partly due to his success in handling New York's financial problems and saving the city from bankruptcy. In 1982 he lost a bid for the Democratic gubernatorial nomination to Mario Cuomo. Defeated as Democratic candidate for mayor in 1989 by David Dinkins, he returned to practice law with Robinson, Silverman, Pearce, Aronsohn & Bowman. A colorful and outspoken character, he also found a place in the news media as a TV talk show host and newspaper columnist. His books include *His Eminence and Hizzoner* (with John Cardinal O'Connor, 1989) and *All the Best, Letters from a Feisty Mayor* (1990).

Koch, Frederick (Henry) (1877–1944) folklorist, educator;

born in Covington, Ky. While teaching English at the University of North Dakota (1905–18), he organized a drama society of students and faculty to produce original plays on regional themes. He then went to the University of North Carolina (1918–44), where, in addition to his classes in drama and playwriting, he organized the Carolina Players, which presented dramas based on folk material and became a training ground for such writers as Thomas Wolfe and Paul Green. Through the establishment of the Bureau of Community Drama (1918), he promoted school and community theater throughout North Carolina; he also encouraged the outdoor pageant plays that Paul Green would make famous.

Koch, Kenneth (Jay) (1925–) poet; born in Cincinnati, Ohio. He studied at Harvard (B.A. 1948) and Columbia University (Ph.D. 1959), where he taught beginning in 1959. A leading figure of the New York school of poetry, he is known for his urban settings, as in *Poems* (1953), and for his witty metaphors, as in "One Train May Hide Another" (1993). He was a lecturer and director of poetry workshops for the elderly and for children, described in *Wishes, Lies, and Dreams* (1970). He also wrote a novel and plays, several of which have been produced off-Broadway.

Koehler, Ted (1894–1973) lyricist; born in Washington, D.C. He played piano in silent film cinemas and began writing songs in the 1920s for vaudeville and Broadway shows. In the 1930s and 1940s he produced floor shows for the Cotton Club and Broadway. With Harold Arlen, Burton Lane, and other composers, he wrote such hits as "I Love a Parade" (1931) and "Stormy Weather" (1933). He also wrote music for such films as *Love Affair* (1939) and *My Wild Irish Rose* (1947).

Koenigsberg, Moses (1878–1945) journalist; born in New Orleans, La. After wide experience as a reporter, he became city editor of William Randolph Hearst's *Chicago American* in 1903. Later a Hearst executive, he established the successful Hearst-owned King Features Syndicate in 1915.

Koffka, Kurt (1886–1941) psychologist; born in Berlin, Germany. He was one of the early proponents of Gestalt psychology, along with Wolfgang Köhler and Max Wertheimer. He emigrated to the United States in the mid-1920s. He was affiliated with Smith College in 1927, becoming professor of psychology in 1932. In 1939 he helped develop tests for impaired judgment and comprehension. He was particularly interested in visual perception and also wrote extensively on art, music, literature, and ethical questions.

Kohlberg, Jerome, Jr. (1925–) lawyer, financier; born in New York City. He graduated from Swarthmore (Pa.) College in 1946 and took a law degree from Columbia University in 1950. He worked as an investment banker for Bear Stearns & Co., before becoming a partner in Kohlberg, Kravis, Roberts & Co. (1976–87), known as "the kings of the leveraged buyout." Their operations helped fuel the "go-go" atmosphere of American business that became synonymous with the Reagan years. He resigned in 1987 to establish an independent firm, Kohlberg & Co.

Kohlberg, Lawrence (1927–87) psychologist; born in Boston, Mass. He taught education and social psychology at the University of Chicago and at Harvard (1968–87). His research posited a series of stages in the formation of conscience from early childhood into adulthood. He set forth his ideas in *The Philosophy of Moral Development* (1981).

Kohler, Foy D. (David) (1908–) diplomat; born in Oakwood, Ohio. He worked as a bank teller before he entered the Foreign Service in 1931; among his various assignments were postings to Greece and the Soviet Union. He directed the Voice of America (1949–52) and was ambassador to the Soviet Union (1962–66). He was assistant secretary of state for European Affairs (1959–62) and he wrote *The Soviet Union: Yesterday, Today, Tomorrow* (1975).

Kohler, Kaufmann (1843–1926) rabbi, scholar; born in Fürth, Germany. During his studies in Munich and Berlin, he moved away from orthodox Judaism. In 1869 he came to the U.S.A. as rabbi of the Beth-El Congregation in Detroit. In 1871 he went to Sinai Temple in Chicago, where, despite fierce criticism, he brought about a number of radical reforms. In 1879 he became rabbi of Temple Beth-El in New York City, where he made similar changes. A series of lectures brought him into conflict with traditionalist scholar Alexander Kohut. On behalf of tradition, Kohut and his followers founded the Jewish Theological Seminary of America in 1887, while Kohler called the Pittsburgh Conference. The Pittsburgh Platform, issued in 1885, eventually became the central document of American Reform Judaism. Kohler became president of Hebrew Union College at Cincinnati (1903–21), where he also taught a number of courses. He was a prolific scholar; his single best-known work is his 1910 book, *Jewish Theology Systematically and Historically Considered.*

Kohler, Walter J. (Jodok), Jr. (1904–76) governor; born in Sheboygan, Wis. Starting as an engineer in his father's plumbing appliance company in 1924 – his father also served as governor of Wisconsin (1929–31) – he became the Kohler company director in 1936, and director of Volrath, stainless steel manufacturer, in 1940. After serving in the U.S. Navy during World War II, he went on to serve as governor of Wisconsin, (Rep., 1951–57); he instituted programs to reduce dairy cattle disease, returning to business afterward.

Köhler, Wolfgang (1887–1967) psychologist; born in Reval, Estonia. He was one of the early proponents of Gestalt psychology along with Kurt Koffka and Max Wertheimer. He emigrated to the United States from Germany in 1935. He became professor of psychology and then research professor of philosophy and psychology at Swarthmore (Pa.) College (1935–58). He developed a physiological theory of perception, which he extended to memory and attention.

Kohn, Walter (1923–) physicist; born in Vienna, Austria. He escaped the Nazis and emigrated to England (1939), then Canada (1940). He came to Harvard in 1946, taught there (1948–50), then moved to the Carnegie-Mellon Institute (1950–60), where he contributed to the theory of electronic structure of metals. He joined the University of California: San Diego (1960–79), and continued his work on the physics of solids. He directed Santa Barbara's Institute for Theoretical Physics (1979–84), then became a physics professor at the University of California: Santa Barbara (1984).

Kohut, Alexander (1842–94) rabbi, scholar; born in Félegyháza, Hungary. Called to New York as rabbi of Congregation Ahavath Chesed in 1885, he soon launched a series of sermons against Reform Judaism. He helped found and taught at the conservative Jewish Theological Seminary of America. A respected scholar, he worked for years on the modernizing of an 11th-century rabbinical dictionary.

Kohut, George Alexander (1874–1933) rabbi, educator; born in Stuhlweissenberg, Hungary. He was the son of Alexander Kohut, whom he accompanied to the U.S.A. in 1885. He was active in a wide range of Jewish educational projects including schools and camps. Though always in frail health, he was a generous and energetic bibliophile, bibliographer, and patron of Jewish scholarship. He founded the Alexander Kohut Memorial Foundation to Foster Jewish Learning in 1915.

Kohut, Rebekah Bettelheim (1864–1951) educator, welfare worker; born in Kaschau, Hungary (now Kosice, Slovakia). Daughter of a rabbi and a schoolteacher, she was brought to the U.S.A. in 1867. Her mother died when Rebekah was six and her father moved to San Francisco, where she experienced a call to become a welfare worker. When in 1887 she married the noted rabbi Alexander Kohut, a widower with eight children, she followed him to New York City and seemed destined to place her career subservient to his needs, although she did do volunteer work, helped to organize Jewish women's groups, and began to teach classes to Jewish immigrants. After Kohut died in 1894, she supported her inherited family with lectures, and, with the financial support of Jacob Schiff, she founded the Kohut School for Girls (1899–1904). When World War I broke out in Europe, she was helping young Jewish women find employment, but once the U.S.A. entered the war in 1917 she was recruited by the federal government to help place women in jobs. After World War I she devoted herself to relief work for Jews in Europe and in 1923 she became president of the World Congress of Jewish Women. She continued to serve as an adviser on employment to Governor Franklin D. Roosevelt of New York and that state's legislature. She was director of Columbia Grammar School in New York City in the late 1930s and remained active in governmental, religious, philanthropic, and women's organizations until her death.

Kolff, Willem J. (Johan) (1911–) surgeon, inventor; born in Leiden, Holland. Educated in Holland, where he taught and practiced medicine, he emigrated to the U.S.A. in 1950. He is the acknowledged inventor of the artificial kidney dialysis machine, and he headed the team that invented and tested a soft-shell artificial heart. He became a professor of surgery at the University of Utah School of Medicine in 1967.

Kolodin, Irving (1908–88) music critic; born in New York City. He wrote for the *New York Sun* from 1932 to 1950 and for the *Saturday Review* from 1947. Best known for the popular *Guide to Recorded Music,* he also wrote program notes for the New York Philharmonic and Metropolitan Opera.

Komarovsky, Mirra (1906–) sociologist; born in Russia. Emigrating as a teenager to the U.S.A., she was educated at Columbia University and taught at Barnard College (1938–74). Pioneering research on leisure time and unemployment, she developed the techniques of repeated interviews and the use of selected case histories. Her books include *Women in College* (1985).

Koop, C. (Charles) Everett ("Chick") (1916–) surgeon, public health official; born in New York City. Surgeon-in-chief of Children's Hospital in Philadelphia, he also taught at the University of Pennsylvania (1948–81). Regarded as a superb pediatric surgeon, his operation separating the Dominican Siamese twins (1974) received international attention. Appointed by President Reagan as Surgeon General of the United States (1981–89), he was at first assumed to be conservative in his views, but proved to be an independent and gradually surprised everyone by his views on such matters as smoking and AIDS. On leaving public office he joined the faculty of Dartmouth College and continued to be much in demand as a speaker on issues of public health.

Koopmans, Tjalling C. (Charles) (1910–85) economist; born in the Netherlands. Educated in his native land, he emigrated to the U.S.A. in 1940. After working in a shipping firm, he became a professor of economics at the University of Chicago (1948–55), then moved to Yale in 1955 where he remained until his retirement in 1981. He won the Nobel Prize in economics (1975) for the development of "linear programming," or "activity analysis," sharing the prize with Soviet mathematician-economist, Leonid V. Kantorovich. Linear programming is used to analyze the relationship between maximum output of a business and all possible combinations of inputs.

Kopp, Sheldon (Bernard) (1929–) psychologist; born in New York City. He studied at New York University, Brooklyn College, and the New School for Social Research (Ph.D. 1960). He practiced clinical psychology at New Jersey and District of Columbia psychiatric facilities (1955–66) and conducted a private practice in psychotherapy from 1962. A member of the Humanistic Psychology Institute, he wrote *If You Meet a Buddha on the Road, Kill Him* (1972).

Koppel, (Edward James) Ted (1940–) television journalist; born in Lancashire, England. Son of German-Jewish refugees, he came to the U.S.A. in 1953 and became an American citizen in 1963. He earned degrees from Syracuse and Stanford. Originally a newscaster for WABC radio (1963–67), he switched to television reporting while covering the Vietnam War, becoming ABC's chief diplomatic correspondent in 1971 and anchor for the *Saturday Night News* in 1975. Anchor for *Nightline,* the distinguished ABC late-night news show begun during the Iran hostage crisis in 1979 (originally called *America Held Hostage*) he is known for consistently knowledgeable and sometimes piercing interviews.

Korff, Serge A. (Alexander) (1906–89) astrophysicist; born in Helsinki, Finland. He fled the Bolsheviks with his professor father and arrived in the U.S.A. in 1918. He performed research at Mt. Wilson Observatory (1931–33) and the California Institute of Technology (1933–35), then joined New York University (1941–74). He was a pioneer in the investigation of cosmic radiation, and made worldwide expeditions using observatories, balloons, and aircraft during the 1930s, 1940s, and 1950s.

Kornberg, Arthur (1918–) biochemist; born in New York City. He began working with enzymes at the National Institutes of Health (1942–53) with his wife and lifetime collaborator, Sylvy (Levy). At Washington University (St. Louis) (1953–59), he discovered the enzyme DNA polymerase, with which he synthesized nonreplicating DNA (1957). With mentor Severo Ochoa, he received the 1959 Nobel Prize in physiology for this breakthrough in molecular biology. Kornberg moved to Stanford (1959–88), where he succeeded in creating biologically active viral DNA (1967).

Korngold, Erich Wolfgang (1897–1957) composer; born in Brno, Moravia. A famous composer in Germany from his teens, he went on to considerable acclaim for such operas as *Die tote Stadt* (1920). He emigrated to Hollywood in 1934 and became one of the finest of screen composers, with scores including *Robin Hood* (1938) and *The Sea Hawk*

(1940). After World War II he returned to composing serious concert music.

Korty, John (1936–   ) film director; born in Lafayette, Ind. By age 16 he was making amateur films; in college he made animated television commercials. In the mid-1960s he was writing, directing, and producing low-budget movies such as *Crazy Quilt* (1966). The documentary *Who Are the De Bolts? . . . And Where Did They Get 19 Kids?* (1977) won him an Oscar. He also made television films.

Kosciusko, (Tadeusz Andrzej Bonawentura) Thaddeus (1746–1817) soldier, revolutionary; born in Lithuania. The son of a small landowner, he developed an ambition for military glory and became a captain in the Polish army. When the American Revolution broke out, he got Benjamin Franklin to recommend him for military service. He arrived in Philadelphia in August 1776 and was soon commissioned a colonel in the engineers; he made major contributions to the victory at Saratoga (1777), the fortifications along the Hudson River, and to the Carolinas campaign and was promoted to brigadier general in 1783. He returned to Poland in 1784 and led rebellions against Russian occupying forces in 1792 and 1794. Although he had been forced to forswear fighting against Russia, he continued to agitate for Polish independence from exile in America and France until his death. His will directed that the 500 acres in Ohio granted him by the U.S. Congress in 1797 be sold and the money used to free slaves; instead it was used to found the Colored School of Newark, N.J., one of the earliest schools for African-Americans in the U.S.A.

Kosinski, Jerzy (Nikodem) (1933–91) writer; born in Lodz, Poland. He had a horrific childhood hiding from the Nazis during World War II, and a tenuous existence under the Stalinists in Poland. He studied at the University of Lodz (B.A. 1950; M.A.s 1953, 1955) and did postgraduate work in sociology at the Polish Academy of Sciences (1955–57). Emigrating to the U.S.A. (1957), he did further postgraduate work at Columbia University (1958–63) and the New School for Social Research (1962–66). After he settled in the U.S.A. he drew upon his past experiences to write semiautobiographical novels with elements of violence, anxiety, and eroticism, as in *The Painted Bird* (1965) and *Steps* (1968). He also wrote several books on sociology under the name of Joseph Novak. He committed suicide in New York City.

Kostof, Spiro (Konstantin) (1936–91) architectural historian; born in Istanbul, Turkey. A Yale-trained proponent of the "new" architectural history stressing the social context of buildings, he became a professor at the University of California: Berkeley and published specialized studies of Roman and Byzantine architecture and urban form, as well as general studies such as *History of Architecture* (1985). He became well known near the end of his life for the Public Broadcasting System television series, *America by Design* (1987).

Koufax, (Sanford) Sandy (1935–   ) baseball pitcher; born in New York City. One of the greatest left-handers in the history of baseball, he won the Cy Young award three times (1963, 1965, 1966) and pitched four no-hit games during his 12-year career (1955–66) with the Brooklyn and Los Angeles Dodgers. A strikeout artist (2,396), he was forced to retire because of an arthritic left elbow. He was elected to baseball's Hall of Fame in 1972.

Koussevitzky, Serge (1874–1951) conductor; born in Vishny-Volochok, Russia. A virtuoso on the double bass, he took up conducting and in 1909 founded his own orchestra and publishing company in Moscow. After the Revolution he emigrated to Paris, where his Concerts Koussevitzky presented important new works by Stravinsky, Prokofiev, Ravel, and others. In 1924 he was named conductor of the Boston Symphony; he would conduct it for 25 years, a legendary era for the orchestra. He continued his historic advocacy of contemporary composers (though tending to conservative ones), commissioning major works from Stravinsky, Hindemith, and Prokofiev, as well as championing American composers including Copland, Piston, and Barber. In the 1930s he developed the orchestra's Tanglewood summer concerts and the associated school called the Berkshire Music Center (1940). After his retirement from the orchestra in 1949, he guest-conducted in Europe and the Americas.

Kouwenhoven, William (Bennett) (1886–1975) educator, electrical engineer; born in New York City. While a professor of electrical engineering at Johns Hopkins, he invented the first practical defibrillator used in the treatment of cardiac arrhythmia. In 1959, he introduced the first-aid technique of external heart massage.

Kovacs, (Ernest) Ernie (1919–62) television comedian; born in Trenton, N.J. After high school, he studied acting, appearing with Long Island, N.Y. stock companies in the 1930s. He wrote a column for the New Jersey *Trentonian* (1945–50). He did much of the writing and producing as well as performing for his three television series – *Time for Ernie* (National Broadcasting Company, 1951), *The Ernie Kovacs Show* (CBS, 1953), and *Kovacs Unlimited* (CBS, 1952–54). He utilized the medium imaginatively through sight gags and apparently improvised zaniness. He brought his slightly wacky personality to the ten movies he appeared in before he died prematurely in a car crash.

Kramer, Amihud (1913–81) food scientist; born in Austria-Hungary. He came to the University of Maryland (1934) where he stayed through his Ph.D. (1942). He worked at the National Canners Association developing an objective method for measuring food quality (1941–44) and then for the National Research Council to revise nutrient tables (USDA *Handbook No. 8*) before returning to teach at the University of Maryland (1948–80). He coauthored *Quality Control for the Food Industry* (1970, 1973). He died unexpectedly during a game of tennis.

Kramer, Hilton (1928–   ) art critic; born in Gloucester, Mass. He studied at Syracuse (B.A. 1950), the New School of Social Research (1950), Columbia University (1950–51), Harvard (1951), and Indiana University (1951–52). He was an art critic and editor for many periodicals, including *Arts Magazine* (1955–58) and the *New York Times* (1965–82), and he was the founder-editor of *New Criterion* (1982). Considered an important art journalist, he published many essays and books on 19th- and 20th-century artists.

Kramer, (John Albert) Jack (1921–   ) tennis player; born in Las Vegas, Nev. After winning the U.S. Open (1946–47), and Wimbledon (1947), he turned professional, and, more than any other player, legitimized the professional game. Through his active promotion, he eventually saw in 1968 the creation of "open" (amateur and professional) play in the major tennis championships.

Kramer, Paul J. (Jackson) (1903–   ) plant physiologist; born in Brookville, Ind. He was an assistant botanist at Ohio State University (1928–31), then moved to Duke (1931–74), continuing his research and writing after retirement. A pioneer in the physiology of woody plants, especially of the southern U.S.A., he made major contributions to studies of the relationship between plants and water, including investigations of transpiration and salt transfer, root structure, and water stress, both in nature and in the controlled environment known as the phytotron.

Kramer, Samuel Noah (1897–1990) Sumerologist, author, museum curator; born near Kiev, Russia. He came to the United States with his family in 1919 and was educated at Temple University (B.A. 1921) and the University of Pennsylvania (Ph.D. 1929). His career as a leading authority on Sumerian language and literature began with a major expedition to Iraq in 1930–31, during which he excavated and translated Sumerian tablets. He became curator of the tablet collections at Pennsylvania's University Museum in 1950 as well as Clark research professor in Assyriology there (1950–68). His many publications include *History Begins at Sumer* (1959) and *The Cradle of Civilization* (1967).

Krauskopf, Joseph (1858–1923) rabbi; born in Ostrowo, Prussia (now Germany). He came to the U.S.A. in 1872. He was rabbi of Congregation Keneseth Israel in Philadelphia from 1887 until the end of his life. A leader of Reform Judaism, he was also devoted to public service, serving on many civic and government commissions and committees.

Krauss, Ruth (Ida) (1911–93) writer; born in Baltimore, Md. She studied at the Parsons School of Fine and Applied Art, New York, and settled in Westport, Conn. She is known for her innovative children's books, such as *A Hole is to Dig: A First Book of First Definitions* (1952).

Krauth, Charles Porterfield (1823–83) Protestant clergyman, theologian; born in Martinsburg, W.Va. A studious child, he was ordained in the Lutheran ministry at age 19. He became a leader of conservative Lutheranism, helping to revive older European forms of worship, including confession, in America. He edited the journal *Lutheran and Missionary* (1861–67) and from 1868 until his death was a professor at the University of Pennsylvania. His *Conservative Reformation and Its Theology* appeared in 1871.

Krautheimer, Richard (1897–1994) architectural historian; born in Fuerth, Germany. A specialist in early Christian and medieval architecture who later turned to the baroque period, he was an early exponent of architectural iconography. His works include *Corpus Basilicarum Christianarum Romae* (1937–70). He taught at Vassar College (1937–52) and the Institute of Fine Arts, New York University (1952).

Kravis, Henry R. (1944–) investment banker; born in Tulsa, Okla. He developed the method of "junk bond" corporate financing at Bear Stearns (New York City). His own investment firm, Kohlberg, Kravis, Roberts and Co. (KKR) (1976), led the surge of leveraged buyouts of U.S. corporations in the 1980s. KKR specialized in buying, restructuring, and managing or selling off undervalued companies; it became one of the world's largest privately held corporations with such major acquisitions as Beatrice Foods (1986) and RJR Nabisco (1988).

Krebs, Edwin G. (Gerhard) (1918–) biochemist; born in Lansing, Iowa. He was an intern and assistant resident at Barnes Hospital, St. Louis (1944–45), then moved to Washington University, St. Louis (1946–48), where he

worked with biochemists Carl and Gerty Cori. He relocated to the University of Washington: Seattle (1948–68), where he collaborated with biochemist Edmond Fischer to demonstrate that biochemical mechanisms, including those of the immune system, cancer cells, and hormonally-related reactions, are basic to all living cells. This research won Krebs and Fischer the 1992 Nobel Prize in physiology. Krebs became professor of biochemistry and department chairman at the University of California: Davis School of Medicine (1968–77). He returned to Seattle to join the University of Washington School of Medicine (1977–91) and became affiliated with the Howard Hughes Medical Institute, Seattle (1983).

Kreisler, Fritz (1875–1962) violinist; born in Vienna, Austria. At age ten, he won a gold medal at the Vienna Conservatory and in 1887 he won the Grand Prix at the Paris Conservatory. The next year saw his American debut in New York. For some years he pursued medicine and military service, but returned to music in 1899. From then on he was one of the most beloved violinists in the world; he also composed light violin works (which he sometimes attributed to other composers) and two operettas. Having spent much time in the U.S.A., he moved there permanently in 1940 and retired in 1950.

Krenek, Ernst (1900–91) composer; born in Vienna, Austria. Having attracted attention in Germany as a composer, his 1925–26 "jazz opera" *Jonny spielt auf* was an international success and remains his best-known work. Turning to a more rationalized 12-tone idiom around the time of the opera *Karl V* (1931–33), he came to the U.S.A. in 1937, where he became an influential avant-garde composer and teacher.

Kresge, S. S. (Sebastian Spering) (1867–1966) merchant, philanthropist; born in Bald Mount, Pa. After business school he worked as a bookkeeper and a tinware salesman (1890–97). He bought into J. G. McCrory's chain stores, opening stores in Memphis, Tenn., and Detroit, Mich. In 1899 he bought out the Detroit store to begin the S. S. Kresge Company, which sold nothing over ten cents. He expanded to several midwestern cities and incorporated as S. S. Kresge in 1912 with 85 stores; by the mid-1920s there were over 300 stores. In the 1920s he expanded into real estate, bought several other stores, had a $30 million account on Wall Street, and was twice divorced. He also founded the National Vigilance Committee for Prohibition Enforcement and the Kresge Foundation (1924), a philanthropic organization that he endowed with the bulk of his fortune. As chairman of the board from 1925, he continued to play an active role in his company, contributing to the establishment of the Kmart discount stores in 1961 and the Jupiter Stores in 1963.

Kress, S. H. (Samuel Henry) (1863–1955) retailer, art collector, philanthropist; born in Cherryville, Pa. He bought his first two stores in Pennsylvania (1887 and 1890) in collaboration with his brother Claude Washington Kress (1876–1940). By 1900 the brothers owned 12 stores in the South; the chain of 51 five-and-dime stores, S. H. Kress Company, was incorporated in 1916, with headquarters in New York City; at Kress's death the chain numbered 264 stores. An art collector who specialized in works of medieval and Renaissance Italy, he was president of the National Gallery of Art (1945–55) and a director of the Metropolitan Museum of Art in New York City. He donated hundreds of paintings to 14 museums across the United States and gave millions of dollars to restore historic buildings in Italy. He established the Kress Foundation in 1929, to which he bequeathed most of his estate. He suffered a paralytic stroke in 1945.

Kreymborg, Alfred (1883–1966) poet, editor, dramatist; born in New York City. He had little schooling, was a chess prodigy, traveled often, and became a journalist and editor based in New York City. He is known as an initiator of the "little" literary magazine, and, among other ventures, he founded *The Glebe* (1913–14), a publication showcasing the Imagists, and *Others* (1915–19), an experimental periodical. He was also interested in puppets, and with his wife, Remo Buffano, started a puppet theater. In the 1930s he directed poetic dramas for the Federal Theater Project.

Krim, Mathilde (b. Galland) (1926–) geneticist, activist, philanthropist; born in Como, Italy. She moved with her family to Switzerland. She lived for a time in Israel and was a member of the Irgun, a militant Zionist organization. She married Arthur Krim, the American motion picture company executive, and moved to New York City in 1958. Having earned her Ph.D. in genetics (1953), she worked for some years in medical research labs and was possibly the first person ever to see DNA chromosomes through an electron microscope. In 1983 she founded the Acquired Immune Deficiency Syndrome (AIDS) Medical Foundation and became one of the first to devote herself to finding a cure for AIDS. Using her society connections, she was successful in fund-raising for the organization and in raising the public's awareness of the epidemic.

Krimmel, John (Lewis) (1789–1821) painter; born in Würtemberg, Germany. He emigrated to Philadelphia (1810), and became known for his portraits and genre paintings. Influenced by European engravings, primarily of the Dutch genre school, his detailed work is shown in his most famous canvas, *Country Wedding* (1814).

Krinsky, Carol (Herselle) (1937–) architectural historian; born in New York City. She studied at Smith College (B.A. 1957) and at New York University (M.A. 1960, Ph.D. 1965), where she taught from 1965. Initially specializing in the Renaissance, her interest broadened to the modern period and she became a leading expert on twentieth-century architecture. Her books include *Rockefeller Center* (1978), *Synagogues of Europe* (1985), and *Gordon Bunshaft of Skidmore, Owings & Merrill* (1988). She was president of the Society of Architectural Historians (1984–86).

Kripke, Saul (Aaron) (1940–) philosopher, logician; born in Bay Shore, N.Y. Educated at Harvard, he was a fellow and lecturer there (1963–67), then taught at Rockefeller University (1967–76) and Princeton (from 1976). A prodigy in his field, he make remarkable advances in logic in such papers as "Naming and Necessity" (1972).

Krishnamurti, Tiruvalam N. (1932–) meteorologist; born in Madras, India. He came to Illinois in 1953 to study meteorology at the University of Chicago. At Florida State University (1967) he won the Rossby Medal from the American Meteorological Society (1985) for his research in tropical weather systems.

Kristol, Irving (William) (1920–) editor, educator; born in New York City. The son of Jewish immigrants, he graduated from the City College of New York in 1940, became active in left-wing political circles, and saw combat with the U.S. Army in France (1944–45). Gradually moving to the right, he edited *Encounter* magazine from 1953–58, and, beginning in 1965, *The Public Interest* magazine. He taught social sciences at New York University from 1969–88. His *Reflections of A Neoconservative* appeared in 1983.

Kroc, (Raymond A.) Ray (1902–84) restaurateur; born in Chicago. A high school drop out, he was an under-age ambulance driver for the Red Cross during World War I, a jazz pianist, a real estate broker during the Florida land boom (1920s), and a salesman for the Lily Tulip Cup Company. In 1941 he formed a company to sell Mult-A-Mixers, which could make five milkshakes at once. In 1954 he visited the San Bernadino, Calif., restaurant of Mac and Dick McDonald who had bought eight Mult-A-Mixers. Impressed by their volume of business and their assembly-style hamburger operation, he proposed a franchise. He sold his Mult-A-Mixer company and by 1960 had 228 McDonald's restaurants with profits of $37 million. He controlled all facets of franchising, even establishing Hamburger University in Elk Grove, Ill., and requiring that all franchise owners attend to learn how to prepare the food. He was chairman of the board of McDonald's Corporation (1968–77) and senior chairman (1977–84). He bought the San Diego Padres in 1974 and established the Kroc Foundation for charitable giving.

Kroeber, Alfred (Louis) (1876–1960) cultural anthropologist; born in Hoboken, N.J. The son of German-born parents, he grew up in a prosperous, cultured, New York City household, graduated from Columbia University in 1896, and received a Ph.D. under Franz Boas there in 1901. He moved west in 1901 to found the anthropology department at the University of California: Berkeley where he remained until 1946. He practiced psychoanalysis for several years, but returned to his chief scholarly interest, the California Indians. His extensive studies were compiled in his *Handbook of the Indians of California* (1925). He developed the concept of cultures as patterned wholes, each with its own style, and each undergoing a growth process analogous to that of a biological organism. His work, *Cultural and Natural Areas of Native North America* (1939), correlated cultural areas, defined by complexes of traits, with ecological areas. *Configurations of Culture Growth* (1944) documented the rise, triumph, and decay of civilizations in terms of cultural life cycles. His influential *Anthropology* (1923) helped establish anthropology as a professional academic discipline.

Kroeger, Alice Bertha (1864–1909) librarian; born in St. Louis, Mo. A protégée of Melvil Dewey, she taught librarianship at Drexel Institute (Philadelphia) and became the first director of Drexel's Library School (1892–1909). Her *Guide to the Standard Usage of Reference Books* was a widely used text. She was an active suffragist.

Krogman, Wilton M. (Marion) (1903–87) physical anthropologist; born in Oak Park, Ill. He taught at Western Reserve (1931–38), then at the University of Chicago (1938–47), before joining the University of Pennsylvania (1947–71). His examinations of fossil North American human skeletons ascertained their physical typology and cultural patterns. His later paleoanthropological studies (1935–45) elucidated human immigrations to Europe via western Asia. He established the Philadelphia Center for Research in Child Growth (1947), and compiled the "Philadelphia Standards" (1947–71), criteria of anatomical measurements applicable to many aspects of pediatric medicine, especially congenital palatal deformities.

Krol, John (Joseph) (1910–) Catholic prelate; born in Cleveland, Ohio. Ordained in 1937, he earned a doctorate in theology (1942), taught canon law, and held administrative posts in the Cleveland diocese, becoming auxiliary bishop and vicar general (1953). As archbishop of Philadelphia (1961–88), he played a leading, largely conservative role among American prelates at the Second Vatican Council, and was president of the National Conference of Catholic Bishops (1971–74).

Kruesi, John (1843–99) inventor, electrical engineer; born in Heiden, Switzerland. In 1871, under Thomas Edison, he began work on telegraphy, telephones, and microphones. Kruesi produced the first phonograph in 1877. He perfected another idea of Edison's, to insulate wire so it could be laid underground. He became superintendent of the Edison laboratories, and in 1892 the general manager of General Electric.

Krupa, Gene (1909–73) musician; born in Chicago. A drummer, he played with several lesser known bands around Chicago until 1929, when he moved to New York City and worked with Red Nichols for the next two years. He was a sideman in commercial studio bands led by Russ Columbo and Mal Hallet between 1932–34, when he also free-lanced on classic jazz sessions with Bix Beiderbecke and Eddie Condon. Between 1935–38, as a main attraction in Benny Goodman's orchestra, he became the first world-renowned jazz drummer. In 1938, he formed his own successful big band, which he led until 1943, when he played briefly with Goodman and Tommy Dorsey. He led another "big band" between 1945–51, then appeared with Jazz at the Philharmonic throughout the 1950s. He led his own small groups thereafter while operating a drum-tuition school, which he opned with Cozy Cole in New York in 1954. A sensationalized biographical film, *The Gene Krupa Story,* for which he recorded the soundtrack, was released in 1959.

Kruskal, Martin David (1925–) physicist, mathematician; born in New York City. He taught mathematics at New York University (1946–51) before becoming a plasma physicist, astrophysicist, and mathematics professor at Princeton (1951–89). He made advancements in the fields of logic, magnetohydrodynamics, controlled fusion, and relativity. He joined Rutgers' mathematics department in 1989.

Krutch, Joseph Wood (1893–1970) author, critic, naturalist; born in Knoxville, Tenn. He graduated from the University of Tennessee and received a Ph.D. in English from Columbia University in 1923. He taught at Columbia (1937–52) and published critical studies of Samuel Johnson, Edgar A. Poe, and Henry David Thoreau. His *Measure of Man* won a National Book Award in 1954. He was drama critic for *The Nation* from 1924–52. He moved to Tucson, Ariz., for his health in 1952, fell under the spell of the natural environment, and published a number of lyrical works about the life of the desert. Toward the end of his life he wrote and narrated television specials about the Sonora desert, the Grand Canyon, and Baja California.

Kubler, George (A.) (1912–) architectural historian; born in Los Angeles. Teaching at Yale (1938), he published important works on Spanish, Portuguese, and Latin American architecture, notably *Mexican Architecture of the Sixteenth Century* (1948) and *The Art and Architecture of Ancient America* (1962), as well as a theoretical work, *The Shape of Time* (1962).

Kubrick, Stanley (1928–) film director; born in the Bronx, N.Y. At age 17 he was a staff photographer for *Look* magazine, and in 1950 he made his first film, a documentary – *Day of the Fight*. His first directorial feature was *Fear and Desire* (1953). A meticulous master of technique and visual composition, his successes include *Lolita* (1962), *Dr. Strangelove* (1964), *2001: A Space Odyssey* (1968), and *A Clockwork Orange* (1971). Often filming in Britain to avoid the commercial pressures of Hollywood, he is seen by his admirers as one of the true American cinema artists, but others find his movies intellectually pretentious and emotionally sterile.

Kuchel, Thomas H. (Henry) (1910–) U.S. senator; born in Anaheim, Calif. He served in the California assembly and senate before his initial appointment and then election to the U.S. Senate (Rep., Calif.; 1953–69). He was Republican whip from 1959–69.

Kuebler-Ross, Elisabeth (1926–) psychiatrist; born in Zurich, Switzerland. She studied at the University of Zurich (M.D. 1957) and moved to the United States shortly thereafter. She taught psychiatry at the Universities of Colorado and Chicago and began her pioneering research into the experience of dying in 1965. Her publications include *On Death and Dying* (1969) and *Death: The Final Stage* (1974) and she is credited with having brought Americans to a new level of consciousness about this stage of life.

Kuhn, Bowie K. (1926–) lawyer, baseball commissioner; born in Takoma Park, Md. (descendant of Jim Bowie, 1796–1836). He earned his law degree at the University of Virginia (1950) and went on to the firm of Wilkie, Farr and Gallagher (1950–69) where he counseled several baseball clients. After representing the major league baseball club owners in negotiations in 1968, he was chosen to be commissioner of baseball (1968–84). During his term, the salaries, prestige, and arrogance of all concerned with professional baseball attained new heights and he was the recipient of both praise and blame. He was forced out in 1984 and told his story in *Hardball: The Education of a Baseball Commissioner* (1987). He returned to private practice in New York City, but his firm, Myerson and Kuhn, got involved in some questionable practices and went bankrupt (1989); threatened with legal action, Kuhn took refuge in Florida.

Kuhn, (Margaret E.) Maggie (1905–) social activist; born in Buffalo, N.Y. She taught junior high school briefly and then worked for the Young Men's Christian Association (1926–37) and the United Presbyterian Church in New York City (1945–70). She founded the Consultation of Older and Younger Adults for Social Change in 1971, which was soon renamed the Gray Panthers. She worked for nursing home reform, fought ageism, and claimed that "old people constitute America's biggest untapped and undervalued human energy source."

Kuhn, Thomas (Samuel) (1922–) philosopher, historian of science; born in Cincinnati, Ohio. Trained as a physicist, he became interested in the historical development of science and in 1962 published *The Structure of Scientific Revolutions,* a study of how scientific theories are formed, judged, and supplanted; its proposition that even the most "objective" scientific theories are influenced by external factors has had wide currency in many areas of contemporary thought. He taught at Harvard (1948–57), the University of California: Berkeley (1957–64), Princeton (1964–79), and Massachusetts Institute of Technology (from 1979).

Kuhn, (Walter Francis) Walt (1877–1949) painter; born in New York City. He had a varied career as a bicycle shop owner and cartoonist before exhibiting at the Armory Show in New York (1913). From then on he experimented with different styles, particularly those of French painters such as Cézanne, Matisse, and Picasso. His mature work, which specialized in portraits of clowns and other circus performers, conveyed an emotionally charged, often stoic message, as seen in *The Blue Clown* (1931).

Kuiper, Gerard Peter (1905–73) astronomer; born in Harenkarspel, Holland. He arrived in California as a fellow at the Lick Observatory (1933–35), and attained citizenship in 1937. He directed the Yerkes and McDonald Observatories (1947–49, 1957–60) and finally the Lunar and Planetary Laboratory at the University of Arizona: Tucson. A principal investigator of the National Aeronautics and Space Administration's Ranger program, he also researched planetary atmospheres.

Kumin, Maxine (b. Winokur) (1925–) poet, writer; born in Philadelphia. She studied at Radcliffe (B.A. 1946; M.A. 1948), and married in 1946. She taught at Tufts (1958–61; 1965–68), Princeton (1977; 1979; 1981–82), and the Massachusetts Institute of Technology (1984) among other institutions. A writer of fiction, children's books, essays, and poetry, she was named poetry consultant to the Library of Congress (1981–82). She is best known for poems of the Northeast, as in *Up Country: Poems of New England* (1972). She lived in Warner, N.H.

Kundla, John (1916–) basketball coach; born in Star Junction, Pa. He coached the Minneapolis Lakers for 11 years (1949–59), and led his club to four National Basketball Association titles (1950, 1952–54). He later coached at the University of Minnesota (1960–68).

Kunhardt, Dorothy (b. Meserve) (1901–79) author, illustrator; born in New York City. Based in New York City and Beverly, Mass., she began writing in the 1930s and became famous for a new concept of touch-and-feel books for young children, notably *Pat the Bunny* (1940), a popular classic.

Kunin, Madeleine (b. May) (1933–) governor; born in Zurich, Switzerland. Emigrating to New York at age six, she worked as a journalist in Burlington, Vt., writing freelance articles while raising her children (1961–71). Elected to the Vermont house of representatives (Dem., 1973–78), she chaired the Appropriations Committee, becoming lieutenant governor (1979–82). As Vermont's governor (1985–91) she reduced state debt, enforced strict environmental codes, and actively recruited women to work in state government.

Kunitz, Stanley (Jasspon) (1905–) poet, editor; born in Worcester, Mass. He studied at Harvard (B.A. 1926; M.A. 1927), and taught at many institutions, notably Columbia beginning in 1967. He is known for his finely crafted poetry, as in *Poems 1928–1978* (1979), and his editorship of reference works on American and European literature.

Kuniyoshi, Yasuo (1893–1953) painter, graphic artist; born in Okayama, Japan. He emigrated to America (1906), studied at the Los Angeles School of Art and Design and at the Art Students League, New York, under Kenneth Hayes Miller (1916). He settled in New York, and his later work was marked by sinister fantasy, as seen in the well-known canvas, *Juggler* (1952).

Kunstler, William M. (Moses) (1919–) lawyer, social activist, professor; born in New York City. A Yale graduate and veteran of World War II, he graduated from Columbia University School of Law and in 1949 formed a law partnership with his brother. During the 1950s he mainly practiced estate and business law, but in the early 1960s his social conscience and commitment were aroused when he began to represent the Congress of Racial Equality (CORE), Martin Luther King's Southern Christian Leadership Conference, and the Student Non-Violence Coordinating Committee (SNCC). He soon became known as the legal voice of "the Movement" – the more radical groups opposing the Vietnam war, mistreatment of blacks, and other perceived flaws in American society. His clients included the Black Panthers, the Catonsville Nine, and the Roman Catholic militants Philip and Daniel Berrigan, but his most celebrated case was that of the Chicago Seven, charged with inciting the violence associated with the 1968 Democratic convention; he himself was sentenced to jail for contempt of court (but he won on appeal). In the years that followed, he continued to remain in the public eye as the defender of those from all walks of life who he felt would not get a fair trial; his outspoken, even provocative manner often placed him in the limelight, but no one ever denied his passion for obtaining justice for all. Throughout his career as a trial lawyer, he taught at New York University Law School and published many books, including legal texts such as *The Law of Accidents* (1954), and more popular works such as *Beyond a Reasonable Doubt* (1961) and *Deep in My Heart* (1966), all written with a certain literary flair.

Kupfer, David J. (1941–) psychiatrist; born in New York City. In 1973 he joined the University of Pittsburgh School of Medicine, becoming chairman of psychiatry in 1983. His primary contribution was in the diagnosis and treatment of mood disorders, particularly sleep disorders and the biological causes of depression.

Kuralt, Charles (1934–) radio/television correspondent; born in Wilmington, N.C. A newspaper writer in North Carolina, he joined CBS News in 1957, becoming a foreign correspondent in 1959. After 10 years abroad, he began exploring America in his *On the Road* series. In 1979 he began anchoring CBS's *Sunday Morning*. He published his memoirs, *A Life on the Road* (1990).

Kurath, Gertrude Prokosch (1903–92) musicologist; born in Chicago. She danced and taught professionally as "Tula" (1922–46) before turning to the study of Indian dance. She did extensive fieldwork and published writings on Iroquois, Pueblo, Six Nations, and Great Lakes Indian dance; she also contributed to dance theory and notation. She founded the Dance Research Center, Ann Arbor, Mich. (1962).

Kurland, (Robert) Bob (1924–) basketball player; born in St. Louis, Mo. Basketball's first dominating seven-foot center, his shot blocking ability led to a ban on goaltending in 1944 while he was a three-time All-American at Oklahoma A&M (1944–46). A member of two gold medal Olympic teams (1948, 1952), he was elected to basketball's Hall of Fame in 1961.

Kurzweil, Raymond C. (1948–) computer scientist, entrepreneur; born in New York City. He developed a print-to-speech reading machine for the blind (1976) and a computer music keyboard (1984). A pioneer in automated speech-recognition, he founded Kurzweil Applied Intelligence (1982), which introduced the Kurzweil Voicesystem (1985), technology to transfer speech directly to a computer. His VoiceMED technology for voice-controlled patient reporting (1986) has been widely used by physicians and hospitals.

Kusch, Polykarp (1911–93) physicist; born in Blankenburg, Germany. Taken to the U.S.A. in 1912, he was naturalized in 1922. He taught at Columbia University (1937–41, 1946–72), performing military research during World War II. He shared the 1955 Nobel Prize in physics (with Willis Lamb) for his precise determination of the magnetic moment of the electron. His last academic position was at the University of Texas (1972–82).

Kuter, Lawrence Sherman (1905–79) aviator; born in Rockford, Ill. A 1927 West Point graduate, he transferred to the Air Corps in 1930 and rose to command a bomber wing in England (1942–43). He held a series of senior commands during the 1950s, including the North American Air Defense Command. He retired in 1962 to become a vice-president of Pan American World Airways, and later, a consultant to the aviation industry.

Kuznets, Simon (1901–85) economist; born in Kharkov, Ukraine. In 1922 he emigrated to the U.S.A. and was educated at Columbia University. He worked at the National Bureau of Economic Research (1927–61) and taught at the University of Pennsylvania (1930–54), Johns Hopkins (1954–60), and Harvard (1960–71). His major contributions include developing national income accounts and performing the historical research necessary to reconstruct that data for the U.S.A. back to 1869. His work advanced the acceptance of Keynesian economics during and after World War II. His major publication was *National Income and Its Composition, 1919–1938* (1941). In 1971 he received the Nobel Prize in economics.

Kyrk, Hazel (1886–1957) consumer economist; born in Ashley, Ohio. A University of Chicago Ph.D., she taught economics there (1925–52) and became a forceful advocate for consumer protection. She wrote the classic *Theory of Consumption* (1923) and contributed to the Bureau of Home Economics' 20-volume *Consumer Purchases Study* (1938–41), which established a baseline for what became the Consumer Price Index.

Kyser, (James King Kern) Kay (1906–85) bandleader; born in Rocky Mount, N.C. He formed his first band in college in the late-1920s; it toured widely and later expanded. In the early-1930s he performed at the Blackhawk Restaurant in Chicago and in 1937 he began broadcasting his popular radio show, *Kay Kyser's College of Musical Knowledge;* it appeared on television from 1949 to 1951, the year he retired. He appeared in several films and released many hit records.

L

Laborde, Alden James (1915–) oil executive; born in Vinton, La. He spent his career in the oil industry. He was founder and president of Ocean Drilling & Exploration Co. (1953–74; CEO and chairman 1974–77), where he invented the mobile offshore oil drilling rig (1954). He was later an industry consultant (1977–85) and CEO and chairman of Gulf Island Fabrication Co. (1985).

Labuza, Theodore P. (1940–) food scientist; born in New York City. He taught food engineering at the Massachusetts Institute of Technology (1965–71), his *alma mater,* before going to the Food Science and Nutrition Department at the University of Minnesota (1971). He wrote 12 textbooks, hundreds of articles, and edited the *Journal of Food Processing and Preservation* (1976–84). During Desert Storm, he worked for the Department of Defense task force on food quality problems associated with a hot environment.

Lachaise, Gaston (1882–1935) sculptor; born in Paris, France. He studied at the École des Beaux-Arts beginning in 1898, worked for René Lalique, then emigrated to Boston (1906), and settled in New York City (1912) to work with Paul Manship and set up his studio. In 1918 he married Isabel Dutard Nagle, the inspiration for much of his work, and created many monumental female nudes, as in *Standing Woman* (1912–27). He died of leukemia at the height of his career.

Ladd, Edwin Fremont (1859–1925) educator, U.S. senator; born in Starks, Maine. As a chemist and president of North Dakota State Agricultural College, he led a statewide campaign for pure food testing. A progressive, he was elected to the U.S. Senate (Rep., N.Dak.; 1921–25).

Ladd, William (1778–1841) sea captain, farmer, pacifist; born in Exeter, N.H. A sea captain turned farmer, turned abolitionist, there is no historical record of his transformation to fulltime pacifism (1819). He founded new peace groups, appointing able lieutenants. He lectured and wrote peace propaganda and was one of the first to link the goals of pacifists with those fighting for women's rights. Founding the American Peace Society (1828), he became a Congregational clergyman (1837) as a means of furthering his cause. The same year he forced the American Peace Society to condemn all war, defensive and offensive. Developer of many techniques of pacifist propaganda, he was the first to make pacifism a political issue in America. In his *Essay on a Congress of Nations* (1840) he was one of the first to predict that there would someday be an international organization like the United Nations.

Ladd-Franklin, Christine (1847–1930) psychologist, logician; born in Windsor, Conn. She studied mathematics at Johns Hopkins University, where she married faculty member Fabian Franklin (1882). In 1883 she proposed the "antilogism," a syllogism concluding that if any two premises are true, the third must be false. Her experiments in psychological optics began in 1886, and she presented her theory of color vision to the International Congress of Psychologists in London in 1892. She taught at Columbia University from 1910 to 1930.

Laemmle, Carl, Sr. (1867–1939) motion picture producer; born in Laupheim, Germany. He emigrated to New York City in 1884 and held various jobs until 1906, when he opened a nickelodeon in Chicago. He soon became a leading film distributor and founded his own studio (1909) in defiance of the powerful Motion Picture Patents Company trust; his Independent Motion Picture Company (IMP) acquired smaller companies to form the Universal Film Manufacturing Company in 1912. He was one of the most aggressive of the early movie producers, luring stars away from other companies, heavily publicizing them, and showing that feature length and sensational movies could be profitable. He appointed some 70 relatives to executive posts at Universal, including his son, Carl Laemmle Jr., who became production chief at age 21; he also hired the 19-year-old Irving Thalberg, son of a friend, and soon entrusted him with running Universal's production studios in Hollywood. By 1935, Laemmle was forced to sell Universal, due to a combination of the Depression and his son's extravagances.

LaFarge, John (1880–1963) Catholic priest, social activist; born in Newport, R.I. A Jesuit who did pastoral work among African-American Catholics in Maryland (1911–26), he devoted much of his later life to promoting racial justice and interracial cooperation, through a network of Catholic interracial councils and as a writer and longtime editor (1926–63) for the Jesuit magazine *America*.

La Farge, John (1835–1910) painter, multi-media artist; born in New York City. After study with Couture in Paris (1856), and William Morris Hunt in Newport, R.I. (1859), he maintained a studio in New York City. He worked as a sculptor, muralist, oil and water color painter, and stained glass designer. He decorated many churches, notably Trinity Church, Boston (1876), and among other accomplishments, invented opaline glass, an iridescent form of milk glass. His most famous painting, *Manua Our Boatman* (1891), produced after a trip to the South Seas with Henry Adams (1890), is a striking and original work.

La Farge, Oliver (Hazard Perry) (1901–63) anthropologist, author; born in New York City. An architect's son, he graduated from Harvard in 1924, and with a background of three field trips into Navajo country, he became an assistant in ethnology at Tulane in 1925. With a coauthor, he published *Tribes and Temples,* an ethnology of the Guatemalan Indians, in 1927. His novel *Laughing Boy* won a Pulitzer Prize in 1929. He continued to write prolifically. He headed the Association of American Indian Affairs, and in the 1950s became a prominent champion of Native American political and social causes.

Lafayette, Marie Joseph Paul Yves Roch Gilbert du Motier, Marquis de (1757–1834) statesman, soldier; born in Auvergne, France. Scion of a wealthy, aristocratic family – his father was killed in the Seven Years' War against England – he entered the French army in 1771 and resigned in 1776 to join the Revolutionary forces in America, where he was commissioned a major general and joined the staff of George Washington. He participated in several battles and was wounded at Brandywine. He served as a liaison officer when the French and Americans became allies in 1778; he went back to France in 1779 where he was treated as a hero, then returned in 1780 to fight with the American forces, playing a crucial role in the final victory at Yorktown (1781). Back in France in 1782, he would often work to promote America's interests – he revisited the U.S.A. in 1784 and then made a triumphal final tour in 1824 – meanwhile becoming a major player in French political life.

Lafever, Minard (1798–1854) builder/architect; born near Morristown, N.J. His five builders' guides (1829–56) spread the Greek Revival style nationwide, while his many New York City churches popularized various other revival styles, notably Gothic.

Laffite, Jean (?1780–?1825) pirate; probably born in France. He came to New Orleans by 1809 and led a band of smugglers and pirates. He and his men were pardoned by President James Madison after they manned artillery during the battle of New Orleans (1815). He founded Galveston, Texas, and reverted to piracy. After a U.S. naval force dispersed the colony, he sailed away and passed into legend.

La Follette, Belle Case (1859–1931) social reformer, journalist; born in Summit, Wis. She graduated from the University of Wisconsin, and after teaching and marrying her college classmate, Robert La Follette (1881), she became the first woman to graduate from that university's law school (1885). She never actually practiced law but used her legal training in her work with her husband. Until her husband's election as governor, she devoted herself to various social reforms, especially those involving women and children. She then became his close adviser and assistant. In 1909, they founded *La Follette's Weekly Magazine* (a monthly after 1914) to promote their progressive agenda; she edited the "Women and Education Department" and wrote many articles; in 1911–12, she wrote a nationally syndicated column. She took the lead in getting wives of Congressmen in Washington to undertake socially useful tasks and was herself in demand nationally as a speaker. She opposed war and was active in several women's peace and disarmament organizations during and after World War I. On her husband's death in

1925, she was urged by many to fill his seat but she declined, working instead to see her son elected. She continued to promote a progressive agenda as associate editor of *La Follette's Magazine.*

La Follette, Philip Fox (1897–1965) governor; born in Madison, Wis. (son of Robert Marion La Follette Sr.) A lawyer, he served as governor (Rep., Wis.; 1931–33, Prog., 1935–39), pushing through the first state unemployment insurance plan. He founded the ill-fated National Progressive Party in 1938, losing his own reelection campaign. After serving on General MacArthur's staff, he practiced law, becoming president of Hazeltine electronics (1955–59).

La Follette, Robert M. (Marion), Sr. (1855–1925) governor, U.S. senator; born in Primrose, Wis. Born into a poor pioneer family, he worked his way through the University of Wisconsin and became a lawyer (1880). (He married his college classmate, Belle Case, herself a lawyer; she remained his solid colleague throughout his career.) A Republican, he served three terms in the U.S. House of Representatives (1885–91), then broke with his state party's "stalwart" establishment and launched his own statewide movement, calling for a broad program of progressive social and economic reforms such as direct primary elections, control of railroad rates, and more equitable taxation. As governor (1901–06) he was eventually successful enough that reformers of the U.S.A. were advocating the "Wisconsin Idea." Moving on to the U.S. Senate (1906–25), he continued to advance his progressive agenda, but when Theodore Roosevelt drew the progressive Republicans into his Bull Moose party in the 1912 election, La Follette felt betrayed. Often on the outs with the establishment – he was known as "Battling Bob" – he opposed America's entry into World War I but supported the various war bills. He also opposed America's joining the League of Nations and the World Court. He ran for president on his own Progressive party ticket in 1924 and got one-sixth of the popular vote.

La Follette, Robert Marion, Jr. (1895–1953) U.S. senator; born in Madison, Wis. Born into a political family, he was elected to the U.S. Senate (Rep., Wis.; 1925–47) to serve out his father's unexpired term. A staunch liberal, he supported tax reform, social security, farm relief, and foreign aid. He was defeated in the Republican primary in 1946 by Joseph R. McCarthy.

La Guardia, Fiorello (Henry) (1882–1947) mayor, lawyer, U.S. representative; born in New York City. After working from age 17 to 23 in the U.S. consulates in Budapest, Trieste, and Fiume (Rijeka), he served as an interpreter on Ellis Island while attending New York University law school (LL.B. 1910). After graduating, he began his long career of social activism, doing *pro bono* work for immigrants. In 1916 he was elected to the U.S. House of Representatives (Rep., N.Y.), which he left early in 1918 to serve in the armed forces in Italy. Resuming his seat later that year, he served in Congress – with time out to serve on New York City's Board of Aldermen (1920–22) – until he was elected to the first of three terms as mayor of New York in 1933. His work for housing and welfare reform, as well as his "common touch," demonstrated by his reading of the Sunday comics on the radio during a newspaper strike, earned him the love of millions of New Yorkers, who knew him as "the Little Flower," an apt nickname since he stood only 5'2". La Guardia was a maverick in many ways – a Republican, despite his liberal philosophies, and an Episcopalian, though born to a Jewish mother and Italian father. After his mayorship, he served as head of the U.S. Office of Civilian Defense (1941) and director general of the United Nations Relief and Rehabilitation Agency (1946).

Lahey, Frank Howard (1880–1953) surgeon; born in Haverhill, Mass. He taught at Harvard (1912–15) and Tufts (1913–24). In 1923 Harvard and Tufts established an unprecedented joint chair for him. A surgeon of international renown, he pioneered a team approach to complicated procedures in lessening trauma. The clinic he opened in 1923 is also famed for using the team approach to diagnosis. President of the American Medical Association (1941–42), he represented the "old guard" and in 1949 he opposed Truman's compulsory national health insurance plan.

Lahm, Frank (Purdy) (1877–1963) aviator; born in Mansfield, Ohio. The son of a balloonist, he graduated from West Point in 1901, served in the cavalry, and transferred to the Signal Corps in 1907. A pioneer aviator, he trained with Wilbur Wright and in 1909 became one of the army's first two certified pilots. Lahm organized the American Expeditionary Force in France in 1917. In the 1930s he served as attaché for air in France, Spain, and Belgium. He retired from the service in 1941.

Lahr, Bert (1895–1967) actor; born in New York City. A comedian with a loveably ugly face, he mugged and gagged his way through impossible situations that he created for his characters. After touring in vaudeville with his wife (1916–27), he appeared on Broadway in *Hold Everything* (1928). A musical comedy star (1928–64), he also appeared in films (1931–67), including *The Wizard of Oz* (1939) where he played the Cowardly Lion. In 1956, he played Estragon in *Waiting for Godot*.

Lajoie, (Napoleon) Nap (1874–1959) baseball player; born in Woonsocket, R.I. During his 21-year career as a second baseman (1896–1916), mostly with the Cleveland Indians, he posted a lifetime batting average of .339. In 1901, he batted .422, highest ever in a season in the American League. He was elected to baseball's Hall of Fame in 1937.

Lake, Simon (1866–1945) engineer, inventor; born in Pleasantville, N.J. He became interested in designing underwater vessels. He competed with John P. Holland's design in 1893 and launched his gasoline engine-powered *Argonaut*, which became the first submarine to successfully operate in the open sea (1898). He established the Lake Torpedo Boat Company in Bridgeport, Conn. (1900) and the U.S. government bought his submarine *Seal* in 1911. He also worked as a submarine consultant to the Russian, German, and British governments.

Lamar, Joseph R. (Rucker) (1857–1916) Supreme Court justice; born in Elbert County, Ga. He served on the Georgia state legislature (1886–89) and on the state supreme court (1904–06) before his appointment to the U.S. Supreme Court (1911–16) by President Taft.

Lamar, Lucius Quintus Cincinnatus (1825–93) Supreme Court justice; born in Putnam County, Ga. He served the U.S. House of Representatives (Miss.; 1857, 1872–77) and was elected to the U.S. Senate (Dem., Miss.; 1876). He was secretary of the interior (1885–87) before President Cleveland named him to the U.S. Supreme Court (1888–91).

Lamar, Mirabeau Buonaparte (1798–1859) soldier, public official; born in Louisville, Ga. After working as a politician and journalist in Georgia, he moved to Texas and com-

manded the Texas cavalry at San Jacinto (1836). He was vice-president (1836–38) and then president (1838–41) of the Republic of Texas. He founded the capital at Austin (1840) and after 1844 he supported statehood for Texas.

Lamb, Joseph (Francis) (1877–1960) composer; born in Montclair, N.J. As a young white man, he studied the published scores of the African-American ragtime composers such as Scott Joplin and James Scott. He then published his own rag, "Sensation," in 1908 and by 1919 had composed 12 more that ensured his later reputation. He remained unknown for years while working in the New York textile trade. He resumed composing in 1949, occasionally performing his works, and first recorded in 1959.

Lamb, Willis E. (Eugene), Jr. (1913–) physicist; born in Los Angeles, Calif. He taught at Columbia University (1938–52), Stanford (1951–56), Oxford (1956–62), Yale (1962–74), and the University of Arizona (1974). He expanded English physicist Dirac's electron theory by demonstrating a change in hydrogen atom energy levels, now known as the Lamb shift (1947). When notified of winning the 1955 Nobel Prize in physics for his research into the hydrogen spectrum, he taught his scheduled class before publicizing his award. He continued to make advances in nuclear structure and laser theory.

Lambdin, James (Reid) (1807–89) painter; born in Pittsburgh, Pa. He studied with Thomas Sully (1823), and became a portrait painter and miniaturist. He settled in Philadelphia (1837), and his subjects included Presidents Lincoln and Grant.

Lambeau, (Earl Louis) "Curly" (1898–1965) football player, coach; born in Green Bay, Wis. As coach of the Green Bay Packers, the team he founded in 1919, he won six National Football League championships in 31 seasons.

Lamberg-Karlovsky, C. C. (Clifford Charles) (1937–) anthropologist, archaeologist; born in Prague, Czechoslovakia. A childhood immigrant to the U.S.A., he became a curator (1969–77) and director (1977) of the Peabody Museum while concurrently a Harvard faculty member. He specialized in prehistoric Mesopotamian and Indus Valley civilizations, particularly trade; he wrote *Ancient Civilizations* (1979) and reports of his extensive excavations at Tepe Yahya, Iran (1970, 1986).

Lambert, Walter Davis (1879–1968) geodesist; born in West New Brighton, N.Y. His work with the U.S. Coast and Geodetic Survey expanded knowledge of the earth's shape, interior, and tides.

Lamm, Norman (1927–) rabbi; born in New York City. He graduated from Yeshiva University in 1949 and earned his Ph.D. there in 1966. He was the founder and editor of *Tradition: A Journal of Orthodox Jewish Thought* (1957). He began teaching Jewish philosophy at Yeshiva University (New York City) in 1959, then became its president (1976).

Lamme, Benjamin (Garver) (1864–1924) electrical engineer, inventor; born near Springfield, Ohio. Interested in mechanics and mathematics as a boy, he graduated from Ohio State University with an engineering degree in 1888. He went to work for Westinghouse Corp. the following year and soon became the company's chief designer of electrical machinery. The New York, New Haven and Hartford Railway adopted his single-phase electric rail system in 1905. A lifelong bachelor, he was Westinghouse's chief engineer from 1903 until his death.

L'Amour, Louis (b. Louis Dearborn LaMoore) (Tex Burns, Jim Mayo, pen names) (1908–88) writer; born in Jamestown, N.D. Leaving school when young, he traveled throughout western America and the world and held a number of jobs, ranging from lumberjack to elephant handler. He published a book of poetry (1939), but it was his first Western novel, *Hondo* (1953), that gained him instant success. Although he would write a nonfiction book about the frontier and numerous film and television scripts, it was his many Westerns that gained him great popularity among a wide spectrum of readers.

Lancaster, (Burton Stephen) Burt (1913–94) movie actor, producer; born in New York. A former circus and vaudeville acrobat, he returned from World War II overseas duty and appeared on Broadway in *A Sound of Hunting* (1945). His first movie was *The Killers* (1946); he went on to become a major Hollywood star, ranging from acrobatic swashbucklers to brooding dramas that gained him four Academy Award nominations with one Oscar for *Elmer Gantry* (1960). In his later years his reputation was even higher among international directors and audiences.

Land, Edwin (Herbert) (1909–91) inventor; born in Bridgeport, Conn. While an undergraduate at Harvard, he made discoveries in the field of polarized light. He organized the Polaroid Corporation in 1937, producing, among other items, sunglasses with polarized lenses. He also developed optical systems for military use during World War II. In 1947 he announced the invention of a photographic process and camera with which a complete photo could be produced within 60 seconds of exposure. Although he did original research on such fields as color vision, and held over 150 patents, he became most widely known for the giant commercial empire he built based on his original instant-photo camera.

Lander, Frederick West (1821–62) explorer, soldier; born in Salem, Mass. He studied engineering and led or participated in five transcontinental surveys for transportation routes (1853–60). He was a Union brigadier general of volunteers (1861–62) and he wrote many patriotic poems during the Civil War.

Landers, Ann (b. Esther Pauline Friedman) (1918–) journalist; born in Sioux City, Iowa. In 1955 she inherited her job as a Chicago-based advice columnist from a previous "Ann Landers," creating an international institution while competing with her twin sister, "Abigail Van Buren." She earned a devoted following for her guidance and advice to the perplexed, weathering her own 1975 divorce along the way; she also won many public service awards for her open discussions of medical issues.

Landis, James (McCauley) (1899–1964) legal scholar; born in Tokyo, Japan (to American missionary parents). He served as an adviser to three U.S. presidents and as a professor (1926–33) then dean (1937–46) at Harvard Law School. He was appointed to the Securities and Exchange Commission by President Roosevelt (1933–37), he chaired the Civil Aeronautics Board under President Truman (1946–47), and he acted as a special assistant to President Kennedy. His untimely death by drowning came coincidentally during a one-year suspension from practicing law for non-payment of his federal income taxes.

Landis, Kenesaw Mountain (1866–1944) judge, baseball commissioner; born in Millville, Ohio. A lawyer appointed federal district judge in Chicago in 1905, Landis gained attention for his dramatic $30-million ruling against Standard Oil (later reversed) and for patriotic cases connected with the Espionage Act of 1917. As baseball's autocratic first commissioner (1920–44), he banned for life eight players who had previously been acquitted in the "Black Sox" scandal of 1919. He earned his reputation for integrity and for reestablishing the reputation and integrity of baseball, but his insistence on excluding African-Americans from organized baseball prevented their participation in the national pastime until after his death. He was inducted into the Baseball Hall of Fame in 1939.

Landon, (Alfred Mossman) Alf (1887–1987) governor; born in West Middlesex, Pa. (father of Nancy Landon Kassenbaum). Starting A. M. Landon & Company to produce oil in 1912, he had become a millionaire by 1929. As governor of Kansas (Rep., 1933–37), he supported the New Deal, but opposed labor unions. After losing the 1936 presidential election, he returned to his oil firm.

Landon, H. C. (Harold Chandler) Robbins (1926–) musicologist; born in Boston, Mass. Landon studied music at Swarthmore and then in Boston with Karl Geiringer. He went to Vienna in 1948 to pursue Haydn research, which finally led to the monumental *Symphonies of Joseph Haydn* (1955). While continuing as a leading Haydn scholar and editor of the symphonies, he also wrote on other composers of the period including Beethoven and Mozart.

Landon, Michael (b. Eugene Maurice Orowitz) (1936–91) television actor; born in New York City. After appearing in small roles in television westerns and drama series including *Playhouse 90*, he made his film debut in *I Was a Teenage Werewolf* (1957). He endeared himself to audiences as Little Joe in the television western series, *Bonanza* (1959–73), and as Charles Ingalls in the television series based on Laura Ingalls Wilder's *Little House on the Prairie* (1979–82). He occasionally wrote and directed for the series he starred in, including *Stairway to Heaven* (1984–88). He had just completed the pilot for *Us* before his sudden death from cancer.

Landowska, Wanda (Aleksandra) (1877–1959) harpsichordist, music teacher; born in Warsaw, Poland. After studying at the Warsaw Conservatory, she became a prominent concert pianist in Europe until about 1910 when she decided to devote her career to playing the harpsichord. She taught in Berlin and then in Paris, promoting older music, particularly that of Bach, and commissioning new works for the harpsichord. Although she made her first concert tour in the U.S.A. in 1923, she did not move there permanently until 1940, coming first to New York City and then to Connecticut (1949). Teaching, playing, recording, writing, and proselytizing extensively – and often imperiously – she is regarded as a leader in the 20th century's revival of the harpsichord.

Landrum, Phillip Mitchell (1907–90) U.S. representative; born in Stephens County, Ga. A high school superintendent (1937–41) and lawyer, he ran for Congress before enlisting in the army. After serving in Europe, he worked for the Veterans' Administration and for Georgia, as assistant attorney general and executive secretary to the governor. In the U.S. House of Representatives (Dem., 1953–77) he cosponsored the Landrum-Griffith Bill to limit labor union picketing and boycotts. He retired to Jasper, Ga.

Landry, (Thomas Wade) Tom (1924–) football player,

coach; born in Mission, Texas. An outstanding defensive back with the National Football League's New York Giants, he became head coach of the Dallas Cowboys in their first year (1960) and remained through 1988. His teams featured a tricky, multiple offense and his creation, the flex defense. During his 29 seasons, the Cowboys won 18 division championships and appeared in five Super Bowls, winning two.

Landsberg, Helmut Erich (1906–85) climatologist; born in Frankfurt-am-Main, Germany. He came to Pennsylvania State University in 1934 to teach, then worked at the University of Chicago and in the federal government before settling at the University of Maryland in 1967. He wrote prolifically about the effects of air pollution on humans. At the time of his death he was with the World Meteorological Organization Commission for Climatology in Switzerland.

Landsteiner, Karl (1868–1943) immunologist; born in Vienna, Austria. He was a microbiologist and immunologist in Europe (1891–1922). He discovered the four basic human blood groups – A, B, O, and AB (1900). He also designed (with Julius Donath) the Donath-Landsteiner test for the red cell disease paroxysmal nocturnal hemoglobinuria (1904), developed darkfield microscopy for the diagnosis of syphilis (1905–06), proposed a viral origin for poliomyelitis (1909–12), and demonstrated the existence of haptens, small-molecular-weight antigens conjugated to a larger protein carrier (1918–20). In 1922 he came to the U.S.A. to the Rockefeller Institute (now Rockefeller University) (1922–39), where he and Philip Levine discovered the blood factors M, N, and P. For his blood group research, Landsteiner won the 1930 Nobel Prize in physiology. In 1940, he and Alexander Wiener discovered the rhesus (Rh) factor in human blood and developed serological tests necessary to avoid Rh-mediated transfusion reactions or neonatal illness. From 1930–32, Landsteiner propagated the typhus organism in living cultures, and, remaining active after retirement, demonstrated that drug allergy is an immunological process (1935–41).

Lane, Burton (b. Burton Levy) (1912–   ) composer; born in New York City. In the 1930s he contributed songs to Broadway revues and was a free-lance composer in Hollywood. He wrote his first complete score with E. Y. Harburg for the Broadway musical *Hold On to Your Hats* (1940) and in 1947 he and Harburg wrote the Broadway classic, *Finian's Rainbow*. From 1957 to 1967 he was president of the American Guild of Authors and Composers and he continued writing songs throughout the 1970s and 1980s.

Lane, Gertrude Battles (1874–1941) editor; born in Saco, Maine. She edited the *Woman's Home Companion* (1911–41), expanding its scope and successfully bucking stiff competition in the field of women's magazines.

Lane, Henry (Smith) (1811–81) U.S. representative/senator; born in Sharpsburg, Ky. A Whig appointee from Indiana, he served in Congress (1840–43), then left to fight in the Mexican-American war. Joining the Republican Party in support of its antislavery policy, he championed the candidacy of Abraham Lincoln in 1860. He was a one-term senator (1861–67) who returned to being a banker and Republican Party activist in Indiana.

Lane, Joseph (1801–81) governor, legislator; born in Buncombe County, N.C. A farmer and merchant in Indiana, he emerged a hero from the Mexican War and was appointed first territorial governor of Oregon (1848–50). He was a member of the House of Representatives (Dem., Ore.; 1851–59) and the Senate (1859–61). In 1860 he ran for vice-president on the Democratic ticket that favored secession, thus ending his public career.

Lane, (Nathaniel Rogers) Fitz Hugh (1804–65) painter, lithographer; born in Gloucester, Mass. Except for a brief foray to Boston, he spent most of his life in Gloucester. He began his career as a lithographer, a skill that influenced his later oil paintings. He influenced many other painters, such as Frederick Church, who admired his ability to record the clarity of light and sky. In the late 20th century he was rediscovered as a painter of seascapes; his *Owl's Head, Penobscot Bay, Maine* (1862) reveals his skill.

Lane, William Preston, Jr. (1892–1967) governor; born in Hagerstown, Md. A lawyer and World War I veteran, he purchased newspapers in Hagerstown in 1922. A crusading Maryland attorney general (1930–34), he prosecuted a white lynch mob in 1933. As governor (Dem., 1947–51), he outlawed Communist Party gatherings. He later chaired the Herald Mail Publishing Company.

Laney, Lucy Craft (1854–1933) educator; born in Macon, Ga. Her parents were independent-minded slaves who purchased their freedom. After graduating from Atlanta University (1873), Laney founded the ground-breaking Haines Normal and Industrial Institute in Augusta for African-American children. She devoted her life to providing education for and improving the living conditions of African-Americans.

Langdell, Christopher (Columbus) (1826–1906) legal scholar; born in New Boston, N.H. He is best known for pioneering the case study method of teaching law and for his trend-setting book, *Casebook on Contracts* (1871). He practiced law in New York City before joining the faculty at Harvard (1870). As dean of Harvard Law School (1875–95) he raised the school's standards by broadening the curriculum and imposing more rigid scholastic requirements.

Lange, Dorothea (b. Nutzhorn) (1895–1965) photographer; born in Hoboken, N.J. Originally a studio portraitist, her searing pictures of migrant workers in California led to her work as a photographer for the Federal Resettlement Administration (1935–42).

Langer, Susanne (Katherina b. Knauth) (1895–1985) philosopher; born in New York City. After graduating from Radcliffe College and earning a 1926 doctorate from Harvard, she taught at Radcliffe (1927–42) and held posts at Columbia University (1945–50) and Connecticut College (1954–61). Her seminal work, *Philosophy in a New Key* (1942), portrayed symbolism as the key in uniting such fields as logic, psychology, and art. She traced the development of mind in *Mind: An Essay in Human Feeling* (1967, 1972, 1982). She was also an accomplished amateur cellist.

Langer, William (1886–1959) governor, U.S. senator; born in Everest, N.D. A lawyer and Republican attorney general (1916–20) he enforced prohibition laws in North Dakota. Elected governor in 1933, he was removed in 1934 for soliciting funds from state employees, but was cleared and reelected (1937–39). Serving in the U.S. Senate (1941–59), he supported social welfare legislation but he opposed American involvement in World War II, the Marshall Plan, and U.S. membership in the United Nations.

Langer, William (Leonard) (1896–1977) historian; born in Boston, Mass. After taking his B.A. from Harvard (1915) and service with a poison-gas unit in World War I, he took his Ph.D. from Harvard (1922). (Between 1921–42 he was married to Susanne Knauth Langer, the well-known philosopher.) After teaching at Clark University (1923–27), he spent the rest of his career on the Harvard faculty (1927–64), becoming one of the nation's leading authorities on European diplomatic history, military history, and U.S. foreign policy. During World War II he worked with the Office of Strategic Services (OSS) (1942–45) – for which he received the Medal of Merit – and in peacetime he served as an adviser to several governmental agencies, including the Central Intelligence Agency (CIA), the State Department, and the President's Foreign Intelligence Advisory Board. The author of many scholarly works, he was widely known as the editor of *An Encyclopedia of World History* (numerous editions since 1940) and of the *Rise of Modern Europe* series.

Langford, Nathaniel Pitt (1832–1911) explorer, conservationist; born in Westmoreland, N.Y. He moved to Minnesota (1854) and then to Bannack, Mont. (1862) where he led a group of Mormon vigilantes, described in *Vigilante Days and Ways* (1890). He explored the Yellowstone area (1870) and after playing an influential role in having it designated a national park (1872), he served, without pay, as the first superintendent of Yellowstone Park (1872–76).

Langley, Samuel (Pierpoint) (1834–1906) inventor, aeronautical pioneer; born in Roxbury, Mass. Although he had no formal higher education, he served for twenty years as director of the Allegheny Observatory (1867–87). While director, he created a system of regulating railroad time that became standard. In 1878 he invented a bolometer, an electrical thermometer, which he used to conduct experiments on solar and lunar radiation. From 1887 to 1906 he served as secretary of the Smithsonian Institution. He built several models of heavier-than-air mechanically propelled flying machines, and in 1896 he achieved the first free flights. His subsequent attempt to build and fly a man-carrying machine failed.

Langlie, Arthur (Bernard) (1900–66) lawyer, governor; born in Lanesboro, Minn. A Republican attorney, he was a budget cutting mayor of Seattle, Wash. (1939–41). As Washington's governor (1941–45, 1949–57), he opposed social welfare funding and fought against the Columbia Valley regional utilities plan. After losing a vicious senatorial campaign, he became a publishing executive with the McCall Corporation in New York City (1957–65).

Langmuir, Irving (1881–1957) chemist; born in Brooklyn, N.Y. After teaching chemistry at the Stevens Institute of Technology (1906–09), he began work at the General Electric laboratory under Willis Whitney (1909). Langmuir's first major contribution was to show that a nitrogen-filled light bulb burned more brightly than a vacuum bulb. He went on to the study of vacuums, inventing the mercury pump (1916), which enabled the creation of very low pressures needed to produce vacuum tubes. At that time, he also began investigating molecular activity occurring in film surfaces that were just one molecule thick. In addition to his various laboratory discoveries, he made theoretical contributions with his explanation of the phenomenon of adsorption; he also developed concepts fundamental to the field of thermonuclear fusion and coined the term *plasma* to describe ionized gas. He was awarded the Nobel Prize in chemistry

(1932) for his work in surface chemistry. That same year he was named associate director of the General Electric labs, where he remained until his retirement (1950). During World War II he worked for the U.S. military on problems of ice formation on aircraft wings; this led to his 1946 discovery of a method to produce rain by seeding clouds with dry ice and silver iodide.

Langston, John Mercer (1829–97) educator, public official; born in Louisa County, Va. The son of a plantation owner and his emancipated slave, he was educated at Oberlin College (B.A. 1849), where he read theology and law, passing the Ohio bar exams in 1854. He was elected township clerk in 1855, the first African-American elected to public office. During the Civil War, he worked to recruit black troops and after the war he was inspector general of the Freedmen's Bureau (1868). He then moved to the newly-founded Howard University, where he served as dean and vice-president, and was one of the founders of the law school (1869–77). He served in the U.S. diplomatic service (1887–85), before successfully standing in the House of Representatives from Virginia (Rep., 1889–91). He had to resort to the courts to have his election upheld, and his bid for reelection was unsuccessful. He published his autobiography, *From the Virginia Plantation to the National Capital* (1894).

Lanier, Sidney (1842–81) writer, poet, musician; born in Macon, Ga. He studied at Oglethorpe University, Ga. (1857–60), was a Confederate soldier (1861–65), and contracted tuberculosis while a prisoner of war. He worked as a law clerk, then decided to devote himself to art. He moved to Baltimore where he played the flute for the Peabody Orchestra (1873–81), taught at Johns Hopkins University, and composed poems such as "Corn" and "Symphony" (1875). In addition to his poetry, which was often based on his feeling for music, he published a novel and other books on literature, versification, and music.

Lanin, Lester (1911–) band leader/contractor; born in Philadelphia, Pa. His brothers Sam Lanin and Howard Lanin were also dance band leaders and band contractors. In 1937 Lester formed his own dance band in Philadelphia, playing strict-tempo danceable music – often known as society-style because of the fashionable people who preferred it. By the late 1940s Lester had emerged as the most prominent of the Lanins, and he was asked to play at so many occasions that he had begun to contract out a series of bands under his name. (He showed up at the most important events.) He played at every U.S. presidential inaugural ball beginning with President Eisenhower's as well as at British royal weddings and other fashionable events. By 1978 he employed some 1,650 musicians in 45 bands as the Lester Lanin Music Corporation; he remained active into the 1990s. His recordings on various labels were also hits.

Lanman, Charles (1819–95) painter, writer; born in Monroe, Mich. He studied engraving with Asher B. Durand in New York City, and exhibited paintings at the National Academy. He settled in Washington, D.C. (1849), and is remembered for his publication of the *Dictionary of the United States Congress* (1859).

Lansing, Robert (1864–1928) cabinet member; born in Watertown, N.Y. An Amherst graduate, he practiced international law (1892–1915) and edited the *Journal of International Law* (1907–28). As secretary of state (1915–20), he angered the Chinese by giving Japan favorable trading rights. He did not support the League of Nations and was fired for running cabinet meetings during President Wilson's illness.

Lansky, Aaron (1955–) cultural activist; born in New Bedford, Mass. He graduated from Hampshire College (1977) and holds an M.A. from McGill University (1980). As founder of the National Yiddish Book Center in South Hadley, Mass. (1980), he rescued some 850,000 discarded Yiddish books in an effort to preserve and revitalize Yiddish culture. A winner of many awards from Jewish organizations, he received a MacArthur Fellowship in 1989.

Lanston, Tolbert (1844–1913) inventor; born in Troy, Ohio. He served in the Civil War and then became a clerk in the U.S. Pension Office (1865–87). In his spare time, he invented and patented several mechanical works. In 1887, he received the first patents for his "monotype" machine – which was really two machines for composing and casting type. He formed the Lanston Monotype Manufacturing Company and continued to make various improvements on his machines.

Lantz, Walter (1900–94) animator; born in New Rochelle, N.Y. The creator of Woody Woodpecker, he spent 50 years with Universal, winning an honorary Oscar in 1979.

Lanza, Mario (b. Alfredo Arnold Cocozza) (1921–59) tenor; born in Philadelphia. Discovered while working in the family's grocery business, he auditioned for Serge Koussevitzky in 1942 and appeared that summer at Tanglewood. His career was interrupted by service in World War II and afterward he went on to Hollywood to appear in several musicals, including his most famous role in *The Great Caruso* (1951). Never a truly disciplined artist, he refused to restrain either his personality or his appetites and died of a heart attack in Rome.

Lapchick, (Joseph Bohomiel) Joe (1900–70) basketball coach; born in Yonkers, N.Y. He played in the American Basketball League during basketball's formative years (1927–31). One of the game's greatest coaches, he coached 20 years at St. John's University between 1937 and 1965. He also coached nine seasons with the National Basketball Association New York Knicks (1948–56). He was elected to basketball's Hall of Fame in 1966.

Laporte, Otto (1902–71) physicist; born in Mainz, Germany. He came to the U.S.A. on a postgraduate fellowship to work for the National Bureau of Standards (1924–26), then became a professor at Michigan (1926–71). A pioneer in plasma physics and atomic spectroscopy, he was also a visiting professor in Japan (1928, 1937), and a science attaché with the American Embassy in Tokyo (1960–63).

LaPorte, William (Frederick) (1913–) consumer products executive; born in New York City. He joined American Home Products in 1938 and for more than 20 years in the 1960s and 1970s headed this multi-billion-dollar consumer products manufacturer. His dictatorial tenure was marked by stringent financial discipline and single-minded focus on profits; he was known for his disdain of accepted management techniques like corporate communications and strategic planning.

Lappé, Frances Moore (1944–) reformer, author; born in Pendleton, Ore. Her best-selling *Diet for a Small Planet* (1971) linked world hunger to economic injustice and urged that agriculture in developed countries shift from meat to vegetable production. She founded the Institute for Food and Development Policy (San Francisco) (1975) and wrote

and lectured widely on economic development, population, and related issues.

Lardner, John Abbott (1912–60) journalist; born in Chicago. Son of writer Ringgold (Ring) Lardner, he was a World War II correspondent and a writer on diverse subjects, noted for his light style and quiet humor.

Lardner, Ring, Jr. (1915–) screenwriter; born in Chicago. He started out as a newspaper reporter and began writing Hollywood scripts in 1937. He won an Oscar for *Woman of the Year* (1942), but during the Communist witch hunts of the 1940s he was named one of the Hollywood Ten and sentenced to a year in jail. On his release, he was blacklisted and had to write scripts under pseudonyms; he regained his true name and reputation with his script for the film *M*A*S*H* (1970).

Lardner, (Ringgold Wilmer) Ring (1885–1933) journalist, writer; born in Niles, Mich. He began as a sportswriter in 1905, and worked for several papers in Indiana, Chicago, Boston, and St. Louis. While a sportswriter and columnist for the Chicago *Tribune* (1913–19), he wrote a series of baseball short stories for the *Saturday Evening Post,* collected in a volume titled *You Know Me Al: A Busher's Letters* (1914). These satirical stories, featuring the letters of an egotistical Chicago White Sox pitcher, Jack Keefe, were praised by Virginia Woolf among many others. Lardner wrote two more books featuring Keefe – *Treat 'Em Rough* (1918) and *The Real Dope* (1919) – and several other collections of stories featuring characters from Broadway, sports, and the workaday world, including *Gullible's Travels* (1917) and *How to Write Short Stories* (1924). He also collaborated with George M. Cohan and George S. Kaufman on plays. One of America's great sardonic humorists, his use of the American vernacular – especially in a story like "Hair Cut" (1929) – has rarely been surpassed.

Larkin, Thomas Oliver (1802–58) merchant, diplomatic agent; born in Charlestown, Mass. He went to California in 1832 and became the U.S. consul to California (1844–48) and a confidential agent of the U.S. government (1845–48). On behalf of President James Polk, he launched a propaganda campaign to separate California from Mexico.

Larned, (William Augustus) Bill (1872–1926) tennis player; born in Summit, N.J. He won the U.S. lawn tennis championships seven times (1901–02, 1907–11), a record shared with two others.

Larsen, Don (James) (1929–) baseball pitcher; born in Michigan City, Ind. He was known during his 21 years in organized baseball as a colorful, old-fashioned, fun-loving player of average major league abilities. But on October 8, 1956, in the fifth game of the New York Yankees-Brooklyn Dodgers World Series, with his 97th and final pitch of the day, Larsen struck out Dodgers pinch-hitter Dale Mitchell and became the only pitcher in baseball history ever to pitch a perfect World Series game (2–0). During his career Larsen pitched for nine major league teams and had a mediocre 81–91 record. Upon retirement (1968) he became a salesman for the Blake-Moffit & Towne paper company of San Francisco.

Larsen, Jack Lenor (1927–) textile designer; born in Seattle, Wash. He started a successful firm (1953) to mass produce textiles with a handwoven quality for such commissions as Lever House and Sears Tower.

Larson, Gary (1950–) cartoonist; born in Tacoma, Wash. He is the creator of the irreverent, often anthropomorphic, sometimes macabre cartoon panels, *The Far Side,* which first appeared in syndication in 1984.

Lashley, Karl S. (Spencer) (1890–1958) psychologist; born in Davis, Va. He studied zoology at the Universities of West Virginia and Pittsburgh and was influenced by John Watson's behaviorism at Johns Hopkins (Ph.D. 1914). He held teaching and research positions at the Universities of Minnesota (1917–26) and Chicago (1929–35) and was research professor of neuropsychology at Harvard (1935–58). He directed the Yerkes Laboratories for Primate Biology in Orange Park, Fla., and made valuable contributions to the study of localization of brain function.

Lasker, Albert (Davis) (1880–1952) advertising executive, philanthropist; born in Freiburg, Germany. Raised in Texas, he joined the Chicago advertising agency, Lord and Thomas in 1898; as sole owner after 1912 he built the firm into a major agency. A gifted copy editor, he was instrumental in shifting advertising from information to persuasion. (It was Lasker who proposed the institution of an independent commissioner of baseball after the Black Sox scandal of 1919.) He dissolved the agency in 1942 (when it became Foote, Cone and Belding). He devoted himself to art collecting and philanthropy and instituted the Lasker awards for medical research and public health.

Lasker, Gabriel W. (Ward) (1912–) physical anthropologist; born in Huntington, York, England. He received his higher education in the U.S.A. (1928–45), then taught at Wayne State University (1946–82). He compared the physical characteristics of Chinese, Mexicans, and Peruvians, and wrote extensively on population genetics in Britain as traced by surnames.

Lasker, Mary (b. Woodward) (1900–94) philanthropist; born in Watertown, Wis. She worked as an art dealer and started a dress pattern line called Hollywood Patterns (1932). In 1942 she and husband Albert Lasker founded the Albert and Mary Lasker Foundation using some of the money from the sale of Albert's successful advertising agency, Lord and Thomas Company. The foundation has influenced and supported medical research and public health initiatives in a number of ways, including the coveted Albert Lasker Medical Research Awards. Much honored, she is a member of the French Legion of Honor, and she holds the 1969 American Medal of Freedom and the 1989 Congressional Gold Medal. A pink tulip was named for her to honor her urban beautification efforts in New York City and Washington, D.C.

Lassaw, Ibram (1913–) sculptor; born in Alexandria, Egypt. Born of Russian parents, he emigrated to New York City (1921) and was a founder (1936) and president (1946–49) of the American Abstract Artists group. He lived in East Hampton, N.Y. He specialized in architectural sculpture and abstract welded wire works, as in *Galactic Cluster #1* (1958).

Lasswell, Harold D. (Dwight) (1902–78) political scientist; born in Donnellson, Ill. His behavioral approach to politics included work on decision-making processes or "policy sciences" that incorporated psychology, political science, and sociology. He taught at the University of Chicago (1922–38) and at Yale Law School (1946–70).

Lathrop, Julia Clifford (1858–1932) social worker; born in Rockford, Ill. Daughter of affluent but reform-minded parents, she graduated from Vassar College (B.A. 1880) and then worked for some ten years in her father's law office. In 1890 she joined Jane Addams at the newly founded Hull House in Chicago and stayed there until 1909; her main work was not at the Chicago house itself but in visiting social welfare institutions throughout Illinois and in promoting reforms in the treatment of people in public institutions for the insane, indigent, delinquent, and children. She especially pioneered in more humane treatment of the mentally ill, and in 1899 she helped establish the first juvenile court in the U.S.A. From 1903 to 1904 she also helped organize the courses in social work that became the Chicago School of Civics and Philanthropy. After a world tour (1910–11), she was appointed the first head of the federal Childrens' Bureau (1912–21) and she made major reforms in legislation and general treatment of children. Retiring to Rockford, Ill., with her sister, she remained engaged as president of the Illinois League of Women Voters (1922–24) and served as U.S. commissioner to the Child Welfare Committee of the League of Nations (1925–31).

Lathrop, Rose Hawthorne (Mother Alphonse) (1851–1926) Catholic nun; born in Lenox, Mass. (daughter of Nathaniel Hawthorne). Raised and educated abroad, she married George Parsons Lathrop in 1871 and with him converted to Catholicism (1891); they later separated. After his death in 1898 she became a Dominican nun and founded a home for terminally ill cancer patients (eventually moved to Hawthorne, N.Y.) and a community of nuns devoted to their care. She wrote poems and other works, including (with her husband) *Memories of Hawthorne* (1897).

Latimer, Lewis Howard (1848–1928) inventor, engineer; born in Chelsea, Mass. After serving in the U.S. Navy during the Civil War, he studied drafting, eventually becoming chief draftsman for both General Electric and Westinghouse. He invented a "water closet for railroad cars" (1873) and drafted the patent drawings for Alexander Graham Bell's first telephone. In 1881 he devised a method to make a carbon filament for a light bulb made by one of Edison's competitors and then supervised that firm's installation of electric lights in New York, Philadelphia, Montreal, and London. In 1884 he went to work for Thomas Edison's company.

Latrobe, Benjamin Henry (1764–1820) architect; born in Fulneck, Yorkshire, England. Having trained in England as an engineer and then as an architect with Samuel Pepys Cockerell, Latrobe enjoyed a successful practice there before emigrating to America in 1795. His early work included the monumental Greek Revival Bank of Pennsylvania (1798–1800) and the earliest American city water system (1799–1801), both in Philadelphia. Latrobe was appointed surveyor of the U.S. Capitol (1803–17) and supervised the construction of William Thornton's plans, making interior alterations; after the burning of the Capitol by the British in 1814, he submitted new designs. He designed numerous other buildings in Washington, D.C., mastering the Federal style and spearheading the popularity of Greek Revival public architecture in America. His largest building was the Cathedral of the Assumption, Baltimore (1805–21), the first vaulted church in the U.S.A.

Lattimore, Owen (1900–89) scholar; born in Washington, D.C. He spent his boyhood in China and was educated in Europe before returning to China (1919–27), primarily to inner Asia, the subject of many of his later books. He edited *Pacific Affairs* (1934–41) (resulting in the charge by Senator Joseph McCarthy in 1950 that he had "lost" China) and taught at the Johns Hopkins University (1938–63) and the University of Leeds, England (1963–75).

Lattimore, Richmond (Alexander) (1906–84) classicist, poet; born in Paotingfu, China (to Protestant missionary parents). He was educated at Dartmouth (B.A. 1926), Christ Church, Oxford (where he was a Rhodes scholar), and the University of Illinois (Ph.D. 1935). He spent virtually his entire teaching career at Bryn Mawr (1935–84), although he held visiting appointments in the United States, England, and Greece. His many translations from Greek into English, notably *Pindar* (1947) and the *Iliad* (1951), made him the best-known and most highly regarded translator of his day. With David Greene, he edited the translation of *The Complete Greek Tragedies* (1967–68). In 1962 he won the Bollingen Translation Prize for his translation of Aristophanes's *Frogs,* and in 1984 he won the award of the American Academy of Poets.

Laubach, Frank (Charles) (1884–1970) missionary, pioneer educator; born in Benton, Pa. A Protestant missionary sent to evangelize the Moro tribespeople of the Philippines (1915–36), he began to combat illiteracy by devising his own system of phonetic symbols and pictures and by promoting his motto, "Each one teach one." As he and his work became known, he was invited by governments to introduce his methods in various countries of Southern Asia, Latin America, and India (where he overcame the initial skepticism of Mohandas Gandhi). In addition to over 200 texts in some 165 languages, he wrote *India Shall be Literate* (1940), *Teaching the World to Read* (1948), and other books.

Lauder, Estée (b. Josephine Esther Mentzer) (?1908–) beautician, business executive; born in Corona, Queens, N.Y. Her Youth Dew beauty oil (1953) launched Estée Lauder, Inc., which became a billion-dollar-a-year business selling cosmetics through top department stores; her marketing innovations included free product samples. She was married twice (1930–39, 1942–83) to Joseph Lauder, her business partner.

Laughlin, James (1914–) publisher; born in Pittsburgh, Pa. Drawing on his family's fortune (from the Jones and Laughlin Steel Co.), in 1936 he founded New Directions Press, which specializes in publishing quality literary works deemed unlikely to gain a mass audience; Dylan Thomas and Ezra Pound were among its authors.

Laughlin, William S. (Sceva) (1919–) physical anthropologist; born in Canton, Mo. He was a faculty member of several universities before joining the University of Connecticut in 1969. He compared skeletal characteristics of Eskimo-Aleuts and Indians, and wrote extensively on Aleut evolution and culture.

Laughton, Charles (1899–1962) stage and film actor; born in Scarborough, England. After working in his family's hotel business, he turned to the English stage (1926). He came to the U.S.A. (1932) to appear in Hollywood movies, and remained to star in many stage and film roles. At home in Shakespeare and modern horror pictures, he also directed and starred in such legendary productions as Shaw's *Don Juan in Hell* and Brecht's *Galileo.*

Laurance, John (1750–1810) U.S. representative/senator; born in Cornwall, England. Coming to America in 1767, he became a lawyer and the son-in-law of Alexander MacDougall. He served as judge advocate general of the Continental army during the American Revolution and

presided over the trial of Major John Andre. He was a member of the Continental Congress (1785–87). As a Federalist from New York he served in the U.S. House of Representatives (1789–93) and in the U.S. Senate (1796–1800).

Laurel, Stan See under LAUREL AND HARDY.

Laurel and Hardy movie comedy team, consisting of **Stan Laurel (b. Arthur Stanley Jefferson)** (1890–1965) movie actor; born in Ulverston, England; **and Oliver (Norvell) Hardy (Jr.)** (1892–1957) movie actor; born in Harlem, Ga. Laurel had been on stage in England and was Charlie Chaplin's understudy when his troupe toured the U.S.A. in 1910 and 1912. He began making movies with *Nuts in May* (1917). Hardy began as a singer at age eight. In 1914 he made his movie debut in *Outwitting Dad.* Although they chanced to appear in the short movie, *Lucky Dog,* in 1917, they did not form their comedy team until 1927 with *Slipping Wives.* Together for three decades, they made more than 100 films, 27 of them features. They were slapstick clowns but with their own subtle variations on the theme of their basic characters. Hardy was fat, pretentious, and blustering; Laurel was bullied, confused, and emotional. Laurel, the creative mind behind the foolishness, outlived Hardy to accept a special Oscar in 1960.

Lauren, Ralph (b. Ralph Lifshitz) (1939–) fashion designer; born in the Bronx, N.Y. As a fledgling designer, he changed his name in the mid-1950s. He founded Polo for men (1968) and Ralph Lauren women's collections (1971). His casual, expensive ready-to-wear was distinguished by classic designs and a rich mixture of fabrics, texture, and color and won him eight Coty Awards. His clothing, housewares, and accessories brilliantly evoked old money and country house life for upwardly mobile America. He became known for expensive advertising that promoted the Lauren image as well as the products.

Laurens, Henry (1724–92) merchant, Revolutionary politician; born in Charleston, S.C. A wealthy businessman, he entered the second Continental Congress in 1777 and served as its second president (1777–78). In 1780 he was captured by the British while on his way to the Netherlands on a diplomatic mission. He was imprisoned and finally exchanged for General Charles Cornwallis (1782). He immediately went on to serve at the peace conference that produced the Treaty of Paris (1783). He served as an unofficial ambassador to England until returning to his estate in South Carolina (1784).

Lauritsen, Charles C. (Christian) (1892–1968) physicist; born in Holstebro, Denmark. He came to the U.S.A. in 1917. He designed and produced radios, until R. A. Milliken influenced him to join the California Institute of Technology (1926–68). Lauritsen helped develop what was then the most powerful X-ray tube extant for cancer therapy (1928). He was a pioneer in nuclear astrophysics and rocketry for most of his career, and produced components for the atomic bomb (1944). He was an outspoken opponent of nuclear testing during the 1950s.

Lavin, Irving (1927–) art historian; born in St. Louis (husband of Marilyn Lavin). He studied at Cambridge, England (1948–49), Washington University, St. Louis (B.A. 1949), New York University (M.A. 1952), and Harvard (M.A. 1952; Ph.D. 1955). He taught at several institutions, notably at the Institute for Advanced Study, Princeton

(1973), and specialized in ancient art, and Renaissance and Baroque sculpture.

Lavin, Marilyn (b. Aronberg) (1925–) art historian; born in St. Louis (wife of Irving Lavin). She studied at Washington University, St. Louis (B.A. 1947; M.A. 1949), the Free University of Brussels (1952), and New York University (Ph.D. 1973). She taught primarily at Princeton (1975) and specialized in Italian Renaissance paintings.

Lawes, Lewis Edward (1883–1947) prison administrator, reformer; born in Elmira, N.Y. Son of a prison guard, he worked as an apprentice reporter at the Elmira (N.Y.) *Telegram,* spent three years in the army (1901–04), and worked temporarily in the insurance business until offered a position as a guard at Clinton Prison, Dannemora, N.Y. (1905). He then became a guard at New York's Auburn prison (1906) and at Elmira Reformatory (1906–15), where he was chief guard and later head records clerk. He was named overseer of the New York City Reformatory (1915) and then was allowed to establish a new reformatory at New Hampton in Orange County, N.Y. As warden of the notorious prison Sing Sing, Ossining, N.Y. (1920–41), he introduced extensive educational and recreational programs, transforming Sing Sing into one of the most progressive prisons of its time. He literally broadcast his reform message on the radio, wrote several books, and coauthored a prison melodrama that had a brief Broadway run. Pragmatic as he was humanitarian, an opponent of the death penalty who, nevertheless, presided over 302 executions, he was one of America's most liberal prison wardens.

Lawless, Theodore Kenneth (1892–1971) physician; born in Thibodaux, La. A leading dermatologist, he taught dermatology and syphilology at Northwestern Medical School (1924–41). He was one of the first physicians to use radium as a treatment for cancer. He was influential in financing African-American businesses in Chicago.

Lawrence, David (Leo) (1889–1966) mayor; born in Pittsburgh, Pa. After working for William J. Brennan, Democratic chief of Allegheny County, he became active in state and national Democratic Party affairs. He went on to serve an unprecedented four terms as mayor of Pittsburgh (1946–59). In concert with Richard K. Mellon and other civic leaders, he helped clean and build up the city. He became the first Catholic governor of Pennsylvania (1959–63). In 1963 President John F. Kennedy, whose nomination he had helped to secure, appointed him chairman of the Committee on Equal Opportunity for Housing.

Lawrence, Ernest O. (Orlando) (1901–58) physicist; born in Canton, S.D. He began his career at Yale (1925–28), then transferred to the University of California: Berkeley (1928–58). His invention of the cyclotron (1929), which accelerates atomic particles to produce artificial radioactivity fundamental to later applications in nuclear physics and medicine, won him the 1939 Nobel Prize. He produced most of the uranium used in the Hiroshima atomic bomb. The element lawrencium is named for him.

Lawrence, Jacob (Armstead) (1917–) painter; born in Atlantic City, N.J. He studied under Charles Alston at the Art Workshop, Harlem, N.Y. (1932–39), and at the Harlem Art Center and the American Artists School, New York (1937–39). Considered a leading black artist, he worked in gouache, an opaque water color, and tempera, a mixture of pigment and a binder. He lived in Brooklyn, N.Y., and is famous for the distinctive flat surfaces of his narrative paintings depicting social problems, as in *The Migration of the Negro* (1940–41), and *Struggle: From the History of the American People* (1955).

Lawrence, James (1781–1813) naval officer; born in Burlington, N.J. He served with distinction in the Tripolitan War and won a notable victory over the British *Peacock* In 1813. He was defeated and mortally wounded in the HMS *Shannon*–USS *Chesapeake* duel in the same year. His famous appeal, "Don't give up the ship!" became a rallying cry for United States sailors.

Lawrence, Paul R. (Roger) (1922–) organizational behavior educator; born in Rochelle, Ill. A Harvard M.B.A. and D.C.S., he taught at the Harvard Business School (1947), where he was named Donham professor of organizational behavior (1968). His books include *Renewing American Industry* (coauthored, 1983) and *Behind the Factory Walls* (1990).

Lawrie, Lee (O.) (1877–1963) sculptor; born in Rixdorf, Germany. When very young he and his family emigrated to Chicago. He became an assistant to Augustus Saint-Gaudens (1894) and attended Yale (B.F.A. 1910), where he later taught (1908–18). Based in Easton, Md., he is known for his numerous architectural sculptures, such as his bronze *Atlas* at the International Building, Radio City, N.Y. (c. 1939).

Laws, G. (George) Malcolm (Jr.) (1919–) folklorist; born in Philadelphia. He earned undergraduate and graduate degrees from the University of Pennsylvania, where he joined the English faculty in 1942, becoming emeritus in 1960. His work on American and British ballads and folk songs and 19th-century English literature includes *Native American Balladry* (1950, revised 1964), *American Balladry from British Broadsides* (1957), and *The British Literary Ballad* (1972).

Lawson, Andrew C. (Cowper) (1861–1952) geologist; born in Anstruther, Scotland. He came to the U.S.A. to study at Johns Hopkins while concurrently serving the Geological Survey of Canada (1882–90), then became a professor at the University of California: Berkeley (1890–1928). He made major contributions to seismology and pre-Cambrian rock classification, then devoted his research to the relationship of isostasy to mountain and deep basin formation. He was privately a poet, a collector of paintings, and a designer of earthquake-proof buildings.

Lawson, Ernest (1873–1939) painter; born in San Francisco, Calif. He studied at the Art Students League, New York, with J. Alden Weir and John Twachtman (1891), and later in Paris at the Académie Julien (1893). Upon his return to America he settled in upper Manhattan and produced his famous impressionistic urban landscapes that linked him to the Ashcan school. His typical use of thick, intense color, often applied with a palette knife, is seen in his major work, *Spring Night, Harlem River* (1913).

Lawton, Henry Ware (1843–99) soldier; born near Toledo, Ohio. A Civil War veteran, he commanded cavalry on the western plains and took part in the campaign (1885–86) that ended in Geronimo's capture. He commanded a division that fought in Cuba during the Spanish-American War and he was killed leading a division in the Philippine insurrection.

Lazarsfeld, Paul (Felix) (1901–76) sociologist; born in Vienna, Austria. He studied mathematics, law, and social psychology at the University of Vienna, where he established a social psychology research center before emigrating to the U.S.A. in 1933. At Columbia University (1940–69) he founded (1945) the Bureau of Applied Social Research. He later taught at the University of Pittsburgh (1970–76). A quantitative methodologist, he was an early researcher of the listening habits of radio audiences and of American popular culture. He became a leading authority on the mass media and voting patterns; the latter work formed the basis of modern voting projection techniques. He devised Latent Structure Analysis, a mathematical technique used in sociological analysis. His books include several regarded as classics: *The Unemployed of Marienthal* (1933), *The People's Choice* (1944), and *Voting* (1954).

Lazarus, Charles (1923–) retailing executive; born in Washington, D.C. As a young man he shifted his father's Washington retail store to toys; he created the Toys "R" Us chain, which became the country's largest toy retailer by using a sophisticated centralized information system to manage large inventories of discounted quality-brand toys. He survived bankruptcy reorganization (1978) to diversify into Kids "R" Us clothing stores (1983).

Lazarus, Emma (1849–87) poet, writer; born in New York City. Educated privately, she lived in New York City. She translated the poetry of Heinrich Heine (1881), wrote a prose romance, and composed poetry including *Songs of a Semite* (1882), an impassioned indictment of Jewish persecution during the Russian pogroms of 1879–83. She remains best known for her sonnet, "The New Colossus" (1883), which is inscribed on the base of the Statue of Liberty.

Lazear, Jesse (William) (1866–1900) physician; born in Baltimore, Md. After graduating from Columbia's medical school and working at the Pasteur Institute in Paris, he gained a reputation for his work in bacteriological research. An outbreak of yellow fever in Cuba led to his being appointed an assistant surgeon in the U.S. Army and assigned to a Yellow Fever Commission with Walter Reed, James Carroll and Aristides Agramonte. Sent to Cuba early in 1900, they investigated and soon proved that the disease was transmitted by the bite of a mosquito; however, Lazear was bitten accidentally by an infected mosquito and died, while Carroll, who had allowed himself to be bitten as part of the experiment, survived.

Lea, Henry Charles (1825–1909) historian, publisher; born in Philadelphia. He took an active role in his father's publishing house (1843–80) until he retired to devote himself to his scholarly interests. A specialist in medieval and church subjects, his *History of the Inquisition of the Middle Ages* (1888) became important (in its French translation) during the Dreyfus trial. As an advocate of reforming city government and the civil service, he received many honors in the United States, but as a historian he was better known among European scholars.

Leacock, (Richard) Ricky (1921–) documentary filmmaker; born in the Canary Islands, Spain. Born to British parents, he began making films at age 14, then came to the U.S.A. at age 17. After serving as a combat cameraman with the U.S. Army in World War II, he worked with Robert Flaherty and other important American documentary filmmakers. He was among the pioneers in using portable equipment and the *cinéma vérité* style. He founded the film department at the Massachusetts Institute of Technology. Among his best known films is *Monterey Pop* (1968).

Leadbelly See LEDBETTER, HUDDIE.

Leahy (Francis William) Frank (1908–73) football coach; born in Portland, Ore. A former Notre Dame tackle under Knute Rockne, he returned to his alma mater and won five national championships in eleven seasons (1941–53).

Leahy, William (Daniel) (1875–1959) naval officer, public official born in Hampton, Iowa. As a naval commander in World War I, he became a close friend of assistant secretary of the navy Franklin D. Roosevelt. He was chief of naval operations (1937–39), ambassador to Vichy France (1940–42), and chief of staff to Roosevelt (1942–45) and Truman (1945–49). He took part in virtually all of the top-level Allied war conferences and became admiral of the navy in 1944 – the first naval officer to achieve five-star rank since George Dewey in 1899.

Lear, Norman (Milton) (1922–) television producer; born in New Haven, Conn. After spending only one year at Emerson College in Boston, he launched a television writing career in 1950 on *The Ford Star Review*. In 1959 he formed Tandem Productions with Bud Yorkin, producing a series of successful movies as well as popular television shows. *All in the Family,* which was derived from a British television program but drew on memories of his father, was televised from 1971 to 1983; it focused on a bigoted blue-collar worker named Archie Bunker; his wife Edith, whom he called "dingbat"; his daughter Gloria; and his liberal son-in-law, Mike Stivic. It was a multiple Emmy winner and the most popular sitcom of its time. Other of his television hits include *Sanford and Son, Maude, Good Times,* and *The Jeffersons.* His syndicated soap opera satire *Mary Hartman, Mary Hartman* (1976–77) developed a cult following. He broke new television ground by introducing substantive issues, controversy, and strong language to sitcoms. An outspoken liberal, he dedicated some of his immense earnings to founding People for the American Way (1981), a group that sponsors mailings, advertisements, and other outlets to combat what it regards as threats from the extreme Right.

Lear, William (Powell) Sr. (1902–78) inventor, industrialist; born in Hannibal, Mo. Leaving home at age 16, he entered the navy and studied radio. He held over 150 patents on inventions such as the automatic pilot for planes, eight-track stereo cartridges, and the car radio. Until 1967 he was the owner of the Lear Jet Corporation, pioneers in the manufacturing of small corporate jets.

Lease, Mary Elizabeth (b. Clyens) (1853–1933) lecturer, political activist; born in Ridgway, Pa. Eventually settling with her family in Wichita, Kans., she passed the bar, lectured on women's suffrage and farmers' welfare, and stumped widely for the People's Party in the 1890s, urging American farmers to "raise less corn and more hell." Her most famous work, *The Problem of Civilization Solved* (1895), contained elements of both Marxism and racism. A fiery, uncompromising figure, she frequently feuded with other activists, and after the election of 1896, moved to New York City, where she was a political writer for the *World* and practiced law on the Lower East Side. She allied herself briefly with the Theosophists, and, for a time, with Christian Science, and she was a member of the Socialist Party from 1899.

Leavenworth, Henry (1783–1834) soldier; born in New Haven, Conn. A lawyer by training, he became a colonel during the War of 1812. While on almost continual frontier duty during 1819–34, he built Forts Leavenworth and Snelling. He died of bilious fever while trying to negotiate peace among the warring Indian tribes of the southwestern frontier.

Leavitt, Henrietta Swan (1868–1921) astronomer; born in Lancaster, Mass. She attended Radcliffe College and volunteered at the Harvard College Observatory before joining the staff in 1902. As head of the photographic photometry department until 1921, she studied the brightness of stars and showed how that variable could be used to judge their distance.

Lebrun, (Federico) Rico (1900–64) painter; born in Naples, Italy. He emigrated to Illinois (1924) as a stained glass designer, and by 1938 settled in California and worked for the Walt Disney Studios as an animator (1939). In his later work he became known for his surrealistic, often morbid subject matter, as seen in his mural, *Genesis* (1960), located at Pomona College, Claremont, Calif.

Lechford, Thomas (fl. 1629–42) lawyer; probably from Surrey, England. He was practicing law in London before 1629, emigrated to Boston in 1638, and was the first lawyer in Massachusetts Bay Colony. He opposed the prevailing politics and religion of the colonial establishment, was debarred, and returned to London in 1641 to practice law there. In 1642 he published *Plain Dealing: or Newes from New-England.*

LeClercq, Tanaquil (1929–) ballet dancer; born in Paris. Trained at the School of American Ballet, in 1946 she joined Ballet Society, which became New York City Ballet. One of its most exciting soloists, her career was cut short when she contracted polio in 1956.

LeConte, John (1818–91) scientist, teacher; born in Liberty County, Ga. (brother of geologist Joseph LeConte). Trained as a physician, he taught physics at the University of California (1869–91). The author of numerous papers, his most important contribution was the discovery of sensitive flames (1858), as well as studies of the speed of sound (1864) and underwater vibrations (1882).

Ledbetter, Huddie (real name of "Leadbelly") (?1885–1949) musician; born near Morringsport, La. A legendary singer and guitarist, he was raised near Shreveport, La., worked on farms in Texas, and began performing in Dallas, Texas, as a protégé of Blind Lemon Jefferson in the 1910s. (Leadbelly got his own nickname because of his deep bass voice.) In 1917 he was sentenced to prison on a murder conviction; eight years later he literally sang a plea of mercy to the Texas governor and was pardoned. A similar episode occurred in 1935: In 1930 he had been sentenced to ten years for wounding a group of men with a knife; in 1934 Leadbelly composed a song for the Louisiana governor, and, with the intervention of the folklorists John and Alan Lomax, won a reprieve. Over the next year, Leadbelly traveled with John Lomax and recorded hundreds of songs that formed a cornerstone of the Library of Congress folklore archives. In 1938 he moved permanently to New York City, where he recorded for Columbia Records and became a celebrated figure in literary and political circles. His best-known songs include "Irene, Good Night," "Rock Island Line," and "Midnight Special."

Lederberg, Joshua (1925–) geneticist; born in Montclair, N.J. He joined the University of Wisconsin (1947–58), moved to Stanford (1959–78), then became president of Rockefeller University (1978–90), where he remained as a professor. He shared one-half the 1958 Nobel Prize in physiology for his work as Edward Tatum's graduate student at Yale (1944–47), where he discovered that bacteria can reproduce sexually, and for his subsequent contributions to the science of bacterial genetics. His discovery of transduction in bacterial genes engendered the possibility of genetic engineering. He was a consultant for the U.S. space program, and wrote extensively on evolution and the future of humanity.

Lederer, Jerome (1902–) aerospace engineer; born in New York City. From 1929 until 1940 he was an aeronautical engineer; he then became director of the safety bureau of the Civil Aeronautics Board. Following 1947 he worked as director of safety for several organizations including the National Aeronautics and Space Administration, retiring in 1972. He wrote numerous books and articles on aviation and space safety.

Lederman, Leon M. (Max) (1922–) physicist; born in New York City. He taught and performed research at Columbia University (1951–79), before becoming director of the Fermi National Accelerator Laboratory (1979–89). He shared the 1988 Nobel Prize with Melvin Schwartz and Jack Steinberger for their discovery (1960–62) of a new subatomic particle, the muon neutrino. A prolific researcher in particle physics, Lederman retired from Fermi to teach at the University of Chicago (1989).

Ledley, Robert Steven (1926–) radiologist, inventor; born in New York City. He held a variety of research posts in government and academia before becoming a professor of radiology at the Georgetown University Medical Center in 1970. His pioneering work in the use of computers in medicine included the invention of the CT diagnostic X-ray scanner. The device made medical imaging and three-dimensional reconstructions possible, and led to improvements in radiation therapy for cancer patients.

Ledyard, John (1751–89) explorer, adventurer; born in Groton, Conn. He joined a British regiment and sailed with Captain James Cook (1776–80). Back in London, he refused to fight against the American colonists so he spent two years confined to barracks (1780–82). He had seen the possibility of a fur trade in northwestern North America and spent several years unsuccessfully trying to organize expeditions there. In 1786, he got the notion of walking across Siberia. Setting out from St. Petersburg in 1787, he was stopped by officials (under order from Empress Catherine) at Irkutsk, Siberia, in 1788. He returned to London and the next year died in Cairo while planning an expedition to the sources of the Niger River.

Ledyard, William (1738–81) soldier; born in Groton, Conn. An active patriot in the years before the American Revolution, he became a captain in the Connecticut militia in 1776. In September 1781 he surrendered Fort Griswold, Conn., after a spirited defense, and was killed, along with 85 other survivors of the battle, by British troops run amok.

Lee, Ann (b. Lees) (1736–84) religious leader, visionary; born in Manchester, England. A blacksmith's daughter, she was working in the textile mills when she joined a new group of Protestants known as "Shakers" because of their agitation during worship services. She married (1762) but the death of her four children in infancy led to self-mortification, ending in a revelation that cohabitation of the sexes was the source of all evil. By about 1770 she was dedicating herself to preaching her new gospel and was twice imprisoned; there she had a "grand vision" that was later interpreted by her followers as the "second coming of Christ." When the Shakers received a "revelation" that they should be spreading their message in New England, she and eight followers went to New York in 1774. By 1778 she and her followers had settled in Watervliet, near Albany; by then known as Mother Ann or Mother of the New Creation, she traveled throughout eastern New York State and New England to spread her message and gain converts to the Shaker faith. Imprisoned briefly in 1780 because of her pacifist teachings, she was also opposed to slavery; it was her insistence on celibacy, however, that proved both to distinguish and ultimately doom her Shaker church.

Lee, Canada (b. Leonard Lionel Cornelius Canegata) (1907–52) actor; born in New York City. He grew up in Harlem and left home at age 14, seeking to be a jockey. Failing in that, he took up boxing and won over 200 bouts (1925–30) until his eyesight was impaired. He took up acting in 1934 and played several important stage roles, including the controversial Bigger Thomas in *Native Son* (1941). He was the first African-American to play a "white" role on stage (in *The Tempest,* 1946) and he achieved success in four movies including *Body and Soul* (1947) and *Cry, The Beloved Country* (1952). He was blacklisted from radio, television and films in the Communist purge of the entertainment industry in the 1950s, primarily because of his associations with admitted Communists and left-wing organizations.

Lee, Charles (1731–82) soldier; born in Cheshire, England. A British officer and soldier of fortune who settled permanently in America in 1773, he was appointed a major general in the Continental army (1775) and participated in several actions. Taken prisoner by the British in December 1776, he was held in New York City for a year and seems to have given the British a plan to defeat the Americans. Exchanged in 1778, he was allowed to return to duty, but after he led his troops in a retreat during the battle of Monmouth, he was court-martialed (1778), found guilty on three counts, and suspended from the army for one year. Having for some time regarded George Washington as his enemy, he used his persuasive powers to gain some supporters in the Continental Congress, but after fighting a duel with Col. John Laurens, a defender of Washington's name, and writing an insulting letter to Congress, he was dismissed from the army in 1780.

Lee, David M. (Morris) (1931–) physicist; born in Rye, N.Y. A researcher and professor at Cornell University (1959), he made major contributions to condensed matter and low-temperature physics with his pioneering investigations of solid and superfluid phases of helium.

Lee, Doris (b. Embrick) (1905–86) painter; born in Aledo, Ill. She studied with Ernest Lawson at the Kansas City Art Institute (1928–29), and studied in Paris (1930). She began her work as an abstract painter, but after settling in Woodstock, N.Y., she focused on whimsical American narrative scenes, such as *Thanksgiving* (1936).

Lee, Eugene (1933–) stage designer; born in Beloit, Wis. He designed for a wide range of theaters, including the American National Theatre Academy Playhouse in New York and the Kennedy Center for the Performing Arts in Washington, D.C.

Lee, Fitzhugh (1835–1905) soldier; born in Fairfax County, Va. (nephew of Robert E. Lee). An 1856 West Point graduate, he led Confederate cavalry in the Virginia theater during the Civil War. He was governor of Virginia (1886–90), U.S. consul general to Cuba (1896–98), and commanded the U.S. VII Corps in Cuba following the Spanish-American War (1899–1901).

Lee, Gypsy Rose (b. Louise Rose Hovick) (1914–70) stripper, actress, writer; born in Seattle, Wash. Starting as a 4-year-old in vaudeville with sister June Havoc, she became the best-known stripper of the 1930s. She made some films (first as Louise Hovick) and wrote two mystery stories as well as an autobiography that was the basis of the musical, *Gypsy.* Stylish and witty, she was briefly a talk-show host (1966).

Lee, Henry (1756–1818) soldier, public official; born in Prince William County, Va. Known as "Light Horse Harry," he led a mixed force of Continental cavalry and infantry in the storming of Paulus Hook, N.J. (1779), and fought with distinction in the southern theater under Nathanael Greene. Lee composed the famous eulogy of his friend George Washington, whom he called "First in war, first in peace and first in the hearts of his countrymen." The father of Robert E. Lee, he had a poor head for business, speculated unwisely, and spent a term (1808–09) in debtors' prison.

Lee, Jason (1803–45) missionary, Oregon pioneer; born in Stanstead, Canada (then part of Vermont). He led a Methodist mission to the Flathead Indians (1834) and settled near present-day Salem, Ore. He contributed to the creation of a provisional government for Oregon (1843), then returned to his home town (1844) after being removed from leadership of his mission.

Lee, Manfred B. See under DANNAY, FREDERIC.

Lee, Ming Cho (1930–) set designer, water colorist; born in Shanghai, China. After his youth in Shanghai and Hong Kong, he attended Occidental College in Los Angeles. He served a five-year apprenticeship with Jo Mielziner, and beginning in 1958 went on to make a name for himself with his imaginative sets for scores of productions on and off Broadway, opera, and dance; for many years he was the principal designer for the New York Shakespeare Festival. He also designed the interiors of theaters and displayed his water colors.

Lee, (Nelle) Harper (1926–) writer; born in Monroeville, Ala. She attended Huntington College (1944–45), studied law at the University of Alabama (1945–49), and attended Oxford University for one year. She was an airline reservation clerk in New York City during the 1950s before returning to Monroeville. Her first and only novel, *To Kill a Mockingbird* (1960), received critical acclaim and was made into a highly successful movie in 1962.

Lee, Peggy (b. Norma Dolores Engstrom) (1920–) popular singer, songwriter, movie actress; born in Jamestown, N.D. She grew up milking cows and made her singing debut on a local radio show. She went on to sing with dance bands in the late-1930s, finally joining Benny Goodman's band, with which she recorded her first hit, "Why Don't You Do Right?" (1942). In 1944 she embarked on a successful solo career, singing in nightclubs, on television, and on recordings; eventually she gained recognition for singing with jazz combos. She also collaborated on or wrote over 500 songs. She appeared in several movies as a guest singer and/

or actress, including *The Jazz Singer* (1953) and *Pete Kelly's Blues* (1955), and was the sound track voice for such movies as *Lady and the Tramp* (1955) and *Pieces of Dreams* (1970).

Lee, Rensselaer Wright (1898–1984) art historian; born in Philadelphia. He studied at Princeton (B.A. 1920; Ph.D. 1926). He taught at many institutions, notably at Princeton (1956–66), and specialized in the Renaissance and baroque periods of art.

Lee, Rex E. (1935–) lawyer, university president; born in Los Angeles, Calif. He practiced with Jennings, Strouss & Salmon (1964–72) and was founding dean of Brigham Young University's law school (1972–81). He was the U.S. Solicitor General (1981–85). He solidified his reputation as the premier constitutional lawyer while practicing with Sidley & Austin in Washington, D.C. (1985–89), before becoming president of Brigham Young University (1989).

Lee, Richard Henry (1732–94) legislator, Revolutionary statesman; born in Westmoreland County, Va. He strenuously opposed the Stamp Act and the Townshend Acts. He became a leader of the radical wing of the Virginia House of Burgesses, where he was associated with Thomas Jefferson and Patrick Henry. In June 1776, he introduced the resolution in Congress which led directly to the drafting of the Declaration of Independence. Later, he continued to serve in Congress, but he refused to attend the Constitutional Convention (1787) and vigorously opposed the new Constitution. As a United States senator (1789–92) he worked for the ideas that were embodied in the Bill of Rights (1791).

Lee, Robert E. (Edward) (1807–70) soldier; born in Westmoreland County, Va. (son of Henry "Lighthorse Harry" Lee). His father, a Revolutionary War hero, had fallen into debt and Robert grew up in modest circumstances in Alexandria, Va. Graduating second in his West Point class of 1829 (and without a single demerit), he married a great-granddaughter of Martha Custis Washington and seems to have consciously emulated George Washington in several respects. He held assignments with the Army Corps of Engineers and then distinguished himself in combat during the Mexican War (1846–47) where he fought alongside many of the officers he would later fight against in the Civil War. He returned to duty as an engineer, served as superintendent of West Point (1852–55), transferred to the cavalry and served on the Texas frontier, and commanded the troops that put down John Brown's raid in Harpers Ferry, Va., in 1859. Lee opposed secession in 1861, but resigned from the U.S. Army in order to fight with his state of Virginia, having turned down Lincoln's offer to command U.S. forces in the field. He held a variety of posts with Confederate forces until July 1, 1862, when he succeeded Gen. Joseph E. Johnston in command of the troops soon known as the Army of Northern Virginia. He then proceeded on a series of campaigns and battles that – because of their sheer boldness, dynamism, flexibility – continue to be admired by all students of military history: the Seven Days' battles that forced the federals to retreat down the Virginia peninsula; the victory at the Second Bull Run (August 1862); the invasion of Maryland that ended in the standoff Battle of Antietam (September 1862); the great defensive victory of Fredericksburg (December 1862); and the battle known as his masterpiece, Chancellorsville (May 1863). After the latter victory he resolved upon a bold gamble, a second invasion of

the North that he hoped would end the war; after three days of savage fighting at Gettysburg (July 1863), he conceded the gamble had failed and led his badly damaged army back to Virginia. With diminishing resources, Lee fought Ulysses S. Grant's forces in a series of brilliant but costly defensive struggles; these continued through the winter of 1864–65, and by the beginning of Grant's spring offensive, Lee commanded an army doomed by the overwhelming numbers and resources of the Union; finally trapped at Appomattox Courthouse, Va., Lee surrendered on April 9, 1865, effectively ending the Confederacy's fight. Although indicted for treason, he was never tried, and he urged all Southerners to take the oath of allegiance to the United States and get on with the rebuilding of one nation. Decisive and willing to run large risks to get at "those people," as Lee called his opponents, he ranks among the greatest of battlefield commanders, although he has been faulted for a strategic short-sightedness that placed his native Virginia at the center of importance. After Appomattox he became president of Washington College (now Washington and Lee) in Lexington, Va. He died there of a heart ailment, already an object, as he would remain, of his countrymen's veneration; because of the way he conducted himself in defeat as well as in victory, he became many Americans' ideal of the gentleman Christian soldier. Among his many notable words were those as he looked over the forces at Fredericksburg before the carnage: "It is well that war is so terrible – we would grow too fond of it."

Lee, Samuel Phillips (1812–97) naval officer; born in Fairfax County, Va. (grandson of Richard Henry Lee). He commanded the North Atlantic blockading squadron (1862–64) and the Mississippi Squadron (1864–65). He became a rear admiral in 1870 and retired in 1873.

Lee, (Shelton Jackson) "Spike" (1957–) movie producer/director/actor; born in Atlanta, Ga. Growing up in a relatively well-off African-American family, he was making amateur movies by age 20 and went on to graduate from the New York University Film School in 1982. He became a director of promise with *She's Gotta Have It* (1986) and made a major move forward in both critical and popular reception with *Do The Right Thing* (1989). No stranger to controversy for certain provocative elements in both his movies and public statements, he stirred up even more than usual with his *Malcolm X* (1992). From 1992–93 he taught a course in film at Harvard University.

Lee, Sherman E. (Emery) (1918–) art historian, museum director; born in Seattle, Wash. After studying at American University (B.A. 1938, M.A. 1939) and Case Western Reserve University (Ph.D. 1941), he was a curator at the Detroit Institute of Fine Art (1941–46). Already known for his knowledge of Asian art, he served in Tokyo with the civil information and education section, Allied Powers (1946–48). He was associated with the Seattle Museum (1948–52) before joining the Cleveland Museum of Art in 1952; as its director (1958–83), he was widely credited with turning it into one of the major museums in the U.S.A. He was also on the art faculty at Case Western Reserve University (1962–83). As a scholar, his specialty was Far Eastern art and his books include *History of Far Eastern Art* (1964, revised several times).

Lee, Tsung Dao (1926–) physicist; born in Shanghai, China. He fled Japanese invaders to study at the National

Southwest University in Kunming (1945), where he first met his friend and later colleague, Chen Ning Yang. Lee came to the U.S.A. in 1946 when he was awarded a scholarship to the University of Chicago. He joined the University of California: Berkeley (1950–51), moved to the Institute for Advanced Studies (IAS), Princeton, N.J. (1951–53), then went to Columbia University (1953), becoming, at age 29, their youngest full professor (1956–60). While at Columbia in the early 1950s, Lee worked jointly with Yang, then at IAS, to challenge and disprove the seemingly irrefutable parity conservation principle that subatomic particles and their mirror images obey the same physical laws. This revolutionary achievement won Lee and Yang the 1957 Nobel Prize in physics. Lee returned to IAS (1960–63), then continued his research at Columbia (1963) to further investigate parity nonconservation, relativity, creation of superdense matter (1974), statistical mechanics, and gravity. A humble and reserved scientist, he stated that thinking left him no time for hobbies.

Lee, Willis A. (Augustus), Jr. (1888–1945) naval officer; born in Natlee, Ky. The highlight of his naval career (1904–45) was his command of the South West Pacific task force during the naval battle of Guadalcanal (November, 1942). He used radar to defeat the Japanese in a night battle.

Lee, Yuan T. (1936–   ) chemist; born in Hsinchu, Taiwan. He came to the United States in 1962. Working with Dudley Herschbach at the University of California: Berkeley, he designed the crossed-molecular-beam apparatus that hastened the understanding of chemical reactions. He shared the Nobel Prize in chemistry (1986) for his contributions concerning dynamics of elementary chemical processes.

Leeser, Isaac (1806–68) rabbi, author; born in Neuenkirchen, Westphalia (now Germany). He came to the U.S.A. in 1824. Founder of the first Hebrew school in Philadelphia and of Maimonides Training College, he was editor of *The Occident and Jewish Advocate,* a strong voice in Conservative Judaism. He translated the Hebrew Bible into English (1853) and was the first rabbi to preach in English.

Leffel, James (1806–66) inventor; born in Botetourt County, Va. Taken to Ohio as an infant, he grew up on the frontier and received only intermittent schooling. As a young man he designed, built, and operated a water-powered sawmill near Springfield, Ohio. Over the years he perfected several improved types of waterwheel. He also patented two types of cooking stoves and achieved local fame as a breeder of poultry.

Lefkowitz, Mary Rosenthal (1935–   ) classicist; born in New York City. She was educated at Wellesley (B.A. 1957) and Radcliffe (Ph.D. 1961) and was professor of Greek and Latin at Wellesley (1975). Along with Sarah Pomeroy's *Goddesses, Whores, Wives and Slaves: Women in Classical Antiquity* (1975), Lefkowitz's *Women in Greece and Rome* (1977), *Heroines and Hysterics* (1981), and *Women's Life in Greece and Rome* (1982) were among the first influential works published in the field of women's history in antiquity.

Lefrak, Samuel J. (Jayson) (1918–   ) real estate developer; born in New York City. He joined his father's Brooklyn construction firm, expanding the Lefrak Organization (president 1948, chairman 1975) through the construction of such major housing, industrial, and commercial developments as King's Bay Houses, Brooklyn (1957), Lefrak City, Queens (1960), and later urban renewal projects. The owner of 94,000 New York apartments, he was long the city's largest private residential landlord.

Lefschetz, Solomon (1884–1972) mathematician; born in Moscow, Russia. He emigrated to America to work as an engineer (1905). Obtaining a Ph.D. (1911), he taught longest at Princeton (1924–53) and chaired its mathematics department (1945–53). Best known for linking topology to algebraic geometers, he also contributed to fixed-point theory and differential equations. Editor of *Annals of Mathematics* (1928–58), editor/founder of the *Journal of Differential Equations,* he was an author of math texts and founded a math center (1957) that was later moved to Brown University and named the Lefschetz Center for Dynamical Systems.

Le Gallienne, Eva (1899–1991) stage actress; born in London, England. Making her stage debut in London at age 15, she came to the U.S.A. the next year and thereafter spent most of her professional career in America, as both a versatile actress in serious plays and as an intelligent director and producer. She founded the Civic Repertory Theatre in New York (1926–32) and later the American Repertory Theater Company. In addition to translations and stage adaptations, she published her memoirs and a study of Eleonora Duse.

Legaré, Hugh Swinton (1797–1843) lawyer, public official; born in Charleston, S.C. Left permanently crippled after a childhood bout with smallpox, he graduated first in his class at the University of South Carolina, studied law in Europe, and served several terms in the state legislature in the 1820s. He opposed Calhoun and nullification in 1828. A man of wide learning and broad views, he served as coeditor of the influential *Southern Review* (1828–32). He served two years as his state's attorney general (1830–32), sat in the U.S. House of Representatives (Whig, 1837–39); and was attorney general in President Tyler's cabinet (1841–43).

LeGuin, Ursula (b. Kroeber) (1929–   ) writer; born in Berkeley, Calif. (daughter of Alfred Kroeber). She studied at Radcliffe (B.A. 1951) and Columbia University (M.A. 1952). She taught French at Mercer University, Ga. (1954–55) and at the University of Idaho (1956). She was a visiting lecturer and writer at many institutions, and her writing includes novels, children's books, poetry, and short stories. Based in Portland, Ore., she is best known for her science fiction/fantasy novels, notably *The Left Hand of Darkness* (1969) and *The Earthsea Trilogy* (1968–72).

Lehman, Adele Lewisohn (1882–1965) philanthropist, art collector, painter; born in New York City (daughter of Adolph Lewisohn). She studied at Barnard (1900) and married Arthur Lehman, an investment banker (1901). She became active in the Federation of Jewish Philanthropies, of which her husband was a founder; after he died she founded the Arthur Lehman Counseling Service to help people needing psychiatric services. Herself an heiress, her philanthropies extended to many activities, from the woman suffrage movement to handicapped children. She and her husband collected Italian art works, many of which became part of various museum collections. She also painted landscapes and still lifes.

Lehman, Herbert (Henry) (1878–1963) banker, governor, U.S. senator, philanthropist; born in New York City. He became a partner in his family's banking business in 1908 and served the government in various capacities during World War I. After serving as lieutenant governor of New York (1929–33) he succeeded Franklin Roosevelt as governor

(1933–42) and combined fiscal benefits with liberal legislation. During World War II he directed the United Nations Relief and Rehabilitation Administration (1943–46). He served in the U.S. Senate (Dem., N.Y.; 1949–57) and was outspoken in his opposition to McCarthyism and in support of civil rights. Among his various philanthropies were child welfare and Jewish resettlement programs.

Lehman, Robert (1891–1969) banker, art collector; born in New York City (son of Philip Lehman). He studied at Yale (B.A. 1913), managed his father's art collection (1913–17), served in the army (1917–19), and joined the family banking business, Lehman Brothers (1919). He became principal partner (1921–64), and financed a variety of major enterprises, such as department stores, airlines, and movie and television companies. A generous art patron, he lived in New York City and Long Island. His art collection – strong in Gothic tapestries and European paintings among other works – was donated to the Metropolitan Museum of Art (1969), where it is displayed in a replica of his New York apartment.

Lehmann, Karl (1894–1960) classical archaeologist; born in Rostock, Germany. He received his Ph.D. from the University of Berlin, then taught in Berlin and Heidelberg. During World War I he was an interpreter for the Turkish navy. In 1935 he began teaching at the Institute of Fine Arts at New York University. He became a U.S. citizen in 1944. Beginning in 1938 he directed the expedition to excavate the ancient Greek sanctuary at Samothrace. In 1954 he directed the building of a museum there. He wrote the definitive work on Trajan's Column (1926), a book on ancient ports, and several books on Samothrace, including *Samothrace: a Guide to the Excavations and the Museum* (1960).

Lehmann, Phyllis (b. Williams) (1912–) classical archaeologist; born in New York City. She graduated from Wellesley College (1934) and received her Ph.D. from New York University (1943). She taught at Smith College from 1946 until her retirement in 1978. She was assistant field director of the excavations in Samothrace, of which her husband, Karl Lehmann, was director. She wrote a number of books, articles, and catalogs for exhibitions of classical art. With her husband, she wrote *Samothracian Reflection: Aspects of the Revival of the Antique* (1973).

Lehmer, Derrick Henry (1905–) mathematician; born in Berkeley, Calif. A Cambridge University professor (1940–72) and professor emeritus of mathematics at the University of California: Berkeley (1972), he is known for work in numbers theory, computing devices, mathematical tables, and other aids to computation.

Lehninger, Albert L. (Lester) (1917–86) biochemist; born in Bridgeport, Conn. He taught at the Universities of Wisconsin (1942–45) and Chicago (1945–52) before moving to Johns Hopkins (1952–86). In 1948, Lehninger and E. P. Kennedy discovered that cellular organelles called mitochondria are the main sites of cell respiration. An authority on cellular energy systems, he made major contributions to enzymology, the bioenergetics of normal and cancer cells, and the results of calcification. He was the author of many textbooks on biochemistry, including the well-known *Biochemistry: The Molecular Biology of Cell Structure,* which sold over 600,000 copies.

Lehrer, (James Charles) Jim (1934–) television journalist; born in Wichita, Kans. A former *Dallas Morning News*

reporter and *Dallas Times Herald* editor, he joined the Public Broadcasting Service in 1972, creating with Robert MacNeil an award-winning, hour-long alternative to network news, the *MacNeil/Lehrer Report.* He is known for his low-key, informal broadcast style. He also turned to writing, publishing several novels, such as *Short List* (1992), and plays, including *Church Key Charlie Blue* (1987).

Leib, Michael (1760–1822) physician, U.S. representative/ senator; born in Philadelphia. A surgeon, he served in the U.S. House of Representatives (Dem.-Rep., Pa.; 1799–1806) and U.S. Senate (1809–14). He was known for attacking his political opponents and their policies so fiercely that he ended up hurting his own party.

Leibenstein, Harvey (1922–) economist; born in Yanishpol, Ukraine, U.S.S.R. Emigrating as a child to Canada, he came to the U.S.A. to attend Northwestern University. After teaching positions at Illinois Institute of Technology, Princeton, and the University of California: Berkeley, he joined the faculty of Harvard (1967), taking emeritus status in 1989. He also served in numerous other capacities; he was a visiting scholar or professor at many foreign universities and consultant to international and national organizations. His early work focused on development economics, especially in backward economies and in relation to population growth; he summed up his groundbreaking ideas in *Economic Backwardness and Economic Growth* (1957). His major contribution to economic theory was his "X-efficiency factor," which took into account such elements as managerial skills and labor relations to explain productivity. First advanced in 1966, his theory was fully set forth in *Beyond Economic Man* (1976) and has since been applied to business organizations.

Leiber, Jerry (1933–) lyricist, producer; born in Baltimore, Md.; **and Stoller, Mike** (1933–) composer, producer; born in Belle Harbor, N.Y. They met as teenagers, shared an affinity for African-American music, and began writing popular rock classics of the 1950s and 1960s such as "Kansas City" (1951) and "Stand By Me" (1961). They also wrote the music and title songs for several Elvis Presley films including *Jailhouse Rock* (1957). As producers they were instrumental in fusing traditional black rhythm-and-blues with popular music styles and using Latin percussion and strings.

Leidy, Joseph (1823–91) zoologist, paleontologist; born in Philadelphia. He was a trained medical doctor and professor of anatomy at the University of Pennsylvania (1853–91). A scientist of unusual range, Leidy published a classic anatomical text and important works on parasitology and protozoa. In addition he is regarded (along with Edward Drinker Cope and O. C. Marsh) as a founder of American vertebrate paleontology; dismayed by his colleagues' contentiousness, however, he abandoned that field after publishing his major work, "The Extinct Mammalian Fauna of Dakota and Nebraska" (1869).

Leighly, John (Barger) (1895–1986) geographer; born in Adams County, Ohio. He taught at the University of California: Berkeley (1923–60). He published widely on a variety of subjects, with his work in meteorology and climatology gaining special attention. He edited *Land and Life: A Selection from the Writings of Carl Ortwin Sauer* (1963, 1967).

Leinsdorf, Erich (1912–93) conductor; born in Vienna, Austria. After musical studies in Vienna, he became an assistant to Bruno Walter and Toscanini at the Salzburg Festival (1934–37). He came to New York in 1938 to conduct at the Metropolitan Opera and was especially acclaimed for his Wagner. He conducted the Rochester Philharmonic from 1947–56, the New York City Opera and Metropolitan from 1955–62, and the Boston Symphony from 1962–69; the latter were his most notable years. He then guest-conducted widely.

Leisler, Jacob (1640–91) colonial leader; born in Frankfurt, Germany. He led a rebellion in New York City during the period following the Glorious Revolution in England (1689–91). As the unofficial chief executive of New York, he called the first intercolonial congress in 1690 to oppose possible French incursions. Following the arrival of English soldiers in 1691, he was tried, convicted of treason, and hanged.

Lejeune, John A. (Archer) (1867–1942) marine officer; born in Pointe Coupee Parish, La. A brilliant combat commander and a reforming commandant, this rugged, charismatic marine oversaw the corps' conversion in the 1920s from a colonial police agency into a modern expeditionary force. The son of a sugar planter, he graduated from the U.S. Naval Academy in 1888, served in Panama and the Philippines and in command of marine detachments at sea, and in 1914 led the marine brigade that assisted in the capture of Vera Cruz, Mexico. In 1918, he took command of the 2nd Infantry Division of the American Expeditionary Force and led it in the battles of St. Mihiel, Blanc Mont, and the Meuse-Argonne. Appointed commandant of the corps in 1920, he developed amphibious doctrine and tactics that were to be applied in the great Pacific campaigns of World War II. He retired in 1929 to become superintendent of the Virginia Military Institute (1929–37).

Leland, Charles Godfrey (Hans Breitmann, pen name) (1824–1903) writer; born in Philadelphia. He studied at the College of New Jersey (now Princeton) (1841–45), and in Heidelberg, Munich, and Paris. He returned to Philadelphia, and after studying law he turned to a career as a journalist for periodicals in New York, Boston, and Philadelphia. While he was the editor of *Graham's Magazine* in 1857, he published a German dialect poem, "Hans Breitmann's Party." This was so well received that he continued to write other verses and ballads under his pen name; several collections were published, such as *Hans Breitmann About Town* (1869). He was also an advocate of introducing industrial and craft arts into American schools. From 1869 on he lived mostly in Europe; he settled in London (1884) and died in Florence, Italy. An accomplished linguist and historian, he wrote on a variety of subjects, including books on the gypsies of Europe and on the ancient Etruscans; he was also known for his translations of Heine's works.

LeMay, Curtis (Emerson) (1906–90) aviator; born in Columbus, Ohio. Commissioned in 1928 from the Reserve Officers' Training Corps at Ohio State University, he earned a reputation as an excellent pilot during the 1930s. From August 1944 he commanded the heavy bomber force that carried out long-range attacks on the Japanese home islands; he helped plan the atomic bomb missions of August 1945. He directed the U.S. airlift of supplies to Berlin in 1948, he led the Strategic Air Command, and he served as Air Force chief of staff (1961–65). An outspoken "hawk" on Vietnam, he ran for vice-president on George Wallace's independent ticket in 1968.

Lemke, William (Frederick) (1878–1959) U.S. representative; born in Albany, Minn. Son of a homesteader, he practiced law in Fargo, N.D. (1905–20) where he joined the populist Nonpartisan League to create institutions that would benefit small farmers. He turned to business after conservatives attacked the league and had a second political career in the U.S. House of Representatives (Rep., N.D., 1933–59) where he sponsored the Farm Mortgage Moratorium Act of 1935. An isolationist, he supported conservation measures after the war.

Lemmon, (John Uhler, III) Jack (1925–) movie actor; born in Boston, Mass. At Harvard College he appeared in the Hasty Pudding Club shows. After Navy service, he went to New York City where he found work as a radio actor, in off Broadway productions, and on television. He first came to wider acclaim in a Broadway revival of *Room Service* (1953) and he made his movie debut in *It Should Happen to You* (1954). He went on to make a long series of popular movies, winning an Oscar as best supporting actor in *Mister Roberts* (1955) and as best actor in *Save the Tiger* (1973). Moving deftly between comic and serious roles, he proved to be one of Hollywood's most versatile and personable actors. He also returned to Broadway as the father in O'Neill's *Long Day's Journey into Night* (1986).

LeMond, (Gregory James) Greg (1961–) bicycle racer; born in Lakewood, Calif. He began to cycle in 1975 and dropped out of high school to pursue his sport professionally. He went to Europe as a member of the U.S. national cycling team (1980). He won the Tour de France in 1986, the first American ever to win the grueling 2,500-mile event. He suffered multiple wounds in a hunting accident (1987) but recovered and won the Tour de France again in 1989 and 1990. He and his family divided their time between Minnesota and Belgium.

L'Enfant, Pierre Charles (1754–1825) architect, city planner; born in Paris, France. He trained as an artist at the Royal Academy of Painting and Sculpture, Paris, and came to America in 1777 to fight the British in the American Revolution. In New York after 1786, he designed ceremonial and monumental works, introducing symbolic and allegorical European decorative motifs to America; he remodeled Federal Hall (1788–89), where Washington took the presidential oath. At George Washington's invitation he submitted a plan (1791) for the new federal capital in the District of Columbia; its integration of the natural features of the site and the symbolism and placement of the major buildings made it an influential model of urban planning and helped popularize the Federal style. Although L'Enfant's output was modest and he spent his last years in straitened circumstances, his plan for the capital assured his reputation for posterity.

L'Engle, Madeleine (b. Camp) (1918–) writer; born in New York City. She graduated from Smith College (1941), worked in the theater in New York (1941–47), taught school for many years, and remained in New York City. By 1960 she began her career as a novelist for young readers, and became famous for her moral fantasies, such as *A Wrinkle in Time* (1962).

Lenox, James (1800–80) book collector, philanthropist; born in New York City. A wealthy merchant and real estate investor, he amassed an impressive collection of Bibles, 15th-century books, and art, which he donated to the Lenox

Library in New York City (incorporated in 1870, and now a part of the New York Public Library). He also donated large funds and gifts of land to churches and other institutions.

Lenski, Gerhard E. (Emmanuel, Jr.) (1924–) sociologist; born in Washington, D.C. He earned undergraduate and graduate degrees at Yale and taught at the Universities of Michigan (1950–63) and North Carolina (1963–73). His books include *Human Societies* (coauthored, 1960, frequently revised) and *Power and Privilege* (1966).

Lenz, Sidney (Samuel) (1873–1960) games expert; born in Chicago. A prosperous lumberman who retired at age 31, he won an unmatched 1,100 whist prizes, innumerable table-tennis tournaments, and the first national auction-bridge title, and was considered the country's best amateur magician. His first book, *Lenz on Bridge* (1926), was a best-seller.

Leonard, Elmore (John, Jr.) (1925–) writer; born in New Orleans. He studied at the University of Detroit (Ph.B. 1950). He was a copywriter in Detroit (1950–61), and a writer of educational and industrial films (1961–63). He founded the Elmore Advertising Company (1963–66) before turning to writing full-time. He began by writing Western novels, then concentrated on hard-boiled crime novels, such as *Glitz* (1985). He lived in Birmingham, Mich.

Leonard, (Walter Fenner) "Buck" (1907–) baseball player; born in Rocky Mount, N.C. As a first baseman for the Homestead Grays (1934–50), he was known as the "Lou Gehrig" of the black baseball leagues. Teamed with Josh Gibson, he helped the Grays win the Negro National League pennant nine years in a row (1937–45). A solid .340 hitter with power, he was elected to baseball's Hall of Fame in 1972.

Leone, Mark P. (Paul) (1940–) anthropologist, archaeologist; born in Waltham, Mass. A University of Arizona Ph.D., he joined the faculty of the University of Maryland (1976). He published a number of works on contemporary American religions including *Roots of Modern Mormonism* (1979). As an archaeologist he is best known for his detailed analyses of pre-Columbian residence patterns and what they reveal about social organization and interaction.

Leontief, Wassily W. (1906–) economist; born in St. Petersburg, Russia. Emigrating to the U.S.A. in 1931, he joined the faculty at Harvard (1931–75). From 1975 to 1984 he was director of the Institute of Economic Analysis at New York University. His interest was narrowly focused on the development and refinement of input-output analysis. A promoter of the importance of raw data, he used it to show how the economy is broken into sectors; by systematically recording the flows of goods and services among industries, he explained their interrelationships. He received, among other honors, the Nobel Prize in economics (1973).

Leopold, (Rand) Aldo (1887–1948) conservationist, ecologist; born in Burlington, Iowa. He grew up a sportsman and a naturalist, graduated from Yale in 1908, and after a year in Yale's forestry school, joined the U.S. Forest Service. Assigned to the Arizona-New Mexico district, he spent 15 years in the field, rising to chief of the district. By 1921 he had begun to campaign for the preservation of wildlife areas for recreational and aesthetic purposes. (In 1924 the government, adopting his views on preservation, set aside 574,000 acres in New Mexico as the Gila Wilderness Area – the first of 78 such areas totaling 14,000,000 acres.) He was with the U.S. Forest Products Laboratory from 1924–28 and then spent three years surveying game populations in the north-central states. In

1933 he became professor of wildlife management at the University of Wisconsin, a position created specifically for him. Over the years, in addition to his pioneering research in game management, he worked out a philosophical concept he called "the land ethic." The concept, he wrote, "simply enlarges the boundaries of the (human) community to include soils, waters, plants, and animals, or collectively the land." After retiring from the university he bought a farm in the Wisconsin Dells. There, after several years of intense observation, he expanded his philosophy in a book, *A Sand County Almanac* (published posthumously in 1949), which became the "bible" of environmental activists of the 1960s and 1970s. He died of a heart attack while fighting a brush fire on a neighbor's farm.

Lerner, Alan Jay (1918–86) lyricist, librettist; born in New York City. Son of a wealthy owner of a women's clothing store chain, he enjoyed the privileges of a cultured family. He began piano lessons at age five and wrote his first songs as a teenager, but his father planned for him to enter the diplomatic service. While at Harvard he contributed to the Hasty Pudding Club Shows in 1938 and 1939; during the summers of 1936 and 1937 he studied at Juilliard. An accident in a boxing match cost him sight in his left eye, and after graduation (1940) he went to New York City determined to write for the theater. He wrote radio scripts and contributed to satirical revues, and in 1942 he met composer Frederick Loewe. They began their collaboration on such hit musicals as *Brigadoon* (1947), *My Fair Lady* (1956), and *Gigi* (1958). Lerner also collaborated on other works, writing the libretto and lyrics for *Love Life* (1948), music by Kurt Weill, and the screenplay for *An American in Paris* (1951). He rejoined Loewe for *Camelot* (1960) but they had a falling-out and went their own ways. Lerner wrote the words for two other musicals, *On A Clear Day You Can See Forever* (1965) and *Coco* (1969). He rejoined Loewe in 1973 to make a stage version of their film musical, *Gigi,* and then for their last collaboration, *The Little Prince* (1974). Lerner's final musicals were not successful but he had earned his place as one of the most meticulous wordsmiths in the history of American musicals.

L'Esperance, Elise (b. Strang) (?1878–1959) physician, pathologist, clinic founder; born in Yorktown, N.Y. Best known for her work in cancer on women and cancer prevention, she founded several New York clinics, both individually and with her sister May Strang (d. 1952), to address these problems. Three clinics, staffed entirely by women, provided the first organized attempts to prevent cancer through testing and early diagnosis of seemingly healthy women. The Strang clinics quickly spawned similar cancer-prevention clinics for women nationwide and made acceptable the "Pap" smear for diagnosis of cervical cancer. She was affiliated with Cornell University for 40 years (1910–50), and was finally named a full clinical professor of preventive medicine before retiring in the early 1950s. Involved in promoting equality for women in medicine, she was active in several women's medical associations. She was editor of the *Medical Woman's Journal* (1936–41) and the first editor of the *Journal of the American Medical Women's Association* (1946–48). She raised and showed hackney horses for sport and collected unique carriages.

Le Sueur, Meridel (b. Wharton) (1900–) writer; born in Murray, Iowa. She was adopted by her stepfather, Alfred Le

Sueur, and she attended high school in Fort Scott, Kans., and studied at the American Academy of Dramatic Art. She worked in Hollywood as a stuntwoman and actress, then returned to the Midwest. She worked as a journalist, labor reporter, and as a writing instructor at the University of Minnesota. A social and cultural activist, she was blacklisted during the McCarthy era. Her work has been rediscovered by feminist readers, and she is honored for her poetry, essays, short stories, a biography of her parents, and novels such as *The Girl* (1939).

Letterman, David (1947–) television comedian; born in Indianapolis, Ind. He studied radio and television at Ball State University (Muncie, Ind.) (B.A. 1970), then worked as a television weatherman and radio talk-show host in Indiana before coming to New York to write comedy material for several major television comedians and specials. He became well known as a brash guest host for Johnny Carson on the *Tonight Show* during the 1978–80 seasons. His own weekly *David Letterman Show* on NBC-TV in 1980 failed to take off, but in 1982 NBC-TV gave him the time slot following Johnny Carson: *Late Night with David Letterman* soon became popular with young people by mixing the usual talk-show ingredients of celebrity guests and music with his irreverent manner and zany comic stunts. After NBC-TV rejected him as the replacement for the retiring Johnny Carson, in 1993 he moved to CBS-TV to host the *Late Show with David Letterman*.

Letterman, Jonathan (1824–72) surgeon; born in Canonsburg, Pa. An army surgeon, he tended soldiers injured during skirmishes with Native Americans (1849–62). Between 1862–64, he served as medical director of the Union's Army of the Potomac; his organization of the medical field service, including mobile hospitals and ambulances, laid the foundations for armies since then. In private practice in San Francisco following the war, he wrote *Medical Recollections of the Army of the Potomac* (1866).

Leuchtenburg, William E. (Edward) (1922–) historian; born in Ridgewood, N.Y. Educated at Cornell (B.A. 1943) and Columbia (Ph.D 1951) Universities, he taught at Smith College, Harvard, Columbia (1952–75), and the University of North Carolina: Chapel Hill (1982). A participant in 20th-century liberal Democratic politics as well as historian, he received Bancroft and Francis Parkman prizes for *Franklin D. Roosevelt and the New Deal, 1932–40* (1963). He held executive positions with the Americans for Democratic Action (1948–49); was a delegate at the 1952 Democratic National Convention; elections analyst for the National Broadcasting Company (1962, 1964, 1968, 1972); member of the National Study Commission on Records and Documents of Federal Officials (1975–77); and served as adviser to the Social Security Administration and on the editorial advisory boards of *Political Science Quarterly* and *American Heritage*.

Leutze, Emanuel (Gottlieb) (1816–68) painter; born in Gmünd, Germany. He emigrated to America (1825), but went back to Europe many times to study (1841–c. 1861). When he returned, he lived in New York and Washington, D.C. His famous historical paintings have been reproduced countless times, especially *Washington Crossing the Delaware* (1851). His popular mural, *Westward the Course of Empire Takes Its Way* (1862), is in the Capitol, Washington, D.C.

Levant, Oscar (1906–72) pianist, actor; born in Pittsburgh, Pa. He studied piano with Sigismund Stojowski and composi-

tion with Schoenberg, but his close friendship with Gershwin was the determining factor in his career; he became one of the foremost Gershwin interpreters and an occasional composer. At the same time, Levant had an active career as a screen and radio humorist and author; his films include *An American in Paris* (1951), and his books include *Memoirs of an Amnesiac* (1965).

Leveille, Gilbert A. (1934–) food scientist; born in Fall River, Mass. He researched protein and lipid metabolism for the U.S. Army Medical Research and Nutrition Laboratory (1960–66) before joining the faculty at the University of Illinois: Urbana (1966–71) where he continued researching obesity. In 1971 he moved to Michigan State University (1971–80) where he established the Department of Food Science and Nutrition. He joined General Foods Corporation (1980–86) and then the Nabisco Foods Group (1986). His books include *Nutrients in Foods* (1983) and *The Setpoint Diet* (1985).

Levertov, Denise (1923–) poet; born in Ilford, Essex, England. Educated privately, she emigrated to America in 1948. She taught at many institutions, notably at Stanford (1982), and is known for her poetry of political and social activism, as in *Candles in Babylon* (1982).

Levi, Edward H. (Hirsch) (1911–) attorney general, university president; born in Chicago. Considered a "product of the University of Chicago," he was the grandson of Rabbi Emil G. Hirsch, one of the school's early faculty members. He began teaching at Chicago (1936) and returned to the school (1945) after serving as special assistant to the United States attorney general. He was an adviser to the so-called "Chicago school" of physicists and assisted in the drafting of the U.S. Atomic Energy Act (1946), leading to establishment of the Atomic Energy Commission. Considered a brilliant antitrust lawyer, he became dean of the University of Chicago Law School (1950–62), university provost (1962–67), and president (1967–75), one of the first scholars of the Jewish faith to be chosen head of a major American university. In the aftermath of the Watergate scandals, he was persuaded to help restore Americans' respect for government by serving as the U.S. attorney general (1975–77). He was the author of many books and articles.

Levi, Isaac (1930–) philosopher; born in New York City. After earning a doctorate from Columbia University (1957) and teaching at Case Western Reserve (1957–62, 1964–70) and City College of New York (1962–64), he became a professor at Columbia in 1970. His main interests were the philosophies of science and social science. His works include *Gambling With Truth* (1967).

Levi-Montalcini, Rita (1909–) neurobiologist; born in Turin, Italy. While a practicing physician, she resisted German occupation by hiding in Florence and aiding war refugees (1943–45). She taught at the University of Turin (1945–47), then came to the U.S.A. to join Washington University (St. Louis) (1947–77). Her studies of nerve growth factor, isolated in 1952 from cultures of mouse tumor cells, won Levi-Montalcini and collaborator Stanley Cohen the 1986 Nobel Prize in physiology or medicine. She divided her time between the U.S.A. and the National Research Council in Rome (1961–89), then moved to Rome permanently to be with her twin sister (1989).

Levin, Harry (Tuchman) (1912–94) scholar, literary critic; born in Minneapolis, Minn. Precocious as an undergraduate at Harvard, he never bothered with a Ph.D. but stayed on as professor of comparative literature (1939–83). Noted for his somewhat mannered style, he wrote perceptively on Elizabethan drama, the modern novel, and French literature. He was also famous for his highly composed lectures: once, as a guest lecturer at Oxford, he timed his quoting of the line from Marlowe's *Dr. Faustus* about the clock striking so that it came just as Christ Church College's "Great Tom" struck noon.

Levine, Arthur E. (Elliot) (1948–) educator, academic administrator; born in New York City. He was senior fellow at Carnegie Council on Policy Studies in Higher Education (University of California: Berkeley) (1975–80); senior fellow of the Carnegie Foundation (1980–82); president of Bradford (Mass.) College (1982–89); and chair of the Institution of Education Management, Harvard (1989). His books include *Reform of Undergraduate Education* (coauthored, 1973), *Why Innovation Fails* (1980), and *Shaping Higher Education's Future* (1989).

Levine, David (1926–) caricaturist; born in New York City. He studied at the Hans Hofmann School in New York, and became best known as an illustrator for the *New York Review of Books, New York Magazine* and *Esquire.* Considered the most influential caricaturist after Al Hirschfeld, he worked in pen and ink and watercolor, and produced revealing portraits of public figures.

Levine, Jack (1915–) painter; born in Boston, Mass. He studied at the Boston Museum School (1929), moved to New York City, and painted scenes of social comment and protest. His satirical cautionary attitude, conveyed through an exaggerated baroque surrealism, is seen in *The Feast of Pure Reason* (1937), and in *Gangster's Funeral* (1952–53). He also painted works dealing with contemporary Jewish life.

Levine, James (1943–) conductor; born in Cincinnati, Ohio. From a musical family, he studied piano in childhood and soloed with the Cincinnati Symphony at age ten. After studies in piano and conducting at the Juilliard School of Music (from 1961), he became assistant conductor of the Cleveland Orchestra. He made his opera debut conducting *Tosca* at the Metropolitan Opera in 1971; two years later he became the house's principal conductor and in 1976 its music director. In that position he built the Met orchestra into one of the finest in the world, and he guest-conducted orchestras and opera companies internationally.

Levine, Lena (1903–65) psychiatrist, gynecologist; born in New York City. An early advocate in the 1920s and 1930s of family planning, she promoted sex education, egalitarian marriages, and contraception. A Freudian from the early 1940s, she counseled women in New York City and wrote widely on such subjects as menopause, frigidity, and sexual relations in marriage.

Levine, Philip (1928–) poet; born in Detroit, Mich. He studied at Wayne State University (B.A. 1950; M.A. 1955), the University of Iowa (M.F.A. 1957), and Stanford (1957). He taught at California State University: Fresno (1981), edited and translated volumes of poetry, and won many awards for his own work. He is known for his spare, reflective poetry, as in *What Work Is* (1991).

Levine, Philip (1900–87) immunohematologist; born in Kletsk, Russia. He came to Brooklyn with his parents in 1908. He was a research assistant at the Rockefeller Institute (1925–32), where, in 1928, he and Nobel laureate Karl Landsteiner codiscovered the M, N, and P human blood groups. Levine taught and performed bacteriological research at the University of Wisconsin (1932–35), was a bacteriologist and serologist at Beth Israel Hospital, Newark, N.J. (1935–44), and actively endorsed laws ordering blood tests for paternity at both institutions. In 1940, with Landsteiner and Alexander Weiner, he discovered the Rh factor in human blood and was the first to publish results of subsequent research on fetal-maternal isoimmunization due to this factor. He became director (1944–66), emeritus director (1966–75), then consultant (1975–85) at the Ortho Research Foundation, Raritan, N.J., whose immunohematology division was renamed the Philip Levine laboratories shortly after his arrival.

Levine, Stephen (1937–) writer/publisher on psychology and spirituality; born in Albany, N.Y. He attended the University of Miami (Fla.) and worked as a journalist before founding Unity Press in San Francisco (1965). He collaborated with psychologist Richard Alpert (Ram Dass) and psychiatrist Elisabeth Kuebler-Ross on work with the sick and dying and their families, using meditative techniques to alleviate pain and grief. His own writings include *A Resonance of Hope* (1959) and *Healers on Healing* (1990).

Levinson, Daniel Jacob (1920–) psychologist; born in New York City. He studied at the University of California: Berkeley and taught at Western Reserve University in Cleveland, Ohio (1947–50). In 1950 he joined Harvard University as a professor and research associate (to 1966). He was a professor of psychiatry at Yale (1966) and wrote *The Authoritarian Person* (1950), *Patienthood in the Mental Hospital* (1964), and *The Seasons of a Man's Life* (1978).

Levitt, Helen (1918–) photographer; born in New York City. She studied at New York's Art Students' League while working as a free-lance photographer (from 1939) and making some short films. Her primary subject was New York street life, and her work was exhibited at galleries and museums including New York's Museum of Modern Art, the Metropolitan Museum of Art, and Yale University. Her publications include *A Way of Seeing: Photographs of New York,* with text by James Agee (1961).

Levitt, William J. (Jaird) (1907–94) builder; born in New York City. He was educated at New York University. With his brother and father he formed Levitt and Sons (1929), a construction company, himself serving as president and managing the business operations as it successfully built nearly 3,000 houses in its first 11 years. The firm built mass-produced housing for the U.S. Navy during World War II and found a successful civilian adaptation in Levittown, Long Island, N.Y., where he built 17,500 small but equipped, landscaped, and affordable houses and associated public and community buildings (1947–51). A second Levittown in Bucks County, Pa., followed. He called his firm "the General Motors of the housing industry." He attracted controversy for racially discriminatory sales policies (upheld by the Pennsylvania courts, 1955). He sold the company to International Telephone and Telegraph in 1968. His later career was marred by failures in foreign projects in the 1970s, and in the 1980s, by three disastrous Levittown-like Florida projects and accusations of misappropriation of funds.

Levy, Gustave Lehman (1910–76) investment banker; born

in New Orleans. He left Tulane University because his widowed mother could not afford tuition, moved to New York City, and in 1933 joined Goldman, Sachs & Co. He became a partner in 1945 and rose to chairman of the management committee in 1969, making him one of the most powerful figures on Wall Street. He also served as chairman of the New York Stock Exchange board of governors (1967–69). He supported charitable and artistic activities and was a top fund raiser for the Republican Party.

Lewin, Kurt (1890–1947) psychologist; born in Mogilno, Prussia (now Poland). Part of the German Gestalt psychology movement, his particular interests were group dynamics and memory. He emigrated to the United States in 1932. He taught at Cornell (1933–35), the University of Iowa (1935–44), and the Massachusetts Institute of Technology (1944–47), where he also directed the research center for group dynamics. He attempted to analyze behavior using laboratory techniques. He saw behavior in terms of forces in the psychological "field" and described individual behavior in terms of the interaction of internal and environmental psychological forces. He compared, for instance, the effect of democratic and authoritarian behavior on groups.

Lewis, C. I. (Clarence Irving) (1883–1964) philosopher; born in Stoneham, Mass. Directed to social problems by his father, a shoemaker blacklisted for union activities, and encouraged in philosophy by an elderly woman he met during a summer job, he graduated from Harvard in 1905, having studied under William James and Josiah Royce. After earning a Ph.D. (1910) he taught at the University of California: Berkeley (1911–20) and Harvard (1920–53). He developed a logic of strict implication, a pragmatic theory of knowledge, and a naturalistic value theory; his works include *An Analysis of Knowledge and Valuation* (1946).

Lewis, David K. (Kellogg) (1941–) philosopher; born in Oberlin, Ohio. Receiving a Harvard doctorate (1967), he taught at the University of California: Los Angeles (1966–73) and then at Princeton. He made important contributions to semantics and the philosophy of science.

Lewis, Delano E. (1938–) lawyer, communications business executive, broadcasting executive; born in Arkansas City, Kans. He took his B.A. in political science and history at the University of Kansas in 1960 and his law degree from Washburn School of Law in 1963. That year he was appointed an attorney for the U.S. Department of Justice; in 1965 he joined an office of the U.S. Equal Opportunity Commission. Between 1965–69 he served in Africa with the Peace Corps; from 1969–73 he was a legislative assistant to Walter Fauntroy, U.S. representative from the District of Columbia. In 1973 he joined C&P Telephone Company, a Bell Atlantic subsidiary; he rose in responsibilities and rank until in 1988 he became its president and chief executive officer, one of the highest such positions held by an African-American. In 1993 he left C&P to become head of the Public Broadcasting Corporation. He was active in numerous civic, public service, and cultural activities and was the recipient of many honors.

Lewis, Dixon Hall (1802–48) U.S. representative/senator; born in Dinwiddie County, Va. He practiced law in Alabama and as member of the house of representatives (Dem., Ala.; 1829–44) he championed states' rights. In the senate (1844–48) he opposed the United States Bank. A man of extraordinary weight, he required special arrangements to travel and to sit in assemblies.

Lewis, Flora (?1923–) journalist; born in Los Angeles. A longtime foreign correspondent for the *New York Times,* she was Paris bureau chief in the 1970s; later, as chief foreign affairs columnist, she became widely known for her independent-minded views.

Lewis, (Frederick Carlton) Carl (1961–) track and field athlete; born in Birmington, Ala. A stand-out all-around athlete at Houston University (1979–82), he went on to win four gold medals in the 1984 Olympics (100-meter, 200-meter, 4 × 100 meter relay, and long jump), two more in the 1988 Games (100-meter and long jump), and an unprecedented third consecutive gold medal in the long jump in the 1992 Olympics. Although he was awarded the gold medal for the 100-meter dash in the 1988 Olympics only after it was taken from Ben Johnson (because he used drugs), Lewis held the world record in the 100-meter dash and dominated the long jump for many years. Although his independent, sometimes distant manner alienated some journalists, he remained a charismatic figure to track fans. He was a fierce competitor and is widely acknowledged to be one of the sport's all-time greatest athletes.

Lewis, George (William) (1882–1948) aeronautical engineer; born in Ithaca, N.Y. As aeronautical research director of the National Advisory Committee of Aeronautics (1924–47), he helped produce national requirements for aircraft design. By the time he retired, his department had three laboratories, 40 wind tunnels, and 6,000 employees. The Lewis Flight Propulsion Laboratory, Cleveland, Ohio, was named for him (1948).

Lewis, Gilbert N. (Newton) (1875–1946) physicist, chemist; born in Weymouth, Mass. He taught chemistry at Harvard (1899–1906), joined the Massachusetts Institute of Technology (1907–11), then moved to the University of California: Berkeley (1912–46). He developed the valence theory of chemical reactions (1923). With his student, Harold Urey, he discovered "heavy" water (1933), and, in the same year, collaborated with E. O. Lawrence to invent the cyclotron. Lewis made fundamental contributions to acid-base theory, thermodynamics, and research on atomic structure and relativity. After 1941, he undertook studies of glaciation and early American civilization.

Lewis, (Harry) Sinclair (1885–1951) writer; born in Sauk Center, Minn. He studied at Yale (1903–06), left to join Upton Sinclair's socialist colony in New Jersey, then returned and finished at Yale (1908). For the next few years he worked as a journalist, editor, and free-lance writer in San Francisco, Washington, D.C., and New York City, but by 1916 he was devoting himself to his own writing, which would fall into three distinct periods. His first novels and short stories – all eminently forgettable – were a search for subject matter and a style. His second phase, essentially the 1920s, produced virtually all his important works, several of which provided names that would become proverbial stereotypes: *Main Street* (1920), a satirical portrait of a conservative small town in the Midwest; *Babbitt* (1922), equally satiric in its portrait of a conservative American businessman; *Elmer Gantry* (1927), also satirical in its portrait of religious hypocrisy. He won the Pulitzer Prize for *Arrowsmith* (1925) but refused it because he felt his views of American life did not conform to the idealized view of America espoused by the Pulitzer panel. He did, however, accept the Nobel Prize in literature (1930), the first

American so honored. His fiction thereafter went into marked decline on the literary scale, although in such works as *It Can't Happen Here* (1935) and *Kingsblood Royal* (1947), he did anticipate certain social issues. He was married to the journalist, Dorothy Thompson, from 1928 to 1942, but theirs was a stormy relationship, aggravated by his severe alcoholism. He spent the last two decades of his life traveling around the U.S.A. and Europe – he died in Rome – as though avoiding the one place he truly knew, the American Midwest.

Lewis, Jerry (b. Joseph Levitch) (1926–) film actor, director, producer; born in Newark, N.J. A zany, mugging, sentimental comic, he worked as a one-night-stand entertainer until he met singer Dean Martin in 1946. The team made their first screen appearance in *My Friend Irma* (1949). After 16 more films, they split up. Lewis began producing and then directing his own movies, becoming a special favorite in France. A dedicated campaigner for charitable causes, he became closely identified with the annual fundraising telethons for the Muscular Dystrophy Association.

Lewis, Jerry Lee (1935–) musician; born in Ferriday, La. A singer and pianist, he emerged in 1956 as one of the most fervent and blues-flavored of the rock 'n' roll originators. He began singing in Assembly of God churches and Bible schools before working as a session musician at Sun Records in Memphis, Tenn. His first recordings for Sun, "Whole Lotta Shakin' Goin' On" and "Great Balls of Fire," caused a sensation and became classics of rock. In 1958, he starred in the film *High School Confidential,* but later that year, when he married his 14-year-old cousin, Myra, he was effectively boycotted by television and radio. Personal controversy and drug addiction continually dogged his career. He made a successful switch to a career in country music in the 1960s and 1970s, but remained widely celebrated for his contributions to rock. In 1986, Lewis became an inaugural member of the Rock 'N' Roll Hall of Fame. *Great Balls of Fire,* a major film biography dramatizing the early years of Lewis's career, was released in 1989.

Lewis, John (Aaron) (1920–) jazz musician; born in La Grange, Ill. As a pianist and arranger, he was employed by numerous bandleaders between 1945–51, including Dizzy Gillespie, Charlie Parker, Miles Davis, Illinois Jacquet, and Lester Young. In 1952 he recorded with vibraphonist Milt Jackson and other members of the original Gillespie band's rhythm section. By 1954 this group had coalesced as the Modern Jazz Quartet, with Lewis serving as its musical director and arranger, and Jackson as its principal soloist. Lewis also composed for movie soundtracks and ballet, and was a proponent of the fusion of jazz and classical elements known as "third-stream."

Lewis, John L. (Llewellyn) (1880–1969) labor leader; born in Lucas, Iowa. He went to work in the coal mines at age 16. After serving as president of his local of the United Mine Workers of America (UMWA), UMWA state lobbyist in Illinois (1909–10), American Federation of Labor (AFL) field representative (1910–16), and UMWA vice-president (1917–19), he was appointed acting president, and then elected UMWA president (1920–60). During the 1920s he won a reputation as an autocratic and aggressive leader, but he could not stanch the decline in UMWA membership. However, in 1933 he launched an organizing drive that rebuilt a powerful UMWA. He played a central role in the organization of the Congress of Industrial Organizations (CIO), serving as its president (1936–40). He backed Franklin Roosevelt in 1936, but in 1940 switched to the Republicans, and resigned his CIO presidency when Roosevelt was reelected for a third term. Lewis went back to leading the UMWA, taking the miners out on strikes that twice got him convicted for contempt of federal orders. By the mid-1950s he had become an advocate of cooperation between the miners and mine owners, but he could never shake his reputation as an old-fashioned labor leader, famed for his bushy eyebrows and fiery rhetoric.

Lewis, Lucy M. (1895–) potter; born in Acoma Pueblo, N.M. A leading artisan of her era, she learned her craft by watching her great-aunt Helice Valeo. She is noted for her hand-built, unglazed red earthenware ornamented with a variety of ancient motifs, especially from the Mimbres and Zuni traditions.

Lewis, (Mary) Edmonia (b. Wildfire) (?1844–?1911) sculptor; born near Albany, N.Y. The daughter of a Chippewa Indian mother and a black father, she was orphaned early and was raised by her mother's tribe. Her brother, Sunrise, a California gold miner, sent her to Oberlin College, Ohio (1859–62), and she changed her name. There she was tried for the attempted murder of two of her classmates, was severely beaten by townspeople, was acquitted, and then moved to Boston (1863). She traveled to Europe (1865), settled permanently in Rome (1867), and was known for her neoclassical work, as seen in her abolitionist sculpture *Forever Free* (1867).

Lewis, Meriwether (1774–1809) explorer, soldier; born in Albemarle County, Va. He became President Thomas Jefferson's private secretary (1801) and was chosen, with William Clark, to lead an overland expedition to the Pacific Ocean. He and Clark made careful observations of the wildlife and lands that they passed through on their journey (1804–06). Lewis was governor of the Louisiana Territory (1806–09) and died mysteriously while on his way to Washington, D.C., in 1809.

Lewis, Oscar (1914–70) anthropologist; born in New York City. He founded the anthropology department at the University of Illinois: Urbana (1948), where he spent his career. His powerful best-selling oral histories of Mexican villagers, Mexican and Puerto Rican slumdwellers, and the Cuban revolution led to his controversial theory of poverty as a transnational subculture and brought widespread public attention to the poor.

Lewis, Reginald F. (1942–93) lawyer, financier; born in Baltimore, Md. A Harvard Law School graduate, he specialized in venture capital in his New York law career. He became one of the country's richest businessmen through his brief but profitable ownership of McCall Pattern Company (1983–87) and his $1 billion acquisition of the Beatrice Companies (1987). He was sometimes criticized for not taking a more prominent and activist role on behalf of his fellow African-Americans, but he preferred to serve as a role model and work quietly behind the scenes.

Lewis, Sinclair See LEWIS, (HARRY) SINCLAIR.

Lewis, W. (William) Arthur (1915–91) economist; born in St. Lucia, West Indies. He completed his formal education in England and accepted a professorship at Princeton in 1963. The thrust of his contribution examines the economics of developing countries and their "dual economies" – small, urban, industrialized economic sectors surrounded by vast, rural, traditional areas. His work also dealt with the supply of labor in developing countries. In 1979 he shared the Nobel Prize in economics with Theodore Schultz.

Lewis, Warren K. (1882–1975) chemical engineer, educator; born in Laurel, Del. On the faculty of the Massachusetts Institute of Technology (1910–48), he was a leader in establishing chemical engineering as a discipline. His own work advanced the production and refining of petroleum.

LeWitt, Sol (1928–) sculptor, conceptual artist; born in Hartford, Conn. He attended Syracuse University, N.Y. (B.F.A. 1949), settled in New York City, and taught at many institutions, including the Museum of Modern Art School (1964–67). He became known for his serial compositions and conceptual sculptures, as in *Untitled Cube* (1968).

Lewontin, Richard C. (Charles) (1929–) geneticist; born in New York City. He was a biometrician at Columbia University (1953–54), an assistant professor at North Carolina State College (1954–58), and a professor at the Universities of Rochester (1958–64) and Chicago (1964–73), and at Harvard (1973). A prolific writer and a former editor of scientific journals, he made major contributions to studies of population genetics, evolution, and philosophical and social aspects of human behavior. He is also known as a controversial critic of his professional colleagues and a commentator on the applications of biological knowledge to broader issues.

Ley, Willy (1906–69) rocket scientist, writer; born in Berlin, Germany. He studied science at German universities, but abandoned his plan to be a geologist after reading (1926) a work by the rocket scientist, Hermann Oberth. Ley took the lead in founding the German Society for Space Travel (1927), made it the center of international activity in rocket research, brought Wernher von Braun and others into the group, conducted important experiments, and in particular helped develop the liquid-fuel rocket. When the Nazis forced rocket research into military applications, he fled to the U.S.A. (1935). Unable to find financial support for rocket research and space travel, he turned to writing about all aspects of science, from astronomy to zoology, and became widely known as a popularizer of science. But he never lost his faith in space travel, writing numerous science-fiction and nonfiction accounts, including the award-winning *Conquest of Space* (1949). He advised filmmakers from Fritz Lang to Walt Disney on space travel. During World War II he advised Americans on bombs and explosive devices.

Leyendecker, J. C. (Joseph Christian) (1874–1951) illustrator; born in Montabour, Germany. His family emigrated to Chicago (1882), he worked as an engraver, and studied at the Art Institute of Chicago and Paris (1896–98). He and his illustrator brother, Frank Leyendecker, moved to New York City (1900), and then to a mansion in New Rochelle, N.Y. Joseph became famous for his advertisements for the "Arrow Collar Man," and his stylized covers for such periodicals as *Collier's* and *The Saturday Evening Post*.

Leypoldt, Frederic (1835–84) publisher; born in Stuttgart, Germany. Emigrating in 1854, he established a publishing firm with Henry Holt in 1866. He was editor and publisher (from 1868) of the journal that became *Publishers' Weekly* and (from 1870) of an annual catalog of published books.

Lhevinne, Josef (1874–1944) **and Rosina** (1880–1976) pianists, teachers; Josef born in Orel, Russia, and Rosina in Kiev, Russia. After gaining fame as soloists in Russia and Europe, they came to the U.S.A. in 1919. While they continued to concertize, they both taught at Juilliard; although he had the more prominent concert career, she lived on to become legendary for teaching an endless succession of prominent pianists including Van Cliburn.

Lhevinne, Rosina See under LHEVINNE, JOSEF.

Libbey, Edward Drummond (1854–1925) glassmaker, philanthropist; born in Chelsea, Mass. After attending Boston University, he worked for the New England Glass Company (1874), becoming president (1883–86). He opened the Libbey Glass Company in Toledo, Ohio, in 1888, sponsoring a demonstration plant at the Chicago exposition of 1893. His success depended heavily on the inventions of Michael Owens; Libbey later founded the Owens Bottle Machine Company (1903) with exclusive rights to manufacture glass bottles, and the Libbey-Owens Sheet Glass Company (1916), serving as president of both firms. He organized the Toledo Art Museum in 1901, serving as its president (1901–25), funding building construction, and bequeathing to the museum his collection of Dutch and English art.

Libby, Willard (Frank) (1908–80) chemist; born in Grand Valley, Colo. He studied at the University of California: Berkeley and was teaching there when World War II took him to Columbia University to work on the atom bomb; he then taught at the University of Chicago (1945–54) before joining the faculty of the University of California: Los Angeles (1959–76). He served on the Atomic Energy Commission (1954–59). He was awarded the Nobel Prize in chemistry (1960) for his role in developing (beginning in 1939 at Berkeley) the carbon-14 method of determining the age of ancient objects crucial to archaeology.

Liberace, (Walter) (b. Wladziu Valentino) (1919–86) pianist; born in Milwaukee, Wis. Self-avowed mama's boy and child prodigy, he was a consummate performer (1950–86), playing in flamboyant costumes on ornate pianos, sometimes with symphony orchestras, but more often at Las Vegas or on television. He ended his career somewhere between a cult figure and a parody of himself.

Liberman, Alex (Alexander Semeonovitch) (1912–) artist, fashion editor; born in Kiev, Russia. Educated in England and France, he moved to New York to become art director of *Vogue* (1941). As art director (1943–62) and then editorial director (1962) of Condé Nast Publications, he oversaw such prestigious magazines as *House and Garden* and *Vanity Fair*. He was also a noted photographer, painter, and sculptor.

Lichtenstein, Roy (1923–) painter, sculptor; born in New York City. He studied at the Art Students League under Reginald Marsh (1940), and became a leader of the New York City based pop art movement, which used objects and images from mass culture and advertising. Based in New York City, he adapted painting techniques from comic strips, commercial printing, stenciling, and projected images. His decorative and witty canvases, such as *Whaam!* (1963), and *Big Painting VI* (1965) brought him fame. During the 1960s he produced elegant sculptures that revived the forms of the 1930s, as seen in *Modern Sculpture with Glass Wave* (1967).

Lichtenstein, Tehilla (1893–1973) religious leader; born in Jerusalem, Palestine (now Israel). She received a B.A. from Hunter College and an M.A. from Columbia University. The leader of the Society of Jewish Science, she was the head of the Congress of Jewish Science and the first woman to occupy a Jewish pulpit in the U.S.A. She was the author of a number of books, including *What it Means to Be a Jew* (1943) and *Choosing Your Way to Happiness* (1954).

Lick, James (1796–1876) financier, philanthropist; born in Fredericksburg, Pa. A piano-maker by training, he spent many years in South America (1820–37) and then moved to San Francisco. He made a fortune in the real estate boom there and bequeathed much of his fortune to public purposes; most notably he left $700,000 to produce the most powerful telescope made to that date, and to house it he founded the Lick Observatory on Mount Hamilton in Santa Clara, Calif.

Licklider, Joseph (Carl Robnett) (1915–90) computer scientist; born in St. Louis, Mo. He was among the first in the 1960s to recognize the potential for user-friendly computers. He published a series of papers in which he outlined the "man-computer symbiosis." He was affiliated with the Massachusetts Institute of Technology (1950–85) and made contributions in the application of computers to libraries and information storage and retrieval.

Lieb, (Frederick George) Fred (1888–1980) sportswriter; born in Philadelphia. A foremost sportswriter for over 50 years, he covered baseball for the *New York Press* beginning in 1911 and wrote articles for the *Sporting News* beginning in 1935. Author of nine books on baseball, he held Card No. 1 in the Baseball Writers Association of America.

Lieber, Francis (1800–72) political reformer, editor, political scientist; born in Berlin, Germany. As a youth he fought against Napoleon in the Battle of Waterloo. Persecuted, even imprisoned, as a liberal in Prussia, he fled in 1826 and arrived in Boston in 1827. Proposing to translate a German encyclopedia, he so enlarged and revised it that he ended up editing a new *Encyclopedia Americana* (13 vols. 1829–33). He taught at the University of South Carolina (1835–57) and Columbia University (1857–72). Two of his works, *Manual of Political Ethics* (1838–39) and *On Civil Liberty and Self-Government* (1853) provided the first thorough analysis of American government since its inception. Known for his ideas on prison reform, he also drafted a *Code for the Government of the Armies of the United States* (1863), which was adopted by the Union army; essentially the first code of international law governing war, it was later used as the basis for the Hague Convention.

Lieberman, Saul (1898–1983) scholar; born in Motol, Poland. He studied the Talmud in Jerusalem and became Professor of Talmud at the Jewish Theological Seminary of America in New York in 1940. He published many scholarly works, most importantly a critical edition of the Tosefta (1955–73), a supplement to the Talmud.

Liebes, Dorothy Wright (1899–1972) textile designer; born in Guerneville, Calif. Opening her own studio (1930) to design handwoven textiles for decorators and architects, she pioneered the use of machine techniques and exotic colors and materials.

Liebling, A. J. (Abbott Joseph) (1904–63) writer; born in New York City. A *New Yorker* staff writer from 1935 until his death, he was a World War II correspondent, did a regular feature criticizing the press, and wrote on such diverse topics as France, New York life, boxing, horse racing, and food.

Liebman, Joshua Loth (1907–48) rabbi, author; born in Hamilton, Ohio. He entered college at age 13, and graduated from the University of Cincinnati at 19. Following his ordination at Hebrew Union College in Cincinnati, he became a lecturer there in Greek philosophy. He was rabbi of Temple Israel in Boston from 1939 until his death. An active Zionist and public speaker, he preached on the radio and served on many national government and religious groups. His 1946 book, *Peace of Mind*, was a best-seller.

Lienau, Detlef (1818–87) architect; born in Utersen, Germany. He emigrated to New York (1848), where he introduced the French Second Empire style and espoused neoclassicism throughout the mid-19th century. He helped found the American Institute of Architects (1857).

Lifton, Robert Jay (1926–) psychiatrist, author; born in New York City. He taught at Yale (1961) and was director of the Center on Violence and Human Survival at John Jay College (New York City) (1985). His main interest throughout his career was to understand and write about how disturbing historical events and processes affect the individual. His best-known writings are in the form of psychohistories. For example, he wrote *Death in Life: Survivors of Hiroshima* (1968) as a way of understanding the coping mechanisms and psychoses of survivors – the way we experience and think about death, possibilities for the future, or our very place in the world, he argued, has been irrevocably changed by Hiroshima. He also wrote *Home from the War: Vietnam Veterans – Neither Victims nor Executioners* (1973), *The Nazi Doctors: Medical Killing and the Psychology of Genocide* (1986), and a number of other books.

Liggett, Hunter (1857–1935) soldier; born in Reading, Pa. A tailor's son, he saw service on the western frontier, and in the Spanish-American War and the Philippine insurrection. Recognized for his intelligent professionalism, he served as president of the Army's War College (1912–17). In World War I, he led a division and a corps in France through several major actions, then commanded the U.S. First Army in the Meuse-Argonne offensive (autumn 1918), in which Allied forces pierced the Hindenburg Line. He commanded the Army of Occupation in Germany (1918–19) and retired in 1921.

Ligutti, Luigi (Gino) (1895–) religious leader; born in Udine, Italy. Emigrating to the U.S.A. as a child and ordained in 1919, he was an Iowa pastor for many years (1920–41). As executive director of the National Catholic Rural Life Conference (1939–60), he promoted greater awareness of Third World needs; he also served as Vatican ambassador to the United Nations Food and Agriculture Organization (1948–71).

Likert, Rensis (1903–81) psychologist, management theorist; born in Cheyenne, Wyo. At the University of Michigan (1946–70) he was founding director of the Institute for Social Research (1949–70). He worked on large organizations and theories of management. His major contributions included the development of a survey methodology that laid the groundwork for probability sampling, the "Likert scale" for measuring attitudes, and a theory of participatory management.

Lilienthal, David (Eli) (1899–1981) lawyer, government official; born in Morton, Ill. A Chicago lawyer, he rewrote Wisconsin's public utility statutes (1931–33). As the most visible and active official of the Tennessee Valley Authority (TVA) (board member from 1933, chairman 1941–46), he enlisted local support for centralized regional planning, fought to keep the TVA free of political ties, and tried to combine sound conservation policies with the TVA's primary goals of flood control and cheap electricity. Chairman of the Atomic Energy Commission (1946–55), he founded and headed the Development and Resources Corporation (1953–79), providing technical assistance to underdeveloped countries.

Lillehei, C. (Clarence) Walton (1918–) surgeon; born in Minneapolis, Minn. He commanded a Mobile Army Surgical Hospital during World War II for three campaigns (1941–44), then returned to the University of Minnesota. He also spent eight years at the Cornell Medical Center (1967–75), returning again to Minnesota. His advances in cardiac surgery include codevelopment of the disposable bubble oxygenator (1955), for which he is dubbed "father of open heart surgery."

Lillie, Frank R. (Rattray) (1870–1947) embryologist; born in Toronto, Canada. He came to the U.S.A. to complete his graduate studies (1891). He taught and performed research at the University of Michigan (1894–99), Vassar College (1899–1900), and the University of Chicago (1900–35). He concurrently served the Woods Hole (Mass.) Marine Biology Laboratory as a researcher and administrator (1893–1942); he developed its Oceanographic Institution and became the institution's first director (1930–39). His major contributions include studies of fertilization in ova of marine organisms, classical investigations of chick embryo morphogenesis, definitive explanations of the development of hormonally-induced freemartinism in heterosexual cattle twins, and developmental research on feather regeneration in poultry. He was the only person to hold simultaneously the presidencies of the National Academy of Science and the National Research Council (1935–36).

Lillie, Gordon William ("Pawnee Bill") (1860–1942) frontiersman, showman; born in Bloomingdale, Ind. Enchanted by stories of the Old West, he left home at age 15 and lived among the Pawnee Indians and learned their language. He held various jobs in Oklahoma and Texas – buffalo hunter, teacher, cattle rancher – and after 1883 he traveled with Buffalo Bill's show and similar "wild west" shows as an interpreter and guardian of the Pawnee who were with the shows. In 1888 he set out with his own show, "Pawnee Bill's Historic Wild West," but it soon failed. Settling in Wichita, Kans., he led "boomers" in the opening of the Oklahoma Territory (1889). He regrouped his wild west show in 1890 and it was extremely popular until 1909, when it merged with Buffalo Bill's. He feuded with Buffalo Bill and in 1913 retired to his 2,000 acre ranch near Pawnee, Okla., where he bred cattle and participated in civic affairs.

Lilly, Eli (1838–98) manufacturer, philanthropist; born in Baltimore, Md. He opened his first drug store in 1860 and then served in the Civil War. His pharmaceuticals manufacturing company in Indianapolis (established in 1876) became one of the largest in the U.S.A. He demonstrated his public spiritedness through forming the Consumers' Gas Trust Company (1888) and through his presidency of the Commercial Club of Indianapolis (1890–95). His "Indianapolis plan of relief" (1894) became a model for helping the unemployed.

Lilly, Josiah Kirby (1861–1948) pharmaceutical manufac- turer; born in Greencastle, Ind. (son of Eli Lilly). He graduated from the Philadelphia College of Pharmacy (1882) and entered his father's firm, Eli Lilly and Company. He was director of the laboratories (1882–98), president of the company (1898–1932), and chairman of the board (1932–48). The company played a major role in the advances of chemotherapy in the early 20th century; during World War I the firm grew belladonna and stramonium plants used to make much-needed medicines. He collaborated with Frederick Banting to market the first commercially produced insulin in the U.S.A. (1923). He and his sons set up the Lilly Endowment, Inc. (1937) to channel funds to charitable, educational, and religious causes.

Liman, Arthur L. (1932–) lawyer; born in New York City. With New York's Paul, Weiss, Rifkind, Wharton & Garrison (1957), he handled many high-profile clients. He was counsel to the McKay Commission on New York's Attica prison riot (1972) and to the U.S. Senate committee investigating the Iran-Contra affair (1987).

Limon, José (1908–72) modern dancer, choreographer; born in Culiacan, Mexico. At age 20, after abandoning a career as a painter, he began studying with Doris Humphrey and Charles Weidman, and he performed with their company until 1940. He formed his own company in 1945, with Humphrey as artistic director, and earned a reputation as the finest male dancer of his time.

Lin, Chia Chiao (1916–) physicist; born in Foochow, China. He came to the U.S.A. to study at the California Institute of Technology (Ph.D. 1944), taught there (1943–45), then moved to Brown (1945–47) before joining the Massachusetts Institute of Technology (1947–87). He made major contributions to the theory of hydrodynamic stability (1955), turbulent flow (1963), mathematics, and astrophysics.

Lin, Maya (Ying) (1960–) landscape architect, sculptor; born in Athens, Ohio. At age 21, and a graduate student at Yale's School of Architecture, she was the center of a major controversy when her design for a memorial to those who died in Vietnam was chosen to be erected in Washington, D.C. In 1990 her memorial to the civil rights movement was dedicated in Montgomery, Ala.

Lincoln, Abbey (b. Anna Marie Wooldridge) (1930–) jazz singer, composer/arranger, movie actress; born in Chicago, Ill. While a teenager she sang at school and church functions and then toured locally with a dance band. At age 19 she won an amateur singing contest in Michigan and went to California where she sang in nightclubs (under her name, Anna Marie). She went to Hawaii as a resident club singer, but in 1954 returned to sing in clubs around Hollywood, now using the name "Gaby Lee." In 1956 she changed her name to "Abbey Lincoln" and made her first album under that name. In the early 1960s she began to work with drummer Max Roach and his band – she and Roach were briefly married (1962–70) – and she not only turned to jazz singing but also became more involved in African-Americans' struggle for civil rights. She recorded Roach's *Insist! Freedom Now Suit* (1960). As her career took off, she toured worldwide as a soloist and appeared on radio and television; she costarred in the movie *Nothing But a Man* (1963) but it was ahead of its time; she also starred in *For Love of Ivy* (1968). Traveling and performing in Africa in the early 1970s, she decided to adopt a new name, "Aminata Moseka," in tribute to her African roots, but then she seemed to drop out of sight professionally. In the early 1990s, however, as Abbey Lincoln again, she revived her career, with both recordings and live performances; she was the subject of a Public Broadcasting System documentary, "*You Gotta Pay the Band*" (1992); and she came to be recognized as one of the truly fine jazz singers of her generation.

Lincoln, Abraham (1809–65) sixteenth U.S. president; born near Hodgenville, Ky. Born in a log cabin to a modest farm family, he moved early with his family to Indiana. His mother died in 1818 and his stepmother, Sarah Bush Johnston, provided a fine model who inspired the ambitious but unschooled boy to discipline and educate himself. The Lincolns moved to Illinois in 1830, and, after twice sailing a flatboat to New Orleans, he settled in New Salem, Ill., where he pursued workaday jobs while studying law on his own. In the 1832 Black Hawk War he served as a volunteer but saw no action. In 1835 he entered the Illinois state legislature as a Whig; after unremarkable service, Lincoln left the legislature in 1841. In 1837 he had begun what would become a successful law practice in Springfield, the capital of Illinois; in 1842 he married Mary Todd, of a prominent Springfield family. His position as a prominent Whig in Illinois took him to the U.S. House of Representatives in 1847–49, where he again had a lackluster record despite his opposition to the war in Mexico. Back in Springfield he gradually began to prosper as a lawyer, often representing business interests, but his eloquently-stated if moderate antislavery views gained him increasing attention. This came to a head during his unsuccessful race (1858) for the U.S. Senate against Stephen A. Douglas, who led the Democratic accommodation to slave interests; the historic debates between the two men secured Lincoln a national following, which led to his becoming the presidential nominee of the new antislavery Republican Party in 1860. Although he received only 40% of the popular vote, due to a split in the Democratic party Lincoln won a majority of the Electoral College votes. Although he had stated his willingness to tolerate slavery where it currently existed, his election precipitated the secession of Southern states and the formation of the Confederacy. In the years of civil war that followed, the inexperienced Lincoln proved to be one of the most extraordinary leaders, both political and moral, the U.S.A. has ever seen. First defining the war as being fought over secession rather than slavery, he oversaw the creation of the Union army. When the political time was right, Lincoln announced the Emancipation Proclamation in September 1862, thereby interpreting the war as a crusade against slavery; he later oversaw the passage of the Thirteenth Amendment (1865), which legally ended slavery. With his immortal Gettysburg Address (November 1863), Lincoln further defined the war as the struggle for preservation of the democratic idea, which he called "government of the people, by the people, for the people." Meanwhile, he took a direct interest in the conduct of the war, hiring and firing generals, getting daily reports from the battlefields, and visiting the troops in the front lines. All this time, too, he had to mediate between the pressures of radical and conservative elements of the North, using an astute combination of suppression and conciliation, and barely surviving the election in 1864. Having seen the victory of the Union forces in April 1865, Lincoln was beginning to plan a generous reconstruction policy when he was assassinated by Southern fanatic John Wilkes Booth. His body was taken by train from Washington to be buried in Springfield, Ill., as the nation he had refounded mourned their "Father Abraham." Master of both a Biblical eloquence and a homespun vernacular, a natural at combining practical politics with moral principles, in only four years as president he had established why he is one of the few Americans who truly "belong to the ages."

Lincoln, Benjamin (1733–1810) soldier, politician; born in Hingham, Mass. A farmer's son, modestly educated, he took an early interest in militia and public affairs, serving in the Massachusetts legislature (1772–73) and as secretary of the Provincial Congress (1775). In 1777, as a major general of continental forces, he operated effectively on the flank of the British army in upstate New York, contributing to the American victory at Saratoga. He did not, however, prove a success in a senior independent command. Leading Washington's southern forces, he withdrew his army into Charleston, S.C., where, besieged, he surrendered in May 1779. Exchanged later in the year, Lincoln fought at Yorktown (1781), served a term as war secretary (1781–83), and led militia forces against Daniel Shays's rebels (1787). He was lieutenant governor of Massachusetts (1788) and collector of the port of Boston (1789–1809).

Lincoln, Mary (b. Todd) (1818–82) First Lady; born in Lexington, Ky. She married Abraham Lincoln in 1842. She was emotionally immature and she became mentally unbalanced as the years passed. As first lady, it seemed that she could do nothing right; she overspent, was exceedingly jealous of Lincoln's affections, and was accused of Confederate sympathies. Following the loss of her son Willie in 1862, and Lincoln's assassination in 1865, she had a mental breakdown and was briefly treated in a sanitarium in 1875. After a tour of Europe, she returned to Springfield, Ill.

Lindbergh, Charles (Augustus) (1902–1974) aviator; born in Detroit, Mich. Pilot, inventor, author, and environmentalist, he made the first solo transatlantic airplane flight in 1927 and returned to America a hero and celebrity of unsurpassed dimension. The son of a Minnesota congressman, Lindbergh showed early mechanical aptitude as well as physical daring. He brought a war surplus Curtiss "Jenny" biplane in 1923 and barnstormed the Midwest and South, completed army flight training in 1925, and worked as an airmail pilot on the pioneering St. Louis-Chicago run. In pursuit of a $25,000 prize, he lifted off from Roosevelt Field, N.Y., in a monoplane named *Spirit of St. Louis* on May 20, 1927, crossed the Atlantic, and landed at LeBourguet Field near Paris after 33 1/2 hours – a flight of 3,600 miles. "The Lone Eagle," as he became known, made a series of epic flights during the 1930s, many with his wife Anne Morrow Lindbergh. In one of America's most notorious crimes, the couple's infant son was kidnapped and murdered in 1932; four years later Bruno Hauptman, protesting his innocence to the last, was put to death for the crime. Lindbergh worked with Dr. Alexis Carrel on experiments that led to the development of an artificial heart. Impressed by German military power, especially in the air, he campaigned for American neutrality in the years leading up to World War II. During the war years he served as a consultant for Ford and the United Aircraft Company. Shy, and at periods almost reclusive, Lindbergh began to appear more often in public in later years as a spokesman for environmental conservation. His autobiography, *The Spirit of St. Louis* (1932), won a Pulitzer Prize; his wife was the best-selling author of *Gift from the Sea* (1955) and other books.

Linder, Richard (1901–78) painter; born in Hamburg, Germany. He emigrated to America (1941), became an illustrator for popular magazines in New York City, and taught at the Pratt Institute, Brooklyn, N.Y. (1952–65). By 1952 he was producing his highly stylized erotic and surrealistic works that linked Pop Art with a symbolic tradition, as seen in *Ice* (1966).

Lindgren, Waldemar (1860–1939) geologist; born in Kalmar, Sweden. He emigrated in 1883 to study mining in the western U.S.A. He performed field work with the U.S. Geological Survey (1884–1915), while concurrently teaching at the Massachusetts Institute of Technology (1908–33). He made major contributions to knowledge of the genesis of ore deposits.

Lindsay, John (Vliet) (1921–) mayor, U.S. representative; born in Queens, N.Y. A graduate of Yale University and Yale Law School, he was executive assistant U.S. attorney general (1955–56) and a three-term member of the House of Representatives from New York City's "Silk Stocking" district on the Upper East Side (Rep., 1959–65). A liberal Republican in 1971 during his first term as mayor of New York (1966–74), he changed his affiliation to Democrat, then ran unsuccessfully in the 1972 presidential primaries. He left public life for a law practice. In 1984, he became a presiding partner in the law firm of Webster & Sheffield. He wrote several books including *The City* (1970).

Lindsay, (Nicholas) Vachel (1879–1931) poet, writer; born in Springfield, Ill. He studied at Hiram College, Ohio (1897–1900), prepared for the ministry, then studied art in Chicago (1901) and New York (1905). He traveled throughout the U.S.A. reciting his poetry to earn a living (1906–12); after the publication of his first major poem, "General William Booth Enters Into Heaven" (1913), he became an extremely popular lecturer and recitalist (1913–31). In works such as "The Congo" (1914), he employed rhythmic effects to capture the spirit of places and people that ordinary Americans could relate to. Despite his success he became severely depressed. He returned to Springfield and committed suicide.

Lindsay, Robert Bruce (1900–85) physicist; born in New Bedford, Mass. He taught at Yale (1923–30) before joining Brown (1930–71). A specialist in acoustics (particularly underwater sound), he was a prodigious writer of textbooks, encyclopedia articles, and historical and philosophical analyses of science.

Lindsey, Benjamin Barr (1869–1943) jurist, reformer; born in Jackson, Tenn. The son of a debt-ridden, depressive confederate officer, he moved with his family to Denver, Colo., at age 11. When his father killed himself five years later, he went to work as an office boy for a lawyer; studying in his free time, he was admitted to the Colorado bar in 1894. He became a crusader for the juvenile court movement, pushing through legislation that created the first such court in the U.S.A. As juvenile court judge for more than a quarter-century (1900–27), he held that economic injustice caused crime and that juvenile offenders should be treated rather than punished. He also established the principle that adults may be legally responsible for contributing to the delinquency of a minor. He moved to California in 1928 and

became a Superior Court judge in Los Angeles in 1934. In later years he campaigned for sex education, contraception, and the liberalization of divorce laws. His autobiography, *The Dangerous Life,* appeared in 1931.

Lindsley, Philip (1786–1855) Protestant clergyman, educator; born near Morristown, N.J. He graduated from the College of New Jersey (now Princeton) in 1804, and after his theological studies, he received a Presbyterian license to preach in 1810. He returned to Princeton to assume both teaching and administrative duties before becoming president of the newly chartered University of Nashville (Tenn.) (1824–50). He shaped this institution into a strong undergraduate college while advancing higher education throughout the region. He accepted the presidency of the New Albany (Ind.) Theological Seminary in 1850 and remained there until his death.

Lineberger, William C. (Carl) (1939–) physicist; born in Hamlet, N.C. A chemist and astrophysicist at the University of Colorado: Boulder (1968), he made major contributions to studies of negative ion structure, molecular fluorescence, and tunable lasers.

Ling, James (Joseph) (1922–) electronics manufacturer, conglomerate organizer; born in Hugo, Okla. His Dallas electrical contracting firm (formed 1946) acquired numerous electronics and aircraft companies and became the conglomerate Ling-Temco-Vought Corporation (LTV) (1961), which in turn he diversified into the largest conglomerate in the country. After his removal as chairman (1970) he managed other holding companies.

Link, Arthur S. (Stanley) (1920–) historian; born in New Market, Va. Educated at the University of North Carolina (Ph.D. 1945), he taught at Princeton University (1945–49), then at Northwestern University, returning to Princeton in 1960, where he retired as professor emeritus in 1991. Editor of *The Papers of Woodrow Wilson* from 1966, he authored many books on 20th-century American history.

Link, Edwin (Albert) (1904–81) inventor, aviation executive; born in Huntington, Ind. While working in his father's piano factory, he and his brother built a flight simulator to help them learn to fly. In 1935 Edwin founded Link Aviation Inc., which produced flight simulators and other apparatus. He also invented equipment for deep-sea exploration, including a mobile unmanned television camera.

Linn, Lewis Fields (1795–1843) physician, U.S. senator; born near Louisville, Ky. A surgeon in the War of 1812, he set up his practice in Missouri, and was then appointed to serve that state in the U.S. Senate (Dem., 1833–43). An exponent of "manifest destiny," his Oregon Bill of 1843 provided liberal land grants and military defense of that territory.

Linowitz, Sol (Myron) (1913–) lawyer, diplomat; born in Trenton, N.J. He graduated from Cornell Law School (1938) and worked for the Office of Price Administration (1942–44) before entering private practice. He was the general counsel and chairman of the board for Xerox Corporation (1958–66) and chief executive officer of Xerox International (1966). He was the U.S. ambassador to the Organization of American States (1966–69), then became a senior partner with the international law firm of Coudert Brothers (1969–77). He was a conegotiator for the Panama Canal Treaties (1977–78) and President Carter's personal ambassador during the Middle East negotiations (1979–81). He wrote a memoir, *The Making of a Public Man* (1985).

Linton, Ralph (1893–1953) cultural anthropologist; born in Philadelphia. Son of a restaurateur, raised a Quaker, he graduated from Swarthmore College in 1915, saw combat in France during World War I (which led to his dismissal from his family's Friends Meeting), and received a Ph.D. from Harvard in 1925. Fieldwork took him to Polynesia in the early 1920s. He taught at the University of Wisconsin, Columbia University, where he succeeded Franz Boas, and Harvard. He introduced the terms "status" and "role" to social science and influenced the development of the culture-and-personality school of anthropology. His works, such as *The Study of Man* (1936) and *The Tree of Culture* (1955), are regarded more as popularizations of anthropology than as original scholarship.

Linz, Juan J. (José) (1926–) sociologist; born in Bonn, Germany. He earned a Ph.D. at Columbia University (1959) and went on to become Stirling professor of political and social science at Yale. His work on political and comparative sociology and development modernization focused on Spain and Latin America and included such titles as *Los empresarios ante el poder publico* (1966) and *El sistema de particos en Espana* (1976).

Lipchitz, Jacques (b. Chaim Jacob) (1891–1973) sculptor; born in Druskienki, Lithuania. He studied in Paris (1909–11), established a studio (1913), and became a master of cubism, as in *Joy of Life* (1927). In 1941 he emigrated to New York City, and his work became more emotional and fluid, as in *Prometheus Strangling the Vulture II* (1944–45). He lived in Hastings-on-Hudson, N.Y. (1947–63) and in Italy (1963–73).

Lipman, Jean (b. Herzberg) (1909–) folk art collector, author; born in New York City. She studied at Wellesley and New York University. She worked for *Art in America,* a magazine devoted to the decorative arts. She and her husband, Howard Lipman, purchased the magazine and she became editor-in-chief (1941–71). As husband and wife they amassed several major folk art collections, while maintaining homes in Wilton, Conn., New York City, and Arizona. She became a trustee emeritus of the Museum of American Folk Art, and wrote and coauthored numerous books, notably *The Flowering of American Folk Art,* with Alice Winchester (1974).

Lipmann, Fritz (Albert) (1899–1986) biochemist; born in Koenigsberg, Germany (now Kaliningrad, Russia). He performed research in cell energy metabolism in Europe (1927–39), taking a year (1931–32) as fellow at the Rockefeller Institute (now Rockefeller University). Fearing the rise of Nazism, he emigrated to the U.S.A. to join Cornell (1939–41), then moved to Harvard and the Massachusetts General Hospital (Boston) (1941–57). Beginning in 1945, he continued his studies of carbohydrate-fueled energy systems, discovered coenzyme A, necessary for cellular energy generation, and further clarified the Krebs citric acid energy cycle. For his pioneering work in cellular biochemistry, he shared the 1953 Nobel Prize in physiology with English biochemist Hans Krebs. In 1957 he returned to Rockefeller, pursuing research on phosphate compounds, cancer cells, thyroid hormones, and bodily energy systems until his death.

Lippard, George (1822–54) writer; born in West Nantmeal Township, Pa. His family moved to Philadelphia (1824), and he studied for the ministry at the Classical Academy, Rhinebeck, N.Y. Rejecting the ministry, he became a journalist, then a free-lance writer. He wrote many historical romances, but is best known for his books indicting the corruption of big cities, such as *The Monks of Monk Hall* (also known as *The Quaker City*) (1844), an exposé of Philadelphia in the fantasy genre. He was the founder of the Brotherhood of the Union (later known as the Brotherhood of America) in 1850, a religious and philosophical organization that attempted to eliminate social exploitation.

Lippincott, Joshua (Ballinger) (1813–86) publisher; born in Juliustown, N.J. Starting as a bookseller in Philadelphia, he founded J. B. Lippincott & Company in 1836; the company prospered as a diversified publisher of religious and medical works, deluxe editions, and other works.

Lippisch, Alexander (Martin) (1894–1976) aeronautical engineer; born in Munich, Germany. Developer of the first delta-wing aircraft (1931), the Messerschmitt-163A fighter plane, and the Me-163B, a rocket interceptor, he pioneered supersonic flight. Emigrating to America as a Defense Department consultant (1946), he founded Lippisch Research Corp. (1965) and developed a wingless aircraft called the aerodyne; he also assisted in the creation of award-winning documentaries on flight.

Lippmann, Walter (1889–1974) writer, editor; born in New York City. He was perhaps the most influential political commentator of his time, sought after by world leaders and followed by millions of loyal readers. After graduating from Harvard (1910), where he studied philosophy, political science, and economics, and was influenced by George Santayana, Lippmann assisted Lincoln Steffens in muckraking research and briefly served as aide to a Socialist mayor. His first book, *A Preface to Politics* (1913), led Herbert Croley to recruit him in 1914 as an editor for the influential *New Republic*. During World War I, Lippmann collaborated in research for a postwar peace conference, in which he later participated. In 1921 he joined the *New York World,* becoming editorial page editor (1923–29) and editor (1929–31). Meanwhile, in *Public Opinion* (1922), he analyzed opinion formation and questioned the public's ability to evaluate complex issues, and in *A Preface to Morals* (1929) he stressed the importance of "disinterestedness." He joined the *New York Tribune* in 1931; his column, "Today and Tomorrow," became widely syndicated and won two Pulitzer Prizes. Later he wrote a column for *Newsweek.* Never doctrinaire, he promoted a pragmatic liberalism in *The Good Society* (1937) and criticized the New Deal for collectivist tendencies. Late in life he backed President Lyndon Johnson's domestic programs but split with him over the Vietnam War.

Lippold, Richard (1915–) sculptor; born in Milwaukee, Wis. He studied at the University of Chicago (1933–37), worked as an industrial designer (1937–41), moved to New York City (1944), then settled in Locust Valley, N.Y. He is known for constructed wire sculptures as in *Variation Number 7: Full Moon* (1950).

Lipscomb, William (Nunn) (1919–) physical chemist; born in Cleveland, Ohio. He was affiliated with the California Institute of Technology (1941–50), the University of Minnesota (1950–59), and Harvard (1959). Between 1946–53, he developed new techniques for studying the volatile boron compounds and determined their structure; this work led him to new understandings of chemical bonding and reactivity and stimulated research in a variety of chemical problems. He was awarded the Nobel Prize in chemistry (1976).

Lipset, Seymour Martin (1922–) social scientist; born in New York City. His distinguished career in academia and public policy included faculty appointments at the University of California: Berkeley (1956–66), Harvard (1965–75), and Stanford's Hoover Institution (1975–92). He wrote and edited many important works on class structure, elites, and comparative politics, most notably *Agrarian Socialism* (1950), *Class, Status and Power* (1953) and *Political Man* (1960).

Lipton, Seymour (1903–86) sculptor; born in New York City. He studied dentistry at Columbia University (D.D.S. 1927) and combined that career for a time with sculpting. He taught at various institutions and is known for his organic metal sculptures such as *Archangel* (1964).

Lisa, Manuel (1772–1820) fur trader; born in New Orleans. Active in the St. Louis fur trade, he built Fort Lisa near present-day Montana and Fort Lisa near present-day Omaha, Nebr. (1812). He was a leader of the Missouri Fur Company from 1808 and was sub-agent for the Indian tribes along the Missouri River (1814–20).

List, Eugene (1918–85) pianist; born in Philadelphia. Making his debut with the Los Angeles Philharmonic at age 12, he went on to a prominent international career. After World War II he taught at Eastman School of Music (Rochester, N.Y.) and in New York City.

Little, Arthur D. (Dehon) (1863–1935) chemical engineer; born in Boston, Mass. He was an authority on paper technology and chemistry and he formed Little & Walker (1900), which became Arthur D. Little, Inc. (1909). The company became the U.S.A.'s largest private industrial research laboratory, moving from research on paper to leather tanning, petroleum, and other areas of applied science and eventually branching out to include many areas of business management.

Little, (Louis Lawrence) Lou (1893–1979) football coach; born in Boston, Mass. Although he had a losing record overall, he developed several outstanding teams as coach of Columbia University (1930–56), including the Rose Bowl winners of 1934.

Little, Malcolm See MALCOLM X.

Little, Royal (1896–1989) textile manufacturer, conglomerate organizer; born in Wakefield, Mass. (nephew of Arthur D. Little). He founded Special Yarns (1923), renamed Textron (1944). He invented the conglomerate by acquiring some 70 unrelated firms which eventually replaced Textron's original textile holdings; his success sparked the conglomeration trend of the 1960s. He retired as chairman and CEO in 1960 and founded a venture capital firm.

Little, William (Lawson, Jr.) (1910–68) golfer; born in Newport, R.I. He won both British and American amateur championships (1934–35), and after turning professional in 1936, he won the U.S. Open (1940).

Little Crow (b. Taheton Wakawa Mini) (?1820–63) Mdewakanton (Santee) Sioux; born near present-day St. Paul, Minn. Friendly with whites to the point of helping them track down "hostile" Indians, he was said by some to have been boastful and often drunk. But in 1862, rebelling against his people's deteriorating condition, he was one of the leaders in an uprising of the Sioux centered around New Ulm, Minn. Some 200 to 300 white settlers were reported killed; within six weeks, some 1,000 Sioux were captured by volunteer forces and eventually 39 were executed. Little Crow escaped capture, only to be killed by a white settler some months later while picking berries with his son.

"Little Richard" (Penniman, Richard Wayne) (1935–) musician; born in Macon, Ga. One of the early and most flamboyant stars of rock 'n' roll, he sang and played piano in church choirs and with gospel groups throughout his childhood, performing in medicine shows on the Southern vaudeville circuit. He made his recording debut with RCA in 1952 in Atlanta, and continued to record in a blues style for independent labels in Houston and New Orleans over the next four years. In 1956 he had a breakthrough single, "Tutti Frutti," which sold 3 million copies and established his basic style of histrionic singing and manic piano playing. Over the next three years, he sold over 18 million records and appeared in several motion pictures, but in 1960 he became a minister in the Seventh Day Adventist church and renounced rock 'n' roll and his own homosexuality. He returned to rock in 1963, touring England with the Beatles and Rolling Stones, and he straddled the worlds of pop music and evangelism over the next 30 years. In 1986, he became an inaugural member of the Rock 'n' Roll Hall of Fame. In 1989, "Tutti Frutti" was named the official rock song of the state of Georgia.

Littleton, Harvey (Kline) (1922–) glassmaker; born in Corning, N.Y. Following service in World War II, he received an M.F.A. in ceramics from Cranbrook Academy, where he studied with Maija Grotell (1951), then taught ceramics at the University of Wisconsin (1951–77). In 1962 he, together with Dominick Labino, pioneered the studio glass movement in Toledo, Ohio. He continued to create free-form glass sculptures in his studio in Spruce Pine, N.C. (1977).

"Little Walter" (Jacobs, Marion Walter) (1931–68) musician; born in Marksville, La. He is widely regarded as the most influential harmonica player in blues history, and as a major innovator of 1950s Chicago blues. As a teenage runaway, he began playing on the streets of New Orleans and made his first appearance on the King Biscuit Time radio program in Helena, Arkansas in 1944. He settled in Chicago in 1946, where he played with leading musicians Big Bill Broonzy and Memphis Slim. He made his first recordings in 1947, and for the next five years he was a sideman with Muddy Waters' pioneering electric blues band. In 1952, he formed his own group, the Jukes, and began a 14-year association with Chess Records, for which he recorded numerous blues hits. He toured with rhythm-and-blues package shows throughout the 1950s, and worked with the annual American Folk Blues Festival tours of England and Europe between 1962–67. He died at age 37 from head injuries sustained in a street fight, though alcoholism had severely hampered his career for at least ten years before his death.

Liveright, Horace (Brisbin) (1886–1933) publisher; born in Osceola Mills, Pa. In 1917, with Albert Boni, he launched the profitable Modern Library series of reprinted classics, sold in 1925 to Bennett Cerf and Donald Klopfer. Liveright also published original titles, with widely varying results; he was financially ruined by the 1929 stock market crash.

Livermore, Mary Ashton Rice (1820–1905) temperance worker, women's rights activist, lecturer, author; born in Boston, Mass. Brought up by a strict Calvinist father, she attended various schools in Boston and began teaching even before graduating from a female seminary in 1831. She then spent three years as a tutor for a family in North Carolina where she saw firsthand the horrors of slavery. In 1842 she took up teaching at a new private coeducational school in Duxbury, Mass., where she met and married (1845) Daniel P. Livermore, a Universalist minister. As a housewife for many years, she wrote stories and poems and became active in the temperance movement. In 1857 she and her husband settled in Chicago and she assisted him in editing a Universalist monthly magazine (1858–69). During the Civil War, she volunteered to serve with the Sanitary Commission and toured military hospitals, raised money in speaking tours and at fairs, and collected vast quantities of supplies for the armed forces. After the war, she became active in the women's suffrage movement and in 1869 founded her own suffrage paper, the *Agitator;* it merged with the *Woman's Journal* (1870–72) when Lucy Stone invited her to become editor of the new magazine of the American Woman Suffrage Association. The Livermores moved to Melrose, Mass., in 1870, the same year that she embarked on what would be a 25-year career on the lecture circuit. She earned substantial sums of money as she traveled the country, becoming famous for such lectures as "What Shall We Do With Our Daughters?" (answer: educate them). She served as president of the American Women's Suffrage Association (1875–78) and was a founder and friend of the Massachusetts Women's Christian Temperance Union (1875–85). She published many articles and two books that enjoyed considerable popularity, *My Story of the War* (1887) and *The Story of My Life* (1897).

Livingston, Edward (1764–1836) lawyer, statesman; born in Columbia County, N.Y. A member of the distinguished Livingston family, he studied law and went on to serve in the U.S. House of Representatives (Dem.-Rep., N.Y.; 1795–1801). He held the offices of U.S. attorney and mayor of New York City simultaneously (1801–04) but resigned when a business associate all but ruined him financially. He moved to New Orleans and began to practice law and pay off his debts when he was unfairly implicated in Aaron Burr's conspiracy to set up an independent nation (1806). For many years he was involved in a legal dispute over real estate that eventually led him into conflict with Thomas Jefferson. During the War of 1812 he took a lead in the defense of New Orleans (1814–15). He spent many years and gained a wide reputation for his work on attempting to reform the penal laws of Louisiana. He went back to the U.S. House of Representatives (Dem.-Rep., La.; 1823–29) and then to the U.S. Senate (1829–31). His old friend, President Andrew Jackson, appointed him secretary of state (1831–33) and then ambassador to France (1833–35); his major accomplishment in these offices was to oversee the negotiations that led to France's repaying American citizens for losses suffered during the Napoleonic wars.

Livingston, Goodhue (1867–1951) architect; born in New York City. He trained at Columbia College School of Mines. Among the many dignified neoclassical buildings he designed in his New York partnership with Breck Trowbridge (1894–1940s) were the St. Regis Hotel (1901–04) and B. Altman & Company Department Store (1905–14).

Livingston, Henry Brockholst (1757–1823) Supreme Court justice; born in New York City. He fought in the American

Revolution before serving on the New York Supreme Court (1802–06). An outspoken opponent of federalism, he was named by President Jefferson to the U.S. Supreme Court (1806–23).

Livingston, M. (Milton) Stanley (1905–86) physicist; born in Brodhead, Wis. He taught and performed research at Cornell University (1934–38), then moved to the Massachusetts Institute of Technology (1938–70). Concurrently, he consulted and performed atomic research at Brookhaven (1946–48), Harvard (1956–67), the Fermi National Accelerator Laboratory (1967–70), and Los Alamos (1950–86). A lifelong leader in atomic particle accelerator design, he developed the first cyclotron with E. O. Lawrence (1931).

Livingston, Peter van Brugh (1710–92) merchant, patriot; born in Albany, N.Y. (brother of Philip and William Livingston). He prospered in New York City by privateering and by supplying various military expeditions during the French and Indian wars. He was a supporter of his brother William's Whig politics and supported the patriot cause during the American Revolution.

Livingston, Philip (1716–78) Revolutionary patriot; born in Albany, N.Y. He had cultural, intellectual, and political interests and was one of the founders of King's College (later Columbia) and N.Y. Society Library. He served in the Continental Congress (1774–78) and signed the Declaration of Independence.

Livingston, Robert R. (1746–1813) lawyer, diplomat; born in New York City. He practiced law before entering the Continental Congress (1775–76, 1779–81, 1784–85). He was the secretary of the Department of Foreign Affairs (1781–83), and as ambassador to France (1801–04), he scored a diplomatic coup by seizing the opportunity to make the Louisiana Purchase agreement with France. As chancellor of New York (1777–1801), he played a major role in state affairs, helping to write its constitution and getting its support for the new federal constitution. He also subsidized Robert Fulton's experiments that led to the successful voyage of the steamboat *Clermont*.

Livingston, William (1723–90) legislator, governor; born in Albany, N.Y. After graduating from Yale in 1741, he chose law instead of the family business, joining the liberal New York firm of James Alexander, noted for championing freedom of the press. In a series of newspaper and magazine articles (1751–52), Livingston attacked a plan to charter King's College (New York City) under the Episcopalians, becoming a leader of the Whigs supporting the separation of church and state. His party won control of the Assembly in 1758, but lost power in 1769 when the "Sons of Liberty" demanded more radical opposition to the Stamp Act. Retreating to his country estate in New Jersey, he soon reemerged as a leader, joining a Committee of Correspondence before representing New Jersey at the First and Second Continental Congresses. In 1776, he briefly commanded the New Jersey militia. As New Jersey's first governor (Fed., 1776–90), he opposed paper currency and treated Loyalists moderately. As a delegate to the Constitutional Convention of 1787, he supported the compromises that would ease its acceptance.

Llewellyn, Karl (Nickerson) (1893–1962) legal scholar; born in West Seattle, Wash. He taught at the law schools of Yale and Columbia University (1930–51) before joining that of the University of Chicago (1951– 62). His specialty was unifying state laws and he helped write the Uniform Commercial Code, but he also became an authority on Native Americans' law. He wrote several books setting forth his broader approach to the law, one that stressed the common law and drew on sociology and anthropology – what he called "realistic jurisprudence": *The Bramble Bush* (1930); *The Cheyenne Way* (with E. A. Hoebel, 1941); and a collection of essays, *Jurisprudence: Realism, Theory and Practice* (1962).

Lloyd, Alice Spencer (b. Geddes) (1876–1962) educator; born in Athol, Mass. A Massachusetts newspaper editor, lecturer, and free-lance writer, she became disabled by spinal meningitis and – her brief marriage having failed – moved in 1916 to impoverished Knott County, Ky. With her mother she founded many elementary and secondary schools, and tuition-free Carey Junior College (later Alice Lloyd College) (1922), many of whose graduates became leaders in Appalachia. Along with a strict curriculum, she enforced almost puritanical rules at her college. The college was supported by gifts she solicited and staffed by college graduates who were attracted by her ideals. She left there only once – in 1951, to appear on the TV program, "This is Your Life," which helped raise $50,000.

Lloyd, Harold (Clayton) (1893–1971) movie actor; born in Burchard, Nebr. Beginning in movies in 1912 as a bit-player and extra, he appeared in a one-reel comedy series as "Willie Work," then did another series as "Lonesome Luke"; both were done under Hal Roach. In subsequent movies Lloyd fine-tuned his persona as a shy, colorless, average man – always wearing oversize horn-rimmed glasses – who makes his way through the minefields of life with a combination of pluck and ingenuity. Dubbed the "king of daredevil comedy," he performed his own stunts and from 1914 to 1947 kept movie fans suspended between hilarity and terror – and made himself a fortune. In 1952 he received a Special Academy Award for being a "master comedian and a good citizen," the latter recognizing his many contributions to charities and service organizations.

Lloyd, Henry Demarest (1847–1903) journalist, author; born in New York City. Disappointed with reform politics in New York City, he joined the *Chicago Tribune* (1872), where, as financial editor and editorial writer he concentrated on the emerging trusts and growing labor movement. He exposed misuses of power by the Standard Oil Company monopoly (1881), becoming the first of the new "muckrakers." Deciding to devote his life to reform, he left the *Tribune* (1885) and traveled to Europe, where he met with political and industrial leaders. On his return he successfully sought commutation of the death sentences of two of the convicted Haymarket rioters (1886). His extensively documented work, *Wealth Against Commonwealth* (1894), forcefully condemned business monopolies. He was nominated by the People's Party for a congressional seat from Chicago, but was heavily defeated. He backed the miners in a 1902 coal strike and officially joined the Socialist Party shortly before his death.

Lloyd, James (Tighman) (1857–1944) U.S. representative; born in Canton, Mo. A sheriff and prosecuting attorney, he went to the U.S. House of Representatives (Dem., Mo.; 1897–1917), serving as minority whip for eight years before leaving to practice law in Washington, D.C.

Locke, Alain Le Roy (1886–1954) teacher, editor, author; born in Philadelphia. He graduated from Harvard (B.A. 1907), and was the first African-American to attend Oxford University as a Rhodes Scholar (B.Litt. 1910). He studied philosophy at the University of Berlin (1910–11) and attended lectures by Henri Bergson in Paris. Returning to America, he taught philosophy at Howard University (1912–17), gained his Ph.D. at Harvard (1918), and resumed his teaching career at Howard as professor of philosophy (1918–53). He first became known as the editor of *The New Negro: An Interpretation* (1925), an anthology of African-American writers associated with the Harlem Renaissance. He published other anthologies featuring the literary work of African-Americans, as well as books, essays, and reviews that were influential in defining African-Americans' distinctive traditions and culture and the role they might play in bringing blacks into mainstream American society. In *The Negro and His Music* (1936) he placed African-Americans' music into the spectrum of African and world folk music, while his *Negro in Art* (1941) was one of the first works to stress the influence of African art on modern Western painting and sculpture.

Locke, Bessie (1865–1952) educator; born in West Cambridge, Mass. She attended kindergarten, public schools, and studied business at Columbia University. About 1892 she visited a kindergarten in New York City run by a friend for children from the slums. She was so impressed by the progress made by these children in manners and appearance that she organized the East End Kindergarten Union of Brooklyn and then the Brooklyn Free Kindergarten Society, of which whe was a trustee and financial secretary (1896–1923). She also organized at the state and national level the New York Kindergarten Society (1899) and the National Association for the Promotion of Kindergarten Education (1909), which became the National Kindergarten Association (1911) and in which she stayed active until her death. From 1913 to 1919 she helped form a kindergarten division within the United States Bureau of Education and worked for better teacher training courses. From 1917 she published a series of home-education articles that by her death had attained international distribution. She helped open more than 3,000 kindergartens benefiting more than 1.6 million children.

Locke, David Rose (Petroleum Vesuvius Nasby, pen name) (1833–88) journalist, writer; born in Vestal, N.Y. He had little formal education, but when very young (1843–50), was an apprentice journalist in Cortland, N.Y. He then worked as an itinerant printer and became a founder of the *Plymouth Advertiser* in Ohio (1852). When he was editor of the *Jeffersonian* in Findlay, Ohio, he gained popularity by printing the Nasby letters (1861); his assumed persona, the Reverend Petroleum Vesuvius Nasby, was an illiterate advocate of slavery and of everything that Locke detested. President Lincoln enjoyed the letters and was said to read them aloud to his Cabinet. Locke became editor and principal owner of the *Toledo Blade* (1865–88) and was a popular lecturer. He continued to publish his satiric letters until 1887, first collected in 1864 as *The Nasby Papers*.

Lockheed, Allan Haines See under LOCKHEED, MALCOLM.

Lockheed, Malcolm (b. Loughead) (?1887–1958) **and Allan Haines Lockheed** (1889–1969) aircraft executives; both born in Niles, Calif. The two brothers became automobile mechanics in San Francisco. Together they built their first airplane (named Model G) and made their first flight (1913). They flew exhibition flights at the Panama-Pacific International Exposition (1915) and they founded (1916) and ran the Loughead Aircraft Manufacturing Company. Malcolm left the company (1919) and disappeared from public life. Allan cofounded the Lockheed Aircraft Company (1926); he legally changed his last name to Lockheed in 1934, but it had been pronounced that way even before. He built the Vega aircraft and left the company just prior to the stock market crash (1929). He worked as a consultant and an aircraft company vice-president and in real estate.

Lockwood, Belva (Ann Bennett) (1830–1917) lawyer; born in Royalton, N.Y. She began teaching by age 15, and after meeting Susan B. Anthony, became more dedicated to fighting for women's rights. Moving to Washington, D.C. (1866), she applied for admission to a law school and was eventually awarded her degree (1873); her first petition to practice before the Supreme Court (1876) was denied, but in 1879, after getting Congress to pass a bill to support her, she became the first woman admitted to practice before the Supreme Court. She did practice law – in 1906 she won a $5 million award to the Cherokees – but she became best known for her activities on behalf of women's rights; in 1884 and 1888 she ran for president of the U.S.A. on the Equal Rights Party ticket. She lectured widely, worked for world peace, and served on the nominating committee for the Nobel Peace Prize.

Lockwood, Charles A. (Andrews) (1890–1967) naval officer; born in Midland, Va. He served aboard submarines (1914–28) and commanded submarines of the South West Pacific Force (1942–43) and of the Pacific Fleet (1943–45). He was the naval inspector general (1946–47).

Loden, Barbara (1932–80) actress, film director; born in Marion, N.C. Commencing her Broadway career in 1957, she enjoyed her greatest success playing the Marilyn Monroe-inspired role in Arthur Miller's *After the Fall* (1964); its director, Elia Kazan, became her (second) husband in 1967. She appeared in a few movies and television dramas, but turned to writing and directing her own films, including *The Frontier Experience* and *Wanda* (1970); the latter has gained considerable acclaim for its anticipation of feminist themes. She also directed off-Broadway plays and before her premature death she was starring in and codirecting *Come Back to the Five and Dime, Jimmy Dean.*

Lodge, George Cabot (1873–1909) poet; born in Boston, Mass. (son of Henry Cabot Lodge). He studied at Harvard (1891–95), in France and Berlin (1895–97), then became secretary to his father (1897), and to a Senate Committee in Washington, D.C. He is known for his sonnets, as in *The Song of the Wave, and Other Poems* (1898).

Lodge, Henry Cabot (1850–1924) U.S. representative/senator, historian; born in Boston, Mass. After obtaining his Ph.D. in political science from Harvard (1876), he joined the faculty and published several historical studies, including *Alexander Hamilton* (1882) and *George Washington* (1888). Active as a Republican in Massachusetts, including a term in the Massachusetts legislature, he served in the U.S. House of Representatives (1887–93) and then in the U.S. Senate (1893–1924). A champion of civil service reform and retaining the gold standard, he also helped secure the adoption of treaties allowing the construction of the Panama Canal. Although a conservative in many ways – he opposed

women's suffrage and the direct election of senators – he was also a close associate of the progressive Republican Theodore Roosevelt. But he is remembered in history because, as chairman of the Senate Foreign relations Committee, he led the opposition to the acceptance of the peace treaty after World War I and specifically President Woodrow Wilson linking it to the U.S.A.'s entry into the League of Nations.

Loeb, Jacques (1859–1924) physiologist; born in Mayen, Germany. He taught and performed research in Germany (1886–91), where his controversial research on caterpillars (1888) demonstrated that animals, like plants, possess similar mechanistic physiological responses (tropisms) to environmental stimuli. In 1899, he discovered artificial parthenogenesis in sea urchin eggs. Frustrated by Bismarck's oppressive regime, Loeb came to the U.S.A. to teach at Bryn Mawr (Pa.) College (1891–92). He moved to the University of Chicago (1892–1902), to the University of California: Berkeley (1902–10) before becoming a physiology professor at the Rockefeller Institute (1910–24). His studies on protein chemistry (1918–24) revealed that proteins can react as acids or bases. His philosophy of psychological and physiological tropisms is summarized in his most-read book, *The Mechanistic Conception of Life* (1912).

Loeb, James (1867–1933) banker, philanthropist, philhellene; born in New York City. He was a member of the family banking firm of Kuhn, Loeb, and Company from 1888 until his father's death in 1901. Thereafter, he lived abroad, primarily in Germany. In 1902, he endowed the Charles Eliot Norton traveling fellowship for Harvard and Radcliffe graduates to attend the American School of Classical Studies in Athens. In 1910, he endowed the Loeb series of texts and English translations of the principal Greek and Latin authors.

Loeb, Leonard B. (Benedict) (1891–1978) physicist; born in Zurich, Switzerland. Brought to the U.S.A. as an infant, he grew up in California. He served in World War I, studied in England, then at the University of Chicago (1919–23). He spent the rest of his career at the University of California: Berkeley, remaining active after his retirement in 1958. He was a specialist in gaseous electronics, authored 12 textbooks and approximately 180 scientific papers, and was a beloved mentor for his students throughout his career as a professor.

Loeffler, Charles Martin (Tornow) (1861–1935) composer, violinist; born in Mülhausen, Alsace. European trained, he came to the U.S.A. in 1881 and after beginning with Leopold Damrosch in New York City, he became affiliated with the Boston Symphony (1882–1903). He enjoyed some acclaim in his time for his colorfully impressionistic and often "neo-archaic" music, such as *Pagan Poem* (1901–07), but although admired by many American musicians, he never truly adopted an American musical idiom.

Loening, Grover (1888–1976) aircraft designer; born in Bremen, Germany (where his father was U.S. consul). He held three degrees from Columbia University including the first ever awarded in aeronautics. As owner of two different companies, he made a variety of contributions to aviation such as the creation of the rigid strut bracing system and the retractable undercarriage.

Loesser, (Henry) Frank (1910–69) lyricist, composer; born in

New York City. As a songwriter in Hollywood in the 1930s and 1940s he wrote such hits as "Heart and Soul" (1938, with Hoagy Carmichael), "Baby, It's Cold Outside" (1947), and "On a Slow Boat to China" (1948). After a modest success with *Where's Charley?* (1948), he scored his greatest triumph, with both critics and the public, with the Broadway classic, *Guys and Dolls* (1950), for which he wrote both words and music; it earned him a Tony Award. He then wrote the semi-operatic *The Most Happy Fella* (1956) and in 1962 he won the Pulitzer in drama for the musical *How to Succeed in Business Without Even Trying* (1961). He also ran a music publishing firm that helped support young composers.

Loevinger, Jane (1918–) psychologist; born in St. Paul, Minn. She studied at the universities of Minnesota and California: Berkeley (Ph.D. 1944). She joined the department of psychology at Washington University, St. Louis, as an instructor in statistics (1946) and became a research associate at its school of medicine (1960). Her research into the psychology of ego development resulted in many publications, including the two-volume *Measuring Ego Development* (1970, with Ruth Wessler and Carolyn Redmore).

Loewe, Frederick ("Fritz") (1904–88) composer; born in Vienna, Austria. Son of Edmund Loewe, an operetta tenor, at age 13 he was the youngest pianist to solo with the Berlin Symphony. At age 15 he composed "Katrina" (1919), which sold two million copies of sheet music in Europe. Although he had studied with great European masters of the piano, when he came to the U.S.A. in 1924 he failed as a piano virtuoso. He took up a series of odd jobs – prospecting for gold, professional boxing – but by the mid-1930s he had launched his career as a composer for the musical theater. Not until he teamed up with lyricist Alan Jay Lerner in 1942, however, did he find his true talent; their first big success was *Brigadoon* (1947) and this was followed by such classic stage and film musical scores as *My Fair Lady* (1956), *Gigi* (1958), and *Camelot* (1960). This last led to their falling-out and they did not collaborate again until in 1973 when they made a stage version of their film musical, *Gigi*. Their last collaboration was *The Little Prince* (1974), after which Loewe retired.

Loewy, Raymond (Fernand) (1893–1987) industrial designer; born in Paris, France. A World War I hero with an engineering degree, he came to New York in 1919 to pursue free-lance illustration. A flamboyant personality and keen businessman, he started his own international design firm (1929), working for Coca-Cola, United Airlines, Exxon, IBM, Greyhound, and others. Memorable are his 1947 Studebaker Starlight Coupe, the Coca-Cola bottle, and the Lucky Strike Cigarette package. In later years he designed Air Force One and NASA space equipment.

Logan (b. Tahgahjute) (also known as James Logan, probably named for the Quaker James Logan) (?1723–80) Indian leader; born in Shamokin (present-day Sunbury), Pa. (son of Chief Shikellamy). He was a friend of the whites until his family was killed at the Yellow Creek Massacre (Ohio, 1774). Dedicating himself to revenge, he refused to attend a peace meeting; instead he allegedly sent a reply that was given by a speaker and quoted in newspapers (and later used by Thomas Jefferson in his *Notes on the State of Virginia,* 1800), including the eloquent plaint: "There runs not a drop of my blood in the veins of any living creature . . .

Who is there to mourn for Logan? Not one!" Logan continued to attack white settlements and during the American Revolution brought scalps and prisoners to the British at Detroit. He was killed by a fellow Indian near Lake Erie.

Logan, James (1674–1750) colonial statesman, judge; born in Lurgan, Ireland. A Scottish schoolmaster's son, he worked as a merchant in Bristol, England; becoming William Penn's secretary in 1699, Logan emigrated with him to Pennsylvania that year. He held a series of government appointments in the colony, and sat on and eventually presided over the ruling Provincial Council (1702–47). He also accepted a judgeship in 1726, and was chief justice of the colony's supreme court (1731–39). He advised Penn's descendants for five decades and himself made a fortune in land speculation and trade with the Indians. He had long shown an interest in translating classical literature such as *M. T. Cicero's Cato Major,* printed in 1744 by Benjamin Franklin; after retiring from public life in 1747, he devoted his final years to his scholarly interests, including a notable work on botany.

Logan, John Alexander (1826–86) soldier, U.S. representative/senator; born in Jackson County, Ill. A lawyer, he volunteered to fight in the Mexican War, then served in the U.S. House of Representatives (Dem., Ill.; 1859–62). During the Civil War, .he held high commands with the Union Army of Tennessee, despite occasional charges that he was a Southern sympathizer. After the war he initiated the first Decoration (Memorial) Day, May 30, 1868. Switching to the Republican Party, he served Illinois as a U.S. representative again (1867–71) and then as senator (1871–77, 1879–86) and ran an unsuccessful campaign for the vice-presidency (1884).

Logan, Joshua (Lockwood III) (1908–88) theater/movie director, playwright; born in Texarkana, Texas. He studied at Princeton and in the late 1920s organized a summer stock company on Cape Cod that launched the careers of actors such as James Stewart and Henry Fonda. He then studied at the Moscow Art Theater under Constantin Stanislavsky and began to direct and act on Broadway as well as work on Hollywood movies. His schedule led to a nervous collapse in the early 1940s but he recovered and served with the U.S. Air Force Combat Intelligence in World War II. He returned to direct a series of hit plays and musicals including *Annie Get Your Gun* (1946), *Mister Roberts* (also cowrote stage version) (1948), *South Pacific* (also cowrote book) (1949); he also directed several successful movies including *Picnic* (1955), *Bus Stop* (1956), and *Camelot* (1967). In 1977 he acted and sang in his own nightclub show at the Rainbow Grill in New York City.

Lohman, Joseph D. (1910–68) criminologist, sociologist; born in New York City. Executive secretary of the National Committee on Segregation in the Nation's Capitol (1946–48), he served on corrections and parole committees in Illinois and was sheriff of Cook County, Ill. (1954–58). Teaching longest at the University of California: Berkeley, where he was dean of the School of Criminology (1961–68), he was consultant to foundations on crime and delinquency, author of numerous books, and appeared on several television series about delinquency and penitentiaries.

Loloma, Charles (1921–91) jewelry maker; born on Hotevilla Hopi Reservation, Ariz. After study at Alfred (N.Y.)

University, he returned to Arizona where he attained international standing with his innovative jewelry designs using Hopi motifs.

Lomax, Alan (1915–) folksong scholar; born in Austin, Texas. Son of folk music scholar John Lomax, he traveled with his father collecting and recording folksongs in prisons and elsewhere throughout the South; among their many discoveries was Huddie Ledbetter, or "Leadbelly," whom they brought to New York City in 1934. Alan joined his father in the Archive of American Folksong at the Library of Congress in 1937 and was responsible for the first recordings of such American originals as Jelly Roll Morton and Muddy Waters. He produced educational radio programs and traveled the world recording and studying folk music. He published *The Land Where the Blues Began* (1993), biographies of African-Americans, and collections of American folk songs – some in collaboration with his sister, Bess Lomax Hawes – that have provided valuable records of and insight into several areas of American folk culture.

Lomax, John A. (Avery) (1867–1948) folklorist; born in Goodman, Miss. He was raised in Texas, where as a teenager he began writing down cowboy songs. He taught and worked while earning his B.A. from the University of Texas (1895) and then got M.A.s in English from Texas (1906) and Harvard (1907). Encouraged by Harvard faculty and enabled by Harvard fellowships, he began systematically collecting cowboy songs at a time when most academics looked down on such an interest; his *Cowboy Songs and Other Frontier Ballads* (1910) was a landmark compilation. In order to support his family, for 20 years he moved back and forth from work in university administration to investment and banking institutions, but he continued to collect and lecture on folksongs. In 1932 he finally began to receive adequate financial aide so that he could take to the road full-time; assisted by his son Alan Lomax, he traveled mostly throughout the south and west; he replaced the old horn-and-cylinder recording machine with a battery powered microphone and disc-cutting machine, and over the years they recorded some 10,000 songs, eventually deposited in the Library of Congress Archives of American Folksong, of which he was named the first curator. Among his many discoveries were such songs as "Home on the Range" and "John Henry," and in 1933 the singer Huddie "Leadbelly" Ledbetter. His *American Ballads and Folk Songs* (1934) and *Our Singing Country* (compiled with his son, 1941), popularized folk music and inspired the folksong movement of the following decades.

Lombard, Carole (b. Jane Alice Peters) (1908–42) movie actress; born in Fort Wayne, Ind. Raised in California from age six, she made her screen debut at age 12. Her movie career was interrupted by an automobile accident but she recovered to appear in a series of Mack Sennett slapstick comedies, beginning with *The Girl from Everywhere* (1927). She went on to become one of the most unusual combinations in Hollywood's history – a beautiful, intelligent, stylish, natural actress, adept at sophisticated comedy. She made several films with her first husband, William Powell, and one with her second husband-to-be, Clark Gable. John Barrymore, with whom she made *Twentieth Century* (1934), called her "perhaps the greatest actress I have ever worked with." She finished *To Be or Not to Be* with Jack Benny (1942) just two weeks before her death in a plane crash when returning from a war bond drive.

Lombardi, (Vincent Thomas) Vince (1913–70) football coach; born in New York City. A starting guard for Fordham's "Seven Blocks of Granite" line in the 1930s, he won great respect as a National Football League (NFL) assistant coach before being named head coach of the Green Bay Packers in 1959. He proved a driving, charismatic leader, winning five NFL championships in only nine seasons. His Packers were victors in Super Bowls I and II. His supposed maxim, "Winning isn't the most important thing; it's the only thing," is probably a misquote of his statement on making the effort to win.

Lombardo, (Gaetano Alberto) Guy (1902–77) bandleader; born in London, Ontario. His band began performing in the United States in 1923. As Guy Lombardo and the Royal Canadians, they went to New York in 1929 and were featured at the Roosevelt Grill for 33 years. In addition to touring extensively and making many successful recordings, the band appeared on radio, television, and in films and appeared live on television every New Year's Eve for many years.

London, Fritz (Wolfgang) (1900–54) physicist; born in Breslau, Germany (now Wroclaw, Poland). While a student in Zurich, he published his pioneering quantum theory of chemical bonding (1927); in 1930 his quantum mechanical interpretation of the Van der Waals intramolecular forces made them known as "London forces." Fleeing the Nazis (1933), London and his physicist brother Heinz London went to Oxford where the two developed the London equations on superconductivity (1935). Fritz London came to Duke University (1939), where he continued his contributions to studies of superfluidity and cryogenics (1939–54).

London, George (b. Burnstein) (1919–85) bass-baritone; born in Montreal, Canada. He studied voice in Los Angeles and made his operatic debut at the Hollywood Bowl in 1941. After years of further study and touring he joined the Vienna State Opera in 1949 and the Metropolitan Opera in New York in 1951. There his rich voice and dramatic abilities illuminated roles including *Boris Gudunov,* which he also sang to acclaim in Moscow. Illness ended his singing career in the mid-1960s; his last years were spent heading opera organizations.

London, (John Griffith) Jack (1876–1916) writer; born in San Francisco. He is said to be the illegitimate son of William Henry Chaney, an astrologer; his mother, a spiritualist, married John London shortly after Jack was born. He had little formal schooling although he was an avid reader, and he spent much of his youth on the Oakland, Calif., waterfront, where he worked at a variety of jobs, some of which – such as oyster pirating – were illegal. In 1893 he worked on a ship that hunted seals from the Arctic to Japan. From 1894–95 he traveled as a hobo and oddjobber throughout Canada and the U.S.A. – at one point joining "Coxey's army" in its march to Washington – and was arrested for vagrancy in New York City. His experiences and reading (including the "Communist Manifesto") convinced him that he was a socialist, and on returning to California he briefly enrolled at the University of California and tried to sell his early writings. Beginning his restless wanderings again, he worked as a goldminer in the Klondike, Yukon Territory (1897–98). Returning to San Francisco, he began to sell stories, novels, and nonfiction, much of it drawing on his experiences in the North; the best known of these are *The Call of the Wild* (1903), *The Sea Wolf* (1904), and *White Fang* (1906). In 1902 he visited the slums of London, and this inspired his book *The People of the Abyss* (1903). In 1904 he covered the Russo-Japanese War for the Hearst newspapers and in 1914 he covered the Mexican Revolution for *Collier's*. In 1907 he went to the South Pacific in a small sailboat, a trip described in *The Cruise of the Snark* (1907). His peripatetic life was the major source for his fiction, especially his thinly autobiographical novels, *Martin Eden* (1908–09) and *John Barleycorn* (1913). From 1905 on he was based on his large ranch in Glen Ellen, Calif., but he often traveled on the lecture circuit. His work earned him over a million dollars but he never seemed able to deal with his success; he promoted explicit socialist views in both fictional and nonfictional works, even while exalting the life of the primitive and self-sufficient. He was an alcoholic and by 1909 he was plagued by a variety of ailments; dependent on painkillers, he died from a (possibly self-inflicted) overdose of morphine.

London, Meyer (1871–1926) lawyer, politician, public official; born in Suwalki, Poland. He emigrated to New York City in 1891, and working by day and studying at night, earned admission to the bar in 1898. A specialist in labor law, he became active in leftist politics and helped found the Socialist Party of America. Elected to the U.S. House of Representatives as a socialist (N.Y., 1915–19, 1921–23), he fought for labor reform and other progressive causes. He initially opposed U.S. participation in World War I. He was killed in an automobile accident.

Long, Crawford (Williamson) (1815–78) surgeon, anesthetist; born in Danielsville, Ga. Practicing in rural Georgia, he was the first doctor to use sulphuric ether as an anesthetic in an operation (1842) – he was removing a tumor from a patient's neck. Although he operated several more times with ether before 1846, he was apparently unaware of its full significance and did not publish a description of his procedure until 1849. By that time, W. T. G. Morton of Boston had filed a patent for discovery of ether in 1846 and Long would never get much credit or gain from claim to priority.

Long, Earl (Kemp) (1895–1960) governor; born in Winnfield, La. (brother of Huey Long). A salesman (1912–27) and tax attorney, he served as his brother's campaign strategist and lobbyist but became a bitter foe when Huey would not pick him as the candidate for lieutenant governor of Louisiana. A Democrat, he got himself elected lieutenant governor on his own in 1936, then moved up to governor (1939–40) because of a political scandal. Returning as the elected governor (1948–52, 1956–60), he passed populist health and education measures, and opposed segregationists, but became increasingly eccentric in his personal life. He was elected to the U.S. House of Representatives in 1960 but died 10 days later.

Long, Huey P. (Pierce) (1893–1935) governor, U.S. senator, political boss, demagogue; born in Winnfield, La. Admitted to the bar in 1915, he came to prominence during his ten years with the Louisiana Railroad (later Public Service) Commission, where he gained the reputation of being a populist who worked on behalf of the rural poor. As a Democrat, he was elected governor of Louisiana (1928–32) and to the U.S. Senate (1932–35), all the while building up a formidable political machine. Adored by his constituents for the services he delivered, "the Kingfish" was reviled both in

the state and nationally for corruption and dictatorial practices; by 1934 he literally controlled every level of government in Louisiana. A founder of the "Share the Wealth" movement, he announced his plan to run for president of the U.S.A. but was assassinated in 1935, allegedly by a doctor opposed to his corrupt ways.

Long, John Davis (1838–1915) governor, secretary of the navy; born in Buckfield, Maine. He was governor of Massachusetts (1880–82) and a U.S. representative (Rep., Mass.; 1883–89). As secretary of the navy (1897–1902) he worked closely with President McKinley and was partly responsible for the navy's sterling performance during the Spanish-American War.

Long, Russell B. (Billiu) (1918–) U.S. senator; born in Shreveport, La. (son of Huey Long). Raised in a completely political environment, he served in the U.S. Senate (Dem., La.; 1948–87). He served as chairman of the Finance Committee and the Joint Committee on Internal Revenue Taxation. From 1965–69 he was the Democrats' majority leader, but a "revolt" by Northern liberals replaced him with Edward Kennedy.

Long, Stephen Harriman (1784–1864) soldier, explorer, engineer; born in Hopkinton, N.H. A Dartmouth graduate, he entered the army in 1814. In 1817 he established Fort Smith, now a city in Arkansas. He then began to lead expeditions for the army: In 1820 he led an exploration party into the Rocky Mountains (discovering the peak outside Denver, Colo., named after him), and in 1823 he explored the sources of the Minnesota River and helped survey the border between the U.S.A. and Canada. After 1827, as a consulting engineer for railroads, he surveyed railroad routes, including that of the Baltimore & Ohio, drew up a manual with curves and gradients, and built railroad bridges. In 1861 he joined the Federal government as chief of the topographical engineers.

Longfellow, Henry Wadsworth (1807–82) poet; born in Portland, Maine. After graduation from Bowdoin College (1825), he studied languages in Europe (1826–29) and became professor and librarian at Bowdoin (1829–35). After further study in Europe, he was appointed Smith Professor of French and Spanish at Harvard (1836–54). A collection of poetry, *Voices in the Night* (1839), contained the poems "A Psalm Life," "Hymn to the Night," and "The Light of the Stars," which soon became widely known. *Ballads and Other Poems* (1841), including such immensely popular works as "The Village Blacksmith," "The Wreck of the Hesperus," and "Excelsior," and his longer narrative poems, *Evangeline* (1847), *The Song of Hiawatha* (1855), and *The Courtship of Miles Standish* (1858), further served to make him the best-known American poet of the century. His *Tales of a Wayside Inn* (1863) opens with "Paul Revere's Ride," which has ever since been a national favorite. The widespread knowledge of these works and their inclusion in school curricula throughout the country did much to establish the popular notion of poetry in the U.S.A. well into the 20th century. For spiritual solace after the accidental death of his second wife in 1861, he translated *The Divine Comedy of Dante Alighieri* (1865–67) and produced a series of six sonnets, "Divina Commedia," which are among his finest poems. Although his work later came to be regarded as saccharine and didactic, there is no denying that he long played one of the traditional roles of a poet.

Longman, (Mary) Evelyn Beatrice (1874–1954) sculptor; born near Winchester, Ohio. She studied with Lorado Taft at the Institute of Chicago (1893–1900), moved to New York City, became the assistant of Daniel Chester French (c. 1901–04), and is known for her beaux-arts style in such commissioned works as *Genius of Electricity* (also known as *The Spirit of Communication*) (1916). In 1926 she married Nathaniel Batchelder and lived in Windsor, Conn.

Longstreet, Augustus Baldwin (1790–1870) lawyer, author, educator, editor; born in Augusta, Ga. He graduated from Yale (1813) and attended the Litchfield (Conn.) Law School (1813–14) before being admitted to the Georgia bar (1815) and settling in Greensboro, Ga. He served in the state legislature (1821) and then as a Georgia Superior Court judge (1822–25) before returning to Augusta to practice law. He wrote a series of 18 humorous sketches for the *Southern Recorder* that were first published anonymously in 1835 as *Georgia Scenes, Characters and Incidents Etc., in the First Half Century of the Republic* (republished under his name in 1840). Popular in their day, they have little literary standing but are known for foreshadowing the frontier vernacular writings of others such as George Washington Harris and Mark Twain. Ordained as a Methodist minister in 1838, he turned to a career as college president: Emory College (Ga.) (1839–48), Centenary College (La.) (1849), the University of Mississippi (1849–56), and the University of South Carolina (1857–65). He had already declared his sympathies when he founded and edited the *Augusta State Rights Sentinel* (1834–36); he supported secession and after the Civil War he wrote articles justifying the Southern position. He also wrote short stories and a novel.

Longstreet, James (1821–1904) soldier; born in Edgefield District, S.C. Raised in Georgia and Alabama, he graduated from West Point (1842) and saw service during the Mexican War. He resigned his U.S. Army commission to join the Confederate army in June 1861. One of Lee's chief lieutenants, he was an outstanding combat officer but was sometimes overcautious as a commander; his delays at Gettysburg led to his being blamed for the Confederate failure there (although Lee and students of the battle have not confirmed this). After the Civil War he became a Republican – even backing Ulysses Grant for president – and he was shunned by many southerners; many years later, he would air his differences with Lee's decisions in his book, *From Manassas to Appomattox* (1896). After several years in private business, he held several federal appointments, including minister resident to Turkey (1880–81).

Longworth, Nicholas (1869–1931) U.S. representative; born in Cincinnati, Ohio. Son of a wealthy, prominent Cincinnati family, he graduated from Harvard University and the University of Cincinnati Law School. He entered Republican politics, serving in the Ohio house (1899–1901) and senate (1901–03) before going to Congress (Rep., Ohio; 1903–13 and 1915–31). In 1906 he made a brilliant match when he married Alice Lee Roosevelt, daughter of Theodore Roosevelt, in the White House. He studied parliamentary procedures and was Republican floor leader before being elected Speaker (1925–31). He advocated strong leadership, adherence to House rules, and cooperation. His fairness endeared him to Democrats and he eliminated the use of personal invective in congressional debates. A natural mediator, he did not hesitate to oppose his father-in-law when he supported Taft's presidential bid in 1912. A talented musician, he and his wife were much admired in Washington, D.C., society.

Lookout, Fred (b. Wahtsake Tumpah) (?1860–1949) Osage chief; born near Independence in present-day Kansas. He was elected to the tribal council in 1896 and head chief, for the first of nine terms, in 1913. When oil was discovered on the reservation he kept much of the money within the tribe.

Loomis, Elias (1811–89) astronomer, mathematician; born in Willington, Conn. He taught math at Western Reserve College (1837–44), and natural history at the University of the City of New York (1844–60) and Yale (1860–89). He wrote books on math and astronomy, determined the speed that electrical current travels in wire, and calculated elements of the orbit of Halley's comet.

Loos, Anita (?1893–1981) writer, playwright; born in Sisson (now Mt. Shasta), Calif. Her father was involved in theatrical companies, and as the family moved, she was a child actress in San Francisco, Los Angeles, and San Diego. She wrote scenarios and dialogue cards for silent movies, married John Emerson (1919), and moved to New York City. She continued to write scores of films and plays, often with the assistance of her husband. They moved to Europe in the 1920s, and, after the stock market crash of 1929, returned to Hollywood. There and in New York City, she wrote screenplays for talking pictures. She is best known for her satiric story collection, *"Gentlemen Prefer Blondes": The Illuminating Diary of a Professional Lady* (1925). The escapades of the protagonist, Lorelei Lee, were adapted as a play, two musicals and movies.

Lopez, Aaron (1731–82) merchant; born in Portugal. He came to Newport, R.I. (1752) and began to practice his Jewish faith. He soon had a large merchant fleet that traded along the Atlantic coast and in the West Indies but the American Revolution ruined his business. Greatly respected in Newport for his honesty and reliability, he drowned at sea.

Lopez, Nancy (1957–) golfer; born in Torrance, Calif. After an outstanding career in amateur golf, she turned professional in 1977 and won the Ladies' Professional Golf Association (LPGA) championship the following year. She was voted LPGA player of the year four times (1978–79, 1985, 1988). She was married to former baseball star, Ray Knight.

Lord, Alfred Bates (1912–91) scholar of oral traditions; born in Boston, Mass. He was educated at Harvard (B.A. 1934, M.A. 1936; Ph.D. 1949), where he was a member of the faculty from 1940 until his retirement as the Arthur Kingsley Porter professor of Slavic and Comparative Literature in 1983. In the 1930s, along with Milman Parry, he recorded and transcribed more than 12,000 oral epics of Serbo-Croatian singers, work which he continued after Parry's death in 1935. Parry and Lord's work with the Serbo-Croatian oral poets led them to conclude that Homer was an oral poet, a theory that revolutionized Homeric studies. His publications include *Serbo-Croatian Folk Tales* (with Bela Bartok, 1951), *Singer of Tales* (1960), and *Epic Singers and Oral Tradition* (1991). His numerous awards include the Order of the Yugoslav Flag with Golden Wreath (1988).

Lord, Daniel A. (Aloysius) (1881–1955) Catholic author, editor; born in Chicago. Ordained a Jesuit priest in 1923, he wrote numerous plays, pageants, and religious books and pamphlets and played a key role in reviving the devotional

Sodality movement in the United States and broadening its scope.

Lorde, Audre (Geraldin[e]) (1934–92) poet, writer; born in New York City. She studied at the University of Mexico (1945), Hunter College (B.A. 1959), and Columbia University (M.L.S. 1961). Based in the Virgin Islands, she taught at many institutions, including Hunter (N.Y.C.) (1980). She was an African-American activist and lesbian feminist who explored the dimensions of modern life in poetry, a novel, and nonfiction, as in *The Cancer Journals* (1980).

Lorentz, Pare (1905–) documentary filmmaker; born in Clarksburg, W.Va. A journalist and movie critic, he became the film adviser to the U.S. Resettlement Administration under President Franklin Roosevelt; for this he wrote and directed two classic documentaries: *The Plow that Broke the Plains* (1936) and *The River* (1937). As head of the new U.S. Film Service, he made *The Fight for Life* (1940); in 1941 he made some short subjects for RKO, then some documentaries for the military in World War II; and from 1946–47 he was chief of the film section of the War Department's Civil Affairs Division.

Lorenz, Edward N. (1917–) meteorologist; born in West Hartford, Conn. Working at the Massachusetts Institute of Technology (1946), he was the first to describe what is known as "deterministic chaos" as a shaper of weather; the impact of his work on scientists' view of nature has been compared in importance to that of Isaac Newton. Among other major meteorology awards, he received the 1991 Kyoto Prize.

Lorimer, George Horace (1868–1937) editor; born in Louisville, Ky. After early success in a meat-packing company and early failure as a retail grocer, he turned to reporting, and, in 1898, won a job from Cyrus H. K. Curtis as literary editor of Curtis's newly acquired *Saturday Evening Post*. He was soon promoted to editor in chief. In his long tenure (1899–1936) he attracted such talented contributors as Mary Roberts Rinehart, Ring Lardner, Sinclair Lewis, Kenneth Roberts, and John P. Marquand. Aided by a solid instinct for public taste, he succeeded in reaching a broad audience that, at the peak of the *Post*'s popularity, exceeded 3 million people. His editorials reflected a basically conservative view, and his vision of America was typified in the popular wholesome *Post* covers, especially those drawn by Norman Rockwell. Lorimer thought himself closely in tune with the American public and was dismayed toward the end of his career by the popularity of New Deal policies.

Loring, William W. (Wing) (1818–86) soldier; born in Wilmington, N.C. He interrupted a Florida state legislative career for military service in the Seminole, Mexican, and Mormon Wars. For most of the Civil War he was a Confederate corps commander. Later he commanded the defenses of the Khedive of Egypt (1869–79), who designated him a pasha. He returned to the U.S.A. for his final years.

Lorsch, Jay W. (William) (1932–) human relations educator; born in St. Joseph, Mo. He earned a D.B.A. at Harvard, where he joined the business school faculty (1965). Known for his application of behavioral science to organizations, he wrote many books on organizational behavior and development including *Understanding Management* (1978) and *Handbook of Organizational Behavior* (1987).

Losey, Joseph (1909–84) movie director; born in La Crosse, Wis. He began directing short subjects, graduating to features with *The Boy With Green Hair* (1948), revealing his interest in social commentary. In exile as a result of the Communist witch hunt of the early 1950s, he settled in England and made a number of quintessentially British movies such as *The Servant* (1963).

Loss, Louis (1914–) legal scholar; born in Lancaster, Pa. Son of Russian immigrants, he decided early to become a lawyer, and after majoring in pre-law at the University of Pennsylvania (1934), he went to Yale Law School. On graduation (1937), he joined the Securities and Exchange Commission (SEC) in Washington, D.C., and gradually became the authority on the laws and regulations pertaining to securities. After teaching securities law part time at the law schools of Yale and George Washington University, he joined the faculty of Harvard Law School in 1952, resigning from the SEC later that year. He published the one-volume *Securities Regulation* (1941), thereby coining that very term as well as laying the intellectual foundations of the legal discipline, and then coauthored (with Joel Seligman) its 11-volume update, *Securities Regulation* (1993), the definitive treatise on the subject. Through his courses and writings on securities law, he trained generations of American lawyers and judges in this subject. His 700-page codification of all American securities laws, regulations, and court decisions only awaits passage by Congress to introduce some standards and simplification into this otherwise confused and confusing field.

Lothrop, Harriet Mulford (b. Stone) (Margaret Sidney, pen name) (1844–1924) writer; born in New Haven, Conn. She attended private school in New Haven, married Daniel Lothrop, founder of the Lothrop publishing company (1881), and settled in the former home of Louisa May Alcott and Nathaniel Hawthorne in Concord, Mass. She is remembered, among many other works, for the *Five Little Peppers and How They Grew* (1881) series for children.

Lothrop, S. K. (Samuel Kirkland) (1892–1965) anthropologist, archaeologist; born in Milton, Mass. He was a Harvard-trained curator of Andean archaeology at the Peabody Museum. After 1915 he conducted extensive fieldwork, notably in Tierra del Fuego, Guatemala, and Mexico. His books include *Coclé* (1937, 1941), *Chichén Itzá* (coauthored, 1951), and *Pre-Columbian Art* (1957).

Loudon, Samuel (ca. 1727–1813) printer, publisher; probably born in Ireland. He arrived in New York City by 1753 and began to publish *The New York Packet and the American Advertiser* in 1776. Although he was a stout patriot, some of his writings were burned by the radical New York Committee of Mechanics (1776). He printed the first constitution of New York (1777), *Laws of the State of New York* (1786), and Noah Webster's *American Magazine* (1787–88). He also operated a bookstore and a circulating library.

Louganis, (Gregory) Greg (1960–) diver; born in San Diego, Calif. One of the greatest divers in history, he won platform and springboard gold medals at both the 1984 and 1988 Olympics.

Louis, Joe (b. Joe Louis Barrow) (1914–81) boxer; born in Lafayette, Ala. His reign as heavyweight champion of 11 years, eight months, is the longest in boxing history (1937–49). He turned professional in 1934 and won the heavyweight title in 1937 with a knockout of James J. Braddock in the eighth round. He defended his title 25 times, a record for any weight division, and posted a career record of 68 wins, three losses, with 54 knockouts. Nicknamed, "The

Brown Bomber," he was a devastating puncher with either hand. His grace and seeming invincibility inspired African-Americans and won him fans throughout the world. Poor management of his earnings, however, left him practically destitute in his later years and he was often dependent on charitable gifts and such jobs as a "greeter" at a gambling casino. His autobiography, *Joe Louis: My Life*, was published in 1978.

Louis, Morris (Bernstein) (1912–62) painter; born in Baltimore, Md. He studied at the Maryland Institute of Fine and Applied Arts (1929–33), and remained in the Baltimore and Washington, D.C. area. His work was strongly influenced by the work of Helen Frankenthaler, and he adapted her staining method to produce a group of paintings called *Veils* (c. 1954–59), and another collection of florals, *Aleph Series* (c. 1960). A prolific and inventive artist, his last series, *Unfurleds* (c. 1960), used broken diagonals.

Lounsbury, Floyd (1914–) linguist; born in Stevens Point, Wis. Educated at Yale (Ph.D. 1949), he later taught there while pursuing research in linguistics and ethnology. He did fieldwork among the Oneida, Cherokee, and Seneca tribes and is the author of *Comparative Indian Morphology*.

Lourie, Richard (1940–) translator, literary critic, novelist; born in Cambridge, Mass. Known for his extensive critical analysis of Russian dissident author Andrew Sinyavsky, he was a prolific translator of Russian and Polish texts, including the works of Soviet writer Vladimir Voinovich and Nobel laureate Czeslaw Milosz. He was founder of Kontakt, a company specializing in Russian/American publishing, and was editor in chief of Governor Mario Cuomo's project to translate Abraham Lincoln's writings into Polish. Recipient of the 1971 Joseph Henry Jackson Award for fiction, he often wrote plots involving cold war topics.

Love, Alfred Henry (1830–1913) radical pacifist, merchant; born in Philadelphia, Pa. A pioneering pacifist of highest principles, he was a wool merchant who resisted the Civil War by refusing to sell his goods for army use; when drafted (1863), he refused to serve or procure a substitute. Founder of the Universal Peace Society (1866) (later the Universal Peace Union), he and its members worked for a reconciliation between North and South and other human rights issues. He pioneered the concept of arbitration and served as a strike mediator (1880s). An uncompromising opponent of militarism, he fought for an international court, but by the eve of the Spanish-American war was considered impractical by fellow pacifists and he was even burned in effigy.

Lovecraft, H. P. (Howard Philips) (Lawrence Appleton, Houdini, John J. Jones, Ames Dorrance Rowely, Edgar Softly, among many pen names) (1890–1937) writer; born in Providence, R.I. He was self-educated and lived in Providence all his life, working as a free-lance writer, journalist, and ghostwriter. From 1914 until 1918 he was an astrology columnist for the *Evening News* (Providence) and was the publisher of *The Conservative* magazine (1915–19; 1923). He was also president of the United Amateur Press Association (1917–18; 1923). Using many pen names, he contributed his supernatural/horror and science fiction/fantasy stories to various pulp magazines, but his reputation as a writer rests mainly on the 60 or so stories he published in *Weird Tales* starting in 1923. Although not much appreciated in his day, he came to attract a small, sometimes fanatical following both in America and abroad, particularly France.

Lovejoy, Arthur O. (Oncken) (1837–1962) philosopher, intellectual historian; born in Berlin, Germany. Brought by his American parents to Boston in 1874, he took his M.A. from Harvard where he studied under Josiah Royce and William James, and then went on to the Sorbonne in Paris. After teaching philosophy at Stanford (1899–1900), Washington University (St. Louis) (1901–09), and the University of Missouri (1909–10), he spent the rest of his career at Johns Hopkins (1910–38). He turned away from the traditional concerns of philosophy to concentrate on tracing the historical evolution of certain fundamental concepts – effectively founding the modern discipline of the history of ideas. He founded and was first editor of the *Journal of the History of Ideas* and was one of the pioneers in encouraging an interdisciplinary approach to scholarship. His masterwork was *The Great Chain of Being* (1936), which proved to be highly influential well beyond philosophy faculties. Other works include *Primitivism and Related Ideas in Antiquity* (with George Boas, 1935) and *Essays in the History of Ideas* (1948). He was also active in settlement work, academic freedom issues, and antifascist organizations during both world wars.

Lovejoy, Elijah (Parish) (1802–37) abolitionist; born in Albion, Maine. Ordained a Presbyterian minister (1833), he went to St. Louis, Mo., to preach and edit the Presbyterian *St. Louis Observer,* enlisting the paper in the fight against slavery, intemperance, and "popery." Harassed for promoting even gradual abolitionism, in 1836 he moved to Alton, Ill., to relocate his paper as the *Alton Observer.* Although some citizens supported his views on slavery, others were adamantly opposed and they threw three successive printing presses into the local river. The final straw came when he called for establishing an auxiliary of the American Anti-Slavery Society (1837). He was shot during a mob attack as he was defending the arrival of yet another printing press.

Lovejoy, Esther Pohl (b. Clayson) (1869–1967) physician, health administrator; born near Seabeck, Washington Territory. Raised on the frontier and with little formal education, she was determined to be a doctor and got herself admitted to the medical school of the University of Oregon, becoming its second woman graduate (1894). After practicing obstetrics in Portland, she and her husband, Emil Pohl, also a doctor, went to Alaska to practice. She returned to Portland in 1899, and while continuing her practice, she also became interested in the women's suffrage movement. From 1905–09, the last two years as director, she was on the Portland Board of Health, and she set sanitation standards that gained her and Portland a national reputation. She continued her private practice and from 1917–18, as a member of the American Women's Medical Association, she worked for the American Red Cross in France. She helped set up the American Women's Hospital and returned to France in 1919 to set up the first of their clinics. Back in Portland she continued her crusade for women's right to vote, ran unsuccessfully for Congress (1920), worked for the medical relief of people throughout the world, and promoted the role of women in medicine. She endowed the Pohl scholarships at the University of Oregon (1936) and wrote several books.

Lovejoy, Owen (1811–64) abolitionist, statesman; born in Albion, Maine. Preparing for the Presbyterian ministry under his minister/editor brother, Elijah, he was there the night that Elijah was killed by an anti-abolitionist mob in Alton, Ill., while defending his printing press. Vowing to fight slavery to vindicate his brother, he spoke fearlessly for this cause (1840–50) despite an Illinois law prohibiting abolition meetings. Elected to the Illinois legislature as an abolitionist (1854), and an early booster of Abraham Lincoln, he was elected to the U.S. House of Representatives (Rep. Ill.; 1857–64) where he sponsored the bill calling for an end to slavery in the United States.

Lovett, Robert (1895–1986) secretary of defense; born in Huntsville, Texas. A Yale graduate and an investment banker, Lovett served in many governmental positions including under secretary of state (1947–49) before becoming secretary of defense (1951–53). He was a director of the Union Pacific Railroad for over fifty years.

Lovins, Amory (Bloch) (1947–) physicist, author; born in Washington, D.C. Educated at Harvard and Oxford, he resigned a physics research fellowship at Merton College, Oxford, to work for Friends of the Earth. A consultant on energy issues, he published widely on energy and other environmental issues, including *Non-Nuclear Futures* (1975), of which he was coauthor. In 1982 he became director of research for the Rocky Mountain Institute in Old Snowmass, Colo. He wrote a syndicated newspaper column on environmental issues and was also a published poet.

Low, Isaac (1735–91) merchant, Loyalist; born at Raritan Landing, N.J. A successful New York City merchant, he was a moderate in the First Continental Congress (1774–75). He cooperated with the British occupation forces (1776–83) and his property was confiscated by patriots (1779). A founder of the New York Chamber of Commerce, he moved to England in 1783.

Low, Juliette (1860–1927) founder of the Girl Scouts; born in Chicago, Ill. From a prominent Savannah, Ga., family, she was educated at private schools and traveled widely. Inspired by the Girl Guides of England, she established the Girl Scouts of America in 1912. Her charm, conviction, and hard work ensured the Girl Scouts' early success.

Low, Mary (Louise b. Fairchild) MacMonnies (1858–1946) painter; born in New Haven, Conn. She studied at the Académie Julien in Paris and married Frederick MacMonnies (1888). After her divorce she married Will Low (1909), and returned to America to live in New York City. During her stay in France she painted sunny impressionistic scenes, such as *Five O'Clock Tea* (1891).

Low, Seth (1850–1916) college president, merchant; born in Brooklyn, N.Y. A successful merchant, he developed public schools and transportation and a permanent civil service as mayor of Brooklyn (1881–86) and New York City (1901–03). As president of Columbia College (later University) (1890–1901) he bought the Morningside Heights site. Columbia's Low Library is named after him.

Low, Will (Hicok) (1853–1932) painter; born in Bronxville, N.Y. He studied in Paris with Gérôme (1872–77), and was a friend of Robert Louis Stevenson. The second husband of Mary MacMonnies Low (1909), he was known as a popular decorative painter.

Lowden, Frank Orren (1861–1943) lawyer, U.S. representative, governor; born near Sunrise City, Minn. He grew up in Iowa where he worked on a farm and taught school. Educated in Iowa and then Chicago, he established a lucrative law practice in Chicago, married George Pullman's

daughter, and began managing the Pullman railroad industries in 1897. Serving in the U.S. House of Representatives (Rep., Ill.; 1906–11), he worked to reform in the State Department. As governor of Illinois (1917–21), he created a state budget bureau and initiated other reforms. He retired to his farm outside Chicago and declined all offers by his fellow Republicans to run for or accept higher office, although he did campaign for measures beneficial to agriculture and improving public administration. During the Great Depression he favored extensive federal aid to farmers.

Lowe, Thaddeus (Sobieski Coulincourt) (1832–1913) aeronaut, inventor; born in Jefferson Mills (now Riverton), N.H. Heading the Union Army's aeronautic section during the Civil War, he sent the first telegraph message from an airborn balloon (1861) and was the first American to take a photograph while airborne. He created a device to measure longitude and latitude (1860) and directed construction of an incline railway at Echo Mountain, California (1891–94), later renamed Mount Lowe. He was also active in manufacturing artificial ice and in improving the manufacture of gas and coke.

Lowell, A. (Abbott) Lawrence (1856–1943) political scientist; born in Boston, Mass. (brother of Amy Lowell and Percival Lowell). After practicing law (1880–97), he taught at Harvard (1897–1909) and served as its president (1909–33). As president, he revamped the undergraduate curriculum and pioneered the opening of Harvard's graduate schools of architecture, business administration, education, and public health. He wrote on a variety of subjects including American education, European history and government, a biography of his astronomer brother, Percival, and his own autobiography. Due to public outcry in 1927, he and two others were asked by the governor of Massachusetts to review the Sacco and Vanzetti murder verdict and subsequent death sentence; the "Lowell Committee" upheld the court's verdict and the execution took place, leaving Lowell a permanent villain in certain circles.

Lowell, Amy (Lawrence) (1874–1925) poet; born in Brookline, Mass. (sister of Percival and Abbott Lawrence Lowell). She was educated privately, traveled widely, and settled in her childhood home. She suffered nervous breakdowns, but from 1902 on, found stability in writing literary criticism, "polyphonic prose," and, most importantly, Imagist and free verse poetry, as in *Sword Blades and Poppy Seed* (1914). In the last decade of her life, she was one of the most prominent and outspoken figures in American arts.

Lowell, Francis Cabot (1775–1817) textile manufacturer; born in Newburyport, Mass. (son of Judge John Lowell). He worked in import-export trade and observed textile machinery in Lancashire while on a visit to England (1810–12). On his return, he started the Boston Manufacturing Company in Waltham, Mass. (1813) with the assistance of his brother-in-law Patrick Tracy Jackson, Paul Moody, and Nathan Appleton. It was the first mill ever to combine all the operations of making finished cloth from raw cotton. He pushed for high duties on imported cotton cloth. He died prematurely and his partners named their new factory town, Lowell, Mass., after him.

Lowell, James Russell (1819–91) editor, diplomat, poet; born in Cambridge, Mass. He studied at Harvard (B.A. 1838; L.L.B. 1840), became an editor (1843), and was a staunch abolitionist and opponent of the war in Mexico. He taught intermittently at Harvard (1855–86), was the first editor of the *Atlantic Monthly* (1857–61), and became the ambassador to Spain (1877–80) and England (1880–85). His derivative serious poetry is largely forgotten today, but his satiric verse in *The Biglow Papers* (1st series, 1848; 2nd series, 1867) and *A Fable for Critics* (1848) provides a still lively memento of his times.

Lowell, Josephine (b. Shaw) (1843–1905) charitable worker; born in West Roxbury, Mass. (sister of Robert Gould Shaw). Influenced by her family's progressive leanings, she raised funds for freedmen's welfare after the Civil War, in which she was widowed, and reported on social conditions for the New York Charities Aid Association; her treatise, *Public Relief and Charity* (1884), reflected a belief that low wages were a root cause of social problems. She cofounded the Charity Organization Society (1902) and the Consumers League of New York (1890).

Lowell, Percival (1855–1916) astronomer; born in Boston, Mass. (brother of Abbott and Amy Lowell). Born to wealth, he prospered in business, then spent the years 1883–93 in Asia, which he wrote about in such books as *Soul of the Far East* (1888). By the early 1890s he was concentrating on astronomy, and he used his personal fortune to build and staff an observatory (now the Lowell) in Flagstaff, Ariz. From 1894 on, he directed important research there, but he became most famous for predictions: the existence of another planet, confirmed by the discovery of Pluto in 1930; and the existence of intelligent life on Mars, nullified by space probes.

Lowell, Robert (Traill Spence, Jr.) (1917–77) poet; born in Boston, Mass. He studied at Harvard (1935–37), and Kenyon College, Ohio (B.A. 1940). A conscientious objector in World War II, he served a prison sentence (1943–44). He taught at many institutions, was Consultant in Poetry, Library of Congress (1947–48), and wrote several plays and translations. A troubled man and brilliant poet, he combined his two beings in launching the so-called confessional school of poetry, and has been honored for his disquieting works, as in *Notebook 1967–1968* (1969; augmented 1970).

Lowen, Alexander (1910–) psychiatrist; born in New York City. He studied law at Brooklyn Law School (1934) and received the M.D. from the University of Geneva, Switzerland, in 1951. In 1954 he became executive director of the Institute for Bio-Energetic Analysis in New York City. He wrote extensively on the mind/body relationship, including *The Betrayal of the Body* (1967) and *The Language of the Body* (1971).

Lowe-Porter, H. T. (b. Helen Tracy Porter) (1876–1963) translator; born in Towanda, Pa. (niece of Charlotte Endymion Porter). She became internationally recognized for translating all of Thomas Mann's works from *Buddenbrooks* (1924) onward, usually in close collaboration with Mann. In 1911 she married the paleographer E. A. Lowe; they lived in Oxford, England, and after 1937 in Princeton, N.J.

Lowery, Joseph E. (1924–) Methodist clergyman, civil rights activist; born in Huntsville, Ala. His first congregation was at the Warren Street Church in Birmingham, Ala. (1952–61). He resigned to become administrative assistant to Bishop Golden (1961–64). He was pastor of St. Paul Church in Atlanta (1964–68) and was named minister of the Central United Methodist Church in Atlanta (1968–86). He succeeded the Rev. Ralph Abernathy as president of the Southern Christian Leadership Conference (SCLC) (1977) and received national and international attention when he led a SCLC delegation on a fact-finding mission to the Middle East (1979) and met with Palestine Liberation Organization (PLO) leaders; Israeli officials refused to meet with the SCLC delegation or its president. Under the leadership of this generally soft-spoken and unassuming man, the SCLC reinstituted Operation Breadbasket to encourage black businesspeople to reinvest in the black community, lobbied on behalf of Haitians interned by the American government after seeking asylum here, and sponsored a march from Selma, Ala., to Washington, D.C., to push the Voting Rights Act of 1982. He often spoke on anti-apartheid issues and made a tentative bid for the Democratic presidential nomination (1984).

Lowey, Susan (1933–) biochemist, physical chemist; born in Vienna, Austria. She performed research at Harvard (1957–59), moved to the Children's Cancer Research Foundation (Boston) (1959–72), then joined Brandeis University (1972). She made significant contributions to the physical chemistry of muscle proteins.

Lowie, Robert (Harry) (1883–1957) cultural anthropologist; born in Vienna, Austria. The son of a merchant who brought his family to America in 1893, he graduated from the City University of New York (1901), taught in the public schools, and took a Ph.D. at Columbia University under Franz Boas (1908). From 1907–21 he was on the staff of the American Museum of Natural History in New York City. He taught at the University of California: Berkeley from 1921–50. His research interests involved North American Indian societies, particularly the Crow. His most influential general works were *Primitive Society* (1920), *Primitive Religion* (1924), and *Social Organization* (1948). In later years he also applied his ethnological approach to studies of Germany in such works as *Toward Understanding Germany* (1954).

Lowndes, William (1782–1822) U.S. representative; born in St. Bartholomew, S.C. A plantation owner and gifted orator, he was elected to Congress (Rep., S.C.; 1811–22) with his friend John Calhoun, pressing for war against England and chairing the Committee on Naval Affairs. While chairman of the Committee of Ways and Means, he supported creation of the second U.S. bank in 1815. Declining diplomatic appointments because of poor health, he supported the Missouri compromise to allow that state its own constitution.

Lowrie, Walter (1784–1868) Protestant administrator, U.S. senator; born in Edinburgh, Scotland. He emigrated to Pennsylvania with his family in 1792. He taught school in Butler, Pa., and entered local politics, holding several small offices before winning election to the U.S. Senate; he spoke out against slavery during his single Senate term (Dem., 1819–25). From 1825–36 he was secretary of the Senate. From 1836 on he directed the activities of the Board of Foreign Missions of the Presbyterian Church. Three of his sons became foreign missionaries.

Lowry, Bates (1923–) art historian; born in Cincinnati, Ohio. He studied at the University of Chicago (Ph.B. 1944; M.A. 1953; Ph.D 1956). He taught at many universities, including New York University (1957–59), Brown (1963–68), and the University of Massachusetts (1971). He served as director of the Museum of Modern Art (1968–69), and wrote several books on architecture.

Loy, Myrna (b. Myrna Williams) (1905–93) actress; born in Raidersburg, Mont. She began her film career as an exotic vamp, but her gift for comedy emerged in *The Thin Man* (1934). By 1936 she was the top feminine box-office draw, and she was awarded an honorary Oscar in 1991. Offscreen she was never associated with the world of Hollywood glamour and scandal, but she did have a lively social conscience and during the McCarthy era she was among the few actors who protested the treatment of actors by the House Committee on Un-American Activities.

Lozowick, Louis (1892–1973) painter, printmaker; born in Ludvinovka, Russia. He emigrated to America (1906), and studied at the National Academy of Design, New York (1912–15). He concentrated on industrial themes in his graphic designs and was the author of *Modern Russian Art* (1925).

Lubin, David (1849–1919) agriculturalist; born in present-day Klodowa, Poland. His family settled in New York City in 1855. At age 16 he drifted west to San Francisco. In 1874 he opened a successful dry goods store with his half-brother in Sacramento, Calif. In 1884, on a visit to Palestine, he had a vision that his life should serve justice as did the prophet Israel's. Returning to Sacramento, he found a calling in agriculture. He fought the railroads over practices that benefited the middlemen over the growers. He proposed that government subsidize the cost of shipping produce overseas and was called a "crank." In 1896 at the International Agricultural Congress in Budapest, he realized that justice for the American farmer depended on justice for all farmers. For 12 years he sought a sovereign state to support an International Institute of Agriculture; in 1910 Italy agreed and the Institute's treaty was ratified by 46 nations. He was the United States delegate to the Institute until his death.

Lubitsch, Ernst (1892–1947) movie director; born in Berlin, Germany. He began directing movies in Germany in 1914, and was brought to Hollywood by Mary Pickford. A specialist in sophisticated comedies and costume epics, his films include *Ninotchka* (1939) and *Heaven Can Wait* (1943).

Luboff, Norman (1917–87) choral conductor/arranger; born in Chicago. After work in film and television, he formed the Norman Luboff Choir in 1963, which toured and recorded both popular and classical music.

Lucas, Anthony Francis (1855–1921) geologist, engineer; born in Spalato, Austria. He came to the U.S.A. in 1879. Drawing on his geological knowledge, he drilled for and struck oil at Spindletop, near Beaumont, Texas, in 1901, the first of the great Texas oil finds. He became world famous, but received small financial reward for his work.

Lucas, George (1945–) movie director/producer; born in Modesto, Calif. After injuring himself as a high school car racer, he became interested in moviemaking and at the Cinema School of the University of Southern California he made a prize-winning science fiction short, *THX-1138* (1965). He became a protégé and assistant of Francis Ford Coppola and was one of the cameramen on the documentary, *Gimme Shelter* (1970). He turned his student film, *THX-1138,* into a full-length movie (1971), gained considerable recognition with *American Graffiti* (1973), and then attained phenomenal success with *Star Wars* (1977), the first

of a series of science fiction films. With virtually unlimited resources as a result of the success of his *Star War* movies, he became increasingly involved in developing state-of-the-art special effects and in producing the works of other young filmmakers.

Lucas, Jerry (Ray) (1940–) basketball player; born in Middletown, Ohio. After playing at Ohio State University (1959–62), he played forward for ten years in the National Basketball Association (NBA) (1964–73), mostly for the Cincinnati Hawks. He was named to the All-NBA first team three times (1965–66, 1968), and in 1979 he was elected to basketball's Hall of Fame.

Lucas, Robert E., Jr. (1937–) economist; born in Yakima, Wash. He was a professor of economics at Carnegie Mellon (1970–74) before joining the faculty at the University of Chicago (1974). He was a supporter of the rational expectations theory, which concludes that because expectations of economic agents are "rational," monetary and fiscal policy only affect output and unemployment for a short time.

Lucas, Scott (Wike) (1892–1968) U.S. senator; born near Chandlerville, Ill. Elected to the U.S. House of Representatives (Dem., Ill. 1935–39) and to the U.S. Senate (1939–1951), he supported the New Deal, serving as Democratic whip and Senate majority leader. His liberal beliefs left him politically vulnerable in the McCarthy era, and he was defeated in his bid for reelection to a third term.

Luce, Clare Boothe (1903–87) playwright, journalist, public official; born in New York City. She was an editor of *Vogue* and *Vanity Fair* before enjoying considerable success with plays such as *The Women* (1936) and *Kiss the Boys Goodbye* (1938). Her personal life often kept her in the limelight, as when she married Henry R. Luce (1935) and converted to Catholicism (1946). An outspoken Republican, she served in the U.S. House of Representatives (Rep., Conn.; 1943–47) and as ambassador of Italy (1953–56). She was especially known for the acerbic wit of both her speech and writings.

Luce, Henry R. (Robinson) (1898–1967) publisher, editor; born in Tengchow, China. In 1923, scraping together $86,000 in capital, he and former Yale University classmate Briton Hadden founded the weekly newsmagazine *Time,* the first of its kind and the first of Luce's several highly innovative and lucrative magazine ventures; after Hadden's death, Luce completed launching of the upscale business magazine *Fortune* (1930), which succeeded despite the ongoing Depression; he also acquired *Architectural Digest* (1932). In 1936 Luce started the picture magazine *Life,* launching the modern era of photojournalism. *Sports Illustrated,* created in 1954, became successful as *Life* began to decline. Luce's communications empire, Time, Inc., also included broadcasting stations, real estate, a magazine export business, and Time-Life Books – which broke new ground in mail order bookselling. He was an active editor, and his magazines often embodied his views as a conservative Republican and ardent supporter of Nationalist China. His second wife was journalist and playwright Clare Boothe Luce.

Luce, Stephen Bleecker (1827–1917) naval officer; born in Albany, N.Y. He served in the Mexican and Civil wars. His *Seamanship* (1863) became a classic textbook. He was deeply interested in the training of seamen and naval officers. His interest led to the establishment of the Naval College at Newport (1884). As the college's first president, he appointed Capt. Alfred T. Mahan to the faculty.

Luciano, (Charles) "Lucky" (b. Salvatore Lucania) (1897–1962) Mafia boss; born in Lercara Friddi, Sicily. He came to New York City at age nine and worked briefly in a hat factory. He engaged in criminal pursuits and rose to become the undisputed king of the New York City Mafia by the early 1930s. He was convicted on 62 counts of compulsory prostitution (1936) but his sentence was commuted in 1946 and he was deported to Italy. (It has been alleged – but denied by officials – that while in prison, he assisted the U.S. military in its plans to invade Sicily in 1943.) He became involved in the Italian black market and international narcotics traffic. He died in Naples but his body was buried in New York City.

Luckman, Charles (1909–) corporate executive, architect; born in Kansas City, Mo. He was an executive and then president of Pepsodent (1943–46) and its parent, Lever Bros. (1946–50). He hired architects, Skidmore, Owings, and Merrill, to design Lever House in New York; at his request they designed an elevated building that left most of the street level open to pedestrians and created the illusion of a floating form for the award-winning skyscraper. Originally trained as an architect, he returned to his Los Angeles-based architecture practice and headed development ventures whose projects included Madison Square Garden, New York; Prudential Center, Boston; and the Manned Space Craft Center, Houston.

Luckman, (Sydney) Sid (1916–) football player; born in New York City. The National Football League's first great T-formation quarterback, he led the Chicago Bears to four championships including the famous 73-0 title game victory over Washington in 1940.

Ludlam, Charles (1943–87) playwright, actor, director; born in Floral Park, N.Y. Cofounder in 1967 of the Ridiculous Theatrical Company, he received an Obie in 1969. Known for his outrageous, campy portrayals, often of female characters, he also received an Obie in 1973 for his roles in *Corn* and *Camille*.

Ludlow, Daniel (1750–1814) merchant, banker, Loyalist; born in New York City. He learned accounting and banking in Holland (1765–?69) and was a Loyalist during the American Revolution. He then prospered with his general importing business on Wall Street. He was president of the Bank of the Manhattan Company (1799–1808). His importing house declared bankruptcy in 1808 and he retired to Skaneateles, N.Y.

Ludlum, Robert (Jonathan Ryder, Michael Shepherd, pen names) (1927–) writer, actor; born in New York City. He served in the Marine Corps (1944–46) and studied at Wesleyan (B.A. 1951). He became a Broadway and television actor (1952–60), and a theater producer in New Jersey (1957–70) and New York City (1960–69). With the publication of his first espionage novel, *The Scarlatti Inheritance* (1971), he became a successful full-time writer of suspense fiction. He lived in Hartford, Conn.

Ludwig, Daniel K. (Keith) (1897–1992) shipper, financier, entrepreneur; born in South Haven, Mich. At age 19 he entered the freight business. His company, National Bulk Carriers (New York City) (founded 1936), became the country's largest shipping corporation and a major oil transporter. He fostered the development of modern supertankers in the 1950s. His diversified international business interests made him one of the world's richest individuals.

Luening, Otto (1900–) composer; born in Milwaukee, Wis. He pursued a long teaching career with schools including Bennington (Vt.) College, Columbia University, and Juilliard. He composed in several styles and in the 1950s was an American pioneer in electronic music.

Lugosi, Bela (b. Bela Ferenc Denzso Blasko) (1882–1956) movie actor; born in Lugos, Hungary. He studied at the Academy of Performing Arts in Budapest and played on the Hungarian stage (from 1901) and in Hungarian movies (sometimes under the name of Arisztid Olt) (from 1917). After making several movies in Germany, he came to the U.S.A. in 1921 and began playing character parts on stage and in films. His biggest success came in a stage play, *Dracula* (1927), which he repeated in the 1931 movie, but this typecast him as a villain and doomed him to playing in a series of low-budget horror films that finally turned him into a parody of himself. Reduced to promoting himself by such gimmicks as giving interviews while lying in a coffin, and constantly with money or marital problems, he became a drug addict and had himself committed to the California State Hospital in 1955. He returned to make three bad movies, including *Plan 9 from Outer Space* (1956), and when he died he was buried in his Dracula cape.

Luhan, Mabel Dodge (b. Ganson) (1879–1962) hostess, promoter of art and social causes, author; born in Buffalo, N.Y. Born into a moderately wealthy family, she studied briefly in New York City and near Washington, D.C., before entering Buffalo society (1897). As expected of such a young woman, she married a young man of her class (1900), but shortly after the birth of their son her husband died in an accident. Suffering from a nervous breakdown, she was sent to Europe, and on the ship she met Edwin Dodge, an architect from Boston; they married in Paris (1905) and went off to Florence, Italy, where she took on the first of her several personas: the "renaissance" hostess of a salon where she entertained a steady flow of celebrities and artists such as Getrude Stein and André Gide. By 1912, more neurasthenic and erratic than ever – she had twice attempted suicide – she returned to New York, separated from her husband (they were divorced in 1916) and adopted her new persona: the radical/avant-garde hostess. Her salon on the edge of Greenwich Village now became a celebrated gathering place of a new stream of artists and social activists; she supported both the famous Armory Show of 1913 and the Paterson Strike Pageant, an extravaganza at Madison Square Garden to support striking textile workers in New Jersey; she spoke out for everything most modern, from Gertrude Stein's prose to Freud's psychology; she supported all kinds of radical causes and individuals while having an intense affair with the revolutionary John Reed. It was the end of this relationship that caused her to attempt suicide again and then to retreat from New York City and adopt her new persona: the leader of a new community. In 1917 she married Maurice Sterne, a painter, and in 1918 they moved to Taos, N.M. She was immediately drawn to the Pueblo Indian culture and for much of the rest of her life she spent her energies trying to become one with the Pueblo Indians, trying to help their community, and trying to bring other artists to join her there. She even went so far as to divorce Sterne and marry Antonio Lujan (1923), a Pueblo Indian (he became Tony Luhan to her). She did manage to pull some artists into her circle – D. H. Lawrence, Georgia O'Keeffe, and Robinson Jeffers – but all soon found her personality too much for long or close relationships. In the 1930s she took up her final persona: the writer-recorder of her own life and ideas, publishing such works as *Lorenzo in Taos* (1932) – about D. H. Lawrence – and *Winter in Taos* (1935). In addition to a fair amount of published work, she left volumes of unpublished materials (now at Yale University's library), and although no single work, idea, contribution, or "persona" of Mabel Dodge Luhan may seem that important, the totality of her life in search of identity and community have gained her some standing as an archetypal 20th-century American woman.

Luisetti, (Angelo) "Hank" (1916–) basketball player; born in San Francisco. He revolutionized basketball by popularizing the one-handed jump shot as a two-time All-American forward at Stanford University (1935–38). He was the first college player to score 50 points in one game. Following college he played Amateur Athletic Union basketball. Although he never played professional basketball, he was elected to basketball's Hall of Fame in 1959.

Luke, Frank, Jr. (1897–1918) aviator; born in Phoenix, Ariz. He enlisted in 1917, learned to fly, and joined the 27th Aero Squadron in France, where in six weeks of furious combat he destroyed 20 German aircraft. Attacked by six German airplanes on Sept. 29, 1918, Luke crash-landed his craft and fought off approaching enemy soldiers until he was mortally wounded.

Lukens, Glen (1887–1967) ceramist; born in Cowgill, Mo. The developer of raw alkaline glazes from natural materials and ceramics professor at the University of Southern California, he was a leader in the West Coast ceramics movement.

Lukens, Rebecca Webb (b. Pennock) (1794–1854) businesswoman; born in Chester County, Pa. She was the oldest of nine children in a Quaker family. She married Dr. Charles Lukens in 1813; he joined her father, Isaac Pennock, in Pennock's ironworks firm in Brandywine, Pa. Following the deaths of her father (1824) and her husband (1825), Rebecca Lukens managed the commercial aspects of the iron business (1825–54). She triumphed over many difficulties and died with an estate valued at over $100,000. The Lukens Steel Company lasted long after her death.

Luks, George (Benjamin) (1867–1933) painter, graphic artist; born in Williamsport, Pa. He studied at the Pennsylvania Academy of the Fine Arts (1884), and traveled widely. He became a graphic artist for the Philadelphia *Press* (1894), war correspondent in Cuba for the *Evening Bulletin* (1895), and a cartoonist for the *World* (1896). His painting style was earthy, realistic, and energetic, as may be seen in *Hester Street* (1905), and he was a member of "the Eight," more popularly known as the Ashcan school.

Lumet, Sidney (1924–) movie director; born in Philadelphia. Originally a child actor, then a television director, he made his first feature film in 1957 – *Twelve Angry Men*. Known for making movies that combine popular elements with serious themes, his greatest commercial triumph was *Network* (1976).

Lunceford, (James Melvin) Jimmie (1902–47) jazz musician; born in Fulton, Mo. He was a music teacher in Memphis who formed a band in 1929 and gradually developed it into an outstanding Swing era orchestra.

Lund, Daryl B. (1941–) food scientist; born in San Bernadino, Calif. He received his Ph.D. and began teaching at the University of Wisconsin: Madison, his *alma mater,* in 1968. In 1984 he chaired the food science department and then removed to Rutgers University (1988) where he again chaired the food science department for two years. In 1991 he was named Executive Dean of Agriculture and Natural Resources and Dean of Cook College (part of Rutgers State University of N.J.) He wrote many scientific papers on food engineering including thermal and aseptic processing of food.

Lundeberg, Harry (1901–51) labor leader, born in Oslo, Norway. A sailor, he immigrated to the U.S.A. in 1923. He joined the Sailors' Union of the Pacific in 1926 and was a leader of the 1934 San Francisco waterfront strike. He was founder and first president (1938–51) of the Seafarers International Union and led a series of strikes that greatly improved sailors' wages and working conditions. A radical in his early days, he became known as a fierce opponent of Communists in the labor movement but he never gave up wearing the clothes of a working sailor.

Lundy, Benjamin (1789–1839) abolitionist; born in Sussex County, N.J. Observing slavery as a saddler in Virginia (1808–12), he formed a pioneering antislavery group soon after settling in St. Clair, Ohio (1815) and, risking harm, published several abolitionist papers, including *The Philanthropist* (with abolitionist Charles Osborne) and *The Genius of Universal Emancipation* (1821). He journeyed to such places as Haiti and Canada seeking colonies for freed slaves, and, though more of a gradualist, was an early influence on William Lloyd Garrison who coedited the latter paper for a time. In 1836 Lundy started *The National Enquirer and Constitutional Advocate of Universal Liberty,* which opposed the annexation of Texas as a slaveholders' plot. After racist mobs destroyed all of his papers, he briefly reestablished *The Genius* shortly before his death.

Lunn, George Richard (1873–1948) minister, mayor, social reformer, public official; born in Lenox, Iowa. An ordained Presbyterian minister, his first pastorate was in 1903 in Schenectady, N.Y. He quickly moved in the direction of social action, founding a People's Church when his more conservative congregation rebelled. He continued in the ministry until 1915. For a time he ran his own reformist newspaper, and was then recruited by the Socialist party, on whose ticket he was elected mayor of Schenectady. As mayor (1912–14, 1916–17), he instituted a number of social reforms, establishing a municipal employment bureau, a lodging house, and a farm, but his independence caused him to be expelled from his own party. He served one term in the U.S. House of Representatives as a Democrat (1917–19), and was again elected mayor of Schenectady in 1919 and 1921, resigning that post when he won the state's lieutenant governorship in 1922 on the Alfred E. Smith ticket. After a reelection defeat in 1924, Lunn was appointed to the state's Public Utilities Commission, where he served until 1942.

Lunsford, Bascom Lamar (1882–1973) folklorist; born in Mars Hill, N.C. He was a North Carolina lawyer and farmer who, although he lacked formal musical training, became well known for collecting, recording, and performing Appalachian folk music. His commercial and archival recordings eventually numbered 3,000 items. He founded among other festivals the annual Mountain Dance and Folk Festival, Asheville, N.C. (1928).

Lunt, Alfred (David) (1892–1977) stage actor; born in Milwaukee, Wis. Although he played some serious parts, he is best known for his roles in the sophisticated modern comedies. After his 1912 debut in Boston, his first success was in the title role of Booth Tarkington's *Clarence* in 1919. In 1922 he married Lynn Fontanne, after which the two usually appeared together, beginning with *Sweet Nell of Old Drury*. Performing with the Theatre Guild, the couple appeared in many distinguished plays including *Arms and the Man* and *Pygmalion*. He appeared alone as the bootlegger in *Ned McCob's Daughter* (1926), and as Marco Polo in *Marco's Millions* (1928). He performed together with Fontanne as Essex in *Elizabeth and Essex* in 1930. The two spent the war years of 1942–45 playing in England. Their last performance was in 1958, Duerrenmatt's *The Visit,* in New York's Globe Theatre (later renamed the Lunt-Fontanne).

Lupino, Ida (1918–   ) movie actress/director/producer; born in London, England. A descendant of a celebrated British theatrical family, she began her film career in England with *Her First Affaire* (1933). She went to Hollywood where she had a number of minor roles until she appeared in *The Light that Failed* (1940), which led to her playing a series of rather tough women, as in *Beware My Lovely* (1952). By the 1950s she began to concentrate more on writing, directing, and producing movies and television films. She made several movies and a television series, *Mr. Adams and Eve,* with her third husband, Howard Duff.

Luria, Salvador (Edward) (1912–91) virologist; born in Turin, Italy. At the Curie Laboratory of the Institute of Radium, Paris (1938–40), he studied the effects of radiation on bacteriophages (viruses that infect bacteria). He then fled the Fascists by emigrating to teach at Columbia University (1940–42). As a research fellow at Vanderbilt (1942–43), he began at informal collaboration with bacteriophage scientists Max Delbrück and Alfred Hershey. Luria pursued his bacteriophage research at the Universities of Indiana (1943–50) and Illinois (1950–59), demonstrating both the effects of bacteriophage genetic material on host bacteria, and spontaneous mutations in bacteriophages. With Delbrück and Hershey, Luria won the 1969 Nobel Prize in physiology. He joined the Massachusetts Institute of Technology (MIT) (1959–78) and was founding director of MIT's Center for Cancer Research (1972–85). He published *General Virology,* the first text of virology as an independent science (1953), was an editor and adviser to many professional journals, and remained active after retirement, as both a scholar and a peace activist.

Lurton, Horace Harmon (1844–1914) Supreme Court justice; born in Newport, Ky. He taught law at Vanderbilt University (1898–1910) and spent many years as a judge, including seventeen years in the U.S. court of appeals, sixth circuit. President Taft named him to the U.S. Supreme Court (1910–14).

Luska, Sidney See HARLAND, HENRY.

Luther, Seth (?1797–?1848) carpenter, reformer; born in Providence, R.I. After working as a carpenter and millhand in the mill towns of New England, he spent some 15 years in the Mississippi Valley, where he observed slavery firsthand. Returning about 1830, he began lecturing and writing pamphlets that denounced abuses of the factory system and championed the ten-hour day. Largely ignored by the press, he influenced community leaders and helped secure passage in Massachusetts of the nation's first child labor law (1842); the same year, he was imprisoned for participating, with Thomas Dorr, in an attack on Rhode Island's arsenal, but he was pardoned in 1843. A victim of mental illness and poor health in later years, he apparently died in a lunatic asylum.

Lyman, Theodore (1833–97) zoologist, soldier; born in Waltham, Mass. He graduated from Harvard in 1855 and worked under Louis Agassiz. He was one of the first trustees of the Museum of Comparative Zoology and he pursued his studies both at home and abroad. He volunteered during the Civil War and was present at several important occasions; his letters to his wife, published as *Meade's Headquarters, 1863–65, Letters of Col. Theodore Lyman from the Wilderness to Appomattox* (1922) are a valuable source for students of the Civil War. He was a member of the House of Representatives (Ind., Mass.; 1883–85).

Lyman, Theodore (1874–1954) physicist; born in Boston, Mass. He taught at Harvard (1907–25), then became director of Harvard's Jefferson Physical Laboratory (1910–47). He discovered the fundamental "Lyman" series of hydrogen wavelengths in the vacuum ultraviolet (1914), and continued to investigate the range of ultraviolet spectra to increasingly shorter wavelengths.

Lynch, Charles (1736–96) soldier, judge; born in Bedford County, Va. A well-to-do landowner, he became a justice of the peace in 1766 and later served in the Virginia House of Burgesses, where he campaigned for independence. He commanded volunteers under Nathanael Greene during the American Revolution. Lynch had a reputation for high-handedness and extralegality in dealing with Tories, especially during the early years of the Revolution, but a legislative investigation concluded (1782) that he acted out of military necessity. (The claim that the word "lynch" – to punish an alleged criminal without due process of law – comes from his name is dubious.)

Lynch, Kevin (Andrew) (1918–84) planner; born in Chicago. Lynch studied at Yale and Taliesin with Frank Lloyd Wright before graduating from the Massachusetts Institute of Technology (1947) where he was a professor of city planning (1949–84). He wrote numerous books on city planning including *The Image of the City* (1960) and *Site Planning*. In his Boston firm, Carr Lynch Associates (1977–84), he designed Boston's Government Center and Waterfront, as well as housing projects.

Lynd, Robert Staughton (1892–1970) sociologist; born in New Albany, Ind. Seminary trained, he began as a missionary in Montana and then turned to sociology and anthropology in the 1920s. He later taught at Columbia University (1931–60). In 1921 he married Helen Merrell, a professor at Sarah Lawrence College. The first of their many collaborations was *Middletown* (1929), a landmark empirical study of urban American culture (actually Muncie, Ind.); with its 1937 sequel, this work was instrumental in bringing an anthropological perspective to the practice of contemporary sociology.

Lynn, Loretta (1937–   ) country music singer; born in Butcher Hollow, Ky. Married at age 13, she had her first child at 14, and was a grandmother by 28. She did not begin singing in public until her mid-twenties but in 1960 she appeared on the "Grand Ole Opry" and recorded her first hit, "I'm a Honky Tonk Girl." She went on to release over 60 singles and 50 albums with many of her own songs including "Coal Miner's Daughter," the title song from the 1980 film based on her best-selling autobiography. She became widely popular for her music and admired as a working-class woman who had triumphed over adversity.

Lyon, Mary (1797–1849) educator; born in Buckland, Mass. After teaching in Massachusetts and New Hampshire seminaries, she was the planner and founding principal (1837–49) of the first permanent women's college in the U.S.A., Mount Holyoke Female Seminary (later College). Lyon modeled the curriculum on that of Amherst College, but hired only female permanent faculty.

Lyon, Nathaniel (1818–61) soldier; born in Ashford, Conn. A West Point graduate (1841), he served in the Mexican War. The North's first hero of the Civil War, his prompt action as commander of the garrison in St. Louis saved the city for the Union. Lyon led a campaign to drive Confederate forces out of Missouri and was killed in action at Wilson's Creek on August 10, 1861.

M

Ma, Yo-Yo (1955–   ) cellist; born in Paris, France. Coming to New York City with his family at age seven, Ma enrolled at Juilliard at age nine, and after studies at Harvard, he ascended rapidly to the highest rank of international soloists. He is noted for warmth of playing joined with superlative technique, a repertoire stretching from Bach to the moderns, and a youthfully enthusiastic stage presence.

Maazel, Lorin (Varencove) (1930–   ) conductor; born in Neuilly, France. Brought as a child to the U.S.A. and raised in Los Angeles and Pittsburgh, he was a child prodigy as a violinist, pianist, and conductor; he made his conducting debut at age eight and at age 12 he conducted the New York Philharmonic. He stepped out of the limelight to study at the University of Pittsburgh and then embarked on further musical training and guest conducting, mostly in Europe; in 1960 he became the first American to conduct at Bayreuth. For many years he was based in Berlin – as musical director of the Deutsche Oper (1965–71) and the Berlin Radio Symphony Orchestra (1965–75) – but he moved on to a series of conductorships, including the Cleveland Orchestra (from 1972), the Orchestre National de France, the Vienna Philharmonic, and the Pittsburgh Symphony (from 1986). He is known for his exacting musicianship and intense interpretations of the classical repertoire.

Mabley, (Jackie) Moms (b. Loretta Mary Aiken) (1894–1975) comedienne; born in Brevard, N.C. A teenage runaway, she played a raunchy grandma on the "Chitlin' circuit" in Northern ghettos for 40 years until whites discovered her in the 1960s.

MacArthur, Arthur (1845–1912) soldier; born in Springfield, Mass. (father of Douglas MacArthur). After seeing extensive combat with a Wisconsin infantry regiment during the Civil War, he served for many years on garrison duty in the West. He led combat forces in the Philippines during the Spanish-American War (1898) and then served as military governor during the insurrection in the Philippines (1900–01). He spent his final eight years in the army commanding departments in the U.S.A.

MacArthur, Charles (1895–1956) playwright, screenwriter, movie director; born in Scranton, Pa. (husband of Helen Hayes, father of James MacArthur). After working as a reporter, he collaborated with Ben Hecht on the classic newspaper play, *Front Page* (1928), and then on *Twentieth Century* (1932), both Broadway hits. He went on to write, alone or in collaboration, several other popular plays and screenplays, usually sophisticated comedies. He codirected several movies with Hecht.

MacArthur, Douglas (1909–   ) diplomat; born in Bryn Mawr, Pa. (nephew of General Douglas MacArthur). As a diplomatic secretary to Vichy France, he was imprisoned for 16 months by the Germans. He was a State Department counselor and ambassador to Japan (1957–61) where he negotiated a second security pact between Japan and the U.S.A. He was ambassador to Belgium (1961–65), Austria (1967–69), and Iran (1969–72). He later served as a business consultant.

MacArthur, Douglas (1880–1964) soldier; born in Little Rock, Ark. The son of a Union army hero during the Civil War (they are the only father and son to win the Congressional Medal of Honor) and a mother ambitious for his success, he graduated from West Point in 1903, rose steadily in the army, and demonstrated his bravado on a secret mission to Mexico in 1914. In World War I he commanded a brigade in combat in France (1918), where he earned a reputation for bravery (wounded three times) as well as foppery – he carried a muffler and a riding crop into the line, but not a helmet or a gas mask. After serving as the superintendent of West Point (1919–22), he completed his second tour of duty in the Philippines. Appointed army chief of staff in 1930 (the youngest ever), he offended liberal-minded people by characterizing as "communists" the Bonus Army veterans he evicted from Washington in 1932. From 1935–41 he served as the military adviser to the Philippine government; in July 1941 he was named commander of U.S. forces in the Far East; overwhelmed by the Japanese after Pearl Harbor, he was ordered to leave his forces on Bataan peninsula (with his promise, "I shall return!") and go to Australia. From 1942 to 1945, as commander of the Southwest Pacific area, MacArthur organized an island-hopping offensive that resulted in the return of U.S. forces to the Philippines in October 1944. As supreme commander of the Allied powers, he presided over the Japanese surrender on September 2, 1945. As military governor of Japan (1945–50), he was a benevolent dictator in forcing Japan to purge itself of its militarism and to adopt more democratic ways. On the outbreak of the Korean War in July 1950, he became commander of United Nations forces in Korea, in which capacity he directed the Inchon offensive that forced the invading North Koreans to surrender most of their gains. When Chinese forces began fighting alongside the North Koreans in November 1950, he forcefully advocated an extension of the war into China. This led to conflict with President Truman, who relieved MacArthur from command on April 11, 1951. This caused great controversy; MacArthur returned home to the hero's welcome he had not yet enjoyed and concluded his address to Congress with his citation of an old military song, "Old soldiers never die, they just fade away." Talk of his running for president came to nothing, and after serving as chairman of the board of Remington Rand, Inc., he lived out his final years as a much-honored hero. Flamboyant, vain – some would say pompous – and bold, he ranks as an imaginative, sometimes brilliant military commander; his troops generally respected him for the care he took with their lives. But most observers agree that his political instincts were stillborn and his ambitions, perhaps fortunately, were kept in check by his superiors.

MacArthur, John D. (1897–1978) businessman, philanthropist; born in Pittson, Pa. He made a fortune through selling cheap life insurance policies. He expanded into real estate and became the largest landowner in Florida. He left most of his wealth to the John D. and Catherine T. MacArthur Foundation, famous for making grants to "geniuses" for prolonged independent projects.

MacArthur, Robert Helmer (1930–72) ecologist; born in Toronto, Canada. He moved to the U.S.A. at age 17, studied mathematics and zoology, and earned a Ph.D. in the latter field from Yale. From 1965 he was a professor of biology at Princeton. Building on an early interest in birds, he developed influential theories about natural selections in animal populations.

MacCurdy, George Grant (1863–1947) anthropologist; born in Warrensburg, Mo. He earned a Ph.D. at Yale, where as professor of prehistoric archaeology and curator of anthropological collections at the Peabody Museum (1898–1931) he wrote widely on American and Old World prehistory and influenced developing academic and museum programs in the new discipline of anthropology.

Macdonald, Dwight (1906–82) essayist, critic; born in New York City. Entering journalism after graduating from Yale, he eventually became a staff writer for the *New Yorker* (1951–71). His essays and political, social, and literary criticism, renowned for their ironic wit, were collected in several volumes including *The Memoirs of a Revolutionist* (1957) and *Against the American Grain* (1962). A lifelong left-wing activist, he often publicly debated political issues; he lectured widely, for example, against the Vietnam War.

MacDonald, Jeanette (1907–65) soprano; born in Philadelphia. Five years after her 1920 debut in a Broadway chorus, she began appearing in films. Although she occasionally sang opera, she was best known for roles opposite Nelson Eddy in film operettas such as *Naughty Marietta* (1935) and *Rose Marie* (1936).

MacDonald, Peter (1937–) Navajo leader; born in Arizona. A trained aerospace engineer, he served as tribal chairman in 1970, 1974, 1978, and 1986, stressing self-sufficiency and tribal enterprise. He worked to extend tribal control over education and mineral leases; toward the latter end he cofounded the Council of Energy Resource Tribes (CERT) (1975), which favored accelerated development of energy resources on the reservation. In 1989 he was removed from office pending the results of criminal investigations. He was sent to prison in 1990 and within several years was convicted of more crimes including fraud, extortion, riot, bribery, and corruption.

MacDonald, Ranald (1824–94) adventurer; born in Fort George, Ore. Of half-Indian, half-white descent, he ran away to sea at age 17. He "shipwrecked" himself in Japan in 1848, and during his year-long imprisonment, he was the first teacher of English there. In the 1850s and 1860s he surfaced in Australia, Canada, and the U.S.A. as a businessman and explorer, at one point participating in the Canadian gold rush. He later retired to a Washington homestead.

MacDonald, Ross See MILLAR, KENNETH.

MacDonald, Thomas Harris (1891–1957) civil engineer; born in Leadville, Colo. Between 1907–19 he developed the state highway system in Iowa. In 1919 he became chief of the federal Bureau of Public Roads, a position he held until his retirement in 1953.

MacDonough, Thomas (1783–1825) naval officer; born in New Castle County, Delaware. He entered the navy in 1800 and served in the Tripolitan War. During the War of 1812, he built and commanded a small fleet on Lake Champlain. He won a decisive victory against a British fleet at Plattsburgh (1814). He died at sea while returning from command of the Mediterranean Squadron.

MacDowell, Edward (Alexander) (1860–1908) composer; born in New York City. He studied in France and Germany and taught piano at the Darmstadt Conservatory, where he became a protégé of Liszt. Returning to the U.S.A in 1888, he lived and worked in Boston and then headed Columbia University's new department of music (1896–1904). While his music is essentially European-Romantic, he also flirted with American nationalistic materials in works such as the *Indian Suite* (1895). The most popular American composer of his era, he succeeded both in ambitious works, such as the *Piano Concerto No. 2* (1889), and in parlor pieces for piano, such as the *Woodland Sketches* (1896). His widow established the MacDowell Colony at their farm in Peterborough, N.H., to serve as a summer residence for artists in various fields.

Macelwane, James B. (Bernard) S. J. (1883–1956) seismologist; born near Port Clinton, Ohio. He took Jesuit vows (1905), joined the faculty of St. Louis University (1912–21), and performed seismological research at the University of California: Berkeley (1921–25) before returning to St. Louis (1925–56). His studies of earthquake waves, epicenters, the earth's micro-oscillations, and blast-induced vibrations were basic to the science of systematic seismology.

MacFadden, Bernarr (b. Bernard Adolphus McFadden) (1868–1955) publisher; born in Mill Spring, Mo. In 1899 he founded *Physical Culture* magazine to promote his ideas on self-help, fitness, and healthy living; he built a publishing empire that included the first confessions magazines and the *New York Evening Graphic,* a sex- and scandal-filled tabloid of the 1920s.

Machen, John Gresham (1881–1937) Protestant theologian; born in Baltimore, Md. A graduate of Johns Hopkins (1901) and Princeton Theological Seminary (1905), he taught at Princeton and was ordained a Presbyterian minister in 1914. He served overseas with the Young Men's Christian Association during World War I. A leading conservative during the controversy over fundamentalism in the 1920s, his *Christianity and Liberalism* (1923) argued that liberal theology and Christian faith were incompatible. In 1929 he was forced out of Princeton for his views and was suspended from the ministry as a schismatic in 1935.

Machlup, Fritz (1902–83) economist; born in Vienna, Austria. Educated in Vienna, he came to the U.S.A. in 1933 and taught at several universities including the University of Buffalo (1935–47), Johns Hopkins (1947–60), Princeton (1960–71), and New York University (1971–83). He was an exceptional writer on many subjects including Keynesian economics, the philosophy of economics and the patent system.

Macintosh, Douglas Clyde (1877–1948) Protestant theologian; born in Breadalbane, Ontario, Canada. He taught in country schools, studied at McMaster University (Canada) and the University of Chicago, and taught theology at Yale for many years. His modernist "empirical theology" sought to use scientific and philosophical methods to preserve the essence of Christian belief. His *Theology as an Empirical Science* appeared in 1917. He was denied U.S. citizenship in 1931 for refusing to promise in advance to bear arms in the event of war.

MacIntyre, Alasdair (Chalmers) (1929–) philosopher; born in Glasgow, Scotland. After several positions at British universities, he came to the United States in 1969, teaching at Brandeis (1969–72), Wellesley (1972–82), Vanderbilt (1982–88), and Notre Dame (from 1988). His works include *Marxism and Christianity* (1954), *After Virtue* (1981), and other influential writings on ethics and philosophy of mind.

Mack, Connie (b. Cornelius Alexander McGillicuddy) (1862–1956) baseball manager/executive; born in East Brookfield, Mass. He managed more games (7,878), won more games as manager (3,776), and lost more games (4,025) than any manager in the history of baseball. He managed the Pittsburgh Pirates (1894–96) and the Philadelphia Athletics for an incredible 50 years (1901–50), during which time he was also a part or full owner of the club. His Athletics won nine pennants and five World Series. He was one of only a few managers ever to manage from the dugout in civilian clothes. One of the most respected figures in history of the game, he was elected to baseball's Hall of Fame in 1937.

Mack, Julian (William) (1866–1943) jurist, community leader; born in San Francisco. He earned his law degree at Harvard and taught law at Northwestern University (1895–1902) and at the University of Chicago (1902–11). He served as a U.S. circuit court judge from 1913 until his death. President of the Zionist Organization of America (1918–21), he was leader of the "Brandeis-Mack group," which favored investment rather than philanthropy for Palestine.

MacKay, John William (1831–1902) miner, capitalist; born in Dublin, Ireland. He came to the U.S.A. as a boy and became an expert in timbering Nevada mines. He made a fortune by reworking the Comstock Lode with new equipment. After striking it rich again with the "Big Bonanza" mine, he became a banker and railroad director and broke the Jay Gould – Western Union communications monoply in 1886.

Mackaye, Benton (1879–1975) regional planner; born in Stamford, Conn. A graduate of Harvard, where he studied geography, he joined the Forestry Service (1905–17). In 1921 he published his proposal for the Appalachian walking trail from Georgia to Maine. A founder of the Regional Planning Association of America, 1923, he did studies for planning commissions (1925–45) including the Tennessee Valley Authority. His farsighted plans to reduce urban congestion and pollution unfortunately were not put into effect.

MacKaye, (James Morrison) Steele (1842–94) actor, playwright, designer, inventor; born in Buffalo, N.Y. Although 19 of his plays were produced in New York, he is best known as a dreamer and deviser of technical innovations, many of which never became reality. In pursuit of a more naturalistic mode of presentation, he reopened the Fifth Avenue Theatre in New York in 1879 as the Madison Square Theatre, introducing a double moving stage as well as overhead and indirect lighting. After opening the Lyceum in 1885, he founded a school of acting there, which became the American Academy of Dramatic Arts. He planned a "Spectatorium" for the 1893 Chicago Columbian Exposition, a vast, technically advanced auditorium, but it was never built. Most of his plays were commercially successful, but only *Won at Last, Hazel Kirke,* and *Paul Kauvar* survived to be performed into the 20th century. A biography, *Epoch* (1927), was written by his son, Percy MacKaye.

MacKaye, Percy (Wallace) (1875–1956) playwright, poet; born in New York City. He graduated from Harvard (1897), taught in New York City (1900–04), then settled in Cornish, N.H. He had a strong interest in pageants and in amateur community theater. His pageant *The Canterbury Pilgrims* (1903) was made into an opera by Reginald De Koven (1917). Other plays using historical material were *Jeanne D'Arc* (1906), *Sappho and Phaon* (1907), and *The Scarecrow* (1908), based on Hawthorne's story "Feathertop." Several works produced in the 1920s drew on tales and folklore collected in Kentucky by him and his wife. In 1949 he produced *The Mystery of Hamlet: King of Denmark,* a series of four verse plays that develop the characters and plot to a point that precedes the action of Shakespeare's *Hamlet.*

Mackendrick, Paul (Lachlan) (1914–) classicist; born in Taunton, Mass. He was educated at Harvard (B.A. 1934; M.A. 1937; Ph.D. 1938) and taught at the University of Wisconsin (1946–84). He became widely known for a series of books – *The Mute Stones Speak* (1960), *The Greek Stones Speak* (1962), *Roman France* (1972), *The Dacian Stones Speak* (1975), *The North African Stones Speak* (1980) – that were popular introductions to the archaeology of specific regions.

MacKinnon, Catharine A. (Alice) (1946–) legal scholar; born in Minneapolis, Minn. She graduated from Smith College (1969) and Yale Law School (1977), later taking a graduate degree in political science from Yale (1987). Even before graduating from law school, she had begun to focus on women's social and legal inequality; expanding a student paper, she published a landmark study, *Sexual Harassment of Working Women: A Case of Sex Discrimination* (1979), arguing that sexual harassment in the workplace constitutes a violation of civil rights statutes; her ideas became the law of the land in a 1986 Supreme Court ruling. Her other, more controversial focus was to urge that pornography be recognized as another form of sex discrimination; she and Andrea Dworkin, a prominent feminist writer, conceived and drafted an ordinance that would allow women who can prove they are harmed by pornography to sue pornographers; adopted by two city councils, it was vetoed (in Minneapolis) and overturned by the courts (in Indianapolis). In addition to sexual harassment and pornography, she pioneered the approach to law from the perspective of women's experience of sex inequality. From this perspective she addressed other gender-related issues including rape and abortion, and her views, cogently and forcefully expressed in articles and lectures (some gathered in *Femininism Unmodified,* 1987), have gained her the reputation of being both iconoclastic and "the central figure in feminist legal thought." Throughout these years of public engagement (1977–89), she practiced law and taught at seven prestigious law schools before accepting a tenured post at the University of Michigan Law School (1989).

MacLaine, Shirley (b. Shirley MacLean Beatty) (1934–) movie actress, author; born in Richmond, Va. (sister of Warren Beatty). Having begun studying ballet at age two, she left for New York after graduating from high school; her first Broadway experience was in the chorus line of *Me and Juliet* (1953). Understudy to Carol Haney in *The Pajama Game* (1954), she replaced the injured Haney after the third performance and was almost immediately signed up by Hollywood, making her screen debut in *The Trouble with Harry* (1955). She proved to be a versatile actress in movies ranging from musicals such as *Irma La Douce* (1963) to sentimental dramas such as *Terms of Endearment* (1983), for which she won an Oscar as best actress. She led an equally varied career offscreen as an activist for liberal causes, leader of the first American women's delegation to China (which resulted in her documentary, *The Other Half of the Sky: A China Memoir,* 1975), a tireless tourer in her one-woman variety shows, and author of several best-sellers. She was also the butt of much teasing for her professed belief in reincarnation.

Maclay, William (1765–1825) U.S. representative; born in Lurgan Township, Pa. Educated in country schools, he became a lawyer in Chambersburg, Pa., where he also served as county commissioner. A Republican member of the Pennsylvania house (1807–08), he was the associate judge for the Cumberland District before going to the U.S. House of Representatives (1815–19), returning to Lurgan afterward.

MacLeish, Archibald (1892–1982) poet, writer, public official; born in Glencoe, Ill. He studied at Yale (B.A. 1915) and served in World War I before receiving an L.L.B. from Harvard (1919). He practiced law in Boston (1920–23) before setting off to Europe to concentrate on his writing, which came under the influence of T. S. Eliot and Ezra Pound. He returned to the U.S.A. to become editor of *Fortune* in New York City (1928–38) and then Librarian of Congress (1939–44) and assistant secretary of state (1944–45), among other posts. In 1932 he received a Pulitzer Prize for his epic poem *Conquistador,* about the Spanish conquest of Mexico. Much of his poetry in this period shows a pronounced concern for national life, culture, social issues, and the preservation of democracy, and he became known as "the poet laureate of the New Deal." He was Boylston professor at Harvard from 1949 to 1962. In 1952 he won a second Pulitzer Prize for his *Collected Poems, 1917–1952* and a third in 1958 for his drama *J. B.,* a modernized treatment of the story of Job.

Macmahon, Arthur W. (1881–1980) political scientist; born in Brooklyn, N.Y. A longtime teacher at Columbia University (1913–58), he cultivated the acceptance of public administration as an academic discipline. He served as an adviser on the Council of National Defense during World War I, the New York City Charter Revision Commission (1921–23), the President's Committee on Administrative Management (1936), and the Commission on Inter-Government Relations (1955).

MacMillan, Whitney (1929–) corporate executive; born in Minneapolis, Minn. He worked his way through the grain division and corporate ranks of the family business, Cargill, Inc., becoming president (1975–76), CEO (1976), and chairman (1977). Besides expanding this giant grain merchant and processor into the world's largest grain trader, he diversified the company into retail consumer markets, insurance, and commodity investment services.

MacMonnies, Frederick William (1863–1937) sculptor; born in Brooklyn, N.Y. An assistant of Augustus Saint-Gaudens (1880 and 1887–89), he studied in Paris (1884), worked there (1889–1915), then returned permanently to New York City. He created many public naturalistic sculptures, such as *Civic Virtue* (1919), located in City Hall Park, New York City.

MacMullen, Ramsay (1928–) historian; born in New York City. Educated at Harvard (B.A. 1950; M.A. 1953; Ph.D. 1957), he taught at Yale (1967). His many publications, including *Soldier and Civilian in the Later Roman Empire* (1963), *Roman Social Relations* (1974), *Paganism in the Roman Empire* (1981), *Christianizing the Roman Empire* (1984), *Corruption and the Decline of Rome* (1990), and *Paganism and Christianity* (1992), concentrated on social history and the period of late antiquity.

MacNeil, Robert ("Robin") (1931–) television journalist/anchor; born in Montreal, Canada. After starring in a Canadian Broadcasting Corporation TV children's show, he worked for Reuters in London, then joined the National Broadcasting Company as a correspondent (1960–65). Co-anchor for WNBC in New York, he left to work as reporter for *Panorama,* a British Broadcasting Corporation documentary series (1966–70). Senior correspondent for Public Broadcasting System TV (1971–75), he anchored the *MacNeil/Lehrer Report* (1975–94). He published *The Story of English* (1986) with Robert McCrum and William Cran, based on a TV documentary, and *Wordstruck* (1989), an informal history of the English language.

MacNeish, Richard S. (Stockton) ("Scotty") (1918–) archaeologist; born in New York City. After graduating from Colgate University (B.A. 1940), he did his graduate work at the University of Chicago. He was the anthropologist and chief archaeologist at the National Museum of Canada (1949–64) and director of the Peabody Foundation for Archaeological Research (1968–83); in 1983 he incorporated himself as the Andover Foundation for Archaeological Research in order to facilitate fund raising and support for his various projects. His most famous excavations were during the 1960s at the site of Tehuacan, Mexico, and he spent much of his career in the field, from Eskimo sites in the Yukon, through northeastern and southwestern U.S.A., and well down into South America. In later years he worked to prove that the arrival of ancestors of the American Indians in the New World was well before 12,000 years ago, and in the early 1990s he directed a search in China for the origins of rice agriculture. A prolific writer on the prehistory of the Americas, he is especially known for his work on the transition from hunting-and-gathering societies to agricultural communities.

Macomb, Alexander (1782–1841) soldier; born in Detroit,

Mich. Son of a prosperous trader, he received a regular army commission in 1799; he then became one of the first to train at West Point and was promoted captain after graduation. He served with the Corps of Engineers (1805–12), working on coast fortifications in the Carolinas and Georgia. In 1814 he defeated a larger British force at Plattsburg, N.Y. By 1821 he was head of the Corps of Engineers and he became commanding general of the entire U.S. Army from 1828–41.

Macon, Nathaniel (1757–1837) U.S. representative/senator; born in Edgecombe, N.C. Although he came north to serve in the New Jersey militia in 1777, he opposed the Constitution. He served in the North Carolina senate (1780–84) before going to the U.S. House of Representatives (Rep., N.C.; 1791–1815) and Senate (1815–28). A defender of slavery, he led the Republican opposition to any Federalist proposals, becoming known for his negative votes. After his retirement he championed states' rights and Van Buren's candidacy.

Macready, John Arthur (1887–1979) aviator; born in San Diego, Calif. A Stanford graduate, he became the first pilot to demonstrate the potential of crop dusting (1922) and went on to set early altitude, endurance, and distant records. He authored one of the first private pilot training manuals, directed the Shell Oil Company's aviation department, and was a cattle rancher and property developer in California.

MacVeagh, Lincoln (1890–1972) publisher, diplomat; born in Narragansett Pier, R.I. He entered publishing in 1915 and founded the Dial Press in 1923. He was ambassador to Greece (1933–41, 1944–47) and the first U.S. ambassador to Iceland (1941–42), then served as ambassador to South Africa, Portugal, and Spain.

Macy, Rowland H. (?1822–77) merchant; born in Nantucket, Mass. A whaler at age 15, when he returned from sea four years later he went into dry goods in Boston. After two failed attempts to run his own shop, he joined the gold rush in California and returned to Boston with $3,000, but again failed at running his own store. In 1857 he moved to New York City where he set up a dry goods store at a good location. With a cash-only policy and competitive pricing, he found success. An especially talented marketer and advertiser, he continued expanding his inventory until by 1872 he was a one-stop department store carrying everything from books to baby carriages and gourmet foods. He used clearance sales as a regular feature to maintain a high inventory turnover. At his death in 1877, he had 400 employees, sales of $1.6 million, and had set the standard for modern department stores.

Madden, Martin (Barnaby) (1855–1928) U.S. representative; born in Darlington, England. Emigrating at age 5, he was a self-made quarryman who opposed machine politics in Chicago. In congress (Rep., Ill.; 1905–28) he created the bureau of the budget.

Maddox, Lester (Garfield) (1915–) governor; born in Atlanta, Ga. A high school dropout, he ran the Pickrick Restaurant in Atlanta (1947–64), closing it rather than serving African-Americans. As Democratic governor of Georgia (1967–71), he instituted early prison release and fought against school desegregation. While lieutenant governor (1971–75), he thwarted Governor Jimmy Carter's government reform measures, opening another Pickrick Restaurant afterward.

Madeleva, Sister Mary (b. Mary Evaline Wolff) (1887–1964) poet, educator; born in Cumberland, Wis. Joining the Sisters of the Holy Cross (1908), she earned a doctorate in English from the University of Southern California at Los Angeles (1925) and was president of St. Mary's College (Notre Dame, Ind.) (1934–61). A medieval scholar, she won distinction for her literary essays and poetry.

Madison, Dolley (b. Payne Todd) (1768–1849) First Lady; born in New Garden, N.C. After her first husband died, she married James Madison in 1794. Extremely popular as first lady, she was a great asset to Madison's political career. In 1814 she saved many state papers and a portrait of George Washington from the advancing British soldiers. In later life she retained a place in Washington society and was granted a lifelong seat on the floor of the House of Representatives.

Madison, James (1751–1836) fourth U.S. president; born in Port Conway, Va. After his education at the College of New Jersey (later Princeton), he returned to Virginia and in 1774 assumed the first of several positions in state government. In 1780 he began three years as a state delegate to the Congress under the Articles of Confederation, where he advocated a stronger national government. As a member of the Virginia House of Delegates (1784–86), he secured passage of Thomas Jefferson's landmark religious freedom bill. A primary mover behind the Constitutional Convention of 1787, Madison imprinted many of his ideas on the final document; he stressed the need for a strong central government; he skillfully managed many of the necessary compromises; although not the official secretary, he kept the most complete record of the convention; and he would be instrumental in adding the Bill of Rights; for these contributions, history has dubbed him "father of the Constitution." Although Madison joined with Federalists Alexander Hamilton and John Jay in contributing to the *Federalist* papers, he moved thereafter to the more liberal Jeffersonian Republican side. He served in the U.S. House of Representatives (1789–97) and then as President Jefferson's secretary of state (1801–09). Elected president (1809–17), he was unable to resist the forces, both domestic and foreign, that led to the War of 1812, which produced the burning of Washington and no real victory. Nonetheless, he left office in 1817 enjoying considerable popularity. Living on his estate at Montpelier (Va.), he was Jefferson's successor as rector of the University of Virginia (1826–36). He opposed such doctrines as nullification and peaceful secession that would eventually lead to the Civil War.

Madonna (b. Madonna Louise Ciccone) (1959–) pop singer, songwriter, movie actress; born in Rochester, Mich. She won a scholarship in high school to study dance at the University of Michigan. She left in the late 1970s and moved to New York City where she studied and danced with Alvin Ailey and Pearl Lang, acted in underground films, and performed with rock bands. Her albums *Madonna* (1983) and *Like a Virgin* (1984) sold over a million copies each and included several hit singles. Her movie performances, except for that in *Desperately Seeking Susan* (1985), were less well-received. Known for her provocative stage and video performances, a somewhat ambiguous symbol of a new feminism in her combination of vulgarity and shrewdness, she was arguably the best-known woman in the world at the height of her popularity. Her 1992 venture, the book *Sex,* photographs of her in pornographic poses plus her texts of erotic musings, seemed to have put a temporary cap on her career as a media superstar, but she continued to draw adoring crowds wherever she appeared.

Magnes, Judah Leon (1877–1948) rabbi, educator; born in San Francisco. Educated at the Hebrew Union College in Cincinnati, he became a Reform rabbi and an ardent Zionist. From 1906 to 1910 he was rabbi at Temple Emanu-El in New York, after which he tried to create a Jewish community structure in New York, known as a Kehilla (1910–22), with the goal of coordinating Jewish religious cultural and other activities. In 1923 he moved to Jerusalem and became the first chancellor of the Hebrew University (1925–35). He supported the idea of an Arab-Jewish state, often criticized Zionist policies, and opposed the 1947 partition of Palestine.

Magoun, Horace Winchell (1907–91) neuroscientist; born in Philadelphia. He taught at Northwestern University Medical School (1934–50) and the University of California Medical School at Los Angeles (1950–72). He did important work in neurology and psychopharmacology and was a leader in the creation of a multidisciplinary approach to the study of the nervous system.

Magruder, John Bankhead (1810–71) soldier; born in Winchester, Va. An 1830 West Point graduate and Mexican War veteran, he gained the nickname "Prince John" from his courtly manner and style of entertainment. Resigning his commission to become a colonel with the Confederate army, he led his forces to victory at Big Bethel, Va., in June 1861, regarded as the first land battle of the Civil War. Failing to prove aggressive enough in the Seven Days Battles (1862), and quarreling with Robert E. Lee, he was transferred to Texas, where he served without distinction until the war's end. He then went to Mexico and became a general under Emperor Maximilian, but in 1867 he returned to the U.S.A. where he lectured on his military experiences.

Mahan, Alfred Thayer (1840–1914) naval officer, author; born in West Point, N.Y. He served in the Civil War and 20 years of routine sea duty before becoming a lecturer of naval history and tactics at the new Naval War College (1885). He twice served as the College's president (1886–89, 1892–93) and published numerous books; the best-known were *The Influence of Sea Power upon History: 1660–1783* (1890) and *The Influence of Sea Power upon the French Revolution and Empire, 1793–1812* (1892). The books brought him an international readership and reputation; he was publicly honored by the British government and thoroughly studied by German naval officers. He was elected president of the American Historical Association (1902) and became a rear admiral on the retired list in 1906.

Mahan, Dennis Hart (1802–71) military theorist; born in New York City (father of Alfred Thayer Mahan). A West Point graduate (1824), he went to France to study in an army school, then returned to West Point (1832) where he spent the rest of his career as a professor of civil and military engineering. He was known for his books on fortifications and other aspects of military engineering, but it was his theories – particularly his stress on mobility, boldness, and speed – that heavily influenced senior commanders in both the Mexican War and Civil War.

Mahler, Herbert (1890–1961) labor organizer, radical; born in Chatham, Ontario, Canada. He left home (1910) to find work in the Canadian West, working as a riverboat pilot and logger until he emigrated to America (1915). In the state of Washington he joined the Industrial Workers of the World (IWW), serving as secretary and organizer for several IWW locals in the Seattle area where he assisted longshoremen and loggers. He was secretary-treasurer of the IWW's Everett Defense Committee (1916) and assisted in the acquittal (1917) of Wobblies charged with murder after the "massacre" of November 1916. During World War I he participated in IWW lumber and copper strikes that tied up war materials, even though he believed more in organization of workers than antiwar activities. He was indicted along with 100 IWW leaders in Chicago (1917) and convicted of three counts of espionage and sedition, sentenced to 12 years in prison, and fined \$20,000 (1918). He remained in prison until President Calvin Coolidge commuted the sentences of all IWW inmates still incarcerated (1923). Named secretary of the IWW's General Defense Committee after his release, he became general secretary-treasurer (1931), but resigned (1932) over disputes concerning IWW direction. He continued organizing work outside of IWW auspices, moving to New York, and then organizing the Kentucky Miners Defense Committee (1937). His last public appearance was picketing the *New Republic* (1948) to protest an unsympathetic portrayal of Joe Hill.

Mahler, Margaret Schoenberger (1897–1985) psychoanalyst; born in Sopron (Oedenburg), Hungary. She studied medicine at the German universities of Munich, Heidelberg, and Jena (M.D. 1922), then founded the first psychoanalytic child guidance clinic in Vienna. Married to psychiatrist Paul Mahler in 1925, she left Austria with him to settle in New York City (1938). She was best known for her pioneer work on childhood schizophrenia and the individuation process.

Mailer, Norman (1923–) writer; born in Long Branch, N.J. He grew up in Brooklyn, excelled in the sciences in school, and majored in engineering at Harvard (B.S. 1943); but having written short stories and a novel before graduation, he was already committed to writing. He was drafted into the U.S. Army (1944–46) and volunteered for combat in the Pacific. After the war, he enrolled at the Sorbonne in Paris (1947–49) to take advantage of the G.I. Bill while writing. He became an overnight sensation with his first novel, *The Naked and the Dead* (1948), which at the time seemed rather shocking in its portrayal of men at war. His next two novels – *Barbary Shore* (1951) and *Deer Park* (1955) – pleased neither critics nor readers and he turned to expressing his increasingly more extremist social and political philosophy in magazine essays that were eventually collected in volumes such *Advertisements for Myself* (1959) and *Cannibals and Christians* (1966). After his novel *The American Dream* (1965) was generally dismissed as too outré for realistic Americans, he tended to concentrate on nonfiction works in which he impressed his own self onto public events or into others' lives – from the journey to the moon (*Of a Fire on the Moon*, 1970) to Marilyn Monroe's life (*Marilyn*, 1973). Meanwhile, his real-world doings and persona would often threaten to overwhelm his literary career; he seemed to be constantly engaged in verbal quarrels with such as Gore Vidal, in divorce proceedings with his various wives (one of whom he stabbed), or in contests to prove that he was the world's heavyweight champion of everything (actually engaging in boxing matches, running for mayor of New York City in 1960, and generally promoting himself as the heir of Ernest Hemingway). He also got distracted by becoming a producer, director, and actor in several bad movies. When he was at his best, however, as in the march on the Pentagon to protest the Vietnam War, an event that led to his Pulitzer Prize-winning *Armies of the Night* (1968), he was still an inimitably potent voice. Although his later novels, such as *Ancient Evenings* (1984) and *Harlot's Ghost* (1991), seemed like bids for the Nobel Prize, many would agree that he deserved it anyway, for his total work represents a truly resonant and creative attempt to probe the mysteries of contemporary individuals and society.

Maiman, Theodore (Harold) (1927–) physicist, inventor; born in Los Angeles. After serving with the U.S. Navy in World War II, he studied engineering physics at the University of Colorado (B.S. 1949) and took his Ph.D. from Stanford (1955). He joined the Hughes Electronics Research Laboratories in 1955. Charles Townes had proposed the maser in 1951 and by 1954 he and his associates had a working model; in 1958 Townes and Arthur Schawlow proposed an optical maser, or laser. Maiman made some improvements in the solid-state maser, and then, using a synthetic ruby crystal, constructed the first operable laser in 1960. From 1975–83 he was with TRW, where he had responsibility for the development of new technological ventures.

Mainbocher (b. Main Rousseau Bocher) (1891–1976) fashion designer; born in Chicago. He studied art and music in Chicago, then served in World War I. After the war, he stayed in Paris, working as a fashion artist with *Harper's Bazaar*, then as editor of French *Vogue* until 1929. He started a couture house there in 1930. He designed the wedding dress for Wallis Simpson, Duchess of Windsor (1937) as well as stage clothing for stars such as Mary Martin, Ruth Gordon and Tallulah Bankhead. He opened a ready-to-wear salon in New York in 1940, and returned to Paris in 1971.

Makemie, Francis (c. 1658–1708) Protestant clergyman; born in County Donegal, Ireland. He was ordained about 1682 and sent to America as a missionary. He evangelized in North Carolina, Virginia, Maryland, and Barbados before settling down as a successful merchant and pastor at Rehobeth on Maryland's eastern shore; he founded the first presbytery in America in 1706. Regarded as the main founder of the Presbyterian Church in America, he encountered much official opposition in an era of religious intolerance and was arrested for his activities on at least two occasions.

Malamud, Bernard (1914–86) writer; born in New York City. His Russian-Jewish parents ran a small grocery store, and he would use such biographical material in much of his writing. He studied at the College of the City of New York (B.A. 1936), and Columbia University (M.A. 1942). He worked for the Census Bureau in Washington, D.C. (1940), and then taught English at New York City evening schools (1940–49). He then moved up to college teaching, first at Oregon State (1949–61), then at Bennington (1961–86). His first novel, *The Natural* (1952), is regarded as launching the modern tradition of serious baseball fiction, while many of his later novels, such as *The Assistant* (1957) and *The Fixer* (1966), were contemporary morality tales based on the Jewish experience.

Malbone, Edward (Greene) (1777–1807) painter; born in Newport, R.I. He painted miniature portraits in Providence, R.I. (1794), traveled to London (1801), and settled in Savannah, Ga. His miniature on ivory of Washington Allston (1801), is detailed and delicate.

Malcolm, Norman (Adrian) (1911–90) philosopher; born in Selden, Kans. Earning a Harvard doctorate, he joined the Princeton faculty in 1940; after serving in the U.S. Navy (1942–45), he spent most of his remaining American career at Cornell (1947–58), then emigrated to Britain. He wrote a 1958 memoir of Ludwig Wittgenstein, who greatly influenced his own philosophy.

Malcolm X (b. Malcolm Little) (1925–65) African-American activist; born in Omaha, Nebr. Malcolm claimed his father, a minister and follower of Marcus Garvey, was murdered by racists in Lansing, Mich. (1931) (but at least one researcher claims his father died accidentally). Moving to Boston, Malcolm turned to pimping and drugs as a teenager. He was sentenced to ten years in prison for burglary (1946) where he discovered the antiwhite Black Muslims. Joining the Muslims (1952), he became a recruiter, changed his name, and came to national attention with his writings and through a television documentary (1959), both of which tended to portray him as a threat to white people. Breaking with the Muslims (1964), he founded the Muslim Mosque in an effort to internationalize the Afro-American struggle and journeyed to Muslim lands abroad where he was impressed with their lack of racial bias. Returning to the U.S.A. convinced that whites were not inherently racist, he called himself El-Hajj Malik El Shabazz and formed the Organization of African American Unity, hoping to cooperate with progressive white groups. Before his assassination in the Audubon Ballroom in New York City (March 1965), he came to believe that leaders of the Nation of Islam and powerful elements within the U.S. government wanted him dead; the only legal trial put all the blame on members of the Nation of Islam. Alex Haley helped immortalize him as coauthor of *The Autobiography of Malcolm X* (1965), and Spike Lee's 1992 film renewed interest in the man and his message. He proved as powerful after his death as alive, influencing disparate movements with his positions on black power and neocolonialism, and transforming the consciousness of a generation of African-Americans.

Mall, Franklin Paine (1862–1917) anatomist, embryologist; born in Belle Plaine, Iowa. After taking his M.D. at the University of Michigan (1883), he studied in Europe and then went to the Johns Hopkins Hospital. After stints at Clark University (1889–92) and the University of Chicago (1892), he returned to Johns Hopkins Medical School (1893). As a medical educator, he revolutionized the study of anatomy in the United States; as a researcher, he made significant contributions, revealing the muscular system of the heart and greatly increasing the knowledge of the intestines. He led the establishment of the *American Journal of Anatomy* (1901) and the department of embryology at the Carnegie Institution (1912), which he directed and turned into one of the world's major repositories for specimens.

Mallon, Mary ("Typhoid Mary") (?1870–1938) typhoid carrier; born in the U.S.A. or Ireland. Working as a private cook while carrying the bacteria that cause typhoid fever, she infected wealthy New York families with the disease (1904–07). Never ill herself, she was finally tracked down and hospitalized in New York City (1907–10) to protect others. Discovered cooking again for a New Jersey sanatorium in 1914, she was hospitalized for life. Although she herself never had the disease, she evidently passed it on to over 50 people, three of whom died.

Mallory, (Anna Margrethe Bjurstedt) "Molla" (1892–1959) tennis player; born in Oslo, Norway. After immigrating to the United States in 1914, she won the U.S. women's national titles eight times (1915–18, 1920–22, 1926).

Mallory, Stephen Russell (1812–73) secretary of Confederate navy; born in Trinidad. He served in the U.S. Senate (Dem., Fla.; 1851–61) and became the secretary of the Confederate navy in 1861. He worked feverishly to convert the USS *Merrimac* into the CSS *Virginia*. He anticipated the coming era of torpedoes and submarines.

Malone, Dumas (1892–1986) historian; born in Coldwater, Miss. He received his doctorate from Yale University (1923) and began teaching there. He was editor (1929–31) and editor-in-chief (1931–36) of the *Dictionary of American Biography,* and editor-in-chief of Harvard University Press (1936–43). The fifth volume of his great six-volume work, *Jefferson and His Time* (1948–81), received the Pulitzer Prize in 1975. He taught at Columbia University (1945–59) and the University of Virginia (1959–62) before retiring to concentrate on his writing.

Malone, Moses (Eugene) (1954–) basketball player; born in Petersburg, Va. He came right out of high school into professional basketball at age 19. After playing two years in the American Basketball Association (1974–75), he played center for the National Basketball Association (NBA) Houston Rockets, Philadelphia 76ers, Washington Bullets, Atlanta Hawks, and Milwaukee Bucks and won the Most Valuable Player award three times (1979, 1982, 1983). An outstanding rebounder, he holds the NBA's alltime offensive rebound record and is the fourth highest alltime point scorer.

Maloof, Sam (1916–) furniture maker; born in Chino, Calif. After working in architectural drafting, graphic arts, and industrial design, he became an independent woodworker in the 1940s. A master of joinery, sculptural organic forms, and functional simplicity, he produced some 100 pieces a year from his Alta Loma, Calif., workshop. Beginning in 1970, he taught in the summers at the Penland School for Crafts in North Carolina.

Maltz, Albert (1908–85) writer; born in New York City. He studied at Columbia University (B.A. 1930), and at Yale's drama school (1930–32). He began his career as a playwright and teacher (1937–40). He moved to Hollywood (1941), and wrote numerous screen plays, such as *This Gun for Hire* (1941). He also wrote short stories, radio plays, and novels. He was a member of the "Hollywood Ten," a group that refused to answer Senator Joseph McCarthy's questions about membership in the Communist Party. He was imprisoned for contempt of Congress (1950–51), and, like many others in the entertainment industry of that era, was blacklisted; he was unable to find work in his field for almost 20 years and therefore concentrated on novels and short stories.

Mamet, David (1947–) playwright; born in Flossmore, Ill. A founder and playwright-in-residence of Chicago's St. Nicholas Theatre Company, his best-known works are *American Buffalo* (1977) and *A Life in the Theater* (1977).

Man Ray (b. Emmanuel Rudnitsky) (1890–1976) painter, photographer; born in Philadelphia. A self-taught artist, he took odd jobs in advertising before leaving for Paris, where he was a commercial photographer (1921–39). Inspired by

Dadaism, he used the Rayogram, a photo developed by sunlight, to combine painting and photography, defying the conventions of both. He taught photography in Hollywood (1939–50) before returning to Paris for good.

Mancini, Henry (1924–94) composer; born in Cleveland, Ohio. In the late-1940s and 1950s he was a pianist-arranger for the Glenn Miller band, a Hollywood arranger, and a composer for television dramas. With lyricist Johnny Mercer he wrote the Oscar-winning standards "Moon River," for the film *Breakfast at Tiffany's* (1961) and the title song for *Days of Wine and Roses* (1962). He wrote the well-known score for *The Pink Panther* (1964) and won an Oscar for *Victor/Victoria* (1982).

Mandel, Marvin (1920–) governor; born in Baltimore, Md. A Democratic lawyer, he served in the Maryland House of Representatives (1952–69), becoming Speaker in 1963. Replacing Spiro Agnew as governor (1969–77), he was an efficient administrator, but in 1975 he was indicted on federal corruption charges, serving 19 months in prison beginning in 1980. He worked in real estate development afterward.

Mandell, Arnold (Joseph) (1934–) psychiatrist; born in Chicago. A Tulane University M.D., he spent his career on the University of California's psychiatry faculty, mostly at San Diego (1969). His extensive bibliography includes many works on the neurobiology of mental disorders, psychopharmacology, and drug abuse, a specialty in which he served on several national commissions. He was awarded a MacArthur Foundation Fellowship (1984).

Mangas Coloradas (b. Dasoda-hae) (?1791–1863) Mimbreño Apache war chief; born in the southwest of present-day New Mexico. Repeated offenses against his family and his people caused a turnabout of this one-time friend to the whites. He and his son-in-law, Cochise, were largely successful in keeping whites out of their territory. In 1863, while carrying a flag of truce, he was arrested, tortured, and killed.

Manheim, Ralph (?1907–92) translator; born in New York City. Regarded as the dean of American professional translators, he produced more than 100 English translations of works by Freud, Jung, Heidegger, Brecht, Grass, Hesse, Proust, and other French and German writers. His many prizes included a MacArthur Foundation "genius" award (1983). He lived after 1950 in Paris and after 1985 in England.

Mankiewicz, Herman J. (1897–1953) screenwriter, movie producer; born in New York (brother of Joseph Mankiewicz). He began as a newspaperman, first as a foreign correspondent in Berlin, then as a New York drama editor. He moved to Hollywood in 1926, writing many screenplays and adaptations and serving as an executive producer on various films. He became embroiled in a controversy over the Academy Award-winning script for *Citizen Kane* (1941), which Orson Welles originally claimed to have written, but for which knowledgeable people insist Mankiewicz deserves most credit.

Mankiewicz, Joseph L. (Leo) (1909–92) movie director/producer, screenwriter; born in Wilkes-Barre, Pa. (brother of Herman J. Mankiewicz). As a foreign correspondent in Berlin, he began translating German silent film titles into English, then went to Hollywood in 1929 to write titles and screenplays for Paramount. By 1936 he was a producer for Paramount, then Fox, directing his first film *Dragonwyck* in 1946. He went on to direct a series of literate, if overly literary films, winning Oscars for both screenplay and direction for both *A Letter to Three Wives* (1949) and *All About Eve* (1950).

Mann, Horace (1796–1859) educator, public official; born in Franklin, Mass. He overcame limited educational opportunities, attended Brown University, and practiced law in Dedham and Boston, Mass. (1821–37). As Massachusetts state representative, senator, and senate president (1827–37), he worked to establish the first state hospital for the mentally ill and a state board of education. As head of the new board, his 12 annual reports (1837–48) comprehensively established the basis for universal, nonsectarian public education. Using his legal skills, he established public high schools, built teacher-training schools, curbed child labor, gained acceptance for women teachers, and fended off opposition from religious and business interests. After serving in the U.S. Congress (Whig, Mass.; 1848–53), he became president of Antioch College (1853–89), which was nonsectarian and open without regard to sex or race. The public school system he established in Massachusetts served as the nation's model, hence his appellation, "the father of American public education."

Mann, James (Robert) (1856–1922) U.S. representative; born in Bloomington, Ill. A successful attorney from Chicago, he was a Republican congressman (1897–22), skilled in legislation and parliamentary tactics, a protégé of Joseph Cannon. Among the acts he sponsored are the Mann-Elkins Act, which regulated railroad rates, the Pure Food and Drugs Act (1906), and the Mann Act to prohibit transporting minors across state lines. As minority leader (1912–18), he successfully impeded Democratic legislation, but never became Speaker.

Mann, Margaret (1873–1960) cataloguer; born in Cedar Rapids, Iowa. She taught library science at her alma mater, Chicago's Armour Institute, and was a cataloguer at the Carnegie Library in Pittsburgh (1903–19). She organized and recatalogued the Engineering Society Library in New York City (1919–24) and taught at the Paris (France) Library School (1924–26). While teaching at the University of Michigan, she authored the first basic text for librarianship, *Introduction to Cataloging and the Classification of Books* (1930).

Manners, Miss See MARTIN, JUDITH.

Mannes, David (1866–1959) violinist, educator, conductor; born in New York City. Concertmaster of the New York Symphony and a conductor and recitalist, in 1916 he opened the music school in New York City that bears his name.

Manning, Warren Henry (1860–1938) landscape architect; born in Reading, Mass. Son of a nurseryman, he joined the Olmsteds as a horticulturalist in 1888, becoming a design assistant before opening his own firm (1896–1938). Enormously successful, he delighted in training young designers and actively promoted the American Society of Landscape Architects. His commissions included a parkway system for Harrisburg, Pa., the Hampton Institute in Virginia, and the Jamestown Exposition of 1907.

Mansfield, Arabella (b. Belle Aurelia Babb) (1846–1911) lawyer, college teacher; born in Burlington, Iowa. She graduated from Iowa Wesleyan University (Mt. Pleasant, Iowa) (1866) and in 1868 married John Mansfield, a professor there. She joined the college's faculty and she and her husband read law together; they applied for admission to the Iowa bar and both were admitted – she thereby becoming the first woman regularly admitted to the practice of law in the U.S.A. – but neither ever practiced law. They went off to study in Europe and after returning to Iowa Wesleyan, they left to teach at Indiana Asbury (later DePauw) University (1879). Her husband suffered a mental breakdown (and died in 1894) but she went on at DePauw, becoming dean of the schools of art (1893–1911) and music (1894–1911).

Mansfield, (Michael Joseph) Mike (1903–) educator, U.S. representative/senator, diplomat; born in New York City. Raised in Montana, he dropped out of school at age 14 and served with the U.S. military from 1917 to 1922. He earned a B.A. and an M.A. from Montana State University where he taught history and political science (1934–43). He served in the U.S. House of Representatives (Dem., Mont.; 1943–53) and then in the U.S. Senate (1953–77), where as majority leader (1961–77) he became an influential critic of the U.S. role in the Vietnam War. President Carter named him ambassador to Japan (1977).

Mansfield, Richard (1854–1907) stage actor; born in Berlin, Germany. Son of English parents, he came to the U.S.A. in 1872 and thereafter alternated between America and England, first attracting attention in light opera productions in London, then moving over to the New York theater in 1883. One of the last in the fading style of romantic acting, his most famous roles were as Dr. Jekyll and Mr. Hyde (1887), Beau Brummel (1890), and Cyrano de Bergerac (1898). He struggled to bring new plays, including Shaw's, to the American stage, but had more success with revivals.

Manson, Charles (1934–) cult leader; born in Cincinnati, Ohio. Released from prison in 1967, he set up a commune based on free love and devotion to himself. Members of his cult conducted a series of grisly murders in California in 1969. He and his accomplices were sentenced to death, but were spared the death penalty due to a Supreme Court ruling against capital punishment.

Mantle, Mickey (Charles) (1931–) baseball player; born in Spavinaw, Okla. During his 18-year career as an outfielder for the New York Yankees (1951–68), the switch-hitting slugger hit 536 homeruns and was voted the American League Most Valuable Player three times (1956–57, 1962). In 1956 he won the American League triple crown with 52 homeruns, 130 runs batted in, and a .353 batting average. He became a restaurateur and television commentator after retiring from baseball. A fan favorite, he was elected to baseball's Hall of Fame in 1974.

Manuelito (b. Hastin Ch'ilhajinii or Hashkeh Naabah) (?1818–94) Navajo war leader; born in present-day Utah. He was the last chief to hold out against a scorched-earth campaign by the U.S. government to defeat the Navajo. After surrendering his starving people (1865), he led them to exile where thousands died due to deplorable conditions. In 1876 he journeyed to Washington, D.C., to plead for a reservation nearer his people's homeland. The principal chief from 1870–85, he was also selected in 1872 to head the Navajo Indian Police Force.

Maranville, (Walter James Vincent) "Rabbit" (1891–1954) baseball player; born in Springfield, Mass. During his 23-year career as an infielder (1912–35), mostly with the Boston Braves, he established many fielding records with his colorful play, including most lifetime putouts by a shortstop (5,133). He was elected to baseball's Hall of Fame in 1954.

Maravich, (Peter Press) Pete (1948–88) basketball player; born in Aliquippa, Pa. He was a three-time National Collegiate Athletic Association scoring leader at Louisiana State University (1968–70), virtually rewriting the National Collegiate Athlete Association record book; among his many records, he averaged 44.2 points per game. He went on to play for the National Basketball Association Atlanta Hawks, New Orleans Jazz, and Boston Celtics, where he averaged 24.2 points per game over ten years. Nicknamed "Pistol Pete," he was elected to basketball's Hall of Fame in 1987.

Marbut, Curtis (Fletcher) (1863–1935) soil scientist, geographer; born in Lawrence County, Mo. After receiving his M.A. from Harvard (1894), he taught geology at the University of Missouri (1895–1913). As chief of the U.S. Soil Survey (1913–33), he developed an international standard for studying soil, known as pedology. He translated *The Great Soil Groups of the World and Their Development* (1927) from the German and wrote the *Soils of the United States* (1935).

Marcantonio, Vito (Anthony) (1902–54) U.S. representative; born in New York City. A political activist in high school, he became Fiorello LaGuardia's protégé: a law clerk in his congressional office, assistant United States attorney general (1930–34), and member of the U.S. House of Representatives (Rep., N.Y.; 1935–37, 1939–51). An overt leftist, he was a critical supporter of the New Deal. In 1947 he raged against the House Committee on Un-American Activities; his opposition to the Korean War led to his defeat in 1951.

March, Francis Andrew (1825–1911) philologist; born in Millbury, Mass. Inspired by the lectures of Noah Webster at Amherst College, he went on to teach for 49 years at Lafayette College in Easton, Pa. (1855–1906), where in 1857 he was appointed to the chair of English language and philology, the first professorship of its kind. His text, *A Comparative Grammar of the Anglo-Saxon Language* (1870), details the Indo-European origins of the language and laid the foundation for the future study of the English language and historical grammar. He directed the American readers for the *Oxford English Dictionary* during the 1870s and 1880s and he was active in the spelling reform movement. With his son (Francis Andrew) he edited an English-language dictionary and a thesaurus.

March, James G. (Gardner) (1928–) social scientist, educator; born in Cleveland, Ohio. An academic and business consultant, he joined the Stanford University faculty (1970), teaching management, higher education, political science, and sociology. His published works are similarly varied and include *Organizations* (1958), *A Behavioral Theory of the Firm* (1963), and *Rediscovering Institutions: The Organizational Basis of Politics* (coauthored, 1989).

March, Peyton Conway (1864–1955) soldier; born in Easton, Pa. Son of a philologist, he graduated from Lafayette College, then from West Point (1888). He served in the Spanish-American War and then in putting down the Philippine insurrection. In 1917 he was made chief of artillery of the American Expeditionary Force in World War I. Appointed army chief of staff in 1918, he reformed and improved army logistics in support of the enormous buildup of American troops and matériel in France. A rival of Gen. John Pershing, the American field commander who favored limits on the powers of the chief of staff, March left the army in 1921. In 1932 he published *The Nation at War,* which continued his feud with Pershing.

Marciano, "Rocky" (b. Rocco Francis Marchegiano) (1923–69) boxer; born in Brockton, Mass. After he failed at becoming a professional baseball player, he took up boxing, winning 27 of 30 amateur bouts before turning professional in 1947. After being only the second boxer ever to knock out Joe Louis (no longer the champion), he won the heavyweight title in 1952 by knocking out "Jersey Joe" Walcott in the 13th round. He successfully defended his title six times before retiring in 1955, the only undefeated heavyweight champion in boxing history; his professional record was 49 victories (43 knockouts). Only 5 feet 11 inches tall, he had an aggressive style and a devastating punch. He died in a small airplane crash.

Marckwardt, Albert (Henry) (1903–75) linguist; born in Grand Rapids, Mich. A graduate of the University of Michigan (1925; Ph.D. 1933), he became professor of English there (1928–62) and then at Princeton (1963–72). He wrote several influential textbooks on the English language, including *Introduction to the English Language* (1942) and *American English* (1958). He was president of the American Dialect Society (1962–64), the Linguistic Society of America (1962), and the National Council of Teachers of English (1967), and he served as a consultant on language and education to the U.S. Information Agency, the U.S. Office of Education, and the Foreign Service Institute of the Department of State.

Marcosson, Isaac Frederick (1876–1961) journalist; born in Louisville, Ky. A writer for the *Saturday Evening Post* for most of his career, he was noted for his interviews with political and industrial leaders, from Lloyd George to Sun Yat-sen. Aided by a legacy, he retired from active journalism in 1936.

Marcus, (Harold) Stanley (1905–) retail executive; born in Dallas (son of Herbert Marcus). An inspired marketer, he transformed his father's Dallas store, Neiman-Marcus, into a national retailer known for its exclusivity, millionaire clientele, and extravagant Christmas catalogue. He was president (1950–72) and chairman (1972–75). After 1977 he was a Dallas-based marketing consultant.

Marcus, Rudolph A. (Arthur) (1923–) physical chemist; born in Montreal, Canada. He did his university work at McGill University in Montreal, taking his Ph.D. in 1946, then worked for the National Research Council of Canada (1946–49) before becoming a research associate in theoretical chemistry at the University of North Carolina (1949–51). After teaching posts at the Polytechnic Institute of Brooklyn and the University of Illinois: Urbana, he became the A. A. Noyes professor of Chemistry at the California Institute of Technology in Pasadena (1978). During his career he was a guest professor at many institutions and the recipient of many awards, including the Wolf Prize in chemistry (1984). He received the 1992 Nobel Prize in chemistry for his mathematical analysis of how the overall energy in a system of interacting molecules changes and induces an electron to jump from one molecule to another; his findings have important implications for many complex chemical reactions from plant photosynthesis to corrosion. Although he performed his work between 1956 and 1965, it took 30 years for experimental confirmation to convince many chemists of the validity of his conclusions.

Marcuse, Herbert (1898–1979) political philosopher; born in Berlin, Germany. Fleeing Hitler, he came to the U.S.A. in 1934 and was naturalized in 1940; much of his career was spent at Brandeis University (1954–65) and the University of California: San Diego (1965–70). A committed but critical Marxist, he made a synthesis of Marx and Freud in *Eros and Civilization* (1955). After the publication of *One-Dimensional Man* (1964), which criticized capitalist societies as repressive, he won notoriety as an inspiration to and apologist for the New Left movement of the 1960s. He retired in La Jolla, Calif., continuing to travel and lecture; in 1971 he was shouted down by European radicals, and he died in Germany where he had gone to lecture.

Marcy, William Learned (1786–1857) lawyer, public official; born in Southbridge, Mass. Instrumental in the powerful "Albany Regency" Democratic machine, he was New York comptroller (1823–29), state supreme court justice (1829–31), U.S. senator (1831–32), and a capable governor of New York (1833–39). As senator he coined the phrase, "to the victor belong the spoils of the enemy." He served as President James Polk's secretary of war (1845–49) during the Mexican War. As secretary of state under President Franklin Pierce (1853–57), he negotiated 24 treaties and various other delicate international cases, including the Gadsden Purchase (1853–54). His reputation as one of the nation's ablest public officials has survived the test of time.

Marden, Brice (1938–   ) painter; born in Bronxville, N.Y. After studies at Yale University School of Art and Architecture with Esteban Vincente and Alex Katz (1961–63), he lived and worked in New York City. He is praised for his minimalist work in oil and wax, as seen in *For Pearl* (1970), whose three panels are covered with color tonalities.

Margenau, Henry (1901–   ) physicist; born in Bielefeld, Germany. He came to the U.S.A. as a graduate student, taught at the University of Nebraska (1926–27), then spent his career at Yale (1929–69). He made advances in spectroscopy and studies of intramolecular and intranuclear forces, wrote extensively on the philosophy of science, and was a consultant for the *Time-Life* science series.

Margulis, Lynn (Alexander) (1938–   ) cell biologist; born in Chicago. She taught and performed research at Boston University (1966–88), and became a Distinguished University Professor at the University of Massachusetts (Amherst) (1988). She made major contributions to the origin, morphogenesis, cytoplasmic genetics, and evolution of slime molds and other protists. She is a proponent of the controversial Gaia hypothesis, which views planet Earth as a homeostatic physicochemical system whose surface is actively influenced by the actions of all living organisms.

Marin, John (1870–1953) painter; born in Rutherford, N.J. He worked as an architect (1893), studied at the Pennsylvania Academy of the Fine Arts (1899–1901), and traveled to Paris (1905–09). Upon his return to New York City, he exhibited at Alfred Stieglitz's gallery (1909–10). He spent summers in Maine and lived in New Jersey. Working primarily in water colors, he was a leading abstract painter in America, as seen in his seascape *Maine Islands* (1922).

Marion, Francis (c. 1732–95) soldier; born in Berkeley County, S.C. A planter, he had fought against the Cherokees in 1759 and 1761, and when the American Revolution began, he volunteered and led "irregulars" in several engagements; because his sprained ankle had led him to leave Charleston, S.C., before its surrender to the British, he was available to command the remaining resistance in South Carolina after the colonials' loss at Camden, S.C. Known as the "Swamp Fox" because the British Col. Tarleton called him "this damned old fox" and because he operated out of a secret hideout on a river island, he used guerrilla tactics to strike at stronger British and Loyalist forces, disrupting enemy communications, capturing supplies, and freeing prisoners before disappearing into the wilderness. From 1781 on he led his troops under Gen. Nathanael Greene. After the war, he served in the South Carolina senate and commanded Fort Johnson in Charleston harbor (1784–90).

Maris, Roger (Eugene) (1934–85) baseball player; born in Hibbing, Minn. During his 12-year career as an outfielder (1957–68), mostly with the New York Yankees and St. Louis Cardinals, he hit a career 275 homeruns and was twice voted the American League Most Valuable Player (1960–61). In 1961 he slammed 61 homeruns to break Babe Ruth's single season record of 60 homeruns set in 1927; the reaction to his breaking Ruth's records was so extreme – and often threatening – that Maris seemed an unhappy man for the rest of his life.

Marisol (Escobar) (1930–   ) sculptor, painter, graphic artist; born in Paris, France. Of Venezuelan parents, she studied in Paris (1949), settled in New York City (1950), and studied at the Art Students League (1950), the New School (1951–54), and the Hans Hofmann School (1951–54). She is known for her witty satirical carvings and assemblages in wood, plaster, paint, and other materials, such as *Woman and Dog* (1964).

Mark, Herman Francis (1895–1992) chemist; born in Vienna, Austria. He emigrated to the United States in 1938. He was a pioneer in polymer chemistry. He became director of I. G. Farben in Germany (1928) and director of the Chemical Institute at the University of Vienna (1933). In 1944, he became director of the Polymer Institute of the Polytechnic University in Brooklyn, which under him became a center for polymer research.

Markham, (Charles Edward Anson) Edwin (1852–1940) poet, editor; born in Oregon City, Ore. He studied briefly at Christian College, Santa Rosa, Calif., then taught in California (1875–1901). After the sudden success of "The Man with the Hoe" (1899), a poem inspired by Jean-Francois Millet's painting, and "Lincoln, the Man of the People" (1901), he moved to Staten Island, New York, and spent the rest of his life writing and lecturing but never again attaining the recognition he gained from these two poems.

Markowitz, Harry Max (1927–   ) economist; born in Chicago. He worked in the private sector (International Business Machines, 1974–83) as well as academia, settling at Rutgers University as the Marvin Speiser Distinguished Professor of Economics and Finance (1982). His principal interest was in the theory of rational behavior in relation to portfolio and investment analysis and planning. He designed and developed several computer programming languages including SIMSCRIPT and EAS-E.

Marlatt, Abby Lillian (1869–1943) home economist, educator; born in Manhattan, Kans. She pioneered the teaching of high school home economics in Rhode Island (1894–1909) before joining the home economics department at the

University of Wisconsin's School of Agriculture (1909). As its director (1913–39), she built it into one of the largest and most influential in the country.

Marler, Peter (Robert) (1928–   ) animal behaviorist; born in London, England. He was a research fellow at Jesus College, Cambridge University (1954–56), then came to the U.S.A. to join the University of California: Berkeley (1957–66). He was a professor at Rockefeller University (1966–89) before moving to the University of California: Davis (1989). Although trained as a botanist, he rekindled his childhood interest in ornithology early in his career. He made major contributions to behavioral studies of animal (including primate) vocalization, especially regarding the social function of birdsongs.

Marlowe, Julia (b. Sarah Frances Frost) (1866–1950) actress; born in Caldbeck, England. Brought to the U.S.A. at age four, she first performed in 1879 at age 12 under the name of Fanny Brough. Her adult debut in 1887 as Parthenia in *Ingomar* was an immediate success. After a start in musical comedies and in comic roles, she was eventually best known as a slender, pale Shakespearean, playing opposite Richard Taber and E. H. Sothern, to whom she was successively married.

Marquand, Allan (1853–1924) art historian; born in New York City. He graduated from Princeton (1874), studied theology, then studied at the University of Berlin (1877–78), and Johns Hopkins (Ph.D. 1880). He taught at Princeton beginning in 1881, and specialized in cataloguing the works of the Della Robbia family of Italy.

Marquand, J. P. (John Philips) (1893–1960) writer; born in Wilmington, Del. He studied at Harvard (B.A. 1915), and after serving with the U.S. Army in World War I he became a journalist and free-lance writer (1916–20). He worked as a copywriter for an advertising agency in New York City (1921–22), then concentrated on his fiction writing after the success of his first novel, *The Unspeakable Gentleman* (1922), printed first in the *Ladies Home Journal.* He continued to publish short stories in various magazines during the next 15 years; the best-known of these stories involved a Japanese detective, Mr. Moto. With the publication of *The Late George Apley* (1937), he commenced his career as a satirical novelist of affluent upper-middle-class WASPS. Although never taken that seriously by the academic-intellectual establishment, such novels as *H.M. Pulham, Esquire* (1941) and *Sincerely, Willis Wade* (1955) gained him a large and respectable readership. He lived most of his final four decades in Newburyport, Mass.

Marquard, (Richard William) "Rube" (1889–1980) baseball pitcher; born in Cleveland, Ohio. A star left-hander during his 18-year career (1908–25), mostly with the New York Giants, he won a record 19 straight games on his way to winning 26 games in 1912. He was elected to baseball's Hall of Fame in 1971.

Marquette, Jacques (1637–75) Catholic missionary, explorer; born in Laon, France. As a young man and as a Jesuit priest, his hero was St. Francis Xavier. He came to Quebec, Canada (1666), learned Indian languages, and proceeded to do missionary work among the Ottawa and Huron Indians in the Great Lakes region. In 1673, he and Louis Jolliet (French explorer, 1645–1700), searched for and found (June 17, 1673) the waters of the Mississippi River; they were the first white men to follow the course of the river. They went as far as the mouth of the Arkansas River and then returned. Marquette preached among the Illinois Indians (1674–75) until he died prematurely from ailments aggravated by his exertions. His journals remain an invaluable record of the region in these years. Wisconsin placed his statue in the U.S. Capitol.

Marquis, Don (b. Donald Robert Perry Marquis) (1878–1937) author, humorist; born in Walnut, Ill. A columnist from 1913 to 1925 for the *New York Sun* and then the *New York Herald Tribune,* he created such characters as "archy" (the literary cockroach) and "mehitabel" (the cat) to satirize fads and pretensions. His humor also helped him surmount personal misfortunes such as the early deaths of his first wife and his two children.

Marriott, J. (John) Willard (1900–85) restaurant/hotel executive; born near Ogden, Utah. His first Hot Shoppe in Washington, D.C. (1927) quickly grew into a chain of family-style drive-ins. Marriott Corporation became a major U.S. hospitality company after diversifying into airline catering (1937) and motels (1957). His son John Willard Marriott Jr. succeeded him as president in 1964, CEO in 1972, and chairman in 1985.

Mars, Forrest (Edward) (1904–   ) candy manufacturer; birthplace unknown. After disagreeing with his father, who had invented the Milky Way bar, he went to Great Britain where he became a leading pet food manufacturer. Returning to the U.S.A. during World War II, he introduced M&M's and purchased the Uncle Ben's Rice Company. He merged with his father's business, Mars Inc., in 1964. During the 1970s he produced at least half of the country's leading candy bars, including the perennial favorite, Snickers. A secretive billionaire, he turned his business over to his sons when he retired.

Marsalis, Wynton (1961–   ) jazz musician; born in New Orleans. Raised in a musical family (including his brother Branford Marsalis), he became a trumpeter who mastered both jazz and classical music; in 1984 he won Grammy Awards for recordings in both fields. He joined Art Blakey's Jazz Messengers in 1980, where he was first heralded for his commitment to pure acoustic jazz styles, and left in 1982 to form the first in a succession of small ensembles. In the following years he became one of the most visible American musicians, maintaining a constant touring schedule and conducting numerous clinics through which he sought to expose public school students to jazz and encourage their pursuit of it as a livelihood. The makeup of his own bands reflected his success in this area, as he brought an impressive number of young musicians to the fore throughout the 1980s. He also turned increasingly to composition, writing short and extended pieces that showed the influence of Duke Ellington and reflected his interest in early jazz styles.

Marsh, George Perkins (1801–82) linguist, diplomat, conservationist; born in Woodstock, Vt. A master of several languages by the time he graduated from Dartmouth (1820), he taught before shifting to the law (1825); with a prosperous practice in Burlington, Vt., he entered politics, eventually serving in the U.S. House of Representatives (Whig, Vt.; 1843–49), where he opposed slavery and the Mexican War. He resigned to serve as ambassador to Turkey (1849–54). He had continued his studies of various languages, such as Icelandic, and as an ambassador was noted for his ability to converse with foreigners in many languages. Back in

Vermont he pursued a variety of interests – writing a book on introducing the camel into the U.S.A. (1856) and lecturing and publishing on the history of the English language. In 1861 he went off to the new kingdom of Italy as first American ambassador, a post he held with great respect until he died in Italy in 1882. While there he published *Man and Nature: Or, Physical Geography as Modified by Human Action* (1864); it was heavily revised and republished as *The Earth as Modified by Human Action* (1874). Although it did not receive much attention in its day, it was rediscovered in the 1930s, and with its thesis that humans have abused the land and must therefore restore it, it has come to be regarded as "the fountainhead of the conservation movement."

Marsh, O. C. (Othniel Charles) (1831–99) paleontologist; born in Lockport, N.Y. He was educated at Yale and Yale's Sheffield School and in Germany. A paleontology professor at Yale (1866–99) and chief vertebrate paleontologist of the U.S. Geological Survey (1882–92), he discovered more than 1,000 fossil vertebrates on expeditions to the western territories, amassing extensive collections for Yale's Peabody Museum. Marsh helped establish and popularize the new science of vertebrate paleontology; his classification and descriptions of extinct vertebrates helped confirm Darwinian theories of evolution and occasioned a fierce rivalry with Edward Drinker Cope. He described the earliest mammals then known, 80 new species of dinosaurs and the first fossil serpents and flying reptiles found in western America; he established the reptilian origin of birds; and he established both the evolution of the horse and the presence of early primates in North America. His publications include "Introduction and Succession of Vertebrate Life in America" (1877) and *The Dinosaurs of North America* (1896). He was president of the National Academy of Sciences (1883–95).

Marsh, Reginald (1898–1954) painter; born in Paris, France. His parents were American artists who returned to America (1900). He studied at Yale University (B.A. 1920), became a cartoonist and illustrator for periodicals, and lived in New York City. Known for his water colors and egg tempera paintings of contemporary urban life, he combined the baroque with a realistic style, as seen in *The Bowery* (1930), and *Negroes on Rockaway Beach* (1934).

Marshak, Robert E. (Eugene) (1916–92) physicist, educator; born in New York City. He taught at Rochester (1939–70), was president of City College, N.Y. (1970–79), then became a Distinguished Professor at Virginia Polytechnic Institute (1979–87). He proposed his pioneering meson theory in 1947, and published his discovery of a universal weak force in subatomic particle behavior in 1957. After observing the effects of the atomic bomb he helped design, he worked to promote international peace.

Marshall, George C. (Catlett), Jr. (1880–1959) soldier, secretary of state; born in Uniontown, Pa. Son of a well-to-do coal dealer, he graduated from the Virginia Military Institute (1901), received a commission in the army the next year, saw service in the Philippines insurrection campaign (1902–03), and proved himself to be an outstanding staff officer in a series of appointments leading up to World War I. One of the first officers to go to France, he was chief of operations of the 1st Infantry Division and then held the same post with the First Army; his brilliant transfer of troops in the Meuse-Argonne campaign caught the attention of Gen. John Pershing, and Marshall became his principal aide

(1919–24). Tall, confident, soft-spoken, and politically adept, Marshall continued to advance his reputation as an administrator; he served in China (1924–27), organized the Civilian Conservation Corps, and was chief of the war plans division and deputy chief of staff (1938–39). As World War II commenced, he became the chief of staff of the U.S. Army, a post he held until 1945; although not the most glamorous of jobs, all recognize that Marshall played a crucial role in training the massive new army, drawing up strategic plans, appointing top military personnel (it was Marshall who advanced Dwight Eisenhower to command the operations in North Africa and Sicily), and balancing out the competing goals of Allied political and military leaders. Marshall wanted to direct the invasion of France but President Franklin Roosevelt preferred to use his talents in Washington; by the war's end, he had earned Winston Churchill's accolade, "the true organizer of victory." After an unsuccessful effort to establish a coalition government in China (1946), he was named secretary of state by President Harry Truman (1947–49), in which post he implemented the postwar recovery plan for war-ravaged Europe that was known as "the Marshall Plan" (although he himself never claimed to have initiated it). He won the Nobel Peace Prize in 1953 for his many contributions to the postwar world (the only professional soldier to be so honored). Resigning in 1949 because of poor health, he served as head of the American Red Cross (1949–50). With the outbreak of the Korean War, he returned to government service as secretary of defense (1950–51). In 1951, Senator Joseph McCarthy charged that Marshall had been "soft on Communism" in connection with his effort to mediate the civil war in China (1945–47), but members of both parties and numerous other prominent Americans defended Marshall vigorously and he has retained his reputation as one of the finest individuals ever to serve America.

Marshall, James (Edward) (1942–92) writer, illustrator; born in San Antonio, Texas. He studied at the New England Conservatory of Music, Boston, remained in the city, taught French (1968–70), and became a free-lance illustrator. He is known for his picture books, such as the *George and Martha* hippopotamus series (1972), and another series beginning with *The Stupids Step Out* (1974), produced in collaboration with Harry Allard.

Marshall, James (Wilson) (1810–85) gold finder; born in Hunterdon County, N.J. After some 14 years in Indiana, Illinois, and Kansas Territory, he arrived at Sutter's Fort (present day Sacramento) in 1845. After losing his land and livestock, he was building a sawmill for John Sutter, near present-day Coloma, Calif. (1848), when he discovered gold; this launched the California "gold rush" of 1849. The government refused to recognize the land claims of Sutter and Marshall. Marshall, who made almost nothing from his discovery, spent his final years bitter, resentful, and working as a gardener.

Marshall, John (1755–1835) Supreme Court justice; born in Prince William (now Fauquier) County, Va. Born in a log cabin, with little formal education, he fought in the American Revolution and studied law briefly (1779–80) before setting up a practice and getting elected to the Virginia legislature (1782). An outspoken advocate of the Federalists' position on the need for a strong central government, he was asked by President George Washington

(1795) to be the U.S. attorney general but he declined because of his financial difficulties. After helping to negotiate Jay's Treaty in France (1797–98), he was elected to the House of Representatives (Fed., Va.; 1799–1800) but left when President John Adams appointed him chief justice of the U.S. Supreme Court (1801–35). During his 34 years, the "Marshall court" profoundly shaped the law and government of the U.S.A. by testing and defining the powers of the new Constitution. Perhaps his most important decision was *Marbury* v. *Madison* (1803), in which he laid down the concept of "judicial review" – namely, that federal courts had the final say in deciding whether congressional legislation was constitutional. In various other decisions over the years, he enforced his view of the supremacy of a strong federal government over the demands of states and their legislatures; presiding over the treason trial of Aaron Burr (1807), he went out of his way to attack the anti-Federalist positions of President Thomas Jefferson (a distant relative). Often the focus of political controversy, autocratic in his dominance of the court – it was he who imposed the practice of issuing a single majority opinion – he had a casual frontier manner but the keenest of intellects. The Liberty Bell in Philadelphia cracked when ringing for the funeral of Marshall.

Marshall, Louis (1856–1929) lawyer, civic leader; born in Syracuse, N.Y. Educated in public schools and at Columbia Law School (1877), he practiced in Syracuse, N.Y., and, from 1894, in New York City, where he became a notable for his defense of minorities in civil rights cases. He also accepted many immigration and labor cases and he successfully argued many cases before the U.S. Supreme Court. A cofounder of the American Jewish Committee, he attended the Paris Peace Conference in 1919 and worked to get antidiscrimination clauses into various treaties. He helped Jewish refugees settle in Palestine in the 1920s, in hopes that the country, then a British protectorate, would become a permanent homeland for Jews.

Marshall, Paule (b. Burke) (1929–) writer; born in New York City. She studied at Brooklyn College (B.A. 1953), and Hunter College (1955). She worked as a librarian and as a staff writer for *Our World* magazine (1953–56). Based in New York City, she became a free-lance writer in 1956. She also taught at Yale (1970), and lectured on Black literature at many institutions. She is known for her stories and novels that celebrate the lives of African-Americans and individuals living in the West Indies and Barbados, as in *Praisesong for the Widow* (1983).

Marshall, Robert (1901–39) forester, conservationist; born in New York City. A field researcher for the U.S. Forest Service in Montana and Alaska, he became director of forestry for the Bureau of Indian Affairs (1933) and worked to involve Native Americans more fully in the management of their forests and ranges. He was a forceful advocate of government ownership of commercial timber lands. As a private citizen, he helped found the Wilderness Society in 1935.

Marshall, Thomas R. (Riley) (1854–1925) vice-president, governor; born in North Manchester, Ind. He served as Woodrow Wilson's vice-president (1913–21), the first vice-president to serve for two full terms in nearly one hundred years. During Woodrow Wilson's illness (1919–21), he refused to take any action that might have led to his replacing the incapacitated president.

Marshall, Thurgood (1908–93) civil rights advocate, Supreme Court justice; born in Baltimore, Md. The great-grandson of a slave, he graduated as valedictorian from Howard University Law School (1933) and soon began to represent civil rights activists. Becoming a counsel for the National Association for the Advancement of Colored People in 1938, during the next 23 years he won 29 of the 32 major cases he undertook for that organization; several of the cases set constitutional precedents in matters such as voting rights and breaking down segregated transportation and education. His finest moment came with *Brown* v. *Board of Education* (1954), which overturned *Plessy* v. *Ferguson* (1896) and its "separate but equal" ruling that perpetuated segregated institutions and facilities. President John F. Kennedy named him to the U.S. Court of Appeals, a seat he finally took over the resistance of Southern senators (1962–65); President Lyndon Johnson appointed him U.S. solicitor general (1965–67) and then to the U.S. Supreme Court, the first African-American to hold such an office (1967–91). Consistently voting with the liberal block, he found himself increasingly isolated as the court's makeup changed and he was forced by ill health to retire and see his seat taken by the conservative Clarence Thomas.

Martin, Agnes (Bernice) (1912–) painter; born in Maklin, Saskatchewan, Canada. After studying art at Columbia University (M.A. 1954), she settled in New York City. Known for her use of acrylic paint in her delicate and quiet grids, she is associated with the minimalist school, as seen in *Play* (1966). She lived in New Mexico from 1967.

Martin, Allie Beth Dent (1914–76) librarian; born in Annieville. After working at several librarian positions in Arkansas and getting an M.A. from the Columbia University School of Library Service (1949), she went with her husband to Tulsa, Okla., and began working in the Tulsa Public Library system. She became director of the Tulsa City-County Library (1963) after campaigning vigorously for improved library services. The Tulsa library was transformed into a model system and Martin, along with architect Charles F. Ward, formed a consultant firm, Library Design Associates, Inc., active throughout the Southwest. She was president of the Southwestern Library Association (1969–70) and was president of the American Library Association (1975–76).

Martin, Francois-Xavier (1762–1846) jurist, author; born in Marseilles, France. At about the age of 19 he appeared in New Bern, N.C., where he taught French while learning English. He began working in a printing shop and moved up to become a publisher. He was admitted to the North Carolina bar in 1789 and began to publish and edit legal texts. In 1809 he was appointed a federal judge for the Mississippi Territory and was reassigned to the Territory of Orleans in 1810; as soon as the latter became the state of Louisiana, he became the state's attorney general (1813–15) and then a judge on the state supreme court (1815–46, chief justice 1836–46). As Louisiana law was based on Spanish and French law, he worked hard to bring the state's law into line with the prevailing American practices based more on English law. He published a total of 34 volumes, including many reports of legal decisions and histories of Louisiana and North Carolina.

Martin, Glenn (Luther) (1886–1955) aircraft manufacturer; born in Macksburg, Iowa. In 1909, using his own airplane,

Martin taught himself to fly, becoming the third person in the United States to do so. Nicknamed "the Dude," he barnstormed from 1909 to 1915 to raise money. In 1912, using a plane built in his California factory, he flew from Los Angeles to Catalina Island and back, a record 32 miles; in 1917 he relocated to Cleveland and designed the MB-2 bomber; in 1929 he moved to Baltimore, producing the B-10 bomber and the China Clipper flying boat as well as other aircraft. In World War II his factory created the B-26 Marauder and the Mariner and Mars flying boats. Following the war his company experienced economic difficulty and in 1952 the navy took over control. Extremely close to his mother, he died shortly after her.

Martin, Homer (Dodge) (1836–97) painter; born in Albany, N.Y. He moved to New York City (1862), traveled in England (1876) and France (1881–86), and settled in St. Paul, Minn. He is known for his impressionistic landscapes, such as *Honfleur Light* (1892).

Martin, John (1893–1985) dance critic, author; born in Louisville, Ky. Appointed as the first dance critic for the *New York Times* in 1927, Martin championed nontraditional dance in his reviews and essays until his retirement in 1962. He wrote several dance books including the classic, *The Modern Dance*.

Martin, John Rupert (1916–) art historian; born in Hamilton, Ontario, Canada. He studied at McMaster University (B.A. 1938), emigrated to America (1941), and attended Princeton (M.A. 1941; Ph.D. 1947). He taught primarily at Princeton beginning in 1947, and specialized in northern baroque art.

Martin, (Johnny Leonard Roosevelt) "Pepper" (1904–65) baseball player; born in Temple, Okla. A third baseman/outfielder for the St. Louis Cardinals (1928–44), he was one of the stars of the famous "Gas House Gang" that won pennants in 1928, 1931, and 1934. Nicknamed, "the Wild Horse of the Osage," he batted .500 in the 1931 World Series in a performance that endures in baseball folklore.

Martin, Joseph (William), Jr. (1884–1968) U.S. representative; born in North Attleboro, Mass. Son of a blacksmith, he turned down a Dartmouth scholarship to become a journalist, buying the *North Attleboro Evening Chronicle* in 1908. A Republican, he served in the Massachusetts legislature (1911–17) before going to the U.S. House of Representatives (1925–67), serving as Speaker, 1947–49. He forged a coalition with conservative Democrats to limit New Deal legislation, and in 1946 he helped pass the Taft-Hartley Act over President Truman's veto.

Martin, Judith Sylvia (b. Perlman) ("Miss Manners," pen name) (1938–) authority on etiquette; born in Washington, D.C. She began as a *Washington Post* reporter and critic (1960–83). The arch wit in her syndicated etiquette column (1978) and books such as *Miss Manners' Guide to Excruciatingly Correct Behavior* (1982), led to her reputation as the first "postmodern" etiquette expert.

Martin, Lawrence (1880–1955) geographer; born in Stockbridge, Mass. He specialized in physiography prior to World War I, teaching at the University of Wisconsin (1906–19), then turned his attention to political and historical geography. From 1924–46 he was chief of the division of maps in the Library of Congress. His knowledge of the history of cartography and Antarctic exploration was remarkable for its thoroughness.

Martin, Lillien Jane (1851–1943) psychologist; born in Olean, N.Y. She studied science at Vassar and taught high school until 1894, when she went to Germany to study experimental psychology at the University of Göttingen. She taught and conducted research at Stanford University for 17 years, published nine books, founded the first mental health clinic for normal children (at Mt. Zion Hospital, San Francisco, 1920), and became an authority on gerontology. At age 78, she established the world's first old-age counseling center, and in 1937 she opened a farm in Alameda County, Calif., "to give employment and restore self-confidence to a group of elderly men." She was active there until her death at the age of 93.

Martin, Lowell (Arthur) (?1912–) librarian; born in Detroit, Mich. After several years as an academic librarian, he became an executive at Grolier, Inc. (1959), where he supervised the publication of a number of new encyclopedias and reference works.

Martin, Luther (c. 1748–1826) lawyer; born in New Brunswick, N.Y. After graduating from the College of New Jersey (later Princeton) (1766), he worked as a teacher while reading law, eventually being admitted to the Virginia bar (1771). He served as attorney general of Maryland (1778–1805, 1818–22) and as a delegate from Maryland to the Continental Congress (1785). He went to the Constitutional Convention in 1789, but as an opponent of a strong central government, he left the convention and then unsuccessfully tried to prevent Maryland from ratifying the new constitution. He got into a legal quarrel with Thomas Jefferson and went over to the Federalist Party, helping Justice Samuel Chase in his impeachment trial (1804) and Aaron Burr in his treason trial (1807). His final years were marked by family problems, his own health problems, and his alcoholism; he ended up destitute and living with his former client, Aaron Burr.

Martin, Mary (Virginia) (1913–90) stage and film actress; born in Weatherford, Texas. Beginning with her 1938 debut in *Leave It to Me*, where she sang the showstopping "My Heart Belongs to Daddy," she was known for her down-to-earth portrayals. She starred in several huge hits, most notably as Nellie Forbush in *South Pacific* (1949), ("I'm Gonna Wash That Man Right Outa My Hair" and other songs), *Peter Pan* (1954), and *The Sound of Music* (1959).

Martin, Paul Sidney (1899–1974) anthropologist; born in Chicago. He spent his career at Chicago's Field Museum of Natural History, much of it as head curator (1935–64), and taught at the University of Chicago (1942–74). He directed numerous Field Museum expeditions to the American Southwest (1930–66); his fieldwork there and in the Midwest and Yucatán resulted in numerous publications.

Martin, Steve (?1945–) comedian, actor; born in Waco, Texas. He wrote television comedy for others before perfecting his own wacky routines for national television in 1975. After 1978 he became a successful film actor and director, drawing on a mix of slapstick and absurdism.

Martin, Thomas Staples (1847–1919) U.S. senator; born in Scottsville, Va. Leader of the Democratic machine in Virginia, he served in the U.S. Senate (1895–1919), where he became chairman of the Committee on Appropriations during World War I. He was renowned for his honesty, hard work, and conservatism.

Martin, William McChesney, Jr. (1906–) stockbroker,

government official; born in St. Louis, Mo. The son of a banker who helped draft the Federal Reserve Act during the Wilson Administration, he graduated from Yale in 1928, worked in a St. Louis brokerage, and returned east in 1931 to take a seat on the New York Stock Exchange (NYSE). In 1938 he became the exchange's first salaried president. He joined the government as an assistant treasury secretary before becoming chairman of the Federal Reserve Board in 1951. Associated with conservative monetary policies during his long tenure on the board, he served on a committee to reorganize the NYSE, and sat on several corporate boards after his retirement from government service in 1970.

Martinez, Maria (1884–1981) potter born in San Idelfonso Pueblo, N.M. Together with husband Julian Martinez, she rediscovered the technique of ancient Pueblo black pottery. After Julian's 1943 death, she continued to produce these traditional wares alone and with her family. Invited to the White House by four presidents, and the recipient of two honorary doctorates, she was asked to lay the cornerstone for Rockefeller Center.

Martino, Donald (James) (1931–) composer; born in Plainfield, N.J. After studies at Princeton and in Italy, he taught at schools including Princeton and Harvard (from 1983). A leading exponent of serial compositional technique, he won the Pulitzer Prize in 1974 for *Notturno*.

Martins, Peter (1946–) ballet dancer, choreographer; born in Copenhagen, Denmark. He trained at the School of the Royal Danish Ballet, and performed in its company (1965–69) before joining the New York City Ballet (1970). Key roles and a celebrated partnership with Suzanne Farrell propelled him to prominence as a dancer. He began choreographing with *Calcium Light Night* (1977); in 1983 he was appointed co-ballet master-in-chief with Jerome Robbins and retired from dancing. He became the sole master-in-chief in 1990. He choreographed several pieces a year, such as *Songs of the Auvergne* (1986). In 1993 he restaged *Sleeping Beauty* after Petipa and produced a much-acclaimed retrospective of George Balanchine's works.

Martiny, Philip (1858–1927) sculptor; born in Strasbourg, France. He studied in France with Augustus Saint-Gaudens, emigrated to New York City (1876), lived in Bayside, N.Y., and became known for architectural sculptures, such as the bronze doors of St. Bartholomew's Church, N.Y.C.

Marty, Martin (Emil) (1928–) Protestant church historian; born in West Point, Nebr. He had extensive training in theology before taking a Ph.D. from the University of Chicago. Ordained in the Lutheran Church in 1952, he held pastorates in Illinois; in 1963 he became professor of the history of modern Christianity at Chicago. He was one of the editors of the liberal *Christian Century* (1956–85) and lectured widely in Roman Catholic and evangelical circles. His extensive list of publications includes *A Short History of Christianity* (1959), *Righteous Empire* (1980), and *Protestantism in the United States* (1985).

Marx, Chico See under MARX BROTHERS.

Marx, Groucho See under MARX BROTHERS.

Marx, Gummo See under MARX BROTHERS.

Marx, Harpo See under MARX BROTHERS.

Marx, Zeppo See under MARX BROTHERS.

Marx Brothers, comedy team; all born in New York City. The three most prominent were **Chico** (b. Leonard) (1886–1961); **Harpo** (b. Adolph, but known as Arthur) (1888–

1964); and **Groucho** (b. Julius Henry) (1890–1977). Early in its career, the team included **Gummo** (b. Milton) (1893–1977) and **Zeppo** (b. Herbert) (1901–77). Sons of German immigrants, they were pushed on the stage by their mother, Minnie Marx (sister of Al Shean of the vaudeville duo, Gallagher & Shean), and began their career in vaudeville as a musical team before switching to the anarchic, surrealist comedy that became their trademark – a mixture of verbal and physical nonsequiturs. Gummo left the act early on and was replaced by Zeppo. The four hit Broadway in 1924 in *I'll Say She Is* and went on to make their first movie, *The Cocoanuts* in 1929. Zeppo left the team after their first five films, but the remaining three had hit after hit until 1950, with *Duck Soup* (1933) and *A Night at the Opera* (1935) arguably their best movies. Chico retired early and Harpo cut back to guest appearances on television, but Groucho remained active, appearing in movies and as the host of a popular television quiz show, *You Bet Your Life* (1950–61). In his later years, Groucho became something of a cultural institution, writing several well-received autobiographical books, and making guest appearances with his much-imitated manner but inimitable quips; he was revered by film buffs and paid homage to by individuals as disparate as Johnny Carson and T. S. Eliot.

Maslow, Abraham (Harold) (1908–70) psychologist; born in New York City. A professor at Brooklyn College (1937–51) and Brandeis University (1951–61), he is regarded as the founder of humanistic psychology. His seminal *Motivation and Personality* (1954) explicated the new humanistic model and introduced such soon-to-be standard psychological concepts as the need hierarchy, self-actualization, and peak experience.

Mason, Daniel Gregory (1873–1953) composer; born in Brookline, Mass. (grandson of Lowell Mason). He studied at Harvard and in Paris (with D'Indy) before returning to the U.S.A. and joining the Columbia University faculty in 1910, where he remained until his 1942 retirement. A well-known pedagogue, author of many books including *Music in My Time* (1938), he was conservative and European-oriented in his music and opinions; his work includes three symphonies and much chamber music.

Mason, George (1725–92) public official, planter; born in Fairfax County, Va. He wrote Virginia's first constitution and declaration of rights (1776) which were later used as models for both the Declaration of Independence and the Bill of Rights. He was a member and the treasurer of the Ohio Company (1752–73) and was interested in western settlement. Although he considered himself to be a private citizen rather than a politician, he served in the Virginia House of Delegates (1776–88), the House of Burgesses (1759–76), and was a member of the July Convention (1775) and a delegate to the Constitutional Convention (1787). He opposed the new Constitution because it presented such a strong federal government.

Mason, James (Murray) (1798–1871) U.S. senator, diplomat; born in Georgetown, D.C. (grandson of George Mason). As U.S. senator from Virginia (1847–61), he supported Southern rights and drafted the Fugitive Slave Act (1850). In 1861, en route to England on a mission to seek English diplomatic recognition for the Confederacy, he and John Slidell were taken by Union forces from the British ship *Trent;* held briefly in what threatened an international crisis, they were released and Mason spent the next four years in England. Although he had considerable success in purchasing naval and military supplies, he never gained diplomatic recognition. After the war, he lived in Canada until 1868 when he returned to Virginia.

Mason, John (c. 1600–72) soldier, public official; born in England. He emigrated to Massachusetts around 1633. Commanding militia, Mason broke the power of the Pequot Indian tribe in 1637 with an attack on an encampment at Mystic, Conn., in which more than 600 Pequots, including women and children, were slaughtered. He later served as a magistrate and as deputy governor of Connecticut.

Mason, Lowell (1792–1872) composer, educator; born in Medfield, Mass. He had been a church organist/choir director when he published a successful hymn collection in 1822, some of its melodies adopted from classical composers. In 1832 he cofounded the Boston Academy of Music, which gave instruction to adults and children. A pedagogue of great influence and importance for American music, he remained a prolific arranger and composer of hymns, his familiar tunes including "Nearer, My God, to Thee" and "From Greenland's Icy Mountains."

Mason, Stevens Thomson (1760–1803) U.S. senator; born in Stafford County, Va. (nephew of George Mason). An aide to Gen. Washington, he was elected to the U.S. Senate from Virginia (Dem.-Rep., 1794–1803). He won fame for publicizing the secret contents of the Jay Treaty.

Mason, Stevens Thomson (1811–43) governor; born in Loudoun County, Va. At age 19 he took over for his father as secretary of the Michigan Territory (1831–36); he led the statehood movement, winning the Upper Peninsula in a boundary dispute. As first governor of Michigan (Dem., 1837–40), he lost popular support when he failed to renegotiate state bonds during the banking crisis of 1837.

Mason, Warren P. (Perry) (1900–) physicist; born in Colorado Springs, Colo. He worked at Bell Telephone Laboratories (1921–65) before going to teach at Columbia University (1965). He made major contributions to the field of piezoelectricity and studies of vibration-induced metal fatigue, and received over 200 patents on telephone equipment.

Massasoit (also known as Ousamequin) (?1580–1661) Wampanoag chief; born at Pawkunnakut in present-day Rhode Island. Although he befriended the Pilgrims (1621), to whom he taught planting methods – and actually joined them for the first Thanksgiving dinner – he came to resent their geographical expansion. His son was Metacomet.

Masselos, William (1920–92) pianist; born in Niagara Falls, N.Y. Juilliard-trained and a formidable technician, he played a broad repertoire but was best known for his performance of Ives and other modern composers.

Massey, Jack C. (Carroll) (1904–90) venture capitalist, entrepreneur; born in Tennille, Ga. In 1964, after a career in the medical supply industry, he bought Kentucky Fried Chicken from its founder, Harland Sanders, for $2 million. Seven years later he sold it for $239 million. His Hospital Corporation of America (founded 1968) became the nation's largest chain of for-profit hospitals. After 1978 he transformed Winners Corporation into a major fast-food franchise operation.

Masters, Edgar Lee (1868–1950) poet, playwright; born in Garnett, Kans. He studied at Knox College, Ill. (1889), became a lawyer (1891), and practiced in Chicago (1891–

1921). He moved to New York upon retirement (1921), and continued to write plays and poetry. His only success was *Spoon River Anthology* (1915; revised 1916), a volume of "epitaphs," poetic portraits of smalltown Americans.

Masters, Sybilla (b. Righton) (?–1720) inventor, retailer; birthplace unknown, but probably Bermuda. Daughter of a merchant seaman who by about 1690 had an estate on the Delaware River, she married Thomas Masters, a Quaker merchant and public official in Philadelphia (mayor in 1707–08). She raised four children, and although her husband was very prosperous, she took an interest in products and activities around her. About 1712 she went to London where she would receive two patents – in her husband's name but credited to her. The first (1715) was for a device for "cleaning and curing the Indian corn"; the cornmeal was later sold in Philadelphia as "Tuscarora Rice" and promoted as a cure for consumption, but it never caught on. The second patent (1716) was for "a new way of working and staining" the straw and palmetto leaf used in making women's hats. She stayed briefly in London to sell her products but by May 1716 she was back in Philadelphia and her patents were registered in Pennsylvania in 1717. She has been called the first female inventor in America and she certainly showed exceptional commercial enterprise for a woman of her day.

Masters, William (Howell) (1915–) biologist, sexual therapist; born in Cleveland, Ohio. He took an M.D. at the University of Rochester School of Medicine and Dentistry. At Washington University (St. Louis), he began in 1944 to establish scientific credentials in reproductive biology before launching his research into all aspects of human sexual activity in 1954. In 1957 he hired a psychologist, Virginia Johnson, to provide the necessary female perspective. They proceeded to investigate the physiological responses to sexual stimulation in actual men and women, and their first report, *Human Sexual Response* (1966), despite its technical nature, created a tremendous controversy. Later works such as *Human Sexual Inadequacy* (1970) and *Homosexuality in Perspective* (1979) proved almost as controversial. In 1964 he founded the Reproductive Biology Research Foundation; renamed the Masters and Johnson Institute, it increasingly concentrated on treating couples' sexual problems and training therapists. Masters and Johnson married in 1971 but divorced in 1992.

Masterson, (William Barclay) "Bat" (1853–1921) law enforcer, sports journalist; born in Iroquois County, Ill. Moving to Kansas with his family at age 17, he engaged in the activities of frontier youths – hunted buffalo, fought the Indians, served as an army scout – until in 1876 he became a deputy marshal at Dodge City, Kansas. For the next quarter century he was one of the most famous of the frontier law enforcers, from Deadwood, S.D., to Tombstone, Ariz., associated at one point with Wyatt Earp. Masterson himself was a gambler and a boxing enthusiast, and in 1902 he went to New York City to be a sports writer for the *New York Morning Telegraph*. President Theodore Roosevelt admired Masterson and appointed him a federal deputy marshal (1905–07) but he resigned to concentrate on journalism, eventually becoming sports editor of the *Telegraph*. Hollywood movies would later make him into an American legend.

Mather, Cotton (1663–1728) clergyman, author; born in Boston, Mass. (son of Increase Mather). He entered

Harvard at age twelve and graduated when he was fifteen. He was ordained in 1685 and held office at Boston's Second Church for the rest of his life (as his father's colleague until 1723). He advocated rebellion against the unpopular Sir Edmund Andros with his political writings (1689). He supported the new Massachusetts charter (1691) and the new royal governor, Sir William Phips, of whom he wrote a biography, *Pietas in Patriam* (1697). His writings on witchcraft may have increased the mind-set that led to Salem witch trials (1692), but he believed that fasting and prayer were the proper methods for fighting witchcraft. His political popularity declined after 1692, but his religious leadership remained strong and he began to sponsor Yale, rather than Harvard, as the center for Congregational education. He wrote over 450 books during his lifetime.

Mather, Frank Jewett, Jr. (1868–1953) art historian, museum director; born in Deep River, Conn. He studied at Williams College (B.A. 1889), Johns Hopkins (Ph.D. 1892), and in Paris (1897–98). He taught at Williams (1893–1900), then became a journalist in New York City (1901–06) and Italy (1906–10). Considered the foremost American art critic of his day, he published on a variety of subjects, from *History of Italian Painting* (1923) to *Modern Painting* (1927). He taught at Princeton (1910–33), and became the director of the Museum of Historic Art (now Princeton University Art Museum) (1922–46), a repository of his collection.

Mather, Increase (1639–1723) religious leader, educator; born in Dorchester, Mass. He finished his education in Ireland (1658) and remained in England until the Stuart restoration (1660) made Puritanism uncomfortable there. He returned to Massachusetts and became the teacher of the Second Church of Boston (1664–1723) and the president of Harvard (1685–1701). He protested the revocation of the Massachusetts charter (1684), led negotiations for a new charter, and nominated Sir William Phips as the first royal governor. After 1701 he left the political arena, but he remained an important leader of New England Congregationalism. He wrote approximately 130 books and pamphlets on history, science, and politics.

Mather, Richard (1596–1669) Protestant minister, writer; born in Lancashire, England (father of Increase Mather; grandfather of Cotton Mather). He was educated locally and taught school nearby before attending Brasenose College, Oxford. He was ordained as a minister (1619) but was twice suspended (1633, 1634) by the Anglican Archbishop Laud due to his nonconformist beliefs. He emigrated to Boston (1635), served the Dorchester Church (1635–69), and is noted for his collaborating on translations of the Psalms in the *Bay Psalm Book* (1640). He took the lead in defining New England Congregationalism, as seen in such works as *Church Government and Church-Covenant Discussed* (1643) and *Platform of Church Discipline* (1649). He was the chief advocate of the Half-Way Covenant (1662) that, by allowing for less than total spiritual conversion, broadened New England's established church membership and maintained the church's power.

Mather, Stephen Tyng (1867–1930) conservationist; born in San Francisco. A descendant of the Mathers of early colonial Massachusetts, he graduated from the University of California at Berkeley in 1887 and worked as a newspaper reporter in New York City before going to work for the Pacific Coast

Borax Company in 1893. He later became president of the Sterling Borax Company. In 1915 he joined the Interior Department as assistant to the secretary and two years later was named first director of the National Park Service. He organized and expanded the park system during his 12-year tenure, adding, among others, Grand Canyon, Rocky Mountain, Grand Teton, and Great Smoky Mountain National Parks.

Matheson, Scott Milne (1929–) governor; born in Chicago. A Utah lawyer, he worked for the Union Pacific Railroad (1958–76), becoming solicitor general in 1972. As Democratic governor of Utah (1977–85), he led a coalition of western governors who demanded involvement in federal planning for land use, particularly water conservation, energy development, and missile placement. He returned to practicing law afterward.

Mathews, John Joseph (c. 1894–1979) writer; born in Pawhuska, Okla. An Osage Indian, he studied at the University of Oklahoma (B.A. 1920) and Oxford (B.A. 1923). He lived in Pawhuska much of his life, and is noted for his historical and biographical texts about the life of the Osage Indians, as in *Wah 'Kon-Tah: The Osage and the White Man's Road* (1932).

Mathewson, (Christopher) Christy (1878–1925) baseball pitcher; born in Factoryville, Pa. During his 17-year career with the New York Giants (1900–16), the right-hander won 373 games, third most in major league history. Four times he won 30 or more games in a season, and he posted an earned run average (ERA) of 1.99 or less six times. He was manager of the Cincinnati Reds (1916–18). Nicknamed "Big Six", he was one of the original five players elected to baseball's Hall of Fame in 1936.

Mathis, (John Royce) Johnny (1935–) popular singer; born in San Francisco, Calif. He sang in a college jazz band and later won a recording contract and engagements at prestigious New York clubs after an audition in San Francisco in 1955. His suave ballad singing helped him survive the dominance of rock in the popular music industry and he remained a successful nightclub performer in the United States and Britain. With Dionne Warwick he recorded a favorite hit, "Friends in Love" (1982).

Matthes, François (Emile) (1874–1948) geographer; born in Amsterdam, Netherlands. He came to the U.S.A. in 1891, studied at the Massachusetts Institute of Technology, and worked with the U.S. Geological Survey (1896–1947). An authority on glaciers and glaciation, he is most highly regarded for his superbly drawn topographic maps, especially of the mountainous area that became Glacier National Park, the upper Grand Canyon, and the Yosemite Valley. As chairman of the committee on glaciers of the American Geophysical Union (1932–46), he developed an international program to study glaciers.

Matthew, William Diller (1871–1930) paleontologist; born in St. John, New Brunswick, Canada. He was on the staff of the American Museum of Natural History (1895–1927); among his major contributions to the mammalian paleontology of Asia and North America was his theory of the northern origin of the mammalian orders.

Matthews, (Albert) Franklin (1858–1917) journalist; born in St. Joseph, Mich. As reporter and editor of the *New York Sun* (1890–1912), he covered the Spanish-American War and the around-the-world cruise of the U.S. Navy's "Great White

Fleet" (1907–08). From 1912 to his death he taught at the Columbia School of Journalism.

Matthews, Herbert (1900–77) journalist; born in New York City. A foreign correspondent and, later, editorialist for the *New York Times* (1922–67), he reported on the Spanish civil war of the 1930s and the Cuban revolution of the 1950s; he was often accused of a leftist bias, especially toward Fidel Castro.

Matthews, Stanley (1824–89) Supreme Court justice; born in Cincinnati, Ohio. An ardent abolitionist, he served as U.S. attorney general in Ohio (1858) and in the U.S. Senate (Rep., Ohio; 1877–79). The Senate rejected his first nomination to the U.S. Supreme Court but approved a second nomination by President Garfield (1881–89).

Matthias, Bernd T. (Teo) (1918–80) physicist; born in Frankfurt-am-Main, Germany. He studied in Rome and Zurich before coming to the U.S.A. (1947) to work at Bell Telephone Laboratories (1947–80); he also worked concurrently at the University of California: San Diego (1961–80). He discovered more superconductive elements and compounds than any other scientist; his 1954 niobium-tin alloy became the primary superconducting material before the advent of ceramics.

Matthiessen, F. O. (Francis Otto) (1902–50) literary critic, educator; born in Pasadena, Calif. He taught at Harvard (1929–50) until he committed suicide. Among his many works on American authors, his *American Renaissance* (1941) was a landmark in American cultural history and helped establish American literature as an academic subject.

Matthiessen, Peter (1927–) writer; born in New York City. He studied at the Sorbonne, Paris (1948–49), and at Yale (B.A. 1950). He was a cofounder of the *Paris Review* (1951) and continued as an editor for the periodical. Long resident in Sagaponack, Long Island, N.Y., he captained a charter fishing boat (1954–56), and was a member of numerous expeditions to Akaska, Canada, Peru, Nepal, East Africa, and New Guinea. His novels, *At Play in the Fields of the Lord* (1965) and *Far Tortuga* (1975), as well as short fiction, won critical acclaim, but he was best noted for his nonfiction work, such as *The Snow Leopard* (1978). In later years he became an eloquent spokesperson for saving the world's natural environments and wildlife.

Matzeliger, Jan Earnst (1852–89) inventor; born in Dutch Guiana. Child of a black mother and white father, he emigrated to the U.S.A. about 1872. Although uneducated, he invented a shoe-making machine (1891) and shoe-nailing machine (1896), which revolutionized the shoe industry. His inventions formed the basis of the United Shoe Machinery Corp. He died of tuberculosis at age 37.

Mauch, Gene (William) (1925–) baseball player/manager; born in Salina, Kans. He played shortstop or second base for six different teams (1944–57). From 1960 to 1987 he was manager of the Philadelphia Phillies, Montreal Expos, Minnesota Twins, and California Angels. Upon his retirement, he had managed more years (26) without winning a league championship than any other manager in history.

Mauchly, John William (1907–80) physicist, computer inventor; born in Cincinnati, Ohio. He taught for several years after graduating from Johns Hopkins University, then joined John P. Eckert at the University of Pennsylvania in the development of ENIAC, the first practical electronic digital computer. Their improved version, UNIVAC I, was acquired for use by the U.S. Census Bureau in 1951. These early Eckert-Mauchly machines helped launch the computer revolution of the second half of the 20th century.

Maurer, Alfred (Henry) (1868–1932) painter; born in New York City. He worked as a lithographer, traveled to Paris (1897), and was influenced by Matisse. He returned to New York and worked in an expressionistic and cubistic style, as seen in *Still Life with Doily* (c. 1930). He is considered one of the first modernists working in America.

Maurin, (Aristide) Peter (1877–1949) Catholic social activist; born in southern France. After a decade as a Christian Brother (1893–1903), he became an itinerant worker, emigrating to Canada and then the U.S.A. (1911). In 1932 he met Dorothy Day in New York City and helped shape her views; together they founded the Catholic Worker movement, which promoted grass roots social action to aid the poor; he also wrote for the movement's newspaper.

Maury, Matthew Fontaine (1806–73) oceanographer; born near Fredericksburg, Va. He entered the U.S. Navy (1825) and spent the next nine years on worldwide sea voyages. In 1839 a stagecoach accident left him permanently lamed. Considered unfit for active duty, in 1842 he was appointed superintendent of the Naval Observatory's Depot of Charts and Instruments. There he compiled information from numerous ships' logs, and gained an international reputation for his research in navigation, oceanography, and meteorology. By interpreting the crossing of the trade winds at the equator, he designed shipping routes which shortened an Atlantic-Pacific crossing by 40 days. In his most famous work, *The Physical Geography of the Sea* (1855), he proposed a transatlantic telegraph cable to be constructed on a level sea-floor plateau he had discovered between Newfoundland and Ireland. In 1861 Maury became a commodore in the Confederate Navy; while working to perfect underwater mines, he went to Europe where he also purchased and outfitted cruisers for the Confederate navy. After a brief self-exile in Mexico and Europe (1865–68), he returned to the U.S.A. to teach at the Virginia Military Institute (1868–73). He is known as the "Pathfinder of the Seas."

Maverick, Fontaine (Maury) (1895–1954) U.S. representative; born in San Antonio, Texas. A lumberman and highly decorated World War I veteran, he served in the U.S. House of Representatives (Dem., Texas; 1935–39) and chaired the War Production Board (1941–46).

Maxim, Hiram (Stevens) (1840–1916) engineer, inventor; born near Sangerville, Maine. Mechanically gifted, he learned several trades as a young man and obtained his first patent, for a hair-curling iron, in 1866. By 1884, working in London, he had produced a devastatingly effective automatic machine gun capable of firing 660 rounds per minute. Every major power adopted the Maxim gun. The company he established to manufacture his invention, with several mergers, eventually became the British defense firm, Vickers Ltd.

Maxwell, Hamish (1926–) tobacco executive; born in Scotland. He came to the U.S.A. after World War II and spent his career at Phillip Morris (1954–91). As variously president, CEO, and chairman of Philip Morris International (1978–85), Philip Morris, Inc. (1983–85), and Philip Morris Cos., Inc. (1985–91), he was renowned for achieving high earnings and diversification through acquisitions such as Kraft Foods (1988).

Maxwell, J. D. (Johnathon Dixon) (1864–1928) car manufacturer; born near Russiaville, Ind. A trained mechanic, he was hired to assist Elwood Haynes in building one of the first American automobiles (1894–99) (now in the Smithsonian Institution). He worked with Ransom Eli Olds in developing the early Olds vehicles (1900–02). He directed the Maxwell-Briscoe Company in Tarrytown, N.Y. (1904–12). Leading the J. D. Maxwell Motor Company (1912–25), he designed a car that incorporated all 19 of his innovative patents. His company was later absorbed by Chrysler Corporation (1925).

May, Rollo (Reese) (1909–94) psychoanalyst; born in Ada, Ohio. He studied psychology at Columbia University, theology under Paul Tillich, and psychoanalysis with Erich Fromm. He taught at various universities throughout his career, but starting in 1958 was most regularly affiliated with the William Alanson White Institute of Psychiatry in New York City. Influenced by Tillich's book *The Courage to Be* (1952), an introduction to European existentialism, he became a pioneer of humanistic psychology with the publication of *Existence: A New Dimension in Psychiatry and Psychology* (with E. Angell and H. F. Ellenberger, 1958). In contrast to cognitive psychology, he emphasized individual values and uniqueness in the practice of psychotherapy. With such books as *Psychology and the Human Dilemma* (1967), *Love and Will* (1969), and *Freedom and Destiny* (1981), he reached a broad public and found himself frequently quoted and honored in his later years.

Maybank, Burnett Rhett (1899–1954) governor, U.S. senator; born in Charleston, S.C. He was elected governor of South Carolina (Dem., 1939–41) and U.S. Senator (1941–54). As chairman of the Senate Appropriations Committee, he was interested in public housing and education issues.

Maybeck, Bernard (Ralph) (1862–1957) architect; born in New York City. He studied at the École des Beaux-Arts, Paris, and established his own office in Berkeley, California (1902). He designed mostly Bay Area suburban houses and community projects, although his best-known works include the Palace of Fine Arts, San Francisco (1913–15). His uniquely inventive designs drew on various traditions and showed unusual diversity of form, scale, and materials.

Maybury-Lewis, David (Henry Peter) (1929–) cultural anthropologist; born in Hyderabad, Pakistan. He served in the British army (1947–48) before going to Oxford (B.A. 1952) and Cambridge (Ph.D. 1956). Pursuing the career of a cultural anthropologist, he emigrated to the U.S.A. in 1960 to join the Harvard faculty. In 1972, with Harvard colleagues, he founded Cultural Survival, Inc., a private organization that aims to protect historical and cultural sites around the world. In 1992 his 10-part series, *Millennium: Tribal Wisdom and the Modern World,* appeared on public television with himself serving as host; a comparative study of different cultures around the world, the series attracted most attention because of its controversial staging or dramatization of certain "native" activities.

Mayer, (Eliezer or Lazar) Louis B. (Burt) (1885–1957) film executive; born in Minsk, Russia. His family emigrated to the U.S.A. when he was three, then to Canada. He worked in the scrap metal field until he bought a movie theater in Haverhill, Mass., and soon owned the largest theater chain in New England. Moving into production, his first film was *Virtuous Wives* (1918). A cofounder of Metro-Goldwyn-Mayer, he was responsible for such films as *Grand Hotel* (1932), the Andy Hardy Series, and *Ninotchka* (1939).

Mayer, Maria Goeppert See GOEPPERT-MAYER, MARIA.

Mayhew, Jonathan (1720–66) Protestant clergyman; born on Martha's Vineyard, Mass. A minister's son, he graduated from Harvard in 1744 and became pastor of West Church, Boston, three years later. He was a theological liberal opposed to Calvinist notions of predestination, and is acknowledged as a forerunner of Unitarianism. A political liberal, too, he delivered a sermon on the Stamp Act (1765) that advocated resistance to unjust laws, thus helping to create a climate in which the independence movement could flourish.

Mayhew, Thomas (1593–1682) Protestant missionary, colonist; born in Wiltshire, England. He settled in Medford, Mass., before 1632 and purchased Martha's Vineyard in 1641, establishing his son as head of a colony there. The elder Mayhew continued and expanded his son's missionary work among the Indians after the latter was lost at sea in 1657. As governor of Martha's Vineyard he was a benevolent dictator; a grandson succeeded him as missionary and chief magistrate of the island.

Maynard, Robert C. (Clyve) (1937–93) journalist, publisher; born in New York City. Son of immigrants from Barbados, he decided early he wanted to be a writer. He quit school at age 16 and began to work as a reporter for the *New York Age,* an African-American weekly, obtaining his first job on a white newspaper in 1961, the *York Gazette and Daily* (Pa.). He spent 1966 as a Nieman Fellow at Harvard, returned to the *Gazette,* and in 1967 joined the *Washington Post* as its first black national correspondent; in 1972 he was named an associate editor of the *Post* and his stature was such that he was one of three journalists invited to question President Gerald Ford and Jimmy Carter in their 1976 campaign debate. Since 1972 he had been codirector of a program at Columbia University School of Journalism to train minority journalists; this program ended in 1974, so in 1977 he left the *Post* and went to establish (with his wife, Nancy Hall Hicks, also a journalist) a similar program at the University of California: Berkeley, the Institute for Journalism Education. In 1979 he became the editor of the *Oakland Tribune* (Calif.), the first African-American to direct editorial operations for a major daily paper. In 1983 he became the first African-American to own and publish a major daily newspaper when he bought controlling interest in the *Tribune.* Eroding circulation and advertising forced him to sell it to the Alameda Newspaper Group in 1992 but he remained as publisher/editor. A Pulitzer Prize juror, and a leader in various professional organizations, he took greatest pride in helping scores of minority youths enter journalism, an effort that earned him the description of "the Jackie Robinson of publishing."

Mayo, Charles Horace (1865–1939) physician; born in Rochester, Minn. After taking his M.D. from Chicago Medical College (1888), he joined his father and older brother William Mayo in founding the clinic at St. Mary's Hospital in Rochester, Minn., and he was soon performing surgery on patients from ever widening areas of the U.S.A. and the world. His own specialties became the thyroid, the nervous system, and eye operations; he was also known for reducing the death rate in goiter surgery. With his brother William he established the Mayo Foundation for Medical

Mayo

Education and Research (1915), to which they donated large sums of money. He became a professor of surgery at the University of Minnesota's Mayo Graduate School of Medicine (1915–36). He was health officer of Rochester from 1912–37 and served in the U.S. armed forces during World War I. He was said to have complemented his brother by being more relaxed and accessible.

Mayo, (George) Elton (1880–1949) psychologist; born in Adelaide, Australia. He lectured on logic, ethics, and psychology in Australia before emigrating to the U.S.A. (1922), where he taught at Harvard Business School (1926–47). He is best remembered for his experimental studies at Western Electric's Hawthorne (Ill.) plant (reported in *The Human Problems of an Industrial Civilization* (1933)), which determined productivity to be dependent on workers' morale.

Mayo, Henry Thomas (1856–1937) naval officer; born in Burlington, Vt. He was the central American figure in the Tampico Incident of 1914 that led to the U.S. naval capture of Veracruz, Mexico. He was commander of the Atlantic Fleet (1916–19), in charge of all naval forces in Atlantic and European waters during World War I. He represented the U.S.A at the Allied naval conference in London (1917).

Mayo, Katherine (1867–1940) journalist, author; born in Ridgway, N.J. She was educated by tutors, in private schools and through travels in Europe. She spent much of the time between 1899 and 1907 in Dutch Guiana with her mining-engineer father, and there and in New York City she pursued a variety of activities – writing magazine articles, collecting insects, researching for a biography of John Brown. In 1910 she commenced what would be a lifelong relationship with M. Moyca Newell, an orphaned heiress; they would build an estate in Bedford Hills, N.Y., travel widely, and collaborate on certain writings. Freed of financial worries, Mayo began to dedicate herself to rather unusual causes such as calling for a state police force for the countryside or exposing the American Legion lobby. In two books, however, she found topics of broader concern – *Isles of Fear* (1925), about the chaotic conditions in the Philippines, and *Mother India* (1927), an exposé of what she saw as the sexual obsessions and the subjugation of women in that land. Behind much of her advocacy, however, lay her own preoccupations with Anglo-Saxon racial superiority and male sexual habits, so she never attained the status of a major social reformer.

Mayo, William James (1861–1939) physician; born in Le Sueur, Minn. After studying under his father, he took his M.D. from the University of Michigan (1883). He joined his father and brother, Charles Mayo, as surgeon at St. Mary's Hospital in Rochester, Minn., and with them he cofounded (1889) what would in 1903 become the Mayo Clinic. The brothers traveled widely to observe the new developments in surgery, and then back in Rochester introduced innovations of their own. William James became especially known for his surgical skills and innovations in stomach, gall bladder, and cancer operations. In 1915 he and his brother founded the Mayo Foundation for Medical Education and Research, to which they donated large sums of money; the foundation became affiliated with the University of Minnesota, where the two brothers also established the Mayo Graduate School of Medicine, which drew students from around the world. William served in the Army Medical Corps during World

War I. Of the two brothers, he was said to be the more reserved and controlling.

Mayo, William Worrall (1819–1911) physician; born in Manchester, England. He emigrated to the U.S.A. in 1845, and after taking his M.D. from the University of Missouri, he settled in Minnesota Territory in 1855. As a prominent physician and surgeon based in Rochester, Minn., he helped build St. Mary's Hospital there after a destructive cyclone (1885). In 1889 he and his two sons, Charles and William Mayo, founded a clinic at that hospital that soon became a surgical center for the region and gradually a surgical hospital and teaching center of world renown. It was also a pioneer in medical group practice – cooperation among several specialists. It was named the Mayo Clinic in 1903. William Worrall was also active in politics, helping to organize the Minnesota Territory as a state (1858), serving as mayor of Rochester for several terms, and as a state senator. In 1862 he served as an army surgeon during the uprising of the Sioux.

Mayr, Ernst (Walter) (1904–) ornithologist, evolutionist; born in Kempten, Germany. He was assistant curator of zoology at the museum of the University of Berlin (1926–32). During 1928–30, wishing to "follow in the footsteps of Darwin," he made three expeditions to New Guinea and the Solomon Islands, which led to his demonstrating that the development of separate species in higher animals depends on the geographic isolation of precursor populations. He came to the U.S.A. to be associate curator, then curator, of the Whitney-Rothschild Collection of the American Museum of Natural History (1932–53). His research on avian paleozoology, evolution, and taxonomy resulted in his seminal redefining of the term "species" to describe an interbreeding natural population reproductively isolated from other such groups (1940). He founded the Society for the Study of Evolution (1946) and was the founding editor of the journal *Evolution* (1949). He relocated to Harvard to become Agassiz professor of zoology (1953–75) and director of Harvard's museum of comparative zoology (1961–70). His philosophical writings on biological evolution emphasize that classification of organisms, unlike descriptive lists of inanimate objects, must be based on their existence as products of evolution. His theory of "peripatetic speciation" states that new species may arise via a few organisms moving beyond their species' range and establishing a new population, which evolves due to environmental differences and inbreeding of genes. After his retirement, his writings emphasized his belief that the future of human evolution depends on education.

Mays, Willie (Howard, Jr.) (1931–) baseball player; born in Westfield, Ala. During his 22-year career (1951–73) primarily with the New York and San Francisco Giants (he played most of his last two seasons with the New York Mets), he hit 660 homeruns, third highest in major league history, and twice won the league Most Valuable Player award (1954, 1965). Famous for his "basket" catches, he was one of the greatest defensive center fielders in the game's history. Nicknamed "the Say Hey Kid," his engaging personality made him a fan favorite. He was elected to baseball's Hall of Fame in 1979.

Maysles, Albert (1926–) **and David** (1932–87) film directors; born in Brookline, Mass. After military service, Albert taught at Boston University, making his first documentary,

Psychiatry in Russia, in 1955. David, after military service, worked as the assistant to the producer of *Bus Stop* (1956) and *The Prince and the Showgirl* (1957). They began collaborating on documentaries in 1957, and became famous for their *cinéma vérité* techniques (which they called "direct cinema"). Their best films have been *Salesman* (1969, about a Bible salesman), *Gimme Shelter* (1970, about the Rolling Stones), and *Grey Gardens* (1975, about an eccentric elderly lady and her daughter). They also turned out industrial and promotional movies, and Albert worked as a cameraman on many documentaries of other filmmakers.

Maysles, David See under MAYSLES, ALBERT.

Mazia, Daniel (1912–   ) cell biologist; born in Scranton, Pa. He taught at the University of Missouri (1938–50), where he performed research on the enzymatic digestion of chromosomes and the role of the nucleus in cell physiology. He moved to the University of California: Berkeley (1951–79), concurrently serving the marine biology laboratory at Woods Hole, Mass. (1950–58). With Katsuma Dan, he isolated the "major protein" of the mitotic microtubules (1952). Mazia joined Stanford (1979), continuing his research on cellular biochemistry. He made significant advances in cellular ion dynamics, chromosome chemistry, and centrosome function.

Mazur, Paul Meyer (1892–1979) investment banker; born in Boston, Mass. He graduated from Harvard in 1914 and served in the army from 1917–19. He was a partner of Lehman Brothers from 1927–69, and a limited partner from 1969 until his death. He authored several books on banking, including *Unfinished Business: A Banker Looks at the Economy* (1973).

Mazzuchelli, Samuel (Charles) (1806–64) Catholic missionary priest; born in Milan, Italy. He emigrated to the U.S.A. (1828) as a Dominican seminarian and was ordained in Cincinnati (1830). After missionary work among Indians in the Mackinac Island area, he established parishes, designed churches and public buildings, and ministered to settlers over a vast area of the Mississippi valley.

McAuliffe, (Sharon) Christa (b. Corrigan) (1948–1986) teacher; born in Framingham, Mass. Community-minded and socially conscious, she started teaching in 1970. National Aeronautics and Space Administration (NASA) officials were impressed with a course she developed for Concord (N.H.) High School entitled "The American Woman." The first teacher selected for the NASA Teacher in Space program, she died along with the crew when their space shuttle *Challenger* blew up not long after launching.

McBain, Ed See HUNTER, EVAN.

McBride, Patricia (1942–   ) ballet dancer; born in Teaneck, N.J. She studied ballet as a child and at the School of American Ballet. She joined New York City Ballet in 1959 and two years later became the youngest principal dancer in the company's history. Partnered with Edward Villela, she performed such high-speed works as *Harlequinade* (1965). A favorite with audiences, she combined technical perfection with an exciting performance style.

McCall, Samuel Walker (1851–1923) U.S. representative, governor; born in East Providence, Pa. A Dartmouth graduate and attorney in Boston (1875–92), he served in the U.S. House of Representatives (Rep., Mass; 1893–1913). Politically independent, he opposed the annexation of the Philippines and spoke against increased federal power during

Theodore Roosevelt's presidency. He left to run for senator and was governor of Massachusetts (1916–18). Author of political biographies, he lectured about government at Ivy League colleges (1902–15).

McCall, (Thomas Lawson) Tom (1913–83) journalist, governor; born in Egypt, Mass. After serving in World War II as a U.S. Navy correspondent, he became a television journalist in Portland, Ore., and produced *Pollution in Paradise*. A Republican, he became Oregon's secretary of state (1964–66). As Oregon's governor (1967–75), he passed 100 environmental protection bills, including the first state fuel conservation plan, in 1974. He later chaired environmental foundations.

McCallum, Daniel C. (Craig) (1815–78) engineer, railroad builder; born in Johnston, Scotland. His parents emigrated to Rochester, N.Y., when he was a boy. He completed elementary school, began working, and became an architect and engineer. In 1851 he patented an inflexible arched truss bridge, and in 1855 he became general supervisor of the New York & Erie Railway. In 1858 he founded McCallum Bridge Company. During the Civil War he was appointed military director of the Union railroads; he managed a vast operation of tracks and personnel that played a crucial role in such Union campaigns as Gen. Sherman's march to Atlanta. He was promoted to major general for his work. He also wrote poetry and published *The Water-Mill and Other Poems* (1870).

McCardell, Claire (1905–58) fashion designer; born in Frederick, Md. She graduated from Parsons School of Design, and in a long career with Townley Frocks (1932–58) she revolutionized American fashion with her casual and comfortable women's clothes, achieving a popular name and recognition then rare for American fashion designers. Her innovations included separates, the wrap-and-tie "popover" housedress (1942) and swimsuit (1943), the leotard, and a widespread use of wool jersey and cotton.

McCarran, Patrick (Anthony) (1876–1954) judge, U.S. senator; born in Reno, Nev. A prominent lawyer and judge, he was elected to the U.S. Senate (Dem., Nev.; 1933–54). A conservative opponent of the New Deal, he won fame in the McCarthy era as an outspoken anti-Communist, sponsoring the Internal Security Act of 1950 and the Immigration and Nationality Act of 1952.

McCarthy, John (1927–   ) mathematician, computer specialist; born in Boston, Mass. He was affiliated with Dartmouth (1955–58), the Massachusetts Institute of Technology (1958–62), and Stanford (1962). He is considered one of the fathers of artificial intelligence, having developed the programming language LISP (1958–62), and he helped develop ALGOL. He also did early work in robotics (1969).

McCarthy, Joseph R. (Raymond) (1909–57) U.S. senator; born in Grand Chute, Wis. After taking his law degree at Marquette University (1935), he served as a judge in Wisconsin (1939–42), then served with the U.S. Marines in World War II. Elected to the U.S. Senate (Rep., Wis.; 1947–57), he remained an obscure figure in his early years in Washington. But in February 1950 he won lasting notoriety by charging that the U.S. State Department had been infiltrated by Communists. His wild, unsubstantiated charges and headline-grabbing investigations of Communists in the foreign service, the U.S. Information Agency, and the military over the next few years led historians to label the early 1950s the "McCarthy era"; the use of unsubstantiated accusations and unfair investigative practices in order to charge disloyalty or enforce conformity has become known as "McCarthyism." Censured by his Senate colleagues in December 1954, he lost influence quickly, and died of alcoholism-related ailments in 1957.

McCarthy, (Joseph Vincent) Joe (1887–1978) baseball manager; born in Philadelphia. He was manager of the Chicago Cubs (1926–30), New York Yankees (1931–46), and Boston Red Sox (1948–50). His Yankee clubs, led by Lou Gehrig and Joe DiMaggio, appeared in eight World Series and won seven of them. Nicknamed "Marse Joe," he was elected to baseball's Hall of Fame in 1957.

McCarthy, Mary (Therese) (1912–89) woman of letters; born in Seattle, Wash. A Vassar graduate, she began her career as a reviewer for the *Nation, New Republic,* and *Partisan Review,* and in the course of a career embracing journalism, fiction, and autobiography, she became America's preeminent woman of letters. McCarthy chronicled decades of American intellectual life in satirical fiction, engaged other writers in public feuds, and repeatedly took contentious literary and political stands in print. The second of her four husbands was Edmund Wilson (married 1938–46).

McCauley, Charles Stewart (1793–1869) naval officer; born in Philadelphia. He was the commandant of the Norfolk, Va., navy yard (1860–61). He ordered the yard to be destroyed rather than allow it to fall into Confederate hands (1861). His efforts were only partly successful as the Confederates gained much matériel from the site.

McCauley, Mary Hays (b. Ludwig) (?1754–1832) Revolutionary heroine, prime candidate to be "Molly Pitcher"; born near Trenton, N.J. In 1778, she joined her first husband, John Hays, at his army encampment in New Jersey. During the battle of Monmouth, she carried water to the American troops, earning the sobriquet "Molly Pitcher"; when her husband was wounded at his cannon, she is said to have taken over and continued firing. After the American Revolution, she returned to Carlisle, Pa., and after her second husband died, she was voted an annuity for her "services" rather than as a veterans' widow, suggesting that she had seen action. She was said to have "sworn like a trooper" and chewed tobacco. Later her story would sometimes be confused with that of Margaret Corbin.

McCawley, Charles G. (Grymes) (1827–91) Marine officer; born in Philadelphia. He took part in the capture of Mexico City in 1847, and, during the Civil War, in the destruction of Fort Sumter and the seizure of forts Wagner and Gregg near Charleston, S.C. His appointment as Marine Corps colonel commandant in 1876 capped a long and exemplary service career.

McCay, Winsor (Zenic) (1869–1934) cartoonist, animator; born in Spring Lake, Mich. In 1905 he created the newspaper comic strip, *Little Nemo in Slumberland,* which he adapted to the animated cartoon, *Little Nemo,* in 1911. His early experimentation with animated films resulted in the landmark cartoon, *Gertie, The Trained Dinosaur* (1909), which permanently established the animated cartoon as an original art form. In 1918 he completed the live-action/animated film, *The Sinking of the Lusitania,* which was a first of its kind. In later life, he drew editorial cartoons for the Hearst newpapers, thereby establishing himself as an eminent cartoonist in three different disciplines.

McClellan, George (1796–1847) surgeon; born in Woodstock, Conn. (father of George Brinton McClellan). A brilliant teacher and surgeon in Philadelphia, he founded Jefferson Medical College (1825) with much dissent from the University of Pennsylvania. The trustees dissolved the faculty in 1839, so he left and founded the medical college of Pennsylvania College (Gettysburg, Pa.).

McClellan, George Brinton (1826–85) soldier; born in Philadelphia. The son of a prominent surgeon, he graduated second in his West Point class (1846) and served during the Mexican War. He taught at West Point (1848–51) then went with Marcy's expedition that explored the sources of the Arkansas River (1852). In 1855 he went to Europe to study the European military systems but resigned from the army in 1857 and went to work as an engineer/administrator with railroads; by 1860 he was president of the Ohio and Mississippi Railroad. With the outbreak of the Civil War, he was commissioned a major general of the Union forces in Ohio (May 1861); after the loss at First Bull Run, he was called to Virginia to command the Army of the Potomac; when he maneuvered Confederate forces out of western Virginia, he became the first Union hero of the war. In November 1861 he replaced Gen. Winfield Scott as general-in-chief of the army; self-confident (and self-important), he was still fondly known as "Little Mac" as he reorganized and trained the army, but he delayed committing it to battle. After much prodding from Lincoln, he launched the Virginia Peninsula Campaign (spring 1862); after its failure, he returned to Washington, his responsibilities reduced. He fought Lee to a standstill at Antietam (September 1862) but was removed from field command for failing to pursue the retreating Confederates. Increasingly more open in his criticism of Lincoln's conduct of the war, he became the Democratic candidate and challenged Lincoln for the presidency in 1864. He left the army and became an engineer for the New York City department of docks (1870–72) and then served as governor of New Jersey (1878–81). No one disputed his intellectual talents or administrative abilities, but the consensus has been that he lacked the instinct for decisive, prompt action in the face of combat.

McClelland, David C. (Clarence) (1917–) psychologist; born in Mt. Vernon, N.Y. A Yale Ph.D., he taught at Wesleyan University (1946–56) and Harvard (1956). He is best known for his works on motivation and achievement including *The Achieving Society* (1963) and *Motivating Economic Achievement* (coauthored, 1969).

McClendon, Rose (b. Rosalie Virginia Scott) (1885–1936) actress, singer; born in Greenville, N.C. In 1927 she was Serena in DuBose Hayward's play, *Porgy.* She helped plan the Black Federal Theatre Project troupe in 1935.

McClintock, Barbara (1902–92) geneticist; born in Hartford, Conn. She joined Cornell (1927–36), then served the National Research Council (1931–33) and the Guggenheim Foundation (1933–34). She joined the University of Missouri (1935–41), then became a staff member of the Carnegie Institution's laboratory in Cold Spring Harbor, N.Y. (1942–67), where she remained after her retirement. A solitary person, she devoted her life to the genetics of maize. Her discoveries in the 1940s and 1950s, that genes can control the behavior of other genes and can transpose themselves ("jump") on the chromosome, were belatedly recognized in her 1983 award of the Nobel Prize in physiology.

McCloskey, James (1943–) minister, social activist; born in Philadelphia, Pa. After achieving success as a businessman, he entered Princeton Theological Seminary in 1979 and as student chaplain at Trenton State Prison, he came into contact with death row prisoners. Founding Centurion Ministries in Princeton, N.J., in 1983, he dedicated himself to freeing prisoners he was convinced had been unjustly sentenced. Using old-fashioned detective work, he coordinated the successful appeals of a growing number of prisoners condemned to long sentences or death.

McCloy, John (Jay) (1895–1989) lawyer, government official; born in Philadelphia, Pa. A corporate lawyer and presidential adviser, he served as assistant secretary of war (1941–45). President of the World Bank (1947–49) and U.S. high commissioner of Germany (1949–50), he provided loans and oversaw Germany's return to statehood. After serving as chairman of the Chase Bank (1953–60), he became principal negotiator on the president's Disarmament Committee (1961–74).

McClure, Samuel S. (Sidney) (1857–1949) editor, publisher; born in County Antrim, Ireland. Emigrating in 1866, he established one of the earliest U.S. newspaper syndicates in 1884 and in 1893 founded *McClure's* magazine, which he made especially successful with the introduction of muckraking journalism after the turn of the century. From 1897 to 1899 he was a partner with Frank Nelson Doubleday in a book publishing firm.

McClurg, Alexander Caldwell (1832–1901) bookseller; born in Philadelphia. After winning renown as an officer in the Union army, he established a major bookselling business in Chicago.

McCollum, Elmer Verner (1879–1967) organic chemist; born near Fort Scott, Kans. He started the first white rat colony in the U.S.A., devoted to studying nutrition (ca. 1907). On the basis of this work, he demonstrated the existence of vitamins A and B (reported 1915). In 1917 he became a biochemist at Johns Hopkins, where he also did work on vitamin D.

McCone, John A. (Alex) (1909–91) businessman, government official; born in San Francisco. An engineer, later president of Consolidated Steel (1929–37), he formed Bechtel-McCone, an international engineering firm, in 1938. He was chairman of the Atomic Energy Commission (1958–60), and as President Kennedy's Central Intelligence Agency director (1961–65), he discovered the Cuban-bound missile shipments that led to the October 1962 crisis. He left to head International Telephone and Telegraph (1965–73).

McConnell, David Hall (1858–1937) business executive; born in Oswego, N.Y. He began his career with a batch of perfume in 1886 and founded California Perfume Company (later Avon Products) to sell perfume, toiletries, and cosmetics door-to-door. The company sales force numbered 5,000 within 12 years and 30,000 by the 1930s. He was Avon's owner, president, and chairman until his death.

McCord, David James (1797–1855) editor, agitator; born in St. Matthew's Parish, S.C. A lawyer turned editor of the *Columbia Telescope* (1823), he turned this newspaper into an extremely zealous advocate of nullification. He, in turn, became an influential state leader who was elected to the U.S. House of Representatives (1833–37). Elected president of the Columbia branch of the Bank of the State (1837–41), he lost his position after supporting the Whig Party. Hot-tempered and impulsive as well as frank and cheerful, he was a trustee of South Carolina College and a new state mental hospital, and he wrote numerous articles.

McCormack, John (1884–1945) tenor; born in Athlone, Ireland. With no formal training, McCormack won a gold medal at the 1902 National Irish Festival; following studies and recitals he made his operatic debut in London in 1907, with instant success. His American debut came two years later in New York; he became a favorite around the U.S.A., after 1914 primarily as a concert singer specializing in sentimental Irish songs. He became an American citizen in 1919.

McCormack, John (William) (1891–1980) U.S. representative; born in Boston, Mass. A public school graduate who studied law privately, he became a lawyer in 1913 and a power in Democratic politics after he returned from the army in 1918; he served in both the Massachusetts House and Senate (1920–26) before going mid-term to the U.S. House of Representatives (1928–71). A skilled tactician, he was majority leader and minority whip before becoming Speaker of the House (1961–69), in which positions he proved a loyal supporter of presidents John F. Kennedy and Lyndon B. Johnson.

McCormick, Anne Elizabeth (b. O'Hare) (1882–1954) journalist; born in Yorkshire, England. She won esteem as a European correspondent for the *New York Times,* especially for prescient stories in the 1930s on the rise of Benito Mussolini in Italy. She joined the paper's editorial board in 1936, and the following year, was the first woman to win a major Pulitzer Prize. She interviewed many world leaders, from Adolf Hitler to Harry Truman.

McCormick, Cyrus Hall (1809–84) inventor, manufacturer; born in Rockbridge County, Va. His father, Robert McCormick (1780–1846), patented several agricultural implements, but abandoned his efforts to develop a mechanical reaper in 1831. The son took up the project and patented a reaper in 1834, a year after the U.S. Patent Office had recognized a similar machine. McCormick and his competitors engaged in a fierce rivalry, but the McCormick Harvesting Machine Company emerged dominant due to constant improvements on his reaper, his use of labor-saving machinery in his factory, and his adoption of new marketing methods, such as deferred payments and guarantees. He used some of his vast wealth to support a Presbyterian theological seminary (after 1886, the McCormick Theological Seminary) and other institutions, and was active in Illinois Democratic politics. In 1902 his manufacturing firm became the International Harvester Company.

McCormick, Robert Rutherford (1880–1955) publisher; born in Chicago (grandson of Joseph Medill). A World War I veteran, Colonel McCormick inherited and ran the *Chicago Tribune* with his cousin Joseph Medill Patterson, assuming sole control as Patterson became preoccupied with the *Daily News* in New York. He was an ultraconservative isolationist, whose views were reflected on the editorial page and sometimes in news coverage.

McCosh, James (1811–94) college president, philosopher; born in Ayrshire, Scotland. He left a professorship at Queen's College, Belfast, Ireland (1852–68), and as president (1868–88), he revitalized the College of New Jersey (later Princeton University) after its post-Civil War decline. A member of the Scottish school of philosophy, he wrote

Intuitions of the Mind (1860) and *Examination of . . . Mill's Philosophy* (1866).

McCoy, Elijah (1843–1929) inventor, manufacturer; born in Canada. His African-American parents had fled from Kentucky to escape slavery. He showed an early talent for mechanical innovations, and in 1870, in Ypsilanti, Mich., he devloped lubricators for steam engines. In 1882 he moved to Detroit where he perfected his lubricating cup, still widely used to provide a steady supply of oil to machinery. He opened the Elijah McCoy Manufacturing Company in 1920 and patented an improved airbrake lubricator, one of the some 50 patents he obtained during his lifetime.

McCoy, Joseph (Geating) (1837–1915) cattleman; born in Sangamon County, Ill. A cattleman, he developed Abilene, Kansas, on the Kansas Pacific railroad, as the main shipping point for cattle to the East. This ushered in the Long Drive (for cattle) over the Chisholm Trail from Texas (1866–75). He set up other cattle drives and served as an agent for the Cherokee. His *Historic Sketches of the Cattle Trade* (1874) is a basic picture of the period. Some claim his brand was the source of the expression "the real McCoy."

McCracken, James (1926–88) tenor; born in Gary, Ind. A fireman's son, he was a steelworker and sang on Broadway before making his Metropolitan Opera debut in 1953. After performing in Europe, he made a triumphant return to the Met in 1963 in the lead of *Otello* and became a leading tenor there.

McCrory, John G. (Graham) (1860–1943) businessman; born in East Wheatfield Township, Pa. In 1882 he opened his first 5 & 10 cent store in Scottdale, Pa., and by 1901 he had 20 stores with annual sales of $498,000. He incorporated in 1915 with 118 stores. When he retired in 1933, there were 244 McCrory's in the eastern and southern states. Four months after he retired the company declared bankruptcy; by 1943 the chain had dwindled to 197 stores.

McCullers, Carson (b. Lula Carson Smith) (1917–67) writer; born in Columbus, Ga. She studied at Columbia and New York University (1935–36). She was an accomplished pianist and intended to study at Julliard, but due to poor health, she studied writing instead. She married J. Reeves McCullers (1937), was divorced (1940), and remarried him in 1945. Her first novel, *The Heart Is a Lonely Hunter* (1940), drew upon her Southern background and explored themes of loss and isolation also seen in her later works. *Reflections in a Golden Eye* (1941), was followed by the short novel *The Ballad of the Sad Café* (1943), and the novel, *The Member of the Wedding* (1946; stage adaptation 1950). She suffered several strokes in 1947, was operated on for breast cancer (1961), and died of a stroke in Nyack, N.Y.

McDavid, Raven (loor), Jr. (1911–84) linguist; born in Greenville, S.C. While teaching English at the University of Chicago, he edited several distinguished linguistic atlases. He and his wife, Virginia Glenn McDavid, advanced the scholarship on English language usage.

McDonald, William C. (1858–1918) cattle baron, governor; born in Jordanville, N.Y. He taught school and studied law in New York before moving to Kansas (1880) and then New Mexico (1881). He was a U.S. deputy mineral surveyor (1881–90) and then entered the cattle business. A strong Democrat, he was pushed to accept his party's nomination and was elected as the first governor of New Mexico (1912–

17). He took no campaign contributions and owed nothing to any factions. He retired to his ranch near Carrizozo, N.M.

McDonnell, James (Smith) (1899–1980) aerospace industrialist; born in Denver, Colo. After earning degrees at Princeton and the Massachusetts Institute of Technology, he worked as an aeronautical engineer, pilot, and stress analyst, setting up an airplane company in 1928. In 1939 he founded the McDonnell Aircraft Corporation, manufacturer of military and naval aircraft and Mercury and Gemini space capsules.

McDougall, Alexander (1732–86) Revolutionary agitator, soldier, politician; born in Islay, Inner Hebrides, Scotland. Emigrating to America with his family (1738), he commanded two privateers (1756–63). He was an educated merchant and came to public attention by issuing a broadside attacking the New York General Assembly (1769); sued for libel, then jailed (1770–71), he attracted a major radical following. As a founder of the Sons of Liberty who took the lead in prewar agitation, he presided over the famous mass meeting in the "Fields" (1774) that called for New York to send delegates to the First Continental Congress. Appointed colonel of the first New York regiment (1775), and later a brigadier and major-general (1777), he played a major role in the war, relieving Benedict Arnold in command of West Point. He represented New York in the Continental Congress (1781–82, 1784–85), and was an organizer and president of the Bank of New York.

McDowell, Ephraim (1771–1830) surgeon; born in Rockbridge County, Va. He attended medical lectures at the University of Edinburgh (1793–94) before returning to Danville, Ky., (1795) where he became known as the best surgeon west of Philadelphia. Often regarded as the "father of abdominal surgery," he never got a medical degree. At his office in 1809, he successfully removed a twenty-pound tumorous ovary without incurring peritoneal infection. His most famous patient was James K. Polk, in whose pre-presidential abdomen he removed bladder stones and stitched up a hernia. He gave the ground for the Danville Episcopal Church, gave free medical service to those who could not pay, and was a founder and trustee of Centre College (in Danville, Ky.).

McDowell, Irvin (1818–85) soldier; born in Columbus, Ohio. A West Point graduate (1838), he served in the Mexican War, on the frontier, and at army headquarters in Washington. At the outbreak of the Civil War, he was given command of the Union troops assigned to defend the nation's capital – his first true command position – and political demands for a quick victory forced him to commit an unready Union army to battle at Bull Run (Manassas) in July 1861; the resulting defeat cost him the top command. He continued to command units within the Army of the Potomac but after his performance at Second Bull Run (August 1862), he was removed and never again led troops in the field. However, he continued in the army in various administrative posts until 1882. Later he served as parks commissioner of San Francisco, Calif.

McDowell, Mary Eliza (1854–1936) social reformer; born in Cincinnati, Ohio. Educated in Illinois' public and private schools, she became a renowned public health reformer as director of the University of Chicago Settlement House (1894–1929). She also campaigned for women's rights, labor organizations, and interracial cooperation.

McDuffie, John (1883–1950) U.S. representative; born in River Ridge, Ala. Tutored at home, he was a lawyer (1908–

19) and congressman (Dem., Ala.; 1919–35), serving as minority and majority whip before becoming U.S. district court judge in Alabama (1935–50).

McElhenny, Hugh (Edward, Jr.) (1928–) football player; born in Los Angeles. Called "the King" for his many long-distance runs, he was All-American at the University of Washington (1951) and a star National Football League halfback (1952–64).

McElroy, Neil (Hosler) (1904–72) business executive, cabinet officer; born in Berea, Ohio. Harvard educated, he spent his career at Procter & Gamble Co., Inc., Cincinnati (1925–72), where he rose through the advertising and promotion ranks to become president (1948–57) and chairman (1959–72). He was U.S. secretary of defense (1957–59).

McEnroe, John (Patrick, Jr.) (1959–) tennis player; born in Wiesbaden, Germany (to an American military family). He trained at Port Washington Tennis Academy (New York) and at age 18 became the youngest man to reach the Wimbledon finals (1977). He won four U.S. Open singles titles (1979–81, 1984) and three Wimbledon singles titles (1981, 1983–84) and was an invaluable member of the American Davis Cup team (1978–85). His skill as a player was often overshadowed by his fierce emotional outbursts on court and his frequent wrangling with umpires, which always attracted the attention of the media and led to professional censure and fines on several occasions.

McFarland, Ernest W. (William) (1894–1984) judge, U.S. senator, governor; born near Earlsboro, Okla. A state superior court judge, he was elected to the U.S. Senate (Dem., Calif.; 1941–53), where he served as majority leader (1951–53). He later served as governor of Arizona (1955–59).

McGee, Anita Newcomb (1864–1940) physician; born in Washington, D.C. Appointed assistant army surgeon in 1898, the first woman to hold such a position, she organized the Army Nurse Corps (1898–1900) for service in the Spanish-American War and thereafter.

McGhee, (Walter Brown) "Brownie" (1915–) guitarist, singer, songwriter; born in Knoxville, Tenn. As a child, he learned banjo and guitar, played organ, and sang in church, and at age 14 he began to play music in traveling shows. In the 1930s he played with blues singer Blind Boy Fuller and met harmonica player Sonny Terry. In the 1940s he performed and recorded extensively with Terry, becoming known in folk and blues circles around the world. He also performed in Broadway shows and cut many solo albums.

McGillicuddy, Cornelius See MACK, CONNIE.

McGillivray, Alexander (b. Hippo-ilk-mico) (?1759–93) Creek leader, trader; born along the Coosa River in present-day Alabama. The son of a Scottish merchant and an Indian, he was raised among the Creek but his father saw that he was also educated in some of the white people's ways. With the outbreak of the American Revolution, he was appointed a colonel by the British and he encouraged Indian attacks on American settlements. After the Revolution, he would spend the rest of his life trying to build up a "united front" of the Indians of the Southeast against the encroaching white settlements; it is agreed that he was also in part motivated by his desire to protect his own trading enterprise. To do this he made a treaty with Spain (1784) and then encouraged the Creeks to war against the frontier settlements (1785–87). He achieved some success,

but in 1790 he went to New York City and signed a peace treaty; in 1792 he repudiated this and signed another treaty with Spain. In each of these treaties, he made sure that he was paid a generous sum for his support and he died a rich man.

McGivney, Michael (Joseph) (1852–90) Catholic priest; born in Waterbury, Conn. As a parish priest in New Haven, Conn., he founded the Knights of Columbus (1882), a Catholic men's fraternal organization, serving as its national chaplain until his death.

McGovern, George (Stanley) (1922–) U.S. representative/ senator; born in Avon, S.D. He was an Air Force pilot during World War II and then became a professor of history and government at the University of South Dakota. He served in the U.S. House of Representatives (Dem., S.D.; 1956–61) and the U.S. Senate (Dem., S.D.; 1963–81). As the Democratic presidential nominee (1972), he was targeted as a radical populist and lost the election by a wide margin. He wrote *The Colorado Coal Strike* (1953) and *A Time of War, A Time of Peace* (1968).

McGowan, William G. (George) (1927–92) telecommunications executive; born in Ashley, Pa. A Harvard-trained management consultant and venture capitalist, he took over Microwave Communications, Inc. (MCI) (1968), and as chairman and CEO he led the firm's successful challenge of the telephone monopoly, American Telephone & Telegraph (AT&T). He won the largest antitrust settlement in history against AT&T in 1980 and built MCI into a $8-billion company. He retired as CEO in 1991.

McGrath, James Howard (1903–66) governor, U.S. senator, attorney general; born in Woonsocket, R.I. A three-term Rhode Island governor (1940–45), he was named solicitor general of the United States (1945) and elected U.S. senator from Rhode Island (Dem., 1947–49). As chairman of the Democratic National Committee he managed Harry S. Truman's upset victory over Thomas Dewey (1948) and desegregated the committee's headquarters. Named attorney general (1949), he was known as a strong civil rights advocate if sloppy administrator. He resigned (1952) after stonewalling an investigation of alleged Justice Department corruption and never again served in public office.

McGraw, John (Joseph) (1873–1934) baseball player/ manager; born in Truxton, N.Y. During a 16-year career as a third baseman (1891–1906), mostly with the famous Baltimore Orioles of the 1890s, he compiled a lifetime batting average of .334; but it is as one of baseball's greatest managers that he is best remembered. After managing Baltimore for three years, he was manager of the New York Giants for 31 years (1902–32), winning ten league pennants, three world championships, and more major league games (2,840) than any manager except Connie Mack. Nicknamed "the Little Napoleon," he was a stern taskmaster and a brilliant discoverer of baseball talent. He was elected to baseball's Hall of Fame in 1937.

McGregor, Douglas M. (Murray) (1906–64) management theorist, educator; born in Detroit, Mich. He taught psychology and industrial management at the Massachusetts Institute of Technology (1937–48, 1954–64) and was president of Antioch College (1948–54). His *Human Side of Enterprise* (1960) changed American management practices and led to the human potential movement by postulating "Theory Y," a humanistic view of behavior and motivation, in sharp contrast to the traditional "Theory X" view of workers as lazy, unmotivated, and needing strict control.

McGuane, Thomas (Francis III) (1939–) writer; born in Wyandotte, Mich. He studied at the University of Michigan, Olivet College, Michigan State (B.A. 1962), Yale (M.F.A. 1965), and Stanford (1966–67). He began his writing career as a flamboyant satirist, as seen in *The Bushwacked Piano* (1971). After a serious auto accident (1972), he worked as a scriptwriter in Hollywood and directed the screen adaptation of his novel, *Ninety-two in the Shade* (1973). He wrote about his newly hedonistic lifestyle in *Panama* (1977), and married for the third time in the same year. He settled down on a ranch in McLeod, Mont., and continued to write.

McGuffey, William (Holmes) (1800–73) educator; born near Claysville, Pa. Largely self-educated through secondary school, McGuffey became a professor of moral philosophy at the University of Virginia (1845–73). He compiled the famous *McGuffey Readers,* six elementary schoolbooks (1836–57), that sold 122 million copies and became standard texts for generations of 19th-century American children.

McHarg, Ian (1920–) landscape architect; born in Clydebank, Scotland. Landscape architecture drew McHarg to the United States, first as a teenage apprentice (1936–39), and then as a student at Harvard University after World War II (1946–50). Edinburgh's (Scotland) first landscape architect (1950–54), he returned permanently to create the University of Pennsylvania's department of landscape architecture (1954–82). In *Design with Nature* (1969) he wrote that ecological considerations should determine architectural decisions. His nationwide firm, Wallace, McHarg, Roberts and Todd (1960–81), did projects from Texas to Africa.

McHugh, (James Francis) Jimmy (1896–1969) composer; born in Boston, Mass. In the 1920s and 1930s he wrote songs for Broadway revues and Harlem's Cotton Club. With lyricist Dorothy Fields he wrote the hits "I Can't Give You Anything but Love, Baby" (1928), "On the Sunny Side of the Street" (1929), and "I'm in the Mood for Love" (1935). He also worked with lyricists Gus Kahn, Ted Koehler and Harold Adamson. In the 1950s and 1960s he performed in nightclubs and television shows.

McHugh, Paul R. (1931–) psychiatrist, neurologist, educator; born in Lawrence, Mass. He became psychiatrist-in-chief at Johns Hopkins Hospital (1975) and director of the Blades Center for Clinical Practice and Research in Alcoholism (1992). An authority on biological bases of behavior, his teaching and research have centered on biopsychology and the mind-brain problem.

McIntire, Samuel (1757–1811) carpenter, builder/architect; born in Salem, Mass. A carpenter and builder, he began his career by repairing ships. From 1780 he built Georgian and Federal style houses for Salem merchants as well as local churches and civic buildings. His designs for brick houses continued to be copied after his death. He was also a woodcarver and a designer of interiors noted for their restrained ornamental woodwork. He designed the Gardner-Pingree House (Essex Institute) (1804–05) and South Congregational Church (1805), both in Salem, Mass. In modern times his furniture has commanded some of the highest prices of any American work.

McIntosh, William (?1775–1825) Indian leader, soldier; born in what is now Carroll County, Ga. Son of a British officer and a Creek Indian, he led the Lower Creeks in alliance with U.S. forces during the War of 1812 and served under Andrew Jackson in the Seminole campaign in Florida (1817–18). A party of Upper Creeks, incensed by his conciliatory policies toward white settlers, killed him at his home on May 1, 1825.

McKay, Clarence Hungerford (1874–1938) businessman, philanthropist; born in San Francisco (son of John W. McKay). He studied in Paris and graduated from Beaumont College, England (1892). He entered his father's business and worked on completing an international telegraph and cable system. He donated large sums of money to various projects, was a famous host at his home in Roslyn, Long Island, and collected medieval armor. He lost his fortune in the stock market crash of 1929.

McKay, Claude (b. Festus Claudius McKay) (1889–1948) writer, poet; born in Sunny Ville, Jamaica. He had already published two volumes in Jamaican dialect before he came to the U.S.A. to study at Tuskegee Institute, Ala. (1912) and Kansas State (1912–14). He moved to New York City, began to publish his poems under the pen name "Eli Edwards," and held several jobs before he went to London (1919–20) where he briefly worked for a communist newspaper. He returned to New York City and published his major work, *Harlem Shadows* (1922). By this time he was having an influence on the "Harlem Renaissance" and was also widely respected abroad. He lived abroad (1922–34), returned to New York in poor health, but continued to travel and write until the end. In addition to his poetry, his prolific output included novels such as *Home to Harlem* (1928), short stories (as in the collection *Gingertown*, 1932), an autobiography, *A Long Way from Home* (1937), and the sociological study, *Harlem: Negro Metropolis* (1940).

McKay, Donald (1810–80) ship builder; born in Shelbourne, Nova Scotia, Canada. Apprenticed in New York, he moved to Newburyport, Mass., and began to build ships. In 1845 he moved his yard to Boston, where he produced clipper ships for the China trade and other purposes; several of his clippers held the world record for speed under sail. He built naval vessels during the Civil War.

McKay, Gordon (1821–1903) inventor; born in Pittsfield, Mass. He was a railroad engineer and a machine repairman (1837–52). He bought the patent for Lyman Blake's machine that sewed the soles of shoes to upper parts (1859); he improved the machine's capabilities, took out a new patent (1862), and formed the McKay Association, which made army shoes during the Civil War. He made a fortune on royalties from leasing his machines (1862–80) and he joined his company with Charles Goodyear's in 1880. He sold his interest in 1895 and retired to Newport, R.I. He made many benefactions, notably the McKay Institute to provide for the education of young African-Americans.

McKechnie, (William Boyd) Bill (1886–1965) baseball manager; born in Wilkinsburg, Pa. During his 25-year career as manager (1915–46), mostly with the Pittsburgh Pirates, Boston Braves, and Cincinnati Reds, he won four league pennants and two world championships. Nicknamed "Deacon," he was elected to baseball's Hall of Fame in 1962.

McKellar, Kenneth (Douglas) (1869–1957) U.S. representative/senator; born in Richmond, Ala. Elected to the U.S. House of Representatives (Dem., Tenn.; 1911–17) and to the U.S. Senate (1917–53), he exercised power through his positions on crucial committees. He gained his greatest public exposure through his strong opposition to the appointment of David E. Lilienthal to head the Tennessee Valley Authority and then the Atomic Energy Commission.

McKenna, Joseph (1843–1926) Supreme Court justice; born in Philadelphia. He served the California state legislature (1875–76) and the U.S. House of Representatives (1884–92), resigning to accept a federal judgeship. He served as U.S. attorney general (1897) and was appointed by President William McKinley to the U.S. Supreme Court (1898–1925).

McKie, Judy (b. Kensley) (1944–   ) furniture designer; born in Boston, Mass. A graduate in painting from the Rhode Island School of Design (1966), she first worked as a graphic designer and made cloth wall-hangings (several of which were used as tents at Woodstock). In 1971, she began making furniture for her own use; then in 1971 she joined the New Hamburger Cabinetworks Cooperative (then in Boston) and began learning about the techniques and tools of woodworking. By the mid-1970s she was selling her individually designed pieces and by 1979 was gaining national recognition in shows, commissions, and awards. Her fascination with primitive stylized animal motifs as seen in pre-Columbian, African, and Native American art expresses itself in unique whimsical sculptural furniture incorporating carved and colorful animal forms. By the early 1990s she had taken to making some tables and benches in cast bronze.

McKim, Charles Follen (1847–1909) architect; born at Isabella Furnace, Pa. He studied at Harvard and the École des Beaux-Arts, Paris. The addition of Stanford White to his partnership with William Rutherford Mead launched McKim, Mead and White (1879), designers of more than 1,000 public, commercial, and residential buildings. McKim was an elegant classical designer; his work includes the Boston Public Library (1887–95) and the Pierpont Morgan Library, New York (1902–07).

McKinley, Ida (b. Saxton) (1847–1907) First Lady; born in Canton, Ohio. She married William McKinley in 1871. Following the untimely deaths of her mother and two daughters in 1873–1875, she developed epilepsy and became an invalid. McKinley remained devoted to her; he carefully tended to her, even while he was president.

McKinley, John (1780–1852) Supreme Court justice; born in Culpeper County, Va. He served the Alabama legislature (1820, 1831), the U.S. Senate (Dem., Ala.; 1826, 1836), and the U.S. House of Representatives (Dem., Ala.; 1832). He was appointed to the U.S. Supreme Court by President Martin Van Buren (1838–52).

McKinley, William (1843–1901) twenty-fifth U.S. president; born in Niles, Ohio. After briefly teaching, then serving in the Civil War, he studied law in Ohio and began practice in 1867. His interest in politics took him to the U.S. House of Representatives (Rep., Ohio; 1877–91), where his campaign for a protective trade policy finally resulted in the high McKinley Tariff of 1890. Although that tariff contributed to his losing his seat in 1890 (and the Republicans' losing the presidency in 1892), he became governor of Ohio (1891–97). In 1896 he ran a successful presidential campaign with the help of big business and Republican kingmaker, Mark Hanna. A new high tariff soon appeared, but more urgent matters took precedence; reluctantly giving in to widespread militant sentiment, he declared war on Spain in 1898. After a short war, America found itself a colonial nation in possession of Puerto Rico, Guam, and the Philippines, and McKinley was soon endorsing international initiatives from Cuba to China. He was reelected in 1900 with Theodore Roosevelt as vice-president, but on September 6, 1901, he was shot by an anarchist, Leon F. Czolgosz, and died eight days later. Although personally decent, honest, and well intentioned, McKinley would always be associated with the special interests of big business and party politics.

McKissick, Floyd B. (1922–   ) civil rights leader, lawyer, business executive; born in Asheville, N.C. After receiving a bachelor's degree at North Carolina Central University, with the legal help of Thurgood Marshall he entered the University of North Carolina Law School at Chapel Hill and became its first black recipient of a law degree (1951). He practiced law in Durham, N.C., (1952–66), and specialized in hundreds of civil rights cases brought before the courts in the 1960s. He was legal counsel for the Congress of Racial Equality (CORE) before becoming CORE's national chairman (1966). He left CORE (1968) to launch Floyd B. McKissick Enterprises, Inc. – a corporation involved in organizing and financing businesses. An arm of that company, Warren Regional Planning Corp., was formed to develop Soul City in North Carolina. He was author of *Three-fifths of a Man* (1968).

McLaughlin, Mary Louise (1847–1939) ceramist; born in Cincinnati, Ohio. A pioneer of the art pottery movement, she founded the Cincinnati Pottery Club (1879) and received international awards for her china painting and decorative metalwork.

McLaws, Lafayette (1821–97) soldier; born in Augusta, Ga. A West Point graduate (1842), he served in the Mexican War and in the West. He went over to the Confederate army in 1861 and as a regimental, brigade, and finally division commander, he fought at Antietam, Fredericksburg, Chancellorsville, and Gettysburg. He was relieved of command and court-martialed for his failure to relieve Knoxville, Tenn. (November 1863) but was exonerated. After the war he served as postmaster of Savannah, Ga.

McLean, John (1785–1861) U.S. representative, Supreme Court justice; born in Morris County, N.J. His career included service in the U.S. House of Representatives (Dem., Ohio; 1812–16) and as an Ohio Supreme Court judge (1816–22). As postmaster general (1823–29), he streamlined the national postal system. He was named to the U.S. Supreme Court by President Andrew Jackson (1830-61).

McLoughlin, John (1784–1857) fur merchant; born in Rivière du Loup, Quebec, Canada. Of Scotch-Irish descent, he studied medicine in Scotland and then came back to join the Canadian North West Fur Company, becoming a partner in 1814. When this company merged with the Hudson's Bay Company (1821), he was placed in charge (1825–46) of the far western region (including the present-day states of Washington and Oregon), whose capital was Fort Vancouver. He effectively monopolized the fur trade for the British, but he was also extremely helpful to the first American settlers in the territory, providing both the material aid and financial support that allowed many to survive, and gaining the reputation of a benevolent despot. After the treaty of 1846 that established the boundary between the U.S.A. and Canada at the 49th parallel (farther north than he and the Hudson's Bay Company had hoped), he retired from the company and began to develop a large tract of land in

Oregon that he now claimed as his own. He was engaged in legal controversy with the American authorities to his death, but he became a U.S. citizen and was honored as "the father of Oregon" when that state placed his statue in the U.S. Capitol. (The land was assigned to his heirs in 1862.)

McLoughlin, (Maurice Evans) Maury (1890–1957) tennis player; born in Carson City, Nev. He won seven tournaments in 1912, including the U.S. singles championship.

McMaster, James A. (Alphonsus) (1820–86) religious journalist; born in Duanesburg, N.Y. An archconservative Catholic convert and antiabolitionist, he founded the Catholic *Freeman's Journal* (1848) and edited it thereafter. In 1861 he was imprisoned, and his journal temporarily suppressed, for attacks on Abraham Lincoln.

McMillan, Edwin (Mattison) (1907–91) physicist; born in Redondo Beach, Calif. Working at the University of California: Berkeley, primarily at their Lawrence Radiation Laboratory (1934–73), he and Glenn Seaborg discovered plutonium (1941) and other transuranium elements. McMillan improved the design of the cyclotron (1945) and built the first synchrotron. He shared the Nobel Prize in chemistry with Seaborg (1951).

McMullen, Clements (1892–1959) aviator; born in Largo, Fla. A civil engineer, he entered the air service after the U.S.A. entered World War I. In 1930 he completed a then-record flight from New York to Buenos Aires. He held several key air support and logistics posts in the U.S.A. and the Pacific during World War II.

McMurtry, Larry (Jeff) (1936–) writer; born in Wichita Falls, Texas. He studied at North Texas State College (now University) (B.A. 1958), Rice University (M.A. 1960), and at Stanford (1960). He taught at several institutions and was co-owner of a book store in Washington, D.C. (1970), where he lived. He drew upon his early years in Texas to write many successful novels, such as *The Last Picture Show* (1966), *Terms of Endearment* (1975), and *Lonesome Dove* (1985).

McNair, Lesley (James) (1883–1944) soldier; born in Verndale, Minn. A West Point graduate (1904), he served with Gen. John Pershing's expedition into Mexico (1916–17) and then at Pershing's headquarters in France in World War I. Making his way through a series of command posts, by March 1942 he was commanding general of the army ground forces; he supervised the mobilization and training of more than 3 million U.S. soldiers and exercised his authority to keep the infantry at the core of the army. As commanding general of the First Army group, he went to Normandy, France, after the invasion, and was killed there July 25, 1944, by American bombs falling short of their target.

McNair, Ronald E. (1950–) astronaut, physicist; born in Lake City, S.C. While earning a Ph.D. in physics at the Massachusetts Institute of Technology (1976), he helped develop the chemical HF/DR and high-pressure CO lasers. Later research at the Hughes Research Laboratories, Malibu, Calif., included research on electro-optic laser modulation for satellite-to-satellite space communications. Selected as an astronaut (1978), he served on Space Shuttle Mission 41-B (1984). The mission marked the first flight of the manned maneuvering unit and the first use of the Canadian arm, which he operated. He also supervised numerous experiments as well as the filming of the mission.

McNamara, Joseph D. (1934–) police chief, detective writer, research fellow; born in New York City. Known for his best-selling detective novels, he spent 35 years in active law enforcement, which included serving as police chief of Kansas City, Mo. (1973–76), and police chief of San Jose, Calif. (1976–91). He was a criminal justice fellow at Harvard Law School (1969) and was named a research fellow at the Hoover Institution, Stanford University (1991). In addition to detective thrillers such as *Fatal Command,* he was the author of *Safe and Sane,* a crime prevention textbook, several other nonfiction works, and numerous articles.

McNamara, Robert (Strange) (1916–) businessman, public official; born in San Francisco. After air force service during World War II, he joined the Ford Motor Company, becoming its president in 1960. As secretary of defense (1961–67), he introduced private industry's cost-efficiency techniques to the Pentagon. He was also a principal spokesman for the Kennedy and Johnson administrations' policies in Vietnam, although he eventually resigned when he lost heart for President Johnson's pursuit of the war. As president of the World Bank (1968–81), he championed support for developing countries.

McNamee, Graham (1888–1942) broadcaster; born in Washington, D.C. A pioneer radio sportscaster, he covered the World Series as early as 1923, and in 1927 he was the announcer for the first coast to coast broadcast of the Rose Bowl. He also covered the Republican national convention in 1924, the first national political convention ever broadcast.

McNarney, Joseph (Taggart) (1893–1972) aviator; born in Emporium, Pa. He graduated from West Point in 1915, attended aviation school the following year, and took command of the 1st Aero Squadron in France in August 1917. After serving in various staff and line posts during the interwar years, McNarney became deputy chief of staff under George Marshall in March 1942. Considered dour and colorless but effective, he served as deputy supreme allied commander in the Mediterranean (1944) and succeeded George Patton as commander of U.S. forces in Europe (1945). McNarney retired in 1952 to become president of Consolidated Vultee Aircraft, later the Convair Division of General Dynamics Corp.

McNary, Charles (Linza) (1874–1944) U.S. senator; born near Salem, Ore. Originally appointed and then elected to the U.S. Senate (Rep., Ore.; 1917–44), he prompted legislation involving agriculture, reforestation, irrigation, and hydroelectric power. As Senate minority leader, he opposed some of President Franklin Roosevelt's New Deal measures, but supported others such as Social Security. He was Wendell Wilkie's vice-presidential running mate in 1940.

McNeill, William H. (Hardy) (1917–) historian; born in Vancouver, Canada. He studied at the University of Chicago (B.A. 1938; M.A. 1939) and at Cornell (Ph.D. 1947), and, except for occasional visiting professorships elsewhere, he taught his entire career at the University of Chicago (1947). Running counter to the trend of his contemporary academics, who tended to specialize in ever smaller periods and topics, he took on a wide variety of subjects in such books as *Venice: The Hinge of Europe, 1081–1797* or *The Metamorphosis of Greece since World War II* (1978). Beyond such studies, he became one of the few modern historians since Arnold Toynbee who dared to take on the world's history, and in books such as *The Rise and Fall of the West: A History of the Human Community* (1963; National Book Award, 1964) and *The Human Condi-*

tion: An Ecological and Historical View (1980), McNeill recognized the ambiguity of human experience while expressing the hope that historical studies might enhance practical wisdom. He also served as editor-in-chief of *Readings in World History* (ten vols. 1968–73).

McNicholas, John T. (Timothy) (1877–1950) Catholic prelate; born in County Mayo, Ireland. Emigrating to the U.S.A. as a child, he was ordained a Dominican priest in 1901. He was a New York City pastor and national director of the Holy Name Society before becoming bishop of Duluth, Minn. (1918). Named archbishop of Cincinnati in 1925, he was also an official of the National Catholic Welfare Conference and an influential Catholic voice, especially on matters relating to education.

McNichols, Stephen L. R. (1914–) lawyer, governor; born in Denver, Colo. Briefly an FBI agent, he practiced law in Denver before joining the navy in World War II (1942–46). An assistant U.S. attorney general (1946–48), he became a Colorado state senator (Dem., 1948–54). As governor (1957–63), he improved conditions for migrant workers and established a state resources development office. He later opened a Denver law firm.

McNickle, (William) D'Arcy (1904–77) Salish/Flathead author, historian, anthropologist; born in Saint Ignatius, Mont. A founding member of the National Congress of American Indians (1944), he also worked for the Bureau of Indian Affairs (1936–52), taught at the University of Saskatchewan (Canada) (1965–71), and served as the founding director of Chicago's Newberry Library Center for the History of the American Indian. His novels, which emphasized the importance of tribalism, include *The Surrounded* (1936) and *Runner in the Sun* (1954).

McNulty, John Augustine (1895–1956) journalist, author; born in Lawrence, Mass. A longtime reporter, he launched a new career writing stories and articles especially for the *New Yorker,* after the success of his 1941 story "Atheist Hit by a Truck."

McPartland, Marian (b. Turner) (1920–) jazz musician; born in Windsor, England. A versatile pianist, she moved to the U.S.A. in 1945 and led a trio from 1951. In 1973 she began an adjunct career as the host of jazz radio programs.

McPhee, John (Angus) (1931–) writer; born in Princeton, N.J. He studied at Princeton (B.A. 1953) and at Cambridge University, England (1953–54). He worked as a television playwright for *Robert Montgomery Presents* (1955–57) and as an associate editor for *Time* magazine (1957–64). In 1964 he became a staff writer for the *New Yorker;* he also taught journalism at Princeton (1975). His nonfiction books, acclaimed for their cool precision, were usually based on articles written for the *New Yorker;* they cover a wide variety of subjects – everything from oranges to ecology, from canoemakers to Alaska; in later years he pursued an interest in geology through a series of books beginning with *Basin and Range* (1981).

McPherson, Aimee (Elizabeth Kennedy) Semple (1890–1944) evangelist; born near Ingersoll, Ontario, Canada. Daughter of a Salvation Army soldier, she married a Pentacostal missionary and was widowed in China in 1910. She returned to North America with her daughter and set out on a career as an evangelist, offering a fundamentalist message of hope and salvation that brought in enormous money contributions over the course of some 25 years. She married and divorced, married and divorced again. Often accompanied by her mother, she traveled around the U.S.A. to conduct her revival meetings. Flamboyant and innovative, she expanded her Los Angeles-based (after 1918) evangelical empire by adding a radio station, a Bible school, and a magazine. She was often accused of improprieties, but nothing was ever proved. She died in Oakland, Calif., of an overdose of sleeping powders.

McPherson, James (Birdseye) (1828–64) soldier; born in Sandusky County, Ohio. First in his class at West Point (1853), he served with the Corps of Engineers. He joined Gen. Ulysses Grant's staff as chief engineer in the Tennessee campaign (1862), then commanded successively a division, a corps, and an army in the western campaigns of 1862–64. Regarded as one of the more aggressive of the Union generals, he was killed during the advance on Atlanta on July 22, 1864.

McQuaid, Bernard (John) (1823–1909) Catholic prelate; born in New York City. Raised in a Catholic orphanage after his parents died, he was ordained in 1848. He was a cofounder (1856) and first president of Seton Hall University (South Orange, N.J.) before being named bishop of Rochester, N.Y. (1868). Regarded as a conservative, he opposed the Knights of Labor as a secret society and led a clerical faction that strongly promoted parochial schools while attacking "godless" public education.

McReynolds, James Clark (1862–1946) Supreme Court justice; born in Elkton, Ky. As assistant U.S. attorney general (1903–07) and as a federal prosecutor, he gained a reputation as a "trustbuster." President Woodrow Wilson named him attorney general (1913–14) and appointed him to the U.S. Supreme Court (1914–41). A strict constructionist, he wrote over 100 dissenting opinions that often opposed New Deal measures.

McShann, Jay (1909–) jazz musician; born in Muskogee, Okla. A distinctive pianist, he led a Kansas City swing band between 1937–47 (which included Charlie Parker in 1940–41) and his own small combos thereafter.

Mead, George Herbert (1863–1931) philosopher, social psychologist; born in South Hadley, Mass. Son of a Congregationalist pastor, he studied at Harvard and in Europe, taught at the University of Michigan (1891–94), and was a professor at the University of Chicago from 1894. He published little, but his lectures, edited posthumously, formed the basis of four books, including *Mind, Self, and Society* (1934). His "social behaviorism" eliminated "mentalistic" categories and portrayed the self as developing from a process of social interaction and communication.

Mead, Margaret (1901–78) cultural anthropologist, author; born in Philadelphia. Daughter of a University of Pennsylvania economist and a feminist political activist, she graduated from Barnard College in 1923 and went on to take a Ph.D. in Franz Boas' program at Columbia University in 1929. Appointed assistant curator of ethnology at the American Museum of Natural History in 1926, she retained the museum connection for more than a half-century. After expeditions to Samoa and New Guinea, she published *Coming of Age in Samoa* (1928) and *Growing Up in New Guinea* (1930). Altogether, she made 24 field trips among six South Pacific peoples. She was married and divorced three times; her third husband (1936–50) was anthropologist Gregory Bateson, with whom she collaborated in field research. Her later works included *Male and Female* (1949) and *Growth and Culture* (1951), in which she argued that personality characteristics, especially as they differ between men and women, were shaped by cultural conditioning rather than heredity. Some critics called her field work impressionistic, but her writings have proved enduring and have made anthropology accessible to a wider public. In her later years she became one of the best known individuals in America, her presence and opinions sought for every possible occasion.

Meade, George Gordon (1815–72) soldier; born in Cadiz, Spain. The son of a U.S. naval agent, he graduated from West Point (1835), saw action in Mexico, served as a military engineer, and received command of a Pennsylvania brigade at the outbreak of the Civil War; he assumed increasingly larger commands in many major battles – the Peninsular Campaign, Antietam, Fredericksburg, Chancellorsville. After Gen. Joseph Hooker resigned his post abruptly, Meade was assigned command of the Army of the Potomac on June 28, 1863; three days later his army found itself engaged at Gettysburg. Meade has been praised for his handling of troops on the defensive at Gettysburg and criticized for failing to pursue the beaten Confederates in the aftermath of the battle. Although he retained his command when Ulysses S. Grant came east in the spring of 1864, Grant took effective operational control of the army and Meade performed loyally in a difficult situation. After the war, he commanded the army's Division of the Atlantic, with a brief interruption to command the then military district that included Alabama, Georgia, and Florida. He died of complications from a wound he sustained during the Peninsula campaign of 1862. His blunt, often intemperate manner did not endear him to his fellow officers, but he gained a reputation as a serviceable soldier.

Meadows, Audrey (b. Cotter) (?1922–) television comedienne; born in Wu Chang, China. Daughter of American missionaries, trained as a singer, she was featured on radio in the *Bob and Ray Show,* then appeared on television's *Jackie Gleason Show* (1952–55). She played Ralph Cramden's long-suffering wife, Alice, on the *Honeymooners* (1955–56). A regular on television comedy shows, she later appeared on *Murder She Wrote* in the 1980s and on CBS's *Uncle Buck* (1990–91).

Means, Gaston Bullock (1879–1938) swindler, spy; born near Concord, N.C. He sold data on Allied shipping to the German embassy (1914) and swindled wealthy people. He was convicted of grand larceny after a ransom money swindle in the Lindbergh kidnapping case.

Means, Russell (1939–) Oglala Sioux activist; born in Pine Ridge, S.D. In Cleveland (1970) he founded the second chapter of the American Indian Movement (AIM). His flair for guerrilla theater, including the seizure of the Mayflower II on Thanksgiving (1970) and the Trail of Broken Treaties (1972), helped bring AIM to national attention. In response to clashes between police and AIM supporters in South Dakota, he and 200 followers seized control of Wounded Knee (1973) for 71 days. In 1974 he was defeated in a runoff election by Richard Wilson for the Sioux Tribal Council presidency; although two federal probes sustained charges of threats, bribery, and ballot-stuffing, the Bureau of Indian Affairs failed to order a new election. He continued his calls for action at places such as the Black Hills and the Custer

Battlefield National Monument. In 1992 he appeared in the movie, *The Last of the Mohicans*.

Meany, George (1894–1980) labor leader; born in New York City. Active first in the plumber's union, then in the New York state federation of labor, he was elected secretary-treasurer of the American Federation of Labor (AFL) in 1939, its president in 1952, and president of the AFL-CIO (Congress of Industrial Organizations) (1955–80).

Meason, Isaac (1742–1818) ironmaster; probably born in Virginia. He arrived in western Pennsylvania about 1771 and established Union Furnace by 1791. Here and at other locations, he manufactured the kitchenware and tools needed by the thousands of people coming over the Allegheny mountains. He contributed to the start of western Pennsylvania's iron and coal industry.

Mecham, Evan (1924–) businessman, governor; born in Duschesne, Utah. A World War II army veteran, he made millions as president of Mecham Pontiac in Glendale, Ariz. (1950–88). After serving in the state senate (Rep., 1960–62), he became American Newspaper Group publisher (1963–74). A controversial governor of Arizona (1987–88) – most notorious for refusing to recognize Martin Luther King's birthday as a state holiday – he was impeached for accepting a $350,000 loan from a real estate developer, Barry Wolfson.

Mechem, Edwin (Leard) (1912–) governor, lawyer; born in Alamogordo, N.M. A lawyer in Las Cruces, N.M. (1939–50), he also worked as an FBI agent (1942–45) and served on the State Police Commission. The first Republican governor in twenty years (1951–55, 1957–59, 1961–62), he was popular despite limited legislative success, retiring to fill out a term in the United States Senate (1963–64). He later resumed his law practice.

Medill, Joseph (1823–99) publisher, editor; born in New Brunswick, Canada. Raised mainly in Ohio and partially self-taught, he became a lawyer, bought and ran two papers, and in 1855 acquired part interest in the *Chicago Tribune,* with which he was associated as owner and editor for most of his later years. He built it into a highly professional, influential, and successful paper, though markedly illiberal (one infamous editorial advocated administering arsenic to derelicts and the unemployed). He also served in public life, notably as mayor of Chicago in the early 1870s.

Meek, Joseph L. (1810–75) trapper, pioneer; born in Washington County, Va. He trapped throughout the Great West (1829–40) and settled in Oregon in 1840. After the Marcus Whitman massacre (1847), he went to Washington, D.C., and asked for protection for the people of Oregon. He served as a U.S. marshal and then turned to farming.

Meeker, Nathan Cook (1817–79) journalist, Indian agent; born in Euclid, Ohio. He became the agricultural editor of the *New York Tribune* in 1865 and founded Union Colony at Greeley, Colo. in 1869. He was killed by Ute Indians while serving as an Indian agent.

Mees, Charles Edward Kenneth (1882–1960) scientist, research administrator; born in Wellingborough, England. In 1913 Kodak brought Mees to America to head their research laboratory where he developed new products with a staff that grew from 20 to 1,000 (1913–53).

Meese, Edwin, III (1931–) lawyer, cabinet member; born in Oakland, Calif. A conservative deputy district attorney (1958–67) and California legal affairs secretary (1967–74), he prosecuted antiwar students for Governor Ronald Reagan. Director of the San Diego Center for Criminal Justice (1977–80), he became Reagan's presidential counsel (1981–85). As attorney general (1985–88), he was accused of impeding the Iran-Contra investigation by allowing conspirators to destroy evidence. He returned to California and took up the private practice of law.

Meggers, Betty J. (Jane) (1921–) anthropologist; born in Washington, D.C. After earning a Ph.D. at Columbia University she joined the staff of the Smithsonian Institution (1954). She did extensive fieldwork in South America, focusing particularly on prehistoric lowlands cultures, cultural ecology, and trans-Pacific contracts, and she published widely.

Meier, Richard (Alan) (1934–) architect; born in Newark, N.J. He graduated from Cornell University and established a New York practice (1963), designing houses and housing projects, commercial buildings, and, particularly in the 1970s and 1980s, museums. His modernist designs were typically simple, often sculptural forms in which space is extended vertically and exteriors are painted white. He designed the Bronx Developmental Center (1970–76), the High Museum, Atlanta, and the new Getty Center, Brentwood, Calif.

Meigs, Josiah (1757–1822) lawyer, educator, public official; born in Middletown, Conn. A Yale graduate (1778), he returned to Yale as a tutor (1781–84), meanwhile helping to launch and edit the *New Haven Gazette* (1784–88), which published the "Hartford Wits." Admitted to the bar in 1783, he practiced law in Bermuda for several years before becoming professor of mathematics and natural philosophy at Yale in 1794. Disputatious and difficult, he left Yale for the presidency of the University of Georgia (1801–10). He was not lamented when he resigned that office in 1810. Appointed surveyor general of the U.S.A. in 1812, he was a founder of the Columbian Institute, later George Washington University.

Meigs, Montgomery Cunningham (1816–92) soldier; born in Augusta, Ga. A West Point graduate (1836), as a member of the Engineering Corps he worked on federal projects including the Capitol's dome and wings. He became quartermaster general of Union forces in May 1861 and served efficiently in that demanding post through the war.

Meiklejohn, Alexander (1872–1964) educator, philosopher; born in Rochdale, England. A childhood immigrant to the U.S.A., he greatly improved the academic quality of Amherst College during his turbulent presidency (1912–23); he directed a short-lived experimental college at the University of Wisconsin (1927–32); and, in retirement, he pioneered adult education in San Francisco.

Meinzer, Oscar Edward (1876–1948) geologist, hydrologist; born in Davis, Ill. His extensive research in Utah, New Mexico, and Arizona on groundwater, water tables, aquifers, and artesian wells, especially as applied to agriculture and economic geology, has made him the recognized father of groundwater hydrology. He was chief of the Division of Ground Water of the U.S. Geological Survey from 1913 until his retirement in 1946.

Meir, Golda (b. Golda Mabovitch) (1898–1978) Israeli politician; born in Kiev, Ukraine. She emigrated to the U.S.A. in 1906 and became a teacher and Zionist activist in Milwaukee. She emigrated to Palestine in 1921 after her marriage to Morris Myerson (she Hebraized her married name in 1956) and worked as a Zionist and labor activist.

Elected to the Israeli parliament in 1949, she held labor (1949–56) and foreign affairs (1956–66) cabinet portfolios and was Israel's fourth prime minister (1969–74). Although credited with strengthening Israel through immigration policies and construction programs, she was forced to resign in the wake of Israel's losses in the October 1973 war.

Meiss, Millard (Lazare) (1904–75) art historian; born in Cincinnati, Ohio. He studied at Princeton (B.A. 1926), Harvard (1928), and New York University (M.A. 1931; Ph.D. 1933). He worked as a building superintendent in New York City, then taught at several institutions, and was a curator of the Fogg Museum (1954–58), specializing in the Renaissance and baroque periods. From 1958 until 1974 he taught at the Institute for Advanced Study, Princeton.

Melcher, Frederic Gershom (1879–1963) editor, publisher; born in Malden, Mass. A contagiously enthusiastic book lover, he won prominence as manager of an Indiana bookstore (1913–18) that became a mecca for writers and artists. He was longtime coeditor of *Publisher's Weekly* magazine (1918–58) and also served as president of its parent company, R. R. Bowker (1934–59). An early promoter of quality children's literature, he established the Newbery and Caldecott Medals for children's books.

Melchers, (Julius) Gari (1860–1932) painter; born in Detroit, Mich. He spent much of his life in Europe, studying in Dusseldorf (1877–80), and he established studios in Paris and Holland (1884). He returned and settled in Fredericksburg, Va. (1914), and continued to paint impressionistic landscapes and portraits.

Melchert, James (1930–) ceramist; born in New Bremen, Ohio. A leader in developing ceramics as a sculptural art medium, he taught at San Francisco Art Institute and is known for pieces combining incongruous elements.

Melchior, Lauritz (Lebrecht Hommel) (1890–1973) tenor; born in Copenhagen, Denmark. Beginning as a baritone (1913) he went on to become arguably the foremost Wagnerian tenor of the century. He sang in Bayreuth (1924–31) and regularly at the Metropolitan Opera (1926–50). In the late 1940s and early 1950s he appeared in several Hollywood movies.

Mellette, Arthur Calvin (1842–96) governor; born in Henry County, Ind. A Republican lawyer, he ran the *Muncie Times* and served in the Indiana legislature (1872–73). Moving to the Dakota Territory, he served on the constitutional convention (1883), establishing state budget limits. First South Dakota governor (1889–93), he used his own money to repay funds stolen by the state treasurer.

Mellon, Andrew (William) (1855–1937) financier, public official, philanthropist; born in Pittsburgh, Pa. Taking over his father's banking house in 1882, he built a business empire by shrewdly anticipating growth industries. He helped found the Union Trust Company of Pittsburgh (1898), the Gulf Oil Corporation (1895), the Pittsburgh Coal Company (1899), the Aluminum Company of America, and the company that built the Panama Canal locks. A conservative Republican, as secretary of the treasury under presidents Warren Harding, Calvin Coolidge, and Herbert Hoover (1921–32), he stressed policies aimed at reducing the national debt. He drew fire by cutting income tax rates substantially as part of a tax-revision program to aid business and the wealthy. He forged agreements with European governments for repayment of their World War I debts and served as ambassador to Britain

(1932–33). In 1913 he established the Mellon Institute for Industrial Research and he endowed the National Gallery of Art (1937).

Mellon, Paul (1907–) art collector, philanthropist; born in Pittsburgh, Pa. (son of Andrew Mellon). A graduate of Yale University (1929), he also studied English literature at Cambridge University, starting his art collection there. Presiding over his father's Washington art collection (1937–39), he served in the cavalry during World War II. As chairman of two foundations, set up to dispense the family fortune, he made generous gifts to several universities, also serving as president of the National Gallery of Art (1963–79). He gave Yale his $35 million collection of British and French art in 1966, with additional funding to build and maintain an art study complex (1966). He was also a noted horseman; horses from his stables have won many of the world's major races.

Melton, James (1904–61) tenor; born in Moultrie, Ga. After college, he studied voice at Vanderbilt and in Berlin, making his opera debut in Cincinnati in 1938. His eight-year Metropolitan Opera career began in 1942, and he was also widely heard on the radio and in concerts. Beyond being one of the first American males to become a major opera star, he conveyed a "down-home" quality offstage that made grand opera seem more accessible to a new generation.

Melville, George Wallace (1841–1912) naval officer, Arctic explorer; born in New York City. As chief of the Bureau of Steam Engineering (1887–1903), he supervised the design of the machinery of 120 naval ships and introduced the water-tube boiler and triple-screw systems. He performed heroic services during an Arctic expedition (1879–81) and wrote *In the Lena Delta* (1885), an account of the voyages.

Melville, Herman (1819–91) writer; born in New York City. He left school when he was 15 and worked as a bank clerk (1834), farmhand, and schoolteacher. In 1837 he served as a cabinboy on a ship bound for Liverpool. In 1841 he set sail on the whaler, *Acushnet,* for the South Pacific; he deserted at the Marquesas Islands with a friend and lived for a short time with the Typee cannibals; he escaped to Tahiti and enjoyed an idyllic period there before he enlisted in the U.S. Navy and returned to Boston (1844). The publication of *Typee* (1846), based on his Marquesas Islands adventure, and *Omoo* (1847), derived from his stay in Tahiti, made him famous; *Mardi* (1849), *Redburn* (1849), and *White-Jacket* (1850), also based on his sea travels, were not quite as successful. He married Elizabeth Shaw (1847), moved to New York City, and traveled to England and Paris (1849). He settled in Pittsfield, Mass., and while writing *Moby Dick* there he became a friend of Nathaniel Hawthorne, dedicating his epic to him. *Moby Dick* (1851) is considered a masterpiece of American literature, but it was not well received by either readers or critics, who found it difficult and unsettling. The autobiographical *Pierre* (1852) also failed to win over the public. Discouraged, Melville traveled to the Holy Land in search of inspiration (1856–57). Such works as *Israel Potter* (1855), *The Piazza Tales* (1856), and *The Confidence Man* (1857) also found few readers, while his poetry would prove even more elusive. Withdrawing from the quest for literary recognition, in 1863 he moved to New York City again and worked there as a customs inspector (1866–85). His last significant work, *Billy Bud, Foretopman,* finished just before his death, was not published until 1924. He died poor and in obscurity; it was the 1920s before Americans recognized his achievements and elevated him to his rank as one of the greatest of all American creative artists.

Menard, H. (Henry) William, Jr. (1920–86) oceanographer; born in Fresno, Calif. He was an oceanographer with the U.S. Navy Electronics Laboratory (1949–55) before joining the Scripps Institution of Oceanography (1955–78). He became director of the U.S. Geological Survey in Reston, Va. (1978–81). He was one of the first to use the aqualung to observe the geology of the ocean floor. His Pacific discoveries of submerged seamounts and vast seafloor displacements (1950) made him a pioneer in plate tectonics.

Menard, Pierre (1766–1844) fur trader, public official; born in St. Antoine, Quebec, Canada. He moved to Indiana (1787) and became a partner in the St. Louis Missouri Fur Company. With Andrew Henry, he led the first organized group of trappers to the Three Forks of the Missouri River (1810). He was the first lieutenant-governor of Illinois and served as an Indian commissioner (1828–29).

Mencken, H. L. (Henry Louis) (1880–1956) editor, writer; born in Baltimore, Md. He left school after his father's death (1899) to become a reporter for the *Baltimore Morning Herald,* later serving as drama critic, city editor, and then managing editor of the *Baltimore Evening Herald.* Soon after the *Herald* folded in 1906, he joined the Baltimore *Sun;* he remained associated with the *Sun* as editor, columnist, or contributor for most of his career, but he also wrote for many other publications. Early on, Mencken published studies of George Bernard Shaw (1905) and Friedrich Nietzsche (1908), both of whom he admired. From 1914 to 1923, with George Jean Nathan he coedited a satirical magazine, *The Smart Set;* in 1924 he and Nathan cofounded the *American Mercury,* a cultural magazine for "a civilized minority," which he coedited for nine years. Social rebels admired Mencken's clever, iconoclastic attacks on the middle-class "booboisie," prudery, and organized religion and politics. As a reviewer and critic he lambasted second-rate authors and championed such writers as Theodore Dreiser, Sinclair Lewis, and Joseph Conrad. Many of his essays and reviews were collected in six volumes of *Prejudices* (1919–27). In a different vein, his detailed study, *The American Language* (1919), traced the developments of a distinctive American idiom. During the 1930s, Mencken's cynicism and his antipathy to the New Deal appeared less in tune with the times, and he turned more toward the past, writing three volumes of memoirs, beginning with *Happy Days* (1940). He also added two supplements to his *American Language* (1945, 1946). A stroke in 1948 left him incapacitated during his last years.

Mendenhall, Dorothy (b. Reed) (1874–1964) physician; born in Columbus, Ohio. A dedicated researcher and physician, she is best known for her early research on Hodgkin's disease and contributions to maternal and child health care while a medical officer at the United States Children's Bureau (1917–36). Her numerous articles greatly influenced the diet of pregnant women and children.

Mendes, Henry Pereira (1852–1937) rabbi; born in Birmingham, England. He came to the U.S.A. in 1877 to serve in the Spanish and Portuguese Synagogue Shearith Israel in New York, where he stayed until 1920. He was involved in local and national politics, arguing for more liberal immigration laws and for less sectarian schools. He was instrumental in organizing many philanthropic and educational institutions, including the first Young Women's Hebrew Association. A founder in 1887 of the Jewish Theological Seminary of America and the Union of Orthodox Jewish Congregations of America, he was an early Zionist and a prolific writer. His brother, Frederic de Sola Mendes (1850–1937), was a scholarly rabbi, who served Congregation Shaaray Tefila in New York from 1874–1920.

Mennin, Peter (b. Mennini) (1923–83) composer; born in Erie, Pa. After studies at Oberlin and Eastman, he was director of Baltimore's Peabody Conservatory of Music (1958–62), then served as president of Juilliard from 1962 until his death. He is best known for his nine symphonies in a mildly modernistic idiom.

Menninger, Charles Frederick (1862–1953) physician; born in Tell City, Ind. (father of Karl and William Claire Menninger). He taught a variety of subjects, including German and physics, before getting a degree in homeopathic medicine in 1887, then took an M.D. in conventional medicine (1908). Inspired by the Mayo clinic he had visited, he founded a clinic in Topeka, Kans., which was originally designed to treat a range of basic medical problems. When his son Karl joined him in 1919, the Menninger Clinic began to shift its focus to psychiatric cases. His son William joined the Clinic in 1925 and it soon became one of the premier psychiatric hospitals in the U.S.A. In 1914 the three of them formed the Menninger Foundation to support training, research, and other programs in the field of psychiatry.

Menninger, Karl (Augustus) (1893–1990) psychiatrist; born in Topeka, Kans. After receiving his medical degree from Harvard Medical School (1917), he worked for two years at the Boston Psychopathic Hospital. In 1919, he returned to Topeka and cofounded the Menninger Diagnostic Clinic (1920) with his father, Charles Frederick Menninger, who had become convinced of the advantages of group medical practice after visiting the Mayo Clinic (1908). At first practicing conventional medicine, Karl's training and interest led him to treat emotional problems. When his brother William received his medical degree, the two cofounded the Menninger Sanitarium and Psychopathic Hospital (1925). The Menningers pioneered intensive milieu therapy, the use of the hospital's social environment as a key part of the therapeutic process. In his best-selling book, *The Human Mind* (1930), Karl Menninger put forward the position that the difference between normality and mental illness was only one of degree. In other books – such as *Man Against Himself* (1938) and *The Crime of Punishment* (1968) – he argued for a humane approach to most of people's failings; he would have a major impact on the reform of Kansas's and other state's mental health programs and he would serve as an adviser to many federal agencies. Although not a strict Freudian, he borrowed some of Freud's ideas for his own eclectic approach to mental illness. In 1931, the Menninger Sanitarium became the first institution licensed to train psychiatric nurses, and in 1933 opened a psychiatric residency program for physicians. In 1941 the family founded the Menninger Foundation, which Karl headed until his death.

Menninger, William Claire (1899–1966) physician, psychiatrist; born in Topeka, Kans. He joined the Menninger Clinic in Topeka, which his brother, Karl, and their father had founded in 1919–20. He directed the Menninger Hospital in the 1930s, which became a model psychiatric hospital. He was influential in gaining public acceptance for psychiatry. During World War II he was chief consultant on psychiatry to the Surgeon General of the U.S. Army, and he was also a leader in the Boy Scout movement. His books include *Psychiatry in a Troubled World* (1948).

Menotti, Gian-Carlo (1911–) composer; born in Cadegliano, Italy. He had written his first opera even before he came to the U.S.A. to study at the Curtis Institute in Philadelphia (1927). Following his first success, the opera *Amelia Goes to the Ball* (1937), he became the most popular of opera composers living in America. His other well-known operas (all with his own librettos), conservative and Italianate in style, include *The Old Maid and the Thief* (1939) and *The Consul* (1950), which won two Pulitzer Prizes. His opera *Amahl and the Night Visitors* premiered on television in 1951 and was broadcast annually at Christmas for many years. Although not as well known as his operas, his other works include a madrigal ballet, *The Unicorn, the Gorgon and the Manticore* (1956) and a symphonic poem, *Apocalypse* (1951). In 1958 he founded the Festival of Two Worlds in Spoleto, Italy; in 1977 it was expanded to a similar annual festival of art in Charleston, S.C.

Mentschikoff, Soia (1915–84) law educator; born in Moscow, Russia. Child of American citizens, she was brought to the U.S.A. as a child and took her law degree at Columbia University (1937). She practiced law in New York City (1937–49) and taught at Harvard Law School (1947–49) and the University of Chicago Law School (1951–74). She was dean of the University of Miami law school (1974–82). A member of various legal commissions and organizations, she was president of the Association of American Law Schools (1974). She published articles in legal journals and several books including (with coauthor Nicholas Katzenbach) *International Unification of Private Law* (1961).

Menuhin, Yehudi (1916–) violinist; born in New York City. He grew up in San Francisco, where he began violin study at age three and made his public debut at age seven. Within a few years he had been acclaimed as a prodigy, finding resounding successes in Europe (where he studied with Georges Enesco) and playing the Beethoven Violin Concerto in New York in 1927. The next year, at age 12, he performed concertos by Beethoven, Brahms, and Bach in one concert of the Berlin Philharmonic. In the early 1930s a world tour took him to 73 cities in 13 countries. During World War II he concertized tirelessly for Allied troops. Largely based in Switzerland and England after the war, he conducted as often as he played, becoming a fixture of music festivals and, from 1969, director of England's Windsor Festival. In the 1960s he helped popularize Indian music in the West. Besides playing the standard repertoire, he commissioned and played important works from composers including Bartók and Walton.

Menzel, Donald Howard (1901–76) astrophysicist; born in Florence, Colo. At Harvard (1932–76), he directed the Observatory (1954–66), and became an authority on the sun's chromosphere. A prolific author of such titles as *Fundamental Formulas of Physics* (1955), *The Universe in Action* (1957), *A Field Guide to the Stars and Planets* (1964), he wrote that flying saucers were optical illusions.

Mercer, Henry Chapman (1856–1930) archaeologist, antiquarian, tile maker; born in Doylestown, Pa. After training as a lawyer, he shifted his interest to the archaeology of the earliest Native American remains in the eastern United States, especially in the Delaware Valley of Pennsylvania. In 1894 he became curator of the Museum of American Prehistoric Archaeology at the University of Pennsylvania, but he retired in 1897 to have more time for fieldwork; he published at least 55 scientific papers, mostly on Native Americans. Meanwhile, he had developed and patented a new method of making tiles that reproduced various illustrations, often by famous Old Masters; these became much sought after in the early years of the 20th century and were widely used in churches and in private homes. He established his Moravian Tile Works in Doylestown, Pa. (1898), where he set up a museum at his home, Fonthill, to display his tiles to the public.

Mercer, (John H.) Johnny (1909–1976) lyricist, composer; born in Savannah, Ga. He collaborated with the great songwriters of his day on such popular hits as "That Old Black Magic" (1942), "Ac-cent-tchu-ate the Positive" (1944), "Come Rain or Come Shine" (1946), and "Moon River" (1961). In 1942 he was a founder and first president of Capitol Records. He wrote some 1,500 songs for films and Broadway musicals, including the hit musical *L'il Abner* (1956).

Merck, George W. (Wilhelm Emanuel) (1894–1957) chemicals executive; born in New York City. A Harvard-trained chemist, he joined Merck and Co., the family chemical firm, in 1915; he was president (1925–50) and chairman (1949–57). He developed the aggressive research program that shifted Merck's focus to pharmaceuticals and made it a leader in manufacturing vitamins, sulfa drugs, and cortisone. He directed the War Research Service during World War II.

Meredith, James (Howard) (1933–) civil rights activist, business executive; born in Kosciusko, Miss. After serving in the U.S. Air Force, he became the first African-American to enroll in the University of Mississippi (1962), but only after he had weathered campus riots (which left two dead) and the resistance of state officials. Federal troops had to protect him on campus until he graduated (1963). He published his autobiographhical *Three Years in Mississippi* (1966) and not long after was shot while on the March Against Fear in Mississippi. He recovered and completed the march, but soon thereafter dropped out of the civil rights movement. He worked as a stockbroker, in real estate, and as an investor (1967) while attending Columbia University Law School (1968). He became president of Meredith Enterprises (1968), lectured on racial problems, and was an unsuccessful Republican candidate for the U.S. House of Representatives (1972). Always a somewhat diffident loner, he never seemed interested in assuming the roles that were thrust upon him.

Meredith, Scott (1923–93) literary agent; born in New York City. He tried his hand at writing short stories before founding the Scott Meredith Literary Agency with his brother in 1946. P. G. Wodehouse was his first prominent client; he later represented many best-selling authors including Norman Mailer. He introduced the concept of auctioning a book to the highest bidding publisher. His *Writing to Sell*, a how-to guide for aspiring authors, was still in print at the time of his death.

Merganthaler, Ottmar (1854–99) inventor; born in Hachtel, Germany. After an apprenticeship in watch- and clock-making, he emigrated to the U.S.A. (1872) and began working in a scientific instrument shop in Washington, D.C.; he moved with his employer to Baltimore, Md., in 1876, becoming a full partner in 1880. In 1876 Merganthaler was asked to help improve a new machine that James Clephane had designed to help in the printing process; this led Merganthaler to spend much of his time during the next few years in trying to invent a totally new machine for setting type. After starting his own shop in 1883, he came up with the first machine that could cast type in bars of molten lead – the so-called linotype machine. It was patented in 1884 and Clephane, with whom Merganthaler had been working, helped set up the National Typographic Company to manufacture it, along with the Merganthaler Printing Company. Merganthaler was forced out of the business in 1888 over policy disagreements, but he never ceased to work at improving his machine, taking out over 50 patents and effectively revolutionizing the printing industry. He was recognized in his lifetime for his important contribution but he died prematurely of tuberculosis.

Meritt, Benjamin Dean (1899–1989) epigrapher, ancient historian; born in Durham, N.C. Along with Albert Einstein, he was one of the original members of Princeton's Institute for Advanced Study, where he was professor of Greek epigraphy, the study of ancient inscriptions (1935–69). He published widely on topography and epigraphy and his *Athenian Tribute Lists* (with M. F. McGregor and H. T. Wade-Gery, 1939–53) made possible detailed study of the growth of the Athenian empire in the 5th century B.C. His work on the Athenian calendar culminated in *The Athenian Year* (1961).

Merman, Ethel (b. Zimmerman) (1908–84) actress, singer; born in Astoria, N.Y. Gutsy, powerful musical comedy performer, she is remembered for her showstopping performances in *Annie Get Your Gun* (1946) and *Call Me Madam* (1950).

Mermin, N. David (1935–) physicist; born in New Haven, Conn. He performed research at the University of Birmingham (1961–63) and the University of California: San Diego (1963–64), before joining Cornell (1964). A theoretical and solid state physicist, he criticized the Nobel Prize system for fostering competition among scientists rather than encouraging pure research (1989).

Merriam, Charles E. (Edward), Jr. (1874–1953) political scientist; born in Hopkinton, Iowa. While teaching at the University of Chicago from 1900 until his final months, he effectively established political science as a discipline at that university and he had a national reputation as the founder of the behavioral school of political science. He was also involved in Chicago's reform politics; he drafted legislation, served as alderman (1909–17), and ran unsuccessfully for mayor in 1911. A strong proponent of social science research and planning, he was the founder and president of the Social Science Research Council (1924–27) and led the National Resources Planning Board (1933–43). His many publications include *New Aspects of Politics* (1925).

Merriam, Clinton Hart (1855–1942) naturalist; born in New York City. The son of a wealthy merchant, he grew up in Locust Grove, N.Y., within view of the Adirondacks. Educated at Yale, he earned a medical degree from Columbia University and practiced medicine for several years before turning full time to natural history. As director of the U.S. Biological Survey from 1885–1910, he oversaw research projects, expeditions, and the building of permanent plant and animal collections. He left government service to pursue his own research interests, and he published works on birds, bears, and Indian folktales.

Merriam, Mansfield (1848–1925) educator, writer, civil engineer; born in Southington, Conn. He taught civil engineering, first at Yale (1877–78), then at Lehigh University until 1907. During this period he was often a consulting engineer on hydraulic and bridge problems. He wrote and edited numerous books and articles on engineering.

Merrifield, R. (Robert) Bruce (1921–) biochemist; born in Fort Worth, Texas. He joined the staff at Rockefeller Institute (later University) in 1949. In the early 1960s he developed the method of manufacturing proteins in the laboratory known as "solid phase peptide synthesis." He was awarded the Nobel Prize in chemistry (1984).

Merrill, Charles Edward (1885–1956) stockbroker, investment banker; born in Green Cove Springs, Fla. Son of a physician, he spent two years at Amherst College, played professional baseball briefly, worked in several investment houses, and established his own firm in 1914. A year later he took in a partner, Edward Lynch. Retiring in 1930, he helped found the magazine, *Family Circle*. In the 1940s he returned to Wall Street to create what became the nation's largest brokerage, first known as Merrill, Lynch, Pierce, Fenner and Beane. The firm built a reputation for conservative investment advice to middle-income clients, an approach widely copied during the 1950s. He left some $25 million at his death to establish the charitable Merrill Trust.

Merrill, Frank (Dow) (1903–55) soldier; born in Hopkinton, Mass. He served as an intelligence officer early in World War II before being assigned to raise the volunteer unit known as "Merrill's Marauders," which fought in the Burma jungle behind the Japanese lines (1943–44).

Merrill, James (Ingram) (1926–) poet, writer; born in New York City. Son of the wealthy stockbroker Charles Merrill, he studied at Amherst (B.A. 1947). He lived abroad – in Greece and elsewhere – for many years, but maintained a home in Stonington, Conn. He wrote plays and novels, but is best known for his elegant, elliptical poetry as in *The Changing Light at Sandover* (1982), which also revealed his involvement with the occult.

Merrill, Robert (1917–) baritone; born in New York City. American-trained, Merrill sang popular music before making his operatic debut in 1944. He joined the Metropolitan Opera in 1945 and remained a favorite there for 30 years. He also appeared in recitals, with orchestras, in films, and in musical comedy.

Merritt, LeRoy Charles (b. LeRoy Charles Schimmel-pfennig) (1912–70) library educator; born in Milwaukee, Wis. Appointed librarian and associate professor of librarianship at Longwood College in Virginia (1942–46), he was also in charge of library materials at the U.S. Army Special Services Headquarters in Paris, France (1944–45). He moved to the University of California School of Librarianship at Berkeley (1946–66) and then became the first dean of the Library School of the University of Oregon (1966–70). Many of his publications are in the area of book selection, library administration, and intellectual freedom. He was editor of the American Library Association *Newsletter on Intellectual Freedom* from 1962 until 1970.

Merritt, Wesley (1834–1910) soldier; born in New York City. He grew up in Illinois, and after graduating from West Point (1860), he saw service as a cavalry officer during the Civil War, including Gettysburg. From 1866 to 1879, he served on the western frontier; he was superintendent of West Point (1882–87). After years at various administrative posts, he was given command of the army forces that captured Manila from the Spanish in 1898. He briefly served as military governor of the Philippines (1898–99) before retiring from the army in 1900.

Merton, Robert K. (King) (1910–) sociologist; born in Philadelphia. Educated at Temple and Harvard Universities, he was long on the faculty of Columbia University (1941–79), where he was associate director of the Bureau of Applied Social Research (1942–71). He helped to establish the sociology of science as a discipline and wrote on a variety of topics including social deviance, mass persuasion, bureaucracy, and social theory.

Merton, Thomas (James) (1915–68) Catholic monk, writer; born in Prades, France. Following his mother's early death, he was raised in France, England, and the U.S.A. After earning bachelor's and master's degrees in English from Columbia University, he converted from agnosticism to Catholicism and in 1941 entered a Trappist monastery at Gethsemani, Ky., taking the name Louis; his autobiography, *The Seven Storey Mountain* (1948), became a best-seller and made him a Catholic folk hero. He continued to write poetry and religious works, and after ordination (1949), he served as master of students, then master of novices. In later life he was increasingly preoccupied with social concerns and he became a major figure in the 1960s antiwar movement. Also drawn to solitude, he won permission to live as a hermit on his monastery's grounds (1965). In 1968 he was allowed to pursue a growing interest in Oriental mysticism by visiting the Far East; while attending a religious conference in Thailand he was apparently electrocuted by a faulty fan in his hotel room.

Mertz, Edwin T. (Theodore) (1909–) agriculturist; born in Missoula, Mont. He was a research chemist at Armour & Co. in Chicago (1935–37) and worked at several Midwestern universities before settling at Purdue in 1946. In his first decade there he discovered high lysine corn, now called Quality Protein Maize (1953), and determined the protein requirements for fast-growing pigs. From 1956 to 1976 he consulted for the Indiana State Hospitals and developed biochemistry research departments at several facilities. In 1976 he attained emeritus status and began consulting on a sorghum research program at Purdue. His publications include *Quality Protein Maize* (1992).

Merwin, W. S. (William Stanley) (1927–) poet; born in New York City. He studied at Princeton (B.A. 1947), tutored Robert Graves' son in Majorca (1950), and was based in England, France, and Hawaii. He is known for his plays, prose parables, and translations as well as for his surrealistic poetry, as in *Opening the Hand* (1983).

Meserve, Frederick Hill (1865–1962) collector; born in Philadelphia. A businessman, he built up in his leisure an extraordinary collection of 19th-century photographs and negatives, many related to Abraham Lincoln. He acquired a large part of Mathew Brady's work.

Messersmith, George S. (Strausser) (1883–1960) diplomat; born in Fleetwood, Pa. Due to his personal reticence, his early family life remains obscure. He taught in the Delaware public schools and entered the Foreign Service in 1914. After a series of consular appointments, he was ambassador to Cuba (1940–42), Mexico (1942–46), and Argentina (1946–47); in this last post he worked closely with President Juan Perón and he resigned as a result of his opposition to the State Department's position on Argentina's role in World War II. He ran the Canadian-owned Mexican Power and Light Company (1947–55).

Messmer, Sebastian (Gebhard) (1847–1930) Catholic prelate; born in Goldach, Switzerland. Ordained in 1871, he emigrated to the U.S.A. where he taught theology and became bishop of Green Bay, Wis. (1891), then archbishop of Milwaukee (from 1903). He exerted great influence among German Catholics in the Midwest.

Metacomet See PHILIP, KING.

Metcalf, Keyes (Dewitt) (1889–1983) librarian, educator; born in Elyria, Ohio. As director of the Harvard University Library (1936–54), he expanded the holdings and services of Widener Library and added two important smaller libraries, Houghton and Lamont.

Metcalfe, Ralph (Harold) (1910–78) U.S. representative, athlete; born in Atlanta, Ga. Winner of Olympic track medals in 1932 and 1936, track coach, and army veteran, he was a Chicago alderman (1955–67) and congressman (Dem., Ill.; 1971–78).

Metz, Christian (1794–1867) religious reformer; born in Neuwied, Prussia. A carpenter by trade, he participated in a religious revival (1817) and became the leader of a group of German mystic-pietists known as Inspirationists. In 1842 he led some 800 followers to America and purchased 5,000 acres near Buffalo, N.Y. They moved west (1854) and bought 18,000 acres in Iowa, which became incorporated as the Amana Church Society (1859). He wrote voluminously and impressed many people with his patience, tolerance, and administrative skills. The Amana Society eventually spread to seven adjacent villages, all run under a system of communal property, labor and activities – originally agricultural but gradually expanding into manufacturing. It is often regarded as the most successful of the utopian-communist experiments in America. In 1932, the secular affairs of the group were reorganized as a kind of joint stock corporation. The Amana brand of appliances is their best-known product.

Meyer, Adolph (1866–1950) psychiatrist; born near Zürich, Switzerland. He emigrated to the United States in 1892. As professor, and later director, he turned the Phipps Psychiatric Clinic at Johns Hopkins into the premier psychiatric training center in the country (1910–41). One of the most important early psychiatrists in America, he developed new treatment methods, including the interview. He was an influential proponent of a holistic psychobiology.

Meyer, Albert (Gregory) (1902–65) Catholic prelate; born in Milwaukee. After studies and ordination in Rome (1926), he did parish work, was a seminary teacher and rector, and became bishop of Superior, Wis. (1946), and archbishop of Milwaukee (1953). In 1958 he was named archbishop of Chicago (1958), becoming a cardinal the next year. He promoted building programs, lay involvement, and desegregation; he also served on Vatican commissions and was a leading liberal voice at the Second Vatican Council.

Meyer, Karl (1899–1990) biochemist; born in Kerpen, Germany. He left Germany (1930) for the University of California: Berkeley before joining Columbia University to direct the department of biochemistry at the Eye Institute (1933–67). His research team identified and analyzed basic chemical components of connective tissues. On retirement, he spent ten years at Yeshiva University in Israel, returning to Columbia as emeritus.

Mich, Daniel Danforth (1905–65) editor; born in Minneapolis, Minn. As editorial director of *Look* magazine (1942–50, 1954–64), he stressed the use of pictures to broaden the reader's perception of the news.

Micheaux, Oscar (1884–1951) motion picture producer; born in Metropolis, Ill. He worked as a Pullman porter, farmer, and rancher and wrote novels before he produced the first motion pictures for African-American audiences (from 1919). During the 1920s he produced *Within Our Gates,* a treatment of the Leo Frank lynching in Atlanta, Ga.; *The Brute,* featuring the black boxer Sam Langford; *The Symbol of the Unconquered,* an indictment of the Ku Klux Klan, and many other silent films. Always hampered by lack of funds and poor distribution, he lapsed into bankruptcy in the early 1940s.

Michel, Robert (Henry) (1923–) U.S. representative; born in Peoria, Ill. He was a combat infantryman in Europe during World War II (1943–46), receiving two Bronze Stars and the Purple Heart. After graduating from college, he worked for Representative Harold Velde (1949–56). Elected to the U.S. House of Representatives (Rep., Ill.; 1957), he served as minority whip (1975–79) and minority leader (1981–95).

Michel, Virgil (b. George Francis Michel) (1890–1938) religious leader; born in St. Paul, Minn. A Benedictine priest with a doctorate from Catholic University, he was a pioneer of Catholic liturgical reform, and while teaching at St. John's College (Minn.), he founded the liturgical periodical *Orate Fratres* (later, *Worship*) (1926). Other concerns, also reflected in his writings, included Indian welfare (he worked among Chippewa Indians from 1930 to 1933), Thomistic philosophy, and social welfare; from 1935 he directed the St. John's Institute for Social Studies.

Michelson, Albert A. (Abraham) (1852–1931) physicist; born in Strelno, Germany (now Strzelno, Poland). His family moved to California when he was two years old. He served in the U.S. Navy, then taught at the Naval Academy (1873–79). After studying in Europe, he taught at several American universities before joining the University of Chicago (1892–1929). The Michelson-Morley experiment (with Western Reserve physicist E. W. Morley) used Michelson's invention, the interferometer, to measure the speed of light in relation to "ether drift." For this and other pioneering work in optical instrumentation, he became the first American scientist to win a Nobel Prize (1907).

Michener, James (Albert) (1907–) writer; born in New York City. A foundling, he was raised by his adoptive parents, Edwin and Mabel Michener, in Doylesville, Pa. He studied at Swarthmore College (B.A. 1929) and at European universities (1931–33), taught in Pennsylvania, then took his M.A. at Colorado State College (now University of Northern Colorado) (1936), where he taught history until 1939. With a reputation as both a theorist and teacher of social studies, he was a visiting professor at Harvard (1939–41), then became a book editor in New York City (1941–49), with time out for service with the U.S. Navy in the Pacific (1944–

45). This experience provided him with the material for his first popular success, *Tales of the South Pacific* (1947), adapted by Rodgers and Hammerstein for the even more successful musical, *South Pacific* (1949). Michener was now free to devote himself to writing his trademark epics – fictionalized histories of such places as Hawaii, Africa, Afghanistan, America, and Israel, as well as straightforward nonfiction works on such topics as Japanese prints (1959) and the role of sports in modern life. To keep up his vast output, he employed teams of researchers, and although critics complained that his later works revealed the seams of his methods, his books continued to satisfy a large public. An outspoken liberal Democrat, he gave generously of his immense earnings.

Middleton, Troy Houston (1889–1976) soldier, educator; born in Mississippi. He left the army in the 1930s to serve as a senior administrator at Louisiana State University (LSU). Recalled in 1942, he commanded an infantry division in combat in Sicily and Italy, and led a corps in France, Belgium, Luxemburg, and Germany from 1944 to 1945. He returned as president of LSU from 1951 to 1962.

Midgley, Thomas, Jr. (1889–1944) inventor, engineer; born in Beaver Falls, Pa. From 1916 to 1921 he worked at the Dayton Engineering Laboratories on the problem of engine "knocking"; he developed the use of tetra-ethyl lead as a gasoline additive and devised the octane number for rating gasoline. As president of the Ethyl Corp. from 1923, he introduced Freon 12 as a refrigerant.

Mielziner, Jo (1901–76) set/theater designer; born in Paris, France. In the course of his career, he designed the sets for over 400 Broadway plays, most of the major productions from the 1930s to the 1950s. Turning his back on the earlier tradition of theatrical realism, he often employed mere suggestions of settings, using scrims and isolated scenic units to create further effects. His use of lighting to change the dramatic focus from one scene to another has been described as "cinematic." Among his works are *The Guardsman* (with Alfred Lunt and Lynn Fontanne, 1924), *Strange Interlude* (1928), *Romeo and Juliet* (with Katharine Cornell, 1934), *Hamlet* (with John Gielgud, 1936), *The Glass Menagerie* (1945), *Death of a Salesman* (1949), *Guys and Dolls* (1950), and *The King and I* (1951). He was the designer of the Washington Square Theatre and (with Eero Saarinen) the Vivian Beaumont Theatre at Lincoln Center.

Mielziner, Moses (1828–1903) rabbi, scholar; born in Schubin, Germany. He came to the U.S.A. in 1865 to be a rabbi in New York. He taught the Talmud at Hebrew Union College, Cincinnati (1879–1903), and became its president (1900–03). He wrote widely on behalf of the Reform movement, including his *Introduction to the Talmud* and *Slavery among the Ancient Hebrews*.

Mies van der Rohe, Ludwig (b. Ludwig Mies) (1886–1969) architect; born in Aachen, Germany. As a young architect and designer in Berlin, he foreshadowed modern architecture with innovative designs for tubular-steel furniture (the cantilevered Barcelona chair (1929)) and steel and glass skyscrapers. He directed the Bauhaus, Dessau (1930–33), which he closed after Nazi threats. Though he had built only 19 buildings, he was internationally famous when he came to the U.S.A. in 1937; he founded and directed the architecture department at the Armour Institute, Chicago (later Illinois Institute of Technology) (1938–58), and designed the insti-

tute's master plan and a number of campus buildings. Mies celebrated contemporary technology and materials; under his influence, skyscraper construction switched from masonry to metal and glass. Following his credo, "less is more," his buildings were characterized by accessible, simple designs devoid of applied ornament and were composed of spaces rather than masses. A founder of the International style, his influence on 20th-century architecture can hardly be overestimated. His starkly simple German Pavilion at the International Exposition in Barcelona in 1929 crystallized public acceptance of modern architecture. His buildings include the glass Lake Shore Drive Apartments, Chicago (1948–51), the Seagram Building, New York (with Philip Johnson, 1954–58), and the Museum of Fine Arts, Houston (1958, 1973).

Mifflin, Thomas (1744–1800) soldier, governor; born in Philadelphia. One of the most radical members of the First Continental Congress, he became quartermaster general of the Continental army (1775–78). After supporting a plot to replace George Washington with Gen. Horatio Gates, he disavowed it; but under criticism for his actions as quartermaster, he resigned. A Democratic-Republican in the Confederation Congress (1782–84), he attended the Constitutional Convention in 1787 and supported the new Constitution. He became governor of Pennsylvania (1790–99) and pursued Jeffersonian policies; reluctantly calling for action against those involved in the so-called Whiskey Rebellion (1794), he dealt leniently with its leaders.

Mikan, George (Lawrence) (1924–) basketball player; born in Joliet, Ill. He was a three-time All-American at DePaul University (1944–46) before playing center for the Minneapolis Lakers (1948–56), where he averaged 22.6 points per game over nine years. One of the National Basketball Association's first superstars, he led the Lakers to five titles in six years and was instrumental in establishing professional basketball in the U.S.A. In 1967 he became the first commissioner of the American Basketball Association. He was voted "the greatest player in the first half-century" by the Associated Press and was elected to basketball's Hall of Fame in 1959.

Milam, Carl Hastings (1884–1963) librarian; born in Harper County, Kans. He was director of the Birmingham (Ala.) Public Library (1913–19), where he opened the first branch for service to African-Americans. During World War I, he was assistant director and then general director of the American Library Association's Library War Service (1917–20). In 1920 he became secretary of the American Library Association and his career in this post for 28 years gave rise to his nickname, "Mr. ALA." In 1948 he became director of the newly formed United Nations Library, where he served until retiring in 1950.

Miles, Nelson (Appleton) (1839–1925) soldier; born in Westminster, Mass. A clerk in a crockery store when the Civil War broke out, he obtained a commission in the 22nd Massachusetts and fought in nearly every major engagement of the Army of the Potomac, ending the war as a brigadier general (and with the Congressional Medal of Honor). After the war, he was Confederate President Jefferson Davis's jailer at Fortress Monroe, Va., and was criticized for keeping Davis shackled in his cell. From 1869 to 1891 he fought the Indians on the western frontier; among other actions, he captured Chief Joseph in 1877 and Geronimo in 1886, but his reputation would never recover from allowing the massacre at Wounded Knee (1890). During the 1894 Pullman strike in Chicago, he was called in to command the troops that controlled the protesters. He became commander-in-chief of the army in 1895, and after directing the training of troops for the Spanish-American War, he led the U.S. forces that occupied Puerto Rico in 1898. He retired from the army in 1903.

Milgram, Stanley (1933–84) social psychologist; born in New York City. He studied at Harvard and Princeton and taught at Yale (1960–63) and the City University of New York (1967–84). He is best known for the study described in *Obedience to Authority: An Experimental View* (1974): Research subjects were ordered to administer "electric shocks" of varying intensity to people in another room; most did so on command, despite the simulated pain and apparent danger to their fellow subjects.

Mili, Gjon (1904–84) photographer; born in Kerce, Albania. He emigrated to the United States in 1923 and studied electrical engineering at the Massachusetts Institute of Technology (MIT) (B.S. 1927). He did research in lighting at Westinghouse Electric in Cambridge (1928–38) and worked on experiments in high-speed photography with Harold E. Edgerton at MIT. Mili would become best known for introducing the results of such advanced technological developments to the general public with his dramatic "stop-action" photographs. A free-lance photographer for *Life* and other magazines, from 1939 he lived in New York City, where his work was frequently exhibited. His many books and articles include *The Magic of the Opera* (1960) and *Homage to Picasso* (1967).

Milk, Harvey (1930–78) public official; born in New York City. He moved to San Francisco in 1969 and at first operated a camera store. But as an experienced financial analyst, he was elected to San Francisco's Board of Supervisors in 1977. Instrumental in passing the city's gay rights ordinance, he was the first acknowledged homosexual official in the city. He was shot to death by a former city supervisor, who also killed Mayor George Moscone. When their assassin was given a light sentence, San Francisco's homosexual community rioted.

Milken, Michael (Robert) (1946–) investment entrepreneur; born in California. As a boy growing up in suburban Los Angeles, he helped his accountant father prepare returns at tax time. He married his high school girlfriend after graduating from the University of California: Berkeley and joined Drexel, Burnham, Lambert in 1970. He led the firm into the 1980s, using high-risk, high-yield bonds to finance corporate takeovers. Condemned by some for virtually inventing these "junk bonds" – bonds secured by little more than the future promises of the very companies the bonds were being used to take over – he was praised by others for shaking up complacent American businesses. In April 1989 he admitted to fraud and racketeering charges and served time in prison before being freed in 1993.

Millar, Kenneth (John Macdonald, John Ross Macdonald, Ross Macdonald, pen names) (1915–83) writer; born in Los Gatos, Calif. He studied at the University of Western Ontario (B.A. 1938), the University of Toronto (1938–39), and the University of Michigan (M.A. 1943; Ph.D. 1951). He taught history and English at the Kitchener Collegiate Institute, Ontario (1939–41), and at the University of Michigan (1942–44; 1948–49). Best known as Ross Mac-

donald, he is credited with turning the detective novel genre into a literary form. His best-known creation, the hard-boiled detective, Miles Archer, is named after Sam Spade's partner in *The Maltese Falcon* by Dashiell Hammett. Millar won many awards for such work as *The Wycherly Woman* (1961), *The Zebra-Striped Hearse* (1962), and *The Chill* (1964). Beginning in 1945 he lived in Santa Barbara, Calif.

Millay, Edna St. Vincent (m. Boissevain) (Nancy Boyd, pen name) (1892–1950) poet, writer; born in Rockland, Maine. She graduated from Vassar (1917), married (1923), and worked as a free-lance writer in New York City. She lived in Greenwich Village, wrote plays for the Provincetown Players, and is known for her self-absorbed lyrical poetry, as in her best work, *Renascence and Other Poems* (1917).

Millbank, Jeremiah (1887–1972) business executive, philanthropist; born in New York City. He established his own investment firm on Wall Street in 1926. He founded the Institute for the Crippled and Disabled (1917) – the first rehabilitation center in the U.S.A. – and financed studies on infantile paralysis and diptheria. He financed the production of *King of Kings* (1926–27), the first film on the life of Jesus Christ.

Miller, Aleck "Rice" See WILLIAMSON, SONNY BOY.

Miller, (Alton) Glenn (1904–44) musician; born in Clarinda, Iowa. A trombonist, he attended the University of Colorado before joining Ben Pollack's orchestra in Chicago in 1924. He moved to New York in 1928, where he free-lanced for the next nine years as a studio musician and worked as a sideman with a succession of bandleaders, including Red Nichols, the Dorsey Brothers, and Ray Noble. After his first band failed in 1937, he put together a second orchestra in 1938. For the next four years, with hits such as "Moonlight Serenade" and "In the Mood," it was the most successful dance band of the period. In 1942, he joined the U.S. Air Force, for which he organized the Glenn Miller Army Air Force Band to entertain the troops. While stationed in Europe, he died on a flight from England to France in a plane that disappeared over the English Channel.

Miller, Arthur (1915–) playwright; born in New York City. He graduated from the University of Michigan (1938), where he won a prize for playwrighting. After serving in the U.S. Army in World War II, he enjoyed his first success with a novel, *Focus* (1945). His first play, *The Man Who Had All the Luck* (1944), was a flop, but *All My Sons* (1947) won the New York Drama Critic Circle Award. Two years later, *Death of a Salesman* won both the Drama Critics Circle Award and the Pulitzer Prize; the play, considered his most enduring work and an American classic, depicts the corrosive effects of self-deception on an ordinary man and his family. *An Enemy of the People* (1950) was a new translation of the Ibsen play. *The Crucible* (1953) told of the witch trials in Salem and was seen as a metaphor for his views on contemporary McCarthyite Red-baiting. Later plays include *A View from the Bridge* (1955) and *After the Fall* (1964), widely assumed to be based on his marriage to Marilyn Monroe (1956–60). He wrote an original screenplay, *The Misfits* (1961), which starred Monroe. His later works, including *The American Clock* (1980), met with little enthusiasm in the U.S.A., but he continued to enjoy a wide following in England and his plays are done in translations throughout the world.

Miller, David Hunter (1875–1961) lawyer, diplomat; born in

New York City. A prominent New York lawyer, he commenced his long association with the U.S. State Department as a special assistant (1917–19). He was an adviser to the U.S. delegation to the Paris Peace Conference (1919), and, with Cecil J. B. Hurst, he wrote the final draft of the Covenant of the League of Nations. He was an editor of treaties (1924–44) and a historical adviser to the State Department (1931–38).

Miller, Dorie (1919–43) Pearl Harbor hero; born near Waco, Texas. An African-American messman aboard the USS *Arizona,* he voluntarily manned a machine gun and downed four Japanese planes during the attack on Pearl Harbor (1941). He was awarded the Navy Cross and was killed in action in 1943.

Miller, Henry (Valentine) (1891–1980) writer; born in New York City. Of German-American parentage (young Henry mainly spoke German until he began school), he briefly attended City College of New York (1909), then worked at a variety of jobs, including Western Union (1920–24). He had married in 1917 (and had a daughter in 1919) but was divorced in 1924, immediately marrying his second wife, June Smith, a dancer. He had long aspired to be a writer and had begun to publish book reviews by 1919, but it was 1922 before he commenced writing a novel (never published). Quitting his job in 1924, he turned to anything to support himself as a writer – selling poems door-to-door, managing a speakeasy in Greenwich Village – and then in 1928 went off to Europe hoping to find a publisher. He returned to New York, wrote a third novel (never published), and, his marriage failing, went to Paris in 1930 where he would live famously for the entire decade. Subsisting largely on handouts and some journalism, he became involved with Anaïs Nin, who helped him publish (in Paris) his first major work, *Tropic of Cancer* (1934), heavily autobiographical and so sexually explicit that it was banned in English-speaking countries. (The first American edition did not come out until 1961.) Subsequent books such as *Black Spring* (1936) and *Tropic of Capricorn* (1939) were also banned. As World War II began, he went off to Greece to visit with an early admirer, the writer Lawrence Durrell; out of this came Miller's *Colossus of Maroussi* (1941). Back in the U.S.A., he toured the country – describing the experience in *The Air-Conditioned Nightmare* (1945) – before settling in Big Sur, Calif., in 1944. By now he was living off advances from James Laughlin of New Directions Press, but several of his books began to sell. His *Sexus* (1949) was the first part of a promised trilogy on his life, called *The Rosy Crucifixion,* but only *Nexus* (1960) appeared. By the late-1950s he was finding himself increasingly honored by the literary establishment, and with the legal decision that *Tropic of Cancer* was not obscene, his works began to be republished. He also began to receive some recognition as a water colorist. By the end of his life, he was widely recognized both for breaking down the barriers of censorship and for opening up the possibilities of modern fiction.

Miller, J. (Joseph) Irwin (1909–) automotive manufacturing executive; born in Columbus, Ind. In a 43-year career with the multinational diesel manufacturer, Cummins Engine Company (Columbus, Ind.), he was president (1947–51) and chairman (1951–77). Through the company's foundation, he sponsored designs by distinguished architects for many of the public buildings that make Columbus a mecca for students of modern architecture.

Miller, Jean Baker (1927–) psychiatrist; born in New York City. She taught at Boston University and the State University of New York Upstate Medical Center. Her interest in female psychology resulted in several ground-breaking books, including (as editor) *Psychoanalysis and Women: Contributions to New Theory and Therapy* (1973) and her *Toward a New Psychology of Women* (1976).

Miller, Joaquin (b. Cincinnatus Hiner [or Heine] Miller) (1839–1913) poet, writer; born in Liberty, Ind. He moved to Oregon (1850) and drifted around mining camps in northern California before he became a lawyer (1861). He practiced law (1863–66), and was a judge (1866–70), by which time his poetry was gaining him some reputation. He moved to London (1870–71), then traveled for many years before settling in California (1887). Most of his plays, novels, and poetry drew on themes of the American West and his reputation as a serious poet did not long survive.

Miller, Joyce (Dannen) (1928–) labor leader; born in Chicago. A staff member of the Amalgamated Clothing Workers in Chicago (1952–1972), she was elected international vice-president of the Amalgamated Clothing and Textile Workers Union in 1976, and president of the Coalition of Labor Union Women in 1977.

Miller, Kelly (1863–1939) civil rights activist, educator; born in Winnsboro, S.C. Son of a slave mother and a free black father, he graduated from Howard University (1886), and after studying science at Johns Hopkins, returned to teach at Howard (1890–1934). He earned a law degree from the school (1903). For most of his career at Howard he chaired the sociology department; he was also dean of the College of Arts and Sciences and held other posts. He assisted W. E. B. DuBois in editing the journal, *Crisis,* and he wrote many essays and several books, including *Out of the House of Bondage* (1917), emphasizing the progress African-Americans had made since emancipation and the role of education in attaining full equality. One of the major African-American spokesmen and teachers of the early 20th century, he was considered a voice of reason and moderation in the struggle for equal rights.

Miller, Kenneth Hayes (1876–1952) painter, teacher; born in Oneida, N.Y. He traveled in Europe (1900), returned to New York City, continued to paint, and, most importantly, began his intermittent teaching career at the Art Students League (1911–51). His paintings are classically composed with richly glazed colors, as in *The Fitting Room* (1931). He was a teacher who influenced many artists, including Isabelle Bishop, Edward Hopper, and Reginald Marsh.

Miller, Marvin (Julian) (1917–) economist, labor leader; born in New York City. His father helped to organize fellow employees in retail stores where he worked and young Marvin grew up as a Dodger fan before taking his B.S. degree in economics from Miami University (Ohio) (1938). During World War II he was an economist and disputes hearing officer for the Wage Stabilization Board. After working for the International Association of Machinists (1947–50) he went to Pittsburgh to work for the United Steel Workers of America (1950–66), where he gained a national reputation for his intelligent negotiations between labor and management. In 1966 he was chosen executive director of the somewhat dormant Major Leagues Baseball Players' Association; with the club owners reluctantly going along, he set up collective bargaining procedures, helped to establish free agency and arbitration, and greatly increased salaries and pensions for the players. In 1972 he directed the first general strike in baseball history (resulting in 86 canceled games) and again in 1981 he led a players' strike that lasted 59 days (713 games canceled). He retired from the post in 1983, having led baseball players through the most expansive period in the history of the game.

Miller, Merton H. (1923–) economist; born in Boston, Mass. With Franco Modigliani he established the controversial "Modigliani-Miller theorems," which applied economic theory to the field of finance. The theorems assert that under perfect competition both the market value of a firm and the cost of capital to the firm are independent of its debt-equity ratio as well as its dividend-payout ratio. He was on the faculty of the University of Chicago beginning in 1965.

Miller, (Mitchell William) Mitch (1911–) oboist, conductor, record producer; born in Rochester, N.Y. Throughout the 1930s and 1940s he played the oboe with distinction for symphony orchestras and as a free-lancer. His contacts with recording companies led him in 1950 to join Columbia Records and he moved from the classical repertoire to scouting and producing such popular performers as Doris Day and Johnny Mathis; his greatest hit single was "Yellow Rose of Texas" (1955). From 1961–66, he had his own television program on the National Broadcasting Company, "Sing Along With Mitch"; with its folksy choristers and his own robust manner, it initiated a brief fad in singing along with traditional music before rock music took over. He went on to become a guest conductor with various symphony orchestras.

Miller, Perry (Gilbert Eddy) (1905–63) literary historian, educator; born in Chicago. He was educated at the University of Chicago and taught American history at Harvard (1931–63), with time out to serve in World War II. He pioneered the serious historical study of colonial literature and theology in his most influential work, *The New England Mind: The Seventeenth Century* (1939), reinterpreting the Puritans through the lens of intellectual history. His studies of Jonathan Edwards (1949), and Roger Williams (1953) and other published works established Miller as a preeminent American intellectual historian.

Miller, Samuel (1769–1850) Protestant clergyman, educator; born near Dover, Del. He studied at the University of Pennsylvania and held Presbyterian pastorates in New York City before becoming a professor at Princeton Theological Seminary, which he helped found. In a long scholarly life he published widely on religion and history, including *Thoughts on Public Prayer* (1849).

Miller, Samuel Freeman (1816–90) Supreme Court justice; born in Richmond, Ky. Initially a medical doctor, he read law and was admitted to Kentucky's bar in 1847. He was an early organizer of the Republican Party and was named to the U.S. Supreme Court by President Abraham Lincoln (1862–90).

Miller, Webb (1892–1940) foreign correspondent; born near Pokagon, Mich. His reports from Mexico during the Pancho Villa crisis helped land him, in 1916, a lifelong job with the United Press. A World War I correspondent, he became general manager for European news in the crucial years preceding World War II. His book *I Have Found No Peace* (1936) expressed disillusionment with modern technology and politics.

Miller, William (1782–1849) religious leader; born in Pittsfield, Mass. A farmer, minor officeholder, and militia veteran of the War of 1812, he underwent a religious conversion around 1816 and convinced himself – and, eventually, thousands of followers – that the Second Coming of Christ was imminent. He became a licensed Baptist preacher in 1833. His Millerite (Adventist) movement peaked in 1843 and declined rapidly when Christ failed to appear as predicted between the period March 1843 to March 1844. His followers, however, organized the Seventh Day Adventist movement in 1863.

Millet, Francis (Davis) (1846–1912) painter, writer; born in Mattapoisett, Mass. He studied art in Antwerp, Belgium (1871–73), and traveled widely, but was based in New York City. A war correspondent for several periodicals during the Russo-Turkish War (1877) and in the Philippines (1899), he painted historical genre scenes. He was the coauthor, with Poultney Bigelow, of *From the Black Forest to the Black Sea* (1893). He died when the ocean liner *Titanic* sank (1912).

Millett, (Katherine Murray) Kate (1934–) writer, political activist, artist; born in St. Paul, Minn. Her Columbia University Ph.D. dissertation, published as *Sexual Politics* (1970), catapulted her to national prominence in the feminist movement. A professor, prolific author, and artist, she founded the Women's Art Colony Farm and exhibited her paintings internationally.

Millikan, Clark (Blanchard) (1903–66) physicist, aerodynamicist; born in Chicago, Ill. Enthusiastic and outgoing, he played a major role in the worldwide development of aeronautical and space programs. He helped the California Institute of Technology become a major force in aeronautical education and research (1928–66), establishing a graduate school of aeronautics (1925), offering the first course in jet propulsion (1945), and cofounding the Jet Propulsion Laboratory.

Millikan, Robert A. (Andrews) (1868–1953) physicist; born in Morrison, Ill. He was a faculty member at the University of Chicago (1896–1921), then moved to the California Institute of Technology (1921–46). He determined the charge on the electron (1909), then confirmed Einstein's quantum photoelectric equation. These two achievements won Millikan the 1923 Nobel Prize in physics. In 1925 he coined the term "cosmic rays," and proposed, but later rejected, their function as the "building blocks" of atoms.

Milliken, Roger (1915–) textile executive; born in New York City. He spent his career at Milliken & Co., the family textile manufacturer and wholesaler. As president (1947–83) and chairman and CEO (1983), he made Milliken an industry leader by promoting research and development and pioneering automated manufacturing. He was a noted antiunion employer who fought an unfair labor practice suit for 24 years before finally losing in the Supreme Court in 1980.

Milliken, William (1922–) governor; born in Traverse City, Mich. An army veteran, he ran his family's department store (1946–60), then served in the Michigan senate. Republican lieutenant governor (1964–69), he succeeded George Romney as governor (1969–83), increasing state funding for education and social welfare programs; a supporter of women's rights, he backed the equal rights amendment. After leaving office he became a consultant in Traverse City.

Millikin, Eugene D. (Donald) (1891–1958) U.S. senator; born in Hamilton, Ohio. He practiced law in Denver, Colo., before he was appointed and then elected to the U.S. Senate (Rep., Colo.; 1941–57). Politically unknown before his appointment, he soon became recognized as a thorough conservative and isolationist. He espoused Colorado's irrigation needs while he was on the Interior Committee.

Mills, C. (Charles) Wright (1916–62) sociologist; born in Waco, Texas. A radical humanist and professor of sociology at Columbia University (1946–62), he was a leading critic of American society who became controversial for his rejection of value-free, scientific sociology in favor of socially responsible social science. He was in the vanguard of the 1950s radical revival. His important works include *White Collar* (1951), *The Power Elite* (1956), *The Sociological Imagination* (1959), and "Letter to the New Left" (1960).

Mills, Clark (1810–83) sculptor, bronze founder; born near Syracuse, N.Y. He had little formal education, moved to Charleston, S.C. (1837), and settled in Washington, D.C. (1850). He is known for establishing an early bronze foundry where he cast his sculptures, such as the equestrian statue of Gen. Andrew Jackson (1853), situated in Lafayette Square, Washington, D.C.

Mills, Donald See under MILLS BROTHERS.

Mills, Enos Abijah (1870–1922) naturalist, author; born near Kansas City, Kans. A frail child, he went to Colorado for his health at age 14, fell under the spell of the mountains, and settled in a homesteader's cabin at the foot of Long's Peak. A chance meeting with John Muir turned him to the systematic study of natural history. He became a writer, lecturer, mountain guide, and, from 1901, innkeeper – his Long's Peak Inn became a haven for nature lovers. His lobbying efforts led to the establishment of the Rocky Mountain National Park in 1915.

Mills, Florence (1895–1927) entertainer, singer; born in Washington, D.C. She was appearing in musicals by age 5, toured with two sisters in vaudeville at age 15, then gained notice in 1916 singing in the Panama Trio. Her big break came when she replaced the lead in the all-black hit musical, *Shuffle Along* (1921); she went on to star in such Broadway musicals as *Plantation Revue* (1922) and *Dixie to Broadway* (1924); by this time she was also a star in London and Paris. She was most famous for her rendition of "I'm a Little Blackbird Looking for a Bluebird" but she also sang a solo written especially for her in William Grant Still's orchestral work, *Levee Land* (1926). Petite, gorgeous, completely in command on stage, she was greatly mourned when she died prematurely.

Mills, Harry See under MILLS BROTHERS.

Mills, Herbert See under MILLS BROTHERS.

Mills, John Jr., See under MILLS BROTHERS.

Mills, Robert (1781–1855) architect; born in Charleston, S.C. America's first native-born professional architect, he trained with Hoban and Latrobe and was a chief exponent of the Greek Revival style. He was South Carolina state engineer and architect (1820–30) and architect of public buildings in Washington, D.C. (1836–42). His humane and enlightened designs for hospitals were used nationwide for 40 years. Mills designed the Washington Monument, Washington, D.C. (1848–84).

Mills, Roger Quarles (1832–1911) U.S. representative, senator; born in Todd County, Ky. A Confederate Army Colonel, he served in the U.S. House of Representatives (Dem., Texas; 1873–92), chairing the Committee on Ways and Means. He left to fill a vacancy in the Senate (1892–99), retiring to Corsicana, Texas.

Mills, Wilbur (Daigh) (1909–92) U.S. representative; born in Kensett, Ark. A graduate of Harvard University law school, he was a Democratic county and probate judge in White County, Ark. (1934–38) before going to the U.S. House of Representatives (1939–77). He chaired the powerful Committee on Ways and Means (1957–73) and the Joint Committee on Internal Revenue before personal scandal forced him to resign. In 1977 he became a tax consultant for the Washington office of a New York law firm.

Mills Brothers, The: John, Jr. (1910–36) born in Bellefontaine, Ohio; **Herbert** (1912–89) born in Piqua, Ohio; **Harry** (1913–82) born in Piqua, Ohio; **Donald** (1915–   ) born in Piqua, Ohio; vocal group. Famous for their smooth harmonies and for imitating instruments with their voices, from the 1930s to 1950s they appeared in films and had many hit songs, including "Paper Doll" (1943). Although not especially innovative, the Mills Brothers were among the early African-American musical groups that enjoyed a following among mainstream white Americans. Not generally known is that when John, Jr. died in 1936, his father, John, Sr. (1882–1967; born in Bellefont, Pa.) stepped in until the mid-1950s; thereafter the surviving brothers performed as a trio into the 1970s.

Milner, (Moses Embree) "California Joe" (1829–76) frontier figure, scout; born near Stanford, Ky. He went west in 1849 and served in the Civil War. He was a scout for Gen. George Custer (1868), Col. Dodge (1875), and the Fifth Cavalry (1876). He was killed by a civilian who bore him a grudge. He was known as an "invaluable guide and Indian fighter" while sober.

Milnes, Sherrill (Eustace) (1935–   ) baritone; born in Downers Grove, Ill. American-trained, Milnes made his Metropolitan Opera debut in *Faust* in 1965 and became one of the favorites at that house. He is admired as much for his dramatic abilities as for his striking voice, his celebrated roles including Don Giovanni and Iago.

Milnor, John W. (Willard) (1931–   ) mathematician; born in Orange, N.J. A noted teacher, he was at the Institute for Advanced Study, Princeton, beginning in 1970. Recipient of the National Medal of Science (1967) and member of the National Academy of Science, his specialties were the topology of manifolds and dynamical systems.

Milosz, Czeslaw (1911–   ) poet, man of letters; born in Szetejnie, Lithuania. A founder of the "catastrophist" school of Polish poetry, cofounder of the literary periodical *Zagary,* and author of a book of essays called *The Captive Mind,* he was a leader of the avant-garde before World War II. During the war he worked for the Warsaw underground and was a member of the Polish diplomatic service (1946–50). Rejecting the Communist government, he exiled himself to Paris to write (1951–60); he won the Prix Littéraire Européen (1953). He emigrated to America (1960) where he joined the University of California: Berkeley faculty as a professor of Slavic languages and literature (1961), and was named professor emeritus (1978). Although his poetry was considered dense and full of cultural-linguistic allusions, its depth of soul won over the literary critics who awarded him the Nobel Prize in literature (1980). He continued to write and do translations in retirement, publishing 11 books (1980–91).

Milstein, Nathan (1904–92) violinist; born in Odessa, Russia. After childhood studies, he toured Russia with pianist Vladimir Horowitz. Making his American debut in St. Louis in 1929, he remained based in the U.S.A. while pursuing an international career as a virtuoso noted for his technical mastery, especially in the Romantic repertoire.

Minarik, Else Holmelund (1920–   ) writer; born in Denmark. Her family emigrated to the United States (1924), and she studied at Queens College and New Paltz College of the State University of New York. She worked as a reporter and teacher, then became known for her children's books, primarily the *Little Bear* (1957) series, illustrated by Maurice Sendak.

Mingus, Charles (1922–79) jazz musician; born in Nogales, Ariz. He was a virtuoso bassist and innovative composer who worked as a sideman with Louis Armstrong, Lionel Hampton, and Red Norvo between 1941 and 1953. He formed his first band in 1954 and led large and small ensembles, which he called Jazz Workshops, thereafter. He was a passionate campaigner for civil rights. His autobiography, *Beneath the Underdog,* was published in 1971.

Minnelli, Vincente (1910–86) film director; born in Chicago (husband of Judy Garland, father of Liza Minnelli). He left school at age 16 and by 1933 was art director of Radio City Music Hall. He became a Broadway director in 1935, and went to Hollywood in 1940, becoming an outstanding director of film musicals of sweeping scope and lavish visual style. He also did comedy and drama. Among his films were *The Clock* (1945), *Kismet* (1955), and his Oscar winner *Gigi* (1958).

Minoka-Hill, Lillie Rose (1876–1952) physician; born on the St. Regis reservation in New York State. Daughter of a Mohawk mother and Philadelphia physician, Joshua G. Allen, she was raised on the reservation until age 5, then was educated in Philadelphia. She attended the Woman's Medical College of Pennsylvania (graduating 1899). She worked at a clinic and in private practice before marrying an Oneida, Charles Hill, in 1905; he took her to his farm in Oneida, Wis., expecting her to give up her career but gradually she returned to practicing medicine. She served the Oneida people of Wisconsin until 1952 with a combination of Western and Native American medicine.

Minor, Robert (1884–1952) cartoonist, radical activist; born in San Antonio, Texas. A distant relative of Sam Houston, he was an editorial cartoonist for the *St. Louis Post-Dispatch* (1904) who joined the Socialist Party (1907), but was drawn to anarchism. After visiting France (1912), he became a cartoonist for the *New York World* (1913), but was fired after doing a cartoon for the radical *Mother Earth.* He was hired by the Socialist *New York Call* (1915) and then joined John Reed and Boardman Robinson, covering the Eastern Front in Europe. He visited Mexico to cover the Pancho Villa episode (1916) and went to Moscow (1918), where he became disillusioned with Leninism, if not Lenin, whom he met. Visiting France, he was almost executed by the United States military there on charges of undermining military morale. Speaking and writing on the Russian Revolution (1920), he joined the new Communist Party and soon became a member of its hierarchy. He attended the Communist International as a delegate (1922–24), edited the *Daily Worker* (1928–30), and championed the cause of American blacks and the unemployed. He was arrested for illegal assembly after a labor demonstration in New York's Union Square, and was sentenced to three years in prison (1930); he served about six months. He ran unsuccessfully as the Communist candidate for governor of New York (1932) and the next year for the mayor of New York City. An unsuccessful candidate for one of New York's U.S. Senate seats (1936), he went to Spain as both a war correspondent for the *Daily Worker* and as the American Party's commissar in the International Brigades. Returning home (1937), he became acting general secretary of America's Communist Party (1940); he promoted U.S. involvement in World War II and worked with the Roosevelt administration to change U.S. policy toward Chinese Communists. Repudiating many of his earlier beliefs after the war, he lost credibility in the party, but assisted in defense of its leaders who had been arrested under the Smith Act of 1940 and were jailed (1951).

Minot, George R. (Richards) (1885–1950) hematologist; born in Boston, Mass. He was on the medical staff of several American hospitals (1912–23) before joining Harvard Medical School (1928–48). Minot and colleague William Murphy shared one-half the 1935 Nobel Prize in physiology for their successful treatment of heretofore fatal pernicious anemia with dietary liver and liver extract. Minot's other major contributions to hematology include developing iron treatment for hypochromic anemia (1931–32) and demonstrating that hemophilia is related to the absence of a plasma globulin (1946).

Minow, Martha L. (Louise) (1954–   ) legal scholar; born in Highland Park, Ill. She taught at Harvard (1981) and is best known for her work on family law. Her major publication is *Making All the Difference* (1990).

Minow, Newton (Norman) (1926–   ) lawyer, communications executive; born in Milwaukee, Wis. A Chicago lawyer, he was named chairman of the Federal Communications Commission (FCC) by President Kennedy (1961–63). He gained unexpected publicity for such a post by attacking the quality of television broadcasting and threatening to revoke broadcast licenses based on programming. Returning to his law practice afterward, he joined the Public Broadcasting System board in 1973, becoming chairman in 1978. In 1987 he became director of the Annenberg Communications Program in Washington.

Minsky, Marvin (1927–   ) electrical engineer, mathematician, educator; born in New York City. A pioneer in the field of artificial intelligence, as early as 1951 he built a "learning machine" to try to demonstrate that what we call mind is composed of mindless parts. In 1958 he became an assistant professor of mathematics at the Massachusetts Institute of Technology, and in 1974, professor in the department of electrical engineering and computer science.

Minton, Sherman (1890–1965) Supreme Court justice; born near Georgetown, Ind. As a U.S. senator (Dem., Ind.; 1935), he promoted New Deal legislation and rose to assistant majority whip. He became a judge on the U.S. Circuit Court of Appeals (1941–49) until President Harry Truman named him to the Supreme Court (1949–56).

Mintz, Beatrice (Stein) (1921–   ) embryologist; born in New York City. She taught at the University of Chicago (1946–60), then joined the Fox Chase Institute of Cancer Research in Philadelphia (1960). She made major advances in studies of experimental genetic control of skin pigment phenotypes in mouse embryo chimeras, and explored the implications of totipotency in mouse tumor cells.

Minuit, Peter (?1580–1638) colonist; born in Wesel, Rhenish Prussia (now Germany). He became the first director-general of New Amsterdam. In 1626 he purchased Manhattan Island from Algonquin Indians for 60 guilders (24 dollars). Later, he led an expedition under the Swedish flag and created the short-lived "New Sweden" in present-day Delaware.

Mises, Richard Von (1883–1953) mathematician; born in Lemberg, Austria. Emigrating to America to teach (1939), he settled at Harvard (1944–53). A major contributor to the mechanics of powered flight, he also worked in probability and statistics, developing the Von Mises limiting-frequency theory. His statistical writings are considered semipopular.

Mitchel, John (Purroy) (1879–1918) mayor; born in Fordham, N.Y. Grandson of the ardent Irish nationalist, John Mitchel, he was a lawyer who came to prominence as a special investigator of New York City officials (1906). Running as a fusion candidate, he won the New York mayoralty in 1913, the youngest mayor in the city's history. He introduced a number of much-needed civic reforms, including a program of tax relief, but he was brought down in the 1917 election by the perception that he was undemocratic, along with allegations of scandal. He died in an airplane accident while training for the Aviation Corps in World War I.

Mitchell, Arthur (1934–) ballet dancer, choreographer; born in New York City. Trained at the School of American Ballet, he became the first African-American dancer to become a full member of the New York City Ballet (1956). In 1968 he began working toward his vision of a classical ballet school for young African-Americans; by 1970 he was opening the Dance Theater of Harlem, which soon was producing dancers capable of performing both classic and original dances. He continued to direct the internationally renowned school and company.

Mitchell, Arthur W. (Wergs) (1883–1968) U.S. representative; born near Lafayette, Ala. Growing up on a farm, in 1897 he went to Tuskegee Institute, where he worked as an office boy for Booker T. Washington. He taught in rural schools in Georgia and Alabama and then founded and served ten years as president of the Armstrong Agricultural School in West Butler, Ala. He studied law, was admitted to the bar in 1927, and began practicing in Washington, D.C., before moving to Chicago (1929), where he engaged in the real estate business while practicing law. Like most African-Americans up to that time, he had entered political life as a Republican, but with President Roosevelt's New Deal he switched to the Democratic Party. In 1934 he defeated the venerable Republican African-American Oscar De Priest, to become the first Democratic African-American in the U.S. House of Representatives (Ill., 1935–43). An outspoken liberal, he denounced the Italian invasion of Ethiopia and nominated black youths to the U.S. military academies. After he had been forced out of a Pullman car in Arkansas, he sued for the right of African-Americans to receive the same accommodations as whites in interstate transportation, and argued his case before the U.S. Supreme Court (*Mitchell vs. United States et al.*, 1941), although it was 1955 before the practice was changed. He continued to fight for the rights of African-Americans – in 1942 proposing to outlaw all poll taxes on the grounds that if blacks could fight for the U.S. they were entitled to vote. On leaving the House he settled in Petersburg, Va., and remained active as a lecturer and with such organizations as the Southern Regional Council.

Mitchell, Charles E. (Edwin) (1877–1955) banker; born in Chelsea, Mass. An Amherst graduate (1899), in 1906 he joined the Trust Company of America in New York City, then ran his own investment house, C. E. Mitchell Company (1911–16). Becoming vice-president of National City Company, an affiliate of National City Bank in 1916, he turned it into a private investment banking firm with 50 branches in the U.S.A. and Europe. By 1921 he was president of both the investment affiliate and the National City Bank; by 1929 he was chairman of the parent organization. A bullish speculator, he flaunted a $25 million advance to traders when the Federal Reserve Bank was attempting to curb speculation in 1929; after the great crash, he was investigated by a U.S. Senate committee and admitted to speculating on the bank's securities. Forced to resign in 1933, he was the first witness in the Gray-Pecora Wall Street probe (1932–34), which uncovered abuses by Mitchell and the National City Bank that appalled even the financial community and brought an end to ownership of investment affiliates by commercial banks. In 1938 he paid the government $1.4 million in interest and penalties for tax evasion. But his investment banking career continued with Blyth and Company (chairman of the board, 1935) and C. E. Mitchell, Incorporated (until 1941) and he held directorships with the National Bank of Haiti and the ITT Corporation, among other companies.

Mitchell, George (John) (1933–) U.S. senator; born in Waterville, Maine. Having served as U.S. attorney and U.S. district judge in Maine, he was elected to the U.S. Senate (Dem., Maine; 1980–95). Elected senate majority leader in 1989, he actively supported environmental legislation and liberal tax reform measures. He achieved national fame during the Senate's Iran-Contra investigation for his skillful interrogation of Oliver North.

Mitchell, Joan (1926–) painter; born in Chicago. Child of a physician father and a mother who was a poet and coeditor of *Poetry* magazine, she studied for two years at Smith College, then transferred to the Art Institute of Chicago to paint full time. Coming to New York City in 1947, she became one of the early abstract expressionists and gained considerable recognition. In 1959 she moved to Paris, then in 1967 to Vetheuil, a village about one hour northwest of Paris where Monet once lived (1878–81). She continued to paint in the abstract expressionist manner, although adopting a sunnier palette and more lyrical mode, and in her attempts to convey the realm of nature – as in *No Birds* (1987–88) or *Wind* (1990) – she seemed to echo French impressionism.

Mitchell, John (1870–1919) labor leader; born in Braidwood, Ill. Having worked in coal mines from the age of 12, he joined the Knights of Labor in 1885. He was a founding member of the United Mine Workers (1890), helped in its first successful national strike (1897), and served as its president (1899–1908), a period in which the union expanded its membership tenfold. He was chairman of the New York State Industrial Commission (1915–19).

Mitchell, John (Galvin) (1931–) writer; born in Cincinnati, Ohio. He graduated from Yale (B.A. 1954) and became a journalist for a variety of newspapers, including the *New*

York Journal-American (1958–65). A science editor and swing writer for *Newsweek* (1965–68), he was a member of the New York City Landmarks Preservation Commission (1966–68). His essays, articles, and historical sketches have appeared in numerous periodicals, notably in *Audubon,* where he was a free-lance editor (1976–91). A writer specializing in natural resource interpretation and historical geography, he is noted for such books as *The Hunt* (1980), and *The Man Who Would Dam the Amazon and Other Accounts From Afield* (1990). He lived in Redding, Conn.

Mitchell, John, Jr. (1863–1929) publisher, banker; born in Laburnam, Va. He left high school in 1880 and taught until he and several others were dismissed for protesting in the *Planet,* a Richmond newspaper started by 13 former slaves, the expected dismissal of several African-American principals (1884). Mitchell became editor and manager of the *Planet,* for which he organized the Planet Printing Company. After a creditor's suit and sale of the newspaper for $400 to a friend, the newspaper was turned over to Mitchell who edited it until 1929, used it to attack the race question, and made it one of the few successful African-American newspapers of its time. In 1890 he entered politics, becoming political boss of the African-American section of Richmond (Jackson Ward) and prominent in the Knights of Pythias (a parallel organization to the white one bearing the same name) and its related orders (1898–1929). Then, in a move around which there is considerable mystery, in 1899 or 1900, he abdicated his position among African-Americans and began supporting his white associates. In 1902 he founded Mechanics Savings Bank, which failed in 1922 resulting in criminal charges against him that were later dropped. In 1920 he ran for governor of Virginia on an all-black ticket and was defeated.

Mitchell, John (Newton) (1913–88) lawyer, cabinet member; born in Detroit, Mich. A wealthy New York investment lawyer (1936–68), he specialized in municipal bonds. Richard Nixon's 1968 campaign manager and attorney general (1969–73), he used illegal surveillance methods against student radicals and black activists. Convicted of obstruction of justice in the Watergate investigation, he served two years in prison (1977–79).

Mitchell, Joni (b. Roberta Joan Anderson) (1943–) singer, songwriter; born in Fort McLeod, Alberta, Canada. Emerging in the 1960s as one of the more sensitive of the folk/ballad singers, she wrote most of her own lyrics and music and had several hits such as "The Circle Game" (1966), "Both Sides Now" (1967), and "Woodstock" (1969). During the 1970s she toured and produced best-selling albums such as *Ladies of the Canyon* (1971), and began adding pop and jazz elements to her style. This new phase was not well received, and in the 1980s she went back to her original style of poetic-personal songs, which by then had influenced a whole generation of women singers.

Mitchell, Lucy (b. Sprague) (1878–1967) educator; born in Chicago. Child of a wealthy businessman, she had a difficult youth but she gradually obtained an education and came to know and be influenced by John Dewey, Jane Addams, and Alice Freeman Palmer, herself a prominent educator. It was the latter who encouraged Lucy Sprague to come to attend Radcliffe College in 1896. After graduation, she went to California where in 1906 she became dean of women and assistant professor of English at the University of Califor-

nia: Berkeley. After her marriage in 1912 to Wesley Clair Mitchell, an economist, the couple moved to New York City where she concentrated on the education of children – specifically, on investigating the best and most up-to-date approaches. With the support of her cousin, Elizabeth Sprague Coolidge, she cofounded the Bureau of Educational Experiments in 1916 and directed it until 1956; by 1950 it had become the Bank Street College of Education. She also cofounded (1931) the Cooperative School for Teachers. Both institutions had widespread influence in educational practice. She also wrote or coauthored or edited 20 books for children and six books for adults, including an autobiography/biography *Two Loves: The Story of Wesley Clair Mitchell and Myself* (1953).

Mitchell, Margaret (Munnerlyn) (Peggy Mitchell, Margaret Mitchell Upshaw, Elizabeth Bennett, pen names) (1900–49) writer; born in Atlanta, Ga. She studied at Smith (1918–19), married Berrien Upshaw (1922; annulled 1924), and became a journalist for the *Atlanta Journal* (1922–26). She married John Marsh in 1925 and in 1926 began working on fiction. After several false starts, she wrote what was to become one of the all-time best-selling American novels, *Gone With the Wind* (1936). It won the Pulitzer Prize (1937) and was made into an immensely popular film (1939). She never wrote another novel and died prematurely after being struck by an automobile.

Mitchell, Maria (1818–89) astronomer; born in Nantucket, Mass. Daughter of an amateur astronomer, she grew up with a love of mathematics and practical experience in astronomical observations. In 1836 she became librarian of the Nantucket Atheneum, and her 20 years there would provide the intellectual stimulus in lieu of a college education. She continued to help her father make observations of stars, work recognized by the U.S. Coast Survey. Then in 1847 she discovered a new comet, and this led to a gold medal from the King of Denmark as well as her becoming the first woman elected to the American Academy of Arts and Sciences (1848), the American Association for the Advancement of Science (1850), and the American Philosophical Society (1869). After a trip to Europe (1857–58), she was presented with a fine telescope by a group of progressive women. When the Vassar Female College was founded, she became the first professor of astronomy there (1865–88) and while earning the reputation as an inspiring teacher – many of her students became prominent in the sciences and other professions – she continued her own researches, mainly into the solar system. A founder of the Association for the Advancement of Women (1873), she was its president (1875–76) and chaired the science committee until her death. She continued to stress the desirability of including both women and the scientific method in all aspects of life.

Mitchell, Sidney Z. (Zollicoffer) (1862–1944) public utility executive; born in Dadeville, Ala. A graduate of the U.S. Naval Academy (1883), he resigned his commission in the navy (1885) – where he installed incandescent lights aboard his ship – and moved to Seattle as Thomas Edison's Northwest sales representative. There he organized 13 lighting companies. Challenged by the problem of financing costly utility development, he helped establish the Electric Bond & Share Company (1905), a utility holding and financial management company; by 1924 it controlled over 10 percent of the U.S. electric utility business. He established the

American & Foreign Power Company (1923), which controlled utility companies throughout Latin America.

Mitchell, Silas Weir (1829–1914) physician, writer, poet; born in Philadelphia. After taking his M.D. from Jefferson Medical College, he continued his medical studies in France, then returned to Philadelphia to practice. During the Civil War, he served as a surgeon for the Union army and collaborated on an important work, *Gunshot Wounds and Other Injuries of Nerves* (1864). In the ensuing decades he specialized in neurology and wrote some 120 articles in that field, but he also did work in toxicology, physiology, and pharmacology. He was a pioneer in advocating the "rest cure" and other psychological approaches to nervous conditions, and he made the Philadelphia Orthopedic Hospital into a major center for treating nervous disorders. Meanwhile, he had been writing fiction and poetry since the end of the Civil War; his first published story, "The Case of George Dedlow" (1866), was notable for conveying the mental state of a soldier about to enter combat. His collected works would eventually add up to 16 volumes, including once widely read novels such as *Roland Blake* (1886) and *Hugh Wayne, Free Quaker* (1897), greatly admired for their psychological insights.

Mitchell, (William) "Billy" (1879–1936) aviation pioneer; born in Nice, France. Son of a U.S. senator, he grew up in Milwaukee, enlisted for service in the Spanish-American War and received a Signal Corps commission in 1901. Assigned to the aviation section in 1916, Mitchell learned to fly the following year and immediately became a forceful and outspoken advocate of military air power. In France in September 1918, he commanded the largest concentration of aircraft – some 1,500 warplanes – in aviation's brief history. In 1921 and 1923 the energetic Mitchell arranged for aircraft to demonstrate the potential of the new arm by sinking obsolete warships at sea; unconvinced, the authorities continued to grade air power low on the priority list. Mitchell provoked a court-martial by his continuing and insistent criticism of his superiors, whom he accused of negligence and even treason. Convicted of insubordination, he resigned from the army in February 1926. As a civilian, he continued to promote his vision of air power's importance in warfare. World War II brought him full posthumous vindication.

Mitchill, Samuel (Latham) (1764–1831) U.S. representative/senator, physician; born in North Hempstead, N.Y. He earned his M.D. in Edinburgh, Scotland, in 1786, then returned to New York to study law. In 1792 he was named to a chair at Columbia University, first in natural history, chemistry, and agriculture, then in botany. He edited the *Medical Repository* (1797–1820), wrote many books including the *Explanation of the Synopsis of Chemical Nomenclature and Arrangement* (1801), and made contributions to the study of sanitary and industrial chemistry. He was elected to the U.S. House of Representatives (Rep., N.Y.; 1801–04), leaving midterm for the U.S. Senate (1804–09), then returning to the House (1809–13). He taught at the College of Physicians and Surgeons in New York (1807–26) and in 1826 helped found Rutgers Medical College.

Mitropoulos, Dimitri (1896–1960) conductor; born in Athens, Greece. Trained first in Athens, he held conducting posts in Berlin and Paris before making his American debut with the Boston Symphony in 1936. From 1937 to 1949 he conducted the Minneapolis Symphony, then became coconductor of the

New York Philharmonic, its principal conductor from 1951 to 1957. He frequently conducted opera and died during a rehearsal at La Scala in Milan. He was noted for his remarkable technical abilities and for his advocacy of progressive composers. He was also a notable pianist and composer.

Mitscher, Marc (Andrew) (1887–1947) naval aviator; born in Hillsboro, Wis. The son of an Indian agent, he graduated from the Naval Academy in 1910, became an early convert to aviation, and commanded naval air stations during World War I. Taking charge of the new aircraft carrier, USS *Hornet,* in October 1941, "Pete" Mitscher became one of the great carrier group commanders of World War II. From January 1944 on, his Central Pacific carrier force operated as a powerful, self-supporting vanguard as U.S. forces swept toward Japan. Mitscher's force is perhaps best remembered for the "Marianas turkey-shoot" of June 19–21, 1944, in which 400 Japanese aircraft were shot down on the first day of the battle.

Mix, (Thomas) Tom (1880–1940) movie actor; born in Mix Run, Pa. He had been a champion rodeo rider, a soldier, and a cowboy in Oklahoma before he began to make short Western movies in 1909. (Studio publicists would later invent an even more glamorous past – fighting in the Spanish-American War, service with the Texas Rangers, and other such mythical feats.) He went on to star in more than 400 low-budget Westerns with his faithful horse, Tony; there was a daily 15-minute radio show about Tom Mix, enemy of all that was bad in the Old West; in the late 1930s he toured with the Tom Mix Circus. He became very rich and extremely famous, was married five times, and died in a car crash.

Model, Lisette (b. Seybert) (1906–83) photographer, teacher; born in Vienna, Austria. Known for the stark realism of her photos, she emigrated to New York in 1938, free-lancing (1941–53) before becoming a master teacher at the New School (1950–83).

Modigliani, Franco (1918–) economist; born in Rome, Italy. He emigrated to the U.S.A. after receiving a degree from the University of Rome in 1939. He taught at several universities before moving to the Massachusetts Institute of Technology in 1962. In the early 1950s, he originated the "lifecycle hypothesis" which provided a microeconomic foundation in individual behavior for patterns of national savings. With Merton Miller, he established the "Modigliani-Miller theorems," which applied economic theory to the field of finance. He was awarded the Nobel Prize in economics (1985).

Moffett, William (Adger) (1869–1933) naval aviator; born in Charleston, S.C. An 1890 Naval Academy graduate, he served with Admiral George Dewey's fleet at the battle of Manila Bay (1898). Well advanced in a traditional naval career by the second decade of the 20th century, Moffett became an early supporter of naval aviation. As chief of the new Bureau of Aeronautics (1921) he expanded navy flying programs and improved training and equipment; too old to learn to fly, he qualified as an aerial observer instead. He perished in the crash of the dirigible *Akron* in a storm off the New Jersey coast on April 4, 1933.

Moholy-Nagy, László (1895–1946) painter, photographer, sculptor, teacher; born in Bacsbarsod, Hungary. He started painting in Europe (1917), and beginning in 1923, he taught at the Bauhaus School, Germany. Among other projects, he produced abstract photograms, and mobile sculptures, such as *Light-Space Requisite* (1922–30). He emigrated to America, and from 1937 until his death, was the director of the Bauhaus School of Design in Chicago (later called the Chicago Institute of Design) (1939). The author of *Vision in Motion* (1947), he influenced many commercial and design artists.

Moiseiwitsch, Tanya (1914–) set designer; born in London, England. Starting with designs for Dublin's Abbey Theatre between 1935 and 1939, she became associated with the Old Vic, the Shakespeare Memorial Theatre in Stratford-upon-Avon, and the Stratford (Ontario) Festival. From its opening in 1963, she was affiliated with the Guthrie Theatre in Minneapolis. She also designed a number of London's contemporary West End productions.

Moissief, Leon S. (Solomon) (1872–1943) bridge engineer; born in Riga, Latvia. He studied at the Baltic Polytechnic Institute in Riga before emigrating to New York City with his family in 1891. There he studied civil engineering at Columbia University (1892–95) and worked with the New York Department of Bridges (1898–1910). He helped design the Williamsburg, Manhattan, and Queensboro Bridges. As an independent consulting engineer (1915–40), he was involved with suspension-bridge projects including the Delaware River Bridge (Philadelphia); the George Washington, Triborough, and Bronx-Whitestone (N.Y.C.); the Tacoma Narrows (Tacoma, Wash.); and the Mackinac Straits (Mich.). He published numerous influential papers on the design and construction of long-span bridges.

Moley, Raymond (Charles) (1886–1975) lawyer, political scientist; born in Berea, Ohio. A law professor at Columbia University (1928–54), he was Governor Franklin D. Roosevelt's representative on the New York Justice Commission (1931–33). An early member of Roosevelt's "brain trust" in 1933, he commuted from New York City to Washington while helping draft New Deal legislation. A contributing editor to *Newsweek* (1937–68), he became disillusioned with Roosevelt, criticizing him in *After Seven Years* (1939).

Momaday, N. (Navarre) Scott (1934–) Kiowa writer, educator; born in Lawton, Okla. Educated first in Indian schools, he received a Ph.D. from Stanford University in 1963. Committed to preserving in print the oral traditions of many tribes, he won many academic and literary awards and honors. His books include *House Made of Dawn* (1968), which won a Pulitzer Prize, and *The Way to Rainy Mountain* (1969).

Monaghan, Thomas S. (Stephen) (1937–) food franchiser; born in Ann Arbor, Mich. With his brother he took over an ailing Ypsilanti, Mich., pizzeria called Dominick's (1960) and parlayed it into the Domino's Pizza chain – the country's second largest, with 4,200 stores by 1988. He owned the Detroit Tigers baseball team (1983). Among his various interests and philanthropies is his dedication to preserving the work of Frank Lloyd Wright.

Mondale, Walter F. (Frederick) (1928–) vice-president, senator; born in Ceylon, Minn. A follower of Hubert Humphrey, he was appointed to Humphrey's vacant Senate seat in 1964. He supported the Great Society social programs and compiled a strong liberal voting record. As Jimmy Carter's vice-president (1977–1981), he was involved in White House decision-making. He ran for the vice-presidency in 1980 and for the presidency in 1984, losing both elections to the conservative Republican ticket of Reagan-Bush.

Mondell, Frank (Wheeler) (1860–1939) U.S. representative; born in St. Louis, Mo. Orphaned at age seven, he was raised by a minister in rural Iowa before heading west where he prospected for coal and discovered the Cambria coal mine in the late 1880s. In the U.S. House of Representatives (Rep., Wyo.; 1895–97, 1899–1923) he advocated rapid expansion in the West and opposed the conservation efforts of the Forest Service, thereby angering President Theodore Roosevelt.

Monis, Judah (1683–1764) scholar; born in Algiers or Italy. Educated in Jewish schools in Europe, he became a free citizen in New York in 1715 or 1716. The first Jew to earn a degree from Harvard College, he was granted an M.A. there in 1720 on the basis of his draft of a Hebrew grammar, the first to be published in America (1735). He became a Christian convert in 1722 and afterward taught Hebrew at Harvard until 1760.

Monk, Meredith (1943–) dancer, choreographer, musician; born in Lima, Peru. Born while her American mother, a singer, was on tour, she grew up in a musical household. After graduating from Sarah Lawrence College, she joined the Judson Dance Theater (New York City) in the mid-1960s, later founding her own performing arts group, the House (1968). She was a leading member of the "next wave" dance movement and her multimedia "opera epics," *Vessel* (1971) and *Quarry* (1975), which both won Obies, have arresting primitive music composed and "sung" by Monk, whose unique voice spans several octaves. In the 1980s she produced several new multimedia pieces, making her Carnegie Hall debut with *Book of Days* (1985), an ambitious work in progress.

Monk, Thelonious (Sphere) (1917–82) jazz musician; born in Rocky Mount, N.C. He was raised in New York and received piano lessons at age 11. Two years later he accompanied his mother's singing at a local Baptist church and began playing piano at parties in Harlem. He led a trio at a neighborhood bar around 1934, then spent two years touring with an evangelist. He attended Juilliard briefly in the late 1930s and between 1939 and 1944 he worked as a sideman with Keg Purnell, Kenny Clarke, Lucky Millinder, and Kermit Scott. As one of the key innovators of modern jazz, he also appeared regularly in the early 1940s at Minton's Playhouse, Clark Monroe's, and other Harlem after-hours clubs and rehearsal sessions where the rudiments of the new style were being developed. He made his recording debut with Coleman Hawkins in 1944, appearing with the saxophonist's quintet for two years, then played with Dizzy Gillespie's orchestra in 1946. He began leading his own group in 1947 in New York. For the next seven years he recorded for Blue Note and Prestige and was at the height of his creativity as a composer, but he remained an enigmatic, underground figure. In 1951 he was convicted for drug possession and deprived of his cabaret card, which precluded him from working in New York nightclubs for six years. He performed occasionally during this period, including an appearance at the Paris Jazz Fair in 1954, and continue to record as a leader and sideman. In 1957 he returned to New York club work with a celebrated engagement at the Five Spot Cafe featuring his new quartet with John Coltrane, and he appeared on CBS-TV's *The Sound of Jazz* that year. By 1961, when he formed a permanent quartet and began recording for

Columbia Records, many of his compositions had become standards, among them "Round Midnight," "Straight No Chaser," "Blue Monk," and "Ruby My Dear." He toured the U.S.A. continually throughout the 1960s, with first tours of Europe in 1961 and Japan in 1964. In that same year, he was featured in a *Time* magazine cover story, one of only five jazz musicians to have received such distinction. He accepted fewer engagements in the late 1960s, but toured internationally with the Giants of Jazz from 1971 to 1972. He made his last major public appearance at the 1974 Newport Jazz Festival, and thereafter a combination of illness and voluntary inactivity kept him from performing.

Monroe, Earl ("the Pearl") (1944–) basketball player; born in Philadelphia, Pa. After playing at Winston-Salem State University (1964–67), he played as a guard for the Baltimore Bullets and then for the New York Knicks (1971–80), leading the team to a National Basketball Association championship in 1973.

Monroe, Elizabeth (b. Kortright) (1768–1830) First Lady; born in New York City. She married James Monroe in 1786. She was familiar with European society because of Monroe's diplomatic tours. She was considered too aloof and aristocratic during her period as first lady.

Monroe, Harriet (1861–1936) editor, poet; born in Chicago. In 1912 she founded *Poetry: A Magazine of Verse,* the first modern American "little magazine," editing it until 1936 and publishing virtually every American poet of the times. Her own poetry was collected in *Valeria and Other Poems* (1892).

Monroe, James (1758–1831) fifth U.S. president; born in Westmoreland Country, Va. A combat veteran of the American Revolution, he studied law with Thomas Jefferson, who became a lifelong mentor. After serving in the Virginia legislature, Monroe began in 1783 a three-year term in the Confederation Congress; he chaired the committee (1785) that prepared the way for framing the Constitution, though in the end he did not participate in its making and objected to the power it gave the central government. As a U.S. senator (1790–94), he opposed George Washington and the Federalists, but was still appointed ambassador to France (1794–96) until an angry President Washington recalled him for opposing the Jay Treaty. He returned to Virginia as governor (1799–1802); then, as a delegate for President Jefferson in 1803, he helped negotiate the Louisiana Purchase. The next four years were spent in less successful diplomacy in Madrid and London. More offices followed: again governor of Virginia (1811), secretary of state under Madison (1811–17), and also secretary of war (1814–15). Monroe ascended to the presidency in 1817 and was almost unanimously voted a second term in 1820. A popular president in a peaceful time, his administration came to be called "the era of good feeling." Among the notable events of his presidency were gaining Florida from Spain in 1818; the settlement of fishing-rights disputes in Newfoundland and Labrador; and (in 1823) the "Monroe Doctrine," which proclaimed American hostility to any further European colonization or interference in the Americas. The activities of his later years included serving as regent of the University of Virginia (1826–30). His years of public service left him so poor that he had to spend the last months of his life with his daughter in New York City, where he died.

Monroe, Margaret (Ellen) (1914–) librarian; born in New York City. As a public librarian and professor of library science at Rutgers University, she became a recognized authority on adult library services.

Monroe, Marilyn (b. Norma Jean Mortenson) (1926–62) movie actress; born in Los Angeles. For most of her childhood and teen years she was in foster homes or an orphanage because her father abandoned her, while her mother, Gladys Monroe Baker, had to work and then was in a mental hospital. (Norma Jean grew up using her mother's last name, Baker, and at age 16 discovered that her father was probably not Mortenson.) In 1942 she married James Dougherty, an aircraft factory worker, and when he went to sea in the merchant marine she took a job in a target airplane factory. Asked to model to illustrate an article in *Yank* magazine, she soon quit her job to become a full-time model and in 1946, after divorcing Dougherty, she went to Hollywood to try to become an actress. Signed by Twentieth-Century Fox, she changed her name to Marilyn Monroe, but for the next few years she had only minor roles in several movies; during one period of unemployment she posed nude for a pin-up calendar that would later become a collector's item. Not until her small roles in two 1950 movies – *The Asphalt Jungle* and *All About Eve* – did her career take off, and, promoted as a slightly ditzy blonde exuding a breathless sexuality, she became a star and celebrity. She was married to former baseball star Joe DiMaggio for about nine months during 1954, and then, determined to shed her image as a sex symbol, she began to study at Lee and Paula Strasberg's Actors Studio in New York City. She did give two of her more sophisticated performances – in *Bus Stop* (1956) and *Some Like It Hot* (1959) – and she was married to the playwright Arthur Miller (1956–61) and even starred in a movie he wrote for her, *The Misfits* (1961); but her life continued in its roller coaster fashion: she was briefly hospitalized in a mental clinic, she was dropped from a movie for failure to show up on time, and she was taking drugs for her various problems. She took her own life with an overdose of barbiturates, and after several years in which she was discussed almost entirely in terms of a sex goddess, she came to be perceived as a symbol of the exploitation of women by Hollywood and men in general.

Monroe, (William Smith) Bill (1911–) country music singer, mandolin player; born near Rosine, Ky. He played with his uncle, Pen Vandiver, and other local musicians before moving to Chicago in 1929. In 1932, he joined an exhibition square dance team sponsored by radio station WLS, and between 1934 and 1938, he and his brother Charlie Monroe gained national popularity as hillbilly radio singers. In 1938 he formed the Blue Grass Boys and the following year he joined the Grand Ole Opry. Throughout the 1940s and 1950s, he made numerous hit recordings of instrumentals, religious, and secular songs. His innovative string-band style became known as bluegrass music in the mid-1950s, and in the 1960s he was a central figure in the establishment of bluegrass festivals nationwide. Among his songs, "Uncle Pen" is a country music classic, and "Blue Moon of Kentucky" was recorded by Elvis Presley for his first release in 1954. He was elected to the Country Music Hall of Fame in 1970, and he was awarded a National Heritage Fellowship by the National Endowment for the Arts in 1981.

Montagu, Ashley (b. Israel Ehrenberg) (1905–) cultural anthropologist; born in London, England. Educated in London, he studied at Florence (Italy) and Columbia

University (New York City), then stayed in the U.S.A. to teach at New York University, the Hahnemann Medical College in Philadelphia, and Rutgers, where he headed the anthropology department from 1949–55. His many publications include *Coming into Being among the Australian Aborigines* (1937), *The Natural Superiority of Women* (1953), and *The Elephant Man* (1971). In his work, he argued forcefully against the view that cultural phenomena are genetically determined and he published many popular articles and books applying his ideas to such contemporary issues as racism.

Montague, William Pepperell (1873–1953) philosopher; born in Chelsea, Mass. A longtime teacher at Barnard College and Columbia University (1903–47), he was one of the "new realists" to coauthor a famous 1912 article expounding an alternative to the idealism then dominant in philosophy. He gave important lecture series and chaired American delegations to international philosophical meetings; his works include *The Ways of Knowing* (1925).

Montana, (Joseph C., Jr.) Joe (1956–) football player; born in Monongahela, Pa. A former Notre Dame quarterback, he led the San Francisco 49ers to victories in four Super Bowls during the 1980s and was selected Most Valuable Player (MVP) in three (XVI, XIX, XXIV). An inspirational leader and talented passer, he was named National Football League (NFL) MVP in 1989 when he led the NFL in passing, and he was chosen all-league many times.

Monteux, Pierre (Benjamin) (1875–1964) conductor; born in Paris, France. He studied violin before becoming the conductor of the famous Ballets Russes in 1911; he conducted their legendary world premiere of Stravinsky's *Le sacre du printemps* (1913). He went to America in 1917 and held the podium of the Boston Symphony from 1919 to 1924. Returning to Paris he founded the Orchestre Symphonique de Paris and remained as its head until 1938. Meanwhile, in 1936 he also began a tenure as conductor of the San Francisco Symphony that lasted until 1952. In 1941 he established a summer school for conductors at Hanover, N.H. From 1960 until his death he worked with the London Symphony. He was known as a restrained but impeccable conductor, looking for the essence of the work rather than imposing himself on the music.

Montezuma, Carlos (b. Wassaja) (?1867–1923) Yavapai physician, leader, editor; born in the Superstition Mountains in present-day Arizona. Sent to Chicago by his adoptive father, he received his M.D. from Chicago Medical School in 1888. He worked all his life for the elimination of the reservation system and the Bureau of Indian Affairs (BIA), advocating instead citizenship for Indians. In 1896 he began private practice in Chicago. In 1906 he declined to serve as head of the BIA. In 1916 he started *Wassaja,* an Indian affairs magazine.

Montgomery, Edmund Duncan (1835–1911) philosopher; born in Edinburgh, Scotland. After retiring as a physician, he emigrated to the U.S.A. (1870), spending two years at a Georgia colony for resettlement of African-Americans. He then bought a plantation in Texas, where he performed research on protoplasm. His study, *Philosophical Problems in the Light of Vital Organization* (1907), analyzed mind and body as aspects of one underlying reality.

Montgomery, Richard (1738–75) soldier; born in County Dublin, Ireland. Commissioned in the British army in 1756, he saw service in America during the French and Indian War, then resigned to settle in America (1773). He married the daughter of the wealthy New Yorker, Robert Livingston (1718–75), and supported the patriots in their resistance to Britain. He became a brigadier general in the Continental army in June 1775, and as second in command in Gen. Philip Schuyler's expedition to Canada, he led the forces that captured Montreal. He lost his life during the assault on Quebec on December 31.

Moody, (Arthur Edson) Blair (1902–54) journalist, U.S. senator; born in New Haven, Conn. After winning acclaim as a Washington, D.C. correspondent for the *Detroit News,* he was appointed to the U.S. Senate (Dem., Mich.; 1951–53). He continued to support an international role for the U.S.A. as he had in his columns and as had the senator whose seat he filled, Arthur Vandenberg, but he failed to be reelected.

Moody, Dwight Lyman (1837–99) Protestant evangelist; born in Northfield, Mass. A shoe salesman in Chicago, he established a church school for slum children in 1858; two years later he decided to devote his life to evangelism. Never ordained, he had a wide influence as a preacher of a simple, conservative, and personal Christianity. With a colleague, hymnist Ira David Sankey, he completed two successful tours of Britain, and they often worked together in America. He founded the Northfield Seminary (1879), the Mount Hermon School (1881), and the Moody Bible Institute in Chicago (1889).

Moody, Helen (Newington) Wills (1905–) tennis player; born in Centerville, Calif. She graduated from the University of California (1927) and from then until her retirement in 1939 she dominated women's tennis. She won her first U.S. women's singles title in 1923, then went on to win it six more times by 1931. She also won the Wimbledon singles championship eight times, the French singles four times, various doubles championships, and two gold medals in the 1924 Olympics. Married to Frederick Moody, she competed between 1929–39 as Helen Wills Moody; divorced and remarried, she competed in senior tournaments as Mrs. Roark.

Moody, Paul (1779–1831) inventor; born in Newbury, Mass. The son of a Revolutionary War officer, he went to work in a woolen mill at age 12 and soon became an expert mechanic. Beginning in 1814, he built and repaired mill machinery in partnership with Francis C. Lowell. Moody designed a series of mechanical improvements that sped the development of the New England textile industry. He was a champion of the temperance movement in Massachusetts.

Moody, Raymond A. (Avery, Jr.) (1944–) psychiatrist; born in Porterdale, Ga. Educated in philosophy at the University of Virginia (B.A. 1966; M.A. 1967; Ph.D. 1969), he received his medical degree (M.D.) from the Medical College of Georgia (1976). He taught philosophy at Eastern Carolina University and the University of Virginia, and published several books of humanistic psychology for a popular audience, such as *Laugh After Laugh: The Healing Power of Humor* (1978). His greatest success, however, came from his *Life After Life* (1975), which, with its accounts of "near-death" experiences, launched the late-20th-century fascination with claims that people could experience bodily death and then return to life.

Moody, William Henry (1853–1917) Supreme Court justice; born in Newbury, Mass. He prosecuted for Massachusetts in the Lizzie Borden murder trial and was elected to the U.S. House of Representatives (Rep., Mass.; 1895). President Theodore Roosevelt named him secretary of the navy (1902–04), attorney general (1904–06), and to the U.S. Supreme Court (1906–10).

Moody, William Vaughn (1869–1910) educator, poet, playwright; born in Spencer, Ind. He began as a teacher at the University of Chicago (1895–1907), then turned to the theater. His poetic plays were not produced; he is known, rather, for his serious social dramas, including *The Great Divide* (1906). At the time of his premature death, he was regarded as the great hope of a new and mature American school of drama.

Mooney, Edward (Francis) (1882–1958) Catholic prelate; born in Mt. Savage, Md. Ordained in 1909, he was a theology professor, seminary spiritual director, and Vatican diplomat before becoming bishop of Rochester, N.Y. (1933). As an official of the National Catholic Welfare Conference, he was a major Catholic spokesman on social issues. Named archibishop of Detroit (1937) and made a cardinal (1946), he promoted workers' rights and bolstered church finances.

Mooney, James (1861–1921) ethnologist; born in Richmond, Ind. The son of Irish immigrants, he became absorbed by North American Indian culture at an early age. He worked as a newspaperman in his hometown before moving to Washington, D.C., in 1885, where he found employment in the Bureau of American Ethnology. He remained there for the rest of his life, studying and writing about the language, lore, and mythology of the Cherokee, Kiowa, and Sioux tribes. He helped prepare the *Handbook of American Indians* (1907–10).

Mooney, Thomas (Joseph) (1882–1942) labor radical; born in Chicago, Ill. Son of a coal miner, he was converted to socialism on a trip to Europe (1907). Settling in San Francisco (1911), he became dedicated to left-wing unity and affiliated with various radical and labor groups including the International Workers of the World and the left-wing faction of the San Francisco Socialists. He helped publish their newspaper, *Revolt,* and ran as Socialist candidate for superior court judge and for sheriff (1911). He was tried and acquitted for carrying explosives (1914) in connection with a strike against the Pacific Gas and Electric Company, but was tried and convicted under questionable circumstances for a San Francisco bombing (1917). After tremendous furor from members of organized labor of all persuasions, California Governor William D. Stephens commuted the sentence from hanging to life imprisonment (1918). Vain and imperious, he hampered efforts to secure his release, but was finally pardoned (1939). After his release he went on tour briefly under labor auspices, but spent his last years in St. Luke's Hospital, San Francisco, suffering from bleeding ulcers.

Moore, Alfred (1755–1810) Supreme Court justice; born in New Hanover County, N.C. He fought in the American Revolution (1776–81) and served as North Carolina's attorney general (1782–91), and on the state legislature (1782) before President John Adams named him to the U.S. Supreme Court (1799–1804).

Moore, Anne Carroll (1871–1961) librarian; born in Limerick, Maine. She studied at the Pratt Library Institute in Brooklyn, N.Y., and directed their pioneer children's program. From 1906–41 she headed children's services at the New York Public Library. A renowned children's book critic, she led the movement to judge children's books on their literary merit rather than on their moral message.

Moore, Archie (b. Archibald Lee Wright) (?1913–) boxer; born in Benoit, Wis., or Collinsville, Ill. He began boxing professionally in 1936, but it was 1952 before he gained a world title, the light heavyweight (1952–62). He twice fought for the heavyweight championship, losing to "Rocky" Marciano in 1955 and to Floyd Patterson in 1956. As articulate as he was clever, as colorful as he was tough, he fought until the age of 49, compiling one of the most astonishing records in boxing history, with 199 victories (145 knockouts), 26 losses, and 8 draws.

Moore, Bessie B. (Boehm) (1902–) librarian; born in Owensboro, Ky. She was a public school administrator who served as the executive director of the Arkansas Council in Economic Education (1962–79).

Moore, Charles W. (Willard) (1925–93) architect, educator; born in Benton Harbor, Mich. He taught widely, notably at Yale (1965–75) and the University of California: Los Angeles (1975–85). In several partnerships, notably Moore Lyndon Turnbull Whitaker (1962–70), he produced designs juxtaposing disparate historical and cultural references.

Moore, Clarence Bloomfield (1852–1936) archaeologist; born in Philadelphia. He was a wealthy socialite and international traveler who toured Europe and Asia Minor, crossed the Andes, and navigated the Amazon before turning to archaeology. He proved a meticulous fieldworker; of his many studies of Indian mounds throughout South-eastern U.S.A., his excavations of the St. John's shell middens in Florida (1892–94) were of particular value.

Moore, Clement (Clarke) (1779–1863) educator, Hebraist, poet; born in New York City. He graduated from Columbia College (1798), became a Hebrew scholar, wrote *A Compendious Lexicon of the Hebrew Language* (1809), and was a founder of and professor at the General Theological Seminary, New York City (1823–50). He is generally known for a poem written for his children, "A Visit From St. Nicholas" (1822), later known as "The Night Before Christmas." The work was copied down by a guest at his home and given, without his knowledge or permission, to a newspaper in Troy, N.Y., for publication in 1823, and was copied by other newspapers throughout the country; it was only in 1844 that Moore was acknowledged as the author. His other claim to fame is that in 1807 he discovered Lorenzo Da Ponte, the librettist of three of Mozart's greatest operas, in a New York City bookstore, and was instrumental in Da Ponte's new career as a teacher of Italian language and literature.

Moore, Douglas (Stuart) (1893–1969) composer, educator; born in Greenport, Long Island. He had a long teaching career at Columbia University (1926–62) and is best known for his "Americana" operas, especially *The Ballad of Baby Doe* (1956).

Moore, Eliakim Hastings (1862–1932) mathematician; born in Marietta, Ohio. Founder and chairman of the University of Chicago mathematics department (1896–1931), he helped shape the university and was a noted "teacher of teachers." He is also known for work in integral equations and general analysis and as a key shaper of 20th-century mathematics.

Moore, Gabriel (1785–1845) U.S. representative/senator; born in Stokes County, N.C. A lawyer, congressman (Dem., Ala.; 1821–29), and governor (1829–31), he began the Muscle Shoals Canal and the state university before going to the Senate (1831–35).

Moore, Grace (1901–47) soprano; born in Jellico, Tenn. After vocal studies in Maryland, she appeared in musical comedy in New York during the 1920s, then pursued further studies in France before making her Metropolitan Opera debut in 1928. She went on to a celebrated international career and appeared in several films. She died in a plane crash near Copenhagen.

Moore, James (1737–77) soldier; born in New Hanover County, N.C. (brother of Maurice Moore). A French and Indian War veteran, he served in the provincial legislature; as relations with Britain deteriorated, he sided with the Whig patriots who opposed the Loyalist Tories in North Carolina. He took command of Continental forces in North Carolina in 1776 and directed them to their first victory, over Loyalist forces at Moore's Creek Bridge (February, 1776). He died at Wilmington, N.C., the following year from "a fit of gout in the stomach."

Moore, John Bassett (1860–1947) international jurist; born in Smyrna, Del. He combined public service with legal scholarship as a professor of law and diplomacy at Columbia University (1891–1924). At the U.S. State Department (1885–91), he dealt with all major American consular business; he was assistant secretary of state during the Spanish-American War and a State Department counselor (1913–14). He was the first U.S. judge on the World Court (1921–28). Among his extensive writings and compilations was *Digest of International Law* (8 vols. 1906).

Moore, Marianne (Craig) (1887–1972) poet; born in Kirkwood, Mo. She studied at Bryn Mawr (B.A. 1909) and Carlisle Commercial College, Pa. (1910), and worked at the U.S. Indian School, Pa. (1911–15). She settled in New York City (1919), living first in Greenwich Village and then in Brooklyn, and worked as a librarian, editor, and lecturer. A modernist poet, she is famous for her mildly eccentric public persona, a devotion to baseball, and her impeccably intelligent poetry, as seen in *The Complete Poems* (1967).

Moore, Mary Tyler (1934–   ) television actress; born in New York City. A professional dancer, she began her career as a comic actress on *The Dick Van Dyke Show* (1960–65). She then starred in *The Mary Tyler Moore Show* (1970–77), a CBS situation comedy that gained her the nickname, "American's girl friend." She founded MTM productions (1970–81) with her then husband, Grant Tinker. She subsequently worked as a dramatic actress in the movie *Ordinary People* (1980) and in made-for-television movies such as *Thanksgiving Day* (1990).

Moore, R. C. (Raymond Cecil) (1892–1974) paleontologist, geologist; born in Roslyn, Washington. This University of Chicago Ph.D. was a member of the U.S. Geological Survey (1913–49) and a Kansas state geologist (1916–54); he taught at the University of Kansas (1916–70). He published widely on petroleum, structural geology, stratigraphy, and invertebrate paleontology, but is best remembered for organizing and directing the 27-volume *Treatise on Invertebrate Paleontology* (1948).

Moore, Robert Lee (1882–1974) mathematician; born in Dallas, Texas. He was associate editor of the American Mathematical Society's *Transactions* (1914–27). A noted professor, he taught longest at the University of Texas (1923–1968) and was credited for using axiomatics as a tool in set-theoretic topology, what he called point-set topology.

Moore, Sally Falk (1924–   ) cultural anthropologist; born in New York City. She graduated from Barnard College in 1943 and received a Ph.D. from Columbia University in 1957. She taught at the University of Southern California and the University of California: Los Angeles before joining the Harvard faculty in 1981. She served as dean of Harvard's Graduate School of Arts and Sciences (1985–89). Among other works, she wrote *Power and Property in Peru* (1958) and *Social Facts and Fabrications* (1986).

Moore, Stanford (1913–82) biochemist; born in Chicago. He was affiliated with Rockefeller Institute for most of the years from 1939 until his death. Using ion-exchange chromatography, he and William Stein analyzed the amino acids present in a variety of proteins; in 1960, they mapped out the complete amino acid sequence of ribonuclease. He shared the Nobel Prize in chemistry with William Stein for this work (1972).

Moore, William H. (Henry) (1848–1923) capitalist; born in Utica, N.Y. Admitted to the bar in Wisconsin, he moved to Chicago to practice corporate law (1872) but he left law to work at corporate mergers and stock manipulation with his brother, James Hobart Moore (1852–1916). In 1890 they merged several cracker manufacturers into the New York Biscuit Company and engineered a price war with the American Biscuit and Manufacturing Company that resulted in the brothers' monopolistic National Biscuit Company (1898). They formed the American Steel Hoop Company (1899), the American Sheet Steel Corporation (1900), and several other metal-based companies; when these were absorbed into the United States Steel Corporation (1901), the brothers became immensely rich. The Moores then had themselves elected to the board of directors of the Chicago, Rock Island, & Pacific Railway (1901) and undertook a series of dubious transactions; by 1914 the once healthy Rock Island was in receivership. An investigation by the Interstate Commerce Commission (1916) charged the Moores, among others, with looting the railroad, and William was ejected from the board. In retirement he raised horses, becoming a four-in-hand driver of international renown.

Moorer, Thomas H. (Hinman) (1912–   ) naval officer; born in Mount Willing, Ala. During World War II he narrowly escaped death twice – his airplane was shot down and the ship that rescued him was torpedoed (1942). He was commander of the Atlantic Fleet (1965–67), chief of naval operations (1967–70), and chairman of the Joint Chiefs of Staff (1970–74) before he retired in 1974.

Morais, Sabato (1823–97) rabbi; born in Leghorn (now Livorno), Italy. He came to the U.S.A. in 1851 and became rabbi of the Mikveh Israel Congregation of Philadelphia, where he served until his death. An abolitionist, he later concerned himself with raising funds for the Russian Jews who settled in America. In opposition to the rising tide of Reform Judiasm, he helped found the Jewish Theological Seminary in New York in 1886, where he taught until his death.

Moran, Thomas (1837–1924) painter; born in Bolton, Lancashire, England. He emigrated to Philadelphia, which became his home (1844), and was apprenticed to an engraver. After revisiting England (1862), he returned to America and traveled with various expeditions to the Western states. His spectacular panoramic paintings, such as the famous *Grand Canyon of the Yellowstone* (1893–1901), brought him critical acclaim.

More, Paul Elmer (1864–1937) critic, philosopher; born in St. Louis, Mo. He was educated at Washington University (St. Louis), and Harvard. With Irving Babbitt he led the New Humanism movement, promoting a neo-Christian philosophy which, he claimed, continued the platonic tradition; his narrow and pedantic views provoked strong reactions from H. L. Mencken and many others. His principal essays on literature and philosophy were collected in *The Greek Tradition* (4 vols. 1917–27) and *Shelburne Essays* (11 vols. 1904–21).

Morehead, Alfred (Hodges) (1909–66) bridge player, author, editor; born in Flintstone, Ga. He helped the Culbertson team beat the British for the prestigious Schwab Cup (1934), became the first bridge editor of the *New York Times* (1935–63), and supervised production of the International Laws of Bridge (1943).

Morel Campos, Juan (1857–96) composer, conductor; born in Ponce, Puerto Rico. He was the most important figure in Puerto Rican music of the 19th century. He composed countless *danzas,* the dance (along with the *bomba* and *plena*) most closely associated with Puerto Rico. He conducted concerts, operas, and operettas throughout Puerto Rico and South America, and died conducting one of his own *zarzuelas* at his beloved La Perla theater in Ponce.

Moreno, Jacob L. (1892–1974) psychiatrist; born in Romania. Educated in Vienna (M.D. 1917), he founded a theater there in which would-be actors could improvise roles and dialogue. This evolved into the method of group psychotherapy he called "psychodrama." After emigrating to the United States, he introduced the term "group therapy" (1932) and established the Psychodramatic Institute in New York (1942). From 1947, he edited the journal *Group Pyschotherapy* (originally *Sociatry*). Psychodrama as a therapeutic technique never spread much beyond a few small centers.

Morey, Charles (Rufus) (1877–1955) art historian; born in Hastings, Mich. He studied at the University of Michigan (B.A. 1899; M.A. 1900; Ph.D. 1938), the University of Chicago (Ph.D. 1941), New York University (D.F.A. 1942), and Yale (Ph.D. 1951). Beginning in 1918 he taught at Princeton and in Rome, specializing in early Christian art.

Morey, Samuel (1762–1843) inventor; born in Hebron, Conn. He was a successful lumberman and became the town engineer for Bellows Falls, Vt. He and his older brother experimented with steamboats after 1790; none were commercially successful but Morey later claimed that Robert Fulton had stolen his ideas. He took out more than 20 patents in all, some of which were well ahead of their time – most notably his American Water Burner (1817–18) and the first American patent (1826) for an internal combustion engine.

Morgan, Agnes Fay (b. Jane Agnes Fay) (1884–1968) biochemist, nutritionist; born in Peoria, Ill. Educated at the University of Chicago (B.S., M.S., Ph.D.), she taught at the University of California: Berkeley (1915–54), where she helped organize (1919) what was to become a nationally outstanding home economics department. A founder of the

science of nutrition, Morgan's research focused on the analysis of nutrients in foods, the stability of vitamins and proteins during food processing, and the physiological effects of vitamin deficiencies; especially noteworthy was her discovery of the role of pantothenic acid in adrenal function and pigmentation. Her work for government and private agencies included the development of improved methods of dehydrating foods.

Morgan, Arthur E. (Earnest) (1878–1976) engineer, educator; born in Cincinnati, Ohio. He worked on drainage flood protection projects from 1905 into the 1920s, and was chairman of the Tennessee Valley Authority (1933–38). He became president of Antioch College (1920) and initiated the Antioch Plan of work-study.

Morgan, Daniel (1736–1802) soldier; probably born in Hunterdon County, N.J. The son of an ironmaster who had settled in the Shenandoah Valley, Va., he had served with the British forces in the French and Indian War and against Pontiac's rebellion (1763–64). He joined the Revolutionary forces on the outbreak of war and fought at Quebec in December 1775, where he was captured. Exchanged in 1776, he led a crack regiment of sharpshooters that played an important role in the victory at Saratoga (1777). He then served under George Washington in Pennsylvania. After briefly resigning (1779–80) in dissatisfaction over his lack of promotion, he rejoined the army to command troops in western North Carolina; on January 17, 1781, a force under his command defeated the British at Cowpens, S.C., in one of the war's decisive battles. In 1794, commanding Virginia militia, Morgan helped suppress the Whiskey Rebellion in western Pennsylvania. He served in the U.S. House of Representatives (Fed., Va.; 1797–99).

Morgan, Edmund S. (Sears) (1916–   ) historian; born in Minneapolis, Minn. Educated at Harvard University (Ph.D. 1942) and the London School of Economics (1937–38), he focused on early New England, pre-Revolutionary, and Revolutionary history. His *Roger Williams: The Church and State* (1967) emphasizes the interplay between colonial theological thought and political institutions. He taught at the University of Chicago (1945–46), Brown (1947–55), and Yale (1955).

Morgan, Garrett A. (1877–1963) inventor; born in Paris, Ky. Born into poverty and with only a fifth-grade education, he moved to Cleveland, Ohio, and worked as a sewing machine mechanic. By 1907 he had a patent for an improved sewing machine and began his own sewing machine business. In 1909 he discovered a substance that straightened hair (temporarily) and by selling it to African-Americans through his own G. A. Morgan Hair Refining Company he achieved the financial security to allow him to pursue his other interests. In 1914 he patented his "breathing device," a hood that allowed the wearer to breathe safely in the presence of smoke, gases, and other pollutants. He worked hard to market this device, especially to fire departments, and often himself demonstrated its reliability in fires; in the South, where there was resistance to buying such a device made by an African-American, he demonstrated as an Indian, "Big Chief Mason"; and in a famous tunnel accident in Cleveland in 1916, where he rescued several men, he was denied a medal from the Carnegie Hero Fund. In World War I his hood was adopted and then adapted to serve as a gas mask. He patented his automatic traffic signal (1923) and sold it to the General Electric Company. In the 1920s he also collaborated in starting a newspaper for African-Americans, the *Cleveland Call* (later the *Call and Post*). He was also active in the Cleveland Association of Colored Men and the National Association for the Advancement of Colored People.

Morgan, John (1735–89) physician; born in Philadelphia. After serving an apprenticeship under the great John Redman of Philadelphia, he continued his medical studies in Great Britain and Italy. On returning, he took the lead in founding the medical school at the College of Philadelphia (University of Pennsylvania) in 1765; he joined the faculty and wrote his influential *Discourse upon the Institution of Medical Schools in America* (1765). After the American Revolution had begun, Congress appointed him medical director of the hospitals and chief physician of the colonial army (1775); he insisted on such charges in the medical department and upon such high standards that his subordinates rebelled and Congress finally removed him (1777). He returned to teaching at the Pennsylvania Hospital and to his private practice, but not without publishing a defense of his conduct.

Morgan, John Hunt (1825–64) soldier; born in Huntsville, Ala. He had fought as a volunteer in the Mexican War and then, as a businessman in Lexington, Ky., he supported a militia group. When the Civil War broke out, he sided with the Confederacy; made a captain, he was assigned a cavalry scouting unit; bold and energetic, he led three daring penetrations from 1862 to 1863, disrupting Union communications in Tennessee and Kentucky and tying down large enemy forces with his relatively small units. Captured during a fourth raid, into Indiana and Ohio in July 1863, Morgan escaped from a federal penitentiary in November and resumed his raiding career. Federal forces surprised and killed Morgan in Greenville, Tenn., the following year.

Morgan, (John Pierpont) Jack (1867–1943) financier, philanthropist; born in Irvington, N.Y. Shortly after graduating from Harvard he married and became a partner in his father's firm, J. P. Morgan & Company. In London (1893–1901) he studied banking at his grandfather's firm, J. S. Morgan & Company. At his father's death (1913), Jack became president and positioned the firm as the sole purchasing agent of more than $3 billion of arms and munitions for the British and French. In 1915 he organized a syndicate of more than 2,000 banks to underwrite loans for the Allies. He served on a committee of bankers reviewing the German war reparations (1922) and was on the 1929 Owen D. Young reparations conference. His philanthropies included the Red Cross, the Episcopal Church, and the New York Lying-In Hospital. In 1923 he established an endowment to make a permanent museum for the extensive rare books and manuscripts of the Morgan Library.

Morgan, J. P. (John Pierpont) (1837–1913) financier, art collector, philanthropist; born in Hartford, Conn. He worked in various banking houses, including his father's (Junius Spencer Morgan) in London, until 1871 when he established Drexel, Morgan & Co. with Anthony J. Drexel. The firm – known as J. P. Morgan & Co. after 1895 – became one of the most powerful banking houses in the world. In 1873 the U.S. treasury allowed his firm to secure part of a government loan, thereby breaking a monopoly held by the unscrupulous Jay Cooke, and although Morgan

definitely worked to advance his own fortune, he established a reputation as a positive force for the nation's financial and industrial base. He helped stabilize the railroads, for instance, and in 1895 he stanched the gold drain from the U.S. treasury reserves. In 1901 he bought out Andrew Carnegie's and others' companies to form the United States Steel Corporation. By this time he was the best known, richest, and most influential financier America had ever seen, and inevitably he was attacked by many, but he emerged from a 1912 Congressional investigation with his reputation largely intact. He gave away large sums to a variety of institutions. A knowledgeable collector of art, he was a major benefactor of the Metropolitan Museum of Art. His large and superb collection of books, manuscripts, and drawings were left to the Morgan Library in New York City.

Morgan, Julia (1872–1957) architect; born in San Francisco. Practicing independently in San Francisco, she designed more than 800 buildings, including Hearst's estates at San Simeon (1919–39) and Wyntoon (1931–42), and she influenced regional styles through her use of redwood shingle and Spanish revival style.

Morgan, Junius S. (Spencer) (1813–90) banker; born in West Springfield, Mass. (father of John Pierpont Morgan, 1837–1913). He grew up in Hartford and worked as a clerk in a dry goods house. He joined the London firm of George Peabody & Company (1854) which became J. S. Morgan & Company (1864–90). Although he spent more than half his life abroad, he remained influential in New York and Connecticut. His firm sided with the Union during the Civil War and secured an important $50 million loan for France during the Franco-Prussian War (1870). Among his philanthropies, he founded a free library in Hartford.

Morgan, Lewis Henry (1818–81) cultural anthropologist, legislator; born near Aurora, N.Y. He graduated from Union College in 1840, became a railroad lawyer, and served in the New York state assembly (1861) and senate (1868), all the while conducting investigations of native North American Indians, beginning with the customs and institutions of the Iroquois. He published his early results in *The League of the Iroquois* (1851); he had become so popular among one clan that he was adopted into it in 1847. His *Systems of Consanguinity and Affinity of the Human Family* (1869) formed the basis of the modern anthropological study of kinship. Karl Marx hailed his *Ancient Society* (1877), a study of the origins and evolution of government and property, as confirming the Marxist materialist theory of history. He is also remembered for his authoritative work, *The American Beaver and His Works* (1868), in which he argued that animals possess powers of rational thought. A temperance advocate and a strong Presbyterian, he was said to fear that his ethnological work was subversive of religion.

Morgan, Thomas Hunt (1866–1945) geneticist; born in Lexington, Ky. Trained as an embryologist, he became a biology professor at Bryn Mawr (1891–1904), where he wrote his first major book, *Regeneration* (1901). He became a professor at Columbia University (1904–28), and began his revolutionary genetic investigations of the fruit fly *Drosophila* (1908). Initially skeptical of Gregor Mendel's research, Morgan performed rigorous experiments which demonstrated that genes were indeed discrete chromosomal units of heredity. In 1910 he discovered sex-linkage in *Drosophila*, and postulated a connection between eye color in fruit flies and human color blindness. With his "fly room" colleagues, he mapped the relative positions of genes on *Drosophila* chromosomes, then published his seminal book, *The Mechanisms of Mendelian Heredity* (1915). Followed by some of his Columbia group, he moved to the California Institute of Technology (Caltech) (1928) to continue *Drosophila* research. In 1933 he received the Nobel Prize in physiology for his studies of the role of chromosomes in heredity. He remained at Caltech until his death, performing administrative duties and pursuing investigations of inheritance in *Drosophila,* mammals, birds, and amphibians.

Morganstern, Oskar (1902–77) economist; born in Silesia, Germany. He was a member of the "Vienna Circle" of philosophers and mathematicians. When the Nazis occupied Vienna in 1938, he emigrated to the U.S.A. and joined the faculty at Princeton University (1938–70). He promoted the application of a game theory approach to economics and coauthored with John von Neumann the pioneering book on this subject.

Morgenthau, Hans J. (Joachim) (1904–80) political scientist; born in Coburg, Germany. He left Germany in 1932 and immigrated to the U.S.A. in 1937. He taught at several universities including the University of Chicago, where he was director of the Center for the Study of American Foreign and Military Policy (1944–61). He emphasized a "realistic approach" to foreign policy, one in which national interests preside over global concerns. He was a fierce critic of U.S. involvement in Vietnam.

Morgenthau, Henry, Jr. (1891–1967) farmer, cabinet member; born in New York City. A wealthy farmer in Dutchess County, N.Y., he published the *American Agriculturist* (1922–33). He stopped farm foreclosures as head of the Farm Credit Administration (1933). Secretary of the Treasury (1934–45), he drafted the Lend-Lease Act and helped found the World Bank, returning to farming afterward.

Morgenthau, Robert M. (Morris) (1919–   ) government attorney; born in New York City. After practicing with the New York firm of Patterson, Belknap, & Webb (1949–61), he served as U.S. attorney for the Southern District of New York (1961–70), targeting white-collar crime. Serving as the district attorney of Manhattan beginning in 1975, he prosecuted numerous important cases and provided extraordinary training for trial lawyers.

Morison, Samuel Eliot (1887–1976) historian, naval officer; born in Boston, Mass. He received a Ph.D. from Harvard (1913) and then served as a private during World War I. He joined the faculty at Harvard (1925–55) and engaged in a lifetime of research and writing on naval, colonial, and exploration history. An active sailor himself, he displayed his intimate knowledge of the sea, ships, navigation, and other realities in his historical writings. He wrote more than 25 books, including two that won Pulitzer Prizes, *Admiral of the Ocean Sea: A Life of Christopher Columbus* (1942) and *John Paul Jones* (1959). He became the historian of U.S. naval operations (1942) and observed naval operations firsthand (1942–45) before writing his 25-volume *History of U.S. Naval Operations in World War II* (1946–62). He retired from the navy as a rear admiral (1951) and received the Presidential Medal of Freedom (1964).

Morley, Christopher (Darlington) (1890–1957) writer; born in Haverford, Pa. His family moved to Baltimore (1900), he

graduated from Haverford College (1910), and he studied at Oxford as a Rhodes Scholar (1910–13). He worked as a journalist in New York City for many years, and lived in Roslyn Heights, Long Island. He wrote many novels, essay collections, and poetry; his best-known novel is *Kitty Foyle* (1939). As an editor he is credited with promoting the works of Joseph Conrad and Sherwood Anderson, among others, and as a longtime judge for the Book-of-the-Month Club (1926–54) he influenced a generation of Americans' reading habits.

Morley, Edward Williams (1838–1923) chemist, physicist; born in Newark, N.J. He taught at Western Reserve University (1869–1906). His important contributions came through his genius in making new instruments for the precise measurements required in modern science. With one of these he was able to measure accurately the oxygen content of the atmosphere (1870s); later he determined the atomic weight of oxygen relative to hydrogen in forming water; he also made a new manometer to measure the thermal expansion of air and its constituent gases. He also worked with A. A. Michelson in developing the interferometer they used to measure lengths in terms of the wavelengths of light. The so-called Michelson-Morley experiment (1887) led to the refutation of the ether hypothesis and contributed to Einstein's theory of relativity.

Morley, Sylvanus Griswold (1883–1948) archaeologist; born in Chester, Pa. He trained as a civil engineer before studying archaeology at Harvard. He obtained major funding for Maya research from the Carnegie Institution, and after 1914 he conducted annual excavations for nearly 40 years, notably at Copán, Honduras; Petén, Guatemala; and (1924–34) Chichén Itzá, Mexico. He wrote important works on Mayan hieroglyphics.

Morphy, Paul (Charles) (1837–84) chess player; born in New Orleans. The son of a wealthy Irish-American father (the family name was originally Murphy) and French-Creole mother, he graduated from Spring Hill (Ala.) College with the school's highest honors ever and received a law degree from the University of Louisiana at age 18. Ineligible to practice until 21, he turned to chess. After winning the American championship and beating the strongest masters in Europe in 1857–59, he came home to a hero's welcome as unofficial world champion (title play was not formalized until 1886). Foreshadowing the career of fellow U.S. champion Bobby Fischer, who called him "perhaps the most accurate chess player who ever lived," he returned to New Orleans, failed to set up a law practice, and went into seclusion. After abandoning all but friendly chess games and suffering from paranoia, he died from a stroke while taking a bath.

Morrill, Justin Smith (1801–98) U.S. representative; born in Strafford, Vt. Son of a blacksmith, he ran a general store in Strafford (1831–48), turned to farming, then went to the U.S. House of Representatives (Whig, Rep., Vt.; 1855–67). A member of the Ways and Means Committee, he sponsored the Land-Grant College Act of 1862, providing public lands for agricultural colleges. In the Senate (Rep., 1867–98) he provided funds for their survival in the Second Morrill Act of 1880.

Morris, Esther Hobart (b. McQuigg) Slack (1814–1902) women's suffrage activist; born in Tioga County, N.Y. An orphan seamstress, she married a civil engineer in 1841 and moved to Illinois after his death. There she married again.

The family emigrated to Wyoming in 1869, her husband opening a saloon in a gold rush settlement called South Pass City. She became involved in the woman's suffrage movement, and in 1870, after the Wyoming legislature had granted women the vote (1869), she was briefly a justice of the peace. A big woman, blunt in speech, she attracted national attention and tried some 70 cases. She called her tenure a successful test "of a woman's ability to hold public office." She separated from her husband in 1871 and moved to Laramie, where one of her sons edited a newspaper. Although the extent of her contribution is debated, she became a legendary figure in the suffrage movement. Late in her life she was dubbed "the Mother of Woman Suffrage," and the state of Wyoming officially commemorated her role as a leading suffragist in 1890.

Morris, George Pope (1802–64) journalist, poet; born in Philadelphia. His periodical, the *New-York Mirror and Ladies Literary Gazette* and its successor, the *New Mirror,* were vehicles for William Cullen Bryant and other New York writers of the 1840s. He later edited the *Evening Mirror* and the *Home Journal,* and he published many of his own popular poems, including the familiar "Woodman, Spare That Tree"; critics generally found his verse insipid and sentimental.

Morris, Gouverneur (1752–1816) statesman, diplomat; born in Morrisania (now part of New York City), N.Y. Fundamentally conservative, he nevertheless served as a N.Y. delegate to the Continental Congress (1777–79) and supported the move for independence; failing to be reelected, he moved to Philadelphia. There he became assistant superintendent of finances under Robert Morris (no relation) and helped plan the decimal coinage system (1781–85). He was a delegate to the Constitutional Convention in 1787, but he advocated almost absolute powers for the president. Returning to his family home in New York in 1788, he went to Europe and served as U.S. ambassador to France during the period of the French Revolutionary terror (1792–94). Back in the States, he served as senator from New York (1800–03). As a Federalist, he constantly found himself opposed to the direction taken by the fledgling democracy.

Morris, John M. (McClean) (1915–93) gynecologist, medical researcher; born in Kuling, China. Son of a Presbyterian missionary, he studied at Princeton, then took his M.D. at Harvard (1940). After a year's expedition studying the birds of the Pacific for the National Geographic Society and the American Museum of Natural History, he served four years during World War II with the U.S. Navy's medical corps. He spent most of his professional career as a professor and chief of gynecology at Yale University School of Medicine (1952–87). He first established his name by identifying a rare sexual disorder, testicular feminization, since known as "Morris's syndrome," but he became best known for developing (along with Dr. Gertrude Van Wangen) the so-called morning-after birth-control pill during the 1960s, a pill that caused a woman's body to eject a fertilized egg by preventing its implantation in the womb. He also developed new techniques in pelvic surgery, was an early advocate in the U.S.A. of radiation therapy for cancer, and was an outspoken proponent of the need to control the growth in the world's population.

Morris, Mark (1956–) choreographer, modern dancer; born in Seattle, Wash. He performed with such choreographers as Eliot Feld and Twyla Tharp before making an informal New York debut with his company in 1980. Rapidly achieving international recognition for his brash and innovative style, his company held a permanent residency in Brussels, Belgium, in 1988–91. In 1990 he began collaborating with Mikhail Baryshnikov on the White Oak Dance Project, based in Florida, while continuing to tour with his own company.

Morris, Nelson (1838–1907) meatpacker; born in Hechingen, Germany. Brought to America as a boy, he came to Chicago in the 1850s and took a job at the Union Stock Yard. In 1874 he formed Morris & Waixel, which eventually became Morris & Company, one of the first packing houses at the Union Stock Yards. Later he would establish packing houses in Missouri and Kansas. He pioneered the shipping of dressed beef from Chicago to the East Coast and Europe. One of the first to import Polled Angus, he raised cattle in Texas and the Dakotas, operating one of the largest feeding operations in the world. Among his other interests, he founded the Nelson Morris Institute of Pathological Research in Chicago.

Morris, Richard (Valentine) (1768–1815) naval officer; born at Morrisania, N.Y. He commanded the Tripoli Squadron (1802–03). A court of inquiry found, somewhat unjustly, that he had been insufficiently diligent in his duty. He was dismissed from the navy in 1804.

Morris, Robert (1734–1806) merchant, banker, public official; born in or near Liverpool, England. He came to Maryland about 1747 to work for his father, a tobacco exporter, then went to Philadelphia where he joined the Willings' shipping firm; by 1754 he had formed a partnership with Thomas Willing, and their mercantile firm became one of the most prosperous in the colonies. Although by no means a radical patriot, he objected to the Stamp Act of 1765; by 1775 he was recognizing a need for some action, but sent to the Continental Congress he only reluctantly signed the Declaration of Independence (1776). During the war, he remained in Philadelphia and provided crucial support, both moral and material, to George Washington; although Morris personally ended up profiting, he risked much of his own money in buying needed armaments for the colonial forces; he was acquitted (1779) by a congressional committe of charges that he had engaged in improper financial transactions. When the colonies realized they were on the brink of bankruptcy, the Continental Congress appointed him superintendent of finance and for three and one-half years (1781–84) he instituted strict financial policies – collecting taxes from the colonies, arranging for a loan from France, and securing the money to transport Washington's army to Yorktown, Va.; again, though, he mixed his own finances with those of the government – buying military supplies, for instance, with notes backed only by his own fortune. He remained active in public life, attending the Constitutional Convention of 1787 and then serving a term as one of Pennsylvania's first two senators (Fed., 1789–95). His speculations in western land led to the collapse of his financial empire and he spent three and one-half years in debtors' prison in Philadelphia (1798–1801). On his release he lived out his final years in poor health and was all but forgotten by his countrymen.

Morris, Robert (1931–) sculptor, mixed media artist; born in Kansas City, Mo. He studied engineering and art, moved to San Francisco (1950), was active as a painter and in improvisatory theater, then settled in New York City (1961). There he specialized in minimalist works, earthwork projects, and scatter pieces.

Morris, Wright (Marion) (1910–) writer, photographer; born in Central City, Nebr. He studied at Crane College (1929) and Pomona College (1930–33). He was a lecturer at numerous institutions and a professor at California State University: San Francisco (1962–75). Praised by the critics but ignored by the general public, his novels, short stories, and critical essays gained him the reputation of a "writer's writer." He is also noted for his photographs, which, like his best fiction, have a spare, understated tone. His best known works are *The Field of Vision* (1956), and *Plains Song: For Female Voices* (1980).

Morrison, Jim (1943–71) rock singer, songwriter; born in Melbourne, Fla. He wrote poetry and studied film at the University of California: Los Angeles where he met keyboard player Ray Manzerek with whom he formed the rock band, The Doors, in 1965. With such hit songs as "Light My Fire" (1967) and "Hello, I Love You" (1968), they were one of the most popular bands of the 1960s. A controversial figure who had been arrested on obscenity charges during a live performance, Morrison died of a heart attack in Paris in 1971.

Morrison, Toni (b. Chloe Anthony Wofford) (1931–) writer, editor; born in Lorain, Ohio. She studied at Howard University (B.A. 1953) and Cornell (M.A. 1955). She taught English at Texas Southern University (1955–57) and at Howard (1957–64); later she would teach at the State University of New York: Purchase (1971–72) and Albany (1984–89), and at Princeton (1989). She married Harold Morrison (1958) and was divorced in 1964. In 1965 she became a senior editor for Random House in New York City. Her novels, which capture the deep passions and rhythms of African-American life, include *Sula* (1973), *Song of Solomon* (1977), and *Beloved* (1987); the last named won the Pulitzer Prize (1988). Recognized as a major American novelist, respected by critics and readers alike, she was awarded the Nobel Prize in literature in 1993.

Morrow, Dwight (Whitney) (1873–1931) lawyer, banker, diplomat; born at Huntington, W.Va. U.S. ambassador to Mexico (1927), U.S. senator from New Jersey (1930–31), financial and legal adviser to presidents and generals, he was also the father of Ann Morrow, who shared her husband Charles Lindbergh's love of flying. A governmental backer of aviation, he chaired a presidential study of aeronautics and its application to national defense (1925) that led to the separation of regulations for commercial and military aircraft.

Morrow, Jeremiah (1771–1852) U.S. representative/senator, governor; born in Gettysburg, Pa. A self-educated surveyor who promoted Ohio's statehood in 1800, he sponsored legislation for affordable public land sales in Congress (Rep., Ohio; 1803–13) and the Senate (1813–19); as governor (1823–26) he promoted public education and canal-building programs. He returned to Congress as a Whig (1840–43).

Morse, C. W. (Charles Wyman) (1856–1933) entrepreneur, swindler; born in Bath, Maine. He left the ice business in Maine for New York City (1897) where he built an ice monopoly and doubled the price of ice. Resulting litigation revealed stock deals involving the Tammany Hall leaders and the mayor. Morse got out of the ice business $12 million richer and moved into shipping. By 1907 he was so close to a monopoly in East Coast shipping that President Theodore Roosevelt intervened. His involvement in banking became the focus of the panic of 1907 and resulted in his being sentenced to 15 years in prison for fraudulent bookkeeping. Calling himself merely a scapegoat, he got out of prison after two years (1910–12) by deceiving doctors into believing he had only weeks to live, and acquiring a pardon from President Taft. He returned to shipping, again attempting to build a monopoly, and garnered U.S. ship building contracts during World War I. In 1922 he was investigated for war fraud by the Harding administration, but was indicted for mail fraud in another case. In 1925 a civil suit against his Virginia Shipbuilding Company resulted in a $11.5 million judgment for the United States. In the mail fraud case he was found too ill to stand trial and in 1926 was placed under guardianship as incompetent to handle his own affairs.

Morse, Jedidiah (1761–1826) minister, geographer; born in New Haven, Conn. Graduating from Yale (1783), he stayed there to study for the ministry, teaching school to support his studies, and writing the first American geography textbook, *Geography Made Easy* (1784), later reprinted in some 25 editions. After several short-term preaching assignments, he settled in the First Congregation Church, Charlestown, Mass. (1789–1819). He defended orthodox Calvinist tenets in the church, publishing the *Panopolist* (1805–10) and establishing the Andover Theological Seminary (1808). He also continued writing about geography, becoming known as the "father of geography," for such texts as *The American Geography* (1789) and *The American Universal Geography* (2 vols. 1796). He helped found the American Bible Society (1816).

Morse, Marston (1892–1977) mathematician; born in Waterville, Maine. A member of the newly founded Institute for Advanced Study in Princeton (1935–62), he specialized in mathematical analysis. Honored after World War I – for his military service – and World War II – for his contributions to ordnance – he was a representative at the United Nations Atoms for Peace Conference (1952). He was known for his love of playing the piano, of sports, and of France.

Morse, Samuel F. B. (Finley Breese) (1791–1872) painter, inventor; born in Charlestown, Mass. He began as a painter, studying in England under Washington Allston and Benjamin West (1811). He returned to New England (1815), and settled in New York City (1823), where he founded the American Academy of Design (1826). His historical painting, *The Old House of Representatives* (1822), and his well-received portrait of Lafayette (1825–26), did not lead to the government art commissions he sought. His last major work, *The Exhibition Gallery of the Louvre* (1832), was based on another trip abroad (1829–32). In New York again (1832), he began his many electrical experiments. From 1835 to 1838 he invented the telegraph, a method of transmitting a series of dots and dashes, representing the alphabet, over telegraph lines by means of electromagnets. Special telegraph lines were constructed to carry messages using the Morse code from Washington, D.C., to Baltimore, Maryland (1844), to prove the practical worth of the invention. He also introduced the daguerreotype, a photographic process, to America (1839). Today he is honored for his work as both a painter and an inventor.

Morse, Wayne (Lyman) (1900–74) U.S. senator; born in Madison, Wis. Dean of the University of Oregon law school, he won fame as a labor arbitrator before being elected to the U.S. Senate (Rep., Ore.; 1945–69). Renowned for his support of human rights, education, progressive farm policies, and environmentalism, he found himself at odds with the Republican Party, declared himself an independent in 1953, and won reelection in 1956 as a Democrat. His leadership of a Senate subcommittee on Latin America influenced President John Kennedy's creation of the Alliance for Progress. He was one of two Senators to vote against the Gulf of Tonkin resolution in 1964, and remained a resolute opponent of the war in Vietnam for the remainder of his career. Defeated for reelection in 1968, he was making a new bid for the Senate when he died.

Mortimer, Charles G. (Greenough) (1900–78) corporate executive; born in New York City. Drawing on previous advertising and merchandising experience, he rose through the corporate ranks of General Foods (1928–65), of which he was variously president, CEO, and chairman (1954–65). He was notable for developing such popular products as Birdseye frozen vegetables and Dream Whip topping, and for greatly expanding General Foods' international sales.

Morton, (Ferdinand Joseph) "Jelly Roll" (1890–1941) jazz musician; born in New Orleans, La. A nomadic figure, legendary braggart, and self-proclaimed "creator of jazz in 1902," he was actually an important pianist and prolific composer who recorded many landmarks of small group classic jazz with his Red Hot Peppers in the 1920s. His colorful life story, related to Alan Lomax of the Library of Congress in 1939, was published as *Mister Jelly Roll* in 1950.

Morton, Julius Sterling (1832–1902) agriculturalist; born in Adams, N.Y. After college he relocated to Nebraska City where he edited the town's newspaper (1854). Active in the territory of Nebraska's politics, he served on the territorial legislature (1855–58) and was appointed secretary of the territory by President James Buchanan (1858–61). He loved trees and in 1872 he had Nebraska observe an "arbor day" on which to plant trees. In 1885 the Nebraska legislature established his birthday, April 22, as Arbor Day (since observed by other states on different days). In 1893–97 he was appointed secretary of agriculture by President Grover Cleveland. He conceived and mapped out *The Illustrated History of Nebraska* (ed. Albert Watkins, 3 vols. 1905–13) and began publication of the *Conservative,* a journal of politics and economics, which was suspended after his death.

Morton, Levi P. (Parsons) (1824–1920) vice-president, businessman; born in Shoreham, Vt. He began work as a store clerk and became extremely wealthy. He was a representative (Rep., N.Y.; 1879–81) and ambassador to France (1881–85) before becoming Benjamin Harrison's vice-president (1889–93). He was a conscientious vice-president, but was dropped from the ticket in 1892. He was governor of New York (1895–96) and continued to manage his extensive business interests.

Morton, Nathaniel (1613–85) Pilgrim chronicler; born in Leyden, Netherlands. Son of the Pilgrim leader, George Morton (1585–1624), he came to Plymouth in 1624 and entered the family of his uncle by marriage, William Bradford. Very close to Bradford for many years, Morton was secretary of the Plymouth Colony (1647–85). He drafted laws and copied notices and was active in the Plymouth leadership during King Philip's War. He prepared *New England's Memoriall* (1669), the major source for Pilgrim history until Bradford's *History of Plimoth Plantation* was recovered in 1855.

Morton, Oliver (Hazard) Perry (Throck) (1823–77) public official; born in Salisbury, Ind. He left the Democratic Party to help found the new Republican Party. As the Republican wartime governor of Indiana (1861–66) he triumphed over an unruly legislature bent on frustrating his support of the Federal war effort. Partially paralyzed (1865), he went to France for treatment; while there, he helped to persuade the French to withdraw their troops from Mexico. He served in the U.S. Senate (Rep., Ind.; 1867–77) and was one of President Grant's trusted advisers.

Morton, Samuel George (1799–1851) physician, naturalist; born in Philadelphia. Of Irish background, Quaker educated, he took a medical degree from the University of Pennsylvania in 1820 and also studied medicine at Edinburgh. His research interests extended to geology, paleontology, and zoology, and he was one of the early advocates of open-air treatment for consumptives. He built a famous collection of human skulls to aid his research in comparative anthropology. Among his published works is *Human Anatomy* (1849). His theories on the diverse origins of races were attacked as subversive of Christian belief.

Morton, Thomas (c. 1590–1647) adventurer; born in England. He settled in present-day Quincy, Mass. and pursued a licentious and convivial life at Merrymount. He was arrested three times by Pilgrim and Puritan leaders, and was twice deported to England.

Morton, William (Thomas Green) (1819–68) dentist, anesthetist; born in Charlton, Mass. He studied dentistry in Baltimore and practiced in Connecticut before setting up a dental practice in Boston in 1842, in partnership with Horace Wells. Wells had been experimenting with nitrous oxide ("laughing gas") as an anesthesia while removing teeth. But in 1844, at the suggestion of his landlord, Professor Charles T. Jackson, Morton first used sulfuric ether to anesthetize a patient before drilling a tooth. After experiments on himself, a goldfish, and his dog, he used it during a tooth extraction (September 1846). The subsequent newspaper report caught the attention of a Massachusetts General Hospital surgeon, Dr. John Warren, who sponsored several surgical demonstrations with Morton as anesthetist. At first he tried to keep secret the nature of his anesthesia, calling it "letheon," but to receive a patent he was forced to describe it in a medical journal. Morton soon found himself in conflict with not only Wells and Jackson but also Crawford W. Long of Georgia over the issue of priority, and he would spend the rest of his life trying to establish himself as the discoverer of ether and in trying to profit from its use. He died a poor man but he came to be recognized as the first to introduce ether into general use as an anesthesia.

Mosby, John Singleton (1833–1916) soldier; born in Edgemont, Va. As a student at the University of Virginia, he had shot a fellow student; while in jail he began to read law under his defense lawyer. He was practicing law when the Civil War began and he joined the Confederate forces in Virginia, fighting at First Bull Run and scouting for Jeb Stuart. From January 1863 to the end of the Civil War, he operated as a partisan ranger in western Virginia, leading hit-and-run raids against scattered outposts of the federals, who viewed him as an outlaw. (His most famous incident involved his surprising Union Gen. Edwin Stoughton in bed and slapping him on the behind.) He was noted for his gray cape, lined with scarlet, and the large ostrich plume on his hat. He lost popularity in the South for supporting Ulysses Grant for president. He briefly served as U.S. consul in Hong Kong and practiced law in California, but returned to Virginia to a long career as a lawyer.

Moscone, George (1929–78) lawyer, mayor; born in San Francisco. After serving in the navy, he worked as a lawyer. He was elected to the San Francisco Board of Supervisors in 1963, then served as state senator (1967–77). Elected mayor of San Francisco in 1977, he supported a variety of liberal policies. He was shot to death by a former city supervisor, who also killed Supervisor Harvey Milk.

Mosconi, (William Joseph) Willie (1913–93) pocket billiards player; born in Philadelphia. After pocketing $75 in a Depression tournament, he took the first of many world titles in 1941. A tireless promoter of the game, he was technical adviser for the movie *The Hustler* (1961), and he authored *Willie Mosconi on Pockets Billiards* (1959).

Moscoso, Teodoro (1910–93) pharmacist, public official; born in Barcelona, Spain. He was an early ally of Luis Muñoz Marín and assisted in the foundation of the Popular Democratic Party (1938). He was best known for his work for economic reform in Puerto Rico, particularly the *Fomento Económico* (Operation Bootstrap), which he headed from 1942–60 and 1973–76. In 1961 President Kennedy first appointed him ambassador to Venezuela and then head of the Alliance for Progress, which channeled U.S. aid to Latin America.

Moses, (Anna Mary Robertson) Grandma (1860–1961) painter; born in Washington County, N.Y. She and her husband were farmers in Virginia and in Eagle Bridge, New York, where they settled (1907). The mother of ten children, she became a painter at the age of 78. Her distinctive folk paintings, such as *Hoosick Falls in Winter* (1943), and *Thanksgiving Turkey* (1943), have made her a popular artist throughout the world.

Moses, Edwin (Corley) (1955–) track athlete; born in Dayton, Ohio. The greatest 400-meter hurdler in track history, he won 122 consecutive races (1977–87), gold medals in the 1976 and 1984 Olympics, and a bronze in the 1988 Games.

Moses, Robert (1889–1981) public administrator; born in New Haven, Conn. Independently wealthy (he seldom accepted any salary), he was educated at Yale, Oxford, and Columbia Universities as a political scientist. He began his government career in New York City's Bureau of Municipal Research (1913) with an attempt to reform the civil service along the lines of his graduate thesis. In 1919 he became chief of staff of New York State's reconstruction commission under Governor Al Smith, who would long be his chief sponsor. In 1924 he was appointed head of both the New York State Council of Parks and the Long Island State Park Commission; using these and numerous other positions – in particular, New York City Parks commissioner (1934–60) and the Triborough Bridge and Tunnel authorities (1934–68) – he radically changed the city and its environs, creating a system of parkways to get New Yorkers to the outskirts, to Jones Beach (his pet project), and to the many state parks (which he also set up); by the end of his career he was credited with building 416 miles of parkway, 13 major bridges, and 658 playgrounds as well as setting aside over 2,000,000 acres of parkland. He did not succeed at everything; he was soundly defeated in his one bid for public office, when he ran as the Republican candidate for governor (1934); and he lost out in his efforts to stop Joseph Papp from performing Shakespeare in Central Park (1959). By the time of his last major project, the New York World's Fair (1964–68), he had fallen into disfavor with many other social thinkers and urban planners because his approach had so often involved razing entire neighborhoods and laying down tons of concrete. Autocratic by temperament and in his operations, he spent his last years defending his achievements, but even his critics agreed that his impact had been irreversible and unique.

Moskowitz, Belle Lindner (Israels) (1877–1933) social worker, political adviser; born in Harlem, N.Y. After a year at Teachers College of Columbia University (1894–95), she held various posts in progressive urban reform organizations for the next twenty years. In 1918 she became an aide to Alfred E. Smith and served him as a close political adviser during his terms as governor of New York (1919–21, 1923–29) and his campaign as the Democratic Party nominee for president in 1928.

Most, Johann Joseph (1846–1906) anarchist; born in Augsburg, Germany. Product of a brutal childhood, disfigured in his youth, he became an ardent European Socialist. He edited Socialist newspapers in Switzerland and Germany (1868–78), was elected twice to the German parliament, lectured frequently, wrote many pamphlets and labor songs, and was expelled from Austria and Germany. Turning anarchist, he was expelled from the German Socialist Party (1880). His paper, *Die Freiheit,* published in London, was suppressed (1881) after publishing an article glorifying the assassination of Czar Alexander II. Emigrating to America (1882), he was greeted as a radical martyr, and he traveled extensively, advocating a violent overthrow of capitalists and the ruling class. A magnetic speaker filled with hatred and invective, a brilliant writer with a biting, sarcastic wit, he became the leader of an extreme faction of American anarchists and composed the declaration adopted by the Pittsburgh convention (1883) that became the manifesto of communist anarchism in America. Imprisoned several times for inciting violence (1886–1901), he repudiated violent intervention and lost his influence.

Mother Ann See LEE, ANN.

Mother Jones See JONES, MARY B.

Motherwell, Robert (1915–91) painter; born in Aberdeen, Wash. He studied at the California School of Fine Arts, San Francisco (1932), majored in philosophy at Stanford University (1932–36) and Harvard (1937–38), and worked under Meyer Schapiro at Columbia University (1940–41). He was based in New York City, and his first paintings were influenced by Piet Mondrian, as in *Spanish Picture with Window* (1942). By 1948 he began his black and white oils, *Elegies to the Spanish Republic* (1948–68). A later series, *Open* (1968–75), is based on an exploration of windows and walls. His reputation as a theorist and painter within the astract expressionist school continues to grow.

Motley, Arthur H. (Harrison) ("Red") (1900–84) publisher, business executive; born in Minneapolis. He joined Crowell-Collier publishers in 1928, and as publisher of *American Magazine* (1941–46), he tripled circulation while increasing advertising revenue, a formula he repeated in resuscitating

Parade Magazine (president, 1946–70). He was president of the U.S. Chamber of Commerce (1960–61).

Motley, Constance Baker (1921–) lawyer, judge; born in New Haven, Conn. While a student at Columbia University (LL.B. 1946), she clerked for the National Association for the Advancement of Colored People's legal defense and education fund, for which she worked full time (1946–65). While there, she successfully argued nine cases before the U.S. Supreme Court, including those of James Meredith and Autherine Lucy. In 1964 she became the first African-American woman to be elected to the New York state senate; she became president of Manhattan Borough (1965–66). In 1966 she became the first black woman federal judge when President Lyndon Johnson appointed her to the U.S. District Court for the southern District of New York. From 1982–86 she served as chief judge, until becoming senior judge in 1986.

Motley, John Lothrop (1814–77) historian, diplomat; born in Dorchester, Mass. Son of a wealthy family, he graduated from Harvard (1831), then spent several years in Germany, Britain, and elsewhere in Europe where he got to know the intellectual and political elite, including Otto von Bismarck. Back in Boston in 1835, he married and decided on a literary career. His first two novels were not successful, so after several months as secretary to the U.S. embassy in St. Petersburg, Russia (1841), he decided to devote himself to writing history – specifically, the history of the Netherlands in the 16th and 17th centuries. He published the work for which he remains best known, *The Rise of the Dutch Republic* (1856). He served as ambassador to Austria (1861–67) and Britain (1869–70) while publishing *The History of the United Netherlands, 1584–1609* (four vols. 1860–67), but died before he could bring his history to its climax in 1648. Although composed in an engaging style, his history has been regarded by most scholars as a highly personal interpretation of events.

Motley, Marion (1920–) football player; born in Leesburg, Ga. A four-time all-league fullback for the Cleveland Browns (1946–53), he played on five league championship teams and led the National Football League in rushing in 1950.

Motley, Willard (Francis) (1912–65) writer; born in Chicago. Schooled in Chicago, he held a variety of jobs, including ranch hand, cook, and interviewer for the Chicago Housing Authority. After deciding to become a writer and settling in Chicago's slums, he wrote *Knock on Any Door* (1947), a naturalistic account of the degradation of a young boy. His subsequent novels were not as well-received, but his final novel, *Let Noon Be Fair,* published posthumously (1966), won critical praise. Although an African-American, Motley said, "My race is the human race." He died of gangrene in Mexico City, Mexico, where he lived.

Mott, C. S. (Charles Stewart) (1875–1973) automobile executive, philanthropist; born in Newark, N.J. He studied mechanical engineering and served in the Spanish-American War. He ran the Weston-Mott automobile parts company (1899–1913) and was a leading executive at General Motors (1913–67). He formed the Mott Foundation (1926) to finance cultural, educational, and health programs, especially in Flint, Michigan. In response to speculations about his wealth, he answered, "What I'm worth is what I am doing for other people."

Mott, John Raleigh (1865–1955) religious leader; born in Sullivan County, N.Y. He grew up in Iowa and returned to New York for college, graduating from Cornell in 1888. In 1891 he became foreign secretary for the Young Men's Christian Association (YMCA) and was the organization's general secretary from 1915–31. He oversaw the Y's welfare programs for Allied servicemen during World War I. An influential ecumenical leader for all his long life, he became honorary president of the World Council of Churches in 1948. He published 15 books, including *The Larger Evangelism* (1944).

Mott, Lucretia Coffin (1793–1880) women's rights activist, abolitionist, religious reformer; born in Nantucket, Mass. A child of Quaker parents, she was early impressed by her mother's and other Nantucket women's active roles while menfolk were away on voyages. The family moved to Boston in 1804 and she attended and then taught at a Quaker boarding school in Poughkeepsie, N.Y. (1808–09). After she moved again with her family to Philadelphia, she married James Mott, a former teacher at the Poughkeepsie school who had now joined her father's hardware firm. By 1821, she became a Quaker minister, noted for her speaking abilities, and in 1827 she and her husband went over with the more progressive wing of the Friends. She had become strongly opposed to slavery and one of the chief advocates of not buying any products of slave labor; her husband, always her supporter, had to get out of the cotton trade about 1830. She became an early supporter of William Lloyd Garrison and his American Anti-Slavery Society, and she often found herself threatened with physical violence due to her radical views. She and her husband attended the famous World's Anti-Slavery Convention in London in 1840, the one that refused to allow women to be full participants. This led to her joining Elizabeth Cady Stanton in calling the famous Seneca Falls Convention, N.Y., in 1848 (at which, ironically, James Mott was asked to preside), and from that point on Lucretia Mott was dedicated to women's rights. She wrote her influential *Discourse on Woman* (1850). While remaining within the Society of Friends, in practice and beliefs she actually identified increasingly with more liberal/progressive trends in American religious life, even helping to form the Free Religious Association in Boston (1867). While keeping up her commitment to women's rights, she also maintained the full routine of a mother and housewife. She continued after the Civil War to work for advocating the rights of African-Americans. She helped to found Swarthmore College (1864), continued to attend women's rights conventions, and when the movement split into two factions in 1869, she tried to bring the two together.

Mott, Valentine (1785–1865) surgeon; born in Glen Cove, N.Y. After taking his medical degree from Columbia University and studying surgery in Great Britain, he opened practice in New York City (1809) and was associated with various colleges. Rapid, skillful, and ambidextrous, he pioneered various circulatory surgeries and procedures; his fame as a bold, innovative surgeon became international. He authored no major works, but bequeathed his substantial library and a surgical and pathological museum to the New York medical profession.

Mould, Jacob Wrey (1825–86) architect and designer; born in Chislehurst, Kent, England. In New York (1852) he was an early practitioner of English High Victorian Gothic and introduced polychrome construction, including polychrome interiors. He also designed public parks.

Moulthrop, (Edwin Allen) Ed (1916–) woodworker; born in Rochester, N.Y. A professor of both architecture and physics at Georgia Institute of Technology, as well as a practicing architect, he had been turning wood since he was 15; in 1976 he began to devote full time to the craft. He is noted for his large bowls that he would treat and finish after turning them out of green Southern woods; his largest stands 45 inches high, is 30 inches in diameter, and weighs 75 pounds. Basic in shape, they are almost sculptural in the purity of their form and material, and his works are owned by many museums and private collectors.

Moulton, Forest Ray (1872–1952) astronomer; born in Le Roy, Mich. A professor at the University of Chicago (1898–1926), he proposed (with Thomas Chamberlin) a hypothesis – no longer accepted – explaining the origins of the solar system. As administrative secretary at the American Academy for the Advancement of Sciences (1937–48), he edited 25 symposium volumes. He authored nine books including *Consider the Heavens* (1935) and many articles.

Moultrie, William (1730–1805) soldier, governor; born in Charleston, S.C. A soldier, he directed military strategy in South Carolina during the American Revolution, defending Charleston in 1776. Becoming a brigadier general, he defeated the British at Beaufort in 1779, then was taken prisoner of war after the fall of Charleston in 1780. As South Carolina's governor (1785–87, 1792–94), he reorganized the militia, reestablished state credit, and improved the waterways.

Mount, William Sidney (1807–68) painter; born in Setauket, Long Island, N.Y. A student at the National Academy of Design, New York (1826), he spent most of his life in Stony Brook, Long Island, and is considered the first established genre painter in America. A popular artist, he is currently acclaimed for his sensitive studies of black Americans, as in *Eel Spearing at Setauket* (1845) and *The Banjo Player* (1858).

Mourning Dove (b. Humishima or Christine Quintasket) (1888–1936) Okanogan/Colville writer, activist; born in Bonner's Ferry, Ida. A migrant worker in Washington most of her adult life, she wrote one of the few early novels by a Native American woman, *Cogewea, the Half-Blood* (1927), as well as *Coyote Stories* (1933). She also cofounded the Colville Indian Council (1930) and in 1935 became the first woman elected to the Colville Tribal Council.

Movius, Hallam L. (Leonard, Jr.) (1907–87) archaeologist; born in Newton, Mass. He was a Harvard professor (1930–77) and curator at the Peabody Museum (1950–77). A leading authority on Stone Age Ireland and France, he was best known for his work on Périgordian and Aurignacian cultures in France, where his annual excavations at Abri Pataud (1958–73) became a celebrated training ground for students.

Mowatt, Anna Cora (b. Ogden) (1819–70) actress, playwright; born in Bordeaux, France. Daughter of a well-to-do American merchant, she came to the U.S.A. at age seven. She started out as a playwright, and her social satire, *Fashion,* was a success in 1845. Despite earlier ill health, she then became an actress, debuting as Pauline in *The Lady of Lyons*. She later formed her own company, which traveled to London.

Mowbray, Henry (Siddons) (1858–1928) painter; born in Alexandria, Egypt. His English parents emigrated to America (1859), and he studied art in Paris under Leon Bonnat (c. 1878). He then settled in New York City (1886), where he was a muralist for many libraries, churches, and courthouses. His most famous work is the decoration of the University Club, New York (c. 1901).

Moxham, Arthur J. (James) (1854–1931) steel manufacturer; born at Neath, Wales. He came to Louisville, Ky., in 1869 and worked in an iron foundry until 1878. In Alabama, he organized the Birmingham Rolling-Mill Company, which he ran until 1883 when he moved to Johnstown, Pa., to build iron girder rails with their inventor, Tom L. Johnson. Moxham directed the town's rebuilding effort after the infamous flood of 1889. The Johnson Company later moved to Ohio and became the Lorain Steel Company, merging in 1899 to form the Illinois Steel Company (which in 1901 became part of U.S. Steel). He also helped found the Dominion Iron & Steel Company in Nova Scotia (1901), was an executive at E. I. du Pont de Nemours Powder Company (1902–14), and formed the Aetna Explosives Company (1914–17).

Moy, Seong (1921–) graphic artist; born in Canton, China. He and his family emigrated to St. Paul, Minnesota (1927). He studied at the St. Paul School of Art (1936–40), the Art Students League (1941–42), and at the Hans Hofmann School, New York (1941–42). He taught at numerous schools and is known for his expressive and abstract color woodcuts, such as *Classical Horse and Rider* (1953).

Moyer, Andrew Jackson (1899–1959) microbiologist, inventor; born in Star City, Ind. Working for the U.S. Agriculture Department laboratory, he developed techniques for the large-scale production of penicillin that are credited with saving thousands of lives during World War II. His discoveries, particularly the use of corn steep liquor, were essential for the development of all other antibiotic fermentation processes.

Moyers, (Billy Don) Bill (1934–) public official, television journalist/producer; born in Hugo, Okla. While still in high school he worked for his local (Marshall, Texas) newspaper. While in college, he wrote to Senator Lyndon Johnson and got himself a summer internship, soon becoming a trusted aide; he went back to Texas to work at Mrs. Johnson's radio and television station while attending the University of Texas. After a year at the University of Edinburgh, Scotland, he earned his degree in divinity from Southwestern Theological Seminary (Waco, Texas) (1959), but he joined Senator Johnson's staff. When Johnson became vice-president, Moyers became his top assistant, but after a month he resigned to become an associate director of the new Peace Corps; he was made its deputy director in 1962. As president, Johnson appointed Moyers a special assistant (1964–65) then press secretary (1965–67). Moyers left to become the publisher of *Newsday* (1967–70). In 1971 he hosted WNET's (New York City's public television station) *This Week,* followed by *Bill Moyers Journal* (1971–76, 1978–81), with a break to serve as a correspondent for *CBS Reports* (1976–78); he returned to CBS to do news analysis (1981–86). He returned to public television where he began to produce a series of shows based on interviewing leading thinkers from various fields. Two of his series, *Joseph Campbell and the Power of the Myth* (1988) and *A World of Ideas* (1989–90), were also converted into best-selling books. His 1992 television series, *Healing and the Mind,* which examined alternatives to traditional medicine, continued his commitment to imbue contemporary issues with questions of ultimate values.

Mr. Wizard See HERBERT, DON.

"Mr. X" See KENNAN, GEORGE F.

Mrak, Emil M. (1901–87) food scientist; born in San Francisco. He grew up on a prune-producing farm in Santa Clara Valley, Calif. In 1937 he joined the faculty at the University of California: Berkeley, his *alma mater,* became chairman of the food science department in 1948, and stayed with the department when it moved to the Davis campus (1951). In 1959 he was named chancellor at Davis. Retired in 1969, he focused on world food problems in developing nations. An internationally recognized yeast specialist, he was also an expert at drying fruit.

Mudd, Samuel (Alexander) (1833–83) physician; born in Charles County, Maryland. A Maryland physician and Confederate sympathizer, he set John Wilkes Booth's broken leg after Lincoln's assassination. He was sentenced to life imprisonment after being convicted of abetting Booth's escape; although he had met Booth at church, he never was implicated in any way in the plot to kill Lincoln. He heroically nursed fellow prisoners at Fort Jefferson (off Key West, Florida) through a yellow fever epidemic before his 1869 pardon and return to Maryland. Continual efforts by his descendants to have his guilty conviction set aside – on grounds that he was only doing his duty as a doctor – continue to this day, but have so far been unavailing.

Mudge, Isadore Gilbert (1875–1957) librarian, bibliographer; born in Brooklyn, N.Y. After graduating from Cornell, she took a degree in library science at the leading such school, the New York State Library School in Albany, N.Y. (1900). She was a librarian at the University of Illinois: Urbana and Bryn Mawr, and after a trip to Europe in 1907–08, she held part-time posts until she became the head reference librarian at Columbia University (1911–41). Over the years she also taught at the library schools of Simmons College (1910–11), the New York Public Library, and Columbia University (1926–42). She edited four editions of the *Guide to Reference Works* (1917, 1923, 1929, 1936), reviewed reference works for the *Library Journal,* and wrote numerous articles, book reviews, and scholarly bibliographies. In many of her written works she was assisted by her longtime professional colleague and personal companion, Minnie Earle Sears. Mudge is credited with virtually creating modern American academic and reference library services.

Muhammad, Elijah (b. Elijah Poole) (1897–1975) religious movement leader; born near Sandersville, Ga. Son of former slaves and sharecroppers, he left home at age 16 and went to Detroit, where he worked in a Chevrolet auto plant. Having had his own spiritual revelation about 1930, he fell in with the Nation of Islam, a movement founded by W. D. Fard (or Farad), a somewhat mysterious African-American who was working as a salesman in Detroit, but whose followers believed he had come from Mecca to save blacks from the "white devils." When Fard disappeared from Detroit in 1934, Poole took over, changed his name to Elijah Muhammad, proclaimed himself the "Messenger of Allah," and made a national movement out of the Black Muslims (a name that Muhammad and his followers neither used nor liked). Muhammad stressed the need for separation of the races and scorned attempts of the civil rights movement to bring about integration; he even called for an all-black state or territory within the United States. He stressed the need for African-Americans to establish their own economic power-base, and he required strict obedience to certain tenets of Islam; although never implicated in any improprieties, he definitely imposed one-man rule. Most Americans were totally unaware of Muhammad and his movement until the 1960s, when its most noted convert, Malcolm X, drew attention to Black Muslims; it was at this time that they gained an undeserved reputation for threatening white people. When Elijah Muhammad died, his son Wallace Poole took over; he soon led the movement closer to traditional Islam and changed its name to the World Community of Islam in the West. But certain of Elijah Muhammad's teachings – the goals of hard work, discipline, self-support, and self-esteem for African-Americans – came to be accepted by increasing numbers outside his movement.

Muhlenberg, Frederick Augustus (Conrad) (1750–1801) U.S. representative, clergyman; born in Trappe, Pa. Sent to school in Germany as a teenager, he returned to Philadelphia in 1770 to become a Lutheran minister. He traveled to rural parishes and spent three years at Christ Church in New York, fleeing from Gen. William Howe's British forces in 1776. His career as a clergyman ended in 1779 when he was appointed to the Continental Congress. After a three-year term, he continued in local political offices and presided over his state's convention ratifying the new U.S. Constitution (1787). With partners, he formed importing and sugar refining businesses. A Federalist member of the House (1789–97), he served as speaker during the first three Congresses, an urbane representative of the middle states. However, he worked well with Jeffersonian Republicans, and shortly before he died he threw his support to the Republican party, which appointed him receiver-general of the Pennsylvania Land Office.

Mühlenberg, Henry Melchior (1711–87) Protestant religious leader; born in Einbeck, Germany. He studied theology at Göttingen, taught at an orphan's school in Halle, and was ordained a Lutheran minister in 1741. The following year he emigrated to Pennsylvania, where he became pastor of three congregations, and, in 1748, organized the first Lutheran synod in America. As head of the synod he traveled extensively in the colonies. He retired from the active ministry in 1779.

Muhlenberg, John Peter Gabriel (1746–1807) minister, soldier, U.S. representative; born in Trappe, Pa. (son of Henry Melchior Mühlenberg). Having taken Anglican orders, he served as pastor of a Lutheran parish in Woodstock, Va. (1771–76). He raised and led the 8th Virginia Regiment (largely composed of German-Americans) in the Revolutionary War, and as a result of his several brave actions, was breveted major-general in 1783. As vice-president of Pennsylvania (1785–88), he worked to adopt the U.S. Constitution. He served Pennsylvania in the U.S. House of Representatives (Dem.-Rep., 1789–91, 1793–95, 1799–1801) and one month in the U.S. Senate (Dem.-Rep., 1801). He was collector of customs at Philadelphia (1802–07). Pennsylvania placed his statue in the U.S. Capitol.

Muir, John (1838–1914) explorer, naturalist, conservationist; born in Dunbar, Scotland. Brought by his family to Wisconsin in 1849, he grew up on a farm; he studied at the University of

Wisconsin (1859–63; no degree, as he refused to take required courses). He was an ingenious inventor of mechanical devices but he lost an eye in 1867 in an industrial accident and so turned to his other interest – natural history. He had already walked through parts of the Midwest and Canada, and in 1867 he walked from Indianapolis to the Gulf of Mexico. In 1868 he moved to California and for the next 12 years he studied the natural world he saw on his extensive travels – going up to Alaska (where in 1879 he discovered Glacier Bay and the glacier later named after him) and to South America, Africa, and Australia – but with a special concern for California's Yosemite Valley. In 1880 he married Louie Wanda Strentzel, the daughter of an Austrian who established the Californian fruit and wine industries, and he spent the next 11 years successfully engaged in growing fruit trees. Meanwhile, he led the campaign that culminated with the act of Congress establishing Yosemite and Sequoia National Parks (1890). In 1891 Congress also passed a bill authorizing the setting aside of forest preserves; opposition by commercial interests forced Muir to continue campaigning, through speeches and magazine articles, to save the forests, but it wasn't until he persuaded President Theodore Roosevelt that any substantial acreage was set aside. In 1892, Muir had also founded the Sierra Club and was the first president of this leading conservationist organization. In addition to his many articles, he published several books during his lifetime – *The Mountains of California* (1894), *Our National Parks* (1901) – while others were published posthumously – *Travels in Alaska* (1915), *A Thousand-Mile Walk to the Gulf* (1916). A sequoia forest near San Francisco was named Muir Woods in his honor, and the John Muir Trust to acquire wild land in Britain was established in 1984.

Muldoon, William A. (1845–1933) physical trainer, wrestler; born in Belfast, N.Y. A champion professional wrestler, he developed the concept of a health spa and trained many celebrities, including two U.S. presidents, William Howard Taft and Theodore Roosevelt.

Mulholland, William (1855–1935) civil engineer; born in Belfast, Ireland. He came to the U.S.A. about 1872 and settled in California in 1877. Between 1886 and 1928 he designed and built the water system that supplies Los Angeles, including the 500-mile long aqueduct from the Sierra Nevada to Los Angeles (1913–19) and a series of 27 earth dams for storage. He retired in 1928.

Muller, Hermann J. (Joseph) (1890–1967) geneticist; born in New York City. He was one of Thomas H. Morgan's graduate students at Columbia University, then taught at the Rice Institute (1915–18) where he used the fruit fly *Drosophila* to discover that X-rays can produce mutations. He returned to Columbia (1918–20), where he theorized that self-replicating genes can control the function of all other cellular components, then became a professor at the University of Texas (1920–32), where he continued his work on the mutagenic effects of X-rays. For his pioneering work in radiation genetics, he was awarded the 1946 Nobel Prize in physiology. He took leave from the University of Texas to perform research in Moscow (1933–37), but left after disagreeing with Stalin's endorsement of an environmental, rather than genetic, explanation of inherited traits. He became a lecturer and researcher at the University of Edinburgh, Scotland (1937–40), then returned to the U.S.A. as a researcher at Amherst College (1940–45). He joined the

University of Indiana (1945–64), and remained active as a visiting professor at various institutions until his death. From 1935 on, he was a proponent of his controversial "positive human eugenic" belief that unusually healthy and gifted men should donate their sperm for the betterment of future generations.

Mullett, Alfred B. (Bult) (1834–90) architect; born in Taunton, England. A childhood immigrant, he was trained by Isaiah Rogers. Mullett was supervising architect of the Treasury Department (1866–74) and designed the State, War and Navy Building (1871–88), now the Old Executive Office Building.

Mulligan, (Gerald Joseph) Gerry (1927–   ) jazz musician; born in New York City. An important baritone saxophonist associated with cool jazz, he began as an arranger for Gene Krupa in 1947 and Claude Thornhill in 1948, then played on the historic Miles Davis Nonet recordings in 1949. He gained considerable success with the quartet he formed with Chet Baker in 1952, and he led ensembles of various sizes thereafter.

Mulliken, Robert S. (Sanderson) (1896–1986) molecular chemist; born in Newburyport, Mass. He spent most of his career as a professor at the University of Chicago (1928–65). His major contribution was his "molecular orbital" theory (first proposed in 1928), which, in its explanation of the bonds between atoms forming molecules, has had great impact in both basic science and applied research. He was awarded the Nobel Prize in chemistry (1966).

Mullis, Kary B. (Banks) (1944–   ) biochemist; born in Lenoir, N.C. A molecular biologist at Cetus Corporation of Emeryville, Calif. (1979–86), his discovery of how to multiply fragments of DNA while at Cetus (the polymerase chain reaction, or PCR) was the basis for the science fiction thriller *Jurassic Park*. From 1986–88 he was with Xytronyx Inc., San Diego, as director of molecular biology. In 1988 he began consulting to various labs in genetic engineering projects. He and Canadian Michael Smith were awarded the 1993 Nobel Prize in chemistry for progress in genetic engineering technology; Mullis's contribution was inventing the technique that allows for detailed examination of minute amounts of DNA.

Mumford, L. (Lawrence) Quincy (1903–82) librarian; born in Pitt County, N.C. The first professionally trained Librarian of Congress (1954–74), he oversaw completion of the Library's James Madison Memorial Building and greatly expanded its foreign procurement processes.

Mumford, Lewis (1895–1990) social thinker, writer; born in Flushing, N.Y. A student at both City and Columbia Universities (1912–18) who never graduated, he wrote for *New Republic* and *Harper's* in the 1920s before publishing his first book, *Sticks and Bones* (1924). A charter member of the Regional Planning Association of America (1924), he became architectural critic for the *New Yorker* in the 1930s. He produced a series of books about the debilitating effects of technology on city life, including the four-volume study *The Renewal of Life* (1934–51), *The Culture of Cities* (1938), and *The City in History* (1961). Seen as a visionary by some and a prophet of doom by others, he continued to offer plans for dealing with the chaos of urban life. He was a planning professor at the University of Pennsylvania (1952–61), and visiting professor at other universities, including the University of California: Berkeley and the Massachusetts Institute of Technology.

Munch, Charles (1891–1968) conductor; born in Strasbourg, France. After a long career as a violinist, he made his conducting debut in Paris in 1932 and three years later organized his own orchestra there. He became conductor of the Boston Symphony in 1949 and stayed until 1962. In the latter year he organized the Orchestre de Paris; he died on tour with that group in Virginia. Munch was known for allowing his players room to express themselves, producing warm and musical performances.

Munday, Richard (c. 1685–1739) builder/architect. His biographical details are sketchy. He helped transform Newport, R.I., into an elegant, modern town in the 1720s and 1730s with buildings influenced by Christopher Wren – Trinity Church (1725–26) and Old Colony House (1739).

Mundelein, George (William) (1872–1939) Catholic prelate; born in New York City. After studies in the U.S.A. and in Rome, where he was ordained (1895), he held administrative posts in the diocese of Brooklyn, becoming an auxiliary bishop (1909). In 1915 he was appointed archbishop of Chicago, becoming a cardinal in 1924. He was a vigorous advocate of Catholic interests and had close ties to President Franklin D. Roosevelt.

Muni, Paul (b. Frederick Weisenfreund) (1895–1967) stage and film actor; born in Lemberg, Austria. He debuted in Chicago's Yiddish theater. A superb character actor, he won two Oscars, one in 1936 for *The Story of Louis Pasteur.*

Munk, Walter H. (Heinrich) (1917–) oceanographer; born in Vienna, Austria. He came to the U.S.A. in 1932, and became a professor of geophysics at the Scripps Institution of Oceanography (1947). He made major contributions to research on ocean acoustics, tides, and the earth's rotation.

Muñoz Marín, Luis (1898–1980) journalist, commonwealth governor; born in San Juan, Puerto Rico. Son of Luis Muñoz Rivera, who had helped to liberate Puerto Rico from Spain, he was educated in the United States. While at Georgetown University, he began writing free-lance articles, translating American poetry into Spanish, and published his own poetry, *Borrones and Madre Haraposa,* in 1917. Returning to Puerto Rico in 1926, he published *La Democracia,* championing Puerto Rican independence. He brought New Deal funding to Puerto Rico as a Liberal Party member of the Puerto Rican senate (1932–38). After founding the Popular Democratic Party in 1938, he campaigned for land redistribution from large landowners to small farmers, becoming senate president (1938–48). Claiming islanders were not yet ready for economic independence, he began "Operation Bootstrap," to attract mainland business investment through the Puerto Rican Industrial Development Corporation. As Puerto Rico's first elected governor (1949–65), he helped draft its constitution and in 1952 presided over its attaining the status of a self-governing Commonwealth. He received a U.S. presidential medal of freedom in 1963.

Munroe, Charles Edward (1849–1938) chemist; born in Cambridge, Mass. Based at the Naval Torpedo Station and War College in Newport, R.I. (1886–92), he was the foremost explosives chemist of his time, inventing smokeless gunpowder (c. 1890) and discovering important properties of guncotton that led to the development of bazookas and shaped charges in World War II. He also played a role in the development of armor-piercing shells.

Munsel, Patrice (Beverly) (1925–) soprano; born in Spokane, Wash. She debuted at the Metropolitan Opera in 1943 and became a staple there until 1958; she later appeared in operetta and musical comedy.

Munsterberg, Hugo (1916–) art historian; born in Berlin, Germany. He emigrated to the U.S.A. (1935) earned a Ph.D. at Harvard, and taught at the State University of New York: New Paltz (1958–78) and Bard College (1978–88). His many books on Japanese, Chinese, and Indian art range from landscape painting to ceramics, folk art, and modern art.

Murchison, Clinton (Williams) "Clint" (1895–1969) entrepreneur, oil executive; born in Athens, Texas. He made a fortune in his twenties drilling Texas oil wells; he founded the natural gas industry with Southern Union Gas Company (1929–50); and he built and ran a succession of large oil companies. He also organized a large conglomerate. His later railroad ventures included a celebrated takeover of the New York Central Railroad (1954).

Murdock, George Peter (1897–1985) cultural anthropologist; born in Meriden, Conn. He studied at Yale and taught there (1928–60) and at the University of Pittsburgh (1960–71). Working out of the mainstream of the Boasian tradition of his time, he initiated the cross-cultural survey, later known as "human relations area files," as an instrument of anthropological generalization. His best-known work, *Social Structure* (1949), focused on family and kinship organization over a wide range of societies.

Murie, Olaus (Johann) (1889–1926) conservationist; born in Moorhead, Minn. He worked as an Oregon game warden, as a field naturalist for the Carnegie Museum in Pittsburgh, and as a researcher for the U.S. Biological Survey. He carried out important research in wildlife conservation in Alaska, Canada, and New Zealand and served on the council of the Wilderness Society from 1937 until his death. His definitive *Elk of North America* appeared in 1951.

Murieta or Murrieta, Joaquín (?–?1853) bandit; birthplace unknown. There were almost certainly several individuals known by this name. A California state law (1850) prohibited Californians of Mexican descent from mining for gold. In retribution, Mexicans attacked several settlements and mining camps, and the leaders of the raids were always said to be Joaquín Murieta. In 1853, a Californian posse killed two Mexicans and displayed the decapitated head of one of them to claim a $1000 reward for the death of Murieta. Murieta's story was popularized by a book by the Cherokee half-breed, Yellow Bird John (also known as Rollin Ridge) in 1854.

Murphree, Eger V. (1898–1962) chemical engineer, petroleum executive; born in Bayonne, N.J. He was affiliated with Standard Oil Development Co. (1934–62), becoming its president (1947). He was a leader in the development of synthetic toluene, hydrocarbon synthesis, and fluid catalytic cracking, hydroforming, and coking. He became involved in the U.S. guided missile program (1956).

Murphy, Audie (1924–71) soldier, actor; born near Kingston, Tenn. The most decorated American soldier of World War II, he won the Congressional Medal of Honor during the fighting in the Colmar Pocket, Germany, in 1945. He appeared in the war adventure films *Beyond Glory* (1948) and *To Hell and Back* (1948).

Murphy, Frank (1890–1949) Supreme Court justice; born in Harbor Beach, Mich. His diverse political career included posts as mayor of Detroit (1930), as governor general then high commissioner of the Philippines (1933–35), and as U.S. attorney general (1939–40). President Franklin D. Roosevelt nominated him to the U.S. Supreme Court (1940–49).

Murphy, Gardner (1895–1979) social psychologist; born in Chillicothe, Ohio. Educated at Yale, Harvard, and Columbia Universities, he taught at Columbia (1921–40) and married psychologist Lois Barclay (1926). After teaching at City College of New York (1940–52), he served as director of research at the Menninger Clinic and Foundation for 15 years. His best-known work is *Personality: A Biosocial Approach to Origins and Structures* (1947).

Murphy, Gerald (Clery) (1888–1964) painter, businessman, patron; born in Boston, Mass. A wealthy painter, he lived near New York and in France (c. 1921), and took over his father's firm, the Mark Cross Company, New York (1931). A patron of the arts, he was the friend of Zelda and F. Scott Fitzgerald.

Murphy, John Benjamin (1857–1916) surgeon; born near Appleton, Wis. He spent his medical career in Chicago, where, in addition to his surgical practice, he taught at Rush Medical College and Northwestern University Medical School and was on the surgical staff at Mercy Hospital and Cook County Hospital. He was one of the first to investigate the cause and treatment of peritonitis following appendicitis, and he developed the "Murphy button" (1892), a device used in abdominal surgery. He also made notable contributions to lung, nerve, and bone/joint surgery.

Murphy, Lois Barclay (1902–) psychologist; born in Lisbon, Iowa. Educated at Vassar, Union Theological Seminary, and Columbia University, she married social psychologist Gardner Murphy in 1926. They collaborated on 16 books, including her important *Asian Psychology* (1968) and *Western Psychology* (1969). She taught at Sarah Lawrence College for 24 years and did major research in child development, including 15 years as director of developmental studies at the Menninger Clinic and Foundation (1952–67) and seven as a consultant to Operation Headstart (1968–74). Her writings include *Personality in Young Children* (2 vols. 1956) and *Vulnerability, Coping and Growth* (1976).

Murphy, Patrick V. (Vincent) (1920–) police commissioner, foundation head; born in New York City. Son of a New York City police officer, he rose through the ranks of the New York City Police Department to deputy chief (1964–65) and then police commissioner (1970–73). In between active police duty, he administered the Justice Department's Law Enforcement Assistance Administration (1968–69). After leaving the commissioner's post, he headed the national Police Foundation (1973–85), taught at John Jay College of Criminal Justice (1985–87), and was a consultant to the United States Conference of Mayors (1985).

Murphy, Robert D. (Daniel) (1894–1978) diplomat, business executive; born in Milwaukee, Wis. His long diplomatic career began in 1920. He helped to negotiate with Vichy France (1940) and was ambassador to Belgium (1949–52) and Japan (1952). He was President Eisenhower's personal representative in Lebanon (1958). He later served as a chairman and director for Corning Glass International.

Murphy, Timothy (1751–1818) soldier; born in Pike County, Pa. A legendary Continental army sharpshooter, he enlisted in June 1775 and fought at Boston and in the New Jersey campaign, served with Gen. Daniel Morgan in the campaign against John Burgoyne (1777), and saw action at Yorktown

(1781). Murphy's inability to read and write did not bar him from postwar successes in local politics.

Murphy, William P. (Parry) (1892–1987) hematologist; born in Stoughton, Wis. He was a staff member of several New England hospitals before starting private practice in Brookline, Mass. (1923–87), concurrently working at Peter Bent Brigham Hospital, Boston (1923–73) and Harvard Medical School (1923–58). Murphy and collaborator George Minot received one-half the 1934 Nobel Prize in physiology for devising dietary liver and liver extract therapy for patients with pernicious anemia. Murphy continued to practice hematology, remaining active at Harvard and Brigham after retirement.

Murray, Henry A. (Alexander) (1893–1988) psychologist; born in New York City. He studied medicine at Columbia University and became interested in psychology upon meeting Carl Jung during the 1920s. He taught psychology at Harvard (1927–62) and directed its Psychological Clinic, where he conducted the research that culminated in the book *Explorations in Personality* (1938). He also published (with Christiana Morgan) the projective Thematic Apperception Test, which measures psychogenic needs.

Murray, James Edward (1876–1961) U.S. senator; born near St. Thomas, Ontario, Canada. He studied law at New York University. He became a U.S. citizen (1901) and set up a law practice in Butte, Mont. He served in the U.S. Senate (Dem., Mont.; 1934–61) where he supported Roosevelt's policies. He was ahead of his time in his advocacy of national health insurance and conservation measures.

Murray, John (1741–1815) Universalist clergyman; born in Alton, England. The son of strict Calvinist parents, he emigrated to the U.S.A. in 1770 and for two years was an itinerant evangelist preaching a decidedly non-Calvinist doctrine of universal salvation. Considered the founder of Universalism in America, he held pastorates in Gloucester, Mass., and Boston. He suffered a paralytic stroke in 1809 and passed the last years of his life as an invalid.

Murray, John Courtney (1904–67) Catholic theologian; born in New York City. A Jesuit priest with a doctorate in theology from Gregorian University in Rome (1937), he taught at a Jesuit seminary in Maryland, was religion editor of the Jesuit magazine *America,* and edited the journal *Theological Studies.* An advocate of ecumenism and freedom for all religions, he was silenced for a time by church conservatives but he strongly influenced the stand on religious liberty adopted at the Second Vatican Council.

Murray, Joseph E. (Edward) (1919–) surgeon; born in Milford, Mass. Trained as a plastic surgeon, he joined Peter Bent Brigham Hospital, Boston (now Brigham and Women's Hospital) (1951–86). He became interested in treatments for kidney failure in the 1950s, and performed the first human kidney transplant between identical twins in 1954. After investigating the effects of immunosuppressant drugs, he then performed the first human kidney transplant from an unrelated donor in 1962. For this lifesaving research, Murray won one-half the 1990 Nobel Prize in medicine. He became professor of surgery at Harvard (1970), and returned to plastic surgery, treating facial defects in children at Children's Hospital Medical Center, Boston (1972–85).

Murray, Philip (1886–1952) labor leader; born in New Glasgow, Scotland. A coal miner from age 10, he emigrated to the U.S.A. in 1902. He held numerous offices within the

United Mine Workers Union, climaxing with that of vice-president (1920–42). He and John L. Lewis founded the Committee of Industrial Organizations (1935). He was president of the Steel Workers Organizing Committee (1936) and succeeded Lewis as president of the Congress of Industrial Organizations (CIO) (1940–52). Although he was a strong proponent of labor's cooperation with the government during World War II and the Korean War, he never abandoned the struggle to improve the situation of laborers. His tact and personal skills kept the CIO together during the difficult war years.

Murrow, Edward R. (b. Egbert Roscoe Murrow) (1908–65) broadcast journalist; born near Greensboro, N.C. He grew up in Washington, where he worked in logging camps while attending Washington State College. As assistant director of the Institute of International Education (1932–35), he traveled abroad extensively, then went to work for CBS in 1935. Appointed director of CBS's European bureau in 1937, he personally described the Nazi takeover of Vienna for radio audiences. His broadcasts from London rooftops during the German bombing raids made him famous, along with the salute, "Good night, and good luck." He returned to New York to be a CBS vice-president and director of public affairs (1946–47). With Fred Friendly, he produced and narrated a weekly radio program, *Hear It Now* (1950–51). An episode from his acclaimed television series, *See It Now* (1951–58), helped turn public opinion against the anti-Communist Senator Joseph McCarthy. For the television series *Person to Person* (1953–59), Murrow interviewed celebrities. In 1961, he became director of the U.S. Information Agency but retired in 1964; his premature death from cancer was probably hastened by his trademark, the ever-present cigarette. He was both an eloquent and direct speaker whose courage and integrity set the standard for the profession.

Musgrave, Richard Abel (1910–) economist; born in Konigstein, Germany. He emigrated to the U.S.A. in 1933, took his Ph.D. at Harvard (1937), and continued to teach there. His book, *The Theory of Public Finance* (McGraw-Hill, 1959), provided a definitive text that incorporates the economics of public finance into economic theory as a whole.

Musgrove, Mary (b. Coosaponakeesa) (?1700–?63) Creek interpreter, trader, political leader; born near the Chatta-hoochee River in present-day Alabama. Serving as James Oglethorpe's interpreter and emissary, she played an important role in the founding of the state of Georgia.

Musial, (Stanley Frank) Stan (1920–) baseball player; born in Donora, Pa. During his 22-year career as a first baseman/outfielder for the St. Louis Cardinals (1941–63), he posted a lifetime batting average of .331, hit 475 home runs, and won the league Most Valuable Player award three times (1943, 1946, 1948). Nicknamed "Stan the Man," he was one of baseball's greatest and most consistent players. On retiring he served as general manager, then senior vice-president of the St. Louis Cardinals and he was elected to the Hall of Fame in 1969.

Muskie, Edmund S. (Sixtus) (1914–) governor, U.S. senator, cabinet officer; born in Rumford, Maine. The first Democratic governor of Maine (1955–59), he then became the first Democrat to represent Maine in the U.S. Senate (1959–80). An unsuccessful vice-presidential candidate (un-der Hubert Humphrey) in 1968, he lost a bid for the presidential nomination in 1972. He served as secretary of state during the final eight months of President Carter's administration and later as a member of the Tower Commission investigating the Iran-Contra scandal.

Musmanno, Michael Angelo (1897–1968) judge, author; born in Stowe Township, Pa. He served in both World War I (infantryman) and World War II (lieutenant commander to rear admiral). He earned a total of seven academic degrees and was a successful, if controversial, lawyer in Pittsburgh, Pa. He tried to reverse the verdict that condemned Sacco and Vanzetti to death (1927), was a member of the team appointed to ascertain whether Adolf Hitler had died in Berlin, was a judge at the Nuremberg War Trials (1946), and was a witness for the prosecution in the trial of Adolf Eichmann (1961). He was judge of the court of common pleas in Allegheny County, Pa. (1934–40), and a member of the Pennsylvania Supreme Court (1951–68). A staunch anti-Communist, he cowrote the Communist Control Act of 1954. He also wrote *Ten Days to Die* (1956) and *Columbus Was First* (1966).

Muste, A. J. (Abraham Johannes) (1885–1967) Protestant clergyman, social activist; born in Zierikzee, the Netherlands. His father, a coachman to a nobleman, brought his family over to Michigan in 1891. A. J. – as he was later known – grew up, he would say, surrounded by the spirit of Abraham Lincoln, and became a minister in the Dutch Reformed Church (1909). As the minister of a church in New York City, he became exposed both to social problems and to socialist thinkers such as Norman Thomas and Eugene Debs; rejecting strict Calvinism and Biblical literalism, he became a minister in a Congregational church in Newtonville, Mass. (1915–17). His pacifism during World War I led him to become a Quaker. He was also a founder of the American Civil Liberties Union. For the next decades, he was involved in a variety of pacifist, social action, and labor groups. In 1933 he helped found a Marxist workers' party, but in 1936 he had an experience that brought him back to Christianity. Thereafter he became active with the Quaker-sponsored Fellowship of Reconciliation, and although opposed to the U.S. participating in World War II, he worked with the government to find alternative service for conscientious objectors. After World War II, while actively opposing nuclear buildup, he continued in his nonviolent protests: in 1959 he served a nine-day jail sentence for scaling a fence at a missile site. He became one of the leaders of the protest against America's involvement in the Vietnam War and only a few weeks before dying he visited Hanoi to try to help negotiate peace with Ho Chi Minh. Martin Luther King Jr., was among the many who paid tribute to Muste as America's Gandhi, the leader of the U.S. nonviolent action movement.

Muybridge, Eadweard (1830–1904) photographer; born in Kingston-upon-Thames, England. Emigrating to America at age 20, he invented a photographic shutter to capture images of animal and human locomotion which were viewed on zootropes (1877–87).

Myers, Jerome (1867–1940) painter; born in Petersburg, Va. Based in New York City (1886), he studied with George De Forest Brush at the Art Students League (c. 1888) before he traveled to Paris (1896). He returned to New York and began his joyful paintings of children and emigrants such as *The Tambourine* (1905).

Myers, (Lawrence Eugene) Lon (1858–99) track athlete; born in Richmond, Va. Considered by many the greatest American track athlete of the 19th century, Myers dominated all running events from 100 yards to the mile from 1878 to 1885. For a time he held the American records at all those distances, though he excelled particularly at the middle distances, running the quarter mile in 48.8 seconds and the half mile in 1:55.4, all during a period when tracks were apt to be composed of an uneven surface of loose cinders. His only serious rival was the great English runner, Walter George, whom he defeated six of the nine times they raced.

N

Nabokov, Vladimir (Vladimirovich) (1899–1977) writer; born in St. Petersburg, Russia. He studied at the Prince Tenishev School, St. Petersburg (1910–17), and at Trinity College, Cambridge (B.A. 1922). To escape the Bolshevik Revolution, he and his family left Russia (1919) and moved to Berlin, Germany. He taught English and tennis, as well as composed crossword puzzles for the Russian emigré newspaper, *Rul* (1922–37), and gained a reputation as a fiction writer (in Russian) under the pen name, V. Sirin. He moved to Paris (1937–40), then, fleeing the Nazis, emigrated to the United States with his wife and child (1940). He taught at Stanford during the summer of 1941 and at Wellesley (1941–48); as an authority on butterflies, he became a research fellow in entomology at Harvard's Museum of Comparative Zoology (1942–59). From 1948 until 1959 he also taught at Cornell. An accomplished linguist, he had known English since his childhood but did not begin writing in it until after he settled in the U.S.A. His varied work includes poetry, fiction, drama, autobiography, essays, translations, and literary criticism, as well as works on butterflies and chess problems. He is most widely known for his novel, *Lolita* (1955), conveying the infatuation of a middle-aged man with a 12-year-old girl; many critics and moralists attacked the novel, but it became a best-seller, if for all the wrong reasons. With the financial security that followed the success of *Lolita* and several later novels, he retired from teaching and settled at the Palace Hotel in Montreux, Switzerland, and continued issuing his literary works and pronouncements until his death.

Nadelman, Elie (1882–1946) sculptor; born in Warsaw, Poland. He studied at the Warsaw Art Academy (1899) and in Paris, where he lived until 1914, then emigrated to New York City and lived in Riverdale, N.Y. He was known for many styles, such as primitivism, cubism, and neoclassicism, as in *Ideal Head* (c. 1915).

Nader, Ralph (1934–) lawyer, consumer advocate; born in Winsted, Conn. He graduated from Princeton (1955) and Harvard Law School (1958), then established a practice in Hartford. Convinced that automobile injuries were often due to unsafe vehicle design, he wrote *Unsafe at Any Speed* (1965, rev. 1972), which aroused public interest and led to passage of the 1966 National Traffic and Motor Vehicle Safety Act. He was chiefly responsible for passage of the 1967 Wholesome Meat Act, imposing federal standards on slaughterhouses. His professional associates, known (sometimes derisively) as "Nader's Raiders" published reports on many subjects, including baby food, insecticides, mercury poisoning, radiation dangers, pension reform, and coal-mine safety. He founded the Center for Responsive Law, Public Citizen Inc., and other groups. Idealistic and modest, he became known for spartan personal habits and long workdays. His many books include *The Menace of Atomic Energy* (1977) and *Who's Poisoning America?* (1981).

Nagel, Ernest (1901–85) philosopher; born in Czechoslovakia. Emigrating to the U.S.A. as a child in 1911 and naturalized in 1919, he was a longtime philosophy teacher at Columbia University (1931–70). One of the first Americans influenced by European analytic philosophy, he wrote important works on logic and the philosophy of science, including *The Structure of Science* (1961).

Nagel, Thomas (1937–) philosopher; born in Belgrade, Yugoslavia. After receiving a Harvard doctorate (1963), he taught at the University of California: Berkeley (1963–66) and Princeton (1966–80), then became a professor and department chairman at New York University. His specialties include ethics, philosophy of mind, and ancient philosophy; his books include *Mortal Questions* (1978).

Nagurski, (Bronislaw) "Bronko" (1908–90) football player; born in Rainy River, Ontario, Canada. Chosen All-American at the University of Minnesota in 1929 at both tackle and fullback, he became the archetype pile-driving fullback of the 1930's with the National Football League Chicago Bears. Although never the league's rushing leader, the powerful, 235-pound runner was nearly impossible to stop without a gain. Ironically, his jump pass to "Red" Grange won the 1932 championship for the Bears.

Naismith, James (1861–1939) physical education teacher, inventor of basketball; born in Almonte, Ontario, Canada. A graduate of McGill (Montreal), he was at the Young Men's Christian Association Training School (now Springfield College) in Springfield, Mass., when he was invited by Luther Gulick, head of the school's physical education department, to devise some form of indoor team sport for the winter, one that would not involve expensive equipment; he devised a game (based on 13 rules) that required throwing balls through hoops – half-bushel peach baskets were used at first, thus providing the name "basketball." The game spread quickly, eventually attaining international popularity; its Hall of Fame is located in Springfield, Mass. Naismith moved on to teach physical education at the University of Kansas (1898–1937).

Nakashima, George (1905–90) furniture maker; born in

Spokane, Wash. Following early work as an architect in Tokyo and India, he moved to New Hope, Pa., in the mid-1940s to begin making sculptural furniture by hand. His creations were informed by Japanese grace and Shaker design. Known as the dean of 20th-century American woodworkers because of his high professional standards, he wrote a book describing his reverence for wood, *The Soul of a Tree* (1981).

Nakian, Reuben (1897–1986) sculptor; born in Long Island, N.Y. He studied at the Art Students League (1912), was an apprentice to Paul Manship (1916), shared a studio with Gaston Lachaise (1920–23), then moved to Stamford, Conn. (1944). He specialized in animal and heroic subjects, and later, expressionistic sculptures, such as *The Dance of Death* (1967).

Namath, (Joseph William) Joe (1943–) football player; born in Beaver Falls, Pa. After starring at the University of Alabama, he signed with the New York Jets of the American Football League in 1965 for a then-record $400,000. Called "Broadway Joe" for his enjoyment of night life, in 1967 he became the first professional to pass for more than 4,000 yards, and he quarterbacked the Jets to victory in Super Bowl III the next year. After retiring from football (1977), he pursued a career in movies and broadcasting.

Nampeyo, Dextra Quotskuyva (b. Tsu Mana) (?1859–1942) Hopi potter; born at Hanu Pueblo in present-day Arizona. Her revival of ancient designs led to a renaissance of Hopi pottery, transforming its quality and leading to its elevation as an art form.

Nancarrow, Conlon (1912–) composer; born in Texarkana, Ark. He pursued both jazz and classical studies in his youth and in 1937 fought in the Spanish Civil War. Three years later he settled in Mexico City, where he created a series of unique, highly complex works for pianola by working directly on the piano rolls. He emerged from relative obscurity by way of a 1982 "genius" award from the MacArthur Foundation.

Nasby, Petroleum See LOCKE, DAVID ROSS.

Nash, Charles W. (Williams) (1864–1948) automobile manufacturer; born in De Kalb County, Ill. When his parents separated in 1870 he was bound out to a farmer in Michigan. He ran away at age 12 and worked various jobs. Married in 1884, he moved to Flint, Mich., in 1891 for his wife's medical needs and ended up at the Durant-Dort Carriage Company trimming upholstery. Promoted rapidly, he became plant supervisor and then general manager (1904), replacing William C. Durant who went on to Buick and General Motors (GM). Under Durant the companies almost went bankrupt, and Nash, who had been making Buick auto bodies, was asked to take over (1912). By 1915 he had restored financial order to GM, although partially by foregoing the stockholder's dividends. Durant regained control of GM (1916), and Nash left for Wisconsin where he bought the company that made the Rambler, renaming it the Nash Motor Company. This he merged with the Kelvinator Company (1937), manufacturer of household appliances like refrigerators, to diversify and stay competitive. He was active in civic affairs in Kenosha, Wis., but retired to Beverly Hills after World War II.

Nash, John F. (Forbes, Jr.) (1928–) mathematician; born in Bluefield, Va. He attended Carnegie Institute of Technology (now Carnegie-Mellon University), switching from chemical engineering to mathematics; he took both a B.A. and M.A. in mathematics in 1948, then earned his Ph.D. in mathematics at Princeton in 1950. Joining the mathematics faculty of Massachusetts Institute of Technology in 1951, he was promoted to associate professor when in 1959 mental illness forced him to resign. Thereafter he resided in Princeton, N.J., for much of that time as a visiting research scholar at Princeton University, but at times as a visiting scholar at the Institute for Advanced Study. His doctoral thesis, "Noncooperative Games" was published in the early 1950s and is regarded as laying the mathematical foundations for game theory. This field of analysis, which uses mathematics to predict how people will behave in all kinds of situations involving rivalries, was invented in the 1940s by John von Neumann and Oskar Morgenstern. Since the 1950s, game theory has been applied by economists in studying strategic behavior, specifically in the organization of industry for competitive situations. Nash shared the 1994 Nobel Prize in economic science with two other major contributors to game theory, John C. Harsanyi, an American, and Reinhard Selten, a German.

Nast, Condé (Montrose) (1873–1942) publisher; born in New York City. After working for *Collier's Weekly* (1898–1907), he bought *Vogue* (1909), which was then a small New York society magazine. He transformed *Vogue* into America's premier fashion magazine, then turned *Vanity Fair* into a sophisticated magazine for all that was stylish; he eventually owned a stable of high-class magazines, including *House and Garden*, British and French *Vogue,* and *Glamour.* Nearly ruined in the Great Depression, he spent his last years struggling to regain his early prosperity.

Nash, (Frediric) Ogden (1902–71) poet, writer; born in Rye, N.Y. He studied at Harvard (1920–21), taught briefly, and was a bond salesman in New York (1924). After he got a job in publishing, he began to contribute his humorous poems to magazines including the *New Yorker,* whose editorial staff he joined in 1932. He soon became known as one of America's most sophisticated as well as popular poets. His poetry's ingenious rhymes and witty juxtapositions soon gained him a reputation with both sophisticates and the general public. In addition to plays and prose pieces, he collaborated with S. J. Perelman on the libretto for the musical *One Touch of Venus* (1943) and the inimitable verses for a recording of Saint-Saëns "Carnival of the Animals."

Nast, Thomas (1840–1902) cartoonist; born in Landau, Germany. When he was five years old, his family migrated to America, and at an early age he studied at the Academy of Design in New York City. He became a draftsman for *Frank Leslie's Illustrated Newspaper* at age 15, and in 1861 he was engaged with *Harper's Weekly* (1861–86), where he defined the genre of the political cartoon. His crusade against the corrupt New York political machine known as the Tweed Ring in 1871 resulted in the removal from office of virtually every member of Tammany Hall. He also created such cartoon icons as the Republican elephant and the Democratic donkey, and he helped form the American notion of Santa Claus.

Nathans, Daniel (1928–) geneticist; born in Wilmington, Del. He was a clinical associate at the National Cancer Institute (1955–57), then a medical resident at Columbia-Presbyterian Medical Center (1957–59). He became a guest investigator at Rockefeller University (1959–62) before joining Johns Hopkins (1962). His studies using restriction enzymes led to the first genetic map of the DNA molecule and made possible the laboratory synthesis of microbial recombinant DNA. He was awarded one-third of the 1978 Nobel Prize in physiology for this pioneering research.

Nation, Carry (Amelia b. Moore) (1846–1911) temperance reformer; born in Garrard County, Ky. Her alcoholic first husband left her with an abiding hatred for liquor and saloons. She conducted a series of hatchet-swinging, saloon-smashing missions in Kansas and in large cities throughout the country. She was arrested 30 times before her retirement due to poor health. Even supporters of the temperance movement found her a difficult person.

Natzler, Gertrud (Amon) (1908–71) **and Otto** (1908–) ceramicists; both born in Vienna, Austria. She was a potter and he was a self-taught glazer when they began to collaborate in Vienna in 1933. They founded a studio in 1935 to produce the elegant thin-walled pots, bowls, vases, and other vessels "thrown" by Gertrud and glazed by Otto; Natzler vessels have richly textured surfaces – some distinctively pock-marked – often painterly in color but never with figural imagery; he would develop over 2,000 glaze formulas, most by trial-and-error in the kiln. In 1938 they fled just as the Nazis took over Vienna and managed to get to Los Angeles with some of their tools and some vessels. They taught for three years in Los Angeles and quickly became known for their high professional and aesthetic standards. After Gertrud's death and some 25,000 works together, Otto turned to making ceramic constructions of geometric forms with metallic glazes.

Natzler, Otto See under Natzler, Gertud Amon.

Nauman, Bruce (1941–) sculptor, mixed media artist; born in Fort Wayne, Ind. He studied at the Universities of Indiana and California: Davis (M.F.A. 1966); after living in California (1964–79), he settled in New Mexico (1979). He is known for his sculptures incorporating aspects of the human body, as in *From Hand to Mouth* (1967), and his subsequent performance pieces utilizing film, video tapes, and neon lighting.

Navarro, (Theodore) "Fats" (1923–50) jazz musician; born in Key West, Fla. He was a brilliant and influential trumpeter and a sideman with Andy Kirk, Billy Eckstine, and Tadd Dameron before his death from tuberculosis.

Navratilova, Martina (1956–) tennis player; born in Prague, Czechoslovakia. After defecting to the U.S.A. from Czechoslovakia in 1975, she provided tennis with one of its greatest rivalries with her many fierce competitions with Chris Evert from 1975 to 1989. Holder of many of the major records in women's tennis, she won the Wimbledon singles nine times (a record), the U.S. singles four times, the Australian three times, and the French twice. In 1992, Navratilova won her 158th professional singles title, an all-time record. As one of the first major sports figures to be open about her lesbianism, she gained respect from many but she also found herself involved in occasional controversies. She retired in 1994.

Nazimova, Alla (1879–1945) stage actress; born in Yalta, Russia. A leading performer with the Moscow Art Theatre, she debuted in New York in 1905 in a Russian play; within six months she learned enough English to play Hedda Gabler. Credited as one of the first to take a psychological approach to acting, she was best known for her Ibsen and Chekhov roles on stage but later she made a few movies.

Neagle, John (1796–1865) painter; born in Boston, Mass. He studied with Bass Otis (c. 1813), married Thomas Sully's niece (1826), and lived in Philadelphia. He became a prominent painter, and his most famous work is *Pat Lyon at the Forge* (c. 1829).

Needham, James Joseph (1926–) accountant, financier; born in Woodhaven, N.Y. He studied at Cornell and St. John's University (New York City) and worked as an accountant for Price, Waterhouse from 1947–54; he later became a partner in the firm R. T. Hyer & Company. Named chairman and chief executive officer of the New York Stock Exchange in 1972, the first chosen from outside the industry, he served until a boardroom coup toppled him in 1976. He later became a consultant, taught at St. John's, and was active in Republican politics and Roman Catholic charitable causes.

Nef, John Ulric (1862–1915) chemist; born in Herisau, Switzerland. Coming to the U.S.A. as a child in 1866, he did his graduate work in Germany. As a professor at Purdue (1887–89), Clark (1889–92), and the University of Chicago (1892–1915), he was a pioneer in the transfer of German university traditions in organic chemistry. His particular field was the study of bivalent carbon compounds such as quinone and the action of alkaline oxidizing agents on sugars.

Neff, Pat Morris (1871–1952) governor, educator; born near McGregor, Texas. An attorney, he served in the Texas house of representatives (Dem., 1901–05), becoming Speaker in 1903. As governor of Texas (1921–25), he founded Texas Technological College and South Texas State Teachers College. He used martial law to control the Limestone and Freestone County oil boom. He later became Baylor University president (1932–47).

Neiman, LeRoy (1927–) illustrator; born in St. Paul, Minn. He studied at the Art Institute of Chicago (1946–50) and the University of Illinois (1951). Based in New York City, he is recognized as the consummate sports artist of the 20th century. In 1972 he was named the official artist for the Olympic games. He was designated the outstanding sports artist in America by the Amateur Athletic Union (1976) and was given the Olympic Artist of the Century Award in 1979.

Nelson, (Eric Hilliard) Rick(y) (1940–85) popular singer; born in Teaneck, N.J. He sang on his parents' television show, *The Adventures of Ozzie and Harriet*, in 1957, and that year had his first hit songs "I'm Walking" and "A Teenager's Romance." In the late-1950s and early-1960s his hits were regularly on the radio. After a decline in his popularity, his single, "Garden Party" (1972), sold over a million copies. He died in a plane crash.

Nelson, George (1907–1986) industrial designer; born in Hartford, Conn. After architecture studies at Yale, Catholic University, and the American Academy in Rome, he founded his own industrial design firm (1946) and became design director at Herman Miller Furniture Company. Among his original concepts were the pedestrian mall (1942), storage wall (1946), and office work station (1947). He edited *Architectural Forum* (1935–44), *Design Journal* (1968–73), and various design books.

Nelson, Jerry Earl (1944–) astrophysicist; born in Glendale, Calif. This maker of gadgets from boyhood solved the physical problems that had long inhibited building the largest telescope in the world. A researcher at the Lawrence Berkeley Laboratory beginning in 1975, his honeycomb mirror concept and project direction enabled the construction of the 33-foot-wide Keck telescope on Hawaii's Mauna Kea volcano.

Nelson, (John) Byron, Jr. (1912–) golfer; born in Ft. Worth, Texas. He twice won the Masters (1937, 1942) and the Professional Golfers' Association (PGA) title (1940, 1945). He won eleven consecutive tournaments on his way to winning 19 tournaments in 1945.

Nelson, Marjorie Maxine (1909–62) biochemist; born in Kansas City, Mo. A University of California: Berkeley Ph.D., she was a staff biochemist at the Institute of Experimental Biology there (1944–58). She was among the first to study environmental factors in fetal development; her research demonstrated that malnutrition causes fetal damage.

Nelson, Nels Christian (1875–1964) anthropologist; born near Fredericia, Jutland, Denmark. He emigrated to the U.S.A. in 1892. Joining the American Museum of Natural History in 1912, he was curator of prehistoric archaeology (1928–43). He pioneered stratigraphic excavation techniques in his extensive international fieldwork and promoted the hypothesis of age-and-area, the outward diffusion of human culture.

Nelson, Samuel (1792–1873) Supreme Court justice; born in Hebron, N.Y. A supporter of women's suffrage and a long-time friend of James Fenimore Cooper, he sat as a judge on the Circuit Court (1823–31) and Supreme Court (1831–45) of New York before President John Tyler named him to the U.S. Supreme Court (1845–51).

Nelson, Willie (Hugh) (1933–) country music singer, songwriter; born in Fort Worth, Texas. Before he was a teenager he sang gospel in a Baptist church and played guitar in polka bands, but he also absorbed both pop and jazz music. Writing songs in Nashville in the 1960s, he helped the country music revival, but he did not get much recognition for his own singing. He relocated to Austin, Texas, and also reconstructed his image, adopting his trademark beard, headband, earring, and blue jeans. At first he won over a largely youthful audience, especially with his annual "picnics," like mini-Woodstocks, but gradually he broadened his appeal to an adult public. A widely popular, eclectic performer, he recorded jazz standards, country-rock, and gospel in his distinctive singing style, with its bluesy, off-beat phrasing. In the late 1980s he was briefly in trouble with the Internal Revenue Service for falling behind in his taxes, but he resolved that problem and resumed his role as something of a national country-music icon, in part because of his generous appearances at benefit concerts.

Nemerov, Howard (Stanley) (1920–91) poet, writer; born in New York City. He studied at Harvard (B.A. 1941), and taught at many institutions such as Bennington (1948–66) and, beginning in 1967, Washington University, St. Louis. He was named Consultant in Poetry (1963–64) and Poet Laureate by the Library of Congress (1988), and is known for his literary prose works and blank verse, as in *Collected Poems* (1977).

Nemir, Rosa Lee (m. Audi) (1906–92) pediatrician; born in Waco, Texas. One of the first women to become a full professor of pediatrics, she spent her career at the New York University medical school (1930–91). A pulmonary and pediatrics specialist, she studied the effects of steroids on tuberculosis and was the first to use the drug rifampin to treat the disease. She promoted medical careers for women through various national and international organizations.

Nerinckx, Charles (1761–1824) religious leader; born in Belgium. Ordained in 1785 and forced underground after the French Revolution, he emigrated to the U.S.A. in 1804 and became a missionary in the wilderness frontier of Kentucky. Zealous and accused of excessive rigorism, he cofounded the Sisters of Loretto (1912), imposing on them a stringent rule of life.

Nestor, Agnes (1880–1948) labor leader; born in Grand Rapids, Mich. A gloveworker in Chicago, she led her sister gloveworkers in a drive for a union shop in 1898 and became president of the all-female local in 1902. She rose through the ranks to become president of the International Gloveworkers Union (1913–15). She was also active in the National Women's Trade Union League (1913–48). Beyond her varied labor union activities, she was a highly regarded proponent of progressive social legislation and she served on various state and national boards and commissions.

Neuberger, Richard Lewis (1912–60) journalist, author, U.S. senator; born in Portland, Ore. He worked as a journalist for the *Portland Oregonian* and as Pacific Northwest correspondent for the *New York Times* and wrote several books and many articles about the Pacific Northwest. He served in the state legislature before his election to the U.S. Senate (Dem., Ore.; 1955–60).

Neugebauer, Otto (?–1990) astronomer/mathematical historian; born in Austria. Fleeing Nazism, he came to America (1939) to teach at Brown University where he became known as a devoted teacher, mathematical and astrological historian, and founder of *Mathematical Reviews*. A member of the National Academy of Sciences, he was an intensely private man.

Neuhaus, Richard John (1936–) minister, author; born in Pembroke, Ontario, Canada. A minister's son, he left home at age 14 and succeeded in business before he became the Lutheran pastor of a largely black congregation in Brooklyn, N.Y. (1961–78). Active in the protest movements of the 1960s, he became more conservative in response to later events, maintaining that the Moral Majority groups were correct in their emphasis, if not in their methods. He converted to Catholicism and wrote *The Catholic Moment* (1987). He became director of the Center on Religion and Society (1984).

Neumann, Franz Leopold (1900–54) political scientist; born in Katowice, Upper Silesia (now Poland). He escaped Nazi persecution in Germany and emigrated to New York in 1936. He served as an adviser to the State Department during World War II and taught at Columbia University (1947–54). His controversial analysis, *The Structure and Practice of National Socialism* (1942), used Marxist analysis to demonstrate how Nazism ultimately served to strengthen capitalism.

Neumann, John (Nepomucene) (1811–60) Catholic prelate, saint; born in Bohemia. After seminary studies he emigrated, virtually penniless, to New York City, where he was accepted for ordination in 1836. Following pastoral work in the Buffalo, N.Y., region, he took vows as a Redemptorist (1842), served in Baltimore and Pittsburgh, and was a Redemptorist vice-provincial (1847–51). As bishop of Philadelphia (from 1852), he built many schools and churches, wrote doctrinal books in German for children, and was well known as a preacher, retreat master, and champion of the poor. Admired for sanctity in his lifetime, he was beatified in 1963 and canonized in 1977.

Neutra, Richard (1892–1970) architect, author; born in Vienna, Austria. He emigrated in 1923, and, working with R. M. Schindler and alone, designed uncompromisingly modernist houses and schools, mostly in California, incorporating such innovations as steel framing (Lovell (Health) House (1929), Los Angeles). Later, with Robert Alexander (1949–mid-1960s), he tackled larger public projects. His books include *Survival Through Design* (1954), which promoted "biorealism," a balance among buildings, people, and the environment.

Nevelson, Louise (b. Berliawsky) (1900–88) sculptor; born in Kiev, Russia. She and her family emigrated to Maine (1905). She married (1920) and then settled in New York City where she studied at the Art Students League (1929–30). She then studied with Hans Hofmann in Munich (1931) and worked in New York City as an assistant to Diego Rivera (1932). Her first sculptures were figural and cubist in mixed media, and by 1950 she had focused on her famous boxed assemblages and constructions, as in *Moon Garden + One* (1957–60). Her architectural environments and fantasies were often of painted wood; later she utilized Plexiglas, aluminum, formica, and steel.

Nevers, (Ernest Alonzo) Ernie (1903–76) football player; born in Willow River, Minn. A triple-threat fullback, he was a unanimous 1925 All-American at Stanford and scored a record 40 points in one National Football League game in 1929.

Nevin, Ethelbert (Woodbridge) (1862–1901) composer; born in Edgeworth, Pa. After studies in America and Europe, he pursued a career of composing sentimental parlor songs and piano pieces such as "The Rosary."

Nevins, (Joseph) Allen (1890–1971) historian, journalist; born in Camp Point, Ill. He attended the University of Illinois (M.A. English, 1913); began his professional career as a journalist in New York City; taught history at Columbia University (1928–58); and was senior research associate at Huntington Library (1958–71). He twice took time out to serve as a U.S. foreign officer (1943–46; 1965). His numerous awards include Pulitzer Prizes in 1932 and 1937 for *Grover Cleveland: A Study in Courage* and *Hamilton Fish: The Inner History of the Grant Administration*. Known for his ground-breaking books on the Civil War, he founded Columbia's Oral History Project (1948) and was a founder of *American Heritage* magazine.

Newberry, John Strong (1822–92) geologist, paleontologist; born in Windsor, Conn. As a physician-naturalist, he accompanied several army exploring expeditions to the American West in the 1850s; in his *Report Upon the Colorado River . . .* (1861) he attributed the formation of the Grand Canyon to erosion; he later published important work on fossil fishes and fossil plants in North American coalbeds. While on the faculty of the Columbia School of Mines (1866–92), he helped establish the institution's outstanding scientific reputation.

Newcomb, Simon (1835–1909) astronomer, mathematician; born in Wallace, Nova Scotia. Born to New England parents who had moved to Nova Scotia, he immigrated to America in his teens; eventually finding work at the office of the *American Ephemeris and Nautical Almanac,* then located at Harvard College, he took a degree from the college's

Lawrence Scientific School (1858). Appointed a professor of mathematics by the U.S. Navy in 1861, he was assigned to the Naval Observatory in Washington, D.C.; he remained affiliated there until 1897; he also served as professor at Johns Hopkins University (1884–94, 1898–1900). Although he made telescopic observations, his major contributions came through his complex mathematical calculations; with these he effectively recalculated and corrected all the known positions and motions of the bodies of the solar system and the major celestial reference objects, a monumental accomplishment that was accepted throughout the world. He also did pioneer work in calculating the sun's parallax, and, with A. A. Michelson, determined the velocity of light. In addition to his scientific writing he published popular texts, *Reminiscences of an Astronomer* (1903), and three novels. He helped found and was first president of the American Astronomical Society (1899–1905) and was the recipient of many honors abroad as well as in America.

Newell, Frederick Haynes (1862–1932) civil engineer; born in Bradford, Pa. He was appointed hydrographer to the U.S. Geological Survey in 1888. He helped prepare bills including the Reclamation Act of 1902 and became director of the Reclamation Service (1907–1914). He later consulted on numerous natural resource projects and wrote on the subject.

Newell, Norman Dennis (1909–) paleontologist, geologist; born in Chicago. Simultaneously professor of geology at Columbia University and curator of fossils at the American Museum of Natural History (1945–77), Newell led many international expeditions and specialized in coral reefs and South American geology.

Newhall, Beaumont (1908–93) photohistorian; born in Lynn, Mass. A Harvard-trained art historian, Newhall was librarian at the Museum of Modern Art (1935–42) where he wrote the catalogue for the exhibition, *Photography 1893–1937,* before becoming its first curator of photography in 1940. An officer for U.S. Air Force photographic intelligence in Egypt, North Africa, and Italy (1942–45), he began his teaching career at Black Mountain College (1946–48). In 1947 he received a Guggenheim grant which he used to write his classic text, *History of Photography,* first published in 1949. Curator of the International Museum of the George Eastman House (GEH) during its formative years, he became editor of *Art in America* (1957–65) and was director of GEH (1958–71). The preeminent teacher of photohistorians, he was a professor of art at New York State University in Buffalo (1968–71) and taught at the University of New Mexico from 1971. In 1984 he received a MacArthur Foundation grant.

Newhall, Nancy (b. Parker) (1908–74) writer, photographer; born in Swampscott, Mass. An art student who married Beaumont Newhall, she was curator of photography at the Museum of Modern Art (1942–45), writing books with Ansel Adams and Edward Weston.

Newhart, (George Robert) Bob (1929–) television comedian; born in Chicago. An accountant who created monologues as a diversion, he became famous with a best-selling recording of his first night club engagement, *The Button-Down Mind of Bob Newhart* (1960). A low-key satirist, he starred in a series of television sitcoms, *The Bob Newhart Show* (1971–78), *Newhart* (1982–90), and *Bob* (1992).

Newhouse, S. I. (Samuel Irving) (1895–1979) publisher;

born in New York City. Starting as an aide to a New Jersey judge, he became manager of the judge's local paper, acquired control of his own newspaper, the *Staten Island Advance,* and built a large chain of papers through acquisitions; he kept them going through cost-cutting economies and often dealt harshly with unions. A major philanthropist, he founded the Newhouse School of Public Communications at Syracuse University in 1964.

Newman, Alfred (1901–70) film composer; born in New Haven, Conn. From 1930 he scored some 200 films including *Arrowsmith* (1931), *Wuthering Heights* (1939), *All About Eve* (1950), and *Airport* (1970). He won eight Oscars.

Newman, Barnett (1905–70) painter, sculptor; born in New York City. He studied at the Art Students League (1922–26), and joined his father's clothing manufacturing business (1927–37). He lived in New York City, and by 1944 began his series of cosmic landscapes using stripes, circles, and color divisions, as seen in *Genetic Moment* (1947). He was one of the founders, along with William Baziotes, Mark Rothko and Robert Motherwell, of an art school, Subjects of the Artist, New York (1947). A leader of color-field painting, as seen in *Onement I* (1948), he stressed the use of color and mythology. His sculptures have a classical composure, as in *Broken Obelisk* (1967).

Newman, Paul (1925–) film actor, director, producer; born in Cleveland (husband of Joanne Woodward). After World War II service in the navy, he discovered theater at Kenyon College, going on to Yale Drama School and the Actors Studio in New York. His first Broadway role in *Picnic* (1953) led to a Hollywood contract and he was soon launched on a long string of popular hits that exploited his peculiar blend of blue-eyed masculinity, ironic humor, obvious intelligence, and a dash of rebelliousness; despite several Oscar nominations, he won his first for *The Color of Money* (1986). In addition to directing and producing movies, he was also a serious motor racer and he lent his name to food products (the profits going to a camp for children with terminal illnesses). Outspoken in endorsing liberal political and social causes, in 1978 he even served as a U.S. delegate to a UN disarmament conference.

Newman, Randy (1943–) composer, lyricist; born in Los Angeles, Calif. The nephew of three successful Hollywood composers and conductors, he began studying the piano at age seven and was writing songs professionally when he was 17. After letting others such as Judy Collins, Peggy Lee, Ella Fitzgerald, and Joni Mitchell sing his songs, he took to performing at colleges and night clubs in the late 1960s and earned a reputation for both his inimitable piano/vocal style, which combined the casual with highly mannered effects, and for his lyrics, which sardonically dissected politics and society. He composed film scores such as *Cold Turkey* (1970), *Ragtime* (1981), and *The Natural* (1984), and released several popular albums including *Sail Away* (1972) and *Little Criminals* (1978). A revue based on his songs played in various theaters between 1981–84 and he performed his old and new songs occasionally.

Newport, Christopher (c. 1565–1617) seaman, colonist; born in England. In 1606 he was given charge of the Virginia Company's expedition to America. He made a total of five voyages to Jamestown (1607–11) and served as the intermediary between the Virginia Company and the new colonists in Virginia.

Newton, Isaac (1800–67) agriculturalist; born in Burlington County, N.J. By his mid-20s he was managing two farms in Springfield, Pa., so successfully that he opened a confectionery shop and sold ice cream made from his dairy surplus. Active in the state and national Agricultural Society, he urged Congress to establish a department of agriculture. In 1861 President Lincoln appointed him supervisor of the agricultural division of the Patent Office. In 1862 Congress created the Department of Agriculture with Newton as its first commissioner. In his annual reports he emphasized the importance of weather and climate to agriculture. He died from the effects of a sunstroke he received while working in the department's experimental field.

Neyland, (Robert Reese, Jr.) Bob (1892–1962) football coach; born in Greenville, Texas. The University of Tennessee coach for 21 years, he made the Vols into a major power and won the national championship in 1951.

Ng Poon, Chew (1866–1931) minister, editor, lecturer; born in South China. He studied under a Taoist priest before he emigrated to San Francisco (1881). He converted to Christianity (1882) and was a Presbyterian minister to Chinese congregations in California (1892–99). He left the ministry and founded the *Chinese Western Daily* (1900), the first Chinese daily paper in the U.S.A. He lectured for the Chautauqua and Lyceum groups (1915–31) and promoted better understanding of Chinese culture in the U.S.A. He became a Mason and a Shriner.

Nicholas, John (?1757–1819) U.S. representative; born in Williamsburg, Va. A graduate of William and Mary and a lawyer, he served in Congress (Rep., Va.; 1793–1801), leaving to pursue farming and preside as common pleas judge (1806–19) in rural New York.

Nicholas, Wilson Cary (1761–1820) U.S. representative/ senator, governor; born in Williamsburg, Va. Son of Robert Carter Nicholas, a prominent Virginian official, he served with George Washington's personal guard unit in the closing years of the American Revolution. After serving in the Virginia Assembly (1784–89, 1794–99), he then represented Virginia in the U.S. Senate (Dem.-Rep.; 1799–1804) and in the U.S. House of Representatives (Dem.-Rep.; 1807–09). While governor of Virginia (1814–17), he assisted his friend Thomas Jefferson in establishing the University of Virginia, but he also nearly bankrupted Jefferson, who had cosigned a loan for his speculation in western lands.

Nichols, Ernest F. (Fox) (1869–1924) physicist; born in Leavenworth, Kans. He was affiliated with Colgate (1892–98), Dartmouth (1898–1903; president, 1909–16), Yale (1916–20), and Nela Research Laboratories, Cleveland (1921–24). He made major advances in studies of infrared radiation (1890s), and quantitatively measured the pressure of light (1901).

Nichols, Kyra (1958–) ballet dancer; born in Berkeley, Calif. Trained by her mother, Sally Streets, and at the School of American Ballet, Nichols joined the New York City Ballet in 1976. Recognized for her fluidity, strength, and speed, she became a principal dancer with the company in 1979.

Nichols, Mike (b. Michaael Igor Peschkowsky) (1931–) stage/film director, writer, comedian; born in Berlin, Germany. Brought to the U.S.A. as a child to escape the Nazis, he emerged out of the cross-fertilizing of the university and the improvised theater of Chicago in the 1950s; he first came to national attention with *An Evening with Mike Nichols and*

Elaine May (1960), with its wry spoofs of everyday and unusual relationships. He went on to direct numerous stage plays – including *Barefoot In the Park* (1963), and *The Odd Couple* (1965) – and films, including *The Graduate,* which won an Oscar as the year's best in 1967. In later years he earned a reputation as a "doctor" who was often brought in to rescue stage or movie productions in trouble.

Nichols, Thomas Low (1815–1901) dietitian, author, reformer; born in Orford, N.H. As a journalist and prolific author he promoted health foods, free love, and spiritualism, among other reforms. After earning a medical qualification (1850) he joined his wife, physician Mary Grove Nichols, in training hydropathic physicians. They lived in England and Europe after 1861.

Nicholson, Francis (1655–1728) colonial governor; born in Yorkshire, England. He had a broad, far-ranging career, as governor or lieutenant-governor of five colonial areas (New York, Virginia, Maryland, Nova Scotia, South Carolina) during 1688–1722. He supported the founding of the College of William and Mary. He directed the conquest of Port Royal (1710), which established British supremacy in Nova Scotia.

Nicholson, Jack (1937–) film actor; born in Neptune, N.J. At age 17 he began as an office boy at Metro-Goldwyn-Mayer and joined a theater group; after a few stage and television roles, he made his first film, a Roger Corman cheapie, *The Cry Baby Killer* (1958). After years of producing, writing, and acting in little-regarded movies, he became an instant success in *Easy Rider* (1969). Thereafter he made a career out of playing explosive nonconformists who combine mordant humor with menacing charisma. He won Oscars for *One Flew Over the Cuckoo's Nest* (1975) and *Terms of Endearment* (1983). His efforts at directing feature films were not so well received, but his presence in many films such as *Batman* (1989) guarantees excitement.

Nicklaus, Jack (William) (1940–) golfer; born in Columbus, Ohio. Considered the greatest golfer in history, he won more major tournaments (21) than any other player. After a successful amateur career at Ohio State University, he turned professional and won the U.S. Open in 1962. Nicknamed, "the Golden Bear", the blond-haired golfer won the Masters six times, the U.S. Open four times, and the British Open three times, between 1962 and 1986. The oldest player ever to win the Masters at age 46, he was voted Golfer of the Century in 1988 by the Professional Golfer's Association (PGA). His various product endorsements and varied business interests – particularly in golf courses – made him a very wealthy man.

Nicolson, Marjorie Hope (1894–1981) literary critic; born in Yonkers, N.Y. She revealed the effect of philosophy and scientific discoveries on 17th-century poetry in such scholarly works as *Newton Demands the Muse* (1947). She taught at Smith College (1926–41) and Columbia University (1941–62).

Niebuhr, H. (Helmut) Richard (1894–1962) Protestant theologian; born in Wright City, Mo. (brother of Reinhold Niebuhr). The son of a pastor, he graduated from Elmhurst College, Ill., in 1912, worked briefly for a newspaper, and held a pastorate in St. Louis before beginning a long academic career. As a professor of theology at Yale from 1931 on, he had an enormous influence on generations of students. His writings, which apply the insights of the social sciences to the problems of Christianity, include *The Meaning of Revelation* (1941) and *Radical Monotheism and Western Culture* (1960).

Niebuhr, Reinhold (1892–1971) Protestant theologian; born in Wright City, Mo. The son of a clergyman and brother of theologian Helmut Richard Niebuhr, he was educated at Elmhurst College (Ill.), Eden Theological Seminary (Mo.), and the Yale Divinity School. Initially a theological liberal and an active Socialist, his experience as pastor of working-class Bethel Evangelical Church in Detroit (1915–28) gradually turned his thinking in a rightward direction – toward what he called Christian realism. He questioned the adequacy of the Christian "gospel of love" in a world of conflict, criminality, and totalitarianism; given human nature, the stern doctrines of sin and repentance were essential. By the end of World War II he had entirely shed his earlier socialism, and he roundly condemned totalitarian Communism. Professor of Christian ethics (1928–60) and dean (1950–60) at Union Theological Seminary, he wrote *Moral Man and Immoral Society* (1932), *Faith and History* (1949), *Structures of Nations and Empires* (1959), and many other books. In his later years he was America's best-known serious theologian, who managed to combine his somber, almost existential philosophy with a concern for contemporary political and social issues.

Nielsen, A. C. (Arthur Charles, Sr.) (1897–1980) product and radio/television audience analyst; born in Chicago. He was trained as an electrical engineer at the University of Wisconsin. He founded the A. C. Nielsen Company (1923) to evaluate the performance of industrial equipment for manufacturers. During the Depression he began the Nielsen Food and Drug Index, which tracked retail sales of national food and drug brands; this remained his largest operation. Using mechanical "audimeters" attached to radio sets, he began measuring radio audiences' listening behavior in the late 1930s, launching in 1942 his National Radio Index for broadcasters and advertisers. He became the dominant force in his field in 1950 by absorbing C. E. Hooper, Inc., and adding a television rating service. "Nielsen ratings," produced by international affiliates, helped the company grow into the largest market research company in the world.

Nier, Alfred O. C. (Otto Carl) (1911–) physicist; born in St. Paul, Minn. He was a fellow at Harvard (1936–38), taught at the University of Minnesota (1938–43), and became a physicist at Kellex Corporation, N.Y., before returning to Minnesota as a professor (1945–80). He developed the high-resolution mass spectrometer to study rare isotopes, and (1940) separated and determined the fissionability of uranium-235.

Nierenberg, William Aaron (1919–) oceanographer; born in New York City. He graduated from the City College of New York in 1939, worked on the Manhattan Project from 1942–45, received a Ph.D. from Columbia University, and taught physics there and at the Universities of Michigan and California: Berkeley. He directed the Scripps Institute of Oceanography in La Jolla, Calif., from 1965–86. For many years he served as a government adviser on scientific issues.

Nieuwland, Julius Arthur (1878–1936) Roman Catholic clergyman, chemist, botanist; born in Hansbeke, Belgium. His family emigrated to the U.S.A. in 1880. Ordained in the Congregation of the Holy Cross (1903), he taught at his alma mater, Notre Dame, from 1904 on. Starting as a chemist, he discovered the reaction between acetylene and arsenic trichloride (1904), which others developed into lewisite, a poison gas. As a result, he almost quit chemistry, turning to botany until the end of World War I. After 1925, further chemical experiments led to a collaboration with DuPont that yielded neoprene, the first commercially successful synthetic rubber.

Nikolais, Alwin (1912–93) choreographer; born in Southington, Conn. After training with Hanya Holm, he worked as a choreographer in Connecticut before moving to New York in 1948. At the Henry Street Playhouse he developed innovative theatrical concepts in children's theater and in his own company, the Nikolais Dance Theater. His avant-garde works are especially noted for their exotic costumes and arbitrary movements.

Niles, Hezekiah (1777–1839) journalist; born in Jefferis's Ford, Pa. After editing the *Baltimore Evening Post* (1805–11), he founded *Niles' Weekly Register,* an influential paper especially in economic policy, editing it until 1836.

Niles, John Jacob (1892–1980) folksinger, song collector; born in Louisville, Ky. After musical training in the U.S.A. and France, he studied Southern Appalachian and other folk music, publishing hundreds of songs and performing internationally.

Niles, Thomas (1825–94) publisher; born in Boston, Mass. Called the "boldest printer in Boston," he cofounded a printing house in 1855; putting out a pirated edition of Thomas De Quincey's *Klosterheim* ahead of another publisher, he soon developed a substantial list. In 1863 he joined Robert Brothers and built that firm into a leading publisher with his savvy acquisitions, including works of the popular (now-forgotten) English poet Jean Ingelow, inspirational novels by J. H. Ingraham, and Robert Louis Stevenson's *Treasure Island.* He also commissioned Louisa May Alcott to write *Little Women.*

Nimitz, Chester (William) (1885–1966) naval officer; born in Fredericksburg, Texas. He supervised the construction of the navy's first diesel ship engine (1913–16). He was chief of staff to the commander of the Atlantic fleet submarine division in World War I. He was chief of the Bureau of Navigation (1939–41) and became commander-in-chief of the Pacific Fleet after Pearl Harbor (1941). In 1942 he was named commander of all land, sea, and air forces in the Pacific. He refused to attack until U.S. forces were fully ready, in spite of pressure from Congress and the newspapers. He developed much of the strategy of "island hopping" while leading the fleet to many victories. He signed for the U.S.A. at the Japanese surrender ceremonies, which took place aboard his flagship, the USS *Missouri,* in 1945. He served as chief of naval operations after the war (1945–47).

Nims, John Frederick (1913–) poet; born in Muskegon, Mich. He studied at the University of Notre Dame (B.A. 1937; M.A. 1939) and University of Chicago (Ph.D. 1945). He taught at numerous institutions, including Notre Dame (1939–45; 1946–62), the University of Illinois: Urbana (1961–64), and at the Chicago branch (1965–73; 1977–85). The editor of *Poetry* magazine (1978–84), he also served as a poetry judge for the National Book Awards (1969), the American Book Awards (1970; 1971), and the Bollingen Prize (1987). He has been praised for his translations of the Greek tragedies, and for his intelligent, witty poetry, as in *Of Flesh and Bone* (1967) and *Selected Poems* (1982).

Nin, Anaïs (1903–77) writer; born in Paris, France. Child of a Spanish father and French-Danish mother, she and her mother moved to New York City (1914) where she attended Catholic schools. She left school when 16, worked as a model, studied dance, and returned to Europe (1923). (In 1923 she married a New York banker, Hugh Guiler; although he would later illustrate some of her novels under the name "Ian Hugo," little is known of how long this marriage survived.) She investigated psychoanalysis under the tutelage of Otto Rank, and briefly practiced the discipline under his supervision and on her own in New York City (1934–35). She returned to France (1935), and helped establish a publishing house, Siana Editions, because no one would publish her erotically charged works. She returned to New York City (1939) and continued writing but it would be the 1960s before she began to be discovered by the literary world at large. She would eventually become best-known for her series of intensely personal journals begun in 1931, *The Diary of Anaïs Nin* (10 vols. 1966–83); additional journals have since been published. She is also known for her intimate relationships with Henry Miller and Lawrence Durrell, among many others described in her writings. She also wrote novels, short stories, and erotica, all clearly drawing on the contents of her journals.

Nirenberg, Marshall W. (Warren) (1927–) biochemist; born in New York City. He taught while a student at the University of Florida (1945–52), then joined the National Institutes of Health (1957). Beginning in 1960, knowing that the genetic code consists of 64 nucleotide base "triplets" that code for 20 amino acids, Nirenberg synthesized successions of nucleic acids with a known base sequence, then determined which amino acid each triplet represented. For his pioneering work in deciphering the genetic code, he was awarded one-third the 1968 Nobel Prize in physiology. After this research, he concentrated on studies of cellular control, neuromuscular differentiation, and genetic evolution.

Nisbet, Robert A. (Alexander) (1913–) sociologist; born in Los Angeles. He had a long academic career, mostly at the University of California: Berkeley (1939–53) and the University of California: Riverside (1953–72). He repeatedly returned to the importance of community in works such as *The Quest for Community* (1953), *History of the Idea of Progress* (1980), *Prejudices* (1982), and *Teachers and Scholars* (1992).

Nixon, Richard (Milhous) (1913–94) thirty-seventh U.S. president; born in Yorba Linda, Calif. Born to Quaker parents, he graduated from Whittier College (Calif.) (1934) and Duke University Law School (1937). He practiced law in Whittier, Calif., and briefly served with the Office of Price Administration (1942) before enlisting in the U.S. Navy during World War II (1942–46). He won a seat in the U.S. House of Representatives (Rep., Calif.; 1947–51) in a campaign noted for his accusation that his Democratic opponent was supported by Communists. As a member of the House Committee on Un-American Activities, he gained fame for his part in the Alger Hiss spy case. He then went on to the U.S. Senate (1951–53), again after suggesting that his Democratic opponent was tainted by Communist associations. He became Eisenhower's vice-president in 1952 and was unusally visible and active in that role. In 1958 he faced down hostile demonstrations in Peru and Venezuela, and in 1959 he had his famous "kitchen debate" with Khrushchev at an American exhibit in Moscow. After narrowly losing the presidency to Kennedy in 1960, he lost a bid for governor of California in 1962, apparently ending his political career. But he came back to win the presidency in 1968, promising a quick end to the Vietnam war; in reality he enlarged and continued America's active role until 1973. His administration was marked by social unrest at home, but he had some accomplishments in foreign relations, notably a 1972 arms treaty with the U.S.S.R. and opening of relations with Communist China. Reelected by a landslide in 1972, Nixon was brought down by revelations of administration misdeeds collectively known as "Watergate." Facing certain impeachment, in August 1974 he became the first U.S. president to resign. He retired from public life for some years and concentrated on writing a series of books on political affairs; but eventually he began to make public appearances at home and abroad, in person and in the media, and he ended by attaining something of the status of an "elder statesman."

Nixon, (Thelma Catherine b. Ryan) Pat (1912–93) First Lady; born in Ely, Nev. Following a difficult childhood, she taught in a California high school before marrying Richard Nixon in 1940. She felt the strain of being a political wife acutely and she was not an active first lady.

Nizer, Louis (1902–94) lawyer, author; born in London, England. He immigrated to the U.S.A. at age three. Noted for this oratorical skills as a youth, he graduated from Columbia University's law school (1924). He formed the law firm Phillips, Nizer, Benjamin & Krim in 1926 and remained with it throughout his career. He soon came to represent the New York association of movie companies and then represented many famous entertainers such as Charlie Chaplin and Mae West; he became the general counsel for the Motion Picture Association of America; he also became a recognized authority on contracts, copyright, and plagiarism law. Perhaps his best-known case was the successful libel suit by Quentin Reynolds against Westbrook Pegler (1954). A man of many talents, he was a caricaturist and painter, he wrote both words and music of songs, he was much in demand as a toastmaster, and he wrote many articles and books, including *My Life in Court* (1961) and *The Jury Returns* (1966).

Noah, Mordecai Manuel (1785–1851) playwright, journalist; born in Philadelphia. He started out as a reporter in Harrisburg, Pa., and wrote several plays between 1802 and 1822. In 1813 he was sent to Tunis as consul to negotiate for the release of Americans held by pirates there. In 1817, he became editor of the *National Advocate* in New York. In 1825 he unsuccessfully tried to found a Jewish refuge on an island in the Niagara River. He was sheriff of New York (1822), surveyor of the Port of New York (1829), and an associate judge of the New York court of sessions (1841). He was founder and editor of several New York newspapers.

Noble, Thomas Satterwhite (1835–1907) painter, teacher; born in Lexington, Ky. He studied with Couture in Paris (1856–59), served in the Confederate Army (1862–65), established a studio in New York (1866–69), and headed the McMicken School of Design (later the Cincinnati Art Academy) (1869–1904). He studied in Munich (1881–83), and retired to Bensonhurst, Long Island (1904). A historical, genre, and seascape painter, he is primarily known for his sympathetic portrayals of black Americans, as in *The American Slave Mart* (1865) and *The Price of Blood* (1868), a scene of a plantation owner selling his mulatto son.

Nochlin, Linda (b. Weinberg) (1931–) art historian; born in New York City. She studied at Vassar (B.A. 1951), Columbia University (M.A. 1952), and New York University (NYU) (Ph.D. 1963). She taught art at Vassar (1952–80), City University of New York (1980–90), Yale (1990), and at NYU's Institute of Fine Arts (1992). She specialized in painting and sculpture of the 19th and 20th centuries, and was one of the first scholars to define feminist issues in 19th-century painting.

Nock, Arthur Darby (1902–63) classicist; born in Portsmouth, England. He was educated at Trinity College, Cambridge (B.A. 1922; M.A. 1926) and the University of Birmingham (L.L.D. 1934). He taught at Harvard (1929–63) and became an American citizen in 1936. Charmingly eccentric even in a world of eccentrics, he is best remembered for his books *Conversion* (1933), *Saint Paul* (1938), and many articles on ancient religion. He was editor of the *Oxford Classical Dictionary* (1949) and a contributor to the *Cambridge Ancient History*.

Noguchi, Hideyo (1876–1928) bacteriologist, immunologist; born in Inawashiro, Japan. From a poor family, he served as an apprentice to a surgeon and graduated from Tokyo Medical College (1897). He emigrated to the U.S.A. in 1899 and worked with Simon Flexner at the University of Pennsylvania, where his exhaustive research made him the authority on the action of snake venom. He went to the Rockefeller Institute (1904–28) where he made a number of crucial contributions to medical research: he developed the methods for growing pure cultures of spiral organisms such as the syphilis spirochete; he demonstrated the presence of the syphilis parasite, *Treponema pallidum,* in the cerebral cortex of deceased patients, identifying it as the cause of certain diseases; he contributed to the study of Rocky Mountain spotted fever, poliomyelitis, and trachoma. Regarded as the major microbiologist of his generation, he died prematurely from the African yellow fever he was studying.

Noguchi, Isamu (1904–88) sculptor; born in Los Angeles, Calif. He and his Japanese father and American mother moved to Japan (1906), but he returned to study in Indiana (1917) and was briefly apprenticed to Gutzon Borglum. He became a premedical student at Columbia University (1923), then studied sculpture (1924), was an assistant of Brancusi in Paris (1927–29), traveled to China and Japan, and settled in New York City (1932). He created ballet sets for Martha Graham (1935), designed furniture and public gardens, and was known for his organic abstract stone carvings, such as *Even the Centipede* (1952).

Noland, Kenneth (1924–) painter; born in Ashville, N.C. He studied at Black Mountain College, North Carolina (1946–48, 1950), and with Ossip Zadkine in Paris (1948–49). He taught at the Institute of Contemporary Art (1949–51), and at Catholic University in Washington, D.C. (1951–60), before moving to South Salem, New York. His acrylic paintings, such as *Par Transit* (1966), demonstrate geometric forms and dominant color bands.

Noll, (Charles Henry) "Chuck" (1932–) football coach; born in Cleveland, Ohio. Named coach of the Pittsburgh Steelers in 1969, his teams won four Super Bowls during the 1970s. In 1990 he won his 200th National Football League game. He left the Steelers at the end of the 1991 season.

Noll, John (Francis) (1875–1956) Catholic prelate; born in Fort Wayne, Ind. Ordained in 1898, he did pastoral work in

Connecticut and in Indiana, where he founded *Our Sunday Visitor* (1912), a diocesan newspaper that expanded into a large chain. In 1925 he began a long tenure as bishop (later archbishop) of Fort Wayne, Ind.

Norden, Carl Lucas (1880–1965) mechanical engineer; born in Semarang, Java. He emigrated to the U.S.A. from Switzerland in 1904. He worked for Sperry Gyroscope (1911–17) but formed his own company in 1915. In 1911 he developed the first gyrostabilizing equipment for U.S. ships. He is known for contributions to military hardware. In 1927 he produced the first Norden bombsight, which allowed precision bombing.

Nordica, Lillian (b. Norton) (1857–1914) soprano; born in Farmington, Maine. She studied in Boston and began singing publicly in 1876. Following further studies in Milan, she made her operatic debut there in 1879 (and allowed her name to be changed to Nordica) and went on to successful appearances around Europe and England. Her Metropolitan Opera debut came in 1890; there and elsewhere she was acclaimed above all for her Wagnerian roles. Leaving the Met in 1909, she made concert tours until her retirement in 1913, and died in Java after a shipwreck.

Nordstrom, Ursula (1910–88) editor, executive; born in New York City. She began her career at Harper & Row publishers (1936–70) as an editor of children's books, headed the children's book department (1940), and became the company's first female vice-president in 1973. She was an innovative editor who established the careers of such writers and illustrators as E. B. White, Maurice Sendak, and Shel Silverstein.

Norman, Jessye (1945–) soprano; born in Augusta, Ga. After musical studies in America, she went to Europe, making her 1969 operatic debut in Berlin. She first appeared in America in 1972, in a concert performance of *Aida* at Hollywood Bowl; her debut at the Metropolitan Opera came in *Les Troyens* in 1983. She pursued regular concert work as well. She was widely admired for the opulent tone she brought to a repertoire ranging from Mozart to Wagner and African-American spirituals.

Norman, Marsha (b. Williams) (1947–) playwright, director; born in Louisville, Ky. A writer and director for Actors' Theatre in Louisville, her 1983 play, *'night Mother*, about a daughter's suicide, won a Pulitzer Prize.

Normand, Mabel (b. Mabel Fortesque) (1894–1930) movie actress; born in Boston, Mass. Daughter of a vaudeville pianist, she was a model at age 13 and made her screen debut at age 16. By 1912 she was starring in Mack Sennett comedies and her performance opposite Charlie Chaplin in *Tillie's Punctured Romance* (1914) made her one of the stars of silent movies for a decade. Scandals involving drugs and two murder cases put a strain on her life and career and she died prematurely of pneumonia and tuberculosis.

Norris, (Benjamin Franklin, Jr.) Frank (1870–1902) writer; born in Chicago. His family moved to California (1884), and he studied art in London and Paris. His interest in art waned and he returned to study at the University of California (1890–94), and Harvard (1895). He worked as a journalist and covered the Boer War for the *San Francisco Chronicle* (1895–96); in 1896 he became a staff member for *The Wave* (1896), a San Francisco literary magazine. He moved to New York City, covered the Spanish-American War for *McClure's* magazine (1898), and worked for Doubleday, Page & Company

beginning in 1899. He was influenced by the naturalistic work of Émile Zola, as seen in his best-known fiction, *McTeague: A Story of San Francisco* (1899) and *The Octopus* (1901). He died shortly after an appendix operation.

Norris, George William (1861–1944) U.S. representative/senator; born in York Township, Ohio. He received a law degree in 1882. Moving to Nebraska in 1885 to practice law, he served as a county prosecuting attorney (1892–96) and state judge (1896–1902). In 1902 he was elected to the U.S. House of Representatives (Rep., Nebr.; 1903–13). In 1913 he began a stormy 30-year career in the U.S. Senate (1913–43). A progressive in domestic matters, he gained national notoriety for his opposition to U.S. entry into World War I and to U.S. participation in the League of Nations. In the 1930s he was a firm supporter of the New Deal. He was a sponsor of the Norris-LaGuardia Anti-Injunction Act of 1932, which protected labor's right to organize; his long years of work for public control of hydroelectric resources culminated in the Tennessee Valley Authority Act of 1933. In 1936 he was elected to the Senate as an Independent, but he was defeated for reelection in 1942.

Norris, Kathleen (b. Thompson) (1880–1966) writer; born in San Francisco. She was educated locally, and after the death of her parents (1899), she worked at a hardware store and a library to help support her siblings. She spent a few months at the University of California: Berkeley (1903), and wrote society columns for local newspapers. She married the writer Charles Gilman Norris (1909), and moved to New York City, although she maintained a home in California. She became known for her many (about 80) sentimental novels – including *Mother* (1911), *The Venables* (1941), and *Through a Glass Darkly* (1957) – and was such a success that she was reputed to be the highest paid American writer of her day. She also wrote serialized stories for national magazines and soap operas for radio.

Norris, William C. (1911–) computer engineer, entrepreneur; born in Red Cloud, Nebr. He helped found Engineering Research Associates in St. Paul, Minn. (late 1940s), which merged with Sperry Rand. He headed Sperry Rand's Univac Division until 1957, when he founded Control Data Corporation in Minneapolis; he retired as its chairman and CEO in 1986. He also became an advocate of government/business cooperation, job creation, efficiency, and technological innovation.

Norstad, Lauris (1907–88) aviator; born in Minneapolis, Minn. Commissioned into the cavalry after graduation from West Point in 1930, he transferred to the Air Corps the following year, and by August 1942 had risen to the post of deputy chief of staff of the 12th Air Force in North Africa. Returning to Washington in 1944, he had direct responsibility for planning the atomic bomb missions. He later commanded U.S. air forces in Europe (1950) and NATO forces in Europe (1956). He retired in 1963 to become president of Owens-Corning Glass.

North, Alex (1910–91) film composer; born in Chester, Pa. After studies at Curtis and Juilliard, he began his screen career scoring *A Streetcar Named Desire* (1952); later credits include *Spartacus* (1960) and *Who's Afraid of Virginia Woolf?* (1966).

North, Douglass C. (Cecil) (1920–) economic historian; born in Cambridge, Mass. As an editor of the *Journal of Economic History* in the 1960s, he supported the new discipline, *cliometrics,* which applies economic and quantitative methodology to history resulting in significantly different interpretations of the past. A member of the faculty at Washington University (St. Louis) from 1950, he wrote widely about the importance of institutions in a field that has concentrated on markets. His books include *Structure and Change in Economic History* (1981). In 1993 he and Robert Fogel, whose work he first published in his journal, were awarded the Nobel Prize in economics for their contribution to economic history.

North, Simeon (1765–1852) engineer, manufacturer; born in Berlin, Conn. Between 1799–1813 he pioneered the manufacture of pistols with interchangeable parts, mostly under government contract. From 1828 to his death, he produced rifles.

Northrop, John (Howard) (1891–1987) biochemist; born in Yonkers, N.Y. He spent most of his career pursuing viral and enzyme research at the Rockefeller Institute (later University) (1924–61), with time out to serve as professor of bacteriology at the University of California: Berkeley (1949–58). During the 1930s, he and his colleagues isolated the enzymes trypsin and chymotrypsin. In 1939 he was the first to isolate a bacterial virus, and in 1940 he crystallized diphtheria antitoxin. He shared the Nobel Prize in chemistry (1946).

Northrop, John (Knudsen) (1895–1981) aircraft designer; born in Newark, N.J. He worked for both the Douglas and Lockheed corporations before forming Northrop Aircraft Inc., in 1939. His airplane designs included the Vega, the A-17 attack plane, and the P-61 night fighter. He retired in 1952 but continued to consult with Northrop.

Norton, Andrew (1786–1853) Biblical scholar, Unitarian theologian; born in Hingham, Mass. He graduated from Harvard in 1804, held a pastorate in Maine for a time, and returned to Harvard as a tutor in 1813. He was professor of divinity at Harvard (1819–30), and afterward an independent scholar. His *Evidences of the Genuineness of the Gospels* (3 vols. 1837–44) was one of the earliest critical studies of the Bible published in America.

Norton, Charles Eliot (1828–1908) editor, author, teacher; born in Cambridge, Mass. A cosmopolitan man of letters and profoundly influential teacher, he edited the works of Dante, Carlyle, and other writers, helped found *The Nation* (1865), and pioneered the teaching of art history at Harvard (1873–97).

Norton, Eleanor Holmes (1937–) civil rights activist; born in Washington, D.C. A lawyer by profession, as assistant director of the American Civil Liberties Union (1965–70), she defended both Julian Bond's and George Wallace's freedom of speech rights. Chairman of the New York Human Rights Commission (1970–77), she championed women's rights and anti-block-busting legislation. She then went to Washington to chair the Equal Employment Opportunities Commission (1977–83). In 1982 she became a law professor at Georgetown University.

Norton, (Joshua Abraham) "Emperor" (?1819–80) legendary eccentric; born in England or South Africa. Nothing is known of his life before he arrived in San Francisco along with others from around the world in the wake of discovery of gold in 1848. But it appears that he had at least spent some time in South Africa and that he arrived as a relatively successful businessman; instead of trying to make his fortune by prospecting, he apparently turned to speculating in rice, a valuable commodity at the time, but ended up losing everything. This evidently drove him into some delusional state if not outright madness and he is said to have vanished for awhile. What is known for sure is that in 1857 he reappeared in San Francisco wearing a costume suspiciously like France's Napoleon III's, and announced that he was "Emperor Norton." For the next 13 years he paraded around the city in his uniform, issuing "proclamations" and official-looking banknotes (which were honored in some restaurants) and appearing at many official functions. Still an "open" frontier town, San Francisco tolerated him with good humor, and when he died, thousands showed up at his funeral. Numerous books, plays, and musical dramas have been written about him, the most notable being Henry Mollicone's opera, *Emperor Norton* (1981).

Norton, Mary Alice (b. Peloubet) (1860–1928) home economist; born in Lanesville, Mass. She was a Smith College graduate and associate of Ellen H. Richards, whom she helped to prepare *Home Sanitation* (1887). She taught domestic science in New England schools and at the University of Chicago (1900–13), and edited the *Journal of Home Economics* (1915–21).

Norton, Mary Teresa (b. Hopkins) (1875–1959) U.S. representative; born in Jersey City, N.J. A secretary (1896–1909) before marriage, she set up day-care nurseries for working mothers after her child died. Entering politics in 1920, she was one of the first women in the U.S. House of Representatives (Dem., N.J.; 1924–51). She chaired the House Labor Committee (1937–46), shepherding through the Wages and Hours Bill; she resigned from the committee to fight against the antilabor Taft-Hartley Act of 1947.

Norval, Morris (1923–) criminologist, scholar; born in Auckland, New Zealand. He served in the Australian Army in the Pacific (1941–45), and, becoming a lawyer, practiced before the Victorian Supreme Court, the South Australian Supreme Court, and the High Court of Australia. He emigrated to America to teach law and criminology at the University of Chicago (1964). Adviser to the Federal Bureau of Prisons, he chaired the National Institute of Corrections (1986–89). He was coeditor of *Crime and Justice: An Annual Review of Research,* and author of numerous articles and books including a book of short stories, *The Brothel Boy and Other Parables of The Law* (1992).

Norvo, Red (b. Kenneth Norville) (1908–) jazz musician; born in Beardstown, Ill. He was a xylophonist and vibes player who worked as a sideman with Victor Young's Radio Orchestra in Chicago in 1927 and Paul Whiteman's Orchestra between 1928–32. After two years of free-lance recording work in New York, he led his own orchestra, featuring his wife, vocalist Mildred Bailey, until 1944. He alternated thereafter between leading his own small groups and appearing as a featured sideman with Benny Goodman and various All Star swing ensembles.

Notman, John (1810–65) architect; born in Edinburgh, Scotland. Practicing in Philadelphia after 1831, he early adopted the Italianate style and incorporated technological innovations like residential central heating and plumbing. He helped found the American Institute of Architects (1857).

Nott, Eliphalet (1773–1866) college president; born in Ashford, Conn. He was a nationally famous Presbyterian preacher in Albany, N.Y., before beginning an extraordinary career as president of Union College, Schenectady (1804–66). He restored the college's financial viability through state lotteries, established engineering and medical schools, and brought Union a reputation for intellectual quality.

Nourse, Edwin (Griswold) (1883–1974) economist, government official; born in Lockport, N.Y. An academic, he directed economic research at the Brookings Institute (1929–46), publishing a study that recommended lowering prices and increasing wages. As Council of Economic Advisors head (1946–53), he irritated President Truman by refusing to champion the administration's economic policies. He then retired to private life.

Novak, Michael (John) (1933–) Catholic educator, author; born in Johnstown, Pa. He graduated from the Georgian University in Rome (1958) and later taught at Stanford University (1965–68), the State University of New York (1968–73), and other schools. He wrote numerous books on Catholicism, identity, and spiritual growth, and became an increasingly more prominent, and outspoken, conservative critic of contemporary trends in American society. His best-known works are *The Experience of Nothingness* (1970) and *The Rise of the Unmeltable Ethnics* (1972). In *Choosing Our King* (1974) he proposed that there should be two presidents of the United States – one with the power, another with the ceremonial role.

Novello, Antonia C. (1944–) pediatrician, public health official; born in Fajardo, Puerto Rico. She graduated from medical school at the University of Puerto Rico (1970) and had her residency and subspecialty training in pediatric nephrology at the University of Michigan (1974) and Georgetown University (1975). In 1978 she left private practice to join the U.S. Public Health Service; she was appointed its director and surgeon general of the United States (1990), the first woman and the first Hispanic to hold the position.

Noyce, Robert N. (1927–90) electrical engineer; born in Burlington, Iowa. He founded Fairchild Semiconductor Corp. (1957) and coinvented the integrated circuit with Jack Kilby. He cofounded Intel Corp. (1968), which developed the silicon-gate MOS process that allows several thousand transistors to be integrated on a single silicon chip.

Noyes, Eliot (Fette) (1910–77) designer, architect; born in Boston, Mass. At the Harvard Graduate School of Design (1938), he was influenced by Gropius, Breuer and Le Corbusier. In 1940 he set up and directed the industrial design department of the Museum of Modern Art. He worked for stage designer-architect Norman Bel Geddes (1893–1958), then established his own practice in New Canaan, Conn., in 1948. Best known for his industrial design, he oversaw the design of products and buildings for International Business Machines (IBM), including the well-known IBM typewriter. At Mobil Corporation, he redesigned and streamlined the American gas station.

Noyes, John Humphrey (1811–86) minister, social reformer; born in Brattleboro, Vt. A first cousin of President Rutherford B. Hayes, he was inspired by revivalist preacher Charles Grandison Finney and he abandoned law to study divinity, eventually at Yale. Founding a revivalist "free" church there, he maintained that Christ's Second Coming had already occurred and that some beings could now live in "perfect" holiness. Forced to leave Yale, and deprived of a license to preach, he formed a community of Bible communists (1836) in Putney, Vt., to realize his message, which also included advocacy of spousal sharing. To escape prosecution for adultery, he fled to central New York and formed the Utopian Oneida Community (1848). He wrote extensively on social and economic experiments and advocated limiting the permission to procreate to an advanced elite; in 1879 he fled to Canada to avoid a charge of statutory rape. Oneida, the most successful of the American Utopian communities, was later reorganized as a business community.

Noyes, William Albert (1857–1941) chemist; born in Independence, Iowa. From 1886–1903 he studied camphor derivatives at Rose Polytechnic Institute (Terre Haute, Ind.), becoming chief chemist at the National Bureau of Standards (1903–07). There he determined atomic weights and obtained the hydrogen:oxygen weight ratio. He became director of the chemical laboratories at the University of Illinois (1907–26).

Nozick, Robert (1938–) philosopher; born in New York City. After earning a 1963 doctorate from Princeton, where he taught (1962–65), he held posts at Harvard (1965–67) and Rockefeller University (1967–69) before becoming a professor at Harvard in 1969. His seminal study, *Anarchy, State and Utopia* (1974), which won a National Book Award, stressed the primacy of individual rights, and he was generally associated with a conservative critique of trends in contemporary thought and society.

Nunn, (Samuel Augustus, Jr.) Sam (1938–) U.S. senator; born in Perry, Ga. After serving in the Georgia legislature (Dem., 1968–72), he was elected to the U.S. Senate (1972). As chairman of the Senate Armed Forces Committee, he attained national prominence as an expert on defense issues. Regarded as a moderate among the Democratic Party leadership, he won the respect of the party's liberals during the administration of Ronald Reagan for his role in the Iran-Contra hearings, his opposition to the nomination of John Tower as Secretary of Defense, and his criticisms of the Strategic Defense Initiative (Star Wars) program. He played a pivotal role in the negotiations that ensued when President Clinton announced his intention of allowing homosexuals to serve openly in the military.

Nurse, Elizabeth (1859–1938) painter; born in Cincinnati, Ohio. A descendant of Rebecca Nurse who was burned at the stake in Massachusetts (1692), Elizabeth studied at the McMicken School of Art (later the Cincinnati Art Academy) with T. S. Noble (1874–81, 1885–86). She studied in Paris (1887), became an expatriate there, painted forceful scenes of European peasant life, as in *Peasant Woman of Borst* (1891), and is considered an early social realist.

Nurse, Rebecca (b. Towne) (1621–92) witchcraft victim; born in Yarmouth, England. She was excommunicated and executed in 1692 at the height of the witch craze in Salem, Massachusetts. In 1712, the same pastor who had excommunicated her formally and publicly canceled the excommunication.

Nuttall, Thomas (1786–1859) botanist, ornithologist; born in Settle, Yorkshire, England. He worked in a Liverpool print shop before emigrating to Philadelphia in 1808. Taking up the study of botany, he accompanied scientific expeditions on the Missouri River (1809–11), the Arkansas and Red Rivers (1818–20), and the Columbia River (1834–35). He published a study of American plant life in 1818 and an ornithological manual in 1832. From 1822–32 he was curator of the Botanical Garden of Harvard. In 1842 he inherited a small estate near Liverpool and returned to England where, a bachelor and recluse, he spent his remaining years cultivating rare plants.

Nuttall, Zelia Maria Magdalena (1857–1933) archaeologist, ethnologist; born in San Francisco. Daughter of an Irish-born physician, she was educated in Europe and would later live there for many years. She used family wealth to pursue archaeological interests throughout her life, although she was associated at one period with Harvard's Peabody Museum. She published important findings in pre-Columbian and colonial Mexican culture and is credited with the discovery of two ancient Mexican codices (one of which is known as the *Codex Nuttall*). The character of "Mrs. Norris" in D. H. Lawrence's *Plumed Serpent* is based on her.

Nutting, Mary Adelaide (1858–1948) nurse educator; born in Waterloo, Quebec, Canada. She left her impoverished family in 1889 to enter nursing school at Johns Hopkins (Baltimore), becoming head nurse in 1891, and superintendent of nurses training (1894–1907). There she commenced what would be her life's work – advancing the professional education of nurses. Moving on to the Columbia University Teachers College, she established the department of hospital economics (1907) and the department of nursing and health, which she chaired (1910–25), making it a leader in the education of nurses. She helped establish the *American Journal of Nursing* (1900) and coauthored *History of Nursing*

(4 vols. 1907–12). Her basic writings are collected in *A Sound Economic Basis for Schools of Nursing* (1926). She was also active in the woman suffrage movement.

Nutting, Wallace (1861–1941) Congregational minister, antiquarian, photographer, author; born in Marlboro, Mass. Poor health led him to give up the ministry in 1904, and to support himself he began to sell his atmospheric photographs of rural New England. By 1912 he was collecting genuine period furniture to place in four old houses he was restoring; seeing a demand, he began in 1917 to manufacture reproductions of mainly American colonial furniture. He became the spokesman for the colonial revival movement among collectors and home furnishers but his reputation remained somewhat compromised by his willingness to make reproductions. He wrote and provided photographs for a number of books including *Furniture Treasury* (3 vols. 1928–33), which remains a useful survey of American furniture.

Nye, Gerald P. (Prentice) (1892–1971) U.S. senator; born in Hortonville, Wis. Originally appointed and then elected to the U.S. Senate (Rep., N.D.; 1925–45), he chaired a special committee in 1934–36 investigating arms sales in World War I.

Nye, James Warren (1815–76) governor, U.S. senator; born in Madison County, New York. A gifted orator, he was appointed governor of the Nevada Territory (Rep.; 1861–64), where he helped suppress the pro-slavery forces. He then served Nevada as one of its first two U.S. senators (1864–73).

O

Oakley, Annie (b. Phoebe Anne Oakley Mozee or Moses)
(1860–1926) markswoman, rodeo performer; born in Darke
County, Ohio. Only five feet tall as an adult, she began
shooting at age nine, and after she bested vaudeville star
shooter Frank Butler, they married and toured together in
Buffalo Bill's Wild West Show (1885–1922). Her specialty
was shooting airborne playing cards, thus the name "Annie
Oakleys" to free tickets (because of holes punched in them).
Her life inspired the musical, *Annie Get Your Gun.*

Oates, Joyce Carol (Rosamond Smith, pen name)
(1938–) writer, poet; born in Lockport, N.Y. She studied
at Syracuse University (B.A. 1960) and the University of
Wisconsin (M.A. 1961), and taught at the University of
Windsor, Ontario (1967–78) and Princeton (1978). A prolific
writer, she published literary criticism, plays, short stories,
and poetry, but is best known for her violent visionary
novels.

O'Bannon, Presley (Neville) (1776–1850) Marine officer;
born in Fauquier County, Va. Leading the Marine detachment in the expedition to capture Derna, Libya, during the
Tripolitan War in April 1805, he helped raise the first
American flag ever to fly over foreign soil – hence the
"shores of Tripoli" reference in the "Marine Hymn." He
resigned in 1807 and lived quietly in Kentucky for more than
four decades.

O'Brien, Fitz-James (1828–62) writer; born in Cork, Ireland.
Seeking money and adventure, he emigrated to New York
City (1852). There, he continued his work as a journalist and
free-lance writer, and wrote poetry, short stories, and plays.
He is best known for his macabre horror stories, as in "The
Diamond Lens," first published in the *Atlantic Monthly*
(1858). Volunteering for service in the Union army in the
Civil War, he was wounded and died of tetanus.

O'Brien, Jeremiah (1744–1818) Revolutionary hero; born in
Kittery, Maine. He ably defended Machias, Maine (then part
of Massachusetts) against British vessels and captured the
British *Margaretta* in what as counted as the first naval battle
of the American Revolution. He commanded privateers
(1777–80) and was captured and briefly imprisoned in
England (1780).

O'Callaghan, (Donald Neil) "Mike" (1920–) governor;
born in La Crosse, Wis. A Korean War army hero (he lost
one leg), he became Southern Nevada Amateur Athletic
Union president in 1959. After directing state and federal
agencies, he opened a consulting firm in 1969. As governor
of Nevada (Dem., 1971–79), he passed a fair housing law

and strong antipollution measures. He joined the *Las Vegas
Sun* afterward.

Occom, Samson (1723–92) Mohegan educator, Presbyterian
religious leader; born near present-day New London, Conn.
Ordained by the Long Island Presbytery (1759), he traveled
to England in 1765 to raise money for Wheelock's Indian
Charity School (later Dartmouth College), becoming the
first Native American to preach in that country. He helped to
create the Brotherton Community of Indians in Oneida
County, New York (1786).

Ochoa, Severo (1905–93) molecular biologist; born in
Luarca, Spain. He taught and performed research in Europe
before coming to the U.S.A. to join Washington University
(St. Louis) (1941–42). At New York University (NYU)
(1942–74), he described the mechanism of the Krebs citric
acid cycle, which generates cellular energy (1940s–1950s). In
1955 he isolated a bacterial enzyme with which he performed
the first test-tube synthesis of various RNAs, enabling the
eventual deciphering of the genetic code. For this he won
one-half the 1959 Nobel Prize in physiology. After retiring
from NYU, he moved to the Roche Institute for Molecular
Biology (New Jersey) (1974–85), then returned to Spain as a
professor at Universidad Autonoma, Madrid (1985).

Ochs, Adolph Simon (1858–1935) publisher; born in Cincinnati, Ohio. He bought the *Chattanooga Times* in 1878 and
the *New York Times* in 1896, lifting the latter from
bankruptcy to become a leading U.S. newspaper.

Ochs, (Philip David) Phil (1940–76) folksinger, songwriter;
born in El Paso, Texas. Inspired by folk legends Woody
Guthrie and Pete Seeger, he dropped out of college to
perform in coffee houses in New York's Greenwich Village.
Such albums as *I Ain't Marchin' Anymore* (1965), with the
songs "Talking Vietnam" and "Draft Dodger Rag," established him as an important protest singer of the period. He
committed suicide.

Ochsner, (Edward William) Alton (1896–1981) surgeon;
born in Kimball, S.D. He chaired the surgical department at
Tulane University (1927–56) and cofounded the Alton
Ochsner Clinic there. A chest surgeon of international
renown, he argued that cigarettes can cause cancer. His
zealous campaign against the tobacco industry included three
books about cancer and smoking. An ardent genealogist, he
discovered that the mother of famed early physician,
Paracelsus (1493–1541), was an Ochsner.

Ocker, William C. (1876–1942) aviator; born in Philadelphia.
He is credited with many advances in instrument flying and

with developing, in 1938, a more efficient type of airplane propeller. He was coauthor of an early manual on the theory and practice of instrument flight.

O'Connell, William (Henry) (1859–1944) Catholic prelate; born in Lowell, Mass. Ordained in 1884, he was rector of the North American College in Rome (from 1895), bishop of Portland, Maine (1901–05), and a Vatican diplomat before becoming archbishop of Boston (1907); he was made a cardinal in 1911. Known for his extensive building program, he was a prominent presence and force in Greater Boston religious life throughout his long term as archbishop.

O'Connor, Carroll (1924–) movie/television actor; born in New York City. Initially a stage actor in Dublin, London, and Paris, he acted in a number of forgettable movies during the 1950s and 1960s. He starred in CBS's *All in the Family* (1971–79) and *Archie Bunker's Place* (1979–83), winning numerous Emmy awards. He played the liberal sheriff on National Broadcasting Company's *In the Heat of the Night* (1987) and appeared in occasional television specials.

O'Connor, John J. (Joseph) (1920–) Catholic prelate; born in Philadelphia. After his ordination (1945) he taught high school, worked with retarded children, and earned advanced degrees in philosophy, psychology, and political science. He then spent 27 years as a U.S. Navy chaplain, becoming chief of chaplains before retiring as a rear admiral (1979). From 1979 to 1983 he was auxiliary bishop of New York, with special responsibility over U.S. military chaplains. After serving briefly as bishop of Scranton, Pa., he was named archbishop of New York in 1984, becoming a cardinal in 1985. A highly influential figure, he espoused generally conservative views; he was outspoken, for instance, in condemning Catholic politicians who took "pro-choice" positions on abortion.

O'Connor, (Mary) Flannery (1925–64) writer; born in Savannah, Ga. She studied at the Women's College of Georgia (now Georgia College; B.A. 1945), and the State University of Iowa (M.F.A. 1947). She lived in Milledgeville, Ga., and suffered from lupus, a disease of the connective tissues, the cause of her father's death (1941) and her own premature death. She was a devout Catholic and her work is infused with visions of powerful spiritual struggles. She is considered a master of the short story form, as seen in her collection, *A Good Man is Hard to Find* (1955). Her acclaimed Gothic Southern novels include *Wise Blood* (1952) and *The Violent Bear It Away* (1960).

O'Connor, Sandra Day (1930–) Supreme Court justice; born in El Paso, Texas. After taking her law degree from Stanford (1952), she had a private practice in Arizona; serving in the Arizona Senate (1969–74), she was the first woman in America to be elected majority leader of a state senate (1972–74). She was elected to a county superior court (1974–79) and was then appointed to the Arizona Court of Appeals (1979–81). When President Ronald Reagan selected her, she became the first woman to serve on the U.S. Supreme Court (1981). Generally conservative in her legal views, she occasionally took independent positions and for long held the "swing vote" on the issue of abortion.

O'Daniel, Wilbert Lee ("Pappy") (1890–1969) musician, governor, U.S. senator; born in Malta, Ohio. A businessman and radio music performer, he composed scores of songs; one, "Them Hillbillies are Politicians Now," led to a campaign that climaxed with his election as governor of Texas (Dem., 1939–41). He went on to serve in the U.S. Senate (1941–49). Although famed for his campaigning techniques, he espoused such conservative views that he had little influence in the Senate.

O'Day, Caroline Love (b. Goodwin) (1875–1943) U.S. representative; born in Perry, Ga. A widely exhibited artist, trained in Europe, she moved with her husband to New York where she became active in social issues and a friend of Eleanor Roosevelt. State associate chairman of the Democratic Party (1932–42), she became commissioner of the N.Y. Board of Social Welfare (1923–34) before going to the U.S. House of Representatives (1935–43), where she regularly supported the New Deal except for military legislation.

Odets, Clifford (1906–63) playwright, film director, actor; born in Philadelphia. Leaving high school to be a poet, he took up acting, appearing on the radio and in repertory theater. In 1931 he helped found the Group Theatre, which in 1935 produced his *Waiting for Lefty* and *Awake and Sing!* These plays immediately established him as a major American social realist and spokesman for the downtrodden, but he himself was soon enjoying the good life in Hollywood where he wrote screenplays and eventually turned to directing films, including *None But the Lonely Heart* (1949) and *Wild in the Country* (1961). He also continued to write a series of realistic and increasingly disillusioned dramas such as *Golden Boy* (1937) and *The Big Knife* (1949).

Odetta (Odetta Holmes Felious Gordon) (1930–) singer, guitarist; born in Birmingham, Ala. During the folk revival of the 1950s and 1960s she was known for her performances of African-American folk music and her albums with a repertory of spirtuals, blues, and children's songs. She toured the Soviet Union and Eastern Europe in 1974 and appeared in films, stage musicals, and on television.

O'Donnell, Emmett, Jr. (1906–71) aviator; born in New York City. A highly decorated bomber commander of World War II, he commanded the Far East Bomber Command in Korea in 1950–51 and became commander-in-chief, Pacific Air Forces, in 1953.

Odum, Eugene Pleasants (1913–) ecologist, educator; born in Lake Sunapee, N.H. The son of a prominent sociologist, he graduated from the University of North Carolina (1934) and received a Ph.D. from the University of Illinois (1939). He was resident biologist at a New York State nature preserve before joining the faculty of the University of Georgia in 1940. He turned from an early interest in birds to ecology; he became one of the founders of a rigorously scientific approach to ecology and was an influential advocate of resource conservation. His *Fundamentals of Ecology* appeared in 1971. He became an emeritus professor at Georgia in 1985.

Oenslager, Donald (Mitchell) (1902–75) set designer; born in Harrisburg, Pa. He began as an actor, but turned to set design in 1924 after studying design in Europe. His early connections were with the Provincetown Players and the Greenwich Village Theatre. Along with Jo Mielziner and Robert Edmond Jones, he is credited as one of the creators of a new kind of less realistic, more symbolic theatrical design, although his designs tended to be decorative and elegant, rather than spare and stripped-down. He designed for opera and ballet as well as drama, and was on the faculty of the Yale School of Drama for nearly 50 years, until the end of his life. Among his productions are *Of Mice and Men*

(1937), *The Doctor's Dilemma,* with Katharine Cornell (1941), *Pygmalion,* with Cedric Hardwicke (1945), *Major Barbara,* with Charles Laughton (1956), and *A Majority of One* (1959), for which he won a Tony Award. He is the author of *Scenery Then and Now* (1936).

Oertel, Johannes (Adam Simon) (1823–1909) painter; born in Fürth, Bavaria. He emigrated to Newark, N.J. (1848), worked as an engraver of banknotes (1852–57), became an Episcopalian deacon (1867), and served in many parishes. Moving frequently, he produced wood carvings and a series of four religious paintings, called the *Redemption* series (c. 1867–1902).

Oerter, (Alfred A.) Al (1936–) track and field athlete; born in Astoria, N.Y. The greatest discus thrower in track and field history, he won a gold medal in an unprecedented four consecutive Olympics (1956–68).

Offner, Richard (b. Schmeidler) (1889–1965) art historian; born in Vienna, Austria. He emigrated with his family to America (1891), and studied at Harvard (1909–12), the American Academy of Rome (1912–14), and the University of Vienna (Ph.D. 1914). He divided his time between New York City and Florence, Italy, taught at New York University (1923–60), and specialized in Italian Renaissance art.

Ogburn, William F. (Fielding) (1886–1959) sociologist; born in Butler, Ga. A Columbia University Ph.D., he taught at Columbia (1919–27) and the University of Chicago (1927–51). His major contributions were his pioneering application of statistical analysis to the social sciences and his seminal interpretation of social change, particularly the social impact of technological change. His major works were *Social Change* (1922, revised through 11 editions), which introduced the term "cultural lag"; *Recent Social Trends in the United States* (2 vols. 1933); and *Sociology* (1940).

Ogg, Frederic (Austin) (1878–1951) political scientist; born in Solsberry, Ind. A prolific writer, he authored many articles and books on world politics. Two textbooks written with P. O. Ray, *Introduction to American Government* (1922) and *Essentials of American Government* (1932), have been read by generations of students. He taught at the University of Wisconsin (1914–48).

Ogilvy, David (Mackenzie) (1911–) advertising executive; born in West Horsley, Surrey, England. He settled in New York City in 1939. After a varied early career, he founded (1948) the advertising agency that became Ogilvy and Mather, a top creative shop whose trademark snob appeal was exemplified by its Hathaway shirt and "man from Schweppes" campaigns. He retired to France (1973), resigning the chairmanship of Ogilvy and Mather (1973) and the Ogilvy Group (1992).

Oglethorpe, James Edward (1696–1785) soldier, founder of Georgia; born in London, England. As a member of Parliament (1722–54), he opposed debt imprisonment and black enslavement. In 1732 he received a charter to establish the colony of Georgia. He pursued a conciliatory policy with the Indians, but fought consistently against the Spanish in Florida. His military skill and philanthropic bent were crucial to the establishment of the Georgia colony.

Ogletree, Charles J., Jr. (1952–) professor, lawyer; born in Merced, Calif. A graduate of Stanford (1974) and Harvard Law School (1978), he worked with the District of Columbia Public Defender Service (1978–82; deputy director, 1984–85), then joined the faculty of Harvard Law School (1985),

becoming director of its Criminal Justice Institute (1990). He became more widely known for his appearances on television programs involving legal issues.

O'Hair, Madalyn Murray (b. Mays) (1919–) social activist; born in Pittsburgh, Pa. She enjoyed a normal, happy childhood, but was overwhelmed when she read the Bible cover-to-cover at age 13. She gradually became an atheist and when her son Bill objected to school prayers, she took the case to the Supreme Court; in a landmark decision outlawing prayers in public schools, she won, in her words, the "unalienable right to freedom *from* religion as well as freedom *of* religion" (1963). She was a cryptographer and second lieutenant during World War II. She and her family (she married twice) were persecuted by their neighbors while the case was being tried.

O'Hara, Edwin (Vincent) (1881–1956) Catholic prelate; born in Lanesboro, Minn. Ordained in 1905, he did pastoral work in Oregon; his concern for fostering religious life and education in sparsely Catholic rural areas led him to found the National Catholic Rural Life Conference (1923), which he directed until 1930, when he became bishop of Great Falls, Mont. In 1939 he was named bishop of Kansas City, becoming archbishop in 1954.

O'Hara, (Francis Russell) Frank (1926–66) poet, art critic; born in Baltimore, Md. He studied at New England Conservatory of Music, Boston (1946–50), Harvard (B.A. 1950), and the University of Michigan (M.A. 1951). He worked for the Museum of Modern Art beginning in 1951, and as an editor for art magazines (1954–64). He wrote plays and art criticism and is noted for his surrealistic poetry, as in *Selected Poems* (1973).

O'Hara, James (1752–1819) soldier, manufacturer; born in Ireland. He arrived in Philadelphia in 1772 and served as a captain in the American Revolution. He was the quartermaster for the U.S. Army (1792–96) and a government contractor (1796–1802). He moved to Pittsburgh and worked to erect that city's first glassworks. He built boats to transport salt and cotton, became involved in the Ligonier iron works, and was engaged in banking.

O'Hara, John (Henry) (1905–70) writer; born in Pottsville, Pa. He attended the Niagara Preparatory School (Niagara Falls, N.Y.). He worked as a reporter in Pottsville (1924–26), then held a variety of jobs, such as steel worker, soda jerk, and gas meter reader. He moved to New York City where he worked as a movie critic, and, using the name of Franey Delaney, as a radio commentator. He was a newspaper editor in Pittsburgh before becoming a press agent for Warner Brothers in Hollywood and a film writer (1934–45). He later settled in Princeton, N.J. A keen observer of the social habits and possessions of his time, he wrote entertaining novels about the sexual exploits and struggles of the upper-middle-class, but never fully gained the critical respect he craved. *Appointment in Samarra* (1934) was his first successful novel, followed by others such as *Butterfield 8* (1935), and *Ten North Frederick* (1955). Another work, *Pal Joey* (1940), became a popular musical.

O'Hare, Kate Richards See CUNNINGHAM, KATE RICHARDS O'HARE.

Ohlin, Lloyd E. (1918–) criminologist, educator; born in Belmont, Mass. A sociologist who focused on both adult and juvenile crime, he taught longest at Harvard (1967). He was special assistant to the secretary for juvenile delinquency,

Office of Health, Education and Welfare (1961–62). He was associate director of the President's Commission on Law Enforcement and Administration of Justice (1966–67), and chairman of the advisory board of the National Institute of Law Enforcement and Criminal Justice (1978). He was the author of numerous books and articles.

Ohr, George Edgar (1857–1918) potter; born in Biloxi, Miss. An eccentric original known as the "mad potter of Biloxi," he set up his own workshop in 1883 and when it burned in 1894, he replaced it with a landmark pagoda-like structure. Far ahead of his time with his twisted, ruffled pots with sinuous handles and with his fondness for visual puns, he stored away his major works in 1900. In 1972 this trove was rediscovered, leading to a new appreciation of his work.

O'Keeffe, Georgia (1887–1986) painter; born in Sun Prairie, Wis. By age 12 she was intent on being an artist. She studied at the Art Institute of Chicago (1904–08) and the Art Students League, New York (1907–08), then taught in Texas (1912–18). Alfred Stieglitz was the first to promote her work; they married (1924) but spent increasingly less time together. While based in New York, she became famous for flower paintings such as *Black Iris* (1926), and cityscapes such as *Radiator Building – Night, New York* (1927). New Mexico, which she visited from 1929 on and where she settled in 1946, inspired the paintings that made her later reputation – stark abstractions from nature, like *Deer's Skull with Pedernal* (1931).

Olah, George A. (Andrew) (1927–) chemist, educator; born in Budapest, Hungary. After taking his Ph.D. at the Technical University of Budapest (1949), he served on its faculty (1949–54), then became the associate director of the Central Chemistry Research Institute of the Hungarian Academy of Sciences (1954–56). He immigrated to Canada where he became a research scientist with Dow Chemical of Canada Ltd. (1957–64) before immigrating to the U.S.A. in 1964 to work with Dow Chemical Co. (1964–65). He then became a professor of chemistry at Case Western Reserve University (1965–69), becoming that institution's C. F. Mabery Professor of Research (1969–77). In 1977 he joined the Hydrocarbon Research Institute at the University of Southern California as the Donald P. and Katherine B. Loker Distinguished Professor of Chemistry. His major work in chemistry opened a new field of hydrocarbon research; in particular, he focused on efforts to stabilize, study, and recombine positively charged fragments of hydrocarbon molecules called "carbocations"; these had long been known to be involved in certain chemical reactions but were too short-lived for chemists to investigate until Olah developed the techniques to stabilize them. His discoveries were important for the development of new fuels and led to the technology that gives gasoline a higher octane rating; they are also applied in making plastics and pharmaceuticals. This work earned him the 1994 Nobel Prize in chemistry.

Oldenburg, Claes (Thure) (1929–) sculptor; born in Stockholm, Sweden. Son of a Swedish diplomat, he grew up in New York State, Oslo, and Chicago (1936). He graduated from Yale (1951), studied at the Art Institute of Chicago (1952–54), and settled in New York City (1956). One of the founders of the pop art movement, he is known for his mixed media sculptures, happenings, soft canvas works, and public monuments.

Oldenburg, Richard (Erik) (1933–) museum director; born in Stockholm, Sweden (brother of Claes Oldenburg). His family emigrated to America (1936), and he studied at Harvard (B.A. 1954). He was manager of the design department for Doubleday & Company, N.Y.C. (1958–61), and was an editor for Macmillan Company (1961–69). He became director of publishing for the Museum of Modern Art (1969–72), and then the director of the museum (1972).

Older, Fremont (1856–1935) journalist; born in Appleton, Wis. As managing editor of the *San Francisco Bulletin* (1895–1918), he waged a crusade against political bosses and the Southern Pacific Railway; he later edited the *San Francisco Call*.

Oldfather, William Abbott (1880–1945) classicist; born in Urumiah, Persia (now Rezaieh, Iran) (to American Presbyterian missionaries). His work was strongly influenced by the classicists at the University of Munich, where he took his Ph.D. (1908). He founded and expanded the classics library at the University of Illinois, where he taught from 1909–45, and he helped turn the university into a major institution. Active in his profession, he was Sather Lecturer (1934), president of the American Philological Association (1937–38), published widely on many aspects of antiquity both in German and in English, and trained many scholars in the field. His work on the topography of Locris remains a classic of its kind.

Oldfield, (Berna Eli) Barney (1878–1946) auto racer; born in Wauseon, Ohio. One of racing's pioneers, he began as a bicycle racer. He was the first to race a car a mile a minute (1903), while driving Henry Ford's famous "999" racer. A colorful showman who specialized in short "match" races on dirt tracks, he also established a land speed record in 1910 for a one-mile distance at over 131 miles per hour.

Oldfield, William Allan (1874–1928) U.S. representative; born in Franklin, Ark. A Spanish-American War veteran and lawyer (1900–09), in congress (Dem., Ark.; 1909–28), he chaired the Committee on Patents and became minority whip.

Olds, Leland (1890–1960) economist, public official; born in Rochester, N.Y. He was an industrial editor for the Federated Press news service (1922–29). Head of the New York State Power Authority (1931–39) and the Federal Power Commission (1939–49), he drafted utility regulations. Poised to reduce natural gas prices, he was denied reappointment by pro-oil senators who cited his "leftist" writings of earlier decades. He later founded Energy Research Associates.

Olds, Ransom (Eli) (1864–1950) automobile manufacturer; born in Geneva, Ohio. His father opened a machine shop in Lansing, Mich., in which Ranson became a partner (1885). There he developed an internal combustion engine that he incorporated into a car. In 1897 he opened the Olds Motor Vehicle Company and, replacing his father's shop, the Olds Gasoline Engine Works. The vehicle company sputtered, but the engine company succeeded. In 1899 Olds moved to Detroit, formed the Olds Motor Works, and designed and produced the popular Oldsmobile. With its low price, easy assembly, and stylish curved dashboard, this was the first car to be produced in quantity. When his backer wanted a more expensive car, Olds quit to form Reo Motor Car Company and organized subsidiary companies to supply him with parts. In 1915, after a softening in the auto market, Olds formed the Ideal Power Lawn Mower Company to manufacture his newest invention. He dabbled in securities and real estate, particularly a Florida planned community, the unsuccessful Oldsmar (1916). A Baptist, his philanthropies included establishing an interdenominational home for retired ministers in Daytona Beach, Fla.

Olitsky, Jules (1922–) painter; born in Snovsk, Russia. Emigrating with his parents to America in 1924, he studied in New York City (1940–42) and in France (1949–51), and he lived in New York and Meredith, New Hampshire. A color-field painter using staining techniques and spray paint, he taught at C. W. Post College, N.Y. (1956–63), and at Bennington College, Vt. (1963–67).

Oliver, Jack E. (Ertle) (1923–) seismologist; born in Massillon, Ohio. He was an adviser to the president (1958–59) and the U.S. Air Force (1960–69), a member of the Atomic Energy Commission (1969–74), and the Irving Porter Church Professor of Engineering at Cornell University (1971). His seismic profiles of the eastern U.S.A. have supported his conviction that seismology is the key to obtaining new data on the earth's continental crust.

Oliver, Joe "King" (1885–1938) jazz musician; born in Louisiana. Raised in New Orleans, he was a cornetist and a pioneer of jazz. He relocated to Chicago in 1919 and by 1923 his band, which included his protégé Louis Armstrong, had become the most influential in jazz. He continued to lead groups on an intermittent basis until 1935.

Oliver, Peter (1713–91) judge; born in Boston, Mass. A member of one of Boston's first social and political families, he graduated from Harvard (1730), served as a common pleas and superior court judge for 24 years, and became chief justice of the superior court in 1771. He moved to Plymouth County, Mass., in 1774, where he established an ironworks and built an imposing mansion, Oliver Hall. A prominent Loyalist, he left Boston with the British forces in 1776 and lived in Birmingham, England, until his death. American patriots burned his mansion in 1782.

Oller, Francisco (1833–1917) painter; born in Santurce, Puerto Rico. He studied in Spain and France in the 1850s and 1860s, where he was a friend of Courbet, Cézanne, and Pissarro and had paintings exhibited at the Paris salon in 1864–65. He then returned to Puerto Rico, where he painted landscapes and scenes of Puerto Rican life, including his best-known work *El Velorio* ("The Wake") (1893), which was shown at the Paris Salon in 1895.

Olmsted, Frederick Law (1822–1903) landscape architect, writer; born in Hartford, Conn. The father of landscape architecture in America (he literally coined the term), he attended lectures at Yale and studied engineering, then took a year-long voyage to China (1843). He returned to start an experimental farm on Staten Island (1847–57), influenced by the views of his friend, Andrew J. Downing. In 1850 he traveled to England where he was impressed by Birkenhead Park, just completed in gritty Liverpool. Commissioned by the *New York Times,* he traveled through the American South, and his eventual two-volume *Cotton Kingdom* (1861) was the classic work on plantation life. Superintendent of New York City's Central Park from 1857, he and Calvert Vaux, a young English architect, won the competition in 1858 to design the area, which was then mostly wilderness occupied by squatters. Their plans called for creating a pastoral effect – walkways winding around gentle slopes, along broad lawns and through groves of trees, with separate recreational areas and vehicular roads. When the Civil War broke out, he interrupted work on Central Park to become general secretary of the U.S. Sanitary Commission (1861–63), but political problems and ill health led him to go to California with his new family – he had married his brother's widow in 1859 and adopted her children, including John Olmsted. There he managed John C. Frémont's Mariposa properties, designed the Berkeley campus of the University of California, and worked to have Yosemite turned into a state reservation; he was soon among those proposing a system of protected wilderness areas for the U.S.A. Returning to New York (1865), he completed work on Central Park, and with Calvert Vaux, he set up a private firm of landscape architecture, which over ensuing decades designed numerous parks distinguished by his vision of saving natural environments within urban areas, such as Brooklyn's Prospect Park, the Boston park system, Chicago's South Park, and Montreal's Mount Royal Park. The firm also designed hundreds of other projects such as the U.S. Capitol Grounds, the Riverside community outside Chicago, and the grounds of the World's Columbian Exposition in Chicago (1893). In 1888 he moved his office to Brookline, Mass., but his firm retained its supremacy in the field.

Olmsted, Frederick Law, Jr. (1870–1957) landscape architect; born in Staten Island, N.Y. (son of Frederick Law Olmsted). Partner in Olmsted Brothers (1898–1950), he served on the Senate Park Commission to upgrade Washington, D.C. (1901–51), developing the system of regional parks that extends out into the suburbs.

Olmsted, John Charles (1852–1920) landscape architect; born in Geneva, Switzerland. Adopted by his uncle, Frederick Law Olmsted when he was seven, he worked on survey expeditions in Nevada before joining the firm in 1875, becoming a full partner in 1884. Renamed Olmsted Brothers (1898–1920), the firm flourished under his expert management and he designed comprehensive park systems for cities across America. The first president of the Society of American Landscape Architects, he drew up the codes of practice for the profession and championed the preservation of outstanding scenic vistas from haphazard zoning.

Olney, Richard (1835–1917) lawyer, cabinet member; born in Oxford, Mass. A brilliant if forbidding Boston lawyer (1859–93), he was President Grover Cleveland's attorney general (1893–95), best known for ending the Pullman strike led by Eugene Debs; he did, however, go on to support the rights of organized labor. As secretary of state (1895–97), he settled the boundary dispute between Venezuela and British Guiana and defended the rights of American nationals in Cuba and China. He retired to his law practice. He remains best known for setting forth (in 1895) what has become known as "the Olney corollary" to the Monroe Doctrine – namely, that "the United States is practically sovereign on this continent" [of South America].

Olsen, John Charles (1869–1948) chemical engineer, educator; born in Galesburg, Ill. He was on the faculty of the Polytechnic Institute, Brooklyn (1900–14), professor of chemistry at Cooper Union (1914–18), and professor of chemical engineering at the Polytechnic Institute (1918–44). He was a founder of the American Institute of Chemical Engineers.

Olsen, Kenneth (Harry) (1926–) electrical engineer; born in Bridgeport, Conn. He helped build WHIRLWIND and SAGE, two early computers, at the Massachusetts Institute of Technology's Lincoln Laboratory (1950–57). He also supervised the building of the transistorized digital computers TX-O and TX-2. In 1957 he founded and became president of the Digital Equipment Corporation, producing the PDP series of computers. In 1977 he introduced VAX (Virtual Address Extension) machines, and in the 1980s, a series of VAX minicomputers. Digital became one of the largest computer manufacturers in the world, but after the recession of the 1980s struck, he resigned as president and CEO of Digital in 1992.

Olson, Charles (John) (1910–70) poet, writer; born in Worcester, Mass. He studied at Yale, Harvard, and Wesleyan (B.A. 1932; M.A. 1933). He taught at several institutions, including Harvard (1936–39), and, as rector and teacher, at Black Mountain College, N.C. (1948–56). Long based in Gloucester, Mass., he is noted for his difficult experimental poetry, especially the *Maximus* series (1953–68), which used what he called "projective verse."

Olson, Floyd (Bjerstjerne) (1891–1936) governor; born in Minneapolis, Minn. Born in the slums, he became a Minneapolis trial lawyer in 1914, serving as county attorney in the 1920s. As Farmer-Labor Party governor (Minn.; 1931–36), he secured money for unemployment relief measures and issued a two-year moratorium on farm foreclosures, despite a conservative Republican legislature.

Olson, Harry Ferdinand (1902–82) radio engineer, inventor; born in Mount Pleasant, Iowa. He joined RCA laboratories in 1928 and developed the unidirectional microphone. In the late 1940s he established the standards for high-fidelity sound reproduction and in 1955 he developed the first electronic music synthesizer. He was awarded a Pulitzer Prize for his contributions to music in 1971.

O'Malley, (Francis J.) Frank (1911–74) educator; born in Clinton, Mass. He went to Notre Dame as a student and stayed there for the rest of his life. A legendary professor of English, he was a "Mr. Chips" come to life. He nurtured his students with an idiosyncratic care that included the writing of personal checks to reward good performance.

O'Malley, Walter (Francis) (1903–79) baseball executive; born in New York City. He was the owner of the Brooklyn and Los Angeles Dodgers (1950–70). His decision to move the franchise from Brooklyn to Los Angeles in 1958 was controversial but it proved to be eminently successful. His son, Peter O'Malley, assumed the presidency of the Dodgers in 1970.

Onassis, Jacqueline (Lee) Kennedy (b. Bouvier) "Jackie" (1929–94) First Lady; born in Southampton, N.Y. Educated at Vassar, the Sorbonne, and Washington University, she worked as a reporter before marrying John Kennedy (1953). She was not always comfortable with the demands of being the wife of a Kennedy and a politician, but as first lady she promoted her personal agenda of the arts, history, and high style. Her first child was stillborn and she lost an infant in 1963, but the Kennedys publicly enjoyed their two fine children, Caroline (b. 1957) and John (b. 1960). Her stoic behavior at Kennedy's death and funeral enhanced her standing with the public, but she stunned the world when in 1968 she married the Greek millionaire shipping magnate Aristotle Onassis. For some years she was the world's premier celebrity, but after Onassis's death (1975), she worked in New York publishing and went about her private rounds of family, the arts, and social engagements. Her last

illness and death were marked by the same quiet dignity with which she had conducted her public life as the president's wife and widow.

O'Neal(e), Margaret See EATON, PEGGY.

O'Neill, Eugene (Gladstone) (1888–1953) playwright; born in New York City. The son of actor James O'Neill, he toured with his father when young, and studied at Princeton (1906–07) and Harvard (1914–15). He worked as an assistant stage manager for his father (1910), as a sailor and laborer in Buenos Aires, Argentina (1910–11), and as an actor (1912). While spending time in a sanatorium for the treatment of tuberculosis (1912), he began to write the plays that made him an icon of American theater. Beginning in 1916, he was associated with the Provincetown Players, where many of his early plays were produced. A restless man, plagued by depression and an illness later diagnosed as Parkinson's disease, he lived in various locations, including New York City, California, and Boston. He wrote passionate works that were derived from his own obsessions, pain, and spiritual quest, such as *Desire Under the Elms* (1924), *Mourning Becomes Electra* (1931), *The Iceman Cometh* (1946), and *Long Day's Journey Into Night* (1956), among many other important works. He was awarded the Nobel Prize in literature in 1936.

O'Neill, James (1847–1920) actor; born in Kilkenny, Ireland (father of Eugene O'Neill). Brought to the U.S.A. as a child, he became popular in romantic roles – particularly in *The Count of Monte Cristo,* which he performed over 6,000 times. His decline is captured in his son's drama, *A Long Day's Journey Into Night.*

O'Neill, Margaret See EATON, PEGGY.

O'Neill, Rose (Cecil) (1874–1944) cartoonist; born in Wilkes-Barre, Pa. She was the creator in 1905 of the cartoon cupids, *The Kewpies,* which were featured in women's magazines and comic strips until her retirement in 1937. In 1913, the first of the famed Kewpie dolls were manufactured, which sold in the millions throughout the world.

O'Neill, (Thomas Phillip, Jr.) "Tip" (1912–94) U.S. representative; born in Cambridge, Mass. His father, the Cambridge Sewer Commissioner, was an active Democrat and Tip followed in his footsteps, running for the Cambridge City Council while at Boston College. An insurance man when elected to the Massachusetts House (1936–52), he became its youngest Speaker in 1947 before going to the U.S. House of Representatives (1953–1987). John McCormack sponsored his membership in Speaker Rayburn's inner circle meetings and on the powerful Rules Committee. O'Neill pushed liberal legislation while protecting his working class constituents from budget cuts. In 1968 he supported Eugene McCarthy's antiwar candidacy and as majority leader in 1973 he voted to cut off funding of the air war in Vietnam. Elected Speaker (1977–87), he failed to muster an uneasy Democratic alliance of aging Southern committee chairmen and impatient young liberals to resist President Reagan's conservative agenda. After retiring, he appeared in television commercials and cowrote *Man of the House; the Life and Political Memoirs of Speaker Tip O'Neill* (1987).

Onesimus (fl. 1706–21) slave, servant; probably born in Africa. He was first a slave (1706–16) and then a servant (1716–?) to the Puritan minister, Cotton Mather. When Boston had an epidemic of smallpox (1721), Onesimus told Mather of a form of inoculation practiced by his people, the

Guramantese. This knowledge, combined with information regarding inoculation that was being done in Constantinople, convinced Mather to advocate inoculation in Boston. Performed by Dr. Zabadiel Boylston, the inoculations were the first done in the American colonies.

Ong, Walter (Jackson) (1912–) Catholic scholar, educator; born in Kansas City, Mo. A Jesuit priest with a 1955 Harvard doctorate in English, he won esteem for his wide-ranging studies in Renaissance literature, modern poetry and criticism, and other areas. He taught from 1959 at St. Louis University.

Onsager, Lars (1903–76) chemist; born in Oslo, Norway. He came to the U.S.A. about 1928 when he was appointed associate in chemistry at Johns Hopkins; he then taught at Brown (1929–33) before becoming affiliated with Yale (1934–72). He demonstrated mathematically (1931) how simultaneous chemical reactions influence each other in ways now called Onsager's reciprocal relations. He was awarded the Nobel Prize in chemistry (1968).

Oosting, Henry J. (John) (1903–68) botanist; born in Holland, Mich. He taught at the University of Minnesota (1927–32), then moved to Duke (1932–63), conducting full-time research after retiring from academic duties. He was an authority on the plant ecology of the eastern U.S.A., including Maine forest birches and the effects of salt spray on the vegetation of the North Carolina coastal dunes.

Oppen, George (1908–84) poet; born in New Rochelle, N.Y. Educated in public schools in California, he was a founder of the objectivist poetry style and established small printing presses in Paris (1930–33) and New York (1934–36). A Communist, he was investigated by the U.S. government, so he moved to Mexico City (1950); he later settled in San Francisco (1958). He continued to write poetry until he was stricken by Alzheimer's disease.

Oppenheim, James (1882–1932) poet, writer; born in St. Paul, Minn. His family moved to New York City when he was a child, and he was educated in the public schools. He took extension courses at Columbia University, then became a secretary and a teacher. He wrote sentimental stories and novels to support his family before becoming a poet, as seen in *Songs for the New Age* (1914). He was also the editor of a literary magazine, *The Seven Arts* (1916–17), and, after it failed, he became involved in the psychoanalytic theories of Carl Jung. He died of tuberculosis after many years of poverty and illness.

Oppenheimer, J. Robert (1904–67) physicist; born in New York City. During his graduate studies in Europe (1925–29), he and Max Born of Göttingen developed their classical contribution to molecular quantum theory, the "Born-Oppenheimer method" (1926). Returning to the U.S.A., Oppenheimer taught theoretical physics concurrently at the California Institute of Technology and the University of California: Berkeley (1929–42), and investigated electron-positron pairs, cosmic ray theory, and deuteron reactions. He joined the Manhattan Project (1942) and directed the Los Alamos laboratory (1943–45), where his crucial input made him internationally known as the "father of the atomic bomb." During the postwar period, he became a government and UN adviser, proposing international regulation of nuclear power to ensure peace. As director of the Institute for Advanced Studies, Princeton, N.J. (1947–66), he stimulated discussion and research in quantum and relativistic physics. He lost his security clearance in 1953 because of his alleged "disloyalty" but he was vindicated in 1963 when he was given the Atomic Energy Commission's Fermi Award.

Oppenheimer, Jane M. (Marlow) (1911–) developmental zoologist; born in Philadelphia. She held fellowships at Yale (1935–36), the American Association of University Women's Berliner (1936–37), and at the University of Rochester (1937–38) before joining the faculty of Bryn Mawr College (1942–80). She made major contributions to studies of developmental biology and experimental embryology of teleost (bony) fishes, and wrote essays and books on the history of embryology.

Orbison, Roy (Kelton) (1936–88) rock 'n' roll singer, songwriter, guitarist; born in Vernon, Texas. He played in two rockabilly bands and made some unsuccessful recordings before Sun Records released "Ooby Dooby" (1956), his first hit. His song "Claudette" (1958) was a hit for the Everly Brothers and he had a string of hits during the early-1960s such as "Only the Lonely" (1960). Many prominent rock 'n' roll musicians regarded him as an influence and he performed with some popularity until his death.

Ore, Oystein (1899–1968) mathematician; born in Oslo, Norway. He emigrated to America (1927) to teach at Yale (1927–68) where he was department chairman (1936–45). Decorated Knight, Order of St. Olav (1947) for Norwegian relief work, he was coeditor of *Gesammelte Werke of R. Dedekind,* and author of several books on number theory and numerous articles.

O'Reilly, John Boyle (1844–90) writer, editor, poet; born near Drogheda, Ireland. He was apprenticed as a journalist, and worked in Ireland and England. He was arrested and tried (1866) on the charge of being a Fenian and traitor to England; he was convicted, imprisoned, and deported to the penal colony in Australia (1868). He escaped to America (1869), settled in Boston, and resumed his career as a journalist. He became co-owner and editor (1876) of the *Pilot,* an influential Irish newspaper, and was a popular lecturer. He wrote a novel, but is best known for his many books of poetry, such as *Songs, Legends and Ballads* (1878).

O'Reilly, Leonora (1870–1927) labor leader, social reformer; born in New York City. A factory worker, union organizer, socialist, and suffragist, she was active in reform activity in New York City, including the Henry Street Settlement House, the Women's Trade Union League, and the National Association for the Advancement of Colored People.

Ormandy, Eugene (b. Blau) (1899–1985) conductor; born in Budapest, Hungary. A child prodigy on violin, Ormandy came to the U.S.A. to play violin in 1920, then took up conducting. He headed the Minneapolis Symphony (1931–35) before taking the podium of the Philadelphia Orchestra in 1936 (for two years co-conductor with Leopold Stokowski); he remained at that post until his retirement in 1980, maintaining the voluptuousness of sound for which the orchestra was both praised and criticized.

Ornstein, Leo (1892–) composer, pianist; born in Kremenchug, Russia. A child prodigy, he came to America with his family in 1907; in his twenties he was notorious as a "futuristic" pianist and composer. He receded into obscurity for decades before his work was rediscovered in the 1970s.

Ortenberg, Arthur (1926–) fashion executive; birthplace unknown. A textile designer and fashion consultant, he married Liz Claiborne in 1957 and together they founded Liz

Claiborne, Inc., in New York City (1976). As secretary, treasurer, and cochairman, he insured that prompt delivery and quality control were hallmarks of their company, which rose to the Fortune 500 list within a decade. After their retirement, they established the Liz Claiborne and Art Ortenberger Foundation (1989) to support environmental causes.

Ortiz, Alfonso Alex (1939–) educator, cultural anthropologist; born in San Juan Pueblo, N.M. He graduated from the University of New Mexico in 1961 and took a Ph.D. from Chicago in 1967. Author of studies of Pueblo Indian societies, including *The Tewa World* (1969), he also compiled and edited an anthology of Native American Poetry. He taught at Princeton before joining the University of New Mexico faculty in 1970.

Ortiz, Simon (Joseph) (1941–) poet, writer; born in Albuquerque, N.M. An Acoma Pueblo Indian, he was educated through the Bureau of Indian Affairs, attended Fort Lewis College (1961–62), the University of New Mexico (1966–68), and the University of Iowa (1968–69). He served in the army (1963–66) during the Vietnam War. He worked in public relations (1969–70), as a newspaper editor (1970–73), and as a teacher at numerous institutions. He lived in Acoma Pueblo, N.M., and is known for his fiction and poetry such as *A Good Journey* (1977) and *From Sand Creek: Rising in This Heart Which Is Our America* (1981).

Orton, James (1830–77) zoologist, explorer; born in Seneca Falls, N.Y. Originally a Presbyterian minister, he became a professor of natural history at Vassar College (1869). He made three expeditions to South America (1867, 1883, 1876) and described the geology and physical geography of the areas he saw in *The Andes and the Amazon* (1870, 1876).

Osborn, Henry Fairfield (1857–1935) paleontologist, educator; born in Fairfield, Conn. He taught natural sciences at Princeton (1881–91) and biology at Columbia University (1891–1907). In 1891 he organized the department of mammalian paleontology at the American Museum of Natural History. As the museum's president (1908–35), he developed it into the world's largest natural history museum. His bibliography includes more than 600 scientific titles, most notably on reptilian and mammalian evolution; he is credited with originating the term "adaptive radiation."

Osborn, William (Henry) (1820–94) railroad promoter; born in Salem, Mass. A representative of a Boston trading house in Manila, in 1853 he married Virginia Reed Sturges, daughter of Jonathan Sturges, an incorporator of the Illinois Central Railroad. As president of the railroad (1855–82), he improved its financial condition and merged it with the Chicago, St. Louis, & New Orleans. When he retired, he engaged in philanthropy as an active promoter of, among other things, railroad workers' welfare.

Osborne, Thomas B. (Burr) (1859–1929) biochemist; born in New Haven, Conn. He spent his career as director of the Connecticut Agricultural Experiment Station, New Haven (1886–1928), while concurrently appointed to the Carnegie Institution (1904–29) and serving Yale as a research assistant (1923–28). He devoted his research to investigations of the chemical structure, function, and nutritive value of plant (especially grain) proteins. He discovered a necessary fat-soluble substance later found to be vitamin A, and advocated a human diet relatively low in protein.

Osborne, Thomas Mott (1859–1926) manufacturer, prison reformer; born at Auburn, N.Y. After selling his family's agricultural machinery firm to International Harvester (1903), and founding the *Auburn Citizen* (1905), a local newspaper, he devoted himself to Democratic politics on a state and national level. After becoming interested in prison reform, he was named warden of Sing Sing (1914–16). For fighting the corrupt New York prison system, he was indicted by the Westchester County grand jury on trumped-up charges (1915). The case was dismissed, but he resigned his post soon after to become commanding officer of the U.S. naval prison, Portsmouth, N.H. (1917–20). The author of three books on prison reform, as well as international prison studies, he was also devoted to music and dramatics.

Osbourne, Lloyd (1868–1947) writer; born in San Francisco. He was educated privately and at the University of Edinburgh. Appointed vice-consul of Samoa, he served in that post until 1897, then settled in New York City. He and his stepfather, Robert Louis Stevenson, collaborated on *The Wrong Box* (1889) and several other novels. Although he continued to write fiction, Osbourne's work is largely unknown today.

Osceola (also known as Powell) (c. 1800–38) Seminole Indian leader; born in Georgia. Although not a chief, he took the lead in opposing all efforts to remove the Seminole from their Florida homeland. His warriors' killing of a U.S. agent in 1835 touched off the second Seminole War, and he led his people in actively resisting the Federal forces. U.S. forces seized Osceola under a flag of truce and imprisoned him in Fort Moultrie, S.C., where he died.

Oser, Bernard L. (Levussove) (1899–) biochemist; born in Philadelphia, Pa. He worked as a biochemist for the Jefferson Medical College (1920–21) and the Philadelphia General Hospital (1922–26) before joining the Food and Drug Research Laboratories in 1926 as assistant director of the biology laboratory. He was president of the organization at his retirement (1976), after which he started a consulting firm. His pathbreaking research helped develop concepts of bioavailability, ingredient interactions, and residue tolerances in food.

Osgood, James Ripley (1836–92) publisher; born in Fryeburg, Maine. In 1871 he cofounded James R. Osgood & Company, an outgrowth of Ticknor & Fields. While retaining many fine authors, it failed financially, and with Osgood's departure (1880), was dissolved into a company headed by Henry Oscar Houghton.

Osgood, William Fogg (1864–1943) mathematician; born in Boston, Mass. A noted teacher at Harvard (1890–1933), he contributed to development of continuous functions, differential equations, Riemann's theorem, calculus of variations, and space-filling curves. His *Lehrbuch der Fuktionetheorie* (1907) is still a classic. He loved travel, tennis, golf, and cigars.

Osler, William (1894–1919) physician; born in Bond Head, Ontario, Canada. He studied medicine in Canada and in Europe (where in 1873 he was the first to observe blood platelets). He returned to teach at McGill University in Montreal (1875–84). He came to the U.S.A. to teach at the University of Pennsylvania (1884–88); while there he helped found the Association of American Physicians. From 1888–1905 he taught at Johns Hopkins University's new medical school, where he revolutionized American medical teaching by insisting that medical students have responsibilities to patients even as he insisted on more scientific and professional standards in the teaching and practice of medicine. His *Principles and Practice of Medicine* (1891) long remained the standard textbook in medical schools throughout the world. He went to Oxford, England, to take the Regius Chair of Medicine (1905–19), and among many honors in his lifetime he was made a baronet in 1911. A man of incredible energy – he wrote numerous books, gave scores of special addresses, founded various organizations – he was also a medical historian and collector of medical books; his library is housed at McGill University.

O'Sullivan, Mary Kenney (1864–1943) labor leader, social reformer; born in Hannibal, Mo. A laborer from an early age, she organized women binders in Chicago, lobbied successfully for the first protective factory law in Illinois, and was the first woman to serve as an organizer for the American Federation of Labor (1892–93). She also organized factory workers in Boston, was involved in the settlement house movement in Massachusetts and, as a founder of the National Women's Trade Union League (1903), promoted unionization and job safety legislation for women.

O'Sullivan, Timothy H. (c. 1840–82) photographer; born in New York City. A protégé of Mathew Brady, he led photographers covering Gettysburg and Richmond during the Civil War. From 1862 to 1865 he photographed the Army of the Potomac with Alexander Gardner. An expedition photographer (1867–74), he took pictures for various geological surveys with a magnesium torch deep in the Comstock mines, in the rain forests of Panama, and along the Chelley Canyon in Arizona.

Oswald, Lee Harvey (1939–63) assassin; born in New Orleans. After a troubled youth, he served in the U.S. Marine Corps (1956–59). Renouncing his U.S. citizenship, he lived in the Soviet Union (1959–62), then returned with his Russian wife to live in Texas. He shot and killed President John F. Kennedy in Dallas (1963) and two days later was killed by Jack Ruby, a Dallas nightclub owner. The question whether he was acting on his own seemed destined to divide people for the foreseeable future.

Othmer, Donald F. (1904–   ) chemical engineer, educator; born in Omaha, Nebr. Of his more than 150 patents, the Othmer still (1927), which improved the design of distillation plants and processes, is his most important. After five years at Kodak (1927–32), he taught at Polytechnic University in New York. He coedited the *Kirk-Othmer Encyclopedia of Chemical Technology.*

Otis, Bass (1784–1861) painter, lithographer; born in Bridgewater, Mass. He began as a scythemaker, became a portrait painter in New York City (1808), and from 1812, lived in Philadelphia. Considered the first American lithographer, he published a portrait of Reverend Abner Kneeland in a volume of lectures (1818). He also painted portraits of Thomas Jefferson and James Madison.

Otis, Charles R. (Rollin) (1835–1927) manufacturer; born in Troy, N.Y., **and Norton P. (Prentiss)** (1840–1905) manufacturer; U.S. representative; born in Halifax, Vt. Working with his father, Elisha Otis, Charles persuaded him to open his own elevator factory to capitalize on Elisha's crucial inventions. After Elisha's death (1861), Charles continued inventing and patenting improvements at the Yonkers elevator factory, while Norton worked in sales. Otis Brothers &

Company was organized in 1864 with Charles as president and Norton as treasurer. In 1890 Charles retired to travel; Norton assumed the presidency. The company consolidated to Otis Elevator Company in 1898. The brothers accumulated more than 30 patents and installed steam elevators in the Washington Monument (1880) and the Eiffel Tower; they installed the first electric elevator in New York City (1889). Norton, active in civic affairs, served two terms in the U.S. House of Representatives (Rep., N.Y.; 1901–03, 1905–07).

Otis, Elisha (Graves) (1811–61) inventor; born in Halifax, Vt. A master mechanic for a company that made bedsteads in Yonkers, N.Y., in 1853 he developed a system to hoist equipment and workers from one floor to the next, patenting it as an "elevator." Otis was soon taking orders for passenger as well as freight lifts. He patented a steam elevator in 1861, and his sons expanded the business after his death.

Otis, Harrison Gray (1765–1848) U.S. representative/senator; born in Boston, Mass. A prominent Boston lawyer, he made a fortune in land speculation. He served in the U.S. House of Representatives (Fed., Mass.; 1797–1801) and then in the U.S. Senate (Federalist, later Whig; 1817–22). During the furor caused by the Embargo Act of 1807, he became the leader of the states' rights movement in Boston and he was the most prominent member of the Hartford Convention (1814). In the Senate debate over the Missouri Compromise, he opposed the extension of slavery, but he was not an active abolitionist. He was mayor of Boston (1829–31).

Otis, James (1725–83) lawyer, political thinker; born in West Barnstable, Mass. He led the resistance to the revival of the Sugar Act in 1761 and objected to the British use of writs of assistance (general search warrants). He wrote numerous political pamphlets, the most famous being *The Rights of the British Colonies Asserted and Proved* (1764). He was the main political leader in Massachusetts until 1769 when he suffered a severe head injury while scuffling with a British officer. From that point on he became mentally imbalanced and political power passed to others. Although he was a strong defender of colonial rights, he opposed violence and he did not anticipate the coming separation from Great Britain.

Otis, Johnny (b. John Veliotes) (1921–   ) musician; born in Vallejo, Calif. A self-styled "white Negro" who worked with African-American musicians throughout his career, he began as a drummer in Count Matthews' House Rockers and other jump blues bands in Oakland between 1940–45. He formed his first band and released the hit record "Harlem Nocturne" in 1946. For the next 15 years, he was a leading figure in the development of West Coast rhythm-and-blues, operating the Barrelhouse nightclub in Los Angeles and discovering Little Esther, the Robins, and Big Mama Thornton. He recorded for Capitol Records throughout the 1950s, including his last hit, "Willie and the Hand Jive," in 1959. Thereafter, he toured occasionally with his blues revue and ran several small record labels, but concentrated on work as a disc jockey and club owner. His autobiography, *Listen to the Lambs,* was published in 1968.

Otis, Norton P. See under OTIS, CHARLES R.

Ott, (Melvin Thomas) Mel (1909–58) baseball player; born in Gretna, La. With an unusual batting style in which he lifted his front foot as he swung, he hit 511 home runs during his 22-year career as an outfielder for the New York Giants (1926–47). He was one of the few players to go straight to the majors from high school. He was also manager of the Giants from 1942 to 1948. In 1951 he was elected to baseball's Hall of Fame.

Ouimet, Francis (Desales) (1893–1967) golfer, stockbroker; born in Brookline, Mass. As a 20-year-old amateur, he won the U.S. Open in 1913 on the Brookline, Mass., course where he caddied as a youngster. He took up a career as a stockbroker and played his long career as an amateur. He was the U.S. amateur champion in 1914 and 1931 and won many other matches. He was a player or a nonplaying captain for every Walker Cup team from 1922 to 1949 and in 1951 he became the first American elected captain of the Royal and Ancient Golf Club of St. Andrews, Scotland.

Ouray (?1820 or ?1833–80) Uncompaghre Ute chief; born at Taos in present-day New Mexico. Raised among Mexicans, he spoke Spanish as well as his Ute language and English. In 1862 he became chief of the Uncompaghre. In 1863 he negotiated a treaty with the U.S.A., ceding all of the Utes' territory east of the Continental Divide but making him chief of the Western Ute. In 1867, with Kit Carson, he suppressed a revolt led by Kaniatse, a rival chief. In 1879, the esteem in which he was held by both sides helped avert a war after an incident involving the murder of several whites. In 1880 he signed a treaty in Washington, D.C., providing for the final removal of the Utes from Colorado to Utah.

Oursler, (Charles) Fulton (1893–1952) author, editor; born in Baltimore, Md. He wrote plays, novels (especially mysteries under the pseudonym Anthony Abbot), and popular religious books, most notably *The Greatest Story Ever Told* (1949); he was senior editor of *Reader's Digest* from 1944 on.

Outcault, Richard (Felton) (1863–1928) cartoonist; born in Lancaster, Ohio. In 1894 his cartoons depicting children in the New York City slums, titled *Hogan's Alley,* became a regular series for the *New York World.* The cartoons provoked protests from the social establishment but charmed the reading public, which nicknamed the series, "The Yellow Kid," a title that later inspired the term, "yellow journalism," to describe the sensationalistic reporting of the day. In 1902 he introduced a well-to-do but mischievous child in the cartoon series, *Buster Brown,* which appeared in the *New York Journal* each Sunday until 1920.

Outerbridge, Paul, Jr. (1896–1958) photographer; born in New York City. A successful free-lance photographer in New York and Paris (1922–39), he changed fashion photography in 1929 when he introduced color, using a new 3-color process.

Overhauser, Albert W. (Warner) (1925–) physicist; born in San Diego, Calif. He performed research at the University of Illinois (1951–53), moved to Cornell (1953–58), and was a solid state physicist at the Ford Motor Company (1958–73) before joining Purdue (1973). He made many contributions to the study of the behavior of conduction electrons in metals, including discovering the now-called Overhauser effect of dynamic polarization (1953).

Ovington, Mary White (1865–1951) civil rights reformer; born in Brooklyn, N.Y. Her Unitarian upbringing and attendance at the Harvard Annex (later Radcliffe College) (1888–91) inspired her to devote herself to social reforms. She became a settlement house worker in Brooklyn (1895–1903) and also assistant secretary to the Social Reform Club of New York; it was a 1903 speech by Booker T. Washington

at the latter that awakened her to the continuing plight of African-Americans, and it was to improving their lot that she devoted the rest of her life. Her original studies led to *Half a Man: The Status of the Negro in New York* (1911), and to close associations with prominent African-Americans, particularly W. E. B. Du Bois, and she joined him in founding the National Association for the Advancement of Colored People (NAACP) in 1909. She served the NAACP for some 40 years in a variety of posts, including chairperson and treasurer, and in addition to helping organize it and establish its policies during these formative years, she played an invaluable role in mediating between often conflicting personalities in the movement. Although she had been a Socialist since 1905, and spoke against war and colonialism and for women's rights, she was essentially a moderate whose main goal was for the integration of the races. She wrote a syndicated newspaper column in the 1920s and several books dealing with issues of race.

Owen, Robert (Dale) (1801–77) social reformer; born in Glasgow, Scotland. He taught briefly in New Lanark, Scotland, where his family owned the cotton mills, and occasionally he ran the factories in his father's absence. Influenced by Robert Dale (his father), whose theory of social reform was based on cooperation, practical education, and humane working conditions, he emigrated with his father to America (1825) to set up the New Harmony Colony in Indiana. Unfit for manual labor, the son taught school there and edited the *New Harmony Gazette.* The community failed (1827) and he would later criticize its participants as "lazy theorists" and "unprincipled sharpers." (His father returned to England in 1828.) Known for practicality in the application of social ideals, he nonetheless came under the influence of Frances Wright and the "Free Enquirers," a liberal group that advocated an early form of socialism. Moving to New York to join the group's inner circle (1829), he edited the *Free Inquirer* and helped form the Association for the Protection of Industry and for the Promotion of National Education. Joining his father in England (1832), he coedited *The Crisis* with him for six months, then returned to New Harmony where he served three terms in the Indiana legislature (1836–38) and was able to secure large-scale public school funding. He also served two terms in the U.S. House of Representatives (1843–47). Appointed chargé d'affaires at Naples (1853) and then minister (1855–58), he embraced spiritualism in Italy. On his return to the U.S.A. (1858), he became a leading advocate of the emancipation of slaves; commissioned to purchase arms for the state of Indiana (1861–63), he wrote an influential pamphlet, *The Policy of Emancipation* (1863). As chairman of a national committee to study freed slaves, he wrote *The Wrong Slavery* (1864). He was also the author of an autobiography and several novels.

Owen, Robert Latham (1856–1947) U.S. senator; born in Lynchburg, Va. Part Cherokee (through his mother), he was active in tribal affairs in Indian Territory both before and after he became a lawyer (1880). He played a major role in the act of Congress that gave U.S. citizenship to the Native Americans in Indian Territory. As soon as Oklahoma became a state, he was elected to the U.S. Senate (Dem., 1907–25). As a senator he was identified with liberal causes, particularly with progressive labor legislation.

Owen, (Stephen Joseph) "Stout Steve" (1898–1964) football player, coach; born in Cleo Springs, Okla. An all-pro tackle in the 1920s, he coached the New York Giants (1931–53) to eight division titles and two National Football League championships.

Owens, (James or John Cleveland) Jesse (1913–80) track and field athlete; born in Danville, Ala. After setting records as a schoolboy athlete in Cleveland, he attended Ohio State University; on one day (May 25, 1935), he set three world records and tied another in the span of about an hour. (His 26 feet 8¼ inch running broad jump was not broken until 1960.) At the 1936 Olympics in Berlin, Germany, he disproved for the world Adolf Hitler's proclamation of "Aryan supremacy" by achieving the finest one-day performance in track history with four gold medals (100 meters, 200 meters, 4 × 100 meters, running broad jump); Hitler left the stadium to avoid having to congratulate an African-American. Although he gained worldwide publicity for his feat, back in the U.S.A. he gained few financial or social benefits and was reduced to running "freak" races against horses and dogs. After graduating from Ohio State (1937) he went into private business before becoming secretary of the Illinois Athletic Commission (until 1955). He made a goodwill tour of India for the U.S. State Department and attended the 1956 Olympics as President Eisenhower's personal representative. He returned to Illinois to direct youth sports activities for the Illinois Youth Commission. In a belated gesture of national recognition, he was awarded the Presidential Medal of Freedom in 1976.

Oxnam, Garfield Bromley (1891–1963) Protestant religious leader, educator; born in Sonora, Calif. He graduated from the University of California in 1913 and studied at Harvard and abroad. Ordained a Methodist Episcopal minister in 1916, he was a pastor, professor of social ethics, and, from 1928–36, president of DePauw University in Indiana. Elected a bishop in 1936, he served in Omaha, Boston, and, from 1952 until his retirement in 1960, Washington, D.C. A theological and political liberal, he headed the World Council of Churches (1948–54) and authored many books, including *A Testament of Faith* (1958).

Ozawa, Seiji (1935–) conductor; born in Hoten, China. Of Japanese descent, he trained in Japan, Paris, and the U.S.A. He conducted the Toronto and San Francisco Symphonies before beginning in 1973 his long tenure as conductor of the Boston Symphony.

Ozick, Cynthia (b. Hallote) (1928–) writer; born in New York City. She studied at New York University (B.A. 1949), and Ohio State University (M.A. 1950). She worked as an advertising copywriter in Boston (1952–53), taught at New York University (1964–65), and was artist-in-residence at City College (1981–82). She lived in New Rochelle, N.Y., and wrote novels, short stories, essays, literary criticism, and translations. She is known for her mystical and supernatural fiction that often draws on Judaic law and history, as in *The Pagan Rabbi, and Other Stories* (1971), and *Levitation: Five Fictions* (1982).

P

Paar, Jack (Harold) (1918–) television host; born in Canton, Ohio. He quit school at age 16 and began working as a radio announcer in the Midwest. In the U.S. Army in World War II he entertained with service shows in the South Pacific. After the war he had some minor movie roles and then began to appear as host of a series of radio and television shows. In 1957 he was assigned to host the National Broadcasting Company's *Tonight* show, and he proved so successful that it was renamed the *Jack Paar Show* (1958–62). A natural conversationalist and interviewer, with a roster of favorite guests, he was known for his feuds on and off camera. Tiring of the daily grind, he retired and bought a local Maryland television station, and returned only briefly (1973) with a weekly television show.

Paca, William (1740–99) governor; born near Abingdon, Md. An Annapolis lawyer and Maryland legislator, he led opposition to the British poll tax in 1774. In the Continental Congress (1774–79), he signed the Declaration of Independence and paid for troops with his own money. As Maryland's governor (1782–85), he built Washington College (Maryland), becoming a federal district judge afterward (1789–99).

Pach, Walter (1883–1958) painter, art historian; born in New York City. Based in New York City, he was a painter who selected European art for the Armory Show (1913). A leading art historian, he published reviews, translations, and books, such as *Queer Thing, Painting* (1939) and *The Classical Tradition in Modern Art* (1959).

Pack, Robert (1929–) poet; born in New York City. He studied at Dartmouth (B.A. 1951) and Columbia University (M.A. 1953). He taught at Barnard (1957–64) and Middlebury College (Vermont) (1964). Associated with the Bread Loaf Writers Conference, Middlebury, Vt. (1973–93), he won many awards for his poetry. Some critics consider him the heir to the sensibilities of Robert Frost, as seen in *Waking to My Name: New and Selected Poems* (1980).

Packard, Alpheus Spring, Jr. (1839–1905) entomologist, geologist; born in Brunswick, Maine. After graduating from Bowdoin College (1861), he served as an entomologist on the Maine geological survey. His work so impressed geologist Louis Agassiz of Harvard's Lawrence Scientific School that he secured a position as Agassiz's assistant (1861–84) while concurrently earning his M.D. from Maine Medical School (1864). He was an assistant surgeon for the Maine Veteran Volunteers during the Civil War (1864–65), then became librarian and custodian for the Boston Society

of Natural History (1865–66) and curator of the Essex Institute (1866). While director of the Peabody Academy of Science (Salem, Mass.) (1867–78), he founded the journal *American Naturalist* (1867) and served as its editor-in-chief until 1887. He was the State Entomologist of Massachusetts (1871–73), and a member of the U.S. Entomological Commission (1877–82). He then taught entomology at the Massachusetts Agricultural College (1870–78), before becoming a professor of zoology and geology at Brown University (1878–1905). His contributions to taxonomy include descriptions of 50 genera and 580 species of insects and marine invertebrates. He was also an authority on insect embryology, and published articles on glaciation. A naturalist in a time of specialization, he was the best-known American entomologist in both the U.S.A. and Europe at the time of his death.

Packard, David (1912–) electrical engineer; born in Pueblo, Colo. He was an engineer with General Electric (1936–38). With his friend, William Hewlett, he formed Hewlett-Packard (HP) in 1939, producing resistance-capacitance audio oscillators in a garage. He was president of HP (1947–64) and then CEO, with a stint as Deputy Secretary of Defense (1969–71).

Packard, James W. (Ward) (1863–1928) engineer, inventor, manufacturer; born in Warren, Ohio. After college, he worked for the Sawyer-Mann Electric Company, manufacturers of incandescent electric lamps, and acquired several patents. After the company was sold to Westinghouse (1889), he founded the Packard Electric Company in Warren, Ohio, with his brother (William Doud Packard, 1861–1923); later it became the New York & Ohio Company, manufacturing improved electrical equipment such as transformers and fuse boxes. Meanwhile, with his brother he designed and built an automobile in 1899 that resulted in the Packard Motor Car Company, located in Detroit. President until 1915, he stayed in Warren researching and developing many improvements for automobiles. Among his philanthropies was an electrical and mechanical engineering laboratory at his alma mater, Lehigh University.

Packard, Vance (Oakley) (1914–) journalist, writer; born in Granville Summit, Pa. He graduated from Pennsylvania State University (1936) and worked as a reporter and columnist for newspapers and the Associated Press before he became an editor and writer at *American* magazine (1942–56). He wrote a number of books popularizing social issues, including *The Hidden Persuaders* (1957), *The Naked Society*

(1964), and *The People Shapers* (1977). He also taught writing at Columbia and New York Universities.

Paepcke, Walter P. (1897–1960) businessman, philanthropist; born in Chicago. He worked in his father's lumber business before he started the Container Corporation of America in 1926. Believing that businessmen should work to make culture more commercially viable, he developed Aspen, Colo., into a winter resort and cultural center. He was director and trustee of several educational foundations.

Page, Charles (Grafton) (1812–68) physician, inventor; born in Salem, Mass. A Harvard graduate and a trained physician, he practiced medicine, and, in his free time, experimented with electricity. Among his many contributions were a self-acting circuit breaker and a primitive electric locomotive, which had a trial run in 1850. In 1841 he became one of two principal examiners of the U.S. Patent Office. He resigned in 1852, but returned to the patent office in 1861 and remained there until his death.

Page, John (1743–1808) U. S. representative, governor; born in Gloucester County, Va. He fought in the French and Indian Wars and in the Revolutionary Army with George Washington before going to Congress (Rep., Va.; 1789–97), and later served as Virginia's governor (1802–05).

Page, Oran "Hot Lips" (1908–54) jazz musician; born in Dallas, Texas. He was a trumpeter and blues singer who appeared with Walter Page, Bennie Moten, and Count Basie before leading his own New York-based orchestra in 1937 and 1938. From 1941 to 1942, he was a featured sideman with Artie Shaw, and he free-lanced thereafter.

Page, Thomas Nelson (1853–1922) writer, diplomat; born in Hanover County, Va. He studied at Washington College (Lexington, Va.) (1869–72), and the University of Virginia (L.L.B. 1873–74). He practiced law in Richmond, Va. (1874–93), and wrote sentimental southern dialect stories, such as *In Ole Virginia; or, Marse Chan and Other Stories* (1887). He also wrote novels, essays, biographies, and children's books, all set in the South before and after the Civil War. He served as U.S. ambassador to Italy (1913–19), but spent most of his life in Virginia.

Page, Walter Hines (1855–1918) editor, publisher, diplomat; born in Cary, N.C. As editor of the *Atlantic Monthly* (1895–98), he added a political dimension to its coverage, boosting its popularity and prestige. Also a partner in Doubleday, Page & Company publishers from 1899, he served during a crucial period as U.S. ambassador to Britain (1913–18).

Page, William (1811–85) painter; born in Albany, N.Y. He was a student of Samuel F. B. Morse in New York (1826), traveled to Italy (1849–60), and settled in Tottenville, Staten Island, N.Y. Few paintings survive, but his haunting portrait, *Mrs. William Page* (1860), is superb.

Paige, (Leroy Robert) "Satchel" (1906–82) baseball pitcher; born in Mobile, Ala. One of the game's greatest pitchers, he was for many years a star in baseball's black leagues before appearing in the major leagues with the Cleveland Indians in 1948. As a right-hander for the Kansas City Monarchs and other Negro League clubs, he relied on near perfect control and guile for his legendary success; it has been unofficially estimated that he appeared in some 2,500 Negro League games and pitched perhaps 300 shutouts, including 55 no-hitters. Famous for his colorful "Rules For Staying Young" (which included "Don't look back. Something might be gaining on you."), he was instrumental in breaking major league baseball's color barrier. In 1971 he was elected to baseball's Hall of Fame.

Paine, Charles Jackson (1833–1916) yachtsman, lawyer; born in Boston, Mass. He was admitted to the bar in 1856. He rose from Union captain to brigadier general (1861–66) during the Civil War. He owned and raced the legendary yachts, the *Mayflower, Puritan,* and *Volunteer,* in international competition. He later invested in railroad companies.

Paine, John Knowles (1839–1906) composer; born in Portland, Maine. After training in Germany (1857–61), he returned to assume, at Harvard, the first chair of music in an American university (1862–1905). One of the "Boston Classic" school, he composed high-toned music in a European style, such as his Symphony No. 2 (1880).

Paine, Thomas (1737–1809) political theorist; born in Thetford, England. He was a British subject, an American citizen, and then an honorary French citizen. He came to Philadelphia in 1774 and published his pamphlet *Common Sense* in 1776; it sold nearly half a million copies and was distributed in Europe as well as the colonies. He then wrote a pamphlet series, *The Crisis,* which began with the memorable line, "These are the times that try men's souls." The pamphlet series greatly uplifted the spirit of the Continental army and the colonists as a whole. Following the American Revolution, he lived quietly in New York until he returned to Britain in 1787. He wrote the *Rights of Man* (1791–92) in response to Edmund Burke's criticism of the French Revolution. He became an honorary French citizen, was elected to the Revolutionary Convention (1792), and was imprisoned during the height of the Terror in Paris. Later he published *The Age of Reason* (1794, 1796) and returned to New York where he lived in obscurity until his death.

Palade, George E. (Emil) (1912–) cell biologist; born in Jassy, Romania. He practiced medicine and taught anatomy in Bucharest (1933–45), then came to the U.S.A. to join Rockefeller University (1946–73). There he made major advances in electron microscopy of cellular organelles, then began his landmark investigations of cellular protein synthesis and enzyme secretion. At Yale (1973–90), he pursued research in cell membrane physiology. He became a dean and a professor in residence at the University of California: San Diego (1990). His many awards include sharing the 1974 Nobel Prize in physiology for his description of cellular protein chemistry.

Palés Matos, Luis (1898–1959) poet; born in Guayama, Puerto Rico. He was one of the creators of Afro-Antillian poetry, which introduced African rhythms and words into the Puerto Rican poetic idom. Works such as *Tuntún de Pasa y Grifería* and *Últimos Poemas* led many to think him Puerto Rico's most important 20th-century poet. He supported himself by working as a civil servant.

Paley, Albert Raymond (1944–) metalworker; born in Philadelphia. Initially studying jewelry-making at Temple University's Tyler School of Art and becoming a master goldsmith, he turned to large scale metalworking in the late 1960s. Singlehandedly he revived blacksmithing as an art form with the ornamental gates, figurative sculpture, metal furniture, grilles, railings, and other architectural elements made on commission in his Rochester, N.Y., workshop.

Paley, Grace (b. Goodside) (1922–) writer; born in New York City. She studied at Hunter College (1938–39) and New

York University. She taught at Columbia and Syracuse Universities during the 1960s, and became a teacher at Sarah Lawrence College. Early in her career she was a poet, but she is most noted for her mastery of the short story form, as in *Enormous Changes at the Last Minute* (1974) and *Later the Same Day* (1985). A feminist and peace activist, she lived in New York City and Thetford, Vt.

Paley, William S. (Samuel) (1901–91) broadcast executive; born in Chicago. He joined the family business, Congress Cigar Co., in Philadelphia, after graduation in 1922 from the Wharton School of Finance at the University of Pennsylvania. Impressed with the results of advertising the family's La Palina cigars on a fledgling local radio network, he bought the network for $300,000 in 1928. A year later, it became the Columbia Broadcasting System (CBS) and grew into one of the most powerful radio and television broadcasting networks in the nation, with Paley at the helm for 50 years. Among his accomplishments were development of the country's best broadcast news operation and the establishment of Columbia Records as one of the most successful recording companies in the world. He was notorious for his talent raids on competitors like the National Broadcasting Company (NBC), from which he wooed Jack Benny, Red Skelton, and Frank Sinatra. An art connoisseur, he served as president of the Museum of Modern Art.

Palmer, Alexander (Mitchell) (1872–1936) lawyer, U.S. representative, cabinet member; born in Moosehead, Pa. A Quaker lawyer, he was a reformer in the House of Representatives (Dem., Pa.; 1909–15). As Alien Property Custodian (1917–19), he confiscated property worth millions of dollars from noncitizens. As U.S. attorney general (1919–21), he launched the notorious "Palmer's raids" to deport aliens and radicals. He then retired to his law practice.

Palmer, Alice Elvira (b. Freeman) (1855–1902) educator; born in Colesville, N.Y. During her tenure as president (1882–87), she turned Wellesley College from a finishing school into a serious college, improving the quality of the curriculum, faculty, and students. She helped found the precursor of the Association of American University Women (1882). She married the Harvard philosopher George Herbert Palmer (1887).

Palmer, Arnold (Daniel) (1929–) golfer; born in Latrobe, Pa. One of golf's most charismatic players, he was instrumental in popularizing the sport in the United States. After a successful amateur career at Wake Forest College, he turned professional and won the Canadian Open in 1955. Between 1958 and 1964, he won the Masters four times, the British Open twice, and the U.S. Open once. One of the first television-age golfing personalities, he attracted a loyal following known as "Arnie's Army." He won over 80 tournaments in his career. His various business interests and product endorsements helped him capitalize on his popularity.

Palmer, Daniel David (1845–1913) founder of chiropractic; born near Toronto, Canada. He moved to Iowa about 1880. Largely self-taught, he was a small businessman who became interested in alternative forms of medicines such as magnetic healing, osteopathy, and vertebral manipulation. In 1898 he founded the Palmer School of Chiropractic in Davenport, Iowa, the first school to train chiropractors by his system. (Chiropractic – from Greek words meaning "hand-practice," – was suggested to Palmer by an educated

patient.) The school was not at first successful – his son, Bartlett Joshua Palmer, was one of the few graduates – and in 1903 he tried to start another one in Portland, Ore. He returned to Davenport where his son was now running the school. In 1906 he was jailed for six months for practicing medicine without a license. He went back to Portland, Ore., and had to restrict himself to his own private practice. His *Textbook of the Science, Art and Philosophy of Chiropractic* (1910) attacked just about everyone who practiced any kind of medicine, including his son. He returned uninvited to a school reunion and died from injuries after being struck by a car while leading a parade. His son Bartlett and grandson David Daniel persevered to make chiropractic the accepted alternative it has become.

Palmer, Erastus Dow (1817–1904) sculptor; born in Pompey, N.Y. He began as a carpenter, moved to Utica, N.Y. (c. 1840), and settled in Albany (1846). He is known for his idealized marble sculptures, as in *The White Captive* (1859).

Palmer, George Herbert (1842–1933) philosopher; born in Boston, Mass. After graduating from Harvard (1864), he studied abroad, then returned to teach Greek and (1872–1913) philosophy there. He used his well-known ethics course partly to develop his own ideas, but was most noted as a critic and expositor. His writings include *The Nature of Goodness* (1904), studies of Sophocles and Vergil, a 1905 biography of the poet George Herbert (after whom he was named), and a 1930 autobiography.

Palmer, John McAuley (1817–1900) soldier, U.S. senator; born in Scott County, Ky. A lawyer who helped form the Republican Party in Illinois, he commanded a Union division at Stones River (Murfreesboro) (1862) and Chickamauga (1863). In a long postwar career, he served as Republican governor of Illinois (1868–72) and later, as a Democrat, in the U.S. Senate (1891–97). He ran for president as a minor party candidate in 1896.

Palmer, Nathaniel Brown "Captain Nat" (1799–1877) explorer, sea captain; born in Stonington, Conn. He went to sea at age 14 and in 1820 was probably the first to discover the Antarctic Peninsula, long known as Palmer Land. He became a packet captain and commander of clipper ships (1833–50). He was one of the first members of the New York Yacht Club (1845) and he owned 17 yachts.

Palmer, Phoebe Worrall (1807–74) Protestant evangelist; born in New York City. Raised in an atmosphere of strict Methodist piety, she wed a homeopathic physician at age 19, lost her first two babies soon after birth, and turned to her Methodist faith. In 1835 she and her sister, by then living in New York City, began a weekly prayer meeting for women; eventually it would attract evangelicals of both sexes. Out of this activity grew her increasing influence on a branch of Methodism that embraced the doctrine of an attainable Christian perfection. Among several works she would eventually publish, *The Way of Holiness* (1845) established her as a leader of the perfectionist movement. From 1850 on, she and her husband traveled throughout the eastern U.S.A. and Canada, preaching their message at camp meetings and elsewhere; they even preached their message in England (1859–63). She also put her ideas into practice, for many years working as corresponding secretary of the New York Female Assistance Society for the Relief and Religious Instruction of the Sick Poor; she would also visit the prisons and slums and she founded the Five Points Mission (1850), a precursor of settlement houses. In 1862 her husband bought the perfectionist movement's main journal, *Guide to Holiness*, which she edited to her death. Although a moderate when it came to contemporary issues such as slavery and women's rights, she did point the way to social reform through her varied activities.

Palmer, Potter (1826–1902) merchant, real estate entrepreneur; born in Albany County, N.Y. He had his own dry goods stores in upstate New York before he moved to Chicago in 1852 and opened one there. His innovative practices – such as allowing customer returns and advertising and displaying merchandise – became known as the "Palmer system" and led to great success. Overworked and ailing, in 1867 he turned the store over to his partners Marshall Field and Levi Z. Leiter. After three years of recuperating in Europe, he returned to Chicago and became a real estate developer. Most of his early buildings were destroyed in the great fire of 1871 but he went right back to building even more roads, homes, and commercial structures. His Palmer House hotel soon became internationally famous. Active in civic affairs, he was commissioner of the South Side park system and the first president of the Chicago Baseball Club. His wife, Bertha Honoré Palmer, continued to manage his real estate empire and through her many philanthropic and cultural activities she became the "first lady" of Chicago.

Palmer, R. R. (Robert Roswell) (1909–) historian; born in Chicago, Ill. Educated at the University of Chicago and Cornell (Ph.D. 1934), he taught political history at Princeton (1936–63; 1966–69) and Yale (1969). His focus on the French Revolution as the "shaping" event in modern history received recognition with a Bancroft Award (1960) for *The Age of the Democratic Revolution: A Political History of Europe and America, 1760–1800* (volume I, 1959; volume II, 1964).

Panofsky, Erwin (1892–1968) art historian; born in Hanover, Germany. He studied at the Universities of Berlin and Munich (c. 1910–14) and the University of Freiburg (Ph.D. 1914); after military service in World War I, he was a professor of the University of Hamburg (1921–32) and worked as a librarian. He fled Nazi Germany, emigrated to New York City (1934), and taught briefly at New York University (1934–35); from 1935 on he taught at the Institute for Advanced Study, Princeton. Although best known in his field for developing the iconological approach to art – a method of interpreting the meaning of works of art by an intense analysis of the symbolism, history, and other nonaesthetic aspects of the subject matter – he had an interest in a wide variety of subjects from the history of movies and the detective story to the works of Mozart. His many published works – which gained him the reputation as the major art historian of the 20th century – include *Early Netherlandish Painting* (1947), *Preface to Studies in Iconology* (1939), *Pandora's Box* (1956), and *Meaning in the Visual Arts* (1955).

Panofsky, Hans (Arnold) (1917–88) meteorologist; born in Kassel, Germany. His father, art historian Erwin Panofsky, brought the family to the United States in 1934. As a professor at Pennsylvania State University (1951–82), he won two of the highest honors from the American Meteorological Society, the Meisinger Award (1965) and the Rossby Medal (1976). A prolific author, he advanced the understanding of clear-air turbulence and the dispersion of air pollutants.

Panofsky, Wolfgang K. H. (Kurt Hermann) (1919–)

physicist; born in Berlin, Germany. He fled the Nazis' anti-Semitic policies in 1934 and entered Princeton. After working on the Manhattan Project (1941–45) he moved to the University of California: Berkeley (1945–51), then joined Stanford (1951–84). He made major contributions to studies of the subatomic particle pion using gamma-ray spectroscopy. He was a government adviser in the 1950s and 1960s and promoted nuclear arms control.

Paoli, Antonio (1871–1946) opera tenor; born in Ponce, Puerto Rico. He studied in Spain and Italy and was famous throughout Europe and the Americas as "the king of tenors and the tenor of kings" from his 1899 debut at the Paris Opera House in Rossini's *William Tell* until his career was interrupted by a stroke in 1925. He was decorated by most of the crowned heads of Europe, including the Czar of Russia in 1904 and Kaiser Wilhelm in 1912. In 1907 he sang Canio in *I Pagliacci*, the first opera to be completely recorded. He last appeared on the stage in *Aida* and *Il Trovatore* at the Teatro Municipal in San Juan (1928).

Papanek, Victor (1926–) designer, educator; born in Vienna, Austria. He came to this country in 1939, studied with Frank Lloyd Wright in 1949, graduated from Cooper Union (1950), and earned an M.S. from the Massachusetts Institute of Technology (1955). He taught at the University of Toronto, the Rhode Island School of Design, Purdue University, and the California Institute of the Arts, among other places in North America. He also worked, taught, and consulted in England, Yugoslavia, Switzerland, and Australia. In 1981 he became professor of design at the University of Kansas. He specialized in design appropriate to local materials and technology. His best-known book is *Design for the Real World: Human Ecology and Social Change* (1971).

Papanicolaou, George (Nicholas) (1883–1962) anatomist, oncologist; born in Kyme, Greece. After completing his medical studies in Germany, he emigrated to the United States in 1913. He was affiliated with Cornell Medical School for most of his career (1914–49); he went on to become director of the Miami Cancer Institute (since renamed Papanicolaou Cancer Research Institute). During the course of cytological studies of cancer patients' vaginal fluid, he noted neoplastic cells and published his findings (1928). He predicted the technique he developed could be used to screen for cervical cancer. The "Pap test," however, did not become widely used until 1947.

Papp, Joseph (b. Papirofsky) (1921–91) theater producer, director; born in New York City. Son of an emigrant Russian-Jewish trunkmaker and pushcart peddler, his first experience with theater was producing navy shows on a flattop in the Pacific. Back in New York, he worked on off-Broadway plays and in 1954 produced the first of his free, outdoor Shakespeare plays in the Lower East Side. He then moved his free productions to Central Park, founding the still-operating New York Shakespeare Festival, noted for its endless series of Shakespeare plays with often unusual settings, casts, and accents. In 1967 he founded the Public Theatre, committed to productions not usually done in the commercial theater; one such, *Chorus Line,* was so successful that it helped support years of less popular productions. Active until his final months, he maintained a love-hate relationship with many of the theater people who worked with him, but all agreed he was a one-of-a-kind theatrical genius.

Pardes, Herbert (1934–) psychiatrist, educator; born in Bronx, N.Y. He became director of the National Institutes of Mental Health (1978–84) where he focused on improving the public image of psychiatry and increasing research support for psychiatric projects. He became chairman of the department of psychiatry at Columbia University (1984) and president of the American Psychiatric Association (1989).

Pardue, Mary Lou (1933–) cell biologist; born in Lexington, Ky. She joined the Massachusetts Institute of Technology (1972), and concurrently taught molecular biology at several other institutions. She made major advances in studies of chromosome structure and function, gene activity during development, and stress responses in insect muscle cells.

Paredes, Américo (1915–) folklorist, educator; born in Brownsville, Texas. After 15 years as a journalist, he joined the University of Texas faculty to teach English and anthropology (1951–85) and direct the Folklore Center (1957–70). His work on Mexican and Mexican-American folk arts and artists includes *Folktales of Mexico* (1970), *A Texas Mexican Cancionero* (1976), and *George Washington Gomez* (1990).

Paretsky, Sara (1947–) writer; born in Ames, Iowa. She studied at the University of Kansas (B.A. 1967), and the University of Chicago (M.A. 1977; Ph.D. 1977). Based in Chicago, she was a publications manager for Urban Research Corporation (1971–74), a free-lance business writer (1974–77), and an advertising and direct mail marketing manager (1977–85). She is the author of many mystery novels featuring V. I. Warshawski, a female hard-boiled private investigator, as seen in *Blood Shot* (1988). She is the founder of Sisters in Crime (1987), a women's group that hopes to gain wider recognition for women mystery writers.

Parini, Jay (Lee) (1948–) poet, writer; born in Pittston, Pa. He studied at Lafayette (B.A. 1970) and the University of St. Andrews (Scotland) (B.Phil. 1972; Ph.D. 1975). He was a faculty member at Dartmouth (1975–82) before teaching at Middlebury (1982) and the Bread Loaf Writers' Conference (1982). He is known for his critical essays, novels, such as *The Last Station* (1990), based on the life of Leo Tolstoy, and his poetry collections, as in *Town Life* (1988).

Parish, Mrs. Henry, II ("Sister") (1910–) interior decorator; born in Morristown, N.J. When the stock market crash brought an end to an early life of privilege, she started her own decorating firm (1933). She created an unpretentious aura of upper class comfort for wealthy clients. For her 1962 commission to redo the Kennedy White House, she brought in Albert Hadley as a partner.

Park, Maud (May) Wood (1871–1955) suffrage leader; born in Boston, Mass. A graduate of Radcliffe College (1895), she founded the College Equal Suffrage League with Inez Haynes Gillmore Irwin (1901). After the death of her husband, Charles Edward Park, she secretly married Robert Hunter, a theatrical agent. She campaigned for the 19th Amendment, which gave women the vote in 1920. She was the first president of the League of Women Voters (1919–24) and headed the Women's Joint Congressional Committee. She traveled and lectured all her life. Her book *Front Door Lobby* (published 1960) tells of her Washington years.

Park, Robert E. (Ezra) (1864–1944) sociologist; born in Harveyville, Pa. A University of Michigan graduate, he was a metropolitan journalist for 11 years before earning graduate degrees at Harvard and the University of Heidelberg (1904). He studied southern blacks while assisting Booker T. Washington at the Tuskegee Institute (1905–13), and he became a pioneering authority on race relations, later writing such important studies as *Race and Culture* (1950). As a University of Chicago professor (1913–29), he concentrated on urban sociological problems, a study for which he coined the term "human ecology"; he helped to found urban sociology as a discipline (and also introduced the terms "collective behavior" and "marginal man"). He was an outstanding teacher of graduate students, directing numerous important studies at Chicago and in visiting appointments abroad. His work on collective behavior was perhaps his prime contribution, but he also wrote on social psychology, the community, ethnic relations, and other topics, and his *Introduction to the Science of Sociology* (with E. W. Burgess, 1921) was influential in promoting empirical research methods. In his later years he was a visiting professor at universities in Asia and at Fisk University (1935–37).

Park, Roswell (1852–1914) surgeon, pathologist, author; born in Pomfret, Conn. At the University of Buffalo School of Medicine (1883–1914), he became chief surgeon for Buffalo General Hospital. A great surgeon, he promulgated important advances in bacteriology and pathology such as Lister's antiseptic technique. He researched malignant tumors and wrote widely on both the practice and history of medicine; his works include *The Principles and Practice of Modern Surgery* (1907) and *The Evil Eye, Thanatology and Other Essays* (1912).

Parker, Arthur C. (Caswell) (b. Gawasowaneh) (1881–1955) Seneca anthropologist, museum director; born in Cattaraugus, N.Y. A Harvard-trained anthropologist, in 1906 he was appointed state archaeologist for the New York State Museum (1906–25). He helped found the *American Indian Magazine* (1911–16) and in 1925 was named director of the Rochester Museum of Arts and Sciences. He wrote extensively about the Iroquois.

Parker, Bonnie See under BARROW, CLYDE.

Parker, (Charles, Jr.) Charlie ("Bird" or "Yardbird") (1920–55) jazz musician; born in Kansas City, Kans. (Note: His name sometimes appears as Charles Christopher Parker Jr., a misnomer.) An only child, he was raised by his mother in Kansas City, Mo., an important center of jazz and blues activity in the 1930s. He received his first music lessons on the baritone horn in the public schools in 1931; three years later he dropped out of school to concentrate on mastering the alto saxophone and watching Lester Young, Count Basie, Hot Lips Page, and other locally based musicians. In 1936 he spent the summer playing in the Ozarks with George E. Lee's band; that same year, he entered the first of his four legal or common law marriages, became a father, and developed an addiction to heroin. Between 1937 and 1939, he played in Kansas City with Lawrence Keyes, Tommy Douglas, Harland Leonard, and his mentor Buster Smith, and he was an inveterate participant in the city's competitive jam sessions. He spent most of 1939 in New York, where he frequently heard the virtuoso pianist Art Tatum and began working out the rhythmic and harmonic ideas that would form the basis of modern jazz. Between 1940 and 1942 he began gaining attention as a featured sideman on recordings and broadcasts with Jay McShann. In 1943 to 1944, he played briefly with the big bands of Earl Hines and Billy Eckstine, where he was a galvanizing figure among his rebellious colleagues, including Dizzy Gillespie. The year 1945 marked a turning point in his career: he led his own group in New York, made numerous combo recordings in the new and controversial bebop style, and played extensively with Gillespie. In December 1945 they played an unsuccessful engagement in Hollywood, but Parker remained in Los Angeles. In June 1946, he suffered a nervous breakdown related to his drug addiction and alcoholism, and he was confined for six months at Camarillo State Hospital. He made a triumphant return to New York in 1947 and formed his celebrated quintet featuring Miles Davis and Max Roach. For the next four years, he worked almost exclusively in New York and recorded the majority of his most famous performances. He toured in Europe in 1949 and 1950, and was showcased in a variety of settings, including a string ensemble, a big band, and Afro-Cuban bands in New York clubs and concert halls and on records. By 1951 he was the most influential jazz musician in the world, but his notoriety as a heroin addict had also become legendary, and the New York police withdrew his cabaret card, a requisite to working in New York nightclubs. Thereafter, he adopted a more itinerant lifestyle, playing with pick-up groups in Boston, Newark, Philadelphia, Chicago, and in California, and appearing as guest soloist with bands led by Woody Herman and Stan Kenton. His cabaret card was reinstated in late 1953, but by then he was beset by sporadic employment, debt, and failing physical and mental health. He twice attempted suicide in 1954 and voluntarily committed himself to Bellevue Hospital in New York. His last public appearance was on March 5, 1955, at Birdland, the club that had been named in his honor in 1949. He died seven days later. His chaotic life formed the basis for the 1987 Clint Eastwood-directed dramatic film *Bird*.

Parker, Dorothy (b. Rothschild) (1893–1967) poet, writer; born in West End, N.J. She attended Catholic and private schools, then became an editor and writer for several periodicals in New York City, notably the *New Yorker* (1925–57). She was a member of the famous Algonquin Hotel Round Table luncheon group (1920s), and was known for her caustic wit. She moved to Hollywood, Calif., in the 1930s, wrote stage and screen plays, fiction, and poetry, and later returned to New York.

Parker, Horatio (William) (1863–1919) composer, teacher; born in Auburndale, Mass. After studies in the U.S.A. and Germany, he joined the Yale faculty (1894–1919). Primarily an organist, drawing on the conservative European traditions, he composed many works with a generalized religious element, such as *Hora Novissima* (1893).

Parker, Isaac (1768–1830) judge; born in Boston, Mass. A goldsmith's son, he graduated from Harvard with high honors in 1786, taught school, then moved to Castine, Maine, where he set up a law practice. He served a term in Congress (1797–99) before accepting an appointment as U.S. marshal for Maine. Named to the Massachusetts Supreme Court in 1806, he became chief justice in 1814, a position he held until his death. He was a steady if unspectacular jurist, and many of his decisions were acknowledged as authoritative in federal and other state courts. In 1817 he drew up a plan for what became Harvard Law

School, at which he was a professor and overseer for several years.

Parker, Isaac Charles (1838–96) judge, public official; born in Belmont Co., Ohio. He attended country schools, taught himself law, and opened a practice in St. Joseph, Mo., where he held various local offices and served in the U.S. House of Representatives (Rep., Mo.; 1871–75). In 1875 President Ulysses S. Grant appointed him to a judgeship in Arkansas with jurisdiction over the Indian Territory to the west, then a haven for renegades and fugitives from justice. He approached his task with such energy that he became known as the "hanging judge." He is said to have issued more than 160 death sentences in 21 years on the bench; some 80 were actually carried out. Not so fierce off the bench, he supported charitable causes and was president of the Fort Smith, Ark., school board for several years.

Parker, Louis (1906–) electrical engineer, inventor; born in Budapest, Hungary. He emigrated to the U.S.A. in 1923 and studied at the City College of New York. He worked on radio direction finders for aircraft, designed portable transmitters for military use, and developed an inexpensive sound system used in television receivers worldwide – his most famous invention. His Parker Instrument Corp. produced some instruments used in the Apollo moon project.

Parker, Quanah See QUANAH.

Parker, Samuel (1779–1866) missionary, explorer; born in Ashfield, Mass. A Congregational clergyman, he went to Oregon in 1835, seeking to convert the Flathead and Nez Percé Indians. After his return to New England by way of Hawaii and Cape Horn, he published *Journal of an Exploring Tour Beyond the Rocky Mountains* (1838).

Parker, Theodore (1810–60) Unitarian clergyman, reformer; born in Lexington, Mass. He overcame a background of poverty to graduate from Harvard Divinity School in 1836. Serving as Unitarian minister in West Roxbury, he was an associate of William Ellery Channing, Ralph Waldo Emerson, and other Transcendentalists, and became a leader of liberal theological thought; his progressive views forced him to resign his first pastorate (1845) and he became a minister at a new church in Boston. He was active, too, in social movements, including school and prison reforms, temperance, and the abolition of slavery. He gradually withdrew from public life after his health began to fail in 1857.

Parker, Willard (1800–84) surgeon; born in Lyndeborough, N.H. He switched from the ministry to medicine and took his medical degree at Harvard (1830). He settled in New York City where he developed a large practice and inspired students at the College of Physicians and Surgeons (1839–70). Noted for his bold operations, he was the first American to operate successfully on an abscessed appendix (1867). He also supported the temperance and public health movements.

Parker, William H. (1902–66) police chief, criminology adviser; born in Lead, S.D. An attorney with specialized police training, he joined the Los Angeles Police Department (1931). Near the close of World War II he developed the Police and Prisons Plan for the Army, as well as introducing democratic police systems to the German cities of Frankfurt and Munich. Returning to Los Angeles (1945), he was named police chief (1950–66) and earned a reputation for separating police work from political control; he also received worldwide attention for innovations in law enforcement. He was appointed honorary chief of the National

Police of the Republic of Korea (1953) and the State Department chose him to redevelop police procedures in India (1964).

Parkhurst, Charles Henry (1842–1933) clergyman, reformer; born in Framingham, Mass. Born on a farm, he became a high school principal and then was ordained (1874) as a Presbyterian minister. He preached in New York City (1880–1918). Although scholarly and reserved, he made a tremendous impact with two sermons (February 1892; March 1892) in which he attacked the political corruption of New York City government. Backed by the evidence he collected, his statements led to the defeat of Tammany Hall and to subsequent reforms. He wrote *Our Fight with Tammany* (1895).

Parkman, Francis (1823–93) historian; born in Boston, Mass. Son of a wealthy old Massachusetts family, he graduated from Harvard College (1844) and Law School (1846), but he never intended to practice law. Always one who pursued outdoors experiences, he immediately headed West and set out on the Oregon Trail (1846), getting to know various American Indians and frontier types. His health suffered during the trip and on his return that October it worsened. He published a series of articles in the *Knickerbocker Magazine* (1847) that came out in a single volume, *The California and Oregon Trail* (1849), now regarded as an American classic (as simply *The Oregon Trail*). He then began what would be his life's work: the eight-volume *France and England in North America:* the first volume was *History of the Conspiracy of Pontiac* (1848), the last was *A Half-Century of Conflict* (1892). During many of those years he suffered from poor eyesight and a nervous disability that made it difficult to work on anything for long. During some of those periods, he developed his interest in horticulture, published his *Book of Roses* (1866), and even taught horticulture at Harvard in 1871. He also wrote a novel, *Vassal Morton* (1856). His mastery of massive quantities of materials, the polish and resonance of his prose, and his insights into nature, history, and people, all combined to create his enduring reputation as one of the greatest of American historians.

Parks, Gordon A. (Alexander Buchanan) (1912–) photographer, writer, movie director, composer; born in Fort Scott, Kans. During World War II, he worked as a correspondent for various organizations. He joined *Life* magazine as a photojournalist (1949–70) and wrote several books, including *The Learning Tree* (1966) and *Born Black* (1971). In 1976 he went to Metro-Goldwyn-Mayer (MGM), where he directed *Shaft* (1971) and *The Super Cops* (1973). He moved to Paramount Pictures as a staff director in 1976. He also composed numerous popular songs and sonatas, including *Symphonic Set: A Piece for Piano and Wind Instruments* and *The Learning Tree Symphony*.

Parks, Rosa (Lee McCauley) (1913–) civil rights activist; born in Tuskagee, Ala. After briefly attending Alabama State University, she married and settled in Montgomery, Ala., where by 1955 she was working as a tailor's assistant in a department store. Contrary to most early portrayals of her as merely a poor, tired seamstress, who on the spur of the moment refused to surrender her seat in a bus to a white passenger, she had long been a community activist – she had served as secretary of the local chapter of the National Association for the Advancement of Colored People and she

had worked for the Union of Sleeping Car Porters. She had also been involved in previous incidents when refusing to leave a bus seat. By forcing the police to remove, arrest, and imprison her on this occasion, and then agreeing to become a test case of segregation ordinances, she played a deliberate role in instigating the Montgomery bus boycott (1955–56). She was fired from her job at the department store and in 1957 she became a youth worker in Detroit, Mich. As she eventually earned recognition as the "midwife" or "mother" of the civil rights revolution, she became a sought-after speaker nationally.

Parks, William (c. 1698–1750) printer, publisher; probably born in Shropshire, England. Emigrating to the U.S.A., he set up presses and founded papers in Virginia and Maryland, starting with the *Maryland Gazette* (1727). He was also a skilled typographer.

Parley, Peter See GOODRICH, SAMUEL.

Parran, Thomas (1892–1968) physician; born in St. Leonard, Md. In 1926, as chief of the division of venereal diseases in the U.S. Public Health Service, he laid the foundation for his campaign while Surgeon General (1936–48) against syphilis and other social diseases. He established and was dean of the graduate school of public health, University of Pittsburgh (1948–58), and he cofounded the World Health Organization.

Parrington, V. L. (Vernon Louis) (1871–1929) literary historian; born in Aurora, Ill. Parrington revolutionized the study of American literature by regarding literary works in the context of intellectual history, most influentially in his 3-volume *Main Currents in American Thought* (1927–30).

Parris, Alexander (1780–1852) builder-architect; born in Hebron, Maine. This Boston architect is known for his neoclassical designs and monumental masonry such as the governor's residence, Richmond, Va. (1812). He is also credited with a number of coastal engineering works.

Parrish, (Frederick) Maxfield (1870–1966) illustrator, painter; born in Philadelphia. He studied at the Pennsylvania Academy of the Fine Arts under Howard Pyle (1891–93), later joining the well-known art colony in Cornish, N.H. (1898). He became famous for his technically skilled and highly decorative illustrations, bookcovers, murals, and best-selling color prints like *Daybreak* (1920). Retiring from illustration in the 1930s, he spent the rest of his life painting rural landscapes, reproduced on calendars and greeting cards.

Parry, Milman (1902–35) philologist; born in Oakland, Calif. Educated in both the United States and France, he pioneered in establishing that the *Iliad* and *Odyssey* were the works of a preliterate oral poetic tradition involving the use of repeated epithets. With Albert Bates Lord (*Singer of Tales,* 1960) he worked on the living oral tradition in Yugoslavia (1933–35), collecting more than 12,000 texts. He taught at Harvard from 1930 until his sudden death (possibly suicide) in 1935. In 1971, his son Adam Parry, also a promising classicist who died young, published *The Making of Homeric Verse: The Collected Papers of Milman Parry.*

Parsons, Albert Richard (1848–87) anarchist, labor activist; born in Montgomery, Ala. Orphaned early, he went to work as a printer's devil (1861) and fought with the Confederate army. He later embraced socialism, campaigning unsuccessfully for several offices, then joined the radical International Working People's Association and began editing its paper (1884). A speaker at the Haymarket rally in Chicago where a bomb killed several people (May 1886), he was tried, and, despite a lack of evidence, convicted, with several others, of conspiracy to commit murder. He refused to seek clemency, and amid outpourings of appeals on his behalf, he was hanged.

Parsons, Betty (b. Pierson) (1900–82) art dealer, painter; born in New York City. She studied painting and sculpture privately, lived in France for many years, and then worked as a director for several galleries (1936–46). In 1946 she established the Betty Parsons Gallery in New York City and was an early promoter of the abstract expressionists. She also exhibited her own paintings and sculptures throughout the United States.

Parsons, Elsie (Worthington Clews) (1875–1941) sociologist, anthropologist, folklorist; born in New York City. She flouted the expectations of her socially prominent family by earning a Columbia University Ph.D. and working as an independent scholar. She wrote feminist sociological works before 1915, then turned to fieldwork-based ethnological studies of southwestern Indians, including the landmark *Mitla* (1936) and *Pueblo Indian Religion* (2 vols. 1939). She was an early field collector of African-American as well as Native American folktales.

Parsons, James B. (Benton) (1913–) judge; born in Kansas City, Mo. An administrator and teacher at Lincoln University (Mo.) (1934–40), a public school teacher in Greensboro, N.C. (1940–42), he served in the Navy in World War II, then took a law degree at the University of Chicago (1949). He joined a Chicago law firm (1949–51), became assistant U.S. district attorney in Chicago (1951–60), and then Cook County Superior Court judge (1960–61). As a U.S. district court judge in Illinois (1961–92), he was the first African-American to serve as a federal judge.

Parsons, Talcott (1902–79) sociologist, educator; born in Colorado Springs, Colo. Educated at Amherst College, the London School of Economics, and the University of Heidelberg, he spent his long academic career at Harvard (1927–73), where he founded the department of social relations (1946) and trained three generations of students. His first book, *The Structure of Social Action* (1937), launched a lifelong effort to supplant traditional empirical sociology with a theoretical approach that synthesized existing theories from all the social sciences. Further developed in such works as *The Social System* (1951) and *Toward a General Theory of Action* (with E. A. Shils, 1951), this general theory of human action and social systems was abstract, complex, and controversial; few claimed to understand it fully, but his interdisciplinary theoretical approach exerted a strong influence on academic sociology.

Parsons, Theophilus (1797–1882) legal scholar; born in Newburyport, Mass. On the faculty of Harvard (1848–69), he was a popular lecturer and wrote several important textbooks including *The Law of Contracts* (1853–55).

Parsons, Theophilus (1750–1813) judge; born in Byfield, Mass. He graduated from Harvard in 1769, practiced law in Maine and Massachusetts in the 1770s, and his ideas heavily influenced Massachusetts' Federalist constitution of 1780. His reputation grew steadily, and by the beginning of the 19th century he was considered the leading lawyer in the United States. An important legal scholar, he is given credit for rooting the U.S. legal system in English common law precedents rather than French ones. From 1806 to 1813 he served as chief justice of the Massachusetts Supreme Court.

Notoriously untidy, legend held that he relied on his wife to dress him for public appearances.

Partch, Harry (1901–74) composer; born in Oakland, Calif. Mostly self-taught, he worked out his ideas partly during years of wandering as a hobo. His music involves microtonal scales of his own invention, played on instruments he designed and built.

Partridge, Earl (Everard) (1900–) aviator; born in Winchenden, Mass. He enlisted in 1918 and served as a foot soldier in France, then obtained a West Point cadetship, graduating in 1924. He held a series of staff and line posts in the Air Corps during the interwar years. In June 1944 he took command of the Third Bombardment Division, with responsibility for the air offensive in Europe. After the war, he commanded the Fifth Air Force in Japan (1954) and the newly formed North American Air Defense Command (1957–59).

Pastor, Tony (b. Antonio) (1837–1908) actor and manager; born in New York City. A performer and entrepreneur, he first appeared with Phineas Barnum. He worked successfully to clean up the image of vaudeville, banning the sale of liquor and getting rid of the cruder acts. He opened several theaters and introduced such stars as Weber and Fields and Lillian Russell. He ran the Fourteenth Street Theatre until his death.

Pastorius, Francis Daniel (?1651–?1720) lawyer; born in Sommerhausen, Germany. He studied at several European universities and practiced law in Frankfurt, Germany, where he met friends of William Penn. In 1683, acting as agent for a group of German Quakers, he journeyed to Philadelphia, bought 15,000 acres from Penn, and laid out the settlement of Germantown. He was the first mayor of the new town and master of the Germantown school from 1702–19. In 1688 he signed the first antislavery petition to circulate in the English colonies.

Pasvolsky, Leo (1893–1953) economist, government official; born in Pavlograd, Russia. He came to the U.S.A. in 1905. After completing his studies at Columbia University, he covered the Paris Peace Conference (1919) for two New York City newspapers. He joined the Institute of Economics (later part of Brookings Institution) (1922) and then became a special assistant to Secretary of State Cordell Hull (1934–46). He was instrumental in organizing the United Nations and in drawing up its charter. He worked to get the U.S.A. to join the U.N. and attended the Bretton Woods Conference (1945). He was director of international studies at Brookings Institution (1946–53).

Patch, Alexander (McCarrell) (1889–1945) soldier; born in Fort Huachuca, Ariz. The son of an army officer, he graduated from West Point (1913), commanded a battalion in France in 1918, and, between the wars, held a series of posts at army educational institutions and unit commands. After Pearl Harbor, he was given command of a task force to help the French defend New Caledonia. In 1943 he led the American forces that crushed Japanese resistance on Guadalcanal. In August 1944 Patch commanded the Seventh Army in the Allied invasion of southern France; he led his army up the Rhone Valley, over the Rhine, and across southern Germany to accept the surrender of major German units in Bavaria on May 5, 1945. He was reassigned to prepare for duty in the Pacific; when Japan surrendered, he headed a board to study the reorganization of the army, but he died of pneumonia shortly thereafter.

Patch, Sam (?1807–29) stunt diver; born in Rhode Island. Accompanied on his travels by a fox and a small bear, he dived from cliffs, bridges, and ships' masts (1827–29). He became a figure of popular legend after his death from a jump into the Genesee River, near Rochester, N.Y.

Paterno, (Joseph Vincent) Joe (1926–) football coach; born in New York City. As a quarterback at Brown at the end of the 1940s, he set several school records. As head coach of Penn State University (1966) he not only took the Nittany Lions to numerous bowl games and national championships in 1982 and 1986, he also became widely admired for his loyalty to the school.

Paterson, William (1745–1806) Supreme Court justice; born in northern Ireland. He came to the U.S.A. when he was two. He served as New Jersey's first attorney general (1776–83), in the first U.S. Senate (N.J.; 1788), and as governor of New Jersey (1790–93) before President George Washington named him to the U.S. Supreme Court (1793–1806).

Patrick, Mason (Mathews) (1863–1942) soldier, aviator; born in Lewisburg, W.Va. The son of a Confederate army surgeon, he graduated from West Point in 1886 as a classmate of John Pershing. Patrick pursued a quiet career as an army engineer until 1917, when Pershing put him in charge of the American Expeditionary Force's air service. From 1921, as chief of the postwar air service, Patrick fostered experimentation in aircraft design and established a chain of air facilities. He supported the 1926 reorganization that gave the aviation section a new name – the Army Air Corps – and a measure of autonomy.

Patten, Gilbert (b. George William Patten) (Burt L. Standish, William West Wilder, among many pen names) (1866–1945) writer; born in Corinna, Maine. He ran away when he was 16, worked in a machine shop, and attended Corinna Union Academy. He began selling dime novels, moved to New York City (1891), and wrote Westerns. From 1896 to 1913 he wrote his Frank Merriwell series for *Tip Top Weekly* under the pen name of Burt L. Standish. Frank Merriwell became a popular paradigm of youth, virtue, wealth, education, good looks, and athletic ability, a mythological American juvenile hero who had little in common with his creator or readers. Patten lived in New York City and Camden, Maine, until he moved to California in 1941.

Patterson, Floyd (1935–) boxer; born in Waco, Texas. He grew up in Brooklyn, N.Y., and ended up in a correctional institution where he took up boxing. He won the gold medal in the middleweight class in the 1952 Olympics. Turning professional, he knocked out Archie Moore in 1956 to take the heavyweight title (vacated by Rocky Marciano). He successfully defended it four times before losing it to Ingemar Johansson of Sweden in 1959; he knocked out Johansson in a bout in 1960, thereby becoming the first heavyweight champion to regain his title. He defeated Johansson again in 1961 but lost the title for good to Sonny Liston in 1962. He continued to box for another decade.

Patterson, John H. (Henry) (1844–1922) manufacturer; born near Dayton, Ohio. He served in the Union army during the Civil War and then attended Dartmouth College; although he graduated (1867), he seems to have acquired a dislike of college education and graduates. He worked at various jobs until 1884 when he bought a major interest in the National Manufacturing Company, a purchase for which he was so ridiculed he tried to buy his way out. When that failed, he renamed it the National Cash Register Company, and as president until 1921, he turned it into an international industry leader by improving its physical plant and product, and by an innovative advertising and education campaign to generate a market. Above all, he pioneered in the development of a sales force, by the use of everything from sales conventions and exclusive sales territories to required calisthenics and generous employee benefits.

Patterson, Joseph Medill (1879–1946) newspaper publisher; born in Chicago. Sharing ownership and control of the *Chicago Tribune* with his cousin, Robert McCormick, he cofounded the *Illustrated Daily News* (later the *New York Daily News*) with him in 1919, and, in 1925, moved to New York to assume management of that paper, the first of the sensational mass-audience tabloids.

Patterson, Robert (1792–1881) soldier; born in County Tyrone, Ireland. Immigrating to the U.S.A. as a boy, he served in the War of 1812 with the Pennsylvania militia and in the Mexican War as a major general of volunteers. He prospered from the sugar industry and cotton mills and was a promoter of the Pennsylvania Railroad. Reactivated as a major general, he commanded Union forces around Harpers Ferry, Va., in 1861 and was criticized for failing to attack the Confederates in his front, leaving them free to reinforce Gen. Beauregard at Bull Run (July 1861). He left the army a few days after the battle.

Pattie, James Ohio (1804–c. 1850) trapper, author; born in Bracken County, Ky. He published a semifictional *Personal Narrative* (1831) regarding his travels to Mexico and California. He joined the gold rush in 1849 and disappeared while camping in the Sierra Nevadas.

Patton, George (Smith), Jr. (1885–1945) soldier; born in San Gabriel, Calif. Descendant of an old Virginia family, he graduated from West Point (1909); he placed fifth in the military pentathlon in the 1912 Olympics. He was an aide to Gen. Pershing in the punitive expedition to Mexico in 1916 and then accompanied him to France in 1917; there he learned from the French and British how to employ the new weapon, the tank, and he distinguished himself by leading his tank brigade through battle. Unconventional to the point of flamboyance, he held to his notion that tanks were the weapons system of the future and by April 1941 he was commander of the Second Armored Division; by January 1942 he was commanding general of I Armored Corps, and in October 1942 he directed the amphibious landings near Casablanca and the ensuing campaign across North Africa. By July 1943 he commanded the U.S. Seventh Army in the Allied invasion of Sicily; he excelled militarily there with a bold campaign that beat the British into Palermo, but the notorious incident in which he verbally abused two ailing soldiers, one of whom he also slapped, nearly cost him his career. He was eventually assigned to lead the Third Army, which led the breakout from Normandy in July–September 1944; after diverting his forces to relieve the Americans trapped in the Battle of the Bulge, he crossed the Rhine in March 1945 and advanced through the heart of Germany into Czechoslovakia. A staunch anticommunist, after the German surrender Patton argued for a combined Allied-German campaign against the Soviet Union. When he then argued for keeping former Nazis in administrative and other positions, he was removed from command of the Third

Army. Severely injured in an automobile accident on Dec. 9, 1945, he died 12 days later. Probably the most admired and the most controversial of all American generals in World War II, he was known for carrying ivory-handled pistols, for racy language, and an intemperate manner, but he was also regarded as one of the most successful American field commanders of any war. The 1971 film, *Patton,* starring George C. Scott in the title role, provoked renewed interest in this complex man.

Paul, Alice (1885–1977) social reformer, lawyer; born in Moorestown, N.J. Influenced by her Quaker family, she graduated from Swarthmore (1905) and went on to do graduate work in New York City and England. While in London (1906–09) she worked in a settlement house and was jailed on three occasions for suffragist actions. She took her Ph.D. from the University of Pennsylvania in 1912, the same year she became chairperson of the congressional committee of the National American Suffrage Association; impatient with its policies, in 1913 she helped to found the more militant Congressional Union for Woman Suffrage, which merged in 1917 to form the National Woman's Party; she would become this party's chairperson in 1942. After women won the right to vote with the 19th Amendment (1920), she devoted herself to gaining equal rights for women and in 1923 introduced the first equal rights amendment in Congress. She had meanwhile studied the law and broadened her field to the international arena, and although she did not live to see an equal rights amendment to the U.S. Constitution, she did get an equal rights affirmation in the preamble to the United Nations charter.

Paulding, James Kirke (1778–1860) writer, public official; born in Great Nine Partners (now Putnam County), N.Y. He had little formal schooling. He became a friend of Washington Irving, and moved to New York City (c. 1796) to live with Washington's brother, William Irving. He worked as a public official, and from 1807–08, he and Washington Irving collaborated on *Salmagundi,* a literary magazine. His public career included his appointment as secretary of the board of navy commissioners under President James Madison (1815–23); navy agent for New York for President James Monroe (1824–38); and secretary of the navy in President Martin Van Buren's cabinet (1838–41). He is best known for his popular and humorous essays, his burlesque of the British, as in *John Bull in America* (1825), and novels, such as *Westward Ho!* (1832). In 1846 he retired and settled near Hyde Park, N.Y.

Pauley, Jane (1950–) television anchor; born in Indianapolis, Ind. (married to Garry Trudeau). Briefly a reporter and WMAQ-TV coanchor in Chicago, she joined National Broadcasting Company (NBC)'s *Today* show in 1976, becoming coanchor in 1982. Resigning after a younger female host was added in 1989, she began an NBC weekly magazine series, *Real Life with Jane Pauley,* later renamed *Dateline.*

Pauling, Linus (Carl) (1901–94) chemist; born in Portland, Ore. After taking his Ph.D. at the California Institute of Technology (1925) and then two years of study abroad, he returned to that institution for most of his professional career (1927–63). In his later years he was associated with the Center for the Study of Democratic Institutions (1963–69), the University of California: San Diego (1967–69) and Stanford University (1969). His early research used X-ray crystallography to study the nature of chemical bonding; in 1928 he published his resonance theory of bonding, and his work on molecule structure opened up new areas to modern chemistry. This work would win him the Nobel Prize in chemistry in 1954. In the 1930s he turned his attention to biochemistry, and among other achievements, he correctly postulated that the shapes of antigens and their antibodies are complementary; his pioneering work on complex organic molecules such as proteins also led to his discovery that sickle-cell anemia resulted from a hereditary defect in blood hemoglobin. As the arms race between the United States and the Soviet Union led to tests of atomic weapons (1950s), Pauling and other scientists became increasingly concerned about the potential genetic damage from the radioactive fallout. In 1957 he drew up an appeal, eventually signed by more than 11,000 scientists in 49 countries, to halt the tests. His efforts led to a temporary moratorium (beginning in 1958) and then to a treaty banning above-ground testing (1963); for this effort he was awarded the Nobel Peace Prize (1962), thereby becoming the first person to win two unshared Nobel prizes. In the late 1960s, he became interested in the biological effects of vitamin C, which led him to his controversial theory of orthomolecular medicine, with its claim that massive doses of vitamin C could prevent or cure various diseases.

Payne, John Howard (1791–1852) actor, playwright, composer; born in New York City. Enamoured of the stage as a youth, he debuted as an actor in 1809 and enjoyed a string of successes that included being the first American to play Hamlet (1809). He spent the years 1813 to 1832 mainly in England and France where he had only modest success as an actor and playwright; among his many plays and adaptations were some ten collaborations with Washington Irving, such as *Charles the Second; or, The Merry Monarch* (1824). It was for one of his operettas, *Clari* (1823), that he wrote the only words (to the music of Henry Rowley Bishop) for which he would be remembered, "Home, Sweet Home." Always fighting off his creditors (he spent a short time in an English debtor's prison), he returned to the U.S.A. and undertook a variety of projects, including a campaign to help the Cherokee. With his theatrical career stalled, friends got him appointed U.S. consul to Tunis from 1842 to 1845, then again in 1851, and he died there the next year.

Payne, Sereno Elisha (1843–1914) U.S. representative; born in Hamilton, N.Y. A graduate of the University of Rochester, he had a law practice in Auburn, N.Y. (1866–1914) before going to Congress (Rep., N.Y.; 1883–85, 1887–1914). Focusing on protective tariffs, he became chairman of the Ways and Means Committee in 1899. A loyal lieutenant to Speaker Joseph Cannon, he cosponsored the unpopular Payne-Aldrich Tariff of 1906. He successfully argued for fair rates in the House but the Senate tacked on high fees.

Payton, Walter (Jerry) "Sweetness" (1954–) football player; born in Columbia, Miss. A fast, powerful running back, he became the National Collegiate Athletic Association's leading career scorer at Jackson State University in 1974 with 464 points. He is the NFL's (National Football League) leading lifetime rusher, with 16,726 yards for the Chicago Bears (1975–87). Extremely consistent, he had 77 NFL games in which he rushed for 100 or more yards and ten seasons of at least 1,000 yards.

Peabody, Elizabeth Palmer (1804–94) publisher, educator; born in Billerica, Mass. In 1839 she opened a Boston bookstore where the transcendentalists' *Dial* magazine was published. She started the first U.S. kindergarten in 1860 in Boston.

Peabody, Endicott (1857–1944) educator; born in Salem, Mass. Born into a patrician New England family, he was the founding headmaster of the elite Groton School in Massachusetts (1884–1940). Peabody decisively shaped the school, which offered a conventional curriculum, stressed athletics, and instilled into its students a strict moral code and sense of social responsibility.

Peabody, Francis Greenwood (1847–1936) Unitarian clergyman, educator; born in Boston, Mass. A clergyman's son, he graduated from Harvard in 1869 and from Harvard Divinity School three years later. Ordained a Unitarian, he held a pastorate in Cambridge for several years and from 1881 taught theology at Harvard, where he offered one of the first systematic courses in Christian social ethics in an American university. Optimistic, convinced of the possibility of establishing the kingdom of God on earth, he supported various reform movements in theory and in practice. He continued to lecture at Harvard for many years after his retirement in 1913.

Peabody, George (1795–1869) banker, philanthropist; born in South Danvers (now Peabody), Mass. (uncle of Othniel C. Marsh). A Baltimore merchant turned London merchant banker, he amassed a fortune, financed O. C. Marsh's research, and founded among other organizations the Peabody Institutes in Baltimore and Peabody, Massachusetts, the Peabody Museums at Harvard and Yale, and the Peabody Educational Fund.

Peabody, Lucy Whitehead (b. McGill) (1861–1949) mission leader; born in Belmont, Kans. As an officer of the Woman's American Baptist Foreign Missionary Society (1890–1906), and chair of the Central Committee on the United Study of Missions (1902–29), she fostered the rise of women's and ecumenical missionary societies and Christian education. Her fundraising in the 1920s helped found seven women's colleges in Asia.

Peabody, Robert Swain (1845–1917) architect; born in New Bedford, Mass.; His partnership (1870–1917) with John Goddard Stearns Jr. (1843–1917) was the foremost Boston firm for 30 years, completing more than 1,000 stylistically diverse commissions and training numerous young architects.

Peale, Charles Willson (1741–1827) painter, naturalist, museum founder (brother of James Peale); born in Queen Annes County, Md. He began as a saddler (1762), studied with John Hesselius in Philadelphia (c. 1762), and with Benjamin West in London (1767–69). He settled in Annapolis, Maryland (1769–75), and painted many portraits. After service in the Continental army (1775–78), he established himself in Philadelphia (c. 1778), and was a member (Dem.) of the Pennsylvania Assembly (1779–80). He established the Portrait Gallery of the Heroes of the Revolution (1782), and founded the Peale Museum of natural history and technology (1786). His most famous painting is *The Staircase Group* (1795), an illusionist work portraying his sons Raphaelle and Titian Peale. Married three times, he had 17 children, many of whom were artists. A respected and prominent advocate of neoclassical ideals and social and political justice, Peale's work is highly regarded.

Peale, James (1749–1831) painter; born in Chestertown, Md. His older brother, Charles Willson Peale, was his teacher. He served in the Continental army (1776–79), and painted historical scenes, miniatures on ivory, and landscapes until his eyesight failed (1818). Living in Philadelphia, he helped run the Peale Museum.

Peale, Norman Vincent (1898–93) Protestant religious leader, author; born in Bowersville, Ohio. The son of a pastor-physician, he graduated from Ohio Wesleyan University in 1920 and was ordained a Methodist Episcopal minister two years later. He held pastorates in Rhode Island and New York before beginning his long association with Marble Collegiate Reformed Church in New York City, where he was pastor from 1932 to 1984. In 1937 he established a psychiatric clinic, the American Foundation of Religion and Psychiatry, as part of his ministry. Known in later years for a somewhat Pollyannish version of Christianity, he authored many best-selling books, including *The Art of Loving* (1948), *The Power of Positive Thinking* (1952), and *The Tough-Minded Optimist* (1962), and was an influential lecturer, radio broadcaster, syndicated newspaper columnist, and host of the television program *What's Your Problem?* In 1969 he became president of the Reformed Church in America. He directed his many pastoral activities from his Foundation for Christian Living in Pawling, N.Y.

Peale, Raphaelle (1774–1825) painter; born in Annapolis, Md. (son of Charles Willson Peale). Based in Philadelphia, he helped his father run the Peale Museum (1790s and 1800). He produced silhouettes (c. 1802), and illusionist still-life paintings which he called "deceptions," as seen in *After the Bath* (1823).

Peale, Rembrandt (1778–1860) painter; born in Bucks County, Pa. (son of Charles Willson Peale). Based in Philadelphia, he traveled widely in Europe and was a founder of the Pennsylvania School of the Fine Arts (1805), and president of the American Academy of Fine Arts, New York (1826). His most famous allegorical painting is *Court of Death* (1820).

Peale, Sarah (Miriam) (1800–85) painter; born in Philadelphia (daughter of James Peale). She lived in Philadelphia, moved to Baltimore, Maryland (1831), then to Washington, D.C. (1840–43), and was a portrait painter. She relocated to St. Louis, Missouri (1847–77), returned finally to Philadelphia (1877–85), and painted still-life pictures.

Peale, Titian (Ramsay) (1799–1885) painter; born in Philadelphia (son of Charles Willson Peale). He was trained as a naturalist and artist by his father at the Peale Museum in Philadelphia, where he became director in 1833. He is known for his naturalist illustrations, as seen in *American Ornithology* (1825–33) by Charles Lucien Bonaparte, and his own work, *Lepidoptera Americana* (1833).

Pearlstein, Philip (1924–   ) painter, teacher; born in Pittsburgh, Pa. He studied at the Carnegie Institute of Technology, Pittsburgh (1946–49), and at the Institute of Fine Arts, New York University (1951–55). Based in New York, he was a teacher at Pratt Institute (1959–63) and Brooklyn College (1963). He is best known for his portraits and nudes, in which he presents the subject in a harsh light and without any idealization of their features. Typical works are *Two Nudes on a Mexican Blanket with Mirror* (1972) and *Two Models in Bamboo Chairs* (1981).

Pearson, Drew (Andrew Russell) (1897–1969) journalist;

born in Evanston, Ill. Fired as the *Baltimore Sun*'s Washington bureau chief after being unmasked as an anonymous coauthor of a political exposé, the *Washington Merry-Go-Round* (1931), he began a syndicated muckraking column of the same name, in partnership at first with the book's coauthor, Robert Allen; he also carried on a popular radio show. After Pearson's death the column was taken over by Jack Anderson, its associate writer since 1947.

Pearson, Thomas Gilbert (1873–1943) ornithologist, conservationist; born in Tuscola, Ill. The son of a Quaker farmer, he graduated from the University of North Carolina (1899), taught school, and published *Stories of Bird Life* in 1901. He organized the North Carolina Audubon Society in 1902 and three years later helped found the National Association of Audubon Societies. As president of the association (1920–34), he lobbied for laws protecting birds and for the creation of bird sanctuaries. His autobiography, *Adventures in Bird Protection,* appeared in 1937.

Peary, Robert E. (Edwin) (1856–1920) explorer, naval officer; born in Cresson, Pa. He graduated from Bowdoin College and joined the U.S. Coast and Geodetic Survey in 1879. He surveyed a proposed ship canal through Nicaragua (1884–88) and began his Arctic journeys during a six-month leave in 1886. He traveled through Greenland (1891, 1893–95, 1896, 1897) and then named the North Pole as his goal. He surveyed northern routes and passages (1898–1902) and sledged to within 175 miles of the Pole in 1906. On his final Arctic journey (1908–09), he, Matthew Henson, and four Eskimos reached the North Pole on April 6, 1909. On returning to the U.S.A. he learned that Frederick A. Cook claimed to have reached the Pole one year earlier. Peary's claim was eventually vindicated and he received the thanks of Congress and the rank of rear admiral. He became interested in aviation and organized the National Aerial Coast Patrol Commission at the start of World War I. In the 1980s it was revealed that he and Matthew Henson had fathered children by Eskimo women during their years in the Arctic.

Peck, (Eldred) Gregory (1916–) movie actor; born in La Jolla, Calif. He was a premed student at the University of California: Berkeley when he became interested in acting. He studied with New York's Neighborhood Playhouse before making his Broadway debut in *Morning Star* (1942). A spinal injury prevented him from serving in World War II and he made his Hollywood debut in a war movie, *Days of Glory* (1943). He went on to star in a long string of serious films, winning an Oscar for best actor in *To Kill a Mockingbird* (1962). Durable and sympathetic rather than glamorous and sexy, he earned the respect of his fellow professionals and his public for his high-minded actions on and off the screen.

Peck, M. (Morgan) Scott (1936–) psychiatrist; born in New York City. He received his M.D. from Case Western Reserve University (1963) and served in the U.S. Army (1963–72), retiring after two years as assistant chief of psychiatry and neurology at the office of the surgeon general. He practiced psychiatry in New Preston, Conn. (1972–84), and eventually and reluctantly attained the status of a guru due to the success of his book, *The Road Less Traveled: A New Psychology of Love, Traditional Values and Spiritual Growth* (1978). It focused on personal integrity and community building and although dismissed by some as merely "inspirational," it spoke to many people (attested by its presence on best-seller lists for some 15 years). He followed up its success with such books as *People of the Lie* (1983) and *The Different Drum* (1987).

Peckham, Rufus Wheeler (1838–1909) Supreme Court justice; born in Albany, N.Y. He served on New York's supreme court (1883–86) and court of appeals (1886–95). President Grover Cleveland named him to the U.S. Supreme Court (1896–1909) where he wrote almost 400 opinions.

Pederson, Charles J. (1904–89) chemist; born in Fusan, Korea. His father was Norwegian, his mother Japanese. He came to the United States in 1927 and became a research chemist at DuPont (1927–69). He developed the compounds called crown ethers in the 1960s, initiating a field known as host-guest chemistry. He shared the Nobel Prize in chemistry (1987).

Peerce, Jan (b. Jacob Pincus Perelmuth) (1904–84); born in New York City. After years of singing popular music, he made his operatic debut in Philadelphia in 1938 and his Metropolitan Opera debut in 1941. He remained at the Met as a favorite "tenor-for-all-roles" until 1962, then was active as a recitalist.

Pegler, (Francis) Westbrook (1894–1969) journalist; born in Minneapolis, Minn. As a columnist for the Hearst-owned King Features Syndicate (1944–62), he won a 1941 Pulitzer Prize for exposing labor corruption but became more noted for vitriolic attacks on public institutions and figures; one target, journalist Quentin Reynolds, sued him and won $175,001. Quitting his column in a dispute over editing, Pegler later wrote for *American Opinion,* an organ of the ultraconservative John Birch Society.

Pei, I. M. (Ieoh Ming) (1917–) architect; born in Canton, China. He emigrated to the U.S.A. (1935) and studied at the Massachusetts Institute of Technology and with Walter Gropius at Harvard. He was director of architecture with the contracting firm Webb and Knapp (1948–55) before establishing his own New York firm (1955), later to become Pei, Cobb Freed and Partners. From the outset Pei was associated with large-scale multipurpose developments, often connected with urban revitalization; his designs include some of the principal commercial, cultural, and educational buildings of the late 20th century, including the Hancock Building (1972) and John F. Kennedy Library (1979), both in Boston; the East Building of the National Gallery of Art, Washington, D.C. (1978); and the controversial glass pyramid entrance to the Louvre, Paris (1983–89); in recent years he undertook major buildings in China and Hong Kong. Pei's buildings are characterized by their carefully, often dramatically arranged masses, use of exterior landscape in interior design through thoughtful siting, and technological innovation (he pioneered, for example, all-glass curtain walls).

Peirce, Benjamin (1809–80) astronomer, mathematician; born in Salem, Mass. (father of Charles Sanders Peirce). Encouraged by Nathaniel Bowditch as a youth, he went on to become a professor of mathematics and astronomy at Harvard (1833–80), founder of the Harvard Observatory (1843), and an organizer of the Smithsonian Institution (1847). He was a consulting astronomer to the *American Nautical Almanac* (1849–67) and was affiliated with the U.S. Coast Survey (1852–74, superintendent from 1867), with which he organized several expeditions. Most of his many publications dealt with astronomy, mechanics, and geodesy –

including his corrected revision (1829–39) of Bowditch's translation of Laplace's work on celestial mechanics – but his major contribution was to American mathematics, in part through his publications such as *Linear Associative Algebra* (1870), but more importantly as a teacher who inspired generations of other young mathematicians.

Peirce, Charles Sanders (1839–1914) philosopher, logician, mathematician; born in Cambridge, Mass. He was the son of Harvard mathematics professor, Benjamin Peirce; although his father early cultivated his intellectual abilities and he was obviously brilliant, he did not do all that well at Harvard. After a temporary post with the U.S. Coast Survey (1859), he remained associated with it for 30 years (1861–91). He performed important experiments with the pendulum and contributed to gravity theory, the use of the wavelength of light as a standard unit of measure, and to conformal map projections. He also lectured at Harvard (1864–65, 1869–70) and Johns Hopkins (1879–84), but his difficult presentations appealed only to the brightest students. Highly temperamental, careless in dress, unsociable to an extreme, he was divorced in 1883; when he inherited some money, he retired in 1887 to an isolated part of Pennsylvania, spending his time writing down his diverse and complex ideas; in his later years he turned to writing book reviews and encyclopedia entries to support himself. During his lifetime he published only one book, *Photometric Researches* (1879), but he produced a prodigious number of papers; his works were collected and published in eight volumes (1931–58). Not a systematic philosopher, he ranged over an incredible variety of topics and singlehandedly anticipated several of the main currents of modern logic, mathematics, and philosophy. He developed the work of the 19th-century Englishman, George Boole, to help lay the foundation of the logical basis of modern mathematics. He set forth ideas since regarded as the beginning of semiotics, the study of the use of signs and symbols. He is probably best known as one of the founders of pragmatism, the quintessentially American school of philosophy – the idea that the real value of any idea lies in its practical effects, its real consequences. Little known and less understood in his day, Peirce has come to be recognized as one of the most important of all American thinkers.

Pelham, Henry (1749–1806) engraver; born in Boston, Mass. (son of Peter Pelham and half-brother of John Singleton Copley). A Loyalist, he studied engraving and painting, and joined John Singleton Copley in London (1776). He worked as an engineer and estate agent in Ireland, and is known for his historical line engraving, *The Boston Massacre* (1770).

Pelham, Peter (c. 1695–1751) engraver; born in London, England. He apprenticed as a mezzotint engraver (1713–26), and emigrated to Boston (1727), where he worked as a schoolmaster and engraver. The stepfather of John Singleton Copley, father of Henry Pelham, and colleague of John Smibert, he is considered the first mezzotint engraver in America, as in his portrait of Cotton Mather (1728).

Pelikan, Jaroslav (Jan, Jr.) (1923–) historian of religion; born in Akron, Ohio. Descended from Eastern European ministers, he was extremely precocious. He started to write at age two, entered high school at age nine, and earned his Ph.D. at 22. He taught at Yale University (1962). He wrote 22 books, including the monumental five-volume *Christian Tradition* (1971, 1974, 1978, 1984, 1989). His *Riddle of Roman Catholicism* (1959) sold many copies during the

presidential campaign of John Kennedy in 1960. He called for dialogue between Christianity and Judaism.

Peltier, Leonard (1944–) Ojibwa-Lakota activist; born in Grand Forks, N.D. Growing up poor, he was moved to action by the abuse and suffering of his people. He participated in the Trail of Broken Treaties (1972) as a member of the American Indian Movement. He was arrested (1976) and convicted (1977) and sentenced to two life terms in prison for the murder of two FBI agents in a shoot-out near Pine Ridge, S.D. His controversial trial was criticized in works such as Peter Mathieson's *In the Spirit of Crazy Horse* (1980) and his continued presence in jail was claimed by some as a symbol of injustice and political oppression. Many appeals were made for his release but none succeeded.

Pelton, Lester Allen (1829–1918) inventor, engineer; born in Vermillion, Ohio. During the California gold rush (1849), Pelton devised an improved undershot waterwheel powered by a jet of water striking pairs of hemispherical cups. Adaptations of Pelton wheels were used in the generation of hydroelectric power.

Pemberton, John Clifford (1814–81) soldier; born in Philadelphia. Although of Quaker ancestry, he served in the Seminole War, the Mexican War, and on the frontier. Married into a Virginia family, he entered the Confederate army after Fort Sumter. By October 1862 he was a lieutenant general and assigned responsibility for the defense of the Mississippi River stronghold of Vicksburg; besieged there by May 1863, he was outgeneraled by Ulysses S. Grant and surrendered on July 4 in one of the decisive Union victories of the Civil War. Because of his roots, Pemberton was criticized by some in the South as having betrayed the Confederacy. He resigned his general's commission and served as a colonel of ordnance for the rest of the war, after which he took up farming in Virginia, eventually returning to Philadelphia.

Pendergast, Thomas (Joseph) (1872–1945) political boss; born in St. Joseph, Mo. Although he held only minor offices, he became a Democratic ward boss in Kansas City by 1910; by the 1920s he had extended his political control through much of Kansas by various corrupt practices. Harry S. Truman started out under his wing. Pendergast expanded his influence during the New Deal by controlling public works projects. In 1939 he was convicted of income tax evasion and served 15 months in Leavenworth Prison.

Pendleton, Edmund (1721–1803) jurist, Revolutionary patriot; born in Caroline County, Va. His father died the year he was born. He worked as a law clerk and was admitted to the bar in 1745. Although he did not come from wealth, he led the conservatives' party in Virginia and opposed Patrick Henry on almost every question except the goal of American freedom. He sat in the Continental Congress (1774, 1775) and was president of the Virginia convention of 1776 that called for a declaration of independence. He was Speaker of the House of Delegates (1776), president of the Virginia constitutional convention (1788), and worked for the adoption of the new federal Constitution. He served as president of the Virginia Supreme Court of Appeals (1779–1803).

Pendleton, George Hunt (1825–89) U.S. representative/senator; born in Cincinnati, Ohio. Known as "Gentleman George," he traveled abroad in Europe and the Middle East in 1844 before returning to the United States where he married Alice Key, the daughter of Francis Scott Key. A Democrat, he served in the Ohio state senate (1853–56) before going to Congress (1857–65). With Stephen Douglas he led the peace wing of the Democratic Party, favoring compromise and states' rights. Although he supported the war, he opposed Lincoln's wartime powers – for example, suspension of habeas corpus. He espoused greenback payment instead of coins for government bonds, causing eastern Democrats to block his presidential nomination in 1868. President of Kentucky Central Railroad (1869–89), he served Ohio again in the U.S. Senate (1879–85) where he supported a bill that created the civil service commission and competitive exams despite the protest of the victorious Democratic congressman. He was President Grover Cleveland's ambassador to Germany (1885–89).

Pendleton, John B. (1798–1866) lithographer; born in New York City. He worked with Charles Willson Peale, traveled to France (1824), where he learned the technique of lithography, and established a lithography business in Boston (1825) and then in New York City (1829). After selling the business to his pupil, Nathaniel Currier (1834), he became a carpenter and established a planing mill (1835–51). He is recognized as the founder of the lithographic process in America.

Penn, William (1644–1718) religious leader, colonist; born in London, England. The son of Admiral Sir William Penn, he was attracted to first the Puritan, then the Quaker faiths. A devout and active Quaker, he wrote *No Cross, No Crown* (1669) and *The Great Case of Liberty of Conscience* (1670). In 1681 King Charles II made Penn the sole proprietor of the land north of Maryland in payment for loans made by Admiral Penn to the crown (the land was named Pennsylvania for the late Admiral). Penn wrote a Frame of Government (1682), which granted religious freedom. He cultivated and maintained warm, friendly relations with the Indians. Although he is known as the founder of the Pennsylvania colony, he lived there only briefly (1682–83, 1699–1701) due to the necessity of defending his proprietorship to King William after the Glorious Revolution in England. After granting a permanent Charter (1701), he returned to England and did not return to his colony.

Pennebaker, D. A. (Donn Alan) (1930–) filmmaker; born in Evanston, Ill. After navy service and starting his own electronics firm, he began making experimental and documentary films, such as *Daybreak Express* (1953) and *Keep on Rockin'* (1973).

Pennell, Joseph (1857–1926) lithographer; born in Philadelphia. He studied at the Pennsylvania Academy of the Fine Arts (1878–80), moved to London (1884), and settled in New York City (1922) to teach at the Art Students League. Highly admired for his book illustrations, he is also known for his publications, *Lithography and Lithographers* (1900), and an authorized biography of Whistler (1908).

Penney, J. C. (James Cash) (1875–1971) retailer, philanthropist; born in Hamilton, Mo. In 1897 he moved to Colorado for health reasons. There he worked in a local dry goods store, moving to Wyoming when his partners opened a branch in Kemmerer, Wyo. (1902). He opened his own store in 1904; in 1907 he bought the two stores of his partners; by 1911 he owned a chain of 22 stores. He went public in 1927, giving shares of stock to all managers and including all employees in profit-sharing. By 1971, J. C. Penney had 1,660 stores and $4 billion in sales, making it the second-largest nonfood retailer in the U.S.A. A devout Christian – he published *50 Years with the Golden Rule* (1950) – he gave generously to his favorite charities and maintained an active role in his company until his death.

Penniman, Richard Wayne See LITTLE RICHARD.

Pennington, Mary Engle (1872–1952) chemist, refrigeration specialist; born in Nashville, Tenn. Persisting in her youthful desire to become a chemist, she eventually obtained a Ph.D. from the University of Pennsylvania, and then started her own laboratory for bacteriological analyses in Philadelphia (1898). This led to her becoming a lecturer at the Women's Medical College of Pennsylvania and the head of the city health department's laboratory. Her pioneer work in methods of preserving dairy products, particularly by refrigeration, led to her being named head of the U.S. Department of Agriculture's new Food Research Laboratory (1908–19); among her several practical innovations was the design of refrigerated railroad cars. After 1919 she worked in private industry and as a consultant, traveling throughout the U.S.A. to dispense the most advanced advice on keeping foods cold or frozen, on handling poultry and eggs, and on processing and preserving foods.

Pennington, William (1796–1862) U.S. representative, governor; born in Newark, N.J. A Princeton graduate and lawyer, he became embroiled with Congress when as Whig governor of New Jersey (1837–43) he affixed his "Broad Seal" to dubious election returns. He later went to the U.S. House of Representatives (1859–62), serving an undistinguished term as compromise Speaker (1859–62).

Penrose, Boies (1860–1921) U.S. senator; born in Philadelphia, Pa. After graduating from Harvard (1881), he published a scholarly text, *The City Government of Philadelphia* (1887). He then turned to politics, and although a member of a prosperous upper-class Philadelphia family, he proved to be as tough as any boss, running the Pennsylvania Republican machine from 1904 until his death. As a member of the U.S. Senate (Rep., Pa.; 1897–1921), he was ineffective as a Speaker, but was good at conferences and committee work. A conservative, he favored high tariffs and opposed women's suffrage and progressive reform policies in general.

Penrose, Richard A. F. (Alexander Fullerton), Jr. (1863–1931) geologist; born in Philadelphia, Pa. He surveyed mineral deposits in Texas (1888) and Arkansas (1889), then taught economic geology at the University of Chicago (1892–1911). He investigated the Cripple Creek, Colo, gold mine for the U.S. Geological Survey (1894), and gained an international reputation in the 1920s for his work on the geology of ores and mining.

Penzias, Arno (Allan) (1933–) radio astronomer; born in Munich, Germany. He immigrated to the United States as a boy and became a citizen in 1946. Educated at Columbia University, he joined American Telephone & Telegraph Bell Laboratories in 1961. In 1978 he won the Nobel Prize in physics for his work with colleague Robert Wilson in discovering cosmic microwave background radiation that supports the "big bang" theory. As vice-president of research at Bell Labs, his work focused on revolutionary new communications technology.

Pepper, Beverly (b. Stoll) (1924–) sculptor, environmental artist; born in New York City. She studied at the Pratt Institute (1940) and in Paris (1949), painted and traveled extensively, and settled in Italy (c. 1952). She is known for totem figures, steel sculptures, mirrored works, and environmental earth constructions, as in *Amphisculpture* (1947–76).

Pepper, Claude D. (Denson) (1900–89) U.S. senator and representative; born near Dudleyville, Ala. A pro-labor liberal, he was elected to the U.S. Senate (Dem., Fla.; 1936–50), where he supported Roosevelt's domestic and foreign policies. After losing his seat in an election marked by anticommunist hysteria, he was elected to the U.S. House of Representatives (1962–89). Congress's oldest member in his last years, he defended Social Security and opposed retirement restrictions.

Pepper, George Wharton (1867–1961) U.S. senator, lawyer; born in Philadelphia, Pa. After practicing, teaching, and writing about the law, he was appointed to the U.S. Senate (Rep., Pa.; 1922–27). He wrote the U.S. Code, a codification of all statutes passed by Congress. Later he would argue several important cases before the Supreme Court involving the constitutionality of New Deal legislation.

Pepper, William (1810–64) physician; born in Philadelphia. One of the elite group of American physicians who studied in France in the 1830s, he returned to Philadelphia to work at the Wills Eye Hospital (1839) and the Institute for Instruction of the Blind (1841) before joining the staff of the Pennsylvania Hospital (1842–58). A keen diagnostician, he went on to teach at the medical school of the University of Pennsylvania (1860–64).

Pepper, William (1843–98) physician; born in Philadelphia. His first case following graduation (1864) was his father, William Pepper Sr. (1810–64), a famous Philadelphia surgeon and diagnostician who died that autumn. The son began teaching at the University of Pennsylvania Medical School in 1868 and continued teaching there until 1895. Along with his pioneer contributions to medicine – his description of malarial parasites, the role of bone marrow in pernicious anemia, and the modern treatment of tuberculosis – he is remembered for significant reforms in medical education. His efforts resulted in a remarkable number of American firsts from the University of Pennsylvania Medical College; the first teaching hospital affiliated with a university medical school (1874), the first nurses training school (1887), and the first laboratory of clinical medicine (1894). As provost of the University of Pennsylvania (1880–94), he led it through an extensive period of growth, effectively creating the modern University of Pennsylvania with its various graduate schools and programs such as extension courses. In addition to his teaching, administrative chores, and clinical practice, he wrote such books as *Text-Book of the Theory and Practice of Medicine* (1893–94) and still found time to give of his leadership and money toward the cultural development of Philadelphia.

Pepperberg, Irene M. (Maxine) (1949–) animal behaviorist, ornithologist; born in New York City. Although she maintained her early interest in interspecies communication and comparative animal behavior, she chose graduate studies in chemistry and chemical physics. She taught and performed research in chemistry at Harvard (1971–76), then relocated to Purdue University (1977–84), where she began her extensive studies of avian communication in the African grey parrot. She became a visiting assistant professor in the Department of Anthropology at Northwestern University (1984–91), then joined the University of Arizona as an assistant professor of ecology and evolutionary biology (1991). She made major contributions to studies of parrot communication, speech physiology, cognition, and tool use, and championed the idea that these birds' speech skills are not merely imitative, but resemble the communication ability of chimpanzees who are trained to use sign language and computers.

Pepperrell, Sir William (1696–1759) colonial leader; born in Kittery, Maine. He was a successful merchant, a chief justice, and an amateur soldier. Following the Yankee capture of Fort Louisbourg under his leadership, Pepperrell was made a baronet.

Perahia, Murray (1947–) pianist; born in New York City. He won the prestigious Leeds International Competition in 1972 and soon entered the highest ranks of international soloists, especially admired for his Mozart performances.

Percy, Walker (1916–90) writer; born in Birmingham, Ala. After the suicide of his father (1929) and death of his mother (1931), he and his brothers and sisters were adopted by their father's cousin, William Percy, who lived in Greenville, Miss. Walker studied at the University of North Carolina (B.A. 1937), and Columbia University (M.D. 1941). He worked as a pathologist in New York City, contracted tuberculosis, and spent three years in a sanatorium. He returned to Columbia to teach pathology (1944), suffered a relapse, and left medicine and New York City. He married (1946), converted to Catholicism (1947), and settled in Covington, La., to write. Starting with his first and best-known work, *The Moviegoer* (1961), he published several novels characterized by his conservative disillusionment with contemporary American life and values. A philosophic-intellectual man, he collected his essays on language in *The Message in the Bottle* (1975).

Perdue, (Franklin Parsons) Frank (1920–) food executive; born in Salisbury, Md. He left college to join his father's chicken farm in Salisbury, Md., in 1939, succeeding him as president (1952) and transforming Perdue Farms into one of the country's largest poultry processors. In 1971 he revolutionized chicken merchandising by labeling what had previously been an anonymous product and by starring in an extensive national advertising campaign. He retired as CEO in 1988.

Pereira, Irene (b. Rice) (1907–71) painter; born in Chelsea, Mass. She supported her family when young, then became an abstract painter on glass and parchment, depicting what she called "infinity," as seen in *Undulating Arrangement* (1947). Based in New York City, she moved to the coast of Spain during her last years.

Perella, Joseph Robert (1941–) investment banker; born in Newark, N.J. A graduate of Lehigh University (1964) and the Harvard Business School (1972), he joined the First Boston Corp. in New York City in 1972, rising to vice-president. There, with colleague Bruce Wasserstein, he helped ignite the 1980s corporate takeover boom. He and Wasserstein formed their own partnership, Wasserstein, Perella & Co., in 1988; it quickly became one of the country's leading takeover firms.

Perelman, Ronald (Owen) (1935–) financier; born in Greensboro, N.C. He began sitting in on the board meetings of his father's firm, Belmont Industries, at age 11, and joined the family concern after graduation from the University of Pennsylvania (1964) and Penn's Wharton School. In 1978 he moved to New York City and set up his own business. By taking over ailing businesses (such as Revlon, Inc., in 1985) and returning them to profitability by focusing on their core products, he built a financial empire that made him at one point, reputedly, the richest man in America.

Perelman, S. J. (Sidney Joseph) (1904–79) writer; born in New York City. After graduating from Brown (1925), he returned to New York City to work as a cartoonist and writer for various periodicals (1925–29). The first collection of his pieces, *Dawn Ginsbergh's Revenge* (1929), attracted the attention of Hollywood, and in the next quarter-century he would write 11 film scripts, including parts of some Marx Brothers movies. Starting in 1931, he also began to publish the first of what proved to be hundreds of pieces in the *New Yorker*, many of them biting satires of contemporary American mores and manners, but all written with his inimitable mix of baroque language, tongue-in-cheek parody, and zany wit. They were periodically collected in such volumes as *The Most of S. J. Perelman* (1958). Although he settled in Bucks County, Pa., in his later years, he was an inveterate traveler and published several books about his travels, such as *Westward Ha! or Around the World in Eighty Cliches* (1948).

Perkins, Carl (1932–) rock 'n' roll singer, songwriter, guitarist; born in Lake City, Tenn. He performed with his brothers Jay Perkins and Clayton Perkins at country dances and in 1955 began recording for Sun Records. In 1956 the brothers recorded Carl's own "Blue Suede Shoes," which reached the top of the country, pop, and rhythm-and-blues charts. A highly regarded musician, in the 1960s he performed with Johnny Cash and in the 1970s and 1980s he recorded with such artists as Paul McCartney and Bob Dylan.

Perkins, Charles E. (Elliott) (1840–1907) railroad executive; born in Cincinnati, Ohio. In 1859, at the advice of his cousin, John Murray Forbes, he clerked for the Burlington & Missouri Railroad, working his way up to superintendent by 1865. He became vice-president of the Chicago, Burlington & Quincy in 1876. The two railroads consolidated in 1880 and he became president in 1881. When he resigned in 1901 the financially sound system comprised over 7,000 miles of track.

Perkins, Dexter (1952–) geologist; born in Boston, Mass. A University of Michigan Ph.D., he joined the geology faculty of the University of North Dakota (1981). His research focused on high grade rocks in the pre-Cambrian shield, the thermodynamics of minerals and mineral systems, and the evolution of the earth's crust.

Perkins, Frances (b. Fannie Coiralie Perkins) (1880–1965) cabinet member; born in Boston, Mass. Graduating from Mount Holyoke College (1902), she taught, worked in settlement houses, and came to favor a greater role for the federal government in aiding the poor. Soon after earning a graduate degree in political science from Columbia University, she witnessed the Triangle Shirtwaist Fire (1911) that killed 146 factory workers; the event further inspired her crusade for safe working conditions and other labor reforms. She won passage of landmark labor legislation as New York State industrial commissioner (1926–32). As longtime U.S. labor secretary and the first woman member of a federal cabinet (1932–45), she helped develop major New Deal reforms, including Social Security (1935) and a federal Fair Labor Standards Act that imposed a minimum wage (1938).

She later served on the Civil Service Commission (1946–53) and taught at Cornell (from 1957).

Perkins, Jacob (1766–1849) inventor; born in Newburyport, Mass. An apprentice goldsmith, he developed steel plates as a replacement for copper in the bank note engraving process, the use of which made counterfeiting more difficult. Perkins and his partner moved to England (1818) where they established the engraving factory that produced the first penny postage stamps (1840). Perkins also experimented with high-pressure steam boilers and invented an early form of water tube boiler.

Perkins, Marion (1908–61) sculptor; born in Marche, Ark. His parents died when he was young and he was raised by an aunt in Chicago. He worked as a janitor, dishwasher, and postal worker before discovering his passion for sculpture in the late 1930s. Largely self-taught, he was inspired by African art. His best-known work, *Man of Sorrows* (1950), depicted a black Christ. Although such works as *John Henry* (1943) and *Ethiopia Awaking* (1948) brought him some reputation, he was unable to earn a living from his art, and he worked as a freight handler to support his family.

Perkins, Maxwell (Evarts) (1884–1947) editor, publisher; born in New York City. Joining Charles Scribner's Sons as an editor in 1914 (and later holding various corporate offices there as well), he showed a genius for recognizing and fostering talent, publishing early works by F. Scott Fitzgerald, Thomas Wolfe, Ernest Hemingway, and others. He is widely considered the best editor in the trade.

Perkins, Thomas (Handasyd) (1764–1854) merchant, philanthropist; born in Boston, Mass. He made his fortune trading in Santo Domingo (1785–92) and China (1792–1838), and was a prominent Federalist state legislator (1805–24). His generous local philanthropy benefited Massachusetts General Hospital, the Boston Athenaeum, and the Perkins Institution for the Blind, renamed for him after a major benefaction in 1833.

Perle, George (1915–) composer, theorist; born in Bayonne, N.J. After musical studies in Chicago and at New York University, he taught at several schools before settling at Queens College (1961–84). He was a leading exponent and theorist of serial composition, his books including *Serial Composition and Atonality* (5th ed. 1982), his compositions including three symphonies and much chamber music.

Perlman, Itzhak (1945–) violinist; born in Tel Aviv, Israel. Crippled by polio in childhood, he took up the violin with enthusiasm and made his public debut at age nine. Four years later he came to New York to study at Juilliard, where his teachers were Ivan Galamian and Dorothy Delay. After winning first prize in the Leventritt Competition in 1964, he entered the highest rank of international violin soloists. The combination of his brilliance in the standard repertoire – with occasional forays into the moderns – and his engaging personality made him one of the most popular soloists of his time.

Perls, (Frederick Salomon) Fritz (1893–1970) psychiatrist; born in Berlin, Germany. He left Germany in 1933, but did not settle in the U.S.A. until 1946. He was a founder and the most influential practitioner of Gestalt psychotherapy, which he explained in *Ego, Hunger, and Aggression* (1947), *Gestalt Therapy* (1951), *Gestalt Therapy Verbatim* (1969), and other books. In the 1960s, he was resident psychiatrist at the

Esalen Institute at Big Sur, Calif., in which role he gained the reputation of being something of a faddish "guru," although he was in fact a most serious professional.

Perot, H. (Henry) Ross (1930–) business executive, public figure; born in Texarkana, Texas. He graduated from the U.S. Naval Academy (1953) but resigned from the Navy as soon as his required tour of duty ended (1953–57). He went to work as a salesman for International Business Machines (IBM) and soon realized that his future lay not in hardware but in the expertise behind using the growing capabilities of computers. He quit IBM and founded Electronic Data Systems (EDS) in Dallas (1962), becoming a multimillionaire by providing the software and services for organizations that owned computers, a billionaire after he took the company public in 1968. In 1969 he commenced his efforts to obtain the release of American POWs in Vietnam; in 1978 he organized a commando brigade that helped to rescue two EDS employees from jail in Teheran, Iran (an escapade popularized in a book and movie, *On Wings of Eagles.*) He sold his company to General Motors in 1984 and went over to join in the management, but he soon fell out with the top executives there, so resigned (1986) and started Perot Systems (1988). In 1992 – by then one of the richest men in the world, with personal assets of $3.5 billion – he presented himself as a populist candidate for the presidency of the United States against Bill Clinton and George Bush; reviving an organization he had founded during the Vietnam War, "United We Stand," as his own third party, he ran a controversial campaign but ended up with 19 percent of the popular vote.

Perry, Antoinette (1888–1946) actress, director; born in Denver, Colo. A director of many plays, she became chairman of the American Theatre Wing. In 1947 the Antoinette Perry Awards (the Tonys) were founded in her memory.

Perry, (Fletcher Joseph) Joe (1927–) football player; born in Stevens, Ark. "The Jet," a San Francisco fullback, led the National Football League in rushing in 1953 and 1954, becoming the first to rush for 1,000 yards in consecutive years.

Perry, Lilla Cabot (1848–1933) painter, poet; born in Boston, Mass. A member of prominent Boston families, the Lowells and Cabots, she studied in Boston (c. 1885–88) and Paris (1888), summered in France, next door to Monet in Giverny (1889–1899), and lived in Japan (1893–1901). Based in Boston, she helped introduce impressionism to America, as seen in *The Trio, Tokyo* (1898–1901), and published four volumes of poetry (1886–1923).

Perry, Mary Chase (1867–1967) ceramist; born in Hancock, Mich. Developer of the Revelation kiln and founder of Pewabic Pottery (1903), both with Horace Caulkins, she later became wealthy from her architectural tile commissions.

Perry, Matthew Calbraith (1794–1858) naval officer; born in South Kingston, R.I. (younger brother of Oliver Hazard Perry). He entered the navy in 1809 and served in the War of 1812. He was the second officer of the New York navy yard (1833–37), became a captain in 1837, and commanded the first American steam warship, the USS *Fulton* (aboard which he conducted the navy's first gunnery school). He commanded the Africa Squadron (1843–46) and the Home Squadron during the last phase of the Mexican War (1847–48). Following four years of shore duty in New York, he

sailed for Japan aboard the USS *Mississippi* in 1852. He arrived off Edo (now Tokyo) in 1853 and demanded that Japan accept diplomatic relations and trade with the U.S.A. He returned to Japan in 1854 and accepted a treaty signed at Yokohama. His report of the expeditions were published as *Narrative of the Expedition of an American Squadron to the China Seas and Japan.*

Perry, Oliver Hazard (1785–1819) naval officer; born in South Kingston, R.I. He became a lieutenant (1807) and commanded coastal gunboats (1807–09) and the USS *Revenge* on the south Atlantic coast (1809–11). Promoted to master commandant (1812), he went to Presque Isle (now Erie), Pa., to build an American fleet for use on Lake Erie during the War of 1812. Leading the fleet against the British fleet in September 1813, he won the battle (although he had to transfer his flag from the USS *Lawrence* to the USS *Niagara*) and sent a famous message to Gen. William Henry Harrison, "We have met the enemy and they are ours." He transported Harrison's army across Lake Erie and led a cavalry charge at the battle of the Thames. After the war he commanded a squadron sent to Venezuela (1819) where he died of yellow fever. His remains were brought to Newport, R.I., in 1826.

Perry, Pettis (1897–1965) Communist; born near Marion, Ala. Son of black sharecroppers, he was a drifter until he joined the Communist Party's International Labor Defense Committee (1932). He moved to New York (1948) to head the party's National Negro Work Commission, was appointed head of the party's Farm Commission (1950), and the same year became a member of the party's leading triumvirate. He was one of 29 Communists out of 141 indicted under the Smith Act (1951) to serve a sentence (1952–55). He ultimately failed in his mission to make the Communist Party attractive to American blacks and was thrust into a leadership role more out of necessity than because of leadership abilities. He died in Moscow where he had gone for medical treatment.

Perry, Ralph Barton (1876–1957) philosopher; born in Poultney, Vt. Earning a Harvard doctorate (1899), he taught briefly at Williams and Smith Colleges, then returned to Harvard, where he taught from 1902 to 1946. He was a key advocate of the "new realism" and of philosophical clarity and precision. He outlined a naturalistic value theory in such works as *The General Theory of Value* (1926). His *Puritanism and Democracy* (1944) was a classic, and his 1935 biography of his teacher and colleague, William James, won a Pulitzer Prize. He was a U.S. Army major during World War I; later he supported the New Deal and campaigned for formation of the United Nations.

Persechetti, Vincent (1915–87) composer; born in Philadelphia. A teacher at Juilliard from 1947, he was a prolific composer of mildly modernistic scores.

Pershing, John J. (Joseph) (1860–1948) soldier; born near Laclede, Mo. Son of a railroad worker turned merchant, he graduated from West Point in 1886. After several years of cavalry service on the frontier, he taught military science (and fencing) at the University of Nebraska; he then went to teach at West Point, where he gained the nickname "Black Jack" because he had commanded a black cavalry unit in Montana. He left West Point to fight in Puerto Rico and Cuba during the Spanish-American War in 1898; from 1899 to 1903 he fought in the Philippines. Rising rapidly, he became a brigadier general in 1906, promoted over the heads of 800 senior officers. He spent the years from 1906 to 1914 in the Philippines; at his next assignment in San Francisco, his wife and three of his four children perished in a fire (1915). This left Pershing a grave and taciturn man, but he pursued his profession assiduously, leading the expedition against Pancho Villa (1916–17). On May 26, 1917, he became commander of the American Expeditionary Force and he led the buildup and training of American forces in France; against intense pressure from the British and French commanders, he also insisted that the American troops should remain intact as units to fight independently and with their own tactics. By September 1918, he launched the U.S. First Army against St. Mihiel in the first independent offensive by American forces; he then cooperated in the Meuse-Argonne offensive that led to the collapse of the Germans and the armistice. He returned to the U.S.A, and in September 1919 was named general of the army; he served as chief of staff until his retirement (1921–24). He served as chairman of the American Battle Monuments Commission and in several honorary diplomatic positions. His memoir, *My Experiences in the World War* (1931), won the Pulitzer Prize in history. Although too old to take any active role in World War II, he did consult with Chief of Staff George Marshall. A child in the Civil War, he was the first of the modern American generals, excelling in personnel, supply, and finance as well as battlefield tactics.

Persons, Wallace R. ("Buck") (1909–) business executive; born in Cleveland, Ohio. He worked his way through the sales hierarchy at Lincoln Electric Co., Cleveland (1934–53). As president, chairman and CEO of Emerson Electric Co., St. Louis (1954–74), he masterminded an acquisition program that turned a manufacturer of fans into a technologically oriented conglomerate admired for its prudent management and high earnings.

Pert, Candace B. (1946–) neuroscientist; born in New York City. She earned a Ph.D. in pharmacology at Johns Hopkins School of Medicine and after 1975 was associated with the National Institute of Mental Health, where she was chief of the brain chemistry section (1982–88). Her early work on receptor molecules in the brain led to the discovery of endorphins, the subject of much of her later research.

Pesotta, Rose (b. Peisoty) (1896–1965) labor leader; born in Derazhnya, Ukraine. The daughter of grain merchants, she was well educated and as a young girl adopted anarchist views. In 1913 she emigrated to New York City and worked in a shirtwaist factory. She soon joined a local of the International Ladies Garment Workers Union (ILGWU). She worked to advance the education of the workers and was elected to the ILGWU's executive board in 1920. In the late 1920s she was sent to Los Angeles to help organize garment workers there; her success led to her being named a vice-president of the ILGWU in 1934 and for the next eight years she continued to organize workers from Seattle to San Juan, from San Francisco to Montreal. In 1942, however, angry because she was the sole woman on the ILGWU's executive board – when 85% of the union's members were women – she went back to being a sewing machine operator. She resigned from the ILGWU board in 1944 but participated in some union activities. Her *Bread Upon the Waters* (1944) told of her union organizing experiences; her *Days of Our Lives* (1958) recounted her youth in Russia.

Peter, Johann Friedrich (1746–1813) composer, organist, teacher, minister; born in Heerendijk, Holland. Trained as both a Moravian minister and a musician, he came to Nazareth, Pa., in 1769. In 1770 he became organist at the Brethrens' House in Bethlehem, Pa., and in addition to directing performances of the music of contemporary Europeans such as Mozart, Handel, and Haydn, he himself composed over 30 anthems. He is regarded as the most sophisticated of the Pennsylvanian Moravian composers and ranks as one of the first serious composers in America.

Peters, (Thomas J.) Tom (1942–) author, lecturer, management consultant; born in Baltimore, Md. He was a McKinsey and Co. associate (1974–81) before founding the Tom Peters Group. His best-seller, *In Search of Excellence* (coauthored, 1982), dissected successful corporate practices and became a business bible. As a ubiquitous and popular author, lecturer, and newspaper columnist, he helped formulate competitive American management practices.

Peterson, Oscar (Emmanuel) (1925–) jazz musician; born in Montreal, Canada. A virtuoso pianist, he won immediate acclaim upon his U.S. debut at Carnegie Hall in 1949. He was then a regular attraction of "Jazz at the Philharmonic" as well as a prolific recording artist and accompanist to other mainstream jazz figures.

Peterson, Roger Tory (1908–) ornithologist; born in Jamestown, N.Y. He began observing and drawing birds as a boy, and pursued an artist's education in New York City at the Art Students League and the National Academy of Design. He taught art and science in Brookline, Mass., for several years before publishing his *Field Guide to the Birds of Eastern North America* in 1934. With its novel and easy-for-the-novice pointers on how to identify birds, this guide became a major best-seller. It also helped him obtain a job with the National Audubon Society; he was art editor for *Audubon* magazine from 1934–43. During World War II, the Army Air Force adapted his bird-spotting methods to aircraft identification. From the late 1940s, he edited a series of field guides, lectured, and continued to publish his own works, among them *Birds over America* (1948), *How to Know the Birds* (1949), and *A Bird Watcher's Anthology* (1957). *Wild America* (1957), written in collaboration with James Fisher, was an account of a journey along the Atlantic, Gulf, and Pacific coasts from Maine to Alaska. Peterson's guides and other work gave him wide influence in building popular awareness of wildlife conservation and environmental protection. He founded the Roger Tory Peterson Institute for the Study of Natural History in 1986.

Petigru, James Louis (1789–1863) lawyer, politician; born in Abbeville District, S.C. A graduate of South Carolina College, he taught school while studying law, was admitted to the bar in 1812, and established a thriving practice in Charleston. An opponent of nullification, he served in the state legislature and as attorney general. He left public service in the 1830s, (with brief service as a federal district attorney, 1851–53) but remained for many years the state's leading lawyer. Although he opposed secession, he ardently supported the Confederacy when war came in 1861.

Peto, John Frederick (1854–1907) painter; born in Philadelphia. Drawn to art and music as a youth, he studied at the Pennsylvania Academy of the Fine Arts (c. 1877) and adopted the trompe l'oeil style associated with the then popular William Harnett. His illusionistic still-lifes portrayed objects like advertising cards, photographs, and worn objects in such paintings as *Ordinary Objects in the Artist's Creative Mind* (1887). By 1889 he had settled in Island Heights, N.J., where his work became more brooding, and he faded from public view. Not until the art historian Alfred Frankenstein discovered his works in the 1940s did he gain a reputation as a true artist.

Petri, Angelo (1883–1961) vintner; born in Marseilles, France. He emigrated to the U.S.A. in 1895, joining the family cigar business; under his presidency, Marca Petri became America's leading brand of cigar. In 1933 he revived the family wine business, which thrived through innovative marketing and by his retirement (1956) had become United Vintners, the world's largest wine distributor.

Pettigrew, Richard Franklin (1848–1926) U.S. senator; born in Ludlow, Vt. He moved to Wisconsin and then to the Dakota Territory (1869), which he helped to survey. He was a territorial delegate to the U.S. House of Representatives (1881–83) and he advocated dividing the territory into two separate states. Chosen as South Dakota's first U.S. senator (Rep., 1889–1901), he became a thorough nonconformist in his party; he opposed the annexations of Hawaii and the Philippines and the entry of the U.S.A. into World War I (for which he was indicted, but not tried). He wrote *The Course of Empire* (1920) and *Triumphant Plutocracy* (1922), in which he blasted every U.S. president since the Civil War.

Pettit, (Robert E. Lee) Bob (1932–) basketball player; born in Baton Rouge, La. After he was an All-American at Louisiana State University, he played forward with the Milwaukee and St. Louis Hawks (1954–65), where he was an All-NBA (National Basketball Association) first team selection ten times and Most Valuable Player twice (1956, 1959). The first player to score 20,000 points in a career, he was elected to basketball's Hall of Fame in 1970.

Petty, Richard (1937–) auto racer; born in Level Cross, N.C. Beginning professional auto racing in 1958, he became the holder of numerous National Association for Stock Car Auto Racing (NASCAR) records. He won the Daytona 500 and the NASCAR national championship each seven times between 1964 and 1981. With over 200 victories, he started more races, won more races, and made more money than any stock car driver in history. His great popularity and financial success earned him the nickname "King Richard," and on his final professional race in 1992, President George Bush made a point by being present.

Pew, Joseph N. (Newton), Jr. (1886–1963) industrialist, philanthropist; born in Pittsburgh, Pa. He studied mechanical engineering at Cornell and invented a gyroscopic instrument for use in oil wells. Following in his father's footsteps, he was vice-president (1912–47) and president (1947–63) of Sun Oil. An economic conservative, he opposed all government regulation of industry. He made large contributions to the Republican Party over three decades and was influential at both the 1940 and 1944 Republican conventions. He and his siblings created a trust fund in memory of their father that continues to make gifts to many charitable and educational organizations.

Peyton, Patrick (1909–92) Catholic priest; born in County Mayo, Ireland. Emigrating to the U.S.A. at age 19 and ordained in 1941, he promoted family prayer, especially the rosary, through massive rallies and radio and television programs, often featuring Hollywood stars. He coined the saying "the family that prays together stays together."

Pforzheimer, Carl H. (Howard) (1879–1957) investment banker, book collector, philanthropist; born in New York City. After graduating from New York City College (1896), he opened his own investment firm in 1901; by 1915 he was so successful that he moved to Purchase, N.Y., where he took an active role in Westchester County affairs. Meanwhile, his great passion was English literature and he collected an immense quantity of manuscripts, first editions, journals, letters, and memorabilia. With his wife he established the Carl and Lily Pforzheimer Foundation in the 1930s, which in turn established the Carl H. Pforzheimer Library in New York City; for many years it was in a separate building and open only to select scholars. In 1986, a major segment of his collection – all works of English literature from 1425 to 1700, including the first work printed in English – was put up for sale; it was acquired for $15 million (through the generosity of H. Ross Perot) by the Harry Ransom Humanities Center at the University of Texas: Austin. In 1987, the segment focusing on the English Romantics – particularly Shelley and his circle – was donated to the New York Public Library so that it, too, would be accessible to a broader public.

Phelan, James (Duval) (1861–1930) mayor; born in San Francisco. He studied law at the University of California, but never became a lawyer. A three-term mayor of San Francisco (1896–1902), he attacked the board of supervisors and helped create a new city charter. He worked to beautify the city and to secure an improved water supply. He served one term in the U.S. Senate (Dem., Calif.; 1915–21).

Phelan, John J. (1931–) financier; born in New York City. Son of a member of the New York Stock Exchange's governing board, he graduated from Adelphi Unversity and became associated with the Exchange in the 1960s. Rising to chairman and chief executive officer, he led the Exchange during a transformation period (1982–90), trying to follow generally conservative policies in an era of investment excess.

Philip, King (b. Metacomet) (?1639–76) Wampanoag leader; born at Pawkunnakut in present-day Rhode Island. Son of Massasoit, he became chief in 1661, and although he did not at first engage in open hostilities, he gradually came to resent the English colonists' increasing restrictions on the Indians' use of their own lands. In 1675 an Indian informer told the English he was planning a revolt; when the informer was killed, supposedly by three Wampanoag, the colonists executed them, and this led to immediate war by angry Wampanoags. Although this war came to be known as "King Philip's War," there is some question as to whether he actually was the initial or major leader. In any case, it soon led to a major uprising of tribes from Rhode Island all the way to the Connecticut River in western Massachusetts; 12 colonial settlements were completely destroyed, and thousands of settlers were killed, but the English gradually wore down the Indians. In the final battle in April 1676 near Mt. Hope (now Bristol, R.I.), Philip was killed (by another Indian fighting for the colonists). The colonists' victory effectively broke up the tribal structures and ended Native Americans' resistance in southern New England.

Philipson, David (1862–1949) rabbi; born in Wabash, Ind. At age 13 he entered the first class of the new Hebrew Union College in Cincinnati, where he was ordained in 1883. He was the rabbi at Har Sinai Temple in Baltimore (1884–88) but served most of his career as rabbi at Bene Israel in Cincinnati (1888–1938). A widely published writer, he became a leader in American Reform Judaism. In 1889 he helped found the Central Conference of American Rabbis. An opponent of Zionism, he saw Judaism as a religious, not a political community.

Phillips, Ammi (1788–1865) painter; born in Colebrook, Conn. An itinerant folk painter, he worked in the area bordering New York, Connecticut, and Massachusetts. He is known for his early dream-like paintings, such as *Harriet Leavens* (c. 1815), and his later stylized work, as in *Girl in Red Dress with Cat and Dog* (1834–36).

Phillips, David Graham (1867–1911) journalist, novelist; born in Madison, Ind. After graduating from the College of New Jersey (later Princeton), he became a journalist, eventually on the *New York World* (1893–1902), where he wrote editorials for publisher Joseph Pulitzer and went on special assignments, such as covering the Greco-Turkish War (1897). After the success of his first novel, *The Great God Success* (1901), he became a free-lance writer, publishing more than 20 others. His novels often depicted corruption in government or industry; some, such as *Susan Lenox: Her Rise and Fall* (published posthumously in 1917), dealt with such issues as the place of women in society. He also wrote articles, especially for the *Saturday Evening Post* – most notably a series attacking corruption in the U.S. Senate; a disparaging reference to this series by President Theodore Roosevelt led to the first use of the term "muckraking." In 1911 Phillips was shot to death by a deranged man angered by one of his novels. Phillips's fiction, though popular at the time, later fell into oblivion.

Phillips, Duncan (Clinch) (1886–1966) art collector, museum founder; born in Pittsburgh, Pa. His maternal grandfather was one of the founders of the Jones and Laughlin steel company. He worked as an essayist, book reviewer, and art lecturer. To display his art collection, in 1918 he founded the Phillips Memorial Gallery in Washington, D.C. (now the Phillips Collection) in honor of his father and brother. He directed the gallery (1918–66) and wrote several books on art, notably *The Artist Sees Differently* (1931).

Phillips, Irna (1901–73) radio/television writer; born in Chicago. After graduating from the University of Illinois (B.S., 1923), she taught speech and drama at the college level. In 1930, for Chicago radio station WGN, she created and performed in *Painted Dreams* (1930–32), generally regarded as the first "soap opera." She moved on to the National Broadcasting Company and wrote *Today's Children* (1932–38), the first network daytime serial. In 1937 she began two more, *The Road of Life* and *Guiding Light;* by 1943 she had five serials on the air and was one of the highest paid women in America. The coming of television did not faze her; in 1949 she wrote the first TV "soap," *These Are My Children,* and she went on to write or co-author several more during the next two decades, including *As the World Turns* (1956), one of the most enduring daytime serials. She is credited with devising many of the now standard elements of soap operas. Although her female characters went through a wide range of experiences, marriage and family were always central to her stories. She herself never married but she adopted two children.

Phillips, James C. (Charles) (1933–) physicist; born in New Orleans, La. He worked at Bell Telephone Laborato-

ries (1956–58), the University of California: Berkeley (1858–59), Cambridge (1959–60), and Chicago (1960–68), before returning to Bell (1968). He made advances in studies of crystals and high-temperature superconductivity.

Phillips, Sam (1923–) music producer; born in Florence, Ala. He began his career as a disc jockey playing gospel music and blues at radio stations in Alabama and Tennessee. In 1950 he opened the Memphis Recording Service, recording black singers, including B. B. King and Howlin' Wolf, and leasing their material to labels in Los Angeles and Chicago. In 1952 he formed the Sun Record Company, and continued making records by a wide variety of black bluesmen and vocal groups, but he sought to record black material by white singers. Elvis Presley was the first of his discoveries in this new "rockabilly" style, and he released the singer's first ten songs before selling his contract to RCA for the then exceptional sum of $35,000. His subsequent discoveries included Johnny Cash, Jerry Lee Lewis, Carl Perkins, Charlie Rich, and Roy Orbison. Phillips sold his controlling interest in Sun Records in 1969.

Phillips, Wendell (1811–84) orator, reformer; born in Boston, Mass. A graduate of Harvard College (1831) and Law School (1834), he soon abandoned his legal practice, and, influenced by his abolitionist wife (Ann Terry Greene) and his Calvinist upbringing, dedicated himself to lecture on behalf of abolition, even at the expense of dissolving the Union; in many respects he was the most radical of the abolitionists. He also espoused such causes as women's rights and humane treatment of the mentally ill, earning a national reputation on the lecture circuit. After the Civil War, Phillips, unlike many abolitionists, turned to seeking social justice for blacks, succeeding William Lloyd Garrison as president of the American Anti-Slavery Society (1865). He grew concerned with the welfare of all workers, and, becoming increasingly radical, he upheld violence as a labor tactic and denounced corporate wealth and the wage and profit system.

Phillips, William (1878–1968) diplomat; born in Beverly, Mass. His long diplomatic career (1905–49) included assignments with both the Foreign Service and the State Department. He was ambassador to Italy (1936–40) and wartime ambassador to India (1942–44) (where he was not allowed to meet with Gandhi). He was a pivotal member of the Anglo-American Committee on Palestine (1946) and he wrote his memoirs, *Ventures in Diplomacy* (1952).

Phips, Sir William (1650–95) adventurer, royal governor; born in Maine. He discovered a Spanish treasure wreck, led a New England fleet against Quebec City (1690), and was the royal governor of Massachusetts. He was the first American to receive knighthood (1687).

Phyfe, Duncan (1768–1854) furniture maker; born in Lock Fanich, Scotland. With his family, he emigrated to Albany, N.Y. (c. 1783), where he apprenticed to a cabinetmaker. He moved to New York City in 1792 and by 1815 his workshops occupied three buildings. A master of design who specialized in mahogany, his early works took their inspiration from English Sheraton and French Directoire furniture, evolving into his own distinctive American Empire style by 1818. Although he derided his work after 1830 as being heavy "butcher furniture," he was the most successful cabinetmaker of his era, leaving the business to his son James when he retired in 1847.

Physick, Philip Syng (1768–1837) surgeon; born in Philadelphia. His desire to be a goldsmith was thwarted by his father's ambitions for him to pursue a medical career. After studying at the University of Pennsylvania and in London, he took his M.D. at the University of Edinburgh, Scotland. Back in Philadelphia he built up a private practice while also serving with the Pennsylvania Hospital (1794–1816) and teaching surgery at the University of Pennsylvania (1801–19). Meanwhile, he drew on his mechanical skills to improve medical instruments, including such inventions as the needle forceps, the guillotine/snare for performing tonsillectomies, and improved splints and traction devices for treatment of dislocations.

Piatigorsky, Gregor (1903–76) cellist; born in Ekaterinoslav, Russia. He played cello in Moscow orchestras before emigrating to Warsaw and then Berlin, where he became first chair in the Philharmonic (1924–28). Moving to America in 1929, he began a long and distinguished career as a soloist, teacher, and chamber musician, gaining a reputation as perhaps the finest player of the cello after Pablo Casals. He went into semiretirement in the 1970s.

Piccard, Jean Felix (1884–1963) aeronautical engineer, organic chemist; born in Basel, Switzerland (twin brother of Auguste Piccard). Emigrating to America to teach chemistry at the University of Chicago (1916), he later joined the University of Minnesota's Department of Aeronautical Engineering (1936–52) where he was best known for his research with high-altitude balloons. He wrote over 70 papers, translated Einstein's *Physics and Reality* into English (1936), and helped develop astronauts' pressurized suits for the National Aeronautics and Space Administration.

Pickens, Andrew (1739–1817) soldier; born near Paxtang, Pa. The son of Irish immigrants, he settled in South Carolina in 1763. In the American Revolution, he helped defeat the Loyalist forces at Kettle Creek, Ga., contributed to the decisive victory at Cowpens, S.C. (1781), and commanded the forces that captured Augusta, Ga.

Pickens, T. (Thomas) Boone, Jr. (1928–) oil company executive, financier; born in Holdenville, Okla. Son of an oil company lawyer who claimed a distant kinship to frontiersman Daniel Boone, he worked as a well-site geologist before establishing his own drilling enterprise, Mesa Petroleum Co., in 1964. From this base he became a feared corporate raider, practicing what his critics called "greenmail" – buying large blocks of a corporation's stock, threatening to take over that company, then selling them back for enormous profits. Even his failures, such as his aborted bids in the 1980s to seize Gulf and Unocal, earned him vast sums. Away from the boardroom, he became a noted crusader against drugs.

Pickering, Edward Charles (1846–1919) astronomer; born in Boston, Mass. (brother of William Henry Pickering). After graduating from Harvard's Lawrence Scientific School (1865), he taught physics at the Massachusetts Institute of Technology (1867–76) where he pioneered in teaching physics by emphasizing laboratory experiments. He then became the director of the Harvard College Observatory (1877–1919), where he pioneered in applying the knowledge and tools of physics to the study of stars – using photometry to calculate the magnitude of stars, using spectroscopy to study star composition. He supervised a large staff – many of them women – to catalogue and compute the magnitude of

80,000 stars and built up a collection of some 300,000 photographs of stars.

Pickering, John (?1776–1846) linguist, philologist, attorney; born in Salem, Mass. (son of Timothy Pickering). He graduated from Harvard (1796) and spent several years in Europe with the United States Diplomatic Corps. After returning to Masssachusetts, he practiced law and served in the state senate. He wrote many books and articles on language, including the first collection of American word usages (1816) and a Greek-English dictionary (1st edition, 1826). He was also a leading authority on the languages of North American Indians.

Pickering, William Henry (1858–1938) astronomer; born in Boston (brother of Edward Charles Pickering). A Massachusetts Institute of Technology graduate, he joined Harvard's astronomy department (1887–1924). He pioneered dry-plate celestial photography and took important early photographs of Mars (1888) and the moon (1900). He was the first to discover a satellite by photography when he located Phoebe, Saturn's ninth moon (1899). His published analyses of Martian canals and his independent prediction of Pluto's existence (1919) rivaled Percival Lowell's work. Pickering established Harvard observatories at Arequipa, Peru (1891) and in Jamaica (1900), and Percival Lowell's observatory at Flagstaff, Ariz. (1894).

Pickett, George Edward (1825–75) soldier; born in Richmond, Va. An 1846 West Point graduate (he ranked last in his class of 59), he served in the Mexican War (1846–47) and later fought Indians on the frontier. Resigning in 1861 to enter Confederate service, he saw combat at Seven Pines and Gaines's Mill and was promoted to major general. At Gettysburg on the third day, he was ordered by Gen. James Longstreet, himself under Gen. Robert E. Lee, to form the brigades for one last desperate charge across an open field; the Confederates suffered disastrous casualties while being repulsed, and although he had participated, it was thereafter unfairly known as "Pickett's Charge." He continued to see action – at New Bern, N.C., Drewry's Bluff, Va., and at Five Forks, Va. – right to the end of the Appomattox campaign. Greatly respected, after the war he turned down a commission from the Khedive of Egypt and a U.S. marshal's post from President Ulysses S. Grant and remained an insurance agent in Virginia.

Pickett, Joseph (1848–1918) painter; born in New Hope, Pa. An untrained artist and owner of a general store in New Hope, Pa., he painted primitive landscapes using house paint and sand, as in his detailed and charming *Manchester Valley* (c. 1914–18).

Pickford, Mary (b. Gladys Mary Smith) (1893–1979) film actress; born in Toronto, Canada, (wife of Douglas Fairbanks Sr.). Her stage debut was made at age five, and her film debut was in 1909. Her childlike charm, her golden curls, and her feminine wiles turned her into "America's Sweetheart." She played Cinderella parts until her retirement in 1933. A cofounder of United Artists, she won an Academy Award for *Coquette* (1929).

Picotte, Susan La Flesche (1865–1915) physician, tribal leader; born on the Omaha reservation in Nebraska. Daughter of Omaha Chief Joseph La Flesche (Iron Eye), she was educated in New Jersey and then at the Hampton Institute (Va.), graduating in 1886 with high honor. She then studied at the Women's Medical College of Pennsylvania, graduating in 1889, and returned to her tribe as a physician (1890–94) and all-around medical overseer. In 1894 she married Henry Picotte (half Sioux, half French) and they moved to Bancroft, Nebr., where she continued her medical practice while raising two children. With the founding of the town of Walthill in the Omaha reservation, she became so active in community and child affairs, as well as a medical doctor, that she was effectively the leader of the Omahas. The hospital she founded (1913) was named after her upon her death.

Pierce, Franklin (1804–69) fourteenth U.S. president; born in Hillsborough, N.H. A lawyer, he steadily ascended the political ladder as a Democrat, moving from the state legislature (1829–33) to the U.S. House of Representatives (1833–37) to the U.S. Senate (1837–42). He returned to private law practice in New Hampshire. Expansionist in sentiments, he served as an officer in the Mexican War (1846–47). A staunch Democrat, in 1852 he was nominated as a compromise presidential candidate – a Northerner sympathetic to the South – and he defeated the Whigs' Gen. Winfield Scott. Pierce then proved unable to mediate the issues boiling around slavery, signing the Kansas-Nebraska Act (1854) (giving settlers the right to vote for slavery), and enforcing the Fugitive Slave Act. The successes of his administration included a treaty with Japan and the Gadsden Purchase from Mexico, which added 20,000 square miles to the U.S.A., but these did not distract people from the turmoil he unleashed in Kansas. The Democrats ignored the unpopular Pierce at the 1856 convention, and he largely retired from politics, although he revived his unpopularity by attacking Abraham Lincoln during the Civil War.

Pierce, Jane (b. Means Appleton) (1806–63) First Lady; born in Hampton, N.H. She married Franklin Pierce in 1834. Tubercular and melancholic from the loss of three sons in childhood, she played little role in her husband's political career and was known as the "Shadow in the White House."

Pierce, John Robinson (1910–) electrical engineer; born in Des Moines, Iowa. Pierce worked in the Bell Telephone Laboratories (1936–71), subsequently becoming professor at the California Institute of Technology. In the 1950s he was one of the first to see the possibilities of satellite communication and played a role in the research that resulted in the launch of *Echo* (1960) and *Telstar* (1962).

Piercy, Esther June (1905–67) librarian; born in Los Angeles. A graduate of the University of Illinois Library School, she spent ten years in the cataloging department at the University of New Mexico (1934–44). At the Enoch Pratt Free Library in Baltimore she planned a complete recataloging and reclassifying system, which became a model for schools and small public libraries.

Piercy, Marge (m. Wood) (1936–) poet, writer; born in Detroit, Mich. She studied at the University of Michigan (B.A. 1957) and Northwestern (M.A. 1958). She held a number of jobs before she could earn her living as a writer. After living in many cities from San Francisco to Paris, she settled in Wellfleet, Mass. Active as a progressive and feminist, she is known for poetry that focuses on social problems, as in *To Be of Use* (1973), and for her novels with feminist themes, such as *Women on the Edge of Time* (1976). Much of her work also deals with Jewish themes.

Pierpont, Francis Harrison (1814–99) governor; born in Morgantown, Va. (now W.Va.). A lawyer and an active Whig, he supported the Union when the Civil War broke out. When Virginia seceded (1861), he organized a mass meeting at Wheeling and became the provisional governor of Western Virginia (1861–63). When West Virginia was admitted as a state (1863), he became governor of the "restored" state of Virginia, the counties still controlled by the Federal government. With the end of the Civil War, he became governor of Virginia (1865–68) and sought to heal the wounds between Yankees and Confederates in his state. West Virginia placed his statue in the U.S. Capitol.

Pike, Albert (1809–91) lawyer, journalist, soldier; born in Boston, Mass. Leaving New England to seek his fortune in the West in 1831, he taught school, wrote for and later owned an Arkansas newspaper, and was admitted to the bar in 1837. He took a break from the law to serve in the Mexican War. By the 1850s he had become a popular poet as well as a successful lawyer. An opponent of secession, he nevertheless obtained a brigadier's commission in the Confederate army and commanded Indian troops at the battle of Pea Ridge (1862). A dispute with a superior led to his arrest and then his resignation in 1863. After the war, he practiced law in Memphis, Tenn., and Washington, D.C. A prominent Freemason, he headed the southern branch of the Scottish Rite from 1859 until his death, and he rewrote the rituals in a book, *Morals and Dogma of the . . . Scottish Rite of Freemasonry* (1872; revised several editions).

Pike, Zebulon (Montgomery) (1779–1813) soldier, explorer; born in Lamberton, N.J. As an army officer, he led several parties of western exploration, including a trip to the headwaters of the Arkansas and Red Rivers (1806–07) during which he approached the Colorado peak that bears his name. Pike was killed leading the successful American assault on British forces at York (now Toronto), Ontario, on April 27, 1813.

Pilbeam, David R. (Roger) (1940–) physical anthropologist; born in Brighton, England. He came to the U.S.A. to teach at Yale (1968–81), then joined the Harvard faculty (1981). A paleoanthropologist and biometrician, he wrote extensively on human and nonhuman primate evolution, including primate dentition and mastication.

Pilcher, Joshua (1790–1843) trader, Indian agent; born in Culpeper County, Va. He was president of the Missouri Fur Company (1820–31) and he trapped and traded (1827–30, 1831–37). He was the U.S. superintendent for Indian affairs (1839–41).

Pillow, Gideon (Johnson) (1806–78) soldier; born in Williamson County, Tenn. A criminal lawyer, he was the law partner of James K. Polk who, when president, appointed him to commands in the Mexican War, much to the annoyance of Gen. Winfield Scott and other American military men. A Democrat, he hoped to avoid secession by compromise, but once the war began he went with the Confederacy. He fought at Belmont and in February 1862 he escaped from Fort Donelson, Tenn., with the garrison commander, leaving the third in command to surrender to Ulysses S. Grant. Vain and fractious, he was never given an important command thereafter. After the war he returned to practicing law.

Pillsbury, Charles Alfred (1842–99) flour miller; born in Warner, N.H. In 1869, shortly after joining his uncle, John Sargent Pillsbury, in Minneapolis, he bought into a flour mill. An innovative manager and marketer, he acquired new milling technology and within a few years the Pillsbury Mill was flourishing. In 1872, with his father and uncle, he organized C. A. Pillsbury & Company and expanded to six more mills in 10 years; by the early 1900s the Pillsbury flour mills were the largest such enterprise in the world. Involved in all aspects of the grain trade, he supported favorable freight rates accorded dealers who brought their grain to Minneapolis, and the development of the Minneapolis, Saulte Sainte Marie, & Atlantic Railway, actions he was able to facilitate as a state senator from 1878–85. When the Pillsbury company was sold in 1889 to an English syndicate, he remained as managing director. Known as a speculator in the wheat market who lost vast sums, he was also generous to his employees and to charities.

Pillsbury, Harry Nelson (1872–1906) chess player; born in Somerville, Mass. The best American since Paul Morphy, he beat an unprecedented field including the world champion, the ex-champion, and the champions of six countries, in Hastings, England (1895). Before dying of apoplexy, he twice beat Jackson Showalter for the U.S. title (1897, 1898).

Pillsbury, John E. (Elliott) (1846–1919) oceanographer; born in Lowell, Mass. He was a career U.S. Navy officer (1867–1908) who retired as a rear admiral. An authority on naval hydrography and geodesy, he determined the axis of the Gulf Stream in the Straits of Florida and off Cape Hatteras, and elucidated the geophysical laws regulating this current's flow.

Pillsbury, John Sargent (1828–1901) governor; born in Sutton, N.H. (uncle of Charles A. Pillsbury). A Minnesota hardware dealer (1855–75) and state senator, he rescued the state university from bankruptcy in 1864. Joining his nephew in founding Pillsbury Mill to grind wheat in 1872, he amassed a fortune. As Minnesota's governor (Rep., 1876–82), he streamlined government, redeemed outstanding railroad bonds, and eliminated corruption. He returned to helping run Pillsbury Mill afterward and dedicated much of his great fortune to funding numerous charities.

Pinchback, Pinckney (Benton Stewart) (1837–1929) governor; born in Macon, Ga. Son of a free black mother and white father, he was educated in Ohio. He organized a Union company of black volunteers in New Orleans in 1862. As a Republican, he became president of the Louisiana Senate (1869–71), then America's first African-American governor (1872–73). He lost contested elections to the U.S. House of Representatives and Senate, later earning a law degree.

Pinchot, Gifford (1865–1946) forester, conservationist, public official; born in Simsbury, Conn. The son of a well-to-do merchant, raised in a cosmopolitan atmosphere, he studied forestry in France after graduating from Yale in 1889. In 1896, as a member of the National Forest Commission, he helped prepare a conservation plan for government woodlands. Two years later he became chief of the U.S. Agriculture Department's Division of Forestry, but was fired in 1910 in a dispute with his superior, a foe of conservation; this break with President William Taft's administration was among the chief causes for Pinchot's old friend Theodore Roosevelt's leaving the Republican Party, and in 1912 Pinchot helped form the Progressive Party that nominated Roosevelt for president. A nonresident member of the faculty at Yale's School of Forestry (1903–36), founded with a grant from his father, he was free to enter politics and served two terms as a reform governor of Pennsylvania (Rep., 1922–26, 1931–35). His autobiography, *Breaking New Ground,* appeared the year after his death.

Pinckney, Charles (1758–1824) governor, U.S. senator, diplomat; born in Charleston, S.C. (second cousin of Thomas Pinckney). After serving as a Revolutionary soldier, he was a South Carolina delegate to the Continental Congress (1784–87), and then to the Constitutional Convention in 1787; although he contributed to the Constitution, it was not as much as he would later claim. He was elected governor of South Carolina several times (Fed., 1789–92; Dem.-Rep., 1797–99, 1807–09). As governor, he extended suffrage to all white males, obtained civil rights for Jews, and established free schools. As U.S. senator (Dem.-Rep., S.C.; 1799–1801), he was a supporter of Jefferson, who named him ambassador to Spain (1801–05); he negotiated Spain's acceptance of the Louisiana Treaty. He also served South Carolina in the U.S. House of Representatives (Dem.-Rep.; 1819–21).

Pinckney, Elizabeth Lucas (c. 1722–93) colonial planter; probably born in Antigua. Her British father was the lieutenant-governor of Antigua, and, after being educated in England, she arrived with her family in South Carolina in 1738. In her father's absence, she managed three family plantations and successfully planted indigo seeds – the first such in North America (1741–44). She married a lawyer, Charles Pinckney (1744), and upon his death in 1758, she again managed plantations on her own. She imported cocoons and raised silk worms. She had a strong influence upon the careers of her sons, Thomas and Charles Cotesworth Pinckney.

Pinckney, Thomas (1750–1828) diplomat, soldier; born in Charleston, S.C. He studied law in London but returned to South Carolina and served with distinction in the American Revolution. He was governor of South Carolina (1787–89) and ambassador to Great Britain (1792–96). He negotiated the San Lorenzo, or Pinckney, Treaty with Spain, which established territorial and traffic rights on the Mississippi River (1795), and served in the House of Representatives (Fed., S.C.; 1797–1801). A scientific planter, he employed agricultural methods that he had observed in Holland. He was a major general in the War of 1812.

Pincus, Gregory (Goodwin) ("Goody") (1903–67) endocrinologist; born in Woodbine, N.J. He taught at four Massachusetts universities – Harvard (1931–38), Clark (1938–45), Tufts (1946–50), and Boston University (1950–67). In 1944 he cofounded the Worcester Foundation for Experimental Biology, one of the first laboratories set up expressly to channel scientific discoveries directly into commercial development. He concentrated on studying hormones and other factors in mammalian reproduction and – with financial support brought in thanks to Margaret Sanger – he became one of the prime developers of an oral contraception pill (1951). An author of books and scientific papers, he published *The Eggs of Mammals* (1936) and *The Control of Fertility* (1965).

Pine, Robert (Edge) (c. 1742–88) painter; born in London, England. He emigrated to America (1784), and lived in Philadelphia. A noted portrait painter, his subjects included George Washington and his family.

Pingree, Hazen (Stuart) (1840–1901) businessman, mayor, governor; born in Denmark, Maine. After serving in the Civil War, he went to Detroit where he became a successful shoe manufacturer. As reform Republican mayor of Detroit (1890–96), he made several major reforms that benefited the citizenry instead of special interests; most notable was his providing gardens for the unemployed, nationally known as "Pingree's Potato Patches." He served as governor (1897–1901) where he attempted to extend his reforms to the railroads.

Pinkerton, Allan (1819–84) detective, Union secret service chief; born in Glasgow, Scotland. Son of a policeman, he became a barrelmaker before emigrating to the U.S.A. in 1842 and settling in Illinois. His abolitionist sympathies led him to aid the "underground railroad" for escaping slaves. After helping to capture a gang of counterfeiters, he was elected a deputy sheriff of his county (1846); in 1850 he moved to Chicago and became the deputy sheriff of Cook County and a detective on the Chicago police force. In 1852 he formed his own private detective agency and gained considerable fame for solving a series of train robberies. In 1861 he discovered a plot to assassinate Abraham Lincoln while he was to travel by railroad to the inauguration in Washington, D.C.; Pinkerton personally guarded Lincoln on this trip. As a result, Gen. George McClellan got Pinkerton named to head the Federal army's new secret service; under the alias "Major E. L. Allen," Pinkerton came up with some intelligence, but its quality was so poor that it was said to have contributed to McClellan's failed Peninsula Campaign; when McClellan lost his command, Pinkerton also lost his post. He continued, however, to investigate damage claims against the government (1862–65). After the Civil War, he went back to Chicago and expanded his own detective agency to other cities. It became known for organizing groups of armed men and hiring them out to help management break strikes by the new labor unions. (In 1892 it was "Pinkerton men" who were called in for the infamous Homestead affair.) He published ten volumes about his experiences as a detective.

Pinkham, Lydia E. (Estes) (1819–83) manufacturer; born in Lynn, Mass. A young schoolteacher in Lynn, she became a member of the Female Anti-Slavery Society and a lifelong friend of Frederick Douglass; she took up various causes including temperance, phrenology, and Grahamism until 1843, when she married Isaac Pinkham. In 1875 Isaac went broke speculating on real estate and Lydia began selling an herbal remedy she had concocted called "Mrs. Lydia E. Pinkham's Vegetable Compound." The remedy was registered in 1876 with the U.S. Patent Office and she herself marketed it with her own advertisements. She did not live long enough to see it achieve its phenomenal success, but for some 50 years it was one of the most popular "patent medicines" in America. It was promoted especially for "women's weakness," but the American Medical Association dismissed all its claims as fraudulent.

Pinkney, William (1764–1822) lawyer, diplomat, U.S. representative/senator; born in Annapolis, Md. Forced to leave school because of his poverty, he read law on his own. Admitted to the bar in 1786, he gained a reputation as one of the most talented trial lawyers of his day, noted for his oratory and vanity as well as for hiding his extensive preparations behind a facade of casualness. He spent 16 years abroad – as a commissioner negotiating maritime disputes with Britain (1796–1804) and then as ambassador, first to Great Britain (1806–11) and later to Russia (1816–18). As U.S. attorney general (1811–14), he strongly supported the War of 1812 and was wounded serving with the

Maryland militia at the battle of Bladensburg (1814). He served Maryland as a Federalist in the U.S. House of Representatives (1791, 1815–16) and the U.S. Senate (1819–22), where he championed the slave-holding states during the debate that led to the Missouri Compromise of 1820. Almost to the end of his life he argued cases before the U.S. Supreme Court.

Pinto, Isaac (1720–91) merchant, scholar, patriot; birthplace unknown. A Sephardic Jew, he appeared first as a merchant in Connecticut and then to have settled in New York City by 1751. He translated the *Evening Service of Roshashanah and Kippur* (1761) and the *Prayers for Shabbath, Rosh-Hashanah, and Kippur* (1766), the first Jewish prayer books to be printed in America. An ardent patriot, he signed the Non-Importation Act (1765). Although he moved about over the years, he was buried in New York City.

Pinza, Ezio (b. Fortunio) (1892–1957) bass; born in Rome, Italy. After gaining fame in Italy he became a favorite at the Metropolitan Opera from 1926 to 1948. He later appeared in Broadway shows and films including *South Pacific*.

Piper, Charles V. (Vancouver) (1867–1926) agronomist; born in Victoria, British Columbia. His parents moved to Washington soon after he was born. Between his bachelor's and master's degrees from the University of Washington (1885, 1892), he worked in his father's bakery and collected plants from the Puget Sound and Mount Rainier area. From 1893 to 1903 he taught botany at State College of Washington in Pullman. With an assistant, he collected and classified plants in Washington, Idaho, and Oregon; this work resulted in a series of classic books such as *Flora of the State of Washington* (1906). As director of the office of forage crops for the United States Department of Agriculture (1903–26), he sought grass samples worldwide to replace the poor Johnson grass; named for its country of origin, the Sudan grass he found was drought resistant and has remained vitally important for American hay crops. Among his other books, he coauthored *Turf for Golf Courses* (1917) and *The Soybean* (1923).

Piper, William (Thomas) (1881–1970) airplane manufacturer; born in Knapps Creek, N.Y. After graduating from Harvard (1903), he worked in construction and then for his family's Pennsylvania oil business. In 1931 he took over a bankrupt airplane company and began producing small affordable planes, "Cubs," for ordinary people. During his lifetime, the Piper Aircraft Corporation produced more airplanes than any other company.

Pippin, Horace (1888–1946) painter; born in West Chester, Pa. An African-American primitive painter who lived in West Chester, Pa., he began painting when he was 43 years old. The bold characteristics of his work are seen in *John Brown Going to His Hanging* (1942).

Pirsson, Louis V. (Valentine) (1860–1919) geologist; born in New York City. He taught at the Sheffield Scientific School (Yale) (1882–1919), while spending summers doing field-work in Montana and New Hampshire for the U.S. Geological Survey. A pioneer in petrology, he devised a new system of classifying igneous rocks.

Piston, Walter (Hamor) (1894–1976) composer; born in Rockland, Maine. He trained as an artist and first took a serious interest in music at Harvard (1920–24). After studies in Paris under Nadia Boulanger, he taught at Harvard (1926–60). A favorite of the conductor Serge Koussevitzky, Piston was noted for his solid craftsmanship in neoclassic works including eight symphonies and five string quartets. He also wrote several popular textbooks, including *Harmony, Counterpoint,* and *Orchestration.*

Pitcher, Molly See CORBIN, MARGARET and McCAULEY, MARY.

Pitchlynn, Peter (b. Hatchootucknee) (1806–81) Chocktaw leader; born in Hushookwa, Miss. A graduate of Nashville University, he was elected to the Chocktaw council where he worked to encourage education and to end polygamy and alcohol drinking. He was elected principal chief in 1860, after which time he traveled often to Washington, D.C., to lobby for the return of his people's homeland.

Pitney, Mahlon (1858–1924) Supreme Court justice; born in Morristown, N.J. He served the U.S. House of Representatives (Rep., N.J.; 1895–99) and in the New Jersey legislature (1899–1901). He was a state supreme court judge (1901–08) when President William Taft appointed him to the U.S. Supreme Court (1912–22). He was a known conservative and opposed organized labor.

Pittman, Key (1872–1940) U.S. senator; born in Vicksburg, Miss. He joined the Alaskan gold rush (1897–1901) and was a lawyer who specialized in mining law. He served in the U.S. Senate (Dem., Nev.; 1913–40). As chairman of the Senate Foreign Relations Committee, he strongly supported President Franklin Roosevelt's foreign policy. Above all, he looked after the interests of the silver-mining states and used his legal skills to see that the price of silver was kept up through government purchases.

Placzek, Adolph K. (Kurt) (1913–) architectural librarian/historian; born in Vienna, Austria. He began as a medical student at the University of Vienna, then shifted to its Institute of Fine Arts. Emigrating to the U.S.A. in 1940, he attended Columbia University, where he became the assistant librarian of Avery Architectural Library (1948–60); he was promoted to Avery Librarian (1960–80) and also held a post at Columbia as adjunct professor of architecture (1971–80). As the director of the foremost American architectural library, he shared his vast knowledge of architectural history with several generations of scholars and students. A longtime member of the Society of Architectural Historians, he served as its president during 1978–80. He was editor of the *Macmillan Encyclopedia of Architects* (1982) and contributed articles to various encyclopedias, books, and periodicals. He was a member of the New York City Landmarks Preservation Commission (1984).

Plank, Charles J. (1915–) chemist, inventor; born in Calcutta, India (the son of American missionary parents). Educated at Purdue University, he joined a forerunner of the Mobil Oil Corporation in 1941. With Edward J. Rosinski, he invented the first commercially applicable apparatus for the cracking of hydrocarbons, a necessary process in petroleum production. In 1970 he became senior scientist at Mobil Oil, the company's highest scientific post.

Plantinga, Alvin C. (Carl) (1932–) philosopher; born in Ann Arbor, Mich. After teaching at Yale (1957–58), where he earned his doctorate, and at Wayne State University (1958–63) and Calvin College (Grand Rapids, Mich.) from 1963, he became a professor at Notre Dame in 1982, specializing in philosophical theology. His works include *God and Other Minds* (1967).

Plaskow, Judith (1946–) writer, educator; born in New York City. She graduated from Clark University (1968) and earned a Ph.D. from Yale University in religious studies. Cofounder and coeditor of the *Journal of Feminist Studies in Religion* (1983), she was appointed professor of religious studies at Manhattan College in 1990. She wrote *Standing Again at Sinai: Judaism from a Feminist Perspective* (1990), as well as many scholarly and popular articles.

Plath, Sylvia (1932–63) poet; born in Boston, Mass. A graduate of Smith College, she had a Fulbright Scholarship to Oxford, where she met and married the English poet, Ted Hughes. She had written poetry since childhood; her first volume of poems, *A Winter Ship* (1960), was published anonymously; her next volume was *The Colossus and Other Poems* (1960); her autobiographical novel, *The Bell Jar* (1963), appeared just before her suicide (1963); other volumes of her poetry appeared posthumously. She was generally regarded as belonging to the modern "confessional school" because of the highly personal nature of her intense, often anguished poetry.

Platt, Charles A. (1861–1933) landscape architect; born in New York City. A painter, he became interested in architecture when he studied Italian villas in 1880. An East Coast architect (1897–1930), he created unified designs for buildings and grounds, notably at Deerfield and Phillips Andover Academies.

Platt, Robert (Swanton) (1891–1964) geographer; born in Columbus, Ohio. A faculty of the University of Chicago (1919–57), he made nine extended field trips to Latin America. These provided the basis for his major book, *Latin America: Countrysides and United Regions* (1942). His keen interest in field study is also revealed in his *Field Study in American Geography* (1959).

Platt, Thomas Collier (1833–1910) political boss, U.S. representative/senator; born in Owego, N.Y. He started in business as a druggist and eventually rose to become president of the United States Express Company (1880–1910). His political career began in 1870 through his alliance with Roscoe Conkling. Although Platt served in both the U.S. House of Representatives (Rep., N.Y.; 1873–77) and in the U.S. Senate (Rep., N.Y.; 1881, 1897–1909), he was most effective in state politics. He ran the powerful New York Republican machine through patronage and power plays (1881–1902). His political downfall came as the star of Theodore Roosevelt ascended in New York; Platt worked to have Roosevelt sidetracked as vice-president in 1900, but Roosevelt soon became president and Platt lost much of his power.

Plimpton, George Arthur (1855–1936) publisher, book collector; born in Walpole, Mass. As chairman of Ginn and Company starting in 1914, he expanded the publishing company worldwide; as an avocation, he assembled a remarkable collection of manuscripts and books illuminating the history of education.

Plumer, William (1759–1850) U.S. senator, governor; born in Newburyport, Mass. He was a Federalist when he served New Hampshire in the U.S. Senate (1802–07), but he became a Democratic-Republican by the time he served as New Hampshire's governor (1812–13, 1816–19). In retirement he wrote influential articles signed "Cincinnatus" and "Veritas."

Plummer, Henry (1837–64) bandit; place of birth unknown. Nothing is known of his early years. He became the marshal of Nevada City, Calif. (1856), but turned to banditry after he murdered a man there. He organized a bandit group that terrorized the Washington Territory and southern Montana (1862–64). He masqueraded as the sheriff of Bannack, Mont., before being apprehended and hanged by a group of vigilantes.

Plunkett, Roy J. (1910–94) chemist, inventor; born in New Carlisle, Ohio. In 1938, after only two years as a research chemist for E. I. du Pont de Nemours & Co., he discovered Teflon, a breakthrough that led to many new fluorochemical products now widely used in the electronics, plastics, and aerospace industries. He remained an effective manager of research, development and production for du Pont until he retired in 1975.

Pocahontas (b. Matoaka) (?1595–1617) Powhatan historical figure; born in present-day Virginia. She reportedly interceded with her father, Chief Powhatan, to spare the life of John Smith of Jamestown colony (1608). After adopting Christianity, she married John Rolfe (1614) and traveled to England in 1616. She died (possibly of smallpox) on the trip back. Through her son, Thomas Rolfe, she is an ancestor of the Randolph family of Virginia.

Podlaski, (Ronald Paul) Ron (1946–   ) veteran/social activist; born in New York City. Born into a single-parent welfare family with seven siblings, he joined the U.S. Army in 1966, and as a volunteer Green Beret, conducted special operations in Vietnam, Laos, and Cambodia. In 1969 he returned to the U.S.A. and after working at several jobs studied child psychology at the University of Maine (1977–79). He then worked at the Maple Hill School (Vt.), a school for abused and troubled children. In 1986 he became vice-president of the Vietnam Veterans of America Foundation (VVAF) and began working with Southeast Asian refugees and Amerasian children in the U.S.A. In 1991, under the auspices of the VVAF, he established a prosthetics clinic in Cambodia, especially for Cambodians injured by land mines laid down during the wars there. In 1992 he began an agricultural and fish-farming program for which the amputees are responsible. A 1994 Petra Foundation Fellow, he lived with his family in Phnom Penh, Cambodia.

Poe, Edgar Allan (1809–49) poet, writer; born in Boston, Mass. He was abandoned by his father when a baby and his mother died before he was three, so he was taken as a foster child into the home of John Allan, a Richmond (Va.) tobacco merchant whose business took him to Great Britain, where Poe was educated (1815–20). Returning to Virginia, he continued his education (1823–25) and attended the University of Virginia (1826); having quarrelled with his foster father (although he chose "Allan" as his middle name) over his gambling debts and refusal to study law, he then went to Boston, where, anonymously and at his own expense, he published *Tamerlane and Other Poems* (1827). He served in the U.S. Army under a false name (Edgar A. Perry) and incorrect age (1827–29) and then attended West Point (1830–31), but got himself dismissed when he realized he would never be reconciled with his foster father. He then went to Baltimore to live with his aunt, Mrs. Maria Clemm; he would marry her daughter and his own cousin, 13-year-old Virginia Clemm, in 1836. His third volume of poetry (1831) brought neither fame nor profit, but a prize-winning short story, "A MS Found in a Bottle" (1833), gained him the editorship of the *Southern Literary Messenger* (1835–36). During the next

several years he was a journalist and editor for a variety of periodicals in New York City, Philadelphia, and then back in New York City, where he settled in 1844 and continued working as an editor while nursing schemes of starting his own magazine. All this while he was gaining some reputation for his short stories, poems, reviews, and essays; such stories as "The Fall of the House of Usher" (1839), "Murders in the Rue Morgue" (1841), and "The Goldbug" (1843), would later be regarded as classics of their genre. He gained some fame from the publication in 1845 of a dozen stories as well as of *The Raven and Other Poems,* and he enjoyed a few months of calm as a respected critic and writer. After his wife died in 1847, however, his life began to unravel even faster as he moved about from city to city, lecturing and writing, drinking heavily, and courting several older women. Just before marrying one, he died in Baltimore after being found semiconscious in a tavern – possibly from too much alcohol, although it is a myth that he was a habitual drunkard and drug addict. Admittedly a failure in most areas of his personal life, he was recognized as an unusually gifted writer and was admired by Dostoevsky and Baudelaire, even if not always appreciated by many of his other contemporaries. Master of symbolism and the macabre, he is considered to be the father of the detective story and a stepfather of science fiction, and he remains one of the most timeless and extraordinary of all American creative artists.

Pohl, Frederik (Elton V. Andrews, Paul Fleur, Warren F. Howard, Cyril Judd, Ernst Mason, and several other pen names) (1919–   ) writer, editor; born in New York City. He attended the public schools in New York City and then went to work as a writer and editor for popular magazines (1939–43, 1946–49), with time out to serve with the U.S. Army Air Force (1943–45). He had set himself up as a literary agent in 1946 and by 1953 his own works were successful enough to allow him to become a free-lance writer. He published a steady stream of short stories and novels, often coauthoring works with other science fiction writers under joint pen names. With Cyril Kornbluth, for instance, he wrote as "Cyril Judd" and produced a modern sci-fi classic, *The Space Merchants* (1953). A pioneer in "sociological sci-fi," which tends to postulate alternative societies, he also helped introduce more sophisticated literary techniques into what had long been regarded as "pulp" fiction. One of his classic works is *Gateway* (1977). He returned to editing science fiction, first at *Galaxy Magazine* (1961–69), then at Ace Books (1971–72), and finally at Bantam Books (1973–79). As the winner of many awards, both for his fiction and as an editor, he lectured widely in the U.S.A. and abroad and appeared on many radio and television programs to discuss science fiction.

Poindexter, Miles (1868–1946) U.S. representative/senator; born in Memphis, Tenn. Settling in the state of Washington in 1891, he practiced law and became active as a Democrat, then shifted to the Republican Party and served as a state judge (1904–08). He was elected to the U.S. House of Representatives (Rep., Wash.; 1909–11) and to the U.S. Senate (1911–23). Although he began as a Progressive, he opposed President Woodrow Wilson's international policies and became leader of the anticommunist "Red Scare" of 1919. He was U.S. ambassador to Peru (1923–28).

Poinsett, Joel Roberts (1779–1851) cabinet member, diplomat; born in Charleston, S.C. After studying medicine and languages in Britain, he traveled widely (1801–08). President Madison sent him as a special agent to observe and deal with independence movements in Latin America (1810–15). He was a member of the U.S. House of Representatives (Dem., S.C.; 1821–25) and the first U.S. ambassador to Mexico (1825–29), where his machinations made him highly unpopular. (An amateur botanist, he developed a plant that he brought back from Mexico and it was named after him, the poinsettia.) He opposed the nullification movement in South Carolina (1830–32). All his life he had hoped for a military career but the closest he came was when President Van Buren named him secretary of war (1837–41). A man of wide interests, he was happy to return to his estate in South Carolina. He opposed the Mexican War and the secession movement that began to emerge in the South after 1847.

Poirier, Richard (1925–) literary critic, educator, writer; born in Gloucester, Mass. A professor at Rutgers (1963) and author of studies of Henry James, Norman Mailer and Robert Frost, he cofounded the Library of America (1979), an ongoing and comprehensive published collection of American literary and historical works.

Poitier, Sidney (1924–) movie actor; born in Miami, Fla. Raised in the Bahamas, he joined the American Negro Theater and appeared on Broadway in 1946. He helped to break the race barrier in Hollywood, beginning with *No Way Out* (1950), and became the number one African-American actor in movies such as *In the Heat of the Night* (1967) and *Guess Who's Coming to Dinner* (1967); he was the first African-American to win an Academy Award, as best actor in *Lilies of the Field* (1963). He later directed a number of movies.

Poland, Luke (Potter) (1815–87) U.S. representative, senator; born in Westford, Vt. A brilliant, self-taught lawyer, he was a Whig Supreme Court justice in Vermont (1848–65), Republican senator (1865–67), and congressman (1867–75) who revised the statute law of the United States.

Polglase, Van Nest (1898–1968) movie art director; born in New York City. Arriving in Hollywood in 1919, he designed sets for countless movies, from *Stage Struck* (1925) and *Top Hat* (1935), to *The Hunchback of Notre Dame* (1939), and his masterpiece, *Citizen Kane* (1941). His sets were noted for their combination of style and atmosphere.

Polk, George (1913–48) journalist; born in Fort Worth, Texas. After three years at Virginia Military Institute, he left to work as a journalist. In 1937 he went to Alaska where he became the city editor of the *Fairbanks Daily News;* while there he completed his college education at the University of Alaska. After two years on the *Shanghai Evening Post* (China) (1938–39), he joined the *Herald Tribune* in Paris, France; in 1940 he went to New York City to work on that paper's foreign news desk. In 1941 he was commissioned in the U.S. Naval Reserve and served as a pilot in the South Pacific; wounded in action, he spent a year in a hospital before leaving the service in 1944. He returned to the *Herald Tribune* as a Washington correspondent and in 1945 he joined CBS radio as an overseas news correspondent. By 1948 he was CBS's chief Middle East correspondent, married to a Greek woman, and based in Athens, and that May he set off for Salonika in northern Greece, evidently to interview a leader of the Communist forces then fighting a civil war; a few days later Polk's body was found washed ashore on Salonika Bay. There were a series of investigations by both

Greek and U.S. authorities and also by private American interests convinced that there was a cover-up; Greek pro-government and Communist supporters charged each other with an assassination; although no findings have ever been agreed on by all parties, later investigations suggest Polk was killed on the orders of pro-government individuals, annoyed at his reports of their failings. Before 1948 ended, Long Island University initiated the George Polk Awards, given each year since to honor journalistic achievements (both print and broadcast).

Polk, James Knox (1795–1849) eleventh U.S. president; born in Mecklenburg County, N.C. Son of a prosperous farmer, he moved in childhood to Tennessee, was admitted to the bar there in 1820, and by 1825 had gained election as a Democrat to the U.S. House of Representatives. He became Speaker of the House (1835–39), where he was a powerful advocate of Jacksonian policies and expansionism. After serving as governor of Tennessee (1839–41), he beat Henry Clay for the presidency as a "dark horse" in 1844, mainly on his promise to seize Mexican territory in the southwest. An efficient and determined executive, he did as promised by provoking the Mexican War, which in 1848 secured for the victorious U.S.A. undisputed possession of Texas, and 500,000 square miles including the future states of California, Arizona, Nevada, Utah, and parts of Wyoming, Colorado, and New Mexico. Meanwhile he peacefully settled the Oregon boundary dispute with England. Exhausted, attacked from all sides because of his opposition to both extremes on the issue of slavery, and holding to a campaign pledge, he did not run for reelection and died three months after leaving office.

Polk, Leonidas (1806–64) clergyman, soldier; born in Raleigh, N.C. He graduated from West Point (1827), but having been converted in his senior year, he resigned his commission shortly after graduating and studied for the Episcopalian ministry. By 1841 he was the Episcopal Bishop of Louisiana, where he also owned a sugar plantation with 400 slaves. He helped establish the University of the South at Sewanee, Tenn. His West Point classmate, Jefferson Davis, urged him to accept an appointment as a general, and he soon found himself in the thick of action, defeating Grant at Belmont, commanding large forces at Shiloh, Perryville, Stone's River (all 1862), and Chickamauga (1863). Gen. Braxton Bragg ordered him to be court-martialed for not following orders at Chickamauga, but President Davis reinstated him. Polk was killed in action near Pine Mountain, Ga., in June 1864, and although Davis lavished the highest praise on him as a military leader, most of his peers felt his real talents lay in his ministry.

Polk, Sarah (b. Childress) (1803–91) First Lady; born in Murfreesboro, Tenn. She married James K. Polk in 1824. Well-educated, she served as Polk's personal secretary and the two often worked together until late at night. Polk died two months after his presidency, but she remained admired and respected by both sides during the Civil War and afterward.

Pollack, Ben (1903–71) musician; born in Chicago. He was a drummer, an ambitious bandleader, and a discoverer of young talent, his distinguished sidemen including Benny Goodman, Glenn Miller, Jack Teagarden, and Harry James. He played with the New Orleans Rhythm Kings from 1922 to 1924, then led his own band in Chicago and New York between 1924 and 1940. He worked thereafter as a music businessman and restaurateur in Hollywood.

Pollard, (Frederick Douglas) "Fritz" (1894–1986) football player; born in Chicago. The second African-American (after Bill Lewis of Harvard, 1892–93) to be named consensus All-America, his running led Brown University to the 1916 Rose Bowl. In the 1920s he played and coached in the National Football League.

Pollock, (Paul) Jackson (1912–56) painter; born in Cody, Wyo. He grew up in Wyoming and California, moved to New York City, and studied intermittently with Thomas Hart Benton at the Art Students League (c. 1929–32). His paintings of the 1930s, such as *Birth* (1937), anticipate the turbulent impasto and sexual imagery of his later work. His first major exhibition was organized by Peggy Guggenheim (1943) when he was using mythological themes, as seen in *The She Wolf* (1943). Around 1946 he settled in Easthampton, Long Island, and began his critically acclaimed abstract work exemplified by *Full Fathom Five* (1947). The spatter-and-drip technique used on his large canvases (1945–55) established his reputation as a major abstract expressionistic painter. He explored figurative studies, but shortly before his death in an automobile accident, he reclaimed his interest in action painting.

Polya, George (1887–1985) mathematician; born in Budapest, Hungary. Emigrating to America for professional reasons (1940), this noted teacher settled at Stanford University (1940–53) and specialized in probability, complex analysis, and combinational theory. Author of ten books, including *How to Solve It,* he also wrote over 250 articles on mathematics.

Pomeroy, Marcus Mills ("Brick") (1833–96) newspaper editor/publisher, propagandist; born in Elmira, N.Y. Working as a journeyman-printer turned journalist at several midwest papers, he settled in Wisconsin at the *La Crosse Democrat* (1860–66), and then in New York he published the *New-York Democrat,* which he sold to William M. Tweed (1870). Back at the *New York Democrat* (1876–80), he worked for the Greenback cause, organized, promoted, and was president of the Atlantic-Pacific Railway Tunnel (1890), and published the general news monthly, *Advance Thought.* Known for his sensational, intensely personal, and independent journalism, he gained national attention for championing the political underdog and the people.

Pons, Lily (Alice Joséphine) (1898–1976) soprano; born in Draguignan, France. Making her operatic debut in 1928, she sang primarily in provincial French theaters before her highly successful Metropolitan Opera debut in New York (1931). A fine dramatic coloratura, she had a glamorous international career during the 1930s and gave concerts until 1972. She also appeared in several 1930s films.

Ponselle, Rosa (b. Ponzillo) (1897–1981) soprano; born in Meriden, Conn. She made her operatic and Metropolitan Opera debut at once, with Enrico Caruso, in 1918, and stayed with the Met until retirement in 1936. She was celebrated for her opulent voice, one of the finest America has produced.

Pontiac (?1720–69) Ottawa chief; born in present-day Ohio. Nothing is known of his early years, but according to the 19th-century historian Francis Parkman, he was an Ottawa chief who favored the French in their struggle with the English. Opposing the British takeover of the Old North-

west, about 1762 he organized a coalition of Indian tribes against them. He led the year-long siege of Fort Detroit (1763–64) while other Indian forces captured eight British forts before they were eventually defeated. Pontiac agreed to peace in 1766. He was apparently murdered by a Peoria warrior in the pay of an English trader. Historians are unsure whether Pontiac actually led what is called "Pontiac's conspiracy" or "rebellion," or if he was only one of several Indian leaders; his role was dramatized and highlighted by Parkman.

Ponzi, Charles (1877–1949) swindler; born in Italy. He came to the U.S.A. in 1899. He ran a financial scheme in Boston (1919–20) that brought him a fortune from unsuspecting, small investors and gained him the name "Get Rich Quick" Ponzi. Convicted of mail fraud and theft, he served prison sentences before being deported to Italy (1934). He moved to Brazil and died with an estate of $75.

Poole, William Frederick (1821–94) librarian, historian; born in Salem, Mass. As a student at Yale, where he graduated in 1849, he maintained and expanded a project indexing useful materials in books and magazines. This index was published in 1848 and was the forerunner to *Poole's Index to Periodical Literature.* He was librarian of the Boston Athenæum (1856–69) and he then helped to establish the library of the U.S. Naval Academy and the Cincinnati Public Library. In 1874 he became the first librarian of the Chicago Public Library and in 1887 he helped organize Chicago's Newberry Library, where he remained until his death. He is also known for his contributions to the profession of library administration.

Poor, Henry Varnum (1821–1905) economist; born in East Andover, Maine. A lawyer and member of the Whig Party, he campaigned for William Henry Harrison before leaving law, and Maine, to join his brother (John Alfred) in New York City and edit the first commercial periodical on railroads, *American Railroad Journal* (1849–62). He collaborated on and authored several important compilations of railroad statistics and histories culminating in the so-called "Poor's Manual," *Manual of Railroads in the United States* (1868), an annual publication which he wrote with his son, Henry William (1844–1915). In 1867 he opened the firm H. V. & H. W. Poor to import rails and railway supplies. He wrote many other books on economics, including *Resumption and the Silver Question* (1878), and argued in favor of protectionist tariffs.

Poor, Henry Varnum (1888–1971) ceramist; born in Chapman, Kans. Following study at Stanford University and in London and Paris art schools, he returned in 1912 to the U.S.A. to teach art. In 1920 he established a studio in Rockland County, N.Y. His first ceramics exhibit (1922) earned a reputation that brought him such commissions as creating painted vases and lamps for Radio City Music Hall (1932).

Popé (?–1690) Tewa Pueblo medicine man, revolutionary leader; probably born on the San Juan Pueblo in present-day New Mexico. He first came to the attention of the Spanish when in 1675 he led the resistance against the Spaniard's treatment of Native American medicine men. Then in 1680 he masterminded and led a successful Indian revolt against the Spanish rulers in New Mexico. After many Spanish were killed and most others fled, he and his followers eradicated every visible trace of the Spanish presence in their region and tried to return to a traditional way of life. He ruled in an arbitrary manner and alienated many of his people as well as neighboring tribes; he was deposed and died soon afterward. Although the Spanish reconquered the area (1692), Popé had led what was probably the most successful revolt by Native Americans.

Pope, Albert A. (Augustus) (1843–1909) manufacturer; born in Boston, Mass. He was decorated for "gallant conduct" during the Civil War. He opened a shoe supplies factory and became wealthy by 1877. He opened the Pope Manufacturing Company in Hartford, Conn., which made small, patented articles, but eventually specialized in bicycles, especially the popular "Columbia" brand. He energetically promoted bicycling and founded *The Wheelman* (1882), which was changed into *Outing* (1883). Known as the "founder of the American bicycle industries," he ventured into the automobile business (1896) and for a time manufactured gasoline and electric cars in Toledo, Hartford, and Indianapolis.

Pope, John (1822–92) soldier; born in Louisville, Ky. A West Point graduate (1842) and Mexican War veteran, he did valuable survey work with the Army topographical engineers in the Southwest and West. Staying with the Union, he led the Army of the Mississippi in a campaign that opened the great river nearly to Memphis (1862). This success, plus the siege of Corinth, brought him to the attention of President Lincoln, who promoted Pope to command the Army of Virginia. He alienated some of his subordinates by his famous address (July 1862) – in which he implied that the Union forces in the East had not been aggressive enough – and he inspired some mockery when, asked where his headquarters would be, he replied, "In the saddle." His failures after the peninsular campaign and at Second Bull Run (August 1862), precipitated his replacement by Gen. George McClellan. Pope never again held a field command, even though he remained in the army until 1886.

Pope, John Russell (1874–1937) architect; born in New York City. A prolific New York architect, he revived Gothic, Georgian, and classical styles. Among his neoclassical designs are the National Archives (1933–35) and the Jefferson Memorial (1937–43), both in Washington, D.C.

Popham, George (?–1608) colonist; born in England. A sea captain, he and Sir Ferdinando Gorges proposed the idea of a Northern Virginia colony. Popham and Raleigh Gilbert commanded the two ships that landed off the coast of Maine in 1607. They stayed the winter at the mouth of the Kennebec River, but Popham died in February and the colony was abandoned that summer.

Porter, A. (Arthur) Kingsley (1883–1933) architectural historian; born in Stamford, Conn. He taught at Yale (1915–19) and Harvard (1920–33). His survey, *Medieval Architecture: Its Origins and Development* (1909), the first scholarly history of its subject by an American, freshly illuminated Lombard Romanesque architecture in what had been regarded as the cultural void between Roman and Renaissance art. Also an expert on Romanesque sculpture, he is regarded as perhaps the greatest American historian of medieval art.

Porter, Cole (Albert) (1891–1964) composer, lyricist; born in Peru, Ind. Born into a family of some wealth and social standing, he showed a talent for music early, publishing a song by age 11. He graduated from Yale (1913) – where he wrote the famous Yale fight song, "Bulldog, Bulldog" – and

after briefly studying law at Harvard, shifted to music. He went off to Paris to continue his music studies (1920–21), and from then on tended to spend much of his time with the rich international set who moved between the U.S.A. and Europe. In 1937 he was left seriously injured by a riding accident but he continued to travel and to compose. Although his first forays into musicals in the early 1920s were box-office failures, several songs were made popular by well-known performers. He composed his first full score for *Paris* (1928), which included the risqué "Let's Do It," and for almost three decades he wrote a dazzling series of successful film scores and Broadway musicals. From the musical, *Gay Divorce* (1932), came the classic "Night and Day," which he said was inspired by Moroccan drums and an Islamic chant. The standard "I've Got You Under My Skin" was first heard in the film *Born to Dance* (1936). Adapted from Shakespeare, his most famous musical, *Kiss Me, Kate* (1948), enjoyed a long Broadway run and was made into a popular film. His last Broadway musicals, *Can-Can* (1953) and *Silk Stockings* (1955), also enjoyed successful runs. *High Society* (1956) was his most successful film musical. Although many of his works reflect the brittle sophistication of his social circle, no American composer ever quite topped the sheer artistry, elegance, and wit of his music and lyrics.

Porter, David Dixon (1813–91) naval officer; born in Chester, Pa. He went to sea at age ten (1823) and served as a midshipman in the Mexican navy (1826–29) before he joined the U.S. Navy (1829). He served as a lieutenant in the Mexican War, and after a furlough (1849–55) he returned to active service and became a commander in the Union navy in 1861. He helped to plan a naval offensive against New Orleans and received the surrender of the Confederate forts there (1862). In command of the Mississippi Squadron (1862–64), he ferried Ulysses S. Grant's army across the Mississippi River, leading to the capture of Vicksburg (1863). He commanded the North Atlantic Blockading Squadron (1864–65) and launched troops to capture Confederate Fort Fisher in Wilmington, N.C. He was superintendent of the Naval Academy (1865–69) and adviser to the secretary of the navy (1869–70). He became a full admiral in 1870 and was the senior American naval officer until his death.

Porter, Edwin S. (Stanton) (1869–1941) film director; born in Connellsville, Pa. He held various odd jobs until serving in the navy, and on his return he marketed the Edison Vitascope, setting up the first screening of motion pictures in 1896. The most prominent innovator in early American films, he began with Edison in 1900, directing and editing most of the Edison Company's output. He pioneered trick photography, special effects, double exposures, split screens, and stop-motion. His greatest triumph was *The Great Train Robbery* (1903).

Porter, Eleanor (b. Hodgman) (Eleanor Stuart, pen name) (1868–1920) writer; born in Littleton, N.H. She studied at the New England Conservatory of Music, Boston, married (1892), and was a concert singer, teacher, and writer beginning in 1901. She is remembered for her series of books for young readers, beginning with *Pollyanna* (1913), so excessive in their cheerfulness that the name has become a synonym for an irrepressible or even irritatingly optimistic individual.

Porter, Eliot (Furness) (1901–90) photographer; born in

Winnetka, Ill. Although he had photographed natural subjects as a youth, he studied chemical engineering at Harvard and then took his M.D. degree at the Harvard Medical School (1929). He taught biochemistry at Harvard and Radcliffe (1929–39) and practiced photography as an amateur. After the first showing of his work (1938) at An American Place, Alfred Stieglitz's gallery in New York, he was persuaded to devote himself full time to photography. He was a pioneer in the use of color pictures and became especially noted for the almost microscopic closeups on the details of natural objects. By 1946 he settled in Sante Fe, N.M., although he was known for his landscape pictures of Maine. Among his dozen major books of photography, often with pertinent texts, are *The Flow of Wildness* (1968), *The Tree Where Man Was Born* (1972), and *Birds of North America – A Personal Selection* (1972). In later years he donated much of his work to the Sierra Club, which spread its conservation message with posters of his brilliant photos and in particular with his book, *In Wildness Is the Preservation of the World* (1962).

Porter, Fitz-John (1822–1901) soldier; born in Portsmouth, N.H. A West Point graduate (1845), he fought in the Mexican War and served on the frontier. Appointed brigadier general after the Civil War began, he fought in numerous battles in northern Virginia. After the Union's loss at the battle of Second Bull Run (August 1862), he was charged by Gen. John Pope with having refused to obey orders; after a celebrated court-martial, he was convicted and discharged in 1863. Military historians still dispute the fairness of the charge; in any case, Porter, after a long campaign, obtained reinstatement in 1886, then resigned.

Porter, (Geneva Grace) Gene Stratton (?1863–1924) writer, photographer, illustrator; born in Wabash County, Ind. Born on a farm, she and her family moved to Wabash, Ind. (1874), where she continued her schooling until 1883. She married in 1886, and settled in Geneva, Ind. She was a nature photographer, illustrator, and writer of sentimental novels, incorporating nature lore, as in *A Girl in the Limberlost* (1909). She also wrote nonfiction nature books.

Porter, John Luke (1813–93) naval architect; born in Portsmouth, Va. He reconditioned the hull of and constructed an armored deck shield for the CSS *Virginia* (formerly the USS *Merrimac*) (1861–62). As a Confederate naval constructor (1862–65), he created plans for more than 40 ironclad or partly armored vessels.

Porter, Katherine Anne (1890–1980) writer; born in Indian Creek, Texas. After being schooled mainly at home, she worked as a journalist in Denver, Colo., and Chicago. She would later elaborate on and exaggerate certain aspects of her life but she does seem to have lived in Mexico and in Europe for some years and would marry three times. Her first collection of short stories, *Flowering Judas, and Other Stories* (1930), gained her considerable acclaim, and for many years she was admired entirely for short stories and novellas, often drawing on Roman Catholic symbolism from her past while expressing her liberal views on present society. With her best works somewhat relegated to schools as minor classics, she astonished the literary world with the publication of her only novel, *Ship of Fools* (1962), a rather bitter and ironic view of humanity. This gained her a final round of appreciation as her *Collected Stories* (1965) won both the Pulitzer and National Book Award, and she fired a parting shot with her critical account of the Sacco-Vanzetti trial and execution, *The Never-Ending Wrong* (1977).

Porter, Keith R. (Roberts) (1912–) cell biologist; born in Yarmouth, Nova Scotia, Canada. He came to the U.S.A. for graduate studies (1934), and became a research fellow at Princeton (1938–39). At the Rockefeller Institute (1939–61), he adapted tissue culture cells for electron microscopy to observe the microanatomy of cellular organelles. He joined Harvard (1961–67), then the University of Colorado (1968–84). He became chairman of the biological science department at the University of Maryland (1984–88), then moved to the University of Pennsylvania (1989). A prolific author and adviser to many scientific journals, he made major advances in studies of experimental embryology and tissue culture technique.

Porter, Noah (1811–92) clergyman, college president; born in Farmington, Conn. A Congregational pastor, he became professor of moral philosophy (1846–92) and president of Yale (1871–86). Among his many philosophical works, *The Human Intellect* (1868) enjoyed the widest success; in *American Colleges and the American Public* (1871) and elsewhere he expounded a conservative educational philosophy.

Porter, Rufus (1792–1884) inventor, editor; born in Boxford, Mass. He left home early and led an eventful, wandering life, playing the fife and violin, and painting portraits. He wandered from Maine to Virginia and back to Connecticut and invented (but did not patent) numerous devices. In New York City, he was editor of the *American Mechanic* (the first scientific newspaper in the U.S.A.) and he began the *Scientific American* (August 28, 1845). He sold the latter within six months and later wrote his scientific prophecy, *Aerial Navigation . . . New York and California in Three Days* (1849). He resumed his wanderings and little is known of the rest of his life.

Porter, Russell Williams (1871–1949) explorer, astronomer, telescope maker; born in Springfield, Vt. He participated in ten Arctic voyages (1894–1904) and was once marooned in the Arctic for nearly two years. Inspired by his celestial observations, he made his own telescope and helped to design the 200-inch telescope on Palomar Mountain in California; he also contributed to the design of the astrophysical laboratory at the California Institute of Technology. He designed landing craft, rockets, and fuses for the U.S. Navy during World War II.

Porter, Sylvia (Field b. Feldman) (1913–91) journalist; born in Patchogue, N.Y. Gaining know-how by working at an investment house, she launched her popular financial column in the *New York Post* in 1935, at first using initials to conceal her gender. She switched to the *Daily News* in 1978.

Porter, William Sydney (originally Sidney) (O. Henry, Oliver Henry, S. H. Peters, pen names) (1862–1910) writer; born in Greensboro, N.C. He was schooled in Greensboro and worked in a drug store there (c. 1877–82). He held a variety of other jobs, such as ranch worker (1882–84), bookkeeper and draftsman (1884–91), and bank teller (1891–94) in Texas. He was a journalist and owner of a weekly newspaper, *Rolling Stone,* in Austin, Texas, but in 1896 he fled to Honduras to escape charges he had embezzled money from the bank he had worked in. He returned when he learned his wife was seriously ill; convicted (1897), he was imprisoned at Ohio State Penitentiary (1898–

1901) where he began to write short stories. Upon his release he settled in New York City. Writing about little incidents in the lives of ordinary people, he became known for his sentimental stories with ironic endings, such as "The Gift of the Magi" and "The Furnished Room." Originally published in magazines, his stories were regularly collected in a series of highly successful volumes (1904–17).

Posner, Richard A. (Allen) (1939–   ) judge, legal scholar; born in New York City. He held several government positions prior to his teaching posts at the law schools of Stanford (1968–69) and the University of Chicago (1969). In 1981 he was appointed judge of the U.S. Court of Appeals for the Seventh Circuit, sitting in Chicago, by which time he is said to have made a fortune as a legal consultant. He became known for his economic approach to legal issues such as antitrust law; he is also known for expressing his views on many subjects outside the narrow confines of law, publishing many articles and books, including *Problems of Jurisprudence* (1990). He is credited with having inspired a new, more interdisciplinaary orientation in contemporary American law schools. Regarded by some as a conservative, he preferred to see himself as a legal pragmatist, somewhat skeptical of many of the broad claims for the role of law and the courts in modern society.

Post, Charles William (1854–1914) cereal manufacturer; born in Springfield, Ill. He dropped out of the University of Illinois and held several jobs until his health failed in 1884. In 1891 he established La Vita Inn in Battle Creek, Mich., an institute for healing by mental suggestion. He began experimenting with breakfast foods and in 1895 invented Postum, a coffee substitute after which he named his company, Postum Cereal Co., Ltd. He also invented Grape Nuts (1897) and Post Toasties (1904). He fought what he called the "tyrannical and dangerous" tactics of union organizers and insisted on an open shop. In 1902 he founded the anti-union Citizen's Industrial Alliance (president, 1905–08) and in 1910 the National Trades' and Workers' Association. In 1914, while recuperating from an appendectomy in his California winter home, he fell into a depression and killed himself.

Post, Emil Leon (1897–1954) mathematician, logician; born in Augustow, Poland. Emigrating to America as a child, he lost his left arm (age 12) and rejected a career in astronomy. He did pioneering work in proof theory and multivalued logics and was cofounder of the theory of recursive functions. He was a founding member of the Association for Symbolic Logic.

Post, Emily (b. Price) (1872–1960) authority on etiquette; born in Baltimore, Md. Daughter of a wealthy New York architect, she wrote society fiction and essays before writing her classic *Etiquette – The Blue Book of Social Usage* (1922). In her ten editions of *Etiquette,* and her syndicated etiquette column and radio show, she defined good manners for millions of Americans, dispensing relaxed yet serious advice that was striking in its flexible response to changing social mores.

Post, George B. (Browne) (1837–1913) architect; born in New York City. In New York he designed residences, pioneering skyscrapers (including the city's first "elevator building"), and classical revival commercial buildings. He received the American Institute of Architects' Gold Medal in 1911.

Post, Richard F. (Freeman) (1918–   ) physicist; born in Pomona, Calif. He taught at Pomona College (1940–42), performed underwater sound studies at the Naval Research Laboratory (1942–46), then moved to Stanford (1947–51) before joining the Lawrence Livermore National Laboratory (1951–87). He made major contributions to particle accelerator research, nuclear fusion, and high-temperature plasma physics.

Post, Wiley (1900–35) aviator; born in Grand Saline, Texas. From 1924 to 1931 he gave flying exhibitions, flew passenger flights, and worked as a test pilot. In 1931 he flew around the world in eight days, 15 hours, and 51 minutes, breaking the previous record of 21 days. He died with Will Rogers in an Alaskan air crash.

Potofsky, Jacob (Samuel) (1894–1979) labor leader; born in Radomisl, Ukraine. Emigrating to the United States in 1905, he took part in the Hart, Schaffner and Marx strike in Chicago in 1910. A founder of the Amalgamated Clothing Workers (ACWA), he worked as an organizer in the 1930s, served as ACWA secretary-treasurer (1940–46), and then president (1946–72).

Potter, David M. (Morris) (1910–71) historian; born in Augusta, Ga. Educated at Emory (A.B. 1932), Yale (M.A. 1933; Ph.D. 1940), and Oxford (M.A. 1947), he taught at the University of Mississippi (1936–38), Yale (1942–61), and Stanford University (1961–71). A revered mentor and one of the preeminent historians of his generation, he is known primarily for his books, articles, and lectures on the American South, especially on the causes of the Civil War; his interdisciplinary work on the American character, historiography, and other subjects led to his reputation as one of the last "Renaissance men" in his discipline. He made his mark with his first book, *Lincoln and His Party in the Secession Crisis* (1942). Completed and edited by Stanford colleague Don E. Fehrenbacher and published posthumously, *The Impending Crisis* (1976) received the Pulitzer Prize in history for 1977.

Potter, Edward T. (Tuckerman) (1831–1904) architect; born in Schenectady, N.Y. (half brother of William Potter). He was a New York architect known for his English High Victorian churches, his use of iron construction, and his model tenement housing.

Potter, William A. (Appleton) (1842–1909) architect; born in Schenectady, N.Y. (half brother of Edward T. Potter). Practicing in New York, he specialized in collegiate buildings and suburban estates and was identified with the American High Victorian Gothic and Richardsonian styles.

Pound, Ezra (Weston Loomis) (1885–1972) poet, writer; born in Hailey, Ida. Brought up in Pennsylvania, he studied at Hamilton College, N.Y. (B.Ph. 1905), and the University of Pennsylvania (M.A. 1906). He taught at Wabash College, Ind. (1906), traveled in Europe (1906–07), then lived in London (1908–20), Paris (1920–24), and Italy (1924–45). He was arrested and jailed for treason by the United States (1945) because he had made public broadcasts in Italy during World War II supporting anti-Semitism and Fascism. Judged insane, he was committed to St. Elizabeth's Hospital, Washington, D.C., and was released in 1958. He then returned to Italy. He was a founder of the imagist poetry movement, and was editor of several intellectual periodicals, such as *Poetry* (1912–19), *The Little Review* (1917–19), and *The Exile* (1927–28). A prolific translator, literary critic, and poet, both as an editor and mentor he helped shape the poetry of the 20th century – playing a major role, for instance, in the final version of T. S. Eliot's "The Wasteland." Of his own work, he is most apt to be remembered for *Hugh Selwyn Mauberly* (1920) and for his *Cantos,* a series of poems written from 1917 to 1970.

Pound, Louise (1872–1958) linguist, folklorist, athlete; born in Lincoln, Nebr. (sister of Roscoe Pound). Educated by her mother at home, she entered the University of Nebraska where she received a B.L. in music in 1892 and an A.M. in English in 1895. During this time she also became the women's state and regional tennis champion and she won a men's varsity letter in tennis at the university. She obtained a Ph.D. from the University of Heidelberg in only two semesters and returned to the University of Nebraska, where she taught for 45 years. For many of these years she was also a ranking golfer, including state champion in 1916. Her work on the origins of the ballad form, her studies of American folk songs and folklore in the Middle West, and especially her inquiries into developments in American English, were significant contributions toward the scholarly recognition of folklore and American speech as legitimate fields of study. In 1955 she became the first woman president of the Modern Language Association and also the first woman elected to the Nebraska Sports Hall of Fame. She was a founder and senior editor of *American Speech* (1925–33).

Pound, Robert V. (Vivian) (1919–) physicist; born in Ridgeway, Ontario, Canada. He came to the U.S.A. with his parents in 1923. He was a researcher with the Submarine Signal Company (Mass.) (1941–42), then performed radiation research at the Massachusetts Institute of Technology (1942–46), before joining Harvard (1945–89). Pound made pioneering studies of nuclear magnetic resonance (1940s–50s), and extensive relativistic gravitational investigations using gamma rays (1950s–60s).

Pound, Roscoe (1870–1964) legal scholar, botanist; born in Lincoln, Nebr. Considered one of the nation's leading jurists outside the Supreme Court, he taught for many years at the University of Nebraska (1892–1903), at Northwestern (1907–09), at the University of Chicago (1909–10), and then at Harvard Law School (1910–47). During his early career as a botanist, he discovered a rare lichen thereafter named "Roscopoundia." He advanced the idea of sociological jurisprudence and his "theory of social interests" influenced several New Deal programs. The theory took actual societal conditions into account rather than maintaining strict adherence to legal codes. However, he later felt that many New Deal programs were grossly mismanaged and thus promoted a welfare or "service state." He set forth these misgivings in *Justice According to Law* (1951). Gifted with boundless energy and an encyclopedic memory, he authored many books including *Readings on the History and System of the Common Law* (1904), *Law and Morals* (1924), and *Jurisprudence* (5 vols. 1959).

Poussaint, Alvin (Francis) (1935–) psychiatrist; born in East Harlem, N.Y. Affiliated with the Harvard Medical School from 1969, he became senior associate professor of psychiatry at Children's Hospital/Judge Baker Children's Center in Boston (1978). A recognized expert on race relations and the psychological and sociological dynamics of prejudice, he consulted widely to corporations and government on issues of race. Because of his belief in the power of media, he gave many public interviews and was script

consultant to the National Broadcasting Company's *Cosby Show* (1984–92).

Powderly, Terence (Vincent) (1849–1924) labor leader, public official; born in Carbondale, Pa. He went to work on the railroads at age 13, then became a machinist (1869–77) and joined the Machinists' and Blacksmiths' National Union, becoming its president in 1872. He also joined the then secretive Noble Order of the Knights of Labor (1874), and, rising quickly, became its leader (1879–93). His ideal was a union open to all, and he disliked confrontational measures, preferring labor-management cooperation. Under his leadership the Knights of Labor achieved its peak of strength and influence, with 1,000,000 members in 1886, the year Samuel Gompers took his cigar-makers' union to join the American Federation of Labor; thereafter the Knights declined. Entering politics, Powderly joined the Greenback-Labor Party and was mayor of Scranton, Pa. (1878–84). He was admitted to the Pennsylvania bar (1894) and served as federal immigration commissioner (1897–1902) and head of the information division of the Bureau of Immigration (1907–21).

Powdermaker, Hortense (1896–1970) cultural anthropologist; born in Philadelphia. The daughter of a businessman, she graduated from Goucher College in 1919, worked as a union organizer, and studied at the London School of Economics. A pioneer among women archaeologists for working alone in exotic places, her *Life in Lesu,* based on research in a Pacific island village, appeared in 1933. She taught at Queens College, New York City, from 1938–68, and did anthropological studies of life in a Mississippi town and in Hollywood, Calif.; the latter resulted in *Hollywood, The Dream Factory* (1950). She published her memoirs, *Stranger and Friend: The Way of an Anthropologist,* in 1966.

Powell See OSCEOLA.

Powell, Adam Clayton, Jr. (1908–72) U.S. representative, minister; born in New Haven, Conn. After earning a Masters of Social Work degree from Columbia University, he ran social and welfare programs at Harlem's Abyssinian Baptist Church, following his father as minister in 1931. Elected to New York's City Council in 1941, the flamboyant Powell went to the U.S. House of Representatives (Dem.; 1945–69) where he fought to outlaw Jim Crow laws. Chairman of the House Committee on Education and Labor (1960–67), he sponsored 48 major pieces of legislation including the Minimum Wage and National Defense Education Bills. However, his absentee rate and eight-year legal battle with a Harlem woman who sued him for libel lost him support in Congress. When he moved to Bimini in 1966 to escape payment, the House voted to exclude him from Congress. After paying libel charges, he returned in 1969, vindicated by a Supreme Court decision that his exclusion had been invalid; however, he was defeated in 1970 by Charles Rangel.

Powell, Adam Clayton, Sr. (1865–1953) Protestant clergyman; born in Franklin Co., Va. The son of a recently freed slave and a German planter killed during the Civil War, he migrated to Ohio in 1884 and was converted at a revival meeting. He graduated from Wayland Seminary, Washington, D.C., in 1892 and held pastorates in New Haven, Conn. and, from 1908–37, at the Abyssinian Baptist Church in New York City, where he preached racial pride and became a leader of the African-American community. He helped found the Urban League and was a member of the National

Association for the Advancement of Colored People's first board of directors.

Powell, Colin (Luther) (1937–) soldier; born in New York City. He graduated from the City University of New York and received a second lieutenant's commission in 1958. Decorated for service in Vietnam, Powell subsequently held a series of senior commands and was a presidential assistant for national security affairs (1987–89). The first African-American to become chairman of the Joint Chiefs of Staff (1989), he had overall responsibility for the U.S. military effort against Iraq (operations Desert Shield and Desert Storm) in 1990–91.

Powell, (Earl) "Bud" (1924–66) jazz musician; born in New York City. He was the most influential pianist in jazz between 1945 and 1960, but his career was severely hampered by recurrent mental instability. He appeared with Cootie Williams from 1943 to 1944 and began leading his own trio in 1947. Between 1959 and 1964 he was based in Paris.

Powell, John Wesley (1834–1902) geologist, geographer; born in Mount Morris, N.Y. Moving throughout the Midwestern states with his family, he attended Oberlin College where he realized his interest was in geology. He volunteered for the Union army when the Civil War broke out and had his right arm amputated at the elbow after being wounded at Shiloh. Taking up a career as a professor of geology, in 1867 he began the first of many field trips with his students into the Rocky Mountain region. Then in 1869 he led a professional expedition, financed by the U.S. government, that climaxed with a 900-mile journey down the Colorado River and through the Grand Canyon. He made other government-sponsored expeditions and in 1875 became director of the U.S. Geographical and Geological Survey of the Rocky Mountain Region; in 1879 this merged with the U.S. Geological Survey and he became its second director (1881–94). In his seminal work, *Report on the Lands of the Arid Region of the United States* (1878), he set forth a land classification program and a survey of irrigation potential; he was one of the first to call for the federal government to play a role in developing the western territories. In his trips he had also become a close student of the Native Americans; he was the first to attempt to classify their languages; and in 1897 he became the first director of the Smithsonian Institution's Bureau of American Ethnology, which he headed until his death. He published on a wide variety of subjects and beyond that promoted publications and projects that advanced both scientific knowledge and popular awareness of the pre-Columbian American West.

Powell, Lawrence Clark (1906–) librarian, author, critic; born in Washington, D.C. He was raised in California where his father, a noted agronomist, managed Sunkist Growers. After spending most of his career as a library administrator at the University of California: Los Angeles, he moved to the University of Arizona (1971) to teach English and write about the American Southwest. A recognized expert on the works of poet (and fellow Occidental College graduate) Robinson Jeffers, he wrote hundreds of articles and reviews and more than a dozen books, including *The Alchemy of Books* (1954) and *Books in My Baggage* (1960).

Powell, Lewis (Franklin), Jr. (1907–) Supreme Court justice; born in Suffolk, Va. His early civic posts included chairing the Richmond, Va., School Board during integra-

tion (1952–61). President Nixon named him to the U.S. Supreme Court (1972–87), where, although known as a conservative, he cast the deciding vote with the liberal majority in *Roe* v. *Wade* (1973).

Power, Effie Louise (1873–1969) children's librarian, author; born in Conneautville, Pa. Beginning her career as an assistant in the Cleveland (Ohio) Public Library, she opened the first children's room in this library in 1898. She also served in the children's department of the Carnegie Library in Pittsburgh (1909–11, 1914–20) and in St. Louis Public Library (1911–14), returning to the Cleveland Library as director of work with children (1920–37). In 1926 in Cleveland, she introduced the "Book Caravan," a forerunner of the bookmobile. She lectured on children and libraries throughout the country; she became a storyteller and instructor in storytelling; and during the 1930s she published several collections of stories for children.

Powers, Hiram (1805–73) sculptor; born in Woodstock, Vt. He and his family settled in Cincinnati, Ohio, where, starting at age 17, he worked in a clock and organ factory. In 1829 he went to work for the Western Museum to install mechanisms in the displays for their "chamber of horrors," but he discovered he had a talent for sculpting the wax figures and this led him to do portrait busts of Cincinnati worthies. He moved to Washington, D.C., in 1834 and was soon making plaster portrait busts of leading figures including President Andrew Jackson and Chief Justice John Marshall. Wealthy patrons financed his move to Florence, Italy, in 1837, originally to improve his artistic skills, but he would stay there for the rest of his life, his home and studio eventually becoming a mecca for many prominent Americans. In 1843 he completed his life-size marble nude woman called *The Greek Slave* and it quickly became one of the best-known and most controversial statues of the century, praised by artists and writers but condemned by preachers and prudes. None of his subsequent works would ever gain the same attention, but his bronze statue of Daniel Webster was placed in front of the Massachusetts State House and his marble statues of Benjamin Franklin and Thomas Jefferson were placed in the U.S. Capitol. He did other monumental statues but is best known for his many marble portrait busts.

Powers, J. F. (James Farl) (1917–) writer; born in Jacksonville, Ill. A socially concerned Catholic, he was jailed during World War II for resisting induction on pacifist grounds; he was also stirred by injustices against blacks. His major interest in fiction became the realistic, often wryly ironic depiction of priests' lives and conflicts, as in his prize-winning novel *Morte d'Urban* (1962) and in *Wheat that Springeth Green* (1988). He lived at intervals in Ireland but mostly in Minnesota, where he taught as St. John's College.

Powers, John R. (Robert) (1893–1977) model agency director; birthplace unknown. He founded commercial modeling by opening the world's first modeling agency in New York City (1920). His glamorous models included Henry Fonda and Barbara Stanwyck. He later established a national chain of modeling schools and a cosmetics business.

Powhatan (b. Wahunsonacock) (?1550–1618) Pamunkey Powhatan chief; born near present-day Richmond, Va. He inherited the chieftainship of the so-called Powhatan Confederacy from his father, but he greatly extended his "empire" until, by the arrival of the English (1607), it was an alliance of roughly 30 tribes, over 100 villages, or 9,000 people. The first Native American leader known to have contact with English settlers in North America, he was reputed to be ruthless in dealing with his fellow Indians, and in the early years of the English in Virginia, he proved to be inhospitable if not downright hostile. He was the chief, who, according to John Smith's account, was about to execute John Smith until his daughter Pocahontas interceded. After Pocahontas married the English planter John Rolfe in 1614, Powhatan made peace with the colonists, but soon after his death both the peace and his Confederacy disintegrated.

Pratt, Benjamin (1710–63) judge; born in Cohasset, Mass. The son of poor parents, he was to have learned a trade when, crippled by the loss of a limb, he was sent to Harvard instead. A successful lawyer with political interests, he represented Boston in the Massachusetts General Court from 1757 to 1759. He served briefly as chief justice of New York, a post a political ally helped him obtain. He had begun to collect material for a projected history of New England at the time of his death.

Pratt, Charles (1830–91) oil merchant, philanthropist; born in Watertown, Mass. One of 11 children, he grew up in adverse circumstances. He went to work at age 10 and moved to New York City in 1851. He specialized in paints and oils (1854–67) before he formed Charles Pratt & Company to refine crude oil at Greenpoint, N.Y. The resultant product was marketed worldwide as an illuminant. He sold his firm to John D. Rockefeller (1874) and then became immensely wealthy while working for Rockefeller's Standard Oil Company. He founded Pratt Institute in Brooklyn (1887) and the Pratt Institute Free Library and gave generously to various educational institutions.

Pratt, Enoch (1808–96) iron merchant, capitalist, philanthropist; born in North Middleborough, Mass. He worked as a clerk in Boston before he moved to Baltimore (1831). He ran a wholesale iron establishment for many years and was a leader of the Maryland Steamboat Company (1872–92). He also engaged in banking and insurance. He supported the (unpopular) Union cause in Baltimore during the Civil War. He used his wealth to support many causes, including the improvement of conditions of African-Americans, but his most notable benefaction was establishing the Enoch Pratt Free Library in Baltimore. Andrew Carnegie later said he was influenced by Pratt's example of branch libraries.

Pratt, Francis Asbury (1827–1902) inventor; born in Woodstock, Vt. He was an apprentice, journeyman, and finally a contractor in the machinist trade. He met Amos Whitney at the Colt armory in Hartford, Conn. (1852), and the two did machine work together and then formed Pratt & Whitney (1865). They made machine tools for making guns and sewing machines. He promoted the use of interchangeable parts and sold guns to many European nations (1865–75). He worked to establish a standard system of gauges and patented a number of important machine tools.

Pratt, Henry (Conger) (1882–1966) aviator; born in Fort Stanton, N.M. A 1904 West Point graduate, he served in the cavalry and transferred to the air service in 1920. As commander of the Air Corps Tactical School from 1936–38, Pratt trained hundreds of aviators who would serve during World War II. He held several defense commands in the U.S.A. and Caribbean during the war.

Pratt, Matthew (1734–1805) painter; born in Philadelphia.

Based in Philadelphia, he painted portraits there in 1758. He studied under Benjamin West in London (1764–66), worked in England (1766–68), and visited England and Ireland (1770). His most famous painting *The American School* (1765), depicts artists in West's studio.

Preble, Edward (1761–1807) naval officer; born in Falmouth (now Portland), Maine. He commanded the Tripoli squadron against the Barbary pirates (1803–04) and authorized the burning of the captured USS *Philadelphia*. He had virtually defeated the Tripolitans when he was replaced in 1804. He had created the first working tactical naval squadron and was a hero to many young officers who later distinguished themselves in the War of 1812.

Prelutsky, Jack (1940–) writer; born in New York City. He attended Hunter College and studied voice at various music schools. He worked as a taxi driver, actor, singer, sculptor, laborer, and carpenter, among other jobs, before becoming a popular poet and storyteller for young readers. His imaginative books have caused controversy at times due to their subject matter, but readers continue to enjoy such works as *Nightmares: Poems to Trouble Your Sleep* (1976), and *The Baby Uggs Are Hatching* (1982). He lived in Olympia, Wash.

Preminger, Otto (1906–86) movie director/producer; born in Vienna, Austria. He abandoned a career as a lawyer to act and work in the theater with Max Reinhardt, and he directed his first movie in 1931. Coming to the U.S.A. in 1933 to direct *Libel* on Broadway, he moved to Hollywood but quarreled with Darryl Zanuck, who prevented him from directing movies. During World War II, with Zanuck away, he got both to act (playing Nazis, although Jewish himself) and direct in three movies and then was allowed to produce and direct *Laura* (1944), which was a big success. In the early 1950s he became an independent producer/director and enjoyed considerable success with such movies as *Anatomy of a Murder* (1959) and *Exodus* (1960). Although most of his movies were simply popular entertainment, his *The Moon is Blue* (1953) broke new ground with its use of what was then regarded as sexually explicit language ("virgin" and "pregnant") while *The Man with the Golden Arm* (1957) was the first Hollywood movie to deal so explicitly with drug addiction.

Prendergast, Maurice (Brazil) (1859–1924) painter; born in St. John's, Newfoundland, Canada. He arrived in Boston (1861) and was apprenticed to a show-card painter when young. Later he studied at the Académie Julien, Paris (1891–95), and returned to Boston where he set up an art studio (1897). He made sporadic trips to Europe as his reputation as an artist grew, and was a member of the Eight (1908), although his water colors and oils didn't reflect the harsh realism of some of the other members of the group. He experimented with style, but his work always had an impressionistic vitality, as in *Central Park* (1900). He lived above the studio of William Glackens in New York (1914–24).

Prescott, Samuel Cate (1872–1962) food scientist; born in South Hampton, N.H. At the Massachusetts Institute of Technology (MIT) (1895), he worked with William Lyman Underwood to understand the scientific basis for canning food. He also led the crusade for sanitary milk and was a major in the Army Sanitary Corps during World War I. As Dean of the School of Science at MIT (1932–42), he helped break down barriers between the sciences to make interdisciplinary studies, like food science, possible. He was the first president of the Institute of Food Technology (1939–41).

Prescott, William H. (Hickling) (1796–1859) historian; born in Salem, Mass. Descended from a prominent and wealthy New England family, he was blinded in the left eye (when hit by a crust of bread thrown by a fellow student) at Harvard College and his right eye was then weakened by inflammation. After touring Europe (1815–17), he was determined to pursue a career of research and writing; he utilized assistants who read to him and a noctograph that guided his hand while he took notes. His *History of the Reign of Ferdinand and Isabella the Catholic* (1837; 1838 on title page) was followed by his *History of the Conquest of Mexico* (three vols. 1843), and his *History of the Conquest of Peru* (1847) gained him an international public for his dramatic narratives; on a visit to England in 1850 he was treated like a celebrity. He died having published only three out of his projected ten-volume work on the reign of King Philip the Second of Spain. Although historians since his day have inevitably come up with much new data, his general themes and insights have generally held up.

Presley, Elvis (Aaron, orig. Aron) (1935–77) popular singer, movie actor; born in Tupelo, Miss. An only child (a twin brother was stillborn), he was raised in a religious home. As a boy he sang with his local Assembly of God church choir, which emulated the style of African-American psalm singing. At age ten he won a school singing contest and taught himself the rudiments of the guitar (although he never really could read music). In 1948 he moved with his family to Memphis, Tenn., where he graduated from high school in 1953 and began working as a truck driver and studying evenings to be an electrician. Later that year he made a private recording for his mother at the Memphis Sound Studio, where he attracted the attention of proprietor Sam Phillips, who also operated Sun Records, a fledgling blues label. In July 1954 Phillips had Presley record his first single, "That's All Right, Mama" and "Blue Moon of Kentucky," a synthesis of rhythm-and-blues and country-and-western that was for awhile described as "rockabilly." The record made an immediate impression on local listeners, who were bewildered to learn that Presley was white, but their enthusiasm for his style of dress, bodily movements, and music signaled the beginnings of rock 'n' roll. He toured the South as the Hillbilly Cat and performed on a Shreveport, La., radio station, and after releasing his first national hit on Sun Records, he moved to RCA Records under the tutelage of his ambitious personal manager, "Colonel" Tom Parker. His first national television appearance was actually in 1955 on Jackie Gleason's *Stage Show,* but it was his 1956 appearance on Ed Sullivan's *Talk of the Town* that made him a national sensation: his pelvic gyrations were considered so scandalous that he was shown only from the waist up. That same year he released his first million-selling single, "Heartbreak Hotel," and starred in *Love Me Tender,* the first of 33 relatively bland movies he eventually made. He was forced to interrupt his career while serving in the U.S. Army (1958–60) but he returned to his recording and movie careers with undimmed success and solidified what became virtually an industry. He scored his last chart-topping single in 1969 but in 1973 his television special, "Elvis: Aloha from Hawaii," was broadcast to a potential worldwide audience of over a billion

people and he carved out a new career as a flashy nightclub performer even as he broadened his repertoire to include traditional and religious songs. In 1973, following his divorce from his wife Priscilla Presley, he became increasingly drug-dependent and overweight, and he spent his last years living reclusively at his Memphis home, Graceland. His death at age 42 shocked his many admirers, who have never given up on the music, mementoes, and memory of the man they regard as "the King of rock 'n' roll."

Press, Frank (1924–   ) seismologist, governnment science adviser; born in New York City. He held faculty positions at Columbia University (1949–55), the California Institute of Technology (1955–65), and the Massachusetts Institute of Technology (1965–77); he was president of the National Academy of Science from 1981. As director of the California Institute of Technology's seismological laboratory, Press and his colleagues first identified the "free oscillations" of the earth – the persistent global vibrations arising from earthquakes and other geological disturbances. During his service on the International Geophysical Year glaciology and seismology panel (1955–59), he helped determine the thickness of the earth's North American crust, while his polar research confirmed Antarctica to be a true continent. He was a consultant for the National Aeronautics and Space Administration, the U.S. military, and the State and Defense Departments; a delegate to the Nuclear Test Ban Conference in Geneva; a member of the President's Science Advisory Committee (1961–64); and director of the U.S. Office of Science and Technology Policy (1977–81).

Presser, Theodore (1848–1925) music publisher, philanthropist; born in Pittsburgh, Pa. After studying music at the New England Conservatory in Boston and then in Leipzig, in 1883 he founded a monthly musical magazine, *Etude* (which ran until 1957). That same year he founded a music publishing firm that grew to become one of the major American publishers of a wide spectrum of serious music. Prospering early, he founded in Philadelphia the Presser Home for Retired Musicians and in 1916 the Presser Foundation for support of various music-related causes.

Preston, Andrew W. (Woodbury) (1846–1924) fruit producer, merchant; born in Beverly, Mass. He worked in a shoemaking factory before he began selling fruit and produce in 1870. In 1882 he established the Boston Fruit Company to import bananas with nine other investors. Incorporated in 1887 with Preston as general manager, it merged with the United Fruit Company (UFC) in 1899, with Preston as president until 1924. In the 1890s he bought vast acres of Caribbean land, which he turned into banana plantations, and created a distribution network that included a fleet of refrigerated steamers. His company grew into a huge conglomerate with hotels, schools, hospitals, and other amenities for its employees as well as a communication and a transportation system, agricultural research facilities, and subsidiaries in England and France. The largest landowner in several Latin American countries – including 89,000 acres of sugar cane in Cuba – UFC wielded a significant influence on the governments of those countries. Preston was also a director of a number of banks and other companies such as the First National Bank of Boston and the U.S. Smelting, Refining and Mining Company.

Preston, Ann (1813–72) physician; born in Westgrove, Pa. She was raised in a Quaker family who were antislavery and pro-women's rights and she briefly attended Quaker schools, but she had to help raise her siblings and to educate herself by reading and attending public lectures. After some teaching of physiology and hygiene to local women and girls in the early 1840s, she became a medical apprentice in 1847 and eventually became a member of the first class to graduate from the Female (later Women's) Medical College of Pennsylvania (1851), becoming a professor there in 1853. When the Philadelphia doctors refused to let the new female doctors gain access to the hospitals, she helped found Women's Hospital of Philadelphia in 1861. In 1866 she became dean of the Women's Medical College and she gradually won acceptance for female physicians in Philadelphia, although she had to fight opposition constantly. As both teacher and administrator, she remained with the hospital and medical college until her death.

Preston, Lewis Thompson (1926–   ) banker; born in New York City. He joined J. P. Morgan & Co. (later Morgan Guaranty Trust) after graduating from Harvard in 1951, and rose through the ranks to become president (1978–80) and chairman and chief executive officer (1980–89), before taking charge of the International Bank for Reconstruction and Development in Washington, D.C.

Preston, William Campbell (1794–1860) U.S. senator; born in Philadelphia, Pa. Elected to the U.S. Senate (Dem., S.C.; 1833–42), he supported states' rights and slavery. He resigned from the Senate and switched to the Whigs. He became president of the College of South Carolina (1845–51).

Prestopino, Gregorio (1907–84) painter; born in New York City. Based in New York, he studied at the National Academy of Design. He used social themes painted in an expressionist style, as in his *Harlem* series (1957), which became an award-winning Cannes Film Festival film, *Harlem Wednesday* (1958).

Preuss, Arthur (1871–1934) Catholic writer; born in St. Louis, Mo. An important voice in the German-American Catholic community, he launched the *Catholic Review* (later, *Catholic Fortnightly Review*) (1894) and from 1896 was literary editor of B. Herder, a German Catholic publishing company. He wrote widely for the Catholic press and translated theological works from German.

Previn, André (1929–   ) conductor, composer; born in Berlin, Germany. After studying music in Berlin and Paris, he fled the Nazis with his Russian-Jewish family, who went to Los Angeles where his great-uncle was musical director at Universal Studios. He continued to study music, played jazz piano, and began to work as an orchestrator and composer for Metro-Goldwyn-Mayer. During his army service in 1950, he began to study conducting with Pierre Monteux and made his debut with the St. Louis Symphony in 1963. He went on to become conductor of various orchestras – Houston, London, Pittsburgh, the Royal Philharmonic, and, in 1986, the Los Angeles Philharmonic. In addition to Oscar-winning film scores, he composed musicals (such as *Coco,* (1969) and concert works; he also continued to play jazz and was an articulate promoter of all types of music.

Pribram, Karl (1919–73) neuropsychologist; born in Vienna, Austria. His family came to the United States in 1925, and he studied medicine at the University of Chicago under neurologist and brain surgeon Percival Bailey. He turned from the private practice of brain surgery to research (1948) after working with Karl Lashley at the Yerkes Laboratories in Orange Park, Fla. At Yale (to 1958) and at Stanford University (1958–73) he did valuable research on cerebral function.

Price, Gwilym A. (Alexander) (1895–1985) corporate executive; born in Canonsburg, Pa. Trained as a lawyer, he was briefly president of the Peoples-Pittsburgh Trust Company before becoming president and CEO (1946–60) and chairman (1960–63) of Westinghouse Electric Corporation. His tenure at Westinghouse was marked by the company's pioneering work on atomic energy.

Price, (Mary Violet) Leontyne (1927–   ) soprano; born in Laurel, Miss. Price studied at Juilliard in New York before finding success on Broadway in *Four Saints in Three Acts* in 1952 and the female lead in *Porgy and Bess* the same year. In 1954 she presented a recital in New York's Town Hall, where she premiered Samuel Barber's *Hermit Songs*. She went on to an outstanding international career on both operatic and concert stages, especially admired for her Italian opera roles; her Metropolitan Opera debut came in 1961. For a time she was married to baritone William Warfield.

Price, (Samuel Blythe) Sammy (1908–92) jazz musician; born in Honey Grove, Texas. He was a versatile pianist, singer, and dancer who began his career with Alphonso Trent from 1927 to 1930 and served as house pianist for Decca Records between 1938 and 1950. Thereafter he freelanced in music while becoming active in Harlem politics and various business ventures.

Price, Thomas Frederick (1860–1919) Catholic missionary; born in Wilmington, N.C. Ordained in 1886, he preached missions and edited a magazine of apologetics. In 1910 he met Father James Walsh, with whom he founded the Maryknoll Foreign Mission Society (1911). In 1918 he went to China with the first group of Maryknoll missionaries; he died of appendicitis the next year.

Pride, Charley (1938–   ) country music singer; born in Sledge, Miss. Born into a family of poor cotton-pickers, he was drawn to country music as a youth, but he first tried a career in baseball. He made it to the minors in Helena, Mont., in 1960, but failed in a tryout with the California Angels. He had done some singing at a country music bar in Helena so he returned there; his singing in local clubs gained him an audition in Nashville, and by 1964 he was under contract with RCA. His first hit was "Snakes Crawl by Night" (1965), followed by "Just Between You and Me" (1966) and many others including "Did You Think to Pray" (1971). The first African-American to break into country music, he was introduced to the "Grand Ole Opry" in 1967 and went on to win many music awards. He toured and appeared on television in the 1970s and 1980s.

Pridham, Edwin S. (1881–1963) electrical engineer; born in Downers Grove, Ill. He cofounded the Commercial Wireless and Development Co. with Peter Jensen and Richard O'Connor (1911) and with Jensen he codeveloped the first dynamic horn loudspeaker. They named their speaker "Magnavox" and then their company became Magnavox. Pridham was chief engineer and remained with Magnavox throughout his career.

Priesand, Sally Jane (1946–   ) rabbi; born in Cleveland, Ohio. She earned a B.A. from the University of Cincinnati and an M.A. from Hebrew Union College in Cincinnati. She was ordained a Reform rabbi in 1972, the first woman to be so ordained in this country. She was named rabbi of Temple Beth El in Elizabeth, N.J., and went to the Monmouth Reform Temple, Tinton Falls, N.J., in 1981. Active in many civic and religious organizations, she wrote *Judaism and the New Woman* (1975).

Priest, James Percy (1900–56) U.S. representative; born in Carters Creek, Tenn. A schoolteacher (1920–26) and journalist (1926–40) before going to Congress (Dem., Tenn.; 1941–56), he served as majority whip (1945–47) and chaired the Interstate and Foreign Commerce Committee.

Priestley, Joseph (1733–1804) scientist, educator, Unitarian minister; born in Leeds, England. In 1794, already famous as a scientist, teacher, and dissident minister, he emigrated in search of religious freedom and because his defense of the French Revolution had made him so many enemies. Settling in Pennsylvania, he became an early promoter of Unitarianism in America. A pioneer in the physics of electricity and the chemistry of gasses, in America he concentrated on writing his theological works, notably *A General History of the Christian Church* (1789–1802), but he became a friend and supporter of Thomas Jefferson and the Democratic-Republicans.

Primakoff, Henry (1914–83) physicist; born in Odessa, Russia. He came to the U.S.A. in 1923, and taught and performed research at several New York City institutions. He then moved to Washington University, St. Louis (1946–60), and the University of Pennsylvania (1960–83). He was an inspirational educator who made major contributions to the physics of wave theory, cosmic rays, solid helium, and weak particle interactions. The "Primakoff effect" deals with the short lifespan of the meson, a subatomic particle.

Primus, Pearl (?1919–94) modern dancer, choreographer; born in Trinidad, British West Indies. Coming to the U.S.A. as a child, she took premed science courses at Hunter College in New York City, and fell into dancing almost by chance while looking for laboratory work in 1940. The first African-American accepted by the New Dance Group, she made her solo debut in 1944 to great critical acclaim. A powerful and dramatic dancer, she gave many performances based on West Indian and African dances, forming her own group with her husband, Percival Borde. She won a Rosenwald fellowship to study the dances of Africa (1948–51) and earned a Ph.D. in anthropology from Columbia University. She was the first director of the Liberian performing arts center (1959) and in the 1970s her works were presented by the Alvin Ailey American Dance Theater.

Prince (b. Prince Rogers Nelson) (1960–) rock singer, songwriter; born in Minneapolis, Minn. Defiantly basing himself in his hometown, he did not gain much of a following with his first albums from 1978 and 1979, but his popularity rose with *Dirty Mind* (1980). Subsequent albums include *Controversy* (1981) and *1999* (1983), with the hit "Little Red Corvette." In 1984 he starred in the movie *Purple Rain,* which yielded a Grammy Award-winning album and the hit "When Doves Cry." Subsequent movies did not do as well. After his North American tour in 1984, he withdrew again to work in Minneapolis, where he built expensive recording and film facilities.

Prince, (Harold Smith) Hal (1928–) theater producer, director; born in New York City. Along with his frequent associate, Stephen Sondheim, he was associated with some of Broadway's most successful musicals, winners of many awards. His shows include *Pajama Game* (1954), *West Side Story* (1957), *A Funny Thing Happened on the Way to the Forum* (1962), *Fiddler on the Roof* (1964), *A Little Night Music* (1973), and *Sweeney Todd* (1979).

Pringle, Henry Fowles (1897–1958) biographer, journalist; born in New York City. A muckraking reporter of the 1920s, he wrote a somewhat deflating Pulitzer Prize biography of Theodore Roosevelt (1931) and an ambitious two-volume biography of William Howard Taft (1939).

Pringle, Joel (Roberts Poinsett) (1873–1932) naval officer; born in Georgetown County, S.C. He served in the Spanish-American War and was the senior American officer at Queenstown, Ireland, during World War I (1917–19). He held several other naval appointments and died while serving as commander of the battleships, U.S. Fleet.

Printz, Johan Bjornsson (1592–1663) Swedish colonial governor; born in Bottnaryd, Sweden. After a successful career in the Swedish army, he was appointed the governor of New Sweden (in the Delaware River Valley) from 1642 to 1653. A giant of a man (some accounts say he weighed 400 lbs.), he was a talented and energetic leader, but his forceful manner caused a group of settlers to try to petition to Sweden regarding their grievances. He viewed this as rebellion, and hanged the leader of the movement, Anders Johnsson (1653). Soon afterward, he gave the government to his deputy and returned to Sweden.

Prior, William Matthew (1806–73) painter; born in Bath, Maine. An itinerant folk artist, he lived in Portland, Maine (1831–40), and worked throughout New England and in Baltimore, Md., before settling in Boston (1841). His skillful paintings, such as *Little Girl with Big Dog* (1848), are highly respected.

Prip, John (1922–) metalsmith; born in New York City. After study in Copenhagen, he returned to the U.S.A. (1948) to teach at Alfred University and Rhode Island School of Design (1963–80), while creating jewelry and tableware designs.

Pritchard, James Bennett (1909–) archaeologist; born in Louisville, Ky. His lifelong study of the Middle East included expeditions to Jericho (1951), el-Jib (1956–62), and Tell es-Sa'idiyeh, Jordan (1964–67), and yielded such publications as *The Ancient Near East* (2 vols. 1958–1975). He ended a long teaching career in the U.S.A. and the Middle East at the University of Pennsylvania (1962–78).

Pritchett, Henry (Smith) (1857–1939) foundation executive; born in Fayette, Mo. He was a German-trained astronomy professor who became president of the new Carnegie Foundation for the Advancement of Teaching (1905–30), where he established the principle of pensions for college teachers, set standards for secondary schools and colleges, and sponsored important studies on professional education, college athletics, and testing programs.

Pritchett, William Kendrick (1909–) classicist; born in Atlanta, Ga. He was educated at Johns Hopkins (Ph.D. 1942) and taught at the University of California: Berkeley (1948–76). He was an expert on Greek epigraphy (the study of inscriptions), warfare, and topography, and his publications include *Studies in Greek Topography I–IV* (1965, 1969, 1980, 1982), *The Greek State at War I–III* (1974; 1979) and *Ancient Greek Military Practices* (1971).

Pritzker, A. N. (Abram Nicholas) (1896–1986) hotel executive; born in Chicago. He worked for his father's Chicago law firm until 1936. With his brother Jack Pritzker (1904–79), he founded the Marmon Group, a family-owned corporate empire that came to include, among other companies, the Hyatt Hotels, Braniff Airlines, and *McCall's* magazine. A noted philanthropist, he funded the University of Chicago's Pritzker School of Medicine.

Pritzker, Jay (Arthur) (1922–) entrepreneur, conglomerate organizer; born in Chicago (son of Abram Nicholas Pritzker). Trained as a lawyer, he early diversified the Chicago-based family business, the Marmon Group, into lumber, and with his engineer brother, Robert Pritzker (1926–), he built a portfolio of 60 diversified industrial corporations. He created the Hyatt Hotel chain (1957) with his brother Donald Pritzker (1932–72) and owned Braniff Airlines (1983–88). In 1979 he established the Pritzker Prize, a $100,000 prize awarded annually to living architects for their career work.

Procter, William C. (Cooper) (1862–1934) manufacturer; born in Glendale, Ohio. He lived in Cincinnati his entire life and joined the family soap-making firm founded by his father, William Alexander. Introduced in 1879, Ivory Soap became the most famous product with the advertising slogan "It floats" and "99 44/100 per cent pure." In 1890 the firm Procter & Gamble incorporated with William C. as general manager and the company boomed. (It was William C.'s brother Harley Procter, however, who is credited with devising the advertising and marketing campaigns that would make Ivory Soap the leader in its field.) By 1934 it counted seven factories, including locations in England and Canada. William C., who became president in 1907, instituted many labor reforms, such as half holidays on Saturdays (1887), profit sharing, and pensions. In 1923 the company guaranteed 48 hours of work a week to all employees. Active in Cincinnati civic affairs, his main philanthropies were hospitals and schools, especially Children's Hospital.

Proctor, Alexander Phimister (1862–1950) sculptor; born in Bozanquit, Ontario, Canada. He studied in New York City at the National Academy of Design and the Art Students League (1887), worked with Augustus Saint-Gaudens (1894), and lived in Connecticut and the western states. He was known for his Western subjects, such as *Bronco Buster* (1918).

Proctor, Bernard Emerson (1901–59) biochemist; born in Malden, Mass. He joined the faculty of the Massachusetts Institute of Technology in 1926 and chaired the department of food technology from 1952 until his death. In the late 1940s he began studying the use of radiation to preserve food. He consulted for the U.S. Public Health Service in 1951 and wrote many papers including four on the microbiology of the upper atmosphere. In 1937 he coauthored *Food Technology*.

Professor Longhair (pseudonym of Henry Roeland Byrd) (1918–80) blues musician; born in Bogalusa, La. As a pianist and singer, he was an innovator of postwar New Orleans rhythm-and-blues. He worked outside music as a stuntman, dancer, boxer, and gambler until 1947, when he formed his first band. In 1949, he made several recordings in his prototypical style, but performed only sporadically for the next two decades. In 1971, his appearances at major festivals in New York and New Orleans led to a renewal of touring and recording activity, which he maintained until his death.

Progoff, Ira (1921–) psychologist; born in New York City.

Educated at the New School for Social Research (Ph.D. 1951), he taught there before joining Drew University (N.J.) (1959) as director of the Institute for Research in Depth Psychology. A humanistic psychologist, he created "process meditation" and "intensive journaling" as methods of spiritual growth. His books include *Life-Study: Experiencing Creative Lives by the Intensive Journal Method* (1983).

Proskouriakoff, Tatiana (Avenirovna) (1909–85) archaeologist, illustrator; born in Tomsk, Russia. A childhood immigrant to the U.S.A., she trained as an architect, and, starting out as an archaeological illustrator, became a pioneer scholar of Maya culture, making outstanding contributions on Maya hieroglyphics and monuments. She held posts at the Carnegie Institution (1939) and Harvard's Peabody Museum (1958–77). She won the 1962 Kidder Medal.

Prosser, Gabriel (?1775–1800) slave insurrectionist; probably born in Henrico County, Va. Other than being a coachman belonging to Thomas Prosser of Henrico County, Va., little was known of his early life and how he came to plan a major slave revolt (1800). Richmond, Va., the state capital, where slaves outweighed whites four-to-one, was chosen as the site of the rebellion. He planned to kill all slave owners, but spare the French and Quaker inhabitants he felt were sympathetic to the black cause, along with women and children. He hoped the remaining 300,000 slaves in Virginia would follow his lead and take over the state. A severe rainstorm the night of the uprising cut off bridges and roads; Prosser and about 1,000 followers were prevented from reaching Richmond, and two house slaves, loyal to their master, informed on the conspirators. Panic swept Richmond, martial law was declared, and some 34 slaves implicated in the conspiracy were rounded up and hanged. Prosser was captured in the hold of the schooner *Mary* when it docked at Norfolk. Brought back to Richmond in chains, he was interrogated by Governor James Monroe, but refused to divulge any information on the conspiracy. He was hanged on October 7, 1800.

Prosser, William Lloyd (1898–) legal scholar; born in New Albany, Ind. A Harvard graduate, he earned a law degree at the University of Minnesota. He was a member of the law faculties of the University of Minnesota (1929–42) and Harvard (1947–48) before becoming dean of the law school at the University of California: Berkeley (1948–63). He published books on torts.

Proxmire, (Edward) William (1915–) U.S. senator; born in Lake Forest, Ill. During his long career in the U.S. Senate (Dem., Wis.; 1957–89), he was considered a maverick politician. He served as chairman of the Committee on Banking as well as chairman of the Committee of Housing and Urban Affairs. He was known as an opponent of wasteful government spending and as a "hawk" during the Vietnam War.

Prudden, T. (Theophil) Mitchell (1849–1924) pathologist; born in Middlebury, Conn. After graduating from Yale Medical School, he continued his medical studies in Europe. As a professor of the College of Physicians and Surgeons in New York City, he was the first American to make the diphtheria antitoxin, used to check an epidemic. In 1901 he became a scientific director of the Rockefeller Institute. He coauthored the *Handbook of Pathological Anatomy and*

Histology (1885), and, an avid amateur paleontologist, wrote *On the Great American Plateau* (1906).

Prudhomme, Paul (1940–) chef; born in Opelousas, La. The youngest of 13 children, he began cooking with his mother by age seven. In his early teens he set off on a 12-year apprenticeship with chefs around the U.S.A., then returned to Louisiana and started the first of several restaurants, Big Daddy's Patio. In 1979, he and his wife, K Hinrichs Prudhomme, opened K-Paul's Louisiana Kitchen in New Orleans, which soon became widely known for both its traditional cajun and creole cooking and his own innovations (such as blackened fish and meats). He himself became internationally honored as one of America's greatest chefs, a reputation furthered through his ebullient personality, and his frequent television appearances, cooking videos, best-selling cookbooks (such as *Paul Prudhomme's Louisiana Kitchen,* 1984), many awards, benefit and fundraising efforts, and invitations to cook at various functions including the 1983 Economic Summit Meeting at Williamsburg, Va. He also marketed his line of Magic Seasoning Blends and seasoned and smoked meats.

Pryor, Richard (1940–) comedian; born in Peoria, Ill. He worked in small clubs before being discovered by Johnny Carson in 1966. He appeared in Las Vegas and in films including *The Lady Sings the Blues* (1972) and *Uptown Saturday Night* (1974). With his expressive face, speedy wit, and raunchy language, he created a variety of characters on stage and screen, but his drug addiction derailed his career; he retired in the late 1980s. He developed multiple sclerosis.

Pryor, Roger Atkinson (1829–1919) U.S. representative; born in Petersburg, Va. A journalist (1852–59), he served in Congress (Dem., Va.; 1859–61), resigning to join the Confederate army. He later was a lawyer and judge (1866–1919) in New York City.

Puente, (Ernesto Antonio) Tito (1920–) bandleader, percussionist, composer; born in New York City. Of Puerto Rican parentage, he served in World War II and then studied at Juilliard. In 1947 he formed what became the Tito Puente Orchestra and became a leader of the mambo and cha-cha-cha fads in the 1950s. From the 1960s to the 1980s he made over 40 albums, some fusing Latin with other musical styles and traditions. He left his big band in 1980 and moved into more jazzlike music with a smaller ensemble, performing at the Monterey Jazz Festival in 1984. But he continued to be popular as North America's grand old man of Latin American music and appeared as himself in the movie, *The Mambo Kings* (1992).

Pulitzer, Joseph (1847–1911) publisher; born in Mako, Hungary. Arriving in the U.S.A. in 1864 to fight in the Union army, he then won such prominence as a reporter for a German-language daily paper in St. Louis, Mo., that he was nominated and elected to the state legislature at age 22. After studying law and joining the bar, he turned again to journalism, acquiring the *St. Louis Dispatch* and merging it with the *Post;* the crusading paper won a solid reputation and wide readership. In 1883 he purchased the *New York World;* in it he combined intelligent, crusading editorials with coverage that grew increasingly sensational as Pulitzer, plagued by nervous and physical disorders, including encroaching blindness, sought to compete with William Randolph Hearst's *Journal.* In his last years, Pulitzer began molding the *World* into a respected paper, and he provided in his will for establishing the Columbia School of Journalism and the Pulitzer Prizes.

Puller, Lewis (Burwell) (1898–1971) marine officer; born in West Point, Va. Noted for his tactical skill and his bravery under fire, "Chesty" Puller personified the tough, hard-driving marine combat commander. His father, a wholesale grocer, died when the boy was ten; he hunted, trapped and fished to help support the family before enlisting in 1918. He served in the Haitian constabulary from 1919 to 1924, and fought guerrillas in Nicaragua from 1928 to 1933. Given command of a batallion in the Seventh Marine Regiment shortly before the outbreak of World War II, he led the unit in a brilliant defense of Henderson Field on Guadalcanal Island in 1942. In 1950, as commander of the First Marine Regiment, he led the seaborne assault on Inchon in Korea, participated in the drive to the Yalu River, and commanded the rear guard in the subsequent retreat from the Chosin Reservoir.

Pullman, George Mortimer (1831–97) inventor, businessman; born in Brocton, N.Y. He spent 1848–55 working with his brother, a cabinetmaker in Albion, N.Y., before moving to Chicago. In 1858 he remodeled two of the day coaches of the Chicago & Alton Railroad into sleepers, a long-time dream of his. He remodeled a third in 1859. The three cars were popular with travelers but not with the railroads, so Pullman left for Colorado, ran a general store (1859–63), and continued revising his plans for sleeper cars. Back in Chicago (1864) he and friend Ben Field patented the folding upper berth, and built their first sleeping car, *Pioneer* (1865); its success led to their starting the Pullman Palace Car Company (1867). Other cars designed and built by Pullman and Field included a dining car (1868), the parlor car (1875), and the vestibule car (1887). Pullman plants were located in several cities, with headquarters in Pullman, Ill., a town built expressly for his employees (1881). (It is now part of Chicago.) For many years the Pullman Company built, staffed, and operated most of the sleeping cars on U.S. railroads and his cars were adopted by many railroads throughout the world.

Pumpelly, Raphael (1837–1923) geologist; born in Owego, N.Y. He expanded his childhood interest in geology by studies and travels in Europe (1854–60). He investigated Arizona's silver mines (1860), then embarked on frequently hazardous geological expeditions to eastern Asia (1861–65). He taught mining at Harvard (1866–73) while concurrently exploring Lake Superior mineral deposits (1866–77). After directing various geological surveys (1879–90), Pumpelly investigated the geology and archaeology of central Asia (1903–04). He made major contributions to the fields of coal and mineral mining, glaciology, and rock disintegration.

Pupin, Michael (Idvorsky) (1858–1935) physicist, inventor; born in Idvor, Austria-Hungary. Of Serbian parentage, he landed penniless in New York in 1874; supporting himself by doing odd jobs, he managed to graduate from Columbia University nine years later. After study in Europe, he returned to become a professor of electromechanics at Columbia (1901–31). Among his inventions were the fluoroscope, by which X-rays can be observed and photographed, and the Pupin inductance coil, which made long-distance telephone service possible by amplifying the signal at intervals along the line. He remained interested in Serbian affairs, and in 1919 he served as an adviser to the

Yugoslav delegation to the Paris Peace Conference. In addition to his scientific writings, he published such books as *The Serbian Orthodox Church* (1918), and his autobiography, *From Immigrant to Inventor,* won a Pulitzer Prize in 1924.

Purcell, Edward M. (Mills) (1912–) physicist; born in Taylorville, Ill. He taught at Harvard (1938–40), was a group leader at the Massachusetts Institute of Technology's Radiation Laboratory (1941–45), then returned to Harvard (1946–80). He was awarded the 1952 Nobel Prize in physics (with Felix Bloch) for his work on the magnetic moments of atomic nuclei, then continued applying nuclear magnetic resonance to help develop the radio telescope.

Purcell, John (Baptist) (1800–83) Catholic prelate; born in Mallow, Ireland. As bishop (from 1833) and archbishop (from 1850) of Cincinnati, he presided over a period of tremendous growth. A temperance advocate and opponent of ethnic parishes, he resigned because of an 1879 diocesan financial scandal, in which he, however, was not implicated.

Purdy, James (Amos) (1923–) writer; born in Ohio. He studied at the Universities of Chicago and Puebla, Mexico. He taught at Lawrence College (Wisc.) (1949–53), worked as an interpreter in France, Spain, and Latin America, and maintained a home in Brooklyn, N.Y. After early failures at being published in America, he was aided by Dame Edith Sitwell and his career was launched in England. He is known for his satiric novels, such as *Malcolm* (1959), as well as for short stories, poetry, and plays.

Pursh, Frederick (1774–1820) botanist, explorer; born in Grossenhain, Saxony. He came to the U.S.A. in 1799 and managed a botanical garden near Philadelphia (1802–05). He undertook two botanical explorations of the territory from North Carolina to Vermont (1806, 1807). He wrote *Flora Americae Septentrionalis* (1814) which included many new species discovered by Lewis and Clark and was the most complete account to that time of the flora of the United States.

Puryear, Martin (1941–) sculptor; born in Chicago. He studied at Catholic University of America (B.A. 1963), Yale (M.F.A. 1971), and taught at the University of Illinois at Chicago Circle (1970, 1978–88). He is known for his work in exotic woods and architectural wall pieces. Although he spoke out on behalf of his fellow African-Americans, his early work at least aimed for an abstract purity rather than social realism.

Pushmataha (?1764–1824) Choctaw chief of the Kinsahahi Clan; born at Noxubee Creek in present-day Mississippi. Elected principal chief of the Choctaw in 1805, he urged peace with and ceded much tribal land to the U.S.A. He opposed Tecumseh's attempts to form a confederacy of Indian tribes and he fought for the U.S.A. in the War of 1812. As a chief he invested money in education based on methods of European settlers.

Putnam, Frederic Ward (1839–1915) archaeologist, naturalist; born in Salem, Mass. He studied zoology with Louis Agassiz at Harvard and became interested in archaeology as a curator at Harvard's Peabody Museum (1875–1909), one of numerous museum affiliations that included the Essex Institute (1856–94) and the American Museum of Natural History (1894–1909). Author, pioneering excavator of Indian sites, and Harvard professor (1886–1909), he virtually founded North American anthropology by developing univer-

sity programs, initiating museum-sponsored excavations, and helping to found Chicago's Field Museum of Natural History.

Putnam, George Haven (1844–1930) publisher, writer; born in London, England. Emigrating as a child, he capably succeeded his father, George Palmer Putnam, as president of G. P. Putnam & Son in 1872. In 1896 he organized the International Copyright League to lobby for copyright legislation. His own writings included several volumes on the Civil War and a popular children's book, *The Little Gingerbread Man* (1910).

Putnam, George Palmer (1814–72) publisher; born in Brunswick, Maine. In 1866, having operated an agency to sell American books in London, and having published his own magazine, *Palmer's Monthly Magazine,* he started the firm that became G. P. Putnam & Son, known for its high literary standards. He fought energetically for reforms in copyright law.

Putnam, Herbert (1861–1955) librarian; born in New York City. As Librarian of Congress (1899–1939), he instituted the Library of Congress classification scheme and preprinted index cards.

Putnam, Hilary (1926–) philosopher, logician; born in Chicago. He earned a doctorate from the University of California: Los Angeles (1951), and after teaching at Rockefeller University (1951–52), Northwestern (1952–53), Princeton (1953–61), and the Massachusetts Institute of Technology (1961–65), he became a professor at Harvard (1965). A prominent analytic philosopher, he dealt with both technical problems and broader questions; his works include *Mind, Language, and Reality* (1965).

Putnam, Israel (1718–90) soldier; born in Salem Village (now Danvers), Mass. A veteran of service with Connecticut militia during the French and Indian War, he became an early opponent of British rule. Appointed major general of Continental forces (1775), Putnam fought at Bunker Hill but proved unequal to subsequent command responsibilities. A paralytic stroke forced his retirement from the army in 1779.

Putnam, Rufus (1738–1824) soldier, Ohio pioneer; born in Sutton, Mass. After serving in the French and Indian War and the American Revolution, he became superintendent of the Ohio Company. He was surveyor general of the U.S.A. (1796–1803) and an influential figure in Ohio until his death.

Puzo, Mario (1920–) writer; born in New York City. He served in the army during World War II, and studied writing at the New School for Social Research and Columbia University during the late 1940s and early 1950s. He worked at a variety of jobs and wrote serious but unsuccessful fiction until he became famous as the author of *The Godfather* (1969). He also wrote the subsequent screen adaptation of his novel (1972). Based on Long Island, N.Y., he wrote several other novels and additional screenplays.

Pyle, Ernie (Ernest Taylor) (1900–45) journalist; born near Dana, Ind. Leaving college to become a reporter for the *La Porte (Ind.) Herald,* he held various other jobs, including that of managing editor of the *Washington (D.C.) News.* In the late 1930s he devoted himself to reporting, especially as a correspondent in Latin America. During World War II he accompanied Allied forces in the invasions of North Africa, Italy, and Normandy, and reported from the front lines with personal stories of soldiers and their lives. His reports, collected in *Here Is Your War* (1943) and *Brave Men* (1944), won great popularity and earned him a Pulitzer Prize. Pyle was killed by Japanese gunfire during the U.S. landing on Okinawa and became a national hero.

Pyle, Howard (1853–1911) illustrator, teacher; born in Wilmington, Del. He studied in Philadelphia (1869–72), illustrated historical events and characters for major publishers and periodicals, established a studio in New York (1876–80), returned to Wilmington (1880), and established the Brandywine School (1900). His pupils included Maxfield Parrish and N. C. Wyeth.

Pyles, Thomas (1905–80) philologist; born in Frederick, Md. He graduated from the University of Maryland in 1926 (M.A. 1927) and received a Ph.D. from Johns Hopkins University in 1938. He taught English at the Universities of Maryland (1927–44), Oklahoma (1944–48), Florida (1948–66), and at Northwestern University (1966–71). An authority on English language and usage, he was the author of several books on language, including *The Origins and Development of the English Language* (1964, later editions revised by John Algeo) and *Words and Ways of American English* (1952). He also served as an adviser to several of the major dictionary publishers in the U.S.A.

Pynchon, Thomas (Ruggles, Jr.) (1937–) writer; born in Glen Cove, N.Y. He studied at Cornell (B.A. 1958), lived in Greenwich Village for a year, and worked on the house publication of Boeing Aircraft (Seattle, Wash.). He moved to Mexico while finishing his first novel, *V.* (1963), and later settled in California. An intensely private writer, he refused to be interviewed or photographed. He is best known for his novel, *Gravity's Rainbow* (1973), an ingenious examination of language and an attempt to organize the ideas and systems of modern life. A collection of short stories, *Slow Learner* (1984), has also been published.

Pynchon, William (c. 1590–1662) trader, colonist; born in England. Emigrating to the Massachusetts Bay Colony in 1630, he would add to his wealth in the New World by fur trading and land dealing. In 1635 he was appointed as one of the commissioners to govern a new settlement at present-day Springfield, Mass. He served as a magistrate of Connecticut from 1636 to 1637, but following a conflict with Thomas Hooker, he supported the claims of the Bay colony to Springfield. From 1638 to 1652 he practically governed Springfield and he increased his already considerable wealth.

Q

Quanah (also known as Parker Quanah) (?1845–1911) Comanche leader; born at Cedar Lake, Texas. He was the son of a Comanche chief and Cynthia Ann Parker, a captive white woman (taken back by whites in 1860). He grew up to become a bold warrior and in 1867 was made war chief of the Comanche. For the next eight years he led an alliance of various tribes in raids against frontier settlements in Texas. After finally surrendering in 1875, he quickly accommodated himself to the white culture by learning Spanish and English, adopting new agricultural methods, and promoting education for his fellow Indians. He himself prospered as both a farmer and the managing agent for business deals between whites and Indian tribes – he was reputed in later years to be the wealthiest Native American in North America – but he also created wealth for fellow Indians by getting them to lease surplus tribal lands to white cattlemen. In 1886 he became a judge of the Court of Indian Affairs; by 1890 he was principal chief of all Comanche bands; he was also a major figure in the peyote religion. He rode beside Geronimo in the inaugural parade of President Theodore Roosevelt (1905).

Quantrill, William (Clarke) (1836–65) guerrilla chief, bandit; born in Canal Dover, Ohio. He had been living on the frontier as a gambler and thief, and after settling in Kansas (c. 1857), he exploited the disturbance between proponents of slavery and free soil. When the Civil War broke out, he formed a group of irregulars, known as Quantrill's Raiders, that robbed mail coaches, fought skirmishes, and attacked Union communities – the most notorious raid being the massacre of some 150 free-soilers in Lawrence, Kans., in August 1863. As the war was ending, he set out for Washington, D.C., evidently to assassinate President Lincoln, but Federal troops mortally wounded him in Kentucky.

Quayle, (James Danforth) Dan (1947–   ) vice-president, senator; born in Indianapolis, Ind. Born into an influential newspaper-owning family, he was elected to the U.S. Senate in 1981 and became George Bush's vice-president in 1989. Generally conceded to have been selected because of his standing with conservatives, he was ridiculed by opponents and some journalists for a series of alleged gaffes betraying ignorance and immaturity, but defended by others who applauded his endorsement of "family values."

Queen, Ellery See DANNAY, FREDERIC.

Quesada, Elwood (Richard) (1904–93) aviator; born in Washington, D.C. He enlisted in the army in 1924 and received a commission after completing flight training the following year. Among other assignments in the 1930s, he flew as chief pilot on the New York-Cleveland airmail run. During World War II, he commanded the Ninth Fighter Command in England (1943), and, as head of the Ninth Tactical Air Command, he directed thousands of sorties in preparation for the Allied landings in Normandy of June 6, 1944. Quesada retired from the service in 1951. In 1959 he became the first head of the newly formed Federal Aviation Administration, and from 1961 to 1962 he was president of the company that owned the Washington Senators baseball team.

Quidor, John (1801–81) painter; born in Tappan, N.Y. His family moved to New York City (c. 1811), he painted signs for fire coaches, and he studied with John Wesley Jarvis (c. 1814–22). He lived on a farm in Illinois (c. 1847), where he painted religious themes; later he moved to Jersey City. His work is surrealistic and based on the literary themes of James Fenimore Cooper and Washington Irving, as in *Ichabod Crane Pursued by the Headless Horseman* (c. 1828).

Quill, Michael J. (Joseph) (1905–66) labor leader; born in County Kerry, Ireland. He emigrated to the United States in 1926, where he worked on the New York subways. A founder of the Transport Workers Union (TWUA), he was elected its president (1935–66). He served three terms on the New York City Council (1937–39, 1943–47). In his later years he became a familiar "character" in New York City, known for his aggressive tactics and feisty manner on behalf of his union's members.

Quincy, Josiah (1772–1864) public official, university president; born in Braintree, Mass. He served four terms in the U.S. House of Representatives (Fed., Mass.; 1805–13), becoming the minority leader, but resigned following the American invasion of Canada. He returned to Boston and was elected to the state senate (1813–20). As six-term mayor of Boston (1823–29), he cleaned the streets, started work on water and sewer systems, separated paupers from criminals, prosecuted gambling and prostitution, filled pestilential tidal flats, and built the Faneuil Hall market. As president of Harvard University (1829–45), he improved food service and began calling students "Mr.," but occasional riots continued; he made notable appointments like Henry Wadsworth Longfellow and Benjamin Peirce; he greatly increased the faculty, endowment, and student body; and he wrote what became the standard history of Harvard, as well as other historical and cultural works. A lifelong Federalist and opponent of slavery, he supported President Abraham

Lincoln and the war, especially in his last public speech at age 91.

Quine, Willard V. (Van Orman) (1908–) philosopher, logician; born in Akron, Ohio. After earning degrees from Oberlin College and Harvard and studying in Prague under Rudolf Carnap, he taught philosophy at Harvard from 1936 to 1978 with some interruptions, including U.S. Navy service in World War II and posts at Oxford (1953–54, 1973–74). Much of his work, especially at first, was highly technical, but he also examined broader issues within a systematic linguistic framework. Though sympathetic to logical positivism, he rejected such tenets as the analytic-synthetic distinction. His influential writings appear in such books as *From a Logical Point of View* (1953) and *Word and Object* (1960).

Quinn, Anthony (1915–) film actor; born in Chihuahua, Mexico. Of Irish-Mexican parentage, he grew up in the U.S.A., and after a few stage roles, he made his movie debut in *Parole!* (1936). For many years he was confined to small parts as an ethnic or exotic, usually as a menacing foreigner or Indian. The status of his roles changed when he won an Oscar for *Viva Zapata* (1952) and gained critical acclaim in Fellini's *La Strada* (1954), but his looks and manner kept him playing exotics, the most notable being *Zorba the Greek* (1964); he later appeared in a musical version of this and he starred in the television series, *The Man and the City.* He was also a serious painter for many years.

Quintero, José (1924–) theatrical director; born in Panama City, Panama. Educated in Los Angeles, he became producer and director of Circle in the Square Theater in New York City in 1951. He compiled a long and distinguished list of credits, including many 20th-century American dramatic works, particularly those of Eugene O'Neill. He also directed television and radio plays. He won a Tony Award for his production of Eugene O'Neill's *A Moon for the Misbegotten.*

R

Rabassa, Gregory (1922–) translator; born in Yonkers, N.Y. He taught at Columbia University (1947–68) and Queens College (1968). His National Book Award for his first translation, Julio Cortazar's *Hopscotch* (1966), was the first of many honors for dozens of translations bringing contemporary Latin American literature to American readers.

Rabe, David (1940–) playwright; born in Dubuque, Iowa. After returning from military service in Vietnam, he wrote several plays based on that war, including *The Basic Training of Pavlo Hummel* and *Sticks and Bones,* both produced in 1971 at the New York Shakespeare Festival.

Rabi, I. I. (Isidor Isaac) (1898–1988) physicist; born in Rymanow, Austria (now Poland). Brought to the U.S.A. in infancy, he tutored at City College of New York (1924–27), studied in Europe (1927–29), then joined Columbia University (1929–67). He performed most of his pioneering research in radar and the magnetic moment associated with electron spin in the 1930s and 1940s. He won the 1944 Nobel Prize in physics for his method of measuring magnetic properties of atoms, molecules, and atomic nuclei which led to the invention of the laser, the atomic clock, and diagnostic uses of nuclear magnetic resonance. Although he observed the first atomic bomb test, he declined practical work on the Manhattan Project, believing that radar offered more advantage to the war effort. A government adviser and proponent of nuclear arms control, he originated the idea for the CERN nuclear research center in Geneva (founded 1954).

Racker, Efraim (1913–91) biochemist; born in Neu Sandez, Poland. A Jewish physician, he fled the Nazis and went to Wales to study brain metabolism (1938–40). He came to the U.S.A. to be a research associate at the University of Minnesota (1941–42), completed his medical residency at Harlem Hospital, N.Y. (1942–44), then moved to New York University (1944–52) and Yale (1952–54). He was chief of nutrition and physiology at the Public Health Research Institute, N.Y. (1943–66), before joining Cornell (1966–91). A pioneer in the biochemistry of cancer, he made major contributions to studies of cellular respiration, enzyme activity, and membrane physiology.

Radbourn, (Charles Gardner) "Old Hoss" (1854–97) baseball pitcher; born in Rochester, N.Y. A right-hander who primarily pitched for Providence and Boston during his 12-year career (1880–91), he established the major league record for most wins in a season (60) in 1884. Nicknamed for his indefatigable willingness to pitch (he pitched in 678

innings in 1884), he was elected to baseball's Hall of Fame in 1939.

Radford, Arthur (William) (1896–1973) naval officer; born in Chicago. He commanded a carrier group that played a notable role in the Gilbert and Marshall Islands campaigns. He was vice-chief of naval operations (1948–49) and commander of the Pacific Fleet (1949–53). He protested what he saw as a reduction of the navy's importance and was chairman of the Joint Chiefs of Staff (1953–57).

Radin, Paul (1883–1959) cultural anthropologist, linguist; born in Lodz, Poland. His father, a rabbi, took the family to Elmira, N.Y., in 1884 and he went on to graduate from the City College of New York in 1902. He studied under Franz Boas at Columbia and received a Ph.D. in 1911. He did extensive fieldwork among the Ojibwa and Winnebago Indians and in Mexico. His *Primitive Man as Philosopher* appeared in 1927. He taught at the University of California: Berkeley, Fiske College, and Black Mountain College (N.C.) and from 1957 until his death, he headed the anthropology department at Brandeis University.

Radner, Gilda (1946–89) comedienne; born in Detroit, Mich. (married to Gene Wilder). After working with the Second City comedy troupe, she appeared on the National Lampoon Radio Hour in 1974. On National Broadcasting Company's *Saturday Night Live* (1975–80), she created zany characters whom she brought to Broadway in *Gilda Radner Live from New York* (1979). She wrote *It's Always Something* (1989) about the ovarian cancer that ended her life prematurely.

Raeff, Marc (1923–) Russian specialist, educator; born in Moscow, Russia. Emigrating to America to escape World War II (1941), he finished his education and taught history first at Clark University, Worcester, Mass. (1949–61). He taught longest at Columbia University (1961), where he focused largely on Russian history and was named Bakhmeteff Professor of Russian Studies (1973). He was a member of the U.S. delegation to the Soviet-American Historical Colloquium (1972) and to the Polish-American Historical Colloquium (1974). He was the author of numerous books on Russia.

Rafinesque, Constantine (Samuel) (1783–1840) naturalist; born in Galata, Turkey. Son of a German mother and French father, he came to the U.S.A. in 1802 and worked in a Philadelphia countinghouse. An amateur naturalist, he traveled to the west and his work brought him into contact with President Thomas Jefferson. In 1805 he went to Palermo, Sicily, where he engaged in commercial and scientific activities. He returned to the U.S.A. in 1815 (arriving naked and penniless after his ship wrecked off Connecticut) and after serving as a tutor in the wealthy New York Livingston family, he obtained a post as professor of botany, natural history, and modern languages at Transylvania University (Lexington, Ky.). He continued his travels as a naturalist and in 1826 returned to Philadelphia where he died in poverty. Drawing on his extensive travels and observations, he had published some 1,000 articles and books, but for all their occasional insights – he somewhat prefigured Darwin's ideas on the origin of species – his work often betrayed his lack of formal scientific education and discipline.

Rainer, Yvonne (1934–) modern dancer, choreographer, filmmaker; born in San Francisco. She trained at the Martha Graham School in New York and with Ann Halprin in California before studying with Merce Cunningham and Robert Dunn in the early 1960s. A pivotal member of the Judson Dance Theatre, she choreographed and appeared in the majority of their works. In 1970 she choreographed *Continuous Project – Altered Daily* for her own company. She then turned to making experimental films such as *Lives of Performers* (1972) and *Privilege* (1990). In 1990 she won a MacArthur Foundation grant.

Rainey, Henry Thomas (1860–1934) U.S. representative; born in Carrollton, Ill. A lawyer, he was master in chancery for Greene County, Ill. (1887–95). A Democrat in the U.S. House of Representatives (1903–21), he would spend most of his life in Congress, with one break as a farmer after his only election loss. Returning to the House (1923–34), he became majority leader, then Speaker of the House (1933–34), before his untimely death.

Rainey, Joseph (Hayne) (1832–87) U.S. representative; born in Georgetown, S.C. A barber with little formal education, he was the first elected black U.S. congressman (Dem., S.C.; 1871–79), afterward working as a banker and broker in Washington, D.C.

Rainwater, (Leo) James (1917–86) physicist; born in Council, Ida. He taught at Columbia University (1939–42), worked on the Manhattan Project (1942–46), then returned to Columbia (1946–86). With Aage Bohr and B. R. Mottelson, he produced a nuclear model unifying the two prevailing theories of nuclear structure. The three shared the 1975 Nobel Prize in physics for this work.

Raisz, Erwin (Josephus) (1893–1968) cartographer, geographer; born in Locse, Hungary. He came to the U.S.A. in 1923, working first for the American Geographical Society in New York City, and later for Harvard's Institute of Geographical Exploration (1930s to 1950s), producing hand drawn maps with great character and elegant calligraphy. His *General Cartography* (1938) was the first book of its kind in the English language and remained so for approximately 15 years. His *Principles of Cartography* was published in 1962.

Raitt, Bonnie (Lynn) (1949–) singer, guitarist; born in Burbank, Calif. Daughter of John Raitt, a musical theater star, she learned guitar when she was 12, inspired by blues musicians Mississippi Fred McDowell and Buddy Guy. She played with McDowell and Howlin' Wolf before she released albums such as *Sweet Forgiveness* (1977) which contained the hit "Runaway." Widely popular during the 1970s for her earthy singing style of rhythm-and-blues, rock, and folk, she

fell into an eclipse until her albums *Nick of Time* (1989) and *Luck of the Draw* (1991) marked a comeback.

Ramo, Simon (1913–) engineer, aerospace executive; born in Salt Lake City, Utah. He developed microwave technology at General Electric and made Hughes Aircraft a major defense contractor before cofounding the Los Angeles-based Ramo-Wooldridge Corporation (later TRW) and Bunker Ramo. As chief scientist of the U.S. intercontinental ballistic missile program (1954–58) he helped to develop the Atlas, Titan, and Minuteman missiles. Retired in 1978, he won the Presidential Medal of Freedom (1983).

Rampton, Calvin Lewellyn (1913–) governor; born in Bountiful, Utah. A Bronze Star veteran of World War II, he practiced law in Salt Lake City, (1946–64), serving as assistant attorney general (1946–48). As Democratic governor of Utah (1965–77), he promoted business and tourism, reduced state debt, and enforced the Fair Employment Practice Act. Declining a fourth term, he returned to his law practice.

Ramseur, Stephen Dodson (1837–64) soldier; born in Lincolnton, N.C. A West Point graduate (1860), he joined the Confederate army and fought in the Seven Days' Battles and Malvern Hill. He led a North Carolina brigade at Chancellorsville, Gettysburg, the Wilderness, and Spotsylvania, where his attack drove Union forces from the famous "Bloody Angle." He was mortally wounded in action at Cedar Creek, Va., having learned of the birth of his daughter only the day before.

Ramsey, Norman F. (Foster), Jr. (1915–) physicist; born in Washington, D.C. He taught at the University of Illinois (1940–42) and Columbia University (1942–47) before joining Harvard (1947). Influenced by his graduate adviser, I. I. Rabi, he pursued his interest in the atom, sharing the 1989 Nobel Prize in physics for his research leading to the development of the cesium atomic clock (1960).

Ramspeck, Robert C. (Word) (1890–1972) U.S. representative; born in Decatur, Ga. A government employee, realtor, and lawyer (1920–29), he served in Congress (Dem., Ga.; 1929–45) where he was majority whip, leaving to become vice-president of Eastern Air Lines (1953–61).

Ran, Shulamit (1949–) composer, pianist; born in Tel Aviv, Israel. After studies at Mannes College and privately, she taught at schools including the University of Chicago. In 1991 she became the second woman to win the Pulitzer Prize in music.

Rand, Ayn (1905–82) writer, philosopher; born in St. Petersburg, Russia. As an adolescent during the Bolshevik Revolution, she saw people stripped of property and massacred. After graduating from the University of Leningrad (1926), she fled to the U.S.A., which she considered the "country of the individual," becoming a citizen in 1931. Starting as a screenwriter and dramatist, she eventually won fame for her novels, such as *The Fountainhead* (1943) – also made into a film she scripted – and *Atlas Shrugged* (1957), the bible of her "objectivism." This philosophy, promoted in books such as *The Virtue of Selfishness* (1957) and through an institute set up by her disciple Nathaniel Brandon, glorified self-assertion and competition.

Rand, Edward Kennard (1871–1945) classicist, medievalist; born in Boston, Mass. He was educated at Harvard (B.S. 1894) and the University of Munich (Ph.D. 1900), and taught at Harvard (1901–42), where he was Pope professor of Latin

(1931–42). He was founder and first president of the Medieval Academy of America (1925), founder and first editor of *Speculum,* and president of the American Philological Association (1922–23). He published more than 100 articles and the popular and influential *Founders of the Middle Ages* (1925), one of the first works in English to look seriously at the period of late antiquity.

Rand, Sally (b. Hazel Beck) (1904–79) dancer; born in Hickory County, Mo. A circus acrobat and film actress (1926–34), she was best known for her long-running striptease act, in which she moved ostrich plumes to reveal different parts of her body (1932–79).

Randall, Samuel Jackson (1828–90) U.S. representative; born in Philadelphia. From a prominent family, he owned an iron and coal company before serving on the city council (1852–56) and in the state senate. In the U.S. House of Representatives (Dem., Pa.; 1863–90) he supported high tariffs and fought against Reconstruction measures like the Civil Rights and Force Bills of 1875. Elected Speaker of the House (1876–81), he codified House rules, but eventually lost Democratic support because of his adherence to high tariffs.

Randi, James (b. Randall James Hamilton Zwinge) (1928–) magician, lecturer, skeptic; born in Toronto, Canada. He dropped out of high school at age 17 and soon became an adept escape artist and magician. Upset by the claims of Uri Geller to have paranormal powers, he founded the Committee for the Scientific Investigation of Claims of the Paranormal (1973). He went on to expose many frauds, notably the television evangelist Peter Popoff (1986) who claimed to hear God's voice. He received a "genius" grant from the MacArthur Foundation and became a naturalized U.S. citizen in 1987. He continued his mission to expose trickery among magicians and others who claimed they possessed supernatural powers.

Randolph, A. (Asa) Philip (1889–1979) labor leader, social activist; born in Crescent City, Fla. Son of a minister, he worked at a variety of jobs while getting an education in Florida and then at City College of New York. He began his efforts on behalf of African-American laborers when, while working as a waiter on a coastal steamship, he organized a protest against their living conditions. In World War I he tried to unionize African-American shipyard workers in Virginia and elevator operators in New York City; in 1917 he founded the *Messenger,* a magazine initially designed to encourage African-American laborers to demand higher wages. After the war, he became more convinced than ever that unions would be the best way for African-Americans to improve their lot. In 1925 he founded the Brotherhood of Sleeping Car Porters and would serve as the president until 1968. A civil rights leader as well as a labor leader, he organized the March on Washington movement in 1941, which forced the government to set up the Fair Employment Practices Committee, and he is credited with pressing President Truman to integrate the armed forces in 1948. He was a principal organizer of the 1963 March on Washington.

Randolph, Edmund (Jenings or Jennings) (1753–1813) lawyer, cabinet officer; born in Williamsburg, Va. (grandson of Sir John Randolph and descendant of Pocahontas). A lawyer and briefly an aide to Gen. George Washington (1775), he served in the Continental Congress (1779–82). As a delegate to the Constitutional Convention (1787), he proposed the Virginia (or Randolph) Plan (basing representation solely on population) and then refused to sign the final version of the Constitution because it was not "republican" enough; later, however, he advocated that Virginia ratify it. Washington named him the first attorney general (1789–94) and then the second secretary of state (1794–95). As the latter, he tried to hold to a neutral path but found himself challenged when Alexander Hamilton got John Jay to negotiate a treaty with the British (1794); intercepted letters from the French ambassador, Fauchet, intimated that Randolph was receptive to bribery; although both Fauchet and Randolph denied this, Randolph was forced to resign. He returned to his law practice and was Aaron Burr's chief counsel when he was tried for treason (1807).

Randolph, John (1773–1833) U.S. representative, orator; born in Prince George County, Va. (second cousin of Edmund Randolph). Educated initially by his stepfather, he proved himself a restless but brilliant student who never stayed long with a particular college or tutor. A reckless horseman, he cut a swashbuckling pose in the U.S. House of Representatives (Dem.-Rep., Va.; 1799–1813), defending the Jeffersonians against the Federalists as chairman of the Standing Committee on Ways and Means. A sarcastic and witty speaker, he was really a party of one who alienated Northern Democrats and quarreled with Jefferson, then opposed the War of 1812, which cost him the next election. Returning to the House (1815–17, 1819–25), he strongly opposed the Missouri Compromise. After an erratic two years in the Senate (1825–27) – during which time he fought a duel in 1826 with Henry Clay over some political insult – he returned to the House (1827–29) leading the opposition to John Quincy Adams. He served briefly as President Andrew Jackson's ambassador to Russia in 1830, returning to his rustic home, "Roanoke," where chronic ill health drove him to drink and opium. At his death, he freed his slaves.

Randolph, Peyton (1721–75) lawyer, statesman; born in Williamsburg, Va. He was King's attorney for Virginia from 1748 to 1766 and continuously from 1748 to 1775. Although fundamentally conservative, he supported the rising tide of colonial protest and was appointed to the first Continental Congress where he served as its first president.

Randolph, Vance (1892–1980) folklorist; born in Pittsburg, Kans. He was a free-lance writer in Missouri and Arkansas who had to undertake much pseudonymous hackwork to finance his collecting and study of Ozark folklore. His many volumes of Ozark lore, mostly published in the 1940s and 1950s, include *Ozark Folksongs* (4 vols. 1946–50) and *Pissing in the Snow* (1976) and are credited with helping to broaden the content and contextual consideration of folklore studies.

Rangel, Charles (Bernard) (1930–) U.S. representative; born in New York City. He served as legal counsel to state and federal agencies and then as state assemblyman (Dem.; 1966–70) from Harlem. One of the more outspoken African-American politicians, he went to Congress in 1971 and eventually chaired the Select Committee on Narcotics Abuse and Control.

Rankin, Jeannette (b. Pickering) (1880–1973) U.S. representative; born in Missoula, Mont. A graduate of the University of Montana (1902) and of the New York School for Social Work (1909), she fought for women's suffrage and helped obtain it in Montana (1914). Running on a platform that called for prohibition and "preparedness that will make for peace" (1916), she was the first woman elected to the U.S. House of Representatives (Rep., Mont.; 1917–19) and became one of only 57 members to vote against U.S. entry into World War I. After losing a reelection bid, she devoted herself to pacifism and women's and children's causes. Serving again in the House (1941–43), she was the only member of Congress to vote, on December 8, 1941, against U.S. entry into World War II. She continued to lobby for peace in later years, particularly during the Korean and Vietnam Wars; in 1967 a group of women formed the Jeannette Rankin Brigade to oppose the latter war.

Ranney, (Joseph) Austin (1920–) political scientist; born in Courtland, N.Y. He taught at Yale (1945–47) and the University of Illinois (1946–63) before joining the faculty at the University of Wisconsin: Madison (1963). He is best known for his analysis of the impact of reform movements on political parties.

Ransom, John Crowe (1888–1974) literary critic, poet, educator; born in Pulaski, Tenn. He was educated at Vanderbilt and Oxford Universities. While teaching at Vanderbilt (1914–37), he joined the Fugitive group of southern writers, founded *Fugitive*, and wrote most of the poetry that was to spark the southern literary renaissance and win the Bollingen Poetry Prize (1951). Even more influential as a critic, in *The New Criticism* (1941) and later essays, Ransom advanced a critical practice based on close textual analysis that was to dominate American universities for 30 years. He became closely identified with Kenyon College as a professor of poetry (1937–58; his students included Allen Tate, Cleanth Brooks, Robert Penn Warren and numerous other poets and critics) and as editor of the *Kenyon Review* (1939–58).

Ransome, F. L. (Frederick Leslie) (1868–1935) geologist; born in Greenwich, England. He emigrated to San Francisco with his family in 1870. After teaching geology at Harvard (1986–97), he joined the U.S. Geological Survey (1897–1923) where he made field investigations of western U.S. metal mining. He joined the University of Arizona (1923–27), then taught part-time at the California Institute of Technology (1928–35). He made major contributions to studies of water and dam management and the importance of foreknowledge of geological faults in mining projects.

Rantoul, Robert (1805–52) lawyer, reformer; born in Beverly, Mass. He practiced law in Salem and Boston and helped shape Democratic Party policy. As a member of the state legislature and in speeches and articles, he advocated free trade, religious tolerance, public education, collective bargaining, and temperance; he opposed slavery, corporate wealth, and the death penalty. He served briefly in the U.S. Senate (Dem., Mass.; 1851) and House of Representatives (Dem., Mass.; 1851–52).

Raphall, Morris Jacob (1798–1868) rabbi; born in Stockholm, Sweden. He completed his doctorate in Germany, then moved to England. In 1841 he became rabbi of the Birmingham Hebrew Congregation, where he fought for equal rights for Jews. In 1849 he came to New York City as rabbi of Congregation B'nai Jeshurun; serving there until 1865, he promoted conservative Judaism in the face of the reform movement. He published many scholarly works and was active in Jewish charitable work, but he was best known

as an orator and was the first Jewish rabbi to open a session of the U.S. House of Representatives with a prayer.

Rapoport, Judith Livant (1933–) child psychiatrist; born in New York City. She became chief of the child psychiatry branch, National Institutes of Mental Health (1984), and was the author of *The Boy Who Couldn't Stop Washing* (1989). Her research has covered aspects of child psychiatry, including diagnosis, hyperactivity, pediatric psychopharmacology, and the obsessive-compulsive disorder.

Rapp, George (1757–1847) Protestant religious leader; born in Iptingen, Germany. A farmer's son, he studied the Bible on his own and became the leader of a group of 200 like-minded families; as Protestant separatists they were subject to persecution. In 1803 he established a communistic settlement in Pennsylvania, called the Harmony Society, with himself as dictator. In 1814 the community migrated to Posey County, Ind., encountered hostility, and returned in 1824 to settle at Economy, (now Ambridge), Pa. There the colony prospered, becoming famous for its wines, spirits, and woolen goods. As one of its tenets was celibacy, the community gradually and inevitably declined.

Rathbone, Monroe J. (Jackson) (1900–76) oil executive; born in Parkersburg, W.Va. (great-nephew of General Thomas "Stonewall" Jackson). He finished a 44-year career with Standard Oil of New Jersey (later Exxon) as president (1954–65), CEO, and chairman of the board (1963–65), having greatly expanded the company's overseas production and sales. "Mr. Jack" was the most influential individual in his industry. His technical innovations included the fluid catalytic cracking process.

Rather, Dan (Irvin) (1931–) television anchorman; born in Wharton, Texas. After reporting for local television in Houston, he joined CBS's Dallas bureau in 1962. He served as CBS White House correspondent (1964–65, 66–74), covering Watergate with special reports like *The White House Tapes: The President's Decision*. One of the initial correspondents on *60 Minutes* (1975–81), he was a tenacious interviewer, becoming *CBS Evening News* anchor in 1981, also anchoring *48 Hours* (1988).

Rathje, William L. (Laurens) (1945–) anthropologist, garbologist; born in South Bend, Ind. He took his Ph.D. in anthropology at Harvard in 1971 and returned to the University of Arizona, his undergraduate alma mater, to teach anthropology. In 1973 he formed the Garbage Project, initially as a method by which student anthropologists could analyze aspects of the local community. In the years following, he not only demonstrated how garbage can be used in this way, but also made certain discoveries; garbage and refuse, he found, decompose much more slowly in modern dumps than thought. He is credited with coining the term "garbology," the study of a society by the examination of its refuse. Among his many publications, he coauthored *Rubbish! The Archaeology of Garbage* (1992) and "Beyond the Pail," a 1991 essay in *Garbage* magazine.

Ratner, Sarah (1903–) biochemist; born in New York City. She taught and performed research at Columbia University (1937–46), moved to New York University (1946–54), then joined New York City's Public Health Research Institute (1954). Her elegant contributions to studies of nitrogen metabolism have led to increased understanding of human disorders of urea synthesis.

Rattner, Abraham (1895–1978) painter; born in Poughkeepsie, N.Y. He studied at the Pennsylvania Academy of the Fine Arts (1917, 1919), and lived in Paris (1920–40) before returning to New York. He taught at several schools, including the New School, New York (1947–55) and Yale University (1952–53). He is known for his surrealistic and religious paintings, such as *Moses* (1957).

Rauschenberg, Robert (1925–) painter; born in Port Arthur, Texas. He studied at the Kansas City Art Institute (1946–47), the Académie Julien, Paris (1947), and with Josef Albers and John Cage at Black Mountain College, North Carolina (1948–50). Traveling widely, he was based in New York City since 1950, where he and Joseph Albers paved the way for pop art of the 1960s. He worked with the Merce Cunningham Dance Company, New York, as costume and stage designer (1955–64). An imaginative and eclectic artist, he used a mix of sculpture and paint in works he called "combines," as seen in *The Bed* (1955). From the late 1950s he incorporated sound and motors in his work, such as *Broadcast* (1959), and silk screen transfers, as seen in *Flush* (1964).

Rauschenbusch, Walter (1861–1918) Protestant religious leader; born in Rochester, N.Y. The son of an immigrant German clergyman, he studied in Germany and returned home to graduate from the Rochester Theological Seminary in 1887. His experience as pastor of an impoverished German immigrant parish in New York City turned him to the Social Gospel movement, of which he became a leader. In 1897 he left parish work to become a professor at the Rochester seminary. His book, *A Theology for the Social Gospel*, appeared in 1917.

Raven, Peter H. (Hamilton) (1936–) botanist; born in Shanghai. Son of an American businessman temporarily in China, he grew up in the U.S.A. He was a National Science fellow at the British Museum of Natural History (1960–61), and a taxonomist and curator at the Rancho Santa Ana Botantical Garden (1961–62) before joining Stanford (1962–71). He became Engelmann Professor of botany at Washington University, St. Louis, and director of the Missouri Botanical Garden (1971). An authority on plant taxonomy, especially of the fuschia family, he also made major contributions to the ethnobotany of Mayan Mexico, co-evolution of both plants and animals, and population ecology. He was an outspoken advocate of conservation of rainforests. He received a MacArthur Fellowship (1985) for his life's work.

Ravitch, Diane (b. Silvers) (1938–) educator, historian; born in Houston, Texas. An educational historian at Teachers College, Columbia (1975), she was appointed Assistant Secretary of Education (1991). She helped define the neoconservative agenda for school reform in such works as *The Troubled Crusade* (1983), *The Schools We Deserve* (1985), and *What Do Our Seventeen-Year-Olds Know?* (coauthored, 1987).

Rawle, William (1759–1836) lawyer; born in Philadelphia. A Loyalist, he studied law in England during the American Revolution but returned to his native city and served as U.S. attorney for Pennsylvania (1791–1800). He was a member of the Maryland Society against slavery (1792–1836), its president from 1818. He was a longtime trustee of the University of Pennsylvania and belonged to several other cultural and legal organizations. His *View of the Constitution of the United States* (1825) was a popular textbook and he also wrote on a variety of other subjects.

Rawlings, Marjorie (b. Kinnan) (1896–1953) writer; born in Washington, D.C. She graduated from the University of Wisconsin: Madison (1918), worked as a publicist in New York (1918–19), wrote verses for United Features syndicate (1926–28), and settled in Florida (1928), first in Cross Creek and later in St. Augustine (1941). Her first novel for young readers, *The Yearling* (1938), won the Pulitzer Prize (1939), and continues to be praised by readers of all ages.

Rawls, John (Bordley) (1921–) philosopher; born in Baltimore, Md. After earning a Ph.D. from Princeton (1950) and teaching at Princeton (1950–52) and Cornell (1953–76), he became a professor at Harvard. His articles in the 1950s and 1960s, culminating in his widely discussed study *A Theory of Justice* (1971), revolutionized political philosophy by reviving a form of the social contract theory.

Ray, Dixie Lee (1914–) biologist, governor; born in Tacoma, Wash. Associate marine biology professor at the University of Washington (1947–72), she also directed the Pacific Science Center of research and public education in Seattle (1963–72). The first woman on the Atomic Energy Commission, as chairman (1973–75) she championed nuclear power plant construction. As an Independent governor of Washington (1977–81), she feuded with aides and refused to close the Hanford nuclear dump, becoming an engineering consultant afterward.

Ray, James Earl (1928–) assassin; born in Alton, Ill. He served in the U.S. Army (1946–48) and was in prison for armed robbery (1960–67). He escaped in 1967 and shot and killed Martin Luther King Jr. (1968). In 1969 he was sentenced to 99 years in prison. Although few doubted he had fired the fatal shot, many questioned whether he acted alone.

Ray, Nicholas (b. Raymond Nicholas Kienzle) (1911–79) film director; born in La Crosse, Wis. After studying architecture under Frank Lloyd Wright, he became an actor and sometime director for radio and the stage. His film directorial debut came with *They Live by Night* (1949). A specialist in movies of social rebellion, characterized by tense and restless camera movement, he directed such movies as *Knock on Any Door* (1949), *Rebel Without a Cause* (1955), and *55 Days at Peking* (1963). With this last film he effectively retired from Hollywood (although he worked with New York State University students in filming *You Can't Go Home Again*, finished in 1976), but his reputation continued to increase due primarily to the tributes from foreign students of films and from many Hollywood insiders.

Ray, Robert D. (1928–) governor; born in Des Moines, Iowa. An army veteran and lawyer, he chaired Iowa's Republican Party (1963–68). As governor of Iowa (1969–83), he funded state university construction, established an environmental agency, and reformed the state's judicial system. As governor of a major grain-producing state, he protested President Carter's decision to cancel grain shipments to the U.S.S.R. to protest the invasion of Afghanistan. On leaving office he joined a Cedar Rapids insurance company.

Rayburn, (Samuel Taliaferro) Sam (1882–1961) U.S. representative; born in Roane County, Tenn. A farm boy, he worked his way through Mayo Normal College and taught school while earning his law degree at night. A powerful Democrat in the Texas House (1906–12), he quickly rose to prominence in the U.S. House of Representatives (1913–61) on the Committee on Interstate and Foreign Commerce, aided by John Nance Gardner. A Southern populist, he sponsored New Deal legislation including the Securities and Exchange Act of 1934 to regulate Wall Street. He took special pride in the Rural Electrification Act of 1936. Elected Speaker of the House (1940–61), he was politically more influential in Washington than in Texas, where oil men had assumed power. He supported Roosevelt's and Truman's foreign policies, but his and Senator Lyndon Johnson's policy of moderation and compromise during the 1950s ultimately alienated liberal Democrats, who backed John Kennedy in 1960. Rayburn aided President Kennedy's liberal legislative package by enlarging the House Rules Committee.

Raymond, (Alexander Gillespie) Alex (1909–56) cartoonist; born in New Rochelle, N.Y. He was the creator of the science fiction newspaper comic strip, *Flash Gordon* (1934), the action-adventure strip, *Jungle Jim* (1934), and *Rip Kirby* (1946), the popular adventures of a police officer.

Raymond, Henry Jarvis (1820–69) journalist, politician; born in Lima, N.Y. He rose to prominence as Horace Greeley's chief assistant on the *New York Tribune* (1841–43) and in 1851 he cofounded the paper that became the rival *New York Times;* he edited the *Times* for the rest of his life, building its reputation for objectivity and fairness in an age noted for more personal journalism. He was also a Speaker of the New York State Assembly, lieutenant governor of New York (1855–57), and a one-term U.S. congressman (1865–67).

Reach, (Alfred James) Al (1840–1928) baseball player/manager; born in London, England. After immigrating to the U.S.A at an early age, he played baseball for the Philadelphia Athletics (1871–72) and served as player-manager during the latter two years. In the 1870s he founded a sporting goods company that manufactured equipment used in professional baseball.

Read, Daniel (1757–1836) composer; born in Attleboro, Mass. He was a singing teacher in New Haven and a writer-collector of some 400 hymn tunes he published in several collections.

Read, Jacob (1752–1816) U.S. senator; born in Christ Church, S.C. After serving in the Continental Congress (S.C., 1783–85), he served in the U.S. Senate (Federalist, 1795–1801). He was one of the so-called "midnight judges," appointed by President John Adams as he left office; following the repeal of the act and the *Marbury v. Madison* case, Read never actually served.

Read, Nathan (1750–1849) engineer; born in Warren, Mass. As a pharmacist, he worked on adapting Watt's steam engine to boats and road carriages. By 1791 he shared a patent for a chain-wheel method of using paddle wheels to propel a steamboat, but he never got financing to build it. He turned to iron manufacturing and in 1795 invented a machine for curring and heading nails. After 1800 he was active in politics.

Reagan, Nancy (b. Davis) (1923–) First Lady; born in New York City. After majoring in drama at Smith College, she became an actress in Hollywood where she met Ronald Reagan; they married in 1952. Fiercely protective of Reagan, she was criticized by some for her interference in White House decision-making, but others pointed out that she provided a realistic counterweight to her husband's more casual and conservative approach.

Reagan, Ronald (Wilson) (1911–) fortieth U.S. president, movie actor; born in Tampico, Ill. A graduate of Eureka College (Ill.) (1932), he worked as a sportscaster for several radio stations in the Midwest. Discovered by a Hollywood agent, he joined Warner Brothers, making his debut in *Love is On the Air* (1937); he appeared in a total of 52 feature movies, his best roles being in *Brother Rat* (1938), *Dark Victory* (1939), and *Kings Row* (1941). He made training films for the Air Force in World War II. He served as a spokesman for the General Electric Company (1952–62), also hosting and occasionally acting on the television series, *General Electric Theater;* from 1962–65 he was host of the television series, *Death Valley Days.* Shifting from his Democratic Party affiliation, he moved into Republican politics and with the 1964 presidential election he emerged as a Goldwater Conservative. In 1966 he was elected governor of California; in his two terms (1967–75) he carried out a generally conservative agenda. In 1968 and 1976 he failed in bids for the Republican presidential nomination; successful in 1980, he easily beat Jimmy Carter in the election with promises of reducing taxes and government regulation while building up the military; four years later he defeated Walter Mondale by a landslide. In office (1981–89) Reagan fulfilled those promises with varied results, including a snowballing national deficit, a shaky financial infrastructure, and an increasing concentration of wealth in the hands of the few. In foreign affairs, he maintained an adversarial approach to the U.S.S.R. and communism everywhere. With little interest in or command of the details of government, he appealed to Americans with his genial manner and laissez-faire approach to the country's problems. Meanwhile, members of his administration, with at least his tacit approval, pursued secret and illegal arms-for-hostages deals with Iran, an enemy of the U.S.A. Reagan departed office still immensely popular, leaving the future to determine the value of his legacy.

Reasoner, Harry (1923–91) radio/television correspondent; born in Dakota City, Iowa. Originally a newspaper writer, he worked on local television news in Minneapolis in the 1950s, joining CBS News as a reporter in 1956. A founding coeditor of *60 Minutes* in 1968, he left to anchor the ABC evening news (1970–78). Returning to *60 Minutes* (1978–91), he published *Before the Colors Fade* (1981).

Rebay, Hilla (b. Baroness Hildegard Anna Agusta Elisabeth Rebay von Ehrenweisen) (1890–1967) painter, curator; born in Strasbourgh, Alsace, France. An abstract painter, she emigrated to New York City (1927), and was instrumental in establishing and directing (1939–51) the Guggenheim Museum of Non-Objective Painting (1939), which became the Solomon R. Guggenheim Museum.

Rebennack, (Malcolm John) "Dr. John" (1940–) musician; born in New Orleans. A versatile pianist and distinctive singer, he was one of the first white musicians associated with the rhythm and blues style of his hometown. He worked as a songwriter and session player between 1957–64, played with a variety of rock bands until 1981, and concentrated on classic jazz and blues styles as a solo performer thereafter.

Reber, Grote (1911–) radio astronomer; born in Wheaton, Ill. An amateur ham radio operator, he was so intrigued by reports of Karl Jansky's "cosmic static" that he built a parabolic dish, the first radio telescope, in his yard in Wheaton (1937). As the world's first radio astronomer, he published a radio map of the sky in 1944. He moved to Tasmania (1954) where he presided over a field of dipoles (antennas) 3,500 feet in diameter while continuing his private research.

Rechy, John (Francisco) (1934–   ) writer; born in El Paso, Texas. He studied at the University of Texas: El Paso (B.A.), and at the New School for Social Research, New York City. He taught creative writing at several institutions and lived in Los Angeles and New York City. His novels primarily dealt with the search for love and identity by homosexual and bisexual characters, as in *City of Night* (1963) and *Bodies and Souls* (1983).

Red Cloud (b. Makhpiya-luta) (1822–1909) Oglala Sioux chief; born near the Platte River in present-day Nebraska. He was chosen chief over the hereditary candidate because of his intelligence, strength, and bravery. Between 1865–68, he led and effectively won "Red Cloud's war," closing the Bozeman trail (in present-day Montana), and forcing the U.S. government to destroy its forts along the trail and to sign the Fort Laramie Treaty (1868), in which the latter accepted the territorial claims of the Sioux in exchange for peace. Although he did not hesitate to criticize the conduct of the U.S. government and its agents, Red Cloud never again went to war against the U.S.A. He made several visits to Washington, D.C., and did speaking tours in Eastern cities, lecturing in 1870 at the Cooper Institute in New York City. Despite his peaceful ways, he was removed by the government from his position as chief in 1877, and he and his people were removed to the Pine Ridge Agency in South Dakota.

Redding, (Jay) J. Saunders (1906–77) educator, literary critic, author; born in Wilmington, Del. After beginning at Lincoln University, he took his degrees at Brown (B.A. 1928, M.A. 1932). As both a professor of literature and an astute observer of the situation of African-Americans, he taught at Morehouse College (Atlanta, Ga.) (1928–31), the Louisville Music Conservatory (1934–36), Southern University (New Orleans) (1936–38), and the Hampton Institute (1943–66). He was a director of the National Endowment for the Humanities (1966–70) and he went on to teach at Cornell until his death. In various critical works, he set forth his views, often at odds with both the white and black establishments. In *Stranger and Alone* (1950), he exposed conditions in America's all-black colleges, charging that the students are trained to be submissive and thus are being educated for failure. And although he became known as "the dean of Afro-American studies," he himself preferred the word "Negro" and distrusted "Black Studies": he wanted to free African-Americans from all special categories and achieve a truly pluralistic and assimilationist society. He wrote over one thousand reviews of books by writers of all colors and his many books include *To Make a Poet Black* (1939), *They Came in Chains* (1950), and *The Lonesome Road* (1958).

Redding, Otis (1941–67) vocalist; born in Dawson, Ga. One of the most influential soul singers of the 1960s, he was raised in Macon, Ga., where he began as an imitator of Little Richard's manic style. He sang with Johnny Jenkins and the Pinetoppers between 1959–62 playing colleges in the Southeast and making several singles for regional labels. In 1962

he made "These Arms of Mine" in his signature ballad style for Stax Records in Memphis. His performance at the Apollo Theatre in Harlem in 1963 confirmed him as a leader in the rhythm-and-blues field, but he did not gain mainstream acceptance until his appearance at the Monterey Pop Festival in 1967. He died in a plane crash in December of that year. The posthumously-released ballad "Dock of the Bay" became his first number one hit early in 1968.

Redfield, Alfred Clarence (1890–1983) oceanographer; born in Philadelphia, Pa. He was a professor at Harvard (1921–57), and concurrently a researcher at the Woods Hole Oceanographic Institution (1930–56). He made major contributions to studies of marine ecology, salt marshes, and tides.

Redfield, Robert (1897–1958) cultural anthropologist; born in Chicago. Son of a corporation lawyer, he studied at the University of Chicago, served as an ambulance driver in France during World War I, and returned to study biology at Harvard and law at Chicago. His father-in-law, sociologist Robert Ezra Park, encouraged him in his desire to give up the law for anthropology. He took a Ph.D. at Chicago in 1928 and spent his entire career there. His field research in Mexico and Central America made him a leading authority on peasant societies. His major works included *The Primitive World and Its Transformation* (1953), *The Little Community* (1955), and *Peasant Society and Culture* (1955).

Redford, (Charles, Jr.) Robert (1937–   ) movie actor, director, producer; born in Santa Monica, Calif. He started out wanting to be a painter, studying art at the Pratt Institute in Brooklyn, but turned to studying acting at the American Academy of Dramatic Arts. He had some small roles on television and the stage, with *Barefoot in the Park* (1963) being his only real Broadway success. Meanwhile, he had begun his movie career in *War Hunt* (1962). His All-American good looks at first threatened to typecast him as another matinee idol, but he began to use his status as a superstar to become a director of serious films such as *Ordinary People* (1980), which won him an Oscar as director. He also became a generous investor in new and untried moviemakers through his Sundance Festival, and was an outspoken supporter of liberal causes and environmental campaigns.

Redman, (Donald Matthew) Don (1900–64) jazz musician; born in Piedmont, W.Va. He was a woodwind player and an innovator of swing-style jazz orchestration. Between 1923 and 1927, he wrote arrangements for Fletcher Henderson, and then led McKinney's Cotton Pickers and his own band until 1941. He served as music director for Pearl Bailey in the 1950s.

Redpath, James (1833–91) reformer, journalist; born in Berwick-on-Tweed, Scotland. His family came to Michigan in the 1850s. Vehemently abolitionist, he wrote for the New York *Tribune* and defended John Brown's Harper's Ferry Raid in *The Public Life of Captain John Brown* (1860). He reported on the war in the South, and became superintendent of schools in Charleston, S.C. (1865). His clients at his Redpath Lecture Lyceum Bureau included Emerson, Thoreau, and Julia Ward Howe. He was assistant editor of the *North American Review* in the 1880s, and supported Henry George for mayor of New York (1886). He was run over by a streetcar in New York.

Redstone, Sumner (Murray) (1923–   ) entertainment executive; born in Boston, Mass. He was a government and private lawyer who through his investments in the entertainment industry came to control an empire of movie houses and television production and distribution companies. As president, CEO, and chairman of National Amusements (1967) and chairman of Viacom International, he pioneered multiplex cinemas and owned the MTV, Showtime, and Nickelodeon television channels.

Reece, Brazilla Carroll (1889–1961) U.S. representative; born in Butler, Tenn. A professor of business administration and distinguished World War II veteran, he served several terms as a congressman (Rep., N.Y.; 1921–31, 1933–47, 1951–61), joining in the 1950s crackdown on communists.

Reed, David Aiken (1880–1953) U.S. senator; born in Pittsburgh, Pa. A lawyer and veteran of World War I, he was originally appointed and then elected to the U.S. Senate (Rep., Pa.; 1922–35). He wrote the national origins clause in the Reed-Johnson Immigration Act (1924). A conservative, he opposed the New Deal yet supported Roosevelt's defense policies.

Reed, Ishmael (Scott) (Emmett Coleman, pen name) (1938–) writer, poet; born in Chattanooga, Tenn. He studied at the University of Buffalo (1956–60), and was a founder of the *East Village Other,* a newspaper in New York (1965). He moved to Berkeley, Calif., and established the Yardbird Publishing Company (1971) and a communications company (1973). He began as a poet, but is best known for his freewheeling satirical novels using African-American themes and linguistic styles.

Reed, John Shepard (1939–) banker; born in Chicago. He was raised in Buenos Aires, Argentina, where his father worked as an Armour Company executive. After overcoming dyslexia, which caused him problems in school as a child, he earned engineering and management degrees from the Massachusetts Institute of Technology. He joined Citicorp in 1965 and rose rapidly; he became a senior vice-president in 1969, and by helping to pioneer the development of, among other things, automatic teller machines, he directed Citicorp's successful venture into commercial banking in the 1970s. He became chairman and chief executive officer of Citicorp in 1984. In the late 1980s he led Citicorp through a period of retrenchment, scaling back peripheral operations and selling off real estate in an effort to avoid financial trouble.

Reed, John (Silas) (1887–1920) journalist, activist; born in Portland, Ore. A lifelong radical, he was a World War I correspondent and later observed the Russian Revolution firsthand, describing it in *Ten Days That Shook the World* (1919). Indicted for sedition in 1919, he fled to the Soviet Union, where he contracted a fatal case of typhus.

Reed, Joseph (1741–85) governor; born in Trenton, N.J. A prosperous Philadelphia lawyer and businessman, married to an Englishwoman, he tried to change British attitudes through correspondence, but by 1775 came to believe that independence was worth a revolution. Washington's military secretary (1775), and later the adjutant general, he helped guide the troops through the arduous campaign that moved across New Jersey and Pennsylvania. He served in the Continental Congress (1777–78). As president of the Supreme Executive Council of Pennsylvania (1778–81), he abolished slavery, provided veterans' benefits, and prosecuted Benedict Arnold for embezzlement.

Reed, Luman (1787–1836) businessman, art patron; born in Austerlitz, N.Y. His family moved to Coxsackie, N.Y. (c. 1789), and he was schooled locally and worked in his father's store. He was a trader on the Hudson River, then joined a New York City grocery business. By 1815 he was a wealthy merchant. He subsidized and encouraged such artists as Asher B. Durand, Thomas Cole and William Sidney Mount. Upon his death his collection was donated to the New-York Historical Society.

Reed, Stanley Forman (1884–1980) Supreme Court justice; born in Minerva, Ky. He served the Kentucky legislature (1912–16), and as general counsel to the Federal Farm Board (1929–32) and the Reconstruction Finance Corporation (1932–35). He was U.S. solicitor general (1935–38) when President Franklin D. Roosevelt named him to the U.S. Supreme Court (1938–57).

Reed, Thomas (Brackett) (1839–1902) U.S. representative; born in Portland, Maine. After working his way through Bowdoin College, he went to California where he became a lawyer in 1863, returning to Maine to practice law and serve in the state legislature. A Republican attorney general (1870–73), he was elected to the U.S. House of Representatives (1876–99). A fierce debater, he used his prosecutorial skills to uncover Democratic fraud in the 1876 presidential elections in Louisiana, connecting Samuel Tilden's nephew to dirty tricks, thereby guaranteeing a Republican victory in 1880. In the reconstruction period, he supported the passage of laws to guarantee blacks' voting rights and opposed funds to compensate the College of William and Mary for war damage. Fiscally conservative, he opposed measures to increase currency through greenbacks or free silver. A member of the Committee on Rules, he supported measures to limit filibustering by the Democrats, thereby securing passage of a protectionist tariff bill in 1883.

Reed, Walter (1851–1902) physician, soldier; born in Belroi, Va. He received a medical degree from the University of Virginia in 1869 and served an internship in Brooklyn; commissioned assistant surgeon in 1875, he spent 11 years in frontier garrison posts. A transfer in 1890 gave Reed the opportunity to pursue bacteriological research at Johns Hopkins University in Baltimore, and in 1893 he became professor of bacteriology at the newly established Army Medical School. In 1897 he began the study of the transmission of yellow fever, the work for which he is remembered, and headed the army's Yellow Fever Commission, which investigated outbreaks of the disease in army camps in Cuba. Experimenting on volunteers, Reed and his colleagues (including Jesse Lazear and James Carroll) proved conclusively that the *Aedes aegypti* mosquito spread yellow fever. Attacks on mosquito breeding places cut the number of cases from 1,400 in Havana in 1900 to 37 in all of Cuba the following year. Walter Reed Army Hospital in Washington, D.C., is named in his honor.

Reed, Willis (Jr.) (1942–) basketball player; born in Hico, La. After playing at Grambling College (1961–64), the six-foot ten-inch center played for the New York Knicks (1965–74), where he led the Knicks to National Basketball Association titles in 1970 and 1973. He coached the Knicks and the New Jersey Nets, and in 1981 he was elected to basketball's Hall of Fame.

Reeve, Tapping (1744–1823) law professor, jurist, author; born in Brookhaven, N.Y. After graduating from (1763) and teaching at (1764–71) the College of New Jersey (later

Princeton), he practiced law in Litchfield, Conn. In 1784 he established the Litchfield Law School, one of the first two law schools in America and for many years the most influential. When he became a judge of the Connecticut Superior Court (1798–1814), he assigned many of the school's functions to James Gould. Reeve was a staunch Federalist who was once indicted (1801) for having libeled President Jefferson in one of his vitriolic newspaper articles. Reeve was also a devout Christian and was responsible for bringing the Reverend Lyman Beecher to Litchfield. He wrote extensively on the law.

Reeves, Ruth (1892–1966) designer; born in Redlands, Calif. After studying painting, she created art deco textile designs, notably for Radio City Music Hall, and was appointed coordinator of the Index of American Design (1936).

Regan, Donald (Thomas) (1918–) stockbroker, cabinet member; born in Cambridge, Mass. After serving as a Marine Corps officer in World War II, he started in 1946 as a trainee at the stockbrokerage firm, Merrill Lynch, rising to chief executive officer in 1973. After serving as President Reagan's secretary of the treasury (1981–85), he became the White House chief of staff (1985–87), and was so domineering that he alienated first lady Nancy Reagan. He was forced to resign after the Tower Commission's report on the Iran "arms for hostages" policy blamed him for the "chaos that descended upon the White House" after disclosure of this disastrous policy. His *For the Record* (1988) is an exposé of White House politics.

Rehan, Ada (b. Crehan) (1860–1916) actress; born in Limerick, Ireland. A great beauty and especially suited to comic roles, she came to the U.S.A. as a child. She debuted at age 14 in Mrs. John Drew's stock company in Philadelphia. An early program misprint caused her to change her name to Rehan. She gained popularity in both New York and London, appearing to greatest acclaim in the role of Katherina in *The Taming of the Shrew*.

Rehn, Frank (Knox Morton) (1848–1914) painter; born in Philadelphia, Pa. He studied at the Pennsylvania Academy of the Fine Arts, moved to the coast of New Jersey where he was known for his marine paintings, and settled in New York City in 1881.

Rehnquist, William H. (Hubbs) (1924–) Supreme Court chief justice; born in Milwaukee, Wis. As assistant attorney general in the Nixon administration (1969–71), he promoted a conservative anticrime position and opposed civil rights measures. President Nixon named him to the U.S. Supreme Court despite opposition from liberal members of Congress. He served as associate justice (1972–86) until President Reagan named him chief justice (1986).

Reich, Steve (1936–) composer; born in New York City. After musical studies at Juilliard and Mills College (with Berio and Milhaud), he formed a New York ensemble in 1965 to perform his stripped-down, highly repetitive music that was part of the "minimalist" movement. From the small ensembles of his early music, he extended his forces (the *Music for 18 Musicians* of 1975) and continued to use electronic and mixed-media means (the *Different Trains* of 1988, for live and taped strings).

Reich, Wilhelm (1897–1957) psychiatrist, author; born in Vienna, Austria. He studied medicine in Vienna, and, becoming interested in Freud's theories of sexuality, he became associated with Freud's Psychoanalytic Polyclinic in

Vienna. Reich developed his own theory that regular orgasms were essential to mental and emotional health, a view he set forth in *The Function of the Orgasm* (1927; English trans. 1942). He also sought to achieve a synthesis of psychoanalysis and Marxism, asserting that abolition of the bourgeois family would free people of sexual inhibitions; his stress on this led to a break with Freud by 1934. In 1939 he fled the Nazis and came to the U.S.A., where he taught in New York City at the New School for Social Research (1939–41) before setting up his own organization, the Orgone Institute (1942). This was to promote his own theories about the "orgone" energy that permeates the universe; he also invented the "orgone box" (about the size of a porto-toilet), which he claimed collected orgone particles and transmitted them to the person within the box to the alleged benefit of the user's sexuality and mental health. This was declared a fraud by the federal government, and after being found guilty of violating the Food and Drug law, he was sentenced to two years in 1956; he died while still in prison.

Reichard, Gladys Amanda (1893–1955) cultural anthropologist; born in Bangor, Pa. Daughter of a physician of Quaker background, she taught in public schools for six years before enrolling at Swarthmore, from which she graduated in the classics in 1919. She went on to Columbia University, where Franz Boas became her mentor, and received a Ph.D. in 1925. She made a lifelong study of the language and culture of the Navaho, presenting the results of her fieldwork in a series of studies, including *Social Life of the Navaho Indians* (1928), *Spider Woman* (1934), and *Navaho Religion: A Study of Symbolism* (1950). She taught at Barnard College from 1923 to the end of her life.

Reichenbach, Hans (1891–1953) philosopher; born in Hamburg, Germany. He returned from service in World War I to study at the University of Berlin, at one point under Albert Einstein, and in 1926 became a physics professor there. He also made close contact with the Vienna Circle of logical positivists. Fleeing Adolf Hitler, he went to Turkey (1933) and to America (1938), where he taught at the University of California: Los Angeles from then on. His works include *The Rise of Scientific Philosophy* (1951).

Reichl, Ernst (1900–81) book designer; born in Leipzig, Germany. Emigrating in 1926, he became one of the greatest American book designers and established a press to issue his Roman Press and other fine editions, known for their originality and freshness of design.

Reid, Daniel G. (Gray) (1858–1925) financier; born in Richmond, Ind. He began as a clerk in the Second National Bank of Richmond and was vice-president by 1895. In 1891 he and friend William B. Leeds, taking advantage of the high tax on imported tin, bought a small tin plate mill in Elwood, Ill., forming the American Tin Plate Company of Illinois with Reid as president. They acquired a second company in 1898 and changed their name to the American Tin Plate Company. They also organized subsidiaries – the National Steel Company, the American Sheet Steel Company, the American Steel and Wire Hoop Company. In 1901 they sold the entire organization to J. P. Morgan who was forming U.S. Steel, for $140 million. Reid moved to New York City and acquired controlling interest in the American Can Corporation, where he chaired the board until 1923. His other interests included railroads and the $50 million Tobacco

Products Company, which he formed in 1912, as president, with Henry Clay Frick and others.

Reid, Harry Fielding (1859–1944) seismologist; born in Baltimore, Md. He was professor of dynamic geology and geography at Johns Hopkins University (1911–30). He was appointed by President Woodrow Wilson to the National Academy of Sciences in 1915 to investigate the possible control of earthslides in the Panama Canal, and then was sent to work with British and French scientists in 1917 on a map-making survey of changes arising from World War I.

Reid, Whitelaw (1837–1912) journalist, diplomat; born near Xenia, Ohio. He was a Civil War correspondent for the *Cincinnati Gazette,* and after abortive attempts with cotton plantations in the South (1865–67), he joined the *New York Tribune* (1868), becoming its editor-in-chief and eventually its principal owner (1872–1905). As the leading Republican editor in the U.S.A., he was overtly involved in Republican politics and supported expansionism in Cuba, Hawaii, the Philippines, and Panama. Known to harbor political ambitions, he was nominated for the vice-presidency (1892), but had to settle for being appointed ambassador to France (1889–92) and Great Britain (1905–12), and for retiring as a wealthy man.

Reik, Theodor (1888–1969) psychoanalyst; born in Vienna, Austria. He became a close friend and protégé of Sigmund Freud after they met in 1910. He took a Ph.D. in psychology from the University of Vienna, and after serving in the German army during World War I, he practiced as a psychoanalyst in Vienna (1918–28), where he participated in Freud's famous Wednesday evening meetings. After 1928 he taught at the Berlin Psychoanalytic Institute until 1933, when he fled the Nazis to The Hague, Holland. In 1938 he emigrated to the U.S.A. where he established a private practice in New York City. He became a U.S. citizen in 1944. In 1946 he established the National Psychological Association for Psychoanalysis when the American Psychoanalytic Association refused him full membership due to his not being a physician – even though Freud himself had written a famous essay in 1926, defending Reik's right to practice. Reik emphasized the role of intuition in a psychoanalyst's treatment and diverged from certain orthodox Freudian views, including the emphasis on the sexual nature of human beings, but maintained his friendship with Freud until the latter's death. His many works included *Listening With the Third Ear* (1948), *Of Love and Lust* (1957), and *Curiosities of the Self* (1965).

Reiner, Fritz (1888–1963) conductor; born in Budapest, Hungary. Reiner conducted opera in Budapest and Dresden before coming to the U.S.A. in 1922 to take over the Cincinnati Symphony. He left Cincinnati in 1931 to guest-conduct and teach at the Curtis Institute, then took the podium of the Pittsburgh Symphony (1938–48). After several seasons with the Metropolitan Opera in New York, Reiner found his greatest acclaim leading the Chicago Symphony between 1953 and 1962. A ruthless taskmaster, he was admired for his impeccable performances of a wide range of music.

Reinhardt, (Adolph Dietrich Friedrich) Ad (1913–67) painter, teacher; born in Buffalo, N.Y. He studied at Columbia University (1931–35, 1936–37), and at New York University (c. 1946–50). Based in New York, he was a member of the American Abstract Artists group (1937–47).

He taught at Brooklyn College, New York (1947–67), and worked as an art critic, illustrator, and cartoonist for various periodicals. Influenced by oriental art, he traveled to Asia in 1958. He began as an abstract minimalist and colorist and remained so. In the 1940s he painted bright abstractions, went on to his red and black period, as seen in *Red Painting* (1952), and from 1952 he concentrated on his "black" paintings, which combine subtle color tonalities.

Reinhold, Meyer (1909–   ) classicist, historian; born in New York City. After retiring as professor of classical studies from the University of Missouri, he became professor of classical studies at Boston University (1983). He was the founder of the International Society for the Classical Tradition (1991), editor of the *Annual Bibliography of the Classical Tradition* (1980), and coeditor, with Wolfgang Haase, of the projected seven-volume *Classical Tradition and the Americas* (1992). His *Roman Civilization: Selected Readings* (3rd edition, 1990), an anthology of source material in translation done with Napthali Lewis, introduced generations of students to Roman history. His extensive publications have ranged over all aspects of Greek and Roman history and civilization, but he is best known for his pioneering and comprehensive work on the classical tradition in America.

Reischauer, Edwin O. (Oldfather) (1910–90) diplomat, scholar born in Tokyo, Japan. The son of an American missionary, he was raised in Japan and earned a B.A. at Oberlin College and a Ph.D. at Harvard. An expert on Japanese language, culture, and politics, he taught at Harvard (1938–81). He and his colleague, John K. Fairbank, established themselves as the country's preeminent East Asia experts, collaborating on two classic textbooks, *East Asia: The Great Tradition* (1960) and *East Asia: The Modern Transformation* (1965). Married to a Japanese woman, Reischauer served with great skill as U.S. ambassador to Japan at a difficult time (1961–66), when Japan criticized escalating American military involvement in Vietnam. He returned to Harvard, joining the foreign policy debate as an opponent of the Vietnam War and an early advocate of restoring diplomatic relations with communist China. His other books include *The Japanese Today* (1988), the final revision of his classic study.

Reisinger, Hugo (1856–1914) businessman, art collector; born in Wiesbaden, Germany. He graduated from the high school in Wiesbaden and became a sales manager for the Siemens Glass works in Dresden. After his second sales trip to America, (1882, 1884), he settled in New York City as an importer and exporter. As he grew in wealth, he collected contemporary German and American paintings to further cultural relations between the two countries. His collection formed the core of Harvard University's Busch-Reisinger Museum.

Reisner, George Andrew (1867–1942) archaeologist, Egyptologist; born in Indianapolis, Ind. After studying Semitics and Egyptology, he devoted his life to directing excavations in Egypt, Palestine, and Sudan for various American institutions (1898–1942). His fieldwork at Napata, Giza, and elsewhere earned him a reputation as America's first great archaeologist and excavator, and set the standard for scientific excavation techniques. Although he spent most of his career excavating abroad, he was on the Harvard faculty (1896–97, 1905–42) and was also curator of Egyptian art at the Boston Museum of Fine Arts (1910–42).

Remington, Eliphalet (1793–1861) manufacturer; born in Suffield, Conn. He stayed on his father's farm even after marriage. In 1816 the family removed to Herkimer County, N.Y., where the father built a water-powered forge to make agricultural tools. Eliphalet made rifle barrels, a task at which he became highly skilled. By his father's death in 1828, the Remingtons' reputation for excellence was established and Eliphalet built a factory in upstate New York in what was called Remington's Corners (now Ilion). Business grew; he purchased the machinery and contracts from Ames Co., in Springfield, Mass. (1845) and in 1847 introduced the Remington pistol. With his three sons the factory expanded to produce agricultural implements in 1856. The Civil War had just brought a great demand for Remington firearms when Eliphalet died. Son Philo Remington (1816–89) became president and reorganized the business, separating out the gun manufactuary (E. Remington & Sons) in 1865. Expansions included sewing machines (1870) and typewriters (1873), but in 1887 the company had retrenched, selling off all factories except those making firearms.

Remington, Frederic (Sackrider) (1861–1909) painter, sculptor, illustrator; born in Canton, N.Y. He studied at the Yale Art School (1878–79) and the Art Students League, New York (c. 1885). He moved west (1880) and became a cowboy and rancher. Offered a commission to illustrate Geronimo's Apache campaign for *Harper's Weekly* (1882), he began his career as a painter of the American West. Traveling frequently, he was based in New Rochelle, New York, from 1886. He recorded the Indian Wars of 1890–91, created his first bronze sculpture, *Bronco Buster* (1895), and was a correspondent during the Spanish-American War (1898). He painted nearly 3,000 oils and made 15 bronze sculptures, capturing both his subject matter and the imagination of the public. He also wrote and illustrated several books that recounted his adventures.

Remond, Sarah Parker (1826–?87) abolitionist, physician; born in Salem, Mass. A child of free African-Americans, she grew up in a comfortable home, surrounded by both blacks and whites opposed to slavery. Her brother Charles Remond became an early antislavery lecturer, and in 1853 Sarah came to public notice when she went to court in Boston after being forced out of a hall to which she held a ticket. In 1856 she became an agent of the American Anti-Slavery Society, and after lecturing in the Northeast, in 1859 she went to Great Britain, where for several years she played a prominent role in exposing the evils of slavery. While there she also studied at the Bedford College for Ladies (now part of the University of London). In 1866 she went on to Florence, Italy, where after apparently studying medicine at a hospital, she practiced as a physician. She seems to have married a man named Pintor, but nothing much is known of her later years and the last dated record of her presence anywhere was in an 1887 letter from her old friend, Frederick Douglass, who saw her on a visit to Italy.

Remsen, Ira (1846–1927) chemist, educator; born in New York City. German-educated, he founded the chemistry department at Johns Hopkins (1876–1913), where he trained a generation of eminent chemists. He was founding editor of the *American Chemical Journal* (1879–1914) and wrote several important textbooks. As Johns Hopkins' president (1901–13), he founded the school of engineering.

Rentschler, Frederick (Brant) (1887–1956) aircraft manufacturer; born in Hamilton, Ohio. He graduated from Princeton in 1909 and served as an engineer during World War I. In 1925 he took over the buildings and name of Pratt and Whitney, which eventually became part of United Aircraft Corporation. As chairman of the board of United, he produced Sikorsky helicopters, Hamilton standard propellers, and Pratt and Whitney engines.

Renwick, James (1818–95) architect; born in New York City. Famous for their stylistic versatility and mechanical and material innovations, his many buildings include Grace Church (1843–46) and St. Patrick's Cathedral (1858–88), New York, and the Smithsonian "Castle" (1847–55), Washington, D.C.

Renwick, James, Sr. (1792–1863) engineer, educator; born in Liverpool, England. Coming to the U.S.A. as a child, he graduated from Columbia University, becoming a professor there (1820–53). A highly respected authority in engineering and science, he contributed particularly to canal and railroad building and to problems relating to the steam engine. He developed the use of inclined planes for transporting canal boats over elevations.

Repplier, Theodore S. (Silkman) (1899–1976) advertising executive; born in Yonkers, N.Y. He was a copywriter at Young and Rubicam (1931–42), among other advertising agencies, and was president and director of the Advertising Council (1946–66).

Reshevsky, Samuel (Herman) (1911–92) chess player; born in Ozorkow, Poland. After emigrating to America at age eight, he was seven times the U.S. champion; his world title hopes were stalled by World War II, then by Soviet-dominated candidates' matches. Eclipsed by Bobby Fischer in 1957, he worked as an investment analyst and insurance salesman.

Resnik, Regina (1922–) mezzo-soprano; born in New York City. She made her concert debut as a soprano in Brooklyn in 1942 and her operatic debut that year in New York; her first Metropolitan Opera appearance came in 1944. After a successful decade of singing internationally, she began doing mezzo-soprano roles in 1955, with comparable success. While performing into the 1970s, she also began directing opera in 1971. Her 1982 documentary film, *The Historic Ghetto of Venice*, won a prize in Italy.

Resor, Stanley (Burnet) (1879–1962) advertising executive; born in Cincinnati, Ohio. He joined the J. Walter Thompson advertising agency in 1908. Soon buying out its founder, as president and chairman (1916–61) he built it into the world's largest advertising agency, renowned for its use of scientific market research and insistence on sales results. In 1917 he married Helen Lansdowne Resor (?1887–1964), a copywriter and pioneer of testimonial advertising who was a vice-president and director of J. Walter Thompson for more than 40 years.

Reston, James (Barrett) "Scotty" (1909–) journalist; born in Clydebank, Scotland. Joining the *New York Times* Washington bureau in 1939, he became an outstanding reporter and political analyst, winning two Pulitzer Prizes (1945, 1957). In the 1960s he became associate and then executive editor of the *Times,* while also writing a regular column.

Retton, Mary Lou (1968–) gymnast; born in Fairmont, W.Va. In the 1984 Olympics at Los Angeles, she won a gold medal in the women's all-around by earning a perfect score of ten in the vault, the final event of the competition. She also won two silver and two bronze medals in individual and team competitions. Her wholesome exuberence won her many commercial endorsements, including an appearance on the front of a Wheaties cereal box.

Reuther, Walter (Philip) (1907–70) labor leader; born in Wheeling, W.Va. He worked at a Ford plant (1927–32) and then went to the Soviet Union to work at the Gorki Auto plant (1933–35). On return to the U.S.A. he became one of the founders of the United Auto Workers (UAW) and took an active role in forcing General Motors to recognize the UAW. During World War II he solidified his reputation as a responsible labor leader and was elected UAW vice-president (1942–46) and then president (1946–70). After World War II he became an outspoken opponent of Communists in the Congress of Industrial Organizations (CIO), to which the UAW belonged, and in 1952 he was elected president of the CIO. He worked for the merger with the AFL in 1955, but by 1968 he led the UAW out of the AFL-CIO because of differences with George Meany.

Revel, Bernard (1855–1940) rabbi, educator; born in Pren, Lithuania. He came to the U.S.A. in 1906 and earned an M.A. from New York University and a Ph.D. from Dropsie College (Philadelphia). He became the head of the Rabbi Isaac Elchanan Yeshiva in New York in 1915, and in 1928 he helped found Yeshiva College, the first Jewish liberal arts institution. He was influential in the modern Orthodox movement.

Revelle, Roger (Randall Dougan) (1909–91) oceanographer, sociologist; born in Seattle, Wash. He worked at the Scripps Institution of Oceanography, where his tectonic studies of the Pacific Ocean led to major contributions to the theory of seafloor spreading. After his interests broadened, Revelle became a professor of population policy at Harvard (1964–76), then joined the University of California: San Diego to be professor of science and public policy (1976–91). He served on U.S. and international committees on world population and the environment.

Revels, Hiram Rhodes (1827–1901) Protestant minister, U.S. senator, educator; born in Fayetteville, N.C. Born to free parents (of Indian as well as African-American descent), he attended Knox College (Galesburg, Ill.). Ordained a minister in the African Methodist Episcopal Church (1845), he served in various churches and capacities in several states before accepting a pastorate in Baltimore in 1860. Early in the Civil War he helped to recruit two black regiments in Maryland, then served as the chaplain in such a regiment in Mississippi, where he organized black churches. In 1863 he established a school for freedom in St. Louis. After serving in different churches, in 1866 he settled in Natchez, Miss., where he soon gained elective offices. On January 20, 1870, he was chosen by a vote of the Mississippi legislature to fill the unexpired term of Jefferson Davis in the U.S. Senate, and although many in the Senate came up with legal objections, he was finally allowed to take his seat on February 25. In a little over a year in the Senate, he took an active role in trying to advance the rights of African-Americans, while at the same time calling for moderation in treatment of former Confederates. He was not chosen to succeed himself after March 1871 but he became the first president of Alcorn University, the first land-grant college in the U.S.A. for black students. Feuds with more radical

Republicans led to his temporary step-down from his post at Alcorn (1874–76) and his siding with the Democrats in the election of 1875, but he returned as president of Alcorn until 1882. In his later years he was also pastor of a church at Holly Springs, Miss., and taught at Shaw (later Rust) College.

Revere, Joseph Warren (1812–80) naval officer, army general; born in Boston, Mass. (grandson of Paul Revere). A true adventurer, he joined the U.S. Navy as a midshipman (1828). As a naval lieutenant, he raised the U.S. flag at Sonoma during the Mexican War (1846). He resigned from the navy (1850), and while ranching and trading in California, he organized the artillery of the Mexican army (1851–52). He rose to the rank of army general during the Civil War, but was dismissed for removing his men from the battle of Chancellorsville (1863). (Lincoln revoked his sentence and he was allowed to resign.) He wrote *Keel and Saddle: A Retrospective of Forty Years of Military and Naval Service* (1872).

Revere, Paul (1735–1818) patriot, silversmith; born in Boston, Mass. He was an excellent silversmith and ardent patriot, but a mediocre military leader. A member of the Sons of Liberty, he became the primary express rider for the Boston Committee of Safety. His famous ride to Lexington in 1775 was only the best-known of the many courier services he performed. He later was court-martialed and acquitted for his leadership during the failed Penebscot Bay expedition of 1779. After the American Revolution, he continued his silversmith trade with great success. He provided materials for the U.S.S. *Constitution* and worked with Robert Fulton in developing copper boilers for steamboats.

Revson, Charles (Haskell) (1906–75) business executive; born in Boston, Mass. With two partners he founded Revlon Inc. (1932), of which he was president (1932–62) and chairman (1962–75). Revlon introduced opaque nail polish and matching colors for lips and nails. Largely through Revson's flair for new product development and brilliant magazine advertising, it became the largest retail cosmetics and fragrance company in the U.S.A.

Rexroth, Kenneth (1905–82) poet, writer, painter; born in South Bend, Ind. He moved to Chicago (1917), studied at the Art Institute there, then at the New School of Social Research and the Art Students League in New York City. He moved to Santa Barbara, Calif. (1958). Although he had several occupations, including journalism, he is best known for his critical essays and his naturalistic erotic poetry.

Reynolds, David Parham (1915–   ) metals executive; born in Bristol, Tenn. (son of Richard S. Reynolds Sr.). He joined the family firm, Reynolds Metals Co. (1937), eventually becoming variously chairman and CEO (1976–88). His innovative marketing – including the introduction of Reynolds Wrap (1947), aluminum soft-drink cans, and inexpensive metal recycling – created major growth in the post-World War II aluminum industry.

Reynolds, John Fulton (1820–63) soldier; born in Lancaster, Pa. A West Point graduate (1841), he served in the Mexican War and on the exploration and Indian-fighting expeditions in the West; he was commandant of cadets at West Point when the Civil War began, but was soon assigned to help defend Washington, D.C. Starting in spring of 1862 he held command positions in a series of battles and was considered one of the best generals in the Army of the Potomac – many believe he rather than Meade should have succeeded Hooker as its commander on the eve of Gettysburg. Instead he was killed by a Confederate sharpshooter at Gettysburg on July 1, 1863.

Reynolds, Quentin (1902–65) journalist, author; born in Bronx, N.Y. He served as a European-based World War II correspondent for *Collier's* magazine and wrote several books on his observations, including *The Wounded Don't Cry* (1941). His career was dampened by accusations of laxity and cowardice by columnist Westbrook Pegler, whom he successfully sued for heavy damages in a celebrated libel case.

Reynolds, Robert Rice (1884–1963) U.S. senator; born in Weaverville, N.C. A lawyer, he served in the U.S. Senate (Dem., N.C.; 1932–45). As chairman of the Senate Military Affairs Committee and a member of the Senate Committee on Foreign Relations, he opposed the U.S. entering World War II.

Reznikoff, Charles (1894–1976) poet, writer; born in Brooklyn, N.Y. He studied at the University of Missouri (1910–11), settled in New York City, and earned a law degree from New York University (1915). He worked in publishing much of his life, and is noted for his spare poetry of the objectivist school. He often dealt with the role of Judaism in his life, as in *Poems 1937–75* (1977).

Rhead, Frederick Hurten (1880–1942) potter; born in Hanley, Staffordshire, England. A descendant of six generations of potters, he emigrated to the U.S.A. (1902) to work as a designer at Weller Pottery and Roseville Pottery. After teaching at University City Pottery and Arequipa Pottery, he opened Rhead Pottery in Santa Barbara, Calif. (1913). In 1927 he joined the Homer Laughlin China Company, West Virgina, as art director. There he created the art deco line of dishware, Fiestaware.

Rhett, Robert Barnwell (b. Robert Barnwell Smith) (1800–76) U.S. representative/senator, political idealogue; born in Beaufort, S.C. A South Carolina planter, he served in the state legislature (1827–32) and was the state's attorney general (1832–37). (It was in 1837 that he adopted the surname of an ancestor.) Inspired by the political rhetoric of the American Revolution, he became a "fire-eater" secessionist and was briefly John C. Calhoun's protégé. He served South Carolina in the U.S. House of Representatives (Dem., S.C.; 1837–49) and in the U.S. Senate (1850–52) and opposed all attempts at compromise over the issues of slaves (of which he owned many) and states' rights. He also carried on his campaign through the columns of the *Charleston Mercury*, which he owned. He was a central delegate at the South Carolina secession convention (1860) and wrote an "Address to the Slaveholding States" to encourage secession. After he failed to become president of the Confederate States of America, he vocally opposed President Jefferson Davis and his conduct of the war. He moved to Louisiana in 1867 and although he was a delegate to the Democratic national convention in 1868, he never abandoned his belief in a "separate and free" South.

Rhine, Joseph (Banks) (1895–1980) psychologist, parapsychologist; born in Juniata County, Pa. After taking his Ph.D. in botany at the University of Chicago, he studied under William McDougall at Duke University, where he became professor of psychology (1937). He cofounded the Parapsychology Laboratory there (1930) and the Institute of Parapsychology in Durham, N.C. (1964) and is generally recognized as the founder of modern studies of psychical phenomena. His experiments involving packs of specially designed cards used by subjects in different rooms established the phenomena of extrasensory perception (ESP) and telepathy on a statistical basis. In addition to coining the term "extrasensory perception," he coined the term "psychokinesis" (PK) to describe mental influence on external events. He founded and edited the *Journal of Parapsychology* and his publications include *New Frontiers of the Mind* (1937). On retiring from Duke (1965), he continued his often controversial work at the Foundation for Research on the Nature of Man.

Rhines, Peter B. (Broomell) (1942–) oceanographer; born in Hartford, Conn. He worked at the Woods Hole Oceanographic Institution (1972–84) before joining the University of Washington (1984). He made major contributions to studies of ocean circulation and the movement of trace chemicals in the seas.

Rhodes, John (Jacob) (1916–) U.S. representative; born in Council Grove, Mo. A World War II veteran, he was judge advocate of the Arizona National Guard (1947–52) before going to Congress (Rep., 1953–83) where he was minority leader for eight years.

Ricci, Ruggiero (1918–) violinist; born in San Francisco. He made a sensational debut at age ten and went on to an international solo career with an enormous repertoire, including advanced moderns.

Rice, Anne (b. Howard Allen O'Brien) (Anne Rampling, A. N. Roquelaure, pen names) (1941–) writer; born in New Orleans. Named after her father, she legally changed her name (c. 1947). She studied at Texas Women's University (1959–60), San Francisco State College (B.A. 1964; M.A. 1971), and at the University of California: Berkeley (1969–70). After a variety of jobs, such as waitress, cook, and insurance claims examiner, she began her career as a writer of erotica and vampire novels. Living in New Orleans, she gained a vast cult readership for both her supernatural novels, such as the *Vampire Chronicles* (1989), a trilogy, and for her sadomasochistic erotica, as in *Beauty's Punishment* (1984). She also wrote mainstream fiction, using the pen name of Anne Rampling.

Rice, Dan (b. Daniel McLaren) (1823–1900) clown; born in New York City. Originally a stableboy and jockey, Rice's act featured his trick horse, Excelsior, weight lifting, and homespun orations during his heyday in the 1860s and 1870s. His crackerboy commentaries on the contemporary scene prefigured many later comedians' routines.

Rice, (Henry) Grantland (1880–1954) sportswriter; born in Murfreesboro, Tenn. A graduate of Vanderbilt University, he began as a reporter with the *Nashville News* (1901); after working as a sportswriter for other Southern newspapers, he joined the *New York Mail* in 1910, then joined the *New York Tribune* (later the *Herald Tribune*) (1911–30), with time out for service in France during World War I (1918–19). After leaving the *Tribune*, he wrote a widely syndicated column, "The Sportlight," made a series of short films on sports, and was in charge of selecting the All-American football team for *Collier's* magazine (1926–54). Considered the dean of American sportswriters, his syndicated columns included some of sport's most memorable phrases, including those describing Notre Dame's football backfield as "The Four

Horsemen". A prolific versifier, one of his poems included the famous line, "When the One Great Scorer comes to write against your name/He marks – not that you won or lost – but how you played the game."

Rice, Henry Mower (1816–94) pioneer, U.S. senator; born in Waitsfield, Vt. He moved to Michigan (1835) and then to Minnesota (1839). He traded with the Winnebago and Chippewa Indians and obtained large land cessions from the latter (1847–51). He was a territorial delegate to Congress (1853–57) and served as one of the new state's first two U.S. senators (Dem., Minn.; 1858–63). He was a U.S. commissioner in several Indian treaty negotiations (1887–88). Minnesota placed his statue in the U.S. Capitol.

Rice, Joseph (Mayer) (1857–1934) educational innovator; born in Philadelphia. A New York physician, he became an educational researcher, publishing a major study, *The Public School System of the United States* (1893). He also reported public schools' standardized test results as editor of the *Forum* (1897–1907) and founded the Society of Educational Research (1903).

Rice, (Leopold) Elmer (b. Reizenstein) (1892–1967) playwright; born in New York City. A lawyer by training, for a time he specialized in courtroom dramas; his first, *On Trial* (1914), was notable for its use of flashbacks. Winner of a Pulitzer Prize in 1929 for *Street Scene,* he had 24 plays produced on Broadway. His later, less successful work dealt with current political events – the Depression (*We the People,* 1933) and the Reichstag trial (*Judgment Day,* 1934).

Rice, Thomas Dartmouth ("Daddy") (1808–60) minstrel performer; born in New York. He was a little-known entertainer when sometime about 1828–31 (it is generally believed although cannot be absolutely proven) he first performed in Louisville, Ky., in blackface (from burnt cork) and rags, a routine he called "Jump Jim Crow." He was supposedly mimicking a crippled black slave (of a Mr. Crow in Louisville) he had observed entertaining his fellow workers in a stable. The song instantly became popular; Rice made the song and his dance the centerpiece of his full-scale musical shows he called "Ethiopian operas" with which he toured widely in the U.S.A. and British Isles to great acclaim (1836, 1838, 1843). To promote himself he adopted the name "Jim Crow" and some believe this is the origin of the name used to refer to African-Americans, specifically when referring to segregation laws. Although he was not the first white man to perform in blackface, the popularity of his singing-dancing-comic routines is said to have led to the minstrel shows of the 1840s. He played the leading role in the New York production of *Uncle Tom's Cabin* in 1854, but died in poverty.

Rich, Adrienne (Cecile) (1929–) poet; born in Baltimore, Md. She studied at Radcliffe (B.A. 1951), lived briefly in the Netherlands, and taught at many institutions, notably Cornell (1981). Based in New York City, she won many awards and is known for her highly personal poetry, such as *Diving into the Wreck: Poems 1971–1972* (1973).

Richard, Gabriel (1767–1832) Catholic missionary; born in Saintes, France. Ordained a Sulpician priest (1791), he emigrated to the U.S.A. during the French Revolution and did missionary work in Illinois, Wisconsin, and Michigan; from 1798 he was based in Detroit. He founded several Catholic schools and in 1817 cofounded the University of Michigan in Detroit (which moved to Ann Arbor in 1837).

He acquired a printing press (1808) with which he published a newspaper and various books, and he also imported textile machinery to promote industry. Imprisoned by the British in the War of 1812, he later became the first Catholic priest to serve as a delegate (before Michigan was a state) to the U.S. House of Representatives (1822). He died while ministering to victims of a cholera epidemic in Detroit.

Richards, A. N. (Alfred Newton) (1876–1966) pharmacologist; born in Stamford, N.Y. He taught at Columbia (1904–08) and Northwestern (1908–10) Universities before settling at the University of Pennsylvania (1910–46). In World War II he chaired the Committee on Medical Research, which made penicillin available for widespread use.

Richards, Ann (b. Dorothy Ann Willis) (1933–) governor; born in Lakeview, Texas. She taught in a junior high school (1955–57) and managed the campaign of Sarah Weddington (the lawyer who won the *Roe* v. *Wade* case) in 1972. As an active Democrat, she became a county commissioner (1977–82), the state treasurer (1983–91), and finally governor of Texas (1991), Texas's first female governor since "Ma" Ferguson (1933–35). Although her early career had been plaqued by alcoholism, she recovered and gained national respect for her rousing nomination speeches at the Democratic National Conventions of 1988 and 1992.

Richards, Dickinson W. (Woodruff) (1895–1973) cardiologist; born in Orange, N.J. He was a research fellow in London, England (1927–28), then joined Columbia University (1928–61). There he collaborated with André Cournand (1936–41) to expand German physician Werner Forssmann's cardiac catheterization technique to investigate cardiovascular and pulmonary diseases, for which Richards (with Cournand and Forssmann) won the 1956 Nobel Prize in physiology. In 1944 Richards and Cournand determined that whole blood is preferable for treatment of hemorrhagic shock. After World War II, Richards was a clinician at Bellevue Hospital, New York City (1945–61), where he studied the effects of the heart stimulant digitalis, and classified the progress of pulmonary insufficiency. He was an outspoken advocate of hospital modernization, health care for the elderly, and legalization of narcotics for addicts.

Richards, Ellen Henrietta (b. Swallow) (1842–1911) chemist, sanitation engineer, educator, home economist; born in Dunstable, Mass. She graduated from Vassar and then became the first woman admitted to the Massachusetts Institute of Technology (MIT); after graduating from there (1873) she was refused a doctorate but in 1876 she established and taught at the Woman's Laboratory at MIT. She also set up programs in the Boston public schools to prepare young women for education in the sciences. Finally admitted to the regular MIT faculty when women were admitted to regular classes, she taught sanitary chemistry there (1884–1911); after conducting a pioneer survey of Massachusetts' inland waterways (1878–90), she established the first program in sanitary engineering at MIT. In her later years she also became a leader in establishing a scientific basis for home economics, with such projects as her studies in the adulteration of groceries and the arsenic content in wallpaper and fabrics, as well as her promotion of good nutrition. She conceived and directed the Lake Placid Conference on Home Economics (1899–1908), which coined the term "home economics" and developed standards for training professionals. Although she published various works, including *The Chemistry of Cooking and Cleaning* (1882) and *Food Materials and Their Adulteration* (1885), her major claim to fame now rests on her having opened up scientific education and professions to women.

Richards, Lloyd (1923–) stage director, actor; born in Toronto, Ontario, Canada. He began his career as a radio then television actor. Later, he mainly directed – the Great Lakes Drama Festival; the Northland Playhouse, Detroit; *A Raisin in the Sun* (1959) in New York; and a number of television productions. He served as artistic director of the Eugene O'Neill Theater Center and until 1991 was dean-artistic director of the Yale School of Drama and Repertory Theater, where he introduced many new American playwrights and theater people.

Richards, (Robert Eugene) Bob (1926–) track and field athlete, Protestant minister; born in Champaign, Ill. A juvenile delinquent as a teenager, he found himself through religion and sports. He was ordained a minister in the Church of the Brethren in 1946, and then became the only two-time Olympic gold medalist in the pole vault (1952, 1956). He accepted the pastorate of a Brethren church in Long Beach, Calif., in 1957, but continued as an advocate of physical fitness in the U.S.A.

Richards, Theodore (Williams) (1868–1928) chemist; born in Germantown, Pa. He was affiliated with Harvard from his graduate studies to his death (1885–1928). He had begun by trying to establish precisely the relation of the atomic weights of hydrogen and oxygen, and he devoted the first half of his career to correcting the errors in the accepted atomic weights of 21 elements. It was this work that won him the Nobel Prize in chemistry in 1914. He then turned his attention to thermochemistry and thermodynamics, producing not only immense amounts of new data, but also elucidating a number of fundamental properties and processes. Regarded as the foremost experimental chemist of his day, he remains important for establishing the modern era of accuracy in physico-chemical analysis.

Richards, William Trost (1833–1905) painter; born in Philadelphia. A draftsman, he studied abroad (1853–56), lived in Germantown, Pa., then settled in Newport, R.I. (1890). He is known for his precise seascapes, such as *On the Coast of New Jersey* (1883).

Richardson, Elliot (Lee) (1920–) lawyer, cabinet member; born in Boston, Mass. A lawyer, he was Massachusetts' lieutenant governor (1965–67) and attorney general (1967–69). After serving as Nixon's secretary of Health, Education, and Welfare (1970–73), he served briefly as secretary of defense (1973). He became attorney general in 1973, but resigned in protest for the firing of Watergate prosecutor, Archibald Cox. Secretary of Commerce (1976–77), he was the chief U.S. negotiator for the international Law of the Sea (1978–80) before returning to private practice. He was the only man in U.S. history to have held four different cabinet posts.

Richardson, H. H. (Henry Hobson) (1838–86) architect; born in Priestley Plantation, La. He graduated from Harvard (1859) and studied at the École des Beaux-Arts, Paris. He returned to open his practice in New York in 1866, in an early partnership (1867–78) with Charles Dexter Gambrill, designing chiefly churches. His design for Trinity Church, Boston (1872–77), won him national recognition. Practicing independently after 1878 in Brookline, Mass., he designed a number

of small suburban libraries and railroad stations, Harvard residence halls, commercial buildings, and private houses, and collaborated on the New York State Capitol, Albany (1876–86). His final works were the Allegheny County Courthouse and Jail, Pittsburgh (1883–88), and the Marshall Field Wholesale Store, Chicago (1885–87), completed by assistants after Richardson's death. Richardson's designs progressively refined Romanesque forms into a style termed "Richardsonian," inspiring the American Romanesque revival. He was widely influential also through his sensitive handling of materials, his mastery of interior decoration, and his introduction of the Queen Anne style to America, as in the William Watts Sherman House, Newport, R.I. (1874–76). He trained a generation of architects including John Galen Howard, Charles McKim, George Shepley, and Stanford White. Some scholars rate him the greatest architect of his age.

Richardson, James Montgomery (1858–1925) U.S. representative; born in Mobile, Ala. Educated in common schools, he became editor of the *Glasgow Times* (Ky.) (1878–1900). After serving as congressman (Dem., Ky.; 1905–07), he returned to his paper and the postmaster's job in Glasgow.

Richardson, Sid (Williams) (1891–1959) oil executive, philanthropist; born in Athens, Texas. He became an independent oil producer in Fort Worth (1919). He speculated in the cattle business and brought in major oil fields in Texas and Louisiana during the 1930s. Known for his down-home style, he collected western art, particularly that of Frederic Remington, and established the Sid Richardson Foundation.

Richberg, Donald (Randall) (1881–1960) lawyer, government official; born in Knoxville, Tenn. A progressive lawyer, he handled Chicago's litigation to reduce gas rates (1915–27) and served as counsel to the Railway Labor Executive's Association (1926–33). A supporter of President Franklin Roosevelt's New Deal, he served as general counsel of the National Recovery Administration in 1933, eventually becoming director of the National Emergency Council (1934–36). He moved on to practice law and teach at the University of Virginia's Law School and turned against Roosevelt's social welfare programs.

Richmond, Julius Benjamin (1916–) physician, child psychiatrist, educator; born in Chicago. He was psychiatrist-in-chief of the Judge Baker Guidance Center in Boston (1971–77) and then served as surgeon general of the United States (1977–81). He pioneered the introduction of psychosocial development in pediatric education. His career was marked by his interest in the development of health policies, particularly those aimed at children and families.

Richmond, Mary Ellen (1861–1928) social worker; born in Belleville, Ill. Raised mainly by women relatives in Baltimore, Md., and with only a few years of formal education through high school, she took a clerical job in New York City (1878–80) and then returned to Baltimore to work as a bookkeeper. Taking a job with the Baltimore Charity Organization Society in 1889, she soon impressed its male leaders with her abilities and was appointed its general secretary in 1891. An early advocate of the need to fully understand the problems of the poor and to train professional social workers, she was one of the first Americans to employ the British term "case work" for this new approach to social work. In 1900 she became the general secretary of the Philadelphia Society for Organizing Charity and soon gained a national reputation – through both her own policies and her writings – for her progressive and professional views on social work. In 1909 she was named director of the Charity Organization Department of the Russell Sage Foundation. Her book, *Social Diagnosis* (1917), laid the theoretical foundation for many of the modern practices of social work.

Richter, Burton (1931–) physicist; born in New York City. Joining Stanford in 1956, he became director of its Linear Accelerator Center (1984). He received the 1976 Nobel Prize in physics (shared with simultaneous and independent codiscoverer S. C. C. Ting) for his discovery of the J/psi hadron, a new heavy elementary particle that provided experimental evidence for the existence of charmed quarks.

Richter, Charles F. (Francis) (1900–85) seismologist; born in Hamilton, Ohio. He was a theoretical physicist until 1927, when he joined the seismological laboratory at the California Institute of Technology. With colleague Beno Gutenberg, he devised the scale of earthquake magnitude that has been the standard for measuring earth tremors since 1935; he never himself referred to it as the "Richter scale."

Richter, Gisela (Marie Augusta) (1882–1972) art historian; born in London, England. Educated in England, she emigrated to the United States in 1905 and was naturalized in 1917. She was an influential curator at the Metropolitan Museum of Art in New York City (1906–48) whose publications included *Roman Portraits* (1948), *Archaic Greek Art* (1949), *Three Critical Periods in Greek Sculpture* (1951), and *A Handbook of Greek Art* (1959), for many years the standard introduction to the topic.

Rickard, (George Lewis) "Tex" (1870–1929) boxing promoter; born in Kansas City, Mo. A colorful, buccaneering character, he ran a gambling business in Texas, made and lost a fortune in the Yukon in the 1890s, and arranged his first prize fight in 1906. He promoted matches during boxing's "golden age," including the Jack Dempsey-George Carpentier bout in 1921 – boxing's first $1 million gate – and the famous Dempsey-Gene Tunney match in 1927.

Rickenbacker, (Edward Vernon) Eddie (1890–1973) aviator; born in Columbus, Ohio. A skilled race-car driver, he became General Pershing's chauffeur during World War I but applied for aviation service. He shot down 26 enemy aircraft in seven months, receiving the Congressional Medal of Honor and the nickname, "Ace of Aces." In 1921 he founded the Rickenbacker Motor Company; it failed in 1927 and he went to work for General Motors (GM). The company employed him to rescue one of their divisions, Eastern Airlines. During his initial management year (1934), the airline turned the first profit in the history of aviation. GM divested the company in 1938; Rickenbacker bought the controlling interest and became president, general manager, and director. In 1942, while on an inspection of military bases in the Pacific, his plane crashed; he spent 22 days adrift on a raft before being rescued. After retiring in 1963, he continued to be a public figure as an advocate of conservative causes.

Ricketts, Howard Taylor (1871–1910) pathologist; born in Findlay, Ohio. After taking his M.D. from Northwestern (1897), he continued his studies in Vienna and Paris, then in 1902 joined the department of pathology at the University of Chicago. A brilliant researcher, he wrote *Infection, Immu-* *nity, and Serum Therapy* (1906). He discovered the vectors of both Rocky Mountain Fever (tick) and typhus (louse) as well as the culprit microorganisms, which were named *Rickettsia* in his honor. He died of typhus in Mexico City while researching the disease.

Rickey, George (Warren) (1907–) sculptor; born in South Bend, Ind. He studied at Trinity College, Scotland (1921–26), at Oxford (1926–29), and in Paris (1929–30). He taught widely in the United States but was based in East Chatham, N.Y. He is known for his outdoor kinetic sculptures, often in polished aluminum, with parts that swing around a fulcrum in response to breezes.

Rickey, (Wesley) Branch (1881–1965) baseball manager/executive; born in Lucasville, Ohio. After playing four years in the majors and a ten-year career as a manager of the St. Louis Browns and Cardinals (1913–25), he became vice-president of the Cardinals (1925–42) and created a "farm system" of 32 minor-league teams that supplied countless star players for the parent major-league club. A religious man, he never played, attended or managed games on Sundays. As vice-president of the Brooklyn Dodgers (1942–50), he established the spring training complex in Vero Beach, Fla., and fulfilled his intention to break baseball's color line; in 1947 he signed Jackie Robinson to a major-league contract despite the vigorous opposition of other club owners. He was general manager (1951–55) and then chairman of the board of directors of the Pittsburgh Pirates (1956–59). He organized the aborted Continental League that led to the founding of the New York Mets in 1962. Nicknamed "the Mahatma" because of his reputation as a baseball sage, he was elected to the Hall of Fame in 1967.

Rickover, Hyman (George) (1900–86) naval officer; born in Makow, Russia (now in Poland). He came with his parents to Chicago (1906) and graduated from the Naval Academy in 1922. He was chief of the electrical division of the Bureau of Ships during World War II. He became convinced that an atomic-powered submarine was both feasible and necessary. As chief of the nuclear power division, Bureau of Ships, and head of the naval reactors branch of the Atomic Energy Commission, he was the driving force behind the launching of the USS *Nautilus* (1954), the world's first nuclear-powered submarine. He helped to develop an experimental nuclear electric-power plant (1956–57) and wrote a number of books including *Education and Freedom* (1959) and *American Education: A National Failure* (1963). His call for the training of more engineers and scientists was heeded in Congress, which sometimes supported him against his naval superiors. He received the Medal of Freedom in 1980.

Riddiford, Lynn M. (Moorhead) (1936–) entomologist; born in Knoxville, Tenn. She was a research fellow at Harvard (1961–63), then taught at Wellesley College (1963–65). She returned to Harvard (1965–73), then relocated to the University of Washington (1973). She made major contributions to studies of the hormonal control of insect development, insect embryogenesis, and the effects of insect olfaction and pheromones.

Riddle, Nelson (1921–87) musician; born in Oradell, N.J. He studied piano and trombone, but from the outset of his career he worked primarily as an arranger, beginning in the late 1930s with Jerry Wald, Tommy Dorsey, and Alvino Rey. After playing with a U.S. Army band during World War II, he joined Bob Crosby and went with him to Los Angeles, where he became a staff arranger for National Broadcasting Company-TV in 1948. Between 1950 and his death, he worked as a free-lance arranger and conductor on hundreds of popular recordings, including classics by Nat King Cole, Frank Sinatra, and Ella Fitzgerald.

Ride, Sally (Kristen) (1951–) astronaut, astrophysicist; born in Encino, Calif. Selected for the National Aeronautics and Space Administration's (NASA) astronaut program out of 1,000 female candidates (1978), she became the first American woman in space on the space shuttle *Challenger* (1983). Known for solving difficult engineering problems and being a team player, she served on a presidential commission investigating the Space Shuttle *Challenger* accident (1986), and as special assistant to the administrator, NASA (1987).

Rider, (Arthur) Fremont (1885–1962) editor, publisher, librarian; born in Trenton, N.J. He graduated from Syracuse University (Ph.B. 1905), but left the New York State Library School without graduating in 1907 to work with Melvil Dewey on revising the Decimal Classification System. He became editor of the *Monthly Book Review* (1909–17), and the *American Library Annual* (1912–17), and managing editor of *Publisher's Weekly* (1910–17) and the *Library Journal* (1914–17). His Rider Press (1914–32) published various periodicals, including the *International Military Digest* (1915–18), and he was vice-president of Arrow Publishing Corporation. He also produced a series of guide books to New York City, Bermuda, Washington, and California. In 1933 he became librarian at Wesleyan University (Conn.) and retired in 1953 after greatly expanding the library's resources. Among many other technical innovations, he invented the microcard, which he refused to patent out of a desire that it be freely available.

Ridgway, Matthew (Bunker) (1895–1993) soldier; born in Fort Monroe, Va. A 1917 graduate of West Point, he served in various overseas posts, and at the outbreak of World War II, was with the War Plans Division of the War Department. He commanded the 82nd Airborne Division in Sicily and Italy (1943) and in the Normandy invasion (1944), and led an airborne corps in northwest Europe (1944–45). Ridgway replaced MacArthur as commander of United Nations forces in Korea (1951), and he succeeded Eisenhower as head of NATO (1952) – thereby becoming the first American to hold the supreme commands in both the Pacific and Atlantic areas. As army chief of staff (1953–55), he argued successfully against commitment of U.S. forces in Vietnam. After retiring from the army, he served as chairman of the Mellon Institute of Industrial Research (1955–60).

Ridgway, Robert (1850–1929) ornithologist; born in Mount Carmel, Ill. At age nine he was making colored drawings of birds he shot. He was the protégé of the zoologist Spencer Baird, who when he became secretary of the Smithsonian Institution appointed Ridgway curator of birds at the U.S. National Museum (1880–1929). He did field studies but it was his writings that gained him the reputation as the country's leading ornithologist. He systematized the color system for bird identification and wrote *Color Standards and Nomenclature* (1886, 1912) and *The Birds of North and Middle America* (8 vols. 1901–19).

Riding, Laura (b. Reichenthal; m. Gottschalk and Jackson) (Madeleine Vara, pen name) (1901–91) poet, writer; born in New York City. She studied at Cornell (1918–21), as well as several other schools, and adopted "Riding" as her surname in 1926. She spent much of her life in Europe and in New York City, but later moved to Wabaso, Fla. A prolific writer of criticism, translations, and prose works, she is noted for her collaborations with the British writer, Robert Graves, and her metaphysical poetry, as in *Selected Poems: In Five Sets* (1970).

Ridley, Clarence Eugene (1891–) city manager; born in Armada, Mich. He earned a national reputation as the progressive city manager of Bluefield, W. Va. (1921–25) and was the first director of the International City Managers' Association (1929–56). Known as "Mr. City Manager," he established the Public Administration Service (1933) and *The Municipal Year Book* (1934) and he developed standards for municipal services.

Riegger, Wallingford (1885–1961) composer; born in Albany, Ga. After extended studies and creative work in Germany, he returned to teach and compose both many rent-paying items, and serious, avant-garde, but still communicative works.

Riesman, David (Jr.) (1909–) sociologist, educator; born in Philadelphia. After a law career, he joined the social science faculty of the University of Chicago (1946–58) and Harvard (1958–80). He gained national prominence with *The Lonely Crowd* (coauthored, 1950). His other works, many on the sociology of higher education, include *On Higher Education* (1980).

Rifkin, Jeremy (1945–) social activist, author; born in Chicago, Ill. He graduated from the Wharton School of Finance at the University of Pennsylvania and the Fletcher School of Law and Diplomacy of Tufts University, but America's role in the Vietnam War so disturbed him that he helped organize the first national rally against the war (1967). He then founded and directed the People's Bicentennial Commission (1971–76) to counter the official, establishment bicentennial celebrations. He went on to lecture and write vigorously about a variety of issues, usually stressing the "true story" hidden from most people, as in shaky pension funds, but most especially the dangers of technology and science, such as genetic splicing. To advance his message, in 1977 he established the Foundation on Economic Trends, which he financed by a continual round of lectures and many books. Among these are *The Emerging Order* (1979), *Entropy* (1980), *Algeny* (1983), *Declaration of a Heretic* (1985), and *Beyond Beef* (1992). Often dismissed as a pest by the sci-tech/corporate establishment, but admired as a useful gadfly by others, he raised important issues in the contemporary debate over the role of science and technology.

Rifkin, Joshua (1944–) musicologist, pianist, conductor; born in New York City. After studies in the U.S.A. and Germany, he taught at Brandeis (1970–82) and pursued a range of activities from early music scholarship and performance to arranging popular music. As a pianist he was a leading figure in the Scott Joplin ragtime revival.

Riggs, Elias (1810–1901) linguist, missionary; born in New Providence, N.J. His gift for languages emerged by age 11; he eventually made use of seven ancient and 14 modern languages. He graduated from Andover Theological Seminary (1832) and embarked upon an extensive missionary career that took him to Greece (1832–38), Turkey (1838–44), Armenia (1844–53), Constantinople (1853–56), and Turkey (1859–62). He translated the Scriptures into Armenian (1853) and Bulgarian, and worked on a joint translation into the Turkish language (1878). Three of his sons became ministers and ten of his grandchildren became missionaries.

Riggs, (Robert Larimore) Bobby (1918–) tennis player; born in Los Angeles. He began playing tennis seriously by age 11 and was tutored in his early years at tennis by two women, Dr. Esther Bartosh and the coach Eleanor Tennant. As an amateur, he helped the U.S.A. win the Davis Cup in 1938, then won the Wimbledon and U.S. singles in 1939; after winning the U.S. singles again in 1941, he turned professional and played for another ten years. In 1973 he emerged from retirement when he claimed that any half-decent male player could defeat even the best female players; he challenged Margaret Smith Court, then a leading woman player, to a winner-take-all match on national television and defeated a "psyched" Court (6–2, 6–1); pressing his point, later that year he played Billie Jean King, who routed him in three straight sets. But even though he was humiliated before millions of television viewers, he was smiling all the way to the bank, for it was known that he was an inveterate gambler and these television performances had netted him a handsome payoff; he continued to enjoy the limelight for some time as an over-the-hill hustler-player.

Riis, Jacob (August) (1849–1914) photographer, social reformer; born in Ribe, Denmark. Son of a journalist, he emigrated to New York City in 1870, where he worked as a laborer before joining the *New York Tribune* in 1873. As the *Evening Sun Crime* reporter in 1888, he took stunning pictures of night life in the slums using a magnesium flash. Riis's *How the Other Half Lives* (1890) moved Police Commissioner Theodore Roosevelt to help the tenement reform movement.

Riker, William H. (Harrison) (1920–93) political scientist; born in Des Moines, Iowa. He taught at Lawrence College (1948–62) before joining the University of Rochester (1962). He is best known for three works: *The Theory of Political Coalitions* (1962), *Liberalism Against Populism* (1982), and *The Art of Political Manipulation* (1986).

Riley, James Whitcomb (Benjamin F. Johnson, of Boone, pen name) (1849–1916) poet; born in Greenfield, Ind. He left school at age 16, worked as a house and sign painter (1870–71), and as a lecturer (1872–76). After working in his father's law office (1875–76), he moved to Indianapolis (1879) and worked as a journalist (1879–88); many of his poems were first published in the *Indianapolis Journal*. He was a popular, sentimental poet, often using a Hoosier (Indiana) dialect, as in "Little Orphant Annie" and "When the Frost is on the Punkin'."

Riley, Terry (1935–) composer; born in Colfax, Calif. After university musical studies, jazz experience, and studies in Indian music, he became one of the founders of the "minimalist" school, his music involving hypnotic repetition of ideas.

Riley, William Bell (1861–1947) Protestant evangelist; born in Greene County, Ind. The son of a pro-slavery Democrat who moved south of Ohio River at the outbreak of the Civil War, he grew up on farms in Kentucky, graduated from Hanover College (Ind.) in 1885, and launched a career as a Baptist preacher in Chicago in 1893. From 1897 to 1942 he was pastor of the First Baptist Church, Minneapolis. A leader of the fundamentalist movement, he spoke out against divorce, dancing, Darwinian biology, New Deal social programs, and communism. The Northwestern Bible Training School,

which he founded in 1902, became a center of evangelical fundamentalism.

Rillieux, Norbert (1806–94) engineer, inventor; born in New Orleans. Son of a wealthy sugar plantation owner and one of his slaves, he was fully accepted by his father and given the educational, cultural, and material advantages of a white youth. He was sent to Paris to obtain an engineering degree and stayed on to teach at his college, *L'Ecole Central*. During the next few years, while publishing a series of papers on steam engines, he invented a special steam-based device to evaporate the juice of the sugar cane to produce sugar. He returned to New Orleans and obtained a patent for his device in 1843. He also took a job with a plantation owner and made a prototype of his evaporator; it had many problems, but he worked on improving it and took another patent in 1846. This improved version soon caught on in Louisiana and the West Indies and helped to increase sugar production; it is the basis of the vacuum pan evaporators used in many agricultural products processes to this day. Rillieux enjoyed a modest profit from his invention and turned his attention to improving the sewage disposal system of New Orleans. But since he was still subjected to the discriminatory laws against African-Americans, in 1854 he went back to Paris and took up his faculty post at *L'Ecole Central* and eventually became its headmaster. He continued to be a highly regarded engineer in France and Europe and in later years contributed to the decipherment of Egyptian hieroglyphics. He was conveniently dropped from American history until in 1934 a plaque honoring his contribution was placed in the Louisiana State Museum in New Orleans.

Rimmer, William (1816–79) painter, sculptor; born in Liverpool, England. His family emigrated to the Boston area (1818), and his father claimed he was the lost Dauphin of France, a claim William also made. William grew up in poverty, and after working as a typesetter, cobbler, and self-taught doctor, he became a sculptor, painter, and respected teacher in New York and Boston. He is best known for his publication, *The Elements of Design* (1864), and for his mystical and enigmatic paintings, such as *Flight and Pursuit* (1872).

Rincón de Gautier, Felisa (1897–1994) mayor; born in Ceiba, Puerto Rico. She assisted Luis Muñoz Marín in forming the Popular Democratic Party in the 1930s, but was best known for being the first woman mayor of San Juan (1946–69). Her weekly open-houses at her official residence and such gestures as flying snow to San Juan for children's Christmas parties made her enormously popular. In 1953 the League of American Women gave her its Woman of the Year Award.

Rindlaub, Jean (b. Wade) (1904–91) advertising executive; born in Lancaster, Pa. She joined the New York advertising agency BBDO in 1930 as a copywriter, working on the General Mills and Campbell's Soup accounts among others; she organized innovative market research panels that were prototypes of focus groups. As a BBDO vice-president (from 1946) and board member (from mid-1950s) she became one of the most influential women in advertising.

Rinehart, Mary (b. Roberts) (1876–1958) writer; born in Pittsburgh, Pa. Born into a strict religious family with limited financial means (her father would commit suicide), by age 15 she was selling stories to a Pittsburgh newspaper. She graduated from the Pittsburgh Training School for Nurses (1896), then married a doctor and had three children by age 25. In 1903 she took up writing short stories to help support her family, and her first novel, *The Circular Staircase* (1908), launched her career as an immensely successful author of a new genre that combined humorous elements and some romance with a mystery story. During World War I she went to Europe as a journalist and later wrote several books promoting women's contributions to the war effort. While turning out her endless succession of popular mysteries, she also collaborated on several successful plays with Avery Hapgood (including *The Bat* (1920), an adaptation of *The Circular Staircase*); she was also something of a proto-feminist, supporting women's suffrage, writing articles about women's new roles in society, even telling in a national magazine as early as 1947 about her surgery for breast cancer. With her support – and her best-selling books as a mainstay – her sons, Stanley Marshall Rinehart Jr. and Frederick Rinehart, founded a publishing firm, Farrar and Rinehart, in 1927 (becoming Rinehart and Company in 1946). Although constantly on the best-seller list in her day – she sold over 10 million copies – her works had little literary merit and soon faded from view.

Rinehart, William Henry (1825–74) sculptor; born in Union Bridge, Md. He worked in a marble quarry and as a stone cutter in Baltimore (1846), studied at the Maryland Institute (1846–51) and in Italy (1855–57), and became an expatriate sculptor in Rome, specializing in neoclassical marble works, such as *Hero* (1869).

Ringgold, Faith (1930–) painter, soft sculptor, performance artist, social activist; born in New York City. She earned B.A. (1948) and M.A. (1959) degrees at City College of New York and began to paint seriously after a trip to Europe in 1961. She soon put aside European influences, however, and began to represent her African-American heritage. A strong feminist, she stated that her art had "taken its direction" from her awareness of herself as a woman artist. From the 1970s, she increasingly concerned herself with representations of black women, often creating cloth and bead female figures with traditional African craft techniques. She also did wall hangings and quilts, appeared on stage in her own performance pieces, and wrote and illustrated two books. Her work hangs in many private collections and American museums, including New York's Museum of Modern Art.

Ringgold, Samuel (1800–46) soldier; born in Washington County, Md. The son of a congressman, he graduated from West Point in 1818. At the head of a corps of "flying artillery," he advanced his guns to within 100 yards of the Mexican lines at Palo Alto (May 8, 1846); mortally wounded there, he died a few days later.

Ripley, George (1802–80) transcendentalist, reformer, editor, literary critic; born in Greenfield, Mass. Ordained a Unitarian minister (1826) after studies at Harvard College and Cambridge Theological Seminary, he ministered to a Boston congregation while studying German idealism. In his *Discourses on the Philosophy of Religion* (1836), he espoused a transcendentalist philosophy stressing individual intuition and the presence of the divine in all; he and his wife, Sophia Dana Ripley, also hosted meetings of a Transcendentalist Club. His philosophical views, combined with a strong belief in social reform, led him to leave the church, and, with his wife and others, to establish a community at Brook Farm (on the edge of Boston) (1841); under his influence, Brook Farm developed into an agricultural commune modeled after the ideas of French socialist Charles Fourier. In 1845 Ripley began editing the *Harbinger,* a journal that propagated Fourierism. After the collapse of Brook Farm (1847) he moved to New York, where he wrote for the *New-York Tribune,* soon becoming a prominent literary critic; he also helped found *Harper's New Monthly Magazine* (1850) and was editor (1858–63) of the *New American Cyclopaedia.* Ripley prospered as a major stockholder in the *Tribune* and was president of the Tribune Association after the death of Horace Greeley (1872).

Ripley, Robert (b. LeRoy) (1893–1949) illustrator, cartoonist, writer; born in Santa Rosa, Calif. He began as a tombstone polisher, worked on newspapers in San Francisco (1909–13), and moved to New York City to work for the *Globe* (1913). He changed his first name and began his *Believe It or Not!* cartoons of oddities (1918). His syndicated feature made him wealthy, and he lived on an island in Long Island Sound he called Bion, an acronym of *Believe It or Not!*

Ritchey, George Willis (1864–1945) optical instrument maker, astronomer; born in Tupper's Plains, Ohio. A onetime teacher of woodworking, he became an optical innovator and oversaw the construction of instruments at Chicago's Yerkes Observatory, where he adapted a 40-inch telescope to photography for George Ellery Hale (1896). After working with Hale in constructing the Mt. Wilson Observatory (1904–09), he headed its optical shop (1909–19); in 1917 he photographed a nova that helped establish the existence of galaxies far from the Milky Way. In later years he worked with the major observatory in Paris, France, where he solved a common mirror-distortion problem by collaborating on the design of the Ritchey-Chretien telescope with the U.S. Naval Observatory in Washington, D.C.

Ritchie, Albert (Cabell) (1876–1936) governor; born in Richmond, Va. A successful Baltimore lawyer, as assistant counsel to the Public Service Commission (1910–15) he won utility rate reductions, becoming Maryland's attorney general (1915–19). As Democratic governor (1919–34), he improved health and education services in the state while reducing taxes. He campaigned against national prohibition laws.

Ritchie, Dennis M. (1941–) computer scientist; born in Bronxville, N.Y. At the American Telephone & Telegraph Co. Bell Laboratories in Murray Hill, N.J., which he joined in 1967, he worked on the design of computer languages and operating systems. He and Kenneth Thompson developed C language, which was the basis for their UNIX multi-user operating system (1973). He continued to refine and add to UNIX.

Ritchie, William A. (Augustus) (1903–) archaeologist; born in Rochester, N.Y. He was on the staff of the Rochester Museum of Arts and Sciences (1924–49), served as New York state archaeologist (1950–71), and joined the Carnegie Museum (1973). Among his important works on northeast American prehistoric archaeology is *The Archaeology of New York State* (1965, revised several times).

Rittenhouse, David (1732–92) instrument maker, inventor, astronomer; born in Paper Mill Run, Pa. Largely self-taught, he was a mathematical prodigy and showed a talent for mechanics; by the age of 19 he was an innovative clockmaker; during his early twenties he was making telescopes; he is credited with being the first to introduce the use of cross hairs (spider web) in transit telescopes. Using his own instruments, he became a student of astronomy and would make several important contributions including a calculator of the sun's parallax. As a surveyor, he was responsible for establishing the basis of what became the Mason and Dixon line demarking Pennsylvania from Maryland; this led to his employment as a surveyor to settle boundary disputes. About 1770, when he moved to Philadelphia, he constructed two orreries that displayed planetary motions. (One survives at the Franklin Institute in Philadelphia.) He continued to work at and publish a variety of scientific and mathematical problems. During the American Revolution he served with the Philadelphia Committee of Safety, and oversaw the manufacture of arms and munitions. A member of the convention that produced Pennsylvania's constitution (1776), he was state treasurer (1777–89), a teacher of astronomy at the University of Pennsylvania (1777–89), a commissioner who set up the First Bank of the United States (1791), and first director of the U.S. Mint (1792–95). In 1791 he succeeded Benjamin Franklin as president of the American Philosophical Society and in 1795 he was elected a fellow of the Royal Society. At his death he was regarded as the foremost American scientist/mathematician of the day.

Rittenhouse, Jessie Bell (1869–1948) critic, anthologist, poet; born in the Genesee Valley, New York. She graduated from the Genesee Wesleyan Seminary in Lima, N.Y. (1890) with a strong literary interest. She soon began reviewing books of poetry for newspapers in Buffalo and Rochester, N.Y. In 1899 she moved to Boston to devote her time fully to literary criticism. She published *The Younger American Poets* (1904), a volume of critical essays. She became a regular reviewer for the *New York Times Review of Books* (1905–15) and in New York she helped found the Poetry Society of America (1910). In 1913 she published the first of six innovative poetic anthologies, *The Little Book of Modern Verse*. Her own poetry, showing the influence of her friend Sarah Teasdale, was published in *The Door of Dreams* (1918), *The Lifted Cup* (1921), and *The Secret Bird* (1930).

Ritter, (Woodward Maurice) Tex (1905–74) country music singer and songwriter; born in Murvaul, Texas (father of John Ritter). While studying at the University of Texas he became interested in cowboy songs and folklore; he started law school at Northwestern University but left to take up a career as a folksinger. By 1930 he had his first role on Broadway; in 1936 he made his first movie; during the 1930s he appeared in more Broadway musicals and began to record cowboy songs. From 1936 to 1945 he appeared in 60 Hollywood Westerns as a singing cowboy, becoming known as "America's Most Beloved Cowboy." As his film popularity declined, he toured in live shows with his horse, White Flash, and continued his recording career; his several hit singles included the title song for the movie *High Noon* (1952); in the 1950s he hosted a radio dance show. He moved to Nashville to join the "Grand Ole Opry" in 1965. In 1970 he was unsuccessful in his bid for the Republican nomination for U.S. senator from Tennessee.

Rivera, Chita (1933–) actress, dancer; born in Washington, D.C. At age 16, Rivera won a scholarship to Balanchine's School of American Ballet in New York City, made her professional debut in *Call me Madam* (1952), and had her first important part in *Guys and Dolls* (1953). Perhaps her best-known role was as Anita in *West Side Story* (1957). Already twice nominated for a Tony, she won the award for the first time for *The Rink,* in which she co-starred with Liza Minnelli (1984), although many considered her finest role to be in the Broadway production of *Kiss of the Spider Woman* (1992).

Rivera, Geraldo (1943–) television journalist; born in New York City. An antipoverty lawyer in New York City (1968–70), he joined WABC *Eyewitness News* (1970–74), gaining fame for producing his exposé of a state home for the retarded, *Willowbrook: The Last Disgrace.* In 1974 he joined ABC, doing pieces for their magazine shows like *20/20.* Starting *Geraldo,* a daytime talk show, in 1987, he pioneered in what came to be known as television tabloid journalism, featuring offbeat topics and sleazy individuals on his show and on at least one occasion scuffling with his guests.

Rivers, Joan (b. Molinsky) (1933–) television comedienne, host; born in New York City. During the 1960s she developed her brash insult-comedy style in small clubs. Discovered by Johnny Carson in 1965, she became a nightclub star, writing a national column (1973–76), as well as books. *Tonight Show* permanent guest-host (1983–86), she left to host her own late-night show (1986–87), and after it failed, she began a daytime *Joan Rivers* show. She published *Still Talking* (1991).

Rivers, Larry (b. Larry Grossberg) (1923–) painter, sculptor; born in New York. A professional musician, he studied at the Julliard School of Music (1944–45) before studying art with Hans Hofmann (1947–48). He traveled widely, but was based in Southampton, Long Island from 1953. A teacher at many schools, he is known for ironic historical works, such as *Washington Crossing the Delaware* (1953), and realistic paintings, such as *Double Portrait of Birdie* (1955). He also worked as a sculptor, specializing in figure studies. An abstract expressionist as well as a predecessor of pop art, he is respected for his versatility as an artist.

Rivers, Lucius Mendel (1905–70) U.S. representative; born in Gumville, S.C. A lawyer and Democratic state assemblyman in South Carolina (1933–36), he served in Congress (1941–70), chairing the powerful Committee on Armed Services during the Vietnam War.

Rivers, Thomas Milton (1888–1962) virologist; born in Jonesboro, Ga. After graduating from Johns Hopkins Medical School (1915), with which he remained affiliated until 1919, he headed the infectious disease ward at Rockefeller Institute for Medical Research (1922–37), becoming the institute's director (1937–56). After retiring he remained active with the Rockefeller Foundation (1956–62). His work in the 1930s and 1940s contributed to making the institute a leader in viral research. As chairman of committees on research and vaccine advisory for the National Foundation for Infantile Paralysis, he oversaw the clinical trials of Jonas Salk's vaccine. He served in the armed forces medical corps during both World Wars and edited *Viral and Rickettsial Infections of Man* (1948).

Rivington, James (1724–1803) publisher; born in London, England. A prosperous English publisher, he emigrated in 1760, ran a bookselling business in Philadelphia with branches in Boston and New York, and in 1773 founded *Rivington's New York Gazette.* Initially, the *Gazette* generally sought to present both sides of issues. But in 1775 the plant was destroyed by Patriots and Rivington returned to England for two years; in 1777 the *Gazette* resumed as a strongly pro-Tory paper, sharply ridiculing the Patriots and their cause, often with inaccuracy. After the American Revolution, his paper failed and he died in poverty.

Rivlin, Alice (Mitchell) (1931–) economist, government official; born in Philadelphia. Daughter of a nuclear physicist, she graduated from Bryn Mawr (1952) and earned a Ph.D. from Radcliffe (1958). She became a staff member of the Brookings Institution in Washington, D.C. (1957), was deputy assistant at the Department of Health, Education and Welfare (1966–69), and then became the first director of the Congressional Budget Office (1975–83). She then became director of economic studies at the Brookings Institution (1983–87). In 1993 she was appointed deputy director of the Office of Management and Budget in the Clinton administration. A respected analyst of the U.S. economy, she wrote several studies of economic problems, including *Economic Choices* (1987) and *Caring for the Disabled Elderly: Who Will Pay?* (1988).

Rix, Julian Waldbridge (1850–1903) painter; born in Peacham, Vt. His family moved to San Francisco (1855), he worked as a decorative painter, illustrator, and landscape artist, and then moved to Patterson, N.J., and New York City (1889). He is known for his impressionist landscapes, as in *Pompton Plains, New Jersey* (1898).

Rizzo, Frank L. (1920–91) police official, mayor; born in Philadelphia. Working up through the ranks of the Philadelphia Police Department, he was named police commissioner (1967–71). He came to political prominence as the self-described "toughest cop in America," dedicated to stopping the decay of the inner cities. His controversial tactics as police commissioner were hailed by white ethnic constituents but were denounced by civil rights groups, creating racial polarization despite low crime rates. He was elected mayor of Philadelphia for two terms (1972–80), only to lose two general mayoral elections to W. Wilson Goode, (1983, 1987) Philadelphia's first black mayor.

Roach, Hal (1892–1992) film producer, director, screenwriter; born in Elmira, N.Y. After a life as a muleskinner and gold prospector in Alaska, he became a stunt man and extra in the movies in 1911. In 1915 he began producing short comedy films featuring Harold Lloyd. An expert in the mechanics of screen humor and slapstick, he fostered the careers of Will Rogers and Laurel and Hardy, as well as creating the "Our Gang" comedies. He won Oscars for two shorts, *The Music Box* (1932) and *Bored of Education* (1936), as well as a special Academy Award in 1983.

Roach, (Maxwell) Max (1924–) jazz musician; born in New Land, N.C. The premier modern jazz drummer, he was raised in Brooklyn, attended the Manhattan School of Music, and recorded with Coleman Hawkins in 1943. Over the next four years, he was a sideman with Benny Carter, Dizzy Gillespie, Stan Getz, and Hawkins. He joined Charlie Parker's trailblazing quintet from 1947–49, then free-lanced as a session player and with Jazz at the Philharmonic and the Lighthouse All-Stars until 1954. Between 1954–56, he and Clifford Brown coled one of the most highly regarded groups in modern jazz. After Brown's death, Roach maintained a succession of groups while pursuing a wide range of activities as a composer and educator, particularly as a professor of music at the University of Massachusetts (1972).

Robards, Jason, Jr. (1922–) stage/movie actor; born in Chicago. Son of a once-famous stage and movie actor, Jason Robards Sr. (1892–1963), he served seven years in the U.S.

Navy, survived the attack on Pearl Harbor, and was awarded the Navy Cross. He came to New York City and supported himself by taxidriving and teaching while gaining experience in television dramas, radio soap operas, and bit parts in plays. He gained public and critical acclaim as a stage actor in Eugene O'Neill's *The Iceman Cometh* (1956) and *Long Day's Journey Into Night* (1957), and would continue to create a number of distinguished roles on stage over the next four decades. He made his film debut in *The Journey* (1959) and would also portray a series of outstanding characters in many movies, winning Oscars as best supporting actor in *All the President's Men* (1976) and *Julia* (1977).

Robbins, Frederick C. (Chapman (1916–) virologist, pediatrician; born in Auburn, Ala. After completing his medical studies, he served the army as an epidemiological investigator (1942–46). At Children's Hospital, Boston (1946–50), he joined John F. Enders and Thomas Weller in devising tissue culture techniques for cultivating the poliomyelitis virus, thus enabling the development of a polio vaccine. This breakthrough won Robbins and his two colleagues the 1954 Nobel Prize in physiology. He moved to Harvard Medical School (1950–52), then became a professor of pediatrics at Case Western Reserve (1952–80). After his retirement, he became president of the Institute of Medicine, National Academy of Sciences (1980–85).

Robbins, Harold (b. Francis Kane) (1916–) writer; born in New York City. Abandoned as an infant, he was adopted in 1927 and took the name of Harold Rubin. (When he began his writing career, he legally changed his name to Harold Robbins.) He studied at a high school in New York City, then held a variety of jobs, such as clerk, cashier, and bookies' runner (1927–31). He made a fortune in the food distribution business (1930s) and lost it speculating. He worked as a warehouse clerk for Universal Pictures in New York (1940–41) but soon became a director of budget and planning there (1942–57). He then took up writing and produced a series of best-sellers, mostly violent and sexually charged adventure novels such as *The Carpetbaggers* (1961). In later years he lived in Cannes, France.

Robbins, Jerome (b. Rabinowitz) (1918–) choreographer, ballet dancer; born in New York City. Trained in modern dance and ballet, Robbins joined Ballet Theatre in 1940 and choreographed his first ballet in 1944. In 1949 he joined New York City Ballet, danced principal roles, and choreographed nine ballets before he formed Ballet: USA, in 1959. He choreographed such celebrated Broadway shows as *West Side Story* (1957) and *Fiddler on the Roof* (1964) and returned to City Ballet in 1969. There he choreographed such major works as *The Goldberg Variations* (1971) and *Glass Pieces* (1983), and became co-ballet master (1983–89). His retrospective *Jerome Robbins's Broadway* was a 1989 hit.

Robert, Christopher Rhinelander (1802–78) merchant, philanthropist; born near Brook Haven, N.Y. He was an importer (1835–62) and president of the Delaware, Lackawanna and Western Railroad (1858–63). A benefactor of religious and educational institutions including Beloit College and Auburn Theological Seminary, he founded (1863) and financially supported the secular Robert College near Istanbul, Turkey, which remains one of the major institutions of higher education for young people from this region of the world.

Robert, Henry Martyn (1837–1923) military engineer; born in

Robertville, S.C. A graduate of West Point (1857), in 1858 he participated in operations against Indians in the Northwest. During the Civil War he served with the Union army and constructed defenses for Washington, D.C. During the next 36 years he served with the Corps of Engineers, constructing many river and harbor improvements as well as fortifications. After the 1900 tidal wave in Galveston, Texas, he helped build its sea wall. His name remains in current usage, however, for other than his engineering feats. Asked to preside at a meeting about 1862, he could not find a guide to the proper procedures, so he drew up his own; after several editions and revisions, it was published as *Robert's Rules of Order* (1915) and remains the standard authority for virtually all official meetings in the U.S.A.

Roberts (Edward Glenn, Jr.) "Fireball" (1931–64) auto racer; born in Apopka, Fla. At his death, he was the all-time stock car money winner. He died from burns suffered in a race crash in 1964.

Roberts, (Granville) Oral (1918–) Protestant evangelist; born in Ada, Okla. The son of a Pentacostal preacher, he had little formal education and endured poor health as a youth. After a dozen years as a pastor and evangelist in a succession of Southern towns, he became a faith healer in 1947. He went on to establish a multimillion dollar evangelical empire and to found Oral Roberts University in Tulsa. He had television and radio programs and published several books, including *Don't Give Up* (1980). In the later 1980s, when his enterprises encountered financial troubles, he made widely publicized appeals for aid.

Roberts, Joseph Jenkins (1809–76) first president of Liberia; born in Petersburg, Va. Of mixed black and white heritage, he emigrated to Liberia with his widowed mother and three brothers in 1829. He became a successful merchant and caught the eye of Liberia's white governor, who appointed Roberts as his successor. The first African-American governor of Liberia, Roberts went on to become the first president of the new country in 1847, serving six terms in all. His major accomplishments include gaining the recognition of Liberia from most European nations and halting the slave trade on Liberia's borders.

Roberts, Kenneth (Lewis) (1885–1957) writer; born in Kennebunk, Maine. He studied at Cornell (B.A. 1908), where he was the editor of the humor magazine. He became a reporter and columnist for the *Boston Sunday Post* (1909–17), and also wrote verse, plays, and editorials. He was a reporter for the *Saturday Evening Post* during the 1920s, then began working on the first of many historical novels. He is best known for *Arundel* (1930), *Northwest Passage* (1937), and *Lydia Bailey* (1947). Several of his works incorporated his often conservative, antiestablishment views. He lived in Kennebunkport, Maine, and, in later years, wrote several books about locating water with a divining rod.

Roberts, Lydia Jane (1879–1965) home economist, educator; born in Hope, Mich. She entered the University of Chicago at age 36, earning a Ph.D. and becoming professor of home economics there (1919–44). Author of the classic *Nutrition Work with Children* (1927), she specialized in children's and community nutrition and nutrition education; she developed standards for dietary requirements and lobbied for vitamin enrichment of flour and bread.

Roberts, Owen J. (Josephus) (1875–1955) Supreme Court justice; born in Philadelphia. He gained prominence when President Calvin Coolidge appointed him to prosecute in the Teapot Dome oil scandal (1924). President Herbert Hoover named him to the U.S. Supreme Court (1930–45). He retired from the court and became dean of the University of Pennsylvania Law School (1948–51).

Roberts, Richard J. (John) (1943–) molecular biologist; born in Derby, England. He took his B.Sc. and Ph.D. at Sheffield University, England. He came to Harvard University in 1969 as a research fellow and in 1972 joined the Cold Spring Harbor Laboratory on Long Island. There he led research to identify enzymes and, in 1977, helped to revolutionize molecular biology by discovering that the messages on DNA are not continuous as had been thought. For this 1977 discovery of "split genes" he and Phillip A. Sharp, who made the same discovery independently at the Massachusetts Institute of Technology, were awarded the 1993 Nobel Prize in medicine. Beginning in 1992 Taylor directed eukaryotic research at New England Biolabs in Beverly, Mass.

Robertson, James (1742–1814) frontiersman; born in Brunswick County, Va. The "Father of Tennessee," he led the first group of settlers to present-day Nashville in 1780. He proved to be an excellent Indian fighter and a maker of peace treaties with the Chickasaw (1781) and Cherokee (1798, 1807) tribes. He impressed both whites and Indians with his fairness and personal integrity.

Robertson, James Brooks Ayers (1871–1938) governor; born in Keokuk County, Iowa. A schoolteacher and lawyer, he served on the Oklahoma Supreme Court Commission (1911–14). As Democratic governor of Oklahoma (1919–23), he built highways and used the National Guard to end a miner's strike. Indicted for bribery, he avoided conviction by a legal tactic and returned to his law practice.

Robertson, Oscar (1938–) basketball player; born in Charlotte, Tenn. A three-time college player of the year at the University of Cincinnati (1958–60), he co-captained the 1960 U.S. Olympic team to a gold medal. He played guard for the Cincinnati Royals (1960–70) and Milwaukee Bucks (1970–74), where he was a nine-time All-NBA (National Basketball Association) first team selection. Nicknamed "the Big O," his 9,887 lifetime assists is second best in NBA history, and his 26,710 career points is fourth on the all-time list. A broadcaster after retiring from the game, he was elected to basketball's Hall of Fame in 1979.

Robertson, Pat (Marion Gordon) (1930–) Protestant evangelist; born in Lexington, Va. The son of a conservative Democrat who served 34 years in the U.S. House and Senate, he graduated from Washington and Lee (1950), took a law degree from Yale, and was ordained a Southern Baptist minister in 1961 after being "born again." He established the Christian Broadcasting Network in Virginia (1961) where he appeared as an evangelical preacher. His network eventually reached 30 million cable television subscribers in the U.S.A.; it enabled him to launch a career as a leader of the religious right. After an unsuccessful bid for the Republican presidential nomination in 1988, he returned to his television ministry.

Robeson, George Maxwell (1829–97) lawyer, public official; born at Oxford Furnace, N.J. His administration while serving as secretary of the navy (1869–77) was criticized for favoritism. He was a Republican congressman from New Jersey (1879–83).

Robeson, Paul (Bustill) (1898–1976) stage actor, singer, political activist; born in Princeton, N.J. At Rutgers University, he was a 4-letter man, a 2-year All-American in football, valedictorian, and a Phi Beta Kappa at a time when few African-Americans even attended college. He took a law degree at Columbia University, but turned to singing and acting, appearing in plays throughout the world, in movies, on concert stages, and on recordings. He was especially known for his renditions of black spirituals, while his most famous stage role was in *Othello*. By the late 1930s, he had become increasingly more active and outspoken on behalf of racial justice, social progress, and international peace; when he defied charges that he was a Communist, the government canceled his passport. He spent most of the next 13 years living in Russia and London, returning to the U.S.A. (1963) to live out his last years in poor health.

Robin, Leo (1895–1984) lyricist; born in Pittsburgh, Pa. He studied dramatics in college and was a reporter before writing lyrics for the Broadway musical, *Hit the Deck* (1927). In 1928 he moved to Hollywood where for three decades he wrote songs for over 100 films with such composers as Jerome Kern and Harold Arlen. With Jule Styne he collaborated on the musical *Gentlemen Prefer Blondes* (1949) and the television special *Ruggles of Red Gap* (1954).

Robineau, Adelaide Alsop (1865–1929) ceramist; born in Middletown, Conn. Beginning as a china decorator, she studied painting with William Merritt Chase. Marriage to Samuel E. Robineau (1899) led to their publication of the periodical *Keramik Studio* and a 1901 move to Syracuse, N.Y., where they established her studio, Four Winds. In 1903 she began making fine porcelain vases in the art nouveau style, specializing in delicate carved and openwork decoration. At the 1911 Turin exposition, her 55 porcelains, notably her *Scarab Vase,* were declared best in the world. Her artistry and dedicated teaching drew numerous awards and honors.

Robins, Eli (1921–) psychiatrist, biochemist, educator; born in Houston, Texas. He became head of the department of psychiatry at Washington University (St. Louis, Mo.) (1963–75). A proponent of biological psychiatry, he built one of the country's leading psychiatry departments. He left the university to devote himself full-time to research on suicide and biological aspects of mental illness, areas in which he became a leading expert.

Robins, Margaret Drier (1868–1945) labor activist; born in Brooklyn. The daughter of successful immigrants, she was president of the Women's Trade Union League during its formative years (1907–22), effectively organizing working women, training them for leadership in unions, and winning protective legislation. She and her husband moved to Florida in 1925, where she supported charitable activities and progressive politics.

Robinson, Abraham (1918–74) logician/mathematician; born in Waldenburg, Germany (now Walbrzych, Poland). Fleeing Nazism, he worked with the British during the war on aerodynamics. This study led him to Princeton (1960–61) where he made his best-known discovery, nonstandard analysis. Teaching at the University of California: Los Angeles (1962–67) and Yale (1967–73), he is known for work in algebra and model theory.

Robinson, Bill "Bojangles" (b. Luther Robinson) (1878–1949) tap dancer; born in Richmond, Va. He began dancing professionally at age eight in Louisville, Ky., then moved to New York City in 1891 to dance in the popular musical, *The South Before the War.* He performed in vaudeville and later was one of the few black dancers to star on the Keith circuit. He first performed on Broadway in 1928, becoming the first African-American to star in a Ziegfield Follies. He danced in the first movie to have its own original musical score, *Dixiana* (1930), and during the 1930s and 1940s he danced in black revues and musicals. He appeared in four films with Shirley Temple, including *The Little Colonel* (1935); although extremely popular in their day, these films would later be criticized for forcing this superb dancer into the role of a shuffling servant. He starred in the movie *Stormy Weather* (1943). Known as "the King of Tapology," he was one of the first performers to tap dance on his toes (as opposed to flat-footed), he led in using tap dance to create rhythmic sound, and is credited with originating the routine of tapping up and down stairs.

Robinson, Boardman (Mike) (1876–1952) illustrator, lithographer; born in Somerset, Nova Scotia. He studied at the Massachusetts Normal Art School (1894–97), in France (1898–99, 1901–04), and lived in New York City. He became known for his Socialist political cartoons and his book illustrations for such writers as Dostoyevsky, Edgar Lee Masters, and Herman Melville. He became the director of the Colorado Springs Fine Arts Center (1930–47), where he initiated an influential lithography program.

Robinson, Charles (1818–94) governor; born in Hardwick, Mass. An agent of the New England Emigrant Aid Company, he unified the antislavery movement in Kansas Territory's Free-State Party (1855–59). Briefly territorial governor, he served as the new state of Kansas's first governor (Rep., 1861–63). Accused of tampering with state bond sales, he fought off impeachment, running without success for representative and governor afterward.

Robinson, Claude (Everett) (1900–61) public opinion analyst; born in Portland, Ore. He pioneered scientific public opinion research. After publishing an influential book on the 1928 presidential election (1932), he developed new scientific sampling techniques for the Gallup Poll (1936–38) and his own Princeton, New Jersey-based Opinion Research Corporation (1938–60). He published important studies of public attitudes and industry in the 1940s and 1950s.

Robinson, Edward (1794–1863) philologist, geographer, biblical scholar; born in Southington, Conn. He trained in Hebrew studies and geography at Hamilton College and in Germany. After touring the Holy Land, he published the first scholarly investigation of the region, *Biblical Researches in Palestine . . .* (3 vols. 1841), an epoch-making work of historical geography. After 1837 he was professor of biblical literature at Union Theological Seminary, New York.

Robinson, Edward G. (b. Emmanuel Goldenberg) (1893–1973) movie actor; born in Bucharest, Romania. Coming to the U.S.A. at age 10, he took up acting at City College of New York; he made his stage debut in 1913 and his Hollywood debut in 1923. Short, squat, with an inimitable mouth and imitable voice, he became a star in *Little Caesar* (1931) and for some years seemed typecast as a criminal. But he moved on to play a wide variety of roles and although his career was set back when he was attacked in the early 1950s by the House Un-American Activities Committee, he recovered and was voted a Special Academy Award in 1972.

He was also known as a collector of 19th- and 20th-century art, although he had to sell it in 1956 to satisfy a divorce settlement.

Robinson, (Edward Gay) Eddie (1919–) football coach; born in Jackson, La. After graduation from college and working at a feed mill, he realized his boyhood ambition by becoming head football coach at Louisiana Negro Normal and Industrial Institute (1941) (since renamed Grambling State University). Henceforth he guided the Tigers to fame, sending over 300 players to professional football camps, compiling the all-time best record as a college football coach and winning numerous awards.

Robinson, Edwin Arlington (1869–1935) poet; born in Head Tide, Maine. He grew up in Gardiner, Maine, studied at Harvard (1891–93), was a free-lance writer (1893–96), and lived in New York City (1896). He was secretary to the president of Harvard (1897), returned to New York, and held various jobs, notably clerk of the Customs House (1904–10). Until President Theodore Roosevelt wrote in praise of his work in 1905, his poetry attracted little attention – he had self-published his early work. He won numerous awards and remains famous for his ironic, psychological profiles such as "Richard Cory" and "Miniver Cheevy"; but in his day he was also acclaimed for his long poems on Arthurian themes, such as *Tristram* (1927).

Robinson, Frank (1935–) baseball player/manager; born in Beaumont, Texas. During his career as a player (1956–76), he played outfield, first base, and designated hitter (DH), mostly for the Cincinnati Reds and Baltimore Orioles. He was the first DH to hit a homer and his 586 career home runs place him fourth in the history of the majors. He became the first to win the Most Valuable Player Award once in both leagues. In 1975 he was named manager of the Cleveland Indians, the first African-American to manage in the majors; he went on to manage the San Francisco Giants (1981–84) and the Baltimore Orioles (1988–91).

Robinson, G. (George) Canby (1878–1960) physician; born in Baltimore, Md. After taking his M.D. from Johns Hopkins (1903), he went on to assist in the organizing of four major medical education institutions: the hospital of the Rockefeller Institute (1910–13), the medical schools of Washington University (1913–20) and Vanderbilt University (1920–28), and the joining of Cornell University Medical College to New York Hospital (1928), where he stayed as director until 1934. With publication of *The Patient as a Person* (1939), he raised the issue of medical humanism. He published memoirs, *Adventures in Medical Education,* in 1957.

Robinson, Gerold (Tanquary) (1892–1971) Slavic studies specialist; born in Chase City, Va. A member of the editorial boards of the *Dial* (1919) and the *Freeman* (1920–24), he was best known for his research on agrarian Russia while teaching at Columbia University (1924–71). During World War II he was chief of the U.S.S.R. Division, the Research and Analysis Branch of the Office of Strategic Services (1941–45), and was awarded the Medal of Freedom (1947). He was author of *Rural Russia Under the Old Regime* (1932), and numerous other books and articles.

Robinson, (Jack Roosevelt) Jackie (1919–72) baseball player; born in Cairo, Ga. A four-sport star at the University of California: Los Angeles (UCLA), he became the first African-American baseball player in the modern era major leagues when he was brought up as an infielder for the Brooklyn Dodgers in 1947. His indomitable personality and competitive nature served him admirably during the first difficult years with the Dodgers, where he was a frequent target of beanballs and the racial epithets of opposing players and fans alike. An excellent fielder, clutch hitter, and base runner, he led the Dodgers to six National League championships and their first ever World Series victory in 1955. During his ten-year career (1947–56), he won the National League batting title with an average of .342 in 1949 and was named the league's Most Valuable Player. After retiring from baseball he was an active spokesperson for civil rights, and in 1962 he was elected to baseball's Hall of Fame.

Robinson, James Harvey (1863–1936) historian; born in Bloomington, Ill. Educated at Harvard University (B.A., 1887; M.A. 1888) and receiving his doctorate in Germany, he taught European history at Columbia University (1895– 1919), where his espousal of "intellectual history" greatly influenced students of the day. He collaborated on textbooks with Charles Beard and James Breasted and helped found the New School for Social Research (1919–21). His popular *Mind in the Making* (1921) displays his innovative historical methodology, emphasizing the development of human understanding as opposed to conventional political and economic events.

Robinson, Joseph Taylor (1872–1937) U.S. senator; born near Lonoke, Ark. After serving in the U.S. House of Representatives (Dem., Ark.; 1903–12), he was elected governor but resigned after serving a few weeks to fill an expired term in the U.S. Senate (1913–37). He was Senate minority leader (1923–33) and majority leader thereafter. He was Al Smith's vice-presidential running mate in 1928. In the Senate he supported the progressive policies of both President Woodrow Wilson and President Franklin D. Roosevelt.

Robinson, Randall (1946–) lawyer, lobbyist; born in Richmond, Va. He attended Virginia Union University and graduated from Harvard Law School in 1970. Going to Washington, D.C., he served as the administrative assistant to several U.S. representatives and was awarded a Ford Fellowship. In 1986 he became executive director of TransAfrica, a Washington-based organization (founded 1977) dedicated to protecting and advancing the political, social, and human rights of people of African descent throughout the world, whether through publications and meetings, overt public and political pressure, or behind-the-scenes lobbying. Robinson was most visible in calling for maintaining a boycott of South Africa until black Africans really got their rights.

Robinson, "Sugar Ray" (b. Walker Smith, Jr.) (1921–89) boxer; born in Detroit, Mich. Often considered, "pound for pound, the greatest boxer in history," he acquired his name by using a friend's birth certificate in order to fight while under the minimum age. He began boxing as an amateur in New York City and turned professional in 1940. He was the world welterweight champion (1946–51) and the world middleweight titleholder five different times; he was the first boxer ever to regain a world title after retiring; he won the first middleweight crown in 1951 with a knockout of Jake LaMotta, and the last title in 1958 against Carmen Basilio. With his quickness, balance, and grace, he posted a record of 174 victories (109 knockouts), 19 defeats, and six draws.

Robinson, Theodore (1852–96) painter; born in Irasburg, Vt. After attending the National Academy of Design in New York City (1874) and helping found the Art Students League, he studied in Paris (1876–78) and returned to the U.S.A. Up to this time he painted in a conventional realistic manner, but after a second stay in France (1884–88) – particularly after meeting Claude Monet in 1887 – he embraced and promoted the Impressionist style. He settled in New York City in 1892, determined to apply the Impressionist style to American subjects, as in *Port Ben, Delaware and Hudson Canal* (1893) or *Union Square in Winter* (1895).

Robinson, Wilbert (1863–1934) baseball manager; born in Bolton, Mass. He had a 17-year major league career (1886–1902), mostly as a star catcher with the Baltimore Orioles (1892–99), then went on to manage and coach minor league teams. To demonstrate his catching prowess, he once caught a grapefruit dropped 400 feet from an airplane. As manager of the Brooklyn Dodgers from 1914 to 1931, he was so popular that the Dodgers were sometimes called the "Robins" in his honor. Nicknamed "Uncle Robbie," he was elected to baseball's Hall of Fame in 1945.

Robinson, (William) Smokey (1940–) singer, songwriter, record producer; born in Detroit, Mich. In high school he formed the Miracles, a vocal group; they signed a contract with Berry Gordy of Motown Records in 1958 and released the hit "Shop Around" in 1960. At Motown Robinson composed and produced many hits such as "My Girl" (1965), helping to perfect the "Motown sound" and refine soul music. He went solo in 1972 and released such successful albums as *A Quiet Storm* (1974) and *Touch the Sky* (1983).

Rochberg, George (1918–) composer; born in Paterson, N.J. He taught at the University of Pennsylvania from 1960 to 1983. Having been a prominent 12-tone avant-gardist in his early work, he later began to use traditional material as well, earning the label "neo-Romantic."

Roche, (Eamonn) Kevin (1922–) architect; born in Dublin, Ireland. Trained at the National University of Ireland, he joined Eero Saarinen (1950) soon after emigrating to America. After Saarinen's death, Roche completed his projects with his associate John Dinkeloo, with whom he then formed a partnership (1966) specializing in civic and corporate buildings. Characterized by stark sculptural forms, Roche's work includes the Oakland Museum, Oakland, Calif. (1961–68) and the Jewish Museum, New York (1985).

Rochefort, Joseph J. (John) (1898–1976) naval officer; born in Dayton, Ohio. He enlisted in the U.S. Naval Reserve in 1918 during World War I, became an ensign in 1919, and transferred to the United States Navy where he was made captain. In 1925 he took charge of the cryptographic section of the Office of Naval Communications until 1927 when he went back to sea. In 1929 he went to the American Embassy in Tokyo to study Japanese, and returned to the Office of Naval Intelligence in 1932. By June 1941, he was in charge of the Combat Intelligence Unit located at Pearl Harbor in the Hawaiian territory. He broke the Japanese coded messages and relayed them to Admiral Chester Nimitz prior to and during the battle of Midway during World War II. For this he was given several awards including the Legion of Merit. He retired from the navy in 1947; after being reactivated in 1950 for the Korean War, he retired permanently in 1953. He was a consultant for the movie *Tora, Tora, Tora* (1953). Never a public figure, he was recognized posthumously when Presi-

dent Reagan awarded him the Distinguished Service Medal for his invaluable service in breaking the Japanese code.

Rock, John Swett (1825–66) teacher, physician, lawyer; born in Salem, N.J. A public school teacher (1844–48), he studied dentistry under Dr. Harbert Hubbard and began practicing in Philadelphia (1851), where he designed prize-winning false teeth. In 1852 he graduated from the American Medical College and then moved his dental practice to Boston. Poor health caused him to study law and he became a justice of the peace in 1861. Presented as a potential U.S. Supreme Court lawyer by Senator Charles Sumner (1865) before Chief Justice Salmon P. Chase, he became the first African-American to be so accredited. Proficient in Greek and Latin, he lectured around the country, refuting the racist theory that Negroes were inferior to whites.

Rockefeller, Abby (Greene) Aldrich (1874–1948) philanthropist, art patron; born in Providence, R.I. (daughter of Nelson Wilmarth Aldrich; mother of Nelson A. Rockefeller). A debutante who married John D. Rockefeller Jr. in 1901, she directed much of her generous philanthropy toward art. She was instrumental in founding (1929) the Museum of Modern Art, of which she was a major benefactor. With her husband she helped plan the restoration of colonial Williamsburg, where she initiated the folk art collection that bears her name.

Rockefeller, David (1915–) banker, philanthropist; born in New York City. A member of the famous and powerful family, brother of former New York Governor Nelson Rockefeller, he graduated from Harvard in 1936 and earned a Ph.D. from the University of Chicago four years later. He was secretary to New York City Mayor Fiorello LaGuardia in 1940–41, and joined Chase National Bank (now Chase Manhattan) after World War II, rising to be chief executive officer (1969–80) of what was then the nation's second largest bank. In that capacity, he worked to further American investment in developing countries; in 1981 he became chairman of Chase's International Advisory Committee. He wrote extensively on banking management, served as a senior executive of family-owned enterprises such as Rockefeller Center Properties, Inc., and, from 1951–70, chaired the Council on Foreign Relations. Deeply involved in philanthropic activities, he headed the Rockefeller Institute for Medical Research for many years, and was said to enjoy beetle collecting as a favorite hobby.

Rockefeller, John D. (Davison) (1839–1937) industrialist, philanthropist; born in Richford, N.Y. After only two years of high school, he went to work in 1855 in Cleveland, Ohio, as a bookkeeper for a small food firm. In 1859 he formed Clark & Rockefeller, a food handling firm that prospered during the Civil War. Deeply religious, he began his philanthropies by giving ten percent of his earnings to churches. In 1863 he entered the brand new oil business by settling up a refinery in Cleveland; by 1870 he had expanded to the extent that he formed the Standard Oil Company of Ohio. By 1878 his company dominated the piping, refining, and marketing of American petroleum; it would soon be a major player in the world markets. His monopolistic tendencies led to a famous federal lawsuit (1890–92), whereupon he dissolved the Standard Oil "trust" and transferred control to companies in different states. He maintained control through Standard Oil (New Jersey) until a 1911 Supreme Court decision forced its dissolution and his retirement. By this time Rockefeller had, since the late 1890s, been increasingly less involved with the business and more engaged in his philanthropic activities. His benefactions during his lifetime reached some $550 million and included especially the Baptist Church, the YMCA, the University of Chicago, and the Rockefeller Institute for Medical Research (since 1953 Rockefeller University). He also established the Rockefeller Foundation (1913), which remained the principal disburser of the estate's fortune in ensuing decades. A legend in his own lifetime, for some he remained the supreme American success story, for others he was the symbol of unrestrained capitalism.

Rockefeller, Laurance (Spelman) (1910–) business executive, conservationist; born in New York City. A grandson of the oil magnate, John D. Rockefeller, he graduated from Princeton in 1932, became involved in commercial aviation, and managed several family enterprises, including the Rockefeller Center entertainment and business complex. As director of the nonprofit Jackson Hole Preserve, he oversaw the donation of 33,000 acres of Rockefeller land to the Grand Teton National Park. The preserve also acquired 5,000 unspoiled acres on St. John Island that in 1976 became the Virgin Islands National Park. He headed the Citizens Advisory Committee on Environmental Quality from 1969 to 1973.

Rockefeller, Nelson A. (Aldrich) (1908–79) vice-president, public servant; born in Bar Harbor, Maine (grandson of John D. Rockefeller). He studied economics and managed family oil holdings in Latin America before turning to public service in 1940. He held important government posts during the Roosevelt, Truman, and Eisenhower administrations. He served as governor of New York (1958–1973), and his standing as a progressive governor was damaged when he ordered the controversial attack on the state prison at Attica in 1971. He earnestly wanted to become president, but the goal persistently eluded him. He lost the 1964 nomination to the ultra-conservative Barry Goldwater. In 1974 he was nominated for the vice-presidency by President Gerald Ford; after several months of hearings, he was confirmed. A loyal and active vice-president, he campaigned for Ford in 1976 even after he was dropped from the ticket. He returned to New York City and managed family business enterprises.

Rockefeller, Winthrop (1912–73) governor; born in New York (grandson of John D. Rockefeller). A Yale dropout, he worked for Socony Vacuum Oil (1939–41, 1946–51), with time out to serve in World War II and then resigning to head the IBEC Housing Corporation, a Rockefeller philanthropy providing low-cost housing. Moving to Arkansas in 1953, he started a 3,500-acre cattle ranch, also chairing the Arkansas Industrial Development Commission. As Republican governor (1967–71), he advanced school desegregation and promoted penal reform.

Rockenbach, Samuel Dickerson (1869–1952) soldier; born in Lynchburg, Va. The son of a Confederate army officer, he graduated from the Virginia Military Institute in 1890 and served in the cavalry. As chief of the Tank Corps, American Expeditionary Force in France (1917–19), he became a pioneer of armored warfare.

Rockhill, William Woodville (1854–1914) orientalist, diplomat; born in Philadelphia. Educated in France, he combined Far Eastern studies with a 30-year diplomatic career. He served in the American embassies in China and Korea (1884–87), published a French translation of *The Life of the Buddha* (1884), and made journeys to Mongolia and Tibet for the Smithsonian Institution. He was a special agent in China during the Boxer Rebellion and was minister to China (1905–09), and ambassador to Russia (1909–11) and Turkey (1911–13). His large collection of rare Chinese works is now part of the Library of Congress.

Rockne, Knute (Kenneth) (1888–1931) football coach; born in Voss, Norway. His family came to this country in 1893. From 1905 through 1910, he worked as a night clerk to earn money for college. An end whose pass receiving helped Notre Dame beat Army in 1913, he became coach at his alma mater in 1918 and served until his death, producing six national championships and five perfect-record teams. Perhaps football's most famous coach, and one of the few whose life inspired a movie, "Rock" was known for his preference for speed over brute force, his use of psychology, and his halftime orations. It was during halftime at the 1928 Army game that he inspired his team to victory with his "Win one for the Gipper" story.

Rockwell, George Lincoln (1918–67) political extremist; born in Bloomington, Ill. The son of vaudeville comedians, he was a Navy pilot during World War II, and was a gifted illustrator. He managed an advertising agency in Portland, Maine, served in the Korean War, and, influenced by anti-Semite Gerald L. K. Smith, founded the American Nazi Party (1958). Although its numbers were tiny, under his direction the party staged numerous provocative, if unsuccessful demonstrations. A white supremacist who blamed Jews for the worldwide Communist movement, he called for their extermination along with the deportation of all blacks. He was discharged from the navy reserves for his actions (1960) and ran for governor of Virginia (1965). He was shot to death (1967) by John Patler, a dark-skinned former member of the American Nazi Party who had been expelled from the party for denouncing his more Aryan-appearing colleagues.

Rockwell, Norman (Percevel) (1894–1978) illustrator; born in New York City. Considered the most famous and popular illustrator in America, he studied at the Chase School of Art, Mamaroneck, N.Y. (c. 1908), the National Academy of Design (1909), and the Art Students League (1910), New York. He was an illustrator for major periodicals, such as *St. Nicholas, Collier's, Life, Judge, Look,* and most importantly, the *Saturday Evening Post* (1916–63). He produced calendars for Brown & Bigelow (1924–76), created advertisements, and illustrated such classics as *Tom Sawyer* and *Huckleberry Finn* by Mark Twain. Early in his career he lived in New Rochelle, N.Y., then moved to Arlington, Vt., and finally settled in Stockbridge, Mass. Using oils and an impeccable realistic technique, he idealized small town America and expressed a personal vision that occasionally rose above sentimentality, as in *Breaking Home Ties* (1954) and *Triple Self Portrait* (1960).

Rockwell, Willard Frederick, Jr. ("Al") (1914–92) industrialist; born in Boston, Mass. In a long career in family-owned companies, he created Rockwell International, a major aerospace conglomerate best known under his leadership for its work on the U.S. Apollo space program. He retired from Rockwell in 1984. He founded Astrotech International Corporation (1981) to promote commercial applications of space exploration, retiring finally in 1989.

Rodbell, Martin (1925–   ) biochemist; born in Baltimore, Md. After earning his bachelor's degree in biology at Johns Hopkins University (1949) he took his Ph.D. at the University of Washington (1954). He was a research biochemist at the University of Illinois (1954–56) before going on to the National Institutes of Health, first with the National Heart Institute (1956–61), then with the National Institute of Arthritis, Metabolic and Digestive Diseases (1961–85). In 1985 he became the scientific director of the National Institute of Environmental Health Science, where he headed the laboratory of signal transduction. He retired in 1994, citing a lack of federal funds for his kind of basic research. He shared the 1994 Nobel Prize in medicine or physiology with Alfred G. Gilman for his work in discovering G proteins, substances that help transmit and modulate chemical signals in cells that control fundamental life processes; too many or too few G proteins can lead to diseases from alcoholism and cholera to diabetes and cancer.

Rodgers, (Charles) Richard (1902–79) composer; born in New York City. He attended Columbia University and studied music and by age 17 was collaborating with Lorenz Hart on amateur musicals. With Hart as lyricist, in the 1920s and 1930s he broke from the common Tin Pan Alley musical to develop the musical play. They produced 14 shows containing many popular songs while further integrating libretto, music, and dance. *On Your Toes* (1936), choreographed by George Balanchine, included his first broad arrangement for ballet sequences (including "Slaughter on Tenth Avenue"), while *Pal Joey* (1940) focused on an amoral nightclub owner. Among his many standards with Hart are "My Funny Valentine" (1937) and "Bewitched" (1940). After Hart's death in 1943, Rodgers teamed up with Oscar Hammerstein II and created his most popular stage works. Their masterpiece, *Oklahoma!* (1943), is called the first American vernacular opera and won the Pulitzer Prize in drama. Their next work, *Carousel* (1945), also a classic, contains some of Rodgers' finest music. Their last musicals, *South Pacific* (1949), *The King and I* (1951), and *The Sound of Music* (1959), contained many famous songs and were highly successful on screen as well as stage. After Hammerstein's death (1960), Rodgers either wrote his own lyrics or collaborated with others for another 20 years of works for theater and television.

Rodgers, (James Charles) "Jimmie" (1897–1933) musician; born in Meridian, Miss. Generally acknowledged as "The Father of Country Music," he worked as a railroad brakeman until 1924, when he was stricken with tuberculosis and began to pursue a career in music. A singer and guitarist, he adapted the black country blues to commercial hillbilly music, and developed a unique new form, the blue yodel. He made his first recordings in 1927, and within a year he reached national popularity and was billed as "the Singing Brakeman" and "America's Blue Yodeler." For the next five years, he performed with touring stage shows throughout the U.S.A., and by the time of his death he had recorded 110 titles, representing a diverse repertoire of love ballads, cowboy songs, railroad and hobo songs, and 13 blue yodels. In 1961, Rodgers became the first person elected to the Country Music Association Hall of Fame.

Rodgers, John (1773–1838) naval officer; born near Havre de Grace, Md. He served as a lieutenant in the undeclared war with France. He served in the Tripolitan War and briefly commanded the Mediterranean squadron (1805). He commanded the USS *President* in its defeat of the British *Little Belt* (1811) and became a popular hero. He performed effectively in the War of 1812 and was head of the Board of Naval Commissioners (1815–24, 1827–37).

Rodgers, John (1812–82) naval officer; born near Havre de Grace, Md. (son of John Rodgers, 1773–1838). His naval career (1828–82) encompassed service in the Seminole War and the Civil War. He commanded the Asiatic Squadron (1870–72) and the Mare Island navy yard (1873–77). He was superintendent of the Naval Observatory (1877–82) and was the senior rear admiral on the retired list at the time of his death.

Rodgers, (William Henry) Bill (1947–   ) marathon runner; born in Hartford, Conn. He won the New York and Boston marathons four times each between 1975 and 1980. After retiring from active racing he opened a chain of sports gear shops.

Rodia, Simon (b. Simon Rodilla) (1879–1965) tile setter, craftsman; born in Italy. An immigrant handyman, he began his life work, the 99-foot-high "Watts Towers" in Los Angeles, in 1924. He worked on the triple spire of steel rods, chicken wire, and concrete intermittently until 1954, when he declared the job finished. Critics take the towers seriously as a work of sculpture, and they were designated a national landmark in 1991.

Rodin, Judith (1944–   ) university president, psychologist; born in Philadelphia, Pa. At the psychology department at Yale University (1972–92) she established a link between eating disorders and the relationship between mothers and daughters. She chaired the department (1989–91) and was promoted to dean of the graduate school and then Yale's provost in 1992. She became the first woman president of any Ivy League school in 1994 when she became president of her alma mater, the University of Pennsylvania.

Rodney, Caesar (1728–84) patriot, statesman; born in Dover, Del. He served in Delaware's provincial assembly from 1761 to 1776 with only one break, in 1771. A member of the Continental Congress (1774–76), he rode 80 miles on horseback and arrived in Philadelphia on July 2, 1776, just in time to cast a decisive vote in favor of Richard Henry Lee's resolution on American independence. He signed the Declaration of Independence, served again in the Continental Congress (1777–78), and was president (governor) of Delaware (1778–81). Delaware placed his statue in the U.S. Capitol.

Rodón, Francisco (1934–   ) painter; born in San Sebastián, Puerto Rico. At the Expo 92 World's Fair in Seville, he was named Puerto Rico's most important 20th-century painter and the successor of the island's two previous most important artists: Campeche (18th century) and Oller (19th century). Rodón studied in Spain, France, and Mexico and painted still lifes and landscapes; but he was best-known for his portraits, which constituted a who's who gallery of prominent Latin and South Americans. In 1990, his *Medea* sold for $93,000 at Christie's in New York, then the highest price ever paid for the work of a Puerto Rican painter.

Rodríguez, (Juan) "Chichi" (1937–   ) golfer; born in Río Piedras, Puerto Rico. Born into poverty, Rodríguez began as a caddy at age 6, and practiced on tin cans with a homemade golf club fashioned from a branch of a guava tree. It has been said that Puerto Rican golf was born with "Chichi," who came to prominence in the 1960s, when he was one of the top ten in the Professional Golf Circuit. His Horatio Alger success story, philanthropy, and jovial manner made him a great favorite with the fans. It was said that pound for pound (he weighed between 112 and 130 pounds), he was the longest hitter in the history of golf: his drives averaged 250 yards and he was known to hit 350 yards. In 1967 he published *Chichi's Secrets of Power Golf.*

Rodzinski, Artur (1892–1958) conductor; born in Spalato, Dalmatia. He conducted in Europe before being invited to the U.S.A. in 1925 by Leopold Stokowski to assist at the Philadelphia Orchestra. He went on to conduct the Los Angeles Philharmonic (1929–33), the Cleveland Orchestra (1933–43), the New York Philharmonic (1943–47), and the Chicago Symphony (1947–48). His musicianship was admired, but temperamental clashes in the latter two posts led him back to European work in his last years.

Roebling, John Augustus (1806–69) civil engineer; born in Mühlhausen, Germany. Educated in Berlin, Roebling emigrated to the United States in 1831, settling near Pittsburgh. He worked as an engineer on several river canal projects where he pioneered the development of wire rope for barges and the machinery needed to use it. From 1844 to 1845 he built an aqueduct across the Allegheny River, the first structure ever to be supported with wire cable. This success was followed in 1846 by a wire-supported suspension bridge over the Monongahela River and in 1848 by a series of aqueducts linking the Delaware River and the Hudson canal. In 1855 he completed the Niagara railway suspension bridge. In 1867, Roebling was chosen chief engineer for a bridge across the East River to connect Manhattan and Brooklyn. While making a survey of the project, one of his feet was accidentally crushed. Despite medical attention, Roebling died of tetanus. The Brooklyn Bridge was completed by his son, Washington Augustus Roebling.

Roebling, Washington Augustus (1837–1926) engineer; born in Saxonburg, Pa. He gained experience working for his father, John Augustus Roebling, building wire-rope suspension bridges, before serving with distinction as a Union army engineer (1861–65). Upon his father's death, he superintended the building of the Brooklyn Bridge (1869–83); because of poor health from 1872 on, he directed operations from his home in Brooklyn overlooking the site. Although he continued to head the family's wire-rope manufacturing business for several years, medical problems forced him to retire in 1888.

Roebuck, Alvah C. (Curtis) (1864–1948) watch repairman, businessman; born near Lafayette, Ind. He began repairing watches as a child and helped support his family at age 12 after his father died. He repaired watches for Richard Sears in Chicago until Sears sold the R. W. Sears Watch Company and moved to Iowa. Under the agreement, Sears was to refrain from selling watches in the Chicago area for a specific number of years, so he enticed Roebuck to form A. C. Roebuck & Company, a mail order watch business based in Minneapolis (1891), which Sears then bought back and moved to Chicago as the Sears and Roebuck Company (1893). Roebuck reunited with Sears in 1909 when Sears asked him to modernize the Emerson typewriter; after Roebuck did so, it was renamed the Woodstock and became a great money-earner for Sears and Roebuck Company. Roebuck continued to work on entertainment devices, including a magic lantern. He developed a motion picture company that he sold in 1924. He moved to Florida, lost all his money in real estate speculation, and in 1930 returned to Sears and Roebuck Company as a correspondent and promoter. He retired to California in 1940.

Roemer, Michael (1928–) movie director; born in Berlin, Germany. After spending the war years in Britain, he arrived in the U.S.A. in 1945; he directed his first short subject, *A Touch of the Times* (1947–49), while he was still in college. He worked on a number of educational shorts and documentaries with Louis De Rochemont before making his first fiction feature, *Nothing but a Man* (1964), highly acclaimed for its sensitive depiction of African-American life.

Roesen, Severin (?–1871) painter; born in (?) Cologne, Germany. Trained as a porcelain and enamel painter, he emigrated to America (1848), lived in New York (1850–57), and moved to Williamsport, Pa. (c. 1858–70). He is known for his opulent floral paintings, as seen in *Still Life, Flowers and Fruit* (1848).

Roethke, Theodore (Huebner) (1908–63) poet; born in Saginaw, Mich. He studied at the University of Michigan (B.A. 1924; M.A. 1936) and Harvard (1930–31). He taught at many institutions, notably the University of Washington: Seattle (1947–63). He is known for lyrical poetry of growth and decay, as seen in his posthumous collection, *The Far Field* (1964).

Rogers, Bruce (1870–1957) book designer; born in Lafayette, Ind. A longtime designer of limited editions for Riverside Press, Harvard University Press (1895–1934), and others, he designed over 400 books, including a well-known 1909 edition of *The Compleat Angler*. He also developed the Centaur typeface.

Rogers, Carl (Ransom) (1902–87) psychotherapist; born in Oak Park, Ill. He took his doctorate in psychology at Columbia University (1931) and published his first book, *Clinical Treatment of Problem Children*, in 1939. He taught at the University of Chicago (1945–57), where his research on the one-to-one relationship in therapy resulted in the book *Client-Centered Therapy* (1951). This nondirective approach rejected doctrinaire interpretations of the patient's symptoms and fostered the development of encounter groups in which the therapist acted primarily as a moderator. By the 1960s his method was being widely adopted, from drug treatment centers to business organizations, and he himself became one of the best-known professionals in his field. His other publications include *Psychotherapy and Personality Change* (1954) and *On Becoming a Person* (1961).

Rogers, Edith (b. Nourse) (1881–1960) U.S. representative; born in Saco, Maine. Educated in Paris, she returned to Europe during World War I to inspect military hospitals, and continued that work in the United States, a personal representative of presidents Warren Harding and Calvin Coolidge (1922–25). Elected to her husband's congressional seat after his death (Rep., Mass.; 1925–60), she championed veterans' rights to pensions and disability allowances, sponsoring the GI Bill of Rights after World War II.

Rogers, Everett Mitchell (1931–) sociologist; born in Carroll, Iowa. He earned undergraduate and graduate degrees at Iowa State University, and joined the faculty of the University of Michigan school of journalism (1973). His early work focused on rural sociology. He later turned to communications and the diffusion of innovations.

Rogers, Fred (McFeeley) (1928–) television producer, host; born in Latrobe, Pa. He produced a local children's show in Pittsburgh during the 1950s, becoming a Presbyterian minister in 1962. In 1965, National Educational Television began broadcasting *Mr. Rogers Neighborhood,* which he continued to produce, host, and write, using puppets and songs to talk to preschool children about their feelings on serious issues. He also recorded albums and published books. His distinctive gentle manner made him both a national institution and the subject of frequent comic parodies.

Rogers, Ginger (b. Virginia Katherine McMath) (1911–) movie actress; born in Independence, Mo. She made her professional debut at age 14 with Eddie Foy's vaudeville troupe; by 1928 she was appearing with her first husband, Jack Pepper, as a vaudeville song-and-dance team; she sang with a band, appeared in film shorts and in Broadway musicals, and made her screen debut in *Young Man in Manhattan* (1930). She and Fred Astaire were not given star billing when they first danced together in *Flying Down to Rio* (1933), but they stole the picture and went on to adorn nine more movies. She made several nonmusical roles – winning the Oscar for best actress in *Kitty Foyle* (1940) – and in 1945 was the highest paid performer in Hollywood. She continued in occasional movies until the mid-1960s but then found a new public when she took over the lead in such musicals as *Hello, Dolly!* and *Mame.* She served as a fashion consultant for the J. C. Penney retail stores in the 1970s.

Rogers, Grace Rainey (1867–1943) art collector, philanthropist; born in Cleveland, Ohio. She was educated locally, married (1907), lived in New York City, and was divorced in 1918. She collected French paintings and Persian art, and was involved in many philanthropic activities. She served on the boards of the Metropolitan and Cleveland museums and New York City's Museum of Modern Art, and donated portions of her collection to each one. The Metropolitan Museum's auditorium for concerts and lectures is named in her honor.

Rogers, Harriet Burbank (1834–1919) educator; born in North Billerica, Mass. A Massachusetts teacher, she adopted the European oral method in teaching a deaf pupil, Fanny Cushing, in 1863. Her success gained her the support of Gardiner Hubbard (the Massachusetts businessman whose own deaf daughter would later marry Alexander Graham Bell) and he helped her set up a school for the deaf (1866) in Chelmsford, Mass. When John Clarke of Northampton, Mass., helped endow a new school in that city, Rogers moved there to become the first director at the Clarke School for the Deaf (1867–86). She made this the first U.S. institution to teach the deaf by articulation and lip reading rather than by signing. Her approach was opposed by many but she and her teachers gradually won many over. Poor health forced her to leave Northampton in 1884 and she spent the years after residing in her hometown where she ran a kindergarten for a while.

Rogers, Isaiah (1800–69) architect and inventor; born in Marshfield, Mass. His innovative designs established American preeminence in hotel architecture; he held several patents for bridge designs. He was supervising architect of the Treasury Department (1863–65).

Rogers, John (1648–1721) religious reformer; born in Milford, Conn. His parents were wealthy Connecticut merchants. He converted to the Seventh-Day Baptist faith (1674) but then developed his own small sect, known as the Rogerenes. He wrote *The Book of the Revelation of Jesus Christ* (1720). Persecuted intensely for his persuasions, he was imprisoned seven times, for a total of 15 years. He married three times (1670, 1690, 1714), the second time to a maid-servant without any legal ceremony; she later sued him and was herself imprisoned for bearing a child out of wedlock. He died of smallpox in Boston. Less known than Roger Williams, he was a pioneer of religious freedom.

Rogers, John (Jr.) (1829–1904) sculptor; born in Salem, Mass. He began as a machinist, draftsman, and railroad mechanic in the Northeast and in Missouri. After study in Paris and Rome (1858–59), he established himself in New York City, and by 1877, lived in New Canaan, Conn. He was famous for the mass production of his narrative figural works in plaster, such as *The Fugitive's Story* (1869).

Rogers, Kenny (Ray) (1941–) popular singer, guitarist; born in Houston, Texas. While in high school he performed on American Bandstand and in the 1960s and 1970s played in various jazz, folk, and country-rock groups including Kenny Rogers and the First Edition. On his own as a country singer, he found wide popularity with the hit "Lucille" (1977) and then produced such hits as "Lady" (1980) and "I Don't Need You" (1981).

Rogers, Mary Josephine (1882–1955) Catholic religious foundress; born in New York City. A graduate of Smith College (1905), she volunteered to help the new Maryknoll missionary society (1912) and helped found the Maryknoll Sisters (1920), of which she was mother general until 1947, under the name Mother Mary Joseph.

Rogers, Randolph (1825–92) sculptor; born in Waterloo, N.Y. He grew up in Ann Arbor, Mich., was a dry goods clerk, moved to New York City (c. 1847), studied sculpture in Rome (1848), and settled there. He is known for his Victorian, often sentimental works, such as *Nydia, the Blind Girl of Pompeii* (1855–56), and for the *Columbus Doors* (1855–60) for the United States Capitol.

Rogers, Robert (1731–95) frontiersman, soldier; born in Metheun, Mass. He led colonial troops during the French and Indian War. "Roger's Rangers" fought the French and Indians successfully in the wilderness. He fought on the Loyalist side during the American Revolution.

Rogers, William P. (Pierce) (1913–) lawyer, cabinet officer; born in Norfolk, N.Y. He took his law degree from Cornell (1937). Assistant district attorney in New York (1938–42), he served with the U.S. Navy (1942–46). He became chief counsel of the U.S. Senate Committee investigating corruption in government expenditures (1947–50). Between long years with his New York firm, Rogers & Wells, he served as U.S. attorney-general under President Eisenhower (1957–61), and as U.S. secretary of state under President Nixon (1969–73). Known as a cautious negotiator, he found himself upstaged by Nixon's special assistant on foreign affairs, Dr. Henry Kissinger, but he worked hard and loyally to defend Nixon's policies before returning to his private practice.

Rogers, (William Penn Adair) Will (1879–1935) humorist, stage/film/radio actor; born in Oolagah, Indian territory (now Oklahoma). Part Cherokee, he was a practicing cowboy but went abroad to seek adventure, beginning his career (1902) as a rider and trick roper in Wild West shows in

South Africa and Australia. Returning to the U.S.A. (1904), he moved into vaudeville and Broadway musicals, becoming an especial favorite in the *Ziegfeld Follies* (1916–24), by which time his act had begun to feature his own cracker-barrel wit and homespun philosophy. By 1918 he was making the first of many movies, and soon he projected his persona of the common-but-shrewd man through many mediums – as a popular radio performer, a syndicated newspaper columnist, author of several books, and a presidential candidate on the Anti-Bunk ticket (1928). His trademark line was, "All I know is what I read in the papers," which he used to launch his wry comments on the current scene. When he died with Wiley Post in a plane crash in Alaska, he was mourned as an authentic American folk hero.

Rogosin, Lionel (1924–) documentary producer, film director; born in New York. After navy service, he made a highly acclaimed documentary, *On the Bowery* (1956), and then gained further acclaim for *Come Back Africa* (1959), filmed in South Africa with a concealed camera. He continued promoting avant-garde films through showings at the theater he owned, the Bleecker Street Cinema in New York City.

Rohatyn, Felix (George) (1928–) financier, author; born in Vienna, Austria. His family fled the Nazis in the mid-1930s, settling first in France, then in the United States. He graduated from Middlebury College in 1948, joined Lazard Freres & Co., the investment house, that same year. He became a naturalized U.S. citizen in 1950 and served in the army (including a tour in Korea) from 1951–53. He returned to Lazard and worked for the firm in Europe for several years during the 1950s. Named a general partner at Lazard in 1961, he earned a reputation as a master arranger of corporate deals and mergers. He headed the New York Stock Exchange's crisis committee during a difficult period in 1970–71, working to supply financing to keep tottering companies from collapse. As unsalaried chairman of New York City's Municipal Assistance Corp. in the late 1970s, he was credited with the key role in rescuing the nation's largest city from bankruptcy. In later years he wrote extensively on economic issues, revealing generally liberal sympathies in relating them to America's social problems.

Rohde, Gilbert (1894–1944) furniture/industrial designer; born in New York City. An innovator in modernist furniture and interior design, he concentrated on progressive designs utilizing new materials and manufacturing techniques; he also pioneered in designing for mass produced furniture. He started his own industrial design firm in 1929 and from 1936 to 1937 he codirected the Design Laboratory in New York City, a Bauhaus-like school supported by the Works Progress Administration. He taught at New York University from 1939 to 1943.

Rohde, Ruth Bryan (Owen) (1885–1954) diplomat, U.S. representative, feminist; born in Jacksonville, Ill. (daughter of William Jennings Bryan). She attended school in Illinois and Nebraska University, but left to marry in 1903. Divorced and remarried, with four children, she supported the family through public speaking after her husband became an invalid. In 1926 she ran unsuccessfully for the U.S. House of Representatives from Florida, then was elected in 1928, the first congresswoman from the deep South (Dem., Fla.; 1929–33). In Congress, she continued to lobby for women's rights. She was appointed a special U.S. ambassador to

Denmark and Iceland (1933), the first woman to hold a major diplomatic post. After her marriage to a Dane, she was forced to resign, returning to the U.S.A. to lecture and write. She was an alternate delegate to the United Nations in 1949.

Roheim, Geza (1891–1953) anthropologist, psychoanalyst; born in Budapest, Hungary. Educated in his native city, he became the first occupant of the University of Budapest's chair in anthropology in 1919. His study of psychoanalysis informed his theories of myth, ritual, and dream life, and made him a pioneer in the convergence of this discipline with anthropology. He emigrated to the U.S.A. for political reasons in 1938. A prolific author, his final work, *Magic and Schizophrenia,* appeared posthumously.

Rohlfs, Charles (1853–1936) furniture maker; born in New York City. After working as a stove designer and an actor, he established a Buffalo workshop to produce oak furniture, first in the simpler arts and crafts, then in the more ornate art nouveau styles. International exhibits brought fame and commissions to design interiors, to make furniture for the Adirondacks camps of the wealthy, and even to make a set of chairs for Buckingham Palace.

Rolfe, John (1585–1622) colonist; born in Norfolk, England. His successful cultivation of tobacco led to its becoming the staple crop of Virginia. He married Pocahontas (1614); the union maintained peace with the Indians that lasted until 1622.

Rollins, Carl Purington (1880–1960) printer; born in West Newbury, Mass. As printer for Yale University (1928–48) he designed over 2,000 volumes and lectured on typography; he wrote a column for the *Saturday Review of Literature* called "The Compleat Collector."

Rollins, (Theodore Walter) "Sonny" (1929–) jazz musician; born in New York City. A commanding tenor saxophonist and improvisor, he worked as a sideman with Bud Powell, J. J. Johnson, Thelonious Monk, and Miles Davis between 1949–55, and began recording on a free-lance basis as a leader in 1951. His career was hampered early on by drug addiction, but he emerged in 1957 from a two-year engagement with the Max Roach-Clifford Brown Quintet as the celebrated leader of his own group. His initial renown was in the hard bop style of modern jazz, but his continual incorporation of calypso, soul, and rock elements enabled him to remain an influential figure for the remainder of his career.

Rölvaag (or Roelvaag), O. E. (Ole Edvart) (Paal Moerck, pen name) (1876–1931) writer; born on the Island of Donna, Helgeland, Norway. He gave up his life as a fisherman and emigrated to America (1896) to become a farmhand in South Dakota. He studied at Augusta College, a preparatory school in South Dakota, and graduated from St. Olaf College (Minn.) (1905). After graduate work at the University of Oslo, Norway, he became a professor of Norwegian language and literature at St. Olaf (1907–31). He wrote his work in Norwegian, but helped with the English translations. He is best known for his semiautobiographical novels of Norwegian immigrant pioneers in the U.S.A., such as *Giants of the Earth* (1927), the first of a triology on this theme.

Romano, John (1908–) psychiatrist, educator; born in Milwaukee, Wis. He founded and chaired the department of psychiatry at the University of Rochester (1946–71), one of the first psychiatric facilities built as an integral part of a university hospital. He was a leader in medical and psychiatric education.

Romanoff, Michael ("Prince Mike"; possibly born Harry F. Gerguson) (?1892–1971) restaurateur, impostor; possibly born in Vilna, Lithuania. Among his many fabrications, little is definitely known of his early life. In 1919 he proclaimed himself a Russian prince and lived a glamorous life on credit in Paris and London before opening a celebrity restaurant in Hollywood (1939), the first of a chain that he managed until his 1962 retirement.

Rombauer, Irma (Louise von Starkloff) (1877–1962) cookbook writer; born in St. Louis, Mo. She learned to cook after her marriage to a St. Louis lawyer. At the request of her grown children, she compiled what became *The Joy of Cooking* (1936), the best-selling cookbook of all time and one beloved for its personal tone and encyclopedic range. Her daughter, Marion Rombauer Becker (1903–76), revised later editions.

Romberg, Sigmund (1887–1951) composer; born in Nagy Kaniza, Hungary. He came to the U.S.A. in 1909; his over 70 operettas, which are among the most popular ever written, include *Blossom Time* (1921), *The Student Prince* (1924), and *The New Moon* (1928).

Romer, Alfred Sherwood (1894–1973) zoologist, paleontologist; born in White Plains, N.Y. He was a zoology professor (1934–65), curator of vertebrate paleontology, and director of the Museum of Comparative Zoology at Harvard (1946–61). He pioneered the use of comparative anatomy to study the evolution of fossil vertebrates, specializing in Permian reptiles; his major publications include *Vertebrate Paleontology* (1933, 3rd edition 1966), *The Vertebrate Body* (1949, 4th edition 1970) and *Osteology of the Reptiles* (1956).

Romney, George (Wilcken) (1907–) businessman, governor, cabinet officer; born in Chihuahua, Mexico. Son of American Mormon missionaries, he came to the U.S.A. at age 5 and attended the University of Utah and George Washington University. He started as a salesman with the Aluminum Company in 1930, working his way over and up in the automobile industry, eventually becoming president and chairman of American Motors Corporation (1954–62). Chairman of Citizens for Michigan (1959–62), he organized a constitutional convention. As a moderate Republican governor of Michigan (1963–69) he supported civil rights legislation while putting the state on a sound financial basis. In 1964 he had refused to support the conservative Republican candidate, Barry Goldwater, and was regarded as the frontrunner for the Republican nomination in 1968 until he committed a gaffe by stating that the U.S. leaders in Vietnam tried to "brainwash" him. President Nixon nevertheless appointed him secretary of Housing and Urban Development (1969–73). He later headed the National Center for Voluntary Action and held high positions in the Church of Jesus Christ of Latter-Day Saints.

Rood, Ogden Nicholas (1831–1902) physicist; born in Danbury, Conn. After postgraduaate study in England and Germany, he taught at Troy University (1858–63) before joining Columbia University (1864–1902). He devised a photometer independent of color, was the first to use photography in microscopy, and made major contributions to electrical conductivity and insulators. An accomplished painter, his book *Modern Chromatics* (1879) was an important influence on both physics and impressionism.

Rooney, Mickey (b. Joe Yule, Jr.) (1920–) movie actor; born in New York City. Born to a vaudeville family, he crawled on stage before he was two and made his first movie at age six. He changed his name after starring in a series of short subjects based on a character named Mickey McGuire. He gained serious attention for playing Puck in the motion picture of Shakespeare's *A Midsummer Night's Dream* (1935). In 1937 he launched a popular series (15) of feature films in which he played Andy Hardy. In 1938 his role in *Boys Town* gained him a Special Academy Award and his diminutive size allowed him to play boys until he was about 28 years old. He proved to be multitalented as he moved from musicals to raucous comedy to serious drama. He returned to the stage in 1979 in a long-running tour with *Sugar Babes* and won an Emmy for his television role in *Bill*. Married several times, often down but never out, he proved to be one of the most resilient showbiz characters of his era.

Roosevelt, (Anna) Eleanor (b. Roosevelt) (1884–1962) First Lady, humanitarian; born in New York City (niece of Theodore Roosevelt). Shy and insecure as a child, she was educated privately, and in 1905 she married Franklin D. Roosevelt (a distant cousin). The first sign of her abilities came during World War I when she worked for the Red Cross; after her husband's polio attack and paralysis in 1921, she took an ever more active role on his behalf in New York State politics. With his election as president, she emerged as a truly public figure in her own right, traveling throughout the country, promoting her causes – particularly those helping women, children, and the poor – giving radio broadcasts, and writing a syndicated column, "My Day" (starting in 1935). Although both ridiculed and vilified by some, she continued to speak out even when her views – such as those on racial discrimination – put her well in advance of her husband. During World War II she traveled abroad to visit U.S. servicemen, and following the death of Franklin (1945), she embarked on a new career, serving as a delegate to the UN General Assembly (1945–51), and serving as chairperson of the UN's Human Rights Commission (1946–51) that drafted the Universal Declaration of Human Rights. She remained an active force in Democratic politics and served as a sort of unofficial American ambassador to the world of the downtrodden. In 1961 President John F. Kennedy reappointed her to the U.S. delegation to the UN; she also chaired the Kennedy administration's Commission on the Status of Women. By the time of her death, she was recognized as the most active and influential of all the U.S. presidents' wives and had earned the sobriquet, "first lady of the world."

Roosevelt, Edith (Kermit b. Carow) (1861–1948) First Lady; born in Norwich, Conn. She was Theodore Roosevelt's second wife (the first had died in 1884); they were married in 1886. She promoted a sense of harmony in the White House, using caterers for entertaining and a personal secretary to handle her correspondence. Following Roosevelt's death in 1919, she became active in charity work and remained a firm Republican, openly opposing Franklin Roosevelt's bid for the presidency in 1932.

Roosevelt, Franklin Delano (1882–1945) thirty-second U.S. president; born in Hyde Park, N.Y. Born into the patrician family (of Dutch descent) that produced his distant cousin Theodore Roosevelt, as well as his wife, Eleanor Roosevelt, he was educated in Europe and at Harvard and Columbia Law School. Admitted to the New York bar in 1907, he served as a progressive state senator (1911–13) and assistant navy secretary (1913–20) before running unsuccessfully as vice-president on the 1920 Democratic ticket. After a crippling attack of polio in 1921 (he would never again walk without assistance), he resumed his political career, becoming governor of New York (1929–33) and seeming to take on a new sense of purpose. With the country in a deep depression, he easily defeated Herbert Hoover in 1932. As president, he moved decisively and set the pattern for the modern liberal Democratic Party with a social and economic program called the "New Deal." An array of agencies and departments, many hastily created in his first months in office, were designed to stimulate the economy, put people to work, and simply to create hope – the Tennessee Valley Authority, Civilian Conservation Corps, Securities and Exchange Commission, Work Projects Administration, and the Social Security Administration, among others. Some of these organizations were short-lived; others became fixtures of the American way of life. While the nation's economy did not fully revive until wartime, his actions earned Roosevelt the gratitude of working people that outweighed the hatred of conservatives. In fact, he himself was not all that interested in either the details of his programs nor in any ideological theories; he was motivated largely by a desire to keep the U.S.A. a functioning and fair society, and to this end he surrounded himself with first-rate people; a person of ordinary intellect and tastes, his mixture of casual optimism and natural sympathies managed to appeal to everyone from artsy intellectuals to disenfranchised minorities. Reelected by a landslide in 1936, he won unprecedented third and fourth terms in 1940 and 1944. Having maintained neutrality in the face of European hostilities in the late 1930s, his administration began supplying arms to the allies by 1940 and then led the nation into World War II after the Japanese attack on Pearl Harbor (December 1941). Having seen the nation through the war, and helped plan, with other allied leaders, the postwar world and the United Nations, Roosevelt died less than four weeks before the German surrender. The object of constant attacks during his presidency – he was regarded as everything from "a traitor to his class" to a would-be dictator – he would suffer somewhat from posthumous revelations about an extramarital relationship and by charges that he conceded too much in negotiations with Joseph Stalin and Winston Churchill, but most historians and informed people continue to regard FDR as one of the three or four greatest American presidents.

Roosevelt, Kermit (1889–1943) explorer, army officer; born in Oyster Bay, Long Island (son of Theodore Roosevelt). He hunted and explored with his father (1909, 1913) and served with both the British aand the U.S. armies during World War I. He formed the Roosevelt Steamship Company (1920). With his brother, Theodore Roosevelt Jr., he collected rare animals and birds in Turkestan and China for the Field Museum in Chicago (1925, 1928–29). He died while on intelligence duty with the U.S. Army in Alaska.

Roosevelt, Nicholas (1767–1854) engineer; born in New York. He was a pioneer in steam navigation, first building a model boat in 1782 propelled by side-paddle wheels turned by springs. He later established a foundry and in 1798 built a steamboat there. In 1811 he and Robert Fulton built the *New Orleans,* the first steamboat on the Ohio and Mississippi Rivers.

Roosevelt, Theodore (1858–1919) twenty-sixth U.S. president; born in New York City (fifth cousin of Franklin Delano Roosevelt). Born into a patrician family, he was sickly as a boy but he built up his body and physical abilities. He graduated from Harvard in 1880, and the next year gained election to the New York legislature (Rep., 1882–84). During the 1880s he also began his extensive historical writings, including such works as *The Naval War of 1812* (1882), *Essays on Practical Politics* (1888), and the four-volume *The Winning of the West* (1889–96). In 1884–86 he ran a ranch in Dakota Territory. He went to Washington, D.C., to serve as a U.S. Civil Service commissioner (1889–95). Named president of the New York police board in 1895, his vigorous reformist efforts – and his tendency to get himself into the headlines – gained him a national reputation, which led to his being appointed assistant navy secretary by President William McKinley (1897). When war with Spain broke out in 1898, Roosevelt resigned to lead the "Rough Riders," a volunteer cavalry unit whose celebrated charge up Kettle Hill in the battle outside Santiago, Cuba, made him a national hero; this helped take him to the governorship of New York (1889–1901) and then to the 1900 Republican ticket as McKinley's vice-president. Roosevelt succeeded to the presidency on the assassination of McKinley in 1901, and proved a powerful and effective leader in a time of national expansion, easily gaining reelection in 1904. Citing as his motto, "Speak softly and carry a big stick," he demonstrated American power on the world stage – including machinations that led to the creation of the Panama Canal – and built up the navy. In the "Roosevelt corollary" to the Monroe Doctrine he proclaimed the U.S.A. the policeman of the Western Hemisphere. Equally active on the domestic front, he pioneered in government regulation of big business with his prosecution of corporations for trust violations; he also created national parks, oversaw passage of the Pure Food and Drug Act, and signed the Hepburn Act regulating railroads. During his campaign in 1904, he declared that he would not run again; in 1908, reluctantly, he promoted his protégé William Howard Taft in a successful presidential campaign. He moved on to a life of traveling, hunting, and writing but by 1911 he was clearly unsatisfied with the conservative direction of the government. He made an unsuccessful bid for the presidency in 1912 with the Progressive ("Bull Moose") Party. As World War I proceeded, he began to denounce President Wilson's cautious policy and he was considering another run for the presidency when he died suddenly. Theodore Roosevelt can be claimed as a hero or villain by proponents of many ideologies or causes, but all would agree that he was defiantly one of a kind as both man and president.

Root, Elihu (1845–1937) lawyer, public official, statesman; born in Clinton, N.Y. He rose to prominence as U.S. district attorney for the southern district of New York (1883–85) and legal adviser to Theodore Roosevelt. As secretary of war (1899–1904) he reorganized the army and established governmental systems for Cuba, Puerto Rico, and the Philippines. As secretary of state (1904–09) he cultivated friendly relations with Latin American countries and negotiated the "Gentlemen's Agreement" with Japan

(1908). He represented the U.S.A. before the Hague Court in the American-British dispute over coastal fisheries (1910), and served as Republican senator from New York (1909–15). A leader in the movement for world peace in the U.S.A. and a staunch League of Nations advocate, he received the Nobel Peace Prize (1912) and continued to work to strengthen international law and justice. He served as president of the Carnegie Endowment for International Peace (1910–25).

Root, Elisha King (1808–65) inventor, engineer, manufacturer; born in Ludlow, Mass. In 1849 he became superintendent of the Colt Firearms Company, eventually becoming president. He remained there until his death. Root invented a drop hammer in 1853, which was soon used in every forge. He also invented a revolving cylinder firearm and developed numerous machines for tooling firearms.

Root, George Frederick (1820–95) composer; born in Sheffield, Mass. He received musical training in Boston before teaching singing at several colleges in New York in the 1840s. In 1853 he cofounded the New York Normal Institute to train music teachers; in 1859 he moved to Chicago, where, in addition to teaching music, he was a music publisher until 1871. He composed a number of cantatas popular in their day, and under the name G. Frederick Wurzel he began to write popular songs. In 1863 he composed "The Battle Cry of Freedom," the first of several celebrated Civil War songs, including "Tramp, Tramp, Tramp, the Boys are Marching" and "The Vacant Chair."

Root, Gladys Towles (1905–82) lawyer; born in Los Angeles, Calif. Known for her attire – furs, feathers, oversized jewelry, towering hats with flashing lights – she practiced law in California (1929–82). Her sex and murder cases were often dramatic; her clients were often poor. (Her biography is titled *Defender of the Damned* (1964).)

Root, John Wellborn (1850–91) architect; born in Lumpkin, Ga. The primary designer in a partnership with Daniel H. Burnham (1873–91), he designed innovative iron- and steel-framed Chicago skyscrapers that shaped the Chicago school of architecture in the 1880s.

Root, Waverley (Lewis) (1903–82) journalist, author; born in Providence, R.I. He was a longtime Paris correspondent for newspapers from the *Chicago Tribune* (1927–57) to the *Washington Post* (1957–69). With *The Food of France* (1958), he launched a second, perhaps more memorable career as a food writer; his works include the international dictionary *Food* (1980).

Roper, Elmo (Burns, Jr.) (1900–71) public opinion analyst; born in Hebron, Nebr. A retailer and salesman, he turned to market research, and, founding his own New York firm (1934), pioneered modern public opinion polling techniques. He published *Fortune*'s public opinion surveys (1935–50), broadcast the first live analysis of election returns (on CBS, 1940), and wrote a syndicated newspaper column, "What People are Thinking." He retired in 1966.

Rorem, Ned (1923–) composer, writer; born in Richmond, Ind. After musical studies in Chicago, the Curtis Institute of Music, and Juilliard, and privately with Virgil Thomson and Aaron Copland, he spent most of the 1950s in Paris, then returned to teach briefly at the Universities of Buffalo and Utah. Best known for his many songs in a lyrical and mildly modernist style, he also wrote effective instrumental music such as *Air Music* (winner of the 1976 Pulitzer Prize). In addition to his music, he published a number of his journals, such as *The Paris Diary* (1966), and numerous articles famous for their biting "insider" views of contemporary music and the art world.

Rorer, Sarah Tyson (b. Heston) (1849–1937) educator, author, dietitian; born in Richboro, Pa. She was a popular author and lecturer who helped make cooking a science. Her Philadelphia Cooking School classes (1883–1903) provided cooks, slumdwellers, and medical institutions with programs stressing nutrition and chemistry. She wrote among other cookbooks the *Philadelphia Cook Book* (1886).

Rorimer, James (Joseph) (1905–66) museum director; born in Cleveland, Ohio. He studied at Harvard (B.A. 1927) and worked for New York's Metropolitan Museum of Art in the decorative arts department. He helped plan the Cloisters (completed in 1938); was curator of medieval art (1934–43, 1946–55); served in the U.S. Army (1943–46); was director of the Metropolitan Museum of Art (1955–66); and wrote many books on art preservation, including *Ultraviolet Rays and Their Use in the Examination of Works of Art* (1931).

Rorty, Richard (McKay) (1931–) philosopher; born in New York City. After studying at the University of Chicago and Yale, and teaching at Yale (1954–56), Wellesley (1958–61), and Princeton (1961–82), he became a professor at the University of Virginia. An esteemed analytic philosopher in his youth, he fell briefly into a period of depression and inertia in the early 1970s. Revived by a "conversion" to pragmatism, he made a forceful and controversial attack on traditional and analytic philosophy in *Philosophy and the Mirror of Nature* (1979), calling for a new "postphilosophic" dialogue of many voices. Although regarded by some as iconoclastic and by others as a maverick, he is conceded to have reintroduced American philosophy into the marketplace of contemporary concerns.

Rose, Albert (1910–90) physicist; born in New York City. He joined the staff at Radio Corporation of America (RCA) in 1935 after getting his Ph.D. from Cornell University. While at RCA he invented the image orthicon television camera tube, first used for military purposes during World War II before becoming the electronic eye for all television cameras. In 1955 he directed research at the RCA laboratory in Zurich, returning in 1957 to the RCA-David Sarnoff Research Center. Widely honored, he authored several books including *Vision: Human and Electronic* (1974).

Rose, Billy (b. Samuel Wolf Rosenberg) (1899–1966) entertainment entrepreneur, lyricist; born in New York City. He helped write popular songs in the 1920s but moved on to become a financer and producer of plays and musicals in the 1930s and 1940s. He owned nightclubs and theater-restaurants, and was famous for producing such spectacles as the "aquacades" for New York's World Fair (1939–40) and the San Francisco Golden Gate Exposition (1940). He occasionally was associated with serious efforts such as the production of *Carmen Jones* (1943); he commissioned Stravinsky's *Scènes de Ballet* (1944). A Broadway fixture, he wrote a syndicated newspaper column, appeared on radio in the 1940s and 1950s, and went through five highly publicized marriages.

Rose, Leonard (1918–84) cellist; born in Washington, D.C. After studies at the Curtis Institute of Music, he played in the NBC Symphony under Arturo Toscanini (1938–39) and was first cellist in the Cleveland Orchestra (1939–43) and

New York Philharmonic (1943–51) before becoming an outstanding solo recitalist, teacher, and member of the Istomin-Stern-Rose trio. He taught at Curtis from 1951 to 1962.

Rose, Mary Davies Swartz (1874–1941) nutritionist; born in Newark, Ohio. A Yale Ph.D. in physiological chemistry, she established a department of nutrition and developed nutrition education programs for public schools while teaching at Teachers College, Columbia University (1909–40). Her many publications include the standard *Foundations of Nutrition* (1927).

Rose, (Peter Edward) Pete (1941–) baseball player/manager; born in Cincinnati, Ohio. During his 24-year career as an infielder and outfielder (1963–86), primarily with the Cincinnati Reds and Philadelphia Phillies, he played in more games (3,562) and got more hits (4,256) than any player in history. A switch-hitting leadoff batter, he ran to first base even when he was walked, earning the nickname "Charlie Hustle." He managed the Reds from 1984 to 1989, when the commissioner of baseball, A. Bartlett Giamatti, permanently banned Rose from baseball for his alleged gambling activities. In return for not having the gambling formally proven, Rose agreed to accept the banishment (which rendered him ineligible for induction into baseball's Hall of Fame), but he was found guilty of income tax evasion and served five months in the Federal prison system (1990). He continued to appear at some unofficial baseball shows and bided his time, hoping some of his supporters might find a way to get him into the Hall of Fame.

Rose, Uriah Milton (1834–1913) jurist; born in Bradfordsville, Ky. He graduated from Transylvania University (1853), moved to Arkansas, and practiced law. Although he originally opposed secession, he cast his lot with his state during the Civil War. He traveled widely after 1872. He was delegate to the Second Peace Conference at the Hague (1907). He wrote *Digest of the Arkansas Reports* (1867) and *The Constitution of the State of Arkansas* (1891). Arkansas placed his statue in the U.S. Capitol.

Rose, Wickliffe (1862–1931) public health administrator; born in Saulsbury, Tenn. He taught at the Peabody College for Teachers and the University of Nashville before joining the Peabody Education Fund (1907–14). He directed the Rockefeller Sanitary Commission for the Eradication of Hookworm in the South (1910–23), a task made possible by his tact and diplomacy. As director of the International Health Board of the Rockefeller Foundation (1913–23), his responsibilities increased to include other preventable diseases and resulted in the establishment of schools of public health in 13 cities around the world. As director of the General Education Board and of the International Education Board, he promoted scientific teaching and research.

Rosecrans, William (Starke) (1819–98) soldier; born in Delaware County, Ohio. He graduated from West Point in 1842, endured a succession of routine assignments, and quit the army in 1854 to enter the business world. Returning to the service in June 1861, he rose rapidlly. His Army of the Cumberland withstood a savage Confederate attack at Stone's River in December 1862. After a brilliant campaign of maneuver, Rosecrans occupied Chattanooga in August 1863. A month later at Chickamauga, however, his army collapsed under a powerful Confederate assault, and he retreated into the Chattanooga defenses where the demoral-ized Rosecrans allowed himself to be besieged. Ulysses S. Grant relieved him in October 1863 and he never again commanded in battle. After the war, Rosecrans served as ambassador to Mexico from 1868 to 1869; he represented California as a Democrat in Congress from 1881 to 1885.

Rosen, Charles (1927–) pianist, writer; born in New York City. Rosen studied piano from childhood, and music history and French literature at Princeton; he made his New York debut as a recitalist in 1951. Thereafter he maintained an active performing and teaching career, meanwhile writing books on music including the 1971 *Classical Style,* itself a classic.

Rosen, Joseph A. (1878–1949) agronomist; born in Moscow, Russia. He was arrested in 1894 for being a revolutionary and was sent to Siberia. He escaped, eventually ending up in Michigan (1903), where he worked on a farm and enrolled at Michigan Agricultural College (1905). He wrote a series of articles on American agriculture for a Russian publication, a practice he continued until the Russian Revolution of 1917. In 1909 he gave his alma mater a pound of Russian rye seed; named Rosen rye in his honor, it became the predominant rye grown in the Midwest. In 1921 he joined Herbert Hoover's American Relief Administration, representing the Joint Distribution Committee of the American Jewish Committee. He introduced tractors to the Soviet Union and helped resettle thousands of Jewish farmers in the Ukraine and the Crimea.

Rosenau, Milton Joseph (1869–1946) epidemiologist; born in Philadelphia. After taking his M.D. at the University of Pennsylvania (1889) and studying disease prevention in Europe, he joined the U.S. Public Health Service in 1890, serving as director of its research laboratory (1899–1909). He made notable contributions in several fields, including the study of anaphylaxis, establishing the official unit for diphtheria antitoxin, and studying typhoid fever, malaria, botulism, and various respiratory diseases. In 1906 he defined the process for milk pasteurization. At Harvard Medical School (1909–35) he established the first school for public health officers (1913), inculcated students with vital knowledge about communicable diseases, and published his most important book, *Preventive Medicine and Hygiene* (1913). At the University of North Carolina: Chapel Hill (1935–45), he established a school of public health.

Rosenbach, Abraham (Simon Wolf) (1876–1952) book dealer/collector; born in Philadelphia. After earning his Ph.D. at the University of Pennsylvania, he joined his brother Philip Rosenbach in the antique business (1902), soon branching out to sell rare books and manuscripts. As a dealer, he helped assemble the volumes at the core of such institutions as the Huntington Library, the Widener Library, the Folger Shakespeare Library, and the Harkness collection (now in the Library of Congress). Over the years he also became one of the world's major collectors, owning such items as James Joyce's manuscript copy of *Ulysses.* A legend in the book world, he wrote such works as *A Book Hunter's Holiday* (1936).

Rosenberg, Ethel See under ROSENBERG, JULIUS.

Rosenberg, Julius (1918–53) **and Ethel (b. Greenglass)** (1915–53) convicted spies; both born in New York City. Julius worked as a U.S. army engineer (1940–45) and was fired for lying about his membership in the Communist Party. Julius and Ethel were arrested (1950) and convicted

(1951) of passing on atomic secrets to the Soviet Union (partly on testimony of Ethel's brother David Greenglass). Despite clemency appeals from leaders and protests around the world, they were both electrocuted, the first Americans ever to be executed for espionage during peacetime.

Rosenberg, Paul (1881–1959) art dealer, collector; born in Paris, France. Educated in Paris, he joined his father's antique business and worked in England (1902–05). He returned to Paris to open an art gallery (1911), and became famous as a dealer of such artists as Picasso, Braque, and Matisse. He opened a branch in England (1935). Fleeing from the Germans, he emigrated to New York City (1940), where he opened a gallery that successfully represented contemporary American and European artists.

Rosenblum, Robert H. (1927–) art historian; born in New York City. He studied at Queens College (B.A. 1948), Yale (M.A. 1950), New York University (Ph.D. 1956), and Oxford (M.A. 1971). He taught at several institutions, notably New York University (from 1966) and specialized in neoclassical, romantic, and 20th-century art.

Rosenfeld, Paul (Leopold) (1890–1946) music/art critic, author; born in New York City. After studying at Yale (B.A. 1912) and Columbia University (Litt.B. 1913), he worked as a free-lance writer for many periodicals, and published books on both music and art. A supporter of the modern movement in the arts, his best-known work was *14 American Moderns* (1924), a volume of essays on such notables as Alfred Stieglitz, Albert P. Ryder, and William Carlos Williams. He was especially known as a passionate supporter of modern American composers in such works as *Discoveries of a Music Critic* (1936).

Rosenman, Leonard (1924–) composer; born in New York City. A Schoenberg student, he began scoring films in 1955 with *East of Eden;* others include *Fantastic Voyage* (1966) and *Barry Lyndon* (1975). He also wrote concert works.

Rosenquist, James (1933–) painter; born in Grand Forks, N.D. He studied at the Art Students League, New York (1954–55), settled in New York (1957), and became associated with the pop art movement of the 1960s. He painted billboards in Times Square (1958–60), and used this approach in his most famous work, *F-111* (1965), an antimilitary protest. Beginning in 1963 he created room environments, as in *Horizon Home Sweet Home* (1970).

Rosenthal, Toby (Edward) (1848–1917) painter; born in New Haven, Conn. After study in San Francisco (1861) and Munich, Germany (1865–72), he remained in Munich, teaching and painting sentimental genre subjects.

Rosenwald, Julius (1862–1932) merchant/business executive, philanthropist; born in Springfield, Ill. He was born across the street from Abraham Lincoln's house and was influenced by the Lincoln mystique. He ran a menswear shop in Chicago (1885–95). When the recently formed Sears, Roebuck & Company moved to Chicago (1893), he became its vice-president (1895–1910), then its president (1910–25) and chairman of the board (1925–32). He built it up to become America's largest retail store, pioneering in the mail-order business, and creating one of the first savings and profit-sharing plans for employees. As he himself greatly prospered, by 1917 he had set up the Julius Rosenwald Fund for the "well-being of mankind"; in the following years he gave generously to causes of all kinds, but especially to Jewish groups in Russia, to Germany after World War I, and

to African-American Young Men's Christian Associations and to schools in the southern U.S.A.

Rosinski, Edward J. (1921–89) chemical engineer, inventor; born in Gloucester County, N.Y. The son of Polish immigrant parents, he combined practical laboratory work for the Mobil Oil Company with a night school education that finally earned him a B.S. in chemical engineering from Drexel University in 1956. With Charles J. Plank, he made significant breakthroughs in the technology of hydrocarbon conversions.

Ross, Barnaby See DANNAY, FREDERIC.

Ross, Betsy (b. Elizabeth Griscom) (1752–1836) seamstress; born in Philadelphia. Although she was a well-known seamstress and the official flagmaker for the Pennsylvania Navy, there is no real evidence that she designed or made the first flag of the United States (in 1776). The story was first told in 1870 by a grandson.

Ross, Denman Waldo (1853–1935) teacher, collector; born in Cincinnati, Ohio. He graduated from Harvard (B.A. 1875; M.A. 1880; Ph.D. 1880), worked under Henry Adams, and taught in the architecture and fine arts department at Harvard beginning in 1899. He also worked in the fine arts department of the Fogg Art Museum beginning in 1909. He wrote several theoretical books on art, including *A Theory of Pure Design* (1907). An avid traveler, he collected oriental art, which he donated to both Boston's and Harvard's Fogg Museums.

Ross, Diana (1944–) popular singer, movie actress; born in Detroit, Mich. Lead singer of the extremely successful trio, the Supremes, she went solo in 1969, recording the hits "Reach Out and Touch Somebody's Hand" and "Ain't No Mountain High Enough" in 1970. She portrayed singer Billie Holliday in the movie *Lady Sings the Blues* (1972) and by the late-1970s achieved superstar status with live and televised concerts. Joining RCA in 1981, she recorded the hit "Muscles" (1982), written by Michael Jackson.

Ross, Douglas Taylor (1929–) software executive; born in Canton, China (of American parents). While head of the Computer Applications Group at the Massachusetts Institute of Technology (1952–69), he created the language APT, used in numerically controlled manufacturing. He taught the first course in software engineering (1968) and worked on computer graphics, and computer-aided design (CAD). He founded SofTech (1969).

Ross, Edmund Gibson (1826–1907) U.S. senator, journalist; born in Ashland, Ohio. A newspaper editor-publisher, and framer of the Kansas constitution, he was appointed to the U.S. Senate (Rep., Kans.; 1866–71). He voted against convicting President Andrew Johnson after deciding the trial was not fair. Politically and socially in disgrace as a result, he returned to practice journalism in Kansas, then moved to New Mexico, where he was appointed territorial governor (1885–89).

Ross, Harold (Wallace) (1892–1951) editor; born in Aspen, Colo. In 1925, with financial backing from businessman Raoul Fleischmann, he founded the *New Yorker* as a sophisticated magazine aimed at a metropolitan audience. With meticulous editing and the services of such contributors as E. B. White, S. J. Perelman, James Thurber, John O'Hara, Ogden Nash, Robert Benchley, Dorothy Parker, Edmund Wilson, and others, he guided the magazine to greatness, especially in its short stories, humor, cartoons, and interpretative reporting.

Ross, John (b. Coowescoowe) (1790–1866) Cherokee leader; born on the Coosa River at Tahnoovayah, Ga. His mother was only part Cherokee, his father Scottish. Raised among Christians, he fought in the War of 1812 under Andrew Jackson. He became a member of the Cherokee National Council in 1817 and its president from 1819–26, during which time he helped draft the Cherokee constitution. From 1823–39 he was principal chief of the eastern Cherokee nation. In 1828, he argued and won a case brought before the U.S. Supreme Court designed to prevent U.S. encroachments on Cherokee lands, but President Jackson refused to enforce the decision. Although opposed to land cessions, he signed the Treaty of New Echota in 1838 and led the Cherokee west on the "Trail of Tears." Once in the Indian Territory (present-day Oklahoma), he joined with the western Cherokee and became tribal chief from 1839 until his death.

Ross, Nellie (b. Tayloe) (?1876–1977) governor; born in St. Joseph, Mo. A housewife, she became the first woman governor in U.S. history (Dem., Wyo.; 1925–27), gaining election after her husband died in midterm. (She was inaugurated two weeks before "Ma" Ferguson in Texas.) She remained active in Democratic politics afterward, and was appointed director of the U.S. Bureau of the Mint (1933–53), again becoming the first woman to hold that office, and becoming the first woman to have her likeness on a mint medal. She expanded the bureau's operations, building the mints at Fort Knox, West Point, and San Francisco. After leaving that office she wrote about politics for women's magazines.

Ross, (Robert) Bob (1943–   ) painting instructor; born in Daytona, Fla. Dropping out of school in the ninth grade, he served in the U.S. Air Force where he took his first painting lesson at an Anchorage, Alaska United Service Organizations club. After the service he attended various art schools until he learned the technique of "wet on wet" from William Alexander (later his bitter rival) – applying oil paints directly on one another to produce complete paintings (mostly landscapes) in less than an hour. In 1983 he began his instruction program, "The Joy of Painting," on public television, eventually carried by over 275 stations and spawning an empire that included videos, how-to books, art supplies, and certified Bob Ross instructors, thus making him one of the best-known and most highly paid of all American painters.

Rossbach, Ed (Charles Edmund) (1914–   ) weaver; born in Chicago. After service in World War II and with a 1947 M.F.A. in ceramics and weaving from Cranbrook Academy, he became design professor at the University of California: Berkeley (1950–79). Acclaimed as the "father of contemporary fiber," he led in the development of nonfunctional textiles, the use of unusual materials, and the introduction of basketry techniques to make sculptural forms.

Rossby, Carl-Gustaf (Arvid) (1898–1957) meteorologist; born in Stockholm, Sweden. His early work in meteorology was at the Bergen Institute in Norway under the famous Vilhelm Bjerknes. He came to the United States in 1926 on a one-year fellowship to the U.S. Weather Bureau, married in 1929, and became a U.S. citizen in 1939. (He would return to Sweden in 1950 at the request of the Swedish government to help found the Institute of Meteorology at the University of Stockholm.) His influence in the United States is felt at the Massachusetts Institute of Technology (1928–39) and the University of Chicago (1941–50), where he organized strong meteorological departments. At the U.S. Weather Bureau (1939–41) he redirected scientific efforts to incorporate important Scandinavian advances in the description of weather fronts and storms. He discovered what are now known as Rossby waves, a description of the flow of air within the jet stream, and the Rossby equation, that calculates how fast the flow develops. A medal bearing his name is given by the American Meteorological Society to honor significant research.

Rossi, Alice S. (b. Schaerr) (1922–   ) sociologist, educator; born in New York City. This Columbia University Ph.D. pursued an academic career, mostly at the University of Massachusetts: Amherst (1974–91). She became a leading feminist scholar as the author and editor of works on family, kinship, sex, and gender; she is particularly noted for her studies of personality development at all ages, what sociologists refer to as "life-course" analyses. Her works include *The Feminist Papers* (1973), *Gender and the Life Course* (1985), and *Of Human Bonding* (coauthored, 1990).

Rossiter, Clinton (Lawrence), III (1917–70) political scientist; born in Philadelphia. He taught at Cornell (1946–59) and wrote on subjects including colonial America, crisis management, and presidential power. Based on a series of his lectures, *The American Presidency* (1956) sold over one million copies.

Rostovtzeff, Michael (Ivanovitch) (1870–1952) historian; born in Kiev, Russia. His career divides almost evenly between his years at the University of Saint Petersburg, and then, after the Russian Revolution, at the University of Wisconsin and Yale (1925–52). One of the first historians to use archaeological evidence, he was director of the Yale excavation at Dura-Europus on the Euphrates (1928–38). He concentrated on economic history with a particular interest in ancient agriculture. His own experiences in Russia influenced his interpretation of the *Social and Economic History of the Roman Empire* (1926) as the triumph of barbarism and the lower classes. His *Social and Economic History of the Hellenistic World* (1941) focused attention on a previously neglected era. His bibliography runs to more than 500 entries; he has been called the most important ancient historian of the first half of the 20th century.

Rostow, Walt Whitman (1916–   ) economist; born in New York City. He served as a special adviser to President John F. Kennedy (1961–63) and was chairman of the Policy Planning Council at the State Department (1961–66). He was a strong supporter of the Vietnam War under President Lyndon B. Johnson and later returned to teaching at the University of Texas: Austin (1969). He is known for his expertise in the history of British economics as well as his theory that societies pass through five stages of economic growth.

Roszak, Theodore (1907–81) sculptor, lithographer; born in Poznan, Poland. After emigration to Chicago (1909), he studied at the Art Institute there (1922–25), the National Academy of Design, N.Y. (1926), produced lithographs, studied in Europe (1929–30), and settled in New York City (1931). He became known for his constructivist sculptures, as in the hammered surfaces of *Specter of Kitty Hawk* (1946–47).

Rotberg, Eugene Harvey (1930–   ) investment banker, lawyer; born in Philadelphia. He worked in government and in private banking after graduating from Temple (1951) and the University of Pennsylvania Law School (1955). After serving as a Security and Exchange Commission lawyer (1963–66), he was vice-president and treasurer of the World Bank in Washington, D.C. (1969–87). He left the World Bank for Merrill, Lynch & Company in 1987.

Roth, Henry (1906–) writer; born in Tysmenica, Austria-Hungary. His family moved to New York City when he was an infant, and after graduating from the City College of New York (B.S. 1928), he began writing while holding a variety of jobs in New York. In 1934 he published *Call It Sleep,* his semiautobiographical novel about an immigrant Jewish boy; the novel was relatively unnoticed at the time and Roth went on teaching, and during World War II, worked as a precision metal grinder. In 1945 he moved to Maine and took up raising chickens; in his late years he moved to Albuquerque, N.M. *Call It Sleep* was reissued in 1960 and hailed a minor classic. Although his only other published works were short magazine pieces and his memoirs, *Nature's First Green* (1978), he is said to have destroyed his second novel and started a third.

Roth, Philip (Milton) (1933–) writer; born in Newark, N.J. He studied at Rutgers (1950–51), Bucknell (B.A. 1954), and the University of Chicago (M.A. 1955; further study, 1956–58). He gained overnight acclaim for *Goodbye, Columbus* (1959, National Book Award), a novella, and five short stories, but for many years he combined his writing career with teaching at such institutions as the University of Iowa (1960–62), the University of New York: Stony Brook (1967–68), Princeton (1962–64), and the University of Pennsylvania (1965–80). Many of his writings brought him criticism from his fellow Jewish-Americans for his satiric views of their lives, while his *Portnoy's Complaint* (1969) gained him notoriety in broader circles for its frank sexuality. In *The Great American Novel* (1973) he tried his hand at mythologizing baseball. His trilogy, beginning with *The Ghost Writer* (1979), features his alter-ego, Nathan Zuckerman, and in these and subsequent books he plays with the notions of what is fiction and what is real about his own public self. He was also drawn to issues of censorship and intellectual freedom and for many years edited a series of translations of authors from Eastern European countries. Whatever his final standing in American literature, he clearly entertained and enraged readers in equal measure.

Rothenberg, Susan (1945–) painter, printmaker; born in Buffalo, N.Y. She studied at Cornell University, New York (B.F.A. 1966), and at George Washington University, Washington, D.C. (1967), and settled in New York City (1969). She is known for her expressionistic large canvases, such as *IXI* (1977), a bold image of a red horse.

Rothko, Mark (b. Marcus Rothkovitch) (1903–70) painter; born in Daugavpils (Dinsk), Latvia. His immigrant parents settled in Portland, Ore. (1913). After two years at Yale he settled in New York City, and except for a brief time studying with Max Weber (1925), he became a self-taught painter. During the 1930s he moved through various styles – starting with traditional representational subjects, then mythological themes – and from 1935–37 he was employed by the Federal Arts Project. In the early 1940s he took an interest in surrealism, but by 1947 his works became increasingly more abstract and by 1950 he found his true style in so-called color-field paintings, works with large rectangles of color that express moods, as in *Four Darks in Red* (1958). In 1961

he had a one-man retrospective at the Museum of Modern Art, an honor reserved for the giants of art. In 1970 he had two more major exhibits – at the Museum of Modern Art and the Metropolitan Museum of Art – but he committed suicide that year, shortly after he had completed what some regard as his masterwork, a group of murals for an interdenominational chapel in Houston, Texas.

Rourke, Constance (Mayfield) (1885–1941) historian, folklorist; born in Cleveland, Ohio. Educated at Vassar College where she then taught (1910–15), after 1915 she was an independent scholar based in Grand Rapids, Mich. She published pioneering cultural studies on the relationship between American folk traditions and art, which, while flawed, are regarded as still insightful, particularly her classic *American Humor* (1931), *Charles Sheeler* (1938), and *The Roots of American Culture* (1942).

Rous, (Francis) Peyton (1879–1970) pathologist; born in Baltimore, Md. He taught pathology at the University of Michigan (1906–08), then joined the Rockefeller Institute (1909–45), continuing his research, and publishing 60 scientific papers after his ostensible retirement. In 1911 he began experiments on chickens with malignant tumors; this led to the discovery that these tumors were caused by what is now known as the Rous sarcoma virus. This revolutionary finding was not immediately believed, and Rous went on to formulate the acid-citrate-dextrose solution for preserving human red cells for transfusion (1915), which saved lives in both world wars and is still used in modern blood banks. He also performed research on the gall bladder, liver, and hepatic circulation. He returned to virus-induced tumors in 1933, studying for the next 20 years both the viral origin of the Shope rabbit papilloma (wart), and the possible interplay of viruses and chemicals as carcinogens. Rous received one-half the 1966 Nobel Prize in physiology for his landmark contributions to viral oncogenesis. He became a consultant to the Sloan-Kettering Institute for Cancer Research (1957–70).

Rouse, (Benjamin) Irving (Jr.) (1913–) anthropologist, archaeologist; born in Rochester, N.Y. He held undergraduate and graduate degrees from Yale, where he taught (1939–84) and was associated (1934–85) with the Peabody Museum. A leading archaeologist of the Caribbean and Venezuela, he made important theoretical contributions to the problems of classifying and interpreting artifacts.

Rouse, James W. (1914–) real estate developer, urban planner; born in Easton, Md. He lost both parents to illness in 1930 and attended night classes at the University of Maryland and its law school while holding such jobs as an auditor for a parking garage company. He worked briefly for the Federal Housing Administration before borrowing money to help found Rouse Co. (1939), a mortgage brokerage firm. During World War II he served with the U.S. Navy, then returned to Maryland and got into building when he erected an early shopping mall in Baltimore in the 1950s. In 1958 he made his name with the first completely enclosed shopping mall. In the 1960s he gained a wider reputation by building Columbia, Md., a totally planned city between Baltimore and Washington, D.C., designed eventually to have 100,000 residents. In the 1970s he became still more widely known for his work on restoring run-down focal locales in cities – the Faneuil Hall-Quincy Market in Boston, Mass. (done in collaboration with the architect/planner Benjamin Thompson), which opened in 1976, was the first. Rouse went on to do other such "festival marketplaces" (some in collaboration with Thompson) as Harborplace in Baltimore and South Street Seaport and Fulton Street Market in New York City. Having built the Rouse Co. into the largest publicly held development corporation in the U.S.A., he retired in 1979. But in 1982 he founded the Enterprise Foundation, using some of his fortune to seek innovative ways to provide housing for the poor. Labeled an "icon and visionary," (he is credited with coining the term "urban renewal"), he is better understood as the self-made man, devout churchgoer, and liberal Democrat who brought a no-nonsense approach to all he undertook.

Rowan, Carl (Thomas) (1925–) journalist; born in Ravenscroft, Tenn. One of the most prominent contemporary black journalists, he was a prizewinning reporter for the *Minneapolis Tribune* (1950–61) and later (from 1965) became a nationally syndicated columnist, as well as a radio commentator and panelist on television public affairs programs. In the mid-1960s he served as ambassador to Finland (1963–64) and then director of the U.S. Information Agency (1964–65).

Rowan, John (1773–1843) U.S. representative/senator; born in York, Pa. A lawyer, he represented Kentucky in Congress (Rep., 1807–09), returning to the state legislature (1813–24), and then going to the Senate (1825–39) where he chaired the Judiciary Committee.

Rowe, Leo Stanton (1871–1946) diplomat; born in McGregor, Iowa. He taught political science and international law at the University of Pennsylvania (1896–1917). He became interested in Latin America and served on numerous committees and delegations (1907–17). He was assistant secretary of the treasury (1917–19) and director-general of the Pan American Union (1920–46). He promoted the "good-neighbor" policy toward Latin America.

Rowland, Benjamin, Jr. (1904–72) art historian, artist; born in Overbrook, Pa. He earned a Ph.D. at Harvard, where he taught for more than 40 years. An authority on the art of ancient India, medieval Italy, and modern America, he wrote books including *Art and Architecture of India* (1953, revised several times) and *The Classical Tradition in Western Art* (1963).

Rowland, Henry Augustus (1848–1901) physicist; born in Honesdale, Pa. A civil engineer, he did railroad surveys (1871), then taught at Wooster University (1871–72) and Rensselaer Polytechnic Institute (1872–75). After a year's study in Europe (1875–76), he became the first physics professor at the new Johns Hopkins University (1876–1901). Best known for his invention of the concave spectral grating (1882), he also discovered the magnetic effect of electrical convection (1876–78) and improved on James Joule's work on the mechanical equivalent of heat.

Rowlandson, Mary (b. White) (c. 1635–post-1678) frontier captive; born in England. Her family emigrated to Massachusetts in 1653 and she married Joseph Rowlandson in 1656. She had four children. In 1675, during King Philip's War, Indians attacked Lancaster, Mass., and carried off Mary and three of her children. She survived three months in captivity and met King Philip, the Indian leader. She and two surviving children were ransomed (1676) and the Rowlandson family moved to Connecticut. Her account of her captivity, *The Soveraignty & Goodness of God* . . . (1682), went through 30 editions and remains a classic of the colonial-frontier literary genre of "captivity" accounts.

Rowson, Susanna (b. Haswell) (c. 1762–1824) writer, actress, educator; born in Portsmouth, England. Her mother died when she was born, and Susanna joined her remarried father, a naval lieutenant stationed in Massachusetts. She returned to England (1778), married (1787), and began writing sentimental novels and verse. Her novel, *Charlotte, A Tale of Truth* (1791; published in America in 1794 as *Charlotte Temple*), became the first best-seller in the United States. When her husband's fortunes failed, she turned to acting and produced plays – many of her own – in America (1793–96). In 1797 she founded a girls' boarding school near Boston, Mass., which she conducted until 1822 while writing novels, poetry, and didactic work for children and editing and contributing to various periodicals.

Royall, Anne (b. Newport) (1769–1854) author, journalist, gadfly; born near Baltimore, Md. Her father lost whatever he had because he was a Loyalist when he died (c. 1775), and by 1785 her mother had gone to work as a servant in the home of a wealthy and well-educated gentleman, William Royall. He helped educate young Anne by encouraging her to read, and in 1797, although 20 years older, he married her. After he died in 1813, his relatives eventually succeeded in depriving Anne of his estate; it was 1848 before she got Congress to vote her a Revolutionary veteran's widow's pension (which yielded her only $10). Meanwhile, in the 1820s she set forth, by foot, stagecoach, and steamer, to visit every corner of the United States; this resulted in ten volumes of still revealing travel books (1826–31). In 1830, now settled in Washington, D.C., she began a publishing firm that published a weekly newspaper, *Paul Pry* (1831–36), combining news with gossip and her feisty editorials. Its successor, the *Huntress* (1836–54), was even more aggressive in pursuit of her enemies (corruption, politicians, ministers, the British) and in support of her causes (Catholics, Masons, states' rights). Notorious for her intemperate language and eccentric ways, she died a pauper but with the grudging respect of many contemporaries.

Royce, Josiah (1855–1916) philosopher: born in Grass Valley, Calif. The son of poor parents who had journeyed to California in the 1849 gold rush, he graduated from the University of California (1875), then studied in Germany, where he was influenced by post-Kantian idealism, and at Johns Hopkins University. In 1878, at William James's invitation, he joined the Harvard faculty, becoming one of its most celebrated teachers. In such works as *Religious Aspects of Philosophy* (1885) and *The World and the Individual* (1900–01), he developed a religiously oriented brand of absolute idealism. In later years he devoted increased attention both to technical problems of logic and mathematics and to moral and religious issues of broad interest.

Royce, Ralph (1890–1965) aviator; born in Marquette, Mich. The son of a bookkeeper, he graduated from West Point in 1914, and during the Mexican expedition of 1916, he flew in the first U.S. military air operations. He held a series of operational commands in the 1920s and 1930s. In 1944, after serving in England, the Pacific, and the Middle East, he commanded U.S. tactical air forces in Europe. After leaving the service, he became director of economic development for the state of Michigan.

Royko, Mike (1932–) journalist; born in Chicago. A hard-hitting reporter and columnist associated with various Chicago papers from 1956, he won many awards for coverage of his Chicago beat, including a 1972 Pulitzer Prize for commentary; his books include *Boss: Richard J. Daley of Chicago* (1971).

Royster, Vermont C. (Connecticut) (1914–) journalist; born in Raleigh, N.C. Joining the *Wall Street Journal* (1936), he served as an editorial writer and as the paper's editor (1958–71), after which he wrote a regular column. His commentary won Pulitzer Prizes in 1953 and 1984.

Rozelle, (Alvin Ray) "Pete" (1926–) football executive; born in South Gate, Calif. He was serving as Los Angeles Rams general manager when he was selected as National Football League (NFL) commissioner in 1960. In his 30 years as commissioner (1960–89), he guided the league through a "war" and subsequent merger with the American Football League, fought off challenges by two other rival leagues, and led the NFL to unprecedented respect and financial success. He retired as NFL Commissioner in 1989.

Rozsa, Miklos (1907–) composer; born in Budapest, Hungary. A child prodigy on the violin, he enjoyed some success in Paris as a serious composer. In the 1930s he began scoring films for his fellow Hungarian, Alexander Korda, in London, and then settled in Hollywood in 1939. Notable among his many screen credits are *Spellbound* (1945) and *Ben-Hur* (1959). His noncommercial works were rediscovered by a later generation who formed a society to perpetuate them with recordings.

Rubenstein, Artur (or Arthur) (1887–1982) pianist; born in Lódź, Poland. He began playing in early childhood and completed his studies in Berlin. He was already famous when he made his U.S. debut with the Philadelphia Orchestra in 1906, but his American appearances were not at first successful. With the outbreak of World War II he settled in Hollywood, played for movie sound tracks, and appeared as himself in two films including *Carnegie Hall* (1947). His reputation grew through the years until by the 1950s he was universally considered one of the giants of the keyboard. A supreme interpreter of Chopin and the standard repertoire, he was also acclaimed for his playing of modern Spanish composers. He was a U.S. citizen from 1946. In 1976, as his performances were finally winding down, he was awarded the U.S. Medal of Freedom.

Rubenstein, Mark (1944–) educator, financier; born in Seattle, Wash. A Harvard-educated professor of finance at the University of California: Berkeley, he and two colleagues devised the investment hedging technique known as portfolio insurance, and formed a firm, LOR, to market the strategy in 1981. The technique appeared to be only partly successful in limiting damage during the stock market tumble of 1987.

Rubicam, Raymond (1892–1978) advertising executive; born in Brooklyn, N.Y. A journalist turned copywriter, he cofounded the New York advertising agency, Young and Rubicam (1923), which became the nation's largest advertising agency. His innovations included employing market research, replacing "hard sell" pitches with an indirect approach, involving advertising agencies in producing client-sponsored radio programming, and introducing advertising into Sunday newspaper comics. He retired in 1944.

Rubin, Jerry (1938–94) activist, author, entrepreneur; born in Cincinnati, Ohio. A reporter for the *Cincinnati Post and Times-Star* (1956–61), he was an antiwar organizer and cochairman for the Vietnam Day Committee, Berkeley, Calif. (1965). He ran for mayor of Berkeley (1966). The first person ever to testify before the House Committee on UnAmerican Activities (HUAC) in costume (1966), he was a cofounder of the Youth International Party (Yippie) (1967) and was an activist in Berkeley (through 1972). A vice-presidential candidate on the Peace and Freedom Party ticket (1968), a defendant in the Chicago 7 trial (1969), and author of *Do It!* (1969), he turned to holistic healing, led workshops at Esalen (1973–74), and was a therapist as part of the Fischer-Hoffman Psychic Therapy Process (1974). Repudiating activism, he became a stockbroker and then organized Jerry Rubin's Business Networking Salon in New York (1982). He and former compatriot, Abbie Hoffman, staged about 40 Yippie-versus-Yuppie debates nationwide (1985–86) before Rubin turned to selling vitamins in major newspapers (1990s).

Rubin, Vera Cooper (1928–) astronomer; born in Philadelphia. Barred from the Princeton astrophysics graduate program, which did not admit women until 1971, she pursued graduate education at Cornell and took a Ph.D. from Georgetown University (1954). Widely traveled, she was at the Carnegie Institute from 1965. In 1981 she became one of 75 women elected to the National Academy of Sciences since its founding in 1863. She found the so-called dark matter that keeps stars from spinning off their galaxies. She lists her four children's Ph.D.'s on her résumé and volunteers her time for lectures and demonstrations to students to encourage their interest in science.

Rubin, William (1927–) art historian, curator; born in New York City. He studied at Columbia University (B.A. 1949; M.A. 1952; Ph.D. 1959), and at the University of Paris. He taught at several institutions before joining the Museum of Modern Art in 1967 as curator and director of painting and sculpture. He specialized in dada and surrealist art, and published many books on modern art.

Rubinow, Isaac Max (1875–1936) physician, economic statistician, social reformer; born in Grodno, Russia. Immigrating to New York City in 1893, he took his M.D. from New York University (1898) and practiced mainly among the urban poor. Realizing that poor health had much to do with economics, he quit his practice (1903) and turned to the social sciences, economics, and statistics. Working for the federal government, he provided much of the data behind the worker compensation laws passed by states between 1911–20. He left government service to work on insurance problems for private organizations. As president of the Casualty Actuarial Society (1914–16), he systematized the accident premium system. He also continued to work for "social insurance," reaching a popular audience with *The Quest for Security* (1934) and influencing the adoption of social security. A socialist as a young man, he wrote *Was Marx Wrong?* (1914) before becoming disillusioned with the Russian Revolution in the 1920s. He also devoted significant time to Jewish causes, including directing medical units in Palestine (1919–22).

Rubinstein, Helena (1870–1965) beautician, business executive; born in Cracow, Poland. She attended medical school in Cracow for two years before moving in the 1890s to Australia, where she opened the country's first beauty salon in Melbourne (1902). Her face cream, formulated according to a family recipe, made her a fortune. She studied with European dermatologists and opened salons in London (1908) and Paris (1912). In 1915 she emigrated to New York and launched an international business empire. "Madame" set cosmetic trends, introducing waterproof mascara, foundation makeup, and all-day spa treatments; she stressed the scientific preparation of her products and instruction of clients in their use. Her success was spiced by a 50-year feud with arch-rival Elizabeth Arden. Her many philanthropies included the endowment of a contemporary art museum in Israel and a medical research foundation.

Ruby, Jack L. (b. Rubenstein, Jacob) (1911–67) assassin; born in Chicago. He came from a broken home and engaged in petty crimes such as "scalping" tickets. He served in the U.S. Air Force (1943–46) and operated nightclubs and dance halls in Dallas, Texas. Two days after the assassination of President John F. Kennedy, he shot and killed Lee Harvey Oswald, the alleged assassin of the President. Despite many attempts to link Ruby to some conspiracy, most disinterested students believe he acted on his own. He was sentenced to death (1964) but died while awaiting a second trial.

Rucker, (George Napoleon) Nap (1884–1970) baseball pitcher; born in Crabapple, Ga. During his ten-year career as a left-hander for the Brooklyn Dodgers (1907–16), he won 134 games and established himself as one of the game's most dependable pitchers.

Rudd, Daniel (1854–1933) Catholic religious leader; born in Bardstown, Ky. Rudd founded the *American Catholic Tribune* (1886), an African-American Catholic newspaper, and (from 1889) organized a series of black Catholic congresses; he was an important early voice for African-Americans in the Catholic church.

Rudel, Julius (1921–) orchestra conductor; born in Vienna, Austria. He studied music in Vienna but emigrated to the U.S.A. in 1938, where he entered Mannes School of Music in New York City. He began his long association with the New York City Opera in 1943 as a rehearsal pianist, becoming its general director (1957–79). He began increasingly to guest conduct symphonic orchestras, and when he left the New York City Opera he became the head conductor of the Buffalo Philharmonic (1979–85).

Rudge, William Edwin (1876–1931) printer, publisher, typographer; born in Brooklyn, N.Y. Going to work at age 13 at his father's printing plant, he inherited the business as a young man, and, encouraged by associates at the newly formed American Institute of Graphic Arts, devoted himself to producing fine, beautifully illustrated works, with the aid of such designers such as Frederic Goudy and W. A. Dwiggins. He assembled an excellent library of graphic arts books and specimens of fine printed works.

Rudkin, Margaret (b. Fogarty) (1897–1967) businesswoman; born in New York City. She worked in a brokerage house in New York and in 1923 married one of the firm's partners. In 1929 the Rudkins developed an estate in Connecticut and named it Pepperidge Farm after its black gum trees. In 1937, to help her asthmatic son, she began baking bread using stone ground whole wheat and other "pure" ingredients. Her son improved, and the allergist's suggestion that she bake for other patients engendered a mail order business. By 1938 she was selling 4,000 loaves of Pepperidge Farm Bread a week; her baked goods line expanded and she opened bakeries in

Pennsylvania (1949) and Illinois (1953). In 1960 she sold Pepperidge Farm to Campbell Soups for $28 million in Campbell's stock and continued to run Pepperidge Farm as an independent subsidiary. She published *The Margaret Rudkin Pepperidge Farm Cookbook* in 1963, and, with her son installed as president, she retired three years later.

Rudolf, Max (1902–) conductor; born in Frankfurt, Germany. After an active German career, he came to the U.S.A. in 1940, where he conducted much at the Metropolitan Opera and led the Cincinnati Symphony from 1958 to 1970.

Rudolph, Paul (Marvin) (1918–) architect; born in Elkton, Ky. A late modernist, he established a New York-based international practice specializing in large projects (1965); irregular textured surfaces and dramatic interior spaces characterize his designs.

Rudolph, Wilma (Glodean) (1940–94) track athlete; born in Clarksville, Tenn. After wearing a leg brace as a child, she became the first American woman to win three gold medals in one Olympics, with victories in the 100 meter dash, the 200 meter dash, and the 4 × 100 meter relay at the 1960 games.

Ruffin, Edmund (1794–1865) agriculturist, author; born in Prince George County, Va. Suspended from William and Mary College for bad grades, and bored by the War of 1812, he returned to Coggin's Point, the family estate. There he discovered that depleted soils were acidic and that the high-calcium "marl" could replenish them. In 1832 he published *An Essay on Calcareous Manures,* which grew through five editions to 500 pages. He published the *Farmer's Register* from 1833 to 1843 and promoted local agricultural organizations as well as such "scientific" farming practices as crop rotation, fertilizing, and proper plowing and drainage. An ardent defender of slavery, he was a major advocate of southern secession; he wrote *The Political Economy of Slavery* (1858) and *Anticipations of the Future* (1860) about an independent South. A member of the Palmetto Guards of Charleston, S.C., he is often credited with firing the first shot on Fort Sumter (although the evidence is doubtful). He spent most of the war protecting his estates from "Yankees." In 1865, when the Confederacy collapsed, he killed himself.

Ruffin, George L. (Lewis) (1834–86) lawyer; born in Richmond, Va. Son of free African-Americans, he and his wife, Josephine St. Pierre Ruffin (1842–1924), fled to England after the Dred Scott decision (1857), but soon returned to Boston. While making his living as a barber, he spoke out on matters concerning African-Americans. He read law in Boston and became the first black to graduate from Harvard Law School (1869). While maintaining a thriving practice in Boston, he served in the Massachusetts legislature (1869–71) and Boston City Council (1876–78), and was named a municipal judge (1883). An active Baptist and able speaker, he attended national conventions of African-Americans and was a close friend of many prominent people of his day, including Frederick Douglass. His wife was a partner in his many efforts to improve the lot of fellow African-Americans.

Ruffin, Josephine St. Pierre (1842–1924) social activist, feminist; born in Boston, Mass. Educated at public schools in Salem and Boston, she was instrumental in developing the African-American women's club movement. She organized the Women's Era Club (1874) and helped found the National Association of Colored Women (1896).

Ruggles, Carl (Charles Sprague) (1876–1971) composer;

born in Marion, Mass. He studied at Harvard and then organized and conducted an orchestra in Minnesota (1912–17) before going to New York to compose and promote new music; there he became a close friend of Charles Ives. After teaching at Miami University (1937–47), Ruggles retired to Vermont, spending much of his time painting. Toward the end of his life he finally found acclaim for the eight highly individual, craggy, painstakingly composed works he had completed, notably *Sun-Treader* for orchestra (1926–31).

Rukeyser, Muriel (1913–80) poet, writer; born in New York City. She studied at Vassar and Columbia University (1930–32), and was based in New York City. She taught at Sarah Lawrence (1946; 1956–67), and was a social activist and feminist poet, themes expressed in *The Collected Poems of Muriel Rukeyser* (1979). She also wrote screenplays, and was a dramatist, translator, and a writer of children's books.

Rumford, Count See THOMPSON, BENJAMIN.

Ruml, Beardsley (1894–1960) public official; born in Cedar Rapids, Iowa. At R. H. Macy and Co. (1934–49, chairman 1945–49) and the New York's Federal Reserve Bank (director 1937–47, chairman 1941–47), and as a New Deal adviser, Ruml was an "idea man." He devised the federal tax withholding system (1943) and was instrumental in establishing the International Monetary Fund (1944).

Rummell, Joseph (Francis) (1876–1964) Catholic prelate; born in Baden, Germany. Emigrating to the U.S.A. at age six, he was ordained in the New York archdiocese (1902), where he served before becoming bishop of Omaha (1928) and archbishop of New Orleans (1935–62). He was an efficient builder and administrator but became best known for his stand in the 1950s against racial segregation in schools; he eventually desegregated all Catholic schools in the New Orleans archdiocese, despite heated opposition from a group of Catholics, three of whom he excommunicated.

Rumsey, Charles Cary (1879–1922) polo player/sculptor; born in Buffalo, N.Y. An accomplished polo player, his bronzes of polo ponies and their riders are also internationally known. His monument of an equestrian Pizarro stands in Lima, Peru.

Rumsey, James (1743–92) inventor, engineer; born in Cecil County, Md. A pioneer in steam navigation, he built a model steamboat in 1784, and in 1786 he exhibited a steamboat on the Potomac. He was awarded patents in the U.S.A. and Europe (1792). Had he lived longer, he might have developed a commercially viable steamboat before Robert Fulton.

Runyon, (Alfred) Damon (1884–1946) journalist, author; born in Manhattan, Kans. He wrote a wide-ranging syndicated column, "On the Brighter Side," for the Hearst chain (1918–36), and penned colorful stories about hoodlums, racketeers, bookies, and other eccentric types encountered in New York's Times Square district. His stories, sold for large sums and collected in several books, inspired the 1950 Broadway musical *Guys and Dolls*.

Rupp, Adolph (Frederick) (1901–77) basketball coach; born in Halstead, Kans. During his 42-year career at the University of Kentucky (1930–72), he coached his teams to a record 874 victories, 27 Southeast Conference titles, and four National Collegiate Athletic Association championships. He also coached the U.S. team to a gold medal in the 1948 Olympic games.

Rush, Benjamin (1745–1813) physician, Revolutionary patriot, educator; born in Byberry, Pa. After studying medicine in Philadelphia, he completed his studies at the University of Edinburgh, Scotland (1768). He set up his practice in Philadelphia and taught chemistry at the medical college there; in 1770 he published the first American chemistry text. He also wrote on social and political subjects, and as the American Revolution approached, he attached himself to the patriots; as a member of the Continental Congress, he signed the Declaration of Independence (1776). During the war, he served only a year as surgeon general of the middle department of the Continental army because he had a dispute with his superior (and former professor), Dr. William Shippen, and he was loosely linked to the Conway Cabal, accused of plotting to replace George Washington. He returned to his practice in Philadelphia but helped lead the fight for Pennsylvania to adopt the new U.S. Constitution; he would serve as the treasurer of the U.S. Mint (1797–1813). Meanwhile, he served on the staff of the Philadelphia Hospital (1783–1813) and would also teach at the University of Pennsylvania (1792–1813). He established the first free clinic in the U.S.A. (1786). He helped found the first antislavery society in the U.S.A. (1803), and was outspoken on other social issues, calling for an end to capital punishment, the reform of education and prisons, and the promotion of temperance. He was also forward-looking in his attitudes toward the treatment of mental illness; his *Diseases of the Mind* (1812) presaged some of the ideas of modern mental therapeutics. His ideas on the cause of diseases, however, became so exotic as to be dangerous – he believed that all diseases were caused by the "excitability" of blood vessels and could be cured by bloodletting. He published *Medical Inquiries and Observations* (1789–93) to promote this theory, and when Philadelphia suffered an epidemic of yellow fever in 1793, he put his theory into practice; unfortunately his patients continued to die. This did not stop him from publishing his theories again in *An Account of the Bilious Remitting Yellow Fever. . . .* (1794), in which he actually came closer to the truth when he indicated that unsanitary conditions had also played a role in the epidemic.

Rush, Otis (1934–) blues musician; born in Philadelphia, Miss. A guitarist and singer, he moved to Chicago in 1948 and began playing in local clubs in 1953. In 1956 his debut recording, "I Can't Quit You, Baby," was a major rhythm-and-blues hit, and over the next four years he produced a body of recorded work that is among the greatest in blues history. His playing became inconsistent and his touring schedule sporadic thereafter, but his strong influence on Eric Clapton and other blues-rock musicians helped him maintain a high-profile reputation as a bluesman.

Rush, Richard (1780–1859) lawyer, diplomat; born in Philadelphia (son of Benjamin Rush). He graduated from the college of New Jersey (now Princeton) (1797). Admitted to the bar in 1800, he was the attorney-general for Pennsylvania (1811), comptroller of the U.S. treasury (1811–14), and U.S. attorney general (1814–17). Briefly secretary of state (1817), he negotiated the Rush-Bagot Agreement (which prohibited fortifications on the Great Lakes). As ambassador to Great Britain (1817–25), he was both well-liked and effective, settling issues resulting from the War of 1812 and the disputed Oregon territory; he also played an important role in setting forth the Monroe Doctrine. He was secretary of the treasury (1825–29), and after unsuccessfully running for vice-president on the ticket of John Quincy Adams, in 1828 he retired from political life for many years. From 1836 to 1838 he was in England as a lawyer who helped to secure the bequest of James Smithson that set up the Smithsonian Institution. He returned to public service to serve as ambassador to France (1847–49).

Rush, William (1756–1833) sculptor, woodcarver; born in Philadelphia. Remaining in Philadelphia, he was apprenticed as a ship figurehead carver (1771); setting up his own wood carving shop, he then became a sculptor and produced wood portraits and public works, such as *Water Nymph and Bittern* (1854), a bronze cast from the wood original (1809). He was one of the founders of the Pennsylvania Academy of the Fine Arts (1805) and is considered one of the first American-born sculptors.

Rushing, (James Andrew) Jimmy (1902–72) jazz musician; born in Oklahoma City, Okla. A vocalist with a unique flair for both blues and Tin Pan Alley material, he sang with Walter Page's Blue Devils in 1929 and with Bennie Moten between 1930 and 1934. From 1935 to 1948 he was featured with Count Basie, and he free-lanced thereafter.

Rusie, Amos (Wilson) (1871–1942) baseball pitcher; born in Mooresville, Ind. During his ten-year career (1889–1901), mostly with the New York Giants, he won 243 games. Three times, the right-hander won 30 or more games in a season. He was elected to baseball's Hall of Fame in 1977.

Rusk, Dean (1909–94) public official; born in Cherokee County, Ga. After serving in the Far East during World War II, he joined the state department in 1945, becoming assistant secretary of state in 1949. He was president of the Rockefeller Foundation from 1951 to 1960. As secretary of state under presidents Kennedy and Johnson, he became most identified with the latter's Vietnam War policy. He went on to teach at the University of Georgia in 1969.

Rusk, Howard A. (Archibald) (1903–89) physician, author; born in Brookfield, Mo. After graduating from the University of Pennsylvania Medical School in only two years, he joined the medical faculty at Washington University (1929–42) and commenced what would be his lifelong career, rehabilitating disabled patients. In World War II he enlisted in the U.S. Army and continued his rehabilitation work at the Jefferson Barracks hospital in Missouri. He focused on the patient's needs after "the stitches are out and the fever is down." For soldiers severely disabled by war this meant taking "them back into the best lives they can live with what they have left" through occupational, physical, and other therapies. At New York University in 1946, he started the first comprehensive rehabilitation program in the world; in 1948 it became the Institute of Rehabilitation Medicine (now the Rusk Institute of Rehabilitation Medicine). During the Korean and Vietnam Wars, Rusk helped South Koreans, from whom he got his nickname "Dr. Live-Again," and the South Vietnamese. A columnist for the *New York Times* (1948–69), he also wrote *A World to Care For* (1972), his autobiography.

Russell, Charles Edward (1860–1941) journalist, reformer, Socialist; born in Davenport, Iowa. Convinced that free trade was a cure for social ills, he founded the Iowa Free Trade League (1881). He then combined journalism with reform as city editor of the *New York World* (1894–97), managing editor of the *New York American* (1897–1900),

and publisher of the *Chicago American* (1900–02). In the following years he became a well-known "muckraker," writing magazine articles exposing problems in American society. He became a prominent Socialist (1910), ran three times for office unsuccessfully, wrote 27 books, and won the Pulitzer Prize (for nonfiction) (1927). Widely traveled and cosmopolitan, he combined a world outlook with Midwestern egalitarianism. As a reporter/editor, his wide-ranging curiosity, passion for facts, and boundless optimism influenced a generation, forcing penal reform in Georgia and tenement reforms in New York.

Russell, (Charles Ellsworth) "Pee Wee" (1906–69) jazz musician; born in Maple Wood, Mo. He was an eccentric clarinetist whose unpredictability paralleled the alcoholic turbulence of his personal life. He was a sideman with Red Nichols and many others between 1920 and 1937. For the next 30 years, he was a beloved fixture at Dixieland clubs in New York.

Russell, Charles (Marion) (1864–1926) painter, sculptor, illustrator; born in St. Louis, Mo. Growing up fascinated with sketching and modeling cowboys, Indians, and animals, he went to Montana at age 16 and settled there, worked as a hunter and cowboy, and lived one winter with the Blood tribe of Canada until in 1892 he decided to devote himself to art full-time. Entirely self-taught, working with oils, water colors, pen-and-ink, and clay, he captured the authentic drama and details of the classic American West, but he never gained quite the standing of his contemporary, Frederic Remington.

Russell, Charles Taze (1852–1916) religious leader; born in Pittsburgh, Pa. Raised a Congregationalist, he became a traveling preacher advocating a doctrine of his own devising, and founded the International Bible Student's Association in 1872. Known as Pastor Russell though he was never ordained, he prophesied a long period of worldwide strife followed by the advent of the kingdom of Christ on earth. He founded the the *Watchtower* periodical in 1879. The sect he established changed its name to Jehovah's Witnesses in 1931.

Russell, George (Allan) (1923–) composer, pianist, theorist; born in Cincinnati. Active from his youth in both jazz and classical music, he wrote the influential theory book *The Lydian Chromatic Concept of Tonal Organization* (2nd ed. 1959) and composed in a variety of idioms usually reflecting his own African-American tradition.

Russell, Henry Norris (1877–1957) astronomer; born in Oyster Bay, N.Y. After five years of research at Cambridge University, England (1900–05), he returned to Princeton, his alma mater, to teach astronomy and study cosmogeny and stellar evolution. He directed the Princeton Observatory (1912–47) and then worked as a research associate at the Harvard Observatory (1947–52). In 1913 the so-called Hertzsprung-Russell diagram established the relationship between a star's brightness and its type of spectra. His theory of stellar evolution has since been replaced, but his theory of the composition of stars is still widely accepted. He was among the first to postulate the existence of millions of solar systems and of planets capable of supporting life; he also recognized the major role of hydrogen in the universe. He wrote several important books including the two-volume textbook *Astronomy* (1927), and *Fate and Freedom* (1927) and *The Solar System and Its Origin* (1935). Known as the "dean of American astronomers," he was awarded six gold medals and elected to many scientific societies.

Russell, James Sargent (1903–) aviator; born in Tacoma, Wash. A 1926 U.S. Naval Academy graduate, he helped develop early naval air operations from battleships and aircraft carriers. Retiring with admiral's rank in 1965, he became a consultant for the Boeing Company.

Russell, Lillian (b. Helen Louise Leonard) (1861–1922) actress, singer; born in Clinton, Iowa. Popular star of the musical stage, a flamboyant blonde beauty known for her unreliability, she appeared in 24 musicals between 1881 and 1899.

Russell, Morgan (1886–1953) painter; born in New York City. He settled in Paris (1906), studied with Henri Matisse (1909), returned to America (1946), and died in Philadelphia. He and Stanton McDonald-Wright founded an abstract art movement called *synchromism* (1913) that focused on the use of color.

Russell, Mother Mary Baptist (b. Katherine Russell) (1829–98) Catholic religious leader; born in Killowen, Ireland. In 1854, a few years after being professed in the Sisters of Mercy, she went to California as head of a group of nuns aiding the sick and poor; she opened many charitable and educational institutions in California during 44 years of service.

Russell, Richard B. (Brevard) (1897–1971) governor, U.S. senator; born in Winder, Ga. He served Georgia, first as governor (Dem.; 1931–33), then in the U.S. Senate (1933–71). A master of the filibuster, he was the leader of the Southern Democratic opposition to civil rights. He was an influential hawk during the Vietnam War. In 1952 he made an unsuccessful bid for the Democratic presidential nomination.

Russell, (William Felton) Bill (1934–) basketball player; born in Monroe, La. He was a two-time All-American at the University of San Francisco (1955–56) before playing center for the Boston Celtics (1956–69), where he was an eleven-time All-NBA (National Basketball Association) first team selection and a five-time Most Valuable Player. One of basketball's greatest defensive centers, he led the Celtics to eleven NBA championships in 13 years. His 22.5 rebounds per game and 21,620 career rebounds are second best in NBA history. He was the first African-American head coach in the NBA, and in 1968 and 1969 he coached the Celtics to two successive titles. He also served as coach and general manager of the Seattle Supersonics (1973–77). A broadcaster after retiring from the game, he was elected to basketball's Hall of Fame in 1974.

Russell, William Hepburn (1812–72) Pony Express founder; born in Burlington, Vt. He moved to Missouri, and, with Alexander Majors, formed the Pony Express (April 1860), which carried the mail from Missouri to California in ten days; the telegraph soon put an end to the service (in October 1861). He was involved in an embezzlement scandal (1861) and he lost a fortune when he sold his freight company in 1862.

Russwurm, John Brown (1799–1851) journalist, public official; born in Port Antonio, Jamaica. In 1827, with John Cornish, he published the first U.S. black newspaper, *Freedom's Journal,* dedicated to promoting black freedom and citizenship. Around 1828 he emigrated to Liberia, where he held public office and edited a newspaper.

Rustin, Bayard (1910–87) institute head, civil rights activist; born in West Chester, Pa. Schooled in literature and history at Cheyney State (Pa.) and Wilberforce (Ohio) Colleges, he joined the Young Communist League (1936) and became an organizer (1938). He also sang occasionally at a New York City nightclub with notables Josh White and Leadbelly. He left the Communist Party (1941) and joined the Fellowship of Reconciliation, a nonviolent antiwar group. In 1940–41, he helped A. Philip Randolph plan a threatened march on Washington to demand better job opportunities for blacks in the defense industrry. He served several jail terms in the 1940s; for conscientious objection during World War II (released 1945), for demonstrating in the American Indian independence movement, and for participating in a North Carolina "freedom ride" (1947). He was involved in various pacifist movements (1947–55), then joined the Southern Christian Leadership Conference (SCLC) (1955) as Martin Luther King's special assistant, serving as the organizational coordinator for the SCLC March on Washington (1963). Named executive director of the newly founded A. Philip Randoph Institute (1964–87), he worked to promote programs to cure America's social and economic ills. Although over the years he advocated the orderly seizure of political power by activist blacks, white liberals, religious parties, and labor unions to effect a rebalance of national priorities, he never favored black separatism.

Rutan, (Elbert L.) Burt (1943–) aircraft designer; born in Portland, Ore. In 1975 he founded Rutan Aircraft Factory. He designed over one hundred aircraft including the *Voyager,* the first plane to navigate the world without refueling (1986). He served as a consultant to Beech Aircraft (1985–88) and continued designing experimental planes in Mojave, Calif.

Rutan, Richard Glenn (1938–) aviator; born in Loma Linda, Calif. A test pilot, he served 20 years in the U.S. Air Force before becoming president of Voyager Aircraft Inc., in 1981. In 1987 he set the world record for a closed-circuit, nonstop, nonrefueled around-the-world flight.

Ruth, (George Herman) "Babe" (1895–1948) baseball player; born in Baltimore, Md. He was born in a poor waterfront neighborhood and at age eight was sent by his saloonkeeper father to St. Mary's Industrial School for Boys, where a priest encouraged his interest in baseball. As a teenager, his baseball exploits caught the attention of the minor league Baltimore Orioles, where he starred as a left-handed pitcher in 1914. Later that year, he was promoted to the major league Boston Red Sox, where he remained until 1919, becoming one of the best pitchers of the time. But he was also demonstrating his power with the bat, and, when in 1920 he was sold to the New York Yankees for a record $100,000, he was made a full-time outfielder. With the Yankees (1920–34), he became the game's preeminent player and such a drawing card that the new Yankee Stadium (1923) was dubbed "the house that Ruth built." During the 1920s he was legendary for his large appetite and high living – he even appeared in several movies – and in the decades thereafter he came to assume almost mythic status, nicknamed "The Bambino" and "The Sultan of Swat." In 1927, he slammed 60 homeruns, a record that stood until Roger Maris hit 61 in 1961. Ruth holds most of baseball's important slugging records, including most years leading a league in homeruns (12), and most total bases in a season (457) and highest slugging percentage for a season (.847), both set in 1920. He retired from the Boston Braves in June 1935 with 714 career homeruns, a record that was broken by Hank Aaron in 1974. He was a coach with the Brooklyn Dodgers in 1938 but never achieved his goal of managing a major league team. He gave much of his time in his last years to charitable events. He was one of the first five players elected to the Hall of Fame in 1936. He died of cancer in 1948, leaving much of his estate to the Babe Ruth Foundation, for underprivileged children.

Rutledge, Edward (1749–1800) governor; born in Charleston, S.C. (brother of John Rutledge). A South Carolina lawyer, he served in the First and Second Continental Congresses (1774–76), where he shifted from his Loyalist sympathies to sign the Declaration of Independence. He went back to South Carolina to fight against the British and was briefly their prisoner after the fall of Charleston. A staunch Federalist, he served in the state legislature (1782–98), where he moderated confiscation of Loyalists' property, later becoming governor (1798–1880).

Rutledge, John (1739–1800) governor; born in Charleston, S.C. (brother of Edward Rutledge). Educated in London, he returned to Charleston to become a brilliant lawyer. He was delegate to the First and Second Continental Congresses (1774–75), returning home to join the Council of Safety, to serve as the first president of South Carolina (1776–78), and to fight in the American Revolution. As South Carolina's governor (1779–82), he reestablished civil government in a state that had been torn apart by war. A defender of wealth and privilege – and of the slave trade – he was a delegate to the Constitutional Convention of 1787 and tried to halt the adoption of direct popular election of the president and Congress. He was one of the first associate justices on the new U.S. Supreme Court (1789–91), but stepped down to become South Carolina's chief justice (1791–95). Nominated in 1795 as chief justice of the U.S. Supreme Court, he was rejected by the Senate because of his attacks on the recent Jay Treaty.

Rutledge, Wiley Blount, Jr. (1894–1949) Supreme Court justice; born in Cloverport, Ky. He was a law professor when President Franklin D. Roosevelt named him to the U.S. Court of Appeals (1939–43), and then to the U.S. Supreme Court (1943–49), where he was known for his defense of civil liberties.

Ryan, (Lynn) Nolan (1947–) baseball pitcher; born in Refugio, Texas. Baseball's all-time leader in strikeouts with over 5,000, the right-hander won over 300 games and pitched a record seven no-hitters in his record (all positions) 28 major league seasons (1966–93) with the New York Mets, California Angels, Houston Astros, and Texas Rangers. In addition to his prowess as a pitcher, he had a reputation as a man of irreproachable character and integrity, and although he had in fact made millions from both his product endorsements and salary – enough to buy a bank as well as other enterprises – he seemed one of the last of the old-time players, oblivious to the big-money contracts, and with an eye only on the well-pitched game.

Ryan, (Michael) John Augustine (1869–1945) Catholic priest, social reformer; born in Vermillion, Minn. An ordained priest (1898), he earned a doctorate in sacred theology (1906) while he was teaching at St. Paul Seminary (1902–15); he then taught at Catholic University in Washington, D.C. (1915–39). He published a liberal social-justice platform in the *Catholic World* (1909), lobbied for the minimum wage for women and children in Wisconsin and Minnesota (1913), taught at various Catholic colleges, founded the Catholic *Charities Review* (1917), directed the National Catholic Welfare Council's social action department (1920–45), and was an ardent backer of the New Deal. Through years of teaching, lecturing, writing, and political support of reform candidates, he showed Catholic Americans a means of integrating Catholic principles of social justice into an industrial American society.

Ryan, T. (Tubal) Claude (1898–1982) aircraft manufacturer; born in Parson, Ky. After flying for the Aerial Forest Patrol, in 1922 he formed a flying service that became Ryan Airlines Inc., in 1925. In 1927 he helped build Charles Lindbergh's *Spirit of St. Louis*. In 1933 he formed Ryan Aeronautical to build planes, including jet trainers for the military.

Ryder, Albert Pinkham (1847–1917) painter; born in New Bedford, Mass. He moved to New York (c. 1868), was a founder of the Society of American Artists, New York (1878), traveled to England (1877), settled again in New York, and, by 1900, was a recluse. A religious and mystical man who shunned personal possessions, he painted dreamlike scenes with powerful emotional content, such as *Toilers of the Sea* (1884) and *Moonlight* (1885). About 165 oils survive that suffer deterioration due to his overpainting and to chemical reactions. Nevertheless his important work continues to impress and forgeries are numerous.

Ryerson, Martin Antoine (1856–1932) businessman, collector; born in Grand Rapids, Mich. His family moved to Chicago and he was educated in Paris and Switzerland, then graduated from Harvard Law School (1878). He took over his father's lumber business, was a director of many other companies, and retired from business in the 1890s. He devoted himself to collecting French Impressionist paintings, and to philanthropic activities for the Chicago Institute of Arts, the Field Museum of Natural History, and the University of Chicago. He presented his collection to the Chicago Institute of Art (1901), and endowed their art library.

Ryun, (James Ronald) Jim (1947–) track athlete; born in Wichita, Kans. In 1964, while a high school senior, he ran a 3:55.3 mile. In 1966, while still in his teens, he set a world record time of 3:51.3 for the mile. (In 1967 he lowered this to 3.51.1.) In 1967 he established a world record for the 1,500 meters, clocking 3:33.1. Never as successful in top-class competition as he was against the clock, at the Olympic Games of 1964, 1968, and 1972 he nevertheless won a silver medal in the 1968 1,500 meter run. He turned professional after the 1972 Olympics, but after suffering several injuries, he retired in 1976.

S

Saarinen, Eero (1910–61) architect; born in Kirkknonummi, Finland. Brought to the U.S.A. in 1923 by his father, the Finnish architect/designer Eliel Saarinen, he studied sculpture in Paris and received a graduate degree in architecture from Yale (1934). In partnership with his father (1936–50) he helped define modernist architecture in a series of public, institutional, and commercial buildings known for their innovative technology and use of materials (the stainless steel Gateway Arch, St. Louis (1948–64)); General Motors Technical Center, Warren, Mich. (1951–56); John Deere and Company Building, Moline, Ill. (1957–63). His later sculptural designs are known for their formal imagery (Ingalls Hockey Rink, Yale University (1956–59)); TWA Terminal, Kennedy International Airport, New York (1956–62); Washington Dulles International Airport, Chantilly, Va. (1958–62). His last work and only skyscraper was the CBS Headquarters, New York (1960–64). Outstanding among the second generation of modern American architects, Saarinen viewed "the way [a] building is used" as determinative of its style; his work ranged stylistically from his early essays in the International style to the extreme plasticity of his later buildings, each project exhibiting a unique design solution. Saarinen was posthumously awarded the Gold Medal of the American Institute of Architects in 1962.

Sabath, Adolph J. (1866–1952) U.S. representative; born in Zabori, Bohemia. Emigrating as a teenager, he arrived penniless in Chicago in 1881, going from shoe salesman to lawyer by 1893. Elected to the U.S. House of Representatives (Dem., Ill.; 1907–52), he championed unrestricted immigration and pro-labor measures like workmen's compensation. An internationalist ally to presidents Roosevelt and Truman, he was frustrated in his efforts to support them by the conservative members of his Rules Committee.

Sabin, Albert (Bruce) (1906–93) immunologist; born in Bialystok, Russia (now Poland). He emigrated to the United States with his family in 1920 and began to concentrate on biomedical research even in medical school. At Cincinnati Children's Hospital and the University of Cincinnati (1939–69), he developed the live-virus vaccine against poliomyeltis as well as vaccines against dengue and sandfly fever. The first tests of his polio vaccine were conducted in 1957, outside the United States because American doctors were not convinced that the method was better than Jonas Salk's killed-virus vaccine; the American tests began in 1960, and in the years since, the Sabin vaccine has replaced the Salk vaccine throughout most of the world. At age 77 Sabin was paralyzed for three months by polyneuritis, thus interrupting his research in Mexico on an aerosol measles vaccine. He consulted to the National Institutes of Health on programs to vaccinate children in impoverished areas of the world (1984–86). Among his many awards are the 1971 National Medal of Science and the 1986 Medal of Freedom.

Sabin, Florence (Rena) (1871–1953) physician, medical researcher; born in Central City, Colo. She is best known for her spirited, devoted teaching and for research on blood cells and the lymphatics. The first woman to join the Johns Hopkins University medical faculty (1902), she was also the first woman to be named full professor (1917), the first female president of the American Association of Anatomists (1924), and the first woman elected to the National Academy of Sciences (1925).

Sacagawea (b. Boinaiv, "Grass Maiden") (?1784–?1812) Shoshone interpreter/guide; born in present-day central Idaho or western Montana. Captured as a young girl by enemy Indians, she was sold to a French-Canadian trapper, Toussaint Charbonneau, who married her in 1804. The only woman on the Lewis and Clark expedition of 1804–06, she served as an invaluable intermediary between the whites and local Indians. After accompanying the expedition to the West Coast, she and her husband settled in North Dakota.

Sacco, (Ferdinando) Nicola (1891–1927) born in Torre Maggiore, Italy; **and Vanzetti, Bartolomeo** (1888–1927) born in Villafalletto, Italy; anarchists, accused robbers/murderers. Sacco, son of a landowner, emigrated to the U.S.A. (1908) where he worked in a Milford, Mass., shoe factory (1909–20). Vanzetti, son of a well-to-do farmer, emigrated to the U.S.A. in 1908 and settled in Plymouth, Mass. (1915), where he worked as a fish peddlar. Although lacking in formal education, both read on their own and became interested in Socialism and a philosophical anarchism – both men spent some of 1918–19 in Mexico to avoid the draft because of their opposition to participating in the war. In 1920, Sacco and Vanzetti were charged with murdering two men while robbing a payroll (about $16,000) at a South Braintree, Mass., shoe factory. Although the evidence was largely circumstantial and often controversial, they were convicted in 1921 and sentenced to die. During the long appeals process, there was a worldwide protest, orchestrated mainly by liberals and the left wing, but after a special governor's committee upheld the trial, they were executed (1927), even though another man had since claimed to have committed the crime. The case would never cease to be controversial, for many believe that the men were really punished for being radicals, anarchists, draftdodgers, and Italian immigrants. Countless books and articles as well as many novels, poems, and plays have been written about the case. Although there is no absolute proof or universal agreement, some experts now believe that Sacco was, in fact, guilty, but that Vanzetti was not.

Sachar, Abram L. (Leon) (1899–1993) historian, university president; born in New York City. His immigrant family moved to St. Louis, Mo., in 1906 and (after a year at Harvard) he took his B.A. and M.A. at Washington University in that city. He went to England to do his research on the Victorian House of Lords and gained his Ph.D. at Cambridge University, England (1923). He then taught history at the University of Illinois (1923–48), where he helped start the Hillel Foundation and served as its national director (1933–48) while overseeing its expansion to colleges nationwide; he remained chairman of the National Hillel Foundation (1948–55). When the American Jewish community decided to start a (nonsectarian) college, Sachar was chosen as the first president of Brandeis University (Waltham, Mass.), and during his tenure (1948–58) he effectively built it into a first-class, nationally recognized teaching-research institution by exercising his unusual combination of abilities as an educator, visionary, and fundraiser. On his retirement he became chancellor of Brandeis. During his long career he served on numerous committees and boards, was the recipient of many honors, and published a number of books, including *A History of the Jews* (1929; 5th edition 1965) and *The Course of Our Times* (1972).

Sachs, (Barney) Bernard (1858–1944) neurologist; born in Baltimore, Md. He did his medical studies in Europe (where he adopted the name Bernard), then settled in New York City where he led the development of organic neurology, at the New York Polyclinic Hospital (1885–1905), as editor of the *Journal of Nervous and Mental Disease* (1886–1911), on the faculty of Columbia's medical school, as consulting neurologist at Mount Sinai Hospital, and as president of the American Neurological Association (1894, 1932). He specialized in children's neurological diseases, such as Tay-Sachs, wrote *Nervous Diseases of Children* (1895), and directed the division of child neurology at New York Neurological Institute (1932–42).

Sachs, Curt (1881–1959) musicologist; born in Berlin, Germany. After studies in art and music, he held posts in Berlin including curator of the Museum of Musical Instruments. Driven from Germany by the Nazis in 1933, he settled in the U.S.A. four years later and held posts as a consultant to the New York Public Library (1937–52) and a teacher at Columbia University (from 1953). He also served as president of the American Musicological Society in 1948–50. His books include *The History of Musical Instruments* (1940) and *The Commonwealth of Art* (1946).

Sachs, Jeffrey D. (David) (1954–) economist; born in Detroit, Mich. On the Harvard faculty from 1980, a tenured full professor from 1983, he made his first contributions to international economics with his ideas on loan markets, labor markets, pricing, and hyperinflation. His ideas on streamlining budgets in developing countries drew him out of the academic groves to serve as an adviser to Bolivia (1986–90) and other Latin American governments. His successes there in turn led to his being hired as the architect of economic reform for Poland; the 1990 "Sachs Plan," which called for an immediate conversion to a capitalist economy, became highly controversial. Increasingly drawn to real-world, practical applications of his ideas, he became an adviser to the Russian Parliament under Boris Yeltsin and served as consultant to several international organizations.

Sachs, Paul Joseph (1878–1965) art connoisseur/educator; born in New York City. He studied at Harvard (B.A. 1900), and joined the family investment firm, Goldman, Sachs and Company (1904–14). He abandoned banking and joined the Fogg Art Museum, an adjunct of Harvard, as an assistant director (1915–44). He taught at Harvard (1917–48) and was instrumental in building the new Fogg Museum (1928). He became known for his seminars on museum administration and for his publications on art.

Sack, Israel (1883–1959) antiques dealer; born in Kaunas, Lithuania. He became apprenticed to a cabinetmaker when young, then became a woodworker in England. He emigrated to Boston (1903), worked as a cabinetmaker, and by 1905 had opened his own business. In the 1920s he was an influential antiques dealer and had established additional shops in other areas of Massachusetts, Connecticut, and New York City. In 1939 he consolidated his business in New York City; after 1955 it was managed by his three sons. He was one of the first to appreciate American antique furniture and furnishings and he effectively collected the works for the American wing of New York City's Metropolitan Museum and for Colonial Williamsburg.

Sackler, Arthur M. (1913–87) psychiatrist, art collector; born in New York City. He studied medicine and art history at New York University, and art at Cooper Union. He was a manufacturer of drugs, worked in the fields of medical advertising and trade journals, and ended up an extremely wealthy man. He founded the Laboratories for Therapeutic Research at the Brooklyn College of Pharmacy in Long Island (1958–83). After initial forays in collecting various types of art – particularly Impressionist paintings and pre-Columbian ceramics – he focused on ancient Asian art. He gave generous bequests and art works to many institutions, notably the Metropolitan Museum, the Smithsonian Institution, and Harvard; the two latter institutions have named major museums after him.

Sacks, Oliver (Wolf) (1933–) neurologist, writer; born in London, England. Educated at Oxford, he came to the U.S.A. in 1960, and after completing advanced studies at the University of California: Los Angeles (1960–65), he joined the neurology faculty at the Albert Einstein College of Medicine (Bronx, N.Y.) (1965), and also became a consultant neurologist at various New York hospitals. Even in his first book, *Migraine: Evolution of a Common Disorder* (1970; expanded edition 1985), he was laying forth his unorthodox approach of stressing links between mental/emotional states and physical/bodily afflictions – essentially a holistic approach. Meanwhile, in the late 1960s he had worked in a New York hospital where he encountered some 80 people suffering from a "sleeping sickness" that had spread around the world about 1916 to 1920; he experimented by giving some of them the drug L-DOPA and obtained what at first seemed to be amazing results (for after "awakening," most soon regressed); he described this experience in *Awakenings* (1973), a book that inspired the

Harold Pinter play, *A Kind of Alaska,* and the movie, *Awakenings* (1992). Controversial in his profession for some of his theories, he also published articles on his "cases" in nonprofessional magazines, then collected them in such books as *The Man Who Mistook His Wife for a Hat and Other Clinical Tales* (1985). His book, *A Leg to Stand On* (1984), went even further in his tendency to link the professional and personal, basing his findings on an accident that temporarily cost him the use of a leg, and thereby promoting his notion of the unity of the complex interactions of body, mind, and behavior.

Sadtler, Samuel Philip (1847–1923) educator, chemist; born in Schuylkill County, Pa. He was professor of chemistry and physics at the University of Pennsylvania (1874–78) and professor of chemistry at the Philadelphia College of Pharmacy until 1916. The author of textbooks, he consulted on over 50 patent litigation cases.

Safire, William L. (1929–) journalist; born in New York City. A former public relations writer and a speechwriter and special assistant to President Richard Nixon, he became a Washington-based columnist for the *New York Times* in 1973 and won a 1978 Pulitzer Prize for commentary. A language buff, he also took on a weekly column devoted to verbal oddities.

Sagan, Carl Edward (1934–) astronomer, author; born in New York City. He began teaching at Harvard University (1962–68) while also working as an astrophysicist at the Smithsonian Observatory (1962–68). At Cornell University from 1970, his enthusiasm for space science and the possibility of intelligent life elsewhere in the universe stimulated the public's interest through such works as the television series *Cosmos* (1977) and books like the *Cosmic Connection* (1973) and (with Ann Druyen), *Shadows of Forgotten Ancestors* (1992).

Sage, Kay (Katherine) Linn (1898–1963) painter; born in Albany, N.Y. (wife of Yves Tanguy). Educated in New York, she worked as a translator there (1917–18), lived abroad (1919–39), and returned to settle in Woodbury, Conn. (1941). She was a surrealistic painter of desolate architectural scenes, as in *The Instant* (1941).

Sage, Mrs. Russell (b. Margaret Olivia Slocum) (1828–1918) philanthropist; born in Syracuse, N.Y. She taught school intermittently after she graduated from Troy Female Seminary. In 1869 she married Russell B. Sage (1816–1906), who accumulated one of the major American fortunes through railroads and investments. After his death, she gave grants to schools, colleges, and nature institutions that totaled $80 million, making her the foremost woman philanthropist of her day.

Sage, Russell (1816–1906) financier; born in Oneida County, N.Y. A clerk at his brother's store in Troy (1828), he attended night school, bought out his brother's store (1836), and opened a wholesale grocer's business. Active in local politics from 1845, he served in the U.S. House of Representatives (Whig, N.Y.; 1853–57) where he promoted the preservation of Mount Vernon. His interest in railroads and finance was sparked by a meeting with Jay Gould, with whom he became an ally. In 1863 he moved to New York City to pursue stocks and finance and is credited with originating "puts and calls" on the stock market (1872). He promoted the development of the Atlantic & Pacific Telegraph Company and its consolidation into Western Union, and was

a prodigious money lender. His fortune at his death was estimated at $70 million.

Sahlins, Marshall David (1930–) cultural anthropologist; born in Chicago. Educated at the University of Michigan and Columbia University, he taught at Michigan and Chicago and made important contributions in oceanic ethnography, cultural evolution, and economic anthropology. His major works include *Evolution and Culture* (1960) and *Culture and Practical Reason* (1976).

Said, Edward W. (1935–) author, educator, political activist; born in Jerusalem. A Palestinian, he and his family became refugees during the 1947 partition of Palestine. He came to the U.S.A. and studied at private schools, receiving his Ph.D. from Harvard in 1964. His reading of Joseph Conrad influenced his views on colonialism. He taught English and literature at Columbia University (1963). Intensely involved both in literary scholarship and Palestinian rights, he wrote many books, most notably *Orientalism* (1978) and *Covering Islam* (1981). In the former he argued that the West's view of the Middle East and the Islamic world has been distorted by intellectual romantics; in the latter, he argued that the American view of Arabs was conditioned almost totally by a hostile media. He was a member of the Palestine National Council (1977) and a recognized leader in the Palestinian cause.

Saint-Gaudens, Augustus (1848–1907) sculptor; born in Dublin, Ireland. His parents emigrated to New York City in 1848. He was apprenticed to cameo cutters (1861–67), studied at Cooper Union and the National Academy of Design (1864–67), in Paris (1867), and established a studio in Rome (1870–72). He traveled throughout his life, but set up a studio in New York City (1875–97), and maintained a summer home and studio, Aspet, in Cornish, N.H., later to become a national historic site (1964). Considered the major American sculptor in the beaux-arts style, he created many commissioned works for John La Farge, Stanford White, and Charles McKim, among others, and was a founder of the Society of American Artists (1877). He is honored for his coin designs; *Grief,* his sculpture for the grave site of Mrs. Henry Adams (1886–91); the Robert Gould Shaw Memorial (1884–97), a commemoration of Shaw's leadership of a black Civil War division; and the equestrian sculpture of General Sherman (1897–1903), among many other fine works.

Saks, Gene (b. Jean Michael Saks) (1921–) stage/television actor, director; born in New York City. He is best known as a director of comedies, including *Nobody Loves an Albatross* (1963), *Mame* (1966), and the Tony Award-winning *Biloxi Blues* (1984).

Saladino, John F. (1939–) interior decorator; born in Kansas City, Mo. With a 1963 M.F.A. from Yale, he started a private practice in 1972. His design is noted for sensitive use of colors, styles, and textures.

Salinger, J. D. (Jerome David) (1919–) writer; born in New York City. He graduated from Valley Forge Military Academy (1936) and studied at New York University, Ursinus College, and Columbia University. He began to write when young, worked as an entertainer on a cruise ship (1941), served in the Army (1942–46), and began to publish short stories. *The Catcher in the Rye* (1951), his first and only novel, was an immediate success, generating a cult-like dedication among many readers. His subsequent collections of short stories, many of which first appeared in the *New*

Yorker, such as *Franny and Zooey* (1961) and *Raise High the Roof Beam, Carpenters* and *Seymour: An Introduction* (1963), raised more speculation about the elusive author. Critics have been puzzled by his work – he is considered to be either too intellectual or too sentimental, a supreme stylist or a didactic practitioner of self-absorbed musings. He also ended up as something of a media preoccupation by virtue of his becoming a recluse for most of his adult life; about all that was ever known of his personal life was that he lived and wrote in Cornish, N.H.

Salisbury, Harrison (1908–93) journalist; born in Minneapolis, Minn. Joining the *New York Times* in 1949, he won a 1955 Pulitzer Prize for articles written as a Moscow correspondent. He reported from Hanoi during the Vietnam War and was a top-ranking *Times* editor before his 1973 retirement.

Salisbury, Rollin (D.) (1858–1922) geologist, geographer; born near Spring Prairie, Wis. A protégé of Professor Thomas Chamberlin while at Beloit (Wis.), he succeeded him in the geology department (1881–91) and assisted him at the U.S. Geological Survey. He followed Chamberlin to the University of Chicago, first as head of the geography department (1892–1919), and subsequently as head of the geology department; he also served as dean of the Ogden Graduate School of Science (1899–1922) where he was a demanding but enthusiastic mentor. A lucid writer, he comanaged the *Journal of Geology* (1893–1922) and cowrote *Geology* (3 vols. 1904–06). He specialized in glacial deposits, studying them in South America, the Arctic, and New Jersey.

Salk, Jonas (Edward) (1914–   ) immunologist; born in New York City. He began his pathbreaking studies on viruses and immunization by starting with the influenza virus while at the University of Michigan (1942–47). At the University of Pittsburgh (1947–63) he developed the first vaccination against poliomyelitis, a killed-virus vaccine, introduced to the public in 1953. (By 1961, and after some resistance, Albert Sabin's simpler and stronger live-virus oral vaccine had supplanted Salk's injectable vaccine in the United States; Salk's vaccine is now used only in a few countries around the world.) He is the founder/director (1963) of the Salk Institute for Biological Studies in San Diego, Calif., and is on the board of directors of the Immune Response Corporation, which is pursuing treatment for AIDS and other diseases such as multiple sclerosis. Among his writings are *Man Unfolding* (1972) and *Anatomy of Reality: Merging of Intuition and Reason* (1983). Widely honored, he holds the French Legion of Honor (1955) and the Presidential Medal of Freedom (1977).

Salle, David (1952–   ) artist; born in Norman, Okla. Son of Russian immigrants, raised in comfortable circumstances in Wichita, Kans., he studied at the California Institute of the Arts and began presenting one-man shows in 1975. His large multimedia paintings, characterized by startling juxtapositions, drew mixed critical reception from the start. He became something of an artist/celebrity during the 1980s.

Salmon, Robert (c.1775–c.1843) painter; born in Scotland or England. Active in Scotland and England as a painter (c. 1800), he emigrated to Boston (c. 1828) and painted marine scenes and landscapes, faithfully recording the details of the era, as seen in *Boston Harbor from Constitution Wharf* (1829).

Salomon, Haym (?1740–85) Revolutionary patriot, banker; born in Leszno, Poland. University educated, he supported Polish independence and had to flee, ending up in New York City in 1772 where he began a dry-goods business. With the American Revolution, he undertook to supply the Continental troops; he was twice arrested by the British as a spy but he escaped to Philadelphia in 1778. There he aided Robert Morris by brokering government bonds, raising hundreds of thousands of dollars through loans of his own and others' money. He lost heavily in the post-Revolutionary recession. He also worked to secure equal treatment for his fellow Jews.

Saltonstall, Dudley (1738–96) naval officer; born in New London, Conn. He commanded the USS *Alfred* during the capture of New Providence (1776). He was dismissed from the navy after the failure of the Penobscott Bay operation under his command.

Saltonstall, Leverett (1892–1979) governor, U.S. senator; born in Chestnut Hill, Mass. A member of the Massachusetts legislature (Rep.; 1923–36) and Speaker from 1929, he was elected governor (1939–45). He served in the U.S. Senate (1945–67) and was Republican whip (1949–57). He also served as chairman of the armed services committee.

Samoset (?1590–?1653) Pemaquid diplomat; born on Monhegan Island in present-day Maine. He had learned some English from British fishermen who had worked off the coast of Maine. Thus it was that he was able to say "Welcome, Englishmen!" when he greeted the Pilgrims at Plymouth in March 1621. He then arranged a meeting with them and Squanto and the Wamponoag chief Massasoit and he fostered friendship between the two groups. In 1625 he signed the first deed of land transfer with the whites and he signed another such deed in 1653. After that he disappears from the historical record.

Sampson, Deborah (1760–1827) Revolutionary soldier, lecturer; born in Plympton, Mass. After a youth as a domestic servant and a few months as a teacher, she left town in 1782 to enlist in the American Revolution by disguising herself as a man and adopting the name "Robert Shurtleff" (or Shirtliff). She concealed her identity while participating in several battles, including one near Tarrytown, N.Y., where she was wounded; only when hospitalized with fever did a doctor discover her sex, and she was discharged from the army. After marrying Benjamin Gannett and having three children, she inspired a romanticized biography in 1797, and this led to her making a lecture tour in 1802. Thanks in part to the intercession of Paul Revere, she was awarded a federal pension in 1805, and 11 years after her death Congress voted her husband and heirs special payments in recognition of her military service.

Sampson, William (1764–1836) lawyer, Irish patriot; born in Londonderry, Ireland. Admitted to the Irish bar, he was exiled for treason, eventually arriving in New York (1806). An eloquent advocate of personal rights, he championed the movement to codify common law. Among his writings are a two-volume *History of Ireland* (1833).

Sampson, William Thomas (1840–1902) naval officer; born in Palmyra, N.Y. He was superintendent of the Naval Academy (1886–89) and chief of the Bureau of Ordnance (1893–97). He commanded the North Atlantic squadron which blockaded Santiago and landed American troops on Cuba (1898). He commanded the Boston navy yard (1899–1901).

Samuelson, Joan Benoit (1957–   ) marathon runner; born

in Portland, Maine. After winning the Boston marathon twice (1979, 1983), she won the first ever women's Olympic marathon at the 1984 Games.

Samuelson, Paul (Anthony) (1915–) economist; born in Gary, Ind. By age 26 he had obtained his Ph.D. from Harvard and secured a teaching position at the Massachusetts Institute of Technology. His distinguished career included writings on a wide variety of subjects in economics – international trade, production theory, capital theory, financial analysis, growth theory, and the history of economic thought. His textbook, *Economics* (McGraw-Hill, 1948; 11th ed., 1980) has been translated into over a dozen languages. He received the Nobel Prize in economics (1970).

Sánchez, Luis Rafael (1936–) writer; born in Humacao, Puerto Rico. Prolific essayist, playwright, and novelist, he was the Puerto Rican writer with the greatest international reputation in the second half of the 20th century. In 1963 he won the Paris-based review *Cuadernos* Award for the best Puerto Rican short story published that year and in 1979 he was awarded a Guggenheim. His 1976 novel, *La guaracha del Macho Camacho* (*Macho Camacho's Beat*), in which characters, many caught in a monstrous traffic jam, speculate on life in vivid Puerto Rican vernacular, was a best-seller both in Spanish and English.

Sanchez, Sonia (1934–) poet, writer; born in Birmingham, Ala. She studied at Hunter College (B.A. 1955), and taught at several institutions, such as Temple University, Philadelphia, beginning in 1977. A black nationalist and political activist, she is known for persuasive and metaphorical poetry, as in *homegirls & handgrenades* (1984). She also wrote plays, short stories, and children's books, and edited African-American anthologies.

Sandage, Allan Rex (1926–) astronomer; born in Iowa City, Iowa. An astronomer at the Carnegie Observatory (1956), he was a senior researcher scientist at the Space Telescope Science Institute (1987). In 1950 he deduced the universe's age – 10 billion years – and in 1960 he discovered quasars. He published *The Hubble Atlas of Galaxies* (1961) and compiled *The Carnegie Atlas of Bright Galaxies* with astronomical photographer John Bedke. In 1991, he was awarded the prestigious Crafoord Prize.

Sandage, C. H. (Charles Harold) (1902–) advertising educator; born in Hatfield, Mo. He taught business, marketing, and advertising at Miami University, Ohio (1929–46) and the University of Illinois (1946–68). He was president of the Farm Research Institute, Urbana, Ill. (1946), a marketing firm that studies the needs and wants of American farmers. His first book, *Advertising Theory and Practice* (1936), was a classic text, going through a dozen editions in 50 years. He was elected to the Advertising Hall of Fame in 1985, one of a very few noncommercial achievers to be so honored.

Sandburg, Carl (August) (Militant; Jack Philips, pen names) (1878–1967) poet, writer, folklorist; born in Galesburg, Ill. He studied at Lombard College, Galesburg (1898–1902) – with time out for service in the Spanish-American War (1899) – and in the decades ahead would work as an editor, journalist, copywriter, lecturer, and collector of folk songs. He was an organizer of the Social-Democratic Party (1908), and was secretary to the Socialist mayor of Milwaukee (1910–12). Known for such famous poems as "Chicago" (1914), and "Fog" (1916), he won the Pulitzer Prize (1940)

for the last of his six-volume biography of Lincoln (1926–39). He was ahead of most of his fellow poets in his interest in American folksong and lore; he collected some 300 folksongs and ballads in *The American Songbag* (1927) and he often gave public recitals, accompanying himself on the guitar. He also wrote children's books and a novel, *Remembrance Rock* (1948). Based in Chicago for much of his life, he retired to Flat Rock, N.C.

Sande, Earl (1898–1968) jockey; born in Groton, S.D. He won the Kentucky Derby three times, the Belmont Stakes five times, and in 1930 he rode Gallant Fox to a Triple Crown.

Sanders, Bernie (1941–) mayor, U.S. representative; born in New York City. After working as a free-lance writer, carpenter, and youth counselor, he became the first Socialist mayor of Burlington, Vt. (1982–90). An unsuccessful candidate for governor in 1972, 1976, and 1986, and for the U.S. Senate in 1971 and 1974, he was elected to the U.S. House of Representatives as an Independent (1991).

Sanders, "Colonel" Harlan (1890–1980) food franchiser; born in Henryville, Ind. When he was 12, his mother remarried and his stepfather sent the children away; Harlan became a farmhand in Greenwood, Ind. With a sixth-grade education, he began 25 years of odd jobs, which included service as a U.S. Army soldier in Cuba. In 1929 he opened a gas station and small restaurant in Corbin, Ky. His cooking grew so popular, he closed the gas station to open Sander's Cafe, which soon added a motel. By 1939, with the invention of the pressure cooker, he had discovered the method for cooking chicken quickly. World War II and a new interstate led to a decline in customers and mounting debts required the sale of his restaurant (1956). He began demonstrating the Colonel Sanders method and his secret seasoning to other restaurant owners; in return for his secrets, they became franchises. In the first two years he sold five franchises; by 1960 he had sold 200, and by 1964, when he sold his company to John Y. Brown and Jack Massey, he had sold more than 600. He became a spokesman for the Colonel Sanders enterprise. The Governor of Kentucky conferred on him the honorary title of Colonel in 1936 in recognition of his contribution to the state's cuisine.

Sanders, George Nicholas (1812–73) promoter, revolutionist, Confederate agent; born in Lexington, Ky. A man of means, half idealist, half con artist, he turned his political lobbying skills to good advantage. During the annexation of Texas (1845), he worked as a political and businessperson's go-between, operating as the same for Eastern capitalists who were speculating in Chicago real estate. Committed financially and politically to the revolutionary cause in Europe (1850s), he crusaded for European republicanism through his "Young America" movement, edited the *Democratic Review* (1851), assisted in the issuance of the Ostend Manifesto, and worked as a Confederate agent in Europe and Canada during the Civil War. He was falsely connected with Lincoln's assassination (1865) but throughout his career managed to antagonize as many people as he won over.

Sanders, Marlene (1931–) television reporter/producer; born in Cleveland, Ohio. After working with Mike Wallace on *Night Beat* (1956–58), she became WNEW public affairs director (1962–64) in New York. At ABC (1964–78), she was the first woman to coanchor the news, she produced documentaries (1972–78), and then became vice-president for news in 1977. A *CBS Reports* producer (1978–87), she wrote *Waiting for Primetime* (1988). In 1991 she began hosting *Profiles in Progress* for the Discovery Channel.

Sandoz, Mari (Marie Susette) (m. Macumber) (1901–66) writer, historian; born in Sheridan County, Nebr. The daughter of Swiss emigrants, she grew up on the family ranch, and lost the use of an eye due to snow-blindness when 15. After completing the eighth grade, she skipped high school and became a teacher. She briefly attended a business school, and studied intermittently at the University of Nebraska (1922–31). She researched the history of the Sioux Indians, and was an editor of historical periodicals (1927–35). After settling in New York City, she still maintained her ties to the family ranch. She is noted as a biographer, novelist, and historian whose work usually drew on the life of the Great Plains. *Cheyenne Autumn* (1953) and *The Cattlemen: From the Rio Grande across the Far Marias* (1958) are two of her best-known nonfiction works; *Miss Morissa* (1955) and *The Horsecatcher* (1956) are among her most admired novels.

Sanford, Charles Steadman, Jr. (1936–) banker; born in Savannah, Ga. He graduated from the University of Georgia (1958) and the Wharton School at the University of Pennsylvania (1960) before joining Bankers Trust Co. (New York City), the eighth largest U.S. bank, in 1961. Named president in 1983, he rose to chairman and chief executive officer in 1987. He served as an overseer of the Wharton School.

Sanford, Edward Terry (1865–1930) Supreme Court justice; born in Knoxville, Tenn. He was a U.S. assistant district attorney general (1907–08) and a U.S. district judge (1908–23) before President Harding named him to the U.S. Supreme Court (1923–30).

Sanford, Maria (Louise) (1836–1920) educator, lecturer; born in Saybrook, Conn. Raised in a humble home but taught to respect education, literature, and service, she graduated from the New Britain (Conn.) Normal School (1855) and taught in Connecticut secondary schools for 12 years. She suffered from "deep depression" from the loss of her father and a broken engagement but read more widely under the supervision of a Yale professor. In 1867 she went to Pennsylvania where by 1869 she had become a school principal; she also began to be more widely known for her ideas about introducing "moral training" while engaging the students' interest. She became one of the early female professors in the U.S.A. when she joined the newly opened Swarthmore College as professor of history and rhetoric (1869–79); she also lectured outside the college on such topics as "Honesty in Public and Private Life" and gave slide shows on art. She went on to the University of Minnesota (1880–1909) where in addition to teaching art appreciation and poetry she also lectured to farm wives. In the late 1880s she borrowed heavily to invest in real estate, and after the boom collapsed, she spent much of the rest of her life paying off every last cent of debt. She engaged in various activities until near her end – traveling to Europe to view the art, lecturing nationally, supporting women's suffrage, clearing land in Florida for a retirement home for her missionary niece. Often in trouble because of her unorthodox ways, she was beloved by her many students and eventually given various honors, as when Minnesota placed her statue in the U.S. Capitol.

Sanford, Terry (1917–) governor, U.S. senator; born in Laurinburg, N.C. A World War II army hero, he became a lawyer and state senator in 1953. As governor (Dem., N.C.; 1961–65), he sponsored progressive legislation including the Higher Education Act (1963) and the North Carolina Fund (1963). After writing *Storm over the States* (1967), he became Duke University president (1969–87). He took office as North Carolina's senator in 1987.

Sanger, Margaret (b. Higgins) (1879–1966) birth control advocate; born in Corning, N.Y. The sixth of eleven children, she married architect William Sanger (1902) and had three children before leaving him in 1913. She moved to New York City (1912) where she became active in the women's labor movement and the Socialist Party. She concluded that control over childbearing was the key to female emancipation and was appalled by women's ignorance of contraception, which she experienced first-hand working as a practical nurse in New York City (1912). She wrote newspaper articles on feminine hygiene, put out a militant journal entitled *Woman Rebel,* and published a pamphlet, *Family Limitation* (1914), in which she coined the term "birth control" and called for legalization of contraception; indicted for violating postal laws, she fled to Canada and then England (1914), where she was influenced by sex reformer Havelock Ellis to tone down her radical tactics. After her return (1915), the government dropped its charges and she began lecturing widely, also founding the *Birth Control Review* (1916), which she edited until 1928. She and her sister served 30 days in prison for opening a birth control clinic in Brooklyn (1916), but an appeal judge's decision allowed for doctors to provide birth control information to married women. Her Birth Control Research Bureau (founded in New York in 1923 with the support of her wealthy new husband, J. Noah Slee) was the first doctor-staffed medical clinic in America and a model for the 300 others she helped establish. In 1921 she founded the American Birth Control League; accused of autocratic tactics, she resigned from its presidency in 1928, but it later merged with her Clinical Research Bureau into the organization that in 1942 became Planned Parenthood. She founded a lobbying group (1929) that successfully sued to allow the mailing of contraceptive materials in the U.S.A. She was less active from the 1940s on, but in the 1950s she induced philanthropist Katharine Dexter McCormick to help fund development of a birth control pill, and in 1952 she helped found the International Planned Parenthood Federation. She was undeniably difficult to work with, and close examination of her writings shows that she endorsed birth control in part to maintain the position of the white race, but she was just as certainly a courageous pioneer.

Sanromá, Jésus María (1902–84) pianist; born in Puerto Rico. Trained in the U.S.A. and Europe (with Cortot and Schnabel), he became an active soloist notable for performances of contemporary music.

Santayana, George (b. Jorge Agustín Nicolás) (1863–1952) philosopher, writer; born in Madrid, Spain. Immigrating to Boston as a boy, he studied with William James and Josiah Royce at Harvard, where he himself taught philosophy (1889–1912); among his students were T. S. Eliot, Gertrude Stein, and Felix Frankfurter. Hating academic life and American commercialism and Puritanism, he took advantage of a modest inheritance to retire in 1912; he left the

U.S.A. to live a solitary life in Oxford, Paris, and after 1925 in Rome. He wrote 18 volumes of philosophy, chief among them *The Life of Reason* (5 vols. 1905–06) and *The Realms of Being* (4 vols. 1927–40); his philosophical works are distinguished by their lucid, literary style. In addition he published poetry, literary, and cultural criticism; a novel, *The Last Puritan* (1935), an unexpected best-seller about Cambridge (Mass.) society; and a three-volume autobiography.

Saperstein, (Abraham M.) Abe (1902–66) basketball promoter; born in London, England. He came to the U.S.A. as a boy, and while coaching a boys' basketball team at Welles Park, Ill., he was invited to coach a Negro American Legion team; when this team lost its sponsorship, he kept it together himself, rechristened it the Harlem Globetrotters, had his tailor-father make new uniforms, and arranged for their first game in Hinckley, Ill., in January 1927. In the early years the team toured only in the Midwest and West, and, with Saperstein as owner, promoter, coach, and even occasionally – at 5′ 3″ – as substitute player, they played straight basketball. He coached the team to win the 1940 world professional title and the International Cup in 1943 and 1944, and by 1950 the team was beating some of the best college and professional teams and making tours around the world. With the rise in popularity of college and pro basketball, the Globetrotters gradually provided more of an entertainment than true games, but Saperstein – who was elected into the Basketball Hall of Fame in 1970 – was recognized as having made a special contribution to the game with his team's mixture of comic routines, spectacular plays and shots, and interaction with fans.

Sapir, Edward (1884–1939) anthropologist, linguist; born in Lauenburg, Germany (now Poland). He emigrated to the U.S.A. in 1889 and was raised in an orthodox Jewish family on New York City's Lower East Side. He attended Columbia University (B.A. 1904; Ph.D. 1909) where he came under the influence of Franz Boas. After teaching briefly at the Universities of California and Pennsylvania, he became chief of anthropology for the Canadian National Museum (1910–25), then went on to teach at the University of Chicago (1925–31) and Yale (1931–39). Although he did some work in African linguistics, he is primarily known for his work with Native American languages, classifying them in "families" and stressing their relationships with their cultures. He encouraged scholars to extend their research beyond formal linguistics and pure ethnography to the psychology of individual personality and behavior. With his student, Benjamin Whorf, he developed what became known as the "Sapir-Whorf hypothesis," namely, that the way people perceive and categorize the real world is strongly influenced by the language they speak. His theories on language became an important part of the European structuralist movement. His publications include poetry as well as his specialized writings; his best known work is *Language: An Introduction to the Study of Speech* (1921).

Sarazen, Gene (b. Eugene Saraceni) (1902–) golfer; born in Harrison, N.Y. He won the U.S. Open and the Professional Golfers' Association (PGA) championships in 1922, when he was only 20 years old. He also won the British Open (1932) and the Masters (1935) to become the first to win each of the four major championships that comprise the Grand Slam of golf.

Sardi, (Melchiorre Pio Vincenzo) Vincent (1885–1969)

restaurateur; born in San Marzano Oliveto, Italy. He was a writer in London and (after 1907) in New York City. He opened a restaurant in New York's theater district (1921), and Sardi's became a city landmark, home to an extended family of theater people and a favorite celebrity-watching spot for others. He retired in 1947.

Sarett, Lewis (Hastings) (1917–) chemist, inventor; born in Champaign, Ill. A graduate of Northwestern University with a Ph.D. from Princeton, he went to work as a chemist for Merck Research Laboratories in New Jersey, where in 1944 he prepared the first synthetic cortisone. A collaborator on some 100 technical papers and patents, he rose to senior vice-president for science and technology in a long career at Merck.

Sargent, Charles Sprague (1841–1927) arboriculturist; born in Boston, Mass. A merchant's son, he graduated from Harvard (1862) and served in the Union Army during the Civil War. He was on the faculty of Harvard (1872–1927) and became director of the college's newly founded Arnold Arboretum (in Boston) (1873), a position he held for the rest of his life. In addition to developing the arboretum's collections, he worked for conservation and national parks, and he published important studies of North American trees and (from 1888–97) edited the weekly magazine *Garden and Forest*.

Sargent, Henry (1770–1845) painter; born in Gloucester, Mass. He studied with Benjamin West in London (1793), returned to live in Boston (1797), served as a militia officer, and painted genre scenes, such as *Tea Party* (c. 1820–25).

Sargent, John Singer (1856–1925) painter; born in Florence, Italy. The son of expatriate American parents, he studied in Florence (1871–72) and Paris (1874), visited Boston (1876), traveled, and returned to Paris (1880). He is praised for his portraits, such as *The Daughters of Edward Darley Boit* (1882). A scandal erupted when he exhibited *Madame X* (1884), because the subject, Madame Gautreau, used lavender powder and wore a low-cut gown. Paris was offended, Madame Gautreau refused the painting, and Sargent moved to London (1885). He was influenced by Velázquez, impressionism, and Japanese composition, and his work is noted for its originality, insight, and technical polish. An extensive traveler, he was at home in London and Boston. He painted murals for the Boston Public Library (1890–1916), and for the Museum of Fine Arts, Boston (c. 1918–21). By 1910 he was weary of portrait painting, and he focused on masterful water colors, such as *Two Girls Fishing* (1925). Both his oils and water colors have ensured his fame.

Sargent, Thomas J. (1943–) economist; born in Pasadena, Calif. Along with Robert E. Lucas Jr., he cofounded the "new" classical macroeconomics. His work stressed a "natural rate of unemployment" and emphasized that departures from that natural rate are completely random. He taught at the University of Minnesota (1975–87) before joining the Hoover Institution, Stanford University (1987).

Sarich, Vincent M. (1934–) physical anthropologist; born in Chicago, Ill. He was a professor at Stanford University (1967–81) before joining the University of California: Berkeley (1981). His comparative protein studies engendered his controversial evolutionary theory that humans diverged from African apes as recently as four million years ago.

Sarnoff, David (1891–1971) broadcast pioneer/executive; born in Uzlian, Russia. He emigrated to New York City with his family at age nine and studied electrical engineering at the Pratt Institute. He gained national recognition in 1912 as a Marconi Wireless Telegraph Co. operator by reporting on the sinking of the *Titanic* and then staying at his station for 72 hours to help direct ships to the sinking liner. When the newly formed Radio Corporation of America (RCA) acquired Marconi Wireless, he rose through the ranks, becoming RCA's president and chairman, and retiring in 1970. A man with a clear vision of broadcasting's future, he predicted radio would become a basic household utility and proposed designing "Radio Music Boxes." Foreseeing the need for programming networks, he set up the National Broadcasting Co. in 1926 to stimulate RCA's radio sales. He was responsible for the first American television service, arranging for RCA to televise programs in 1936 to 150 homes in the New York City area. Under his guidance, RCA developed the black-and-white-compatible color television system adopted by the Federal Communication Commission in 1953, and the National Broadcasting Company took the lead in broadcasting color television. A colonel in the U.S. Army Signal Corps from 1924, he was promoted to brigadier general while on active duty in 1944–45 and thereafter enjoyed being called General Sarnoff.

Saroyan, William (1908–81) writer, playwright; born in Fresno, Calif. With unschooled talent, he emerged in the early 1930s from the Armenian community of California that he later depicted in *My Name is Aram* (1940). He created a mild sensation – and defined himself – with his collection of short stories, *The Daring Young Man on the Flying Trapeze* (1934). His second play, *The Time of Your Life* (1939), won a Pulitzer, which he refused because he disapproved of literary prizes. Undisciplined in his writings and life – he gambled away most of his earnings – he cultivated the naive, sentimental, and fantastic and failed to produce much of note after his youthful successes.

Sarton, (Eleanor) May (1912–) poet, writer; born in Wondelgem, Belgium (daughter of George Sarton). She grew up in Cambridge, Mass., and attended Shady Hill School (1917–26). She published poetry early, trained at the Civic Repertory Theatre in New York City (1929–33), and traveled widely. A noted teacher at many institutions, she is known for her poetry, short stories, novels, and memoirs, such as *Endgame: A Journal of the Seventy-Ninth Year* (1992). She settled in York, Maine, and in her later years became something of a cult figure to a circle of women.

Sarton, George Alfred (Léon) (1884–1956) historian; born in Ghent, Belgium. After founding *Isis* (1912), principal journal of the history of science, he emigrated to the United States (1915). Supported by the Carnegie Institution after 1918 and based at Harvard University (1920–51), he became the seminal figure in establishing the history of science as a valid discipline in the U.S.A. In 1936 he founded the journal *Osiris*. His *Introduction to the History of Science* (3 vols. 1927–48) is a classic in its field.

Sasaki, Hideo (1919–) landscape architect, professor; born in Reedley, Calif. Professor of landscape design at Harvard University (1950–70), he promoted and developed regional planning, using civil engineers and urban planners to design Boston's Waterfront Park.

Sassacus (?1560–1627) Massachuset Pequot chief; born near present-day Groton, Connecticut. As a youth he fought the English colonists. Named chief about 1632, he lost roughly 700 people in one battle of the Pequot War. His death coincided with the virtual destruction of the Pequot nation.

Satanta (b. Set-tainte, "White Bear") (1830–78) Kiowa chief; born on the northern Great Plains. Under extreme pressure he signed the Medicine Lodge Treaty of 1867, ceding tribal lands in exchange for a reservation in the Indian Territory. Known for his oratory as well as his bravery, he committed suicide while in prison for a crime he probably did not commit.

Satir, Virginia (Mildred) (1916–88) educator, psychotherapist; born in Neillsville, Wis. She studied at the University of Chicago (M.A. 1948) and pioneered in the development of family therapy by conducting workshops nationwide. She helped found the Mental Research Institute (1959) and established the International Human Learning Resource Network (1979). Her publications include *Peoplemaking* and *Self-Esteem*.

Sauer, Carl (Ortwin) (1889–1975) geographer; born in Warrenton, Mo. A Ph.D. graduate of the University of Chicago, he taught at the University of Michigan (1915–23), later joining the faculty of the University of California: Berkeley, where he spent the rest of his career. A competent linguist with a fine literary style, he published numerous scholarly monographs over the years, most notably *Morphology of Landscape* (1925), and a book of lectures, *Agricultural Origins and Dispersals* (1952). He was largely responsible for shifting the focus of American geography from environmental "determinism" to the study of landscape and cultural geography.

Savage, Edward (1761–1817) painter; born in Princeton, Mass. He studied with Benjamin West in London (1791), worked as an artist in Boston (1794–1801), and moved to New York (1801). He is known for his portraits of George Washington and his family.

Sawyer, Diane (1945–) journalist, television correspondent/anchor; born in Glasgow, Ky. (married to Mike Nichols). Hired as ABC WLKY-TV's weathergirl in 1967, she then became a reporter in Louisville, Ky. Coming to Washington as a Nixon press aide in 1970, she stayed on after Watergate to help with Nixon's memoirs. A CBS news reporter (1978–81), she cohosted the *Morning News with Charles Kuralt* (1981–84), then became the first woman correspondent on *60 Minutes* (1984–89). In 1989 she left to coanchor ABC's *Primetime Live*.

Sawyer, Philetus (1816–1900) U.S. representative/senator; born in Whiting, Vt. He moved to Wisconsin where he became a successful lumberman. He was elected to the U.S. House of Representatives (Rep., Wis.; 1865–75) and to the U.S. Senate (1881-93). Charged with corruption by Robert La Follette, he was defeated for reelection.

Saxton, Joseph (1799–1873) inventor; born in Huntington, Pa. A banker's son, he learned the watchmaker's trade and made a clock for the belfry of Independence Hall in Philadelphia. As an official of the U.S. Mint (1837–43), he designed and built the balances used to verify standard weights. He was superintendent of weights and measures for the U.S. Coast Survey (1843–73). Among other inventions, he patented a deep-sea thermometer and an ever-pointed pencil.

Say, Thomas (1787–1834) entomologist, conchologist; born in Philadelphia. He attended Quaker schools, but expanded his childhood interest in natural history by self-teaching.

After helping to found the Philadelphia Academy of Natural Sciences (1812), he was appointed zoologist for Major Stephen H. Long's expeditions to the Rocky Mountains (1819) and the sources of the Minnesota River (1823). He became curator of the American Philosophical Society (1821–27), then professor of natural history at the University of Pennsylvania (1822–28). He was so inspired by utopologist Robert Owen that he went to Owen's "ideal community" in New Harmony, Indiana (1825). Although this social experiment failed, Say remained in New Harmony for the rest of his life after leaving his professorship. His exclusively descriptive and taxonomic scientific works include many books and professional articles on American insects, birds, and shells. Considered the father of descriptive entomology in America, his two major works were the three-volume *American Entomology* (1817–28) and *American Conchology* (1830–34).

Sayers, Gale (Eugene) (1943–) football player; born in Wichita, Kans. An All-American at the University of Kansas, he was a brilliant breakaway runner. As a rookie with the Chicago Bears, he scored six touchdowns in a 1965 game on his way to the league scoring title. He led the National Football League in rushing twice (1966, 1969), set the record for average kickoff returns, and was all-league five times.

Sayles, John (Thomas) (1950–) writer, movie scriptwriter/director/actor; born in Schenectady, N.Y. After graduating from Williams College, he wrote fiction, publishing prize-winning short stories and the novels *Pride of Bimbos* (1975) and *Union Dues* (1977). These led him to Hollywood and scriptwriting, and he spent several years working on junk movies until he was able to write, direct, and act in *The Return of the Secaucus Seven* (1980), filmed in only 27 days and on a budget of about $60,000. He continued to struggle to make his own movies until he was awarded a MacArthur Foundation grant (1983); this allowed him to continue scripting and directing critically acclaimed independent feature movies, such as *Matewan* (1987) and *Eight Men Out* (1988), while also writing novels.

Scalia, Antonin (1936–) Supreme Court justice; born in Trenton, N.J. He practiced law (1960–67) and taught (1967–71) before joining the Nixon administration as executive counsel (1971–77). President Reagan named him to the U.S. Court of Appeals (1982–86) and to the U.S. Supreme Court (1986).

Scaravaglione, Concetta (Maria) (1900–75) sculptor; born in New York City. She studied at the National Academy of Design, the Art Students League, and later in Rome (1947–50). Using the direct carving technique, she worked with flowing lines and humanistic themes, as in *Group* (1935).

Scarry, Richard (McClure) (1919–94) writer, illustrator; born in Boston, Mass. He studied at the Boston Museum School (1938–41); the Archipenko Art School, Woodstock, N.Y.; and the Eliot O'Hara Watercolor School in Gooserocks Beach, Maine. In 1946 he began to write and illustrate brightly colored and extremely detailed popular books for young children, as in *What Do People Do All Day?* (1968). He was based in New York City until 1969 and then settled in Switzerland.

Schaefer, Vincent J. (Joseph) (1906–93) meteorologist; born in Schenectady, N.Y. He left high school at age 16 to help support his family, and enrolled in the General Electric

(GE) Apprentice School (1922–26). He worked in the GE Research Lab Instrument Shop where he so impressed Irving Langmuir that he became his research assistant (1933–38) and then an associate of Langmuir's (1938–54). For the U.S. government during World War II they designed an efficient smoke generator to screen military operations, improved the filter for gas masks, and tackled the problem of icing on airplane wings. In the course of this project, in 1946, Schaefer caused a cloud to "snow" by seeding it with dry ice from an airplane. This resulted in the five-year government sponsored "Project Cirrus" at GE to study cloud seeding. In 1952 Schaefer became director of research at Munitalp Foundation and in 1959 he joined the faculty at the State University of New York: Albany, where he was instrumental in establishing the Atmospheric Sciences Research Center of which he was the first director (1960–76). He retired in 1976 after receiving two honorary degrees, including Sc.D. from Notre Dame University (1948), and several awards including the prestigious Robert M. Losey Award (1953). He wrote more than 270 scientific papers and was coauthor of *Field Guide to the Atmosphere* (1983).

Schafer, Roy (1922–) psychologist; born in the Bronx, N.Y. Trained at the Menninger Foundation and Austen Riggs Center, he was a staff psychologist for Yale's health service (1961–76) and professor of psychiatry at Cornell University Medical College (1976–79). He established a private practice in New York City (1979). His early work focused on psychological testing; later he wrote on psychoanalysis and psychotherapy in works including *Aspects of Internalization* (1968) and *A New Language for Psychoanalysis* (1976).

Schaff, Philip (1819–93) Protestant theologian; born in Chur, Switzerland. He studied at several German universities and took a theological degree in Berlin in 1841. In 1844 he accepted the chair of theology at the German Reformed seminary in Mercersburg, Pa. In 1870 he became a professor at Union Theological Seminary in New York. An early ecumenicist, he foresaw the eventual unification of diverse Christian sects. He wrote or edited more than 80 works of theology and biblical scholarship, including *The Creeds of Christendom* (1877).

Schalk, (Raymond William) Ray (1892–1970) baseball player; born in Marvel, Ill. During his 18-year career as a catcher (1912–29), primarily with the Chicago White Sox, he established many league records for fielding. Nicknamed "Cracker," he was an honest member of the "Black Sox" club that conspired to lose the 1919 World Series. In 1955 he was elected to baseball's Hall of Fame.

Schaller, George B. (Beals) (1933–) mammalogist; born in Berlin, Germany. He was brought to the U.S.A. (Missouri) as a teenager. After working as a research associate at Johns Hopkins (1963–66), he became a research zoologist at the New York Zoological Society (Bronx Zoo) (1966), and was the director of its international conservation program from 1979 to 1988. He concurrently served as adjunct associate professor at Rockefeller University (1966). He wrote highly acclaimed books on African and Asian mammals based on his own pioneering studies supported by long-term observations of species in their natural habitats. In 1973 he won the National Book Award for *The Serengeti Lion: A Study of Predator-Prey Relations,* and was awarded the 1980 World Wildlife Fund Gold Medal for his contributions to the understanding and conservation of endangered species.

Schally, Andrew V. (Victor) (1926–) endocrinologist; born in Wilno, Poland. He fled to Romania from Poland at the German invasion of 1939 and emigrated to Great Britain via Italy and France. He was a protein chemist in England (1949–52) and an endocrinologist in Canada (1952–57) before coming to the U.S.A. to join Baylor University (1957–62). He then relocated to Tulane and the Veterans Administration Hospital, New Orleans (1962). He spent his career isolating and determining the chemical structures of hypothalamic hormones that regulate pituitary output of hormones affecting the thyroid, adrenals, gonads, and somatic growth. For these contributions, he shared the 1977 Nobel Prize in physiology with collaborator Roger Guellemin and immunologist Rosalyn Yalow.

Schamberg, Morton (Livingston) (1881–1918) painter; born in Philadelphia. He studied architecture at the University of Pennsylvania (1899–1903), art at the Philadelphia Academy of the Fine Arts (1903–06), traveled in Europe (1906, 1908–09), and was based in Philadelphia. He shared a studio with Charles Sheeler and painted abstract paintings of machinery, as in *Machine* (1916).

Schapiro, Meyer (1904–) art historian; born in Shavly, Russia. His family emigrated to America (1907), and he studied at Columbia University (B.A. 1924; M.A. 1926; Ph.D. 1929), where, beginning in 1928, he taught for many years. He also held concurrent positions as a lecturer at other institutions in America and abroad. He specialized in early medieval and modern art, and published several theoretical texts on the symbolic content of art.

Schapiro, Miriam (1923–) painter; born in Toronto, Canada. Born of American parents, she studied at the Museum of Modern Art, New York (1937–41), and at the State University of Iowa (1943–49). Based in New York and California, she was, by 1955, a feminist abstract expressionist, collagist, and cofounder, with Judy Chicago, of the Feminist Art Program in California (1972–75). She was also a founder of Womanhouse (1972), a female art environment in California.

Scharf, John Thomas (1843–98) historian, collector; born in Baltimore, Md. A Confederate soldier, he wrote studies in local history, including his *History of Maryland* (1879), and was a noted collector of Americana.

Schary, Dore (1905–80) screenwriter, movie producer/director; born in Newark, N.J. Originally an actor, he turned to screenwriting in 1932, sharing an Oscar for *Boys Town* (1938). After holding various posts with several film companies, he became Metro-Goldwyn-Mayer's chief of production (1948–56) and when fired he went to New York to write and produce the play *Sunrise at Campobello* (1956). In subsequent years he worked in both the theater and films as a writer, director, and producer, and he held public offices such as national chairman of B'Nai B'rith's Anti-Defamation League and Commissioner of cultural affairs for New York City. He was also outspoken and active in promoting liberal causes and was one of the few who openly resisted the blacklisting that occurred in the McCarthy era.

Schattsschneider, E. E. (Elmer Eric) (1892–1971) political scientist; born in Bethany, Minn. He received his Ph.D. at age 38 and spent most of his teaching career at Wesleyan University (1930–60). He championed political party competition as the anchor of American democracy in books such as *Politics, Pressures and the Tariff* (1935), *The Semisovereign*

People (1960), and *Two Hundred Million Americans in Search of a Government* (1969).

Schawlow, Arthur L. (Leonard) (1921–) physicist; born in Mount Vernon, N.Y. He taught and did microwave research in Toronto (1941–49), then went to Columbia University (1949–51). He performed superconductivity research at Bell Telephone Laboratories (1951–61) before joining Stanford (1961). He used his experience in maser technology to lay the basis for the laser with his brother-in-law, C. H. Townes (1958), and shared half the 1981 Nobel Prize in physics (with N. Bloembergen) for their contribution to laser spectroscopy.

Schechter, Solomon (?1847–1915) Hebraic scholar, educator; born in Focsani, Romania. Educated in Vienna and Berlin, he went to England in 1882, where in 1890 he was appointed lecturer in the Talmud and rabbinical literature at Cambridge University. He gained wide notice for identifying a Hebrew fragment, brought from Egypt, as a lost portion of Ecclesiasticus (one of the Apocrypha of the Bible); he went off to Cairo and located some 50,000 old Hebrew and Arabic manuscripts (including some more parts of Ecclesiasticus) which would provide the basis for many of his subsequent books, such as *Documents of Jewish sectaries* (1910). In 1901 he accepted the post of Jewish Theological Seminary of America (New York City). He soon became the major Jewish scholar in the U.S.A. while the seminary and its lay arm, the United Synagogue of America, became important centers of Conservative Judaism. He wrote what is regarded as the first modern approach to Jewish theology, *Some Aspects of Rabbinic Theology* (1909).

Schein, Edgar H. (Henry) (1928–) psychologist; born in Zurich, Switzerland. He emigrated to the U.S.A. in 1939. An expert on industrial and organizational psychology, he joined the faculty of the Sloan School at the Massachusetts Institute of Technology (1956) and established a private consultancy to government and industry. His books include *Organizational Culture and Leadership* (1985).

Schele de Vere, Maximilian (1820–98) philologist; born in Wexiö, Sweden. He showed an early aptitude for languages and obtained a Ph.D. from the University of Berlin in 1841. He emigrated to America in 1843, and in 1844 he was appointed professor of modern languages at the University of Virginia. He was among the first in this country to embrace the methods of comparative linguistics, leading to his *Outlines in Comparative Philology* (1853). At the founding of the University of Virginia, Thomas Jefferson had advocated the study of Anglo-Saxon and this recommendation was finally realized in the teaching of Schele de Vere, a pioneer in Anglo-Saxon studies. Other significant works are *Studies in English* (1867) and *Americanisms: The English of the New World* (1871).

Schelling, Thomas Crombie (1921–) economist; born in Oakland, Calif. He was a U.S. government economist (1948–53) and a professor at Yale (1953–58) before becoming the Lucius N. Litauer Professor of Political Economics at Harvard. The diverse subjects of his teaching and writing include arms control, crime, and business ethics. His analysis of economic policy in such areas as energy, environmental protection, and nuclear capabilities is widely respected.

Schereschewsky, Samuel (Isaac Joseph) (1831–1906) missionary, translator; born in Tauroggen, Lithuania. He came to the U.S.A. in 1854 as a Christian convert from Judaism, and after seminary training, he went as a missionary to China

(1859). He was Protestant Episcopal Bishop of Shanghai (1877–83) and translated the Bible and the Book of Common Prayer into Chinese. He spent his last decade in Japan.

Schick, Bela (1877–1967) pediatrician; born in Bolgar, Hungary. On the medical faculty at the University of Vienna, Austria (1902–23), he was a pioneer in studying childhood diseases such as scarlet fever, infantile diarrhea, diphtheria, and other diseases such as tuberculosis, serum sickness, and allergies, a new field of medicine. He developed what came to be known as the Schick test (1913), which determines a child's susceptibility to diphtheria. In 1923, he came to Mt. Sinai Hospital (New York City) to direct pediatrics, becoming a U.S. citizen in 1929. Recipient of the Howland Medal (1954), he helped found the American Academy of Pediatrics. In addition to various specialized works, he wrote *Child Care Today* (1933).

Schiff, Jacob (Henry) (1847–1920) financier, philanthropist; born in Frankfurt-am-Main, Germany. He came to New York City at age 18 and was licensed as a stockbroker in 1866; after working in a succession of brokerage houses, he joined the investment banking firm of Kuhn, Loeb & Company in 1874, becoming its president by 1885. He amassed a great fortune, primarily in railroads and insurance companies. He participated in the struggle for control of the Northern Pacific Railroad that precipitated the stock market panic of 1901. He secured a $200-million loan for Japan in the Russo-Japanese War (1904), and then, as a founder of the American Jewish Committee (1906), he worked to abrogate the U.S.-Russian commercial treaty because of Russian treatment of Jews. He also promoted a loan for the Manchurian Railway in China (1911). One of the foremost figures in American Jewry of his day, he supported a wide range of philanthropies, both religious and secular; although not a Zionist, he supported educational institutions in Palestine; his many philanthropies included the Tuskegee Institute, the Henry Street Settlement House, the Red Cross, and Harvard and Cornell Universities.

Schiff, Leonard I. (Isaac) (1915–71) physicist; born in Fall River, Mass. He performed research at the University of California: Berkeley (1937–40), the University of Pennsylvania (1940–45), and Los Alamos (1945–47), before joining Stanford (1947–66). A major contributor to research in theoretical nuclear physics, relativity, and gravitation, he was a proponent of extensive experimental testing of Einsteinian theory.

Schillinger, Joseph (1895–1943) composer/theorist; born in Kharkov, Russia. He began his career in Russia and came to the U.S.A. in 1928. His mathematically-based composition system attracted students including Gershwin.

Schindler, Alexander M. (1925–) rabbi, organization executive; born in Munich, Germany. He came to the U.S.A. in 1937. A graduate of the City College of New York, he was ordained at Hebrew Union College in Cincinnati. He served in the U.S. Army in the 10th Mountain Division in World War II. He was associate rabbi at Temple Emmanuel in Worcester, Mass., from 1959–63. In 1973 he was named president of the Union of American Hebrew Congregations. From 1976–78 he was president of the Conference of Major Jewish Organizations.

Schindler, R. M. (Rudolph Michael) (1887–1953) architect; born in Vienna, Austria. He emigrated in 1914 and worked briefly with Frank Lloyd Wright before establishing a Los Angeles practice. He worked outside the architectural mainstream designing small, low-cost houses characterized by their cubist designs and exploration of spatial relationships. He also designed furniture. Schindler House, Los Angeles (1921–22) and Lovell Beach House, Newport Beach, Calif. (1926) are among his designs.

Schippers, Thomas (1930–77) conductor; born in Kalamazoo, Mich. A brilliant talent, he made his public debut at age 18. During the 1950s he conducted at the Metropolitan Opera and guested internationally; he conducted the Cincinnati Symphony for six years before his death from cancer.

Schirmer, (Friedrich) Gustav (Emil) (1829–93) music publisher; born in Königsee, Germany. Emigrating to America with his family in 1840, he worked in various New York City music-publishing firms before acquiring his own in 1861; in 1866 he renamed it G. Schirmer and it went on to become one of the great international music publishers. A musician himself, he was noted for promoting American musicians while also publishing the new European composers of his day such as Wagner and Tchaikovsky; he gave generously to help Wagner build his Festspielhaus in Bayreuth.

Schirra, Walter (Marty) (1923–) astronaut, naval officer; born in Hackensack, N.J. He was chosen as one of the seven original astronauts (1959). He participated in three missions into space: Sigma 7 (1962), Gemini 6 (1965), and Apollo 7 (1968). He resigned from NASA (1969) and developed his business interests in Denver, Colo.

Schlesinger, Arthur M. (Meier), Jr. (1917–) historian; born in Columbus, Ohio (son of Arthur Meier Schlesinger). After graduating from Harvard (1938) and a year at Cambridge University, England, he went back to Harvard to do the research that led to *The Age of Jackson* (1945) (Pulitzer Prize, 1946). During World War II he served with the Office of War Information (1942–43) and the OSS (Office of Strategic Services) (1943–45). He returned to teach history at Harvard (1946–61) and became widely known for his multivolume history of the Franklin D. Roosevelt era. Long active in politics – he was a founder of Americans for Democratic Action and a speech writer for Adlai Stevenson's 1952 presidential campaign – he left to become special assistant to President John F. Kennedy (1961–63) and then to President Lyndon B. Johnson (1963–64). After publishing his account of the Kennedy years, *A Thousand Days* (1965) (Pulitzer Prize, 1966), he became a Schweitzer professor at the City University of New York (1967). In his later years, he became one of the best-known American historians, both through his own writings on topics of general concern and because of his willingness to comment publicly whenever the media needed an academic to provide some historical perspective.

Schlesinger, Arthur Meier (1888–1965) historian; born in Xenia, Ohio. After receiving his Ph.D. from Columbia University (1917), he taught at Ohio State (1912–19) and the University of Iowa (1919–24) before joining the Harvard faculty (1924–54); during his long career he is credited with training more first-rate historians than any other professor of his generation. His main contribution to American historiography was his emphasis on social and cultural aspects of America's history rather than the traditional political, economic, and military elements. Among his many books are *New Viewpoints in American History* (1922), *The Rise of* *the City, 1878–98* (1933), and *The American Reformer* (1950). He edited (with Dixon Ryan Fox) the *History of American Life* (13 vols. 1927–48).

Schlesinger, Frank (1871–1943) astronomer; born in New York City. An astronomer at the Yerkes Observatory (1903–05), he also directed the University of Pittsburgh's Allegheny Observatory (1905–20) and the Yale University Observatory (1920–41). This much-honored astronomer compiled a catalogue of 4,000 stellar distances (1935) and wrote monographs about photographic methods and stellar parallaxes.

Schlesinger, James R. (Rodney) (1929–) economist, cabinet member; born in New York City. He taught economics at the University of Virginia (1955–63) and then worked at the Rand Corporation (1963–69). He formulated the Bureau of the Budget's energy policy (1969) and was the chairman of the Atomic Energy Commission (1971–73). After briefly directing the Central Intelligence Agency in 1973, he became secretary of defense (1973–75); he supported the 1973 bombing raids on Cambodia. As secretary of energy in the Carter administration (1977–79), he championed atomic testing. He then turned to consulting work in the fields of international finance and relations.

Schley, Winfield Scott (1839–1909) naval officer; born in Frederick County, Md. He commanded the "Flying Squadron" at the start of the Spanish-American War. In the absence of his commanding officer, William Thomas Sampson, he defeated the Spanish fleet (1898). His actions led to a lasting controversy with Sampson. A board of inquiry later reported against Schley's actions in the battle (1901).

Schmidt, Benno (Charles) (1913–) financier; born in Abilene, Texas. He graduated from the University of Texas in 1936 and taught law there and at Harvard before serving in the army during World War II. He joined J. H. Whitney & Co. (New York City) in 1946, rising to become a managing partner. He supported many charitable and artistic causes. A son, Benno Schmidt Jr., was president of Yale University.

Schmidt, Maarten (1929–) astronomer; born in Groningen, Holland. He left the Leiden Observatory (1953–59) for the Hale Observatory and the California Institute of Technology in 1959. He also joined the staff of the Owens Valley Radio Observatory (1970–78) and directed the Hale Observatory (1978–80). His research included the cosmic distribution of quasars.

Schmidt, (Michael Jack) Mike (1949–) baseball player; born in Dayton, Ohio. During his 18-year career as a third baseman for the Philadelphia Phillies (1972–89), he hit 548 home runs and won the league Most Valuable Player Award three times (1980–81, 1986).

Schmitz, William J. (Joseph), Jr. (1937–) oceanographer; born in Houston, Texas. He joined the Woods Hole Oceanographic Institution in 1967, and became a senior scientist there in 1979. He made major contributions to low-frequency ocean circulation.

Schmoke, Kurt (Lidell) (1949–) lawyer, mayor, public official; born in Baltimore, Md. Appointed by President Jimmy Carter to the White House domestic policy staff (1977–78), he served as the U.S. Attorney for the District of Maryland (1978–82), Maryland's state attorney (1982–87) and as Baltimore's mayor (1988). He founded the Baltimore Community Development Financing Corporation in 1988.

Schmucker, Samuel Simon (1799–1873) Protestant religious leader, educator; born in Hagerstown, Md. Trained at the University of Pennsylvania and Princeton Theological Seminary, he became a leader of American Lutherism when in 1820 he cofounded, with his father, the General Synod of Lutheran Churches. In 1826 he was appointed the first professor of the Lutheran seminary, in Gettysburg, Pa. He remained there until 1864. He advocated "American Lutheranism" in contrast to a sterner creed favored by German and Scandinavian immigrants, and was a political liberal, supporting abolition and other reform movements.

Schnabel, Julien (1951–) painter, conceptual artist; born in New York City. He studied at the University of Houston (1969–73), settled in New York City, worked as a cab driver and cook, and traveled in Europe. A controversial avant-garde artist, he used a collage technique incorporating fiberglass, broken crockery, and various other objects on his mammoth canvases.

Schneerson or Schneersohn, Menachem Mendel (1902–94) rabbi; born in Nikolaev, Russia. Descended from a family of leaders in the Hasidic movement, he studied in Berlin and Paris, and came to the U.S.A. in 1941. He was named the world leader of the Chabad-Lubavitch Movement in 1950. An author on scholarly subjects, he established Lubavitch institutions all over the world and some of the Lubavitch Hasidim came to regard him as virtually the Messiah.

Schneider, Alexander (1908–93) violinist; born in Vilna, Lithuania. He had an orchestral career before fleeing the Nazis to the U.S.A. in 1933. He played chamber music, taught, and conducted widely, but is best known as second violin of the Budapest Quartet.

Schneider, David Murray (1918–) cultural anthropologist; born in New York City. He graduated from Cornell (1940) and received a Ph.D. from Harvard (1949). Field trips to Yap Island in the Pacific (1947–48) and among the Mescalero Apache in New Mexico (1955–58) yielded influential studies. He taught at Harvard and Berkeley before becoming professor of anthropology at Chicago in 1960. He is the author of *The American Kinship Universe* (1975), among other works.

Schneiderman, (Rachel) Rose (1884–1972) labor leader, social reformer; born in Savin, Poland. Emigrating to the U.S.A. in 1892, she went to work in her early teens sewing caps. In 1903 she helped organize a New York City local of the United Cloth and Cap Makers and took the lead in getting women elected to the union; in 1904 she was elected to the union's executive board, the highest position yet held by a woman in any American labor organization. In 1905 she joined the Women's Trade Union League (WTUL), the national organization that led the fight to improve conditions of working women; she would remain among the WTUL's most active leaders for 45 years, serving as president from 1926 to 1950. She took a major role in several of the landmark events of the American labor struggle; in 1909 she called for the strike of women waistmakers; that same year she took a role in organizing the garment workers; and she denounced all those who had contributed to the disastrous Triangle Waist Company fire in 1911. In addition to these and many other actions with the WTUL, she worked for women's right to vote; she helped organize the International Congress of Labor; President Franklin Roosevelt appointed her (the only woman) to the Labor Advisory Board of the National Recovery Act (1933–35); she was secretary of the

New York State Department of Labor (1937–43); and she lectured widely before diverse audiences and served on various boards, ending her long life as one of the most respected spokespersons and activists for improving the conditions of laboring people.

Schoenheimer, Rudolf (1898–1941) biochemist; born in Berlin, Gemany. He investigated peptide synthesis and the chemistry of sterols in plants and animals in Germany (1923–32). When Hitler forbade Jews to hold faculty positions in Germany, Schoenheimer accepted an invitation to join the faculty of Columbia University (1933–41). There he performed pioneering research in Harold Urey's laboratory, using Urey's newly discovered deuterium and heavy hydrogen isotopes to demonstrate that many human substances (*e.g.,* depot fats, proteins, and even bone) formerly regarded as static, actually are involved in a steady turnover. Schoenheimer's career abruptly ended when, becoming depressed over both personal problems and the rise of German anti-Semitism, he committed suicide in 1941.

Schofield, John McAllister (1831–1906) soldier; born in Gerry, N.Y. Son of a Baptist clergyman, he graduated from West Point (1853), served in Florida, taught at West Point, and was on leave of absence to teach at Washington University (St. Louis) when the Civil War began. He was assigned to duty in Missouri and held a series of administrative posts during the first years of the war. He commanded the Twenty-third Corps of the Army of the Ohio in the Atlanta campaign (1864) and at the battles of Franklin and Nashville (1864); he also saw action in the final march through the Carolinas. He served as superintendent of West Point (1876–81), and ended his long military career as commanding general of the army (1888–95).

Schomburg, Arthur A. (Alonzo) (1874–1938) scholar; born in San Juan, Puerto Rico. Of African descent, he studied in Puerto Rico and the Virgin Islands. He came to New York City in 1891 and worked as a clerk in the Bankers Trust Company. Incensed and inspired by a former teacher's comment that the Negro people had "no history," he formed the division of Negro Literature History and Prints at the Harlem 135th Street Branch Library (1925). At the request of the Urban League, the Carnegie Corporation purchased the collections in 1926; Schomburg remained as curator until his death. His collections form the basis for a comprehensive library of information on African-Americans.

Schoolcraft, Henry Rowe (1793–1864) explorer, ethnologist; born in Albany County, N.Y. At Union and Middlebury Colleges, he concentrated on geology and minerology, then set off to explore Missouri (1817–18) and the Northwest (with Lewis Cass) (1820); his particular goal was to discover the source of the Mississippi, and in 1832 he discovered and named the source, Lake Itasca, in Minnesota. His extensive relations with Native Americans – he married an Ojibwa woman – led to his appointment as Indian agent for the tribes around lake Superior (1822) and later as superintendent of Indian affairs for Michigan (1836–41). Among his many pioneer works on Indian ethnology is the *Historical and Statistical Information Respecting the . . . Indian Tribes of the United States* (6 vols. 1851–57).

Schopf, J. (James) William (1941–) paleontologist; born in Urbana, Ill. A Harvard Ph.D., he joined the faculty at the University of California: Los Angeles (1968), where he became professor of paleobiology. He was NASA's principal investigator of lunar samples (1969–74). A specialist on the origin of life, Precambrian paleobiology, paleobotany, and fossil and modern microorganisms, he announced in 1980 the discovery in Australia of 3.5 billion-year-old fossil organisms, a find that pushed back the age of life on earth by 1.2 billion years.

Schorr, Daniel (Louis) (1916–) broadcast journalist; born in New York City. He started writing for newspapers in high school; by 1941 he was New York news editor for the Netherlands News Agency, rejoining them in Holland after his army service (1943–45). Recruited by Edward R. Murrow in 1953, he was CBS News diplomatic correspondent until the late 1960s when he began covering American politics. A hard-nosed reporter, he won three Emmys for his Watergate coverage and earned the wrath of several presidents. After leaking a Congressional report on illegal Central Intelligence Agency and FBI operations, he was suspended by CBS News and resigned in 1976. He went on to do commentary for National Public Radio.

Schorsch, Ismar (1935–) scholar, educator; born in Hanover, Germany. He came to the U.S.A. in 1938. He became a rabbi at the Jewish Theological Seminary in New York, served as a chaplain in the U.S. Army, then joined the seminary as a professor of history. In 1986 he became the seminary's chancellor, and he helped found the Seminary for Judaic Studies in Jerusalem.

Schreckengost, Viktor (1906–) ceramist; born in Sebring, Ohio. After studying at the Cleveland Institute of Art, he studied ceramics and sculpture in Vienna, Austria (1929–30), then returned to Cleveland. He had been persuaded to return by R. Guy Cowan of the Cowan Pottery Studio, outside Cleveland; Cowan allowed Schreckengost to teach at the Cleveland Institute of Art while making his own pottery – both his individual pieces and those for mass production. While his bowls and dinnerware as well as architectural ceramics and sculptural works had art deco elements, his pottery often had distinctly American design elements.

Schreiver, Bernard Adolph (1910–) aviator; born in Bremen, Germany. His parents brought him to the U.S.A. as a child. A combat veteran of World War II, Schreiver headed the Air Force's intercontinental ballistic missile program during the formative period 1954 to 1959. After retiring in 1966, he became a consultant to the aerospace industry.

Schrieffer, J. (John) Robert (1931–) physicist; born in Oak Park, Ill. After completing his graduate studies in Europe (1957–58), he went to the Universities of Chicago (1958–59) and Illinois (1959–62). He moved to the University of Pennsylvania (1962–79), then joined the University of California: Santa Barbara (1980). A specialist in solid state physics, he and collaborators John Bardeen and Leon N. Cooper shared the 1972 Nobel Prize for developing the Bardeen-Cooper-Schrieffer (BCS) theory of superconductivity.

Schuchert, Charles (b. Karl) (1858–1942) paleontologist; born in Cincinnati, Ohio. Schuchert, whose formal education ended at age 12, began his scientific career illustrating state geological surveys, and ended it as professor of historical geology at Yale (1904–23), then nationally preeminent in training invertebrate paleontologists and stratigraphers. A pioneer paleogeographer, Schuchert published the classic "Paleogeography of North America" (1910) and the long-lived *Text-Book of Geology* (1915). His last great work was *Historical Geology of North America* (1935–43).

Schufeldt, Robert Wilson (1822–95) naval officer; born in Red Hook, N.Y. He was a Union naval commander in the Civil War and chief of the Bureau of Equipment and Recruiting (1875–78). He negotiated and signed a treaty with Korea (1882), the "Hermit Kingdom's" first treaty with any western nation.

Schulberg, Budd (1914–) screenwriter; born in New York City. Growing up in Hollywood as the son of early film producer Benjamin P. Schulberg, he started working at age 17 as a publicist for Paramount, becoming a scriptwriter at 19. His 1941 novel, *What Makes Sammy Run?* was an inside look at Hollywood. During World War II he made documentary films with John Ford. Having flirted with Communism in the 1930s, he named certain Hollywood colleagues as fellow travelers during the McCarthy era. He won an Academy Award for the screenplay and story for *On The Waterfront* (1954).

Schuller, Gunther (1925–) composer, French hornist, educator, jazz scholar; born in New York City. He became first chair of the Metropolitan Opera Orchestra at age 19. He left that post to pursue composition and teach at Yale (1964–66); from 1966 to 1977 he was president of the New England Conservatory; meanwhile he taught at Tanglewood in the summer, and from 1974 to 1984, he directed the music school there. A prolific composer, his mature work uses 12-tone technique often inflected by his involvement in jazz. His prose writings include the classic 1968 study *Early Jazz.*

Schultz, Adolph H. (Hans) (1891–1976) physical anthropologist; born a citizen of Switzerland, in Stuttgart, Germany. He came to the U.S.A. to teach at the Carnegie Institution (1916–25), then became a professor at Johns Hopkins (1925–51) before going to the University of Zurich (1951–62). His research in human prenatal growth indicated that racial variations and individual differences are demonstrable in fetuses. His award-winning comparative studies on monkeys and apes (1948) showed that similarities in early developmental stages decrease with age due to differing growth rates.

Schultz, Theodore W. (William) (1902–) economist; born in Arlington, S.D. He is best known for his contributions to agricultural economics, his promotion of the human capital theory, and his views on the economics of the family. First focusing his work on U.S. agriculture, he later expanded his work to include the agricultural problems of developing countries. He was part of the "Chicago school" of economic thought as a professor at the University of Chicago (1943–74). After his retirement in 1974, he served as a consultant to the United Nations and in 1980 he shared the Nobel Prize in economics with W. Arthur Lewis.

Schulz, Charles M. (Monroe) (1922–) cartoonist; born in Minneapolis, Minn. After studying art through a correspondence course and contributing free-lance cartoons to the *Saturday Evening Post,* he created in 1950 a newspaper comic strip tentatively titled *Li'l Folks.* The strip was accepted for syndication under the new title, *Peanuts,* and became the most successful cartoon strip in history. The childhood travails of Charlie Brown and his friends, Lucy, Linus, and his dog, Snoopy, have been immortalized in more than 30 animated television specials and three full-length cartoon films, and have made Schulz one of the wealthiest individuals in America.

Schuman, William (Howard) (1910–92) composer, educator; born in New York City. He studied composition under Roy Harris at Juilliard and in 1943 won the first Pulitzer Prize in music (for "Secular Cantata, No. 2"). While remaining prolific as a composer, he headed the Juilliard School of Music from 1945–62 and then New York's Lincoln Center until 1969. His works, for a variety of media and marked by an eclectic technique often with a strong American flavor, include ten symphonies, a number of choral works, and the short opera *The Mighty Casey* (1953); this last-named was turned into a cantata in 1976, retitled *Casey at the Bat,* and was considerably expanded for a production in 1991.

Schumann-Heink, Ernestine (b. Rossler) (1861–1936) contralto; born near Prague, Bohemia. Having come to fame in Europe, especially for her Wagnerian roles (she appeared at Bayreuth between 1896 and 1906), she made her American debut in Chicago in 1898; she would sing with the Metropolitan Opera off and on until 1932. Regarded as the greatest contralto of her time, she concertized with German lieder but would also perform light opera and sing on the radio when it became popular. An American citizen from 1905, she remained in the U.S.A. during World War I and demonstrated her patriotism while sons of her different marriages fought on opposite sides. (Her hyphenated last name was composed of the names of two of her three husbands.) She made one movie, *Here's to Romance* (1935), but died before she could continue with her plans for a film career.

Schumpeter, Joseph Alois (1883–1950) economist; born in Triesch, Austro-Hungary. One of the greatest 20th-century economists, he was born and educated in Austria and served briefly there as the Minister of Finance. He emigrated to the U.S.A. in 1932, accepting a professorship at Harvard University. His early theorizing replaced Marx's view of greed-driven capitalism with dynamic, innovative entrepreneurship, clearly differentiating the capitalist from the entrepreneur. He published several books, although *Capitalism, Socialism, and Democracy* (1942) stands out as his masterpiece. In it, he rejects the Marxist diagnosis of the imminent breakdown of capitalism and at the same time predicts the almost inevitable emergence of socialism due to a betrayal of capitalist values by intellectuals of the western world. His final book, *History of Economic Analysis* (posthumously published in 1954), is considered a brilliant exposition of the history of economic thought.

Schurman, Jacob (Gould) (1854–1942) educator, philosopher, diplomat; born in Freetown, Prince Edward Island, Canada. He studied in Great Britain and Germany before he came to teach philosophy at Cornell University (1886), where he promoted an idealistic approach that applied philosophy to all of human experience. In 1892 he began the *Philosophical Review,* the first scholarly journal of philosophy in the U.S.A. As president of Cornell (1892–1920), he turned Cornell from a small private college into a major university with public as well as private segments. He served as chairman of a U.S. commission that studied conditions in the newly acquired Philippines (1899) and he personally advocated independence. Later he served as ambassador to Greece and Montenegro (1912–13), China (1921–25), and Germany (1925–30).

Schurz, Carl (1829–1906) politician, journalist; born near Cologne, Germany. Fleeing Germany because of revolutionary sympathies, he arrived in the U.S.A. in 1852. An abolitionist and liberal Republican, he was a Civil War general; later, as U.S. senator (1869–75), he attacked corruption in the Grant administration. He was U.S. interior secretary under President Rutherford B. Hayes. A Washington correspondent of the *New York Tribune* in the late 1860s, he also edited several papers, including the *New York Evening Post* (1881–83).

Schuster, Max (Lincoln) (1887–1970) publisher; born in Kalusz, Austria. In 1924, with his friend Richard Simon, he founded Simon and Schuster publishers, with $2,000 in joint capital. One of his contributions to the firm's early success was commissioning Will Durant to write his trend-setting popularization, *The Story of Philosophy* (1926).

Schutz, Alfred (1899–1959) sociologist; born in Vienna, Austria. He emigrated to the U.S.A. in 1939. From 1943 until his death he was on the faculty of the New School for Social Research. He wrote on social science methodology, phenomenology, and the philosophy of Edmund Husserl, William James, and others. His *Collected Papers* (3 vols. 1962–66) and other English translations of his works were published posthumously.

Schuyler, Montgomery (1843–1914) journalist, architectural critic; born in Ithaca, N.Y. He helped found the *Architectural Record* (1891). An authoritative architectural journalist writing for the New York *World* and *New York Times* (1883–1907), he promoted modernism as embodied in skyscrapers.

Schuyler, Peter (1657–1724) soldier, colonial official; born in Beverwyck (present-day Albany), New York. A prosperous merchant, he became the first mayor of Albany in 1686, and held several posts in the colonial government. He organized the defense of the frontier against French incursions. From 1710 to 1711, he took five Iroquois chiefs to London to visit Queen Anne.

Schuyler, Philip John (1733–1804) soldier, landowner, U.S. senator; born in Albany, N.Y. A wealthy New York landowner, he was appointed major general in 1775 and he organized the campaign against British Canada. He successfully used delaying tactics which held up Burgoyne's invasion (1777) until vital Continental reinforcements arrived. Following accusations of negligence, he demanded and received a court-martial (1778) where he was acquitted with honors regarding the loss of Fort Ticonderoga in 1777. He later served as a United States senator (1789–91, 1797–98).

Schwab, Charles M. (Michael) (1862–1939) industrialist; born in Williamsburg, Pa. He began in Andrew Carnegie's Braddock steelworks as an engineer's helper and rose to chief engineer and assistant manager by age 19. Combining an ability to utilize the new technology and methods with an ability to deal with people, he rose in Carnegie's organization until he became president of Carnegie Steel Company (1897). In this post he helped Carnegie sell the properties to J. P. Morgan for the formation of U.S. Steel (1901), of which he became the first president. He resigned in 1903 and joined Bethlehem Steel Corporation, building it into a major steel producer by his progressive management policies. He built submarines for Allied clients in World War I and was drafted by President Wilson to direct the Emergency Fleet Corporation (1918). From 1927–32 he presided over the American Iron and Steel Institute. With a fortune once estimated at $200 million, he died insolvent from a combination of lavish living and bad business investments.

Schwab, Charles R. (1937–) stockbroker; born in Woodland, Calif. A lawyer's son, he sold chickens and eggs door-to-door as a child, graduated from the Stanford School of Business (1959), and worked as a mutual funds manager before establishing his own brokerage house in San Francisco in 1971. He built it into one of the nation's leading brokerages by offering discount fees and other inducements to small investors. He is the author of *How to Be Your Own Stockbroker* (1984).

Schwartz, Arthur (1900–84) composer; born in New York City. While practicing law in the mid-1920s, he began selling songs to vaudeville and Broadway revues. In the 1930s, 1940s, and 1950s he collaborated for Broadway, mainly with lyricist Howard Dietz, and worked as a Hollywood producer and composer with such lyricists as Dorothy Fields and Ira Gershwin on musicals, revues, films, and television. One of his best-known melodies is that for "You and the Night and the Music," and with Dietz he wrote the show-business standard, "That's Entertainment" (1953). From 1958 to 1983 he was director of ASCAP (American Society of Composers, Authors and Publishers).

Schwartz, Benjamin I. (Isadore) (1916–) historian; born in Boston, Mass. A Harvard Ph.D., he taught ancient and modern Chinese history there (1950–74) before becoming Eastman Professor at Oxford University, England (1974). His books include *Communism in China* (1968) and *The World of Thought in Ancient China* (1985).

Schwartz, Delmore (1913–66) poet, writer; born in New York City. He studied at the University of Wisconsin (1931), New York University (1933–35), and Harvard (1935–37). He taught at many institutions, notably Harvard (1941–47), and was the editor of the *Partisan Review* (1941–55), but he spent his final years as an increasingly erratic and reclusive bohemian and he died of a heart attack while living in a Times Square hotel. He is known for his ironic poetry, such as *In Dreams Begin Responsibilities* (1938).

Schwartz, Louis B. (1913–) legal educator, consultant; born in Philadelphia. A pioneer in a generation of legal code reformers, he spent his early career (1935–46) working for the federal Securities and Exchange Commission and Justice Department. He was aide to U.S. Ambassador Chester Bowles in India as an administrator of the Agency for International Development program (1964). He was director of the National Commission on Reform of Federal Criminal Laws (1967–71), and taught at the University of Pennsylvania Law School (1964–83). He also taught law at the University of California: Hastings (1938) and gained a major reputation for championing the exclusionary rule in defense of individual rights and liberties. He was author of *Free Enterprise and Economic Organization* (1983–85, in two volumes) and many other books and papers.

Schwartz, Maurice (1890–1960) stage actor; born in Sedikor, Russia. An intense and impressive figure in the Yiddish theater, he came to this country in 1901. He founded and for many years headed the Yiddish Art Theatre in New York.

Schwartz, Melvin (1932–) physicist; born in New York City. After completing all his university work at Columbia, including his Ph.D. (1958), he worked at Brookhaven National Laboratory (1956–58), taught at Columbia (1958–66), then moved to Stanford as a physics professor (1966–83). Meanwhile, in 1970 he had founded a company, Digital Pathways, Inc., to produce systems that secure computers from outside tamperers, and in 1983 he left academic work to devote himself to this company. Schwartz shared the 1988 Nobel Prize in physics with Leon Lederman and Jack Steinberger for work they had collaborated on while at Columbia (1960–63) – specifically, for an experiment that used an accelerator-created beam of neutrinos to examine the effect of weak nuclear forces at high energies; this in turn led to their discovery that there are two types of neutrinos. In 1991 Schwartz returned to the Brookhaven National Laboratory to take up his work with high energy and nuclear physics.

Schwartzkopf, (H.) Norman (1934–) soldier; born in Trenton, N.J. A 1956 West Point graduate, he served as deputy commander of U.S. forces in the Grenada invasion (1983) and held a series of senior staff and field commands in the United States and Europe. Promoted to full general in 1988, he led the Allied forces in the brief desert war against Iraq in January–February 1991. An overnight national hero, he retired later in 1991.

Schwarz, Harvey Fisher (1905–88) electrical engineer; born in Edwardsville, Ill. At General Electric, he developed the Radiola 44, an advanced-design radio receiver. In 1932 he moved to England where he designed radios and phonographs. During World War II he co-invented the Decca radio-navigation system, first used during the invasion of Normandy in 1944.

Schwarzschild, Martin (1912–) astronomer; born in Potsdam, Germany. He came to Harvard College Observatory as a research fellow in 1937. He served in the U.S. Army in World War II and won the Legion of Merit and a Bronze Star. At Princeton University beginning in 1947, he combined advances in nuclear physics with "balloon astronomy" to develop theories on stellar evolution.

Schwatka, Frederick (1849–92) explorer; born in Galena, Ill. After graduating from West Point (1871) he served as a cavalry lieutenant on the frontier, also studying law and medicine; he then qualified as a lawyer (1875) and a doctor (1876). He led an expedition (1878–80) to uncover the wreckage of the Franklin expedition; he established that all had perished and no records were left behind. After resigning from the army (1885) he explored the Yukon River and opened new territory in Alaska. He lectured widely and wrote about his adventures in such books as *In the Land of Cave and Cliff Dweller* (1893) about the Tarahumari Indians of Chihuahua, Mexico.

Schwinger, Julian S. (Seymour) (1918–94) physicist; born in New York City. He taught and performed research at several American institutions before becoming a professor at Harvard (1945–75). His renormalization technique, a mathematical revision of quantum electrodynamics, made him one of three winners of the 1965 Nobel Prize in physics. He joined the University of California: Los Angeles (1975), and continued to make advances in electromagnetic theory and theoretical particle physics.

Scorsese, Martin (1942–) film director; born in Flushing, N.Y. Small and sickly as a child, he grew up in New York City's Little Italy and entered a Catholic seminary in his early teens; he left after a year to go on to New York University's film school (where he stayed as an instructor until 1970). As a student he made several prize-winning short films; his feature directorial debut was *Who's That Knocking at My Door?* (1968). He made some television documenta-

ries and another feature film but gained his first broad public with *Mean Streets* (1973). From then, many of his films drew upon his Italian-American heritage and often deal with masculine aggression, as in *Taxi Driver* (1976), *Raging Bull* (1979), and *Cape Fear* (1991). Something of a loner and not really a part of the Hollywood crowd, he showed an ability to balance his critically acclaimed films, which seem to question traditional American values, with more commercially viable movies.

Scott, Charlotte Angas (1858–1931) mathematician; born in Lincoln, England. Emigrating to America to head the mathematics department at Bryn Mawr College (1885), she was editor of the American edition of *Arithmetic for Schools,* author of *An Introductory Account of Certain Modern Ideas and Methods in Plane Analytical Geometry* (1894), and other texts.

Scott, Dred (c. 1795–1858) slave, plaintiff; born in Southampton County, Va. After 1827 he lived mostly in St. Louis, being passed among various owners. In a historic test case he sued for his freedom based on a five-year residence in free territories, but the Supreme Court ruled against him (1857). Freed later that year, he became a hotel porter and a minor celebrity in St. Louis.

Scott, George C. (Campbell) (1927–) stage/movie actor; born in Wise, Va. He grew up in Detroit, then served in the U.S. Marine Corps (1945–49). After starting at the School of Journalism at the University of Missouri, he changed to English and drama and began to act in student shows (1949–53). He spent the next four years holding odd jobs as he worked in stock companies in Toledo, Ohio, Washington, D.C., and Ontario, Canada. His New York stage debut in the 1957 Shakespeare Festival brought him such praise that he was soon taking leading roles in both stage plays and movies. In 1963–64 he starred in an admired TV series, *East Side, West Side*. His most celebrated movie role was in *Patton* (1970) for which he received the Oscar as best actor, but he refused to accept it after denouncing the Academy Awards as a "meat parade." In 1971 he also refused the Emmy Award as best actor in a TV production of Arthur Miller's *The Price*. Intense as both an actor and in person, he was particularly known for his portrayal of "angry men," but he has also done both comic and warm-hearted characters. He directed two movies, *Rage* (1972) and *The Savage is Loose* (1974), and occasionally returned to the theater to take on stage roles.

Scott, James Brown (1866–1943) international lawyer, educator; born in Kincardine, Ontario, Canada. He came to the U.S.A. in 1876 and served in the Spanish-American War. After a series of posts at law schools, he organized and was first dean of Los Angeles Law School (1896–99), dean at the law college of the University of Illinois (1899–1903), and professor of law at Columbia University (1903–06). He became the chief legal officer of the State Department (1906–11). He then served as secretary of the Carnegie Endowment for International Peace (1911–40); during those years he taught occasionally at law schools in the capital's region. He was a strong advocate for an international court of justice to settle disputes.

Scott, John Paul (1909–) animal behaviorist; born in Kansas City, Mo. He was a graduate assistant at the University of Chicago (1932–35), moved to Wabash College (1935–45), was a researcher and administrator at Jackson

Memorial Laboratory, Maine (1945–65), then became a professor of psychology at Bowling Green State University (Ohio) (1965–80). An authority on the physiology of aggression, he applied his early interest in behavioral genetics of guinea pigs and fruit flies to the biology, social behavior, and genetics of dogs, mice, and other mammals.

Scott, Norman (1889–1942) naval officer; born in Indianapolis, Ind. Entering the navy in 1907 and graduating from Annapolis in 1911, he served on destroyers in World War I. He served on the U.S. naval commission to Brazil from 1937 to 1939 and was a rear admiral by 1939. Leading a task force against the Japanese in the Solomon Islands campaign, he went down with his ship, the USS *Atlanta*.

Scott, Thomas A. (Alexander) (1823–81) railroad executive; born at Fort Loudon, Pa. He began working in the state toll collector's office at age 17 and continued until 1850 when he became station agent for the Pennsylvania Railroad at Duncansville. As the railroad grew he was transferred and promoted, becoming first vice-president in 1859. (It was Scott who first hired young Andrew Carnegie in 1853 and helped him advance his career.) During the Civil War he was made assistant secretary of war in charge of government railways, troops, and munitions transportation. In 1870, the Pennsylvania Company was organized with Scott as president to direct rail growth west of Pittsburgh. In 1871 he was elected president of the foundering Union Pacific Railroad, a job he passed to Jay Gould when he became president of the Pennsylvania Railroad Company (1874–80). He was also president of the Texas & Pacific Railway Company (1872–80).

Scott, Walter Edward ("Death Valley Scotty") (1872–1954) mining prospector; born in (?) Cynthiana, Ky. His birthplace and early life were mysterious. He rode for Buffalo Bill's Wild West Show and convinced many people that he had discovered a rich gold mine in Death Valley. Supported and financed by the millionaire Albert M. Johnson, he built Scotty's Castle, which became a tourist attraction in Death Valley.

Scott, Winfield (1786–1866) soldier; born near Petersburg, Va. A Virginia patrician, he studied law but then joined the U.S. Army. In the War of 1812, he saw considerable action on the Canadian border, was briefly captured, and after being severely wounded in the battle of Lundy's Lane (near Niagara Falls), he emerged from the war as a national hero. In the peacetime army, he wrote about military tactics and rose in rank; he won a new reputation as a peacemaker for helping to ease the nullification crisis in 1832 and for settling border disputes with Canada; in 1839 he prevented what could have been a bloody conflict by convincing 16,000 Cherokee to accept resettlement beyond the Mississippi. Appointed general in chief of the army in 1841, he was in command of U.S. forces as they went to war against Mexico in 1846; in March 1847 he himself took to the field and captured Vera Cruz; he launched an offensive toward the Mexican capital; after a series of dramatic victories, he led American forces into Mexico City in September 1847. Once more a national hero – affectionately known as "Old Fuss and Feathers" for his weakness for military uniforms and pomp – he ran unsuccessfully for president as a Whig in 1852. When the Civil War broke out, he was still general in chief of the U.S. Army, and although a Virginian, he stayed with the Federal army; everyone agreed that he was too old

and infirm to direct the Union's war, but he formulated what became known as "the anaconda plan" – because it called for a snake-like encirclement and strangulation of the Confederacy – and then retired in October 1861. He wrote his memoirs and traveled to Europe (1864); at his death he was regarded as one of the great men of America's history.

Scott, W. (William) Richard (1932–) sociologist; born in Parsons, Kans. He taught at Stanford University (1960), where he directed the Center for Organizations Research (1988). His many books on organizations include *Organizations: Rational, Natural and Open Systems* (1981, revised 1987) and *Organizational Environments: Ritual and Rationality* (coauthored, 1983).

Scoville, Joseph Alfred (1815–64) journalist, novelist; born in Woodbury, Conn. He was briefly John C. Calhoun's private secretary. After Calhoun's death, he was editor of the *New York Picayune* (1850–52) and the *Pick* (1852–55). His writings provoked Northern outrage during the Civil War but he is now better known for his informal history, *The Old Merchants of New York City* (5 vols. 1863–66), which he published with the pen name, Walter Barrett.

Scribner, Charles (1854–1930) publisher; born in New York City. In 1879 he succeeded his brother, John Blair Scribner, as head of the firm that became Charles Scribner's Sons, acting as president through 1928 and then chairman of the board. Aided by editors such as Maxwell Perkins, Scribner's grew in distinction, publishing works by Edith Wharton, George Santayana, Ernest Hemingway, Theodore Roosevelt, and others.

Scripps, E. W. (Edward Wyllis) (1854–1926) journalist; born near Rushville, Ill. He founded the *Cleveland Penny Press* in 1878, eventually adding some 30 other mass-audience papers in the first major U.S. newspaper chain. In 1907 he founded the United Press news service (later United Press International). A millionaire philanthropist, he left his empire to his son Robert Paine Scripps.

Scudder, Janet (Netta Deweze Frazee) (1869–1940) sculptor; born in Terre Haute, Ind. She studied at the Cincinnati Academy of Art and worked as a furniture carver. After studying with Frederick MacMonnies in Paris (c. 1893–96), she lived most of her life there. She is known for her ornamental garden sculptures, such as *Frog Fountain* (1901–04).

Scudder, (Julia) Vida (Dutton) (1861–1954) social reformer; born in Madura, India. After her missionary father died, she spent her youth in Europe. Educated at Smith College and Oxford University, and committed to Christian socialism and Marxism, she became a renowned social activist. She was a founder of the Women's Trade Union League (1903). She founded Dennison House, a settlement house in Boston (1892), taught at Wellesley College (1887–1928), organized for labor, published 16 books, and wrote her autobiography (1937).

Scull, Robert C. (1917–86) businessman, art collector; born in New York City. His family name was originally "Sokolnikoff," but his father's Russian name was shortened by emigration authorities. Robert attended public schools and attended night school at the Art Students League and the Pratt Institute. He became a free-lance illustrator and then an industrial designer. After his marriage to Ethel Redner, his father-in-law left him a share of a taxi business that he used to establish the Super Operating Corporation, a taxi company whose drivers were called "Scull's Angels." His ability to gain publicity was evident even then, as seen in his well-publicized hiring of Amy Vanderbilt to teach his drivers courtesy. He and his wife purchased many works by artists in the pop art tradition. They sold part of their collection in 1965 and established the Robert and Ethel Scull Foundation in order to subsidize and encourage young unknown artists. They held a second auction in 1973, and by that time they were an extravagant personification of the pop art scene. Robert divorced Ethel Scull (1975), remarried, and moved to a farm in Connecticut. In 1978 he established a new foundation in his name and continued to buy contemporary art.

Scully, Vincent (Joseph, Jr.) (1920–) architectural historian; born in New Haven, Conn. He made major contributions to the history of modern American architecture with his studies of Louis Sullivan's humanism and Frank Lloyd Wright's symbolism and was an early and energetic booster of Robert Venturi's work. His 15 books include *Modern Architecture: The Architecture of Democracy* (1961), *American Architecture and Urbanism* (1969), and an iconographical study of Greek architecture, *The Earth, the Temple, and the Gods . . .* (1962). Scully was a preeminent teacher of architectural history at Yale (1947–91).

Seaborg, Glenn T. (Theodore) (1912–) chemist; born in Ishpeming, Mich. After working as an apricot picker, farmworker, lab assistant, and apprentice linotype operator to pay for tuition, he received his B.A. in chemistry at the University of California: Los Angeles (1934), and his Ph.D. (1937). His early interest was in discovering radioactive isotopes, many of which are used in medical therapy as well as in basic scientific research. In 1939 he turned his attention to the transuranium elements (those with nuclei heavier than that of uranium); working with the cyclotron and his colleagues at the University of California: Berkeley, he eventually produced six such artificial elements. During World War II he worked on the Manhattan Project to develop techniques for the large-scale production of plutonium; the plutonium he produced at a laboratory at the University of Chicago went into the atomic bombs that destroyed Hiroshima and Nagasaki in 1945. In 1946 he returned to his research at Berkeley. He served as chancellor of the University of California (1958–61) and then as chairman of the Atomic Energy Commission (1961–71). He shared the Nobel Prize in chemistry with Edwin McMillan (1951) for his work on transuranium elements.

Seabury, Samuel (1873–1958) lawyer, anticorruption investigator; born in New York City. Elected the youngest judge in New York (1902), he was named to the state supreme court (1907–13) and to the court of appeals (1914–16). Investigating magistrates' courts in New York City (1930–31), he exposed widespread corruption, forcing the resignation of Mayor James J. Walker. Seabury's name became virtually synonymous with exposing municipal corruption and although he returned to private practice in 1932, he played a major role in the reform administration of Mayor Fiorello La Guardia.

Seager, Richard B. (Berry) (1882–1925) archaeologist; born in Lansing, Mich. Son of a propserous lawyer (and brother of a well-known economist, Henry Rogers Seager, 1870–1930) he was forced by a heart condition to leave Harvard. But he recuperated in Germany and then pursued his own studies of classics and archaeology; he would spend most of the rest of his life in Europe. In 1903, in Greece, he met Edith Boyd (Hawes), a young American who had recently begun to excavate Minoan remains on Crete. Seager joined her and soon was in charge of his own site, Vasilike. He continued to excavate for many years on Crete and wrote several important scholarly monographs, particularly on his finds at Pachyammos, Mochlos, and Pseira. He was also a collector of sealstones and other small artifacts, which he donated to various museums. Having originally gone to Egypt to see the discoveries from the tomb of Tutankhamon, he was taken ill on ship returning to Crete and died at sea.

Seale, Bobby (1936–) political activist, educator; born in Dallas, Texas. One of the original Black Panthers (1966), he gained notoriety for his vociferous demonstrations during and after the 1968 Chicago convention. He was jailed in connection with those riots and was one of 13 Panthers held in connection with the alleged execution of suspected Panther informer Alex Rackley. Later adopting a moderate political approach, he ran unsuccessfully for mayor of Oakland, Calif. (1973), resigned as Black Panther chairman (1974), wrote his autobiography, *A Lonely Rage,* and dropped out of the black power movement. An associate in the African-American history department at Temple University (1980s), he wrote a cookbook called *Barbeque with Bobby* (1987) with proceeds going to grassroots political groups.

Seaman, Elizabeth (Nellie Bly, pen name) (b. Cochrane) (c. 1865–1922) journalist; born in Cochrane Mills, Pa. As a reporter for the New York World she won renown for such stories as her expose of conditions in an insane asylum on New York City's Blackwell's Island, where she posed as an inmate. In 1889–90 she made a round-the-world trip in 72 days, bettering the 80-day record of Jules Verne's fictional Phineas Fogg. A pioneering woman journalist, she took her pen name from a Stephen Foster song about a social reformer.

Searle, John R. (Rogers) (1932–) philosopher, linguist; born in Denver, Colo. Educated at the University of Wisconsin (1949–52) and Oxford (B.A. with first class honors, 1955; M.A. and D.Phil. 1959), he taught first at Oxford (1956–59) and then joined the philosophy faculty at the University of California: Berkeley (1959). His many publications include *The Campus War* (1971), a study of the Berkeley student riots, and *Minds, Brains, and Science* (1985), the Reith lectures for 1984. In such works as *Speech Acts* (1969) and *Expression and Meaning* (1979) he expounded a distinctive approach to the study of language and its relation to the mind, one that has greatly influenced linguists and cognitive scientists as well as philosophers. He is perhaps best known for his thesis that computers do not and can not possess genuine artificial intelligence.

Searles, Harold F. (Frederic) (1918–) psychiatrist; born in Hancock, N.Y. After taking his B.A. at Cornell (1940) and his M.D. at Harvard (1943), he interned at the New York Hospital and then served in the United States Army Medical Corps (1945–47). He worked as a psychiatrist for the Veterans Administration Mental Hygiene Clinic in Washington, D.C. (1947–49), and then joined the staff of the Chestnut Lodge Sanitarium (now Hospital) in Rockville, Md. (1949–64). After studying at the Washington Psychoanalytic Institute (1947–53), he began his long affiliation with the faculty of that institute (1955). In addition to other teaching and staff positions in psychiatry and psychotherapy in the Washington, D.C., area and at Columbia University's medical school (1964–73), his other major affiliation was with Georgetown University's medical school (1964–80). He also maintained a private practice of psychoanalysis and psychotherapy for three decades. He published some 65 articles and several books, including *My Work with Borderline Patients* (1986), focusing particularly on psychosis, schizophrenia, and the dynamics of the psychoanalytical process between therapists and patients. He received numerous honors including the Frieda Fromm-Reichmann Award for Research on Schizophrenia (1965).

Sears, (Eleonora Randolph) Eleo (1881–1968) sportswoman; born in Boston, Mass. Born into a patrician family, she was a dynamic tennis player as a young woman and went on to win the national women's doubles championship four times (1911, 1915–17) and the national mixed doubles championship once (1916). She took up squash in 1918, at a time when few women played, and in 1928 won the first women's national championship. She also excelled in equestrian competition, long-distance walking, golf, and aquatic sports. Totally independent in all she did, she pioneered in the movement for women to wear appropriate clothing when participating in sports. She also used her personal fortune to support groups such as the U.S. equestrian team, ice skaters, and the Boston police department's mounted troop.

Sears, Minnie Earl (1873–1933) cataloguer, bibliographer; born in Lafayette, Ind. She had a long career as a cataloguer at Bryn Mawr College (1903–07), the University of Minnesota (1909–14), and the New York Public Library (1914–20), and then in 1923 she joined the H. W. Wilson Company and published her *List of Subject Headings for Small Libraries*. In recognition of her contribution, the sixth edition was retitled the *Sears List of Subject Headings,* and it remains in widespread use. She also edited the American Library Association's *Standard Catalog for Public Libraries* (1927–33) and the second edition of the *Standard Catalog for High School Libraries* (1932). From 1927 to 1931 she taught at the Columbia University School of Library Service.

Sears, (Richard Dudley) Dick (1861–1943) tennis player; born in Boston, Mass. He won the lawn tennis singles championship seven consecutive times (1881–87). He was the first ever champion in both lawn and court tennis, winning the U.S. court title in 1892.

Sears, Richard W. (Warren) (1863–1914) merchant; born in Stewartville, Minn. At age 17 he supported his widowed mother and sisters by working for the Minneapolis and St. Louis railway in Minneapolis. In 1886 while a station agent in Redwood, Minn., he acquired a shipment of watches that had been refused, and he sold them through the mail at considerable profit; he then bought more watches and advertised in the newspaper establishing the mail-order R. W. Sears Watch Company. A success, this "Barnum of merchandising" advertised nationally, moved to Chicago, and hired watch repairman Alvah C. Roebuck. In 1889 he sold the business, retired to Iowa as a country banker, but grew bored, and returned to Minneapolis where he established the A. C. Roebuck mail-order business, selling watches and jewelry. Returning to Chicago in 1893 as Sears, Roebuck & Company, the business grew from a 25-item catalogue to a 1,000-page book in just a few years. As president, Sears directed all the advertising and copy writing

and owed much of his success to buying large amounts of advertising space in newspapers each month. He retired in 1909 to his farm north of Chicago.

Seattle (b. Sealth) (?1788–1866) Suquamish/Duwamish chief; born near present-day Seattle, Wash. An active warrior as a youth, he later converted to Christianity and advocated peace with the whites. For this, the city of Seattle was named in his honor in 1852.

Seaver, (George Thomas) Tom (1944–   ) baseball pitcher; born in Fresno, Calif. During his 20-year career (1967–86), primarily with the New York Mets and Cincinnati Reds, the right-hander won 311 games and the Cy Young Award three times (1969, 1973, 1975). Nicknamed, "Tom Terrific," he was elected to baseball's Hall of Fame in 1992.

Seckler-Hudson, Catheryn (1902–63) political scientist, educator; born in Modale, Iowa. She taught political science and public administration at American University (1933–63), where she served as dean of the school of government (1957–63) and founded the Washington semester program. Her books include *Our Constitution and Government* (1940), which achieved wide international distribution.

Sedgwick, Catherine Maria (1789–1867) writer; born in Stockbridge, Mass. (daughter of Theodore Sedgwick, 1746–1813). She was educated locally and at boarding schools in Boston and Albany. After the death of her mother (1807), she lived with her brother in Albany and with her sister in New York City. After her father's death (1813), she returned to Stockbridge, but continued her visits to her siblings. She published many novels and stories in the romantic-didactic vein then popular and is credited with writing the first American domestic novel, *A New England Tale* (1822). She also wrote several "moral" guidance books. The most popular American female author of her time, she was also held in high regard by such contemporaries as Nathaniel Hawthorne.

Sedgwick, John (1813–64) soldier; born in Cornwall, Conn. A West Point graduate (1837), he saw considerable action in the Seminole War, the Mexican War, and in the West. A brigade, division, and finally corps commander in the Army of the Potomac, he fought on the Virginia Peninsula and at Antietam, Fredericksburg, Chancellorsville, and Gettysburg. A sharpshooter killed him at Spotsylvania on May 9, 1864. Highly popular with the troops – he was known as "Uncle John" – West Point cadets in danger of failing traditionally twirl the rowels of the spurs on his statue there to guarantee passing their exams.

Sedgwick, Theodore (1811–59) legal scholar; born in Albany, N.Y. He practiced law for several years (1934–50) and served as U.S. district attorney for the Southern District of New York (1858–59). He wrote extensively for the popular press as well as *Thoughts on the Annexation of Texas* (1844) and *Statutory and Constitutional Law* (1857).

Seeger, Alan (1888–1916) poet; born in New York City. He graduated from Harvard (1910), and settled in Paris, France (1912). He joined the Foreign Legion during World War I, and was killed during the Battle of the Somme (1916). He is best known for his poem, "I Have a Rendezvous with Death," first published in *The North American Review* (1916).

Seeger, Charles (Louis, Jr.) (1886–1979) ethnomusicologist, composer, teacher; born in Mexico City, Mexico. A Harvard graduate (1908), he taught at schools including the Institute of Musical Art in New York (1921–33), the New School for Social Research (1931–35), and the University of California: Los Angeles (1957–61), and was an administrator of the Works Projects Administration Music Project (1938–40). His studies in folk music and his field collecting helped inspire a generation of folk music performers and scholars, among them his children Pete, Peggy, and Mike. He was married to composer Ruth Crawford.

Seeger, (R. Peter) Pete (1919–) folksinger, songwriter; born in New York City. As a son of Charles Seeger, the musicologist, and stepson of Ruth Crawford-Seeger, the composer, he was raised in a home devoted to American folk music. He studied sociology at Harvard (1936–38) but left to pursue his interest in singing and painting. Influenced by Leadbelly and Woody Guthrie, he formed (with Guthrie) the Almanac Singers in 1941, one of the first such groups to give voice to social issues. In 1949 he joined the Weavers, the first commercially successful folk music group; although it had formally separated by about 1960, it occasionally regrouped for special concerts. Seeger performed for the civil rights and antiwar movements of the 1950s and 1960s (and at one point fell afoul of the U.S. government for his antiwar actions). His best-known original is "Where Have All the Flowers Gone?" (1961). By the 1980s he was lending his voice and reputation to the environmental movement. In addition to performing he wrote scholarly articles on folk music.

Segal, George (1924–) sculptor; born in New York City. After moving with his family to New Jersey (1940), he studied at New York University (B.A. 1950) and Rutgers (M.A. 1963). He specialized in sculptural environments, creating lifelike scenes in isolated situations, such as "Man at a Table" (1961). His unpainted white plaster figures are cast from living people.

Segar, Elzie (Crisler) (1894–1938) cartoonist; born in Chester, Ill. In 1919 he created the newspaper comic strip, *Thimble Theatre*, which initially featured Olive Oyl and her brother Castor, but later starred the hamburger-craving Wimpy, and on January 17, 1929, Popeye the Sailor. Popeye's spinach-eating heroics have been immortalized in a series of Max Fleischer animated cartoons and a 1980 full-length film starring Robin Williams.

Segrè, Emilio (Gino) (1905–89) physicist; born in Tivoli, Italy. He discovered the slow neutron with Enrico Fermi at the University of Rome (1930–35), before moving to the University of Palermo (1935–38). A Jewish anti-Fascist, he left Mussolini's regime for the University of California: Berkeley (1938–72). There his work on synthesizing artificial atoms resulted in his isolation of fissionable plutonium (with Glenn Seaborg, 1940). After serving on the Manhattan Project (1943–46), Segrè discovered the antiproton (with Owen Chamberlain, 1955), for which the two shared the 1959 Nobel Prize in physics. Segrè continued his research in particle physics and worked to promote nuclear weapons bans.

Seidel, George (Lukas Emil) (1864–1947) mayor; born in Ashland, Pa. At age 13 he began working as a woodworker; he became interested in trade unions, and while advancing his woodworking skill in Germany (1886–92), he became a fairly radical Socialist. On returning to Milwaukee, he joined a branch of the Social Democracy of America and served two terms on the city council. Stressing municipal reform, he was elected mayor of Milwaukee in 1910 on a Socialist ticket, the

first Socialist mayor of a major U.S. city. He lost reelection in 1912 partly due to fears of the "red menace." He was also an unsuccessful vice-presidential candidate with Eugene Debs in 1912. Although he held various municipal offices in Milwaukee off and on until 1936, he failed in his attempts to be governor and U.S. senator.

Seidensticker, Edward George (1921–) scholar, translator, educator; born in Castle Rock, Colo. He earned an M.A. at Columbia University and taught Japanese at the University of Michigan (1966–77) and Columbia University (1977–85). He is best known for his masterly translation of the famous 11th-century Japanese novel, *The Tale of Genji* (1976).

Seidl, Anton (1850–98) conductor; born in Budapest, Hungary. A protégé of Wagner, he conducted opera widely before coming to New York's Metropolitan Opera in 1885 to establish the Wagnerian repertoire. He also conducted the New York Philharmonic from 1891.

Seitz, Don Carlos (1862–1935) journalist; born in Portage, Ohio. Capable business manager of the *New York World* from 1898 to 1923, he also wrote biographies of Joseph Pulitzer and Horace Greeley.

Seixas, Gershom Mendes (1746–1816) rabbi; born in New York City. The son of Isaac Mendes Seixas, who emigrated to America from Portugal in 1730, Gershom Seixas was minister of Congregation Shearith Israel in New York for almost 50 years (1768–1816). When British forces took over the city, he removed the synagogue's religious objects from the city. In 1780 he helped found the first synagogue in Philadelphia. He was one of 13 ministers at George Washington's first inauguration. He was a trustee of Columbia College (1787–1815). He urged Jews to enter the mainstream of American society and to this end was the first rabbi to preach sermons in English in an American synagogue.

Selby, Hubert, Jr. (1928–) writer; born in New York City. He studied for one year at Peter Stuyvesant High School, and joined the merchant marine (1944–46). He became an insurance analyst (1950–64), before becoming a writer of short stories and novels. Based in Los Angeles, he is best known for his first collection of short stories, *Last Exit to Brooklyn* (1964). Due to the book's graphic sexual content, it was banned in Italy and an obscenity trial was held in England, but eventually Selby came to be praised as a social critic and prose stylist.

Sellars, Peter (1958–) stage director; born in Pittsburgh, Pa. Commencing as a precocious and controversial director while a Harvard undergraduate, he kept this reputation alive with a variety of iconoclastic theatrical and operatic productions throughout the U.S.A. He is best known for setting productions in periods and locales different from those of the originals.

Sellars, Wilfrid (Stalker) (1912–89) philosopher; born in Ann Arbor, Mich. Educated at Oxford, he taught at the State University of Iowa (1938–46), the University of Minnesota (1947–58), Yale (1958–63), and then the University of Pittsburgh. His works in analytic philosophy, both influential and abstruse, include *Science, Perception and Reality* (1963).

Selleck, Tom (1945–) television/movie actor; born in Detroit, Mich. A talented collegiate athlete, he supported himself as a model, winning bit parts in film and television during the seventies. He starred in CBS's *Magnum, PI*

(1980–88), playing an easy-going private eye. He also appeared in films, including *Three Men and a Baby* (1987).

Sellers, William (1824–1905) manufacturer, engineer; born in Delaware County, Pa. In 1848 he began to manufacture machinists' tools and mill gearing in Providence and in 1886 he formed William Sellers & Co. He developed formulas for machining screw threads and nuts. He was also director of several railroads in the 1860s and 1870s.

Sellin, Thorsten (Johan) (1896–) educator, criminologist; born in Ornskoldsvik, Sweden. He emigrated to America (1915) to study. Teaching longest at the University of Pennsylvania (1920–68), he was named professor emeritus of the sociology department (1968); he also lectured at Columbia University (1935–46). Throughout his academic career he served as an international adviser on crime and penal codes. He advised the Census Bureau on criminal statistics (1931–46), helped construct the Swedish Penal Code (1946–47), was a member of the Prison Labor Compact Authority (1934), and was president of the International Penal and Penitentiary Foundation (1965–71). Serving on the steering committee of the 4th United Nations Congress on Crime Prevention, he was author of several books including *Culture Conflict and Crime* (1938).

Selznick, David O. (Oliver) (1902–65) movie executive; born in Pittsburgh, Pa. Starting as an assistant to his father, Lewis Selznick, an early film producer, he worked for Metro-Goldwyn-Mayer (MGM) (1926–27), then Paramount (1927–31), and then RKO (1931–36) before forming his own company, Selznick International. He produced many successful films, the most famous being *Gone With the Wind* (1939), and later joined in European coproduction. His first wife, Irene Mayer, was the daughter of Louis B. Mayer of MGM; his second wife was Jennifer Jones, star of several of his films. He was renowned for intruding in his productions either through long detailed memos or, in the case of *Gone With the Wind*, actually directing a few scenes.

Selznick, Philip (1919–) sociologist; born in Newark, N.J. A Columbia University Ph.D., he joined the faculty of the University of California: Berkeley (1952), where he chaired the Center for the Study of Law and Society (1961–72). He studied the sociology of large organizations and of law. His many books include the much revised *Sociology* (coauthored, 1955), a standard textbook.

Semmes, Raphael (1809–77) Confederate naval officer; born in Charles County, Md. He served in the U.S. Navy (1826–61) and then the Confederate navy (1861–65). He commanded the CSS *Sumter* which captured numerous Union vessels before being blockaded in Gibraltar. In command of the CSS *Alabama* (1862–64) he captured or destroyed 64 ships worth 6.5 million dollars and led his ship around the world before being defeated by the USS *Kearsarge* off Cherbourg, France (1864).

Semple, Ellen (Churchill) (1863–1932) geographer; born in Louisville, Ky. She studied at Vassar College (1882), later earning an M.A. there before traveling to Leipzig where she audited Friedrich Ratzel's courses (1891–92) because women could not enroll in the university. After founding a girls' school in Louisville with her sister (1893), she pursued a career of writing and field research. Her first book, *American History and Its Geographic Conditions* (1903), gained a broad public and led to her being invited to lecture in America and Europe. Her second and most important

book, *Influences of Geographic Environment on the Basis of Ratzel's System of Anthropo-Geography* (1911), was intended as an interpretation of that German geographer's ideas, but her own thoughts strongly colored the text; in particular, she stressed that physical environment strongly influences not only how humans act but how they view the world. After a world tour of 18 months, she returned to the U.S.A. and taught at various colleges until settling at Clark University (Mass.) (1921–32). She published her third major work, *The Geography of the Mediterranean Region* (1931), just before she died. Although subsequent generations of geographers tend to reject her strict deterministic views, she remains a respected pioneer in her field.

Sendak, Maurice (Bernard) (1928–) illustrator, writer, stage designer; born in New York City. He studied at the Art Students League (1949–51), worked for All American Comics (1944–45), and created window displays in New York City (1944–45). Under the direction of Ursula Nordstrom, he began illustrating picture books. Influenced by Dürer, Hogarth, and Cruikshank, he produced his own, often controversial children's classics, such as *The Nutshell Library* (1962), *Where the Wild Things Are* (1963), *In the Night Kitchen* (1970), and *Outside Over There* (1981). He was also a set and costume designer for operas, such as *The Magic Flute* (1980), and worked on films for television. For many years he lived in Ridgefield, Conn.

Sennett, Mack (b. Michael or Mikall Sinnott) (1880–1960) film director, producer, actor; born in Danville, Quebec, Canada. After appearing on Broadway and in burlesque, he switched to films in 1908. By 1910 he was directing Biograph shorts. A cofounder of Keystone, he made his name with slapstick comedy and later added his skills to romances. The "King of Comedy" received a special Oscar in 1937.

Sequoyah, or Sequoia (?1770–1843) Native American leader, inventor of Cherokee writing system; born in eastern Tennessee. He was born into a Cherokee family respected for its knowledge; he became a silversmith and trader. By 1821, after 12 years of work, he perfected his system of writing to record the Cherokee language; drawing on English, Greek, and Hebrew letters, he came up with 85 or 86 new characters. He traveled about teaching his syllabary to other Cherokee; within a few years it was used to print newspapers and books, including parts of the Bible, in Cherokee. He went to Washington, D.C., in 1828 to negotiate a treaty governing the exchange of the Cherokees' land in Arkansas for land in territory that became Oklahoma; he then worked to improve relations among the Indians forcibly relocated there. The giant trees and then a national park, in California, were named after him. Although Sequoyah was a name given him by Christian missionaries – his Cherokee name was Sogwali – he was usually known to his white contemporaries as George Guess, or Gist (because, it is claimed, he was fathered by a white explorer-soldier, Nathaniel Gist).

Sergeant, John (1779–1852) U.S. representative; born in Philadelphia. A lawyer from Philadelphia and a Federalist congressman (1815–29), becoming a Whig in his last term (1837–41), he chaired the Judiciary Committee and provided legal counsel to the Second Bank of the United States.

Serkin, Peter (1947–) pianist; born in New York City (son of Rudolf Serkin). He studied in childhood with his father and made his public debut at age ten. From his teens he had an active career as a recitalist and performer with orchestras. For some time he concentrated on contemporary music and was a cofounder of the new-music quartet, Tashi. Later he returned to performing the whole range of piano repertoire.

Serkin, Rudolf (1903–91) pianist; born in Eger, Bohemia. In childhood he studied piano and composition in Vienna, making his recital debut at age 12. He became well-known both for his solo performances and for his chamber-music recitals with violinist Adolf Busch. After making his American debut in 1933, he moved to the U.S.A. in 1939 to join the faculty of the Curtis Institute, whose director he became from 1968 to 1976. In 1949 he helped found the important summer music school at Marlboro, Vt. Admired for his insightful performance of the Austro-German classical repertoire, he also successfully played Chopin, Debussy, and Bartók.

Serra, Junipero (1713–84) missionary; born in Petra, Majorca. He entered the Franciscan Order in 1730 and arrived in Mexico City in 1750. He founded nine missions in present-day California (including San Diego and San Francisco) and was responsible for the baptism of over 6,000 Indians. He was beatified by the Roman Catholic Church in 1988.

Serra, Richard (Anthony) (1939–) sculptor; born in San Francisco. He worked in a steel plant during his schooling at the University of California, studied with Josef Albers at Yale (M.F.A. 1964), traveled in Italy (1964–65), and settled in New York City. He is known for his gravity series, such as *Belts* (1966–67), and his large metal plate works, as in *House of Cards* (1969). His minimalist approach to sculpture has not appealed to some viewers, and one of his works, *Tilted Arc* (1981), installed on the plaza of the Jacob Javits Federal Building in New York City, was ordered removed (1985) because of adverse public reactions.

Service, John Stewart (1909–) foreign service officer; born in Chengtu, China. He was raised by his missionary parents in China, where he worked for the U.S. foreign service (1933–45), unsuccessfully recommending America's early recognition of the communists. The government dismissed him for disloyalty for passing documents to the leftist journal *Amerasia* (1945); he was reinstated by the Supreme Court, but retired to teach at the University of California: Berkeley (1962).

Sessions, Roger (Huntington) (1896–1985) composer; born in Brooklyn, N.Y. After studies at Harvard, Yale, and privately with Ernest Bloch, he taught for a while, then spent some years in Europe, meanwhile contributing to the historic Copland-Sessions new-music concerts of 1928 to 1931. Back in the U.S.A. from 1933, he taught at a series of schools including Princeton and Juilliard (from 1965). His early works were neoclassic and later ones 12-tone, all marked by high craft and seriousness; they include the opera *Montezuma* (1959–63) and the Concerto for Orchestra, which won the 1981 Pulitzer Prize.

Seton, Elizabeth Ann (Bayley) (1774–1821) Catholic religious foundress, saint; born in New York City. The daughter of prominent physician Richard Bayley, she married William Seton (1794) and had five children; in 1803 he died of tuberculosis in Rome, where they had journeyed hoping the climate would cure him. Attracted to Catholicism by friends there, she became a convert after her return (1805), alienating many associates, and moved with her children to Baltimore, where she founded an elementary school. In 1809

she pronounced vows as a nun and began forming a religious congregation, formally instituted in Emmitsburg, Md., as the Sisters of Charity (1813). As superior general she founded many religious communities and schools and was renowned for sanctity. She was canonized in 1975, becoming the first American-born saint.

Seton, Ernest Thompson (1860–1946) naturalist, writer, illustrator; born in Durham, England. The 12th of 14 children, he emigrated to Canada with his family in 1866 when his father's shipping business failed. He studied art, but returned to his first love, natural history, writing and illustrating a series of books about birds and animals; critics accused him of humanizing his wild creatures for narrative effect. He was a strong proponent of conservation and of preserving Indian culture and woodcraft skills. A founder of the Boy Scouts of America (1910), he resigned as chief scout in 1915 to protest former President Theodore Roosevelt's campaign to "militarize" scouting. He spent his last years in a country house he built in New Mexico.

Setton, Kenneth M. (1914–) historian; born in New Bedford, Mass. Educated at Boston University (B.A. 1936) and Columbia University (M.A. 1938; Ph.D. 1941), he taught at the University of Manitoba (Canada) (1943–50) and Columbia (1950–65). Professor at the Institute for Advanced Study, Princeton (1968) and one of America's most distinguished medievalists, his works include the five-volume *A History of the Crusades* (editor-in-chief, 1969–85); his four-volume *The Papacy and the Levant, 1204–1571* (1976–84); and *Western Hostility to Islam* (1992).

Seuss, Dr. See GEISEL, THEODOR.

Sevareid, (Arnold) Eric (1912–92) broadcast journalist; born in Velva, N.D. He worked at the Minneapolis *Journal* and was city editor for the *Paris Herald Tribune* before joining CBS Radio in 1939. He served as national correspondent and commentator for the *CBS Evening News* until 1977. Often characterized as the brightest of "Murrow's boys" at CBS, he had a weakness for vaguely "deep" speculations about the human condition, about which he grew increasingly disillusioned as he aged. He published his memoirs, *Not So Wild A Dream* (1976).

Severinsen, (Carl H.) Doc (1927–) musician; born in Arlington, Ore. A trumpeter, he began as a sideman with Ted Fio Rito in 1945. He subsequently worked in the big bands of Charles Barnet in 1947–49, and Tommy Dorsey on and off between 1949–55. He became a staff musician at National Broadcasting Company-TV in 1954, appeared in the series, *The Subject Is Jazz* in 1958, and became a sideman in the *Tonight Show* orchestra in 1962. Between 1967 and *Tonight Show* host Johnny Carson's retirement in 1992, he was the orchestra's leader; he also came to assume the role of a comic foil to Carson by wearing bizarre suits and engaging in banter. During this period, he toured sporadically with his own orchestra, conducted college clinics, and appeared as a soloist with symphony and pop orchestras nationwide.

Sevier, John (1745–1815) soldier, public official; born near present-day New Market, Va. He led militia forces during the American Revolution and was governor of the short-lived state of Franklin (1785–88). He also served as governor of Tennessee (1796–1801, 1803–09). He was twice in the House of Representatives (Dem., N.C.; 1789–91, Dem., Tenn.; 1811–15).

Sewall, Samuel (1652–1730) judge, merchant; born in

Bishopstoke, England. He came to Boston in 1661, married the daughter of a wealthy shipowner, served as a superior court justice, and became the colony's chief justice in 1718. In 1697, he confessed his error in having been partly responsible for sending people to the gallows during the Salem witch trials (1692). He wrote one of the first antislavery tracts and left a diary (1674–77; 1685–1729) that remains an incomparable record of the life, mentality, and world of a Puritan of his era.

Seward, William H. (Henry) (1801–72) public official, cabinet officer; born in Florida, N.Y. A lawyer, he joined the new Whig Party and served as governor of New York (1839–43) and as U.S. senator (N.Y.; 1849–61). Becoming increasingly more liberal, he moved to the new Republican Party for his second term as senator and came to embody Northern antislavery sentiment: he caused a controversy with his claim (1850) that slavery should be excluded from new states by a "higher law than the Constitution." Disappointed in his hopes for the Republican nomination in both 1856 and 1860, he accepted the post of secretary of state in Lincoln's cabinet. After Lincoln squelched his attempts at imposing his own views and policies, Seward settled down to become an excellent secretary of state. He was wounded by one of the conspirators who killed Lincoln (1865), but recovered to continue serving under President Andrew Johnson. He asserted the Monroe Doctrine against French policy in Mexico (1866) and in 1867 bought the area of Alaska from Russia for $67,000,000 – an action that was called "Seward's Folly." He sided with President Johnson and his Reconstruction policies, and with the end of the Johnson Administration (1869), he toured the world and retired to Auburn, N.Y.

Sexton, Anne (b. Harvey) (1928–74) poet; born in Newton, Mass. She studied at Garland Junior College, Boston (1947–48), and was a fashion model (1950–51). Based in Weston, Mass., she married (1948), divorced (1974), and suffered from mental illness. Her autobiographical poetry remains respected and is noted for its highly charged emotional climate, as seen in her first volume, *To Bedlam and Part Way Back* (1960). She committed suicide at the height of her career.

Seymour, Horatio (1810–86) governor; born in Pompey Hill, N.Y. (brother-in-law of Roscoe Conkling). A protégé of William Marcy and an "Albany Regency" Democrat, he served in the New York Assembly (1842, 1844–45) and gained a reputation for compromise and moderation. As Democratic governor (1853–55), he improved the prison system and opposed prohibition. He worked in business but remained a respected figure in Democratic politics. Elected to a second term as New York's governor (1863–65), he provided the Union army with soldiers and financing even though he was initially opposed to the war and to Lincoln's war powers. He made an unsuccessful run for the Democratic nomination for president in 1868, helped force Boss Tweed from power, and helped his own protégé, Grover Cleveland, become president.

Seymour, John (c. 1738–1818) furniture maker; born in England. In 1785 he emigrated to Maine and then arrived in Boston (1794) where together with son Thomas Seymour he became the leading cabinet maker in the federal style.

Shahn, Ben (Benjamin) (1898–1969) painter, photographer, graphic artist; born in Kaunas, Lithuania. He emigrated with his parents to New York (1906), was a lithographer (1913–

30), and studied at the National Academy of Design (1922). After study in Europe (1925–27), he became an activist painter in New York. A sequence of 23 gouaches based on the Sacco-Vanzetti case (1931–32) that ended in the execution of two political anarchists, and his series on the trial of labor leader Tom Mooney (1933), established his reputation. His style was semiabstract and boldly colored, and his posters for activist causes reflect his paintings. As a photographer he recorded the lives of farm workers for the Farm Security Administration (1935–38).

Shalala, Donna (Edna) (1941–) political scientist, educator, cabinet officer; born in Cleveland, Ohio. Of Lebanese descent, she took her B.A. from Western College for Women (Oxford, Ohio) (1962) and then spent two years with the Peace Corps in Iran. She then earned her M.A. and Ph.D. (1970) from Syracuse; while there she participated in programs that taught foreign students and Peace Corps staff. She taught at Bernard Baruch College (N.Y.C.) (1970–72) and then at Teachers College of Columbia (1972–79); she also served with the Municipal Assistance Corporation (1975–77), which helped restore financial stability to New York City. She was assistant secretary for political development and research in the Department of Housing and Urban Development (1977–80). In 1980 she became president of Hunter College (part of the City University of New York City) – the youngest woman ever to head a major college; she greatly increased its endowment, enlarged its faculties, upgraded its student body, and enlarged its building program. In 1988 she moved on to become the chancellor of the University of Wisconsin: Madison, only the second woman (after Hanna Holborn Gray at the University of Chicago) to head a major American research university; she also became a professor of political science and educational policy studies. One of her most publicized programs there was the so-called Madison Plan to deal with racism on campus. In 1993 she was appointed secretary of the Department of Health and Human Services by President Clinton.

Shaler, Nathaniel (Southgate) (1841–1906) geologist, geographer; born in Newport, Ky. After graduating from Harvard (1862), he served with the 5th Kentucky Battery in the Union army, then returned to assist Jean Louis Agassiz at Harvard, studying abroad afterward. In 1868 he returned to Harvard for good, becoming an extremely popular professor, writing magazine articles and books, such as *A First Book in Geology* (1884). He headed the Atlantic Coast Division of the U.S. Geological Survey (1884–1900) and revitalized Harvard's Lawrence Scientific School while dean (1891–1906). Books that reflect his interest in conservation and the environment are *Aspects of the Earth* (1889) and *Man and Earth* (1905).

Shanker, Albert (1928–) union leader; born in New York City. He was a confrontational president of New York City's United Federation of Teachers (1964–86), leading repeated teachers' strikes and becoming a major force in city politics. As national president of the American Federation of Teachers (1974) he supported public school reform and his weekly column in the *New York Times* served as a much-quoted forum for ideas on education.

Shannon, Claude E. (Elwood) (1916–) mathematician; born in Gaylord, Mich. His paper, "The Mathematical Theory of Communication" (1958), marked the beginnings of information theory that underlies modern communications engineering and is at the heart of a still-growing body of mathematical analysis. He was affiliated with Bell Laboratories (1941–72) and was also noted for devising an experiment illustrating the capabilities of telephone relays (1952). A National Medal of Science recipient (1966) and member of the National Academy of Sciences, he taught at a variety of universities.

Shapiro, Harry L. (Lionel) (1902–90) physical anthropologist; born in Boston, Mass. He served the American Museum of Natural History (1926–70), becoming curator and chairman of anthropology in 1942. He performed extensive research on the Pitcairn Islanders (1936), and originated the forensic system of anatomically identifying war dead (1946).

Shapiro, Karl (Jay) (1913–) poet, writer; born in Baltimore, Md. He studied at the University of Virginia (1932–33), Johns Hopkins (1937–39), and Pratt Library School, Baltimore (1940). He taught at many institutions, notably the University of California: Davis (1968). He was an editor of literary periodicals (1950–66), and wrote literary criticism and a novel. He is noted for his direct diction and mastery of poetic forms, as seen in *Collected Poems 1940–1977* (1978).

Shapley, Harlow (1885–1972) astrophysicist; born in Nashville, Mo. To leave the farm, he took a business course, and at age 16 became a reporter for the *Daily Sun* in Chanute, Kans. With only a fifth-grade education, he attended the Presbyterian Carthage Collegiate Institute, graduated in two semesters, and went on to the University of Missouri: Columbia in 1907. The journalism school, his choice, was not yet open so he studied astronomy, an interest that was clinched by a teaching assistantship; in 1910 he graduated; in 1911 he took his Ph.D. at Princeton. He observed at Mt. Wilson Observatory from 1914 to 1921 before going to Harvard College where he directed the observatory from 1921–52. His early work included pioneer studies of binary stars and star clusters. He calculated that our sun is 30,000 light years from the center of the Milky Way, not at its center as was supposed; this resulted in the first realistic assessment of the size of our galaxy. Highly in demand as a lecturer, he wrote both technical works and more popular books such as *Of Stars and Men* (1958). He was active in scientific organizations and was the recipient of many honors.

Sharp, Phillip A. (Allen) (1944–) molecular biologist; born in Falmouth, Ky. He helped pay his Union College (Kentucky) tuition by working on the family farm, took a Ph.D. in chemistry from the University of Illinois: Urbana, went to California Institute of Technology, and then to the Cold Spring Harbor Laboratory. In 1974 he joined the faculty at the Massachusetts Institute of Technology (MIT), where he also directed the Center for Cancer Research and chaired the biology department. In 1977 he discovered that DNA is not continuous as had been thought. For this discovery of "split genes" he shared the 1993 Nobel Prize in medicine with Richard J. Roberts, who independently made the same discovery. In 1978 Sharp helped found Biogen, a Cambridge-based producer of interferon through genetic engineering. In 1990 he accepted and then declined the presidency of MIT after deciding he preferred teaching and research.

Sharpe, William Forsyth (1934–) economist; born in Cambridge, Mass. He is best known for his work in investment management analysis, and especially for his capital asset pricing model. From 1970 he taught at Stanford University Graduate School of Business as the Timken Professor of Finance.

Sharples, James (1751–1811) painter; born in Lancashire, England. He studied for the priesthood, took up painting instead, emigrated to America (1793), and settled in Philadelphia. He was known for his pastel portraits, including those of George and Martha Washington.

Sharswood, George (1810–83) judge; born in Philadelphia. He took his B.A. degree at the University of Pennsylvania (1828), read law, and commenced his private practice in 1831. He was a Pennsylvania district judge (1845–67), then served on the state supreme court (1868–82). Considered a great judge (only 32 out of some 4,000 cases were reversed on appeal), he was also dean of the University of Pennsylvania law school (1852–68), a University of Pennsylvania trustee (1872–83), and director of the Princeton Theological Seminary. He wrote and edited many volumes on law.

Shatner, William (1931–) television/movie actor; born in Montreal, Canada. A graduate of McGill University where he studied acting, he was among the original actors in Tyrone Guthrie's Stratford Shakespeare Festival (1954–57). After working on Broadway and in television, he captained the USS *Enterprise* for television's quintessential science fiction series, *Star Trek* (1966–69) and recreated his roles as Capt. Kirk in a number of successful movies in the 1970s and 1980s. He returned to television in *T. J. Hooker* (1982–86) and *Rescue 911* (1989).

Shattuck, Lemuel (1793–1859) statistician, public health reformer; born in Ashby, Mass. Initially a schoolteacher in New York and Michigan, where he organized the state's first Sunday School in Detroit, he returned to Massachusetts and in 1839 helped found the American Statistical Association. He was instrumental in ensuring accurate recording of births, marriages, and deaths in Massachusetts (1842). He revolutionized census-taking and assisted the federal government in its 1850 census. His *Report* (1850) from the Massachusetts sanitary commission is recognized as the inspiration for future developments in public health works and measures in the U.S.A.

Shaw, Anna Howard (1847–1919) reformer, minister, physician; born in Newcastle-upon-Tyne, England. She came with her family to the U.S.A. in 1851. Her father, an impractical reformer, built a crude log cabin in the Michigan frontier (near Big Rapids) and put his family there in 1859; young Anna had to learn many traditionally male skills to help the family survive. She got an education in a local high school but early felt a "call" to be a preacher, and with the support of a local Methodist woman she began to preach in 1870. In 1876 she went to Boston University from which – after great economic trials – she took her certificate in 1878. She became a minister in a Methodist church in East Dennis, Mass. (1878–85), and after considerable trouble she was ordained in 1880. Meanwhile, she decided she could do more good for women as a doctor and she went to Boston University's medical school, taking her M.D. in 1886. In 1885 she also became a lecturer and organizer for the Massachusetts Woman Suffrage Association; she left that post in 1887 to become a free-lance lecturer. From 1888 to 1892 she worked with the Woman's Christian Temperance Union. Urged by Susan B. Anthony to put her talents as an orator to work for the suffrage movement, in 1891 she became a national lecturer for the newly united National

Woman Suffrage Association (NWSA); in 1892 she became the NWSA's vice-president and in 1904 she became its president. During her decades with the suffrage movement, she became one of the most prominent and eloquent workers for the cause, but she was not a good administrator and gradually a younger generation of women grew restless at the NWSA's failure to offer a strong strategy and leadership. When she resigned from the presidency of the NWSA in 1915 she was somewhat relegated to the sidelines of the suffrage movement; but she worked hard during World War I to coordinate women's activities in the war effort and she continued to speak out for woman suffrage. She died just as she was about to set out on a speaking tour in support of President Woodrow Wilson's peace treaty at the League of Nations.

Shaw, Henry Wheeler (Josh Billings, pen name) (1818–85) writer; born in Lanesboro, Mass. He studied at Hamilton College (1832–33), but was dismissed for removing the clapper from the chapel bell. He then traveled widely, held a variety of jobs, and settled in Poughkeepsie, N.Y. There he became a realtor and auctioneer. Using his pen name, he wrote humorous aphorisms (with crude misspellings), as in *Josh Billings, His Sayings* (1865), and a parody annual, *Farmer's Allminax* (1869–80). Once he was successful, he moved to New York City.

Shaw, Lemuel (1781–1861) judge; born in Barnstable, Mass. The son of a Congregational minister, he was educated at home and worked as a journalist while he read law. Admitted to the bar in 1804, he established a lucrative practice in Boston. As chief justice of the Massachusetts Supreme Court from 1830 to 1860, his rulings on railroad, utility, and other commercial cases had a major impact on the development of the nation's commercial and constitutional law. In 1850 he presided over the sensational trial of Harvard professor John W. Webster, convicted of murdering Dr. George Parkman. His daughter married the novelist Herman Melville.

Shaw, Ralph Robert (1907–72) librarian, educator; born in Detroit, Mich. He served as U.S. Department of Agriculture librarian (1940–54) and founded the Scarecrow Press, publishers of reference and bibliographic materials. His *American Bibliography* indexed 50,000 items published between 1801 and 1819.

Shaw, Robert Gould (1837–63) soldier; born in Boston, Mass. The son of abolitionists, he enlisted in the Union army early in the Civil War. In April 1863 he assumed command – initially with some reluctance – of the Fifty-fourth Massachusetts, the first northern black regiment to see combat. He was killed in July leading a charge on Fort Wagner, South Carolina. He and the events leading to this fateful charge were portrayed in the film *Glory* (1990). Shaw and his regiment are memorialized in a low-relief sculpture by Saint-Gaudens (1884–97) in the Boston Common.

Shaw, Robert (Lawson) (1916–   ) conductor; born in Red Bluff, Calif. Having found fame with his vocal choruses in the 1940s and 1950s, he took up instrumental conducting and from 1967 led the Atlanta Symphony, bringing that orchestra to prominence.

Shawn, (Edwin Myers) Ted (1891–1972) dancer, choreographer, dance festival administrator; born in Kansas City, Mo. Intending to study theology, he took up dance at age 18 as a cure for paralysis. Won over to ballet, he debuted in 1912 and after a tour met and married Ruth St. Denis in 1914. They settled in Los Angeles in 1915 and founded the Denishawn School of Dancing (moved to New York City in 1921) and the Denishawn Dancers. They toured throughout the world, taught many who would become leading figures of modern dance in America, and choreographed their own dances; several of Shawn's drew on Native American themes. By 1932 Shawn and St. Denis were separated and he moved to Lee, Mass., where he began a school just for male dancers (1933–40); he also toured with this company. The school was disbanded with the onset of World War II, but in 1941 he established the Jacob's Pillow Dance Festival (Becket, Mass.) and built it into an internationally recognized summer school and performance showcase. From 1945 on, St. Denis and he performed together again on special occasions. He gave a solo tour in Australia (1947) and led the Jacob's Pillow Touring Company (1952). He wrote several books on dance, including *Dance We Must* (1940).

Shawn, William (1907–92) editor; born in Chicago. As the *New Yorker*'s managing editor (1939–52), and as its skilled if autocratic editor in chief (1952–87), he exercised a strong influence on the magazine's development.

Shawnee Prophet See TENSKWATAWA.

Shays, Daniel (c. 1747–1825) soldier, insurrectionary; probably born in Hopkinton, Mass. His origins were humble and little is known of his early life. He fought at Bunker Hill (1775) and at Saratoga (1777); he resigned from the army in 1780 and settled in Pelham, Mass., where he held several town offices. He led the insurrection in western Massachusetts (1786–87) that grew out of a severe economic depression; armed groups threatened courts charged with the collection of debts, and in January 1787 Shays directed an assault on the Springfield Arsenal. Militia forces repulsed his band and pursued it to Petersham, where the remnants were captured. Shays himself fled to Vermont. Massachusetts authorities condemned him to death for being a leader of the rebellion that bears his name; he received a pardon in 1788. Shays migrated to western New York, where he passed the remainder of his years in obscurity.

Shea, John (Dawson) Gilmary (1824–92) historian; born in New York City. Admitted to the bar (1846), he left to become a Jesuit (1848), then left the order (1852) and devoted himself to studying Catholic history; his works include a pioneering four-volume history of the church (1886–92). Also an expert on Indian languages, he was a cofounder (1884) and first president of the American Catholic Historical Society.

Shearing, George (Albert) (1919–   ) jazz musician; born in London, England. Blind from birth, he played piano with Harry Parry's Radio Rhythm Band and Frank Weir's Orchestra in London during World War II. He moved to New York in 1947 and led a trio and quartet before forming the quintet in 1949 that brought him international fame. He maintained a widespread touring schedule thereafter while making numerous guest appearances with symphony orchestras.

Sheed, Frank (Francis Joseph) (1897–1981) Catholic religious publisher, writer; born in Sydney, Australia. As a soapbox religious lecturer living in England, he married Maisie Ward and with her founded Sheed & Ward to publish high-quality Catholic books (1926). In 1940 the family settled in the U.S.A., where a branch was established (the company was sold in 1973). A forceful apologist for Catholic doctrine,

Sheed wrote several books, most notably *Theology and Sanity* (1947).

Sheehy, Gail (1937–   ) journalist, writer on popular psychology; born in Mamaroneck, N.Y. She attended the University of Vermont (B.S. 1958) and worked as a feature writer on the *New York Herald Tribune* (1963–66) and as an editor on *New York* magazine (1966–77). She wrote a number of best-sellers, including *Passages: Predictable Crises of Adult Life* (1976), *Pathfinders* (1981), and *The Silent Passage* (1992), which excelled in translating the findings and theories of academics and professionals into language and concepts that were meaningful to a broad public.

Sheeler, Charles (1883–1965) painter, photographer; born in Philadelphia, Pa. A leading precisionist painter, he painted industrial structures with an architect's eye and turned to photography to support his art. Successful in both mediums (1912–62), his clients included architects, private patrons, and museums.

Sheen, Fulton J. (John) (b. Peter Sheen) (1895–1979) Catholic prelate; born in El Paso, Ill. After being ordained (1919) and earning graduate degrees in philosophy at Louvain and Rome, he did pastoral work and (from 1926) taught at Catholic University. An enthralling preacher and lecturer with a theatrical style, he won a huge audience for his talks on radio, the *Catholic Hour* (1930–52), and his television series, *Life is Worth Living* (1952–65), and for books such as *Peace of Soul* (1949); he also recruited funds for the missions as national director of the Society for the Propagation of the Faith. After serving as an auxiliary bishop of New York, he was named bishop of Rochester, N.Y. (1966), retiring with the title of archbishop (1969).

Shehan, Lawrence (Joseph) (1898–1984) Catholic prelate; born in Baltimore, Md. Ordained in 1922, he was made bishop of Bridgeport, Conn. (1953), and archbishop of Baltimore (1961), becoming a cardinal in 1965 and retiring in 1974. Known for his ecumenism and for liberal positions on social issues, he played a prominent role at the Second Vatican Council and energetically implemented its changes.

Shelby, Isaac (1750–1826) soldier, public official; born in present-day Washington County, Md. He followed the moving frontier, relocating to Virginia (1773) and Kentucky (1783). He fought in important battles during the American Revolution and became the first governor of Kentucky (1792–96). He returned to the governor's office (1812–16) and led Kentucky volunteers in Michigan and Canada during the War of 1812. He was offered the post of secretary of war (1817) but declined because of his age.

Sheldon, Edward (Brewster) (1886–1946) playwright; born in Chicago. His output is divided between social realism, such as *The Nigger* (1909), which confronts issues of racial purity, and love stories, such as *Romance* (1913), his biggest success.

Sheldon, Sidney (1917–   ) producer, writer; born in Chicago. He studied at Northwestern (1935–36), and held a variety of jobs during the Depression years. He moved to New York City hoping to become a composer, but disappointed in that endeavor, he moved to Los Angeles. He became a noted film and television producer of such shows as *The Patty Duke Show,* and *I Dream of Jeannie.* Beginning in 1970, he also published a number of best-selling suspense novels, such as *The Other Side of Midnight* (1974).

Shepard, Alan (Bartlett), Jr. (1923–   ) astronaut, NASA administrator; born in East Derry, N.H. An Annapolis graduate, after World War II service on a destroyer he became a U.S. Navy pilot. One of the seven original astronauts (1959), he became the first American in space when on May 5, 1961, he rode the capsule "Freedom 7" to an altitude of 117 miles. Grounded because of an ear disorder (1963–69), he directed NASA's astronaut training program (1965–74); when recovered, he commanded the Apollo 15 lunar mission in 1971 and became the fifth astronaut to land on the moon. Promoted to rear admiral, he retired from NASA and the U.S. Navy in 1974 and entered private business in Houston.

Shepard, Anna Osler (1903–73) ceramist; born in Merchantville, N.J. She was largely a self-taught expert on prehistoric ceramics who was affiliated with the Carnegie Institution and the U.S. Geological Survey. She performed rigorous scientific analyses of pottery from the American Southwest and Mesoamerica, often with controversial results. Her books include the standard *Ceramics for the Archaeologist* (1957).

Shepard, Sam (b. Samuel Shepard Rogers VII) (1943–   ) playwright, actor; born in Fort Sheridan, Ill. He was raised in California and studied agricultural science at Mount Antonio Junior College there (1960–61). He moved to New York City (1962), worked as an actor and a rock musician. His career as a playwright began in 1964 with Theatre Genesis's Obie Award-winning productions of *Cowboy* and *The Rock Garden.* Although he won critical acclaim and a small following, his offbeat and off-Broadway plays did not bring him much financial success, and he moved to England (1971–75) where he wrote his rock-drama, *The Tooth of Crime* (1972). He returned to see a steady stream of his stage plays produced – *Buried Child* (1978) won the Pulitzer – while he also wrote film scripts and appeared in several movies, including *The Right Stuff* (1983). Both the critics and public have found it difficult to categorize his iconoclastic approach to drama, agreeing only that it seems disturbingly to reflect the contemporary American scene, and he remains somewhat elusive and ambiguous as a force in the modern theater.

Shepard, Thomas (1605–49) Protestant clergyman; born in Towcester, England. Educated at Emmanuel College, Cambridge, and ordained in 1627, he was silenced for nonconformity and emigrated to Massachusetts in 1635. He espoused a stern Calvinist doctrine as pastor at Newtown (now Cambridge). A promoter of education, he was said to have established the first scholarships for needy students in America. His autobiography provides a detailed portrait of his times.

Shepp, Archie (1937–   ) jazz musician; born in Fort Lauderdale, Fla. Raised in Philadelphia, he studied drama at Goddard College before emerging in 1960 as a saxophonist with Cecil Taylor, whose ensemble was appearing in the off-Broadway production of *The Connection.* Throughout the 1960s he was a spokesman for the jazz avant-garde and a leader of the Jazz Composers Guild and other collectives. In 1964 he began leading his own stylistically eclectic groups which eventually gained a wide following in Europe. In addition to his performing career, he wrote plays and essays, and taught African-American studies at the University of Massachusetts (1973).

Sheppard, Eugenia (?–1984) newspaper columnist; born

near Columbus, Ohio. She revolutionized fashion reporting with her breezy style and stories about the personalities behind the clothes in her work on New York City's *Herald Tribune* (1940–56). Her syndicated column "Inside Fashion" (1956) made her the most influential fashion arbiter of the 1950s and 1960s. Secretive about her age, she was believed to be in her 80s when she died.

Shera, Jesse Hauk (1903–82) librarian, educator; born in Oxford, Ohio. After graduating from Columbia University (Ph.D. 1944) he held successive positions in government and academia. After several years at the University of Chicago Library, he became dean of the Western Reserve University School of Library Science (1952–82) where he established the doctoral program in librarianship and edited the university press. Despite a severe visual handicap, he was a prolific author and a pioneer in the field of information retrieval.

Sheridan, Philip (Henry) (1831–88) soldier; born in Albany, N.Y. The son of Irish immigrant parents, he worked as a store clerk before obtaining a West Point appointment; he was an undistinguished student, and because of a discipline infraction, he graduated in 1853, a year late. When the Civil War began, he was still an obscure lieutenant and was assigned only desk jobs; at one point he was almost court-martialed for violating an administrative regulation. His combat career did not begin until May 1862 when he was appointed colonel in the cavalry; after distinguishing himself in the Union advance on Corinth, Miss., and the battle of Booneville, Miss., he was promoted to general and commanded a division at Perryville and Stone's River (1862); as a corps commander, his troops took part in the charge up Missionary Ridge that won the decisive Battle of Chattanooga (1863). Grant then put him in charge of the cavalry of the Army of the Potomac; he led the raid on Richmond that resulted in the death of Jeb Stuart at Yellow Tavern (May 1864). As commander of the Army of the Shenandoah in 1864, he drove Confederate forces from the Shenandoah Valley and laid it waste (August 1864–February 1865), leaving the inhabitants, as he put it, "with only their eyes to weep with over the war." Sheridan's fabled "ride" occurred on October 19, 1864, when he rallied his routed forces at Cedar Creek. Commanding a combined force of infantry and cavalry, the intense, aggressive, and hard-driving Sheridan led a furious Union pursuit to Appomattox, where he joined Grant in compelling Lee's surrender on April 9, 1865. After the war he proved to be especially severe as a military governor in the South; he also organized punitive campaigns against the Plains Indian tribes. (He is reliably reported as having actually said, "The only good Indians I ever saw were dead.") In 1884 he succeeded Sherman as commander-in-chief of the army.

Sherman, Henry Clapp (1875–1955) food chemist; born in Ash Grove, Va. The bulk of his career was spent at Columbia University (1899–1946) where he taught and researched aspects of food and nutrition. He analyzed digestive enzymes (1910–34) and quantified human requirements for protein. During the 1920s and 1930s, his lab assayed vitamins A, B_1, B_2, and C. With his biochemist daughter Caroline Sherman as collaborator, he studied calcium and debunked spinach's reputation as a health-building vegetable. The results of this research were published in *Science of Nutrition* (1943).

Sherman, James S. (Schoolcraft) (1855–1912) vice-president, U.S. representative; born in Utica, N.Y. He was known as an amicable and parliamentary congressman (1887–91, 1893–1904). Both parties praised his handling of the Senate while he was vice-president under William Howard Taft (1909–12).

Sherman, John (1823–1900) U.S. senator, cabinet officer; born in Lancaster, Ohio (brother of William T. Sherman). A lawyer who became active in the new Republican Party, he served in the U.S. House of Representatives (Rep., Ohio; 1855–61) and the U.S. Senate (1861–77). During these years in the Senate, he concentrated on financial affairs and played a major role in restoring national credit. President Hayes then appointed him secretary of the treasury (1877–81) and he superintended the U.S.'s return to the gold standard. He went back to the U.S. Senate (Rep., Ohio; 1881–97) and made his impact with the Sherman Antitrust Act and the Silver Purchase Act (both in 1890). President McKinley named him secretary of state in 1897 but he resigned a year later to protest the administration's decision to go to war with Spain.

Sherman, Roger (1721–93) statesman, patriot; born in Newton, Mass. He lived in Connecticut from 1743. A tireless legislator, he had the distinction of being the only person to sign all of the following: the Articles of Association (1774), the Declaration of Independence (1776), the Articles of Confederation (1777), and the Constitution (1787). He later served as a senator (1791–93).

Sherman, Thomas West (1813–79) soldier; born in Newport, R.I. The Civil War's "other Sherman," he was a West Point graduate (1836) who fought in Florida, the Mexican War, and on the frontier. A stern disciplinarian and thus unpopular with Civil War volunteer troops, he commanded the Port Royal, S.C., expedition (1861) and afterward fought in Mississippi and Louisiana, where he lost a leg in action at Port Hudson (1863).

Sherman, William Tecumseh (1820–91) soldier; born in Lancaster, Ohio. Orphaned at age nine and raised by a prominent Ohio politician, he graduated from West Point in 1840, saw service in Florida, and, during the Mexican War, in California; he stayed there and in 1853 resigned from the army to become a banker. When the bank failed in 1857, he became superintendent of the Louisiana Military Academy; he resigned when Louisiana seceded early in 1861. Reentering the army, he led a brigade at First Bull Run (July 1861), then was given command of the Union forces assigned to hold Kentucky in the Union; there (late 1861), under pressure from Washington and the press, he had a mild nervous breakdown. Recovered, he was assigned to Ulysses Grant's command and came into his own leading large units at Shiloh (1862), Vicksburg (1863), and Chattanooga (1863). When Grant left to take command of the Federal forces, Sherman assumed command of operations in the west and by September 1864 had captured Atlanta in one of the Civil War's most decisive campaigns. The advocate of a hard, unrelenting war on all fronts – "War is cruelty and you cannot refine it," he said, thus solidifying his reputation as the first modern general – he then set off on his famous March to the Sea. Cutting a wide swath of destruction through Georgia, and, in early 1865, through the Carolinas, by April 1865 he had forced the surrender of the last major Confederate forces. After directing the fight against the Indians as the transcontinental railroad was being built, he succeeded Grant as commander in chief of the army (1869–83). His excellent *Memoirs* were published in 1875. Asked to run for president in 1884, he sent his oft-quoted refusal: "I will not accept if nominated and will not serve if elected."

Sherry, Louis (1856–1926) restaurateur; probably born in St. Albans, Vt. After working in hotels, he opened his first New York City restaurant (1881). Renowned for its attention to detail and meticulous service in rooms hung with tapestries and oil paintings, Sherry's served New York's elite until Prohibition (1919), when he shifted to catering and confectionery.

Sherwood, Robert E. (Emmet) (1896–1955) playwright; born in New Rochelle, N.Y. Beginning as a reviewer of books and movies, he began writing screenplays, including the original script that became the play, *Idiot's Delight* (1936). He won a Pulitzer Prize for this, as well as for two more plays, *Abe Lincoln in Illinois* (1938) and *There Shall Be No Night* (1940). He became a speech writer for President Franklin Roosevelt and served as director of the overseas branch of the Office of War and Information (1942–44); drawing on his inside knowledge, he wrote the Pulitzer Prize-winning study, *Roosevelt and Hopkins* (1948).

Shields, James (1806–79) judge, soldier, U.S. senator; born in Altmore, County Tyrone, Ireland. Setting out for Quebec about 1822, he was shipwrecked on the coast of Scotland, where he spent several years as a tutor. About 1826 he arrived in New York City, then settled in Illinois where he taught, fought in the Black Hawk War, and became a lawyer. As state auditor he was drawn into a quarrel with another lawyer, Abraham Lincoln, whom Shields allegedly challenged to a duel; they resolved the issue and became firm friends. After serving on the Illinois Supreme Court (1843–46), he was briefly the commissioner of the U.S. General Land Office, but resigned to serve in the Mexican War (1846–48), where his actions gained him the brevet rank of major general. He served briefly as governor of the Oregon Territory but resigned to take a seat in the U.S. Senate (Dem., Ill.; 1849–55). He then moved on to the Minnesota Territory and encouraged Irish immigrants there; when Minnesota became a state, he was one of the first two U.S. senators (Dem., Minn.; 1858–59). He volunteered for service with the Union army and saw combat as a brigadier general (1861–63). Settling in Missouri, he lectured on behalf of charitable, religious, and Irish causes; served in the state legislature; and then went back to the U.S. Senate (Dem., Mo.; 1879) – thereby becoming the only person to serve three different states as a U.S. senator. Illinois placed his statue in the U.S. Capitol.

Shinn, Everett (1876–1953) painter, illustrator; born in Woodstown, N.J. He studied at the Pennsylvania Academy of the Fine Arts (1893–97), became an illustrator for various periodicals, and moved to New York (c. 1898). Beginning in 1901 he painted theater scenes and set designs, usually in pastels, as in *London Hippodrome* (1902). He was among the founders of the Eight (1908), a school of painting based on realism.

Shipman, Ellen (b. Biddle) (1870–1950) landscape architect, feminist; born in Philadelphia. Overcoming resistance to women in her profession, she designed gardens for private clients, and employed an all-female staff in her New York City and Cornish, N.H., design firms (1920–50).

Shipstead, Henrik (1881–1960) U.S. senator; born in Burbank, Minn. A dentist, he was elected to the U.S. Senate (Farmer-Labor Party, later Rep., Minn.; 1923–47). A supporter of La Follette and of the New Deal, he was also an isolationist. As a member of the Senate Foreign Relations Committee, he opposed U.S. membership in the United Nations.

Shiras, George, Jr. (1832–1924) Supreme Court justice; born in Pittsburgh, Pa. He spent 25 years at a private Pittsburgh law firm before President Benjamin Harrison named him to the U.S. Supreme Court (1892–1903).

Shirer, William L. (Lawrence) (1904–93) journalist, author; born in Chicago. After working as a correspondent in Europe and (briefly) in India, he joined CBS in 1937 and broadcast on the momentous events in Europe from Vienna, London, Prague, and ultimately Berlin, alerting Americans to the peril of Nazism; at the outset of World War II he covered the German army in the field. He wrote a syndicated column for the *New York Herald Tribune* from 1942 to 1948, Quitting CBS in 1947 in a dispute over the scope for personal opinions, he worked for the Mutual Broadcasting System before turning to writing full-time. His comprehensive study of the Nazi regime and its origins, *The Rise and Fall of the Third Reich* (1960), though called oversensational by some and condemned in West Germany as anti-German, won wide praise and a National Book Award, besides becoming a best-seller. Other books range from *Berlin Diary: The Journal of a Foreign Correspondent, 1934–41* (1941) to *Gandhi: A Memoir* (1979), based on interviews with Mahatma Gandhi in the 1930s. His two-volume memoir, *Twentieth Century Journey,* was published in 1976 and 1984.

Shirlaw, Walter (1838–1909) painter; born in Paisley, Scotland. He and his parents emigrated to New York (1841). He became a bank-note engraver until 1870, studied in Munich (1870–77), and was one of the founders of the Society of American Artists (1877). He painted genre scenes and murals.

Shirley, William (1694–1771) colonial governor; born in Preston, Sussex, England. He came over to Massachusetts in 1731 and served as judge of admiralty and then advocate general before becoming governor of the colony (1741–56). He took a broad view of Britain's colonial policies, and during the war between Britain and France (1744–48), he was perhaps the chief instigator of the operation that led to the English colonists' capture of the French fortress of Louisburg, Nova Scotia (1745). In 1755 he was named the supreme commander of British forces in North America during the French and Indian War, but after the failure of the Niagara expedition, he was recalled to England (1756). He avoided court-martial and was later named governor of the Bahamas (1761–67).

Shockley, William B. (Bradford) (1910–89) physicist; born in London, England (of American parents). He worked at Bell Telephone Laboratories (1936–42), then performed anti-submarine research at Columbia University (1942–44) and the War Department (1944–45). Returning to Bell (1945–54), he collaborated with J. Bardeen and W. Brattain to invent the transistor, for which the three shared the 1956 Nobel Prize in physics. Shockley worked at Beckmann Instruments (1955–58), then founded Shockley Transistor (1958–63) before joining Stanford (1963–74). There he developed his controversial opinions on the relationship of intelligence to the human races, theories he considered more important than his contributions to physics.

Shoemaker, (William Lee) Bill (1931–) jockey; born in Fabens, Texas. The greatest winning jockey in thoroughbred racing history, he won 8,833 races in his 42-year career, including the Kentucky Derby (four times), the Belmont (five times), and the Preakness (twice). After retiring in 1990, he was paralyzed in an auto accident in 1991.

Sholes, Christopher (Latham) (1819–90) printer, inventor; born in Mooresburg, Pa. He learned the printer's trade in Pennsylvania before migrating to Wisconsin, where he edited newspapers in Madison and Milwaukee. He designed and patented a typewriter in 1868 and sold the rights to the Remington Arms Company five years later. By 1876 Remington was manufacturing and marketing typewriters under its own name.

Shores, Louis (1904–81) librarian; born in Buffalo, N.Y. The son of politically progressive German-Jewish immigrants, he taught English at traditionally black Fisk University. In 1933 he became dean of the library school at George Peabody College for Teachers in Nashville, Tenn., where he received his Ph.D. (1934) and pioneered courses in audio-visual materials. Later, he worked concurrently as dean of the library school at Florida State University (1941–67) and as consultant to *Collier's Encyclopedia*.

Shorey, Paul (1857–1934) classicist; born in Davenport, Iowa. After studying in America and Germany, he taught at Bryn Mawr (1885–92) and the University of Chicago (1892–1927), where he was the first professor of Greek. A friend of the great classicist Basil Gildersleeve, he published extensively on Plato and Aristotle, and Greek metrics. He also founded *Classical Philology,* and gave the University of California Sather Lectures in 1916–17, 1918–19, and 1928–29.

Short, (Robert W.) Bobby (1926–) singer, pianist; born in Danville, Ill. Working in obscurity in clubs, he first found success in 1968 with the recording of a concert with Mabel Mercer and his long-term engagement at the Cafe Carlyle, both in New York. He sparked a revival of Cole Porter's music with a series of albums in the 1970s in which he interpreted various composers' music. With his casual but intimate renditions, he remained the quintessential cafe/supper-club singer of his time.

Short, Walter Campbell (1880–1949) soldier; born in Fillmore, Ill. Commissioned in the U.S. Army in 1902, he served on the Mexican punitive expedition (1916–17) and in France during World War I. Between the wars he rose in rank and reputation and in February 1941 was named commander of the army's Hawaiian Department. He was relieved of command for failing to take adequate action against the Japanese attack on Pearl Harbor on December 7, 1941, and he retired from the army in February 1942. He offered his own defense before a congressional committee in 1946 and historians generally came to agree that his failings were only part of a larger pattern among American leaders at the time.

Shorter, Frank (C.) (1947–) marathon runner; born in Munich, Germany. After a distinguished track career at Yale University, he became the first American in 64 years to win a gold medal as a marathoner in the Olympics at the 1972 Games.

Shotwell, James Thomson (1874–1965) historian, internationalist; born in Strathroy, Ontario, Canada. He came to the U.S.A. in 1898 and taught history at Columbia University (1905–42). He was an adviser to President Woodrow Wilson at the Paris Peace Conference (1919); he continued to promote his vision of collective security and this led to the Kellogg-Briand Peace Pact (1928). He served as president of the League of Nations Associates (1935–39), was chairman of the consultants to the U.S. delegation to the United Nations Conference in 1945, and was president of the Carnegie Endowment for International Peace (1949–50). He served as editor of what became the 152-volume work, *Economic and Social History of the World War.*

Shoup, George Laird (1836–1904) governor, U.S. senator; born in Kittanning, Pa. He sold mining goods in Colorado, serving as an army scout in the Southwest during the Civil War (1861–64). Moving to Idaho, he led that territory to statehood, becoming Republican governor (1889–90). In the U.S. Senate (1891–1901), he chaired the Committee on the Territories, supporting Indian rights.

Shouse, Jouett (1879–1968) U.S. representative; born in Woodford County, Ky. A journalist and businessman active in Democratic politics, he served in the Kansas state legislature before going to the U.S. House of Representatives (1915–19) where he sponsored the Federal Farm Loan Act of 1916. Returning to business, he reluctantly became chairman of the Democratic National Committee in 1929, masterminding a Democratic congressional victory. Passed over by Franklin Roosevelt in 1932, he joined the conservative American Liberty League and bred horses in Kentucky.

Shrady, George Frederick (1837–1907) surgeon, medical journalist; born in New York City. He practiced at several hospitals in New York City, gaining some reputation as a plastic surgeon. He attended President Garfield when he was shot and President Grant in his last illness, and wrote about each experience. Perhaps his major influence on his profession was through his advocacy of reform of both doctors' education and medical practices while editor of the *American Medical Times* (1860–64) and the *Medical Record* (1866–1904).

Shreve, R. Norris (1885–1975) chemical engineer, educator; born in St. Louis, Mo. He became affiliated with Purdue University's School of Chemical and Metallurgical Engineering (1930–61), becoming its head (1947–51). During World War II he was involved in the Manhattan Project to produce the atomic bomb. Specializing in the manufacture of dyes, he served as technical director of or consultant to numerous chemical companies.

Shubert, Lee (b. Levi) (?1873–1953) producer, theater manager; born in Shervient, Lithuania. He and his brothers Sam and Jacob Shubert broke the Theatrical Syndicate's monopoly in New York City to become the nation's biggest theater owners and producers.

Shubrick, William Branford (1790–1874) naval officer; born on Bull's Island, S.C. He served as a naval lieutenant during the War of 1812 and on the Pacific coast during the Mexican War. He refused to support the Confederate cause and retired in 1861.

Shull, Clifford G. (1915–) physicist, educator; born in Pittsburgh, Pa. After earning his B.S. at Carnegie Institute of Technology (1937) and his Ph.D. at New York University (1941), he went to work as a research physicist for the Texas Company (1941–46) before joining the Oak Ridge National Laboratory as a chief physicist (1946–55). In 1955 he became a professor of physics at the Massachusetts Institute of Technology, where he took emeritus status in 1986. He began the work for which he is most famous – using neutron beams to probe the structure of atoms – while working at Oak Ridge National Laboratory. His experiments not only proved certain claims made by the theory of quantum mechanics but also provided a tool that has led to major developments in the electronics industry, superconductivity, and other important fields involving physics. He shared the 1994 Nobel Prize in physics with Bertram N. Brockhouse, a Canadian.

Shultz, George (Pratt) (1920–) economist, cabinet member; born in New York City. An economics professor at the Massachusetts Institute of Technology (1946–57) before going to the University of Chicago (1957–69), he served on employment task forces. President Nixon's secretary of labor (1969–70), he averted a national rail strike, later becoming secretary of the treasury (1973–74). President Reagan's secretary of state (1982–88), he championed arms control and was widely admired for his measured approach to foreign affairs.

Shumway, Norman (Edward) (1923–) surgeon; born in Kalamazoo, Mich. A heart surgeon on the faculty of the Stanford University School of Medicine (1958), he pioneered research on heart transplantation, and then moved on to heart-lung transplants by 1981. An author of more than 450 publications on the heart, he was honored worldwide for his work.

Shuster, George (Nauman) (1894–1977) writer, educator; born in Lancaster, Wis. An English professor at Notre Dame (1920–24) and St. Joseph's College for Women (1925–35), he was managing editor of the lay Catholic magazine *Commonweal* (1929–37), before resigning after controversy over his criticisms of the Franco regime in Spain. He wrote fiction and essays on literature, religion, and European affairs, but gained his widest reputation as president of Hunter College (1940–60).

Shuster, Joe See under SIEGEL, (JEROME) JERRY.

Sibley, Henry Hastings (1811–91) public official; born in Detroit. He promoted the organizing of the Minnesota Territory (1849) and was the first governor of Minnesota state (1858–60). He commanded expeditions against the Sioux (1862–64) and acted as a peace commissioner (1865–66). He moved to St. Paul and engaged in private business.

Sickels, Frederick Ellsworth (1819–95) engineer, inventor; born near Camden, N.J. A physician's son, he had a fascination with railroads and went to work as a rodman for the Harlem Railroad at age 16. In 1841 he perfected his first invention, a cut-off for steam engines. His steam-powered steering apparatus for ships was not, however, a success; it worked, but no one would buy it. He migrated west after the Civil War, building railroads and bridges, and later became chief engineer for the waterworks in Kansas City, Mo.

Sickles, Daniel (Edgar) (1825–1914) soldier, U.S. representative; born in New York City. A lawyer and active Democrat, he twice served New York City in the U.S. House of Representatives (1857–61, 1893–95) but his colorful and controversial career lay elsewhere. During his first term in Washington, he killed Barton Key, the son of Francis Scott Key, in a duel (1859) but was acquitted in a trial in which he was the first American defendant to plead temporary insanity. (Young Key had been having an affair with Mrs. Sickles, whom her husband took back after being acquitted.) When the Civil War broke out, he raised a brigade, and, assigned the rank of brigadier general, led it through several campaigns and battles, culminating at Gettysburg where he made a much criticized and risky assault on July 2, 1863; he paid for it with the loss of a leg but was awarded the Congressional Medal of Honor. He was appointed military governor of the Carolinas after the war and stayed in the army until 1869, then served as ambassador to Spain (1869–73). Back practicing law in New York City, he was chairman of the New York State Monuments Commission (1886–1912); he was relieved of this post for mishandling funds, but he is credited with preserving Gettysburg battlefield as a national park.

Sidney, Margaret See LOTHROP, HARRIET MULFORD.

Sieber, (Albert) Al (1844–1907) army scout; born in Baden, Germany. He came with his family to Pennsylvania (1849) and then went to Minnesota (1856). He served as a private in the Civil War and was badly wounded at Gettysburg. He went west (1866), worked as a ranch foreman in Arizona (1868–71), and became an army scout under Col. George Crook in 1871. Sieber commanded the Apache scouts who served with the U.S. Army against Geronimo. Stern and inflexible, he was known as the outstanding scout of the Southwest. Discharged in 1890, he did odd jobs, and was crushed to death in an accident while building a road near the Roosevelt Dam. Called "Man of Iron" by the Indians, he was wounded at least 29 times in his career.

Siebert, Muriel (?1930–) stockbroker, educator; born in Cleveland, Ohio. After three years at Western Reserve University (now Case Western), she joined Bache & Co., in 1954 and moved on to several other investment houses before buying her own seat on the New York Stock Exchange in 1967, thereby becoming its first woman member. She established her own firm, Muriel Siebert & Co., in 1969. After a term as New York State superintendent of banks (1977–82), she ran an unsuccessful campaign for the Republican Senate nomination. She returned to her firm in 1983.

Siegel, (Jerome) Jerry (1914–) cartoonist; born in Cleveland, Ohio; **and Shuster, (Joseph) Joe** (1914–92) cartoonist; born in Toronto, Canada. Shuster's family had moved to Cleveland when he was nine years old and the two youths teamed up to do cartoons and comic strips while still in high school. They first appeared in an amateur comic book in 1935 and enjoyed their first success as professionals with a strip called "Slam Bradley" for *Detective Comics*. Siegel evidently had proposed the idea for a "man of steel" and Shuster had drawn him as early as 1934, but it was 1938 before the latter first appeared as "Superman" in the June issue of *Action Comics*. Although the strip was an immediate success and Siegel (stories) and Shuster (drawings) went on to produce it for many years, they had sold the rights away completely and did not profit from the many spin-offs, including the early serial movies. By 1975, when Warner Communications was clearly making a fortune from the new film version starring Christopher Reeve, there was such a public outcry when it was discovered that Siegel and Shuster were nearly destitute that Warner granted each an annual pension of $20,000, which provided them with modest comfort as well as belated recognition.

Siegmeister, Elie (1909–91) composer; born in New York City. After studies in New York and with Nadia Boulanger in

France, he taught at Hofstra University (New York) from 1949. His music involves an individual adaptation of modernist ideas, with a strong nationalistic element. He also wrote introductory texts on music.

Sigourney, Lydia (b. Lydia Howard Huntley) (1791–1865) poet; born in Norwich, Conn. She was educated and taught school locally (1811–19) until she married (1819), and thereafter lived in Hartford, Conn. Immensely prolific and popular during her time, she wrote pious sentimental poems and edited religious and juvenile publications.

Silcox, Ferdinand Augustus (1882–1939) forester, conservationist; born in Columbus, Ga. The son of a Confederate army veteran, he was educated at the College of Charleston, S.C., and the Yale School of Forestry. He worked for the U.S. Forest Service in Colorado and Montana from 1905 to 1917. Using experience gained in working with labor and management in the forest industries, he built a second career as an industrial relations specialist during the 1920s. Appointed director of the U.S. Forest Service in 1933, he oversaw the addition of more than 13,000,000 acres to U.S. holdings during his six-year tenure.

Silko, Leslie (b. Marmon) (1948–) writer, poet; born in Albuquerque, N.M. Born of Laguna Indian, Mexican, and Anglo-American heritage, she was raised on a Pueblo Indian Reservation, and studied at the University of Mexico (B.A. 1969). She was a teacher and wrote poetry, short stories, and novels, most of which draw on her Laguna heritage. *Ceremony* (1977), a novel, established her reputation as an important writer and she won a MacArthur Foundation "genius" grant in 1981. She lived in Tucson, Ariz.

Silliman, Benjamin, Jr. (1816–85) chemist, geologist; born in New Haven, Conn. Succeeding his father as professor of chemistry at Yale (1853–70), he was an editor of the *American Journal of Science* and the author of several textbooks. He is best known for his chemical analysis of rock oil from central Pennsylvania (1855), effectively launching the modern petroleum industry. He revealed the oil to be a mixture of hydrocarbons that could be separated into various distillations; he explained how to prepare and purify many of the "fractions," and suggested uses for several such as kerosene, paraffin, various lubricants, and an illuminating gas. One fraction, for which he could suggest no purpose at the time, was gasoline.

Silliman, Benjamin, Sr. (1779–1864) chemist, geologist; born in Trumbull, Conn. He was admitted to the bar (1802), but abandoned this career to become professor of chemistry and natural history at Yale (1802–53), devoting his spare time to study these subjects at Philadelphia, Edinburgh, and London. He founded (1818) and edited the *American Journal of Science* (1818–46). An inspirational educator, Silliman popularized the then new science of geology to a generation of students. He made major contributions to mineralogy and the geology of New England.

Sills, Beverly (b. Belle Miriam Silverman) (1929–) soprano; born in New York City. A radio performer from childhood (called "Bubbles"), she began her musical studies at age 12 and made her operatic debut in 1953 in San Francisco. Two years later she began a long association with the New York City Opera, whose manager she became (1979–88) just before her retirement as a singer in 1980. Vivacious in personality and a soprano of the first rank, she performed worldwide to steady acclaim.

Silver, Abba Hillel (1893–1963) rabbi, Zionist leader; born in Sirvintos, Lithuania. He was brought to the U.S.A. in 1902. He was educated at Hebrew Union College in Cincinnati, the University of Cincinnati, and Western Reserve University. He served as rabbi of Congregation Tifereth Israel in Cleveland (1917–63) and published several books, including *Religion in a Changing World* (1930) and *The World Crisis and Jewish Survival* (1941). A militant Zionist, he headed many organizations including the Zionist Organizations of America, American Zionist Emergency Council, United Jewish Appeal, United Palestine Appeal, and Central Conference of American Rabbis. He was president of the World Zionist Organization (1945–48).

Silver, Horace (Ward Martin Tavares) (1928–) jazz musician; born in Norwalk, Conn. An influential pianist and composer, he helped to develop and popularize the hard-bop style in the mid-1950s. He was a sideman with Stan Getz and Coleman Hawkins between 1950 and 1953, a cofounder of the Jazz Messengers in 1954, and the leader of his own groups thereafter.

Silverman, Sime (1873–1933) newspaper publisher; born in Cortland, N.Y. After working on the *New York Morning Telegraph* (1896–1905), he founded *Variety,* a weekly dedicated to show business. It soon became an institution, respected for both its dollars-and-cents approach to the business and its Runyonesque approach to shows, and its slangy and often original style added many words to the language. He remained its publisher and editor to his death, which came right after he had started a Hollywood edition of his paper.

Silverman, Sydel (1933–) anthropologist; born in Chicago. Educated at the University of Chicago and Columbia University (Ph.D. 1963), she taught at Queens College in New York City before becoming president of the Wenner-Gren Foundation for Anthropological Research in 1987. A specialist in Italian peasant society, she is the author of *Peasant Society: A Reader* (1965) and *Three Bells of Civilization: The Life of an Italian Hill Town* (1975).

Silverstein, Shel (Shelby) (Uncle Shelby, pen name) (1932–) poet, cartoonist, composer; born in Chicago. He served in the U.S. armed forces in Japan and Korea as a cartoonist for *Stars and Stripes* (1950s), returned to New York City and became a roving reporter, composer, and folksinger. Encouraged by Ursula Nordstrom, children's editor of Harper & Row, he published several innovative books of verse for readers of all ages, such as *Where the Sidewalk Ends* (1974), and *A Light in the Attic* (1981). He lived in Greenwich Village, New York; Key West, Fla.; and on a houseboat in Sausalito, Calif.

Silvert, Kalman H. (Hirsch) (1921–76) political scientist; born in Bryn Mawr, Pa. He ended a long teaching career at New York University (1967–76). He is credited with introducing quantitative techniques to political analysis, influencing changes in the United States government's Latin America policy in the 1970s, and promoting Latin American studies and social science research. His works include the posthumous *Reason for Democracy* (1977).

Simic, Charles (1938–) poet; born in Belgrade, Yugoslavia. His father escaped from the violence of World War II to New York City, and his family followed him in 1954. Charles studied at New York University (B.A. 1967), and became an editorial assistant for *Aperture,* a photography magazine

(1966–69). He taught at several institutions, notably the University of New Hampshire (1974). He is praised for his translations of the Yugoslavian poets, and for his own evocative and often surrealistic poetry, as in *The Book of Gods and Devils* (1990).

Simkhovitch, Mary (Melinda) (b. Kingsbury) (1867–1951) social reformer; born in Chestnut Hill, Mass. Inspired by work among the poor while a student at Boston University, Radcliffe College, and Columbia University, she worked at New York City settlement houses and in 1902 founded her own, Greenwich House, where she encouraged grass roots activism by residents. She was a leader in urban revitalization efforts, and as president of the Public Housing Conference (1931–43) and vice-chairman of the New York City Housing Authority, she promoted construction of public housing. Her writings include a 1940 autobiography.

Simmons, (Aloysius Harry) Al (b. Aloys Szymanski) (1902–56) baseball player; born in Milwaukee, Wis. During his 20-year career as an outfielder (1924–44), primarily with the Philadelphia Athletics, he posted a lifetime batting average of .334 and hit 307 home runs. Nicknamed "Bucketfoot" because he tended to stride away from a pitched ball, he was elected to baseball's Hall of Fame in 1953.

Simmons, Furnifold (McLendel) (1854–1940) U.S. senator; born in Jones County, N.C. After leading a movement to deny African-Americans the right to vote, he was elected to the U.S. House of Representatives (Dem., N.C.; 1887–89) and to the U.S. Senate (1901–31). He managed to hold control over Democratic politics in North Carolina while advancing his conservative views in the Senate through the committee posts he gained by seniority.

Simms, William Gilmore (1806–70) writer; born in Charleston, N.C. After the death of his mother (1808), he was raised by his maternal grandmother and schooled locally. He was admitted to the bar (1827), but spent his time writing poetry and working as an editor in Charleston. He became a prolific writer of historical romances, notably *The Yamassee: A Romance of Carolina* (1835). He also continued to write poetry, short stories, histories, and essays. A believer in the myth that the South could be a paradise where slaves were treated benevolently, he saw his life and work radically altered by the Civil War.

Simon, Herbert A. (Alexander) (1916–   ) social scientist, economist; born in Milwaukee, Wis. A true interdisciplinarian, his work encompassed psychology and computer science as well as economics. He spent several years as a researcher at the University of California: Berkeley and taught political science at the Illinois Institute of Technology (1942–49) before becoming a professor at Carnegie-Mellon University (1949). He focused his work on administrative behavior and decision making in government and business. He argued that economic action is "bounded" by limited knowledge, information, and resources. In addition to many other awards and distinctions, in 1978 he received the Nobel Prize in economics.

Simon, (Marvin) Neil (1927–   ) playwright; born in New York City. After fulfilling his obligation to the Air Force Reserve in 1946, he took a clerical job with Warner Brothers in New York, but soon began writing comic material for radio and television personalities (1947–60). With his brother Danny Simon he wrote sketches for Broadway shows such as *Catch a Star* (1955) and *New Faces of 1956*. His first

full-length comedy, *Come Blow Your Horn* (1961), was a success but it was *The Odd Couple* (1965) that launched his career as late-20th-century America's most successful writer of comedies. Year in and year out he filled theaters – and eventually the television screen and moviehouses – with his string of popular comedies and musicals (*Sweet Charity,* 1966; *Promises, Promises,* 1969); in 1966 he had four hit shows on Broadway. At the same time, he became increasingly dissatisfied at hearing himself dismissed as a gag-writer, and starting with *The Gingerbread Lady* (1970), he began to deal with more serious themes; with *Chapter Two* (1977), he became autobiographical; and with *Brighton Beach Memoirs* (1983) he began a series of dramas drawing on his youthful years; he was finally given serious recognition with the Pulitzer for *Lost in Yonkers* (1991).

Simon, Norton (Winfred) (1907–93) businessman, art collector; born in Portland, Ore. He spent much of his early years in San Francisco and attended college for a short time. He invested in the stock market, survived the crash of 1929, invested in the Hunt Foods & Industries Company, and made a fortune. His business success was legendary by the time he began collecting art ranging from old masters, sculpture, tapestries, and furniture. He established several tax-exempt foundations and financed a new art museum in conjunction with the Los Angeles County Museum to house his collection (1965). After his divorce from his first wife, Lucille Ellis Simon, he married the actress, Jennifer Jones (1971). In 1974 he moved his collection to the Pasadena Art Museum, and by 1978 had taken over the museum and changed the name to the Norton Simon Museum.

Simon, Paul (1942–   ) singer, composer, lyricist; born in Newark, N.J. Son of teachers (his father also played double bass in a radio orchestra), he got to know **Art Garfunkel** (1942–   ; b. New York City) in the sixth grade at their Queens (New York City) public school. Sharing an interest in sports and pop music, they began to sing together – Simon played the acoustic guitar – and soon were performing at local social functions. By 1957 they were calling themselves "Tom and Jerry" and had a recording contract; one of their songs, "Hey Schoolgirl," became a minor hit. By 1959 they had drifted apart, Simon going to Queens College, Garfunkel to Columbia University, but by their sophomore year they were reunited and turning to folk music. Simon had continued his professional singing career but after taking his B.A. he briefly attended Brooklyn Law School. They cut their first album as Simon and Garfunkel in 1964, and one of its songs, "Sounds of Silence," was so popular that it was issued as a single and became a top hit. This led to a series of highly successful singles and albums, a constant round of appearances at colleges, on television, tours in Europe and the U.S.A., and special concerts. Their music for the movie *The Graduate* (1967) included a new hit, "Mrs. Robinson." "Bridge Over Troubled Waters" (1970) was their next big hit. They split up in 1970 – Simon simply stated that "I didn't want to be half of something"; they appeared together at a political rally in 1972, but then not again until a 1981 concert in Central Park; they toured together in 1982 and 1983 and thereafter appeared infrequently on special occasions. Garfunkel – who for the most part had simply been singing Simon's compositions – went on to pursue a career as a movie actor (as in *Carnal Knowledge,* 1971) although he also continued to record solo albums. Simon continued expanding his musical interests and styles and maintained his standing as one of the major figures in popular music. His recordings, such as *Still Crazy After All These Years* (1975), continued to win awards. He wrote the screenplay and songs as well as starred in the movie *One-Trick Pony* (1980), and had a small role in *Annie Hall* (1977). In 1985 he went to South Africa and recorded with some prominent (black) South African musicians; this led to his highly successful album, *Graceland* (1986), but also to some protests against his being perceived as cooperating with the racist authorities; he denied this and in 1992 was invited by black South Africans to play there. *The Rhythm of the Saints* (1990) reflected his continuing interest in music from other cultures. He was generous with both his money and musical talents in supporting a variety of charitable causes.

Simon, Richard (Leo) (1899–1960) publisher; born in New York City. With his friend, Max Schuster, he founded the publishing firm of Simon and Schuster (1924) and helped develop it through such best-selling ideas as the first crossword puzzle book.

Simon, William (Edward) (1927–) financier, cabinet member, born in Paterson, N.J. An army veteran, he was a partner with Salomon Brothers (1968–72), dealing in government securities and becoming extremely rich. As director of the Federal Energy Office (1973–74), he instituted fuel allotments during the oil crisis. He then served presidents Nixon and Ford as secretary of the Treasury (1974–77). On leaving the government, he wrote *A Time for Action* (1980) and formed Wesray, an investment company, in 1981.

Simon, Yves (René Marie) (1903–61) philosopher; born in Cherbourg, France. After studying in Paris under Jacques Maritain and teaching at the University of Lille, he went to the United States, where he taught at Notre Dame University (from 1938) and the University of Chicago (from 1948); he was a leading Thomistic philosopher.

Simonds, Ossian Cole (1855–1926) landscape architect; born in Grand Rapids, Mich. Trained as a civil engineer, he became superintendent of Chicago's Graceland Cemetery, which he turned into a park-like masterpiece in the 1880s before going into private practice in Chicago.

Simone, Nina (b. Eunice Kathleen Waymon) (1933–) jazz singer, pianist, composer; born in Tryon, N.C. After studying piano and teaching music as a teenager, she attended Juilliard for a year; she failed to gain admission to Curtis Institute (Philadelphia), she believed, on account of her race. She turned to playing the piano and singing in Atlanta, Ga., nightclubs, first using the name "Nina Simone" in 1954, and first won national acclaim with her 1959 recording of Gershwin's "I Loves You, Porgy." She toured the United States and Europe in the 1960s; by this time she had taken up the cause of civil rights and she began to write and perform protest songs such as "To Be Young, Gifted and Black" and "Four Women." In the early 1970s, she expatriated herself, angrily denouncing the treatment of African-Americans in the U.S.A. and eventually settled in the south of France. For many years she was distracted by quarrels with agents, recording companies, and the Internal Revenue Service over money matters, and her occasional performances in the U.S.A. were unevenly given and received. By the late 1980s, however, she seemed to mellow somewhat and she returned to the U.S.A. in 1993 to promote a new album, *A Woman Alone,* and her autobiography, *I Put a Spell on You* (1992). Called the "highpriestess of soul," she remains distinctive for her blending of jazz, pop, and soul with emotional intensity and a classical amplitude.

Simpson, Alan K. (Kooi) (1931–) U.S. senator; born in Denver, Colo. Elected the the U.S. Senate (Rep., Wyo.; 1979), he served as party whip from 1985. A conservative, he was an opponent of government regulation.

Simpson, George Gaylord (1902–84) paleontologist; born in Chicago. After earning a Ph.D. at Yale, Simpson began his long association with the American Museum of Natural History (1927–59), where he was eventually curator of fossil mammals and chairman of the department of geology and paleontology (1942–59). He was later Alexander Agassiz Professor of Vertebrate Paleontology at Harvard (1959–70). Simpson specialized in early fossil mammals, leading expeditions on four continents and discovering in 1953 the 50-million-year old fossil skulls of Dawn Horses in Colorado. He helped develop the modern biological theory of evolution, drawing on paleontology, genetics, ecology, and natural selection to show that evolution occurs as a result of natural selection operating in response to shifting environmental conditions; among his works in this field is the popular *Meaning of Evolution* (1944, revised 1967).

Simpson, Joanne Malkus (1923–) meteorologist; born in Boston, Mass. The first woman to receive a Ph.D. in meteorology (1949), she studied with Carl-Gustaf Rossby at the University of Chicago and trained military forecasters during World War II. Her award-winning research on cumulus clouds and weather modification took her around the country. Her home-base was the Goddard Space Flight Center/NASA since 1979; she was chief scientist for meteorology from 1988.

Simpson, (Orenthal James) "O.J." (1947–) football player; born in San Francisco. A two-time All-American halfback and Heisman Trophy winner at the University of Southern California, he joined the professional Buffalo Bills in 1969 but did not excel until the offense was tailored to showcase his running. He topped 1,000 yards rushing five consecutive years (1972–76) and led the National Football League four times. In 1973 he became the first to rush for over 2,000 yards. After retiring from pro football (1979), he moved on to a profitable career in television commercials and as a sportscaster. When his estranged wife Nicole and Ronald Goldman were murdered, Simpson was charged with the crime in a case that became a sensational media event.

Sims, James Marion (1813–83) gynecologist; born in Lancaster County, S.C. Practicing in Alabama, he gained a reputation by performing difficult and unorthodox surgery – in particular, for dealing with fistulas in women; he perfected his technique after 30 operations on an unanesthetized 17-year-old female slave named Anarcha (1849). His work, published in the *American Journal of the Medical Sciences* (1852), gained him such attention that he went to New York City in 1853, where he taught his procedure to other doctors; this led to the establishment of the New York Woman's Hospital (1857). He spent most of 1861–65 in Europe where he performed various operations to considerable acclaim. Taking up his practice in New York City, he went to France during 1870 to perform surgery in the Franco-Prussian War. His *Clinical Notes on Uterine Surgery* (1866) contributed to the founding of modern gynecology.

Sims, William Snowden (1858–1936) naval officer; born in Port Hope, Ontario, Canada. As the inspector of target practice (1902–09) he brought about great improvements in naval gunnery. He commanded the Atlantic Torpedo Flotilla (1913–15) and was president of the Naval War College (1917). He was named commander of U.S. naval forces in European Waters (1918). He was a coauthor of *The Victory at Sea* (1920) which won a Pulitzer Prize in history.

Sinatra, (Francis Albert) Frank (1915–) singer, movie actor; born in Hoboken, N.J. As a teenager, he organized a singing group, the Hoboken Four, which won first prize on the *Major Bowes Original Amateur Hour*. Following graduation from the Drake Institute, he spent several years singing in New Jersey roadhouses before finding work in the late 1930s as a radio studio singer in New York City. In 1939, while performing at a club in New Jersey, he was heard by Harry James, who signed him to appear with his new swing band. After touring with James in 1939, he rose to prominence with Tommy Dorsey's orchestra (1940–42). Breaking away from Dorsey, in 1943 he began working as a single and serving as emcee on the popular radio program, *Lucky Strike Hit Parade*. He quickly emerged as one of the earliest and most adulated teen idols – the hysteria he engendered in his "bobby-soxer" fans culminated in rioting at the Paramount Theatre in New York on Columbus Day, 1944. He remained a popular radio star throughout the 1940s and recorded numerous hits for Columbia Records between 1943 and 1952, but becoming unhappy with conditions there he moved to Capitol Records (1953–62). His recordings during this period came to epitomize American popular singing at its finest, with a style that maintained fidelity to a song's lyric and mood while imbuing it with subtle elements of jazz beat and phrasing. In 1960 he was a cofounder of Reprise Records, which he recorded for exclusively after 1963. He also had a successful career as a movie actor, beginning as a straight actor in *Higher and Higher* (1943); throughout the 1950s and 1960s he played dramatic roles that brought him considerable acclaim, including *From Here to Eternity* (1953), for which he received an Academy Award as best supporting actor. This work brought him into the Hollywood community, where he became a member of the "Rat Pack," a group that included his occasional concert partners, Sammy Davis Jr., and Dean Martin. During these years he also had highly publicized marriages to movie stars Ava Gardner and Mia Farrow. Regular appearances at Las Vegas and such locales, the lifestyle that inevitably went with such a celebrity (bodyguards, hangers-on), a temperament that involved him in occasional fights, fabulous wealth, and various business ventures – all this added up in some people's minds to alleged involvement with the underworld, but nothing beyond personal acquaintances was ever proven. In practice he was most generous in his gifts to both individuals and organizations, and his overall status in the entertainment industry earned him the title "Chairman of the Board." He announced his retirement in 1971 but he returned for various concerts and tours in the next two decades. Among the many testaments to his special status as a pop superstar was his 1980 recording of "New York, New York," which made him the only singer in history to have hit records in five consecutive decades.

Sinclair, Upton (Beall), Jr. (1878–1968) social reformer, novelist; born in Baltimore, Md. A published writer even before he graduated from the City College of New York (1897), he took up writing for newspapers and completed and published several successful novels. Joining the Socialist Party (1902), he helped found the Intercollegiate Socialist Society (1905) and ran unsuccessfully for a congressional seat from New Jersey (1906). In that year his novel, *The Jungle* shocked the world with its exposure of conditions in the meat-packing industry in Chicago; he had expected the exposé to lead to an improvement in working conditions but instead it led to passage of the Pure Food and Drug Act, to protect consumers. He used royalties from *The Jungle* to help found a cooperative residence, Helicon Hall, in Englewood, N.J. He continued to publish muckraking probes of the capitalist world and for many years was prominent in California politics, running unsuccessfully for several offices as a socialist and for governor (1934) as a Democrat. Author of over 80 books that exposed alleged evils in such institutions as organized religion, the education establishment, and the press, he won a Pulitzer Prize for *Dragon's Teeth* (1942), the third novel in his 11-volume Lanny Budd series, and published his autobiography (1954).

Singer, Isaac Bashevis (Isaac Bashevis, Isaac Warshofsky, pen names) (1904–91) writer; born in Radzmin, Poland (brother of Israel Singer). He attended a rabbinical seminary (1920–27), but decided upon a secular life and worked for the Hebrew and then for the Yiddish press (1923–35). Concerned by the threat of Nazism, he emigrated to New York City (1935), and worked as a staff member for the *Jewish Daily Forward*, where most of his work was first published in Yiddish. He wrote novels, short stories, children's books, plays, and memoirs, first in Yiddish and then translated into English under his supervision. He is best known for his novels and short stories set in the Jewish ghettos of Eastern Europe, as in *The Family Moskat* (1950) and *A Crown of Feathers and Other Stories* (1973). He was awarded the 1978 Nobel Prize in literature.

Singer, Isaac M. (Merritt) (1811–75) inventor, manufacturer; born in Pittstown, N.Y. He worked at unskilled jobs, apprenticed as a mechanic, and then wandered state-to-state working as a mechanic. In Lockport, Ill. (1839), he patented a rock drill, but squandered the profits. In Pittsburgh (1849) he patented a carving machine and found financing to manufacture it, but a boiler explosion destroyed everything, leaving him penniless again. In 1851, asked to repair a crude sewing machine, he immediately saw how it could be greatly improved. He took out patents on his own improvements, and started to manufacture his machine. After Elias Howe brought Singer and others to trial in 1854, Singer had to pay royalties to Howe for infringing on his basic needle patent. But Singer would continue to patent more improvements and build the I. M. Singer company into the world's best-known manufacturer of practical domestic sewing machines, in part by spending large sums on advertising. When he retired from his company in 1863, he went to Europe.

Singer, Israel Joshua (1893–1944) writer; born in Bilgoray, Poland (brother of Isaac Bashevis Singer). He and his family moved to Warsaw (1908), and he was educated to become a rabbi. By the age of 18 he left home and lived a secular life. He held a series of odd jobs, and studied science, language, mathematics, painting, and writing. During World War I he was conscripted into the Russian army, and worked at forced labor during the German occupation (1915). He moved to Kiev, Russia, where he worked as a proofreader for a Jewish newspaper, and wrote stories and plays before returning to Warsaw (1921). His novel, *The Sinner* (1933), was well received in America, and he emigrated to New York City (1934). There he wrote novels depicting the conflict between European and American cultures, as in *The Family Carnovsky* (1943). A master of the Yiddish tradition in America, he is credited for paving the way for his younger brother, Isaac Bashevis Singer.

Singer, June Kurlander (1918–) psychologist; born in Cleveland, Ohio. She studied at Northwestern University and married rabbi and psychoanalyst Richard E. Singer in 1939. Twenty years later, she did graduate work in psychology at the Jung Institute and conducted a private practice in psychology (from 1962). She was associated with the Virginia Frank Child Development Center in Chicago and wrote several books on Jungian psychology, including *Androgyny: Toward a New Theory of Sexuality* (1976).

Singer, S. J. (Seymour Jonathan) (1924–) cell biologist; born in New York City. He was a research fellow at the California Institute of Technology (1947–48), worked for the U.S. Public Health Service (1948–51), moved to Yale (1951–61), then joined the University of California: San Diego (1961). He made major contributions to the physical chemistry of proteins (including antibodies), membrane biology, and chemical cytology.

Singleton, Charles S. (Southward) (1909–85) translator, author, educator; born in McLoud, Okla. He taught 40 years at the Johns Hopkins University and ten years at Yale. A scholar of Italian Renaissance literature, of his many translations, essays, and critical works, the masterwork was the definitive prose translation of Dante's *Divine Comedy* (6 vols. 1970–75).

Sinnott, Edmund W. (Ware) (1888–1968) botanist, educator; born in Cambridge, Mass. He taught at Harvard (1908–15), during which period he made botanical expeditions to Australasia. He then moved to the Connecticut Agricultural College (1915–28), before going on to Barnard College (1928–39), Columbia University (1939–40) and Yale (1940–56). During the 1920s and 1930s he performed extensive research on the genetic determination of fruit morphology, especially squashes. He brought Yale to prominence in botany as director of Yale's Sheffield School (1945–56), and later as dean of the Yale graduate school (1950–56). From 1945 onward, he expounded his philosophy that science can bring about human solidarity.

Sirhan, Sirhan (c. 1943–) assassin; born in Palestine. He came with his family to California in 1956. As a Palestinian, he was enraged by Senator Robert Kennedy's pro-Israeli stance. He shot and killed Kennedy (1968) and was found guilty of premeditated murder. His death sentence was commuted to life imprisonment due to a plea for leniency by Senator Edward Kennedy.

Sirica, John (Joseph) (1904–92) judge; born in Waterbury, Conn. Son of an immigrant Italian barber, he graduated from Georgetown Law School (1926) but tried his hand at boxing before setting up his law practice in Washington, D.C. He moved between government law appointments and private practice before being appointed to the Federal bench by President Eisenhower in 1957. Becoming chief judge in 1971, he assigned the Watergate burglary case to himself in 1973; during two years, he proceeded to push witnesses and lawyers to reveal the facts until he had effectively brought President Richard Nixon to resign in the face of impeachment. Although criticized by some for his often less than judicial manner and methods, he was upheld by the Court of Appeals and became a folk hero of sorts, "the Watergate judge." He retired from the Federal bench in 1986, an unassuming man who once found himself thrust under history's spotlight and had risen to the occasion.

Siskind, Aaron (1903–) teacher, photographer; born in New York City. An English teacher, he started taking photographs in 1930, focusing on the textures of everyday objects. He taught photography at the Illinois Institute of Technology (1951–71).

Sisler, George (Harold) (1893–1973) baseball player; born in Manchester, Ohio. One of the game's greatest hitters, he twice achieved a batting average of over .400 in a season (1920, 1922), and in 1920 he established a major league record for most hits in a season (257). He was also an outstanding defensive first baseman during his 15-year career (1915–30), mostly with the St. Louis Browns. He was elected to baseball's Hall of Fame in 1939.

Sissle, (Lee) Noble (1889–1975) lyricist, singer; born in Indianapolis, Ind. He began singing with the famous Society Orchestra. In 1915 he met Eubie Blake and they toured in vaudeville for several years, performing their own songs including "Good Night, Sweet Angeline" (1916). In 1921 they joined with the vaudeville team in creating *Shuffle Along,* the first black musical to play in a major Broadway theater during the regular season; it spawned a series of similar musicals, several by Sissle and Blake, and also produced Sissle and Blake's classic, "I'm Just Wild about Harry." In the 1930s and 1940s Sissle was a bandleader and cofounder of the Negro Actors Guild. In 1972 he and Blake received Yale University's Ellington medal. Sissle and Blake's songs would continue to be heard in later Broadway musicals such as *Bubbling Brown Sugar* (1976) and *Eubie* (1978).

Sitting Bull (b. Tatanka Yotanka) (?1831–90) Hunkpapa Sioux leader and medicine man; born on the Grand River in S.D. Even as a youth he was known among the Sioux as a warrior; by 1856 he headed the Strong Heart warrior society and in 1866 he became chief of the northern hunting Sioux. Bitterly opposed to white encroachment, he made peace with the U.S. government (1868) when it guaranteed him a large reservation free of white settlers. Following the discovery of gold in the Black Hills (1874), he joined with the Arapaho and Cheyenne to fight against the invaders. Although head of the war council, he remained in the encampment and performed a rite while his warriors defeated Col. George Custer's men at the Little Bighorn (1876). He and his followers attempted to move to Canada, but the Canadian government refused to accept them, and they returned to the U.S.A. in 1881. After serving a two-year imprisonment, he traveled with Buffalo Bill's Wild West Show (1885–86). He was arrested for supporting the Ghost Dance movement and killed by Indian policemen – just prior to the battle of Wounded Knee.

Six, Robert (Forman) (1907–86) airline executive; born in Stockton, Calif. Using family money, he established Valley Flying Service in 1929. In 1937, after having worked in China as a pilot, he borrowed money and bought a 40 percent interest in Varney Speed Lines, renamed Continental Airlines in 1938. Continental successfully competed against industry giants for the 46 years of Six's presidency.

Sizer, Theodore R. (Ryland) (1932–) educator; born in New Haven, Conn. He directed Harvard's Master of Arts in Teaching program (1961–64) and was dean of the graduate school of education at Harvard (1964–72). He was professor of education at Brown University (1984) and chairman of the Coalition of Essential Schools (1984). He wrote *Horace's Compromise* (1984) and *Horace's School: Redesigning the American High School* (1992).

Skinner, B. F. (Burrhus Frederic) (1904–90) psychologist, educator, author; born in Susquehanna, Pa. Forgoing his early goal of being a writer, he earned his doctorate in psychology at Harvard (1931). He stayed on there to continue his research with the so-called Skinner box he developed to test the effects of behavior modification on laboratory animals. He then taught at the University of Minnesota (1936–45) and Indiana University (1945–48). During World War II he worked for the Office of Scientific Research and Development on such projects as training pigeons to guide missiles (never achieved). In 1945 he gained considerable attention when he published an article about an "air crib," a mechanically controlled environment in which his daughter had spent much of her first two years. He then returned to teach and research at Harvard (1948–74) and gained a reputation as the chief American exponent of the behavioral approach to psychology, especially operant conditioning, based on laboratory experiments, chiefly with pigeons, that produced behavior modification through reinforcement (as by the release of food pellets) of certain learned behaviors. The popular application of the theory, as in the "teaching machine" device with its programmed instructions, seemed bizarre at the time it was introduced but in the current age of computer-assisted instruction (CAI) seems merely to have arrived ahead of its time. His many professional writings include *Science and Human Behavior* (1953) and *Verbal Behavior* (1957). In books such as *Walden Two* (1948), a novel, and *Beyond Freedom and Dignity* (1971), his often controversial views on social engineering reached a broader public than did his professional writings. After his retirement from Harvard he accepted a position at Oxford University and before his death composed a record of his work and life in a multivolume autobiography.

Skinner, Otis (1858–1942) stage actor; born in Cambridge, Mass. Called a "flamboyant and scene-filling" actor, he performed in both classic and modern plays. He was the father of Cornelia Otis Skinner.

Slaney, Mary (b. Decker) (1958–) track athlete; born in Bunnvale, N.J. She held several different U.S. records in distance running, from the 800 meter to the 10,000 meter race. Her attempt at an Olympic medal was thwarted in 1984 when she was accidentally tripped by Zola Budd in the 3,000 meter race at Los Angeles.

Slater, John C. (Clarke) (1900–76) physicist; born in Oak Park, Ill. He taught and performed research at Harvard (1924–30), where he introduced a determinantal wave function for multielectron systems. At the Massachusetts Institute of Technology (1930–66), he pursued fundamental research on magnetron design. In the 1950s and 1960s, he returned to quantum mechanical studies of molecular and solid-state theory. His last academic position was at the University of Florida (1964–76).

Slater, Samuel (1768–1835) engineer, inventor; born in Belper, England. The son of a yeoman farmer, he received a modest education, then learned about advanced textile machinery as an apprentice. In 1789 he emigrated to the U.S.A. in disguise and under an assumed name, as Britain had banned the export of textile machinery or details about it. Working from memory, he built up-to-date spinning machines for a Rhode Island cotton mill (1793). He established his own manufacturing firm (1798) and he directed several large mill operations.

Slatkin, Leonard (1944–) conductor; born in Los Angeles. Son of the Hollywood conductor Felix Slatkin, he became an assistant at the St. Louis Symphony in 1968 and music director there in 1979; he became known for his performances of the milder moderns.

Slattery, John (Richard) (1851–1926) Catholic religious leader; born in New York City. Heir to a construction company fortune, he was ordained as a Mill Hill Father (1877). In 1884 he became a missionary among African-Americans in the Richmond, Va., area. As rector of a Boston seminary (from 1888) and founder of the Josephite Fathers (1892), he trained other priests for such missionary work. A progressive concerned with the material as well as the religious needs of blacks, he was stung by the 1899 Vatican condemnation of "Americanism" and in 1906 he left the priesthood, becoming an attorney.

Slick, (Wing) Grace (1939–) rock singer, songwriter; born in Chicago, Ill. She was a fashion model before singing with the group, the Great Society, in 1965. In 1966 she joined Jefferson Airplane, the first popular San Francisco rock band. After releasing such successful albums as *Surrealistic Pillow* (1967) and *Volunteers* (1969) the Airplane disbanded and in 1974 she formed Jefferson Starship which released the best-selling album *Red Octopus* (1975), as well as later albums.

Slidell, John (1793–1871) U.S. senator, diplomat; born in New York City (brother of Alexander Slidell Mackenzie). A wealthy New Orleans lawyer and moderate Democrat, he was the political boss of Louisiana and the power behind the Buchanan administration as a U.S. senator (1853–61). His capture with James Mason by Union forces in November 1861 en route to a Confederate diplomatic mission to Europe on the *Trent* sparked an international crisis. Released on December 30, Slidell went to France but never did succeed in obtaining French support for the Confederacy. He stayed in Paris until 1871, then retired to England where he died.

Slipher, Vesto Melvin (1875–1969) astronomer; born in Mulberry, Ind. At the Lowell Observatory in Arizona (1901–69; director from 1917, emeritus from 1953), this highly honored astronomer led two solar eclipse expeditions, participated in the search that found Pluto (1930), and determined the rotations of several planets.

Sliwa, Curtis (?1954–) social activist; born in New York City. He was a rebellious student in parochial school. While working at a McDonald's restaurant, he organized the Rock Brigade, which evolved into the Magnificent Thirteen and then the Guardian Angels (1979). Originally the Guardian Angels simply wanted to protect subway riders in New York City, but the organization spread to many other cities (eventually to foreign countries) and broadened its goals to protecting people in various public areas. Some regarded the Angels as potentially dangerous vigilantes, but gradually the group came to be accepted by city governments and the public at large. He married Lisa Evers (1981), a karate black belt, who served as his close associate in his expanding organization. There were several attempts on Sliwa's life during the 1980s.

Sloan, Alfred P. (Pritchard), Jr. (1875–1966) industrialist, philanthropist; born in New Haven, Conn. After studying at Brooklyn Polytechnic and the Massachusetts Institute of Technology, he headed Hyatt Roller Bearing Company and then United Motors, a group that supplied parts and accessories to General Motors (GM). When the company was taken over by GM, he joined the executive committee, and became GM's president (1923–37) and chairman (1937–46). He established a model administration, pioneered in trade-in policies, and embarked on diversification with such products as diesel locomotives, turning GM into one of the world's largest manufacturers. On retirement he focused on his philanthropies through the Alfred P. Sloan Jr. Foundation, which continues to make large grants for cancer research, engineering education, improving industrial management, and the general advancement of knowledge of science and technology. He wrote *My Years with General Motors* (1964).

Sloan, Eric (b. Everard Jean Hinrichs) (1905–85) illustrator, painter, author; born in New York City. He studied at the Art Students League, New York, under John Sloan (1930s), whose last name he appropriated. Based in Cornwall, Conn. and, later, in Santa Fe, N.M., he became an expert on everything from agriculture to weather while writing and illustrating books on early American artifacts, such as *The ABC Book of Early Americana* (1963), and *I Remember America* (1971).

Sloan, (James Forman) "Todhunter" (1873–1933) jockey; born in Kokomo, Ind. Often winning as many as five races in a day, he rode 137 winners on 369 mounts in 1897 and an amazing 186 winners on 362 mounts (45.1 percent) in 1898.

Sloan, John (French) (1871–1951) painter, printmaker; born in Lock Haven, Pa. From 1892 he worked as an illustrator for various periodicals, studied at the Pennsylvania Academy of the Fine Arts (1892–93), and became an accomplished etcher beginning in 1902. He moved to New York (1902) and was one of the founders of the Eight (1908), some of whom became known as the Ashcan school for their paintings of urban life. He taught at the Art Students League (1916–38), and his paintings were bold and warmly colored, as in *The City from Greenwich Village* (1922). From the 1930s on he painted female nudes, such as *Nude and Nine Apples* (1937).

Sloan, Samuel (1815–84) architect; born in Beaver Dam, Pa. "The Architect of Philadelphia," he designed public buildings, schools, and churches, and, working with Thomas S. Kirkbride, became an authority on designing insane asylums. He wrote seven influential plan books (1852–73).

Sloat, John Drake (1781–1867) naval officer; born in Goshen, N.Y. Joining the navy in 1800, he served in the undeclared naval war against France, then left the navy to command a merchant vessel (1801–12). He rejoined the navy to fight in the War of 1812 and stayed on, becoming commander of the Pacific Squadron in 1844. Hearing that the U.S.A. was at war with Mexico in May 1846, he sailed his squadron to Monterey, Calif., and after occupying that

Mexican settlement, he proclaimed California to be a possession of the U.S.A. In poor health, he was dismissed in July by Commodore Robert Stockton and went back to Washington, D.C., where he was praised by some and condemned by others. His last nine years of active duty were spent on shore duty.

Slocum, Henry Warner (1827–94) soldier, lawyer, U.S. representative; born in Delphi, N.Y. A West Point graduate (1852), he left the army to practice law. He returned to the service in 1861 and saw action at both Bull Run battles, Antietam, and Chancellorsville. He commanded the Union right-wing corps at Gettysburg and led the Army of Georgia, a component of Sherman's army, through Georgia and the Carolinas in 1864–65. After the war, he took up his law practice in Brooklyn and served three terms in the U.S. House of Representatives (Dem., N.Y.; 1869–73, 1883–85).

Slocum, Joshua (1844–c. 1910) mariner, adventurer, author; born in Wilmot Township, Nova Scotia, Canada. His family was of Loyalist descent. He went to sea as a cook and sailed in the Pacific Ocean. He became a naturalized American citizen and married twice (an Australian and an American). He built an 80-ton steamer in the Philippines (1874) and was prosperous until 1886. After being wrecked off Brazil (1887), he, his wife, and two sons built a 35-foot sailing canoe and returned to New York City. Aboard the 35-foot *Spray,* he sailed around the world alone (1895–98), traveling 46,000 miles. He retired to West Tisbury, Mass., and wrote *Sailing Alone Around the World* (1900). He sailed again in the *Spray* (1909) and was never heard from again.

Slonimsky, Nicolas (1894–   ) conductor, composer, musicologist; born in St. Petersburg, Russia. After studies in piano and composition at the St. Petersburg conservatory, he came to the U.S.A. in 1923 and embarked on a peripatetic career that centered during the 1920s and 1930s on conducting, with an emphasis on modern composers, and occasional composing. He later turned to writing, most notably *Music Since 1900* (4th ed. 1971) and the *Baker's Biographical Dictionary of Music* (starting with the 1958 ed.). His memoirs, *Perfect Pitch,* appeared in 1988.

Slosson, Edwin Emery (1865–1929) chemist, author; born in Albany (now Sabetha), Kans. Based in Chicago (1902) and then Washington, D.C. (from about 1920), he was primarily a popularizer of science, writing 18 books and over 2,000 articles as well as 20 technical bulletins on chemical research.

Smale, John (Gray) (1927–   ) corporate executive; born in Listowel, Ontario, Canada. He spent virtually his entire career at Procter & Gamble, where he launched Crest toothpaste and other new products and acquired Richardson-Vicks and G. D. Searle's over-the-counter drugs. As variously president, CEO, and chairman (1974–90), he rejuvenated Procter & Gamble's stolid corporate culture.

Smale, Stephen (1930–   ) mathematician; born in Flint, Mich. This National Academy of Sciences member contributed largely to topology with his h-cobordism theorem. This work won him the Fields Medal (1966). As a professor at the University of California: Berkeley (1960), his research spanned from n-dimensional geometry to applied science.

Small, Albion W. (Woodbury) (1854–1926) sociologist; born in Buckfield, Maine. He taught history and political economy at Colby College (Maine) before serving as its president (1889–91). He then went to the University of Chicago (1892–

1926), where as founding chairman he developed the nation's first sociology department into a major academic center. He came to be regarded as a founder of American sociology, launching and editing the *American Journal of Sociology* (1895–1926) and publishing more than 300 articles and books, including *General Sociology* (1905) and *Between Eras: From Capitalism to Democracy* (1913).

Smalls, Robert (1839–1915) Civil War hero, sailor, U.S. representative; born in Beaufort, S.C. His mother was an African-American slave, but as he grew up learning the trade of sailmaker and rigger, he became a familiar figure on the Charleston waterfront. Having gained considerable skill at piloting boats along the South Carolina and Georgia coasts, he was forced by the Confederates to pilot the *Planter,* a transport boat that had a crew of African-Americans with a few white officers. On May 13, 1862, with the white officers ashore, he persuaded its African-American crew to sail the ship out of Charleston harbor and then turned it over to the Union navy; its cargo was estimated to be worth several million dollars. Immediately celebrated as a hero in the North, he was hired by the Union army as a pilot and participated in several engagements. In October 1862 he went to New York City to try to get support for a colony of freed slaves at Port Royal, S.C.; he spent nine months in Philadelphia to get a basic education; in June 1864 he attended the Republican Party Convention as part of a delegation of free blacks. After the war he served in the South Carolina legislature and then in the U.S. House of Representatives (Rep., S.C.; 1875–79, 1882–87); struggling constantly against obstacles placed in his way by colleagues, he worked to gain some measures of equity for African-Americans. He was also an officer in the South Carolina militia, rising to the rank of major general. He ended his career as the Federal collector of the port in his native town of Beaufort, S.C. (1889–1913).

Smeal, Eleanor (Marie Cutri) (1939–) social activist; born in Astabula, Ohio. The child of Italian immigrants, she grew up in Pennsylvania and attended Duke University, from which she graduated Phi Beta Kappa in 1961. She married Charles Smeal in 1963. They settled in Pittsburgh where she worked in civic affairs, particularly the League of Women Voters. In 1970 she and her husband joined the National Organization for Women (NOW). By 1973 she was elected to the national board of directors (1973), became board chair in 1975, and then served as president of NOW (1977–82). After leaving NOW because she found it too conservative, she helped found the Women's Political Caucus and the Feminist Majority Foundation.

Smedley, Agnes (1894–1950) journalist, social activist; born in Osgood, Mo. After an early life of deprivation and self-education, she took up revolutionary and pacifist causes, first being jailed in India (1918) for working for liberation from Britain. She went to China for a German newspaper in 1928 and lived there until 1941, openly identifying with the Chinese Communist movement in her reporting and in her best-known book, *Battle Hymn of China* (1943).

Smelser, Neil J. (Joseph) (1930–) sociologist; born in Kahoka, Mo. Educated at Harvard and Oxford Universities and trained as a psychoanalyst, he taught at the University of California: Berkeley (1958). His works on comparative methodology, economic development, social change, and collective behavior include *Sociology of Economic Life* (1963, later revised), *Sociological Theory* (1976), and *Social Paralysis and Social Change* (1991).

Smibert, John (1688–1751) painter; born in Edinburgh, Scotland. He began as a house and coach painter, moved to London (1709), studied portrait painting, moved to Italy (c. 1717–20), and came back to London (1720–28). Emigrating to Newport, R.I., with Bishop Berkeley (1729), he painted his most famous work, *Dean Berkeley and His Entourage* (1729). In 1730 he moved to Boston to spend the next 18 years mainly doing portraits, which were somewhat awkward in style, of upper-class Massachusetts colonists. He designed Faneuil Hall, Boston (1740–42), his sole architectural work.

Smillie, James (1807–85) engraver; born in Edinburgh, Scotland. He emigrated with his family to Quebec, Canada (1821), studied engraving in London (1827), and settled in New York City (1829). He is known for his steel engravings of paintings, such as *The Voyage of Life* series by Thomas Cole (1839–40).

Smillie, Wilson George (1886–1971) epidemiologist; born in Eaton, Colo. He established the first school for public health in South America under the auspices of the Rockefeller Foundation (1917–27), and lost his first wife to the influenza epidemic in Brazil while working there. After ten years at the Harvard School of Public Health (1927–37), he joined Cornell University Medical College (1937–55), and on retiring, published the influential *Public Health – Its Promise for the Future* (1955).

Smith, Alexander (1865–1922) physical chemist, educator; born in Edinburgh, Scotland. He emigrated to the United States in 1894 and became affiliated with the department of chemistry at the University of Chicago (1894–1911). During that period, he did important studies on sulphur and on the formation of solid and liquid forms of sulphur. He also developed methods of measuring vapor pressure at high temperatures. He was head of the chemistry department at Columbia University (1911–19).

Smith, (Alfred Emanuel) Al (1873–1944) political leader; born in New York City. Leaving school at age 12, he worked for the local Democratic organization and with its help was elected to the state assembly (1903). By 1913 he was assembly speaker, and in 1918 he was elected governor of New York; losing his first reelection bid, he won back the state house for the next three two-year terms; he proved an able administrator and surprisingly liberal and internationalist for someone who had emerged from the Democratic machine. After nearly capturing the 1924 Democratic presidential nomination, he won it in 1928, but, handicapped in part by his Catholicism, lost the election overwhelmingly. After unsuccessfully battling Franklin D. Roosevelt for the 1932 nomination, he came to oppose New Deal policies. He received many honors as a Catholic layman.

Smith, (Anthony Peter) Tony (1912–80) sculptor, painter, architect; born in South Orange, N.J. After suffering from tuberculosis when young, he studied at the Art Students League (1933–36) and architecture at Chicago's New Bauhaus (1937–38). He was an apprentice to Frank Lloyd Wright (1938–39) and a practicing architect in New York City (1940–60). He painted and worked on architectural commissions, taught at many institutions, and was associated with the minimalist school of sculpture.

Smith, Bessie (1895–1937) vocalist; born in Chattanooga, Tenn. Beginning her career in the minstrel show of her mentor, Ma Rainey, between 1923–33 she toured extensively throughout the U.S.A. and recorded prolifically. Known as "Empress of the Blues," she established prototypes for both classic female blues singing and the hard-lived life associated with it.

Smith, Bruce (1892–1955) police consultant, criminologist; born in Brooklyn. He worked at the New York Bureau of Municipal Research while completing a degree at Columbia University (1914–16). Through the bureau he was sent to Harrisburg, Pa., to conduct a police study (1923), which led to a career as a police consultant. He created a uniform international system for reporting crime statistics – publishing the first *Uniform Crime Reports* in 1930 – taught at the FBI's national police training school (1935–55), and was director of the Institute of Public Administration (1954–55). He gained national attention during the 1950s for his critical scrutiny of the New York Police Department. Skeptical and pragmatic, he helped survey police departments in 50 American cities and several foreign countries, promoting efficiency and standardized crime reporting. He was also an avid sailor.

Smith, C. R. (Cyrus Rowlett) (1899–1990) aircraft executive; born in Minerva, Texas. After having worked in banking, he became manager of Texas Air Transport, owned by the Texas-Louisiana Power Company. In 1934 this company reorganized, becoming American Airlines. He was chief executive until he retired in 1968, when he served as secretary of commerce for one year.

Smith, Cloethiel Woodard (1910–93) architect; born in Peoria, Ill. Trained in both architecture and city planning, she founded a Washington, D.C. firm bearing her name (1963), specializing in urban planning and renewal and new town residential communities; her work is characterized by small scale and attention to community activities and includes the Southwest Urban Renewal Area and Waterfront, Washington, D.C., and La Clede Town, St. Louis, Mo.

Smith, David Eugene (1860–1944) mathematician; born in Cortland, N.Y. An early career in law (1881–84) was abandoned for mathematics. Teaching longest at Columbia University (1901–26), he was librarian of the American Mathematical Society (1902–20), editor of several mathematical journals and encyclopedias, author of over 40 math texts, and an extensive traveler and book collector.

Smith, David (Roland) (1906–65) sculptor; born in Decatur, Ind. He studied at Ohio University (1924–25), worked as an assembler in a car factory, moved to New York City (1926), and studied at the Art Students League (1927–32) with John Sloan among others. He was influenced by the welded sculptures of Picasso, and by 1933, he was producing his acclaimed welded steel series, such as *Tank Totem V* (1955–56). After travel in Europe, the Middle East, and Russia (1935–36), he established a studio at the Terminal Iron Works, a shipfitting establishment in Brooklyn, settled in Bolton Landing, N.Y. (1938), and continued the Voltri-Bolton, Zig, and Cubi series. He died in an automobile accident in Vermont.

Smith, Edgar Fahs (1854–1928) chemist, educator; born in York, Pa. Affiliated with the University of Pennsylvania for most of his career (1888–1920), he did research on methods of electrochemical analysis, atomic weight determinations, and compounds of rare metals, including tungsten and molybdenum.

Smith, Edmund Kirby (1824–93) soldier; born in St. Augustine, Fla. Resigning from the U.S. Army (1861) after 16 years – including service in the Mexican War and on the frontier – he joined the Confederate army. He led the advance into Kentucky (1862) and fought at the battle of Perryville; he was then reassigned to head the Trans-Mississippi Department. On June 2, 1865, he became the last senior Confederate commander to surrender. He was president of the University of Nashville (1870–75), and then he taught mathematics at the University of the South at Sewanee (1875–93).

Smith, Eli (1801–57) missionary, translator; born in Northford, Conn. He was ordained as a Congregational minister (1826) and went to Malta to work for the American Board of Commissioners for Foreign Missions. He traveled extensively in the Middle East (1829–31) and published his *Missionary Sermons and Addresses* (1833). During the last decade of his life he translated much of the Bible into Arabic. He died of cancer in Beirut and his work was finally completed by Cornelius Van Dyck.

Smith, Elias (1769–1846) Protestant clergyman, author; born in Lyme, Conn. He had little formal education but studied the Bible on his own, joined the Baptist Church and was an itinerant preacher in New Hampshire and Massachusetts. In 1808 he established the *Herald of Gospel Liberty,* the first religious weekly in the U.S.A. He sold the paper in 1818, rejected Calvinist doctrine, and became a Universalist. Rejecting this in turn, he became interested in physical rather than spiritual health and joined forces with a physician to establish a successful private sanatorium.

Smith, Ellison DuRant ("Cotton Ed") (1866–1944) U.S. senator; born near Lynchburg, S.C. Himself a cotton planter, he would devote his long political career to fighting high tariffs and Northern business/financial interests. He served in the U.S. Senate (Dem., S.C.; 1904–44), and after opposing Republican administrations he at first welcomed President Franklin Roosevelt; but he soon opposed the New Deal policies and agencies that he believed were inimical to the Southern way of life. He was also an outspoken white supremacist and during World War II he opposed the national mobilization efforts.

Smith, (Frederick Wallace) Fred (1944–) entrepreneur; born in Marks, Miss. As a junior at Yale he conceived the idea of an overnight intercity delivery service for small packages. He founded the Memphis (Tenn.)-based delivery company Federal Express (1971), creating a computer-directed network of planes and trucks and inventing an innovative "hub and spoke" routing system that, together with aggressive advertising, made it one of the country's fastest growing companies in the 1980s.

Smith, George O. (Otis) (1871–1944) geologist; born in Hodgdon, Maine. He joined the U.S. Geological Survey (1896), and became its director (1907). He maintained his directorship until 1930, except for his one year on the U.S. Coal Commission (1922–23). He became chairman of President Hoover's Federal Power Commission (1930–33). An authority on the coal and oil industries, Smith's advocacy of increased regulation of natural energy helped enact more restrictive legislation on Federal mining and land use.

Smith, Gerrit (1797–1874) philanthropist, reformer; born in Utica, N.Y. Born into a wealthy family (with money from the fur trade and in land dealings), he studied law but would spend most of his life managing the family fortune. He was active nationally as a leader of the antislavery Liberty Party (1824–74), was vice-president of the American Peace Society (1830s), and from 1835 on was a well-known abolitionist (his house was a stop on the Underground Railroad). Elected to one term in the U.S. House of Representatives as an independent (1853–55), he ran unsuccessfully for governor of New York on the People's Party ticket (1858), advocating temperance, abolition, and land reform. Although he had supported John Brown's 1859 raid on the federal arsenal at Harper's Ferry, he denied doing so. He supported the Union and campaigned for Abraham Lincoln in 1864. Although he later backed giving the vote to African-Americans, he also advocated moderate policies toward Southern whites. He donated much of his fortune to building churches and theological schools, as well as to various colleges.

Smith, Hamilton O. (Othanel) (1931–) molecular biologist; born in New York City. He performed research at the University of Michigan (1962–67), then joined Johns Hopkins (1967). In the 1970s he obtained enzymes from bacteria that would split genes to give genetically active fragments; these "restriction enzymes" allowed the possibility of new kinds of genetic engineering, as well as providing a tool for DNA sequencing. For this work he shared the 1978 Nobel Prize in physiology with his associate Daniel Nathans and Swiss molecular biologist Werner Arber. Smith continued to investigate restriction enzymes and their interactions with DNA.

Smith, Harold Dewey (1898–1947) public administrator; born in Haven, Kans. A specialist in fiscal management, he directed the Michigan Municipal League (1928–37), serving as state budget director. Powerful director of President Franklin D. Roosevelt's Bureau of the Budget (1939–45), he reviewed all federal spending and legislation, urging wartime anti-inflation measures. He left to head the World Bank (1946–47).

Smith, Hedrick (1933–) journalist, Slavic specialist; born in Scotland (where his parents were living temporarily). An American citizen raised in the United States, he was a staff reporter for the *New York Times* (1962–68), part of the Pulitzer Prize-winning team that produced the Pentagon Papers series; he also won a Pulitzer Prize for international reporting (1974). Known for combining a readable style with provocative analysis, he was the author of several books on power and politics. He traveled extensively in Russia (1987–92), creating the award-winning documentary series *Inside Gorbachev's USSR,* and established his own documentary film company to produce the series *Challenge to America.*

Smith, Holland M. (McTyeire) (1882–1967) marine officer; born in Seale, Ala. He gave up a law career for a marine commission in 1905, and after serving in the Philippines, Panama, and the Dominican Republic, he saw action in France from 1917 to 1918. During World War II, "Howlin' Mad" Smith led the Fifth Amphibious Corps in the bloody Pacific campaigns of the Gilbert, Marshall, and Mariana Islands, and commanded at Iwo Jima in 1945, scene of the most vicious fighting in Marine Corps history.

Smith, Horton (1908–63) golfer; born in Springfield, Ohio. He won the first Masters Tournament ever held in 1934 and won again in 1936.

Smith, Howard K. (Kingsbury) (1914–) television correspondent/anchorman; born in Ferriday, La. A Rhodes scholar, he joined CBS (1941–61) in Berlin during World War II, returning in 1957 as Washington correspondent and later bureau chief. He moderated the first Kennedy-Nixon debate in 1960, joining ABC in 1961, and later coanchoring *ABC Evening News* (1969–75). Becoming increasingly conservative politically, he later worked as a commentator (1975–79).

Smith, Howard (Worth) (1883–1976) U.S. representative; born in Broad Run, Va. A farmer and judge in Alexandria, he represented Virginia Democrats in Congress (1931–67), chairing the Committee on Rules, whose members blocked progressive legislation.

Smith, James McCune (1813–65) physician; born in New York City. The son of a slave freed by the laws of New York, he got his medical degree from the University of Glasgow, Scotland (1837) and practiced briefly in Paris before returning to New York. He worked 20 years on the medical staff of the Free Negro Orphan Asylum. He devoted his life to the welfare of African-Americans and to insisting on their moral and physical equality with whites. A prolific writer, he opposed the American Colonization Society's plan to repatriate African-Americans and he was active in the Underground Railroad.

Smith, Jedediah Strong (1798–1831) explorer, fur trader; born in Bainbridge, N.Y. Starting in the fur trade with Gen. William Ashley in St. Louis in 1822, he took over Ashley's Rocky Mountain trade in 1826 with two others. From 1826–30, he led exploratory expeditions from Great Salt Lake, Utah, across the Mohave desert into California, where he was nearly imprisoned by the Mexican governor. He then went north through the Sierras and along the Willamette River to Ft. Vancouver, Oregon, surviving an attack by the Umpqua Indians en route. In 1831 he was killed by Comanches after entering the Santa Fe trade. Because he did not write of his trips, he did not get credit for his achievements for many years; but he was, among other firsts, the first American to enter and exit California by the eastern route.

Smith, Jessie Carney (1930–) librarian; born in Greensboro, N.C. A professor of library science at Fisk University, she wrote extensively on African-American library collections and their importance to the black community.

Smith, J. (Joseph) Russell (1874–1966) geographer; born near Lincoln, Va. After earning his Ph.D. in Economics at the University of Pennsylvania, he stayed there to teach at the Wharton School (1903–19). He then became chairman of the division of economic geography at Columbia University's Business School (1919–44). A pioneer in the field of economic geography, he was a prolific writer whose works include *Industrial and Commercial Geography* (1913), *The World's Food Resources* (1919), *North America* (1925), and *Tree Crops* (1929).

Smith, John (1579–1631) explorer, adventurer, colonist; born in Lincolnshire, England. After fighting the Ottoman Turks, he helped to found Jamestown in 1607. He became a member of the governing council and was once captured by the Indians of Powhatan's tribe – he was rescued by the chief's daughter, Pocahontas. From 1608 to 1609 he served as the president of the Jamestown colony, but he was plagued by constant bickering with other settlers. Following a severe injury, he returned to England in 1609. He returned to America in 1614 and explored the coast of what he called

New England. He wrote several books on Virginia, the settlement at Jamestown, New England, and his earlier travels in Europe and Asia. The books induced many settlers to leave for the New England area.

Smith, Joseph (1805–44) religious leader; born in Sharon, Vt. He moved to New York state with his parents in 1816 and received his first "call" as a prophet four years later, at age 15, when he claimed that God confided in him the first of several revelations of the true Christianity. In 1823 an angel told him of a hidden gospel on golden plates, with accompanying stones that would enable him to translate the text from "reformed Egyptian." On September 22, 1827, these records were delivered to him. He published them as *The Book of Mormon* in 1830 and organized the Church of the Latter Day Saints (the Mormons) in April of that year. Despite ridicule, hostility, and occasional violence, Smith's sect gained converts. In 1831 the Mormons established a headquarters in Ohio and later built a community called Zion in Missouri. After an anti-Mormon uprising in Missouri in 1838, Smith founded the community of Nauvoo in Illinois; by the early 1840s nearly 20,000 Mormons had settled there. Meanwhile, Smith introduced the custom of polygamy, and when he announced he would run for the presidency in 1844, he and his brother Hyrum Smith were imprisoned. On June 27 a mob of 150 men broke into the jail at Carthage, Ill., and shot them both dead. The Mormons thereafter migrated westward to Utah under Smith's successor, Brigham Young.

Smith, (Kathryn Elizabeth) Kate (1909–86) singer; born in Greenville, Va. While appearing on Broadway as the contralto lead in *Flying High* (1930), she was discovered by agent Ted Collins. She began her radio show on CBS in 1931, immortalizing *God Bless America* in 1938. During World War II she toured widely to sell war bonds and entertain the troops. Star of the *Kate Smith Hour* (1950–54) on National Broadcasting Company television, she returned with CBS's *Kate Smith Show* in 1960. With her "classic" voice, her large physique, and old-fashioned values, she sustained her popularity during many years when much of the entertainment business was moving in other directions.

Smith, (Lloyd) Logan Pearsall (1865–1946) writer; born in Millvale, N.J. Member of a wealthy Quaker family, he studied at Haverford College (1881–84) and Harvard (1884–85), but took little interest in his family's glass-making business and went off to England in 1888 to pursue his literary interests at Oxford. Financially independent, he was able to devote his life to cultivating his aesthetic ideals, but although he published some fiction (*The Youth of Parnassus*, 1895), he was essentially an appreciator. Most of his published works were essays as in *Trivia* (1902), *Reperusals and Re-Collection* (1936), and *Last Words* (1945). He also became known as an editor and anthologist, and as a defender of the traditional English language and literary values, he published *Milton and His Modern Critics* (1940), an attack on his fellow Americans, T. S. Eliot and Ezra Pound. He spent most of his life in London, becoming a British citizen in 1913, and was a friend of many notable contemporaries – Whistler, Santayana, Henry James, and Berenson – who married Pearsall's sister Mary; another sister, Alys, was Bertrand Russell's first wife. His autobiography, *Unforgotten Years* (1938), was among his most engaging works.

Smith, Merriam (1913–70) journalist; born in Savannah, Ga.

As White House correspondent for United Press International from 1941 until his death, he covered six presidents and wrote several books about the presidency, beginning with *Thank You, Mr. President* (1946). He was riding in the motorcade when President John F. Kennedy was assassinated in 1963 and won a Pulitzer Prize for coverage of the event. Later, plagued with a drinking problem and poor health, he committed suicide.

Smith, Nathan (1762–1829) physician, surgeon, medical educator; born in Rehoboth, Mass. After serving as an apprentice to physicians in Vermont, he began practicing medicine in Cornish, N.H., but, realizing his lack of knowledge, he pursued studies at Harvard (1789–90) and then in Europe (1796–97). Back in Cornish with a flourishing practice, he persuaded nearby Dartmouth College to teach medicine and in 1798 he became the medical school's first professor. When the state legislature failed to support his efforts, he went to Yale in 1813 as its first professor of anatomy, surgery, and obstetrics. He was one of the most advanced American physicians of his day both in his surgical techniques and in emphasizing close observation instead of traditional theory. His most important writing was *Practical Essay on Typhous Fever* (1824).

Smith, Oliver (Lemuel) (1918–94) set designer; born in Waupun, Wis. Winner of many awards including seven Tonys and the Sam S. Shubert Award for Achievement in the Theatre, his designs span all aspects of performance – drama, opera, ballet and film. He began his Broadway career in 1942 with *Rosalinda*. Thereafter he designed for *Brigadoon* (1947), *My Fair Lady* (1956), *West Side Story* (1957), and *The Odd Couple* (1965).

Smith, (Osborne Earl) Ozzie (1954–) baseball player; born in Mobile, Ala. In a career that began in 1978, he established himself as one of the greatest fielding shortstops in baseball history. Nicknamed "the Wizard of Oz," he played for the San Diego Padres and the St. Louis Cardinals.

Smith, Patti (Lee) (1946–) rock singer, songwriter; born in Chicago, Ill. She grew up in New Jersey and attended college on an art scholarship. In 1967 she moved to New York City where she gave poetry readings, wrote songs, and formed a band that defined the early punk culture and its music in the late-1970s. Their biggest hit, "Because the Night" (1978), was written with Bruce Springsteen. In 1979 she abandoned her musical career.

Smith, Reginald Heber (1889–1966) lawyer; born in Fall River, Mass. Managing director of the Boston firm Hale & Dorr (1919–56), he was widely acclaimed for initiating the modern American system of legal aid for those who cannot afford lawyers. He wrote *Justice and the Poor* (1919) and *Survey of the Legal Profession* (1953). He received the American Bar Association's gold medal (1951).

Smith, Robert (1757–1842) secretary of the navy, secretary of state; born in Lancaster, Pa. He served as Thomas Jefferson's secretary of the navy (1801–09). He maintained a blockading squadron against the Barbary pirates with very limited funds. He was secretary of state (1809–11) but he feuded with President James Madison and was forced to resign.

Smith, (Robert) "Buffalo" Bob (1917–) puppeteer, producer; born in Buffalo, New York. A vocalist and pianist on local Buffalo, N.Y., radio in the 1930s and 1940s, he started a children's show on WNBC radio in New York (1947) which became the *Howdy Doody* show (1947–60). One of the first children's television shows, it featured a freckled-faced puppet. He returned with a short-lived revival in 1976.

Smith, Samuel Harrison (1772–1845) journalist; born in Philadelphia. He edited two early newspapers covering congressional activities and backing President Thomas Jefferson.

Smith, Seba (Major Jack Downing, pen name) (1792–1868) journalist, writer; born in Buckfield, Maine. He and his family moved to Bridgton, Maine (1799), and he worked in a grocery store, brick yard and iron foundry. He studied at Bowdoin (1815–18) and traveled in Europe. He became the assistant editor of the *Eastern Argus,* Portland, Maine (1820–26) and founded the *Portland Courier* (1829). There he began the publication of political and satirical commentaries in the form of letters from "Major Downing" (1830–33), published as *The Life and Writings of Major Jack Downing of Downingsville* (1833). The success of Smith's Downing letters led several writers to imitate both the name and style, the most notable being Charles Augustus Davis. Smith moved to Charleston, S.C. (1839), then to New York City to work as an editor and writer; he wrote a second series of Downing letters (1847–59), published as *My Thirty Years Out of the Senate* (1959). His *Way Down East* (1854), stories about typical New Englanders, was another popular work. In 1860 he settled in Patchogue, Long Island, N.Y.

Smith, Sophia (1796–1870) philanthropist; born in Hatfield, Mass. She finished formal schooling at age 14, but educated herself with the many books in her family's house. A shy young woman, she never married; deaf by age 40, she lived her entire life in her family's home with an unmarried sister and brother, Austin Smith. As the last surviving member of her family, she inherited its money, in particular the fortune Austin had accumulated. Guided primarily by the Reverend John Morton Greene, her pastor, she finally decided to leave her money to establish a new college for women – rejecting earlier proposals that she leave it to nearby Amherst or Mt. Holyoke Colleges. She left $393,105 and Smith College opened in Northampton, Mass., in 1875.

Smith, Stephen (1823–1922) surgeon, public health pioneer; born in Onondaga County, N.Y. On the staff at Bellevue Hospital from 1851 until 1911, he wrote several textbooks, of which his *Handbook of Surgical Operations* (1862) was most valuable to Civil War surgeons. The Metropolitan Health Law that he drafted for New York City (1866) served to guide sanitation reforms in cities throughout the U.S.A. An extraordinarily active man, he worked for higher standards in everything from vaccinations to nursing education. He was one of the founders as well as first president of the American Public Health Association (1871).

Smith, Theobald (1859–1934) medical scientist; born in Albany, N.Y. He organized the department of bacteriology at George Washington University (St. Louis) where he then taught (1886–95). He went on to Harvard Medical School and simultaneously served as director of the pathology lab of the Massachusetts Board of Health (1895–1915). His last post was as director of the department of animal pathology at the Rockefeller Institute (1915–29). His early work was on the swine plague, hog cholera, and Texas fever among cattle. He studied the relationship between bovine and human tuberculosis, showed how parasites act as vectors of disease, did important work on a smallpox vaccine and on diphtheria

and tetanus antitoxins, and was the first to record his observations of allergy.

Smith, Thomas (active in Mass. 1650–90) painter. He is identified tentatively as Captain (or Major) Thomas Smith who arrived in Boston from Bermuda (1650). An attributed painting is *Self-Portrait* (c. 1690), showing a navy battle in the background with the artist holding a poem and a skull.

Smith, T. (Thomas) Lynn (1903–76) sociologist; born in Sanford, Colo. He was a professor at the University of Florida (1949–76) where he specialized in population studies, rural and urban sociology, and Latin American cultures and institutions. His more than 50 books and 200 articles include *Sociology of Rural Life* (1940, later revised), *Fundamentals of Population Study* (1960), and studies of Brazil (1946) and Colombia (1967).

Smith, W. (William) Eugene (1918–78) photojournalist; born in Wichita, Kans. Educated in Catholic schools, he left Notre Dame University to work for *Newsweek* magazine in 1937. A photographer with *Life* (1939–41) and war correspondent (1942–54), his photo essays focused on life in small villages from midwives in rural America to "the man of mercy," Dr. Albert Schweitzer, in Africa. In 1971 he captured the suffering of fishing families poisoned by mercury in Japan.

Smith, Walter Bedell (1895–1961) soldier, diplomat; born in Indianapolis, Ind. With no college education, he began as a National Guardsman in 1910 and rose slowly through the ranks of the regular army until Gen. George Marshall brought him to Washington in 1939 to assist in the build-up of the army. By 1942 he was secretary of the Joint Chiefs of Staff and from 1942 to 1945 he was Eisenhower's chief of staff, in which position he helped plan and carry out the invasions of North Africa, Sicily, and Normandy. President Truman appointed him ambassador to the Soviet Union (1946–49) and then director of the Central Intelligence Agency (1950–53). Under President Eisenhower he served as under secretary of state (1953–54).

Smith, (Walter Wellesley) "Red" (1905–82) journalist; born in Green Bay, Wis. Hired away from the *Philadelphia Record* in 1945 by the *New York Herald Tribune,* he became a widely syndicated sports columnist with a national reputation. When the *Tribune* folded in 1967, he found a new base at the *New York Times.* Known for his humor and command of language, he won many awards, including a 1976 Pulitzer Prize.

Smith, William (Loughton) (1758–1812) U.S. representative, ambassador; born in Charleston, S.C. Orphaned at age 12, he was sent to school in London where he became a lawyer in 1774. Returning in 1783, he became a congressman (Fed., S.C.; 1787–97), speculating in government scrip and supporting the federal bank. Ambassador to Portugal (1797–1801), he returned to his law practice and wrote political letters, "The Numbers of Phocion," for the *Charleston Daily Courier.*

Smith, Winthrop (Hiram, Jr.) (1949–) financial services executive; born in New York City. He graduated from Amherst in 1971, took a graduate business degree at the University of Pennsylvania in 1974, and joined Merrill, Lynch, Pierce, Fenner and Smith (now Merrill, Lynch) as an investment banker. He rose through a series of management positions to become the firm's national sales director in 1990.

Smithies, Arthur (1907–81) economist; born in Hobart, Tasmania, Australia. He was educated in Australia and

England before taking his Ph.D. at Harvard (1934). His principal field of expertise was macroeconomics and the U.S. budgetary process. He taught at the University of Michigan (1934–43), served on the U.S. Bureau of the Budget (1943–48), and returned to academia to teach economics at Harvard University (1948). He wrote on a variety of subjects including Schumpeterian economics and location economics.

Smithson, Robert (Irving) (1938–73) sculptor, painter; born in Passaic, N.J. He studied at the Art Students League (1953), traveled throughout the United States, worked as an abstract painter, then focused on conceptual sculptures and large earthworks, such as *Spiral Jetty* (1970). He was killed in a plane accident while working on his last environmental construction, *Amarillo Ramp* (1973).

Smoholla (?1815–1907) Wanapum religious leader; born on the upper Columbia River in present-day Washington. His beliefs that a return to traditional Indian truths would cause the world to revert to a pristine state formed the basis of the "Washani" or "Dreamer Religion" of the Northwest Indians.

Smoot, George Fitzgerald, III (1945–) astrophysicist; born in Yukon, Fla. At the Lawrence Berkeley Laboratory, University of California: Berkeley, from 1971 he led a study of cosmic background radiation that in 1992 resulted in a picture of the universe shortly after the big bang some 15 billion years ago.

Smoot, Reed (Owen) (1862–1941) U.S. senator; born in Salt Lake City, Utah. A prominent Mormon business and religious leader, he was elected to the U.S. senate (Rep., Utah; 1903–33). He became an influential figure in the Senate, advocating protectionist policies, tax reduction, and the creation of national parks. He coauthored the Smoot-Hawley Tariff of 1930, which increased tariff rates. After being defeated in 1932, he returned to Utah to devote himself to his duties as an apostle of the Church of Jesus Christ of Latter-Day Saints.

Smothers, Dick See under SMOTHERS, TOM.

Smothers, (Thomas Bolyn, 3rd) Tom (1939–) and **(Richard) Dick** (1937–) musicians/comedians; born on Governors Island, N.Y. Sons of an army major, they formed a folk singing group, the Casual Quintet, in college. After Tom's satirical asides began to change them from a straight folk group into a comic act, the brothers performed as a duo at New York's Blue Angel in 1961. Discovered by Jack Paar, they appeared on television variety shows in the early 1960s and at Carnegie Hall. The *Smothers Brothers Comedy Hour* (1967–69) was a critical success, but their politically satiric skits were frequently cut by CBS and their show ended when Tom complained publicly. They acted on Broadway in *I Love My Wife* (1978–79) and in movies, including *Terror at Alcatraz* (1982), returning to television with the *Smothers Brothers Special* (1988).

Smyth, Herbert Weir (1857–1938) classicist; born in Wilmington, Del. He spent most of his teaching career (1901–25) at Harvard, where he had earned his B.A. in 1876. His many publications include *The Ionic Dialect* (1894); *Greek Grammar* (1920); his University of California Sather lectures, *Aeschylean Tragedy* (1924); and the Loeb edition of the plays of Aeschylus (1922). After his death, his personal library became the basis of Harvard's classics collection, the Smyth, housed in the Widener Library.

Snead, (Samuel Jackson) Sam (1912–) golfer; born in Hot Springs, Va. Nicknamed, "Slammin' Sammy," his smooth, uncomplicated style won him a wide following and three Masters tournaments (1949, 1952, 1954) and three Professional Golfers' Association (PGA) titles (1942, 1949, 1951). He finished second in the U.S. Open four times but never won. He retired with more PGA tournament victories (84) than any golfer in history.

Snell, Bertrand Hollis (1870–1958) U.S. representative; born in Colton, N.Y. A graduate of Amherst College, he started working as a lumberjack in 1894, becoming the owner of his own lumber company by 1904, before diversifying into other businesses. In the U.S. House of Representatives (Rep., N.Y.; 1915–39), he chaired the House Rules Committee in the 1920s, often frustrating the Democrats. As minority leader during the 1930s, he fought against the New Deal. Afterwards he ran the *Potsdam Courier-Freeman* (N.Y.).

Snell, George D. (Davis) (1903–) immunogeneticist; born in Bradford, Mass. He taught zoology at Dartmouth (1929–30), then performed research at the University of Texas (1933–34), where his studies on mice first demonstrated the mutagenic effects of X-rays on mammals. He moved to Washington University (St. Louis) (1933–34), then joined the Jackson Laboratory, Bar Harbor, Maine (1935). There, using inbred strains of mice, he discovered the genetic histocompatibility locus, a group of closely associated genes responsible for transplant acceptance. This breakthrough won him one-third the 1980 Nobel Prize in physiology. After his retirement from Jackson (1968), he remained as a consultant and continued to contribute to scientific publications.

Snider, (Edwin Donald) "Duke" (1926–) baseball player; born in Los Angeles. During his 18-year career (1947–64), primarily with the Brooklyn and Los Angeles Dodgers, he established himself as one of the game's great center fielders as well as a powerful hitter. In five consecutive seasons (1953–57) he hit 40 or more home runs, a National League record. A broadcaster after retiring from baseball, he was elected to the Hall of Fame in 1980.

Snodgrass, W. D. (William DeWitt) (S. S. Gardons, pen name) (1926–) poet, writer; born in Wilkinsburg, Pa. He studied at Geneva College, Pa. (1943–44; 1946) and the University of Iowa (B.A. 1949; M.A. 1951; M.F.A. 1953). He taught at many institutions, notably the University of Delaware (1980). Based in Erieville, N.Y., he published translations, critical essays, and a play, but he is best known for his first volume of personal poetry, *Heart's Needle* (1959).

Snow, Carmel White (1887–1961) editor; born near Dublin, Ireland. As the talented fashion editor (1932–35) and editor in chief (1935–57) of *Harper's Bazaar,* she helped her readers become "well-dressed women with well-dressed minds."

Snow, Edgar (Parks) (1905–72) journalist, author; born in Kansas City, Mo. After graduating from the Columbia School of Journalism, he went to China as a reporter (1928–40) and for the rest of his life wrote on Chinese affairs. In the first foreign news reports from Yenan in the mid-1930s, collected as *Red Star over China* (1937), he presented the communist revolutionaries as a popular and potentially victorious force at a time when Western governments were committed to Chiang Kai-shek's Nationalists. In his post-China years, he was a writer and lecturer based in the U.S.A., and, after 1959, in Switzerland. His later books, including *The Other Side of the River* (1962) and *The Long Revolution* (1972), provided the West with valuable firsthand information and analysis during China's years of isolation; on his periodic trips to China, he was given exclusive interviews and privileged access as an old and trusted friend of Mao Zedong and Zhou Enlai.

Snowden, Frank (Martin), Jr. (1911–) classicist; born in York County, Va. Educated at Harvard (B.A. 1932; M.A. 1933; Ph.D. 1944) he taught at Howard University (1942–90) and was one of the first African-American classicists. His publications include *Blacks in Antiquity* (1970) and *Before Color Prejudice: Ancient Views of Blacks* (1983).

Snyder, Gary (Sherman) (1930–) poet, writer; born in San Francisco. He studied anthropology at Reed College (B.A. 1951), at Indiana University (1951–52), and at the University of California: Berkeley (1953–56), where he later taught (1964–65; 1986). He also studied Buddhism in Japan (1956; 1959–64; 1965–68), and was a seaman and a forester. Based in Nevada City, Calif., he is known for his association with the Beat poets and for his poetry on mystical and environmental themes, as in *Turtle Island* (1974).

Snyder, Hartland S. (Sweet) (1913–62) physicist; born in Salt Lake City, Utah. He was at Northwestern (1940–47) before joining the Brookhaven National Laboratories (1947–62). With E. Courant and M. S. Livingston, he discovered the alternating gradient focusing principle, which enabled construction of powerful nuclear reactors.

Snyder, Solomon (Halbert) (1938–) psychiatrist; born in Washington, D.C. Affiliated with Johns Hopkins University School of Medicine (1965), he became director of the department of neuroscience in 1980. He made possible many advances in molecular neuroscience by identifying the receptors for neurotransmitters and drugs and elucidating the actions of psychotropic agents (1960s–80s).

Sokolow, Anna (1910–) modern dancer, choreographer, teacher; born in Hartford, Conn. A student and member of Martha Graham's company from 1930–39, she formed her own dance group in 1934. Invited to perform in Mexico in 1939, she stayed on to develop that country's first modern dance company, returning yearly to train dancers during the 1940s; she also helped form an Israeli modern dance company in the 1950s and taught in the United States as well, training some who became leading choreographers. A choreographer for over 50 years, she worked with ballet and modern dance companies, Broadway theater, and the New York City Opera. Many of her pieces have political themes, such as *Rooms* (1955), about the Holocaust, and "Kurt Weill" (1988), about war atrocities.

Soldner, Paul (1921–) ceramist; born in Summerfield, Ill. Influential as ceramics professor at Scripps College (Claremont, Calif.), he is responsible for establishing Japanese *raku* firing techniques in American ceramics through nationwide workshops.

Solecki, Ralph (Stefan) (1917–) anthropologist; born in New York City. He joined the faculty at Columbia University (1959–88). His best-known excavations were at the Neanderthal site at Shanidar Cave in Iraq. His publications include early works on aerial photography and photo-interpretation as well as two volumes on Shanidar (1971, 1972).

Solomon, Hannah Greenebaum (1858–1942) clubwoman, social reformer; born in Chicago. Daughter of a prosperous hardware merchant, she studied piano, beginning with Carl Wolfsohn in 1873. After marrying in 1879, she devoted herself to many social, cultural, and service clubs. In 1890

she organized the Jewish Women's Congress, which became the National Council of Jewish Women; she was its president until 1905 (and then honorary president for life). Increasingly active in welfare and social reform, she established in 1897 the Bureau of Personal Service to help new Jewish immigrants, often working with Jane Addams. She also played an active role in reviving the Illinois Industrial School for Girls. In 1904 she joined Susan B. Anthony and May Wright Sewall as delegates to the International Council for Women in Berlin. She continued to work for civic reform in Chicago, even investigating the city's waste disposal system. She retired in the 1920s and gave her final years to travel, music, and the arts.

Soloveitchik, Joseph Ber (1903–93) rabbi, scholar; born in Pruzhany, Poland (now Belarus). He came from a family of Talmud scholars and was educated in Berlin. He came to the U.S.A. in 1932 and became rabbi of Boston's Orthodox community. In 1941 he joined the faculty of the Rabbi Isaac Elchanan Theological Seminary, affiliated with Yeshiva University in New York. He was chairman of the Rabbinical Council of America's Halakha Commission. Although he published little, he was internationally known as an Orthodox authority and Talmudic scholar.

Solow, Robert Merton (1924–) economist; born in New York City. He is best known for his path-breaking work on capital and growth. His theory of capital concentrates not on the measurement of capital but on how the rate of return on capital is determined. His theory of growth fine-tuned so-called "sources-of-growth accounting" to include estimates of aggregate production functions and technological advances. He taught exclusively at the Massachusetts Institute of Technology (1950) except for one year at Oxford University (1968–69), and he served as chairman of the Federal Reserve Bank in Boston (1975–80). Awarded the Nobel Prize in economics (1987), he was cited for his study of the factors that permit production growth and increased welfare.

Somervell, Brehon Burke (1892–1955) soldier, businessman; born in Little Rock, Ark. A West Point graduate (1914), as an army engineer he worked on various projects including some in France during World War I. On detached duty as chief of the Works Progress Administration in New York City (1936–40), he supervised construction of La Guardia Field. During World War II he headed the army's Services of Supply. After retiring in 1946, he became president of the Koppers Company.

Sondheim, (Joshua) Stephen (1930–) composer, lyricist; born in New York City. He received tutoring from family friend Oscar Hammerstein II and at age 17 was a production assistant for Richard Rodgers and Hammerstein. He wrote some music for television shows and for the play *Girls of Summer* (1956) before making his debut on Broadway by writing lyrics for Leonard Bernstein's *West Side Story* (1957) and Jule Styne's *Gypsy* (1959). He first wrote music as well as words for the successful farce, *A Funny Thing Happened on the Way to the Forum* (1962). With producer-director Harold Prince he wrote both words and music for a string of innovative works, including *A Little Night Music* (1973) – which contained his best-known song, "Send in the Clowns" – and *Pacific Overtures* (1976), which combined elements of the Broadway musical with Japanese Kabuki theater. He won the 1985 Pulitzer Prize in drama for *Sunday in the Park with George* (1984). Known for their often complex wordplay, evocative music, and unconventional subject matter, his works for stage, screen, and television mark him as one of the true artists of modern musical theater, one of the few who could inspire fans to wait overnight in freezing weather for tickets to merely a revue featuring his songs. He himself remained a private person, never courting publicity, and about all the public knew of him is that he enjoyed word-based puzzles and party games.

Sonneborn, Tracy M. (Morton) (1905–81) geneticist; born in Baltimore, Md. He was a National Research Council fellow (1928–30), moved to Johns Hopkins (1930–39), then joined the University of Indiana (1939–76), remaining active after his retirement. He discovered crossbreeding and mating types in paramecia (1937), thus integrating the genetic principles known in multicellular organisms with that of protozoa. He wrote many books and professional articles dealing with mitochondrial inheritance, nuclear differentiation, and the relationship of genetics and the environment.

Sonnenschein, Rosa (1847–1932) editor; born in Hungary. She immigrated to the U.S.A. with her rabbi husband in 1869. She was editor of *American Jewess,* a women's paper, from 1895–99. A moderate liberal, she was sympathetic to Zionism and believed in synagogal rights for women, along with home and marriage. Her 1880 essay, "The Pioneers," described a St. Louis women's literary society.

Son of Many Beads (also Bidaga and Jose Pino) (c. 1866–1954) Navaho leader; born near Glenwood, N.M. He was taught the Navaho traditions, customs, ceremonies – including the curing methods – by his father, Many Beads. A farmer and herder himself, he worked to secure title to land in New Mexico for his people. Meanwhile, he became known to the various archaeologists and anthropologists studying the Navahos and they relied on him for explaining the Navaho culture. In particular, the philosopher John Ladd began to interview him at length and Ladd's *Structure of a Moral Code* (1957), which compares the ethics of the Navaho and the western tradition, owed much to Son of Many Beads.

Sontag, Susan (1933–) critic, writer; born in New York City. She grew up in Arizona and Los Angeles, took degrees from the University of Chicago and Harvard, then did postgraduate work at Oxford before settling in New York City to teach and write. She first gained attention with her essay, "Notes on Camp" (1964), and went on to publish several novels including *The Volcano Lover* (1992); but she is best known for her critical essays and cultural analyses such as *On Photography* (1976) and *Illness as Metaphor* (1978); she also directed her own movie, *Duet for Cannibals* (1969). The nature of her concerns and writings have gained her the reputation as America's answer to "Continental intellectuals." Her son by an early marriage, David Rieff, is the author of *Los Angeles, Capital of the Third World* (1991).

Soper, Alexander (Coburn, III) (1904–93) architectural historian; born in Chicago. Trained as an architect and historian at Princeton, he taught at Bryn Mawr College (1939–60) and the Institute of Fine Arts, New York University (1960). The first American historian of East Asian architecture, he laid the foundations for the study of Chinese and Japanese architecture in the U.S.A. He at first worked on Japanese architecture, turning after the 1960s to Buddhist art. He

wrote *The Art and Architecture of Japan* (with R. Paine, 1955) and *The Art and Architecture of China* (with L. Sickman, 1956) and published numerous translations of art historical texts.

Sorensen, Charles (1881–1968) engineer, automobile executive; born in Copenhagen, Denmark. Brought to the U.S.A. as a child, he began working in Henry Ford's pattern department (1904), rising to become plant superintendent (1925) and vice-president (1941). He helped develop the assembly line (1909–13), the Model T and Model A, and the Ford V-8 engine. During World War I he was involved in airplane production; during World War II, he was blamed for production problems with planes so he resigned (1944) and went to work for Willys-Overland. He had a reputation as a harsh, even ruthless administrator.

Sorenson, Theodore (Chaikin) (1928–) lawyer, government official; born in Lincoln, Nebr. After law school, he became Senator John F. Kennedy's assistant (1953–61), serving as strategist and speech writer during his presidential campaign. As special counsel to President Kennedy (1961–63), he helped write his major addresses. In 1966 he returned to private practice, writing *The Kennedy Legacy* (1969) and editing *Let the Word Go Forth* (1985).

Sorin, Edward (Frederick) (1814–93) religious leader; born in Ahuillé, France. Ordained in 1838, he emigrated to Indiana as a missionary (1841), founded Notre Dame University (1844), and was its president (1844–65). In 1868 he became superior general of his congregation, the Holy Cross Fathers.

Sothern, Edward Askew (1826–81) actor; born in Liverpool, England. The lanky comedian first appeared in England as Douglas Stewart, then as Sothern in Boston in 1852. His greatest fame came as Lord Dundreary in *Our American Cousin* (1858).

Sousa, John Philip (1854–1932) composer, bandmaster; born in Washington, D.C. He studied violin and trombone in childhood and at age 13 joined the U.S. Marine Band (1867–72). After some years of playing in popular orchestras, he returned in 1880 as director of the Marine Band. In 1892 he formed his own band and toured with it much of the rest of his life. His compositions include ten operettas, but he is known chiefly for his over 100 marches, which earned him the title "the March King"; they include classics such as "The Stars and Stripes Forever" and "The Washington Post." He also wrote three novels and an autobiography, *Marching Along* (1928).

Souter, David H. (Hackett) (1939–) Supreme Court justice; born in Melrose, Mass. He spent seven years with the New Hampshire attorney general's office (1971–78) and rose through the state's judiciary (1978–90). After three months on a U.S. Court of Appeals (1990), he was appointed by President George Bush to the U.S. Supreme Court (1990).

Southworth, Albert Sands (1811–94) photographer, inventor; born in West Fairlee, Vt. A partner at Southworth and Hawes (1843–60), he was a tireless experimenter who took photographs of the sun's eclipse and invented a multiple image camera.

Sowell, Thomas (1930–) economist; born in Gastonia, N.C. Educated at Harvard, Columbia University, and the University of Chicago, he taught at Rutgers (1962–63), Howard (1963–64), and Brandeis Universities (1967–70). He left the University of California: Los Angeles in 1972 to direct the Ethnic Minorities Research Project at the Urban Institute in Washington, D.C. His books include *Black Education: Myths and Tragedies* (1972) and *Race and Economics* (1973). During the Reagan administrations of the 1980s he gained considerable publicity for advancing the neoconservative position that affirmative action was bad for the morale of black Americans.

Soyer, Isaac (1907–81) painter; born in Tombov, Russia (brother of Raphael Soyer and Moses Soyer). His parents emigrated to New York (1912), and he studied in New York and Europe. He specialized in city genre scenes, as in *Employment Agency* (1937).

Soyer, Moses (1899–1974) painter; born in Tombov, Russia (twin of Raphael Soyer and brother of Isaac Soyer). His family emigrated to New York (1912), he worked in a factory, studied in New York, and, like his brothers, painted city scenes, as in *Girl at Sewing Machine* (1939–40).

Soyer, Raphael (1899–1987) painter, writer; born in Tombov, Russia (twin of Moses Soyer and brother of Isaac Soyer). His family emigrated to New York (1912), he worked in a factory, studied at Cooper Union (1914–17) and the National Academy of Design (1918–22), and, beginning in 1932, taught at the Art Students League. He was a social realist, as in *Farewell to Lincoln Square* (1959), and a figure painter, as seen in *Standing Nude Female* (1960). His most famous book was *Diary of an Artist* (1977).

Spaatz, Carl (1891–1974) aviator; born in Boyertown, Pa. A 1914 West Point graduate, he shot down three German aircraft as commander of the Thirty-first Aero Squadron in France during World War I. Along with Ira C. Eaker and several relief pilots, "Tooey" Spaatz established an air endurance record of 150-plus hours over Los Angeles in January 1929. His support of air power advocate William Mitchell slowed his progress through the grades, but by July 1941 he had risen to chief of air staff under George C. Marshall. Spaatz went on to command the air arm for Eisenhower in North Africa and Sicily, and became chief of the Strategic Air Force, Europe, in 1944. Blunt and forceful, he argued that air power alone could subjugate the Germans – a theory the Allied invasion of France rendered untestable. After the end of the European war, Spaatz commanded the air force in the Pacific, directing the firebombing and, in August 1945, the atomic bombing of Japanese cities. He became first chief of staff of the independent air force in 1947 and retired the following year.

Spahn, Warren (Edward) (1921–) baseball pitcher; born in Buffalo, N.Y. During his 21-year career (1942–65), primarily with the Boston and Milwaukee Braves, he won 363 games, more than any left-hander in major league history. Thirteen times he won 20 or more games in a season, and in 1973 he was elected to baseball's Hall of Fame.

Spalding, Albert (1888–1953) violinist; born in Chicago. Trained in Europe and the U.S.A., he made his American debut in 1908 at Carnegie Hall, and for several decades thereafter he enjoyed an active international career and reputation, the first American violinist to do so. He taught at Juilliard (1933–44) and also composed for violin and piano.

Spalding, (Albert Goodwill) Al (1850–1915) baseball player, executive, businessman; born in Byron, Ill. One of baseball's major promoters, he pitched for the Boston Red Stockings in baseball's first organized league, the National Association (1871–75). He was instrumental in founding the National League in 1876, the same year he won a league-leading 47 games as a right-handed pitcher for the Chicago White Stockings. He also managed the White Stockings (1876–77) and served as club president (1882–91). He played a leading role in the first visit of a U.S. baseball team to Britain (1874) and then in organizing a round-the-world tour of two baseball teams (1888–89). In 1875 he founded the sporting goods company, A. G. Spalding and Bros., which long was the sole supplier of baseballs used in the major leagues. In 1907 he almost singlehandedly created the myth that Abner Doubleday had "invented" baseball.

Spalding, Catherine (1793–1858) Catholic religious foundress; born in Charles County, Md. In 1813, at Bardstown, Ky., she founded the Sisters of Charity of Nazareth; as longtime mother superior, she established many educational and charitable institutions.

Spalding, John (Lancaster) (1840–1916) Catholic prelate; born in Peoria, Ill. The nephew of Bishop Martin Spalding, he studied theology in Europe, where he was ordained (1863). He became widely known for sermons and writings. As bishop of Peoria (1877–1908) he strongly supported parochial schools and free inquiry; he pressed for the establishment of Catholic University (Washington, D.C.), of which he was a cofounder (1887).

Spalding, Martin (John) (1810–72) Catholic prelate; born in Baltimore, Md. The first American Catholic to win a doctorate in theology (in Rome, 1834), he was a teacher, college president (1838–40), and scholar known especially for his writings on the Protestant Reformation. He served as bishop of Louisville from 1850; as archbishop of Baltimore, from 1864, he played a leading role in national church affairs.

Spargo, John (1876–1966) reformer, museum director; born in Cornwall, England. Leaving the ministry for the labor movement, he attacked the British conduct of the Boer War in his *Barry Herald* (1899), earning the reputation as a socialist intellectual and skilled orator. Emigrating to New York (1901), he worked on behalf of many social causes and exposed childhood poverty in *The Bitter Cry of the Children* (1906). Moving to Bennington, Vt., he wrote extensively on socialism and served on the executive committee of the Socialist Party. During World War I he resigned from the Socialist Party and became a major architect of President Wilson's anti-Bolshevik policy. In 1926 he founded the Bennington (Vt.) Historical Museum and until 1954 served there as a caretaker of American history.

Sparkman, John (Jackson) (1899–1985) U.S. representative/ senator; born in Hartselle, Ala. A farmer's son and a lawyer, he represented Alabama in Congress (Dem., 1937–46) before being elected in 1946 to the Senate, where he served until 1979. A Southern conservative when it came to civil rights, he was moderate enough to be the Democrats' candidate for vice-president in 1952 and he chaired the Foreign Relations Committee (1975–79).

Spaulding, Albert C. (Clanton) (1914–) archaeologist; birthplace unknown. He taught at the University of Michigan (1947–61). His major contribution was to introduce the use of quantitative techniques in archaeology and to develop it as a scientific discipline. His most important publications include works on the archaeology of Native Americans of the Plains and accounts of his investigations in the Aleutian Islands (1962).

Speaker, (Tristram E.) Tris (1888–1958) baseball player; born in Hubbard, Texas. During his 22-year career (1907–28), mostly with the Boston Red Sox and Cleveland Indians, he was considered the greatest defensive center fielder in the game's history. A solid left-handed hitter, he posted a lifetime batting average of .344 and holds the major league record for most doubles in a career (793). He managed the Indians (1919–26) and took them to their first pennant and World Series (1920). Nicknamed "the Grey Eagle," he was elected to baseball's Hall of Fame in 1937.

Spector, Phil (1940–) record producer, songwriter; born in New York City. While a teenager he recorded his first hit song and studied under producers/songwriters Jerry Leiber and Mike Stoller. In 1961 he cofounded Philles Records, became sole owner in 1962, and produced 20 hits in three years working with such artists as the Crystals, Ben E. King, and the Righteous Brothers. As a producer he broke ground by collaborating creatively with musicians and by using multitrack recording and electronic effects to create the famous "wall of sound."

Speer, Robert Elliott (1867–1947) Protestant missionary leader; born in Huntingdon, Pa. The son of a Democratic politician, he decided on a missionary career during his second year at Princeton, became secretary of the Board of Foreign Missions of the Presbyterian Church two years after graduation, and continued as spokesman, chief fund-raiser, and publicist for church missions for nearly 50 years (1891–1937). He believed that Christianity would bring "progress and free government" to all peoples, from the West to the East.

Speicher, Eugene (Edward) (1883–1962) painter; born in Buffalo, N.Y. He studied at the Fine Arts Academy, Buffalo (1902–06), and the Art Students League, New York (1906–08) under Robert Henri and William Merritt Chase. Based in Woodstock, N.Y., he painted landscapes and portraits, such as *Consuela* (1947).

Speiser, Ephraim Avigdor (1902–65) archaeologist, biblical scholar, linguist; born in Skalat, Ukraine, Austria-Hungary. He emigrated to the U.S.A. as a teenager. A research fellow at the University of Pennsylvania (1924–46), he was a leading authority on biblical lands and culture and excavated important Sumerian sites in Iraq. His books include *Mesopotamian Origins* (1930) and, as editor, *At the Dawn of Civilization* (Vol. I, 1965).

Spelling, Aaron (1923–) television producer; born in Dallas, Texas. A television actor in the 1950s, he began producing *Zane Grey Theatre* in 1960, then joined Danny Thomas to produce *The Mod Squad* (1968–73). Continuing with police shows, he introduced *Charlie's Angels* in 1976. During the 1980s his company produced the series, *Dynasty,* and movies of the week for all three networks, making him one of the most successful and prosperous producers in television history.

Spellman, Francis (Joseph) (1889–1967) Catholic prelate; born in Whitman, Mass. Ordained after studies in Rome (1916), he did parish work, worked on Boston's archdiocesan newspaper, served as attaché to the papal secretary of state (1925), and became auxiliary bishop of Boston (1932). In 1939, he was made archbishop of New York and military vicar of U.S. armed forces, becoming a cardinal in 1946. A strong administrator and influential leader, with close ties both to the Vatican and to high U.S. officials, he was a religious conservative and ardent anti-Communist. From 1951 he regularly spent Christmas visiting troops overseas. His writings include a best-selling novel, *The Foundling* (1951).

Spence, (Gerald Leonard) Gerry (1929–) lawyer, author; born in Laramie, Wyo. An honors graduate from the University of Wyoming Law School (1952), he was a county prosecuting attorney in Wyoming (1954–62) and then a partner in various Wyoming law firms (1962–78) before forming Spence, Moriarty & Schuster in Jackson, Wyo., in 1978. During his early years in private practice he concentrated on representing insurance companies, but eventually he took to representing people in a variety of personal liability or criminal cases. Among his more publicized cases that involved large settlements for his clients were the verdict against Kerr-McGee in the Karen Silkwood case on behalf of her children, and a verdict against McDonald's on behalf of a family-owned ice cream company; among his more celebrated defense cases were the acquittal for Imelda Marcos and the acquittal for Randy Weaver in the Idaho standoff case where a federal agent was killed. Spence did not lose a jury case after 1969. He lectured at law schools and conducted seminars for various legal organizations around the U.S.A. and is the author of several books including his autobiography, *Gunning for Justice* (1982), *With Justice for None* (1989), and *From Freedom to Slavery, The Rebirth of Tyranny in America* (1993).

Spence, Janet Taylor (1923–) psychologist; born in Toledo, Ohio. She studied at Yale and the State University of Iowa (Ph.D. 1949). She taught at Northwestern University (1949–60), where she formulated the Taylor Manifest Anxiety Scale, which contributed to both clinical and social psychology. In 1960 she married psychologist Kenneth W. Spence, with whom she collaborated in editing the two-volume *Psychology of Learning and Motivation* (1967–68). She taught and did research at the University of Texas from 1964.

Spence, Jonathan D. (Dermot) (1936–) historian, educator; born in Surrey, England. He came to the U.S.A. in 1959, earning a Ph.D. at Yale and joining its faculty (1966). He freshly illuminated Chinese history, particularly of the 16th and 17th centuries, through his innovative studies of historical characters from Emperor K'ang-hsi to Western missionaries; his *Search for Modern China* (1990) won widespread acclaim.

Spence, Michael A. (Andrew) (1943–) economist; born in Montclair, N.J. He taught at Stanford University (1973–76) and Harvard (1971–73, 1976–90) before returning to Stanford as dean of the business school (1990). His principal contributions include work on the economics of information and in the dynamic aspects of competition.

Spencer, Elizabeth (m. Rushers) (1921–) writer; born in Carrollton, Miss. She studied at Belhaven College (B.A. 1942) and Vanderbilt (M.A. 1943). She lived in Italy (1953–58), married in 1956, and became a writer of novels and short stories. She taught writing at Concordia University, Montreal, Canada (1976–86) and at the University of North Carolina (1986). Her early novels are based in the rural South, and several others are set in Italy, as in *The Light in the Piazza* (1960), but whatever the setting, her works tend to deal with expatriates and outsiders.

Spencer, Joseph (Earle) (1907–84) geographer; born in Bolivar, Mo. After earning his Ph.D. at the University of

California: Berkeley, he spent several years in China. In 1940 he joined the faculty at the University of California: Los Angeles where, with an interruption during World War II, he remained until 1975. With William E. Thomas he wrote *Cultural Geography* (1969), *Asia, East by South* (1971), and *Introducing Cultural Geography* (1973).

Spencer, Lilly (or Lilli) (b. Angelique Marie Martin) (1822–1902) painter; born in Exeter, England. Her French parents emigrated to America (1830) and lived in Marietta, Ohio (1833). She moved to Cincinnati, Ohio (1841), married (1844), and settled in New York City (1848). The breadwinner of her family, she was a genre painter, as in *Picnic, Fourth of July* (c. 1864).

Spencer, Niles (1893–1952) painter; born in Pawtucket, R.I. After study at the Rhode Island School of Design (1913), and with George Bellows and Robert Henri in New York (1915), he traveled frequently in Europe but was based in Provincetown, Mass. He painted abstract landscapes, such as *Two Bridges* (1947).

Spero, Nancy (1926–) painter; born in Cleveland, Ohio (wife of Leon Golub). She studied at the Art Institute of Chicago (1945–49), in Paris (1950–51), worked in Italy (1956–57) and Paris (1959–64), and returned to live in New York City. A founder of Women Artists in Revolution in 1969, she used paper scrolls for a feminist expressionistic collage in *Tortures of Women* (1976).

Sperry, Elmer (Ambrose) (1860–1930) engineer, inventor; born in Cortland, N.Y. A lumber merchant's son, he attended the State Normal School at Cortland and Cornell before founding the Sperry Electric Company (1880), the first of his eight companies, in Chicago. This firm manufactured dynamos and arc lamps. Over the years he invented and produced a wide range of items, including mining machinery, street car equipment, electric automobiles, an arc searchlight, and an autopilot. He began his most important work, in gyroscope development, in 1896, combining electrical and mechanical elements into devices that stabilized ships and aircraft. His gyrocompass, first installed on the battleship USS *Delaware* in 1910, soon became standard equipment in the U.S. Navy. He also developed an electrolytic process for obtaining pure caustic soda from salt and a technique for recovering tin from old cans and scrap. Altogether, the restless and fertile Sperry held more than 400 patents.

Sperry, Roger W. (Wolcott) (1913–) neurobiologist; born in Hartford, Conn. He was a research fellow at Harvard (1941–46), worked at the neurological diseases laboratory of the National Institutes of Health (1952–53), then joined the California Institute of Technology (1954–84). He demonstrated that neural circuitry is specifically "wired" for particular functions, and pioneered experiments in which he severed the connections between the right and left brain hemispheres. These "split-brain" studies led to his view that the mind is an "emergent property" arising from the complexity of the physical brain. He was awarded one-third the 1981 Nobel Prize in physiology.

Sperry, Willard Learoyd (1882–1954) Protestant clergyman, theologian; born in Peabody, Mass. The son of a Congregational minister who became president of Olivet College (Mich.), he graduated from Olivet in 1903 and studied theology at Oxford as one of the first Rhodes Scholars. He held pastorates in Fall River, Mass., and Boston before accepting the deanship of Harvard Divinity School in 1925, where he remained until 1953. A tolerant dean (he admitted Nazarenes, Adventists, and others), he developed an austere theology that sought a middle ground between modern liberal Protestant thought and strict Calvinism.

Spiegelman, (Avarham) Art (1948–) cartoonist; born in Stockholm, Sweden. Brought to the U.S.A. as a three-year-old, he studied cartooning in high school, and while a student at Harpur College (N.Y.) (1965–68), he began creating novelty cards for Tip Top Chewing Gum; in later years he continued to work for them as a creative consultant. In the 1960s and 1970s he contributed a series of comics to underground periodicals, under pseudonyms such as Al Flooglebuckle. Beginning in 1979 he taught a class in comics at the School of Visual Arts in New York City; in 1980, with his wife, he founded *Raw,* a yearly review of avant-garde comics. His reputation was confined to a small circle until he published his comic-book novels, *Maus: A Survivor's Tale* (1986) and *Maus II: And Here My Troubles Began* (1991); drawing on his father's accounts of his experiences during the Holocaust, he defied expectations by drawing the Jews as mice and the Nazis as cats, and somehow his simple drawings enhanced the pathos. In 1992 he won a Pulitzer Prize Special Award for his *Maus* books, the same year he became a contributing editor at the *New Yorker.*

Spielberg, Steven (1947–) film director; born in Cincinnati, Ohio. At age 13 he won a contest with a short feature, *Escape to Nowhere.* He turned to television directing in 1969, and in 1974 he turned out his first feature film, *The Sugarland Express.* He specialized in films of primeval fears or childlike wonder, such as *Jaws* (1975), *Close Encounters of the Third Kind* (1977), and *E.T.* (1982). In 1993 he enjoyed spectacular success with *Jurassic Park,* one of the most popular movies of all time, and *Schindler's List,* his most respected serious film.

Spier, Leslie Ephraim (1893–1961) anthropologist; born in New York City. He was a specialist in American Indian culture, particularly known for his work on the Ghost Dance religion. During a long teaching career ending at the University of New Mexico (1939–55), he helped develop anthropology as an academic discipline and led the application of ethnographical techniques to historical research.

Spillane, (Frank Morrison) Mickey (1918–) writer; born in New York City. He studied at Kansas State College (now University). In the early 1940s he wrote scripts for comic books, then became famous for his first novel, *I, the Jury* (1947). He went on to write a series of highly popular violent, sardonic, and sexually explicit mysteries, most featuring his detective, Mike Hammer. He converted to the Jehovah's Witnesses in 1952, and lived in Myrtle Beach, S.C.

Spingarn, Joel (Elias) (1875–1939) literary critic, writer, social reformer, horticulturist; born in New York City. After taking all his degrees (through the Ph.D.) at Columbia University, he stayed on with the faculty (1899–1911) and gained an international reputation for his scholarly studies of literary criticism; his *The New Criticism* (1911) was among the first American works to draw heavily on the theories of the Italian philosopher Benedetto Croce. When he got into a dispute with Nicholas Murray Butler, president of Columbia, over what he regarded as an issue of free speech, he was dismissed. A man of independent means, he would continue his literary pursuits pretty much on his own, although he occasionally taught at the New School for Social Research. He bought a newspaper in a small town outside New York City, the *Amenia Times,* and served as its publisher; in 1919 he would also help found Harcourt, Brace and Company, serving as its literary adviser until 1924. Spingarn had already shown an interest in the world outside the university – in 1908 he had run unsuccessfully as a Republican for the U.S. House of Representatives – and he would serve as a delegate of the Progressive Party at two national conventions. He had also helped found the National Association for the Advancement of Colored People (NAACP) (1909) and from 1911 on he was active with the NAACP, eventually serving as its president (1930–39). In 1913 he established the Spingarn Medal, still given annually to the African-American who has shown great achievement. During World War I he volunteered for service in the army and succeeded in setting up a special camp to train black officers. He was a delegate to the convention that established the American Legion. He continued to publish his literary studies, his own poetry, and a major anthology of European literature, but he spent most of his later years at his country estate at Amenia, N.Y., where he concentrated on cultivating flowers, becoming a recognized authority on the clematis.

Spink, J. G. (John George) Taylor (1888–1962) publisher, editor; born in St. Louis, Mo. He was the son of Charles Taylor, who had acquired the principal interest in the *Sporting News* (TSN) in 1899 when the founder (1886), Charles's brother Alfred Spink, sold it to him. (Charles had been a farmer in South Dakota when Alfred asked him to join the staff late in 1886.) A weekly tabloid-style periodical, long devoted solely to baseball, it was known for its breezy yet informative contents and soon established itself as the "Bible of baseball." After dropping out of high school in 1909, J. G. went to work for his father as an office boy and by 1914 he succeeded his father as editor and publisher, positions he held until his death. The firm also put out various other sports-related publications, including the standard annual handbook, the *Baseball Register.* Described as a "pint-sized, souped-up bulldozer," J. G. Taylor Spink ran the paper as the autocratic proprietor he was, demanding total commitment from his staff and many correspondents; he was especially notorious for phoning anyone, night or day, wherever they were, whenever he wanted a story. He himself loved to play the horses, but never at the expense of either his work hours or his investment. On his death, his son C. C. Johnson took over as editor/publisher, and in the 1960s, anticipating *TSN*'s financial problems, converted it to an all-sports periodical; in 1977 he sold *TSN* to the Times Mirror publishing group.

Spiro, Melford Elliot (1920–) cultural anthropologist; born in Cleveland. Educated at the University of Minnesota (B.A. 1941) and Northwestern (Ph.D. 1950), he taught at Washington University (St. Louis), the University of Connecticut, and Chicago before becoming chairman of the anthropology department at the University of California: San Diego, in 1968. His publications include *Kibbutz: Venture in Utopia* (1955) and *Kinship and Marriage in Burma* (1977).

Spitz, Mark (1950–) swimmer; born in Modesto, Calif. He won a record seven gold medals at the 1972 Munich Games, dominating a single Olympiad as no athlete ever before. After retiring from competition, he became a sports commentator and enjoyed many product endorsements. He tried to make a comeback for the 1992 Olympics, but failed to make the team.

Spitzer, Lyman, Jr. (1914–) astrophysicist; born in Toledo, Ohio. He was a fellow at Harvard (1938–39), then taught at Yale (1939–42, 1946–47). He investigated military undersea and sonar projects at Columbia University (1942–46), before joining Princeton as head of the department of astrophysical sciences and the observatory (1947). He applied theoretical physics to studies of star formation, and performed pioneering research in controlled nuclear fusion, plasma physics, and the use of artificial satellites as telescope stations. In 1985 he won the prestigious Crafoord Prize for his studies of the Copernicus satellite's findings on the interstellar medium (1972–81), the "stuff" from which stars are formed.

Spock, Benjamin (McLane) (1903–) pediatrician, psychiatrist, author, social activist; born in New Haven, Conn. While in medical school at Yale he rowed for the gold-medal U.S. crew team in the 1924 Olympics. Between 1931 and 1933 he served residencies in New York City hospitals and began a six-year training program with the New York Psychoanalytic Institute. While teaching pediatrics at Cornell University's Medical College in New York City (1933–43), he also maintained a private practice. During 1943 to 1945 he spent two years with the U.S. Navy as a psychiatrist. In 1946 he published *The Common Sense Book of Baby and Child Care;* later retitled *Baby and Child Care,* it became universally known as "Doctor Spock," went through countless editions, was translated into 39 languages, and sold over 40 million copies. It made him both the hero and villain of late-20th-century American childrearing, for his flexible approach was regarded by many as wonderfully humane while others saw it as "permissiveness" and the cause of many behavioral problems. He went on to teach at the medical schools of the Universities of Minnesota and Pittsburgh before settling at Western Reserve University (1955–67), all the while retaining his reputation as the nation's friendly baby doctor through his magazine columns, articles, and various books. In the 1960s he became increasingly prominent for his positions on public issues, working for the National Committee for a Sane Nuclear Policy and opposing the Vietnam War; in 1968 he was tried and convicted for counseling draft evasion, but the conviction was overturned in 1969; he set forth his views on contemporary society in *Decent and Indecent* (1970); in 1972 he was the presidential candidate for the pacifist People's Party (1972). Retiring in 1967, he spent much of the next quarter-century living and sailing on boats. He astonished many when in 1992 he endorsed the claim that cows' milk was bad for children.

Spofford, Ainsworth Rand (1825–1908) librarian; born in Gilmanton, N.H. During his tenure as Librarian of Congress (1865–97), he initiated legislation and transformed the Library of Congress from the library of the legislature to the nation's library.

Spooner, John Coit (1843–1919) U.S. senator; born in Lawrenceburg, Ind. A Civil War veteran and lawyer, he won fame for the railroad litigation cases he successfully argued before the U.S. Supreme Court. Elected to the U.S. Senate (Rep., Wis.; 1885–91, 1897–1907), he was author of a bill authorizing construction of the Panama Canal. The rise of the progressive Republicans drove him out of office and he went into private practice in New York City.

Spotswood, Alexander (1676–1740) colonial official; born in Tangier, Morocco. He was the lieutenant governor of Virginia (1710–22). Identified with frontier expansion, he led several expeditions to the Blue Ridge Mountains area. He negotiated a treaty with the Iroquois Indians to protect Virginia from Iroquois raids.

Spotted Tail (b. Sinte Gleska) (?1833–81) Brûlé Sioux leader; born along the White River in present-day South Dakota or near present-day Laramie, Wyo. A signer of the Fort Laramie Treaty of 1868 – in which the U.S. government accepted the territorial claims of the Sioux in exchange for peace – he traveled often to Washington, D.C., as the government-appointed chief of the agency Sioux.

Sprague, Clifton (Albert Furlow) (1896–1955) naval officer; born in Dorchester, Mass. He fought a remarkable naval action against the Center Force of the Japanese fleet in 1944. His escort carrier group sustained heavy losses but performed the vital service of removing the Center Force from the battle of Leyte Gulf.

Sprague, Frank (Julian) (1857–1934) electrical engineer, inventor; born in Milford, Conn. He developed an interest in electricity while a cadet at the U.S. Naval Academy. As a junior naval officer (1878–83), Sprague experimented with various types of dynamos and motors. He resigned from the Navy to become an assistant to Thomas Edison in 1883 and formed the Sprague Electric Railway and Motor Company the following year. In 1887 he installed the nation's first electric trolley system in Richmond, Va., for which he has been called "the father of electric railway traction." He sold this company to Edison in 1892 and established a concern that manufactured electric elevators, selling it in turn to Otis Elevator Company. He perfected a control system for multiunit trains in 1895, using this as a basis for an automatic train control system he developed. In his later years he produced electric motors for small tools and appliances and coinvented the third rail for electrified rail lines. He served as chairman of committees on shipbuilding and electricity for the Naval Consulting Board during World War I.

Springsteen, Bruce (Frederick Joseph) (1949–) musician; born in Freehold, N.J. A self-taught guitarist, he began performing with a local high school group, the Castiles, in 1965. Over the next five years, he was a sideman in several Asbury Park, N.J., bands before forming his own ten-piece group in 1971 and signing with Columbia Records the following year. Promoted as the new Bob Dylan, his highly-anticipated debut album was released in 1973, but not until his third album, *Born to Run,* released amidst a hail of publicity that included cover stories in *Time* and *Newsweek,* did he enjoy widespread commercial success. Contractual disputes prevented him from recording for the next three years, during which time he developed his celebrated live shows and honed his image as a grass roots musician with working-class values. He resumed regular recording activity in 1978, and by the mid-1980s he had become the world's most popular rock star. He had also become a figure of wide populist appeal: during the 1984 presidential campaign, his endorsement was sought, and his album *Born in the U.S.A.* was quoted by both major candidates. While continuing to record, he gradually reduced his touring schedule after 1985, but made personal appearances at numerous rock benefits such as Live Aid and Amnesty International, as well as local fund-raising concerts in Asbury Park.

Sproul, Allan (1896–1978) banker; born in San Francisco. The son of a Scottish immigrant, he graduated from the University of California: Berkeley in 1919 and joined the Federal Reserve banking system the following year. An authority on the world monetary system, he was president and chief executive officer of the Federal Reserve Bank of New York, the largest of the 12 in the Federal Reserve system, from 1941–56.

Sproul, Robert (Gordon) (1891–1975) university president; born in San Francisco. His 44-year career at the University of California culminated in a presidential term (1930–58) in which the university gained an international reputation for excellence. His unsympathetic treatment of students opposed to the draft in World War II and his acquiescence in the loyalty oath ordered by the Regents in 1949 were controversial.

Spruance, Raymond (Ames) (1886–1969) naval officer; born in Baltimore, Md. He was one of the navy's ablest tactical leaders during World War II. He commanded one of the two task forces that defeated the Japanese fleet at Midway (1942). As commander of the Central Pacific Area and Force (1943–45), he directed operations in the Gilbert and Marshall Islands, and led attacks on Tinian, Guam, and Saipan, the battle of the Philippines, and the final assault on Okinawa. He was president of the Naval War College (1945–48).

Spuhler, James N. (Norman) (1917–) physical anthropologist; born in Tucumcari, N.M. He taught at several universities before joining the University of New Mexico (1967–84). He related genetics to human evolution in studies of inbreeding in Japan and the human biology of the Navaho.

Squanto (?1580–1622) Pawtuxet interpreter; born on Cape Cod. He is thought to have been the same as the Indian named Tisquantum who was first captured along the Maine coast and taken to England; he evidently lived there until 1614, when Captain John Smith took him back to Cape Cod. In 1615, Squanto was captured by another English sea captain and sold into slavery in Spain; he escaped and made his way to England. After a brief visit to Newfoundland, he was taken by another English sea captain to serve as a guide along the New England coast but Squanto escaped and made his way to his Pawtuxet homeland; finding his people wiped out by smallpox, he went to live with the neighboring Wampanoags. In 1621 he was introduced to the Pilgrims at Plymouth; he served as their interpreter in their treaty with Massasoit, showed them how to plant corn, where to fish, and generally helped them survive in an unknown environment. He died from a fever while guiding Governor Bradford's expedition around Cape Cod.

Squibb, Edward Robinson (1819–1900) pharmacologist, manufacturing chemist; born in Wilmington, Del. Four years as a naval surgeon (1847–51) convinced him of the need for better quality pharmaceuticals. As director of the Navy Pharmacy (1853–57), he improved techniques for the manufacture of ether and chloroform and other pharmaceuticals. In 1858 he opened his own firm, Edward R. Squibb, M.D., in Brooklyn; after an explosion destroyed the lab, it was reopened as E. R. Squibb & Sons (1892) and continued to pioneer both the basic research and manufacture of pharmaceuticals. He shared his knowledge in over 100 papers in the *American Journal of Pharmacy* and other publications.

Squier, Ephraim George (1821–88) diplomat, archaeologist; born in Bethlehem, N.Y. In 1845 the American Ethnological

Society commissioned him to survey Ohio Indian mounds; his report (with E. H. Davis, 1848) remained the standard work on Mound Builders for 50 years and helped establish the field of American archaeology. His diplomatic postings to Central and South America (1849–65) yielded further ethnological and archaeological studies.

Staats, Elmer B. (Boyd) (1914–) government official, foundation executive; born in Richfield, Kans. He ended his tenure (1939–53, 1958–66) at the U.S. Bureau of the Budget as deputy director. As U.S. Comptroller General (1966–81), he introduced modern management techniques, including data processing, to government. He later became president of the Harry S. Truman Scholarship Foundation (1984).

Stadtman, Earl R. (Reece) (1919–) biochemist; born in Carrizozo, N.M. He was a research assistant at the University of California: Berkeley (1943–49), and a fellow at Massachusetts General Hospital (1949–50) before becoming a biochemist and physiologist at the National Heart, Lung, and Blood Institute, (Bethesda, Md.) (1950). An authority on enzyme chemistry, he investigated vitamin B_{12} function (with wife and collaborator Thressa Stadtman), membrane transport, protein modification in aging, and oxygen toxicity.

Stadtman, Thressa C. (Campbell) (1920–) biochemist; born in Sterling, N.Y. She was a nutrition assistant at Cornell (1942–43), performed research in food microbiology at the University of California: Berkeley (1943–47), and was a research assistant at Harvard (1949–50) before joining the National Heart, Lung, and Blood Institute (Bethesda, Md.) (1950). She made major advances in studies of amino acid metabolism, vitamin B_{12}-dependent enzymes (with husband and collaborator Earl Stadtman), microbial biochemistry, and the biochemistry of selenium.

Stafford, Jean (1915–79) writer; born in Covina, Calif. She studied at the University of Colorado (B.A. and M.A. 1936), and at Heidelberg University (Germany) (1936–37). She was married three times, notably to Robert Lowell (1940; divorced 1948), taught at several institutions, and won many awards. She wrote novels, children's fiction, and nonfiction, but is best known for her short stories, as in her Pulitzer Prize-winning work, *The Short Stories of Jean Stafford* (1969).

Stagg, Amos Alonzo (1862–1965) football coach; born in West Orange, N.J. An end for Yale, he was named to the first All-America team in 1889 and began his 72-year coaching career the next year. In 1892 he became coach at the University of Chicago, remaining until 1932 when he reached the school's mandatory retirement age of 70. During his tenure there, he produced four undefeated teams and won seven Western Conference titles. From 1933 to 1946, he coached at College of Pacific, winning Coach of the Year honors in 1943 at age 81 when his team won seven games against major competition. After retiring as a head coach, he continued as an assistant until he was 98. Always a spokesman for fair, clean sport, he was nicknamed "Mr. Integrity." He was also a remarkably innovative football coach, inventing dozens of plays, tactics, and strategies that became standard for other coaches.

Stahl, O. (Oscar) Glenn (1910–) writer, lecturer, government official; born in Evansville, Ind. He specialized in public personnel issues in his work at the Federal Security Agency (1941–51) and U.S. Civil Service Commission (1951–69), where he directed bureau policies and standards.

His books include many editions of *Public Personnel Administration* and *Personnel Administration: Standing Up for Government* (1990).

Stamos, Theodoros (1922–) painter; born in New York City. Based in New York, he studied at the American Artists School (1948–49), and traveled abroad. His abstract paintings are symbolic and biomorphic, as in *Aegean Sun Box No. 2* (1965).

Standing Bear, Luther (Chief Standing Bear, pen name) (?1868–?1939) actor, writer; born in Sioux Pine Reservation, N.D. He left the reservation for a tour with Buffalo Bill's Wild West Show, then returned to the reservation. He became a U.S. citizen, settled in Huntington Park, Calif., and worked as an actor. He was a transitional Native American figure who was interested in capturing on paper the beliefs and customs of his people, as well as the difficulties of adapting to white America. He is best known for his autobiography, *My People, My Sioux* (coauthored with E. A. Brininstool, 1928), and *Stories of the Sioux* (1934).

Standish, Burt L. See PATTEN, GILBERT.

Standish, Miles (?1584–1656) soldier, colonist; born in Lancashire, England. He was the military leader of the Plymouth Colony. He learned Indian languages and through skillful negotiations he managed to prevent any serious Indian wars during his tenure in Plymouth.

Stanford, (Amasa) Leland (1824–93) railroad builder, government official; born in Watervliet, N.Y. He practiced law in Wisconsin and then moved to California (1852) where he ran a general store. Successful in business, he became governor of California (1861–63), and more importantly, a founder and president of the Central Pacific Railroad (1863–93). He openly used his political power and ties to assist his railroad's development. After the transcontinental linking with the Union Pacific Railroad (1869), he built up the Southern Pacific Railroad; he eventually joined it with the Central Pacific to form the Southern Pacific Company, which he served as president (1884–90). He made a fortune, and, with his wife, founded and endowed Leland Stanford, Jr., University (1885) in memory of their only son (who died in 1884 at age 15). He served in the U.S. Senate (Rep., Calif.; 1885–93), but had an undistinguished career as a senator primarily interested in keeping the government from interfering in his railroad operations.

Stanley, Francis Edgar (1849–1918) **and Freelan O.** (1849–1940) twin brothers, inventors, manufacturers; both born in Kingfield, Maine. Francis was a portrait painter and a photographer in Maine. The two brothers joined together in 1883 and formed the Stanley Dry Plate Company, but they sold the business to Eastman Kodak Company (1905). They invented the "Stanley Steamer" automobile (1896), the first steam motorcar in New England. They built 100 cars, sold their business (1898), repurchased the business (1902), and organized the Stanley Motor Carriage Company (with Francis as president). They made over 10,000 "Steamers" before they sold the business in 1918, the same year in which Francis died as the result of an automobile accident.

Stanley, Freelan O. See under STANLEY, FRANCIS EDGAR.

Stanley, Henry Morton (b. John Rowlands) (1841–1904) journalist, explorer; born in Denbigh, Wales. After an unhappy youth he came to New Orleans (1859) and received his new name from a merchant who informally adopted him.

During the Civil War he served in the Confederate army and then the Union army and navy; after the war he covered Gen. W. S. Hancock's expedition against the Indians (1867) as a correspondent. He also went to the Middle East as a journalist. Sent by Bennett of the *New York Herald* in 1869 to find the "lost" Scottish missionary, David Livingstone, Stanley found him deep in Africa in 1871 and greeted him with the oft-quoted "Dr. Livingstone, I presume?" On his return to England, Stanley's claims were not at first believed but he went back to Africa and explored extensively (1874–77) and published *Through the Dark Continent* (1878). He helped to organize the Congo Free State (1879–84). After several more expeditions, he went to London and, becoming a British citizen again (1892), was elected to Parliament (1895). His last years were spent in further travel and lecturing, and he died in London.

Stanley, Louise (1883–1954) home economist; born in Nashville, Tenn. A Yale biochemistry Ph.D., she taught home economics at the University of Missouri (1907–23). As chief of the new Bureau of Home Economics at the U.S. Department of Agriculture (1923–43), she directed the massive Consumer Purchases Study (1938–41) and promoted standardized clothing sizes.

Stanley, Wendell (Meredith) (1904–71) biochemist; born in Ridgeville, Ind. Working at the Rockefeller Institute (1931–48), he began his research on the tobacco mosaic virus that would eventually establish the chemical nature of viruses and gain him a share of the Nobel Prize in chemistry (1946). He established the virus lab at the University of California: Berkeley (1948) and remained there until his death.

Stanley, William (1858–1916) electrical engineer, inventor; born in Brooklyn, N.Y. A lawyer's son, he enrolled at Yale as a prelaw student but soon dropped out and returned to New York. In the early 1880s, working as an assistant to Hiram Maxim and, later, to Edward Weston, he became interested in electricity. During his tenure as chief engineer for George Westinghouse, he demonstrated the first practical use of the transmission of high tension electricity, in Great Barrington, Mass. (1886). Stanley left Westinghouse and with two partners devised a large-scale system for the distribution of alternating current to provide electric power for industry. Among his inventions were a condenser, a two-phase motor, and an alternating current watt-hour meter.

Stansbury, Howard (1806–63) soldier, explorer; born in New York City. Educated as a civil engineer, he entered the army in 1838 and engaged in years of survey work. He commanded an expedition that explored and surveyed the Great Salt Lake (1849–50). He later surveyed in the Great Lakes area and built military roads in Minnesota.

Stanton, Edwin (McMasters) (1814–69) lawyer, public official; born in Steubenville, Ohio. A tireless, innovative lawyer who pioneered the temporary insanity defense, he served as attorney general under President Buchanan (1860–61) and – although a Democrat – secretary of war (1862–68) under Presidents Lincoln and Johnson. Although he greatly exceeded his authority both during and after the Civil War, he is credited with establishing effective civilian control of the armed forces. Disagreements with Johnson led to his expulsion from the cabinet, which became the immediate provocation for Johnson's impeachment. President Grant appointed him to the Supreme Court in 1869 but he died before joining the court.

Stanton, Elizabeth Cady (1815–1902) women's rights leader, feminist pioneer; born in Johnstown, N.Y. Daughter of a lawyer who made no secret of his preference for another son, she early showed her desire to excel in intellectual and other "male" spheres. She graduated from the Emma Willard's Troy Female Seminary (1832) and then was drawn to the abolitionist, temperance, and women's rights movements through visits to the home of her cousin, the reformer Gerrit Smith. In 1840 she married a reformer, Henry Stanton (omitting "obey" from the marriage oath), and they went at once to the World's Anti-Slavery Convention in London, where she joined other women in objecting to their exclusion from the assembly. On returning to the U.S.A., Elizabeth and Henry had seven children while he studied and practiced law, and eventually they settled in Seneca Falls, N.Y. With Lucretia Mott and several other women, she called the famous Seneca Falls Convention in July 1848, drew up its "Declaration of Sentiments," and took the lead in proposing that women be granted the right to vote. She continued to write and lecture on women's rights and other reforms of the day (and for awhile adopted the new female clothing promoted by Amelia Bloomer), and after meeting Susan B. Anthony in 1851, she was one of the principals in promoting women's rights in general (such as divorce) and the right to vote in particular. During the Civil War she concentrated her efforts on abolishing slavery, but afterward she became even more outspoken in promoting women suffrage. She became publisher of the *Revolution* (1868–69), a militant weekly paper, and in 1869, with Susan B. Anthony, she formed the National Woman Suffrage Association, of which she was the first president (1869–90). Between 1868 and 1880 she also traveled widely as a popular lecturer on the lyceum circuit. She became one of the chief proponents of a woman suffrage amendment to the U.S. Constitution. She and Susan B. Anthony collaborated on the first three volumes of the *History of Woman Suffrage* (1881–86). When the two leading woman suffrage organizataions united as the National American Woman Suffrage Association, she served as its first president (1890–92). Meanwhile, she had long been critical of the role that the Bible and organized religion played in denying women their full rights, and with her daughter, Harriet Stanton Blatch, she published a critique, *The Woman's Bible* (2 vols. 1895, 1898). This brought considerable protest not only from expected religious quarters but from many in the woman suffrage movement. More so than many other women in that movement, she was able and willing to speak out on a wide spectrum of issues – from the primacy of legislatures over the courts and constitution to women's right to ride bicycles – and she deserves to be recognized as one of the more remarkable individuals in American history.

Stanton, Frank (Nicholas) (1908–) broadcast executive; born in Muskegon, Mich. He received his Ph.D. in psychology from Ohio State University (and thus was often referred to as Dr. Stanton). He was hired by CBS in 1934 when an executive read his dissertation on radio audience research. Coinventor of the Stanton-Lazarsfeld program analyzer, he shepherded CBS through several decades of successful expansion as its president (1946–72). He served as chairman of the American Red Cross (1973–79).

Stanton, Frederick (Perry) (1814–94) U.S. representative, governor; born in Alexandria, Va. A lawyer in Memphis, he went to the U.S. House of Representatives (Dem., Tenn.; 1845–55), chairing the Committee on Naval Affairs before becoming governor of the Kansas territory (1858–61).

Stanwyck, Barbara (b. Ruby Stevens) (1907–90) film actress; born in New York City. A working girl from the age of 13, she debuted on Broadway as a chorus girl at age 15. Beginning in Hollywood in *Broadway Nights* (1927), she established herself as a professional, dependable leading lady, playing both comedy and drama, usually in the role of a no-nonsense lady. In 1965 she switched to television, and was awarded an honorary Academy Award in 1981.

Stapleton, Jean (b. Jeanne Murray) (1923–) stage/television actress; born in New York City. A character actress, she appeared in Broadway shows during the 1950s and 1960s, including *The Bells Are Ringing* (1956) and *The Rhinoceros* (1961). Intelligent, liberal, outspoken in real life, she gained her widest fame while portraying a woman who was virtually her opposite, Edith Bunker in *All in the Family* (1971–79), winning several Emmy awards. She returned to Broadway afterward and acted in the CBS series, *Baghdad Cafe.*

Stapp, John Paul (1910–) aviation physician; born in Salvador, Brazil. The son of American missionary parents, he earned a Ph.D. in biophysics (1939) and a medical degree (1943) before joining the army medical corps, where he began a life's work of research into the limits of human endurance, especially in regard to the physiological effects of high acceleration. As part of his research, he rode a rocket sled to a land speed record of 632 miles per hour in 1954. His work helped speed the manned exploration of space; he served as chief scientist of the Aerospace Medical Team in 1962. Stapp joined the faculty of the University of Southern California after retiring from government service in 1970.

Stark, Harold M. (Mead) (1939–) mathematician; born in Los Angeles, Calif. He began his career at the University of Michigan (1964–72) before joining the Massachusetts Institute of Technology faculty (1972). He specialized in elementary number theory with emphasis on zeta functions and applications in quadratic fields.

Stark, Harold Raynsford (1880–1972) naval officer; born in Wilkes-Barre, Pa. He was chief of naval operations (1939–42). He was censured in a naval investigation (1945) for having failed to forward key intelligence to Admiral Husband Kimmel prior to the Japanese attack on Pearl Harbor (1941).

Stark, John (1728–1822) soldier; born in Londonderry, N.H. He served with Rogers' Rangers in the French and Indian War (1754–63). As colonel of a New Hampshire regiment, he fought at Bunker Hill, helped cover the retreat from Canada (1776), and fought at Trenton and Princeton. He resigned in March 1777 to protest the promotion of junior officers over him, but he was appointed brigadier general; it was a detachment under his command that defeated the British forces at Bennington, Vt. (August 1777), a crucial victory followed by his cutting off Burgoyne's retreat and leading to the British surrender at Saratoga. He continued to fight to the end of the American Revolution but retired from public life after the war.

Stark, Louis (1888–1954) journalist; born in Hungary. A *New York Times* reporter for over 30 years, he specialized in labor news; respected as impartial and knowledgeable, he won a 1942 Pulitzer Prize.

Starr, Ellen Gates (1859–1940) social reformer; born near Laona, Ill. Growing up in an Illinois village, she was influenced by her aunt, Eliza Allen Starr, a writer and lecturer on Christian art who lived in Chicago, to enroll in the Rockford Female Seminary (1877–78) (Rockford, Ill.), where she met Jane Addams. For several years she taught at a girls' school in Chicago, but after years of corresponding with Jane Addams and an 1888 trip with her to Europe, the two women established Hull House (1898), a settlement house in Chicago's West Side. For the next 30 years, she was the principal coordinator for cultural activities at Hull House – promoting everything from great books reading clubs to bookbinding – but she soon broadened her concerns to become an activist for child labor and labor issues in general. She eventually joined the Socialist Party and then in 1920 – after a lifetime of searching for a congenial religion – she joined the Catholic Church. After a crippling ailment, she retired in 1930 to a Catholic convent in New York.

Starr, (Shirley) Belle (b. Myra Belle) (1848–89) bandit queen; born at or near Carthage, Mo. Her brothers were killed while fighting with Quantrill's Raiders in the Civil War and in gunfights. She was romantically linked with Thomas Coleman Younger, James H. Reed, Sam Starr, a Cherokee, and Jim July, also a Cherokee. She was rumored to be the "leader of a band of horse thieves" and was convicted once by "Hanging Judge" Parker (1883). On other occasions, she defended herself and her companions with great legal skill. She was shot and killed – allegedly by a man wanted for murder and who inevitably feared she might turn him in – and she was immortalized in popular literature.

Starzl, Thomas (Earl) (1926–) surgeon; born in Le Mars, Iowa. At the University of Colorado School of Medicine (1962–80) and the University of Pittsburgh Medical Center (1981), he advanced organ transplantation by perfecting both the surgical techniques and the drugs to suppress the body's rejection of transplants. Controversial because of his willingness to take risks and make claims that more conservative surgeons shied away from, he performed the first successful human liver transplant (1963), and the first baboon liver transplantation (1992). His autobiography is titled *The Puzzle People: Memoirs of a Transplant Surgeon* (1992).

Stassen, Harold (Edward) (1907–) governor; born in Dakota City, Minn. After putting himself through college and law school, he practiced law in St. Paul, Minn., serving as county attorney (1930–38). After taking the lead in reforming the Republican Party in Minnesota, he served as governor (1939–43) and reformed the state civil service. After serving in World War II as an aide to Admiral Halsey (1943–45), he was a delegate to the founding conference of the United Nations. Highly regarded as a young liberal Republican, he lost the 1948 nomination to Thomas Dewey, so settled for becoming president of the University of Pennsylvania (1948–53). He directed disarmament studies for Eisenhower (1955–58), practicing law in Philadelphia afterward. He became something of a national joke by announcing that he was running for president during every campaign starting in 1948.

Staubach, Roger (Thomas) (1942–) football player; born in Silverton, Ohio. The 1963 Heisman Trophy winner at the Naval Academy, he fulfilled his naval obligation before turning professional in 1969. Four times National Football

League (NFL) passing leader, he quarterbacked the NFL Dallas Cowboys to four conference titles and victories in Super Bowls VI and XII. His ability to bring his team from behind in the closing minutes won him the nickname "Captain Comeback."

St. Clair, Arthur (1738–1818) soldier, public official; born in Thurso, Scotland. He resigned from the British army in 1762 and settled in western Pennsylvania. He served with the Continental forces at Trenton and Princeton; his withdrawal from Fort Ticonderoga without a battle (1777) drew heavy criticism. He was a Pennsylvania delegate to the Confederation Congress (1785–87; president in 1787). As governor of the Northwest Territory (1787–1802), he commanded the army that was soundly defeated near Fort Wayne by the Miami Indians led by Little Turtle (1791).

St. Denis, Ruth (b. Dennis) (1877–1968) dancer, choreographer; born in Somerville, N.J. Dancing from age six, she began in vaudeville and musicals at age 16 and then became an actress who worked with stage director David Belasco (1898–1905). Convinced that dance was the way for her to express her "noblest thoughts," she studied the cultures and dances of the East (although it is also claimed that she took her inspiration from a poster for Isis cigarettes) and then choreographed her own first dance, *Radha* (1906), based on Hindu mythology and using actual East Indian dancers. An overnight success with her mixture of exotic spectacle and high seriousness, she toured Europe for three years. After returning to the U.S.A., she produced elaborate dance productions based on Egyptian and Japanese elements. In 1914 she met and married dancer Ted Shawn and they went to Los Angeles and founded the Denishawn School of Dancing (moved to New York City in 1921) and the Denishawn Dancers. They toured widely, continued to choreograph independently, and trained many of the leading figures in modern American dance. By 1932 they were separated (although they never divorced). By this time she was increasingly embracing the religious element of dance, founding the Society of Spiritual Arts in 1931 and later the Church of the Divine Dance (1947), convinced that dance was a form of worship. In 1939 she published her autobiography, *An Unfinished Life*. From 1945 on she appeared with Ted Shawn at his Jacob's Pillow Dance Festival and at special events. She continued choreographing and performing dances based on Asian and Egyptian mythology until the mid-1960s, often performing in churches to express her idea of the spiritual nature of her work.

Stebbins, Emma (1815–82) sculptor, painter; born in New York City. She was a painter until 1857, lived and worked in Rome (1857–70), and is famous for *The Angel of the Waters* (c. 1862), installed in Central Park (1873) where it is known as the "Bethesda Fountain." She returned to America and lived in New York City (1870) and in Newport, R.I.

Stebbins, G. (George) Ledyard (1906–   ) botanist; born in Lawrence, N.Y. He was an assistant in botany at Harvard (1929–31), and an instructor at Colgate (1931–35), before joining the University of California: Berkeley (1935–50). He used the plant extract colchicine to create polyploidy (the condition of having more than twice the number of chromosomes) in several species of grasses, and was the first biologist to produce a new species artificially and naturalize it (1944). He was a pioneer in applying modern ideas of evolution to botany, as expounded in his *Variation and Evolution in Plants*

(1950). At the University of California: Davis (1950–73) he researched cytogenetics and parthenogenesis in plants. His creation of fertile hybrids made major contributions to both taxonomy and economic plant breeding.

Steber, Eleanor (1916–90) soprano; born in Wheeling, W.Va. American-trained, she made her Metropolitan Opera debut in 1940 and stayed there until 1966, famed for her sensitive musicality. Thereafter she continued singing recitals and teaching.

Stedman, Edmund Clarence (1833–1908) poet, writer; born in Hartford, Conn. His father died when he was two, and he was raised by his maternal grandfather (1835–39), and by his uncle in Norwich, Conn. He studied at Yale (1849–c. 51), then worked for various newspapers in Connecticut and New York City. He ran his own brokerage house in New York City (1864–1908), and lived in Bronxville, N.Y. He wrote rather imitative sentimental poetry, as in *Poems, Lyrical and Idyllic* (1860), but had some influence with his critical studies and anthologies such as *Poets of America* (1885) and *An American Anthology* (1900).

Steele, Fletcher (1885–1971) landscape architect; born in Rochester, N.Y. In the 1920s and 1930s he introduced French modernism to American landscape design, replacing beaux arts formalism with more experimental designs. From his Boston office (1920–70) he completed some 600 commissions, including Naumkeag in Stockbridge, Mass., where he created sweeping vistas with curving walls and sculpted mounds of earth.

Stefansson, Vilhjalmur (1879–1962) explorer; born in Arnes, Manitoba, Canada. Of Icelandic descent, he grew up in Dakota Territory. He studied theology and anthropology at Harvard (1903–06). He went to Iceland (1904–05) and then to the Arctic three times (1906–07, 1908–12, 1913–18). He reported having found some "blond Eskimos" (1912). After 1920 he wrote and lectured extensively, stressing that the Arctic was not barren and that commercial airplanes could travel over the North Pole. He served as a consultant on Arctic issues to the Allies during World War II.

Steffens, Lincoln (1866–1936) journalist, social reformer; born in San Francisco. After graduating from the University of California and studying in Europe, he became a reporter and, ultimately, city editor for the *New York Post* (1892–98), then city editor on the *New York Commercial Advertiser* (1898–1902). As managing editor of the muckraking *McClure's* magazine (1902–06), he wrote carefully researched articles documenting city government corruption that flourished in the face of public apathy; the articles, which created a sensation, were republished in *The Shame of the Cities* (1904), an epoch-making work in urban reform. Steffens also analyzed corruption and reform on the state level in *The Struggle for Self-Government* (1906). He was associate editor of the *American* (1906–07) and then *Everybody's* magazine (1906–11). Visiting postrevolutionary Communist Russia in 1919, he made the famous comment, "I have seen the future and it works." His classic *Autobiography* (1931) was a pungent, often skeptical commentary on the reform movement of the time.

Stegner, Wallace (Earle) (1909–93) writer, educator; born in Lake Mills, Iowa. The son of Scandinavian immigrants, he lived in a half-dozen western states with his family before they settled in Salt Lake City, Utah. After completing his education at the Universities of Utah (B.A. 1930) and Iowa

(Ph.D. 1935), he began teaching English, a career that would take him to several major universities; for most of it he was at Stanford University where he directed the Creative Writing Center (1945–71). Starting with *Restoring Laughter* (1937), he published over two dozen novels, collections of short stories and essays, and historical works; *The Big Rock Candy Mountain* (1943) was among his most popular novels while *Angel of Repose* (1972) won the Pulitzer Prize in fiction. His nonfiction works include biographies of John Wesley Powell, Joe Hill, and Bernard DeVoto. Most of his works dealt with the American West, which he viewed with a mixture of skepticism about its stereotypes, yet respect for its strengths. In his later years he increasingly expressed his concern for the damage being done to the natural environment of the West.

Steichen, Edward (1879–1973) photographer, curator; born in Luxembourg (brother-in-law of Carl Sandburg). Emigrating to the United States as a toddler, he was apprenticed to a Milwaukee lithographic design company in 1894. His strong sense of design led to studies in painting and photography and attracted the attention of Stieglitz in 1905, for whom he designed gallery shows and the magazine *Camera Work*. Commander of aerial photography during World War I, he abandoned art photography to become chief photographer for *Vogue* and *Vanity Fair* (1923–38). Hired by the U.S. Navy to photograph World War II at sea, he was promoted from lieutenant commander to captain and organized the *Road to Victory* exhibit in 1941. From 1947 to 1961, he was director of photography at the Museum of Modern Art, curating some 50 exhibits including *The Family of Man* (1955). In 1963 he was awarded the Presidential Medal of Freedom by President Kennedy.

Steig, William (1907–) artist, cartoonist, writer; born in New York City. He studied in New York at City College (1923–25) and the National Academy of Design (1925–29). In 1930 he began to make wood sculptures and to work as a free-lance artist, notably for the *New Yorker*. Late in his life he began writing as well as illustrating children's books, many of them classics of the genre, such as *Roland, The Minstrel Pig* (1968), *Sylvester and the Magic Pebble* (1969), and *The Amazing Bone* (1976).

Stein, Gertrude (1874–1946) writer, art patron; born in Allegheny, Pa. Daughter of a wealthy merchant, she lived in Europe with her family (1874–79). Upon their return, the family settled in Oakland, Calif. She attended Radcliffe College (B.A. 1898), where she studied psychology under William James (and would remain greatly influenced by his ideas) and at Johns Hopkins Medical School (1897–1901). She followed her brother, Leo Stein, first to London and then Paris (1903), where they began collecting post-impressionist paintings, thereby helping several leading artists such as Matisse and Picasso. She and Leo established a famous literary and artistic salon at 27 rue de Fleurus. Leo moved to Florence, Italy, in 1912, taking many of the paintings, but from 1909 Gertrude had as her assistant Alice B. Toklas, who would remain as Gertrude's lifelong companion. She had been writing for several years and began to publish her innovative works: *Three Lives* (1909), *The Making of Americans: Being a History of a Family's Progress* (written 1906–11; published 1925), and *Tender Buttons: Objects, Food, Rooms* (1914). Intended to employ the techniques of abstraction and cubism in prose, much of her work was virtually unintelligible to even educated readers. During World War I she bought her own Ford van and she and Toklas served as ambulance drivers for the French. After the war, she maintained her salon (although after 1928 she spent much of the year in the village of Bilignin, and in 1937 she moved to a more stylish location in Paris) and served as both hostess and inspiration to such American expatriates as Sherwood Anderson, Ernest Hemingway, and F. Scott Fitzgerald. (She is credited with coining the term, "the lost generation.") She lectured in England in 1926 and in 1933 published her only commercial success, *The Autobiography of Alice B. Toklas*, written by Stein from Toklas's point of view. She made a successful lecture tour of the U.S.A. in 1934 but returned to France where she spent World War II; with the liberation of Paris in 1944, she was visited by many Americans. In addition to her other novels and memoirs, she wrote librettos to two operas by Virgil Thomson, *Four Saints in Three Acts* (1934) and *The Mother of Us All* (1947). Although critical opinion is divided on her various writings, the imprint of her strong, witty personality survives as does her influence on contemporary literature.

Stein, Leo (Daniel) (1872–1947) art collector, critic; born in Allegheny, Pa. (brother of Gertrude Stein). He studied at Harvard (1892–94), and Johns Hopkins (1897), then moved to Paris (1902). His sister, Gertrude, lived with him beginning in 1903, and they began collecting paintings by such contemporary artists as Cézanne, Matisse, and Picasso. By 1912 he and his sister parted company and he returned to America to work as a journalist. He and his wife settled near Florence, Italy (1921). His writings include *Appreciation: Painting, Poetry, and Prose* (1947). He is remembered as an influential promoter of 20th-century paintings.

Stein, William (Howard) (1911–80) biochemist; born in New York City. Beginning in 1938 at the Rockefeller Institute, he and Stanford Moore set about analyzing the amino acids in proteins; by 1960 they had determined the amino acid sequence of ribonuclease. Stein and Moore shared the Nobel Prize in chemistry (1972) with Christian Anfinsen. Stein remained affiliated with Rockefeller University until about 1970.

Steinbeck, John (Ernst) (Amnesia Glasscock, pen name) (1902–68) writer; born in Salinas, Calif. He studied sporadically at Stanford (1919–25) before working in New York City as a reporter and bricklayer. He returned to California and worked at a variety of jobs until he could support himself as a writer. His fourth novel, *Tortilla Flat* (1935), was the first to gain him any critical or financial recognition; it was followed by *In Dubious Battle* (1936), an account of a California strike, and his well-known moral fable, *Of Mice and Men* (1937); the last named was adapted for a successful stage play and movie. He lived and worked with Oklahoma migrants who were heading for California (1937–39), and forged what is considered his masterpiece, *The Grapes of Wrath* (1939), from that experience. The novel revealed, once again, his love of the land, sympathy for the human condition, and his intolerance of the corruption and exploitation of the weak by powerful commercial interests. He worked as a foreign correspondent during World War II and during the Vietnam War (1966–67). His critical reputation declined in his later years – despite such popular works as the novel *East of Eden* (1952) and a travel/memoir, *Travels with Charley* (1962) – but he had written a number of modern classics and was awarded the Nobel Prize in literature in 1962.

Steinberg, (Hans Wilhelm) William (1899–1978) conductor; born in Cologne, Germany. He was a prominent conductor before being driven from Germany by the Nazis in 1933. From 1945 he had a distinguished American career with the symphonies of Buffalo, Pittsburgh and Boston.

Steinberg, Leo (1920–) art historian; born in Moscow, Russia. He studied at the Slade School, London (1940), and emigrated to New York City to study at New York University (Ph.D. 1960). He taught at Hunter College (1961–75), and the University of Pennsylvania (1975). A noted critic as well as scholar, he specialized in Renaissance, baroque, and contemporary art.

Steinberg, Malcolm S. (Saul) (1930–) developmental biologist; born in New Brunswick, N.J. He was a research fellow at the Carnegie Institution (1956–58), moved to Johns Hopkins (1958–66), then joined Princeton (1966). He concurrently taught embryology at the Woods Hole (Mass.) Marine Biology Laboratory (1967–72, trustee 1969–77). He made major contributions to studies of animal morphogenesis and cell assembly and adhesion.

Steinberg, Saul (1914–) graphic artist; born in Ramnicul-Sarat, Romania. He studied sociology and psychology in Bucharest (1932) and received his doctorate in architecture in Italy (1932–40). His drawings began appearing in American periodicals (1940), notably in the *New Yorker.* He escaped from Fascism to the Dominican Republic (1941) and emigrated to New York City (1942). After service in the United States Navy during World War II, he returned to New York and became an influential observer and satirist of modern culture, as seen in *Manassas, Virginia: Main Street* (1978). He won many awards for his pen and ink drawings and watercolors, and his publications, such as *The Passport* (1954) and *The New World* (1965) reinforced his international reputation as a modern master of the graphic arts.

Steinberg, Saul Phillip (1939–) financial executive; born in New York City. A 1959 graduate of the Wharton School at the University of Pennsylvania, he engineered one of the first modern corporate raids at age 28, when, borrowing heavily, he took over Reliance Insurance Co. of Philadelphia. He built Reliance Group Holdings, a financial services firm, on the base of the insurance company. In 1969, he failed in a spectacular attempt to take over the giant Chemical Bank (New York City).

Steinberger, Jack (1921–) physicist; born in Bad Kissigen, Germany. He fled the Nazis with his brother and came to the U.S.A. in 1935. After performing research at Princeton (1948–49) and the University of California: Berkeley (1949–50), he joined Columbia University (1950–72). He, L. Lederman, and M. Schwartz shared the 1988 Nobel Prize for their 1960–62 accelerator-created beam of neutrinos and subsequent discovery that neutrinos exist in two types. Steinberger continued his subatomic particle research at the European Organization for Nuclear Research (CERN) (1968–86), then became a professor at the Scuola Normale, Pisa (1986).

Steinbrenner, George (Michael III) (1930–) businessman, baseball executive; born in Rocky River, Ohio. Chairman of the Cleveland-based American Shipbuilding Co., he became the principal owner of the New York Yankees (1973) and served as club president (1979–90). His pursuit of free agent players resulted in a World Series championship (1979) but he was constantly involved in controversies with his players and managers, usually ending in their abrupt departure. He was suspended from baseball (1990–92) for conduct detrimental to the game, but returned to manage the franchise (1993), promising to keep a somewhat lower profile.

Steinbrugge, Karl V. (Vathauer) (1919–) engineering seismologist; born in Tucson, Ariz. He was a structural designer (1942–50) before joining the University of California: Berkeley (1950–78). He advised national and state organizations on the environmental impact of earthquakes, and made major contributions to the U.S. Public Health Earthquake Hazards Reduction Act (1977).

Steinem, Gloria (1934–) writer, feminist, social reformer; born in Toledo, Ohio. After graduating from Smith College (1956), she went to India on a scholarship and stayed on to write newspaper articles and a guidebook. Determined to be a journalist, she returned to the U.S.A. and worked (1958–60) for the Independent Research Service (later revealed as secretly subsidized by the CIA). She went to New York City and began as a free-lancer, first attracting attention with her article, "I Was a Playboy Bunny," an exposé based on her own undercover work in a New York City Playboy Club. She was soon publishing her articles and becoming something of a celebrity, often seen with celebrity males; she also began to write some television comedy material. In 1968 she was invited to write a column, "The City Politic," for a new magazine, *New York,* thus beginning her career as a serious social commentator. She also became affiliated with a radical women's group, the Redstockings, and published her first overtly feminist piece, "After Black Power, Women's Liberation" (1968). In 1971 she joined other prominent feminists in forming the National Women's Political Caucus and took the lead in launching *Ms.* magazine (an insert in *New York* in December 1971, first independent issue in January 1972). About this time she began to come under fire from some feminists, in part because of her work with the Independent Research Service, in part because some questioned whether anyone so glamorous could be a serious feminist. But she continued on her own way, speaking out, lecturing widely, organizing various women's functions, and editing *Ms.* until 1987. In 1986 she published *Marilyn,* a biographical study of Marilyn Monroe's life from a feminist perspective. In 1992 she became controversial once again when she published *Revolution from Within: A Book of Self-Esteem,* which seemed to some feminists to be a retreat from social action.

Steiner, (Maximilian Raoul) Max (1888–1971) film composer; born in Vienna, Austria. In 1929 he came to Hollywood from Broadway and went on to score over 200 films, his credits including *King Kong* (1933), *Gone with the Wind* (1939), and *The Treasure of the Sierra Madre* (1948).

Steinitz, (Wilhelm) William (1836–1900) chess player; born in Prague, Czechoslovakia. Discovering an interest and talent for chess while a student in Vienna, he began to devote his life to the game and by 1866 he was recognized as the world champion. Resident in England from 1862, where he edited a chess column in an English magazine while defending his world championship, he emigrated to America in 1883, where he edited the *International Chess Magazine,* wrote chess columns, and published a basic text, *The Modern Chess Instructor* (2 vols. 1889, 1895). His loss of the world championship in 1894 so disturbed him that he spent much of the rest of his life in mental institutions.

Steinmetz, (b. Karl August Rudolf) Charles Proteus (1865–1923) electrical engineer, inventor; born in Breslau, Germany. Deformed from birth, he devoted his energy to school and diverse intellectual interests. After graduating from Zurich Polytechnic, he emigrated to the U.S.A. in 1889. His first major accomplishment was the publication in 1892 of data showing how magnets lose power in the process of generating alternating current. In 1893 he introduced a new formula for calculating alternating current. In that year he started work at General Electric (GE), becoming chief consulting engineer in 1910. GE gave Steinmetz unrestricted latitude in his experiments and an open-ended salary. Steinmetz advanced research by substituting laboratory methods based on mathematical principles for the older practice of developing a theory and building a model to test it. For many years he studied transient electrical phenomena such as lightning, unexpected electrical discharges that can damage circuits, and he became widely known for his demonstrations of man-made lightning. His classes at Union College (Schenectady, N.Y.), many inventions, several books, and numerous honors made him one of the best-known scientists in America in his day.

Stella, Frank (Philip) (1936–) painter; born in Malden, Mass. (nephew of Joseph Stella). He studied art at Princeton (1954–58), settled in New York City (1958), and worked as a house painter. He produced abstract "pin-stripe" works (1959), such as *The Marriage of Reason and Squalor* (1959), painted his "black" series (c. 1960), and soon was experimenting with shaped canvases and copper and aluminum paint. From 1964 to 1965 he created his *Notched V* series and, later, began his large sculptural wall reliefs, *The Indian Bird Series* (1977–78). Later his work was three dimensional.

Stella, Joseph (b. Giuseppe) (1877–1946) painter; born in Muro Lucano, Italy (uncle of Frank Stella). He emigrated to New York City (1896), studied at the New York School of Art under William Merritt Chase (1898), and was an illustrator for many periodicals. He traveled to Europe (1910–12), and was influenced by the Italian futurists, who stressed a dynamic and kinetic approach to art. He returned to New York (1913), traveled frequently, but settled in Queens, New York (1935). His brightly colored and energetic canvases, such as *Battle of Lights, Coney Island* (1913), were followed by a series of abstract panels, as in *The Bridge* (1926), and later, by symbolic paintings.

Stelze, Charles (1869–1941) Protestant clergyman, reformer; born in New York City. The son of poor immigrant Germans, he grew up in tenements and took his first sweatshop job at age eight. Ordained a Presbyterian minister in 1900, he worked in inner city missions in Minneapolis, New York City, and St. Louis. From 1906 to 1913 he headed the Presbyterians' social gospel arm, the Department of Church and Labor. His book, *Christianity's Storm Center: A Study of the Modern City* (1907), called for aggressive evangelism in working-class districts. From 1913 until the end of his life he was a free-lance publicist for religious and social causes, including temperance.

Stengel, (Charles Dillon) Casey (1891–1975) baseball player/manager; born in Kansas City, Mo. One of baseball's authentic "characters" and a manager of eccentric genius, Stengel abandoned dental school and began his distinguished six-decade career in Kankakee, Ill., in 1910. From 1912–25 he played outfield in the major leagues (1925–31 in the minors) compiling career averages of .964 for fielding and .284 for batting. Coaching and managing after 1932, as manager of the Yankees (1948–60) he won ten pennants and seven World Series championships; in the five seasons from 1949 to 1953, he won five consecutive pennants and Series. He managed the New York Mets from 1962–65 and was inducted into the Baseball Hall of Fame in 1966. Known for his encyclopedic knowledge of players and for making strategic choices "against" the averages, his famous quotable malapropisms and "Stengelese" attained legendary proportions in the 1958 Senate subcommittee hearings examining baseball's trust-exempt status.

Stephens, Alexander H. (Hamilton) ("Little Ellick") (1812–83) Confederate vice-president, U.S. representative, governor; born near Crawfordville, Ga. He was admitted to the bar (1834) and served Georgia in the U.S. House of Representatives (Whig, 1843–53; Dem., 1853–59), where he opposed the war with Mexico but strongly supported the Compromise of 1850. As more extremist Southerners began to call for secession, he opposed it, but at the same time he defended the institution of slavery. When Georgia seceded, he went along with it and somewhat reluctantly he found himself elected vice-president of the Confederate States of America (1861–65). During the Civil War, he often opposed Jefferson Davis's policies, but in the end had little impact on events. He led the Confederate delegation to the unsuccessful peace conference at Hampton Roads, Va. (February 1865). He was imprisoned for five months in Boston Harbor, Mass., and on returning to Georgia was elected to the U.S. Senate in 1866 but was refused his seat. He then wrote a controversial defense of the Confederate position, *A Constitutional View of the Late War Between the States* (2 vols, 1868–70). He did return to the U.S. House of Representatives (Dem., Ga.; 1873–82) and then served briefly as governor of Georgia (1882–83).

Stephens, John Lloyd (1805–52) traveler, author, promoter; born in Shrewsbury, N.J. A New York lawyer, he began a series of exotic journeys in 1834 and through his books became known as the "American traveler." He wrote *Incidents of Travel in Egypt, Arabia Petraea and the Holy Land* (1837) and *Incidents of Travel in Greece, Turkey, Russia, and Poland* (1838). During 1839–41, he traveled in Central America and Mexico with the English artist Frederick Catherwood. His two books on their travel and discoveries, beautifully illustrated by Catherwood, were among the first to publicize Mayan remains and effectively founded the field of Mayan archaeology. He later promoted both steamboat and railroad companies, notably the Panama Railroad (1849–51). He died prematurely from a disease he contracted in Panama.

Stern, Isaac (1920–) violinist; born in Kremenets, Russia. Brought in infancy to the U.S.A. by his family, he grew up in San Francisco and took up the violin at age eight, later studying at the city's conservatory (1928–31) and debuting with the orchestra at age 11. After years of further study and growth, he achieved an outstanding success at his Carnegie Hall debut in 1943. He went on to a career in the highest rank of international violinists – the only one to have been entirely trained in America. From 1961 he often played chamber music with pianist Eugene Istomin and cellist

Leonard Rose; for many years he was president of New York's Carnegie Hall, which he helped save from demolition. An intense and individual player, he both mastered the standard repertoire and introduced many new works. As a cultural ambassador he made tours of Russia in 1956 and of China in 1979.

Stern, Otto (1888–1969) physicist; born in Sorau, Germany. After completing his graduate work in physical chemistry at the University of Breslau, Germany (Ph.D. 1912), he worked with Albert Einstein at the Kaiser Wilhelm Institute in Berlin. In 1919 he went to work with Max Born at the Institute for Theoretical Physics in Frankfurt, Germany, and it was there, during the 1920s, that Stern developed the use of molecular beams to study the magnetic properties of atoms; he proved the existence of atomic magnetic moments and measured their magnitudes. It was this work that gained him the 1943 Nobel Prize in physics. In 1933, forced by the Nazis to leave Germany, he emigrated to the U.S.A. and there, thanks to a grant from the Buhl Foundation, he took up his work at the Carnegie Institute of Technology in Pittsburgh (now Carnegie-Mellon University). He became a U.S. citizen in 1939 and, with time out for government research during World War II, he remained affiliated with that institution until he retired in 1946.

Stern, Robert A. M. (Arthur Morton) (1939–) architect, author; born in New York City. He broke with the International style to design "modern traditional" residential, commercial, and institutional buildings. He was a widely published professor of architecture at Columbia University (1970).

Sternberg, George Miller (1838–1915) bacteriologist, epidemiologist; born in Otsego County, N.Y. As a surgeon in the Union army during the Civil War, he was present at several battles, but spent the final months on hospital duty after he contracted typhoid fever. He remained in the army, and during the 1870s he became an authority on yellow fever. Assigned to the Havana Yellow Fever Commission (1879–80), he was one of the first to use photomicrography in the course of his investigations. He would go on to be the co-discoverer (with Louis Pasteur) of the pneumococcus, the plasmodium of malaria, and the bacilli of tuberculosis and typhoid fever. His research on microorganisms reinforced his interest in disinfection, resulting in his essay *Disinfection and Individual Prophylaxis against Infectious Diseases* (1886). As the pioneer American bacteriologist, he laid down the basics of the science, summed up in his major text, *A Manual of Bacteriology* (1892). Promoted to surgeon general of the U.S. Army (1893–1902), he oversaw the establishment of the Army Medical School, the Army Nurse Corps, the Army Dental Corps, the Typhoid Fever Board (1898), and the Yellow Fever Commission, headed by Walter Reed (1900).

Sterne, Maurice (1878–1957) painter; born in Libau, Latvia. He and his widowed mother emigrated to New York City (1889), where he studied under Thomas Eakins at the National Academy of Design (1894–99). Although he often traveled, he remained based in New York. He is best known for his landscapes, influenced by Gaugin and Cézanne.

Stetson, John B. (Batterson) (1830–1906) manufacturer; born in Orange, N.J. Born into a family of hatters with 11 siblings, Stetson learned the trade and set out on his own. Ill health forced him west where a life outdoors restored him, and in 1865 he moved to Philadelphia and opened a hat factory. He achieved success by relying on his own taste for style and by building a reputation for quality. At his death, he left an industrial plant employing 3,500, with production of two million hats and employee benefits such as profit-sharing, bonuses, and a company hospital. An active and generous Baptist, he wintered in De Land, Fla., where he supported the De Land Academy whose name was changed to the John B. Stetson University.

Stettheimer, Florine (1871–1944) painter; born in Rochester, N.Y. In the 1890s she studied at the Art Students League, in Europe (1906–14), and settled in New York. She created the sets and costumes for *Four Saints in Three Acts* (1934), an opera by Virgil Thomson and Gertrude Stein. Her paintings were satiric, theatrical, and symbolic.

Stettinius, Edward R. (Reilly) (1900–49) corporation executive, cabinet member; born in Chicago, Ill. At General Motors (1920–34), he established a workers' insurance plan before going to the United States Steel Corporation (1934–40), where as chairman of the board he recognized the steel workers' union. He was with the Office of Production Management (1941–43); as secretary of state (1944–46), he spearheaded negotiations to establish the United Nations; he then served as chairman of the American delegation to the first meetings of the United Nations (1945–46).

Steuben, Baron von (Friedrich Wilhelm Ludolf Gerhard Augustin) (1730–94) soldier; born in Magdeburg, Prussia (now Germany). The son of an army officer, he saw service during the Seven Years War and became an aide to Frederick the Great; his title came from service under a minor German prince. After meeting Benjamin Franklin in Paris, he was given letters of introduction to George Washington and went to America in December 1777. He joined Washington at Valley Forge and immediately began to introduce European methods of training and discipline. In May 1778 he was appointed inspector general of the Continental army, in which post he helped shape the raw American colonials into a credible military force. He himself saw action at Monmouth and Yorktown. He helped Washington plan for the demobilization of the Continental army and the future defense of the states, and Washington's final official act as commander was to commend Steuben for his service. He became an American citizen by act of the Pennsylvania legislature in 1783 and several states gave him large tracts of land. He spent most of his final years in New York, regarded as one of the true heroes of the American Revolution.

Steuben, John (b. Itzak Rijock) (1906–57) union organizer, radical activist, labor editor; born in Brailov, Ukraine. After he emigrated to America with his father (1923), little is known of his life until he became active in the American labor movement in the 1930s. He was an organizer for the Communist-run Steel and Metal Workers Industrial Union (1930s) and played a major role in the "Little Steel" Strike (1936–37). After serving in World War II, he edited *March of Labor* (1950–54) and published *Strike Strategy* (1950). In later years he suffered FBI harassment despite repudiating the Soviet state.

Steunenberg, Frank (1861–1905) governor; born in Keokuk, Iowa. A typesetter, he bought the *Caldwell Tribune* in 1866 with his brother, later serving in the Idaho legislature. As Democratic governor of Idaho (1897–1901), he called in the federal authorities to put down the Western Federation of Miners strike (1899). Returning to publishing, he was killed by a bomb outside his home, placed there by a union member.

Stevens, Edwin Augustus (1795–1868) engineer, financier; born in Hoboken, N.J. Son of John Cox Stevens, he managed his father's business for many years but he was also interested in armored coverings and their application to naval warfare. One of the boats he outfitted, the *Naugatuck,* attacked the *Merrimac* during the Civil War. Stevens ran the Camden & Amboy Railroad from 1830 until his death. He provided the land and money for what became the Stevens Institute of Technology.

Stevens, George (1904–75) director; born in Oakland, Calif. He directed two-reelers for Hal Roach beginning in 1930, and began making features in 1933. A versatile director, he won Oscars for *A Place in the Sun* (1951) and *Giant* (1956).

Stevens, Harry (Mozley) (1855–1934) business executive; born in London, England. He emigrated to Ohio in 1882, winning in 1887 the first of the baseball park concessions that would launch him as the preeminent food concessionaire at America's ballparks, racetracks, and convention centers. In the early 1900s he introduced frankfurters in rolls at the New York Polo Grounds; he became the "hot dog king" by shifting baseball fare from lemonade and ice cream to franks, peanuts, and soda. His son Frank M. Stevens (1880–1965) continued expanding the business.

Stevens, Isaac Ingalls (1818–62) soldier, public official; born in Andover, Mass. He was an army engineer in the Mexican War and was governor of the Washington Territory (1853–57). He directed the exploration for the Pacific Railroad surveys and ruthlessly suppressed an Indian rebellion within the Territory (1855). He served in the House of Representatives (Dem., Washington Territory; 1857–61) and, as a Union brigadier general, was killed in the Civil War.

Stevens, John Cox (1749–1856) engineer, inventor; born in New York City. After serving in the American Revolution, Stevens joined the growing group of men interested in steam power, especially as applied to ships. He designed boilers and engines that received some of the first American patents (1791) and he collaborated with such pioneers in steamboats as Nicholas Roosevelt and Robert R. Livingston. In 1803 he built the *Little Juliana,* which was propelled by twin Archimedean screws; it served as a ferry between Manhattan and Hoboken, N.J. Design problems led him to revert to paddle wheels, but Robert Fulton's *Clermont* sailed up and down the Hudson River (1807) before Stevens' *Phoenix* was ready (1809). The *Phoenix* sailed to Philadelphia, however, becoming the world's first ocean-going steamboat. Stevens then turned his interest to steam-powered railways and in 1825 he operated the first steam locomotive in America. He proposed several other engineering projects that would not be accomplished for many decades.

Stevens, John Paul (1920–) Supreme Court justice; born in Chicago. After several years in private practice, he was named by President Nixon to the U.S. Court of Appeals, Seventh Circuit (1970–75). President Ford named him to the U.S. Supreme Court (1975) where he became known as a moderate.

Stevens, Risé (1913–) mezzo-soprano; born in New York City. After finding her first successes in Prague, she debuted at the Metropolitan Opera in 1938, where she remained popular for many years, meanwhile appearing internation-

ally. From 1975 to 1978 she was president of the Mannes College of Music.

Stevens, Robert Livingston (1787–1856) naval architect, engineer, inventor; born in Hoboken, N.J. He assisted his father, John Cox Stevens, in the design and construction of steamboats, for which he invented numerous improvements. Joining his brother as president and chief engineer of the Camden & Amboy Railroad, he also invented several improvements for railroads including the T-rail, the hook-headed railroad spike, and the cowcatcher; he was the first to burn anthracite in a locomotive. He also made contributions to military ordnance and naval armoring.

Stevens, Thaddeus (1792–1868) U.S. representative; born in Danville, Vt. Congenitally lame, he grew up with an intense empathy for society's poor and disenfranchised. He graduated from Dartmouth College, then studied law, setting up practice in Gettysburg, Pa. (1816). He served in the state's house of representatives (1833–41) but the formative experience of his years in Gettysburg inspired his passionate antipathy to slavery. He went to the U.S. House of Representatives (1849–53) as a Whig but left in impatience over the party's stand on slavery. After helping to form the new Republican Party in Pennsylvania, he returned to the House (1859–68); as chairman of the Ways and Means Committee, he exerted major influence on the conduct of the war, often differing with Lincoln. Almost fanatical in advocating harsh policies against the Confederate states, he emerged as the leader of the Radical Republicans and got himself appointed to the joint committee on reconstruction. His idea of treating the South as what he called "a conquered province" brought him into open conflict with President Andrew Johnson. Stevens led the move to impeach Johnson, then died soon after Johnson's acquittal. He remains one of the most problematic of American politicians – his espousal of the rights of African-Americans spoiled by his intolerance of those who disagreed with his approach.

Stevens, Wallace (1879–1955) poet, insurance executive; born in Reading, Pa. He took a special course at Harvard (1897–1900) and published some poems while there. He went to New York City to work as a journalist (1900–01) but didn't care for journalism and went to New York University Law School (1901–03). He practiced law in New York City (1904–16) and in 1916 joined the legal staff of the Hartford Accident and Indemnity Company, with which he remained until his death (becoming a vice-president in 1934). While in New York City he had come to know many of the leading writers and artists, and he published his first poems as an adult in 1914, with "Sunday Morning" appearing in *Poetry* magazine in 1915. His verse play, "Three Travelers Watch a Sunrise," (1916) won a *Poetry* prize and was produced by New York's Provincetown Playhouse (1917). His first collection of poetry, *Harmonium,* was published in 1923, and though selling less than 100 copies, received some acclaim from fellow poets. More collections followed throughout the 1930s and 1940s, but not until the 1950s did he begin to receive wider recognition, reflected in literary awards, publication of his essays and addresses, and tributes to him as a major modern poet. After his death his influence on poets and serious readers of poetry only increased, for they found in the meticulous language and daring metaphors of such poems as "The Emperor of Ice Cream" and "The Man with the Blue Guitar" – decidedly difficult as they are – the creative imagination that allows humans to face the reality Stevens valued.

Stevenson, Adlai E. (Ewing) (1835–1914) vice-president, politician; born in Christian County, Ky. (grandfather of Adlai Stevenson). As first assistant postmaster (1885–89), he supported patronage and fired thousands of people. As vice-president during Grover Cleveland's second term (1893–97), he made many friends and presided gracefully over the Senate. He ran unsuccessfully for the vice-presidency in 1900 and the governorship of Illinois in 1908.

Stevenson, Adlai (Ewing), II (1900–65) governor, government official; born in Los Angeles, Calif. (grandson of vice-president Adlai E. Stevenson). After studying history and literature at Princeton University (1918–22), he worked at the Bloomington, Ill., *Daily Pentagraph* while earning a Northwestern University law degree. He joined a conservative Chicago law firm, Cutting, Moore, and Sidley, in 1927, taking time out to work as special counsel for the Agricultural Adjustment Administration (1933–35) and serving as president of the Chicago Council of Foreign Relations. He returned to Washington during World War II as attorney for Navy Secretary Frank Knox (1941–44). Special assistant to Secretary of State Edward Stettinus Jr., (1945–47), he mustered public support for the United Nations at the San Francisco conference, subsequently serving as senior adviser for the first General Assembly meeting. As Democratic governor of Illinois (1949–53), he doubled funding for public education, ended political appointments to the state police department, and vetoed a state "antisubversive" squad. Drafted for president at the 1952 Democratic convention, he campaigned eloquently for principled politics, but lost to General Eisenhower. After traveling in Asia and the Middle East, he published *A Call to Greatness* (1954). Campaigning for president again in 1956, he championed the suspension of nuclear testing and focused on race relations and conservation issues, but he lost heavily to the popular Eisenhower. After founding the Democratic Advisory Council in 1957, he returned to his Chicago law firm. As President Kennedy's United Nations ambassador (1961–65), he was largely ignored during the Bay of Pigs invasion planning and was later foiled by Lyndon Johnson after trying to initiate peace talks with Hanoi. Greatly admired by liberals, he proved to be one of America's "lost causes" as a national political leader. He died of a heart attack while walking alone on a street in London.

Stevenson, Andrew (1784–1857) U.S. representative, ambassador; born in Culpeper County, Va. Son of a minister, he was a lawyer in Richmond and a member of the Virginia house of delegates (1809–21). In Congress (Dem., Va.; 1821–34, as Speaker, 1827–34), he alienated Whigs with his partisan committee appointments and Southern Democrats with his opposition to nullification. Appointed ambassador to Britain (1834–41), he returned to become president of the Virginia agricultural society and rector at the University of Virginia.

Stevenson, James (?1929–) cartoonist, writer; born in New York City. He graduated from Yale and was a reporter for *Life* magazine until 1955. From 1956 to 1963 he was a cartoonist and writer for the *New Yorker*. Thereafter he illustrated and wrote numerous books for children, such as *Could Be Worse!* (1977), and *Worse Than Willy!* (1984). He lived in Connecticut.

Stevenson, James (1840–88) explorer, ethnologist; born in Maysville, Ky. He joined the U.S. Geological Survey and, with Dr. Ferdinand Hayden, explored the Missouri, Columbia, and Snake Rivers to their sources. He participated in the Yellowstone region survey (1871) and was probably the first white man to climb the Great Teton (1872). After 1879 he worked for the U.S. Bureau of Ethnology; he studied the languages and customs of the Blackfeet, Navaho, Zuni, Hopi, and Pueblo Indians, and he collected and catalogued a great deal of their cultural materials.

Steward, Julian (Haynes) (1902–72) anthropologist; born in Washington, D.C. He founded cultural ecology, the study of social systems in terms of their environment, with such works as *Theory of Culture Change* (1955, revised 1973) and *Evolution and Ecology* (1977), and edited the encyclopedic *Handbook of South American Indians* (7 vols. 1946–59). He ended his teaching career at the University of Illinois: Urbana (1952–72).

Stewart, Alexander T. (Taylor) (1803–76) merchant; born in Lisburn, Ireland. He came to New York City around 1820 after the death of his grandfather who had raised him to be a minister, a job for which he had no inclination. With a $5,000 inheritance, he invested in Irish lace and in 1823 opened his first shop. He expanded rapidly, in part by purchasing the goods of merchants who failed during the panic of 1837. By 1850 his was the largest establishment of its kind in New York; by 1862 his retail business covered an entire city block, the largest store in the world. His interests encompassed textile mills in New England, and real estate in New York, including the Garden City development for the middle class on Long Island. Although penurious about wages, his acts of charity included sending food to Ireland during the 1847 famine and bringing back a boat-load of immigrants for whom he found jobs. In 1878 his coffin was stolen and his remains were ransomed to his widow. They were returned in 1880 and reinterred in Garden City.

Stewart, Ellen (1931–) theater producer, director; born in Alexandria, La. Starting out as an elevator operator and clothing designer, she set up her own little theater in a New York tenement basement in 1962; growing from this, her companies – known variously as La Mama, Cafe La Mama, and La Mama ETC (Experimental Theater Club) – performed countless plays by avant-garde, international, and young American playwrights; toured widely and to great acclaim; and set up branches throughout the world. Self-taught in the drama and theatrical arts, married five times, she is recognized as a major influence in late-20th-century theater.

Stewart, George F. (1908–82) food scientist; born in Arizona. Before joining the faculty at the University of California: Davis in 1951, he was a research chemist in the food industry and a faculty member at Iowa State University. In 1959 he was named chair of the combined food science and dairy industry departments at Davis; from 1965 to 1970 he was the first director of the Food Protection and Toxicology Center at Davis. He conducted crucial research in poultry preservation and dehydrated egg products. A prolific writer, he coedited with Emil M. Mrak, *Advances in Food Research*.

Stewart, James (Maitland) (1908–) film actor; born in Indiana, Pa. He was a magician and accordionist when he was a boy, and while he was attending Princeton University he appeared in campus productions. After graduation he joined a repertory company in Massachusetts, where two of his coperformers were Henry Fonda and Margaret Sullavan. This tall, gangly, drawling young man arrived in Hollywood in 1935, where he appeared in *The Murder Man,* but it wasn't until he starred in such films as *Mr. Smith Goes to Washington* (1939) that filmmakers realized how appealing he was to the American public. In 1940 he won an Academy Award for *The Philadelphia Story.* He was a bomber pilot in World War II, flying 20 missions over Germany and attaining the rank of colonel. After the war, he returned, once again playing the quintessential small-town man in *It's a Wonderful Life* (1947), a movie revived every Christmas on television. He went on to a variety of roles – cowboys, detectives, and other masculine types. He was given an honorary Oscar in 1984.

Stewart, Potter (1915–85) Supreme Court justice; born in Jackson, Mich. He was in private practice and involved in Cincinnati politics when he was appointed to the U.S. Court of Appeals (1954–58). President Eisenhower named him to the U.S. Supreme Court (1959–81) where he took independent and moderate judicial positions.

Stewart, T. (Thomas) Dale, Jr. (1901–) physical anthropologist; born in Delta, Pa. He was curator, director, and senior scientist of the National Museum of Natural History (1927–71). His research on fossil and modern skeletons demonstrated normal and pathological osseous development in prehistoric North Americans, the Neanderthals of Iraq, and the Korean War dead.

Stewart, William Morris (1827–1909) lawyer, public official; born in Goshen, N.Y. He dropped out of Yale to join the California gold rush (1850), and after a period of prospecting, he settled down to practice law. He made a fortune in legal fees by representing the successful claimants to the Comstock Lode in Nevada in 1859, and went on to serve as Republican U.S. senator from Nevada (1864–75, 1887–1905). Always at the service of the silver interests, he endorsed Democrat William Jennings Bryan for president in 1896 on the basis of Bryan's support of a silver standard for currency. He was an early supporter of federal aid to reclaim arid lands for agriculture.

Stibitz, George Robert (1904–) computer engineer; born in York, Pa. He began work at the Bell Labs (1930) on problems relating to the calculation of complex numbers. In 1937 he built a binary-based relay switch system that made possible a computer to perform simple calculations (1939). In 1940 he transmitted computer work over the telephone. He worked for the government during World War II. In 1964, using computer modeling to study human physiology, he became a research associate at Dartmouth Medical School. He was named professor in 1965 and retired in 1973.

Stickley, Gustav (1858–1942) furniture craftsman, designer, editor; born in Osceola, Wis. Son of a stonemason, he learned and practiced the trade until about 1875 when he went to work in an uncle's chair factory in Brandt, Pa. By 1880 he had taken over the firm, and, with his younger brothers Charles Stickley and Albert Stickley, formed Stickley Brothers, a furniture manufacturing firm, which they moved to Binghamton, N.Y., in the 1880s. Gustav at one point became involved with promoting electric streetcars – and was evidently the first to operate one in the U.S.A. – but he concentrated his energies on improving the design of furniture and homes, not just for aesthetic reasons, but also because he believed that his new

functionalism would improve the lives of both the workers and users of his products. In this he was influenced by the ideas of the Englishmen John Ruskin and William Morris, and the British Arts and Crafts movement, and in the late-1890s he traveled in Europe to observe the new styles. On return, in 1898 he started a factory in Eastwood, N.Y., where furniture was made – using machines when feasible – in a style he called "Craftsman": mostly "fumed" oak, plain rectilinear lines, usually leather for seats, simple finish. After being exhibited at a trade fair in 1900, the new furniture came to be widely known as "Mission style," because it looked like the furniture made for the Catholic missions in the Southwest, although Stickley himself claimed the name arose because his furniture was designed to fulfill its "mission of usefulness." (In the spirit of medieval craftsmen, he placed his motto on his furniture, *als ik kan,* – "as I can" – borrowed from the 14th-century artist Jan van Eyck.) In 1901 he founded a magazine, *Craftsman,* to promote his ideas about home furnishings and social reforms; he remained its publisher and editor until it stopped publication in 1916. In 1902 *Craftsman* began printing home designs, usually for small bungalows with built-it furniture; mail-order firms such as Sears, Roebuck sold the complete materials for building these. Stickley, meanwhile, after briefly turning his company into a profit-sharing cooperative (1901–05), greatly expanded his manufacturing capacity, established his corporate headquarters in the Craftsman Building in New York City, and in 1908 established Craftsman Farms in New Jersey as a model for growing and serving food. The Craftsman movement seemed to be everywhere, but in 1915 his overextended empire collapsed into bankruptcy as a result of World War I and changing tastes, and Gustav Stickley never regained his influence. Two of his brothers, Leopold and J. George Stickley, who had already been making furniture in Gustav's style in Fayetteville, N.Y., purchased his factory at Eastwood and continued making furniture under the Stickley name.

Stickney, A. B. (Alpheus Beede) (1840–1916) railway builder; born in Wilton, Maine. He left a career as a lawyer in Minnesota (1862–69) to start working for the railroads. He was involved in several of the midwestern and northwestern railways until 1883, when he organized and began construction of the Minneapolis & Northwestern Railroad; he was the company's president, and when it merged with the Chicago, St. Paul & Kansas City (1887), he became president of both. In 1892, as chairman of the board, he reorganized roads as the Chicago Great Western Railroad, which he led until 1908 when the road went bankrupt and he was appointed receiver. In 1909 he retired. The financial methods with which he tried to manage the railroads were new to America, ideas he acquired in England and set forth in *The Railway Problem* (1891), but which could not protect the road from an insufficient earning power.

Stiegel, (Heinrich Wilhelm) Henry William (1729–85) ironmaster, glassmaker; born in Cologne, Germany. In 1750 he emigrated to Philadelphia and by 1758 he was operating an iron manufactory in Lancaster County, Pa., which soon was one of the most successful in the colonies. In 1764 he began the first of his three glass factories; in addition to making standard sheet glass, he employed German, Venetian, and English glassblowers to make some of the most widely marketed glass tableware of the time. Although his glass wares were not signed and there are several varieties of

"Stiegel ware" – including those colored wine-red, amethyst, and blue, and some with molded patterns – purists prefer to limit the term to a fine flint or green variety of glassware with engraved or enameled decoration. Legendary for his lavish expenditures, by 1774 he was bankrupt and imprisoned for debt, and his business never truly recovered after that.

Stieglitz, Alfred (1864–1946) photographer, curator; born in Hoboken, New Jersey. He traveled to Berlin, Germany, in 1881 to study mechanical engineering and came back to New York in 1890 a photographer and admirer of avant-garde art. Partner in a photogravure business (1890–95), he continued taking photographs and edited *Camera Notes* for the Camera Club (1897–1902). He resigned in 1902, founding the photo-secession movement to express his belief that photography was an art form, equal to painting. Editor of *Camera Work,* he opened the "291" gallery (its name merely the address on 5th Avenue) to exhibit art from Europe (1905–17). In 1917 he met and began photographing the artist Georgia O'Keeffe, whom he married in 1924. A leader of the "pictorialist" approach to photography, he achieved his painterly effects by filming at night, in the snow and rain, instead of retouching in the lab. Winner of 150 awards for his own photography, he championed the careers of artists and photographers at the American Place Gallery (1929–46).

Stieglitz, Julius (1867–1937) chemist; born in Hoboken, N.J. (brother of Alfred Stieglitz). He was affiliated with the University of Chicago (1892–1933). His research in such fields as molecular rearrangements and stereochemistry helped lay the foundations of physicoorganic chemistry. During World War I, he advised the government on how to overcome shortages of chemicals which had come from Germany.

Stigler, George J. (Joseph) (1911–91) economist; born in Renton, Wash. A leader of the Chicago school of economic thought, he taught at several colleges and universities before joining the faculty of the University of Chicago (1959–91). He wrote on economic theory, industrial organization, and the history of economic thought. His analysis of labor markets was a prototype for all later work on "search models" of unemployment. His examination of pricing policies in industry and public utilities is highly respected. For his work on the theory of market forces and economic regulation he received the Nobel Prize in economics (1982).

Stiglitz, Joseph E. (1942–   ) economist; born in Gary, Ind. He completed his Ph.D. from the Massachusetts Institute of Technology at age 24, and went on to teach at several universities before settling at Princeton (1979). He is known best by other economists for his highly technical analysis of the competitive process.

Stiles, Charles W. (Wardell) (1867–1941) medical zoologist, public health reformer; born in Spring Valley, N.Y. He did his graduate studies at several major European universities before going to Washington, D.C., as a zoologist with the Department of Agriculture's bureau of animal industry (1891–1902); there he investigated diseases in animals in slaughterhouses, pork trichinosis, and parasitic worms in livestock. In 1895 he was one of five elected to the International Commission on Zoological Nomenclature, serving as its secretary from 1898–1936. Transferring to the Hygienic Laboratory of the U.S. Public Health and Marine Hospital Service, he served as chief of its zoology division

(1902–31); he also taught medical zoology at Georgetown (1892–1906) and at Johns Hopkins (1897–1937). His major contribution was his discovery of a variety of hookworm and confirming it as endemic in the southern United States (1902); his work led to the formation of the Rockefeller Sanitary Commission (1909) and its campaign to eradicate hookworm disease in the U.S. He investigated the health problems in various work sites and performed experiments on soil pollution caused by pathogens in groundwater. Another of his major contributions – which occupied him from the 1890s to the mid-1930s – was coauthoring the *Index-Catalog of Medical and Veterinary Zoology* (vols. 1–4, 1902–20; and supplements).

Stiles, Ezra (1727–95) scholar, clergyman; born in North Haven, Conn. Besides conducting his Newport, R.I., ministry (1755–86), he was a theologian and scientist reputed to be the most learned scholar in New England. He wrote the charter founding Rhode Island College (1764) (later Brown University) and taught ecclesiastical history during his tenure as a secularizing president of Yale (1778–95).

Still, Clyfford (1904–80) painter; born in Grandin, N.D. He was raised in Canada and Spokane, Wash., studied at Washington State University (1935), taught there until 1941, moved to San Francisco, and began teaching at the California School of Fine Arts in 1946. In New York he was one of the founders of the Subjects of the Artist teaching group (1948–49), settled in Maryland (1966), and continued to teach. He painted abstract organic canvases in the 1940s, and by the 1950s, he achieved recognition as an abstract expressionist, as in *Painting* (1951).

Still, William Grant (1895–1978) composer; born in Woodville, Miss. Called "the dean of Afro-American composers," he worked with W. C. Handy and graduated from Oberlin College. His music, while classical in technique, grew out of black life; his works include the *Afro-American Symphony* (1931).

Stillé, Alfred (1813–1900) physician; born in Philadelphia. After completing his medical studies in Europe, he practiced in Philadelphia and taught at the Pennsylvania Medical College (1854–59) and the University of Pennsylvania (1864–83). A founder of the American Medical Association (1847), he was also a prolific writer. His *Elements of General Pathology* (1848) was the first American text on pathology, and his *Epidemic Meningitis or Cerebro-Spinal Meningitis* (1867) was a pioneering work on this subject.

Stilwell, Joseph (Warren) (1883–1946) soldier; born in Palatka, Fla. A 1904 West Point graduate, he served as an intelligence officer in France from 1917 to 1918, and during three tours in China in the 1920s and 1930s, he became an expert on the Chinese and proficient in the language. During his term at the Infantry School, Fort Benning, Ga. (1929–33), he also acquired his nickname, "Vinegar Joe," because of his often caustic manner, the same that poisoned so many of his dealings with others throughout his controversial career. Named commander of American forces in the China-Burma-India Theater in February 1942, he succeeded in overseeing the construction of a road (later named after him) to link China with India. His other mission – to improve the fighting efficiency of the Chinese Army – led him to clash repeatedly with Chiang Kai-shek, whom he considered more interested in amassing power and fighting Communists than in defeating the Japanese. Stilwell also fell out with the

British military but it was Chiang's displeasure that finally led to his recall in October 1944. He was assigned to serve the Army's ground forces under Gen. MacArthur and he succeeded Gen. Buckner to command the Tenth Army's final victory on Okinawa. He finished out his career in command of the Sixth Army in California but his proudest moment was to be awarded the Combat Infantrymen Badge.

Stilwell, (Simpson Everett) "Jack" (1848–1903) scout, peace officer; born in Tennessee. He moved to New Mexico and was an army scout (1867–81). He served under Col. Custer and other leaders in exceptionally dangerous ventures. He was a U.S. deputy marshal and a police judge in Oklahoma.

Stimson, Henry (Lewis) (1867–1950) lawyer, public official; born in New York City. A graduate of Yale and Harvard, he joined Elihu Root's law firm (1893) and was appointed U.S. district attorney for the Southern District of New York by President Theodore Roosevelt in 1906. After failing as Republican candidate for governor, he served as secretary of war in the Taft administration (1911–13), delegate-at-large to the New York constitutional convention, and governor general of the Philippines (1927–29). As secretary of state under President Hoover (1929–33) he drew fire for his "Stimson Doctrine" of nonrecognition of Japanese rule in Manchuria (1931). Despite his Republican affiliation, he was chosen by President Franklin Roosevelt as secretary of war (1940–45) and he supervised mobilization, training, and general war operations with energy and skill. As chief presidential adviser on atomic policy, he advised President Truman to drop the atomic bomb on Japanese cities of strategic importance (1945).

Stine, Charles (Milton Altland) (1882–1954) chemical engineer; born in Norwich, Conn. He worked for DuPont from 1907 until his retirement in 1945. He conducted research into dye stuffs, explosives, propellants, paints, varnishes, stains, and various organic chemicals. He developed processes for manufacture of nitric acid and enamels.

Stix, Thomas H. (Howard) (1924–   ) physicist; born in St. Louis, Mo. A plasma physicist at Princeton (1953), he made advances in controlled fusion, waves and instabilities, and plasma heating and confinement.

St. John, Adela Rogers (1894–1988) journalist; born in Los Angeles. Daughter of criminal lawyer Earl Rogers – the subject of her 1962 best-seller, *Final Verdict* – she reported for the Hearst syndicate on such stories as the Leopold-Loeb murder trial and wrote fiction and confessional-style celebrity interviews.

Stock, Frederick August (1872–1942) conductor; born in Jülich, Germany. Trained in Germany, he came to the U.S.A. and in 1895, a protégé of Theodore Thomas, joined the Chicago Symphony as a viola player. He succeeded Thomas as conductor in 1905 and served until his death, making the orchestra a major cultural force for the whole Midwest through its educational programs and varied repertoire.

Stockbridge, Levi (1820–1904) agriculturalist; born in Hadley, Mass. His early interest in improving agriculture was fostered on his family's farm. He was active in local and state civic affairs serving three terms in the state legislature (1855, 1870, 1883), 12 years on the State Board of Agriculture, and 22 years as state cattle commissioner (1869–91). In 1867 he joined the newly opened Massachusetts Agricultural College (now the University of Massachusetts) to teach and supervise

the farm. From 1880 to 1882 he presided over the College, after which he retired. His experiments in fertilizers led to the development of Stockbridge Formulas, and his investigations into plant leaching and the value of soil mulch were published in "Experiments in Feeding Plants" (1876).

Stockton, Frank (Francis Richard) (Paul Fort, John Lewees, pen names) (1834–1902) writer, editor; born in Philadelphia, Pa. He was a wood engraver, then became the assistant editor of *St. Nicholas Magazine* in New York (1873–81). He wrote for adults, notably his short story, "The Lady or the Tiger?" (1882), and books for children, such as *The Bee-Man of Orn, and other Fanciful Tales* (1887). Later he lived in New Jersey (1890), and settled in Charles Town, W. Va. (1899).

Stockton, John Potter (1826–1900) U.S. senator; born in Princeton, N.J. After serving as U.S. ambassador to Italy, he was elected to the U.S. Senate (Dem., N.J.; 1865–66), but his right to take the seat was challenged. Forced to forfeit his seat, he was later reelected (1869–75). He then returned to New Jersey where he served as attorney general (1877–97).

Stockton, Richard (1730–81) Revolutionary patriot; born in Princeton, N.J. He graduated from Princeton College (1748) and practiced law in New Jersey (1754–66). He was on the executive council for the province of New Jersey (1768–76). He served in the Continental Congress (1776) and signed the Declaration of Independence. Taken prisoner by Tories in late 1776, he was released after an imprisonment in New York, but the experience had broken his health. New Jersey placed his statue in the U.S. Capitol.

Stockton, Robert (Field) (1795–1866) naval officer; born in Princeton, N.J. Joining the navy in 1811, he fought in the War of 1812 and against the Barbary pirates. Leaving the navy in 1828, he spent the next ten years in New Jersey, where he prospered from canal construction and railroad investments; he had also been active in trying to get freed slaves to return to Africa and helped to find the territory that later became Liberia. Rejoining the navy in 1838, he supported John Ericsson by commissioning and commanding the navy's first screw-propeller driven ship, the USS *Princeton*. Sent to reinforce the U.S. forces in California when war with Mexico seemed imminent, he arrived in Monterey in July 1846; he relieved Commodore John Sloat, put himself in command of all naval and land forces, and by mid-August was declaring California a territory of the U.S.A. After losing out in a dispute with General Stephen Kearny over who exercised authority in California, Stockton returned to the East and resigned from the navy in 1850. After brief service as a senator (Dem., N.J.; 1851–53) he spent his last years as president of a canal company. Stockton, Calif., was named after him in 1850.

Stoddard, Solomon (1643–1729) Protestant theologian; born in Boston, Mass. He graduated from Harvard in 1662 and became the first librarian there, serving from 1667 to 1674. From 1672 until his death he was pastor of the Congregational church at Northampton, Mass. (where his grandson Jonathan Edwards succeeded him). He helped develop the controversial Half-way Covenant, which permitted church membership to those who, without a full conversion experience, nevertheless showed qualities of godliness. His theological writings, including *The Doctrine of Instituted Churches* (1700), were important documents in the development of American Protestantism.

Stoddert, Benjamin (1751–1813) public official; born in Charles County, Md. He was a Revolutionary militia captain and secretary to the Board of War of the Continental Congress (1779–81). As the first secretary of the navy (1798–1801) he added 50 vessels to the navy, pushed for the construction of docks and naval yards, and promoted the construction of a naval hospital at Newport, R.I. His business affairs suffered after 1801 and he died deeply in debt.

Stoeckel, Carl (1858–1925) music patron; born in New Haven, Conn. Son of a music professor at Yale, in 1895 he married Ellen Battell Terry, an heiress from Norfolk, Conn. Together they made their home a center of music and the arts and they provided funds for various local cultural institutions, particularly glee clubs and choral groups. In 1899 they sponsored the first of a series of annual concerts that in 1906 moved to the "music shed" on their Norfolk estate. Attracting major performers and conductors – including Jan Sibelius in 1914 – and commissioning new works, this series has continued ever since as a summer music festival.

Stokes, Carl (Burton) (1927–) mayor, judge; born in Cleveland, Ohio. He served as assistant city prosecutor (1958–62), state representative (1963–68), and as mayor of Cleveland (1968–72), the first African-American mayor of a major U.S. city. He worked as a television anchor (1972–80) and he became a judge in the Cleveland Municipal Court (1983).

Stokes, Louis (1925–) U.S. representative; born in Cleveland, Ohio. An army veteran and lawyer from Cleveland, he served in the U.S. House of Representatives (Dem., 1963), becoming chairman of the Select Committee on Intelligence in 1989.

Stokes, Thomas Lunsford, Jr. (1898–1958) journalist; born in Atlanta, Ga. A popular Washington reporter and columnist, he won a 1938 Pulitzer Prize for influential articles exposing corruption in the New Deal Works Progress Administration.

Stokowski, Leopold (b. Antoni Stanislaw Boleslawowicz) (1882–1977) conductor; born in London, England. After musical studies in London, Paris, and Germany, Stokowski came to the U.S.A. in 1905 and four years later was named conductor of the Cincinnati Symphony. He left that post in 1912 for a long and celebrated tenure as conductor of the Philadelphia Orchestra, in which he cultivated a popular but later dated creaminess of sound. Stokowski became the great matinee idol of conductors – that despite his bold championing of advanced composers including Varèse, Berg, and Schoenberg – and was for awhile linked with Greta Garbo. Resigning from Philadelphia in 1938, he went on to conduct for shorter periods orchestras including the NBC Symphony, Hollywood Bowl Symphony, New York Philharmonic, Houston Symphony (1955–62), and American Symphony (1962–73), the latter of which he founded. His popularity is reflected in the fact that he appeared in several movies, notably *One Hundred Men and a Girl* (1937) and *Fantasia* (1940).

Stoller, Mike See under LEIBER, JERRY.

Stolzman, Richard (1942–) clarinetist; born in Omaha, Nebr. Raised in San Francisco from age four, he had a father who played alto saxophone on weekends with a dance band; Richard started clarinet lessons in school at age eight. Turned down by Eastman School of Music and Juilliard conservatory, he went to Ohio State and played in the football band and with Dixieland jazz groups. Going to Yale on a scholarship to take a master's degree in music (1967), he was converted to the classical repertoire, although he retained his love and feel for jazz. In 1970 he went to teach at the California Institute of the Arts (Valencia, Calif.), but at the summer Marlboro Festivals (Vt.) he joined with Peter Serkin and two string players to form the Tashi Quartet and soon came to be known for his virtuoso playing. In 1981 he won a Grammy for the best chamber music performance and that same year he presented a solo clarinet recital at Carnegie Hall, the first in its history. Although some fellow clarinetists questioned his use of vibrato and dynamic changes (which gave a more emotional tone than is traditional in classical music), and certain other liberties he took in his interpretations, he is acknowledged to be a master of the instrument; without ever having held a chair in any major orchestra, he became a full-time solo clarinetist, performing a constant round of recitals and with symphonic orchestras and chamber music groups.

Stommel, Henry M. (Melson) (1920–) oceanographer; born in Wilmington, Del. He was a physical oceanographer at the Woods Hole Oceanographic Institution (1944–59) before joining the Massachusetts Institute of Technology (MIT) (1959–60). He left MIT to teach at Harvard (1960–63), returned to MIT (1963–78), then moved back to Woods Hole as senior scientist (1979). He was considered the leading authority on Gulf Stream dynamics. Using physical models, he developed the first theory of this Atlantic current, which he later expanded into his definitive book, *The Gulf Stream* (1955). From 1954–76, Stommel established numerous long-term international projects to gather data on the world's ocean currents and geochemistry of the sea. Working with various colleagues, he made major contributions to studies of cumulus clouds, oceanic salinity and thermal gradients, and plankton distribution. In recognition of his profound influence on geophysical hydrodynamics and climatology, he shared Sweden's prestigious Crafoord Prize in 1983.

Stone, Barton Warren (1772–1844) Protestant religious leader; born in Port Tobacco, Md. He studied law, then underwent a religious conversion and became an evangelist. He held several Presbyterian pastorates before breaking with that denomination to establish several independent churches in Kentucky and Ohio. His "Christian" churches eventually merged with the Disciples of Christ. In 1826 he founded the periodical *Christian Messenger,* and varied his editorial duties with evangelical activities in Illinois and Missouri.

Stone, Charles A. (Augustus) (1867–1941) electrical engineer; born in Newton, Mass., **and Webster, Edwin S. (Sibley)** (1867–1950) electrical engineer; born in Roxbury, Mass. They met at the Massachusetts Institute of Technology; both studied electrical engineering, becoming such close friends that they were always known as "Stone and Webster." Discouraged from going into business together by a Massachusetts Institute of Technology professor, Stone worked for a welding and then a manufacturing company, and Webster worked for Kidder, Peabody & Company. Then in 1889, with a loan from their parents, they opened the Massachusetts Electrical Engineering Company, a consulting firm. The first project was a hydroelectric plant to supply a Maine paper mill (1890). They managed public utilities from

1895; established a securities department in 1902 to finance utility companies; and continued engineering and construction. By 1912 they occupied an 8-story building with about 600 consultants and employees, yet they kept their desks side-by-side, and signed their correspondence "Stone & Webster." Among their notable achievements was the Los Angeles Big Creek transmission system (1913). In 1920 they incorporated as Stone & Webster, Inc., and in subsequent years they established subsidiary firms to manage various aspects of their operations – the sale of securities, the engineering and construction projects, the management of public utilities. By the 1930s Stone & Webster had completed more than $1 billion in construction, significantly advancing the electrification of America. Among their personal interests, Webster was a horticulturalist, and Stone raised horses.

Stone, Edward Durell (1902–78) architect; born in Fayetteville, Ark. After studying at the University of Arkansas, Harvard, and the Massachusetts Institute of Technology, he began teaching at New York University (1927–42) before setting up his practice in New York City (1935–78). Later he also taught at Yale (1946–52). More eclectic than innovative, he moved from a modernist style to a more ornamented style, often using grillwork and deliberately echoing the local/cultural environment. His many public buildings include the U.S. Embassy in New Delhi, India, and the John F. Kennedy Center for the Performing Arts in Washington, D.C.

Stone, Harlan Fiske (1872–1946) Supreme Court justice and chief justice; born in Chesterfield, N.H. He taught (1898–1924) and was dean (1910–24) of Columbia Law School. He briefly served as U.S. attorney general (1924) before President Calvin Coolidge named him associate justice to the U.S. Supreme Court (1924–41). President Franklin Roosevelt promoted him to chief justice (1941–46). His views were generally liberal.

Stone, I. F. (Isidor Feinstein) (1907–89) journalist, publisher; born in Philadelphia. After serving on the *New York Post* and *The Nation* (1933–46), he founded the radical journal, *I. F. Stone's Weekly* (later, *Biweekly*), which he edited until 1971; there and elsewhere he was an early voice of what became the New Left and an early opponent of U.S. policy in Vietnam. A true "gadfly" journalist, he often printed government statements in juxtaposition with contradictory quotes from the same official source.

Stone, Irving (b. Tannenbaum) (1903–89) writer; born in San Francisco. He changed his surname legally, and was educated at the University of California: Berkeley (B.A. 1923) and the University of Southern California (M.A. 1924). He taught economics at the college level (1923–26), lectured and taught at several other institutions (1948–85), and lived in Los Angeles. Early in his career he wrote plays and detective stories, but after a stay in France, he became a highly successful writer of biographical novels. He is noted for *Lust for Life* (1934), based on the life of Vincent Van Gogh, and a biography of Michelangelo, *The Agony and the Ecstasy* (1961).

Stone, John Augustus (1800–34) actor, playwright; born in Concord, Mass. He is best known for his play *Metamora; or, The Last of the Wampanoaqs* (1829), which won actor Edwin Forrest's contest for a play whose hero was "aboriginal of this country."

Stone, Lucy (1818–93) abolitionist, women's rights activist; born in West Brookfield, Mass. The eighth of nine children of a farmer and tanner who believed that women had few rights, she early determined to get an education; she finally was able at age 25 to enter Oberlin College (Ohio); when she graduated in 1847 she was the first Massachusetts woman to have earned a college degree. Within months she was appointed a lecturer for the American Anti-Slavery Society, but she was soon concentrating on women's rights. In 1850 she was a leader in calling a women's rights convention at Worcester, Mass.; her speech there both won over Susan B. Anthony to the cause and inspired John Stuart Mill to write "The Enfranchisement of Woman." She traveled widely throughout North America to lecture on women's rights. In 1855 she married Henry Blackwell (brother of the pioneer doctors, Elizabeth and Emily Blackwell, and brother-in-law of Antoinette Brown Blackwell, the first woman ordained a minister in the U.S.A.), but she kept her own name and he joined her in protesting against contemporary marriage laws. Although she retired for a few years after the birth of her daughter (1857), she emerged after the Civil War as a leader in the women's rights movement. A schism developed between her and the two more radical feminist leaders, Susan B. Anthony and Elizabeth Cady Stanton, and she ended up founding the American Woman Suffrage Association (AWSA) (1869). She then founded the *Woman's Journal* (1870), and she and her husband effectively financed as well as edited it from 1872 on. In 1890 she led the AWSA to unite with the Stanton-Anthony group to form the National American Woman Suffrage Association; she served as chairperson of its executive committee until her death. In keeping with her independent spirit, she was the first person in New England to be cremated.

Stone, Melville Elijah (1848–1929) journalist; born in Hudson, Ill. In 1875 he founded the *Chicago Daily News* as a one-penny, mass-circulation paper. After selling it in 1888 and serving as a bank president, he became general manager of the Associated Press (AP) (1893–1921) and expanded AP news gathering operations worldwide.

Stone, Oliver (1946–) movie director, screenwriter; born in New York City. Dropping out of Yale in 1965, he taught English and history in Saigon, Vietnam, as a civilian; he returned to Vietnam with the U.S. Army (1967–68) and was wounded in combat. He studied at the film school of New York University and went on to write screenplays; he won a 1978 Oscar for *Midnight Express* but subsequent screenplays were for mostly forgettable action films. He then wrote and directed two highly regarded movies, *Salvador* (1986) and *Platoon* (1987); the latter won him Oscars for best director and best picture. Established as a serious director, he produced and directed a series of commercially successful but often edgy movies, the most controversial being *JFK* (1991), his highly partisan account of the assassination of President Kennedy.

Stone, Robert (Anthony) (1937–) writer; born in New York City. He studied at New York University (1958–60), and Stanford (1962–64). He worked for the *New York Daily News* as a copyboy and caption writer (1958–60), and held a variety of other jobs until he became a free-lance writer in England, California, and South Vietnam (1967–71). He taught at Princeton, Amherst, and Stanford, among other institutions. He is noted for his pessimistic but carefully crafted novels, such as *Dog Soldiers* (1974). He lived in California.

Storer, Francis Humphreys (1832–1914) chemist; born in Boston, Mass. (son of David Humphreys Storer). After leaving Harvard, he served as a chemist with the U.S. North Pacific expedition (1853–54); he then worked with the Boston Gas Light Company (1858–71) and was affiliated with the Massachusetts Institute of Technology (1865–71); his brother-in-law, Charles William Eliot, president of Harvard, appointed him to Harvard's Bussey Institution, an agricultural school (1869–1907). Storer did important research on soils, fertilizers, forage crops, and a variety of agricultural and horticultural products.

Storer, Maria Longworth Nichols (1849–1932) ceramicist, arts patron; born in Cincinnati, Ohio. Born into the wealthy Longworth family, she married at age 19 George Ward Nichols and together they promoted the musical institutions of Cincinnati. Impressed by the Japanese pottery she saw at the Philadelphia Centennial Exposition (1876), she began to experiment with making pottery. In 1880 she established Rockwood Pottery (in Cincinnati), which became famous for its vases and jugs with a rich glaze that she had developed. Her Rockwood ware won a gold medal at the 1889 Paris Exposition. She withdrew from the business in 1890 and embarked on a new life with her second husband (her first having died in 1885), Bellamy Storer (a lawyer who went on to serve in the U.S. House of Representatives, Rep., Ohio; 1891–95). Through their friendship with Presidents William McKinley and Theodore Roosevelt, he was appointed ambassador to Austro-Hungary in 1902. Meanwhile, having been converted to Catholicism by Cincinnati's Archbishop John Ireland, the Storers tried to pressure the Vatican to appoint him a Cardinal, but their machinations led them to break with Roosevelt, who then dismissed Storer (1906). Maria then refused to attend the wedding of her nephew Nicholas Longworth to Roosevelt's daughter Alice Roosevelt. She lived out her final years in Paris, Boston, and Cincinnati, writing on various subjects and taking part in charitable activities.

Stormer, Horst L. (Ludwig) (1949–) physicist; born in Frankfurt-am-Main, Germany. He was educated in Germany and came to the U.S.A. to work at American Telephone & Telegraph Bell Laboratories (1977). A solid-state physicist, Stormer pursued investigations of magnetic and transport properties of electrons in liquids and solids.

Storrs, John (Henry Bradley) (1885–1956) sculptor; born in Chicago. He traveled extensively, studied in Berlin and Paris (1907–10, 1914–16), and in the United States in Chicago, Pennsylvania, and Boston. After becoming an expatriate in Paris, he was interred in a Nazi concentration camp during World War II. He is known for his innovative cubist sculptures, such as *Composition Around Two Voids* (1932).

Story, Joseph (1779–1845) Supreme Court justice; born in Marblehead, Mass. He was serving on the Massachusetts legislature (1805–07, 1811–12) when President Madison named him to the U.S. Supreme Court (1812–45). Along with chief justice John Marshall, he promoted nationalism and a strong central government.

Story, William Wetmore (1819–95) sculptor, poet, lawyer; born in Salem, Mass. (son of Justice Joseph Story). He studied at Harvard, practiced law, and studied sculpture in Italy (1847) before settling there permanently (1856). He

wrote poetry and became close friends of Robert and Elizabeth Browning and Henry James. He is known for his literary interests and related sculptures, such as *Cleopatra* (1858).

Stouffer, Samuel (Andrew) (1900–60) sociologist; born in Sac City, Iowa. A Harvard M.A. in literature, he earned a University of Chicago Ph.D. (1930) after several years of managing a family newspaper. He taught at the Universities of Wisconsin and Chicago and was the first director of Harvard's Laboratory of Social Relations (1946–60). A specialist in public opinion research who promoted quantitative research methods – he introduced the use of "sample surveys" – he became the leading sociologist of his generation. He directed or made major contributions to the Social Science Research Council's research on social aspects of the Depression (1930s), a Carnegie Commission study of African-Americans (1940), and a Ford Foundation study of public attitudes toward communism (1955). Under his leadership, the War Department's wartime research on soldiers (1941–46) yielded the classic *Studies in Social Psychology in World War II* (4 vols. 1949–50); this work led to the key theories of "relative deprivation" and "reference groups." Although insisting on quantified data, he believed in applying the knowledge to solving social problems.

Stouffer, Vernon B. (Bigelow) (1901–74) business executive; born in Cleveland, Ohio. He graduated from the Wharton School of Business, University of Pennsylvania, soon afterwards opening his first restaurant in Cleveland; from this he built the multimillion-dollar Stouffer Corporation, a national chain of restaurants, inns, and food processors and distributors.

Stout, Rex (Todhunter) (1886–1975) writer; born in Noblesville, Ind. His family moved to Topeka, Kans., when he was young, and he was schooled locally. He joined the navy (1906–08), then held a variety of jobs in different locations. He lived in Paris (1927–29), and upon his return, began a long and successful writing career. His first mystery novel, *Fer-de-Lance* (1934), introduced Nero Wolfe, a fat, brilliant, orchid-loving detective, and Archie Goodwin, his assistant and man-about-town. Stout lived in Brewster, N.Y., served on many patriotic committees and boards, and was a radio broadcaster during World War II. He was also a founder and director of Vanguard Press.

Stowe, Harriet (Elizabeth) Beecher (1811–96) writer; born in Litchfield, Conn. (daughter of Lyman Beecher). Raised by her severe Calvinist father, she was educated and taught at the Hartford Female Seminary (founded by her sister Catherine Beecher). Moving to Cincinnati with her father in 1832, she began to write sketches and short fiction; she married in 1836 but persevered in her writing while raising seven children. In 1850 her husband took up a post as professor of religion at Bowdoin College, Maine, and there she began work on *Uncle Tom's Cabin*. It appeared in weekly installments in the *National Era* (1851–52) and was published as a two-volume novel in 1852; it became an instant and controversial best-seller, both in the U.S.A. and abroad. She made three trips to Europe during the 1850s where she was befriended by major literary figures. The novel had a major impact on Northerners' attitudes toward slavery and by the beginning of the Civil War had sold more than a million copies. She followed this spectacular success with numerous works of fiction, biography, children's books, travelogues, theological works, temperance tracts, and practical works on housekeeping (including coauthoring with sister Catherine, *The American Woman's Home,* 1869), but nothing she wrote ever approached the success of her first novel.

Strand, Mark (1934–) poet, writer; born in Summerside, Prince Edward Island, Canada. His family moved to the United States (1938), and he attended Antioch (B.A. 1957), Yale (B.F.A. 1959), and the University of Iowa (M.A. 1962). He taught at many institutions, notably the University of Utah (1981), received a MacArthur Foundation Grant (1987), and was named poet laureate by the Library of Congress (1990). He wrote fiction, criticism, and children's books, and worked as a translator and editor. He is best known, however, for his lyric poetry, as in *Selected Poems* (1980).

Strand, Paul (1890–1976) photographer; born in New York City. Originally a portrait photographer (1912–22) whose work was exhibited by Stieglitz, he began photographing machines, rocks, and plants to capture their abstract shapes and forms. In 1921 he filmed *Manhatta,* an abstract tribute to Manhattan. President of Frontier films (1937–42), he made leftist documentaries including *The Plow that Broke the Plains* (1936). He moved to Orgeval, France, in 1951 to escape McCarthyism.

Strasberg, Lee (b. Israel Strassberg) (1901–82) theater director; born in Budzanov, Austria-Hungary (now Budanov, Ukraine). Brought to America as a child, he had a brief acting career, then was one of the founders of the Group Theatre in 1931, directing a number of plays there. But his greatest influence was through the Actors Studio where he became director in 1950. A proponent of "method" acting, he influenced several generations of actors, from Marlon Brando to Dustin Hoffman.

Stratemeyer, Edward L. (Arthur M. Winfield, Horatio Alger Jr., Captain Ralph Bonehill, Nick Carter, and many other pen names) (1862–1930) writer, book syndicate operator; born in Elizabeth, N.J. After graduating from high school and working in his father's tobacco shop, he began writing juvenile fiction, selling his first story in 1888. During the next decade he contributed to and edited various magazines while commencing (1894) his prolific output of series books, combining Horatio Alger sentiments with formulaic adventure plots. In 1906 he founded the Stratemeyer Literary Syndicate in New York (later moving to New Jersey); he supplied the characters, plots, and authors' pen names to a team of writers who over the years wrote more than 800 books under some 60 pseudonyms, including the *Tom Swift* series (by Victor Appleton), the *Bobbsey Twins* series (by Laura Lee Hope) and the *Hardy Boys* series (by Franklin W. Dixon). Stratemeyer himself probably wrote a total of another 220 books. After his death the syndicate was directed by his daughter, Harriet S. Adams, who herself had created the *Nancy Drew* series (under the name of Carolyn Keene).

Stratemeyer, George Edward (1890–1969) aviator; born in Cincinnati, Ohio. The son of an army officer, he graduated from West Point in 1915 and earned his wings two years later. During the interwar period he held staff and operational posts, and in 1943 he became commander of air forces in the India-Burma theater. He later directed air operations in China. He commanded air forces in Korea in 1950 and 1951

before health problems forced him from the service. After retirement he became a supporter of Red-baiting U.S. Senator Joseph McCarthy.

Stratton, (Charles Sherwood) "General Tom Thumb" (1838–83) celebrity; born in Bridgeport, Conn. His parents were of normal height, but he grew to only 40 inches and weighed only 70 pounds. He joined P. T. Barnum's museum at the age of four; at age six, Barnum took him to Europe where he entertained royalty and caused a sensation. He toured the U.S.A. (1847–52) and then went into semiretirement. He married Lavinia Warren, another dwarf, in 1863; they had one daughter who died young. On his death it was found that he had squandered the fortune he had made.

Stratton, Samuel (Wesley) (1861–1931) educator; born in Litchfield, Ill. He studied mechanical engineering at the University of Illinois, and by 1891 was teaching physics. In 1892 he went to the newly opened University of Chicago, taught physics, researched its application to engineering, and planned and supervised the construction of Ryerson laboratories. In 1900 the secretary of the treasury asked him to write a proposal for a Bureau of Standards. His proposed legislation was adopted in 1901. The Bureau was located within the Department of Commerce with Stratton as its first director. In 1923 he became president of the Massachusetts Institute of Technology, becoming chairman of the corporation in 1930. He died suddenly on the same day as his friend Thomas Alva Edison, while dictating Edison's eulogy.

Straus, Isidor (1845–1912) merchant; born in Otterberg, Germany (brother of Nathan and Oscar S. Straus). His mother, Sara, brought the family to join her husband, Lazarus, in Georgia in 1854. Isidor clerked in his father's Atlanta store, and then traveled to Europe (1863) on commission to purchase supplies for the Confederacy. Stranded in Liverpool, England, with southern ports blockaded, he sold cotton shares and Confederate bonds and returned to New York (1865). There, he and his father formed L. Straus & Sons, a crockery and glassware firm that in 1874 bought into R. H. Macy and Company. In 1888 Isidor and brother Nathan became partners of Macy's and in 1896 its sole owners. They also developed Abraham & Straus, another department store. Active in civic affairs, Isidor was an influential friend of President Grover Cleveland on whom he prevailed to pursuade Congress to adopt a gold standard. He served in the U.S. House of Representatives (Dem., N.Y.; 1894–95) but declined renomination. His philanthropies included the Montefiore Home and the American Jewish Committee, and he was president of the Educational Alliance (1893–1912), a settlement house on New York City's Lower East Side. He and his wife, Ida Blun, were aboard the S. S. *Titanic;* both drowned when Ida refused to be separated from her husband of 40 years, and he refused a seat on a life boat while women remained aboard the ship.

Straus, Nathan (1848–1931) merchant, philanthropist; born in Otterberg, Germany (brother of Isidor and Oscar S. Straus). His mother, Sara, brought the family to join her husband, Lazarus, in Georgia in 1854. They moved to New York after the Civil War and in 1866 Nathan joined L. Straus & Sons, the family's crockery and glassware firm. In 1888 he and his brother Isidor became partners of R. H. Macy and Company, becoming its sole owners in 1896. Nathan established employee amenities such as restrooms, medical care, and a lunchroom. He and Isidor also helped develop

Abraham & Straus, another department store. He was New York City park commissioner (1889–93) and president of the board of health (1898). By 1914 he had retired from involvement with Macy's. An active philanthropist, he helped the poor acquire food, coal, and shelter through the winters of 1892–93, 1893–94. In 1892 he began a campaign for the pasteurization of milk, opening almost 300 milk depots around the country and abroad. He was President Taft's delegate to the Third International Congress for the Protection of Infants (1911, Berlin). In 1925 the League of Nations recognized him as a layman pioneer in public health. His other passion was the welfare of the Jewish people in Palestine, to which he gave nearly two-thirds of his fortune; he built schools, public kitchens, and clinics. In 1927 the cornerstone to his last health center in Jerusalem proclaims it for all the people of the land, "Christian, Moslem, and Jew." Widely honored, President Taft called him "a great Jew and the greatest Christian of us all."

Straus, Oscar Solomon (1850–1926) diplomat, author; born in Otterberg, Germany (brother of Isidor and Nathan Straus). His mother Sara brought the family to join her husband Lazarus in Georgia in 1854. After they moved to New York City in 1866, Oscar studied and practiced law until he joined the family's crockery and glassware firm, L. Straus & Sons, in 1881. In 1887, at the suggestion of Henry Ward Beecher, President Grover Cleveland appointed him ambassador to Turkey (1887–89), a post he returned to twice (1898–1900, 1909–10). He was appointed a member of the Permanent Court of Arbitration at the Hague in 1902, and was reappointed in 1908, 1912, and 1920. President Theodore Roosevelt appointed him secretary of commerce and labor (1906–09). He headed the Progressive ticket as the unsuccessful candidate for governor of New York (1912). He spoke out consistently for the safety of Russian and European Jews, backed the Zionist movement, and supported President Wilson in his efforts for the League of Nations at Versailles. He gave generously to Jewish charitable and cultural causes. He wrote many books including *Roger Williams, The Pioneer of Religious Liberty* (1894) and his own memoirs, *Under Four Administrations: From Cleveland to Taft* (1922).

Straus, William L. (Louis), Jr. (1900–81) physical anthropologist; born in Baltimore, Md. He taught at Johns Hopkins (1927–66), where he made detailed anatomical and neuromuscular studies of apes and monkeys. He investigated the evolution of erect bipedal posture.

Strauss, Leo (1899–1973) political scientist; born in Kirchhain (Hesse), Germany. Educated in Germany, he emigrated to the U.S.A. in 1938. He taught at the New School for Social Research until 1949, then at the University of Chicago (1949–67). Known for his fierce allegiance to the study of classical political philosophy, he shunned the new behavioral and quantitative approaches to political science.

Strauss, Levi (?1830–1902) clothing manufacturer; born in Bavaria, Germany. He came to New York City in 1847 and worked as a peddlar before moving to San Francisco in 1850 when gold was discovered in California. He began to sell cloth and soon opened a dry goods store with supplies shipped in by his brothers in New York. When miners wanted a sturdy pair of pants, he tried making them out of tent canvas; he then shifted to a cotton imported from France, *serge de Nimes*, which was known in America as "denim." Dyed indigo blue and with copper rivets at the stress points, these pants soon became known as "Levi's" and were soon adopted as the work pants for many in the West; from there they spread throughout the U.S.A. and eventually throughout the world. A bachelor, Strauss turned the business over to two nephews; one passed it on to his son-in-law Walter Haas Sr., in whose family it largely remained throughout the 20th century.

Strauss, Lewis (Lichtenstein) (1896–) banker, cabinet member; born in Charleston, W.Va. After working on Belgian relief with Herbert Hoover (1917–19), he joined New York investment bankers Kuhn, Loeb & Co. (1929–45). A reservist, he was appointed naval rear admiral for distinguished service in 1945. He became an Atomic Energy Commission member (1946–50), later chairman (1953–58), championing the hydrogen bomb and denying Robert Oppenheimer security clearance. Briefly secretary of commerce (1958–59), he wrote *Men and Decisions* (1962).

Strauss, Robert (Schwartz) (1918–) lawyer, government official; born in Lockhart, Texas. After working for the Federal Bureau of Investigation (1941–45), he formed a profitable Dallas law firm. He served as Democratic Party chairman (1972–77), then was President Carter's Middle Eastern envoy in 1979 and campaign manager in 1980. Respected by Republicans, he served as ambassador to Russia (1991–92) to facilitate economic growth and encourage American investments.

Stravinsky, Igor (Fyodorovich) (1882–1971) composer, conductor; born in Oranienbaum, near St. Petersburg, Russia. Son of an admired bass in the Imperial Opera, he studied piano and composition as a boy. Although he studied law at St. Petersburg University, he was far more interested in music; between 1903–06 he studied composition under Rimsky-Korsokov and became a member of that composer's circle. In 1909 the Russian ballet impresario Sergei Diaghilev invited him to compose for his company, the Ballets Russes; in 1910 the company danced Stravinsky's first major work, *The Firebird,* and for the next 20 years he was closely associated with Diaghilev's company; their premiere of Stravinsky's *Le Sacre du Printemps* ("the rite of spring") in 1913 caused a tremendous commotion. After 1910 Stravinsky essentially settled in Western Europe – first Switzerland, then Paris – where he toured as a conductor and pianist in performances of his own music; after the Russian Revolution in 1917, he regarded himself as an exile. In 1926 he rejoined the Russian Orthodox Church and his devout Christianity inspired many of his subsequent works. After three tours in the U.S.A. and several American commissions, he moved there in 1939, settled in Los Angeles, and became a naturalized citizen in 1945. Although he continued to be an international neoclassicist in his musical style, he did show some recognition of his American environment, writing his famous *Circus Polka* (1942) for the elephants of the Barnum and Bailey Circus and his *Ebony Concerto* (1945) for Woody Herman; his various efforts at movie music ended up being used in other compositions. The climax of his neoclassical style was his opera, *The Rake's Progress* (1951). The young American conductor, Robert Craft, became Stravinsky's inseparable assistant from 1948 on; Craft not only aided Stravinsky in his various musical projects but helped him assemble several books; Craft also introduced Stravinsky to the serialist school of music and, from the early 1950s, Stravinsky composed in his own adaptation of this style. By this time, he was generally recognized as the leading composer of his era and he toured throughout the world conducting his own and others' works; in 1962 his 80th birthday was widely celebrated and he made a triumphant return to Russia. He settled in New York City in 1969 and died there, but was buried in Venice near Diaghilev's grave.

Strayer, Joseph Reese (1904–87) medievalist, educator; born in Baltimore, Md. Known for his work on the origins of representative government and the beginning of modern administrative systems. he taught longest at Princeton University (1929) where he was named professor emeritus (1973) and chaired the history department (1941–61). President of the Medieval Academy of America (1966–69), a fellow of the American Academy of Arts and Scientists, he was the author of numerous books on the medieval period.

Strayhorn, (William) Billy (1915–67) jazz musician; born in Dayton, Ohio. He was the composer of "Lush Life," "Take the 'A' Train," and many songs and extended works associated with Duke Ellington, for whom he was a staff arranger, lyricist, and key collaborator from 1938 until his death.

Streep, Meryl (1951–) movie actress; born in Basking Ridge, N.J. After majoring in drama at Vassar College and attending Yale's School of Drama, she appeared in several Broadway plays and with the New York Shakespeare Festival. Her film debut in *Julia* (1977) led to a succession of strong roles, many of which gained her Academy Award nominations and Oscars – the latter for best supporting actress in *Kramer vs. Kramer* (1979) and best actress in *Sophie's Choice* (1982). A radiant, serious actress, she became legendary for the perfectionist approach she brought to linguistic and other details of each role.

Street, J. C. (Jabez Curry) (1906–89) physicist; born in Opelika, Ala. He worked as an electrical engineer (1927–28), then joined the Bartol Foundation (1931–32) before beginning his lifelong investigations of cosmic rays at Harvard (1932–76) and, concurrently, at the Massachusetts Institute of Technology (1941–45). Best known for his codiscovery (with E. C. Stevenson) of the muon, a chief component of cosmic rays, he also made major contributions to studies of particle physics, ionization and cloud chambers, radar, and electrical discharges in gases.

Streisand, (Barbara Joan) Barbra (1942–) film actress, singer; born in New York City. She began her career as a nightclub singer and made her Broadway debut in *I Can Get It For You Wholesale* (1962). With her less-than-classic face and throbbing voice, she made her first film, *Funny Girl* (1968), for which she won the Academy Award. She won another Oscar for the music for the song "Evergreen" in the film *A Star Is Born* (1977). Notorious for her demanding ways, she maintained her status as a superstar with her occasional films, recordings, and television specials, later moving on to producing and directing movies.

Strengell, Marianne (1909–) textile designer; born in Helsinki, Finland. In 1937 she came to the U.S.A. to teach weaving and design at Cranbrook Academy (1937–61, 1967–68). As a free-lance designer she developed the Strengell Loom to weave carpets and thin textiles. She collaborated with leading architects, industrial clients, and even automo-

bile design studios who were attracted by her experiments with new materials, textures, and abstract designs.

Strickland, William (1788–1854) architect, engineer; born in Navesink, N.J. He apprenticed with Benjamin Latrobe and also became a skilled artist, engraver, and engineer. He launched the Greek revival in America with a series of Philadelphia public buildings in the 1820s and 1830s, notably the Second Bank of the United States (1818–24); he completed public engineering projects including the Delaware Breakwater (1828–40); and he was designer and supervising architect of the Tennessee State Capitol, Nashville (1845–59).

Strong, Anna Louise (1885–1970) journalist; born in Friend, Nebr. A radical, she lived mostly in China and the Soviet Union, where she started English-language newsletters and wrote books and articles promoting the Communist cause.

Strong, Ann (Louise) (1930–) regional planner, lawyer; born in New Amsterdam, New York. A professor of planning at the University of Pennsylvania where she taught from 1959, she specialized in land use management, finding ways to preserve farmlands and waterways while putting up low-cost housing in nearby Chester County.

Strong, Augustus Hopkins (1836–1921) Protestant theologian, educator; born in Rochester, N.Y. The son of a newspaper publisher, he graduated from Yale (1857) and the Rochester Theological Seminary (1859) and held Baptist pastorates in Massachusetts and Ohio. President of the Rochester Seminary from 1872 to 1912, he produced theological works, including *Systematic Theology* (3 vols. 1886), that sought a middle ground between conservative and liberal doctrine. He helped interest John D. Rockefeller, a former parishioner, in higher education; Rockefeller later founded the University of Chicago.

Strong, George Templeton (1820–75) lawyer, diarist; born in New York City. A precocious child, he read history at age six and had soon mastered Greek, Latin, and many classic works. He was a lawyer, a trustee of Columbia College, and helped to found that institution's law school. He was treasurer of the U.S. Sanitary Commission during the Civil War. Most notably, he kept an extensive, humorous, and insightful diary (October 5, 1835–June 25, 1875), now recognized as a treasure trove of information about the events and personalities of 19th-century America. The diary was not published until 1952.

Strong, Josiah (1847–1916) Protestant religious leader; born in Napierville, Ill. A graduate of Western Reserve College (1869), he was ordained in 1871 and held several pastorates before writing the highly influential *Our Country* (1885), in which he proposed religious solutions for social and economic problems. He developed his Social Gospel themes in the *New Era* (1893). He founded the League for Social Service in 1902, under whose auspices he continued to lecture and write to promote Christian responsibility for curing social ills.

Strong, William (1808–95) Supreme Court justice; born in Somers, Conn. He served in the U.S. House of Representatives (Dem., Pa.; 1847–51) then returned to practice law. He sat on the Pennsylvania Supreme Court (1850–68) before President Grant named him to the U.S. Supreme Court (1870–80).

Strong, William Barstow (1837–1914) railroad official; born in Brownington, Vt. An 1855 graduate of Bell's Business

Strong

College in Chicago, he began working for the Milwaukee & St. Paul Railroad as a station agent. Between 1867 and 1877 he worked for several railroads with increasing responsibility until he became vice-president of the Atchison, Topeka & Santa Fe Railroad, in charge of its expansion program. During his tenure (president 1881–89), he turned the railroad into one of the largest in the country at just under 7,000 miles. At his retirement he took up farming.

Strong, William D. (Duncan) (1899–1962) archaeologist, anthropologist; born in Portland, Ore. After various academic posts he joined the faculty at Columbia University (1937–62). An authority on South American Indians, he led many North and South American expeditions and discovered the tomb of the war god Ai apaec in Peru (1946). He won the 1955 Viking Fund Medal.

Struever, Stuart (McKee) (1931–) archaeologist; born in Peru, Ill. He taught at Northwestern University and the University of California. An authority on the "new" archaeology known for his work on field methods, research design, and the origins of cultivation in prehistoric North America, he directed excavations at the Koster site in Illinois.

Strunsky, Simeon (1879–1948) journalist; born in Vitebsk, Russia. A longtime editorial writer and columnist for the *New York Post* and (1924–48) *New York Times*, he was an ardent liberal, known for his pungent style and light touch.

Stryker, Roy Emerson (1893–1975) government official; born in Grand Junction, Colo. An economist, he was chief of the Farm Security Administration's (FSA) historical section (1935–43), where he developed an outstanding team of photographers to document harsh conditions in rural America. He made sure that FSA photos were widely used in books and periodicals and included in major museum exhibits. He directed a documentary project for Standard Oil of New Jersey from 1943 to 1950.

Stuart, Gilbert (Charles) (1755–1828) painter; born in North Kingston, R.I. Showing an early talent for drawing, he followed the Scottish painter Cosmos Alexander to Edinburgh (1772); returning to Rhode Island (1773), he was unable to advance with his painting so he went to London (1775) where, between 1775 and 1782 he studied with Benjamin West. His *Portrait of a Gentleman Skating* (1782) gained such praise that he was soon busy painting portraits of wealthy British. Extravagant and careless in his spending habits, he fled London (1787) to avoid debtors prison; in Dublin, Ireland, he repeated the pattern – a successful portraitist but also a debtor. He returned to America (1793), settling in Philadelphia where he painted two life portraits of George Washington; the third, the famous unfinished *Athanaeum Head* was painted in nearby Germantown, Pa. (1796). He moved his studio to Washington, D.C. (1803–05), then settled permanently in Boston. Known for his wit and knowledgeable talk but also for his touchiness and taking snuff, his reputation as a portraitist remains as high as ever, especially for his luminous coloring effects.

Stuart, (James Ewell Brown) Jeb (1833–64) soldier; born in Patrick County, Va. An 1854 West Point graduate, he fought against Indians on the frontier and was Robert E. Lee's aide in the assault against John Brown and his men at Harpers Ferry. He began his career as the Confederacy's best-known cavalry commander with a well-timed charge that stopped a federal assault at First Bull Run (1861). In June 1862 he led 1,200 troopers in a famous ride around McClellan's army; as

often turned out to be the case with Stuart, the raid was more spectacular than productive. He led his cavalry in most of the other famous campaigns in northern Virginia, but received much criticism for losing contact with Lee, who called him "the eyes of the army," for a critical week during the Gettysburg campaign (June 1863). A dramatic figure in his gaudy uniforms and famous plumed hat (he was called "Beauty" by fellow officers), he was mortally wounded in a clash with Sheridan's troopers at Yellow Tavern on May 11, 1864.

Stuart, John Leighton (1876–1972) Protestant missionary, educator; born in Hangchow, China. The son of Presbyterian missionaries, he graduated from Hampden-Sydney College, was ordained a Presbyterian minister, and returned to China in 1904. He was a professor at Nanking Theological Seminary from 1908 to 1919; in the latter year he became first president of Yenching University in Peking. Named U.S. ambassador to China in 1946, he returned to the U.S.A. in 1949 after the consolidation of Communist power. His memoir, *Fifty Years in China,* appeared in 1954.

Stuart, Moses (1780–1852) Protestant clergyman, educator; born in Wilton, Conn. A farmer's son, studious as a child, he graduated from Yale in 1799 at the head of his class. He was pastor of a New Haven Congregational church (1806–10), and from 1810 to 1848 he was professor of sacred literature at Andover Theological Seminary, where he learned Hebrew and published the first Hebrew grammar in America. He also publicized German advances in biblical scholarship. He taught more than 1,500 ministers over his long career.

Stuart, Robert (1785–1848) trader; born in Callander, Scotland. He emigrated to Canada (1807) and joined the Pacific Fur Company (1810). He was active in the Astoria colony (1810–12) and headed the American Fur Company in the upper Great Lakes area (1820–34). He settled in Detroit and became superintendent of Indian affairs for Michigan (1841–45).

Studebaker, Clement (Clem) (1831–1901) manufacturer; born near Gettysburg, Pa. He helped his father in his small wagon-building shop until 1852, when he and his older brother Henry Studebaker with just $68 and some blacksmith tools, established H & C Studebaker in South Bend, Ind. They put their name on their extremely well-made wagons and received many contracts. In 1868 the company became the Studebaker Brothers Manufacturing Company with Clem as president. In 1870, with three more brothers in the firm, they opened a branch in St. Joseph, Mo., to outfit pioneers headed west, and became the largest horse-drawn carriage company in the world. By 1897 Clem was experimenting with gasoline-powered automobiles, which his company began to manufacture shortly after his death. Active in the Republican Party, he was appointed a delegate to the 1889 Pan American Congress by President Harrison. He was also an active Methodist both with the Chautauqua Association and as a trustee and benefactor of De Pauw University.

Sturges, Preston (b. Edmund Preston Biden) (1898–1959) film director, screenwriter, playwright; born in Chicago. Educated in America and Europe, he enlisted in the Air Corps in World War I and later worked in the cosmetics industry, inventing a "kiss-proof" lipstick. He turned to writing plays, and his biggest Broadway hit was *Strictly Dishonorable* (1929). In 1933 he was in Hollywood, working as a screenwriter, and in 1940 he persuaded Paramount to let him direct his own screenplay, *The Great McGinty,* which won him the screenwriter's Oscar. Then came a brief run of directorial successes with inventive, freewheeling comedies that combined wit, slapstick, and social concerns, such as *Sullivan's Travels* (1941) and *Hail the Conquering Hero* (1944). After 1944 his career went into a precipitous decline, and he spent his last ten years in Paris.

Sturgis, John Hubbard (1834–88) architect; born in Macao. His Boston partnership (1866–88) with Charles Brigham (1841–1925) was best known for residential designs and interiors; they introduced the English Arts and Crafts tradition to Boston.

Sturgis, Russell (1836–1909) architect, architectural critic; born in Baltimore, Md. He abandoned his architectural practice in 1880 after completing a series of buildings at Yale and became the foremost architectural critic of his day. In periodicals, books, encyclopedia articles and lectures, he championed Louis Sullivan and sparked a national awareness of art and architecture. His monumental four-volume *History of Architecture* (1906–15) was unfinished at his death.

Sturtevant, Alfred H. (Henry) (1891–1970) geneticist; born in Jacksonville, Ill. As a research assistant in Thomas H. Morgan's "fly room" at Columbia University (1915–28), he used the fruit fly *Drosophila* to determine that genes are arranged in linear order. His analysis of these "linkage groups" in reference to two other genes on the same chromosome (1913) became the classical method for chromosome mapping. He moved with Morgan to the California Institute of Technology (1928–62), where he remained an active lecturer and visiting professor after his retirement. Sturtevant's major contributions to genetics include the genetic role in sexual selection and development, and the importance of chromosomal "crossing over" in mutations. His research on lethal genes influenced his later writings on the effects of atomic bomb tests on human evolution. Having grown up on a farm, he also had a lifelong interest in animals, especially in the social insects.

Sturtevant, Benjamin (Franklin) (1833–90) inventor; born in Norridgewock, Maine. Raised on a farm in near poverty, he learned the cobbler's trade and, as a labor-saving device, invented a shoe-pegging machine. He lost the rights to this invention through misadventure, but his rotary exhaust fan, which he developed to clear dust out of shoe factories, made his fortune. By 1878 his manufacturing company was turning out 5,000 fans a year and selling to a worldwide market.

Stuyvesant, Petrus (?–1672) colonial governor; born in Friesland, Netherlands. He became governor of New Netherland in 1647. He worked to save the colony from the disastrous policies of his predecessor, Willem Kieft. He was frustrated by the people of New Amsterdam who won the right of independent municipal government (1653) and by the capture of New Netherland by English forces (1664).

Styne, (b. Julius Kerwin Stein) Jule (1905–94) composer, producer; born in London, England. He immigrated to the United States in 1912 and attended the Chicago College of Music. In the 1920s and 1930s he led his own bands and played piano with Benny Goodman and Glenn Miller. His first Broadway scores were for *High Button Shoes* (1947) and *Gentlemen Prefer Blondes* (1949). He did the music for *Bells are Ringing* (1956) with librettists-lyricists Betty Comden and

Adolph Green, and he wrote *Gypsy* (1959) with lyrics by Stephen Sondheim. He also wrote *Funny Girl* (1964), with lyrics by Bob Merrill. He wrote popular songs for over 80 films, including "Three Coins in a Fountain" (1954), words by Sammy Cahn. He was also the producer of several plays and musicals. In the 1980s he taught songwriting at New York University.

Styron, William (1925–   ) writer; born in Newport News, Va. He attended Duke (B.A., 1947) and studied writing at the New School for Social Research. He was an associate editor for McGraw-Hill Book Company in New York City (1947). He gained critical praise for his first novel, *Lie Down in Darkness* (1951), and went on to write such notable works as *The Confessions of Nat Turner* (1967), and *Sophie's Choice* (1979). He lived in Roxbury, Conn., and summered in Vineyard Haven, Mass.

Sublette, William Lewis (?1799–1845) fur trader, merchant; born in Lincoln County, Ky. He moved to Missouri around 1818 and made a fortune in the fur trade. In partnership with Jedediah Strong Smith and David E. Jackson, he brought the first wagons over the Oregon Trail to the Rocky Mountains (1830).

Sullivan, Anne (b. Joanna Mansfield Sullivan) (1866–1936) teacher of Helen Keller; born in Feeding Hills, Mass. Nearly blind from a childhood fever, she was educated at the Perkins Institution in Waltham, Mass. She returned there in 1887 to teach the newly-admitted seven-year-old Helen Keller and broke through Helen's isolation by spelling out words on her hand (a story made famous by *The Miracle Worker,* 1957). For the rest of her life Sullivan remained Keller's companion while establishing her own reputation as an author, lecturer, and advocate for the deaf.

Sullivan, (Edward Vincent) Ed (1902–74) journalist, television host; born in New York City. Originally a sportswriter, he began his syndicated Broadway gossip column at the *New York Daily News* in 1934. He hosted the CBS variety series, *The Ed Sullivan Show* (1948–71). Much parodied for his stiff manner and his opening line, "We've got a reeeally big shew tonight," he was the first to give national exposure to many entertainers, in particular Elvis Presley and the Beatles.

Sullivan, Harry Stack (1892–1949) psychiatrist; born in Norwich, N.Y. In 1922, he began working at Saint Elizabeth's Hospital in Washington, D.C., a major center for psychiatry. While there, he became aware of the therapeutic effects of psychiatric interviews. He moved to Baltimore and worked and taught at Sheppard and Enoch Pratt Hospital (1923–31), coming under the influence of Adolph Meyer at Johns Hopkins. In 1932 he moved to New York City to set up his clinical practice but he continued to teach at the University of Maryland School of Medicine (1933–43), Yale, and at the Georgetown School of Medicine. Although influenced by Freudian psychoanalysis, he believed that "personality" only has meaning in the context of cultural patterns and interpersonal relations, and that psychiatry is the study of those relations. He saw mental illnesses as problem-solving efforts that could lead to greater emotional integration. Sullivan demonstrated, for instance, that even severe schizophrenics display symbol activity that is human and therefore understandable. He was the first editor of *Psychiatry* (1938–49), and wrote *Conceptions of Modern Psychiatry* (1947). After World War

II, he applied his theories to understanding international relations, but the "Sullivanians" never gained the status that he had hoped for.

Sullivan, James (1744–1808) legal scholar; born in Berwick, District of Maine. He was initially King's counsel for York County in Maine but took an active role in support of the American Revolution. For many years he was a prominent Boston lawyer and Massachusetts statesman; he served on the state supreme court (1776), as state attorney general (1790–1807), and as governor (1807–08).

Sullivan, James E. (Edward) (1860–1914) sports administrator; born in New York City. He was one of the founders of the Amateur Athletic Union (AAU) in 1888 and its secretary from 1889–96. The James E. Sullivan Memorial Trophy is awarded to the outstanding amateur athlete each year.

Sullivan, John (1740–95) soldier, public official; born in Somersworth, N.H. A lawyer and militia officer, he sat as a delegate to the First and Second Continental Congresses and fought at Trenton and Princeton (1777). He led the expedition to Newport, R.I. (1778), which failed largely because of the absence of naval support. Poor health forced him to leave the army in November 1779. After the American Revolution, Sullivan served three terms as governor of New Hampshire and as a federal judge.

Sullivan, John L. (Lawrence) (1899–1982) lawyer, public official; born in Manchester, N.H. He was the assistant secretary of the treasury (1939–44) and worked actively on the wartime finances. His tenure as secretary of the navy (1947–49) was cut short when he resigned in protest over the cancellation of the navy's first supercarrier.

Sullivan, John L. (Lawrence) (1858–1918) boxer; born in Roxbury, Mass. He began his amateur career boxing around New England and became known as the "Boston Strong Boy." The last bare-knuckle world heavyweight champion, he held the title from 1882 to 1892. In 1892 he lost his crown to James J. Corbett by a knockout under the newly adopted Queensbury rules requiring padded gloves. A colorful personality who often boasted in a tavern that he could "beat any man in the house," the "Great John L's" career record was 31 victories (16 knockouts), one loss, three draws, and one no decision. After retiring, he renounced his former lifestyle and became a temperance advocate.

Sullivan, Leon (Howard) (1922–) civil rights activist, Baptist minister; born in Charleston, W.Va. Ordained in 1939 while still in high school and encouraged by Adam Clayton Powell Jr., he studied at the Union Theological Seminary (1943–45) and then Columbia University (Master's in Religion 1947). He joined the Abyssinian Baptist Church in Harlem and supported the "Don't buy where you can't work" boycott. As pastor at Zion Baptist Church in North Philadelphia (1950–88), he espoused "evangelistic materialism" and led boycotts of Philadelphia businesses that refused to hire African-Americans. Among the organizations he founded to assist African-American economic development was the Opportunities and Industrial Centers of America, located in an abandoned jailhouse purchased by the congregation (1964). In 1971 he was elected to the board of directors of General Motors Corporation. The "Sullivan Principles" (1977) became guidelines for American corporations doing business in South Africa with the intent of destroying apartheid. Widely honored, he was given the Freedom Foundation Award (1960), made pastor emeritus at his church

(1988), and awarded a Medal of Freedom (1991). He began a $40-million aid program for Africa in 1992.

Sullivan, Louis Henri (1856–1924) architect; born in Boston, Mass. He studied architecture for one year each at the Massachusetts Institute of Technology and the École des Beaux-Arts, Paris, but gained most of his training in architects' offices in Philadelphia and Chicago. In partnership with Dankmar Adler (1881–95), Sullivan became perhaps the foremost exponent of the Chicago school, producing 120 buildings including such landmarks as the Auditorium (1886–90), Schiller (1891–93), and Stock Exchange (1893–94) Buildings and the Transportation Building at the World's Columbian Exposition of 1893, all in Chicago, and the Wainwright Building, St. Louis (1890–91). Sullivan's distinctive midwestern skyscrapers and office blocks were innovative and influential in their experimental skeleton construction, vertical articulation, and intricate low-relief ornamentation. After the partnership broke up, Sullivan designed a series of small midwestern banks and the Schlesinger and Mayer (Carson, Pirie, Scott) Building, Chicago (1899–1904); but he produced almost nothing in his last fifteen years and died in relative obscurity. He published a series of books elaborating, if not always clearly explaining, the revolutionary architectural philosophy ("form follows function") that made him the "Father of Modernism." Frank Lloyd Wright was his student. Sullivan was awarded the Gold Medal of the American Institute of Architects in 1944.

Sullivan, Mark (1874–1952) journalist; born in Avondale, Pa. A muckraking writer for *McClure's* and *Collier's* magazines (1905–14), he edited *Collier's* for a few years and, from 1923, wrote a syndicated column for the *New York Tribune* (later, *Herald Tribune*). He wrote a popular multivolume social history of the United States in the early 20th century, called *Our Times*.

Sully, Thomas (1783–1872) painter; born in Horncastle, Lincolnshire, England. He and his family emigrated to Charleston, South Carolina (1792); he received art instruction from family members and began his portrait painting career (1801) in Richmond and Norfolk, Va. He worked with Gilbert Stuart in Boston (1807), moved to Philadelphia (1808), and studied with Benjamin West in London (1809), where he was influenced by Sir Thomas Lawrence. Returning to Philadelphia (1810), he painted technically polished and elegant portraits, such as *Fanny Kemble as Beatrice* (1833), and was often compared to Gilbert Stuart.

Sulzberger, Mayer (1843–1923) judge, scholar; born in Hildesheim, Germany. In 1848 he came to Philadelphia, where he was educated and became a lawyer in 1865. He became a judge of the court of common pleas (1895–1916). He was active in Jewish philanthropies, especially education. Throughout his life he published scholarly religious works.

Sulzer, William (1863–1941) U.S. representative, governor; born in Elizabeth, N.J. A New York City lawyer and assemblyman (1890–94), he served in the U.S. House of Representatives (Dem., N.Y.; 1895–1913); there he supported such progressive policies as the graduated income tax and direct election of senators while opposing American intervention in Mexico. Governor of New York in 1913, he began investigating corruption in state politics only to be impeached himself for investing campaign contributions in the stock market. Although he served one more term in the state assembly (1914–16), his attempts at higher office failed and he returned to his law practice.

Sumner, Charles (1811–74) U.S. senator; born in Boston, Mass. An exceptional law student, he originally rejected a law practice and political career to become a lecturer at Harvard Law School and an editor of legal textbooks. Between 1835–37 he traveled in Europe. He emerged as a public figure when he denounced the Mexican War at an Independence Day speech in Boston in 1845 and he toured as a lyceum lecturer. He then entered the U.S. Senate through a coalition of Free Soilers and Democrats (Mass., 1851–54), later becoming the Republican senator (1854–97). He became an outspoken abolitionist and was physically assaulted by Representative Preston Brooks (S.C.) while sitting at his Senate desk (1856) and was left slightly crippled for life. He continued to advocate the emancipation of slaves, and as a Radical Republican after the Civil War, he pressed for imposing harsh terms on the former Confederate states and for the impeachment of President Andrew Johnson. He soon fell out with President Ulysses Grant's administration, but he remained a voice of moral integrity until his death.

Sumner, James (Batcheller) (1887–1955) biochemist; born in Canton, Mass. He was affiliated with Cornell for his entire career (1915–55). He was the first researcher to isolate and crystallize an enzyme, the plant enzyme urease, and confirm that it consists of protein (1926). He shared the Nobel Prize in chemistry (1946) with John Northrop and Wendell Stanley.

Sumner, William Graham (1840–1910) sociologist, educator; born in Paterson, N.J. Son of an immigrant English workman who read and thought about social and economic issues, he took a B.A. from Yale in 1863 and then went to Europe to study for the ministry. In 1869 he was ordained as a priest in the Protestant Episcopal Church and by 1870 he was rector of the Church of the Redeemer in Morristown, N.J. Desiring to speak out on social and economic issues of the day, in 1872 he accepted a professorship in political and social science at Yale, a post he held until his death. He was one of the most influential teachers of his era, famed for his independent thought, innovative classes, and rigorous standards. Usually labeled a proponent of *laissez-faire* capitalism, he was a man of strong moral convictions and opposed all forms of shoddy thinking. He saw all aspects of society as interrelated and as he worked on what was to be his major book, he became sidetracked on a supporting study of the underlying customs of societies through the ages; he published this as *Folkways* (1907). Thus his major work, *Science of Society,* came out in four volumes posthumously in 1927, heavily edited by Yale professor Albert G. Keller. A man of immense energies, in addition to his teaching he participated in community activities, working in particular to improve Connecticut's public education. In his day he was also widely known for his lively essays and public lectures, perhaps the most notable being one called "The Forgotten Man," what a later generation would call "the silent majority" of average people who "are never mentioned in the newspapers, but just work and save and pay."

Sumter, Thomas (1734–1832) soldier, public official; born in Hanover County, Va. Raised on the frontier, a veteran of the French and Indian War, he settled in South Carolina in 1765. During the American Revolution he led a partisan campaign against the British in the Carolinas and the success of his small force gained him the nickname, "Gamecock of the Revolution" (and led to his name being given to the island-fort off Charleston where the Civil War began). After the war, Sumter sat in the U.S. House of Representatives and the Senate.

Sunday, (William Ashley) Billy (1862–1935) Protestant evangelist; born in Ames, Iowa. He grew up in poverty but managed to complete high school before joining the Chicago White Sox baseball team in 1883. He underwent a religious conversion in 1887, and, after retiring as a player in 1891, went to work for the YMCA in Chicago. His fabulously successful career as an evangelist began in 1896. A flamboyant fundamentalist, his denunciations of science, liquor, and political liberalism attracted an enormous following, especially in rural areas. Although his influence began to decline after about 1920, he continued preaching to the end of his life.

Sunstein, Cass R. (Robert) (1954–) legal scholar; born in Salem, Mass. He served as an attorney adviser to the Department of Justice (1980) and taught at the University of Chicago (1981). Known for his work in administrative law, civil procedure, and constitutional law, his major publications are *Constitutional Law* (with Stone, Seidman, and Tushnet) (1986) and *After the Rights Revolution* (1990).

Sununu, John H. (Henry) (1939–) engineer, governor; born in Havana, Cuba. Born during his American parents' business trip, he became an engineer, forming J. H. S. Engineering Co. (1965–82) and teaching at Tufts (1966–82). As governor of New Hampshire (Rep., 1983–89), he opposed taxes, recruited new businesses, and supported the controversial Seabrook nuclear plant. As President Bush's chief of staff (1989–91), he offended many with his brusque manner and became the center of several controversies; he was asked to resign. For a time he appeared as a television news commentator.

Suomi, Verner (Edward) (1915–) meteorologist; born in Eveleth, Minn. Inventor of the Spinscan weather satellite camera (1963), he began as a Minnesota public school teacher (1938–42). At the University of Wisconsin: Madison (1948) he helped found the Space Science and Engineering Center in 1967 and helped develop the man-computer interactive data access system (McIDAS).

Suppes, Patrick (1912–) philosopher, educator; born in Tulsa, Okla. After serving in the U.S. Air Force (1942–46) and earning a doctorate in philosophy from Columbia University (1950), he joined the Stanford University faculty in 1948; in 1959 he became director of Stanford's Institute for Mathematical Studies in the Social Sciences. As president of the American Educational Research Association (1973–74), he was a pioneer in computer-assisted instruction and contributed to logic and probability theory.

Surratt, Mary Eugenia (b. Jenkins) (1817–65) **and John Harrison, Jr.** (1844–1916) alleged assassination conspirators; born in Waterloo, Md. Mrs. Surratt was widowed in 1864 and she opened a boarding house in Washington, D.C. It was here that John Wilkes Booth allegedly plotted the assassination of President Lincoln with his colleagues; her young son John, who had served as a message runner for the Confederacy, was alleged to have been involved in some way. Following Lincoln's assassination, John escaped to Canada while his mother was arrested and tried (May 10–

June 30, 1865) for participating in the conspiracy. Although she insisted she had no part in the plot, she was hanged on July 7, 1865 (along with three others). John returned to the U.S.A. and was acquitted by a civil court in 1867. He later was a freight agent for the Baltimore Packet Company.

Susskind, David (1920–87) television/stage/movie producer; born in Brookline, Mass. Forming Talent Associates in 1947 to package creative personnel, he produced live television dramas, like *Armstrong Circle Theatre,* during the 1950s, and Broadway plays, including *Rashomon* (1959). In 1958 he launched *Open End,* an issue-oriented panel television program, and he also produced films like *Raisin in the Sun* (1961). He continued to moderate discussion on *The David Susskind Show* (1967–86).

Sutherland, Earl W. (Wilbur), Jr. (1915–74) biochemist; born in Burlingame, Kans. At Washington University (St. Louis) (1940–53), he identified the role of the enzyme phosphorylase in glucose metabolism. At Case Western Reserve (1953–63), he discovered how adrenaline regulates carbohydrate metabolism in the liver (1955). In 1956 he isolated a cyclic adenosine monophosphate (cyclic AMP), then demonstrated its activation by hormones. For this accomplishment, he won the 1971 Nobel Prize for physiology. After moving to teach at Vanderbilt (1963–73), he relocated to the University of Miami Medical School (1973–74).

Sutherland, Edwin Hardin (1883–1950) sociologist, criminologist; born in Gibbon, Nebr. Son of a college president, he taught longest at the University of Indiana (1935–50), chairing the sociology department (1935–49). His textbook, *Criminology* (1924), became a standard, undergoing four editions by 1947. This work codified the "multiple factors" known to be associated with crime and criminality and argued that criminal behavior was learned. He shattered the class-oriented study of crime with *The Professional Thief* (1937) and *White Collar Crime* (1949), coining the term "white collar crime."

Sutherland, George (1862–1942) Supreme Court justice; born in Stony Stratford, Buckinghampshire, England. He came to the U.S.A. at age two. He was a member of Utah's first legislature (1896), the U.S. House of Representatives (Rep., Utah; 1901–03), and the Senate (Rep., Utah; 1905–17). President Harding named him to the U.S. Supreme Court (1922–38) where he frequently voted against New Deal measures.

Sutter, John Augustus (1803–80) California colonist; born in Kandern, Baden (now Germany). A Swiss citizen, he came to the U.S.A. in 1834 and by 1839 had made his way to Mexican California. He obtained large land grants from the Mexican authorities and set up a colony on the American River near present-day Sacramento. Known for his helpfulness to American settlers, he was ruined by the events that followed the discovery of gold on his property. Gold-seekers and squatters took over his land, and he went bankrupt in 1852, spending most of his remaining years asking the state and federal governments to arrange compensation; except for a brief and modest pension, he never received anything and he died a disillusioned man.

Sutton, Walter S. (Stanborough) (1877–1916) geneticist, surgeon; born in Utica, N.Y. While he was a graduate student in Edmund B. Wilson's laboratory (Columbia University, 1901–03), he used grasshopper cells to prove that chromosomal behavior in meiosis is responsible for observed Mendelian phenomena. Although his achievements in cell research were and still are recognized as classic, Sutton pursued his goal of becoming a physician, received an M.D. from Columbia (1907), then practiced surgery in Kansas City, Kans., and Kansas City, Mo., until his death.

Suzzallo, (Anthony) Henry (1875–1933) educator; born in San Jose, Calif. As its president (1915–26), he developed the University of Washington: Seattle into a major university designed to meet the state's needs. During his presidency (1930–33), the Carnegie Foundation for the Advancement of Teaching issued major reports on higher education in California and federal involvement in education.

Swadesh, Morris (1909–67) linguist; born in Holyoke, Mass. Child of immigrant Russian Jews, he grew up knowing Russian and Yiddish. He took his B.A. and M.A. at the University of Chicago under Edward Sapir, who in 1931 brought Swadesh with him to Yale, where Swadesh took his Ph.D. (1933). He spent part of every year throughout the 1930s doing fieldwork with Native Americans and became familiar with many of their languages. He taught at the University of Wisconsin (1937–39), then went to Mexico to head a program of education for native Mexicans while serving as professor at the Instituto Politecnico Nacional de Mexico (1939–41). During World War II he served in the language section of the U.S. Army (1942–46) and edited dictionaries and teaching materials for several languages. After teaching one year at the City College of New York (1948–49), he was fired due to the McCarthyism that drove out academics with "leftist sympathies." Supported by various grants, he worked for several years on an ambitious project to trace the relationships among all American Indian languages, one of his major concerns and contributions. He returned to Mexico as a professor at the Universidad Nacional Autonoma and at the Escuela Nacional de Antropologia e Historia (1956–67). Honored as among the first generation to develop modern linguistic analysis in the U.S.A., he initiated or was associated with many new approaches such as phonemics, pattern analysis of linguistic structure, and glottochronology. Author of 22 books and over 130 articles, he was especially known for his work on the origin and evolution of language, effectively founding what is known as prehistoric linguistics.

Swann, Thomas (1809–83) businessman, governor, U.S. representative; born in Alexandria, then part of the District of Columbia. After a successful career in the railroad business, he became mayor of Baltimore (1856–58). He served as Union Party governor of Maryland (1866–69). He supported Reconstruction, but also worked to restore the franchise to southern sympathizers. He later served four terms in the U.S. House of Representatives (1869–76).

Swanson, Claude (Augustus) (1862–1939) U.S. representative; born in Swansonville, Va. After his father's business reverses, he worked to earn his college and law school tuition, going to the U.S. House of Representatives (Dem., Va.; 1893–1905) where he championed free rural postal service. As governor of Virginia (1905–10), he advanced public school education. Appointed to the U.S. Senate (1910–33), he became an authority on the navy, attending the General Disarmament Conference in Geneva before becoming secretary of the navy (1933–39).

Swanson, Gloria (b. Gloria Josephine Mae Swenson or Svensson) (1897–1983) movie actress; born in Chicago. Of Swedish-Italian descent, she was hired as an extra in a

Chicago movie studio (1915); there she met movie actor Wallace Beery, whom she married in 1916 and accompanied to Hollywood. She made numerous short romantic films for Mack Sennett and then a series of sentimental dramas for Triangle Productions before being hired by Cecil B. De Mille. By the mid-1920s, she had become the most popular and glamorous of Hollywood actresses (and was on her third husband). Backed by Joseph Kennedy, father of the later president, she began producing her own movies but lost heavily on von Stroheim's *Queen Kelly* (1938). She made a few talkies, retired in 1934, made a single film in 1941, *Father Takes a Wife,* and then made a sensational comeback in *Sunset Boulevard* (1950), where she played an evocation of her actual self. She made a few more movies, promoted cosmetics, fashions, and health foods, starred on Broadway in *Butterflies are Free* (1971), and took a sixth husband (1976), but was never able to recapture what *Sunset Boulevard* had so vividly portrayed.

Swanton, John Reed (1873–1958) anthropologist, folklorist; born in Gardiner, Maine. He pioneered ethnohistorical research techniques while working for the Bureau of American Ethnology (1900–44). He published prolifically; among his most important works are *Indian Tribes of the Lower Mississippi Valley* (1911), *Indians of the Southeastern United States* (1946), and studies of the Tlingit (1908) and Caddo (1942) Indians. He won the Viking Fund Medal.

Swarthout, Gladys (1904–69) mezzo-soprano; born in Deepwater, Mo. American trained and highly attractive, she appeared at the Metropolitan Opera between 1929 and 1945, meanwhile concertizing and appearing in films during the 1930s.

Swasey, Ambrose (1846–1937) mechanical engineer; born in Exeter, N.H. In 1880 he joined a Cleveland company to make machine tools and optical instruments. He specialized in large telescopes, including the 36-inch Lick (1888), the 40-inch Yerkes, and many others. His company also provided high-quality instruments to the military during World War I.

Swayne, Noah Haynes (1804–84) Supreme Court justice; born in Frederick County, Va. His abolitionism prompted a move from Virginia to Ohio, where he served as U.S. district attorney (1830–39). He was practicing law privately when President Lincoln named him to the U.S. Supreme Court (1863–81).

Swayze, John Cameron, Sr. (1906–) television newscaster; born in Wichita, Kans. An editorial staffer with Missouri's *Kansas City Journal Post* (1930–40), he began broadcasting radio news there. At the National Broadcasting Company in New York he began the *Camel News Caravan* (1948–56), one of the earliest television news shows. He worked as an announcer, panel show host, and commercial spokesperson afterward, publishing the *Art of Living* (1979).

Sweeney, James Johnson (1900–86) museum director, art historian/critic; born in New York City. He studied at Georgetown University (B.A. 1922) and at several other institutions. In Paris during the 1920s he was an editor on the literary magazine *Transition*. He was a journalist in Chicago (1931–32), director of exhibitions at the University of Chicago (1933–34), and lectured at New York University (1935–40). He was curator at the Museum of Modern Art (1945–46), director of the Guggenheim Museum (1952–59), and director of the Museum of Fine Arts, Houston (1961–68). In the 1970s he chaired the executive committee of the

Israel Museum, Jerusalem. His specialty was 20th-century avant-garde art and his numerous publications include the book *Plastic Redirections in Twentieth Century Art* (1934).

Sweeney, Orland R. (1883–1958) chemical engineer; born in Martin's Ferry, Ohio. He developed uses for agricultural products and waste and became head of the chemical engineering department at Iowa State University in Ames (1921). He helped establish the U.S. Department of Agriculture Farm Byproducts Utilization Lab at Ames (1930).

Sweetser, Arthur (1888–1968) diplomat; born in Boston, Mass. He was the U.S.A.'s unofficial ambassador to the League of Nations (1919–39). He was deputy director of the Office of War Information (1942–45) and chairman of the United Nations Information Bureau (1945–53). In 1954 he founded the International Schools Foundation.

Swift, Gustavus Franklin (1839–1903) meat packer; born near Sandwich, Mass. He worked in the butcher trade from age 14 in his brother's shop. By 1859 he was purchasing, slaughtering, dressing, and peddling his own steer to Cape Cod residents. His reputation as a shrewd judge of beef grew. In 1872 he became partners with a renowned Boston meat dealer. As a buyer, Swift followed the cattle market, moving steadily west until he got to Chicago (1875). He revolutionized the meatpacking industry by shipping east dressed beef instead of live steer (1877). His partnership dissolved, he independently hired an engineer to invent a refrigerator car for summer shipments. In 1885 he incorporated as Swift & Company and pioneered in the use of waste products to make glue, oleomargarine, soap, and fertilizer. The company expanded internationally and by 1903 was worth more than $25 million.

Swift, Zephaniah (1759–1823) U.S. representative, jurist; born in Wareham, Mass. He studied and practiced law in Windham, Conn. He served in Connecticut's general assembly (1787–93, 1820–22) and in the U.S. House of Representatives (Fed., 1793–97). He opposed slavery and sat on the Connecticut Superior Court (1801–19); he fell into disfavor after participating in the Hartford Convention (1814) that threatened secession in opposition to the War of 1812. He wrote some of the first American law texts and was eulogized for making laws intelligible.

Swindler, Mary Hamilton (1884–1967) classical archaeologist; born in Bloomington, Ind. She earned her B.A. and M.A. at Indiana University (1905, 1906), then came to Bryn Mawr College, where she earned her Ph.D. (1912), and stayed most of her life. She founded a museum at Bryn Mawr to teach students from original classical artifacts. Her book *Ancient Painting* (1929) was her major work. An authority on Crete and the Aegean world, she became a professor of classical archaeology in 1931. The first woman editor of the *American Journal of Archaeology* (1932–46), she expanded its scope and brought it international reputation. After her retirement she continued to teach at Bryn Mawr and elsewhere.

Swing, Raymond (Edwards) Gram (1887–1968) journalist; born in Cortland, N.Y. A correspondent in Berlin during World War I, he later became widely known as a radio commentator for the British Broadcasting System and the Mutual Broadcasting System.

Swope, Gerard (1872–1957) engineer, businessman, public official; born in St. Louis, Mo. He joined Western Electric Company in 1895 and by 1913 had become vice-president in charge of domestic sales and international operations, reorganizing Western Electric's foreign interests. A parallel concern of Swope's was social justice. From 1897 to 1899 he lived and worked at Hull House in Chicago, marrying a social worker who also worked there. In 1919 he joined General Electric as the first president of its subsidiary International General Electric, where he promoted international corporate support for European reconstruction following World War I. As president of General Electric in 1922, with Owen D. Young chairing the board, he recognized a corporation's responsibility to its employees, customers, and the industry. His "new capitalism" vision, called the Swope Plan (1931), became the basis for the National Industrial Recovery Act of 1933 and he helped implement the New Deal. He headed community chest campaigns, founded the National Health and Welfare Retirement Association, and retiring in 1939, chaired the New York City Housing Authority. His causes included cooperative housing, health insurance, and Zionism. In 1951 he chaired the Institute of Pacific Relations.

Swope, Herbert Bayard (1882–1958) journalist; born in St. Louis, Mo. A World War I correspondent for the *New York World,* he won a 1917 Pulitzer Prize for his dispatches. As executive editor of the *New York World* in the 1920s, he promoted numerous crusades and developed a widely imitated Op Ed page. An associate of Bernard Baruch, he reportedly coined the phrase "cold war," usually credited to Baruch.

Sykes, Lynn Ray (1937–) seismologist; born in Pittsburgh, Pa. He was a researcher and professor at the Lamont-Doherty Geological Observatory, Columbia University (1962). He made major contributions to the seismic investigation of underground nuclear testing, and the relationship of earthquakes to tectonic movement.

Sylvis, William H. (1828–69) labor leader; born in Armagh, Pa. An iron molder, he joined a local molder's union in Philadelphia in 1857. In 1860 he helped organize the Iron Molder's International Union (IMIU), and served as its president (1863–69). In 1866 he founded the National Labor Union, and served as its president (1868–69). Although he looked to the English cooperative labor movement and was opposed to strikes, he took an active role in fighting for labor's rights.

Symington, Stuart (1901–88) U.S. senator; born in Amherst, Mass. He served in the army during World War I, attended Yale (1919–23), and worked as an executive for several companies, becoming in 1939 the president and chairman of the Emerson Electric Manufacturing Company in St. Louis. He was assistant secretary of War for Air and then the first secretary of the air force during the first Truman administration. He ran for the Senate from Missouri in 1952 and was reelected three times. He retired in 1975.

Szarkowski, (Thaddeus) John (1925–) writer, museum director; born in Ashland, Wis. A professor of art history and photography at Albright College in Buffalo, he won a Guggenheim in 1954 to do a photographic study of architect Louis Sullivan. Director of photography at the Museum of Modern Art (1962–91), he wrote books to establish criteria for evaluating the seemingly casual snapshot photographs of renegades like Diane Arbus and Lee Friedlander and he exhibited their work.

Szasz, Thomas (Stephen) (1920–) psychiatrist, author; born in Budapest. He emigrated to the United States in 1938 and became professor of psychiatry at the State University of New York Health Science Center at Syracuse, N.Y. (1956). Long regarded as a maverick within his field, he argued that mental illness (as opposed to organic disturbance) does not exist, but is rather a metaphor. Mental illness should rather be seen as "problems of living." Psychiatry, he claimed, simply glosses over this difference. In line with this belief, he opposed use of the insanity plea in criminal cases, arguing that criminal law should be allowed to work unimpeded when a person has committed a dangerous act. Most controversially, he took the position that psychiatry is a repressive arm of the modern bureaucratic state and a tool for social control because it can be used to imprison innocent people by "civil commitment" simply because their thought patterns are considered aberrant. The author of many books, including *The Myth of Mental Illness* (1974), he did much to alert the public to potential dangers of coercive practices masked by psychiatric rationales.

Szell, George (1897–1970) conductor; born in Budapest, Hungary. A child prodigy as pianist and composer, he made his conducting debut with the Berlin Philharmonic at age 17, conducting his own music. He went on to lead various opera orchestras including the Berlin State Opera (1924–29). After conducting the Scottish Orchestra in Glasgow for three years, he came to the U.S.A. in 1939 and guest-conducted widely. Named conductor of the Metropolitan Opera in 1944, he left two years later to take over the Cleveland Orchestra, which in the decades until his death he built into one of the great ensembles of the world, his interpretations marked by a remarkable clarity and elegance of playing – achieved by means of a famously dictatorial approach. During his Cleveland tenure Szell continued to guest-conduct worldwide, notably at the Salzburg Festivals (1949–68).

Szent-Györgyi, Albert (von Nagyrapolt) (1898–1986) biochemist; born in Budapest, Hungary. Trained as an anatomist, he worked at several European institutions, publishing studies of bacteriology and quantum mechanics before concentrating on biochemistry. He won the 1937 Nobel Prize in physiology for his discovery of the oxidation-preventing action of vitamin C, which he termed ascorbic acid. He also discovered the controversial vitamin P, plant pigments that reduce capillary fragility and protect against radiation damage. Harassed because of his anti-Nazi activities, he was granted protective citizenship at the Swedish embassy in Hungary. He refused the presidency of Hungary, emigrating to the U.S.A. in 1947 because of his dislike of postwar Soviet dominance of his native country. He joined the Marine Biology Laboratories at Woods Hole, Mass. (1947–86), and founded its Institute for Muscle Research (1947). There he continued research on heart muscle based on his 1940 discovery of the contractile muscle protein, actomyosin. He concurrently served the National Foundation for Cancer Research (1980–86). He authored several books and over 200 scientific papers, and was actively opposed to the Vietnam war.

Szilard, Leo (1898–1964) physicist; born in Budapest, Hungary. He fled from Nazi Germany to England (1933), and emigrated to the U.S.A. to work on nuclear physics at Columbia University (1938–52). Influenced by Enrico Fermi, he convinced Albert Einstein to write the famous 1939 letter to President Franklin Roosevelt urging military development of atomic physics. Szilard was sent to the University of Chicago (1942–64), where he became a central figure in the Manhattan Project. He became an active advocate of peaceful uses of atomic energy, and turned his research toward bacteriology and investigations of human memory and aging. He joined the Salk Institute of Biological Studies in 1964.

Szold, Benjamin (1829–1902) rabbi; born in Nemeskér, Hungary. Educated in Vienna and Breslau (Poland), he came to the U.S.A. in 1859 to be rabbi of Congregation Oheb Shalom in Baltimore, which he served for more than 40 years. He edited a popular revised prayer book in 1863. A notable scholar, he was also an early Zionist and was devoted to public causes, including abolition.

Szold, Henrietta (1860–1945) educator, reformer, Zionist leader; born in Baltimore, Md. (daughter of Benjamin Szold). Raised by her father to speak several languages, she graduated from a Baltimore high school and then taught for almost 15 years at a private academy for girls in that city while also teaching in her father's synagogue. She also became active in assisting the integration of Jewish immigrants into the U.S.A. and organized a night school to help them become "Americanized" (1889–98). Using the pen name "Sulamith," she contributed articles to the *Jewish Messenger* in New York City. She was editor of the Jewish Publication Society (1893–1916) and the most active editor of the *American Jewish Year Book* (1904–08). After her father died, in 1903 she and her mother moved to New York City where she continued as an editor. Disappointed in love, she took a trip abroad and visited Palestine (1910) and from then on was devoted to Zionism in general – the settling of Jews in Palestine – and in particular to improving the health of the inhabitants of Palestine. She had been a member of a Zionist society in Baltimore since 1893, but now she organized and became first president of the national Hadassah (1912–26); she would become the first woman member of the Palestine Zionist executive of the World Zionist Organization (1927). She spent many of the years between 1920–45 in Palestine or in traveling to Europe to facilitate the immigration of Jews, especially those faced with the growing menace of the Nazis. She continued her activities into her eighties; the recipient of countless honors, none was more significant than "mother of the Yishuv," referring to the Jewish settlement of Palestine. Although an ardent Zionist, she always hoped to foster friendly relations between Jews and Arabs in Palestine.

T

Taber, John (1880–1965) U.S. representative; born in Auburn, N.Y. A graduate of Yale, he practiced law and served as a judge in Cayuga, N.Y., before going to the U.S. House of Representatives (Rep., N.Y.; 1923–63) where he chaired the Committee on Appropriations (1949–55).

Tabern, Donalee L. (1900–74) chemist, inventor; born in Bowling Green, Ohio. He joined Abbott Laboratories in 1926 after two years as an instructor at Cornell. His researches led to the development of many sleep-producing drugs, including the famous Nembutal and, in cooperation with Ernest Volwiler, Pentothal. He later headed Abbott's research efforts in the use of radioactive materials in biology and medicine.

Tabor, Horace (Austin Warner) (1830–99) prospector, merchant; born in Holland, Vt. He moved to Colorado and made a fortune from a silver mine (1878). He built a hotel and two opera houses in Colorado. He filled an unexpired term in the U.S. Senate (Rep., Colo.; 1883). He lost his fortune and was penniless by 1893; he was made postmaster of Denver to spare him the humiliation of total destitution. His second wife was "Baby Doe," who in 1935 ended her life freezing to death in the shack at the mouth of the mine that she was convinced would still yield more silver.

Tafoya, Margaret (1904–) potter; born in Santa Clara Pueblo, N.M. Member of a multigenerational Tewa pottery family, she is noted for her polished black-and-red ware, often incised with the traditional bear paw design.

Taft, Helen (b. Herron) (1861–1943) First Lady; born in Cincinnati, Ohio. She married William Howard Taft in 1886. A vigorous supporter of her husband, she pushed him to seek the presidency in 1908. In 1909 she suffered a stroke that impaired her speech and kept her out of the public eye for eighteen months.

Taft, Lorado (Zadoc) (1860–1936) sculptor, educator; born in Elmwood, Ill. A graduate of the University of Illinois (B.A. 1879; M.A. 1880) he studied at the École des Beaux Arts in Paris (1880–83), then taught sculpture at the Chicago Art Institute (1886–1906), where he introduced marble carving. His commissions came slowly and in 1903 he published *History of American Sculpture,* which led to lucrative lecture tours. In the 1910s he began sculpting a series of monumental fountains such as Columbus Fountain (1912) in Washington, D.C. An advocate for art education, he lectured high school students and created "Peep Shows" of sculptors at work for children. He continued creating large scale pieces until the end of his life.

Taft, Robert A. (Alphonso) (1889–1953) U.S. senator; born in Cincinnati, Ohio (son of President William Howard Taft). He graduated from Yale and Harvard Law School. During World War I he worked with Herbert Hoover in the U.S. Food Administration and then for postwar European relief efforts. He entered politics in Ohio, serving in the state legislature, and as a prominent conservative Republican he went on to serve in the U.S. Senate (Ohio; 1938–53). An isolationist in foreign affairs and an opponent of "New Deal" and "Fair Deal" domestic programs, he was a candidate for the Republican presidential nomination in 1940, 1948, and 1952. Known as "Mr. Republican," he coauthored the Taft-Hartley Act, which imposed new restrictions on labor, defended Senator Joseph McCarthy, and continued to oppose the U.S.A.'s internationalist actions.

Taft, William Howard (1857–1930) twenty-seventh U.S. president; born in Cincinnati, Ohio. Having studied at Yale and practiced law in Cincinnati, he gravitated to Republican politics and held several appointments and a judgeship in Ohio. In 1890 he began two years as U.S. solicitor-general under President Benjamin Harrison, then became a federal circuit judge (1892). He left that position in 1900 when President William McKinley sent him to the Philippines, where he became civil governor. In 1904 President Theodore Roosevelt made Taft the secretary of war and his chosen successor. An extremely large man, easy-going and conciliatory, Taft did not really want to be president but he was elected in 1908. He had an uneasy tenure as president; although he pursued antitrust prosecutions like his predecessor, he was perceived to be allied with conservative Republicans. That led to Roosevelt's party-splitting run in 1912, ensuring a victory for the Democrat, Woodrow Wilson. After some years of teaching at Yale Law (1913–21), Taft was named chief justice of the Supreme Court in 1921, a position he enjoyed far more than being president. He served until one month before his death, and although known more for his reform of court operations, he participated in several major decisions.

Tait, Arthur Fitzwilliam (1819–1905) painter; born in Livesey Hall near Liverpool, England. He emigrated to New York City (1805), summered in the Adirondacks, and became known for his works of the American West, as well as sporting scenes, many of which were made into lithographs by Currier & Ives.

Takaezu, Toshiko (1929–) ceramist; born in Pepeekeo, Hawaii. After study under Maija Grotell at Cranbrook, she taught at Cranbrook, other schools, and then at Princeton University (1966). In 1968 she established a studio in Quakertown, N.J. With her biomorphic forms of the 1950s, her explorations of sound by enclosing clay pebbles in pots, and the more recent closed cracked vessels, she drew on Zen ideas and abstract expressionist forms.

Takamine, Jokichi (1854–1922) chemist, industrialist; born in Takaoka, Japan. Already well established as a leading industrialist chemist in Japan, he married an American and moved to the U.S.A. in 1885. Working mainly with Parke, Davis & Co., he also continued to aid Japan in the development of its chemical research and industries. He is best known for developing the enzyme known as takadiastase and for being the first to isolate a pure hormone, adrenaline (epinephrine), from the suprarenal gland (1901).

Talbot, Marion (1858–1948) home economist, educator; born in Thun, Switzerland. She was raised and educated in Boston. She joined the faculty of the University of Chicago, teaching sanitary science, and, as the nation's first dean of women, developing the women's house system (1892–1925). With Ellen H. Richards she edited *Home Sanitation* (1887); other works include *The Education of Women* (1910) and *The Modern Household* (1912).

Tallchief, Maria (b. Betty Marie) (1925–) ballet dancer, teacher, artistic director; born in Fairfax, Okla. Raised in Los Angeles, she studied with Ernest Belcher and Bronislav Nijinska. One of the Ballet Russe de Monte Carlo's four Native American stars in the early 1940s, she married George Balanchine and returned with him to the United States. Known for her elegance and brilliance as a dancer, she performed with New York City Ballet until 1965. The ballet troupe and school she formed to serve the Chicago Lyric Opera in 1974 became the Chicago City Ballet in 1980.

Talma, Louise (1906–) composer; born in Arachon, France. She studied in New York and with Nadia Boulanger in France and taught at Hunter College (1946–76). Her music is typically neoclassic, later mixed with serialism, but always personal; she has been called "the dean of women composers." Her works include the 1955–56 opera *Alcestiad,* based on a Thornton Wilder text.

Talmadge, Edwards (1747–1821) glove manufacturer; born in England, near the Scottish border. He came to America in 1770 and fought on the American side during the Revolution. He started his own tannery in Johnstown, N.Y. (1783), and he taught leather tanning to glovemakers. This began the glove and mitten industry in the U.S.A. He originated the "oil-tan" method for preparing buckskin.

Talmadge, Eugene (1884–1946) governor; born in Forsyth, Ga. A Georgia farmer and lawyer, he entered state politics as Democratic commissioner of agriculture (1927–33). A states rights governor (Dem., 1933–37), he attacked individuals and agencies opposed to him, and, with Huey Long, he led Southern opposition to President Franklin Roosevelt, even mounting an abortive campaign to replace Roosevelt in 1936. He returned to farming, practicing law, and publishing his own weekly paper, the *Statesman.* Governor again (1941–43), he lost favor after demanding that the University of Georgia regents fire a pro-integration dean. He was re-elected governor in 1946 but died before assuming office.

Talmadge, Herman Eugene (1913–) governor, U.S. senator; born in Telfair, Ga. (son of Eugene Talmadge). A lawyer, he served as Georgia's governor (Dem., 1947–55), increasing funding for schools, highways, and hospitals. In the U.S. Senate (1957–81), he opposed civil rights legislation and supported defense spending, becoming Agriculture and Forestry Committee chair. Charged in 1979 with financial misconduct, he returned to his Georgia law practice.

Tammany (?1625–?1701) Delaware chief; born near the Delaware River near present-day Bucks County, Pa. According to legend, he welcomed William Penn to America in 1682; little is known about him except for his name in several contemporary texts. For his legendary character and loyalty to the whites, he became known as Saint Tammany, the patron saint of America and a symbol of the American resistance to the British. Several American organizations subsequently took his name, the most famous being New York City's Society of Saint Tammany (1789), originally so named to reflect the members' disdain for pretentious Americans; later it became known as Tammany Hall, which functioned as Democratic Party organization of New York.

Tandy, Jessica (1909–94) stage and film actress; born in London, England. Starting her career in England, she first came to act in the U.S.A. in 1930; not until playing Blanche in the original production of *Streetcar Named Desire* (1947) did she begin to be perceived as an American actress. After her marriage to Hume Cronyn (1942) they were often together on stage, where she was noted for her incisive portrayals of a wide range of modern and classic roles. Her film career never amounted to much until she won an Oscar (1989) as leading actress in *Driving Miss Daisy.*

Tanenbaum, Marc H. (1925–92) rabbi, publicist; born in Baltimore, Md. An ordained rabbi, he became national director of the department of interreligious affairs for the American Jewish Committee in 1961. He spent much of his life as a religious consultant to print and broadcast media as well as government and civic agencies.

Taney, Roger (Brooke) (1777–1864) Supreme Court chief justice; born in Calvert County, Md. A member of a prosperous landowning family, he practiced law and then became active in Maryland politics, serving in the state senate (1816–21) and as state attorney general (1827–31). His opposition to the Bank of the United States gained him the favor of President Andrew Jackson, who named him U.S. attorney general (1831–33) and secretary of the treasury (1833); however, the Senate refused to confirm him for the latter post or for his first nomination to the U.S. Supreme Court (1835). Upon Chief Justice John Marshall's death (1836), Jackson renominated Taney to replace him and the Senate confirmed him (1836–64). His tenure was marked by decisions on foreign relations matters as well as on issues regarding relations between federal and state courts. The opinion for which he is best known is in the case of *Dred Scott* v. *Sandford,* in which he not only declared that an African-American could not be a citizen but also that Congress had no authority to ban slavery from the territories. This made him a target for the new Republican Party and during the Civil War his decisions against several Federal war measures made him further suspect.

Tanguay, Eva (1878–1947) actress; born in Marbleton, Canada. A whirlwind of energy on stage, she was an oversized vaudevillian with a big voice (1901–24), who delighted in shocking audiences with outrageous costumes and lyrics. Her signature song was "I Don't Care" from *The Chaperones* (1903).

Tanguy, Yves (1900–57) painter; born in Paris, France. A former merchant marine officer, he became a self-taught surrealistic painter (c. 1925). He emigrated to America (1939) with his wife, Kay Sage, and lived in Woodbury, Conn. He is known for his mysterious and fantastic paintings, such as *Fear* (1949).

Tannenbaum, Frank (1893–1969) historian; born in Brod, Galicia, Austria-Hungary. He emigrated to the U.S.A. in 1905, two years later enrolling in night classes at the radical Ferrer School. As a young member of the Industrial Workers of the World, or "Wobblies," he worked as a labor activist and was briefly imprisoned. He later earned degrees at Columbia College and the Brookings Institution. During his long career as a Latin American historian at Columbia University (1935–61), he originated (1945) and for 25 years directed Columbia's famous University Seminar Program. His interests and contributions were unusually diverse, ranging from prison reform to race relations. His *Crime and the Community* (1938) became a standard text; his most famous book, *Slave and Citizen* (1947), was a pioneering work on the historiography of American slavery. Long interested in Mexican history, particularly the revolution, he came to be regarded as the dean of North American Mexicanists; his awards included the Mexican government's National Order of the Águila Azteca.

Tanner, Henry Ossawa (1859–1937) painter; born in Pittsburgh, Pa. A major 19th-century black painter of religious and genre scenes, he studied with Thomas Eakins (1880–82). Tormented by racial persecution, he settled in Paris, France (1891) and only briefly returned to America (1902–04). His early atmospheric genre works, such as *The Banjo Lesson* (c. 1893), have been recently rediscovered and praised by the art world.

Tappan, Arthur (1786–1865) merchant, philanthropist, abolitionist; born in Northampton, Mass. (brother of Benjamin and Lewis Tappan). Brought up in a strict religious home, he succeeded in the import business and started (1826) a prosperous silk jobbing venture in New York City soon involving his brother Lewis as partner. In 1827 he founded the *New York Journal of Commerce* to be a model of decent and reform-minded journalism. Both brothers devoted time and money to causes ranging from temperance to abolitionism. Arthur backed many theological seminaries and colleges, as well as William Lloyd Garrison's abolitionist newspaper, *The Liberator*, and similar journals. In 1833 he cofounded the American Anti-Slavery Society and became its first president. Later breaking with other abolitionists because of their linking of abolitionism with other issues, such as feminism, he helped found the American and Foreign Anti-Slavery Society (1840); he also cofounded the American Missionary Society (1846), which included abolition as one of its goals.

Tappan, Henry (Philip) (1805–81) university president, philosopher; born in Rhinebeck on the Hudson, N.Y. He gained international recognition as a philosopher with his works on free will in the 1830s and 1840s. As president (1852–63) he helped develop the University of Michigan into a great research institution modeled on German universities.

Tappan, Lewis (1788–1873) merchant, abolitionist; born in Northampton, Mass. (brother of Benjamin and Arthur Tappan). In 1828 he entered into partnership with Arthur as a silk jobber in New York and succeeded him as editor of the *New York Journal of Commerce*, which he sold in 1831. He 1841 he set up the first commercial credit-rating agency in the U.S.A. With Arthur he helped fund and direct antislavery societies, and he actively sought close links with abolitionists abroad. With his brother he founded the American and Foreign Anti-Slavery Society (1840) and the American Missionary Association (1846). Like his brother he gradually became more radical as an abolitionist, and in 1855 he left the American and Foreign Anti-Slavery Society to become an officer in the Abolition Society, which called for elimination of slavery in existing slave states.

Tarbell, Edmund (Charles) (1862–1938) painter; born in West Croton, Mass. He was based in Boston, studied at the Boston Museum School (1879), where he later taught (1889–1913), and in France (1883–88). He was a member of the Ten (1898), largely an impressionist group, and his paintings, such as *In the Orchard* (1891), have recently been reevaluated and praised.

Tarbell, Ida (Minerva) (1857–1944) journalist, historian; born in Erie County, Pa. A staff writer for the muckraking *McClure's* magazine (1894–1906), she published her explosive denunciation of John D. Rockefeller's fortune-building methods in *History of the Standard Oil Company* (1904). From 1906 to 1915, with other *McClure's* writers, she edited the *American* magazine. Her other books include *The Business of Being a Woman* (1912) and *The Nationalizing of Business*, on post-Civil War economic growth.

Tarkenton, (Francis Asbury) Fran (1940–) football player; born in Richmond, Va. Famous for his ability to scramble with the football, he nevertheless set National Football League career passing records for attempts, completions, yards, and touchdowns (1961–78).

Tarkington, (Newton) Booth (1869–1946) writer, playwright; born in Indianapolis, Ind. He studied at Purdue (1890–91) and Princeton (1891–93). He hoped to become a painter but, lacking skill, he turned to writing popular novels and plays; the best known of the latter is *Monsieur Beaucaire* (1901), an adaptation of his own novel. He is best known for the novels, *The Magnificent Ambersons* (1918) and *Alice Adams* (1921), as well as for his children's novels, such as *Penrod* (1914) and *Seventeen* (1916). He was popular during the early part of the 20th century, but today his work seems dated and insubstantial. He lived in Kennebunkport, Maine.

Tarr, Ralph (Stockman) (1864–1912) geologist, geographer; born in Gloucester, Mass. He studied geology and physiography at Harvard under Nathaniel Shaler and William Davis, graduating in 1891. He taught at Cornell (1892–1912), publishing textbooks like *Elementary Physical Geography* (1895). He organized the Cornell Greenland Expedition that traveled with Peary (1896) and led the National Geographic Society's expeditions to Alaska (1909, 1911), later writing *Alaskan Glacier Studies* (1912).

Tarski, Alfred (1901–83) mathematical logician; born in Warsaw, Poland. Fleeing Nazism, he eventually settled at the University of California: Berkeley (1942) where he was an inspiring teacher. A member of the National Academy of Science, he discovered interconnections between logic, algebra, set theory, and measure theory. He also brought clarity to the semantics of mathematical logic, legitimizing semantic concepts such as truth and definability with his work on definitions of truth in formalized languages (1933–

35). He was known especially for the mathematicians he influenced as a professor.

Tate, James (Vincent) (1943–) poet; born in Kansas City, Mo. He studied at the University of Missouri (1963–64), Kansas State (B.A. 1965), and the University of Iowa (M.F.A. 1967). He taught at several universities, including Columbia (1969–71) and the University of Massachusetts: Amherst (1971). He lived in Pelham, Mass. He is known for his preoccupation with the use of language, seen in such books as *The Lost Pilot* (1967) and *Constant Defender* (1983).

Tate, (John Orley) Allen (1899–1979) man of letters; born in Winchester, Ky. As a student at Vanderbilt University he joined the Fugitive group of southern writers; he later became the preeminent representative of the Southern Agrarian school. Best remembered for measured, classical poems like his well-known "Ode to the Confederate Dead" (he won the Bollingen poetry prize in 1956), he was also a prominent New Critic, an essayist, and the teacher of John Berryman and Theodore Roethke, among many others. He was married (1924–59) to the novelist Caroline Gordon.

Tattnal, Josiah (1795–1871) naval officer; born near Savannah, Ga. While serving in the U.S. Navy (1812–61) he compromised American neutrality by assisting a hard-pressed British squadron in its attack on a Chinese fort (1859). He explained that "blood is thicker than water" and his action was upheld by the U.S. government. As a Confederate naval officer (1861–65) he commanded the coastal defenses of Georgia and South Carolina and gave the order for the CSS *Virginia* to be burned rather than allow her to fall into Northern hands.

Tatum, (Arthur) Art (1909–56) jazz musician; born in Toledo, Ohio. Near-blind from birth, he was established as a jazz pianist in New York by 1932 and worked mainly as a soloist thereafter. He was a keyboard virtuoso whose overwhelming technique and harmonic imagination strongly influenced jazz pianists and the bebop style of the following generation.

Tatum, Edward L. (Lawrie) (1909–75) geneticist; born in Boulder, Colo. At Stanford (1935–45), he worked with George W. Beadle using the bread mold *Neurospora* to discover the relationship between genetic mutation and the synthesis of essential cellular chemicals (1941). At Yale (1945–78), Tatum and his graduate student Joshua Lederberg found that similar mutations could be demonstrated after sexual reproduction in the bacterium *Escherichia coli* (1947). Tatum, Beadle, and Lederberg shared the 1958 Nobel Prize in physiology or medicine for their pioneering work in microbial genetics. Tatum was a professor and educator at Rockefeller University (1957–75).

Taube, Henry (1915–) chemist; born in Neudorf, Saskatchewan, Canada. After taking his B.S. and M.S. at the University of Saskatchewan, he went on to take his Ph.D. in chemistry at the University of California: Berkeley (1940). He became a U.S. citizen in 1942. While teaching at Cornell (1941–46), he worked during World War II at the National Defense Research Committee (1944–45). He then taught at the University of Chicago (1946–61). In 1962 he joined the faculty of Stanford University, becoming the Marguerite Blake Wilbur Professor of Chemistry in 1976 (emeritus in 1988). During his career he was the recipient of many of the highest awards his profession of inorganic chemistry offers, including the National Medal of Science (1977), the Welch Award (1983), and the Priestly Medal of the American Chemical Society (1985). He won the 1983 Nobel Prize in chemistry for discovering the basic mechanism of chemical reactions that lie behind everything from enzymes to batteries. He was specifically cited for his work in electron transfer reactions, especially in metal complexes, work that has applications in the chemical industry, but it was also noted that he had made at least 18 major discoveries in his field.

Taubman, A. Alfred (1925–) real estate developer, auction house owner, art collector; born in Pontiac, Mich. He attended the University of Michigan and the Lawrence Institute of Technology (Mich.), where he studied architecture. In 1951 he formed his own company in Oak Park, Mich., a suburb of Detroit, and concentrated on commercial construction; by the late 1940s he moved into designing and building retail stores and "strip" malls. In 1964 he opened his first major shopping center, Southland, in Hayward, Calif., and in the ensuing years he built a vast empire of shopping malls. With this as his financial base, he branched out to acquire a restaurant chain (A&W), a broadcast network (the Broadcast Group), a department store chain (Woodward & Lathrop), even a football team (the Michigan Panthers of the U.S. Football League). His most publicized acquisition was the 1983 purchase of Sotheby Parke Bernet, the great London-based art auction house; although many English people spoke as though the barbarians had finally toppled British civilization – the flamboyant Taubman was known to work out daily in his own gym with a prizefighter – he was in fact a serious art collector and art museum trustee who had the best interests of the firm at heart. In 1988 and 1992 he sold off large parts of his share in the firm, just as he also (1992) took his shopping mall company public.

Taussig, Helen (b. Brooke) (1898–1986) physician; born in Cambridge, Mass. Specializing in congenital malformations of the heart, she is best known as codeveloper of the famous "blue-baby" operation (1944) along with the late Dr. Alfred Blalock. The Blalock/Taussig procedure helped pave the way for open heart surgery using the heart-lung machine, accounting for major progress in cardiac surgery. She was also instrumental in blocking the use of thalidomide in the United States. She conducted her research both at Harriet Lane Home, Baltimore – where she was the physician in charge of the children's cardiac clinic (1930–63) – and concurrently as a member of the Johns Hopkins medical school faculty (1930–63) where she was named professor emeritus of pediatrics (1963–86). As caring a physician as she was an exacting researcher, she followed her cardiac patients into adulthood and remained concerned for their well-being. A National Academy of Sciences member, she received over 20 honorary degrees.

Taussig, Joseph (Knefler) (1877–1947) naval officer; born in Dresden, Germany (while his American father served in the European Squadron). Wounded during service in China's Boxer Rebellion, he commanded destroyers in World War I. Between 1920 and 1936 he served mainly at the Naval College or in staff positions, and although he seemed marked for the navy's top post, a longstanding feud with Franklin Roosevelt sidelined his career. In 1943 he was recalled to active service to head the naval clemency board.

Tawney, James Albertus (1855–1919) U.S. representative; born near Gettysburg, Pa. A blacksmith who became a lawyer in 1882, he served in the Minnesota Senate. In the U.S. House of Representatives (Rep., 1893–1911) he was majority whip and chairman of the Committee on Appropriations.

Tawney, Lenore (1925–) weaver; born in Lorain, Ohio. After studying sculpture, she began weaving in 1948. In 1957 she left Chicago for New York. She influenced a generation of American weavers with her nonfunctional hangings. Her 1950s work influenced by abstract expressionism gave way to figurative pieces with religious themes, then to sculptural shapes in the 1960s and then again in the 1970s to the exploration of new materials such as paper and feathers, and assemblage techniques. Her weavings for architectural commissions were often of monumental size.

Tax, Sol (1907–) cultural anthropologist; born in Chicago. Educated at the Universities of Wisconsin and Chicago (Ph.D. 1935), he carried out field studies among the North American, Guatemalan, and Mexican Indians, and had a long career as a professor of anthropology at Chicago. As a longtime associate at the Wenner-Gren Foundation for Anthropological Research, he promoted many expeditions and field campaigns. His publications include *Evolution after Darwin* (3 vols. 1960). He was editor of *American Anthropologist* from 1953–56.

Taylor, Albert Davis (1883–1951) landscape architect; born in Carlisle, Mass. Trained by Warren Manning, he opened a firm in Cleveland, Ohio (1916–51), drafting plans that combined naturalistic parks with formal gardens near buildings for clients like the Pentagon and Forest Hill Park in Cleveland.

Taylor, Barry N. (Norman) (1936–) physicist; born in Philadelphia, Pa. He taught at the University of Pennsylvania (1963–66), then became a physicist at RCA Laboratories, N.J. (1966–70) before joining the National Bureau of Standards (1970). He made key advances in precision measurements and fundamental constants, absolute electrical measurements, and superconductivity.

Taylor, Bayard (1825–78) traveler, journalist, writer; born in Kennett Square, Pa. Brought up as a Quaker, he traveled widely in Europe (1844–45) and the Near and Far East (1851–53); he became a master's mate aboard Commodore Perry's expedition to Japan (1853). He wrote and lectured extensively about his travels. Meanwhile, he continued to publish poetry and novels and his translation of Goethe's *Faust* (2 vols. 1870–71). He was serving as U.S. ambassador to Germany when he died.

Taylor, Cecil (Percival) (1933–) jazz musician; born in New York City. A conservatory-trained pianist, he emerged in 1955 as a bandleader with an uncompromising, abstract approach to jazz language and harmony. He worked sporadically until the 1970s, but eventually won recognition, particularly among Europeans, for his style of extended, nontonal free improvisation.

Taylor, Edward (1645–1729) Protestant clergyman, poet; born near Coventry, England. Refusing to take the oath of conformity required of English schoolteachers, he emigrated to Massachusetts in 1668, graduated from Harvard three years later, and became a physician/pastor in Westfield, Mass., where he remained to the end of his life. At his death, he left a manuscript of his "Poetical Works." His poems, many on religious themes, were not published until the late 1930s, at which time he was recognized as the finest American poet of the 17th century. A comprehensive edition, *The Poems of Edward Taylor,* appeared in 1960.

Taylor, Elizabeth (1932–) movie actress; born in London, England. Just before World War II, the Taylors (who were American) returned to the U.S.A. Groomed by her mother to be a movie star, she made her screen debut in *There's One Born Every Minute* (1942) and already showed her star quality in *National Velvet* (1944). After a series of relatively light roles, she parlayed her beauty and popularity into an increasingly serious acting career, and although her first Oscar – best actress, in *Butterfield 8* (1960) – was voted for sentimental reasons (she had just survived a major illness), her second – for *Who's Afraid of Virginia Woolf?* (1966) – was well deserved. Her private life, meanwhile, became as theatrical as her roles – she would marry seven men, including Richard Burton (twice) – and her treatment for alcohol addiction, her weight problems, and her propensity for expensive jewelry and tough talk made her the epitome of the old-fashioned Hollywood celebrity whose every move was reported. In the 1980s she appeared on stage and on television and then took on a new role as outspoken advocate of AIDS sufferers.

Taylor, Francis Henry (1903–57) museum director; born in Philadelphia. He studied at the University of Pennsylvania (B.A. 1924) and various other institutions. He was the assistant curator (1927–28) and then the curator of medieval art (1928–31) at the Philadelphia Museum of Art. He was director of the Worcester Museum of Art (1931–40), which he turned into the best small city museum in America. As director of the Metropolitan Museum (1940–55), he undertook a series of international loans from European collections that were unsettled during World War II; the museum's attendance soared and its membership almost tripled. He wrote *The Taste of Angels* (1948).

Taylor, Frederick Winslow (1856–1915) efficiency engineer; born in Germantown, Pa. After an apprenticeship at a hydraulic works in Philadelphia (1874–78), he went to work at Midvale Steel Company, where he codeveloped the Taylor-White system for heat treating chrome-tungsten tool steel. While there, Midvale introduced piece work in the factory and Taylor became interested in the most efficient way to perform specific tasks. By closely observing the workers' procedures and measuring the output, he developed methods for maximizing each operation as well as for selecting the man best suited for each job, thereby improving both labor relations and company profits. Chief engineer beginning in 1884, he left Midvale in 1890, opening a consulting firm in 1893. While he is most associated with efficiency engineering of people – long known throughout the world as "Taylorism" – he also developed machines and processes that would help speed up work. He promoted his ideas on efficiency engineering in *Principles of Scientific Management* (1911) and in several other books.

Taylor, Graham (1851–1938) Protestant clergyman, civic reformer; born in Schenectady, N.Y. Ordained (1873), he served the Dutch Reformed church in Hopewell, N.Y. (1873–80). Becoming the pastor of the Fourth Congregational Church in West Hartford, Conn. (1880–92), he worked with wayward men and was appointed a professor at the Hartford Theological Seminary (1888) where he taught urban missionary techniques. He left Hartford to head a new department of Christian sociology at the Chicago Theological Seminary – the first institution in the United States to establish such a department (1892–1924). Eager to adapt Christianity to urban problems and involve students, he saw the creation of a settlement house as a means of accomplishing both goals. He and his family and four students were the first inhabitants of Chicago Commons (1894), which eventually occupied a new building and became a model of settlement house design. Equally active in the seminary and in the settlement house movement, he became convinced of the need for trained social workers and helped initiate the first professional course in social work at the University of Chicago (1903). While at the seminary he wrote his first book, *Religion in Social Action* (1913). He declined the presidency of the seminary (1906) but served as acting president for two years. He appointed his daughter director of Chicago Commons (1921) while continuing to formulate policy and raise funds and work on other civic projects involving labor mediation, education, politics, and social reform.

Taylor, Henry Osborn (1856–1941) historian; born in New York City. He studied American history under Henry Adams at Harvard University (1874) and law at Columbia University and Leipzig; his *Treatise on the Law of Private Corporations* (1884) became a standard text. Turning from legal theory to the evolution of human ideals, his *Mediaeval Mind* (1911) was considered a classic of intellectual history. In later years he wrote primarily about philosophy.

Taylor, John ("of Caroline") (1753–1824) political philosopher, U.S. senator, agriculturist; born in Caroline County, Va. He fought in the American Revolution and served several terms in the Virginia House of Delegates (1779–81, 1782–85) as well as the U.S. Senate (1792–94, 1803, 1822–24). A Jeffersonian Democrat, he opposed the Federal Constitution because it did not sufficiently protect individual and states' rights. In 1798 he introduced the "Virginia Resolutions" supporting delegated powers and asserting that states' rights take precedence in cases of the "dangerous exercise of other powers." He wrote numerous pamphlets, books, and articles such as *An Inquiry into the Principles and Policy of the Government of the United States* (1814), proposing divided powers of government to best serve the people and opposing a permanent national debt. Owner of several plantations in Caroline County, he also wrote a series of essays on agriculture, collected in *The Arator* (1813).

Taylor, (Joseph) Deems (1885–1966) composer, writer/ broadcaster on music; born in New York City. After graduating from New York University, he enjoyed some success with such compositions as *Through the Looking Glass* (1917). Continuing to compose, he also took up an active career as a music critic for various publications and later as a promoter of serious music on radio, becoming widely known as the intermission commentator for the New York Philharmonic broadcasts (1936–43); he even appeared in the Disney film *Fantasia* (1940). His music remained relatively conservative; several works, including the opera *Peter Ibbetson* (1931), were well-received in their time but have since fallen into neglect.

Taylor, Joseph H., Jr. (1941–) radio astronomer; born in Philadelphia. After studying at Haverford (B.A. 1963) and Harvard (Ph.D. 1968), he joined the faculty of the University of Massachusetts: Amherst (1969–80). In 1974 he and a graduate assistant, Russell A. Hulse, discovered the first

binary pulsar using the radio telescope at the Arecibo Observatory in Puerto Rico; for this discovery and its contribution to understanding gravitation, they would be awarded the Nobel Prize in physics in 1993. Taylor helped found the Five College Radio Observatory, where further research on pulsars confirmed in 1978 Einstein's theory of gravitational waves, thus adding to the understanding of the laws governing the universe. In 1980 Taylor joined the physics faculty at Princeton University.

Taylor, Lance (Jerome) (1940–) economist; born in Montpelier, Ida. Educated at California Institute of Technology and Harvard, he taught at Harvard before joining the faculty of the Massachusetts Institute of Technology in 1974. He was a consultant for the World Bank, the United Nations, and several foreign governments, and is the author of *Macro Models for Developing Countries* (1979) and other works.

Taylor, Lily Ross (1886–1969) classicist, ancient historian; born in Auburn, Ala. A student of Tenney Frank, she spent most of her teaching career at Bryn Mawr (1927–52). Both her teaching and her scholarship received many honors; *Life* magazine cited her as one of the country's great teachers, and her *Voting Districts of the Roman Republic* (1962) won the Goodwin Award of the American Philological Association. Her seven books and more than 70 articles focused on Roman politics and political institutions, including the cults of Ostia and Etruria. Her *Divinity of the Roman Empire* (1931) was the first extensive study of that subject and remains a classic. At the time of her death in a car accident at age 83, she was working on a study of the Roman Senate.

Taylor, Lucy Beaman (b. Hobbs) (1833–1910) dentist; born in western New York. The first American woman to earn a dental degree (1866), she did so only after years of being refused admission to dental schools (1859–65). Practicing with her husband in Lawrence, Kans. (1867–86), she was the first woman to be admitted into a state dental association.

Taylor, Margaret (Mackall b. Smith) (1788–1852) First Lady; born in Calvert County, Md. She married Zachary Taylor in 1810. She went to Washington reluctantly and was little-known as first lady. Following Taylor's death in office she lived with her son in Mississippi.

Taylor, (Marshall W.) "Major" (1878–1932) bicycle racer; born in Indianapolis, Ind. The first widely recognized black American athlete, he won national championships at the height of cycling's popularity from 1899 to 1904.

Taylor, Maxwell D. (Davenport) (1901–87) soldier; born in Keystesville, Mo. A West Point graduate (1922), he was among those who set up the first airborne units. In World War II, he commanded the 101st Airborne Division and was the first general to land in Normandy on D-Day. He was superintendent of West Point (1945–49) and served as military governor of Berlin (1949–51). He commanded the U.S. Eighth Army in the Korean War (1953–55) before taking over as commander of the U.S. and United Nations Far East commands. He was army chief of staff (1955–59) before retiring, but President John F. Kennedy called him out of retirement in 1961 and appointed him chairman of the Joint Chiefs of Staff (1962–64). He took an active role under presidents Kennedy and Johnson in escalating the U.S. commitment to South Vietnam and served as ambassador to South Vietnam (1964–65). Regarded as more cosmopolitan than the average army officer, he was fluent in several languages and the author of four books on military issues.

Taylor, Moses (1806–82) banker; born in New York City. He began as a clerk at an importing house in the City and by 1832, with $15,000, opened his own business handling the Cuban sugar trade. In 1855 he became president of City Bank in New York where his policy was to hold large cash reserves. He dabbled in railroads, public utilities, and helped the Lincoln administration finance the Civil War. He also joined with Cyrus W. Field in the first Atlantic cable venture and supported the project until it saw success.

Taylor, Nathaniel William (1786–1858) Protestant theologian; born in New Milford, Conn. He graduated from Yale in 1807, was ordained in 1812, held a Congregational pastorate in New Haven for ten years, and from 1822 until a few weeks before his death was professor of theology at Yale. His "New Haven theology," long assailed as heresy, denied the Calvinistic doctrine of sin as depravity. He contributed controversial articles to the *Christian Spectator* and other journals and was a persuasive, eloquent preacher and teacher.

Taylor, Paul (1930–) choreographer, modern dancer; born in Pittsburgh, Pa. He danced with Merce Cunningham (1953–54) and Martha Graham (1958–62) before forming his own company in 1957. Known for his singularly lyrical style, he is recognized as one of America's leading choreographers.

Taylor, Peter (Hillsman) (1917–94) writer; born in Trenton, Tenn. He studied at Vanderbilt (1936–37), Southwestern (1937–38), and Kenyon (B.A. 1940). He served in the army (1941–45) and taught at the University of North Carolina (1946–67) and the University of Virginia (1967). He wrote novels and plays, but is best known for his short stories, as in *The Collected Stories of Peter Taylor* (1969). He was consistently praised for his mastery of the form and his use of Southern settings.

Taylor, Robert Love (1850–1912) U.S. representative/senator, governor; born in Carter County, Tenn. Elected to the U.S. House of Representatives (Dem., Tenn.; 1879–81), governor of Tennessee (1887–91, 1897–99), and to the U.S. Senate (1907–12), he won fame and fortune as a popular speaker.

Taylor, (Vernon) James (1948–) folk/ballad singer, songwriter; born in Boston, Mass. Brother of pop-folk musicians, Alex, Kate and Livingston Taylor, as a teenager he turned to the guitar and played with brother Alex's band. In 1965 he committed himself to a psychiatric hospital for ten months. He went to New York City and played with a folk-rock group, the Flying Machine. He first gained wide popularity with his album *Sweet Baby James* (1970) and went on to record several successful singles and albums, often singing others' songs and often with other well-known singers. In 1972 he and singer-songwriter Carly Simon were married (later divorced). His music mixed folk, rock, and blues and is known for its easygoing rhythms and crooning style of singing; his own lyrics were often in the confessional vein.

Taylor, Walter W. (Willard) (1913–) archaeologist; born in Chicago, Ill. His *Study of Archaeology* (1948) attacked traditional taxonomic methodology and called for more stringent excavations and analysis of material. A specialist in the neolithic and chalcolithic archaeology of Western Europe, he was also known for his North American fieldwork. He taught at Southern Illinois University (1958–74).

Taylor, Zachary (1784–1850) twelfth U.S. president; born in Orange County, Va. With little formal education, he volunteered for the army in 1806, was commissioned lieutenant in 1808, and enjoyed a long military career that saw distinguished service in the War of 1812, the Black Hawk War (1832), and the Seminole Wars. Already known nationwide as "Old Rough and Ready," he provoked the opening hostilities of the Mexican War (1846–47) and won celebrated victories at Palo Alto, Resaca de la Palma, Monterrey, and Buena Vista. The Whigs adopted this politically inexperienced war hero as their presidential candidate in 1848 and he and Millard Fillmore won the election. The main issue facing Taylor and the nation was the question of slavery; he took a position against abolition but also against the spread of slavery into new states – which satisfied no one; meanwhile, Henry Clay proposed the Compromise of 1850, which put the issue on hold for the time being, and Taylor died in office amidst these unresolved controversies.

Tchelitchew, Pavel (1898–1957) painter; born in District of Kaluga, Russia. After study in Russia, he worked in Berlin (1921–23), moved to Paris (1923–c. 1934), where he was a scenic designer for ballets, and moved to New York City (1934). Known for his intricate surrealistic work, as in *Hide and Seek* (1940–42), he settled in Italy in 1950.

Teagarden, (Weldon John) Jack (1905–64) jazz musician; born in Vernon, Texas. He was a trombonist and singer whose relaxed, melodic instrumental style was highly influential. He was a featured sideman with Ben Pollack and Paul Whiteman (1927–38), led his own big band (1939–46), appeared with Louis Armstrong's All-Stars (1947–51), and led small groups thereafter.

Teague, Walter Dorwin (1883–1960) industrial designer; born in Decatur, Ind. After study at New York's Art Students League and subsequent free-lance illustrating, graphic, and typographic work, he founded an industrial design office (1926) whose clients included Kodak, Corning Glass, Ford, US Steel, Texaco, and Du Pont. Among his notable designs were the 1928 Kodak Bantam Special camera, the 1935 Texaco gas station, Pyrex ovenware, and the Boeing 707 airplane interior.

Teale, Edwin Way (1899–1980) naturalist, author; born in Joliet, Ill. The only child of a railroad mechanic, his lifelong interest in natural history grew out of childhood summers on his grandfather's northern Indiana farm. He graduated from Earlham College in 1922 and was a staff writer for *Popular Science* magazine from 1928 to 1941. His first nature book, *Grassroots Jungles*, appeared in 1937 and he helped promote an appreciation of the environment long before it became a cause. *Wandering through Winter*, the final volume in his natural history of the four seasons in America, won a Pulitzer Prize in nonfiction in 1965.

Teasdale, (b. Sarah Trevor) Sara (1884–1933) poet; born in St. Louis, Mo. She was educated privately, traveled in Europe and the Middle East (1905–07), married (1914–29), and settled in New York City (1916). Her early poetry, such as *Love Songs* (1917), was marked by a delicate lyricism, but her later poems, as in *Strange Victory* (1933), reveal a more intense core. Afflicted with bouts of depression, she committed suicide in New York City.

Tecumseh (b. Tecumtha) (?1768–1813) Shawnee chief; born on the Mad River near present-day Springfield, Ohio. One of the most sophisticated Native American opponents of the encroaching United States, Tecumseh was a highly skilled warrior, orator, and statesman who advocated "civilized" resistance. He was undoubtedly influenced by the fact that his father and two brothers were killed while fighting American colonists. In 1795 he refused to sign the Treaty of Greenville, which ceded much of present-day Ohio to American settlers. In the late 1790s, he became involved with a white woman named Rebecca Galloway, with whom he studied many prominent works of Western civilization; as a condition of marriage, however, she insisted he give up his Indian ways, and the relationship ended. In 1808 he established, with his brother Tenskwatawa, known as the Shawnee Prophet, a pan-Indian headquarters on the banks of the Tippecanoe River (now known as Prophet's Town, Ind.). Tecumseh spent the next several years attempting to build an alliance, based on the idea of a common ownership of land, among dozens of tribes in the trans-Appalachian west. In 1811, with Tecumseh away, the unfinished alliance suffered a profound setback when Indiana Territory Governor William Henry Harrison defeated Tenskwatawa's forces at Tippecanoe. But Tecumseh persisted and during the War of 1812 he persuaded thousands of Indians to join with the British; given the rank of brigadier general, he commanded his own and other troops brilliantly, but his dream of an independent Indian nation died with him at the Battle of the Thames.

Tefft, Thomas Alexander (1826–59) architect; born in Richmond, R.I. In his brief architectural career (1851–56) he designed 150 east-coast buildings of various types and in popular styles, including the Railroad Station, Providence, R.I. (1848).

Tekakwitha, Blessed Kateri (1656–80) Indian Catholic convert; born in Ossernenon, in Mohawk territory (now Auriesville, N.Y.) When she was three years old, a smallpox epidemic killed her mother (a Catholic but not allowed to practice) and father; she herself was scarred and partially blinded by the disease. Raised by an anti-Catholic uncle, but inspired by Jesuit missionaries, she took instruction and was baptized a Catholic at age 20. To escape continuing persecution she fled a year later to a Christian Indian village near Montreal, where, in her brief remaining life, she became noted for religious fervor and extreme asceticism. She was beatified in 1980.

Telemaque See VESEY, DENMARK.

Teller, Edward (1908–) physicist; born in Budapest, Hungary. He studied theoretical physics in Europe before emigrating to the U.S.A. (1935). At George Washington University, he collaborated with George Gamow in classifications of rules for beta decay, and applications of astrophysics to controlled thermonuclear reactions. Teller worked on the atomic bomb (1941–46), then became a physicist at the University of Chicago (1946–52). After joining the University of California: Berkeley (1953–75), he repudiated Oppenheimer's moral qualms and took the lead in developing the hydrogen bomb (1954). Throughout his career as a physicist and as a government adviser, Teller was an advocate of defensive atomic weaponry and often found himself engaged in controversies.

Teller, Henry Moore (1830–1914) U.S. senator; born in Granger, N.Y. He went out to the Colorado Territory during its gold rush period and practiced law in Central City (where the main hotel is named for him). Elected as one of the new state's first two senators (Rep., Colo.; 1877–82), he resigned to serve as secretary of the interior under President Chester Arthur (1882–85). He returned to the U.S. Senate (1885–1909), the first three terms as a Republican; his advocacy of bi-metalism – the use of silver as well as gold to back U.S. money – led him to switch to the Democratic Party for his final term. Although he introduced the 1898 resolution that led the U.S.A. into the Spanish-American War, he opposed the U.S.A. pursuing war in the Philippines, and in his later years he supported more progressive social policies.

Temin, Howard M. (Martin) (1934–94) virologist; born in Philadelphia. He spent his career at the University of Wisconsin (1960). Working with RNA viruses (1970), he isolated the enzyme reverse transcriptase that transcribes viral RNA into the host cell's DNA. For this achievement, he won one-third the 1975 Nobel Prize in physiology. His later research includes major contributions to studies of tumor viruses, enzyme chemistry, AIDS, and viral evolution.

Temple, Shirley (1928–) movie actress, diplomatic official; born in Santa Monica, Calif. Precociously talented, she was "discovered" at a dancing school and at age three and a half was appearing in a series of short films. In 1934 she made nine movies, leaping to stardom with *Little Miss Marker,* and winning a special Academy Award for her "outstanding contributions to screen entertainment" that year. For the next six years she was not only one of the most popular and best paid of all movie stars, she inspired a virtual cult of adulation and name-brand products. As she moved into her teens, her appeal and career faltered and she effectively retired from the movies in 1950; attempts to revive her career on television in 1958 and in 1960 also failed. Married to business executive Charles Black in 1950, as Shirley Temple Black she unsuccessfully ran as a Republican for U.S. representative and senator from California. She was appointed a U.S. representative to the United Nations (1969), ambassador to Ghana (1974–75), White House chief of protocol (1976–77), and ambassador to Czechoslovakia (1989–92).

Templeton, Sir John (Marks) (1912–) investment counselor, philanthropist; born in Winchester, Tenn. After graduating from Yale, he went as a Rhodes Scholar to Balliol College, Oxford. He became an executive with a petroleum prospecting firm, the National Geophysical Company of Dallas and New York (1937–40), and formed his own investment house, Templeton, Dobbrow and Vance, Inc. (1940–65); he then established Templeton Growth Fund, and in ensuing years, several other large international investment funds. Having made a large fortune, he increasingly gave his money and energies to various worthwhile organizations and causes. Originally a Presbyterian, he became especially interested in promoting ecumenical dialogue among all the world's religions; in addition to donating money and support to various religious institutions, in 1972 he initiated the Templeton Prize for Progress in Religion, regarded as the Nobel Prize for those who have contributed the most to religious life. In addition to many articles in financial and religious journals, he wrote several books, including *The Humble Approach* (1982) and *Riches for the Mind and Spirit* (1990). In 1987 he accepted a British knighthood, and he made the Bahamas his legal residence.

Ten Broeck, Richard (1812–92) horseman; born in Albany, N.Y. The first American to win on the English turf (1856), he owned such champion thoroughbreds as Lexington, Starke, and Prioress.

Tennent, Gilbert (1703–64) Protestant evangelist; born in County Armagh, Northern Ireland. He emigrated to America with his father about 1718 and entered the ministry in 1725. A fiery, persuasive preacher, he helped foment the religious revival known as the Great Awakening, during which he traveled through the northern colonies with English evangelist George Whitefield. His dismissive views on the pastorate and on the church as an institution provoked a schism among New Jersey Presbyterians in the 1740s. Mellowing in later years, when he served in Philadelphia, he helped to heal the breach he had largely created.

Tenney, Tabitha Gilman (1762–1837) anthologist, writer; born in Exeter, N.H. Raised in a Puritanical, bookish, and somewhat secluded atmosphere in a noted New Hampshire family, she acquired the intellectual and gentlewomanly accomplishments expected of her. In 1788 she married Samuel Tenney, a surgeon who turned to politics after the American Revolution, serving in the U.S. House of Representatives (1800–07). In 1799 she published *The Pleasing Instructor,* an anthology of poetry and selections from classical writers intended to improve the character and conduct of young women; no copies have survived. She remains known chiefly for her two-volume novel, *Female Quixotism: Exhibited in the Romantic Opinions and Extravagant Adventures of Dorcasina Sheldon* (1801), a satire on literary tastes and an expression of American intellectual independence.

Tenskwatawa (b. Lauliwasikau) (?1768–?1837) Shawnee resistance leader; born on the Mad River near present-day Springfield, Ohio (brother of Tecumseh). A vision in 1805 led him to believe that Indians must reject the ways of whites and return to their traditions; his prediction of a solar eclipse in 1806 was largely responsible for his fame as "The Prophet." He worked with his brother Tecumseh to unite Indians as common owners of the land throughout the then Northwest Territory. In 1811, with Tecumseh away, he led his people to defeat in the Battle of Tippecanoe. His credibility gone, he moved to Canada but returned in 1826 to move west with his people.

Terhune, Albert Payson (1872–1942) writer; born in Newark, N.J. His mother was Mary Virginia Hawes Terhune ("Marion Harland") (1830–1922), a successful writer of books on household management such as *Common Sense in the Household* (1871). Albert and his family lived in Europe (1876–78), returned to Springfield, Mass. (1878–84), and settled in Brooklyn, N.Y. His father was a minister, and the family summered at Sunnybank, in Pompton Lakes, N.J., the setting of many books by Terhune. After study at Columbia University (B.A. 1893), he toured Europe and the Near East with his mother, then returned to New York City to work as a reporter for the *Evening World* (1894–1914). From 1912 on, he lived at Sunnybank. He wrote many magazine stories and is best known for his collie stories for young readers, such as *Lad, A Dog* (1919).

Terkel, (Louis) "Studs" (1912–) interviewer, actor, writer; born in New York City. His studies at the University of Chicago culminated in a law degree (1934) but after failing the bar exams, he took a job with the federal government as a statistician. He returned to Chicago in 1935, joined the Federal Writer's Project, wrote weekly radio shows for WGN, and also played the villain in several radio soap operas. In the late 1930s he acted with the Chicago Repertory Theater, where he continued through the 1940s and the 1950s while renaming himself "Studs" after the James T. Farrell character, Studs Lonigan. In the 1940s he broadcast news and sports, and as a disc jockey, he promoted, among others, Mahalia Jackson. From about 1949–53 he hosted *Stud's Place,* a Chicago television program where he played a bartender who interviewed various distinguished guests. He was blacklisted in 1953 for "signing an anti-Jim Crow petition," and, unable to get work, he turned to a socially progressive radio station, WFMT. Practically a volunteer in the beginning, he developed the hour-long radio program that became the *Studs Terkel Show* and which in 1962 won the prestigious Pre-Italia Award. In 1967 his lifelong fascination with "the man of inchoate thought" yielded the first of his oral histories called *Division Street: America.* It was followed by a series of edited interviews, including *Hard Times: An Oral History of the Great Depression* (1970), *Working: People Talk About What They Do All Day and How They Feel About What They Do* (1974), and *Race: How Blacks and Whites Feel and Think About the American Obsession* (1991).

Terman, Frederick E. (Emmons) (1900–82) electrical engineer, educator; born in English, Ind. During World War II he helped develop antiradar devices, including noise transmitters and the aluminum foil "window," and electronic jammers used during the invasion of Normandy. From 1925 to 1965 he was associated with Stanford University.

Terman, Lewis (Madison) (1877–1956) educational psychologist; born in Johnson County, Ind. This Stanford University professor (1910–42) coined the term "I.Q.," developed intelligence tests for the army during World War I, and published the widely used Stanford-Binet intelligence test in *The Measurement of Intelligence* (1916). The last volume of Terman's classic 30-year study of gifted children was published in 1959.

Terrell, Mary Church (1863–1954) civil rights activist; born in Memphis, Tenn. The daughter of former slaves, Terrell's life spanned the period from the Emancipation Proclamation to the Supreme Court's decision in *Brown* v. *Board of Education* that school segregation was illegal. After graduating from Oberlin College (1884), she taught for several years, then moved to Europe seeking greater freedom both as an African-American and as a woman. Returning to the United States after two years, she founded the National Association of Colored Women (NACW) in 1896; as NACW president, she spearheaded attempts to aid mothers and children. After decades of quiet service, in the 1950s she led the fight to desegregate restaurants in Washington, D.C., picketing with the aid of a cane. On June 8, 1953, the district court declared Washington's segregated restaurants illegal.

Terry, Alfred Howe (1827–90) soldier; born in Hartford, Conn. A Connecticut militia officer, he commanded federal forces from First Bull Run (July 1861) to the final battles in the Carolinas. One of 15 officers to receive the "Thanks of Congress" (for taking Fort Fisher, N.C.), he remained in the regular army after the Civil War and saw extensive service on the frontier. He was in command of the expedition against the Sioux when Custer met his fate at Little Big Horn in June 1876. He sat on several boards that negotiated treaties with Native Americans.

Terry, David Smith (1823–89) judge; born in Todd County, Ky. He served with the Texas Rangers in the Mexican War and then settled in Stockton, Calif., where he read and practiced law. He was elected associate justice (1855) and chief justice (1857) of the California Supreme Court. Often rash and violent, he killed Senator David Broderick in a duel but was acquitted of murder (1859). He commanded a Confederate regiment and brigade in Texas; with the end of the Civil War, he went to Mexico but he returned to practice law in Stockton, Calif. (1869–89). He was shot and killed by a bodyguard assigned to protect a California judge whom Terry had threatened after a particularly complicated divorce case (in which Terry had married the woman involved).

Terry, Eli (1772–1852) inventor, clock manufacturer; born in East Windsor, Conn. After an apprenticeship (1786–92), he made his first clocks by hand. He turned to using water power to drive his tools (1800) when he established the U.S.A.'s first clock factory in Plymouth, Conn. In 1807 he formed a partnership with Seth Thomas and their factory eventually produced 10,000–12,000 clocks per year. Terry himself patented ten improvements in clockworks and introduced several popular innovations in clock design.

Terry, Sonny (b. Sanders Terrel) (1911–86) blues singer, harmonica player; born in Greensboro, Ga. He learned harmonica as a child and began earning a living in the streets at a young age. In 1938 he performed at the "From Spirituals to Swing" concert at Carnegie Hall, displaying a unique virtuosity that involved bending and modulating notes. From the 1940s into the 1980s he performed widely with guitarist Brownie McGhee but also cut many solo albums.

Terzaghi, Karl (1868–1963) engineer; born in Prague, Czechoslovakia. After graduating from an Austrian technical college, he practiced engineering in Vienna; in 1916 he went to Istanbul to teach and in 1918 joined the faculty of Robert College there. He first came to the U.S.A. in 1925 to teach at the Massachusetts Institute of Technology (1925–29), then went to Vienna to teach (1929–38), returning to the U.S.A. in 1939; he became a citizen in 1943 and taught at Harvard (1946–56). His entire career was devoted to establishing the modern discipline of soil mechanics – the behavior of soil under stress – and foundation engineering, thereby enabling engineers to design safe foundations, earth dams, etc., on a scientific basis.

Tesla, Nikola (1856–1943) electrical engineer, inventor; born in Smiljan Lika, Croatia. Educated in Austria and Czechoslovakia, he worked as an electrical engineer in Paris before coming to the U.S.A. (1884) to seek support for one of his inventions. He went to work for Thomas Edison but resigned in 1885 and set up his own laboratory. Never good at personal relations or business, he was forced out of his firm, but he started another in 1887 and finally succeeded with his original invention, an electro-magnetic motor that would be the basis of most alternating-current machinery. He sold the patents to Westinghouse in 1888, but after working with that company for a year, he quit and thereafter worked on his own. He continued to produce some important inventions involving high-frequency electricity – the Tesla coil, a resonant air-core transformer, being one such – and his alternating-current system illuminated the Chicago World's Fair (1893) and led to the construction of the Niagara Falls hydroelectric generating plant (1896). His reputation among both scientists and the

public was now at its peak but he became increasingly more reclusive and eccentric. He continued to come up with new inventions, including one for wireless transmission of electricity and one for radio controlled craft; he also anticipated pulsed radar, harnessing solar power, and radio communication with other planets, but his eccentricities prevented him from getting either a fair hearing or profits. Although he could well have used the money, in 1912 he refused the Nobel Prize in physics because he claimed that corecipient Thomas Edison was not a true scientist. He spent his final years feeding and housing pigeons and living mainly off an annual honorarium from his homeland. The *tesla,* a unit of magnetic flow density, is named after him.

Thacher, John Boyd (1847–1909) book collector, public official, writer; born in Albany, N.Y. Associated with his family's manufacturing firm for most of his life, he was also a state senator and mayor of Albany and, as a hobby, collected incunabula and valuable materials on Christopher Columbus, of whom he wrote a biography.

Thalberg, Irving G. (Grant) (1899–1936) movie executive; born in New York City. Sickly as a youth, he mastered shorthand and typing and at age 19 became the secretary to Carl Laemmle, head of Universal Film Manufacturing. His understanding of the film business led Laemmle to put him in charge of reorganizing Universal's Hollywood studios in 1919. In 1923 he was hired by Louis B. Mayer, becoming supervisor of production for the newly formed Metro-Goldwyn-Mayer (MGM). Despite his youth, he combined strong administrative decisiveness with a genius for recognizing what made a successful movie and he helped to make MGM a leading studio, involving himself in every detail and demanding excellence. He introduced the "sneak preview" to gauge audience response before releasing a film. A 1932 heart attack forced him to retire prematurely, but since 1937 the Academy of Motion Pictures has honored outstanding producers with the Irving G. Thalberg Award.

Tharp, Twyla (1941–   ) choreographer, modern dancer; born in Portland, Ind. Trained in ballet and modern dance, she performed with the Paul Taylor Dance Company (1963–65) before forming her own company. Her early abstract works such as *Push Comes to Shove* (1975), and dances for the movies *Hair* (1979) and *White Knights* (1985), have evolved into more popular works for ballet companies. After disbanding her company in 1987, she worked as artistic associate for the American Ballet Theatre for two years, subsequently choreographing pieces for other leading ballet companies. In 1992 she performed her pieces with a "pickup" troupe of outstanding dancers, assembled for a two-week engagement in New York City, and published her autobiography, *Push Comes to Shove.*

Tharpe, Sister Rosetta (b. Nubin) (1915–73) gospel musician; born in Cotton Plant, Ark. She began singing and playing guitar in church and by 1938 was a featured soloist in Cotton Club revues backed by Cab Calloway and Lucky Millinder. Beginning in 1944 she developed a huge following in the burgeoning gospel market, which she maintained for the rest of her life.

Thayer, Abbot (Handerson) (1849–1921) painter; born in Boston, Mass. He attended the National Academy of Design, New York (c. 1868), and studied in Paris (1875–79). After his return to New York (1879–1901), he settled in Dublin, N.H. (1901). A sentimental genre painter, he is remembered for his theories concerning the protective coloration of animals, known as "Thayer's Law."

Thayer, Ernest Lawrence (1863–1940) poet, businessman; born in Lawrence, Mass. His father owned several woolen mills, one in Worcester, Mass., where Ernest grew up. At Harvard he was regarded as a brilliant philosophy student of William James; he also contributed to the annual Hasty Pudding plays and was an editor of the Harvard *Lampoon.* After graduating with honors (1885), he went to Paris, where his classmate/friend, William Randolph Hearst, invited him to contribute a humor column to the *San Francisco Examiner;* Thayer did so under the by-line "Phin" (1886–88), writing a series of humorous ballads that included *Casey* (appearing June 3, 1888, and for which he was paid $5). It went generally unnoticed until William De Wolf Hopper, a vaudeville comedian/comic opera singer of the day, began to recite it (starting late 1888 or early 1889); it so caught on that he recited it over 10,000 times in the ensuing years. Thayer returned to Worcester in 1887 and unenthusiastically managed one of the family's mills; he retired after about 20 years, and ended up in Santa Barbara, Calif., in 1912, where he married a widow and spent the rest of his life. As *Casey at the Bat* (its widely known title) increased in popularity, many tried to claim authorship (and many ballplayers claimed to have been the original Casey), but Thayer is recognized as the true author. His only other published poems were several more humorous ballads for Hearst's *New York Journal* (1896–97). For many years he found it a nuisance to be associated with the ballad, but in his final years he came to accept that he had written a classic of its kind. It has inspired many musical works, movies, paintings, sculptures and – above all – endless parodies and variations.

Thayer, James Bradley (1831–1902) jurist; born in Haverhill, Mass. Educated at Harvard, he was admitted to the Boston bar in 1856 and conducted a private practice while contributing to legal volumes. He then became a professor of law at Harvard (1874–1902) and was one of those who introduced the case system to the law school. He wrote *Cases on Constitutional Law* (1895), *A Preliminary Treatise on Evidence* (1898), and numerous other works. Off the bench he urged tariff reform and allotment of lands to Native Americans. He published a variety of nonlegal works, including reviews of translations from Latin and Greek and a biography of John Marshall.

Thayer, Nathaniel (1808–83) financier, philanthropist; born in Lancaster, Mass. He came from a family that included many distinguished ministers. He became a partner in a Boston commerce house, trading with the West Indies (1829). He joined his brother in banking at John E. Thayer & Brother (1840). He became the principal director (1857), and through railroad financing, became one of the wealthiest men in New England. An overseer of Harvard College (after 1866), he contributed generously to that institution.

Thayer, Sylvanus (1785–1872) engineer, educator; born in Braintree, Mass. After graduating from Dartmouth and a year at West Point, he served by constructing fortifications (1809–15). Appointed superintendent of West Point (1817–33), he totally transformed it into a first-rate institution – thereby becoming known as "the father of West Point" – but his rigid discipline led to so much unrest among cadets that he was forced to resign. From 1833 on he supervised the construction of harbor improvements and coastal fortifications in New England.

Theiler, Max (1899–1972) physician; born near Pretoria, South Africa. He emigrated to the United States in 1922. In 1927 he and two other medical researchers proved that yellow fever is caused by a virus, not bacteria. Between 1936 and 1940, he developed and tested a safe and effective vaccine against yellow fever. He was affiliated with Harvard Medical School (1922–30), the Rockefeller Institute (1930–64), and Yale Medical School (1964–67). He was awarded the Nobel Prize in medicine (1951).

Theobald, Robert Alfred (1884–1957) naval officer; born in San Francisco. He engaged in heated debates with Captain Richmond K. Turner at the Naval War College (1936–38) regarding the relative importance of naval and air forces. He commanded the North Pacific Force (1942–43). He criticized President Franklin Roosevelt in *The Final Secret of Pearl Harbor* (1954).

Theroux, Paul (Edward) (1941–) writer; born in Medford, Mass. He studied at the University of Maine (1959–60), the University of Massachusetts (B.A. 1963), and Syracuse University (1963). He was a lecturer in English in Malawi as a member of the Peace Corps (1963–65), but was expelled on the charge of spying. He continued to teach in Uganda (1965–68), and in Singapore (1968–71). He settled in London, England, and wrote novels, short stories, children's books, a screenplay, and numerous travel books. He wrote of the expatriate life, and won critical praise for travel accounts, such as *The Great Railway Bazaar: By Train Through Asia* (1975), and for novels, notably *The Mosquito Coast* (1982). He also wrote a critical appraisal of his teacher and mentor in *V. S. Naipaul: An Introduction to His Works* (1972).

Thimann, Kenneth Vivian (1904–) plant physiologist; born in Ashford, England. He taught in London (1926–30), then came to the U.S.A. to join the California Institute of Technology (1930–35). There, he and Frits Went codiscovered natural auxin, a hormone regulating both growth and its selective inhibition in plants; Thimann also demonstrated auxin-like functions in certain synthetic substances. At Harvard (1935–65), he investigated the physiology of bacteria, fungi, protozoa, and forest trees. He published his studies of plant senescence (1980) while at the University of California: Santa Cruz (1965–84).

Thomas, Augustus (1857–1934) playwright; born in St. Louis, Mo. Praised for his use of distinctly American material, his first popular success was *Alabama* (1891), based on a family conflict in the wake of the Civil War. He wrote or adapted over 65 plays, mostly conventional in technique and narrow in appeal and all forgotten, but he led the way in establishing a true American drama.

Thomas, (Christian Friedrich) Theodore (1835–1905) conductor; born in Esens, Germany. Thomas studied violin before coming the U.S.A. with his family in 1845. After peripatetic years playing violin around the country, he made his conducting debut in New York in 1860; two years later he founded the Thomas Orchestra, which played in New York and toured the U.S.A. until 1878, all to immense acclaim. From 1862 Thomas was also co-conductor of the Brooklyn Philharmonic, and in 1877 took over the New York Philharmonic. Except for 1878 to 1880, when he served as president of an institution he founded, the Cincinnati College of

Music, Thomas conducted in New York and Brooklyn until 1891. In that year he was named conductor of the Chicago Orchestra (later Symphony), where he remained until his death. He was a dynamic apostle of the symphony orchestra in the U.S.A., perhaps doing more to foster classical music than any other in the country's history; besides establishing the older European repertoire, he introduced to the U.S.A. the music of Tchaikovsky, Dvořák, Bruckner, Richard Strauss, and many others.

Thomas, Clarence (1948–) Supreme Court justice; born in Pin Point, Ga. Shaped by his poor-but-proud family and his Catholic schooling, he went on to graduate from Holy Cross College and Yale Law School and to espouse conservative views on the situation of his fellow African-Americans. He worked as assistant secretary of education (1981) and then headed the Equal Employment Opportunity Commission (1981–89). President Bush appointed him to the federal court of appeals (1990–91) and to the U.S. Supreme Court, where, only after a highly controversial Senate hearing and vote, did he become the second African-American to take a seat (1991).

Thomas, Cyrus (1825–1910) entomologist, ethnologist; born in Kingsport, Tenn. He was a lawyer and minister turned scientist. As state entomologist he wrote a report on Illinois insects (1877–82). Appointed archaeology chief of the Bureau of American Ethnology (1882), he directed a major survey of Indian mounds and pioneered Maya studies.

Thomas, E. (Edward) Donnall (1920–) surgeon, oncologist; born in Mart, Texas. He was a practicing hematologist and researcher at several northeastern hospitals before joining Columbia University (1956–63); he then moved to the University of Washington (1963). He began his pioneering studies of bone marrow transplants for treatment of human leukemia in the 1950s. He performed the first successful brother-sister bone marrow transplant in 1970, after persevering with his research on histocompatibility typing and use of immunosuppressant drugs. He shared the 1990 Nobel Prize in medicine with kidney transplant innovator Joseph Murray.

Thomas, George Henry (1816–70) soldier; born in Southampton County, Va. A West Point graduate (1840), he fought in the Seminole War, on the western frontier, and in the Mexican War. After teaching at West Point (1851–55) he joined a new cavalry division. Although a Virginian, he stayed with the Union and commanded units at several major campaigns and battles. His greatest moment came at Chickamauga (1863), where his stubborn defense earned him the sobriquet "Rock of Chickamauga." Forces under Thomas's command stormed Missionary Ridge at Chattanooga (1863), and his Army of the Cumberland decisively defeated a Confederate army under Hood at Franklin and Nashville, Tenn. (Nov.–Dec. 1864), for which he was one of 15 officers voted "Thanks of Congress." He stayed in the army after the war and died in San Francisco while in command of the Military Division of the Pacific.

Thomas, Isaiah (1749–1831) printer, publisher; born in Boston, Mass. The foremost 18th-century American publisher, he learned his trade as a young apprentice and in 1770 cofounded in Boston a tabloid called the *Massachusetts Spy;* soon becoming sole owner, he made it a pro-patriot organ. After fighting in the American Revolution, he returned to build up a prosperous printing, publishing, and retail bookselling business, centered in Worcester, Mass., with branches in several cities. Thomas published over 400 titles, including the most important literary works of the time. He published the first English-language Bible and first dictionary printed in America, the first American edition of the popular *Mother Goose's Melody,* and a speller that sold 300,000 copies. He was the first major U.S. publisher of children's books. Retiring in affluence in 1802, he wrote a well-regarded two-volume *History of Printing in America* (1810) and in 1812 founded the American Antiquarian Society.

Thomas, Jesse Burgess (1777–1853) U.S. senator; born in Sheperdstown, Va. (now W.Va.) He settled in Indiana Territory about 1803 and held several offices while working to separate Illinois as an independent territory. Appointed a federal judge in the new Illinois Territory (1809–18), he then became one of the new state's first two senators (Dem., Ill.; 1818–29). He proposed the amendment calling for admission of Maine and Missouri but prohibiting slavery above 36° 30′ that became part of the Missouri Compromise Bill (1820). After leaving the Senate, he moved to Ohio and saw service in the Black Hawk War (1832) and managed his wife's extensive property there; he committed suicide less than two years after her death.

Thomas, John Charles (1891–1960) baritone; born in Meyersdale, Pa. He was a well-known recitalist and musical comedy singer when he made his operatic debut in 1924; he sang at the Metropolitan Opera from 1934 to 1943.

Thomas, John Parnell (b. Feeney, Jr.) (1895–1970) U.S. representative; born in Jersey City, N.J. A counterespionage officer during World War I, he sold bonds at Paine Webber (1924–41). A Republican mayor and New Jersey assemblyman before going to the U.S. House of Representatives (1937–49), he joined the conservative Dies Committee in 1939 and chaired the notorious House Un-American Activities Committee (1947–50), punishing "unfriendly" witnesses from Hollywood with prison terms. Indicted for padding his congressional payroll in 1949, he served time in federal prison, then retired to Florida.

Thomas, Lewis (1913–93) physician, author, educator; born in Flushing, N.Y. A surgeon's son, he graduated from Princeton (1933) and Harvard Medical School (1937) and taught medicine at Johns Hopkins, Tulane, the University of Minnesota, New York University, and Yale before becoming a professor of medicine at the Medical School of Cornell in New York City in 1973. He served as chief executive officer of the Sloan-Kettering Cancer Center, New York City, from 1973–80 and was a member of many public and private advisory agencies. A best-selling author, he discussed the place of humans in the biological world in such books as *The Lives of a Cell* (1974), *Late Night Thoughts on Listening to Mahler's Ninth Symphony* (1983), and *The Fragile Species* (1992). *The Lives of a Cell* won a National Book Award in 1975.

Thomas, Lorenzo (1804–75) soldier; born in New Castle, Del. A West Point graduate (1823), he fought in the Seminole War and Mexican War. He was adjutant general of the Federal Army (1861–63) before being assigned to recruit and organize freed slaves for Union service (1863–65). Reappointed adjutant general (1868), he became involved in an unseemly power struggle with Secretary of War Edwin Stanton that led to the impeachment of President Andrew Johnson in 1868.

Thomas, Lowell (Jackson) (1892–1981) news commentator, author; born in Woodington, Ohio. After earning two M.A.s (University of Denver and Princeton), and working as a reporter and teacher, he took a trip to Alaska (1915). His resultant travelogue led President Woodrow Wilson to commission him to film and record ongoing World War I events; this led to his contacts with Colonel T. E. Lawrence in the Middle East and eventually to his best-selling book, *With Lawrence in Arabia* (1924). Immediately after the war he began a career as a lecturer and as a world traveler; his encircling the entire globe by airplane during 1926–27 was one of the first promotions of the potential of aviation. From 1930–76 he was a radio newscaster, but he managed to travel to exotic places around the world, narrate Movietone newsreels (1935–52) and travelogues for Twentieth Century-Fox, and write numerous books. He broadcast from many combat zones during World War II and in 1949 he was invited to Tibet by the Dalai Lama. He profiled outstanding historical figures on Public Broadcasting System's *Lowell Thomas Remembers* (1976–79) and published a two-part autobiography, *Good Evening Everybody* (1977) and *So Long Until Tomorrow* (1978).

Thomas, (Martha) Carey (1857–1935) educator, feminist; born in Baltimore, Md. She was dean (1885–1908) and president (1894–1922) of the new Bryn Mawr College, where she pioneered graduate study for women. By insisting on rigorous academic standards, she led the drive to improve standards of higher education generally. Imposing the condition of women's admission, Thomas helped found Johns Hopkins Medical School.

Thomas, Michael Tilson (1944–) conductor; born in Hollywood, Calif. A precocious talent, he was thrust into fame at age 25 when as an assistant he took over a concert of the Boston Symphony from ailing William Steinberg. He went on to guest-conduct widely and led the Buffalo Philharmonic (1971–79) and the London Symphony (1988).

Thomas, Norman (Mattoon) (1884–1968) reformer, socialist; born in Marion, Ohio. An ordained Presbyterian minister (1911), he served among the poor of New York City and became convinced that traditional religions and political parties were not satisfying contemporary American needs. He helped establish the Civil Liberties Bureau of the American Union Against Militarism (1917), the precursor to the American Civil Liberties Union (ACLU), which he helped found in 1920. Drawn to socialism, he officially joined the Socialist Party (1918) and gave up his pastorate, although he remained a minister through 1931. Associate editor of the *Nation* (1921–22) and codirector of the League for Industrial Democracy (1922–37), he ran unsuccessfully as a Socialist for a series of offices in New York. As the leader of the Socialist Party after 1926, he ran for president six times (1928–48). A pacifist, he tentatively supported World War II after Pearl Harbor, protested Japanese-Americans' internment, was critical of America dropping the atomic bomb, and founded the Post-War Council to support world peace. Devoted to a democratic socialism, he was opposed to Communists and purged them from the ranks of the ACLU (1940). He opposed the Vietnam War. To the end of his life he remained an active lecturer and a "presence" on the American public stage. Criticized as a poor organizer for failing to heal factional wounds or attending to party work, he was charged with the demise of socialism in this country, but historians argue that socialism had been defeated by the New Deal before he took control of the party. He has also been credited with working for many social reforms long before they became accepted and put into law.

Thomas, Seth (1785–1859) clockmaker; born in Wolcott, Conn. He started out as a skillful woodworker invited to manufacture clocks in partnership with Eli Terry and Silas Hoadley (1807–12). He began his own factory in 1812 and in 1814 bought the rights to Terry's popular shelf clock, developing a highly successful business, which he incorporated as Seth Thomas Clock Company in Plymouth, Conn. (an area which was later renamed Thomaston in his honor). He became extremely rich from his clock manufacturing and other enterprises including a cotton mill and a brass-rolling and wiremaking factory.

Thomas, William I. (Isaac) (1863–1947) sociologist; born in Russell County, Va. He began as an English professor at Oberlin College (1889–95) before getting a Ph.D. in sociology at the University of Chicago. Dismissed from the University of Chicago faculty (1894–1918) after a sex scandal, he never again held a permanent appointment, but obtained research funding and visiting professorships. An empiricist, he helped to make sociology a scientific discipline; he also pioneered the study of social psychology. His most important books were *Source Book for Social Origins* (1909) and *The Polish Peasant in Europe and America* (coauthored, 5 vols. 1918–20).

Thompson, Benjamin (1919–) architect, urban designer; born in St. Paul, Minn. He attended the University of Virginia before graduating from Yale, then served in the U.S. Navy in World War II (1941–45). After the war, he and some young architect friends at Harvard's architecture school invited the school's head, Walter Gropius, to start a firm with them; it was known as Architects' Collaborative and took the lead in designing classic modern buildings. In 1953, Thompson and his wife Jane Thompson, an editor and curator, started Design Research, a Cambridge (Mass.)-based firm that imported and sold the latest in European furnishings and housewares. Thompson is credited with suggesting (about 1967) that Boston renovate its fading Faneuil Hall-Quincy Market neighborhood to attract people. He and his firm won the design competition (and developer James Rouse became their collaborator). Their success in Boston led to the firm – now Benjamin Thompson Associates – to take on other renovation projects such as the Union Station in Washington, D.C., and the Ordway Theatre in St. Paul, Minn. Thompson won the American Institute of Architects' gold medal in 1992.

Thompson, Benjamin (often called by title, Count Rumford) (1753–1814) scientist, administrator; born in Woburn, Mass. He showed a youthful aptitude for mathematics and science, and after a three-year apprenticeship with a Salem, Mass., merchant, he studied medicine and taught school briefly. In 1772 he married a wealthy widow and accepted a British commission as major in a New Hampshire regiment. As the American Revolution began to heat up, he seemed unable to join one side or the other, but when he was denied a commission in the Continental army, he cast his lot with the Loyalists; after the British evacuated Boston (March 1776), he fled to England (and left his wife behind). Always adept at ingratiating himself with the powerful, he got himself elected to the prestigious Royal Society (1779). He returned to America as a lieutenant colonel (1781–83) and saw some combat – he would be knighted in 1784 – and then went on to serve the Prince of Bavaria for many of the next 18 years. While in Munich, he helped improve conditions for both the Bavarian army and the poor and unemployed; for his services he was made a count of the Holy Roman Empire – choosing for his title the name of his former wife's hometown, Rumford (now Concord), N.H. Between 1795–1802 he spent much time in England, but in 1803 he settled permanently in France; he was briefly married to the widow of the great French chemist, Lavoisier. Although something of a dilettante-tinkerer – he invented a calorimeter, a photometer, and the drip-coffee maker – he did carry on scientific and mechanical experiments, and in his studies of heat he made a major contribution: by observing the boring of cannons in Munich, he was the first to understand that heat is a form of motion. Never shy about promoting himself, he endowed the Rumford Medals of the Royal Society *and* the American Academy of Arts and Sciences as well as the Rumford chair of science at Harvard.

Thompson, Bob (1937–66) painter; born in Louisville, Ky. He studied at the Boston Museum School (1955), the University of Louisville (1955–58), traveled extensively, and lived in many places including New York and Paris. A surrealist artist, he died of a lung hemorrhage when he was 29 years old.

Thompson, Clara (Mabel) (1893–1958) psychoanalyst; born in Providence, R.I. She attended Pembroke, the women's college affiliated with Brown University (1912–16), and received her M.D. from Johns Hopkins University (1920). She was influenced by William Alanson White, Harry Stack Sullivan, Sandor Ferenczi, Karen Horney, and other neo-Freudians, and taught at the New York Psychoanalytic Institute (1933–41). In a famous schism in the American psychoanalytic community, in 1943 she helped establish the William Alanson White Institute (director, 1946–58), a training school. She continued her private practice and made her major contributions to psychoanalysis through her influence on students and colleagues. She did, however, publish some original work on women and sexuality, her best-known book being *Psychoanalysis: Evolution and Development* (with Patrick Mullahy, 1950).

Thompson, Dorothy (1894–1961) journalist; born in Lancaster, N.Y. A foreign correspondent in Vienna and Berlin during the 1920s, she later wrote a syndicated column (1936–57) and espoused vehemently anti-Nazi views prior to World War II. Her books include *New Russia* (1928) and *Let the Record Speak* (1939). She was married to Sinclair Lewis from 1928 to 1942.

Thompson, Edward Herbert (1856–1935) explorer, archaeologist; born in Worcester, Mass. Untrained in archaeology, geology, or fieldwork, he managed to get himself sent as U.S. consul to Mexico (1885), expressly to investigate Maya sites, and for 40 years he sent back a stream of valuable artifacts and information, particularly from Chichén Itzá. His popular books stimulated public interest in Maya culture.

Thompson, Homer (Armstrong) (1906–) archaeologist; born in Devlin, Ontario, Canada. He was educated at the University of Michigan (Ph.D. 1929) and became a naturalized U.S. citizen. He was simultaneously professor of classical archaeology at the Institute for Advanced Study at Princeton and field director of the Athenian agora (1947–77). An expert on the history and monuments of Athens, his

Guide to the Athenian Agora (1976) was admired by both scholars and nonspecialists.

Thompson, James D. (David) (1920–73) sociologist; born in Indianapolis, Ind. He climaxed a long academic career in sociology and business administration teaching at Vanderbilt University (1968–73). He specialized in social organization and organizational change and development. His many publications include *Organizations in Action* (1967).

Thompson, James R. (1936–) governor; born in Chicago. A lawyer, he was assistant state's attorney for Cook County (1959–64), arguing criminal civil rights cases before the Illinois and U.S. Supreme Courts. A Northwestern assistant law professor (1964–69), he became U.S. attorney (1971–75), prosecuting corrupt public officials. As Republican governor of Illinois (1977–87), he passed a "Class X" crime law, mandating a minimum six-year sentence for violent crimes. He left office and returned to practicing law.

Thompson, Jerome B. (1814–66) painter; born in Middleboro, Mass. He began as a sign painter, moved to New York City (1835), and became a portrait painter. After travel in England (1852), he settled in New Jersey and painted rural genre scenes, as in *Apple Gathering* (1856).

Thompson, J. (James) Walter (1847–1928) advertising executive; born in Pittsfield, Mass. He served in the Union navy in the Civil War. In 1867 he joined William Carlton's New York advertising agency, which he bought in 1878 and turned into the most successful agency in history. He virtually created modern advertising, transforming advertising into a primary sales tool by persuading magazines and major clients (Eastman Kodak, Prudential Insurance) of its respectability; his success in placing advertising in magazines made national product campaigns possible. Believing that advertising had peaked, he sold the agency in 1916 and devoted himself to such interests as yachting.

Thompson, Kay (1912–) actress, singer, writer; born in St. Louis, Mo. She began her career as a pianist (1928), and built a career as a singer, arranger, composer, choreographer, and actress. Based primarily in Beverly Hills, Calif., she launched a second career with her children's series, beginning with *Eloise: A Book for Precocious Grown Ups* (1955).

Thompson, Kenneth L. (1943–) computer scientist, engineer; born in New Orleans. With Dennis Ritchie, he developed C language and UNIX (1973) at American Telephone & Telegraph Bell Laboratories in Murray Hill, N.J., which he joined in 1966. His research centered on programming languages, operating systems, and computer games. He codeveloped several chess-playing machines.

Thompson, Llewellyn E., Jr. (1904–72) diplomat, Kremlinologist; born in Los Animas, Colo. He entered the Foreign Service in 1929 and served in Switzerland, the Soviet Union, and Great Britain (1929–46). An expert on Eastern European and Soviet affairs, he helped to negotiate the Austrian State Treaty (1952–55). As ambassador to the Soviet Union (1957–62, 1967–69) he was known for his tact and "quiet diplomacy." He maintained an excellent rapport with the top Soviet leaders during tense moments such as the U-2 incident and the Berlin crisis.

Thompson, Oscar (1887–1945) music critic; born in Crawfordsville, Ind. He began with *Musical America* in 1919 and later wrote for the *New York Evening Post* and *New York Sun;* he also taught at Curtis Institute. His books include *Debussy, Man and Artist* (1937).

Thompson, Randall (1899–1984) composer; born in New York City. Harvard-educated, he taught at various schools including Harvard (1948–65) while composing genteel, often nationalistic works that were popular mainly in the 1940s and 1950s.

Thompson, Samuel (1769–1843) holistic physician; born in Alstead, N.H. Lame from birth, son of a farmer, he preferred studying the curative powers of plants to working on the farm. With minimal formal education, he developed a theory of disease and a curative process (relying on such plants as *lobelia* and cayenne pepper) which he patented in 1813 and 1823. Author of *Learned Quackery Exposed* (1824), he franchised his system and fought litigious attacks from old-school physicians. Although his knowledge was flawed, he anticipated certain modern theories of health and medicine.

Thompson, Smith (1768–1843) Supreme Court justice; born in Amenia, N.Y. He served the New York legislature (1800–02) and the state supreme court (1802–18). President Monroe named him secretary of the navy (1818–23) and to the U.S. Supreme Court (1823–43). An antinationalist, he often dissented from the majority of the court.

Thompson, Stith (1885–1976) folklorist; born in Bloomfield, Ky. At Indiana University (1921–55) he created a preeminent center for folklore studies. He established folklore as an academic discipline and founded the Folklore Institutes of America. Among his numerous publications his major contribution was the seminal *Motif-Index of Folk-Literature* (6 vols. 1932–36, revised 1955–58), which catalogues all the recurrent subjects, characters, themes, etc., in the folklore of the world.

Thompson, Victor A. (Alexander) (1912–   ) political scientist; born in Hannah, N.D. He earned a Ph.D. from Columbia University. His academic career began at Illinois Institute of Technology (1950–62) and ended at the University of Florida: Gainesville (1971–81). His books on bureaucracy and public administration include *Bureaucracy and Innovation* (1969) and *Bureaucracy and the Modern World* (1976).

Thompson, Waddy (1798–1868) U.S. representative; born in Pickensville, S.C. A lawyer in Greenville, he was a Whig member of the South Carolina legislature (1826–30) who sought to nullify federal influence over his state. In Congress (Whig; 1835–41) he opposed antislavery petitions. As ambassador to Mexico (1842–44), he successfully negotiated the release of some 300 North American prisoners from the war between Texas and Mexico; he also opened the door for American immigration into California and generally improved relations between the two countries. He returned to South Carolina to practice law and opposed the war with Mexico. He also opposed secession but he lost his fortune during the Civil War.

Thompson, William (Hale) ("Big Bill") (1869–1944) mayor; born in Boston, Mass. Born to wealth, he tried his hand at ranching in the West, then returned to Chicago where – except for a brief term as an alderman – he showed little interest in anything except sports. Backed by Chicago's political boss, Fred Lundin, he got himself elected mayor for two terms (1916–24); he dropped out of politics because Lundin was indicted for fraud and race riots marred his term, but he got himself reelected for another term (1928–32), this time backed by Al Capone, the crime boss. Thompson's

campaign to purge the school board and school libraries of all "pro-British" elements resulted in his being derided throughout America. His political career faded out and he was the target of a number of suits charging corruption.

Thomson, Elihu (1853–1937) electrical engineer, inventor; born in Manchester, England. He emigrated to America with his family at age 5 and attended Philadelphia schools. With the support of Edwin J. Houston (1847–1914), a teacher at a Philadelphia high school where Thomson also taught (1870–76), Thomson began experimenting with electricity. Thomson and Houston together invented an arc street-lighting system (patented 1881) and established a company to manufacture this and other innovations. Thomson stayed on as a consultant when in 1892 the firm merged with the Edison General Electric Co. to become General Electric Co. He became a lecturer at the Massachusetts Institute of Technology (MIT) in 1894 and was acting president at MIT from 1920–22. In a long and industrious life he patented some 700 inventions and designs. He was the inventor of electric welding and a centrifugal cream separator, among many other devices, and he helped to develop stereoscopic x-ray pictures.

Thomson, J. (John) Edgar (1808–74) engineer, railroad president; born in Springfield Township, Pa. He learned engineering from his father, started with the Pennsylvania Engineer Corps, and by 1830 was in charge of an engineering division. After studying advanced transportation in Europe, he became chief engineer of the Georgia Railroad (1832). In 1847 he joined the newly incorporated Pennsylvania Railroad to locate the tracks through the Allegheny Mountains, a feat that opened a route from Philadelphia to Pittsburgh by 1854. President of the railroad (1852–74), he bought the state's system of canals and rails (1857) and acquired other railroads that extended the Pennsylvania Railroad to Chicago. He was also instrumental in the creation of the American Steamship Company (1870). Active in Philadelphia civic affairs, he established a foundation, supported by his estate, called the St. John's Orphanage to educate and maintain the daughters of railroad men killed while on duty.

Thomson, Keith Stewart (1938–   ) zoologist; born in Heanor, England. He received his Ph.D. from Harvard (1961), then returned to England to teach and perform research at University College, London University (1963–65). He then joined the Peabody Museum of Natural History at Yale (1965–87) to teach biology and become curator of vertebrate zoology. A Darwinist and specialist on the history of science, he made major contributions to studies of the biology of lower vertebrates, paleozoology, and the morphogenesis and evolution of tetrapods, and wrote for both a lay and scientific readership on "living fossil" fishes such as the coelacanth. He became president of the Academy of Natural Sciences, Philadelphia, in 1987.

Thomson, (Robert Brown) Bobby (1923–   ) baseball player; born in Glasgow, Scotland. He came to the U.S.A. at age two. He participated in one of baseball's most memorable moments in 1951 when he hit a home run – called "the shot heard around the world" – in the ninth inning of a deciding play-off game against the Brooklyn Dodgers to win the National League pennant for the New York Giants. A fine outfielder, he hit 20 or more home runs eight times during his 15-year career (1946–60).

Thomson, Virgil (Garnett) (1896–1989) composer, music

critic; born in Kansas City, Mo. Studying piano and organ as a youth, he grew up knowing the traditional Protestant hymns before going off to continue his music studies at Harvard, in Paris (1922), and at the Mannes Music School in New York City (1923–24). Returning to Paris in 1925, he lived there for the next ten years and developed a style characterized by a sophisticated simplicity, often drawing on American folk themes. He composed symphonies, ballets, choral and chamber music; over 100 musical "portraits" of well-known individuals; two operas with librettos by Gertrude Stein – *Four Saints in Three Acts* (premiered 1934) and *The Mother of Us All* (1947); and several film scores, notably *Louisiana Story* (which won the 1948 Pulitzer Prize). When he returned to the U.S.A., he became the music critic of the *New York Herald Tribune* (1940–54) and continued to "hold court" at his apartment in the Chelsea Hotel in New York City to the end.

Thoreau, Henry David (b. David Henry Thoreau) (1817–62) writer, poet; born in Concord, Mass. After graduating from Harvard (1837), where he began his lifelong habit of keeping journals, he taught briefly in Concord but resigned to protest the disciplinary whipping of students. He helped in his father's pencil factory, and then, with his brother John Thoreau, opened a private school in Concord (1838), based on Transcendentalism, the literary/philosophical movement espoused by Ralph Waldo Emerson, Bronson Alcott, and Orestes Brownson. When John became fatally ill, the school was closed and Thoreau lived in Emerson's home as a sort of handyman while he maintained his practice of writing in his journal; he published a few pieces in the *Dial*, the Transcendentalist journal, wrote poetry, and lectured at the Concord Lyceum. In 1843–44 he went to Staten Island, N.Y., to tutor the children of Emerson's brother, William Emerson, and upon his return built a small structure on Emerson's land alongside Walden Pond. During his stay there – July 4, 1845–Sept, 6, 1847, although by no means every night – he was jailed one night for refusing to pay a poll tax meant to support America's war in Mexico; in 1849 he would publish an essay on this experience, "Resistance to Civil Government" (later known as "On the Duty of Civil Disobedience"), which in its call for passive resistance to unjust laws was to inspire Gandhi and Martin Luther King Jr. (Thomas Carlyle called it the one truly original American contribution to civilization.) During this time he completed the manuscript for *A Week on the Concord and Merrimack Rivers* (1849), a ruminative account of a trip he had taken with his brother John in 1839. The journal he kept at Walden became the source of his most famous book, *Walden, Or Life in the Woods* (1854), in which he set forth his ideas on how an individual should best live to be attuned to his own nature as well as to nature itself. After leaving Walden, he lived with Emerson (1847–49) and then for the rest of his life in his family home; he occasionally worked at the pencil factory and did some surveying work while he made brief trips to such places as Cape Cod, Maine, and (in 1861) as far as Minnesota. By the 1850s he had become greatly concerned over slavery, and having met John Brown in 1857, he would write passionately in his defense. He lived out his final years knowing he had tuberculosis and spent much of his time preparing his journals and manuscripts for what indeed proved to be their posthumous publication. Little known outside his circle in his day, it was not until later in the 20th century that he came to be regarded as one of America's major literary thinkers.

Thornburg, Richard (Lewis) (1932–) governor, cabinet member; born in Pittsburgh, Pa. A corporate lawyer (1959–69) and Pennsylvania's attorney general (1969–75), he became an assistant attorney general in Washington after Watergate (1975–79). As governor of Pennsylvania (Rep., 1975–87), he oversaw evacuation and cleanup after the Three Mile Island nuclear disaster, blocking efforts to reopen the reactor. As Bush's attorney general (1988–91), he prosecuted drug criminals, leaving to make an unsuccessful run for the Senate. He returned to practicing law.

Thorndike, E. L. (Edward Lee) (1874–1949) educational psychologist, author, lexicographer; born in Williamsburg, Mass. Influenced by William James while at Harvard, he took his Ph.D. at Columbia University with a thesis that pioneered the study of animal learning. He then taught at the Teachers College of Columbia University (1899–1941). He was one of the founders of modern educational psychology, applying scientific principles and quantitative treatment to psychological research and by developing a theory of stimulus-response-based learning. His work influenced the curriculum and teaching and evaluation methods of public schools by advocating the accommodation of differing aptitudes among students and by developing some of the first aptitude, achievement, and intelligence tests. He provided the basis for school readers used by a generation of American teachers. His records of Teachers College adult night school students proved that the capacity to learn does not diminish significantly with age; this finding led to an increase in adult education programs. Immensely prolific, he published some 450 books and articles; among the most influential of his 78 books are *Educational Psychology* (3 vols. 1913–14), *The Measurement of Intelligence* (1927), and *The Fundamentals of Learning* (1932). In his later years he also applied his theories to language usage and oversaw the *Thorndike Century* junior (1935) and senior (1941) dictionaries. Along with John Dewey, he was one of the most influential forces on American education in the 20th century.

Thorndike, Israel (1755–1832) sailor, merchant; born in Beverly, Mass. He went to sea at an early age and commanded a privateer during the American Revolution. He became active in the early China trade and was elected to the Massachusetts legislature 13 times. He moved to Boston (1810) and his mansion became a center for political and social discourse.

Thorndike, Lynn (1882–1965) historian; born in Lynn, Mass. (brother of Edward Lee Thorndike). After taking his Ph.D. at Columbia University (1905), he taught at Northwestern (1907–09) and Western Reserve (1909–24) before returning to Columbia as a professor (1924–50). His early reputation as a medievalist came from his teaching and his textbook, *History of Medieval Europe* (1917); but he came to international prominence when he began publishing the first of what proved to be his eight-volume masterwork, *A History of Magic and Experimental Science* (1923–58), in which he was among the first to explore such activities as astrology, alchemy, and magic and their relationships to the development of modern science. He was prolific as an author, admired as a trainer of other professors, and active in various professional groups, including the founding of the History of Science Society (1924).

Thornthwaite, Charles (Warren) (1899–1963) climatologist, geographer; born in Bay County, Mich. He took his Ph.D. at the University of California: Berkeley in 1930, taught at the University of Oklahoma (1927–34), and spent several years with the climatic division of the U.S. Soil Conservation Service. In 1946 he established the Laboratory of Climatology with Seabrook Farms, N.J., where he made important contributions to his field.

Thornton, Charles B. (Bates) ("Tex") (1913–81) conglomerate organizer; born in Haskell, Texas. After developing the armed forces' first statistical management control system during World War II, he led the "Whiz Kids" team that modernized Ford's management (1946–49) and restructured Hughes Aircraft's management (1949–53) before cofounding the electronics company (1953) that became Litton Industries. Through dozens of mergers, Litton became one of the country's first conglomerates. Thornton was president until 1961, then chairman and CEO.

Thornton, William (1759–1828) architect, physician; born in Tortola, British West Indies. After emigrating in 1786 he became a Philadelphia physician. In 1793 he won the competition to design the U.S. Capitol (1793–1827, completed by others); his architectural output was otherwise meager.

Thorpe, (James Francis) Jim (1888–1953) athlete; born near Shawnee, Okla. Voted in 1950 by an Associated Press panel as the greatest athlete of the century, he attended the Carlisle Indian Industrial School in Pennsylvania from 1903 to 1912, where he starred as an All-American football halfback (1911–12). In 1912 he won gold medals in the Olympic decathlon and pentathlon but was later forced to return the medals because he had played semi-professional baseball in 1909, thereby losing his amateur status on a technicality. He excelled at every sport he played, including the traditional Native American sport of lacrosse. He played major league baseball as an outfielder for six years (1913–19) and dominated professional football during its formative years (1917–29). As first president (1920) of the American Professional Football Association, he helped found the National Football League (1922). After retiring from competition, he appeared in movie westerns and spoke on behalf of Native American education. It was not until 1984 that the International Olympic Committee returned the gold medals to Thorpe's family. The Jim Thorpe Memorial is located in Yale, Okla.

Thumb, Tom See STRATTON, CHARLES.

Thurber, James (Grover) (1894–1961) author and cartoonist; born in Columbus, Ohio. One of America's great humorists, he wrote short stories and drew witty cartoons as a staff member of the *New Yorker* magazine from 1927 to 1933 and thereafter as a contributor until his death in 1961. He portrayed the preposterousness and frustrations of modern life in such collections as *The Owl in the Attic and Other Perplexities* (1931), *The Seal in the Bedroom and Other Predicaments* (1932), and *Fables For Our Time* (1940), which included his illustrations and such memorable stories as *The Secret Life of Walter Mitty*. He was also the author of children's books, including *The Thirteen Clocks* (1950), and coauthored with Elliot Nugent the Broadway comedy, *The Male Animal* (1940). As a youngster he lost the sight in his

left eye, and in his mid-forties he eventually lost the vision in his other eye, thereby writing as many of his stories while blind as when he enjoyed vision.

Thurmond, J. (James) Strom (1902–   ) U.S. senator; born in Edgefield, S.C. A teacher and superintendent of education before turning to the law, he was judge of the state's circuit court (1938–42). Volunteering for service with the U.S. Army in World War II (1942–45), he returned and served as governor of South Carolina (Dem., 1947–51). Although relatively progressive as a governor, especially in matters of education – even for African-Americans – he was staunchly opposed to the civil rights program of the Democrats in 1948; at that year's convention he led the walkout of the Southern Democrats and ran as presidential candidate of the State's Rights Democratic Party or "Dixiecrats." Originally appointed a Democrat to the U.S. Senate in 1954, he was elected on his own in 1956; switching to the Republican Party in 1964, he continued to be reelected and became a prominent force in the emergence of a conservative Republican Party in the South.

Thurow, Lester (Carl) (1938–   ) economist; born in Livingston, Mont. He was a Rhodes scholar (1960–62) and earned his Ph.D. at Harvard in 1964. He taught at the Massachusetts Institute of Technology (MIT) (1968) and was an economic adviser to Democratic presidential nominee George McGovern (1972). He gained wide exposure in both the print and sound media. In *The Zero-Sum Society* (1980), he argued that the United States was losing ground against its economic competitors. He was dean of the Sloan School of Management at MIT (1987).

Thurston, Howard (1869–1936) magician; born in Columbus, Ohio. An illusionist, he was one of the first to float a woman in 1920 and performed elaborate card tricks that baffled even fellow magicians.

Thurston, Robert Henry (1839–1903) mechanical engineer, educator; born in Providence, R.I. He was a pioneer and innovator in technical education. In 1871 he was asked to organize the department of mechanical engineering at the newly-formed Stevens Institute of Technology, Hoboken, N.J. He drew up a four-year course of instruction that included training students on actual research. To this end, he solicited research commissions from industrial firms and used the resultant income to purchase further equipment for the school lab. When he was appointed secretary of the U.S. Board to Test Iron, Steel, and Other Metals in 1875, the students at Stevens did much of the work as part of their studies. In 1885 he was hired by Cornell University to reorganize Sibley College and make it a first-rate college of mechanical engineering. He remained there until his death. His own research was primarily on the reciprocating steam engine.

Thurstone, Louis L. (Leon) (1887–1955) psychologist; born in Chicago. After studying electrical engineering at Cornell, he did graduate work in psychology at the University of Chicago (Ph.D. 1917). He taught statistics and mental test theory there (1924–52) while directing the psychometric laboratory he had founded with his wife, psychologist Thelma G. Thurstone. They joined the University of North Carolina in 1952 and founded its psychometric laboratory. He is known for his contributions to the measurement of intelligence and attitudes and he developed some of the tests used by the U.S. Army and American educational institutions.

Thwing, Charles (Franklin) (1853–1937) college president; born in New Sharon, Maine. As president of Western Reserve University, Cleveland (1890–1921), he orchestrated great expansion, inaugurating new graduate schools, extension studies, and adult education. He helped to found the Cleveland School of Education. His many publications include *History of Higher Education in America* (1906).

Thye, Edward John (1896–1969) governor, U.S. senator; born in Frederick, S.D. A farmer all his life, he became the deputy commissioner of agriculture for Minnesota (1938–42). Elected lieutenant governor (Rep., 1943), he became governor (1943–45) when Harold Stassen left to serve in the navy and was elected for a full term (1945–47). He moved on to the U.S. Senate (Rep., Minn.; 1947–59) where he supported civil rights and aid to education.

Tibbett, Lawrence (1896–1960) baritone; born in Bakersfield, Calif. After experience as an actor and in light opera, he studied voice in New York and made his Metropolitan Opera debut in 1923, going on to be a favorite there until his retirement in 1950. He was admired both for his roles in Italian classics and in new operas, and also appeared in films and recitals, and on radio.

Tibbles, Susette La Flesche (b. Inshtatheumba, "Bright Eyes") (1854–1903) Omaha reformer, author, illustrator; born in present-day Nebraska (sister of Susan La Flesche Picotte). Both grandfathers were Caucasians, both grandmothers were Native Americans; her father was an Omaha chief, her mother was more involved with the world of whites. After studying at a girls school in Elizabeth, N.J., Susette returned to the reservation and became a teacher in a government school. In an infamous affair in its day, the Ponca Indians were forcibly removed from their lands in 1877; in the national protest that followed, Susette La Flesche traveled to the East as translator for the Ponca chief, Standing Bear, on a lecture tour organized by an Omaha newspaperman, Thomas Tibbles. (She coauthored, with Standing Bear, *Ploughed Under: The Story of an Indian Chief*, 1882.) She and Tibbles were married in 1881 and their crusade led to the passage of the Dawes Act of 1887. The Tibbles also traveled to England to present the case for Native Americans' claims to their land. Thereafter she lectured occasionally, wrote various articles, and gained a minor reputation as an artist-illustrator. She and her husband lived most of their years in Nebraska where she died on her native land.

Ticknor, William Davis (1810–64) publisher; born in Lebanon, N.H. In 1832 he founded the Boston firm that, with the able partnership of James Fields, became one of the most distinguished American publishing companies.

Tiffany, Louis Comfort (1848–1933) glass maker, interior designer; born in New York City. After early study with painter George Innes, he founded an interior design collaborative in 1879, which decorated in richly orientalist fashion important residences, including the Mark Twain house. But it was his exquisite *art nouveau* glass that brought international acclaim. His iridescent favrile glass (patented in 1894) – used in making his stained glass windows, chandeliers, tiles, and vessels in flowing organic forms – came from the Tiffany Furnaces (started in 1892) and the Tiffany Studios (1902–32). He also designed lamps, furniture, textiles, ceramics, and wallpaper, and in his later years turned to jewelry. He was an officer of Tiffany & Company, the jewelers, and he set up a foundation to support artists (1919).

Tilden, Samuel Jones (1814–86) lawyer, public official; born in New Lebanon, N.Y. In poor health as a boy, he had little formal education, though he did manage to attend Yale for one term and law school in New York City. Admitted to the bar in 1841, he built a prosperous practice and became active in Democratic politics, leading the Free-Soil wing of the party and supporting the Union on the outbreak of the Civil War. After taking a leading role in breaking up Boss Tweed's "ring," he was elected governor of New York on a reform platform (1875–77). He ran for president as a Democrat in 1876 and won the popular vote in a close race; when an electoral commission awarded the disputed election to Rutherford B. Hayes, he returned to New York City and resumed his law practice. He left a Tilden Trust to support what became the New York Public Library.

Tilden, (William Tatem, Jr.) "Big Bill" (1893–1953) tennis player; born in Germantown, Pa. The dominant tennis player during sports' "golden age" of the 1920s, he won seven U.S. Open championships (1920–25, 1929), three Wimbledon titles (1920–21, 1930), and led the U.S. Davis Cup team to seven consecutive victories (1920–26). Turning professional in 1931, he won several pro titles, including the doubles title in 1945. He was publisher and editor of *Racquet* magazine, wrote several books on tennis, including, *The Art of Lawn Tennis* (1920), and made numerous short films on tennis. A 1950 poll overwhelmingly voted him the greatest tennis player of the first half of the 20th century.

Tilghman, Tench (1744–86) soldier; born in Talbot County, Md. A Philadelphia merchant, he abandoned his business interests in 1776 to become a volunteer aide on George Washington's staff. Washington recognized Tilghman's contributions when he assigned him to carry news of Cornwallis' surrender to the Continental Congress (1781).

Tilghman, William (1756–1827) jurist; born in Talbot County, Md. A Loyalist, he sat out the Revolutionary War reading law at his family's estate in Maryland. Member of the Maryland assembly (1788–90) and senate (1791), he moved to Philadelphia to practice law (1795). He was on Pennsylvania's court of appeals (1805), then chief justice of the Pennsylvania Supreme Court (1806–27). Trustee of the University of Pennsylvania (1802–27) and president of the American Philosophical Society (1824–27), he is credited with trying to apply more objective equity to Pennsylvania law.

Tilghman, William (Matthew) (1854–1924) lawman; born in Fort Dodge, Iowa. An outstanding lawman in Kansas and Oklahoma (1877–1914), he also supervised the production of a motion picture, *The Passing of the Oklahoma Outlaws*. He came out of retirement during the Prohibition period and was killed in Cromwell, Okla.

Tillich, Paul (Johannes) (1886–1965) theologian, philosopher; born in Starzeddel, Prussia. Educated in theology and philosophy and ordained a Lutheran minister (1912), he was a chaplain in World War I, then pursued an academic career, but his religiously grounded socialism and opposition to Hitler led to suspension from the University of Frankfurt in 1933. Emigrating to America, he held posts at Union Theological Seminary (1933–55), Harvard (1955–62), and the University of Chicago (1962–65). He emerged in lectures, sermons, and writings as an "apostle to the skeptics," seeking to harmonize Christianity and modern culture. His existentially oriented work, *The Courage to Be* (1952), focusing on God as object of "ultimate concern," was one of several that reached a wide audience; he became perhaps the century's best-known American theologian. His principal work was the three-volume *Systematic Theology* (1951, 1957, 1963).

Tillman, (Benjamin Ryan) "Pitchfork Ben" (1847–1918) farmer, governor, U.S. senator; born in Ropers, S.C. Himself a farmer, he led a Farmers Association that promoted reforms in agricultural and industrial education. Once elected governor of South Carolina (Dem., 1890–94), he took over South Carolina politics and government. Although a populist-progressive in some matters – taxation, education – he also framed an article in a new state constitution that practically denied African-Americans the right to vote. Campaigning for the U.S. Senate in 1894, he shouted, "Send me to Washington and I'll stick my pitchfork into [President Cleveland's] old ribs!" and gained the inimitable nickname by which he would thereafter be known. In the Senate (Dem., S.C.; 1895–1918), he became an even more outrageous figure, opposing liberal Republicans such as President Theodore Roosevelt, yet advocating increased naval spending and the Hepburn Rate Bill. All the while he resisted extending any civil rights to African-Americans – even justifying lynching and calling for repeal of the 15th amendment. Meanwhile, he continued to control affairs in South Carolina (getting his nephew acquitted in 1903 of assassination of a political foe). After 1902 he became more irascible and quarrelsome than ever but a paralytic stroke in 1909 limited his ability to harangue people; he stayed in the Senate, however, to the end.

Tillstrom, Burr (1917–85) puppeteer; born in Chicago. With Fran Allison, he created the *Kukla, Fran, and Ollie Show* on television (1947–57) which featured a cast of hand puppets. It won two Peabody Awards and three Emmys.

Tilly, Charles (1929–) sociologist; born in Lombard, Ill. Harvard-educated, he taught at institutions including the University of Michigan (1969–84) and the New School for Social Research (1984), where he directed the Center for Studies of Social Change. He combined sociological, political, and historical analysis in his studies of early capitalism, war, and social action. He wrote among other works *The Contentious French* (1986).

Tilson, John (Quillin) (1866–1958) U.S. representative; born in Clear Branch, Tenn. After working his way through Yale law school, he practiced law in New Haven (1897), and was a Connecticut representative (1905–08). He challenged the Republican Party's candidate and was elected to the U.S. House of Representatives (1909–11, 1915–31). Republican majority leader (1925–31), his ambitions to be Speaker were thwarted in 1931 and he opened a Washington law office, later serving as chairman of Save the Children.

Timken, Henry (1831–1909) inventor; born in Bremen, Germany. He came to America as a child and, disliking life on a Missouri farm, learned the wagonmaker's trade. By 1855 he had established his own carriage-making business in St. Louis. Most of his patents were for carriage improvements, including the "Timken spring" that made his fortune. He also invented and gave his name to a tapered roller bearing. He continued in the carriage business until 1897, when he retired to California.

Timoshenko, Stepan (Stephan) Prokofyevich (1878–1972) civil engineer, educator; born in St. Petersburg, Russia. He worked as a railway engineer, then in 1906 lectured at Kiev University. He fled the Soviet Union, emigrating to the U.S.A. in 1922. He taught structural engineering at Stanford (1936–54) and contributed to theoretical and applied mechanics.

Ting, Samuel Chao Chung (1936–) physicist; born in Ann Arbor, Mich. He was raised in China and Taiwan, coming to the U.S.A. to study at the University of Michigan (1956–62). He performed nuclear research in Geneva (1963–64), then taught at Columbia University (1964–69). While on leave from Columbia, he went to Hamburg, where he began his pioneering studies of subatomic particles. Returning to the U.S.A., he joined the Massachusetts Institute of Technology (1967), where, in 1974, he discovered the long-lived particle, "J," later proved identical to independent discoverer Burton Richter's psi particle. Ting and Richter shared the 1976 Nobel Prize in physics for their codiscovery of the particle they agreed to term "J/psi."

Tinker, Grant (1926–) television producer; born in Stamford, Conn. After working in advertising, he was a National Broadcasting Company (NBC) programmer (1961–67), moving to Universal Studios to be near his then wife, Mary Tyler Moore. They formed MTM productions in the 1970s, producing other comedy shows as well. As NBC chairman (1981–86), he pulled the network from last to first place. After resigning, he founded GTG Entertainment (1986).

Tiomkin, Dimitri (1894–1980) composer; born in Russia. A piano virtuoso, he toured Europe and the United States in the 1920s. In 1930 he began writing theme music for Hollywood films; he eventually earned Oscars for the background music to *High Noon* (1952), *The High and the Mighty* (1954), and *The Old Man and the Sea* (1958). His last film was the Soviet-produced *Tschaikowsky* (1970), for which he scored the composer's music.

Tisch, Laurence A. (Alan) ("Larry") (1923–) corporate executive; born in Bensonhurst, N.Y. He was the president (1946–74) and investment strategist of Tisch Hotels, a partnership with his brother Robert Tisch (1926). They were later known for buying failing companies and making them profitable through massive lay-offs and strategic shifts. Their major takeovers included Loews Corporation (1961), Lorillard (1968), and CBS (1986), where his immediate cuts at CBS News caused controversy.

Tishler, Max (1906–89) chemist, inventor; born in Boston, Mass. Educated at Tufts and Harvard, he developed in the late 1930s a synthesis of riboflavin that made the large-scale production of vitamin B_2 economical. The practical synthesis of other vitamins resulted from this breakthrough. After a long career as a research chemist, he became a professor of chemistry at Wesleyan University, Connecticut, in 1969.

Titchener, Edward Bradford (1867–1927) psychologist; born in Chichester, England. Before coming to the United States in 1892, he studied at Oxford (England) and Leipzig (Germany), where he was influenced by Wilhelm Wundt. He taught at Cornell University (1892–1927) and became the nation's leading exponent of experimental psychology, founding the Society of Experimental Psychologists in 1904. His major works include the four-volume *Experimental Psychology* (1901–05) and *The Psychology of Feeling and Attention* (1908).

Titcomb, Timothy See HOLLAND, JOSIAH GILBERT.

Tjian, Robert (Tse Nan) (1949–   ) geneticist; born in Hong Kong, China. He was a staff investigator at Cold Spring Harbor Laboratory, N.Y. (1976–79), then became a professor of biochemistry at the University of California: Berkeley (1979). One of the most-cited contemporary biochemists in the world, he made major contributions to research on genetic transcription and gene expression in both fruit flies and in mammalian cells infected with cancer-causing viruses. It was his laboratory that developed sequence-specific DNA affinity chromatography, the technique necessary for purifying genetic transcription factors.

Tobey, Mark (1890–1976) painter; born in Centerville, Wis. A self-taught artist, he moved to New York (1911) and became a commercial artist and portraitist. He converted to Bahá'í (1918), a Near Eastern-based religion, which influenced his "white writing," a calligraphic technique used in his abstract tempera and gouache paintings, such as *Broadway* (1936). He traveled widely and lived in Seattle, Washington, and Switzerland.

Tobin, James (1918–   ) economist; born in Champaign, Ill. A professor at Yale University from 1955, he maintained an adamant belief in Keynesian economic theory. His work included interest-elasticity of monetary demands, consumer economics, and the incorporation of money and business cycles in growth models. He received the Nobel Prize in economics (1981).

Toch, Ernst (1887–1964) composer; born in Vienna, Austria. He had a prominent career in Germany before fleeing the Nazis and coming to the U.S.A. in 1935. He wrote some film scores and taught privately, meanwhile composing a substantial body of music in a post-Romantic style with touches of modernism.

Todd, (Michael) Mike (b. Avrom Hirsh Goldbogen) (1900–58) showman; born in Minneapolis, Minn. (married to Elizabeth Taylor). The son of a rabbi, he specialized in producing spectaculars, developing three dimensional film for his Academy Award-winning *Around the World in Eighty Days* (1956).

Todd, Thomas (1765–1826) Supreme Court justice; born in King and Queen County, Va. He advocated for Kentucky's statehood and served its court system as a clerk (1792–1801), a judge (1801–06), and as chief justice (1806–07). President Jefferson named him to the U.S. Supreme Court (1807–26).

Toland, Gregg (1904–48) cinematographer; born in Charleston, Ill. He entered films at the age of 15 and became an assistant cameraman the next year. By 1929 he had distinguished himself as an inventive and creative artist. Working mainly for Samuel Goldwyn, he won the Oscar for his camera work in *Wuthering Heights* (1939).

Tolley, Howard Ross (1889–1958) agricultural economist; born in Howard County, Ind. In 1912 he moved to Washington, D.C., as a mathematician for the Coast and Geodetic Survey, then started working for the U.S. Department of Agriculture (1915). At the Office of Farm Management he initiated research on economic aspects of farming. When the Bureau of Agricultural Economics (BAE) opened (1923), he helped develop a research program to generate data as well as techniques for analyzing farm problems. He left in 1930 for the University of California's Giannini Foundation for Agricultural Economics, but returned to Washington at President Franklin Roosevelt's request to assist with New Deal farm programs. At the Agricultural Adjustment Administration he developed a conservation-oriented plan (1933–35). In 1944 he administered the AAA and in 1946 returned to the BAE as its chief. He advocated cash supports, quota systems, and restricted acreage for certain crops. He helped organize the Food and Agriculture Organization (FAO) of the United Nations (1943) and was one of its chief economists. He quit to join the Ford Foundation as director of the Washington office (1951–54). He wrote *The Farmer, Citizen at War* (1943) and articles for the *Journal of Farm Economics.*

Tolman, Edward Chace (1886–1959) psychologist; born in West Newton, Mass. He studied at the Massachusetts Institute of Technology, Harvard, and Yale, and taught at Northwestern University before joining the University of California: Berkeley (1918–54). In his first book, *Purposive Behavior in Animals and Men* (1932), he broke with the rigid stimulus-response behaviorism of John B. Watson to postulate such variables as goals, cognition, and behavioral supports within the environment. During the 1930s and 1940s, he was one of the nation's leading theorists in the field of cognitive psychology.

Tolton, Augustine (1854–97) Catholic priest; born in Ralls County, Mo. The first Catholic priest whose parents were both African-Americans, he escaped from slavery with family members at age seven. He overcame poverty and frequent rejections to obtain backing and permission to study for the priesthood in Rome, where he was ordained (1886). He returned to work as a struggling pastor among poor black Catholics in Illinois.

Tombaugh, Clyde (William) (1906–   ) astronomer; born in Streator, Ill. In 1930, while at the Lowell Observatory in Flagstaff, Ariz. – and before he had earned his bachelor's degree – he found the ninth planet, Pluto, the existence of which had been predicted by Percival Lowell. He would also discover a globular star cluster, hundreds of asteroids, and a supercluster of galaxies. After stints at Arizona State College (1943–45), the University of California: Los Angeles (1945–46), and the White Sands Missile Range (1946–51), he settled at New Mexico State University where he concentrated on studying the planet Mars.

Tomlin, Bradley (Walker) (1899–1953) painter; born in Syracuse, N.Y. He traveled in Europe often, settled in New York City (1927), became a commercial artist, and taught at Sarah Lawrence College (1932–41). By 1937 he was working in a cubist manner and, later, used a calligraphic style, as in *Number 20* (1949).

Tomlin, Lily (b. Mary Jean Tomlin) (1939–   ) comedienne; born in Detroit, Mich. Performing in cabarets while doing temporary work, she became successful on television's *Laugh-In* (1969–73) with her repertoire of off-beat characters. She also appeared in movies and network specials. In 1985 her one-woman stage show (coauthored with Jane Wagner), *In Search for Signs of Intelligent Life in the Universe,* won a Tony award.

Tompkins, Daniel D. (1774–1825) vice-president, governor; born in Fox Meadows (now Scarsdale), N.Y. He was governor of New York (1807–17). During his vice-presidency under James Monroe (1817–25), he was plagued by charges that he had mishandled New York state finances during the War of 1812. After his death, audits showed that the state owed money to the Tompkins family and his descendants received $92,000.

Tonty, Henri de (1650–1704) explorer; probably born in Paris, France (evidently son of the Neapolitan banker Lorenzo Tonti). He joined the French army at age 18 and in 1678 went with Robert Cavelier, Sieur de La Salle, to explore in North America. The Native Americans would call Tonty "Iron Hand" because of a metal hand that replaced the right one lost fighting in France. He supervised building of the *Griffon,* the first sailing vessel on the Great Lakes. He survived extreme deprivation – and a wound from an Indian raid – in the Illinois country (1680) and then went with La Salle to discover the mouth of the Mississippi River (1682). Between 1683 and 1700, based mainly in Illinois, he was effectively commander of France's possessions and settlements in the Mississippi Valley. After 1700 he joined the French colony at New Orleans and died of yellow fever near present-day Mobile, Ala.

Tooker, George (Clair, Jr.) (1920–   ) painter; born in New York City. He studied at the Art Students League, New York (1943–44), and privately with Paul Cadmus. Based in New York, he used egg tempera as his medium to paint surrealistic urban scenes in a style called "magic realism," as in *The Subway* (1950).

Toombs, Robert (Augustus) (1810–85) U.S. representative/ senator, Confederate cabinet member, soldier; born in Washington, Ga. A lawyer and wealthy plantation owner, he served Georgia in the U.S. House of Representatives (Whig, 1845–53) and in the U.S. Senate (Dem., 1853–61), and was one of the more active and outspoken proponents of preserving slavery and states' rights. He led Georgia to secession, then became the Confederate secretary of state, but he soon became impatient for action and resigned in July 1861 to take on a brigadier general's commission. Seriously wounded at Antietam in 1862, he resigned from the army for many of the same reasons he resigned his cabinet post and attacked Davis's administration: Toombs was ambitious and argumentative and above all was impatient with the caution of other Confederate leaders. He volunteered with the Georgia militia when Sherman was advancing on Atlanta (1864) and fled to Cuba and then England when the Confederacy collapsed. He returned to Georgia and prospered as a lawyer, but his life ended sadly when his wife died insane and he became blind and turned to drink.

Toomer, Jean (Eugene Nathan) (1894–1967) poet, writer; born in Washington, D.C. He studied at the University of Wisconsin (1914), and City College, N.Y. (1917), and worked briefly as a superintendent of a black rural school in Georgia (1921). He studied with a mystic in France (1924), lived in Harlem (1925) and Chicago (1926–33), then married and settled in Pennsylvania (1934). An important writer of the Harlem Renaissance, he is best known for *Cane* (1923), a work combining poetry, fiction, and drama.

Tormé, (Melvin Howard) Mel (1925–   ) vocalist, composer, author; born in Chicago. He was involved in show business from age four, singing with the Coon-Sanders Orchestra in 1929 and Buddy Rogers in the early 1930s. He studied drums and songwriting while acting in radio soap operas between 1934–40. His first song, "Lament to Love," was recorded by Harry James in 1941. "The Christmas Song" and "Born to be Blue" are among his other songs. In 1942–43, he sang and played drums with Chico Marx, then led his own vocal group, the Mel-Tones, in California until 1947. Thereafter, as the epitome of Cool School jazz singers, he toured as a headlining concert performer and recorded a string of hit records throughout the 1950s. He also appeared as an actor in numerous dramatic television series. He is the author of biographies of Judy Garland and Buddy Rich, and an autobiography, *It Wasn't All Velvet.*

Torrey, John (1796–1873) botanist; born in New York City. His interest in botany began in 1810, when he first met American naturalist Amos Eaton. Although he received his M.D. (1818) and practiced medicine (1818–24), he preferred botany, and published results of a two-year survey of wild plants found within a 30-mile radius of New York City. His scientific papers on plants of the northeastern U.S.A. brought him to fame, and large numbers of specimens collected by expeditions to the American West were sent to him for study and identification. He became dissatisfied with the Linnaean classification system and introduced a more natural botanical system to his classifications of U.S. flora. After marrying in 1824, he taught chemistry, mineralogy, and geology at the U.S. Military Academy at West Point (1824–27). From then on, his knowledge of chemistry provided the financial support to continue his primary interest, systematic botany. He returned to New York City to teach chemistry and botany at the College of Physicians and Surgeons (1827–55), concurrently serving the College of New Jersey (now Princeton University) during the summers of 1830–54. In 1834 he met the young Asa Gray, and was sufficiently impressed to invite Gray to assist him on his projected multivolume work, *A Flora of North America,* of which two volumes were published (1838, 1843) before the work was abandoned upon Gray's move to Harvard (1842). Torrey became chief assayer at the U.S. Assay Office, N.Y. (1854–73), which was then receiving large amounts of gold from California, and continued to expand his botanical collection while traveling on business to the western U.S.A. In 1856 he became a trustee of Columbia University; his library and herbarium were transferred to the New York Botanical Garden in 1899 (which he had helped to found). In addition to his pioneering contributions to the classification of American plants, he was an inspiring educator who influenced the careers of many future botanists. The Torrey Botanical Society, Torrey Peak in Colorado, the genus *Torreya* in the yew family, and the mineral torreyite are named in his honor.

Toscanini, Arturo (1867–1957) conductor; born in Parma, Italy. He was a cellist before the night in 1886 when he took over the baton from an indisposed conductor in Rio de Janeiro and stayed on the podium for the rest of his career. After years of journeyman work in Italian opera houses, he became conductor of Milan's La Scala in 1898. In 1909 he came to the U.S.A. to lead the Metropolitan Opera orchestra; his subsequent career took him to positions in Europe, England, and the U.S.A., including the podium of the New York Philharmonic from 1928 to 1936. In 1937 the NBC Symphony, primarily a broadcasting and recording orchestra, was created for Toscanini; he led it until 1954, cementing his reputation as one of the most revered conductors in the world. He helped pioneer a new performance tradition that proclaimed an end to Romantic interpretive excesses and substituted absolute fidelity to the score; in practice, that made for clean, sinewy performances, achieved partly by his legendary tantrums in rehearsals. He was equally admired for his performances of Beethoven and other 19th-century classics and of modern composers including Stravinsky, Debussy, and Richard Strauss.

Tourel, Jennie (b. Davidson) (1910–73) mezzo-soprano; born in St. Petersburg, Russia. She studied voice in Paris, making her operatic debut there in 1933. Coming to the U.S.A. in 1940, she joined the Metropolitan Opera in 1944. She excelled in a wide range of styles including contemporary opera, and was an active recitalist.

Tourgée, Albion (Winegar) (1838–1905) writer, judge, editor; born in Williamsfield, Ohio. He studied at the University of Rochester (N.Y.), served as a Union soldier in the Civil War (1861–63), and was admitted to the Ohio bar (1864). In 1865 he moved to North Carolina, where he briefly edited a newspaper and was elected judge of North Carolina's superior court (1868–74). As an ardent supporter of the Reconstruction policies and a foe of the Ku Klux Klan, he was regarded as the epitome of the carpetbagger – a Northerner who lived in the South for political advantage after the Civil War – but he seems to have been a sincere proponent of reform and justice. He wrote at least two novels there, including *A Fool's Errand* (1879), then moved to New York City in 1879. He edited *Our Continent* (1882–84), a magazine in which he continued to champion the rights of blacks and to expose the Ku Klux Klan; he failed in his efforts to start another magazine in Buffalo, N.Y. Along with his political essays and newspaper articles, he continued to publish his novels, none except *Hot Ploughshares* (1883) receiving much respect. From 1897–1905 he was the U.S. consul in Bordeaux, France.

Toussaint, Pierre (1766–1853) philanthropist; born in Santo Domingo. Brought to New York City as a slave (1787), he worked as a hairdresser; supporting his owner's wife when she became widowed and impoverished, he was emancipated in 1807. A devout Catholic who became highly successful in business, he spent much of his money on charities and personally nursed and housed people in need.

Tower, John (Goodwin) (1925–91) U.S. senator; born in Houston, Texas. He served in the navy during World War II and then studied at the London School of Economics. He was the first Republican ever elected to the U.S. Senate from Texas (1961–85). He specialized in defense matters and was chairman of the Armed Services Committee. He chaired the Iran-Contra investigation (1986–87). In 1989 he was nominated for secretary of defense, but his nomination was rejected by the Senate after allegations of alcoholism and womanizing, charges he vigorously denied. He died in an airplane crash.

Towers, John (Henry) (1885–1955) naval aviator; born in Rome, Ga. A 1906 Naval Academy graduate, in 1911 he became the third naval officer to qualify as a pilot. In May 1919, forced down off the Azores while attempting a transatlantic flight in the seaplane NC-3, Towers rigged a sail and made port after a two-day voyage. After commanding the carriers *Langley* and *Saratoga,* he became chief of the Bureau of Aeronautics in 1939. He served in senior staff positions during World War II; this naval aviation pioneer finally saw sea duty in 1945 as commander of the Second Carrier Task Force. He commanded the Pacific Fleet before retiring from the service in 1947. He served as a vice-president of Pan American World Airways from 1949 to 1953.

Towle, Charlotte Helen (1896–1966) social work educator; born in Butte, Mont. Growing up in a mining town, she heard her family discuss labor and management issues, and by the time she graduated from Goucher College (Md.) (1919), she was already determined to be a social worker. She worked for the Red Cross and the Veterans Bureau, then in a neuropsychiatric hospital in Tacoma, Wash. (1924–26) before studying at the New York School of Social Work (1926–27). Dissatisfied with the by-then conventional casework approach of the day, she was drawn to a more psychological approach to social work, working in Philadelphia and then returning to New York City (1928–32). She then went to the University of Chicago, where, as a professor at the School of Social Service Administration (1932–62), she was a pioneer in establishing the psychosocial approach to social work. Through her classes, articles, and such books as *Social Case Records from Psychiatric Clinics* (1941) and *The Learner in Education for the Professions* (1954), her influence spread far beyond Chicago's school to other social work schools in the U.S.A. and England. In 1945 she gained some notoriety when she wrote a government manual, *Common Human Needs,* in which she asserted that all people had a right to food, shelter, and health care; it was attacked by some as advocating socialism and the government ceased printing it; but the American Association of Social Workers continued to print it. She held many key posts with professional and governmental organizations.

Towne, Henry Robinson (1844–1924) engineer, manufacturer; born in Philadelphia. He began his career during the Civil War, supervising the installation of ship engines and machinery. In 1868 he was a partner at the Yale Lock Manufacturing Company and became president in 1869. He held that position until 1915. He introduced modern manufacturing processes to the lock industry.

Townes, Charles H. (Hard) (1915–) physicist; born in Greenville, S.C. He taught at the California Institute of Technology (1937–39), then moved to Bell Telephone Laboratories (1939–47). While at Columbia University (1948–61), he invented the maser (1953–54); for the scientific work behind this he was awarded the 1964 Nobel Prize in physics (shared with two Russian physicists). With his brother-in-law Arthur Schawlow he also laid the basis for the laser. Townes served as science adviser to both the federal government and private industry. He continued his research at the Massachusetts Institute of Technology (1961–66) and at the University of California: Berkeley (1967), applying maser-laser technology to astrophysics.

Townsend, Francis E. (Everett) (1867–1960) physician, social reformer; born near Fairbury, Ill. He moved to Belle Fourche, S.D., to practice medicine (1903) and served as a physician in World War I. After an acute attack of peritonitis, he moved to Long Beach, Calif., with his family (1919). Appointed assistant health officer of Long Beach, he remained in this position until he was ousted in a local political upheaval (1933). His health remained a problem and he lost most of his savings during the Great Depression. Almost destitute, he conceived of his old-age revolving pension plan for the elderly; its essential feature was that every American over 60 would be given a pension to be financed by a national sales tax. Within two years the so-called Townsend plan spawned a social movement with 2.25 million members throughout the U.S.A. and its own newspaper (1935). Several bills incorporating the Townsend plan were introduced in Congress in 1935–36. Accused of profiting from the misery of others – the organization's finances were in disarray, due largely to Townsend's chief associate, Robert Clements – the essentially naive Townsend allied himself with the Reverend Gerald L. K. Smith, national organizer of Huey Long's Share-the-Wealth program, and through him became involved with an unsavory lot seeking to unseat President Franklin D. Roosevelt. Townsend faced a jail term for refusing to answer Congressional questioning about his organization of "Townsend Clubs," but Roosevelt commuted the sentence (1937). Although he attempted to modernize the plan, the return to prosperity and World War II eventually killed his movement.

Townsend, Lynn Alfred (1919–) business executive; born in Flint, Mich. A University of Michigan M.B.A., he worked for accounting firms before joining Chrysler Corporation as comptroller (1957). He rapidly moved into Chrysler's international operations, becoming president and CEO (1961–66) and chairman and CEO (1967–75).

Townsend, Robert (Chase) (1920–) business executive; born in Washington, D.C. He had an early career in investment and international banking at American Express Co. (1948–62) before moving over to Avis Rent-a-Car. As president and chairman, he introduced the "We Try Harder" advertising campaign that built the firm into a major industry competitor (1962–65). He was later advisor and senior partner of *Congressional Monitor* (1969), and after publishing his best-selling *Up the Organization* (1970), he enjoyed great popularity as an advocate of reforming American business.

Tozzer, Alfred (Marston) (1877–1954) anthropologist; born in Lynn, Mass. He earned undergraduate and graduate degrees from Harvard, where he taught for over 40 years. Tozzer's most important works on the Maya include *Maya Grammar* (1921) and *Chichén Itzá and its Center of Sacrifice* (1957), a major synthesis of American prehistory.

Trabert, (Marion Anthony) Tony (1930–) tennis player; born in Cincinnati, Ohio. He won ten Grand Slam tournaments between 1950 and 1955 – five in singles and five in doubles competition.

Tracy, Benjamin F. (Franklin) (1830–1915) public official; born near Owego, N.Y. He became a brevet brigadier general in the Civil War and was a U.S. attorney for New York (1866–73). As secretary of the navy (1889–93) he instituted administrative reforms and began building a powerful modern navy.

Tracy, Spencer (1900–67) movie actor; born in Milwaukee, Wis. After World War I service in the Navy, he played the lead in a college play and then enrolled in drama school, making his Broadway debut in a bit part in 1922. His feature film debut was in *Up the River* (1930). He first played gangster roles, graduated to priests and friends of the hero, and ended up playing gruff, humorous men with integrity. He won an Oscar for *Captains Courageous* (1937) and *Boys Town* (1938). In 1942 he began an intimate relationship with Katharine Hepburn that would remain a well-known secret until his death, but as a devout Catholic he would not divorce his wife of some 20 years.

Train, Arthur C. (Cheney) (1875–1945) lawyer, author; born in Boston, Mass. Twice assistant district attorney in New York (1901–08), 1913–15), he began publishing his "court stories" in 1904; after 1922 he devoted full time to writing stories, urbane novels, and nonfiction works based on courtroom experiences. His well-loved character, Ephraim Tutt, appeared as lawyer-hero in over eighty stories (1919–45); the fictional *Yankee Lawyer: The Autobiography of Ephraim Tutt* (1943) was so convincing that *Who's Who* asked Tutt to fill out its form.

Trampler, Walter (1915–) violinist/violist; born in Munich, Germany. He briefly played violin in the Boston Symphony before founding the New Music String Quartet (1947–56), in which he played viola. He later taught at Juilliard and Boston University, meanwhile concertizing into the 1990s.

Trapp, Martin Edwin (1877–1951) governor; born in Robinson, Kans. A lawyer, he served as Oklahoma state auditor (1907–11) and lieutenant governor (1914–23) before replacing impeached Governor John Walton. As Democratic governor (1923–27), he established hunting, forestry, and conservation commissions, and reduced the Ku Klux Klan's power through an "antimask law." He later became a dealer in investment securities.

Traubel, Helen (1899–1972) soprano; born in St. Louis, Mo. American-trained, she made her Metropolitan Opera debut in 1939 and stayed until 1953, meanwhile touring internationally. She was a leading Wagnerian soprano of her time.

Travers, (Jerome Dunstan) Jerry (1887–1951) golfer; born in New York City. Dominating golf between 1907 and 1915, he was the only golfer other than Bobby Jones to win four U.S. Amateur titles. He won the U.S. Open as an amateur in 1915.

Travis, Walter (John) (1862–1927) golfer; born in Malden, Victoria, Australia. One of golf's pioneers, he immigrated to the United States at age 23 and won three U.S. Amateur titles (1900–01, 1903). He founded *American Golfer* magazine in 1905.

Travis, William Barret (1809–36) lawyer, soldier; born in Edgefield County, S.C. He grew up in South Carolina and Alabama, studied law privately, and was admitted to the bar before he turned 20. Migrating to Texas in the early 1830s, he became active in the movement agitating for independence from Mexico. In 1835 he led a small band of Texans in open revolt; in early 1836 Mexican forces besieged his little command inside the Alamo fortress. The Alamo fell on March 6, 1836, and all its defenders, including Travis, were killed.

Traylor, Bill (1854–1947) folk artist, plantation worker; born in Alabama. Born a slave, he worked on a plantation near Selma, Ala., until his early eighties; he then moved to Montgomery, Ala. He had begun drawing the world around him in a bold, primitive, but often strikingly original way. In the last two decades of his life he produced over 1,000 works, but it was not until the 1980s that he was discovered; his work has been exhibited around the world and he is the subject of a biography (1992).

Trevino, Lee (Buck) (1939–) golfer; born in Dallas, Texas. He twice won each of three major championships – the U.S. Open (1968, 1971), the Professional Golfers' Association (PGA) title (1974, 1984), and the British Open (1971–72). A popular member of the PGA tour, as the first Latino to become a major golfer he was affectionately known as "Super Mex."

Tribe, Laurence H. (Henry) (1941–) legal scholar; born in Shanghai, China, to Russian-Jewish parents. His father was a naturalized American and the family moved to San Francisco when Tribe was five years old. He is considered a brilliant Supreme Court litigator and legal scholar. In addition to his teaching career at Harvard (1969), he served as a consultant to several government committees including the U.S. Senate Committee on Public Works (1970–72). In 1978 he helped write a new constitution for the Marshall Islands. Perhaps he is best known for his frequent Congressional testimony, particularly in regard to Supreme Court nominees (he influenced the failure of Robert H. Bork's nomination in 1987). He warned against "presidential court-packing" in his book, *God Save This Honorable Court* (1985). His expertise was in legal, constitutional, and jurisprudential theory; the role of law in shaping technological development; and the uses and abuses of mathematical methods in policy and systems analysis. His major publications are *Legal Process and Technological Change* (1980), and *American Constitutional Law* (1978).

Trillin, Calvin (Marshall) (1935–) author; born in Kansas City, Mo. A Yale graduate, he was a *New Yorker* staff writer (1963) and columnist for the *Nation* and national syndication (1978). His essays reported sympathetically on ordinary American life and passionately on food and were collected in such volumes as *American Fried* (1974).

Trilling, Lionel (1905–75) literary critic; born in New York City. Long associated with Columbia University as a student (B.A., M.A., Ph.D.) and teacher (1931–75), he was a literary critic of international stature and held guest professorships at various universities in the U.S.A. and abroad. A liberal humanist, he equated literary criticism with moral evaluation and cultural criticism. He wrote prolifically on 19th- and 20th-century writers, publishing important studies of Matthew Arnold (1939) and E. M. Forster (1943); his collected essays include *The Liberal Imagination* (1950), *Beyond Culture* (1965), and *Sincerity and Authenticity* (1972). His one novel, *The Middle of the Journey* (1957), was regarded as having been inspired by events in the life of Whittaker Chambers. His wife (m. 1929) was critic Diana Trilling.

Trimble, Robert (1777–1828) Supreme Court justice; born in Augusta County, Ga. He served Kentucky's court of appeals (1807–09) and as district attorney (1813–17). President James Madison named him to a federal court (1817–26) and President John Q. Adams named him to the U.S. Supreme Court (1826–28).

Trippe, Juan (Terry) (1899–1981) airline executive; born in Sea Bright, N.J. He graduated from Yale in 1922, after having flown with the navy. In 1923 he organized Long Island Airways, which became Pan American Airways in 1927. Under his strong leadership, the company compiled many firsts, including flying across the Atlantic and the Pacific, using American-made jets commercially and offering round-the-world service in 1947. After World War II he championed low-cost air fares and introduced two classes. In 1966 he ordered the first 747s. He retired as CEO in 1968.

Trist, Nicholas (Philip) (1800–74) lawyer, diplomat; born in Charlottesville, Va. He attended West Point but left to study law in the office of Thomas Jefferson (whose granddaughter he married). He entered the State Department in 1828 and was consul in Havana, Cuba (1833–41). Chief clerk of the State Department from 1845, he went to Mexico in 1847 to negotiate an end to the war with Mexico; when charges that he was conceding too much reached Washington, he was ordered back, but he stayed and ended up signing the treaty of Guadalupe Hidalgo (1848). This ended his diplomatic career, and he returned to practice law in Virginia.

Tristano, (Leonard Joseph) Lennie (1919–78) jazz musician; born in Chicago. Blind from childhood, he was a conservatory-trained pianist, leader of his own small groups in New York from 1946, and a strong influence on Bill Evans. As a music teacher and theorist, he developed a small but distinguished following among musicians.

Trivers, Robert L. (1943–) sociobiologist; born in Washington, D.C. He was a consultant and research writer at the Education Development Center, Cambridge, Mass. (1965–72) before joining the faculty of Harvard (1971–78). A person of flamboyant temperament, who, while Caucasian, has identified with blacks since childhood, he espoused black culture, joined the Black Panthers in 1979, and contrasted the "effeteness" of Harvard with the more "real" life of Jamaica. After being denied tenure at Harvard, he moved to the University of California: Santa Cruz (1978). He defended the controversial theory that human behavioral traits (e.g., mate selection and altruism) are genetically determined, and he made significant contributions to studies of "selfish" genes, blood parasites and sexual selection in Jamaican lizards, biology and the law, and studies of symmetry in humans and other animals.

Trott, Benjamin (c. 1770–c. 1841) painter; born in (?) Boston. An artist in New York (c. 1791), he moved to Philadelphia (c. 1794–97), then traveled continuously, painting miniatures, until he settled in Baltimore, Md. (c. 1839).

Trotter, Mildred (1899–) physical anthropologist; born in Monaca, Pa. She studied and taught at Washington University School of Medicine, St. Louis, Mo. (1920–67). She quantified anatomical variations in American blacks and whites, particularly regarding hair distribution and skeletal weight differences due to aging.

Trotter, William Monroe (1872–1934) civil rights leader; born near Chillicothe, Ohio. Raised in Boston, he was an honors student at Harvard. He founded the *Guardian* (1901) as "propaganda against discrimination." He opposed Booker T. Washington, and he helped W. E. B. DuBois in founding the Niagra Movement (1905). He found the National Association for the Advancement of Colored People too moderate. He formed the National Equal Rights League and protested discrimination. He went to the Paris Peace Conference (1919) and tried to persuade the delegates to outlaw racial discrimination. Largely unrecognized during his lifetime, he employed methods – notably nonviolent protest – that were adopted by later 20th-century civil rights activists.

Trova, Ernest (Tino) (1927–) sculptor, painter; born in St. Louis, Mo. Based in St. Louis, he began as a painter influenced by Willem de Kooning (1940s and 1950s), then started his *Falling Man* sculpture series, using chrome plated bronze, silver Plexiglas, glass, and epoxy. By 1980 he began his *Poet* sculptures, an exploration of man's relationship to the environment.

Trowbridge, (Samuel) Breck (Parkman) (1862–1925) architect; born in New York City. He trained at Columbia College School of Mines and the École des Beaux-Arts, Paris. In a 30-year New York partnership with Goodhue Livingston he designed elegant neoclassical banks, hotels, public buildings, and residences for wealthy clients.

Trudeau, Edward Livingston (1848–1915) physician; born in New York City. He switched to medicine from the navy after nursing his brother who died of tuberculosis (1868), graduating from the New York College of Physicians and Surgeons (1871). In 1873, ill with tuberculosis himself, he recuperated seven years in the Adirondack Mountains (New York); remaining there to practice medicine and study tuberculosis, he founded the Adirondack Cottage Sanatorium (later famous as the Trudeau Sanitarium) at Saranac Lake (1884). In 1894 he established the Saranac Laboratory, the first such to study tuberculosis and where he was the first American physician to conduct experiments for tuberculosis immunity. He died of tuberculosis, as did his daughter before him, and the Trudeau Sanitarium closed in 1957, thanks to new antituberculosis therapy which his contributions helped to advance.

Trudeau, Garry B. (1948–) cartoonist; born in New York City. While an undergraduate at Yale University, he created a comic strip, "Bull Tales," which later became *Doonesbury*, a comic strip characterized by its wry humor and satiric presentation of contemporary events. The strip became nationally syndicated and in 1975 it won Trudeau a Pulitzer Prize. *Doonesbury* was occasionally so controversial that papers refused to run certain installments. Trudeau took a "vacation" (1982–84) and then returned to syndication in September 1984.

Truman, David B. (Bicknell) (1913–) political scientist; born in Evanston, Ill. He taught at several colleges including Harvard, Cornell, and Columbia University (1951–59), and served as president of Mount Holyoke College (1969–78). He authored several important books, including *Administrative Decentralization* (1940), *The Governmental Process* (1951), and *The Congressional Party* (1959).

Truman, (Elizabeth Virginia b. Wallace) Bess (1885–1982) First Lady; born in Independence, Mo. The daughter of a farmer, she and Harry Truman were childhood sweethearts; they married in 1919. Although a private person, she exerted considerable influence over Truman's public career. The Trumans had one child, Margaret Truman, who after a brief career as a singer, retired to marry; later she became a writer. Following the presidency, Bess lived quietly until her death.

Truman, Harry S. (1884–1972) thirty-third president; born in Lamar, Mo. A farm boy, he could not afford college but he was commissioned a lieutenant with the National Guard when he went off to France to fight in World War I. He returned to help run a Kansas City, Mo., clothing store that proved unsuccessful. In the 1920s he joined the local Democratic Party machine, which put him in several county offices; although he never took a law degree, he read law and served as presiding judge on a county court (1926–34); this post did not involve judicial duties but was more like a county administrator. He then was elected to the U.S. Senate (1935–45). His personal integrity helped him get reelected in 1940 despite the exposure of the Missouri machine's corruption. He came to national attention heading what was called the Truman Committee, which investigated government wartime production and saved taxpayers millions. That prominence brought him to office as Franklin D. Roosevelt's new vice-president in 1944. When Roosevelt died the next

April, Truman became president; he would go on to win a close election in 1948. This apparently colorless "everyday American" surprised everyone with his boldness in a troubled time: he dropped the first atom bonbs on Japan; authorized the Marshall Plan to aid postwar Europe; proposed the "Truman Doctrine" of Communist containment and support for free peoples; organized the Berlin Airlift (1948–49); ordered the desegregation of the armed forces (1948); established NATO (1949); sent U.S. troops to deal with the Communist invasion of South Korea in 1950; and dismissed the popular General MacArthur for insubordination in Korea. His visionary, Roosevelt-style social program, which he called the "Fair Deal," was largely stymied by a conservative Congress. Truman declined to run in 1952 and settled in Independence, Mo., for a long retirement of writing and speaking his mind. The motto of the man and the politician was on the plaque on his desk – "The buck stops here" – and with each passing decade, Truman has come to be regarded by both historians and ordinary Americans as one of their favorite and even greatest presidents.

Trumbo, (James) Dalton (1905–76) screenwriter, writer; born in Montrose, Colo. A former newspaperman, he began screenwriting in 1935. As one of the Hollywood Ten during the Communist witch hunt of the late 1940s, he spent ten months in jail, then moved to Mexico; during the period when he was blacklisted, he wrote 18 screenplays under pseudonyms, one of which, *The Brave One* (1956), won an Oscar for "Robert Rich". In 1960 his real name was allowed back on the credits for such films as *Spartacus* and *Exodus*. In 1971 he wrote and directed the film of his own antiwar novel, *Johnny Got His Gun* (1939).

Trumbull, John (1756–1834) painter; born in Lebanon, Conn. (son of Jonathan Trumbull (1710–85)). He served intermittently in the Continental Army (1775–77, 1778) but spent most of the years 1777–79 studying art in Boston. He went to London to study with Benjamin West (1780); he was briefly imprisoned in retribution for the hanging of Major Andre as a spy. Released from prison, he went to Amsterdam and painted a full-length portrait of George Washington; its engraved version gave Europeans their first view of the American Revolution's leader. He returned to the U.S.A. (1782–83) and then went back to Benjamin West (1783–89). He returned to America (1789–94), was John Jay's private secretary (1793–94), and then returned to England (1794–1804). He established a studio in New York (1804–08), then returned to London (1808–15), and finally settled in New York City (1815). During these years he tended to specialize in portraits that are an authentic, if not especially stylish, record of the age. In 1817 he was commissioned to paint four pictures for the Rotunda of the U.S. Capitol; his *Surrender of General Burgoyne at Saratoga, Surrender of Lord Cornwallis at Yorktown, Declaration of Independence,* and *Resignation of Washington,* were completed in 1824. Although not as impressive as some of his other works (including the original smaller versions), these works established him as the artist of the American Revolution – millions of American schoolchildren have seen the Revolution through his eyes.

Trumbull, John (1750–1831) poet, lawyer; born in Watertown, Conn. (second cousin of Jonathan Trumbull). Extremely precocious as a child, he studied at Yale (B.A. 1767; M.A. 1770) and taught there (1771–73). He then studied law with John Adams (1773), practiced law in New Haven and Hartford (1774–1825), and was a judge of the Connecticut state courts (1801–19). He was associated with the "Hartford (or Connecticut) Wits," an informal group, Federalist in their politics but promoting a new American spirit in their writing; although he published a number of satirical essays and poems, he is known today solely for one work, *M'Fingle* (1775–82), a burlesque epic poem satirizing the pro-British Tories in America.

Trumbull, Jonathan (1740–1809) merchant, governor; born in Lebanon, Conn. (brother of John Trumbull, painter). He was a Continental army paymaster (1775–78), the first comptroller of the treasury (1778–79), and George Washington's secretary (1781–83). He served as a congressman (1789–94; Speaker of the House 1791–94) and senator (1795–96) before becoming governor of Connecticut (1797–1809). In 1809 he refused to deploy Connecticut militiamen to enforce the Embargo Act.

Trumbull, Jonathan (1710–85) patriot, governor; born in Lebanon, Conn. (father of John Trumbull, the painter, and of Jonathan Trumbull, the governor). Originally a successful merchant, he was governor of Connecticut (1769–84). He was the only colonial governor to adopt a radical stance at the start of the American Revolution. He made Connecticut a principal source of supplies for the Continental army.

Trumbull, Lyman (1813–96) U.S. senator, jurist; born in Colchester, Conn. He first went to Georgia to teach school (1833–37), but after studying law he moved to Illinois to practice there and was named to that state's supreme court. Originally a Democrat, he opposed his party on the slavery issue and was appointed to the U.S. Senate as a free-soil Democrat (Ill.; 1855–61). He was reelected senator as a Republican (1861–67) but after the Civil War he came to reject the Radical Republicans' policies, voted to acquit President Johnson, and returned to the Democratic Party for his final term (1867–73). He served as Samuel Tilden's lawyer during the contested presidential election of 1876 and he ran unsuccessfully as the Democratic candidate for governor of Illinois in 1880.

Trumka, Richard (1949–) union leader; born in Nemacolin, Pa. Son of an Italian-American mother and a Polish-American coalminer, Richard himself spent some seven years of his youth working in the coal mines. He took an active role in the local of the United Mine Workers (UMW) but he left the mines to take a degree in accounting from Pennsylvania State University and then a law degree from Villanova. In 1974 he went to Washington to serve on the legal staff of the UMW where he soon became dissatisfied with the way the union was being operated. Running as an insurgent, he was elected president in 1982, winning by a clear 2–1 majority. As the fourth president in ten years of a union long associated with violence and corruption, he brought a new stability; as a "technocrat," he spoke for the new breed of highly skilled miners; and as a man of the highest personal standards, he was expected to bring a new integrity to the UMW.

Trump, Donald (John) (1946–) real estate developer; born in New York City. He was the son of a New York City residential real estate developer, whose Trump Organization he took over. He greatly expanded its holdings and built increasingly grandiose buildings including the Trump Tower, New York (1982) and Atlantic City casinos. His high-profile political dealmaking and enthusiastic self-promotion made him a 1980s celebrity who suffered a spectacular crash into near-bankruptcy in 1990.

Truscott, Alan (Fraser) (1925–) bridge player, writer; born in London, England. He won several Oxford University chess titles and was European bridge champion (1961). Named bridge editor of the *New York Times* in 1964, he became the only U.S. newspaper columnist to regularly cover events as well as provide instruction.

Truscott, Lucien King, Jr. (1895–1965) soldier; born in Chatfield, Texas. He taught school for several years before receiving a commission in 1917 and rose through the grades to command U.S. assault forces in the invasion of southern France in August 1944. He led the Fifth Army from December 1944 until the end of the war.

Truth, Sojourner (b. Isabella) (?1797–1883) abolitionist, women's rights activist; born in Ulster County, N.Y. Born to slaves of a wealthy Dutch-American estate owner – she grew up speaking Dutch – she herself served as a slave in the Dumont family (1810–27) and had at least five children (two daughters were sold away from her). She fled her owners' household in 1827 and found refuge in the home of the Van Wageners and took their name. She successfully sued to get her son back from slavery in Alabama, and about 1829 she settled in New York City with him and a daughter. A religious mystic by this time, for the next few years she was heavily involved with some questionable religious evangelicals; after a scandal in which she was an innocent bystander, she withdrew to raise her children and to work as a domestic. Then in 1843 she announced that "voices" had commanded her to assume the name "Sojourner Truth" and to set out as a preacher. She ended up in Northampton, Mass., with a utopian community and stayed there until about 1850 when she settled in Battle Creek, Mich. By that time she had also added lectures on abolition and women's rights to her public appearances. (Extremely tall, she was accused of being a man and is said to have bared her breast at a women's rights convention to prove she was a woman.) She was received by President Lincoln at the White House in 1864. After the war she advocated a "Negro State" and promoted the emigration of African-Americans to the West. She continued to travel throughout much of the northeast, lecturing on a variety of inspirational and social reform topics, retiring to Battle Creek, Mich., in her later years.

Truxtun, Thomas (1753–1822) naval officer, merchant captain; born near Hempstead, N.Y. He was successful as a privateer in the American Revolution and as a captain in the China trade. He became a naval captain (1794) and supervised the construction of the USS *Constellation* at Baltimore. During the undeclared war with France he captured the French *Insurgente* (1799) and defeated *La Vengeance* in a five-hour battle (1800). He wrote books on navigation and naval tactics and left a record of success for the new U.S. Navy.

Tryon, Thomas (1926–) actor, writer; born in Hartford, Conn. He studied at Yale (B.A. 1949), and in New York City at the Art Students League and the Neighborhood Playhouse. Using the name of Tom Tryon, he was an actor (1952–71) on Broadway, and television, as well as in Hollywood films. He gave up on acting to become a successful novelist. He wrote compelling horror fiction, as in *The Other* (1971), and *Harvest Home* (1973), before writing novels set in

Hollywood, such as *All That Glitters: Five Novellas* (1986). He lived in New York City.

Tryon, William (1729–88) colonial governor, Loyalist; born in Surrey, England. He served as governor of North Carolina (1765–71) and of New York (1771–75). Later, he led Loyalist attacks on Connecticut (1780). Although a capable administrator, he was too prone to use force.

Tuan, Yi-Fu (1930–) geographer; born in Tients'in, China. He emigrated to England in 1946 and to the United States in 1951. He studied at Oxford and the University of California: Berkeley before becoming a professor at the University of Wisconsin: Madison (1983). One of the newer generation of geographers concerned with broader philosophical issues of the subject, he was a prolific author; his books include *Topophilia* (1974), *Space and Place* (1977), *Landscapes of Fear* (1979), and *Morality and Imagination: Paradoxes of Progress* (1989).

Tubb, Ernest (1914–84) country music songwriter, performer; born near Crisp, Texas. After recording for RCA Victor and Decca, he joined the "Grand Ole Opry" in 1943. His own radio program, *Midnight Jamboree*, helped launch the careers of the Everly Brothers and Elvis Presley. Tubb's drawling vocal style, unaffected lyrics, and espousal of the electric guitar made him a major influence on honky tonk music. He was elected to the Country Music Hall of Fame in 1965.

Tubman, Harriet (b. Ross) (c. 1820–1913) abolitionist; born in Bucktown, Md. Reared in slavery, she married a free black, John Tubman, in 1844. He opposed her plans to flee north, so she escaped alone via the Underground Railroad (1849); over the next decade she led nearly 300 Maryland slaves to safety, including several siblings and her elderly parents. Known as "the Moses of her people," she was devoutly religious and a believer in decisive action. She helped John Brown organize his 1859 raid on Harper's Ferry, Va., but was prevented by illness from accompanying him. During the Civil War she repeatedly went behind enemy lines to spy for the Union and recruit slaves to fight in the army. In her later years, living in Auburn, N.Y., she helped support relatives and other former slaves and raised money for freedmen's schools and a home for elderly blacks.

Tuchman, Barbara (1912–89) historian; born in New York City. After graduating from Radcliffe College (1933) and reporting on the Spanish Civil War for the *Nation* (1937–38), she turned to the study of history. Her career as a nonacademic, best-selling historian began in earnest with her fourth book, the Pulitzer Prize-winning *The Guns of August* (1962). *Stillwell and the American Experience in China, 1911–45* (1971) won a second Pulitzer. Her six best-sellers sold many millions of copies.

Tuchman, Maurice (1936–) museum curator; born in New York City. He graduated in art history from City College of New York in 1957 and took a master's degree from Columbia University two years later. He became curator of 20th-century art at the Los Angeles County Museum (1964). An expert on contemporary art, he wrote extensively for professional journals.

Tucker, Benjamin (Ricketson) (1854–1939) anarchist, reformer; born in South Darmouth, Mass. Although he attended the Massachusetts Institute of Technology (1870–73), he was more drawn to social reform than engineering and became a convert to individualist anarchism (1872).

Leaving school, he traveled to France to study the works of French socialist Pierre Joseph Proudhon, on whom he became an authority. He translated and published at his own expense Proudhon's celebrated work under the title *What is Property?* (1876). He founded the *Radical Review* (1877), but his most famous publication was the broadsheet, *Liberty,* which was issued regularly (1881–1908) and became a widely read clearinghouse for unorthodox thought. A brilliant polemicist, he wrote much of *Liberty* himself while on the staff of the *Boston Globe* (1878) and then as editor of the *Engineering Magazine* in New York City (1892). An outspoken, at times literary voice for individualist anarchism, he defied police arrest by selling banned books. His publishing venture collapsed (1908) when his New York establishment was destroyed by fire. He moved to France and never again found much of a public for his writings. He and his family moved to Monaco (1926) and letters from the 1930s reflect a growing despair at the rise of totalitarianism.

Tucker, Henry St. George (1780–1848) jurist; born in Chesterfield County, Va. (son of St. George Tucker). Member of the Virginia house and senate and the U.S. House of Representatives (Dem.-Rep., Va; 1815–19), and a superior court judge (1824–31), he was elected president of the Virginia Supreme Court in 1831. In 1841 he became professor of law at the University of Virginia, initiating its "Honor System." A soldier in the War of 1812 and the author of light verse, he wrote important legal commentaries.

Tucker, John Randolph (1823–97) lawyer, professor, congressman; born in Winchester, Va. (son of Henry St. George Tucker, 1780–1848). Attorney general of Virginia (1857–65), professor and dean at Washington & Lee University (1870–74, 1889–97), U.S. Representative (Dem., Va.; 1875–87), he maintained a law practice (1865–97), often appearing before the U.S. Supreme Court. He championed states' rights, tariff reform, and the Constitution.

Tucker, Richard (b. Reuben Ticker) (1913–75) opera tenor; born in New York City. He started singing in synagogues as a child and was working as a fur salesman in New York when he married the sister of established tenor, Jan Peerce, who challenged him to take voice lessons. He made his Metropolitan Opera debut in 1945, becoming an internationally popular lyric tenor. He continued to sing as a cantor on special occasions.

Tucker, Robert (C.) (1918–) Slavic specialist, educator; born in Kansas City, Mo. A guiding force in the analysis of the modern Soviet state, he taught longest at Princeton University (1962) where he was named professor emeritus (1984). He was chairman of the Council on International and Regional Studies (1977–80) and director of the Program in Russian Studies (1963–73, 1980–82). A member of the American Academy of Arts and Sciences (1975), he was the author of a number of books on the former Soviet Union and Stalinism. These included *Politics As Leadership* (1983), *Political Culture and Leadership in Soviet Russia: From Lenin to Gorbachev* (1987), and *Stalin in Power: The Revolution from Above (1929–41)* (1992).

Tucker, Sophie (b. Sonia Kalish) (1884–1966) singer, entertainer; born in Russia. Brought to the U.S.A. as a child, she first performed on vaudeville in blackface, singing ragtime melodies. She almost stole the show in the *Ziegfield Follies of 1909* and returned as a star to vaudeville, abandoning blackface but continuing in the African-American style. She helped popularize songs of black composers such as Eubie Blake and was also known for her racy songs. She enjoyed great success on tour to England in 1922 and went on to appear in several stage and movie musicals, but was especially known as a nightclub torch singer. In her later years she billed herself as "The Last of the Red-Hot Mamas."

Tucker, St. George (1752–1827) jurist; born in Port Royal, Bermuda. He emigrated to Virginia in his late teens. A lieutenant-colonel at Yorktown, he became judge of the general court in Virginia (1788) and professor at William and Mary (1800). He sat on the Virginia Supreme Court (1803–11) and was federal judge for Virginia (1813–27). His important works include his *Dissertation on Slavery: with a Proposal for its Gradual Abolition in Virginia* (1796) and an annotated *Blackstone's Commentaries* (1803).

Tuckerman, Edward (1817–86) botanist; born in Boston, Mass. (brother of Frederick G. Tuckerman). After receiving a law degree from Harvard (1839), he studied lichens in Europe (1841–42) under the Swedish lichen specialist Elias Fries. He became museum curator at Union College (1842–43), then returned to Harvard, earning a bachelor's degree (1847) and a degree in divinity (1852). He wrote many historical and theological articles after joining Amherst College as a lecturer in history (1854–58) and a professor of botany (1858–86). He was the first botanist to explore the New England mountains for lichens; his *Genera Lichenum: An Arrangement of North American Lichens* (1872) is considered his greatest book on this topic. Tuckerman Ravine in New Hampshire is named for him.

Tuckerman, Frederick Goddard (1821–73) poet; born in Boston, Mass. He studied at Harvard (1841) and at the Law School there (1839–42); although admitted to the bar (1844), he practiced only briefly. A wealthy man, he retired to Greenfield, Mass., to study literature, botany, and astronomy (1847). Rediscovered as a poet in 1931, he is known for his sonnets and narrative poetry, notably "The Cricket," a study of the relationship of man and nature.

Tuckerman, Henry Theodore (1813–71) art/literary critic; born in Boston, Mass. He attended Harvard (1832–33), withdrew due to poor health, and traveled abroad (1833–34). He returned to Boston, published books on Italy, and settled in New York City (1845). Independently wealthy, he is regarded today as a pedantic and sentimental critic of the arts, but during his lifetime he was highly praised. Of his many books, only one or two, such as *Book of the Artists: American Artist Life* (1867), now have much of interest.

Tudor, David (1926–) pianist, composer; born in Philadelphia. A formidable technician, he gravitated to music on the edge of the avant-garde and is best known for performing John Cage's music.

Tudor, Frederic (1783–1864) businessman; born in Boston, Mass. He developed and pursued the practice of sending cargoes of ice from Boston to the tropical ports of Havana, Charleston, New Orleans, and eventually Calcutta, India (1833). Known as the "Ice King," he prospered and became a leading citizen in Boston.

Tudor, Tasha (b. Starling Burgess) (1915–) writer, illustrator; born in Boston, Mass. She studied at the Boston Museum of Fine Arts School. Her mother, Rosamond Tudor, was a portrait painter, and Tasha changed her first name and adopted her mother's maiden name. She also elected to live a 19th-century lifestyle in Marlboro, Vt., where she raised all her food, lived without inside plumbing, and made her own candles. Her illustrations are reminiscent of Kate Greenaway, and her immensely popular books for children, such as *Tasha Tudor's Favorite Stories* (1965), and her illustrations for the work of other writers, continue to delight young and adult readers.

Tufte, Edward R. (Rolf) (1942–) political scientist, statistician, information designer; born in Kansas City, Mo. After taking his Ph.D. at Yale (1965), he taught public policy at Princeton (1967–71), then joined the faculty at Yale (1971) where he became a professor of political science and statistics (1977). In addition to publishing various specialized monographs in his field, such as *Political Control of the Economy* (1978), he became more widely known as a pioneer proponent of using graphs, charts, diagrams, and other visual elements – on both the printed page and computers – to convey significant information with more clarity. In furtherance of this he started his own firm, Graphics Press, to publish his own handsomely designed books, *The Visual Display of Quantitative Information* (1983) and *Envisioning Information* (1990), in which scientific and aesthetic elements combine to advance his ideas about making the complex more comprehensible.

Tufts, John (1689–1750) minister, hymnologist; born in Medford, Mass. A Harvard-educated minister, he published the pioneering instruction book, *A Very Plain and Easy Introduction to the Art of Singing Psalm Tunes* (1721). It went through 11 editions in the next 24 years and helped to make music acceptable to Americans emerging from a Puritan tradition.

Tugwell, Rexford (Guy) (1891–1979) economist, public official; born in Sinclairville, N.Y. An economics professor at Columbia University when recruited to join Franklin Roosevelt's "Brain Trust" in 1932, he became head of the Resettlement Administration in 1935. He pushed through an ambitious program to resettle rural poor in new greenbelt towns before resigning in 1936. He was governor of Puerto Rico (1941–46) and taught economics at the University of Chicago (1946–57).

Tune, Tommy (b. Thomas James Tune) (1939–) actor, director, choreographer; born in Wichita Falls, Texas. Choreographer and codirector of *The Best Little Whorehouse in Texas* (1978), he won Tony Awards for his acting and choreography.

Tunney, (James Joseph) "Gene" (1898–1978) boxer; born in New York City. Although he boxed as a youth, he came to notice when he won the light heavyweight title of the American Forces serving in Europe in World War I (he was in the U.S. Marines). He was the world heavyweight champion (1926–28) and twice defeated Jack Dempsey during the 1920s "golden age" of sports. He was the beneficiary of a controversial "long count" in the second Dempsey bout in 1927 when he was knocked down and given a delayed count before coming back to defeat Dempsey on points. Cultivated and well spoken, he posted a career record of 65 victories (43 knockouts), two defeats, and one draw. In World War II he served in the U.S. Navy as director of its physical fitness program. His son, John V. Tunney, was U.S. Senator from California (1971–77).

Tureck, Rosalyn (1914–) pianist, harpsichordist; born in Chicago. She made her debut at age 11 with the Chicago

Symphony and joined the Juilliard faculty in 1943. She was among the century's leading Bach interpreters.

Turekian, Karl K. (Karekin) (1927–) oceanographer; born in New York City. A professor of geology and geophysics at Yale (1956), he made major contributions to prehistoric glaciology and the geochemistry of oceanic trace elements.

Turnbull, Colin (1924–) anthropologist; born in Harrow, England. He studied at Oxford University (B.A. 1947, M.A. 1949, B.Litt. 1957, D.Phil. 1964). He conducted fieldwork first in India (1949–51), then among the Mbuti pygmies of Zaire. He worked at the American Museum of Natural History in New York (1959–69), then became professor at George Washington University in 1976. He wrote several books on Africa, including *The Forest People* (1961), *Wayward Servants* (1965), and *The Human Cycle* (1983).

Turner, Frederick Jackson (1861–1932) historian; born in Portage, Wis. Taking his Ph.D. from Johns Hopkins (1890), he taught at the University of Wisconsin (1889–1910) and at Harvard (1910–24). When he read a paper, "The Significance of the Frontier in American History," at the American Historical Association's meeting at Chicago World's Columbian Exposition (1893), he gained almost overnight prominence among his colleagues as well as the subject of his life's work. His paper was printed in 1894, and after he had spent his career developing and supporting it, he presented its final form in the Pulitzer Prize-winning *Significance of Sections in American History* (1932). His thesis, simply stated, is that Americans' history, culture and psychology derived less from their European heritage and more from their distinctive frontier – the free land and its resources that allowed for new kinds of interactions among the emerging nation's inhabitants. He spent the next 40 years exploring and teaching his thesis and won several generations of specialists and observers over to it; although it would eventually come under attack from revisionists, "the frontier" remains one of the touchstones of American history and indissolubly associated with Turner.

Turner, (Joseph) "Big" Joe (1911–85) jazz vocalist; born in Kansas City, Mo. A major influence on blues and rock musicians, he began as a blues-shouting bartender and came to prominence at the "Spirituals to Swing" concert at Carnegie Hall in 1938. He teamed with boogie-woogie pianist Pete Johnson until 1955 and appeared in many jazz all-star contexts thereafter.

Turner, Nat (1800–31) leader of slave insurrection; born in Southampton County, Va. He was born on the Virginia plantation of Benjamin Turner, who allowed him to be instructed in reading, writing, and religion. Sold three times in his childhood and hired out to John Travis (in the 1820s), he became a fiery preacher and leader of African-American slaves on Benjamin Turner's plantation and in his Southampton County, Va., neighborhood, claiming that he was chosen by God to lead them from bondage. Believing in signs and hearing divine voices, he was convinced by an eclipse of the sun (1831) that the time to rise up had come and he enlisted the help of four other slaves in the area. An insurrection was planned, aborted, and rescheduled; then, on August 21–22, he and six other slaves killed the Travis family, managed to secure arms and horses, and enlisted about 75 other slaves in a disorganized insurrection that resulted in only the murder of 51 white people. Afterwards, he hid nearby successfully for six weeks until his discovery, conviction, and hanging at

Jerusalem, Va., along with 16 of his followers. The incident put fear in the heart of Southerners, ended the organized emancipation movement in that region, resulted in even harsher laws against slaves, and deepened the schism between slaveholders and free-soilers that would culminate in the Civil War.

Turner, Ralph H. (Herbert) (1919–) sociologist; born in Effingham, Ill. He earned his Ph.D. at the University of Chicago and spent his long academic career at the University of California: Los Angeles (1948–90). He specialized in collective behavior and social movements, and wrote *Collective Behavior* (coauthored, 1957, later revised) and several works on community response to disasters, particularly earthquakes.

Turner, Richmond K. (Kelly) (1885–1961) naval officer; born in Portland, Ore. He served on battleships during World War I and was on the staff of the Naval War College (1935–38). He commanded the amphibious forces that launched the grueling Guadalcanal campaign (1942). He planned and directed amphibious landings at Makin and Tarawa (1943), in the Marshall Islands (1944), and at Iwo Jima and Okinawa (1945). He was the naval representative on the United Nations Military Staff Committee (1945–47).

Turner, (Robert Edward III) Ted (1938–) communications tycoon; born in Cincinnati, Ohio. Expelled from Brown University for having women in his room, he took over the family's Atlanta-based billboard enterprise in 1963 after his father's suicide and began building his media empire. In 1970 he bought an independent Atlanta UHF station and built it into the first satellite-transmitted superstation. His programming strategy was based on sports broadcasts of the Atlanta Braves and Hawks, the baseball and basketball teams he owned. He developed the Cable News Network, turning it into a worldwide news network with 24-hour coverage. In the late 1980s he created Turner Broadcasting System, the first new network since the advent of public television in the 1960s, as well as a cable service, Turner Network Television. A man of boundless energy and ambitious ideals – an accomplished sailor, he set himself the goal of winning the America's Cup and did so in 1977 – he set out to improve relations with the then U.S.S.R. by establishing the Goodwill Games in 1985 and later turned his attention to promoting environmental issues. His third marriage in 1991 was to movie star Jane Fonda, and the impact of his various enterprises was such that *Time* named him "Man of the Year" that year.

Turner, Roscoe (1895–1970) aviator; born in Corinth, Mass. He served in the Balloon Service during World War I and then worked as a circus lion tamer, parachute jumper, and stunt flyer. In the 1930s Turner, a colorful personality, broke transcontinental speed records seven times and won many awards for his flying.

Turner, Thomas Wyatt (1877–1978) social activist; born in Charles County, Md. An African-American Catholic who taught biology at Howard University (from 1913), he organized and chaired a Committee for the Advancement of Colored Catholics (later Federated Colored Catholics) to combat racial discrimination in the church; it was active especially from 1919 until 1932, when it was splintered by a dispute over Turner's then-controversial emphasis on protest and confrontation.

Turner, Victor Witter (1920–) cultural anthropologist; born

744

in Glasgow, Scotland. Educated at the Universities of London and Manchester, he taught at Manchester before becoming professor of anthropology at Cornell University in 1963. An authority on rituals and social processes, he taught social thought at the University of Chicago (1968–77), and moved on to the University of Virginia in 1977.

Tuttle, Merlin D. (Devere) (1941–   ) mammalogist; born in Honolulu, Hawaii. He was codirector of the Venezuelan Research Project of the Smithsonian Institution (1965–67), performed research on population ecology at the University of Minnesota (1972), then became curator of mammals at the Milwaukee Public Museum (1975–86). He made major contributions to studies of predator/prey interaction and foraging behavior in mammals, and the energetics of thermoregulation, hibernation, and migration in bats. He founded Bat Conservation International (1982) in Austin, Texas, to promote a positive image of bats and encourage their preservation, and he relocated to Austin (1986) to work exclusively for this cause.

Twachtman, John Henry (1853–1902) painter, etcher; born in Cincinnati, Ohio. He began as a window shade decorator and studied under Frank Duveneck at the McMicken School of Design, Cincinnati, Ohio (1871). After study in Munich (1875–77), and living in Venice (1877) and Paris (1883–85), he returned to settle in Greenwich, Conn. (1889). His work was influenced by James Whistler and impressionism, as seen in *Araques-la-Bataille* (1885). He taught at the Art Students League, New York (1889–1902), and was a founder of the Ten (1898), an impressionist group.

Twain, Mark See CLEMENS, SAMUEL LANGHORNE.

Tweed, (William Marcy) "Boss" (1823–78) U.S. representative, political boss; born in New York City. He apprenticed as a saddler and then became an officer in a volunteer fire company. He was a city alderman and then served in the U.S. House of Representatives (Dem., N.Y.; 1853–55). By 1857, he was emerging as the major power in New York City's Tammany Hall Democrats, controlling patronage and nominations to public offices. By 1868 he was sitting in the state senate and he also became commissioner of public works for New York City, positions that further advanced his control of graft and corruption; the gigantic profits of the "Tweed Ring" were estimated at between 30 and 200 million dollars. He also joined Jay Gould and James Fisk in the illegal financial transactions that looted the Erie Railroad. Although everyone knew of his doings, he remained popular because of his generosity, but by 1871 reformers were able to organize against him. Finally convicted in 1873, he escaped to Cuba and Spain (1875–76) but was extradited and returned to jail, where he died.

Twining, Nathaniel (Farragut) (1897–1982) aviator; born in Monroe, Wis. A 1918 West Point graduate, he served eight years in the infantry before transferring to the air service. Promoted rapidly on the outbreak of World War II, he took command of the newly formed 13th Air Force in the Southwest Pacific in 1942; in January 1944 he went to the Mediterranean as commander of the Fifteenth Air Force, which carried out the famous Ploesti oilfield raids under his direction. Twining returned to the Pacific in August 1945 to command the Twentieth Air Force in the final phase of the air offensive against Japan. He ended a long service career as chairman of the joint chiefs of staff (1957–60).

Twitty, Victor C. (Chandler) (1901–67) zoologist; born near Loogootee, Ind. He taught zoology at Yale (1929–31), became a National Research Council fellow at the Kaiser Wilhelm Institute, Berlin (1931–32), then joined Stanford University (1932–63). During his career investigating the biology of salamanders, he made major contributions to studies of their skin pigmentation and organ and tissue differentiation, discovered new species of the western newt, and demonstrated homing behavior in these animals using artificial hybridization.

Twombly, Cy (1928–   ) painter; born in Lexington, Va. He studied at the Boston Museum School (1948–49), and at the Black Mountain College, N.C., with Franz Kline and Robert Motherwell (1951–52). He traveled in Europe and Africa (1952–53) before settling permanently in Italy (1957), and is known for his calligraphic–like work, as in *Leda and the Swan* (1961).

Tworkov, Jack (1900–82) painter; born in Biala, Poland. He emigrated to New York (1913), studied at Columbia University (1920–23), and at the National Academy of Design (1923–25). Based in New York and Provincetown, Mass., he taught at many schools and was part of the New York school of painting in the 1940s and 1950s, as seen in *The Wheel* (1953).

Tyler, Anne (m. Modarressi) (1941–   ) writer; born in Minneapolis, Minn. She studied at Duke (B.A. 1961) and Columbia (1961–62) Universities. She worked as a Russian bibliographer at Duke (1962–63), and as a library assistant at McGill University, Montreal (1964–65). Reynolds Price encouraged her to write when she attended Duke, but it was only when she settled in Baltimore (1967) with her psychiatrist husband and children that she began to produce her highly acclaimed short stories and novels. She is best known for such novels as *Dinner at the Homesick Restaurant* (1982), and *The Accidental Tourist* (1985).

Tyler, Harold R. (Russell), Jr. ("Ace") (1922–   ) lawyer; born in Utica, N.Y. In New York City private practice most of 1950–62, he was U.S. district judge (1962–75) and deputy U.S. attorney general (1975–77). In 1977 he joined Patterson, Belknap, Webb & Tyler, representing corporate clients.

Tyler, John (1790–1862) tenth U.S. president; born in Charles City County, Va. Trained as a lawyer, Tyler steadily ascended the political ladder, gaining the state legislature in 1811, the U.S. House of Representatives (1816–19), the Virginia governorship (1825–27), and the U.S. Senate (1827–36). Highly active as a senator, he maintained a states' rights position and resisted all attempts to regulate slavery; he resigned from the Senate to protest President Jackson's antinullification measures. Gravitating to the anti-Jackson Whigs, Tyler won election as Benjamin Harrison's vice-president in 1840, then ascended to the presidency on Harrison's death in April 1841. He soon alienated his Whig supporters by resisting a new national bank; at one point he had to lead the White House staff in holding off a violent mob, and in 1843 the Whigs even threatened to impeach him. Nonetheless, his term saw the Webster-Ashburton Treaty fixing the borders of the U.S. and Canada; he also encouraged the move to annex Texas. Long out of the public eye after failing to be nominated in 1844, Tyler headed a Southern peace mission to find a compromise to avoid splitting the Union in 1861. When that failed, he voted for Virginia to secede and was elected to the Confederate House of Representatives just before his death.

Tyler, Julia (b. Gardiner) (1820–89) First Lady; born on Gardiner's Island, N.Y. She married the widower John Tyler in 1844 and they had seven children. She was an energetic first lady – the first one to have her own press secretary.

Tyler, Letitia (b. Christian) (1790–1842) First Lady; born in New Kent County, Va. She married John Tyler in 1813. A quiet, modest person, she died after a stroke, the first president's wife to die in the White House.

Tyler, Royall (1757–1826) lawyer, judge, playwright; born in Boston, Mass. After reading law, he served in the American Revolution and then took up the practice of law, first in Portland, Maine (1780–85) and then in Boston (1785–91). He volunteered for service in the force that quelled Shays Rebellion in 1787, the very year that his comedy, *The Contrast,* became the first professionally produced play (in New York City) by an American. It included a character, Jonathan, the first of many similar no-nonsense Yankees who would appear on stage. His comic opera, *May Day in Town,* was also produced in New York in 1787, and he wrote several other plays, some of them now lost. In 1791 he moved to Vermont where he eventually served as the state's chief justice (1807–13) and was also a professor of jurisprudence at the University of Vermont (1811–14). Meanwhile, he continued his literary career. Under the pen name of Spondee, he collaborated with Joseph Dennie to write satirical prose and verse for several publications. He also published one novel, *The Algerine Captive* (1797).

Tyner, McCoy (Alfred) (1938–　) jazz musician; born in Philadelphia, Pa. An influential pianist, he began with the Jazztet in 1959 and then emerged between 1960 and 1965 as a dynamic keyboard artist in the historic John Coltrane Quartet. He free-lanced as a sideman with various singers until 1972, and went on to lead his own ensembles.

Typhoid Mary See MALLON, MARY.

Tyson, Cicely (1942–　) actress; born in New York City. Daughter of immigrants from the Caribbean island of Nevis, she was raised in poverty. She worked as a secretary and a model while establishing herself as an actress. With Arthur Mitchell, she cofounded the Dance Theatre of Harlem. Her stage and television credits include the film *Sounder* (1972), the miniseries *Roots* (1977), and the television movie *The Autobiography of Miss Jane Pittman* (1974), for which she won an Emmy. She was briefly married to jazz trumpeter Miles Davis.

U

Udall, Stewart (Lee) (1920–   ) conservationist, public official; born in St. John, Ariz. Son of a jurist who became chief justice of Arizona, he served in the air force during World War II. He practiced law for several years before winning election to the U.S. House of Representatives (Dem., Ariz.; 1955–61) where he developed a reputation as a conservation advocate. As secretary of the interior in the Kennedy and Johnson administrations (1961–69), he curbed abuses in the sale and exploitation of public lands and reformed the Bureau of Indian Affairs. He became a private conservation consultant in 1969.

Ueberroth, Peter (Victor) (1937–   ) businessman, baseball commissioner, Olympics chairman; born in Evanston, Ill. He was both athletic and entrepreneurial from an early age, and after graduation from college he went on to become the operations manager and vice-president of the Trans International Airline (1959–62). He then formed his own company, Transportation Consultants International (1963–79). Invited in 1979 to head the Los Angeles Olympics Organizing Committee, he used his marketing and business talents to turn the 1984 games into a self-supporting event and was named "Man of the Year" by *Time* for 1984. That same year he became commissioner of baseball, but he soon became disenchanted by his inability to have a decisive impact on affairs and in 1989, after one term, he stepped aside and went back to the private business world. In the wake of the Los Angeles riots (1992), he headed a task force of public and private institutions determined to remove the economic and social causes of such episodes, an assignment even more frustrating than dealing with the owners of major league baseball teams.

Ulam, Adam (Bruno) (1922–   ) Russian specialist, educator; born in Lwow, Poland. Emigrating to America to teach government at Harvard University (1947), he directed the Russian Research Center (1973–74). He was a research associate for the Center for International Studies, Massachusetts Institute of Technology (1953–55). Although many of his books focused on the Russian political system of the cold war era, he also wrote *The Fall of the American University* (1972) and contributed to many professional journals.

Ullman, Edward (Louis) (1912–76) geographer; born in Chicago, Ill. A Ph.D. graduate from the University of Chicago (1942), he worked for U.S. government agencies in the 1940s, including the Office of Special Services and the Joint Chiefs of Staff (1943–46). Professor of geography at the University of Washington (1951–76), he was a specialist in

cities and transportation networks, serving as director for the Center for Urban and Regional Research (1967–69) and publishing *The Economic Base of American Cities* (1969).

Ulrich, Edward Oscar (1857–1944) geologist, paleontologist; born in Cincinnati, Ohio. He was curator of the Cincinnati Society of Natural History (1877–81), paleontologist for geological surveys of the U.S. Midwest (1885–96), and geologist for the U.S. Geological Survey (1897–1932). He made significant contributions to marine invertebrate paleozoology and chronologic stratigraphy.

Uncas (?1606–82) Pequot/Mohegan leader; born in present-day Connecticut. He led rebellions against his father-in-law, Sassacus, the Pequot leader, eventually taking over part of the Pequot lands and ruling its people under their new tribal name, the Mohegans. He maintained power throughout much of his life with the help of the English colonists, whom he supported in the Pequot War (1636–37) and King Philip's War (1675–76).

Uncle Sam See WILSON, SAMUEL.

Underhill, John (?1597–1672) soldier; born in England. He fought in the Pequot War in New England (1637); served as governor of the colony at Dover, N.H. (1638–40); and participated in the war against Holland (1664–65) that added New Amsterdam to English possessions in America.

Underwood, Oscar (Wilder) (1862–1929) U.S. representative/ senator; born in Louisville, Ky. He practiced law in Birmingham before going to the U.S. House of Representatives (Dem., Ala.; 1897–1915). A brilliant man, destined for higher office, his fight with William Jennings Bryan over tariff reductions in 1911 cost him the critical votes in the 1912 presidential convention. In the U.S. Senate (1915–27) he masterminded wartime appropriations. A second bid for the presidency ended in 1923 when he demanded the Democratic convention denounce the Ku Klux Klan.

Underwood, William (1787–1864) food processor; born in London, England. He apprenticed at Cross & Blackwell's factory before moving to Boston (1819) to open William Underwood & Co. (1822), the first canning factory in New England. He expanded his fruit line to include pickles, milk, and sauces (1828), and canned tomatoes (1835). In 1839 he began substituting tin cans for glass jars and found them less expensive and more adaptable. He opened a lobster canning business in Harpswell, Maine, in 1844, and an oyster canning plant in Boston in 1850. As competition increased, he focused on specialty foods such as deviled ham, clams, and sardines. In 1860 he purchased the rights to advanced sterilization methods, and during the Civil War he canned roast beef for Union soldiers.

Unitas, (John Constantine) Johnny (1933–) football player; born in Pittsburgh, Pa. The Pittsburgh Steelers cut the former University of Louisville quarterback in their 1955 training camp, but he signed with the Baltimore Colts in 1956 and led them to National Football League championships in 1958 and 1959. An exceptional leader and passer who thrived on pressure, he threw at least one touchdown pass in 47 consecutive games. Often all-pro, he passed for 40,239 yards in 19 seasons.

Unruh, Jesse M. (Marvin) (1922–87) public official; born in Newton, Kans. A sharecropper's son, he put himself through college on the G.I. bill, working for a railway freight company afterward. As a Democratic Californian assemblyman (1951–69), he increased the assembly's power and professionalism, becoming speaker in 1961. A shrewd politician, he managed Pat Brown's and Robert Kennedy's campaigns in California. He became state treasurer in 1974.

Unser, Al (1939–) auto racer; born in Albuquerque, N.M. He won the Indianapolis 500 four times (1970–71, 1978, 1987). His brother, Bobby Unser, won the Indianapolis 500 three times (1968, 1975, 1981). His son, Al Unser Jr., became a champion auto racer.

Untermeyer, Samuel (1858–1940) lawyer; born in Lynchburg, Va. He grew up in Virginia and New York City and graduated from Columbia Law School in 1878. He opened a law office the following year and gradually established himself as the leading trial lawyer of his time. Much involved in forming large corporations early in his career, he later argued many cases aimed at breaking up the concentration of economic power. As special counsel for a congressional committee that investigated (1912–13) the so-called "Money Trust," he helped prepare the ground for the Federal Reserve Act, the Federal Trade Commission Act, and the Clayton Anti-Trust Act. A lifelong Democrat (though he never ran for office), he was a strong supporter of Franklin D. Roosevelt's New Deal of the 1930s.

Updike, Daniel Berkeley (1860–1941) printer, scholar; born in Providence, R.I. In 1893 he founded Merrymount Press, which printed finely made books, mostly for other publishers, and greatly influenced development of the graphic arts. A scholar of printing, he wrote *Printing Types: Their History, Forms, and Use* (1922).

Updike, John (Hoyer) (1932–) writer, poet, critic; born in Shillington, Pa. He studied at Harvard (B.A. 1954) and the Ruskin School of Drawing and Fine Arts, Oxford (1954–55); although he would not develop his youthful talents as an artist, he never lost his interest in art. He worked on the staff of the *New Yorker* for two years; while maintaining his relationship with that periodical, he became, over the years, a highly successful novelist, short story writer, poet, and essayist, eventually settling in Georgetown, Mass. His first novel, *The Poorhouse Fair* (1957), initiated the critical dispute about his writing: some critics would praise his wit, style, use of language, and his affinity for the middle class and their spiritual and sexual angst; others complain about his plots, the sexual content of his work, and the alleged lack of substance. For most readers, Updike became associated with such popular works as *The Witches of Eastwick* (1989) and his contemporary American Everyman, Harry "Rabbit" Angstron in *Rabbit Run* (1960), *Rabbit Redux* (1971), *Rabbit*

is Rich (1981), and *Rabbit at Rest* (1990). Some readers and critics feel that *The Centaur* (1963), an early mythic novel about a teacher in a small town, is his best work. He is also admired for his many reviews and essays on a wide range of writers, artists, and cultural issues.

Upjohn, Richard (1802–78) architect; born in Shaftesbury, Dorset, England. He emigrated (1829) and worked with Alexander Parris in Boston (1834–38). His first major building and the one by which he is best remembered was Trinity Church, New York (1839–46), which definitively linked the Protestant Episcopal Church with the Gothic Revival style. Upjohn designed many residences and public buildings promoting medieval and Italianate forms; his primary reputation as a church architect rests on a series of large and small urban and rural churches characterized by their adaptation of the English Gothic style to local materials, his own favorite being Trinity Chapel, New York (1853). His later ecclesiastical architecture incorporated Romanesque and Italianate forms. He published a pattern book, *Rural Architecture* (1852). Upjohn trained many young architects including Leopold Eidlitz. He was a founder and first president of the American Institute of Architects (1857–76).

Upjohn, William E. (Erastus) (1853–1932) physician, manufacturer; born in Richland Township, Mich. Following his father in a medical career, he graduated from the University of Michigan in 1875 and set up a pharmaceutical laboratory in addition to his private practice. He developed a process for making pills and granules that resulted in the Upjohn Pill and Granule Company (1885), organized with the help of his three brothers. By 1902 the firm, renamed the Upjohn Company, expanded into a full line of pharmaceutical products. By 1909 his brothers withdrew from the firm and William continued sole management until his death. Civic-minded, he helped charter the city of Kalamazoo, Mich. (1914), and was elected to its first commission and as its first mayor. He also donated the 17-acre Upjohn Park to the city.

Upshur, Abel Parker (1791–1844) legislator, jurist; born in Northampton County, Va. A Virginia Supreme Court judge (1826–41) he held pro-slavery, states' rights views. He was secretary of the navy (1841–43) and secretary of state (1843–44) before his death from a gun explosion aboard the USS *Princeton*.

Upton, Emory (1839–81) soldier, military theorist; born near Batavia, N.Y. An 1861 West Point graduate, he earned rapid promotion. At Spotsylvania (1864) his tactical innovations led to a penetration of forbidding Confederate defenses. He later published important works on tactical theory. He committed suicide after he discovered he had contracted a fatal disease.

Urban, Joseph (1872–1933) architect, set designer; born in Vienna, Austria. Pursuing a successful career in Europe as an architect, interior designer, and stage designer, he first came to America as designer of the Austrian pavilion at the St. Louis Exposition in 1904. In 1911 he returned to settle in the U.S.A., first working for the Boston Opera Company, then moving to New York to design sets for the *Ziegfield Follies* (1915–32) as well as for the Metropolitan Opera. Perhaps best known as designer of the egg-shaped Ziegfield Theatre, he continued to design houses and public buildings as well as interiors, furniture, and industrial products; he also illustrated children's books. Although regarded as a borrower and popularizer of different styles, he had considerable influence on other designers.

U'Ren, William Simon (1859–1949) lawyer, reformer; born in Lancaster, Wis. Raised in Wisconsin, Nebraska, and Colorado, he worked as a miner and blacksmith before reading law. He was admitted to the Colorado bar in 1881 but gave up his legal practice after a few years because of poor health. After several years of various jobs in different states and Hawaii, he settled in Oregon and opened a law office in Portland. As a leader of powerful citizen lobbies, he pressed successfully for such political reforms as initiative and referendum, direct primaries, and direct election of U.S. senators – innovations that soon spread to other states. His favorite innovation, however, the single tax advocated by Henry George, was never accepted, and after his failed 1914 run for governor of Oregon on this platform, he withdrew from active politics. He kept up a modest law practice until shortly before his death.

Urey, Harold (Clayton) (1893–1981) chemist; born in Walkerton, Ind. With great persistence he managed to get a college education, and then, after working for a chemical company during World War I, he finally obtained his Ph.D. in physical chemistry from the University of California: Berkeley (1923). He worked on the theory of atomic structure with Niels Bohr in Copenhagen before joining the faculty at Columbia University (1929–45). He won the 1934 Nobel Prize in chemistry for separating the isotope deuterium from hydrogen; instead of attending the prize ceremony, he stayed at home to attend the birth of his third daughter. During World War II he directed the search to separate uranium-235 from uranium-238 for the Manhattan project. After the war he took the lead in questioning the ethics of using nuclear weapons. At the Enrico Fermi Institute of Nuclear Studies (University of Chicago, 1945–58), he pondered the origin of the elements, their abundance in stars, and the derivation of planets. Among his other important contributions was a technique that used oxygen isotope-bearing minerals to date geological formations and to measure annual water temperatures. His publications include *The Planets: Their Origin and Development* (1952). At the University of California: San Diego (1958–81) he analyzed lunar rocks from the Apollo missions. Highly regarded, he won more than 30 awards as well as honorary degrees from 25 universities.

Uris, Leon (Marcus) (1924–   ) writer; born in Baltimore, Md. He studied at local public schools, delivered newspapers by truck for the *San Francisco Call-Bulletin,* and served in the Marine Corps (1942–45). Eventually settling in Aspen, Colo., he wrote popular best-sellers such as *Exodus* (1957). He also wrote many screenplays, including *Gunfight at the O.K. Corral* (1957).

V

Vagelos, P. (Pindaros) Roy (1929–   ) business executive, physician; born in Westfield, N.J. A Columbia-trained surgeon and biochemist, he was associated with the National Institutes of Health (1956–66) and the Washington University School of Medicine (1966–75) before joining Merck, Sharp & Dohme Research Labs, Rahway, New Jersey (president 1976–84). As president and CEO (1985) and chairman (1986) of Merck & Company, Inc., he was widely admired for attracting top research scientists who developed many major new drugs.

Vail, Theodore (Newton) (1845–1920) telephone and utilities executive; born near Minerva, Ohio. He moved to New Jersey (1847) where he learned to operate the telegraph while a clerk in a drugstore. By age 19 he was at Western Union Telegraph Company in New York City. In 1866 he moved with his family to Iowa and by 1869 was working for the U.S. Post Office Department. He inaugurated the Fast Mail, the first train to carry only mail, between New York and Chicago (1875), and by 1876 was general superintendent of the railway mail service. He became general manager of the new Bell Telephone Company (1878–87) where he directed the expansion of local exchanges, anticipated technical developments, and organized financing of the system. He also made possible a long distance system by connecting all the existing companies into the American Telephone & Telegraph Company (AT&T) (1885) with himself as president. Exhausted, he retired to a Vermont farm in 1889. From 1894–1907 he helped develop utilities in Argentina. He was called back to AT&T in 1907 to deal with the problems that ensued when the Bell patents expired in 1893–94. He successfully reunified the phone companies and pushed research and development; in 1915 the first transcontinental telephone line was opened. He retired to chair the board of directors (1919). He was a cousin of Alfred Vail, telegraph pioneer and partner of Samuel Morse.

Vaillant, George Clapp (1901–45) archaeologist; born in Boston, Mass. His Harvard Ph.D. thesis established a chronology of Maya ceramics; his later work established the historical sequence of cultures in pre-Columbian Mexico. At the American Museum of Natural History (1927–41) he directed the museum's Mexican excavations. His major work was *The Aztecs of Mexico* (1941).

Vaillant, George (Eman) (1934–   ) psychiatrist; born in New York City. In 1967 he became involved with the Grant Study of 268 Harvard students, begun in 1937; this ongoing longitudinal study focused on the adaptations and defense mechanisms that allow people to live their lives successfully. He discussed his findings and observations in *Adaptations to Life* (1977). An authority on alcoholism, which he began researching in 1972, he wrote *The Natural History of Alcoholism* (1983).

Valenti, (Joseph) Jack (1921–   ) motion picture executive; born in Houston, Texas. He was a decorated bomber pilot during World War II. He cofounded and ran an advertising agency (1952–63). He helped to coordinate Lyndon B. Johnson's inauguration (1963) and then became the president's special assistant (1963–66). He was president of the Motion Picture Association of America (1966). He cowrote a new code for movies (1966) which intended to reflect, rather than dictate, public values.

Vallandigham, Clement Laird (1820–71) politician; born in New Lisbon, Ohio. Of southern ancestry, a supporter of state's rights, and an ardent antiabolitionist, he served in the U.S. House of Representatives (Dem. Ohio; 1858–63) opposing the Republicans at every step. After the outbreak of the Civil War he became a leader of the Peace Democrats – better known as the Copperheads. A military court convicted him of treason in May 1863, and Lincoln ordered him banished from the North. He ran for governor of Ohio in absentia later in 1863 and was soundly defeated. Returning to Ohio in June 1864 via Canada and the South, he prepared the peace plank in the Democrats' 1864 presidential platform. He worked after the war for reconciliation between the North and South.

Vallee, (Hubert Prior) Rudy (1901–86) band leader, singer; born in Island Pond, Vt. Intending to become a pharmacist, he took up the saxophone; while at the University of Maine and then Yale he formed his own band. After graduation he continued with his band and by the late 1920s he began to enjoy great popularity as a vocalist with a genteel style that made him the first to be called a "crooner." One of his first hits was "The Vagabond Lover," which became his nickname and the title of his first movie (1929). He was also known for carrying a little megaphone. For three decades he enjoyed a successful career on radio, in movies, in Broadway musicals, and with a solo nightclub act. During World War II he joined the Coast Guard and conducted a band. His style of singing went out of fashion by the late 1950s but he enjoyed a reprise in the 1961 hit musical, *How to Succeed in Business Without Really Trying;* he recreated the role in the 1967 movie version. He also formed a talent agency and music publishing company.

Van Allen, James (Alfred) (1914–) physicist; born in Mount Pleasant, Iowa. Educated at Iowa Wesleyan and the University of Iowa, he was a fellow in nuclear physics at the Carnegie Institution of Washington's department of terrestrial magnetism (1939–41). He spent several years at Johns Hopkins University in the 1940s before returning to head the department of physics and astronomy at the University of Iowa (1951). As one of the major planners of the International Geophysical Year (1957–58), he proposed the experiment that, using data from the Explorer I and Pioneer III space probes of the region known as the magnetosphere, revealed the existence of the radiation belts – concentrations of electrically charged particles known since as "the Van Allen belts." He was the principal investigator on 23 other space probes and in 1989 he was awarded the Crafoord Prize.

Van Allsburg, Chris (1949–) writer, illustrator, sculptor; born in Grand Rapids, Mich. He graduated from the University of Michigan (1972) and the Rhode Island School of Design (1975), where he taught illustration beginning in 1977. Based in Providence, R.I., he worked as a fine artist, sculptor, and creator of award-winning books for children, such as *The Polar Express* (1985).

Van Anda, Carr Vattel (1864–1945) journalist; born in Georgetown, Ohio. Associated for 16 years with the *New York Sun*, he was hired by *New York Times* publisher Adolph Ochs in 1904 as that paper's brilliant managing editor; from then until his retirement in 1932, he played a key role in developing the *Times* into one of the nation's great papers, especially in its coverage of science and exploration, fields in which Van Anda was particularly interested.

Van Buren, Abigail (Pauline Esther Philips b. Friedman) (1918–) journalist; born in Sioux City, Iowa. The twin of rival "sob sister" Ann Landers, she launched her own "Dear Abby" advice column in 1956; it, too, became an internationally syndicated column, and she too gained a dedicated following as well as many public service awards, particularly for publicizing public health issues.

Van Buren, Hannah (b. Hoes) (1783–1819) wife of Martin Van Buren; born in Kinderhook, N.Y. She died in 1819, long before Van Buren's presidency. Van Buren's daughter-in-law, Abigail Singleton Van Buren, served as White House hostess.

Van Buren, Martin (1782–1862) eighth U.S. president; born in Kinderhook, N.Y. After studying law in a law office, he began a local practice and soon became active in the Democratic-Republican party. He entered the N.Y. state senate (1812–20), concurrently serving as state attorney general from 1816–19. In 1821 he entered the U.S. Senate and in 1828 was elected governor of New York, by which time he was a leader of the so-called Albany Regency. In 1829 he was named secretary of state by President Andrew Jackson, whom Van Buren had staunchly supported with his New York political machine. After effective service in the cabinet, he became Jackson's vice-president and heir apparent (1833–37). Elected president as a Democrat in 1836, Van Buren soon had to deal with the financial panic of 1837, to which he responded with the Independent Treasury Act. Meanwhile he tolerated slavery but opposed its spread into the territories, and he maintained neutrality during the Canadian rebellion of 1837. Two unpopular policies – his refusal to annex Texas and his war against the Seminoles – contributed to his defeat in 1840 by the anti-Jackson Whigs. Van Buren's later political life was marked by several attempts to regain the presidency, but his opposition to the annexation of Texas and then to the spread of slavery left him on the sidelines.

Van Buren, Steve (1920–) football player; born in La Ceiba, Honduras. Although known for his blocking at Louisiana State University, he proved a bruising, all-pro runner for the Philadelphia Eagles. He led the National Football League in rushing four times (1945, 1947–49), becoming the first man to run for over 1,000 yards in two different seasons. His powerful rushes helped his team win league championships in 1948 and 1949.

Vance, (Clarence Arthur) "Dazzy" (1891–1961) baseball pitcher; born in Orient, Iowa. During his 16-year career (1915–35), mostly with the Brooklyn Dodgers, he won 197 games and the Most Valuable Player Award in 1924, yet he did not win his first major league game until age 31. A right-hander with an exceptional fastball, he led his league in strikeouts for seven consecutive seasons, a National League record. He was elected to baseball's Hall of Fame in 1955.

Vance, Cyrus (Roberts) (1917–) lawyer, cabinet member; born in Clarksburg, W.Va. A corporate and government lawyer in New York (1947–61), he became secretary of the army (1961–64). As deputy defense secretary (1964–68), he went on peace missions to Panama, Santa Domingo, and Cyprus. President Carter's secretary of state (1977–80), he could not resolve the Iranian hostage crisis and resigned when Carter undertook a helicopter rescue mission against his advice. In 1992 he led a mission to negotiate peace in Yugoslavia.

Vance, Harold (Sines) (1890–1959) automobile executive, government official; born in Port Huron, Mich. He ended his 45-year career at the Everitt-Metzger-Flanders Company and its successor, Studebaker Corporation, which he led out of receivership (1933–35), then becoming chairman until its 1954 merger with Packard. On the Atomic Energy Commission (1955–59), he promoted the industrial use of nuclear energy.

Vance, Zebulon Baird (1830–94) governor; born in Buncombe County, N.C. A Know-Nothing in the U.S. House of Representatives (N.C., 1858–61), he campaigned against secession. Once the war was underway, however, as Conservative Party governor (1862–65) he had to lead a divided state and he gave limited support to the Confederacy. Reelected governor (Dem., 1877–79), he restored the state economy and improved public education. In the U.S. Senate (1880–94), he served on the Finance Committee.

Van de Graaff, Robert J. (Jemison) (1901–67) physicist; born in Tuscaloosa, Ala. He conceived the idea for his constant-potential electrostatic generator (later known as the Van de Graaff generator) while he was a Rhodes scholar at Oxford (1926–28), and constructed its first working model at Princeton (1929–31). At the Massachusetts Institute of Technology (1931–60), he developed his generator for use as a particle accelerator, but was unsuccessful in using it to bombard uranium and other heavy ions. He invented the insulating-core transformer in the late 1950s.

Vandegrift, Alexander (Archer) (1887–1973) marine officer; born in Charlottesville, Va. He commanded the First Marine Division at Guadalcanal in August 1942 in America's first large-scale offensive against Japan, and won the Medal of Honor for directing a brilliant defense against repeated enemy counterattacks.

Vandenberg, Arthur (Hendrick) (1884–1951) U.S. senator; born in Grand Rapids, Mich. A reform-minded journalist and editor of the *Grand Rapids Herald,* he was appointed and then elected to the U.S. Senate (Rep., Mich.; 1928–51). He conceived of the federal bank deposit insurance system, and led a successful fight for congressional reappointment. His greatest fame came in foreign affairs. Originally the leader of the isolationist bloc in the Senate, he coauthored the 1937 Neutrality Act. During World War II he abandoned isolationism, and helped secure American membership in the United Nations. As the ranking Republican member of the Senate Foreign Relations Committee, he proved a valuable supporter of President Truman's cold war policies.

Vanderbilt, Amy (1908–74) authority on etiquette; born in Staten Island, N.Y. (cousin of Commodore Cornelius Vanderbilt). She studied journalism at New York University and worked in advertising, publicity, and journalism before Doubleday invited her to write an etiquette manual. *Amy Vanderbilt's Complete Book of Etiquette* (1952, frequently revised) established her as the leading American authority on good manners, a position maintained for two decades by her popular books and television and radio programs and her syndicated etiquette column (1954–74), which reached 40 million readers.

Vanderbilt, Cornelius (1843–99) businessman, philanthropist; born near New Dorp, N.Y. The eldest son of William H. Vanderbilt, he was a favorite of the "Commodore" and became an assistant treasurer of the New York & Harlem Railroad in 1867, serving as its president from 1886–99. Patriarch of the Vanderbilts from 1885, he directed the family investments with the aid of his brother William Vanderbilt, and he served on the boards of many corporations. Among his benefactions was the New York College of Physicians and Surgeons (Columbia University), the New York General Theological Seminary, and Yale University.

Vanderbilt, Cornelius ("Commodore") (1794–1877) steamship and railroad developer, financier; born in Port Richmond, N.Y. He began as a ferryman between Staten Island and New York City (1810), then worked for Thomas Gibbons (1818–29) and assisted him in his fight against the steamboat monopoly before establishing his own steamboat business. By 1846 he was one of the richest men in America. In 1849 he started a steamship line to California that involved traveling overland through Nicaragua; when his employees tried to cheat him out of his business with the aid of American filibuster William Walker, Vanderbilt helped eject Walker from Nicaragua (1857) and regained control of his line; he then sold it to the Pacific Mail Steamship Company. Shifting his interest to railroads, by 1862 he was buying stock in the New York & Harlem Railroad; soon he was extending its service and became president; he then acquired the Hudson River Railroad and the New York Central and by 1872 had consolidated them as the New York Central. In the next few years he acquired even more lines and extended his railroad empire into Michigan and Canada. Although his success definitely rested in part on his insistence on providing the best service and on using the best equipment, he could be a ruthless competitor. His most famous business battles were fought against Daniel Drew, first over steamships, then railroads. In 1868, Drew, along with Jay Gould and James Fisk, defeated Vanderbilt's attempt to add the Erie Railroad to his well-run rail system

by their fraudulent stock manipulations known as the "Erie Wars." Never one for giving to charity, he made an exception near the end of his life with gifts totaling $1 million to Central University in Nashville, Tenn.; it renamed itself Vanderbilt University (1873). When he died with an estate of some $100 million, he was the wealthiest man in America.

Vanderbilt, George Washington (1862–1914) capitalist, forestry pioneer, agriculturist; born on Staten Island, N.Y. (grandson of Cornelius Vanderbilt, son of William Henry Vanderbilt). He was privately tutored and a world traveler, speaking eight languages. In 1889, in love with the Appalachian Mountains of North Carolina, he began buying acreage (130,000 total) near Asheville, N.C., and proceeded to study forestry, architecture, and landscape gardening. The architect of his $3 million estate, "Biltmore," was Richard Morris Hunt; Frederick Law Olmsted was his landscape gardener; Gifford Pinchot was placed in charge of the forest. Moving to "Biltmore" in 1896, Vanderbilt became a pioneer in forestry science; on his acreage he founded the Biltmore nursery, which specialized in trees and plants of the Appalachian region, and the Biltmore School of Forestry. He also bred hogs and cows and sold the meat and dairy products, and his advanced agriculture, forestry, and animal husbandry practices served to inspire similar reforms throughout the South. Among his benefactions was the Jackson Square branch of the New York Public Library, and the ground on which Columbia University's Teacher's College was built.

Vanderbilt, Gloria (Gloria Morgan Vanderbilt-Cooper) (1924–) artist, socialite; born in New York City. An heiress involved in a widely publicized "poor little rich girl" custody suit at age 10, she achieved later notoriety for her four marriages, but considerable respect for her work as a painter, stage and film actress, author, and, after the late 1960s, designer of housewares and fashion.

Vanderbilt, Harold Stirling (1884–1970) bridge innovator; born in Oakdale, N.Y. A Harvard Law School graduate and railroad magnate, he helped contract bridge spread from 1926 to 1929 by espousing the game, and modernized it with bidding and scoring changes. He presented the Vanderbilt Cup team trophy in 1928 and twice won it.

Vanderbilt, William H. (Henry) (1821–85) railroad developer, financier; born in New Brunswick, N.J. His father, "Commodore" Vanderbilt, regarded him as incapable of playing a role in his business empire, but after William succeeded at running a farm on Staten Island and then at turning around the bankrupt Staten Island Railroad (1857–63), his father appointed him vice-president of the New York & Harlem Railroad (1864). He soon became his father's closest aide and an able administrator, and after his father's death (1877), he became president of the New York Central and expanded the railroad system even further with the purchase of other lines. Like his father, he gave good service and invested in good equipment, but also like his father he could be ruthless in pursuit of profit. He gave special rates to favored commercial customers, he bribed officials when they threatened to expose the illegal tactic, and he fought government regulation whenever he could. Although he was, unlike his father, generous with gifts during his lifetime, he remains best known for his 1882 crack, "The public be damned!" When he saw that the tide was turning against such vast monopolies as his, he sold large amounts of stock in 1879. In poor health, he resigned as president of the New

York Central Railroad in 1883 and gave his final years to his philanthropies and his interest in horses. By his death, he had doubled the already vast family fortune, which he left to his three sons.

Vanderbilt, William K. (Kissam) (1849–1920) businessman, sportsman; born near New Dorp, N.Y. Son of William H. Vanderbilt, he was an executive in the family railroads (1869–1903) and helped his brother Cornelius Vanderbilt manage the family investments. In 1903 he turned over control of the New York Central system to the Rockefeller-Morgan-Pennsylvania group. An enthusiastic yachtsman, he owned and sailed the *Defender* in international yacht races with England (1895); he actively supported the Metropolitan Opera and collected paintings.

Van der Donck, Adrien (1620–55) Dutch colonist; born in Breda, Netherlands. A lawyer, he came to America in 1641 to serve as the officer of justice for the Van Rensselaer family; when he fell out with the estate's manager, he established a new settlement at present-day Yonkers, N.Y. In 1650, he wrote the "Remonstrance," in which he listed the grievances of the Dutch colonists against their leaders in Holland. When he took it to The Hague, he was detained for almost three years; he returned to New Netherland in 1653, but was restricted to providing only legal advice. His action led to the organization of city government in New Amsterdam.

Van Deren, Coke (Frank) (1921–) photographer, gallery director; born in Lexington, Ky. Inspired by Ansel Adams, he left his business, Van Deren Hardware (1946–55), to pursue a career in the arts, earning a M.F.A. from Indiana University in 1958. His photographs won prizes in international competitions (1955–60) and he taught at Harvard, Arizona, and New Mexico State Universities. From 1979 to 1987 he was director of the San Francisco Museum of Modern Art's photography department.

Vanderlyn, John (1775–1852) painter; born in Kingston, N.Y. He studied with Gilbert Stuart in Philadelphia (1795–96), in Paris (1796–1801), returned briefly to New York (1801–03), and lived in Rome and Paris (1803–15). He is known for portraits and historical subjects such as *Ariadne Asleep on the Isle of Naxos* (1812). He returned to New York, produced cycloramas, the *Palace and Gardens of Versailles* (1816–19), and retired to Kingston, N.Y. (1829).

Vanderpool, Eugene (1906–89) archaeologist; born in New Jersey. He first came to Greece in 1927, returned briefly to the United States to finish his B.A. at Princeton (1929), and thereafter spent virtually his entire life in Greece. No one knew more about Greek epigraphy and topography, especially the topography of Attica; his knowledge led the Germans to inter him during World War II. He was a beloved and revered teacher and mentor at the American School of Classical Studies, where he was an agora excavator (1932–67), deputy director (1947–67), and professor of archaeology (1949–71).

Van der Rohe, Ludwig Mies See MIES VAN DER ROHE, LUDWIG.

VanDerZee, James (1886–1983) photographer; born in Lenox, Mass. After attending the public schools in Lenox, he went to New York City about 1906 and held a series of jobs as a waiter and elevator operator. Between 1909 and 1915, he played in Fletcher Henderson's band and the John Wanamaker Orchestra (and in an orchestra that accompa-

nied silent movies). Attracted to photography, he got a job as a darkroom assistant, and after learning the fundamentals of photography he opened his own studio in Harlem in 1916. On the upper end of Manhattan, Harlem was only then becoming a haven for African-Americans and during the next fives decades he would photograph African-Americans of all social classes and occupations. He took thousands of pictures – mostly indoor portraits, although he occasionally went out and photographed the Harlem scene. Although he photographed many of the African-American celebrities who passed through Harlem, most of his work was of the straightforward commercial studio variety – weddings and funerals (including pictures of the dead for grieving families), family groups, teams, lodges, clubs, people simply wanting to have a record of themselves in fine clothes. He often supplied props or costumes and in his developing – which he did himself – he would add pictorial touches with an air brush or double-printed images. Forgotten for many years, he had retired and was reduced to poverty when in 1969 the Metropolitan Museum of Art mounted an exhibit called *Harlem on My Mind* that brought him and his work renewed attention and rewards. He took up photography again in 1980 until his death.

Van Devanter, Willis (1859–1941) Supreme Court justice; born in Marion, Ind. His involvement in frontier politics led to his appointment as assistant U.S. attorney general (1897–1903) and as a federal judge (1903–10). President Taft named him to the U.S. Supreme Court (1911–37). As a conservative, he often opposed President Franklin Roosevelt's New Deal measures.

Vandiver, H. S. (Harry Schultz) (1882–1973); mathematician; born in Philadelphia. Spending most of his teaching career at the University of Texas: Austin (1924–66), he wrote 173 papers (1900–63), concentrating on number theory, cyclotomy, and commutative algebra. He is best known for his work on Fermat's last theorem. He was also known for his criticism of public education and for his love of classical music.

Van Doren, Carl (Clinton) (1885–1950) writer, critic; born in Hope, Ill. (brother of Mark Van Doren). He studied at the University of Illinois (B.A. 1907), and Columbia University (Ph.D. 1911). He taught at the University of Illinois (1907–08), and Columbia (1911–30), and was headmaster of the Brearley School (New York City) (1916–19). Editor of the *Nation* (1919–22), *Century* (1922–25), and the *Library Guild* (1926–34), he wrote for many prestigious periodicals and reference works. He wrote poetry when young, but is best known for his translations, literary criticism, and distinguished biographies, such as *Swift* (1930), and *Benjamin Franklin* (1938), a winner of a Pulitzer Prize. He lived in New York City.

Van Doren, Irita (b. Bradford) (1891–1966) editor; born in Birmingham, Ala. A leading light in New York literary society, she was literary editor of the *New York Herald Tribune* (1926–63). Married for a time to Carl Van Doren, she later was a longtime companion to Wendell Willkie.

Van Doren, Mark (1894–1972) poet, teacher, writer; born in Hope, Ill. (brother of Carl Van Doren). He studied at the University of Illinois (B.A. 1914; M.A. 1915), and Columbia University (Ph.D. 1920), where he taught English (1920–59). He also taught at St. John's College (Maryland) (1937–57), and Harvard (1963). A prolific scholar and writer, he wrote children's books, critical studies, and plays, notably *The Last Days of Lincoln* (1959). He is best known for his carefully crafted poetry, as in *Collected and New Poems, 1924–1963* (1963). He lived in New York City and Falls Village, Conn.

Van Dorn, Earl (1820–63) soldier; born near Port Gibson, Miss. A West Point graduate (1842), he saw considerable action fighting in the Mexican War, the Seminole War, and against the Indians (he was wounded four times in one engagement). As a major general of the Confederate cavalry, he was defeated at Pea Ridge, Ark. (March 1862) and Corinth, Miss. (Oct. 1862); he retrieved his military reputation leading Confederate cavalry against Grant during the Vicksburg campaign (1862–63). A civilian enemy – said to be a jealous husband – shot and killed Van Dorn as he sat working in his tent.

Van Duyn, Mona Jane (1921–) poet; born in Waterloo, Iowa. Born and educated in Iowa, she had a successful career both as an academic and a poet. From 1950, she taught mainly at Washington University (St. Louis, Mo.). In 1971 her *To See, To Take* won the National Book Award and *Near Changes* won the Pulitzer Prize in 1991. Her poems have appeared in a wide range of publications, including the *New Yorker, Kenyon Review,* and *Atlantic.* From the 1980s, Van Duyn increasingly appeared in anthologies of American poetry. Critics have praised her for her accurate depiction of the everyday world, her graceful use of rhyme, and her ability to make the ordinary seem extraordinary. In 1992–93 she was poet laureate of the U.S. Library of Congress.

Van Dyck, Cornelius (Van Allen) (1818–95) scholar, medical missionary; born in Kinderhook, N.Y. He graduated from Jefferson Medical College (1839) and became a medical missionary for the American Board of Commissioners for Foreign Missions. He studied Arabic intensively and ran a high school in Lebanon (1843–49). In 1857, he took up the uncompleted work of Eli Smith; by 1865 he had made the first modern translation of the Bible into Arabic. He was a professor of pathology at Syrian Protestant College (1867–83). His last work was a translation of *Ben Hur* into Arabic.

Van Dyke, Dick (1925–) television/movie actor, comedian; born in West Plains, Mo. He appeared in television variety shows during the 1950s, making his Broadway debut in *Bye, Bye Birdie* (1960). Star of the *Dick Van Dyke Show* on CBS (1961–66), he also danced and sang in the films *Mary Poppins* (1965) and *Chitty, Chitty, Bang, Bang* (1968). After *The New Dick Van Dyke Show* (1971–74), he appeared infrequently, due to alcoholism, but after conquering this he returned in 1991 with television mystery movies.

Van Dyke, Henry (1852–1933) Protestant clergyman, author; born in Germantown, Pa. The son of a Presbyterian minister, he grew up in New York City, was educated at Princeton, and held pastorates in Newport, R.I., and New York City. From 1899 to 1923 he was a professor of English at Princeton. His publications included poetry, essays, and short stories on religious and secular themes. He was American ambassador to the Netherlands and Luxembourg from 1913 to 1916 and served as a naval chaplain during World War I.

Van Dyke, Willard Ames (1906–86) filmmaker, photographer; born in Denver, Colo. Trained by Edward Weston, he changed to film in 1939, producing, directing, and photographing social documentary films with American Documentary Film (1940–68).

Van Fleet, James (Alward) (1892–1992) soldier; born in Coytesville, N.J. A West Point graduate (1915), during World War I he commanded a machine gun battalion in France, and in World War II he held successively higher commands, culminating with that of the Third Corps. In 1948–50 he was in Greece to train and equip the Greeks fighting the Communist forces there. From 1951–53, he served in Korea, commanding the U.S. Eighth Army during the grueling period of hard fighting for little gain while the armistice talks dragged on. Although he retired in 1953, he was recalled to active duty in 1961–62 to help train U.S. Army guerrilla fighters. He then lived a quiet life to reach the age of 100.

Van Heusen, James (b. Edward Chester Babcock) (1913–90) composer; born in Syracuse, N.Y. In the 1930s his first popular songs were performed and recorded. He joined lyricist Johnny Burke in 1940 and began writing scores for many Bing Crosby films with such hit songs as "It's Always You" (1941) and "Swinging on a Star" (1944). With lyricist Sammy Cahn he wrote many popular songs of the 1950s for film and television, including "High Hopes" (1959), and wrote the musical, *Skyscraper* (1965). He retired in the 1970s.

Van Hise, Charles (Richard) (1857–1918) college president, geologist; born in Fulton, Wis. A specialist in pre-Cambrian and metamorphic geology and a member of the U.S. Geologic Survey, he taught at the University of Wisconsin (1879–1903). As Wisconsin's president (1903–18), he oversaw a major expansion and developed an extension service, creating an influential model for other state universities.

Van Orstrand, C. E. (Charles Edwin) (1870–1959) geophysicist; born near Manito, Ill. He served the U.S. Geological Survey (1901–40), where he made major contributions to a series of mathematical tables, then patented instruments for determining temperatures in deep wells and oil fields.

Van Rensselaer, Mariana (b. Griswold) (1851–1934) art critic; born in New York City. She was educated privately and traveled extensively in Germany. She married (1873), lived in New Brunswick, N.J., and returned to New York City after her husband's death (1884). She published many books on art and architecture, including the first work on a contemporary American architect, *Henry Hobson Richardson and His Works* (1888). She is primarily known for her scholarly work, *History of the City of New York in the Seventeenth Century* (2 vols. 1909).

Van Rensselaer, Martha (1864–1932) home economist; born in Randolph, N.Y. A rural schoolteacher and school commissioner, she joined the faculty of Cornell University (1900). There she organized extension programs; co-chaired the new home economics department, where she created a degree program; and became codirector (1925) of the New York State College of Home Economics.

Van Rensselaer, Stephen (1764–1839) public official, soldier, philanthropist; born in New York City. Having inherited his father's vast upstate New York estate, he was the last of the fully empowered Dutch patroons and, being independently wealthy, was free to devote himself to public service. From 1789 to 1798 he held various state offices – in the legislature and senate and as lieutenant governor; he was a member of the state's constitutional conventions (1801, 1821); and he was active in advancing the construction of the

Erie Canal. He became a major general in the New York State militia, and during the War of 1812 he led the disastrous attack on Queenston Heights, Ontario, He was a regent of the University of the State of New York (1819–39), set up the first state agricultural board, and personally paid for the state's first geological survey. He served in the U.S. House of Representatives (Fed., N.Y.; 1822–29) and when the presidential election of 1824 came to the House he cast the deciding vote for John Quincy Adams. In 1824 he founded the school that became the Rensselaer Polytechnic Institute (Troy, N.Y.) and donated to various other educational institutions.

Vansina, Jan (Maria Jozef) (1929–) historian, cultural anthropologist, linguist; born in Antwerp, Belgium. He came to the U.S.A. to join the University of Wisconsin faculty in 1960. His fieldwork in Africa yielded studies of Bushoong grammar (1959) and historical studies of Rwanda (1962) and the Kuba of Zaire (1963, 1964). He pioneered in developing the field of oral history, based on interviews with people whose recollections can be recorded, and described the method in *De la Tradition Orale* (1961), subsequently revised and published in English as *Oral Tradition as History* (1985). His later works include *Paths in the Rainforests* (1990).

Van Vechten, Carl (1880–1966) writer, photographer; born in Cedar Rapids, Iowa. He studied at the University of Chicago (1899–1903), and worked for the *Chicago American* newspaper (1903–06). He moved to New York City and became a music critic, then Paris correspondent for the *New York Times* (1908–09). A longtime friend of Gertrude Stein, he became friendly with many of her circle. He wrote novels about life in New York City such as *Nigger Heaven* (1926), a work that renewed interest in the cultural life of African-Americans during the Harlem Renaissance of the 1920s. He also became an accomplished photographer in the 1930s, specializing in documentary portraits.

Van Vleck, Edward Burr (1863–1943) mathematician; born in Middletown, Conn. Son of mathematician John Van Vleck, he taught longest at the University of Wisconsin (1906–29). An early editor of the American Mathematical Society's *Transactions* (1906–10) and a National Academy of Sciences member, he helped lay the foundation for the growth of mathematical research.

Van Vleck, John H. (Hasbrouck) (1899–1980) physicist; born in Middletown, Conn. Educated entirely in the U.S.A., he taught at Harvard (1922–23) and the University of Minnesota (1923–28), where, in 1926, he expanded English physicist Paul Dirac's quantum mechanics to explain the electric and magnetic properties of atoms. His classical treatise, *The Theory of Electric and Magnetic Susceptibilities* (1932), published while he was teaching at the University of Wisconsin (1928–34), earned Van Vleck the title "father of modern magnetism." He promoted the union of physics and chemistry, applying his discoveries to chemical bonding in crystals. Returning to Harvard (1934–69), he used his theory in studies of nuclear magnetic resonance and in the development of computer memory systems. He shared the 1977 Nobel Prize in physics (with Philip Anderson and Nevill Mott) for his pioneering research. His colleagues knew him as a patient, gentle man whose personal interests included collecting detailed information of U.S. and European railroad timetables.

Van Waters, Miriam (1887–1974) penologist, prison reformer; born in Greensburg, Pa. She was known for transforming institutions for women offenders into models of prisoner rehabilitation. As superintendent of the Massachusetts State Reformatory for Women (1932–57), she made that institution one of the most progressive in the United States. She previously headed detention homes in Portland, Ore. (1914–17) and Los Angeles, Calif. (1917–20) and was author of the highly acclaimed *Youth in Conflict* (1925).

Vanzetti, Bartolomeo See under SACCO, NICOLA.

Varèse, Edgar (1883–1965) composer; born in Paris, France. While studying engineering in Paris, he also pursued musical studies with prominent teachers. There and during a stay in Berlin (1908–15), he made a name as a composer and conductor and numbered Debussy among his sponsors. A visit to New York in 1915 turned into a lifetime's stay; meanwhile all his early pieces were lost or destroyed. In the U.S.A. he became a leader of the avant-garde, helping found the International Composers' Guild and the Pan-American Society. He composed a handful of works of spectacular originality and aggressive modernism, including *Amériques* (1921–22), *Offrandes* (1921), and one of the first all-percussion works, *Ionisation* (1931). Audience rejection and personal depression led to a long creative hiatus, but in the 1950s he emerged to become a prime influence on the new generation. Later works included the *Poème électronique*, written for the 1958 Brussels World's Fair.

Varmus, Harold E. (Elliot) (1939–) virologist, oncologist; born in Oceanside, N.Y. He was an associate chemist at the National Institutes of Health (1968–70), then joined the University of California: San Francisco (1970), where he met collaborator J. Michael Bishop. The two scientists' investigations on oncogenic (cancer-causing) viruses demonstrated that a normal cell may transform into a cancer cell if a tumor virus inserts its oncogenic genes into the host cell's DNA. This breakthrough in cancer research earned Varmus and Bishop the 1989 Nobel Prize in physiology.

Varnay, Astrid (1918–) soprano; born in Stockholm, Sweden. Brought to the U.S.A. in childhood, she studied first with her mother. She made her first Metropolitan Opera appearance (in *Die Walküre*) in 1941 and her last in 1974. She was admired internationally, especially for her Wagnerian roles.

Varnedoe, (John) Kirk (Train) (1946–) museum curator, teacher; born in Savannah, Ga. He studied at Williams College (B.A.) and Stanford (M.A., Ph.D.). He taught at Stanford (1973–77), Columbia University (1974–80), and at the Institute of Fine Arts, New York University (1980–88). He headed the department of painting and sculpture of the Museum of Modern Art, and in addition to his numerous articles and lectures on art topics, he has become known for his imaginative exhibits.

Vauclain, Samuel (Matthews) (1856–1940) engineer, inventor; born in Port Richmond, Pa. His father helped Matthias Baldwin build his first locomotive. After an apprenticeship with the Pennsylvania Railroad shops, the younger Vauclain joined the Baldwin Locomotive Works in Philadelphia (1883) and remained with the company for the rest of his life. He perfected a series of improvements to locomotives and became a world authority on locomotive design. As president (from 1919) and later board chairman (from 1929) of Baldwin, he was noteworthy for his hostility to labor unions, once firing 2,500 workers he considered to be "agitators."

Vaughan, Henry (1846–1917) architect; born in Cheshire, England. In 1881 he emigrated to Boston, where he led the "Boston Gothicists," designing primarily churches and schools. His late American Gothic Revival influenced Ralph Adams Cram, among others.

Vaughan, Sarah (Lois) (1924–90) jazz vocalist; born in Newark, N.J. She began singing in church, won an Apollo Theatre talent contest in 1942, and was featured with Earl Hines from 1944 to 1945. Influenced by bebop and possessing operatic range, she emerged as an original stylist by the late 1940s and established a solo career as an internationally acclaimed artist thereafter.

Vaughan, Stevie Ray (1954–90) rock musician; born in Dallas, Texas. A virtuoso guitarist, he played with teenage bands in Dallas before moving to Austin in 1972, where he played with a succession of local blues bands. In 1981 he formed Double Trouble, a blues-rock trio, and performed at the Montreux Jazz Festival in Switzerland, attracting widespread acclaim. He recorded with David Bowie in 1982, and the following year released his first album. He toured on a continual basis until his death in a helicopter accident following a concert performance in Wisconsin.

Vaughan, Thomas Wayland (1870–1952) geologist, paleontologist, oceanographer; born in Jonesville, Texas. Educated at Harvard (A.B., A.M., Ph.D.), he was an authority on marine sediments, fossil and recent corals, and American Tertiary stratigraphy. He was a researcher with the U.S. Geological Survey (1894–1939) and custodian of madreporian corals (1903–23) at the U.S. National Museum. Under his directorship (1924–36), Scripps Institute, La Jolla, Calif., became a leading oceanographical research center.

Vaux, Calvert (1824–95) landscape designer, architect; born in London, England. Emigrating at age 25 to work with Andrew Jackson Downing, he designed country houses and published *Villas and Gardens* (1852). A pioneer in the public parks movement, he joined Frederick Law Olmsted (1857–72) and together they produced the winning design for New York City's Central Park (1858–76). Vaux also contributed to Brooklyn's Prospect Park. After leaving Olmsted, he designed Ottawa's Parliament grounds, which influenced Canadian landscape design.

Vaux, Roberts (1786–1836) penology reformer, philanthropist; born in Philadelphia. A Quaker, he made his fortune as a merchant before retiring about 1814 to devote himself to social reforms. He helped found Philadelphia's free public school system, the Eastern Penitentiary, the Frankford Asylum, institutions for the blind and deaf, the Linnaean Society, Franklin Institute, the Athenaeum, and others. He advocated temperance but his most important work was in improving the prison system. In the last months of his life he served as justice of the Court of Common Pleas.

Veblen, Oswald (1880–1960) mathematician; born in Brooklin, Maine (nephew of Thorstein Veblen). Known for developing the school of mathematics at the Institute for Advanced Study, Princeton (1932–50), he had considerable influence on many mathematicians including Robert Lee Moore, Joseph Wedderburn, Alonzo Church, and J. H. C. Whitehead. His greatest contribution to mathematics was to geometry, particularly the development of analysis situs.

Veblen, Thorstein (Bunde) (1857–1929) economist, social critic; born in Cato, Wis. Educated at Carleton College, he took his Ph.D. in philosophy from Yale University in 1884. Having little use for neoclassical economics, he is best known for his sharp criticism of modern industrial civilization in such works as *The Theory of the Leisure Class* (1899), *The Instinct of Workmanship* (1914), *Imperial Germany and the Industrial Revolution* (1915), *The Higher Learning in America* (1918), and *Absentee Ownership* (1923). He argued in favor of economics as an evolutionary science, intending an inquiry into the genesis and growth of economic institutions. His writings drew on history, psychology, and anthropology, and he had a tendency to devise colorful phrases such as "conspicuous consumption," "pecuniary emulation," and "ostentatious display." He found it difficult to secure a permanent teaching job – his eccentric teaching style and unorthodox personal life led to his dismissal from both the University of Chicago and Stanford. His last work was practically indecipherable, and despite a small but loyal following, he died in relative obscurity in 1929, but his books and ideas have since continued to be widely cited.

Vedder, Elihu (1836–1923) illustrator, painter; born in New York City. He studied in Paris (1856), toured Europe, returned to New York (1861–66), then settled in Rome (1866). He is known for his paintings, such as *The Questioner of the Sphinx* (1863), illustrations of the *Rubaiyat of Omar Khayyam* (1884), and murals for the Library of Congress, Washington, D.C. (1896–97).

Veeck, (William Louis, Jr.) Bill (1914–86) baseball executive; born in Chicago. He was the son of William Veeck who owned the Chicago Cubs (1919–33). He lost a leg in an injury in World War II. He was the owner of the Cleveland Indians (1947–49), St. Louis Browns (1951–53), and Chicago White Sox (1959–61, 1976–80). In 1947 he signed Larry Doby as the first African-American to play in the American League. An unabashed promoter, he was responsible for the "exploding" scoreboard at Comiskey Park in Chicago, and in 1952 he sent a midget, Eddie Gaedel, to bat in a game for the Browns. He was elected to baseball's Hall of Fame in 1991.

Veiller, Lawrence Turner (1872–1959) social worker, housing expert; born in Elizabeth, N.J. Working as a volunteer for the University Settlement and Charity Organization Society (COS) of New York (1890s) and as a plan examiner in the city buildings department, he came to view housing as key to social improvement. He established and was executive officer of the Tenement House Committee (1898–1907) under the auspices of COS, rising to national prominence as secretary of the New York State Tenement House Commission (1900–01), and transforming the nation's housing reform movement through the use of propaganda and political strategy. These efforts led to the New York State Tenement House Law (1901), which banned the worst forms of multifamily housing. He was founder and director of the National Housing Association (1911–36), author of housing reform tracts that influenced local and state legislation through the 1920s, and a proponent of zoning, but lost his reputation as the nation's leading housing reformer when he opposed the government's public housing policies.

Velikovsky, Immanuel (1895–1979) physician, psychoanalyst, cosmologist, writer; born in Vitebsk, Russia. As a young man he studied in Moscow, mastering several disciplines and learning several languages; he then studied botany and zoology at the University of Edinburgh, Scotland; he took a medical degree in Moscow and did postgraduate medical studies in Berlin. After marrying in 1923, he lived in Paris and then Palestine (1928–38) before settling in New York City in 1939. Working as a psychoanalyst and independent scholar, he burst upon the scholarly/scientific world in 1950 with his book, *Worlds in Collision,* which claimed that a fragment of the planet Jupiter – later known as Venus – had careened through space in 1500 B.C. and brushed against Earth, causing various phenomena that in turn impacted on history (events recorded in the Bible and elsewhere). Attacked by most scientists, he gained at least some sympathy when it was revealed that the scientific establishment had tried to force his publisher to drop the book. Capitalizing on his notoriety, he lectured widely and wrote articles and books – including *Ages in Chaos* (1952) and *Oedipus and Akhnaton: Myth and History* (1960) – mostly promoting his equally heretical views on the links between natural phenomena, legends, history, and the human psyche. Although his theories convinced a small circle of true believers – and may contain some kernels of truth here and there – they have generally not held up to scientific scrutiny. Undoubtedly a brilliant polymath, he appears to have contributed more to understanding human psychology than to the advancement of science.

Vendler, Helen (Hennessy) (1933–) literary critic, educator; born in Boston, Mass. A professor at Boston University (1966–85) and Harvard (1981), she became the *New Yorker*'s poetry critic (1978); through her numerous reviews there and in the *New York Review of Books* she exerted a powerful influence over the reputations and publications of contemporary poets.

Venturi, Robert (1925–) architect, author; born in Philadelphia. A Princeton graduate, he worked for Louis Kahn before establishing (1958) the Philadelphia firm that became Venturi, Rauch, Scott Brown and Associates. As both architect and theorist, Venturi spearheaded the reaction against modernism by embracing historical and popular architectural styles, most famously the common commercial strip. His seminal *Complexity and Contradiction in Architecture* (1966) and *Learning from Las Vegas* (with his wife and partner, Denise Scott Brown, and Steven Izenour, 1972) have been as influential as his buildings, including the recent Sainsbury Wing of the National Gallery, London (1991). He won the Pritzker Prize (1991).

Verdon, (Gwyneth Evelyn) Gwen (1926–) stage actress; born in Culver City, Calif. Remembered for singing and dancing "Whatever Lola Wants (Lola Gets)" in *Damn Yankees* (1955), she starred in a number of other Broadway musicals.

Verhoogen, John (1912–) geophysicist; born in Brussels, Belgium. He obtained his Ph.D. in volcanology from Stanford University (1936), became a prospector and engineer in the Belgian Congo (Zaire) (1940–46), then joined the University of California: Berkeley (1947–77). He performed thermodynamic investigations of the earth's internal convection currents, then specialized in the paleomagnetism of iron-titanium oxides.

Vermeule, Emily Townsend (1928–) classicist, art historian, archaeologist; born in New York City. One of relatively few women full professors at Harvard (1970), she gave the University of California Sather lectures in 1975 and was director of the Harvard Cyprus expedition (1971). Her wide-ranging publications include *Euripides V. Electra* (1959), *Greece in the Bronze Age* (1964), and *Death in Early Greek Art and Poetry* (1978).

Very, Jones (1813–80) poet, writer; born in Salem, Mass. He sailed with his ship captain father, then attended Harvard (B.A. 1836), where he was a tutor in Greek. He studied at Harvard Divinity School (1836–38), but resigned and spent a month in an asylum. After working briefly as a minister, he retired to Salem and became a transcendentalist poet admired by Ralph Waldo Emerson.

Vesey, Denmark ("Telemaque") (?1767–1822) insurrection leader; born probably on St. Thomas, West Indies. The property of Captain Vesey, a Charleston, S.C., slave trader and planter, he spent 20 years sailing with his master. In 1800 he purchased his freedom (allegedly having won a lottery), took up carpentry in Charleston, and prospered at his trade. By 1818 he was preaching to slaves at plantations throughout the region, and drawing on the Bible, he told them that, like the Israelites, they would gain their freedom. Although he would later deny it, he allegedly held meetings at his home to collect arms for an uprising he was planning for as many as 9,000 African-Americans in South Carolina. The plan was betrayed by several fearful slaves and he and others were seized. He defended himself ably at his trial but was sentenced and hanged along with about 35 blacks; some 35 others were sold to West Indian plantation owners. It would have been the largest slave revolt in U.S. history but its end result was the passing of even stricter laws against African-Americans.

Vestal, Albert (Henry) (1875–1932) U.S. representative; born in Frankton, Ind. A prosecuting attorney before going to the U.S. House of Representatives (Rep., Ind.; 1917–32), he chaired the Committee on Weights and Measures, also serving as majority whip (1925–32).

Vidal, (Eugene Luther) Gore (Edgar Box, pen name) (1925–) writer; born in West Point, N.Y. He studied at Exeter Academy, and served in the Army during World War II. His novel, *The City and the Pillar* (1948), was one of the first serious works by an American to deal explicitly with homosexuals. He wrote a number of successful novels, plays, short stories, books of literary criticism, essays, and, using the pen name of Edgar Box, mystery novels. He ran unsuccessfully for the U.S. House of Representatives (1960), and the U.S. Senate (1982); he drew on the former experience for his play, *The Best Man* (1960). Said to have originated the idea of the Peace Corps, he was an often vitriolic commentator on the American political and social scene. Such fictional works as *Myra Breckenridge* (1968) display his capacity for irreverent wit, while in a semifictional work such as *Lincoln* (1984), and in his prolific output of reviews and essays, he displayed the vast range of his knowledge alongside his generally disaffected attitudes toward American society.

Vidor, King (Wallis) (1894–1982) film director; born in Galveston, Texas. Taken with movies as a youth, he worked as a projectionist, then filmed local news events. With his new bride, Florence Arto, he went off to Hollywood in 1915; her career as an actress quickly took off, but King Vidor didn't direct his first feature film until 1919, establishing his reputation with *The Big Parade* (1925). In many of his early films, such as *The Crowd* (1929), he was truly innovative in his use of camera techniques and sound effects, but in subject and mood he was somewhat naive; in *Our Daily Bread* (1934) he extolled nature and cooperative farming. Thereafter he turned to more commercially acceptable films like *Duel in the Sun* (1947), retiring abruptly in 1959. He taught graduate filmmaking at the University of California: Los Angeles in the 1960s and in 1979 he received an honorary Oscar for his "incomparable achievements as a cinematic creator and innovator."

Viereck, George Sylvester (1884–1962) writer, propagandist; born in Munich, Germany. He emigrated to New York with his family (1896). A published poet (1904), he became a writer and editor with German language publications, defending Germany at the outbreak of World War I. Questioned by the U.S. government in 1918 for receiving money from a former German minister, he was not prosecuted, despite public outrage. Known for his interviews of international figures – including Hitler (1923) – he was a Nazi apologist who was indicted (1941) under the Foreign Agents Registration Act; he served four years in prison (1943–47). He wrote two novels and a memoir in his later years.

Vignelli, Massimo (1931–) designer; born in Milan, Italy. In collaboration with wife Lella Vignelli, he started a New York firm (1965) creating modernistic graphics, tableware, furniture, public interiors, and product designs.

Villard, Henry (b. Ferdinand Heinrich Gustav Hilgard) (1835–1900) financier, publisher; born in Speyer, Germany. From a prominent Bavarian family, he left for America after political disagreements with his father. He changed his name to avoid being forced back to Germany, landed in New York in 1853, and traveled to relatives in Illinois, where he read law and learned English. In 1858 he covered the Lincoln-Douglas debates for a German-language newspaper in New York City, the *Staats-Zeitung*. He soon began to write for several other papers, including the *New York Herald* and *Tribune*. In 1868 he became secretary of the American Social Science Association in Boston, enabling him to study public and corporate finance and sparking his interest in railway finance. Going to Oregon in 1874 as the representative of German bondholders of the Oregon & California Railroad, he soon took over as president. When in 1876 he was also made the receiver of the Kansas Pacific Railway, he decided to form a transportation monopoly in the Pacific Northwest. Although large debts forced him out of control in 1884, he is considered one of the most important railway promoters of the 1880s. Meanwhile he had shifted his interests back to the East, buying the *New York Evening Post* (1881) and helping found the Edison General Electric Company (1889). He expanded his publishing company to acquire the *Nation* and generally supported liberal and progressive causes.

Villard, Oswald Garrison (1872–1949) journalist; born in Wiesbaden, Germany. In 1900 he became owner and editor of the *New York Post*, inherited from his father, Henry Villard; his pacifist positions later adversely affected circulation and he sold the paper in 1918, but retained the *Nation*, which he edited until 1932.

Villella, Edward (1936–) ballet dancer, artistic director; born in Bayside, N.Y. Trained at the School of American Ballet and a welterweight boxing champion in college, he joined New York City Ballet in 1957. His athletic style helped dispel the myth that ballet was "unmasculine." After a hip injury he became artistic director of the Eglevsky Ballet Company in 1979 and founded the Miami City Ballet in 1985.

Vincent, (Francis Thomas, Jr.) Fay (1938–) lawyer, baseball commissioner; born in Waterbury, Conn. An aspiring athlete, he suffered a back injury in college and was forced to pursue a more cerebral career. He took his law degree at Yale (1963) and practiced law in New York City and Washington, D.C. (1963–78). As a corporate lawyer, he moved over to become president and chief executive officer of Columbia Pictures Industries (1978–83) and head of Coca-Cola's entertainment division (1983–88). Invited in 1989 by his old friend A. Bartlett Giamatti to assist him as commissioner of baseball, on Giamatti's premature death Vincent was named commissioner (1989–92). A series of crises – including the earthquake in San Francisco that cast a shadow across the 1989 World Series; a spring lockout in 1990; the activities of Yankees' owner George Steinbrenner that led Vincent to suspend him – made Vincent unpopular with some team owners. After he unilaterally announced that some National League teams would be realigned in their divisions, he was asked in September 1992 to resign by a 18–9 vote of the owners. Although at first vowing to fight, he soon resigned and returned to private law practice, thereafter becoming a prominent commentator on broader public issues.

Vincent, John Carter (1900–72) diplomat; born in Seneca, Kans. He started his diplomatic career in 1925, headed the office of Far Eastern Affairs (1945), and was ambassador to Switzerland (1947). In 1952–53 he was named as the "number two" State Department employee on Senator Joseph McCarthy's list of suspected Communists. A board of inquiry found "reasonable doubt" as to his loyalty to the U.S.A. and he retired. He was never officially rehabilitated, but later commentators described him as an ideal diplomat, public servant, and loyal American.

Viner, Jacob (1892–1970) economist; born in Montreal, Canada. Educated in the U.S.A., he is known as a leading interwar price and trade theorist as well as a historian of economic thought. While teaching at the University of Chicago (1916–46), he also served as a Special Assistant to the U.S. Treasury (1934–39), then moved to Princeton University where he remained until his retirement (1946–60).

Vinson, Carl (1883–1981) U.S. representative; born in Milledgeville, Ga. (grand-uncle of Samuel Augustus Nunn). A lawyer, prosecuting attorney, and judge, he served in the Georgia House of Representatives (1912–14) before moving on to the U.S. House of Representatives (Dem., 1914–65). As chairman of the Committee on Naval Affairs (1933–47) he prepared the Navy for World War II, and became chairman of the Armed Services Committee (1949–63). He retired to Milledgeville, Ga.

Vinson, Frederick M. (Moore) (1890–1953) Supreme Court chief justice; born in Louisa, Ky. He served in the U.S. House of Representatives (Dem., Ky.; 1923–29, 1931–38) and was appointed to the U.S. Court of Appeals (1938). He directed the Office of Economic Stabilization (1943–45) and was secretary of the treasury (1945–46) before President Truman named him chief justice of the U.S. Supreme Court (1946–53).

Vizenor, Gerald (1934–) Chippewa writer; born in Minneapolis, Minn. A professor at the University of California: Berkeley, his poetry and fiction reflected his childhood experiences of desertion and death. His books include *Darkness in Saint Louis Bearheart* (1978), *Dead Voices* (1992), and the screenplay *Harold of Orange*.

Vizetelly, Frank (Francis) Horace (1864–1938) lexicographer, editor; born in London, England. Born into a family of printers, Vizetelly came to the United States in 1891 after his father suffered imprisonment and financial loss on charges of obscenity for publishing the works of Émile Zola. He began work at Funk & Wagnalls during the preparation of *A Standard Dictionary of the English Language* (1894) and was the managing editor of the *New Standard Dictionary* (1913). He wrote a weekly column for *Literary Digest* for over thirty years, explaining questions of grammar, etymology, and usage. He wrote enthusiastically on matters of language in his own books, in interviews and letters to the editors of the New York newspapers, and he served as a language usage adviser to numerous radio stations.

Vlastos, Gregory (1907–) classicist; born in Istanbul, Turkey. He was educated at Robert College, Istanbul (B.A. 1925) and Harvard (Ph.D. 1931) and became a naturalized U.S. citizen. He taught at Cornell (1948–55), Princeton (1955–76), and the University of California: Berkeley (1976–82). He was highly regarded for his publications in the field of Greek philosophy, which included *Platonic Studies* (1973) and *Plato's Universe* (1975).

Voegelin, Eric (Herman Wilhelm) (1901–85) political philosopher; born in Cologne, Germany. After studying and teaching law in Europe, he emigrated to the U.S.A. to escape Nazism, teaching at Louisiana State University (1942–58) and elsewhere in the U.S.A.; he was naturalized in 1944. He taught at the University of Munich (1958–69) before becoming a senior research fellow at the Hoover Institution in Stanford, Calif. He sought to develop a comprehensive philosophy of history and society, notably in his masterwork *Order and History,* published starting in 1956.

Vogel, Ezra F. (1930–) scholar, educator; born in Delaware, Ohio. He earned a Ph.D. at Harvard before joining its faculty (1961). He wrote on East Asian industry and repeatedly analyzed Japanese business practices and policy to argue for an American industrial policy in such works as *Japan as Number One* (1979) and *The Four Little Dragons* (1991).

Vogt, William (1902–68) ornithologist, ecologist; born in Mineola, N.Y. He worked as a bird sanctuary curator and as a field naturalist and editor for the National Audubon Society before turning in the 1940s to the problems posed by the pressures of the human population on the environment. From 1943–50 he headed the conservation section of the Pan American Union. His book *Road to Survival* (1948) became a best-seller. He headed the Planned Parenthood Federation, America's largest birth control organization, from 1951–61.

Volcker, Paul A. (1927–) economist; born in Cape May, N.J. After many years in government banking, he served as the highly influential chairman of the Federal Reserve Board (1979–87). He then became the Frederick H. Schultz Class of 1951 Professor of International Economics at Princeton University as well as a partner in the investment firm of James D. Wolfensohn, Inc.

Vollmer, August (1876–1955) criminologist; born in New Orleans. After service in the Spanish-American War, he

became the chief of police in Berkeley, Calif. (1905–32). He reorganized the police department of San Diego (1917) and Los Angeles (1923–24) and established professional police administrations at the Universities of Chicago and California. He wrote *The Criminal* (1949), *Crime and the State Police,* and other books.

Volner, Jill Wine (1943–) lawyer; born in Chicago. A trial attorney with the U.S. Department of Justice pursuing organized crime (1969–73), she became assistant special prosecutor for the Watergate prosecution (1974–75). After serving as general counsel of the Department of the Army (1977–79), she returned to practice law in Chicago.

Volstead, Andrew (John) (1860–1947) U.S. representative; born in Kenyon, Minn. Trained to be a Lutheran minister, he became a lawyer instead (1884) and entered Republican politics in Granite Falls, Minn. In the U.S. House of Representatives (1903–23) he guarded the interests of wheat farmers. In 1919 he persuaded Congress to override President Wilson's veto to secure passage of the Volstead Act, which prohibited the sale of alcoholic beverages until repealed in 1933. He worked to enforce prohibition after leaving Congress.

Volwiler, Ernest H. (1893–) chemist, inventor; born in Hamilton, Ohio. Educated in Ohio and Illinois, he joined Abbott Laboratories in 1918 and rose to become director of research by 1930. With Donalee Tabern, he discovered Pentothal in 1936, a drug widely used for minor procedures requiring anesthesia. He became president of Abbott in 1950 and chairman of the board in 1958.

Von Braun, Wernher (1912–77) engineer, rocket expert; born in Wirsitz, Germany. Developer of the V-2 flying bomb that was deployed against Britain (1944), he was one of the most important of the German weapons specialists to work on rocketry and jet propulsion in America after the war. Hitler personally released him when he was imprisoned on espionage charges after refusing to cooperate with Gestapo Chief Heinrich Himmler's attempted takeover of the V-2 project. Von Braun never approved of the military use of the rocket and surrendered willingly to American troops (1945). Signing a one-year contract with the U.S. Army, he was flown to America where he eventually became technical director of the U.S. Army Ordnance Guided Missile Project in Alabama (1950). He was chiefly responsible for the manufacture and launching of the first American artificial earth satellite, Explorer I (1958). As director of the Marshall Space Flight Center (1960–70), he developed the Saturn rocket for the Apollo 8 moon landing (1969). Good-looking and outgoing, he was occasionally the butt of both humorous and serious attacks aimed at the very notion of former German scientists working for the U.S. space program.

Von Hagen, Victor Wolfgang (1908–) naturalist, explorer, ethnographer; born in St. Louis, Mo. During a lifetime of adventure and exploration he discovered live quetzals in Honduras (1937–38), studied the fauna of the Galapagos Islands (1936–63), and led expeditions along the Inca Highway (1953–55) and the Royal Persian Road (1973–75). His popular books include *Jungle in the Clouds* (1940).

Von Mises, Ludwig (1881–1973) economist; born in Austro-Hungary. He taught at the University of Vienna (1913–34) while also serving as a principal economic adviser to the Austrian government. He left Austria in 1934 due to the turmoil provoked by the Nazis, going first to Geneva, and in

1940 to the U.S.A., where he taught at New York University (1945–69). A leader in the Austrian school of economics, he wrote and lectured extensively on behalf of economic liberalism.

Vonnegut, Kurt (Jr.) (1922–   ) writer; born in Indianapolis, Ind. He studied at Cornell (1940–42), the Carnegie Institute of Technology (1943), and the University of Chicago (1945–47; M.A. 1971). He served in the U.S. Army (1942–45), and his experiences as a prisoner of war in Dresden, Germany, influenced his future work, specifically his novel, *Slaughterhouse-Five* (1969). He was a police reporter in Chicago (1947), worked for General Electric Company's public relations (1947–50), and taught at numerous institutions. He eventually settled in New York City, and produced a steady stream of novels, short stories, nonfiction, and plays. He was labeled as a science fiction writer early in his career, but soon began to appear more as a social satirist with such works as *Cat's Cradle* (1963). He is best known for his irony, wild inventive humor, and themes such as the uneasy balance between technology and humanity.

Von Neumann, John (b. Johann) (1903–57) mathematician; born in Budapest, Hungary. Son of a wealthy Jewish banker, he emigrated to America (1933) to join the new Institute for Advanced Study, Princeton. He contributed to the creation of the atomic and hydrogen bombs and became a member of the Atomic Energy Commission (1955). He is considered one of the last representatives of a group of great mathematicians who were equally at home in pure and applied mathematics and who produced steadily in both directions throughout their careers. Known for an exceptional ability to digest an enormous amount of extremely diverse material with amazing rapidity, he contributed to almost every facet of the mathematics of the 1930s, and was a founder of game theory, and worked in early computer science, theoretical physics, and numerical weather prediction. He is the coauthor of *The Theory of Games and Economic Behavior* (with Oskar Morgenstern, 1944) and of numerous articles.

Vonnoh, Bessie (Onahotema) Potter (1872–1955) sculptor; born in St. Louis, Mo. She studied with Lorado Taft at the Art Institute of Chicago (1890), became one of his assistants, opened her own studio (1894), married the painter, Robert Vonnoh (1899), and lived in New York City, Connecticut, and France. She is known for her plaster and bronze statuettes, such as *The Young Mother* (1896).

Vonnoh, Robert William (1858–1933) painter; born in Hartford, Conn. (husband of Bessie Potter Vonnoh). He grew up in Boston, studied in Paris (1881–90), established studios in New York and Los Angeles, and taught painters such as Robert Henri and William Glackens.

Von Stade, Frederica (1945–   ) mezzo-soprano; born in Somerville, N.J. American-trained, she made her Metropolitan Opera debut in 1970 and by the end of the decade was an international favorite, her celebrated roles including Cherubino and Mélisande.

Von Sternberg, Josef (1894–1969) film director; born in Vienna, Austria. In New York at age 17, he became a film patcher for World Film. In 1917 he joined the Army Signal Corps and made training films. His first movie was *The Salvation Hunters* (1925). He became the master of the American screen with his pictorial compositions and light and shadow effects. Among his films were *The Blue Angel* (1930), *The Scarlet Empress* (1934), and *Macao* (1952).

Von Stroheim, Erich (b. Erich Oswald Stroheim) (1885–1957) actor, motion-picture director; born in Vienna, Austria. Regarded by later generations of moviemakers and critics as an early genius of American film whose abilities were sacrificed to commercialism, in his brief eight-film career von Stroheim established himself as one of the silent era's most prominent directors. Although he claimed he was a Prussian aristocrat and cavalry officer, he was actually the son of a Jewish hatter for whom he worked before emigrating to the U.S.A. sometime between 1906–09. After arriving in Hollywood (1914), he worked for D. W. Griffith. In 1917 he played the first of the autocratic Prussian officer roles for which he became known as "the Man You Love to Hate." He directed his first movie, *Blind Husbands* (1919), his 42-reel, seven-hour masterpiece, *Greed* (1923), and his last Hollywood film, *Queen Kelly* (1928). Shunned by the studios for his profligate style and resistance to formula, after working as a character actor he moved to France and enjoyed considerable acting success, playing the hateful German officer in Renoir's *The Grand Illusion* (1937). After his last American role, in *Sunset Strip* (1950), he returned to France, unsuccessful in securing directing projects, but legendary as the director whose meticulous realism and mature themes anticipated the sound era.

Von Wiegand, Karl Henry (1874–1961) journalist; born in Hesse, Germany. A once famous foreign correspondent for United Press (1911–17) and the Hearst newspapers (from 1917), he covered a dozen wars and roamed the globe in search of scoops, though his stories often were seen to lack depth.

Voorsanger, Jacob (1852–1908) rabbi, scholar; born in Amsterdam, the Netherlands. Educated in Amsterdam, he came to the U.S.A. in 1873, serving congregations in several major cities. From 1889 until his death, he was rabbi of Temple Emanu-El in San Francisco. He was a Semitic scholar who helped found the Semitic department at the University of California. A gifted writer, speaker, and public figure, he helped organize relief after the earthquake of 1906.

Vorenburg, James (1928–   ) lawyer, educator; born in Boston, Mass. He began his legal career as law clerk to Justice Felix Frankfurter (1953–54) and received public recognition as assistant special prosecutor to the Watergate Special Prosecution Force (1973–75) that led to the resignation of President Richard Nixon. A professor at Harvard Law School from 1962 and dean from 1981, he was executive director of the federal Committee on Law Enforcement and Administration of Justice (1965–67) and was a trustee of the National Association for the Advancement of Colored People (NAACP) Legal Defense Fund.

Vose, Seth Morton (1831–1910) art dealer; born in Stoughton, Mass. He bought the Westminster Art Gallery, Providence, R.I. (c. 1850), and by 1852 was importing paintings by Corot, thus introducing the Barbizon School of painters to America. He later opened another gallery in Boston that is still run by his descendants.

Vought, Chance (Milton) (1890–1930) aircraft designer/manufacturer; born in New York City. He was taught to fly by the Wright brothers (c. 1910) and was chief engineer of the Wright company until forming his own firm (1917).

Ambitious, daring, and extremely mechanical, he had an intuitive sense for designing clean, streamlined aircraft. Among his famous designs were the Vought-Wright Model V military biplane (1916), the Vought VE-7 (1919), the Vought UO-1 military observation plane (1922–25), and the FU-1 single-seat high-altitude supercharged fighter (1925). He helped unite major aircraft companies into United Aircraft & Transport Corp. (1929).

Voulkos, Peter (1924–   ) potter; born in Bozeman, Mont. A West Coast potter and sculptor, he led in the development of pottery as an art form, while influencing numerous students and achieving international status. With an M.F.A. from California College of Arts and Crafts (1952), he taught at Black Mountain College (1953) where he was exposed to the avant-garde. On the University of California: Berkeley faculty from 1959, he is known for his slashed and cracked pots.

Vreeland, Diana (Dalziel) (c. 1901–89) fashion journalist; born in Paris, France. The daughter of wealthy parents, she moved to New York as a teenager. She dispensed extravagant advice to snobs in her famous "Why Don't You . . ." in *Harper's Bazaar* (1936); as fashion editor of *Harper's* (1937–62), she became "the high priestess of style," a trend-setter who coined the term "beautiful people" and cultivated her reputation for wit. She was editor in chief of *Vogue* (1962–71) and, after her retirement, mounted major annual fashion exhibitions at the Metropolitan Museum, New York.

W

Waddell, James (Iredell) (1824–86) naval officer; born in Pittsboro, N.C. He served in the U.S. Navy (1841–62) and then the Confederate States Navy (1862–65). He commanded the Confederate raider *Shenendoah* on a 58,000-mile, around-the-globe voyage (1864–65) and decimated the New England whaling fleet in the Pacific Ocean. Following an amnesty, he returned to the U.S.A. and engaged in commercial sailing.

Wade, Benjamin Franklin (1800–78) lawyer, public official; born in Springfield, Mass. Raised on a farm, he moved to Ohio at age 21, taught school and read law, and was admitted to the bar in 1831. He built a thriving practice before entering public life in the antislavery cause. Elected to the U.S. Senate (Whig, Ohio; 1851–56; Rep., 1856–69), he joined with congressional Radical Republicans to press for the emancipation of slaves and, after the Civil War, a punitive peace for the former Confederacy. As chairman of the powerful Joint Committee on the Conduct of the War, he participated in investigations of every aspect of the federal war effort. He was among those who pursued the impeachment of President Andrew Johnson most vehemently; as president pro tempore of the Senate he would have succeeded Johnson as president and was so sure of a conviction that he actually began to select his cabinet. He retired from public life in 1869, resumed the practice of law, and became general counsel for the Northern Pacific Railway.

Wade, Leigh (1896–) aviator; born in Cassopolis, Mich. He learned to fly in Canada in 1917 and became a pioneer test pilot, participating in many air races and international competitions during the 1920s. He was a member of the army's first round-the-world flight. He later held senior management positions for several aviation companies.

Wagley, Charles (Walter) (1913–91) anthropologist; born in Clarksville, Texas. He earned his A.B. and Ph.D. under Franz Boas at Columbia University, where he spent most of his career teaching (1946–71, 1965–71 as the first Franz Boas professor of anthropology) and directing the Institute of Latin American studies (1961–69). A social anthropologist, he worked in the 1930s among the descendants of the Maya in Guatemala; in the 1940s he was among the first Americans to work in the South American lowlands, beginning the work on Brazil for which he is best known. His community and aboriginal studies in northern and central Brazil include published studies of Tapirape (1940, 1943) and Tenetehara (1949). His other works include the frequently revised *Introduction to Brazil* (1963) and *The Latin American Tradition* (1968).

Wagner, (John Peter) "Honus" (1874–1955) baseball player; born in Carnegie, Pa. During his 21-year career as an infielder (1897–1917), mostly with the Pittsburgh Pirates, he was widely considered the greatest all-around player to have ever played the game and he is still regarded as one of the greatest shortstops. An outstanding right-handed hitter with exceptional speed, he holds the National League record for most consecutive seasons batting .300 or more (17). After his retirement, he served as coach for the Pirates for 19 years (1933–51). Nicknamed "the Flying Dutchman," he was elected to baseball's Hall of Fame in 1936.

Wagner, Robert F. (Ferdinand) (1877–1953) U.S. senator; born in Hesse-Nassau, Germany. He immigrated to the U.S.A. in 1896 and took a law degree from New York Law School (1900). Active in the New York State legislature, he became lieutenant governor in 1914. He was elected to the New York Supreme Court in 1918 and to the U.S. Senate (Dem., N.Y.; 1927–49). He won fame as an advocate of labor rights. While in the New York legislature he was chairman of the committee that investigated the Triangle Shirtwaist Fire of 1911 and he helped establish new legal protections for worker safety. As a senator during the Great Depression, his hand touched practically every piece of important relief and labor legislation, including the National Industrial Recovery Act, the National Labor Relations Act (or Wagner Act), the Social Security Act, the Wagner-Steagall Act (concerning public housing), and the Home Loan Act. A leader in postwar planning, he was the prime mover behind the Public Housing Act of 1949; he also helped shape the GI Bill and Veteran Placement Service.

Wagner, Robert F., Jr. (1910–91) mayor, diplomat; born in New York City. He was the son of U.S. Senator Robert F. Wagner. He graudated from Yale University (1933) and Yale Law School (1937). He was a decorated intelligence officer in the Army Air Corps and served in the New York State Assembly. As three-term mayor of New York City (1954–65), he was known for his cautious consensus-building. An advocate of programs for the poor, he introduced significant reforms in education and housing. He served as ambassador to Spain (1968–69) and emissary to the Vatican (1978–80).

Wagstaff, (Samuel, Jr.) Sam J. (1921–89) curator, collector; born in New York City. He graduated from Yale, served in the Navy during World War II, and studied Renaissance art at New York University's Institute of Fine Arts. He worked as a curator at the Wadsworth Atheneum (1961–68) and at the Detroit Institute of Arts (1968–71). Beginning in 1973 he assembled a vast photography collection that he sold to the J. Paul Getty Museum (1984). He then began to collect 19th-century American silver.

Wainwright, Jonathan (Mayhew) (1883–1953) soldier; born in Walla Walla, Wash. He graduated from West Point in 1906, saw combat service in France in World War I, and held a series of staff appointments before being assigned to the Philippines in 1940. He led the withdrawal into the Bataan defense lines, where U.S. and Filipino forces surrendered to the Japanese in April 1942; Wainwright himself held out on Corregidor for another month. He spent three years in a Japanese prisoner of war camp.

Waite, Morrison Remick (1816–88) Supreme Court chief justice; born in Lyme, Conn. He practiced corporate and railroad law before serving on the Ohio Supreme Court (1863–71). He was President Grant's third choice for chief justice of the U.S. Supreme Court after Congress refused to confirm two prior nominees. His tenure on the Supreme Court (1874–88) was marked with important cases involving the new Fourteenth Amendment.

Wakoski, Diane (1937–) poet; born in Whittier, Calif. She studied at the University of California: Berkeley (B.A. 1960), taught in New York City (1963–66), then at several colleges, notably Michigan State University (1976). She is known for her literary criticism and her autobiographical poetry, as in *The Collected Greed: Parts I–XIII* (1984).

Waksman, Selman A. (Abraham) (1888–1973) soil microbiologist; born in Priluka, Ukraine. He came to the U.S.A. in 1910 and lived with relatives on a New Jersey farm. He became a soil microbiologist at Rutgers (1918–58), while concurrently working at the New Jersey Agricultural Experiment Station (1921–54) and at the Woods Hole Oceanographic Institute as a marine bacteriologist (1931–42). After early research on peat and humus, he focused on fungus-like soil bacteria called actinomycetes, classifying them and extensively investigating their chemistry. To determine why the tuberculosis bacillus does not survive in soil, Waksman and his staff examined over 10,000 soil microorganisms. He coined the term "antibiotic" for antibacterial microbial metabolites, and in 1943 he discovered streptomycin, effective against not only the tuberculosis bacillus but also sulfa- and penicillin-resistant bacteria. For this accomplishment, Waksman won the 1952 Nobel Prize in physiology. He continued to isolate other antibiotics and brought soil microbiology to scientific prominence. His autobiography, *My Life with the Microbes* (1954), was translated into many languages.

Walcott, Charles Doolittle (1850–1927) geologist, paleontologist; born in New York Mills, N.Y. He worked for the U.S. Geological Survey (1879–1907, director 1894–1907) and was secretary of the Smithsonian Institution (1907–27). Walcott's voluminous publications on trilobites, brachiopods, fossil jellyfish and western fossils established him as a leading authority on Cambrian rocks and fossils. His discovery of fossilized soft-bodied organisms in British Columbia (1909) ranks among the greatest ever fossil finds.

Wald, George (1906–) biochemist; born in New York City. He was a research fellow at the University of Chicago and in Europe (1932–34), then joined Harvard (1934–77). While in Berlin (1933), he discovered vitamin A in the retina; in

subsequent research he determined how the retinal rod cells enable black-and-white night vision. During the late 1950s, his investigations of the three types of retinal cone cells demonstrated that these cells' color reception is due to the presence of three different protein pigments. For this work, he shared the 1967 Nobel Prize in physiology. He was a dedicated and popular lecturer who believed that the natural world is "of chance, but not accident," and described a scientist's ongoing intellectual development as that of a "learned child." He was active against the Vietnam war, the arms race, and the development of nuclear power plants.

Wald, Lillian D. (1867–1940) public health nurse, settlement leader; born in Cincinnati, Ohio. Among the greatest of a generation of outstanding social workers, she was a gifted fundraiser, a pacifist, and a child welfare activist, and is best known as a founder of public health nursing and related services through establishment of the Nurses' Settlement at 265 Henry Street, New York City (1895). She created the first public school nursing program in the United States (1902), assisted in establishing a nursing program for industrial policyholders by the Metropolitan Life Insurance Company, and was a prime mover (1910) in the establishment of a nursing and health department at Teachers College of Columbia University. At her initiative, the American Red Cross established the precursor to the Town and Country Nursing Service (1912). She was the first president and one of the founders of the National Organization for Public Health Nursing (1912). Equally influential in social service, by 1913 her Henry Street Visiting Nurses Service had a staff of 92, making 200,000 visits annually, along with first aid stations and convalescent facilities. Concerned for children, she was a founder of the National Child Labor Council (1904). Optimistic, warm, unselfconsciously tolerant, she is also known for her realistic understanding of the complexities of community life.

Waldo, Samuel Lovett (1783–1861) painter; born in Windham, Conn. A portrait painter active in Hartford, Conn. (c. 1799), he became an itinerant artist. He studied with Benjamin West and John Singleton Copley in London (1806–08), then settled in New York City (1809) and, after 1820, was the painting partner of William Jewett.

Walgreen, Charles R. (Rudolph) (1873–1939) drug store chain owner; born near Galesburg, Ill. An accident in a shoe factory led to the loss of part of a finger on his left hand; the doctor who treated him persuaded him to become a druggist's apprentice. In 1893 he went to Chicago, became a registered pharmacist (1897) and then fought in the Spanish-American War. He returned to Chicago and worked as a pharmacist for druggist Issac W. Blood, whom he bought out in 1902 when Blood retired. He acquired his second store in 1909 and organized C. R. Walgreen and Company. In 1916 the name was changed to Walgreen Company, with seven stores. His drugstore innovations included lunch counters that had soda fountains, and he is credited with introducing the "malted milk." A talented retailer, he continued to manufacture some of his drugs to keep prices competitive and quality high; by 1939, 25,000 different articles were being manufactured by Walgreen. In 1927 he had 110 stores. He established the Charles R. Walgreen Foundation for the Study of American Institutions at the University of Chicago (1937).

Walker, (Aaron Thibeaux) "T-Bone" (1910–75) blues musician; born in Linden, Texas. A pioneering electric guitarist, he worked as a lead-boy for Blind Lemon Jefferson in Dallas before teaching himself guitar in the mid-1920s. He toured with a variety of medicine shows throughout the South and made his first recording in 1929. Between 1930–35 he toured with Ida Cox, Ma Rainey, Cab Calloway, and Milt Larkins, then appeared as a sideman with Les Hite's Orchestra for five years, during which time he developed a prototypical style for electric blues. His 1942 Capitol recording "Call It Stormy Monday" was the first of many blues standards he recorded over the next 25 years. He toured with his own band thereafter, but also appeared with the American Folk Blues Festival and all-star jazz groups on annual tours of Europe between 1962–74.

Walker, (Addison Mortimer) Mort (1923–) cartoonist; born in El Dorado, Kans. In 1940 he created the popular newspaper comic strip, *Beetle Bailey*, featuring a shiftless soldier and his friends. He also created and served as author of *Hi and Lois, Fitz's Flats,* and *Boner's Ark.*

Walker, Alan (Cyril) (1938–) physical anthropologist; born in Leicester, England. He lived and worked in Africa before coming to the U.S.A. in 1973. He taught at Harvard (1973–78), then joined Johns Hopkins (1978). His extensive field research on the evolutionary implications of Kenyan fossils includes his discoveries of a 1.6-million-year-old *Homo erectus* (1984), and a 2.5-million-year-old "hyper-robust" *Australopithecus boisei* (1985).

Walker, Alice (Malsenior) (1944–) writer, poet; born in Eatonville, Ga. She studied at Spelman College (1961–63) and Sarah Lawrence (B.A. 1965). She worked in Georgia registering voters, with the Head Start program in Mississippi, and the welfare department in New York City. She settled in San Francisco but taught at many institutions. She won wide acclaim for her poetry and fiction, notably *The Color Purple* (1982), a novel that explores the experience of American black women. This work won the Pulitzer Prize (1983) and was made into a successful movie (1985). Much of her later writing revolves around racial and "womanist" concerns.

Walker, Amasa (1799–1875) businessman, economist, U.S. representative; born in Woodstock, Conn. Retiring from business (1840), he devoted himself to study and public service. He was president of the Boston Temperance Society (1839), founder and first secretary of the Boston Lyceum, and a founder of Oberlin College where he lectured on economics (1842–49). He attended two International Peace Congresses (England 1844, Paris 1849). A specialist in the monetary system, he wrote widely on this topic. He was elected to the Massachusetts House of Representatives (1848, 1859) and the state Senate (1849); he was secretary of the state of Massachusetts (1851–53); and he filled out a term in the U.S. House of Representatives (1862–63), where he continued to exert influence on monetary issues. His *Science and Wealth* (1866) was a popular textbook in economics for many years.

Walker, David (1785–1830) African-American leader; born in Wilmington, N.C. Born a free man in the South, he traveled widely and became greatly concerned over the conditions of his fellow blacks. Moving to Boston (1827), he established a second-hand clothing business. In 1829 he issued *Walker's Appeal,* an antislavery pamphlet that urged slaves to rise up against their oppressors, and slaveholders to repent. Appear-

ing in the South (1830), the *Appeal* raised fear among slaveholders, and a price was set on his head throughout the region. After issuing an even more militant appeal to end slavery, he died of natural causes.

Walker, (James John) Jimmy (1881–1946) mayor, songwriter; born in New York City. Having graduated law school, he was more interested in writing lyrics for popular songs (his only memorable one being "Will You Love Me in December as You Do in May?", 1905). Turning to politics, he got the support of the Democratic machine and by 1914 was serving in the New York state senate. From 1921–25 he was the leader of Democrats in the senate and so was picked to run for mayor of New York City. As mayor (1926–32) he supported an expanded transit system and created a department of sanitation, but he became best known for his dapper appearance and a lifestyle that embodied the Roaring Twenties. Despite his popularity, revelations of financial improprieties, both personal and in his administration, forced him to resign. In 1940, Mayor Fiorello La Guardia, who had lost to Walker in 1928, named him arbiter in garment industry disputes.

Walker, (Joseph) Joe (1892–1985) cinematographer; born in Denver, Colo. Working in Hollywood from the late 1910s, he began to get his first credits in the 1920s and eventually filmed many well-known films, in particular those of Frank Capra. He became an expert in optics and pioneered the zoom lens. In the early 1950s he retired to pursue his research and he invented the Elektra-Zoom, used on television cameras.

Walker, Joseph Reddeford (1789–1876) explorer, trapper, guide; born in Virginia. He engaged in extensive fur trapping and trading in the upper Missouri region (1820–40), giving his name to Walker Lake and Walker's Pass. He served as a guide for several exploratory expeditions between 1832 and 1860. He guided prospectors during the 1849 Gold Rush and settled in California, but in 1861 he set out for Arizona on the final expedition of his long career, discovering rich ore deposits near what is now Prescott.

Walker, Kenneth N. (1898–1943) aviator; born in Cerillos, N.M. An early advocate of bombing as a prime strategic weapon, Walker was killed leading a raid on Japanese shipping at Rabaul, New Britain, and was a posthumous winner of the Congressional Medal of Honor.

Walker, Maggie Lena (Draper) (1867–1934) activist, businesswoman; born in Richmond, Va. Daughter of a former slave (and evidently a white Northern father), she assisted her mother in running a laundry out of her home. She graduated from a normal school (teachers' training) for African-Americans (1883) and then taught school until she married in 1886. Thereafter she dedicated herself to what became the Independent Order at St. Luke, an African-American fraternal and insurance cooperative; becoming its executive secretary-treasurer in 1899, she almost singlehandedly built it into a prosperous nationwide organization. In 1903 she founded the St. Luke Penny Savings Bank in Richmond, Va., thereby becoming the first female bank president in the U.S.A.; her bank gradually absorbed other African-American banks and became a major bank (1929). She was also active in several other organizations and programs dedicated to improving economic and social conditions for African-Americans. An accident in 1907 eventually left her unable to walk, but she continued her many activities with the aid of a wheelchair, a chauffeured automobile, and an elevator in her home.

Walker, Mary E. (Edwards) (1832–1919) physician, feminist; born in Oswego Town, N.Y. Graduating from Syracuse Medical College (1855), she married a medical student who also became a physician. An activist on behalf of women's dress reform, she wore "bloomers" at the ceremony; the word "obey" was omitted from her vows, and she kept her own name. (They separated in 1859.) During the Civil War she was an assistant surgeon (1863–64), was imprisoned by the Confederates (1864), and won a Congressional Medal of Honor for Meritorious Service (1865). Afterward she lectured on such issues as dress reform and women's suffrage, but did not support a proposed suffrage amendment, contending the right to vote was already contained in the Constitution. The government questioned her medical credentials and withdrew her medal in 1917, but she continued to wear it (and it was posthumously restored in 1977).

Walker, Moses Fleetwood (1856–1924) born in Mt. Pleasant, Ohio; **and Welday Wilberforce Walker** (1860–1937) born in Steubenville, Ohio; baseball players, businessmen, civil rights pioneers. Sons of an Ohio physician, as students the Walker brothers helped organize and played on the Oberlin College varsity baseball team. In 1883 "Fleet" played on Toledo's Northwestern League team; when Toledo was accepted in the American Association in 1884, he became the first African-American in the major leagues, batting .263 in 42 games and earning respect as a catcher. Welday played five games as a major league outfielder in 1884, batting .182. In 1887 the International League voted to bar contracts with blacks, and the Walker brothers' careers soon declined. In 1889 "Fleet," playing with Syracuse in the International League, became the last African-American in that league. In 1895 he killed a man in self-defense in a racial attack in Syracuse, and although exonerated, he left town and went to Steubenville, Ohio, where his brother Welday followed him. They managed a hotel there and eventually owned some motion picture theaters. Meanwhile the brothers had become increasingly open in their opposition to the growing segregation in American society, and Moses became the editor of the *Equator,* a periodical devoted to African-American concerns. In 1908 the brothers published *Our Home Colony – A Treatise on the Past, Present and Future of the Negro Race in America,* now regarded as ranking among the earliest of the 20th-century works to advocate the return of African-Americans to Africa. The Walker brothers even set up a travel office to aid African-Americans to go to Liberia.

Walker, Ralph Thomas (1889–1973) architect; born in Waterbury, Conn. He was known for his 1920s art deco skyscrapers; later he designed hundreds of labs and research centers. He was acclaimed in 1957 by the American Institute of Architects as "the architect of the century" and by Frank Lloyd Wright as "the only other architect in America."

Walker, Sarah Breedlove (Madame C. J. Walker) (1876–1919) businesswoman, philanthropist; born in Delta, La. Orphaned at the age of six, she was raised by an elder sister and married to "Mr. McWilliams" at age 14 in Vicksburg. Widowed at age 20 with a daughter, A'Lelia Walker, she moved to St. Louis and attended public night schools and worked days as a washerwoman. In 1905 she invented a method for straightening African-Americans' "kinky" hair:

her method involved her own formula for a pomade, much brushing, and the use of heated combs. Encouraged by her success, she moved to Denver, Colo., where she married Charles J. Walker; she promoted her method and products by traveling about the country giving lecture-demonstrations. Her business became so successful that she opened an office in Pittsburgh (1908), which she left in charge of her daughter. In 1910 she settled in Indianapolis, where she established the headquarters of Madame C. J. Walker Laboratories to manufacture cosmetics and train her sales beauticians. These "Walker Agents" became well known throughout the black communities of the U.S.A. and the Caribbean, and they in turn promoted Madame Walker's philosophy of "cleanliness and loveliness" as aids to advancing the status of African-Americans. An innovator, she organized clubs and conventions for her representatives which recognized not only successful sales, but also philanthropic and education efforts among African-Americans. At her death she was sole owner of her business; one-third of her multi-million dollar estate went to her daughter – who herself became well known as a supporter of the Harlem Renaissance – the remainder to various philanthropies.

Walker, Thomas (1715–94) physician, explorer, legislator; born in King and Queen County, Va. After practicing as a doctor he became interested in seeking out new land for speculation. As chief agent for the Loyal Land Company, he led explorers into present-day Kentucky (1750–51). He served numerous terms in the Virginia House of Burgesses and represented Virginia at the Fort Stanwix Indian treaty (1768). He was a guardian for Thomas Jefferson and, as a member of the Virginia Committee of Safety (1776), took an active role in advancing the American Revolution.

Walker, Thomas Barlow (1840–1928) businessman, collector, philanthropist; born in Xenia, Ohio. He had little formal education, sold grindstones, moved to Minneapolis, and eventually became a wealthy lumberman. He used his fortune to benefit art, religious, and charity institutions. Among other philanthropic projects, he established what became Minneapolis's Walker Art Center in 1879, where he housed his eclectic art collection.

Walker, Timothy (1802–56) legal scholar; born in Wilmington, Mass. In 1833 he founded a private law school which later affiliated with Cincinnati College (1835). His book, *Introduction to American Law* (1837), was highly acclaimed and published in several editions.

Walker, Walton (Harris) (1889–1950) soldier; born in Belton, Texas. A combat veteran of both World War I and World War II, he commanded United Nations ground forces in Korea in 1950. He directed the defensive battle of the Pusan Perimeter, then led the counteroffensive that drove North Korean forces northward to the Manchurian border. He was killed when his jeep collided with a truck near Seoul on December 23, 1950.

Walker, Welday Wilberforce See under WALKER, MOSES FLEETWOOD.

Walker, William (1824–60) adventurer, filibuster; born in Nashville, Tenn. With degrees in medicine and law, he failed to find success practicing law. In 1853 he gained notoriety by attempting to seize and govern the Mexican province of Lower California. In 1855 he led a small band of mercenaries to Nicaragua, and after overthrowing the government, he briefly served as president (1856–57). With visions of uniting all the Central American republics under his control, he announced plans to build a canal linking the Atlantic and the Pacific, but he was ousted in 1857 by agents of Cornelius Vanderbilt, whose commercial interests he had opposed; an attempt to return to Nicaragua later that year was foiled. In 1860, he landed in Honduras with yet another scheme to seize power; but he was arrested, and after a Honduran court martial, was shot by a firing squad.

Walker, William H. (1869–1934) chemical engineer; born near Pittsburgh, Pa. He organized and directed the department of chemical engineering at the Massachusetts Institute of Technology (1905). He conducted research on cellulose and coinvented a method of manufacturing artificial silk (1905). During World War I he was instrumental in setting up the chemical warfare program.

Walkowitz, Abraham (c. 1878–1965) graphic artist, painter; born in Tyumen, Russia. He emigrated to New York City (c. 1889), studied at the National Academy of Design (1894, 1898), in Paris (1906–07), and returned to New York. A modernist, he was influenced by the French artists called Fauvists ("wild beasts"). Noted for his ability to use line to convey motion, he did thousands of drawings of Isadora Duncan.

Wallace, George (Corley) (1919–   ) governor; born in Clio, Ala. A University of Alabama Law School graduate, he served as an army air force flight engineer during World War II. A Democratic assistant attorney general in Alabama (1946–47), he served in the legislature (1947–53). Elected a state circuit judge (1953–59) he defied the U.S. Civil Rights Commission with his segregationist rulings. After returning to private practice, he became Alabama's governor (1963–67), proclaiming "segregation forever." In 1963 he achieved national notoriety when he stood in the doorway of the administration building of the University of Alabama, denying two black students admission until President Kennedy brought in the national guard. Succeeded as governor by his wife Lurleen Wallace, he ran for president in 1968 on the American Independent Party ticket, championing rural Southern values and states' rights. A strong third, he received over nine million votes, winning in five southern states. He would serve three more terms as governor (1971–79, 1983–87) but he was in a wheelchair most of those years: In 1972, while campaigning for the Democratic presidential nomination, he was shot and paralyzed, thus ending his national political ambitions. He had always insisted he was not a racist and in later years he did in fact align himself with a more liberal agenda and civil rights leaders.

Wallace, Henry A. (Agard) (1888–1965) vice-president; born in Adair County, Iowa. He switched from the Republican to the Democratic Party in the late 1920s. Appointed secretary of agriculture in 1933, he carried out policies mandated by the Agriculture Adjustment Act of 1933. In 1940 he was nominated for vice-president after Franklin Roosevelt made it clear that he wanted Wallace. An active vice-president, he advocated cooperation with the Soviet Union and economic assistance to underdeveloped countries. He was dropped from the ticket in 1944 but still campaigned for Roosevelt. He was named secretary of commerce in 1945, but was later fired by President Truman for his outspokenness regarding American relations with the Soviet Union. In 1948 he ran unsuccessfully for president as the Progressive Party candi-date. In 1952 he published *Why I Was Wrong,* which explained his new distrust of the Soviet Union.

Wallace, Henry Cantwell (1866–1924) journalist, cabinet member; born in Rock Island, Ill. (father of Henry A. Wallace). A farmer and professor of dairying at Iowa State Agricultural College, with his family he published *Wallace's Farmer* (1894–1924). His political and scientific writings influenced farm organizations. Secretary of agriculture (1921–24), he emphasized matching farm production to consumption, championed agricultural education, and instituted the Bureau of Agricultural Economics, the Bureau of Home Economics, and radio market reports.

Wallace, John Hankins (1822–1903) horseman, publisher; born in Allegheny County, Pa. He compiled the standard book on pedigree trotting horses, *American Trotting Register* (1871), and wrote a major history on standardbreds, *The Horse in America* (1897).

Wallace, Lewis (1827–1905) author, soldier; born in Brookville, Ind. He served with volunteer troops in the Mexican War, practiced law and was active in political and militia affairs in Indiana, and commanded a division under Grant at Shiloh (1862). His novel, *Ben Hur,* a story of Christians in the Roman Empire, has been in print continuously since it first appeared in 1880.

Wallace, Lila (Bell) Acheson (1889–1984) editor/publisher, art collector, philanthropist; born in Virden, Manitoba, Canada. Her father was a Presbyterian minister who brought his family to the U.S.A. when she was a girl and she grew up in the Midwest. She graduated from the University of Oregon (1917), taught school for two years, and then worked for the Young Women's Christian Association. She married DeWitt Wallace in 1921 and was directly involved in launching the *Reader's Digest* in 1922. As the publication quickly caught on after its first issue of 5,000 copies, she served as cochairman of the company until 1973, and as a director until 1984. Although she gradually withdrew from the day-to-day operations, she was known to exercise indirect influence on the *Digest*'s editorial agenda. She assembled an extensive collection of art – strong in French Impressionists – and placed original paintings throughout the *Digest*'s offices; she was also a lover of gardening and flowers and among the many millions she donated to the Metropolitan Museum of Art was a fund to provide fresh flowers daily to the museum's Great Hall. Among her benefactions were the restoration of Giverny, Monet's home in France; the gallery for the Abu Simbel temple at the Metropolitan; the Bird House at the New York Zoological Society's Bronx Zoo; and millions to various hospitals and churches as well as to such arts institutions as the Juilliard School of Music. Altogether she gave away some $60 million in her lifetime, and since they had no children, she and her husband left their fortune to foundations that continue to donate millions to various causes.

Wallace, (Myron Leon) Mike (1918–   ) broadcast journalist; born in Brookline, Mass. A University of Michigan graduate, he entered broadcasting on a Michigan radio station. Hardest-hitting of the adversary interviewers, he won fame with ABC's *Mike Wallace Interview* (1957–60), later becoming the mainstay for the long-running CBS TV news magazine, *60 Minutes* (1968).

Wallace, William (1825–1904) inventor, manufacturer; born in Manchester, England. He emigrated to America with his parents as a boy and eventually they settled in Derby, Conn. There the elder Wallace went into the wire-drawing business. His son became president upon his death and built a large and flourishing copper, brass, and wire enterprise. In 1874 Wallace introduced dynamo-electric machinery into his factory. Eventually his dynamos could copper-plate 100 miles of steel wire at a time. He later designed the first commercial arc light. He sold his business and retired to Washington, D.C., in 1896.

Wallace, (William Roy) De Witt (1889–1981) publisher; born in St. Paul, Minn. He was son of the dean (later president) of Macalaster College, which he attended, and later married his roommate's sister, Lila Bell Acheson (1889–1984; born in Manitoba, Canada). Working as a book salesman, he got the idea of a magazine that printed digests of other publications' articles. The first issue of the pocket-sized magazine, *Reader's Digest,* appeared in February 1922; sold only through the mail, it soon caught on, eventually becoming the world's largest circulation magazine, printed in 17 languages for 31 million readers in 168 countries; the firm also branched out into condensed books, original books, and recordings, all sold only through the mail.

Wallack, Lester (John Johnstone) (1820–88) actor, manager; born in New York City. Tall and elegant and well-received in both comic and romantic roles, he also successfully managed several New York theaters.

Wallance, Donald A. (1909–90) designer; born in New York City. In independent practice since the 1940s, he designed auditorium seating for Lincoln Center, hospital furniture, and household goods such as stainless steel tableware.

Waller, (Thomas Wright) "Fats" (1904–43) jazz musician; born in New York City. Composer of "Ain't Misbehavin'," "Honeysuckle Rose," and other standards, and a leading exponent of the "stride" piano style, he began as an organist at the Abyssinian Baptist Church in Harlem, where his father was pastor. He played New York cabarets and theatres in the 1920s, and though hampered by alcoholism, he achieved wide popularity during the 1930s as an irrepressible singer, songwriter, and stage and screen personality.

Wallerstein, Immanuel (Maurice) (1930–) sociologist; born in New York City. He studied at Columbia University (B.A. 1951; M.A. 1954; Ph.D. 1959), and at Oxford (1955–56). He taught at Columbia (1958–71), McGill University, Montreal, Canada (1971–76), and State University of New York: Binghamton (1976), where he was distinguished professor of sociology and director of the Fernand Braudel Center for the Study of Economics, Historical Systems, and Civilizations. He wrote many texts dealing with the economy and political systems of the world, including *The Modern World-System* (2 vols. 1974, 1980), *The Politics of the World Economy* (1984), and *Geopolitics and Geoculture* (1991).

Walling, William English (1877–1936) labor reformer, socialist; born in Louisville, Ky. A man of independent means, educated at the University of Chicago and Harvard Law School, he rejected his privileged, liberal heritage and deliberately chose to become a factory inspector in Illinois (1900–01). He then moved to New York City and lived in the tenement district (1901–05) and cofounded the National Women's Trade Union League (1903). He spent much of the years 1905–08 in Russia where he got to know leading revolutionary figures; on his return he published *Russia's Message* (1908). After witnessing a race riot (1908), he

helped found the National Association for the Advancement of Colored People (NAACP) and joined the Socialist Party (1910–17), but resigned because of its antiwar stance. He worked full-time for the American Federation of Labor, wrote for the *American Federationist,* ran unsuccessfully for Congress in Connecticut (1924), and was executive director of the Labor Chest (1935). Although he moved back and forth on the left-wing spectrum, he mainly supported reform as opposed to revolution.

Walsh, (Edward Augustine) "Big Ed" (1881–1959) baseball pitcher; born in Plains, Pa. During his 14-year career (1904–17), mostly with the Chicago White Sox, he won 40 games in 1908 and 195 games overall. A right-hander who threw a spitball when the pitch was allowed, he was elected to baseball's Hall of Fame in 1946.

Walsh, James A. (Anthony) (1867–1936) Catholic prelate; born in Boston, Mass. Ordained in 1892, he cofounded the Catholic Mission Bureau (1906) to support foreign missions and, with Father Thomas Price, won approval for a seminary for missionaries (1911). Walsh was the first superior of the new Catholic Foreign Mission Society of America (Maryknoll), which dispatched its first missionaries in 1918. He was consecrated a bishop in 1933.

Walsh, Lawrence E. (Edward) (1912–) lawyer; born in Port Maitland, Nova Scotia, Canada. He emigrated to the U.S.A. in 1914 and took his law degree at Columbia University (1935). District judge of New York (1954–57), U.S. deputy attorney general (1957–60), and deputy head of the U.S. delegation on Vietnam (Paris 1969), he was a partner in the Washington firm of Davis, Polk and Wardwell (1961–81) before joining Oklahoma City's Crowe & Dunlevy (1981). From 1986–92 he was the independent counsel heading the investigation of the Iran/Contra affair, and as such found himself both hotly attacked and defended for his persistence in pursuing those involved.

Walsh, (William Ernest) Bill (1931–) football coach; born in Los Angeles. The most successful professional coach of the 1980s, he guided the San Francisco 49ers to victories in Super Bowls XVI, XIX, and XXIII. After coaching the 49ers (1979–89) he spent two years as a sportscaster and then took up coaching at Stanford (1992).

Walter, Bruno (b. Bruno Walter Schlesinger) (1876–1962) conductor; born in Berlin, Germany. A protégé of Mahler, he was in charge of the Munich Opera in 1913–22 and from 1919 was chief conductor of the Berlin Philharmonic. International tours won him a worldwide reputation before he fled the Nazis in 1938. Settling in the U.S.A. the next year, he guest-conducted widely over the next two decades, including many appearances at the Metropolitan Opera. In 1947–49 he led the New York Philharmonic. He was best known for his performances and recordings of the Viennese classics from Mozart and Beethoven to Brahms and Mahler.

Walter, Francis (Eugene) (1894–1963) U.S. representative; born in Easton, Pa. A lawyer before going to the U.S. House of Representatives (Dem., Pa.; 1933–65) he came to prominence when, as chairman of the Subcommittee on Immigration, he sponsored the McCarran-Walter Act of 1952, which favored Northern Europeans over other immigrants. In 1955 he became chairman of the House Un-American Activities Committee, casting a broad net to round up "subversives" and successfully resisting attempts to curb the committee's power.

Walter, Thomas U. (Ustick) (1804–87) architect; born in Philadelphia. After designing mostly Greek Revival buildings in Philadelphia, he became famous for designing the U.S. Capitol wings and dome (1851–65). He was a founder and president (1876–87) of the American Institute of Architects.

Walters, Barbara (1931–) television journalist/interviewer; born in Boston, Mass. After graduation from Sarah Lawrence College, she went to work for the National Broadcasting Company's publicity department, then moved to the *Today Show*. Successful despite a slight lisp (later parodied on *Saturday Night Live*), she developed the reputation for intelligent and probing – if not confrontational – interviews. In 1976, ABC gave her a million-dollar-a-year contract – making her the highest-paid television journalist at the time – and the opportunity to be the first woman coanchoring the network evening news; however, under pressure from her coanchor Harry Reasoner, the network eased her out in 1979. She then moved to ABC's *20/20* where she became coanchor with Hugh Downs (1984). Her occasional *Barbara Walters Specials* (1976) established her as one of television's most skilled interviewers – known for her ability to elicit candid remarks from normally wary subjects – and she helped break the stereotype of women television journalists as merely pretty faces.

Walters, William Thompson (1820–94) businessman, art collector; born in Liverpool, Pa. He studied as a civil and mining engineer in Philadelphia, and worked at iron furnaces. He settled in Baltimore (1841) and ran a produce trading company. By 1883 he was involved in the coordination of railroads ranging from Washington, D.C., south to Florida and west to St. Louis, a project carried on by his son, Henry Walters. During a stay in Paris (1861–65), he collected paintings by such artists as Corot and Millais, and later added two galleries to his home to house his collection, now part of Baltimore's Walters Art Gallery. He was also interested in breeding stock animals and is credited with introducing the Percheron horse to America.

Walton, (Anthony John) Tony (1934–) set/costume designer; born in Walton-on-Thames, Surrey, England. Dividing his career between London and New York, he designed for drama, musicals, ballet, opera, films, and television.

Walton, John C. (1881–1949) governor; born near Indianapolis, Ind. An engineer, he served as Oklahoma City's commissioner of Public Works (1917–19) and mayor (1919–23). As Democratic governor in 1923, he used martial law to stop Ku Klux Klan violence in Tulsa County, extending it statewide to block his opponents. Impeached after ten months in office for abusing his powers, he later served on the Oklahoma Corporation Commission (1932–39).

Walton, (Samuel Moore) Sam (1918–92) retail executive; born in Kingfish, Okla. Raised in Missouri, he graduated from the University of Missouri. In 1945 he opened the first of a chain of Ben Franklin five-and-dime franchises in Arkansas, and in 1962, his first Wal-Mart discount store. Headquartered at Bentonville, Ark., he created a national chain of Wal-Mart stores in small towns and rural areas, selling brand-name goods in high volume at low prices (and often ruining local Main Street merchants). The company went public (1970), and thanks to a unique decentralized distribution system and his charismatic leadership and celebrated hands-on management style, it grew exponen-

tially in the 1980s. In 1991 Wal-Mart became the nation's largest retailer, with 1,700 stores; he was reported by *Forbes* to be the richest man in the country. He was president and CEO until 1988 and chairman until his death. The family business empire included Arkansas and Oklahoma banks and newspapers. He was awarded the Medal of Freedom shortly before his death.

Walton, (William Theodore) Bill (1952–) basketball player; born in LaMesa, Calif. As a 6'11" center, he was a three-time college player of the year (1972–74) for the University of California: Los Angeles, where he led the Bruins to two undefeated seasons and two National Collegiate Athletic Association championships (1972–73). In a National Basketball Association career beset by injuries, he led the Portland Trail Blazers to a title in 1977 and was the Most Valuable Player in 1978. He had a brief second career with the Boston Celtics. After retiring from basketball, he became a television color commentator.

Wanamaker, John (1838–1922) merchant; born in Philadelphia. After a few years as secretary of the Philadelphia Young Men's Christian Association, he and his new brother-in-law, Nathan Brown, opened a men's clothing store called "Oak Hall" (1861). In 1869, a year after Brown's death, Wanamaker opened the more fashionable John Wanamaker & Company; he turned this store over to his brothers to manage when in 1876, in time for the centennial, he opened the "Grand Depot," a huge dry goods and men's clothing store located in a former Pennsylvania Railroad depot. Unable to attract other merchants to open shop under his roof, in 1877 he opened a number of 'specialty shops' that flourished after a year. He expanded into New York City (1896) and continued enlarging his innovative "department" stores. He advertised effectively in newspapers and implemented a money-back customer guarantee. An enthusiastic Presbyterian and Republican, he founded the Bethany Sunday School (1858), supported temperance and the Pennsylvania Blue Laws, and unsuccessfully ran for various political offices. He required military drill of his male clerks and offered to release them for service during the Spanish-American War and World War I, but he provided business classes and benefits for his employees. As a reward for his support of Benjamin Harrison, he was made Postmaster General (1889) and introduced several improvements.

Wanamaker, Sam (1919–93) actor, director; born in Seattle, Wash. He first appeared on the stage in Chicago and then on Broadway, where he appeared in a number of hits during the 1940s. In the 1950s he moved to England, where he made his permanent home, and turned from acting to directing. His credits include the play, *Children from their Games* (1962); the film, *The Spy Who Came in from the Cold* (1965); and episodes of the television series *Columbo* during the 1970s. He will probably be longest remembered, however, as the force behind the rebuilding of Shakespeare's Globe Theater on the south bank of London's Thames River. At the time of his death, the Globe was half-reconstructed, but he had supervised its first stage production.

Waner, Paul (Glee) (1903–65) baseball player; born in Harrah, Okla. During his 20-year career as an outfielder (1926–45), mostly with the Pittsburgh Pirates, he posted a lifetime batting average of .333, compiled 3,152 hits, and won the Most Valuable Player Award in 1927. He was nicknamed "Big Poison." His brother, Lloyd Waner (1906–

82), who was called "Little Poison," played outfield for the Pirates as well. Both have been elected to baseball's Hall of Fame.

Wang, An (1920–90) electrical engineer, applied physicist; born in Shanghai, China. He emigrated to the United States in 1945. In 1948 he invented magnetic core memory, a key element in computer technology. In 1951 he founded Wang Laboratories in Boston, which he took public in 1955; for many years his firm took the lead in providing office computers, but by the 1980s the competition had caught up with him; he turned the firm over to his son in 1986. A generous philanthropist, he donated to numerous cultural and educational institutions.

Wanger, Walter (b. Walter Feuchtwanger) (1884–1968) film producer; born in San Francisco (husband of Joan Bennett). After service in World War I, he joined Paramount as a producer, later moving to Columbia and MGM before going independent. Among his more ambitious films were *Stagecoach* (1939) and *Joan of Arc* (1948).

Wannier, Gregory H. (Hugh) (1911–83) physicist; born in Basel, Switzerland. He taught at the University of Geneva (1935–36), then came to the U.S.A. as an exchange student at Princeton (1936–37). After teaching at several American universities, he became a physicist in private industry (1946–60), then returned to academic life at the University of Oregon (1961–77). Wannier made major advances in solid state physics, including molecular and crystal structure, magnetism, and statistical methods.

Warburg, Edward M. M. (Mortimer Morris) (1908–92) arts patron; born in White Plains, N.Y. In 1928, as an undergraduate at Harvard, he and three others, including Lincoln Kirstein, founded the Harvard Society for Contemporary Art, which rented rooms to exhibit paintings of Klee, O'Keeffe, Matisse, and others. Warburg was an early supporter of the Museum of Modern Art (1929) as a trustee (1932–58, honorary 1958–86). With Kirstein, he also helped found the American Ballet (1933), holding the first George Balanchine production in his home. He remained an active patron of the arts and ballet in New York City. During World War II he organized displaced persons camps following D-Day and helped refugees from the concentration camps, for which he earned the Bronze Star.

Ward, Aaron Montgomery (1843–1913) merchant; born in Chatham, N.J. His parents moved to Niles, Mich., where he worked odd jobs until 1865 when he moved to Chicago and clerked for Field, Palmer, & Leiter. By about 1870 as a traveling salesman for a dry goods wholesaler, he noted the disparity between the cash prices farmers received and the high cost of retail products. In 1872, with partner George Thorne, Ward put out a single-sheet catalogue of dry goods at reasonable prices and guaranteed customer satisfaction. Success was immediate – by 1876 the catalogue was 150 illustrated pages, and sales reached $1 million by 1888. With the completion of the Ward Tower in Chicago (1900), Montgomery Ward's attracted national attention, with sales of $40 million by his death. The company passed to Thorne's five sons since Ward had none. Ward's wife later bequeathed more than $8 million to Northwestern University for a medical and dental school. His foresight is credited with securing Chicago's Grant Park as a public lakefront area.

Ward, Arch (Burdette) (1896–1955) sportswriter; born in Irwin, Ill. As a sportswriter and editor for the *Chicago Tribune* (1925–51), he created the annual baseball All-Star game as a promotion for the 1933 World's Fair in Chicago. In 1934 he also created the annual college All-Star football game.

Ward, Artemus See BROWNE, CHARLES FARRAR.

Ward, Douglas Turner (Douglas Turner, actor name) (1930–) actor, playwright, director, producer; born in Burnside, La. Cofounder of the Negro Ensemble Company (1968), he also appeared in films and on television.

Ward, Frederick Townsend (1831–62) soldier of fortune; born in Salem, Mass. Sent to sea at age 15 as punishment by his father, he soon became a mercenary – with William Walker in Mexico, with Garibaldi in Italy, and with the French in the Crimean War. In 1859 he arrived in a China torn by civil war; he offered his services to the Manchu Dynasty leaders and during the next three years he led Chinese troops to many victories. Quick to adopt new methods of warfare and armor, concerned for his troops, he was fearless and tireless in combat (he was wounded 15 times) and was killed in a battle at Tzeki.

Ward, (John Montgomery) Monte (1860–1925) baseball player, lawyer; born in Bellefonte, Pa. A pitcher and infielder for 17 years (1878–94), mostly with the New York Giants, he led an unsuccessful effort to repeal baseball's reserve clause, which bound a player to a team through a self-renewing contract. After retiring from baseball, he became an attorney and frequently represented players in their grievances against major league baseball. He was elected to baseball's Hall of Fame in 1964.

Ward, John Quincy Adams (1830–1910) sculptor; born near Urbana, Ohio. He studied with Henry Kirke Brown and became his assistant (1849–56) before opening his own studio in New York City (1861). He is known for his naturalistic equestrian statues and historical and commemorative portrait sculptures, such as *Freeman* (1863), which depicts Lincoln and a freed slave.

Ward, Joseph (1838–89) minister, educator; born in Perry Center, N.Y. He graduated from Andover Theological Seminary (1868). Known as the "Father of Congregationalism" in Dakota Territory, he founded Yankton Academy (1872) which became Yankton College (1881), the first college in the upper Mississippi River valley. He was president of the college (1881–89) and is credited with establishing the public education system in South Dakota. South Dakota placed his statue in the U.S. Capitol.

Ward, Lester Frank (1841–1913) sociologist, geologist; born in Joliet, Ill. Raised on the frontier, he briefly attended the Susquehanna Collegiate Institute in Towanda, Pa., before serving in the Union army during the Civil War (1862–64). While working for the United States Treasury Department (1865–81), he earned three degrees at Columbian College (now George Washington University); he then worked for the United States Geological Survey (1881–1905) as a geologist, biologist, and paleontologist. While working as a scientist, he was caught up in the current debate over evolution and the conflict between science and religion; increasingly more concerned with social issues, in 1883 he published *Dynamic Sociology,* the first of his several once influential texts on sociology. He spent his final years as a professor of sociology at Brown University (1906–13). Liberal, humanitarian, and democratic in his ideals, he saw education, economics, and government actions as the key to most of society's problems. His six-volume "mental autobiography," *Glimpses of the Cosmos,* was published posthumously (1913–18).

Ward, Maisie (1889–1975) religious publisher, author; born in England. Descended from prominent English Catholics, she married Frank Sheed in 1926 and with him founded the Catholic publishing company, Sheed & Ward. From 1940 they lived in the U.S.A., where a branch was established. Her own works include a biography of G. K. Chesterton.

Ward, Nathaniel (?1578–1652) Protestant religious leader; born in Haverhill, England. A member of a notable Puritan family, he studied at Emmanuel College (Boston) and Cambridge University, practiced law, and entered the Anglican ministry in 1618. He served a London parish from 1624–33, was dismissed for nonconformism, emigrated to Massachusetts, and in 1634 accepted the pastorate of Agawam (now Ipswich). In the late 1630s he helped compile the first code of laws for Massachusetts. Returning to England in the mid-1640s, he held the pastorate of Shenfield until his death.

Ward, Robert (De Courcy) (1867–1931) climatologist, geographer; born in Boston, Mass. Associated with Harvard University (1890–1913), he was an American pioneer in climatology, publishing a much-needed student text, *Practical Exercises in Elementary Meteorology* (1899). Editor of the *American Meteorological Journal* (1892–96), he helped found the Immigration Restriction League in 1894. The first professor of climatology in the U.S.A. (1910), he published his best known work, *The Climates of the United States,* in 1925.

Ward, Samuel (1786–1839) banker; born in Warwick, R.I. His family moved to New York City (1790) and at age 14 he began working at the prominent banking house of Prime & Sands. By 1808 he made partner, and was soon a head of the firm whose name changed to Prime, Ward & King. During the panic of 1837, he led New York's wealthiest financiers to forestall a repudiation of specie (script) payments by the state and in 1838 he arranged a loan of $5 million in gold bars from the Bank of England for the New York banks. In 1839 he helped found and became first president of the Bank of Commerce. The strain of attempting to control a second specie payment crisis in Philadelphia, as well as among some Southern states that October, broke his health and he died at the end of the month.

Warde, Frederic (b. Arthur Frederick Warde) (1894–1939) typographer; birthplace unknown. Influenced by European craftsmen on his travels abroad, he produced classically attractive works for Princeton University Press and the Limited Editions Club, as well as under his own Pleiad imprint.

Warde, Mother Mary Francis Xavier (b. Frances Teresa Warde) (1810–84) religious leader; born in Mountrath, Ireland. A wealthy Dubliner, she did charitable work and joined the newly formed Sisters of Mercy in 1831. In 1843 she brought a group of these nuns to the U.S.A., where she founded institutions and led religious communities in Pennsylvania, Rhode Island, New Hampshire, and elsewhere. She was a pioneer in adult religious education.

Ware, William R. (Robert) (1832–1915) educator, architect; born in Cambridge, Mass. He founded and directed architectural programs at the Massachusetts Institute of Technology (1865–81) and Columbia University (1881–1903) and practiced (1863–81) with Henry Van Brunt (1832–1903).

Warfield, David (b. Wollfeld or Wohlfelt) (1866–1951) stage actor; born in San Francisco. Starting with depictions of East Side Jews, he was known as a talented character actor, with his longest-running role in *The Music Master* (1904–07).

Warfield, Paul (D.) (1942–) football player; born in Warren, Ohio. An all-pro pass receiver for the undefeated Miami Dolphins of 1972, he averaged more than 20 yards per catch over 13 National Football League seasons.

Warfield, Wallis See WINDSOR, WALLIS WARFIELD.

Warfield, William (Caesar) (1920–) baritone; born in Helena, Ark. He graduated from the Eastman School of Music in 1946 and in 1950 began a celebrated international career as a recitalist. Among his operatic roles was his lead in productions of *Porgy and Bess* during the 1950s, alongside his then-wife, soprano Leontyne Price. In 1974 he began teaching at the University of Illinois.

Warhol, Andy (b. Andrew Warhola) (1928–87) painter, filmmaker; born in Pittsburgh, Pa. A founder of the pop art movement of the 1960s, he studied at the Carnegie Institute of Technology, Pittsburgh (1945–49) and by 1950 had settled in New York City working as a commercial artist. By 1957 he began his series of silkscreen paintings based on comic strips, advertisements, and newspaper photos of public personalities; by 1961 his painted replicas of Campbell's Soup cans made him into a celebrity, and from then on his works and words ("In the future everyone will be famous for 15 minutes.") kept him constantly in the headlines although he cultivated an image that was both elusive and evasive. Much of his work was collaborative and produced in a loft called "the Factory." He also turned to making underground films such as *Chelsea Girls* (1966), deliberately coarse amalgams of sexuality and banality; these were coproduced and primarily directed by Paul Morrissey. In 1968 Warhol was shot and wounded by Valerie Solanis, who had appeared in his films. In 1969 he began to publish *Interview,* a magazine of fashion news and gossip. He then embarked on his serial portraits of international personalities, becoming extremely rich from selling silkscreen multiples of such as Mao Zedong (1974). He amassed a fabulous collection of antiques and collectibles (such as cookie jars), auctioned after his death for a small fortune. Said to have been a devout Catholic, he remained personally enigmatic despite his years in the public spotlight.

Waring, (Frederick Malcolm) Fred (1900–84) conductor, songwriter, inventor; born in Tyrone, Pa. By age 16 he was conducting his first small group of musicians, "the Banjazzatra," and while an engineering student at Pennsylvania State, he formed the Pennsylvanians with his brother Tom Waring. The group performed throughout the 1920s and even made the first all-musical movie, *Syncopation* (1929), but it was thanks to his many appearances on radio during the 1930s that Waring's Pennsylvanians became a national institution. His was also the first orchestra to have its own television show (starting in 1949). His soft melodies and lush orchestrations struck a chord with mainstream Americans and he was often invited by President Eisenhower to play at White House functions; although his style of music was pretty much overwhelmed by later developments, he gave his farewell concert at President Reagan's inaugural concert in 1981. Waring prospered greatly from his music-making; he also composed about 200 songs and formed the Shawnee Press, a major publisher of choral and band music. More surprisingly, he is also the man behind the Waring Blendor, one of the first electric food processors, which he patented in 1937 and perfected and marketed for many years.

Waring, James (1922–75) modern and ballet dancer, choreographer; born in Alameda, Calif. Trained in the Graham technique as well as in classical ballet, he created a distinctive form of pictorial theater for his own company (1954–69) and others. He became a major influence on postmodern dance, with *Phrases* and *Amoretti* among his best known works.

Warmoth, Henry Clay (1842–1931) governor; born in Mac-Leansboro, Ill. A self-taught lawyer, he fought for the Union with the Missouri Volunteers (1862–65). He moved to New Orleans in 1865, where he specialized in military and government law. As the Republican governor of Louisiana (1868–72), he squandered state money on the railroads and alienated both white and black voters with his lukewarm support for civil rights. Impeached in 1872, he left public life to run his sugar plantation and refinery.

Warner, Albert See under WARNER BROTHERS.

Warner, Charles Dudley (1829–1900) writer; born in Plainfield, Mass. He studied at Hamilton (B.A. 1851), worked as a railroad surveyor in Missouri (1853–54), then returned to school to take a law degree at the University of Pennsylvania (1858). He practiced law in Chicago until 1860 before moving to Hartford, Conn., to work as an editor for the *Evening Press* (which merged with the *Hartford Courant* in 1867). He traveled to Europe often and wrote numerous travel sketches and essays, but is remembered now for only his first novel, which he coauthored with Mark Twain, *The Gilded Age* (1873).

Warner, Edward (Pearson) (1894–1958) aeronautical engineer, international civil servant; born in Pittsburgh, Pa. Teaching at the Massachusetts Institute of Technology (1920–26), he influenced aeronautic pioneers. As assistant secretary of the navy for aeronautics (1926–29), he assisted the growth of American aviation. He was editor of *Aviation* (1929–34), an adviser to the Civil Aeronautics Board (CAB), and head of the International Civil Aviation Organization (1947–57).

Warner, Glenn (Scobey) "Pop" (1871–1954) football coach; born in Springville, N.Y. Although he studied law at Cornell, he practiced only a few months before embarking on a 44-year coaching career in 1895. He coached at the University of Georgia, Cornell, and Temple, but his most successful tenures were at Carlisle Indian School (1899–1903, 1907–14), where he coached Jim Thorpe; the University of Pittsburgh (1915–23), where he produced three undefeated teams; and Stanford University (1924–32), where he developed three Rose Bowl teams. He ranked his 1925 Stanford fullback, Ernie Nevers, as a greater player than Thorpe. He retired with 312 victories, more than any other coach. Contemplative and creative, he was credited with inventing numerous plays, strategies, and improvements in equipment. His greatest claim to fame was his development of both the single- and double-wing offensive formations into versatile and deceptive offensive attacks that were copied for years.

Warner, Harry (Morris) See under WARNER BROTHERS.

Warner, Jack (Leonard) See under WARNER BROTHERS.

Warner, John W. (William) (1927–) U.S. senator, cabinet officer; born in Washington, D.C. He served in the U.S. Navy (1944–46) and Marines (1949–52). He worked for the department of justice (1954–60). He was undersecretary (1969–72) and then secretary (1972–74) of the navy. He was the administrator of the American Revolution Bicentennial Administration (1974–76) and then a senator from Virginia (Rep., 1979). He was married twice, to Catherine Mellon (1957–1973) and to Elizabeth Taylor (1976; separated in 1981).

Warner, Olin (Levi) (1844–96) sculptor; born in Suffield, Conn. He studied in Paris (1869–72), settled in New York City (1872), and was one of the founders of the Society of American Artists (1877). He traveled in the Northwest Territory (1889) and died in New York after a bicycle accident. He is known for his portrait medallions and busts, such as *J. Alden Weir* (1880).

Warner, Samuel See under WARNER BROTHERS.

Warner, Susan (Bogert) (Elizabeth Wetherell, pen name) (1819–85) writer; born in New York City. After economic setbacks, she and her family lived on Constitution Island in the Hudson River near West Point. To help earn money for the family, she wrote many novels and books for children; her sister, Anna B. Warner, would collaborate on some of her books. She is best known for her first novel, *The Wide Wide World* (1852), about a young orphan and her spiritual development. Her work was characterized by piety, sentimentality, a lack of action, and an overabundance of tears – a popular mix in that era.

Warner, W. (William) Lloyd (1898–1970) anthropologist, sociologist; born in Redlands, Calif. His doctoral dissertation, *A Black Civilization* (1937, several times revised), was a major work on aboriginal tribal kinship systems. Warner applied anthropological research methods to contemporary American society in his studies of class structure, symbol systems, and industrial relations. He taught at the University of Chicago (1935–59) and Michigan State University (1959–70).

Warner Brothers (b. Eichelbaums) movie executives; **Harry (Morris)** (1881–1958), born in Krasnashiltz, Poland; **Albert** (1884–1967), born in Baltimore, Md.; **Samuel** (1887–1927), born in Baltimore, Md.; **Jack (Leonard)** (1892–1978), born in London, Ontario, Canada. The parents immigrated to the U.S.A. in the mid-1880s. By 1903 the brothers and a sister had a nickelodeon in Newcastle, Pa., and then expanded into a movie distribution company; they moved into production with *Perils of the Plains* (1910) and in 1919 formed their own Hollywood production company, Warner Brothers Pictures (incorporated in 1923). Their firm grew slowly, but their gamble on the first sound feature movie with synchronized songs and dialogue, *The Jazz Singer* (1927), launched them as a major studio. Although Warner Brothers movies often had a relatively austere look, as the brothers were not especially noted for either financial extravagance or high style, they would produce some of the classic American films. During the 1930s the studio specialized in gangster films, musicals, and historical biographies; by the 1940s they were strong in adventure movies, melodramas, and mystery dramas. In the 1950s the company suffered from the loss of their theater chain (due to government action) and the growth of television, and by 1969 the surviving brother, Jack, had lost control.

Warren, Earl (1891–1974) Supreme Court chief justice; born in Los Angeles. He was district attorney in Alameda County, Calif. (1920–39), state attorney general (1939–43), and served three terms as governor of California (1942–53) before President Eisenhower appointed him chief justice of the U.S. Supreme Court (1953–69). To many people's surprise, the liberal "Warren Court" actively used its judiciary powers to decide several landmark cases that affected civil rights, criminal procedure, and religious practice. *Brown* v. *Board of Education* (1954) desegregated public schools and ruled segregation "inherently unequal." *Miranda* v. *Arizona* (1966) ensured the rights of criminal suspects. The court shocked the country when it found required prayer in public schools to breach the separation of church and state. At the special request of President Lyndon Johnson, he headed the investigation of President Kennedy's assassination; the "Warren Commission" found that Lee Harvey Oswald acted alone.

Warren, Harry (Salvatore) (1893–1981) composer; born in Brooklyn, N.Y. Of Italian-American descent, he was completely self-taught as a musician and as a young man supported himself playing the piano in dance halls and movie houses. After writing songs in the 1920s for Broadway revues, he moved to Hollywood where from 1932 to 1957 he worked with such lyricists as Al Dubin and Mack Gordon on over 75 films including *Forty-Second Street* (1933) and *Just for You* (1952); his songs won three Oscars and more than 100 achieved national popularity, among them "We're in the Money" (1933), "Lullaby of Broadway" (1935), and "Jeepers, Creepers" (1938). Demand for his work declined during the 1960s rock era, but the Broadway musical hit of 1980, *Forty-Second Street,* used 17 of Warren's songs.

Warren, John (Collins) (1778–1856) surgeon; born in Boston, Mass. Son and nephew of famous Boston doctors, he studied surgery with his father (John Warren, 1753–1815) and then completed his studies in Europe. He set up a practice in Boston (1802) and was on the faculty of the Harvard Medical School for most of his career (1809–47). Active in reforming medical education and practice in America, he was one of the founders of Massachusetts General Hospital, where on October 16, 1846, he performed the first operation using ether as an anesthesia (with William Morton administering it). The first American to operate on a strangulated hernia, he wrote an important book on his specialty, *Surgical Observations on Tumours* (1837).

Warren, John Collins (1842–1927) surgeon; born in Boston, Mass. (grandson of John Warren, 1778–1856). He studied three years in Europe before returning (1869) to take up a practice in Boston. He was associated with the Harvard Medical School and Massachusetts General Hospital for most of his professional career. His most important book, *Surgical Pathology and Therapeutics* (1895), drew on his studies of infectious bacteria.

Warren, Joseph (1741–75) physician, Revolutionary patriot; born in Roxbury, Mass. Meeting John Adams while inoculating him for smallpox, he turned revolutionary, making a number of anti-British speeches at Faneuil Hall, writing articles and mediating for removal of troops after the Boston Massacre (1770). One of three chosen to write a report on colonists' rights (1772), he dispatched Paul Revere and William Dawes (1775) on their famous rides. He was chosen president pro tempore of the Provincial Congress (1775). Head of the committee to organize a colonial army and major general, he was shot dead at Breed's Hill.

Warren, Leonard (b. Varenov) (1911–60) baritone; born in New York City. After studies in the U.S.A. and Milan, he made his Metropolitan debut in 1939 and became an acclaimed Verdi interpreter. He died while performing in Verdi's *La forza del destino* at the Met.

Warren, Mercy Otis (1728–1814) historian, poet; born in Barnstable, Mass. (sister of James Otis, aunt of Harrison G. Otis). She married James Warren (1754) and had five sons. In addition to publishing poetry and plays, she published historical works including *Observations on the New Constitution* (1788) and *History of the Rise, Progress, and Termination of the American Revolution* (1805). She corresponded at length with Abigail Adams, John Adams, and other leading political figures and is arguably America's first major female intellectual.

Warren, Robert Penn (1905–89) poet, writer; born in Guthrie, Ky. He studied at Vanderbilt University (B.A. 1925), the University of California: Berkeley (M.A. 1927), Yale (1927–28), and Oxford as a Rhodes Scholar (B. Litt. 1930). At college he had joined with other poets known as the "Fugitives" or "Southern agrarians" to promote Southern conservative values, even defending segregation in *I'll Take My Stand* (1930), but from the 1950s on he was outspoken in demanding that the South change its ways. He taught at many institutions, primarily Yale (1961–73), and was named the first official Poet Laureate of the United States (1986), among many other honors. Based in Fairfield, Conn., he worked as an editor, wrote critical essays, poetry, and novels; the most famous of his novels is *All the King's Men* (1946), based on the career of Huey Long. He was also a founder and editor of the *Southern Review* (1935–42) and an advisory editor of *Kenyon Review* (1938–68).

Warren, William, (Jr.) (1812–88) actor; born in Philadelphia. Son of the actor-manager William Warren, he was a superb comedian who spent the largest part of his career performing classic and contemporary roles at the Boston Museum between 1847 and 1882. While there, he played nearly 600 different parts, including Sir Peter Teazle, Polonius, and Tony Lumpkin.

Warwick, Dionne (b. Warwicke) (1941–) popular/soul singer; born in East Orange, N.J. She sang in a gospel trio before recording her first hit songs on Scepter, including "Walk On By" (1964) and "I Say a Little Prayer" (1967). After a lull in her career in the 1970s, her album *Dionne* (1979) sold a million copies. She went on to release the albums *Heartbreaker* (1982) and *How Many Times Can We Say Goodbye?* (1983).

Washakie (?1804–1900) Shoshone chief; born in the Green River Valley of present-day eastern Utah and southern Wyoming. He assisted early trappers, traders, and settlers, and fought with the U.S.A. in their wars with the Sioux and other tribes that had been traditional enemies of the Shoshone. In 1868 he exchanged Shoshone lands for a reservation at Wind River, Wyo. He served as a chief through the 1870s. The epitaph on his grave is most telling: "Always loyal to the Government and to his white brothers."

Washburn, Cadwallader Colden (1818–82) land agent, industrialist, miller, U.S. representative, governor; born in Livermore, Maine. In 1839 he traveled west to Davenport, Iowa, where he held several jobs and read law. In 1842 he opened a law office in Mineral Point, Wis., and in 1844 he formed a partnership with Cyrus Woodland to buy up valuable public land, which they then sold to settlers; the partnership dissolved in 1855 but Washburn continued as a developer. A Republican, he served in the U.S. House of Representatives (Wis., 1855–61), where he opposed attempts to make slavery legal. During the Civil War, he organized and led a volunteer cavalry from Wisconsin. After the war he served in the U.S. House of Representatives again (1867–71) and as governor of Wisconsin (1872–73). Although he was involved in a variety of businesses throughout his career, including lumber and railroads, he made his greatest contribution with his Minneapolis Mill Co., which became one of the largest flour-millers in the U.S.A. Among his philanthropies were the University of Wisconsin's Washburn Observatory, a public library in La Crosse, Wis., and an orphan asylum in Minneapolis, Minn.

Washburn, Emory (1800–77) legal scholar; born in Leicester, Mass. He taught at Harvard Law School (1855–76), served on the Massachusetts House of Representatives (1826–27, 1838, 1876–77), and was governor of Massachusetts (1853–54). He wrote several important books including, *Judicial History of Massachusetts* (1840), *Treatise on the American Law of Real Property* (1862), and *Lectures on the Study and Practice of the Law* (1871).

Washburn, Israel (1813–83) U.S. representative, governor; born in Livermore, Maine. The eldest of 11 children, he studied law with an uncle, becoming a lawyer (1834–50) before going to the U.S. House of Representatives (Whig, Maine; 1851–61). He left the Whig Party to form the antislave Republican Party in 1854 (and is credited with coining the party's name). As governor of Maine (1861–63), he provided extra volunteers and money to support the Union war effort. An unsuccessful senatorial candidate, he was a port collector (1863–78) and railroad president (1878–83) in Portland.

Washburn, Margaret Floy (1871–1939) psychologist; born in New York City. She entered Vassar College at age 16, graduated in 1891, and received her Ph.D. from Cornell in 1894. After teaching at Wells College for Women and other institutions, she returned to teach at Vassar (1903–37). She was a pioneer in introducing experimental research and faculty-student collaboration into the psychology department at an undergraduate liberal arts college. Her publications include her major work on animal behavior, *The Animal Mind* (1908), and her book on the motor theory of mental functions, *Movement and Mental Imagery* (1916).

Washburn, Sherwood L. (Larned) (1911–   ) physical anthropologist; born in Cambridge, Mass. Educated at Harvard, he later taught at Columbia University (1939–47), the University of Chicago (1947–58), and the University of California: Berkeley (1958–79). A leading authority on primate and human evolution, he stressed the importance of field studies for modeling the behavior of extinct hominids. He edited *Social Life of Early Man* (1962), and published several books on human evolution.

Washburn, William (Drew) (1831–1912) U.S. representative/senator; born in Livermore, Maine. A Republican lawyer and U.S. surveyor general in Minnesota, he served in the U.S. House of Representatives (1879–85) and in the Senate (1889–95), working to improve the Mississippi River and its tributaries.

Washington, Booker T. (Taliaferro) (b. Booker Taliaferro) (1856–1915) educator; born in Hale's Ford, Va. He was born into slavery and adopted the name "Booker Washington" as a schoolboy; he graduated from Hampton Institute, Virginia (1875). As its first principal (1881–1915), Washington built Tuskegee Institute, Alabama, into a major black institution offering "industrial education," or vocational training, to its own students and, through its extension programs, to rural blacks. His teaching, writing, and lecturing – particularly a famous address in Atlanta in September 1895 – established him as America's foremost black leader, although his promotion of education and economic progress rather than demanding equal rights as the key to progress alienated many African-American intellectuals. He was the founder and first president (1900–15) of the National Black Business League. The first of his three autobiographical volumes was *Up from Slavery* (1901).

Washington, Bushrod (1762–1829) Supreme Court justice; born in Westmoreland County, Va. (nephew of George Washington). He fought in the American Revolution and served the Virginia legislature (1787). President John Adams named him to the U.S. Supreme Court (1798–1829) where he usually concurred with Chief Justice John Marshall's decisions.

Washington, Dinah (b. Ruth Jones) (1924–63) jazz vocalist; born in Tuscaloosa, Ala. An original stylist rooted in gospel music, she began with the Sara Martin Singers and was featured with Lionel Hampton between 1943–46. Despite her turbulent personal life and premature death, she developed a successful solo career and was a pervasive influence on female soul and rock singers beginning in the 1950s.

Washington, George (1732–99) first U.S. president; born in Westmoreland County, Va. His father, a prosperous planter and iron foundry owner, died when he was 11, and George moved in with his elder half-brother Lawrence, who owned the plantation Mount Vernon. In 1748 George did surveying for Lord Fairfax, a relative of Lawrence by marriage, meanwhile reading widely in Mt. Vernon's library. In 1751 Washington accompanied the ailing half-brother to Barbados and on his death the next year was left guardian of Lawrence's daughter at Mt. Vernon, which Washington would inherit in 1761 after her death. Having studied military science on his own, in 1753 he began several years' service with the Virginia militia in the French and Indian Wars, taking command of all Virginia forces in 1755 and participating in several dangerous actions. Commissioned as aide-de-camp by Gen. Edward Braddock in 1755, he barely escaped with his life in the battle that took Braddock's life. He resigned his commission in 1758, following his election to the Virginia House of Burgesses (1759–74). When in 1759 he married wealthy widow Martha Custis, Washington's fortune and social position was secured. (They had no children together but raised her two children and then her two grandchildren.) After a period of living the sociable life of a gentleman farmer, however, Washington risked it all by casting his lot with those rebelling against British rule, although his original motives probably had less to do with high principles and more to do with his personal annoyance with British commercial policies. In 1774 he participated in the First Continental Congress and took command of the Virginia militia; next year the Second Congress, impressed with his military experience and commanding personality, made him commander in chief of the Continental army (June 1775). With remarkable skill, patience, and courage,

Washington led the American forces through the Revolution, struggling not only with the British but with the stingy Continental Congress and also on occasion with resentful fellow officers. Notable among his achievements were his bold crossing of the Delaware to rout enemy forces at Trenton on Christmas night of 1776 and his holding the army together during the terrible winter encampment at Valley Forge in 1777–78. His victory over the British at Yorktown (1781) effectively ended the war, but for almost two more years he had to strive to keep the colonists from splintering into selfish enterprises. Washington returned to Mount Vernon in 1783, but maintained his presence in the debate over the country's future; he solidified that role when he chaired the Philadelphia Constitutional Convention of 1787. In 1789, the first electors unanimously voted Washington as president; he was reelected in 1793. A natural leader rather than a thinker or orator, he had great difficulty coping with an unruly new government, futilely resisting the growing factionalism that resolved into the forming of Hamilton's Federalist Party – to which Washington finally gravitated – and Jefferson's liberal Democratic-Republican Party. In 1796 Washington announced he would not run again (thus setting a precedent for only two terms) and retired from office the next year. In 1798 he accepted command of a provisional American army when it appeared there would be war with France, but the threat passed. The following year he died at Mount Vernon and was mourned around the world. He immediately began to attain almost legendary status so that succeeding generations throughout the world could bestow no higher accolade than to call their own national hero, "the George Washington" of their country.

Washington, Harold (1922–87) U.S. representative, mayor; born in Chicago. A decorated air force veteran of World War II, he was a member of the Illinois legislature (1966–76), the state senate (1978–80), and the U.S. House of Representatives (Dem., Ill.; 1981–83). Running for mayor of Chicago as a Democrat, but largely without party backing, he defeated Bernard Epton to become the city's first African-American mayor (1984–87). In the 1987 election, with voting going largely along racial lines (and with both sides accused of fraud), Washington won over former mayor Jane Byrne's challenge but he died before he could begin a second term.

Washington, Martha (b. Dandridge) Custis (1731–1802) First Lady; born in New Kent County, Va. Daughter of a wealthy landowner, she became even wealthier when her first husband, Daniel Parke Custis, died in 1757. She married George Washington in 1759. She had four children by her first marriage, two of whom died in childhood; George Washington helped raise the other two, and when the son, John Custis, died in 1781, his two youngest children were raised at Mount Vernon. During the American Revolution, she spent winters in army camps with her husband and organized a women's sewing circle to mend clothes for the troops. At Mount Vernon she proved a pleasant hostess, although she dressed very plainly and did not enjoy being first lady.

Wasserstein, Bruce (1947–   ) investment banker; born in New York City. A graduate of the University of Michigan (1967) and Harvard Business School (1971), he joined the First Boston Corp. in 1977, rising to managing director and becoming, with colleague Joseph Perella, a noted leveraged buyout specialist. He and Perella formed their own firm, Wasserstein, Perella & Co., in 1988. The author of *Corporate Finance Law,* he was a brother of Pulitzer Prize-winning playwright Wendy Wasserstein.

Waterhouse, Benjamin (1754–1846) physician; born in Newport, R.I. One of the best educated American physicians of his time, he studied in Europe for seven years before joining the new Harvard Medical Department in 1783. Following the latest claims by Edward Jenner, he imported cowpox vaccine for his son and a servant boy (1799); the servant boy was then inoculated with smallpox and survived. Waterhouse continued vaccinating with success, but in the rush to follow him, others administered impure vaccine and some people died; there was a backlash against him but he was cleared by a committee of physicians (1802). Stressing the necessity of pure vaccine, he continued to promote vaccination and was instrumental in its success in America. After differences with colleagues at the Harvard Medical School turned bitter, he was forced to resign (1812) and he spent several years (1813–20) as superintendent of army posts in New England. In later years he traced the cause of moral decline in youth to intemperance.

Waterman, Alan (Tower) (1892–1967) physicist, scientific administrator; born in Cornwall, N.Y. He expanded radar's military applications in the Office of Scientific Research and Development (1942–46) and assigned scientists to military units. He was with the Office of Naval Research (1946–51). As the first director of the National Science Foundation (1951–63), he funded basic science research with an annual budget that grew to $500 million.

Waters, Ethel (1900–77) stage actress/singer; born in Chester, Pa. An eloquent performer, she began in both black and white vaudeville, then debuted on Broadway in 1927. She is remembered for her role in *The Member of the Wedding* (1950).

Waters, Muddy (b. McKinley Morganfield) (1915–83) musician; born in Rolling Fork, Miss. One of the last of the great country blues singers and a primary innovator of modern Chicago blues, he was raised on the Stovall Plantation in Clarksdale, Miss., where he began playing harmonica and guitar while working as a sharecropper. In 1941 and 1942, he was recorded by Alan Lomax, the folklorist of the Library of Congress, and, emboldened by this experience, he moved to Chicago in 1943 seeking a career in music. Over the next several years, he gradually developed an ensemble blues style while performing in neighborhood bars in Chicago's South Side ghetto. In 1946 he recorded an unissued session for Columbia, and for the next three years he recorded in a country blues style for Aristocrat Records. In 1950 he gained his first national success with "Rolling Stone," the inaugural release of Chess Records, the rhythm-and-blues label with which his name was virtually synonymous for the next 25 years. In 1952 he made his first recordings with his six-piece combo, which pioneered the electronically-amplified Chicago blues style. Featuring Little Walter, Jimmy Rogers, and Otis Spann, this group released several rhythm-and-blues hits, including "Hoochie Coochie Man" and "Got My Mojo Working," and toured extensively on the black nightclub circuit throughout the 1950s. He made the first of several annual tours of England in 1958, during which he exerted a profound influence on the early British rock scene. He appeared at the Newport Jazz Festival in 1960, and was a central figure in the folk-blues revival of the mid-1960s. By the late 1960s, his songs were widely covered in rock; several headlining bands, including the Rolling Stones and Eric Clapton, featured him on their tours. He was a perennial Grammy winner throughout the 1970s, and his appearance in The Band's farewell concert, filmed as *The Last Waltz,* was widely hailed. He was inducted into the Rock 'n' Roll Hall of Fame in 1987.

Watie, Stand (1806–71) Cherokee leader, Confederate soldier; born near the site of Rome, Ga. (brother of Elias Boudinot). He published a Cherokee newspaper with his brother, and when they and two others signed the treaty in which southeastern Cherokees agreed to resettle west of the Mississippi, Watie alone escaped killing by angry tribesmen. Siding with the Confederacy, he was appointed colonel of the Cherokee Mounted Rifles and fought in many engagements including Wilson's Creek (1861) and Pea Ridge (1862); later he served as a raider and light cavalry commander. When most of his people decided to support the Union in 1863, he led those Cherokee who stayed with the Confederacy and was among the last Confederate officers to surrender. He spent his final years as a planter and tobacco processor.

Watkins, Carleton E. (1829–1916) photographer; born in Oneonta, N.Y. Lured to California by the gold rush, he took odd jobs before learning photography in San Francisco. He photographed Yosemite with stereoscopic and special wideview cameras (1861–67), winning a gold medal at the Paris Exposition in 1868. Unfortunately few of his negatives remain, as they were lost to creditors in the 1870s; he reshot, but lost them again in the 1906 San Francisco earthquake.

Watson, Charles Roger (1873–1948) missionary, educator; born in Cairo, Egypt. Of Scottish descent, he went to the U.S.A. in 1889 and earned his Presbyterian divinity degree at Princeton University (1899). He directed the activities of the United Presbyterian Board of Foreign Missions (1902–16). He founded Cairo Christian University (1919) – later renamed the American University in Cairo. He was the school's president (1920–45). He succeeded in persuading many wealthy Americans to support the school. He retired to the U.S.A. in 1945.

Watson, Elkanah (1758–1842) promoter, agriculturist; born in Plymouth, Mass. He was indentured to John Brown, the Rhode Island merchant, from 1773–79. He carried money and dispatches to France where he found a partner and opened a business, which failed in the financial crisis of 1783; after settling his debts he traveled to Holland to see the canals and returned to America (1785). After another business failure in 1789 he moved to Albany, N.Y., founded a bank, and began promoting his vision – a canal system. He promoted two canal companies, one of which was chartered in 1798 to build a canal around Niagara Falls. After a falling out with the bank directors, he moved to Pittsfield, Mass., where he bought a farm and sponsored a cattle show in 1810, the predecessor of the Berkshire Agricultural Society and the first county fair in the country. He wrote several books including his memoirs and *History of the Rise and Progress, and Existing Condition of the Western Canals in the State of New York* (1820).

Watson, James D. (Dewey) (1928–   ) geneticist; born in Chicago, Ill. After studying under geneticist Hermann J. Muller at the University of Indiana, he worked on DNA in bacterial viruses as a research fellow in Copenhagen (1950–

51). At a symposium in Naples (1951), he was inspired by English scientist Maurice H. F. Wilkins, whose X-ray diffraction studies would contribute to elucidating the structure of the DNA molecule. Watson went to Cambridge (1951–53), where he and the English geneticist Francis Crick delineated the molecular structure of DNA and explained the mechanism of its replication (1953); in 1962, Watson, with Crick and Wilkins, shared the Nobel Prize in physiology for this work. Watson joined the California Institute of Technology (1953–55), then returned to work with Crick at Cambridge (1955–56). Differences in personality between the two caused Watson to join Harvard (1956–76), where he performed research on RNA and protein synthesis. In 1968, Watson, still associated with Harvard, became director of the Cold Spring Harbor Laboratory (N.Y.) (1968–88); he then became director of the National Center for Human Genome Research at the National Institute of Health (1989). His popular account of the discovery of DNA structure, *The Double Helix* (1968), achieved wide fame for its candid revelations about the personalities and politics behind scientific endeavors.

Watson, James Eli (1864–1948) U.S. representative/senator; born in Winchester, Ind. A lawyer, he served in the U.S. House of Representatives (Rep., Ind.; 1895–97, 1899–1909) and the Senate (1916–33), becoming majority leader (1929–33). A party loyalist, he supported big business, isolationism, and restrictions on immigration.

Watson, John B. (Broadus) (1878–1958) psychologist, advertising executive; born in Greenville, S.C. Educated at the University of Chicago (Ph.D. 1903), he taught at Johns Hopkins University (1908–20) where he made a radical departure from the psychology of mental processes to found the movement called "behaviorism." (He first used the term in a 1913 article.) His studies in medicine, biology, and animal behavior led him to postulate that man and other animals functioned purely from physiological and physical bases; behaviorism stresses "stimulus–response" as its basic tenet. Rejecting such notions as motivation or innate abilities, he claimed that given the proper environment, a normal child could acquire any skill. His book *Psychology from the Standpoint of a Behaviorist* (1919) ushered in a period of major growth and controversy in the field of psychology. Forced to resign from Johns Hopkins in 1920 after he divorced his wife to marry a former student, he went to New York City and entered the field of commercial advertising, but he continued to write about and promote his behaviorist school.

Watson, Thomas Edward (b. Edward Thomas) (1856–1922) U.S. representative/senator, populist politician; born near Thomson, Ga. The grandson of a wealthy slaveowner, he saw his family fortunes destroyed during the Civil War. He became a successful criminal lawyer, and positioning himself as an agrarian reformer, he opposed the new capitalists and industrialists who were betraying the "Old South." He served in the U.S. House of Representatives (Pop., Ga.; 1891–93), where he won the first appropriation for free delivery of rural mail. He was nominated for vice-president by the Populist Party (1896) and for president by the People's Party (1904). He became a ferocious supporter of segregation and obsessively opposed to such minorities as Catholics, Jews, and Socialists. He violently opposed U.S. entrance into World War I and his magazines were banned from the U.S.

mail. Elected on a platform of opposition to the League of Nations, he served only briefly in the U.S. Senate (Dem., Ga.; 1921–22). His career was celebrated in a ballad, the "Thomas E. Watson Song."

Watson, Thomas John (1874–1956) business executive; born in Cambell, N.Y. He worked at National Cash Register in Dayton, Ohio (1896–1911), becoming general sales manager. During that period he learned the punch-card industry. Sales became the driving force in all he did, particularly after he formed International Business Machines (IBM) by merging several other companies (1924). By 1929, IBM controlled 20 percent of the punch device market. In the 1930s, Wallace Eckert, Howard Aiken, and others convinced IBM to back computer research; however, Watson was slow to embrace the new technology in the 1940s because of the competition it represented to his mechanical devices. It was not until the early 1950s that his son convinced him to enter the computer market and by then he had turned IBM's operations over to his son.

Watson, Thomas (John), Jr. (1914–93) business executive; born in Dayton, Ohio. Son of the founder of International Business Machines (IBM), he joined the firm in 1937, then served with the U.S. Air Force in World War II (1941–45). During the late 1940s, his father began grooming him to take over IBM and he became convinced that the company should enter the computer market. He was named president of IBM (1952–61) and he placed the company at the center of the industry. As chairman (1961–71) he committed IBM to a new line of computers in 1962, the S/360s, which revolutionized the industry. He was chairman of the executive committee (1971–79) and remained active at IBM into the 1980s, with two years out (1979–81) to serve as U.S. ambassador to the Soviet Union.

Watterson, Henry (1840–1921) journalist, politician; born in Washington, D.C. The son of a U.S. congressman, he grew up personally familiar with many presidents and passionately interested in politics. As progressive-minded editor of the *Louisville (Ky.) Courier-Journal* (1868–1902) and then editorial writer (through 1919), he became the most influential voice in southern journalism. He himself served briefly in the U.S. House (1876–77). In 1917 he won a Pulitzer Prize in journalism for editorials urging U.S. entrance into World War I.

Watterson, (William) Bill (1958–) cartoonist; born in Chagrin Falls, Ohio. After graduating from Kenyon College (1980), where he had done political cartooning, he spent five years trying to find his niche. Starting in 1985 he produced the syndicated newpaper comic strip, *Calvin and Hobbes,* featuring a mischievous six-year-old boy and his toy tiger come-to-life.

Wattleton, Faye (1943–) nurse, social service advocate; born in St. Louis, Mo. A nurse who studied midwifery at Columbia University Medical School in 1964, she started as president of the Dayton, Ohio, Planned Parenthood chapter in 1967, becoming national president in 1978. As an African-American spokeswoman for abortion rights, she revamped the agency, making it a much more dynamic advocate for change in the nation's health, social, and political practices. In 1992 she left to host a television talk show.

Watts, Alan (Wilson) (1915–73) mystic, writer, lecturer; born in Chislehurst, England. He became fascinated with Asian art and literature during his adolescence. He graduated from

King's School (1932) and emigrated to the U.S.A. in 1939. He was an Episcopal chaplain (1944–50) but then left the church and became an independent writer. Believing that most churches were limiting, he advocated Asian mysticism as the alternative to ego-based consciousness. He wrote many books, including *The Spirit of Zen* (1936) and *Psychotherapy East and West* (1961). Somewhat reluctantly, he was adopted as a "guru" by counter-culture youths during the 1960s.

Watts, André (1946–) pianist; born in Nuremberg, Germany. Son of an African-American soldier and a Hungarian mother, he studied piano in Philadelphia and appeared with the Philadelphia Orchestra at age nine. He was catapulted to fame in 1963, when he played on national television with the New York Philharmonic. After his first world tour in 1967, he became an international favorite, primarily noted for his elegant handling of the 19th-century repertoire.

Wattson, Lewis Thomas (Father Paul James Francis) (1863–1940) Catholic religious leader; born in Millington, Md. After a decade as an Episcopalian pastor, he cofounded, with Lurana Mary White, the Society of the Atonement, a Franciscan-type religious congregation, at Graymoor in Garrison, N.Y. (1898). There he sheltered homeless men, started a religious magazine, the *Lamp,* and launched the Church Unity Octave to pray for Christian unification. The society became Catholic in 1909 and he became a Catholic priest. A tireless fundraiser, he authorized missions in southwestern United States and abroad and cofounded (1924) the Catholic Near East Welfare Association.

Wauchope, Robert (1909–79) archaeologist, anthropologist; born in Columbia, S.C. He was the influential director of the Middle American Research Institute, Tulane University (1942–75). A specialist in Latin American prehistory and the archaeology of the American Southwest, he wrote such important works as *House Mounds of Uaxactun* (1934) and edited the comprehensive *Handbook of Middle American Indians* (16 vols. 1964–76).

Waugh, Frederick Judd (1861–1940) painter; born in Bordentown, N.J. He studied at the Pennsylvania Academy of the Fine Arts, in Paris (1882–83), and worked in Europe as an illustrator (1892–1907). Returning to America, he lived in Connecticut (1915) and Provincetown, Mass. (1927), focusing on marine paintings.

Waxman, Franz (b. Wachsmann) (1906–67) film composer; born in Königshütte, Germany. Coming to Hollywood in 1934, Waxman scored many films (specializing in suspense and horror) including *The Bride of Frankenstein* (1935), *Rebecca* (1940), and *Sunset Boulevard* (1950).

Wayland, Francis (1826–1904) lawyer, educator; born in Boston, Mass. (son of Francis Wayland, 1796–1865). A Massachusetts and Connecticut lawyer trained at Harvard Law School, he was dean of Yale Law School (1873–1903), where he revitalized and expanded the school and introduced the first American graduate law degrees.

Wayland, Francis (1796–1865) clergyman, educator; born in New York City. He wrote the classic *Moral Dignity of the Missionary Enterprise* (1823). As president of Brown University (1827–55), he greatly strengthened the faculty and curriculum; his influential *Report on the Condition of the University* (1850) advocated a higher education responsive to democracy's needs. He planned the Rhode Island public school system (1828).

Wayne, Anthony (1745–96) soldier; born in Wayneboro, Pa. A Revolutionary war hero, he was often called "Mad Anthony" because of his courage on the battlefield. He fought in numerous important battles during 1775–78 and demonstrated his military excellence in his surprise attack on and capture of Stony Point in 1779. In 1780 he took quick action that prevented a British seizure of West Point after Benedict Arnold's betrayal of the post. Following his retirement in 1783, he was recalled to military service in 1792 to meet a threat from Indians in the Ohio River valley. He campaigned cautiously in 1793 before winning a decisive battle at Fallen Timbers in 1794. He forced the Indian chiefs to accept the Treaty of Greenville, which opened up new areas to white settlers.

Wayne, James Moore (1790–1867) Supreme Court justice; born in Savannah, Ga. He served as mayor of Savannah, as a circuit court judge (1824–29), and in the U.S. House of Representatives (Ga.; 1829). President Jackson named him to the U.S. Supreme Court (1835–67) where he had a long but undistinguished career.

Wayne, John (b. Marion Michael Morrison) (1907–79) film actor; born in Winterset, Iowa. This tough, tall, strong-but-silent he-man made his first film in *Hangman's House* (1928) and graduated to a long succession of small parts in low-budget movies until he got his big break in *Stagecoach* (1939). He became the quintessential mythical movie hero, and finally won an Oscar for *True Grit* (1969) after some 250 films. His final movie was *The Shootist* (1976). He became known in later years for his outspokenness on behalf of conservative political causes, particularly for his support of America's role in Vietnam.

Wayne, June (1918–) lithographer; born in Chicago, Ill. Self-taught, she was an industrial designer and radio writer (1939–43), worked in France (1957–59), and returned to New York City. She strongly influenced the resurgence of lithography in the 1960s and is known for her illustrations for *John Donne, Songs and Sonnets* (1958). She was the founder of the Tamarind Lithography Workshop in Los Angeles, Calif. (1960–70), later organized as the Tamarind Institute at the University of New Mexico in Albuquerque (1970).

Weaver, Earl (Sidney) (1930–) baseball manager; born in St. Louis, Mo. During his 17-year career as a tempestuous manager of the Baltimore Orioles (1968–86), he won four league championships and a World Series in 1970. He holds the record for ejections from games (98).

Weaver, James (Baird) (1833–1912) U.S. representative; born in Dayton, Ohio. A brigadier general in the Union army and a district attorney, he was elected by the Greenback Party in Iowa to the U.S. House of Representatives (1879–81, 1885–89). He was the Populist Party's presidential candidate in 1892.

Weaver, Robert (1924–) illustrator; born in Pittsburgh, Pa. Considered the forerunner of modern expressive illustrators, he studied at Carnegie Tech (Pittsburgh) and in Italy (1949–51), and worked as an illustrator for such periodicals as *Fortune, Esquire, Life* and *Playboy*. He influenced many commercial artists and is known for his innovative use of multiple images, as in *Jason Robards Rehearsing* Huey (1982).

Weaver, Robert (Clifton) (1907–) housing administrator, cabinet member; born in Washington, D.C. A member of President Franklin Roosevelt's informal "Black Cabinet" (1933–42), he became a New York housing commissioner (1954–59) and Federal Housing Agency administrator (1961–66), coauthoring *The Dilemma of Urban America* (1965). As President Lyndon Johnson's secretary of housing and urban development (1966–69) – the first African-American cabinet member in U.S. history – he promoted "demonstration cities" funding. He then became president of Bernard Baruch College in New York City.

Weaver, (Sylvester L.) Pat (1908–) television executive; born in Los Angeles, Calif. (father of Sigourney Weaver). A radio writer and producer, he served as a Young and Rubicam advertising manager in the 1940s. Joining National Broadcasting Company in 1949, he became president (1953–55), later chairman, creating the *Today* and *Tonight* shows. In 1956 he returned to advertising, later founding Subscription Television in Los Angeles.

Weaver, Warren (1894–1978) mathematician; born in Reedsburg, Wis. A mathematics teacher early in his career, he is noted for promoting scientific research, especially as director of natural sciences for the Rockefeller Foundation (1932–55) and adviser to other foundations (1956–78). A past president of the National Academy of Sciences and defense department adviser, he is the author of an autobiography, mathematics texts, and *Alice in Many Tongues,* a book that reflects his fascination with Lewis Carroll.

Weaver, William (1923–) writer, translator, music critic; born in Washington, D.C. In 1948 he moved to Italy and, as a writer and European newspaper correspondent, eventually became known in America as a lecturer and opera broadcaster. He won international awards for his English translations of French and Italian operas and modern Italian prose, including Umberto Eco's *The Name of the Rose* (1983).

Webb, Electra Havemeyer (1888–1960) museum founder; born in New York City (daughter of Louisine Elder Havemeyer). She studied at a commercial college, learned outdoor sports from her father, and married J. Watson Webb (1910). Immensely wealthy, the couple lived in New York City and Westbury, Long Island. They settled in Shelburne, Vt. (1949), building a house on the Webb land holdings. Two years earlier, Electra had founded the Shelburne Museum, a center for American folk art, paintings, and crafts. She collected numerous artifacts and buildings, which she reconstructed on site. Considered an important resource of Americana, the Shelburne Museum was personally supervised by Electra Webb until her death.

Webb, Jack (Randolf) (1920–1982) television actor, director, producer; born in Santa Monica, Calif. He created *Dragnet,* a documentary style police radio show in 1949, starring in and directing the show when it moved to National Broadcasting Company-TV (1952–59). His company, Mark VII, Ltd., produced a series of police shows, including a revival of *Dragnet* (1967–70), and *Adam-12* (1968–75).

Webb, James (Edwin) (1907–92) business executive, government official; born in Granville County, N.C. A Sperry Gyroscope executive (1936–41) and Marine Corps major, he served as President Truman's budget director (1946–49), balancing the budget before joining the state department (1949–52). As the National Aeronautics and Space Administration director (1961–68), he put American astronauts ahead of the Russians, leaving to head a science foundation.

Webb, James Watson (1802–84) journalist, diplomat; born in Claverack, N.Y. After serving in the U.S. Army, where he won a reputation as a duelist, he bought the *New York Morning Courier* in 1827, soon merging it with the *Enquirer,* and eventually took over editorship of the merged paper, retaining that role until 1861. A strong partisan, he originally supported Andrew Jackson but later became a prominent Whig. As a diplomat he helped secure French withdrawal from Mexico in 1865 and from 1861 to 1869 was U.S. ambassador to Brazil.

Webb, (William Henry) "Chick" (1909–39) musician; born in Baltimore, Md. A hunchback from birth, he was a highly acclaimed drummer who began playing on Chesapeake Bay pleasure steamers with the Jazzola Orchestra in 1924. Moving to New York City, he was a sideman with Edgar Dowell in 1925, then formed his own combo in 1926. He gradually developed a big band while playing in Harlem nightclubs during the late 1920s and early 1930s. In 1931, he began playing long regular seasons at the Savoy Ballroom, a venue with which his name was virtually synonymous during the swing era. In 1935, he introduced his vocalist, Ella Fitzgerald, who assumed leadership of the band upon his death from tuberculosis of the spine.

Webb, William Snyder (1882–1964) physicist, archaeologist; born in Greendale, Ky. He was long on the faculty of the University of Kentucky (1904–50), where he headed the departments of physics and anthropology and archaeology. He was archaeologist of the Tennessee Valley Authority (1934–37) and during World War II aided the U.S. atomic bomb effort at Oak Ridge, Tennessee.

Webber, Charles Wilkins (1819–56) explorer, journalist; born in Russellville, Ky. He served in the Texas struggle for independence and went to New York City to become a journalist. His acquaintance with John James Audubon influenced his writing, which included *The Hunter-Naturalist* (1851). He tried but failed to organize exploration expeditions in the Southwest and died in Nicaragua after joining the filibuster expedition of William Walker.

Weber & Fields See WEBER, JOSEPH (MORRIS).

Weber, Joseph (Morris) (1867–1942) **and Fields, (Lewis Maurice) Lew** (1867–1941) vaudeville comedians, theatrical producers; both born in New York City. Starting together as schoolboys in the Lower East Side, they perfected a long-running act (1877–1904) that involved song-and-dance, dialect, slapstick, and sometimes blackface routines in which Fields was the bullying partner and Weber the fall-guy – the inspiration for many such duos as Laurel and Hardy and Abbott and Costello. At their peak they comanaged Weber and Fields Music Hall, parodying serious plays and musicals. Splitting in 1904, they took up again in 1912 and went on to musicals and even films but never regained their original popularity.

Weber, Kem (1889–1963) designer; born in Berlin, Germany. Stranded in California by World War I, he became a leading West Coast art deco and modernist free-lance designer of interiors and furniture.

Weber, Max (1881–1961) painter, sculptor; born in Bialystok, Russia. Emigrating with his family to Brooklyn (1891), he studied at the Pratt Institute (1898–1900), in Paris with Matisse (1908), then settled in New York (1909). His paintings and sculptures were influenced by expressionism, as seen in *The Geranium* (1911), and by cubism, as in *Chinese Restaurant* (1915). He moved to Garden City, Long Island (1920) and began his representational period. By the

late 1930s he focused on religious subjects, as in *Adoration of the Moon* (1944).

Webster, (Benjamin Francis) Ben (1909–73) jazz musician; born in Kansas City, Mo. He was an outstanding tenor saxophonist who played with Bennie Moten and Fletcher Henderson during the 1930s and emerged as a featured soloist with Duke Ellington between 1940–43. He free-lanced thereafter and spent the last ten years of his life in Copenhagen.

Webster, Beveridge (1908–) pianist; born in Pittsburgh, Pa. He studied with his father and in Paris before his 1934 American debut with the New York Philharmonic. While concertizing widely, he taught at Juilliard from 1946.

Webster, Daniel (1782–1852) U.S. representative/senator, orator; born in Salisbury, N.H. He graduated from Dartmouth College and taught school while studying law. Admitted to the bar in 1805, he gained a local reputation as an orator and came to wider notice as an opponent of the U.S. undertaking the War of 1812. He was then elected to the U.S. House of Representatives (Fed., N.H.; 1813–17) where he became a leader in opposing the policies of the Democratic-Republication administration. He then moved to Boston to pursue his law career, including appearances before the U.S. Supreme Court. Elected again to the U.S. House of Representatives, but now from Massachusetts (Fed., 1823–27), he was a strong supporter of John Quincy Adams. Elected to the U.S. Senate (National Republican, 1827–41), he was a supporter of the National Bank, a protectionist, and a champion of the nascent New England woolen cloth industry, as well as an opponent of the annexation of Texas and the Mexican war. Although opposed to slavery, he was denounced by abolitionists for his support of compromises on sectional issues involving the slavery issue. Devoutly pro-union, he denounced the nullification arguments by states' rights advocates in a famous debate in 1830. As secretary of state (1841–43) he negotiated treaties settling a border dispute with Canada (Webster-Ashburton Treaty, 1842) and establishing relations with Chicago. He was reelected to the U.S. Senate (Whig, Mass.; 1845–50) where he delivered his famous speech (March 7, 1850) supporting the Compromise of 1850. This led to his being attacked by the antislavery forces, but he left the Senate to serve again as secretary of state (1850–52). He died in that office, greatly admired for his oratory, integrity, and commitment to preserving the union, but never having obtained the broad support that would have gained him the presidency he coveted.

Webster, Edwin S. (Sibley) See under STONE, CHARLES A.

Webster, Noah (1758–1843) lexicographer; born in West Hartford, Conn. The son of a dairy farmer, he graduated from Yale College in 1778 and served under his father as a private in the American Revolution. He was admitted to the bar in 1781, but earned his living for some years as a teacher. In 1783 he published the first volume of *A Grammatical Institute of the English Language.* This small volume, in later editions titled *The American Spelling Book,* became widely known as *The Blue-Backed Speller.* It was immensely popular and continued in use in schools throughout the country well into the 20th century. Webster was an ardent patriot and Federalist and entered into his speller many of those spelling forms that continue to distinguish American from British writing. He also worked for the passage of the first U.S. copyright law in 1790. For ten years he served as editor for Federalist newspapers in New York City, but from 1803 he devoted himself largely to the study of language. *A Compendious Dictionary of the English Language* (1806) established his reputation as a lexicographer, but it was the appearance of a much expanded work in 1828, *An American Dictionary of the English Language,* that assured his preeminence in the field. As even the title hints, Webster recognized in his dictionary American contributions to the language in both new vocabulary and the development of new meanings. Although the dictionary was his main occupation for over 20 years, he also found time for other interests, including writing works on diseases, agriculture, and scientific subjects. During a ten-year residency in Amherst, Mass. (1812–22), he helped to found Amherst College (1821) and he served two terms in the Massachusetts legislature. In his later years he continued to revise his dictionaries, campaign for unified copyright laws, and write essays. In 1833 he published a somewhat expurgated revision of the *Authorized Version of the Bible.* After his death, Webster's dictionary was seen through subsequent editions by his son-in-law, Chauncey Allen Goodrich.

Webster, William H. (Hedgcock) (1924–   ) lawyer, government official; born in St. Louis, Mo. A St. Louis lawyer (1949–60) and United States attorney (1960–71), he was an outstanding federal court of appeals judge (1971–78). Hired to restore integrity to the FBI (1978–87), he used electronic surveillance to pursue organized crime. He followed William Casey as director of the Central Intelligence Agency (1987–91).

Wechsler, David (1896–1981) psychologist; born in Lespedi, Romania. He came to the United States as a youth and was chief psychologist at New York City's Bellevue Hospital for 35 years. He devised a series of intelligence tests that became standard diagnostic tools, including the Wechsler-Bellevue Intelligence Scale. In 1970 he began teaching at New York University's medical school, where he had been a clinical psychologist since World War II.

Wedderburn, Joseph H. (Henry) (1887–1948) mathematician; born in Forfar, Scotland. He emigrated to America to join the Princeton faculty (1909–45). He is best known as a contributor to the *Annals of Mathematics* (starting 1911). During World War I he was a British army captain.

Wedemeyer, Albert C. (Coady) (1897–1989) soldier; born in Omaha, Nebr. He graduated from West Point in 1918 and served with distinction in Tientsin, China (where he studied Mandarin Chinese) (1930–32) and the Philippines (1932–34). He was the first American officer to study at the *Kriegsakadamie* (German general staff school) since World War I. He was commander of all U.S. forces in the China theater (1944–45). He retired from the army in 1951 and wrote the *Wedemeyer Reports* (1954). He then worked as a business executive.

Weeden, Donald Edward (1930–   ) stockbroker; born in Oakland, Calif. He graduated from Stanford (1951) and in 1956 joined Weeden & Co., the investment house his father founded. A leading "third market" firm, Weeden & Co., by the late 1960s handled some eight percent of the total business in stocks listed on the New York Stock Exchange (NYSE), effectively challenging the NYSE's monopoly. He became chairman of the family firm in 1970.

Weegee See FELLING, ARTHUR.

Weems, Mason Locke (1759–1825) clergyman, bookseller, writer; born in Ann Arundel County, Md. Criticized for his sprightly informality as an Episcopal clergyman, "Parson Weems" was well-known for his uplifting sermons, moral tracts, and fictionalized biographies, especially for his best-selling life of George Washington, which went through 86 editions between 1800 and 1827. The fifth edition (1806) saw the first appearance in print of the story of young Washington and the cherry tree. From about 1794 on, Weems traveled between New York and Georgia to sell books and preach sermons.

Weems, Ted (b. Wilfred Theodore Weymes) (1901–63) bandleader; born in Pitcairn, Pa. He played trombone in college and with his own band had a first hit record with "Somebody Stole My Gal" (1923). The band toured the Midwest and settled in Chicago in 1929. He became popular on radio and recorded many hits throughout the 1930s. After serving in World War II he formed a successful new band, but his popularity eventually declined and in the 1950s he worked as a disc jockey and band agent.

Weidenmann, Jacob (1829–93) landscape architect; born in Winterthur, Switzerland. An engineer and architect in Panama and South America, he immigrated to the U.S.A. in 1861 to be superintendent of parks in Hartford, Conn., where he designed the Cedar Hill Cemetery. In 1870 he joined Frederick Olmsted in New York, designing the Schuykill Reservoir in Philadelphia among other projects. Publishing *Modern Cemeteries* in 1888, he advocated park-like grounds minimizing monuments.

Weidenreich, Franz (1873–1948) physical anthropologist; born in Edenkoben, Germany. He received his M.D. from the University of Strassburg (1899), then served at several German universities until Nazi anti-Semitism forced him to emigrate to the U.S.A. The University of Chicago sent him to China (1934–41), where his excavations of the fossil Peking (Beijing) Man resulted in a series of definitive monographs. Returning to the U.S.A., Weidenreich continued his work at the American Museum of Natural History.

Weidman, Charles (Edward, Jr.) (1901–75) modern dancer, choreographer; born in Lincoln, Nebr. He trained at the Denishawn school and performed with the company for eight years, before forming his own with Doris Humphrey in 1928. Known for dramatic as well as comic portrayals, his best choreography included *Atavisms* (1936) and *A Home Divided* (1945). He founded Dance Theater Company in 1948 and encouraged the development of many male dancers.

Weigel, Gustave A. (1906–64) Catholic priest, theologian; born in Buffalo, N.Y. A Jesuit, he was a theology professor in Chile (1937–48) and at a Jesuit seminary in Maryland (from 1949). He was a pioneering advocate of ecumenism and played a key role as interpreter and liaison for non-Catholics at the Second Vatican Council.

Weill, Kurt (1900–50) composer; born in Dessau, Germany. Son of a rabbi, after a moderately successful career as a musical avant-gardist he teamed with playwright Bertolt Brecht to create a series of popular theater works that joined radical social ideas to jazz-influenced music; most notable was the 1928 *Threepenny Opera,* which became a sensation across Europe and its best-known song "Mack the Knife" an international classic. Driven from Germany by the Nazis, he and his actress wife Lotte Lenya moved permanently to the U.S.A. in 1935; three years later came his first Broadway hit,

Knickerbocker Holiday, which introduced the immortal "September Song." After other Broadway successes including *Lady in the Dark* (1941) and *One Touch of Venus* (1943), he wrote the "folk opera" *Down in the Valley* (1948), which used traditional Kentucky tunes. He died suddenly while working on a musical version of *Tom Sawyer.*

Wein, George (Theodore) (1925–) music producer; born in Boston, Mass. A pianist, he worked as a sideman with Edmond Hall, Bobby Hackett, and other mainstream jazz artists between 1944 and 1949. He had a dual career after 1950, when he opened Storyville, the best-known of the Boston nightclubs that he operated throughout the 1950s. In 1954 he inaugurated the three-day Newport Jazz Festival in Rhode Island, an annual production that expanded to a ten-day event when it moved to New York City in 1972. In 1959, he began producing festivals at various sites in the U.S.A. and in 1974 he established Festival Productions, Inc., to manage these activities on an international scale. He produced the Newport Folk Festival between 1963 and 1968. He also recorded and conducted occasional tours with his Newport All-Stars, which he began leading in 1957.

Weinberg, Harry (1908–90) real estate/transit companies businessman, philanthropist; born in Galicia, Austro-Hungarian Empire. In 1912 he was brought to Baltimore, Md., where his father already was operating an auto-repair shop. He quit school at age 12 and worked in his father's shop. By his twenties he was investing in Baltimore real estate; he then used his profits to buy bus companies and made a major fortune when his Fifth Avenue Coach Line was bought by New York City in 1962. From 1950 on he gradually shifted his business interests and residence to Hawaii, where he amassed more real estate; he permanently settled in Hawaii in 1968. In later years he also engaged in corporate buyouts. Known as a tempestuous, tough-talking, reclusive man, he shunned all the trappings of wealth – flying coach class and buying his clothes off the rack. At his death he left close to $1 billion to a charitable trust to benefit the poor.

Weinberg, John Livingston (1925–) investment banker; born in New York City. He graduated from Princeton (1948), took a graduate degree at Harvard (1950), and joined Goldman, Sachs & Co., where his father was a senior partner. He himself rose to partner in 1956 and senior partner in 1976. Named senior chairman of the firm in 1990, he continued Goldman, Sachs's traditionally conservative policies. A Marine Corps veteran (1942–46; 1951–52), he served as a Princeton trustee.

Weinberg, Steven (1933–) physicist; born in New York City. He was an instructor at Columbia University (1957–59) before moving to the University of California: Berkeley (1959–69). In 1967 he produced a gauge symmetry theory that correctly predicted that electromagnetic and weak nuclear forces are identical at extremely high energies. The theory also predicted the weak neutral current, confirmed by particle accelerator experiments in 1973. As this theory was also independently developed by Pakistani physicist Abdus Salam, and extended by Sheldon Glashow, all three scientists shared the 1979 Nobel Prize in physics. Weinberg pursued his theoretical investigations in the unification of the fundamental forces of the universe at the Massachusetts Institute of Technology (1969–73) and Harvard (1973–83). He joined the University of Texas (1982) and concurrently became a consultant at the Smithsonian Astrophysical Laboratory (1983).

Weinberger, Caspar (Willard) (1917–) lawyer, cabinet member; born in San Francisco. A California corporate lawyer (1947–69), he became Office of Management and Budget director (1970–73) and Nixon's secretary of health, education, and welfare (1973–75). President of Bechtel Power Company (1975–80), he returned as Reagan's secretary of defense (1981–87), championing costly defense systems. Returning to the law, he was indicted in 1992 for abetting the Iran-Contra arms deals.

Weinman, Adolph Alexander (1870–1952) sculptor; born in Karlsruhe, Germany. He and his widowed mother emigrated to New York City (1880), where he was apprenticed to a wood and ivory carver (1885) before studying at Cooper Union (1886) and with Augustus Saint-Gaudens at the Art Students League. He opened a studio (1904) and became known for his coin designs, such as the Mercury dime and the Liberty half-dollar, as well as for his architectural works, notably the interior and facade of New York City's Pennsylvania Station.

Weinstein, Jack (1921–) judge; born in Wichita, Kans. A graduate of Brooklyn College (1943), he served in the navy before receiving a law degree from Columbia University (1948). He achieved a reputation as a distinguished legal scholar while a member of Columbia's faculty from 1952 to 1967. Appointed a federal judge for the Eastern District of New York (1967), he became known for his liberal, humanitarian rulings, and issued landmark decisions in several civil rights cases. In 1985 he oversaw a multimillion-dollar settlement of Vietnam veterans' health claims growing out of exposure to the defoliant Agent Orange.

Weinstein, Nathan See WEST, NATHANIEL.

Weir, J. (Julian) Alden (1852–1919) painter; born in West Point, N.Y. He studied in Paris (1873), traveled in Europe (1873–83), worked in New York, and settled in Connecticut (1883). A founder of the Ten (1898), an impressionist group, he is remembered for his paintings such as *Idle Hours* (1888). In 1991 his property in Wilton/Ridgefield, Conn., was named a National Historic Site, the first artist's home so designated.

Weiser, Johann Conrad (1696–1760) Indian agent; born near Herrenberg, Germany. He emigrated to New York before settling in Pennsylvania in 1729. He learned the dialects of the Iroquois tribes and pursued good relations with them. In response to the threat of war with French Canada, he arranged formal conferences with the Indians in Philadelphia in 1731 and 1736 and made the Iroquois alliance binding with the treaty of 1742.

Weisgall, Hugo (David) (1912–) composer; born in Ivancice, Moravia. American-trained, he taught at the Jewish Theological Seminary, Juilliard, and at Queens College. He is best known for his operas, including *Six Characters in Search of An Author* (1956).

Weisman, Frederick R. (1912–) businessman, art collector, philanthropist; born in Minneapolis, Minn. Child of Russian immigrants, he moved to Los Angeles in the 1930s, entered the produce business, joined Hunt Foods, and eventually became the president of the giant food conglomerate (and married the daughter of its founder, Norton Simon). In 1970 he established Mid-Atlantic Toyota Distributors, which imported Toyota vehicles into the mid-Atlantic; when he sold the distributorship in 1990 he further increased his already large fortune. For many years he had been collecting paintings and sculpture – mostly modern American – some of which he donated to museums; but about 350 prime works remained in his mansion in Holmby Hills, outside Los Angeles, which he intended to remain as a private museum. He gave such large sums to various other museums that at least four assigned his name to them. He also donated large sums to various medical institutions, particularly to the Venice (Calif.) Family Clinic that serves the poor and homeless.

Weiss, Paul A. (Alfred) (1898–1989) developmental biologist; born in Vienna, Austria. He taught and performed research in Vienna and Germany (1922–30) before coming to Yale (1931–33). He joined the University of Chicago (1933–54), then moved to Rockefeller University (1954–64), remaining active as an adviser and visiting professor in his retirement. His proof of nerve regeneration became instrumental in surgical transplant techniques during and after World War II. He made major contributions to studies of cell organization in both developing embryos and mixed cells in culture (1950s–60s).

Weisskopf, Victor F. (Frederick) (1908–) physicist; born in Vienna, Austria. While a graduate student in Germany, he and E. P. Wigner made advancements in quantum electrodynamics in their studies of light emission by electrons. With Wolfgang Pauli he postulated the existence of charged particles without spin (1934); experimental evidence for this theory occurred in 1946 with the discovery of the meson. Weisskopf fled the Nazis in 1937 and joined the University of Rochester (1937–43). He became a group leader of the Manhattan Project at Los Alamos (1943–46), then moved to the Massachusetts Institute of Technology (1946–74), where he continued his research on the nucleus and subatomic particles. He concurrently served CERN:Geneva as its director-general. An accomplished pianist and lover of classical art and music, he published numerous books, including textbooks and autobiographical accounts of life as a physicist.

Weissmuller, (Peter John) Johnny (1904–84) swimmer, actor; born in Windber, Pa. He attended schools in Chicago and the University of Chicago, and during the 1920s was the best all-around amateur swimmer in the U.S.A. After winning three gold medals in the 1924 Olympics and two more at the 1928 Games, he parlayed his celebrity in a career as a movie actor. (Hollywood publicists would later claim he was born in Hungary but had hidden this fact in order to compete for the U.S. Olympic team.) After appearing in some short subjects and swimming extravaganzas, he starred in 12 *Tarzan* movies in the 1930s and early 1940s including *Tarzan, the Ape Man* (1932); when he was replaced by a younger actor, he made a series of *Jungle Jim* movies. He formed a swimming pool company and continued to make occasional appearances in trash films.

Weitzel, Godfrey (1835–84) soldier; born in Cincinnati, Ohio. A West Point graduate (1855), he constructed harbor defenses and taught engineering at West Point. As a Union officer, he was in charge of various fortifications, including those at Cincinnati and Washington, D.C. He served as chief engineer of the Union force that occupied New Orleans (April 1862), then commanded a division in Louisiana and a corps in the Army of the James in Virginia, participating in the siege of Petersburg and the Appomattox campaign. His mostly black XXV Corps led the Union entry into Richmond, the Confederate capital, on April 3, 1865. He remained in the army until his death.

Welch, James (1940–) Blackfeet/Gros Ventre writer; born in Browning, Mont. His writing explored both the pride of heritage and the deep sense of loss experienced by many Indians. His books include *Winter in the Blood* (1974), *The Death of Jim Loney* (1979), and *Fools Crow* (1986).

Welch, John F. (Frances), Jr. ("Jack") (1935–) electronics executive; born in Salem, Mass. He joined General Electric (GE) after earning his Ph.D. in chemical engineering (1960). Through his aggressive marketing of the company's plastics, materials, and consumer goods and services, he earned steady promotions (vice-president 1972, senior vice-president 1977–79, vice-chairman 1979–81) before becoming GE's youngest-ever chairman and CEO (1981). Regarded as a master of strategic planning, if a ruthless executive, he redefined GE's areas of concentration and mandated that the company be number one or two at everything it did. Enterprises that either fell outside the strategic orbit or failed to perform were sold. The result was 132,000 layoffs, 73 plant closings, and more than 200 sales of products or businesses, and a major acquisition – RCA (1985). He became one of the country's most respected and influential business leaders for transforming an industrial giant into a flexible, entrepreneurial organization.

Welch, Joseph Nye (1890–1960) lawyer; born in Primghar, Iowa. A graduate of Grinnell College (1914) and Harvard Law School (1917), he went into private practice in Boston and established a reputation as an excellent trial lawyer. In 1954, as special counsel for the army, he conducted a televised duel with Senator Joseph McCarthy in congressional hearings called to consider McCarthy's allegations that evidence of an army communications spy ring had been covered up. Welch gained a clear advantage in the exchanges through his old-fashioned moral indignation as well as his legal expertise, and the Senate voted a few months later to censure McCarthy. Welch returned to private practice, emerging briefly to narrate a television series on constitutional history and to play the trial judge in the 1959 movie *Anatomy of a Murder*.

Welch, William Henry (1850–1934) pathologist, medical educator, public health pioneer; born in Norfolk, Conn. After taking his M.D. from the New York College of Physicians (1875), he spent three years studying in Europe with some of the most important medical researchers of the day. Back in New York City, he began work as a pathologist at the Bellevue Hospital and Women's Hospital. Accepting a post as professor of pathology at Johns Hopkins University (1883), he returned to Europe briefly to study bacteriology under Robert Koch, then organized a pathological laboratory at Johns Hopkins; he would eventually serve as first dean of the Johns Hopkins Medical School (1893–98) and was responsible for introducing many of the reforms and individuals who made Johns Hopkins a major medical center. In an advisory capacity, he also implanted his ideas on medical schools, education, and research in the newly founded Rockefeller Institute of Medical Research and the Carnegie Foundation. Meanwhile, he had become increasingly more interested in issues of public health, serving as president of the Maryland Board of Health (1898–1922), advising the surgeon general of the army during World War

I, and becoming the first dean of the new School of Hygiene and Public Health at Johns Hopkins (1918–26). Through all these years he also made notable contributions to medical research, including his discovery that cholera and typhoid were spread by microorganisms, not miasmas (1887); his book *Thrombosis and Embolism* (1899); his discovery of a bacillus (named after him) that produces "gas gangrene" in wounded soldiers; and other work that advanced the fields of pathology and bacteriology in the U.S.A.

Weld, Theodore Dwight (1803–95) abolitionist; born in Hampton, Conn. After attending Hamilton College and the Oneida Institute, which stressed manual labor in education, he was influenced by Presbyterian evangelist Charles Grandison Finney to devote himself to promoting reforms and he went to study at the Lane Seminary in Cincinnati (1834). For about ten years thereafter, as an ardent abolitionist, he gave forceful lectures, trained workers for the American Anti-Slavery Society, and wrote influential pamphlets, although, being very retiring, he permitted nothing to be published under his own name. He was an adviser to an antislavery bloc in Congress in the early 1840s and recruited prominent people to abolitionism. He and his wife later opened two schools in New Jersey that stressed the importance of manual labor; many abolitionists' children went there. After the Civil War he became a crusader for women's rights.

Welk, Lawrence (1903–92) bandleader; born in Strasburg, N.D. In the 1920s he developed what he called a sweet-sounding "champagne music" with his orchestra. He toured and appeared on radio in the 1930s and 1940s and in 1951 began hosting his own television show. Carried on network television until 1971, the show featured such traditional forms as tap and ballroom dancing, ragtime piano, and a variety of singing. He was a major publisher of music and the author of several books.

Wellek, René (1903–) literary critic; born in Vienna, Austria. He came to America in 1939 and taught at Yale (1946). His *Theory of Literature* (with Austin Warren, 1949) became a manual of New Criticism; he wrote the monumental 7-volume *History of Modern Criticism* (1955–91).

Weller, Thomas H. (Huckle) (1915–) virologist, parasitologist; born in Ann Arbor, Mich. After becoming a pediatrician, he taught and performed research at Harvard Medical School (1940–41, 1948–85). He shared the 1954 Nobel Prize in physiology for discovering that poliomyelitis virus can grow in tissue culture, thus enabling development of a polio vaccine. He isolated and investigated two worms parasitic in humans, demonstrated that chicken pox and shingles are caused by the same virus, cultivated the mumps and Coxsackie viruses, and isolated the viral agents of rubella and cytomegalic inclusion disease.

Welles, (Benjamin) Sumner (1892–1961) diplomat; born in New York City. Independently wealthy, he joined the Foreign Service in 1915. Specializing in Latin America, he supervised American withdrawal from the Dominican Republic (1922–25). In the state department (1933–43), he championed the Good Neighbor Policy, renegotiating the Panama Canal treaty (1934–36). Resigning after an alleged homosexual incident, he later wrote about foreign affairs.

Welles, (George) Orson (1915–85) stage/movie actor, director; born in Kenosha, Wis. Son of a wealthy inventor and a concert pianist, he was a precocious child who staged miniproductions of Shakespeare in his house. When his mother died in 1925, he went on a world tour with his father, then attended a private school in Illinois where he continued to direct plays (1926–31). With his father's death in 1927, he became the ward of a Chicago physician, Dr. Maurice Bernstein. Welles turned down college and set off for Ireland on a sketching tour – he had shown talent as an artist – and ended up acting with Dublin's famous Gate Theatre (1931). He returned to the U.S.A. in 1932, toured with Katharine Cornell's road company, and made his Broadway debut – as Tybalt in *Romeo and Juliet* – in 1934, the year he also gave his first radio performance. With John Houseman, he collaborated on productions for the Phoenix Theatre Group and the Federal Theater Project; they then founded the Mercury Theatre in 1937, noted for such productions as an all-African-American *Macbeth*. In 1938, Welles and Houseman began to produce plays on their *Mercury Theatre on the Air;* that October 30, as a Halloween spoof, they broadcast a dramatization of H. G. Wells's *War of the Worlds,* so realistic in conveying a Martian invasion that it led to a literal panic in the Northeast. His growing reputation led to his being hired by RKO in Hollywood but none of his initial projects got into production. Then he made *Citizen Kane* (1941), which despite its success with critics and a few metropolitan audiences, was not all that successful at the time. Two more movies, *The Magnificent Ambersons* (1942) and *The Lady from Shanghai* (1948), were heavily edited by the studios and only years later recognized as superb works. From this point on, Welles suffered from his reputation as an erratic filmmaker who couldn't hold to budgets or schedules, and he would spend the rest of his life forced to seeking financing for his projects. By about 1946, he was effectively in exile in Europe where he continued to act in others' movies (*The Third Man,* 1949) to earn money so that he could make his own (*Othello,* 1952; *Chimes at Midnight/Falstaff,* 1966). Back in the U.S.A. by the mid-1970s, he found himself honored as one of the true geniuses of American movies, but thereafter he was reduced to appearances in grade-B movies, television talk shows, and television commercials. Several times divorced, overweight, with a resume that included many failed projects, he would have seemed a failure at his death had his rich life not produced so many original works.

Welles, Gideon (1802–78) secretary of the navy, journalist, politician; born in Glastonbury, Conn. As part owner and editor of the *Hartford Times* (1826–36), he endorsed Jacksonian democracy. Although he failed in his efforts to become a representative, senator, and governor, he held several state political offices (1826–44) until becoming chief of the U.S. Navy's Bureau of Provisions and Clothing (1846–49). Opposed to slavery, he left the Democratic Party in 1854 and helped organize the new Republican Party, founding the *Hartford Evening Press* to promote the Republicans' goals. The newly elected President Lincoln, knowing he needed a New Englander in the cabinet, appointed Welles to his cabinet. As secretary of the navy (1861–69), he managed the department with great energy, enterprise, and economy, gaining a reputation for freeing it as far as possible from political favoritism. Under his leadership, the navy quickly expanded, adopted the ironclads and other new technology, successfully blockaded the Confederacy, and contributed greatly to the eventual Union victory. He did not get on with all his fellow cabinet members and he deplored Lincoln's suspension of habeas corpus in 1863, but he supported

Lincoln's moderate plans for reconstruction and backed Andrew Johnson when he was impeached. After leaving the cabinet, he wrote a series of important magazine articles; one of these was expanded to become *Lincoln and Seward* (1874); his diary of the Civil War period (revised by him in later years; not published until 1911) provides a revealing glimpse of the times.

Welles, Roger (1862–1932) naval officer, explorer; born in Newington, Conn. A graduate of the U.S. Naval Academy (1884), he served in three Arctic explorations and wrote *English-Eskimo and Eskimo-English Vocabularies* (1890). He explored the Orinoco River (South America) (1891), served with distinction in the Spanish-American War, and was the director of naval intelligence during World War I.

Wellman, Walter (1858–1934) journalist, explorer, aeronaut; born in Mentor, Ohio. A journalist given to making sensational expeditions – in 1891 he erected a monument on Watling Island, or San Salvador, where he said Columbus had first landed – he made two failed attempts to reach the North Pole in an airship (1907, 1909). In 1910 he was one of a crew of six who set off in another large airship to try to cross the Atlantic; within hours, the dirigiblelike craft went down off Cape Hattaras, but it had broken existing world records for time and distance flown by any aircraft; while in flight, too, it had received the first wireless messages sent to an airship above water. He recounted his adventures in *The Aerial Age* (1911).

Wells, Horace (1815–48) dentist, anesthetist; born in Hartford, Vt. He was a dentist in Hartford, Conn., when about 1840 he became interested in the possibility of using nitrous oxide – "laughing gas" – as a painkiller while extracting teeth. In 1841 he formed a partnerhip with a Boston dentist, William T. G. Morton, a dentist who was looking into ether as an anesthetic. In December 1844, Wells had one of his own teeth extracted while under nitrous oxide and he extracted several more from patients without pain. However, when he attempted to demonstrate the gas's efficacy for surgery at the Harvard Medical School in 1845, it failed. In 1846 Morton successfully demonstrated the use of ether, first (September) for teeth extraction and then (October) for surgical operations at Massachusetts General Hospital. In December 1846, Wells published a claim in the *Hartford Courant* that he had discovered the anesthetic effect of both nitrous oxide and ether; in 1847 he elaborated his claims in a pamphlet. Morton, meanwhile, had filed patent claims for ether, which was at once regarded as superior for protracted operations. Wells moved to New York City, and continuing his investigations into anesthetics, had taken chloroform; in jail for creating a disturbance while under its influence, he committed suicide.

Wells, Kitty (b. Muriel Ellen Deason) (1919–) country music singer, songwriter; born in Nashville, Tenn. In the 1930s and 1940s she sang on several radio programs. In 1952 she joined the "Grand Ole Opry" and recorded her first hit songs for Decca (later MCA). By 1963 she had released 461 singles and 43 albums. Her songs address such social problems as drinking and divorce and her career paved the way for other female country music singers.

Wells-Barnett, Ida Bell (1862–1931) civil rights advocate; born in Holy Springs, Miss. Born a slave, she attended Rust College after emancipation and taught school in Memphis, Tenn. (1884–91); she was fired for writings critical of segregated education. In 1892, as part-owner and editor of a Memphis newspaper, she published articles denouncing the lynching of three acquaintants; warned to stay out of town, she went to the Northeast and became a renowned antilynching activist, and she published works on the subject. After her marriage to a Chicago editor and lawyer (1895), she was secretary of the National Afro-American Council (1898–1902) and helped found the National Association for the Advancement of Colored People (1910) – which she found too conservative. She also campaigned for women's suffrage.

Welsh, Matthew E. (1912–) governor; born in Detroit, Mich. A Democratic lawyer, he served in the Indiana house (1941–43), and senate (1955–59), becoming Democratic minority leader. As governor (1961–65), he established the Indiana Fair Employment Commission and Youth Training Centers. Joining an Indianapolis law firm afterward, he also chaired the United States–Canada International Joint Committee (1966–70).

Welty, Eudora (1909–) writer; born in Jackson, Miss. She studied at Mississippi State College for Women (1926–27), the University of Wisconsin (B.A. 1929), and Columbia's Graduate School of Business (1930–31). She worked for newspapers and a radio station in Mississippi, as a publicity agent for the Works Progress Administration (WPA), and lectured at several colleges. She lived most of her life in Jackson, Miss. She is praised for her finely tuned Southern "gothic" novels, such as *The Optimist's Daughter* (1972), and the keen sense of the local place in her short fiction, as seen in *The Collected Stories of Eudora Welty* (1980). Her publications also include *One Time, One Place* (1971), a collection of photographs taken when she worked for the WPA, and several collections of essays.

Welwood, John (1943–) psychologist; born in Boston, Mass. A University of Chicago Ph.D., he joined the faculty of the California Institute of Integral Studies, San Francisco (1979) while maintaining a private psychotherapy practice. He sought to integrate eastern religious and psychological traditions into western psychotherapy (*The Meeting of the Ways,* 1979). His later work focused on intimate relationships (*Challenge of the Heart,* 1985).

Wengenroth, Stow (1906–78) lithographer; born in New York City. He studied at the Art Students League and the Grand Central School of Art, and lived in Greenport, Long Island, and Rockport, Maine. Known as a celebrated New England lithographer, as in *Black Weather* (1932) and *Untamed* (1947), he was praised by Andrew Wyeth as "the greatest black-and-white artist in America."

Went, Frits W. (Warmolt) (1903–90) plant physiologist; born in Utrecht, Netherlands. He performed research in Java (1928–32), then came to the U.S.A. to join the California Institute of Technology (1933–58), where he codiscovered (with K. V. Thimann) the plant growth hormones known as auxins; he devoted 20 years of research to these substances. He invented the phytotron, a specialized greenhouse for investigations of the controlled effects of climate on plants. He became director of the Missouri Botanical Garden (1958–63), then was a professor at Washington University (St. Louis) (1963–65). He relocated to the University of Nevada: Reno (1965–85), where he made major contributions to studies of the environmental effects of volatile substances produced by desert plants.

Wertheimer, Max (1880–1943) psychologist; born in Prague.

In 1912, he published the results of a two-year study on the perception of movement, undertaken with Kurt Koffka and Wolfgang Köhler, which marked the beginning of the Gestalt psychology movement. He emigrated to the United States in 1933. During his ten years in the United States, he played an active role in the development of the New School for Social Research.

Weschler, Herbert (1909–) assistant attorney general, criminal law adviser; born in New York City. As assistant attorney general he helped establish the International Military Tribunal at Nuremburg (1945) and served as technical adviser to the tribunal judge. Counsel in many important Supreme Court cases, a professor at Columbia Law School (1933), he assisted drafting the federal rules of criminal procedure and the revised penal law and code of criminal procedure for New York State, as well as assisting in revision of the federal appellate court system. He directed the Institute of American Law for 20 years and was author of many books and articles.

Wescott, Glenway (1901–87) writer, poet; born in Kewaskum, Wis. He studied at the University of Chicago (1917–19). Independently wealthy, he began his writing career as a poet, but is best known for his short stories and novels, especially *The Grandmothers* (1926). He lived in Germany (1921–22), and in France (c. 1925–33), where he mixed with Gertrude Stein and the American expatriate community. (Robert Prentiss, a character in Hemingway's *The Sun Also Rises,* is based on him.) He returned to America and settled near Hampton, N.J. His novel, *The Pilgrim Hawk: A Love Story* (1940), was praised by the critics, and was followed by *Apartment in Athens* (1945), a popular success. From then on he ceased to write fiction, although he published his essays and edited the works of others.

Wesselman, Tom (1931–) painter; born in Cincinnati, Ohio. He studied at the Art Academy of Cincinnati, at Cooper Union (c. 1961), and remained in New York City. A pop artist, he specialized in paintings of everyday objects, collages, and, beginning in the 1960s, erotic themes, as in his continuing series, *The Great American Nude.*

Wesson, Daniel Baird (1825–1906) gunsmith; born in Worcester, Mass. After serving an apprenticeship with his brother, he engaged in the making of firearms. His long association with Horace Smith (1853–55, 1857–73) was profitable for both men; they patented a new type of repeating pistol (1854) and the Smith and Wesson revolver (1857). After Smith's retirement (1873), Wesson worked alone (1873–83) and then brought two of his sons into the business. Wesson's most notable achievement was his development of the first metal cartridge used in ordnance – making breech-loading rifles possible.

West, Benjamin (1738–1820) painter, teacher; born in Springfield, Pa. He painted portraits in Philadelphia (1756), traveled to Rome (1759–62), where he was influenced by the classical German painter Anton Mengs, then settled in London (1763). There he became a charter member of the Royal Academy (1768; president in 1792), and was appointed historical painter to George III (1772). *Death of Wolfe* (1771), his depiction of Gen. James Wolfe in the siege of Quebec during the French and Indian Wars, brought him fame. Throughout his long career in London he promoted and taught visiting American artists, such as Matthew Pratt, Charles W. Peale, Gilbert Stuart, S. F. B. Morse, Washing-

ton Allston and Thomas Sully. Later West's historical subjects waned in popularity, but his allegorical *Death on a Pale Horse* (1802) influenced the emerging French school of romantic painting.

West, Cornel (1953–) educator, philosopher; born in Sacramento, Calif. Educated at Harvard and New York's Union Theological Seminary, he became a noted writer and speaker on what he called "prophetic pragmatism," a philosophy that sought to fuse the life of the mind with public affairs in the areas of racial oppression, sexism, violence, and homophobia. His books include *The American Evasion of Philosophy* (1985) and *Race Matters* (1993). In 1988 he became director of the highly regarded African-American Studies program at Princeton University.

West, Jerry (Alan) (1938–) basketball player; born in Cheylan, W.Va. He was an All-American at the University of West Virginia (1956–60) and he co-captained the U.S. Olympic team to a gold medal in 1960. He then played for the Los Angeles Lakers (1960–74), where he was a ten-time All-NBA (National Basketball Association) first team selection. One of the game's greatest guards, he averaged 27 points per game, fourth best in NBA history, and became known as "Mr. Clutch" for his ability to score when the game was on the line. A Lakers general manager after retiring from the game, he was elected to basketball's Hall of Fame in 1979.

West, Joseph (?–1692) colonist; born in England. He was the agent and storekeeper for the new settlement at Albemarle Point, South Carolina. He became governor in 1671 and led the fledgling colony through a year of scarcity. After a brief interruption, he served again as governor (1674–82) and the center of the colony was moved to New Charles Town (present-day Charleston).

West, Mae (1893–1980) actress; born in Brooklyn, N.Y. Starting in vaudeville, she appeared on Broadway (1911–28) before becoming a film star in the 1930s. She wrote much of her own dialogue, replete with sexual innuendo. A mistress of comic timing, she was a sultry siren who befuddled her co-stars – Cary Grant in *She Done Him Wrong* and W. C. Fields in *My Little Chickadee.* The "Mae West" life-jacket is named after her buxom figure.

West, Nathanael (b. Nathan Wallenstein Weinstein) (1903–40) writer; born in New York City. He studied at Tufts (1921) and Brown (Ph.B. 1924), and lived in Paris for two years where he finished his first novel. He changed his name legally in 1926. Until 1933 he was a manager of various inexpensive hotels belonging to his father in New York City and he continued to write. He settled in California (1935) to become a screenwriter (1936–40). His fiction was largely neglected until after he and his wife died in an automobile accident. His work was revived by critics between 1947 and 1957, and he is praised for its sensitive mix of mordant humor and pathos, as in the novels *Miss Lonelyhearts* (1933), and *The Day of the Locust* (1939).

West, Robert C. (Cooper) (1913–) geographer; born in Enid, Okla. He taught at Louisiana State University (1948–80). He specialized in the historical geography of Latin America, cultural geography and ethnography of Latin American blacks and Indians, and the biogeography of the humid tropics. His works include *Pacific Lowlands of Colombia* (1957) and the first volume of *Handbook of Middle American Indians* (co-edited, 1964).

Westinghouse, George (1846–1914) engineer, inventor,

manufacturer; born in Central Bridge, N.Y. After serving in the Union forces during the Civil War, he turned his attention to the development of a railroad braking system, patenting an air brake in 1869 that soon became widely used. He also combined his own inventions and patents he purchased to introduce electrically controlled signal and switching systems for the railroads. He also invented the gas meter and a system of conducting natural gas through pipes safely into homes. He was a pioneer in the development of means to transmit alternating current over distances to provide electric power for domestic and industrial use. He founded the Westinghouse Electric Company in 1886; by the turn of the century, his enterprises employed more than 50,000 workers and were among the most powerful and successful in the U.S.A. By 1907 he had lost some of his power and he retired in 1911, but he continued to experiment with various new devices.

Westmoreland, William C. (Childs) (1914–) soldier; born in Spartanburg County, S.C. A 1936 West Point graduate, he saw extensive combat duty in World War II and the Korean War. He was superintendent of the U.S. Military Academy (1960–63). In 1964 he became commander of U.S. forces in Vietnam and oversaw the buildup of U.S. forces to a total of 500,000 by 1968, but his "search and destroy" strategy proved unsuccessful against the communist Vietnamese, and after the Tet offensive of 1968, he was recalled to the U.S.A. to serve as army chief of staff. He retired from the army in 1972 and failed in his bid for the Republican gubernatorial nomination in South Carolina in 1974.

Weston, Edward (1886–1958) photographer; born in Highland Park, Ill. Fascinated by the landscapes, produce, and people of California and Mexico, he took portraits to support his art, setting up the first of many studios in 1911. Commercially successful, in 1927 he began his studies to capture in close-ups the sensuousness of nudes and vegetables. From 1928 to 1933 he took landscape pictures of deserts, sand dunes, and beach foliage, receiving the first photographer's Guggenheim in 1937.

Wexler, Haskell (1925–) cinematographer, movie director; born in Chicago. After making industrial and educational movies for some ten years, he broke into feature films as cameraman for the semidocumentary *The Savage Eye* (1959). He went on to film a number of notable movies, culminating in *Who's Afraid of Virginia Woolf?* (1966), for which he won an Academy Award. He also branched out into writing, directing, and producing movies, most of which were documentaries that allowed him to express his own progressive political sympathies; the best known of his own films, *Medium Cool* (1969), mixed a fictional plot with documentary footage. He won another Academy Award for the cinematography of *Bound for Glory* (1976).

Wexler, Jacqueline (b. Grennan) (1926–) college president; born in Sterling, Ill. Raised on a farm, she became a Roman Catholic nun and a college administrator. While president of the Roman Catholic Webster College (Mo.) (1965–69), she was released from her vows and turned the governance of the college over to laypeople. She wrote *Where I Am Going* (1968). She married in 1969 and then served as president of Hunter College (New York City) (1970–79). She was noted for her fund raising skills.

Wexler, Jerry (1917–) record producer; born in New York City. An aficionado of the black music that he heard in New York jazz clubs in the 1930s, he served in the U.S. Navy during World War II and worked for BMI and the publishing division of MGM between the late 1940s and early 1950s. Between 1948 and 1951, he wrote a column for *Billboard* in which he reported on black popular music and coined the term "rhythm-and-blues." In 1953, he became a co-owner of Atlantic Records, the most important mainstream record label to give exposure to black music in the 1950s and 1960s. During the 1950s he produced seminal, gospel-influenced recordings by Ray Charles, the Clovers, and Lavern Baker, and in the 1960s his work with Otis Redding, Aretha Franklin, and Wilson Pickett helped establish the soul music idiom. In the 1970s he promoted the careers of Dr. John, Dusty Springfield, and José Feliciano. After the sale of Atlantic in 1978, he joined Warner Brothers as an executive vice-president and continued to produce recordings until his retirement in 1982. His autobiography, *The Rhythm and the Blues,* was published in 1993.

Wexner, Leslie (Herbert) (1937–) entrepreneur; born in Dayton, Ohio. He worked briefly for his father's Ohio clothing store before opening his own Columbus sportswear store, The Limited (1963). The company went public six years later and rapidly became one of the country's largest women's sportswear retailers through innovative merchandising and the acquisition of such chains as Lane Bryant and Victoria's Secret.

Weyerhaeuser, Frederick E. (Edward) (1872–1945) lumberman, financier; born in Rock Island, Ill. Born into an extended family of lumberjacks and sawmill operators, his father Frederick Weyerhaeuser had formed scores of joint ventures involving timberland and sawmill operations throughout the Pacific northwest and along the Mississippi in Louisiana and Arkansas. After Yale, and a four-year apprenticeship, son Frederick became president of Southern Lumber Company in Arkansas (1900). At his father's office in St. Paul (1903), he managed finances and founded the Weyerhaeuser Sales Company to market lumber from competing, yet associated, mills (1916). He held various directorships and served as treasurer (1906–28) and president (1928–45) of the Weyerhaeuser Timber Company. A Presbyterian, he actively supported the Union Gospel Mission and the Young Men's Christian Association.

Weyerhaeuser, George (Hunt) (1926–) lumber executive; born in Seattle, Wash. A Yale graduate, he joined Tacoma-based Weyerhaeuser Company, the family business, in 1949, working as a mill foreman and branch manager before joining the executive ranks in 1957. Variously president, CEO, and chairman (1966), he rejuvenated the company through restructuring, expansion, diversification, and aggressive marketing.

Whalen, Grover (Michael Aloysius) (1886–1962) promoter, merchant, public official; born in New York City. His long business career included positions at John Wanamaker (1914–34), Schenley, and Coty. As the city's official greeter (1919–53), he originated ticker tape parades in staging welcoming ceremonies for, among others, Charles Lindbergh, the Prince of Wales, and returning soldiers from both world wars. He was a member of the New York-New Jersey Bridge-Tunnel Commission (1919–23); chairman of New York City's Board of Purchasing (1919–24); police commissioner (1928–29); and president of the group that organized the New York World's Fair of 1939–40.

Wharton, Edith (Newbold b. Jones) (1862–1937) writer; born in New York City. Raised in a wealthy "old" family, she was privately educated and traveled often in Europe, where she met her lifelong friend and mentor, Henry James. She married a Boston banker, Edward Robbins Wharton, in 1885 and they divided their time among homes in New York City, Newport, R.I., Lenox, Mass., and Europe. Her husband was ten years older than she and gradually deteriorated from a mental illness, so she devoted herself to her early passion for writing (she had privately printed a volume of her poems in 1878). Her first book was *The Decoration of Houses* (coauthored with Ogden Codman Jr., 1897), literally about interior decoration but also prefiguring her concern with the social mores of her class. Her first novel was *The Valley of Decision* (1902), but her first popular novel was *The House of Mirth* (1905). Her next popular work – and still a minor classic – was *Ethan Frome* (1911). By 1907 she had effectively settled in France; she divorced Wharton in 1913 and during World War I she was active in relief work in France; she also traveled extensively – eventually writing about her travels in Italy and Morocco – over her lifetime she was friendly with many of the most notable men of the time, from Bernard Berenson to Theodore Roosevelt. Perhaps her most admired collection of short fiction, *Xingu and Other Stories,* was published in 1916; her *Age of Innocence* (1920) won the Pulitzer Prize, the first in fiction awarded to a woman. She continued to publish both short fiction and novels; in 1925 she published her thoughts on literature, *The Writing of Fiction* (1925), and in 1934 her autobiography, *A Backward Glance.* She was noted for her polished prose and for her ability to capture the psychological realities of her characters; as for her themes, she attacked the hypocrisies and rigidities of the old society she came from, but she also had little liking for the new monied class she saw emerging around her.

Wharton, Samuel (1732–1800) merchant, land speculator; born in Philadelphia. A prominent merchant by 1763, he was a central figure in three attempts to gain large land grants west of the Alleghenies: the Grand Illinois Venture (1764–72), Indiana Grant (1768–69), and Vandalia (1770–75). None of the projects were ultimately successful; the start of the American Revolution in 1775 wrecked the Vandalia scheme. Wharton served in the Continental Congress (1782–83) and was a justice of the court of common pleas in Southwark, Pa. (1790–91).

Wharton, William H. (1802–39) Texas Revolution leader; born in Albemarle County, Va. Marrying into the wealthy Groce family of Texas, he and his wife turned their plantation on "Eagle Island" into a meeting ground for those who molded the future state. Pushed out by Stephen Austin for leadership of the colonization forces (1832), he was president of the convention (1833) that wrote a preliminary Texas constitution. He was named judge-advocate of the separatist army (1835), but resigned and went east to promote Texas's revolution (1835–36). Santa Anna was captured in his absence and the revolution nearly complete, but he tried to negotiate Texas's inclusion into the United States (1836–37); he did not live to see annexation completed.

Whatmough, Joshua (1897–1964) linguist; born in Rochdale, Lancashire, England. He was educated in England at the Universities of Manchester and Cambridge before becoming chairman of the department of comparative philology (1926–51) and a member of the linguistics department (1951–63) at Harvard. He was an influential editor of *Harvard Studies in Classical Philology* (1932–34; 1941–48) whose many publications included *Foundations of Roman Italy* (1937) and *Dialects of Ancient Gaul* (1970).

Wheatley, Phillis (c. 1753–84) poet; born in Africa, possibly Senegal. She was sold in slavery to the John Wheatley family in Boston (1761), was educated by them – even learning Latin and Greek – and by the age of 13 was composing poems so sophisticated that many people charged she could not have written them. Sent to London with the Wheatley's son (1778), she was received in society, published her first volume of poems, then returned to Boston. She was freed, married, and had three children, none of whom survived her. A collection of her poetry and prose, *Memoirs and Poems of Phillis Wheatley,* was printed in 1834. Although her poems are now regarded as generally derivative in their neoclassical manner, they were often cited in the 19th century by those pointing out that African-Americans needed only to be educated in order to become the equal of their fellow Americans.

Wheaton, Henry (1785–1848) lawyer, diplomat; born in Providence, R.I. A graduate of Rhode Island College (now Brown), he practiced in Providence before moving to New York City (1812), where he edited the *National Advocate,* a Jeffersonian journal, and was a Marine Court justice (1815–19). As reporter for the U.S. Supreme Court (1816–28), he published two volumes of highly regarded reports that bear his name. He was U.S. chargé d'affaires in Denmark (1827–35) and ambassador to Prussia (1835–46), and in both posts he negotiated important treaties. Among his several legal works, *Elements of International Law* (1836) had the greatest impact on his contemporaries.

Wheeler, Anna Pell (b. Johnson) (1883–1966) mathematician; born in Hawarden, Iowa. The first female mathematician to address the American Mathematical Society, she fostered women's participation in mathematics. Teaching longest at Bryn Mawr (1918–48) where she also chaired the mathematics department, she specialized in integral equations. She was also an avid bird watcher and wildflower enthusiast.

Wheeler, Benjamin (Ide) (1854–1927) university president; born in Randolph, Mass. A University of Heidelberg Ph.D., he was a professor of Greek and comparative philology. As president of the University of California (1899–1919), he guided extensive expansion, adding 20 departments, attracting an internationally renowned faculty, and strengthening graduate divisions and research activities.

Wheeler, Burton K. (Kendall) (1882–1975) U.S. senator; born in Hudson, Mass. After taking a law degree from the University of Michigan (1905), he began to practice law in Butte, Montana (1906–11). He was federal district attorney for Montana (1913–18). Elected to the U.S. Senate (Dem., Mont.; 1934–47), he was an outspoken progressive in the 1920s and helped expose the scandals of the Harding administration. He grew more conservative in the 1930s, leading the fight against President Franklin Roosevelt's "court packing" plan in 1937 and against American intervention in World War II. After losing the election of 1946, he returned to private law practice in Montana.

Wheeler, Candace (1827–1923) designer; born in Delhi, N.Y. Founder of the Society of Decorative Art (1877), she designed textiles and wallpaper for the decorative collaborative, Associated Artists, which she headed from 1893 to 1907.

Wheeler, Joseph (1836–1906) Confederate soldier; born in Augusta, Ga. Wheeler's cavalry was practically the sole organized Confederate force that contested Sherman's March to the Sea (1864). He represented Alabama in Congress (1884–1900); appointed to command a volunteer division in 1898, he saw action against the Spanish in Cuba.

Wheeler, Ruth (1877–1948) physiological chemist; born in Plains, Pa. She taught high school science before earning a Ph.D. at Yale and becoming a professor of chemistry, nutrition, and physiology at Vassar (1926–44). She headed the American Red Cross nutrition service (1917–32) and wrote the *American Red Cross Textbook on Food and Nutrition* (1927).

Wheeler, Wayne Bidwell (1869–1927) lawyer, activist; born in Trumbull County, Ohio. He graduated from Oberlin College in 1895 and became a lawyer as a means of working for prohibition through the Anti-Saloon League. Deeply involved all his life in league activities in Ohio and the nation, he became a powerful lobbyist for prohibition. By 1920, when national prohibition went into effect, he and his allies already had campaigned successfully for restrictive liquor legislation in 33 states.

Wheeler, William (Almon) (1819–87) vice-president, businessman; born in Malone, N.Y. Following an impoverished youth, he became a lawyer and businessman. Known as a scrupulously honest congressman, he was elected vice-president under Rutherford B. Hayes (1877–81) but displayed little enthusiasm for the office.

Wheeler, William Morton (1865–1937) zoologist, entomologist; born in Milwaukee, Wis. He was curator of the Milwaukee Public Museum (1887–90), taught morphology and embryology at Clark University (Mass.) (1890–93), then studied for a year in Europe before becoming an assistant professor at the University of Chicago (1894–99). At the University of Texas (1890–1903), he began the work on ants that engaged him for the rest of his life; he was the principal authority on ants and social insects at his death. As curator of invertebrate zoology at the American Museum of Natural History (1903–08), he designed the Hall of the Biology of Invertebrates. He was professor of entomology at Harvard (1908–34) and dean of Harvard's Bussy Institute for Research in Applied Biology (1915–29). He authored over 450 scientific publications, mostly on ants, although he did extend his theories to include other social animals, including humans.

Wheelock, Eleazar (1711–79) college president; born in Windham, Conn. A Congregational minister, he founded Moor's Indian Charity School in Lebanon, Conn. (1754), moving the school to Hanover, N.H., in 1770 and reestablishing it as Dartmouth College; he was president until his death. He wrote a *Narrative of the Indian School at Lebanon* (1762–75).

Wheelock, Lucy (1857–1946) educator; born in Cambridge, Vt. She was a leader in the kindergarten movement. Herself a kindergarten teacher, she was founding director (1896–1939) of Wheelock School (later College), where she developed a three-year kindergarten teacher-training course incorporating current educational theories.

Wheelwright, John Brooks (1897–1940) poet; born near Boston (descendant of John Wheelwright, 1592–1679). He

attended Harvard and studied architecture at the Massachusetts Institute of Technology. He was known as a radical socialist in Boston, and wrote poetry accompanied by his own prose interpretations. He privately printed three volumes of his poems. *The Collected Poems of John Wheelwright* (1972) was published posthumously.

Wherry, Kenneth (Spicer) (1892–1951) U.S. senator; born in Liberty, Nebr. Active in state politics, he was elected to the U.S. Senate (Rep., Nebr.; 1943–51). A thorough conservative and isolationist, he served as Republican floor leader (1947–51).

Whipple, Fred Lawrence (1906–) astronomer; born in Red Oak, Iowa. Educated at California University, he spent most of his career teaching at Harvard (1945). He wrote the standard *Earth, Moon and Planets* (1941). His 1950 theory that comets are like dirty snowballs in composition and behavior was not questioned until the 1990s. He brought the Smithsonian Astrophysical Observatory to Cambridge (1955).

Whipple, George H. (Hoyt) (1878–1976) pathologist; born in Ashland, N.H. He taught and performed research at Johns Hopkins (1905–07), served as a pathologist at Ancon Hospital, Panama (1907–08), then returned to Johns Hopkins (1909–14). He moved to the University of California: Berkeley (1914–21), then joined the University of Rochester (1921–55), where he became the first dean of the Rochester School of Medicine and Dentistry (1921–53), bringing that institution into scientific prominence. He shared the 1934 Nobel Prize in physiology for his research (1918–25) that resulted in his proposal that dietary liver be used for treatment of pernicious anemia. He made major advances in investigations of protein metabolism in humans, in addition to studies of tuberculosis, pancreatitis, malaria, and the rare intestinal lipid disorder now known as Whipple's disease.

Whipple, Henry Benjamin (1822–1901) Episcopal bishop, Indian advocate; born in Adams, N.Y. Ordained in 1850 after a brief career as a merchant, he held rectorships in New York, Florida, and Illinois before becoming Episcopal bishop of Minnesota in 1859. He established missions among the Indians, who called him Straight Tongue, and spoke out for more civilized treatment of the tribes. After the 1862 uprising of the Minnesota Sioux, he convinced President Lincoln to commute death sentences of more than 300 (but 38 Sioux were hanged). In his last years he was presiding bishop of the American Episcopal Church.

Whipple, Squire (1804–88) civil engineer; born in Hardwick, Mass. He worked on canals and railroads until 1841 and devised several new apparatuses. In 1840 he devised an apparatus for weighing canal boats and later a weighing lock scale. In 1841 he patented the bowstring iron truss bridge, then the Whipple trapezoidal bridge. Beyond his actual structures, he made his major contribution with *A Work on Bridge Building* (1847), a pioneer work of scientific engineering with its method for computing stress.

Whistler, George (Washington) (1800–49) soldier, engineer; born in Fort Wayne, Ind. At the United States Military Academy at age 14, he distinguished himself as a draftsman. After graduating he assisted in various topographical projects and helped in the location of several railroads, including the Baltimore & Ohio. He resigned from the army to become the engineer to the Proprietors of Locks and Canals at Lowell, Mass. (1833–37). From 1840–42, as chief engineer of the Western Railroad, he located a difficult section of track through the Berkshire Mountains in Massachusetts. This feat attracted the attention of Tsar Nicholas I who hired him to be consulting engineer for a railroad between St. Petersburg and Moscow. He began in 1842, received the decoration of the Order of St. Anne in 1847, and died of Asiatic cholera before he could finish the project. His son, George William Whistler, continued his father's work in Russia until his death in 1869. His other son, James A. M. Whistler returned to the U.S.A. and went on to become the famed painter.

Whistler, James Abbott McNeil (1834–1903) painter, etcher; born in Lowell, Mass. Son of an engineer who was employed by the Czar, after his father's death in St. Petersburg, Russia (1849), he returned to America and attended West Point (1851–54) but failed academically. He moved to Paris (1855–59), then to London where he spent most of the rest of his life. (He never did return to the U.S.A.) By 1862 he was showing his *White Girl*, a portrait of his mistress, Joanna Heffernan, the first of many controversial works that increasingly depended on subjective coloring and spatial relationships and which he called "symphonies" or "nocturnes"; the most famous of these was *Arrangement in Grey and Black No. 1* (1871), more familiar to millions as "Whistler's Mother." In addition to his many oils, watercolors, and pastels, he did several fine series of etchings: *The French Set* (1858–59); *The Thames Set* (1859–71); *The Venice Set* (1880, 1886). He painted the interior of the exotic Peacock Room for the London home of F. R. Leyland (1876–77). After the noted British critic John Ruskin cast aspersions on his art and character, Whistler sued for libel; he won the case for a farthing but was left bankrupt; he made some money from his book about the trial, *The Gentle Art of Making Enemies* (1890). His flamboyant and acerbic manner often distracted from the genuine artistry behind his work, but in later years the latter has come to be recognized.

Whitcomb, Richard (Travis) (1921–) aeronautical engineer; born in Evanston, Ill. While associated with the Langley Aeronautical Laboratory (1943–58) he vastly improved American supersonic aircraft with development of his "wasp-waist" plane that allowed for a minimum of drag in the transonic speed range. Heading the National Aeronautics and Space Administration's Transonic Aerodynamics Board (1958–80), he became a research associate at Langley (1980).

White, Andrew (1579–1656) missionary; born in London, England. A Jesuit theology professor who came under fire for political activities and for his rigidly Thomistic philosophy, he went to Maryland (1634) as head of a band of Jesuit missionaries and evangelized among the Indians, also writing an Algonquin grammar and catechism. He was expelled by Puritans and sent back in chains to England (1645), where he was forced to remain.

White, Andrew Dickson (1832–1918) university president, diplomat, historian; born in Homer, N.Y. A historian of Europe, he planned and was the first president of Cornell University (1867–85), where his innovations included integrating natural sciences and technical arts and recruiting eminent "nonresident professors." Later a U.S. diplomat posted to Germany and Russia, he was president of the International Peace Conference at the Hague (1899).

White, Bailey (June) (1950–) writer; born in Thomasville, Ga. She studied at Florida State University (B.A. 1973), taught first grade in Thomasville, and lived in the same house where she was born. Beginning in 1990 she was a commentator for National Public Radio's *All Things Considered*. A popular essayist and storyteller, she has received critical praise for her humorous writings in *Mama Makes Up Her Mind, and Other Dangers of Southern Living* (1993).

White, Byron (Raymond) ("Whizzer") (1917–) Supreme Court justice; born in Fort Collins, Colo. After an All-American football career at the University of Colorado, he played professional football for one season (1938) with the Pittsburgh Pirates (now Steelers) before going to Oxford as a Rhodes Scholar; he returned to the U.S.A. to attend Yale Law School (1940) and he played two seasons with the Detroit Lions before serving with the U.S. Navy in World War II. He practiced law in Colorado before his old friend John F. Kennedy named him deputy U.S. attorney general (1961–62) and then appointed him to the U.S. Supreme Court (1962). Despite his adventurous past, he turned out to be fairly conservative in his legal opinions. He retired from the Court in 1993.

White, Canvass (1790–1834) civil engineer; born in Whitesboro, N.Y. In 1816 he became an assistant to Benjamin Wright, chief engineer of the Erie Canal. In 1817–18 he was sent to England to study construction methods, and on his return he surveyed improved routes for the canal. He also developed a high-quality cement, patented in 1820, and he worked on other canals and water projects.

White, Clarence Hudson (1871–1925) photographer, teacher; born in West Carlisle, Ohio. A groceryman, in 1906 he came to New York where he was a colleague of Alfred Stieglitz and later opened his own school of photography (1914–25).

White, E. B. (Elwyn Brooks) (1899–1985) writer, editor; born in Mount Vernon, N.Y. He attended Cornell University (1917–21), worked as a reporter on the *Seattle Times* (1922–23), then settled in New York City as an advertising copywriter (1924–25). From 1926 on he was a contributing editor of the *New Yorker* magazine, and became known for his impeccable prose style and his personal and ironic essays. Married to *New Yorker* fiction editor, Katherine White (1929), he moved with her to North Brooklin, Maine (1938), writing a column for *Harper's* magazine, "One Man's Meat" (1938–43), and numerous pieces for the *New Yorker*. He wrote children's classics, such as *Stuart Little* (1945), *Charlotte's Web* (1952), and *The Trumpet of the Swan* (1970). He also published books of poetry, essays, and a revision of a grammar and composition text originally written by William Strunk, Jr., *The Elements of Style* (1959).

White, Edmund (Valentine, III) (1940–) writer; born in Cincinnati, Ohio. He studied at the University of Michigan (B.A. 1962), before settling in New York City and becoming an editor (1962–73). He also taught at Johns Hopkins (1977–79) and Columbia University (1981–83), among other institutions. He is best known for his novels that deal explicitly with homosexual themes, such as *A Boy's Own Story* (1982), and for his nonfiction, notably *States of Desire: Travels in Gay America* (1980).

White, Edna Noble (1879–1954) home economist, educator; born in Fairmount, Ill. She was recruited from the Ohio State University faculty to direct the Merrill-Palmer Institute, Detroit (1919–47), where she pioneered interdisciplinary child development research and originated longitudinal studies and the study of families. Its laboratory nursery school made important contributions to the parent education movement.

White, Edward Douglass (1845–1921) Supreme Court justice/chief justice; born in Lafourche Parish, La. He was active in Louisiana politics and helped found Tulane University. He served one term in the U.S. Senate (Dem., La.; 1891) before his nomination by President Cleveland to the U.S. Supreme Court (1894–1910); President Taft appointed him chief justice (1910–21).

White, Ellen Gould (b. Harmon) (1827–1915) religious leader; born in Gorham, Mo. A fragile, nervous child, she was tutored at home but had no formal education. She converted to Adventism after hearing William Miller preach (1842); when the Second Coming of Christ failed to take place as predicted, in 1844 the Millerites faded, but she almost singlehandedly – and then with her husband James White (1821–81) – kept the Adventist movement alive by traveling and preaching. During her life she claimed to have experienced 2,000 visions and prophetic dreams. She became head of the Seventh Day Adventist Church when it was formally established in 1863, and one of her religious books, *Steps to Christ,* has by now sold more than 20 million copies. Settling in Battle Creek, Mich. (1855), she also grew dedicated to a healthy diet and hydrotherapy, and in 1861 helped open the Western Health Reform Institute there. She helped found Battle Creek College (1874), the first U.S. Adventist educational institution, and in 1904 cofounded the College of Medical Evangelists in California. From 1891 to 1900 she lived in Australia as a missionary.

White, Gilbert (Fowler) (1911–   ) geographer, educator; born in Chicago. A graduate of the University of Chicago, he researched flood problems for President Franklin Roosevelt's administration (1934–42). As a conscientious objector, he served during World War II with the Friends Service Society. He was president of Haverford College (1946–55) and then went on to teach geography at the University of Chicago (1955–69). He left there (1970) to direct the Institute of Behavioral Science (Boulder, Colo.), where he concentrated on exploring behavioral responses to potential natural hazards like floods and fires. Among his numerous published works are *Human Adjustment to Floods* (1942), *Science and the Future of Arid Lands* (1960), and *Strategies of American Water Management* (1969).

White, Henry (1850–1927) diplomat; born in Baltimore, Md. The heir to a distillery fortune, he was well-received in London society. He was a secretary in the U.S. embassy in London (1883–93, 1897–1905) and ambassador to Italy (1905–07) and France (1907–09). He was an influential member of the Peace Commission at the end of World War I, accompanied President Wilson to the Paris Peace Conference (1919), and tried to get the U.S.A. to join the League of Nations.

White, John (fl. 1585–93) painter, cartographer, colonial governor; born in England. Nothing is known of him until he sailed with Sir Martin Frobisher's second expedition to Baffin Island (1577). In 1585 he was sent by Sir Walter Raleigh to Roanoke Island (now in North Carolina) as artist and mapmaker; he came back with a set of watercolors that remain the primary source for the study of the flora, fauna, and indigenous inhabitants of this part of North America. It is now generally accepted that he was the John White sent as governor on the second expedition to Roanoke (1587); it was this White's daughter who gave birth to Virginia Dare, the first British child born in the New World. After going to England for more support (1587), he returned (1590) to find the colony had totally vanished. He sailed back and reportedly lived in Newtowne in Kylmore, Ireland, by 1593.

White, Joseph M. (1781–1839) lawyer, U.S. representative; born in Franklin County, Ky. Knowledge of French and Spanish gained him clients in Pensacola, and he represented Floridians in the U.S. House of Representatives (Dem., 1825–37). An eloquent speaker, he also published *New Collection of Laws, Charters, etc., of Great Britain, France, and Spain* (1839).

White, (Joshua Daniel) Josh (1915–69) blues/gospel/folk singer, guitarist; born in Greenville, S.C. As a child he learned from street singers in the southeast and Chicago; he soon joined in with street evangelists and gospel singers and became a prodigious guitarist. At age 13 he recorded with Blind Joe Taggart. In the 1930s he recorded such blues and gospel songs as "There's a Man Goin' Around Taking Names" (1933). In 1939 he formed his own group, the Josh White Singers. A favorite of President Franklin Roosevelt, he performed at the White House. In New York City in the 1940s he appeared in several musicals such as *John Henry* (1940) and *A Long Way from Home* (1948). In the 1950s he performed with his group, the Carolinas, and with such artists as Woody Guthrie and Paul Robeson. In moving between gospel/blues and folk music and between the white and black worlds, he prefigured a whole generation of other African-American musicians.

White, Leonard D. (Dupee) (1891–1958) political scientist, historian; born in Acton, Mass. He pioneered higher education in public administration at the University of Chicago (1920–56), himself writing a standard introductory text (1926, several times revised). As U.S. Civil Service Commissioner (1934–37), he developed civil service examinations and training for university graduates. His books include four volumes of history of American public administration (1948–58).

White, Leslie A. (Alvin) (1900–75) social anthropologist; born in Salida, Colo. He studied at Columbia University, the New School for Social Research, and the University of Chicago, and he taught at the University of Michigan for more than 30 years. He carried out extensive fieldwork among the Pueblo Indians from 1926 to 1957. In his book *The Science of Culture* (1949), and other works, he propounded a theory of cultural evolution – in particular, that culture advances as technological efficiency in using environmental energy sources increases. Although not immediately adopted, White's theory came to be one of the more influential attempts at explaining early New World societies.

White, Lynn (Townsend), Jr. (1907–87) historian, college president; born in San Francisco, Calif. An internationally known medieval scholar specializing in medieval technology and the religious background of industrialism, he attended Stanford University (B.A. 1928), Union Theological Seminary (M.A. 1929) and Harvard (M.A. 1930; Ph.D. 1934). He taught at Princeton and Stanford (1933–43), was president of Mills College (1943–58), then taught at the University of California: Los Angeles (1958–74). His books include

Medieval Technology and Social Change (1962) and *Medieval Religion and Technology* (1978).

White, Minor (1908–76) teacher, editor; born in Minneapolis, Minn. His career began slowly with part-time teaching jobs (1937–41) until he came to Columbia University to study art and aesthetics in 1945. Hired as photographer for the Museum of Modern Art, he founded *Aperture* magazine in 1952 and began lecturing on how to "read" a photograph. He taught at the George Eastman House (1952–57) and at Rochester Institute of Technology (1955–64).

White, Paul Dudley (1886–1973) cardiologist; born in Boston, Mass. Regarded as one of the world's premier authorities on heart disease, he preached the preventive value of diet, exercise, and weight control. He was the first American to make wide use of electrocardiograms (1914) and wrote the standard text, *Heart Disease* (1931). He was affiliated with Massachusetts General Hospital (1911–73) while serving on many committees and foreign missions.

White, Pearl (Fay) (1889–1938) movie actress; born in Green Ridge, Mo. She began as a child actress and with her earnings bought a horse; by age 13 she rode well enough to join a circus as an equestrienne; an accident forced her to quit the circus so she returned to acting. Working as a secretary for a film company, she was signed to replace a lead in a Western, *The Life of Buffalo Bill* (1910). She appeared in dozens of movies, mostly short features, and then in 1914 commenced the series that she became most famous for, *The Perils of Pauline*. These and other "cliffhangers" (in which she did many of her own stunts) made her one of Hollywood's most popular actresses. In 1920 she tried more serious roles, but was not very successful; in 1924, having made what proved to be her last movie in France, she retired there for the rest of her life.

White, Peregrine (1620–1703) colonist; born on the *Mayflower* in Cape Cod Bay. His parents were William and Susanna White. He was the first English child born in New England (another child, Oceanus Hopkins, had been born at sea). He became a captain of militia and settled in Marshfield, Mass.

White, Robert M. (1923–) meteorologist; born in Boston, Mass. (brother of Theodore White). As chief of the U.S. Weather Bureau (1963–65), he supported advances in the weather warning system through the use of satellites and computers. He led efforts to save the whales as U.S. Commissioner of the International Whaling Commission (1973–77) and became president of the National Academy of Engineering in 1983.

White, Stanford (1853–1906) architect; born in New York (son of Richard Grant White). A self-taught artist, he apprenticed with H. H. Richardson. During his partnership in McKim, Mead and White (1879–1906), the firm became the largest architectural office in the world. White was a prolific designer of furniture, interiors, jewelry, and even magazine covers; his graceful decorations complemented McKim's classical forms. He designed the first Madison Square Garden, Washington Arch, and the Metropolitan Club (all in New York City). A bon vivant, his relationship with Evelyn Nesbit (beginning when she was fourteen years old), who subsequently married Harry K. Thaw, fueled Thaw's jealousy of White's eminence and panache, and Thaw shot Stanford White to death on the rooftop of Madison Square Garden in June 1906.

White, Thomas (Dresser) (1901–65) aviator; born in Walker, Minn. He graduated from West Point in 1920, completed aviation training in 1925, and carried out a series of staff and line assignments, including tours as air attaché in the Soviet Union, Italy, and Brazil. As deputy commander of the Thirteenth Air Force, he took part in the reconquest of the Philippines (1944); he commanded the Seventh Air Force during the Iwo Jima and Okinawa campaigns. He served as air force chief of staff during the late 1950s, a period of intensive development of missile-borne strategic weapons systems.

White, Tim (Timothy) Douglas (1950–) physical anthropologist; born in Los Angeles, Calif. A professor at the University of California: Berkeley (1970), his excavation of protohominid footprints in Tanzania (1978) led to his codiscovery (with D. C. Johanson) of "Lucy," the earliest human ancestor (*Australopithecus afarensis*) (1978–79).

White, Wallace H. (Humphrey), Jr. (1877–1952) U.S. senator; born in Lewiston, Maine. He served in the U.S. House of Representatives (Rep., Maine; 1917–31). Elected to the U.S. Senate (1931–49), he was minority leader (1944–47) and majority leader (1947–49).

White, Walter (Francis) (1893–1955) civil rights leader, author; born in Atlanta, Ga. Fair-skinned, blond, and blue-eyed although part black, he could pass for white but chose to champion the cause of the black race after experiencing a race riot in Atlanta, Ga. (1906). (In 1926 he published his novel *Flight*, based on his experiences of "passing.") As an insurance company cashier, he took the lead in establishing a branch of the National Association for the Advancement of Colored People (NAACP) in Atlanta (1916). He was named assistant secretary of the NAACP (1918–31) and NAACP executive secretary (1931–55). One of the most ardent antilynching proponents in America, he investigated more than 40 lynchings and eight race riots. As a Guggenheim Fellow he conducted a study of lynching in the United States, the basis of his *Rope and Faggot: A Biography of Judge Lynch* (1929). He became acting secretary of the NAACP the same year and continued to promote his antilynching efforts, along with launching campaigns against segregation in public facilities, white primaries, and the poll taxes, and against educational discrimination. Author of several other books and numerous articles, he was awarded the Spingarn Medal (1937) in recognitioon of his efforts on behalf of African-Americans. Because of his efforts and those of A. Philip Randolph, President Franklin Roosevelt prohibited discrimination in the defense industries and established the Fair Employment Practices Commission (1941). Journalistic research he conducted in Europe, published as *A Rising Wind* (1945), influenced President Harry Truman's decision to desegregate the armed forces. In 1946 he pressured President Truman to set up the President's Committee on Civil Rights, and this led the Democrats to adopt the divisive civil rights platform in 1948. Also concerned with worldwide prejudice, he was less successful on this front and was criticized as an autocrat inside the NAACP. Although he retained his post until his death, from 1949 on his powers were limited.

White, William Allen (1868–1944) journalist, author; born in Emporia, Kans. He quit college to become business manager of the *El Dorado Republican* and, later, an editorial writer for the *Kansas City Star*. In 1895, borrowing $3,000, he bought the small, rural *Emporia Gazette,* which he published and edited for the rest of his life, besides contributing articles and short stories to many other publications. His 1896 editorial attacking populism was widely circulated by Republicans during that year's presidential campaign and made him famous; he came to be regarded as an independent-minded, commonsensical spokesman for small-town America. A 1921 essay on his daughter's death in a riding accident became a classic, and a 1922 editorial supporting striking railroad workers brought him a Pulitzer Prize. He also wrote novels and biographies of Woodrow Wilson (1921) and Calvin Coolidge (1925, 1938). His autobiography, published in 1946, won a posthumous Pulitzer Prize.

White (William DeKova) Bill (1934–) baseball player, sportscaster, baseball executive; born in Lakewood, Fla. He attended college on an academic (not athletic) scholarship. After a 13-year career as a first baseman (1956–69), mostly for the St. Louis Cardinals, he was a television sportscaster (1971–88) and then baseball's first African-American league president – of the National League – (1988–93).

White, William S. (Smith) (1906–) journalist; born in De Leon, Texas. After working for the Associated Press for almost 20 years, he became a Washington reporter for the *New York Times* (1945–58). His biography of Senator Robert Taft won a 1955 Pulitzer Prize.

Whitefield, George (1714–70) Protestant evangelist; born in Gloucester, England. An innkeeper's son, he entered Oxford in 1732, came under the influence of John Wesley, and turned to evangelism after an intense religious experience in 1735. A powerful preacher, he ran afoul of English ecclesiastical authorities and sailed for Georgia, U.S.A., in 1737 to assist the Wesleys in their mission there. In that and subsequent visits he helped touch off the Great Awakening religious revival. He continued to evangelize in England and America until his death, which came at Newburyport, Mass., while he was on a preaching tour.

Whitehead, John Cunningham (1922–) investment executive; born in Evanston, Ill. Son of a telephone lineman, educated at Haverford College and Harvard, he joined Goldman, Sachs & Co. in 1947, became a partner in 1956, and was senior partner and co-chairman from 1976–84. He served as a deputy secretary of state in the Reagan Administration (1985–89) before returning to the private sector as chairman of AEA Investors, Inc. (New York City).

Whitehead, Wilbur C. (Cherrier) (1866–1931) bridge authority; born in Cleveland, Ohio. President of the Simplex Automobile Company, he turned to bridge in 1910 and played on the 1928 Vanderbilt Cup winners. He helped popularize bridge by competing in games described on radio and invented many standard conventions of bidding and play.

Whiteman, Paul (1890–1967) bandleader; born in Denver, Colo. He was a violinist in the Denver Symphony Orchestra between 1912 and 1915 and the San Francisco Symphony Orchestra until 1918. After brief service in the U.S. Navy during World War I, he became the leader of the orchestra at the Fairmont Hotel in San Francisco in 1919. He moved this band to engagements in Atlantic City and New York in 1920, toured with it in Europe in 1923, made numerous recordings, and was credited with raising the standards for popular orchestras. He gained wide renown as the conductor of the 1924 premiere of *Rhapsody in Blue,* one of George

Gershwin's experiments in "symphonic jazz" that Whiteman commissioned. He was promoted thereafter as the "king of jazz," though he is best known in jazz circles as the employer of several influential musicians, including Bix Beiderbecke, Jack Teagarden, and the Dorsey brothers. He led his orchestra throughout the mid-1940s, then worked as the music director of ABC in New York until his retirement.

Whiting, Arthur Battelle (1861–1936) pianist, composer; born in Cambridge, Mass. Trained in Boston and Munich, he played chamber music widely and was an American pioneer of the original-instrument movement.

Whiting, John W. M. (1908–) sociologist, psychologist; born in Chilmark, Martha's Vineyard, Mass. Educated at Yale (B.A. 1931; Ph.D. 1938), he worked as a researcher for Yale's Institute of Human Relations from 1938–47, using anthropological and psychoanalytical perspectives to inform his work on child development and socialization. Later associated with Harvard, he also directed the Child Development Research Unit of the University of Nairobi (1966–73). He published *Child Training and Personality* in 1953.

Whitlock, Brand (1869–1934) mayor, author, diplomat; born in Urbana, Ohio. A journalist and lawyer, he served four terms as mayor of Toledo (1906–14), running on a nonpartisan reform platform and keeping the government free of graft. He was much honored for his service as American minister, later ambassador to Belgium, during and after World War I. He wrote 18 books, both fiction and nonfiction.

Whitman, C. O. (Charles Otis) (1842–1910) zoologist; born in Woodstock, Maine. He was a professor at the Imperial University of Japan (1880–81), where his four students became their country's pioneers in zoology. He performed research at the Naples Zoology Station (1882), became an assistant at the Museum of Comparative Zoology, Harvard (1883–85), then directed the Allis Lake Laboratory, Milwaukee (1886–89), where he founded the *Journal of Morphology* (1887). He moved to Clark University (Worcester, Mass.) (1889–92), then became a professor and curator of the Zoological Museum at the University of Chicago (1892–1910), while concurrently serving as director of the Marine Biology Laboratory, Woods Hole (Mass.), from its founding in 1888 until 1908. A dedicated educator who preferred to teach a few research students at a time, he made major contributions in the areas of evolution and embryology of worms, comparative anatomy, heredity, and animal behavior.

Whitman, Cedric (Hubbell) (1916–79) classicist, poet; born in Providence, R.I. After taking his B.A. (1943) and Ph.D. (1947) at Harvard, he joined the faculty, serving as Eliot Professor of Greek Literature from 1974 until his death in 1979. His *Sophocles: A Study in Heroic Humanism* (1951) won the Award of Merit of the American Philological Association (1952); *Homer and the Heroic Tradition* (1958) won the Christian Gauss Prize given by Phi Beta Kappa to the best book published that year and was one of the postwar era's most influential books of literary criticism on Homer.

Whitman, Marcus (1802–47) physician, missionary; born in Rushville, N.Y. He established a mission near present-day Walla Walla, Wash., in 1836. After returning east, he brought over 900 settlers to Washington in 1843. Following a measles epidemic in which many Indians died but most whites survived, he and his wife were killed by Cayuse Indians.

Whitman, (Walter) Walt (1819–92) poet, writer; born in West Hills, Huntington, Long Island, N.Y. He was educated in Brooklyn (1825–30) where his father, a carpenter and farmer, had moved about 1823. He left school about age 12, and after working as an office boy, at age 13 he became a printer's assistant on several papers around New York City. While exposing himself to opera and theater, he began to contribute occasional pieces to newspapers (including some of the earliest reports of baseball games); at one stage he taught in various schools on Long Island (1836–41). In 1838 he was the founder/editor of a Huntington, Long Island, newspaper, *The Long Islander.* He continued educating himself through his reading and between 1841–48 contributed to various magazines – both fiction and commentary – and worked as an editor on several newspapers in and around New York City, most especially the *Brooklyn Eagle* (1846–48); he was fired from this last post because of his outspoken antislavery views. He then journeyed to New Orleans where for three months he wrote for the *New Orleans Crescent.* On returning to Brooklyn, he continued writing for and editing various newspapers (1848–62), and occasionally helping his father build houses. Meanwhile, about 1848 he had begun writing poetry in earnest. In 1855 he gathered 12 of these relatively long poems and self-published them as *Leaves of Grass.* Its radically free-flowing style and intensely personal subject matter did not engage the public or critics – although when Ralph Waldo Emerson wrote, "I greet you at the beginning of a new career," Whitman stamped that on the cover of an enlarged second edition (1856). In December 1862 he went to Virginia to find his brother who had been wounded in a battle; he stayed in Washington, D.C., to serve as a nurse in hospitals with wounded Civil War soldiers. He obtained a job as clerk in the Department of the Interior in 1865 but was soon fired when it was discovered he was the author of *Leaves of Grass,* already regarded as scandalous because of its frank sexual allusions. (His second volume of poems, *Drum Taps* (1865), was more acceptable to the public.) He then found a job in the attorney general's office (1865–73) but when he suffered a paralytic stroke he moved to Camden, N.J. He continued to write and publish larger editions of *Leaves of Grass* (his deathbed edition appearing in 1892) and also published the second of his prose works, *Specimen Days* (1882; his first was *Democratic Vistas,* 1877). Revered by a small band as "the Good Gray Poet," he held court in Camden, his reputation actually higher in Europe. It was only in the decades after his death that Whitman came to be recognized as one of the major American creative forces.

Whitmore, Frank Clifford (1887–1947) organic chemist; born in North Attleboro, Mass. After teaching at several universities, he became affiliated with Pennsylvania State College (later University) from 1929 to 1947. There he did his most important work, on the nature of intramolecular rearrangements of organic molecules.

Whitney, Anne (1821–1915) sculptor, poet; born in Watertown, Mass. Educated by tutors, she published poetry (1847–59), studied anatomy with William Rimmer in Boston (1862–64), and opened a studio there (1871). She made several trips to Europe and Italy (1867–76) and utilized her abolitionist and suffragist beliefs in her sculptures, as in *Roma* (1869). She returned to Boston and worked until her early eighties.

Whitney, Asa (1797–1872) merchant, railroad promoter; born in North Groton, Conn. A dry goods merchant, he became head of his own firm in 1836. After suffering financial losses and the death of his wife in 1840, he traveled to China where he became very wealthy as an agent for several New York firms and envisioned the value of an American transcontinental railroad to trade with China. He devised a plan for its construction which he presented to Congress in 1844, and spent the next seven years lobbying the public through newspapers, speeches, and pamphlets, including *A Project for a Railroad to the Pacific* (1849). In 1852 he remarried and retired to his Washington estate. He died shortly after the first transcontinental railroad was completed.

Whitney, Asa (1791–1874) inventor, manufacturer; born in Townsend, Mass. A railroad superintendent and canal commissioner, he patented a locomotive steam engine in 1840. Settling in Pennsylvania, he later started a company, Asa Whitney & Sons, that became the country's largest manufacturer of train wheels.

Whitney, Eli (1765–1825) inventor, engineer; born in Westboro, Mass. Whitney showed early mechanical skill, manufacturing nails at home by age 15. Determined to get an education, he taught school to pay for his way at Yale (1789–92). Moving to Savannah, Ga., to teach, he found the post filled but he was invited to stay on the plantation belonging to Gen. Nathanael Green's widow. After learning of the problems of local cotton growers, by Spring of 1793 he had developed the cotton gin for separating cotton from its seeds, a machine that could perform the work of 50 slaves. He soon ran into patent difficulties, and although he eventually won in court (1807), he profited very little from his invention. Deciding to turn to the manufacture of rifles, in 1798 he obtained a contract from the U.S. government and opened a factory near New Haven, Conn.; it was the manufacturing of firearms that led to his considerable fortune. And although now popularly associated with the cotton gin, he is actually more important for inventing machines that produced interchangeable gun parts, the basis for his reputation as the originator of mass production.

Whitney, Gertrude Vanderbilt (1875–1942) sculptor, art patron; born in New York City. She studied with tutors and with various sculptors. Married to Henry Payne Whitney (1896), she established and ran a hospital in France during World War I. She lived in Greenwich Village and was an influential art patron. She established the Whitney Museum of American Art in New York City (1930) and is also known for her architectural sculptures, such as "Titanic Memorial," Washington, D.C. (1931).

Whitney, Hassler (1907–) mathematician; born in New York City. Noted for his work in topology analysis, he joined the Princeton faculty (1933) and became a professor emeritus at the Institute for Advanced Study (1977). A member of the National Academy of Sciences, awarded the National Medal of Science (1976), he specialized in manifolds, integration theory, and analytic varieties.

Whitney, John Hay ("Jock") (1904–82) financier, publisher; born in Ellsworth, Maine. Member of a patrician family and a Yale graduate (1926), he had a varied career in motion pictures, publishing, and finance. He was chairman of Selznick International Pictures from 1936–40, during which the company produced one of the most popular movies of all time, *Gone with the Wind.* A senior partner in J. H. Whitney

& Co., investment bankers, he was publisher of *The New York Herald Tribune* from 1957–66 and served as U.S. ambassador to Great Britain from 1956–61.

Whitney, William Collins (1841–1904) lawyer, politician; born in Conway, Mass. He practiced law in New York City and reorganized the city's corporation counsel's office. As secretary of the navy (1885–89) he fought against outmoded concepts of ship design and supported the aims of the Naval War College.

Whitney, William Dwight (1827–94) philologist, lexicographer; born in Northampton, Mass. After graduating from Williams College (1845), and working briefly as a bank teller, he studied languages at the University of Breslau (Ph.D. 1861). He taught Sanskrit at Yale and was appointed head of both that department and the modern language department. He translated the Vedas (the ancient Hindu sacred scriptures), authored a Sanskrit grammar, and contributed to an important Sanskrit dictionary. He served as the first president of the American Philological Association (1869) and edited the 6-volume *Century Dictionary* (1889–91). His interest in the origin and growth of languages, as detailed in his *Language and the Study of Language* (1867) and *The Life and Growth of Language* (1875), helped popularize the study of language. Recognizing the central importance of usage in governing language change, he was one of the first modern grammarians. His *Essentials of English Grammar* (1877), although never as popular as some other 19th-century grammars, is widely regarded as a pathbreaking work.

Whitney, Willis Rodney (1868–1958) chemical/electrical engineer; born in Jamestown, N.Y. While teaching at the Massachusetts Institute of Technology (1896–1904), he began to work with General Electric (GE) (1901) and ended up staying with the firm until 1954, at one stage serving as vice-president (1928–41). He was director of research at GE in Schenectady, N.Y., where he founded its laboratory and helped make GE a leader in lighting and other applications of electricity. His innovations in such items as the tungsten filament and the X-ray tube led to his holding over 40 patents.

Whittaker, Charles Evans (1901–73) Supreme Court justice; born near Troy, Kans. He practiced law in Kansas City for 30 years before presiding over a U.S. district court (1954–56) then a U.S. Court of Appeals (1956–57). President Eisenhower named him to the U.S. Supreme Court (1957–62) where he wrote no major opinions.

Whittaker, Robert H. (Harding) (1920–80) botanist, ecologist; born in Wichita, Kans. He taught zoology at Washington State College (1948–51), then became a senior scientist in biology at Hanford (Wash.) Atomic Products Operations (1951–54). He moved to Brooklyn College (1954–64), then was a visiting biologist at Brookhaven National Laboratory, N.Y. (1964–66). He moved to the University of California: Irvine (1966–68), then joined Cornell (1968–80). He made major contributions to the ecological niche theory in his classifications of plant communities.

Whitten, Charles Arthur (1909–) geodesist; born in Redfield, S.D. A member of the U.S. Coast and Geodetic Survey (1930–68) and its chief geodesist (1968–72), his computations and analysis of the earth's crustal movements furthered the international prominence of U.S. geodesy.

Whitten, Jamie (Lloyd) (1919–) U.S. representative; born in Cascilla, Miss. A state representative and district attorney, he served in the U.S. House of Representatives (Dem., Miss.; 1941–89) chairing the Joint Committee on Budget Control and the Committee on Appropriations.

Whittier, John Greenleaf (1807–92) poet, writer; born in Haverhill, Mass. Although he had little formal education, he studied for one year at Haverhill Academy (1827) and then taught there (1827–28). He began writing poetry as a youth, but had to start making his living as a newspaper editor (1829–32). A devout Quaker, he thereafter directed much of his energies throughout the Civil War to promoting abolitionism, both as an editor of several antislavery periodicals, and through his poetry, such as his collection, *Voice of Freedom* (1846). He also spent one term in the Massachusetts legislature (1835–37) and ran unsuccessfully for the House of Representatives (1842). He opposed the Mexican War and was one of those who proposed founding the Republican Party. He was one of the founders of the *Atlantic Monthly* (1857) and remained a contributor. After the Civil War he lived (from 1876 on) in Amesburg and Denvers, Mass. Although he wrote a fair amount of critical essays and some fiction, he was highly popular in his day as one of the so-called household poets; several of his ballads and genre poems – "Barefoot Boy" (1856), "Barbara Fritchie" (1864), and "Snow-Bound" (1866) – survive as classic Americana.

Whittlesey, Derwent (Stainthorpe) (1890–1956) geographer; born near Rockford, Ill. He first taught at the University of Chicago (1920–28) before joining the Harvard faculty (1928–56). He contributed much to political geography and historical geography; in 1929 he introduced the term for which he was long best known, "sequent occupance." He also had a keen interest in Africa.

Whittredge, Thomas Worthington (1820–1910) painter; born in Springfield, Ohio. A sign painter in Cincinnati (1838–39), he became a landscape artist (1843), studied in Europe (1849–59), returned to New York (1859), and settled in the Catskill Mountains. Known as a Hudson River School painter, as seen in *Trout Pool in the Catskills* (1875), he moved to Summit, N.J., in 1880.

Whitworth, (Kathrynne Ann) Kathy (1939–) golfer; born in Monahans, Texas. She won more professional tournaments (88) than any golfer in history, male or female, including three Ladies' Professional Golf Association (LPGA) titles (1967, 1971, 1975).

Whorf, Benjamin Lee (1897–1941) linguist, chemical engineer; born in Winthrop, Mass. After receiving his B.S. in chemical engineering from the Massachusetts Institute of Technology (1918), he began a lucrative lifelong career at the Hartford Fire Insurance Company (1919–41), where he specialized in fire hazards and prevention. In 1925 he renewed a childhood interest in Central America and in 1930 he traveled to Mexico. In 1931 he enrolled in Edward Sapir's American Indian linguistics course at Yale University. Through his work in comparative linguistics in studies of Hebrew, Mayan, Aztec, and Hopi languages and cultures, he developed the "Whorf-Sapir hypothesis" – that the grammatical structure of a language affects the culture of its speakers by conditioning the ways in which they think.

Whyte, William H. (Hollingsworth), Jr. ("Holly") (1917–) urban sociologist, writer; born in West Chester, Pa. Writer and editor at *Fortune* magazine (1946–59), he wrote *The Organization Man* (1956), a popular sociological tract that identified a new type of modern men who shape their lives to the requirements of organizational employers. He explored the dangers of urban sprawl in *The Last Landscape* (1960) and the vitality of urban spaces in *City: Rediscovering the Center* (1989), both drawing heavily on his well-known tactic of "hanging around" cities to observe behavior. In later years he also became identified with his activities for conservationist and preservationist groups.

Wickenden, William Elgin (1882–1947) electrical engineer, educator; born in Toledo, Ohio. He taught at the Massachusetts Institute of Technology (1909–18). From 1918–24 he held various personnel positions at Bell Telephone and American Telephone & Telegraph Co. From 1924 to 1929 he studied methods of engineering education and was president of Case School of Applied Science from 1929 to his retirement in 1941.

Wickersham, George Woodward (1858–1936) lawyer, cabinet member; born in Pittsburgh, Pa. A successful New York corporate lawyer, as President Taft's attorney general (1909–13) he aggressively pursued antitrust indictments and had a major role in shaping the Taft administration's policies. Returning to corporate law, he served as legal adviser to the League of Nations (1924–29). As head of the so-called Wickersham Committee (1929–31), he proposed numerous reforms of the federal judicial system. He also concluded that the 18th amendment, prohibiting the sale of alcoholic beverages, should be retained even though it had led to a breakdown in law enforcement; this was so controversial that nothing came of his other suggestions.

Wideman, John Edgar (1941–) writer; born in Washington, D.C. He earned degrees from the University of Pennsylvania and Oxford University, England (where he was a Rhodes Scholar), then attended the Iowa Writers' Workshop. He taught at the Universities of Pennsylvania (1966–74), Wyoming (1974–85) and Massachusetts (1986). His complex and literate fiction often drew on the African-American urban culture of his youth, and includes *Hurry Home* (1970), *The Lynchers* (1973), *Sent for You Yesterday* (1983, P.E.N./Faulkner Award for fiction), *Philadelphia Fire* (1990, P.E.N./Faulkner Award) and *Stories* (1992). He was awarded a MacArthur Foundation "genius" grant (1993).

Widener, Harry Elkins (1885–1912) book collector; born in Philadelphia. Born into a wealthy family, he graduated from Harvard University and devoted himself to book collecting. Returning from researches in London, he lost his life on the *Titanic;* his mother established a library in his name at Harvard University.

Wiener, Norbert (1894–1964) mathematician, communication theorist; born in Columbia, Mo. A child prodigy, he graduated from Tufts College at age 14, did graduate work at Harvard and Cornell, read philosophy at Cambridge University under Bertrand Russell, and then worked as an editor and taught philosophy and engineering at the Massachusetts Institute of Technology before settling into its mathematics department (1919–64). During World War I he had done some special mathematics for the U.S. Army and in World War II he worked on developing high-speed electronic computer radar. Most of his early work in such fields as stochastic processes and harmonic analysis were too esoteric and complex for the public, but in 1948 he published *Cybernetics* – he coined the word from the Greek for "steersman," and "cyber-" would become a commonly used prefix. Although it relied on such terms as "feedback," "input," "output," and "homeostasis," the book was written in a relatively accessible way and was the first work to inform an only dimly aware public of what was to be the wave of the future – the communication theory that would underlie the handling of information by electronic devices, namely computers. Known for various personal quirks, he had a reputation for being a terrible lecturer and a poor listener, and he could be both inappropriately pompous and playful. His fellow mathematicians would often criticize his work but he remained a bridge between the leading edge of scientific thought and a broader public with such books as *The Human Use of Human Beings* (1950) and *Gold and Golem, Inc.* (1964). He was awarded the National Medal of Science (1964) in recognition of his pathbreaking work.

Wiesel, (Eliezer) Elie (1928–) writer; born in Sighet, Romania. When he was 16, the Jews of his town were taken to Nazi concentration camps. The rest of his family died at Auschwitz and Buchenwald, but he managed to survive. After the war he studied at the Sorbonne in Paris and worked for Israeli, American, and French newspapers. He settled in the U.S.A. in 1956. He taught at City College of New York and became professor of humanities at Boston University (1976). His life was devoted to writing and speaking about the Holocaust, with the aim of making sure that it is never forgotten; he was one of the principal forces behind establishing the Holocaust Memorial Museum in Washington, D.C. His first novel, *Night* (1956), was first published in Yiddish, and is based on his experiences in the death camps. Other novels include *Dawn* (1961) and *Jews of Silence* (1967). He also wrote plays, retellings of biblical stories, and Hasidic tales. In 1986 he received the Nobel Peace Prize for his work as a "messenger to mankind."

Wiesel, Torsten N. (Nils) (1924–) neurobiologist; born in Uppsala, Sweden. He taught in Stockholm (1954–55), then came to the U.S.A. to join Johns Hopkins (1955–59). He relocated to Harvard (1959–83), where he performed pioneering research on the visual cortex of the brain. He and collaborator David Hubel shared half the 1981 Nobel Prize in physiology for their discovery of how the brain interprets the messages it receives from the eyes. After retiring from Harvard, Wiesel joined Rockefeller University (1983).

Wiggin, Albert H. (Henry) (1868–1951) banker; born in Medfield, Mass. After several Boston-area jobs in banking, he became vice-president of the National Park Bank in New York City (1899–1904). There he helped organize the Banker's Trust Company (1903). In 1904 he became the youngest vice-president in the history of Chase National Bank; by 1911 he was president; in 1917 he chaired the board; in 1930 he chaired the governing board. Under his leadership the Chase National Bank grew to one of the world's largest. Circumventing regulations that prohibited commercial banks from trust business, he established the Mercantile Trust Company; to handle stocks and bonds he established the Chase Securities Corporation (both in 1917). He enhanced his and the bank's position by serving on 59 corporate boards, and arranged seven mergers, the largest of which was with the Equitable Trust Company. His reputation was damaged by a Congressional probe (1933), which found that Chase, like other banks, circumvented the law through its affiliates, and that Wiggin had used his "official and fiduciary position for private profit." He was sued by stockholders and chose to settle out of court.

Wiggin, Kate Douglas (Smith) (1856–1953) author, educator; born in Philadelphia, Pa. Raised in Maine, where her widowed mother moved to, she attended various schools in the Northeast before moving to California (1873) with her mother and stepfather. She took a course to be a kindergarten teacher and from 1877 on was active in operation of kindergartens and promoting the kindergarten movement in California. She married in 1881, moved to New York City in 1884, and after her husband's death in 1889 she began to concentrate on writing. Among her numerous books for children, her best known are *Rebecca of Sunnybrook Farm* (1903) and *Mother Carey's Chickens* (1911). She also wrote some books for adults drawing on her many trips to Europe, and with her sister, Nora Smith, she wrote a three-volume book about the kindergarten movement, *The Republic of Childhood* (1895–96).

Wigginton, (B.) Eliot (1942–) educator, author; born in Wheeling, W.Va. As a high school teacher in Rabun Gap, Ga., he initiated "Foxfire," an innovative program of student-initiated projects based on regional folklore. His Foxfire Fund (established 1966) and *Foxfire* manuals of traditional crafts and folklore (1972) helped to document southern Appalachian culture, train teachers, and establish similar programs nationwide.

Wigglesworth, Michael (1631–1705) Protestant clergyman, poet; born in Yorkshire, England. He emigrated to Massachusetts as a boy, graduated from Harvard in 1751, and was a fellow and tutor at Harvard before being ordained in Malden, Mass., in 1656. His epic poem "Day of Doom" (1662) has been described as conservative Calvinist theology in readable form; it was an early American best-seller. He continued his pastorate in Malden, and also practiced medicine there to the end of his life.

Wight, Peter B. (Bonnett) (1838–1925) architect, inventor; born in New York City. He helped rebuild the commercial center of Chicago after the 1871 fire; designed furniture and interiors; and invented fireproof construction techniques.

Wightman, Hazel (Virginia Hotchkiss) (1886–1974) tennis player; born in Healdsburg, Calif. She won the U.S. women's singles, doubles, and mixed doubles three times each (1909–11), a record shared by only two others. Nicknamed the "Queen Mother of Tennis," she won a total of 45 national championships.

Wigmore, John Henry (1863–1943) law educator; born in San Francisco. Educated at Harvard, fluent in many languages, he taught law in Tokyo (1889–92). In 1893 he became a law professor at Northwestern University, becoming dean of its law school (1901–29). He was noted for his prolific legal writings, chief of which is his ten-volume *Treatise on the Anglo-American System of Evidence* (3rd ed. 1940). He was a founder and first president of the American Institute of Criminal Law and Criminology (1909–10).

Wigner, Eugene P. (Paul) (1902–) physicist; born in Budapest, Hungary. He taught and performed research in Germany (1926–30), then emigrated to the U.S.A. (1930). He taught at Princeton (1930–36), spent a year at the University of Wisconsin, then returned to Princeton (1938–71). While his earlier research concentrated on rates of chemical reactions, the theory of metallic cohesion, and group theory in quantum mechanics, he later focused on nuclear structure, including studies of nuclear resonance, electron spin, and the mirror nuclides now known as Wigner nuclides (one of several atomic phenomena given his name). Taking leave from Princeton (1942–45), he joined Enrico Fermi in Chicago, where his calculations were essential to the design of the first atomic bomb. After World War II, Wigner became an advocate of nuclear arms control. He won the 1963 Nobel Prize for his many contributions to nuclear physics and elementary particles. After retiring, he continued his interest in the effect of nuclear technology on society.

Wilbur, Ray Lyman (1875–1949) physician, educator, public official; born in Boonesboro, Iowa. After taking his B.A. and M.A. at Stanford, he went on to get his M.D. (1899) and began practicing medicine in San Francisco; starting in 1900 he would become associated with Stanford for most of his career – with time out for government service – as a professor (1900–16), dean of the medical school (1911–16), and university president (1916–29). During World War I he assisted his former Stanford classmate/friend, Herbert Hoover, as administrator of food supplies; Wilbur coined the slogan "food will win the war" for the American war effort (1917). As a prominent Republican physician, he attended President Harding on his deathbed (1923). President Hoover appointed him secretary of the interior (1929–33), after which he returned to being president of Stanford (1933–43) and then its chancellor (1943–49). He is credited with making Stanford into a major university, establishing graduate and engineering schools.

Wilbur, Richard (Purdy) (1921–) poet, writer; born in New York City. He studied at Amherst (B.A. 1942), and Harvard (M.A. 1947) and taught at many institutions, notably Wesleyan (1957–77). Based in Cummington, Mass., he won acclaim for his poetry translations as well as for his own elegant lyrical poetry, as in *New and Collected Poems* (1988). He is also widely known for his often performed translations of Molière and for his lyrics to the musical *Candide* (1956). He was named Poet Laureate of the United States in 1987.

Wilcox, Ella Wheeler (1850–1919) poet, writer; born in Johnstown Center, Wis. Although she studied briefly at the University of Wisconsin (1867–68), she was largely self-educated and her sentimental, inspirational verse, although immensely popular in its day, never found favor among serious students of poetry. Her *Poems of Passion* (1883) gained her early notoriety for writing "immoral" poetry; her poems thereafter tended to be on such subjects as temperance and, in later years, on religion and spiritualism. She wrote a daily poem in a newspaper syndicate for some years. She also wrote fiction and essays. After marrying (1884), she lived with her husband in Meriden, Conn., and New York City; they also traveled widely.

Wilczek, Frank A. (Anthony) (1951–) physicist; born in New York City. He taught and performed research at Princeton (1974–80) before joining the University of California: Santa Barbara as an astrophysicist (1980). Using mathematical calculations, he discovered the nature of the "glue" that holds nuclear subparticles together while he was a graduate student at Princeton (1972–73). His continued research includes high energy physics, quantum field theory, and cosmological studies of matter and antimatter.

Wild, Earl (1915–) pianist; born in Pittsburgh, Pa. A child prodigy, he began performing as a teenager and made his New York debut in 1944. He became an international virtuoso noted for extraordinary technical skill and the breadth of his repertoire.

Wildavsky, Aaron B. (Bernard) (1930–93) political scientist; born in New York City. He taught at Oberlin (Ohio) College (1958–63) and at the University of California: Berkeley (1963). His contributions include numerous books and articles that focus on public policy, budgeting, the presidency, and the process of political analysis.

Wilder, (Alexander Lafayette Chew) Alec (1907–80) composer, arranger; born in Rochester, N.Y. He began songwriting and arranging in New York in the 1930s for such artists as Cab Calloway, Bing Crosby, Ethel Waters and Mabel Mercer. In 1939 he composed a series of innovative octets that combined classical and popular musical forms. In the 1950s he began writing chamber and orchestral music and opera and in the 1970s he hosted a series of radio programs on American popular music. Although appreciated by jazz and classical musicians, his work is not very well known by the public.

Wilder, Billy (b. Samuel Wilder) (1906–) film director, screenwriter, producer; born in Vienna, Austria. After a time as a law student at the University of Vienna, he turned to newspaper work in Vienna and then in Berlin. He began his film career as the cowriter of *Menschen am Sonntag* (1929). Fleeing Hitler in 1933, he went to France, then to America, working on movie scripts with Charles Brackett. An American citizen from 1934, he made his Hollywood directorial debut with *The Major and the Minor* (1942), which he also cowrote. He became a specialist in cowriting and directing incisive dramas, acerbic comedies, and bittersweet romances, then later turned to farce. In the late 1950s he became his own producer. His Academy Awards came with *The Lost Weekend* (1945, for director and screenwriter), *Sunset Boulevard* (1950, screenwriter), and *The Apartment* (1960, director and screenwriter).

Wilder, Burt Green (1841–1925) zoologist, neurologist, composer; born in Boston, Mass. After interrupting his education at Harvard to serve as a Union surgeon during the Civil War, he completed his M.D. (1866). From 1867 to 1910 he was a professor of neurology and vertebrate zoology at Cornell University. He was widely known for his meticulous studies of vertebrate brains, although science has rejected his premise that the contours of brains reveal the characteristics of the owner. He encouraged the donation of brains of intellectual leaders to balance the preponderance of those of the criminal and insane that were the basis of so many studies (and his own brain was added to his collection after his death). A man of wide interests – he was an ardent advocate of temperance and a member of the Non-Smokers' Protective League and the Simplified Spelling Board – he was an amateur musician who composed hymns and an orchestral setting of "Old Ironsides" by his fellow physician, Oliver Wendell Holmes. His varied publications include *What Young People Should Know* (1874) and *The Brain of Sheep* (1903).

Wilder, Laura (b. Ingalls) (1867–1957) writer; born in Pepin, Wis. She attended school in various states as her family of pioneers moved around the West. She taught in the Dakota Territory (1882–85) and married Almanzo Wilder (1885); they farmed in De Smet, S.D., until 1894, then moved to Mansfield, Mo. Drawing on her own and her husband's family experiences, she began writing the *Little House* books when in her sixties; the fourth in the series of nine is the classic *Little House on the Prairie* (1935).

Wilder, Thornton (Niven) (1897–1975) novelist, playwright; born in Madison, Wis. Raised in China where his father was with the U.S. consular service, he graduated from Yale, took an M.A. from Princeton, then taught English at the Lawrenceville School and University of Chicago (1930–37), until he could afford to be a full-time writer. He wrote several novels, including the Pulitzer Prize-winning *Bridge of San Luis Rey* (1927). But he is best known for his Pulitzer Prize-winning plays, *Our Town* (1938), a story of small-town life, and *The Skin of Our Teeth* (1942), an allegory about humankind's close calls. *The Matchmaker* (1954) was reincarnated as the hit musical *Hello, Dolly!* in 1964.

Wiley, Alexander (1884–1967) U.S. senator; born in Chippewa Falls, Wis. A lawyer, he was elected to the U.S. Senate (Rep., Wis.; 1939–63), where he rose to chairman of the Senate Foreign Relations Committee and the Judiciary Committee. He was a sponsor of the GI Bill. Originally an isolationist, he embraced internationalist policies after World War II, supporting foreign aid, the United Nations, and disarmament.

Wiley, Charles (1782–1826) publisher; born in New York City. Opening a print shop in 1807, he began a publishing business in 1814, putting out works by Washington Irving, James Fenimore Cooper, and other New York literary figures.

Wiley, Harvey Washington (1844–1930) chemist, food reformer, government official, author; born in Kent, Ind. A log-schoolhouse graduate, he became a chemistry professor at Purdue University (1874–83). As chief chemist for the U.S. Department of Agriculture (1883–1912), he campaigned against then widespread food adulteration, championing passage and enforcement of the Pure Food and Drug Act (1906). He also taught agricultural chemistry at George Washington University (1899–1914). He lectured widely and wrote several books, including *Foods and Their Adulteration* (1907) and *Not by Bread Alone* (1915).

Wilhelm, (James) Hoyt (1923–) baseball pitcher; born in Huntersville, N.C. During World War II he distinguished himself in combat during the Battle of the Bulge (1944). During his 21-year career (1952–72), mostly as a reliever for the New York Giants and Chicago White Sox, he appeared in more games (1,070) than any other pitcher in history. A right-handed knuckleballer, he was elected to baseball's Hall of Fame in 1985.

Wilkes, Charles (1798–1877) naval officer, explorer; born in New York City. He commanded a naval scientific expedition which surveyed the Antarctic coast, islands of the Pacific, and the American northwest coast (1838–42). He was the first explorer to name Antarctica as a continent, and returned home after circling the globe. He instigated the *Trent* affair (1861) which nearly brought Great Britain into the Civil War on the Confederate side. He was court-martialed in 1864 for violating neutral powers in pursuit of Confederate ships. Following his suspension from duty (1864–65) he became a retired rear admiral.

Wilkins, Leslie T. (1915–) criminologist, statistician; born in England. Starting his career as a statistician and researcher with the British Civil Service (1945–64), he worked for the United Nations in the Far East (1964–66). He came to the United States to teach criminology at the University of California: Berkeley (1966–68) where he was acting dean (1968–69), but he taught longest at the State University of New York at Albany School of Criminal Justice and was named professor emeritus (1981). He is the author of many books and articles on criminology.

Wilkins, Roy (1910–81) journalist, civil rights leader; born in St. Louis, Mo. Reared by an aunt and uncle in St. Paul, Minn., he was editor of his school paper (1923) and after graduation edited an African-American weekly, the *St. Paul Appeal,* before joining the staff of the *Kansas City Call,* a leading black weekly. He left the *Call* (1931) to serve as executive assistant secretary of the National Association for the Advancement of Colored People (NAACP) and editor of the organization's newspaper, *Crisis* (1934–49). He was named acting secretary of the NAACP (1949) and executive secretary (1955–77). He was considered one of the most articulate spokesmen for the more moderate wing of the civil rights movement, eventually winning praise from Jesse Jackson and other younger African-American leaders.

Wilkinson, (Charles Burnham) "Bud" (1915–) football coach; born in Minneapolis, Minn. He coached the University of Oklahoma (1947–64) to three national titles, twelve consecutive Big Eight titles, and a National Collegiate Athletic Association record 47-game winning streak (1953–57). He headed President John F. Kennedy's Physical Fitness Program and in 1964 he ran unsuccessfully for U.S. senator from Oklahoma.

Wilkinson, James (1757–1825) soldier, conspirator; born in Calvert County, Md. He served in the American Revolution under Benedict Arnold and Horatio Gates and joined the Conway Cabal, the group that schemed against Washington. Seemingly a conspirator by nature, he intrigued with Aaron Burr to establish a separate nation on the western frontier; when the plot was discovered, he had the effrontery to order Burr's arrest. Leader of the failed expedition to Montreal (1813), Wilkinson left the army in 1815.

Wilkinson, Jemima (1752–1819) Protestant religious leader; born in Cumberland, R.I. The pretty, clever daughter of a prosperous farmer, she became deeply religious after hearing George Whitefield preach at age 18. Some years later she claimed to have fallen into a trance, died, and awakened with a new soul, that of a prophetess. Calling herself the "Public Universal Friend," she drew large crowds preaching in New England. Encountering increasing antagonism, she established a religious colony, Jerusalem, in western New York (1789–90). Her followers increasingly objected to her dictatorial ways, and she lived out her late years estranged and alone.

Will, George (Frederick) (1941–) journalist; born in Champaign, Ill. An Oxford graduate with a doctorate from Princeton, he taught political science, was a congressional aide, and joined *National Review* as an editor (1973–76) before becoming a syndicated columnist (1974), a *Newsweek* contributing editor, and a commentator for ABC (from 1981). A conservative known for his dry wit and erudition, he won a 1977 Pulitzer Prize. His books include the 1990 best-seller, *Men at Work,* on his avocation, baseball.

Willard, Emma Hart (1787–1870) educator; born in Berlin, Conn. Raised by a father who, while a farmer, encouraged her to read and think for herself, she attended a local academy (1802–04) and then began to teach. In 1807 she went to Middlebury, Vt., to head a female academy there, marrying a local doctor in 1809. In 1814 she opened her own school, the Middlebury Female Seminary, to provide advanced education that young women were denied by colleges. Her *Address . . . Proposing a Plan for Improving Female Education* (1819) was a much admired and influential proposal to get public support for advanced education for young women. In 1821 she moved to Troy, N.Y., where she opened the Troy Female Seminary; with both boarding and day students, in some respects it was the first U.S. institution of serious learning for young women although even it recognized that most of its graduates would be housewives, not professionals, and most of its students came from families of means. The school actually made a profit and she also earned money from textbooks she wrote. (She also wrote poetry; only "Rocked in the Cradle of the Deep" remains known.) Her husband died in 1825 and she ran the school until 1838. Her second marriage proved disastrous and she separated within nine months. Her later years were spent in traveling to promote education for women. She returned to Troy in 1844. (The seminary was renamed the Emma Willard School in 1895.)

Willard, Frances (Elizabeth Caroline) (1839–98) temperance and suffrage leader; born in Churchville, N.Y. Growing up on the frontier in Wisconsin Territory, she persevered against her father's opposition to get any education as a girl. She spent a year at the North Western Female Seminary in Evanston, Ill. (1858–59), and held a series of teaching posts in the Northeast (1859–68). She then traveled for two years in Europe with a wealthy friend, Kate Jackson. Returning to Evanston, she became affiliated with Northwestern University as dean of women students and a professor of English (1871–74). She then transferred her interest to the temperance movement, becoming the corresponding secretary of the National Women's Christian Temperance Union (WCTU) (1874–77). She ran into conflict with other women in the temperance movement by insisting on linking its goals with women's right to vote, but by 1879 she had gained enough support through her writings and eloquence to be elected president of the WCTU, a position she held until her death. She became a national figure through her personal appearances and her energy, broadening the WCTU's agenda to embrace women's suffrage and other progressive social causes. She also led the WCTU to become an international organization, becoming president of the World WCTU (1891–98). She tried to link the temperance and suffrage movements to political parties and candidates through a "Home Protection" Party and then through other political parties but never succeeded in uniting many women in this effort. She spent most of the years 1892 to 1896 in England and shifted her emphasis to the need for a socialist approach to economic reforms and an educational approach to eliminating the social effects of alcohol.

Willard, Nancy (1936–) poet, writer; born in Ann Arbor, Mich. She studied at the University of Michigan (B.A. 1958; Ph.D. 1963), Stanford University (M.A. 1960), and in Paris and Oslo. Beginning in 1965, she taught at Vassar, lived in Poughkeepsie, N.Y., and from 1975 she was an instructor at Bread Loaf Writer's Conference, Middlebury, Vt. She wrote literary criticism and adult novels, but is best known for her poetry, as in *Water Walker* (1990), and for her juvenile books, such as *The Mountains of Quilt* (1987).

Willard, Simon (1753–1848) clock maker; born in Grafton, Mass. Establishing his clock factory in Roxbury, Mass., about 1778, he would turn out over 5,000 timepieces by the time he retired in 1839. He patented the "Willard Patent Timepiece" (1802), still familiar as the banjo wall clock, and an alarm clock (1819). His clocks were widely used and admired in public places.

Willey, Gordon R. (Randolph) (1913–) anthropologist, archaeologist; born in Chariton, Iowa. Bowditch Professor of Archaeology at Harvard (1950–83), he was a leading archaeologist and theorist of New World prehistory known particularly for his settlement pattern studies. His published works include reports on Peruvian, Panamanian, and Maya archaeology and *An Introduction to American Archaeology* (2 vols. 1966–71). He won the 1974 Kidder Medal.

Williams, Anna (Wessels) (1863–1954) physician, bacteriologist; born in Hackensack, N.J. Best known for research on infectious diseases and discovery of an effective diphtheria immunization, she fought to advance the cause of women doctors. Besides teaching at the New York Infirmary (1891–95; 1902–05), she was assistant director of the New York City Research Laboratories (1905–34) and a prolific writer.

Williams, Clarence (1898–1965) composer, publisher; born in Plaquemine, La. When he was 13 he traveled as a singer and dancer with a minstrel show from New Orleans. He settled in New York and in the 1920s supervised an exceptional series of small-band recordings with Louis Armstrong, Sidney Bechet and other notable musicians. He was an important promoter and publisher of such artists as Fats Waller, Willie "the Lion" Smith and Spencer Williams.

Williams, Daniel Hale (1858–1931) surgeon, medical educator; born in Hollidaysburg, Pa. One of the first African-Americans to graduate from medical school (Chicago Medical College/Northwestern University, 1883), he organized Provident Hospital in Chicago (1891), establishing training programs for the medical education of African-American men (interns) and women (nurses). While there he performed the first successful surgical closure of a wound to the heart and the pericardium (1893); he perfected the suture technique for stopping hemorrhage from the spleen; he was also an early advocate of asepsis. President Grover Cleveland appointed him surgeon-in-chief at Freedmen's hospital in Washington, D.C. (1893–98), where he established a second training program for African-American men and women. He then became a professor of clinical surgery at Meharry Medical College in Nashville, Tenn. (1899). In 1913, he was a charter member – and the only African-American so honored – of the American College of Surgeons, and for many decades he was regarded as the premier African-American in the medical profession.

Williams, Edward Bennett (1920–88) lawyer, sports executive; born in Hartford, Conn. After practice with the Washington, D.C., law firm of Hogan & Hartson (1945–49), he opened his own office to focus on cases involving civil liberties and constitutional guarantees. Starting in the 1950s, he was often vilified for defending such controversial clients as Senator Joseph McCarthy, gambler Frank Costello, industrialist Bernard Goldfine, Teamster boss James R. Hoffa, Congressman Adam Clayton Powell Jr., and Robert G. "Bobby" Baker, secretary to the senate Democrats. Bennett's exuberant self-confidence was justified by his patience, persistence, and accomplishments as a legal artist and power broker. He was owner of the Baltimore Orioles baseball team and president of the Washington Redskins football team (1965–85). He wrote *One Man's Freedom* (1962) and *You in Trial Law* (1963).

Williams, (Egbert Austin) Bert (?1874–1922) stage actor, singer, songwriter; born in Nassau, Bahamas, British West Indies. Part African in descent, he was raised in Los Angeles and went on the road with the Mastadon Minstrels in 1891; he was so light-skinned that he had to use blackface to maintain his role as an African. In 1893 he formed a partnership with another African-American song-and-dance man, George Walker; their New York City premiere in 1896 in the farce, *The Gold Bug,* made them into a hit team and they appeared in a number of musicals until Walker retired in 1909. Williams was the first black comic to record with Victor Records (starting in 1901); he was one of those behind the early all-black musical, *In Dahomey* (1902); and he was one of the founders of the first African-American actors' society (1906). Williams continued as a solo act and became the most celebrated "black" actor on Broadway, appearing in the annual *Ziegfield Follies* between 1910–19 (except for 1913 and 1918). His last Broadway appearance was in *Broadway Brevities* in 1920. Although he had appeared in blackface throughout his career and often played a shuffling fall-guy, he was credited as one of the first African-Americans to defy some of the stereotypes of the minstrel-show Negro, especially in his own songs such as "Nobody" and "That's a-Plenty." He was the subject of Duke Ellington's "Portrait of Bert Williams" (1940).

Williams, Eleazar (c. 1789–1858) missionary; born in Caughnawaga, Canada. Of part Iroquois descent, educated in Massachusetts, he established a mission among the Oneida Indians and translated an Episcopal prayer book into the Iroquois language. In 1822 he led a group of Oneidas to new lands in Wisconsin, though he eventually had to abandon his dream of establishing an Indian empire in the West. After 1839 he maintained that he was Louis XVII, the "Lost Dauphin" of France, a claim he never renounced.

Williams, (Hiram) Hank (1923–53) composer, lyricist; born in Olive Hill, Ala. As a young boy he joined the local church choir, taught himself guitar (and, legend claims, learned music from a local African-American street singer). In 1937 he won an amateur music contest and soon began singing on radio. In 1939 he formed Hank Williams and His Drifting Cowboys and began performing at honky-tonks and square dances. He worked in shipbuilding during World War II and reunited the Drifting Cowboys in 1944. He moved to Nashville, Tenn., in 1946 and became a regular performer on *Louisiana Hayride,* a country music radio show in 1947. In 1949 he began recording for MGM Records and caused a sensation at the "Grand Ole Opry" when he sang "Lovesick Blues" (1922, by Irving Mills and Cliff Friend), his recording of which reached No. 1 on the country music charts. Many hits followed, including "Hey, Good Lookin' " (1951) and "Your Cheatin' Heart" (1953). Called the "hillbilly Shakespeare," he wrote simple melodies mixing gospel, blues, and country, and his words and singing evoked a powerful sense of emotion; as much as anyone he was responsible for country music's being taken up by a broader public. Unsettled by a chronic back condition and a broken marriage, in 1953 he died of a heart attack attributed to drugs, alcohol, and insomnia, leaving a legacy of over 100 classic country songs. His son, Hank Williams Jr., became a popular country singer in the 1960s.

Williams, John (1664–1729) clergyman, author; born in Roxbury, Mass. He was captured in the French and Indian raid on Deerfield where he was the town's minister. Following two years in captivity in Canada (1704–06), he returned to Massachusetts and wrote *The Redeemed Captive Returning to Zion* (1707).

Williams, John (Alfred) (J. Dennis Gregory, pen name) (1925–) writer; born in Jackson, Miss. He studied at Syracuse (B.A. 1950; graduate study 1950–51). He worked in Syracuse for the county welfare department, and in public relations (1952–54), and in Hollywood and New York City he worked in television and radio (1954–55). He also worked in publishing for a variety of employers in New York City (1955–59), and as a correspondent in Africa for *Newsweek* (1964–65). A teacher at numerous institutions, including Rutgers (1979), he lived in Teaneck, N.J. He wrote nonfiction and numerous novels, and is known for his opposition to American racism, as seen in *!Click Song* (1982).

Williams, John (Sharp) (1854–1932) U.S. representative/senator; born in Memphis, Tenn. A lawyer and cotton plantation owner, he was minority leader in the U.S. House of Representatives (Dem., Miss.; 1893–1909), and chairman of the Library and University Committees in the Senate (1911–23).

Williams, John (Towner) (1932–) film composer, conductor; born in New York City. He is the leading screen composer of his generation, his films including the *Star Wars* series and *Close Encounters of the Third Kind*. In 1980 he became conductor of the Boston Pops, retiring from that post in 1992 to devote his time to composing.

Williams, (Joseph Goreed) Joe (1918–) jazz vocalist; born in Cordele, Ga. An outstanding jazz singer and popular show business figure, he began his career in Chicago in the late 1930s with Jimmie Noone, toured with King Kolax, and gained prominence with Count Basie between 1954–60. He free-lanced thereafter as a solo attraction and with all-star jazz groups.

Williams, Margery (Winifred) (1881–1944) writer; born in London, England. She came to America in 1890, attended schools in Pennsylvania, married, spent many years traveling between England, Paris, and Italy, and then settled in New York City (1921). She wrote many books for adults (using her married name, Margery Bianco) and children, notably *The Velveteen Rabbit; or How Toys Become Real* (1922), and *Poor Cecco* (1925).

Williams, Mary Lou (b. Mary Elfrieda Scruggs) (1910–81) jazz musician; born in Atlanta, Ga. She was an important arranger and pianist with Andy Kirk from 1929–41, and wrote arrangements for Duke Ellington and Benny Goodman in the 1930s and 1940s. She later embraced the bebop style and wrote several sacred works, including "Mary Lou's Mass" in 1970.

Williams, Michael (1877–1950) journalist; born in Halifax, Nova Scotia. Emigrating to the U.S.A. as a penniless youth, he was a newspaper reporter in Boston, New York, and San Francisco before a 1912 conversion to active Catholicism, which he recounted in a colorful memoir, *The Book of High Romance* (1918). Seeking to create a Catholic intellectual periodical under lay auspices, he cofounded *Commonweal* magazine (1914) and was its editor until 1937.

Williams, Paul Revere (1894–1980) architect; born in Los Angeles. Educated at the University of Southern California, he established an independent practice (1923). He designed Los Angeles civic buildings and the M.C.A. (now Litton Industries) Building, Beverly Hills, but is best remembered as a prominent society architect who designed hundreds of elegant houses in period styles for wealthy California clients.

Williams, Robert Ray (1918–) aviator; born in Evanston, Wyo. A West Point graduate, he organized the first Army Aviation Unit in 1946, as the Army Air Force prepared to become the independent U.S. Air Force. He commanded the Army Aviation Center (1962–63) and advised South Vietnamese forces (1966–67).

Williams, Robert (Runnels), Jr. (1886–1965) chemist, inventor; born in Nellore, India. The son of American Baptist missionaries, he graduated from the University of Chicago in 1907. As a researcher in the Bureau of Science in Manila, the Philippines (1909–14), he sought a cure for beriberi. Returning to the U.S.A., he worked as chemical director for the Bell Telephone Co. for many years, doing vitamin research in his spare time. He isolated thiamine in 1933 and synthesized vitamin B_1 two years later. He channeled the profits from his vitamin patents to the Williams-Waterman Fund for the Combat of Dietary Disease.

Williams, Roger (?1603–83) religious leader; born in London, England. By 1629 he had become a Church of England minister but his sympathy for the Puritans led him to emigrate to Massachusetts in 1630. His unorthodox views on religious toleration and on the rights of Indians brought about his banishment by the Massachusetts General Court in 1635. With a few followers, he founded Providence, the first Rhode Island settlement, in 1636. In 1639, he became a Seeker – one who had no specific creed, but adhered to the basic beliefs of Christianity. As the first president of Rhode Island (1654–57), he welcomed religious groups – Jews and Quakers – that were persecuted in Massachusetts. Although he remained a firm friend to the Narragansett Indians, he served as a captain in King Philip's War. His numerous writings on religious matters, and the political structure he gave Rhode Island show that he was far ahead of his time in his views on tolerance and liberty.

Williams, Samuel Wells (1812–84) scholar, diplomat; born in Utica, N.Y. A printer's son, he directed an American mission press in Canton aand Macao (1833–45) and was secretary and interpreter to the American legation in China (1856–76). The leading sinologist of his day, he published several Chinese dictionaries, and his *Middle Kingdom* (1848, revised 1883) was for decades the standard English-language work on China.

Williams, Talcott (1849–1928) journalist; born in Turkey. After experience as a political reporter and editor, he became in 1912 the first director of the Columbia University School of Journalism and helped develop its innovative curriculum.

Williams, Tennessee (b. Thomas Lanier Williams) (1911–83) playwright; born in Columbus, Miss. From an old Tennessee family (he adopted his first name by 1939 while in New Orleans), he was raised under the influence of his clergyman-grandfather. Moving with his family to St. Louis in 1913, he went on to several colleges, graduating from the State University of Iowa in 1938. He moved around the country for many years, working at odd jobs while he wrote short plays and getting occasional productions in community theaters; in 1943 he briefly worked as a scriptwriter for Metro-Goldwyn-Mayer. He gained sudden success with the New York production of *The Glass Menagerie* (1945) and his next and greatest success came with *A Streetcar Named Desire* (1947), which won a Pulitzer Prize. Although Williams' life was marked by personal disarray, mental stress, and drug addiction, he enjoyed long-term relationships with male companions and continued to be productive. In 1968 he converted to Catholicism. His later plays include *Summer and Smoke* (1948), *The Rose Tattoo* (1950), *Cat on a Hot Tin Roof* (1955, Pulitzer Prize), *Sweet Bird of Youth* (1959), and *Night of the Iguana* (1961). He also published two novels and a fair amount of poetry. Several of his plays were made into successful movies, but his later works were not well received and he became disaffected from the New York professional theater. He died by choking on the cap of a bottle of pills. His best work is distinguished by a poetry, intensity, and compassion that guarantee him a permanent place as a major artist-dramatist.

Williams, (Theodore Samuel) Ted (1918–) baseball player; born in San Diego, Calif. During his 19-year career as an outfielder for the Boston Red Sox (1939–60), he hit 521 home runs and posted a lifetime batting average of .344, sixth highest in major league history; his career total walks (2,019) are second only to Babe Ruth's. In 1941 he batted .406, a mark not bested in over 50 years. He managed the Washington Senators (1969–71) and the Texas Rangers (1972). One of the finest hitters in the game's history, he lost five years of his baseball career due to active military service as a combat pilot in World War II and the Korean conflict. Nicknamed "the Splendid Splinter," he was elected to baseball's Hall of Fame in 1966.

Williams, William (c. 1727–c. 1791) painter; born in Bristol, England. A seaman, he arrived in Philadelphia (1747), painted, and constructed a theater in Philadelphia (1759). He wrote an autobiographical novel, *The Journal of Llewellyn Penrose, a Seaman* (1776), and produced fine portraits, such as *Deborah Hall* (1766). He returned to Bristol (1776), and died in an almshouse.

Williams, William Carlos (1883–1963) poet, writer, physician; born in Rutherford, N.J. He studied in Switzerland and Paris (1897–99), the University of Pennsylvania's medical school (M.D. 1906), and did postgraduate work in pediatrics in Leipzig (1909–10). Returning to Rutherford, N.J., he would combine the writing of poetry with the practice of medicine (1910–51). He was associated with the Imagists early in his career, but preferred to call his approach "objectivism." He went on to create a revolutionary modernist approach to prose and poetry; his masterpiece is generally regarded to be the five-volume semiautobiographical epic poem, *Paterson* (1946–58). He was also a novelist, playwright, critic, and translator, and was appointed Consultant in Poetry, Library of Congress, Washington, D.C. (1952), although he declined to serve.

Williamson, Sonny Boy (b. Aleck Ford; also known as Aleck "Rice" Miller) (?1899–1965) harmonica player; born in Glendora, Miss. Eventually becoming a legendary singer and harmonica player, he began by performing as "Little Boy Blue" in the Mississippi Delta region throughout the 1920s and 1930s. In 1941 he began broadcasting on *King Biscuit Time,* a daily radio program in Helena, Ark.. which

he remained associated with until his death. Following John Lee "Sonny Boy" Williamson's murder in 1948, he became the second harmonica player in blues to record under this name, first with Trumpet Records (1951–54), then with Chess Records (1955–64). Between 1963–65 he made annual tours of Europe, performing with Eric Clapton and other emerging rock musicians.

Willing, Thomas (1731–1821) merchant, banker; born in Philadelphia. He studied law in London and then prospered at various commercial pursuits (1749–93), joining with Robert Morris to form Philadelphia's major mercantile firm. Patriotic but not radical, as a delegate to the Continental Congress (1775–76) he voted against the initial resolution for independence. He was president of the Bank of North America (1781–91), supported the new constitution, and then served as the first president of the Bank of the United States (1791–97).

Willis, Bailey (1857–1949) geologist; born in Idlewild-on-Hudson, N.Y. He served the U.S. Geological Survey (1884–1916), taking leaves to explore China (1902) and Argentina (1911–15). He joined Stanford (1915), where his lectures and research on seismology earned him the sobriquets "the earthquake professor" and "Earthquake Willie." After his retirement (1922), he traveled to seismic centers of the world. His conclusion that earthquakes cannot be predicted led to his proposals for better building codes in earthquake-intensive areas.

Willis, Nathaniel Parker (Roy, Cassius, Philip Slingsby, pen names) (1806–67) poet, writer, editor; born in Portland, Maine. He and his family moved to Boston (1812), and he studied at Yale (B.A. 1927), where he was known as a poet. He became a journalist and founded the *American Monthly* magazine (1829). After moving to New York City, he worked as a foreign correspondent for the *New York Mirror* until 1836, and eventually became coeditor there. He traveled to England often, maintained a home by the Hudson River, and was noted for epistolary essays, as seen in *Pencillings by the Way* (1844).

Williston, Samuel (1861–1963) jurist; born in Cambridge, Mass. He was professor (1890–1938) and active professor emeritus (1938–63) at Harvard Law School. He continued in private practice into his nineties and became Harvard's oldest living alumnus. His five-volume *Law of Contracts* (1920–22) became a standard. He codified commercial law that was adopted by most American states. The American Bar Association awarded him its first gold medal (1929).

Williston, Samuel Wendell (1851–1918) paleontologist, entomologist; born in Roxbury, Mass. The leader of numerous western expeditions, Williston published important work on Cretaceous and Permian amphibians and reptiles and, reflecting lifelong research, three editions of his classic *Manual of North American Diptera* (1888–1908). He taught at the University of Chicago (1902–18).

Willkie, Wendell (1892–1944) businessman, presidential candidate; born in Elwood, Ind. Trained as a lawyer, he practiced briefly before entering the Army in World War I. An active Democrat, he was delegate to the 1924 national convention. In the 1930s, as president of an Indiana utilities holding company, Commonwealth and Southern Corp., he battled public ownership of that industry under Franklin Roosevelt's New Deal programs such as the Tennessee Valley Authority. Though not widely known outside the business community, he was recruited as the "dark horse" Republican candidate against Roosevelt in 1940. He lost the election, but tallied the greatest number of popular votes of any Republican to that date. During World War II he supported Roosevelt's Lend-Lease program to Britain, promoted an organization to protect world peace, and fought to improve civil liberties in the U.S.A. In 1942 Roosevelt named him goodwill ambassador to the Middle East, China, and the Soviet Union. His 1943 book *One World* was a best-seller. In 1944, he was defeated in the presidential primaries, well behind the eventual Republican candidate, Thomas E. Dewey.

Willoughby, Westel Woodbury (1867–1945) political scientist; born in Alexandria, Va. After practicing law for several years, he taught at Johns Hopkins University (1897–1933) and served as a technical adviser to the government of China.

Wills, Helen See MOODY, HELEN WILLS.

Wills, (James Robert) Bob (1905–75) country music fiddler, singer, bandleader, songwriter; born in Kosse, Texas. He played in bands in the late-1920s. In 1934 he formed the Texas Playboys, a band popular in the Southwest, before moving to California in 1942 to perform in movies and dance halls. Although he was a traditional hoedown fiddler, his band helped popularize western swing in the 1950s and 1960s with an eclectic repertory of country, jazz, blues, and pop. His own best-known compositions include "Faded Love," "Maiden's Prayer," and "San Antonio Rose."

Willson, Meredith (1902–84) composer, lyricist; born in Mason City, Iowa. He studied in New York City for a career in serious music and after touring with the John Philip Sousa band (1921–23), he became the principal flutist of the New York Philharmonic Symphony Orchestra (1924–29). In the 1930s and 1940s he was music director of several radio programs including *The George Burns and Gracie Allen Show.* He also composed film scores (including Chaplin's *The Great Dictator,* 1940) and both words and music for popular songs; his biggest hit would be "May the Good Lord Bless and Keep You" (1950). Even this was eclipsed by the success of his musical, *The Music Man* (1957), for which he wrote the book as well as lyrics and music. His other successful musical was *The Unsinkable Molly Brown* (1960), for which he wrote lyrics and music. He also composed some concert music.

Willys, John N. (North) (1873–1935) industrialist; born in Canandaigua, N.Y. He attempted law, but preferred business, and in 1897 bought a factory in Elmira, N.Y., where he specialized in bicycles. Successful, he organized a car sales company and in 1907 bought out the Overland Company in Indiana and moved it to an abandoned factory in Toledo, Ohio; by 1910 he had produced and sold 18,200 Willys-Overland cars. In 1919 he organized the Willys Corporation, a short-lived holding company; financial troubles in the car business forced its liquidation in 1921. Having sold his Willys-Overland Company stock for $25 million in 1929, he became U.S. ambassador to Poland (1930–32). In 1933 his financially-troubled car company went into receivership with Willys as receiver and president; he died suddenly without resolving the company's finances.

Wilmot, David (1814–68) U.S. representative/senator; born in Bethany, Pa. Son of a prosperous merchant, he was a lawyer and became a congressman (Dem., Pa.; 1845–51). For an 1846 bill to appropriate money for settling the war with Mexico, he drew up an amendment that would prohibit slavery in any territory acquired by federal funds. Known as the Wilmot Proviso, this amendment was continually defeated over the years and led to his losing the 1850 election. He served as a judge (1851–61) and helped to found the Republican Party in 1854. Appointed a senator (1861–63), he lost in the 1862 election – although that was the year the Wilmot Proviso finally passed – and Lincoln appointed him to the court of claims.

Wilson, Alexander (1766–1813) ornithologist; born in Paisley, Scotland. Raised in poverty, he supported himself as a weaver and peddler before emigrating to the U.S.A. in 1794. Settling in Philadelphia, he taught school and took up the study of birds. In 1808 he published the first volume of his *American Ornithology,* completing six more volumes over the next five years. His assistant completed the project after his death. Wilson also published two volumes of poetry, including a collection in the Scots dialect.

Wilson, August (1945–) playwright; born in Pittsburgh, Pa. A writer who never finished high school, he won two Pulitzer Prizes for his plays, which depict the black experience in America: *Fences* (1987) and *The Piano Lesson* (1990). His goal was to write a cycle of plays, one set in each decade of the 20th century. He founded Minnesota's Black Horizons Theatre Company. His *Ma Rainey's Black Bottom* won a New York Drama Critics Circle Award (1984–85).

Wilson, Charles E. (Erwin) ("Engine Charlie") (1890–1961) automobile executive, cabinet member; born in Minerva, Ohio. An electrical engineer, he designed automobile products for Westinghouse (1912–21), then became president of Delco Remy (1926–28). As vice-president of General Motors (1928–41), then president (1941–52), he recognized the United Auto Workers union, championed cost-of-living wage increases, and led his company through World War II as a major producer of military vehicles. President Eisenhower's outspoken secretary of defense (1953–57), he began by angering liberals with his claim that "what was good for our country was good for General Motors and vice-versa," and ended by angering the military with severe cuts in the defense budget.

Wilson, Charles Edward ("Electric Charlie") (1886–1972) corporate executive; born in New York City. He ended a 51-year career with General Electric (GE) as its president (1940–50), known for his tough anti-union policies and willingness to close plants in communities dependent on GE for jobs. He directed the War Production Board (1942–44). An influential government adviser during Truman's presidency, he became chairman of W.R. Grace and Co. (1952).

Wilson, (Charles) Kemmons (1913–) entrepreneur, hotel executive; born in Osceola, Ark. A Memphis builder and realtor, he built his first Holiday Inn in 1952; his uniformly clean, dependable family motels replaced tourist courts on U.S. highways and transformed the lodging industry. By 1978 he had built the world's largest lodging chain. He retired in 1979.

Wilson, Edith (b. Bolling Galt) (1872–1961) First Lady; born in Wytherville, Va. Widow of a Washington jeweler, she met and married the widower President Woodrow Wilson in 1915. Although she lacked an advanced formal education, she was intelligent and immediately became the mainstay of Wilson's personal life. After his stroke in 1919, she served as the liaison between him and government officials – even guiding his hand when he signed documents – but she probably did not make the important decisions as she is sometimes accused of doing. After his death in 1924 she kept his ideals alive through the Woodrow Wilson Foundation.

Wilson, Edmund (1895–1972) writer, editor; born in Red Bank, N.J. After taking his B.A. at Princeton (1916) and serving with the U.S. Army in World War I, he went to New York City and became an editor for such periodicals as *Vanity Fair* (1920–21) and the *New Republic* (1926–31); he was the regular book reviewer for the *New Yorker* (1944–48) and thereafter contributed occasional reviews. He wrote a novel, plays, poems, and short stories, but except for a collection of the last named, *Memoirs of Hecate County* (1946), his creative work did not command much attention. Instead, he gained his reputation as the dean of American letters through his erudite and trenchant nonfictional works. As he became interested in various topics, he would learn whatever languages were necessary, and after immersing himself in the subject, he would produce his own original interpretations, such as *To the Finland Station: A Study in the Writing and Acting of History* (1940) and *The Scrolls from the Dead Sea* (1955). His major reputation rests on his literary criticism, exhibited in such works as *Axel's Castle: A Study in the Imaginative Literature of 1870–1930* (1931) and *Patriotic Gore: Studies in the Literature of the American Civil War* (1962). He edited the uncollected works of his Princeton classmate, F. Scott Fitzgerald (1954), and wrote countless magazine articles, essays, and reviews. He published two autobiographical works, and after his death a series of memoirs were extracted from his diaries and notebooks. He was married four times, including to Mary McCarthy (1938–46). Based in New York City for much of his life, he also spent parts of each year in Wellfleet, Mass., and at his family home in upstate New York.

Wilson, Edmund B. (Beecher) (1856–1939) geneticist; born in Geneva, Ill. After studying in Europe (1882–83), he taught at Williams College (1883–84), then moved to the Massachusetts Institute of Technology (1884–85). He became the first professor of biology at Bryn Mawr (1885–91), where he published his research on earthworm embryology and studies of movement in the invertebrate *Hydra*. In the 1890s he began the first of nearly 50 summers investigating marine biology at Wood's Hole, Mass., realizing the importance of live specimens in his research. His work at Columbia University (New York City) (1891–1928) brought that institution to prominence in genetics and cytology. Inspired by Thomas H. Morgan, he developed the theory of sex determination via X and Y chromosomes (1905–12), and recognized what came to be known as sex-linked inheritance. His monumental book, *The Cell in Development and Inheritance* (1896), became a mainstay of classrooms and underwent several revisions. He was a respected educator and an accomplished flautist and cellist.

Wilson, Edward O. (Osborne) (1929–) entomologist, sociobiologist; born in Birmingham, Ala. He was a biologist with the Alabama State Department of Conservation (1949), then moved to Harvard (1953), becoming Mellon Professor of Science (1990). In the 1950s, he combined evolutionary theory with classification methods to revise the ant genus *Lasius*. He found that ants communicate via chemical substances known as pheromones, and discovered that these insects have a social caste system (1953). With colleague William L. Brown, he coined the phrase "character displacement" (1956) to explain the evolutionary divergence and adaptation occurring when two closely related species first come into contact. In 1967 he described a fossil ant of the Mesozoic Age. He specialized in ants and other social insects until he published his book *Sociobiology: The New Synthesis* (1975), which propounded the controversial theory that biology determines basic social behavior in humans and other animals. His later writings, including the Pulitzer Prize-winning *On Human Nature* (1978) and *Promethean Fire: Reflection on the Origin of the Mind* (1983, with physicist Charles J. Lumsden), expanded his theory that many human cultural traits, such as the incest taboo, can be explained by genetic factors and evolutionary theory.

Wilson, Ellen (Louise b. Axson) (1860–1914) First Lady; born in Savannah, Ga. Originally a painter, she married Woodrow Wilson in 1885. She was a great asset to Wilson; she translated German books for use in his scholarly work. As first lady, she worked for the improvement of the Washington slums and for better sanitary facilities for women in government offices. She died of Bright's disease while in the White House.

Wilson, Gill (Robb) (1893–1966) aviator, journalist; born in Clarion County, Pa. A Presbyterian minister as well as an early private pilot, he advocated military preparedness and became New Jersey's director of aviation in 1930. He was the first executive officer of the Civil Air Patrol. During World War II he was a correspondent for the *Herald Tribune*.

Wilson, Halsey William (1868–1954) bibliographer, publisher; born in Wilmington, Vt. As the owner of a Minneapolis bookstore, he and his wife Justina Wilson, a prominent suffragist, compiled and in 1898 began publishing the *Cumulative Book Index,* which continues as an authoritative bibliographic reference work. In 1901 he began publishing the *Reader's Guide to Periodical Literature,* followed in 1905 by the *Book Review Digest.* These and the *Wilson Library Journal* (1914) remain standard works in the field. In 1913 he moved the H. W. Wilson Company to White Plains, N.Y., and then to the Bronx, New York City, where it remains a major publisher of reference works.

Wilson, Henry (b. Jeremiah Jones Colbath) (1812–75) vice-president, abolitionist; born in Farmington, N.H. A poor farm laborer with little formal schooling, at age 21 he renamed himself and went off to Massachusetts where he soon had a successful shoe factory. After a trip to Virginia exposed him to slavery (1836), he devoted the rest of his life to abolishing it, frequently changing political affiliations until he found a party, the new Republican Party, opposed to slavery. He represented Massachusetts in the Senate (1855–73), when he became Ulysses S. Grant's second-term vice-president; but after two strokes he died in office.

Wilson, Hugh R. (Robert) (1885–1946) diplomat; born in Evanston, Ill. After a series of posts with the U.S. Foreign Service (1911–27), he was ambassador to Switzerland (1927–37) and an American delegate to the London Naval Conference (1930). He was assistant secretary of state (1937) and the last pre-war ambassador to Germany (1938–39); following his recall to protest Nazi treatment of the Jews, he was not replaced. During World War II he worked in the Office of Strategic Services (1941–45). He wrote *The Education of a Diplomat* (1938) and *Diplomat Between Wars* (1941).

Wilson, (Jack Leroy) Jackie (1934–84) vocalist; born in Detroit, Mich. A rhythm-and-blues singer who performed with acrobatic showmanship, he began with a local gospel group, the Ever Ready Singers, after deciding against a career in boxing. In 1951, he joined Billy Ward's Dominoes, a doo-wop group, and two years later he replaced his idol, Clyde McPhatter, as the group's unbilled lead singer. He remained with the Dominoes until 1957, exerting a strong influence on Elvis Presley and other emerging rock 'n' roll stars, but still unknown to the general public. He recorded his first hit record "Reet Petite" in 1957, and until 1967, when he released his last hit, "Higher and Higher," he toured regularly and made frequent appearances on Dick Clark, Ed Sullivan, and other television shows. In 1975 he suffered severe brain damage as the result of a fall during a performance on a Dick Clark revival show in Camden, N.J., where he remained hospitalized until his death. He was inducted into the Rock 'n' Roll Hall of Fame in 1987.

Wilson, James (1742–98) lawyer, political thinker, U.S. Supreme Court justice; born in Carskerdo, Scotland. He emigrated from Scotland in 1765, and after reading law under John Dickinson, he began a practice in 1768; by 1773 he had also begun the first of his lifelong speculations in land purchases. In 1774 he distributed to members of the First Continental Congress his pamphlet, *Considerations on the Nature and Extent of the Legislative Authority of the British Parliament,* in which he rejected any authority of the British Parliament over the colonies. He signed the Declaration of Independence and was a central figure at the Constitutional Convention (1787) where he argued strongly for popular election of both houses of Congress and the President. In 1789 he became one of the first six justices of the Supreme Court. His most important decision was in *Chisholm v. Georgia,* in which he was able to reaffirm his long-standing belief that sovereignty lay with the people of the U.S.A., not with the state. He had continued his land speculations even as a justice and was being threatened both by creditors and with impeachment when he died.

Wilson, James Harrison (1837–1925) soldier; born near Shawneetown, Ill. A hard-hitting Union cavalry commander, he defeated Nathan Forrest at Franklin, Tenn. (1864); a detachment of his command captured Jefferson Davis in Georgia in May 1865. Wilson volunteered on the outbreak of the Spanish-American War and saw service in China during the Boxer Rebellion (1900).

Wilson, James Q. (Quinn) (1931–) sociologist, criminologist; born in Denver, Colo. A Chicago Ph.D., he taught at Harvard (1961–87) and the University of California: Los Angeles (1987). He became identified as a neoconservative social scientist in works on criminals and the police, including *Varieties of Police Behavior* (1968) and *Thinking about Crime* (1975).

Wilson, Joseph C. (Chamberlain, II) (1909–71) manufacturer; born in Rochester, N.Y. (son of Joseph Robert Wilson). He joined the Haloid Company, his father's photographic paper business (founded in 1907), in 1933. As president (1946–66), he directed its long but successful development of the xerographic process, which after 1960 revolutionized U.S. office routines and made the company, renamed Xerox in 1961, a corporate giant.

Wilson, Kenneth G. (Geddes) (1936–) physicist; born in Waltham, Mass. He was a fellow at Harvard (1959–62) and

CERN, Geneva (1962–63). He moved to Cornell (1963–88), then joined Ohio State (1988). He won the 1982 Nobel Prize in physics for using the mathematical process of renormalization to explain phase transitions of matter. His later work involved applying renormalization to quark theory and computer simulations.

Wilson, Lanford (1937–) playwright; born in Lebanon, Mo. A founder of the Circle Repertory Company in New York (1969), he had several of his plays performed there, including *The Hot 1 Baltimore* (1972), which earned the off-Broadway record of 1,166 performances for a nonmusical. *The Fifth of July* (1978) and the Pulitzer Prize-winning *Talley's Folly* (1979), depict the post-Vietnam War world of the same Southern family.

Wilson, (Lewis Robert) "Hack" (1900–48) baseball player; born in Elwood City, Pa. During his 12-year career as an outfielder (1923–34), mostly with the Chicago Cubs, he hit 56 home runs and batted in the major league record 190 runs in 1930. Small for a slugger (5'6"), he led his league in home runs four times. He was elected to baseball's Hall of Fame in 1979.

Wilson, Louis (Round) (1876–1979) librarian, educator; born in Lenoir, N.C. He graduated from the University of North Carolina (Ph.D., 1905) and stayed on to plan the library school and develop the university's extensive Carolina history collection; he also served as dean of the extension program and editor of the university press. He spent ten years (1932–42) as the first dean of the University of Chicago Graduate Library School before returning to the University of North Carolina until his retirement in 1959.

Wilson, Orlando W. (1900–72) criminologist, educator; born in Veblen, S.D. Police chief of Fullerton, Calif. (1925–56) and Wichita, Kans. (1928–39), and superintendent of police in Chicago (1960–67), he became president of the Society for the Advancement of Criminology (19451–49). He taught at the University of California: Berkeley (1939–60) where he was dean of the school of criminology (1950–60). He was author of numerous books, including *Police Records* (1942) and *Police Administration* (1950), and editor of *Parker on Police* (1956).

Wilson, Richard (1926–) physicist; born in London, England. He came to the U.S.A. in 1950 to be a research associate at Rochester (1950–51) and Stanford (1951–52) while concurrently teaching at Christ Church, Oxford (1948–53). He joined Harvard in 1955. A specialist in both elementary particles and environmental physics, he was an outspoken advocate of the need for atomic power.

Wilson, Robert (1941–) playwright, theatrical director/producer/designer, sculptor; born in Waco, Texas. Trained as an artist, he became a creator of plotless, operatically scaled, highly stylized avant-garde theater works. His productions, which tend to investigate history, science and cultural identity, are often very long (*The Life and Times of Joseph Stalin* lasts 12 hours). His career was more active and his reputation far higher in Europe than in the United States. His sculpture won the Golden Lion at the 1993 Venice Biennale.

Wilson, Robert R. (Rathbun) (1914–) physicist; born in Frontier, Wyo. He was affiliated with Princeton (1940–46) when he took leave to become head of the experimental nuclear division that developed the atomic bomb at Los Alamos, N.M. (1944–46). He continued his research at

Cornell (1947–67), then moved to the University of Chicago (1967–80), where he designed the Fermi National Accelerator Laboratory and became its first director (1967–78). He also taught at Columbia University (1980–83).

Wilson, Robert W. (Woodrow) (1936–) physicist, radio astronomer; born in Houston, Texas. He was a fellow in radio astronomy at the California Institute of Technology (1962–63), then joined Bell Laboratories (1963). In 1964 he and his collaborator Arno Penzias detected microwave noise in the constellation Cassiopeia that proved to be residual radiation from the "big bang" at the creation of the universe. This discovery won Wilson and Penzias half the 1978 Nobel Prize in physics. Wilson also investigated the presence of interstellar carbon monoxide, and the composition of dark gas clouds of the Milky Way.

Wilson, Samuel "Uncle Sam" (1766–1854) meat packer; born in West Cambridge (now Arlington), Mass. A Revolutionary War veteran, he started a meatpacking plant in Troy, New York. The meat that he shipped to the army during the War of 1812 was stamped "U.S." The U.S. referred to U.S. properties but was then somewhat humorously said to stand for "Uncle Sam" Wilson. As the term "Uncle Sam" came into more widespread use as a symbol of the United States (after 1815), it has been generally claimed that it owes its origin to Samuel Wilson's nickname.

Wilson, (Theodore Shaw) Teddy (1912–86) jazz musician; born in Austin, Texas. He was a brilliant pianist who became the first black musician to work with a prominent white band when he joined Benny Goodman in 1936. He led numerous all-star recordings in the 1930s, fronted a big band and combo in the 1940s, worked on the staff of CBS in the 1950s, and free-lanced as a soloist and conservatory teacher thereafter.

Wilson, (Thomas) Woodrow (1856–1924) twenty-eighth U.S. president; born in Staunton, Va. Son of a Presbyterian minister, he studied at Princeton and Johns Hopkins, gaining his Ph.D. with the first of his major books on American government, *Congressional Government* (1885). After teaching at Bryn Mawr and Wesleyan (1885–90), he moved to Princeton, whose president he became in 1902 and where his reforms had a wide impact on American university education. In 1910, Wilson entered politics as a Democrat and was elected governor of New Jersey (1911–13); his liberal reforms brought him national attention and the Democratic presidential nomination in 1912 (although only on the 46th ballot). With the Republicans split between Taft and Theodore Roosevelt, Wilson won by a landslide. He effectively continued a reformist program he called the "New Freedom"; his initiatives included lowering tariffs, a graduated income tax, the Federal Reserve Act, the Federal Trade Commission, the Clayton Antitrust Act, the eight-hour workday, and landmark laws against child labor. On the international front he was less successful, especially in his attempts to intervene in Mexican politics. He won reelection in 1916 with a pledge to keep America out of the European war, but found the U.S.A. inexorably drawn in; declaring war on Germany in April 1917, he proposed a peace in the form of the "Fourteen Points," which brought Germany to the bargaining table in late 1918. Much of the world now hailed him as virtually a savior, but at the Versailles Peace Conference he was confronted by the compromises of *Realpolitik*. On his return to America his dream of a League of Nations – largely due to his refusal to compromise – went down to defeat in Congress as his health collapsed. He spent his last months in office incapacitated (his wife served as his intermediary for many decisions) and in 1921 retired to seclusion. Undeniably one of the most intelligent and high-minded presidents the U.S. has had, he was also rigid in certain ways and unresolved in others so that when it came to the climax of his life's work – America's entry into a League of Nations – he was unable to make the appropriate moves.

Wilson, (William Griffith) "Bill W." (1895–1971) founder of Alcoholics Anonymous; born in East Dorset, Vt. Alcoholism ran in his family and he suffered from a strong sense of inferiority and separation from other people. He was an artillery officer in World War I and a successful stockbroker during the 1920s, but he found his only true relief in alcohol. He experienced a spiritual recovery from alcoholism in 1934 and founded – with Dr. Robert H. Smith – Alcoholics Anonymous in 1935. Several of the premises and procedures of "AA" – regular meetings of people from all walks of life, identifying oneself only by a first name, full confession of one's weakness and misdeeds, the "12-step program" towards recovery – have been subsequently adopted by many other recovery programs such as Gamblers Anonymous and Overeaters Anonymous. Wilson himself remained known only as "Bill W." until later years when the program began to achieve widespread recognition.

Wilson, William Julius (1935–) sociologist; born in Derry Township, Pa. He earned his Ph.D. at Washington State University and joined the faculty of the University of Chicago (1971). He studied the ghetto poor and the cycle of poverty in America and developed city programs in Chicago to help urban African-Americans. His works include *Power, Racism and Privilege* (1973), *Through Different Eyes* (1973), and *The Truly Disadvantaged* (1987).

Wilson, (Woodrow) Olly (1937–) composer; born in St. Louis, Mo. After graduate work at the University of Iowa, he studied native music in Africa and taught at schools including Oberlin (Ohio) College and University of California: Berkeley (from 1970). He was a prominent composer in a modernist idiom, his music often reflecting his African-American background.

Winans, Ross (1796–1877) inventor, manufacturer; born in Sussex County, N.J. He had his first exposure to railroads while selling horses to the Baltimore & Ohio in 1828, and he soon designed an improved wheel for rail cars that set the standard for a full century. Winans worked for the B&O for a time before establishing his own railroad machinery business. He later produced a streamlined hull design for steamships. He acquired some local fame as a philanthropist and as the author of a series of unorthodox works on religion.

Winant, John G. (Gilbert) (1889–1947) governor, government official; born in New York City. Member of a wealthy family, he became a history teacher at his former prep school, St. Paul's School, in Concord, N.H. (1911–17). As a moderate Republican, he also served in the New Hampshire legislature (1916–17). He served in the American Air Service (1917–18). He returned to St. Paul's until 1920 when he went to the state senate, and then served as governor (1925–27, 1933–35). Although a Republican, he was recognized as sympathetic to labor, and President Franklin Roosevelt got him appointed to the International Labor

Organization (ICO) in Geneva (1935); he came back to Washington after a few months to head the newly created Social Security Board. On returning to the ICO in 1937, he became its director in 1939. Roosevelt named him ambassador to England (1940–46) and he helped plan the Three-Power Foreign Ministers Conference in Moscow (1943). In 1946 President Truman appointed him a representative to the Economic and Social Council of the UN.

Winchell, Walter (b. Winchel) (1897–1972) journalist; born in Chicago. Father of the newspaper gossip column, which he pioneered in the 1920s along with many slangy neologisms, Winchell also was a familiar voice on radio, from 1929 through the mid-1950s, with his staccato delivery punctuated by the sound of teletype keys.

Winchester, Oliver (Fisher) (1810–80) manufacturer; born in Boston, Mass. He worked at various jobs until 1837 when he opened a men's clothing store in Baltimore that manufactured and sold shirts. In 1847 he moved to New York City where he and a partner made men's shirts by a new method Winchester had patented; business was so successful that in 1850 they opened a factory in New Haven, Conn. By 1856 he had become the principal stockholder and owner of Volcanic Repeating Arms Company, which as president he reorganized as the New Haven Arms Company (1857). The company was superintended by the well-known armaments inventor, Tyler Henry, and Winchester acquired the rights to manufacture pistols and rifles under the patents of Henry and others. By 1860 he was manufacturing a new, superior repeating rifle, used by both sides in the Civil War; by acquiring still more inventions and patents, Winchester greatly improved the rifle in subsequent years. His company had been reorganized as the Winchester Repeating Arms Company in 1866. Active in politics, he served as lieutenant governor of Connecticut (1866–67). He made generous gifts to Yale.

Windom, William (1827–91) U.S. representative/senator; born in Belmont, Ohio. A lawyer before going to the U.S. House of Representatives (Rep., Minn.; 1859–69), he went mid-term to the Senate (1870–83). He practiced law in New York City, then became Secretary of the Treasury (1889–91).

Windsor, Wallis Warfield, Duchess of (b. Bessie Wallis Warfield) (1896–1986) socialite; born in Blue Ridge Summit, Pa. Her father, a member of an old established family, died when she was an infant, and her early years were spent in genteel poverty. Bills for her Baltimore private schools, Arundell and Oldfields, were paid by a prosperous uncle. She became a popular member of a transatlantic social set. In 1930, while married to her second husband, British-born Ernest Simpson, she met Edward, Prince of Wales. Their relationship became an international *cause célèbre* and soon after his accession as Edward VIII in 1936, he abdicated in order to marry her. Shunned by most of the British royal family, the Windsors lived among the international social elite, mainly in France.

Winfrey, Oprah (Gail) (1954–) television talk show host; born in Kosciusko, Miss. A television coanchor while in college, she cohosted *Baltimore is Talking* (1977–84). Taking over ABC's *A.M. Chicago* in 1984, she surpassed veteran Phil Donahue with her confessional style talk show, syndicated as the *Oprah Winfrey Show* (1986). She received an Academy Award nomination for her role in *The Color Purple* (1985). Intensely energetic and immensely rich, she

founded her own production company, allowing herself to do movies and television shows she personally believed in.

Winnemucca, Sarah (b. Thocmetony) (?1844–91) Northern Paiute educator, interpreter, writer; born near Humboldt Lake, Nev. She served often as an interpreter with the U.S. Army, looking to it for fair treatment for Indians and urging her people to keep the peace. She worked tirelessly, although ultimately unsuccessfully, for a permanent Paiute reservation. In 1884 she published *Life Among the Paiutes*.

Winogrand, Garry (1928–84) photographer, teacher; born in New York. Between assignments as a commercial photographer in New York City (1952–69), he started shooting street scenes, and from 1969 he taught photography and used grants to pursue his art.

Winokur, George (1925–) psychiatrist; born in Philadelphia. He was professor of psychiatry at Washington University (St. Louis) (1966–71) and professor of psychiatry at the University of Iowa College of Medicine (1991). His primary area of research was in the genetic epidemiology of manic depressive (bipolar) illness, unipolar depressive illness, and alcoholism.

Winslow, Charles-Edward (Amory) (1877–1957) bacteriologist, public health expert; born in Boston, Mass. A leader in the nascent American public health movement, his career combined roles of researcher, educator, and civil servant. He took an M.S. at the Massachusetts Institute of Technology where he then taught while heading the sewage experiment station (1899–1910). He taught at the College of the City of New York (1910–14), then joined the faculty of Yale (1915–57). He was also curator of public health at the American Museum of Natural History (1910–22) (where his first exhibit was of giant models of house flies and other insect disease vectors). In 1926 he was president of the American Public Health Association and in the 1950s he served as a consultant to the World Health Organization. In addition to promoting public health and preventive medicine, he advocated national health insurance. An author of more than 600 titles, including *Cost of Sickness and the Price of Health* (1951), he was the first editor of the *Journal of Bacteriology* (1916), and editor of the *Journal of Public Health* (1944–54).

Winslow, Edward (1595–1655) Pilgrim leader, author; born in Droitwitch, England. He negotiated with Indians on behalf of the Plymouth colony and was the governor for three terms (1633, 1636, 1644). His accounts of the Plymouth settlement (published in England, 1622, 1624) were the first to be written in America.

Winsor, Justin (1831–97) historian, librarian; born in Boston, Mass. Stemming from his early interest in history, his first book, *A History of the Town of Duxbury,* was published in 1849 during his freshman year at Harvard. He left Harvard in 1852 without taking a degree and traveled in Europe. He returned to Boston in 1854 and began writing criticism, poetry, and fiction for various periodicals. He became a trustee and then director (1868–77) of the Boston Public Library. During his 20-year tenure as librarian of Harvard College (1877–97), he became the first president of the American Library Association (1876–85) and a cofounder of the *American Library Journal*. As a historian, he wrote such groundbreaking works as *The Reader's Handbook of the American Revolution* (1880), *A Narrative and Critical History of America* (1884–89), *The Mississippi*

Basin (1895), and *The Westward Movement* (1897). His interest in and use of maps made him the leading historical cartographer of his day.

Winter, Paul (Theodore) (1939–) bandleader, composer; born in Altoona, Pa. A child musician, he learned saxophone and toured with the Ringling Brothers Circus at age 17. In 1961 his college sextet won a 23-country tour of Latin America. He formed the Paul Winter Consort in 1967 and began mixing folk, classical, ethnic, and jazz forms, creating what he called "Earth music," a prototype of New Age music. Dedicated to worldwide cultural and environmental issues, the Consort performs in many benefit concerts and has won many humanitarian awards.

Winter, William Forrest (1923–) governor, lawyer; born in Grenada, Miss. A lawyer, he served in the Mississippi house of representatives (Dem., 1948–56), becoming state treasurer in 1964 and lieutenant governor (1972–76). As governor (1980–84), he tried to improve Mississippi's image, inviting intellectuals to the governor's mansion, courting high technology industry, and mandating compulsory school attendance. He returned to his law firm, Ludlum, Winter, and Stennis.

Winters, (Arthur) Yvor (1900–68) poet, literary critic; born in Chicago. He taught at Stanford University (1928–66), where he received his Ph.D. (1934). In the 1930s he began writing literary criticism; later works include *In Defense of Reason* (1947) and *The Function of Criticism* (1957). He won the Bollingen Prize (1961) for his taut, formalistic poetry. A controversial critic, he attacked popular literary icons ranging from Walt Whitman to Henry James.

Winthrop, John (1714–79) astronomer, mathematician; born in Boston, Mass. (descended from John Winthrop, colonial governor). The first thorough American scientist, he was a professor of mathematics and natural philosophy at Harvard (1738–79). He kept a detailed journal of the weather in Cambridge during 1742–79, and he predicted the return of Halley's comet in 1759. He performed advanced studies in astronomy and introduced algebra and calculus to the Harvard curriculum. He was an ardent patriot during the American Revolution.

Winthrop, John (1587–1649) first governor of Massachusetts Bay; born in Edwardstone, England. A Puritan lawyer, he decided to emigrate. He signed the Cambridge agreement (1629) and was chosen as governor of the expedition while he was still in England. He arrived at Salem in 1630 and soon relocated the colony to Boston. He remained the preeminent leader of the colony, serving as governor during four periods (1629–34, 1637–40, 1642–44, 1646–49). He came into conflict with the "freemen" of the colony who resented his belief that governors and magistrates should rule as they best saw fit (he was a theocrat, not a democrat). He demonstrated the harsh and forbidding aspect of Puritan rule when he exiled Anne Hutchinson and her followers for their unorthodox views. He ably defended the colony's charter in a letter to the Lords Commissioners of Plantations (1638) and was elected as the president of the Confederation for the United Colonies in 1643. He became less popular in his last years as governor but he had piloted the Massachusetts Bay colony through its first years and had left a deep imprint upon its character. He wrote a journal that was published in part as *A Journal of the Transactions and Occurrences in the Settlement of Massachusetts . . . 1630 to 1644*. Throughout his career, his main intent was to erect a pious, godly, Puritan commonwealth.

Winthrop, John ("Fitz-John") (1638–1707) soldier, colonial governor; born in Ipswich, Mass. Son and grandson of colonial governors, he commanded Connecticut militia against the Dutch (1673) and the French (1690) and served as governor of Connecticut from 1698–1707.

Winthrop, John, Jr. (1605–76) colonial governor; born in Groton, Suffolk, England (son of John Winthrop, 1587–1649). He served as governor of Connecticut (1657–58, 1659–76) and obtained a liberal charter for Connecticut in 1662. His scientific interests – chemistry and medicine – led to his becoming a member of the Royal Society (1663).

Winthrop, Robert Charles (1807–94) U.S. representative/senator; born in Boston, Mass. After studying law in Daniel Webster's office, he served in the state legislature before his election to the U.S. House of Representatives (Whig, Mass.; 1840–50). He was Speaker of the House from 1847–49. Appointed to succeed Daniel Webster in the U.S. Senate (1850–51), he was defeated for reelection by antislavery forces the following year. A scholar and orator, he published a biography of his illustrious ancestor, John Winthrop.

Wirt, William (1772–1834) lawyer, cabinet officer, author; born in Bladensburg, Md. Son of Swiss-German tavernkeepers, he read law and began his practice in Virginia. After three terms as clerk of Virginia's House of Delegates (1800–02), he gained fame as assistant prosecuting attorney in Aaron Burr's treason trial (1807). As U.S. attorney general (1817–29) under both President James Monroe and John Quincy Adams, he argued landmark cases. He was the reluctant presidential candidate of the Anti-Masons in 1832. With some ambition to have a literary reputation, he enjoyed considerable popularity with *The Letters of the British Spy* (1803), observations on society supposedly written by an English visitor. Less successful was his *Sketches of the Life and Character of Patrick Henry* (1817).

Wirz, Henry (1822–65) physician, army officer; born in Switzerland. A Louisiana physician, he was wounded at Fair Oaks and Seven Pines (May 1862). After some time in Europe as a Confederate agent, in January 1864 he became superintendent of Andersonville prison in South Carolina; it became notorious for its appalling conditions and high death rate. He was later convicted of conspiring to murder prisoners and hanged in November 1865 – the only person executed after the Civil War for war crimes.

Wise, Henry Alexander (1806–76) U.S. representative; born in Drummondtown, Va. A Virginia lawyer, he served as a Jacksonian, Whig, and Democratic member of the U.S. House of Representatives (1833–44), resigning to become ambassador to Brazil (1844–47) and governor of Virginia (1856–60).

Wise, Isaac Mayer (1819–1900) rabbi; born in Steingrub, Bohemia, (now Czech Republic). He studied in Vienna and settled in the U.S.A. in 1846. Rabbi of Orthodox congregations in Albany, N.Y., and Cincinnati, he changed them into Reform synagogues, and soon became the preeminent leader of Reform Judaism in the U.S.A. In 1873 he organized the Union of American Hebrew Congregations; in 1875 he founded the Hebrew Union College in Cincinnati and served as its president until his death; and in 1889 he established the Central Conference of American Rabbis. He was founder and editor of the *American Israelite* and *Deborah*. A prolific writer, he published many historical and religious works, including *History of the Israelitish Nation* (1854), as well as novels, plays, and a memoir, *Reminiscences* (1901).

Wise, John (1652–1725) Congregational clergyman, theologian, author; born in Roxbury, Mass. A Harvard graduate (1673), he served as a preacher in Branford, Conn. (1675–76), in Hatfield, Mass. (1677–78), and in Ipswich, Mass., where he was ordained in 1683. He spent the rest of his life in Ipswich (with the exception of service as chaplain of the 1690 expedition to Quebec) and became embroiled in battles against colonial taxes. He also protested against the centralization of church government, as seen in *The Vindication of the Church Government of New-England Churches* (1717). Known for his independent views and lively prose, he also defended those accused of witchcraft (1703) and promoted smallpox vaccinations. His egalitarian "democratic" views made him a popular writer for both American Revolutionaries and abolitionists.

Wise, Stephen Samuel (b. Weiss) (1874–1949) rabbi, social activist, Zionist leader; born in Budapest, Hungary. Brought to the U.S.A. as a baby by his rabbi father, he grew up in New York City, studied to be a rabbi there and in Vienna, and by age 19 was the rabbi of New York's Congregation B'nai Jeshurun. Outspoken in his sympathies for labor and other social causes, he refused an offer to be rabbi of New York's most prestigious temple, Emanu-El; instead he founded his own Free Synagogue (1907), where until his death he preached a message that combined liberal Judaism with calls for social justice. Along with openly siding with labor, he attacked everyone from corrupt politicians to the Ku Klux Klan. He was one of the founders of the National Association for the Advancement of Colored People (1909) and the American Civil Liberties Union (1920). He was one of the founders of the Federation of American Zionists (1893), was the first president of the new Zionist Organization of America (1918), and in 1919 went to France to argue for the goal of a Jewish homeland in Palestine. During the 1930s he spoke out against Hitler's treatment of Jews; in the 1940s, with World War II raging, he took the lead in demanding that the Allies stop the extermination of the Jews. Not unexpectedly in such a man, he could be contentious, and in his final years he lost his leadership of the American Zionist movement; but for half a century he had been one of the strongest voices for and from the American Jewish community.

Wiseman, Frederick (1930–) documentary filmmaker; born in Boston, Mass. After teaching law, he turned to making his own distinctive kind of documentaries, starting with *Titicut Follies* (1967) and continuing through a long series that focused on American institutions, such as *Model* (1980), and then increasingly on broader experiences, as in *Near Death* (1989). The hallmark of a Wiseman documentary is its apparently nonintrusive ability simply to record on film and in sound the minutiae of the subject and to leave all interpretation to the viewer. He formed his own film company and in later years accepted commissions from television companies and other organizations.

Wissler, Clark (Clarkson Davis) (1870–1947) anthropologist; born in Wayne County, Ind. He spent his career at the American Museum of Natural History (1902–47). He wrote a landmark text, *The American Indian* (1917), popularized anthropology as an academic discipline, and formulated the concept of North American "culture areas" and the "age-area" theory of the diffusion of culture.

Wistar, Caspar (1761–1818) physician; born in Philadelphia (grandson of Caspar Wistar, 1696–1742). After completing his medical studies at Edinburgh, Scotland, he returned to Philadelphia and started a practice. In 1789 he succeeded Benjamin Rush as professor of chemistry at the medical school of the College of Philadelphia (later University of Pennsylvania), then became professor of anatomy and midwifery (1792–1810). He published *System of Anatomy*, the first American anatomy textbook (1811). Elected to the American Philosophical Society in 1787, he succeeded Thomas Jefferson as president (1815–18). Wistar parties, the discussion groups he was noted for sponsoring, continued after his death, and in 1818 a genus of vines, *Wistaria* (now *Wisteria*), was named in his honor.

Wistar, Caspar (1696–1752) glass manufacturer; born near Heidelberg, Germany. He created a window and bottle glassmaking factory in West Jersey in 1740. It was the earliest successful workers' co-operative venture in the colonies.

Wister, Owen (1860–1938) writer; born in Germantown, Pa. He graduated from Harvard (1882) before studying music composition in Paris (1882–84). Suffering from ill health, he spent summers in the American West, and these visits profoundly affected his future writing. He studied law at Harvard (1885–88), and settled in Philadelphia, where he practiced law. By 1891 he devoted himself to writing biographies, essays, and novels. He is remembered for his Western novels, notably *The Virginian* (1902), a book containing the prototype of the American cowboy in subsequent fictions and films.

Withers, Frederick C. (Clarke) (1828–1901) architect; born in Shepton Mallet, Somerset, England. His wide New York practice was identified with ecclesiastical and institutional architecture and the High Victorian Gothic style. In partnership with Calvert Vaux and Frederick Law Olmsted (1864–71), he worked on Central Park, New York.

Witherspoon, John (1723–94) Protestant clergyman, Continental Congressman, educator; born in Gifford, Scotland. Educated at the University of Edinburgh, he served two Scottish parishes before emigrating to America in 1768 to become president of the College of New Jersey (now Princeton). During his long tenure (until 1794) he greatly strengthened both the college and the American Presbyterian Church. A firm supporter of the colonies in the dispute with Britain, he was the only clergyman to sign the Declaration of Independence. He served in the Continental Congress (1776–82) and, after the American Revolution, in the New Jersey legislature. Not widely known as a "founding father," he played an influential role in establishing several major American institutions.

Wittkower, Rudolf (1901–71) architectural historian; born in Berlin, Germany. After twenty years at the Warburg Institute, London, he taught at Columbia University (1956–69). His major scholarly contributions included his explication of religious symbolism in Renaissance architecture in *Architectural Principles in the Age of Humanism* (1949) and his distinction between mannerism and baroque architecture.

Wittwer, Sylvan H. (Harold) (1917–) agronomist; born in Hurricane, Utah. He taught at his alma mater, the University of Missouri (1943–46), before moving to Michigan State University (1946–83) to teach horticulture and direct the

Agriculture Experiment Station (1965–83). An international authority on raising greenhouse tomatoes, he wrote several books including *Greenhouse Tomatoes, Lettuce, and Cucumbers* (1979). As the only American member of the Lenin All Union Academy of Agricultural Sciences, he consulted to Russia's president on agricultural matters in 1991.

Wolcott, Oliver (1760–1833) cabinet member, governor; born in Litchfield, Conn. A lawyer, he became a U.S. treasury auditor (1789–91), then U.S. comptroller (1791–95). He won the support of Alexander Hamilton, whom he succeeded as secretary of the treasury (1795–1800), but caught between the machinations of his friend Hamilton and other Federalists, and frustrated by his inability to improve the nation's financial situation, he retired from the treasury. Moving to New York City about 1803, he turned to business and then became president of the Bank of America (1812–15). He then returned to Litchfield, Conn., where he became a gentleman farmer. Having switched to the Democratic-Republican Party, he became governor of Connecticut (1817–27) and during those years he introduced such major reforms as separation of governmental powers and separation of church and state, and generally introduced new democratic policies.

Wolf, Eric R. (Robert) (1923–) anthropologist; born in Vienna, Austria. He emigrated to the U.S.A. in 1940. His academic career included teaching at Herbert Lehman College, City University of New York (1971). His work on peasant cultures and their integration into industrialized societies included fieldwork in Puerto Rico, Mexico, and Italy. He wrote *Peasants* (1966) and *Peasant Wars of the Twentieth Century* (1969).

Wolfe, Thomas (Clayton) (1900–38) writer, playwright; born in Ashville, N.C. Son of a stonecutter, he studied at the University of North Carolina (B.A. 1920), and Harvard (M.A. 1922; graduate study 1923). He taught intermittently at New York University (1924–30), and lived in Brooklyn, N.Y. He traveled in Europe several times, began his career writing plays, but turned to writing novels during his turbulent affair with an older woman who was married and a mother. His novels were fictionalized biographies, and his writing habits, influenced by excessive drinking, were haphazard and undisciplined. His early work, *Look Homeward, Angel: A Story of the Buried Life* (1929), benefited from extensive editing by Maxwell Perkins at Scribner's. That novel and *Of Time and the River: A Legend of Man's Hunger in His Youth* (1935), *The Web and the Rock* (1939), and *You Can't Go Home Again* (1940) (the latter two published posthumously after being heavily edited by Edward C. Aswell) continue to engage modern readers with their mythical portrait of Wolfe as a young writer. He died of tuberculosis of the brain.

Wolfe, (Thomas Kennerley) Tom (1931–) writer, artist; born in Richmond, Va. He received his doctorate in American Studies from Yale University in 1957 and began a career as a reporter for the *Springfield Union* (1956–59); the *Washington Post* (1959–62); and the *New York Herald Tribune* (1962–66). The originator of such phrases as "radical chic," and "the me decade," his "new journalism" essays were collected under such titles as *The Kandy-Kolored Tangerine-Flake Streamline Baby* (1965). His other nonfiction titles include the *Electric Acid Koolaid Test* (1968), *The Right Stuff* (1979), and *From Bauhaus to Our*

House (1981). An artist, he had two one-man shows in New York City (1965, 1974) and published a collection of his drawings called *In Our Time* (1980). *The Bonfire of the Vanities,* his first novel, was published in 1987. Cultivating his "dandy" image with such affectations as his trademark white suit and arch mannner, he seemed genuinely committed to his conservative stance against a generally liberal New York intellectual world.

Wolfes, Felix (1892–1971) music teacher, composer; born in Hanover, Germany. Forced by the Nazis to abandon a promising career as an opera conductor and transcriber of modern operas for piano, he came to New York and was assistant conductor at the Metropolitan Opera (1938–47). In 1948 he joined the faculty of the New England Conservatory of Music; there, at Tanglewood, and in private lessons in New York he taught two generations of American singers. He composed over 200 *Lieder* in the classic vein, which are now being published and increasingly sung in public.

Wolfskill, William (1798–1866) trapper, California pioneer; born near Richmond, Ky. He trapped along the Rio Grande and became a Mexican citizen in 1830. He pioneered the western Spanish trail from Taos to California (1830–31) and settled in Los Angeles. He planted the first private orange grove in that area and was the first person there to ship oranges commercially.

Wollaston, John (active 1736–70) painter; born in London, England. He emigrated to New York (1749), painted portraits, and worked for the British East India Company in Bengal (1758–67). He moved to Charlestown, S.C. (1767), then returned to London. Approximately 300 unsigned portraits are attributed to him, such as *Cornelia Beekman* (c. 1750–55).

Wolpe, Joseph (1915–) psychiatrist; born in Johannesburg, South Africa. He earned an M.D. at the University of Witwatersrand, South Africa, and taught there before moving to the psychiatry faculties of the University of Virginia (1960–65) and Temple University (1965–84). His therapeutic techniques for curing phobias and anxiety and his published works, such as *The Practice of Behavior Therapy* (1969, later revised), provided the basis (with B. F. Skinner's work) for modern behavior therapy, which cures emotional problems by changing patients' behavior.

Wolpe, Stefan (1902–72) composer; born in Berlin, Germany. Active in German theater productions with Brecht and others in the 1920s, he studied with Busoni and Webern before fleeing the Nazis in 1934. In the U.S.A. from 1938, he taught in various schools including Black Mountain (1952–56) and Long Island University (1957–68). From a variety of influences ranging from jazz to 12-tone technique, he composed in a highly controlled and increasingly complex style.

Wolper, David L. (Lloyd) (1928–) television/film producer; born in New York. Most famous for his television documentaries, he went into feature films with such movies as *Willy Wonka and the Chocolate Factory* (1971) and *Visions of Eight* (1973).

Wolpoff, Milford H. (Howell) (1942–) physical anthropologist; born in Chicago, Ill. He taught at Case Western Reserve (1968–70) before becoming a professor at the University of Michigan (1970). He made extensive studies of fossil hominid evolution, tool-making, and dental variation.

Wonder, Stevie (b. Steveland Judkins) (1950–) musician; born in Saginaw, Mich. A premature baby, he was blinded by receiving too much oxygen in the incubator. He began playing the harmonica at an early age and was signed to a long-term contract with Motown Records in 1960. In 1963 he released his first album, *Little Stevie Wonder: The 12 Year Old Genius,* and its single release "Fingertips - Pt. 2," became his first million seller. During the 1960s, while attending the Michigan School for the Blind, he had numerous hit records in the classic Motown rhythm-and-blues style. In 1971, upon his 21st birthday, he renegotiated his contract and gained full artistic control over his work. Throughout the 1970s, he became proficient in the use of synthesizers and electronic keyboards and he released a series of innovative, commercially successful albums featuring a fusion of progressive rock and soul, biting social commentary, and sentimental ballads. In 1976, he signed a contract with Motown for $13 million, the largest negotiated in recording history at that date. In the 1980s and 1990s, he was increasingly engaged in children's and civil rights causes, and he led the campaign to make Martin Luther King's birthday a national holiday. He was inducted into the Rock 'n' Roll Hall of Fame in 1989.

Wood, Beatrice (1893–) ceramist; born in San Francisco. After art study at Académie Julian in Paris, she returned in 1914 to New York where she joined Marcel Duchamp's circle. In 1928 she moved to Los Angeles and began to study ceramics with Glen Lukens and the Natzlers. She established a studio in Ojai, Calif., in the 1940s. There she continued to produce her famed luster glaze pots well into her 90s.

Wood, Benjamin (1820–1900) journalist; born in Shelbyville, Ky. As editor of the mass-audience *New York Daily News* (1860–1900), he helped it attract the largest readership of any U.S. paper. He was controversial because of his support for the Confederate cause in the Civil War.

Wood, Bryce (1909–86) political scientist; born in Everett, Wash. He promoted research on Latin America as executive associate of the Social Science Research Council (1949–73) while himself writing such influential works on American foreign policy and international relations as *The United States and Latin American Wars, 1932–1942* (1966) and two studies of the Good Neighbor policy (1966, 1985).

Wood, Devolson (1832–97) civil engineer, educator, author; born in Smyrna, N.Y. He designed an ore dock in 1866 and invented an air compressor and a steam rock drill. He taught from 1872 to 1897 at Stevens Institute of Technology, Hoboken, N.J. He was the author of works on mechanics, bridge construction, and mathematics.

Wood, Edith Elmer (1871–1945) housing reformer; born in Portsmouth, N.H. After graduating from Smith College (1890), she wrote fiction, undertook settlement house work, and married before launching her influential, life-long career in housing reforms. As lobbyist, writer, and government consultant, she helped define New Deal housing policy.

Wood, Fernando (1812–81) U.S. representative, mayor, businessman; born in Philadelphia. As a Tammany Hall Democrat, he served New York City in the U.S. House of Representatives (1841–43). He then made a fortune as a merchant from the California gold rush of 1849. Again as a Tammany candidate, he served as mayor of New York City (1855–59) and although he achieved some good things – notably in helping to create Central Park – his administra-tion was marked by widespread graft and crime. Tammany Hall rejected him so he formed his own ticket, which he called Mozart Hall, and was elected for a third term (1859–61). Opposed to the Civil War, he joined with C. L. Vallandigham to form the Peace Democrats in 1863. He went on to serve in the U.S. House of Representatives (Dem., N.Y.; 1863–65, 1867–81), and although he often opposed his own party, he managed to gain leadership roles and overcome the dubious associations of his past.

Wood, Grant (1892–1942) painter; born in Anamosa, Iowa. After working as a farmer, silversmith, and designer, he made four trips to Europe in the 1920s where he was exposed to the late medieval primitive painting style that would later influence his work. He settled back in Cedar Rapids, Iowa, becoming a painter who captured the idiosyncratic aspects of the people and landscape there, thus becoming a founder of the so-called regional movement. His most famous works, such as *American Gothic* (1930) and *Daughters of Revolution* (1932), are characterized by a flat, almost abstract surface and ironic subtext. From 1934 on, he taught painting at the University of Iowa.

Wood, Harland G. (Goff) (1907–91) biochemist; born in Delavan, Minn. He performed research at the University of Wisconsin (1935–36), where he and E. L. Tatum discovered that vitamin B_{12} is necessary to bacteria growth. He moved to Iowa State (1936–43), then became a professor at the University of Minnesota (1943–46). He joined Case Western Reserve (1946–78), remaining active in professional societies and in education after his retirement. He made major contributions to studies of biological energy systems, including the discovery that carbon dioxide is utilized by heterotrophic organisms.

Wood, Leonard (1860–1927) soldier and physician; born in Winchester, N.H. A Harvard medical graduate (1884), he participated in the campaign against Geronimo (1886), served as President McKinley's physician and, with Theodore Roosevelt, organized the first U.S. Volunteer Cavalry – the Rough Riders – for action against the Spanish in Cuba (1898). Wood arose to army chief of staff (1910) but was passed over for command of the American Expeditionary Force during World War I.

Wood, Robert E. (Elkington) (1879–1969) retail executive; born in Kansas City, Mo. The son of a Kansas homesteader, he graduated from West Point and served in the army until 1915. For his last ten years in uniform he was quartermaster and eventually director of the Panama Railroad Company during the construction of the Panama Canal. During World War I he was the army's quartermaster general. He began his 30-year career with Sears, Roebuck and Co. in 1924. As vice-president (1924–28), president (1928–39), and chairman (1939–54), he built Sears into the world's largest general merchandiser. Supervising the opening of Sears' first retail stores in 1925, he redirected the company's focus from mail order to chain store retail operations. He helped to establish the largest employee savings and profit-sharing pension plan in the country and formed the subsidiary Allstate Insurance Co. (1931; chairman 1939–54). A prominent Republican, he strongly supported Senator Joseph McCarthy's anti-Communist campaign in the 1950s, led the America First Committee, and cofounded what became the Manion Forum for the propagation of arch-conservative political views (1954).

Wood, Robert W. (Williams) (1868–1955) physicist; born in Concord, Mass. He taught at Wisconsin (1897–1901), then joined Johns Hopkins (1901–38), where he served after his retirement as research professor until 1953. An authority on spectroscopy, he helped develop color photography, devised practical uses for infrared and ultraviolet light, and also performed research on sound waves. He wrote over 200 scientific articles, some science fiction, and an illustrated book of nonsense verse, *How to Tell the Birds from the Flowers* (1907).

Woodberry, G. E. (George Edward) (1855–1930) literary critic; born in Beverly, Mass. An inspiring teacher at Columbia University (1891–1904) and elsewhere, he wrote essays (notably *Heart of Man* (1899)) and biographies of Poe, Hawthorne, and Emerson but published little in his last, reclusive years.

Woodbridge, F. J. E. (Frederick James Eugene) (1867–1940) philosopher, educator; born in Windsor, Ontario. Raised in Michigan, he graduated from Amherst College (1889) and Union Theological Seminary, but decided against the ministry and studied philosophy in Germany (1892–94). After teaching at the University of Minnesota, where he built a respected philosophy department, he became a professor at Columbia University (1902–39) and dean of graduate studies (1912–29), playing a key role in Columbia's development. In 1904 he cofounded the *Journal of Philosophy,* an organ of anti-idealist philosophy, which he edited thereafter. He was a realist in the tradition of Aristotle; his works include *The Purpose of History* (1916) and *The Realm of Mind* (1926).

Woodbury, Levi (1789–1851) cabinet member, Supreme Court justice; born in Francestown, N.H. He served as a New Hampshire Superior Court judge (1817–23), as governor (1823–24), and in the U.S. Senate (N.H.; 1825–31, 1841–45). He served Presidents Jackson and Van Buren as secretary of the navy (1831–34) and secretary of the treasury (1834–41). President Polk named him to the U.S. Supreme Court (1845–51).

Wooden, John (Robert) (1910–   ) basketball coach; born in Martinsville, Ind. He was a three-time All-American guard on Purdue University's basketball teams (1930–32). During his career as coach at the University of California: Los Angeles (1948–75), his teams won a record ten National Collegiate Athletic Association championships, seven of them consecutively (1967–73). He is a member of the Basketball Hall of Fame, and in 1977 an annual award was established in his name to honor the outstanding college basketball player-student of the year.

Woodhull, Victoria Claflin (1838–1927) **and Claflin, Tennessee Celeste** (1845–1923) spiritualists, entrepreneurs, activists; both born in Homer, Ohio. One of the more outrageous "sister acts" in American history, as young girls they traveled with their dubious father as part of a family medicine show, claiming cures for whatever ailed. In 1853 Victoria married a Dr. Canning Woodhull and would have two children by him; he would come and go in her life and in 1866 she divorced him and took out a marriage license with Col. James Harvey Blood, a spiritualist/faddist. That same year, Tennessee, after having been charged with manslaughter for the death of one of her "patients," married a gambler. In 1868 Victoria was "visited" by a spirit who told her to go to New York City, and the whole family followed her there. The sisters, both physically attractive, gained the support of Commodore Cornelius Vanderbilt and soon were running Woodhull, Claflin & Company, the first stock brokerage owned by women; they prospered through their investments. Victoria then came under the influence of Stephen Pearl Andrews, a utopian intellectual, and in 1870 she announced she was a candidate for the president of the U.S.A. – the first woman to do so. She also started *Woodhull & Claflin's Weekly,* which for the next six years published a mixture of muckraking, fads, scandals, and surprises including the first English translation in the U.S.A. of Marx's Communist Manifesto. She delivered a statement to a Congressional committee on the right of women to vote (1871) and was briefly adopted by the women suffrage movement, but she was dropped in 1872 and so formed her own Equal Rights Party. Meanwhile, she had publicly charged the Reverend Henry Ward Beecher with committing adultery with a parishioner and by election time the sisters were in jail, accused of sending obscenity through the mails; they were acquitted in mid-1873. After somewhat tempering her radical views, Victoria went off to England in 1877, accompanied by Tennessee, and began lecturing on "The Human Body The Temple of God." By 1883 she was marrying a proper Englishman, John Martin; Tennessee married a prosperous merchant (1885), and when he was made a baronet, she became Lady Cook. They continued their crusading, both in England and on visits to the U.S.A. – Victoria published (1892–1901) a periodical promoting eugenics, *Humanitarian* – and lived out their years as notorious relics of an unorthodox past.

Woods, Arthur (1870–1942) public official, businessman; born in Boston, Mass. His career ranged from teaching, reporting, and running a lumber business in Mexico (1907), to police work and philanthropy. Named deputy police commissioner of New York City (1907–09), he became police commissioner (1909–14). During World War I he helped direct the U.S. propaganda efforts abroad, was staff director of military aeronautics, and later helped to reestablish servicemen in civilian life (1919). After chairing the president's Committee for Employment (1930–31), he became the first chairman of Colonial Williamsburg and author of several books.

Woods, Granville T. (1856–1910) inventor; born in Ohio. Born to free African-Americans, he received only sketchy schooling, quitting in his early teens to start a variety of jobs – in a railroad machine shop, as a railroad engineer, in a steel mill, as an engineer on a British ship, and then back on the railroad. But somewhere along the way – evidently in New York City between 1876–78 – he had taken some courses in electricity, which he evidently realized held the key to the future, and in 1881 he settled in Cincinnati, Ohio, where he eventually was able to set up his own company to develop, manufacture, and sell electrical apparatus. His first invention was for an improved steam boiler furnace, but thereafter his patents were mainly for electrical devices, such as his second invention, an improved telephone transmitter. The patent for his device combining the telephone and telegraph was bought by Alexander Graham Bell and the payment freed Woods to devote himself to his own researches. One of his most important inventions was the "troller," or grooved metal wheel, that allowed street cars (soon known as "trolleys") to collect electric power from overhead wires. His most important invention (1887) was the multiplex telegraph (also known as the induction telegraph, or block system); he defeated Thomas Edison's legal suit that challenged his patent, then turned down Edison's offer to make him a partner. Thereafter Woods was often known as "the black Edison." After receiving the patent for the multiplex telegraph, he reorganized his Cincinnati company as the Woods Electric Co., but in 1890 he moved his own research operations to New York City, where he was joined by a brother, Lyates Woods, who also had several inventions of his own. Granville's next most important invention (1901) was the power pick-up device that is the basis of the so-called "third rail" used by electric-powered transit systems. Between 1902–05 he received patents for an improved air-brake system. By the time of his death he had some 60 patents, many of them assigned to the major manufacturers of electrical equipment that is a part of everyone's daily life.

Woods, William Burnham (1824–87) Supreme Court justice; born in Newark, Ohio. He served the Union Army and fought in several major Civil War battles, earning the rank of brigadier general. He was appointed a U.S. circuit judge for Georgia (1869–80) until President Hayes named him to the U.S. Supreme Court (1881–87).

Woodson, Carter G. (Godwin) (1875–1950) historian, educator; born in New Canton, Va. Impoverished and lacking formal schooling until age 17, he went on to earn a Ph.D. from Harvard (1912). He devoted his life to promoting African-American education and history in the hope of improving American race relations. He founded the *Journal of Negro History* (1916), the black-owned Associated Publishers press (1921), and the popular *Negro History Bulletin* (1937). He inaugurated Negro History Week (1926), collected and edited primary documents of black history and, a prolific author of popular and scholarly books, created widespread public interest in black history, laying the groundwork for the later development of African-American studies.

Woodville, Richard Caton (1825–c. 1855) painter; born in Baltimore, Md. He studied medicine (c. 1842), painting in Düsseldorf, Germany (1845–51), and became an expatriate in Paris and London. He is known for genre works, such as *Politics in an Oyster House* (1848).

Woodward, C. (Comer) Vann (1908–) historian; born in Vanndale, Ark. Educated at Emory (B.A. 1930), Columbia University (M.A. 1932) and the University of North Carolina (Ph.D. 1937), he taught at several universities before serving in the navy during World War II (1943–46). After the war he taught at Johns Hopkins (1946–61) and then at Yale (1961–77; emeritus, 1977) while occasionally serving as visiting professor at various institutions. His half-century of scholarship and publications, focusing on the American South since the Civil War and race relations in the broader sphere, established him as one of the country's most eminent interpreters of the American experience. *Tom Watson: Agrarian Rebel* (1938) and *Origins of the New South, 1877–1913* (1951) set the tone for his career by challenging the entrenched notion that post-Civil War political struggles in the South raged between agrarian landowners and Northern industrial-capitalistic forces; his contention that the struggle was primarily internal, fueled by Southern industrialists, and that economic recovery never really occurred in the post-Reconstruction "New South," set the agenda for Southern historiography for decades. *The Strange Career of Jim Crow* (1955) showed that legal racial segregation was a 20th-century phenomenon and that Southern discrimination against African-Americans was less a result of immutable "folkways" than of political and economic expediency. He received a Pulitzer Prize for his edition of *Mary Chesnut's Civil War* (1981) and he served as general editor of the multivolume *Oxford History of the United States* (1982). As a historian who believed that accurate knowledge of the past can contribute to social change, in later years he increasingly brought his authority and knowledge to expressing his views about contemporary issues.

Woodward, Henry (c. 1646–c. 1686) settler, agent, pioneer; birthplace unknown, possibly Barbados. He went to the settlement near Cape Fear (present-day North Carolina) in 1664, but was captured (1666) and held by the Spanish in Florida. He escaped (1668) and went to South Carolina (1670) where he was the first English settler and the interpreter and Indian agent for the proprietors of the colony. He opened the inland Indian trade after 1674 and expanded the trading frontier to the Chattahoochee River (the border of Georgia and Alabama) where he laid the basis for an alliance with the Lower Creek Indians.

Woodward, Joanne (1930–) film actress; born in Thomasville, Ga. (wife of Paul Newman). After starting on Broadway and in television dramas, she made her first film in 1955, later winning the Academy Award for *The Three Faces of Eve* (1957). She starred in two films directed by her husband – *Rachel Rachel* (1968) and *The Effect of Gamma Rays on Man-in-the-Moon Marigolds* (1972) – and has also been an activist on behalf of liberal social and political causes.

Woodward, Robert B. (Burns) (1917–79) biochemist; born in Boston, Mass. After graduating from the Massachusetts Institute of Technology, he was affiliated with Harvard throughout his entire career (1938–79); because of the practical applications of his work, he would also serve as a consultant for various companies. During World War II he achieved the first synthesis of quinine, and he went on to become world famous for his synthesis of various organic compounds including steroids, alkaloids, chlorophyll, tetracycline, and vitamin B_{12}. In 1947 he joined units of amino acids into polypeptide chains; these would be used in the manufacture of plastics and artificial antibiotics. Beyond his specific discoveries, he changed the field of biochemistry by his application of the techniques of physical chemistry. He was awarded the Nobel Prize in chemistry (1965).

Woodward, (Robert Upshur) Bob (1943–) journalist; born in Geneva, Ill. A *Washington Post* reporter (1971–78), later metropolitan editor, and assistant managing editor (from 1981), he was best known for unmasking, with Carl Bernstein, the Watergate scandal and cover-up; their coverage of the investigative story of the century won almost every major journalistic prize including a 1973 public service Pulitzer Prize for the paper. Woodward wrote the controversial "insider" books such as *The Brethren* (with Scott Armstrong, 1979), *Wired* (1984), and *The Commanders* (1991).

Woodward, William (F.) (1876–1953) horseman, banker; born in New York City. Owner of Woodward's Belair Stud Farm, he produced such Triple Crown winning thoroughbreds as Gallant Fox (1930) and Omaha (1935).

Woodworth, Robert S. (Sessions) (1869–1962) psychologist; born in Belchertown, Mass. Influenced at Harvard by William James, he did graduate work in psychology at Columbia University, where he taught from 1903 to 1942. He conducted psychophysical experiments focused on stimulus-response and added the term "drive" to psychology's vocabulary. His publications include *Dynamic Psychology* (1918), *Experimental Psychology* (1938), and *Dynamics of Behavior* (1958).

Wool, John Ellis (1784–1869) soldier; born in Newburgh, N.Y. He raised a company of volunteers in Troy, N.Y., in the War of 1812 and fought so well that he was commissioned a colonel in the regular army in 1816 and made inspector general. When the war with Mexico began in 1846, he organized another large group of volunteers in Ohio. He then led an epic 900-mile march of 1,400 troops from San Antonio, Texas, and effectively ensured the U.S. victory at Buena Vista. He continued to hold important commands in the peacetime army, and after the Civil War broke out, he (at age 77) kept Fort Monroe from falling to the Confederates (Aug. 1861); in 1862 he occupied Norfolk and Portsmouth, Va., when the Confederates evacuated them. He held other major staff commands until retiring in July 1863.

Woollard, George P. (Prior) (1908–79) geophysicist; born in Savannah, Ga. He taught at Princeton (1940–47) before joining the University of Wisconsin (1948–76). He was an authority on gravitational aspects of geology. He also advanced the application of acoustical science to oceanography.

Woolley, Mary Emma (1863–1947) college president; born in South Norwalk, Conn. One of Brown University's first female graduates (1894), she became a leading educator of women. As president of Mount Holyoke College (1901–37) she strengthened the curriculum and the faculty and instituted honors and graduate programs. She was a prominent advocate for women's rights and international peace.

Woolman, John (1720–72) Protestant preacher, reformer; born in Rancocas, N.J. The son of a farmer, he received a Quaker education and became a Quaker in 1743. A tailor by trade, he turned to preaching and traveled for some 30 years through the colonies – and also in England – spreading Quaker views. An early advocate of the abolition of slavery, he also called for the prohibition of liquor sales to Indians. He died of smallpox while on a visit to England. His famous *Journal,* much reprinted, first appeared in 1774.

Woolman, Mary (Raphael) (b. Schenck) (1860–1940) home economist; born in Camden, N.J. She was educated at Columbia University and taught domestic economy at Teachers College, Columbia University (1893–1912). A well-known lecturer and author, she specialized in vocational education and textiles, publishing among other works *Textiles: A Handbook for Students and Consumers* (1913) and *Clothing: Choice, Care, Cost* (1920).

Woolsey, Theodore Dwight (1801–89) educator, political scientist; born in New York. A valedictorian at Yale (1820), he attended Princeton Theological Seminary until 1823, then completed his theological studies at Yale and Europe. He was professor of Greek at Yale (1831–46), then became its president (1846–71), during which time he taught history, political science, and international law. He was chairman of the American committee for the revision of the New Testament (1871–81). Aside from editions of Greek classics,

he also wrote an *Introduction to the Study of International Law* (1860) and *Political Science* (1878).

Woolson, Abba Louise (b. Goold) (1838–1921) fashion reformer; born in Windham, Maine. She was a teacher and author of essays on women and literature. She was an early and effective critic of women's fashions; in her *Dress-Reform* (1874) she decried the discomfort and unhealthiness of women's clothing and offered examples of less constricting designs.

Woolson, Constance Fenimore (Anne March, pen name) (1840–94) writer; born in Claremont, N.H. (great-niece of James Fenimore Cooper). Her family moved to Cleveland, Ohio, when she was young, and she studied there and in New York City. She traveled with her mother in various parts of America and wrote travel sketches and regional stories for periodicals, such as *Castle Nowhere: Lake Country Sketches* (1875). She lived in Europe beginning in 1879, where she became a friend of Henry James (who portrayed her in *The Aspern Papers*). She also wrote novels, including *For the Major* (1883), short stories, and poetry. After a serious illness she committed suicide in Venice.

Woolworth, Frank W. (Winfield) (1852–1919) merchant; born in Rodman, N.Y. As a store clerk, he was a failure; in 1875, at a "ninety-nine cent store" in Port Huron, Mich., his wages were reduced, and he went home sick to Watertown, N.Y. He did, however, have ability in merchandising and convinced Moore & Smith, where he was a clerk (1878), to try a counter of items all priced at five cents. It succeeded, but a five-cent store in Utica, promoted by his boss and run by Woolworth, failed. In 1879 a second store in Lancaster, Pa., with the addition of a line of ten-cent goods, succeeded. He, his brother, a cousin, and later two others became partners, running their own five and dime store chains. By 1912, all five chains were absorbed into the F. W. Woolworth Company. He built the Woolworth building in New York City, then the tallest in the world (1913). At his death his company owned more than a thousand stores across North America with a volume of more than $107 million.

Worcester, Joseph E. (Emerson) (1784–1865) lexicographer; born in Bedford, N.H. He worked on the family farm until he entered Phillips Academy at age 21, and then received a B.A. from Yale College in 1811. While teaching school he began the compilation of several gazetteers and textbooks in geography and history. In 1828 he published a revision of Samuel Johnson's famous *Dictionary of the English Language* and the next year, under the direction of Noah Webster's son-in-law, Chauncey Goodrich, he edited an abridged version of Webster's *American Dictionary of the English Language.* On the heels of this work he published his own *Comprehensive Pronouncing and Explanatory Dictionary of the English Language* (1830), against which Webster leveled a charge of plagiarism, thus beginning an acrimonious rivalry known as the "dictionary wars." His most important work is the *Dictionary of the English Language* (1860), which reflects traditional British style in contrast to Webster's recognition of American vocabulary, spelling, and usage.

Worden, John Lorimer (1818–97) naval officer; born in Westchester County, N.Y. He commanded the new ironclad USS *Monitor* in its epic but indecisive battle with the CSS *Virginia* in 1862; he was temporarily blinded during the battle. He later became the superintendent of the Naval

Academy (1869–74) and commander of the European Squadron (1875–77).

Work, Henry Clay (1832–84) printer, composer; born in Middletown, Conn. In the 1860s he became an editor and composer for the periodical, *Song Messenger of the Northwest*. He became nationally known, both for his temperance song, "Come Home, Father" (1864), and then for his stirring Civil War songs, including the still-sung "Marching Through Georgia" (1865). After the war his writing declined, but in the mid-1870s he wrote "Grand-father's Clock," which sold 800,000 copies. In his last years he wrote still more songs that gained him fame and respect.

Work, Milton C. (1864–1934) authority on card games; born in Philadelphia. After taking degrees in arts, finance, and law at the University of Pennsylvania, he practiced law for 20 years and authored *Whist of Today* (1895). Considered the leading bridge authority (1917–31), he wrote popular source-books and lectured widely.

Workman, Fanny (b. Bullock) (1859–1925) explorer, mountain climber; born in Worcester, Mass. She married William Hunter Workman, a prominent physician (1881). The couple lived in Europe (1889–98) and bicycled through the Mediterranean area and the Middle East. They engaged in exploration, mountain climbing, mapping and photographing in the Himalayan mountains (1899–1912). She lectured extensively and they published many books, including *In the Ice World of the Himalaya* (1900).

Worth, Irene (1916–) stage actress; born in Nebraska. Beginning as a teacher, she made her New York debut in 1943. She performed widely, with praise for her comic and tragic roles in both modern and classic productions.

Worthington, Henry (Rossiter) (1817–80) hydraulic engineer, inventor; born in New York City. He trained as a hydraulic engineer. Among his early inventions was a feeding pump for steam boilers, and he later designed a direct steam pump that was widely used in water supply systems and for pumping oil through pipelines. He was a founder of the American Society of Mechanical Engineers.

Worthington, L. (Lawrence) Valentine (1920–) oceanographer; born in London, England. He came to the U.S.A. in 1938. He spent his professional career at Woods Hole Oceanographic Institution (1941–82) except for his three years in the U.S. Navy (1943–46). He made major contributions to the study of deep-water North Atlantic currents.

Wouk, Herman (1915–) writer; born in New York City. He studied at Columbia University (B.A. 1934) before he was employed in New York City as a jokewriter for radio comedians (1934–35) and as a scriptwriter for Fred Allen (1936–41). He wrote plays, but is best known for best-selling novels, such as *The Caine Mutiny: A Novel of World War II* (1951), *Marjorie Morningstar* (1955), and *The Winds of War* (1971).

Wovoka (?1858–1932) Paiute visionary, founder of the Ghost Dance religion; born on the Walker River in present-day Nevada. His father, a religious mystic, died when Wovoka was about 14 and he went to work with a white family, the Wilsons; he was known to whites as Jack Wilson. At the end of 1888, he had a vision that drew on a mixture of Indian and Christian religious teachings: he claimed that the Messiah would return Native Americans to a pre-contact existence – and rid the continent of whites – if Indians would live in harmony and in traditional ways and, above all, dance the Ghost Dance. His message spread quickly among the tribes of the Great Plains and the Northwest and they began to adopt the Ghost Dance and regard Wovoka as a great deliverer. The Sioux became especially fervent in their adoption of this cult; their restiveness culminated in the murder of Sitting Bull and the massacre at Wounded Knee. The Ghost Dance cult lost its appeal for most Indians, and during the next decade, Wovoka moderated his message and advised Indians to accommodate themselves to the whites' ways. He spent his final years on a reservation in Nevada.

Wozniak, Stephen (Gary) ("the Woz") (1950–) electrical engineer, computer inventor; born in San Jose, Calif. Son of an engineer at Lockheed who worked on satellites, he enrolled at the University of California: Berkeley in 1971, the same year he began to collaborate with another young man, Steven Jobs, in building "blue boxes" that allowed people to make free long-distance calls. They then began to make computers out of borrowed "chips," and working out of a family garage, he and Jobs designed a more "user-friendly" alternative to the new computers being introduced by International Business Machines (IBM). Wozniak was now working for Hewlett-Packard and when that company refused to back the new computer, he and Jobs formed Apple Computer (1976) to make their Apple I. In the ensuing years, Wozniak played a major role in designing later Apple models, Lisa and Macintosh. He took several years off (it is claimed that he suffered from amnesia after crashing in a small plane), returned to Apple in 1983, but left in 1985 after a series of disagreements with Jobs. In 1985 he started a new company, MBF, to explore new possibilities for electronics. He also became involved in other projects, including UNUSON ("unite us in song"), with its goal of eliminating international enmities by using new communication devices. In 1990 he also joined Mitchell Kapor in establishing the Electronic Frontier Foundation to provide legal aid for computer hackers facing criminal prosecution and to research the legal aspects of computer communication.

Wright, Arthur Frederick (1913–76) historian; born in Portland, Ore. A Harvard Ph.D., he taught at Stanford (1947–59) and Yale (1959–76) Universities and was a leading Asia scholar of his generation. He focused on pre-modern Chinese social and intellectual history in works including *Buddhism in Chinese History* (1959, revised 1971) and *The Sui Dynasty* (1978).

Wright, Benjamin (1770–1842) civil engineer; born in Wethersfield, Conn. He was chief engineer on the Erie Canal (1817–25), the first major engineering project in the U.S.A. He also built the original St. Lawrence Ship Canal and the Chesapeake and Ohio Canal (1825–31). He subsequently became a railroad engineer.

Wright, Charles A. (Alan) (1927–) legal scholar; born in Philadelphia. He taught at the University of Minnesota (1950–55) before joining the faculty at the University of Texas: Austin (1955). His major publications are *Handbook of the Law of Federal Courts* (1963) and *Federal Practice and Procedure: Criminal* (four vols. 1969).

Wright, Chauncey (1830–75) philosopher; born in Northampton, Mass. Graduating from Harvard after studies in mathematics and science (1852), he worked for the American Ephemerist and Nautical Almanac, until a legacy in 1872 allowed him to retire. He lived a simple, often melancholy bachelor's existence in Cambridge, where he associated with William James and C. S. Peirce as senior member of a discussion group ironically titled the Metaphysical Club. A stimulating conversationalist, Wright wrote scientific and philosophical essays in an empirical vein; most of these – including his most significant one, "Evolution of Self-Consciousness," – appeared in the *North American Review*. He has been praised as anticipating 20th-century trends in philosophy, but he was overshadowed by James and others. He taught sporadically at Harvard (1870, 1874–75).

Wright, Elizur (1804–85) abolitionist, insurance reformer; born in South Canaan, Conn. After graduating from Yale he taught in the early 1830s at Western Reserve (Ohio), but hostility toward his abolitionist activism led him to resign. Moving to New York, he helped found and became secretary of the New York Anti-Slavery Society (1833), edited its publications, and resigned (1839) to serve briefly as editor of a Massachusetts abolitionist journal. In 1846 he founded and became editor of *The Weekly Chronicle* (later purchased by the Free Soil Party); in this capacity, and later, as Massachusetts' insurance commissioner (1859–66), he fought for and won the enactment of insurance reforms that had wide impact on the U.S. insurance industry, including those that required companies to maintain adequate reserves. Although his reforms got him forced from his state office position by the industry, he worked as an actuary for insurance companies. He was also active in conserving the natural environment.

Wright, Frances ("Fanny") (1795–1852) abolitionist, social activist, author; born in Dundee, Scotland. Having lost both parents while a child, she was raised by relatives; she read on her own and by her twenties was writing romantic poetry and plays with progressive themes. She came to the U.S.A. in 1818 with a younger sister and had her play *Altorf* produced in New York City; when it failed, she traveled throughout the Northeast and then returned to Britain (1820). Her *Views of Society and Manners in America* (1821) became one of the best-known traveler's accounts of the day, distinguished by its almost embarrassing praise for everything in the New World. She went over to France in 1821 and began a somewhat ambiguous relationship with the aging Marquis de Lafayette, almost 40 years her senior; when he made his famous "farewell tour" of America in 1824–25, she followed him around. She stayed on in the U.S.A. and took on the cause of abolishing slavery; she purchased 640 acres near Memphis, Tenn., and set up a plantation, Nashoba, on which she intended to demonstrate a method for liberating slaves; her scheme ended in scandal, but through highly controversial lectures, she continued attacking not only slavery but also organized religion and laws forbidding marriage between the races; although she thus antagonized most Americans, the freethinking, bold-talking "Fanny Wright" gained the respect of others such as the young Walt Whitman. By 1829 she was settling in New York City; she had by this time linked up with Robert Dale Owen of the utopian community at New Harmony, Ind., and she joined him in publishing the *Free Enquirer* in which she promulgated her increasingly more radical views about religion, education, and other social issues. She went off to Paris in 1830, married a French doctor and reformer (1831), and in 1835 returned to the U.S.A. with him and their child, settling this time in Cincinnati, Ohio, but continuing to lecture until

1839. In her last book, *England, the Civilizer* (1848), she called for a sort of united nations that would impose peace on the world; in its vague theorizing, it was an instance of the idealism and impracticality that characterized so much of her life and work.

Wright, Frank Lloyd (1867–1959) architect; born in Richland Center, Wis. His irregular education included briefly studying civil engineering at the University of Wisconsin. After five years in Louis Sullivan's office he started his own Chicago practice (1893). Wright's early work spearheaded the Prairie School; he designed houses influenced by the Arts and Crafts movement and characterized by horizontal lines, overhanging roofs, asymmetrical composition, and use of regional materials (Ward Willits House, Highland Park, Ill. (1902); Taliesin, Spring Green, Wis. (1911)). Two Berlin publications of his work (1910–11) spread his influence to Europe. The second phase of his career (1918–36) saw only one major building, the Imperial Hotel, Tokyo (1916–22). Finding little work during the Great Depression, Wright designed experimental projects, lectured widely, published his *Autobiography* (1932), and established the Taliesin Fellowship, a program under which he was to train numerous young architects at Taliesin West. In his prolific third phase (1936–59), Wright designed many of his most famous buildings (Falling Water, Bear Run, Pa. (1936); the Guggenheim Museum, New York (1943–46, 56–59); Taliesin West, Scottsdale, Ariz. (begun 1938)), and developed the compact, "Usonian" house. A gifted designer – he designed most of the interior details and even the furniture of many of his projects – Wright was uniquely influential through his love of natural textures (he favored unplaned wood and rough-quarried stone), mastery of organic architecture that, as he said, "*develops* from within outward," and conception of architectural space and open planning. Autocratic, opinionated, often infuriating, he never saw some of his more grandiose visions – such as a mile-high building – beyond the drawing board; but even his drawings came to be treasured as works of art. He received the American Institute of Architects' Gold Medal (1949).

Wright, George (1847–1937) baseball player; born in Yonkers, N.Y. One of baseball's pioneers, as a shortstop he was the star player on the famed Cincinnati Red Stockings of 1869, baseball's first admittedly professional club, which was managed by his brother, Harry Wright. He played in the first seven years of the National League's existence (1876–82), and in 1937 he was elected to baseball's Hall of Fame. On retiring from baseball he formed a sporting goods manufacturing firm, Wright and Ditson.

Wright, Harold Bell (1872–1944) writer; born in Rome, N.Y. His family settled in Sennett, N.Y., where he was schooled. His mother died in 1883, and he became an itinerant worker before studying for the ministry (1894–96). Although he was not ordained, he preached at a variety of churches, and settled on a farm near Escondido, Calif. He wrote popular melodramatic religious novels, such as *The Shepherd of the Hills* (1907).

Wright, (James Claude, Jr.) Jim (1922–   ) U.S. representative; born in Fort Worth, Texas. An army veteran with a Distinguished Flying Cross, and an amateur boxer, he served in the Texas legislature (1947–49) and was Democratic mayor of Weatherford, Texas (1950–54) before going to the U.S. House of Representatives (1955–89). A member of the

Public Works Committee, he protected Texas oil interests and ran unsuccessfully for Lyndon Johnson's Senate seat in 1961. In 1976 he won the majority leadership from three other deadlocked candidates and was unopposed when he became Speaker of the House in 1986. His legislative blitzkrieg and opposition to Reagan's Central American policy roused the ire of Republicans including the conservative Newt Gingrich, who charged him with taking advantage of his position to earn royalties on his biography, *Reflections of A Public Man* (1984), and to benefit a stockyard and banks in which he held investments. Although Wright denied any wrongdoing, he was forced to resign in 1989.

Wright, John J. (Joseph) (1909–79) Catholic prelate; born in Boston, Mass. Ordained in Rome, where he earned a doctorate in theology (1939), he taught philosophy and was secretary to the Boston archbishop before becoming auxiliary bishop of Boston (1947), bishop of Worcester, Mass. (1950), and finally bishop of Pittsburgh (1958). Doctrinally conservative, he was a liberal on social issues and a strong promoter of ecumenism and of retreats for laypeople. He was made a cardinal (1969) and appointed prefect of the Sacred Congregation of Clergy, becoming the highest-ranking American in the Vatican.

Wright, John Kirtland (1891–1969) geographer; born in Cambridge, Mass. He grew up in an academic atmosphere and as a child came to know William Morris Davis, the Harvard professor who more than any other American provided a disciplined structure for geography. Wright studied geography and history at Harvard and at the graduate level was allowed to offer the history of geographical knowledge as his special field; his own dissertation was published as *The Geographical Lore of the Time of the Crusades: A Study in the History of Medieval Science and Tradition in Western Europe* (1925, republished 1965). In 1920, Isaiah Bowman, director of the American Geographical Society, hired Wright as his librarian and he spent most of his career affiliated with that society; he never held a university faculty post – only in his later years did he give a few seminars – but functioned much as a research associate, editor, and mentor to many geographers. Although he did not publish that many books, he wrote countless articles, geographical record items, and book reviews; many of his essays – some collected in *Human Nature in Geography* (1966) – had considerable impact on the field. His special interests included the history of the discipline, the role of human nature in geography, maps and atlases, and "geosophy."

Wright, Joseph (1756–93) painter, dies-inker; born in Borderstown, N.J. He studied in London (c. 1772), returning to settle in Philadelphia (1782). He painted portraits, notably of George Washington (1783), who appointed him first draftsman and dies-inker of the United States mint (1792).

Wright, (Mary Kathryn) "Mickey" (1935–   ) golfer; born in San Diego, Calif. She won the Ladies' Professional Golf Association (LPGA) championship and the U.S. Open four times, twice in the same year (1958, 1961). She had 82 career tournament wins, including a record 13 victories in 1963.

Wright, Orville See under WRIGHT, WILBUR.

Wright, (Philip) Quincy (1890–1970) legal scholar; born in Medford, Mass. Educated at Lombard College (1912) and the University of Illinois (Ph.D. 1915), he taught at Harvard (1916–19) and the University of Minnesota (1919–23). From 1923 to 1956 he taught at the University of Chicago. He was an adviser to the U.S. State Department (1943–45) and to the Nuremberg Tribunal (1945). Among other books, he wrote *The Enforcement of International Law through Municipal Law in the U.S.* (1916), *The Causes of War and the Conditions of Peace* (1935) and *The Role of International Law in the Prevention of War* (1961).

Wright, Richard (Nathaniel) (1908–60) writer, poet; born near Natchez, Miss. The grandson of slaves and son of a sharecropper, he went to school in Jackson, Miss., through only the ninth grade, but got a story published at age 16 while working at various jobs in the South. In 1927 he went to Chicago and worked briefly in the post office, but, forced on relief by the Depression, he joined the Communist Party (1932). With two more minor works published, he found employment with the Federal Writers Project; his *Uncle Tom's Children* (1938), a collection of four stories, was highly acclaimed. In 1937 he moved to New York City where he was an editor on the Communist newspaper, *Daily Worker,* but the publication of *Native Son* (1940) brought him overnight fame and freedom to write; a stage version (by Wright and Paul Green) followed in 1941 (and Wright himself later played the title role in a movie version made in Argentina). *Black Boy* (1945) advanced his reputation, but after living mainly in Mexico (1940–46), he had become so disillusioned with both the Communists and white America that he went off to Paris where he lived the rest of his life as an expatriate. He continued to write novels – such as *The Outsider* (1953) and *The Long Dream* (1958) – and nonfiction – such as *Black Power* (1954) and *White Man, Listen!* (1957) – and was regarded by African-American writers such as James Baldwin as an inspiration. His naturalistic fiction no longer has the standing it once enjoyed, but his life and works remain exemplary.

Wright, Russel (1904–76) industrial designer; born in Lebanon, Ohio. Beginning with his spun aluminum bar wares, his successful free-lance designs included the 1932 Wurlitzer radio redesign, Modern Living furniture (1935), and American Modern ceramic tablewares (1937). He operated his own firm, Russel Wright Associates (1954–67).

Wright, Sewall (1889–1988) geneticist; born in Melrose, Mass. He worked in the Animal Husbandry Division of the U.S. Department of Agriculture (1915–25), where he began his fundamental studies of the frequently negative genetic effects of inbreeding in guinea pigs. He expanded his research to demonstrate the improvement of livestock populations by crossbreeding, offspring selection, and purposeful inbreeding. At the University of Chicago (1926–54), he did most of his theoretical work on mathematical theories of population genetics. He then moved to the University of Wisconsin (1955–60), where he remained active as an emeritus professor until his death from a fall during one of his habitual walks. He is known for his theory of genetic drift, which explained the role of small populations in evolution due to random fluctuations of gene frequencies. He integrated his own research with the work of Darwin and Mendel to establish a mathematical model for the genetic evolution of human and animal populations.

Wright, Wilbur (1867–1912) born near Millville, Ind., **and Orville** (1871–1958) born in Dayton, Ohio; aviation pioneers, inventors. The sons of a minister (later bishop) of the United Brethren Church, they showed mechanical genius from boyhood, although neither bothered to graduate from high school. In 1892 they opened a bicycle sales and repair shop in Dayton, Ohio, and soon were making and selling their own bicycles. Reading about experiments with gliders spurred their interest in flight, and they built their first glider in 1899, a biplane kite with wings that could be twisted mechanically. The brothers made their first trip to Kitty Hawk, N.C., in 1900 to conduct glider experiments on the sand hills there. Back in Dayton they built the first wind tunnel and prepared their own tables of lift-pressures for various wing surfaces and wind speeds. They also built a powerful four-cylinder engine and an efficient propeller, and in September 1903 they returned to Kitty Hawk. Bad weather delayed the testing of this aircraft until December 17, 1903, when Orville piloted it on a flight of 12 seconds and 120 feet; Wilbur flew later in the day, staying aloft for 59 seconds to cover 852 feet. The brothers built two sturdier, more reliable planes over the next two years and in 1906 received a U.S. patent for a powered aircraft. Initially they sold their plane to the British and French governments, but in 1908 the U.S. War Department contracted for a Wright flying machine for the army. In 1909 they formed the American Wright Company and proceeded to manufacture their improved planes and to train pilots. Wilbur, a bachelor as was his brother, died of typhoid in May 1912. In 1915 Orville – who had continued to test fly all his planes – retired from the aircraft manufacturing business to pursue his own research interests. During World I he accepted a commission as a major to serve as a consultant to the army air service and he served for many years on the National Advisory Committee for Aeronautics.

Wright, (William Henry) Harry (1835–95) baseball manager; born in Sheffield, England. He immigrated to the U.S.A. with his family while an infant and played cricket throughout his youth. In 1858 he joined the Knickerbocker Club of New York City, one of baseball's first organized teams. In 1869 he was manager of the famed Cincinnati Red Stockings, baseball's first admittedly professional club, which featured his brother, George Wright, at shortstop. He was a National League manager for 18 years (1876–93), starting with the league's first year of existence. One of baseball's true pioneers, he was elected to the Hall of Fame in 1953.

Wrigley, Philip K. (Knight) (1894–1977) corporate executive, baseball team owner; born in Chicago (son of William Wrigley Jr.) He joined Wrigley's, his father's chewing gum firm, as a teenager, and was for 52 years variously president, CEO, and chairman. His progressive labor practices included guaranteed worker incomes (1934) and a gradual retirement plan (1950). As principal owner and president of the Chicago Cubs (1934–77), he became a celebrated holdout against night baseball games. During World War II he was the prime mover in organizing the All-American Girls Professional Baseball League, which played a cross between softball and baseball; it played in Midwest cities for a few years, but did not long survive the revival of baseball after the war ended.

Wrigley, William, Jr. (1861–1932) businessman; born in Philadelphia. He left his father's soap factory in 1891 when he moved to Chicago. There his uncle supplied seed money on the condition Wrigley take a cousin as partner, and they started manufacturing soap, baking powder, and later, chewing gum; the gum became so popular, they dropped the

other products. In 1899 he introduced spearmint gum, which lagged in sales until a major advertising campaign in 1907; within a year spearmint gum sales increased tenfold. In 1911 he bought Zeno Manufacturing Company, the company that contracted to make his gum, and the William Wrigley, Jr., Company was founded. In 1916 he bought a controlling interest in the Chicago National League baseball team, the Cubs, and purchased outright minor league teams in Los Angeles and Reading, Pa. (The Cubs ballpark was renamed Wrigley Field in 1926.) In 1919 he bought Santa Catalina Island, off the California coast, which he developed into a resort and on which he is buried.

Wriston, Walter Bigelow (1919–) banker; born in Middletown, Conn. Son of a historian who later became president of Brown University, he graduated from Wesleyan College (1941) and served four years in the Army before joining First National City Bank (later Citibank) in 1946. As president (1967–70) and chairman (1970–84) of Citibank, he held sway as one of the nation's most influential bankers. He led the move to expand Citibank's commercial operations, including home mortgages and credit card services, before retiring in 1984. He chaired President Reagan's Economic Policy Advisory Board (1982–89) and wrote *Risk and Other Four Letter Words*.

Wu, Chien-Shiung (1929–) physicist; born in Shanghai, China. She came to the U.S.A. for graduate study (1936), taught at Smith College and Princeton, then joined Columbia University (1944–81). She performed experiments on the parity principle in beta emission (1957, 1963). Her later research included studies of muonic and pionic X-rays, spectroscopic examinations of hemoglobins, and ultra-low temperature physics.

Wunsch, Carl Isaac (1942–) oceanographer; born in New York City. He taught at the Massachusetts Institute of Technology (1966) and was a visiting professor at several other universities. He made major contributions to research on ocean acoustics, waves, circulation, and tides.

Wuorinen, Charles (1938–) composer; born in New York City. He began composing in childhood and studied at Columbia University, later teaching there and at the Manhattan School. He was a prolific, well-known, sometimes controversial exponent of the serial compositional technique.

Wurster, Catherine See BAUER, CATHERINE.

Wyeth, Andrew (Newell) (1917–) painter; born in Chadds Ford, Pa. (son of N. C. Wyeth). Son of the well-known illustrator, he grew up in the atmosphere of an artist's studio and the natural world; a sinus condition kept him from attending school and he was tutored privately. He began drawing as a youth but not until about age 15 did he begin to get instructions from his father. By 1937 he had a one-man show of his watercolors at a New York gallery and found instant acceptance. In addition to watercolors he took up egg tempera as a medium and the dry-brush method, and working with a relatively restrained spectrum of colors, he proceeded to produce some of the best-known and most popular works of art by any American of his time – *Christina's World* (1948), *The Trodden Weed* (1951) and numerous other of his "typical" works that combine both a familiar vision of Americana along with suggestive themes and moods. Museum shows of his work have set records for attendance, and reproductions of his work have created an entire industry. He himself spent almost his entire life moving between Chadds Ford, Pa., and his summer home at Cushing, Maine. He first went to Europe in 1977 to be inducted into the French Academy of Fine Arts – the only American since Sargent to be so honored; the Soviet Academy of the Arts made him an honorary member in 1978. Although he was widely honored by official and popular circles, professional artists and critics tended to ignore or dismiss him as a popular/sentimental realist, but this does not seem to explain either his art or its appeal. Virtually a recluse, he surprised everyone when he released his series, *The Helga Pictures* (1971–85), which renewed speculations about his life and work.

Wyeth, N. C. (Newell Convers) (1883–1945) illustrator, painter; born in Needham, Mass. (father of Andrew Wyeth). He studied at the Mechanic Arts School, Boston (1899), briefly at the Normal Arts School, Boston, and at the Howard Pyle School of Art, Wilmington, Del. (1902–11). Using oils, he painted thousands of illustrations for periodicals, posters, and books, such as *Treasure Island* and *Kidnapped* by Robert Louis Stevenson, *The Deerslayer* and *Last of the Mohicans* by James Fenimore Cooper, and *Robinson Crusoe* by Daniel Defoe. Devoted to a life in the country, he spent winters in Chadds Ford, Pa., and summered in Port Clyde, Maine. He and his young grandson died in a railroad accident near his home in Chadds Ford.

Wyeth, Nathaniel (Jarvis) (1802–56) trader, explorer; born in Cambridge, Mass. He was active in the ice business of Frederic Tudor. A follower of Hall Kelley, he attempted to settle a commercial and agricultural colony in Oregon (1832–34). He built Fort Hall, but later sold it to the Hudson's Bay Company and returned to the East and selling ice to people in hot climates.

Wyler, William (1902–81) director; born in Mulhouse, Germany (now France). Of Swiss parentage, he studied business in Switzerland, then the violin in Paris; there he met Carl Laemmle, head of Universal Pictures, who invited him to New York in 1922 to write publicity. Moving to Hollywood in 1923, he made his directorial debut in 1925 and went on to a long and distinguished career, climaxing with such Academy Award-winning films as *Mrs. Miniver* (1942), *The Best Years of Our Lives* (1946), and *Ben Hur* (1959). During World War II he enlisted in the U.S. Air Force and made two documentaries, *Memphis Belle* (1944) and *Thunderball* (1945). Noted for his total control – he was called "90-Take Wyler" because of his insistence on reshooting until he got each scene perfect – he was honored for the craftsmanship and high style of his pictures.

Wylie, Elinor (Morton Hoyt) (1885–1928) poet, writer; born in Somerville, N.J. She attended private schools and was a debutante. After leaving her first husband, she went off to England with Horace Wylie (1910–14); on returning to America, they were married in 1915. In 1921, she left Wylie and moved to New York City where in 1923 she married William Rose Benét. All of her writing was published in the final seven years of her life. She is best known today for her delicate poetry, as in *Angels and Earthly Creatures* (1929), but, in addition, for her critical essays, reviews, and four published novels; all the latter were comic fantasies; two – *The Orphan Anvil* (1926) and *Mr. Hodge and the Hazard* (1928) – drew on her fascination with Percy Bysshe Shelley.

Wyman, Jeffries (1814–74) anatomist, ethnologist; born in Chelmsford, Mass. The leading anatomist of his day, Wyman lectured among other institutions at Harvard, where he was curator of what became the Peabody Museum (1866–74). His published work, renowned for its precision and accuracy, included the first description of the gorilla's skeletal structure, but he is best known by later archaeologists for his pioneering excavations and reports of shell middens in Florida.

Wyman, Jeffries (1901–) molecular biologist; born in West Newton, Mass. Grandson of Harvard anatomist and zoologist Jeffries Wyman (1814–74), he taught and performed research at Harvard (1928–51), became a scientific adviser to the U.S. Embassy, Paris (1951–54), then directed UNESCO's Middle East Science Office (1955–59). He relocated to the Regina Elena Institute in Rome (1960–84), where he remained active in research and scientific writing. He made major contributions to studies of allosteric enzymes and hemoglobin and published extensively in scientific journals on the relationship of thermodynamics and electrostatics to biology.

Wyman, Seth (1784–1843) burglar; born in Goffstown, N.H. He stole almost from infancy but he was first brought to justice about the age of 20. He was later convicted of larceny in Maine (then part of Massachusetts) but pardoned in 1818 in order to shift the cost of maintaining him and his wife and 6 children. He served 3 years in New Hampshire for stealing cloth and then returned to Goffstown. He publicized his career in *The Life and Adventures of Seth Wyman . . .* (1843).

Wythe, George (1726–1806) judge, law educator; born in Hampton, Va. He served as the colony of Virginia's attorney general and in the House of Burgesses, but he opposed Britain's Stamp Act (1764) and was a signer of the Declaration of Independence. He was sole justice of Virginia's High Court (1789–1801). He defended judicial review, and at the College of William and Mary, he was the first professor of law in the United States (1779–90), teaching John Marshall, James Monroe, Henry Clay, and others who would become influential lawyers and government officials. He died from poisoning by a grandnephew seeking to secure a legacy.

XYZ

Yakobson, Sergius O. (1901–79) foreign affairs specialist, author; born in Moscow, Russia. Emigrating to America to escape the onslaught of World War II, he was a Russian affairs specialist for the Library of Congress (1941), and then director of the Slavic and Central Europe division when it was established (1951). A frequent contributor to journals, he was the author of *Conflict and Change in Soviet Historical Scholarship*.

Yale, Caroline Ardelia (1848–1933) educator of the deaf; born in Charlotte, Vt. She spent more than 60 years at the Clarke Institute for the Deaf, Northampton, Mass., as a teacher and principal (1886–1922). She helped devise the "Northampton Vowel and Consonant Charts," a widely used teaching aid, and helped gain national acceptance of the oral method of teaching in deaf schools.

Yale, Elihu (1649–1721) merchant, benefactor; born in Boston, Mass. He went with his father to London (1652) and became an agent in the East India Company (1671–99). He served in India and was accused of profiting at the expense of the company (1692). He was recalled in 1699. At the request of both Jeremiah Dummer and Cotton Mather, he gave books and other articles (1714, 1718) to the Collegiate School at Saybrook, Conn., which was renamed Yale College in 1718.

Yale, Linus (1821–68) inventor, manufacturer; born in Salisbury, Conn. He tried his hand at portrait painting and then began to assist his father in improving bank locks. By 1849 he had set up a small lock factory in Shelburne Falls, Mass., and began to invent and manufacture a continuous series of improved locks, both for banks and private use. In 1851 he patented the first "double lock" – two locks within one case, operated by a key. About 1862 he began to sell the "Monitor Bank Lock," the first dial-operated combination lock. In 1863 he patented the Yale Double Dial Bank Lock, the basis of bank safe locks still in use. In 1861 he patented a small cylinder lock with pin tumblers, operated by a key; this was the first modern pin-tumbler lock, although it was based on a mechanism used by the Egyptians as early as 2000 B.C. In 1865 he patented an improved cylinder lock, the basis of Yale locks still in use. With his Massachusetts factory busy making bank locks, in 1868 he formed a partnership with John H. Towne and his son Henry R. Towne and set up the Yale Lock Manufacturing Company in Stamford, Conn., to make cylinder locks. Yale died soon after the factory began production.

Yalom, Irvin D. (David) (1931–) psychiatrist, educator; born in Washington, D.C. A Boston University M.D., he taught psychiatry at Stanford's medical school (1962), where he also directed the Adult Psychiatry Clinic (1973). He was an influential proponent of the existential approach to psychotherapy. His books include *The Theory and Practice of Group Psychotherapy* (1970, later revised) and *Existential Psychotherapy* (1980).

Yalow, Rosalyn (b. Sussman) (1921–) medical physicist; born in New York City. She earned her Ph.D. at the University of Illinois (1945) and taught at Hunter College (New York City) (1946–50). In association with Dr. Solomon A. Berson, she developed radioimmunoassay (RIA) – using radioactive "tracers" to measure minute amounts of hormones, antibodies, and other substances in the body. For her contributions to explaining the role of hormones in body chemistry, she shared the Nobel Prize in medicine (1977), only the second woman to receive the award in this field. She did her research at the Veterans Hospital in the Bronx (1950–80) and the City University of New York (1968–74).

Yancey, William Lowndes (1814–63) U.S. representative, diplomat; born in Ogeechee, Ga. He was a leading Alabama lawyer who resigned after an unsatisfying congressional term (Dem., 1844–46) to promote his unyielding views on states' rights and secession across the South; he is largely credited with shaping southern public opinion to favor secession. He died in office as a Confederate senator (1862–63).

Yang, Chen Ning (1922–) physicist; born in Hofei, China. The son of a mathematics professor, he came to the U.S.A. to study at the University of Chicago (1945). There he renewed his friendship with Tsung Dao Lee, whom he knew in China when the Japanese forced both men to change schools. Yang became a professor at the Institute for Advanced Studies, Princeton, N.J. (1949–66), regularly meeting with Lee, then a professor at Columbia University. Their conversations regarding particle spin variations on the "mirror symmetry," or parity law, brought the two to collaborate on research disproving the validity of a physical law formerly held inviolate. This breakthrough won Yang and Lee the 1957 Nobel Prize. Yang continued investigations into symmetry principles and statistical mechanics at the State University of New York: Stony Brook (1966). Calling himself "Frank" to Americans (in honor of Benjamin Franklin), he visited China annually to promote mutual understanding between Americans and Chinese.

Yankelovich, Daniel (1924–) sociologist, public opinion analyst; born in Boston, Mass. Educated at Harvard and the

Sorbonne, Paris, he became president (1958–81) and chairman (1981) of the New York public polling firm that became Yankelovich, Skelly and White/Clancy Shulman, Inc. He specialized in measuring social and cultural trends and analyzing their effect on government and industry; he established the importance of social research in corporate planning. His books of social analysis include *Ego and Instinct* (1970) and *New Rules* (1981).

Yanofsky, Charles (1925–) molecular biologist; born in New York City. After being with the biology department of Western Reserve University (1954–58), he moved to Stanford University, where he continued his research on genetics using *E. Coli*. His many honors include the Albert Lasker Award in Basic Medical Research (1971).

Yastrzemski, Carl (Michael) (1939–) baseball player; born in Southampton, N.Y. During his 23-year career as an outfielder for the Boston Red Sox (1961–83), he hit 452 home runs and won the league Most Valuable Player Award in 1967. Nicknamed "Yaz," he was elected to baseball's Hall of Fame in 1989.

Yawkey, (Thomas Austin) Tom (1903–76) baseball executive; born in Detroit, Mich. Nephew of Bill Yawkey who had once owned the Detroit Tigers, and heir to a multimillion-dollar fortune, he attended Yale (where he played second base) and had been looking for a major league team to own when the Boston Red Sox came up for purchase in 1933. He was actively involved in running the Red Sox until his death (his 44 years was the second longest any major league team had been owned by one individual) and he was willing to spend his own money in pursuit of a world series championship that always eluded him. He was elected to the Hall of Fame in 1980.

Yeager, (Charles Elwood) Chuck (1923–) aviator, test pilot; born in Myra, W.Va. A fighter pilot ace during World War II, he became the first to break the sound barrier, when he flew the Bell X-1 rocket 670 mph in level flight (October 14, 1947). He held various air force command assignments between 1954–62. He was vice-commander of the Ramstein, Germany, Air Base (1968–69), U.S. defense representative to Pakistan (1971–73), and director of aerospace safety at Norton Air Force Base in California (1973–75). His autobiography, *Press On,* was published in 1985. He appears as the main character in Tom Wolfe's book, *The Right Stuff,* and as the epitome of that virtue he appeared in numerous commercial endorsements.

Yerby, Frank (Garvin) (1916–91) writer; born in Augusta, Ga. He studied at Paine College (B.A. 1937), Fisk University (M.A. 1938), and at the graduate level at the University of Chicago (1939). He taught English in the South (1939–41), and worked as a laboratory technician (1941–44), and as chief inspector for Fairchild Aircraft in Jamaica, N.Y. (1944–45). He lived in Florida in the early 1950s, before settling in Madrid, Spain in 1955. He first gained recognition for his short stories about racial injustice, but he turned to writing best-selling romantic adventure novels, such as *The Foxes of Harrow* (1946). The child of a racially mixed couple, he was chided by some African-American critics for not focusing on racial issues, but he did deal with Black Africa in *The Dahomean: An Historical Novel* (1971).

Yerkes, Charles T. (Tyson) (1837–1905) railway financier; born in Philadelphia. He opened his own brokerage firm and joined the stock exchange (1859), started his own banking house (1862), and by 1866 had established his brilliance in municipal finance. When a financial "panic" followed the Chicago fire of 1871, Yerkes was caught short as Philadelphia's bond salesman and imprisoned for "technical embezzlement," a two-year sentence of which he served seven months and was pardoned. He recouped his losses, but his reputation in Philadelphia society never recovered. In 1881 he divorced, remarried, and moved to Chicago (1882). There he engineered the construction of the Downtown Union Loop, replacing the old horse-drawn lines with modern rail transportation; but his methods of financing were so corrupt that Illinois took steps to establish municipal, not private, ownership of street railways. Politically and socially ostracized for his "rapacity," he left Chicago in 1899. In 1900 he went to London where he headed the syndicate that built the subway. His main philanthropy was an observatory given to the University of Chicago (1892). Theodore Dreiser's "Cowperwood trilogy" – *The Financier* (1912), *The Titan* (1914), and *The Stoic* (1947) – was based on the life of Yerkes.

Yerkes, Robert (Mearns) (1876–1956) psychobiologist, primate researcher; born in Breadysville, Pa. He studied at Harvard, where he taught comparative psychology (1901–17). During World War I, at the University of Minnesota, he promoted the development of intelligence tests for servicemen. With Edward L. Thorndike and John B. Watson, he was among the first American advocates for the study of animal behavior. He developed refined experimental methods for determining how animals learn and how this learning is related to their basic drives. He became professor of psychobiology at Yale University in 1929 and established the Yerkes Laboratories for Primate Biology in Orange Park, Fla. (The center is now at Emory Unniversity, Atlanta, Ga.) His most influential works on primate behavior include *The Mental Life of Monkeys and Apes* (1916), *The Mind of a Gorilla* (1927), and *The Great Apes* (1929). In 1944 he was named professor emeritus at Yale.

Yezierska, Anzia (?1885–1970) writer; born in Plinsk, Poland. She emigrated to New York City with her parents (c. 1901), and studied domestic science at Columbia University. She lived in the ghetto of the Lower East Side, taught cooking (1905–13), was reportedly romantically involved with John Dewey, educator and philosopher, and was married twice. She wrote short stories, notably *Hungry Hearts* (1920), and on the basis of that publication moved to California, where her collection was made into a silent movie. After a brief stint as a screenwriter, she moved back to New York City, and continued to write novels about Russian Jewish immigrants, such as *Salome of the Tenements* (1922). She published her autobiography, *Red Ribbon on a White Horse* (1950), but her novels having gone out of fashion, she died in poverty.

Yolen, Jane (Hyatt) (1939–) writer, poet, editor; born in New York City. After graduating from Smith College (1960), she worked for various periodicals and publishers in New York before becoming a free-lance writer in 1965. Based in Hatfield, Mass., from 1974, she published many fine books for children, such as *The Girl Who Cried Flowers and Other Tales* (1974) and *The Moon Ribbon and Other Tales* (1976). She was also known as a tireless lecturer, teacher, editor, and promoter of imaginative writing for children.

York, Alvin (Cullum) (1887–1964) soldier, popular hero; born in Pall Mall, Tenn. His fundamentalist Christian religion taught him to disapprove of killing and war, but he resolved his doubts after being inducted into the army in 1917. In France on Oct. 8, 1918, York led a small detachment against a German machine gun emplacement; firing his rifle 17 times, he killed 17 of the enemy; out of bullets, he killed 8 more with his pistol; his marksmanship induced 132 Germans to surrender. The greatest American hero of World War I was awarded the Congressional Medal of Honor and returned home to a ticker tape parade. He was a founder of the American Legion and Gary Cooper portrayed him in the movie *Sergeant York* (1941).

Yorke, Peter (Christopher) (1864–1925) Catholic priest, journalist, activist; born in Galway, Ireland. Ordained in Baltimore (1887) after study in Ireland and the U.S.A., he was chancellor of the San Francisco archdiocese (1894–99) and editor of its newspaper, which fought anti-Catholic bigotry. He also founded and edited (from 1902) a controversial weekly paper championing Irish nationalism and the rights of labor. A prominent civic leader, he held pastorates in Oakland and San Francisco (1903–25).

Yost, Fielding (Harris) "Hurry Up" (1871–1946) football coach; born in Fairview, W.Va. He coached the University of Michigan (1901–23, 1925–26) to ten Western Conference titles. His 1901 team won the first Rose Bowl.

You, Dominique (c. 1772–1830) pirate; born either in Haiti or France. He may have served in the French navy. By 1810 he was prominent among a group of smugglers and pirates at Barataria Bay, just off the Louisiana coast, under Jean Laffite's leadership. He served with distinction in the American artillery at the Battle of New Orleans (1815); for this he was pardoned by President Madison. He settled in New Orleans by 1817 and by the time of his death had become a legend in Louisiana.

Youmans, (Millie) Vincent (Jr.) (1898–1946) composer; born in New York City. Abandoning the chance to go to Yale and then a job on Wall Street, he went to work as a song plugger on Tin Pan Alley. After serving with the navy in World War I, he returned to work as an accompanist and composer. His music for *Wildflower* (1923), *No, No, Nanette* (1925), *Hit the Deck!* (1927), and *Great Day!* (1929) included such popular songs as "Tea for Two," "Sometimes I'm Happy," and "Without a Song." For the film *Flying Down to Rio* (1933) he also wrote such melodies as "Carioca" and "Music Makes Me." During the 1930s, his finances, marriage, and health all collapsed, although his music would always be played, and he never enjoyed much success after 1933. Said to have been the model for Abe North in F. Scott Fitzgerald's *Tender is the Night*, he died prematurely of tuberculosis.

Young, Ammi B. (Burnham) (1798–1874) architect; born in Lebanon, N.H. He designed the Vermont State House, Montpelier (1832), and the Customs House, Boston (1837–47). As the first supervising architect of the Treasury Department (c. 1852–62) he designed many Greek Revival and Italianate public buildings; although traditional in his design, he pioneered in the use of iron in construction.

Young, Andrew (Jackson), Jr. (1932–) civil rights activist, Protestant minister, public official; born in New Orleans, La. As a minister, he joined the Southern Christian Leadership Conference (SCLC) in 1960 and came to be one of the closest associates of Martin Luther King Jr.; as the SCLC's executive director (1964–70), he took an active role in working at

desegregation. Elected to the U.S. House of Representatives (Dem., Ga.; 1973–77), he was the first African-American to represent Georgia in Congress since 1871. In 1977 he resigned from Congress to accept an appointment from President Carter as U.S. Representative to the United Nations; he was forced to resign in 1979 after it was revealed that he had met secretly with members of the Palestinian Liberation Organization. He served as mayor of Atlanta, Ga. (1981–89) and continued to be an exponent of moderation and reform within the African-American community.

Young, Brigham (1801–77) religious leader, colonizer of Utah; born in Whitingham, Vt. He was an undirected farmer and house painter in upstate New York until he was baptized into the Mormon church in 1832. He led converts to Kirtland, Ohio, and was recognized as a successful missionary when Joseph Smith chose him as one of the Twelve Apostles in 1835. He directed the Mormons' move to Nauvoo, Ill., and led a successful mission to England (1839–41). After the death of Joseph Smith (1844), he became the leader of the Mormons and directed the move to the valley of the Great Salt Lake (1846–48). A tireless and efficient administrator, he instituted irrigation systems, agricultural programs, and construction projects, all the while encouraging a steady flow of immigrants to the colony the Mormons called Deseret. Appointed by the U.S. Congress as the first territorial governor of Utah (1850), he refused to step down when the Federal government replaced him in 1857, leading to the "Mormon War" (1857–58); he remained the Mormons' effective leader until his death. More the founder of the economic and social structures of the Mormons than a spiritual leader, he was a virtual despot in his administration, but a congenial in his private life; he had numerous wives and 56 children.

Young, Coleman (Alexander) (1918–) mayor; born in Tuscaloosa, Ala. A graduate of Detroit Eastern High School, he served in the Army Air Corps (1942–46). A Michigan state senator (1964–74), he became the longest serving mayor of Detroit (1974–94). His tenure as mayor often reflected the city's racial, economic, and political problems.

Young, (Denton True) "Cy" (1867–1955) baseball pitcher; born in Gilmore, Ohio. During his 22-year career (1890–1911), mostly with the Cleveland Indians and Boston Red Sox, he won 511 games, the major league record. One of the game's legendary pitchers, the right-hander won 20 or more games for 14 consecutive seasons. An annual award is named in his honor; it is presented to the best pitcher in each league. Called "Cy" for cyclone, he was elected to baseball's Hall of Fame in 1937.

Young, Ewing (?–1841) Oregon pioneer, trapper; born in eastern Tennessee. He trapped in New Mexico before traveling throughout California (1832–34). With Hall Jackson Kelley, he went to Oregon in 1834. He became a leader in the Oregon area, building a sawmill and extending the cultivation of his lands.

Young, George (1870–1935) bibliophile, book collector; born near South Boston, Va. A son of former slaves, he worked for many years as a pullman porter – collecting, in his travels, a library of 9,000 books related to black history and culture (now in the New York Public Library).

Young, Lester (Willis) "Prez" (1909–59) jazz musician; born in Woodville, Miss. He was an innovative tenor saxophonist who inspired the bebop movement and a new school of saxophone playing. After extensive sideman work, he gained prominence with Count Basie from 1936 to 1940 and appeared on numerous recordings with Billie Holiday. He led his own groups thereafter, but his later performances were markedly diminished by his alcoholism.

Young, M. (Merwin) Crawford (1931–) political scientist; born in Philadelphia, Pa. A Harvard Ph.D., he spent his academic career at the University of Wisconsin, as Rupert Emerson Professor of Political Science after 1969. He specialized in politics and development in developing countries, particularly Africa. His works include *The Politics of Cultural Pluralism* (1976), *Ideology and Development in Africa* (1982), and *The Rise and Decline of the Zairian State* (coauthored, 1985).

Young, Mahonri MacKintosh (1877–1957) sculptor, art critic; born in Salt Lake City (grandson of Brigham Young). He studied in Salt Lake City (1897), moved to New York City (1899), and studied at the Art Students League (1899–1900) and in Paris (1901–05). He taught at the Art Students League intermittently (1916–43), lived in New York City and Ridgefield, Conn., and was known for his sculptures of working men, boxers, such as *Groggy* (1926), and Mormon subjects, such as *This Is the Place* (1947), in Utah. He also wrote articles and books on art.

Young, Owen D. (1874–1962) lawyer, businessman, public official; born in Van Hornesville, N.Y. He worked in a Boston law firm after college and became a partner in 1907. In 1913 he joined General Electric (GE) as general counsel and vice-president to settle patent and labor disputes. Sensitive to corporate social responsibilities, he served on President Woodrow Wilson's National Industrial Conferences (1919, 1920) and President Warren Harding's Unemployment Conference (1921). In 1919 he organized and chaired the board of the Radio Corporation of America (RCA) and helped establish America's commercial lead in the burgeoning radio technology. He became board chairman of GE in 1922 and helped found the National Broadcasting Company (NBC) in the mid 1920s. Forced by the federal courts to choose between GE or RCA, he chose GE (1933). Teamed with Gerald Swope as president, he directed GE in making progress in public and labor relations while focusing on manufacturing electrical equipment, particularly consumer goods. An international diplomat, Young helped devise the Dawes Plan (1923–24) to ease the World War I debt payments crippling Germany. He chaired the 1929 Reparations Conference, which established, among other things, the Bank for International Settlements. He was also instrumental in plans for a state university system in New York.

Young, Robert (b. George Young) (1907–) movie/ television actor; born in Chicago. A graduate of the Pasadena Playhouse, he appeared as a leading man in Hollywood films of the 1930s and 1940s including *And Baby Makes Three* (1949). He starred in two television series, *Father Knows Best* (1954–62), winning two Emmies, and *Marcus Welby, M.D.* (1969–76). Thereafter he appeared in occasional television films.

Young, Robert Ralph (1897–1958) railroad executive, financier; born in Canadian, Texas. A financial manager turned stockbroker and speculator, he purchased the Alleghany Corporation, thus gaining control of the Chesapeake and Ohio Railroad (1933). As chairman (1942–54), he was a leader in the modernization of U.S. railroads. After a highly publicized proxy fight, he gained control of the New York Central (1954).

Young, Stark (1881–1963) drama critic, novelist; born in Como, Miss. Giving up his career as an academic – at the University of Texas: Austin (1903–14) and Amherst College (1915–21) – he turned to writing as an editor of *New Republic* (1922–47) and *Theatre Arts Magazine* (1922–48). He also contributed theater criticism to the *New York Times*. He was regarded as one of the first serious American critics of current theater; the best work was collected in *Immortal Shadows* (1949). His own plays had little success but one of his novels, *So Red the Rose* (1934), was popular and was made into a movie (1935).

Young, Victor (1900–1956) composer, conductor, violinist; born in Chicago, Ill. A classically trained violinist, in the 1920s he worked as an orchestra arranger for Ted Fiorito and as a musical director for movie theaters and vaudeville. He became musical director for Brunswick Records in 1931 and in 1935 he moved to Hollywood where for 20 years – as composer, arranger, conductor – he worked on over 225 film scores.

Young, Whitney M., Jr. (1922–71) social reformer; born in Lincoln Ridge, Ky. He earned a masters degree in social work from the University of Minnesota (1947) and became dean of the Atlanta School of Social Work (1954–61). While a visiting scholar at Harvard University (1960–61) he was named executive director of the Urban League (1961–71). Author of *To Be Equal* (1964) and *Beyond Racism* (1969), and recipient of a Presidential Medal of Freedom (1969), he worked quietly to improve African-Americans' condition in the community and at the workplace until his untimely death by drowning while on an African visit.

Younger, Irving (b. Yoskowitz) (1932–88) lawyer, law professor, judge, author; born in New York City. He attended the Bronx High School of Science, graduated from Harvard (1953), and after two years in the army went on to take his degree from New York University Law School (1958). After working with a private New York law firm (1958–60), he served as an assistant U.S. attorney in Manhattan (1960–62) before opening his own law firm with his wife, Judith Weintraub Younger, herself later a professor and dean at the law school of Syracuse University. He served as a judge on the Civil Court in New York City (1969–74) and taught law at New York University before joining the law faculty at Cornell (1974–81); he also held guest professorships at Columbia, Georgetown, and Harvard Universities. He joined the Washington, D.C., law firm of Williams and Connelly (1981–84), and then became a professor at the law school of the University of Minnesota (1984–88). A leading scholar of evidence and an authority on trial techniques and civil procedure, he made many audio and video tapes on these topics, used by generations of law students in preparation for their exams; his tapes inspired the popular series of lectures by "star" college professors. He was famous for his ability to cross-examine witnesses and was also well known for his wit and theatrics in lectures and the courtroom. A man of broad learning, with a deep feeling for music, theater, and literature, he published many articles and several books, including *The Art of Cross-Examination* (1976), *Principles of Evidence* (with Michael Goldsmith,

1984), and he wrote a column on persuasive writing for the *American Bar Association Journal.*

Younger, (Thomas Coleman) "Cole" (1844–1916) bandit; born in Jackson County, Mo. He was one of "Quantrill's Raiders" during the Civil War. He joined with Jesse James and formed the James-Younger band, which included Cole and his two brothers, James Younger and Robert Younger. Shot and captured during a failed bank raid in Northfield, Minn., the three brothers were sentenced to life imprisonment. Robert died in 1889 of tuberculosis, Cole and James were paroled in 1901, and James committed suicide in 1902. Cole was pardoned in 1903 and remained a law-abiding citizen in his old age.

Youngerman, Jack (1926–) painter; born in Louisville, Ky. He studied art and lived in Europe (1947–56), returned to New York City, and specialized in ragged-edge abstract paintings, such as *Black, Yellow, Red* (1964). He was the designer of stage sets for Jean Genet's *Deathwatch* (1958), created stainless steel sculptures and wooden cut-outs (1971–72) and, beginning in 1982, taught at New York University.

Yount, George (Concepcion) (1794–1865) California pioneer, trapper; born in Dowden Creek, N.C. He trapped along the Arizona rivers before going to California with William Wolfskill (1830–31). He became a Mexican citizen (1835) and settled in Sacramento in 1836.

Yung Wing (1828–1912) Chinese official, educational reformer; born in Nam Ping, Pedro Island, China. He was the first Chinese to graduate from an American college (Yale, 1854); his memoir, *My Life in China and America* (1909), reflects his divided life thereafter. As commissioner of the Chinese Educational Mission (1870–81), he brought other Chinese students to America until a counter-reform Chinese government stopped his efforts.

Yunkers, Adja (1900–83) printmaker, painter; born in Riga, Latvia. He studied in St. Petersburg, Berlin, Paris, and London, maintained a studio in Stockholm, Sweden (1942–45), emigrated to America, and lived in Albuquerque, N.M. Considered an important woodcut artist working in color, he used a painterly approach to his medium, as seen in the polyptych called *Magnificat* (1953).

Zah, Peterson (1937–) Navajo leader; born on the Navajo reservation, Arizona. His childhood in a remote part of the reservation helped shape his concerns as Tribal Chairman (1982, 1990) for the more traditional elements of Navajo society. His political career began with his leadership of People's Legal Services (1972). Other themes of his chairmanship included better relations with the Hopi Indians, reorganizing tribal government to make it more accountable, and reconciliation after the bitterly divisive late-1980s.

Zaharias, "Babe" (b. Mildred Ella Didrikson) (1914–56) athlete; born in Fort Arthur, Texas. One of the greatest all-around athletes of all time, she was an All-American in high school basketball. In the 1932 Olympics, she won gold medals in the javelin and the 80-meter hurdles and a silver in the high jump. (She had set a world record in the high jump that was disqualified because she had used the then unacceptable "western roll.") In 1933 she turned to golf, and after winning various amateur championships, she turned professional in 1948 and won the U.S. Open golf championship three times (1948, 1950, 1954). She also excelled at swimming, tennis, and rifle shooting. She died prematurely of cancer, which she had been fighting since 1952.

Zahm, John (Augustine) (1851–1921) Catholic priest, science educator, author; born in New Lexington, Ohio. A science professor at Notre Dame (1875–92), he lectured widely, defending the compatibility between Christian doctrine and evolutionary theory, but his study, *Evolution and Dogma* (1896), was condemned by the Vatican. After serving as U.S. provincial of the Holy Cross Fathers (1898–1906), he traveled in the western hemisphere – sometimes with Theodore Roosevelt – often recording his observations under the pen name J. H. Mozans.

Zahniser, Howard Clinton (1906–64) conservationist, editor; born in Franklin, Pa. A clergyman's son, he graduated from Greenville (Ill.) College (1928), taught high school English, and joined the U.S. Fish and Wildlife Service (1931), where he was an editor, writer, and broadcaster on wildlife research and conservation. In 1945 he became secretary (later executive director) of the Wilderness Society and editor of its magazine, positions he held until his death. He was also the book editor of *Nature* magazine (1935–59). In the 1950s he led a successful campaign to defeat the proposed Green River Dam, which would have flooded wilderness areas in Dinosaur National Monument on the Colorado-Utah line.

Zakrzewska, Marie Elizabeth (1829–1902) physician; born in Berlin, Germany. A midwife and teacher, she met such opposition to her holding a position in Berlin that in 1853 she emigrated to America, determined to become a doctor. With Dr. Elizabeth Blackwell as mentor, she attended Cleveland Medical College, graduating in 1856. In 1857, she and Blackwell opened the New York Infirmary for Women and Children, the first staffed totally by women. In 1859 she went to Boston to join the just-founded New England Female Medical College, but she quit over its lax standards (1862); she then opened the New England Hospital for Women and Children, staffed by female M.D.s and run by herself until 1899 when she retired. She and her hospital are credited with training many of the finest women physicians of the time and with advancing the acceptance of women in medicine. She also conducted an extensive private practice in Boston and found time to work for such causes as the abolition of slavery and for woman suffrage.

Zaks, Jerry (1946–) actor, director; born in Stuttgart, Germany. In the 1970s he acted in *Grease* and in *Talley's Folly.* In 1985 he won an Obie for directing *The Foreigner* and *The Marriage of Bette and Boo.*

Zamecnik, Paul C. (Charles) (1912–) biochemist; born in Cleveland, Ohio. He performed research in Copenhagen (1939–40), returned to the U.S.A. for a fellowship at the Rockefeller Institute (1941–42), then joined Harvard (1942–79) in association with the Massachusetts General Hospital (1956–79). He won international acclaim for his research in protein synthesis, nucleic acid metabolism, and oncogenic (cancer-causing) RNA viruses. He became principal scientist at the Worcester (Mass.) Foundation for Experimental Biology (1979).

Zane, (Elizabeth) Betty (?1766–?1831) heroine; probably born in present-day West Virginia. Her brother, Col. Ebenezer Zane, built Fort Henry in present-day Wheeling, W.Va. During a fierce Indian attack (1782) she is reputed to have run from the fort to a nearby powder magazine, under Indian fire, to replenish the supply of the defenders. She married two times and had seven children.

Zanuck, Darryl F. (Francis) (1902–79) film executive, producer, screenwriter; born in Wahoo, Nebr. He played a little Indian in a Western film at age eight, and in 1923 he joined Warners as a screenwriter. In 1933 he founded Twentieth Century, which merged with Fox in 1934. He became an independent producer in 1956. Among his films were *Little Caesar* (1930), *How Green Was My Valley* (1941), and *The Sound of Music* (1965); he won the Thalberg Award three times (1937, 1944, 1950).

Zappa, Frank (b. Francis Vincent) (1940–93) rock songwriter, guitarist, composer; born in Baltimore, Md. He played guitar in a high school blues and rock band and briefly studied music theory in college. In the 1960s he joined the Mothers of Invention, a band known for its outrageous satire and eclectic sound. In the 1970s and 1980s he produced and recorded several albums and composed and conducted his own concert music for various symphony orchestras.

Zare, Richard N. (Neil) (1939–) chemical physicist; born in Cleveland, Ohio. He was a research assistant at the University of Colorado (1964–65), taught at the Massachusetts Institute of Technology (1956–66), then returned to Colorado (1966–69). He became a chemistry professor at Columbia University (1969–77), where he developed laser fluorescence in the 1970s. He moved to Stanford (1977) and pursued research on fluorescence, chemiluminescence, and the applications of laser fluorescence to chemistry and biology.

Zariski, Oscar (1899–) mathematician; born in Kobrin, U.S.S.R. Emigrating to America to teach at Johns Hopkins (1927), he later joined the Harvard faculty (1969) and specialized in algebraic geometry, modern algebra, and topology. A member of the National Academy of Sciences, he received the National Medal of Science (1965) and the Cole Prize.

Zaturenska, Marya (1902–82) poet; born in Kiev, Russia. She emigrated to America (1909), and studied at Valparaiso University (1922–23) and the University of Wisconsin (1923–25). She married the poet, Horace Gregory (1925), and herself became a highly respected anthologist and lyric poet, as seen in her Pulitzer Prize-winning (1938) *Cold Morning Sky* (1937). She wrote a biography, *Christina Rossetti* (1949). In her later years she lived in Shelburne Falls, Mass.

Zeckendorf, William (1905–76) real estate developer; born in Paris, Ill. He spent his career in real estate, after 1938 with Webb & Knapp, New York, of which he became sole owner in 1949. Before the company's spectacular bankruptcy in 1965, he embodied glamorous real estate dealmaking: he put together the United Nations site in New York, initiated major urban renewal developments, and employed architects such as I. M. Pei and Le Corbusier.

Zeisler, Claire (1903–91) weaver; born in Cincinnati, Ohio. She studied at Columbia University, Chicago's Institute of Design, and with Alexander Archipenko and Moholy-Nagy in the 1940s. She was among the first to introduce multiple off-loom techniques to make free-standing sculptural fiber forms; she was also noted for her large three-dimensional hangings.

Zener, Clarence (Melvin) (1905–93) physicist; born in Indianapolis, Ind. He taught at several American universities (1930–42), then became a physicist at the Watertown (Mass.) Arsenal (1942–45). He moved to Chicago (1945–51), was a physicist and engineer at Westinghouse (1951–65), then joined Texas A&M (1966–68). He then went on to Carnegie-Mellon (1968). He made seminal contributions to studies of superconductivity, metallurgy (1935–50), wave

function, and the uses of oceanic thermoclines as sources of electrical power (1973).

Zenger, John Peter (1697–1746) printer, journalist; born in Germany. He emigrated to New York and formed a printing partnership. As editor of the *New-York Weekly Journal,* he was arrested and tried for libelous statements against the administration of Governor William Cosby. The sentence of not guilty was the first major victory for the freedom of the press.

Ziegfeld, Florenz, Jr. (1867–1932) theater manager, producer; born in Chicago. Best known as creator of the Ziegfeld Follies in 1907, he was also responsible for many other Broadway productions, staged after 1927 in the Ziegfeld Theatre. Ziegfeld's shows were opulent events, featuring beautiful women and rich settings. Himself an extravagant character, he was married first to actress Anna Held, then to comedienne Billie Burke.

Zimbalist, Efrem (1889–1985) violinist, composer; born in Rostov, Russia. Already a famous soloist when he settled in the U.S.A. in 1914, he soloed widely and headed the Curtis Institute (1941–68).

Zimmerman, Robert See DYLAN, BOB.

Zinder, Norton David (1928–) geneticist; born in New York City. His entire research career was spent at the Rockefeller University (1952), where he was a professor involved in the international genome project, a 15-year effort to map every gene on every human chromosome and break the genetic code.

Zinn, Howard (1922–) historian; born in New York City. Educated at New York (B.A. 1951) and Columbia (M.A., 1952; Ph.D., 1958) Universities, he taught at Upsala College (1953–56), Spelman College (1956–63), and Boston University (1964–88; professor emeritus 1988). He received an Air Medal and battle stars for service in the U.S. Army Air Forces (1943–45). Active in social and political affairs throughout his life and an authority on the history of American civil disobedience, he participated with the Student Nonviolent Coordinating Committee (SNCC) during the civil rights movement of the 1960s and 1970s. As a prominent protester of American aggression in Vietnam, he helped secure the release of the first three American prisoners of war. He drew upon personal experience to discuss civil rights in *SNCC: The New Abolitionists* (1964); and American militarism in *Vietnam: The Logic of Withdrawal* (1967). His work, *A People's History of the United States* (1980), approaches history from the viewpoint of working class and minority groups. His *LaGuardia in Congress* (1959) received the Beveridge Prize.

Zinnemann, Fred (1907–) film director; born in Vienna, Austria. He arrived in Hollywood in 1929, becoming a director of short subjects in 1937. He went on to win Oscars for *That Mothers Might Live* (1938, short subject), *From Here to Eternity* (1953), and *A Man for All Seasons* (1966).

Zinsser, Hans (1878–1940) physician, bacteriologist, author; born in New York City. He was a bacteriologist at New York City's Roosevelt Hospital (1906–10) while teaching the subject at Columbia University, then taught at Stanford (1910–13). Thereafter he was affiliated with Columbia's (1913–23) and Harvard's (1923–40) medical schools. He observed the typhus epidemic in Serbia in 1915 and an epidemic in Russia in 1923. These experiences were the impetus for his studies on epidemics as well as his classic best-seller, *Rats, Lice and History* (1935). He also made important contributions to the field of immunology and to understanding such diseases as tuberculosis, syphilis, and typhus fever.

Ziolkowski, Korczak (1908–82) sculptor; born in Boston, Mass. He was the assistant to sculptor Gutzon Borglum in the creation of the National Monument at Mount Rushmore. In 1948, Ziolkowski began his own life-work: the carving out of a granite mountain (near Custer, S.D.), of a 563-foot high statue of Sioux warrior Crazy Horse, as a memorial to the American Indians. Ziolkowski's work was intended to surpass Mount Rushmore (22 miles away) in size, and stand as the single largest work of sculpture in the world. Ziolkowski founded the nonprofit Crazy Horse Memorial Foundation Commission; after his death, several of his ten children worked to finish the gigantic project.

Zook, George (Frederick) (1885–1951) educator; born in Fort Scott, Kans. In a distinguished government career he was U.S. Commissioner of Education (1933–34) and president of the American Council on Education (1934–50). He was a leading and influential advocate of expanding government aid to higher education and of developing junior colleges.

Zorach, William (1887–1966) sculptor, painter; born in Eurburick-Kovno, Lithuania. His family emigrated (1891) and settled in Cleveland, Ohio (1894), where he was an apprentice to a lithographer. He moved to New York City (1907), attended the Art Students League and the National Academy of Design (1908–09), and, after study in France (1910–11), produced Fauvist-style paintings. Based in New York, he focused on sculpture (1922), carving directly in stone and wood, as in *Floating Figure* (1922). He also taught at the Art Students League (1929–60) and wrote several books on sculpture.

Zuckerman, Pinchas (1948–) violinist; born in Tel Aviv, Israel. After studies with Galamian at Juilliard, he won the Leventritt Competition in 1967 and pursued a glamorous solo career. He conducted the St. Paul Chamber Orchestra from 1980 to 1987.

Zukofsky, Louis (1904–78) poet, writer; born in New York City. He studied at Columbia University (M.A. 1924), and taught at many institutions, notably Colgate (1947–66). He was a translator, but is best known for his innovative and textually demanding Objectivist poetry, as in his series, *A* (1940–79).

Zumwalt, Elmo R. (Russell), Jr. (1920–) naval officer; born in San Francisco. He joined the navy in 1942 and directed arms control and (as of 1963) contingency planning regarding Cuba. He commanded the U.S. naval forces in Vietnam (1968–70) and was chief of naval operations (1970–74); in this latter office, he became famous for firing off "Z-grams," directives and orders designed to bring the navy more up to date in personnel matters, in particular to break down some of the traditional barriers between the races. In 1968 he collaborated with his son, Elmo Zumwalt III, on *My Father, My Son,* a book recounting his son's experiences with cancer, evidently acquired after being exposed to Agent Orange while serving in Vietnam – the very chemical defoliant his father had given orders to disperse.

Zuppke, (Robert Carl) Bob (1879–1957) football coach; born in Berlin, Germany. The Zuppke family immigrated to Milwaukee in 1881. Although a football sub in high school and the University of Wisconsin, he became a successful high school coach. He coached the University of Illinois (1913–41) to four national championships and seven Western Conference titles. He developed many great players, including "Red" Grange.

Zwilich, Ellen Taafe (1939–) composer; born in Miami, Fla. After studies in violin and composition, she received the first Juilliard doctorate awarded to a woman (1975). She went on to an active career of composing modernistic but communicative music and in 1982 became the first woman to win the Pulitzer Prize in music.

Zworykin, Vladimir (Kosma) (1889–1982) physicist, inventor; born in Murom, Russia. Trained in physics in Russia and France, he emigrated to the U.S.A. in 1919 and worked for the Westinghouse Corp. until 1929. In that year he demonstrated a television receiver with a cathode ray tube of his invention that contained the main features of modern picture tubes. Joining RCA (1929–54), he continued to perfect his invention. He later contributed to the development of the electron microscope.

Zygmund, Antoni (1900–) mathematician; born in Warsaw, Poland. Fleeing Nazism, he emigrated to America (1940) where he taught longest at the University of Chicago (1964). A National Academy of Sciences member and recipient of the National Medal of Science (1986), he did pioneering research in hard analysis. He wrote six books and over 180 papers.

OCCUPATIONAL INDEX

The following index lists all headword entries according to one or more occupations or subjects with which they were chiefly associated or by which they are today most often remembered. It is intended as a guide to the reader in several ways: first, as an aid in locating a specific name when the reader cannot recall it but knows the individual's occupation; second, as a means of extending one's knowledge of significant figures in a particular field; and thirdly, as a way of indicating the range of coverage provided in a subject.

Advertising Ayer, Francis Wayland; Barton, Bruce; Bates, Ted; Belding, Don; Bernays, Edward L.; Bernbach, William; Borden, Pete; Brophy, Thomas D'Arcy; Burnett, Leo; Byoir, Carl; Calkins, Elmo; Cone, Fax; Dillon, Tom; Duffy, Ben; Durstine, Roy; Fitz-Gibbon, Bernice Bowles; Hooper, C.E.; Lasker, Albert; Ogilvy, David; Powers, John R.; Repplier, Theodore S.; Resor, Stanley; Rindlaub, Jean; Rubicam, Raymond; Sandage, C. H.; Thompson, J. Walter; Watson, John B.

Aeronautics and Space Acosta, Bert; Aldrin, "Buzz"; Allen, William; Angel, Jimmy; Armstrong, Neil; Balchen, Bernt; Beech, Walter; Bell, Lawrence; Bellanca, Giuseppe Mario; Bennett, Floyd; Bingham, Hiram; Boeing, William; Bradley, Mark E.; Byrd, Richard; Cessna, Clyde; Chanute, Octave; Chapelle, Dickey; Chidlaw, Benjamin Wiley; Cochran, Jacqueline; Collins, Michael; Cooper, Kenneth H.; Crane, Carl J.; Crossfield, Scott; Curtiss, Glenn; De Seversky, Alexander; Doolittle, James; Douglas, Donald, Sr.; Dryden, Hugh; Eaker, Ira; Earhart, Amelia; Ely, Eugene; Fairchild, Sherman; Frye, Jack; Geiger, Roy S.; Glenn, John, Jr.; Goddard, George William; Goddard, Robert; Grumman, Leroy; Guthrie, Janet; Heinemann, Edward H.; Hughes, Howard; Hunsaker, Jerome; Ide, John; Jastrow, Robert; Johnson, Clarence L. "Kelly"; Karman, Theodore von; Keys, Clement; King, Samuel; Klemin, Alexander; Langley, Samuel; Lear, William; Lederer, Jerome; Lewis, George; Ley, Willy; Lindbergh, Charles; Lippisch, Alexander; Lockheed, Malcolm; Loening, Grover; Lowe, Thaddeus; Macready, John Arthur; Martin, Glenn; McAuliffe, Christa; McDonnell, James; McMullen, Clements; McNair, Ronald E.; Millikan, Clark; Mitchell, "Billy"; Moffett, William; Morrow, Dwight; Norstad, Lauris; Northrop, John; Ocker, William C.; Piccard, Jean Felix; Piper, William; Post, Wiley; Quesada, Elwood; Ramo, Simon; Rentschler, Frederick; Rickenbacker, Eddie; Ride, Sally; Rockwell, Willard Frederick, Jr.; Rutan, Burt; Rutan, Richard Glenn; Ryan, T. Claude; Schirra, Walter; Shepard, Alan; Six, Robert; Smith, C.R.; Stapp, John Paul; Suomi, Verner; Towers, John; Townsend, Robert; Trippe, Juan; Turner, Roscoe; Von Braun, Wernher; Vought, Chance; Wade, Leigh; Walker, Kenneth N.; Warner, Edward; Wellman, Walter; Whitcomb, Richard; Williams, Robert Ray; Wilson, Gill; Wright, Orville; Wright, Wilbur; Yeager, Charles Elwood

Agriculture Ackerman, James S.; Allston, Robert; Babcock, Stephen Moulton; Baldwin, Loammi; Bennett, Hugh Hammond; Borlaug, Norman; Brannan, Charles F.; Burbank, Luther; Campbell, George; Carver, George Washington; Chandler, Robert F.; Chapman, John, real name of "Johnny Appleseed"; Clark, William Smith; Crevecoeur, Jean de; Deere, John; Dunbar, William; Haugen, Gilbert; Hoard, William Dempster; Hopkins, Cyril George; House, John Henry; Johnson, Samuel William; Jones, D.F.; Kelley, Oliver Hudson; Kellogg, W.K.; Kleberg, Robert J., Jr.; Lubin, David; Mertz, Edwin T.; Morgenthau, Henry, Jr.; Morton, Julius Sterling;

Jefferson, Thomas; Jenney, William Le Baron; Jensen, Jens; Johnson, Philip; Jones, E. Fay; Jones, Robert Trent, Sr.; Jordy, William H.; Joseph, Mother; Kahn, Louis I.; Kiesler, Frederick John; Kiley, Dan; Kimball, Fiske; Kostof, Spiro; Krautheimer, Richard; Krinsky, Carol; Kubler, George; Lafever, Minard; Latrobe, Benjamin Henry; L'Enfant, Pierre Charles; Levitt, William J.; Lienau, Detlef; Lin, Maya; Livingston, Goodhue; Lowry, Bates; Luckman, Charles; Lynch, Kevin; Mackaye, Benton; Manning, Warren Henry; Mather, Henry Mather; Maybeck, Bernard; McHarg, Ian; McIntire, Samuel; McKim, Charles Follen; Meier, Richard; Mies van der Rohe, Ludwig; Mills, Robert; Moore, Charles W.; Morgan, Julia; Moses, Robert; Mould, Jacob Wrey; Mullett, Alfred B.; Mumford, Lewis; Munday, Richard; Nelson, George; Neutra, Richard; Notman, John; Noyes, Eliot; Olmsted, Frederick Law; Olmsted, Frederick Law, Jr.; Olmsted, John Charles; Parris, Alexander; Peabody, Robert Swain; Pei, I.M.; Placzek, Adolph K.; Platt, Charles A.; Pope, John Russell; Porter, A. Kingsley; Post, George B.; Potter, Edward T.; Potter, William A.; Pritzker, Jay; Renwick, James; Richardson, H. H.; Roche, Kevin; Rogers, Isaiah; Root, John Wellborn; Rouse, James W.; Rudolph, Paul; Saarinen, Eero; Sasaki, Hideo; Schindler, R.M.; Schuyler, Montgomery; Scully, Vincent; Shipman, Ellen; Simonds, Ossian Cole; Sloan, Samuel; Smith, Cloethiel Woodard; Smith, Tony; Soper, Alexander; Steele, Fletcher; Stern, Robert A.M.; Stickley, Gustav; Stone, Edward Durell; Strickland, William; Strong, Ann; Sturgis, John Hubbard; Sturgis, Russell; Sullivan, Louis Henri; Taubman, A. Alfred; Taylor, Albert Davis; Tefft, Thomas Alexander; Thompson, Benjamin; Thornton, William; Trowbridge, Breck; Upjohn, Richard; Urban, Joseph; Vanderbilt, George Washington; Van Rensselaer, Mariana; Vaughan, Henry; Vaux, Calvert; Veiller, Lawrence Turner; Venturi, Robert; Walker, Ralph Thomas; Walter, Thomas U.; Ware, William R.; Weidenmann, Jacob; White, Stanford; Whyte, William H., Jr.; Wight, Peter B.; Williams, Paul Revere; Withers, Frederick C.; Wittkower, Rudolf; Wright, Frank Lloyd; Young, Ammi B.; Zeckendorf, William

Art Abbey, Edwin Austin; Adams, Herbert Samuel; Albers, Josef; Albright, Ivan; Aldrich, Larry; Alexander, John; Allston, Washington; Alpers, Svetlana; Altman, Benjamin; Ames, Ezra; Andre, Carl; Anshutz, Thomas; Archipenko, Alexander; Arensberg, Walter; Arnheim, Rudolf; Artzybasheff, Boris; Audubon, John James; Avery, Milton; Avery, Samuel Putnam; Bache, Jules S.; Bacon, Peggy; Badger, Joseph; Ball, Thomas; Bannister, Edward; Barnard, George Grey; Barnes, Albert Coombs; Barr, Alfred, Jr.; Barthe, Richmond; Bartlett, Paul; Bascove; Baskin, Leonard; Baziotes, William; Beal, Gifford; Beardon, Romare; Beaux, Cecilia; Bellows, George; Belmont, August; Benbridge, Henry; Benglis, Lynda; Benson, Frank; Benton, Thomas Hart; Berenson, Bernard; Berman, Eugene; Bertoia, Harry; Bierstadt, Albert; Bingham, George Caleb; Birch,

William Russell; Bischoff, Elmer; Bishop, Isabel; Bitter, Karl; Blackburn, Joseph; Blakelock, Ralph; Blashfield, Edwin; Bliss, Lizzie Plummer; Block, Herbert; Bluemner, Oscar; Blum, Robert; Blume, Peter; Blythe, David; Bohrod, Aaron; Borglum, Gutzon; Bourgeois, Louise; Bridgeman, Frederick; Brooks, Romaine; Brown, Henry Kirke; Brown, J.G.; Brown, John Carter; Brown, Mather; Brumidi, Constantino; Brush, George; Burchfield, Charles; Burroughs, Bryson; Burton, Scott; Cadmus, Paul; Cahill, Holger; Calder, Alexander; Calder, A. Stirling; Cary, Elisabeth Luther; Casilear, John William; Cassatt, Mary; Castelli, Leo; Catlett, Elizabeth; Catlin, George; Cesnola, Luigi Palma di; Champney, Benjamin; Chapman, John; Chase, William Merritt; Chavez, Edward; Chicago, Judy; Christy, Howard Chandler; Chryssa; Church, Frederick; Clark, Francine Clary; Clark, Robert Sterling; Clarke, Thomas Benedict; Close, Chuck; Cole, Thomas; Coleman, Charles; Colman, Samuel, Jr.; Cone, Claribel; Cone, Etta; Copley, John Singleton; Corcoran, William Wilson; Cornell, Joseph; Cortissoz, Royal; Cox, Kenyon; Crane, Bruce; Craven, Wayne; Crawford, Thomas; Cropsey, Jasper; Currier, Nathaniel; Curry, John; Dale, Chester; Dallin, Cyrus; Davidson, Jo; Davies, Arthur; Davis, Stuart; Dawkins, Henry; de Creeft, Jose; de Kooning, Willem; De Lue, Donald; De Menil, Dominique; de Montebello, Philippe Lannes; Demuth, Charles; de Rivera, Jose; de Tolnay, Charles Erich; De Vinne, Theodore Low; de Weldon, Felix; Dewing, Thomas; D'Harnoncourt, Rene; Di Suvero, Mark; Dickinson, Preston; Diebenkorn, Richard; Diller, Burgoyne; Dine, Jim; Doughty, Thomas; Dove, Arthur; Dreier, Katherine; du Bois, Guy Pene; Duchamp, Marcel; Duncanson, Robert; Dunlap, William; Durand, Asher; du Simitiere, Pierre; Duveneck, Frank; Eakins, Thomas; Earl, Ralph; Eberle, Abastenia St. Leger; Edmonds, Francis; Edmondson, William; Eichenberg, Fritz; Eilshemius, Louis; Eitner, Lorenz; Ellsworth, David; Emmerich, Andre; Epstein, Jacob; Ernst, Max; Esherick, Wharton; Estes, Richard; Ettinghausen, Richard; Evergood, Philip; Fasanella, Ralph; Feiffer, Jules; Feke, Robert; Fenollosa, Ernest Francisco; Ferber, Herbert; Field, Erastus; Flagg, James Montgomery; Flannagan, John Bernard; Flavin, Dan; Force, Juliana Rieser; Francis, Sam; Frank, Mary; Frankenthaler, Helen; Frankfurter, Alfred; Fraser, James Earle; Frazee, John; Fredericks, Marshall; Freedberg, Sydney Joseph; Freer, Charles Lang; French, Daniel Chester; Frick, Henry C.; Friedlaender, Walter; Frieseke, Frederick; Frishmuth, Harriet Whitney; Fuertes, Louis Agassiz; Fuller, George; Gabo, Naum; Gardner, Isabella Stewart; Geldzahler, Henry; Getty, J. Paul; Gibran, Khalil; Gifford, Sanford; Glackens, William; Goldwater, Robert; Golub, Leon; Goodrich, Lloyd; Goodyear, Anson Conger; Gorky, Arshile; Gorman, R.C.; Gottlieb, Adolph; Grabar, Oleg; Graves, Morris; Graves, Nancy; Greenough, Horatio; Grooms, Red; Gropper, William; Grosman, Tatyana; Gross, Chaim; Grosz, George; Guggenheim, Peggy; Guggenheim, Solomon Robert; Guglielmi, Louis;

Art (*cont.*)

Guston, Philip; Gwathmey, Robert; Haberle, John; Hale, Lilian Westcott; Hale, Philip Leslie; Halpert, Edith Gregor; Hambridge, Jay; Hamilton, George Heard; Hammer, Armand; Hanson, Ann; Hare, David; Harnett, William; Hart, Charles Henry; Hart, Frederick E.; Hart, George "Pop"; Hartigan, Grace; Hartley, Marsden; Hartt, Frederick; Hassam, Childe; Havemeyer, Henry O.; Havemeyer, Louisine Waldron; Hawthorne, Charles; Heade, Martin; Healy, George; Held, Al; Held, John, Jr.; Henri, Robert; Henry, Edward; Herbert, Robert Louis; Hesse, Eva; Hesselius, Gustavus; Hesselius, John; Hibbard, Howard; Hicks, Edward; Higgins, Eugene; Hirshhorn, Joseph H.; Hoffman, Malvinia Cornell; Hofmann, Hans; Holmes, William Henry; Holt, Elizabeth Basye; Homar, Lorenzo; Homer, Winslow; Hopper, Edward; Hosmer, Harriet Goodhue; Houser, Allen C.; Hovenden, Thomas; Hoving, Thomas; Howe, Oscar; Hoxie, Vinnie; Hunt, Richard; Hunt, William Morris; Huntington, Anna Vaughn; Hurd, Nathaniel; Indiana, Robert; Inman, Henry; Inness, George; Isham, Samuel; Ives, Chauncey Bradley; Jackson, Martha; Janis, Sidney; Janson, H.W.; Jarves, James Jackson; Jennewein, Carl Paul; Jewett, William; Johns, Jasper; Johnson, Eastman; Johnson, John Graver; Johnson, Joshua; Johnson, Sargent; Johnson, William H.; Johnston, Henrietta; Johnston, John Taylor; Johnston, Joshua; Johnston, Thomas; Jouett, Matthew; Judd, Donald; Kabotie, Fred; Kahn, Otto; Kane, John; Kaprow, Allan; Karfiol, Bernard; Karp, Ivan C.; Katz, Alex; Kelly, Ellsworth; Kensett, John; Kent, Rockwell; Kienholz, Edward; Kiesler, Frederick John; King, Charles; Kitaj, R.B.; Kitzinger, Ernst; Kline, Franz; Kramer, Hilton; Kress, S.H.; Krimmel, John; Kuhn, Walt; Kuniyoshi, Yasuo; Lachaise, Gaston; La Farge, John; Lambdin, James; Lane, Fitz Hugh; Lanman, Charles; Lassaw, Ibram; Lavin, Irving; Lavin, Marilyn; Lawrence, Jacob; Lawrie, Lee; Lawson, Ernest; Lebrun, Rico; Lee, Doris; Lee, Rensselaer Wright; Lee, Sherman Emery; Lehman, Adele Lewisohn; Lehman, Karl; Lehman, Phyllis; Lehman, Robert; Leutze, Emanuel; Levine, Jack; Lewis, Edmonia; LeWitt, Sol; Liberman, Alex; Lichtenstein, Roy; Lin, Maya; Linder, Richard; Lipchitz, Jacques; Lipman, Jean; Lippold, Richard; Lipton, Seymour; Longman, Evelyn Beatrice; Louis, Morris; Low, Mary MacMonnies; Low, Will; Lowry, Bates; Lozowick, Louis; Luhan, Mabel Dodge; Luks, George; MacMonnies, Frederick William; Malbone, Edward; Man Ray; Marden, Brice; Marin, John; Marisol; Marquand, Allan; Marsh, Reginald; Martin, Agnes; Martin, Homer; Martin, John Rupert; Martiny, Philip; Mather, Frank Jewett, Jr.; Maurer, Alfred; Meiss, Millard; Melchers, Gari; Mellon, Paul; Miller, Kenneth Hayes; Millet, Francis; Mills, Clark; Mitchell, Joan; Moholy-Nagy, Laszlo; Moran, Thomas; Morey, Charles; Morgan, J.P.; Morris, Robert; Morse, Samuel F.B.; Moses, Grandma; Motherwell, Robert; Mount, William Sidney; Mowbray, Henry; Moy, Seong; Munsterberg, Hugo; Murphy, Gerald; Myers, Jerome; Nadelman, Elie; Nakian, Reuben; Nast, Thomas;

Nauman, Bruce; Neagle, John; Neiman, LeRoy; Nevelson, Louise; Newman, Barnett; Noble, Thomas Satterwhite; Nochlin, Linda; Noguchi, Isamu; Noland, Kenneth; Nourse, Elizabeth; Oertel, Johannes; Offner, Richard; O'Keeffe, Georgia; Oldenburg, Claes; Oldenburg, Richard; Olitsky, Jules; Oller, Francisco; Otis, Bass; Pach, Walter; Page, William; Palmer, Erastus Dow; Panofsky, Erwin; Parrish, Maxfield; Parsons, Betty; Peale, Charles Willson; Peale, James; Peale, Raphaelle; Peale, Rembrandt; Peale, Sarah; Peale, Titian; Pearlstein, Philip; Pelham, Henry; Pelham, Peter; Pendleton, John B.; Pennell, Joseph; Pepper, Beverly; Pereira, Irene; Perkins, Marion; Perry, Lilla Cabot; Peterson, Roger Tory; Peto, John Frederick; Phillips, Ammi; Phillips, Duncan; Pickett, Joseph; Pine, Robert; Pippin, Horace; Pollock, Jackson; Porter, A. Kingsley; Powers, Hiram; Pratt, Matthew; Prendergast, Maurice; Prestopino, Gregorio; Prior, William Matthew; Proctor, Alexander Phimister; Puryear, Martin; Pyle, Howard; Quidor, John; Rattner, Abraham; Rauschenberg, Robert; Rebay, Hilla; Reed, Luman; Rehn, Frank; Reinhardt, Ad; Reisinger, Hugo; Remington, Frederic; Richards, William Trost; Richter, Gisela; Rickey, George; Rimmer, William; Rinehart, William Henry; Ringgold, Faith; Rivers, Larry; Rix, Julian Waldbridge; Robinson, Boardman; Robinson, Theodore; Rockefeller, Abby Aldrich; Rockwell, Norman; Rodon, Francisco; Roesen, Severin; Rogers, Grace Rainey; Rogers, John; Rogers, Randolph; Rorimer, James; Rosenberg, Paul; Rosenblum, Robert H.; Rosenfeld, Paul; Rosenquist, James; Rosenthal, Toby; Ross, Bob; Ross, Denman Waldo; Roszak, Theodore; Rothenburg, Susan; Rothko, Mark; Rowland, Benjamin, Jr.; Rubin, William; Rumsey, Charles Cary; Rush, William; Russell, Charles; Russell, Morgan; Ryder, Albert Pinkham; Ryerson, Martin Antoine; Sachs, Paul Joseph; Sack, Israel; Sackler, Arthur M.; Sage, Kay Linn; Saint-Gaudens, Augustus; Salle, David; Salmon, Robert; Sargent, Henry; Sargent, John Singer; Savage, Edward; Scaravaglione, Concetta; Scarry, Richard; Schamberg, Morton; Schapiro, Meyer; Schapiro, Miriam; Schnabel, Julien; Scudder, Janet; Scull, Robert C.; Segal, George; Sendak, Maurice; Serra, Richard; Shahn, Ben; Sharples, James; Sheeler, Charles; Shinn, Everett; Shirlaw, Walter; Simon, Norton; Sloan, Eric; Sloan, John; Smibert, John; Smillie, James; Smith, David; Smith, Thomas; Smith, Tony; Smithson, Robert; Soyer, Isaac; Soyer, Moses; Soyer, Raphael; Speicher, Eugene; Spencer, Lilly; Spencer, Niles; Spero, Nancy; Spiegelman, Art; Stamos, Theodoros; Stebbins, Emma; Steig, William; Stein, Gertrude; Stein, Leo; Steinberg, Leo; Steinberg, Saul; Stella, Frank; Stella, Joseph; Sterne, Maurice; Stettheimer, Florine; Still, Clyfford; Storrs, John; Story, William Wetmore; Stuart, Gilbert; Sully, Thomas; Sweeney, James Johnson; Swindler, Mary Hamilton; Szarkowski, John; Taft, Lorado; Tait, Arthur Fitzwilliam; Tanguy, Yves; Tanner, Henry Ossawa; Tarbell, Edmund; Taubman, A. Alfred; Taylor, Francis Henry; Tchelitchew, Pavel; Thayer, Abbot; Thompson, Bob; Thompson, Jerome B.;

Tobey, Mark; Tomlin, Bradley; Tooker, George; Traylor, Bill; Trott, Benjamin; Trova, Ernest; Trudeau, Garry B.; Trumbull, John; Tuchman, Maurice; Tuckerman, Henry Theodore; Tudor, Tasha; Twachtman, John Henry; Twombly, Cy; Tworkov, Jack; Van Allsburg, Chris; Van Rensselaer, Mariana; Vanderlyn, John; Varnedoe, Kirk; Vedder, Elihu; Vermeule, Emily Townsend; Vonnoh, Bessie; Vonnoh, Robert William; Vose, Seth Morton; Wagstaff, Sam J.; Waldo, Samuel Lovett; Walker, Thomas Barlow; Walkowitz, Abraham; Wallace, Lila Acheson; Walters, William Thompson; Warburg, Edward M. M.; Ward, John Quincy Adams; Warhol, Andy; Warner, Olin; Waugh, Frederick Judd; Wayne, June; Weaver, Robert; Webb, Electra Havemeyer; Weber, Max; Weinman, Adolph Alexander; Weir, J. Alden; Weisman, Frederick R.; Wengenroth, Stow; Wesselman, Tom; West, Benjamin; Whistler, James Abbott McNeil; White, John; Whitney, Anne; Whitney, Gertrude Vanderbilt; Whittredge, Thomas Worthington; Williams, William; Wilson, Robert; Wolfe, Tom; Wollaston, John; Wood, Grant; Woodville, Richard Caton; Wright, Joseph; Wyeth, Andrew; Wyeth, N.C.; Young, Mahonri MacKintosh; Youngerman, Jack; Yunkers, Adja; Ziolkowski, Korczak; Zorach, William

Astronomy Adams, Walter; Angel, James; Baade, Wilhelm Heinrich; Banneker, Benjamin; Barnard, Edward Emerson; Bok, Bart; Bond, William Cranch; Bowditch, Nathaniel; Bowen, Ira Sprague; Brashear, John Alfred; Burnham, Sherburne Wesley; Campbell, William Wallace; Cannon, Annie Jump; Chandrasekhar, Subrahmanyan; Clark, Alvan; Davidson, George; Douglass, Andrew Ellicott; Drake, Frank; Fleming, Williamina Paton Stevens; Fowler, William Alfred; Gamow, George; Giacconi, Riccardo; Gold, Thomas; Goldberg, Leo; Gould, Benjamin Apthorp; Greenstein, Jesse Leonard; Hale, George Ellery; Hall, Asaph; Hill, George William; Holden, Edward Singleton; Hubble, Edwin; Jansky, Karl Guthe; Jastrow, Robert; Keeler, James Edward; Korff, Serge A.; Kuiper, Gerard Peter; Leavitt, Henrietta Swan; Loomis, Elias; Lowell, Percival; Menzel, Donald Howard; Mitchell, Maria; Moulton, Forest Ray; Nelson, Jerry Earl; Neugebauer, Otto; Newcomb, Simon; Peirce, Benjamin; Penzias, Arno; Pickering, Edward Charles; Pickering, William Henry; Porter, Russell Williams; Reber, Grote; Ritchey, George Willis; Rittenhouse, David; Rubin, Vera Cooper; Russell, Henry Norris; Sagan, Carl Edward; Sandage, Allan Rex; Schlesinger, Frank; Schmidt, Maarten; Schwarzschild, Martin; Shapley, Harlow; Slipher, Vesto Melvin; Smoot, George Fitzgerald, III; Spitzer, Lyman, Jr.; Taylor, Joseph H., Jr.; Tombaugh, Clyde; Van Allen, James; Velikovsky, Immanuel; Whipple, Fred Lawrence; Wilson, Robert W.; Winthrop, John

Banking See under FINANCE AND BANKING.

Bibliography and Libraries Adler, Elmer; Allibone, Samuel Austin; Andrews, William Loring; Asheim, Lester Eugene; Avram, Henriett D.; Ayer, Edward Everett; Baker, Augusta; Beach, Sylvia Woodbridge; Billings, John Shaw; Bontemps, Arna; Bowker, Richard Rogers; Brown, John Carter; Carey, Mathew; Carnovsky, Leon; Chappell, Warren; Cheney, Frances Neel; Cleland, Thomas Maitland; Clements, William Lawrence; Cogswell, Joseph Green; Cutter, Charles; Dana, John Cotton; Day, Stephen; Dewey, Melvil; Draper, Lyman Copeland; Dwiggins, William Addison; Eastman, Linda Anne; Evans, Charles; Fainsod, Merle; Fiske, Daniel Willard; Folger, Emily Clara; Folger, Henry Clay; Gottheil, Richard James Horatio; Green, Samuel; Greenaway, Emerson; Haines, Helen Elizabeth; Hardison, O. B.; Harrison, Peter; Haviland, John; Henne, Frances E.; Hewins, Caroline Maria; Hoe, Robert; Hutton, Laurence; Isham, Ralph Hayward; Jewett, Charles Coffin; Jones, Clara; Josey, E.J.; Knox, Henry; Kohut, George Alexander; Kroeger, Alice Bertha; Lansky, Aaron; Lenox, James; Leypoldt, Frederic; Mann, Margaret; Martin, Allie Beth Dent; Martin, Lowell; McNickle, D'Arcy; Melcher, Frederic Gershom; Merritt, LeRoy Charles; Meserve, Frederick Hill; Metcalf, Keyes; Milam, Carl Hastings; Mitchell, Maria; Monroe, Margaret; Moore, Anne Carroll; Moore, Bessie B.; Mudge, Isadore Gilbert; Mumford, L. Quincy; Peabody, Elizabeth Palmer; Pforzheimer, Carl H.; Piercy, Esther June; Placzek, Adolph K.; Plimpton, George Arthur; Poole, William Frederick; Powell, Lawrence Clark; Power, Effie Louise; Pratt, Enoch; Putnam, Herbert; Reichl, Ernest; Rider, Fremont; Rockhill, William Woodville; Rosenbach, Abraham; Schomburg, Arthur A.; Sears, Minnie Earl; Shaw, Ralph Robert; Shera, Jesse Hauk; Shores, Louis; Smith, David Eugene; Smith, Jessie Carney; Smyth, Herbert Weir; Spofford, Ainsworth Rand; Thacher, John Boyd; Thomas, Isaiah; Tilden, Samuel Jones; Weems, Mason Locke; Widener, Harry Elkins; Wilson, Halsey William; Wilson, Louis; Winsor, Justin; Young, George

Biochemistry See BIOLOGY; CHEMISTRY.

Biology Abel, John J.; Alexander, Hattie Elizabeth; Asimov, Isaac; Audubon, John James; Avery, Oswald T.; Axelrod, Julius; Ayala, Francisco J.; Baltimore, David; Beadle, George W.; Beebe, William; Benacerraf, Baruj; Bishop, J. Michael; Bloch, Konrad E.; Blumberg, Baruch S.; Bonner, James; Bonner, J.T.; Bridges, Calvin B.; Briggs, Robert William; Brower, Lincoln P.; Brown, Donald D.; Brown, Michael S.; Cade, Thomas J.; Carr, Archibald; Carroll, James; Carson, Rachel; Catesby, Mark; Chance, Britton; Chang, M.C.; Chapman, Frank; Child, Charles M.; Chittenden, Russell H.; Clark, Eugenie; Claude, Albert; Cohen, Carolyn; Cohen, Stanley; Cohn, Edwin J.; Cohn, Mildred; Conklin, Edwin G.; Cori, Carl F.; Cori, Gerty T. b. Radnitz; Cormack, Allan MacLeod; Delbruck, Max; Dethier, Vincent G.; Dick, Gladys; Ditmars, Raymond; Dobzhansky, Theodosius; Doisy, Edward A.; Dubos, Rene J.; Dulbecco, Renato; Dunn, L.C.; Du Vigneaud,

Biology (*cont.*)

Vincent; Eagle, Harry; Eakin, Richard M.; Edelman, Gerald M.; Edsall, John R.; Ehrlich, Paul R.; Eisner, Thomas; Elion, Gertrude B.; Emerson, Rollins A.; Enders, John F.; Erlanger, Joseph; Fankhauser, Gerhard; Fischer, Edmond H.; Folin, Otto; Forbes, Stephen Alfred; Fruton, Joseph S.; Gajdusek, D. Carleton; Gall, Joseph G.; Gans, Carl; Garn, Stanley, M.; Gasser, Herbert S.; Gilbert, Walter; Goldschmidt, Richard B.; Goldstein, Joseph L.; Gould, James L.; Gould, Stephen Jay; Grant, Peter R.; Griffin, Donald R.; Guillemin, Roger; Hamburger, Viktor; Harrison, Ross B.; Hart, Edwin Bret; Hartline, H. Keffer; Harvey, E. Newton; Heinrich, Bernd; Henderson, Lawrence J.; Hershey, Alfred D.; Hitchings, George H.; Holley, Robert W.; Holtfreter, Johannes; Hrdy, Sarah Blaffer; Hyman, Libbie; Inouye, Shinya; Jaffe, Lionel F.; Janzen, Daniel H.; Jennings, Herbert S.; Jordan, David Starr; Just, Ernest E.; Kandel, Eric Richard; Keeton, William T.; Kendall, Edward C.; Kennedy, Eugene P.; Khorana, Har Gobind; Kinsey, Alfred; Kirschner, Marc Wallace; Kornberg, Arthur; Krebs, Edwin G.; Krim, Mathilde; Landsteiner, Karl; Lederberg, Joshua; Lehninger, Albert L.; Levi-Montalcini, Rita; Lewontin, Richard C.; Lipmann, Fritz; Lowey, Susan; Luria, Salvador; Margulis, Lynn; Marler, Peter; Masters, William; Mayr, Ernst; Mazia, Daniel; McClintock, Barbara; McCollum, Elmer Verner; Merrifield, R. Bruce; Meyer, Karl; Moore, Stanford; Morgan, Agnes Fay; Morgan, Thomas Hunt; Moyer, Andrew Jackson; Muller, Hermann J.; Mullis, Kary B.; Murphy, William P.; Nabokov, Vladimir; Nathans, Daniel; Nelson, Marjorie Maxine; Nirenberg, Marshall W.; Noguchi, Hideyo; Northrop, John; Ochoa, Severo; Oppenheimer, Jane M.; Osborne, Thomas B.; Oser, Bernard L.; Packard, Alpheus Spring, Jr.; Palade, George E.; Pardue, Mary Lou; Pauling, Linus; Pepperberg, Irene M.; Porter, Keith R.; Proctor, Bernard Emerson; Racker, Efraim; Ratner, Sarah; Ray, Dixie Lee; Riddiford, Lynn M.; Ridgway, Robert; Robdell, Martin; Roberts, Richard J.; Robins, Eli; Salk, Jonas; Say, Thomas; Schaller, George B.; Schoenheimer, Rudolf; Schopf, J. William; Scott, John Paul; Sharp, Phillip A.; Singer, S.J.; Smith, Hamilton O.; Sonneborn, Tracy M.; Sperry, Roger W.; Stadtman, Earl R.; Stadtman, Thressa C.; Stanley, Wendell; Stein, William; Steinberg, Malcolm S.; Sturtevant, Alfred H.; Sumner, James; Sutherland, Earl W., Jr.; Sutton, Walter S.; Szent-Gyorgyi, Albert; Tatum, Edward L.; Temin, Howard M.; Thomson, Keith Stewart; Tjian, Robert; Trivers, Robert L.; Tuttle, Merlin D.; Twitty, Victor C.; Waksman, Selman A.; Wald, George; Watson, James D.; Weiss, Paul A.; Wheeler, William Morton; Whitman, C.O.; Wiesel, Torsten N.; Williams, Anna; Wilson, Edmund B.; Wilson, Edward O.; Wood, Harland G.; Woodward, Robert B.; Wright, Sewall; Wyman, Jeffries; Yanofsky, Charles; Yerkes, Robert; Zamecnik, Paul C.; Zinder, Norton David

Botany Allard, Harry A.; Ames, Oakes; Anderson, Edgar S.; Arnon, Daniel I.; Bailey, Irving W.; Bailey, Liberty Hyde, Jr.; Bartram, John; Bartram, William; Berry, Edward Wilber; Bessey, Charles Edwin; Bigelow, Jacob; Blakeslee, Albert Francis; Bogorad, Lawrence; Bonner, James; Braun, E. Lucy; Briggs, Winslow R.; Britton, Nathaniel L.; Burbank, Luther; Carver, George Washington; Chase, Agnes; Clausen, Jens; Clements, Frederick Edward; Colden, Cadwallader; Coulter, John Merle; Cowles, Henry Chandler; Cronquist, Arthur; Eaton, Amos; Eaton, Daniel Cady; Emerson, Rollins A.; Esau, Katherine; Fairchild, David Grandison; Fernald, Merritt L.; Galston, Arthur W.; Garner, W.W.; Gray, Asa; Heiser, Charles B.; Hiesey, William M.; Jepson, Willis Linn; Keck, David D.; Kramer, Paul J.; Nuttall, Thomas; Oosting, Henry J.; Piper, Charles V.; Pound, Roscoe; Pursh, Frederick; Raven, Peter H.; Sinnott, Edmund W.; Stebbins, G. Ledyard; Thimann, Kenneth Vivian; Torrey, John; Tuckerman, Edward; Went, Frits W.; Whittaker, Robert H.

Business and Industry Ackoff, Russell L.; Adams, Alvin; Albright, Horace Marden; Aldrich, Larry; Allen, William; Altman, Benjamin; Ammons, Elias Milton; Anderson, Joseph R.; Anderson, Robert O.; Andreas, Dwayne; Anthony, Robert N.; Appleton, Nathan; Arden, Elizabeth; Asch, Moses; Ash, Roy L.; Astor, John Jacob; Avery, Sewell; Bache, Richard; Bache, Theophylact; Baer, George Frederick; Ball, C. Olin; Ball, Frank Clayton; Barker, Jacob; Barnard, Chester; Barnes, Albert Coombs; Batten, William; Bean, L.L.; Bechtel, Stephen Davison; Beckman, Arnold; Beech, Walter; Behn, Sosthenes; Bell, Lawrence; Bennis, Warren; Bernays, Edward L.; Billings, Frederick; Bingham, William; Birdseye, Clarence; Bissel, George Henry; Blanchard, Kenneth H.; Bloch, Henry Wollman; Bloomingdale, Alfred S.; Blough, Roger M.; Bludhorn, Charles G.; Boeing, William; Borie, Adolph Edward; Bower, Marvin; Bradley, Milton; Bradshaw, Thornton F.; Brady, "Diamond Jim"; Bren, Donald L.; Bridges, Robert; Brookings, Robert Somers; Brown, Alexander; Brown, Charles L.; Brown, George; Brown, Moses; Bryan, John Henry, Jr.; Budd, Edward G. Gowen; Buick, David Dunbar; Burke, James Edward; Busch, Adolphus; Busch, August A., Jr.; Busch, August Anheuser III; Cable, Ransom R.; Cabot, George; Cabot, Godfrey Lowell; Caldwell, Philip; Cameron, Simon; Candler, Asa; Carlson, Curtis LeRoy; Carnegie, Andrew; Carnegie, Dale; Carrier, Willis; Case, Jerome; Casey, James E.; Cessna, Clyde; Chapin, Roy Dikeman; Chess, Leonard; Chevrolet, Louis; Chisum, John Simpson; Chrysler, Walter P.; Churchman, C. West; Claflin, Tennessee Celeste; Claiborne, Liz; Clark, Edward; Clark, William Andrews; Coffin, Charles A.; Colbert, Lester; Collins, Edward Knight; Colt, Samuel; Combs, Moses; Cone, Moses H.; Conover, Harry; Converse, Edmund Cogswell; Cooper, Peter; Coors, Adolph; Cope, Thomas Pym; Cord, Errett Lobban; Cordiner, Ralph Jarron; Corliss, George Henry; Cornell, Ezra; Corning, Erastus; Couzens, James; Coxey, Jacob; Crawford, Frederick C.; Crocker, Charles; Crow, Trammel; Crowell, Henry P.; Cudahy, Edward A.;

Cudahy, Michael; Cunningham, Harry; Curtice, Harlowe H.; Curtiss, Glenn; Cushing, John Perkins; Daly, Marcus; Davis, Arthur Vining; Deere, John; De Lorean, John; Deming, W. Edwards; Depew, Chauncey Mitchell; DePree, Max O.; Derby, Elias Hasket; Deringer, Henry, Jr.; De Seversky, Alexander; DeVos, Richard; Dick, A.B.; Dillon, Sidney; Disney, Walt; Dodge, Horace; Dodge, John; Doherty, Henry Latham; Doriot, Georges F.; Dorrance, John T.; Douglas, Donald, Sr.; Dows, David; Drake, Edwin L.; Drucker, Peter; Dryden, John Fairfield; Duer, William; Duesenberg, Fred; Duke, James; DuMont, Allen B.; Dun, R. G.; du Pont, Alfred I.; du Pont, E.I.; du Pont, Henry Francis; du Pont, Pierre S.; Durant, William C.; Duryea, Charles E.; Eastman, George; Eccles, Marriner; Engelberger, Joseph F.; Ertegun, Ahmet; Evans, Oliver; Fairless, Benjamin F.; Faneuil, Peter; Fargo, William George; Ferre, Luis Antonio; Fiedler, Fred E.; Field, Cyrus W.; Field, Marshall; Filene, Edward A.; Firestone, Harvey; Fisher, Donald G.; Fisher, Frederick John; Fiske, Haley; Fitzhugh, William; Folger, Henry Clay; Follett, Mary Parker; Forbes, John Murray; Forbes, Robert Bennet; Ford, Henry; Ford, Henry II; Forten, James; Freer, Charles Lang; Frick, Henry C.; Frye, Jack; Funston, Keith; Gadsden, James; Gallo, Ernest; Gallo, Julio; Galvin, Robert W.; Gantt, Henry Laurence; Gates, Frederick T.; Gates, William H.; Gault, Stanley C.; Geneen, Harold; Gerber, Frank; Getty, J. Paul; Gilbreth, Frank; Gillette, King C.; Gimbel, Isaac; Girard, Stephen; Goizueta, Roberto; Goldwyn, Samuel; Goodnight, Charles; Goodrich, Benjamin F.; Goodyear, Anson Conger; Gordy, Berry, Jr.; Gould, Gordon; Grace, William Russell; Graham, Bill; Grant, W.T.; Gratz, Barnard; Gray, Bowman; Gray, Harry; Greenway, John Campbell; Griffin, Merv; Grinnell, Henry; Griswold, John A.; Guggenheim, Daniel; Guggenheim, Simon; Guggenheim, Solomon Robert; Haas, Walter A., Jr.; Haggin, James Ben Ali; Hall, J.C.; Hammer, Armand; Hammond, George H.; Hammond, John; Hancock, Thomas; Handwerker, Nathan; Hanna, Mark; Harland, Thomas; Harlow, Bryce N.; Harper, Mike; Harriman, Edward H.; Hartford, George Huntington; Havemeyer, Henry O.; Haynes, Elwood; Heckscher, August; Hefner, Hugh; Heineman, Ben; Heinz, Henry John; Heinz, Howard; Helmsley, Leona; Hershey, Milton; Hill, James J.; Hilton, Conrad; Hobbs, Alfred Charles; Hoe, Richard March; Hoe, Robert; Hoffman, Paul; Holman, Eugene; Hoover, William Henry; Hopkins, Johns; Hopkins, Mark; Hopson, Howard C.; Hormel, George A.; House, "Colonel"; Hoving, Walter; Howell, Albert Summers; Hoyt, Jesse; Hudson, J.L.; Hughes, Howard; Humphrey, George; Hunt, H.L.; Huntington, Collis P.; Hurok, Sol; Iacocca, Lee; Icahn, Carl; Inman, Samuel Martin; Insull, Samuel; Iverson, Ken; Jackson, Patrick Tracy; Jacobsen, Alfred; Jacuzzi, Candido; Jeffers, William Martin; Jensen, Peter Laurits; Jobs, Steven; Johnson, Eldridge Reeves; Johnson, Howard; Johnson, John Harold; Johnson, Robert Wood; Johnson, Tom Loftin; Johnston, John Taylor; Jones, Jesse Holman; Jones, Reginald Harold;

Jones, Samuel Milton; Joy, James F.; Judah, Theodore; Juilliard, Augustus D.; Kaiser, Henry J.; Kalmus, Natalie; Kapor, Mitchell; Kappel, Frederick R.; Kauffman, Ewing M.; Kellogg, John Harvey; Kellogg, W.K.; Kelly, William; Kendall, Donald M.; Kerr, Robert Samuel; Kettering, Charles; King, William; Kluge, John W.; Knight, Philip H.; Knox, Rose Markward; Knudsen, William S.; Kresge, S.S.; Kress, S.H.; Kroc, Ray; Kurzweil, Raymond C.; Laborde, Alden James; Landon, Alf; LaPorte, William; Lauder, Estee; Lauren, Ralph; Lawrence, Paul R.; Lazarus, Charles; Lear, William; Lefrak, Samuel J.; Levitt, William J.; Lewis, Delano E.; Libbey, Edward Drummond; Lilly, Eli; Lilly, Josiah Kirby; Ling, James; Little, Arthur D.; Little, Royal; Lockheed, Allan Haines; Lockheed, Malcolm; Lopez, Aaron; Low, Seth; Lowell, Francis Cabot; Luce, Henry R.; Luckman, Charles; Ludlow, Daniel; Ludwig, Daniel K.; Lukens, Rebecca Wade; MacArthur, John D.; MacKay, John William; MacMillan, Whitney; Macy, Rowland H.; Marcus, Stanley; Marriott, J. Willard; Mars, Forrest; Martin, Glenn; Masters, Sybilla; Maxwell, Hamish; Maxwell, J.D.; McCallum, Daniel C.; McCone, John A.; McConnell, David Hall; McCormick, Cyrus Hall; McCoy, Elijah; McCrory, John G.; McDonnell, James; McElroy, Neil; McGowan, William G.; McGregor, Douglas M.; McKay, Clarence Hungerford; McKay, Donald; McLoughlin, John; McNamara, Robert; Mecham, Evan; Merck, George W.; Merganthaler, Ottmar; Millbank, Jeremiah; Miller, J. Irwin; Milliken, Roger; Mitchell, Sidney Z.; Monaghan, Thomas S.; Morris, Nelson; Morse, C.W.; Mortimer, Charles G.; Mott, C. S.; Moxham, Arthur J.; Murchison, Clinton; Murphy, Gerald; Murphy, Robert D.; Nash, Charles W.; Newhouse, S.I.; Nielsen, A.C.; Norris, William C.; North, Simeon; Northrop, John; O'Hara, James; Olds, Ransom; O'Malley, Walter; Ortenberg;, Arthur; Osborn, William Henry; Osborne, Thomas Mott; Otis, Charles R.; Otis, Norton P.; Packard, James W.; Paepcke, Walter P.; Paley, William S.; Palmer, Potter; Patterson, John H.; Penney, J.C.; Perdue, Frank; Perkins, Charles E.; Perkins, Thomas; Perot, H. Ross; Persons, Wallace R.; Peters, Tom; Petri, Angelo; Pew, Joseph N. Jr.; Pickens, T. Boone, Jr.; Pillsbury, Charles Alfred; Pinckney, Elizabeth Lucas; Pingree, Hazen; Pinkham, Lydia E.; Pinto, Isaac; Piper, William; Pope, Albert A.; Post, Charles William; Powers, John R.; Pratt, Charles; Pratt, Enoch; Preston, Andrew W.; Price, Gwilym A.; Pritzker, A. N.; Pritzker, Jay; Procter, William C.; Pullman, George Mortimer; Quanah; Ramo, Simon; Rathbone, Monroe J.; Redstone, Summer; Reed, Luman; Reid, Daniel G.; Reisinger, Hugo; Remington, Eliphalet; Rentschler, Frederick; Revson, Charles; Reynolds, David Parham; Richardson, Sid; Rickenbacker, Eddie; Rickey, Branch; Robert, Christopher Rhinelander; Rockefeller, John D.; Rockefeller, Laurance; Rockwell, Willard Frederick, Jr.; Roebuck, Alvah C.; Romney, George; Root, Elisha King; Rosenwald, Julius; Ross, Douglas Taylor; Rubinstein, Helena; Rudkin, Margaret; Ryan, T. Claude; Ryerson, Martin

Business and Industry (*cont.*)

Antoine; Sanders, "Colonel" Harlan; Sardi, Vincent; Sarnoff, David; Schein, Edgar H.; Schwab, Charles M.; Scott, Thomas A.; Scott, W. Richard; Scull, Robert C.; Sears, Richard W.; Sellers, William; Selznick, David O.; Selznick, Philip; Simon, Norton; Singer, Isaac M.; Six, Robert; Sloan, Alfred P., Jr.; Smale, John; Smith, C.R.; Smith, Fred; Somervell, Brehon Burke; Sorensen, Charles; Spalding, Al; Squibb, Edward Robinson; Stanford, Leland; Stanley, Francis Edgar; Stanley, Freelan O.; Steinbrenner, George; Stetson, John B.; Stettinius, Edward R.; Stevens, Harry; Stewart, Alexander T.; Stickney, A.B.; Stouffer, Vernon B.; Straus, Isidor; Straus, Nathan; Strauss, Levi; Strong, William Barstow; Studebaker, Clement; Sublette, William Lewis; Swann, Thomas; Swift, Gustavus Franklin; Swope, Gerard; Takamine, Jokichi; Talmadge, Edwards; Tappan, Arthur; Tappan, Lewis; Taubman, A. Alfred; Taylor, Frederick Winslow; Teague, Walter Dorwin; Terry, Eli; Thomas, Seth; Thomson, J. Edgar; Thornton, Charles B.; Tisch, Laurence A.; Towne, Henry Robinson; Townsend, Lynn Alfred; Townsend, Robert; Trippe, Juan; Trumbull, Jonathan; Trump, Donald; Tudor, Frederic; Turner, Ted; Ueberroth, Peter; Underwood, William; Upjohn, William E.; Vagelos, P. Roy; Vail, Theodore; Vance, Harold; Vanderbilt, Cornelius; Vanderbilt, Cornelius ("Commodore"); Vanderbilt, William H.; Vanderbilt, William K.; Vought, Chance; Walgreen, Charles R.; Walker, Maggie Lena; Walker, Sarah Breedlove; Walker, Thomas Barlow; Walters, William Thompson; Walton, Sam; Wanamaker, John; Wang, An; Ward, Aaron Montgomery; Washburn, Cadwallader Colden; Watson, Thomas John; Watson, Thomas, Jr.; Webb, James; Weinberg, Harry; Weisman, Frederick R.; Welch, John F., Jr.; Wesson, Daniel Baird; Westinghouse, George; Wexler, Jerry; Wexner, Leslie; Weyerhaeuser, Frederick E.; Weyerhaeuser, George; Whalen, Grover; Wharton, Samuel; Whitney, Asa (1791–1874); Whitney, Asa (1797–1872); Williams, Eleazer; Willing, Thomas; Willkie, Wendell; Willys, John N.; Wilson, Charles E.; Wilson, Charles Edward; Wilson, Joseph C.; Wilson, Kemmons; Winans, Ross; Winchester, Oliver; Wistar, Caspar; Wood, Robert E.; Woods, Arthur; Woolworth, Frank W.; Wright, Elizur; Wrigley, Philip K.; Wrigley, William, Jr.; Wyeth, Nathaniel; Yale, Elihu; Yale, Linus; Yerkes, Charles T.; Young, Owen D.; Young, Robert Ralph; Zeckendorf, William

Chemistry Adams, Roger; Altman, Sidney; Anfinsen, Christian; Atwater, Wilbur Olin; Babcock, Stephen Moulton; Baekeland, Leo; Bancroft, Wilder Dwight; Berg, Paul; Bolton, Henry Carrington; Brown, Herbert; Calvin, Melvin; Carothers, Wallace; Carr, Emma Perry; Castner, Hamilton; Cech, Thomas R.; Chance, Britton; Chandler, Charles Frederick; Cohn, Mildred; Colton, Frank Benjamin; Conant, James Bryant; Cooke, Joseah Parsons, Jr.; Coolidge, William David; Corey, Elias J.; Cottrell, Frederick Gardner; Cram, Donald; Debye, Peter; Dorr, John Van Nostrand; Dow, Henry; Draper, John William;

Duncan, Robert Kennedy; Du Vigneaud, Vincent; Edsall, John R.; Ellis, Carleton; Fischer, Edmond H.; Flory, Paul John; Folin, Otto; Franklin, Edward Curtis; Frasch, Herman; Fruton, Joseph S.; Giauque, William; Gomberg, Moses; Guillemin, Roger; Hale, William Jay; Hanford, William Edward; Hare, Robert; Hauptman, Herbert; Henderson, Lawrence J.; Herschbach, Dudley R.; Hoffmann, Roald; Holley, Robert W.; Holmes, Donald Fletcher; Horsford, Eben Norton; Ipatiev or Ipatieff, Vladimir; Jackson, Charles Thomas; James, Charles; Johnson, Samuel William; Jones, Harry Clary; Julian, Percy; Karle, Jerome; Kennedy, Eugene P.; Kharasch, Morris; Kirkwood, John G.; Kornberg, Arthur; Krebs, Edwin G.; Langmuir, Irving; Lee, Yuan T.; Lehninger, Albert L.; Lewis, Gilbert N.; Lewis, Warren K.; Libby, Willard; Lipmann, Fritz; Lipscomb, William; Little, Arthur D.; Loeb, Jacques; Lowey, Susan; Marcus, Rudolph A.; Mark, Herman Francis; McCollum, Elmer Verner; Merck, George W.; Merrifield, R. Bruce; Meyer, Karl; Moore, Stanford; Morgan, Agnes Fay; Morley, Edward Williams; Mulliken, Robert S.; Mullis, Kary B.; Munroe, Charles Edward; Nef, John Ulric; Nelson, Marjorie Maxine; Nieuwland, Julius Arthur; Nirenberg, Marshall W.; Northrop, John; Noyes, William Albert; Olah, George A.; Olsen, John Charles; Onsager, Lars; Osborne, Thomas B.; Oser, Bernard L.; Othmer, Donald F.; Pauling, Linus; Pederson, Charles J.; Pennington, Mary Engle; Plank, Charles J.; Plunkett, Roy J.; Proctor, Bernard Emerson; Racker, Efraim; Ratner, Sarah; Remsen, Ira; Richards, Ellen Henrietta; Richards, Theodore; Rodbell, Martin; Rosinski, Edward J.; Sadtler, Samuel Philip; Sarett, Lewis; Schoenheimer, Rudolf; Seaborg, Glenn T.; Sherman, Henry Clapp; Shreve, R. Norris; Silliman, Benjamin, Jr.; Silliman, Benjamin, Sr.; Slosson, Edwin Emery; Smith, Alexander; Smith, Edgar Fahs; Squibb, Edward Robinson; Stadtman, Earl R.; Stadtman, Thressa C.; Stanley, Wendell; Stein, William; Stieglitz, Julius; Stine, Charles; Storer, Francis Humphreys; Sumner, James; Sutherland, Earl W., Jr.; Sweeney, Orland R.; Szent-Gyorgyi, Albert; Tabern, Donalee L.; Takamine, Jokichi; Taube, Henry; Tishler, Max; Urey, Harold; Waksman, Selman A.; Wald, George; Walker, William H.; Wheeler, Ruth; Whitmore, Frank Clifford; Whitney, Willis Rodney; Wiley, Harvey Washington; Williams, Robert, Jr.; Wood, Harland G.; Woodward, Robert B.; Zamecnik, Paul C.; Zare, Richard N.

Colonial Settlements in America Alden, John; Allen, Ethan; Andros, Sir Edmund; Argall, Sir Samuel; Bacon, Nathaniel; Bartram, John; Berkeley, Sir William; Bienville, Jean Baptiste le Moyne, Sieur de; Bonner, John; Boylston, Zabdiel; Bradford, William (1590–1657); Bradford, William (1663–1752); Bradstreet, Anne; Brent, Margaret; Brewster, William; Bridges, Robert; Brown, Moses; Byrd, William; Cabot, George; Calvert, Leonard; Carter, Robert "King"; Carteret, Philip; Chittenden, Thomas; Church, Benjamin; Claiborne, William; Coddington, William; Copley, Lionel; Cotton, John; Croghan,

George; Dare, Virginia; Davenport, John; Davies, Samuel; Deane, Silas; DeLancey, James; Dickinson, John; Dinwiddie, Robert; Dudley, Joseph; Dudley, Thomas; Dulany, Daniel; Dummer, Jeremiah; Dunmore, John Murray, Earl of; Dustin, Hannah; Dyer, Mary; Edwards, Jonathan; Eliot, John; Endecott, John; Fairfax, Thomas; Fitzhugh, William; Galloway, Joseph; Gardiner, Lion; Gist, Christopher; Gorton, Samuel; Gosnold, Bartholomew; Hamilton, Andrew; Hancock, Thomas; Harvard, John; Henderson, Richard; Hill, William; Hooker, Thomas; Hornblower, Josiah; Hull, John; Hurd, Nathaniel; Hutchinson, Anne; Hutchinson, Thomas; Johnson, Edward; Johnson, Sir William; Kieft, Willem; King, Rufus; Lechford, Thomas; Leisler, Jacob; Lincoln, Benjamin; Livingston, William; Logan, James; Lopez, Aaron; Low, Isaac; Ludlow, Daniel; Martin, Luther; Mason, George; Mason, John; Masters, Sybilla; Mather, Cotton; Mather, Increase; Mayhew, Jonathan; Mayhew, Thomas; Minuit, Peter; Morris, Gouverneur; Morton, Nathaniel; Morton, Thomas; Muhlenberg, Frederick Augustus; Muhlenberg, Henry Melchior; Newport, Christopher; Nicholson, Francis; Nourse, Rebecca; Oglethorpe, James Edward; Oliver, Peter; Otis, James; Paca, William; Pastorius, Francis Daniel; Penn, William; Pepperrell, Sir William; Phips, Sir William; Pinckney, Elizabeth Lucas; Pinto, Isaac; Popham, George; Pratt, Benjamin; Printz, Johan Bjornsson; Pynchon, William; Randolph, Peyton; Reeve, Tapping; Rogers, John; Rogers, Robert; Rolfe, John; Schuyler, Peter; Seixas, Gershom Mendes; Sewall, Samuel; Shepard, Thomas; Shirley, William; Smith, John; Smith, Thomas; Spotswood, Alexander; Standish, Miles; Steigel, Henry william; Stuyvesant, Petrus; Thompson, Benjamin; Tryon, William; Van der Donck, Adrien; Weiser, Johann Conrad; West, Joseph; White, Andrew; White, John; White, Peregrine; Wigglesworth, Michael; Williams, John; Williams, Roger; Winslow, Edward; Winthrop, John (1587–1649); Winthrop, John (1638–1707); Winthrop, John (1714–1779); Winthrop, John, Jr. (1605–1676); Wise, John; Wistar, Caspar; Woodward, Henry; Yale, Elihu; Zenger, John Peter

Conservation See ENVIRONMENTAL STUDIES.

Crafts Albers, Anni; Arneson, Robert; Autio, Rudy; Babbit, Isaac; Belter, John Henry; Binns, Charles Fergus; Carder, Frederick; Castle, Wendell; Chihuly, Dale; Duckworth, Ruth; Dummer, Jeremiah; du Pont, Henry Francis; Eckhardt, Edris; Ellis, Harvey; Ellsworth, David; Esherick, Wharton; Frankl, Paul T.; Frey, Viola; Frid, Tage; Fulper, William H.; Gregory, Waylande; Grotell, Maija; Grueby, William H.; Guermonprez, Trude; Harper, William; Heaton, Maurice; Herter, Christian; Hicks, Sheila; Hitchcock, Lambert H.; Hubbard, Elbert; Hurd, Nathaniel; Lewis, Lucy M.; Libbey, Edward Drummond; Liebes, Dorothy Wright; Littleton, Harvey; Loloma, Charles; Lukens, Glen; Maloof, Sam; Martinez, Maria; McIntire, Samuel; McKie, Judy; McLaughlin, Mary Louise; Meason, Isaac; Melchert, James; Mercer,

Henry Chapman; Moulthrop, Ed; Nakashima, George; Nampeyo, Dextra Quotskuyva; Natzler, Gertud Amon; Natzler, Otto; Nelson, George; Nutting, Wallace; Ohr, George Edgar; Paley, Albert Raymond; Perry, Mary Chase; Phyfe, Duncan; Poor, Henry Varnum; Prip, John; Revere, Paul; Rhead, Frederick Hurten; Robineau, Adelaide Alsop; Rodia, Simon; Rohde, Gilbert; Rohlfs, Charles; Rossbach, Ed; Sack, Israel; Schreckengost, Viktor; Seymour, John; Shepard, Anna Osler; Soldner, Paul; Steigel, Henry William; Stickley, Gustav; Storer, Maria Longworth Nichols; Tafoya, Margaret; Takaezu, Toshiko; Tawney, Lenore; Thomas, Seth; Tiffany, Louis Comfort; Urban, Joseph; Voulkos, Peter; Webb, Electra Havemeyer; Wigginton, Eliot; Wood, Beatrice; Zeisler, Claire

Crime and Espionage Allen, Francis A.; Arnold, Benedict; Augustus, John; Bancroft, Edward; Barrow, Clyde; Berkman, Alexander; Best, Roy; Boesky, Ivan; Bonney, William H.; Booth, John Wilkes; Borden, Lizzie; Boyd, Belle; Brockway, Zebulon Reed; Brown, Lee P.; Burns, William J.; Calley, William L.; Capone, Al; Chambers, Whittaker; Chessman, Caryl; Cicotte, Eddie; Claflin, Tennessee Celeste; Cressey, Donald R.; Crippen, Hawley Harvey; Cushman, Pauline; Czolgosz, Leon; D'Aquino, Iva Ikuko Toguri; Dillinger, John; Donovan, William; Duffy, Clinton T.; Gates, Daryl F.; Gillars, Mildred; Glueck, Eleanor Touroff; Glueck, Sheldon; Greenhow, Rose O'Neal; Guiteau, Charles Julius; Harrison, John, Jr.; Hearst, Patricia; Hinckley, John W. Jr.; Hiss, Alger; Hoffa, Jimmy; Hoover, J. Edgar; Imbau, Fred E.; Kidd, Captain; Kirchwey, George Washington; Laffite, Jean; Lawes, Lewis Edward; Lohman, Joseph D.; Luciano, "Lucky"; Manson, Charles; Masterson, "Batt"; McCloskey, James; McNamara, Joseph D.; Means, Gaston Bullock; Milken, Michael; Morse, C.W.; Murieta or Murrieta, Joaquin; Murphy, Patrick V.; Norval, Morris; Ohlin, Lloyd E.; Osborne, Thomas Mott; Oswald, Lee Harvey; Parker, Bonnie; Parker, William H.; Pinkerton, Allan; Plummer, Henry; Ponzi, Charles; Quantrill, William; Ray, James Earl; Rosenberg, Ethel; Rosenberg, Julius; Ruby, Jack L.; Sacco, Nicola; Sellin, Thorsten; Sirhan, Sirhan; Smith, Bruce; Starr, Belle; Surratt, Mary Eugenia; Sutherland, Edwin Hardin; Van Waters, Miriam; Vanzetti, Bartolomeo; Vaux, Roberts; Vollmer, August; Vorenburg, James; Weschler, Herbert; Wilkins, Leslie T.; Wilson, James Q.; Wilson, Orlando W.; Wirz, Henry; Wyman, Seth; You, Dominique; Younger, "Cole"

Dance Adams, Diana; Ailey, Alvin; Arpino, Gerald; Ashley, Merrill; Astaire, Fred; Baker, Josephine; Balanchine, George; Baryshnikov, Mikhail; Bennett, Michael; Berkeley, Busby; Bolger, Ray; Brown, Trisha; Chase, Lucia; Christensen, Lew; D'Amboise, Jacques; Davis, Sammy, Jr.; de Mille, Agnes; Denby, Edwin; Duncan, Isadora; Dunham, Katherine; Fagan, Garth; Farrell, Suzanne; Feld, Elliot; Forsythe, William; Fosse, Bob; Fuller, Loie; Graham, Martha; Gregory, Cynthia; Hawkins, Erick; Hayden, Melissa;

OCCUPATIONAL INDEX

Dance (*cont.*)
Holder, Geoffrey; Holm, Hanya; Humphrey, Doris; Jamison, Judith; Joffrey, Robert; Jones, Bill T.; Kaye, Nora; Kelly, Gene; Kent, Allegra; Kidd, Michael; Kirkland, Gelsey; Kirstein, Lincoln; Kistler, Darci; Kurath, Gertrude Prokosch; LeClercq, Tanaquil; Limon, Jose; Martin, John; Martins, Peter; McBride, Patricia; Mitchell, Arthur; Monk, Meredith; Morris, Mark; Nichols, Kyra; Nikolais, Alwin; Primus, Pearl; Rainer, Yvonne; Rivera, Chita; Robbins, Jerome; Robinson, Bill "Bojangles"; Shawn, Ted; Sokolow, Anna; St. Denis, Ruth; Tallchief, Maria; Taylor, Paul; Tharp, Twyla; Tune, Tommy; Tyson, Cicely; Villella, Edward; Warburg, Edward M. M.; Waring, James; Weidman, Charles

Design and Fashion Adrian; Arden, Elizabeth; Baldwin, Billy; Beene, Geoffrey; Bel Geddes, Norman; Bertoia, Harry; Blass, Bill; Bloomer, Amelia; Bradley, Will H.; Breuer, Marcel; Brodovitch, Alexey; Brown, Eleanor McMillen; Buatta, Mario; Burton, Scott; Butterick, Ebenezer; Carnegie, Hattie; Cassini, Oleg; Chwast, Seymour; Claiborne, Liz; Codman, Ogden; Conover, Harry; Cumming, Rose Stuart; Dache, Lilly; de la Renta, Oscar; Demorest, Ellen Louise Curtis; Deskey, Donald; de Wolfe, Elsie; Draper, Dorothy; Dreyfuss, Henry; Dwiggins, William Addison; Eames, Charles; Ellis, Harvey; Esherick, Wharton; Fuller, Buckminster; Galanos, James; Gibson, Charles Dana; Glaser, Milton; Godey, Louis Antoine; Gorey, Edward; Halston; Hampton, Mark; Head, Edith; Klein, Anne; Klein, Calvin; Knoll, Florence; Liberman, Alex; Liebes, Dorothy Wright; Loewy, Raymond; Mainbocher; McCardell, Claire; McKie, Judy; Mielziner, Jo; Nelson, George; Noyes, Eliot; Oenslager, Donald; Ortenberg;, Arthur; Papanek, Victor; Parish, Mrs. Henry, II; Phyfe, Duncan; Reeves, Ruth; Rohde, Gilbert; Saladino, John F.; Sheppard, Eugenia; Smith, Oliver; Snow, Carmel White; Strengell, Marianne; Teague, Walter Dorwin; Tiffany, Louis Comfort; Vignelli, Massimo; Vreeland, Diana; Wallance, Donald A.; Weber, Kem; Wheeler, Candace; Woolson, Abba Louise; Wright, Russel

Diplomacy Acheson, Dean; Adams, Charles Francis; Annenberg, Walter; Armstrong, Hamilton Fish; Badeau, John S.; Bancroft, George; Barlow, Joel; Baruch, Bernard; Belmont, August; Blakeslee, George H.; Bloch, Henry Wollman; Bohlen, Charles E.; Boker, George Henry; Borchard, Edwin Montefiore; Braden, Spruille; Bruce, David K. E.; Buell, Raymond Leslie; Bullitt, William C.; Bunche, Ralphe J.; Bunker, Ellsworth; Burlingame, Anson; Cabot, John M.; Carlucci, Frank Charles; Choate, Joseph H.; Christopher, Warren M.; Clay, Cassius Marcellus; Conant, James Bryant; Cordier, Andrew W.; Crocker, Chester; Cross, Samuel Hazzard; Cushing, Caleb; Daniels, Josephus; Dawes, Charles G.; Day, William Rufus; Deane, Silas; Depew, Chauncey Mitchell; Dodd, William Edward; Dodge, Augustus; Dulles, Allen; Dulles, John Foster; Edge, Walter Evans; Eichelberger, Clark M.; Everett, Edward; Fortas,

Abe; Franklin, Benjamin; Gadsden, James; Gallatin, Albert; Grew, Joseph Clark; Habib, Philip C.; Hare, Raymond A.; Harriman, Averell; Hay, John; Henderson, Loy W.; Hill, David Jayne; Hornbeck, Stanley K.; House, "Colonel"; Hughes, Charles Evans; Hunt, William Henry; Hunter, Ellsworth; Hurley, Patrick J.; Izard, Ralph; Jay, John; Johnson, Nelson Trusler; Johnson, Reverdy; Johnson, U. Alexis; Kellogg, Frank; Kennan, George F.; Kennedy, Joseph; King, Rufus; Kohler, Foy C.; Larkin, Thomas Oliver; Laurens, Henry; Leahy, William; Linowitz, Sol; Livingston, Robert R.; Lowell, James Russell; MacArthur, Douglas; MacVeagh, Lincoln; Mansfield, Mike; Marcy, William Learned; Marsh, George Perkins; Mason, James; Mellon, Andrew; Messersmith, George S.; Miller, David Hunter; Moore, John Bassett; Morris, Gouverneur; Moscoso, Teodoro; Motley, John Lothrop; Murphy, Robert D.; Page, Thomas Nelson; Page, Walter Hines; Phillips, William; Pinckney, Charles; Pinckney, Thomas; Pinkney, William; Poindexter, Miles; Poinsett, Joel Roberts; Reid, Whitelaw; Reischauer, Edwin O.; Rockhill, William Woodville; Rohde, Ruth; Rowe, Leo Stanton; Rush, Richard; Samoset; Schurman, Jacob; Service, John Stewart; Shotwell, James Thomson; Shultz, George; Slidell, John; Smith, Walter Bedell; Smith, William; Squier, Ephraim George; Stevenson, Adlai II; Stevenson, Andrew; Stockton, John Potter; Straus, Oscar Solomon; Strauss, Robert; Sweetser, Arthur; Temple, Shirley; Thompson, Llewellyn E., Jr.; Thompson, Waddy; Trist, Nicholas; Vance, Cyrus; Van Dyke, Henry; Vincent, John Carter; Webb, James Watson; Webster, Daniel; Welles, Summer; Wheaton, Henry; White, Andrew Dickson; White, Henry; Whitlock, Brand; Whitney, John Hay; Williams, Samuel Wells; Willkie, Wendell; Wilson, Hugh R.; Winant, John G.; Yancey, William Lowndes; Young, Owen D.

Earth Sciences Abbe, Cleveland; Adams, Leason Heberling; Agassiz, Louis; Allen, Clarence Roderic; Anderson, Don Lynn; Andrews, Roy Chapman; Anthes, Richard; Barton, Donald C.; Benioff, Hugo; Bentley, Wilson; Berry, Edward Wilber; Birch, Francis; Bjerknes, Jacob; Bolt, Bruce A.; Boucot, Arthur James; Bowen, Norman; Bowie, William; Bryson, Reid A.; Bucher, Walter H.; Byerly, Perry; Chamberlin, T.C.; Charney, Jule Gregory; Cornell, C. Allin; Cox, Allan V.; Cressman, George; Daly, Reginald Aldworth; Dana, James D.; Davis, William; Day, Arthur L.; DeGolyer, Everette Lee; Dietz, Robert Sinclair; Drake, Charles; Dutton, Clarence Edward; Dziewonski, Adam Marian; Emmons, S.F.; Espy, James; Ewing, Maurice; Ferrel, William; Fleming, John A.; Fujita, Tetsuya or Theodore; Gilbert, G.K.; Gould, Stephen Jay; Gregory, Herbert; Griggs, David T.; Gutenberg, Beno; Guyot, Arnold; Hall, James, Jr.; Hallgren, Richard E.; Hansen, William Peat; Hartt, C. Fred; Haskell, Norman; Hatcher, John Bell; Hayden, Ferdinand V.; Hayford, John F.; Heck, Nicholas H.; Hedberg, Hollis Dow; Heiland, C.A.; Heilprin, Angelo; Hess, H.H.;

Hitchcock, Edward; Hobbs, William; Hosler, Charles; Houghton, Henry; Hubbert, M. King; Johnson, Douglas; Karcher, J.C.; King, Clarence; Knopf, Adolph; Knopoff, Leon; Krishnamurti, Tiruvalam N.; Lambert, Walter Davis; Landsberg, Helmut Erich; Lawson, Andrew C.; Lewis, Warren K.; Lindgren, Waldemar; Lorenz, Edward N.; Lucas, Anthony Francis; Macelwane, James B., S.J.; Marbut, Curtis; Marsh, O.C.; Marshall, James; Matthew, William Diller; Maury, Matthew Fontaine; Meinzer, Oscar Edward; Menard, H. William, Jr.; Moore, R.C.; Munk, Walter H.; Murphree, Eger V.; Newberry, John Strong; Newell, Frederick Haynes; Newell, Norman Dennis; Nierenberg, William Aaron; Oliver, Jack E.; Packard, Alpheus Spring, Jr.; Panofsky, Hans; Penrose, Richard A.F., Jr.; Perkins, Dexter; Pillsbury, John E.; Pirsson, Louis V.; Powell, John Wesley; Press, Frank; Pumpelly, Raphael; Ransome, F. L.; Redfield, Alfred Clarence; Reid, Harry Fielding; Revelle, Roger; Rhines, Peter B.; Richter, Charles F.; Rossby, Carl-Gustaf; Salisbury, Rollin; Schaefer, Vincent J.; Schmitz, William J., Jr.; Schopf, J. William; Schuchert, Charles; Shaler, Nathaniel; Silliman, Benjamin, Jr.; Silliman, Benjamin, Sr.; Simpson, George Gaylord; Simpson, Joanne Malkus; Smith, George O.; Steinbrugge, Karl V.; Stommel, Henry M.; Suomi, Verner; Sykes, Lynn Ray; Tarr, Ralph; Terzaghi, Karl; Thornthwaite, Charles; Turekian, Karl K.; Ulrich, Edward Oscar; Van Hise, Charles; Van Orstrand, C.E.; Vaughan, Thomas Wayland; Verhoogen, John; Ward, Lester Frank; Ward, Robert; White, Robert M.; Whitten, Charles Arthur; Willis, Bailey; Williston, Samuel Wendell; Woollard, George P.; Worthington, L. Valentine; Wunsch, Carl Isaac

Ecology See ENVIRONMENTAL STUDIES.

Economics Adelman, Irma; Andrews, John Bertram; Arrow, Kenneth; Baer, Werner; Bain, Joe S.; Barro, Robert; Baumol, William; Becker, Gary; Bergson, Abram; Berle, A.A.; Berry, Sara S.; Boulding, Kenneth; Bowles, Samuel; Brimmer, Andrew Felton; Buchanan, James M.; Burns, Arthur F.; Carey, Henry; Chamberlin, Edward Hastings; Chenery, Hollis; Clark, John Bates; Coase, Ronald; Commons, John Rogers; Conklin, George T., Jr.; Corey, Lewis; Debreu, Gerard; Domar, Evsey D.; Dornbusch, Rudiger; Douglas, Paul H.; Dunlop, John Thomas; Eckstein, Otto; Enthoven, Alain; Feldstein, Martin S.; Fink, Albert; Fisher, Irving; Fogel, Robert W.; Friedman, Milton; Galbraith, John Kenneth; George, Henry; Georgescu-Roegen, Nicholas; Greenspan, Alan; Griliches, Zvi; Hadley, Arthur Twining; Hansen, Alvin Harvey; Harsanyi, John C.; Hirschman, Albert O.; Homer, Sidney; Hotelling, Harold; Isard, Walter; Jorgenson, Dale W.; Kaufman, Henry; Kerr, Clark; Keyserling, Leon H.; Klein, Lawrence Robert; Knight, Frank Hyneman; Koopmans, Tjalling C.; Kuznets, Simon; Kyrk, Hazel; Leibenstein, Harvey; Leontief, Wassily W.; Lewis, W. Arthur; Lucas, Robert E., Jr.; Machlup, Fritz; Markowitz, Harry Max; Martin, William McChesney, Jr.; Miller, Marvin; Miller,

Merton H.; Modigliani, Franco; Morganstern, Oskar; Musgrave, Richard Abel; North, Douglass C.; Nourse, Edwin; Olds, Leland; Pasvolsky, Leo; Poor, Henry Varnum; Rivlin, Alice; Rohatyn, Felix; Rostow, Walt Whitman; Rubinow, Isaac Max; Sachs, Jeffrey D.; Samuelson, Paul; Sargent, Thomas J.; Schelling, Thomas Crombie; Schlesinger, James R.; Schultz, Theodore W.; Schumpeter, Joseph Alois; Sharpe, William Forsyth; Shultz, George; Simon, Herbert A.; Smithies, Arthur; Solow, Robert Merton; Sowell, Thomas; Spence, Michael A.; Stigler, George J.; Stiglitz, Joseph E.; Taylor, Lance; Thurow, Lester; Tobin, James; Tugwell, Rexford; Veblen, Thorstein; Viner, Jacob; Volcker, Paul A.; Von Mises, Ludwig; Walker, Amasa

Education Adams, Charles Kendall; Adams, Herbert Baxter; Adler, Mortimer J.; Alcott, Bronson; Alder, Cyrus; Alegria, Ricardo E.; Andrews, Benjamin; Angell, James; Arbuthnot, May Hill; Asheim, Lester Eugene; Astin, Alexander W.; Atherton, George Washington; Aydelotte, Frank; Badeau, John S.; Bailey, Stephen; Barnard, Frederick A.P.; Barnard, Henry; Baron, Salo; Barzun, Jacques; Beadle, William Henry Harrison; Beecher, Catherine Esther; Belkin, Samuel; Bell, Alexander Graham; Bell, Terrel; Benitez, Jaime; Bennett, William J.; Berlitz, Charles; Berry, Martha McChesney; Berry, Mary Frances; Bestor, Arthur Eugene; Bestor, Arthur; Bethune, Mary McLeod; Bliss, Howard Sweetser; Bok, Derek; Bowman, Isaiah; Boyer, Ernest; Bragg, Mabel Caroline; Brainard, Daniel; Breckinridge, Sophonisba Preston; Brinton, Crane; Brown, Hallie Quinn; Butler, Nicholas Murray; Cabot, Hugh; Capen, Samuel; Carnovsky, Leon; Carver, George Washington; Chamberlain, Joshua; Chamberlin, T.C.; Chase, Gilbert; Clark, William Smith; Clarke, Francis Devereux; Cohen, Gerson D.; Cohen, Stephen F.; Coleman, James; Commoner, Barry; Conant, James Bryant; Conway, Jill Ker; Cooke, Joseah Parsons, Jr.; Cooney, Joan Ganz; Cooper, Thomas; Coppin, Fanny Marion Jackson; Cordier, Andrew W.; Counts, George S.; Crandall, Prudence; Cremin, Lawrence; Cross, Wilbur; Cubberley, Ellwood Patterson; Curry, Jabez; Damrosch, Walter; Daniels, Robert; Deloria, Vine, Jr.; Dewey, John; Dornbusch, Rudiger; Doyle, Sarah Elizabeth; Duncan, Robert Kennedy; Durand, William; Durant, Henry; Dwight, Timothy; Dyer, Wayne W.; Eddy, Henry; Edsall, David Linn; Eisenman, Peter D.; Eliot, Charles William; Elkin, Stanley; Erskine, John; Evans, Daniel Jackson; Fernow, Bernhard Eduard; Fess, Simeon Davidson; Finkelstein, Louis; Finley, John H., Jr.; Finley, Robert; Finn, Chester Evans, Jr.; Finney, Charles Grandison; Flanagan, Hallie; Flexner, Abraham; Flexner, Simon; Flint, Austin; Fox, Dixon; Freund, Paul Abraham; Fulbright, J. William; Funston, Keith; Gallaudet, Edward Miner; Gallaudet, Thomas; Gardner, John; Gates, Henry Louis, Jr.; Gates, Thomas S.; Giamatti, A. Bartlett; Gibbons, James; Gilman, Daniel Coit; Glueck, Nelson; Goldsmith, Grace Arabell; Goldstein, Max Aaron; Goodlad, John; Goodman, Paul;

Gantt, Henry Laurence; Gates, William H.; Gatling, Richard Jordan; Gibbs, James Ethan Allen; Gilbreth, Frank; Gilbreth, Lillian; Gillette, King C.; Ginsburg, Charles P.; Glidden, Joseph; Goethals, George Washington; Goldmark, Peter; Goodyear, Charles; Gorrie, John; Gould, Gordon; Gray, Elisha; Greatbatch, Wilson; Greene, Leonard Michael; Greenway, John Campbell; Grumman, Leroy; Hale, William Jay; Hall, Charles Martin; Hallidie, Andrew; Hamming, Richard W.; Hanford, William Edward; Hansen, William Peat; Happer, William, Jr.; Haupt, Herman; Hawes, Josiah Johnson; Haynes, Elwood; Heinemann, Edward H.; Hewlett, William R.; Hillier, James; Hoe, Richard March; Holland, Clifford; Holland, John Philip; Hollerith, Herman; Holley, Alexander Lyman; Holmes, Donald Fletcher; Hornblower, Josiah; Hotchkiss, Benjamin Berkeley; Houdry, Eugene Jules; House, Royal; Howe, Elias; Howell, Albert Summers; Humphreys, Joshua; Hunsaker, Jerome; Hussey, Obed; Hyatt, John; Isherwood, Benjamin; Ives, Frederick Eugene; Jackson, Dugald; Jacuzzi, Candido; Jenney, William Le Baron; Jensen, Peter Laurits; Jervis, John B.; Jewett, Frank Baldwin; Jobs, Steven; Johnson, Clarence L.; Johnson, Eldridge Reeves; Jones, Thomas P.; Jones, William Richard; Judah, Theodore; Julian, Percy; Kalmus, Herbert T.; Kalmus, Natalie Mabelle; Kapor, Mitchell; Karman, Theodore von; Kelly, William; Kennelly, Arthur Edwin; Kernighan, Brian W.; Kettering, Charles; Kilby, Jack S.; King, Clarence; Klemin, Alexander; Knuth, Donald E.; Kolff, Willem J.; Kouwenhoven, William; Kruesi, John; Kurzweil, Raymond C.; Lake, Simon; Lamme, Benjamin; Land, Edwin; Langley, Samuel; Lanston, Tolbert; Latimer, Lewis Howard; Lear, William; Lederer, Jerome; Ledley, Robert Steven; Leffel, James; L'Enfant, Pierre Charles; Lewis, George; Lewis, Warren K.; Licklider, Joseph; Link, Edwin; Lippisch, Alexander; Little, Arthur D.; Loening, Grover; Loewy, Raymond; Long, Stephen Harriman; Lowe, Thaddeus; Lucas, Anthony Francis; MacDonald, Thomas Harris; MacKaye, Steele; Maiman, Theodore; Masters, Sybilla; Matzeliger, Jan Earnst; Mauchly, John William; Maxim, Hiram; McCallum, Daniel C.; McCarthy, John; McCormick, Cyrus Hall; McCoy, Elijah; McDonnell, James; McKay, Gordon; Mees, Charles Edward Kenneth; Melville, George Wallace; Merganthaler, Ottmar; Merriam, Mansfield; Midgley, Thomas, Jr.; Minsky, Marvin; Moissief, Leon S.; Moody, Paul; Morey, Samuel; Morgan, Arthur E.; Morgan, Garrett A.; Morley, Edward Williams; Morse, Samuel F.B.; Mulholland, William; Murphree, Eger V.; Newell, Frederick Haynes; Norden, Carl Lucas; Norris, William C.; North, Simeon; Northrop, John; Noyce, Robert N.; Olsen, John Charles; Olsen, Kenneth; Olson, Harry Ferdinand; Othmer, Donald F.; Otis, Elisha; Packard, David; Packard, James W.; Page, Charles; Parker, Louis; Pelton, Lester Allen; Perkins, Jacob; Piccard, Jean Felix; Pierce, John Robinson; Plank, Charles J.; Plunkett, Roy J.; Porter, Rufus; Pratt, Francis Asbury; Pridham, Edwin S.; Pullman, George Mortimer; Pupin, Michael; Ramo,

Simon; Read, Nathan; Renwick, James, Sr.; Rillieux, Norbert; Ritchey, George Willis; Robert, Henry Martyn; Roebling, John Augustus; Roebling, Washington Augustus; Roebuck, Alvah C.; Rogers, Isaiah; Roosevelt, Nicholas; Root, Elisha King; Rosinski, Edward J.; Rumsey, James; Sarett, Lewis; Saxton, Joseph; Schaefer, Vincent J.; Schwarz, Harvey Fisher; Sellers, William; Sholes, Christopher; Shreve, R. Norris; Sickels, Frederick Ellsworth; Singer, Isaac M.; Slater, Samuel; Sorensen, Charles; Sperry, Elmer; Sprague, Frank; Stanley, Francis Edgar; Stanley, Freelan O.; Stanley, William; Steinbrugge, Karl V.; Steinmetz, Charles Proteus; Stevens, Edwin Augustus; Stevens, John Cox; Stevens, Robert Livingston; Stibitz, George Robert; Stine, Charles; Stone, Charles A.; Strickland, William; Sturtevant, Benjamin; Swasey, Ambrose; Sweeney, Orland R.; Swope, Gerard; Tabern, Donalee L.; Taylor, Frederick Winslow; Terman, Frederick E.; Terry, Eli; Terzaghi, Karl; Tesla, Nikola; Thayer, Sylvanus; Thompson, Benjamin; Thompson, Kenneth L.; Thomson, Elihu; Thomson, J. Edgar; Thurston, Robert Henry; Timken, Henry; Timoshenko, Stepan Prokofyevich; Towne, Henry Robinson; Vauclain, Samuel; Volwiler, Ernest H.; Von Braun, Wernher; Walker, William H.; Wallace, William; Wang, An; Waring, Fred; Warner, Edward; Webster, Edwin S.; Wesson, Daniel Baird; Westinghouse, George; Whipple, Squire; Whistler, George; Whitcomb, Richard; White, Canvass; Whitney, Asa; Whitney, Eli; Whitney, Willis Rodney; Wickenden, William Elgin; Wight, Peter B.; Willard, Simon; Williams, Robert, Jr.; Winans, Ross; Wood, Devolson; Woods, Granville T.; Worthington, Henry; Wozniak, Stephen; Wright, Benjamin; Wright, Orville; Wright, Wilbur; Yale, Linus; Zworykin, Vladimir

Entertainment Allen, Fred; Bailey, James; Bailey, Pearl; Baker, Josephine; Barnum, P.T.; Belushi, John; Benny, Jack; Berle, Milton; Blackstone, Harry; Borge, Victor; Brice, Fanny; Bruce, Lenny; Buck, Frank; Cantor, Eddie; Christy, Edwin Pearce; Clark, Bobby; Cody, William Frederick; Cook, Joe; Cosby, Bill; Davis, Sammy, Jr.; Disney, Walt; Dixon, George Washington; Eltinge, Julian; Emmett, Daniel; Fields, Lew; Fleming, Peggy; Forepaugh, Adam; Foxx, Redd; Foy, Eddie; Garland, Judy; Goldin, Horace; Gregory, Dick; Harrigan, Edward; Hayes, Peter Lind; Henie, Sonja; Herrmann, Alexander; Holm, Eleanor; Houdini, Harry; Irwin, Bill; Janis, Elsie; Kellar, Harry; Kelley, Emmett; Kitt, Eartha; Knievel, "Evil"; Lee, Gypsy Rose; Liberace; Lillie, Gordon William; Mabley, Moms; Madonna; Martin, Steve; Mills, Florence; Oakley, Annie; Rand, Sally; Rice, Dan; Rice, Thomas Dartmouth; Rivers, Joan; Rogers, Will; Rose, Billy; Smothers, Dick; Smothers, Tom; Stratton, "General Tom Thumb"; Tanguay, Eva; Thurston, Howard; Todd, Mike; Tucker, Sophie; Weber, Joseph; Wein, George; West, Mae; Williams, Bert

Environmental Studies Abbey, Edward; Agassiz, Alexander; Albright, Horace Marden; Allard, Harry A.; Austin, Mary; Babbitt, Bruce; Bachman, John;

OCCUPATIONAL INDEX

Environmental Studies (*cont.*)

Baird, Spencer Fullerton; Bennett, Hugh Hammond; Bigelow, Henry B.; Brand, Stewart; Braun, E. Lucy; Broecker, Wallace S.; Brower, David; Brown, Lester; Burroughs, John; Carson, Rachel; Catesby, Mark; Clements, Frederick Edward; Colby, William Edward; Commoner, Barry; Cowles, Henry Chandler; Craig, Harmon; Dall, William Healey; Davis, Russ E.; Dilg, Will; Doubleday, Neltje de Graff; Douglas, Marjory Stoneman; Edge, Rosalie; Edwin, James; Ehrlich, Paul R.; Ewing, Maurice; Fernow, Bernhard Eduard; Fleming, Richard H.; Fofonoff, Nicholas Paul; Forbes, Stephen Alfred; Fossey, Dian; Fuertes, Louis Agassiz; Fuglister, Frederick C.; Grinnell, George Bird; Hardin, Garrett; Harris, Rollin Arthur; Hornaday, William Temple; Isaacs, John D.; Iselin, Columbus O'Donnell; Johnson, Martin W.; Johnson, Robert Underwood; Krutch, Joseph Wood; Langford, Nathaniel Pitt; Leopold, Aldo; Lovins, Amory; MacArthur, Robert Helmer; Marshall, Robert; Mather, Stephen Tyng; McCall, Tom; Merriam, Clinton Hart; Mills, Enos Abijah; Muir, John; Murie, Olaus; Odum, Eugene Pleasants; Pearson, Thomas Gilbert; Pinchot, Gifford; Rafinesque, Constantine; Redfield, Alfred Clarence; Revelle, Roger; Rockefeller, Laurance; Sargent, Charles Sprague; Seton, Ernest Thompson; Silcox, Ferdinand Augustus; Teale, Edwin Way; Udall, Stewart; Vogt, William; Von Hagen, Victor Wolfgang; Zahniser, Howard Clinton

Exploration and Pioneer Settlements Akeley, Carl; Akeley, Mary Lee; Andrews, Roy Chapman; Applegate, Jesse; Armstrong, John; Baldwin, Evelyn Briggs; Bandelier, Adolph; Bartlett, Robert; Beale, Edward Fitzgerald; Becknell, William; Beckwourth, Jim; Bidwell, John; Bienville, Jean Baptiste le Moyne, Sieur de; Bingham, Hiram; Boone, Daniel; Bozeman, John M.; Brannan, Samuel; Burnham, Frederick Russell; Byrd, Richard; Carson, Kit; Chisolm, Jesse; Clark, George Rogers; Clark, William; Cody, William Frederick; Colter, John; Cook, Frederick Albert; Cuffe, Paul; De Long, George Washington; Dixon, "Billy"; Dodge, Henry; Dunbar, William; Edwin, James; Ellsworth, Lincoln; Emory, William H.; Fairchild, David Grandison; Filson, John; Freeman, Thomas; Fremont, John; Gibson, Paris; Gimbel, Peter; Gist, Christopher; Gosnold, Bartholomew; Gray, Robert; Greely, Adolphus Washington; Grinnell, Josiah; Hall, Charles Francis; Hayes, Isaac Israel; Heilprin, Angelo; Henderson, Richard; Henson, Matthew; Hubbard, Bernard Rosecrans; Ives, Joseph Christmas; Johnson, Martin; Johnson, Osa; Joseph, Mother; Kane, Elisha Kent; Kelley, Hall, J.; Kennan, George; Kino, Eusebio Francisco; Lander, Frederick West; Langford, Nathaniel Pitt; Ledyard, John; Lee, Jason; Lewis, Meriwether; Lillie, Gordon William; Long, Stephen Harriman; Marquette, Jacques; Meek, Joseph L.; Melville, George Wallace; Milner, Moses Embree; Muir, John; Newport, Christopher; Orton, James; Palmer, Nathaniel Brown; Parker, Samuel; Peary, Robert E.; Pike, Zebulon; Porter, Russell Williams; Pursh, Frederick; Putnam, Rufus; Rice, Henry Mower;

Robertson, James; Roosevelt, Kermit; Sacagawea, Boinaiv; Schoolcraft, Henry Rowe; Schwatka, Frederick; Sieber, Al; Smith, Jedediah Strong; Smith, John; Stanley, Henry Morton; Stansbury, Howard; Stefansson, Vilhjalmur; Stevenson, James; Sutter, John Augustus; Thompson, Edward Herbert; Tonty, Henri de; Von Hagen, Victor Wolfgang; Walker, Joseph Reddeford; Walker, Thomas; Webber, Charles Wilkins; Welles, Roger; Wellman, Walter; Wharton, Samuel; Whitman, Marcus; Wilkes, Charles; Williams, Roger; Wolfskill, William; Woodward, Henry; Workman, Fanny; Wyeth, Nathaniel; Young, Ewing; Yount, George

Fashion See under DESIGN AND FASHION.

Film Alda, Alan; Allen, Woody; Altman, Robert; Anderson, Judith; Anger, Kenneth; Arthur, Jean; Arzner, Dorothy; Astaire, Fred; Avery, Tex; Bacall, Lauren; Ball, Lucille; Bankhead, Tallulah; Bara, Theda; Barbera, Joseph; Barrymore, Ethel; Barrymore, John; Barrymore, Lionel; Beery, Wallace; Behrman, S.N.; Belushi, John; Benchley, Robert; Benny, Jack; Berkeley, Busby; Bernstein, Elmer; Bikel, Theodore; Bitzer, Billy; Bogart, Humphrey; Bow, Clara; Boyd, William; Brackett, Charles; Brando, Marlon; Brennan, Walter; Brooks, Louise; Burnett, Carol; Burnett, Charles; Burr, Raymond; Burroughs, Edgar Rice; Cagney, James; Cain, James M.; Capra, Frank; Carmichael, Hoagy; Carroll, Diahann; Cassavetes, John; Chaney, Lon; Chaplin, Charlie; Chayefsky, Paddy; Clark, Bobby; Clarke, Shirley; Clift, Montgomery; Cohn, Harry; Colbert, Claudette; Conner, Bruce; Constantine, Eddie; Cooper, Gary; Coppola, Francis Ford; Corman, Roger; Crawford, Joan; Cronyn, Hume; Crosby, Bing; Cukor, George; Curtiz, Michael; Dassin, Jules; Davis, Ossie; Davis, Bette; Day, Doris; Dean, James; Dee, Ruby; De Mille, Cecil B.; De Niro, Robert; Dietrich, Marlene; Disney, Walt; Donaldson, Walter; Dressler, Marie; Dumont, Margaret; Duvall, Robert; Eastman, P.D.; Eastwood, Clint; Eddy, Nelson; Fairbanks, Douglas, Sr.; Falk, Peter; Fejos, Paul; Field, Sally; Fields, W. C.; Fishburne, Larry; Flaherty, Robert J.; Fleming, Victor; Flynn, Errol; Fonda, Henry; Fonda, Jane; Foote, Horton; Ford, John; Frank, Robert; Freed, Arthur; Freeman, Morgan; Freleng, Fritz; Gable, Clark; Garbo, Greta; Garfield, John; Garland, Judy; Gibbons, Cedric; Gimbel, Peter; Gish, Lillian; Glover, Danny; Goldberg, Whoopi; Goldwyn, Samuel; Gramatky, Hardie; Grant, Cary; Griffith, D.W.; Hanna, William; Hardy, Oliver; Harlow, Jean; Hart, William S.; Hawks, Howard; Hayes, Helen; Hays, Will; Hayworth, Rita; Hecht, Ben; Henie, Sonja; Hepburn, Katharine; Herrmann, Bernard; Heston, Charlton; Hoffman, Dustin; Hope, Bob; Horne, Lena; Houseman, John; Howe, James Wong; Howell, Albert Summers; Hughes, Howard; Huston, John; Ince, Thomas H.; Ives, Burl; Ivory, James; Iwerks, Ub; Jarmusch, Jim; Johnson, Nunnally; Jolson, Al; Jones, Chuck; Jones, James Earl; Jones, Quincy; Julia, Raul; Kael, Pauline; Kalmus, Herbert T.; Kalmus, Natalie

Mabelle; Kander, John; Karloff, Boris; Kaye, Danny; Kazan, Elia; Keaton, Buster; Kelly, Gene; Kelly, Grace; Kern, Jerome; King, Stephen; Koehler, Ted; Korty, John; Kovacs, Ernie; Kubrick, Stanley; Laemmle, Carl, Sr.; Lahr, Bert; Lancaster, Burt; Lantz, Walter; Lanza, Mario; Lardner, Ring, Jr.; Laughton, Charles; Laurel, Stan; Laurel and Hardy; Leacock, Ricky; Lee, Canada; Lee, "Spike"; Lemmon, Jack; Levant, Oscar; Lewis, Jerry; Lloyd, Harold; Loden, Barbara; Logan, Joshua; Lombard, Carole; Lorentz, Pare; Losey, Joseph; Loy, Myrna; Lubitsch, Ernst; Lucas, George; Lugosi, Bela; Lumet, Sidney; Lupino, Ida; MacArthur, Charles; MacDonald, Jeanette; MacLaine, Shirley; Madonna; Maltz, Albert; Mancini, Henry; Mankiewicz, Herman J.; Mankiewicz, Joseph L.; Martin, Mary; Martin, Steve; Marx, Chico; Marx, Groucho; Marx, Gummo; Marx, Harpo; Marx, Zeppo; Marx Brothers; Mayer, Louis B.; Maysles, Albert; Maysles, David; McCay, Winsor; Micheaux, Oscar; Minnelli, Vincente; Mix, Tom; Monroe, Marilyn; Muni, Paul; Murphy, Audie; Newman, Alfred; Newman, Paul; Nichols, Mike; Nicholson, Jack; Normand, Mabel; North, Alex; Odets, Clifford; Parks, Gordon A.; Peck, Gregory; Pennebaker, D.A.; Perelman, S.J.; Pickford, Mary; Poitier, Sidney; Polglase, Van Nest; Porter, Edwin S.; Preminger, Otto; Presley, Elvis; Previn, Andre; Pryor, Richard; Quinn, Anthony; Rainer, Yvonne; Ray, Nicholas; Reagan, Ronald; Redford, Robert; Roach, Hal; Robards, Jason, Jr.; Robin, Leo; Robinson, Edward G.; Roemer, Michael; Rogers, Ginger; Rogers, Will; Rogosin, Lionel; Rooney, Mickey; Ross, Diana; Rozsa, Miklos; Sayles, John; Schary, Dore; Schulberg, Budd; Scorsese, Martin; Scott, George C.; Selleck, Tom; Selznick, David O.; Sennett, Mack; Shepard, Sam; Simon, Neil; Sinatra, Frank; Spielberg, Steven; Stanwyck, Barbara; Steiner, Max; Stevens, George; Stewart, James; Stone, Oliver; Streep, Meryl; Streisand, Barbra; Sturges, Preston; Susskind, David; Swanson, Gloria; Tandy, Jessica; Taylor, Elizabeth; Temple, Shirley; Thalberg, Irving G.; Tiomkin, Dimitri; Toland, Gregg; Tomlin, Lily; Tracy, Spencer; Trumbo, Dalton; Valenti, Jack; Van Dyke, Dick; Van Dyke, Willard Ames; Van Heusen, James; Vidor, King; Von Sternberg, Josef; Von Stroheim, Erich; Walker, Joe; Wanger, Walter; Warhol, Andy; Warner, Albert; Warner, Harry; Warner, Jack; Warner, Samuel; Warner Brothers; Warren, Harry; Waters, Ethel; Waxman, Franz; Wayne, John; Weissmuller, Johnny; Welles, Orson; West, Mae; West, Nathanael; Wexler, Haskell; White, Pearl; Wilder, Billy; Williams, John; Wiseman, Frederick; Wolper, David L.; Woodward, Joanne; Wyler, William; Young, Robert; Young, Victor; Zanuck, Darryl F.; Zinnemann, Fred

Finance and Banking Ames, Oakes; Angermueller, Hans; Appleton, Nathan; Astor, John Jacob; Astor, William Backhouse; Babson, Roger; Bache, Jules S.; Baker, George F.; Barker, Jacob; Baruch, Bernard; Batten, William; Belmont, August; Biddle, Nicholas; Birk, Roger Emil; Boesky, Ivan; Bogle, John Clifton; Brady, "Diamond Jim"; Brown, James; Brown, John A.;

Buffett, Warren; Bulfinch, Thomas; Chouteau, Rene Auguste; Clausen, Alden Winship; Conklin, George T., Jr.; Cooke, Jay; Corcoran, William Wilson; Dale, Chester; DeNunzio, Ralph Dwight; Dodge, Joseph M.; Donaldson, William Henry; Drew, Daniel; Drexel, Anthony Joseph; Duer, William; Dun, R. G.; du Pont, Coleman; du Pont, Pierre S.; Field, Cyrus W.; Fisk, James; Flagler, Henry M.; Forbes, John Murray; Funston, Keith; Gallatin, Albert; Garrett, Robert; Gary, Elbert Henry; Gates, Thomas S.; Giannini, Amadeo P.; Girard, Stephen; Gladwin, Harold S. Jay; Green, Hetty; Guggenheim, Meyer; Harriman, Averell; Harriman, Edward H.; Havemeyer, William Frederick; Hayden, Charles; Higginson, Henry L.; Hill, James J.; Hirshhorn, Joseph H.; Hock, Dee Ward; Holladay, Ben; Homer, Sidney; Hopson, Howard C.; Icahn, Carl; Inman, John Hamilton; Insull, Samuel; Johnson, Edward Crosley III; Kahn, Otto; Katzenbach, Nicholas; Kaufman, Henry; Kennedy, Joseph; Kohlberg, Jerome, Jr.; Kravis, Henry R.; Lehman, Herbert; Lehman, Robert; Levy, Gustave Lehman; Lewis, Reginald F.; Lick, James; Loeb, James; Ludwig, Daniel K.; MacKay, John William; Martin, William McChesney, Jr.; Massey, Jack C.; Mazur, Paul Meyer; Mellon, Andrew; Merrill, Charles Edward; Milken, Michael; Mitchell, Charles E.; Mitchell, John, Jr.; Moore, William H.; Morgan, John "Jack" Pierpont; Morgan, J.P.; Morgan, Junius S.; Morris, Robert; Needham, James Joseph; Peabody, George; Perella, Joseph Robert; Perelman, Ronald; Pforzheimer, Carl H.; Phelan, John J.; Pickens, T. Boone, Jr.; Preston, Lewis Thompson; Reed, John Shepard; Regan, Donald; Reid, Daniel G.; Rockefeller, David; Rockefeller, John D.; Rohatyn, Felix; Rotberg, Eugene Harvey; Rubenstein, Mark; Ruml, Beardsley; Sage, Russell; Salomon, Haym; Sanford, Charles Steadman, Jr.; Schiff, Jacob; Schmidt, Benno; Schwab, Charles R.; Siebert, Muriel; Simon, William; Smith, Winthrop; Sproul, Allan; Steinberg, Saul Phillip; Stevens, Edwin Augustus; Strauss, Lewis; Taylor, Moses; Templeton, Sir John; Thayer, Nathaniel; Vanderbilt, Cornelius; Vanderbilt, George Washington; Vanderbilt, William H.; Villard, Henry; Ward, Samuel; Wasserstein, Bruce; Weeden, Donald Edward; Weinberg, John Livingston; Weyerhaeuser, Frederick E.; Whitehead, John Cunningham; Whitney, John Hay; Wiggin, Albert H.; Willing, Thomas; Woodward, William; Wriston, Walter Biglow; Yerkes, Charles T.; Young, Robert Ralph

First Ladies See under PRESIDENTS, VICE PRESIDENTS, and FIRST LADIES, U.S.

Food and Nutrition Atwater, Helen Woodard; Ball, C. Olin; Beard, James; Bevier, Isabel; Birdseye, Clarence; Blunt, Katharine; Borden, Gail; Bryan, John Henry, Jr.; Child, Julia; Claiborne, Craig; Corson, Juliet; Cruess, William; Davis, Adelle; Delmonico, Lorenzo; Diat, Louis Felix; Dorrance, John T.; Farmer, Fannie; Fellers, Carl R.; Fisher, M.F.K.; Fletcher, Horace; Franey, Pierre; Gallo, Ernest; Gallo, Julio; Gerber, Frank; Goizueta, Roberto; Graham,

Foster; du Pont, Coleman; Du Pont, Pierre Samuel, IV; Duvall, Gabriel; Dwight, John Wilbur; Eastland, James O.; Eastman, Joseph Bartlett; Eaton, Charles Aubrey; Eccles, Marriner; Edge, Walter Evans; Edgerton, Sidney; Edison, Charles; Edmunds, George F.; Elders, M. Joycelyn; Ellsworth, Oliver; Englebright, Harry; Ervin, Sam, Jr.; Evarts, William Maxwell; Everett, Edward; Fainsod, Merle; Farley, Jim; Ferguson, Homer; Ferraro, Geraldine; Ferre, Luis Antonio; Ferry, Orris Sanford; Fess, Simeon Davidson; Fessenden, William Pitt; Fish, Hamilton; Fitzgerald, John Francis; Flanders, Ralph; Foley, Thomas; Foote, Henry Stuart; Foraker, Joseph Benson; Ford, Wendell H.; Fordney, Joseph Warren; Forrestal, James; Frazier, Lynn Joseph; Frye, William Pierce; Fulbright, J. William; Gallatin, Albert; Gallinger, Jacob H.; Garrett, Finis; Gear, John Henry; George, James Zachariah; George, Walter F.; Gephardt, Richard Andrew; Gerry, Peter; Gibson, Paris; Gillett, Frederick Hunting; Gilmer, John Adams; Gingrich, Newt; Glass, Carter; Glenn, John, Jr.; Goldberg, Arthur J.; Goldwater, Barry M.; Goodhue, Benjamin; Gore, Thomas Pryor; Grasso, Ella; Gray, William H. III; Green, James Stephen; Green, Theodore; Greenspan, Alan; Greenwood, Arthur Herbert; Gresham, Walter Q.; Griffin, Robert P.; Griswold, John A.; Gross, Harold; Grow, Galusha Aaron; Gruening, Ernest; Grundy, Felix; Guffey, Joseph F.; Guggenheim, Simon; Haig, Alexander; Haldeman, H. R.; Hale, Eugene; Halleck, Charles; Hamilton, Alexander; Hamilton, Charles; Hampton, Wade (1751–1835); Hampton, Wade (1818–1902); Hanna, Mark; Hanson, John; Harlan, James; Harlow, Bryce N.; Harper, Robert Goodloe; Harriman, Averell; Harrison, Byron; Hart, Gary; Hart, Philip A.; Hartley, Fred, Jr.; Hastings, Alcee; Hatch, Carl A.; Haugen, Gilbert; Hawkins, Augustus; Hawkins, Benjamin; Hawley, Joseph Roswell; Hay, John; Hayne, Robert Young; Hearst, William Randolph; Hebert, Felix; Heflin, James; Helms, Richard; Henderson, David; Hennock, Frieda B.; Hepburn, William; Herbert, Hilary Abner; Hershey, Lewis; Hill, J. Lister; Hinds, Asher Crosby; Hiss, Alger; Hoar, George; Hoar, Samuel; Hobby, Oveta Culp; Hoffman, Paul; Hooks, Benjamin; Hoover, J. Edgar; Hopkins, Harry; Hopkinson, Francis; Houston, Sam; Howard, Jacob Merritt; Howe, Louis M.; Hufstedtler, Shirley; Hughes, Charles Evans; Hull, Cordell; Humphrey, George; Humphrey, Hubert H.; Hunt, William Henry; Hurley, Patrick J.; Ickes, Harold L.; Ingalls, John James; Izard, Ralph; Jackson, Henry M.; Javitz, Jacob K.; Jay, John; Johnson, Hiram W.; Johnson, Hugh; Johnson, Louis; Johnson, Reverdy; Johnson, Tom Loftin; Johnston, Joseph Eggleston; Jones, Jesse Holman; Jones, John P.; Jones, Wesley L.; Jordan, Barbara; Kahn, Julius; Katzenbach, Nicholas; Kefauver, Estes; Kelley, William Darrah; Kellogg, Frank; Kellogg, William Pitt; Kenna, John; Kennedy, Edward M. "Ted"; Kennedy, John Pendleton; Kennedy, Robert F.; Kent, Joseph; Kenyon, William Squire; Kern, John W.; Kerr, Robert Samuel; Keyserling, Leon H.; Kilgore, Harley M.; King,

Rufus; Kirkpatrick, Jeanne; Kirkwood, Samuel Jordon; Kissinger, Henry; Kitchin, Claude; Knowland, William F.; Knox, Frank; Knox, Philander Chase; Knudsen, William S.; Knutson, Harold; Koch, Edward I.; Koop, C. Everett; Kuchel, Thomas H.; Ladd, Edwin Fremont; La Follette, Robert M., Sr.; La Follette, Robert Marion, Jr.; LaGuardia, Fiorello; Lamar, Lucius Quintus Cincinnatus; Landis, James; Landrum, Phillip Mitchell; Lane, Henry; Lane, Joseph; Langer, William; Langston, John Mercer; Lansing, Robert; Laurance, John; Leahy, William; Lee, Richard Henry; Legare, Hugh Swinton; Lehman, Herbert; Leib, Michael; Lemke, William; Lewis, Dixon Hall; Lilienthal, David; Lindsay, John; Linn, Lewis Fields; Livingston, Edward; Lloyd, James; Lodge, Henry Cabot; Logan, John Alexander; London, Meyer; Long, Huey P.; Long, John Davis; Long, Russell B.; Longworth, Nicholas; Lovejoy, Owen; Lovett, Robert; Lowden, Frank Orren; Lowndes, William; Lowrie, Walter; Lucas, Scott; Luce, Clare Boothe; Maclay, William; MacLeish, Archibald; Macon, Nathaniel; Madden, Martin; Mallory, Stephen Russell; Mann, Horace; Mann, James; Mansfield, Mike; Marcantonio, Vito; Marcy, William Learned; Marsh, George Perkins; Marshall, George C., Jr.; Martin, Joseph, Jr.; Martin, Thomas Staples; Martin, William McChesney, Jr.; Mason, George; Mason, James; Mason, Stevens Thomson; Mather, Stephen Tyng; Maverick, Fontaine; Maybank, Burnett Rhett; McCall, Samuel Walker; McCarran, Patrick; McCarthy, Joseph R.; McCloy, John; McCone, John A.; McCormack, John; McDuffie, John; McElroy, Neil; McFarland, Ernest W.; McGovern, George; McGrath, James Howard; McKellar, Kenneth; McLean, John; McNamara, Robert; McNary, Charles; Meese, Edwin III; Metcalfe, Ralph; Michel, Robert; Millikin, Eugene D.; Mills, Roger Quarles; Mills, Wilbur; Mitchell, Arthur W.; Mitchell, George; Mitchell, John; Mitchill, Samuel; Mondale, Walter F.; Mondell, Frank; Moody, Blair; Moore, Gabriel; Morgenthau, Henry, Jr.; Morrill, Justin Smith; Morris, Gouverneur; Morris, Robert; Morrow, Dwight; Morrow, Jeremiah; Morse, Wayne; Morton, Julius Sterling; Morton, Oliver Perry; Moyers, Bill; Muhlenberg, Frederick Augustus; Muhlenberg, John Peter Gabriel; Murray, James Edward; Muskie, Edmund S.; Newton, Isaac; Nicholas, John; Nicholas, Wilson Cary; Norris, George William; Norton, Mary Teresa; Nourse, Edwin; Novello, Antonia C.; Nunn, Sam; Nye, Gerald P.; Nye, James Warren; O'Daniel, Wilbert Lee; O'Day, Caroline Love; Oldfield, William Allan; Olds, Leland; Olney, Richard; O'Neill, "Tip"; Otis, Harrison Gray; Owen, Robert; Owen, Robert Latham; Page, John; Palmer, Alexander; Palmer, John McAuley; Parker, Isaac Charles; Pasvolsky, Leo; Paulding, James Kirke; Payne, Sereno Elisha; Pendleton, George Hunt; Pennington, William; Penrose, Boies; Pepper, Claude D.; Pepper, George Wharton; Perkins, Frances; Pettigrew, Richard Franklin; Phelan, James; Pilcher, Joshua; Pinchot, Gifford; Pinckney, Charles; Pittman, Key; Platt, Thomas Collier; Plumer, William; Poindexter, Miles; Poinsett, Joel Roberts; Poland, Luke; Powderly,

OCCUPATIONAL INDEX

Government, National (*cont.*)

Terence; Powell, Adam Clayton, Jr.; Preston, William Campbell; Priest, James Percy; Proxmire, William; Pryor, Roger Atkinson; Quincy, Josiah; Rainey, Henry Thomas; Rainey, Joseph; Ramspeck, Robert C.; Randall, Samuel Jackson; Randolph, Edmund; Randolph, John; Rangel, Charles; Rankin, Jeanette; Rayburn, Sam; Read, Jacob; Reece, Brazilla Carroll; Reed, David Aiken; Reed, Thomas; Regan, Donald; Revels, Hiram Rhodes; Reynolds, Robert Rice; Rhett, Robert Barnwell; Rhodes, John; Rice, Henry Mower; Richardson, Elliot; Richardson, James Montgomery; Richberg, Donald; Richmond, Julius Benjamin; Rittenhouse, David; Rivers, Lucius Mendel; Rivlin, Alice; Robeson, George Maxwell; Robinson, Joseph Taylor; Rogers, Edith; Rogers, William P.; Rohde, Ruth; Romney, George; Root, Elihu; Ross, Edmund Gibson; Ross, Nellie; Rowan, Carl; Rowan, John; Ruml, Beardsley; Rusk, Dean; Russell, Richard B.; Sabath, Adolph J.; Saltonstall, Leverett; Sanders, Bernie; Sanford, Terry; Sawyer, Philetus; Schlesinger, James R.; Schmoke, Kurt; Schurz, Carl; Schuyler, Philip John; Sergeant, John; Sevier, John; Seward, William H.; Shalala, Donna; Sherman, John; Sherman, Roger; Shields, James; Shipstead, Henrik; Shoup, George Laird; Shouse, Jouett; Sickles, Daniel; Simmons, Furnifold; Simon, William; Simpson, Alan K.; Slidell, John; Slocum, Henry Warner; Smalls, Robert; Smith, "Cotton Ed"; Smith, Harold Dewey; Smith, Howard; Smith, Robert; Smith, William; Smoot, Reed; Snell, Bertrand Hollis; Sorenson, Theodore; Sparkman, John; Spooner, John Coit; Staats, Elmer B.; Stahl, O. Glenn; Stanton, Edwin; Stanton, Frederick; Stephens, Alexander H.; Sternberg, George Miller; Stettinius, Edward R.; Stevens, Isaac Ingalls; Stevens, Thaddeus; Stevenson, Adlai II; Stevenson, Andrew; Stewart, William Morris; Stimson, Henry; Stockton, John Potter; Stokes, Louis; Strauss, Lewis; Stryker, Roy Emerson; Sullivan, John L.; Sulzer, William; Sumner, Charles; Sumter, Thomas; Sununu, John H.; Swanson, Claude; Swift, Zephaniah; Symington, Stuart; Taber, John; Taft, Robert A.; Talmadge, Herman Eugene; Tawney, James Albertus; Taylor, John; Taylor, Robert Love; Teller, Henry Moore; Thomas, Jesse Burgess; Thomas, John Parnell; Thompson, Waddy; Thornburg, Richard; Thurmond, J. Strom; Thye, Edward John; Tillman, "Pitchfork Ben"; Tilson, John; Tolley, Howard Ross; Toombs, Robert Augustus; Tower, John; Tracy, Benjamin F.; Trumbull, Lyman; Tucker, John Randolph; Tugwell, Rexford; Tweed, William Marcy "Boss"; Udall, Stewart; Underwood, Oscar; Upshur, Abel Parker; Vallandigham, Clement Laird; Vance, Cyrus; Vance, Zebulon Baird; Vandenberg, Arthur; Vestal, Albert; Vinson, Carl; Volstead, Andrew; Wade, Benjamin Franklin; Wagner, Robert F.; Walker, Amasa; Wallace, Henry Cantwell; Walter, Francis; Warner, John W.; Washburn, Cadwallader Colden; Washburn, Israel; Washburn, William; Washington, Harold; Waterman, Alan; Watson, James Eli; Watson, Thomas Edward; Watterson, Henry; Weaver, James; Weaver, Robert; Webb, James; Webster, Daniel; Webster, William H.; Weinberger, Caspar; Welles, Gideon; Wheeler, Burton K.; Wherry, Kenneth; White, Joseph M.; White, Leonard D.; White, Wallace H.; Whitney, William Collins; Whitten, Jamie; Wickersham, George Woodward; Wilbur, Ray Lyman; Wiley, Alexander; Williams, John; Wilmot, David; Wilson, Charles E.; Windom, William; Winthrop, Robert Charles; Wirt, William; Wise, Henry Alexander; Wolcott, Oliver; Wood, Fernando; Woodbury, Levi; Wright, Jim; Yancey, William Lowndes; Young, Andrew, Jr.

Government, State and Local Adams, Sherman; Alexander, Lamar; Alger, Russell Alexander; Allen, Henry Justin; Allen, William; Altgeld, John Peter; Ames, Adelbert; Ammons, Elias Milton; Andrew, John Albion; Arnall, Ellis; Askew, Reubin; Austin, Stephen; Aycock, Charles Brantley; Baker, Edward Dickinson; Barbosa, Jose Celso; Barron, William Wallace; Barry, Marion S., Jr.; Bartlett, "Bob"; Bartlett, Josiah; Berrios Martinez, Ruben; Bidwell, John; Big Foot; Black Hawk; Black Kettle; Blanton, Ray; Blount, William; Bond, Julian; Boreman, Arthur I.; Bowdoin, James; Bradley, Tom; Brant, Joseph; Bridges, Styles; Brown, Edmund G. "Pat"; Brown, Jerry; Brown, Lee P.; Burke, John; Burnett, Peter; Burns, John Anthony; Burnside, Ambrose; Burton, Harold; Butler, David C.; Byrne, Jane; Byrnes, James F.; Carey, Joseph Maull; Cermak, Anton; Chaffee, John H.; Chamberlain, Joshua; Chandler, "Happy"; Chittenden, Thomas; Cisneros, Henry; Clark, William; Clarke, James Paul; Clayton, Powell; Clement, Frank; Clinton, De Witt; Cochise; Coddington, William; Combs, Bert; Corning, Erastus; Cornplanter; Corwin, Thomas; Cox, George Barnsdale; Crazy Horse; Crazy Snake; Croker, Richard; Cross, Wilbur; Crow Dog; Crump, "Boss"; Cuomo, Mario; Curley, James Michael; Daley, Richard; Davis, Alice Brown; Dekanawida; Dennis Wolf Bushyhead; Dewey, Thomas E.; Diego, Jose de; Dinkins, David; Dodge, Henry Chee; Dorr, Thomas; Driscoll, Alfred; Dukakis, Michael; Dull Knife; Du Pont, Pierre Samuel IV; Edge, Walter Evans; Edgerton, Sidney; Edison, Charles; Egan, William; Evans, Daniel Jackson; Everett, Edward; Evers, Charles; Fagan, Mark; Fargo, William George; Ferguson, James Edward; Ferguson, "Ma"; Ferre, Luis Antonio; Ferry, Elisha Peyre; Fish, Hamilton; Fitzgerald, John Francis; Folsom, James; Foote, Henry Stuart; Foraker, Joseph Benson; Ford, Wendell H.; Foss, Joseph; Frazier, Lynn Joseph; Gall; Gardner, O. Max; Gaynor, William; Gear, John Henry; Geary, John White; Geronimo; Gilpin, William; Giuliani, Rudolph W.; Glick, George Washington; Goebel, William; Goldwater, Sigismund; Goode, Wilson; Grace, William Russell; Grasso, Ella; Green, Theodore; Hague, Frank; Hall, David; Hamilton, Andrew; Hampton, Wade; Hancock, John; Handsome Lake; Harrison, Benjamin; Harrison, Carter Henry; Hatcher, Richard; Havemeyer, William Frederick; Hayden, Tom; Hayne, Robert Young; Henry Roe Cloud; Hiawatha; Hoan, Daniel Webster; Hoard, William Dempster; Hobby, William Pettus;

Stone, Melville Elijah; Strong, Anna Louise; Strunsky, Simeon; Sullivan, Ed; Sullivan, Mark; Swayze, John Cameron, Sr.; Swing, Raymond Gram; Swope, Herbert Bayard; Tarbell, Ida; Thomas, Lowell; Thompson, Dorothy; Tucker, Benjamin; Van Anda, Carr Vattel; Van Buren, Abigail; Van Vechten, Carl; Vanderbilt, Amy; Villard, Oswald Garrison; Von Wiegand, Karl Henry; Vreeland, Diana; Walker, Mort; Wallace, Henry Cantwell; Wallace, Mike; Walters, Barbara; Ward, Arch; Watterson, Henry; Watterson, Bill; Webb, James Watson; Webber, Charles Wilkins; Welles, Gideon; Wellman, Walter; White, William Allen; White, William S.; Will, George; Williams, Michael; Williams, Talcott; Wilson, Gill; Winchell, Walter; Wolfe, Tom; Wood, Benjamin; Woodward, Bob; Zenger, John Peter

Labor Anderson, Mary; Andrews, John Bertram; Barry, Leonora; Bellanca, Dorothy; Bloor, Ella "Mother Bloor"; Bridges, Harry; Brimmer, Andrew Felton; Carey, James; Carey, Ronald; Chavez, Cesar; Commons, John Rogers; Conboy, Sara; Curran, Joseph; Darrow, Clarence; Debs, Eugene V.; De Leon, Daniel; Dreier, Mary Elizabeth; Dubinsky, David; Dunlop, John Thomas; Fasanella, Ralph; Feldman, Sandra; Flynn, Elizabeth Gurley; Foster, William Z.; Fraser, Douglas; Frey, John; Furuseth, Andrew; Garretson, A.B.; Gold, Ben; Goldberg, Arthur J.; Gompers, Samuel; Gotbaum, Victor H.; Gould, William B. IV; Green, William; Hartley, Fred, Jr.; Haywood, William Dudley; Hill, Joe; Hillman, Sidney; Hoffa, Jimmy; Howard, Charles P.; Hutcheson, William; Jones, Casey; Jones, Mary B. "Mother Jones"; Kerr, Clark; Keyserling, Leon H.; Kirkland, Lane; Lewis, John L.; London, Meyer; Lundeberg, Harry; Mahler, Herbert; Meany, George; Miller, Joyce; Miller, Marvin; Mitchell, John; Mooney, Thomas; Murray, Philip; Nestor, Agnes; O'Reilly, Leonora; O'Sullivan, Mary Kenney; Parsons, Albert Richard; Perkins, Frances; Pesotta, Rose; Potofsky, Jacob; Powderly, Terence; Quill, Michael J.; Randolph, A. Philip; Reuther, Walter; Robins, Margaret Dreier; Schneiderman, Rose; Shanker, Albert; Stark, Louis; Steuben, John; Sylvis, William H.; Trumka, Richard; Walling, William English

Landscape Architecture See ARCHITECTURE.

Law Abrams, Floyd; Ackerman, Bruce A.; Adams, Brooks; Allen, Florence Ellinwood; Altgeld, John Peter; Ames, James Barr; Amsterdam, Anthony G.; Angell, Joseph K.; Angermueller, Hans; Arnold, Thurman; Auchincloss, Louis; Augustus, John; Babbitt, Bruce; Baer, George Frederick; Bailey, F. Lee; Baldwin, Henry; Barbour, Philip Pendleton; Bazelon, David; Belin, David; Bell, Derrick, Jr.; Bell, Griffin B.; Belli, Melvin M.; Benedict, Kirby; Benjamin, Judah; Ben-Veniste, Richard; Biddle, Francis; Billings, Frederick; Binney, Horace; Black, Hugo; Black, Jeremiah; Blackmun, Harry A.; Blair, John; Blakey, G. Robert; Blatchford, Samuel; Bonaparte, Charles Joseph; Borchard, Edwin

Montefiore; Bork, Robert H.; Boudin, Leonard B.; Brackenridge, Henry Marie; Brackenridge, Hugh Henry; Bradley, Joseph P.; Bradwell, Myra; Brandeis, Louis D.; Brennan, William J., Jr.; Brewer, David J.; Breyer, Stephen G.; Bristow, Benjamin Helm; Brown, Henry Billings; Brown, Ron; Buckner, Emory; Burger, Warren; Burton, Harold; Butler, Pierce; Byrnes, James F.; Calabresi, Guido; Campbell, John Archibald; Cardozo, Benjamin; Carter, James Coolidge; Catron, John; Chaffee, Zechariah; Chambers, Julius L.; Chase, Salmon P.; Chase, Samuel; Chayes, Abram; Chesnutt, Charles W.; Chipman, Nathaniel; Choate, Joseph H.; Civiletti, Benjamin R.; Clark, Edward; Clark, Grenville; Clark, Tom C.; Clarke, John H.; Clifford, Nathan; Clinton, Hilary Rodham; Cohen, Benjamin V.; Cohn, Roy M.; Coleman, William T., Jr.; Collamer, Jacob; Combs, Bert; Cooley, Thomas; Corbin, Arthur L.; Corbin, Arthur Linton; Corboy, Philip H.; Cox, Archibald; Cranch, William; Crater, Joseph Force; Crittenden, John J.; Cromwell, William N.; Cummings, Homer; Curtis, Benjamin R.; Curtis, George Ticknor; Cushing, Caleb; Cushing, William; Cutler, Lloyd N.; Dallas, Alexander James; Dana, Richard Henry; Dane, Nathan; Daniel, Peter V.; Darrow, Clarence; Davis, David; Davis, John William; Day, William Rufus; Dean, Arthur H.; Dees, Morris, Jr.; DeLancey, James; Deloria, Vine, Jr.; Dershowitz, Alan M.; Devens, Charles Jr.; Dodd, S.C.T.; Doe, Charles; Dole, Sanford; Dorsen, Norman; Douglas, William O.; Du Ponceau, Peter Stephen; Duvall, Gabriel; Dworkin, Ronald; Edelstein, David Norton; Ellsworth, Oliver; Evarts, William Maxwell; Fessenden, William Pitt; Field, David Dudley; Field, Martha A.; Field, Stephen J.; Fiske, Haley; Flom, Joseph H.; Foreman, Percy; Fortas, Abe; Frank, Jerome; Frank, John P.; Frankfurter, Felix; Freund, Ernst; Freund, Paul Abraham; Fuller, Melville W.; Garrett, Finis; Garrity, Arthur, Jr.; Gary, Elbert Henry; George, James Zachariah; Gesell, Gerhard; Ginsburg, Ruth Bader; Giuliani, Rudolph W.; Glendon, Mary Ann; Goetz, Cecelia H.; Goldberg, Arthur J.; Gordon, Robert W.; Gould, William B. IV; Gray, Horace; Gray, John Chipman; Greenberg, Jack; Greenleaf, Simon; Gresham, Walter Q.; Grier, Robert C.; Gunther, Gerald; Haggin, James Ben Ali; Hamilton, Andrew; Hand, Augustus Noble; Hand, Learned; Harlan, John Marshall (1833–1911); Harlan, John Marshall (1899–1971); Harper, Robert Goodloe; Harris, Paul Percy; Hart, Charles Henry; Hastie, William Henry; Hastings, Alcee; Haynes, Richard; Hays, Arthus Garfield; Hazard, Geoffrey C., Jr; Hennock, Frieda B.; Higgenbotham, A. Leon, Jr.; Higgins, George; Hill, Anita; Hillquit, Morris; Hoar, Ebenezer Rockwood; Hoar, Samuel; Holmes, Oliver Wendell, Jr.; Hooks, Benjamin; Hopkinson, Francis; Horsmanden, Daniel; Houston, Charles H.; Hudson, Manley Ottmer; Hufstedtler, Shirley; Hughes, Charles Evans; Hughes, Richard; Hulett, Alta M.; Hunt, Ward; Hurst, James Willard; Hutchinson, Thomas; Imbau, Fred E.; Ingersoll, Robert; Iredell, James; Jackson, Howell E.; Jackson, Robert; Jaworski, Leon; Jay, John; Jessup, Philip Caryl; Johnson, Frank, Jr.;

Law (*cont.*)

Johnson, James Weldon; Johnson, John Graver; Johnson, Reverdy; Johnson, Thomas; Johnson, William; Jones, Leonard; Jones, Sam Houston; Kadish, Sanford; Kamisar, Yale; Karst, Kenneth L.; Katzenbach, Nicholas; Kaufman, Irving; Kay, Herma Hill; Kellogg, Frank; Kelsen, Hans; Kennedy, Anthony M.; Kennedy, Flo; Kennedy, Robert F.; Kent, James; Kilgore, Carrie; Kirchwey, George Washington; Kohlberg, Jerome, Jr.; Kuhn, Bowie K.; Kunstler, William M.; Lamar, Joseph R.; Lamar, Lucius Quintus Cincinnatus; Landis, James; Landis, Kenesaw Mountain; Langdell, Christopher; Lechford, Thomas; Lee, Rex T.; Legare, Hugh Swinton; Levi, Edward H.; Lewis, Delano E.; Lewis, Reginald F.; Lieber, Francis; Lilienthal, David; Liman, Arthur L.; Lindsey, Benjamin Barr; Linowitz, Sol; Livingston, Edward; Livingston, Henry Brockholst; Livingston, Robert R.; Llewellyn, Karl; Lockwood, Belva; Logan, James; London, Meyer; Loss, Louis; Lowden, Frank Orren; Lurton, Horace Harmon; Mack, Julian; MacKinnon, Catharine A.; Mansfield, Arabella; Marshall, John; Marshall, Louis; Marshall, Thurgood; Martin, Francois-Xavier; Martin, Luther; Matthews, Stanley; McKenna, Joseph; McKinley, John; McKissick, Floyd B.; McLean, John; McNichols, Stephen L. R.; McReynolds, James Clark; Mechem, Edwin; Meese, Edwin III; Mentschikoff, Soia; Miller, David Hunter; Miller, Samuel Freeman; Minow, Martha L.; Minow, Newton; Minton, Sherman; Mitchell, John; Moley, Raymond; Moody, William Henry; Moore, Alfred; Moore, John Bassett; Morgenthau, Robert M.; Motley, Constance Baker; Murphy, Frank; Musmanno, Michael Angelo; Nader, Ralph; Nelson, Samuel; Nizer, Louis; Norton, Eleanor Holmes; Norval, Morris; O'Connor, Sandra Day; Ogletree, Charles J., Jr.; Oliver, Peter; Olney, Richard; Otis, James; Palmer, Alexander; Parker, Isaac; Parker, Isaac Charles; Parsons, James B.; Parsons, Theophilus (1750–1813); Parsons, Theophilus (1797–1882); Paterson, William; Peckham, Rufus Wheeler; Pendleton, Edmund; Pepper, George Wharton; Petigru, James Louis; Pike, Albert; Pinkney, William; Pitney, Mahlon; Poland, Luke; Posner, Richard A.; Pound, Roscoe; Powell, Lewis, Jr.; Pratt, Benjamin; Prosser, William Lloyd; Randolph, Edmund; Randolph, Peyton; Rantoul, Robert; Rawle, William; Reed, Stanley Forman; Reeve, Tapping; Rehnquist, William H.; Richardson, Elliot; Richberg, Donald; Roberts, Owen J.; Robinson, Randall; Rock, John Swett; Rogers, William P.; Root, Elihu; Root, Gladys Towles; Rose, Uriah Milton; Ruffin, George L.; Rush, Richard; Rutledge, John; Rutledge, Wiley Blount, Jr.; Sampson, William; Sanford, Edward Terry; Scalia, Antonin; Schwartz, Louis B.; Scott, James Brown; Seabury, Samuel; Sedgwick, Theodore; Sewall, Samuel; Seward, William H.; Sharswood, George; Shaw, Lemuel; Shields, James; Shiras, George, Jr.; Sirica, John; Smith, Reginald Heber; Sorenson, Theodore; Souter, David H.; Spence, Gerry; Stanton, Edwin; Stevens, John Paul; Stewart, Potter; Stewart, William Morris; Stimson, Henry; Stone, Harlan Fiske; Story,

Joseph; Strauss, Robert; Strong, William; Sullivan, James; Sulzberger, Mayer; Sunstein, Cass R.; Sutherland, George; Swayne, Noah Haynes; Swift, Zephaniah; Taft, William Howard; Taney, Roger; Terry, David Smith; Thayer, James Bradley; Thomas, Clarence; Thompson, Smith; Tilghman, William (1756–1827); Tilghman, William (1854–1924); Todd, Thomas; Tribe, Laurence H.; Trimble, Robert; Trist, Nicholas; Trumbull, John; Trumbull, Lyman; Tucker, Henry St. George; Tucker, John Randolph; Tucker, St. George; Tyler, Harold R. "Ace"; Tyler, Royall; Untermeyer, Samuel; U'Ren, William Simon; Van Devanter, Willis; Vincent, Fay; Vinson, Frederick M.; Volner, Jill Wine; Vorenburg, James; Wade, Benjamin Franklin; Waite, Morrison Remick; Walker, Timothy; Walsh, Lawrence E.; Warren, Earl; Washburn, Emory; Washington, Bushrod; Wayland, Francis; Wayne, James Moore; Webster, William H.; Weinstein, Jack; Welch, Joseph Nye; Weschler, Herbert; Wheaton, Henry; Wheeler, Wayne Bidwell; White, Byron; White, Edward Douglass; White, Joseph M.; Whitney, William Collins; Whittaker, Charles Evans; Wickersham, George Woodward; Wigmore, John Henry; Williams, Edward Bennett; Williston, Samuel; Wilson, James; Winter, William Forrest; Wirt, William; Woodbury, Levi; Woods, William Burnham; Wright, Charles A.; Wright, Quincy; Wythe, George; Younger, Irving

Libraries See under BIBLIOGRAPHY AND LIBRARIES.

Linguistics and Lexicography Andrews, Stephen; Anthon, Charles; Barnhart, Clarence L.; Bartlett, John; Berlitz, Charles; Bloomfield, Leonard; Bolinger, Dwight; Brinton, Daniel Garrison; Cassidy, Frederic G.; Chomsky, Noam; Cross, Samuel Hazzard; Deloria, Ella Cara; Duckert, Audrey R.; Du Ponceau, Peter Stephen; Flexner, Stuart Berg; Fodor, Jerry A.; Frank, Tenney; Friedman, William Frederick; Fries, Charles C.; Funk, Isaac; Gildersleeve, Basil; Goffman, Erving; Goodrich, Chauncey Allen; Goodwin, William Watson; Gottheil, Richard James Horatio; Greenberg, Joseph H.; Gumperz, John; Guralnik, David B.; Haas, Mary; Hall, Edward Twitchell, Jr.; Harper, William Rainey; Harrington, John Peabody; Haugen, Einar Ingvald; Hymes, Dell; Kittredge, George Lyman; Lounsbury, Floyd; March, Francis Andrew; Marckwardt, Albert; Marsh, George Perkins; McDavid, Raven, Jr.; Mencken, H. L.; Meritt, Benjamin Dean; Monis, Judah; Oldfather, William Abbott; Parry, Milman; Pickering, John; Pound, Louise; Pyles, Thomas; Riggs, Elias; Safire, William L.; Sapir, Edward; Schele De Vere, Maximilian; Searle, John R.; Sequoyah; Shorey, Paul; Smyth, Herbert Weir; Squanto; Swadesh, Morris; Thorndike, Edward L.; Vansina, Jan; Vizetelly, Frank Horace; Webster, Noah; Whatmough, Joshua; Whitney, William Dwight; Whorf, Benjamin Lee; Williams, Samuel Wells; Worcester, Joseph E.

Literary Criticism and Theory Abrams, Meyer; Allen, Hervey; Appleton, William W.; Babbitt, Irving; Barzun, Jacques; Bate, Walter Jackson; Bingham,

Millicent; Blackmur, R.P.; Bloom, Harold; Bourne, Randolph; Brooks, Cleanth; Brooks, Van Wyck; Brustein, Robert; Burke, Kenneth; Bush, Douglas; Campbell, Joseph; Cary, Elisabeth Luther; Chapman, John Jay; Child, Francis James; Clausen, Wendell; Cowley, Malcolm; Crane, R.S.; DeVoto, Bernard; Edel, Leon; Eliot, T.S.; Ellmann, Richard; Fiedler, Leslie; Fuller, Margaret; Gardner, John; Gardner, Martin; Gass, William; Gates, Henry Louis, Jr.; Greenblatt, Stephen; Griswold, Rufus Wilmot; Hadas, Moses; Heller, Maximilian; Highet, Gilbert; Howe, Irving; Howells, William Dean; Huneker, James Gibbons; Jarrell, Randall; Kael, Pauline; Kazin, Alfred; Keene, Donald; Knox, Bernard; Krutch, Joseph Wood; Lattimore, Richard; Levin, Harry; Locke, Alain Le Roy; Lourie, Richard; Macdonald, Dwight; Matthiessen, F.O.; McCarthy, Mary; Mencken, H. L.; Miller, Perry; Milosz, Czeslaw; Moore, Anne Carroll; More, Paul Elmer; Nabokov, Vladimir; Nicolson, Marjorie Hope; Norton, Charles Eliot; O'Hara, Frank; Parrington, V.L.; Poirier, Richard; Pound, Ezra; Powell, Lawrence Clark; Ransom, John Crowe; Redding, J. Saunders; Rittenhouse, Jessie Bell; Said, Edward W.; Shapiro, Karl; Smith, Logan Pearsall; Sontag, Susan; Spingarn, Joel; Stedman, Edmund Clarence; Tate, Allen; Tenney, Tabitha Gilman; Thompson, Stith; Trilling, Lionel; Tuckerman, Henry Theodore; Updike, John; Van Doren, Carl; Vendler, Helen; Vidal, Gore; Warren, Robert Penn; Wellek, Rene; Whitman, Cedric; Wilson, Edmund; Winters, Yvor; Woodberry, G.E.

Literature Abu Madi, Ilya; Adamic, Louis; Agee, James; Aiken, Conrad; Albee, Edward; Alcott, Louisa May; Aldrich, Thomas Bailey; Alger, Horatio; Algren, Nelson; Allen, Hervey; Allen, Paula Gunn; al-Rayhani, Amin; Ammons, A.R.; Anderson, Maxwell; Anderson, Robert; Anderson, Sherwood; Angell, Roger; Angelou, Maya; Antin, Mary; Arida, Nasib; Asch, Sholem; Ashbery, John; Asimov, Isaac; Athertonn, Gertrude; Auchincloss, Louis; Auden, W.H.; Austin, Mary; Bacon, Delia Salter; Baker, Ray Stannard; Baldwin, James; Baraka, Imamu Amiri; Barlow, Joel; Barnes, Djuna; Barney, Natalie Clifford; Barry, Philip; Barth, John; Barthelme, Donald; Barzun, Jacques; Bates, Katherine Lee; Baum, Frank; Beecher, Catherine Esther; Bellamy, Edward; Bellow, Saul; Bemelmans, Ludwig; Benchley, Robert; Benet, Stephen Vincent; Berrigan, Daniel J.; Berry, Wendell; Berryman, John; Bierce, Ambrose; Biggers, Earl Derr; Bishop, Elizabeth; Bishop, John Peale; Blackmur, R.P.; Blume, Judy; Bly, Robert; Bodenheim, Maxwell; Bogan, Louise; Boker, George Henry; Bonnin, Gertrude Simmons; Bontemps, Arna; Botkin, B.A.; Botta, Anne Charlotte; Boucicault, Dion; Boudinot, Elias; Bowles, Jane; Bowles, Paul; Boyesen, H.H.; Boyle, Kay; Brackenridge, Hugh Henry; Bradbury, Ray; Bradstreet, Anne; Bragg, Mabel Caroline; Braithewaite, William Stanley; Brautigan, Richard; Brodkey, Harold; Brodsky, Joseph; Bromfield, Louis; Brooks, Gwendolyn; Brougham, John; Brown, Charles Brockden; Brown, Margaret Wise; Brown, Rita Mae;

Brown, Sterling; Brown, William Wells; Browne, Charles Farrar; Bryant, William Cullen; Buck, Pearl; Buckley, William F., Jr.; Bukowski, Charles; Bulfinch, Thomas; Bullins, Ed; Burgess, Gelett; Burgess, Thornton W.; Burke, James Lee; Burke, Kenneth; Burnett, Francis Hodgson; Burroughs, Edgar Rice; Burroughs, John; Burroughs, William S.; Cabell, James Branch; Cable, George Washington; Cahan, Abraham; Cain, James M.; Caldwell, Erskine; Calisher, Hortense; Canby, Henry Seidel; Cantwell, Robert; Capote, Truman; Carver, Raymond, Jr.; Cather, Willa; Chandler, Raymond; Chapman, John Jay; Chayefsky, Paddy; Cheever, John; Chesnut, Mary; Chesnutt, Charles W.; Chessman, Caryl; Chopin, Kate; Ciardi, John; Cleary, Beverly; Cleaver, Eldridge; Clemens, Samuel Langhorne; Coatsworth, Elizabeth; Codrescu, Andrei; Connell, Evan S., Jr.; Connelly, Marc; Conroy, Jack; Cooke, John; Coolbrith, Ina; Cooper, James Fenimore; Coover, Robert; Corso, Gregory; Cozzens, James Gould; Crane, Hart; Crane, Stephen; Crapsey, Adelaide; Crawford, Francis Marion; Creeley, Robert; Crevecoeur, Jean de; Crosby, Caresse b.; Crosby, Harry; Cross, Wilbur; Cullen, Countee; cummings, e.e.; Cunningham, J.V.; Curtis, George William; Dahlberg, Edward; Dana, Richard Henry; Dannay, Frederic; Davenport, Guy; Davis, Ossie; Davis, Owen; Davis, Rebecca Harding; Davis, Richard Harding; Day, Clarence; de Burgos, Julia; De Forest, John William; DeLillo, Don; del Rey, Lester; de Paola, Tomi; Deutsch, Babette; DeVries, Peter; Dick, Philip K.; Dickey, James; Dickinson, Emily; Didion, Joan; di Donato, Pietro; Diego, Jose de; Doctorow, E.L.; Dodge, Mary Elizabeth b.; Doolittle, Hilda; Douglas, Lloyd C.; Douglas, Marjory Stoneman; Dove, Rita; Dreiser, Theodore; Dunbar, Paul Lawrence; Duncan, Robert; Dunlap, William; Eastman, P.D.; Eberhart, Richard; Edel, Leon; Eiseley, Loren; Eliot, T.S.; Elkin, Stanley; Ellis, Edward; Ellison, Ralph; Emerson, Ralph Waldo; Erdrich, Louise; Erskine, John; Everson, William Antonius; Farrell, James T.; Fast, Howard; Faulkner, William; Fauset, Jessie R.; Faust, Frederick Shiller; Fearing, Kenneth; Ferber, Edna; Ferlinghetti, Lawrence; Field, Eugene; Fields, James Thomas; Fisher, Dorothy Canfield; Fisher, M.F.K.; Fitch, Clyde; Fitzgerald, F. Scott; Fletchner, John Gould; Foote, Shelby; Forbes, Esther; Frank, Waldo; Frederic, Harold; Freeman, Mary; Freneau, Philip Morin; Friedan, Betty; Frost, Robert; Fuller, Henry Blake; Gaddis, William; Gaines, Ernest J.; Gale, Zona; Gardner, Erle Stanley; Gardner, John; Gardner, Martin; Garland, Hamlin; Gass, William; Geisel, Theodor Seuss; Gibran, Khalil; Gilder, Richard Watson; Gillette, William; Ginsberg, Allen; Giovanni, Nikki; Glasgow, Ellen; Glaspell, Susan; Gold, Michael; Goodman, Paul; Goodrich, Samuel Griswold; Gordon, Caroline; Gorey, Edward; Gould, Stephen Jay; Grafton, Sue; Gramatky, Hardie; Greeley, Andrew M.; Green, Julien; Greenberg, Blu; Gregory, Horace; Grey, Zane; Gruelle, Johnny; Guare, John; Gunther, John; Guthrie, Ramon; Hadas, Moses; Hale, Edward Everett; Hale, Nancy; Haley, Alex; Hall,

OCCUPATIONAL INDEX

Literature (*cont.*)

Donald; Halleck, Fitz-Greene; Hamilton, Edith; Hammerstein, Oscar II; Hammett, Dashiell; Hammon, Jupiter; Hansberry, Lorraine; Hapgood, Isabel Florence; Harkness, Georgia Elma; Harland, Henry; Harper, Frances Ellen Watkins; Harper, Michael; Harris, Joel Chandler; Harte, Bret; Hartmann, Carl Sadakichi; Hawkes, John; Hawthorne, Nathaniel; Hayden, Robert; Hearn, Lafcadio; Hecht, Anthony; Hedge, Frederic Henry; Heilbrun, Carolyn; Heinlein, Robert; Heller, Joseph; Hellman, Lillian; Hemingway, Ernest; Herbert, Frank; Herbst, Josephine; Hergesheimer, Joseph; Herne, James A.; Hersey, John; Heyward, DuBose; Higgins, George; Highet, Gilbert; Highsmith, Patricia; Hillerman, Tony; Hillyer, Robert; Himes, Chester; Hoffer, Eric; Hoffman, Charles Fenno; Holland, Josiah Gilbert; Holmes, John Clellon; Holmes, Oliver Wendell; Howard, Bronson; Howard, Richard; Howard, Sidney; Howe, Julia Ward; Howells, William Dean; Hoyt, Charles Hale; Hubbard, L. Ron; Hughes, Langston; Humphrey, William; Humphries, Rolfe; Hunter, Evan; Hunter, Robert; Hurst, Fannie; Hurston, Zora Neale; Ignatow, David; Ingraham, Prentiss; Irving, John; Irving, Washington; Jackson, Helen Hunt; Jackson, Shirley; James, Alice; James, Henry; Jarrell, Randall; Jastrow, Marcus; Jeffers, Robinson; Jewett, Sarah Orne; Johnson, James Weldon; Johnson, Nunnally; Johnson, Osa; Johnson, Robert Underwood; Jones, James; Jong, Erica; Jordan, June; Judson, Edward Zane Carroll; Kallman, Chester; Kanin, Garson; Kazin, Alfred; Keats, Ezra Jack; Keeley, Edmund; Keene, Donald; Keillor, Garrison; Kennedy, Adrienne; Kennedy, John Pendleton; Kennedy, William; Kenyon, Jane; Kerouac, Jack; Key, Francis Scott; Kincaid, Jamaica; King, Stephen; Kingsley, Sidney; Kingston, Maxine; Kinnell, Galway; Kizer, Carolyn; Koch, Kenneth; Kosinski, Jerzy; Krauss, Ruth; Kreymborg, Alfred; Kumin, Maxine; Kunhardt, Dorothy; Kunitz, Stanley; La Farge, Oliver; L'Amour, Louis; Lanier, Sidney; Lardner, Ring; Lattimore, Richard; Lazarus, Emma; Lee, Harper; Lee, Manfred B.; LeGuin, Ursula; Leland, Charles Godfrey; L'Engle, Madeleine; Leonard, Elmore; Le Sueur, Meridel; Levertov, Denise; Levine, Philip; Lewis, Sinclair; Ley, Willy; Lindsay, Vachel; Lippard, George; Lodge, George Cabot; London, Jack; Longfellow, Henry Wadsworth; Longstreet, Augustus Baldwin; Loos, Anita; Lord, Daniel A.; Lorde, Audre; Lothrop, Harriet Mulford; Lourie, Richard; Lovecraft, H.P.; Lowe-Porter, H.T.; Lowell, Robert; Ludlum, Robert; MacKaye, Percy; MacLeish, Archibald; Mailer, Norman; Malamud, Bernard; Maltz, Albert; Mamet, David; Manheim, Ralph; Markham, Edwin; Marquand, J.P.; Marshall, James; Marshall, Paule; Masters, Edgar Lee; Mathews, John Joseph; Matthiessen, Peter; McCarthy, Mary; McCullers, Carson; McGuane, Thomas; McKay, Claude; McMurtry, Larry; McNamara, Joseph D.; McPhee, John; Melville, Herman; Meredith, Scott; Merrill, James; Merton, Thomas; Merwin, W.S.; Michener, James; Millar, Kenneth; Millay, Edna St. Vincent; Miller, Arthur; Miller, Henry; Miller,

Joaquin; Milosz, Czeslaw; Minarik, Else Holmelund; Mitchell, John; Mitchell, Margaret; Mitchell, Silas Weir; Momaday, N. Scott; Monroe, Harriet; Moody, William Vaughn; Moore, Clement; Moore, Marianne; Morley, Christopher; Morris, Wright Marion; Morrison, Toni; Motley, Willard; Mourning Dove; Mowatt, Anna Cora; Mumford, Lewis; Nabokov, Vladimir; Nash, Ogden; Nemerov, Howard; Neuberger, Richard Lewis; Nims, John Frederick; Nin, Anais; Norris, Frank; Norris, Kathleen; Oates, Joyce Carol; O'Brien, Fitz-James; O'Connor, Flannery; Odets, Clifford; O'Hara, Frank; O'Hara, John; Olson, Charles; Oppen, George; Oppenheim, James; O'Reilly, John Boyle; Ortiz, Simon; Osbourne, Lloyd; Oursler, Fulton; Ozick, Cynthia; Pack, Robert; Packard, Vance; Page, Thomas Nelson; Pales Matos, Luis; Paley, Grace; Paretsky, Sara; Parini, Jay; Parker, Dorothy; Parks, Gordon A.; Patten, Gilbert; Paulding, James Kirke; Peale, Norman Vincent; Percy, Walker; Perelman, S.J.; Piercy, Marge; Pike, Albert; Plath, Sylvia; Poe, Edgar Allan; Pohl, Frederik; Porter, Eleanor; Porter, Gene Stratton; Porter, Katherine Anne; Porter, William Sydney; Pound, Ezra; Powers, J.F.; Prelutsky, Jack; Pringle, Henry Fowles; Purdy, James; Puzo, Mario; Pynchon, Thomas; Rabassa, Gregory; Rabe, David; Rand, Ayn; Ransom, John Crowe; Rawlings, Marjorie Kinnan; Rechy, John; Reed, Ishmael; Rexroth, Kenneth; Reznikoff, Charles; Rice, Anne; Rice, Elmer; Rich, Adrienne; Riding, Laura; Riley, James Whitcomb; Rinehart, Mary; Rittenhouse, Jessie Bell; Robbins, Harold; Roberts, Kenneth; Robinson, Edwin Arlington; Roethke, Theodore; Rolvaag, O.E.; Roth, Henry; Roth, Philip; Rowson, Susanna; Rukeyser, Muriel; Runyon, Damon; Sacks, Oliver; Sagan, Carl Edward; Salinger, J.D.; Sanchez, Luis Rafael; Sanchez, Sonia; Sandburg, Carl; Sandoz, Mari; Saroyan, William; Sarton, May; Sayles, John; Scarry, Richard; Schulberg, Budd; Schwartz, Delmore; Sedgwick, Catherine maria; Seeger, Alan; Seidensticker, Edward George; Selby, Hubert, Jr.; Sendak, Maurice; Sexton, Anne; Shapiro, Karl; Shaw, Henry Wheeler; Sheldon, Edward; Sheldon, Sidney; Sherwood, Robert E.; Shuster, Joe; Siegel, Jerry; Sigourney, Lydia; Silko, Leslie; Silverstein, Shel; Simic, Charles; Simms, William Gilmore; Simon, Neil; Sinclair, Upton, Jr.; Singer, Isaac Bashevis; Singer, Israel Joshua; Singleton, Charles S.; Slosson, Edwin Emery; Smith, Logan Pearsall; Smith, Seba; Snodgrass, W.D.; Snyder, Gary; Sontag, Susan; Spencer, Elizabeth; Spiegelman, Art; Spillane, Mickey; Stafford, Jean; Standing Bear, Luther; Stedman, Edmund Clarence; Stegner, Wallace; Steig, William; Stein, Gertrude; Steinbeck, John; Steinem, Gloria; Stevens, Wallace; Stevenson, James; Stockton, Frank; Stone, Irving; Stone, John Augustus; Stone, Robert; Stout, Rex; Stowe, Harriet Beecher; Strand, Mark; Stratemeyer, Edward L. Allen; Taylor, Bayard; Taylor, Edward; Taylor, Peter; Teale, Edwin Way; Teasdale, Sara; Tenney, Tabitha Gilman; Terhune, Albert Payson; Thayer, Ernest Lawrence; Theroux, Paul; Thomas, Augustus; Thomas, Lewis; Thompson, Kay; Thoreau, Henry David; Thurber,

Medicine (*cont.*)

Michael; L'Esperance, Elise; Letterman, Jonathan; Levi-Montalcini, Rita; Levine, Lena; Levine, Philip; Lillehei, C. Walton; Linn, Lewis Fields; Loeb, Jacques; Long, Crawford; Lovejoy, Esther Pohl; Luria, Salvador; Magoun, Horace Winchell; Mall, Franklin Paine; Mayo, Charles Horace; Mayo, William James; Mayo, William Worrall; McClellan, George; McDowell, Ephraim; McGee, Anita Newcomb; Mendenhall, Dorothy; Menninger, Charles Frederick; Menninger, William Claire; Minokaa-Hill, Lillie Rose; Minot, George R.; Mintz, Beatrice; Mitchell, Silas Weir; Montezuma, Carlos; Morgan, John; Morris, John M.; Morton, Samuel George; Morton, William; Mott, Valentine; Moyer, Andrew Jackson; Mudd, Samuel; Murphy, John Benjamin; Murphy, William P.; Murray, Joseph E.; Nemir, Rosa Lee; Nichols, Thomas Low; Noguchi, Hideyo; Novello, Antonia C.; Nutting, Mary Adelaide; Ochsner, Alton; Osler, William; Page, Charles; Palade, George E.; Palmer, Daniel David; Papanicolaou, George; Park, Roswell; Parker, Willard; Parran, Thomas; Pepper, William (1810–1864); Pepper, William (1843–1898); Pert, Candace B.; Physick, Philip Syng; Picotte, Susan La Flesche; Pincus, Gregory; Pope; Preston, Ann; Pribram, Karl; Prudden, T. Mitchell; Reed, Walter; Richards, A.N.; Richards, Dickinson W.; Richmond, Julius Benjamin; Ricketts, Howard Taylor; Rivers, Thomas Milton; Robbins, Frederick C.; Robinson, G. Canby; Rock, John Swett; Rose, Wickliffe; Rosenau, Milton Joseph; Rous, Peyton; Rubinow, Isaac Max; Rush, Benjamin; Rusk, Howard A.; Sabin, Albert; Sabin, Florence; Sachs, Bernard; Sacks, Oliver; Salk, Jonas; Schally, Andrew V.; Schick, Bela; Shattuck, Lemuel; Shaw, Anna Howard; Shrady, George Frederick; Shumway, Norman; Sims, James Marion; Smillie, Wilson George; Smith, James McCune; Smith, Nathan; Smith, Stephen; Smith, Theobald; Snell, George D.; Sperry, Roger W.; Spock, Benjamin; Stapp, John Paul; Starzl, Thomas; Sternberg, George Miller; Stiles, Charles W.; Stille, Alfred; Sutton, Walter S.; Tabern, Donalee L.; Taussig, Helen; Taylor, Lucy Beaman; Temin, Howard M.; Theiler, Max; Thomas, E. Donnall; Thomas, Lewis; Thompson, Samuel; Townsend, Francis E.; Trudeau, Edward Livingston; Upjohn, William E.; Vagelos, P. Roy; Van Dyck, Cornelius; Varmus, Harold E.; Velikovsky, Immanuel; Wald, Lillian D.; Walker, Mary E.; Walker, Thomas; Warren, John; Warren, John Collins; Warren, Joseph; Waterhouse, Benjamin; Watson, James D.; Wattleton, Faye; Welch, William Henry; Weller, Thomas H.; Wells, Horace; Whipple, George H.; White, Paul Dudley; Whitman, Marcus; Wiesel, Torsten N.; Wilbur, Ray Lyman; Williams, Anna; Williams, Daniel Hale; Winslow, Charles-Edward; Wistar, Caspar; Wood, Leonard; Yalow, Rosalyn; Zakrzewska, Marie Elizabeth; Zinsser, Hans

Military Abrams, Creighton W., Jr.; Aguinaldo, Emilio; Alger, Russell Alexander; Allen, Terry; Almond, Edward Mallory; Ames, Adelbert; Anderson, George W.; Anderson, Robert; Andrews, Frank; Angel, Jimmy; Armstrong, Harry George; Armstrong, John; Arnold, Benedict; Arnold, "Hap"; Atkinson, Henry; Babcock, Orville E.; Bacon, Nathaniel; Bainbridge, William; Baldwin, Loammi; Banks, Nathaniel Prenties; Barney, Joshua; Barron, James; Barry, John; Barton, Clara; Beale, Edward Fitzgerald; Beau, Louis Victor; Beauregard, Pierre G.T.; Bee, Barnard; Benson, William Shepherd; Biddle, James; Biddle, Nicholas; Black Hawk; Bliss, Tasker; Bong, Richard; Bonneville, Benjamin Louis Eulalie de; Boone, Daniel; Borie, Adolph Edward; Bowie, James; Boyington, "Pappy"; Bradley, Mark E.; Bradley, Omar; Bragg, Braxton; Brant, Gerald Clark; Brant, Joseph; Brereton, Lewis; Brooke, John Mercer; Brown, George; Brown, Jacob; Buchanan, Franklin; Bucher, Lloyd; Buckner, Simon Bolivar; Buckner, Simon Bolivar, Jr.; Buell, Don Carlos; Buford, John; Bullard, Robert Lee; Burdett, Allen Mitchell, Jr.; Burke, Arleigh A.; Burnside, Ambrose; Burrows, William; Butler, Benjamin; Butler, Smedley D.; Callaghan, Daniel; Calley, William L.; Canby, Edward Richard Sprigg; Carlson, Evans F.; Carson, Kit; Cass, Lewis; Chafee, Adna; Chaffee, John H.; Chaffee, Roger B.; Chamberlain, Joshua; Chandler, William Eaton; Chauncey, Issac; Chennault, Claire; Chidlaw, Benjamin Wiley; Chouteau, Rene Auguste; Church, Benjamin; Clark, George Rogers; Clark, Mark; Clark, William; Clay, Cassius Marcellus; Clay, Lucius; Cleburne, Patrick; Cochise; Collins, J. Lawton; Conner, David; Conner, Fox; Conolly, Richard L.; Corbin, Margaret; Craig, Malin; Crazy Horse; Crockett, "Davy"; Crook, George; Custer, George Armstrong; Dade, Francis Langhorne; Dahlgren, John; Dale, Richard; Dargue, Herbert; Davis, Benjamin, Jr.; Davis, Benjamin Oliver, Sr.; Davis, Charles Henry; Davis, Jefferson; Davis, Jefferson Columbus; Dean, William; Dearborn, Henry; Decatur, Stephen (1752–1808); Decatur, Stephen (1779–1820); De Long, George Washington; Denby, Edwin; Denfeld, Louis; Denton, Jeremiah A., Jr.; Devens, Charles, Jr.; Devers, Jacob; Dewey, George; Dickman, Joseph; Dix, Dorothea; Dodge, Grenville; Dodge, Henry; Doniphan, Alexander William; Donovan, William; Doolittle, James; Doubleday, Abner; Douglas, James Henderson, Jr.; Drum, Hugh; Duerk, Alene; Dull Knife; Du Pont, Samuel Francis; Eaker, Ira; Early, Jubal; Echols, Oliver P.; Edson, Merritt A.; Eisenhower, Dwight D.; Elliott, Jesse Duncan; Ellis, Earl H.; Emory, William H.; Evans, Robley; Ewell, Richard Stoddart; Farragut, David; Fetterman, William Judd; Fiske, Bradley Allen; Fitch, Aubrey; Fletcher, Frank J.; Flipper, Henry Ossian; Foote, Andrew Hull; Forrest, Nathan Bedford; Foss, Joseph; Foulois, Benjamin D.; Fox, Gustavus Vasa; Fredenall, Lloyd R.; Fremont, John; Friedman, William Frederick; Funston, Frederick; Gabrieski, Francis Stanley; Gadsden, James; Gall; Gates, Horatio; Gavin, James; Geary, John White; Geiger, Roy S.; George, Harold Huston; George, Harold Lee; George, James Zachariah; Geronimo; Ghormley, Robert Lee; Girty, Simon; Goethals, George Washington; Goldsborough, Louis; Gorgas, Josiah; Gorgas, William Crawford; Grant, Ulysses S.;

Graveley, Samuel Lee, Jr.; Gray, Alfred M.; Greely, Adolphus Washington; Greene, Nathanael; Gridley, Charles; Grierson, Benjamin Henry; Groves, Leslie; Haig, Alexander; Hale, Nathan; Halleck, Henry; Halsey, William "Bull"; Hammond, William A.; Hampton, Wade; Hampton, Wade; Hancock, Winfield Scott; Hansell, Haywood Shepherd Jr.; Hardee, William Joseph; Harkins, Paul Donal; Harlan, Josiah; Harmar, Josiah; Harrison, William Henry; Hart, Thomas; Haupt, Herman; Hawley, Joseph Roswell; Hayes, Ira; Hays, "Jack"; Henderson, Archibald; Herbert, Hilary Abner; Herkimer, Nicholas; Herres, Robert Tralles; Hershey, Lewis; Hewitt, Henry; Heywood, Charles; Higginson, Thomas Wentworth; Hill, Ambrose; Hill, William; Hines, Frank; Hines, John Leonard; Hitchcock, Ethan Allen; Hitchcock, Tommy; Hobby, Oveta Culp; Hobson, Richmond; Hodges, Courtney; Hood, John Bell; Hooker, Joseph; Hopkins, Esek; Hopper, Grace Murray; Horner, Charles Albert; Houston, Sam; Howard, Oliver Otis; Howze, Hamilton Hawkins; Hull, Isaac; Hull, William; Humphreys, Joshua; Hunt, William Henry; Ingersoll, Royal; Isherwood, Benjamin; Jackson, "Stonewall"; James, Daniel, Jr.; Johnson, Hugh; Johnson, Louis; Johnston, Albert Sidney; Johnston, Joseph Eggleston; Jones, Catesby Ap Roger; Jones, John Paul; Jones, Thomas ap Catesby; Kalb, Johann; Kearny, Lawrence; Kearny, Philip; Kearny, Stephen Watts; Kenney, George; Kent, Jacob; Kent, Jacob Ford; Kimmel, Husband Edward; Kincaid, Thomas; King, Ernest J.; Knerr, Hugh Johnston; Knox, Henry; Knudsen, William S.; Kosciusko, Thaddeus; Kuter, Lawrence Sherman; Lafayette, Marie Joseph Paul Yves Roch Gibert du Motier; Lahm, Frank; Lamar, Mirabeau Buonaparte; Lander, Frederick West; Lawrence, James; Lawton, Henry Ware; Leahy, William; Leavenworth, Henry; Ledyard, William; Lee, Charles; Lee, Fitzhugh; Lee, Henry; Lee, Robert E.; Lee, Samuel Phillips; Lee, Willis A., Jr.; Lejeune, John A.; LeMay, Curtis; L'Enfant, Pierre Charles; Lewis, Meriwether; Liggett, Hunter; Lincoln, Benjamin; Lockwood, Charles A.; Logan, John Alexander; Logan; Long, John Davis; Long, Stephen Harriman; Longstreet, James; Loring, William W.; Luce, Stephen Bleecker; Luke, Frank Jr.; Lyman, Theodore; Lynch, Charles; Lyon, Nathaniel; MacArthur, Arthur; MacArthur, Douglas; MacDonough, Thomas; Macomb, Alexander; Magruder, John Bankhead; Mahan, Alfred Thayer; Mahan, Dennis Hart; Mangas Coloradas; Manuelito; March, Peyton Conway; Marion, Francis; Marshall, George C., Jr.; Mason, John; Mayo, Henry Thomas; McCauley, Charles Stewart; McCauley, Mary Hays; McCawley, Charles G.; McClellan, George Brinton; McDougall, Alexander; McDowell, Irvin; McIntosh, William; McLaws, Lafayette; McNair, Lesley; McNarney, Joseph; McPherson, James; Meade, George Gordon; Meigs, Montgomery Cunningham; Melville, George Wallace; Merrill, Frank; Merritt, Wesley; Middleton, Troy Houston; Mifflin, Thomas; Miles, Nelson; Miller, Dorie; Mitchell, "Billy"; Mitscher, Marc; Moffett, William; Montgomery, Richard; Moore, James;

Moorer, Thomas H.; Morgan, Daniel; Morgan, John Hunt; Morris, Richard; Mosby, John Singleton; Moultrie, William; Murphy, Audie; Murphy, Timothy; Nimitz, Chester; Norstad, Lauris; O'Bannon, Presley; O'Brien, Jeremiah; O'Donnell, Emmett, Jr.; Oglethorpe, James Edward; O'Hara, James; Paine, Charles Jackson; Palmer, John McAuley; Partridge, Earl; Patch, Alexander; Patrick, Mason; Patterson, Robert; Patton Jr., George; Peary, Robert E.; Pemberton, John Clifford; Perry, Matthew Calbraith; Perry, Oliver Hazard; Pershing, John J.; Pickens, Andrew; Pickett, George Edward; Pike, Albert; Pike, Zebulon; Pillow, Gideon; Pinckney, Thomas; Polk, Leonidas; Pope, John; Porter, David Dixon; Porter, Fitz-John; Porter, John Luke; Powell, Colin; Pratt, Henry; Preble, Edward; Pringle, Joel; Puller, Lewis; Putnam, Israel; Putnam, Rufus; Quanah; Quesada, Elwood; Radford, Arthur; Ramseur, Stephen Dodson; Red Cloud; Reed, Walter; Revere, Joseph Warren; Reynolds, John Fulton; Rickenbacker, Eddie; Rickover, Hyman; Ridgway, Matthew; Ringgold, Samuel; Robert, Henry Martyn; Robeson, George Maxwell; Rochefort, Joseph J.; Rockenbach, Samuel Dickerson; Rodgers, John (1773–1838); Rodgers, John (1812–1882); Rogers, Robert; Roosevelt, Kermit; Rosecrans, William; Royce, Ralph; Russell, James Sargent; Rutan, Richard Glenn; Saltonstall, Dudley; Sampson, Deborah; Sampson, William Thomas; Schirra, Walter; Schley, Winfield Scott; Schofield, John McAllister; Schreiver, Bernard Adolph; Schufeldt, Robert Wilson; Schuyler, Peter; Schuyler, Philip John; Schwartzkopf, Norman; Scott, Norman; Scott, Winfield; Sedgwick, John; Semmes, Raphael; Sevier, John; Shaw, Robert Gould; Shays, Daniel; Shelby, Isaac; Shepard, Alan; Sheridan, Philip; Sherman, Thomas West; Sherman, William Tecumseh; Shields, James; Short, Walter Campbell; Shubrick, William Branford; Sickles, Daniel; Sims, William Snowden; Sitting Bull; Sloat, John Drake; Slocum, Henry Warner; Smalls, Robert; Smith, Edmund Kirby; Smith, Holland M.; Smith, Robert; Smith, Walter Bedell; Somervell, Brehon Burke; Spaatz, Carl; Sprague, Clifton; Spruance, Raymond; St. Clair, Arthur; Standish, Miles; Stansbury, Howard; Stark, Harold Raynsford; Stark, John; Steuben, Baron von; Stevens, Isaac Ingalls; Stilwell, Joseph; Stimson, Henry; Stockton, Robert; Stoddert, Benjamin; Stratemeyer, George Edward; Stuart, Jeb; Sullivan, John; Sullivan, John L.; Sumter, Thomas; Tattnal, Josiah; Taussig, Joseph; Taylor, Maxwell D.; Taylor, Zachary; Terry, Alfred Howe; Terry, David Smith; Thayer, Sylvanus; Theobald, Robert Alfred; Thomas, George Henry; Thomas, Lorenzo; Thompson, Benjamin; Tilghman, Tench; Toombs, Robert Augustus; Towers, John; Tracy, Benjamin F.; Travis, William Barret; Truscott, Lucien King Jr.; Truxtun, Thomas; Turner, Richmond K.; Twining, Nathaniel; Underhill, John; Upshur, Abel Parker; Upton, Emory; Vandegrift, Alexander; Van Dorn, Earl; Van Fleet, James; Van Rensselaer, Stephen; Waddell, James; Wainwright, Jonathan; Walker, Walton; Wallace, Lewis; Ward, Frederick Townsend; Warner, John W.; Washington, George;

Military (*cont.*)

Wayne, Anthony; Wedemeyer, Albert C.; Weitzel, Godfrey; Welles, Roger; Westmoreland, William C.; Wheeler, Joseph; Whistler, George; White, Thomas; Wilkes, Charles; Wilkinson, James; Williams, Robert Ray; Wilson, James Harrison; Winthrop, John; Wood, Leonard; Wool, John Ellis; Worden, John Lorimer; York, Alvin; Zumwalt, Elmo R., Jr.

Miscellaneous Adair, James; Adler, Polly; Ashmun, Jehuda; Astor, Brooke; Atlas, Charles; Austin, Moses; Austin, Stephen; Baca, Elfego; Bean, "Judge" Roy; Beidler, John Xavier; Bent, Charles; Bottineau, Pierre; Breen, Patrick; Bridger, James; Bridgman, Laura Dewey; Brunvand, Jan Harold; Burk, Martha Jane; Campbell, Robert; Caniff, Milt; Carmack, George Washington; Carroll, Anna Ella; Cayce, Edgar; Comstock, Henry; Converse, Harriet Maxwell; Corey, Martha; Crawford, "Captain Jack"; Crumb, R.; Culbertson, Ely; Culbertson, Josephine; Darrow, Charles B.; Eaton, "Peggy"; Eisner, Will; Farnham, Russel; Farnham, Thomas Jefferson; Fink, Mike; Fischer, Bobby; Fitzpatrick, Thomas; Frietschie or Fritchie, Barbara; Glass, Hugh; Goren, Charles; Gould, Chester; Gray, Harold; Gregg, Josiah; Hale, Clara "Mother"; Hamilton, Charles; Hayes, William Henry; Henry, Andrew; Herriman, George; Hickok, "Wild Bill"; Holt, Berta Marian; Hoppe, Willie; Ishi; Jacobs, Harriet Ann; Jones, Louis C.; Keckley, Elizabeth; Kelly, Walt; King, Richard; Larson, Gary; Laws, G. Malcolm; Lenz, Sidney; Lisa, Manuel; Little Crow; Low, Juliette; MacDonald, Ranald; Mallon, Mary, "Typhoid Mary"; McCoy, Joseph; Meir, Golda; Morehead, Alfred; Morphy, Paul; Mosconi, Willie; Norton, "Emperor"; Norton, Mary Alice; Onesimus; Patch, Sam; Pendergast, Thomas; Pettie, James Ohio; Pillsbury, Harry Nelson; Pocahontas; Randi, James; Reshevsky, Samuel; Roberts, Joseph Jenkins; Rockwell, George Lincoln; Ross, Betsy; Rowlandson, Mary; Russell, William Hepburn; Scott, Dred; Scott, Walter Edward; Slocum, Joshua; Stanley, Louise; Steinitz, William; Stephens, John Lloyd; Stilwell, "Jack"; Stuart, Robert; Tabor, Horace; Truscott, Alan; Vanderbilt, Gloria; Vanderbilt, Harold Stirling; Walker, William; Watson, Elkanah; Whitehead, Wilbur C.; Wilson, Samuel, "Uncle Sam"; Windsor, Duchess of, Wallis Warfield; Woodhull, Victoria Claflin; Work, Milton C.; Zane, Betty

Motion Pictures See FILM.

Music, Classical: Abravanel, Maurice; Adams, John; Adler, Larry; Adler, Richard; Amram, David; Anderson, Marian; Antheil, George; Argento, Dominick; Ax, Emanuel; Babbitt, Milton; Bampton, Rose; Barber, Samuel; Battle, Kathleen; Bauer, Harold; Beach, Amy; Becker, John J.; Berger, Arthur; Bergsma, William; Bernstein, Leonard; Billings, William; Blitzstein, Marc; Bloch, Ernest; Bolcom, William; Borge, Victor; Brant, Henry; Brown, Earle; Browning, John; Buck, Dudley; Bumbry, Grace; Burleigh, Henry Thacker; Cadman, Charles Wakefield;

Cage, John; Caldwell, Sarah; Callas, Maria; Carpenter, John Alden; Carr, Benjamin; Carter, Elliott; Chadwick, George Whitefield; Chase, Gilbert; Christie, William; Cliburn, Van; Cohen, Joel; Colgrass, Michael; Cook, Will Marion; Coolidge, Elizabeth Sprague; Copland, Aaron; Corigliano, John; Cowell, Henry; Crawford-Seeger, Ruth; Crumb, George; Dahl, Ingolf; Damrosch, Leopold; Damrosch, Walter; Davis, Anthony; DeGaetani, Jan; Dello Joio, Norman; Del Tredici, David; Densmore, Frances; DePreist, James; Dett, R. Nathaniel; Diamond, David; Diaz, Justino; Ditson, Oliver; Dixon, Dean; Dorati, Antal; Downes, Olin; Druckman, Jacob; Duke, Vernon; Dwight, John Sullivan; Eddy, Nelson; Einstein, Alfred; Ellington, Duke; Elman, Mischa; Erskine, John; Farrar, Geraldine; Farrell, Eileen; Farwell, Arthur; Fiedler, Arthur; Finck, Henry Theophilus; Fine, Irving; Fine, Vivian; Finney, Ross Lee; Fischer, Carl; Fleischer, Leon; Floyd, Carlisle; Foote, Arthur; Foss, Lucas; Friml, Rudolf; Fuchs, Joseph; Gabrilowitsch, Ossip; Galli-Curci, Amelita; Garden, Mary; Geiringer, Karl; Gershwin, George; Gilbert, Henry F.; Gilman, Lawrence; Gilmore, Patrick; Glass, Philip; Gluck, Alma; Godowsky, Leopold; Goldovsky, Boris; Goodman, Benny; Gottschalk, Louis Moreau; Gould, Morton; Graffman, Gary; Grainger, Percy; Graupner, Johann; Greenberg, Noah; Griffes, Charles Tomlinson; Grofe, Ferde; Hale, Philip; Hamlisch, Marvin; Hanson, Howard; Harbison, John; Harris, Roy; Harrison, Lou; Hayes, Roland; Heifetz, Jascha; Heinrich, Anthony Philip; Herbert, Victor; Herrmann, Bernard; Hill, Patty Smith; Hillis, Margaret; Hitchcock, H. Wiley; Hofmann, Josef; Homer, Louise; Hopkinson, Francis; Horne, Marilyn; Hovaness, Alan; Huneker, James Gibbons; Hurok, Sol; Imbrie, Andrew; Istomin, Eugene; Ives, Charles; Janis, Byron; Johannesen, Grant; Juilliard, Augustus D.; Kalisch, Gilbert; Kallman, Chester; Kay, Hershy; Kay, Ulysses; Kirchner, Leon; Kirsten, Dorothy; Kneisel, Franz; Kolodin, Irving; Korngold, Erich Wolfgang; Koussevitzky, Serge; Kreisler, Fritz; Krenek, Ernst; Kurath, Gertrude Prokosch; Landon, H.C. Robbins; Landowska, Wanda; Lanza, Mario; Leinsdorf, Erich; Levant, Oscar; Levine, James; Lhevinne, Josef; Lhevinne, Rosina; List, Eugene; Loeffler, Charles Martin; London, George; Luboff, Norman; Luening, Otto; Ma, Yo-Yo; Maazel, Lorin; MacDonald, Jeanette; MacDowell, Edward; Mannes, David; Marsalis, Wynton; Martino, Donald; Mason, Daniel Gregory; Mason, Lowell; Masselos, William; McCormack, John; McCracken, James; Melchior, Lauritz; Melton, James; Mennin, Peter; Menotti, Gian-Carlo; Menuhin, Yehudi; Merrill, Robert; Milnes, Sherrill; Milstein, Nathan; Mitropoulos, Dimitri; Monteux, Pierre; Moore, Douglas; Moore, Grace; Morel Campos, Juan; Munch, Charles; Munsel, Patrice; Nancarrow, Conlon; Nordica, Lillian; Norman, Jessye; Ormandy, Eugene; Ornstein, Leo; Ozawa, Seiji; Paine, John Knowles; Paoli, Antonio; Parker, Horatio; Partch, Harry; Peerce, Jan; Perahia, Murray; Perle, George; Perlman, Itzhak; Persechetti, Vincent; Peter, Johann Friedrich; Piatigorsky, Gregor; Pinza,

Ezio; Piston, Walter; Pons, Lily; Ponselle, Rosa; Presser, Theodore; Previn, Andre; Price, Leontyne; Ran, Shulamit; Read, Daniel; Reich, Steve; Reiner, Fritz; Resnik, Regina; Ricci, Ruggiero; Riegger, Wallingford; Rifkin, Joshua; Riley, Terry; Rochberg, George; Rodzinski, Artur; Romberg, Sigmund; Rorem, Ned; Rose, Leonard; Rosen, Charles; Rosenfeld, Paul; Rosenman, Leonard; Rubenstein, Artur; Rudel, Julius; Rudolf, Max; Ruggles, Carl; Russell, George; Sachs, Curt; Sanroma, Jesus Maria; Schillinger, Joseph; Schippers, Thomas; Schirmer, Gustav; Schneider, Alexander; Schuller, Gunther; Schuman, William; Schumann-Heink, Ernestine; Seeger, Charles; Seidl, Anton; Serkin, Peter; Serkin, Rudolf; Sessions, Roger; Shaw, Robert; Siegmeister, Elie; Sills, Beverly; Slatkin, Leonard; Slonimsky, Nicolas; Sousa, John Philip; Spalding, Albert; Steber, Eleanor; Steinberg, William; Stern, Isaac; Stevens, Rise; Still, William Grant; Stock, Frederick August; Stoeckel, Carl; Stokowski, Leopold; Stolzman, Richard; Stravinsky, Igor; Swarthout, Gladys; Szell, George; Talma, Louise; Taylor, Deems; Thomas, Theodore; Thomas, John Charles; Thomas, Michael Tilson; Thompson, Oscar; Thompson, Randall; Thomson, Virgil; Tibbett, Lawrence; Toch, Ernst; Toscanini, Arturo; Tourel, Jennie; Trampler, Walter; Traubel, Helen; Tucker, Richard; Tudor, David; Tureck, Rosalyn; Varese, Edgar; Varnay, Astrid; Von Stade, Frederica; Walter, Bruno; Warfield, William; Warren, Leonard; Watts, Andre; Webster, Beveridge; Weill, Kurt; Weisgall, Hugo; Whiting, Arthur Battelle; Wild, Earl; Wilder, Alec; Wilson, Olly; Wolfes, Felix; Wolpe, Stefan; Wuorinen, Charles; Zimbalist, Efrem; Zuckerman, Pinchas; Zwilich, Ellen Taafe

Music, Popular Acuff, Roy; Adderley, "Cannonball"; Addington, Maybelle; Adler, Richard; Alpert, Herb; Andrews, LaVerne; Andrews, Maxine; Andrews, Patti; Andrews Sisters, The; Armstrong, Louis "Satchmo"; Asch, Moses; Atkins, Chet; Bacharach, Burt; Baez, Joan; Bailey, Mildred; Bailey, Pearl; Baker, Chet; Baker, Josephine; Balliett, Whitney; Barnet, Charlie; Basie, Count; Bechet, Sidney; Beiderbecke, Bix; Benson, George; Berigan, "Bunny"; Berlin, Irving; Bernstein, Elmer; Berry, "Chu"; Berry, Chuck; Bikel, Theodore; Blake, Eubie; Blakey, Art; Block, Martin; Bolden, Buddy; Brice, Fanny; Broonzy, "Big Bill"; Brown, Clifford; Brown, James; Brubeck, Dave; Burns, Ralph; Butterfield, Paul; Byrne, David; Cahn, Sammy; Calloway, Cab; Cantor, Eddie; Carmichael, Hoagy; Carroll, Diahann; Carter, A.P.; Carter, Benny; Carter Family, The; Cash, Johnny; Charles, Ray; Chenier, Clifton; Chess, Leonard; Christian, Charlie; Christy, June; Clark, Dick; Cleveland, James L.; Cline, Patsy; Cohan, George M.; Cole, Nat King; Coleman, Cy; Coleman, Ornette; Coltrane, John; Comden, Betty; Como, Perry; Condon, Eddie; Conover, Willis; Constantine, Eddie; Cooder, Ry; Cook, Will Marion; Crosby, Bing; Crosby, Bob; Cugat, Xavier; Curtis, Natalie; Dameron, Tadd; Darin, Bobby; Davis, Anthony; Davis, Miles; Davis, Sammy, Jr.; Day, Doris; Diddley, Bo; Dietz, Howard; Dolphy, Eric; Domino,

"Fats"; Donaldson, Walter; Dorsey, Tommy; Dougherty, Sara; Duke, Vernon; Dyer-Bennett, Richard; Dylan, Bob; Eckstine, Billy; Eldridge, Roy "Little Jazz"; Ellington, Duke; Emmett, Daniel; Ertegun, Ahmet; Evans, Bill; Evans, Gil; Fields, Dorothy; Fitzgerald, Ella; Flanagan, Tommy; Foster, Stephen Collins; Franklin, Aretha; Freed, Alan; Freed, Arthur; Friml, Rudolf; Garcia, Jerry; Garfunkel, Art; Garland, Judy; Garner, Errol; Gaye, Marvin; Gershwin, George; Gershwin, Ira; Getz, Stan; Gillespie, "Dizzy"; Goodman, Benny; Gordon, Dexter; Gordy, Berry, Jr.; Graham, Bill; Granz, Norman; Gray, Glen; Green, Al; Green, Johnny; Grossman, Albert B.; Guthrie, "Woody"; Haley, "Bill"; Hamlisch, Marvin; Hammond, John; Hampton, Lionel; Hancock, Herbie; Handy, W.C.; Harbach, Otto; Harburg, E.Y.; Harney, Benjamin Robertson; Hart, Lorenz; Hawkins, Coleman; Hays, William Shakespeare; Henderson, Fletcher; Hendricks, Jon; Hendrix, "Jimi"; Herman, Jerry; Herman, Woody; Hernandez, Rafael; Hill, Joe; Hines, Earl "Fatha"; Hodges, Johnny "Rabbit"; Holiday, Billie "Lady Day"; Holly, Buddy; Holyoke, Samuel; Hooker, John Lee; Hope, Bob; Horne, Lena; Howlin' Wolf; Humes, Helen; Hutchinson, Abby; Hutchinson, Asa; Hutchinson, Jesse; Hutchinson, John; Hutchinson, Judson; Hutchinson Family, The; Ives, Burl; Jackson, Mahalia; Jackson, Michael; Jacquet, "Illinois"; James, Harry; Jarrett, Keith; Jefferson, "Blind" Lemon; Johnson, Lonnie; Johnson, "J.J."; Johnson, James P.; Johnson, Robert; Jolson, Al; Jones, George; Jones, Quincy; Jones, "Spike"; Joplin, Janis; Joplin, Scott; Jordan, Louis; Kahn, Gustav Gerson; Kander, John; Kaye, Danny; Kenton, Stan; Kern, Jerome; King, B.B.; King, Carole; Kirk, Rahsaan Roland; Kitt, Eartha; Koehler, Ted; Krupa, Gene; Kyser, Kay; Lamb, Joseph; Lane, Burton; Lanin, Lester; Ledbetter, Huddie; Lee, Peggy; Leiber, Jerry; Lerner, Alan Jay; Lewis, Jerry Lee; Lewis, John; Liberace; Lincoln, Abbey; "Little Richard"; "Little Walter"; Loesser, Frank; Loewe, Frederick; Lomax, Alan; Lomax, John A.; Lombardo, Guy; Luboff, Norman; Lunceford, Jimmie; Lunsford, Bascom Lamar; Lynn, Loretta; Madonna; Mancini, Henry; Marsalis, Wynton; Mathis, Johnny; McClendon, Rose; McGhee, Brownie; McHugh, Jimmy; McPartland, Marian; McShann, Jay; Mercer, Johnny; Merman, Ethel; Miller, Glenn; Miller, Mitch; Mills, Donald; Mills, Florence; Mills, Harry; Mills, Herbert; Mills, John, Jr.; Mills Brothers; Mingus, Charles; Mitchell, Joni; Monk, Meredith; Monk, Thelonious; Monroe, Bill; Morrison, Jim; Morton, "Jelly Roll"; Mulligan, Gerry; Navarro, "Fats"; Nelson, Rick; Nelson, Willie; Nevin, Ethelbert; Newman, Alfred; Newman, Randy; Niles, John Jacob; North, Alex; Norvo, Red; Ochs, Phil; O'Daniel, Wilbert Lee; Odetta; Odetta, Gordon, Odetta Holmes Felious; Oliver, Joe "King"; Orbison, Roy; Otis, Johnny; Page, Oran "Hot Lips"; Parker, Charlie; Perkins, Carl; Peterson, Oscar; Phillips, Sam; Pollack, Ben; Porter, Cole; Powell, "Bud"; Presley, Elvis; Previn, Andre; Price, Sammy; Pride, Charley; Prince; Prince, Hal; Professor Longhair; Puente, Tito; Raitt, Bonnie;

Music, Popular (*cont.*)

Rebennack, "Dr. John"; Redding, Otis; Redman, Don; Riddle, Nelson; Rifkin, Joshua; Ritter, Tex; Roach, Max; Robeson, Paul; Robin, Leo; Robinson, Smokey; Rodgers, Richard; Rodgers, "Jimmie"; Rogers, Kenny; Rollins, "Sonny"; Root, George Frederick; Rose, Billy; Ross, Diana; Rozsa, Miklos; Rush, Otis; Rushing, Jimmy; Russell, George; Russell, Lillian; Russell, "Pee Wee"; Sandburg, Carl; Schuller, Gunther; Schwartz, Arthur; Seeger, Charles; Seeger, Pete; Severinsen, Doc; Shearing, George; Shepp, Archie; Short, Bobby; Silver, Horace; Simon, Paul; Simone, Nina; Sinatra, Frank; Sissle, Noble; Slick, Grace; Smith, Bessie; Smith, Kate; Smith, Patti; Smothers, Dick; Smothers, Tom; Sondheim, Stephen; Sousa, John Philip; Spector, Phil; Springsteen, Bruce; Steiner, Max; Stoller, Mike; Strayhorn, Billy; Streisand, Barbra; Styne, Jule; Tatum, Art; Taylor, Cecil; Taylor, James; Teagarden, Jack; Terry, Sonny; Tharpe, Sister Rosetta; Thompson, Kay; Tiomkin, Dimitri; Torme, Mel; Tristano, Lennie; Tubb, Ernest; Tucker, Sophie; Tufts, John; Turner, "Big" Joe; Tyner, McCoy; Vallee, Rudy; Van Heusen, James; Vaughan, Sarah; Vaughan, Stevie Ray; Walker, "T-Bone"; Waller, "Fats"; Waring, Fred; Warren, Harry; Warwick, Dionne; Washington, Dinah; Waters, Ethel; Waters, Muddy; Waxman, Franz; Webb, "Chick"; Webster, Ben; Weems, Ted; Weill, Kurt; Wein, George; Welk, Lawrence; Wells, Kitty; Wexler, Jerry; White, Josh; Whiteman, Paul; Wilder, Alec; Williams, Bert; Williams, Clarence; Williams, Hank; Williams, Joe; Williams, John; Williams, Mary Lou; Williamson, Sonny Boy; Wills, Bob; Willson, Meredith; Wilson, Jackie; Wilson, Teddy; Winter, Paul; Wonder, Stevie; Work, Henry Clay; Youmans, Vincent; Young, Lester "Prez"; Young, Victor; Zappa, Frank

Nutrition See under FOOD AND NUTRITION.

Philanthropy Annenberg, Walter; Avery, Samuel Putnam; Baker, George F.; Ball, Frank Clayton; Baruch, Bernard; Booth, George G.; Bowen, Louise deKoven; Brace, Charles Loring; Bren, Donald L.; Brookings, Robert Somers; Brown, James; Buck, Beryl H.; Cabot, Godfrey Lowell; Cardin, Shoshana; Carnegie, Andrew; Clark, Edna McConnell; Clark, Francine Clary; Clark, Robert Sterling; Converse, Edmund Cogswell; Coolidge, Elizabeth Sprague; Cope, Thomas Pym; Corcoran, William Wilson; Cornell, Ezra; Couzens, James; Crane, Charles Richard; Davis, Arthur Vining; De Menil, Dominique; Dodge, Geraldine R.; Drexel, Anthony Joseph; Duke, James; Eastman, George; Field, Marshall; Filene, Edward A.; Fiske, Daniel Willard; Flagler, Henry M.; Flexner, Abraham; Folger, Henry Clay; Ford, Henry; Forten, James; Frick, Henry C.; Gates, Frederick T.; Girard, Stephen; Gratz, Rebecca; Grinnell, Henry; Guggenheim, Daniel; Guggenheim, Peggy; Guggenheim, Simon; Guggenheim, Solomon Robert; Hammer, Armand; Harvard, John; Havemeyer, Henry O.; Havemeyer, Louisine Waldron; Hayden, Charles; Heckscher, August; Heinz, Howard; Hershey, Milton;

Higginson, Henry L.; Hirshhorn, Joseph H.; Hoffman, Paul; Hopkins, Johns; Johnson, Robert Wood; Juilliard, Augustus D.; Kauffman, Ewing M.; Kellogg, W.K.; Kettering, Charles; Kluge, John W.; Kresge, S.S.; Kress, S.H.; Lasker, Albert; Lasker, Mary; Lehman, Adele Lewisohn; Lehman, Robert; Lenox, James; Lewis, Jerry; Libbey, Edward Drummond; Lick, James; Lilly, Eli; Loeb, James; Lowell, Josephine; MacArthur, John D.; McKay, Clarence Hungerford; McLoughlin, John; Mellon, Andrew; Mellon, Paul; Millbank, Jeremiah; Morgan, John "Jack" Pierpont; Morgan, J.P.; Mott, C. S.; Newhouse, S.I.; Peabody, George; Penney, J.C.; Perkins, Thomas; Pew, Joseph N., Jr.; Pforzheimer, Carl H.; Pratt, Charles; Pratt, Enoch; Presser, Theodore; Pritzker, A. N.; Richardson, Sid; Robert, Christopher Rhinelander; Rockefeller, Abby Aldrich; Rockefeller, David; Rockefeller, John D.; Rockefeller, Laurance; Rogers, Grace Rainey; Rosenwald, Julius; Ryerson, Martin Antoine; Sackler, Arthur M.; Sage, Mrs. Russell; Schiff, Jacob; Sloan, Alfred P., Jr.; Smith, Gerrit; Smith, Sophia; Stoeckel, Carl; Straus, Nathan; Tappan, Arthur; Templeton, Sir John; Thayer, Nathaniel; Tilden, Samuel Jones; Toussaint, Pierre; Vanderbilt, Cornelius; Van Rensselaer, Stephen; Vaux, Roberts; Walker, Sarah Breedlove; Walker, Thomas Barlow; Wallace, Lila Acheson; Warburg, Edward M. M.; Weinberg, Harry; Weisman, Frederick R.; Whitney, Gertrude Vanderbilt

Philosophy Abbot, Francis; Adler, Mortimer J.; Arendt, Hannah; Barrett, William; Bowne, Boden Parker; Brightman, Edgar Sheffield; Callahan, Daniel; Caplan, Arthur L.; Carnap, Rudolf; Carus, Paul; Cavell, Stanley; Chisholm, Roderick; Church, Alonzo; Cohen, Morris R.; Creighton, James Edwin; Davidson, Donald; Dennett, Daniel; Dewey, John; Edman, Irwin; Emerson, Ralph Waldo; Fodor, Jerry A.; Fromm, Erich; Gibbard, Allan; Goodman, Nelson; Hall, Stanley; Harris, William Torrey; Hempel, Carl; Hickok, Laurens Perseus; Hocking, William Ernest; Hook, Sidney; Howison, George Holmes; James, Henry, Sr.; James, William; Jeffrey, Richard; Johnson, Alexander Bryan; Kripke, Saul; Kuhn, Thomas; Langer, Susanne; Levi, Isaac; Lewis, C.I.; Lewis, David K.; Lovejoy, Arthur O.; Malcolm, Norman; Marcuse, Herbert; McCosh, James; Mead, George Herbert; Montague, William Pepperell; Montgomery, Edmund Duncan; Nagel, Ernest; Nagel, Thomas; Niebuhr, Reinhold; Nozick, Robert; Palmer, George Herbert; Peirce, Charles Sanders; Perry, Ralph Barton; Plantinga, Alvin C.; Porter, Noah; Putnam, Hilary; Quine, Willard V.; Rand, Ayn; Rawls, John; Reichenbach, Hans; Ripley, George; Rorty, Richard; Royce, Josiah; Santayana, George; Schurman, Jacob; Searle, John R.; Sellars, Wilfrid; Simon, Yves; Suppes, Patrick; Tappan, Henry; Tarski, Alfred; Taylor, John; Tillich, Paul; Vlastos, Gregory; Voegelin, Eric; Watts, Alan; West, Cornel; Woodbridge, F.J.E.; Wright, Chauncey

Photography Abbott, Berenice; Adams, Ansel; Adams, Marian Hooper; Arbus, Diane; Avedon, Richard;

Bourke-White, Margaret; Brady, Mathew; Brodovitch, Alexey; Callahan, Harry; Cunningham, Imogen; Curtis, Edward; Day, Fred Holland; De Carava, Roy; Draper, John William; Duncan, David Douglas; Eakins, Thomas; Eastman, George; Eisenstaedt, Alfred; Evans, Walker; Fairchild, Sherman; Felling, "Weegee"; Frank, Robert; Friedlander, Lee; Gardner, Alexander; Goddard, George William; Hare, Jimmy; Hawes, Josiah Johnson; Heinecken, Robert; Hicks, Wilson; Hine, Lewis; Jackson, William Henry; Johnson, Martin; Johnson, Osa; Kasebier, Gertrude; Kertész, André; Lange, Dorothea; Levitt, Helen; Man Ray; Mees, Charles Edward Kenneth; Meserve, Frederick Hill; Mili, Gjon; Model, Lisette; Moholy-Nagy, Laszlo; Morris, Wright Marion; Muybridge, Eadweard; Newhall, Beaumont; Newhall, Nancy; Nutting, Wallace; O'Sullivan, Timothy H.; Outerbridge, Paul, Jr.; Parks, Gordon A.; Porter, Eliot; Porter, Gene Stratton; Riis, Jacob; Shahn, Ben; Sheeler, Charles; Siskind, Aaron; Smith, W. Eugene; Southworth, Albert Sands; Steichen, Edward; Stieglitz, Alfred; Strand, Paul; Stryker, Roy Emerson; Szarkowski, John; Van Deren, Coke; VanDerZee, James; Van Dyke, Willard Ames; Van Vechten, Carl; Wagstaff, Sam J.; Watkins, Carleton E.; Weston, Edward; White, Clarence Hudson; White, Minor; Winogrand, Garry

Physics Adler, Stephen L.; Alvarez, Luis W.; Anderson, Carl D.; Anderson, Philip W.; Atanasoff, John V.; Bardeen, John; Bekesy, Georg von; Bennett, Willard Harrison; Bergmann, Peter G.; Bethe, Hans A.; Bitter, Francis; Bjorken, James E.; Blewett, John P.; Bloch, Felix; Bloembergen, Nicolaas; Brattain, Walter H.; Breit, Gregory; Bridgman, Percy W.; Briggs, Lyman; Brillouin, Leon N.; Chamberlain, Owen; Chandrasekhar, Subrahmanyan; Child, C.D.; Chu, Steven; Coblentz, W.W.; Cohen, Carolyn; Compton, Arthur H.; Condon, E.U.; Cooper, Leon N.; Cormack, Allan MacLeod; Courant, Ernest D.; Cronin, James W.; Dalgarno, Alexander; Damadian, Raymond; Davisson, Clinton J.; Dawson, John M.; Debye, Peter; Dehmelt, Hans G.; Dempster, A.J.; Dicke, Robert H.; Donnelly, Russell J.; Dryden, Hugh; Duane, William; Einstein, Albert; Fairbank, William M., Sr.; Feenberg, Eugene; Fermi, Enrico; Feshbach, Herman; Feynman, Richard; Fitch, Val L.; Fowler, William Alfred; Friedman, Jerome I.; Fritzshe, Hellmut; Furth, Harold P.; Gamow, George; Gell-Mann, Murray; Giacconi, Riccardo; Giaevar, Ivar; Gibbs, J. Willard; Glaser, Donald A.; Glashow, Sheldon L.; Goddard, Robert; Goeppert-Mayer, Maria; Goldhaber, Maurice; Gossard, Arthur C.; Gould, Gordon; Greenstein, Jesse Leonard; Hall, Edwin H.; Hamann, Donald R.; Hansch, Theodor W.; Henley, Ernest M.; Henry, Joseph; Herb, Raymond G.; Herring, Conyers; Hillier, James; Hofstadter, Robert; Hughes, Vernon W.; Hulse, Russell A.; Jastrow, Robert; Kadanoff, Leo P.; Kendall, Henry W.; Kinoshita, Toichiro; Kip, Arthur F.; Kirkpatrick, Paul H.; Kittel, Charles; Kleppner, Daniel; Kohn, Walter; Korff, Serge A.; Kruskal, Martin David; Kusch,

Polykarp; Lamb, Willis E., Jr.; Laporte, Otto; Lauritsen, Charles C.; Lawrence, Ernest O.; LeConte, John; Lederman, Leon M.; Lee, David M.; Lee, Tsung Dao; Lewis, Gilbert N.; Lin, Chia Chiao; Lindsay, Robert Bruce; Lineberger, William C.; Lipscomb, William; Livingston, M. Stanley; Loeb, Leonard B.; London, Fritz; Lovins, Amory; Lyman, Theodore; Maiman, Theodore; Margenau, Henry; Marshak, Robert E.; Mason, Warren P.; Matthias, Bernd T.; Mauchly, John William; McMillan, Edwin; McNair, Ronald E.; Menzel, Donald Howard; Mermin, N. David; Michelson, Albert A.; Millikan, Clark; Millikan, Robert A.; Morley, Edward Williams; Nelson, Jerry Earl; Nichols, Ernest F.; Nier, Alfred O.C.; Oppenheimer, J. Robert; Overhauser, Albert W.; Panofsky, Wolfgang K.H.; Penzias, Arno; Phillips, James C.; Pickering, Edward Charles; Pickering, William Henry; Post, Richard F.; Pound, Robert V.; Priestley, Joseph; Primakoff, Henry; Pupin, Michael; Purcell, Edward M.; Rabi, I.I.; Rainwater, James; Ramsey, Norman F., Jr.; Richter, Burton; Rood, Ogden Nicholas; Rose, Albert; Rowland, Henry Augustus; Schawlow, Arthur L.; Schiff, Leonard I.; Schrieffer, J. Robert; Schwartz, Melvin; Schwinger, Julian S.; Segre, Emilio; Shockley, William B.; Shull, Clifford G.; Slater, John C.; Smoot, George Fitzgerald, III; Snyder, Hartland S.; Spitzer, Lyman, Jr.; Steinberger, Jack; Stern, Otto; Stix, Thomas H.; Stormer, Horst L.; Stratton, Samuel; Street, J. C.; Szilard, Leo; Taylor, Barry N.; Teller, Edward; Ting, Samuel Chao Chung; Townes, Charles H.; Van Allen, James; Van de Graaff, Robert J.; Van Vleck, John H.; Volwiler, Ernest H.; Wang, An; Wannier, Gregory H.; Waterman, Alan; Webb, William Snyder; Weinberg, Steven; Weisskopf, Victor F.; Wigner, Eugene P.; Wilczek, Frank A.; Wilson, Kenneth G.; Wilson, Richard; Wilson, Robert R.; Wilson, Robert W.; Wood, Robert W.; Wu, Chien-Shiung; Yalow, Rosalyn; Yang, Chen Ning; Zare, Richard N.; Zener, Clarence; Zworykin, Vladimir

Physiology See MEDICINE.

Pioneer Settlements See under EXPLORATION AND PIONEER SETTLEMENTS.

Political Science Alexander, Robert J.; Almond, Gabriel; Arendt, Hannah; Bentley, Arthur Fisher; Bloom, Allan David; Brzezinski, Zbiniew; Burgess, John William; Carter, Gwendolyn Margaret; Coleman, James S.; Converse, Philip E.; Corey, Lewis; Corwin, Edward Samuel; Dahl, Robert A.; Eichelberger, Clark M.; Fenno, Richard R., Jr.; Friedrich, Carl J.; Goodnow, Frank Johnson; Gronlund, Laurence; Hamilton, Alexander; Harris, Lou; Herring, E. Pendleton; Hough, Jerry F.; Johnson, John J.; Key, Valdimer Orlando, Jr.; Kirkpatrick, Jeanne; Kissinger, Henry; Lasswell, Harold D.; Lattimore, Owen; Lieber, Francis; Linz, Juan J.; Lippman, Walter; Lowell, A. Lawrence; Macmahon, Arthur W.; Marcuse, Herbert; Merriam, Charles E., Jr.; Moley, Raymond; Morgenthau, Hans J.; Neumann, Franz Leopold; Ogg,

OCCUPATIONAL INDEX

Political Science (*cont.*)

Frederic; Ranney, Austin; Riker, William H.; Rossiter, Clinton III; Schattsschneider, E. E.; Seckler-Hudson, Catheryn; Shalala, Donna; Silvert, Kalman H.; Strauss, Leo; Thompson, Victor A.; Truman, David B.; Tucker, Robert; Tufte, Edward R.; White, Leonard D.; Wildavsky, Aaron B.; Will, George; Willoughby, Westel Woodbury; Wilson, James; Wood, Bryce; Woolsey, Theodore Dwight; Young, M. Crawford

Politics See GOVERNMENT, NATIONAL; GOVERNMENT, STATE AND LOCAL; PRESIDENTS, VICE PRESIDENTS, and FIRST LADIES, U.S.

Presidents, Vice Presidents, and First Ladies, U.S. Adams, Abigail; Adams, John; Adams, John Quincy; Adams, Louisa; Agnew, Spiro T.; Arthur, Chester A.; Barkley, Alben W.; Breckinridge, John; Buchanan, James; Burr, Aaron; Bush, Barbara; Bush, George; Calhoun, John C.; Carter, Jimmy; Carter, Rosalynn; Cleveland, Frances; Cleveland, Grover; Clinton, Bill; Clinton, George; Clinton, Hilary Rodham; Colfax, Schuyler; Coolidge, Calvin; Coolidge, Grace; Curtis, Charles; Dallas, George; Dawes, Charles G.; Eisenhower, Dwight D.; Eisenhower, Mamie; Fairbanks, Charles; Fillmore, Abigail; Fillmore, Millard; Ford, Betty; Ford, Gerald R.; Garfield, James A.; Garfield, Lucretia; Garner, John Nance; Gerry, Elbridge; Gore, Al, Jr.; Grant, Julia; Grant, Ulysses S.; Hamlin, Hannibal; Harding, Florence; Harding, Warren G.; Harrison, Anna; Harrison, Benjamin; Harrison, Caroline; Harrison, William Henry; Hayes, Lucy; Hayes, Rutherford B.; Hendricks, Thomas A.; Hobart, Garret A.; Hoover, Herbert; Hoover, Lou; Humphrey, Hubert H.; Jackson, Andrew; Jackson, Rachel Donelson Robards; Jefferson, Martha; Jefferson, Thomas; Johnson, Andrew; Johnson, Eliza; Johnson, Lady Bird; Johnson, Lyndon Baines; Kennedy, John F.; King, William R.D.; Lincoln, Abraham; Lincoln, Mary; Madison, Dolley; Madison, James; Marshall, Thomas R.; McKinley, Ida; McKinley, William; Mondale, Walter F.; Monroe, Elizabeth; Monroe, James; Morton, Levi P.; Nixon, Pat; Nixon, Richard; Onassis, Jacqueline Kennedy "Jackie"; Pierce, Franklin; Pierce, Jane; Polk, James Knox; Polk, Sarah; Quayle, Dan; Reagan, Nancy; Reagan, Ronald; Rockefeller, Nelson A.; Roosevelt, Edith; Roosevelt, Eleanor; Roosevelt, Franklin Delano; Roosevelt, Theodore; Sherman, James S.; Stevenson, Adlai E.; Taft, Helen; Taft, William Howard; Taylor, Margaret; Taylor, Zachary; Tompkins, Daniel D.; Truman, Bess; Truman, Harry S.; Tyler, John; Tyler, Julia; Tyler, Letitia; Van Buren, Hannah; Van Buren, Martin; Wallace, Henry A.; Washington, George; Washington, Martha Custis; Wheeler, William; Wilson, Edith; Wilson, Ellen; Wilson, Henry; Wilson, Woodrow

Psychiatry Ackerman, Nathan W.; Barchas, Jack D.; Beck, Aaron T.; Bender, Lauretta; Benedek, Therese; Berne, Eric; Bettelheim, Bruno; Brill, Abraham A.; Bruch;, Hilde; Cantwell, Dennis Patrick; Carpenter,

William T.; Clayton, Paula Jean; Cleckley, Hervey Milton; Cloninger, Claude Robert; Coles, Robert Martin; Coyle, Joseph T.; Dunbar, Helen Flanders; Earls, Felton James; Erickson, Milton H.; Erikson, Erik H.; Fink, Max; Frank, Jerome David; Frankl, Viktor; Freedman, Daniel X.; Fromm, Erich; Fromm-Reichmann, Frieda; Grof, Stanislav; Guze, Samuel Barry; Hamburg, David Alan; Hartmann, Heinz; Heninger, George Robert; Horney, Karen; Jelliffe, Smith Ely; Judd, Lewis Lund; Kaufman, Barry Neil; Kety, Seymour Solomon; Klein, Donald Franklin; Klerman, Gerald Lawrence; Kuebler-Ross, Elisabeth; Kupfer, David J.; Leone, Mark P.; Levine, Lena; Lifton, Robert Jay; Lowen, Alexander; Mahler, Margaret Schoenberger; Mandell, Arnold; Masters, William; May, Rollo; McHugh, Paul R.; Menninger, Charles Frederick; Menninger, Karl; Menninger, William Claire; Meyer, Adolph; Miller, Jean Baker; Moody, Raymond; Moreno, Jacob L.; Pardes, Herbert; Peck, M. Scott; Perls, Fritz; Pert, Candace B.; Poussaint, Alvin; Rapoport, Judith Livant; Reich, Wilhelm; Reik, Theodor; Richmond, Julius Benjamin; Robins, Eli; Rogers, Carl; Roheim, Geza; Romano, John; Sackler, Arthur M.; Satir, Virginia; Schafer, Roy; Searles, Harold F.; Snyder, Solomon; Spock, Benjamin; Sullivan, Harry Stack; Szasz, Thomas; Thompson, Clara; Vaillant, George; Winokur, George; Wolpe, Joseph; Yalom, Irvin D.

Psychology Allport, Gordon; Anastasi, Anne; Angell, James; Argyris, Chris; Baltes, Paul B.; Bandura, Albert; Bayley, Nancy; Beers, Clifford; Bennis, Warren; Bradshaw, John; Brothers, Joyce; Bruner, Jerome S.; Buhler, Charlotte; Calkins, Mary Whiton; Chin, Robert; Clark, Kenneth; Clark, Mamie Phipps; Dewey, John; Dyer, Wayne W.; Ellis, Albert; Exner, John E.; Festinger, Leon; Fiedler, Fred E.; Fodor, Jerry A.; Friday, Nancy; Gesell, Arnold; Gilligan, Carol; Haley, Jay; Hall, Stanley; Harlow, Harry; Herzberg, Fred; Hoffman, Lynn; Holt, Edwin Bissell; Hull, Clark L.; James, William; Jensen, Arthur R.; Johnson, Virginia; Jones, Mary Cover; Kagan, Jerome; Kahn, Robert L.; Kandel, Eric Richard; Katz, Daniel; Kegan, Robert G.; Kirkbride, Thomas Story; Koffka, Kurt; Kohlberg, Lawrence; Kohler, Wolfgang; Kopp, Sheldon; Ladd-Franklin, Christine; Lashley, Karl S.; Levine, Stephen; Levinson, Daniel Jacob; Lewin, Kurt; Lifton, Robert Jay; Likert, Rensis; Loevinger, Jane; Martin, Lillien Jane; Maslow, Abraham; Masters, William; Mayo, Elton; McClelland, David C.; Mead, George Herbert; Milgram, Stanley; Murphy, Gardner; Murphy, Lois Barclay; Murray, Henry A.; Pribram, Karl; Progoff, Ira; Reik, Theodor; Rhine, Joseph; Rodin, Judith; Schafer, Roy; Schein, Edgar H.; Sheehy, Gail; Singer, June Kurlander; Skinner, B.F.; Spence, Janet; Taylor, Frederick Winslow; Terman, Lewis; Thorndike, Edward L.; Thurstone, Louis L.; Titchener, Edward Bradford; Tolman, Edward Chace; Velikovsky, Immanuel; Washburn, Margaret Floy; Watson, John B.; Wechsler, David; Welwood, John; Wertheimer, Max; Whiting, John W.M.; Woodworth, Robert S.; Yerkes, Robert

Publishing, Editing and Printing Abbott, Lyman; Allen, Frederick Lewis; Annenberg, Walter; Appleton, Daniel; Armstrong, Hamilton Fish; Bancroft, Hubert Howe; Beach, Moses Yale; Beach, Sylvia Woodbridge; Beadle, Erastus; Beard, "Uncle Dan"; Berlitz, Charles; Blackwell, Betty Talbot; Blumenthal, Joseph; Bok, Edward William; Bonner, Robert; Booth, George G.; Bowker, Richard Rogers; Bradford, William; Bradley, Will H.; Bradwell, Myra; Braithewaite, William Stanley; Brand, Stewart; Brannan, Samuel; Brown, Helen Gurley; Bryant, William Cullen; Buckley, William F., Jr.; Burke, John J.; Cahan, Abraham; Canby, Henry Seidel; Canfield, Cass; Cantwell, Robert; Carey, Henry; Carey, Mathew; Carter, John Mack; Cerf, Bennett; Chappell, Warren; Chase, Edna Woolman; Childs, George William; Chwast, Seymour; Cleland, Thomas Maitland; Conroy, Jack; Cousins, Norman; Cox, James Middleton; Croly, Herbert David; Crosby, Caresse; Crosby, Harry; Crowninshield, Frank; Currier, Nathaniel; Curtis, Cyrus Herman K.; Daniels, Josephus; Darley, Felix; Day, Stephen; Dees, Morris, Jr.; DeGraff, Robert Fair; Dell, Floyd; del Rey, Lester; De Vinne, Theodore Low; DeVries, Peter; Dille, John Flint; Ditson, Oliver; Dodge, Mary Elizabeth; Donovan, Hedley; Doubleday, Frank Nelson; Dwiggins, William Addison; Eastman, Max; Edes, Benjamin; England, John; Evans, Frederick William; Field, Marshall III; Fields, James Thomas; Fischer, Carl; Forbes, Malcolm; Foster, John; Frankfurter, Alfred; Franklin, Benjamin; Fuller, Margaret; Gannett, Frank Ernest; Garrison, William Lloyd; Gibson, Charles Dana; Gilder, Richard Watson; Gillis, James M.; Glass, Carter; Goddard, Sarah; Godey, Louis Antoine; Godkin, Edwin Lawrence; Gold, Michael; Goodrich, Samuel Griswold; Goudy, Frederic William; Graham, Katharine; Greeley, Horace; Green, Samuel; Gregg, John Robert; Griswold, Rufus Wilmot; Grosvenor, Gilbert; Guinzburg, Alfred; Haines, Helen Elizabeth; Haldeman-Julius, Emanuel; Hale, Sarah Josepha; Hall, James; Hapgood, Norman; Harcourt, Alfred; Harper, Fletcher; Harper, James; Harris, Benjamin; Harris, T. George; Hearst, William Randolph; Hecker, Isaac; Hefner, Hugh; Heilprin, Michael; Heuser, Herman J.; Hines, Duncan; Hoard, William Dempster; Hobby, William Pettus; Hodge, Charles; Hoe, Richard March; Hoe, Robert; Holland, Josiah Gilbert; Holt, Henry; Houghton, Henry Oscar; Howells, William Dean; Hutton, Laurence; Ives, James; Jarves, James Jackson; Johnson, John Harold; Johnson, Robert Underwood; Jones, Thomas P.; Jovanovich, William; Kellogg, Paul Underwood; Kenedy, P. J.; Keppler, Joseph; Kiplinger, Willard Monroe; Knopf, Alfred; Knowland, William F.; Kreymborg, Alfred; Kristol, Irving; LaFarge, John; Lane, Gertrude Battles; Lanston, Tolbert; Laughlin, James; Lea, Henry Charles; Leeser, Isaac; Leyendecker, J.C.; Leypoldt, Frederic; Liberman, Alex; Lieber, Francis; Lipman, Jean; Lippincott, Joshua; Liveright, Horace; Locke, David Rose; Lorimer, George Horace; Loudon, Samuel; Lovejoy, Elijah; Lowell, James Russell; Luce, Henry R.; Lundy, Benjamin; Macdonald, Dwight; MacFadden, Bernarr; MacVeagh, Lincoln; Martin, Lowell; Marty, Martin; Maynard, Robert C.; McClure, Samuel S.; McClurg, Alexander Caldwell; McCord, David James; McCormick, Robert Rutherford; Medill, Joseph; Melcher, Frederic Gershom; Mencken, H. L.; Meredith, Scott; Merganthaler, Ottmar; Mich, Daniel Danforth; Mitchell, John, Jr.; Monroe, Harriet; Motley, Arthur H.; Murray, John Courtney; Nast, Conde; Newhouse, S.I.; Ng Poon, Chew; Niles, Thomas; Noah, Mordecai Manuel; Nordstrom, Ursula; Ochs, Adolph Simon; O'Reilly, John Boyle; Osgood, James Ripley; Oursler, Fulton; Page, Walter Hines; Paine, Thomas; Parks, William; Patterson, Joseph Medill; Peabody, Elizabeth Palmer; Pendleton, John B.; Perkins, Maxwell; Plimpton, George Arthur; Pohl, Frederik; Porter, Rufus; Presser, Theodore; Preuss, Arthur; Pulitzer, Joseph; Putnam, George Haven; Putnam, George Palmer; Reichl, Ernest; Rider, Fremont; Ripley, George; Rivington, James; Rogers, Bruce; Rollins, Carl Purington; Ross, Harold; Royall, Anne; Rudge, William Edwin; Schirmer, Gustav; Schuster, Max; Scribner, Charles; Scripps, E. W.; Shawn, William; Sheed, Frank; Sholes, Christopher; Silverman, Sime; Simon, Richard; Snow, Carmel White; Sonnenschein, Rosa; Spink, J. G.; Stockton, Frank; Stone, I. F.; Stratemeyer, Edward L.; Szold, Henrietta; Thomas, Isaiah; Ticknor, William Davis; Tourgee, Albion; Updike, Daniel Berkeley; Van Doren, Carl; Van Doren, Irita; Villard, Henry; Villard, Oswald Garrison; Wallace, De Witt; Wallace, Lila Acheson; Ward, Maisie; Warde, Frederic; White, E.B.; Whitney, John Hay; Wiley, Charles; Williams, Michael; Wilson, Halsey William; Zahniser, Howard Clinton; Zenger, John Peter

Religion Abbot, Francis; Abernathy, Ralph D.; Adler, Samuel; Alder, Cyrus; Alexander, Archibald; Allen, Richard; Arbez, Edward S. S.; Asbury, Francis; Bachman, John; Backus, Isaac; Bacon, Leonard; Badeau, John S.; Badin, Stephen T.; Baker, George; Ballou, Adin; Ballou, Hosea; Baraga, Frederic; Baron, Salo; Beecher, Henry Ward; Beecher, Lyman; Beissel, John Conrad; Belkin, Samuel; Bellamy, Joseph; Benson, Ezra Taft; Bentley, William; Berkeley, Sir William; Berkowitz, Henry; Bernardin, Joseph L.; Berrigan, Daniel J.; Berrigan, Philip F.; Bingham, Hiram; Bishop, William; Black Elk; Blackwell, Antoinette Louisa Brown; Blake, Eugene Carson; Bliss, Daniel; Bliss, Howard Sweetser; Bowne, Boden Parker; Brainerd, David; Brannan, Samuel; Brewster, William; Briggs, Charles Augustus; Brodie, Fawn M.; Brooks, Phillips; Brown, Olympia; Brown, Raymond; Brown, William Adams; Brownson, Orestes; Buchman, Frank; Burke, John J.; Burns, Anthony; Bushnell, Horace; Cabrini, Frances Xavier; Callimachos, Panos Demetrios; Campbell, Alexander; Carroll, John; Cartwright, Peter; Channing, William Ellery; Chauncy, Charles; Chavis, Benjamin, Jr.; Clarke, James Freeman; Clarke, Mary Francis; Cody, John; Coffin, Henry Sloane; Coffin, William Sloane, Jr.; Cohen, Gerson D.; Colman, Benjamin; Cone,

OCCUPATIONAL INDEX

Religion (*cont.*)

James Hal; Connelly, Mother Cornelia; Conwell, Russell; Coppin, Fanny Marion Jackson; Corcoran, James; Corrigan, Michael; Cotton, John; Coughlin, Charles E.; Curran, Charles E.; Cushing, Richard J.; Cutler, Timothy; Dabrowski, Joseph; Daly, Mary; Damien, Father; Davenport, John; David, John Baptist; Davies, Samuel; Day, Dorothy; Delille, Henriette; De Smet, Pierre Jean; Dickenson, Mother Clare Joseph; Douglas, Lloyd C.; Dow, Lorenzo; Drexel, Mother Katharine Mary; Dubois, John; Dubourg, Louis William; Duchesne, Rose Philippine; Duffy, Francis P.; Dwight, Timothy; Dyer, Mary; Eddy, Mary Baker; Edwards, Jonathan; Einhorn, David; Eliade, Mircea; Eliot, John; Elliot, Walter; Ellis, John Tracy; England, John; Evans, Frederick William; Falwell, Jerry; Farrakhan, Louis; Feinstein, Moshe; Felsenthal, Bernhard; Fillmore, Charles; Finkelstein, Louis; Finley, Robert; Finney, Charles Grandison; Fiske, Fidelia; Flaget, Benedict; Flanagan, Edward; Flores, Patricio; Fosdick, Henry Emerson; Fox, Matthew; Franklin, C.L.; Frelinghuysen, Theodorus Jacobus; Friedlaender, Israel; Frothingham, Octavius Brooks; Gates, Frederick T.; Gaudin, Juliet; Gay, Ebenezer; Gibbons, James; Gillis, James M.; Ginzberg, Louis; Gladden, Washington; Glueck, Nelson; Goodrich, Chauncey Allen; Goodspeed, Edgar Johnson; Gordis, Robert; Gordon, George Angier; Gottheil, Richard James Horatio; Gottschalk, Alfred; Graham, Billy; Gray, William H. III; Greeley, Andrew M.; Green, Arthur; Greenberg, Irving; Guilday, Peter; Hale, Edward Everett; Hanna, Edward; Healy, James Augustine; Healy, Patrick F.; Hecker, Isaac; Hedge, Frederic Henry; Heller, Maximilian; Henry Roe Cloud; Henson, Josiah; Hesburgh, Theodore; Heschel, Abraham Joshua; Heuser, Herman J.; Hickok, Laurens Perseus; Higginson, Thomas Wentworth; Hillenbrand, Reynold; Himes, Joshua Vaughan; Hirsch, Emil Gustav; Hodge, Charles; Hodur, Francis; Holmes, John Haynes; Holyoke, Samuel; Hooker, Thomas; Hopkins, Mark; Hopkins, Samuel; House, John Henry; Hubbard, L. Ron; Hughes, John; Huntington, Frederic Dan; Hutchinson, Anne; Ireland, John; Jackson, Jesse; James, Henry, Sr.; Jastrow, Marcus; Jogues, Isaac; Johnson, Samuel; Jones, Rufus; Joseph, Jacob; Joseph, Mother; Judson, Adoniram; Kahane, Meir; Kaplan, Mordecai; Keane, John; Keller, James; Kelley, Francis Clement; Kenkel, Frederick P.; Kenrick, Francis; Kerby, William; Kidder, Daniel P.; King, Henry Churchill; King, Martin Luther, Jr.; King, Thomas Starr; Kino, Eusebio Francisco; Kneeland, Abner; Kohler, Kaufmann; Kohut, Alexander; Kohut, George Alexander; Krauskopf, Joseph; Krauth, Charles Porterfield; Krol, John; LaFarge, John; Lamm, Norman; Lathrop, Rose Hawthorne; Laubach, Frank; Lee, Ann; Lee, Jason; Leeser, Isaac; Lichtenstein, Tehilla; Lieberman, Saul; Liebman, Joshua Loth; Ligutti, Luigi; Lindsley, Philip; Lord, Daniel A.; Lowery, Joseph E.; Lowrie, Walter; Lunn, George Richard; Machen, John Gresham; Macintosh, Douglas Clyde; Magnes, Judah Leon; Makemie, Francis;

Marquette, Jacques; Marty, Martin; Mather, Cotton; Mather, Increase; Mather, Richard; Maurin, Peter; Mayhew, Jonathan; Mayhew, Thomas; Mazzuchelli, Samuel; McCloskey, James; McGivney, Michael; McMaster, James A.; McNicholas, John T.; McPherson, Aimee Semple; McQuaid, Bernard; Meilziner, Moses; Mendes, Henry Pereira; Merton, Thomas; Messmer, Sebastian; Metz, Christian; Meyer, Albert; Michel, Virgil; Miller, Samuel; Miller, William; Moody, Dwight Lyman; Mooney, Edward; Moore, Clement; Morais, Sabato; Morse, Jedidiah; Mott, John Raleigh; Mott, Lucretia Coffin; Muhammad, Elijah; Muhlenberg, Frederick Augustus; Muhlenberg, Henry Melchior; Muhlenberg, John Peter Gabriel; Mundelein, George; Murray, John; Murray, John Courtney; Muste, A.J.; Nerinckx, Charles; Neuhaus, Richard John; Neumann, John; Ng Poon, Chew; Niebuhr, H. Richard; Niebuhr, Reinhold; Nieuwland, Julius Arthur; Nock, Arthur Darby; Noll, John; Norton, Andrew; Nott, Eliphalet; Novak, Michal; Noyes, John Humphrey; Nutting, Wallace; Occom, Samson; O'Connell, William; O'Connor, John J.; O'Hara, Edwin; Ong, Walter; Oxnam, Garfield Bromley; Palmer, Phoebe Worrall; Parker, Samuel; Parker, Theodore; Parkhurst, Charles Henry; Peabody, Francis Greenwood; Peabody, Lucy Whitehead; Peale, Norman Vincent; Pelikan, Jaroslav; Penn, William; Peyton, Patrick; Philipson, David; Pinto, Isaac; Plaskow, Judith; Polk, Leonidas; Powell, Adam Clayton, Jr.; Powell, Adam Clayton, Sr.; Preuss, Arthur; Price, Thomas Frederick; Priesand, Sally Jane; Priestley, Joseph; Purcell, John; Raphall, Morris Jacob; Rapp, George; Rauschenbush, Walter; Revel, Bernard; Revels, Hiram Rhodes; Richard, Gabriel; Richards, Bob; Riggs, Elias; Riley, William Bell; Roberts, Oral; Robertson, Pat; Robinson, Edward; Rogers, John; Rogers, Mary Josephine; Rudd, Daniel; Rummell, Joseph; Russell, Charles Taze; Russell, Mother Mary Baptist; Ryan, John Augustine; Sachar, Abram L.; Schaff, Philip; Schechter, Solomon; Schereschewsky, Samuel; Schindler, Alexander M.; Schmucker, Samuel Simon; Schneerson or Schneersohn, Menachem Mendel; Schorsch, Ismar; Seixas, Gershom Mendes; Serra, Junipero; Seton, Elizabeth Ann; Shaw, Anna Howard; Shea, John Gilmary; Sheen, Fulton J.; Shehan, Lawrence; Shepard, Thomas; Silver, Abba Hillel; Slattery, John; Smith, Eli; Smith, Elias; Smith, Joseph; Smoholla; Soloveitchik, Joseph Ber; Sorin, Edward; Spalding, Catherine; Spalding, John; Spalding, Martin; Speer, Robert Elliott; Spellman, Francis; Sperry, Willard Learoyd; Stelze, Charles; Stiles, Ezra; Stoddard, Solomon; Stone, Barton Warren; Strong, Augustus Hopkins; Strong, Josiah; Stuart, John Leighton; Stuart, Moses; Sullivan, Leon; Sulzberger, Mayer; Sunday, Billy; Szold, Benjamin; Szold, Henrietta; Tanenbaum, Marc H.; Taylor, Edward; Taylor, Graham; Taylor, Nathaniel William; Tekakwitha, Blessed Kateri; Tennent, Gilbert; Tillich, Paul; Tolton, Augustine; Truth, Sojourner; Van Dyck, Cornelius; Van Dyke, Henry; Voorsanger, Jacob; Walsh, James A.; Ward, Joseph; Ward, Maisie; Ward, Nathaniel; Warde,

Mother Mary Francis Xavier; Watson, Charles Roger; Wattson, Lewis Thomas; Weems, Mason Locke; Weigel, Gustave A.; Whipple, Henry Benjamin; White, Andrew; White, Ellen Gould; Whitefield, George; Wigglesworth, Michael; Wilkinson, Jemima; Williams, John; Williams, Roger; Winthrop, John; Wise, Isaac Mayer; Wise, John; Wise, Stephen Samuel; Witherspoon, John; Woolman, John; Wovoka; Wright, John J.; Yorke, Peter; Young, Brigham; Zahm, John

Revolution, U.S. Adams, John; Adams, Samuel; Allen, Ethan; Arnold, Benedict; Attucks, Crispus; Bailey, Anna "Mother Bailey"; Barney, Joshua; Barron, James; Barry, John; Biddle, Nicholas; Bowdoin, James; Brant, Joseph; Bushnell, David; Carroll, Charles "of Carrolton"; Carroll, John; Clark, George Rogers; Colden, Cadwallader; Corbin, Margaret; Cornplanter, also known as John O'Bail; Dale, Richard; Decatur, Stephen; Derby, Elias Hasket; Dickinson, John; Duer, William; Du Ponceau, Peter Stephen; Ellery, William; Etheridge, Anna; Fries, John; Gadsden, Christopher; Gates, Horatio; Girty, Simon; Gratz, Barnard; Greene, Nathanael; Hale, Nathan; Hamilton, Alexander; Hampton, Wade; Hancock, John; Hanson, John; Harrison, Benjamin; Hawkins, Benjamin; Henry, Patrick; Herkimer, Nicholas; Hopkins, Esek; Hull, William; Humphreys, Joshua; Imlay, Gilbert; Izard, Ralph; Jefferson, Thomas; Jones, John Paul; Kalb, Johann; Kent, Jacob; Knox, Henry; Kosciusko, Thaddeus; Lafayette, Marie Joseph Paul Yves Roch Gibert du Motier; Laurance, John; Laurens, Henry; Ledyard, William; Lee, Charles; Lee, Henry; Lee, Richard Henry; Lincoln, Benjamin; Livingston, Peter van Brugh; Livingston, Philip; Livingston, William; Lynch, Charles; Marion, Francis; Marshall, John; McCauley, Mary Hays; McDougall, Alexander; McGillivray, Alexander; Mifflin, Thomas; Monroe, James; Montgomery, Richard; Moore, Alfred; Moore, James; Morgan, Daniel; Morgan, John; Morris, Robert; Moultrie, William; Muhlenberg, John Peter Gabriel; Murphy, Timothy; O'Brien, Jeremiah; O'Hara, James; Page, John; Paine, Thomas; Pendleton, Edmund; Pickens, Andrew; Pinckney, Thomas; Putnam, Israel; Randolph, Edmund; Reed, Joseph; Revere, Paul; Rittenhouse, David; Rodney, Caesar; Rush, Benjamin; Rutledge, Edward; Rutledge, John; Salomon, Haym; Saltonstall, Dudley; Sampson, Deborah; Schuyler, Philip John; Sevier, John; Shelby, Isaac; Sherman, Roger; Stark, John; St. Clair, Arthur; Steuben, Baron von; Stockton, Richard; Stoddert, Benjamin; Sullivan, James; Sullivan, John; Sumter, Thomas; Talmadge, Edwards; Taylor, John; Thomas, Isaiah; Thorndike, Israel; Tilghman, Tench; Trumbull, John; Trumbull, Jonathan (1710–1785); Trumbull, Jonathan (1740–1809); Truxtun, Thomas; Walker, Thomas; Warren, Joseph; Washington, George; Wayne, Anthony; Wilkinson, James; Willing, Thomas; Wilson, James; Witherspoon, John; Wythe, George

Social Reform and Political Activism Abbott, Grace; Abernathy, Ralph D.; Addams, Jane; Aguinaldo,

Emilio; al-Amin, Jamil Abdullah; Albizu Campos, Pedro; Alinsky, Saul; Allen, Florence Ellinwood; Ames, Jessie Daniel; Andrews, John Bertram; Andrews, Stephen; Anthony, Susan B.; Antin, Mary; Astor, Nancy, Viscountess; Augustus, John; Bailey, Gamaliel; Baker, Ella Josephine; Balch, Emily Greene; Baldwin, Roger; Ballou, Adin; Banks, Dennis; Barbosa, Jose Celso; Barney, Nora Stanton; Barton, Clara; Beard, Mary Ritter; Beecher, Henry Ward; Beers, Clifford; Bellanca, Dorothy; Belmont, Alva; Berger, Victor Louis; Bergh, Henry; Berkman, Alexander; Berrigan, Daniel J.; Berrigan, Philip F.; Bethune, Mary McLeod; Bickerdyke, "Mother"; Birney, James Gillespie; Blackwell, Antoinette Louisa Brown; Blair, Emily Jane Newell; Blatch, Harriet Eaton; Bloomer, Amelia; Bloor, Ella "Mother Bloor"; Bonaparte, Charles Joseph; Bond, Julian; Booth, Eva; Boudin, Leonard B.; Bowen, Louise deKoven; Brace, Charles Loring; Bradford, David; Bradwell, Myra; Breckinridge, Sophonisba Preston; Bremer, Edith Terry; Brisbane, Albert; Brown, Hallie Quinn; Brown, John; Brown, Moses; Brown, Olympia; Brown, William Wells; Burr, Aaron; Burritt, Elihu; Cabet, Etienne; Campbell, Helen Stuart; Carmichael, Stokely; Catt, Carrie Clinton; Chapin, Henry Dwight; Chaplin, Ralph Hosea; Charren, Peggy; Chavis, Benjamin, Jr.; Child, Lydia Maria; Chisholm, Shirley; Chomsky, Noam; Claflin, Tennessee Celeste; Clark, Grenville; Clark, Ramsey; Clay, Cassius Marcellus; Cleaver, Eldridge; Coffin, William Sloane, Jr.; Collier, John; Commoner, Barry; Comstock, Anthony; Cooper, Thomas; Coughlin, Charles E.; Coxey, Jacob; Crandall, Prudence; Creel, George; Cuffe, Paul; Cunningham, Kate Richards O'Hare; Curtis, George William; Davis, Angela; Davis, Katherine Bement; Day, Dorothy; Debs, Eugene V.; Dees, Morris, Jr.; Delany, Martin Robison; De Leon, Daniel; Dell, Floyd; Dellinger, David; Deloria, Vine, Jr.; Dennis, Eugene; Devine, Edward Thomas; Dickinson, Anna Elizabeth; Dix, Dorothea; Dock, Lavinia Lloyd; Donnelly, Ignatius; Dorr, Thomas; Douglass, Frederick; Dow, Neal; Dreier, Mary Elizabeth; Du Bois, W.E.B.; Duniway, Abigail Jane; Eastman, Joseph Bartlett; Edelman, Marion; Edge, Rosalie; Edwards, Harry; Evans, Frederick William; Evers, Charles; Farmer, James; Farrakhan, Louis; Flanagan, Edward; Flynn, Elizabeth Gurley; Fonda, Jane; Forten, James; Fortune, Timothy Thomas; Foster, William Z.; Fowle, Elida Baker Rumsey; Franklin, C.L.; Friedan, Betty; Fuller, Margaret; Furuseth, Andrew; Gardner, John; Garrison, William Lloyd; Garvey, Marcus; George, Henry; Gilman, Charlotte; Gilmer, Elizabeth Meriwether; Glueck, Eleanor Touroff; Gold, Ben; Gold, Michael; Goldman, Emma; Goldsmith, Grace Arabell; Goodman, Paul; Gordon, Anna Adams; Graham, Sylvester; Greenberg, Jack; Gregory, Dick; Grimke, Angelina Emily; Grimke, Sarah Moore; Grinnell, Josiah; Gronlund, Laurence; Hall, Gus; Hamilton, Alice; Harper, Frances Ellen Watkins; Havemeyer, Louisine Waldron; Hawes, Harriet Boyd; Hayden, Tom; Henson, Josiah; Herbst, Josephine; Herron, Carrie Rand; Hill, Joe; Hillquit,

OCCUPATIONAL INDEX

Social Reform and Political Activism (*cont.*)
Morris; Hine, Lewis; Hoffman, Abbie; Hoge, Mrs. A.H.; Holmes, John Haynes; Hooks, Benjamin; Howe, Irving; Howe, Julia Ward; Howe, Samuel Gridley; Hunter, Robert; Ingersoll, Robert; Innis, Roy; Jackson, Jesse; Jewett, William Cornell; Johnson, Hiram W.; Johnson, James Weldon; Johnson, William Eugene; Jones, Mary B. "Mother Jones"; Jones, Rufus; Jones, Samuel Milton; Jordan, Vernon, Jr.; Josey, E.J.; Kahane, Meir; Keller, Helen; Kelley, Abby; Kelley, Florence; Kellogg, Paul Underwood; Kenkel, Frederick P.; Kennedy, Flo; Kevorkian, Jack; Kilgore, Carrie; King, Martin Luther, Jr.; Kohut, Rebekah Bettelheim; Krim, Mathilde; Kuhn, Maggie; Kunstler, William M.; Ladd, William; LaFarge, John; La Farge, Oliver; La Follette, Belle Case; Lansky, Aaron; Lappe, Frances Moore; Lathrop, Julia Clifford; Lawes, Lewis Edward; Lease, Mary Elizabeth; Lindsey, Benjamin Barr; Livermore, Mary Ashton Rice; Lloyd, Henry Demarest; Lockwood, Belva; Love, Alfred Henry; Lovejoy, Elijah; Lovejoy, Esther Pohl; Lovejoy, Owen; Lowery, Joseph E.; Lubin, David; Luhan, Mabel Dodge; Lundy, Benjamin; Lunn, George Richard; Luther, Seth; MacDonald, Peter; MacKinnon, Catharine A.; MacLaine, Shirley; Mahler, Herbert; Malcolm X; Marshall, Louis; Marshall, Thurgood; Maurin, Peter; McCloskey, James; McCord, David James; McDowell, Mary Eliza; McKissick, Floyd B.; Means, Russell; Meredith, James; Miller, Kelly; Millett, Kate; Minor, Robert; Montezuma, Carlos; Mooney, Thomas; Morris, Esther Hobart McQuigg Slack; Moskowitz, Belle Lindner; Most, Johann Joseph; Mott, Lucretia Coffin; Mourning Dove; Muste, A.J.; Nader, Ralph; Nation, Carry; Nichols, Thomas Low; Norton, Eleanor Holmes; Noyes, John Humphrey; O'Hair, Madlyn Murray; O'Reilly, Leonora; O'Sullivan, Mary Kenney; Ovington, Mary White; Owen, Robert; Paine, Thomas; Palmer, Phoebe Worrall; Park, Maud Wood; Parker, Theodore; Parkhurst, Charles Henry; Parks, Rosa; Parsons, Albert Richard; Paul, Alice; Peltier, Leonard; Perkins, Frances; Perry, Pettis; Phillips, Wendell; Podlaski, Ron; Pomeroy, Marcus Mills; Preston, Ann; Prosser, Gabriel; Randolph, A. Philip; Rankin, Jeanette; Rantoul, Robert; Redpath, James; Reed, John; Remond, Sarah Parker; Richmond, Mary Ellen; Rifkin, Jeremy; Riis, Jacob; Ripley, George; Robeson, Paul; Robins, Margaret Dreier; Rubin, Jerry; Rubinow, Isaac Max; Ruffin, George L.; Ruffin, Josephine St. Pierre; Russell, Charles Edward; Rustin, Bayard; Ryan, John Augustine; Sacco, Nicola; Said, Edward W.; Sanders, George Nicholas; Sanger, Margaret; Schneiderman, Rose; Scudder, Vida; Seale, Bobby; Shaw, Anna Howard; Shays, Daniel; Simkhovitch, Mary; Simone, Nina; Sinclair, Upton, Jr.; Sliwa, Curtis; Smeal, Eleanor; Smedley, Agnes; Smith, Gerrit; Solomon, Hannah Greenebaum; Spargo, John; Spingarn, Joel; Spock, Benjamin; Stanton, Elizabeth; Starr, Ellen Gates; Steffens, Lincoln; Steinem, Gloria; Stelze, Charles; Steuben, John; Stone, I. F.; Stone, Lucy; Sullivan, Leon; Sumner, Charles; Swope, Gerard; Szold, Henrietta;

Tappan, Arthur; Tappan, Lewis; Taylor, Graham; Terrell, Mary Church; Thomas, Norman; Tibbles, Susette La Flesche; Towle, Charlotte Helen; Townsend, Francis E.; Travis, William Barret; Trotter, William Monroe; Truth, Sojourner; Tubman, Harriet; Tucker, Benjamin; Turner, Nat; Turner, Thomas Wyatt; U'Ren, William Simon; Van Waters, Miriam; Vanzetti, Bartolomeo; Vaux, Roberts; Veiller, Lawrence Turner; Vesey, Denmark; Wald, Lillian D.; Walker, David; Walker, Maggie Lena; Walker, Mary E.; Walker, Moses Fleetwood; Walker, Welday Wilberforce; Walling, William English; Wattleton, Faye; Weld, Theodore Dwight; Wells-Barnett, Ida Bell; Wheeler, Wayne Bidwell; White, Walter; Wiesel, Elie; Wilkins, Roy; Willard, Frances; Wilson, "Bill W."; Wise, Stephen Samuel; Wood, Edith Elmer; Woolman, John; Wright, Elizur; Wright, Frances; Young, Andrew, Jr.; Young, Whitney M., Jr.; Zinn, Howard

Sociology Argyris, Chris; Becker, Howard; Bell, Daniel; Bellah, Robert N.; Bendix, Reinhard; Berger, Peter L.; Bernard, Jessie Shirley; Blau, Peter M.; Blumer, Herbert; Breckinridge, Sophonisba Preston; Brisbane, Albert; Cayton, Horace Roscow; Coleman, James; Cooley, Charles Horton; Coser, Lewis A.; Cressey, Donald R.; Crossley, Archibald M.; Devine, Edward Thomas; Drake, St. Clair; Du Bois, W.E.B.; Duncan, Otis D.; Edwards, Harry; Ehrenreich, Barbara; Erikson, Kai T.; Etzioni, Amitai; Follett, Mary Parker; Gallup, George; Garfinkel, Harold; Glazer, Nathan; Glueck, Eleanor Touroff; Glueck, Sheldon; Goffman, Erving; Greeley, Andrew M.; Harris, Lou; Hochschild, Arlie Russell; Hoffman, Lynn; Homans, George; Hymes, Dell; Kerby, William; Kinsey, Alfred; Komarovsky, Mirra; Kristol, Irving; Lazarsfeld, Paul; Lenski, Gerhard E.; Linz, Juan J.; Lipset, Seymour Martin; Lohman, Joseph D.; Lynd, Robert Staughton; March, James G.; Merton, Robert K.; Milgram, Stanley; Mills, C. Wright; Murphy, Gardner; Nisbet, Robert A.; Ogburn, William F.; Ohlin, Lloyd E.; Park, Robert E.; Parsons, Elsie; Parsons, Talcott; Revelle, Roger; Richmond, Mary Ellen; Riesman, David; Robinson, Claude; Rogers, Everett Mitchell; Roper, Elmo; Rossi, Alice S.; Schutz, Alfred; Scott, W. Richard; Sellin, Thorsten; Selznick, Philip; Simon, Herbert A.; Small, Albion W.; Smelser, Neiler J.; Smith, T. Lynn; Stouffer, Samuel; Sumner, William Graham; Sutherland, Edwin Hardin; Taylor, Graham; Terkel, "Studs"; Thomas, William I.; Thompson, James D.; Tilly, Charles; Turner, Ralph H.; Veblen, Thorstein; Vollmer, August; Wallerstein, Immanuel; Ward, Lester Frank; Warner, W. Lloyd; Whiting, John W.M.; Whyte, William H., Jr.; Wilkins, Leslie T.; Wilson, James Q.; Wilson, Orlando W.; Wilson, William Julius; Yankelovich, Daniel

Sports Aaron, Hank; Abdul-Jabbar, Kareem; Alexander, Grover; Ali, Muhammad; Allen, Mel; Andretti, Mario; Angell, Roger; Anson, "Cap"; Arcaro, Eddie; Arledge, Roone; Armour, Tommy; Armstrong, Henry; Ashe, Arthur; Ashford, Emmet; Auerbach, "Red";

Baer, Max; Baker, Hobey; Barber, "Red"; Barrow, Ed; Barry, Rick; Baugh, Sammy; Baylor, Elgin; Beamon, Bob; Bell, "Cool Papa"; Bench, Johnny; Bender, "Chief"; Berg, Patty; Berra, "Yogi"; Berwanger, "Jay"; Bird, Larry; Blaik, Earl "Red"; Blaikie, William; Blanchard, "Doc"; Blanda, George; Booth, "Albie"; Boston, Ralph; Braddock, James J.; Bradley, Bill; Brickhouse, Jack; Brock, Lou; Brown, Jim; Brown, Paul; Brundage, Avery; Bryant, Paul "Bear"; Budge, Don; Butkus, Dick; Button, Dick; Caldwell, Charlie; Camp, Walter; Campbell, Earl; Carlton, Steve; Cartwright, Alexander, Jr.; Cauthen, Steve; Chadwick, Henry; Chamberlain, Wilt; Chandler, "Happy"; Chevrolet, Louis; Cicotte, Eddie; Clarkson, John; Clemente, Roberto; Cobb, Ty; Cochrane, "Mickey"; Collins, Eddie, Sr.; Comiskey, Charlie; Connolly, Maureen; Connolly, Tom; Connors, Jimmy; Corbett, "Gentleman Jim"; Corbitt, Ted; Cordero, Angel, Jr.; Cosell, Howard; Courtney, Charles; Cousy, Bob; Crawford, Sam; Cromwell, Dean; Crowninshield, George; Cunningham, Glenn; Daley, Arthur; Davis, Dwight; Davis, Ernie; Davis, Glenn "Junior"; Dean, "Dizzy"; Delahanty, Ed; DeMar, Clarence; Dempsey, Jack; Dickey, Bill; DiMaggio, Joe; Dorsett, Tony; Doubleday, Abner; Douglas, Robert L.; Dreyfuss, Barney; Drysdale, Don; Duffy, Hugh; du Pont, Margaret Osborne; Durocher, Leo; Ederle, Gertrude; Edwards, Harry; Erving, Julius; Evert, Chris; Ewry, Ray; Feller, Bob; Fingers, Rollie; Fitzsimmons, Bob; Fitzsimmons, "Sunny Jim"; Fleming, Peggy; Flood, Curt; Ford, "Whitey"; Foreman, George; Fosbury, Dick; Foster, Rube; Foxx, Jimmie; Foyt, A. J.; Fraser, Gretchen; Frick, Ford; Galvin, "Pud"; Gehrig, Lou; Giamatti, A. Bartlett; Gibson, Althea; Gibson, Bob; Gibson, Josh; Gifford, Frank; Gifford, Frank; Gipp, George; Gonzales, "Pancho"; Graham, Otto; Grange, "Red"; Greenberg, Hank; Griffin, Archie; Griffith, Clark; Gumbel, Bryant; Gurney, Dan; Guthrie, Janet; Hagen, Walter; Halas, George "Papa Bear"; Hamill, Dorothy; Harris, "Buck"; Hart, Doris; Hartack, Bill; Harwell, Ernie; Haughton, Percy; Havlicek, John; Hayes, Bob; Hayes, "Woody"; Haynes, Marquis; Heffelfinger, "Pudge"; Heilmann, Harry; Heisman, John; Henderson, Rickey; Henie, Sonja; Hirsh, Maximilian; Hitchcock, Tommy; Hogan, Ben; Holm, Eleanor; Holman, Nat; Hornsby, Rogers; Hornung, Paul; Huggins, Miller; Hulman, Tony; Jackson, Reggie; Jackson, "Shoeless Joe"; Jeffries, James J.; Johnson, Jack; Johnson, Judy; Johnson, "Magic"; Johnson, Rafer; Johnson, Walter; Jones, Bobby; Jones, "Plain Ben"; Jones, Robert Trent, Sr.; Jordan, Michael; Joyner-Kersee, Jackie; Kahanamoku, Duke; Kazmaier, Dick; Keeler, "Wee Willie"; Kelly, Johnny; Kelly, "King"; Ketchel, Stanley; Kiphuth, Robert; Klein, "Chuck"; Klem, Bill; Knight, Bobby; Knight, Philip H.; Koufax, Sandy; Kramer, Jack; Kuhn, Bowie K.; Kundla, John; Kurland, Bob; Lajoie, Nap; Lambeau, "Curly"; Landis, Kenesaw Mountain; Landry, Tom; Lapchick, Joe; Larned, Bill; Larsen, Don; Leahy, Frank; LeMond, Greg; Leonard, "Buck"; Lewis, Carl; Lieb, Fred; Little, Lou; Little, William; Lombardi,

Vince; Lopez, Nancy; Louganis, Greg; Louis, Joe; Lucas, Jerry; Luckman, Sid; Luisetti, "Hank"; Mack, Connie; Mallory, "Molla"; Malone, Moses; Mantle, Mickey; Maranville, "Rabbit"; Maravich, Pete; Marciano, "Rocky"; Maris, Roger; Marquard, "Rube"; Martin, "Pepper"; Masterson, "Batt"; Mathewson, Christy; Mauch, Gene; Mays, Willie; McCarthy, Joe; McElhenny, Hugh; McEnroe, John; McGraw, John; McKechnie, Bill; McLoughlin, Maury; McNamee, Graham; Metcalfe, Ralph; Mikan, George; Monroe, Earl "The Pearl"; Montana, Joe; Moody, Helen Wills; Moore, Archie; Moses, Edwin; Motley, Marion; Muldoon, William A.; Musial, Stan; Myers, Lon; Nagurski, "Bronko"; Naismith, James; Namath, Joe; Navratilova, Martina; Neiman, LeRoy; Nelson, Byron, Jr.; Nevers, Ernie; Neyland, Bob; Nicklaus, Jack; Noll, "Chuck"; Oerter, Al; Oldfield, Barney; O'Malley, Walter; Ott, Mel; Ouimet, Francis; Owen, "Stout Steve"; Owens, Jesse; Paige, "Satchel"; Paine, Charles Jackson; Palmer, Arnold; Paterno, Joe; Patterson, Floyd; Payton, Walter "Sweetness"; Perry, Joe; Pettit, Bob; Petty, Richard; Pollard, "Fritz"; Pound, Louise; Radbourn, "Old Hoss"; Reach, Al; Reed, Willis; Retton, Mary Lou; Rice, Grantland; Richards, Bob; Rickard, "Tex"; Rickey, Branch; Riggs, Bobby; Roberts, "Fireball"; Robertson, Oscar; Robinson, Eddie; Robinson, Frank; Robinson, Jackie; Robinson, "Sugar Ray"; Robinson, Wilbert; Rockne, Knute; Rodgers, Bill; Rodriguez, "Chichi"; Rose, Pete; Rozelle, "Pete"; Rucker, Nap; Rudolph, Wilma; Rumsey, Charles Cary; Rupp, Adolph; Rusie, Amos; Russell, Bill; Ruth, "Babe"; Ryan, Nolan; Ryun, Jim; Samuelson, Joan Benoit; Sande, Earl; Saperstein, Abe; Sarazen, Gene; Sayers, Gale; Schalk, Ray; Schmidt, Mike; Sears, Dick; Sears, Eleo; Seaver, Tom; Shoemaker, Bill; Shorter, Frank; Simmons, Al; Simpson, "O.J."; Sisler, George; Slaney, Mary; Sloan, "Todhunter"; Smith, Horton; Smith, Ozzie; Smith, Red; Snead, Sam; Snider, "Duke"; Spahn, Warren; Spalding, Al; Speaker, Tris; Spitz, Mark; Stagg, Amos Alonzo; Staubach, Roger; Steinbrenner, George; Stengel, Casey; Stevens, Harry; Sullivan, James E.; Sullivan, John L.; Tarkenton, Fran; Taylor, "Major"; Ten Broeck, Richard; Thomson, Bobby; Thorpe, Jim; Tilden, "Big Bill"; Trabert, Tony; Travers, Jerry; Travis, Walter; Trevino, Lee; Tunney, "Gene"; Turner, Ted; Ueberroth, Peter; Unitas, Johnny; Unser, Al; Van Buren, Steve; Vance, "Dazzy"; Veeck, Bill; Vincent, Fay; Wagner, "Honus"; Walker, Moses Fleetwood; Walker, Welday Wilberforce; Wallace, John Hankins; Walsh, "Big Ed"; Walsh, Bill; Walton, Bill; Waner, Paul; Ward, Arch; Ward, Monte; Warfield, Paul; Warner, Glenn "Pop"; Weaver, Earl Johnny; West, Jerry; White, Bill; Whitworth, Kathy; Wightman, Hazel; Wilhelm, Hoyt; Wilkinson, "Bud"; Williams, Ted; Wilson, "Hack"; Wooden, John; Woodward, William; Wright, George; Wright, Harry; Wright, "Mickey"; Yastrzemski, Carl; Yawkey, Tom; Yost, Fielding "Hurry Up"; Young, "Cy"; Zaharias, "Babe"; Zuppke, Bob

Technology See under ENGINEERING AND TECHNOLOGY.

OCCUPATIONAL INDEX

Television and Radio Alda, Alan; Allen, Fred; Allen, Mel; Arledge, Roone; Arness, James; Ball, Lucille; Barber, "Red"; Barrymore, Lionel; Benny, Jack; Berle, Milton; Block, Martin; Bochco, Steven; Bowes, Edward; Brickhouse, Jack; Brokaw, Tom; Brothers, Joyce; Brown, Tony; Buckley, William F., Jr.; Burnett, Carol; Burr, Raymond; Button, Dick; Caesar, Sid; Cantor, Eddie; Carney, Art; Carson, Johnny; Cavett, Dick; Chamberlain, Richard; Chancellor, John; Chayefsky, Paddy; Chung, Connie; Clark, Dick; Coca, Imogene; Conover, Willis; Cooke, Alistair; Cooney, Joan Ganz; Cosby, Bill; Cosell, Howard; Cronkite, Walter; Crosby, Bing; Dana, Charles Anderson; D'Aquino, Iva Ikuko Toguri; Davis, Elmer; Day, Doris; Dean, "Dizzy"; Dewhurst, Colleen; DuMont, Allen B.; Falk, Peter; Faulk, John Henry; Fessenden, Reginald; Fleming, Peggy; Foxx, Redd; Frederick, Pauline; Freed, Alan; Friendly, Fred W.; Garroway, Dave; Gifford, Frank; Gifford, Frank; Gillars, Mildred; Gillis, James M.; Griffin, Merv; Gumbel, Bryant; Harvey, Paul; Harwell, Ernie; Hayes, Peter Lind; Hemsley, Sherman; Herbert, Don "Mr. Wizard"; Hewitt, Don; Hooper, C.E.; Hope, Bob; Johnson, Nick; Jolson, Al; Kaltenborn, H.V.; Keeshan, Bob; Keillor, Garrison; King, Larry; Kluge, John W.; Koppel, Ted; Kovacs, Ernie; Kuralt, Charles; Landon, Michael; Lear, Norman; Lehrer, Jim; Letterman, David; Lewis, Delano E.; MacNeil, Robert; Martin, Steve; McNamee, Graham; Meadows, Audrey; Minow, Newton; Moore, Mary Tyler; Moyers, Bill; Murrow, Edward R.; Namath, Joe; Nelson, Rick; Newhart, Bob; Nielsen, A.C.; O'Connor, Carroll; Paar, Jack; Paley, William S.; Pauley, Jane; Pearson, Drew; Phillips, Irna; Radner, Gilda; Rather, Dan; Reasoner, Harry; Redstone, Summer; Rivera, Geraldo; Rivers, Joan; Robertson, Pat; Rogers, Fred; Rowan, Carl; Saks, Gene; Sanders, Marlene; Sarnoff, David; Sawyer, Diane; Schorr, Daniel; Schulz, Charles M.; Selleck, Tom; Sevareid, Eric; Shatner, William; Sheen, Fulton J.; Sheldon, Sidney; Simpson, "O.J."; Smith, "Buffalo" Bob; Smith, Howard K.; Smith, Kate; Smothers, Dick; Smothers, Tom; Spelling, Aaron; Stanton, Frank; Stapleton, Jean; Sullivan, Ed; Susskind, David; Swayze, John Cameron, Sr.; Swing, Raymond Gram; Taylor, Deems; Terkel, "Studs"; Thomas, Lowell; Tillstrom, Burr; Tinker, Grant; Turner, Ted; Tyson, Cicely; Vallee, Rudy; Van Dyke, Dick; Wallace, Mike; Walters, Barbara; Waring, Fred; Weaver, Pat; Webb, Jack; Welk, Lawrence; Welles, Orson; Winchell, Walter; Winfrey, Oprah; Wolper, David L.; Young, Owen D.; Young, Robert

Theater Abbott, George; Adams, Maude; Ade, George; Adler, Richard; Albee, Edward; Aldredge, Theoni V.; Aldridge, Ira; Anderson, Judith; Anderson, Maxwell; Anderson, Robert; Aronson, Boris; Atkinson, Brooks; Bacharach, Burt; Bailey, Pearl; Baker, George Pierce; Bankhead, Tallulah; Barry, Philip; Barrymore, Ethel; Barrymore, John; Barrymore, Lionel; Barrymore, Maurice; Bay, Howard; Behrman, S.N.; Belasco, David; Bel Geddes, Norman; Bennett, Michael; Berlin, Irving; Berman, Eugene; Bernstein, Aline;

Boker, George Henry; Bolger, Ray; Booth, Edwin Thomas; Booth, John Wilkes; Booth, Junius Brutus; Boucicault, Dion; Brady, William A.; Breuer, Lee; Brougham, John; Brown, William Henry; Brustein, Robert; Bullins, Ed; Carney, Art; Carnovsky, Morris; Carroll, Diahann; Carroll, Vinnette; Chamberlain, Richard; Clark, Bobby; Clurman, Harold; Cohan, George M.; Colbert, Claudette; Coleman, Cy; Comden, Betty; Connelly, Marc; Cook, Will Marion; Cornell, Katharine; Crawford, Cheryl; Cronyn, Hume; Crothers, Rachel; Cushman, Charlotte; Cushman, Pauline; Dalrymple, Jean; Daly, Augustin; Davidson, Gordon; Davis, Ossie; Davis, Owen; Dee, Ruby; Dewhurst, Colleen; Dietz, Howard; Donaldson, Walter; Dressler, Marie; Drew, John; Drew, Louisa Lane; Duke, Vernon; Dunlap, William; Elliott, Maxine; Eltinge, Julian; Evans, Maurice; Feiffer, Jules; Fichandleer, Zelda; Fields, Dorothy; Fiske, Minnie Maddern; Fitch, Clyde; Flanagan, Hallie; Fontanne, Lynne; Foreman, Richard; Fornes, Maria Irene; Forrest, Edwin; Freed, Arthur; Freeman, Morgan; Frohman, Charles; Frohman, Daniel; Fuller, Loie; Gershwin, Ira; Gillette, William; Gilpin, Charles Sidney; Glaspell, Susan; Goldovsky, Boris; Gorelik, Mordecai; Green, Paul; Guare, John; Hammerstein, Oscar; Hammerstein, Oscar, II; Hampden, Walter; Hansberry, Lorraine; Harbach, Otto; Harburg, E.Y.; Harrigan, Edward; Harris, Julie; Hart, Lorenz; Hayes, Helen; Hayes, Peter Lind; Hecht, Ben; Hellman, Lillian; Herbert, Victor; Herman, Jerry; Herne, James A.; Hewlett, James; Hirschfeld, Al; Hopkins, Arthur; Houseman, John; Howard, Bronson; Howard, Sidney; Hoyt, Charles Hale; Hughes, Langston; Hyman, George; Inge, William; Janauschek, Fanny; Jefferson, Joseph; Jones, James Earl; Jones, Robert Edmond; Julia, Raul; Kahn, Gustav Gerson; Kander, John; Kanin, Garson; Karloff, Boris; Kaufman, George S.; Keene, Laura; Keith, B.F.; Kennedy, Adrienne; Kern, Jerome; Kingsley, Sidney; Knott, Sarah Gertrude; Koch, Frederick; Kreymborg, Alfred; Lahr, Bert; Lane, Burton; Laughton, Charles; Lee, Canada; Lee, Eugene; Lee, Ming Cho; Le Gallienne, Eva; Leiber, Jerry; Lemmon, Jack; Lerner, Alan Jay; Loden, Barbara; Loesser, Frank; Loewe, Frederick; Logan, Joshua; Loos, Anita; Luce, Clare Boothe; Ludlam, Charles; Ludlum, Robert; Lugosi, Bela; Lunt, Alfred; MacArthur, Charles; MacKaye, Percy; MacKaye, Steele; Mamet, David; Mansfield, Richard; Marlowe, Julia; Martin, Mary; McClendon, Rose; Mercer, Johnny; Merman, Ethel; Mielziner, Jo; Miller, Arthur; Mills, Florence; Moiseiwitsch, Tanya; Moody, William Vaughn; Mowatt, Anna Cora; Muni, Paul; Nazimova, Alla; Nichols, Mike; Noah, Mordecai Manuel; Norman, Marsha; O'Connor, Carroll; Odets, Clifford; Oenslager, Donald; O'Neill, Eugene; O'Neill, James; Papp, Joseph; Pastor, Tony; Payne, John Howard; Perry, Antoinette; Porter, Cole; Prince, Hal; Quintero, Jose; Rabe, David; Radner, Gilda; Rehan, Ada; Rice, Elmer; Richards, Lloyd; Rivera, Chita; Robards, Jason, Jr.; Robeson, Paul; Robin, Leo; Rodgers, Richard; Rogers, Ginger; Rogers, Will; Rose, Billy; Rowson, Susanna; Russell, Lillian; Saks, Gene;

Saroyan, William; Schary, Dore; Schwartz, Maurice; Scott, George C; Sellars, Peter; Sendak, Maurice; Sheldon, Edward; Shepard, Sam; Sherwood, Robert E.; Shubert, Lee; Silverman, Sime; Simon, Neil; Skinner, Otis; Smith, Oliver; Sondheim, Stephen; Sothern, Edward Askew; Standing Bear, Luther; Stapleton, Jean; Stewart, Ellen; Stone, John Augustus; Strasberg, Lee; Sturges, Preston; Styne, Jule; Tandy, Jessica; Tarkington, Booth; Thomas, Augustus; Thompson, Kay; Tillstrom, Burr; Tomlin, Lily; Tryon, Thomas; Tune, Tommy; Tyler, Royall; Tyson, Cicely; Urban, Joseph; Verdon, Gwen; Wallack, Lester; Walton, Tony; Wanamaker, Sam; Ward, Douglas Turner; Warfield, David; Warren, William; Waters, Ethel; Weill, Kurt; Welles, Orson; Wilder, Thorton; Williams, Bert; Williams, Tennessee; Willson, Meredith; Wilson, August; Wilson, Lanford; Wilson, Robert; Worth, Irene; Youmans, Vincent; Young, Stark; Zaks, Jerry; Ziegfeld, Florenz, Jr.

Zoology Ayala, Francisco J.; Baird, Spencer Fullerton; Beebe, William; Bigelow, Henry B.; Brower, Lincoln P.; Cade, Thomas J.; Carr, Archibald; Carson, Rachel; Chapman, Frank; Child, Charles M.; Clark, Eugenie; Conklin, Edwin G.; Cope, Edward Drinker; Coues, Elliott; Delson, Eric; Dethier, Vincent G.; Ditmars, Raymond; Dobzhansky, Theodosius; Eakin, Richard M.; Ehrlich, Paul R.; Eisner, Thomas; Fankhauser, Gerhard; Forbes, Stephen Alfred; Fossey, Dian; Fuertes, Louis Agassiz; Gans, Carl; Goldschmidt, Richard B.; Goodman, Morris; Gould, James L.; Grant, Peter R.; Gregory, W.K.; Griffin, Donald R.; Grinnell, George Bird; Harlow, Harry; Harrison, Ross B.; Hart, Edwin Bret; Heinrich, Bernd; Hornaday, William Temple; Hrdy, Sarah Blaffer; Hyman, Libbie; Janzen, Daniel H.; Jennings, Herbert S.; Keeton, William T.; Kinsey, Alfred; Leidy, Joseph; Lillie, Frank R.; Lyman, Theodore; Margulis, Lynn; Marler, Peter; Mayr, Ernst; Nuttall, Thomas; Oppenheimer, Jane M.; Orton, James; Packard, Alpheus Spring, Jr.; Pearson, Thomas Gilbert; Pepperberg, Irene M.; Peterson, Roger Tory; Riddiford, Lynn M.; Ridgway, Robert; Romer, Alfred Sherwood; Say, Thomas; Schaller, George B.; Scott, John Paul; Simpson, George Gaylord; Stiles, Charles W.; Thomas, Cyrus; Thomson, Keith Stewart; Tuttle, Merlin D.; Twitty, Victor C.; Vogt, William; Wheeler, William Morton; Whitman, C.O.; Wilder, Burt Green; Williston, Samuel Wendell; Wilson, Alexander; Wilson, Edward O.; Wright, Sewall; Wyman, Jeffries; Yerkes, Robert

INDEX OF NAMES

The following index lists the name of every individual mentioned within an article, and refers the reader to the article or articles where it is mentioned. Thus, the index entry beginning

Boulanger, Nadia   Berger, Arthur; Blitzstein, Marc . . . .

means that Nadia Boulanger is mentioned under the entries for Arthur Berger and for Marc Blitzstein, and all the other names following. Note that the index entry itself may or may not be an entry in the dictionary. In this example, it is not, since Nadia Boulanger was not an American. Names within parentheses at the beginning of some entries – for example, pen names, etc. – are not included. (A relatively few, very common pen names or stage names are included as entries in the main section of the dictionary, with cross-references to the entries under which the corresponding article appears.)

This index vastly expands the coverage of the dictionary to thousands of individuals, without regard to whether they were Americans or not, and increases the usefulness of included entires. One can thus track every mention of Benjamin Franklin's name and discover his relationship with lesser known people about whom one might want to learn more. The index will also serve as *aide-mémoire* when one knows the name of one party to a major event but cannot recall the names of others. The Index of Names is designed to knit together the complex fabric of the book to make more of its information accessible.

Clark, George Rogers Clark, William
Clark, Grenville Buckner, Emory
Clark, Kenneth B. Clark, Mamie Phipps
Clark, Tom C. Clark, Ramsey
Clark, William Lewis, Meriwether; Sacagawea
Clark, W. Van Alan Clark, Edna McConnell
Clarke, John Rogers, Harriet Burbank
Clarke, Kenny Monk, Thelonious
Clausen, Jens Hiesey, William M.; Keck, David D.
Clay, Cassius Ali, Muhammad
Clay, Henry Cheves, Langdon; Clay, Cassius Marcellus; Finley, Robert; Hayne, Robert Young; Jouett, Matthew; Polk, James Knox; Randolph, John; Taylor, Zachary; Wythe, George
Clements, Robert Townsend, Francis E.
Clemm, Maria Poe, Edgar Allan
Clemm, Virginia Poe, Edgar Allan
Clephane, James Merganthaler, Ottmar
Cleveland, Grover Blaine, James Gillespie; Carlisle, John Griffin; Cleveland, Frances; Fuller, Melville W.; Harrison, Benjamin; Hendricks, Thomas A.; Lamar, Lucius Quintus Cincinnatus; Morton, Julius Sterling; Olney, Richard; Peckham, Rufus Wheeler; Pendleton, George Hunt; Seymour, Horatio; Stevenson, Adlai E.; Straus, Isidor; Straus, Oscar Solomon; Tillman, "Pitchfork Ben"; White, Edward Douglass; Williams, Daniel Hale
Cliburn, Van Lhevinne, Josef
Clinton, Bill Alegría, Ricardo E.; Babbitt, Bruce; Bentsen, Lloyd Millard Jr.; Brown, Lee P.; Brown, Ron; Christopher, Warren M.; Cisneros, Henry; Clinton, Hillary Rodham; Elders, M. Joycelyn; Gore, Al, Jr.; Jordan, Vernon, Jr.; Nunn, Sam; Rivlin, Alice; Shalala, Donna
Clinton, George Ames, Ezra; Clinton, De Witt
Clinton, Hillary Edelman, Marion
Clinton, Roger Clinton, Bill
Clovers, the Wexler, Jerry
Cochise Crook, George; Mangas Coloradas
Cockerell, Samuel Pepys Latrobe, Benjamin Henry
Codman, Ogden, Jr. Wharton, Edith
Cody, William F. "Buffalo Bill" Ingraham, Prentiss; Judson, Edward Zane Carroll
Coffin, Howard Chapin, Roy Dikeman
Cohan, George M. Cagney, James; Lardner, Ring
Cohen, Stanley Levi-Montalcini, Rita
Cohn, Jack Cohn, Harry
Cole, Bob Johnson, James Weldon
Cole, Cozy Krupa, Gene
Cole, Eddie Cole, Nat "King"
Cole, Nat "King" Charles, Ray; Riddle, Nelson
Cole, Thomas Church, Frederick; Durand, Asher B.; Reed, Luman; Smillie, James
Coleman, Cy Fields, Dorothy
Coleman, Ornette Ertegun, Ahmet
Coleridge, Samuel Taylor Allston, Washington
Collins, Judy Newman, Randy
Collins, Ted Smith, Kate
Collinson, Peter Bartram, John
Coloradas, Mangas Cochise
Colt, Samuel Hays, "Jack"
Colt, Winchester Remington Hubbard, L. Ron

Coltrane, John Davis, Miles Dewey; Dolphy, Eric; Ertegun, Ahmet; Monk, Thelonious; Tyner, McCoy
Columbo, Russ Krupa, Gene
Columbus, Christopher Irving, Washington; Thacher, John Boyd
Comden, Betty Coleman, Cy; Styne, Jule
Commons, John R. Andrews, John Bertram
Condon, Eddie Krupa, Gene
Cone, Fax Belding, Don
Cone, Herman Cone, Moses H.
Conkling, Roscoe Blaine, James Gillespie; Platt, Thomas Collier; Seymour, Horatio
Connelly, Marc Kaufman, George S.
Conrad, Joseph Crane, Stephen; Mencken, H. L.; Morley, Christopher; Said, Edward W.
Conroy, Jack Bontemps, Arna
Cook, Abbie Mitchell Cook, Will Marion
Cook, Frederick A. Peary, Robert E.
Cook, James Ledyard, John
Cook, Lady Woodhull, Victoria Claflin
Cook, Mercer Cook, Will Marion
Cooke, Jay Morgan, J. P.
Cooke, Sam Alpert, Herb
Coolidge, Calvin Coolidge, Grace; Davis, John William; Dawes, Charles G.; Hoover, J. Edgar; Hughes, Charles Evans; Mahler, Herbert; Mellon, Andrew; Roberts, Owen J.; Rogers, Edith; Stone, Harlan Fiske; White, William Allen
Coolidge, Elizabeth Sprague Mitchell, Lucy
Coon, Carleton Howells, William W.
Cooper, Gary Gehrig, Lou; York, Alvin
Cooper, James Fenimore Darley, Felix; Greenough, Horatio; Nelson, Samuel; Quidor, John; Wiley, Charles; Woolson, Constance Fenimore; Wyeth, N. C.
Cooper, Leon N. Bardeen, John; Schrieffer, J. Robert
Cope, Edward Drinker Leidy, Joseph; Marsh, O. C.
Copeland, Ada King, Clarence
Copland, Aaron Bernstein, Leonard; Bowles, Paul; Brant, Henry; Coolidge, Elizabeth Sprague; Graham, Martha; Koussevitzky, Serge; Rorem, Ned
Copley, John Singleton Badger, Joseph; Earl, Ralph; Hurd, Nathaniel; Pelham, Henry; Pelham, Peter; Waldo, Samuel Lovett
Coppola, Francis Ford Lucas, George
Corbett, James J. Sullivan, John L.
Corbin, John Corbin, Margaret
Corbin, Margaret McCauley, Mary Hays
Corey, Giles Corey, Martha
Cori, Carl Cori, Gerty T.; Krebs, Edwin G.
Cori, Gerty Krebs, Edwin G.
Corman, Roger Coppola, Francis Ford; Nicholson, Jack
Cornell, Katharine Evans, Maurice; Mielziner, Jo; Oenslager, Donald; Welles, Orson
Cornish, John Russwurm, John Brown
Cornwallis, Charles Kalb, Johann; Laurens, Henry; Tilghman, Tench
Corot, Jean-Baptiste-Camille Vose, Seth Morton; Walters, William Thompson
Cortazar, Julio Rabassa, Gregory
Cortez, Hernando Castaneda, Carlos E.
Cosby, William Zenger, John Peter
Costello, Frank Williams, Edward Bennett

INDEX OF NAMES

Matisse, Henri Kuhn, Walt; Maurer, Alfred; Russell, Morgan; Stein, Gertrude; Stein, Leo; Warburg, Edward M. M.; Weber, Max

Matlock, Matty Crosby, Bob

Matson, Norman Glaspell, Susan

Mauchly, John W. Eckert, J. Presper

Maugham, Somerset Frohman, Charles

Maurin, Peter Day, Dorothy

Maverick, Peter Durand, Asher B.

Maxam, Allan Gilbert, Walter

Maxim, Hiram Stanley, William

Maximilian, Emperor Magruder, John Bankhead

Mayer, Irene Selznick, David O.

Mayer, Joseph Goeppert-Mayer, Maria

Mayer, Louis B. Selznick, David O.; Thalberg, Irving G.

Mayo, Charles Mayo, William James; Mayo, William Worrall

Mayo, William Mayo, Charles Horace; Mayo, William Worrall

McAlister, Elizabeth Berrigan, Philip F.

McBain, Ed Hunter, Evan

McCall, Jack Hickok, "Wild Bill"

McCann, Edson del Rey, Lester

McCarthy, Eugene Kennedy, Robert F.; O'Neill, "Tip"

McCarthy, Joseph R. Block, Herbert; Bridges, Styles; Carlson, Evans F.; Cohn, Roy M.; Dassin, Jules; Fairbank, John K.; Finley, M. I.; Flanders, Ralph; Hammett, Dashiell; Jessup, Philip Caryl; Kennedy, Robert F.; La Follette, Robert Marion, Jr.; Lattimore, Owen; Lehman, Herbert; Le Sueur, Meridel; Loy, Myrna; Maltz, Albert; Marshall, George C., Jr.; McCarran, Patrick; Murrow, Edward R.; Schary, Dore; Schulberg, Budd; Stratemeyer, George Edward; Taft, Robert A.; Vincent, John Carter; Welch, Joseph Nye; Williams, Edward Bennett; Wood, Robert E.

McCarthy, Mary Hellman, Lillian; Wilson, Edmund

McCartney, Paul Perkins, Carl

McCauley, Mary Ludwig Hays Corbin, Margaret

McClellan, George Brinton Banks, Nathaniel Prentiss; Curtis, George Ticknor; Hancock, Winfield Scott; Hutchinson Family, The; Jackson, "Stonewall"; McClellan, George; Pinkerton, Allan; Pope, John; Stuart, Jeb

McClintic, Guthrie Cornell, Katharine

McClintock, Barbara Emerson, Rollins A.

McClure, Samuel S. Doubleday, Frank Nelson

McConnell, David Hall Clark, Edna McConnell

McCormack, John Albert, Carl; O'Neill, "Tip"

McCormack, Robert Dirksen, Everett

McCormick, Cyrus Hussey, Obed

McCormick, Katharine Dexter Sanger, Margaret

McCormick, Robert McCormick, Cyrus Hall; Patterson, Joseph Medill

McCullers, J. Reeves McCullers, Carson

McCullough, Paul Clark, Bobby

McDavid, Virginia Glenn McDavid, Raven, Jr.

McDonald, Dick Kroc, Ray

McDonald, Mac Kroc, Ray

McDonald-Wright, Stanton Russell, Morgan

McDougall, William Rhine, Joseph

McDowell, Mississippi Fred Raitt, Bonnie

McDuff, Jack Benson, George

McGhee, Brownie Terry, Sonny

McGlynn, Edward Corrigan, Michael

McGovern, George Dees, Morris, Jr.; Hart, Gary; Thurow, Lester

McGraw, John Foster, Rube

McGregor, M. F. Meritt, Benjamin Dean

McHugh, Jimmy Fields, Dorothy

McIlvaine, John G. Eyre, Wilson

McKay, John W. McKay, Clarence Hungerford

McKenney, Thomas L. Hall, James

McKim, Charles Furness, Frank; Gilbert, Cass; Richardson, H. H.; Saint-Gaudens, Augustus

McKinley, William Cannon, Joseph G.; Czolgosz, Leon; Day, William Rufus; Dirksen, Everett; Fairbanks, Charles; Fuller, Henry Blake; Goldman, Emma; Hanna, Mark; Hoar, George; Hobart, Garret A.; Knox, Philander Chase; Long, John Davis; McKenna, Joseph; McKinley, Ida; Roosevelt, Theodore; Sherman, John; Storer, Maria Longworth Nichols; Taft, William Howard; Wood, Leonard

McKinney, William Redman, Don

McKitrick, Eric Elkins, Stanley M.

McMahon, Ed Carson, Johnny

McMillan, Edwin Seaborg, Glenn T.

McNamara, Robert Califano, Joseph A., Jr.

McPhatter, Clyde Wilson, Jackie

McShann, Jay Parker, Charlie

McVicker, Mary Booth, Edwin Thomas

Mead, Margaret Bateson, Gregory; Benedict, Ruth

Mead, William Rutherford Furness, Frank; Gilbert, Cass; McKim, Charles Follen

Meade, George Gordon Burnside, Ambrose; Reynolds, John Fulton

Meany, George Reuther, Walter

Medill, Joseph McCormick, Robert Rutherford

Melcher, Marty Day, Doris

Mellon, Andrew Mellon, Paul

Mellon, Catherine Warner, John W.

Mellon, Richard K. Lawrence, David

Melville, Herman Robinson, Boardman; Shaw, Lemuel

Memphis Slim "Little Walter"

Mencken, H. L. More, Paul Elmer

Mendel, Gregor Dobzhansky, Theodosius; Eakin, Richard M.; Morgan, Thomas Hunt; Wright, Sewall

Mengs, Anton West, Benjamin

Menninger, Charles Frederick Menninger, Karl

Menninger, Karl Menninger, Charles Frederick

Menninger, William Claire Menninger, Charles Frederick

Menotti, Gian-Carlo Barber, Samuel

Mercer, Johnny Mancini, Henry

Mercer, Mabel Short, Bobby; Wilder, Alec

Merchant, Ismail Ivory, James

Mercouri, Melina Dassin, Jules

Meredith, James Abrams, Creighton W., Jr.; Motley, Constance Baker

Merman, Ethel Berlin, Irving

Merrell, Helen Lynd, Robert Staughton

Merriam, Charles E. Frank, Jerome

Merrill, Bob Styne, Jule

Merrill, Charles Merrill, James

Metacomet Massasoit

Metcalfe, Suzanne Baum, Frank

Taylor, Richard Kendall, Henry W.
Taylor, Zachary Clayton, John Middleton; Davis, Jefferson; Taylor, Margaret
Teagarden, Jack Carmichael, Hoagy; Getz, Stan; Pollack, Ben; Whiteman, Paul
Teasdale, Sarah Rittenhouse, Jessie Bell
Tecumseh Harrison, William Henry; Tenskwatawa
Tei-Shin Fenollosa, Ernest Francisco
Teller, Edward Gamow, George
Temin, Howard Dulbecco, Renato
Temple, Shirley Robinson, Bill "Bojangles"
Tennant, Eleanor Riggs, Bobby
Tenney, Asa Bridgman, Laura Dewey
Tenney, Samuel Tenney, Tabitha Gilman
Tennyson, Alfred, Lord Daly, Augustin
Tenskwatawa Tecumseh
Terhune, Mary Virginia Hawes Terhune, Albert Payson
Terry, Eli Thomas, Seth
Terry, Ellen Fontanne, Lynne
Terry, Ellen Battell Stoeckel, Carl
Terry, Sonny McGhee, "Brownie"
Tevis, Lloyd Haggin, James Ben Ali
Thalberg, Irving Laemmle, Carl, Sr.
Tharp, Twyla Morris, Mark
Thayer, Abbott H. Fuertes, Louis Agassiz
Thigpen, Corbett Cleckley, Hervey Milton
Thimann, K. V. Went, Frits W.
Thomas, Clarence Higgenbotham, A. Leon, Jr.; Hill, Anita; Marshall, Thurgood
Thomas, Danny Spelling, Aaron
Thomas, Dylan Dylan, Bob
Thomas, Lowell Carnegie, Dale
Thomas, Norman Muste, A. J.
Thomas, Seth Terry, Eli
Thomas, Theodore Stock, Frederick August
Thomas, William E. Spencer, Joseph
Thompson, Benjamin Rouse, James W.
Thompson, Clara Horney, Karen
Thompson, Dorothy Lewis, Sinclair
Thompson, Jane Thompson, Benjamin
Thompson, J. Walter Haldeman, H. R.
Thompson, Kenneth Ritchie, Dennis M.
Thompson, Stanley Jones, Robert Trent, Sr.
Thomson, G. P. Davisson, Clinton J.
Thomson, Virgil Bowles, Paul; Rorem, Ned; Stein, Gertrude; Stettheimer, Florine
Thoreau, Henry David Alcott, Louisa May; Emerson, Ralph Waldo; Hawthorne, Nathaniel; King, Martin Luther, Jr.; Krutch, Joseph Wood; Redpath, James
Thoreau, John Thoreau, Henry David
Thorndike, Edward L. Barnhart, Clarence L.; Thorndike, Lynn; Yerkes, Robert
Thorne, George Ward, Aaron Montgomery
Thornhill, Claude Mulligan, Gerry
Thornton, Big Mama Otis, Johnny
Thornton, William Latrobe, Benjamin Henry
Thorpe, Jim Warner, Glenn "Pop"
Thurber, James DeVries, Peter; Ross, Harold
Thurstone, Thelma G. Thurstone, Louis L.
Tibbles, Thomas Tibbles, Susette La Flesche
Tiffany, Louis Comfort Carder, Frederick
Tilden, Samuel J. Carpenter, Matthew Hale; Evarts,

William Maxwell; Hayes, Rutherford B.; Reed, Thomas; Trumbull, Lyman
Tillich, Paul May, Rollo
Timberlake, John Eaton, "Peggy"
Ting, S. C. C. Richter, Burton
Tinker, Grant Moore, Mary Tyler
Tisch, Robert Tisch, Laurence A.
Tisquantum Squanto
Tito, Marshal Josip Adamic, Louis
Todd, David Peck Bingham, Millicent
Todd, John King, Clarence
Todd, Mabel Loomis Bingham, Millicent
Todd, Mary Lincoln, Abraham
Toklas, Alice B. Stein, Gertrude
Tolstoy, Leo Parini, Jay
Tomonaga Feynman, Richard
Tonti, Lorenzo Tonty, Henri de
Torrey, John Gray, Asa
Toscanini, Arturo Barber, Samuel; Leinsdorf, Erich; Rose, Leonard
Tower, John Nunn, Sam
Town, Ithiel Davis, Alexander J.
Towne, Henry R. Yale, Linus
Towne, John H. Yale, Linus
Townes, Charles Gould, Gordon; Maiman, Theodore; Schawlow, Arthur L.
Toynbee, Arnold McNeill, William H.
Tracy, Spencer Hepburn, Katharine
Travis, John Turner, Nat
Trent, Alphonso Price, Sammy
Trent, Robert, Jr. Jones, Robert Trent, Sr.
Tresca, Carlo Flynn, Elizabeth Gurley
Trevor, Claire Bren, Donald L.
Trilling, Diana Trilling, Lionel
Trott, Richard Eisenman, Peter D.
Trowbridge, Breck Livingston, Goodhue
Trudeau, Garry Coffin, William Sloane, Jr.; Pauley, Jane
Truman, Harry S. Albizu Campos, Pedro; Barkley, Alben W. Baruch, Bernard; Bender, George Harrison; Burton, Harold; Byrnes, James F.; Clark, Tom C.; Condon, E. U.; Cooke, Morris; Curley, James Michael; de Weldon, Felix; Dewey, Thomas E.; Harriman, Averell; Hatch, Carl A.; Hopkins, Harry; Hurley, Patrick J.; Ickes, Harold L.; Johnson, Louis; Keyserling, Leon H.; Lahey, Frank Howard; Landis, James; Leahy, William; MacArthur, Douglas; Marshall, George C., Jr.; McCormick, Anne Elizabeth; McGrath, James Howard; Minton, Sherman; Martin, Joseph, Jr.; Nourse, Edwin; Pendergast, Thomas; Randolph, A. Philip; Rayburn, Sam; Rockefeller, Nelson A.; Sabath, Adolph J.; Smith, Walter Bedell; Stimson, Henry; Symington, Stuart; Truman, Bess; Vandenberg, Arthur; Vinson, Frederick M.; Wallace, Henry A.; Webb, James; White, Walter; Wilson, Charles Edward; Winant, John
Truman, Margaret Truman, Bess
Trumbauer, Frankie Beiderbecke, Bix
Trumbull, John Durand, Asher B.; Trumbull, Jonathan
Trumbull, Jonathan Trumbull, John; Trumbull, Jonathan
Tubman, John Tubman, Harriet
Tucker, Henry St. George Tucker, John Randolph
Tucker, St. George Tucker, Henry St. George

Wagner, Richard Damrosch, Leopold; Damrosch, Walter; Finck, Henry Theophilus; Seidl, Anton

Wagner, Jane Tomlin, Lily

Wagner, Robert F. Keyserling, Leon H., Wagner, Robert F., Jr.

Walcott, "Jersey Joe" Marciano, "Rocky"

Wald, George Hartline, H. Keffer

Wald, Jerry Riddle, Nelson

Wald, Lillian Dock, Lavinia Lloyd

Waldo, Samuel Jewett, William

Walker, Admiral Bonner, John

Walker, A'Lelia Walker, Sarah Breedlove

Walker, Alice Bascove

Walker, Charles J. Walker, Sarah Breedlove

Walker, George Williams, Bert

Walker, James J. Seabury, Samuel

Walker, William Cazneau, Jane Maria Eliza Storms; Vanderbilt, Cornelius; Ward, Frederick Townsend; Webber, Charles Wilkins

Wallace, DeWitt Wallace, Lila Acheson

Wallace, George Johnson, Frank, Jr.; LeMay, Curtis; Norton, Eleanor Holmes

Wallace, Henry A. Wallace, Henry Cantwell

Wallace, Lurleen Wallace, George

Wallace, Mike Sanders, Marlene

Waller, Fats Basie, Count; Williams, Clarence

Walsh, James Price, Thomas Frederick

Walter, Bruno Bernstein, Leonard; Leinsdorf, Erich

Walters, Henry Walters, William Thompson

Walters, R. H. Bandura, Albert

Walton, Izaak Bartlett, John

Walton, John Trapp, Martin Edwin

Wanamaker, John VanDerZee, James

Waner, Lloyd Waner, Paul

Ward, Artemus Browne, Charles Farrar

Ward, Billy Wilson, Jackie

Ward, Charles F. Martin, Allie Beth Dent

Ward, John Quincy Adams French, Daniel Chester

Ward, Maisie Sheed, Frank

Ward, Samuel Bates, Katherine Lee

Warfield, David Belasco, David

Warfield, William Price, Leontyne

Waring, Fred Day, Doris

Waring, Tom Waring, Fred

Warner, Anna B. Warner, Susan

Warner, Charles Dudley Clemens, Samuel Langhorne

Warren, Austin Wellek, René

Warren, James Warren, Mercy Otis

Warren, John Warren, John

Warren, John Morton, William; Warren, John Collins

Warren, Lavinia Stratton, "General Tom Thumb"

Warren, Robert Penn Jarrell, Randall; Ransom, John Crowe

Warren, William Warren, William,

Warwick, Dionne Bacharach, Burt; Mathis, Johnny

Washington, Booker T. Fortune, Timothy Thomas; Mitchell, Arthur W.; Ovington, Mary White; Park, Robert E.; Trotter, William Monroe

Washington, Dinah Jones, Quincy

Washington, George Adams, John; Adams, Samuel; Bache, Benjamin Franklin; Barnum, P. T.; Bingham, William; Blair, John; Borglum, Gutzon; Cabot,

George; Chase, Samuel; Clark, George Rogers; Cushing, William; Dinwiddie, Robert; du Simitière, Pierre; Ellsworth, Oliver; Fairfax, Thomas; Freeman, Douglas Southall; Gates, Horatio; Gist, Christopher; Greenough, Horatio; Hamilton, Alexander; Harmar, Josiah; Hawkins, Benjamin; Iredell, James; Irving, Washington; Jefferson, Thomas; Johnson, Thomas; Kalb, Johann; Knox, Henry; Lafayette, Marie Joseph Paul Yves Roch Gilbert du Motier, Marquis de; Lee, Charles; Lee, Henry; Lee, Robert E.; L'Enfant, Pierre Charles; Madison, Dolley; Marshall, John; Mason, Stevens Thomson; Mifflin, Thomas; Monroe, James; Morgan, Daniel; Morris, Robert; Nicholas, Wilson Cary; Page, John; Paterson, William; Pine, Robert; Randolph, Edmund; Rush, Benjamin; Savage, Edward; Sharples, James; Steuben, Baron von; Stuart, Gilbert; Tilghman, Tench; Trumbull, John; Trumbull, Jonathan; Washington, Bushrod; Washington, Martha Custis; Weems, Mason Locke; Wright, Joseph

Washington, Harold Byrne, Jane

Washington, Martha Custis Lee, Robert E.; Sharples, James

Wasserstein, Bruce Perella, Joseph Robert

Wasserstein, Wendy Wasserstein, Bruce

Waters, Ethel Wilder, Alec

Waters, Muddy Butterfield, Paul; Chess, Leonard; "Little Walter"; Lomax, Alan

Watkins, Albert Morton, Julius Sterling

Watson, John B. Jones, Mary Cover; Lashley, Karl S.; Tolman, Edward Chace; Yerkes, Robert

Watson, Thomas A. Bell, Alexander Graham

Watt, James Evans, Oliver; Read, Nathan

Wayland, Francis Wayland, Francis

Wayne, Anthony Clark, William; Harrison, William Henry

Wayne, John Arness, James; Ford, John

Weaver, Randy Spence, Gerry

Weaver, Sigourney Weaver, Pat

Webb, Chick Jordan, Louis

Webb, J. Watson Webb, Electra Havemeyer

Weber, Max Bendix, Reinhard; Bishop, Isabel Wolff; Rothko, Mark

Weber and Fields Pastor, Tony

Webern, Anton Wolpe, Stefan

Webster, Daniel Binney, Horace; Hayne, Robert Young; Powers, Hiram; Winthrop, Robert Charles

Webster, John W. Shaw, Lemuel

Webster, Noah Goodrich, Chauncey Allen; Loudon, Samuel; March, Francis Andrew; Worcester, Joseph E.

Wedderburn, Joseph Veblen, Oswald

Weddington, Sarah Richards, Ann

Weems, Ted Como, Perry

Weidenreich, Franz Howells, William W.

Weidman, Charles Humphrey, Doris; Limon, José

Weill, Kurt Blitzstein, Marc; Gershwin, Ira; Green, Paul; Lerner, Alan Jay

Weinberg, Steven Glashow, Sheldon L.

Weiner, Alexander Levine, Philip

Weir, Frank Shearing, George

Weir, J. Alden Lawson, Ernest

Weld, Theodore Grimké, Angelina Emily; Grimké, Sarah Moore